LAROUSSE

TASCHEN-WÖRTERBUCH

**DEUTSCH
ENGLISCH**

**ENGLISCH
DEUTSCH**

LAROUSSE

ISBN 978-2-0354-2087-9

Sales: Houghton Mifflin Company, Boston
Library of Congress CIP Data
has been applied for

LAROUSSE

POCKET
DICTIONARY

**GERMAN
ENGLISH**
**ENGLISH
GERMAN**

LAROUSSE

Für diese Ausgabe/For this edition

Helen Galloway   Sigrid Koehler
Janice McNeillie

Für frühere Ausgaben/For the previous edition

Helen Bleck   Alexander Behrens   Joaquín Blasco

Anna Canning   Lynda Carey   Stuart Fortey

Helen Galloway   Steffen Krug   Elisabeth Lauer

Dörthe and Günther Lügenbuhl   Friedman Lux

Úna ní Chiosáin   Ruth Noble   Elaine O'Donoghue

Christina Reinicke   Stefan Rosenland   Veronika Schilling

Ingrid Schumacher   Alan Seaton   Liliane Seifert

Katerina Stein   Anna Stevenson   Patrick White

Preface

This dictionary has been designed as a reliable and user-friendly tool for use in all language situations. It provides accurate and up-to-date information on written and spoken German and English as they are used today.

Its 55,000 words and phrases and 80,000 translations give you access to German texts of all types. The dictionary aims to be as comprehensive as possible in a book of this size, and includes many proper names and abbreviations, as well as a selection of the most common terms from computing, business and current affairs.

Carefully constructed entries and a clear page design help you to find the translation that you are looking for fast. Examples (from basic constructions and common phrases to idioms) have been included to help put a word in context and give a clear picture of how it is used.

Vorbemerkung

Dieses Wörterbuch wurde als zuverlässiger und benutzerfreundlicher Begleiter für Schule, Beruf und Freizeit entwickelt. Es gibt schnell und präzise Auskunft über den aktuellen Wortschatz des Englischen und des Deutschen in seiner geschriebenen und gesprochenen Form.

55 000 Wörter und Ausdrücke mit ihren 80 000 Übersetzungen eröffnen den Zugang zu englischen Texten aller Art. Um dieses Nachschlagewerk innerhalb des vorgegebenen Umfangs so umfassend wie möglich zu gestalten, wurden zudem viele Eigennamen und Abkürzungen sowie eine Auswahl der gebräuchlichsten Begriffe aus den Bereichen EDV/Internet, Wirtschaft und Tagespolitik aufgenommen.

Mit großer Sorgfalt gestaltete Einträge und eine übersichtliche Seitengestaltung helfen dem Benutzer, die gesuchte Übersetzung schnell zu finden. Zusätzlich veranschaulichen zahlreiche Beispiele (von grammatischen Basiskonstruktionen und gebräuchlichen Kollokationen bis zu idiomatischen Wendungen) die Benutzung des betreffenden Wortes im Kontext.

Abkürzungen

Abbreviations

Akkusativ	A	accusative
Abkürzung	*abk /abbr*	abbreviation
abwertend	*abw*	pejorative
Adjektiv	*adj*	adjective
Verwaltung	ADMIN	administration
Adverb	*adv*	adverb
Flugwesen, Luftfahrt	AERON	aeronautics, aviation
Landwirtschaft	AGRIC	agriculture
amtssprachlich, formell	*amt*	official language
Anatomie	ANAT	anatomy
Archäologie	ARCHAEOL	archaeology
Architektur	ARCHIT	architecture
Astrologie	ASTROL	astrology
Astronomie	ASTRON	astronomy
Kfz-Technik	AUT(O)	automobile, cars
Hilfsverb	*aux*	auxiliary
Biologie	BIOL	biology
Botanik	BOT	botany
Chemie	CHEM	chemistry
Handel	COMM	commerce, business
ein zusammengestztes Substantiv bildend ein Substantiv, das zur näheren Bestimmung eines anderen dient z.B. **gardening** in **gardening book** oder **airforce** in **airforce base**	*comp*	compound-forming element a noun used to modify another noun, e.g. **gardening** in **gardening book** or **airforce** in **airforce base**
Komparativ	*compar*	comparative
Datenverarbeitung	COMPUT	computers
Konjunktion	*conj*	conjunction
Bauwesen	CONSTR	construction, building trade
Verlaufsform	*cont*	continuous
Kochkunst	CULIN	culinary, cooking
Dativ	D	dative
demonstrativ, hinweisend	*dem*	demonstrative
Determinant	*det*	determiner
Wirstschaft	ECON	economics
Datenverarbeitung	EDV	computers
eigentliche Bedeutung	*eigtl*	literal

Abkürzungen | | **Abbreviations**

Elektrotechnik	ELEKTR/ELEC	electricity, electronics
etwas	*etw*	something
Interjektion	*excl*	exclamation
Femininum	*f*	feminine
umgangssprachlich	*fam*	informal
übertragene Bedeutung	*fig*	figurative
Finanzen	FIN	finance, financial
Flugwesen, Luftfahrt	FLUG	aeronautics, aviation
gehoben	*fml*	formal
Fotografie	FOTO	photography
Fußball	FTBL	football
Genitiv	*G*	genitive
gehoben	*geh*	formal
generell	*gen*	generally
Geografie	GEOGR	geography, geographical
Geologie	GEOL	geology, geological
Geometrie	GEOM	geometry
Grammatik	GRAMM	grammar
Geschichte	HIST	history
humorvoll	*hum*	humerous
Industrie	IND	industry
unbestimmt	*indef*	indefinite
umgangssprachlich	*inf*	informal
Interjektion	*interj*	exclamation
unveränderlich	*inv*	invariable
ironisch	*iron*	ironic
jemand	*jd*	someone (nominative)
jemandem	*jm*	someone (dative)
jemanden	*jn*	someone (accusative)
jemandes	*js*	someone (genitive)
Komparativ	*kompar*	comparative
Konjunktion	*konj*	conjunction
Kochkunst	KÜCHE	culinary, cooking
Rechtswesen	LAW	law
Linguistik	LING	linguistics
eigentliche Bedeutung	*lit*	literal
Maskulinum	*m*	masculine noun
Mathematik	MATH	mathematics
Medizin	MED	medicine
Meteorologie	METEOR	weather, meteorology

Abkürzungen		Abbreviations
Militärwesen	MIL	military
Musik	MUS	music
Mythologie	MYTH	mythology
Schifffahrt	NAUT	navigation
Schifffahrt	NAVIG	nautical, maritime
Norddeutsch	*Norddt*	northern German
Neutrum	*nt*	neuter noun (countries and towns) not used with an article
Zahlwort	*num*	numeral
ohne Plural	*ohne pl*	uncountable noun
sich	*o.s.*	oneself
Ostdeutsch	*Ostdt*	East German
Österreichisch	*Österr*	Austrian German
abwertend	*pej*	pejorative
Perfekt	*perf*	perfect
persönlich	*pers*	personal
Fotografie	PHOT	photography
Redewendung(en)	*phr*	phrase(s)
Physik	PHYS	physics
Plural	*pl*	plural
Politik	POL	politics
besitzanzeigend	*poss*	possessive
Partizip Perfekt	*pp*	past participle
Präposition	*präp*	preposition
Präsens	*präs*	present
Präteritum	*prät*	preterite
Vorsilbe	*pref*	prefix
Präposition	*prep*	preposition
Pronomen	*pron*	pronoun
Psychologie	PSYCH	psychology, psychiatry
Vergangenheitsform	*pt*	past tense
Warenzeichen	®	registered trademark
Eisenbahn	RAIL	railways
Rechtswesen	RECHT	law
reflexives Verb	*ref*	reflexive verb
regelmäßig	*reg*	regular
Religion	RELIG	religion
Redewendung(en)	*RW*	phrase(s)

Abkürzungen

		Abbreviations
salopp	*salopp*	very informal
jemand	*sb*	someone, somebody
Subjekt	*sbj*	subject
Schifffahrt	SCHIFF	navigation
Schule	SCHULE/SCH	school
Schweizerdeutsch	*Schweiz*	Swiss German
Singular	*sg*	singular
Slang	*sl*	slang
Sport	SPORT	sport
Börse	ST EX	stock exchange
etwas	*sthg*	something
Süddeutsch	*Süddt*	southern German
Superlativ	*superl*	superlative
Technik, Technologie	TECH	technology
Telekommunikation, Fernmeldewesen	TELEKOMM/TELEC	telecommunications
Fernsehen	TV	television
Druckwesen	TYPO	printing
Plural	U	uncountable noun
britisches Englisch	UK	British English
Universität	UNIV	university
unregelmäßig	*unr*	irregular
unveränderlich	*unver*	invariable
amerikanisches Englisch	US	American English
Verb	*v/vb*	verb
intransitives Verb	*vi*	intransitive verb
unpersönliches Verb	*vimp/v impers*	impersonal verb
salopp	*vinf*	very informal
vor Substantiv	*vor Subst*	before noun
transitives Verb	*vt*	transitive verb
vulgär	*vulg*	vulgar
Wirtschaft	WIRTSCH	economics
Zoologie	ZOOL	zoology
kulturelle Entsprechung	≃	cultural equivalent
Trennbarkeit des deutschen Verbs	|	indicates separable German verb

Lautschrift

Deutsche Vokale

[a] Affe, Banane
[a:] Arzt, Antrag
[e] Beton
[e:] edel
[ɛ] echt, Händler
[ɛ:] Rätsel, Dessert
[ə] Aktie
[i:] Vier
[i] Radio
[ɪ] Winter
[o] Melodie
[o:] apropos
[ɔ] sollen
[ø] ökologisch
[ø:] Öl
[œ] Köchin, Pumps
[u] Kuvert, aktuell
[u:] Kuh
[ʊ] Kunst
[y] Büchse, System
[y:] Tür

Deutsche Diphthonge

[ai] Deichsel
[aʊ] Auge
[ɔy] EuroCity

Deutsche Nasale

[ã] Chanson
[ã:] Abonnement
[ɛ̃:] Pointe
[õ] Chanson

Halbvokale

Jubiläum [j]
Hardware [w]

Konsonanten

Baby [b]
ich [ç]
Achse, Kaviar [k]
Duett, Medien [d]

Phonetics

English vowels

[ɑ:] barn, car, laugh
[æ] pat, bag, mad
[ɒ] pot, log
[e] pet, tend
[ɜ:] burn, learn, bird
[ə] mother, suppose
[i:] bean, weed
[ɪ] pit, big, rid
[ɔ:] born, lawn
[u:] loop, loose
[ʌ] run, cut
[ʊ] put, full

English diphthongs

[aɪ] buy, light, aisle
[aʊ] now, shout, town
[eɪ] bay, late, great
[ɔɪ] boy, foil
[əʊ] no, road, blow
[ɪə] peer, fierce, idea
[eə] pair, bear, share
[ʊə] poor, sure, tour

Semi-vowels

you, spaniel
wet, why, twin

Consonants

bottle, bib

come, kitchen
dog, did

Lautschrift

Gin	[dʒ]	jet, fridge
Fantasie, Vier	[f]	fib, physical
Algerien, gut	[g]	gag, great
Hobby	[h]	how, perhaps
alphabetisch, Laser	[l]	little, help
Material, Alarm	[m]	metal, comb
November, Angabe	[n]	night, dinner
singen	[ŋ]	sung, parking
Pony, Pappe	[p]	pop, people
Apfel	[pf]	
Revue, rot	[r]	right, carry
Slalom, Soße	[s]	seal, peace
Stadion, Schule	[ʃ]	sheep, machine
Toast, Volt	[t]	train, tip
Konversation	[ts]	
Chili	[tʃ]	chain, wretched
	[θ]	think, fifth
	[ð]	this, with
Vase, Wagen	[v]	vine, livid
Macht, lachen	[x]	
Soße, Sonne	[z]	zip, his
Etage	[ʒ]	usual, measure

Phonetics

Die Betonung der deutschen Stichwörter wird mit einem Punkt für einen kurzen betonten Vokal (z.B. **Berg**) und mit einem Strich für einen langen betonten Vokal (z.B. **Magen**) angegeben.

German headwords have the stress marked either by a dot for a short stressed vowel (e.g. **Berg**) or by an underscore for a long stressed vowel (e.g. **Magen**).

Der Haupton eines englischen Wortes ist durch ein vorangestelltes ['] markiert, der Nebenton durch ein vorangestelltes [ˌ].

The symbol ['] indicates that the following syllable carries primary stress and the symbol [ˌ] that the following syllable carries secondary stress.

Das Zeichen [ʳ] zeigt in der englischen Phonetik an, dass der Endkonsonant „r" ausgesprochen wird, wenn das folgende Wort mit einem Vokal beginnt. Im amerikanischen Englisch wird dieses „r" so gut wie immer mitgesprochen.

The symbol [ʳ] in English phonetics indicates that the final "r" is pronounced only when followed by a word beginning with a vowel. Note that it is nearly always pronounced in American English.

Warenzeichen

Als Warenzeichen geschützte Wörter sind in diesem Wörterbuch durch das Zeichen ® gekennzeichnet. Die Markierung mit diesem Symbol, oder sein Fehlen, hat keinen Einfluss auf die Rechtskräftigkeit eines Warenzeichens.

Trademarks

Words considered to be trademarks have been designated in this dictionary by the symbol ®. However, neither the presence nor the absence of such designation should be regarded as affecting the legal status of any trademark.

Irregular English Verbs

Infinitive	Past Tense	Past Participle	Infinitive	Past Tense	Past Participle
arise	arose	arisen	drive	drove	driven
awake	awoke	awoken	eat	ate	eaten
be	was, were	been	fall	fell	fallen
			feed	fed	fed
bear	bore	born(e)	feel	felt	felt
beat	beat	beaten	fight	fought	fought
begin	began	begun	find	found	found
bend	bent	bent	fling	flung	flung
bet	bet/ betted	bet/ betted	fly	flew	flown
			forget	forgot	forgotten
bid	bid	bid	freeze	froze	frozen
bind	bound	bound	get	got	got
bite	bit	bitten			(*US* gotten)
bleed	bled	bled	give	gave	given
blow	blew	blown	go	went	gone
break	broke	broken	grind	ground	ground
breed	bred	bred	grow	grew	grown
bring	brought	brought	hang	hung/ hanged	hung/ hanged
build	built	built			
burn	burnt/ burned	burnt/ burned	have	had	had
			hear	heard	heard
burst	burst	burst	hide	hid	hidden
buy	bought	bought	hit	hit	hit
can	could	–	hold	held	held
cast	cast	cast	hurt	hurt	hurt
catch	caught	caught	keep	kept	kept
choose	chose	chosen	kneel	knelt/ kneeled	knelt/ kneeled
come	came	come			
cost	cost	cost	know	knew	known
creep	crept	crept	lay	laid	laid
cut	cut	cut	lead	led	led
deal	dealt	dealt	lean	leant/ leaned	leant/ leaned
dig	dug	dug			
do	did	done	leap	leapt/ leaped	leapt/ leaped
draw	drew	drawn			
dream	dreamed/ dreamt	dreamed/ dreamt	learn	learnt/ learned	learnt/ learned
drink	drank	drunk	leave	left	left

Infinitive	Past Tense	Past Participle	Infinitive	Past Tense	Past Participle
lend	lent	lent	sleep	slept	slept
let	let	let	slide	slid	slid
lie	lay	lain	sling	slung	slung
light	lit/ lighted	lit/ lighted	smell	smelt/ smelled	smelt/ smelled
lose	lost	lost	sow	sowed	sown/ sowed
make	made	made			
may	might	–	speak	spoke	spoken
mean	meant	meant	speed	sped/ speeded	sped / speeded
meet	met	met			
mow	mowed	mown/ mowed	spell	spelt/ spelled	spelt/ spelled
pay	paid	paid	spend	spent	spent
put	put	put	spill	spilt/ spilled	spilt/ spilled
quit	quit/ quitted	quit/ quitted	spin	spun	spun
read	read	read	spit	spat	spat
rid	rid	rid	split	split	split
ride	rode	ridden	spoil	spoiled/ spoilt	spoiled/ spoilt
ring	rang	rung			
rise	rose	risen	spread	spread	spread
run	ran	run	spring	sprang	sprung
saw	sawed	sawn	stand	stood	stood
say	said	said	steal	stole	stolen
see	saw	seen	stick	stuck	stuck
seek	sought	sought	sting	stung	stung
sell	sold	sold	stink	stank	stunk
send	sent	sent	strike	struck	struck/ stricken
set	set	set			
shake	shook	shaken	swear	swore	sworn
shall	should	–	sweep	swept	swept
shed	shed	shed	swell	swelled	swollen/ swelled
shine	shone	shone			
shoot	shot	shot	swim	swam	swum
show	showed	shown	swing	swung	swung
shrink	shrank	shrunk	take	took	taken
shut	shut	shut	teach	taught	taught
sing	sang	sung	tear	tore	torn
sink	sank	sunk	tell	told	told
sit	sat	sat	think	thought	thought

Infinitive	Past Tense	Past Participle	Infinitive	Past Tense	Past Participle
throw	threw	thrown	weep	wept	wept
tread	trod	trodden	win	won	won
wake	woke/ waked	woken/ waked	wind	wound	wound
			wring	wrung	wrung
wear	wore	worn			
weave	wove/ weaved	woven/ weaved			

Infinitiv	Präsens	Präteritum	Perfekt
beginnen	beginnt	begann	hat begonnen
beißen	beißt	biss	hat gebissen
bitten	bittet	bat	hat gebeten
bleiben	bleibt	blieb	ist geblieben
bringen	bringt	brachte	hat gebracht
denken	denkt	dachte	hat gedacht
dürfen	darf	durfte	hat gedurft/dürfen
essen	isst	aß	hat gegessen
fahren	fährt	fuhr	hat/ist gefahren
finden	findet	fand	hat gefunden
fliegen	fliegt	flog	hat/ist geflogen
fließen	fließt	floss	ist geflossen
geben	gibt	gab	hat gegeben
gehen	geht	ging	ist gegangen
gelten	gilt	galt	hat gegolten
geschehen	geschieht	geschah	ist geschehen
gießen	gießt	goss	hat gegossen
greifen	greift	griff	hat gegriffen
haben	hat	hatte	hat gehabt
halten	hält	hielt	hat gehalten
heben	hebt	hob	hat gehoben
heißen	heißt	hieß	hat geheißen
helfen	hilft	half	hat geholfen
kennen	kennt	kannte	hat gekannt
kommen	kommt	kam	ist gekommen
können	kann	konnte	hat können/gekonnt
lassen	lässt	ließ	hat gelassen/lassen
laufen	läuft	lief	hat/ist gelaufen
leihen	leiht	lieh	hat geliehen
lesen	liest	las	hat gelesen
liegen	liegt	lag	hat gelegen
lügen	lügt	log	hat gelogen
messen	misst	maß	hat gemessen
mögen	mag	mochte	hat gemocht/mögen
müssen	muss	musste	hat gemusst/müssen
nehmen	nimmt	nahm	hat genommen
nennen	nennt	nannte	hat genannt

Unregelmäßige deutsche Verben

Infinitiv	Präsens	Präteritum	Perfekt
raten	rät	riet	hat geraten
reißen	reißt	riss	hat/ist gerissen
rennen	rennt	rannte	ist gerannt
riechen	riecht	roch	hat gerochen
rufen	ruft	rief	hat gerufen
schieben	schiebt	schob	hat geschoben
schießen	schießt	schoss	hat/ist geschossen
schlafen	schläft	schlief	hat geschlafen
schlagen	schlägt	schlug	hat/ist geschlagen
schließen	schließt	schloss	hat geschlossen
schneiden	schneidet	schnitt	hat geschnitten
schreiben	schreibt	schrieb	hat geschrieben
schreien	schreit	schrie	hat geschrie(e)n
schwimmen	schwimmt	schwamm	hat/ist geschwommen
sehen	sieht	sah	hat gesehen
sein	ist	war	ist gewesen
singen	singt	sang	hat gesungen
sitzen	sitzt	saß	hat gesessen
sprechen	spricht	sprach	hat gesprochen
springen	springt	sprang	hat/ist gesprungen
stehen	steht	stand	hat gestanden
stehlen	stiehlt	stahl	hat gestohlen
sterben	stirbt	starb	ist gestorben
stoßen	stößt	stieß	hat/ist gestoßen
streiten	streitet	stritt	hat gestritten
tragen	trägt	trug	hat getragen
treffen	trifft	traf	hat getroffen
treten	tritt	trat	hat getreten
trinken	trinkt	trank	hat getrunken
tun	tut	tat	hat getan
verlieren	verliert	verlor	hat verloren
waschen	wäscht	wusch	hat gewaschen
werden	wird	wurde	ist geworden/worden
werfen	wirft	warf	hat geworfen
wissen	weiß	wusste	hat gewusst
wollen	will	wollte	hat gewollt/wollen

a, A (*pl a* ODER *-s*) [ɑː] *das* - **1.** [Buchstabe] a, A - **2.** MUS A.

Aal (*pl -e*) *der* eel.

aalglatt *adj abw* slippery.

a.a.O. (*abk für am angegebenen Ort*) loc. cit.

Aas (*pl -e* ODER *Äser*) *das* - **1.** (*pl Aase*) [Kadaver] carrion (*U*) - **2.** (*pl Äser*) *salopp abw* [Luder] devil; **kein Aas** *salopp* not a damned single person.

ab ⟷ *präp* (*+ D*) - **1.** [zeitlich] from; **ab 8 Uhr** from 8 o'clock; **ab 18 (Jahren)** over (the age of) 18 - **2.** [räumlich] from; **ab Werk** ex works; **9.30 ab Köln** leaving Cologne at 9.30 - **3.** [bei einer Reihenfolge] over; **Einkünfte ab 15 000 Euro** incomes over 15,000 euros. ⟷ *adv* - **1.** [räumlich] off; **weit ab gelegen** situated a long way away - **2.** [auffordernd] **ab ins Bett!** get to bed! - **3.** [elliptisch] off; **Hut ab!** *fig* hats off!; *siehe auch* **ab sein.** ⟶ **ab und zu, ab und an** *adv* now and then.

ab|arbeiten *vt* to work off.

Ablart *die* variety.

abartig *adj* deviant.

Abb. (*abk für Abbildung*) fig.

Abbau *der* (*ohne pl*) - **1.** [Demontage - von Bühne, Gerüst] taking down; [- von Maschine] dismantling - **2.** [Reduzierung] reduction - **3.** [beim Bergbau] mining - **4.** CHEM & BIOL breaking down.

ab|bauen ⟷ *vt* - **1.** [abbrechen - Kulissen, Bühne, Zelt] to take down; [- Maschine] to dismantle - **2.** [reduzieren] to reduce - **3.** CHEM & BIOL to break down - **4.** [beim Bergbau] to mine. ⟷ *vi* to go downhill.

ab|bekommen *vt* (*unreg*) - **1.** [Anteil, Partner, Prügel] to get; **Schaden abbekommen** to get damaged; **hast du etwas abbekommen?** [Verletzung] did you get hurt? - **2.** *fam* [Fleck] to get off.

ab|bestellen *vt* to cancel.

ab|bezahlen *vt* to pay off.

ab|biegen (*perf hat/ist abgebogen*) (*unreg*) ⟷ *vi* (*ist*) to turn off; **nach links/rechts abbiegen** to turn left/right. ⟷ *vt* (*hat*) [verhindern - Vorhaben] to avert; [- Thema] to change.

Ablbild *das* picture.

ab|bilden *vt* to depict.

Ablbildung *die* - **1.** [Bild] illustration - **2.** [Wiedergabe] depiction.

ab|binden *vt* (*unreg*) - **1.** [ausziehen] to undo - **2.** MED to ligature.

ab|blasen *vt* (*unreg*) *fam* to call off.

ab|blättern (*perf ist abgeblättert*) *vi* to flake off.

ab|blenden ⟷ *vt* - **1.** [Lampe] to screen - **2.** [Scheinwerfer] to dip *UK*, to dim *US*. ⟷ *vi* - **1.** FOTO to stop down - **2.** AUTO to dip *UK* ODER dim *US* one's headlights.

Abblendllicht *das* dipped *UK* ODER dimmed *US* headlights *Pl.*

ab|blitzen (*perf ist abgeblitzt*) *vi fam:* **bei jm abblitzen** to get short shrift from sb.

ab|blocken *vt* to block.

ab|brechen (*perf hat/ist abgebrochen*) (*unreg*) ⟷ *vt* (*hat*) - **1.** [Stück, Ast] to break off; [Bleistift] to break - **2.** [Vorhaben, Beziehungen, Reise, Studium] to break off; [Streik] to call off. ⟷ *vi* - **1.** (*hat*) [im Gespräch] to break off - **2.** (*ist*) [Geräusch] to stop.

ab|brennen (*perf hat/ist abgebrannt*) (*unreg*) ⟷ *vt* (*hat*) - **1.** [Haus] to burn down - **2.** [Feuerwerk] to let off. ⟷ *vi* (*ist*) to burn down.

ab|bringen *vt* (*unreg*): **jn von seiner Meinung abbringen** to make sb change his/her mind; **jn davon abbringen, aus dem Fenster zu**

springen to stop sb from jumping out of the window; **das bringt uns vom Thema ab** we're getting off the subject.

ab|bröckeln (perf ist **abgebröckelt**) vi to flake off.

Ab|bruch der - **1.** [Ende] breaking off; **einer Sache** (D) **keinen Abbruch tun** fig not to harm sthg - **2.** [Zerstörung] demolition.

abbruchreif adj fit only for demolition.

ab|buchen vt WIRTSCH: **abbuchen (von)** to debit (to).

Abc [a(:)be(:)'tse:] das ABC.

ab|danken vi to abdicate.

ab|decken vt - **1.** [gen] to cover - **2.** [abräumen - Tisch] to clear; [- Dach] to take off.

Abdeckung (pl -en) die - **1.** [zum Schutz] cover - **2.** WIRTSCH covering.

ab|dichten vt [gegen kalte Luft] to insulate; [gegen Wasser] to waterproof; [Gefäß] to make airtight; [Fenster] to draughtproof.

Abdichtung die [gegen kalte Luft] insulation; [gegen Wasser] waterproofing; [von Fenster] draughtproofing; [von Gefäß] making airtight.

ab|drehen (perf **hat/ist abgedreht**) <> vt (hat) - **1.** [Wasser, Gas] to turn off - **2.** [Knopf, Schraube] to twist off - **3.** FILM [Szene] to shoot. <> vi (hat, ist) [den Kurs ändern] to turn away.

Abdruck (pl -**drücke**) der - **1.** [Spur] imprint - **2.** [Druck] printing.

ab|drucken vt to print.

ab|drücken <> vt [abquetschen] to constrict; **jm die Luft abdrücken** to squeeze the breath out of sb. <> vi [schießen] to pull the trigger.
 ➡ **sich abdrücken** ref to leave an impression.

Abend (pl -e) der evening; **am Abend** in the evening; **gestern/heute/morgen Abend** yesterday/this/tomorrow evening; **guten Abend!** good evening!; **zu Abend essen** to have one's dinner ODER evening meal; **bunter Abend** social evening.

Abend|brot das cold supper.

Abend|essen das dinner, evening meal.

Abend|kasse die box office (where tickets may only be bought immediately before performance).

Abend|kurs der evening class.

abendlich adj evening (vor Subst).

Abend|mahl das RELIG (Holy) Communion.

Abend|programm das evening programmes Pl ODER viewing (U).

abends adv in the evening; **spätabends** late in the evening.

Abenteuer (pl -) das - **1.** [Erlebnis] adventure - **2.** [Wagnis] venture - **3.** [Liebesverhältnis] affair.

abenteuerlich adj - **1.** [waghalsig] adventurous - **2.** [fantastisch] fantastic.

Abenteurer, in (mpl -, fpl -nen) der, die adventurer.

aber <> konj but. <> adv: **das ist aber nett!** how nice!; **aber gerne!** of course!; **aber immer!** fam sure!; **jetzt ist aber Schluss!** that's enough now!; **du kommst aber spät!** you're a bit late, aren't you?

Aber|glaube, -n der superstition.

abergläubisch adj superstitious.

ab|fahren (perf **hat/ist abgefahren**) (unreg) <> vi (ist) [losfahren] to leave; [Zug] to depart, to leave; **auf jn/etw abfahren** fam fig to be into sb/sthg. <> vt (hat) - **1.** [Ladung] to take away - **2.** [Strecke] to go over - **3.** [Reifen] to wear down - **4.** [Fahrkarte] to get full use out of.

Ab|fahrt die - **1.** [Start] departure; **Vorsicht bei der Abfahrt des Zuges!** stand clear of the doors, the train is about to depart! - **2.** [Autobahnabfahrt] exit - **3.** [Skiabfahrt] descent.

Abfahrts|zeit die departure time.

Ab|fall der - **1.** [Hausmüll] refuse; [industriell] waste - **2.** (ohne pl) [Rückgang] drop, fall.

Abfall|beseitigung die waste disposal.

ab|fallen (perf ist **abgefallen**) vi (unreg) - **1.** [herunterfallen] to fall off - **2.** [übrig bleiben] to be left over; **was fällt für mich ab?** what do I get out of it? - **3.** [schlechter sein]: **gegen jn/etw abfallen** to suffer by comparison with sb/sthg - **4.** [sich neigen] to slope (down) - **5.** [sich verringern] to drop, to fall.

abfällig <> adj disparaging. <> adv disparagingly.

ab|fangen vt (unreg) - **1.** [Brief, Anruf, Transport] to intercept - **2.** [Person] to catch - **3.** [Schlag] to ward off - **4.** [Flugzeug] to regain control of.

ab|färben vi to run; **auf jn/etw abfärben** fig to rub off on sb/sthg.

ab|fassen vt to write.

ab|fertigen vt - **1.** [Waren] to prepare for dispatch; [Gepäck] to check in; [Schiff, Flugzeug] to prepare for departure - **2.** [Passagier, Antragsteller] to attend to.

Ab|fertigung die - **1.** [von Gepäck] check-in; [von Waren] preparation for dispatch; [von Schiff, Flugzeug] preparation for departure - **2.** [von Passagier, Antragssteller] attending to.

ab|feuern vt [Gewehr, Schuss] to fire; [Rakete] to launch.

ab|finden vt (unreg) [entschädigen]: **jn mit etw abfinden** to give sb sthg in compensation. ➡ **sich abfinden** ref: **sich mit etw abfinden** to come to terms with sthg.

Abfindung (pl -en) die [für einen Verlust] compensation; [für die vorzeitige Entlassung] severance pay.

ab|fliegen (perf ist **abgeflogen**) vi (unreg) to take off.

abl|fließen (*perf* ist **abgeflossen**) *vi* (*unreg*) [Spülwasser] to drain away; [Regenwasser] to run away.

Abl|flug *der* - **1.** [von Flugzeug] take-off - **2.** [Flughafenbereich] departures (*U*).

Abfluss (*pl* -flüsse) *der* - **1.** [Öffnung - von Waschbecken, Dusche] plughole - **2.** [von Kapital] flight - **3.** [von Spülwasser] draining away; [von Regenwasser] running away.

abl|fragen *vt* to call up; **jn (etw) abfragen** to test sb (on sthg).

Abfuhr (*pl* -en) *die*: **jm eine Abfuhr erteilen** to rebuff sb.

abl|führen ◇ *vt* - **1.** [festnehmen] to take away - **2.** [vom Thema] to lead away. ◇ *vi* MED to act as a laxative.

Abführl|mittel *das* laxative.

abl|füllen *vt* - **1.** [Flüssigkeit]: **Wein in Flaschen abfüllen** to bottle wine - **2.** [Flaschen, Säcke] to fill - **3.** *fam* [betrunken machen]: **jn abfüllen** to get sb plastered.

Abgabe (*pl* -n) *die* - **1.** [Übergabe - von Gutachten] handing over; [- von Arbeit] handing in - **2.** [von Stimmen] casting - **3.** [Verkauf] sale - **4.** [von Ball] passing - **5.** [von Wärme, Sauerstoff] giving off. ⬥ **Abgaben** *Pl* [Steuern] taxes.

abgabenfrei *adj* exempt from tax.

abgabenpflichtig *adj* taxable.

Abgangs|zeugnis *das* leaving certificate.

Abgase *Pl* exhaust fumes.

abl|geben *vt* (*unreg*) - **1.** [abliefern - Brief, Geschenk] to hand over; [- Arbeit] to hand in; [- an der Garderobe] to leave - **2.** [verkaufen] to sell - **3.** [teilen]: **jm etw abgeben** to give sb sthg - **4.** [äußern - Erklärung] to make; [- Meinung] to give; [- Stimme] to cast - **5.** [abtreten] to give up - **6.** [darstellen - Figur] to cut; **einen guten Vater abgeben** to make a good father - **7.** SPORT [werfen] to pass - **8.** [ausströmen] to give off - **9.** [abfeuern] to fire. ⬥ **sich abgeben** *ref*: **sich mit etw (nicht) abgeben** (not) to concern o.s. with sthg; **sie gibt sich mit ganz obskuren Typen ab** she mixes with some really dubious types.

abgebrüht *adj* *fam* hard-boiled, tough.

abgedroschen *adj* well-worn, hackneyed.

abl|gehen (*perf* ist **abgegangen**) (*unreg*) ◇ *vi* - **1.** [sich lösen] to come off - **2.** [verlassen]: **von etw abgehen** to leave sthg - **3.** [abfahren] to leave, to depart - **4.** [abgeschickt werden] to go off - **5.** [abgerechnet werden] to be taken off ODER deducted - **6.** [abzweigen] to branch off - **7.** [abweichen]: **von seiner Meinung abgehen** to change one's mind; **von seinen Forderungen abgehen** to drop one's demands - **8.** [verlaufen] to go; **es ist gut abgegangen** it went well; **es geht ab** *salopp* things are really buzzing - **9.** [fehlen]: **ihm geht jedes Feingefühl ab**

he lacks any sensitivity, he has no sensitivity. ◇ *vt* [Strecke, Straße] to walk along; [Grundstück] to walk over.

abgekämpft *adj* worn-out.

abgekartet *adj*: **ein abgekartetes Spiel** a put-up job.

abgelegen *adj* remote.

abgemacht *adj* settled; **abgemacht!** it's a deal!

abgemagert *adj* emaciated.

abgeneigt *adj*: **einer Sache (D) (nicht) abgeneigt sein** (not) to be opposed to sthg.

abgenutzt *adj* [Türgriff, Fußboden] worn; [Gerät] worn-out.

Abgeordnete (*pl* -n) *der, die* [im Bundestag] member of parliament; [im Landtag] representative.

Abl|gesandte *der, die* envoy.

abgeschieden *adj* remote.

Abgeschiedenheit *die* remoteness.

abgesehen *adv*: **abgesehen von jm/etw** apart from sb/sthg. ⬥ **abgesehen davon, dass** *konj* apart from the fact that.

abgespannt *adj* exhausted.

abgestanden *adj* [Bier] flat; [Luft] stale; [Wasser] stagnant.

abgestorben ◇ *pp* ▷ **absterben**. ◇ *adj* - **1.** [Baum, Ast] dead - **2.** [Fuß, Bein] numb.

abgestumpft *adj* - **1.** [gefühllos] hardened - **2.** [apathisch] apathetic.

abgetragen *adj* worn-out.

abl|gewinnen *vt* (*unreg*): **jm etw abgewinnen** to win sthg from sb; **einer Sache (D) Geschmack abgewinnen** to acquire a taste for sthg.

abl|gewöhnen *vt*: **jm etw abgewöhnen** to get sb to give sthg up; **sich (D) etw abgewöhnen** to give sthg up.

abl|grenzen *vt* - **1.** [abtrennen - mit Zaun] to fence off; [- mit Mauer] to wall off - **2.** [unterscheiden] to differentiate. ⬥ **sich abgrenzen** *ref*: **sich von jm/etw abgrenzen** to distance o.s. from sb/sthg.

Abgrenzung (*pl* -en) *die* - **1.** [Grenze] boundary - **2.** [Definition] definition.

Abl|grund *der* abyss; **vor dem Abgrund stehen** *fig* to be on the edge of the abyss.

abgrundtief ◇ *adj* profound, deep. ◇ *adv* profoundly, deeply.

abl|gucken *vt* *fam* to copy; **etw von** ODER **bei jm abgucken** to copy sthg from sb.

abl|hacken *vt* to chop off.

abl|haken *vt* to check off.

abl|halten *vt* (*unreg*) - **1.** [veranstalten] to hold - **2.** [fern halten]: **jn von etw abhalten** to keep sb from sthg.

abhanden *adv*: **mir ist meine Brille abhanden gekommen** my glasses have gone missing.

Ab|handlung *die* treatise.

Ab|hang *der* slope.

ab|hängen ◇ *vt (reg)* - **1.** [Bild] to take down - **2.** [Anhänger, Wagon] to uncouple - **3.** [Konkurrenten, Verfolger] to shake off. ◇ *vi (unreg)* - **1.**: **von jm/etw abhängen** to depend on sb/sthg - **2.** *fam* [sich entspannen] to chill (out).

abhängig *adj*: **von etw abhängig sein** [von Wetter, Geschmack, Zufall] to depend on sthg; [von Hilfe, Vormund] to be dependent on sthg; [von Drogen] to be addicted to sthg.

Abhängigkeit *(pl -en) die* - **1.** [gen] dependence; **Abhängigkeit von etw** dependence on sthg - **2.** [von Drogen] addiction.

ab|härten ◇ *vt* to toughen up. ◇ *vi*: **dieses Wetter härtet ab** this weather toughens you up. ◆ **sich abhärten** *ref* to toughen (o.s.) up.

ab|hauen *(perf ist abgehauen) vi fam* [verschwinden] to clear off.

ab|heben *(unreg)* ◇ *vt* - **1.** [vom Konto] to withdraw - **2.** [am Telefon] to pick up - **3.** [beim Kartenspiel] to cut. ◇ *vi* [abfliegen] to take off. ◆ **sich abheben** *ref*: **sich von jm/etw** *ODER* **gegen jn/etw abheben** to stand out against sb/sthg.

ab|heften *vt* to file away.

ab|hetzen *vt* to drive hard. ◆ **sich abhetzen** *ref* to rush one's socks off.

Abhilfe *die*: **Abhilfe schaffen** to take remedial action.

ab|holen *vt* [Paket, Ware] to collect; [Person] to pick up.

ab|holzen *vt* [Wald, Allee] to clear; [Bäume] to cut down.

ab|hören *vt* - **1.** [heimlich anhören - Gespräch] to listen in on; [- Telefon] to tap - **2.** [abfragen] to test; **jm etw abhören** to test sb on sthg - **3.** [abhorchen] to sound.

Abi *(pl -s) das abk für* **Abitur**.

Abitur *(pl -e) das* ≃ A levels *Pl UK*, ≃ SATs *US*, *final examination at a German "Gymnasium", qualifying pupils for university entrance.*

Abitur|feier *die party at end of school studies.*

Abiturient, in [abituri'ɛnt, ɪn] *(mpl -en, fpl -nen) der, die pupil who is taking/has taken the "Abitur".*

Abitur|zeugnis *das certificate awarded to a pupil who has passed the "Abitur".*

ab|kapseln ◆ **sich abkapseln** *ref* to cut o.s. off.

ab|kaufen *vt* - **1.** [kaufen]: **jm etw abkaufen** to buy sthg from sb - **2.** *fam* [glauben]: **diese Geschichte kaufe ich dir nicht ab!** I'm not buying that story (of yours)!

ab|klappern *vt fam*: **etw (nach etw) abklappern** to scour sthg (for sthg).

ab|klingen *(perf ist abgeklungen) vi (unreg)* [Fieber] to die down.

ab|knöpfen *vt*: **jm etw abknöpfen** to get sthg out of sb.

ab|kochen *vt* to sterilize *(by boiling)*.

ab|kommen *(perf ist abgekommen) vi (unreg)*: **von etw abkommen** [Kurs, Weg] to deviate from sthg; [Thema] to get off sthg; [Gewohnheit, Vorhaben] to give sthg up, to abandon sthg.

Abkommen *(pl -) das* agreement.

abkömmlich *adj* available.

ab|können *vt (unreg) salopp*: **ich kann ihn/es nicht ab** I can't stand *ODER* stick *UK* him/it.

ab|kriegen *vt fam* - **1.** [gen] to get; **das Auto hat was abgekriegt** the car got damaged; **einen/eine abkriegen** to get a man/woman - **2.** [Deckel, Schraube, Fleck] to get off.

ab|kühlen *(perf hat/ist abgekühlt) vi* - **1.** [Temperatur] to cool down - **2.** [Stimmung, Engagement] to cool. ◆ **sich abkühlen** *ref* [Person] to cool down *ODER* off; [Verhältnis] to cool; **es hat sich abgekühlt** it has got cooler.

Abkühlung *die* cooling.

ab|kürzen *vt* - **1.** [Weg]: **den Weg abkürzen** to take a short cut - **2.** [Wort] to abbreviate - **3.** [Besuch, Reise] to cut short; [Verfahren] to shorten.

Ab|kürzung *die* - **1.** [von Weg] short cut - **2.** [von Wörtern] abbreviation.

ab|laden *vt (unreg)* - **1.** [abräumen] to unload - **2.** [erzählen]: **seinen Kummer bei jm abladen** to unburden o.s. to sb.

Ab|lage *die* - **1.** [für Papiere, Akten] filing cabinet - **2.** [Abheften] filing.

Ab|lagerung *die* [Sediment] deposit.

ab|lassen *(unreg)* ◇ *vt* - **1.** [Luft] to let out - **2.** [Wasser] to drain off. ◇ *vi*: **von jm ablassen** [in Ruhe lassen] to leave sb alone; **von etw ablassen** [aufgeben] to give sthg up.

Ab|lauf *der* - **1.** [Verlauf] course; **um den friedlichen Ablauf der Veranstaltung zu gewährleisten** to ensure that the event passes off peacefully - **2.** [Abfluss] drain; [Rinne] outlet - **3.** [Ende] expiry.

ab|legen ◇ *vt* - **1.** [Mantel] to take off - **2.** [sich abgewöhnen] to get rid of - **3.** [Eid, Prüfung] to take - **4.** [Akten] to file. ◇ *vi* - **1.** [Garderobe] to take one's coat/hat/etc off - **2.** [Schiff] to cast off.

Ableger *(pl -) der* - **1.** [von Pflanzen] cutting - **2.** [Filiale] subsidiary.

ab|lehnen *vt* - **1.** [Angebot, Vorschlag] to reject; [Einladung] to refuse, to turn down - **2.** [Rauschgift, Schusswaffen] to disapprove of.

Ablehnung *(pl -en) die* - **1.** [von Angebot] rejection; [von Einladung] refusal; **auf Ablehnung stoßen** to be rejected - **2.** [Missbilligung] disapproval.

ab|leisten *vt*: **den Wehrdienst ableisten** to do one's military service.

ab|leiten *vt* - 1. [Rauch, Gas] to draw off - 2. [folgern, zurückführen]: **etw von** ODER **aus etw ableiten** [Wort, Recht] to derive sthg from sthg - 3. [Gleichung] to differentiate.

Ab|leitung *die* - 1. [von Rauch, Gas] drawing off - 2. [von Wort, Formel] derivation.

ab|lenken *vt* - 1. [zerstreuen] to distract; **jn von der Arbeit ablenken** to put sb off their work - 2. [Aufmerksamkeit, Verdacht] to divert - 3. [weglenken - Angriff] to ward off; [- Bewegung] to deflect.

Ab|lenkung *(pl* -en) *die* - 1. [Zerstreuung] distraction - 2. [Richtungsänderung] deflection.

ab|lesen *vt (unreg)* - 1. [lesen] to read out - 2. [den Stand feststellen] to read - 3. [erraten]: **er liest ihr jeden Wunsch von den Augen ab** he can always tell what she wants from the look in her eyes.

ab|liefern *vt* to deliver.

ab|lösen *vt* - 1. [ersetzen] to take over from - 2. [abmachen] to take off. **⇔ sich ablösen** *ref* - 1. [sich abwechseln] to take turns - 2. [abgehen] to come off.

Ab|lösung *die* - 1. [Zahlung] paying off - 2. [Ersatzperson] relief.

ab|luchsen ['aplʊksn] *vt*: **jm etw abluchsen** to get sthg out of sb.

ABM [ɑːˈbeːˈʔɛm] *(pl* -) *(abk für* **Arbeitsbeschaffungsmaßnahme)** *die* job creation scheme.

ab|machen *vt* - 1. [entfernen] to take off - 2. [verabreden] to agree on; **einen Termin abmachen** to make an appointment.

Ab|machung *(pl* -en) *die* agreement.

ab|magern *(perf* ist **abgemagert)** *vi* to get thinner.

Ab|marsch *der* departure.

ab|marschieren *(perf* ist **abmarschiert)** *vi* [bei Wandern] to set off; MIL to march off.

ab|melden *vt* - 1. [Personen]: **ein Kind von der Schule abmelden** to give notice of a child's removal from school; **sie ist bei mir abgemeldet** *fam fig* I've had it ODER I'm through with her - 2. [Gegenstände - Telefon] to have disconnected; [- Auto] to take off the road. **⇔ sich abmelden** *ref*: **sich polizeilich abmelden** to notify the police that one is moving away; **sich bei einem Verein abmelden** to cancel one's membership of a club.

Ab|meldung *die* - 1. [beim Einwohnermeldeamt] *notification that one is moving away* - 2. [von der Schule] *notification of a child's removal from school.*

ab|messen *vt (unreg)* to measure.

ABM-|Stelle *die* job created as part of a job creation scheme.

ab|mühen ⇔ sich abmühen *ref* to struggle.

ab|nehmen *(unreg)* ◇ *vt* - 1. [herunternehmen - Vorhänge, Wäsche] to take down; [- Hut, Deckel] to take off; [- Hörer] to pick up - 2. [wegnehmen]: **jm etw abnehmen** to take sthg (away) from sb - 3. [entlasten]: **jm etw abnehmen** to relieve sb of sthg - 4. [kontrollieren] to inspect - 5. [kaufen]: **jm etw abnehmen** to buy sthg from sb - 6. [glauben]: **das nimmt dir keiner ab!** nobody will buy that! - 7. [entgegennehmen - Prüfung] to conduct; **jm ein Versprechen abnehmen** to make sb give a promise - 8. [amputieren]: **jm einen Finger abnehmen** to take sb's finger off - 9. [entnehmen]: **jm Blut abnehmen** to take sb's blood - 10. [verlieren - Gewicht] to lose. ◇ *vi* - 1. [leichter werden] to lose weight - 2. [sich verringern - Temperatur, Luftdruck, Ressourcen] to decrease; [- Mond] to wane.

Abnehmer, in *(mpl* -, *fpl* -nen) *der, die* buyer.

Ab|neigung *die* aversion.

ab|nutzen, abnützen *vt* to wear out. **⇔ sich abnutzen, sich abnützen** *ref* to wear out.

Abo *(pl* -s) *das fam abk für* **Abonnement**.

Abonnement [abɔnəˈmãː] *(pl* -s) *das* - 1. [einer Zeitung] subscription - 2. [im Theater] season ticket.

abonnieren *vt* to subscribe to.

ab|packen *vt* to pre-pack.

ab|passen *vt* - 1. [Person] to catch - 2. [Moment] to wait for.

ab|pflücken *vt* to pick.

ab|prallen *(perf* ist **abgeprallt)** *vi* - 1. [zurückspringen - Ball] to bounce back, to rebound; [- Kugel] to ricochet - 2. [Vorwurf, Worte]: **an jm** ODER **von jm abprallen** to make no impression on sb.

ab|putzen *vt* to wipe.

ab|quälen ⇔ sich abquälen *ref* [sich plagen]: **sich mit etw abquälen** to struggle with sthg.

ab|raten *vi (unreg)*: **(jm) von etw abraten** to advise (sb) against sthg.

ab|räumen *vt* [Geschirr] to clear away; [Tisch] to clear.

ab|reagieren *vt*: **etw an jm abreagieren** to take sthg out on sb. **⇔ sich abreagieren** *ref*: **sich an jm abreagieren** to take it out on sb.

ab|rechnen ◇ *vi* [Kassiererin] to cash up; **mit jm abrechnen** [zahlen] to settle up with sb; [sich rächen] to get even with sb. ◇ *vt* [abziehen] to deduct.

Ab|rechnung *die* - 1. [Bilanz, Rechnung] accounts *Pl* - 2. [Rache] reckoning.

ab|reiben *vt (unreg)* - 1. [Schmutz] to rub off - 2. [Hände] to wipe - 3. [Kind, Hund] to rub down.

Abreibung *(pl* -en) *die* thrashing.

Ab|reise *die* departure.

ab|reisen *(perf ist abgereist) vi* to depart.

ab|reißen *(perf hat/ist abgerissen) (unreg)* <> *vt (hat)* - 1. [Papier] to tear off - 2. [Haus] to pull down. <> *vi (ist)* - 1. [Teil, Knopf, Etikett] to come off; [Faden] to break off - 2. [Kontakt] to break off.

ab|richten *vt* to train.

ab|riegeln *vt* - 1. [verschließen] to bolt - 2. [Gelände] to cordon off.

Abriss *(pl -e) der* - 1. [Zerstörung] demolition - 2. [Darstellung] outline.

ab|rollen *(perf hat/ist abgerollt)* <> *vt (hat)* [abspulen] to unwind. <> *vi (ist)* - 1. [von einer Rolle] to unwind - 2. [ablaufen] to go - 3. SPORT to go into a roll.

ab|rücken *(perf hat/ist abgerückt)* <> *vt (hat)* to move away. <> *vi (ist)* [wegrücken]: **von jm/etw abrücken** [sich entfernen] to move away from sb/sthg; [sich distanzieren] to distance o.s. from sb/sthg.

Abruf *der* EDV retrieval. ◆ **auf Abruf** *adv*: **auf Abruf bereitstehen** to be standing by.

ab|rufen *vt (unreg)* EDV to retrieve.

ab|runden *vt* - 1. [Zahl, Summe] to round down - 2. [Ecke, Küche, Programm] to round off.

abrupt <> *adj* abrupt. <> *adv* abruptly.

ab|rüsten <> *vi* to disarm. <> *vt* to get rid of.

Abrüstung *die* disarmament.

ab|rutschen *(perf ist abgerutscht) vi* - 1. [wegrutschen] to slip - 2. [Schüler]: **er ist in Mathematik abgerutscht** his marks in mathematics have gone down.

ab|sacken *(perf ist abgesackt) vi* - 1. [sinken - Flugzeug, Druck] to drop; [- Gebäude] to subside - 2. [Leistung]: **sie ist in Chemie abgesackt** her marks in chemistry have got worse.

Ab|sage *die* - 1. [von Termin, Veranstaltung] cancellation - 2. [Zurückweisung]: **jm/einer Sache eine Absage erteilen** to reject sb/sthg.

ab|sagen <> *vt* to cancel. <> *vi* to cancel.

ab|sägen *vt* - 1. [sägen - Baum] to saw down; [- Brett] to saw off - 2. *fam* [entlassen] to axe.

ab|sahnen *fam* <> *vt* to cream off. <> *vi* to make a killing.

Ab|satz *der* - 1. [von Schuhen] heel - 2. [Verkauf] sales *Pl* - 3. [im Text] paragraph.

ab|saufen *(perf ist abgesoffen) vi (unreg)* - 1. *salopp* [im Wasser - Schiff] to go to the bottom; [- Person] to go to a watery grave - 2. *fam* [Motor] to flood.

ab|schaffen *vt* - 1. [Regelung] to abolish - 2. [aufheben] to do away with - 3. [weggeben] to get rid of.

ab|schalten *vi* & *vt* [ausschalten] to switch off.

ab|schätzen *vt* - 1. [Menge, Zahl] to estimate - 2. [Menschen] to weigh up.

Abscheu *die* ODER *der* disgust, revulsion.

abscheulich <> *adj* disgusting. <> *adv* disgustingly.

ab|schicken *vt* to post UK, to mail US.

ab|schieben *(perf hat/ist abgeschoben) (unreg)* <> *vt (hat)* - 1. [außer Landes] to deport - 2. *fam* [versetzen] to shunt off. <> *vi (ist) salopp abw* [fortgehen] to push off.

Abschied *(pl -e) der* - 1. [Trennung, Weggehen] parting; **von jm/etw Abschied nehmen** to say goodbye to sb/sthg - 2. [Entlassung] resignation; **seinen Abschied nehmen** to resign.

ab|schießen *vt (unreg)* - 1. [Flugzeug] to shoot down - 2. [Kugel, Gewehr] to fire; [Pfeil] to shoot; [Rakete] to launch - 3. [töten] to shoot - 4. [Körperteil]: **ihm ist ein Bein abgeschossen worden** his leg has been shot off - 5. *fam* [entlassen]: **jn abschießen** to give sb the boot, to kick sb out.

ab|schirmen *vt* to shield.

ab|schlachten *vt fam* to slaughter.

ab|schlagen *vt (unreg)* - 1. [verweigern]: **jm etw abschlagen** to refuse sb sthg - 2. [abtrennen - durch Schneiden] to chop off; [- durch Schlagen] to knock off.

abschlägig <> *adj* unfavourable. <> *adv*: **etw abschlägig bescheiden** to refuse sthg.

Abschlepp|dienst *der* (vehicle) recovery service.

ab|schleppen *vt* - 1. [Auto, Schiff] to tow away - 2. *fam* [Person] to pick up.

Abschlepp|seil *das* towrope.

ab|schließen *(unreg)* <> *vt* - 1. [Tür] to lock - 2. [Tätigkeit] to finish - 3. [Geschäft] to conclude; [Vertrag] to sign; [Versicherung] to take out - 4. WIRTSCH to balance. <> *vi* [mit etw enden]: **mit etw abschließen** to finish with sthg; **mit der Vergangenheit abschließen** to draw a line under the past; **mit Verlust abschließen** to show a loss.

abschließend <> *adj* concluding. <> *adv* in conclusion.

Abschluss *(pl Abschlüsse) der* - 1. [Ende] end; **zum Abschluss der Tagung spricht Professor Schulz** Professor Schulz will bring the conference to a close - 2. [von Geschäft] conclusion; [von Vertrag] signing; [von Versicherung] taking out - 3. [Abschlusszeugnis von Hochschule] degree.

Abschluss|zeugnis *(pl -zeugnisse) das* school-leaving certificate.

ab|schmecken *vt* - 1. [würzen] to season - 2. [kosten] to taste.

ab|schmieren <> *vt* - 1. [Motor] to lubricate; [Fahrradkette] to grease - 2. *fam* [abschreiben] to crib. <> *vi fam* [Flugzeug] to nosedive; [Computer, Programm] to crash.

ab|schminken *vt*: **jn abschminken** to remove sb's make-up. ◆ **sich abschminken** *ref*: **sich abschminken** to remove one's make-up.

ab|schnallen (*perf* hat/ist abgeschnallt) *vt* (*hat*) to unfasten. ◆ **sich abschnallen** *ref* to unfasten one's seatbelt.

ab|schneiden (*unreg*) ◇ *vt* - **1.** [Stück] to cut off - **2.** [Weg]: **jm den Weg abschneiden** to block sb's way - **3.** [Wort]: **jm das Wort abschneiden** to cut sb off. ◇ *vi*: **gut/schlecht abschneiden** to do well/badly.

Ab|schnitt *der* - **1.** [im Text, von Strecke] section - **2.** [von Formular, Karte] detachable portion; [von Scheck] counterfoil; [von Eintrittskarte] stub - **3.** [Zeitraum] period - **4.** MATH segment.

ab|schrauben *vt* to unscrew.

ab|schrecken *vt* - **1.** [abhalten] to deter - **2.** [mit kaltem Wasser - Eier] to put into cold water.

Abschreckung (*pl* -en) *die* deterrent.

ab|schreiben *vt* (*unreg*) - **1.** [kopieren] to copy - **2.** WIRTSCH [aufgeben] to write off.

Ab|schrift *die* copy.

Abschuss (*pl* -schüsse) *der* - **1.** [von Flugzeug] shooting down - **2.** [von Gewehr] firing; [von Rakete] launching - **3.** [von Wild] shooting.

abschüssig *adj* sloping.

ab|schütteln *vt eigtl* & *fig* to shake off.

ab|schwächen *vt* to lessen. ◆ **sich abschwächen** *ref* to grow weaker.

ab|schweifen (*perf* ist abgeschweift) *vi* [Gedanken, Blick] to wander; **vom Thema abschweifen** to digress.

ab|schwellen (*perf* ist abgeschwollen) *vi* (*unreg*) - **1.** [Schwellung] to go down - **2.** [Geräusch] to fade (away).

absehbar *adj* foreseeable; **in absehbarer Zeit** in the foreseeable future.

ab|sehen (*unreg*) ◇ *vt* [Folgen] to foresee; **das Ergebnis ist abzusehen** it's possible to tell what the result will be. ◇ *vi* - **1.** [verzichten]: **von etw absehen** to refrain from sthg - **2.** [ausnehmen]: **sieht man davon ab, dass er taub ist, ist er kerngesund** if you ignore the fact that he's deaf, he's perfectly healthy - **3.** [wollen]: **es auf etw (A) abgesehen haben** to be after sthg; **es darauf abgesehen haben, alle zu verärgern** to be intent on annoying everyone - **4.** [ärgern]: **es auf jn abgesehen haben** to have it in for sb.

ab|seifen *vt* [Kind] to soap down.

ab|seilen *vt* to lower down on a rope. ◆ **sich abseilen** *ref* - **1.** [mit einem Seil] to abseil - **2.** *fam* [verschwinden] to leg it.

ab sein (*perf* ist ab gewesen) *vi* (*unreg*) - **1.** [entfernt]: **dieses Dorf ist weit von allem ab** this village is far away from everything - **2.** [abgetrennt] to have come off.

abseits ◇ *präp*: abseits eines Ortes ODER von einem Ort away from a place. ◇ *adv* out of the way; **sich abseits halten** to keep oneself to oneself.

Abseits *das* - **1.** SPORT offside - **2.** [Isolation]: **ins Abseits geraten** to be left out in the cold.

ab|senden *vt* to send off.

Ab|sender *der* - **1.** [Person] sender - **2.** [Adresse] sender's name and address.

Absenderin (*pl* -nen) *die* sender.

ab|setzen *vt* - **1.** [herunternehmen - Hut, Brille] to take off - **2.** [hinstellen, hinlegen] to put down - **3.** [aussteigen lassen] to drop off - **4.** [Betrag]: **etw von der Steuer absetzen (können)** to (be able to) deduct sthg from one's tax - **5.** [Ware] to sell - **6.** [entmachten - König] to depose - **7.** [Aufführung] to drop, to take off - **8.** [Medikament] to come off - **9.** [Kleidung] to trim. ◆ **sich absetzen** *ref* - **1.** [fliehen] to take off - **2.** [sich ablagern] to be deposited - **3.** [sich entfernen]: **sich von etw absetzen** to pull away from sthg - **4.** [sich abheben]: **sich gegen etw absetzen** to stand out against sthg.

ab|sichern *vt* to make safe. ◆ **sich absichern** *ref* to cover o.s.; **sich gegen etw absichern** to protect o.s. against sthg.

Ab|sicht *die* intention; **es war nicht meine Absicht, dir zu schaden** I didn't mean to harm you.

absichtlich ◇ *adj* deliberate, intentional. ◇ *adv* deliberately, intentionally.

absolut ◇ *adj* absolute. ◇ *adv* absolutely; **das gefällt mir absolut nicht** I don't like that at all.

absolvieren [apzɔl'viːrən] *vt* [Kurs] to complete; [Prüfung] to pass.

ab|sondern *vt* - **1.** [Sekret] to secrete - **2.** [isolieren] to isolate. ◆ **sich absondern** *ref* to isolate o.s.

ab|spalten *vt* CHEM to separate. ◆ **sich abspalten** *ref*: **sich (von etw) abspalten** to break away (from sthg).

ab|speisen *vt*: **jn mit etw abspeisen** to fob sb off with sthg.

ab|sperren *vt* - **1.** [abriegeln] to seal off - **2.** [verschließen] to lock.

Ab|sperrung *die* - **1.** [Schranke, Sperre] barrier - **2.** [Absperren] sealing off.

ab|spielen *vt* to play. ◆ **sich abspielen** *ref* to take place.

Ab|sprache *die* arrangement; **nach vorheriger Absprache** after prior consultation.

ab|sprechen *vt* (*unreg*) - **1.** [vereinbaren] to agree on - **2.** [verweigern, aberkennen]: **jm etw absprechen** [Recht] to deny sb sthg; [Fähigkeit] to deny that sb has sthg. ◆ **sich absprechen** *ref*: **wir hatten keine Zeit, uns abzusprechen** we had no time to agree on what to say/do.

ab|springen (*perf* ist abgesprungen) *vi* (*unreg*) - **1.** SPORT to jump - **2.** [sich lösen] to come off - **3.** *fam* [zurücktreten]: **von etw abspringen** to back out of sthg.

ab|spülen ◇ *vt* - **1.** [Geschirr] to wash - **2.** [Schmutz] to wash off. ◇ *vi* to wash up *UK*, to wash the dishes *US*.

ab|stammen *vi*: von jm/etw abstammen to be descended from sb/sthg.

Abstammung *die* descent.

Ab|stand *der* [räumlich] distance; [zeitlich] interval; **50 Meter Abstand** a distance of 50 metres; **von jm/etw Abstand halten** to keep one's distance from sb/sthg.

ab|statten *vt*: jm einen Besuch abstatten to pay sb a visit.

ab|stauben *vt* - **1.** [putzen] to dust - **2.** *fam* [mitnehmen]: etw bei jm abstauben to get sthg off sb.

Abstecher (*pl* -) *der* detour.

ab|stehen (*perf* hat/ist abgestanden) *vi* (*unreg*): von etw abstehen to stick out from sthg.

abstehend *adj*: er hat abstehende Ohren his ears stick out.

ab|steigen (*perf* ist abgestiegen) *vi* (*unreg*) - **1.** [hinunterklettern] to get off - **2.** SPORT to be relegated - **3.** [übernachten] to stay.

ab|stellen *vt* - **1.** [Gerät, Strom, Wasser] to turn off - **2.** [Last] to put down; [Möbel] to store, to put; [Auto, Fahrrad] to park - **3.** [Missstand] to put an end to - **4.** [freistellen]: jn zu etw abstellen to assign sb to sthg.

Abstell|raum *der* storage room.

ab|stempeln *vt* - **1.** [stempeln - Dokument] to stamp; [- Briefmarke] to postmark - **2.** *abw* [anprangern]: jn zu ODER als etw abstempeln to label sb sthg.

ab|sterben (*perf* ist abgestorben) *vi* (*unreg*) to die off.

Abstieg (*pl* -e) *der* - **1.** [vom Berg] descent - **2.** [sozial, finanziell] decline - **3.** SPORT relegation.

ab|stimmen ◇ *vi* [wählen] to vote. ◇ *vt* - **1.** [einstellen]: etw auf jn/etw abstimmen to adapt sthg to sb/sthg; [Farben] to match sthg to sb/sthg - **2.** [absprechen]: etw mit jm abstimmen to agree on sthg with sb. ➠ **sich abstimmen** *ref*: sich mit jm (über etw (A)) abstimmen to agree (on sthg) with sb.

Abstimmung *die* - **1.** [Wahl] vote - **2.** [Koordinierung] coordination - **3.** [Absprache] agreement.

ab|stoßen *vt* (*unreg*) - **1.** [wegdrücken] to push off - **2.** [verkaufen] to sell off - **3.** [anekeln] to repel - **4.** [abnützen - Farbe] to knock off.

abstoßend ◇ *adj* repulsive. ◇ *adv* repulsively.

abstrakt ◇ *adj* abstract. ◇ *adv* in the abstract.

ab|streiten *vt* (*unreg*) to deny.

Ab|strich *der* - **1.** [Einschränkungen] reservation; **Abstriche machen** to make concessions - **2.** MED swab; [von Gebärmutter] smear.

ab|stufen *vt* - **1.** [Löhne, Preise, Farben] to grade - **2.** [Haare] to layer.

ab|stumpfen (*perf* hat/ist abgestumpft) ◇ *vt* (hat) - **1.** [Subj: Lärm, Monotonie] to dull the senses of - **2.** [Subj: Leid, Schmerz] to harden. ◇ *vi* (ist): gegen etw abstumpfen to become inured to sthg.

Ab|sturz *der* crash.

ab|stürzen (*perf* ist abgestürzt) *vi* [Flugzeug & EDV] to crash; [Bergsteiger] to fall.

ab|suchen *vt*: etw (nach jm/etw) absuchen to search sthg (for sb/sthg).

absurd *adj* absurd.

Abt (*pl* Äbte) *der* abbot.

ab|tasten *vt* to feel.

ab|tauen (*perf* hat/ist abgetaut) ◇ *vt* (hat) to defrost. ◇ *vi* (ist) [Eis] to thaw; [Kühlschrank] to defrost.

Abtei (*pl* -en) *die* abbey.

Ab|teil (*pl* -e) *das* compartment.

ab|teilen *vt* to divide off.

Abteilung[1] (*pl* -en) *die* - **1.** [einer Firma, im Kaufhaus] department - **2.** MIL unit.

Ab|teilung[2] *die* [Trennung] dividing off.

Äbtissin (*pl* -nen) *die* abbess.

ab|tragen *vt* (*unreg*) - **1.** [Erde, Steine - Subj: Wind, Wasser] to erode; [Subj: Person] to remove (layer by layer) - **2.** [Kleidung] to wear out - **3.** [Schulden] to pay off.

ab|treiben (*perf* hat/ist abgetrieben) (*unreg*) ◇ *vt* (hat) [Kind]: sie will das Kind abtreiben she wants to have an abortion. ◇ *vi* - **1.** (hat) MED [Abort vornehmen] to carry out an abortion; [Abort vornehmen lassen] to have an abortion - **2.** (ist) [Boot] to be driven off course.

Abtreibung (*pl* -en) *die* abortion.

ab|trennen *vt* - **1.** [abschneiden - Coupon, Blatt] to detach; [- Ärmel, Saum] to cut off - **2.** [abteilen] to divide off.

ab|treten (*perf* hat/ist abgetreten) (*unreg*) ◇ *vt* (hat) - **1.** [Absätze] to wear down - **2.** [Rechte] to relinquish; etw an jn abtreten, jm etw abtreten to let sb have sthg. ◇ *vi* (ist) [fortgehen] to make one's exit.

ab|trocknen *vt* to dry; sich die Hände abtrocknen to dry one's hands. ➠ **sich abtrocknen** *ref* to dry o.s.

ab|verlangen *vt*: jm etw abverlangen to demand sthg from sb.

ab|wägen *vt* to weigh up; zwei Dinge gegeneinander abwägen to weigh up two things against each other.

ab|wählen *vt* - **1.** [Politiker] to vote out (of office) - **2.** [Schulfach] to drop.

ab|wälzen *vt*: etw auf jn abwälzen to shift sthg onto sb.

ab|wandeln *vt* to vary.

ab|wandern (*perf* ist **abgewandert**) *vi* - 1. [fortgehen] to migrate - 2. [Kapital] to be removed.

Ab|wandlung *die* adaptation.

ab|warten ⟺ *vt* to wait for; **ich kann es kaum abwarten, in Urlaub zu fahren** I can hardly wait to go on holiday. ⟺ *vi* to wait and see.

abwärts *adv* downwards; **alle, vom Assistenten abwärts** everyone from the assistant down.

Abwasch *der* (ohne pl) washing-up *UK*, dishes *US Pl.*

ab|waschen (*unreg*) ⟺ *vt* - 1. [Geschirr] to wash - 2. [Schmutz] to wash off. ⟺ *vi* to wash up *UK*, to wash the dishes *US*.

Ab|wasser *das* [von Haushalt] sewage (*U*); [von Industrie] effluent (*U*).

ab|wechseln ['apvɛksln] ⟺ **sich abwechseln** *ref* to alternate; **sich mit jm abwechseln** to take turns with sb.

abwechselnd ['apvɛkslnt] *adv* alternately.

Abwechslung ['apvɛkslʊŋ] (*pl* -en) *die* change.

abwegig *adj* bizarre.

Abwehr *die* - 1. [Widerstand] resistance - 2. SPORT & MIL defence.

ab|wehren ⟺ *vt* - 1. [Schlag, Angriff] to ward off - 2. [Störung] to deter. ⟺ *vi* to refuse.

ab|weichen (*perf* ist **abgewichen**) *vi* (*unreg*): **von etw abweichen** to deviate from sthg; **seine Ansichten weichen von meinen ab** his opinions differ from mine.

abweichend *adj* different.

ab|weisen *vt* (*unreg*) - 1. [ablehnen] to reject - 2. [Person] to turn away.

abweisend ⟺ *adj* unfriendly. ⟺ *adv* dismissively.

ab|wenden *vt* (*unreg*) - 1. [wegdrehen]: **den Kopf abwenden** to turn away; **den Blick abwenden** to look away - 2. [Unglück] to avert. ⟺ **sich abwenden** *ref* to turn away; **sich von jm/etw abwenden** to turn one's back on sb/sthg.

ab|werfen *vt* (*unreg*) - 1. [von Flugzeug] to drop - 2. [Geld]: **Gewinn abwerfen** to yield a profit.

ab|werten *vt* to devalue.

ab|wertend *adj* pejorative.

abwesend ⟺ *adj* - 1. [nicht anwesend] absent - 2. [unkonzentriert] absent, absentminded. ⟺ *adv* absently.

Abwesenheit *die* absence; **in js Abwesenheit** in sb's absence; **durch Abwesenheit glänzen** *iron* to be conspicuous by one's absence.

ab|wickeln *vt* - 1. [Schnur] to unwind - 2. [Geschäft] to complete - 3. [Institution] to wind up, to close down.

Abwicklung (*pl* -en) *die* - 1. [Abschluss] completion - 2. [Auflösung] winding up, closing down.

ab|wiegen *vt* (*unreg*) to weigh out.

ab|wimmeln *vt fam* to get rid of.

ab|wischen *vt* - 1. [Fläche] to wipe - 2. [Dreck] to wipe off.

ab|würgen *vt fam* - 1. [Motor] to stall - 2. [beenden, unterdrücken] to stifle.

ab|zahlen *vt* to pay off.

ab|zählen ⟺ *vt* to count. ⟺ *vi* to use a counting-out rhyme.

Ab|zeichen *das* badge.

ab|zeichnen *vt* to draw. ⟺ **sich abzeichnen** *ref* - 1. [sich ankündigen] to emerge - 2. [sich zeigen] to stand out.

ab|ziehen (*perf* ist/hat **abgezogen**) (*unreg*) ⟺ *vt* (hat) - 1. [Schürze, Mütze] to take off; [Schlüssel] to take out - 2. [subtrahieren - Nummer] to subtract; [- Betrag] to deduct - 3. [Bett] to strip - 4. [Soldaten] to withdraw - 5. [veranstalten]: **eine Schau** ODER **Show abziehen** *salopp* to make a fuss - 6. [Haut]: **einem Kaninchen die Haut abziehen** to skin a rabbit. ⟺ *vi* (ist) - 1. [Gas] to clear - 2. [am Person] to clear off.

Ab|zug *der* - 1. [von Kamin] flue; [Belüftung] vent - 2. [Foto] print; [Druck] proof - 3. [Subtraktion] deduction; **nach Abzug der Unkosten** after costs - 4. [Fortgehen] withdrawal - 5. [am Gewehr] trigger.

abzüglich *präp*: **abzüglich einer Sache** (*G*) less sthg.

ab|zweigen (*perf* hat/ist **abgezweigt**) ⟺ *vi* (ist) to branch off. ⟺ *vt* (hat) to put aside.

Abzweigung (*pl* -en) *die* turning.

Account (*pl* -s) *der* EDV account.

ach *interj* oh!

Achse ['aksə] (*pl* -n) *die* - 1. [Linie & MATH] axis; **auf Achse sein** *fig* to be on the move - 2. [von Auto] axle.

Achsel ['aksl] (*pl* -n) *die* shoulder; **mit den Achseln zucken** to shrug one's shoulders.

achselzuckend ['aksltsʊkn̩t] *adv* with a shrug.

acht *num* eight; *siehe auch* **sechs**.

Acht (*pl* -en) *die* eight; *siehe auch* **Sechs**.

Achte (*pl* -n) *der, die, das* eighth; *siehe auch* **Sechste**.

achte, r, s *adj* eighth; *siehe auch* **sechste**.

Achteck (*pl* -e) *das* octagon.

achtel *adj* (*unver*) eighth; *siehe auch* **sechstel**.

Achtel (*pl* -) *das* - 1. [der achte Teil] eighth - 2. MUS quaver *UK*, eighth note *US*; *siehe auch* **Sechstel**.

achten ⟺ *vt* to respect. ⟺ *vi*: **auf etw achten** to pay attention to sthg; **auf jn achten** to look after sb.

Achter|bahn *die* roller coaster.

achtfach ◇ *adj* eightfold. ◇ *adv* eight times.

Acht geben *vi* ⊳ **Acht**.

achthundert *num* eight hundred.

achtlos ◇ *adj* careless. ◇ *adv* carelessly.

achtmal *adv* eight times.

achttausend *num* eight thousand.

Achtung *die* - 1. [Respekt] respect - 2. [Vorsicht]: **Achtung!** look out!; [formell] attention, please!; **Achtung, Stufe!** mind the step!; **Achtung, fertig, los!** SPORT on your marks, get set, go!

achtzehn *num* eighteen; *siehe auch* **sechs**.

Achtzehn (*pl* -en) *die* eighteen; *siehe auch* **Sechs**.

achtzig *num* eighty; **auf achtzig sein** *fam* to be livid; **jn auf achtzig bringen** *fam* to make sb livid; *siehe auch* **sechs**.

Achtzig *die* eighty; *siehe auch* **Sechs**.

Achtzigerǀjahre, achtziger Jahre *Pl*: **die Achtzigerjahre** the eighties.

ächzen *vi* to groan.

Acker (*pl* Äcker) *der* field.

Ackerbau *der* agriculture; **Ackerbau treiben** to farm.

ADAC [aːdeːʔaːˈtseː] (*abk für* **Allgemeiner Deutscher Automobilklub**) *der* ≃ AA *UK*, ≃ AAA *US*.

addieren *vt* MATH to add up.

Adel *der* nobility.

adelig = **adlig**.

Ader (*pl* -n) *die* vein.

Adjektiv (*pl* -e) *das* adjective.

adjektivisch [ˈatjɛktiːvɪʃ] ◇ *adj* adjectival. ◇ *adv* GRAMM adjectivally.

Adler (*pl* -) *der* eagle.

adlig, adelig *adj* noble.

Admiral (*pl* -e ODER Admiräle) *der* MIL admiral.

adoptieren *vt* to adopt.

Adoption (*pl* -en) *die* adoption.

Adoptiveltern *Pl* adoptive parents.

Adoptivǀkind *das* adopted child.

Adressbuch (*pl* -bücher) *das* - 1. [privat] address book - 2. [von Stadt, Gemeinde] directory.

Adresse (*pl* -n) *die* address.

adressieren *vt* to address; **etw an jn adressieren** to address sthg to sb.

Adria *die*: **die Adria** the Adriatic.

Advent [atˈvɛnt] *der* Advent; **erster/zweiter Advent** first/second Sunday in Advent.

Adventsǀkranz *der* Advent wreath.

Adverb [atˈvɛrp] (*pl* -ien) *das* adverb.

adverbial [atvɛrˈbjaːl] ◇ *adj* adverbial. ◇ *adv* adverbially.

Affäre (*pl* -n) *die* - 1. [Skandal, Liebschaft] affair; **sich aus der Affäre ziehen** to get out of it - 2. [Angelegenheit] matter.

Affe (*pl* -n) *der* - 1. [Tier - klein] monkey; [- groß] ape - 2. *salopp abw* [blöder Kerl] jerk, twit *UK*.

affektiert *abw* ◇ *adj* affected. ◇ *adv* affectedly.

affig *fam abw* ◇ *adj* stuck-up. ◇ *adv* in a stuck-up way.

Afrika *nt* Africa.

Afrikaner, in (*mpl* -, *fpl* -nen) *der, die* African.

afrikanisch *adj* African.

After (*pl* -) *der* anus.

AG [aːˈgeː] (*pl* -s) (*abk für* **Aktiengesellschaft**) *die* ≃ plc *UK*, ≃ corp. *US*

Ägäis *die*: **die Ägäis** the Aegean.

Agent, in (*mpl* -en, *fpl* -nen) *der, die* - 1. [Spion] secret agent - 2. [Vermittler] agent.

Agentur (*pl* -en) *die* agency.

Aggression (*pl* -en) *die* aggression.

aggressiv ◇ *adj* aggressive. ◇ *adv* aggressively.

Agrarǀpolitik *die* agricultural policy.

Ägypten [ɛˈgʏptn] *nt* Egypt.

Ägypter, in (*mpl* -, *fpl* -nen) *der, die* Egyptian.

ägyptisch *adj* Egyptian.

ah *interj*: ah! [Ausdruck der Verwunderung] oh!; [Ausdruck plötzlichen Verstehens] ah!

aha *interj* aha!

Aha-ǀErlebnis *das* revelation.

ähneln *vi*: **jm/einer Sache ähneln** to resemble sb/sthg.

ahnen *vt* - 1. [im Voraus fühlen] to have a premonition of - 2. [vermuten] to suspect.

ähnlich ◇ *adj* similar; **jm/etw ähnlich sein** to be similar to ODER like sb/sthg. ◇ *adv* similarly; **jm/etw ähnlich sehen** to look like sb/sthg; **das sieht dir/ihm ähnlich!** that's just like you/him!

Ähnlichkeit (*pl* -en) *die* similarity.

Ahnung (*pl* -en) *die* - 1. [Vorgefühl] premonition; **ich habe so eine Ahnung, als ob** I have the feeling that - 2. [Vorstellung, Vermutung] idea; **keine Ahnung!** I've no idea!; **keine/nicht die geringste Ahnung haben** to have no/not the faintest idea.

ahnungslos ◇ *adj* unsuspecting. ◇ *adv* unsuspectingly.

Ahnungslosigkeit *die* lack of suspicion.

ahoi *interj* SCHIFF ahoy!

Ahorn (*pl* -e) *der* maple.

Ähre (*pl* -n) *die* ear (of corn).

Aids [ˈeidz] (*abk für* **Acquired Immune Deficiency Syndrome**) *nt* Aids.

Aidsǀkranke *der, die* Aids sufferer.

Aidstest (*pl* -s) *der* Aids test.

Akademie (*pl* -n) *die* academy.

Akademiker, in *(mpl -, fpl -nen) der, die* university graduate.

akademisch *adj* academic.

Akazie *(pl -n) die* acacia.

Akkord *(pl -e) der* chord. ➡ **im Akkord** *adv* WIRTSCH: **im Akkord arbeiten** to do piecework.

Akkordeon *(pl -s) das* accordion.

Akku *(pl -s) der* storage battery; [für Radio, Walkman] rechargeable battery.

Akkumulator *(pl -en) der* - 1. ELEKTR storage battery - 2. EDV accumulator.

Akkusativ *(pl -e) der* accusative.

Akne *die* acne.

Akrobat, in *(mpl -en, fpl -nen) der, die* acrobat.

akrobatisch ◇ *adj* acrobatic. ◇ *adv* acrobatically.

Akt *(pl -e) der* - 1. [Handlung, Aufzug] act - 2. [Bildnis] nude - 3. [Zeremonie] ceremony.

Akte *(pl -n) die* file; **etw zu den Akten legen** to shelve sthg.

aktenkundig *adj*: **ein aktenkundiger Vorgang** an occurrence which is on record.

Aktentasche *die* briefcase.

Aktie ['aktsjə] *(pl -n) die* share; **die Aktien steigen/fallen** share prices are rising/falling.

Aktiengesellschaft *die* ≃ public limited company *UK,* ≃ corporation *US.*

Aktienkurs *der* share price.

Aktion *(pl -en) die* - 1. [Tätigkeit] action; **in Aktion sein/treten** to be in/go into action - 2. [Verkauf] sale; [Werbung] promotion.

Aktionär, in [aktsjo'nɛːɐ̯, rɪn] *(mpl -e, fpl -nen) der, die* shareholder.

aktiv ◇ *adj* active. ◇ *adv* actively.

Aktiv *das* GRAMM active.

aktivieren [akti'viːrən] *vt* - 1. [System, Alarm] to activate - 2. [Person] to mobilize.

Aktivität [aktivi'tɛːt] *(pl -en) die* activity.

Aktualität *die* relevance; **an Aktualität gewinnen** to become topical.

aktuell *adj* - 1. [Theaterstück, Buch] topical; [Thema, Problem] current - 2. [modisch] fashionable.

Akupunktur *(pl -en) die* acupuncture.

Akustik *(ohne pl) die* - 1. PHYS acoustics *(U)* - 2. [Schallverhältnisse] acoustics *Pl.*

akut ◇ *adj* - 1. [vordringlich] urgent - 2. MED acute. ◇ *adv* - 1. [vordringlich] urgently - 2. MED acutely.

AKW [aːkaːˈveː] *(pl -s) das (abk für Atomkraftwerk) das* nuclear power station.

Akzent *(pl -e) der* - 1. GRAMM [Betonung] stress - 2. [Tonfall] accent; **Akzente setzen** to set a new trend.

akzeptieren *vt* to accept.

Alarm *(pl -e) der* alarm; **Alarm schlagen** to raise the alarm; **es war blinder Alarm** it was a false alarm.

Alarmanlage *die* [von Gebäude] burglar alarm; [von Auto] car alarm.

alarmieren *vt* - 1. [aufschrecken] to alarm - 2. [rufen] to alert.

Albaner, in *(mpl -, fpl -nen) der, die* Albanian.

Albanien *nt* Albania.

albanisch *adj* Albanian.

albern ◇ *adj* silly. ◇ *adv* in a silly way. ◇ *vi* to fool around.

Albino *(pl -s) der* albino.

Albtraum *(pl -träume) der* nightmare.

Album *(pl Alben) das* album.

Alge *(pl -n) die* - 1. [Seetang] piece of seaweed; **Algen** seaweed *(U)* - 2. [Algenpest verursachend]: **Algen** algae.

Algebra *die* algebra.

Algerien *nt* Algeria.

Algerier, in [al'geːriɐ, rɪn] *(mpl -, fpl -nen) der, die* Algerian.

algerisch *adj* Algerian.

alias *adv* alias.

Alibi *(pl -s) das* - 1. RECHT alibi - 2. [Ausrede] excuse.

Alimente *Pl* maintenance *(U) UK,* child support *(U) US.*

alkalisch *adj* alkaline.

Alkohol *(pl -e ODER Alkoholika) der* - 1. *(pl Alkohole)* CHEM alcohol - 2. *(pl Alkoholika)* [Getränk] alcohol; **unter Alkohol stehen** *amt* to be under the influence (of alcohol).

alkoholabhängig *adj*: **alkoholabhängig sein** to be an alcoholic.

alkoholfrei *adj* alcohol-free.

Alkoholgehalt *(pl -e) der* alcohol content.

Alkoholiker, in *(mpl -, fpl -nen) der, die* alcoholic.

alkoholisch ◇ *adj* alcoholic. ◇ *adv* alcoholically.

Alkoholismus *der* alcoholism.

all *det* all (of); **all das Warten** all this waiting.

All *das*: **das All** space.

alle, s ◇ *det* - 1. [sämtliche] all; **alle Kleider** all the clothes; **alle beide** both (of them); **alle fünf überlebten** all five survived; **wir alle** all of us - 2. [verstärkend]: **in aller Ruhe** in peace and quiet; **in aller Öffentlichkeit** quite openly; **alle Welt** everyone - 3. [allerlei]: **Getränke aller Art** all kinds of drinks; **alles Mögliche** all kinds of things - 4. [im Abstand von] every; **alle 50 Meter/zwei Wochen** every 50 metres/two weeks. ◇ *pron* - 1. [auf Personen bezogen] all, everyone; **alle sind gekommen** everyone came, they all came; **alles einsteigen! all aboard!** - 2. [auf Sachen bezogen] all, everything; **das ist alles** that's all ODER everything. <> adj fam: **die Milch ist alle** we've run out of milk. ⬦ **trotz allem** adv in spite of everything. ⬦ **vor allem** adv above all.

Allee (pl -n) die [Straße] avenue.

allein <> adj - 1. [für sich] alone; **heute Abend war ich allein zuhause** I was on my own at home this evening - 2. [einsam] lonely. <> adv - 1. [für sich] alone - 2. [selbstständig] on one's own, by oneself - 3. [einsam] alone; **allein zurückbleiben** to stay behind by oneself; **allein herumstehen** to stand around on one's own; **allein dastehen** to be all alone in the world - 4. [nur] only; **allein das Handgepäck wiegt 10 kg** the hand luggage alone weighs 10 kg. <> konj geh however. ⬦ **ganz allein** <> adj - 1. [für sich] all alone - 2. [einsam] all on one's own, all by oneself. <> adv - 1. [für sich, einsam] all alone - 2. [selbstständig] all on one's own, all by oneself. ⬦ **von allein** adv by oneself/itself.

allein erziehend adj: **allein erziehende Mutter** single mother.

Alleingang der single-handed effort. ⬦ **im Alleingang** adv single-handedly.

alleinig adj sole.

allein stehend adj - 1. [ledig] single - 2. [allein wohnend]: **eine allein stehende Person** a person who lives alone.

Alleinstehende (pl -n) der, die - 1. [ledig] single person - 2. [allein wohnend] person who lives alone.

allemal adv fam: **dich schlage ich allemal** I could beat you no sweat; ▷ **Mal**.

allenfalls adv at most.

allerbeste, r, s adj very best.

allerdings adv - 1. [als Antwort] certainly - 2. [einschränkend] though.

allererste, r, s adj very first.

Allergie (pl -n) die allergy.

allergisch <> adj allergic; **gegen etw allergisch sein** MED to be allergic to sthg; [etw nicht ausstehen können] not to be able to stand sthg. <> adv - 1. MED allergically; **auf etw allergisch reagieren** to have an allergic reaction to sthg - 2. [ablehnend]: **auf Lügen reagiere ich wirklich allergisch** I really can't stand people lying.

allerhand <> adj (unver) all sorts of; **das ist ja allerhand!** [erbost] that really is the limit!; [anerkennend] that's not bad at all! <> pron all sorts of things.

Allerheiligen nt All Saints' Day.

allerhöchstens ['alɐˈhøːkstn̩s] adv at the very most.

allerlei det all sorts of.

allerletzte, r, s adj - 1. [letzte] very last - 2. [schlecht] most awful.

Allerletzte das: **das ist ja das Allerletzte!** that's the absolute limit!

Allerseelen (ohne Artikel) All Souls' Day.

allerseits adv: **guten Tag/Abend allerseits** good afternoon/evening everyone.

alles ▷ **alle**.

allesamt adv all together.

Alleskleber der all-purpose glue.

Allgäu das: **das Allgäu** the Allgäu.

allgemein <> adj - 1. [gen] general - 2. [Interesse, Sprachgebrauch] common; [Wehrpflicht, Wahlrecht] universal. <> adv generally. ⬦ **im Allgemeinen** adv in general.

Allgemeinbildung die general education.

allgemein gültig <> adj universal. <> adv universally.

Allgemeinheit (pl -en) die - 1. [Öffentlichkeit] general public - 2. [Undifferenziertheit] generality. ⬦ **Allgemeinheiten** Pl [Floskel] generalities.

Allheilmittel das cure-all, panacea.

Alligator (pl -gatoren) der alligator.

alliiert adj allied.

Alliierte Pl allies; **die Alliierten** HIST the Allies.

alljährlich <> adj annual. <> adv every year.

allmächtig adj almighty.

allmählich <> adj gradual. <> adv gradually.

allseits adv everywhere.

Alltag der everyday life.

alltäglich <> adj - 1. [täglich] daily - 2. [üblich] everyday. <> adv every day.

Alltagstrott der daily grind.

allwissend adj all-knowing, omniscient.

allzu adv far too. ⬦ **allzu sehr** adv far too much. ⬦ **allzu viel** adv far too much.

Alm (pl -en) die mountain pasture.

Almosen (pl -) das alms Pl.

Aloe ['aːloe] (pl -n) die aloe.

Alpen Pl: **die Alpen** the Alps.

Alpenveilchen das cyclamen.

Alpenverein der organization which promotes study of the Alps and organizes mountain hikes etc.

Alpenvorland das (ohne pl) foothills Pl of the Alps.

Alpha (pl -s) das alpha.

Alphabet [alfaˈbeːt] (pl -e) das alphabet.

alphabetisch <> adj alphabetical. <> adv alphabetically.

alpin adj alpine.

Alptraum der = **Albtraum**.

als konj - 1. [zur Kennzeichnung eines Zeitpunkts] when; **als es dunkel wurde** when it got dark; **erst als** only when - 2. [zur Kennzeichnung einer Zeitspanne] as - 3. [bei Vergleich]: **sie ist besser als ihr Bruder** she is better than her brother; **der Wein ist besser, als ich dachte** the wine is better than I thought it would be; **mehr als** more than - 4. [bei Vergleich vor Konjunktiv] as if, as though; **es sieht so aus, als würde es bald regnen** it looks like it's going to rain soon; **als ob** as if, as though - **5.** [zur Kennzeichnung einer Eigenschaft] as; **ich verstehe es als Kompliment** I take it as a compliment; **als Kind** as a child.

also <> *interj* well; **also doch!** so I was right (after all)!; **also gut** ODER **schön!** oh, all right then!; **na also!** what did I tell you!, there you are!; **also dann!** *fam* right then!; **also bitte!** [Unmut ausdrückend] for heaven's sake!; [widerwillig nachgebend] if you must. <> *adv* - **1.** [das heißt] that is - **2.** [demnach] so; **da lag also der Fehler!** so that's where the mistake was - **3.** [endlich] so; **die Sache ist also erledigt** so the matter is settled.

alt (*kompar* **älter**, *superl* **älteste**) *adj* - **1.** [gen] old; **12 Jahre alt** 12 years old; **wie alt bist du?** how old are you?; **zwei Jahre älter** two years older; **dieser alte Schmarotzer!** *abw* the old sponger! - **2.** [antik] antique - **3.** [historisch] ancient; **alte Sprachen** classics, classical languages; **das alte Rom** ancient Rome; **alt aussehen** *salopp* to be up shit creek.

Alt (*pl* **-e** ODER **-**) <> *der* (*pl* **Alte**) MUS alto. <> *das* (*pl* **Alt**) [Bier] *type of dark German beer.*

Altar (*pl* **Altäre**) *der* altar.

Altbau (*pl* **-ten**) *der* old building.

altbekannt *adj* [Methode] well-known.

altbewährt *adj* proven.

Altbier *das type of dark German beer.*

Alte (*pl* **-n**) <> *der, die* - **1.** [alter Mensch] old man (old woman *die*) - **2.** *salopp abw* [Elternteil, Gatte] old man (old girl *die*) - **3.** *salopp abw* [Vorgesetzter] boss, guvnor *UK* - **4.** [Gleiche]: **ganz der/die Alte** exactly the same. <> *das* (*ohne pl*): **alles beim Alten lassen** to leave everything just as it is.

alteingesessen *adj* long-established.

Altenheim = **Altersheim**.

Altentagesstätte *die* old people's day centre.

Alter (*pl*) - *das* - **1.** [Lebensalter] age; **im Alter von 12 Jahren** at the age of 12; **eine Frau mittleren Alters** a middle-aged woman; **bis ins hohe Alter war er gesund** he remained healthy until a ripe old age - **2.** [Altsein] old age.

älter *adj* - **1.** > **alt** - **2.** [ziemlich alt] elderly.

Ältere (*pl* **-n**) *der* **die Ältere** the Elder.

altern (*perf* **hat/ist gealtert**) *vi* - **1.** [Person] to age - **2.** [Cognac, Käse] to mature.

alternativ <> *adj* alternative. <> *adv* - **1.** [wahlweise] alternatively - **2.** [unkonventionell]: **alternativ leben** to have an alternative lifestyle.

Alternative [alterna'tiːvə] (*pl* **-n**) *die* alternative.

altersbedingt *adj* age-related.

Altersgenosse *der* contemporary.

Altersgenossin *die* contemporary.

Altersgrenze *die* - **1.** [Höchstalter, Mindestalter] age limit - **2.** [Rentenalter] retirement age.

Altersgruppe *die* age group.

Altersheim, Altenheim *das* old people's home.

altersschwach *adj* - **1.** [Person] old and infirm - **2.** [Gegenstände] decrepit.

Altersversorgung *die* [privat] provision for one's old age; [vom Staat] provision for the elderly.

Altertum (*pl* **-tümer**) *das* [Antike] antiquity.
> **Altertümer** *Pl* [antike Objekte] antiquities.

Älteste (*pl* **-n**) *der, die* - **1.** [ältestes Kind] eldest - **2.** [älteste Person] eldest person.

althergebracht *adj* traditional.

altklug <> *adj* precocious. <> *adv* precociously.

altmodisch <> *adj* old-fashioned. <> *adv* in an old-fashioned way.

Altpapier *das* paper for recycling; **aus Altpapier** made from recycled paper.

Altpapiercontainer *der* paper recycling bin.

altsprachlich *adj* > **Gymnasium**.

Altstadt *die* old town.

Alu *das fam* aluminium *UK*, aluminum *US*.

Alufolie *die* tinfoil (*U*).

Aluminium *das* aluminium *UK*, aluminum *US*.

am *präp* - **1.** (an + dem) at the; **am Flughafen** at the airport; **am Schönste am Urlaub ist es, lange schlafen zu können** the nicest thing about holidays is being able to sleep in; **ich möchte am Ausflug teilnehmen** I would like to take part in the trip - **2.** (*nicht auflösbar*) [in geografischen Angaben]: **am Meer** by the sea - **3.** (*nicht auflösbar*) [im Datum] on the; **am Abend** in the evening; **am Montag** on Monday; **am 4. Oktober** on 4. October; **am Anfang des Jahres** at the start of the year - **4.** (*nicht auflösbar*) [in Superlativen]: **am schönsten** the most beautiful - **5.** (*nicht auflösbar*) *fam* [vor substantivierten Infinitiven]: **ich bin am Arbeiten** I am working; *siehe auch* **an**.

amateurhaft *abw* <> *adj* amateurish. <> *adv* amateurishly.

Amboss (*pl* **-e**) *der* - **1.** [Schmiedegerät] anvil - **2.** MED incus.

ambulant <> *adj* MED outpatient. <> *adv* MED [behandeln] as an outpatient.

Ambulanz (*pl* **-en**) *die* MED outpatients' department.

Ameise (*pl* **-n**) *die* ant.

Ameisenhaufen *der* anthill.

amen *interj* amen!

Amen *das* [Zustimmung] blessing, approval.

Amerika *nt* America.

Amerikaner, in (*mpl* **-**, *fpl* **-nen**) *der, die* American.

amerikanisch *adj* American.

Ami (*pl* -s) *der fam* Yank.

Amino|säure *die* amino acid.

Ammoniak *das* ammonia.

Amnestie (*pl* -n) *die* amnesty.

Amöbe (*pl* -n) *die* amoeba.

Amok *der*: **Amok laufen** to run amok.

Ampel (*pl* -n) *die* traffic lights *Pl*; **rote Ampel** red light.

Ampere [am'pɛːɐ̯] (*pl* **Ampere**) *das* amp, ampere.

Amphi|theater *das* amphitheatre.

amputieren *vt* to amputate.

Amsel (*pl* -n) *die* blackbird.

Amt (*pl* **Ämter**) *das* - **1.** [Behörde] department; [Gebäude] office; **von Amts wegen** on official orders - **2.** [Stellung] position; [wichtige politische oder kirchliche Stellung] office - **3.** [Pflicht] duty; [Aufgabe] task.

amtierend *adj*: **der amtierende Bundeskanzler** the German chancellor in office.

amtlich ⬦ *adj* official. ⬦ *adv* officially.

Amts|geheimnis *das* official secret.

Amts|gericht *das* ≃ county court *UK*, ≃ district court *US*.

Amts|sitz *der* seat of office.

Amts|sprache *die* official language.

Amts|zeit *die* term of office.

Amulett (*pl* -e) *das* amulet.

amüsieren *vt* to amuse. ➤ **sich amüsieren** *ref* to have fun; **sich über jn/etw amüsieren** [auslachen] to make fun of sb/sthg; [lustig finden] to find sb/sthg funny.

an ⬦ *präp* - **1.** (+ D) [räumlich] at; **an einem Tisch sitzen** to be sitting at a table; **an der Wand** on the wall; **an der Hauptstraße** on the main road; **Lehrer an einem Gymnasium** teacher at a grammar school - **2.** (+ A) [räumlich] to; **sich an den Tisch setzen** to sit down at the table; **etw an die Wand lehnen** to lean sthg against the wall - **3.** (+ D) [zeitlich] on; **an diesem Tag** on that day; **an Fulda 15.09** arriving at Fulda at 15.09 - **4.** (+ D) [stellt Bezug her]: **an Krebs leiden** to have cancer; **an etw zweifeln** to doubt sthg - **5.** (+ D) [aus dieser Menge]: **genug an Beweisen haben** to have enough proof - **6.** (+ D) [mithilfe von] with; **am Stock gehen** to walk with a stick; **jn an der Stimme erkennen** to recognize sb by their voice - **7.** (+ A) *fam* [ungefähr]: **an die 30 Grad** about 30 degrees - **8.** (+ A) [stellt Bezug her]: **an jn denken** to think about sb; **sich an jn/etw erinnern** to remember sb/sthg; **an und für sich** generally; **an sich** in itself. ⬦ *adv* - **1.** [elliptisch]: **Licht an!** turn the light on! - **2.** [zeitlich]: **von jetzt an** from now on.

Analogie (*pl* -n) *die geh* analogy.

Analphabet, in (*mpl* -en, *fpl* -nen) *der*, *die* illiterate (person).

Analyse (*pl* -n) *die* analysis; [von Blut] test.

analysieren *vt* to analyse; [Blut] to test.

Ananas (*pl* - ODER -se) *die* pineapple.

Anarchie (*pl* -n) *die* anarchy.

Anarchist, in (*mpl* -en, *fpl* -nen) *der*, *die* anarchist.

Anästhesie (*pl* -n) *die* anaesthesia.

Anatomie (*pl* -n) *die* anatomy.

an|bahnen *vt* [Geschäft, Treffen] to prepare; [Gespräch] to start. ➤ **sich anbahnen** *ref* to be on the way.

an|bändeln *vi fam*: **mit jm anbändeln** to start going out with sb.

An|bau *der* - **1.** [Gebäudeteil] extension - **2.** [Bauen] building (*of extension*) - **3.** [von Pflanzen] growing.

an|bauen *vt* - **1.** [Gebäude] to add (*as an extension*) - **2.** [Pflanze] to grow.

an|behalten *vt* (*unreg*) to keep on.

anbei *adv* enclosed.

an|beißen (*unreg*) ⬦ *vt* to take a bite of. ⬦ *vi* - **1.** [Fisch] to bite - **2.** *fig* [Käufer] to take the bait.

an|belangen *vt*: **was jn/etw anbelangt** as far as sb/sthg is concerned.

an|beten *vt* to worship.

an|biedern ➤ **sich anbiedern** *ref abw*: **sich bei jm anbiedern** to curry favour with sb.

an|bieten *vt* (*unreg*) to offer. ➤ **sich anbieten** *ref* - **1.** [Mensch] to offer one's services; **sie bot sich an, uns die Stadt zu zeigen** she offered to show us round the city - **2.** [Sache]: **der Montag bietet sich als Termin für das Treffen an** Monday would be the best day for the meeting - **3.** [geeignet erscheinen]: **folgende Möglichkeiten bieten sich an** we have the following possibilities.

Anbieter, in (*mpl* -, *fpl* -nen) *der*, *die* supplier.

an|binden *vt* (*unreg*) to tie (up).

An|blick *der* sight.

an|blicken *vt* to look at.

an|braten *vt* (*unreg*) to brown.

an|brechen (*perf* hat/ist **angebrochen**) (*unreg*) ⬦ *vt* (*hat*) - **1.** [Verpackung] to open - **2.** [Knochen] to crack - **3.** [Geldschein] to break into. ⬦ *vi* (*ist*) *geh* [Tag] to dawn; [Morgen] to break; [Nacht] to fall.

an|brennen (*perf* hat/ist **angebrannt**) (*unreg*) ⬦ *vt* (*hat*) [mit Feuer] to set fire to. ⬦ *vi* (*ist*) [Essen] to burn; **nichts anbrennen lassen** *fam fig* never to let a single chance go by.

an|bringen *vt* (*unreg*) - **1.** [befestigen] to put up - **2.** [Kritik] to make - **3.** *fam abw* [mitbringen] to bring back.

Anbruch *der* [von Epoche] dawning; **bei Anbruch der Dunkelheit** when darkness falls/fell.

an|brüllen vt fam to bawl out; **gegen etw anbrüllen** to shout above sthg.

andächtig ◇ adj reverent. ◇ adv reverently.

an|dauern vi to continue.

andauernd ◇ adj continual. ◇ adv continually.

Andenken (pl -) das - 1. [Erinnerung] memory; **zum Andenken an jn/etw** in memory of sb/sthg - 2. [Gegenstand, Souvenir] souvenir.

andere, r, s ◇ adj - 1. [unterschiedlich] different - 2. [übrig, weitere] other. ◇ pron: **der/die/das andere** the other (one); **ein anderer/eine andere** [bei Dingen] a different one; [bei Personen] someone else; **ich habe noch zwei andere** I've got two others; **unter anderem** among other things.

anderenfalls = andernfalls.

andererseits, andrerseits adv on the other hand.

andermal ◆ **ein andermal** adv another time, some other time.

ändern vt to change; [Kleid] to alter; **das lässt sich nicht ändern** there's nothing to be done about it. ◆ **sich ändern** ref to change.

andernfalls, anderenfalls adv otherwise.

anders ◇ adv - 1. [andersartig, verschieden] differently; **sie sieht ganz anders aus als ihre Schwester** she doesn't look at all like her sister; **anders ausgedrückt** put another way; **so und nicht anders!** this way only! - 2. [sonst] else; **jemand/irgendwo anders** somebody/somewhere else; **niemand anders als du kann uns jetzt noch helfen** only you can help us now. ◇ adj different; **das muss anders werden** this has got to change; **mir wird ganz anders** I feel weird.

andersherum adv the other way round.

anderswo adv elsewhere, somewhere else.

anderthalb num one and a half.

Änderung (pl -en) die [gen] change; [an Kleid] alteration.

anderweitig ◇ adj other. ◇ adv - 1. [anderswo] elsewhere - 2. [auf andere Weise] otherwise.

an|deuten vt - 1. [ansprechen] to hint at; **andeuten, dass ...** to hint that ... - 2. [umreißen, skizzieren] to outline.

Andeutung die hint; **eine Andeutung machen** to drop a hint.

Andrang der crush; **es herrscht großer Andrang** there is a great crush.

an|drehen vt fam [verkaufen]: **jm etw andrehen** to flog sb sthg.

andrerseits = andererseits.

an|drohen vt: **jm etw androhen** to threaten sb with sthg.

Androhung die: **unter Androhung von etw** under threat of sthg.

an|lecken (perf ist angeleckt) vi - 1. [stoßen]: **an etw anecken** to bang against sthg - 2. [sich unbeliebt machen]: **bei jm/überall anecken** to rub sb/everybody up the wrong way.

an|eignen vt: **sich (D) etw aneignen** [lernen] to pick sthg up; abw [nehmen] to take sthg (for o.s.)

aneinander adv [drücken, befestigen] together; [reiben] against one another; [denken] about one another; **sich aneinander gewöhnen** to get used to one another.

aneinander fügen vt to put together. ◆ **sich aneinander fügen** ref to fit together.

aneinander geraten (perf ist aneinander geraten) vi (unreg) to clash.

aneinander grenzen vi [Länder] to border on one another; [Gärten, Wohnungen] to be adjacent.

aneinander hängen vi (unreg) [einander lieben] to be attached to one another.

aneinander legen vt to lay down next to each other.

Anekdote (pl -n) die anecdote.

an|ekeln vt to make sick.

anerkannt adj recognized.

an|erkennen vt (unreg) - 1. [Leistung, Begabung] to acknowledge - 2. [Meinung, Person] to accept - 3. [Autorität, Staat, Vaterschaft] to recognize.

Anerkennung (pl -en) die - 1. [von Leistung, Begabung] acknowledgement - 2. [von Meinung, Person] acceptance - 3. [von Autorität, Staat, Vaterschaft] recognition.

an|fachen vt to fan.

an|fahren (perf hat/ist angefahren) (unreg) ◇ vt (hat) - 1. [bei Unfall] to run into - 2. [Ziel] to approach - 3. [Last] to deliver - 4. [tadeln] to scold. ◇ vi (ist) [losfahren] to start.

An|fall der fit.

an|fallen (perf hat/ist angefallen) (unreg) ◇ vi (ist) [Kosten] to be incurred. ◇ vt (hat) [angreifen] to attack.

anfällig adj: **für etw anfällig sein** to be prone ODER susceptible to sthg.

An|fang der beginning, start; **Anfang April** at the beginning of April; **von Anfang an** from the beginning ODER start; **von Anfang bis Ende** from start to finish.

an|fangen (unreg) ◇ vi - 1. [gen] to begin, to start; **mit etw anfangen** to start sthg, to begin sthg; **wer fängt an?** who's first?; **er fängt schon wieder an!** there he goes again! - 2. [machen]: **er weiß nichts mit sich anzufangen** he doesn't know what to do with himself; **mit etw nichts anfangen können** [verstehen] not to be able to get anywhere with sthg; [gebrauchen] not to be able to use sthg. ◇ vt [beginnen] to begin, to start.

Anfänger, in (*mpl* -, *fpl* -nen) *der, die* beginner; **ein blutiger Anfänger** a total beginner.

anfänglich ◇ *adj* initial. ◇ *adv* initially.

anfangs *adv* at first.

Anfangsbuchstabe *der* [von Wort] first letter; [von Name] initial.

Anfangsstadium *das* initial stages *Pl*.

anfassen ◇ *vt* - **1.** [berühren] to touch - **2.** [behandeln] to treat - **3.** [angehen] to handle. ◇ *vi* [helfen] to lend a hand; **mit anfassen** to lend a hand.

anfechten *vt* (*unreg*) [anzweifeln - Testament] to contest; [- Urteil] to appeal against.

anfertigen *vt* [Anzug, Schrank] to make; [Bericht] to write; [Protokoll] to take down; **ein Porträt anfertigen lassen** to have a portrait done.

Anfertigung *die* (*ohne pl*) [von Anzug, Möbeln] making; [von Bericht] writing; [von Protokoll] taking down.

anfeuchten *vt* [Lippen, Briefmarke] to moisten; [Haut] to moisturize; [Lappen] to wet.

anfeuern *vt* to spur on.

anflehen *vt* to beg.

anfliegen (*perf* hat/ist angeflogen) (*unreg*) ◇ *vt* (*hat*) [Subj: Flugzeug] to approach; [Subj: Fluggesellschaft] to serve, to fly to. ◇ *vi* (*ist*): **angeflogen kommen** to come flying up.

Anflug *der* - **1.** [von Flugzeug, Hubschrauber]: **im Anflug (auf etw (A)) sein** to be approaching (sthg) - **2.** [Spur] hint.

anfordern *vt* to ask for; [per Post] to send off for.

Anforderung *die* - **1.** [Bestellung] request - **2.** [Anspruch] demand; **Anforderungen stellen** to make demands; **einer Anforderung genügen** to meet a requirement; **den Anforderungen einer Sache gewachsen sein** to be up to the demands of sthg.

Anfrage *die* amt enquiry.

anfreunden ◆ **sich anfreunden** *ref* to make friends; **sich mit jm anfreunden** to make friends with sb; **ich freunde mich langsam mit der Idee an** the idea is growing on me.

anfühlen *vt* to feel. ◆ **sich anfühlen** *ref* to feel.

anführen *vt* - **1.** [nennen] to quote - **2.** [täuschen] to take in - **3.** [führen] to lead.

Anführer, in *der, die* leader.

Anführungszeichen *Pl* quotation marks, inverted commas.

Angabe *die* - **1.** [Hinweis] detail - **2.** [Aufschneiderei] showing off.

angeben (*unreg*) ◇ *vt* - **1.** [nennen, zitieren - Personalien, Grund] to give; [- Zeuge] to name - **2.** [bestimmen - Richtung, Kurs] to set - **3.** [behaupten] to claim, to allege. ◇ *vi* [aufschneiden] to show off; **mit etw angeben** to show off about sthg.

Angeber (*pl* -) *der* show-off.

Angeberin (*pl* -nen) *die* show-off.

angeblich ◇ *adj* alleged. ◇ *adv* allegedly.

angeboren *adj* [Krankheit] congenital; [Talent, Abneigung] innate.

Angebot *das* - **1.** [Anbieten] offer; **Angebot und Nachfrage** supply and demand - **2.** [Sortiment] range; **etw im Angebot haben** to offer sthg.

angebracht ◇ *pp* ▷ **anbringen**. ◇ *adj* appropriate.

angebunden ◇ *pp* ▷ **anbinden**. ◇ *adj*: **kurz angebunden sein** to be brusque.

angegriffen ◇ *pp* ▷ **angreifen**. ◇ *adj* [Gesundheit, Position] weakened.

angeheitert *adj* merry.

angehen (*perf* hat/ist angegangen) (*unreg*) ◇ *vi* (*ist*) - **1.** [Licht] to go on; [Feuer] to catch - **2.** [akzeptabel sein]: **es geht nicht an, etw zu tun** it's not on to do sthg - **3.** [vorgehen]: **gegen jn/etw angehen** to fight sb/sthg. ◇ *vt* (*hat*) [betreffen] to concern; **jn etwas angehen** to concern sb; **das geht dich nichts an** it's none of your business.

angehend *adj* future.

angehören *vi*: **einer Sache (D) angehören** to belong to sthg.

Angehörige (*pl* -n) *der, die* - **1.** [Verwandte] relative - **2.** [Mitglied] member.

Angeklagte (*pl* -n) *der, die* defendant.

Angel (*pl* -n) *die* - **1.** [zum Fischen] fishing rod - **2.** [Scharnier] hinge.

angelaufen ◇ *pp* ▷ **anlaufen**. ◇ *adj* [Silber, Messing] tarnished.

Angelegenheit *die* matter; **kümmere dich um deine eigenen Angelegenheiten!** mind your own business!

angeln ◇ *vi* - **1.** [fischen] to fish - **2.** [suchen]: **nach etw angeln** [suchen] to fish around for sthg. ◇ *vt* - **1.** [fischen] to fish for; [fangen] to catch - **2.** [erobern]: **sich (D) jn angeln** to land o.s. sb.

angemessen ◇ *adj*: (**einer Sache (D)**) **angemessen** appropriate (to sthg). ◇ *adv* appropriately.

angenehm ◇ *adj* pleasant. ◇ *adv* pleasantly.

angenommen ◇ *pp* ▷ **annehmen**. ◇ *adj* [Kind] adopted; [Name] assumed. ◆ **angenommen, dass** *adv* assuming (that).

angeregt ◇ *adj* lively. ◇ *adv*: **sich angeregt unterhalten** to have a lively conversation.

angeschlagen *adj* - **1.** [kaputt] chipped - **2.** [krank] groggy; **gesundheitlich angeschlagen sein** to be in poor health.

angesehen ◇ *pp* ▷ **ansehen**. ◇ *adj* respected.

Angesicht *das*: im Angesicht einer Sache (G) in the face of sthg; von Angesicht zu Angesicht face to face.

angesichts *präp*: angesichts einer Sache (G) in view of sthg.

angespannt ◇ *adj* tense. ◇ *adv* closely.

Angestellte (*pl* -n) *der, die* employee; [im Büro] white-collar worker.

angestrengt ◇ *adj* [Miene] strained; [Versuch] concerted. ◇ *adv* [arbeiten, rudern, zuhören] hard.

angetan ◇ *pp* ⊳ **antun**. ◇ *adj*: von jm/etw angetan sein to be keen on sb/sthg.

angewiesen ◇ *pp* ⊳ **anweisen**. ◇ *adj*: auf jn/etw angewiesen sein to be dependent on sb/sthg.

an|gewöhnen *vt*: sich (D) angewöhnen, etw zu tun to get into the habit of doing sthg; jm etw angewöhnen to get sb used to sthg.

An|gewohnheit *die* habit.

angewurzelt *adv*: wie angewurzelt stehen bleiben to stand rooted to the spot.

Angler, in (*mpl* -, *fpl* -nen) *der, die* angler.

Anglistik *die (ohne pl)* English language and literature.

an|greifen (*unreg*) ◇ *vt* - 1. [gen] to attack - 2. [Gesundheit] to affect - 3. [Projekt] to tackle - 4. [Vorrat] to draw on - 5. *Süddt* [anfassen] to touch. ◇ *vi* to attack.

Angreifer, in (*mpl* -, *fpl* -nen) *der, die* attacker.

An|griff *der* attack; etw in Angriff nehmen *fig* to set about sthg.

angriffslustig ◇ *adj* aggressive. ◇ *adv* aggressively.

angst *adj*: mir wird angst und bange I'm scared stiff.

Angst (*pl* Ängste) *die* - 1. [Furcht] fear; vor jm/etw Angst haben to be afraid of sb/sthg; es mit der Angst zu tun bekommen to get scared; jm Angst machen to frighten sb - 2. [Sorge]: Angst um jn/etw haben to be anxious about sb/sthg.

Angst|hase *der fam abw* chicken.

ängstigen *vt* to frighten. ◆ **sich ängstigen** *ref*: sich vor jm/etw ängstigen to be frightened of sb/sthg; sich um jn/etw ängstigen to be anxious about sb/sthg.

ängstlich ◇ *adj* nervous. ◇ *adv* - 1. [furchtsam] nervously - 2. [genau] very carefully.

an|gucken *vt fam* to look at; [Fernsehsendung] to watch; sich (D) etw angucken to look at sthg; [Fernsehsendung] to watch sthg.

an|haben *vt* (*unreg*) - 1. [Kleidung] to have on, to be wearing - 2. [Schaden]: jm/einer Sache nichts anhaben können to be unable to harm sb/sthg.

an|halten (*unreg*) ◇ *vi* - 1. [Fahrzeug] to stop - 2. [Zustand] to last. ◇ *vt* [Bewegung] to stop; [Taxi] to hail; den Atem anhalten to hold one's breath.

anhaltend *adj* lasting.

Anhalter (*pl* -) *der* [Mitfahrer] hitchhiker; per Anhalter fahren to hitchhike.

Anhalterin (*pl* -nen) *die* [Mitfahrerin] hitchhiker.

Anhalts|punkt *der* clue.

anhand, an Hand *präp*: anhand einer Sache (G) with the aid of sthg.

Anhang *der* (*ohne pl*) - 1. [Nachwort] appendix - 2. *fam* [Familie] relatives *Pl*; mit Anhang auf einem Fest erscheinen to go to a party with someone.

an|hängen ◇ *vt* (*reg*) - 1. [Wagen]: etw an etw (A) anhängen [Wagon] to couple sthg to sthg; [Anhänger] to hitch sthg to sthg - 2. [Zeit]: etw an etw (A) anhängen to tag sthg onto sthg - 3. [angebliche Schuld]: jm etw anhängen to pin sthg on sb. ◇ *vi* (*unreg*): einer Sache (D) anhängen to be an adherent of sthg.

Anhänger (*pl* -) *der* - 1. [von Fahrzeugen] trailer; [von Straßenbahn] carriage (*other than front carriage*) - 2. [Person - von Kandidat, Mannschaft] supporter; [- von Sekte] member - 3. [Schmuck] pendant.

Anhängerin (*pl* -nen) *die* [von Kandidat, Mannschaft] supporter; [von Sekte] member.

anhänglich *adj* [Hund, Partner] devoted.

an|hauchen *vt* to breathe on.

Anhäufung (*pl* -en) *die* accumulation.

an|heben *vt* (*unreg*) - 1. [heben] to lift - 2. [vergrößern] to raise.

an|heuern ◇ *vt* - 1. [Matrosen] to sign on - 2. [Arbeitskräfte] to take on. ◇ *vi* [auf einem Schiff] to sign on.

Anhieb ◆ **auf Anhieb** *adv* straight off.

An|höhe *die* rise.

an|hören *vt* - 1. [hören]: sich (D) etw anhören to listen to sthg; etw mit anhören to overhear sthg; ich kann das nicht mehr mit anhören I can't bear to listen to it any longer - 2. [erraten]: jm seine Freude/Wut anhören to hear the joy/anger in sb's voice - 3. *amt* [Zeugen] to give a hearing to. ◆ **sich anhören** *ref* to sound.

Anis *der* aniseed.

an|kämpfen *vi*: gegen jn/etw ankämpfen to fight against sb/sthg.

An|kauf *der* purchase.

Anker (*pl* -) *der* anchor; vor Anker gehen/liegen to drop/be at anchor.

ankern *vi* to anchor; [Anker werfen] to drop anchor; [vor Anker liegen] to be at anchor.

an|ketten *vt* to chain.

An|klage die - 1. [vor Gericht] charge; **gegen jn Anklage erheben** to bring a charge against sb - 2. [öffentlich] accusation - 3. [Kläger] prosecution.

an|klagen vt - 1. [vor Gericht]: **jn (wegen etw) anklagen** to charge sb (with sthg) - 2. [öffentlich] to accuse.

Anklang der: **(bei jm) Anklang finden** to meet with (sb's) approval.

an|kleben vt to stick.

an|klopfen vi to knock.

an|knüpfen <> vt - 1. [Seil]: **etw an etw (A) anknüpfen** to tie sthg to sthg - 2. [Gespräch] to strike up. <> vi [Worte, Vorlesung]: **an etw (A) anknüpfen** to take sthg up.

an|kommen (perf ist angekommen) vi (unreg) - 1. [am Ziel] to arrive; **sie kommt mit dem Auto an** she's coming by car - 2. [näher kommen] to approach - 3. [mit Idee, Vorschlag]: **mit etw ankommen** to come up with sthg - 4. (RW): **bei jm gut/schlecht** ODER **nicht ankommen** to come down well/badly with sb - 5. [sich durchsetzen]: **gegen jn/etw nicht ankommen** to be no match for sb/sthg - 6. [wichtig sein]: **es kommt auf jn/etw an** it depends on sb/sthg; **es kommt darauf an** it depends; **es kommt mir vor allem auf die Qualität an** what matters to me is quality - 7. [riskieren]: **es auf etw (A) ankommen lassen** to run the risk of sthg.

an|kreiden vt: **jm etw ankreiden** to hold sthg against sb.

an|kreuzen vt to mark with a cross.

an|kündigen vt to announce. ◆ **sich ankündigen** ref: **der Herbst kündigt sich an** autumn is on its way.

Ankunft die arrival.

an|kurbeln vt to boost.

an|lächeln vt to smile at.

an|lachen vt - 1. [lachen] to look smilingly at - 2. [erobern]: **sich (D) jn anlachen** to land o.s. sb.

Anlage die - 1. [Park - städtisch] park; [- von Schloss, Gebäude] grounds Pl - 2. [Gelände - militärisch] installation; [- für Sport] facilities Pl - 3. [Geldanlage] investment - 4. [Bau] construction.

Anlass (pl Anlässe) der - 1. [Grund] cause; **dazu gibt es keinen Anlass** there's no call for that - 2. [Ereignis] occasion.

an|lassen vt (unreg) - 1. [eingeschaltet lassen] to leave on - 2. [starten] to start (up) - 3. [anbehalten] to keep on.

Anlasser (pl -) der AUTO starter.

anlässlich präp: **anlässlich einer Sache** (G) on the occasion of sthg.

an|lasten vt: **jm etw anlasten** [verantwortlich machen für] to blame sb for sthg; [Verbrechen, Charakterfehler] to accuse sb of sthg.

Anlauf der - 1. [Schwung] run-up; **Anlauf nehmen** to take a run-up - 2. [Versuch] attempt.

an|laufen (perf hat/ist angelaufen) (unreg) <> vi (ist) - 1. [beginnen] to begin, to start; [Motor, Maschine] to start; FILM to open - 2. [Körperteil]: **rot/blau anlaufen** to go red/blue - 3. [Metall] to tarnish; [Fensterscheibe, Brille] to steam up - 4. [sich nähern]: **angelaufen kommen** to come running up. <> vt (hat) [Hafen] to call at.

an|legen <> vt - 1. [Garten, Park, Beet] to lay out; [Straße] to plan - 2. [Kartei, Sammlung] to start - 3. [Vorrat] to lay in - 4. [beabsichtigen]: **es darauf anlegen, etw zu tun** to be determined to do sthg - 5. [Geld] to invest - 6. [anlehnen]: **etw (an etw (A)) anlegen** to lay sthg (on sthg) - 7. [umbinden] to put on - 8. [Subj: Tier] to lay back; **die Ohren anlegen** to lay back its ears - 9. [Waffe] to raise to one's shoulder - 10. geh [anziehen - Geschmeide] to put on. <> vi - 1. [Schiff] to dock - 2. [mit Gewehr]: **auf jn/etw anlegen** to aim at sb/sthg. ◆ **sich anlegen** ref: **sich mit jm anlegen** to pick a fight with sb.

Anlege|stelle die mooring.

an|lehnen vt - 1. [Tür, Fenster] to leave ajar - 2. [an die Wand] to lean; **etw an etw (A) anlehnen** to lean sthg against sthg. ◆ **sich anlehnen** ref: **sich an etw (A) anlehnen** to lean against sthg; fig to draw upon sthg.

Anlehnung (pl -en) die: **in Anlehnung an einen Roman entstanden** based on a novel.

Anleitung die - 1. [Hinweis] instruction; **unter js Anleitung** under sb's guidance - 2. [Text] instructions Pl.

an|lernen vt to train.

an|liegen vi (unreg) - 1. [sitzen]: **eng anliegen** to be tight - 2. fam [zu erledigen sein]: **was liegt heute an?** what do we have to do today?

Anlieger (pl -) der resident.

an|locken vt [Kunden] to attract; [mit Köder] to lure.

an|lügen vt (unreg) to lie to.

Anm. abk für **Anmerkung**.

an|machen vt - 1. [Gerät] to turn on, to switch on - 2. [Salat] to dress - 3. salopp [ansprechen] to chat up UK, to hit on US.

an|malen vt [bemalen] to paint.

an|maßen vt: **sich (D) anmaßen, etw zu tun** to presume to do sthg.

anmaßend adj presumptuous.

Anmelde|formular das application form.

an|melden vt - 1. [beim Amt - Auto, Wohnsitz, Gewerbe] to register; [- Fernseher] to get a licence for; [- Patent] to apply for - 2. [in Schule, Kurs] to enrol - 3. [zu Termin] to make an appointment for; **sind Sie für heute angemeldet?** do you have an appointment for today? - 4. [Besuch] to announce. ◆ **sich anmelden** ref - 1. [für Kurs] to enrol - 2. [zu Termin] to make an appointment.

Anmeldung *die* - 1. [beim Amt] registration; [eines Patents] application - 2. [in Schule, Kurs] enrolment - 3. [zu Termin] making an appointment - 4. [Rezeption] reception.

anmerken *vt* - 1. [spüren]: **jm etw anmerken** to notice sthg in sb; **sich (D) nichts anmerken lassen** not to show one's feelings - 2. [sagen] to comment.

Anmerkung (*pl* -en) *die* - 1. [im Text] note - 2. [gesprochen] comment.

annähern *vt* to bring closer. ◆ **sich annähern** *ref*: **sich einander annähern** to approach one another.

annähernd *adv* nearly.

Annäherung (*pl* -en) *die* approach; **die Annäherung von Wallonien an Flandern** the rapprochement between the Walloons and the Flemish.

Annahme (*pl* -n) *die* - 1. [Meinung] assumption; **in der Annahme, dass...** on the assumption that... - 2. [von Paket, Brief] receipt; [von Geschenk] acceptance.

annehmbar ◇ *adj* acceptable. ◇ *adv* reasonably (well).

annehmen *vt* (*unreg*) - 1. [empfangen, zustimmen, akzeptieren, zulassen] to accept; [Anruf] to take - 2. [vermuten] to assume - 3. [Staatsangehörigkeit, Namen, Kind] to adopt; [Dialekt, Gewohnheit] to pick up - 4. [Gestalt] to take on.

Annehmlichkeit (*pl* -en) *die*: **Annehmlichkeiten** [Vorteile] advantages; [Bequemlichkeiten] comforts.

Annonce [aˈnɔŋsə] (*pl* -n) *die* advertisement.

annoncieren [anɔŋˈsiːrən] ◇ *vi* to place an advertisement. ◇ *vt* to advertise.

annullieren *vt* [Ehe] to annul; [Vertrag] to cancel.

anlöden *vt fam* to bore to tears.

anonym ◇ *adj* anonymous. ◇ *adv* anonymously.

Anorak (*pl* -s) *der* anorak.

anordnen *vt* - 1. [befehlen] to order - 2. [Gegenstände] to arrange.

Anordnung *die* - 1. [Aufstellung] layout - 2. [Befehl] order; **auf js Anordnung (A)** on sb's orders; **Anordnungen treffen** to make arrangements.

anpacken ◇ *vt* - 1. [mit Händen] to grab - 2. [behandeln]: **jn hart anpacken** to treat sb harshly - 3. [lösen] to tackle. ◇ *vi* [helfen]: **mit anpacken** to lend a hand.

anpassen *vt*: **etw einer Sache (D) anpassen** to adapt sthg to sthg. ◆ **sich anpassen** *ref* to adapt.

Anpassung (*pl* -en) *die* adaptation.

Anpfiff *der* - 1. [im Fußball] kick-off - 2. *fam* [Tadel] ticking-off.

anpflanzen *vt* to plant.

anpöbeln *vt* to shout abuse at.

anprangern *vt* to denounce.

anpreisen *vt* (*unreg*) [Waren] to tout.

Anprobe *die* fitting.

anprobieren *vt* to try on.

anrechnen *vt* - 1. [einbeziehen] to take into account; **jm etw hoch anrechnen** to think highly of sb for sthg - 2. [berechnen] to charge for.

Anrecht *das* - 1. [Recht]: **ein Anrecht auf etw (A) haben** *oder* **besitzen** to have the right to sthg - 2. [Abonnement] subscription.

Anrede *die* form of address.

anreden *vt* - 1. [ansprechen] to speak to - 2. [mit Titel]: **den Chef mit "Herr Professor" anreden** to address the boss as "Professor"; **jn mit seinem Vornamen anreden** to call sb by their first name.

anregen *vt* - 1. [beleben] to stimulate - 2. [empfehlen] to propose - 3. [ermutigen]: **jn anregen, etw zu tun** to encourage sb to do sthg.

Anregung *die* - 1. [Belebung] stimulation - 2. [Anreiz] incentive.

Anreise *die* journey (there).

anreisen (*perf* **ist angereist**) *vi* to travel (there).

Anreiz *der* incentive.

anrempeln *vt* to barge into.

anrichten *vt* - 1. [Abendessen] to prepare - 2. [Schaden] to cause; **da hast du was Schönes angerichtet!** you've really gone and done it now!

anrücken (*perf* **ist angerückt**) *vi* - 1. [Truppen] to move in - 2. *fam* [auftauchen] to show up.

Anruf *der* call.

Anrufbeantworter (*pl* -) *der* answering machine.

anrufen (*unreg*) ◇ *vt* [telefonieren] to call, to phone. ◇ *vi* to call, to phone; **bei jm anrufen** to call *oder* phone sb.

anrühren *vt* - 1. [berühren - Person, Gegenstand] to touch; [- Thema] to touch on - 2. [rühren] to mix.

ans *präp* (**an** + **das**): **ans Fenster klopfen** to knock on the window; *siehe auch* **an**.

Ansage *die* announcement.

ansagen *vt* to announce; **jm/etw den Kampf ansagen** to declare war on sb/sthg.

ansammeln *vt* to collect. ◆ **sich ansammeln** *ref* - 1. [anhäufen, anstauen] to pile up - 2. [versammeln] to gather.

Ansammlung *die* - 1. [Anhäufung] accumulation - 2. [Versammlung] gathering.

Ansatz *der* - 1. [Anfang, Anzeichen] first sign; **im Ansatz stecken bleiben** to fall at the first hurdle; **gute Ansätze zeigen** to show promising signs - 2. [von Körperteil] base - 3. MATH formulation.

ansaugen *vt* to suck in.

an|schaffen vt: sich (D) etw anschaffen to get o.s. sthg.

Anschaffung (pl -en) die acquisition, purchase.

an|schalten vt to turn on.

an|schauen vt to look at; sich (D) etw anschauen to have a look at sthg.

anschaulich ◇ adj clear. ◇ adv clearly.

Anschein der appearance; dem ODER allem Anschein nach apparently; es hat den Anschein, als ob it looks like, it appears that.

anscheinend adv apparently.

an|schieben vt (unreg) to push-start.

Anschlag der - 1. [Attentat - auf Person] assassination attempt; [- auf Botschaft] attack; einen Anschlag auf jn verüben to make an attempt on sb's life; einen Anschlag auf etw (A) verüben to attack sthg - 2. [Zettel, Plakat] notice - 3. [auf der Schreibmaschine] keystroke; 50 Anschläge pro Zeile 50 characters per line - 4. [am Klavier] touch.

an|schlagen (perf hat/ist angeschlagen) (reg) ◇ vt - 1. [Plakat] to put up - 2. [Geschirr] to chip - 3. [wählen] to adopt - 4. [Taste] to strike - 5. [beim Stricken] to cast on - 6. [verletzen]: sich (D) den Kopf an etw (D) anschlagen to knock one's head against sthg. ◇ vi - 1. [wirken] to work - 2. [bellen] to start barking.

an|schließen vt (unreg) - 1. [verbinden - Telefon, Wasserhahn] to connect; [- Elektrogerät] to plug in - 2. [folgen lassen] to add - 3. [festschließen]: etw an etw (A) anschließen to lock sthg to sthg. ◆ sich anschließen ref [mitmachen]: sich jm/einer Sache anschließen to join sb/sthg; sich einer Meinung anschließen to endorse an opinion.

anschließend ◇ adv afterwards. ◇ adj ensuing.

Anschluss (pl -schlüsse) der - 1. [an Zug, Telefon] connection; den Anschluss verpasst haben fig to be left behind; kein Anschluss unter dieser Nummer the number you have dialled has not been recognized - 2. [Telefonapparat] extension - 3. [zu Freunden]: Anschluss finden to meet people - 4. [Folge]: im Anschluss an etw (A) following sthg - 5. POL Anschluss.

an|schmiegen ◆ sich anschmiegen ref: sich an jn/etw anschmiegen to snuggle up to sb/sthg.

an|schnallen vt [Skier, Rollschuhe] to put on; [Sicherheitsgurt] to fasten. ◆ sich anschnallen ref to fasten one's seat belt.

an|schneiden vt (unreg) - 1. [schneiden] to cut into - 2. fig [ansprechen] to broach.

an|schreiben (unreg) ◇ vt - 1. [Schulden]: sie ließ ihre Einkäufe anschreiben she asked to pay for her purchases later - 2. [per Brief] to write to. ◇ vi: anschreiben lassen to pay later.

an|schreien vt (unreg) to shout at.

Anschrift die address.

Anschuldigung (pl -en) die accusation.

an|schwellen (perf ist angeschwollen) vi (unreg) - 1. [Körperteil] to swell - 2. [Gewässer] to rise - 3. [Geräusch] to grow louder.

an|schwemmen vt to wash up.

an|sehen (unreg) ◇ vt - 1. [anblicken] to look at; sich (D) etw ansehen [zur Unterhaltung] to go and see sthg; sich (D) jn/etw ansehen [zur Prüfung] to look at sb/sthg - 2. [erkennen]: man sieht ihm sein Alter nicht an he doesn't look his age; man sieht ihr ihre Müdigkeit nicht an her tiredness doesn't show - 3. [erachten]: jn/etw als etw ansehen to regard sb/sthg as sthg - 4. [ertragen]: etw nicht (mit) ansehen können not to be able to stand sthg. ◇ vi: sieh mal an! fancy that!

Ansehen das [Ruf] reputation.

ansehnlich adj - 1. [groß] considerable - 2. [schön] attractive.

an sein (perf ist an gewesen) vi (unreg) to be on.

an|setzen ◇ vt - 1. [in Stellung bringen - Werkzeug] to place in position; [- Trinkgefäß, Blasinstrument] to raise to one's lips - 2. [Termin] to arrange; [Preis] to fix - 3. [Stück]: etw an etw (A) ansetzen to attach sthg to sthg - 4. [Person]: jn auf etw (A) ansetzen to put sb on sthg - 5. [zubereiten] to prepare - 6. [anlagern]: Rost ansetzen to get rusty. ◇ vi [anfangen] to begin; zum Sprung ansetzen to get ready to jump; das Flugzeug setzte zur Landung an the plane was commencing its descent. ◆ sich ansetzen ref [sich ablagern - Rost, Schimmel] to form; [- Kalk] to accumulate, to build up.

Ansicht (pl -en) die - 1. [Meinung] opinion, view; der gleichen/anderer Ansicht sein to be of the same/a different opinion; meiner Ansicht nach in my view ODER opinion - 2. [Betrachtung]: zur Ansicht [zur Probe] on trial ODER approval - 3. [Abbildung] view. ◆ Ansichten pl opinions, views.

Ansichts|karte die postcard.

ansonsten adv otherwise.

an|spannen vt - 1. [Muskel] to tense; [Seil] to tauten - 2. [anstrengen] to put under strain - 3. [Pferd] to harness.

Anspannung die strain; nervöse Anspannung nervous tension.

an|spielen ◇ vi: auf jn/etw anspielen to allude to sb/sthg. ◇ vt SPORT to play the ball to.

Anspielung (pl -en) die allusion.

an|spornen ['anʃpɔrnən] vt to spur on; jn zu etw anspornen to spur sb on to sthg.

Ansprache (pl -n) die speech.

ansprechbar adj: nicht ansprechbar sein [wegen Krankheit, Ohnmacht, Trunkenheit] to be in no fit state to talk to anybody; [beschäftigt sein] to be unavailable to talk to anybody.

an|springen (perf hat/ist angesprungen) (unreg) <> vt (hat) [angreifen] to pounce on. <> vi (ist) - 1. [Auto, Motor] to start - 2. fam [reagieren]: **auf etw** (A) **anspringen** to jump at sthg.

An|spruch der - 1. [Recht] claim; **auf etw Anspruch haben** to be entitled to sthg - 2. [Forderung] demand; **hohe Ansprüche an jn stellen** to demand a lot of sb; **jn/etw in Anspruch nehmen** to make demands on sb/sthg; **viel Zeit in Anspruch nehmen** to take a lot of time; **ich nahm seine Hilfe gern in Anspruch** I was happy to accept his help.

anspruchslos ['anʃpruxsloːs] adj - 1. [bescheiden] unpretentious; [Leben] simple - 2. [Publikum, Person, Lektüre] undemanding - 3. [Pflanze] easy to look after.

anspruchsvoll ['anʃpruxsfɔl] adj demanding; [Zeitung] serious.

an|stacheln ['anʃtaxln] vt [Ehrgeiz] to fire; **jn zu etw anstacheln** to goad sb into sthg.

Anstalt (pl -en) die - 1. [Institution] institution - 2. [Irrenanstalt] mental hospital, institution.

Anstand der [gutes Benehmen] decency.

anständig <> adj decent; **eine anständige Tracht Prügel** fam a real hiding. <> adv - 1. [ordentlich, integer] decently - 2. fam [kräftig]: **anständig bezahlen** to pay well; **anständig reinhauen** to stuff one's face.

anstandslos adv without hesitation.

an|starren vt to stare at.

anstatt präp: **anstatt js/einer Sache** instead of sb/sthg. <> **anstatt dass** konj: **anstatt dass wir reden** instead of talking. <> **anstatt zu** konj instead of.

an|stecken <> vt - 1. [infizieren, mitreißen] to infect; **jn mit etw anstecken** to infect sb with sthg, to give sb sthg; **er hat uns alle mit seinem Lachen angesteckt** his laughter was infectious - 2. [Zigarette, Kerze] to light; [Haus] to set fire to - 3. [Orden, Brosche] to pin on; [einen Ring] to put on. <> vi to be infectious. <> **sich anstecken** ref: **sich (bei jm) mit etw anstecken** to catch sthg (from sb).

ansteckend adj infectious.

Ansteckung (pl -en) die infection.

an|stehen vi (unreg) - 1. [in Schlange] to queue UK, to stand in line US - 2. [Problem] to be on the agenda; [Termin] to be fixed.

an|steigen (perf ist angestiegen) vi (unreg) to rise.

anstelle präp: **anstelle js/einer Sache**, **anstelle von jm/etw** instead of sb/sthg.

an|stellen vt - 1. [Gerät] to turn on - 2. [Angestellte] to employ, to take on; **in einem Großbetrieb angestellt sein** to work in a big factory - 3. [zustande bringen - Beobachtung, Vergleich] to make; [- Unfug] to get up to; [- Blödsinn] to talk; **sie hat alles Mögliche angestellt** she tried everything; **wie soll ich das anstel-**

len? how am I supposed to do that? <> **sich anstellen** ref - 1. [Schlange stehen] to queue UK, to stand in line US - 2. [sich benehmen] to act; **sie stellte sich sehr geschickt an** she got the hang of it very quickly.

Anstellung die position.

Anstieg (pl -e) der - 1. [Zunahme] rise - 2. [Aufstieg] ascent.

an|stiften vt: **jn zu etw anstiften** to incite sb to sthg.

Anstoß der - 1. [Anlass] impetus (U); **den Anstoß zu etw geben** to provide the impetus for sthg - 2. [Ärger]: **an etw** (D) **Anstoß nehmen** to take offence at sthg - 3. [im Fußball] kick-off.

an|stoßen (perf hat/ist angestoßen) (unreg) <> vt (hat) [mit dem Fuß] to kick; [mit dem Ellenbogen - mit Gewalt] to elbow; [- heimlich] to nudge; **sich das Knie am Tisch anstoßen** to bang one's knee on the table. <> vi - 1. (ist) [anecken]: **mit der Schulter am Schrank anstoßen** to bang one's shoulder on the cupboard - 2. (hat) [angrenzen]: **an etw** (A) **anstoßen** to adjoin sthg - 3. (hat) [mit Gläsern]: **(mit jm) auf jn/etw anstoßen** to drink to sb/ sthg (with sb).

an|strahlen vt - 1. [beleuchten - Bauwerk] to floodlight; [- Schauspieler] to spotlight - 2. [anlächeln] to beam at.

an|streichen vt (unreg) - 1. [streichen] to paint - 2. [kennzeichnen] to mark.

an|strengen ['anʃtrɛŋən] vt - 1. [ermüden] to strain - 2. [Kräfte, Fantasie, Kopf] to use - 3. [Prozess] to start. <> **sich anstrengen** ref [sich bemühen] to make an effort, to try.

Anstrengung (pl -en) die effort.

Anstrich der - 1. [Farbe] coat of paint - 2. [Schein] air; **einer Sache** (D) **einen seriösen Anstrich geben** to lend authority to sthg.

Ansturm der - 1. [Angriff] assault - 2. [Andrang] rush.

an|stürmen (perf ist angestürmt) vi: **gegen etw anstürmen** [Festung] to storm sthg.

Antarktis die Antarctic.

Anteil (pl -e) der - 1. [Teil] share - 2. [Teilnahme]: **an etw** (D) **Anteil haben** to participate in sthg; **an etw** (D) **Anteil nehmen** [bemitleiden] to share in sthg; [sich beteiligen] to participate in sthg.

Anteilnahme die - 1. [Mitleid] sympathy - 2. [Interesse] interest.

Antenne (pl -n) die - 1. TECH aerial - 2. [Gefühl]: **eine/keine Antenne für etw haben** to have a/ no feel for sthg.

Anthrax (pl Anthrax) das anthrax.

Antialkoholiker, in [antialko'hoːlikɐ, rɪn] (mpl Antialkoholiker, fpl -nen) der, die teetotaller.

antiautoritär [antiautori'tɛːɐ̯] <> adj permissive. <> adv permissively.

Antibiotikum [anti'bjo:tikum] (*pl* **-ka**) *das* antibiotic.

antifaschistisch *adj* antifascist.

antik [an'ti:k] *adj* - **1.** [klassisch] classical - **2.** [alt] antique.

Antike [an'ti:kə] *die*: **die Antike** (classical) antiquity.

Antikörper *der* antibody.

an|tippen *vt* - **1.** [Gegenstand] to tap - **2.** [Thema] to touch on.

antiquarisch *adj* second-hand.

Antiquität [antikvi'tɛ:t] (*pl* **-en**) *die* antique.

Antrag ['antra:k] (*pl* **Anträge**) *der* - **1.** [Bitte] application; **einen Antrag auf etw (A) stellen** to apply for sthg - **2.** [im Parlament] motion - **3.** [Formular] application form.

Antragsformular *das* application form.

an|treffen *vt* (*unreg*) to find.

an|treiben *vt* (*unreg*) - **1.** [Wagen] to drive; [Motor, Gerät] to power - **2.** [Person] to urge on; **jn zur Eile antreiben** to urge sb to hurry - **3.** [anschwemmen] to wash up.

an|treten (*perf* hat/ist **angetreten**) (*unreg*) ⟨⟩ *vt* (hat) - **1.** [beginnen] to start - **2.** [Erbschaft] to come into. ⟨⟩ *vi* (ist) - **1.** [sich aufstellen] to line up - **2.** [kämpfen]: **gegen jn antreten** [in Fußball, Tennis] to play sb; [im Boxen] to fight sb; [in Wahl] to stand against sb.

Antrieb *der* - **1.** [Kraft] drive; **mit elektrischem Antrieb** electrically-powered - **2.** [Motivation] impetus; **etw aus eigenem Antrieb tun** to do sthg on one's own initiative.

an|trinken *vt* (*unreg*): **sich** (D) **Mut antrinken** to fill o.s. with Dutch courage.

Antritt *der* (*ohne pl*) - **1.** [Beginn] start - **2.** SPORT: **er hat einen schnellen Antritt** he has a good turn of pace.

an|tun *vt* (*unreg*) - **1.** [Unrecht] to do; **wie konntest du mir das antun?** how could you do that to me?; **sich** (D) **etwas antun** to take one's own life - **2.** [Gutes]: **jm zu viel Ehre antun** to do sb too much justice - **3.** [lieben]: **das Bild hat es mir angetan** I really like the picture.

Antwort ['antvɔrt] (*pl* **-en**) *die* - **1.** [Erwiderung] answer; [auf Brief] reply; **die Antwort auf etw** (A) the answer to sthg; **Antwort/keine Antwort geben** to reply/not to reply - **2.** [Reaktion] response; **als Antwort auf** (+ A) in response to.

antworten ⟨⟩ *vi* - **1.** [erwidern] to answer; **auf etw** (A) **antworten** to answer sthg, to reply to sthg - **2.** [reagieren] to respond. ⟨⟩ *vt* [auf Fragen] to answer.

an|vertrauen *vt*: **jm etw anvertrauen** to entrust sb with sthg. ⟨⟩ **sich anvertrauen** *ref*: **sich jm anvertrauen** to confide in sb.

an|wachsen ['anvaksn] (*perf* ist **angewachsen**) *vi* (*unreg*) - **1.** [festwachsen] to take root - **2.** [wachsen] to increase.

Anwalt ['anvalt] (*pl* **Anwälte**) *der* - **1.** [Rechtsanwalt] lawyer - **2.** *fig* [Fürsprecher] advocate.

Anwältin ['anvɛltɪn] (*pl* **-nen**) *die* - **1.** [Rechtsanwältin] lawyer - **2.** *fig* [Fürsprecherin] advocate.

Anwaltsbüro *das* [Firma] firm of lawyers.

Anwärter, in (*mpl* **-**, *fpl* **-nen**) *der, die*: **ein Anwärter (auf etw** (A)**)** a candidate (for sthg).

an|weisen *vt* (*unreg*) - **1.** [zeigen] to show; **jm etw anweisen** to show sthg to sb - **2.** [beauftragen]: **jn anweisen, etw zu tun** to instruct sb to do sthg.

Anweisung *die* - **1.** [Befehl] instruction; **Anweisung haben, etw zu tun** to have instructions to do sthg - **2.** [Zahlung - per Bank] payment; [- per Post] postal order.

anwendbar *adj*: **(auf jn/etw) anwendbar sein** to be applicable (to sb/sthg).

an|wenden *vt* - **1.** [Hilfsmittel, Gewalt, List] to use - **2.** [Methode, Regel]: **etw auf jn/etw anwenden** to apply sthg to sb/sthg.

Anwendung *die* - **1.** [Verwendung, Einsatz] use - **2.** [von Methode, Regel] application.

an|werben *vt* (*unreg*) to recruit.

anwesend *adj* present; **bei etw anwesend sein** to be present at sthg.

Anwesenheit *die* presence; **in js Anwesenheit** (D)**, in Anwesenheit von jm** in sb's presence.

an|widern ['anvi:dɐn] *vt* to fill with repulsion.

Anwohner, in (*mpl* **-**, *fpl* **-nen**) *der, die* resident.

Anzahl *die* number.

an|zahlen *vt* to pay a deposit on; **100 Euro anzahlen** to pay a deposit of 100 euros.

Anzahlung *die* deposit, down payment.

Anzeichen *das* sign.

Anzeige ['antsaigə] (*pl* **-n**) *die* - **1.** [in Zeitung] advertisement; [Brief] announcement - **2.** [Instrument] display - **3.** [Strafanzeige] charge; **gegen jn Anzeige erstatten** to bring a charge against sb.

an|zeigen *vt* - **1.** [melden] to report - **2.** [zeigen] to show.

Anzeigenteil *der* advertisements section.

an|zetteln ['antsetln] *vt* to instigate.

an|ziehen (*unreg*) ⟨⟩ *vt* - **1.** [Kleidung] to put on; **sich** (D) **etw anziehen** to put sthg on - **2.** [Person]: **jn anziehen** to dress sb - **3.** PHYS [anlocken] to attract - **4.** [Schraube, Tau] to tighten; [Bremse] to apply - **5.** [Körperteil] to draw up. ⟨⟩ *vi* - **1.** [steigen] to rise - **2.** [beschleunigen] to accelerate. ⟨⟩ **sich anziehen** *ref* [Person] to get dressed; **sich warm anziehen** to dress warmly.

anziehend *adj* attractive.

Anziehungskraft *die* - **1.** PHYS (gravitational) attraction - **2.** [Reiz] attractiveness, appeal.

Anlzug der - **1.** [Kleidungsstück] suit - **2.** [Nähern]: **im Anzug sein** to be approaching.

anzüglich ['antsy:kliç] <> adj lewd. <> adv lewdly.

anlzünden vt [Streichholz, Kerze] to light; [Haus] to set fire to.

anlzweifeln vt to doubt.

Apartment = **Appartement**.

Aperitif [aperi'ti:f] (pl -s) der aperitif.

Apfel ['apfl] (pl Äpfel) der apple.

Apfellbaum der apple tree.

Apfellkuchen der apple cake.

Apfellmus das apple sauce (usually eaten as dessert).

Apfellsaft der apple juice.

Apfelsine [apfl'zi:nə] (pl -n) die orange.

Apfellwein der cider.

Apostel [a'pɔstl] (pl -) der apostle.

Apostroph [apo'stro:f] (pl -e) der apostrophe.

Apotheke [apo'te:kə] (pl -n) die pharmacy, chemist's UK, drugstore US.

Apotheker, in (mpl -, fpl -nen) der, die pharmacist, chemist UK, druggist US.

Apparat [apa'ra:t] (pl -e) der - **1.** [Gerät] device - **2.** [Telefon]: **am Apparat!** speaking! - **3.** [von Partei, Staat] apparatus - **4.** salopp [Riesending] whopper.

Appartement [apartə'mã:], **Apartment** [a'partmənt] (pl -s) das [Wohnung] flat UK, apartment US.

Appell [a'pɛl] (pl -e) der - **1.** [Aufruf] appeal - **2.** MIL roll call.

appellieren vi: **an jn/etw appellieren** to appeal to sb/sthg.

Appetit [ape'ti:t] der appetite; **Appetit/keinen Appetit auf etw (A)** haben to feel/not to feel like sthg; **guten Appetit!** enjoy your meal!

appetitlich adj appetizing.

applaudieren [aplau'di:rən] vi to applaud.

Applaus [a'plaus] der (ohne pl) applause; **jm Applaus spenden** to applaud sb.

Aprikose [apri'ko:zə] (pl -n) die apricot.

April der (ohne pl) April; **April, April!** April fool!; siehe auch **September**.

Aprillscherz der April fool's trick.

apropos [apro'po:] adv by the way; **apropos Pizza, hast du Hunger?** talking of pizza, are you hungry?

Aquarell [akva'rɛl] (pl -e) das - **1.** [Bild] watercolour - **2.** [Farbe]: **in Aquarell malen** to paint in watercolours.

Aquarium [a'kva:rjʊm] (pl Aquarien) das aquarium.

Äquator [ɛ'kva:tɔr] der (ohne pl) equator.

Ära ['ɛ:ra] (pl Ären) die era.

Araber, in ['arabɐ, rɪn] (mpl -, fpl -nen) der, die Arab.

Arabien nt Arabia.

arabisch adj [Kultur, Volk, Politik] Arab; [Sprache, Literatur] Arabic; [Halbinsel, Landschaft] Arabian.

Arabisch(e) das (ohne pl) Arabic; siehe auch **Englisch(e)**.

Arbeit ['arbait] (pl -en) die - **1.** [gen] work; **die Arbeiten am Tunnel** the work on the tunnel; **bei der Arbeit sein** to be working; **ihr Wagen ist in Arbeit** your car is being worked on; **zur Arbeit gehen** to go to work - **2.** [Arbeitsstelle] job; **keine Arbeit haben** to be out of work; **Arbeit suchen** to be looking for work ODER a job - **3.** [Leistung, Werk] work - **4.** [Klassenarbeit] test - **5.** [wissenschaftlich] paper.

arbeiten <> vi - **1.** [Person] to work; **bei der Post arbeiten** to work for the Post Office; **zu Hause arbeiten** to work from home; **an etw (D) arbeiten** to work on sthg; **an sich (D) arbeiten** to work hard - **2.** [funktionieren - Maschine] to operate; [- Herz] to function. <> vt to make; **sich (D) die Finger** ODER **Hände wund arbeiten** to work one's fingers to the bone. ◆ **sich arbeiten** ref: **sich nach oben arbeiten** to work one's way up.

Arbeiter (pl -) der worker.

Arbeiterin (pl -nen) die worker.

Arbeitgeber, in (mpl -, fpl -nen) der, die employer.

Arbeitnehmer, in (mpl -, fpl -nen) der, die employee.

Arbeitslamt das job centre UK, employment agency US.

Arbeitslaufwand der: **der Arbeitsaufwand ist zu hoch** it would take too much effort.

arbeitsfrei adj: **zwei arbeitsfreie Nachmittage in der Woche** two afternoons off a week.

Arbeitslkraft die: **sich (D) seine Arbeitskraft erhalten** to keep o.s. fit for work. ◆ **Arbeitskräfte** Pl workers.

Arbeitslkreis der [Lerngruppe] study group; [Ausschuss] working party.

arbeitslos adj unemployed.

Arbeitslose (pl -n) der, die unemployed person; **die Arbeitslosen** the unemployed.

Arbeitslosigkeit die (ohne pl) unemployment.

Arbeitslmarkt der labour market.

Arbeitslplatz der - **1.** [Stellung, Job] job - **2.** [Ort] workplace; **dort am Fenster ist mein Arbeitsplatz** I work over there by the window.

arbeitsscheu adj workshy.

Arbeitslspeicher der EDV RAM.

Arbeitslstelle die - **1.** [Stellung] job - **2.** [Ort, Abteilung] department.

Arbeitsᛁsuche die: auf Arbeitssuche sein to be looking for work ODER a job.

Arbeitsᛁtag der working day.

Arbeitsᛁteilung die division of labour.

Arbeitsᛁunfall der industrial accident.

Arbeitsᛁvermittlung die [private Agentur] employment agency.

Arbeitsᛁweise die [von Person] way of working; [von Maschine] mode of operation.

Arbeitsᛁzeit die working hours Pl.

Arbeitsᛁzimmer das study.

Archäologe [arçɛo'lo:gə] (pl -n) der archaeologist.

Archäologin [aʀçeo'lo:gɪn] (pl -nen) die archaeologist.

Arche ['arçə] (pl -n) die: die Arche Noah Noah's Ark.

Architekt, in [arçi'tɛkt, ɪn] (mpl -en, fpl -nen) der, die architect.

Architektur [arçitɛk'tu:ʀ] die (ohne pl) architecture.

Archiv [ar'çi:f] (pl -e) das archive.

archivieren [arçi'vi:rən] vt to (store in an) archive.

ARD [ɑːɛr'de:] (abk für Arbeitsgemeinschaft der öffentlich-rechtlichen Rundfunkanstalten der Bundesrepublik Deutschland) die German public broadcasting network, responsible for the Erstes Programm TV channel.

Arena [a're:na] (pl Arenen) die arena.

arg [ark] (kompar ärger, superl ärgste) ⬦ adj [schlimm] bad; [sehr schlimm] terrible; js ärgster Feind sb's arch enemy. ⬦ adv [schlimm] badly; [sehr schlimm] terribly.

Argentinien nt Argentina.

Ärger ['ɛrgɐ] der (ohne pl) - 1. [Verärgerung] annoyance; [Zorn] anger - 2. [Problem] trouble; (jm) Ärger machen to cause (sb) trouble.

ärgerlich ⬦ adj - 1. [verärgert] annoyed; [zornig] angry; auf jn/über etw (A) ärgerlich sein [verärgert] to be annoyed with sb/at sthg; [zornig] to be angry with sb/at sthg - 2. [unangenehm] annoying. ⬦ adv [verärgert] angrily.

ärgern vt to annoy. ⬟ sich ärgern ref to get annoyed; sich über jn/etw ärgern to get annoyed with sb/at sthg.

Ärgernis (pl -se) das - 1. [Ärgerliches] nuisance - 2. RECHT: Erregung öffentlichen Ärgernisses offence against public decency.

Argument (pl -e) das argument.

argumentieren vi to argue.

Argwohn der (ohne pl) suspicion.

argwöhnisch ⬦ adj suspicious. ⬦ adv suspiciously.

Arie ['ɑːrjə] (pl -n) die aria.

aristokratisch adj aristocratic.

Arithmetik die (ohne pl) arithmetic.

Arkaden Pl ARCHIT arcade sing.

Arktis die Arctic.

arm (kompar ärmer, superl ärmste) ⬦ adj poor; um etw ärmer sein to have lost sthg; er ist nun um 50 Euro ärmer he's now 50 euros worse off ODER the poorer; arm dran sein fam to be in a bad way. ⬦ adv poorly; jn arm essen to eat sb out of house and home.

Arm (pl -e) der [gen] arm; jn/etw im Arm halten to hold sb/sthg in one's arms; jn auf den Arm nehmen to pull sb's leg; jn mit offenen Armen aufnehmen to welcome sb with open arms. ⬟ Arm in Arm adv arm in arm.

Armatur (pl -en) die [von Maschine, Auto] instrument. ⬟ Armaturen Pl [im Badezimmer] fittings.

Armaturenᛁbrett das AUTO dashboard.

Armᛁband (pl -bänder) das [Schmuck] bracelet; [von Uhr] strap.

Armbandᛁuhr die wristwatch, watch.

Armᛁbinde die armband.

Arme (pl -n) der, die - 1. [Bedauernswerte] poor thing; du Armer! you poor thing! - 2. [Mittellose] poor man/woman; die Armen the poor.

Armee [ar'me:] (pl -n) die army.

Ärmel (pl -) der sleeve; die Ärmel hochkrempeln eigtl & fig to roll up one's sleeves.

Ärmelkanal der: der Ärmelkanal the (English) Channel.

Armᛁlehne die arm, armrest.

ärmlich ⬦ adj [Wohnung, Kleidung] shabby; [Verhältnisse] miserable. ⬦ adv shabbily.

armselig adj - 1. [ärmlich] shabby - 2. [gering] meagre.

Armut die (ohne pl) poverty.

Aroma (pl -s ODER Aromen) das - 1. [Geruch] aroma - 2. [Würze] flavouring.

arrangieren [arãʒ'ʒi:rən] vt [Treffen, Feier, Musik] to arrange. ⬟ sich arrangieren ref: sich mit jm arrangieren [sich verständigen] to come to an understanding with sb.

arrogant ⬦ adj arrogant. ⬦ adv arrogantly.

Arroganz die (ohne pl) arrogance.

Arsch (pl Ärsche) der salopp - 1. [Gesäß] arse UK, ass US - 2. [Blödmann] arsehole UK, asshole US; jm in den Arsch kriechen vulg to lick sb's arse UK ODER ass US.

Arsen das (ohne pl) arsenic.

Art (pl -en) die - 1. [Weise] way; eine einfache Art, etw zuzubereiten a simple way of preparing ODER to prepare sthg; etw auf eine andere Art tun to do sthg another way; auf gesunde Art healthily; auf diese Art wird er nie gewinnen he'll never win like this ODER this way; die Art und Weise(, wie) the way (that); Bratkartoffeln nach Art des Hauses the chef's special fried potatoes - 2. (ohne pl) [Wesen] nature; [Verhalten] behaviour; das entspricht nicht ihrer Art, sich zu beschweren it's not like her to complain - **3.** [Sorte] sort, kind; **eine Art Grippe** a sort *oder* kind of flu; **in dieser Art** in this form; **das Schloss ist in seiner Art einmalig** the castle is the only one of its kind - **4.** BIOL species.

Artensterben *das (ohne pl)* dying out of species.

Arterie *(pl -n) die* artery.

Arteriosklerose *(pl -n) die* arteriosclerosis *(U)*.

Arthritis *die* arthritis.

artig <> *adj* good. <> *adv:* **sie hat den Teller Spinat artig aufgegessen** she ate up all her spinach like a good girl.

Artikel *(pl -) der* - **1.** [in der Zeitung, im Gesetz] article; [im Wörterbuch] entry - **2.** [Ware] item, article - **3.** GRAMM: **der bestimmte/unbestimmte Artikel** the definite/indefinite article.

artikulieren *vt* to articulate.

Artillerie *(pl -n) die* MIL artillery.

Artischocke *(pl -n) die* artichoke.

Artist, in *(mpl -en, fpl -nen) der, die* [im Zirkus] (circus) performer.

artistisch *adj* acrobatic.

Arznei *(pl -en) die* medicine.

Arzt [aːɐ̯t͡st] *(pl Ärzte) der* doctor.

Arzthelfer, in *der, die* doctor's receptionist.

Ärztin ['ɛːɐ̯t͡stɪn] *(pl -nen) die* doctor.

ärztlich *adj* medical.

Arztpraxis *die* doctor's practice.

as *(pl -)*, **As** *(pl -) das* MUS A flat.

As *(pl -se) das* = **Ass.**

Asbest *(pl -e) das* asbestos.

Asche *(pl -n) die* [von Feuer] ashes *Pl*; [von Zigarre, Vulkan] ash.

Aschenbecher *der* ashtray.

Aschenputtel *(pl Aschenputtel) das* Cinderella.

Aschermittwoch *der* Ash Wednesday.

Asiat, in *(mpl -en, fpl -nen) der, die* Asian.

asiatisch *adj* Asian.

Asien *nt* Asia.

asozial <> *adj* antisocial. <> *adv* antisocially.

Aspekt *(pl -e) der* aspect.

Asphalt [as'falt] *(pl -e) der* asphalt.

asphaltieren *vt* to asphalt.

aß *prät* ⊳ **essen.**

Ass *(pl -e) das* [Spielkarte, Person] ace.

Assistent, in *(mpl -en, fpl -nen) der, die* assistant.

assistieren *vi* to assist; **jm bei etw assistieren** to assist sb with sthg.

Ast *(pl Äste) der* branch; **sich** *(D)* **einen Ast lachen** *fam fig* to laugh o.s. silly.

AStA ['asta] *(pl ASten) (abk für Allgemeiner Studentenausschuss) der* students' union.

Aster *(pl -n) die* aster.

Astgabel *die* fork in a branch.

Ästhetik [ɛs'teːtɪk] *(pl -en) die* - **1.** *(ohne pl)* [das Schöne] aesthetic - **2.** [Wissenschaft] aesthetics *(U)*.

Asthma *das* asthma.

Astrologie *die (ohne pl)* astrology.

astrologisch *adj* astrological.

Astronaut, in *(mpl -en, fpl -nen) der, die* astronaut.

Astronomie *die (ohne pl)* astronomy.

Asyl *(pl -e) das* - **1.** *(ohne pl)* [Zuflucht] asylum - **2.** [Obdachlosenasyl] hostel.

Asylant *(pl -en) der* asylum seeker.

Asylantin *(pl -nen) die* asylum seeker.

Asylbewerber, in *der, die* asylum seeker.

Asylrecht *das (ohne pl)* right of asylum.

asymmetrisch *adj* asymmetrical.

Atem *der (ohne pl)* - **1.** [die Atmung] breathing - **2.** [die Atemluft] breath; **außer Atem sein** to be out of breath; **Atem holen** [einatmen] to breathe in; [sich ausruhen] to catch one's breath; **jn in Atem halten** [in Spannung versetzen] to keep sb on tenterhooks.

atemberaubend <> *adj* breathtaking. <> *adv* breathtakingly.

atemlos <> *adj* breathless. <> *adv* breathlessly.

Atemnot *die (ohne pl)* difficulty in breathing.

Atempause *die:* **eine Atempause einlegen** *oder* **machen** to take a breather.

Atemzug *der* breath.

Atheist, in *(mpl -en, fpl -nen) der, die* atheist.

Äther *der (ohne pl)* ether.

Äthiopien *nt* Ethiopia.

Athlet, in *(mpl -en, fpl -nen) der, die* athlete.

athletisch <> *adj* athletic. <> *adv* athletically.

Atlantik *der:* **der Atlantik** the Atlantic (Ocean).

Atlas *(pl -se oder Atlanten) der* - **1.** [Buch] atlas - **2.** *(pl Atlasse)* [Satin] satin.

atmen *vt & vi* to breathe.

Atmosphäre *(pl -n) die* eigtl & fig atmosphere.

Atmung *die (ohne pl)* breathing.

Atoll *(pl -e) das* atoll.

Atom *(pl -e) das* atom.

atomar *adj* - **1.** [von Atomen] atomic - **2.** [mit Atomkraft] nuclear.

Atombombe *die* atom *oder* atomic bomb.

Atomkraft *die (ohne pl)* nuclear power.

Atomkraftwerk *das* nuclear power station.

Atom|krieg *der* nuclear war.

Atom|macht *die* nuclear power *(country).*

Atom|müll *der (ohne pl)* nuclear waste.

Atom|sprengkopf *der* nuclear warhead.

Atom|waffe *die* nuclear weapon.

Attentat *(pl -e) das* [erfolglos] assassination attempt; [erfolgreich] assassination.

Attentäter, in *(mpl -, fpl -nen) der, die* [erfolglos] would-be assassin; [erfolgreich] assassin.

Attest *(pl -e) das* doctor's certificate.

Attraktion *(pl -en) die* attraction.

attraktiv *adj* attractive.

Attrappe *(pl -n) die* dummy.

Attribut *(pl -e) das geh* [Merkmal & GRAMM] attribute.

au *interj* [Ausdruck von Schmerz] ouch!, ow!

Aubergine [oberˈʒiːnə] *(pl -n) die* aubergine *UK,* eggplant *US.*

auch *adv* - 1. [ebenfalls] also, too; **ich auch me too; ich auch nicht** me neither; **auch das noch!** that's the last thing I need! - 2. [sogar] even - 3. [wirklich]: **sie war unkonzentriert, aber es war ja auch schon spät** she couldn't concentrate, but it was late - 4. [verstärkend]: **dass du auch immer kleckern musst!** do you have to make such a mess!; **hast du die Tür auch wirklich zugemacht?** are you sure you closed the door? - 5. [egal]: **wo auch (immer)** wherever; **was auch (immer)** whatever; **wer auch (immer)** whoever; **wie dem auch sei** be that as it may.

Audienz *(pl -en) die* audience.

audiovisuell [audjoviˈzuɛl] *adj* audiovisual.

auf ◇ *präp* - 1. *(+ D, A)* [räumlich] on; **auf dem/den Tisch** on the table; **auf dem Land** in the country; **aufs Land** to the country; **auf einen Berg steigen** to climb a mountain; **auf der Post** at the post office; **auf eine Feier gehen** to go to a party; **auf die Uni gehen** to go to university** - 2. *(+ D)* [zeitlich - während]: **auf der Reise** on the journey; **auf der Hochzeit/Feier** at the wedding/party - 3. *(+ A)* [zur Angabe der Art und Weise]: **auf diese Art** in this way; **auf Deutsch** in German; **auf jeden Fall** in any case - 4. [feste Verbindungen]: **auf Reisen gehen** to go on a tour; **von heute auf morgen** overnight - 5. *(+ A)* [zur Angabe eines Wunsches]: **auf ihr Wohl!** your good health! - 6. [zur Angabe eines Verhältnisses]: **auf ein Kilo Obst kommt ein Kilo Zucker** add a kilo of sugar for every kilo of fruit. ◇ *adv* - 1. [offen] open; **Tür auf!** open the door! - 2. [aufgestanden] up; **ich bin seit zehn Uhr auf** I've been up since ten o'clock - 3. [feste Verbindungen]: **auf einmal knallte es** suddenly there was a bang; **er aß alle Süßigkeiten auf einmal** he ate all the sweets in one go. ◇ *interj* [los, weg]: **auf in die Kneipe!** (let's

go) to the pub! ◆ **auf und ab** *adv* - 1. [herauf und herunter] up and down - 2. [hin und her] back and forth.

auf|atmen *vi* to breathe a sigh of relief.

Aufbau *(pl -ten) der* - 1. *(ohne pl)* [Bauen - von Zelt, Gerüst] putting up; [- von Ruinen] rebuilding - 2. *(ohne pl)* [Gründung] building up - 3. *(ohne pl)* [Struktur] structure - 4. [Anbau] superstructure.

auf|bauen *vt* - 1. [bauen - Zelt, Gerüst] to put up; [- Ruinen] to rebuild - 2. [gründen, schaffen] to build up - 3. [zusammensetzen - Kulissen, Modelleisenbahn] to build; **aus etw aufgebaut sein** to be made up ODER composed of sthg - 4. TELEKOM [Verbindung] to establish - 5. [ordnen] to structure - 6. [fördern]: **jn zu** ODER **als etw aufbauen** to make ODER turn sb into sthg - 7. [trösten]: **jn aufbauen** to give sb strength - 8. [begründen]: **etw auf etw (D) aufbauen** to base sthg on sthg. ◆ **sich aufbauen** *ref fam* [sich hinstellen] to plant o.s.

auf|bäumen ◆ **sich aufbäumen** *ref* - 1. [Pferd] to rear (up) - 2. [Person]: **sich gegen jn/etw aufbäumen** to rebel against sb/sthg.

auf|bauschen *vt* [übertreiben] to blow up.

auf|bekommen *vt (unreg)* - 1. [öffnen] to get open - 2. *fam* [aufessen] to manage (to eat) - 3. [Schulaufgabe] to get for homework.

auf|bereiten *vt* to process; [Trinkwasser] to purify.

auf|bessern *vt* - 1. [verbessern] to improve - 2. [erhöhen] to increase.

auf|bewahren *vt* [in Tresor] to keep; **etw (für jn) aufbewahren** to look after sthg (for sb); **die Milch kühl aufbewahren** to store the milk in a cool place.

Aufbewahrung *die* storage.

auf|bieten *vt (unreg)* - 1. [Kraft] to summon up; [Einfluss] to use - 2. [Polizei, Militär] to call out.

auf|blasen *vt (unreg)* [Ballon, Luftmatratze] to blow up, to inflate; [Backen] to puff out.

auf|bleiben *(perf ist aufgeblieben) vi (unreg)* - 1. [wach bleiben] to stay up - 2. [offen bleiben] to stay open.

auf|blenden ◇ *vt* to turn on full beam *UK* ODER high beam *US.* ◇ *vi* to put one's headlights on full beam *UK* ODER high beam *US.*

auf|blicken *vi* - 1. [hochsehen] to look up - 2. [bewundern]: **zu jm aufblicken** to look up to sb.

auf|blitzen *(perf aufgeblitzt) vi* [Licht] to flash.

auf|blühen *(perf ist aufgeblüht) vi* - 1. [blühen] to blossom - 2. [aufleben] to blossom (out) - 3. [wachsen] to flourish.

auf|brauchen *vt* to use up.

auf|brausen *(perf ist aufgebraust) vi* - 1. [erklingen] to break out - 2. [hochfahren] to flare up.

auf|brechen *(perf hat/ist aufgebrochen)* *(unreg)* ⬦ *vt (hat)* [mit Gewalt öffnen - Tür] to force open; [- Schloss] to force; [- Deckel] to force off; [- Wohnung, Auto, Tresor] to break into. ⬦ *vi (ist)* - 1. [abreisen]: **aufbrechen (nach)** to set off (for) - 2. [aufreißen] to open.

auf|bringen *vt (unreg)* - 1. [beschaffen] to raise - 2. [einsetzen] to summon up - 3. [einführen - Gerücht] to start - 4. [wütend machen] to make angry - 5. [öffnen können] to get open.

Aufbruch *der (ohne pl)* departure.

auf|brummen *vt fam*: **jm etw aufbrummen** [Strafe] to slap sthg on sb.

auf|bürden *vt*: **jm/sich etw aufbürden** [Verantwortung] to burden sb/o.s. with sthg; [Last, Rucksack] to load sb/o.s. down with sthg.

auf|decken *vt* - 1. [aufschlagen] to turn back - 2. [entdecken] to uncover - 3. [Spielkarten]: **seine Karten** ODER **sein Spiel aufdecken** to show one's hand - 4. [im Bett]: **jn aufdecken** to pull the covers off sb.

auf|drängen *vt*: **jm etw aufdrängen** to force sthg onto sb. ⬦ **sich aufdrängen** *ref* - 1. [Person] to impose; **er hat sich uns vor der Reise aufgedrängt** he imposed himself on us before we set off - 2. [Idee]: **dieser Gedanke/ Verdacht drängte sich mir auf** I couldn't help thinking/suspecting that; **diese Idee drängt sich einem ja sofort auf, wenn man seinen Bericht hört** this idea comes immediately to mind on hearing his report.

auf|drehen ⬦ *vt* - 1. [Wasserhahn, Gas] to turn on; [Deckel] to unscrew; [Flasche, Dose] to open - 2. *fam* [laut stellen] to turn up. ⬦ *vi fam* - 1. [schnell fahren] to put one's foot down - 2. [in Stimmung kommen] to get going.

aufdringlich ⬦ *adj* [Person] pushy; [Farbe] loud; [Parfüm] overpowering. ⬦ *adv* insistently.

aufeinander *adv* - 1. [einer auf dem anderen] one on top of the other; **sie liegen aufeinander** they are lying on top of each other - 2. [gegenseitig] one another; **sie passen aufeinander auf** they look out for each other.

aufeinander folgen *(perf sind aufeinander gefolgt)* *vi* to come one after the other.

aufeinander prallen *(perf sind aufeinander geprallt)* *vi* - 1. [zusammenstoßen] to crash into one another - 2. [sich widersprechen] to clash.

aufeinander stoßen *(perf sind aufeinander gestoßen)* *vi (unreg)* - 1. [Köpfe, Wagons] to bump into each other - 2. [Meinungen] to clash.

Aufenthalt *(pl -e)* *der* - 1. [Anwesenheit] stay; **der Aufenthalt im Bereich des Krans ist gefährlich** keep well clear of the crane - 2. [Unterbrechung] stop; **in Köln haben wir eine Stunde Aufenthalt** we'll have an hour to wait in Cologne.

Aufenthalts|genehmigung *die* residence permit.

Aufenthalts|ort *der* place of residence.

Auferstehung *die (ohne pl)* resurrection.

auf|essen *vt (unreg)* to eat up.

auf|fädeln *vt* to string.

auf|fahren *(perf ist aufgefahren)* *(unreg)* ⬦ *vi* - 1. [im Auto]: **dicht auf den Vordermann auffahren** to sit right on the tail of the car in front; **auf jn/etw auffahren** to run into sb/sthg - 2. [erschrecken] to start; **aus dem Schlaf auffahren** to awake with a start. ⬦ *vt* - 1. [heranfahren] to bring up - 2. *fam* [anbieten] to lay on - 3. [aufschütten] to put down.

Auffahrt *(pl -en)* *die* - 1. [zur Autobahn] slip road *UK*, on-ramp *US* - 2. [zu einem Gebäude] drive - 3. [Aufstieg] climb - 4. *Schweiz* [Himmelfahrt] Ascension Day.

Auffahr|unfall *der* rear-end collision.

auf|fallen *(perf ist aufgefallen)* *vi (unreg)* to stand out; **mir ist nichts Besonderes an ihm aufgefallen** nothing in particular struck me about him; **das ist mir aufgefallen** I've noticed that.

auffallend ⬦ *adj* striking. ⬦ *adv* strikingly.

auffällig ⬦ *adj* [Kleidung, Auto] ostentatious; [Farbe] loud; [Verhalten] odd, unusual. ⬦ *adv* [geschminkt] ostentatiously; [häufig] surprisingly.

auf|fangen *vt (unreg)* - 1. [Ball] to catch - 2. [Worte, Spruch, Signal] to pick up - 3. [Stoß, Schlag] to cushion; [Inflation, Preissteigerung] to offset - 4. [sammeln] to collect.

Auffang|lager *das* transit camp.

auf|fassen *vt* to understand; **etw als etw auffassen** to take sthg as sthg.

Auffassung *die* opinion; **zu der Auffassung kommen, dass ...** to come to the conclusion that ...; **nach js Auffassung** in sb's opinion.

Auffassungs|gabe *die (ohne pl)* intelligence; **eine schnelle Auffassungsgabe haben** to be quick on the uptake.

auf|flackern *(perf ist aufgeflackert)* *vi* [leuchten] to flicker into life.

auf|fliegen *(perf ist aufgeflogen)* *vi (unreg)* - 1. [fliegen] to fly up - 2. [sich öffnen] to fly open - 3. *fam* [entdeckt werden - Vorhaben] to be uncovered; [- Bande] to be broken up.

auf|fordern *vt* - 1. [bitten]: **jn zum Platznehmen auffordern** ODER **invite sb to be seated** - 2. [befehlen]: **jn dazu auffordern, etw zu tun** to require sb to do sthg - 3. [zum Tanz] to ask to dance.

Aufforderung *die* - 1. [Bitte] request, invitation - 2. [Befehl] demand.

auf|frischen ⬦ *vt* - 1. [erneuern - Bezug] to freshen up; [- Farbe] to brighten up; [- Möbel] to renovate - 2. [erweitern - Kenntnisse] to brush up on; [- Erinnerung] to refresh. ⬦ vi [Wind] to freshen.

auf|führen vt - 1. [auf der Bühne] to perform - 2. [nennen, auflisten] to give, to list. ➠ **sich aufführen** ref abw [sich benehmen] to behave.

Auf|führung die [Vorstellung] performance.

auf|füllen vt - 1. [nachfüllen] to top up - 2. [füllen] to fill up - 3. [ergänzen] to replenish.

Auf|gabe die - 1. [Pflicht] task; **das ist nicht meine Aufgabe** that's not my responsibility - 2. [Kapitulation] surrender - 3. (ohne pl) [von Geschäften]: **die Einzelhändler wurden zur Aufgabe genötigt** the retailers were forced to give up their businesses - 4. [eines Pakets] posting UK, mailing US; [einer Anzeige] placing - 5. [SCHULE - in Prüfung] question; [- in Mathematik] problem; [- Übung] exercise; [- Schulaufgabe] homework (U).

Aufgaben|bereich der area of responsibility.

Aufgang (pl Aufgänge) der - 1. [Treppe] stairs Pl - 2. [Leuchten] rising.

auf|geben (unreg) ⬦ vt - 1. [Gewohnheit, Stelle, Geschäft] to give up; **das Rauchen aufgeben** to give up smoking - 2. [Person] to give up on; [Plan, Idee, Hoffnung] to give up; [Wettkampf, Spiel] to pull out of; **ich gebe es auf!** I give up! - 3. [auftragen] to set; **jm etw aufgeben** to set sb sthg - 4. [Bestellung] to place; **eine Anzeige aufgeben** to place an advert in the paper - 5. [verschicken] to send. ⬦ vi [aufhören, kapitulieren] to give up.

aufgebläht adj [Ballon, Verwaltungsapparat] inflated; [Bauch] swollen; [Backen] puffed-out.

Auf|gebot das - 1. [an Personen] contingent; [an Maschinen, Waren] array - 2. [für Hochzeit] banns Pl; **das Aufgebot bestellen** to publish the banns.

aufgebracht ⬦ pp ▷ **aufbringen**. ⬦ adj [wütend] angry.

aufgedunsen adj bloated.

auf|gehen (perf ist aufgegangen) vi (unreg) - 1. [Sonne, Mond] to rise - 2. [Knoten, Knopf] to come undone - 3. [sich öffnen] to open - 4. [Rechnung] to work out - 5. [verschwinden]: **in etw (D) aufgehen** to disappear into sthg; **in Flammen aufgehen** to go up in flames - 6. [sich einsetzen]: **in etw (D) aufgehen** to be wrapped up in sthg - 7. [deutlich werden]: **jm aufgehen** to dawn on sb - 8. [Teig, Kuchen] to rise.

aufgehoben ⬦ pp ▷ **aufheben**. ⬦ adj: **(bei jm) gut/schlecht aufgehoben sein** to be/not to be in good hands (with sb).

aufgeklärt adj enlightened.

aufgelegt adj: **gut/schlecht aufgelegt sein** to be in a good/bad mood.

aufgeregt ⬦ adj excited. ⬦ adv excitedly.

aufgeschlossen ⬦ pp ▷ **aufschließen**. ⬦ adj open-minded; **etw gegenüber** ODER **für etw aufgeschlossen sein** to be open to sthg.

aufgeweckt adj bright.

auf|greifen vt (unreg) - 1. [fangen] to pick up - 2. [übernehmen] to take up.

aufgrund präp: **aufgrund einer Sache** (G) because of sthg.

auf|haben (unreg) ⬦ vt - 1. [Hausaufgaben] to have for homework - 2. [tragen] to have on, to be wearing - 3. [offen lassen - Mantel, Tür] to have open; [- Knopf] to have undone. ⬦ vi [geöffnet sein] to be open.

auf|halten vt (unreg) - 1. [offen halten - Tür, Tasche] to hold open; **die Hand aufhalten** to hold out one's hand; **die Augen aufhalten** to keep one's eyes open; **jm etw aufhalten** to hold sthg open for sb - 2. [anhalten - Entwicklung, Inflation] to put a check on - 3. [stören] to hold up; **ich möchte Sie nicht aufhalten** I don't want to keep you. ➠ **sich aufhalten** ref [sich befinden] to stay.

auf|hängen ⬦ vt - 1. [hinhängen - Mantel, Plakat] to hang up; [- Bild] to hang; [- Wäsche] to hang out - 2. [erhängen] to hang - 3. [mit etw begründen]: **etw an etw (D) aufhängen** to base sthg on sthg. ⬦ vi [am Telefon] to hang up. ➠ **sich aufhängen** ref fam [sich erhängen] to hang o.s.

Aufhänger (pl -) der - 1. [Halterung] loop - 2. fig [Grund, Anstoß] pretext.

auf|häufen vt to pile up. ➠ **sich aufhäufen** ref to pile up.

auf|heben vt (unreg) - 1. [nehmen] to pick up - 2. [aufbewahren] to keep; **etw gut aufheben** to keep sthg safe - 3. [Gesetz, Verordnung] to repeal; [Verbot, Embargo] to lift; [Visapflicht] to end - 4. [ausgleichen]: **etw/einander aufheben** to cancel sthg/each other out. ➠ **sich aufheben** ref to cancel each other out.

auf|heitern vt [Person] to cheer up. ➠ **sich aufheitern** ref - 1. [fröhlich werden] to cheer up - 2. [sonnig werden] to clear up.

auf|hellen vt [heller machen] to lighten. ➠ **sich aufhellen** ref - 1. [Gesicht, Miene] to light up - 2. [Wetter, Himmel] to clear up.

auf|hetzen vt to stir up; **jn gegen jn/etw aufhetzen** to stir sb up against sb/sthg.

auf|holen ⬦ vt [Verspätung] to make up. ⬦ vi [Sportler, Wirtschaft] to catch up.

auf|horchen vi - 1. [horchen] to prick up one's ears - 2. [aufmerksam werden] to sit up and take notice.

auf|hören vi - 1. [nicht weitermachen] to stop; **aufhören, etw zu tun** to stop doing sthg; **mit etw aufhören** to stop sthg; **mit dem Rauchen aufhören** to stop smoking - 2. [kündigen] to finish **- 3.** [zu Ende sein - Film, Straße, Weg] to end; [- Lärm, Regen] to stop; [- Nebel] to lift; **da hört sich doch alles auf!** *fig* that's the limit!

auf|klappen *vt* to open.

auf|klären *vt* **- 1.** [Missverständnis] to clear up; [Mord] to solve **- 2.** [informieren]: **jn über etw** *(A)* **aufklären** to tell sb about sthg **- 3.** [über Sexualität informieren] to explain the facts of life to. ➤ **sich aufklären** *ref* **- 1.** [sich auflösen] to be cleared up **- 2.** [sonnig werden] to clear up.

Auf|klärung *die* **- 1.** [von Irrtum] clearing up; [von Verbrechen] solving **- 2.** [Information] informing **- 3.** [Information über Sexualität] sex education **- 4.** HIST Enlightenment.

Auf|kleber *der* sticker.

auf|knöpfen *vt* to unbutton.

auf|kommen *(perf* ist aufgekommen) *vi (unreg)* **- 1.** [entstehen] to arise; [Sturm] to get up; **keine Zweifel aufkommen lassen** to leave no room for doubt **- 2.** [übernehmen, zahlen]: **für jn/etw aufkommen** to pay for sb/sthg **- 3.** [aufstehen können] to get up **- 4.** [landen] to land.

auf|kriegen *vt fam* **- 1.** [öffnen können - Tür, Paket] to get open; [- Knoten] to get undone **- 2.** [aufessen]: **etw nicht aufkriegen** not to eat sthg up.

auf|laden *vt (unreg)* **- 1.** [Lasten]: **etw auf etw** *(A)* **aufladen** to load sthg onto sthg **- 2.** [aufbürden]: **jm/sich etw aufladen** to burden sb/o.s. with sthg **- 3.** [Batterie] to charge.

Auf|lage *die* **- 1.** [von Büchern] edition; [von Zeitung] circulation **- 2.** [Bedingung] condition; **jm zur Auflage machen, dass...** to make it a condition for sb that...

auf|lassen *vt (unreg)* **- 1.** [Tür, Jacke] to leave open; [Knopf] to leave undone **- 2.** [Hut, Mütze] to keep on.

auf|lauern *vi*: **jm auflauern** to lie in wait for sb.

Auf|lauf *der* **- 1.** [Speise] bake **- 2.** [Menschenansammlung] crowd.

auf|laufen *(perf* ist aufgelaufen) *vi (unreg)* **- 1.** [sich festfahren]: **auf etw** *(A)* **auflaufen** to run aground on sthg **- 2.** [abblocken]: **jn auflaufen lassen** SPORT to bodycheck sb **- 3.** [steigen]: **auf etw** *(A)* **auflaufen** to mount up to sthg.

auf|leben *(perf* ist aufgelebt) *vi* **- 1.** [Person] to liven up **- 2.** [Gespräch, Erinnerung] to revive.

auf|legen ◇ *vt* **- 1.** [Tischtuch, Schallplatte, Schminke, Kohle] to put on; [Besteck] to put out **- 2.** [Produkt, Buch] to bring out **- 3.** [am Telefon] to hang up. ◇ *vi* [am Telefon] to hang up.

auf|lehnen *ref*: **sich auflehnen** to rebel against sb/sthg.

auf|leuchten *(perf* hat/ist aufgeleuchtet) *vi* to light up.

auf|listen *vt* to list.

auf|lockern *vt* **- 1.** [Erde, Boden] to break up; [Muskeln] to loosen up **- 2.** [Stimmung, Rede] to

liven up. ➤ **sich auflockern** *ref* **- 1.** [Sportler] to limber up **- 2.** [Bewölkung] to break up; [Knoten] to loosen.

auf|lösen *vt* **- 1.** [in Flüssigkeit, in Bestandteile] to dissolve; **etw in etw** *(D)* **auflösen** to dissolve sthg in sthg **- 2.** [Staatenverbund, Demonstration, Versammlung] to break up; [Vertrag] to cancel; [Verlobung] to break off; [Parlament] to dissolve **- 3.** [Betrieb, Haushalt] to break up. ➤ **sich auflösen** *ref* **- 1.** [Tablette, Kristalle] to dissolve; [Nebel] to lift; [Bewölkung] to break up; **sich in etw** *(D)* **auflösen** to dissolve in sthg; **er hat sich in Luft aufgelöst** he vanished into thin air **- 2.** [Menge, Versammlung] to disperse.

Auf|lösung *die* **- 1.** [in Flüssigkeit, in Bestandteile] dissolving; **ein Bildschirm mit hoher Auflösung** a high-resolution screen **- 2.** [von Koalition, Demonstration, Versammlung] breaking up; [von Vertrag] cancellation; [von Verlobung] breaking off; [von Parlament] dissolving **- 3.** [von Betrieb, Haushalt] breaking up.

auf|machen ◇ *vt* **- 1.** [gen] to open; [Schnur, Knopf, Jacke] to undo **- 2.** [gestalten] to make. ◇ *vi* **- 1.** [öffnen] to open the door; **jm aufmachen** to let sb in **- 2.** [Geschäft] to open. ➤ **sich aufmachen** *ref* [abreisen]: **sich aufmachen (nach)** to set off (for).

Aufmachung *(pl* -en) *die* **- 1.** [Gestaltung] layout **- 2.** [Kleidung] appearance.

aufmerksam ◇ *adj* **- 1.** [konzentriert] attentive; **jn auf jn/etw aufmerksam machen** to draw sb's attention to sb/sthg **- 2.** [höflich] thoughtful. ◇ *adv* attentively.

Aufmerksamkeit *(pl* -en) *die* **- 1.** [Konzentration] attentiveness **- 2.** [Mitbringsel] gift.

auf|muntern *vt* [aufheitern] to cheer up; [ermutigen] to encourage.

Aufnahme *(pl* -n) *die* **- 1.** [Empfang] reception; **Aufnahme in etw** *(A)* [Verein, Intensivstation] admission into sthg **- 2.** [Beginn - von Kontakt] establishment; [- von Arbeit, Gespräch, Verhandlungen] start **- 3.** [Aufzeichnung] recording; [von Diktat] taking down **- 4.** [Fotografie] photograph.

aufnahmefähig *adj* receptive.

Aufnahme|prüfung *die* entrance examination.

auf|nehmen *vt (unreg)* **- 1.** [aufheben, ergreifen] to pick up **- 2.** [empfangen - in Klub] to admit; [- Gast] to receive; [- Asylant] to take in; **Namen auf einer Liste aufnehmen** to include names on a list; **ein Wort im Wörterbuch aufnehmen** to include a word in the dictionary; **jn bei sich** *(D)* **aufnehmen** to take sb in **- 3.** [essen]: **Nahrung aufnehmen** to eat **- 4.** [Informationen] to take in; [Vorschlag] to take up **- 5.** [reagieren auf]: **etw mit Begeisterung aufnehmen** to receive sthg enthusiastically **- 6.** [beginnen - Gespräch, Arbeit, Verhandlungen] to start; [- Thema, Tätigkeit] to take up; **mit jm Kontakt auf-**

nehmen to contact sb - **7.** [konkurrieren]: **es mit jm/etw aufnehmen können** to be a match for sb/sthg - **8.** [sich leihen - Kredit, Hypothek] to get, to obtain; [- Geld, Summe] to borrow - **9.** [Foto] to take - **10.** [auf Tonband] to record.

auf|opfern ◈ **sich aufopfern** ref: **sich für jn/etw aufopfern** to sacrifice o.s. for sb/sthg.

auf|päppeln vt [nach Krankheit] to nurse back to health.

auf|passen vi to pay attention; **auf jn/etw aufpassen** to keep an eye on sb/ sthg; **auf Fehler aufpassen** to watch out for mistakes; **pass bloß auf, wenn ich dich erwische!** just you wait until I catch you!

auf|platzen (perf ist **aufgeplatzt**) vi to burst (open).

Aufprall (pl -e) der impact.

auf|prallen (perf ist **aufgeprallt**) vi: **auf etw (A) aufprallen** to hit sthg.

Auf|preis der extra charge.

auf|pumpen vt to pump up.

Aufputsch|mittel das stimulant.

auf|quellen (perf ist **aufgequollen**) vi (unreg) to swell up.

auf|raffen ◈ **sich aufraffen** ref [sich entschließen]: **sich dazu aufraffen, etw zu tun** to face up to doing sthg.

auf|ragen vi to rise up.

auf|räumen ◇ vt - **1.** [ordnen] to tidy up - **2.** [forträumen] to tidy away. ◇ vi - **1.** [ordnen] to tidy up - **2.** [etw beenden]: **mit etw aufräumen** to put an end to sthg.

auf|rechnen vt: **etw gegen etw aufrechnen** to compare sthg with sthg.

aufrecht ◇ adj - **1.** [gerade] upright - **2.** [Demokrat, Haltung] upstanding. ◇ adv [gerade] upright.

aufrecht|erhalten vt (unreg) to maintain.

auf|regen vt [ärgern] to annoy; [beunruhigen] to upset. ◈ **sich aufregen** ref to get worked up; **sich über jn/etw aufregen** to get worked up about sb/sthg.

aufregend adj exciting.

Auf|regung die excitement; **das schlechte Wahlergebnis versetzte die Partei in Aufregung** the bad election result caused a great stir in the party.

aufreibend adj [anstrengend] exhausting.

auf|reißen (perf hat/ist **aufgerissen**) (unreg) ◇ vt (hat) - **1.** [öffnen - Brief, Verpackung] to tear open; [- Tür, Fenster] to fling open; [- Mund, Augen] to open wide - **2.** salopp [kennen lernen] to pick up. ◇ vi (ist) [Naht] to split; [Wolkendecke] to break up.

aufreizend ◇ adj provocative. ◇ adv provocatively.

auf|richten vt - **1.** [hochziehen - Kranken] to sit up; [- Rücken] to straighten (up) - **2.** [aufstellen] to erect - **3.** [trösten] to lift. ◈ **sich aufrichten** ref [sich hochziehen] to sit up.

aufrichtig ◇ adj sincere. ◇ adv sincerely.

Auf|richtigkeit die (ohne pl) sincerity.

auf|rücken (perf ist **aufgerückt**) vi to move up; **zum Direktor aufrücken** to be promoted to headmaster.

Auf|ruf der appeal.

auf|rufen vt (unreg) - **1.** [nennen, rufen] to call - **2.** [auffordern]: **jn zu etw aufrufen** to appeal to sb for sthg.

Aufruhr (pl -e) der - **1.** [Aufstand] uprising - **2.** [Unruhe] turmoil.

auf|runden vt: **aufrunden (auf (+ A))** to round up (to).

auf|rüsten vi to rearm; **wieder aufrüsten** to rearm.

Auf|rüstung die rearmament.

aufs präp = **auf + das**.

auf|sagen vt [Text] to recite.

auf|sammeln vt to pick up.

aufsässig adj rebellious.

Auf|satz der - **1.** [Schularbeit] essay UK, paper US - **2.** [Abhandlung] paper - **3.** [Aufbau] upper section.

auf|saugen vt to soak up.

auf|schauen vi - **1.** [mit Bewunderung]: **zu jm aufschauen** to look up to sb - **2.** Süddt [aufblicken] to look up.

auf|scheuchen vt - **1.** [verscheuchen] to startle - **2.** fig [stören] to disturb.

auf|schieben vt (unreg) - **1.** [verschieben] to put off - **2.** [öffnen - Tür, Fenster] to slide open; [- Riegel] to slide back.

Auf|schlag der - **1.** [Aufprall] impact - **2.** [auf den Preis] extra charge - **3.** [am Hosenbein] turn-up UK, cuff US; [am Ärmel] cuff - **4.** SPORT serve; **er hat Aufschlag** it's his serve.

auf|schlagen (perf hat/ist **aufgeschlagen**) (unreg) ◇ vt (hat) - **1.** [öffnen - Buch, Zeitung, Augen] to open - **2.** [Ei, Schale] to crack (open); [Eis] to break - **3.** [verletzen]: **sich das Knie aufschlagen** to cut one's knee - **4.** [aufbauen - Bett, Zelt] to put up; [- Lager] to pitch - **5.** [dazurechnen]: **etw auf etw (A) aufschlagen** to add sthg onto sthg. ◇ vi - **1.** (ist) [aufprallen]: **auf etw (A) aufschlagen** to hit sthg - **2.** (hat) SPORT to serve.

auf|schließen (unreg) ◇ vt to unlock. ◇ vi - **1.** [öffnen]: **jm aufschließen** to unlock the door for sb - **2.** [nachrücken] to move up.

Aufschluss der (ohne pl): **über etw (A) Aufschluss geben** to provide information about sthg.

aufschlussreich adj informative.

auf|schneiden (unreg) ◇ vt to cut open. ◇ vi [angeben] to boast.

Auf|schnitt *der* sliced cold meat and/or cheese.

auf|schrauben *vt* [Deckel] to unscrew; [Glas] to screw the lid off.

auf|schrecken *(perf hat/ist aufgeschreckt)* ◇ *vt (hat)* to startle. ◇ *vi (ist)* to start.

Auf|schrei *der eigtl & fig* cry; **ein Aufschrei ging durchs Volk** there was a public outcry.

auf|schreiben *vt (unreg)* - **1.** [notieren] to write down - **2.** [Strafzettel geben] to book.

Auf|schrift *die* inscription.

Auf|schub *der* period of grace; **es duldet keinen Aufschub** it must not be delayed.

auf|schütten *vt* - **1.** [nachfüllen] to pour on - **2.** [anhäufen - Damm, Wall] to build up.

Auf|schwung *der* - **1.** [Auftrieb] upturn; **sein Optimismus gab uns Aufschwung** his optimism gave us a lift - **2.** SPORT swing-up.

auf|sehen *vi (unreg)* [hochschauen] to look up; **zu jm aufsehen** [bewundern] to look up to sb.

Aufsehen *das:* **Aufsehen erregen** to cause a stir; **Aufsehen erregend** sensational.

Aufseher, in *(mpl -, fpl -nen) der, die* [im Gefängnis] warder.

auf sein *(perf ist auf gewesen) vi (unreg) fam* - **1.** [offen sein] to be open - **2.** [wach sein] to be up.

auf|setzen ◇ *vt* - **1.** [gen] to put on - **2.** [schreiben] to draft. ◇ *vi* [landen] to touch down. ◆ **sich aufsetzen** *ref* [sich aufrichten] to sit up.

Auf|sicht *die (ohne pl)* - **1.** [Kontrolle] supervision; **die Aufsicht über jn/etw haben** to supervise sb/sthg - **2.** [Person] supervisor.

auf|sitzen *(perf hat/ist aufgesessen) vi (unreg)* - **1.** *(ist)* [aufsteigen - auf Motorrad] to get on; [- Pferd] to mount - **2.** *(ist)* [sich täuschen lassen]: **jm aufsitzen** to be taken in by sb - **3.** *(hat)* [wach bleiben] to sit up.

auf|spannen *vt* to put up.

auf|sparen *vt:* **sich (D) etw aufsparen** to save sthg.

auf|sperren *vt* - **1.** [aufschließen] to unlock - **2.** [offen halten] to open wide.

auf|spielen ◆ **sich aufspielen** *ref* [angeben] to give o.s. airs; **sich als Chef/Genie aufspielen** to play the boss/genius.

auf|springen *(perf ist aufgesprungen) vi (unreg)* - **1.** [aufstehen]: **aufspringen (vor (+ D))** to jump up (with) - **2.** [sich öffnen - Blüte, Tür] to burst open; [- Haut, Hände] to become chapped - **3.** [springen]: **auf etw (A) aufspringen** to jump onto sthg.

auf|stacheln *vt:* **jn (zu etw) aufstacheln** to spur sb on (to sthg).

auf|stampfen *vi:* **mit dem Fuß aufstampfen** to stamp one's foot.

Auf|stand *der* uprising, rebellion.

aufständisch *adj* rebellious.

auf|stauen *vt* to dam. ◆ **sich aufstauen** *ref* [Wasser] to collect; [Gefühle, Wut] to get bottled up.

auf|stecken *vt* - **1.** [hochstecken] to pin up - **2.** *fam* [aufgeben, abbrechen] to give up.

auf|stehen *(perf hat/ist aufgestanden) vi (unreg)* - **1.** *(ist)* [sich erheben] to get up - **2.** *(hat)* [offen stehen] to stand open.

auf|steigen *(perf ist aufgestiegen) vi (unreg)* - **1.** [auf Motorrad, Fahrrad, Pferd] to get on; **auf etw (A) aufsteigen** [Fahrrad, Pferd] to get on sthg - **2.** [Bergsteiger, Hubschrauber, Ballon] to climb; [Vogel] to soar; **auf einen Berg aufsteigen** to climb a mountain - **3.** [Rauch] to rise; [Nebel] to lift - **4.** [Erfolg haben] to be promoted.

auf|stellen *vt* - **1.** [hinstellen - Schachfiguren, Kegel, Lampe] to set up; [- Schild] to put up - **2.** [aufbauen - Gerüst, Gitter] to put up - **3.** [Liste, Plan] to draw up - **4.** [Theorie, Behauptung] to put forward - **5.** [auswählen] to select - **6.** [Ohren] to prick up; [Stacheln] to raise. ◆ **sich aufstellen** *ref* - **1.** [sich hinstellen] to take up one's position - **2.** [sich aufrichten - Haare] to stand on end.

Auf|stellung *die* - **1.** [Hinstellen - von Schachfiguren, Kegeln, Lampe] setting up; [- von Schild] putting up - **2.** [Aufbau - von Gerüst, Gitter] putting up - **3.** [von Liste, Plan] drawing up - **4.** [von Theorie, Behauptung] putting forward - **5.** [Wahl] selection.

Aufstieg *(pl -e) der* - **1.** [Aufsteigen] ascent - **2.** [Erfolg] promotion.

auf|stocken *vt* - **1.** [höher bauen] to raise the height of - **2.** [vergrößern] to increase.

auf|stoßen *(perf hat/ist aufgestoßen) (unreg)* ◇ *vt (hat)* [öffnen] to push open. ◇ *vi* - **1.** *(ist)* [stoßen]: **mit etw auf etw (D) aufstoßen** to hit sthg with sthg - **2.** *(hat)* [rülpsen] to belch - **3.** *(ist) fam* [unangenehm auffallen]: **sein Verhalten ist mir sauer** ODER **übel aufgestoßen** his behaviour left a nasty taste in my mouth.

aufstrebend *adj* up-and-coming.

auf|stützen *vt* to prop up. ◆ **sich aufstützen** *ref* to support o.s.

auf|suchen *vt* to go to.

Auf|takt *der* - **1.** [Anfang] start - **2.** MUS upbeat.

auf|tanken *vt* [Auto] to fill up; [Flugzeug] to refuel; **Benzin auftanken** to fill up with petrol UK ODER gas US.

auf|tauchen *(perf ist aufgetaucht) vi* - **1.** [aus dem Wasser] to surface - **2.** [sichtbar werden] to appear - **3.** [aufkommen] to arise - **4.** [gefunden werden, ankommen] to turn up.

auf|tauen ◇ *vt (perf hat aufgetaut)* [Lebensmittel] to defrost; [Boden, Eis] to thaw. ◇ *vi (perf ist aufgetaut)* [Lebensmittel] to defrost; [Boden, Eis] to thaw.

auf|teilen vt - **1.** [verteilen] to share out - **2.** [einteilen] to divide up; **etw in etw (A) aufteilen** to divide sthg up into sthg.

Auf|teilung die - **1.** [Verteilung]: **Aufteilung (unter (+D))** sharing out (amongst) - **2.** [Einteilung]: **Aufteilung (in (+A))** division (into).

auf|tischen vt - **1.** [servieren] to serve up - **2.** fam fig [erzählen] to come out with.

Auftrag (pl **Aufträge**) der - **1.** [Befehl, Aufgabe] task; **jm einen Auftrag geben** ODER **erteilen** to give sb a task - **2.** [Bestellung] order; **etw in Auftrag geben** [Untersuchung, Reparatur] to order sthg; [Studie, Gemälde] to commission sthg.

auf|tragen (unreg) <> vt - **1.** [aufstreichen] to apply - **2.** [bestellen]: **jm auftragen, etw zu tun** to tell sb to do sthg; **sie hat mir Grüße an dich aufgetragen** she asked me to pass on her regards to you - **3.** [abtragen] to wear out. <> vi: **dick auftragen** fam [übertreiben] to go over the top.

Auftraggeber, in (mpl -, fpl -nen) der, die [Kunde] client.

auf|treffen (perf **ist aufgetroffen**) vi (unreg) to land.

auf|treiben (perf **hat aufgetrieben**) vt (unreg) (hat) [finden] to find.

auf|treten (perf **ist aufgetreten**) vi (unreg) - **1.** [treten] to tread - **2.** [sich benehmen] to behave - **3.** [erscheinen - Person] to appear; [- Problem, Gefahr, Frage] to arise.

Auftreten das - **1.** [Benehmen] behaviour - **2.** [Erscheinen] occurrence.

Auf|trieb der buoyancy; **jm/einer Sache Auftrieb geben** fig to give sb/sthg a lift.

auf|tun vt (unreg) fam [finden] to come across. ◆ **sich auftun** ref eigtl & fig to open up.

auf|türmen vt to pile up. ◆ **sich auftürmen** ref [Masse, Probleme] to pile up; [Berge] to tower.

auf|wachen (perf **ist aufgewacht**) vi to wake up.

auf|wachsen ['aufvaksn̩] (perf **ist aufgewachsen**) vi (unreg) to grow up.

Aufwand der - **1.** [Einsatz - von Geld] expenditure; **es ist mit viel Aufwand verbunden** it takes a lot of time/effort/etc - **2.** [Luxus] extravagance.

aufwändig <> adj extravagant. <> adv extravagantly.

auf|wärmen vt - **1.** [warm machen] to warm up - **2.** fam fig [wieder erwähnen] to bring up again. ◆ **sich aufwärmen** ref to warm o.s. up.

aufwärts adv upwards; **von 50 cm³ aufwärts** from 50 cm³ up ODER upwards.

aufwärts gehen (perf **ist aufwärts gegangen**) vi (unreg): **mit den Verkaufszahlen geht es aufwärts** the sales figures are looking up.

auf|wecken vt to wake up.

auf|weisen vt (unreg) [zeigen] to show; **der Plan weist Mängel auf** the plan contains flaws.

auf|wenden vt [Geld, Zeit] to spend; [Energie, Kraft] to use (up).

aufwendig adj & adv = **aufwändig**.

auf|werfen vt (unreg) - **1.** [anhäufen - Erde, Kies] to pile up - **2.** [ansprechen] to raise.

auf|werten vt [Währung] to revalue; [Ansehen, Status] to enhance.

auf|wickeln vt to wind up.

auf|wiegeln vt abw to incite; **jn gegen jn aufwiegeln** to stir sb up against sb.

Auf|wind der upcurrent; **Aufwind bekommen** fig to get a boost; **Aufwind haben** to be going strong.

auf|wirbeln vt & vi to swirl up.

auf|wischen vt to mop up.

auf|wühlen vt - **1.** [zerwühlen] to churn up - **2.** [erregen] to stir up.

auf|zählen vt to list.

Auf|zählung die list.

auf|zeichnen vt - **1.** [zeichnen] to draw - **2.** [aufnehmen] to record.

Auf|zeichnung die [Aufnahme] recording. ◆ **Aufzeichnungen** Pl [Notizen] notes; **sich (D) Aufzeichnungen machen** to take notes.

auf|ziehen (perf **hat/ist aufgezogen**) (unreg) <> vt (hat) - **1.** [Uhr, Spielzeugauto] to wind up - **2.** [erziehen - Kind] to bring up; [- Tier] to raise - **3.** [öffnen] to open - **4.** [necken] to tease; **jn mit etw aufziehen** to tease sb about sthg - **5.** fam [organisieren - Geschäft, Arbeitsgruppe] to set up; [- Fest, Kampagne] to organize. <> vi (ist) [Gewitter] to brew; [Wolken] to mass.

Auf|zucht die rearing.

Auf|zug der - **1.** [Lift] lift UK, elevator US - **2.** abw [Aufmachung] get-up - **3.** [Akt] act.

auf|zwingen vt (unreg): **jm etw aufzwingen** to force sthg onto sb. ◆ **sich aufzwingen** ref: **der Gedanke zwingt sich regelrecht auf** the thought is unavoidable.

Auge (pl -n) das - **1.** [Sehorgan] eye; **ein blaues Auge** a black eye; **mit bloßem Auge** with the naked eye; **etw mit eigenen Augen gesehen haben** to have seen sthg with one's own eyes; **ihm wurde schwarz vor Augen** everything went black - **2.** [Würfelpunkt] dot; **(große) Augen machen** to stare wide-eyed; **seinen Augen nicht trauen** not to believe one's eyes; **jn aus den Augen verlieren** to lose touch with sb; **ein Auge zudrücken** to turn a blind eye; **jn/etw im Auge behalten** to keep an eye on sb/sthg; **jn aus den Augen lassen** as I see/he sees/etc it; **jn/etw mit anderen** ODER **neuen Augen sehen** to see sb/sthg differently; **jn/etw nicht aus den Augen lassen** not to take one's eyes off sb/sthg; **unter vier Augen** in private; **etw vor Augen haben** to have sthg in mind.

Augen|arzt, ärztin der, die eye specialist, ophthalmologist.

Augen|blick der moment; **im Augenblick** at the moment; **jeden Augenblick** at any moment, any time.

augenblicklich <> adj - **1.** [sofortig] immediate - **2.** [jetzig] current. <> adv - **1.** [umgehend] immediately - **2.** [jetzig] currently.

Augen|braue die eyebrow.

Augen|farbe die: **welche Augenfarbe hat sie?** what colour are her eyes?

Augen|höhe die: **in Augenhöhe** at eye level.

Augen|winkel der: **jn/etw aus den Augenwinkeln beobachten** to watch sb/sthg out of the corner of one's eye.

Augen|zeuge, zeugin der, die eyewitness.

augenzwinkernd adv with an air of complicity.

August der August; **siehe auch September**.

Auktion [auk'tsio:n] (pl -en) die auction.

Aula (pl -s) die hall.

Aupairmädchen, Au-pair-Mädchen [o'pɛːrmeːtçən] (pl -) das au pair.

aus <> präp (+ D) - **1.** [heraus] out of; **aus dem Haus gehen** to go out of the house, to leave the house; **Rauch kam aus dem Fenster** smoke was coming out of the window - **2.** [zur Angabe der Herkunft] from; **aus Amerika** from America; **ein Lied aus den 70er Jahren** a song from the seventies - **3.** [zur Angabe des Materials]: **aus Plastik** made of plastic; **Möbel aus Eschenholz** ash furniture - **4.** [zur Angabe der Zugehörigkeit]: **einer aus der Gruppe** a member of the group - **5.** [zur Angabe der Entfernung] from; **aus 50 m Entfernung** from 50 m away - **6.** [zur Angabe des Grundes]: **aus welchem Grund?** for what reason?, why?; **aus Spaß** for fun; **aus Habgier** from greed, out of greed. <> adv - **1.** [elliptisch]: **Licht aus!** lights out! - **2.** [zu Ende] over; **aus und vorbei** all over.

Aus das end; **ins Aus gehen** SPORT to go out (of play).

aus|arbeiten vt [Plan, Liste, Vertrag] to draw up; [Methode, Vorschlag] to work out.

Ausarbeitung (pl -en) die [von Plan, Liste, Vertrag] drawing up; [von Methode, Vorschlag] working out.

aus|arten (perf ist ausgeartet) vi to degenerate; **in (+ A) ODER zu etw ausarten** to degenerate into sthg.

aus|atmen vt & vi to breathe out.

aus|baden vt: **etw ausbaden müssen** to pay (the price) for sthg.

Aus|bau der - **1.** [Beseitigung] removal - **2.** [Erweiterung - von Netz, Haus] extension; [- von Dachboden] conversion; [- von Kenntnissen] expansion.

aus|bauen vt - **1.** [beseitigen] to remove - **2.** [erweitern - Netz, Haus] to extend; [- Dachboden] to convert; [- Kenntnisse] to expand; [- Kontakte] to intensify, to strengthen.

aus|bessern vt [Schaden, Zaun] to repair; [Kleidungsstück] to mend.

aus|beulen vt - **1.** [glätten] to beat out - **2.** [verformen] to make baggy.

Aus|beute die gain.

aus|beuten vt to exploit.

aus|bilden vt - **1.** [schulen] to train; **sich zu etw ausbilden lassen** to train to be sthg - **2.** [hervorbringen] to develop.

Ausbilder, in (mpl -, fpl -nen) der, die instructor (instructress f).

Aus|bildung die [beruflich, fachlich] training; [schulisch] education; **in der Ausbildung sein** [beruflich, fachlich] to be a trainee; [schulisch] to be in education.

Ausbildungs|zeit die period of training, traineeship.

aus|bleiben (perf ist ausgeblieben) vi (unreg) - **1.** [Besserung, Katastrophe] to fail to materialize; [Gäste, Touristen] to fail to turn up; **das bleibt nicht aus** that's inevitable - **2.** [nicht nach Hause kommen] to stay out.

Aus|blick der view; **ein Ausblick auf etw (A)** fig a look ahead to sthg.

aus|booten vt to oust.

aus|brechen (perf hat/ist ausgebrochen) (unreg) <> vi (ist) - **1.** [Gefangene, Krieg, Panik, Epidemie] to break out; **aus etw ausbrechen** to break out of sthg - **2.** [verfallen]: **in Gelächter ausbrechen** to burst out laughing; **in Tränen ausbrechen** to burst into tears - **3.** [Auto] to spin out of control - **4.** [Vulkan] to erupt. <> vt (hat) [herausbrechen] to break off.

aus|breiten vt to spread out; **etw über jm/etw ausbreiten** to spread sthg out over sb/sthg. ➤ **sich ausbreiten** ref - **1.** [sich verbreiten] to spread - **2.** fam [sich breit machen] to spread o.s. out.

Aus|bruch der - **1.** [Flucht] break-out - **2.** [Beginn] outbreak; **nach einer Woche kam die Krankheit vollends zum Ausbruch** after a week the disease broke out fully - **3.** [von Vulkan] eruption - **4.** [Gefühlsäußerung] outburst.

aus|brüten vt eigtl & fig to hatch.

Aus|dauer die [Beharrungsvermögen] perseverance; SPORT stamina.

ausdauernd <> adj persevering; **ein ausdauernder Läufer** a runner with a lot of stamina. <> adv untiringly.

aus|dehnen vt - **1.** [Einzugsgebiet, Einfluss] to expand; [Gummiband] to extend; [Kleidungsstück] to lengthen - **2.** [zeitlich] to extend. ➤ **sich ausdehnen** ref [Metall, Handel] to expand; [Feuer] to spread; [Weite] to stretch out; **sich auf etw (A) ausdehnen** [Brand, Hysterie, Aktivitäten] to spread to sthg.

aus|denken vt (unreg): **sich** (D) **etw ausdenken** [Geschichte, Plan] to think sthg up; [Geschenk] to think of sthg; **da musst du dir schon etwas anderes ausdenken!** fam you'll have to do better than that!

Aus|druck (pl -drücke ODER -e) der - **1.** (pl Ausdrücke) [Formulierung] expression - **2.** (ohne pl) [Zeichen] expression; **einer Sache** (D) **Ausdruck geben** ODER **verleihen** geh to express sthg - **3.** (pl Ausdrucke) EDV printout.

aus|drucken vt EDV to print (out).

aus|drücken vt - **1.** [Orange, Schwamm, Saft] to squeeze - **2.** [Zigarette] to stub out - **3.** [aussprechen] to express; **mit einfachen Worten ausdrücken** to put sthg simply - **4.** [zeigen - Gefühle, Dank] to express, to show. ◆ **sich ausdrücken** ref - **1.** [Person] to express o.s. - **2.** [Freude, Gier, Intoleranz] to reveal itself.

ausdrücklich ◇ adj explicit. ◇ adv explicitly.

Ausdrucks|weise die way of expressing o.s.

auseinander adv apart; **auseinander!** break it up!; **die Schwestern sind sechs Jahre auseinander** there's six years between the two sisters.

auseinander fallen (perf ist auseinander gefallen) vi (unreg) to fall apart.

auseinander gehen (perf ist auseinander gegangen) vi (unreg) - **1.** [sich trennen - Gruppe] to break up; [- Wege] to diverge; [- Personen] to part - **2.** [Vorhang] to open - **3.** [Meinungen] to differ - **4.** [Ehe] to break up.

auseinander halten vt (unreg) to distinguish.

auseinander laufen (perf ist auseinander gelaufen) vi (unreg) - **1.** [Gruppe] to disperse - **2.** [Eis, Käse] to melt; [Farbe] to run.

auseinander leben ◆ **sich auseinander leben** ref to drift apart.

auseinander nehmen vt (unreg) to dismantle.

auseinander setzen vt: **jm etw auseinander setzen** to explain sthg to sb. ◆ **sich auseinander setzen** ref - **1.** [sich beschäftigen]: **sich mit etw auseinander setzen** to examine sthg - **2.** [sich streiten]: **sich mit jm auseinander setzen** to argue with sb.

Auseinandersetzung (pl -en) die - **1.** [mit Thema]: **Auseinandersetzung (mit)** examination (of) - **2.** [Streit] argument; [Debatte] debate.

auserwählt adj chosen.

aus|fahren (perf hat/ist ausgefahren) (unreg) ◇ vt (hat) - **1.** [spazieren fahren - im Rollstuhl, Kinderwagen] to take out for a walk - **2.** [ausklappen - Antenne] to extend; [- Fahrwerk] to lower - **3.** [liefern] to deliver - **4.** [sehr schnell fahren] to drive flat out. ◇ vi (ist) - **1.** [spazieren fahren - im Rollstuhl, Kinderwagen] to go for a walk - **2.** [hinausfahren - Zug] to depart.

Aus|fahrt die - **1.** [Stelle] exit; **'Ausfahrt freihalten!'** 'keep clear!' - **2.** [Auslaufen] departure.

aus|fallen (perf ist ausgefallen) vi (unreg) - **1.** [Haare, Zahn] to fall out - **2.** [nicht stattfinden] to be cancelled; [Fußballspiel] to be postponed - **3.** [Verdienst, Einnahme] to be lost - **4.** [Maschine] to break down; [Bremse, Signal] to fail - **5.** [Mitarbeiter] to be absent; [Athlet] to pull out - **6.** [sich erweisen]: **der Sieg fiel deutlich aus** it was a clear victory; **gut/schlecht ausfallen** to turn out well/badly.

ausfallend adj abusive; **ausfallend werden** to become abusive.

Ausfall|straße die arterial road.

aus|fegen ◇ vt to sweep out. ◇ vi to sweep up.

aus|fertigen vt amt [Vertrag, Testament] to draw up; [Pass, Zeugnis, Rechnung] to issue.

ausfindig adv: **jn/etw ausfindig machen** to find sb/sthg.

aus|fließen (perf ist ausgeflossen) vi (unreg) to leak.

Ausflucht (pl Ausflüchte) die excuse; **Ausflüchte machen** to make excuses.

Ausflug der trip; **einen Ausflug machen** ODER **unternehmen** to go on a trip.

Ausflugs|lokal das cafe or pub in the countryside to which you can drive or walk out.

Ausfluss (pl -flüsse) der - **1.** [im Waschbecken] plughole - **2.** [Ausfließen] leaking - **3.** MED discharge.

aus|fragen vt to interrogate.

aus|fressen vt (unreg): **er hat mal wieder etwas ausgefressen** fam he's been up to his tricks again.

Ausfuhr (pl -en) die - **1.** [Ware] export - **2.** [Tätigkeit] exporting.

aus|führen vt - **1.** [spazieren führen - Familie, Hund] to take for a walk - **2.** [exportieren] to export - **3.** [realisieren - Reparatur, Befehl, Plan] to carry out; [- Freistoß, Schritte] to take - **4.** [erklären] to explain.

ausführlich ◇ adj detailed. ◇ adv in detail.

aus|füllen vt - **1.** [Formular, Antrag] to fill in ODER out; [Kreuzworträtsel] to do; [Scheck] to make out - **2.** [füllen] to fill (up) - **3.** [verbringen]: **seine Zeit mit etw ausfüllen** to spend one's time doing sthg - **4.** [zufrieden stellen] to fulfil.

Aus|gabe die - **1.** [Ausgeben] distribution; [von Befehl, Banknoten] issuing; [von Essen] serving - **2.** [von Geld] expenditure; **Ausgaben** expenditure (U) - **3.** [Edition] edition.

Aus|gang der - **1.** [von Gebäude] exit; [von Wald] edge; [von Ort] end - **2.** (ohne pl) [Ausgeherlaubnis] time off; [von Soldaten] pass - **3.** [Ende] outcome.

Ausgangs|lage die starting position.

Ausgangs|punkt der starting point.

Ausgangs|sperre *die* curfew.

aus|geben *vt (unreg)* - **1.** [verteilen] [Lebensmittel, Decken] to hand out; [Befehl, Banknoten] to issue; [Essen] to serve - **2.** [Geld] to spend - **3.** *fam* [zu Drink einladen]: **jm einen ausgeben** *fam* to buy sb a drink - **4.** [bezeichnen]: **sich als jd/etw ausgeben** to pretend to be sb/sthg; **jn/ etw als** ODER **für jn/etw ausgeben** to pass sb/ sthg off as sb/sthg.

ausgebucht *adj* fully booked.

ausgedient *adj:* **dieser Sessel hat nun ausgedient** I/we/*etc* no longer have any use for this armchair.

ausgedörrt *adj* [Kehle, Erde] parched; [Pflanze] withered.

ausgefallen ◇ *adj* unusual. ◇ *adv* unusually.

ausgeflippt *adj fam* weird, freaky.

ausgeglichen *adj* [Mensch, Persönlichkeit] balanced; [Spiel] even; [Klima] stable; [Leistung] steady.

aus|gehen *(perf* ist ausgegangen) *vi (unreg)* - **1.** [ins Kino, in die Disko] to go out - **2.** [verlöschen - Kerze, Lampe] to go out; [- Motor] to stop; [- Heizung, Computer] to go off - **3.** [enden] to end - **4.** [hervorgebracht werden]: **von jm ausgehen** to come from sb - **5.** [zugrunde legen]: **von etw ausgehen** to assume sthg; **davon ausgehen,dass...** to assume (that...) - **6.** [ausfallen] to fall out - **7.** [zu Ende gehen] to run out; **mir gehen die Ideen aus** I'm running out of ideas.

ausgehungert *adj* starved.

ausgelassen ◇ *adj* exuberant. ◇ *adv* exuberantly.

ausgelaugt *adj* worn-out.

ausgemergelt *adj* [Körper, Mensch] emaciated.

ausgenommen *konj* - **1.** [es sei denn] unless - **2.** [außer] except.

ausgeprägt ◇ *adj* pronounced. ◇ *adv* particularly.

ausgerechnet *adv:* **ausgerechnet heute** today of all days; **ausgerechnet mir muss das passieren** it had to happen to me of all people.

ausgereift *adj* perfected.

ausgeschlossen *adj* out of the question.

ausgesprochen ◇ *adj* [Ähnlichkeit, Begabung] definite; [Abneigung, Vorliebe] marked; [Glück, Zufall] real. ◇ *adv* extremely, really.

ausgestorben *adj:* **wie ausgestorben** dead, deserted.

ausgewachsen ['aʊsgəvaksn̩] *adj* [erwachsen] fully-grown.

ausgewogen *adj* balanced.

ausgezeichnet ◇ *adj* excellent. ◇ *adv* excellently.

ausgiebig ◇ *adj* [Beratungen, Untersuchungen] extensive; [Frühstück] large; [Spaziergang] long. ◇ *adv* extensively; **ausgiebig frühstücken** to eat a large breakfast.

aus|gießen *vt (unreg)* to pour out.

Ausgleich *(pl* -e) *der* - **1.** [Gleichgewicht] balance; **er schafft sich einen Ausgleich zu seiner Arbeit, indem er sich sportlich betätigt** he balances out his work by doing sport - **2.** [Wiedergutmachung] compensation; **zum** ODER **als Ausgleich** in return - **3.** SPORT equalizer.

aus|gleichen *(unreg)* ◇ *vt* [Unterschiede, Unregelmäßigkeiten] to even out; [Mängel, Ungerechtigkeit] to make up for; [Gegensätze] to reconcile; [Konflikt] to settle; [Konto] to balance. ◇ *vi* SPORT to equalize. ◆ **sich ausgleichen** *ref* [Unterschiede] to even out; [Konto] to balance.

aus|graben *vt (unreg)* to dig up.

Aus|grabung *die* excavation, dig.

Ausguck *(pl* -e) *der* lookout (post).

Ausguss *(pl* -güsse) *der* drain.

aus|haken *vt* to unhook.

aus|halten *(unreg)* ◇ *vt* - **1.** [ertragen] to stand; **den Vergleich mit etw aushalten** to bear comparison with sthg; **mit ihr ist es nicht auszuhalten** she's unbearable - **2.** *abw* [bezahlen] to keep; **sich von jm aushalten lassen** to be kept by sb. ◇ *vi* [durchhalten] to hold out.

aus|handeln *vt* to negotiate.

aus|händigen *vt* to hand over.

Aus|hang *der* notice.

aus|hängen ◇ *vi (unreg)* [angeschlagen sein] to be up; **die Liste hängt am schwarzen Brett aus** the list is up on the noticeboard. ◇ *vt (reg)* - **1.** [anschlagen] to put up - **2.** [Tür] to take off its hinges.

Aushängeschild *(pl* -er) *das fig* advertisement.

aus|heben *vt (unreg)* - **1.** [ausschaufeln] to dig out - **2.** [aushängen] to take off its hinges - **3.** [Verbrechernest] to raid.

aus|hecken *vt* to think up.

aus|helfen *vi (unreg)* to help out.

Aus|hilfe *die* - **1.** [Aushelfen] assistance; **zur Aushilfe arbeiten** to help out - **2.** [Aushilfskraft] temporary worker; [im Büro] temp.

Aushilfs|kraft *die* temporary worker; [im Büro] temp.

aushilfsweise *adv* on a temporary basis.

aus|höhlen *vt* [Stamm] to hollow out.

aus|holen *vi* - **1.** [mit dem Arm] to move one's arm back - **2.** [beim Erzählen]: **weit ausholen** to go back a long way.

aus|horchen *vt* to sound out.

aus|kennen ◆ **sich auskennen** *ref* to know one's way around; **sich in einer Stadt**

auskennen to know one's way around a town; **sich mit Computern auskennen** to know a lot about computers.

aus\|kippen vt to tip out.

aus\|klammern vt [Thema] to leave aside.

aus\|klappen vt to open out.

aus\|klingen (perf hat/ist ausgeklungen) vi (unreg) (hat, ist) [Musik, Tag, Fest] to come to an end.

aus\|klinken (perf hat/ist ausgeklinkt) <> vt (hat) to release. <> vi (ist) to come free. ➤ **sich ausklinken** ref to come free.

aus\|klopfen vt [Teppich] to beat; [Pfeife] to knock out; [Kleidungsstück] to dust down.

aus\|knipsen vt fam to switch off.

aus\|knobeln vt - 1. fam [auslosen - mit Würfeln] to throw dice to decide - 2. [ausklügeln] to work out.

aus\|kommen (perf ist ausgekommen) vi (unreg) - 1. [genug haben] to get by, to manage; **mit etw auskommen** [Proviant] to make sthg last; [Gehalt] to get by on sthg; [Hilfe] to manage with sthg, to get by with sthg - 2. [sich vertragen] to get on; **mit jm gut/schlecht auskommen** to get on well/badly with sb; **mit jm nicht auskommen** not to get on with sb.

aus\|kosten vt geh to enjoy to the full.

aus\|kratzen vt [Schüssel] to scrape out.

aus\|kundschaften vt to spy out.

Auskunft (pl Auskünfte) die - 1. [Information] information (U); **eine Auskunft bekommen** to get some information - 2. (ohne pl) [Auskunftsschalter] information desk; [Fernsprechauskunft] directory enquiries.

Auskunfts\|schalter der information desk.

aus\|kurieren vt to cure.

aus\|lachen vt to laugh at.

aus\|laden vt (unreg) - 1. [entladen] to unload - 2. [nach einer Einladung]: **jn ausladen** to tell sb not to come.

ausladend adj overhanging; [Hinterteil] protruding; [Bewegung] sweeping.

Aus\|lage die display. ➤ **Auslagen** Pl expenses.

Ausland das (ohne pl): **im Ausland** abroad; **ins Ausland** abroad.

Ausländer (pl -) der foreigner.

ausländerfeindlich <> adj xenophobic. <> adv: **ausländerfeindlich eingestellt sein** to be xenophobic.

Ausländerfeindlichkeit die (ohne pl) hostility to foreigners, xenophobia.

Ausländerin (pl -nen) die foreigner.

ausländisch adj foreign.

Auslands\|gespräch das international call.

Auslands\|korrespondent, in der, die foreign correspondent.

Auslands\|reise die trip abroad.

aus\|lassen vt (unreg) - 1. [Absatz, Einzelheit] to leave out, to miss out; [Chance, Gelegenheit] to miss - 2. [abreagieren]: **etw an jm auslassen** to take sthg out on sb. ➤ **sich auslassen** ref fam [sich äußern]: **sich über jn/etw auslassen** abw to bitch about sb/sthg.

aus\|lasten vt - 1. [Betrieb, Maschine] to run at full capacity - 2. [beanspruchen] to keep fully occupied; **mit etw ausgelastet sein** to be kept fully occupied with sthg.

Auslauf der (ohne pl) room (to run about).

aus\|laufen (perf ist ausgelaufen) vi (unreg) - 1. [Tank, Fass] to leak - 2. [Flüssigkeit] to leak out - 3. [Schiff] to set sail - 4. [Modell, Serie] to be discontinued - 5. [Vertrag, Amtszeit] to expire.

aus\|laugen vt - 1. [Bestandteile entziehen]: **der Boden wurde völlig ausgelaugt** the soil was completely stripped of its nutrients - 2. [erschöpfen] to wear out.

aus\|lecken vt to lick out.

aus\|leeren vt to empty; [Glas, Tasse, Flasche] to drain, to empty.

aus\|legen vt - 1. [Waren] to display; [Köder, Gift] to put down - 2. [auskleiden]: **ein Zimmer mit Teppich auslegen** to carpet a room; **einen Schrank (mit Papier) auslegen** to line a cupboard (with paper) - 3. [vorstrecken]: **jm etw auslegen** to lend sb sthg - 4. [interpretieren] to interpret; **sein Zögern wurde ihm als Ängstlichkeit ausgelegt** his hesitation was interpreted as fear.

aus\|leiern <> vi (perf ist ausgeleiert) [Kleidungsstück] to stretch. <> vt (perf hat ausgeleiert) [Kleidungsstück] to stretch.

Ausleihe (pl -n) die - 1. (ohne pl) [Ausleihen] lending - 2. [Ausleihstelle] issue desk.

aus\|leihen vt (unreg): **jm etw ausleihen** to lend sb sthg; **sich** (D) **etw ausleihen** to borrow sthg.

Auslese die (ohne pl) - 1. [Selektion] selection - 2. [Wein] quality wine made from specially selected grapes.

aus\|liefern vt - 1. [Verbrecher]: **jn jm ausliefern** to hand sb over to sb - 2. [liefern] to deliver.

aus\|liegen vi (unreg) to be on display; [Gift, Köder] to be down.

aus\|loggen vi to log off, to log out. ➤ **sich ausloggen** ref EDV to log off, to log out.

aus\|löschen vt - 1. [löschen] to extinguish, to put out - 2. [vernichten] to erase; [Spuren] to cover; [Bevölkerung] to annihilate.

aus\|losen vt to draw lots for.

aus\|lösen vt - 1. [Alarm, Mechanismus] to set off, to trigger - 2. [Krieg, Panik, Freude] to cause.

Auslöser (pl -) der - 1. FOTO (shutter release) button - 2. [Ursache] trigger.

aus\|machen vt - 1. [Radio, Licht, Motor] to turn off; [Zigarette] to put out - 2. [vereinbaren - Treffen] to arrange; [- Termin] to make; **wir haben ausgemacht, nichts zu verraten** we agreed not to say anything; **ich habe mit ihm ausgemacht, dass wir ins Kino gehen** I arranged to go to the cinema with her - 3. [stören]: **macht es Ihnen etwas aus, wenn ich rauche?** do you mind if I smoke?; **das macht ihm nichts aus** it doesn't matter to him - 4. [betragen] to come to; **der Umweg hat eine Stunde ausgemacht** the diversion took an hour - 5. [bedeuten]: **viel ausmachen** to make a big difference; **wenig ausmachen** not to make much difference - 6. geh [erkennen] to make out - 7. [bilden - Reiz] to be, to constitute.

ausl**malen** vt - 1. [ausfüllen] to colour in - 2. [schildern] to describe vividly - 3. [sich vorstellen]: **sich** (D) **etw ausmalen** to imagine sthg.

Ausl**maß** das extent.

ausl**merzen** vt to eradicate; [Erinnerungen] to obliterate.

ausl**messen** vt (unreg) to measure.

ausl**mustern** vt - 1. MIL: **wegen seines Herzfehlers wurde er ausgemustert** the army rejected him because of his bad heart - 2. [aussondern] to take out of service; [abgetragene Kleidung] to sort out.

Ausnahme (pl -n) die exception; **mit Ausnahme von** with the exception of; **eine Ausnahme machen** to make an exception.

Ausnahmel**zustand** der: **den Ausnahmezustand verhängen** to declare a state of emergency.

ausnahmslos adv without exception.

ausnahmsweise adv: **ausnahmsweise dürfen die Kinder aufbleiben** the children can stay up just this once.

ausl**nutzen, aus**l**nützen** vt - 1. [nutzen] to use, to make use of; [Gelegenheit, Vorteil] to use, to make the most of - 2. [missbrauchen] to take advantage of, to exploit.

ausl**packen** ⟨⟩ vt to unpack; [Paket, Geschenk] to unwrap. ⟨⟩ vi fam to spill the beans.

ausl**plaudern** vt to give away.

ausl**pressen** vt - 1. [Frucht] to squeeze - 2. [ausbeuten] to squeeze dry.

ausl**probieren** vt to try out.

Auspuff (pl -e) der exhaust.

ausl**pumpen** vt to pump out; **jm den Magen auspumpen** to pump sb's stomach out.

ausl**quetschen** vt - 1. [auspressen] to squeeze - 2. fam [ausfragen] to grill; **jn über etw** (A) **ausquetschen** to grill sb about sthg.

ausl**radieren** vt - 1. [durch Radieren] to rub out, to erase - 2. fig [zerstören] to wipe out.

ausl**rangieren** vt fam [Kleidung, Möbel] to throw out; [Fahrzeug] to scrap.

ausl**rauben** vt [Person] to rob; [Geschäft] to loot.

ausl**räumen** vt - 1. [entfernen, leeren] to clear out - 2. fam [ausrauben] to clean out - 3. [Missverständnis] to clear up; [Zweifel] to dispel.

ausl**rechnen** vt to calculate, to work out; **sich** (D) **etw ausrechnen** to work sthg out for o.s.; **sie hatte sich gute Chancen ausgerechnet** she had fancied her chances.

Ausl**rede** die excuse; **faule Ausrede** fam feeble excuse.

ausl**reden** ⟨⟩ vi to finish speaking. ⟨⟩ vt: **jm etw ausreden** to talk sb out of sthg.

ausl**reichen** vi to be enough; **es muss bis März ausreichen** it has to last until March.

ausreichend ⟨⟩ adj - 1. [genügend] sufficient; **eine ausreichende Anzahl von Teilnehmern** enough participants - 2. SCHULE mark 4 on a scale of 1 to 6, indicating a pass, but only just. ⟨⟩ adv sufficiently; **wir haben ausreichend für die Party eingekauft** we bought enough for the party.

Ausl**reise** die: **bei der Ausreise** on leaving the country.

Ausreisel**genehmigung** die exit visa.

ausl**reisen** (perf ist ausgereist) vi: **nach Deutschland ausreisen** to leave for Germany; **aus einem Land ausreisen** to leave a country.

ausl**reißen** (perf hat/ist ausgerissen) (unreg) ⟨⟩ vi (ist) fam to run away. ⟨⟩ vt (hat) [Unkraut] to pull up.

ausl**renken** vt: **jm/sich** (D) **den Arm ausrenken** to dislocate sb's/one's arm.

ausl**richten** vt - 1. [übermitteln]: **jm etw ausrichten** to tell sb sthg; **ich soll Ihnen Grüße von meiner Tante ausrichten** my aunt sends her regards; **kann ich etwas ausrichten?** can I take a message? - 2. [erreichen] to achieve; **ich habe bei der Behörde nichts ausrichten können** I didn't get anywhere with the authorities - 3. [Text] to align - 4. [anpassen]: **etw auf jn/ etw ausrichten, etw nach jm/etw ausrichten** to gear sthg towards sb/sthg.

ausl**rotten** vt [Rasse, Ungeziefer] to exterminate; [Aberglauben] to eradicate.

ausl**rücken** (perf ist ausgerückt) vi - 1. MIL to move out - 2. fam [weglaufen] to run away.

ausl**rufen** vt (unreg) - 1. [rufen] to cry, to exclaim - 2. [öffentlich] to announce; **jn ausrufen lassen** to page sb - 3. [verkünden]: **einen Streik ausrufen** to call a strike.

Ausrufel**zeichen, Ausrufungszeichen** das exclamation mark.

ausl**ruhen** ⟨⟩ vi to rest. ⟨⟩ vt to rest; **die Beine/die Arme ausruhen** to rest one's legs/arms. ➡ **sich ausruhen** ref to rest, to have a rest.

ausl**rüsten** vt [Truppe] to equip; [Schiff] to fit out; **ein Auto mit einem Katalysator ausrüsten** to fit a car with a catalytic converter. ➡ **sich ausrüsten** ref to equip o.s.

Aus|rüstung die - 1. [das Ausstatten - von Truppe] equipping; [- von Schiff] fitting out - 2. [Ausstattung] equipment (U).

aus|rutschen (perf ist ausgerutscht) vi to slip; **das Messer ist ihr ausgerutscht** the knife slipped out of her hand.

Ausrutscher (pl -) der slip.

Aus|sage die - 1. [Äußerung - vor Gericht] statement; **nach Aussage eines Fachmanns** according to an expert - 2. [Inhalt] message.

Aussagekraft die expressiveness.

aus|sagen ⬦ vt - 1. [ausdrücken]: **etw über jn/etw aussagen** to say sthg about sb/sthg, to reveal sthg about sb/sthg - 2. [vor Gericht] to state. ⬦ vi to testify, to give evidence.

aus|schalten vt - 1. [abstellen] to switch off, to turn off - 2. [ausschließen] to eliminate.

Ausschau die (ohne pl): **nach jm/etw Ausschau halten** to look out for sb/sthg.

aus|schauen vi - 1. [ausblicken]: **nach jm/etw ausschauen** to look out for sb/sthg, to be on the lookout for sb/sthg - 2. Süddt & Österr [aussehen] to look; **er schaut gut aus** he looks well; **es schaut mit jm/etw gut/schlecht aus** things are looking good/bad for sb/sthg.

aus|scheiden (perf hat/ist ausgeschieden) (unreg) ⬦ vi (ist) - 1. [aus Gruppe]: **aus etw ausscheiden** to leave sthg - 2. [SPORT - verlieren] to get knocked out; [- wegen Verletzung] to pull out - 3. [wegfallen] to be ruled out. ⬦ vt (hat) [Giftstoff] to reject; [Eiter] to secrete.

aus|schenken vt to serve.

aus|schildern vt to signpost.

aus|schlafen vi (unreg) to have a lie-in.

Aus|schlag der - 1. [auf Haut] rash - 2. [das Entscheidende]: **den Ausschlag geben** to be the decisive factor.

aus|schlagen (perf hat/ist ausgeschlagen) (unreg) ⬦ vt (hat) - 1. [entfernen]: **er hat ihm einen Zahn ausgeschlagen** he knocked out one of his teeth - 2. [ablehnen] to turn down. ⬦ vi - 1. (hat) [treten] to kick out - 2. (hat, ist) [Zeiger, Pendel] to swing - 3. (hat, ist) [Pflanze, Baum] to produce leaves.

ausschlaggebend adj decisive.

aus|schließen vt (unreg) - 1. [Grund, Erklärung, Möglichkeit] to rule out; [Irrtum] to prevent; [Zweifel, Unsicherheit] to remove - 2. [ausstoßen]: **jn von etw ausschließen** to expel sb from sthg - 3. [aussperren] to lock out. ➤ **sich ausschließen** ref - 1. [sich aussperren] to lock o.s. out - 2. [sich fern halten - Person] to rule o.s. out; **diese beiden Möglichkeiten schließen sich gegenseitig aus** these two possibilities rule each other out.

ausschließlich ⬦ adj exclusive. ⬦ adv exclusively. ⬦ präp (+ G) excluding.

Ausschluss (pl -schlüsse) der expulsion; **unter Ausschluss der Öffentlichkeit** RECHT in camera.

aus|schmücken vt - 1. [Raum] to decorate - 2. [Geschichte] to embellish.

aus|schneiden vt (unreg) to cut out.

Aus|schnitt der - 1. [Zeitungsausschnitt] cutting UK, clipping US - 2. [Halsausschnitt] neckline; **ein Kleid mit tiefem Ausschnitt** a low-cut dress - 3. [Auszug] excerpt; [eines Romans] excerpt, extract; [eines Films] clip, excerpt; [eines Bilds] detail.

aus|schöpfen vt - 1. [Schüssel] to scoop out - 2. fig [ausnutzen] to exhaust.

Aus|schreibung die [von Stelle, Wettbewerb] advertisement; [von Projekt] call for tenders.

Ausschreitungen Pl violent clashes.

Ausschuss (pl -schüsse) der - 1. [Gremium] committee - 2. (ohne pl) [Ausschussware] rejects Pl.

aus|schütteln vt to shake out.

aus|schütten vt - 1. [Gefäß] to empty; [Flüssigkeit] to pour out - 2. [auszahlen] to pay out, to distribute.

ausschweifend adj [Fantasie] wild; [Leben] debauched.

aus|sehen vi (unreg) to look; **sie sieht gut aus** she looks good; **es sieht nach Regen aus** it looks like rain; **es sieht danach aus, als würden wir gewinnen** it looks like we will win; **es sieht aus, als ob wir gewinnen werden** it looks as if we will win; **mit dem Zuschuss sieht es gut aus** things are looking good as far as the grant is concerned; **wie sieht's aus?** fam how's things?; **sehe ich danach aus, als würde ich stehlen?** do I look as if I would steal?; **so siehst du aus!** fam fig you can think again!, nothing doing!

aus sein (perf ist aus gewesen) vi (unreg) - 1. [zu Ende sein] to be over; **mit dem Trinken ist es aus** no more drinking for me; **es ist aus mit ihm** he's had it; **es ist aus zwischen ihnen** it is over between them - 2. [nicht an sein] to be out - 3. SPORT to be out - 4. [erpicht sein]: **auf etw (A) aus sein** fam to be after sthg; **sie ist darauf aus, mir etw zu verkaufen** she is out to sell me sthg.

außen adv outside; **von außen** from (the) outside; **nach außen** outwards.

Außen|handel der (ohne pl) foreign trade.

Außen|minister, in der, die foreign minister.

Außen|politik die (ohne pl) foreign policy.

Außen|seite die outside.

Außenseiter, in (mpl -, fpl -nen) der, die outsider.

Außenstehende (pl -n) die, der outsider.

Außen|welt die (ohne pl) outside world.

außer ⬦ präp (+ D) - 1. [außerhalb] out of; **außer Haus sein** to be away from home; **außer Atem sein** to be out of breath; **außer Betrieb** out of order; **außer sich sein (vor)** to be beside o.s. (with) - 2. [abgesehen von] except (for), apart from; **alle außer ihm** everyone except (for) him; **nichts außer** nothing but - 3. [zusätzlich] in addition to, as well as. <> *konj* except; **ich komme, außer es regnet** I'll come, unless it rains.

außerdem *adv* also; **es ist viel zu spät, außerdem regnet es** it's far too late and it's raining too.

äußere *adj* - 1. [Wand, Umstände] external; [Ähnlichkeit, Schein] outward - 2. [auswärtig] foreign.

Äußere *das (ohne pl)* (outward) appearance.

außergewöhnlich <> *adj* - 1. [ungewöhnlich] unusual - 2. [sehr gut] exceptional. <> *adv* exceptionally, remarkably.

außerhalb <> *präp (+ G)* outside; **außerhalb der Stadt** outside town; **außerhalb der Öffnungszeiten** outside opening hours. <> *adv* [nicht im Stadtgebiet] out of town.

außerirdisch *adj* extraterrestrial.

äußerlich <> *adj* - 1. [an der Außenseite] external - 2. [nach außen hin] outward; [oberflächlich] superficial. <> *adv*: **äußerlich war sie ruhig** she was outwardly calm; **die Salbe ist äußerlich anzuwenden** the ointment is for external application; **äußerlich betrachtet** on the face of it.

Äußerlichkeiten *Pl* - 1. [Umgangsform und Aussehen] appearances - 2. [Unwesentliches] trivialities.

äußern *vt* to express. ◆ **sich äußern** *ref* - 1. [seine Meinung sagen]: **sich über jn/etw äußern** to give one's opinion on ODER about sb/sthg; **sich zu etw äußern** to comment on sthg - 2. [sich zeigen]: **sich in etw (D) äußern** to reveal itself in sthg.

außerordentlich <> *adj* extraordinary. <> *adv* extremely, extraordinarily; **der Film hat mir außerordentlich gut gefallen** I thought the film was extremely good.

äußerst *adv* extremely.

außerstande, außer Stande *adj*: **zu etw außerstande sein** to be incapable of sthg.

äußerste *adj* - 1. [Ende] furthest; [Rand] outermost - 2. [größte] extreme; **von äußerster Dringlichkeit** of the utmost urgency, extremely urgent - 3. [Termin] latest possible; [Preis, Angebot] final - 4. [schlimmste] extreme.

Äußerung *(pl -en) die* [offizielle Aussage] statement; [Bemerkung] remark.

aus|setzen <> *vt* - 1. [verlassen] to abandon - 2. [versprechen] to offer - 3. [ausliefern] to expose - 4. [beanstanden]: **dieser Kunde fand an allem etwas auszusetzen** this customer found fault with everything. <> *vi* [Herz] to stop; [Motor] to cut out; **sein Atem setzte kurzzeitig aus** he stopped breathing momentarily; **beim Spiel aussetzen** to miss a go. ◆ **sich aussetzen** *ref*: **sich einer Sache (D) aussetzen** to expose o.s. to sthg.

Aussicht *(pl -en) die* - 1. [Sicht] view - 2. [Zukunftsperspektive] prospect; **sie hat eine Beförderung in Aussicht** she's in line for promotion; **jm etw in Aussicht stellen** to promise sb sthg.

aussichtslos *adj* hopeless.

aussichtsreich *adj* [Vorhaben] promising; **ein aussichtsreicher Kandidat** a candidate who stands a good chance of succeeding.

Aussichts|turm *der* lookout tower.

aus|söhnen *vt* to reconcile. ◆ **sich aussöhnen** *ref*: **sich mit jm/etw aussöhnen** to become reconciled with sb/to sthg.

aus|sortieren *vt* to sort out.

aus|spannen <> *vt* - 1. [ausbreiten] to spread - 2. *fam* [wegnehmen]: **jm die Freundin/den Freund ausspannen** to pinch sb's girlfriend/boyfriend. <> *vi* to relax.

aus|sperren *vt* to lock out.

aus|spielen *vt* - 1. [einsetzen] to bring to bear - 2. [im Sport] to outplay - 3. [manipulieren]: **jn gegen jn ausspielen** to play sb off against sb.

aus|spionieren *vt* - 1. [Geheimnis, Versteck] to uncover - 2. [Person] to spy on.

Aus|sprache *die* - 1. [Artikulation] pronunciation; **eine gute/schlechte Aussprache haben** to have a good/bad accent - 2. [Gespräch] discussion [to resolve a dispute].

aus|sprechen *vt (unreg)* - 1. [artikulieren] to pronounce - 2. [ausdrücken] to express; [Urteil, Strafe] to deliver. ◆ **sich aussprechen** *ref* - 1. [sich äußern]: **sich über etw ausführlich aussprechen** to say what's on one's mind about sthg - 2. [Stellung nehmen]: **sich gegen/für jn/etw aussprechen** to come out against/in favour of sb/sthg - 3. [offen sprechen]: **sich mit jm aussprechen** to talk things through with sb.

aus|spucken <> *vi* to spit. <> *vt* - 1. [spucken] to spit out - 2. *fam* [ausgeben, bezahlen] to cough up - 3. *fam* [erbrechen] to puke up.

aus|spülen *vt* to rinse out.

aus|statten *vt* [mit Gerät] to equip; [mit Lebensmitteln, Kleidung, Geld] to provide.

Ausstattung *(pl -en) die* - 1. [mit Möbeln] furnishing; [mit Geräten] equipping; [mit Lebensmitteln, Kleidung, Geld] provision - 2. [Ausrüstung] equipment; [von Küche, Auto] fittings *Pl* - 3. [Einrichtung] furnishings *Pl*.

aus|stehen *(unreg)* <> *vt* to endure; **jn/etw nicht ausstehen können** *fam* not to be able to stand sb/sthg. <> *vi* [Zahlung] to be outstanding; **die Antwort steht noch aus** we're still waiting for an answer.

aus|steigen *(perf ist ausgestiegen) vi (unreg)* - 1. [heraussteigen] to get out; **aus einem Bus/Zug aussteigen** to get off a bus/train - 2. *fam* [ausscheiden]: **aus einem Geschäft aussteigen** to pull out of a deal - 3. [aus Gesellschaft] to drop out (from society).

Aussteiger, in (mpl -, fpl -nen) der, die drop-out.

aus|stellen vt - **1.** [zeigen - Waren] to display; [- Kunstwerke] to exhibit - **2.** [ausfertigen - Scheck, Rezept] to make out; [- Visum] to issue; **einen Scheck auf jn ausstellen** to make out a cheque to sb - **3.** [ausschalten] to turn off.

Aus|stellung die exhibition.

aus|sterben (perf ist ausgestorben) vi (unreg) [Tierart] to become extinct; [Tradition] to die out.

Aus|steuer die dowry.

Ausstieg (pl -e) der - **1.** [Öffnung] exit - **2.** (ohne pl) [Rückzug]: **sie haben den Ausstieg aus der Kernenergie beschlossen** they have decided to abandon nuclear energy.

aus|stoßen vt (unreg) - **1.** [ausschließen] to expel - **2.** [hervorstoßen - Schrei] to give; [- Seufzer] to heave; [- Fluch] to utter - **3.** [produzieren] to emit.

aus|strahlen <> vt - **1.** [verbreiten] to radiate - **2.** [senden] to broadcast. <> vi [strahlen - Licht] to shine.

Aus|strahlung die - **1.** [Wirkung] charisma - **2.** [Senden] broadcasting.

aus|strecken vt [Zunge] to stick out; [Fühler] to put out; **die Beine/Arme ausstrecken** to stretch one's legs/arms. ◆ **sich ausstrecken** ref to stretch out.

aus|suchen vt to choose; **sich (D) etw aussuchen** to choose sthg.

Aus|tausch der exchange; [von Spielern] substitution.

austauschbar adj interchangeable.

aus|tauschen vt - **1.** [mitteilen] to exchange - **2.** [auswechseln] to replace; **einen Spieler (gegen einen anderen) austauschen** to substitute a player (with another).

aus|teilen vt [Prospekte] to hand out; [Karten] to deal (out); [Essen] to dish out.

Auster (pl -n) die oyster.

aus|toben vt: **seine Wut an jm austoben** to vent one's fury on sb. ◆ **sich austoben** ref to let off steam.

aus|tragen vt (unreg) - **1.** [Zeitung, Post] to deliver - **2.** [ausfechten]: **einen Streit mit jm austragen** to have it out with sb - **3.** [Wettkampf] to hold - **4.** [im Mutterleib] to carry to term. ◆ **sich austragen** ref to sign out.

Australien nt Australia.

Australier, in [aus'tra:ljɐ, rɪn] (mpl -, fpl -nen) der, die Australian.

australisch adj Australian.

aus|treiben vt (unreg) - **1.** [verbannen] to exorcize - **2.** [abgewöhnen]: **jm etw austreiben** to cure sb of sthg.

aus|treten (perf hat/ist ausgetreten) (unreg) <> vt (hat) - **1.** [ersticken - Funken] to stamp out; [- Zigarette] to tread out - **2.** [abnutzen] to

wear down - **3.** [weiten] to break in. <> vi (ist) - **1.** [ausscheiden]: **aus etw austreten** to leave sthg - **2.** [zur Toilette gehen] to answer the call of nature.

aus|trinken (unreg) <> vt [Kaffee, Bier] to drink up, to finish; [Glas] to drain, to finish. <> vi to drink up.

Aus|tritt der [aus Partei] resignation; **die Kirche hat zahlreiche Austritte zu verzeichnen** a lot of people have left the Church.

aus|trocknen <> vi (perf ist ausgetrocknet) [Haut, Brot, Boden] to dry out; [See] to dry up. <> vt (perf hat ausgetrocknet) [Haut, Brot, Boden] to dry out; [See] to dry up.

aus|tüfteln vt to work out.

aus|üben vt [Beruf] to practise; [Amt] to hold; [Einfluss, Druck] to exert; [Macht] to exercise, to wield.

aus|ufern (perf ist ausgeufert) vi to get out of hand.

Aus|verkauf der sale.

ausverkauft adj sold out.

Aus|wahl die - **1.** (ohne pl) [Wahl] choice - **2.** [Auslese] selection - **3.** [Sortiment] range.

aus|wählen vt to choose, to select.

aus|walzen vt - **1.** [walzen] to roll out - **2.** abw [breittreten] to drag out.

aus|wandern (perf ist ausgewandert) vi to emigrate.

Auswanderung die (ohne pl) emigration.

auswärtig adj - **1.** [extern] external - **2.** [aus einem anderen Ort] from another town; [Mannschaft] away (vor Subst) - **3.** [außenpolitisch] foreign.

Auswärtige Amt das foreign ministry.

auswärts adv [spielen, übernachten] away from home; **auswärts essen** to eat out.

aus|waschen vt (unreg) [Fleck] to wash out; [Kleidungsstück] to wash; [Pinsel] to rinse.

aus|wechseln ['ausvɛksln] vt [Reifen, Batterien] to replace; [Spieler] to substitute; **wie ausgewechselt sein** to be a different person.

Aus|weg der way out.

ausweglos adj hopeless.

aus|weichen (perf ist ausgewichen) vi (unreg) - **1.** (+ D) [Fußgänger, Hindernis] to avoid; [Schlag] to dodge; [Auto] to get out of the way of - **2.** (+ D) [Frage, Entscheidung, Blick] to avoid - **3.** [zurückgreifen]: **auf etw (A) ausweichen** to switch to sthg.

ausweichend adj evasive.

aus|weinen ◆ **sich ausweinen** ref: **sich bei jm ausweinen** to cry on sb's shoulder.

Ausweis (pl -e) der [Personalausweis] identity card; [von Mitglied] membership card; [Zugangsberechtigung] pass.

aus|weisen *vt (unreg)* - **1.** [verbannen] to deport, to expel - **2.** [erkennen lassen]: **jn als etw ausweisen** to identify sb as sthg. ◆ **sich ausweisen** *ref* to show one's identification.

Ausweis|kontrolle *die* identity card check.

Ausweispapiere *Pl* papers, identification *(U)*.

Ausweitung *(pl -en) die* - **1.** [Vergrößerung] expansion - **2.** [eines Streiks] spreading.

auswendig *adv* by heart; **etw auswendig wissen** *ODER* **können** to know sthg by heart.

Aus|wertung *die* evaluation.

Aus|wirkung *die* effect, impact; **die Auswirkung auf jn/etw** the effect *ODER* impact on sb/ sthg.

aus|wringen *(prät* **wrang aus,** *perf* **ausgewrungen)** *vt (unreg)* to wring out.

Auswuchs ['ausvu:ks] ◆ **Auswüchse** *Pl* excesses.

aus|zahlen *vt* - **1.** [Gehalt, Lohn] to pay - **2.** [Teilhaber] to buy out; [Arbeiter] to pay off. ◆ **sich auszahlen** *ref* to pay off.

aus|zählen *vt* to count up.

aus|zeichnen *vt* - **1.** [mit Preisschild] to price - **2.** [ehren]: **jm mit einem Preis auszeichnen** to award a prize to sb - **3.** [charakterisieren]: **große Biegsamkeit zeichnet diesen Werkstoff aus** this material is characterized by its great flexibility. ◆ **sich auszeichnen** *ref* [Person] to distinguish o.s.; [Produkt] to stand out.

aus|ziehen *(perf* **hat/ist ausgezogen)** *(unreg)* ◇ *vt (hat)* - **1.** [ablegen] to take off; **die Jacke ausziehen** to take off one's jacket - **2.** [entkleiden] to undress - **3.** [vergrößern - Tisch, Antenne] to pull out - **4.** [herausziehen] to pull out. ◇ *vi (ist)* [umziehen] to move out. ◆ **sich ausziehen** *ref* to undress; **sich die Schuhe ausziehen** to take off one's shoes off.

Auszubildende *(pl -n) der, die* trainee.

Aus|zug *der* - **1.** [Ausschnitt] excerpt - **2.** [Kontoauszug] statement - **3.** [Umzug] move.

auszugsweise *adv*: **ein Roman auszugsweise abdrucken** to publish a novel in instalments.

Auto *(pl -s) das* car; **mit dem Auto fahren** to go by car, to drive.

Auto|atlas *der* road atlas.

Auto|bahn *die* motorway *UK*, freeway *US*.

Autobahn|gebühr *die* toll.

Autobahn|kreuz *das* interchange.

Autobahn|meisterei *(pl -en) die* motorway *UK ODER* freeway *US* maintenance department.

Auto|bus *der* bus.

Auto|fahrer, in *der, die* (car) driver.

autogenes Training *das* autogenics *(U)*, relaxation technique based on self-hypnosis, developed by German neurologist J.H. Schultz.

Autogramm *(pl -e) das* autograph.

Automat *(pl -en) der* [für Getränke, Zigaretten] vending machine.

Automatik *(pl -en) die* automatic mechanism.

Automatik|getriebe *das* automatic transmission.

automatisch ◇ *adj* automatic. ◇ *adv* automatically.

automatisieren *vt* to automate.

Autonomie *(pl -n) die* autonomy.

Autor *(pl -toren) der* author.

Auto|radio *das* car radio.

Auto|rennen *das* - **1.** [Sportart] motor racing - **2.** [Wettkampf] motor race.

Autorin *(pl -nen) die* author.

autoritär *adj* authoritarian.

Autorität *(pl -en) die* authority.

Auto|unfall *der* car accident.

Auto|verkehr *der* car traffic.

avantgardistisch [avɑ̃'gardɪstiʃ] *adj* avant-garde.

Avocado [avo'kɑːdo] *(pl -s) die* avocado.

Axt *(pl* **Äxte)** *die* axe.

Azalee *(pl -n) die* azalea.

Azubi *(pl -s) der, die fam* trainee.

B

b, B *(pl -* ODER *-s)* [beː] *das* - **1.** [Buchstabe] B, b - **2.** [MUS - Note] B flat; [- Vorzeichen] flat. ◆ **B** *(pl* **B)** *(abk für* **Bundesstraße)** *die* ≈ A road *UK*, ≈ state highway *US*.

Baby ['beːbi] *(pl -s) das* baby.

Baby|sitter, in ['beːbisitɐ, rɪn] *(mpl* **Baby**sitter, *fpl* -nen) *der, die* babysitter.

Bach *(pl* **Bäche)** *der* stream; **den Bach runtergehen** *fam* to go down the tubes.

Backbord *das (ohne pl)* SCHIFF port.

Backe *(pl -n) die* [Wange, von Po] cheek.

backen *(präs* **bäckt** ODER **backt,** *prät* **backte** ODER **buk,** *perf* **hat gebacken)** ◇ *vt* - **1.** [im Ofen] to bake - **2.** [braten] to fry. ◇ *vi* to bake.

Backen|zahn *der* molar.

Bäcker *(pl -) der* baker.

Bäckerei *(pl -en) die* bakery.

Bäckerin *(pl -nen) die* baker.

Back|form *die* baking tin.

Back|ofen *der* oven.

Back|pulver *das* baking powder.

Back|stein der brick; **ein Gebäude aus Backstein** a brick building.

bäckt präs ▷ **backen**.

Bad (pl Bäder) das - 1. [Badezimmer] bathroom - 2. [Baden - im Meer] bathing (U); [- in der Wanne] bath; **ein Bad in der Menge nehmen** fig to press the flesh - 3. [Schwimmbad] (swimming) pool - 4. [Kurort] spa town.

Bade|anzug der swimming costume, swimsuit.

Bade|hose die swimming trunks Pl.

Bade|kappe die swimming cap.

Bade|mantel der bathrobe.

Bade|meister, in der, die [im Schwimmbad] pool attendant; [am Strand] lifeguard.

baden ◇ vt [Kind] to bath UK, to bathe US; [Wunde] to bathe. ◇ vi - 1. [in der Wanne] to have a bath - 2. [schwimmen] to swim; **baden gehen** to go for a swim; **wenn das passiert, werde ich bei** ODER **mit meinen Plänen baden gehen** fam if that happens, I can kiss my plans goodbye. ▰ **sich baden** ref to have a bath.

Bade|wanne die bath (tub).

Bade|zimmer das bathroom.

baff adj: **(ganz) baff sein** fam to be gobsmacked.

Bafög ['baːfœk] (abk für **Bundesausbildungsförderungsgesetz**) das [Stipendium] maintenance which is half grant and half loan awarded to students and trainees by the State; **Bafög bekommen** to get a grant.

Bagel (pl Bagel) der bagel.

Bagger (pl -) der mechanical digger.

baggern ◇ vt [Graben] to dig; [Fahrrinne] to dredge. ◇ vi fam [Mädchen anmachen]: **er baggert schon wieder** he's on the pull again.

Bahn (pl -en) die - 1. [Eisenbahn] train; **mit der Bahn fahren** to travel by train ODER rail - 2. [Institution] railway UK, railroad US; **die Bahn** [Deutsche Bahn] German rail company; **bei der Bahn arbeiten** to work for the railways - 3. [Weg] path; **wir haben freie Bahn** AUTO the road is clear, fig the way is clear - 4. [von Rakete, Planet] path - 5. SPORT [in Schwimmbad, Stadion] lane; **40 Bahnen schwimmen** to swim 40 lengths - 6. [Straßenbahn] tram UK, streetcar US - 7. [Streifen - von Stoff] length; [- von Tapete] strip; **auf die schiefe Bahn geraten** to fall into bad ways; **jn aus der Bahn werfen** to shatter sb.

bahnbrechend adj pioneering.

BahnCard® ['baːnkaːd] (pl -s) die card offering 50% discount on German rail fares.

Bahn|damm der railway embankment.

bahnen vt: **jm/sich einen Weg bahnen** to clear a path for sb/o.s.

Bahn|hof der (railway) station.

Bahn|steig (pl -e) der platform.

Bahnsteig|kante die platform edge.

Bahnüber|gang der level crossing UK, grade crossing US.

Bahre (pl -n) die - 1. [für Kranke] stretcher - 2. [für Tote] bier.

Baiser [bɛ'zeː] (pl -s) das meringue.

Bakterien Pl bacteria, germs.

Balance [ba'laŋsə] die balance.

balancieren [balaŋ'siːrən] ◇ vt (perf hat balanciert) to balance. ◇ vi (perf ist balanciert) to balance.

bald adv - 1. [in Kürze, schnell] soon - 2. fam [fast] almost, nearly - 3. fam [endlich]: **hältst du jetzt bald den Mund?** just shut up, will you? ▰ **bis bald** interj see you soon ODER later!

Baldrian (pl -e) der valerian.

balgen vi to tussle. ▰ **sich balgen** ref: **sich (mit jm um etw) balgen** to tussle (with sb over sthg).

Balkan der: **der Balkan** the Balkans.

Balken (pl -) der beam.

Balkon [bal'kɔŋ, bal'koːn] (pl -s ODER -e) der balcony.

Ball (pl Bälle) der ball; **am Ball bleiben** [nicht aufhören] to stick at it; [auf dem Laufenden bleiben] to keep up to date.

Ballade (pl -n) die ballad.

Ballast der ballast.

Ballaststoffe Pl roughage (U).

ballen vt: **die Faust ballen** to clench one's fist. ▰ **sich ballen** ref [Schnee, Lehm]: **sich zu etw ballen** to form into sthg.

Ballen (pl -) der - 1. [Packen] bale - 2. [von Hand] ball of the hand; [von Fuß] ball of the foot.

ballern fam ◇ vi - 1. [schießen] to spray bullets - 2. [schlagen]: **gegen** ODER **an etw (A) ballern** to hammer on sthg. ◇ vt - 1. [ohrfeigen]: **jm eine/ein paar ballern** to sock sb one - 2. [werfen]: **etw gegen etw ballern** to smash sthg against sthg.

Ballett (pl -e) das ballet; **ins Ballett gehen** to go to the ballet.

Ballon [ba'lɔŋ] (pl -s ODER -e) der balloon.

Ball|spiel das ball game.

Ballungs|gebiet das conurbation.

Balsam der eigtl & fig balm.

Balte (pl -n) der native/inhabitant of the Baltic.

Baltikum das: **das Baltikum** the Baltic.

Baltin (pl -nen) die native/inhabitant of the Baltic.

baltisch adj Baltic.

balzen vi to perform a courtship display.

Bambus (pl -se) der bamboo.

banal ◇ adj banal. ◇ adv banally.

Banane (pl -n) die banana.

Bananen|republik *die abw* banana republic.

Banause (*pl* -n) *der abw* philistine.

Banausin (*pl* -nen) *die abw* philistine.

Band[1] [bant] (*pl* **Bänder** ODER **Bände**) ◇ *das* (*pl Bänder*) - 1. [aus Stoff] band; [als Zierde] ribbon - 2. [Tonband] tape; **etw auf Band aufnehmen** to tape sthg - 3. [Fließband] conveyor belt; **am laufenden Band** *fig* continuously - 4. [aus Bindegewebe] ligament. ◇ *der* (*pl Bände*) [Buch] volume; **das spricht Bände** *fig* that speaks volumes.

Band[2] [bɛnt] (*pl* -s) *die* band.

Bandage [ban'dɑːʒə] (*pl* -n) *die* [Verband] bandage.

bandagieren [banda'ʒiːrən] *vt* to bandage.

Band|breite *die* - 1. ELEKTR bandwidth - 2. *fig* [Vielzahl] range.

Bande (*pl* -n) *die* - 1. [von Verbrechern, Kindern] gang - 2. [SPORT - von Bahn, Spielfeld] barrier; [- von Billardtisch] cushion.

bändigen *vt* [Tier] to tame; [Kind] to control.

Bandit (*pl* -en) *der* bandit.

Band|maß *das* tape measure.

Band|nudeln *Pl* tagliatelle (*U.*)

Band|scheibe *die* [Körperteil] disc.

Band|wurm *der* - 1. [Wurm] tapeworm - 2. *fig* [Gebilde]: **dieser Satz ist ein Bandwurm** this sentence is never-ending.

bange *adj* anxious; **mir ist/wird bange** I am/I'm getting worried.

Bange *die*: **keine Bange!** don't worry!

Bank (*pl* **Bänke** ODER -en) *die* - 1. (*pl Bänke*) [in Park, Schule] bench; [in Kirche] pew; **etw auf die lange Bank schieben** *fig* to put sthg off - 2. (*pl Banken*) [Geldinstitut] bank.

Bank|anweisung *die* banker's order.

Bankett (*pl* -e) *das* banquet.

Bank|geheimnis *das* banking confidentiality.

Bankier [baŋ'kjeː] (*pl* -s) *der* banker.

Bank|konto *das* bank account.

Bank|leit|zahl *die* bank sort code.

Bank|note *die* banknote.

Bank|raub *der* bank robbery; **einen Bankraub** to rob a bank.

Bank|räuber, in *der, die* bank robber.

bankrott *adj* bankrupt.

Bankrott (*pl* -e) *der* bankruptcy; **Bankrott gehen** to go bankrupt.

Bank|überfall *der* bank raid.

Bank|verbindung *die* account details *Pl*.

bannen *vt* - 1. [fesseln] to hold spellbound - 2. [Gefahr] to ward off; [bösen Geist] to exorcize.

Banner (*pl* -) *das* banner.

Baptist, in (*mpl* -en, *fpl* -nen) *der, die* Baptist.

bar ◇ *adj* - 1. [mit Bargeld] cash; **bares Geld** cash - 2. [pur - Zufall] pure; [- Unsinn] sheer. ◇ *adv* [in Bargeld] for cash. ◆ **in bar** *adv* in cash.

Bar (*pl* -s) *die* - 1. [Nachtlokal] bar (*often also a brothel*) - 2. [Theke] bar.

Bär (*pl* -en) *der* bear; **jm einen Bären aufbinden** *fig* to pull sb's leg.

Baracke (*pl* -n) *die* hut.

Barbar, in (*mpl* -en, *fpl* -nen) *der, die* barbarian.

barbarisch ◇ *adj* barbaric. ◇ *adv* barbarically.

barfuß *adv* barefoot.

barg *prät* ⟶ **bergen**.

Bar|geld *das* cash.

bargeldlos ◇ *adj* cashless. ◇ *adv*: **bargeldlos zahlen** to use a cashless payment method.

Bariton (*pl* -e) *der* baritone.

Barkeeper ['baːkiːpɐ] (*pl* -) *der* barman.

barock *adj* baroque.

Barock *der* ODER *das* (*ohne pl*) baroque period.

Barometer *das* barometer.

Baron [ba'roːn] (*pl* -e) *der* baron.

Baronesse [baro'nɛsə] (*pl* -n) *die* daughter of a baron.

Baronin [ba'roːnɪn] (*pl* -nen) *die* baroness.

Barrel ['barəl] (*pl* -s ODER -) *das* barrel.

Barren (*pl* -) *der* - 1. [Block] bar - 2. [Turngerät] parallel bars *Pl*.

Barriere [ba'rjeːrə] (*pl* -n) *die* barrier.

Barrikade (*pl* -n) *die* barricade; **sie ging auf die Barrikaden** *fig* she was up in arms.

barsch (*superl* **barsch(e)ste**) ◇ *adj* curt. ◇ *adv* curtly.

Barsch (*pl* -e) *der* [Fisch] perch.

Bar|scheck *der* uncrossed cheque.

Bart (*pl* **Bärte**) *der* - 1. [Gesichtshaar] beard - 2. [Schlüsselbart] bit; **jm um den Bart gehen** ODER **streichen** to butter sb up.

bärtig *adj* bearded.

Bar|zahlung *die* payment in cash.

Basar (*pl* -e), **Bazar** (*pl* -e) *der* bazaar.

Basel *nt* Basel, Basle.

basieren *vi*: **auf etw** (*D*) **basieren** to be based on sthg.

Basilikum *das* basil.

Basis (*pl* **Basen**) *die* - 1. [Grundlage] basis - 2. MIL base - 3. POL grass roots *Pl*; **an der Basis arbeiten** to work at grass-roots level.

Baske (*pl* -n) *der* Basque.

Baskenland *das*: **das Baskenland** the Basque Country.

Basketball ['baːskətbal] *der* basketball.

Baskin (*pl* -nen) *die* Basque.

baskisch adj Basque.

Bass (pl Bässe) der - **1.** [Stimme, Sänger] bass - **2.** [Kontrabass] double bass; [Bassgitarre] bass (guitar).

Bassist, in (mpl -en, fpl -nen) der, die - **1.** [im Orchester] double bass player; [in Rockgruppe] bass player, bass guitarist - **2.** [Sänger] bass.

Bassschlüssel (pl --schlüssel) der MUS bass clef.

Bast der raffia.

Bastelei (pl -en) die - **1.** [Basteln] handicrafts pl - **2.** [Reparaturversuche]: **er hat genug von der ewigen Bastelei** he's had enough of tinkering around all the time.

basteln ⟨> vt to make; **Weihnachtsgeschenke basteln** to make one's own Christmas presents. ⟨> vi to do handicrafts; **sie bastelt gerne** she likes making things herself; **an etw** (D) **basteln** to tinker with sthg.

Bastler, in (mpl -, fpl -nen) der, die handicrafts enthusiast.

BAT [beːaːˈteː] (abk für Bundesangestelltentarif) der statutory salary scale for public employees.

Batterie (pl -n) die - **1.** [Stromspeicher] battery - **2.** [große Menge] array.

batteriebetrieben adj battery-powered.

Batzen (pl -) der fam: **das hat mich einen Batzen Geld gekostet** that cost me a packet.

Bau (pl -ten ODER -e) der - **1.** [das Bauen] construction; **in** ODER **im Bau sein** to be under construction - **2.** (ohne pl) [Baustelle] building site - **3.** (pl Bauten) [Gebäude] building - **4.** (pl Baue) [von Kaninchen] burrow; [von Fuchs] den; [von Dachs] set.

Bauarbeiten Pl construction work (U).

Bauarbeiter, in der, die construction worker.

Bauch (pl Bäuche) der stomach; **sich** (D) **den Bauch voll schlagen** fam to stuff o.s. ODER one's face; **mit etw auf den Bauch fallen** fig to make a botch ODER mess of sthg.

bauchig adj bulbous.

Bauchnabel der navel.

Bauchschmerzen [ˈbauxʃmɛrtsn̩] Pl stomachache (U).

Baudenkmal das listed building.

bauen ⟨> vt - **1.** [anlegen, errichten] to build - **2.** [herstellen] to make; [Auto, Flugzeug] to build, to make - **3.** fam [verursachen - Unfall] to cause; **Mist bauen** to mess up. ⟨> vi - **1.** [arbeiten, bauen lassen] to build; **an etw** (D) **bauen** to be building sthg - **2.** [vertrauen]: **auf jn/etw bauen** to rely on sb/sthg.

Bauer (pl -n ODER -) ⟨> der (pl Bauern) - **1.** [Landwirt] farmer; HIST peasant - **2.** [Schachfigur] pawn - **3.** [Spielkarte] jack. ⟨> das & der (pl Bauer) [Vogelkäfig] (bird) cage.

Bäuerin (pl -nen) die [Frau des Bauern] farmer's wife; [Landwirtin] farmer.

bäuerlich ⟨> adj rural. ⟨> adv: **sich bäuerlich kleiden** to wear rustic clothes.

Bauernfrühstück das fried potatoes with scrambled egg and pieces of bacon.

Bauernhof der farm.

baufällig adj dilapidated.

Baufirma die construction firm, building contractor.

Baugenehmigung die planning permission (U).

Bauland das (ohne pl) development site.

Baum (pl Bäume) der tree.

baumeln vi to dangle; **die Beine baumeln lassen** to dangle one's legs.

Baumschule die (tree) nursery.

Baumstamm der tree trunk.

Baumsterben das forest dieback.

Baumstumpf der tree stump.

Baumwolle die cotton.

Bausatz der kit.

Bausch (pl -e ODER Bäusche) der ball.

bauschen vt [Kleidungsstück] to puff out; [Segel] to fill. ⟨> **sich bauschen** ref [Vorhänge, Segel] to billow; [Ärmel] to puff out.

Bausparkasse die building society UK, savings and loan association US.

Baustein der - **1.** [zum Bauen] brick - **2.** [zum Spielen] building block - **3.** [Bestandteil] constituent part, component.

Baustelle die building site; [auf einer Straße] roadworks pl.

Bauten Pl ⟨> Bau.

Bauunternehmer, in der, die building contractor.

Bauwerk das building.

Bayer, in (mpl -n, fpl -nen) der, die Bavarian.

bayerisch = **bayrisch**.

Bayerisch = **Bayrisch**.

Bayerische = **Bayrische**.

Bayern nt Bavaria.

bayrisch, bayerisch ⟨> adj Bavarian. ⟨> adv like a Bavarian.

Bayrisch, Bayerisch das (ohne Pl) Bavarian (dialect).

Bazille (pl -n) die MED bacillus; **Bazillen** germs.

Bd. (abk für Band) vol.

beabsichtigen vt to intend.

beachten vt - **1.** [befolgen - Vorschriften, Verbot] to observe; [- Ratschläge, Anweisungen] to follow - **2.** [berücksichtigen - Umstände, Gefahr] to take into consideration; **jn nicht beachten** to take no notice of sb.

beachtlich ⟨> adj [Leistung, Verbesserung, Erfolg] considerable; [Position] important. ⟨> adv considerably.

Beachtung *die* - **1.** [Befolgung - von Regeln] observing - **2.** [Berücksichtigung] consideration; **unter Beachtung aller Umstände** taking everything into consideration; **einer Sache** *(D)* **Beachtung schenken** to take sthg into consideration; **jm keine Beachtung schenken** to take no notice of sb; **Beachtung finden** to be taken into consideration.

Beamte *(pl* -n) *der* State employee *(e.g. teacher, policeman, civil servant).*

Beamtenschaft *die (ohne pl)* State employees *Pl.*

Beamtin *(pl* -nen) *die* State employee *(e.g. teacher, policewoman, civil servant).*

beängstigend ⇔ *adj* frightening. ⇔ *adv* frighteningly.

beanspruchen *vt* - **1.** [fordern] to claim - **2.** [Material, Bremsen] to wear out - **3.** [strapazieren - Geduld, Person] to tax; **wir möchten Ihre Gastfreundschaft nicht länger beanspruchen** we don't want to impose on you any longer - **4.** [Raum, Zeit, Energie] to take up.

Beanspruchung *(pl* -en) *die* - **1.** [von Material, Nerven] strain - **2.** [im Beruf] demands *Pl.*

beanstanden *vt* to complain about.

Beanstandung *(pl* -en) *die* complaint.

beantragen *vt* - **1.** [verlangen] to apply for - **2.** [vorschlagen] to propose.

beantworten *vt* to answer.

Beantwortung *(pl* -en) *die:* **die Beantwortung der Frage** the answer to the question.

bearbeiten *vt* - **1.** [mit Werkzeug] to work - **2.** [Text] to edit; [Musikstück] to arrange; **ein Buch für den Film bearbeiten** to adapt a book for the screen - **3.** [betreuen] to deal with - **4.** *fam* [misshandeln - Schlagzeug] to bang away at; **jm mit den Fäusten bearbeiten** to do sb over - **5.** *fam* [beeinflussen] to work on.

Bearbeitung *(pl* -en) *die* - **1.** [von Werkstück, Metall] working - **2.** [von Text] editing; [von Musikstück] arranging; [für Film, Fernsehen] adaptation - **3.** [von Antrag] processing.

beatmen *vt:* **jn künstlich beatmen** to give sb artificial respiration.

Beatmung *(pl* -en) *die:* **künstliche Beatmung** artificial respiration.

beaufsichtigen *vt* to supervise.

beauftragen *vt:* **jn beauftragen, etw zu tun** [bitten] to tell sb to do sthg; [Auftrag erteilen] to commission sb to do sthg; **beauftragt sein, etw zu tun** to be charged with doing sthg.

Beauftragte *(pl* -n) *der, die* representative.

bebauen *vt* [mit Gebäuden] to build on, to develop; **ein Gelände mit Häusern bebauen** to build houses on a site.

beben *vi* - **1.** [durch Explosion] to shake - **2.** [Hände, Person, Stimme] to tremble.

Beben *(pl* -) *das* - **1.** [von Händen, Person, Stimme] trembling - **2.** [Erdbeben] earthquake.

Becher *(pl* -) *der* - **1.** [Kaffeebecher - ohne Henkel, aus Pappe, Styropor] cup; [- ohne Henkel, aus hartem Kunststoff] beaker; [- mit Henkel, aus Porzellan] mug - **2.** [Pokal] goblet - **3.** [für Jogurt] pot; [für Eis] tub.

Becken *(pl* -) *das* - **1.** [Waschbecken] basin; [Spülbecken] sink; [Schwimmbecken] pool - **2.** [Körperteil] pelvis - **3.** [Instrument] cymbal.

bedacht ⇔ *pp* ⊳ **bedenken**. ⇔ *adj* - **1.** [vorsichtig] careful - **2.** [bemüht]: **auf etw** *(A)* **bedacht sein** to be concerned about sthg. ⇔ *adv* [vorsichtig] carefully.

bedächtig ⇔ *adj* - **1.** [langsam] deliberate - **2.** [nachdenklich - Person, Miene] thoughtful; [- Worte] well-considered. ⇔ *adv* - **1.** [langsam] deliberately - **2.** [überlegt - sprechen] with well-considered words.

bedanken ➡ **sich bedanken** *ref* to say thank you; **ich möchte mich herzlich bedanken** thank you very much; **sich bei jm für etw bedanken** to thank sb for sthg.

Bedarf *der* need; **Bedarf an etw** *(D)* **haben** to be in need of sthg. ➡ **bei Bedarf** *adv* should the need arise.

bedauerlich *adj* regrettable.

bedauern *vt* - **1.** [Irrtum, Unüberlegtheit] to regret - **2.** [Person] to feel sorry for; **bedaure!** I'm sorry!

Bedauern *das* - **1.** [Mitleid] sympathy - **2.** [Reue] regret.

bedauernswert *adj* - **1.** [Irrtum] regrettable - **2.** [Person] pitiable.

bedecken *vt* to cover. ➡ **sich bedecken** *ref* [Himmel] to cloud over.

bedeckt ⇔ *pp* ⊳ **bedecken**. ⇔ *adj* [Himmel] overcast.

bedenken *(prät* **bedachte**, *perf* **hat bedacht**) *vt* - **1.** [überlegen] to consider - **2.** *geh* [beschenken - im Testament] to remember.

Bedenken *(pl* -) *das* - **1.** [Nachdenken] consideration - **2.** [Zweifel] doubt.

bedenklich *adj* - **1.** [prekär] serious - **2.** [besorgt] anxious - **3.** [fragwürdig] dubious.

Bedenkzeit *die:* **jm Bedenkzeit geben** to give sb some time to think it over.

bedeuten *vt* - **1.** [gen] to mean; **viel/nichts bedeuten** to mean a lot/nothing; **jm viel/wenig/nichts bedeuten** to mean much/not to mean much/to mean nothing to sb; **das hat nichts zu bedeuten** that doesn't matter - **2.** *geh* [zu verstehen geben]: **jm etw bedeuten** to indicate sthg to sb.

bedeutend ⇔ *adj* - **1.** [wichtig] important - **2.** [groß] considerable. ⇔ *adv* [sehr] considerably.

Bedeutung *(pl* -en) *die* - **1.** [Sinn] meaning - **2.** [Wichtigkeit] importance; **einer Sache** *(D)* **große/keine Bedeutung beimessen** to attach great/no importance to sthg.

bedienen ◇ *vt* - **1.** [Person] to serve; **mit diesem Produkt sind Sie gut bedient** this product is a good deal - **2.** [Maschine] to operate. ◇ *vi* to serve. ◈ **sich bedienen** *ref* to help o.s.; **bedienen Sie sich!** help yourself!

Bedienung (*pl* -en) *die* - **1.** [Versorgung] service - **2.** [Steuerung, Anwendung] operation - **3.** [Kellner] waiter; [Kellnerin] waitress.

Bedienungsanleitung *die* operating instructions *Pl*.

bedingen *vt* [verursachen] to bring about.

Bedingung (*pl* -en) *die* [Voraussetzung] condition; **eine Bedingung stellen** to stipulate a condition; **unter einer Bedingung** on one condition. ◈ **Bedingungen** *Pl* [Umstände] conditions.

bedingungslos ◇ *adj* unconditional. ◇ *adv* unconditionally.

bedrängen *vt* [unter Druck setzen] to pressurize; [mit Truppen] to advance on; **jn mit Fragen bedrängen** to badger sb with questions.

bedrohen *vt* to threaten.

bedrohlich ◇ *adj* [Situation, Aussehen] threatening; [Nähe, Intensität] dangerous. ◇ *adv* [ansehen] threateningly; [nah, schnell] dangerously.

Bedrohung (*pl* -en) *die* threat.

bedrücken *vt* to depress.

bedrückt *adj* - **1.** [Person] depressed - **2.** [Schweigen, Stimmung] oppressive.

Bedürfnis (*pl* -se) *das* need.

bedürftig *adj* needy.

beeilen [bə'ailən] ◈ **sich beeilen** *ref* to hurry; **beeile dich!** hurry up!

beeindrucken [bə'aindrʊkn̩] ◇ *vt* to impress. ◇ *vi* to make an impression.

beeinflussen [bə'ainflʊsn̩] *vt* to influence.

beeinträchtigen [bə'aintrɛçtɪgn̩] *vt* [Bewegungsfähigkeit, Sicht] to impair; [Produktion, Stimmung] to affect adversely; [Wert, Qualität] to reduce; [Gesundheit] to damage; [Konzentration] to hamper.

Beeinträchtigung [bə'aintrɛçtɪgʊŋ] (*pl* -en) *die* [von Bewegungsfähigkeit, Sicht] impairment; [von Produktion, Stimmung] adverse effect; [von Wert, Qualität] reduction; [von Gesundheit] damaging; [von Konzentration] hampering.

beenden [bə'ɛndn̩] *vt* to end.

beengt [bə'ɛŋt] *adv*: **beengt wohnen** to live in cramped conditions.

beerben [bə'ɛrbn̩] *vt*: **jn beerben** to inherit sb's estate.

beerdigen [bə'eːɐdɪgn̩] *vt* to bury.

Beerdigung [bə'eːɐdɪgʊŋ] (*pl* -en) *die* funeral.

Beerdigungsinstitut *das* funeral directors *Pl*.

Beere (*pl* -n) *die* berry.

Beet (*pl* -e) *das* [mit Blumen] flowerbed; [mit Gemüse] vegetable patch.

Beete *die* = **Bete**.

befahl *prät* ▷ **befehlen**.

befahrbar *adj* [Straße, Weg] passable; [Fluss] navigable.

befahren (*präs* befährt, *prät* befuhr, *perf* hat befahren) ◇ *vt* to use. ◇ *adj*: **eine stark befahrene Straße** a busy street.

befangen ◇ *adj* - **1.** [schüchtern] shy - **2.** RECHT partial - **3.** *geh* [gefangen]: **in dem Glauben befangen sein, dass...** to labour under the misconception that... ◇ *adv* shyly.

Befangenheit *die* - **1.** [Schüchternheit] shyness - **2.** RECHT partiality.

befassen (*präs* befasst, *prät* befasste, *perf* hat befasst) *vt*: **jn mit etw befassen** *geh* to assign sthg to sb. ◈ **sich befassen** *ref*: **sich mit einer Frage befassen** to look into a question; **sich intensiv mit einem Thema befassen** to study *ODER* look at a matter in great detail.

Befehl (*pl* -e) *der* - **1.** [Aufforderung] order - **2.** EDV command.

befehlen (*präs* befiehlt, *prät* befahl, *perf* hat befohlen) ◇ *vt* to order; **jm befehlen, etw zu tun** to order sb to do sthg; **du hast mir gar nichts zu befehlen** I don't take orders from you. ◇ *vi*: **über jn/etw befehlen** to command sb/sthg.

Befehlsform *die* GRAMM imperative.

befestigen *vt* - **1.** [anbringen]: **etw an etw (D) befestigen** to attach sthg to sthg; **etw mit Schrauben an der Wand befestigen** to screw sthg to the wall - **2.** [verstärken - Stadt] to fortify; [- Ufer, Damm] to reinforce; [- Straße] to make up.

Befestigung (*pl* -en) *die* - **1.** [das Anbringen] attaching - **2.** [die Verstärkung - von Stadt] fortification; [- von Ufer, Damm] reinforcement; [- von Straße] making up.

befiehlt *präs* ▷ **befehlen**.

befinden (*prät* befand, *perf* hat befunden) *vt*: **etw für gut/richtig befinden** *geh* to deem sthg good/right. ◈ **sich befinden** *ref* to be; **sein Büro befindet sich im ersten Stock** his office is on the first floor.

Befinden *das* (state of) health.

beflecken *vt* to stain.

befohlen *pp* ▷ **befehlen**.

befolgen *vt* [Rat] to follow; [Befehl, Vorschrift] to obey.

befördern *vt* - **1.** [transportieren] to transport - **2.** [im Beruf] to promote.

Beförderung (*pl* -en) *die* - **1.** [Transport] transportation - **2.** [im Beruf] promotion.

Beförderungsmittel *das* means of transport.

befragen *vt* - **1.** [Person, Zeugen] to question - **2.** [Karten, Wahrsagerin] to consult.

Befragung (pl -en) die questioning.

befreien vt [Gefangenen] to free; [Land, Volk] to liberate; [Tier] to set free; **jn von etw befreien** [von Diktatur, Schmerzen] to free sb from sthg; [vom Unterricht] to excuse sb from sthg.

Befreiung die [von Gefangenen, Tier] freeing; [von Land, Volk] liberation; [der Frau] emancipation; **eine Befreiung vom Unterricht kommt nicht infrage** there's no question of you being excused from classes.

befreundet adj [Länder] friendly; **mit jm befreundet sein** to be friends with sb.

befriedigen vt to satisfy.

befriedigend adj - 1. [zufrieden stellend] satisfactory - 2. SCHULE ≈ C, mark equivalent to 3 on scale of 1 to 6.

Befriedigung die - 1. [Zufriedenheit] satisfaction - 2. [Zufriedenstellung] satisfying.

befristen vt to put a time limit on; **ihre Tätigkeit ist auf ein Jahr befristet** her contract only runs for one year.

befristet adj [Vertrag] fixed-term, temporary.

befruchten vt to fertilize.

Befruchtung (pl -en) die fertilization; **künstliche Befruchtung** artificial insemination.

befugt adj: **zur Unterschrift befugt sein** to be authorized to sign.

Befund (pl -e) der [ärztlich] results Pl; [von Fachmann] findings Pl; **'ohne Befund'** MED 'negative'.

befürchten vt to fear.

Befürchtung (pl -en) die fear.

befürworten vt to support.

Befürworter, in (mpl -, fpl -nen) der, die supporter.

begabt adj talented.

Begabung (pl -en) die talent.

begann prät ⊳ **beginnen**.

Begebenheit (pl -en) die occurrence; **eine wahre Begebenheit** something that really happened.

begegnen vi [entgegenkommen, treffen]: **jm begegnen** to meet sb; **etw (D) begegnen** [Gefahr] to face sthg; **einer Person mit Freundlichkeit begegnen** to treat sb in a friendly manner. ◆ **sich begegnen** ref [treffen] to meet.

Begegnung (pl -en) die meeting.

begehen (prät beging, perf hat begangen) vt - 1. [verüben - Mord, Verbrechen] to commit; [- Fehler] to make; **eine Dummheit begehen** to do something stupid - 2. geh [feiern] to celebrate - 3. [benützen] to use.

begehren vt to desire; **sehr begehrt sein** to be much sought after.

begeistern vt: **sie begeisterte das Publikum** she delighted the audience; **man kann ihn für nichts begeistern** you can't make him enthusiastic about anything. ◆ **sich begeistern**

ref: **sich für etw begeistern** [Idee] to be enthusiastic about sthg; FILM [Hobby] really to like sthg.

begeistert ◇ adj [Reiter, Schwimmer] enthusiastic, keen; [Publikum] delighted; **von dieser Idee bin ich gar nicht begeistert** I'm not very enthusiastic about ODER keen on that idea. ◇ adv enthusiastically.

Begeisterung die [über Idee, Beschluss, für Hobby] enthusiasm; [über Leistung] delight.

begierig ◇ adj [Blicke] longing; [Lippen, Hände] eager; **nach etw** ODER **auf etw (A) begierig sein** to be eager for sthg; **darauf begierig sein, etw zu tun** to be eager to do sthg. ◇ adv eagerly.

begießen (prät begoss, perf hat begossen) vt - 1. [mit Wasser] to water - 2. [feiern] to celebrate with a drink.

Beginn der beginning, start. ◆ **zu Beginn** adv at the beginning ODER start.

beginnen (prät begann, perf hat begonnen) ◇ vt to begin, to start. ◇ vi to begin, to start; **mit etw beginnen** to begin sthg, to start sthg.

beglaubigen vt to certify.

Beglaubigung (pl -en) die [Bescheinigung] certificate.

begleiten vt to accompany.

Begleiter, in (mpl -, fpl -nen) der, die companion; [beim Musizieren] accompanist.

Begleiterscheinung die side effect.

Begleitung (pl -en) die - 1. [Begleiten]: **sie kam in Begleitung** she came with someone; **in Begleitung einer Freundin** accompanied by a friend - 2. MUS accompaniment - 3. [Begleitperson] escort; [Freund] companion.

beglückwünschen vt: **jn zu etw beglückwünschen** to congratulate sb on sthg.

begnadigen vt to pardon.

Begnadigung (pl -en) die pardon.

begnügen ◆ **sich begnügen** ref: **sich mit etw begnügen** to make do with sthg.

begonnen pp ⊳ **beginnen**.

begraben (präs begräbt, prät begrub, perf hat begraben) vt - 1. [beerdigen] to bury - 2. [beenden, vergessen - Streit] to bury; [- Hoffnung, Vorhaben] to abandon.

Begräbnis (pl -se) das funeral.

begreifen (prät begriff, perf hat begriffen) vt & vi to understand.

begrenzen vt - 1. [Zeit, Geschwindigkeit] to limit, to restrict - 2. [Fläche, Raum]: **der Park wird vom Fluss begrenzt** the river forms the park's boundary.

Begrenzung (pl -en) die - 1. [von Zeit, Geschwindigkeit] restriction, limit - 2. [von Fläche, Raum] boundary.

Begriff (pl -e) der - 1. [Wort] term - 2. [Vorstellung] idea, concept; **im Begriff sein** ODER **ste-**

hen; **etw zu tun** to be about to do sthg; **jm ein Begriff sein** to mean something to sb; **sich** (D) **einen Begriff von etw machen** to get an idea of sthg.

begriffsstutzig *adj abw* slow.

begründen *vt* - **1.** [erklären] to justify; **sie begründete ihr Verhalten mit persönlichen Problemen** she gave personal problems as the reason for her behaviour - **2.** [gründen - Firma, Stadt, Religion] to found; [- Theorie] to originate.

Begründer, in (*mpl* -, *fpl* -nen) *der, die* [von Religion, Stadt, Firma] founder; [von Theorie] originator.

Begründung (*pl* -en) *die* - **1.** [Angabe von Gründen] reason - **2.** [Gründung - von Firma, Stadt, Religion] founding; [- von Stil] establishment.

begrüßen *vt* - **1.** [grüßen] to greet - **2.** [gut finden] to welcome.

Begrüßung (*pl* -en) *die* greeting; [von Gästen] welcome.

begünstigen *vt* to favour.

begutachten *vt* - **1.** [Subj: Fachmann] to examine and report on - **2.** [betrachten] to have a look at.

begütert *adj* well-to-do.

behaart *adj* hairy.

behäbig *adj* [Mensch] portly; [Ausdrucksweise, Schritte] ponderous.

behaglich ⟨⟩ *adj* [Sessel] comfortable; [Wärme] cosy. ⟨⟩ *adv* comfortably.

behalten (*präs* behält, *prät* behielt, *perf* hat behalten) *vt* - **1.** [nicht abgeben] to keep - **2.** [sich merken] to remember.

Behälter (*pl* -) *der* container.

behandeln *vt* - **1.** [gen] to treat; **jn gut/schlecht behandeln** to treat sb well/badly - **2.** [Problem, Thema] to deal with.

Behandlung (*pl* -en) *die* treatment.

beharren *vi* to insist; **auf etw** (D) **beharren** to insist on sthg.

beharrlich ⟨⟩ *adj* persistent. ⟨⟩ *adv* persistently.

behaupten *vt* - **1.** [versichern] to claim - **2.** [verteidigen - Vorteil, Position] to maintain. ◆ **sich behaupten** *ref* - **1.** [sich durchsetzen] to assert o.s. - **2.** [gewinnen]: **sich gegen jn behaupten** to overcome sb.

Behauptung (*pl* -en) *die* - **1.** [Aussage] claim - **2.** [Verteidigung] maintenance.

beheben (*prät* behob, *perf* hat behoben) *vt* to rectify.

beheimatet *adj*: **beheimatet in** (+ D) [Pflanze, Tierart] native to; [Person] from.

beheizen *vt* to heat.

behelfen (*präs* behilft, *prät* behalf, *perf* hat beholfen) *vi*: **sich** (D) **mit/ohne etw behelfen** to make do with/without sthg.

behelfsmäßig *adj* [Unterkunft, Konstruktion] makeshift; [Ersatz] temporary.

beherbergen *vt* to put up.

beherrschen *vt* - **1.** [Land, Stadt] to rule - **2.** [Leidenschaft, Markt] to control - **3.** [dominieren] to dominate - **4.** [meistern - Pferd, Wagen] to have control of; [- Arbeit, Sport, Instrument] to have mastered; [- Sprache] to have a command of. ◆ **sich beherrschen** *ref* to control o.s.

beherrscht ⟨⟩ *adj* self-controlled. ⟨⟩ *adv* with self-control.

Beherrschung *die* - **1.** [von Leidenschaft] control; **die Beherrschung verlieren** to lose control - **2.** [von Pferd, Wagen] control; [von Instrument] mastery; [von Sprache] command.

beherzigen *vt* to take to heart.

behilflich *adj*: **jm bei etw behilflich sein** to help sb with sthg.

behindern *vt* - **1.** [Verkehr, Sicht] to obstruct - **2.** [Person]: **jn bei etw behindern** to hinder sb in sthg.

behindert *adj* disabled.

Behinderte (*pl* -n) *der, die* disabled person; **die Behinderten** the disabled.

behindertengerecht *adj* *suitable for people with disabilities.*

Behinderung (*pl* -en) *die* - **1.** [Behindern] obstruction - **2.** [Handicap] disability.

Behörde (*pl* -n) *die* authority. ◆ **Behörden** *Pl* authorities.

behutsam ⟨⟩ *adj* careful. ⟨⟩ *adv* carefully.

bei *präp* (+ D) - **1.** [räumlich - nahe] near; [- innen] at; **das Hotel ist gleich beim Bahnhof** the hotel is right next to the station; **Bernau bei Berlin** Bernau near Berlin; **beim Arzt** at the doctor's; **sie arbeitet bei einem Verlag** she works for a publishing company; **bei meiner Tante** at my aunt's; **bei mir** at my house; **die Schuld liegt allein bei mir** *fig* I alone am to blame; **ein Kind bei der Hand nehmen** to take a child's hand, to take a child by the hand - **2.** [zusammen mit einer Person] with; **ich bleibe bei dir** I'm staying with you - **3.** [zeitlich] at; **bei Beginn** at the beginning; **bei der Arbeit** at work; **bei seiner Beerdigung** at his funeral; **Vorsicht beim Ein- und Aussteigen** be careful when getting on and off; **beim Sport brach er sich den Arm** he broke his arm (while) playing sports - **4.** [als Teil einer Menge] among; **einige dieser Stilelemente finden sich auch bei Picasso** some of these stylistic touches are also found in Picasso's work - **5.** [zur Angabe von Umständen]: **bei Tag/Nacht** by day/night; **bei Gelegenheit** some time - **6.** [zur Angabe der Ursache]: **bei Regen fällt der Ausflug aus** if it rains the trip will be cancelled; **bei deinem Talent solltest du Maler werden** with your talent you should be an artist. ◆ **bei sich** *adv*: **hast du Geld bei dir?** have you got any money on you?; **bei sich** (D) **sein** *fig* to be (feeling) o.s.

bei|behalten vt (unreg) [Methode] to keep to; [Gegenstände] to keep.

bei|bringen vt (unreg) - 1. [lehren]: jm etw beibringen to teach sb sthg - 2. [mitteilen]: jm etw (schonend) beibringen to break sthg (gently) to sb - 3. amt [bringen] to produce.

Beichte (pl -n) die confession.

beichten <> vt to confess; jm etw beichten to confess sthg to sb. <> vi to confess.

beide <> pron [zwei] both; die beiden both of them; diese beiden these two; ihr beiden you two. <> adj - 1. [zwei]: die beiden Pferde both (of) the horses, the two horses; diese beiden Exemplare both (of) these copies, these two copies - 2. [alle zwei] both. ➡ **beides** pron both.

beiderlei det both.

beiderseitig adj mutual.

beiderseits präp (+ G) on both sides of.

beidseitig <> adj mutual. <> adv on both sides.

beieinander adv together.

Beifahrer, in (mpl -, fpl -nen) der, die front-seat passenger.

Beifahrer|sitz der passenger seat.

Beifall der applause; Beifall spenden ODER klatschen to applaud.

beifällig <> adj approving. <> adv approvingly.

bei|fügen vt: einer Sache (D) etw beifügen to enclose sthg with sthg.

beige [be:ʃ] adj beige.

Beigeschmack der - 1. [von Esswaren]: das Bier hat einen bitteren Beigeschmack the beer tastes slightly bitter - 2. [von Begriff] connotation; die ganze Affäre hatte einen bitteren Beigeschmack the whole affair left a bitter taste in the mouth.

Beihilfe die - 1. [finanziell] financial aid - 2. [kriminell] aiding and abetting; jm Beihilfe leisten to aid and abet sb.

bei|kommen (perf ist beigekommen) vi (unreg): jm beikommen [fertig werden mit] to get the better of sb.

Beil (pl -e) das axe.

Beilage die - 1. [Speise] side dish; mit Reis als Beilage served with rice - 2. [zu Zeitung] supplement - 3. amt [Beilegen] enclosure.

beiläufig <> adj casual. <> adv casually, in passing.

bei|legen vt - 1. [beifügen]: einer Sache (D) etw beilegen to enclose sthg with sthg - 2. [schlichten] to resolve.

Beileid das (ohne pl) condolences Pl; herzliches ODER aufrichtiges Beileid! my sincere condolences!

beiliegend adj amt enclosed; beiliegend übersenden wir Ihnen please find enclosed.

beim präp (bei + dem): ich bin beim Essen I'm eating at the moment; beim letzten Test in the last test; sie war beim Arzt she was at the doctor's; sie traf ihn beim Einkaufen she met him while she was shopping; beim Rasenmähen helfen to help with mowing the lawn; siehe auch bei.

bei|messen vt (unreg): einer Sache (D) große/keine Bedeutung beimessen to attach great/no importance to sthg.

Bein (pl -e) das leg.

beinah, beinahe adv almost, nearly.

Bei|name der epithet.

bei|nhalten [bəˈɪnhaltn̩] vt to contain.

Beipack|zettel der instruction leaflet.

bei|pflichten vi: jm/einer Sache beipflichten to agree with sb/sthg.

beisammen adv together.

Beisammensein das get-together.

Beisein das: im Beisein von jm, in js Beisein in the presence of sb, in sb's presence.

beiseite adv aside, to one side; beiseite lassen to leave aside ODER to one side; beiseite legen to put aside.

Beisetzung (pl -en) die funeral.

Beispiel das example; sich (D) an jm ein Beispiel nehmen to follow sb's example; sich (D) ein Beispiel an etw (D) nehmen to take sthg as one's example. ➡ **zum Beispiel** adv for example.

beispielhaft <> adj exemplary. <> adv in exemplary fashion.

beispiellos <> adj unprecedented; [Unverschämtheit] unbelievable. <> adv unprecedentedly.

beispielsweise adv for example.

beißen (prät biss, perf hat gebissen) <> vt to bite. <> vi - 1. [mit den Zähnen] to bite; in etw (A) beißen to bite into sthg - 2. [brennen] to sting; Qualm beißt in den Augen smoke makes your eyes sting. ➡ **sich beißen** ref - 1. [mit den Zähnen] to bite each other - 2. [Farben] to clash.

bei|stehen vi (unreg): jm beistehen to stand by sb.

bei|steuern vt: etw (zu etw) beisteuern to contribute sthg (to sthg).

Beitrag (pl Beiträge) der - 1. [Geld, Mitarbeit] contribution; [als Vereinsmitglied] subscription - 2. [Artikel] article.

bei|tragen (unreg) <> vt to contribute. <> vi: zu etw beitragen to contribute to sthg.

bei|treten (perf ist beigetreten) vi (unreg): etw (D) beitreten to join sthg.

Beitritt der [zur EU] entry; [zu Verein] joining.

beizeiten adv in good time.

bejahen vt [Frage] to say yes to; [Standpunkt] to approve of.

bekämpfen vt [Feind, Kriminalität] to fight; [Schädlinge] to control.

Bekämpfung die: die Bekämpfung von etw the fight against sthg; [von Schädlingen] the control of sthg.

bekannt adj well-known.

Bekannte (pl -n) der, die acquaintance.

Bekanntlkreis der circle of acquaintances.

Bekanntlgabe die announcement.

bekannt geben vt (unreg) to announce.

bekanntlich adv as is well known.

bekannt machen vt [Beschluss, Plan] to announce; [Fremde, Gäste] to introduce; jn mit jm bekannt machen to introduce sb to sb; jn/sich mit etw bekannt machen to familiarize sb/o.s. with sthg.

Bekanntschaft (pl -en) die - 1. [Kennen, Bekannte] acquaintance; mit jm Bekanntschaft schließen to make sb's acquaintance - 2. [Bekanntenkreis] acquaintances Pl.

bekehren vt to convert. ➤ **sich bekehren** ref: sich (zu etw) bekehren to convert (to sthg).

bekennen (prät bekannte, perf hat bekannt) vt [Sünde] to confess; [Fehler] to admit. ➤ **sich bekennen** ref: sich zu etw bekennen [Glauben] to profess sthg; [Überzeugung] to declare one's support for sthg; [Attentat] to claim responsibility for sthg.

beklagen vt to mourn. ➤ **sich beklagen** ref: sich (bei jm über jn/etw) beklagen to complain (about sb/sthg to sb).

bekleckern vt: etw mit etw bekleckern to spill sthg on sthg. ➤ **sich bekleckern** ref: sich mit etw bekleckern to spill sthg on o.s.

bekleidet adj: mit etw bekleidet sein to be wearing sthg.

Bekleidung die (ohne pl) - 1. [Kleidung] clothes Pl - 2. geh [von Posten, Amt] tenure.

beklemmend <> adj oppressive. <> adv oppressively.

Beklemmung (pl -en) die anxiety.

beklommen <> adj anxious. <> adv anxiously.

bekommen (prät bekam, perf hat/ist bekommen) <> vt (hat) to get; [Zug, Bus, Krankheit] to catch; ich bekomme noch 100 Euro von dir you owe me 100 euros; was bekommen Sie? what would you like?; was bekommen Sie dafür? how much is it?; es sind keine Karten mehr zu bekommen there are no more tickets available ODER to be had; Prügel/eine Strafe bekommen to be beaten/punished; sie bekommt ein Kind she's expecting (a baby); Besuch bekommen to have visitors; etw geschenkt/geliehen bekommen to be given/ lent sthg; Angst/Hunger bekommen to get frightened/hungry; seine Stimme bekam einen zärtlichen Ton his voice took on a gentle tone. <> vi (ist): jm gut bekommen [Essen] to agree with sb; der Wein ist mir nicht bekommen the wine disagreed with me.

bekräftigen vt [Meinung, Kritik] to confirm, to reinforce; jn in etw (D) bekräftigen to confirm sb in sthg.

bekreuzigen ➤ **sich bekreuzigen** ref to cross o.s.

bekritzeln vt to scribble on.

bekümmert <> adj worried. <> adv worriedly.

belächeln vt abw to laugh at.

beladen (präs belädt, prät belud, perf hat beladen) vt: etw (mit etw) beladen to load sthg (with sthg).

Belag (pl Beläge) der - 1. [von Bremsen] lining; [von Straße] surface; [von Fußboden] covering - 2. [auf Brot] topping - 3. [auf der Zunge] fur; [auf den Zähnen] film.

belagern vt to besiege.

Belagerung (pl -en) die siege.

Belang (pl -e) der [Bedeutung]: von/ohne Belang sein (für jn) to be important/of no importance (to sb). ➤ **Belange** Pl [Interessen] interests.

belangen vt RECHT: jn (für etw) belangen to prosecute sb (for sthg).

belasten vt - 1. [mit Gewicht] to put a load on; etw mit etw belasten to weight sthg down with sthg - 2. [Umwelt] to pollute; [Leber] to put a strain on - 3. [beanspruchen] to weigh heavily on; jn mit etw belasten to burden sb with sthg - 4. [besorgen]: jn belasten to weigh on sb's mind - 5. RECHT to incriminate - 6. [finanziell - Konto] to debit; ein Haus mit einer Hypothek belasten to mortgage a house.

belästigen vt to bother; [sexuell] to harass.

Belästigung (pl -en) die annoyance; [sexuell] harassment.

Belastung (pl -en) die - 1. [mit Gewicht] load - 2. [von Umwelt] pollution - 3. [psychisch] strain - 4. [von Konto] debiting.

belauern vt [Person] to spy on; [Verhalten] to observe secretly.

belaufen (präs beläuft, prät belief, perf hat belaufen) ➤ **sich belaufen** ref: sich auf etw (A) belaufen to amount to sthg.

belauschen vt to eavesdrop on.

belebt adj busy.

Beleg (pl -e) der - 1. [Quittung] receipt - 2. [Nachweis] proof.

belegen vt - 1. [mit Belag]: etw mit etw belegen [Brot] to top sthg with sthg; [Boden] to cover sthg with sthg - 2. [besuchen] to enrol for - 3. [okkupieren] to occupy - 4. [einnehmen]: den ersten/zweiten Platz belegen to come first/second - 5. [nachweisen - Zahlung] to provide proof of; [- Behauptung, Argument] to back up; [- Zitat] to reference.

Belegschaft (*pl* -en) *die* workforce.

belegt *adj* - 1. [mit Aufschnitt]: **belegtes Brot/ Brötchen** open sandwich/roll; **ein belegtes Brot mit Käse** a slice of bread with cheese on it - 2. [Zunge] furred - 3. [besetzt - Zimmer] occupied; [- Hotel, Kurs] full - 4. [Stimme] hoarse.

belehren *vt* to instruct; **jn über etw** *(A)* **belehren** to instruct sb about sthg; [Rechte] to inform sb of sthg; **jn eines Besseren/anderen belehren** to teach sb better/otherwise.

beleibt *adj* corpulent.

beleidigen *vt* [Person] to insult; [Empfinden] to offend.

Beleidigung (*pl* -en) *die* insult; **Beleidigung des guten Geschmacks** offence against good taste.

beleuchten *vt* - 1. [Denkmal, Brunnen] to illuminate; [Straße, Raum] to light - 2. [Thema] to examine.

Beleuchtung (*pl* -en) *die* - 1. [mit Licht] lighting - 2. [Lampen, Scheinwerfer] lights *Pl* - 3. (*ohne pl*) [von Thema, Theorie] examination.

Belgien *nt* Belgium.

Belgier, in [ˈbɛlɡjɐ, rɪn] (*mpl* -, *fpl* -nen) *der, die* Belgian.

belgisch *adj* Belgian.

belichten *vt* to expose.

Belichtung (*pl* -en) *die* FOTO exposure.

Belieben *das*: **nach Belieben** as you like; **das steht** ODER **liegt in deinem Belieben** that is up to you.

beliebig <> *adj* any; **eine beliebige Summe** any amount. <> *adv*: **beliebig viel/viele** as much/many as you like; **beliebig lange** as long as you like.

beliebt *adj* popular; **bei jm beliebt sein** to be popular with sb; **sich bei jm beliebt machen** to make o.s. popular with sb.

Beliebtheit *die* popularity.

beliefern *vt*: **jn (mit etw) beliefern** to supply sb (with sthg).

bellen *vi* to bark.

belohnen *vt* to reward.

Belohnung (*pl* -en) *die* - 1. [Belohnen] rewarding - 2. [Lohn, Entgelt] reward.

Belüftung *die* ventilation.

belügen (*prät* belog, *perf* hat belogen) *vt* to lie to.

bemalen *vt* [anmalen] to paint.

bemängeln *vt* to criticize.

bemerkbar *adj* noticeable; **sich bemerkbar machen** [Person] to attract attention; [Sache] to become apparent.

bemerken *vt* - 1. [wahrnehmen] to notice - 2. [sagen] to remark.

bemerkenswert <> *adj* remarkable. <> *adv* remarkably.

Bemerkung (*pl* -en) *die* remark.

bemitleiden *vt* to feel sorry for.

bemühen *vt* geh [Anwalt, Gutachter] to call on. ◆ **sich bemühen** *ref* - 1. [sich anstrengen] to try; **sich bemühen, etw zu tun** to try to do sthg - 2. [sich kümmern]: **sich um jn bemühen** to take care of sb.

Bemühung (*pl* -en) *die*: **Bemühungen** efforts.

benachbart *adj* [Personen, Dörfer] neighbouring; [Disziplinen] related.

benachrichtigen *vt* to inform.

benachteiligen *vt* to disadvantage; [Minderheiten] to discriminate against.

benehmen (*präs* benimmt, *prät* benahm, *perf* hat benommen) ◆ **sich benehmen** *ref* to behave; **sich gut/schlecht benehmen** to behave well/badly.

Benehmen *das* behaviour.

beneiden *vt*: **jn (um etw) beneiden** to envy sb (sthg).

beneidenswert <> *adj* enviable. <> *adv* enviably.

Benelux-Länder *Pl* Benelux countries.

benennen (*prät* benannte, *perf* hat benannt) *vt* to name; RECHT to call.

Bengel (*pl* -) *der* little rascal.

benommen <> *adj* groggy. <> *adv* groggily.

benoten *vt* to mark.

benötigen *vt* to need.

benutzen, benützen *vt* to use.

Benutzer, in (*mpl* -, *fpl* -nen) *der, die* user.

Benutzung *die* use.

Benzin (*pl* -e) *das* petrol *UK*, gas *US*; **bleifreies/verbleites Benzin** unleaded/leaded petrol *UK* ODER gas *US*; **Benzin tanken** to fill up with petrol *UK* ODER gas *US*.

Benzin|kanister *der* petrol can *UK*, gas can *US*.

beobachten *vt* - 1. [observieren] to observe - 2. [überwachen] to watch - 3. [bemerken] to notice.

Beobachter, in (*mpl* -, *fpl* -nen) *der, die* observer.

Beobachtung (*pl* -en) *die* observation.

bepackt *adj* loaded up.

bequem <> *adj* - 1. [gemütlich] comfortable; **es sich** (D) **bequem machen** to make o.s. comfortable - 2. [faul] lazy - 3. [Lösung, Weg] easy. <> *adv* - 1. [liegen, sitzen] comfortably - 2. [leicht] easily.

Bequemlichkeit (*pl* -en) *die* - 1. [Gemütlichkeit] comfort - 2. [Faulheit] laziness.

beraten (*präs* berät, *prät* beriet, *perf* hat beraten) <> *vt* - 1. [Rat geben] to advise; **jn über etw beraten** to advise sb on sthg - 2. [besprechen] to discuss. <> *vi*: **über etw** *(A)* **beraten** to discuss sthg. ◆ **sich beraten** *ref*: **sich mit jm über etw** *(A)* **beraten** to discuss sthg with sb.

Berater, in *(mpl -, fpl -nen) der, die* adviser.

beratschlagen *vi* to discuss; **über etw** *(A)* **beratschlagen** to discuss sthg.

Beratung *(pl -en) die* - **1.** [Ratgeben] advice - **2.** [Besprechung] discussion.

Beratungslstelle *die* advice centre.

berauben *vt*: **jn einer Sache** *(G)* **berauben** to rob sb of sthg.

berauschend ⬦ *adj* intoxicating. ⬦ *adv*: **berauschend wirken** to have an intoxicating effect.

berechenbar ⬦ *adj* - **1.** [Summe, Größe] calculable - **2.** [Person, Reaktion] predictable. ⬦ *adv* predictably.

berechnen *vt* - **1.** [ausrechnen] to calculate - **2.** [anrechnen] to charge.

berechnend ⬦ *adj* calculating. ⬦ *adv* calculatingly.

Berechnung *(pl -en) die* calculation; **aus Berechnung handeln** to act in a calculating manner.

berechtigen *vt*: **jn zu etw berechtigen** to entitle sb to sthg.

berechtigt *adj* justified.

Berechtigung *(pl -en) die* - **1.** [Genehmigung] right - **2.** [Korrektheit] legitimacy.

bereden *vt* [besprechen]: **etw (mit jm) bereden** to discuss sthg (with sb).

Bereich *(pl -e) der* - **1.** [Gebiet] area - **2.** [Aufgabe, Thema] field.

bereichern *vt* to enrich. ⬥ **sich bereichern** *ref*: **sich (an jm/etw) bereichern** to make money (at sb's expense/from sthg).

Bereicherung *(pl -en) die* enrichment.

bereisen *vt* to travel around.

bereit *adj* - **1.** [fertig]: **bereit sein** to be ready - **2.** [gewillt]: **bereit sein, etw zu tun** to be willing to do sthg; **sich bereit erklären, etw zu tun** to agree to do sthg.

bereitlhaben *vt* to have ready.

bereitlhalten *vt (unreg)* to have ready. ⬥ **sich bereithalten** *ref*: **sich zu** ODER **für etw bereithalten** to be ready for sthg.

bereitlmachen *vt* to get ready. ⬥ **sich bereitmachen** *ref* to get ready.

bereits *adv* already; **bereits um sechs Uhr** as early as six o'clock.

Bereitschaft *die* - **1.** [Wille] willingness - **2.** [Bereitschaftsdienst] emergency service; **Bereitschaft haben** [Polizei, Feuerwehr] to be on standby; [Arzt] to be on call.

bereitlstehen *vi (unreg)* [Fahrzeug, Koffer] to be ready; [Sanitäter, Polizei] to be on standby.

Bereitlstellung *die* provision.

bereitwillig ⬦ *adj* willing. ⬦ *adv* willingly.

bereuen *vt* [Fehler, Worte, Verhalten] to regret; [Sünde] to repent of.

Berg *(pl -e) der* [Erhöhung, große Menge] mountain; [kleiner] hill. ⬥ **Berge** *Pl* mountains; **in die Berge fahren** to go to the mountains.

bergab *adv* downhill; **mit jm/etw geht es bergab** sb/sthg is going downhill.

bergan = **bergauf**.

bergauf, bergan *adv* uphill; **mit jm/etw geht es bergauf** things are looking up for sb/sthg.

Bergbau *der* mining.

bergen *(präs* **birgt,** *prät* **barg,** *perf* **hat geborgen)** *vt* - **1.** [Verunglückte] to rescue; [Leiche, Unfallwagen] to recover; [Boot] to salvage - **2.** *geh* [enthalten]: **etw in sich** *(D)* **bergen** to involve sthg.

Berglführer, in *der, die* mountain guide.

Berglhütte *die* mountain hut.

bergig *adj* mountainous.

Berglmann *(pl -leute) der* miner.

Berglsteigen *das* (mountain) climbing.

Berglsteiger, in *der,* *die* (mountain) climber; [professionell] mountaineer.

Bergung *(pl -en) die* [von Verletzten] rescue; [von Leiche, Unfallwagen] recovery; [von Boot] salvage.

Berglwacht *die (ohne pl)* mountain rescue service.

Berglwandern *das* hill walking.

Berglwerk *das* mine.

Bericht *(pl -e) der* report; **über etw** *(A)* **Bericht erstatten** to report on sthg.

berichten ⬦ *vt* to report. ⬦ *vi* to report; **von jm/etw** ODER **über jn/etw berichten** to report on sb/sthg.

Berichtlerstattung *die* reporting.

berichtigen *vt* to correct.

Berichtigung *(pl -en) die* correction.

Berlin *nt* Berlin.

Berliner *(pl -)* ⬦ *der* - **1.** [Person] Berliner - **2.** [Gebäck] doughnut *(filled with jam)*. ⬦ *adj (unver)* Berlin *(vor Subst)*.

Berlinerin *(pl -nen) die* Berliner.

berlinerisch *adj* Berlin *(vor Subst)*.

Berliner Mauer *die* Berlin Wall.

Berliner Philharmoniker *Pl* Berlin Philharmonic *(sg)*.

Bern *nt* Bern, Berne.

Bernstein *der* amber.

bersten *(präs* **birst,** *prät* **barst,** *perf* **ist geborsten)** *vi* [Schiff, Gebäude] to break up; [Glas, Eis] to shatter.

berüchtigt *adj* notorious; **für** ODER **wegen etw berüchtigt sein** to be notorious for sthg.

berücksichtigen *vt* - **1.** [Vorschlag, Wunsch] to take into consideration; **wenn man berücksichtigt, dass...** considering (that...) - **2.** [Bewerber, Antrag] to consider.

Beruf (*pl* -e) *der* profession; **was sind Sie von Beruf?** what do you do (for a living)?

berufen[1] *adj* - **1.** [fähig] competent - **2.** [bestimmt]: **zu etw berufen sein** to have a vocation as sthg.

berufen[2] (*prät* **berief**, *perf* **hat berufen**) *vt* to appoint; **jn ins Ausland berufen** to post sb abroad. ➠ **sich berufen** *ref*: **sich auf jn/etw berufen** to quote sb/sthg as one's authority.

beruflich ◇ *adj* professional. ◇ *adv* [reisen] on business.

Berufslausbildung *die* vocational training.

Berufslberatung *die* career guidance.

Berufslleben *das* working life.

Berufslschule *die* vocational school (*attended part-time by apprentices*).

Berufslsoldat *der* professional soldier.

berufstätig *adj*: **berufstätig sein** to have a job, to work; **sie ist nicht berufstätig** she doesn't work.

Berufstätige (*pl* -n) *der, die* working person; **die Berufstätigen** the working population.

Berufsverkehr *der* rush-hour traffic.

Berufung (*pl* -en) *die* - **1.** [Ruf] appointment; [ins Ausland] posting - **2.** RECHT appeal; **Berufung einlegen** to appeal - **3.** [Begabung] vocation - **4.** [Bezug] reference; **unter Berufung auf jn/etw** with reference to sthg.

beruhen *vi*: **auf etw** (D) **beruhen** to be based on sthg; **etw auf sich** (D) **beruhen lassen** to let sthg rest.

beruhigen *vt* to calm (down). ➠ **sich beruhigen** *ref* [Person] to calm down; [Lage] to settle down; [Meer] to become calm.

Beruhigung (*pl* -en) *die* [von Person, Meer] calming; [von Lage] settling down.

Beruhigungslmittel *das* sedative.

berühmt *adj* famous; **wegen** ODER **für etw berühmt sein** to be famous for sthg.

Berühmtheit (*pl* -en) *die* - **1.** [Berühmtsein] fame - **2.** [Person] celebrity.

berühren *vt* - **1.** [anfassen] to touch - **2.** [beeindrucken] to move.

Berührung (*pl* -en) *die* - **1.** [Anfassen] touch - **2.** [Kontakt]: **mit jm/etw in Berührung kommen** to come into contact with sb/sthg.

besänftigen *vt* to soothe.

Besatzung (*pl* -en) *die* - **1.** [Personal] crew - **2.** MIL occupying forces *Pl.*

beschädigen *vt* to damage.

Beschädigung (*pl* -en) *die* - **1.** [Beschädigen] damaging - **2.** [Schaden] damage (U).

beschaffen ◇ *vt* to obtain; **jm etw beschaffen** to get sb sthg; **sich** (D) **etw beschaffen** to get sthg. ◇ *adj*: **das Material ist so beschaffen, dass es große Belastungen aushält** the nature of the material is such that it can withstand heavy loads.

Beschaffenheit *die* - **1.** [Art] nature - **2.** [Zustand] condition.

beschäftigen *vt* - **1.** [anstellen] to employ; **er ist bei Siemens beschäftigt** he works for Siemens - **2.** [ablenken] to keep busy - **3.** [beanspruchen - Frage] to preoccupy; **sie ist im Moment sehr beschäftigt** she is very busy at present. ➠ **sich beschäftigen** *ref*: **sie beschäftigt sich intensiv mit Religion** she's heavily involved in religion; **wir beschäftigen uns gegenwärtig mit der Frage, wie** we are currently considering ODER looking at the issue of how to.

Beschäftigte (*pl* -n) *der, die* employee.

Beschäftigung (*pl* -en) *die* - **1.** [Tätigkeit - Arbeit] occupation; [- Hobby] activity - **2.** [Arbeitsstelle] job; **eine Beschäftigung suchen** to be looking for work; **ohne Beschäftigung sein** to be out of work - **3.** [Anstellen] employment - **4.** [Auseinandersetzung]: **Beschäftigung mit etw** [Thema, Problem] consideration of sthg.

Bescheid (*pl* -e) *der* [Entscheidung] decision; **den Bescheid vom Finanzamt erwarten** to be waiting for an answer from the tax office; **Bescheid wissen** to know; **jm Bescheid sagen** ODER **geben** [benachrichtigen] to let sb know; *fam* [jm die Meinung sagen] to give sb a piece of one's mind.

bescheiden ◇ *adj* - **1.** [anspruchslos, einfach] modest; [Benehmen] unassuming - **2.** [Essen] frugal; [Ergebnis, Leistung] mediocre. ◇ *adv* [sich kleiden, leben] simply.

bescheinigen *vt* [mit Zeugnis] to certify; **den Empfang von etw bescheinigen** to sign for sthg; **sich etw bescheinigen lassen** to get sthg confirmed in writing.

Bescheinigung (*pl* -en) *die* - **1.** [bescheinigen] certification - **2.** [Schein] certificate.

bescheißen (*prät* **bescheiss**, *perf* **hat bescheissen**) *vt salopp*: **jn (um etw) bescheißen** to con sb (out of sthg).

Bescherung (*pl* -en) *die* giving of Christmas presents.

beschießen (*prät* **beschoss**, *perf* **hat beschossen**) *vt* to fire on.

beschimpfen *vt* to insult; [mit groben Worten] to swear at.

Beschimpfung (*pl* -en) *die* insult; **Beschimpfungen** abuse (U).

beschissen *vulg* ◇ *pp* ▷ **bescheißen**. ◇ *adj* shitty. ◇ *adv* [sich benehmen] shittily; **es geht mir beschissen** things are going like shit for me.

beschlagen (*präs* **beschlägt**, *prät* **beschlug**, *perf* **hat/ist beschlagen**) ◇ *vt* (hat) [Pferd] to shoe; [Schuhsohlen] to stud. ◇ *vi* (ist) to mist ODER steam up. ◇ *adj* well-informed; **in etw** (D) **beschlagen sein** to be well up on sthg.

beschlagnahmen *vt* to confiscate.

beschleunigen ⬦ vt [Tempo, Schritte] to quicken; [Abreise] to hasten; [Arbeitsprozess] to speed up. ⬦ vi to accelerate.

Beschleunigung (pl -en) die [von Verfahren, Entwicklung] speeding up; [von Auto] acceleration.

beschließen (prät beschloss, perf hat beschlossen) ⬦ vt - 1. [entscheiden] to decide on; beschließen, etw zu tun to decide to do sthg; [Gesetz] to pass; [Vorhaben] to approve - 2. geh [beenden] to end. ⬦ vi [beraten]: über etw (A) beschließen to decide on sthg.

Beschluss (pl -schlüsse) der decision; einen Beschluss fassen to take a decision.

beschmutzen vt [Teppich, Kleidung] to soil; [Wand] to stain; jm/sich das Kleid beschmutzen to get sb's/one's dress dirty.

beschränken vt to limit, to restrict. ⬦ sich beschränken ref: sich auf etw (A) beschränken [Sache] to be confined to sthg; [Person] to confine o.s. to sthg.

beschränkt adj - 1. abw [engstirnig] narrow-minded - 2. [dürftig] limited; in beschränkten Verhältnissen leben to live in straitened circumstances - 3. abw [dumm] slow, dim.

beschreiben (prät beschrieb, perf hat beschrieben) vt - 1. [darstellen, formen] to describe; [Weg] to tell - 2. [voll schreiben] to write on.

Beschreibung (pl -en) die description.

beschriften vt to label; [Brief] to address; [Etikett] to write on.

beschuldigen vt to accuse; jn einer Sache (G) beschuldigen to accuse sb of sthg.

Beschuldigung (pl -en) die accusation.

beschützen vt to protect; jn vor etw (D) beschützen to protect sb from sthg.

Beschützer, in (mpl -, fpl -nen) der, die protector.

Beschwerde (pl -n) die [Klage] complaint. ⬦ **Beschwerden** pl [Schmerzen] trouble (U); Beschwerden im Kreuz haben to have back problems ODER trouble with one's back.

beschweren vt [belasten] to weight down. ⬦ sich beschweren ref: sich (über jn/etw) beschweren to complain (about sb/sthg).

beschwichtigen vt [Person] to placate; [Zorn] to calm.

beschwindeln vt to dupe.

beschwingt adj [Stimmung] lively; [Melodie] lilting.

beschwipst adj tipsy.

beschwören (prät beschwor, perf hat beschworen) vt - 1. [beeiden] to swear to - 2. [erscheinen lassen - Geister] to invoke; [- Bilder] to conjure up; [- Erinnerungen] to evoke - 3. [bitten] to entreat, to implore.

beseitigen vt - 1. [entfernen - Fleck] to remove; [- Abfall] to get rid of, to dispose of; [- Schwierigkeiten, Missbrauch] to eliminate; [- Schnee] to clear away - 2. [ermorden] to eliminate.

Beseitigung (pl -en) die - 1. [Entfernung - von Fleck] removal; [- von Abfall] disposal; [- von Schwierigkeiten, Missbrauch] elimination - 2. [Ermordung] elimination.

Besen (pl -) der broom.

besessen adj - 1. [verrückt]: wie besessen like someone possessed - 2. [begeistert]: von etw besessen sein to be obsessed with sthg.

besetzen vt - 1. [Stelle, Rolle] to fill - 2. [Sitzplatz, Haus, Gebiet, Land] to occupy - 3. [verzieren]: etw mit etw besetzen to trim sthg with sthg.

besetzt adj occupied; [Telefon] engaged; [Sitz] taken; nicht besetzt [Büro] closed.

Besetzung (pl -en) die - 1. [von Posten] filling - 2. [Team - von Schauspielern] cast; [- von Sportlern] team - 3. [von Land, Gebiet, Haus] occupation.

besichtigen vt [Museum] to visit; [Wohnung] to view; [Stadt] to go sightseeing in.

Besichtigung (pl -en) die [von Museum] visit; [von einer Wohnung] viewing; [von einer Stadt] sightseeing; [Führung] tour.

besiegen vt - 1. [Feind] to defeat; [Mannschaft] to beat - 2. [Zweifel, Neugier] to overcome.

Besiegte (pl -n) der, die loser.

Besinnung die: die Besinnung verlieren to lose consciousness.

Besitz der - 1. [Eigentum] property - 2. [Besitzen] possession - 3. [Landgut] estate.

besitzen (prät besaß, perf hat besessen) vt to possess, to own; [Recht, Qualität] to have.

Besitzer, in (mpl -, fpl -nen) der, die owner.

besondere, r, s adj [speziell] special; [außergewöhnlich] particular; besondere Kennzeichen distinguishing features; im Besonderen in particular, especially.

Besonderheit (pl -en) die special feature, peculiarity.

besonders ⬦ adv - 1. [vor allem, sehr] especially, particularly - 2. [gut]: nicht besonders not very well. ⬦ adj: nicht besonders sein to be not very good; der Film ist nicht besonders the film isn't up to much.

besorgen vt - 1. [beschaffen] to get (hold of); jm/sich etw besorgen to get sb/o.s. sthg - 2. [sich um etw kümmern] to see to.

besorgt ⬦ adj worried; um jn besorgt sein to be worried about sb; rührend um jn besorgt sein to be concerned for sb's wellbeing. ⬦ adv anxiously; besorgt aussehen to look worried.

Besorgung (pl -en) die [Einkäufe] purchase; Besorgungen shopping (U).

bespielen vt to record on.

bespitzeln vt to spy on.

besprechen (*präs* **bespricht**, *prät* **besprach**, *perf* **hat besprochen**) *vt* - 1. [erörtern]: **etw (mit jm) besprechen** to discuss sthg (with sb) - 2. [rezensieren] to review - 3. [aufnehmen] to record (one's voice) on. ➼ **sich besprechen** *ref*: **sich (mit jm über etw) besprechen** to confer (with sb about sthg).

Besprechung (*pl* **-en**) *die* - 1. [Beratung] discussion; **in einer Besprechung sein** to be in a meeting - 2. [Rezension] review.

bespritzen *vt* - 1. [nass machen] to splash - 2. [beschmutzen] to spatter.

besser *adj* - 1. [als Komparativ von gut] better; [ziemlich gut] good; **das hier ist schon ein besseres Gerät** this is a pretty good machine; **das Hotel ist eine bessere Absteige** the hotel is just a glorified dosshouse; **besser ist besser** better safe than sorry - 2. [gesellschaftlich gehoben] superior. ◇ *adv* better.

Bessere (*pl* **-n**) *der, die, das* better; **Besseres zu tun haben** to have better things to do.

bessern *vt* to improve; [Verbrecher] to reform. ➼ **sich bessern** *ref* [Wetter, Zustand] to improve; [Mensch] to mend one's ways.

Besserung *die* improvement. ➼ **gute Besserung** *interj* get well soon!

Bestand (*pl* **-stände**) *der* - 1. [Bestehen] continued existence; **Bestand haben** to last - 2. [Vorrat] stock.

bestanden *pp* ▷ **bestehen**.

beständig ◇ *adj* - 1. [dauernd] constant - 2. [gleich bleibend - Wetter] settled; [- Freund] faithful; [- Mitarbeiter] reliable - 3. [widerstandsfähig]: **gegen etw beständig sein** to be resistant to sthg. ◇ *adv* - 1. [dauernd] constantly - 2. [zuverlässig] steadily, reliably.

Bestandsaufnahme *die* stocktaking.

Bestandteil *der* component.

bestätigen *vt* to confirm; [Urteil] to uphold. ➼ **sich bestätigen** *ref* to be confirmed, to prove true.

Bestätigung (*pl* **-en**) *die* confirmation; [von Urteil] upholding.

beste, r, s ◇ *adj* best; **sich bester Gesundheit erfreuen** to enjoy the best of health. ◇ *adv*: **am besten gehe ich jetzt** I'd better go now.

Beste (*pl* **-n**) *der, die, das* best (one); **das Beste aus etw (D) machen** *fig* to make the best of sthg; **es steht nicht zum Besten mit jm/etw** things are not looking good for sb/sthg; **eine Anekdote zum Besten geben** to tell a story; **jn zum Besten halten** *fig* to pull sb's leg.

bestechen (*präs* **besticht**, *prät* **bestach**, *perf* **hat bestochen**) ◇ *vt* to bribe. ◇ *vi*: **sie besticht durch ihre Schlagfertigkeit** she makes an impression with her quick-wittedness.

bestechlich *adj* open to bribery.

Besteck (*pl* **-e**) *das* [Essbesteck] cutlery (*U*); **ein Besteck** a place setting.

bestehen (*prät* **bestand**, *perf* **hat bestanden**) ◇ *vi* - 1. [existieren] to exist; **es besteht there is** - 2. [sich zusammensetzen]: **das Buch besteht aus zehn Kapiteln** the book consists of ten chapters; **der Rahmen besteht aus Kunststoff** the frame is made of plastic - 3. [beinhalten]: **ihre Aufgabe besteht in der Planung des Projekts** her job consists of ODER involves planning the project; **das Problem besteht darin, dass...** the problem is that... - 4. [beharren]: **auf etw (D) bestehen** to insist on sthg - 5. [standhalten]: **vor jm/etw bestehen** to stand up to sb/sthg. ◇ *vt* to pass.

bestehen bleiben (*perf* **ist bestehen geblieben**) *vi* (*unreg*) - 1. [übrig bleiben] to remain - 2. [Vorschrift] to be upheld.

bestellen ◇ *vt* - 1. [anfordern] to order; **sich (D) etw bestellen** to order sthg (for o.s.) - 2. [reservieren] to book, to reserve - 3. [kommen lassen] to summon - 4. [ausrichten]: **jm Grüße bestellen** to give ODER send one's regards to sb; **kann ich ihm etwas (von dir) bestellen?** can I give him a message (from you)? - 5. [bearbeiten] to cultivate; **es ist um jn/etw schlecht bestellt** sb/sthg is in a bad way. ◇ *vi* to order.

Bestellung (*pl* **-en**) *die* - 1. [Anforderung, Waren] order - 2. [Reservierung] booking, reservation - 3. [Bearbeitung] cultivation. ➼ **auf Bestellung** *adv* to order; **wie auf Bestellung** as if by command.

bestenfalls *adv* at best.

bestens *adv* very well.

bestialisch ◇ *adj abw* [Mord, Tat] brutal. ◇ *adv* - 1. *abw* [grausam] brutally - 2. *fam* [unerträglich] dreadfully.

Bestie (*pl* **-n**) *die* - 1. [Raubtier] beast - 2. *abw* [Unmensch] brute.

bestimmen ◇ *vt* - 1. [Preis, Termin] to fix; **jn zum Nachfolger bestimmen** to designate sb as one's successor - 2. [vorsehen]: **für jn/etw bestimmt sein** to be intended for sb/sthg - 3. [ermitteln] to determine; [Pflanze] to classify; [Bedeutung] to define - 4. [Charakter] to determine; [Stadtbild, Atmosphäre] to characterize. ◇ *vi* - 1. [entscheiden] to decide; **sie bestimmt in dieser Firma** she makes the decisions in this firm - 2. [verfügen]: **über etw (frei) bestimmen können** to be able to do what one likes with sthg.

bestimmt ◇ *adj* - 1. [gewiss] certain; [genau] particular - 2. [festgelegt] fixed - 3. GRAMM definite; **der bestimmte Artikel** the definite article - 4. [entschieden] definite, firm. ◇ *adv* - 1. [entschieden] firmly, decisively - 2. [sehr wahrscheinlich] no doubt; [sicher] certainly; **das ist bestimmt kein Problem** I'm sure that won't be a problem; **etw bestimmt wissen** to know sthg for sure ODER certain; **ganz bestimmt** definitely.

Bestimmtheit *die* firmness, decisiveness; **mit Bestimmtheit** [entschlossen] decisively.

Bestimmung *die* - 1. *(ohne pl)* [von Preis, Frist] fixing - 2. *(pl -en)* [Vorschrift] regulation; **eine gesetzliche Bestimmung** a legal provision - 3. *(ohne pl)* [Zweck] (intended) purpose; **ein Schiff seiner Bestimmung übergeben** to launch a ship - 4. *(pl -en)* [Ermitteln] determining; [von Pflanze] classification; [von Begriff, Bedeutung] definition - 5. *(pl -en)* GRAMM modifier.

Best|leistung *die* SPORT best performance; **ihre persönliche Bestleistung** her personal best.

Best.Nr. *(abk für Bestellnummer)* order no.

bestrafen *vt*: **jn (für etw) bestrafen** to punish sb (for sthg); **jn mit Gefängnis bestrafen** to sentence sb to imprisonment.

Bestrafung *(pl -en) die* punishment; [gerichtlich] sentence.

bestreiten *(prät bestritt, perf hat bestritten)* *vt* - 1. [leugnen - Meinung, Aussage] to contest; [- Beschuldigung] to deny; **es lässt sich nicht bestreiten** it is indispensable - 2. [finanzieren] to pay for - 3. [gestalten] to carry.

bestürmen *vt* - 1. MIL to storm - 2. [bedrängen]: **jn mit Fragen bestürmen** to bombard sb with questions.

bestürzt ◇ *adj*: **über etw (A) bestürzt sein** to be dismayed about sthg. ◇ *adv* in dismay.

Best|zeit *die* SPORT fastest time.

Besuch *(pl -e) der* - 1. [Besuchen] visit; [von Schule, Kirche] attendance; **bei jm zu Besuch sein** to be staying with *ODER* visiting sb - 2. *(ohne pl)* [Gast] visitor, guest; [Gäste] visitors *Pl*, guests *Pl*; **wir haben Besuch** we have a visitor/visitors.

besuchen *vt* to visit; [Kirche, Schule, Vorlesung] to attend.

Besucher, in *(mpl -, fpl -nen) der, die* visitor.

besucht *adj*: **gut/schlecht besucht** well/ poorly attended.

betätigen *vt* [Hebel] to operate; [Bremse] to apply. ◆ **sich betätigen** *ref*: **sich politisch/ sportlich betätigen** to engage in politics/ sport.

betäuben *vt* - 1. MED to anaesthetize - 2. [Trauer, Schmerz] to deaden, to dull.

Bete ◆ **Rote Bete** *die* beetroot.

beteiligen *vt*: **jn an etw (D) beteiligen** to give sb a share in sthg. ◆ **sich beteiligen** *ref*: **sich an etw (D) beteiligen** to participate in sthg; [Kosten] to contribute to sthg.

Beteiligung *(pl -en) die* - 1. [Mitwirkung]: **Beteiligung (an etw (D))** participation (in sthg); [an Verbrechen] involvement (in sthg) - 2. [an Gewinn] share.

beten ◇ *vi* to pray; **um** *ODER* **für etw beten** to pray for sthg; **für jn beten** to pray for sb. ◇ *vt* to say.

beteuern *vt* to declare.

Beton [be'tɔŋ] *(pl -s) der* concrete.

betonen *vt* - 1. [aussprechen] to stress - 2. [hervorheben] to emphasize, to stress.

Betonung *(pl -en) die* - 1. [Betonen] stress - 2. [Hervorhebung] emphasis.

Betracht *(ohne Artikel)* ◆ **in Betracht** *adv*: **jn/etw in Betracht ziehen** [erwägen] to consider sb/sthg; [berücksichtigen] to take sb/sthg into account; **(nicht) in Betracht kommen** (not) to be worth considering. ◆ **außer Betracht** *adv*: **etw außer Betracht lassen** to disregard sthg.

betrachten *vt* - 1. [ansehen] to look at; **sich (D) etw (näher) betrachten** to have a (closer) look at sthg - 2. [beurteilen] to regard - 3. [überprüfen] to examine, to consider. ◆ **sich betrachten** *ref* to look at o.s.

Betrachter, in *(mpl -, fpl -nen) der, die* observer.

beträchtlich ◇ *adj* considerable. ◇ *adv* considerably.

Betrachtung *(pl -en) die* - 1. [Betrachten] contemplation - 2. [Überlegung] reflection.

Betrag *(pl Beträge) der* amount *(of money)*.

betragen *(präs beträgt, prät betrug, perf hat betragen) vt* [Preis, Rechnung] to amount *ODER* come to; **die Entfernung von A zu B beträgt 10 Kilometer** A is 10 kilometres away from B. ◆ **sich betragen** *ref*: **sich gut/schlecht betragen** to behave well/badly.

betreffen *(präs betrifft, prät betraf, perf hat betroffen) vt* [angehen] to concern; [Auswirkungen haben auf] to affect; **was mich/diese Angelegenheit betrifft** as far as I am/this matter is concerned.

Betreffende *(pl -n) der, die* person concerned.

betreiben *(prät betrieb, perf hat betrieben) vt* - 1. [vorantreiben] to pursue - 2. [führen - Gewerbe] to carry on; [- Laden] to run - 3. [antreiben]: **mit etw betrieben werden** to be driven by sthg; **diese Anlage wird mit Solarenergie betrieben** this system is solar-powered.

betreten[1] ◇ *adj* embarrassed. ◇ *adv* sheepishly.

betreten[2] *(präs betritt, prät betrat, perf hat betreten) vt* to enter; [Rasen] to walk on; [Bühne] to walk onto.

betreuen *vt* to look after, to take care of; [Sportler] to coach.

Betreuer, in *(mpl -, fpl -nen) der, die* [von Kindern] child-minder; [von Sportlern] coach; [von Touristen] guide; [von Alten] care worker.

Betreuung *die* care; [von Sportler] coaching.

Betrieb *(pl -e) der* - 1. [Unternehmen] company, firm; [Produktionsstätte] plant; **heute ist er nicht im Betrieb** he is not at work today - 2. [Tätigkeit] operation - 3. [Treiben, Verkehr]: **es ist** *ODER* **herrscht viel Betrieb** it is very busy.

in Betrieb adv in operation; **etw in Betrieb setzen** [Maschine] to start (up) sthg; [Fabrik] to commission sthg. **außer Betrieb** adv out of order; **etw außer Betrieb setzen** [Maschine] to stop sthg, to shut down sthg; [Fabrik] to decommission sthg.

betriebsam adj busy.

Betriebs|rat der - **1.** [Gremium] works council - **2.** [Mensch] works council member.

Betriebs|system das EDV operating system.

Betriebs|wirtschaft die business administration.

betrinken (prät betrank, perf hat betrunken) **sich betrinken** ref to get drunk.

betroffen ◇ pp ▭ **betreffen**. ◇ adj - **1.** [bestürzt] shaken, upset; [Schweigen] stunned - **2.** [nicht verschont]: **von etw betroffen sein** to be affected by sthg. ◇ adv: **jn betroffen ansehen** to look at sb in consternation.

betrübt adj [Gesicht] sad; [Stimmung] gloomy; **über etw (A) betrübt sein** to be sad about sthg.

Betrug der fraud; **das ist ja Betrug!** that is daylight robbery!

betrügen (prät betrog, perf hat betrogen) ◇ vt to cheat; [Ehepartner] to cheat on; **jn um etw betrügen** to cheat sb out of sthg. ◇ vi to cheat.

Betrüger (pl -) der conman, con artist.

Betrügerei (pl -en) die swindling.

Betrügerin (pl -nen) die con artist.

betrunken ◇ pp ▭ **betrinken**. ◇ adj drunk.

Bett (pl -en) das - **1.** [gen] bed; **ins** ODER **zu Bett gehen** to go to bed; **das Bett machen** to make the bed - **2.** [Federbett] duvet, quilt.

Bett|decke die [aus Wolle] blanket; [gesteppt] quilt, duvet.

betteln vi to beg; **um etw betteln** to beg for sthg.

betten vt: **jn auf etw (A) betten** to lay sb (down) on sthg.

Bettler, in (mpl -, fpl -nen) der, die beggar.

Bett|tuch (pl -tücher) das sheet.

Bett|wäsche die bed linen.

Bett|zeug das (ohne pl) bedding, bedclothes Pl.

beugen vt - **1.** [Körper, Finger, Gesetz] to bend - **2.** [Substantiv, Adjectiv] to inflect; [Verb] to conjugate. **sich beugen** ref - **1.** [sich lehnen] to lean - **2.** [sich unterwerfen]: **sich einer Sache (D) beugen** to submit ODER bow to sthg.

Beule (pl -n) die [am Kopf] lump; [am Auto] dent.

beunruhigen [bə'ʊnruːɪgn] vt to worry; **über etw (A) beunruhigt sein** to be worried about sthg.

beurlauben [bə'uːɐlaʊbn̩] vt [suspendieren] to suspend.

beurteilen [bə'uːɐtaɪln] vt to judge; [Größe, Qualität] to assess; **jn falsch beurteilen** to misjudge sb.

Beurteilung [bə'uːɐtaɪlʊŋ] (pl -en) die judgement; [von Größe, Qualität] assessment.

Beute die - **1.** [von Einbrecher] loot - **2.** [von Raubtier] prey.

Beutel (pl -) der [Sack] bag.

bevölkern vt - **1.** [bewohnen] to inhabit - **2.** [füllen] to fill.

Bevölkerung (pl -en) die population.

bevollmächtigen vt to authorize.

bevor konj before.

bevor|stehen vi (unreg) to be imminent.

bevorzugen vt - **1.** [vorziehen] to prefer - **2.** [protegieren] to give preferential treatment to.

bewachen vt to guard.

Bewacher, in (mpl -, fpl -nen) der, die guard.

bewaffnen vt to arm. **sich bewaffnen** ref to arm o.s.

Bewaffnung (pl -en) die - **1.** [Ausrüstung] armament, arming - **2.** [Waffen] arms Pl.

bewahren vt - **1.** [Person]: **jn vor etw (D) bewahren** to protect sb from sthg - **2.** [Nerven, Ruhe] to keep.

bewähren **sich bewähren** ref to prove one's/its worth.

bewahrheiten **sich bewahrheiten** ref to prove (to be) true.

Bewährung die - **1.** [Profilierung] test, trial - **2.** RECHT probation; **auf** ODER **mit Bewährung** on probation.

bewaldet adj wooded.

bewältigen vt [Arbeit, Problem] to cope with; [js Tod, die Vergangenheit] to come to terms with; [Papierberge] to get through.

bewässern vt to irrigate.

bewegen¹ (prät bewegte, perf hat bewegt) vt (reg) - **1.** [gen] to move - **2.** [beschäftigen] to concern, to preoccupy. **sich bewegen** ref - **1.** [körperlich] to move; [im Freien] to take ODER get some exercise - **2.** [sich verhalten] to act.

bewegen² (prät bewog, perf hat bewogen) vt (unreg) geh: **jn zu etw bewegen** [veranlassen] to induce sb to do sthg; [überreden] to prevail upon sb to do sthg.

beweglich adj agile; [Hebel] movable.

bewegt adj - **1.** [unruhig - Leben] eventful; [- See, Meer] choppy - **2.** [Stimme, Worte] emotional.

Bewegung (pl -en) die - **1.** [körperlich, politisch] movement; **etw in Bewegung setzen** to set sthg in motion; **sich in Bewegung setzen** *fam* [Person] to get moving; [Zug] to start to move - **2.** [körperlich] exercise.

Bewegungsfreiheit *die* freedom of movement; [Handlungsspielraum] room for manoeuvre.

bewegungslos ⟨⟩ *adj* motionless. ⟨⟩ *adv*: **bewegungslos dastehen** to stand there motionless.

Beweis (*pl* -e) *der*: **ein Beweis** a piece of evidence; **Beweise** evidence, proof.

beweisen (*prät* bewies, *perf* hat bewiesen) *vt* - **1.** [gen] to prove; [Unschuld] to establish - **2.** [Mut] to show.

bewerben (*präs* bewirbt, *prät* bewarb, *perf* hat beworben) ⟫ **sich bewerben** *ref* to apply; **sich bei einer Firma bewerben** to apply for a job with a firm; **sich um etw bewerben** to apply for sthg.

Bewerber, in (*mpl* -, *fpl* -nen) *der, die* applicant.

Bewerbung (*pl* -en) *die* application.

bewerfen (*präs* bewirft, *prät* bewarf, *perf* hat beworfen) *vt*: **jn/etw mit etw bewerfen** to pelt sb/sthg with sthg.

bewerten *vt* to assess, to evaluate; [Klassenarbeit] to mark; **etw zu hoch/niedrig bewerten** to overrate/underrate sthg.

bewilligen *vt* [Antrag] to approve; [Hilfe, Kredit] to grant.

bewirken *vt* to cause; **es bewirkte das Gegenteil** it had the opposite effect; **wir haben bewirkt, dass jetzt Nachtbusse eingesetzt werden** we have managed to get them to lay on a night bus service.

bewohnen *vt* to inhabit.

Bewohner, in (*mpl* -, *fpl* -nen) *der, die* inhabitant.

bewölkt *adj* cloudy, overcast.

Bewölkung *die* (*ohne pl*) - **1.** clouding over - **2.** [Wolken] clouds *Pl*.

bewundern *vt* to admire.

Bewunderung *die* admiration.

bewusst ⟨⟩ *adj* - **1.** [absichtlich] deliberate - **2.** [bedacht] conscious; **ihre Absichten sind mir bewusst** I am aware of her motives; **ihre Absichten wurden mir bewusst** I realized what her motives were; **sich (D) einer Sache (G) bewusst sein** to be aware of sthg. ⟨⟩ *adv* - **1.** [absichtlich] deliberately - **2.** [bedacht] consciously.

bewusstlos *adj* unconscious.

Bewusstlosigkeit *die* (state of) unconsciousness.

Bewusstsein *das* - **1.** [Wissen] awareness - **2.** [geistige Klarheit] consciousness; **bei Bewusstsein sein** to be conscious; **das Bewusstsein verlieren** to lose consciousness.

bezahlen ⟨⟩ *vt* [Ware, Leistung] to pay for; [Person, Miete, Rechnung] to pay. ⟨⟩ *vi* to pay; **wir möchten bitte bezahlen!** may we have the bill please?

bezahlt *adj* paid.

Bezahlung *die* - **1.** [von Ware, Rechnung] payment - **2.** [Entgelt] pay.

bezeichnen *vt* - **1.** [nennen] to call; **jn/etw als etw bezeichnen** to describe sb/sthg as sthg - **2.** [markieren] to mark, to indicate.

bezeichnend *adj* characteristic; **bezeichnend für etw sein** to be characteristic of sthg.

Bezeichnung *die* - **1.** (*pl* -en) [Benennung] name; [Beschreibung] description - **2.** (*ohne Pl*) [Markierung] marking.

beziehen (*prät* bezog, *perf* hat bezogen) *vt* - **1.** [Kissen, Sofa] to cover; **das Bett frisch beziehen** to change the bedclothes - **2.** [Haus, Wohnung] to move into - **3.** [Ware, Zeitung, Einkünfte] to get; [Arbeitslosenhilfe] to receive - **4.** [anwenden]: **etw auf sich (A)/jn beziehen** to understand sthg to refer to o.s./to sb; **eine Aussage auf sich (A) beziehen** to take a remark personally. ⟫ **sich beziehen** *ref* - **1.** [angewendet werden]: **sich auf jn/etw beziehen** to refer to sb/sthg; **meine Kritik bezog sich nicht auf Sie** my criticism wasn't aimed at you - **2.** [sich berufen]: **sich auf etw (A) beziehen** to refer to sthg - **3.** [sich bewölken]: **der Himmel bezieht sich** the sky is clouding over.

Beziehung (*pl* -en) *die* - **1.** [Kontakt - zu Person] relationship; **Beziehungen** [politisch] relations; **gute/schlechte Beziehungen zu jn haben** to be on good/bad terms with sb; **er verfügt über gute Beziehungen** he has lots of contacts - **2.** [Verhältnis] connection - **3.** [Hinsicht] respect.

beziehungsweise *konj* - **1.** [genauer gesagt] or rather, that is - **2.** [oder] or; **die Kinder sind ins Kino beziehungsweise ins Schwimmbad gegangen** the children have either gone to the cinema or gone swimming - **3.** [jeweils] and respectively; **die Uhren kosten 300 beziehungsweise 400 Euro** the watches cost 300 and 400 euros respectively.

Bezirk (*pl* -e) *der* district; [von Kirche] diocese.

Bezug (*pl* Bezüge) *der* - **1.** [Überzug] cover - **2.** [Beziehung]: **auf etw (A) Bezug nehmen** *amt* to refer to sthg; **in Bezug auf etw (A)** with regard to sthg. ⟫ **Bezüge** *Pl* income (*U*).

Bezugsperson *die* person to whom one looks for guidance, support etc.

bezwecken *vt*: **etw mit etw bezwecken** to aim to achieve sthg by sthg.

bezweifeln *vt* to doubt.

BGB [beːgeːˈbeː] (*abk für* **Bürgerliches Gesetzbuch**) *das* German civil code.

BH [beːˈhaː] (*pl* -s) (*abk für* **Büstenhalter**) *der* bra.

Bhf. *abk für* **Bahnhof**.

Bibel (pl -n) die bible.

Biber (pl -) der [Tier] beaver.

Bibliothek (pl -en) die library.

biegen (prät bog, perf hat/ist gebogen) <> vt (hat) to bend. <> vi (ist) [Auto, Fahrer]: **um die Ecke biegen** to go round the corner. ➤ **sich biegen** ref to bend.

Biegung (pl -en) die bend.

Biene (pl -n) die bee.

Bier (pl -e) das beer; **ein großes/kleines Bier** a half-litre/30 cl glass of beer.

Bier|dose die beer can.

Bier|garten der beer garden.

Bier|glas das beer glass.

bieten (prät bot, perf hat geboten) vt - 1. [anbieten] to offer; [Schutz, Chance] to provide; **jm etw bieten** to offer sb sthg; [Gelegenheit, Schutz] to provide sb with sthg - 2. [zeigen] to present; **einen schrecklichen Anblick bieten** to look terrible - 3. [gefallen]: **sich** (D) **etw nicht bieten lassen** not to stand for sthg. ➤ **sich bieten** ref: **es bot sich eine Gelegenheit an** an opportunity came up.

Bikini (pl -s) der bikini.

Bilanz (pl -en) die - 1. WIRTSCH balance; [schriftlich] balance sheet - 2. [Ergebnis] outcome.

Bild (pl -er) das - 1. [gen & TV] picture; [Gemälde] painting; [Zeichnung] drawing; [Foto] photograph - 2. [Anblick] sight - 3. [Vorstellung] idea, impression; **sich** (D) **ein Bild von jm/etw machen** to get an idea of sb/sthg - 4. [Metapher] image; **(über etw** (A)**) im Bilde sein** to be in the picture (about sthg).

bilden <> vt [gen] to form. <> vi: **Lesen bildet** reading improves your mind. ➤ **sich bilden** ref - 1. [sich formen] to form - 2. [sich informieren] to educate o.s.

Bilder|buch das picture book.

Bild|hauer, in (mpl -, fpl -nen) der, die sculptor (sculptress die).

bildlich <> adj - 1. [Darstellung] pictorial - 2. [Wendung, Ausdruck] figurative. <> adv - 1. [darstellen] pictorially - 2. [gesprochen] figuratively.

Bild|schirm der screen.

Bildschirmschoner (pl -) der EDV screen saver.

Bildung (pl -en) die - 1. [Ausbildung] education; **eine umfassende Bildung besitzen** to be well-educated ODER cultured - 2. [Formung] formation.

Bildungs|politik die education policy.

Bildungs|weg der: **der zweite Bildungsweg** second chance for people outside the education system to obtain educational qualifications.

Billard ['bɪljart] das billiards (U).

billig <> adj - 1. [preiswert] cheap - 2. abw [schlecht - Anzug, Papier, Scherz, Trick] cheap; [- Ausrede] feeble. <> adv cheaply; **die Vase habe ich billig gekauft** I got the vase cheap.

Billig|angebot das special offer.

Billiglohn|land das: **Arbeiter aus Billiglohnländer wie Indonesien** cheap labour from countries like Indonesia.

bimmeln vi to ring.

bin präs ▷ **sein**.

Binde (pl -n) die - 1. [Verband] bandage - 2. [über den Augen] blindfold; [um den Arm] armband - 3. [Damenbinde] sanitary towel.

Binde|mittel das binding agent.

binden (prät band, perf hat gebunden) <> vt - 1. [zusammenbinden] to tie together - 2. [festbinden]: **etw an etw** (A) **binden** to tie sthg to sthg - 3. [Krawatte] to knot; [Schleife, Knoten] to tie - 4. [Soße, Buch, durch Vertrag] to bind. <> vi to bind. ➤ **sich binden** ref [heiraten] to get married.

Binde|strich der hyphen.

Bind|faden der string.

Bindung (pl -en) die - 1. [Verbundenheit] bond; [Verpflichtung] commitment - 2. [Skibindung] binding.

Binnen|markt der internal market; [von EU] single market; **der europäische Binnenmarkt** the European single market.

Biochemie die biochemistry.

Biokost die health food.

Biologe (pl -n) der biologist.

Biologie die biology.

Biologin (pl -nen) die biologist.

biologisch adj - 1. [der Biologie] biological - 2. [natürlich - Farben] natural; [- Brot] organic.

Bio|müll der organic waste.

birgt präs ▷ **bergen**.

Birke (pl -n) die birch.

Birn|baum der pear tree.

Birne (pl -n) die - 1. [Frucht] pear - 2. [Glühbirne] light bulb - 3. fam [Kopf] nut.

birst präs ▷ **bersten**.

bis <> präp (+ A) - 1. [zeitlich] until; **wir bleiben bis morgen** we are staying until tomorrow; **von Montag bis Freitag** from Monday to Friday, Monday through Friday US; **bis auf Weiteres** until further notice; **bis bald!** see you soon!; **bis dann!** see you then!; **bis morgen!/später!** see you tomorrow/later! - 2. [spätestens]: **das muss bis Mittwoch fertig sein** it must be ready by Wednesday - 3. [räumlich] to; **es sind noch 200 km bis Berlin** there are still 200 km to go to Berlin; **bis auf die Haut durchnässt** soaked to the skin. <> konj until; **warte, bis ich komme** wait until I'm there. ➤ **bis auf** präp (+ A) except for, apart from. ➤ **bis zu** präp up to; **bis zu 20 Personen** up to 20 people.

Bischof (pl Bischöfe) der bishop.

bischöflich adj episcopal.

bisher adv: bisher hat sie nicht angerufen she hasn't called so far; **wir haben das bisher immer so gemacht** until now we've always done it this way.

bisherig adj [ehemalig] former; **sein bisheriges Verhalten** his behaviour up to now.

bislang adv: bislang hat sie nicht angerufen she hasn't called so far; **wir haben das bislang immer so gemacht** until now we've always done it this way.

Bison (pl -s) der bison.

biss prät ⊳ **beißen**.

Biss (pl -e) der eigtl & fig bite.

bisschen adj [wenig]: **das bisschen Regen macht doch nichts** that little bit of rain won't do any harm. ◆ **das bisschen** pron: **das bisschen kannst du jetzt auch noch essen** you can eat that little bit up. ◆ **ein bisschen** ⟨⟩ adj [etwas] a bit of, a little; **ein bisschen Kaffee** a drop of coffee. ⟨⟩ adv [ein wenig] a bit; **ein bisschen bleiben** to stay a while. ◆ **kein bisschen** ⟨⟩ adj: **wir haben kein bisschen Brot** we have no bread at all. ⟨⟩ adv [nicht] not at all. ◆ **ach du liebes bisschen** interj oh, dear!

Bissen (pl -) der [Stück] bite.

bissig adj eigtl & fig vicious; 'Vorsicht, bissiger Hund' 'beware of the dog'.

bist präs ⊳ **sein**.

Bistum (pl -tümer) das diocese.

bitte ⟨⟩ adv please. ⟨⟩ interj - 1. [als Bitte, Aufforderung] please; **bedient euch, bitte!** please help yourselves!; **bitte! hier ist Ihr Kaffee!** here's your coffee for you; **bitte sehr! kommen Sie herein!** (do) come in!; **bitte schön! was möchten Sie kaufen?** yes Sir/Madam, how can I help you? - 2. [als Antwort]: **danke! - bitte!** thanks! - don't mention it!; **Entschuldigung! - bitte!** sorry! - that's all right!; **kann ich nur einen Apfel nehmen? - bitte!** may I have an apple? - of course!; **bitte sehr ODER schön!** [Antwort auf einen Dank] don't mention it!, you're welcome! - 3. [als Nachfrage] pardon?, sorry?; **wie bitte?** pardon?, sorry? - 4. [am Telefon]: **ja bitte?** hello? - 5. [zur Selbstbestätigung]: **na bitte!** there you are, you see!

Bitte (pl -n) die [Anliegen] request; **eine Bitte um etw** a request for sthg.

bitten (prät bat, perf hat gebeten) ⟨⟩ vt - 1. [höflich auffordern]: **jn bitten, etw zu tun** to ask sb to do sthg; **ich bitte Sie, etwas leiser zu sein!** please be a little quieter!; **jn um etw bitten** to ask sb for sthg; **ich bitte Sie um Aufmerksamkeit!** may I have your attention, please! - 2. [einladen]: **jn zu sich bitten** to ask sb to come round to one's house. ⟨⟩ vi [Bitte aussprechen]: **um etw bitten** to ask for sthg; **ich bitte um Ruhe!** silence, please!

bitter ⟨⟩ adj - 1. [gen] bitter - 2. [Ironie] biting - 3. [Not] desperate; [Armut] abject. ⟨⟩ adv - 1. [gen] bitterly; **bitter schmecken** to taste bitter - 2. [benötigen] desperately.

Bitterkeit die eigtl & fig bitterness.

Bizeps (pl -e) der biceps (sg).

BKA [beːkaːˈʔaː] (abk für **Bundeskriminalamt**) das Federal Office for criminal investigation.

Blähungen pl wind (U).

Blamage [blaˈmaːʒə] (pl -n) die disgrace.

blamieren vt [kompromittieren] to disgrace. ◆ **sich blamieren** ref [sich bloßstellen] to disgrace o.s.

blank adj - 1. [glänzend] shiny - 2. [pur] sheer, pure - 3. [unbedeckt] bare; **blank sein** fam to be broke.

Blase (pl -n) die - 1. [auf der Haut] blister - 2. [Luftblase] bubble - 3. [Harnblase] bladder.

Blasebalg (pl -bälge) der bellows Pl.

blasen (präs bläst, prät blies, perf hat geblasen) ⟨⟩ vt - 1. [gen] to blow - 2. [Trompete, Horn] to play - 3. vulg: **jm einen blasen** to give sb a blow job. ⟨⟩ vi - 1. [gen] to blow - 2. [auf Trompete, Horn] to play.

Blasinstrument das wind instrument.

Blaskapelle die brass band.

blass (kompar blasser ODER blässer, superl blasseste ODER blässeste) adj - 1. [Haut] pale - 2. [Erinnerung, Ahnung] vague; [Hoffnung] faint.

Blässe die paleness.

bläst präs ⊳ **blasen**.

Blatt (pl Blätter) das - 1. [von Pflanzen] leaf - 2. [Papier] sheet - 3. [Seite] page - 4. [Zeitung] paper; **ein unbeschriebenes Blatt sein** [unbekannt] to be an unknown quantity; [unerfahren] to be inexperienced; **kein Blatt vor den Mund nehmen** not to mince one's words; **das Blatt hat sich gewendet** the tide has turned.

blättern (perf hat/ist geblättert) ⟨⟩ vi - 1. (hat) [umschlagen]: **in etw (D) blättern** to leaf through sthg - 2. (ist) [abblättern] to flake (off). ⟨⟩ vt (hat) [Geldscheine] to count out.

Blätterteig der puff pastry.

blau (kompar blauer, superl blau(e)ste) adj - 1. [Farbe] blue - 2. [geprellt]: **ein blaues Auge** a black eye; **ein blauer Fleck** a bruise - 3. [betrunken]: **blau sein** fam to be sloshed - 4. fam [geschwänzt]: **einen blauen Montag machen** to skip work ODER skive off UK work on Monday.

Blau das [Farbe] blue.

blauäugig adj - 1. [Augen] blue-eyed - 2. [naiv] naïve.

Blaubeere die bilberry, blueberry.

Blaue (pl -n) das - 1. [Farbe] blue - 2. [Unbe-kannte]: **ins Blaue** [fahren] with no particular place to go; [reden] aimlessly.

Blaulhelm der blue beret.

bläulich adj bluish.

Blaullicht das [Signal] flashing blue light (on ambulance etc.)

blaulmachen vi fam [schwänzen] to skip ODER skive off UK school/work.

Blazer ['ble:zɐ] (pl -) der blazer.

Blech das - 1. [Metall] sheet metal - 2. [Backblech] baking sheet UK, cookie sheet US - 3. fam [Unsinn] rubbish.

blechen fam vt & vi to fork out.

Blechlinstrument das brass instrument.

Blechlschaden der bodywork damage (U).

Blei das [Metall] lead.

Bleibe (pl -n) die place to stay.

bleiben (prät blieb, perf ist geblieben) vi - 1. [an einem Ort] to stay; **wo bleibst du denn so lange?** [bei Eintreffen] what kept you? - 2. [in einem Zustand] to remain; **sie ist ganz die Alte geblieben** she hasn't changed a bit; **wir bleiben in Kontakt** we keep in touch; **bei etw bleiben** to stick to sthg; **es bleibt also dabei, morgen um zehn Uhr** ten o'clock tomorrow morning, like we said, then?; **das bleibt unter uns** it's strictly between ourselves - 3. [als Übriges] to be left; **uns bleiben nur noch wenige Tage** we only have a few days left.

bleibend adj lasting.

bleiben lassen vt (unreg) - 1. [unterlassen] to leave be - 2. [aufgeben] to give up.

bleich adj pale.

bleifrei adj unleaded.

Bleilstift der pencil.

Bleistiftspitzer (pl -) der pencil sharpener.

Blende (pl -n) die - 1. [vor Fenster] blind, screen; AUTO visor - 2. [FOTO - Objektivöffnung] diaphragm; [- Blendenzahl] aperture.

blenden ⬦ vt eigtl & fig to dazzle. ⬦ vi [Licht] to be dazzling.

blendend ⬦ adj dazzling. ⬦ adv marvellously; **du siehst blendend aus!** you look dazzling!

Blick (pl -e) der - 1. [der Augen] look; [kurz] glance; **den Blick heben/senken** to raise/lower one's eyes; **einen Blick auf etw** (A) **werfen** to glance at sthg; **sie würdigte mich/es keines Blickes** she did not deign to look at me/it - 2. [Ausblick] view - 3. [Urteil] eye; **keinen Blick für etw haben** not to appreciate sthg.

blicken vi to look; **sich (nicht) blicken lassen** (not) to show one's face; **das lässt tief blicken** that explains a lot.

Blicklpunkt der: **im Blickpunkt der Öffentlichkeit** in the public eye.

blieb prät ➪ **bleiben**.

blies prät ➪ **blasen**.

blind ⬦ adj - 1. [gen] blind; **blind für etw sein** to be blind to sthg - 2. [versteckt] ➪ **Passagier** - 3. [falsch] ➪ **Alarm**. ⬦ adv blindly.

Blinddarmlentzündung die appendicitis (U).

Blinde (pl -n) der, die blind man (blind woman die).

Blindenlschrift die braille.

Blindheit die eigtl & fig blindness.

blinken vi - 1. [funkeln - Metall] to gleam; [- Sterne] to twinkle; [- Wasser, Edelstein] to sparkle - 2. [signalisieren - Verkehr] to indicate; [Signal geben] to signal.

Blinker (pl -) der indicator UK, turn signal US.

Blinkllicht das flashing light.

blinzeln vi [mit einem Auge, als Zeichen] to wink; [mit beiden Augen] to blink.

Blitz (pl -e) der - 1. [am Himmel] lightning (U); **ein Blitz** a flash of lightning; **wie der Blitz** like lightning - 2. [Blitzlicht] flash.

Blitzableiter (pl -) der lightning conductor.

blitzblank adj [Geschirr] sparkling clean; [Wohnung] spotless.

blitzen ⬦ vi - 1. [am Himmel]: **es blitzt** there is lightning - 2. [funkeln - Schmuck, Wohnung] to sparkle]; [- Metall] to gleam. ⬦ vt fam [fotografieren] to take a flash photo of; **geblitzt werden** to be caught by a speed camera.

Blitzllicht das flash.

Blitzlschlag der flash of lightning; **vom Blitzschlag getroffen werden** to be struck by lightning.

blitzschnell ⬦ adj lightning. ⬦ adv like lightning.

Block (pl Blöcke ODER -s) der - 1. (pl Blöcke) [Stück] block - 2. (pl Blöcke) [aus Papier] pad - 3. (pl Blöcke, Blocks) [Häuserblock] block - 4. (pl Blocks) [Gruppe - von Staaten] bloc; [Fraktion] faction.

Blockade (pl -n) die blockade.

Blockflöte die recorder.

Blocklhaus das log cabin.

blockieren ⬦ vt - 1. EDV [versperren] to block - 2. [zum Stillstand bringen] to obstruct. ⬦ vi [Motor] to jam; [Räder] to lock.

Blocklschrift die block capitals Pl.

blöd, blöde fam ⬦ adj stupid. ⬦ adv stupidly.

Blödsinn der fam rubbish.

blond adj blond (blonde die).

Blondine (pl -n) die blonde.

bloß ⬦ adv - 1. fam [lediglich] only, just; **jetzt bloß noch etwas drehen** now just turn it some more - 2. [zum Ausdruck von Ratlosigkeit]: **was sollen wir bloß machen?** what on earth shall we do? - 3. [zum Ausdruck von Ärger]: **warum musstest du bloß den Schlüssel stecken lassen?** why did you have to go and leave the key in the lock? - **4.** [zum Ausdruck einer Drohung]: **hau bloß ab!** just push off, all right?; **unterschreib das bloß nicht!** don't you dare sign that! - **5.** [zum Ausdruck einer Aufforderung]: **bloß keine Panik!** just don't panic! - **6.** [zum Ausdruck eines Wunsches]: **hätte ich bloß nichts gesagt!** if only I hadn't said anything! ⟨⟩ adj - **1.** [nackt] bare; **mit bloßen Füßen** barefoot; **mit bloßem Auge** with the naked eye - **2.** [rein] sheer.

bloßIstellen vt to show up; [Betrüger] to unmask.

bluffen [blœfn] abw vt & vi to bluff.

blühen vi - **1.** [Pflanze] to bloom, to flower; [Baum] to blossom - **2.** [florieren] to flourish - **3.** fam [drohen]: **das kann dir auch noch blühen!** you're not out of the woods yet!

blühend adj - **1.** [Pflanze] blooming, flowering; [tree] blossoming - **2.** [frisch] radiant - **3.** [ausufernd]: **eine blühende Fantasie** a vivid imagination.

Blume (pl -n) die [Pflanze] flower.

BlumenIkohl der cauliflower.

BlumenIstrauß der bunch of flowers.

BlumenItopf der flowerpot.

Bluse (pl -n) die blouse.

Blut das blood; **Blut spenden** to give blood; **Blut stillend** styptic.

Blutlabnahme die blood test.

BlutIbad das bloodbath.

BlutIdruck der blood pressure.

Blüte (pl -n) die - **1.** [Pflanzenteil] flower, bloom; [von Baum] blossom - **2.** [das Blühen] flowering, blooming; [von Baum] blossoming; **in voller Blüte** in full flower; [Baum] in full blossom - **3.** [Aufschwung] flowering.

Blutegel (pl -) der leech.

bluten vi to bleed; **aus der Nase bluten** to have a nosebleed.

Bluter, in (mpl -, fpl -nen) der, die haemophiliac.

Blutlerguss der MED haematoma; [blauer Fleck] bruise.

Blütelzeit die - **1.** [von Pflanze] flowering period - **2.** [von Kultur, Reich] heyday.

Blutlgefäß das blood vessel.

Blutlgruppe die blood group.

blutig ⟨⟩ adj bloody. ⟨⟩ adv - **1.** [befleckt]: **jn blutig schlagen** to beat sb to a pulp - **2.** [niederschlagen] bloodily.

Blutlkonserve die unit of stored blood (for transfusions etc.)

BlutIkörperchen (pl Blutkörperchen) das corpuscle; **weiße/rote Blutkörperchen** white/red blood cells.

Blutlkreislauf der blood circulation.

Blutlprobe die - **1.** [Untersuchung] blood test - **2.** [entnommenes Blut] blood sample.

Blutlspender, in der, die blood donor.

Blutlübertragung die blood transfusion.

Blutung (pl -en) die bleeding; MED haemorrhage; [Monatsblutung] period.

blutunterlaufen adj bloodshot.

Blutlwurst die black pudding UK, blood sausage US.

BLZ abk für **Bankleitzahl**.

Bö = **Böe**.

Bock (pl Böcke) der - **1.** [Kaninchen, Reh] buck; [Ziege] billy-goat; [Schaf] ram; **stur wie ein Bock** as stubborn as a mule; **ein geiler Bock** salopp a randy old goat - **2.** SPORT (vaulting) horse - **3.** [Gerüst] trestle; **darauf hab ich keinen Bock** fam I can't be fagged.

Bocklbier das bock, strong dark beer.

bockig adj [trotzig] contrary.

Bockspringen das - **1.** SPORT vaulting - **2.** [Spiel] leapfrog.

Bocklwurst die type of pork sausage, usually boiled and eaten in a bread roll with mustard.

Boden (pl Böden) der - **1.** [Grund] ground; [Erdreich] soil; **auf deutschem Boden** on German soil; **er hat den Boden unter den Füßen verloren** [beim Klettern] he lost his footing; [im Leben] his world has fallen apart - **2.** [Fußboden] floor; **zu Boden gehen** [im Boxsport] to go down - **3.** [von Gefäß, Koffer, Meer] bottom - **4.** [Speicher] loft; **am Boden zerstört** absolutely shattered; **an Boden gewinnen/verlieren** to gain/lose ground.

bodenlos adj - **1.** [tief] bottomless - **2.** [unglaublich] incredible.

Bodenpersonal das ground staff.

Bodenschätze Pl mineral resources.

Bodenturnen das floor exercises Pl.

Böe (pl -n), **Bö** (pl -en) die gust.

bog prät ⟶ **biegen**.

Bogen (pl - ODER Bögen) der - **1.** [Biegung] curve; **dort macht die Straße einen Bogen nach links** the road curves to the left there; **einen Bogen um jn/etw machen** to steer clear of sb/sthg; **in hohem Bogen** [Wasser] in a great arc; **in hohem Bogen hinausgeworfen werden** ODER **hinausfliegen** to be thrown out on one's ear - **2.** [Bauwerk] arch - **3.** [Schusswaffe & MUS] bow - **4.** [Blatt] sheet.

Bogenschießen das archery.

Bohle (pl -n) die thick plank.

Böhmen nt Bohemia.

Böhmerwald der Bohemian Forest.

Bohne (pl -n) die bean; **dicke/grüne Bohnen** broad/green beans; **das interessiert mich nicht die Bohne** fam I'm not in the slightest bit interested in that.

bohnern vt to polish.

bohren ⟨⟩ vt - **1.** [Loch] to drill; [Brunnen, Schacht] to sink - **2.** [hineinstoßen] to stick, to thrust. ⟨⟩ vi - **1.** [mit einem Bohrer] to drill; **nach Öl/Wasser bohren** to drill for oil/water;

in ODER an einem Zahn bohren to drill a tooth; in der Nase bohren to pick one's nose - 2. *fam* [drängen] to keep on. ◆ **sich bohren** *ref* [eindringen]: sich in etw (A) bohren to bore one's way into sthg.

bohrend *adj* [Blick] piercing; [Schmerz] gnawing; [Fragen] probing.

Bohrer (*pl* -) *der* [Gerät] drill.

Bohrlmaschine *die* drill.

Bohrung (*pl* -en) *die* drilling.

böig *adj* gusty.

Boiler [bɔylɐ] (*pl* -) *der* boiler.

Boje (*pl* -n) *die* buoy.

Bolzen (*pl* -) *der* bolt.

bombardieren *vt* to bombard; jn mit etw bombardieren *eigtl* & *fig* to bombard sb with sthg.

Bombe (*pl* -n) *die* bomb.

Bombenlanschlag *der* bombing, bomb attack.

Bombenerfolg (*pl* -e) *der fam* smash hit.

Bombenlstimmung *die fam* wild atmosphere.

Bon [bɔŋ] (*pl* -s) *der* - 1. [Beleg] receipt - 2. [für Speisen und Getränke] voucher.

Bonbon [bɔŋ'bɔŋ] (*pl* -s) *der* ODER *das* sweet.

Bonn *nt* Bonn.

Bonze (*pl* -n) *der abw* bigwig.

Boom [bu:m] (*pl* -s) *der* boom.

Boot (*pl* -e) *das* boat; mit ODER in einem Boot fahren to go by boat; Boot fahren to go boating; wir sitzen alle in einem ODER im selben Boot *fig* we are all in the same boat.

Bord (*pl* -e) ◇ *das* [Brett] shelf. ◇ *der* SCHIFF & FLUG side; von Bord gehen to disembark; alle Vorsicht über Bord werfen to throw caution to the winds. ◇ **an Bord** ◇ *adv* on board; alle Mann an Bord! all aboard! ◇ *präp* (+ G) on board.

Bordell (*pl* -e) *das* brothel.

Bordlkarte *die* boarding card.

Bordsteinlkante *die* kerb.

borgen *vt* - 1. [entleihen] to borrow; etw von ODER bei jm borgen to borrow sthg from sb; sich (D) etw borgen to borrow sthg - 2. [verleihen]: jm etw borgen to lend sb sthg.

Borke (*pl* -n) *die* bark.

Börse (*pl* -n) *die* - 1. [Geldbeutel] purse - 2. WIRTSCH stock market; [Gebäude] stock exchange; das Unternehmen geht an die Börse the company is being floated (on the stock market).

bösartig *adj* - 1. [Verhalten, Mensch, Bemerkung] malicious; [Hund] vicious - 2. [Krankheit] malignant.

Böschung (*pl* -en) *die* bank.

böse ◇ *adj* - 1. [schlecht] bad; [verwerflich] wicked, evil - 2. [wütend]: (über etw (A)) böse

sein/werden to be/get angry (about sthg; auf jn böse sein, jm böse sein to be angry with sb - 4. [frech, ungezogen] naughty. ◇ *adv* - 1. [schlimm] badly; sich böse erkälten to catch a nasty cold - 2. [bösartig]: es war nicht böse gemeint I didn't mean it nastily - 3. [wütend] angrily.

Böse (*pl* -n) ◇ *der, die* villain. ◇ *das*: nichts Böses tun/vorhaben not to do/mean any harm; etw Böses sagen to say sthg nasty; nichts Böses ahnen to be unsuspecting.

Bösewicht (*pl* -er ODER -e) *der* - 1. [Schuft] villain - 2. [Schlingel] rascal.

boshaft ◇ *adj* - 1. [böse] wicked, evil - 2. [höhnisch] malicious. ◇ *adv* [höhnisch] maliciously.

Bosheit (*pl* -en) *die* - 1. [Gesinnung] malice - 2. [Handlung] malicious thing.

Bosnien-Herzegowina *nt* Bosnia-Herzegowina.

bosnisch *adj* Bosnian.

Boss (*pl* -e) *der* boss; [von Bande] leader.

böswillig ◇ *adj* malicious. ◇ *adv* [handeln] maliciously.

bot *prät* ▷ **bieten**.

Botanik *die* botany.

botanisch *adj* botanical ▷ **Garten**.

Bote (*pl* -n) *der* - 1. [gen] messenger; [von Kurierdienst] courier - 2. [Vorbote] herald.

Botin (*pl* -nen) *die* - 1. [gen] messenger; [von Kurierdienst] courier - 2. [Vorbotin] herald.

Botschaft (*pl* -en) *die* - 1. [Mitteilung] message - 2. [diplomatische Vertretung] embassy.

Botschafter, in (*mpl* -, *fpl* -nen) *der, die* ambassador.

Bouillon [bʊl'jɔŋ] (*pl* -s) *die* bouillon.

Boulette = **Bulette**.

Boulevard [bul(ə)'vaːɐ] (*pl* -s) *der* boulevard.

Boulevardlpresse *die* tabloid press, sensationalist press.

Boulevardltheater *das* light theatre.

Boutique (*pl* -n), **Butike** (*pl* -n) [bu'tiːk] *die* boutique.

Bowle ['boːlə] (*pl* -n) *die* punch.

Bowling ['boːlɪŋ] (*pl* -s) *das* bowling.

Box (*pl* -en) *die* - 1. [Lautsprecherbox] speaker - 2. [Kasten] box - 3. [an Rennstrecke] pit; [in Pferdestall] box; [in Garage] space.

boxen ◇ *vi* to box. ◇ *vt* - 1. SPORT to fight - 2. [schlagen] to punch. ◆ **sich boxen** *ref* [kämpfen] to fight.

Boxer (*pl* -) *der* [Hund & SPORT] boxer.

Boxlkampf *der* boxing match.

boykottieren [bɔykɔ'tiːrən] *vt* to boycott.

brach *prät* ▷ **brechen**.

brachte *prät* ▷ **bringen**.

Branche ['brɑ̃ːʃə] (pl -n) die (branch of) industry; [Gewerbe] trade.

Brand (pl Brände) der [großes Feuer] fire, blaze; **etw gerät in Brand** sthg catches fire; **etw in Brand setzen** ODER **stecken** to set fire to sthg, to set sthg on fire; **einen Brand haben** fam to be dying of thirst.

Brandenburg nt Brandenburg.

Brandenburger Tor das Brandenburg Gate.

brandneu adj brand-new.

Brand|stifter, in der, die arsonist.

Brand|stiftung die arson.

Brandung (pl -en) die surf.

Brand|wunde die burn.

brannte prät ▷ **brennen**.

Brannt|wein der spirits Pl; **Whisky ist ein Branntwein** whisky is a type of spirit.

Brasilianer, in (mpl -, fpl -nen) der, die Brazilian.

brasilianisch adj Brazilian.

Brasilien nt Brazil.

brät präs ▷ **braten**.

braten (präs brät, prät briet, perf hat gebraten) vt & vi [in der Pfanne] to fry; [im Ofen mit Fett] to roast; [im Ofen ohne Fett] to bake.

Braten (pl -) der roast.

Brat|hähnchen das roast chicken.

Bratkartoffeln Pl fried potatoes.

Brat|pfanne die frying pan.

Bratsche (pl -n) die MUS viola.

Brat|wurst die (fried) sausage.

Brauch (pl Bräuche) der custom.

brauchbar ◇ adj [Vorschlag] useful; [Material, Kleidung] usable. ◇ adv usefully; **brauchbar arbeiten** to do acceptable work.

brauchen ◇ vt - 1. [benötigen] to need; **jm/ etw für etw brauchen** to need sb/sthg for sthg - 2. [verbrauchen] to use (up) - 3. [verwenden]: **jn/etw (nicht) brauchen können** (not) to be able to use sb/sthg. ◇ aux [müssen] to need; **ihr braucht nicht zu grinsen** there's no need for you to grin.

Braue (pl -n) die brow, eyebrow.

brauen vt [Bier, Tee] to brew; [Trank] to make.

Brauerei (pl -en) die brewery.

braun ◇ adj - 1. [Farbe] brown; **braune Butter** butter melted in frying pan until brown - 2. [nationalsozialistisch] Nazi. ◇ adv [farbig] brown; [braten] until brown; siehe auch **braun gebrannt**.

Braun das brown.

Bräune die suntan.

bräunen (perf hat/ist gebräunt) ◇ vt (hat) - 1. [Körper, Gesicht] to tan - 2. [Zwiebeln] to brown; [Zucker] to caramelize. ◇ vi - 1. (hat) [durch Sonne] to tan - 2. (ist) [Braten] to turn brown. ◆ **sich bräunen** ref [durch Sonne - Person] to get a tan; [- Haut] to go brown; [sonnenbaden] to sunbathe.

braun gebrannt adj tanned.

Braunkohle die brown coal, lignite.

Brause (pl -n) die - 1. [Getränk, Pulver] sherbet - 2. [Dusche] shower.

brausen (perf hat/ist gebraust) vi - 1. (hat) [Meer, Wind] to roar; [Beifall] to thunder - 2. (ist) [sich fortbewegen] to race.

Braut (pl Bräute) die - 1. [am Hochzeitstag] bride - 2. [Verlobte] fiancée - 3. salopp [Mädchen] bird UK, chick US.

Bräutigam (pl -e) der - 1. [am Hochzeitstag] bridegroom - 2. [Verlobter] fiancé.

Braut|paar das bride and groom Pl.

brav adj - 1. [artig] good - 2. [bieder] plain.

bravo ['brɑːvo] interj bravo!

BRD [beːɛrˈdeː] (abk für **Bundesrepublik Deutschland**) die FRG.

brechen (präs bricht, prät brach, perf hat/ist gebrochen) ◇ vt - 1. (hat) [gen] to break; [Ast] to break off; [Rose, Blume] to pluck; [Trotz, Hartnäckigkeit] to overcome; [Ehe] to break up; **jm/ sich den Arm brechen** to break sb's/one's arm - 2. (hat) [erbrechen] to vomit (up). ◇ vi - 1. (ist) [durchbrechen] to break - 2. (hat) [erbrechen] to vomit, to be sick - 3. (hat) [Kontakt abbrechen]: **mit jm brechen** to break off contact with sb - 4. (hat) [Brauch aufgeben]: **mit einer Tradition brechen** to break with a tradition - 5. (ist) [durchkommen] to burst out. ◆ **sich brechen** ref [Schall] to echo; [Licht] to be refracted; [Wellen] to break.

brechend adv: **brechend voll** full to bursting.

Brech|reiz der nausea (U).

Brei (pl -e) der purée; [aus Haferflocken] porridge; [aus Kartoffeln] mashed potatoes Pl; [aus Gries] semolina.

breit ◇ adj - 1. [gen] wide; [Schultern, Gesicht, Hüften, Aussprache] broad; **ein breites Lachen** a guffaw - 2. [allgemein] general. ◇ adv - 1. [seitlich ausgedehnt]: **breit gebaut** sturdily built - 2. [ausgedehnt - darstellen] in great detail; [- lächeln] broadly; **breit lachen** to guffaw.

breitbeinig adv [dastehen] with one's legs apart; **breitbeinig gehen** to walk with a rolling gait.

Breite (pl -n) die - 1. [Ausdehnung] width - 2. [geografische Lage] latitude.

Breiten|grad der (degree of) latitude.

breit machen vt: **die Beine breit machen** fam to spread one's legs. ◆ **sich breit machen** ref fam - 1. [Raum beanspruchen] to take up a lot of room - 2. [sich einquartieren] to make o.s. at home - 3. [sich verbreiten] to spread.

breit|schlagen vt (unreg) fam [überreden] to talk round; **sich zu etw breitschlagen lassen** to let o.s. be talked into sthg.

breitschultrig, breitschulterig *adj* broad-shouldered.

Bremsbelag *der* brake lining.

Bremse (*pl* -n) *die* - 1. [Bremsvorrichtung] brake - 2. [Insekt] horsefly.

bremsen <> *vi* [halten] to brake. <> *vt* - 1. [Fahrzeug] to brake - 2. [Entwicklung, Person] to slow down.

Bremslicht *das* brake light.

Bremspedal *das* brake pedal.

Bremsweg *der* braking distance.

brennbar *adj* flammable.

brennen (*prät* brannte, *perf* hat gebrannt) <> *vi* - 1. [gen] to burn; [Haus, Wald, Gardine] to be on fire, to burn; **es brennt!** fire! - 2. [Lampe, Birne] to be on - 3. [Wunde, Augen] to smart; [Füße] to be sore - 4. [erregt sein]: **auf etw** (A) **brennen** to be dying for sthg. <> *vt* - 1. [Loch] to burn - 2. [Ziegel, Ton] to fire; [Schnaps] to distil; [Mandeln] to roast - 3. *fam* [CD-Rom] to burn.

Brenner *der*: **der Brenner** the Brenner Pass.

Brennholz *das* firewood.

Brennnessel, Brenn-Nessel *die* stinging nettle.

brenzlig *adj* - 1. [Geschmack] burnt; **ein brenzliger Geruch** a smell of burning - 2. *fam* [heikel] dicey.

Brett (*pl* -er) *das* - 1. [aus Holz] plank; **schwarzes Brett** noticeboard - 2. [zum Spielen] board.

Brettspiel *das* board game.

Brezel (*pl* -n) *die* pretzel.

bricht *präs* ⊳ **brechen**.

Brief (*pl* -e) *der* letter.

Brieffreund, in *der, die* pen pal.

Briefkasten *der* - 1. [bei der Post] postbox *UK*, mailbox *US* - 2. [am Hauseingang] letterbox *UK*, mailbox *US*.

Briefkopf *der* letterhead.

Briefmarke *die* stamp.

Brieftasche *die* wallet.

Briefträger, in *der, die* postman (postwoman *die*).

Briefumschlag *der* envelope.

briet *prät* ⊳ **braten**.

Brillant [brɪl'jant] (*pl* -en) *der* brilliant.

Brille (*pl* -n) *die* - 1. [Sehhilfe, Augengläser] glasses *Pl*; **eine Brille tragen** to wear glasses - 2. *fam* [Klosettbrille] toilet seat.

bringen (*prät* brachte, *perf* hat gebracht) *vt* - 1. [herbringen] to bring; **jm etw bringen** to bring sb sthg - 2. [holen] to get, to fetch; **jm etw bringen** to get ODER fetch sb sthg - 3. [befördern] to take, to give a lift to; **ich bringe Sie zum Bahnhof** I'll take you ODER give you a lift to the station - 4. [begleiten] to see; **jn zur Tür bringen** to see sb to the door - 5. *fig* [lenken]: **die Rede auf etw bringen** to bring the conver-

sation round to sthg; **jn auf die Idee bringen, etw zu tun** to give sb the idea of doing sthg; **jn in Gefahr bringen** to put sb in danger - 6. [Ergebnis]: **das bringt nur Ärger** that'll cause nothing but trouble; **jn dazu bringen, dass er etw tut** to make sb do sthg, to get sb to do sthg; **Gewinn bringen** to yield a profit; **das bringt nichts** *fam* that won't achieve anything - 7. [leisten]: **es weit bringen** to go far ODER a long way; **er brachte es bis zum Minister** he made it to minister - 8. [veröffentlichen - in einer Zeitung] to publish; [- im Fernsehen, Radio] to broadcast; FILM to screen; **etw hinter sich** (A) **bringen** to get sthg over and done with; **ich kann es nicht über mich bringen, so etwas zu tun** I can't bring myself to do such a thing; **jn um etw bringen** to do sb out of sthg; **du bringst mich noch mal um den Verstand!** you're driving me mad!

brisant *adj* [heikel] explosive.

Brise (*pl* -n) *die* breeze.

Brite (*pl* -n) *der* Briton, British person; **die Briten** the British; **ich bin Brite** I'm British.

Britin (*pl* -nen) *die* Briton, British person.

britisch *adj* British.

Britische Inseln *Pl* British Isles.

Broccoli, Brokkoli ['brɔkoli] *der* broccoli.

bröckeln (*perf* hat/ist gebröckelt) *vi* - 1. (*hat*) [zerfallen] to crumble - 2. (*ist*) [sich lösen]: **der Putz bröckelt von den Wänden** the plaster is flaking off the walls.

Brocken (*pl* -) *der* - 1. [von Brot, Fleisch] bit, chunk; [von Lehm] lump - 2. *fam* [dicker Mensch] hefty fellow; **ein paar Brocken einer Sprache sprechen** to speak a few words of a language.

brodeln *vi* [Wasser, Suppe, Lava] to bubble.

Brokkoli = **Broccoli**.

Brombeere *die* blackberry.

Bronchien ['brɔnçiən] *Pl* bronchial tubes.

Bronchitis [brɔn'çiːtɪs] *die* bronchitis (*U*).

Bronze ['brɔnsə] *die* bronze.

Brosche (*pl* -n) *die* brooch.

Broschüre (*pl* -n) *die* brochure.

Brot (*pl* -e) *das* - 1. [als Laib] bread; **ein Laib Brot** a loaf of bread - 2. [als Scheibe] slice of bread; **ein belegtes Brot** an open sandwich; **ein Brot mit Schinken** a slice of bread with ham on it - 3. [Lebensunterhalt]: **sich sein Brot verdienen** to earn a living.

Brötchen (*pl* -) *das* (bread) roll.

Browser ['brauzɐ] (*pl* -) *der* EDV browser.

Bruch (*pl* Brüche) *der* - 1. (*ohne pl*) [Brechen] breaking; [von Damm] bursting; **zu Bruch gehen** [Glas] to smash, to shatter - 2. [von Versprechen, Wort] breaking; [von Vertrag] breach - 3. [Trennung]: **ein Bruch mit der Tradition** a break with tradition; **es kam zum Bruch mit seiner Familie** he broke off contact with his family - 4. [MED - von Knochen] fracture; [- von Eingeweide] hernia; **sich einen Bruch heben** to have ODER suffer a hernia - 5. MATH fraction.

brüchig adj [Material] brittle; [Teig] crumbly; [Beziehung] fragile; [Stimme] cracked.

Bruch|landung die crash landing.

Bruch|rechnung die (ohne pl) fractions Pl.

Bruch|strich der line (of a fraction).

Bruch|stück das [von Vase, Werk] fragment.

bruchstückhaft ['bruxʃtykhaft] ◇ adj fragmentary. ◇ adv in fragments.

Bruch|teil der fraction.

Brücke (pl -n) die - 1. [gen] bridge; **eine Brücke schlagen** [Turnübung] to make a bridge - 2. [Teppich] rug.

Bruder (pl Brüder) der - 1. [Geschwister, Mönch] brother - 2. fam [Kerl] guy.

brüderlich ◇ adj brotherly. ◇ adv like brothers.

Brühe (pl -n) die - 1. [Suppe] broth; [zum Kochen] stock - 2. [Wasser] dirty water - 3. abw [Tee, Kaffee] dishwater.

Brüh|würfel der stock cube.

brüllen ◇ vt to roar. ◇ vi [Löwe, Person] to roar; [Stier] to bellow; [Baby, Affe] to screech; **vor Schmerz brüllen** to howl with pain.

brummen vi - 1. [Hummel] to buzz; [Bär] to growl - 2. [Person, Motor] to drone.

brummig ◇ adj [Person] grumpy; [Antwort] bad-tempered, surly. ◇ adv grumpily.

brünett adj: **eine brünette Frau** a brunette.

Brunnen (pl -) der - 1. [zum Wasserholen] well - 2. [Springbrunnen] fountain - 3. [Wasser] mineral water.

Brunst (pl Brünste) die [von Reh] heat; [von Hirsch] rut.

brüsk ◇ adj brusque. ◇ adv brusquely.

Brüssel nt Brussels.

Brust (pl Brüste) die - 1. (ohne pl) [Thorax] chest - 2. [Busen] breast.

brüsten ⟺ **sich brüsten** ref abw: **sich mit etw brüsten** to boast about sth.

Brust|korb der thorax.

Brust|schwimmen das breaststroke.

Brüstung (pl -en) die parapet.

Brust|warze die nipple.

brutal ◇ adj brutal. ◇ adv brutally.

Brutalität (pl -en) die brutality.

brüten vi - 1. [Vögel] to brood - 2. [nachdenken]: **über etw (D) brüten** to ponder sthg.

brutto adv gross.

Bruttosozial|produkt das gross national product, GNP.

brutzeln ◇ vi to sizzle. ◇ vt fam to fry (up).

BSE (abk für Bovine Spongiforme Enzephalopathie) die BSE.

Bube (pl -n) der - 1. [Junge] boy - 2. [Spielkarte] jack.

Buch (pl Bücher) das book; **die Bücher führen** to keep the books; **über etw (A) Buch führen** to keep a record of sthg.

Buchbinder, in (mpl -, fpl -nen) der, die bookbinder.

Buche (pl -n) die beech.

buchen vt - 1. [verbuchen] to enter - 2. [reservieren] to book.

Bücherei (pl -en) die library.

Bücher|regal das bookshelves Pl.

Bücher|schrank der bookcase.

Buch|führung die bookkeeping.

Buchhalter, in (mpl -, fpl -nen) der, die accountant, bookkeeper.

Buch|haltung die accountancy, bookkeeping.

Buch|händler, in der, die bookseller.

Buch|handlung (pl -en) die bookshop.

Buchladen (pl -läden) der bookshop.

Buchse ['buksə] (pl -n) die socket.

Büchse ['byksə] (pl -n) die - 1. [Dose] can, tin UK - 2. [Gewehr] shotgun.

Büchsen|milch die tinned milk UK, canned milk US.

Büchsen|öffner der can opener, tin opener UK.

Buchstabe ['bu:xʃta:bə] (pl -n) der letter; **grosser Buchstabe** capital (letter); **kleiner Buchstabe** lower-case letter; **in fetten Buchstaben** in bold.

buchstabieren [bu:xʃta'bi:rən] vt to spell.

buchstäblich ['bu:xʃtɛ:plıç] adv literally.

Bucht (pl -en) die bay.

Buchung (pl -en) die - 1. [Verbuchung] entry - 2. [Reservierung] booking.

Buchweizen der buckwheat.

Buckel (pl -) der [Rücken] hump; **einen Buckel haben** to be a hunchback; **rutsch mir den Buckel runter!** fam abw get lost ODER stuffed!

bucklig adj [Person] hunchbacked; [Oberfläche, Straße] bumpy.

Bückling (pl -e) der - 1. hum [Verbeugung] bow - 2. [Hering] smoked herring.

Budapest nt Budapest.

buddeln vt & vi to dig.

buddhistisch adj Buddhist.

Bude (pl -n) die - 1. [Verkaufsstand] stall - 2. fam [kleine Wohnung, möbliertes Zimmer] pad; **die Leute rennen ihr die Bude ein** fam she has people queuing on her doorstep - 3. fam abw [Wohnung] dump.

Budget [by'dʒe:] (pl -s) das budget.

Büfett [by'fɛt] (pl -s), **Buffet** [by'fe:] (pl -s) das - 1. [Verkaufstisch] counter - 2. [Speisen]: **kaltes Büfett** cold buffet - 3. [Geschirrschrank] sideboard.

Büffel (*pl* -) *der* buffalo.

Buffet [by'fe:] (*pl* -s) *das Österr & Schweiz* = **Büfett**.

Bug (*pl* -e) *der* [von Schiff] bow; [von Flugzeug] nose.

Bügel (*pl* -) *der* - 1. [Kleiderbügel] (coat) hanger - 2. [Griff] handle - 3. [Steigbügel] stirrup - 4. [Brillenbügel] side-piece.

Bügelbrett *das* ironing board.

Bügeleisen *das* iron.

Bügelfalte *die* crease.

bügeln *vt & vi* to iron.

Buggy (*pl* -s) *der* buggy.

Bühne (*pl* -n) *die* - 1. [Theaterraum] stage - 2. [Theater] theatre.

Bühnenbild *das* set.

buk *prät* ▷ **backen**.

Bukarest *nt* Bucharest.

Bulette (*pl* -n), **Boulette** (*pl* -n) *die* rissole.

Bulgarien *nt* Bulgaria.

bulgarisch *adj* Bulgarian.

Bullauge *das* porthole.

Bulldogge *die* bulldog.

Bulldozer ['buldo:ze] (*pl* **Bulldozer**) *der* bulldozer.

Bulle (*pl* -n) *der* - 1. [Tier] bull - 2. *salopp abw* [Polizist] pig, cop.

Bummel (*pl* -) *der* stroll; **einen Bummel machen** to go for a stroll.

bummeln (*perf* hat/ist gebummelt) *vi* - 1. *(ist)* [spazieren] to stroll - 2. *(hat)* [langsam sein] to dawdle.

Bummelzug *der* slow train.

bumsen (*perf* hat/ist gebumst) ◇ *vi* - 1. *(hat)* fam [knallen] to bang; **es hat gebumst** [Lärm] there was a bang; [bei Unfall] there was a crash - 2. *(ist)* fam [prallen]: **gegen** ODER **an etw** (A) **bumsen** to bang into sthg - 3. *(hat)* fam [koitieren] to get laid, to have it off UK. ◇ *vt* fam to lay, to have it off with UK.

Bund (*pl* Bünde ODER -e) ◇ *der* - 1. (*pl* Bünde) [Zusammenschluss] association - 2. [Bundesrepublik] central government - 3. fam [Bundeswehr]: **der Bund** the army - 4. (*pl* Bünde) [an Kleidung] waistband. ◇ *das* (*pl* Bunde) [von Gemüse] bunch.

Bündel (*pl* -) *das* - 1. [von Wäsche, Anträgen] bundle; [von Geldscheinen] wad - 2. [aus Stroh] bale.

bündeln *vt* - 1. [Heu, Stroh] to bale - 2. [Kleidung, Papier, Banknoten] to tie into bundles - 3. [Produkte] to combine.

Bundesbahn ▷ **Deutsche Bahn**.

Bundesbürger, in *der, die* German citizen.

Bundesgrenzschutz *der* (ohne pl) German border police.

Bundeskanzler, in *der, die* German chancellor.

Bundesland *das* federal state; **die alten/neuen Bundesländer** the old/new federal states.

Bundesliga *die* German national league for football, ice hockey etc.

Bundespost ▷ **Deutsche Bundespost**.

Bundespräsident, in *der, die* - 1. [in Deutschland, Österreich] president - 2. [in der Schweiz] chair of the "Bundesrat".

Bundesrat *der* (ohne pl) [Parlament] Bundesrat, upper chamber of the German Parliament, made up of representatives from each of the German states.

Bundesregierung *die* German ODER federal government.

Bundesrepublik *die* - 1. [Föderation] federal republic - 2. ▷ **Bundesrepublik Deutschland**.

Bundesrepublik Deutschland *die* Federal Republic of Germany.

Bundesstaat *der* federal state.

Bundesstraße *die* ≃ A road UK, ≃ state highway US.

Bundestag ▷ **Deutsche Bundestag**.

Bundeswehr *die* German army.

bundesweit *adj & adv* nationwide (in Germany, Austria).

bündig ◇ *adj* [kurz] concise. ◇ *adv* [kurz] concisely.

Bündnis (*pl* -se) *das* alliance.

Bungalow ['buŋgalo] (*pl* -s) *der* bungalow.

Bunker (*pl* -) *der* [Schutzraum] bunker.

bunt ◇ *adj* - 1. [vielfarbig] colourful - 2. [abwechslungsreich] [Programm] varied; **eine bunte Mischung** a motley assortment; **ein bunter Abend** a social evening - 3. [durcheinander] mixed-up; **jetzt wirds mir zu bunt** I've had enough. ◇ *adv* - 1. [vielfarbig] colourfully - 2. [abwechslungsreich]: **bunt gemischt** assorted; **es zu bunt treiben** to overdo it.

Buntstift *der* coloured pencil.

Burg (*pl* -en) *die* - 1. [Gebäude] castle - 2. [Sandburg] circular wall of sand built on beach by holidaymakers to mark off the area where they are sitting.

Bürge (*pl* -n) *der* guarantee.

bürgen *vi*: **für jn/etw bürgen** *fig* to vouch for sb/sthg; **für jn bürgen** WIRTSCH to stand surety for sb.

Bürger, in (*mpl* -, *fpl* -nen) *der, die* - 1. [Einwohner] citizen - 2. [Mittelständler] middle-class person.

Bürgerinitiative *die* [Gruppe] grass-roots pressure group.

Bürgerkrieg *der* civil war.

bürgerlich ◇ *adj* - 1. [staatlich] civil - 2. [des Bürgertums - Partei, Familie] middle-class; [- Küche] traditional - 3. HIST & POL [spießig] bourgeois. <> *adv* [wie das Bürgertum]: **Ulm ist eine bürgerlich geprägte Stadt** Ulm is a middle-class city.

Bürger|meister, in *der, die* mayor. ◆ **Regierende Bürgermeister** *der* mayor and leader of local government.

Bürgersteig (*pl* **-e**) *der* pavement *UK*, sidewalk *US*.

Bürgertum *das* bourgeoisie.

Bürgschaft (*pl* **-en**) *die* surety.

Büro [by'ro:] (*pl* **-s**) *das* office.

Büro|klammer *die* paper clip.

bürokratisch <> *adj* bureaucratic. <> *adv* bureaucratically.

Bursche (*pl* **-n**) *der* - **1.** [Junge] lad - **2.** [Prachtexemplar]: **ein prächtiger Bursche** a magnificent specimen.

burschikos *adj* [Frau] mannish; [Mädchen] boyish.

Bürste (*pl* **-n**) *die* [Gerät] brush.

bürsten *vt* to brush; **sich** (*D*) **die Haare bürsten** to brush one's hair.

Bus (*pl* **-se**) *der* - **1.** [Omnibus] bus - **2.** [Reisebus] bus, coach *UK*.

Busch (*pl* **Büsche**) *der* [Strauch, Zone] bush.

Büschel (*pl* **-**) *das* [von Gras, Haaren] tuft; [von Stroh] bundle.

buschig *adj* bushy.

Busen (*pl* **-**) *der* bosom.

Bus|fahrer, in *der, die* - **1.** [von Omnibus] bus driver - **2.** [von Reisebus] bus driver, coach driver *UK*.

Bushalte|stelle *die* bus stop.

Business Class *die* (*ohne pl*) business class.

Bussard (*pl* **-e**) *der* buzzard.

büßen <> *vt* - **1.** [Sünden] to atone for - **2.** [Untat] to pay for. <> *vi* - **1.** RELIG: **für etw büßen** to atone for sthg - **2.** [bestraft werden]: **für etw büßen** to pay for sthg.

Buß|geld *das* fine.

Buß- und Bet|tag *der* Day of Prayer and Repentance, *German public holiday in November*.

Büste (*pl* **-n**) *die* bust.

Büsten|halter *der* bra.

Butike = **Boutique**.

Butter *die* butter.

Butter|brot *das* slice of bread and butter.

Butter|dose *die* butter dish.

Butter|milch *die* buttermilk.

BWL [be:ve:'ɛl] (*abk für* **Betriebswirtschaftslehre**) *die* business studies.

Byzanz *nt* HIST Byzantium.

bzg. (*abk für* **bezüglich**) re.

bzw. *abk für* **beziehungsweise**.

C

c (*pl* **-** ODER **-s**), **C** (*pl* **-** ODER **-s**) [tse:] *das* - **1.** [Buchstabe] c, C - **2.** MUS C. ◆ **C** (*abk für* **Celsius**) C.

ca. (*abk für* **circa**) approx.

Cabaret [kaba're:] (*pl* **-s**) *das* cabaret.

Cabrio ['ka:brio] (*pl* **-s**) *das* = **Kabrio**.

Café [ka'fe:] (*pl* **-s**) *das* cafe.

Cafeteria [kafetə'ri:a] (*pl* **-s**) *die* cafeteria.

Callcenter ['kɔ:lsɛntɐ] (*pl* **-s**) *das* TELEKOM call centre.

Calzium ['kaltsjʊm] *das* = **Kalzium**.

campen ['kɛmpn̩] *vi* to camp.

Camping ['kɛmpɪŋ] *das* camping; **zum Camping fahren** to go camping.

Campus *der* (*ohne Pl*) campus.

canceln ['kɛnsl̩n] (*präs* **cancelt**, *prät* **cancelte**, *perf* **hat gecancelt**) *vt* to cancel.

Cape [ke:p] (*pl* **-s**) *das* cape.

Carsharing *das* car sharing.

CB-|Funker [tse:'be:fʊŋkɐ] *der* CB ham.

CD [tse:'de:] (*pl* **-s**) (*abk für* **Compactdisc**) *die* CD.

CD-Brenner (*pl* **-**) *der* CD burner.

CD-ROM [tse:de:'rɔm] (*pl* **-**) (*abk für* **Compact Disk read only memory**) *die* EDV CD-ROM.

CD-Spieler [tse:'de:ʃpi:lɐ] (*pl* **-**) *der* CD player.

CDU [tse:de:'u:] (*abk für* **Christlich-Demokratische Union**) *die* Christian Democratic Union, *major German political party to the right of the political spectrum*.

C-Dur ['tse:du:ɐ] *das* C major.

Cello ['tʃɛlo] (*pl* **-s**) *das* cello.

Celsius ['tsɛlzjʊs] Celsius, centigrade; **10 Grad Celsius** 10 degrees Celsius ODER centigrade.

Cent [(t)sɛnt] (*pl* **-s** ODER **-**) *der* - **1.** [in EU] (euro)cent - **2.** (*pl* **Cents**) [in USA] cent.

Chamäleon [ka'mɛ:leɔn] (*pl* **-s**) *das* chameleon.

Champagner [ʃam'panjɐ] (*pl* **-**) *der* champagne.

Champignon ['ʃampɪnjɔŋ] (*pl* **-s**) *der* mushroom.

Chance ['ʃɑ̃:s(ə)] (*pl* **-n**) *die* [Möglichkeit] chance; **jm eine Chance geben** to give sb a chance.

Chaos ['ka:ɔs] *das* chaos.

chaotisch [ka'o:tɪʃ] <> *adj* chaotic. <> *adv* chaotically.

Charakter [ka'raktɐ] (*pl* **-tere**) *der* character.

charakterisieren [karakteri'zi:rən] *vt* to characterize.

Charakteristik [karakte'rıstık] *(pl -en) die* characteristic.

charakteristisch [karakte'rıstıʃ] <> *adj* characteristic; **für jn/etw charakteristisch sein** to be characteristic of sb/sthg. <> *adv* characteristically.

charakterlich [ka'rakteliç] *adj:* **charakterliche Schwäche** weakness of character.

charakterlos [ka'rakteloːs] <> *adj* unprincipled. <> *adv* without principle.

charmant, scharmant [ʃar'mant] <> *adj* charming. <> *adv* charmingly.

Charme, Scharm [ʃarm] *der* charm.

Charterflug ['tʃartefluːk] *der* charter flight.

Chartermaschine *die* charter plane.

chartern ['tʃarten] *vt* to charter.

Chat [tʃɛt] *(pl -s) der* EDV chat.

Chatroom ['tʃɛt,ruːm] *(pl -s) der* EDV chatroom.

Chauvinismus [ʃovi'nısmus] *der abw* chauvinism.

chauvinistisch [ʃovi'nıstıʃ] *abw* <> *adj* chauvinist. <> *adv* chauvinistically.

checken ['tʃɛkn] *vt* - 1. [untersuchen] to check - 2. *salopp* [verstehen]: **sie checkt es einfach nicht!** she just doesn't get it!

Chef [ʃɛf] *(pl -s) der* [von Firma, Mafiosi] boss; [von Organisation] head.

Chefarzt *der* senior consultant *UK,* specialist *US.*

Cheflärztin *die* senior consultant *UK,* specialist *US.*

Chefin *(pl -nen) die* [von Firma] boss; [von Organisation] head.

Chefredakteur, in *der, die* editor-in-chief.

Chemie [çe'miː] *die (ohne pl)* - 1. [Wissenschaft] chemistry - 2. *fam* [Chemikalien] chemicals *Pl.*

Chemikalie [çemi'kaːljə] *(pl -n) die* chemical.

Chemiker, in ['çeːmike, rın] *(mpl -, fpl -nen) der, die* chemist.

chemisch ['çeːmıʃ] <> *adj* [Reaktion, Zusammensetzung] chemical; **chemisches Labor** chemistry lab; **chemische Reinigung** drycleaning. <> *adv* chemically; **chemisch reinigen** to dry-clean.

Chemotherapie [çemotera'piː] *(pl -n) die* chemotherapy.

Chicorée, Schikoree ['ʃikore] *die ODER der* chicory.

Chiffre ['ʃifrə] *(pl -n) die* - 1. [Zeichen] (code) symbol - 2. [von Anzeigen] box number.

chiffrieren [ʃi'friːrən] *vt* to encode.

Chile ['tʃiːle] *nt* Chile.

Chili ['tʃiːli] *(pl -s) der* - 1. [Schote] chilli (pepper) - 2. [Gewürz] chilli (powder).

China ['çiːna] *nt* China.

Chinakohl *der (ohne pl)* Chinese leaves *Pl UK,* bok choy *US.*

Chinese [çi'neːzə] *(pl -n) der* Chinese (man).

Chinesin [çi'neːzin] *(pl -nen) die* Chinese (woman).

chinesisch [çi'neːzıʃ] *adj* Chinese.

Chinin [çi'niːn] *das* quinine.

Chip [tʃip] *(pl -s) der* [beim Spiel, ELEKTR & EDV] chip.

Chips [tʃips] *Pl* crisps *UK,* chips *US.*

Chirurg [çi'rurk] *(pl -en) der* surgeon.

Chirurgie [çirur'giː] *(pl -n) die* - 1. [Wissenschaft] surgery - 2. [Krankenhausabteilung] surgical unit; **auf der Chirurgie liegen** to be in surgery.

Chirurgin [çi'rurgin] *(pl -nen) die* surgeon.

chirurgisch [çi'rurgıʃ] <> *adj* surgical. <> *adv* surgically.

Chlor [kloːɐ] *das* chlorine.

Cholesterin [koleste'riːn] *das* cholesterol.

Chor [koːɐ] *(pl Chöre) der* MUS & ARCHIT choir; **im Chor** in chorus.

Choreografie *(pl -n),* **Choreographie** *(pl -n)* [koreogra'fiː] *die* choreography.

Christ ['krıst] *(pl -en) der* Christian.

Christbaum *der* Christmas tree.

Christdemokrat, in *der, die* Christian Democrat.

Christentum ['krıstntuːm] *das* Christianity.

Christi Himmelfahrt *(ohne Artikel)* [Feiertag] Ascension Day.

Christin ['krıstin] *(pl -nen) die* Christian.

Christkind *das* - 1. [Jesuskind] baby Jesus, Christ Child - 2. [zu Weihnachten] ≃ Santa Claus.

christlich ['krıstlıç] <> *adj* Christian. <> *adv:* **christlich handeln** to act like a Christian.

Christus ['krıstus] *der* Christ.

Chrom [kroːm] *das* [als Überzug] chrome; CHEM chromium.

Chromosom [kromo'zoːm] *(pl -en) das* chromosome.

Chronik ['kroːnık] *(pl -en) die* chronicle.

chronisch ['kroːnıʃ] *adj* chronic.

chronologisch [krono'loːgıʃ] <> *adj* chronological. <> *adv* chronologically.

circa ['tsırka] *adv* = zirka.

clever ['klɛvɐ] <> *adj* clever, smart. <> *adv* cleverly, smartly.

Clique ['klıka] *(pl -n) die* - 1. [Gruppe] group of friends - 2. *abw* [Interessengemeinschaft] clique; [von Verbrechern] gang.

Clown, in [klaun, ın] *(mpl -s, fpl -nen) der, die* clown.

Club = Klub.

cm *(abk für Zentimeter)* cm.

c-Moll ['tseːmɔl] *das* MUS C minor.

Cocktail ['kɔkteːl] *(pl -s) der* cocktail.

Code ['koːt] *(pl -s) der* = Kode.

Cognac® ['kɔnjak] (pl -s) der cognac.

Cola ['koːla] (pl -s) die ODER das Coke®.

Comer See ['koːmɐ 'zeː] der Lake Como.

Comic ['kɔmɪk] (pl -s) der - 1. [Geschichte] cartoon - 2. [Heft] comic.

Computer [kɔm'pjuːtɐ] (pl -) der computer.

Computer|spiel das computer game.

Container [kɔn'teːnɐ] (pl -) der [gen] container; [für Altglas, Papier] bank.

contra ['kɔntra] präp = **kontra**.

Cord [kɔrt] der = **Kord**.

Couch [kautʃ] (pl -en) die couch.

Count-down ['kaunt'daun] (pl -s) das & der countdown.

Cousin [ku'zɛ̃] (pl -s) der cousin.

Cousine (pl -n), **Kusine** (pl -n) [ku'ziːnə] die cousin.

Cowboy ['kaubɔy] (pl -s) der cowboy.

Creme [kreːm] (pl -s ODER -n), **Krem** [kreːm] (pl -s) die - 1. [Hautcreme] cream - 2. [Speise] confectioner's custard.

cremig, kremig ['kreːmɪç] <> adj creamy. <> adv: etw cremig schlagen to cream sthg.

Crew [kruː] (pl -s) die [Besatzung] crew.

CSU [tseːɛs'uː] (abk für Christlich-Soziale Union) die Christian Social Union, Bavarian political party to the right of the political spectrum, long-time alliance partners of the CDU.

Cup [kap] (pl -s) der SPORT cup.

Curry ['kœri] (pl -s) das - 1. [Gewürz] curry powder - 2. [Gericht] curry.

Curry|wurst die sausage with curry sauce.

CVP [tseːfaupeː] (abk für Christliche Volkspartei (der Schweiz)) die Popular Christian Democratic Party, right-wing political party in Switzerland.

Cyberspace ['saibɐspeɪs] der (ohne pl) cyberspace.

D

d (pl - ODER -s), **D** (pl - ODER -s) [deː] das - 1. [Buchstabe] d, D - 2. MUS D.

da <> adv - 1. [dort] there; **guck mal da!** look over there!; **da kommt der Bus!** here comes the bus!; **das da gefällt mir am besten** I like that one best; **da drüben** over there - 2. [hier] here; **da bin ich!** here I am!; **ist noch etwas Brot da?** is there any bread left?; **ich bin gleich wieder da** I'll be back in a minute - 3. [in diesem Zusammenhang]: **da fällt mir ein** I've just thought - 4. [in dieser Beziehung] there; **da irren**

Sie sich you're wrong there - 5. [unter dieser Bedingung] in that case; **da gehe ich lieber gleich** in that case I'd rather go straight away. <> konj [weil] as, since; **da ihr Vater krank war, musste sie zu Hause bleiben** as her father was ill, she had to stay at home.

DAAD [deːaːaː'deː] (abk für Deutscher Akademischer Austauschdienst) der German Academic Exchange Service, cultural body which organizes academic exchanges for students and staff.

da|behalten vt (unreg) to keep (in ODER back).

dabei, dabei adv - 1. [räumlich]: **waren Sie bei der Auktion dabei?** were you at the auction?; **hast du zufällig eine Briefmarke dabei?** do you happen to have a stamp on you?; **nicht dabei sein** to be missing; **ich bin dabei!** fig count me in! - 2. [zeitlich] at the same time; **sie waren gerade dabei, das Haus zu verlassen** they were just leaving the house - 3. [bei dieser Sache]: **dabei kam heraus, dass...** in the process it came out that...; **mir ist nicht ganz wohl dabei (zumute)** I don't really feel happy about it; **und dabei bleibts!** and that's the end of it!; **es ist nichts dabei** fam fig there's nothing wrong with it - 4. [obwohl] although - 5. [überdies]: **und dabei ist sie auch noch intelligent** and (what is more) she's clever too; **siehe auch dabei sein.**

dabei|haben vt (unreg) [Person] to have with one; [Gegenstand] to have on one; **sie wollten ihn nicht dabeihaben** they didn't want him there.

dabei sein (perf ist dabei gewesen) vi (unreg) - 1. [anwesend sein] to be present ODER there - 2. [im Begriff sein]: **dabei sein, etw zu tun** to be just doing sthg.

da|bleiben (perf ist dageblieben) vi (unreg) to stay.

Dach (pl Dächer) das roof; **das Dach decken** to roof the house; **unterm Dach wohnen** to live in the attic.

Dach|boden der attic; **auf dem Dachboden** in the attic.

Dach|luke die skylight.

Dach|rinne die gutter.

Dachs [daks] (pl -e) der badger.

dachte prät ▷ **denken**.

Dach|ziegel der roof tile.

Dackel (pl -) der dachshund.

Dadaismus [dada'ɪsmus] der Dadaism.

dadurch, dadurch adv - 1. [auf diese Art] because of this; **dadurch, dass... because...**; **dadurch, dass wir uns viel Mühe gaben** because we tried very hard; **dadurch kam es, dass...** that was why... - 2. [räumlich] through it.

dafür, dafür adv - 1. [für etwas] for it; **30 Euro dafür bezahlen** to pay 30 euros for it; **er kann nichts dafür** it's not his fault; **er hat kein Ver-**

ständnis dafür he has no feeling for that - **2.** [bejahend] for it, in favour of it; **dafür spricht, dass** this is confirmed by the fact that - **3.** [als Ausgleich]: **er arbeitet langsam, dafür aber gründlich** he works slowly yet thoroughly - **4.** [im Tausch] in exchange.

dafür|können *vt* (*unreg*): **nichts dafürkönnen** not to be able to help it; **ich kann doch nichts dafür, dass der Zug zu spät kommt!** it's not my fault if the train is late!

DAG [de:ɑ:'ge:] (*abk für* **Deutsche Angestellten Gewerkschaft**) *die* German white-collar union.

dagegen, dagegen *adv* - **1.** [räumlich] against it; **das Auto fuhr dagegen** the car drove into it - **2.** [ablehnend] against it; **etwas dagegen haben** to object; **hast du etwas dagegen, wenn ich rauche?** do you mind if I smoke?; **dagegen lässt sich nichts machen** nothing can be done about it - **3.** [im Gegensatz] in comparison; **sie ist groß, er dagegen ist klein** she's tall, whereas he is short; **dieser ist nichts dagegen!** this is nothing in comparison!

da gewesen <> *pp* ⊳ **da sein**. <> *adj*: **noch nie da gewesen** unheard of.

Daheim *das Südtt, Österr & Schweiz* home.

daher, daher *adv* - **1.** [aus dieser Richtung] from there; **ach, daher weht (also) der Wind!** *fig* so that's the way the wind is blowing! - **2.** [deswegen] that is why; **daher (auch) der Name** hence the name; **daher der ganze Ärger** that's the reason for all the hassle; **daher kommt es, dass...** that is why/how...

dahin, dahin <> *adv* - **1.** [räumlich] there - **2.** [zeitlich]: **bis dahin** until then; **bis dahin sind wir fertig** we'll be ready by then - **3.** [als Ziel]: **seine Bemühungen gehen dahin, sich selbstständig zu machen** he's trying to set up his own business. <> *adj fam* [kaputt, beendet, weg]: **das Kleid ist dahin!** the dress has had it!; **meine Träume sind dahin** my dreams have been shattered.

dahingestellt *pp*: **es bleibt** ODER **sei dahingestellt** it remains to be seen.

dahinten *adv* back there, over there.

dahinter *adv eigtl & fig* behind it.

dahinter kommen (*perf ist dahinter gekommen*) *vi* (*unreg*) *fam* to find out.

dahinter stecken *vi* to be behind it.

dahinter stehen *vi* (*unreg*) to be behind it.

damalig *adj* [Bedingungen, Zustände] at that time; **der damalige Präsident** the then president.

damals *adv* then, in those days; **als ich damals krank wurde** when I got ill; **seit damals** since then.

Damast (*pl* -e) *der* damask.

Dame (*pl* -n) *die* - **1.** [Frau] lady; **der Wettbewerb der Damen** the women's competition;

meine (sehr verehrten) Damen und Herren ladies and gentlemen - **2.** [Spielkarte] queen - **3.** [Spiel] draughts (*U*). ➤ **Damen** *Pl* [Toilette] ladies (*sg*).

Damen|binde *die* sanitary towel *UK*, sanitary napkin *US*.

damenhaft <> *adj* ladylike. <> *adv* like a lady.

Damen|toilette *die* ladies (toilet).

damit, damit <> *konj* so that. <> *adv* - **1.** [mit dieser Sache]: **was soll ich damit?** what am I supposed to do with this?; **sie war damit einverstanden** she agreed to it; **was meinst du damit?** what do you mean by that?; **her damit!** *fam* hand it over!; **hör auf damit!** *fam* stop it! - **2.** [somit] because of that.

dämlich *fam abw* <> *adj* stupid. <> *adv* stupidly.

Damm (*pl* Dämme) *der* [Deich] dam; **wieder auf dem Damm sein** *fam fig* to be up and about again.

dämmern *vi* - **1.** [einsetzen]: **es dämmert** [am Morgen] it's getting light, day is breaking; [am Abend] it's getting dark, night is falling - **2.** [halb schlafen]: **(vor sich hin) dämmern** to doze - **3.** *fam* [bewusst werden]: **eine Ahnung dämmerte ihm** a suspicion dawned on him.

Dämmerung (*pl* -en) *die* [am Morgen] dawn; [am Abend] dusk.

dämmrig, dämmerig *adj* [Licht] dim; [Tag] gloomy, dull.

Dämon (*pl* Dämonen) *der* demon.

dämonisch *adj* demonic.

Dampf (*pl* Dämpfe) *der* [Dunst] steam; **giftige Dämpfe** poisonous fumes; **jm Dampf machen** *fam* to make sb get a move on.

Dampf|bad *das* steam bath, Turkish bath.

dampfen *vi* to steam.

dämpfen *vt* - **1.** [dünsten] to steam - **2.** [Geräusch, Schritte] to muffle; [Instrument, Farbton] to mute; [Licht] to dim; [Stoß] to cushion; [Stimme] to lower - **3.** [Wut, Aufregung] to calm; [Begeisterung] to dampen - **4.** [verringern] to curb.

Dampfer (*pl* -) *der* steamship, steamer.

Dämpfer (*pl* -) *der*: **jm einen Dämpfer aufsetzen** ODER **verpassen** to dampen sb's spirits.

Dampf|maschine *die* steam engine.

Dampf|walze *die* steamroller.

danach, danach *adv* - **1.** [zeitlich] after, afterwards; **zwei Stunden danach** two hours later; **wir können doch erst ins Theater gehen und danach etwas essen** why don't we go to the theatre first and eat afterwards? - **2.** [nach etwas]: **danach schnappen/greifen** to snap/grab at it; **sich danach sehnen** to long for it; **ich habe danach gefragt** I asked about it - **3.** [entsprechend]: **es sieht ganz danach aus** it looks like it; **mir ist jetzt nicht danach (zumute)** I don't feel like it at the moment.

Däne (*pl* -n) *der* Dane.

daneben adv - 1. [räumlich] next to it/him/etc, beside it/him/etc; **gleich daneben** right next to it - 2. [vergleichend] in comparison - 3. [außerdem] in addition (to that).

daneben|benehmen (unreg) ⟺ **sich danebenbenehmen** ref to make an exhibition of o.s.

daneben|gehen (perf ist danebengegangen) vi (unreg) - 1. [danebenzielen] to miss (the target) - 2. fam [misslingen] to fail.

Dänemark nt Denmark.

Dänin (pl -nen) die Dane.

dänisch adj Danish.

dank präp: **dank einer Sache** (G) thanks to sthg.

Dank der (ohne pl) thanks Pl; **zum Dank dafür** as a reward, by way of saying thank you; **vielen Dank!** thank you (very much)!; **schönen** ODER **besten Dank auch!** thank you (very much)!

dankbar ⟨⟩ adj - 1. [voller Dank] grateful; **jm (für etw) dankbar sein** to be grateful to sb (for sthg) - 2. [lohnend] rewarding. ⟨⟩ adv [voller Dank] gratefully.

Dankbarkeit die gratitude.

danke interj thanks!, thank you!; **danke, dass du gekommen bist!** thanks ODER thank you for coming!; **noch einen Kaffee? - danke, gern/im Moment nicht** would you like another coffee? - yes, please/no thanks ODER no thank you, not just now; **danke gleichfalls!** thanks, you too!; **danke sehr** ODER **schön!** thanks (very much)!, thank you (very much)!

danken vi: **jm (für etw) danken** to thank sb (for sthg); **na, ich danke!** fam no thanks!, no thank you!; **nichts zu danken!** don't mention it!

Dankeschön das thank you.

Dank|schreiben das letter of thanks.

dann adv - 1. [gen] then; **bis dann** see you (then) - 2. [außerdem] then; **und dann (noch)** and, on top of that - 3. [konditional] in that case, then. ⟺ **also dann** interj all right then. ⟺ **dann und dann** adv at such and such time. ⟺ **dann und wann** adv now and then.

daran, daran adv - 1. [an diese Sache]: **ich denke gerade daran** I'm just thinking about it; **er arbeitete lange daran** he worked at ODER on it for a long time; **es ist nichts Wahres daran** there is no truth in it; **mir liegt viel daran** it is very important to me; **er war schuld daran** it was his fault - 2. [räumlich]: **er klebte Papier daran** he stuck paper (on)to it; **wir gingen daran vorbei** we went past it; **nahe daran** close to it - 3. [deshalb]: **sie ist daran gestorben** she died of it; **es liegt daran, dass...** it is because...

daran|setzen vt [Energie, Kraft] to use; **alles daransetzen** to do one's utmost.

darauf, darauf adv - 1. [räumlich] on it - 2. [Richtung]: **darauf zielen** to aim at it; **das deutet darauf hin, dass...** fig this implies that... - 3. [zeitlich] after that; **am Tag darauf** the day after, the next day; **bald darauf** soon after(wards) - 4. [als Reaktion] to that; **darauf steht die Todesstrafe** the penalty for that is death - 5. [zum Ausdruck einer Intention]: **sie ist darauf aus, einen Mann zu bekommen** she's out to get a husband; **sie bestand darauf** she was most particular about it; **besonders darauf achten, dass...** to take particular care to...

daraufhin adv - 1. [aus einem Grund] as a result - 2. [zu einem Zweck]: **das Produkt daraufhin prüfen, ob es den Normen entspricht** to test the product (in order) to see if it meets the standards.

daraus, daraus adv - 1. [räumlich] from it, out of it - 2. [aus dieser Sache] from it; **daraus folgt, dass...** from this it follows that...; **mach dir nichts daraus!** don't let it bother you!; **ich mache mir nichts daraus** I'm not very keen on it; **daraus wird nichts!** fam nothing doing! - 3. [aus einem Material] from it, out of it.

darf präs ⟶ **dürfen**.

darin, darin adv - 1. [in etwas] in it, inside - 2. [in diesem Sachverhalt] there.

dar|legen vt to explain.

Darlehen (pl -) das loan.

Darm (pl Därme) der - 1. [Organ] intestine - 2. [Material] gut.

Darm|infektion die bowel infection.

dar|stellen vt - 1. [Subj: Bild] to portray, to depict - 2. [beschreiben] to describe - 3. [Subj: Schauspieler] to play - 4. [sein] to represent, to constitute; **als Wissenschaftler stellt er etwas dar** he is an impressive scientist.

Darsteller, in (mpl -, fpl -nen) der, die actor (actress die); **der Darsteller des Hamlet** the actor playing Hamlet.

Dar|stellung die - 1. [als Bild] depiction, portrayal; **eine grafische Darstellung** a graphic representation - 2. [Bericht] account.

darüber, darüber adv - 1. [räumlich - über etw] above it, over it; [- über etw hinweg] across it, over it; **darüber hinaus** fig in addition; **darüber sind wir schon hinaus** we have already passed that stage - 2. [über diese Sache] about it; **hast du darüber nachgedacht?** did you think about it?; **ich komme nicht darüber hinweg** I can't get over it; **darüber hinwegsehen** to ignore it - 3. [mehr] above that, over that; **nichts geht darüber!** fig there is nothing to beat it.

darum, darum adv - 1. [räumlich] round it - 2. [um diese Sache] about it; **jn darum bitten, etw zu tun** to ask sb to do sthg; **darum geht es nicht** that's not the point; **es geht darum, dass...** the thing is that... - 3. [deswegen] that's why; **ach darum!** so that's why!; **eben darum** for that very reason; **warum? darum!** *fam* why? because!

darunter, darunter adv - 1. [räumlich] under it; **sie hob das Kissen und fand ihre Kette darunter** she lifted the cushion and found her necklace underneath - 2. [unter dieser Sache]: **er leidet darunter** he suffers from it; **was verstehst du darunter?** what do you understand by that?; **darunter kann ich mir nichts vorstellen** that doesn't mean anything to me - 3. [weniger]: **30 Meter oder etwas darunter** 30 metres or a little less - 4. [in dieser Menge] among(st) them; **viele Besucher, darunter auch einige aus dem Ausland** many visitors, including some foreigners.

das ⟨> *det* the; **das Rauchen** smoking. ⟨> *pron* - 1. [Demonstrativpronomen] that; **das da** that one there; **unser Haus? das haben wir verkauft** our house? we've sold it; **das regnet heute wieder wie verrückt** it's raining like mad again today - 2. [Relativpronomen - Person] who, that; [- Sache] which, that.

da sein (*perf* **ist da gewesen**) *vi* (*unreg*) - 1. [vorhanden sein, anwesend sein] to be there; **es ist keine Milch mehr da** there's no more milk, there's no milk left; **ich bin gleich wieder da** I'll be back in a second - 2. [eingetreten sein - Situation] to arise; [- Augenblick] to arrive; **er überbot alles, was bisher da gewesen war** he surpassed everything which had gone before - 3. [leben] to live - 4. *fam* [wach sein] to be with it; **geistig voll da sein** to be all there.

dalsitzen *vi* (*unreg*) - 1. [an einer Stelle] to sit (there) - 2. *fam* [in einer Situation] to be left (there).

dasjenige ⟨> *det* the; **dasjenige Kind, das hingefallen ist** the child who fell. ⟨> *pron*: **dasjenige, was sie am liebsten tut** the thing she likes to do most; **dasjenige, das** the one which.

dass *konj* - 1. [im Objektsatz] that; **ich weiß, dass du gern angelst** I know (that) you like fishing - 2. [im Subjektsatz] the fact that; **du musst bedenken, dass er nicht mehr klein ist** you must remember (that) he's not young anymore - 3. [im Attributsatz] that; **unter der Bedingung, dass...** on (the) condition that...; **es war eine Dummheit, dass er das gesagt hat** it was stupid of him to say that - 4. [in festen Verbindungen]: **anstatt, dass er selbst kam** instead of coming himself; **ohne dass sie etwas gemerkt hat** without her noticing anything.

dasselbe ⟨> *det* the same. ⟨> *pron* the same one; **genau dasselbe hast du gestern gesagt** you said exactly the same thing yesterday.

dalstehen *vi* (*unreg*) - 1. [an Stelle] to stand (there) - 2. [in Situation] to find o.s.; **mit leeren**

Händen dastehen to be left empty-handed; **gut** *ODER* **glänzend dastehen** to be in a good *ODER* splendid position.

Datei (*pl* -en) *die* EDV file.

Daten *Pl* - 1. [Zeiten] ⟹ **Datum** - 2. [Informationen] data; **Daten verarbeitend** data-processing.

Datenautolbahn *die* EDV information superhighway.

Datenbank (*pl* -en) *die* databank.

Datenlnetz *das*: **das Datennetz** the Net; **im Datennetz** on the Net.

Datenschutzlgesetz *das* data protection law.

Datentypist, in (*mpl* -en, *fpl* -nen) *der, die* data inputter.

Datenlverarbeitung *die* data processing.

datieren *vt* to date.

Dativ (*pl* -e) *der* dative.

Datum (*pl* **Daten**) *das* date; **welches Datum haben wir heute?** what's today's date?

Dauer *die* length; **dieses Glück hatte keine Dauer** this happiness did not last; **auf (die) Dauer** in the long term; **seine Ehe war nicht von Dauer** his marriage was short-lived.

dauerhaft ⟨> *adj* [Friede, Freundschaft] lasting; [Material] durable. ⟨> *adv*: **das Problem dauerhaft lösen** to find a lasting solution to the problem.

Dauerlkarte *die* season ticket.

Dauerllauf *der* jog.

dauern *vi* to last; **es dauert zu lange** it's taking too long; **eine Weile wird es schon noch dauern, bis ich fertig bin** it will still be a while before I'm finished.

dauernd ⟨> *adj* constant. ⟨> *adv* constantly.

Dauerlwelle *die* perm.

Dauerlzustand *der* permanent state.

Däumchen (*pl* -) *das*: **Däumchen drehen** *fam* to twiddle one's thumbs.

Daumen (*pl* -) *der* thumb; **am Daumen lutschen** to suck one's thumb; **jm die Daumen drücken** *ODER* **halten** *fig* to keep one's fingers crossed for sb.

Daune (*pl* -n) *die*: **Daunen** down (*U*).

Daunenldecke *die* eiderdown.

davon, davon adv - 1. [räumlich] from it - 2. [von diesem Gegenstand, aus dieser Menge] of it - 3. [von dieser Sache] about it; **er ist nicht davon betroffen** he is not affected by it; **sie ist davon krank geworden** it made her ill; **das kommt davon!** that's what happens!

davonlkommen (*perf* **ist davongekommen**) *vi* (*unreg*) to escape.

davonllaufen (*perf* **ist davongelaufen**) *vi* (*unreg*) to run away; **jm davonlaufen** [Ehepartner, Hausmädchen] to walk out on sb; [Verfolgter] to shake sb off.

davor, davor adv - 1. [räumlich] in front of it - 2. [zeitlich] beforehand; **kurz davor sein, etw zu tun** to be on the point of doing sthg - 3. [vor dieser Sache]: **jn davor warnen** to warn sb of it; **ich habe Angst davor** I'm scared of it.

dazu, dazu adv - 1. [außerdem] in addition, into the bargain; **es schneit und es ist noch kalt dazu** it's snowing, and it's cold too - 2. [zu dieser Sache]: **er hat nicht die Zeit dazu** he hasn't got time for it; **ich habe keine Lust dazu** I don't feel like it; **ich bin nicht dazu gekommen** I didn't get round to it.

dazu|geben vt (unreg) to add.

dazu|gehören vi - 1. [zu etwas gehören] to belong; **gehört der Drucker dazu?** is the printer included? - 2. [nötig sein]: **es gehört Mut dazu, das zu tun** it takes courage to do that.

dazu|kommen (perf **ist dazugekommen**) vi (unreg) - 1. [ankommen] to arrive - 2. [hinzukommen]: **sie ist neu dazugekommen** she's a recent arrival; **kommt noch etwas dazu?** would you like anything else?

dazu|tun vt (unreg) to add.

dazwischen adv - 1. [örtlich, zeitlich] in between - 2. [dabei] among them.

dazwischen|kommen (perf **ist dazwischengekommen**) vi (unreg) - 1. [dazwischengeraten]: **er kam mit dem Finger dazwischen** he got his finger caught in it - 2. [ungeplant passieren]: **mir ist etw dazwischengekommen** sthg has cropped up.

dazwischen|rufen (unreg) ⟨⟩ vt: **etw dazwischenrufen** to interrupt by shouting sthg. ⟨⟩ vi to interrupt by shouting.

DB (abk für **Deutsche Bahn**) German railway company.

DDR [deːdeːˈʔɛr] (abk für **Deutsche Demokratische Republik**) die GDR.

Dealer, in [ˈdiːlɐ, rɪn] (mpl -, fpl -nen) der, die fam pusher.

Debatte (pl -n) die debate; **zur Debatte stehen** to be on the agenda.

debattieren ⟨⟩ vt to debate. ⟨⟩ vi: **über etw (A) debattieren** to debate sthg.

Deck (pl -s) das deck; **unter Deck gehen** to go below. ◆ **an Deck** adv on deck.

Deck|blatt das title page.

Decke (pl -n) die - 1. [Tischdecke] tablecloth - 2. [zum Zudecken - Wolldecke] blanket; [- Steppdecke] quilt, duvet - 3. [Zimmerdecke] ceiling; **(mit jm) unter einer Decke stecken** to be in cahoots (with sb).

Deckel (pl -) der - 1. [von Gefäßen] lid - 2. [von Büchern] cover.

decken ⟨⟩ vt - 1. [bedecken - Haus] to roof; **das Dach decken** [- mit Ziegeln] to tile the roof; [- mit Stroh] to thatch the roof - 2. [Tisch] to lay, to set - 3. [legen] **die Hand über die Augen decken** to cover one's eyes with one's hand - 4. [schützen - Kind, Körperteil, Rückzug] to cov-

er; [- Komplizen] to cover up for - 5. SPORT to mark - 6. [Bedarf] to meet - 7. WIRTSCH [Zoologie] to cover. ⟨⟩ vi - 1. [den Tisch decken] to lay ODER set the table - 2. [Farbe] to cover. ◆ **sich decken** ref [Dreiecke] to be congruent; [Meinungen] to coincide; [Aussagen] to tally.

Deck|name der assumed name.

Deckung (pl -en) die - 1. [Schutz] cover; **in Deckung gehen** to take cover - 2. SPORT [beim Boxen] guard; [Manndeckung] marking; [Verteidigung] defence - 3. [Befriedigung - von Bedarf] covering; **zur Deckung der Nachfrage** in order to meet demand - 4. [Versicherungsschutz, von Scheck] cover - 5. MATH congruence.

deckungsgleich adj [Dreiecke] congruent; [Ansichten, Theorien] matching.

Decoder [deˈkoːdɐ] (pl -) der ELEKTR decoder.

decodieren = **dekodieren**.

defekt adj faulty, defective.

Defekt (pl -e) der fault, defect.

defensiv [defɛnˈziːf] ⟨⟩ adj defensive; [Fahrweise] safe, careful. ⟨⟩ adv defensively; [fahren] safely, carefully.

definieren vt to define. ◆ **sich definieren** ref to be defined.

Definition (pl -en) die definition.

definitiv ⟨⟩ adj final. ⟨⟩ adv: **sich definitiv entscheiden** to make a final decision; **kannst du mir definitiv sagen, ob du kommst?** can you let me know for sure whether you're coming?

Defizit (pl -e) das - 1. [Fehlbetrag] deficit - 2. [Fehlen] shortage.

deformieren vt to deform.

deftig adj - 1. [nahrhaft] substantial, hearty - 2. [derb] coarse.

Degen (pl -) der rapier.

dehnbar adj [Stoff, Gummi, Begriff] elastic; [Metall] ductile.

dehnen vt - 1. [Substanz, Glieder] to stretch - 2. [Laut] to draw out. ◆ **sich dehnen** ref - 1. [gen] to stretch - 2. [Gespräch, Warten] to drag on.

Deich (pl -e) der dyke.

Deichsel [ˈdaɪksl̩] (pl -n) die shafts Pl.

dein, e det your.

deine, r, s ODER **deins** pron yours.

deiner pron (Genitiv von du) of you; **ich erinnere mich deiner** I remember you.

deinerseits adv - 1. [du selbst] for your part - 2. [von dir] on your part.

deinesgleichen pron people like you; **du und deinesgleichen** you and your like.

deinetwegen adv - 1. [dir zuliebe] for your sake - 2. [wegen dir] because of you.

deinetwillen ◆ **um deinetwillen** adv for your sake.

dekadent adj decadent.

Deklination (pl -en) die declension.

deklinieren *vt* to decline.

dekodieren, decodieren [deko'di:rən] *vt* to decode.

Dekolletee (*pl* -s), **Dekolleté** (*pl* -s) [dekɔl'te:] *das* décolleté.

Dekor (*pl* -s ODER -e) ⬦ *das* & *der* [Verzierung] pattern. ⬦ *das* [im Theater, Film] décor.

Dekoration (*pl* -en) *die* - **1.** [Ausschmückung, Auszeichnung] decoration; [von Schaufenster] window-dressing - **2.** [Kulisse] set.

dekorativ *adj* decorative.

dekorieren *vt* [schmücken, auszeichnen] to decorate; [Schaufenster] to dress.

Delegation (*pl* -en) *die* delegation.

Delegierte (*pl* -n) *der, die* delegate.

Delfin (*pl* -e) *der* = **Delphin**.

delikat ⬦ *adj* - **1.** [Speise] delicious - **2.** [Person, Angelegenheit, Lage] delicate. ⬦ *adv* [behutsam] delicately.

Delikatesse (*pl* -n) *die* [Leckerbissen] delicacy.

Delikt (*pl* -e) *das* offence; **ein Delikt begehen** to commit an offence.

Delle (*pl* -n) *die* dent.

Delphin (*pl* -e), **Delfin** (*pl* -e) ⬦ *der* [Säugetier] dolphin. ⬦ *das (ohne Pl)* [Sportart] butterfly.

Delta (*pl* -s) *das* delta.

dem ⬦ *det (Dativ Singular von der, das)*: **mit dem Kind** with the child. ⬦ *pron (Dativ Singular)* - **1.** [Demonstrativ von der, das - Person] to him; [- Sache] to that one; **mit dem** [- Person] with him; [- Sache] with that one - **2.** [Relativpronomen von der, das - Person] to whom; [- Sache] to which; **mit dem** [- Person] with whom; [- Sache] with which.

demaskieren *vt* [entlarven] to unmask.

dementsprechend ⬦ *adj* appropriate. ⬦ *adv* accordingly.

demgegenüber *adv* on the other hand.

demgemäß *adv* accordingly.

demnach *adv* so.

demnächst [de:m'nɛ:st] *adv* soon.

Demokrat (*pl* -en) *der* democrat.

Demokratie (*pl* -n) *die* democracy.

Demokratin (*pl* -nen) *die* democrat.

demokratisch ⬦ *adj* democratic. ⬦ *adv* democratically.

demolieren *vt* to wreck.

Demonstrant, in (*mpl* -en, *fpl* -nen) *der, die* demonstrator.

Demonstration (*pl* -en) *die* demonstration.

demonstrativ *adj* - **1.** [betont auffällig] pointed - **2.** [anschaulich] revealing.

Demonstrativ|pronomen *das* GRAMM demonstrative pronoun.

demonstrieren ⬦ *vi* to demonstrate; **gegen/für etw demonstrieren** to demonstrate against/in support of sthg. ⬦ *vt* to demonstrate.

demoskopisch ⬦ *adj* opinion poll (*vor Subst*); **demoskopische Untersuchung** opinion poll. ⬦ *adv* through opinion polls.

demütig *adj* - **1.** [ergeben] humble - **2.** [unterwürfig] submissive.

demütigen *vt* to humiliate. ◈ **sich demütigen** *ref* to humiliate o.s.

Demütigung (*pl* -en) *die* humiliation.

demzufolge *adv* consequently.

den ⬦ *det* - **1.** *(Akkusativ Singular von der)* the - **2.** *(Dativ Plural von der, die, das)* to the; **mit den Kindern** with the children. ⬦ *pron (Akkusativ Singular)* - **1.** [Demonstrativ von der - Person] him; [- Sache] that one - **2.** [Relativpronomen von der - Person] which.

denen *pron (Dativ Plural)* - **1.** [Demonstrativ von der, die, das] to them; **mit denen** with them - **2.** [Relativpronomen von der, die, das - Personen] to whom; [- Sachen] to which; **mit denen** [- Personen] with whom; [- Sachen] with which.

Denglisch *das* language made up of a mixture of German and English.

Den Haag *nt* The Hague.

denkbar ⬦ *adj* [vorstellbar] conceivable; **nicht denkbar** unthinkable. ⬦ *adv* [äußerst] extremely; **die denkbar besten/schlechtesten Bedingungen** the best/worst conditions imaginable.

denken (*prät* **dachte**, *perf* **hat gedacht**) ⬦ *vi* - **1.** [gen] to think; **es gab mir zu denken** it made me think; **ich denke nicht** I don't think so; **denkst du, er schafft das?** do you think he'll manage?; **an jn/etw denken** to think of sb/sthg; **denk an den Kaffee!** don't forget the coffee!; **er denkt immer nur an sich** he always thinks about himself - **2.** [planen]: **an etw (A) denken** to think about sthg; **ich denke nicht daran, das zu tun** I have no intention of doing it. ⬦ *vt* - **1.** [gen] to think; **wer hätte das gedacht!** who would have thought it! - **2.** [sich vorstellen]: **das hätte ich mir denken können** I might have known; **das habe ich mir schon gedacht!** I thought as much!

denkfaul *adj* mentally lazy; **sei nicht so denkfaul** use your brain.

Denk|fehler *der* mistake in one's reasoning; **einen Denkfehler machen** to make a mistake in one's reasoning.

Denkmal (*pl* -mäler ODER -e) *das* [Monument] monument; **sich (D) ein Denkmal setzen** to ensure one's place in history.

denkmalgeschützt *adj* listed.

Denkmalspflege, Denkmalpflege *die* preservation of historical monuments.

Denkmalsschutz, Denkmalschutz *der* protection of historical monuments.

Denk|weise *die* way of thinking.

denkwürdig *adj* memorable.

Denk|zettel *der* lesson; **jm einen Denkzettel geben** ODER **verpassen** to teach sb a lesson.

denn ⬦ *konj* [weil] because. ⬦ *adv* - 1. [verstärkend] then; **was hast du denn?** so what's wrong?; **warum denn nicht?** why not?; **was ist denn eigentlich passiert?** so what actually happened? - 2. [dann] then.

dennoch *adv* nevertheless.

Deo (*pl* -s) *das* deodorant.

Deodorant (*pl* -s ODER -e) *das* deodorant.

Deponie (*pl* -n) *die* dump.

deponieren *vt* to deposit.

Depp [dεp] (*pl* -en) *der Österr, Schweiz & Süddt fam* twit.

Depression (*pl* -en) *die* depression; **an** ODER **unter Depressionen (D) leiden** to suffer from depression.

depressiv *adj* - 1. MED depressive - 2. [Situation, Stimmung] depressing.

der ⬦ *det* - 1. [Nominativ] the; **der Tod death** - 2. [Genitiv] of the; **der Hut der Frau** the woman's hat; **der Duft der Rosen** the fragrance of the roses - 3. [Dativ] the. ⬦ *pron* - 1. [Demonstrativpronomen - Person] he; **der war es** it was him; **der hat es getan** he did it; **unser Sohn? der geht schon längst in die Schule** our son? he's been at school for a long time - 2. [Demonstrativpronomen - Sache] that one; **der Wein? der war fantastisch** the wine? it was great; **der und der so-and-so** - 3. [Relativpronomen - Person] who, that; [- Sache] which, that; **die Frau, der ich das Buch gab** the woman I gave the book to, the woman to whom I gave the book.

derart *adv* so; **es hat lange nicht mehr derart geregnet** it's a long time since it rained so much; **ein derart teures Auto kann ich mir nicht leisten** I can't afford such an expensive car. ⬦ **derart, dass** *konj* so that.

derartig *adj* such; **eine derartige Frechheit** such (a) cheek.

derb ⬦ *adj* - 1. [kräftig - Stoß, Schlag] hefty; [- Leder] tough - 2. [grob] coarse, crude. ⬦ *adv* - 1. [fest] roughly - 2. [grob] crudely.

deren *det* - 1. [Genitiv Singular von die - Person] her; [- Sache] its - 2. [Genitiv Plural von die, der, das] their - 3. [Relativpronomen - Person] whose; [- Sache] of which.

derentwegen ⬦ *adv* - 1. [ihr zuliebe] for her sake; [ihnen zuliebe] for their sake - 2. [wegen ihr] because of her; [wegen ihnen] because of them. ⬦ *pron* - 1. [der, denen zuliebe - Person] for whose sake; [- Sache] for the sake of which - 2. [wegen der, denen - Person] because of whom; [- Sache] because of which.

dergleichen *pron* that sort of thing.

derjenige ⬦ *det*: **derjenige Mensch, der** the person who. ⬦ *pron*: **derjenige, der das getan hat** whoever did this; **von allen Posten erfordert derjenige des Vorsitzenden besonders viel Einsatz** of all the jobs, the chairman's is the one which requires the most effort; **von allen Teilnehmern erhält derjenige den Preis, der** the prize goes to the contestant who.

dermaßen ⬦ **dermaßen, dass** *konj* so that.

derselbe ⬦ *det* the same. ⬦ *pron* the same one.

derzeit *adv* at the moment, at present.

derzeitig *adj* current.

des *det* (Genitiv von der, das) of the; **der Schwanz des Hundes** the dog's tail.

desertieren (*perf* ist desertiert) *vi* to desert.

desgleichen *adv* likewise.

deshalb *adv* therefore. ⬦ **deshalb, weil** *konj* because.

Desinfektions|mittel *das* disinfectant.

desinfizieren *vt* to disinfect.

Desktop-Publishing ['dεsktɔppʌblɪʃɪŋ] *das* (ohne pl) EDV desktop publishing.

dessen *pron* - 1. [Genitiv Singular von der, das - Person] his; [- Sache] its - 2. [Relativpronomen von der, das - Person] whose; [- Sache] of which.

Dessert [dε'se:ɐ̯] (*pl* -s) *das* dessert; **zum Dessert** for dessert.

destillieren *vt* to distil.

desto *konj*: **je eher, desto besser!** the sooner, the better!

deswegen *adv* therefore; **er ist krank und kann deswegen nicht kommen** he's ill, which is why he can't come; **er ist gerade deswegen nicht gekommen** that's precisely the reason he didn't come; **ach, deswegen!** oh, that's why! ODER **the reason!**; **deswegen, weil** because.

Detail [de'tai] (*pl* -s) *das* detail. ⬦ **im Detail** *adv* [detailliert] in detail.

detailliert ⬦ *adj* detailed. ⬦ *adv* in detail.

Detektiv, in (*mpl* -e, *fpl* -nen) *der, die* detective.

deuten ⬦ *vt* [auslegen] to interpret; [Sterne] to read. ⬦ *vi* - 1. [zeigen]: **auf jn/etw deuten** to point at sb/sthg - 2. [schließen lassen]: **auf etw (A) deuten** to point to sthg, to indicate sthg.

deutlich ⬦ *adj* - 1. [klar erkennbar, leicht verständlich] clear; **jm etw deutlich machen** to make sthg clear to sb - 2. [rücksichtslos offen] blunt; **deutlich werden** to speak one's mind. ⬦ *adv* - 1. [klar, verständlich] clearly - 2. [rücksichtslos offen] bluntly.

Deutlichkeit *die* - 1. [Klarheit] clarity - 2. [Offenheit] bluntness. ⬦ **mit aller Deutlichkeit** *adv* [nachdrücklich] quite clearly.

deutsch ◇ adj German. ◇ adv [in deutscher Sprache] in German; siehe auch **englisch**.

Deutsch das German.

Deutsche (pl -n) ◇ der, die [Person] German; **die Deutschen** the Germans. ◇ das - 1. [deutsche Sprache] German - 2. [deutsche Wesensart]: **das ist das typisch Deutsche an ihm** that is what is typically Deutsche about him; siehe auch **Englische**.

Deutsche Bahn die (ohne pl) German railway company.

Deutsche Bundesbahn die (ohne pl) = **Deutsche Bahn**.

Deutsche Bundesbank die Bundesbank.

Deutsche Bundespost die (ohne pl) = **Deutsche Post**.

Deutsche Bundestag der (ohne pl) Bundestag, lower house of the German Parliament.

Deutsche Demokratische Republik die German Democratic Republic.

Deutsche Gewerkschaftsbund der German Trade Union Federation.

Deutsche Mark die (pl -) German mark, Deutschmark.

Deutsche Post die German postal service.

Deutsche Reich das German Reich.

Deutschland nt Germany.

Deutschlandlied das German national anthem.

deutschsprachig ['dɔytʃʃpraːxɪç] adj - 1. [Bevölkerung] German-speaking - 2. [Unterricht]: **deutschsprachigen Unterricht erteilen** to teach in German.

Deutschunterricht der (ohne pl) German lessons Pl; **Deutschunterricht geben** to teach German.

Devise [de'viːzə] (pl -n) die motto. ◆ **Devisen** Pl foreign currency (U).

Devisenkurs der exchange rate.

Dezember der December; siehe auch **September**.

dezent ◇ adj - 1. [taktvoll] discreet - 2. [unaufdringlich] tasteful. ◇ adv - 1. [taktvoll] discreetly - 2. [unaufdringlich] tastefully.

dezimal adj decimal.

Dezimalsystem das decimal system.

Dezimalzahl die decimal.

DGB [deːgeːˈbeː] (abk für Deutscher Gewerkschaftsbund) der Federation of German Trade Unions.

dgl. abk für **dergleichen**.

d. h. (abk für das heißt) i.e.

Dia (pl -s) das slide.

Diabetes der diabetes (U).

Diabetiker, in (mpl -, pl -nen) der, die diabetic.

Diagnose (pl -n) die fig & MED diagnosis; **die Diagnose auf etw (A) stellen** to diagnose sthg.

diagonal ◇ adj diagonal. ◇ adv: **etw diagonal lesen** to skim-read sthg.

Diagonale (pl -n) die diagonal; **eine Diagonale zeichnen** to draw a diagonal line.

Diakon (pl -e ODER -en) der - 1. [evangelisch] Church welfare worker - 2. [katholisch] deacon.

Diakonisse (pl -n) die - 1. [evangelisch] community nurse (working for the Church) - 2. [katholisch] deaconess.

Dialekt (pl -e) der dialect.

Dialog (pl -e) der dialogue.

Diamant (pl -en) der diamond.

Diaprojektor der slide projector.

Diät (pl -en) die diet; **Diät halten** to be on a diet; **eine Diät machen** to go on a diet; **Diät kochen** to cook dietary meals; **(nach einer) Diät leben** to follow a diet.

Diäten Pl [in der Politik] allowance (sg).

dich pron (Akkusativ von du) - 1. [Personalpronomen] you - 2. [Reflexivpronomen] yourself; **hast du dich umgezogen?** have you changed?; **beeil dich!** hurry up!

dicht ◇ adj - 1. [gegen Luft] airtight; [gegen Wasser] watertight; [Schuhe, Stoff] waterproof; **nicht dicht sein** [Dach] to be leaking; [Schuh] to be letting water in; **nicht** ODER **nicht mehr ganz dicht sein** fam fig & abw to be funny in the head - 2. [Wald, Nebel] dense - 3. [Haar, Gefieder] thick; [Verkehr] heavy. ◇ adv - 1. [undurchlässig]: **dicht schließen** to close tight - 2. [gedrängt] tightly; [bevölkert] densely; **er ist dicht behaart** he is very hairy - 3. [ganz nahe]: **dicht dahinter/daneben** right behind/next to it.

Dichte die - 1. [Undurchlässigkeit] impermeability - 2. [von Wald, Nebel] denseness - 3. [von Bevölkerung & PHYS] density; [von Verkehr] heaviness.

dichten ◇ vt - 1. [in Verse fassen] to write - 2. [gegen Wasser] to make watertight; [gegen Luft] to make airtight; [Fugen] to seal; [Leck] to stop. ◇ vi - 1. [dicht machen] to seal - 2. [Verse schreiben] to write (poetry).

Dichter, in (mpl -, fpl -nen) der, die poet; [von Dramen] writer.

dichterisch ◇ adj poetic. ◇ adv poetically.

Dichtung (pl -en) die - 1. [Kunstwerk] poem - 2. [Literatur] literature - 3. [für Wasserhahn] washer; [im Maschinenbau] gasket.

dick ◇ adj - 1. [gen] thick; [Person, Bauch] fat - 2. [geschwollen] swollen - 3. fam [groß, bedeutend - Auto, Gehalt, Fehler] whacking great; **ein dickes Lob** a big pat on the back; **sie sind dicke Freunde** they're as thick as thieves. ◇ adv - 1. [stark] thickly - 2. fam [sehr] really; **mit jm dick befreundet sein** to be as thick as thieves with sb; **jn/etw dick(e) haben** fam to have had one's fill of sb/sthg; **mit jm durch dick und dünn gehen** to go through thick and thin with sb.

Dicke (pl -n) ⟨⟩ die [gen] thickness; [von Person, Bauch] fatness; **die Wand hat eine Dicke von 20 cm** the wall is 20 cm thick. ⟨⟩ der, die [Person] fatty.

dickflüssig adj thick.

Dickicht (pl -e) das thicket.

Dickkopf der - 1. [Person] pig-headed person - 2. [Haltung]: **einen Dickkopf haben** to be pig-headed.

dickköpfig adj pig-headed.

Dickmilch die sour milk.

die ⟨⟩ det the; **sich** (D) **die Hände waschen** to wash one's hands; **die Natur** nature. ⟨⟩ pron - 1. [Demonstrativpronomen - Person] she, they Pl; [Sache] it; **die war es** it was her; **die hat es getan** she did it; **meine Tochter? die geht schon längst in die Schule** my daughter? she's been at school for a long time - 2. [Demonstrativpronomen - Sache] that one, those ones Pl; **meine Lehre? die habe ich abgebrochen** my training? I've given it up - 3. [Relativpronomen - Person] who, that; [- Sache] which, that.

Dieb (pl -e) der thief.

Diebin (pl -nen) die thief.

diebisch ⟨⟩ adj - 1. [schadenfroh] gloating - 2. [stehlend] thieving. ⟨⟩ adv: **sich diebisch freuen** to gloat.

Diebstahl (pl -stähle) der theft.

diejenige ⟨⟩ det: **diejenige Frau, die** the woman who. ⟨⟩ pron: **unter allen Bewerbungen wurde diejenige ausgewählt, die am originellsten war** the application that was chosen was the most original one.

Diele (pl -n) die - 1. [Flur] hall - 2. [Brett] floorboard.

dienen vi - 1. [nützen]: **einer Sache** (D) **dienen** to help with sthg; **jm dienen** to be of use to sb; **als etw dienen** to serve as sthg; **der Teppich dient nur zur Zierde** the carpet is only for decoration - 2. [behilflich sein] to be of help - 3. [für etw wirken]: **jm/einer Sache dienen** to serve sb/sthg - 4. [Subj: Butler]: **jm dienen** to serve sb - 5. [Soldat sein] to serve.

Diener, in (mpl -, fpl -nen) der, die eigtl & fig servant.

Dienst (pl -e) der - 1. [gen] service; **der öffentliche Dienst** the civil service; **jm seine Dienste anbieten** to offer sb one's services; **jm einen (guten) Dienst erweisen** to serve sb well - 2. [Arbeit, Pflicht] work; [von Arzt, Soldat] duty; **zum Dienst gehen** to go to work; [Arzt, Soldat] to go on duty; **Dienst haben** to be working; [Arzt, Soldat] to be on duty; **Dienst habend** on duty; **Dienst nach Vorschrift** work-to-rule - 3. [Arbeitsverhältnis] post.

Dienstag (pl -e) der Tuesday; siehe auch **Samstag**.

dienstags adv on Tuesdays; siehe auch **samstags**.

Dienstgeheimnis das official secret.

Dienstgrad der rank.

diensthabend adj = Dienst habend.

Dienstleistung die service.

dienstlich ⟨⟩ adj - 1. amt [den Dienst betreffend] business (vor Subst); [Befehl] official - 2. [unpersönlich] impersonal. ⟨⟩ adv amt [verreisen] on business.

Dienstreise die business trip; **auf Dienstreise sein** [geschäftlich] to be away on business; [Politiker] to be away on official business.

Dienststelle die: **die oberste Dienststelle** the highest authority.

Dienstwagen der company car.

Dienstweg der: **den Dienstweg einhalten** to go through the proper channels.

Dienstzeit die - 1. [Dienststunden] working hours Pl - 2. [Soldatenzeit] term of service.

dies pron this, these Pl; **dies und das** ODER **jenes** fig this and that.

diesbezüglich ⟨⟩ adj related (to this). ⟨⟩ adv regarding this (matter).

diese, r, s ODER **dies** ⟨⟩ det this, these Pl; [jene] that, those Pl; **am 9. dieses Monats** on the 9th of this month. ⟨⟩ pron this one, these ones Pl; [jene] that one, those ones Pl.

Diesel (pl -) der diesel.

dieselbe ⟨⟩ det the same. ⟨⟩ pron the same one.

diesig adj misty.

diesjährig adj: **die diesjährige Ernte** this year's harvest.

diesmal adv this time.

diesseits präp [auf dieser Seite]: **diesseits eines Ortes** (G) on this side of a place.

Dietrich (pl -e) der skeleton key.

Differenz (pl -en) die - 1. [gen] difference - 2. [Fehlbetrag] deficit. ☞ **Differenzen** Pl [Meinungsverschiedenheiten] differences.

differenzieren ⟨⟩ vt to differentiate between. ⟨⟩ vi to make distinctions.

digital adj digital.

Digitalanzeige die digital display.

Digitalkamera (pl -s) die digital camera.

Diktat (pl -e) das - 1. [Nachschrift] dictation - 2. geh [Zwang] dictate.

Diktator (pl -toren) der dictator.

Diktatorin (pl -nen) die dictator.

Diktatur (pl -en) die abw dictatorship.

diktieren vt to dictate; **jm etw diktieren** to dictate sthg to sb.

Dill der dill.

Dimension (pl -en) die eigtl & fig dimension; **ungeahnte Dimensionen annehmen** to take on unprecedented proportions.

DIN [diːn] (*abk für* **Deutsche Industrienorm**) *die* DIN.

Ding (*pl* -e ODER -er) *das* - **1.** (*pl* Dinge) [Gegenstand, Angelegenheit] thing; **vor allen Dingen** above all; **über den Dingen stehen** to be above it all; **den Dingen ihren Lauf lassen** to let things take their course; **es ist nicht mit rechten Dingen zugegangen** there was something odd about it; **wie die Dinge liegen** as things stand - **2.** (*pl* Dinger) *fam* [Sache] thing - **3.** (*pl* Dinger) [Mädchen]: **ein junges/dummes Ding** a young/stupid thing; **das ist (ja) 'n Ding!** *fam* would you believe it!, there's a thing!; **ein Ding drehen** *fam* to do a job.

Dings *fam* <> *der, die* [Person] thingy, thingummy. <> *das* [Gegenstand, Ort] thingy, thingummy.

Dinosaurier (*pl* -) *der* dinosaur.

Diözese (*pl* -n) *die* diocese.

Diplom (*pl* -e) *das* - **1.** [akademischer Grad] degree (*in science or technology*) - **2.** [Urkunde] diploma.

Diplomarbeit *die* dissertation (*submitted for a degree*).

Diplomat (*pl* -en) *der* diplomat.

Diplomatie *die* diplomacy.

Diplomatin (*pl* -nen) *die* diplomat.

diplomatisch <> *adj* diplomatic. <> *adv* diplomatically.

Diplomingenieur, in *der, die* qualified engineer.

dir *pron* (Dativ von *du*) (to) you; **das gehört dir** it belongs to you, it's yours; **ich komme mit dir** I'm coming with you; **tun dir die Füße weh?** do your feet hurt?

direkt <> *adj* direct. <> *adv* - **1.** [sofort] straight; TV live - **2.** [nahe] right; **direkt neben** right next to - **3.** [unmittelbar]: **sie kaufen ihre Milch direkt beim Bauern** they buy their milk direct from the farmer - **4.** [unverblümt] directly.

Direktor (*pl* -toren) *der* [von Schule] headmaster UK, principal US; [von Museum] director; [von Strafanstalt] governor UK, warden US; [von Abteilung] manager.

Direktorin (*pl* -nen) *die* [von Schule] headmistress UK, principal US; [von Museum] director; [von Strafanstalt] governor UK, warden US; [von Abteilung] manager.

Direktübertragung *die* live broadcast.

Dirigent, in (*mpl* -en, *fpl* -nen) *der, die* conductor.

dirigieren <> *vt* - **1.** MUS to conduct - **2.** [Unternehmen] to manage, to run; [Verkehr] to direct. <> *vi* to conduct.

Diskettenlaufwerk *das* EDV disk drive.

Disko (*pl* -s) *die* *fam* disco.

Diskontsatz *der* WIRTSCH discount rate.

Diskothek (*pl* -en) *die* discotheque.

Diskretion *die* discretion; **in Bezug auf etw Diskretion wahren** to treat sthg in confidence.

diskriminieren *vt* - **1.** [benachteiligen] to discriminate against - **2.** [herabwürdigen] to disparage.

Diskussion (*pl* -en) *die* discussion.

Diskuswerfen *das* SPORT discus.

diskutieren <> *vi* to discuss; **über jn/etw diskutieren** to discuss sb/sthg. <> *vt* to discuss.

disqualifizieren *vt* to disqualify.

Dissertation (*pl* -en) *die* (doctoral) thesis.

Distanz (*pl* -en) *die* - **1.** [Entfernung] distance - **2.** [persönlicher Abstand] detachment; **etw aus der Distanz heraus beurteilen** to judge sthg from a distance; **jm gegenüber auf Distanz gehen/bleiben** to distance o.s./keep one's distance from sb.

distanziert <> *adj* detached. <> *adv*: **distanziert wirken** to seem distant.

Distel (*pl* -n) *die* thistle.

Disziplin (*pl* -en) *die* discipline.

disziplinarisch <> *adj* disciplinary. <> *adv*: **gegen jn disziplinarisch vorgehen** to take disciplinary action against sb.

diszipliniert <> *adj* disciplined. <> *adv* in a disciplined way.

diverse [diˈvɛrzə] *adj Pl* various.

Dividende [diviˈdɛndə] (*pl* -n) *die* dividend.

dividieren [diviˈdiːrən] *vt*: **etw (durch etw) dividieren** to divide sthg (by sthg).

Division [diviˈzjoːn] (*pl* -en) *die* MATH & MIL division.

Diwan (*pl* -e) *der* divan.

DM (*abk für* **Deutsche Mark**) DM.

D-Mark [ˈdeːmark] (*pl* -) (*abk für* **Deutsche Mark**) *die* German mark, Deutschmark.

d-Moll *das* D minor.

DNA [deːɛnˈʔaː] (*abk für* **desoxyribonucleic acid**) *die* = DNA.

DNS [deːɛnˈʔɛs] (*abk für* **Desoxyribonukleinsäure**) *die* = DNA.

doch <> *konj* [aber] yet, but. <> *adv* - **1.** [trotzdem] anyway; **er wollte erst nicht, aber dann hat er es doch gemacht** at first he didn't want to, but then he did it anyway; **willst du nicht? - doch** don't you want to? - yes, I do; **doch noch** after all - **2.** [verstärkend]: **setzen Sie sich doch!** do sit down!; **das kann doch nicht wahr sein!** I don't believe it!; **aber das konnte ich doch nicht wissen!** but how could I have known! ◆ **nicht doch** *interj* don't do that!

Docht (*pl* -e) *der* wick.

Dock (*pl* -s) *das* dock.

Dogge (*pl* -n) *die* mastiff.

Doktor (*pl* -toren) *der* - **1.** [Titel] doctorate; **seinen Doktor machen** to do one's doctorate - **2.** [Träger des Doktortitels, Arzt] doctor.

Doktorand, in (*mpl* -en, *fpl* -nen) *der, die* PhD student.

Doktorlarbeit *die* doctoral thesis.

Doktorin (*pl* -nen) *die* doctor.

Doktrin (*pl* -en) *die* doctrine.

Dokument (*pl* -e) *das* document.

Dokumentarlfilm *der* documentary.

Dokumentation (*pl* -en) *die* - **1.** [Informationsmaterial] documentation *(U)* - **2.** [Darstellung]: **eine Dokumentation über etw** *(A)* **machen** to document sthg.

Dolch (*pl* -e) *der* dagger.

Dollar (*pl* -s ODER -) *der* dollar.

dolmetschen *vt* & *vi* to interpret.

Dolmetscher, in (*mpl* -, *fpl* -nen) *der, die* interpreter.

Dolomiten *Pl* Dolomites.

Dom (*pl* -e) *der* cathedral.

dominant *adj* dominant.

Dominanz (*pl* -en) *die* dominance.

dominieren <> *vi* to predominate. <> *vt* to dominate.

Dominikaner, in (*mpl* -, *fpl* -nen) *der, die* GEOGR & RELIG Dominican.

Dominikanische Republik *die* Dominican Republic.

Donau *die*: **die Donau** the Danube.

Donner *der* thunder.

donnern (*perf* hat/ist gedonnert) <> *vi* - **1.** (hat) [beim Gewitter]: **es donnert** it is thundering - **2.** (ist) [sich bewegen] to thunder - **3.** (hat) *fam* [schlagen] to hammer - **4.** (ist) *fam* [prallen]: **gegen etw donnern** to slam into sthg. <> *vt* (hat) *fam* to hurl.

Donnerstag (*pl* -e) *der* Thursday; *siehe auch* **Samstag.**

donnerstags *adv* on Thursdays; *siehe auch* **samstags.**

Donnerwetter *das* (ohne *pl*) *fam* almighty row; **Donnerwetter!** my goodness!

doof *fam* <> *adj* stupid. <> *adv* stupidly.

dopen ['do:pn] *vt* [Pferd] to dope. **sich dopen** *ref* [Sportler] to take drugs.

Doping ['do:pɪŋ] (*pl* -s) *das* drug-taking.

Doppel (*pl* -) *das* - **1.** [Kopie] duplicate - **2.** SPORT doubles *(U)*.

Doppellbett *das* double bed.

Doppelldecker (*pl* -) *der* - **1.** FLUG biplane - **2.** [Omnibus] double-decker (bus).

doppeldeutig *adj* ambiguous; **doppeldeutiger Witz** double entendre.

Doppellgänger, in (*mpl* -, *fpl* -nen) *der, die* double.

Doppellhaus *das* pair of semi-detached houses.

Doppellkinn *das* double chin.

Doppellklick (*pl* -s) *der* EDV double click.

Doppellname *der* double-barrelled name.

Doppellpunkt *der* colon.

doppelseitig *adj* - **1.** [Lungenentzündung] double - **2.** [zwei Seiten umfassend] two-page.

doppelt <> *adj* - **1.** [zweifach] double - **2.** [gesteigert] twice as much. <> *adv* twice; **doppelt so viel** twice as much.

Doppellzimmer *das* double room.

Dorf (*pl* Dörfer) *das* [Ort] village; **auf dem Dorf** in the country.

Dorflbewohner, in *der, die* villager.

dörflich *adj* village (vor *Subst*); [Gegend] rural.

Dorn (*pl* -en) *der* [von Rose] thorn; [von Schnalle] prong.

Dornröschen *das* Sleeping Beauty.

Dörrobst *das* dried fruit.

Dorsch (*pl* -e) *der* cod.

dort *adv* there; **dort drüben** over there; **dort, wo wir Fußball spielen** where we play football.

dorther *adv* from there.

dorthin *adv* there.

dortig *adj* local.

Dose (*pl* -n) *die* - **1.** [Behälter] box; [für Zucker] bowl; [für Butter] dish - **2.** [Konservendose] can, tin *UK*; [Bierdose] can; **Erbsen aus der Dose** tinned *UK* ODER canned peas.

dösen *vi* to doze.

Dosenlmilch *die* condensed ODER evaporated milk.

Dosenlöffner *der* can ODER tin *UK* opener.

dosieren *vt* to measure out.

Dosierung (*pl* -en) *die* dosage.

Dosis (*pl* Dosen) *die* dose.

Dotter (*pl* -) *das* & *der* yolk.

Double ['du:bl̩] (*pl* -s) *das* double.

down [daʊn] *adj* *fam*: **down sein** to be down.

downlloaden (*präs* loadet down, *prät* loadete down, *perf* hat downgeloadet) *vt* EDV to download.

Dozent, in (*mpl* -en, *fpl* -nen) *der, die* lecturer *UK*, assistant professor *US*.

dpa [de:pe'ʔaː] (*abk für* Deutsche Presseagentur) *die* German Press Agency.

Dr. (*abk für* Doktor) Dr.

Drache (*pl* -n) *der* dragon.

Drachen (*pl* -) *der* - **1.** [Spielzeug] kite - **2.** *abw* [Frau] dragon.

Draht (*pl* Drähte) *der* wire; **auf Draht sein** *fam* to be on the ball; **einen guten Draht zu jm haben** to be well in with sb.

Drahtseillbahn *die* cable railway.

Drahtzieher, in (*mpl* -, *fpl* -nen) *der, die* [Hintermann] person pulling the strings.

Drama (*pl* Dramen) *das* drama.

dramatisch *adj* dramatic.

dramatisieren *vt* [hochspielen] to play up, to make a big thing of.

Dramaturg, in (*mpl* -en, *fpl* -nen) *der, die* person who selects and adapts plays for the stage.

dran *adv* - 1. *fam* = **daran** - 2. [an der Reihe]: **ich bin jetzt dran** it's my turn; **wer ist als Nächster dran?** who's next?, whose turn is it?; **dran sein** to be for it.

drang *prät* ⊏⟩ **dringen**.

Drängelei (*pl* -en) *die* - 1. *abw* [durch Schieben] pushing (and shoving) - 2. [durch Reden] pestering.

drängeln ⟨⟩ *vi* - 1. [durch Schieben] to push - 2. [durch Reden] to go on (and on). ⟨⟩ *vt* - 1. [durch Schieben] to push - 2. [durch Reden] to pester. ⬥ **sich drängeln** *ref*: **sich nach vorn drängeln** to push one's way to the front.

drängen ⟨⟩ *vi* - 1. [schieben] to push - 2. [nicht warten]: **zum Aufbruch drängen** to insist on leaving; **zur Eile drängen** to urge haste; **auf etw** (*A*) **drängen** to push ODER press for sthg. ⟨⟩ *vt* - 1. [schieben] to push - 2. [antreiben] to urge.

dranhalten ⬥ **sich dranhalten** *ref* (*unreg*) *fam* to get a move on.

drankommen (*perf* **ist drangekommen**) *vi* (*unreg*) - 1. [an die Reihe kommen] to have one's turn; **ich bin als Letzter drangekommen** I was last - 2. [heranreichen] to reach.

drastisch ⟨⟩ *adj* - 1. [einschneidend] drastic - 2. [sehr deutlich] graphic. ⟨⟩ *adv* - 1. [stark] drastically - 2. [sehr deutlich] graphically.

drauf *adv* *fam* = **darauf**; **es kommt drauf an** it depends; **etw drauf haben** [Fähigkeit] to be really good at sthg; **er hatte hundert Sachen drauf** AUTO he was doing a hundred; **gut drauf sein** to be in a good mood; **drauf und dran sein, etw zu tun** to be on the point of doing sthg.

Draufgänger, in (*mpl* -, *fpl* -nen) *der, die* daredevil.

draufgehen (*perf* **ist draufgegangen**) *vi* (*unreg*) *fam* - 1. [umkommen] to buy it - 2. [verbraucht werden] to be used up.

draußen *adv* outside. ⬥ **nach draußen** *adv* outside. ⬥ **von draußen** *adv* from outside.

Dreck *der* *fam* [Schmutz] muck, dirt; **Dreck machen** to make a mess; **das geht dich einen Dreck an** it's none of your damn business; **jn in den Dreck ziehen** to drag sb/sthg through the mud.

Dreckarbeit *die* *fam* - 1. [schmutzige Arbeit] dirty work - 2. [niedere Arbeit] menial jobs *Pl*.

dreckig ⟨⟩ *adj* - 1. [schmutzig, unverschämt] dirty; **sich dreckig machen** to get dirty - 2. *fam* *abw* [gemein]: **du dreckiges Schwein!** you filthy swine! ⟨⟩ *adv* *fam* - 1. *abw* [unverschämt] dirtily - 2. [schlecht]: **ihr geht es dreckig** she is in a bad way.

Dreckspatz *der* *fam* mucky pup.

Drehbuch *das* screenplay.

drehen ⟨⟩ *vt* - 1. [im Kreis bewegen] to turn - 2. [einstellen]: **das Radio laut/leise drehen** to turn the radio up/down - 3. [formen - Seil] to twist; [- Zigarette, Pillen] to roll - 4. TV to film, to shoot. ⟨⟩ *vi* - 1. [wenden] to turn - 2. [am Knopf, Schalter]: **an etw** (*D*) **drehen** to turn sthg; **am Radio drehen** to turn the knob on the radio. ⬥ **sich drehen** *ref* [sich wenden] to turn; **mir dreht sich alles** *fam* my head is spinning; **sich um jn/etw drehen** to be about sb/sthg; **es dreht sich darum, dass...** the thing is...

Drehorgel *die* barrel organ.

Drehscheibe *die* [Knotenpunkt] hub.

Drehstuhl *der* swivel chair.

Drehtür *die* revolving door.

Drehung (*pl* -en) *die* turn.

Drehzahl *die* revs *Pl*.

drei *num* [Zahl] three; **für drei essen** to eat like a horse; *siehe auch* **sechs**.

Drei (*pl* -en) *die* - 1. [Zahl] three - 2. [Schulnote] ≃ C, mark of 3 on a scale from 1 to 6; *siehe auch* **Sechs**.

dreidimensional ⟨⟩ *adj* three-dimensional. ⟨⟩ *adv* three-dimensionally.

Dreieck (*pl* -e) *das* triangle.

dreieckig *adj* triangular.

Dreier (*pl* -) *der* - 1. [Drei] three - 2. [beim Lotto] three correct numbers *Pl* - 3. *fam* [Sprungbrett] three-metre board.

dreierlei *adj* (*unver*) three different; **auf dreierlei Weise** in three different ways.

dreifach ⟨⟩ *adj* triple; **die dreifache Menge** three times as much; **in dreifacher Größe** three times as big; **in dreifacher Ausfertigung** in triplicate; **der dreifache Gewinner** the three times ODER triple winner. ⟨⟩ *adv* three times.

dreihundert *num* three hundred.

Dreikönigsfest *das* Epiphany.

dreimal *adv* three times.

Dreisatz *der* rule of three.

dreißig *num* thirty; *siehe auch* **sechs**.

Dreißig *die* thirty; *siehe auch* **Sechs**.

Dreißigerjahre, dreißiger Jahre *Pl*: **die Dreißigerjahre** the thirties.

dreist ⟨⟩ *adj* impudent. ⟨⟩ *adv* impudently.

Dreistigkeit (*pl* -en) *die* [Wesen, Verhalten] impudence.

dreistöckig *adj* - 1. [Haus] three-storeyed - 2. [Torte] three-tiered.

dreitausend *num* three thousand.

dreiteilig *adj* three-part; [Kostüm, Anzug] three-piece.

drei viertel *num* three quarters; **drei viertel Liter** three-quarters of a litre; **drei viertel acht** a quarter to UK ODER of US eight.

Dreivierteltakt *der* three-four time.

dreizehn *num* thirteen; *siehe auch* **sechs**.

Dreizimmer\wohnung *die* three-roomed flat *UK ODER* apartment *US*.

dreschen (*präs* drischt, *prät* drosch, *perf* hat gedroschen) ⟨⟩ *vt* - **1.** [Getreide] to thresh - **2.** *fam* [prügeln] to thrash. ⟨⟩ *vi fam* [schlagen] to bang.

Dresden *nt* Dresden.

Dress (*pl* -e) *der* - **1.** SPORT kit - **2.** *fam* [Kleidung] outfit.

dressieren *vt* to train.

Dressing (*pl* -s) *das* dressing.

Dressur (*pl* -en) *die* - **1.** [Dressieren] training - **2.** [Pferdedressur] dressage.

drillen *vt* to drill.

drin *adv fam* - **1.** = **darin** - **2.** [möglich]: **drin sein** to be on the cards; **bei diesem Spiel ist noch alles drin** there is still everything to play for in this game - **3.** [gewöhnt]: **drin sein** to have got into the swing of things.

dringen (*prät* drang, *perf* hat/ist gedrungen) *vi* - **1.** (ist) [eindringen]: **durch** *ODER* **in etw** (A) **dringen** to penetrate sthg; **Wasser dringt durch die Decke** water is leaking through the ceiling; **Gas drang in den Raum** gas seeped into the room - **2.** (hat) [drängen]: **auf etw** (A) **dringen** to insist on sthg.

dringend ⟨⟩ *adj* urgent. ⟨⟩ *adv* urgently.

Dringlichkeit *die* urgency.

drinnen *adv* inside; **nach drinnen gehen** to go inside.

drischt *präs* ▷ **dreschen**.

dritt ◆ **zu dritt** *num*: **wir sind zu dritt** there are three of us; **wir sind zu dritt ins Kino gegangen** three of us went to the cinema.

dritte, r, s *adj* third; *siehe auch* **sechste**.

Dritte *der, die, das* third; [außenstehende Person] third party; *siehe auch* **Sechste**.

drittel *adj* (*unver*) third of a; *siehe auch* **sechstel**.

Drittel (*pl* -) *das* third; *siehe auch* **Sechstel**.

dritteln *vt* to divide into three.

drittens *adv* thirdly.

Dritte Reich *das*: **das Dritte Reich** the Third Reich.

Droge (*pl* -n) *die* drug.

drogenabhängig *adj*: **drogenabhängig sein** to be a drug addict.

Drogen\abhängige (*pl* -n) *der, die* drug addict.

Drogen\händler, in *der, die* drug dealer.

Drogerie (*pl* -n) *die* chemist's (shop) (*nondispensing*) *UK*, drugstore *US*.

drohen *vi* to threaten; **drohen, etw zu tun** to threaten to do sthg; **jm (mit etw) drohen** to threaten sb (with sthg).

dröhnen *vi* - **1.** [hallen] to boom - **2.** *salopp* [berauschen] to give you a high.

Drohung (*pl* -en) *die* threat.

Dromedar (*pl* -e) *das* dromedary.

drosch *prät* ▷ **dreschen**.

Drossel (*pl* -n) *die* thrush.

drosseln *vt* [Geschwindigkeit, Leistung] to reduce; [Heizung] to turn down.

drüben *adv* [nebenan] over there.

drüber = **darüber**.

Druck (*pl* -e) *der* - **1.** [Kraft, Zwang] pressure; **Druck hinter etw** (A) **machen** *fam fig* to put pressure on regarding sthg; **Druck auf jn ausüben, jn unter Druck setzen** to put pressure on sb; **Druck machen** to put pressure on; **unter Druck stehen** to be under pressure - **2.** [Drucken] printing - **3.** [Gravur] print.

Druck\buchstabe *der* printed letter; **in Druckbuchstaben schreiben** to print.

Drücke\berger, in (*mpl* -, *fpl* -nen) *der, die abw* shirker.

druckempfindlich *adj* [Körperstelle] sensitive to pressure; **Pfirsiche sind druckempfindlich** peaches bruise easily.

drucken *vt* to print.

drücken ⟨⟩ *vt* - **1.** [pressen] to press; **jn/etw an sich** (A) **drücken** to hold sb/sthg to one - **2.** *fam* [umarmen] to hug, to squeeze - **3.** [mindern] to lower. ⟨⟩ *vi* - **1.** [pressen]: **auf etw** (A) **drücken** to press sthg; **es drückt auf die Laune** it gets you down - **2.** [Schuhe] to pinch - **3.** *salopp* [fixen] to shoot up. ◆ **sich drücken** *ref* - **1.** [sich pressen]: **sich an etw** (A) **drücken** to flatten o.s. against sthg - **2.** [sich entziehen]: **sich vor etw** (D) **drücken** *abw* to get out of sthg.

drückend *adj* - **1.** [Probleme, Sorgen] serious; [Verantwortung, Schulden] heavy; [Armut] grinding - **2.** [Hitze] oppressive.

Drucker (*pl* -) *der* printer.

Drücker (*pl* -) *der* - **1.** [Türdrücker] handle - **2.** [Hausierer] door-to-door salesman; **am Drücker sitzen** *fam* to call the shots.

Druckerei (*pl* -en) *die* printing works, printer's.

Druck\fehler *der* misprint.

Druck\knopf *der* press stud *UK*, snap fastener *US*.

Druck\sache *die* printed matter (*U*).

Druck\schrift *die* block capitals *Pl*.

drum *fam* = **darum**.

drunter *adv fam* = **darunter**; **alles** *ODER* **es geht drunter und drüber** everything is going haywire.

Drüse (*pl* -n) *die* gland.

Dschungel (*pl* -) *der* jungle.

dt. (*abk für* **deutsch**) Ger.

DTP (*abk für* **Desktop-Publishing**) *das* (*ohne pl*) EDV DTP.

du *pron* du; **ach, du bists!** oh, it's you!; **du sagen** to use the du form of address; **mit jm per du sein** ≃ to be on first name terms with sb.

Duale System *das* privately run waste disposal and recycling system.

Dübel (*pl* -) *der* Rawlplug®.

Dublin ['dablin] *nt* Dublin.

ducken ➡ **sich ducken** *ref* to duck.

dudeln *fam abw* <> *vi* [Plattenspieler, Radio] to drone; [auf Instrument] to tootle. <> *vt* [auf Blasinstrument] to tootle on.

Dudel|sack *der* bagpipes *Pl*.

Duell [du'ɛl] (*pl* -e) *das* duel.

Duett [du'ɛt] (*pl* -e) *das* duet.

Duft (*pl* Düfte) *der* scent.

duften *vi* to smell nice; **nach etw duften** to smell of sthg.

dulden *vt* *geh* to tolerate.

dumm (*kompar* dümmer, *superl* dümmste) <> *adj* - 1. [gen] stupid; **dummes Zeug** rubbish, nonsense; **es ist** *ODER* **wird mir zu dumm** I've had enough of it - 2. [unangenehm - Fehler, Zufall] annoying. <> *adv* stupidly.

Dumme (*pl* -n) *der*, *die*: **der Dumme sein** to be the one who loses out.

dummerweise *adv* - 1. [ärgerlicherweise] unfortunately - 2. [aus Dummheit] stupidly.

Dummheit (*pl* -en) *die* - 1. [fehlende Klugheit] stupidity - 2. [Handlung] stupid thing; **mach keine Dummheiten** don't do anything stupid.

Dumm|kopf *der* idiot.

dümmlich <> *adj* stupid. <> *adv* stupidly.

dumpf <> *adj* - 1. [Klang] dull, muffled - 2. [Schmerz] dull; [Befürchtung, Verdacht] vague - 3. [stumpfsinnig] apathetic. <> *adv* - 1. [dunkel] dully - 2. [stumpfsinnig] apathetically.

Düne (*pl* -n) *die* dune.

düngen <> *vt* to fertilize. <> *vi* - 1. [Dung] to act as a fertilizer - 2. [Person] to fertilize one's land/garden/*etc*.

Dünger (*pl* -) *der* fertilizer.

dunkel <> *adj* - 1. [gen] dark; **im Dunkeln tappen** *fig* to grope around in the dark - 2. [Ton, Stimme] deep - 3. [vage] vague; **jn über etw** (A) **im Dunkeln lassen** to keep sb in the dark about sthg - 4. [dubios] shady. <> *adv* - 1. [streichen, färben] in dark colours/a dark colour - 2. [klingen] deep - 3. [unklar] vaguely.

dunkelblau *adj & adv* dark blue.

dunkelblond <> *adj* light brown; [Person] with light brown hair. <> *adv* light brown.

dunkelhaarig *adj* dark-haired.

Dunkelheit *die* darkness.

Dunkel|ziffer *die* number of unreported incidents.

dünn <> *adj* - 1. [gen] thin; **sich dünn machen** [wenig Platz brauchen] to squeeze up - 2. [Ge-

tränk, Stimme] weak - 3. [Haare, Bewuchs] sparse. <> *adv* [bevölkert, bewachsen] sparsely; [auftragen] thinly.

dünnflüssig *adj* thin.

Dunst (*pl* Dünste) *der* - 1. [Nebel] haze, mist - 2. [von Zigaretten] smoke; [in der Küche] steam; **keinen (blassen) Dunst von etw haben** *fam* not to have the foggiest (idea) about sthg.

dünsten *vt* to steam.

dunstig *adj* [neblig] hazy, misty.

Duo (*pl* -s) *das* duo.

Dur *das* major; **eine Sonate in Dur** a sonata in a major key.

durch <> *präp* (+ A) - 1. [räumlich, zeitlich] through; **darf ich mal bitte durch?** excuse me, please!; **durch die Schweiz reisen** to travel across Switzerland; **die ganze Nacht durch** throughout the night - 2. [mittels] by; **durch eigene Schuld** through one's own fault; **durch Ihre Hilfe** with your help; **das Haus wurde durch ein Erdbeben zerstört** the house was destroyed by an earthquake - 3. MATH divided by; **sechs durch drei** six divided by three. <> *adv* - 1. *fam* [später als]: **es ist schon zwölf durch** it's gone *ODER* past twelve - 2. *fam* [durchgebraten] well done - 3. *fam* [beendet]: **bis morgen muss ich mit dem Buch durch sein** I have to finish the book by tomorrow; **durch und durch** through and through; **durch und durch nass** wet through.

durch|arbeiten <> *vt* to work through. <> *vi* to work without a break. ➡ **sich durcharbeiten** *ref*: **sich durch etw durcharbeiten** [Menschenmenge, Text] to work one's way through sthg.

durch|atmen *vi* to breathe deeply.

durchaus, durchaus *adv* - 1. [gut, ohne weiteres] perfectly; **es kann durchaus sein** it is perfectly possible - 2. [unbedingt] absolutely - 3. [absolut, überhaupt]: **durchaus nicht** definitely not, not at all.

durch|blättern *vt* to flick through.

Durch|blick *der fam* overview; **den Durchblick verlieren** to lose track of things.

durch|blicken *vt* to see through.

Durchblutung *die* circulation.

durch|bohren[1] <> *vt* [Brett] to drill through; [Loch] to drill. <> *vi* to drill through.

durchbohren[2] *vt* [Subj: Kugel] to go through; **jn mit Blicken durchbohren** to fix sb with a piercing gaze.

durch|braten *vt* (*unreg*) to cook well *ODER* through.

durch|brechen[1] (*perf* hat/ist durchgebrochen) (*unreg*) <> *vt* (hat) - 1. [zerbrechen] to break in two - 2. [einreißen - Wand] to knock in. <> *vi* (ist) - 1. [zerbrechen] to break in two; [Boden] to give way - 2. [durchdringen] to break through; [Geschwür, Abszess] to perforate.

durchbrechen[2] (*präs* **durchbricht**, *prät* **durchbrach**, *perf* **hat durchbrochen**) *vt* to break through.

durch|brennen (*perf* **ist durchgebrannt**) *vi* (*unreg*) - 1. [Draht] to blow, to go - 2. *fam* [weglaufen] to run away.

Durch|bruch *der* - 1. [Erfolg] breakthrough - 2. [Öffnung] opening.

durch|checken ['dʊrtʃʃɛkn̩] *vt* to check over.

durchdacht *adj* well thought out; **gut/schlecht durchdacht** well/badly thought out.

durch|denken[1] *vt* (*unreg*) to think through.

durchdenken[2] (*prät* **durchdachte**, *perf* **hat durchdacht**) *vt* to think out.

durch|diskutieren *vt* to talk through.

durch|drehen (*perf* **hat/ist durchgedreht**) ◇ *vi* - 1. (*ist*) *fam* [verrückt werden] to crack up - 2. (*hat*) [Räder] to spin. ◇ *vt* (*hat*) to mince.

durch|dringen (*perf* **ist durchgedrungen**) *vi* (*unreg*) [Geräusch, Licht, Nachricht] to get through; [Wasser] to seep through.

durch|drücken *vt* - 1. *fam* [durchsetzen] to push through - 2. [Gelenk] to straighten - 3. [passieren] to press through.

Durcheinander *das* [von Menschen] confusion; [von Dingen] chaos.

durcheinander bringen *vt* (*unreg*) - 1. [Person] to confuse - 2. [Dinge] to muddle up - 3. [verwechseln] to mix up.

durch|exerzieren *vt* to go through.

durch|fahren (*perf* **ist durchgefahren**) *vi* (*unreg*) - 1. [durchqueren] to go *ODER* drive through - 2. [durchgehend fahren] to go *ODER* drive non-stop.

Durch|fahrt *die* - 1. [Durchfahren]: **die Durchfahrt freigeben** to open the road (again) - 2. [Durchreise] way through; **auf der Durchfahrt sein** to be travelling through - 3. [Weg] access road.

Durch|fall *der* - 1. [Diarrhöe] diarrhoea - 2. *fam* [Misserfolg] flop; [bei einer Prüfung] failure.

durch|fallen (*perf* **ist durchgefallen**) *vi* (*unreg*) - 1. *fam* [versagen] to flop; [bei einer Prüfung] to fail - 2. [durch eine Öffnung] to fall through.

durch|forsten *vt* - 1. [durchsuchen - Gegend] to search; [- Textmaterial] to search through - 2. [ausdünnen - Wald] to thin out.

durch|fragen ◆ sich durchfragen *ref* to ask one's way.

durchführbar *adj* practicable.

durch|führen ◇ *vt* to carry out; [Veranstaltung] to hold. ◇ *vi* to go through.

Durch|gang *der* - 1. [Durchgehen]: 'Durchgang verboten' 'no right of way' - 2. [Weg] passage - 3. [Phase] stage; [von Wahl] round.

durchgängig ◇ *adj* [Auffassung] general; **ein durchgängiges Motiv in seinen Werken** a motif that runs through his works. ◇ *adv* universally; **durchgängig gute Leistungen bringen** to achieve consistently good results.

Durchgangsverkehr *der* through traffic.

durch|geben *vt* (*unreg*) to pass on; TV & RADIO to broadcast.

durchgebraten ◇ *pp* ▷ **durchbraten**. ◇ *adj*: **gut durchgebraten** well done.

durchgefroren *adj* frozen through.

durch|gehen (*perf* **ist durchgegangen**) (*unreg*) ◇ *vi* - 1. [gehen] to go through; **bitte durchgehen!** [im Bus] please move to the back of the bus! - 2. [durchdringen] to get through - 3. [Pferd] to bolt; **mit jm durchgehen** [Gefühle] to run away with sb - 4. [andauern - Sitzung, Veranstaltung] to go on non-stop - 5. [akzeptiert werden - Fehler, Gesetzesvorlage] to get through; **jm etw durchgehen lassen** to let sb get away with sthg. ◇ *vt* to go through.

durch|greifen *vi* (*unreg*) - 1. [einschreiten] to take action - 2. [durch eine Öffnung]: **durch etw durchgreifen** to reach through sthg.

durch|halten (*unreg*) ◇ *vi* to hold out. ◇ *vt* [Belastung] to withstand; [Strecke, Wettkampf] to make it to the end of.

Durchhaltevermögen *das* stamina.

durch|kämmen *vt* to comb.

durch|kommen (*perf* **ist durchgekommen**) *vi* (*unreg*) - 1. [durch etw gelangen]: **durch etw durchkommen** to get through sthg - 2. [am Telefon, bei Prüfung] to get through - 3. [Nachricht] to be announced - 4. [durchfahren] to pass through - 5. [durchdringen - Wasser, Sonne] to come through - 6. [überleben] to pull through - 7. [erfolgreich sein]: **mit dieser Idee wirst du beim Chef kaum durchkommen** you won't get anywhere with the boss with that idea.

durch|lassen *vt* (*unreg*) to let through.

durchlässig *adj* [Boden] porous; [Material] permeable; [Grenze] open.

durch|lesen *vt* (*unreg*) to read through.

durch|leuchten *vt* - 1. [röntgen] to X-ray - 2. [untersuchen] to examine, to investigate.

durch|machen ◇ *vt* - 1. [Schwierigkeiten, schwere Zeiten] to go through; **sie hat viel durchgemacht** she's been through a lot - 2. *fam* [feiern]: **eine Nacht durchmachen** to party all night. ◇ *vi fam* to stay up.

Durch|messer *der* diameter.

durch|nehmen *vt* (*unreg*) to do.

durchqueren *vt* [Zimmer, Fluss] to cross; [Land] to go across; [Gegend] to go through.

durch|rechnen *vt* to calculate.

Durch|reise *die*: **Durchreise (durch)** journey through; **auf der Durchreise** passing through.

durch|reißen (*perf* **hat/ist durchgerissen**) (*unreg*) ◇ *vt* (*hat*) [Papier, Stoff] to tear in two; [Faden] to break in two. ◇ *vi* (*ist*) [Stoff] to tear in two; [Faden, Draht] to break in two.

durch|ringen ⟶ **sich durchringen** ref
(unreg): **sich zu etw durchringen** to make up
one's mind finally to do sthg.

durch|rosten (perf **ist durchgerostet**) vi to
rust through.

durch|sagen vt to announce.

durch|schauen[1] vt to look through.

durchschauen[2] vt to see through.

Durch|schlag der - 1. [Kopie] carbon copy
- 2. [Sieb] strainer.

durch|schlagen (perf **hat/ist durchgeschla-
gen**) (unreg) ⟨⟩ vt (hat) [Glas] to smash
through; [Stein, Holz] to split; [Wand] to knock
through; **etw durch etw durchschlagen** to
knock sthg through sthg. ⟨⟩ vi (ist) to show
through. ⟶ **sich durchschlagen** ref
- 1. [durch Gegend] to make it - 2. [durch Zeit] to
struggle through.

durch|schneiden vt (unreg) [Faden, Stoff] to
cut through; [Brot, Blatt Papier] to cut in half;
[Kehle] to cut.

Durch|schnitt der average.

durch|schnittlich ⟨⟩ adj average. ⟨⟩ adv
[im Durchschnitt] on average; abw [mittelmäßig]
averagely.

durch|schütteln vt to shake well; **im Bus
durchgeschüttelt werden** to be shaken about
on the bus.

durch|schwitzen vt to soak with sweat.

durch|sehen (unreg) ⟨⟩ vt to look through.
⟨⟩ vi: **durch etw durchsehen** to see through
sthg.

durch sein (perf **ist durch gewesen**) vi (unreg) fam - 1. [Zug, Kontrolleur] to have come
through; **bei jm unten durch sein** fig & abw to
be in sb's bad books - 2. [mit Buch, Arbeit] to
have finished - 3. [Braten, Kartoffeln] to be done
- 4. [Sohle, Ärmel] to be worn out - 5. [Gesetz] to
have gone through.

durch|setzen vt [Plan, Vorhaben, Reform] to
push through; [Anspruch] to assert. ⟶ **sich
durchsetzen** ref to assert o.s.; [Erfindung] to
gain acceptance.

durch|sichtig adj [Stoff, Folie] transparent.

durch|sprechen vt (unreg) to talk over.

durch|stehen vt (unreg) to come through.

durch|stellen vt to put through.

durch|stöbern vt to rummage through.

durch|stoßen[1] vt (unreg): **etw durch etw
durchstoßen** to push sthg through sthg.

durchstoßen[2] (präs **durchstößt**, prät **durch-
stieß**, perf **hat durchstoßen**) vt to break
through.

durch|streichen vt (unreg) to cross out.

durch|suchen vt to search.

durchtrainiert ['durçtrɛniːɐ̯t] adj in peak
condition.

durch|trennen[1] vt to sever.

durchtrennen[2] vt to sever.

durchtrieben ⟨⟩ adj cunning. ⟨⟩ adv cunningly.

Durchwahl die (ohne pl) extension.

durchweg adv without exception.

durch|wühlen[1] vt [Schublade] to rummage
through; [Zimmer] to ransack.

durch|wühlen[2] vt [Schublade] to rummage
through; [Zimmer] to ransack.

durch|zählen vt to count.

durch|ziehen[1] (perf **hat/ist durchgezogen**)
(unreg) ⟨⟩ vt (hat) - 1. [durch Öffnung] to pull
through; **etw durch etw durchziehen** to pull
sthg through sthg - 2. fam [Plan] to see
through. ⟨⟩ vi (ist) - 1. [durch Gegend] to pass
through - 2. [in Marinade - Fleisch] to marinate;
[- Gemüse] to steep.

durchziehen[2] vt (unreg) to pass through.

Durch|zug der - 1. [von Wetter] passage
- 2. (ohne pl) [Zugluft] draught.

dürfen (präs **darf**, prät **durfte**, perf **hat gedurft** ODER **dürfen**) ⟨⟩ aux (perf **hat dürfen**)
- 1. [als Erlaubnis]: **etw tun dürfen** to be allowed
to do sthg; **darf ich mich setzen?** may I sit
down?; **darf ich fragen?** may I ask?; **darf ich
Ihnen behilflich sein?** geh can I be of help?
- 2. [als Überzeugung, Wunsch]: **das dürfen wir
nicht vergessen** we mustn't forget that; **so etwas darf einfach nicht passieren** such a thing
simply should not happen; **du darfst nicht
traurig sein!** don't be sad! - 3. [Veranlassung ha-
ben]: **man darf davon ausgehen, dass...** we
can assume that... - 4. [als Annahme]: **das dürfte genügen** that should be enough. ⟨⟩ vi
(perf **hat gedurft**): **sie darf nicht ins Schwimmbad** she's not allowed to go swimming. ⟨⟩ vt
(perf **hat gedurft**) fam: **das darf man nicht!**
you're not allowed to do that!; **was darf es
sein?** what can I get you?

dürftig ⟨⟩ adj - 1. [Einkünfte, Bezahlung] meagre - 2. abw [Ergebnis] poor; [Bearbeitung]
sketchy; [Bewuchs] sparse. ⟨⟩ adv - 1. [ent-
lohnt] meagrely; [bekleidet] scantily - 2. abw
[unzureichend] poorly; [sich entschuldigen]
lamely.

dürr adj - 1. [Person] scrawny - 2. [Blatt] dry
- 3. [Worte] blunt.

Dürre (pl **-n**) die drought.

Durst der [Gefühl] thirst; **Durst haben** to be
thirsty.

durstig ⟨⟩ adj thirsty. ⟨⟩ adv thirstily.

Durst|strecke die lean period.

Dusche (pl **-n**) die shower.

duschen ⟨⟩ vi to have a shower. ⟨⟩ vt to
shower. ⟶ **sich duschen** ref to have a
shower.

Dusch|raum der shower room.

Düse (pl **-n**) die nozzle.

düsen (perf **ist gedüst**) vi fam to rush.

Düsen|flugzeug das jet aircraft.

Dussel (pl -) der fam dope.

düster ◇ adj gloomy. ◇ adv gloomily.

Dutzend (pl -) das [zwölf] dozen; **im Dutzend** by the dozen. ➡ **Dutzende** Pl [viele] dozens; **zu Dutzenden** in their dozens.

dutzendmal adv a dozen times.

dutzendweise adv by the dozen.

duzen vt to address someone using the familiar "du" form. ➡ **sich duzen** ref to address each other using the familiar "du" form; **mit jm duzen** to use the "du" form with sb.

DVD (pl -s) (abk für Digital Versatile Disc) die EDV DVD.

Dynamit das dynamite.

DZ abk für Doppelzimmer.

E

e (pl - ODER -s), **E** (pl - ODER -s) [eː] das - 1. [Buchstabe] e, E - 2. MUS E. ➡ **E** der abk für Eilzug.

Ebbe (pl -n) die tide (outgoing); **es ist Ebbe** it is low tide; **bei Eintritt der Ebbe** when the tide is going out.

eben ◇ adj [flach - Gegend, Weg] flat; [glatt - Brett, Boden] smooth. ◇ adv - 1. just; **kannst du mal eben vorbeikommen?** can you just come round for a minute? - 2. [knapp]: **er hat ihn nur so eben berührt** he just touched him; **ich mache das eben zu Ende** I'll just finish it off - 3. [genau]: **eben den Anwalt meine ich** he's the very lawyer I mean; **eben das war es, was ich sagen wollte!** that was exactly what I wanted to say! ◇ interj - 1. [zum Ausdruck von Einverständnis] exactly - 2. [zum Ausdruck von Widerspruch]: **aber du hast doch dein Geld! - eben nicht!** but you've got your money, haven't you! - no I haven't!

Eben|bild das image.

ebenbürtig adj equal; **jm ebenbürtig sein** to be sb's equal; **einer Sache ebenbürtig sein** to be equal to sthg.

Ebene (pl -n) die - 1. [Flachland] plain - 2. PHYS & MATH plane - 3. [Niveau] level; **auf gleicher** ODER **der gleichen Ebene** on the same level; **auf höchster Ebene** at the highest level.

ebenfalls adv as well; **danke, ebenfalls** thanks, same to you.

ebenso adv just as.

ebenso gut adv just as well.

Eber (pl -) der boar.

ebnen vt to level; **jm den Weg ebnen** to smooth sb's path.

ec abk für Eurocheque.

Echo (pl -s) das echo.

Echse ['ɛksə] (pl -n) die lizard.

echt ◇ adj - 1. [unverfälscht] genuine - 2. [wahr, typisch] real. ◇ adv - 1. [rein] real; **echt italienisch essen** to eat real Italian food - 2. fam [wirklich] really.

Echtheit die genuineness.

Ecke (pl -n) die - 1. [gen] corner - 2. fam [Gegend] area; **eine hübsche Ecke!** a pretty spot!; **das ist noch eine ganze Ecke!** it's still quite a way!; **um die Ecke** fam round the corner; **es fehlt (bei uns) an allen Ecken und Enden** we are short of everything.

eckig ◇ adj - 1. [Form] square - 2. [Bewegung] awkward. ◇ adv [ungelenk] awkwardly.

Eck|zahn der canine tooth.

edel adj - 1. geh [Person, Geste] noble - 2. geh [Form] well-formed - 3. [Holz, Wein] fine.

Edel|metall das precious metal.

Edel|stahl der stainless steel.

Edel|stein der precious stone.

EDV [eːdeːˈfau] (abk für elektronische Datenverarbeitung) die data-processing.

Efeu der (ohne pl) ivy.

Effeff das: **etw aus dem Effeff beherrschen** fam to know sthg inside out.

Effekt (pl -e) der effect.

effektiv ◇ adj effective; [Gewinn, Leistung] net. ◇ adv effectively.

Effektivität [ɛfɛktiviˈtɛːt] die effectiveness.

effektvoll ◇ adj effective. ◇ adv effectively.

egal adj: **es ist mir egal** it's all the same to me; **das kann dir doch egal sein** that's no concern of yours; **das ist egal** it doesn't matter. ➡ **egal ob** adv no matter whether.

Egoismus der egoism.

eh ◇ interj fam hey. ◇ adv - 1. [immer]: **wie eh und je** as always - 2. Süddt & Österr fam [sowieso] anyway.

Ehe (pl -n) die marriage.

Ehe|bett das double bed.

Ehe|bruch der adultery (U).

Ehe|frau die wife.

Ehe|leute Pl married couple.

ehelich adj marital; [Recht] conjugal.

ehemalig adj former.

ehemals adv formerly.

Ehe|mann (pl -männer) der husband.

Ehe|paar das married couple.

Ehe|partner der marriage partner.

eher adv - 1. [vorher] earlier, sooner - 2. [lieber] rather - 3.: **das ist schon eher möglich** that is more likely - 4. [vielmehr] more.

Ehe|ring der wedding ring.

Ehe|schließung die marriage ceremony.

Ehre *die* honour; **jm zu Ehren** in sb's honour.

ehren *vt* [Achtung erweisen] to honour; **deine Großmut ehrt dich** your generosity does you credit; **dieses Angebot ehrt mich** I am honoured by this offer.

ehrenamtlich ◇ *adj* honorary. ◇ *adv* in an honorary capacity.

Ehren|bürger, in *der, die* honorary citizen.

Ehren|gast *der* guest of honour.

ehrenhaft ◇ *adj* honourable. ◇ *adv* honourably.

Ehren|mann (*pl* -männer) *der* man of honour.

Ehren|mitglied *das* honorary member.

Ehren|sache *die* point of honour; **das ist doch Ehrensache, dass ich bald wieder zurück bin** you can count on me to be back soon.

Ehrenwort (*pl* -e) *das* word of honour; **(großes) Ehrenwort!** *fam* I/we promise!

Ehrfurcht *die* [Verehrung] reverence; [Scheu] awe.

ehrfürchtig ◇ *adj* reverent. ◇ *adv* reverently.

Ehrgeiz *der* ambition.

ehrgeizig ◇ *adj* ambitious. ◇ *adv* ambitiously.

ehrlich ◇ *adj* honest. ◇ *adv* fairly; **ehrlich gesagt** to be honest.

Ehrlichkeit *die* honesty.

Ehrung (*pl* -en) *die* [das Ehren] honouring (*U*); [Ehre] honour.

ehrwürdig *adj* venerable.

Ei (*pl* -er) *das* - **1.** [gen] egg; **jn/etw wie ein rohes Ei behandeln** to treat sb/sthg with kid gloves - **2.** *vulg* [Hoden] ball.

Eiche (*pl* -n) *die* oak.

Eichel (*pl* -n) *die* - **1.** [Frucht] acorn - **2.** [des männlichen Gliedes] glans (penis).

Eichhörnchen (*pl* -) *das* squirrel.

Eid (*pl* -e) *der* oath. ➡ **unter Eid** *adv* under oath.

Eidechse ['aidɛksə] (*pl* -n) *die* lizard.

eidesstattlich ◇ *adj* sworn. ◇ *adv* solemnly.

Eid|genosse *der* Swiss citizen.

Eid|genossin *die* Swiss citizen.

Ei|dotter *das* & *der* egg yolk.

Eier|becher *der* egg cup.

Eier|kuchen *der* pancake.

Eier|schale *die* eggshell.

Eier|stock *der* ovary.

Eifer *der* eagerness.

Eifersucht *die* jealousy.

eifersüchtig ◇ *adj* jealous; **auf jn eifersüchtig sein** to be jealous of sb. ◇ *adv* jealously.

eifrig ◇ *adj* eager. ◇ *adv* eagerly.

Eigelb (*pl* - ODER -e) *das* egg yolk.

eigen *adj* - **1.** [jm gehörend] own - **2.** [typisch] typical. ➡ **Eigen** *das*: **sich** (*D*) **etw zu Eigen machen** to make sthg one's own.

Eigen|art *die* characteristic.

eigenartig ◇ *adj* strange. ◇ *adv* strangely.

Eigenbedarf *der* (*ohne pl*) personal requirements *Pl*; **für den Eigenbedarf** for one's own use.

eigenbrötlerisch ◇ *adj* reclusive. ◇ *adv* like a recluse.

eigenhändig ◇ *adj* own. ◇ *adv* with one's own hands.

eigenmächtig ◇ *adj* unauthorized. ◇ *adv* on one's own authority.

Eigen|name *der* proper name.

eigennützig ◇ *adj* selfish. ◇ *adv* selfishly.

eigens *adv* specially.

Eigenschaft (*pl* -en) *die* characteristic; [von Auto] feature; **in seiner Eigenschaft als etw** in one's capacity as sthg.

Eigenschaftswort (*pl* -wörter) *das* adjective.

eigensinnig ◇ *adj* stubborn. ◇ *adv* stubbornly.

eigenständig ◇ *adj* independent. ◇ *adv* independently.

eigentlich ◇ *adv* - **1.** [im Grunde, wirklich] really - **2.** [übrigens] by the way; **wer ist eigentlich Petra?** who is Petra(, by the way)? - **3.** [zum Ausdruck von Ärger]: **was erlauben Sie sich eigentlich?** what do you think you're doing? ◇ *adj* [wirklich] real.

Eigen|tor *das* own goal.

Eigentum *das* - **1.** [Besitz] property - **2.** [Besitzrecht] ownership.

Eigentümer, in (*mpl* -, *fpl* -nen) *der, die* owner.

eigentümlich *adj* peculiar.

eigenwillig *adj* - **1.** [eigen] original - **2.** [starrsinnig] obstinate.

eignen ➡ **sich eignen** *ref* to be suitable; **sich zu** ODER **für etw eignen** to be suitable for sthg.

Eignungs|prüfung *die* aptitude test.

Eil|brief *der* express letter.

Eile *die* hurry; **in Eile sein** to be in a hurry; **etw hat Eile/keine Eile** sthg is/is not urgent.

eilen (*perf* hat/ist geeilt) *vi* - **1.** (*ist*) [Person] to hurry - **2.** (*hat*) [Angelegenheit] to be urgent; **eilt!** urgent!; **mit etw eilt es/eilt es nicht** sthg is/is not urgent.

eilig ◇ *adj* - **1.** [Bewegung] hurried; **es eilig haben** to be in a hurry - **2.** [Angelegenheit, Brief] urgent. ◇ *adv* hurriedly.

Eimer (*pl* -) *der* bucket.

ein, e ◇ *num* one; **eine einzelne Rose** a single rose; **ein Uhr** one o'clock; **einer Mei-**

nung sein to have the same opinion; **für alle Mal** fam fig once and for all; **in einem fort** fig non-stop; **js Ein und Alles sein** fig to mean everything to sb. <> **det** a, an (vor Vokal); **ein Hund** a dog; **eine Idee** an idea; **ein Mädchen** a girl; **eines Tages** one day; **da ist eine Frau Schmidt am Apparat** there's a Mrs Schmidt on the phone. <> **pron** - 1. [als Teil einer Menge] one; **hier ist noch eins/eine** here's another one; **ein und dasselbe** one and the same - 2. fam [jemand] someone, somebody; **sieh mal einer an!** well I never!; **das kann einen schon mal passieren** these things can happen to you. <> **adv: ein-aus** on-off; **ein und aus gehen** fig to come and go; **nicht ein noch aus wissen** fig not to know whether one is coming or going.

ein|arbeiten vt [an die Arbeit gewöhnen] to train. ◆ **sich einarbeiten** ref to settle in.

ein|atmen vt & vi to breathe in.

Einbahn|straße die one-way street.

Einband (pl -bände) der book cover.

ein|bauen vt - 1. [Schrank, Bad] to fit; [Motor] to install - 2. [in Text] to incorporate.

Einbau|küche die fitted kitchen.

ein|berufen vt (unreg) - 1. [Sitzung] to summon - 2. [Wehrpflichtige] to call up UK, to draft US.

Einberufung die - 1. [einer Sitzung] summoning (U) - 2. [von Wehrpflichtigen] call-up UK, draft US.

ein|betten vt to wrap.

ein|beziehen vt (unreg): **jn/etw in etw (A) einbeziehen** to include sb/sthg in sthg.

ein|biegen (perf hat/ist eingebogen) (unreg) <> vi (ist) [abbiegen] to turn; **nach rechts/links einbiegen** to turn right/left. <> vt (hat) [verbiegen] to bend.

ein|bilden vt - 1. [sich einreden]: **sich (D) etw einbilden** to imagine sthg; **was bildest du dir eigentlich ein, wer du bist?** who do you think you are? - 2. [stolz sein]: **er bildet sich ganz schön viel ein** he is really full of himself; **sich (D) viel auf etw (A) einbilden** to be conceited about sthg; **darauf brauchst du dir nichts einzubilden** that's nothing to be proud of.

Einbildung (pl -en) die - 1. [Fantasie] imagination - 2. [Hochmut] conceit.

Einbildungskraft die imagination.

ein|binden vt (unreg) - 1. [einschlagen] to bind - 2. [einbeziehen]: **jn/etw in etw (A) einbinden** to integrate sb/sthg into sthg.

ein|bläuen vt: **jm etw einbläuen** to drum sthg into sb.

einbleuen = einbläuen.

Ein|blick der - 1. [Blick]: **Einblick in die Dokumente bekommen** to get a look at the documents; **Einblick in etw (A) nehmen** to examine sthg; **jm Einblick in etw (A) gewähren** to allow sb to examine sthg - 2. [Einsicht] insight.

ein|brechen (perf hat/ist eingebrochen) vi (unreg) - 1. (hat) [gewaltsam eindringen] to break in; **bei jm einbrechen** to burgle sb - 2. (ist) [einstürzen] to fall in - 3. (ist) [Partei, Mannschaft] to come unstuck - 4. (ist) [durchbrechen] to fall through - 5. (ist) [eindringen]: **(in ein Land) einbrechen** to invade (a country) - 6. (ist) geh [Nacht, Dunkelheit] to fall; [Winter] to set in.

Einbrecher, in (mpl -, fpl -nen) der burglar.

ein|bringen vt (unreg) - 1. [Ernte] to bring in - 2. [Gewinn] to bring in; [Anerkennung] to bring; [Erfahrung] to give; **das bringt nichts ein** that's not worth it - 3. [vorlegen] to introduce - 4. amt [einsetzen - Geld, Vermögen] to invest; [- in eine Ehe] to put in.

ein|brocken vt fam: **jm/sich etwas einbrocken** to land sb/o.s. in it; **dieses Problem hast du dir selbst eingebrockt!** you brought this problem on yourself!

Ein|bruch der - 1. [Straftat] break-in; **einen Einbruch begehen** to commit a burglary - 2. [Zusammenbruch] collapse - 3. [Eindringen] penetration - 4. fam [bei Wahl] drubbing - 5. [Beginn - von Winter] onset; **vor Einbruch der Nacht** before nightfall.

einbürgern vt [eine Staatsangehörigkeit verleihen] to naturalize. ◆ **sich einbürgern** ref [üblich werden] to become established.

Ein|buße die loss.

ein|büßen <> vt to lose. <> vi: **an etw (D) einbüßen** to lose sthg.

ein|checken ['aintʃekn] vt & vi to check in.

ein|cremen, einkremen vt to put cream on. ◆ **sich eincremen** ref to put cream on.

ein|dämmen vt - 1. [stauen] to dam - 2. [zurückhalten] to contain.

ein|decken vt fam [überhäufen]: **jn mit etw eindecken** to swamp sb with sthg.

eindeutig <> adj clear. <> adv clearly.

ein|dringen (perf ist eingedrungen) vi (unreg) - 1. [hineingelangen]: **in etw (A) eindringen** [Wasser] to get into sthg; [Messer] to enter sthg - 2. [einbrechen]: **in etw (A) eindringen** [Gebäude] to break into sthg; [Land] to invade sthg.

eindringlich <> adj insistent. <> adv insistently.

Eindringling (pl -e) der intruder.

Eindruck (pl -drücke) der impression; **Eindruck auf jn machen** to make an impression on sb; **einen Eindruck von etw bekommen** ODER **erhalten** to get an impression of sthg; **einen guten/schlechten Eindruck (auf jn) machen** to make a good/bad impression (on sb).

ein|drücken vt - 1. [beschädigen - Kotflügel, Fensterscheibe] to smash in; [- Nase, Kissen] to flatten - 2. [in etw hineindrücken] to press.

eindrucksvoll <> adj impressive. <> adv impressively.

ein|ebnen vt to level.

eineiig ['ain aiiç] *adj*: **eineiige Zwillinge** identical twins.

eineinhalb *num* one and a half.

ein|engen *vt* - **1.** [beschränken] to constrict - **2.** [einschränken] to restrict; **jn in seiner Freiheit einengen** to curb sb's freedom.

einerlei *adj* immaterial; **das ist mir einerlei** that's all the same to me.

einerseits *adv*: **einerseits... andererseits...** on the one hand... on the other (hand)...

einfach <> *adj* - **1.** [leicht, schlicht] simple - **2.** [Fahrkarte, Knoten] single. <> *adv* - **1.** [leicht, schlicht] simply; **ich komme einfach mit** I'll just come with you; **es sich einfach machen** to make it easy for o.s. - **2.** [nicht mehrfach]: **etw einfach falten** to fold sth once.

Einfachheit *die* simplicity.

ein|fädeln *vt* - **1.** [Faden, Nadel] to thread - **2.** [bewerkstelligen]: **sie hat die Sache schlau eingefädelt** she worked things very cleverly.

ein|fahren (*perf* hat/ist eingefahren) (*unreg*) <> *vi* (ist) [Zug] to arrive. <> *vt* (hat) - **1.** [hineinschaffen - Ernte] to bring in - **2.** [beschädigen - Tor, Mauer] to knock down; [- Kotflügel] to smash in - **3.** AUTO to run in *UK*, to break in *US* - **4.** [einziehen - Fahrwerk] to retract.

Ein|fahrt *die* - **1.** [Einfahren] arrival; **der Zug hat noch keine Einfahrt** the train still hasn't arrived - **2.** [Stelle zum Hineinfahren] entrance.

Ein|fall *der* - **1.** [Idee] idea; **ihm kam ein Einfall** he had an idea - **2.** [Einfallen]: **der Einfall von Sonnenstrahlen** the sun's rays shining in - **3.** [Eindringen] invasion; **der Einfall der Römer in Gallien** the invasion of Gaul by the Romans.

ein|fallen (*perf* ist eingefallen) *vi* (*unreg*) - **1.** [in den Sinn kommen]: **ihm fiel nichts Besseres ein** no better idea occurred to him; **ihm fällt immer eine passende Ausrede ein** he always thinks of a suitable excuse; **mir fällt nichts ein, was ich kochen könnte** I can't think of anything that I could cook; **sich** (*D*) **etwas einfallen lassen** to think of something; **was fällt dir/Ihnen ein!** what(ever) are you thinking of! - **2.** [wieder in den Sinn kommen] to remember; **da fällt mir ein** that reminds me - **3.** [hereinkommen] to shine in - **4.** MIL: **in etw** (*A*) **einfallen** to invade sth - **5.** [einstimmen] to join in - **6.** [einstürzen] to collapse.

einfallslos *adj* unimaginative.

einfallsreich *adj* imaginative.

einfältig *adj* - **1.** [arglos] naive; [Lächeln] innocent - **2.** [beschränkt] simple-minded.

Einfamilien|haus *das* house designed for one family.

ein|fangen *vt* (*unreg*) - **1.** [fangen und fest halten] to capture - **2.** *fam* [bekommen]: **sich** (*D*) **etw einfangen** to get sth.

einfarbig *adj* all one colour.

ein|fassen *vt* - **1.** [Stoff] to edge - **2.** [mit Mauer] to enclose - **3.** [Edelstein] to set.

ein|fliegen *vt* (*unreg*) to fly in; **jn/etw einfliegen lassen** to fly sb/sth in.

ein|fließen (*perf* ist eingeflossen) *vi* (*unreg*) [Wasser, Luft] to flow in; **eine Kritik einfließen lassen** to slip in a criticism.

ein|flößen *vt* - **1.** [zu trinken geben] to help to drink - **2.** [erregen]: **jm etw einflößen** [Ehrfurcht, Vertrauen, Angst] to inspire sth in sb.

Einfluss (*pl* -flüsse) *der* influence; **unter Einfluss von Alkohol** under the influence of alcohol; **auf jn/etw Einfluss haben** [Macht] to have influence over sb/sth; [Effekt] to influence sb/sth; **auf jn/etw Einfluss nehmen** to influence sb/sth.

einflussreich *adj* influential.

einförmig *adj* monotonous.

ein|frieren (*perf* hat/ist eingefroren) (*unreg*) <> *vt* (hat) to freeze; [Beziehungen] to suspend. <> *vi* (ist) [Wasserleitung] to freeze; [Teich] to freeze over.

ein|fügen *vt* [gen & EDV] to insert. ➤ **sich einfügen** *ref* [sich anpassen] to fit in.

einfühlsam *adj* sensitive.

Einfuhr (*pl* -en) *die* - **1.** [Einführen] importation - **2.** [Ware] import.

ein|führen *vt* - **1.** [gen] to introduce; **jn in etw** (*A*) **einführen** to introduce sb to sth - **2.** [importieren] to import - **3.** [hineinschieben] to insert, to introduce.

Ein|führung *die* introduction.

ein|füllen *vt* to pour in; **etw in etw** (*A*) **einfüllen** to pour sth into sth.

Ein|gang *der* - **1.** [Eingangstür] entrance - **2.** [von Geld, Post] receipt.

eingangs *adv* at the beginning.

Eingangs|halle *die* entrance hall.

ein|geben *vt* (*unreg*) EDV to enter.

eingebildet *adj* - **1.** [nicht wirklich] imaginary - **2.** [hochmütig] arrogant.

Eingeborene (*pl* -n), **Eingeborne** (*pl* -n) *der, die* native.

eingefleischt *adj* ▷ **Junggeselle**.

ein|gehen (*perf* ist eingegangen) (*unreg*) <> *vi* - **1.** [ankommen]: **bei uns ist noch keine Antwort eingegangen** we have not yet received a reply - **2.** [Tier, Pflanze] to perish - **3.** [Firma] to close down - **4.** [beachten]: **auf jn/etw eingehen** to respond to sb/sth; **auf etw** (*A*) **eingehen** [Angebot, Vorschlag] to agree to sth - **5.** [Kleidung] to shrink - **6.** *geh* [Einzug halten]: **in die Geschichte eingehen** to go down in history. <> *vt* [Bündnis, Ehe, Verpflichtung] to enter into; [Risiko] to take; [Wette] to make.

eingehend <> *adj* detailed. <> *adv* in detail.

eingenommen ◇ pp ▷ **einnehmen**. ◇ adj: **von sich eingenommen sein** to have a high opinion of o.s.; **für/gegen etw eingenommen sein** to be taken with/biased against sthg; **von jm/etw eingenommen sein** to be taken with sb/sthg.

eingeschlossen pp ▷ **einschließen**.

eingetragen ◇ pp ▷ **eintragen**. ◇ adj registered, ▷ **Verein**; siehe auch **Warenzeichen**.

Eingeweide Pl entrails.

ein|gewöhnen ⇒ **sich eingewöhnen** ref to settle in.

ein|gießen vt (unreg) [Tasse, Glas] to pour; **jm etw eingießen** to pour sb sthg.

ein|gliedern vt: **jn/etw in etw (A) eingliedern** to integrate sb/sthg into sthg. ⇒ **sich eingliedern** ref: **sich in etw (A) eingliedern** to integrate into sthg.

ein|graben vt (unreg) - 1. [in den Boden] to bury - 2. [eindrücken - Spuren] to carve. ⇒ **sich eingraben** ref: **sich in etw (A) eingraben** [Tier] to burrow into sthg; [Fluss] to carve (itself) a channel into sthg.

ein|greifen vi (unreg): **(in etw (A)) eingreifen** to intervene (in sthg).

Ein|griff der - 1. [Intervention] intervention - 2. MED operation.

ein|haken ◇ vt to fasten. ◇ vi to interrupt.

ein|halten (unreg) ◇ vt [befolgen, erfüllen - Termin] to keep; [- Plan] to keep to; [- Vorschrift] to observe. ◇ vi [innehalten]: **in ODER mit seinem Tun einhalten** to interrupt what one is doing.

einhändig adv one-handed.

ein|hängen ◇ vt - 1. [in ein Scharnier - Tür] to hang; [- Fenster] to put in - 2. [auflegen - Telefonhörer] to put down. ◇ vi to hang up.

einheimisch adj local.

Einheit (pl -en) die - 1. [Geschlossenheit] unity - 2. MIL [Maßeinheit] unit.

einheitlich ◇ adj - 1. [geschlossen] unified - 2. [gleich] uniform; [Standard] standardized. ◇ adv uniformly; [sich kleiden] in the same way.

einhellig ◇ adj unanimous. ◇ adv unanimously.

ein|holen ◇ vt - 1. [Person, Wagen] to catch up with; [verlorene Zeit] to make up for - 2. [holen] to obtain - 3. [einziehen - Netz] to haul in; [- Leine] to reel in - 4. [einkaufen] to get. ◇ vi: **einholen gehen** to go shopping.

einig adj [einer Meinung]: **(sich) über jn/etw einig sein** to agree about sb/sthg; [vereint] united.

einige ◇ det - 1. [eine gewisse Menge] a few, some; **nach einiger Zeit** after some time; **einige Probleme** a few problems; **nur einige waren da** there were only a few people there

- 2. [beträchtlich] quite a few; **das brachte so einige Probleme mit sich** this caused quite a lot of problems; **so einige waren da** there were quite a lot of people there. ◇ pron a few, some. ⇒ **einiges** pron something; **das hat einiges für sich** there is something to be said for it; **ich könnte dir einiges erzählen** I could tell you a thing or two.

einigen vt to unite. ⇒ **sich einigen** ref: **sich (mit jm) einigen** to reach an agreement (with sb); **sich auf etw (A) einigen** to agree on sthg.

einigermaßen adv fairly.

Einigkeit die - 1. [Eintracht] unity - 2. [Übereinstimmung] agreement.

Einigung (pl -en) die - 1. [Übereinkunft] agreement - 2. [Vereinigung] unification.

Ein|kauf der - 1. [Einkaufen] shopping - 2. [eingekaufte Ware] purchase; **die Einkäufe aus dem Wagen holen** to get the shopping out of the car - 3. WIRTSCH purchasing.

ein|kaufen ◇ vt to buy. ◇ vi: **einkaufen gehen** to go shopping.

Einkaufs|bummel der shopping expedition; **einen Einkaufsbummel machen** to go on a shopping expedition.

Einkaufs|tasche die shopping bag.

ein|kehren (perf ist eingekehrt) vi to stop off.

ein|klammern vt to put in brackets, to bracket.

Einklang der harmony.

ein|kleiden vt to kit out. ⇒ **sich einkleiden** ref: **sich neu einkleiden** to buy o.s. a new wardrobe.

Einkommen (pl -) das income.

Einkommens|steuer die income tax.

ein|kreisen vt - 1. [umzingeln] to surround - 2. [eingrenzen] to pin down - 3. [mit Stift] to circle.

ein|kremen = **eincremen**.

Einkünfte Pl income (U).

ein|laden vt (unreg) - 1. [Gast] to invite; **jn zu etw einladen** [Hochzeit, Party] to invite sb to sthg; **darf ich Sie zu einem Kaffee einladen?** can I buy you a coffee?; **jn in ein Restaurant einladen** to take sb out for a meal - 2. [Last] to load.

einladend ◇ adj inviting. ◇ adv invitingly.

Einladung die invitation.

Ein|lage die - 1. [im Schuh] insole - 2. KÜCHE vegetables, noodles, meat etc added to a clear soup - 3. [im Programm] interlude - 4. WIRTSCH [bei Bank] deposit; [bei Firma] investment.

Einlass der admission.

ein|lassen *vt (unreg)* - **1.** [hereinlassen] to admit - **2.** [Wasser] to run - **3.** [einsetzen] to set. ➤ **sich einlassen** *ref*: sich mit jm/auf etw (A) einlassen to get involved with sb/in sthg.

ein|laufen *(perf hat/ist eingelaufen) (unreg)* ◇ *vi (ist)* - **1.** SPORT: **ins Stadion einlaufen** to enter the stadium; **ins Ziel einlaufen** to cross the finishing line - **2.** [Wasser] to run in - **3.** [einfahren] to come in - **4.** [Stoff] to shrink. ◇ *vt (hat)* [Schuhe] to wear in. ➤ **sich einlaufen** *ref* to warm up.

ein|leben ➤ **sich einleben** *ref* to settle in.

ein|legen *vt* - **1.** [hineintun] to put in; **den ersten Gang einlegen** to go into first gear - **2.** KÜCHE to preserve; [in Essig] to pickle - **3.** [Pause] to have, to take - **4.** [Berufung, Bitte] to lodge; **ein gutes Wort für jn einlegen** to put in a good word for sb.

ein|leiten *vt* - **1.** [beginnen - Untersuchung, Verfahren] to start; [- Schritte] to take; [- Geburt] to induce - **2.** [einführen] to open - **3.** [einlassen]: **Abwässer in den Fluss einleiten** to let effluent into the river.

einleitend ◇ *adj* introductory. ◇ *adv* by way of introduction.

Ein|leitung *die* - **1.** [Einführung] introduction - **2.** [Beginn - von Untersuchung] start.

ein|lenken *vi* to give way.

ein|leuchten *vi*: **es leuchtet mir ein, dass...** I can see that...

einleuchtend ◇ *adj* convincing. ◇ *adv* convincingly.

ein|liefern *vt* [bringen - in psychiatrische Anstalt] to commit; **jn in ein Krankenhaus einliefern** to take sb to hospital.

sich ein|loggen *ref* EDV to log on; **sich ins Internet einloggen** to log on to the Internet.

ein|lösen *vt* - **1.** [Scheck] to cash; [Gutschein] to redeem - **2.** [Versprechen] to keep.

Ein|lösung *die* [von Scheck] cashing; [von Gutschein] redemption.

ein|machen *vt* to preserve.

einmal *adv* - **1.** [ein einzelnes Mal] once; **noch einmal** (once) again - **2.** [irgendwann - zuvor] before; [- in Zukunft] sometime; **haben wir uns nicht schon einmal gesehen?** haven't we met before?; **irgendwann einmal möchte sie nach England ziehen** she'd like to move to England someday - **3.** [mal, bitte]: **komm einmal her!** come here, will you!; **hör mir einmal gut zu!** now listen to me carefully! ➤ **auf einmal** *adv* - **1.** [plötzlich] suddenly - **2.** [zusammen, gleichzeitig] at once. ➤ **nicht einmal** *adv* not even.

Einmaleins *das (ohne pl)* - **1.** [Zahlenreihe] multiplication tables *Pl* - **2.** [Grundwissen] ABC.

einmalig *adj* - **1.** [einzeln - Zahlung] one-off - **2.** [außergewöhnlich] unique - **3.** [wunderbar] fantastic.

ein|marschieren *(perf ist einmarschiert) vi* to invade.

ein|mischen ➤ **sich einmischen** *ref*: sich (in etw (A)) einmischen to interfere (in sthg).

Ein|mischung *die* interference.

ein|münden *(perf hat/ist eingemündet) vi*: **in etw (A) einmünden** [Fluss] to flow into sthg; [Straße] to lead into sthg.

einmütig ◇ *adj* unanimous. ◇ *adv* unanimously.

Einnahme *(pl -n) die* - **1.** [Einkommen] income; [an einer Kasse] takings *Pl*; [vom Staat] revenue - **2.** [von Medikament] taking - **3.** [Eroberung] capture.

ein|nehmen *vt (unreg)* - **1.** [Geld, Medikament, Platz] to take; **viel Raum einnehmen** to take up a lot of room - **2.** [erobern] to capture; **jn für sich einnehmen** *fig* to win sb over.

einnehmend *adj* captivating.

ein|ordnen *vt* to put in its place; [Akten] to file; [Dichter, Politiker] to categorize. ➤ **sich einordnen** *ref* [Auto] to get into the correct lane; [Person] to fit in.

ein|packen *vt* - **1.** [verpacken - Kleidung] to pack; [- Geschenk] to wrap - **2.** *fam* [anziehen] to wrap up.

ein|parken ◇ *vt* to park. ◇ *vi* to park.

ein|passen *vt* to fit.

ein|pflanzen *vt* - **1.** [pflanzen] to plant - **2.** MED to implant.

ein|planen *vt* [Verlust, Verzögerung] to allow for; [Person] to count in.

ein|prägen *vt* - **1.** [eingravieren] to imprint - **2.** [einschärfen]: **sich (D) etw einprägen** to memorize sthg; **jm etw einprägen** to impress sthg on sb.

einprägsam *adj* easily remembered; [Melodie] catchy.

ein|rahmen *vt* to frame.

ein|räumen *vt* - **1.** [einordnen, ordnen - Kleidung, Geschirr] to put away; **den Schrank einräumen** to put things away in the cupboard - **2.** [Frist, Kredit] to grant - **3.** [zugeben] to admit.

ein|reden ◇ *vi*: **auf jn einreden** to keep on at sb. ◇ *vt*: **jm etw einreden** to talk sb into sthg.

ein|reiben *vt (unreg)* to rub in.

ein|reichen *vt* [Antrag] to submit; [Beschwerde] to lodge.

Ein|reise *die* entry.

ein|reisen *(perf ist eingereist) vi* to enter; **nach Deutschland einreisen** to enter Germany.

Einreise|visum *das* entry visa.

ein|reißen *(perf hat/ist eingerissen) (unreg)* ◇ *vt (hat)* - **1.** [Gebäude] to pull down - **2.** [Papier, Stoff] to tear. ◇ *vi (ist)* - **1.** [Papier, Stoff] to tear - **2.** *abw* [Unsitte] to become a habit.

ein|renken vt - 1. MED to put back in its socket - 2. [bereinigen] to sort out. ➤ **sich einrenken** ref to sort itself out.

ein|richten vt - 1. [möblieren] to furnish - 2. [organisieren] **etw so einrichten, dass...** to organize sthg in such a way that... - 3. [Stelle, Institution] to set up. ➤ **sich einrichten** ref - 1. [mit Möbeln] to furnish one's home - 2. [sich einstellen]: **sich auf etw (A) einrichten** to prepare for sthg.

Ein|richtung die - 1. [Möbel] furnishings Pl - 2. [Einrichten] furnishing - 3. [Schaffung] setting up - 4. [Institution] institution.

ein|rücken (perf hat/ist eingerückt) ◇ vi (ist) to enter. ◇ vt (hat) to indent.

eins ◇ num [als Zahl] one; **eins A** top-quality, A-1. ◇ pron one; siehe auch **sechs**.

Eins (pl -en) die - 1. [Zahl] one - 2. [Schulnote] ≈ A, mark of 1 on a scale from 1 to 6; siehe auch **Sechs**.

einsam adj - 1. [Person] lonely - 2. [Haus, Gegend] isolated.

Einsamkeit die - 1. [von Person] loneliness - 2. [von Haus, Gegend] isolation.

ein|sammeln vt [Werkzeug, Spielzeug] to gather up; [Kinder] to pick up; [Klassenarbeiten] to collect in; [Geld] to collect.

Ein|satz der - 1. [Geld] stake - 2. [Einsetzen] use; **unter Einsatz aller Kräfte** with a huge effort; **zum Einsatz kommen** to be used - 3. [Engagement] commitment - 4. MIL mission; **im Einsatz sein** to be in action - 5. [Fach] compartment - 6. MUS entry.

einsatzbereit adj [Truppe] ready for action; [Maschine] ready for use.

ein|schalten vt - 1. [anstellen] to switch on - 2. [hinzuziehen] to call in. ➤ **sich einschalten** ref - 1. [von selbst angehen] to switch on - 2. [eingreifen] to intervene.

ein|schärfen vt: **jm etw einschärfen** to impress sthg upon sb.

ein|schätzen vt [Gefahr, Lage] to assess; [Vermögen, Umsatz] to estimate; [Person] to judge; **jn/etw falsch einschätzen** to misjudge sb/sthg.

Ein|schätzung die [von Gefahr, Lage] assessment; [von Vermögen, Umsatz] estimation; [von Person] judgement.

ein|schenken vt: **jm etw einschenken** to pour sb sthg.

ein|schicken vt to send in.

ein|schieben vt (unreg) - 1. [hineinschieben] to insert - 2. [einfügen] to fit in.

ein|schlafen (perf ist eingeschlafen) vi (unreg) - 1. [aus Müdigkeit] to fall asleep - 2. [Körperteil] to go to sleep - 3. [aufhören] to peter out - 4. [sterben] to pass away.

ein|schläfern vt - 1. [töten] to put to sleep - 2. [in Schlaf versetzen] to send to sleep.

einschläfernd adj soporific.

ein|schlagen (perf hat/ist eingeschlagen) (unreg) ◇ vi - 1. (ist) [treffen] to strike - 2. (hat) [zustimmen] to agree; [mit Händedruck] to shake on it - 3. (hat) [lenken] to steer; **nach rechts einschlagen** to turn right - 4. (hat) [Furore machen - Schallplatte] to be a hit; [- Erfindung] to be a success; [- Enthüllungen] to cause a furore - 5. (hat) [schlagen]: **auf jn einschlagen** to beat sb. ◇ vt (hat) - 1. [Nagel] to knock in - 2. [Glas, Tür] to smash in - 3. [Buch, Geschenk] to wrap (up) - 4. [Weg] to take.

einschlägig ◇ adj [Literatur] relevant; [Methode] appropriate. ◇ adv: **einschlägig vorbestraft sein** to have a previous conviction for a similar offence.

ein|schleichen ➤ **sich einschleichen** ref (unreg) eigtl & fig to creep in.

ein|schleusen vt [Waffen] to smuggle in; [V-Leute] to infiltrate.

ein|schließen vt (unreg) - 1. [einsperren] to lock up - 2. [aufbewahren] to lock away - 3. [umzingeln] to surround - 4. [beinhalten] to include.

einschließlich ◇ präp (+ G) including; **von 1,3 bis einschließlich 5,5** from 1.3 to 5.5 inclusive. ◇ adv: **bis Montag einschließlich** up to and including Monday.

ein|schmeicheln ➤ **sich einschmeicheln** ref: **sich bei jm einschmeicheln** abw to curry favour with sb.

einschneidend ◇ adj drastic. ◇ adv drastically.

ein|schneien (perf ist eingeschneit) vi to get snowed in.

Ein|schnitt der - 1. [Schnitt] cut; [bei Operation] incision - 2. [Zäsur] turning point.

ein|schränken vt to limit; [Rauchen, Trinken] to cut down on; [Menge, Anzahl] to reduce. ➤ **sich einschränken** ref to economize.

Einschränkung (pl -en) die - 1. [Einschränken] limitation; [von Kosten] reduction - 2. [Vorbehalt] reservation.

ein|schreiben vt (unreg) - 1. [hineinschreiben]: **eingeschrieben sein** to be registered - 2. [Brief]: **etw einschreiben lassen** ODER **eingeschrieben schicken** to send sthg recorded delivery. ➤ **sich einschreiben** ref [sich anmelden] to register.

Ein|schreiben das: **etw per Einschreiben schicken** to send sthg recorded delivery.

ein|schreiten (perf ist eingeschritten) vi (unreg) to intervene.

ein|schüchtern vt to intimidate.

Einschüchterung (pl -en) die intimidation.

ein|schulen vt: **eingeschult werden** to start school.

Ein|schulung die [Tag] first day at school.

ein|sehen vt (unreg) - 1. [Fehler, Schuld] to recognize, to admit - 2. [Papiere] to examine.

einseitig ⟨⟩ *adj* - **1.** [subjektiv] one-sided - **2.** [auf einer Seite] on one side - **3.** [Beziehung] unilateral. ⟨⟩ *adv* - **1.** [subjektiv] one-sidedly - **2.** [auf einer Seite] on one side - **3.** [unausgewogen]: **sich einseitig ernähren** to eat an unbalanced diet.

ein|senden (*prät* **sendete ein** *ODER* **sandte ein**, *perf* **hat eingesendet** *ODER* **eingesandt**) *vt* to send in.

ein|setzen ⟨⟩ *vt* - **1.** [hineinsetzen] to put in - **2.** [gebrauchen] to use; **die Polizei/das Militär einsetzen** to bring in the police/army - **3.** [in Amt] to appoint - **4.** [Leben] to risk; [Geld] to stake. ⟨⟩ *vi* to begin; [Sturm] to break. ◆ **sich einsetzen** *ref* to be committed; **sich für jn einsetzen** to stand up for sb; **sich für etw einsetzen** to support sthg.

Ein|sicht *die* - **1.** [Erkenntnis] insight; **zu der Einsicht kommen, dass...** to come to realize that... - **2.** [Einblick]: **in etw (A) Einsicht bekommen** to get a look at sthg.

einsichtig ⟨⟩ *adj* - **1.** [vernünftig] sensible - **2.** [verständlich] clear. ⟨⟩ *adv* - **1.** [vernünftig] sensibly - **2.** [verständlich] clearly.

Ein|siedler, in *der, die* hermit.

einsilbig ⟨⟩ *adj* - **1.** [Person] taciturn - **2.** [Wort, Antwort] monosyllabic. ⟨⟩ *adv* [antworten] in monosyllables.

ein|sinken (*perf* **ist eingesunken**) *vi* (*unreg*) to sink (in).

ein|spannen *vt* - **1.** [Pferd] to harness - **2.** [zur Arbeit] to rope in - **3.** [in Schreibmaschine] to insert.

ein|sparen *vt* to save; [Personal] to cut back on.

ein|sperren *vt* to lock up.

ein|spielen *vt* - **1.** [Geld] to bring in; [Unkosten] to cover - **2.** [Instrument] to play in - **3.** [einfügen] to fit in. ◆ **sich einspielen** *ref* - **1.** [sich aufwärmen] to warm up - **2.** [sich abstimmen] to settle down; **die Kollegen haben sich aufeinander eingespielt** the colleagues are now working well together.

ein|springen (*perf* **ist eingesprungen**) *vi* (*unreg*): **(für jn) einspringen** to stand in (for sb).

Ein|spruch *der* objection; **Einspruch (gegen etw) erheben** to object (to sthg).

einspurig ⟨⟩ *adj* single-lane. ⟨⟩ *adv*: **'nur einspurig befahrbar'** 'single-lane traffic only'.

ein|stecken *vt* - **1.** [in Tasche] to put in one's pocket; **vergiss nicht, Geld einzustecken!** don't forget to take some money with you! - **2.** [Kritik, Niederlage, Verlust] to take - **3.** [Stecker] to plug in - **4.** [Brief] to post *UK*, to mail *US* - **5.** [stehlen] to pocket.

ein|steigen (*perf* **ist eingestiegen**) *vi* (*unreg*) - **1.** [in Auto] to get in; [in Bus, Zug] to get on; **ins Auto/in den Zug einsteigen** to get in the car/on the train - **2.** [anfangen]: **in etw (A) einstei-**

gen [Beruf, Politik] to go into sthg - **3.** [sich einkaufen]: **bei RTL/in eine Firma einsteigen** to buy a share in RTL/a company.

einstellbar *adj* adjustable.

ein|stellen *vt* - **1.** [Angestellte] to take on - **2.** [Gerät, Lautstärke - zum ersten Mal] to set; [- genauer] to adjust; [Sender] to tune into - **3.** [anmachen] to switch on - **4.** [beenden] to stop. ◆ **sich einstellen** *ref* - **1.** [sich vorbereiten]: **sich auf jn/etw einstellen** to prepare for sb/sthg; [sich anpassen] to get used to sb/sthg - **2.** [geh] [anfangen] to begin.

Ein|stellung *die* - **1.** [von Angestellten] appointment - **2.** [von Gerät, Lautstärke - zum ersten Mal] setting; [- genauer] adjustment; [von Sender] tuning - **3.** [Beendigung - von Verfahren, Zahlungen] termination, stopping - **4.** [Meinung, Haltung] attitude - **5.** [Szene] take.

Einstellungs|gespräch *das* interview.

Einstieg (*pl* -e) *der* - **1.** [Beginn] entry - **2.** [in Bus, Zug] boarding.

ein|stimmen *vi* - **1.** [mitsingen, mitspielen]: **(in etw (A)) einstimmen** to join in (sthg) - **2.** [vorbereiten]: **jn auf etw (A) einstimmen** to get sb in the right mood for sthg.

einstimmig ⟨⟩ *adj* - **1.** MUS for one voice - **2.** [übereinstimmend] unanimous. ⟨⟩ *adv* - **1.** MUS in unison - **2.** [übereinstimmend] unanimously.

einstöckig *adj* single-storey.

ein|studieren *vt* to rehearse.

ein|stufen *vt* to categorize; **jn in eine Gehaltsgruppe einstufen** to put sb in an income bracket.

einstündig *adj* one-hour.

Ein|sturz *der* collapse.

ein|stürzen (*perf* **ist eingestürzt**) *vi* - **1.** [Haus, Mauer] to collapse - **2.** [hereinbrechen]: **neue Eindrücke stürzten auf sie ein** she was overwhelmed by new impressions.

Einsturz|gefahr *die*: 'Vorsicht, Einsturzgefahr!' 'danger, building unsafe!'

einstweilig *amt* ⟨⟩ *adj* temporary. ⟨⟩ *adv* temporarily.

eintägig *adj* one-day.

ein|tauchen (*perf* **hat/ist eingetaucht**) ⟨⟩ *vt* (*hat*) to dip; [völlig] to immerse; [Keks] to dunk. ⟨⟩ *vi* (*ist*) to dive in.

ein|tauschen *vt*: **etw gegen etw eintauschen** to exchange sthg for sthg.

eintausend *num* a *ODER* one thousand.

ein|teilen *vt* - **1.** [klassifizieren] to classify - **2.** [unterteilen] to divide up - **3.** [Arbeit, Zeit] to organize - **4.** [einplanen]: **jn für** *ODER* **zu etw einteilen** to assign sb to sthg.

einteilig *adj* one-piece.

Ein|teilung *die* - **1.** [Klassifizierung] classification - **2.** [Unterteilung] division - **3.** [von Arbeit, Zeit] organization.

eintönig ⬦ *adj* monotonous. ⬦ *adv* monotonously.

Eintopf *der* stew.

einträchtig *adv* harmoniously.

Eintrag (*pl* -träge) *der* [Notiz] entry.

ein|tragen *vt* (*unreg*) - 1. [notieren] to write down - 2. *amt* [registrieren] to register - 3. [Geld] to bring in; [Ärger, Sympathie] to bring. ➡ **sich eintragen** *ref* to put one's name down.

einträglich *adj* lucrative.

ein|treffen (*perf* ist eingetroffen) *vi* (*unreg*) - 1. [ankommen] to arrive - 2. [wahr werden] to come true.

ein|treiben *vt* (*unreg*) to collect.

ein|treten (*perf* hat/ist eingetreten) (*unreg*) ⬦ *vi* (ist) - 1. [in Raum, Phase] to enter; **in etw (A) eintreten** to enter sthg - 2. [in Gruppe, Verein]: **in etw (A) eintreten** to join sthg - 3. [sich einsetzen]: **für jn/etw eintreten** to stand up for sb/sthg - 4. [Tod] to occur; [Fall, Umstände] to arise. ⬦ *vt* (hat) to kick in.

Eintritt *der* - 1. [in Raum, Phase] entry; '**Eintritt frei**' 'admission free'; '**Eintritt verboten**' 'no entry' - 2. [Eintrittspreis] admission - 3. [in Gruppe, Verein] joining - 4. [Anfang]: **bei Eintritt der Dämmerung** at dawn.

Eintritts|geld *das* admission fee.

Eintritts|karte *die* ticket.

ein|trüben ➡ **sich eintrüben** *ref* to cloud over; **es trübt sich ein** it's clouding over.

ein|üben *vt* to rehearse.

einverstanden ⬦ *adj*: **mit jm/etw einverstanden sein** to agree with sb/sthg; **sich mit etw einverstanden erklären** to agree to sthg. ⬦ *interj* OK!

Ein|verständnis *das* - 1. [Übereinstimmung] agreement - 2. [Billigung] consent.

Ein|wand *der* objection; **Einwand (gegen etw) erheben** to object (to sthg).

ein|wandern (*perf* ist eingewandert) *vi* to immigrate.

Ein|wanderung *die* immigration.

einwandfrei ⬦ *adj* perfect; [Material] flawless; [Nachweis] irrefutable. ⬦ *adv* perfectly.

einwärts *adv* inwards.

Einweg|flasche *die* non-returnable bottle.

ein|weichen *vt* to soak.

ein|weihen *vt* - 1. [Gebäude] to open - 2. [Wagen, Sofa] to christen, to use for the first time.

Ein|weihung *die* [von Gebäude] opening; [von Wohnung] housewarming party.

ein|weisen *vt* (*unreg*) - 1. [Patienten] to admit - 2. [Anfänger]: **jn in etw (A) einweisen** to introduce sb to sthg.

Ein|weisung *die* - 1. [von Patienten] admission - 2. [von Anfänger] introduction.

ein|wenden *vt*: **einwenden, dass...** to object that...; **dagegen ist nichts einzuwenden** there's no reason why not.

ein|werfen *vt* (*unreg*) - 1. [Münze] to insert; [Brief] to post *UK*, to mail *US* - 2. [Ball, Frage, Bemerkung] to throw in - 3. [kaputtwerfen] to smash.

ein|wickeln *vt* - 1. [einpacken] to wrap up - 2. *fam abw* [überreden] to take in.

ein|willigen *vi*: **(in etw (A)) einwilligen** to agree (to sthg).

Einwilligung (*pl* -en) *die* consent.

ein|wirken *vi* - 1. [Salbe] to take effect - 2. [Person]: **auf jn beruhigend einwirken** to have a calming influence on sb.

Einwohner, in (*mpl* -, *fpl* -nen) *der, die* inhabitant.

Einwohnermelde|amt *das* local government office at which inhabitants of a town must register at the beginning and end of their residency.

Ein|wurf *der* - 1. [Ausspruch] comment - 2. [von Ball] throw-in - 3. [von Münze] insertion; [von Brief] posting *UK*, mailing *US* - 4. [Schlitz] slot.

Einzahl *die* singular.

ein|zahlen *vt* to pay in.

Ein|zahlung *die* deposit.

ein|zeichnen *vt* to mark.

Einzel (*pl* -) *das* singles *Pl*.

Einzel|fall *der* isolated case.

Einzel|gänger, in (*mpl* -, *fpl* -nen) *der, die* loner.

Einzel|handel *der* retail trade.

Einzelheit (*pl* -en) *die* detail; **in allen Einzelheiten** down to the last detail.

Einzel|kind *das* only child.

einzeln ⬦ *adj* - 1. [speziell] individual - 2. [isoliert] single; **jedes einzelne Exemplar** every single copy - 3. [Schuh, Socke] odd. ⬦ *adv* individually; [ankommen, abholen] separately; **einzeln stehend** solitary. ⬦ *det* (*nur pl*) a few.

Einzelne ⬦ *pron sing* - 1. [Person]: **jede/jeder Einzelne** (each and) every one - 2. [Sache]: **jede/jeder/jedes Einzelne** every single one. ⬦ *pron Pl* - 1. [Personen] some (people) - 2. [Sachen] some. ⬦ *der, die* [Mensch] individual. ⬦ *das*: **ins Einzelne gehen** to go into detail; **im Einzelnen** in detail. ➡ **Einzelnes** *pron* some things *Pl*.

Einzel|person *die* single person.

Einzel|stück *das* [Kunstgegenstand] piece.

Einzel|zimmer *das* single room.

ein|ziehen (*perf* hat/ist eingezogen) (*unreg*) ⬦ *vt* (hat) - 1. [Bauch, Netz] to pull in; [Krallen, Fahrgestell] to retract - 2. [Faden, Band] to thread in - 3. [Wand] to put in - 4. [zur Armee] to call up - 5. [Geld, Steuern] to collect - 6. [beschlagnahmen] to confiscate - **7.** [Banknoten, Münzen] to withdraw (from circulation) - **8.** *amt* [Informationen] to gather. <> *vi (ist)* - **1.** [in Wohnung] to move in - **2.** [Einzug halten] to enter - **3.** [Fett, Creme, Flüssigkeit] to be absorbed.

einzig <> *adj (ohne Kompar)* - **1.** [alleinig] only; **nur noch ein einziges Mal** just one more time; **ein einziger Besucher** a single visitor - **2.** *geh* [einzigartig] unique - **3.** [total] complete. <> *adv* only; **einzig und allein** entirely.

einzigartig *adj* unique.

Einzige *der, die, das:* **der/die/das Einzige** [Person] the only one; [Sache] the only thing; **das Einzige, was** the only thing that; **nur ein Einziger erhob sich** only one person stood up.

Einzimmer|wohnung *die* one-room flat *UK* ODER apartment *US*.

Ein|zug *der* - **1.** [von Jahreszeit] arrival - **2.** [von Sportler, Sieger] entrance - **3.** MIL entry - **4.** [in Wohnung] move - **5.** [von Geld, Steuern] collection.

Eis *(pl -) das* - **1.** [Gefrorenes] ice; **etw auf Eis legen** *eigtl & fig* to put sthg on ice - **2.** [Eiscreme] ice cream.

Eis|bahn *die* ice rink.

Eis|bär *der* polar bear.

Eis|becher *der* (ice-cream) sundae.

Eis|bein *das* knuckle of pork.

Eis|berg *der* iceberg.

Eis|café ['aiskafeː] *das* ice-cream parlour.

Eischnee *der:* **das Eiweiß zu Eischnee schlagen** to beat the egg white until stiff.

Eiscreme, **Eiskrem** ['aiskreːm] *die* ice cream.

Eis|diele *die* ice-cream parlour.

Eisen *(pl -) das* [gen] iron.

Eisen|bahn *die* - **1.** [Zug] train; **mit der Eisenbahn fahren** to travel by train - **2.** [Institution] railway *UK*, railroad *US* - **3.** [Modelleisenbahn] train set.

Eisenbahn|netz *das* rail network.

Eisen|erz *das* iron ore.

eisenhaltig *adj* [Erz] iron-bearing, ferrous; [Nahrung] containing iron.

eisern <> *adj eigtl & fig* iron; **eisern bleiben** to remain resolute. <> *adv* [unnachgiebig] resolutely.

eisgekühlt *adj* chilled.

Eis|hockey *das* ice hockey.

eisig <> *adj* - **1.** [eiskalt] freezing - **2.** [abweisend] icy, frosty. <> *adv* - **1.** [eiskalt]: **eisig kalt** freezing cold - **2.** [abweisend]: **eisig lächeln** to give a frosty smile.

eiskalt <> *adj* - **1.** [Körperteil, Getränk, Wind] ice-cold - **2.** [Mensch, Mord] cold-blooded; [Blick] frosty. <> *adv* - **1.** [sehr kalt] ice-cold - **2.** [herzlos] in cold blood.

Eiskrem = **Eiscreme**.

Eiskunstlauf *der* figure skating.

Eis|zapfen *der* icicle.

Eis|zeit *die* Ice Age.

eitel *adj abw* vain.

Eitelkeit *(pl -en) die abw* vanity.

Eiter *der* pus.

eitern *vi* to fester.

eitrig, **eiterig** *adj* [Wunde] festering; [Geschwür] suppurating.

Eiweiß *(pl -e) das* - **1.** [im Hühnerei] egg white - **2.** BIOL & CHEM protein.

Ei|zelle *die* ovum.

EKD [eːkaːˈdeː] *(abk für Evangelische Kirche in Deutschland) die Protestant Church in Germany.*

Ekel *(pl -)* <> *der* [Abscheu] disgust; **Ekel vor etw** *(D)* **empfinden** to find sthg disgusting. <> *das fam abw* [Person] horror.

ekelhaft <> *adj* - **1.** [Ekel erregend] disgusting - **2.** [Arbeit, Chef] nasty. <> *adv* [Ekel erregend] disgustingly.

ekeln *vt:* **das ekelt mich** I find that disgusting. <> **sich ekeln** *ref:* **sich (vor jm/etw) ekeln** to be disgusted (by sb/sthg).

eklig, **ekelig** *adj* - **1.** [Ekel erregend] disgusting - **2.** *fam* [gemein] nasty.

Ekzem *(pl -e) das* eczema *(U)*.

elastisch *adj* - **1.** [Gummi] elastic - **2.** [Körper] supple; [Gang] springy.

Elbe *die:* **die Elbe** the (River) Elbe.

Elch *(pl -e) der* elk.

Elefant *(pl -en) der* elephant; **wie ein Elefant im Porzellanladen** *fam* like a bull in a china shop.

elegant <> *adj* elegant. <> *adv* elegantly.

Eleganz *die* elegance.

Elektriker, in *(mpl -, fpl -nen) der, die* electrician.

elektrisch <> *adj* - **1.** [elektrisch betrieben - Licht, Rasierapparat, *etc*] electric; **elektrisches Gerät** electrical appliance - **2.** [mit Elektrizität zusammenhängend - Widerstand, Ladung] electrical. <> *adv* electrically.

Elektrizitäts|werk *das* power station.

Elektrode *(pl -n) die* electrode.

Elektro|gerät *das* electrical appliance.

Elektro|geschäft *das* electrical goods store.

Elektro|herd *der* electric oven.

Elektro|motor *der* electric motor.

Elektronik *die (ohne pl)* - **1.** [Wissenschaft] electronics *(U)* - **2.** [Teile] electronics *Pl.*

elektronisch <> *adj* electronic. <> *adv* electronically.

Elektrotechnik *die* electrical engineering.

Element *(pl -e) das* element; **in seinem Element sein** to be in one's element; **dunkle** ODER **zwielichtige Elemente** shady characters.

elend ⇔ *adj* - **1.** [erbärmlich] miserable - **2.** [krank] wretched. ⇔ *adv* - **1.** [erbärmlich] miserably - **2.** [schlecht] wretchedly; **sich elend fühlen** to feel wretched.

Elend *das* - **1.** [Unglück] misery - **2.** [Ärmlichkeit] poverty.

Elends|viertel *das* slum.

elf *num* eleven; *siehe auch* **sechs**.

Elf (*pl* -en) ⇔ *die* [Zahl & SPORT] eleven. ⇔ *der* elf; *siehe auch* **Sechs**.

Elfenbein *das* ivory.

elfhundert *num* one thousand one hundred.

Elfmeter (*pl* -) *der* penalty.

elfte, r, s *adj* eleventh; *siehe auch* **sechste**.

Elfte (*pl* -n) *der, die, das* eleventh; *siehe auch* **Sechste**.

elftel *adj (unver)* eleventh; *siehe auch* **sechstel**.

Elftel (*pl* -) *das* eleventh; *siehe auch* **Sechstel**.

Elite (*pl* -n) *die* elite.

Elite|schule *die* prestigious school.

Ellbogen (*pl* -), **Ellenbogen** (*pl* -) *der* elbow.

Elle (*pl* -n) *die* - **1.** [Knochen] ulna - **2.** [Maßeinheit] cubit.

Ellenbogen = Ellbogen.

Elsass *das* Alsace.

elsässisch *adj* Alsatian.

Elster (*pl* -n) *die* magpie.

elterlich *adj* parental.

Eltern *Pl* parents.

Eltern|abend *der* SCHULE parents' evening.

Eltern|haus *das* home.

Eltern|teil *der* parent.

Email [e'mai] *das* enamel.

E-Mail ['i:mɛil] (*pl* -s) *die* EDV e-mail; **jm eine E-Mail schicken** to send sb an e-mail, to e-mail sb.

E-Mail-|Adresse *die* e-mail address.

Emanzipation (*pl* -en) *die* emancipation.

emanzipieren ⇒ **sich emanzipieren** *ref* to become emancipated.

Embargo (*pl* -s) *das* embargo.

Embryo (*pl* -s ODER -onen) *der* embryo.

Emigrant, in (*mpl* -en, *fpl* -nen) *der, die* émigré.

emigrieren (*perf* ist emigriert) *vi* to go into (voluntary) exile, to leave the country.

Emission (*pl* -en) *die* emission.

emotional ⇔ *adj* emotional. ⇔ *adv* emotionally.

empfahl *prät* ⇨ **empfehlen**.

empfand *prät* ⇨ **empfinden**.

Empfang (*pl* Empfänge) *der* - **1.** [Erhalt - von Brief, Ware] receipt; **etw in Empfang nehmen** to receive sthg; **ein Paket für die Nachbarn in Empfang nehmen** to take a parcel for the neighbours - **2.** [Begrüßung] welcome - **3.** [Veranstaltung, Rezeption & TV] reception.

empfangen (*präs* empfängt, *prät* empfing, *perf* hat empfangen) *vt* - **1.** [gen] to receive - **2.** [begrüßen] to greet; **Gäste empfangen** to receive visitors.

Empfänger (*pl* -) *der* - **1.** [Gerät] receiver - **2.** [Adressat] addressee; [von Arbeitslosengeld] recipient.

Empfängerin (*pl* -nen) *die* [Adressat] addressee; [von Arbeitslosengeld] recipient.

empfänglich *adj*: (für etw) empfänglich sein to be susceptible (to sthg).

Empfängnis *die* conception.

Empfängnisverhütung *die* contraception.

Empfangs|bescheinigung *die* acknowledgement of receipt.

empfängt *präs* ⇨ **empfangen**.

empfehlen (*präs* empfiehlt, *prät* empfahl, *perf* hat empfohlen) *vt* to recommend; **jm empfehlen, etw zu tun** to recommend that sb do sthg. ⇒ **sich empfehlen** *ref* - **1.** [sich anbieten] to be recommended; **es empfiehlt sich, etw zu tun** it is advisable to do sthg - **2.** *geh* [sich verabschieden] to take one's leave.

empfehlenswert *adj* - **1.** [gut] recommendable - **2.** [ratsam] advisable.

Empfehlung (*pl* -en) *die* - **1.** [Ratschlag] recommendation; **auf js Empfehlung hin, auf Empfehlung von jm** on sb's recommendation - **2.** [Beurteilung] reference - **3.** *geh* [Gruß] regards *Pl*.

Empfehlungs|schreiben *das* reference.

empfiehlt *präs* ⇨ **empfehlen**.

empfinden (*prät* empfand, *perf* hat empfunden) *vt* to feel; **etw als Kränkung empfinden** to take offence at sthg.

Empfinden *das* feeling; **das Empfinden für Gut und Böse** the sense of good and evil; **für ODER nach meinem Empfinden** if you ask me.

empfindlich ⇔ *adj* - **1.** [Haut, Film, Gemüt] sensitive - **2.** [Gesundheit, Person] delicate - **3.** [Strafe, Verlust] severe. ⇔ *adv* - **1.** [verletzlich] sensitively - **2.** [merklich] severely; **jn empfindlich treffen** to hurt sb badly - **3.** [sehr - kalt] bitterly.

Empfindlichkeit *die* - **1.** [von Haut, Film, Gemüt] sensitivity - **2.** [von Person] susceptibility - **3.** [von Material, Gemüt] delicacy.

Empfindung (*pl* -en) *die* - **1.** [Wahrnehmung] sensation - **2.** [Emotion] feeling.

empfing *prät* ⇨ **empfangen**.

empfohlen *pp* ⇨ **empfehlen**.

empfunden *pp* ⇨ **empfinden**.

empören *vt* to outrage. ⇒ **sich empören** *ref*: sich über etw (A) empören to be outraged by sthg.

empört *adj* outraged.

Empörung *die* outrage.

emsig ◇ *adj* industrious; [Biene] busy; [Treiben] bustling. ◇ *adv* industriously.

Ende (*pl* -n) *das* - 1. [gen] end; **Ende März** at the end of March; **zu Ende sein** to be over; **zu Ende gehen** to come to an end; **ein Ende nehmen** to be over; **kein Ende nehmen** to go on and on - 2. *fam* [Wegstrecke]: **es ist noch ein ganzes Ende** it's still quite a way; **am Ende sein** [körperlich] to be completely exhausted; [nervlich] to be at the end of one's tether UK ODER US; **mit seiner Geduld am Ende sein** to have run out of patience; **mit seiner Weisheit am Ende sein** to be at one's wit's end. ◆ **am Ende** *adv* in the end. ◆ **letzten Endes** *adv* - 1. [am Schluss] in the end - 2. [im Grunde genommen] ultimately, in the final analysis.

Endeffekt *der*: **im Endeffekt** in the end.

enden (*perf* hat/ist geendet) *vi* - 1. (*hat*) [zu Ende gehen] to end; **der Zug endet in Köln** the train terminates in Cologne; **gut/schlecht enden** to have a happy/an unhappy ending; **nicht enden wollend** unending - 2. (*hat, ist*) [sterben] to meet one's end; [schließlich landen]: **im Gefängnis enden** to end up in prison.

End|ergebnis *das* end result.

endgültig ◇ *adj* final; [Antwort] definitive; [Beweis] conclusive. ◇ *adv* finally; [erklären] definitively.

Endivie [ɛn'diːvjə] (*pl* -n) *die* endive.

endlich ◇ *adv* - 1. [nach langem Warten] at last; **wann kommst du denn endlich?** so when are you finally going to come? - 2. [am Ende] finally; **um neun erreichten wir endlich das Ziel** we eventually got there at nine. ◇ *adj* finite.

endlos ◇ *adj* endless. ◇ *adv* interminably; [dauern] for ages.

End|spurt *der* final spurt.

End|station *die* terminus.

Endung (*pl* -en) *die* ending.

Energie (*pl* -n) *die* energy.

Energiebedarf *der* (*ohne pl*) energy requirements *Pl*.

Energie|krise *die* energy crisis.

Energie|verbrauch *der* energy consumption.

energisch ◇ *adj* forceful. ◇ *adv* forcefully.

eng ◇ *adj* - 1. [Raum] narrow; **im Auto ist es eng** it's cramped in the car - 2. [Kleidung] tight - 3. [Auslegung, Interpretation] narrow; **im engeren Sinn (des Wortes)** in the narrowest sense (of the word) - 4. [Beziehung, Freund, Verwandte] close. ◇ *adv* - 1. [dicht gedrängt] close together - 2. [anliegen] tightly - 3. [auslegen, interpretieren] narrowly - 4. [nah] close; **eng mit jm befreundet sein** to be close friends with sb.

engagieren [ãga'ʒiːrən] *vt* to engage. ◆ **sich engagieren** *ref*: **sie engagiert sich**

politisch she's very involved in politics; **sich für jn/etw engagieren** to show commitment to sb/sthg.

Enge *die* - 1. [Schmalheit] narrowness - 2. [Platzmangel] crampedness.

Engel (*pl* -) *der* angel.

England *nt* England.

Engländer, in (*mpl* -, *fpl* -nen) *der, die* Englishman (Englishwoman *die*); **die Engländer** the English.

englisch ◇ *adj* English. ◇ *adv* [sprechen] in English.

Englisch(e) *das* English; **auf/in Englisch** in English.

engstirnig *abw* ◇ *adj* narrow-minded. ◇ *adv* narrow-mindedly.

Enkel, in (*mpl* -, *fpl* -nen) *der, die* grandson (granddaughter *die*); **unsere Enkel** our grandchildren.

Enkel|kind *das* grandchild.

enorm ◇ *adj* enormous, immense. ◇ *adv* tremendously, terribly; **sich enorm anstrengen** to make a tremendous effort.

entarten (*perf* ist entartet) *vi* to degenerate.

entbehren ◇ *vt* - 1. [verzichten auf] to do without - 2. *geh* [vermissen] to miss. ◇ *vi*: **einer Sache (G) entbehren** to lack sthg.

entbehrlich *adj* dispensable.

Entbehrung (*pl* -en) *die* privation.

Entbindung (*pl* -en) *die* - 1. [Befreiung] discharge - 2. [Gebären] delivery.

entblößen *vt* - 1. [Körper] to bare, to expose - 2. [Mensch] to expose; [Gedanken, Gefühle] to reveal. ◆ **sich entblößen** *ref* [sich ausziehen] to undress; [Exhibitionist] to expose o.s.

entdecken *vt* - 1. [gen] to discover - 2. [Fehler] to detect; [Urheber] to identify; **kannst du ihn entdecken?** can you make him out?

Entdecker, in (*mpl* -, *fpl* -nen) *der, die* discoverer.

Entdeckung (*pl* -en) *die* discovery.

Ente (*pl* -n) *die* - 1. [Tier] duck - 2. [Zeitungsmeldung] hoax - 3. *fam* [Auto] Citroën 2 CV.

enteignen *vt* [Mensch] to dispossess; [Vermögen] to expropriate.

enterben *vt* to disinherit.

entfallen (*präs* entfällt, *prät* entfiel, *perf* ist entfallen) *vi* - 1. [vergessen]: **ihr Name ist mir entfallen** her name has slipped my mind - 2. [sich verteilen]: **auf jn entfallen** to fall ODER go to sb.

entfalten *vt* - 1. [öffnen] to unfold - 2. [entwickeln] to develop - 3. [zeigen] to display, to show; [Aktivität] to launch into - 4. [erläutern] to set out. ◆ **sich entfalten** *ref* - 1. [Blüte, Fallschirm] to open; [Segel] to unfurl - 2. [sich verwirklichen] to develop.

Entfaltung (*pl* -en) *die* - 1. [von Persönlichkeit] development; [von Aktivität] launching into; **etw zur Entfaltung bringen** to develop sthg to its full potential - **2.** [von Blüte] opening.

entfernen vt [beseitigen] to remove; **ein Kind von seiner Mutter entfernen** to take a child away from its mother. ◆ **sich entfernen** ref [sich wegbegeben] to leave; **sich von etw entfernen** [weggehen] to leave sthg; [von Pfad, Thema] to stray from sthg.

entfernt ◇ adj - **1.** [fort]: **wenige Kilometer von hier entfernt** a few kilometres away ODER from here; **weit entfernt** a long way away - **2.** [abgelegen] remote; **weit davon entfernt sein, etw zu tun** not to have the slightest intention of doing sthg - **3.** [Verwandte] distant; [Ähnlichkeit] vague - **4.** [Ahnung] faint, vague. ◇ adv - **1.** [weitläufig] distantly, remotely - **2.** [blass, gering] vaguely, faintly. ◆ **Entfernteste** das: **nicht im Entferntesten hatte ich daran gedacht** I didn't have the slightest intention of doing it.

Entfernung (pl -en) die - **1.** [Distanz] distance; **in einer Entfernung von 2 km** at a distance of 2 km; **aus der Entfernung zugucken** to look on from afar - **2.** [Beseitigung] removal - **3.** [Weggehen] departure.

entfremden vt [Person] to alienate; **jn jm/einer Sache entfremden** to alienate ODER estrange sb from sb/sthg.

entführen vt [Mensch] to kidnap; [Flugzeug] to hijack.

Entführer, in (mpl -, fpl -nen) der, die [von Menschen] kidnapper; [von Flugzeug] hijacker.

Entführung (pl -en) die [von Menschen] kidnapping; [von Flugzeug] hijacking.

entgegen präp (+ D) contrary to; **sie kam ihm entgegen** she was coming towards him.

entgegen|gehen (perf ist entgegengegangen) vi (unreg): **jm/einer Sache entgegengehen** to approach sb/sthg; **dem Ende entgegengehen** to draw to a close.

entgegengesetzt adj [Richtung, Seite, Meinung] opposite; **entgegengesetzte Ansichten** conflicting ODER opposing opinions.

entgegen|kommen (perf ist entgegengekommen) vi (unreg) - **1.** [herankommen]: **jm entgegenkommen** to approach sb - **2.** [auf Wünsche eingehen]: **js Wünschen/Erwartungen entgegenkommen** to meet sb's wishes/expectations.

Entgegenkommen das goodwill; **zu großem Entgegenkommen bereit sein** to be ready to make major concessions.

entgegenkommend ◇ adj [Mensch, Verhalten] accommodating, obliging. ◇ adv accommodatingly, obligingly.

entgegen|nehmen vt (unreg) to accept.

entgegen|setzen vt: **jm/etw Widerstand entgegensetzen** to resist sb/sthg; **einer Behauptung Beweise entgegensetzen** to pro-

duce evidence that contradicts a statement; **diesen Vorwürfen habe ich nichts entgegenzusetzen** I have no answer to these reproaches.

entgegen|stehen vi (unreg): **einer Sache (D) entgegenstehen** to stand in sthg's way; **dem steht nichts entgegen** there is no objection to that.

entgegnen vt [antworten] to reply; [barsch] to retort.

entgehen (prät entging, perf ist entgangen) vi - **1.** [entkommen]: **einer Sache (D) entgehen** to escape sthg - **2.** [unbemerkt bleiben]: **dieser Fehler ist mir entgangen** this mistake escaped my notice.

entgleisen (perf ist entgleist) vi - **1.** [Zug] to be derailed - **2.** [taktlos sein] to commit a faux pas.

entgleiten (prät entglitt, perf ist entglitten) vi: **jm ODER js Händen entgleiten** to slip from sb's hands.

enthalten (präs enthält, prät enthielt, perf hat enthalten) vt to contain. ◆ **sich enthalten** ref - **1.** [nicht abstimmen]: **sich der Stimme enthalten** to abstain - **2.** geh [auf etw verzichten] to abstain; **sich einer Sache (G) enthalten** to abstain from sthg.

enthaltsam adj abstemious; **sexuell enthaltsam sein** to abstain from sex.

Enthaltsamkeit die abstinence.

Enthaltung (pl -en) die abstention.

enthüllen vt - **1.** [Denkmal, Gemälde] to unveil - **2.** [Wahrheit, Geheimnis] to reveal.

entkommen (prät entkam, perf ist entkommen) vi to escape; **jm entkommen** to elude sb.

entkräftet adj [kraftlos] exhausted.

entladen (präs entlädt, prät entlud, perf hat entladen) vt [Lkw, Waffe] to unload. ◆ **sich entladen** ref - **1.** [Gewitter] to break - **2.** [Wut, Aggressionen] to erupt - **3.** [Batterie] to discharge.

entlang ◇ präp along; **die Straße entlang, entlang der Straße** along the road. ◇ adv: **am Fluss entlang** along the river.

entlang|gehen (perf ist entlanggegangen) vi & vt (unreg): **etw (A) ODER an etw (D) entlanggehen** to go along sthg.

entlarven [ɛntˈlarfn̩] vt to expose.

entlassen (präs entlässt, prät entließ, perf hat entlassen) vt - **1.** [Kranken, Soldat] to discharge; [Gefangenen] to release - **2.** [kündigen] to sack.

Entlassung (pl -en) die - **1.** [aus dem Krankenhaus, aus der Armee] discharge; [aus dem Gefängnis] release - **2.** [Kündigung] redundancy; [Aktion] sacking.

entlasten vt - 1. [von einer Belastung befreien] to relieve the strain on; [Gewissen] to ease - 2. RECHT to exonerate - 3. WIRTSCH: **sein Konto entlasten** to reduce one's overdraft.

entleeren vt to empty. ⟶ **sich entleeren** ref to empty.

entlegen adj remote.

entleihen (prät entlieh, perf hat entliehen) vt to borrow; **etw von jm entleihen** to borrow sthg from sb.

entlocken vt: **jm etw entlocken** to coax sthg out of sb.

entlüften vt to ventilate.

Entmachtung (pl -en) die removal from power.

entmilitarisieren vt to demilitarize.

entmündigen vt: **jn entmündigen** to declare sb unfit to manage his/her own affairs.

entmutigen vt to discourage, to dishearten.

entnervt adj: **entnervt sein** to have reached the end of one's tether UK ODER rope US.

entreißen (prät entriss, perf hat entrissen) vt [wegnehmen] to snatch away.

entrüsten vt to incense. ⟶ **sich entrüsten** ref: **sich über jn/etw entrüsten** to be incensed by sb/sthg.

Entrüstung die indignation.

entschädigen vt to compensate; **jn für etw entschädigen** to compensate sb for sthg.

Entschädigung (pl -en) die compensation.

entschärfen vt - 1. [Bombe, Debatte] to defuse - 2. [Kritik] to take the sting out of.

entscheiden (prät entschied, perf hat entschieden) ⟷ vi: **über etw (A) entscheiden** to decide on sthg. ⟷ vt [Streit] to settle; [Fußballspiel] to decide. ⟶ **sich entscheiden** vi [sich entschließen] to decide; **sich für/gegen jn/etw entscheiden** to decide on/against sb/sthg.

entscheidend ⟷ adj [Problem, Frage] decisive; [Stimme, Tor] deciding. ⟷ adv decisively.

Entscheidung (pl -en) die decision; [von Jury] verdict; [von Gericht, Ausschuss] ruling; **eine Entscheidung treffen** to make ODER take a decision.

entschieden ⟷ pp ▷ **entscheiden**. ⟷ adj [Verteidiger] staunch, steadfast; [Gegner] firm, strong. ⟷ adv firmly, emphatically; **das geht entschieden zu weit!** that's going far too far!

entschließen (prät entschloss, perf hat entschlossen) ⟶ **sich entschließen** ref to decide; **sich zur Annahme des Angebots entschließen** to decide to accept the offer.

entschlossen ⟷ pp ▷ **entschließen**. ⟷ adj determined, resolute. ⟷ adv without hesitation.

Entschlossenheit die determination, resolution.

Entschluss (pl -üsse) der decision; **einen Entschluss fassen** to make ODER take a decision.

entschlüsseln vt to decipher.

entschuldigen vt to excuse; **entschuldige bitte!** (I'm) sorry!; **entschuldigen Sie bitte!** [vor Frage, Bitte] excuse me!; [tut mir Leid!] (I'm) sorry!

Entschuldigung (pl -en) ⟷ die - 1. [Rechtfertigung] excuse - 2. SCHULE note (from one's parents or a doctor) - 3. [Bitte um Verzeihung] apology - 4. [Nachsicht]: **jn um Entschuldigung bitten** to beg sb's pardon. ⟷ interj [vor Frage, Bitte] excuse me!; [tut mir Leid!] (I'm) sorry!

Entsetzen das horror; **zu js Entsetzen** to sb's horror.

entsetzlich ⟷ adj - 1. [schrecklich] horrible - 2. [stark] terrible. ⟷ adv [sehr] terribly.

entsetzt ⟷ adj horrified; **über etw (A) entsetzt sein** to be horrified at sthg. ⟷ adv in horror, aghast.

entsichern vt to release the safety catch of.

Entsorgung (pl -en) die waste disposal.

entspannen vt to relax. ⟶ **sich entspannen** ref - 1. [Person] to relax - 2. [Situation] to ease.

Entspannung die - 1. [Erholung] relaxation - 2. [von Situationen] reduction of tension.

Entspannungs|politik die policy of détente.

entsprechen (präs entspricht, prät entsprach, perf hat entsprochen) vi - 1. [genügen]: **einer Sache (D) entsprechen** [Tatsachen] to correspond to sthg; [Erwartungen, Anforderungen] to meet sthg; **100° Celsius entsprechen 212° Fahrenheit** 100° Celsius is equivalent to 212° Fahrenheit; **einem Zweck entsprechen** to fulfil a purpose - 2. [nachkommen]: **einer Sache (D) entsprechen** to comply with sthg.

entsprechend ⟷ adj - 1. [angemessen, zuständig] appropriate - 2. [dementsprechend] corresponding. ⟷ adv [angemessen] appropriately; [dementsprechend] correspondingly. ⟷ präp: **einer Sache (D) entsprechend, entsprechend einer Sache (D)** in accordance with sthg.

entspringen (prät entsprang, perf ist entsprungen) vi - 1. [Fluss] to rise - 2. [entstehen aus]: **einer Sache (D) entspringen** to arise from sthg.

entstehen (prät entstand, perf ist entstanden) vi - 1. [geschaffen werden] to come into being; [Gebäude] to be built; [Kunstwerk] to be created; [Beziehung] to develop; [Roman] to be written; [Streit] to arise; **aus etw** ODER **durch etw entstehen** to come about as a result of sthg - 2. [Schaden, Kosten] to be incurred.

Entstehung (pl -en) die - 1. [eines Gebäudes] building; [eines Kunstwerkes] creation; [des Lebens] origins Pl - 2. [von Kosten, Schaden] incurring.

entstellen *vt* - **1.** [Person] to disfigure - **2.** [Sachverhalt] to distort.

enttäuschen ◇ *vt* to disappoint; [Hoffnungen] to dash. ◇ *vi* to be disappointing.

enttäuscht ◇ *adj* disappointed; [Hoffnungen] dashed; **von jm enttäuscht sein** to be disappointed in *ODER* with sb. ◇ *adv* disappointed.

Enttäuschung (*pl* -en) *die* disappointment.

entwaffnen *vt eigtl & fig* to disarm.

Entwarnung (*pl* -en) *die* all-clear (signal).

entwässern *vt* to drain; MED to dehydrate.

entweder ⏵ **entweder... oder...** *konj* either... or...

entweichen (*prät* **entwich**, *perf* **ist entwichen**) *vi* to escape.

entwerfen (*präs* **entwirft**, *prät* **entwarf**, *perf* **hat entworfen**) *vt* [Möbelstück, Kleidungsstück] to design; [Text] to draft; [Programm] to plan.

entwerten *vt* - **1.** [Fahrkarte] to cancel, to validate - **2.** [Geld] to devalue.

entwickeln *vt* to develop; [Gase] to produce. ⏵ **sich entwickeln** *ref* to develop; [Gase] to be produced; **sich aus etw entwickeln** to develop out of sthg; **sich zu etw entwickeln** to develop into sthg, to become sthg.

Entwicklung (*pl* -en) *die* - **1.** [Entfaltung, Ausarbeitung] development; **in der Entwicklung (sein)** (to be) at the development stage - **2.** FOTO developing - **3.** [von Gasen] production.

Entwicklungs|helfer, in *der, die* overseas aid worker.

Entwicklungs|hilfe *die* development aid.

Entwicklungs|land *das* developing country.

entwirren *vt eigtl & fig* to unravel.

entwischen (*perf* **ist entwischt**) *vi fam* to make off; **jm entwischen** to give sb the slip.

entwöhnen *vt* to wean.

entwürdigend ◇ *adj* degrading. ◇ *adv* degradingly.

Entwurf (*pl* -ürfe) *der* - **1.** [Zeichnung] blueprint - **2.** [Konzept] draft.

entwurzeln *vt eigtl & fig* to uproot.

entziehen (*prät* **entzog**, *perf* **hat entzogen**) *vt*: **jm etw entziehen** to withdraw sthg from sb; **einer Sache (D) etw entziehen** to draw *ODER* extract sthg from sthg. ⏵ **sich entziehen** *ref*: **sich jm/einer Sache entziehen** to escape sb/sthg; **sich der Verantwortung entziehen** to evade responsibility; **das entzieht sich meiner Kenntnis** I don't know anything about that.

Entziehungs|kur *die* detox.

entziffern *vt* to decipher.

entzücken *vt* to delight; **sie war von dem Gemälde entzückt** she thought the painting was delightful.

entzückend *adj* delightful, charming.

Entzug *der* withdrawal; **im Entzug sein** to be in detox.

Entzugs|erscheinung *die* withdrawal symptom.

ent|zünden *vt* to light. ⏵ **sich entzünden** *ref* - **1.** [brennen] to catch fire; TECH to ignite - **2.** MED to become inflamed - **3.** [entstehen]: **sich an etw (D) entzünden** to be ignited by sthg.

Entzündung (*pl* -en) *die* inflammation.

Enzian (*pl* -e) *der* [Pflanze] gentian.

Enzyklopädie (*pl* -n) *die* encyclopedia.

Enzym (*pl* -e) *das* enzyme.

Epidemie (*pl* -n) *die* epidemic.

Epik *die* [Gattung] epic poetry.

Epilepsie (*pl* -n) *die* epilepsy.

Episode (*pl* -n) *die* episode.

Epoche (*pl* -n) *die* period, era.

Epos (*pl* **Epen**) *das* epic.

er *pron* he; [bei Sachen, Tieren] it; **er war's!** it was him!

erachten *vt*: **jn/etw als** *ODER* **für etw erachten** to consider sb/sthg (to be) sthg.

Erachten *das*: **meines Erachtens** in my opinion.

erahnen *vt* [im Dämmerlicht] to barely make out; [Absicht] to get an inkling of.

erarbeiten *vt* - **1.** [Stellung, Wissen] to acquire (through one's own efforts) - **2.** [Bericht, Programm] to draw up.

Erbarmen *das* mercy, compassion; **mit jm/etw Erbarmen haben** to take pity on sb/sthg.

erbärmlich ◇ *adj* - **1.** [armselig, unzureichend] wretched, terrible - **2.** *abw* [gemein] despicable - **3.** [sehr groß] terrible. ◇ *adv* [sehr] terribly.

erbarmungslos ◇ *adj* merciless. ◇ *adv* mercilessly.

erbauen *vt* - **1.** [errichten] to build - **2.** *geh* [erheben] to uplift.

Erbauer, in (*mpl* -, *fpl* -nen) *der, die* builder.

Erbe (*pl* -n) ◇ *das* - **1.** [Vermögen] inheritance - **2.** [geistiges Vermächtnis] legacy. ◇ *der* heir.

erben ◇ *vt* to inherit. ◇ *vi* to come into an inheritance.

erbeuten *vt* to capture (as booty).

Erb|folge *die* succession.

Erbgut *das* BIOL genetic make-up.

Erbin (*pl* -nen) *die* heiress.

erbittert ◇ *adj* [Kampf] fierce; [Feind] bitter. ◇ *adv* fiercely.

Erb|krankheit *die* hereditary disease.

erblich ◇ *adj* hereditary. ◇ *adv*: **erblich belastet sein** to have a hereditary condition.

erblinden (*perf* **ist erblindet**) *vi* to go blind.

erbrechen (*präs* **erbricht**, *prät* **erbrach**, *perf* **hat erbrochen**) *vt* to vomit (up). ⏵ **sich erbrechen** *ref* to vomit.

Erbrechen *das* vomiting.

erbringen (*prät* erbrachte, *perf* hat erbracht) *vt* - 1. [ergeben] to result in; [Geldsumme] to bring in; **Leistung erbringen** to produce; **eine notwendige Leistung erbringen** to do some necessary work - 2. [Nachweis] to produce.

Erbschaft (*pl* -en) *die* inheritance.

Erbse (*pl* -n) *die* pea.

Erb|stück *das* heirloom.

Erd|ball *der* globe.

Erd|beben *das* earthquake.

Erd|beere *die* strawberry.

Erd|boden *der* [Boden] ground, earth; **etw dem Erdboden gleichmachen** to raze sthg to the ground; **wie vom Erdboden verschluckt sein** to seem to have vanished from the face of the earth.

Erde *die* - 1. [Erdreich] soil, earth - 2. [fester Boden] ground; **etw aus der Erde stampfen** *fam* [Gebäude] to build sthg overnight; **jn unter die Erde bringen** *fam* [begraben] to bury sb; **du bringst mich noch unter die Erde!** you'll be the death of me! - 3. [Welt] world; **auf der ganzen Erde** in the whole world - 4. [Planet] Earth.

erden *vt* ELEKTR to earth.

erdenklich *adj* conceivable, imaginable. ◆ **alles Erdenkliche** *adv*: **alles Erdenkliche tun** to do one's utmost.

Erd|gas *das* natural gas.

Erdgeschoss (*pl* -e) *das* ground floor *UK*, first floor *US*.

Erd|kugel *die* globe.

Erd|kunde *die* geography.

Erdnuss (*pl* -nüsse) *die* peanut.

Erd|öl *das* (mineral) oil.

erdrosseln *vt* to strangle.

erdrücken *vt* - 1. [zu Tode drücken] to crush to death - 2. [belasten] to overwhelm.

Erd|rutsch *der* landslide.

Erd|teil *der* continent.

erdulden *vt* to endure.

ereifern ◆ **sich ereifern** *ref* to get worked up.

ereignen ◆ **sich ereignen** *ref* to happen; [Unfall] to occur.

Ereignis (*pl* -se) *das* event.

ereignisreich *adj* eventful.

erfahren (*präs* erfährt, *prät* erfuhr, *perf* hat erfahren) ◇ *vt* - 1. [Kenntnis erhalten von] to learn; [hören] to hear; **etw von jm erfahren** to hear sthg from sb; **etw über jn/etw erfahren** to find out sthg about sb/sthg; **etw durch jn/etw erfahren** to find out about sthg from sb/sthg - 2. *geh* [erleben - Glück, Leid] to experience; [- Veränderung] to undergo. ◇ *adj* experienced.

Erfahrung (*pl* -en) *die* - 1. [Kenntnis] experience (*U*) - 2. [durch Nachforschen]: **etw in Erfahrung bringen** to find sthg out.

erfahrungsgemäß *adv* judging from experience.

erfassen *vt* - 1. [Bedeutung] to grasp, to understand - 2. [Daten, Zahlen] to record - 3. [mitreißen - von Fahrzeug] to drag along; [- Wasser] to sweep along - 4. [überkommen]: **Angst erfasste sie** she was overcome with fear.

erfinden (*prät* erfand, *perf* hat erfunden) *vt* to invent.

Erfinder, in (*mpl* -, *fpl* -nen) *der, die* inventor.

Erfindung (*pl* -en) *die* - 1. [Entwicklung] invention; **eine Erfindung machen** to invent something - 2. [Ausgedachtes] fabrication.

Erfolg (*pl* -e) *der* success; **Erfolg haben** to be successful; **mit Erfolg** successfully. ◆ **Erfolg versprechend** *adj* promising. ◆ **viel Erfolg** *interj* good luck!

erfolglos ◇ *adj* unsuccessful. ◇ *adv* unsuccessfully.

erfolgreich ◇ *adj* successful. ◇ *adv* successfully.

Erfolgs|erlebnis *das* feeling of success.

erforderlich *adj* required; **für** ODER **zu etw erforderlich sein** to be required for sthg.

erfordern *vt* to require.

Erfordernis (*pl* -se) *das* requirement.

erforschen *vt* [Wissensgebiet] to study; [Land, Gelände] to explore; [Möglichkeiten] to investigate.

Erforschung (*pl* -en) *die* [von Wissensgebiet] study; [von Land, Gelände] exploration; [von Möglichkeiten] investigation.

erfreuen *vt* to please. ◆ **sich erfreuen** *ref*: **sich an etw** (*D*) **erfreuen** to take pleasure in sthg. ◆ **sehr erfreut** *interj* pleased to meet you!

erfreulich *adj* pleasing.

erfreulicherweise *adv* luckily.

erfrieren (*prät* erfror, *perf* ist erfroren) *vi* to freeze to death; [Blüten] to be killed by frost; **sich die Hände/Füße erfrieren** to suffer frostbite in one's hands/feet.

erfrischen *vt* to refresh; [geistig] to stimulate. ◆ **sich erfrischen** *ref* to refresh o.s.

erfrischend *adj* refreshing; [Gespräch] stimulating.

Erfrischung (*pl* -en) *die* refreshment.

erfüllen *vt* - 1. [Wunsch, Vertrag, Pflicht, Bedingungen] to fulfil - 2. [füllen, ausfüllen] to fill. ◆ **sich erfüllen** *ref* [Wunsch] to come true.

ergänzen *vt* - 1. [vervollständigen] to complete - 2. [hinzufügen] to add. ◆ **sich ergänzen** *ref* to complement one another.

Ergänzung (*pl* -en) *die* - **1.** [Vervollständigung] completion (*U*) - **2.** [Zusatz] supplement; [zu Gesetz] amendment.

ergeben (*präs* ergibt, *prät* ergab, *perf* hat ergeben) *vt* [Ertrag] to produce; [herausfinden] to show; **eins mal eins ergibt eins** one times one is ODER makes one; **das ergibt keinen Sinn** that doesn't make any sense. ◆ **sich ergeben** *ref* - **1.** [erfolgen] to arise; **sich aus etw ergeben** to result from ODER be the result of sthg - **2.** [kapitulieren] to surrender.

Ergebenheit *die* devotion.

Ergebnis (*pl* -se) *das* result.

ergebnislos *adj* unsuccessful.

ergiebig *adj* [Quelle] rich; [Thema] fertile; [Gespräch] productive.

ergießen (*prät* ergoss, *perf* hat ergossen) ◆ **sich ergießen** *ref* to pour.

ergreifen (*prät* ergriff, *perf* hat ergriffen) *vt* - **1.** [packen, Macht] to seize - **2.** [festnehmen] to capture - **3.** [Initiative, Gelegenheit] to take; [Beruf] to take up; [Maßnahmen] to adopt - **4.** [erfassen] to overcome.

ergreifend ◇ *adj* moving. ◇ *adv* movingly.

ergriffen ◇ *pp* ▷ **ergreifen**. ◇ *adj*: **ergriffen sein** to be (deeply) moved.

ergründen *vt* to discover.

erhalten (*präs* erhält, *prät* erhielt, *perf* hat erhalten) *vt* - **1.** [bekommen] to receive, to get - **2.** [bewahren] to preserve; **gut erhalten** in good condition.

erhältlich *adj* available.

Erhaltung *die* preservation; [von Tierarten] conservation.

erhängen ◆ to hang. ◆ **sich erhängen** *ref* to hang o.s.

erheben (*prät* erhob, *perf* hat erhoben) *vt* - **1.** [Arm, Stimme, Glas] to raise - **2.** [Gebühren] to charge; [Steuern] to levy - **3.** [Daten] to gather - **4.** [vorbringen]: **Anklage erheben** to bring charges; **auf etw** (*A*) **Anspruch erheben** to make a claim for sthg; **Einspruch erheben** to raise an objection; **etw zum Prinzip erheben** to make sthg a principle. ◆ **sich erheben** *ref* - **1.** [aufstehen] to rise, to get up - **2.** [losfliegen] to rise - **3.** [rebellieren]: **sich gegen jn/etw erheben** to rise up against sb/sthg - **4.** [überragen]: **sich über jn/etw erheben** to rise above sb/sthg.

erheblich ◇ *adj* considerable. ◇ *adv* considerably.

Erhebung (*pl* -en) *die* - **1.** [Hügel] rise - **2.** [Aufstand] uprising - **3.** [Untersuchung] survey.

erhitzen *vt* - **1.** [heiß machen] to heat - **2.** [erregen] to excite.

erhoffen *vt* to anticipate; **sich** (*D*) **etw von jm erhoffen** to expect sthg from sb.

erhöhen *vt* - **1.** [Preis, Einsatz, Geschwindigkeit] to increase - **2.** [Mauer] to raise. ◆ **sich erhöhen** *ref* [steigen] to increase.

Erhöhung (*pl* -en) *die* increase.

erholen ◆ **sich erholen** *ref*: **sich (von etw) erholen** to recover (from sthg).

erholsam *adj* relaxing.

Erholung *die* [von Krankheit] recovery; [von Anstrengung] rest.

erinnern ◇ *vt* - **1.** [an Aufgabe, Termin]: **jn an etw** (*A*) **erinnern** to remind sb about ODER of sthg - **2.** [an Vergangenheit]: **jn an jn/etw erinnern** to remind sb of sb/sthg. ◇ *vi* - **1.** [an Aufgabe, Termin]: **ich muss daran erinnern, dass...** I must remind you that... - **2.** [an Vergangenes]: **an jn/etw erinnern** to be reminiscent of sb/sthg. ◆ **sich erinnern** *ref* to remember; **sich an jn/etw erinnern** to remember sb/sthg.

Erinnerung (*pl* -en) *die* - **1.** [Eindruck] memory; **Erinnerung an etw** (*A*) memory of sthg - **2.** [Gedenken]: **zur Erinnerung an jn** in memory of sb; **jn/etw in guter/schlechter Erinnerung behalten** to have fond/bad memories of sb/sthg - **3.** [Gedächtnis] memory - **4.** [Andenken] memento.

erkälten ◆ **sich erkälten** *ref* to catch (a) cold.

Erkältung (*pl* -en) *die* cold.

erkennbar *adj* recognizable.

erkennen (*prät* erkannte, *perf* hat erkannt) *vt* - **1.** [sehen können] to make out - **2.** [Person, Fehler] to recognize; **etw zu erkennen geben** to reveal sthg - **3.** [Irrtum] to acknowledge.

erkenntlich *adj*: **sich erkenntlich zeigen** to show one's gratitude.

Erkenntnis (*pl* -se) *die* - **1.** [Entdeckung, Einsicht] realization; **wissenschaftliche Erkenntnisse** scientific discoveries; **zu der Erkenntnis kommen, dass...** to realize that... - **2.** [Erkennen] knowledge.

Erker (*pl* -) *der* bay window.

erklärbar *adj* explicable; **nicht erklärbar** inexplicable; **leicht erklärbar** easily explained.

erklären *vt* - **1.** [erläutern] to explain; **ich kann es mir nicht erklären** I can't explain it - **2.** [bezeichnen] to declare; [Absicht] to state; [Rücktritt] to announce; **etw für ungültig erklären** to declare sthg invalid; **jn für vermisst erklären** to declare sb missing. ◆ **sich erklären** *ref* [sich äußern]: **sich (mit etw) einverstanden erklären** to declare that one is in agreement (with sthg); **er erklärte sich bereit, es zu tun** he said he was willing to do it.

Erklärung (*pl* -en) *die* - **1.** [Erläuterung] explanation - **2.** [Mitteilung] statement.

erklingen (*prät* erklang, *perf* ist erklungen) *vi* [Ton, Instrument] to sound; **am Schluss erklang die Nationalhymne** at the end the national anthem was played.

erkranken (*perf* ist erkrankt) *vi* to fall ill.

Erkrankung (*pl* -en) *die* illness.

erkundigen ◆ **sich erkundigen** *ref* to enquire; **sich nach jm erkundigen** to ask after sb; **sich nach etw erkundigen** to ask about sthg.

Erkundigung (*pl* -en) *die* enquiry; **Erkundigungen über jn/etw einziehen** ODER **einholen** to make enquiries about sb/sthg.

erlangen *vt* to obtain.

Erlass (*pl* -e ODER **Erlässe**) *der* - **1.** [von Befehl] decree - **2.** [von Schulden] remission.

erlassen (*präs* erlässt, *prät* erließ, *perf* hat erlassen) *vt* - **1.** [Befehl] to issue; [Gesetz] to enact - **2.** [Strafe, Schulden] **jm etw erlassen** to let sb off sthg.

erlauben *vt* to allow; **jm etw erlauben** to allow sb sthg; **sich** (*D*) **etw erlauben** [sich herausnehmen] to take the liberty of doing sthg; [sich gönnen] to allow o.s. sthg. ◆ **erlaube mal** *interj* how dare you!

Erlaubnis *die* permission.

erläutern *vt* to explain.

Erläuterung (*pl* -en) *die* explanation.

Erle (*pl* -n) *die* alder.

erleben *vt* - **1.** [erfahren, kennen lernen] to experience; [Abenteuer] to have - **2.** [Geburtstag, Jubiläum] to live to see.

Erlebnis (*pl* -se) *das* experience.

erledigen *vt* - **1.** [Frage, Angelegenheit, Auftrag] to deal with; [Arbeit] to get through; [Einkäufe, Hausaufgaben] to do - **2.** *fam* [töten] to bump off - **3.** *fam* [besiegen] to wipe out. ◆ **sich erledigen** *ref* [sich erübrigen]: **etw erledigt sich (von selbst)** sthg takes care of itself.

erledigt *adj* - **1.** [ausgeführt, beendet - Angelegenheit] settled; [- Auftrag] carried out; [- Arbeit] done - **2.** *fam* [erschöpft]: **erledigt sein** to be worn out.

erleichtern *vt* - **1.** [leichter machen - Arbeit, Situation] to make easier; [- Gepäck] to make lighter; **jm das Verständnis erleichtern** to make it easier for sb to understand - **2.** [Gewissen] to ease.

erleichtert ◇ *adj*: **erleichtert sein** to be relieved. ◇ *adv*: **erleichtert aufatmen** to breathe a sigh of relief.

Erleichterung (*pl* -en) *die* - **1.** [Befreiung] relief - **2.** [von Aufgabe] facilitation (*U*); [von Last] easing (*U*).

erleiden (*prät* erlitt, *perf* hat erlitten) *vt* to suffer.

erlernen *vt* to learn.

erlesen *adj geh* [Gemälde, Porzellan, Wein] fine; [Mahl] choice.

erleuchten *vt* - **1.** [erhellen] to light up - **2.** *geh* [inspirieren] to inspire.

erlischt *präs* ▷ **erlöschen**.

Erlös (*pl* -e) *der* proceeds *Pl*.

erlöschen (*präs* erlischt, *prät* erlosch, *perf* ist erloschen) *vi* - **1.** [Feuer, Licht] to go out; [Vulkan] to become extinct - **2.** [Gefühle] to die; [Anspruch, Mitgliedschaft] to lapse.

erlösen *vt* to rescue; **jn von etw erlösen** [Leid, Schmerz] to release sb from sthg; RELIG to deliver sb from sthg.

ermächtigen *vt*: **jn zu etw ermächtigen** to authorize sb to do sthg.

ermahnen *vt* to remind; **jn zu mehr Vorsicht ermahnen** to remind sb to be more careful.

Ermahnung (*pl* -en) *die* reminder.

ermäßigt *adj* reduced.

Ermäßigung (*pl* -en) *die* reduction.

Ermessen *das* judgement; **das liegt ganz in Ihrem Ermessen** that is entirely up to you.

ermitteln ◇ *vt* to determine; [Schuldige, Täter] to identify; [Sieger] to decide. ◇ *vi* to investigate.

Ermittlung (*pl* -en) *die* [Erkundigung] enquiries *Pl*; [Entdeckung] identification (*U*).

ermöglichen *vt* to make possible.

ermorden *vt* to murder.

Ermordung (*pl* -en) *die* murder; [von Politiker] assassination.

ermüden ◇ *vi* (*perf* ist ermüdet) to tire. ◇ *vt* (*perf* hat ermüdet) to tire.

Ermüdung *die* tiredness.

ermuntern *vt* to encourage.

ermutigen *vt* to encourage.

ernähren *vt* - **1.** [beköstigen] to feed - **2.** [unterhalten] to support. ◆ **sich ernähren** *ref* to eat; **sich vegetarisch ernähren** to eat a vegetarian diet; **sich mit** ODER **von etw ernähren** [Person] to live on sthg; [Tier] to feed on sthg.

Ernährung *die* - **1.** [Ernähren] feeding - **2.** [Mahlzeit] diet; **gesunde Ernährung** a healthy diet.

ernennen (*prät* ernannte, *perf* hat ernannt) *vt* to appoint; **jn zu etw ernennen** to appoint sb (as) sthg.

erneuern [ɛɐ̯'nɔʏɐn] *vt* - **1.** [ersetzen] to replace - **2.** [ausbessern - Gebäude] to renovate; [- Gemälde] to restore; [- kaputten Zaun] to repair - **3.** [Vertrag, Angebot] to renew.

Erneuerung [ɛɐ̯'nɔʏərʊŋ] (*pl* -en) *die* - **1.** [Ersatz] replacement (*U*) - **2.** [Ausbesserung - von Gebäude] renovation (*U*); [- von Gemälde] restoration (*U*) - **3.** [von Vertrag, Angebot] renewal.

erneut ◇ *adj* [Angebot, Vorschlag] new; [Kraft] renewed; [Weigerung] further. ◇ *adv* again.

erniedrigen *vt* to humiliate. ◆ **sich erniedrigen** *ref* [sich demütigen] to lower o.s.

Erniedrigung (*pl* -en) *die* humiliation (*U*).

ernst ◇ *adj* - **1.** [gen] serious; [Verhalten] solemn - **2.** [Absicht, Vorschlag] sincere. ◇ *adv* - **1.** [gen] seriously - **2.** [Absicht, Vorschlag] sincerely; **es mit etw ernst meinen** to be serious about sthg; **jn/etw ernst nehmen** to take sb/ sthg seriously.

Ernst *der* seriousness; **mit etw Ernst machen** to be serious about sthg; **im Ernst?** really?

Ernst|fall *der* (case of) emergency.

ernsthaft <> *adj* serious; [Verhalten] solemn. <> *adv* - **1.** [gen] seriously - **2.** [aufrichtig] sincerely.

ernstlich *adv* - **1.** [gen] seriously - **2.** [beabsichtigen, bereuen] sincerely.

Ernte (*pl* -n) *die* harvest.

ernten *vt* - **1.** [Früchte] to harvest; [Obst] to pick - **2.** [Beifall] to earn; [Undank] to receive.

ernüchtern *vt* [desillusionieren] to bring down to earth.

Ernüchterung (*pl* -en) *die* [Desillusion] disillusionment (U).

erobern *vt* - **1.** [erkämpfen] to conquer - **2.** [gewinnen] to capture.

Eroberung (*pl* -en) *die* conquest.

eröffnen *vt* - **1.** [gen] to open - **2.** [bekannt geben]: **jm etw eröffnen** to reveal sthg to sb - **3.** [Gerichtsverfahren] to institute - **4.** [von Möglichkeit] to open up. ● **sich eröffnen** *ref*: **sich jm eröffnen** to open up to sb.

Eröffnung (*pl* -en) *die* - **1.** [gen] opening (U) - **2.** [Bekanntgabe - unerwartet] revelation (U); [- von Plan] disclosure (U) - **3.** [von Gerichtsverfahren] institution - **4.** [Möglichkeit] opening up (U).

erörtern *vt* to discuss.

Erörterung (*pl* -en) *die* discussion.

Erotik *die* eroticism.

erotisch *adj* erotic.

erpressen *vt*: **jn (mit etw) erpressen** to blackmail sb (with sthg).

Erpresser, in (*mpl* -, *fpl* -nen) *der, die* blackmailer.

Erpressung (*pl* -en) *die* blackmail (U).

erproben *vt* [Maschine, Mittel] to test; [Ausdauer, Zuverlässigkeit] to put to the test; [Methode] to try out.

erraten (*präs* errät, *prät* erriet, *perf* hat erraten) *vt* to guess.

erregen *vt* - **1.** [aufregen - Person] to excite; [- Gemüt, sexuell] to arouse - **2.** [anregen] to stimulate - **3.** [verursachen - Aufmerksamkeit, Aufsehen] to attract; [- Widerspruch] to give rise to; [- Mitleid, Neid] to arouse.

Erreger (*pl* -) *der* MED pathogene.

Erregung (*pl* -en) *die* - **1.** [von Person] excitement (U); [sexuelle] arousal (U) - **2.** [von Nerven] stimulation (U) - **3.** [Verursachen - von Mitleid, Neid] arousing (U); [- von Aufmerksamkeit] attracting (U).

erreichbar *adj* [Person] available; [Ort] within reach.

erreichen *vt* - **1.** [Ort, Person, Geschwindigkeit] to reach; [Ziel] to achieve; [Bahn] to catch - **2.** [telefonisch] to contact; **wo/wann sind Sie zu erreichen?** where/when can you be contacted? - **3.** [durchsetzen] to achieve; **bei ihm kann man nichts erreichen** you'll not get anywhere with him.

errichten *vt* - **1.** [bauen, aufbauen] to erect - **2.** [Herrschaft] to establish.

Errichtung *die* - **1.** [Bau, Aufbau] erection - **2.** [von Herrschaft] establishment.

erringen (*prät* errang, *perf* hat errungen) *vt* [Sieg, Freundschaft] to win; [Vorteil, Mehrheit] to gain.

erröten (*perf* ist errötet) *vi* to blush; **vor Wut erröten** to flush with anger.

Errungenschaft (*pl* -en) *die* achievement; **technische Errungenschaften** technical advances; **meine neueste Errungenschaft** my latest acquisition.

Ersatz *der* - **1.** [Ausgleich] substitute - **2.** [Entschädigung] compensation.

Ersatz|dienst *der* community work done by conscientious objectors instead of military service.

ersatzlos *adv* without substitution; **ersatzlos gestrichen** abolished.

Ersatz|mann (*pl* -männer ODER -leute) *der* [beim Fußball] substitute; [bei der Arbeit] replacement.

Ersatz|rad *das* spare wheel.

Ersatz|teil *das* spare part.

erscheinen (*prät* erschien, *perf* ist erschienen) *vi* - **1.** [kommen, sich zeigen] to appear - **2.** [Buch, Zeitung] to come out - **3.** [wirken] to seem.

Erscheinung (*pl* -en) *die* - **1.** [Ereignis] phenomenon - **2.** [Gestalt] appearance - **3.** [Vision] apparition.

erschießen (*prät* erschoss, *perf* hat erschossen) *vt* to shoot. ● **sich erschießen** *ref* to shoot o.s.

erschlagen (*präs* erschlägt, *prät* erschlug, *perf* hat erschlagen) *vt* to kill; **vom Blitz erschlagen werden** to be struck by lightning.

erschöpft <> *adj* exhausted. <> *adv* [müde] wearily.

Erschöpfung *die* exhaustion.

erschrak *prät* ⊳ **erschrecken**.

erschrecken (*präs* erschreckt ODER erschrickt, *prät* erschreckte ODER erschrak, *perf* hat erschreckt ODER ist erschrocken) <> *vt* (hat) (reg) [überraschen] to startle; [ängstigen] to frighten. <> *vi* (ist) (unreg) [überrascht sein] to be startled; [Angst haben] to be frightened; **über etw (A) erschrecken** to be alarmed by sthg. ● **sich erschrecken** *ref* (unreg) to get a fright.

erschreckend <> *adj* alarming. <> *adv* alarmingly.

erschrickt *präs* ▷ **erschrecken**.

erschrocken *pp* ▷ **erschrecken**.

erschüttern *vt* - 1. [Haus, Person] to shake; **er lässt sich durch nichts erschüttern** he's unflappable - 2. [Vertrauen, Ruf] to shatter.

erschütternd *adj* distressing.

Erschütterung *(pl -en) die* - 1. [von Haus] shaking *(U)* - 2. [von Person] (state of) shock - 3. [von Vertrauen, Ruf] shattering.

erschweren *vt* to make (more) difficult.

erschwinglich *adj* affordable.

ersetzbar *adj* replaceable.

ersetzen *vt* - 1. [auswechseln, ausgleichen] to replace - 2. [erstatten - Auslagen] to reimburse; [- Schaden] to make good.

ersichtlich *adj* obvious.

ersparen *vt* to save.

Ersparnis *(pl -se) die* saving. ❧ **Ersparnisse** *Pl* savings.

erst *adv* - 1. [nicht eher] not until; **er fährt erst morgen los** he's not going until tomorrow; **erst als** only when - 2. [vor kurzem] (only) just; **sie war erst gestern hier** she was here only yesterday - 3. [zuerst] first; [anfänglich] at first - 4. [emphatisierend]: **sie ist ja schon groß, aber ihr Bruder erst!** she is tall but her brother is even taller; **jetzt werde ich es erst recht/recht nicht tun!** now I'm definitely going/not going to do it! ❧ **erst einmal** *adv* - 1. [nur einmal] only once - 2. [zuerst] at first.

erstarren *(perf ist erstarrt) vi* [vor Kälte] to go numb; [vor Schreck] to become paralysed; [Gips] to harden.

erstatten *vt* - 1. [Betrag] to reimburse - 2. [vorbringen]: **gegen jn Anzeige erstatten** to report sb (to the authorities); **Bericht erstatten** to (make a) report.

Erstauf|führung *die* première.

erstaunen *(perf hat/ist erstaunt)* ▷ *vt (hat)* to astonish, to amaze. ▷ *vi (ist):* **über etw** *(A)* **erstaunen** to be astonished ODER amazed at sthg.

Erstaunen *das* astonishment; **jn in Erstaunen (ver)setzen** to astonish ODER amaze sb.

erstaunlich *adj* astonishing, amazing.

erstaunt *adj* [Person] astonished, amazed; [Gesicht, Miene] surprised; **über etw** *(A)* **erstaunt sein** to be astonished by sthg.

erstbeste, r, s *adj:* **kaufe nicht gleich den erstbesten Wagen!** don't just buy the first car you look at! ❧ **Erstbeste** *der, die, das* first thing to come along.

erste, r, s *adj* - 1. [anfänglich] first - 2. [beste - Qualität, Wahl] top; [- Liga, Geige] first - 3. [Ergebnis, Erfolg] initial.

Erste *der, die, das* first; *siehe auch* **Sechste**. ❧ **als Erstes** *adv* first (of all). ❧ **fürs Erste** *adv* for the time being.

erstechen *(präs ersticht, prät erstach, perf hat erstochen) vt* to stab to death.

erste Hilfe *die* first aid.

erstens *adv* firstly, in the first place.

ersticken *(perf hat/ist erstickt)* ▷ *vi (ist)* to suffocate; **wir ersticken zurzeit in Arbeit** we're up to our eyes in work at the moment. ▷ *vt (hat)* [Person, Tier] to suffocate; [Feuer] to put out; **etw im Keim ersticken** to nip sthg in the bud.

erstklassig ▷ *adj* first-class. ▷ *adv* excellently.

erstmalig ▷ *adj* first. ▷ *adv* for the first time.

erstmals *adv* for the first time.

erstrangig ▷ *adj* - 1. [vorrangig] of prime importance - 2. [erstklassig] first-rate. ▷ *adv* as a matter of priority.

erstrebenswert *adj* worthwhile.

erstrecken ❧ **sich erstrecken** *ref* - 1. [jn/etw betreffen]: **sich auf jn/etw erstrecken** to apply to sb/sthg - 2. [sich ausdehnen]: **sich erstrecken bis** [räumlich] to extend as far as; **sich über etw** *(A)* **erstrecken** [zeitlich] to last for sthg; [räumlich] to extend over sthg.

ertappen *vt* to catch; **jn bei etw ertappen** to catch sb doing sthg; **jn auf frischer Tat ertappen** to catch sb red-handed.

erteilen *vt:* **jm etw erteilen** to give sb sthg.

ertönen *(perf ist ertönt) vi* [Instrument] to sound; [Stimme] to ring out; [Geräusch] to be heard.

Ertrag *(pl -träge) der* [an Gemüse, Getreide] yield; [finanziell] profits *Pl*.

ertragen *(präs erträgt, prät ertrug, perf hat ertragen) vt* to bear.

erträglich *adj* [Zustände] tolerable; [Schmerz] bearable.

ertränken *vt* to drown.

ertrinken *(prät ertrank, perf ist ertrunken) vi* to drown.

erübrigen *vt* to spare. ❧ **sich erübrigen** *ref* to be unnecessary.

Erw. *(abk für Erwachsene)* adult.

Erwachen *das* awakening; **das gab ein böses Erwachen** *fig* it was a rude awakening.

Erwachsene [ɛɐˈvaksnə] *(pl -n) der, die* adult.

Erwachsenenbildung *die* adult education.

erwägen *(prät erwog, perf hat erwogen) vt* to consider.

erwähnen *vt* to mention.

erwähnenswert *adj* worth mentioning.

Erwähnung *(pl -en) die* mention *(U)*.

erwärmen *vt* [wärmen] to warm. ❧ **sich erwärmen** *ref* - 1. [sich aufwärmen] to warm up - 2. [sich begeistern]: **ich kann mich für deine Idee nicht erwärmen** I can't generate any enthusiasm for your idea.

erwarten *vt* - 1. [warten auf] to wait for; **ich kann es kaum erwarten!** I can hardly wait! - 2. [mit etw rechnen, erhoffen] to expect.

Erwartung *(pl* -en) *die* expectation. ➡ **Erwartungen** *Pl* expectations; [Anforderung] requirements.

erwartungsvoll <> *adj* expectant. <> *adv* expectantly.

erwecken *vt* - 1. [Ehrgeiz, Misstrauen] to arouse; [Hoffnungen] to raise - 2. [Tote] to awaken.

erweisen *(prät* **erwies,** *perf* **hat erwiesen)** *vt* [Schuld] to prove; **jm einen Dienst** ODER **Gefallen erweisen** to do sb a favour; **es ist erwiesen, dass...** it has been proved that... ➡ **sich erweisen** *ref* [sich zeigen]: **sich als etw erweisen** to prove to be sthg.

erweitern *vt* [Raum, Angebot, Umfang] to extend; [Bekanntenkreis, Wissen] to expand. ➡ **sich erweitern** *ref* [Straße, Angebot] to extend; [Bekanntenkreis, Produktion] to expand; [Pupillen] to dilate.

Erweiterung *(pl* -en) *die* [von Raum, Angebot] extension *(U)*; [von Bekanntenkreis, Wissen] expansion *(U)*; [von Pupillen] dilation *(U)*.

Erwerb *der* - 1. [von Haus, Grundstück] purchase - 2. [von Kenntnissen] acquisition - 3. [aus Geschäft] earnings *Pl.*

erwerben *(präs* **erwirbt,** *prät* **erwarb,** *perf* **hat erworben)** *vt* - 1. [kaufen] to purchase - 2. [erlangen] to acquire.

erwerbslos *adj* unemployed.

erwerbstätig *adj* employed; **die erwerbstätige Bevölkerung** the working population.

erwidern *vt* - 1. [antworten] to reply - 2. [Besuch, Gruß, Gefälligkeit] to return.

erwiesen <> *pp* ▷ **erweisen.** <> *adj* proven.

erwischen *vt* - 1. [ertappen]: **jn (bei etw) erwischen** to catch sb (doing sthg) - 2. [rechtzeitig erreichen] to catch - 3. [bekommen] to get; **ihn hat es erwischt** *fam* [krank sein] he's got it; [verletzt sein] he's hurt; [verliebt sein] he's got it bad; [tot sein] he's dead.

erwog *prät* ▷ **erwägen.**

erwogen *pp* ▷ **erwägen.**

erwünscht *adj* [Gäste, Entwicklung] welcome; [Ergebnis] desired; **nicht erwünscht sein** not to be welcome.

erwürgen *vt* to strangle.

Erz *(pl* -e) *das* ore.

erzählen *vt* [Geschichte, Witz] to tell; **dem werde ich was erzählen!** *fam* I'll give him a piece of my mind!

Erzählung *(pl* -en) *die* - 1. [Bericht] account - 2. [Dichtung] story.

Erz|bischof *der* archbishop.

Erz|engel *der* archangel.

erzeugen *vt* [Produkt] to produce; [Energie, Angst, Druck] to generate.

Erzeugnis *(pl* -se) *das* product.

Erzeugung *die* [von Produkten] production; [von Energie, Druck] generation.

erziehen *(prät* **erzog,** *perf* **hat erzogen)** *vt* [Kinder - in der Familie] to bring up; [- in der Schule] to educate; [Tier] to train; **jn zu jm/etw erziehen** to bring sb up to be sb/sthg.

Erzieher, in *(mpl* -, *fpl* -nen) *der, die* - 1. [Berufsbezeichnung] teacher - 2. [Eltern, Lehrer] educator.

erzieherisch <> *adj* educational. <> *adv* educationally.

Erziehung *die* [in der Familie] upbringing; [in der Schule] education.

Erziehungs|berechtigte *der, die amt* parent ODER guardian.

erzielen *vt* [Kompromiss] to reach; [Ertrag, Gewinn] to make.

erzogen <> *pp* ▷ **erziehen.** <> *adj:* **gut/ schlecht erzogen** well/badly brought up.

erzwingen *(prät* **erzwang,** *perf* **hat erzwungen)** *vt* to force.

es *pron* - 1. [Personalpronomen im Nominativ - bei Sachen] it; [- bei Personen] he (she *die*) - 2. [Personalpronomen im Akkusativ - bei Sachen] it; [- bei Personen] him (her *die*); **ich hoffe es** I hope so; **ich weiß es** I know - 3. [unpersönliches Pronomen] it; **es ist drei Uhr** it's three o'clock; **es regnet/schneit** it's raining/snowing; **es freut mich, dass...** I'm pleased that...; **gestern gab es Nudeln** yesterday we had pasta; **es ist sehr interessant, sich mit Jill zu unterhalten** Jill is very interesting to talk to; **es geht mir gut** I'm fine; **wer war es?** who was it?

Es *(pl* -) *das* - 1. MUS E flat - 2. [Psychologie] id.

Esche *(pl* -n) *die* ash.

Esel *(pl* -) *der* - 1. [Tier] donkey - 2. *fam* [Schimpfwort] ass; **ich Esel!** stupid me!

Eselin *(pl* -nen) *die* she-ass.

Eskimo *(pl* -s) *der* Eskimo.

Espe *(pl* -n) *die* aspen.

Espresso [es'preso] *(pl* - ODER -s) <> *der* espresso. <> *das* [Lokal] coffee bar.

Essay ['εse] *(pl* -s) *das* & *der* essay.

essbar *adj* edible.

essen *(präs* **isst,** *prät* **aß,** *perf* **hat gegessen)** <> *vi* to eat; **essen gehen** to go out for a meal; **warm/kalt essen** to have a hot/cold meal. <> *vt* to eat; **seinen Teller leer essen** to eat everything on one's plate.

Essen *(pl* -) *das* meal; **Essen machen** ODER **kochen** to make ODER cook a meal.

Essig *(pl* -e) *der* vinegar.

Ess|löffel *(pl* -) *der* dessertspoon.

Ess|zimmer *(pl* -) *das* dining room.

Estland *nt* Estonia.

estnisch adj Estonian.

Estragon der tarragon.

Etage [e'tɑːʒə] (pl -n) die floor.

Etagen|wohnung die flat UK, apartment US (in a block).

Etappe (pl -n) die stage.

Etat [e'tɑː] (pl -s) der budget.

Ethik (pl -en) die - 1. [Lehre] ethics (U) - 2. (ohne pl) [Moral] ethics Pl.

ethnisch adj ethnic.

Etikett (pl -e(n) ODER -s) das label.

etliche, r, s det several, quite a few; **etliche Male** several times. ◆ **etliches** pron: etliches zahlen to pay quite a lot; **es gibt etliches zu erwähnen** there are quite a few things to mention.

Etui [ɛt'viː] (pl -s) das case.

etwa adv - 1. [zirka, ungefähr] about; **es funktioniert etwa so** it works roughly like this - 2. [zum Beispiel] for example - 3. [zum Ausdruck der Beunruhigung, eines Vorwurfs in Fragen]: **ist es etwa schon 24 Uhr?** don't tell me it's 12 o'clock already - 4. [zur Bekräftigung]: **Edinburgh ist nicht etwa groß, aber schön** Edinburgh is certainly not big but it is beautiful.

etwaig adj possible; **etwaige Fragen** any questions that might arise.

etwas ◇ det - 1. [gen] something; [in Fragen] anything; **etwas Anderes/Schönes** something else/nice - 2. [ein wenig] some; **möchten Sie noch etwas Kaffee?** would you like some more coffee? ◇ pron something; [in Fragen] anything; **hast du etwas für mich?** have you got anything for me?; **das ist doch wenigstens etwas!** that's something at least!; **so etwas** such a thing. ◇ adv a little; **etwas spät** rather late.

EU (abk für Europäische Union) die EU.

euch pron (Akkusativ und Dativ von ihr) - 1. [Personalpronomen] you; **wir haben es euch gesagt** we told you; **das gehört euch** this is yours, this belongs to you; **mit euch** with you - 2. [Reflexivpronomen] yourselves; **könnt ihr euch das vorstellen?** can you imagine that? - 3. [einander] each other.

euer, e ODER **eure** det your; **alles Gute, Euer Thomas** yours, Thomas.

eure, r, s pron yours.

eurer pron (Genitiv von ihr) you.

eurerseits adv - 1. [Ihr selbst] for your part - 2. [von Euch] on your part.

euretwegen adv - 1. [euch zuliebe] for your sake - 2. [wegen euch] because of you.

eurige (pl -n) pron (mit Artikel) geh yours.

Euro ['ɔyro] (pl -) der euro.

Eurocent ['ɔyrosɛnt] (pl -s) der eurocent.

Eurocheque (pl -s), **Euro|scheck** (pl -s) ['ɔy-rofɛk] der Eurocheque.

Eurocheque-Karte, Euroscheckkarte die Eurocheque card.

Eurocity ['ɔyrositi] (pl -s) der international train linking two or more major European cities.

Euro|land das Euroland.

Europa nt Europe.

Europäer, in (mpl -, fpl -nen) der, die European.

europäisch adj European.

Europa|parlament das European Parliament.

Europarat der Council of Europe.

Euro|scheck = **Eurocheque**.

Euro|zone die euro zone.

ev. abk für **evangelisch**.

e. V. (abk für **eingetragener Verein**), registered society.

evakuieren [evaku'iːrən] vt to evacuate.

evangelisch [evaŋ'geːlɪʃ] adj Protestant.

Evangelium [evaŋ'geːljʊm] (pl -ien) das gospel.

eventuell [evɛn'tʊɛl] ◇ adj possible. ◇ adv maybe, perhaps.

ewig ◇ adj - 1. [nie endend] eternal - 2. fam abw [andauernd] constant. ◇ adv - 1. [endlos] eternally - 2. fam abw [zu lange] constantly. ◆ **auf ewig** adv [für immer] forever.

Ewigkeit (pl -en) die eternity.

EWS [eː'veː'ɛs] (abk für **Europäisches Währungssystem**) das EMS.

exakt ◇ adj exact; [Arbeit] precise. ◇ adv exactly; [arbeiten] with precision.

Exaktheit die precision.

Examen (pl -) das examination; **Examen machen** to take one's examinations.

Exekutive [ɛkseku'tiːvə] die (ohne pl) executive.

Exempel (pl -) das example; **an jm ein Exempel statuieren** to make an example of sb.

Exemplar (pl -e) das example; [von Buch] copy.

Exil (pl -e) das exile (U).

existent adj existing.

Existenz (pl -en) die - 1. [Bestehen] existence - 2. [Existenzgrundlage] livelihood - 3. abw [Person] character.

Existenz|minimum das (ohne pl) subsistence level.

existieren vi - 1. [bestehen] to exist - 2. [auskommen] to live.

exklusiv ◇ adj exclusive. ◇ adv - 1. [vornehm, abgesondert]: **exklusiv leben** to live an exclusive lifestyle - 2. [ausschließlich] exclusively.

Exkursion (pl -en) die study trip.

Exmatrikulation (pl -en) die UNI removal of someone's name from a university register.

Exot (*pl* -en), **Exote** (*pl* -n) *der* [Mensch] exotic person; [Tier] exotic animal.

exotisch <> *adj* exotic. <> *adv* exotically.

Expedition (*pl* -en) *die* expedition.

Experiment (*pl* -e) *das* - **1.** [Versuch] experiment - **2.** [Wagnis] experimentation.

experimentell <> *adj* experimental. <> *adv* experimentally.

experimentieren *vi* to experiment; **mit etw experimentieren** to experiment on sthg.

Experte (*pl* -n) *der* expert.

Expertin (*pl* -nen) *die* expert.

explodieren (*perf* ist **explodiert**) *vi* to explode.

Explosion (*pl* -en) *die* explosion.

explosiv *adj* explosive.

Export (*pl* -e) *der* export.

Exporteur [ɛkspɔr'tøːɐ̯] (*pl* -e) *der* exporter.

Expressionismus *der* expressionism.

extra <> *adv* - **1.** [separat] separately - **2.** [zusätzlich] extra - **3.** [speziell] specially. <> *adj* (*unver*) extra.

Extrakt (*pl* -e) *der* extract.

extrem <> *adj* extreme. <> *adv* [billig, auffällig] extremely; [reagieren, denken] in an extreme way; **extrem rechts stehen** to be on the extreme right.

Extremfall *der* extreme case.

Extremist, **in** (*mpl* -en, *fpl* -nen) *der*, *die* extremist.

Extremsport *der* extreme sports *Pl*.

exzellent <> *adj* excellent. <> *adv* excellently.

Exzess (*pl* -e) *der* excess.

EZ *abk für* **Einzelzimmer**.

EZB (*abk für* **Europäische Zentralbank**) *die* European Central Bank.

F

f (*pl* - *ODER* -s), **F** (*pl* - *ODER* -s) [ɛf] *das* - **1.** [Buchstabe] f, F - **2.** MUS F. ➡ **F** (*abk für* **Fahrenheit**) F.

Fa. (*abk für* **Firma**) Co.

fabelhaft <> *adj* fantastic. <> *adv* fantastically.

Fabrik (*pl* -en) *die* factory.

Fabrikant, **in** (*mpl* -en, *fpl* -nen) *der*, *die* factory owner.

Fabrikarbeiter, **in** *der*, *die* factory worker.

fabrikneu *adj* brand new.

fabrizieren *vt fam abw* [machen] to throw together.

Facette (*pl* -n), **Fassette** (*pl* -n) [fa'sɛtə] *die* facet.

Fach (*pl* **Fächer**) *das* - **1.** [in Möbel, Behälter] compartment; [für Brief, Schlüssel] pigeonhole - **2.** [in Schule, Studium] subject; **vom Fach sein** to be an expert.

Fachabitur *das* exam taken at the end of a secondary vocational school which enables students to enter a "Fachhochschule" but not university.

Facharbeiter, **in** *der*, *die* skilled worker.

Facharzt, **ärztin** *der*, *die* specialist.

Fachausdruck *der* technical term.

Fächer (*pl* -) *der* fan.

Fachgeschäft *das* specialist shop *UK ODER* store *US*.

Fachhochschule *die* college offering primarily vocational courses to the equivalent of bachelor level.

Fachkenntnis *die* specialist knowledge *(U)*.

Fachkraft *die* skilled worker.

fachkundig <> *adj* expert. <> *adv* expertly.

fachlich <> *adj* [Problem] technical; [beruflich] professional. <> *adv* technically; [beruflich] professionally; **sich fachlich weiterbilden** to gain professional qualifications.

Fachmann (*pl* -leute) *der* expert.

fachmännisch <> *adj* expert. <> *adv* expertly.

fachsimpeln ['faxzɪmpl̩n] *vi fam* to talk shop.

Fachwissen *das* specialist knowledge.

Fackel (*pl* -n) *die* torch.

Faden (*pl* **Fäden**) *der* - **1.** [Faser] thread - **2.** MED stitch; **den Faden verlieren** to lose the thread.

fähig *adj* capable; **zu etw fähig sein** to be capable of sthg.

Fähigkeit (*pl* -en) *die* - **1.** [Begabung] talent - **2.** [Können] ability.

fahnden *vi*: **nach jm/etw fahnden** to search for sb/sthg.

Fahndung (*pl* -en) *die* search.

Fahne (*pl* -n) *die* flag; **eine Fahne haben** *fam fig* to smell of drink.

Fahnenflucht *die* MIL desertion.

Fahrausweis *der* - **1.** [Fahrschein] ticket - **2.** *Schweiz* [Führerschein] driving licence *UK*, driver's license *US*.

Fahrbahn *die* road.

Fähre (*pl* -n) *die* ferry.

fahren (*präs* **fährt**, *prät* **fuhr**, *perf* **hat/ist gefahren**) <> *vi* (*ist*) - **1.** [Person - gen] to go; [- mit Auto] to drive; [- mit Fahrrad] to ride; **mit dem Zug/Bus fahren** to go by train/bus; **ins Gebirge fahren** to go to the mountains; **wir fahren**

nach England we're going to England; **durch Wien fahren** to drive through Vienna; **langsam/zu schnell fahren** to drive slowly/too fast; **120 km/h fahren** to drive at 120 km/h; **ein Gedanke fuhr ihm durch den Kopf** a thought flashed through his mind; **was ist denn in dich gefahren?** *fig* what's got into you? - **2.** [Fahrzeug] to go; [Schiff] to sail - **3.** [abfahren] to leave; **wann fährst du?** when are you leaving ODER going?; **der Bus fährt alle 30 Minuten** the bus leaves ODER runs every half hour; **einen fahren lassen** *fam* to fart. ◇ *vt* - **1.** *(hat)* [Fahrzeug] to drive; [Fahrrad] to ride - **2.** *(ist)* [Entfernung, Strecke] to drive; **ich fahre diese Strecke jeden Tag** I drive ODER come this way every day - **3.** *(ist)* SPORT: **Rollschuh fahren** to rollerskate; **Ski fahren** to ski; **Schlitten fahren** to go sledging.

Fahrenheit *nt* Fahrenheit.

Fahrer *(pl -)* der driver.

Fahrerflucht die failure to stop after an accident.

Fahrerin *(pl -nen)* die driver.

Fahr|gast der passenger.

Fahr|geld das fare.

Fahr|karte die ticket.

Fahrkarten|schalter der ticket desk.

fahrlässig ◇ *adj* negligent; **fahrlässige Tötung** manslaughter UK, murder in the second degree US. ◇ *adv* negligently.

Fahrlässigkeit die negligence.

Fahr|plan der timetable.

fahrplanmäßig ◇ *adj* scheduled. ◇ *adv* on schedule.

Fahr|preis der fare.

Fahr|prüfung die driving test.

Fahr|rad das bicycle; **mit dem Fahrrad fahren** to cycle.

Fahr|schein der ticket.

Fahr|schule die driving school.

Fahr|stuhl der lift UK, elevator US.

Fahrt *(pl -en)* die - **1.** [gen] journey; [kurzer Ausflug] trip; **auf der Fahrt nach Berlin** on the way to Berlin; **freie Fahrt haben** to have a clear run - **2.** *(ohne pl)* [Geschwindigkeit] speed; **in Fahrt kommen** ODER **geraten** [in Schwung kommen] to get going; *fam* [wütend werden] to flare up. ◆ **gute Fahrt** *interj* have a good journey!

fährt *präs* ▷ **fahren**.

Fährte *(pl -n)* die trail.

Fahrtkosten, Fahrkosten *Pl* travelling expenses.

Fahrt|richtung die [im Verkehr] direction; [im Zug] direction of travel; **die A9 in Fahrtrichtung Berlin/München** the northbound/southbound section of the A9.

fahrtüchtig *adj* [Person] fit to drive; [Fahrzeug] roadworthy.

Fahr|verbot das driving ban.

Fahr|zeug *(pl -e)* das vehicle.

Fahr|zeughalter, **in** *(mpl Fahrzeughalter, fpl -nen)* der, die registered owner.

fair [fɛːɐ̯] ◇ *adj* fair. ◇ *adv* fairly.

Fairness ['fɛːɐ̯nɛs] die fairness.

Faktor *(pl -toren)* der factor.

Fakultät *(pl -en)* die UNI faculty.

Falke *(pl -n)* der falcon.

Fall *(pl Fälle)* der - **1.** [gen] case; **für alle Fälle** for all eventualities; **klarer Fall!** sure thing!; **jd/etw ist ganz sein Fall** *fam fig* one is very keen on sb/sthg - **2.** *(ohne pl)* [Sturz] fall; **zu Fall kommen** to fall; **jn zu Fall bringen** *fig* to bring sb down; **etw zu Fall bringen** *fig* to thwart sthg. ◆ **auf alle Fälle** *adv* - **1.** [unbedingt] definitely - **2.** [vorsichtshalber] in any case. ◆ **auf jeden Fall** *adv* in any case. ◆ **auf keinen Fall** *adv* under no circumstances. ◆ **für den Fall, dass** *konj* in case.

Falle *(pl -n)* die - **1.** [zum Fangen] trap; **(jm) eine Falle stellen** to set a trap (for sb); **in eine Falle geraten** *fig* to fall into a trap - **2.** *fam* [Bett] bed.

fallen *(präs fällt, prät fiel, perf ist gefallen)* vi - **1.** [gen] to fall; [Preise, Niveau, Temperatur] to drop; [Haare, Stoff] to hang - **2.** [Urteil] to be passed; [Entscheidung] to be made; [Wort] to be spoken; [Schuss] to be fired; **die Würfel sind gefallen** the die is cast; **in Ungnade fallen** to fall out of favour; **durch eine Prüfung fallen** to fail an exam.

fällen *vt* - **1.** [Baum] to fell - **2.** [Urteil] to pass; [Entscheidung] to make.

fällig *adj* due.

Fallobst das *(ohne pl)* windfalls *Pl*.

falls *konj* if; **falls es dir nicht gefällt** in case ODER if you don't like it.

Fall|schirm der parachute.

Fallschirm|springer, **in** der, die parachutist.

fällt *präs* ▷ **fallen**.

Fall|tür die trapdoor.

falsch ◇ *adj* - **1.** [nicht korrekt, nicht passend] wrong - **2.** [imitiert, gefälscht, irreführend - Gebiss, Stolz, Angaben] false; [- Pass, Geldschein] forged. ◇ *adv* - **1.** [nicht korrekt] wrongly; **etw falsch verstehen** to misunderstand sthg; **falsch singen** to sing out of tune; **falsch abbiegen** to take the wrong turning - **2.** [hinterhältig] falsely.

Falsche *(pl -n)* der, die, das [Person] wrong person; [Sache] wrong thing; **an den Falschen** ODER **die Falsche geraten** *fam* to come to the wrong person.

fälschen *vt* to forge.

Fälscher, **in** *(mpl -, fpl -nen)* der, die forger.

Falsch|fahrer, **in** der, die person who drives into oncoming traffic on a motorway.

Falschgeld *das* counterfeit money.

fälschlich <> *adj* false. <> *adv* falsely.

Fälschung *(pl -en) die* - 1. [Fälschen] forging - 2. [Gefälschtes] forgery.

Falte *(pl -n) die* [in Stoff, Papier] fold; [in Hose, Hemd] crease; [in Haut] wrinkle.

falten *vt* [Stoff, Papier, Hände] to fold.

Falter *(pl -) der* butterfly.

faltig *adj* [Haut, Hände] wrinkled; [Hemd, Tischtuch] creased.

familiär <> *adj* [die Familie betreffend] family *(vor Subst).* <> *adv* [zwanglos] informally.

Familie [fa'mi:ljə] *(pl -n) die* family; **Familie haben** to have a family.

Familien|betrieb *der* family business.

Familien|feier *die* family celebration.

Familien|kreis *der (ohne pl)* family circle.

Familien|name *der* surname.

Familien|stand *der* marital status.

famos [fa'mo:s] *fam adj* marvellous.

Fan *(pl -s) der* fan.

Fanatiker, in *(mpl -, fpl -nen) der, die* fanatic.

fand *prät* ▷ **finden**.

Fanfare *(pl -n) die* fanfare.

Fang *der* - 1. [Fangen] catching - 2. [Beute] catch.

fangen *(präs* **fängt**, *prät* **fing**, *perf* **hat gefangen**) *vt* to catch. ➤ **sich fangen** *ref* - 1. [in Falle, Netz] to get caught - 2. [nach Schwierigkeiten] to regain one's composure.

fängt *präs* ▷ **fangen**.

Fantasie *(pl -n)*, **Phantasie** *(pl -n)* [fanta'zi:] *die* - 1. *(ohne pl)* [Vorstellungskraft] imagination - 2. [Vorstellung] fantasy.

fantasielos, phantasielos <> *adj* unimaginative. <> *adv* unimaginatively.

fantasieren, phantasieren *vi* - 1. [irrereden] to be delirious - 2. [träumen] to fantasize.

fantasievoll, phantasievoll <> *adj* imaginative. <> *adv* imaginatively.

fantastisch, phantastisch <> *adj* fantastic. <> *adv* fantastically.

Farb|aufnahme *die* colour photograph.

Farbband *(pl -bänder) das* (typewriter) ribbon.

Farb|drucker *der* EDV colour printer.

Farbe *(pl -n) die* - 1. [Licht, Buntheit] colour; **Farbe bekommen** *fig* to get some colour - 2. [Material] paint - 3. [in Kartenspiel] suit.

farbecht *adj* colourfast.

färben <> *vt* to dye. <> *vi* to run. ➤ **sich färben** *ref* to change colour; **sich rosa färben** to turn pink.

farbenblind *adj* colour-blind.

Farb|fernsehen *das* colour television.

Farb|fernseher *der* colour television.

Farb|film *der* colour film.

Farb|foto *das* colour photo.

farbig <> *adj* - 1. [Druck, Fernsehen] colour - 2. [bunt, lebhaft] colourful - 3. [Person, Papier] coloured. <> *adv* colourfully.

Farbige *(pl -n) der, die* coloured person.

farblich *adv* as regards colour.

farblos *adj* colourless.

Farb|stoff *der* colouring.

Färbung *(pl -en) die* - 1. [Farbgebung] tinge - 2. [Tendenz] slant.

Farn *(pl -e) der* fern.

Fasan *(pl -e ODER -en) der* pheasant.

Fasching *(pl -e ODER -s) der* carnival before Lent.

Faschismus *der* fascism.

Faschist, in *(mpl -en, fpl -nen) der, die* fascist.

Faser *(pl -n) die* fibre.

faserig *adj* [Fleisch] stringy; [Holz] coarse.

Fass *(pl* **Fässer**) *das* barrel. ➤ **vom Fass** *adj* & *adv* draught.

Fassade *(pl -n) die* facade.

fassen *(präs* **fasst**, *prät* **fasste**, *perf* **hat gefasst**) <> *vt* - 1. [anfassen] to take hold of; **jn/etw zu fassen bekommen** to catch hold of sb/sthg - 2. [Dieb] to catch - 3. [Entschluss] to make - 4. [begreifen]: **ich kann es nicht fassen** I can't take it in - 5. [als Inhalt] to hold. <> *vi*: **an** ODER **in etw** *(A)* **fassen** [kurz] to touch sthg; [lang] to feel sthg. ➤ **sich fassen** *ref* to pull o.s. together; **sich auf etw** *(A)* **gefasst machen** *fig* to prepare o.s. for sthg; **sich kurz fassen** to keep it short.

Fassette *die* = **Facette**.

Fassung *(pl -en) die* - 1. [von Glühbirne] socket; [von Perle] setting - 2. [von Text] version - 3. [Selbstbeherrschung]: **jn aus der Fassung bringen** to put sb out.

fassungslos <> *adj* [Person] speechless; [Gesicht] astounded. <> *adv* speechlessly.

Fassungsvermögen *das* capacity.

fast *adv* nearly, almost.

fasten *vi* to fast.

Fasten|zeit *die* - 1. [Zeit religiösen Fastens] fasting period - 2. [vor Ostern] Lent.

Fastnacht *die* carnival before Lent.

fatal *adj* [verhängnisvoll] fatal.

fauchen *vi* to hiss.

faul <> *adj* - 1. [Lebensmittel, Holz] rotten - 2. [Person] lazy - 3. *fam* [Witz, Ausrede] dubious. <> *adv* [träge] lazily.

faulen *(perf* **hat/ist gefault**) *vi* [Holz, Fleisch] to rot; [Zahn] to decay.

faulenzen *vi* to laze around.

Faulheit *die* laziness.

faulig *adj* [Obst] rotten; [Wasser] stagnant.

Fäulnis *die* rot.

Fauna *die* BIOL fauna.

Faust (*pl* **Fäuste**) *die* fist; **auf eigene Faust** *fig* off one's own bat.

Faust|regel *die* rule of thumb.

Faust|schlag *der* punch.

Fax (*pl* - ODER -e) *das* fax.

faxen *vt* to fax.

Faxen *Pl* **fam: die Faxen dick** ODER **satt haben** to have had enough.

FAZ ['ɛfaːtsɛt] (*abk für* **Frankfurter Allgemeine Zeitung**) *die* German newspaper, renowned for its business and financial news.

Fazit (*pl* -s ODER -e) *das* result.

FCKW [ɛfɟyːtseːkaːˈveː] (*abk für* **Fluorchlorkohlenwasserstoff**) *der* (*ohne pl*) CFC.

F.D.P. [ɛfɟydeːˈpeː] (*abk für* **Freie Demokratische Partei**) *die* German liberal party.

Februar *der* February; *siehe auch* **September**.

fechten (*präs* **ficht**, *prät* **focht**, *perf* **hat gefochten**) *vi* to fence.

Fechter, in (*mpl* -, *fpl* -nen) *der, die* fencer.

Feder (*pl* -n) *die* - 1. [von Vogel] feather - 2. [zum Schreiben] nib; **zur Feder greifen** to take up one's pen - 3. [in Maschine, Matratze] spring. ◆ **Federn** *Pl*: **(noch) in den Federn liegen** *fam* to be (still) in bed.

Feder|ball *der* - 1. [Spiel] badminton - 2. [Ball] shuttlecock.

Feder|bett *das* quilt.

federn ◇ *vi* [elastisch sein] to be springy; [bei Sprung, Druck] to spring back; **in den Knien federn** to give at the knees. ◇ *vt* [Fahrzeug]: **gut gefedert sein** [Auto] to have good suspension; [Matratze] to be well sprung.

Federung (*pl* -en) *die* [von Wagen] suspension (*U*); [von Bett] springs *Pl*.

Fee (*pl* -n) *die* fairy.

fegen (*perf* **hat/ist gefegt**) ◇ *vt* (hat) to sweep. ◇ *vi* - 1. (hat) *Norddt* [säubern] to sweep up - 2. (ist) [rasen] to sweep.

fehl *adv*: **fehl am Platz sein** to be out of place.

Fehl|betrag *der* shortfall.

fehlen *vi* - 1. [nicht vorhanden sein] to be missing; **für ein Hobby fehlt ihr die Zeit** she doesn't have time for a hobby; **(in der Schule) fehlen** to miss school; **es fehlt an etw** (D) there is a lack of sthg; **es fehlt ihm einiges an Erfahrung** he is somewhat lacking in experience - 2. [vermisst werden]: **sie fehlt mir** I miss her - 3. [irren]: **weit gefehlt!** far from it! - 4. [erkrankt sein]: **was fehlt dir/Ihnen?** what is the matter with you?

Fehl|entscheidung *die* wrong decision.

Fehler (*pl* -) *der* - 1. [Unrichtigkeit] mistake - 2. [Schwäche] fault; **ist es mein Fehler, dass er geht?** is it my fault that he's leaving? - 3. [Mangel] defect.

fehlerfrei ◇ *adj* perfect. ◇ *adv* perfectly.

fehlerhaft ◇ *adj* [Maschine] defective; [Aussprache] poor. ◇ *adv* [schreiben, arbeiten] poorly; [verarbeitet] defectively.

Fehl|geburt *die* miscarriage.

Fehl|griff *der* mistake.

fehl|schlagen (*perf* **ist fehlgeschlagen**) *vi* (*unreg*) to fail.

Fehl|start *der* - 1. [von Sportlern] false start - 2. [von Rakete] abortive launch.

Fehl|urteil *das* - 1. [Rechtspruch - von Richter] wrong judgement; [- von Geschworenen] wrong verdict - 2. [Beurteilung] misjudgement.

Feier (*pl* -n) *die* party.

Feier|abend *der* evening after work; **Feierabend machen** to finish work; **nach Feierabend** after work; **mit etw ist Feierabend** *fam fig* it's all over with sthg.

feierlich ◇ *adj* - 1. [Akt, Handlung, Stille] dignified - 2. [Erklärung] solemn; **das ist schon nicht mehr feierlich** *fam* that really is too much. ◇ *adv* - 1. [verabschieden, begehen] in a dignified manner - 2. [erklären] solemnly.

Feierlichkeit (*pl* -en) *die* [Würde] solemnity. ◆ **Feierlichkeiten** *Pl* celebrations.

feiern ◇ *vt* - 1. [Fest, Feiertag] to celebrate - 2. [Person] to fête. ◇ *vi* to celebrate.

Feier|tag *der* holiday; **kirchlicher Feiertag** feast day.

feige *adj* cowardly.

Feige (*pl* -n) *die* fig.

Feigheit *die* cowardice.

Feigling (*pl* -e) *der* coward.

Feile (*pl* -n) *die* file.

feilen ◇ *vt* to file. ◇ *vi*: **an etw** (D) **feilen** *fig* to polish sthg up.

feilschen *vi*: **um etw feilschen** to haggle over sthg.

fein ◇ *adj* - 1. [Haar, Spitze, Pulver] fine - 2. *fam* [erfreulich, sympathisch] great - 3. [Gesicht] delicate - 4. [Material, Zutat, Küche] top-quality - 5. [Sinne] keen - 6. [Spott, Nuance] subtle - 7. [Leute] refined; **sich fein machen** to make o.s. smart. ◇ *adv* - 1. [gemahlen, gezeichnet] finely - 2. *fam* [schön, erfreulich]: **fein gemacht!** well done!; **fein sein** *fig* to have done well for o.s. - 3. [sich verhalten] nicely - 4. [vornehm, elegant] elegantly. ◆ **vom Feinsten** *adj* top-quality.

Feind (*pl* -e) *der* enemy; **sich** (D) **Feinde machen** to make enemies.

Feindin (*pl* -nen) *die* enemy.

feindlich ◇ *adj* - 1. [Haltung, Nachbarn] hostile - 2. [Soldaten] enemy (*vor Subst*). ◇ *adv* hostilely.

Feindlichkeit *die* [Gesinnung] hostility.

Feindschaft (*pl* -en) *die* enmity (*U*).

feindselig ◇ *adj* hostile. ◇ *adv* hostilely.

Feindseligkeit (*pl* -en) *die* hostility. ◆ **Feindseligkeiten** *Pl* hostilities.

feinfühlig adj sensitive.

Feinheit (pl -en) die - 1. [Beschaffenheit] fineness - 2. [Vornehmheit] refinement. ◆ **Feinheiten** Pl subtleties.

Feinkost|geschäft das delicatessen.

Fein|schmecker, in (mpl · **Feinschmecker**, fpl -nen) der, die gourmet.

Feld (pl -er) das - 1. [gen] field - 2. [Teil - von Formular] box; [- von Brettspiel] square; **das Feld räumen** to bow out; **jm das Feld überlassen** to make way for sb.

Feld|bett das camp bed UK, cot US.

Feld|flasche die water bottle.

Feld|salat der (ohne pl) lamb's lettuce.

Feld|weg der footpath (between fields).

Feld|zug der campaign.

Felge (pl -n) die - 1. [Teil des Rades] (wheel) rim - 2. [Turnübung] circle.

Fell (pl -e) das [Haarkleid] fur; [von Hund, Pferd] coat; [von Schaf] fleece.

Fels (pl -en) der - 1. (ohne pl) [Gestein] rock - 2. geh [Felsen] cliff.

Felsen (pl -) der cliff.

felsenfest ◇ adj firm. ◇ adv firmly.

felsig adj rocky.

feminin ◇ adj - 1. [gen] feminine - 2. abw [unmännlich] effeminate. ◇ adv - 1. [weiblich] femininely - 2. abw [unmännlich] effeminately.

Femininum (pl -nina) das GRAMM feminine noun.

Feminismus der [Frauenbewegung] feminism.

Feminist, in (mpl -en, fpl -nen) der, die feminist.

feministisch ◇ adj feminist. ◇ adv in a feminist way.

Fenchel der fennel.

Fenster (pl -) das window; **weg vom Fenster sein** fam fig to be out of it.

Fenster|laden der shutter.

Fenster|platz der window seat.

Fenster|scheibe die window pane.

Ferien Pl holiday sing UK, vacation sing US; **die großen Ferien** the summer holidays UK, the summer vacation US; **in die Ferien fahren**, **Ferien machen** to go on holiday UK, to go on vacation US.

Ferien|lager das summer camp.

Ferien|ort der resort.

Ferkel (pl -) das - 1. [Tier] piglet - 2. fam [dreckiger Mensch] mucky pup - 3. fam [unanständiger Mensch] filthy swine.

fern ◇ adj - 1. [räumlich] far-off - 2. [zeitlich] distant. ◇ adv far; **von fern** from a distance. ◇ präp geh: **fern einer Sache** (D) far from sthg.

Fern|bedienung die remote control.

Ferne die (ohne pl) [räumlich]: **ihr Blick schweifte in die Ferne** she stared off into the distance; **in der Ferne** in the distance; **aus der Ferne** [betrachten] from a distance; [Gruß] from far-off lands.

Ferne Osten der Far East.

ferner ◇ konj in addition. ◇ adv geh in future. ◇ adj (Kompar) ⊏ **fern**.

Fern|gespräch das long-distance call.

ferngesteuert adj remote-controlled.

Fern|glas das binoculars Pl.

fern halten vt (unreg): **jn/etw von jm/etw fern halten** to keep sb/sthg away from sb/sthg. ◆ **sich fern halten** ref: **sich von jm/etw fern halten** to keep away from sb/sthg.

Fern|licht das full beam UK, high beam US.

Fern|rohr das telescope.

Fernseh|apparat der television set.

fern|sehen vi (unreg) to watch television.

Fernsehen das television; **im Fernsehen** on television, on TV.

Fernseher (pl -) der - 1. [Gerät] television, TV - 2. [Fernsehzuschauer] viewer.

Fernseh|film der television ODER TV film.

Fernseh|programm das - 1. [Sendungen] television ODER TV programmes Pl - 2. [Programmheft] television ODER TV guide.

Fern|steuerung die remote control.

Fern|straße die trunk road UK, highway US.

Fern|verkehr der long-distance traffic.

Ferse (pl -n) die heel; **jm auf den Fersen sein/bleiben** fig to be/stay on sb's heels.

fertig adj - 1. [vollendet - gen] finished; [- Essen] ready - 2. [bereit]: **fertig sein** to be ready - 3. [am/zu Ende]: **(mit etw) fertig sein** to have finished (sthg) - 4. [müde]: **fertig sein** fam [körperlich] to be worn out; [psychisch] to be shattered; **mit den Nerven fertig sein** to be at the end of one's tether UK ODER rope US; **mit jm fertig sein** fam to be finished ODER through with sb; **mit etw fertig/nicht fertig werden** to cope/not cope with sthg; **mit jm schon/nicht fertig werden** fam to cope/not cope with sb.

fertig bringen vt (unreg) [zustande bringen]: **er hat es fertig gebracht, dass die Familien wieder miteinander reden** he has managed to get the families talking to each other again.

Fertig|haus das prefabricated house.

Fertigkeit (pl -en) die skill. ◆ **Fertigkeiten** Pl skills.

fertig|machen vt - 1. fam [zurechtweisen] to lay into - 2. fam [zur Verzweiflung bringen]: **der macht mich fertig** he does my head in - 3. fam [erschöpfen] to wear out.

fertig machen vt - 1. [abschließen] to finish - 2. [bereitmachen] to get ready - 3. fam [erledigen] to sort out; [zusammenschlagen] to do in. ◆ **sich fertig machen** ref [sich bereitmachen] to get ready.

fertig stellen *vt* to complete.

Fessel *(pl -n) die -* **1.** [Strick, Zwang] bond - **2.** [Körperteil - bei Tieren] pastern; [- bei Menschen] ankle.

fesseln *vt* - **1.** [anketten, binden] to tie up; **jm die Hände fesseln** to tie sb's hands up - **2.** [faszinieren] to grip.

fesselnd <> *adj* gripping. <> *adv* grippingly.

fest <> *adj* - **1.** [gut befestigt - Knoten, Verband] tight - **2.** [Griff, Druck, Meinung] firm - **3.** [Wohnsitz, Angestellte] permanent; [Arbeitszeiten, Gehalt, Termin] fixed - **4.** [Stoff, Schuhe] strong - **5.** [verbindlich - Vereinbarung, Vorgaben] binding; [- Zusage] definite - **6.** [Nahrung] solid - **7.** [entschlossen - Blick, Stimme] steady. <> *adv* - **1.** [haltbar, straff] tightly - **2.** [drücken, ziehen] hard - **3.** [überzeugt - glauben] firmly - **4.** [verbindlich - zusagen, vereinbaren] definitely - **5.** [angestellt] permanently - **6.** [schlafen] soundly - **7.** *fam* [tüchtig - zugreifen] with a will.

Fest *(pl -e) das -* **1.** [Veranstaltung] party - **2.** [Feiertag] festival. **frohes Fest** *interj* happy Christmas!

festangestellt ⊳ **fest**.

Festlbetrag *der* fixed amount.

festlbinden *vt (unreg)* to tie up.

Festlessen *das* banquet.

festlhalten *(unreg)* <> *vt* - **1.** [aufzeichnen] to record - **2.** [feststellen]: **wir können festhalten, dass...** it is clear that... <> *vi*: **an jm festhalten** to stand by sb; **an etw festhalten** to stick to sthg.

fest halten *(unreg) vt* [halten] to hold on to. **sich fest halten** *ref*: **sich an jm/etw fest halten** to hold on to sb/sthg.

festigen *vt* to strengthen. **sich festigen** *ref* to become stronger.

Festiger *(pl -) der* [Schaum] styling mousse; [Spray] hairspray.

Festigkeit *die -* **1.** [Widerstandsfähigkeit] strength - **2.** [Standhaftigkeit] steadfastness.

Festival ['fɛstival] *(pl -s) das* festival.

Festland *das* mainland.

festllegen *vt* - **1.** [bestimmen] to fix - **2.** [verpflichten]: **jn auf etw (A) festlegen** to pin sb down to sthg. **sich festlegen** *ref* [sich binden] to commit o.s.; **sich auf etw (A) festlegen** to commit o.s. to sthg.

festlich <> *adj* [Essen, Veranstaltung] festive; [Kleidung] formal. <> *adv* festively.

Festlichkeit *(pl -en) die* [Atmosphäre] festiveness. **Festlichkeiten** *Pl* festivities.

festlmachen *vt* - **1.** [befestigen] to fix; [Boot] to moor - **2.** [vereinbaren - Termin] to fix; [- Geschäft] to secure.

Festnahme *(pl -n) die* arrest.

festlnehmen *vt (unreg)* to arrest.

Festlnetz *das* TELEKOM land-line telephone network *(as opposed to mobile phones)*.

Festlplatte *die* EDV hard disk.

festlsetzen *vt* - **1.** [bestimmen] to fix - **2.** [verhaften] to arrest. **sich festsetzen** *ref* [Dreck] to collect.

fest sitzen *vi (unreg)*: **es sitzt fest** [Dübel] it won't come out; [Farbe] it won't come off.

Festspiele *Pl* festival *sing*.

festlstehen *vi (unreg)* - **1.** [bestimmt sein] to have been fixed - **2.** [sicher sein] to be definite.

festlstellen *vt* - **1.** [in Erfahrung bringen] to find out; [diagnostizieren] to establish - **2.** [beobachten] to notice; **sie stellte fest, dass er Recht hatte** she realized that he was right - **3.** [anmerken] to state.

Festlstellung *die -* **1.** [Ermittlung] establishing - **2.** [Wahrnehmung] realization; **ich machte die Feststellung, dass...** I realized that... - **3.** [Erklärung] remark.

Festung *(pl -en) die* fortress.

Fete ['feːtə] *(pl -n) die fam* party.

fett <> *adj* - **1.** [Fleisch, Gericht] fatty - **2.** [Person, Tier, Erbe, Beute] fat. <> *adv* [mit viel Fett]: **fett essen** to eat fatty food.

Fett *(pl -e) das* fat; **er hat sein Fett weg** *fam fig* he got what was coming to him.

fettarm *adj* low-fat.

fetten <> *vt* to grease. <> *vi* to be greasy.

fett gedruckt *adj* in bold (type).

fettig *adj* greasy.

Fettnäpfchen *das*: **ins Fettnäpfchen treten** *fam* to put one's foot in it.

Fetzen *(pl -) der* scrap; **etw in Fetzen zerreißen** to tear sthg to pieces; **das Kleid ist ein billiger Fetzen!** that dress is just cheap rubbish!

fetzig *adj fam* [toll] cool.

feucht <> *adj* [Wand, Tuch, Haar] damp; [Hände, Augen] moist; [Klima] humid. <> *adv* [wischen] with a damp cloth.

Feuchtigkeit *die -* **1.** [leichte Nässe] moisture - **2.** [Feuchtsein - von Wand, Tuch, Haar] dampness; [- von Händen, Augen] moistness; [- von Klima] humidity.

feudal <> *adj* - **1.** [den Feudalismus betreffend] feudal - **2.** [aristokratisch] aristocratic - **3.** *fam* [vornehm] grand. <> *adv fam* [vornehm] grandly.

Feuer *(pl -) das -* **1.** [gen] fire; **auf offenem Feuer kochen** to cook over an open fire; **Feuer machen** to light a fire; **im Ofen Feuer machen** to light the oven; **jm Feuer geben** to give sb a light; **Feuer legen** to start a fire; **das Feuer einstellen/eröffnen** to cease/open fire - **2.** *(ohne pl)* [Schwung, Temperament - von Person] passion; [- von Begeisterung, Leidenschaft] fervour;

Feuer fangen *fam* [sich verlieben] to be smitten; **(für jn/etw) Feuer und Flamme sein** *fam* to be really keen (on sb/sthg). <> *interj* fire!

Feueralarm *der* fire alarm.

feuerfest *adj* fireproof; [Backform] oven-proof.

feuergefährlich *adj* flammable.

Feuer|löscher (*pl* **Feuerlöscher**) *der* fire extinguisher.

feuern <> *vt fam* - 1. [entlassen, heizen] to fire - 2. [schleudern] to fling. <> *vi* [schießen]: **auf jn/etw feuern** to fire at sb/sthg.

Feuer|wehr (*pl* -en) *die* fire brigade.

Feuer|wehrmann (*pl* -**männer** ODER -**leute**) *der* fireman.

Feuer|werk *das* - 1. [Veranstaltung] firework display - 2. [Raketen] fireworks *Pl*.

Feuer|zeug *das* lighter.

Feuilleton [fœjə'tɔ̃] (*pl* -s) *das* - 1. [literarischer Teil einer Zeitung] arts section - 2. [literarischer Beitrag] arts feature.

ff. (*abk für* folgende Seiten) ff.

FH [ɛf'haː] (*pl* -s) *die* ⊳ **Fachhochschule**.

ficht *präs* ⊳ **fechten**.

Fichte (*pl* -n) *die* spruce.

Fieber *das* - 1. [hohe Körpertemperatur] temperature; **Fieber haben** to have a temperature; **bei jm Fieber messen** to take sb's temperature - 2. *geh* [Besessenheit] fever.

fieberhaft <> *adj* feverish. <> *adv* feverishly.

fiebern *vi* - 1. [Fieber haben] to have a temperature - 2. [angespannt warten]: **vor Erregung fiebern** to be in a fever of excitement; **nach etw fiebern** to yearn for sthg.

Fieber|thermometer *das* thermometer.

fiel *prät* ⊳ **fallen**.

fies *fam abw* <> *adj* nasty. <> *adv* - 1. [gemein] nastily - 2. [ekelhaft]: **fies schmecken** to taste horrible.

Figur (*pl* -en) *die* - 1. [gen] figure; [männlich] physique - 2. [literarische Darstellung] character - 3. [Spielstein] piece; **eine gute/schlechte Figur abgeben** ODER **machen** to cut a good/poor figure.

Filet [fi'leː] (*pl* -s) *das* fillet.

Filiale (*pl* -n) *die* branch.

Film (*pl* -e) *der* film; **beim Film sein** ODER **arbeiten** to be in the movies.

filmen *vt & vi* to film.

Film|kamera *die* film camera, movie camera *US*.

Film|star ['fɪlmʃtaːɐ̯] *der* film star, movie star.

Filter (*pl* -) *das* & *der* filter.

filtern *vt* to filter.

Filter|tüte *die* filter (paper).

Filter|zigarette *die* filter cigarette.

Filz (*pl* -e) *der* - 1. [Stoff] felt - 2. *abw* [Vetternwirtschaft] jobs *Pl* for the boys.

filzen *vt fam* [Person] to frisk; [Haus, Koffer] to search.

Filz|stift *der* felt-tip (pen).

Finale (*pl* -) *das* - 1. [Endkampf, Endspiel] final - 2. MUS finale.

Finanzamt *das* tax office.

Finanz|beamte *der* tax inspector.

Finanz|beamtin *die* tax inspector.

Finanz|bedarf *der* (*ohne pl*) financial needs *Pl*.

Finanzen *Pl* finances.

finanziell [finan'tsi̯ɛl] <> *adj* financial. <> *adv* financially.

finanzieren *vt* to finance.

Finanzierung (*pl* -en) *die* financing.

Finanz|ministerium *das* finance ministry, ≈ Treasury *UK*, ≈ Department of the Treasury *US*.

finden (*prät* **fand**, *perf* **hat gefunden**) <> *vt* - 1. [gen] to find; **wo finde ich die Post?** where is the post office?; **er fand die Kinder schlafend** he found the children sleeping; **an etw Gefallen finden** to get ODER come to like sthg - 2. [erhalten]: **Verwendung finden** to be used; **Anerkennung finden** to receive recognition - 3. [beurteilen]: **ich finde sie nett** I think she's nice; **wie findest du...?** what do you think of...? <> *vi* - 1. [erfolgreich suchen]: **er hat nicht zu uns gefunden** he couldn't find his way to our place - 2. [beurteilen]: **ich finde, dass...** I think (that...); **ich finde nichts dabei** I don't see anything wrong with it. ⬥ **sich finden** *ref* [wieder auftauchen]: **der Schlüssel hat sich gefunden** I/we found the key; **das wird sich (schon) alles finden!** everything will be all right.

Finder, in (*mpl* -, *fpl* -nen) *der* finder.

Finder|lohn *der* reward (*for finding something*).

fing *prät* ⊳ **fangen**.

Finger (*pl* -) *der* [Glied] finger; **jn in die Finger kriegen** ODER **bekommen** *fam* to get one's hands on sb; **etw in die Finger kriegen** ODER **bekommen** *fam* to get hold of sthg; **lange Finger machen** *fam abw* to be light-fingered.

Finger|abdruck *der* fingerprint.

Finger|hut *der* - 1. [zum Nähen] thimble - 2. [Blume] foxglove.

Finger|nagel *der* fingernail.

Finger|spitze *die* fingertip.

Finger|spitzengefühl *das* sensitivity; **Fingerspitzengefühl haben** ODER **besitzen** ODER **beweisen** to show sensitivity.

Fink (*pl* -en) *der* finch.

finnisch *adj* Finnish; *siehe auch* **englisch**.

Finnisch(e) *das* Finnish; *siehe auch* **Englisch(e)**.

Finnland *nt* Finland.

finster ⟨⟩ *adj* - **1.** [Nacht, Straße, Zimmer, Zeiten] dark - **2.** [Person, Miene] grim, sombre - **3.** [Gegend, Gestalt] sinister. ⟨⟩ *adv* [unfreundlich] grimly.

Finsternis (*pl* -se) *die* darkness.

Finte (*pl* -n) *die* ruse.

Firma (*pl* Firmen) *die* firm, company.

Firmen|name *der* company name.

Firmen|wagen *der* company car.

Firmung (*pl* -en) *die* RELIG confirmation.

First Class *die* first class.

Fisch (*pl* -e) *der* - **1.** [Tier, Gericht] fish - **2.** ASTROL Pisces; **Fisch sein** to be a Pisces. ⟐ **Fische** *Pl* ASTROL Pisces (U).

Fisch|besteck *das* fish knives and forks *Pl*.

fischen ⟨⟩ *vt* - **1.** [fangen] to catch - **2.** [angeln] to fish for - **3.** [holen] to fish out. ⟨⟩ *vi* - **1.** [Fische fangen] to fish; **fischen gehen** to go fishing - **2.** *fam* [greifen]: **nach etw fischen** to fish for sthg.

Fischer, in (*mpl* -, *fpl* -nen) *der, die* fisherman (fisherwoman *die*).

Fischer|boot *das* fishing boat.

Fischerei *die* fishing.

Fischfang *der* fishing.

Fisch|händler, in *der, die* fishmonger *UK*, fish seller *US*.

Fisch|stäbchen ['fɪʃtɛːpçən] *das* fish finger *UK*, fish stick *US*.

Fiskus *der* treasury.

fit *adj* [körperlich] fit; [geistig] sharp, mentally alert; **fit in Chemie sein** *fam* to be good at chemistry.

Fitness ['fɪtnɛs] *die* [körperliche] fitness; [geistige] sharpness, mental alertness.

Fitnesscenter (*pl* -) *das* fitness centre.

fix ⟨⟩ *adj* - **1.** *fam* [schnell] quick - **2.** [Kosten] fixed - **3.** [erschöpft]: **fix und fertig sein** *fam* to be beat ODER knackered *UK*. ⟨⟩ *adv fam* [schnell] quickly.

Fixer, in (*mpl* -, *fpl* -nen) *der, die fam* junkie.

fixieren *vt* - **1.** [anstarren] to stare fixedly at - **2.** [befestigen, konservieren] to fix - **3.** *geh* [festhalten] to record.

FKK [ɛfkaːˈkaː] (*abk für* Freikörperkultur) *das* nudism; **am Strand FKK machen** to sunbathe on the beach in the nude.

flach ⟨⟩ *adj* - **1.** [eben] flat - **2.** [niedrig, dünn - Gebäude, Absätze] low; [- Stein, Schuhe] flat; [- Teller] shallow - **3.** [seicht, oberflächlich] shallow. ⟨⟩ *adv*: **flach atmen** to take shallow breaths.

Fläche (*pl* -n) *die* - **1.** [Gebiet] area - **2.** [geometrisch] plane - **3.** [Seite] surface.

flach|fallen (*perf* ist flachgefallen) *vi* (*unreg*) *fam*: **die Party fällt flach** the party's off; **23 Stellen fallen flach** 23 people are getting the boot.

Flachland *das* (*ohne Pl*) lowlands *Pl*.

flackern *vi* to flicker.

Fladen (*pl* -) *der* - **1.** [Brotfladen] *flat, round loaf* - **2.** [Kuchen] pancake - **3.** [Kuhfladen] cowpat.

Flagge (*pl* -n) *die* flag.

flambieren *vt* to flambé.

Flamingo (*pl* -s) *der* flamingo.

flämisch *adj* Flemish.

Flamme (*pl* -n) *die* - **1.** [Feuer] flame - **2.** [zum Kochen] burner.

Flandern *nt* Flanders *sing*.

Flanell (*pl* -e) *der* flannel.

Flanke (*pl* -n) *die* flank.

Flasche (*pl* -n) *die* - **1.** [Gefäß] bottle; **eine Flasche Sekt** a bottle of champagne - **2.** *salopp abw* [Versager] drip.

Flaschen|bier *das* bottled beer.

Flaschen|öffner *der* bottle opener.

Flaschen|zug *der* block and tackle.

flattern (*perf* ist/hat geflattert) *vi* - **1.** [gen] to flutter - **2.** [schlagen]: **mit den Flügeln flattern** to flutter its wings.

Flaum *der* down.

flauschig *adj* fleecy.

Flausen *Pl*: **Flausen im Kopf haben** always to be up to some trick or other.

Flaute (*pl* -n) *die* - **1.** [wirtschaftlich] slack period - **2.** [Windstille] calm.

Flechte (*pl* -n) *die* - **1.** [Pflanze] lichen - **2.** [Hautausschlag] eczema.

flechten (*präs* flicht, *prät* flocht, *perf* hat geflochten) *vt* [Haare, Zopf] to plait *UK*, to braid *US*; [Korb] to weave.

Fleck (*pl* -e ODER -en) *der* - **1.** [Klecks] stain - **2.** [Stelle] patch; **blauer Fleck** bruise - **3.** [Ort] spot.

fleckenlos ⟨⟩ *adj* spotless. ⟨⟩ *adv* spotlessly.

Fleck|entferner *der* stain remover.

fleckig *adj* - **1.** [schmutzig] stained - **2.** [gefleckt - Haut] blotchy; [- Obst] blemished.

Fleder|maus *die* bat.

Flegel (*pl* -) *der* lout.

flegelhaft ⟨⟩ *adj* loutish. ⟨⟩ *adv* loutishly.

flehen *vi*: (**um etw) flehen** to plead (for sthg).

Fleisch *das* - **1.** [Nahrungsmittel] meat - **2.** [Muskelgewebe, Fruchtfleisch] flesh; **Fleisch fressend** carnivorous.

Fleisch|brühe *die* meat stock.

Fleischer (*pl* -) *der* butcher.

Fleischerei (*pl* -en) *die* butcher's (shop).

Fleischerin (*pl* -nen) *die* butcher.

fleischfressend = **Fleisch**.

fleischig *adj* fleshy.

Fleisch|wolf *der* mincer *UK*, meat grinder *US*.

Fleisch|wurst *die* type of cold pork sausage similar to mortadella.

Fleiß *der* diligence; **viel Fleiß auf etw (A) verwenden** to put a lot of work into sthg.

fleißig <> *adj* [eifrig, arbeitsam] hard-working. <> *adv* - 1. [eifrig, arbeitsam] hard - 2. *fam* [oft, viel] a lot; **fleißig bezahlen** to fork out money.

fletschen *vt*: **die Zähne fletschen** to bare one's teeth.

flicht *präs* ▷ **flechten**.

flicken *vt* to mend.

Flicken *(pl -) der* patch.

Flick|zeug *das (ohne pl)* [für Reifen] repair kit; [für Kleidung] sewing kit.

Flieder *(pl -) der* lilac.

Fliege *(pl -n) die* - 1. [Insekt] fly - 2. [Schleife] bow tie.

fliegen *(prät flog, perf hat/ist geflogen)* <> *vi (ist)* - 1. [gen] to fly - 2. *fam* [stürzen] to fall - 3. *fam* [entlassen werden] to get fired, to get the sack *UK* - 4. [attraktiv finden]: **auf jn/etw fliegen** to be crazy about sb/sthg. <> *vt (hat)* to fly.

Fliegen|pilz *der* fly agaric.

Flieger *(pl -) der* - 1. [Pilot] pilot - 2. *fam* [Flugzeug] plane.

Fliegerin *(pl -nen) die* pilot.

fliehen *(prät floh, perf hat/ist geflohen)* <> *vi (ist)*: **aus dem Gefängnis fliehen** to escape from jail; **vor jm/etw fliehen** to flee from sb/sthg. <> *vt (hat)* to shun.

Fliese *(pl -n) die* tile.

Fließband *(pl -bänder) das* conveyor belt; **am Fließband arbeiten** to be an assembly-line *ODER* a production-line worker.

fließen *(prät floss, perf ist geflossen) vi* to flow; **das Blut fließt aus der Wunde** the blood is flowing from the wound.

fließend <> *adj* - 1. [perfekt] fluent - 2. [ungenau, unscharf - Grenzen, Übergang] fluid - 3. [Verkehr, Material] flowing; [Wasser] running. <> *adv* [sprechen] fluently.

flimmern *vi* - 1. [Luft, Wasser, Oberflächen] to shimmer - 2. [Fernsehbild] to flicker.

flink <> *adj* - 1. [geschickt] nimble - 2. [schnell] quick. <> *adv* - 1. [geschickt] nimbly - 2. [schnell] quickly.

Flinte *(pl -n) die* shotgun.

flirten ['flœrtn̩] *vi*: **(mit jm) flirten** to flirt (with sb).

Flitterwochen *Pl* honeymoon *sing*; **in die Flitterwochen fahren** to go on honeymoon.

flitzen *(perf ist geflitzt) vi fam* [Person, Wagen] to whizz.

flocht *prät* ▷ **flechten**.

Flocke *(pl -n) die* [von Schnee, Getreide] flake; [von Staub] ball; [von Schaum] blob.

flog *prät* ▷ **fliegen**.

floh *prät* ▷ **fliehen**.

Floh *(pl Flöhe) der* flea.

Floh|markt *der* flea market.

Flora *die* flora.

florieren *vi* to flourish.

Floskel *(pl -n) die* cliché.

floss *prät* ▷ **fließen**.

Floß *(pl Flöße) das* raft.

Flosse *(pl -n) die* - 1. [von Fisch, Rückenflosse von Delfin] fin; [Bauchflosse von Delfin und Robbe] flipper - 2. [Schwimmflosse] flipper - 3. *salopp abw* [Hand] paw.

Flöte *(pl -n) die* [Querflöte] flute; [Blockflöte] recorder.

flöten <> *vi* - 1. [Flöte spielen] to play the flute/recorder - 2. [pfeifen - Person] to whistle - 3. *fam abw* [einschmeichelnd sprechen] to speak in honeyed tones. <> *vt* - 1. [spielen] to play on the flute/recorder - 2. [pfeifen] to whistle - 3. *fam abw* [einschmeichelnd sagen]: **sie flötete mir Schmeicheleien ins Ohr** she murmured flattering remarks into my ear.

flott <> *adj* - 1. [schick] smart, stylish - 2. [lebhaft, schnell - Musik, Person] lively; [- Service] speedy; [- Auto] fast - 3. [fahrtüchtig - Wagen] roadworthy; [- Kahn] seaworthy. <> *adv* - 1. [schnell, lebhaft - arbeiten, laufen] quickly; [- tanzen, spielen] in a lively manner; **mach flott!** make it snappy! - 2. [schick] smartly.

Flotte *(pl -n) die* fleet.

Fluch *(pl Flüche) der* - 1. [Schimpfwort] curse - 2. *(ohne pl)* [Verwünschung] curse.

fluchen *vi* to swear.

Flucht *die* [aus dem Gefängnis] escape; **sie sind auf der Flucht** they are fleeing; **die Flucht ergreifen** to take flight.

fluchtartig <> *adj* hurried. <> *adv* hurriedly.

flüchten *(perf hat/ist geflüchtet) vi (ist)* to flee; **vor jm/etw flüchten** to flee from sb/sthg. ⇒ **sich flüchten** *ref (hat)*: **sich in etw (A) flüchten** to take refuge in sthg.

flüchtig <> *adj* - 1. [kurz] fleeting; [Gruß, Abschied] brief - 2. [ungenau - Eindruck] superficial; [- Arbeit] hurried - 3. [flüchtend - Gefangene] escaped; [- Mörder] wanted. <> *adv* - 1. [ungenau] superficially; [arbeiten] hurriedly - 2. [kurz] briefly.

Flüchtigkeits|fehler *der* careless mistake.

Flüchtling *(pl -e) der* refugee.

Flucht|weg *der* escape route.

Flug *(pl Flüge) der* flight.

Flug|bahn *die* [von Rakete] trajectory.

Flug|blatt *das* leaflet.

Flügel *(pl -) der* - 1. [gen] wing - 2. [Musikinstrument] grand piano.

Flug|gast *der* passenger *(on plane)*.

flügge *adj* [Vogeljunge] fully-fledged; **flügge werden** [Kind] to be ready to leave the nest.

Flug|gesellschaft *die* airline.

Flug|hafen *der* airport.

Flug|lotse *der* air traffic controller.

Flug|platz *der* airfield.

Flug|verkehr *der* air traffic.

Flug|zeug *das* plane, aeroplane *UK*, airplane *US*; **mit dem Flugzeug fliegen** to fly.

Flugzeug|träger *der* aircraft carrier.

Flunder *(pl -n) die* flounder.

flunkern *vi* to tell stories.

Fluor *das* fluorine.

Flur *(pl -e ODER -en)* ⬦ *der (pl Flure)* [Korridor] corridor; [am Eingang] hallway. ⬦ *die (pl Fluren)* [Gelände] fields *Pl*.

Fluss *(pl Flüsse) der* - **1.** [Wasserlauf] river - **2.** [Bewegung] flow.

flussabwärts *adv* downstream.

flussaufwärts *adv* upstream.

Flussbett *(pl -en) das* river bed.

flüssig ⬦ *adj* - **1.** [nicht fest] liquid; [Metall] molten; [Butter] melted - **2.** [Stil, Verkehr] flowing; [Ausdruck] fluent - **3.** [zahlungsfähig, verfügbar]: **flüssig sein** to be solvent; **nicht flüssig sein** to be short of money. ⬦ *adv* [sprechen] fluently.

Flüssigkeit *(pl -en) die* liquid.

Flusslauf *(pl -läufe) der* course *(of a river)*.

Flusspferd *(pl -e) das* hippopotamus.

flüstern ⬦ *vi* to whisper. ⬦ *vt* to whisper; **jm etw ins Ohr flüstern** to whisper sthg into sb's ear; **jm was flüstern** *fam fig* to tell sb a thing or two.

Flut *(pl -en) die* - **1.** *(ohne pl)* [Ansteigen des Wasserstandes] tide *(incoming)*; **die Flut kommt** the tide is coming in; **bei Flut** at high tide; **eine Flut von etw** *fig* a flood of sthg - **2.** *geh* [Wassermasse] waters *Pl*.

Flutlicht *das (ohne pl)*: **bei Flutlicht spielen** to play under floodlights.

focht *prät* ⬦ **fechten**.

Fohlen *(pl -) das* foal.

Föhn *(pl -e) der* - **1.** [Wind] *hot, dry wind typical of the Alps* - **2.** [Haartrockner] hairdryer.

föhnen *vt*: **jm/sich die Haare föhnen** [zum Trocknen] to dry sb's/one's hair; **jm die Haare föhnen** [zum Frisieren] to blow-dry sb's hair.

Folge *(pl -n) die* - **1.** [Konsequenz] consequence; **etw zur Folge haben** to result in sthg - **2.** [Fortsetzung] episode - **3.** [Serie] succession - **4.** *amt* [Befolgung]: **jm/einem Befehl Folge leisten** to obey sb/an order; **einer Einladung Folge leisten** to accept an invitation.

folgen *(perf* ist gefolgt*) vi* - **1.** [nachfolgen, verstehen, sich richten nach]: **jm/einer Sache folgen** to follow sb/sthg - **2.** [sich anschließen]: **auf etw** *(A)* **folgen** to follow sthg; **wie folgt** as follows - **3.** [gehorchen]: **(jm/einer Sache) folgen** to obey (sb/sthg) - **4.** [sich logisch ergeben]: **aus etw folgen** to follow from sthg.

folgend *adj* following. ⬦ **Folgende** *das*: **das Folgende** the following. ⬦ **Folgendes** *nt* the following.

folgendermaßen *adv* as follows.

folgern *vt*: **aus etw folgern, dass...** to conclude from sthg that...

Folgerung *(pl -en) die* conclusion.

folglich *adv* consequently.

folgsam ⬦ *adj* obedient. ⬦ *adv* obediently.

Folie ['foːljə] *(pl -n) die* - **1.** [Verpackung - aus Plastik] film; [- aus Metall] foil - **2.** [für Overheadprojektor] transparency.

Folklore *die* - **1.** [Musik] folk music - **2.** [Brauchtum] folklore.

folkloristisch *adj* folkloric; [Musik] folk.

Folter *(pl -n) die* torture; **jn auf die Folter spannen** *fig* to keep sb on tenterhooks.

foltern *vt* to torture.

Fön® *(pl -e) der* = **Föhn**.

fönen = **föhnen**.

Fonetik, Phonetik *die (ohne pl)* phonetics.

fonetisch, phonetisch ⬦ *adj* phonetic. ⬦ *adv* phonetically.

Fontäne *(pl -n) die* - **1.** [von Wasser] jet - **2.** [Springbrunnen] fountain.

Förder|kurs *der* SCHULE extra classes *Pl*.

fordern *vt* - **1.** [verlangen] to demand - **2.** [beanspruchen] to make demands on.

fördern *vt* - **1.** [unterstützen] to support; [Handel, Frieden] to promote; [Begabung] to foster - **2.** [Bodenschätze] to mine.

Forderung *(pl -en) die* - **1.** [Verlangen] demand - **2.** [finanzieller Anspruch] claim.

Förderung *(pl -en) die* - **1.** [Unterstützung] support; [von Handel, Frieden] promotion; [von Begabung] fostering - **2.** [von Bodenschätzen] mining.

Forelle *(pl -n) die* trout.

Form *(pl -en) die* - **1.** [gen] form; **in Form einer Sache** in the form of sthg; **in Form sein** to be in good form; **sich/jn in Form bringen** to get o.s./sb into shape; **die Form wahren** to observe the proprieties - **2.** [Gestalt] shape - **3.** [für Kuchen] baking tin.

formal ⬦ *adj* formal. ⬦ *adv* formally.

Formalität *(pl -en) die* formality.

Format *(pl -e) das* - **1.** [Größe] size; **im Format DIN A 3** in A3 format - **2.** [Niveau - von Person] stature; **die Frau hat Format** she's a woman of stature.

formatieren *vt* EDV to format.

Formation *(pl -en) die* - **1.** [gen] formation - **2.** [Gruppe] group.

Formel *(pl -n) die* formula; **Formel 1** SPORT Formula One.

formell ⬦ *adj* formal. ⬦ *adv* formally.

formen vt - 1. [Material] to shape - 2. [Person] to mould. ➥ **sich formen** ref [sich bilden] to take shape.

formieren vt to form. ➥ **sich formieren** ref [sich aufstellen] to get into formation; [Organisation] to form.

förmlich ◇ adj formal. ◇ adv - 1. [gen] formally - 2. [regelrecht] really.

formlos ◇ adj - 1. [nicht formal] informal - 2. [amorph] shapeless - 3. [ungezwungen] casual. ◇ adv - 1. [nicht formal] informally - 2. [ungezwungen] casually.

Formular (pl -e) das form.

formulieren vt to formulate.

Formulierung (pl -en) die - 1. [Formulieren] formulation - 2. [Textstelle] wording.

forsch ◇ adj self-confident. ◇ adv self-confidently.

forschen vi - 1. [wissenschaftlich untersuchen] to do research - 2. [ermitteln]: **in js Augen forschen** to search sb's eyes; **nach jm/etw forschen** to search for sb/sthg.

Forscher, in (mpl -, fpl -nen) der, die researcher.

Forschung (pl -en) die research; **Forschungen** research.

Förster, in (mpl -, fpl -nen) der, die forest ranger.

fort adv [weg] away; **fort sein** to be gone. ➥ **und so fort** adv and so forth.

fort|bestehen vi (unreg) to continue; [trotz Bedrohung] to continue to exist.

fort|bewegen vt to move. ➥ **sich fortbewegen** ref to move.

Fortbildung (pl -en) die - 1. [Weiterbildung] training; **Fortbildung zur Bekämpfung der Arbeitslosigkeit** lifelong learning as a means of combatting unemployment - 2. [Kurs] training course.

fort|fahren (perf hat/ist fortgefahren) (unreg) ◇ vi - 1. (ist) [wegfahren] to leave - 2. [nicht aufhören] to continue. ◇ vt (hat) [wegfahren] to take away.

fort|führen vt - 1. [weitermachen] to carry on - 2. [fortbringen] to take away.

fort|gehen (perf ist fortgegangen) vi (unreg) - 1. [weggehen] to leave - 2. [weitergehen] to continue.

fortgeschritten ◇ pp ▷ **fortschreiten**. ◇ adj advanced; **zu fortgeschrittener Stunde** at a late hour.

Fortgeschrittene (pl -n) der, die advanced student.

fort|kommen (perf ist fortgekommen) vi (unreg) - 1. [wegkommen] to get away - 2. [fortgebracht werden] to be taken away - 3. [abhanden kommen] to disappear.

fortlaufend adv [ständig] continually; [nummerieren] consecutively.

fort|pflanzen ➥ **sich fortpflanzen** ref - 1. [sich reproduzieren] to reproduce - 2. [sich ausbreiten] to spread.

Fortpflanzung die reproduction.

fort|schreiten (perf ist fortgeschritten) vi (unreg) to progress; [Zeit] to move on; [Krankheit, Prozess] to advance.

Fort|schritt der progress (U); **Fortschritte** progress; **Fortschritte machen** to make progress.

fortschrittlich ◇ adj progressive. ◇ adv progressively.

fort|setzen vt to continue.

Fortsetzung (pl -en) die continuation; [von Film] sequel.

Fossil (pl -ien) das fossil.

Foto (pl -s), **Photo** (pl -s) das photo; **ein Foto machen** to take a photo.

Foto|apparat der camera.

Fotograf (pl -en) der photographer.

Fotografie (pl -n) die - 1. [Fotografieren] photography - 2. [Foto] photograph.

fotografieren ◇ vt to photograph. ◇ vi to take photographs.

Fotografin (pl -nen) die photographer.

Fotokopie (pl -n) die photocopy.

fotokopieren ◇ vt to photocopy. ◇ vi to make photocopies.

Foto|modell das (photographic) model.

Fotozelle (pl -n), **Photozelle** die photoelectric cell, photocell.

Fötus (pl -se ODER -ten) der foetus.

foulen ['faʊlən] ◇ vt SPORT to foul. ◇ vi SPORT to commit a foul.

FPÖ [ɛfˈpeːˈøː] (abk für Freiheitliche Partei Österreichs) die Austrian Freedom Party.

Fr. - 1. [verheiratet] (abk für Frau) Mrs; [unverheiratet] Ms, Miss - 2. (abk für Freitag) Fri.

Fracht (pl -en) die freight; [mit Schiff] cargo.

Frachter (pl -) der freighter.

Fracht|gut das freight.

Frack (pl Fräcke) der tails Pl; **im Frack** in tails.

Frage (pl -n) die question; **eine rhetorische Frage** a rhetorical question; **jm Fragen stellen** to ask sb questions; **in diesen Fragen weiß er am besten Bescheid** he knows most about these issues ODER matters; **das kommt nicht in Frage** that's out of the question; **etw in Frage stellen** [bezweifeln] to question sthg; [gefährden] to jeopardize sthg.

Frage|bogen der questionnaire.

fragen ◇ vt to ask; **jn um Rat fragen** to ask sb for advice; **jn nach jm/etw fragen** to ask sb about sb/sthg; **jn nach seinem Namen/der Uhrzeit fragen** to ask sb his name/the time. ◇ vi to ask; **nach jm fragen** [sich erkundigen] to ask about sb; [Treffen] to ask to see sb; **der Polizist fragte nach dem genauen Hergang** the policeman asked for a precise description of events; **da fragst du noch!** you need to ask? ◆ **sich fragen** *ref* to wonder; **ich frage mich, ob** I wonder if *ODER* whether; **es fragt sich noch, ob** it is debatable whether.

Frage|wort (*pl* -wörter) *das* interrogative pronoun.

Frage|zeichen *das* question mark.

fraglich *adj* - 1. [zweifelhaft]: **es ist fraglich, ob** it is doubtful whether - 2. [infrage kommend] in question.

fragwürdig *adj* dubious.

Fraktion [frak'tsjo:n] (*pl* -en) *die* - 1. [im Parlament] (parliamentary) party - 2. [innerhalb einer Partei] faction.

Franc [frã:] (*pl* -s *ODER* -) *der* franc.

Franken (*pl* -) ◇ *nt* Franconia. ◇ *der* Swiss franc.

Frankfurt *nt*: **Frankfurt am Main/an der Oder** Frankfurt (am Main)/an der Oder.

frankieren *vt* to stamp.

fränkisch *adj* - 1. [aus Franken] Franconian - 2. HIST [westgermanisch] Frankish.

Frankreich *nt* France.

Franse (*pl* -n) *die* strand; **ein Schal mit Fransen** a scarf with a fringe.

Franziskaner, in (*mpl* -, *fpl* -nen) *der, die* Franciscan.

Franzose (*pl* -n) *der* Frenchman; **die Franzosen** the French.

Französin (*pl* -nen) *die* Frenchwoman.

französisch *adj* French; *siehe auch* **englisch**.

Französisch(e) *das* French; *siehe auch* **Englisch(e)**.

fraß *prät* ▷ **fressen**.

Fratze (*pl* -n) *die* [Grimasse] grotesque face; [aus Schmerz, Widerwille] grimace.

Frau (*pl* -en) *die* - 1. [Erwachsene] woman - 2. [Gattin] wife - 3. [als Anrede - verheiratet] Mrs; [- neutral] Ms; **Frau Doktor** Doctor.

Frauen|arzt, ärztin *der, die* gynaecologist.

frauenfeindlich ◇ *adj* misogynistic. ◇ *adv* in a misogynistic way.

fraulich ◇ *adj* feminine. ◇ *adv* in a feminine way.

frdl. ▷ **freundlich**.

frech ◇ *adj* - 1. [gen] cheeky; [unartig] naughty; [Lüge] barefaced - 2. [Minirock] daring. ◇ *adv* [gen] cheekily; [unartig] naughtily.

Frechheit (*pl* -en) *die* - 1. (*ohne pl*) [freches Verhalten] cheek - 2. [freche Bemerkung] cheeky remark.

frei ◇ *adj* - 1. [gen] free; **frei von etw** free of sthg; **ist dieser Stuhl frei?** is this seat free?; **drei Wochen frei haben** to have three weeks off; **bei der Reaktion wird Energie frei** energy is released during the reaction - 2. [Mitarbeiter] freelance - 3. [nackt] bare; **machen Sie sich bit-**

te frei would you mind undressing? ◇ *adv* - 1. [gen] freely; **frei lebende Tiere** animals living in the wild; **frei sprechen** to speak without notes - 2. [gratis] for free; **etw frei Haus liefern** to deliver sthg free. ◆ **im Freien** *adv* in the open (air).

Frei|bad *das* open-air swimming pool.

Freiberufler, in (*mpl* -, *fpl* -nen) *der, die* - 1. [Mitarbeiter] freelancer - 2. [Arzt, Anwalt] doctor/lawyer in private practice.

freiberuflich ◇ *adj* [Journalist, Übersetzer, Fotograf] freelance; **freiberuflicher Mitarbeiter** freelancer. ◇ *adv*: **freiberuflich tätig sein** to be self-employed.

Frei|bier *das* free beer.

frei|geben (*unreg*) ◇ *vt* - 1. [gen] to release - 2. [genehmigen - FILM] to pass as fit for public viewing; [- Straße, Brücke] to open; **jm einen Tag freigeben** to give sb a day off. ◇ *vi* [Freizeit genehmigen]: **jm freigeben** to give sb time off.

freigebig *adj* generous.

Freiheit (*pl* -en) *die* - 1. [Ungebundenheit] freedom; **ein Tier in die Freiheit entlassen** to set an animal free - 2. [Privileg] liberty.

Freiheits|strafe *die* prison sentence.

freiheraus *adv* freely.

Frei|karte *die* free ticket.

Freikörperkultur *die* naturism.

Freiland|ei *das* free-range egg.

frei|lassen *vt* (*unreg*) [Gefangene] to release; [Tier] to set free.

freilich *adv* - 1. [jedoch] admittedly - 2. *Süddt* [sicher] of course.

Freilicht|bühne *die* open-air theatre.

frei|machen ◇ *vt* - 1. [Brief] to stamp - 2. [ausziehen]: **den Oberkörper freimachen** to take one's top off, to strip to the waist. ◇ *vi* to take time off. ◆ **sich freimachen** *ref* - 1. *fam* [als Urlaub] to take time off - 2. [sich ausziehen] to take one's clothes off.

freimütig ◇ *adj* frank. ◇ *adv* frankly.

frei|sprechen *vt* (*unreg*) to acquit.

frei|stehen *vi* (*unreg*) - 1. [Wohnung] to stand *ODER* be empty - 2. [Entscheidung]: **es steht ihm frei, zu gehen oder zu bleiben** it's up to him whether he stays or goes.

frei|stellen *vt* - 1. [entbinden]: **jn von etw freistellen** to exempt sb from sthg - 2. [überlassen]: **jm etw freistellen** to leave sthg up to sb.

Frei|stoß *der* SPORT free kick.

Frei|stunde *die* free period.

Freitag (*pl* -e) *der* Friday; *siehe auch* **Samstag**.

freitags *adv* on Fridays; *siehe auch* **samstags**.

freiwillig ◇ *adj* voluntary. ◇ *adv* voluntarily.

Freiwillige (*pl* -n) *der, die* volunteer.

Frei|zeichen das dial tone.

Frei|zeit die - 1. (ohne pl) [Mußezeit] free time - 2. [Gruppenreise - für Kinder] holiday camp.

freizügig <> adj - 1. [gewagt] daring - 2. [großzügig] generous - 3. [frei] liberal. <> adv - 1. [gewagt] daringly - 2. [großzügig] generously - 3. [frei] liberally.

fremd adj - 1. [ausländisch] foreign - 2. [nicht einem selbst gehörend]: **fremde Angelegenheiten** other people's business; **in einer fremden Wohnung übernachten** to spend the night in someone else's flat - 3. [unvertraut] strange; **er ist fremd in dieser Stadt** he is a stranger to this town.

fremdartig adj strange.

Fremde (pl -n) <> der, die stranger. <> die (ohne plural) foreign parts Pl.

Fremden|führer, in der, die tourist guide.

Fremden|hass der (ohne pl) xenophobia.

Fremden|verkehr der tourism.

Fremdenverkehrs|büro das tourist information office.

Fremden|zimmer das (guest) room.

Fremd|körper der foreign body.

Fremd|sprache die foreign language.

fremdsprachig adj in a foreign language.

Fremdwort (pl -wörter) das foreign word.

Frequenz (pl -en) die - 1. PHYS frequency - 2. MED rate.

fressen (präs frisst, prät fraß, perf hat gefressen) <> vt - 1. [beim Tier] to eat - 2. fam abw [essen] to guzzle, to scoff UK - 3. fam [Strom, Geld] to eat up; **jn gefressen haben** fam not to be able to stand sb, to hate sb's guts. <> vi - 1. [Tier] to feed; **der Vogel frisst einem aus der Hand** the bird will eat out of your hand - 2. salopp abw [Mensch] to stuff one's face - 3. [zehren, nagen]: **an etw (D) fressen** to eat away at sthg.

Freude (pl -n) die joy; **es ist mir eine Freude zu kommen** it would be a pleasure for me to come; **jm die Freude an etw verderben** to spoil sb's enjoyment of sthg; **an etw Freude haben** to take pleasure in sthg; **jm eine Freude machen** to make sb happy.

freudig <> adj - 1. [Begrüßung] joyful - 2. [Überraschung] pleasant. <> adv - 1. [begrüßen] joyfully - 2. [überrascht] pleasantly.

freuen vt to please. ➡ **sich freuen** ref to be pleased; **es freut mich, dass...** I'm pleased that...; **freut mich sehr!** pleased to meet you!; **sich an etw (D) freuen** to get a lot of pleasure from sthg; **sich über etw (A) freuen** to be pleased about sthg; **sich auf etw (A) freuen** to be looking forward to sthg.

Freund (pl -e) der - 1. [guter Bekannter] friend - 2. [Liebhaber] boyfriend - 3. [Anhänger] lover; **ein Freund klassischer Musik** a classical music lover.

Freundin (pl -nen) die - 1. [gute Bekannte] friend - 2. [Geliebte] girlfriend.

freundlich <> adj - 1. [Mensch, Geste, Rat] friendly; **danke für die freundliche Begrüßung** thank you for your kind welcome; **bist du so freundlich und begleitest mich?** would you be so kind as to accompany me? - 2. [Umgebung, Stimmung] nice. <> adv [nett] in a friendly way; **jm freundlich gesinnt sein** to be well-disposed towards sb.

Freundlichkeit (pl -en) die - 1. (ohne pl) [nette Art] friendliness - 2. [Gefälligkeit] favour.

Freundschaft (pl -en) die friendship; **mit jm Freundschaft schließen** to make friends with sb.

freundschaftlich <> adj friendly. <> adv in a friendly way; **jm freundschaftlich verbunden sein** to be friends with sb.

Frieden, Friede der peace; **jn in Frieden lassen** to leave sb in peace; **mit jm Frieden schließen** to make peace with sb.

Friedens|bewegung die peace movement.

Friedens|vertrag der peace treaty.

Fried|hof der cemetery.

friedlich <> adj peaceful. <> adv peacefully.

frieren (prät fror, perf hat/ist gefroren) vi - 1. (hat) [an Kälte leiden] to be cold; **es friert ihn** he is cold; **an den Füßen frieren** to have cold feet; **es friert mich an den Händen** my hands are cold - 2. (hat) [sehr kalt sein]: **es friert** it is freezing - 3. (ist) [gefrieren] to freeze.

Frikadelle (pl -n) die rissole.

frisch <> adj - 1. [gen] fresh; [Verletzung] recent; [Farbe] wet; [Kraft] renewed; **diese Erinnerung ist noch frisch** it's still fresh in my memory - 2. [sauber] clean; **sich frisch machen** to freshen up; **du bist wohl nicht ganz frisch!** salopp are you crazy? - 3. [kühl - unangenehm] chilly; [- angenehm] cool - 4. [in Form] refreshed; **frisch und munter sein** to be bright and cheery. <> adv [gewaschen, zubereitet] freshly; [renoviert] newly; **das Brot kommt frisch vom Bäcker** the bread is fresh from the baker's; **'frisch gestrichen'** "wet paint".

Frische die - 1. [gen] freshness; **in alter Frische** as fresh as ever - 2. [Kühle - unangenehm] chilliness; [- angenehm] coolness.

Frisch|käse der soft cream cheese.

Friseur, in (mpl -e, fpl -nen), **Frisör, in** (mpl -e, fpl -nen) [fri'zøːɐ̯, rɪn] der, die hairdresser.

Friseuse (pl -n), **Frisöse** (pl -n) [fri'zøːzə] die hairdresser.

frisieren vt - 1. [Person]: **jn frisieren** to do sb's hair; **sie ist schick frisiert** she has a trendy hairstyle - 2. fam [Zahlen] to fiddle; **die Bilanzen frisieren** to cook the books - 3. fam AUTO to soup up. ➡ **sich frisieren** ref [sich kämmen] to do one's hair.

Frisör, in = Friseur.

Frisöse = Friseuse.

frisst *präs* ▷ **fressen**.

Frist (*pl* -en) *die*: jm eine Frist von einer Woche geben to give sb a week; bis zur Prüfung bleibt dir noch eine Frist von drei Tagen you still have three days to go until the exam; die Frist wird nicht verlängert the deadline is not being extended; eine Frist einhalten to meet a deadline; innerhalb kürzester Frist in a very short space of time.

fristlos ◇ *adj* immediate. ◇ *adv* without notice, with immediate effect.

Frisur (*pl* -en) *die* hairstyle.

froh *adj* - 1. [vergnügt] happy - 2. [erleichtert] glad; über etw (A) froh sein to be pleased ODER glad about sthg - 3. [Nachricht] good.

fröhlich ◇ *adj* - 1. [Mensch, Lachen] cheerful - 2. [Fest] jolly. ◇ *adv* [vergnügt] cheerfully.

Fröhlichkeit *die* cheerfulness.

fromm (*kompar* frommer ODER frömmer, *superl* frommste ODER frömmste) *adj* - 1. [Mensch, Christ] devout; [Worte, Einstellung] pious - 2. [heuchlerisch] sanctimonious, pious.

Fronleichnam (*ohne Artikel*) Corpus Christi.

Front (*pl* -en) *die* front.

frontal ◇ *adj* - 1. [Zusammenstoß] head-on - 2. [Angriff, Darstellung] frontal. ◇ *adv* - 1. [von vorn] head-on - 2. [angreifen] from the front.

fror *prät* ▷ **frieren**.

Frosch (*pl* Frösche) *der* frog.

Frost (*pl* Fröste) *der* frost.

frösteln *vi* to shiver.

frostig ◇ *adj eigtl* & *fig* frosty. ◇ *adv* frostily.

Frottee [frɔ'te:] (*pl* -s) *der* ODER *das* towelling.

Frucht (*pl* Früchte) *die* fruit; Früchte fruit (U).

fruchtbar *adj* - 1. [Erde, Lebewesen] fertile - 2. [Gespräch, Idee] fruitful.

Fruchtbarkeit *die* fertility.

fruchtig *adj* fruity.

Fruchtsaft *der* fruit juice.

früh ◇ *adj* early; am frühen Morgen/Abend early in the morning/evening; [Tat] premature. ◇ *adv* early; früh am Abend/Morgen early in the evening/morning; er ist früh gestorben he died young; gestern/heute/morgen Früh yesterday/this/tomorrow morning; etw zu früh verkaufen to sell sthg too soon.

früher ◇ *adv* formerly. ◇ *adj* former; in früheren Zeiten in the past.

frühestens *adv* at the earliest.

Frühgeburt *die* - 1. [Geburt] premature birth; eine Frühgeburt haben to give birth prematurely - 2. [Baby] premature baby.

Frühjahr *das* spring; im Frühjahr in spring.

Frühling (*pl* -e) *der* spring; im Frühling in spring.

frühreif *adj* [Kind] precocious.

Frührentner, in *der, die* person who has taken early retirement.

Frühstück *das* breakfast; nach dem Frühstück after breakfast; zum Frühstück for breakfast.

frühstücken ◇ *vi* to have breakfast. ◇ *vt* to have for breakfast.

frustrieren *vt* to frustrate.

Fuchs [fʊks] (*pl* Füchse) *der* - 1. [Tier] fox - 2. [Pelz] fox fur - 3. *fam* [Mensch]: ein schlauer Fuchs a cunning devil.

Fuchsie ['fʊksjə] (*pl* -n) *die* fuchsia.

Füchsin ['fʏksɪn] (*pl* -nen) *die* vixen.

fuchteln *vi*: mit etw fuchteln to wave sthg around.

Fuge (*pl* -n) *die* - 1. [Ritze] gap - 2. MUS fugue.

fügen *vt* [einfügen]: etw an etw (A) fügen to join sthg to sthg; etw in etw (A) fügen to fit sthg into sthg; fest gefügt firmly established. ◆ **sich fügen** *ref* - 1. [hineinpassen] to fit - 2. [sich unterordnen]: sich einer Sache (D) fügen to obey sthg.

fühlbar ◇ *adj* noticeable. ◇ *adv* noticeably.

fühlen ◇ *vt* to feel. ◇ *vi* to feel; nach etw fühlen to feel for sthg. ◆ **sich fühlen** *ref* to feel; sich krank fühlen to feel ill.

Fühler (*pl* -) *der* feeler, antenna.

fuhr *prät* ▷ **fahren**.

Fuhre (*pl* -n) *die* load; [von Taxi] fare.

führen ◇ *vt* - 1. [Person, Tier] to lead; jn zu einem Versteck führen to show ODER lead sb to a hiding-place - 2. [leiten - Firma, Hotel] to run, to manage; [- Partei] to lead; [- Haushalt] to run; [- Truppen] to command; [- Krieg, Kampf] to wage; den Vorsitz führen to be the chairperson - 3. [durchführen - Gespräch] to hold; ein Ferngespräch führen to make a long-distance call; das Protokoll führen to take the minutes; ein langes Gespräch geführt haben to have had a long conversation; einen Prozess gegen jn führen to take legal action against sb - 4. [Gegenstand]: etw mit sich ODER bei sich führen to carry sthg - 5. [Ware] to stock - 6. [Liste] to keep; sie wird als Mitglied geführt she's listed as a member - 7. [Touristen] to show around - 8. [Name, Titel] to have - 9. [bewegen] to handle. ◇ *vi* - 1. SPORT to lead; knapp führen to be just in the lead; mit 1:0 führen to be leading 1-0, to be 1-0 up - 2. [Straße] to lead - 3. [zu einem Ergebnis]: zu etw führen to lead to sthg; zum Erfolg führen to bring success; das führt zu nichts that won't get us anywhere. ◆ **sich führen** *ref* to behave.

führend *adj* leading.

Führer, in (*mpl* -, *fpl* -nen) *der, die* - **1.** [Anführer] leader; **der Führer** [Hitler] the Führer - **2.** [Fremdenführer, Buch] guide.

Führer|schein *der* driving licence *UK*, driver's license *US*.

Führung (*pl* -en) *die* - **1.** [das Führen - von Firma, Hotel] running, management; [- von Truppen] command; [- von Partei] leadership; [- von Haushalt] running; **unter (der) Führung von** under the direction of - **2.** [Personen - von Firma] management; [- von Partei] leadership - **3.** [führende Stellung] lead; **in Führung liegen** to be in the lead ODER ahead; **in Führung gehen** to take the lead - **4.** [Besichtigung] guided tour - **5.** [Verhalten]: **wegen guter Führung** on the grounds of good conduct - **6.** [Handhabung, Steuerung] operation.

Führungs|zeugnis *das*: **polizeiliches Führungszeugnis** *police certificate stating that holder has no criminal record.*

Fülle *die (ohne pl)* [Menge, Übermaß] abundance.

füllen *vt* - **1.** [gen] to fill; [Geflügel, Tomate] to stuff - **2.** [hineingeben]: **etw in etw (A) füllen** to put sthg into sthg; **den Saft in Flaschen füllen** to fill the bottles with juice. ⬥ **sich füllen** *ref* [voll werden]: **sich mit etw füllen** to fill up with sthg.

Füller (*pl* -) *der* fountain pen.

Füllfeder|halter *der* fountain pen.

füllig *adj* plump.

Füllung (*pl* -en) *die* [von Geflügel, Tomate] stuffing; [von Gebäck, in Zahn] filling.

fummeln *vi* - **1.** *fam* [tasten]: **nach etw fummeln** to fumble about for sthg; **an etw (D) fummeln** to fumble around with sthg - **2.** *salopp* [sexuell berühren] to make out.

Fund (*pl* -e) *der* - **1.** [Objekt] find - **2.** [Handlung] discovery.

Fundament (*pl* -e) *das* - **1.** [Grundmauer] foundations *Pl*; **bis auf die Fundamente abgerissen** to be razed to the ground - **2.** [Grundlage] basis.

Fund|büro *das* lost property office *UK*, lost-and-found office *US*.

Fund|grube *die* treasure trove.

fundiert *adj* [Wissen, Firma] sound; [Kritik, Überlegungen] well-founded; [Vortrag, Bericht] well-reasoned.

fündig *adj*: **fündig werden** to make a find.

Fund|sache *die*: **Fundsachen** lost property (*U*).

fünf *num* five; *siehe auch* **sechs**.

Fünf (*pl* -en) *die* - **1.** [Zahl] five - **2.** [Schulnote] ≈ E, mark of 5 on a scale from 1 to 6; *siehe auch* **Sechs**.

fünffach ⬦ *adj*: **die fünffache Menge** five times as much; **in fünffacher Größe** five times

as big; **der fünffache Gewinner** the five-times winner. ⬦ *adv* [aufdern] five times; **fünffach gelagert** with five bearings.

fünfhundert *num* five hundred.

Fünf|kampf *der* pentathlon.

fünfmal *adv* five times.

fünftausend *num* five thousand.

fünfte *num* fifth; *siehe auch* **sechste**.

Fünfte (*pl* -n) *der, die, das* fifth; *siehe auch* **Sechste**.

fünftel *adj (unver)* fifth; *siehe auch* **sechstel**.

Fünftel (*pl* -) *das* fifth; *siehe auch* **Sechstel**.

fünfzehn *num* fifteen; *siehe auch* **sechs**.

Fünfzehn (*pl* -en) *die* fifteen; *siehe auch* **Sechs**.

fünfzig *num* fifty; *siehe auch* **sechs**.

Fünfzig *die* fifty; *siehe auch* **Sechs**.

Fünfzigerjahre, fünfziger Jahre *Pl*: **die Fünfzigerjahre** the fifties.

Funk *der* [Übermittlung] radio.

Funke (*pl* -n), **Funken** (*pl* -) *der* spark; **keinen Funken von etw haben** ODER **besitzen** not to have a scrap of sthg.

funkeln *vi* [Licht] to sparkle; [Stern] to twinkle; [Gold] to glitter.

funken ⬦ *vt* to radio. ⬦ *vi*: **bei ihm hat es endlich gefunkt** *fam* [er versteht] he finally got it; **bei den beiden hat es gefunkt** *fam* [sie sind verliebt] they've fallen for each other.

Funken = Funke.

Funk|gerät *das* radio set; [tragbar] walkie-talkie.

Funk|haus *das* broadcasting centre.

Funktion [fʊnk'tsjoːn] (*pl* -en) *die* - **1.** MATH [Aufgabe] function; [Tätigkeit] functioning - **2.** [Position] position.

Funktionär, in (*mpl* -e, *fpl* -nen) *der, die* official.

funktionieren *vi* to work.

für *präp* (+ *A*) - **1.** [gen] for; **sich für etw entschuldigen** to apologize for sthg; **sich für Geschichte interessieren** to be interested in history; **für jn einspringen** to stand in for sb; **jn für dumm halten** to think sb is stupid; **einen Mantel für 700 Euro kaufen** to buy a coat for 700 euros; **für ein halbes Jahr** for half a year; **für immer** for ever, for good; **für sein Alter ist er noch recht munter** he's still very sprightly for his age - **2.** [Unterstützung - ausdrückend] in favour of; **für die Abschaffung der Todesstrafe sein** to be in favour of abolishing the death penalty; **früh aufstehen hat etwas für sich** there is something to be said for getting up early - **3.** [zur Angabe der Folge]: **Wort für Wort** word by word; **Tag für Tag** day after day.

Furcht *die* fear; **Furcht haben (vor jm/etw)** to be afraid (of sb/sthg); **aus Furcht vor jm/etw** for fear of sb/sthg. ⬥ **Furcht erregend** ⬦ *adj* frightening. ⬦ *adv* frighteningly.

furchtbar ◇ *adj* terrible. ◇ *adv* [sehr] terribly; **sich furchtbar anstrengen** to make an enormous effort.

fürchten ◇ *vt* to fear; **ich fürchte, dass der Wagen kaputt ist** I'm afraid the car is out of action; **er fürchtet, zu spät zu kommen** he's afraid of arriving late. ◇ *vi*: **um etw fürchten** to fear for sthg. ➡ **sich fürchten** *ref*: **sich (vor) jm/etw fürchten** to be afraid (of sb/sthg).

fürchterlich ◇ *adj* terrible. ◇ *adv* [sehr] terribly; **sich fürchterlich anstrengen** to make an enormous effort.

furchtsam *adj* [Person, Tier] easily frightened; [Blick] fearful.

füreinander *adv* for each other.

Furnier (*pl* -e) *das* veneer.

fürs *präp* (*für* + *das*) ➡ **für**.

Fürsorge *die* - 1. [menschliche Unterstützung] care - 2. [Sozialhilfe] social security *UK*, welfare *US* - 3. [Sozialamt] social services *Pl UK*, welfare services *Pl US*.

fürsorglich ◇ *adj* attentive. ◇ *adv* attentively.

Für|sprecher, in *der, die* advocate.

Fürst (*pl* -en) *der* prince.

Fürstentum (*pl* -tümer) *das* principality.

Fürstin (*pl* -nen) *die* princess.

fürstlich ◇ *adj* - 1. [von einem Fürsten]: **das fürstliche Schloss** the prince's castle - 2. [Bezahlung] handsome. ◇ *adv* [bezahlen] handsomely; **fürstlich leben** to live like a prince.

Fuß (*pl* Füße) *der* - 1. [Körperteil, von Berg] foot - 2. [tragender Teil - von Lampe, Gefäß] base; [- von Möbeln] leg; **auf eigenen Füßen stehen** to stand on one's own two feet; **(festen) Fuß fassen** to find one's feet. ➡ **zu Fuß** *adv* on foot; **ich gehe oft zu Fuß zur Arbeit** I often walk to work.

Fuß|ball *der* - 1. SPORT football *UK*, soccer *US* - 2. [Ball] football *UK*, soccer ball *US*.

Fußballer, in (*mpl* -, *fpl* -nen) *der, die* footballer *UK*, soccer player *US*.

Fußball|mannschaft *die* football team *UK*, soccer team *US*.

Fußball|platz *der* football ground *UK*, soccer ground *US*.

Fußball|spiel *das* football match *UK*, soccer game *US*.

Fußball|spieler, in *der, die* football player *UK*, soccer player *US*.

Fuß|boden *der* floor.

Fussel (*pl* - ODER -n) *die* ODER *der* fluff (*U*); Fusseln fluff.

fusseln *vi* to go bobbly.

Fußgänger (*pl* -) *der* pedestrian.

Fußgängerin (*pl* -nen) *die* pedestrian.

Fußgänger|über|weg *der* pedestrian crossing *UK*, crosswalk *US*.

Fußgänger|zone *die* pedestrian precinct *UK* ODER zone *US*.

Fuß|gelenk *das* ankle.

Fuß|note *die* footnote.

Fuß|sohle *die* sole (*of the foot*).

Fuß|spur *die* footprint.

Fuß|tritt *der* kick.

Fuß|weg *der* footpath.

futsch *adj fam*: **futsch sein** [fort] to have all gone; [kaputt] to be bust.

Futter (*pl* -) *das* - 1. [für Haustiere] food; [für Vieh] feed; [Heu] fodder - 2. [Stoff] lining.

futtern *fam* ◇ *vt* to feed. ◇ *vi*: **sie kann viel futtern** she can put away a lot of food.

füttern *vt* - 1. [gen] to feed - 2. [Kleidung] to line.

Futur (*pl* -e) *das* GRAMM future (tense).

G

g (*pl* - ODER -s), **G** (*pl* - ODER -s) [ge:] *das* - 1. [Buchstabe] g, G - 2. MUS G. ➡ **g** (*abk für* Gramm) g.

gab *prät* ➡ **geben**.

Gabe (*pl* -n) *die* [Geschenk, Talent] gift.

Gabel (*pl* -n) *die* - 1. [Besteckteil, beim Fahrrad] fork - 2. [in der Landwirtschaft] pitchfork - 3. [vom Telefon] cradle; **den Hörer auf die Gabel legen** to hang up.

Gabelung (*pl* -en), **Gablung** (*pl* -en) *die* fork.

gackern *vi eigtl & fig* to cackle.

gaffen *vi fam abw* to gawp.

Gag [ge(:)k] (*pl* -s) *der* - 1. *fam* [Witz] gag - 2. [Besonderheit] gimmick.

Gage ['ɡɑːʒə] (*pl* -n) *die* fee.

gähnen *vi eigtl & fig* to yawn.

Gala (*pl* -s) *die* - 1. [Galavorstellung] gala - 2. [Kleidung] formal dress.

Galaxis (*pl* -xien) *die* - 1. [Milchstraße]: **die Galaxis** the Galaxy - 2. [Sternsystem] galaxy.

Galerie (*pl* -n) *die* gallery.

Galgen (*pl* -) *der* gallows (*sg*).

Galgenfrist *die* grace.

Galle (*pl* -n) *die* - 1. [Organ] gall bladder - 2. [Flüssigkeit] bile; **mir kommt die Galle hoch** *fam* it makes my blood boil.

Galopp (*pl* -s ODER -e) *der* gallop; **im Galopp** [beim Pferd] at a gallop; *fam* [schnell] at top speed.

galoppieren (*perf* hat/ist galoppiert) *vi* to gallop.

galt *prät* ▷ **gelten**.

gammeln *vi fam* - 1. *abw* [nichts tun] to loaf around - 2. [verderben] to go off.

Gämse (*pl* -n) *die* chamois.

Gang [gaŋ] (*pl* Gänge) *der* - 1. [Gangart] gait; **er hat einen Gang wie John Wayne** he walks like John Wayne - 2. [Spaziergang, Ausgang] walk - 3. [Flur, Weg] corridor; [in Flugzeug] aisle; **unterirdischer Gang** underground passage - 4. [beim Kfz] gear; **im ersten Gang** in first gear - 5. [Bewegung]: **etw in Gang bringen** ODER **setzen** [gen] to get sthg going; [Maschine] to start sthg up; **der Motor ist/kam in Gang** the engine is running/started up; **die Diskussion kam erst nach einer Stunde in Gang** it was an hour before the discussion got going - 6. [Ablauf] course; **im Gange sein** to be going on - 7. [Speisegang] course.

Gang² [gɛŋ] (*pl* -s) *die* gang.

gängig *adj* - 1. [üblich] common - 2. [aktuell] current - 3. [handelsüblich] popular.

Gangway ['gɛŋweː] (*pl* -s) *die* [von Schiff] gangway; [von Flugzeug] steps *Pl*.

Ganove [ga'noːvə] (*pl* -n) *der* crook.

Gans (*pl* Gänse) *die* goose; **dumme Gans!** *fam* silly goose!

Gänse|blümchen *das* daisy.

Gänse|braten *der* roast goose.

Gänse|füßchen *Pl fam* quotation marks.

Gänse|haut *die* (ohne *pl*) goose-pimples *Pl* UK, goosebumps US.

Gänse|marsch *der*: **im Gänsemarsch** in single file.

Gänserich (*pl* -e) *der* gander.

ganz ◇ *adj* - 1. [komplett] whole, entire; **den ganzen Tag** all day, the whole day; **eine ganze Zahl** a whole number; **ganze Note** MUS semibreve *UK*, whole note *US* - 2. [alle] all; **der ganze Kaffee** all the coffee; **ganz Paris** the whole of Paris - 3. *fam* [heil] whole, intact; **die Tasse ist noch ganz** the cup is still intact ODER in one piece - 4. [nur]: **wir haben ganze zehn Minuten dafür gebraucht** it took us no more than ten minutes - 5. [verstärkend] **eine ganze Menge** quite a lot; **was soll der ganze Quatsch!** what's all this nonsense about? ◇ *adv* - 1. [sehr] really; **er ist ein ganz seltsamer Mensch** he's a very strange person; **ganz viel/ wenig** very much/little - 2. [völlig] completely; **er kommt ganz bestimmt** he is sure to come; **ganz und gar** completely; **ganz und gar nicht** not at all - 3. [einschränkend] quite; **der Film war ganz gut** the film was quite good.

Ganze *das* - 1. [Einheit] whole; **eine Sache als Ganzes beurteilen** to judge sthg as a whole - 2. [alles] whole thing; **das Ganze war eine Far-**ce the whole thing was a farce; **aufs Ganze gehen** to go for it; **es geht ums Ganze** it's all or nothing.

gänzlich ◇ *adj* complete. ◇ *adv* completely.

ganztägig ◇ *adj* all-day; **ein ganztägiger Ausflug** a day trip. ◇ *adv* [geöffnet] all day; [arbeiten] full-time.

ganztags *adv*: **ganztags arbeiten** to work full-time.

Ganztags|schule *die* school attended in the morning and afternoon, rather than just in the morning as with most German schools.

gar ◇ *adv*: **gar kein** no/not at all; **es war gar keiner da** there was no one there at all; **auf gar keinen Fall** under no circumstances at all; **gar nicht** not at all; **aber du hast doch gar nicht gefragt!** but you didn't even ask!; **gar nichts** nothing at all. ◇ *adj* [Speise] done.

Garage (*pl* -n) *die* garage.

Garantie (*pl* -n) *die* guarantee.

garantieren ◇ *vt* to guarantee. ◇ *vi*: **für etw garantieren** to guarantee sthg.

garantiert ◇ *adv fam*: **er hat garantiert verschlafen** I bet he's overslept; **wir werden garantiert gewinnen** we're bound to win. ◇ *adj* guaranteed.

Garderobe (*pl* -n) *die* - 1. [in der Wohnung] hallstand - 2. [in öffentlichen Räumen] cloakroom *UK*, checkroom *US* - 3. (ohne *pl*) [Kleidung] clothes *Pl* (except underwear); **eine neue Garderobe kaufen** to buy a new wardrobe - 4. [für Künstler] dressing room.

Garderoben|ständer *der* coatstand.

Gardine (*pl* -n) *die* net curtain; **hinter schwedischen Gardinen** *fam* behind bars.

garen *vt* to cook.

gären (*prät* **gor** ODER **gärte**, *perf* **hat/ist gegoren** ODER **gegärt**) *vi* - 1. (ist) (*unreg*) [in Gärung sein] to ferment - 2. (hat) (*reg*) [Unzufriedenheit, Ärger]: **es gärte im Volk** the people were growing restless.

Garn (*pl* -e) *das* [zum Nähen] thread; [zum Weben] yarn.

Garnele (*pl* -n) *die* shrimp.

garnieren *vt* to garnish.

Garnitur (*pl* -en) *die* - 1. [Satz] set; **eine Polstermöbelgarnitur** a three-piece suite - 2. [Garnierung] garnish.

Garten (*pl* Gärten) *der* garden. ➤ **botanische Garten** *der* botanical gardens *Pl*, botanical garden. ➤ **zoologische Garten** *der* zoo.

Garten|arbeit *die* gardening.

Garten|bau *der* horticulture.

Garten|schere *die* [klein] secateurs *Pl*; [Heckenschere] shears *Pl*.

Gärtner (*pl* -) *der* gardener.

Gärtnerei (*pl* -en) *die* - **1.** [Betrieb] nursery - **2.** [Gartenarbeit] gardening.

Gärtnerin (*pl* -nen) *die* gardener.

Gar|zeit *die* cooking time.

Gas (*pl* -e) *das* - **1.** [gen] gas - **2.** [Gaspedal] accelerator *UK*, gas pedal *US*; [Treibstoff] petrol *UK*, gas *US*; **(das) Gas wegnehmen** to take one's foot off the accelerator *UK* ODER gas *US*; **Gas geben** to accelerate.

Gas|flasche *die* gas cylinder.

gasförmig *adj* gaseous.

Gas|hahn *der* gas tap.

Gas|heizung *die* gas heating.

Gas|herd *der* gas cooker *UK*, gas stove *US*.

Gas|kocher *der* camping stove, Primus stove®.

Gas|maske *die* gas mask.

Gas|pedal *das* accelerator *UK*, gas pedal *US*.

Gas|pistole *die* pistol that fires gas cartridges.

Gasse (*pl* -n) *die* alley; **die Menschenmenge bildete eine Gasse für das Fahrzeug** the crowd parted to let the vehicle through.

Gast (*pl* Gäste) *der* - **1.** [Eingeladene] guest; **bei jm zu Gast sein** to be sb's guest; **Gäste haben** to have guests; **wir haben heute Abend Freunde zu Gast** we are having some friends round ODER over this evening - **2.** [im Hotel] guest; [im Lokal] customer - **3.** [Tourist] visitor.

Gast|arbeiter, in *der, die* foreign worker.

Gäste|buch *das* visitors' book.

Gäste|zimmer *das* guest room.

gastfreundlich *adj* hospitable.

Gast|geber, in (*mpl* -, *fpl* -nen) *der, die* - **1.** [Einladende] host - **2.** [heimische Mannschaft] home team.

Gast|haus *das* inn.

Gast|hof *der* inn.

Gast|hörer, in *der, die* UNI auditor *US*, *person permitted to attend university lectures without being registered as a student.*

gastieren *vi* to give a guest performance.

Gast|land *das* [für Veranstaltung] host country.

Gast|mannschaft *die* away team.

Gastronomie *die* - **1.** [Gewerbe] catering - **2.** [Kochkunst] gastronomy.

Gast|spiel *das* guest performance.

Gast|stätte *die* rustic restaurant with pub attached.

Gatter (*pl* -) *das* - **1.** [Tor] gate - **2.** [Zaun] fence.

Gattung (*pl* -en) *die* - **1.** BIOL genus - **2.** [Art, Untergruppe] kind, type; [von Literatur, Kunst, Musik] genre.

GAU [gau] (*pl* -s) (*abk für* größter anzunehmender Unfall) *der* MCA, *maximum credible accident.*

Gaumen (*pl* -) *der* palate.

Gauner (*pl* -) *der* - **1.** [Betrüger] crook - **2.** *fam* [Spitzbube] cunning devil.

Gaunerin (*pl* -nen) *die* crook.

Gazelle (*pl* -n) *die* gazelle.

geb. - **1.** (*abk für* geborene) née - **2.** (*abk für* geboren) b.

Gebäck (*pl* -e) *das* pastries *Pl*.

gebacken ◇ *pp* ▷ **backen**. ◇ *adj* baked.

gebar *prät* ▷ **gebären**.

gebären (*präs* gebärt ODER gebiert, *prät* gebar, *perf* hat geboren) *vt* to give birth to.

Gebär|mutter *die* womb.

Gebäude (*pl* -) *das* - **1.** [Bauwerk] building - **2.** [gedanklich] structure; [aus Lügen] web.

geben (*präs* gibt, *prät* gab, *perf* hat gegeben) ◇ *vt* - **1.** [gen]: **jm etw geben** to give sb sthg, to give sthg to sb; **jm einen Kuss geben** to give sb a kiss, to kiss sb; **Unterricht geben** to teach; **eine Party geben** to have a party; **sein Einverständnis geben** to agree, to give one's consent - **2.** [platzieren]: **den Teig in die Kuchenform geben** to put the dough in the baking tin - **3.** [vorhanden sein]: **es gibt** there is/are; **hier gibt es viele Studenten** there are a lot of students here; **die schönsten Fresken gibt es in Italien** the most beautiful frescoes can be found in Italy; **was gibt es heute zum Mittagessen?** what's for lunch today?; **was gibts?** *fam* what's up?; **das gibts doch nicht!** *fam fig* I don't believe it! - **4.** [eine Bedeutung beimessen]: **viel/wenig auf etw** (A) **geben** *fam* to set a lot of/little store by sthg - **5.** [telefonisch]: **geben Sie mir bitte die Personalabteilung!** can you put me through to the personnel department, please? - **6.** [kausal]: **die Kuh gibt Milch** the cow produces milk; **das gibt doch nie etwas** nothing will ever come of that; **das Buch gibt mir nichts** *fam* I didn't get much out of the book. ◇ *vi* [beim Kartenspielen] to deal; **du gibst!** it's your deal.

Gebet (*pl* -e) *das* prayer; **ein Gebet sprechen** to say a prayer.

gebeten *pp* ▷ **bitten**.

Gebiet (*pl* -e) *das* - **1.** [Region, Gegend] area - **2.** [Bereich] field, area.

gebieten (*prät* gebot, *perf* hat geboten) *vt* - **1.** [befehlen]: **jm gebieten, etw zu tun** to command sb to do sthg - **2.** [verlangen]: to call for; **Vorsicht ist geboten** caution is called for.

gebieterisch ◇ *adj* imperious. ◇ *adv* imperiously.

Gebilde (*pl* -) *das* structure.

gebildet ◇ *adj* educated. ◇ *adv* eruditely.

Gebirge (*pl* -) *das* mountains *Pl*; [Bergkette] mountain range; **im Gebirge** in the mountains.

gebirgig *adj* mountainous.

Gebirgspass (*pl* -pässe) *der* mountain pass.

Gebiss (pl -e) das - **1.** [Zähne] teeth Pl - **2.** [Zahnersatz] dentures Pl.

gebissen pp ▷ **beißen**.

Gebläse (pl -) das fan.

geblasen pp ▷ **blasen**.

geblieben pp ▷ **bleiben**.

geblümt adj [Kleid, Stil] flowery.

gebogen ◇ pp ▷ **biegen**. ◇ adj curved.

geboren ◇ pp ▷ **gebären**. ◇ adj born; **Frau Maier, geborene Müller** Mrs. Maier, née Müller; **dazu geboren sein, etw zu tun** fig to be born to do sthg.

geborgen ◇ pp ▷ **bergen**. ◇ adj safe; **sich (bei jm) geborgen fühlen** to feel secure ODER safe with sb.

Geborgenheit die security.

geborsten pp ▷ **bersten**.

Gebot (pl -e) das - **1.** [Befehl] directive; [moralisch] precept; [göttlich] commandment - **2.** [Erfordernis] requirement; **das Gebot der Stunde** the needs of the moment - **3.** [Angebot] bid.

geboten ◇ pp ▷ **bieten, gebieten**; (RW) **etw für sein Geld geboten bekommen** to get sthg for one's money. ◇ adj necessary, requisite.

gebracht pp ▷ **bringen**.

gebrannt ◇ pp ▷ **brennen**. ◇ adj burnt; **gebrannte Mandeln** toasted almonds.

gebraten ◇ pp ▷ **braten**. ◇ adj [in der Pfanne] fried; [im Backofen] roast.

Gebrauch [gə'braʊx] (pl -bräuche) der use; **etw in Gebrauch nehmen** to start using sthg.

gebrauchen vt to use; **ich könnte etwas zu essen gebrauchen** I could use something to eat.

gebräuchlich adj - **1.** [verbreitet] common - **2.** [üblich] usual.

Gebrauchs|anweisung [gə'braʊxsanvaɪzʊŋ] die instructions Pl.

gebrauchsfertig [gə'braʊxsfɛrtɪç] adj ready-to-use.

Gebrauchs|gegenstand [gə'braʊxsgə:gŋʃtant] der everyday object.

gebraucht adj second-hand.

Gebraucht|wagen der used ODER second-hand car.

gebrochen ◇ pp ▷ **brechen**. ◇ adj broken. ◇ adv [unvollkommen]: **er spricht gebrochen Italienisch** he speaks broken Italian.

Gebrüll das (ohne pl) [von Löwe, Menschenmenge] roaring; [von Stier] bellowing; [von Kind, Affe] screeching.

Gebühr (pl -en) die charge; [für Arzt, Anwalt] fee; [für Autobahn] toll; [für Post] postage.

gebührend ◇ adj [Strafe, Belohnung] suitable; [Sorgfalt] due. ◇ adv [strafen, belohnen] suitably; **etw gebührend sorgfältig machen** to do sthg with due care.

Gebühren|einheit die TELEKOM unit.

gebührenfrei adj & adv free of charge.

gebührenpflichtig adj subject to a charge.

Geburt (pl -en) die birth; **er ist von Geburt kein Deutscher** he is not German by birth.

gebürtig adj: **sie ist gebürtige Bayerin, sie ist aus Bayern gebürtig** she's Bavarian by birth.

Geburts|datum das date of birth.

Geburts|ort der place of birth.

Geburts|tag der - **1.** [Jahrestag] birthday; **wann hast du Geburtstag?** when is your birthday?; **jm zum Geburtstag gratulieren** to wish sb a happy birthday; **alles Gute zum Geburtstag!** happy birthday! - **2.** amt [Geburtsdatum] date of birth.

Geburtstags|feier die birthday party.

Geburtstags|kind das birthday boy/girl.

Geburts|urkunde die birth certificate.

Gebüsch (pl -e) das bushes Pl.

gedacht ◇ pp ▷ **denken**. ◇ adj: **das Geschenk ist als Trost gedacht** the present is meant to be a consolation; **eigentlich war das anders gedacht** actually that's not what was intended.

Gedächtnis (pl -se) das memory; **kein Gedächtnis für Zahlen haben** to have no head for numbers; **zum Gedächtnis an jn** in memory of sb.

Gedächtnis|feier die commemoration.

gedämpft adj [Licht, Musik, Stimmung] subdued; [Geräusch, Schritte] muffled; [Farbton, Musikinstrument] muted; [Stimme] low.

Gedanke (pl -n) der - **1.** [Gedachte, Überlegung] thought; **sich (D) Gedanken über etw (A) machen** to think about sthg; **js Gedanken lesen können** to be able to read sb's mind; **er hat sich entschlossen, keinen Gedanken daran zu verschwenden** he decided not to waste any time thinking about it; **der bloße Gedanke, dass...** the very idea that... - **2.** [Vorstellung, Vorhaben] idea; **mit dem Gedanken spielen, etw zu tun** to toy with the idea of doing sthg - **3.** [Sorge]: **sich (D) Gedanken über jn/etw machen** to be worried about sb/sthg.

gedankenlos ◇ adj [ohne nachzudenken] thoughtless; [unaufmerksam] absent-minded. ◇ adv [ohne nachzudenken] without thinking; [unaufmerksam] absent-mindedly.

Gedanken|strich der dash.

gedankenverloren adv lost in thought.

Gedeck (pl -e) das - **1.** [Geschirr und Besteck] place setting - **2.** [Speisenfolge] set meal.

Gedenk|minute die minute's silence.

Gedenk|stätte die memorial.

Gedenk|tafel die plaque.

Gedicht (pl -e) das poem.

Gedränge das crush.

gedrängt ◇ adj [Bericht, Beschreibung] succinct; [Zeitplan] busy. ◇ adv succinctly.

gedroschen *pp* ▷ **dreschen**.

gedrückt *adj* depressed.

gedrungen ◇ *pp* ▷ **dringen**. ◇ *adj* stocky.

Geduld *die* patience; **mit jm Geduld haben** to be patient with sb; **die Geduld verlieren** to lose one's patience.

geduldig ◇ *adj* patient. ◇ *adv* patiently.

Geduldsfaden *der*: **ihm reißt (gleich) der Geduldsfaden** he's losing his patience.

gedurft *pp* ▷ **dürfen**.

geeignet *adj* suitable; **für etw geeignet sein** to be suitable for sthg; **nicht geeignet** unsuitable; **er ist zum Lehrer geeignet** he'd make a good teacher.

Gefahr (*pl* -en) *die* danger; **es besteht die Gefahr eines Unfalls** there's the risk of an accident; **außer Gefahr sein** no longer to be in danger; **Gefahr laufen, etw zu tun** to be in danger of doing sthg.

gefährden *vt* [Gesundheit, Leben, Mensch] to endanger; [Unternehmen, Projekt] to jeopardize.

gefahren *pp* ▷ **fahren**.

gefährlich ◇ *adj* dangerous. ◇ *adv* dangerously.

gefahrlos ◇ *adj* safe. ◇ *adv* safely.

Gefälle (*pl* -) *das* - 1. [von Straße, Dach] slope - 2. [Unterschied] difference.

gefallen (*präs* gefällt, *prät* gefiel, *perf* hat gefallen) *vi* - 1. [gut finden]: **er/es gefällt mir** I like him/it - 2. [ertragen]: **sich** (D) **etw gefallen lassen** to put up with sthg; **sich** (D) **nichts gefallen lassen** not to put up with any nonsense; **das lasse ich mir gefallen!** *fam* I can handle this!

Gefallen (*pl* -) *der* favour; **jm einen Gefallen tun** to do sb a favour; **jn um einen Gefallen bitten** to ask sb a favour.

gefällig *adj* - 1. [entkommend] helpful; **jm gefällig sein** to be of help to sb - 2. [angenehm] pleasant - 3. [genehm]: **noch ein Bier gefällig?** would you like another beer?

Gefälligkeit (*pl* -en) *die* [Gefallen] favour.

gefälligst *adv* kindly.

Gefangene (*pl* -n) *der*, *die* prisoner.

gefangen nehmen *vt* (*unreg*) - 1. [festnehmen] to capture - 2. [in Bann ziehen] to captivate.

Gefangenschaft *die* captivity.

Gefängnis (*pl* -se) *das* - 1. [Haftanstalt] prison - 2. [Haftstrafe] imprisonment.

Gefängnisstrafe *die* prison sentence.

gefärbt *adj* dyed.

Gefäß (*pl* -e) *das* - 1. [Behältnis] container - 2. [von Lebewesen] blood vessel.

gefasst ◇ *adj* - 1. [gelassen] composed - 2. [vorbereitet]: **auf etw** (A) **gefasst sein** to be prepared for sthg; **du kannst dich darauf gefasst machen, dass...** *fam* you'd better start getting used to the idea that...; **sonst kannst du dich auf was gefasst machen** *fam* otherwise you're in for it. ◇ *adv* [gelassen] calmly.

Gefecht (*pl* -e) *das* skirmish.

Gefieder (*pl* -) *das* feathers *Pl*.

geflogen *pp* ▷ **fliegen**.

geflohen *pp* ▷ **fliehen**.

geflossen *pp* ▷ **fließen**.

Geflügel *das* poultry.

Geflüster *das* whispering.

gefochten *pp* ▷ **fechten**.

Gefolge *das* entourage; [bei Beerdigung] cortege.

Gefolgschaft (*pl* -en) *die* - 1. (*ohne pl*) [Loyalität] allegiance; **jm die Gefolgschaft verweigern** to stop supporting sb - 2. [Anhängerschaft] followers *Pl*.

gefragt *adj* popular; **sehr gefragt sein** to be very much in demand.

gefräßig *adj abw* greedy.

Gefreite (*pl* -n) *der* lance corporal *UK*, private first class *US*.

gefressen *pp* ▷ **fressen**.

gefrieren (*prät* gefror, *perf* hat/ist gefroren) *vi* (*ist*) to freeze; **es hat gefroren** there has been a frost.

Gefrierfach *das* freezer (compartment).

Gefriertruhe *die* (chest) freezer.

gefroren ◇ *pp* ▷ **frieren**, **gefrieren**. ◇ *adj* frozen.

Gefühl (*pl* -e) *das* - 1. [gen] feeling; **seine Beine sind ohne Gefühl** he's got no feeling in his legs; **er kennt keine Gefühle** he doesn't have any feelings; **etw im Gefühl haben** to know sthg instinctively - 2. [Gespür] sense; **ein Gefühl für etw** a sense of sthg.

gefühllos ◇ *adj* - 1. [taub] numb - 2. [herzlos] callous. ◇ *adv* [herzlos] callously.

Gefühlsleben *das* emotional life.

gefühlsmäßig ◇ *adj* emotional. ◇ *adv* emotionally.

gefunden *pp* ▷ **finden**.

gegangen *pp* ▷ **gehen**.

gegebenenfalls *adv* if necessary.

Gegebenheit (*pl* -en) *die* condition, circumstance.

gegen *präp* (+ A) - 1. [gen] against; **gegen die Tür hämmern** to bang on the door; **das Schiff fährt gegen die Strömung** the ship is sailing upstream; **gegen etw sein** to be opposed to ODER against sthg; **heute spielt Leipzig gegen Bremen** Leipzig are playing Bremen today; **ein Mittel gegen Grippe** a flu remedy, a medicine for flu - 2. [zeitlich]: **gegen fünf Uhr** at about five o'clock; **gegen Abend wurde es kühler** it cooled down towards evening

- 3. [im Austausch für] for; **gegen bar** for cash
- 4. [im Vergleich zu] in comparison to, compared with.

Gegen|argument das counterargument.

Gegend (pl -en) die - 1. [Gebiet, Bereich] area; **in der Gegend** nearby; **in der Gegend von** near; **in der Nierengegend** in the region of the kidneys; **hier in der Gegend** round here - 2. [Nachbarschaft] neighbourhood; **so in der Gegend** fam thereabouts.

Gegen|darstellung die conflicting account.

gegeneinander adv against one another ODER each other.

Gegenfahr|bahn die opposite side of the road.

Gegen|gewicht das counterbalance; **ein** ODER **das Gegengewicht zu etw bilden** to counterbalance sthg.

Gegen|gift das antidote.

gegenläufig <> adj opposite. <> adv in the opposite direction.

Gegen|leistung die **als Gegenleistung (für etw)** in return (for sthg).

Gegen|maßnahme die countermeasure.

Gegen|mittel das antidote.

Gegen|richtung die opposite direction.

Gegen|satz der contrast; **im Gegensatz zu** in contrast to; **im Gegensatz zu etw stehen** to contrast with sthg.

gegensätzlich <> adj conflicting. <> adv completely differently.

Gegen|seite die - 1. [Gegenpartei] opposing side; [vor Gericht] opposing party; SPORT opposition - 2. [andere Seite] other side.

gegenseitig <> adj mutual. <> adv each other, one another; **sich gegenseitig helfen** to help each other ODER one another.

Gegen|spieler, in der, die - 1. [Gegner] opponent - 2. [im Theater] antagonist.

Gegensprechan|lage die intercom.

Gegen|stand der - 1. [Ding, Objekt] object - 2. [Thema] subject.

gegenständlich adj [Kunst] representational.

Gegen|stimme die - 1. [Stimme dagegen] vote against - 2. [abweichende Meinung] dissenting voice.

Gegen|teil das opposite; **das Gegenteil von jm/etw sein** to be the opposite of sb/sthg. **im Gegenteil** adv on the contrary; **ganz im Gegenteil** quite the reverse ODER opposite.

gegenteilig adj opposite.

gegenüber <> präp (+ D) - 1. [räumlich] opposite; **gegenüber der Kirche** opposite the church; **mir gegenüber** opposite me - 2. [zur Angabe einer Beziehung] towards; **so kannst du dich den Schülern gegenüber nicht verhalten** you can't behave like that towards the pupils - 3. [zur Angabe eines Vergleichs] compared with; **gegenüber der alten Wohnung** compared with the old flat UK ODER apartment US. <> adv opposite; **der Garten gegenüber** the garden over ODER across the road.

Gegenüber das person sitting opposite.

gegenüber|liegen vi (unreg) to be opposite; **das gegenüberliegende Gebäude** the building opposite; **einander gegenüberliegen** to face one another ODER each other. **sich gegenüberliegen** ref to face one another ODER each other.

gegenüber|stehen vi (unreg) - 1. [zugewandt stehen]: **jm/einer Sache gegenüberstehen** to be facing sb/sthg - 2. [gegenübergestellt sein]: **einer Sache (D) gegenüberstehen** to be faced with sthg; **jm feindlich gegenüberstehen** to have a hostile attitude towards sb. **sich gegenüberstehen** ref - 1. [sich zugewandt stehen, gegeneinander spielen] to face one another ODER each other - 2. [in Konflikt stehen] to clash.

gegenüber|stellen vt - 1. [mit jm konfrontieren]: **dem Zeugen die Verdächtigen gegenüberstellen** to line the suspects up in front of the witness - 2. [nebeneinander halten]: **das Alterswerk eines Autors seinen frühen Romanen gegenüberstellen** to compare the late works of an author with his early novels.

gegenüber|treten (perf **ist gegenübergetreten**) vi (unreg) **jm gegenübertreten** to face sb.

Gegenverkehr der oncoming traffic.

Gegenwart die - 1. [Zeitpunkt] present; **die Kunst der Gegenwart** contemporary art; **bis in die Gegenwart** up to the present day - 2. [Präsenz] presence; **in js Gegenwart** in sb's presence - 3. GRAMM present (tense).

Gegen|wert der equivalent amount.

Gegen|wind der headwind.

gegessen pp |> **essen**.

geglichen pp |> **gleichen**.

geglitten pp |> **gleiten**.

geglommen pp |> **glimmen**.

Gegner, in (mpl -, fpl -nen) der, die - 1. [Widersacher, im Sport] opponent - 2. [Feind] enemy.

gegnerisch adj opposing.

gegolten pp |> **gelten**.

gegoren <> pp |> **gären**. <> adj fermented.

gegossen pp |> **gießen**.

gegraben pp |> **graben**.

gegriffen pp |> **greifen**.

Gehabe das abw affected behaviour.

gehabt pp |> **haben**.

Gehackte das mince UK, mincemeat US.

Gehalt (pl **Gehälter**) <> das salary. <> der - 1. [Inhalt] content - 2. [Anteil]: **ein geringer Gehalt an Gold** a low gold content.

gehalten pp ▷ **halten**.

Gehaltsablrechnung die salary statement.

gehandikapt [gəˈhɛndikɛpt] adj handicapped.

gehangen pp ▷ **hängen**.

gehässig ◇ adj spiteful. ◇ adv spitefully.

Gehäuse (pl -) das - 1. [von Uhr, Fotoapparat, Radio] casing; [von Schnecke] shell - 2. [von Apfel, Birne] core.

gehbehindert adj disabled (used of people who have difficulty walking).

Gehege (pl -) das reserve; [im Zoo] enclosure.

geheim ◇ adj - 1. [heimlich] secret - 2. [geheimnisvoll] mysterious. ◇ adv [nicht offen] in secret; **geheim abstimmen** to vote by secret ballot. ● **im Geheimen** adv secretly.

Geheimldienst der secret service.

geheim halten vt (unreg) to keep secret.

Geheimnis (pl -se) das - 1. [Geheimgehaltenes] secret - 2. [Unbekanntes] mystery.

geheimnisvoll ◇ adj mysterious. ◇ adv mysteriously.

Geheimlnummer die [von Telefon] ex-directory number UK, unlisted number US; [von Scheckkarte] PIN (number); [von Tresor] combination.

Geheimlpolizei die secret police.

geheißen pp ▷ **heißen**.

gehen (prät ging, perf ist gegangen) ◇ vi - 1. [Fortbewegung] to go; **einkaufen gehen** to go shopping; **in die Stadt gehen** to go into town; **zur Armee gehen** to join the army; **in Serienproduktion gehen** to go into mass production - 2. [weggehen, abfahren] to go; **ich gehe jetzt** I'm off now; **mein Zug geht um acht Uhr** my train leaves ODER goes at eight o'clock - 3. [zu Fuß gehen] to walk; **mit jm gehen** fam [eine Beziehung haben] to go out with sb - 4. [verkehren] to go; **der Bus geht drei Mal täglich** the bus goes ODER runs three times a day - 5. [ergehen]: **wie geht es dir/Ihnen?** how are you?; **es geht mir gut/schlecht** I'm well/not very well; **der Firma geht es gut/schlecht** the company is doing well/badly - 6. [sich handeln um]: **es geht um deine Mutter** it's about your mother; **worum geht es in diesem Buch?** what's this book about?; **es geht darum, alle Karten loszuwerden** the idea is to get rid of all your cards; **darum geht es nicht** that's not the point - 7. [annehmbar sein]: **wie gefällt es dir? - es geht** how do you like it? - it's OK - 8. [funktionieren - gen] to work; [- Uhr, Auto] to go; **das Geschäft geht gut** business is going well - 9. [zur Beschreibung von Vorgängen]: **wie geht das mit der Anmeldung?** how's the application going?; **das geht doch ganz einfach** it's quite simple; **was geht denn hier vor sich?** what's going on here, then? - 10. [möglich, erlaubt sein] to be OK; **aber das geht doch nicht!** you can't do that!; **ginge es vielleicht, dass wir...?** do you think we could possibly...? - 11. [sich erstrecken]: **das Wasser ging ihm bis zu den Knien** the water came up to his knees; **die Straße geht bis zum Rathaus** the street goes as far as the town hall; **das geht über unsere Mittel** that's beyond our means - 12. [passen]: **in/durch etw gehen** to go in/through sthg - 13. [sich richten]: **es kann nicht immer nur nach dir gehen** you can't always have things your own way; **wenn es nach mir ginge** if I had my way - 14. [ein Arbeitsverhältnis beenden] to leave - 15. [Teig] to rise. ◇ vt to walk. ● **sich gehen** ref: **sich gehen lassen** to let o.s. go.

geheuer adj: **das ist mir nicht (ganz) geheuer** [Furcht einflößend] I find that (rather) eerie; [unwohl] I'm not (too) sure about that; [verdächtig] I find that (rather) odd ODER suspicious.

Geheul, Geheule das - 1. [Heulen] howling - 2. fam abw [Heulerei] wailing.

Gehilfe (pl -n) der - 1. [Ausgebildeter] qualified assistant (who has successfully completed an apprenticeship) - 2. [Helfer] assistant.

Gehilfin (pl -nen) die - 1. [Ausgebildete] qualified assistant (who has successfully completed an apprenticeship) - 2. [Helferin] assistant.

Gehirn (pl -e) das - 1. [Hirn] brain - 2. (ohne pl) fam [Verstand] brain, brains Pl; **sich das Gehirn zermartern** to rack one's brain ODER brains.

Gehirnlerschütterung die concussion (U).

gehoben ◇ pp ▷ **heben**. ◇ adj - 1. [höher - Position, Stellung] senior; [- Einkommen, Erwartung] higher - 2. [exklusiv] sophisticated - 3.: **in gehobener Stimmung** in high spirits.

geholfen pp ▷ **helfen**.

Gehör (pl -e) das hearing; **ein schlechtes Gehör haben** to be hard of hearing; **nach dem Gehör** by ear; **jm/einer Sache Gehör/kein Gehör schenken** to listen/not to listen to sb/sthg.

gehorchen vi to obey; **jm gehorchen** to obey sb; **der Vernunft gehorchen** to listen to reason.

gehören vi - 1. [einer Person]: **jm gehören** to belong to sb - 2. [an Ort] to belong; **wohin gehört das Werkzeug?** where does this tool belong? - 3. [als Bestandteil]: **zu etw gehören** to be part of sthg; **sie gehört zum Krankenhauspersonal** she's a member of the hospital staff - 4. [als Notwendigkeit]: **zum Reiten gehört viel Geschick** riding requires a lot of skill; **es gehört Mut dazu, dies zu tun** it takes a lot of courage to do it - 5. [müssen]: **solche Leute gehören eingesperrt** such people ought to be locked up. ● **sich gehören** ref: **es** ODER **das gehört sich nicht** it's not the done thing.

gehörig ◇ adj - 1. [gebührend] proper - 2. [beachtlich] considerable; **mit einer gehörigen Portion Mut** with a good deal of courage.

◇ *adv* - 1. [gebührend] properly - 2. [beacht-
lich - steigen, erhöhen] considerably; **jn gehörig
durchprügeln** to give sb a good thrashing.
Gehörlose (*pl* -n) *der, die* deaf person; **die
Gehörlosen** the deaf.
gehorsam *adj* obedient.
Gehorsam *der* obedience; **jm den Gehorsam
verweigern** to refuse to obey sb.
Gehorsamkeit *die* obedience.
Geh|weg *der* - 1. [Gehsteig] pavement *UK*,
sidewalk *US* - 2. [Weg] footpath.
Geige (*pl* -n) *die* [im Orchester] violin; [in Folk]
fiddle.
geil *adj* - 1. *fam* [begierig auf Sex] horny; **er war
geil auf sie** he wanted to get into her knickers
- 2. *abw* [lüstern - Mann] lecherous; [- Blick, Ge-
danke] lewd - 3. *fam* [toll] wicked.
Geisel (*pl* -n) *die* hostage.
Geisel|nahme (*pl* -n) *die* hostage-taking.
Geist (*pl* -e *ODER* -er) *der* - 1. [Verstandeskraft]
mind; **den Geist aufgeben** *fam* to give up the
ghost; **jm auf den Geist gehen** *fam* to get on
sb's nerves - 2. [Intellekt] intellect - 3. [Gesin-
nung] spirit - 4. (*pl* Geiste) [Spirituose] *schnapps
distilled from fruit, especially berries* - 5. (*pl*
Geister*) [Person, Genie] mind - 6. (*pl* Geister*)
[überirdische Wesenheit]: **der Heilige Geist** the
Holy Ghost - 7. (*pl* Geister*) [Gespenst] ghost.
Geister|fahrer, *in der, die person who
drives into oncoming traffic on a motorway*.
geistesabwesend ◇ *adj* absent-minded.
◇ *adv* absent-mindedly.
Geistes|blitz *der* flash of inspiration.
geistesgegenwärtig ◇ *adj* quick-witted.
◇ *adv* with great presence of mind.
geistesgestört *adj* mentally disturbed *ODER*
unbalanced.
geisteskrank *adj* mentally ill.
Geistes|kranke *der, die* mentally ill person;
[im Krankenhaus] mental patient.
Geistes|wissenschaft *die* arts subject; **die
Geisteswissenschaften** the arts.
geistig ◇ *adj* - 1. [intellektuell - Mensch, Freiheit, Vermächtnis] intellectual; [- Anstrengung,
Kraft, Fähigkeit] mental - 2. [alkoholisch] alcoholic. ◇ *adv* [intellektuell - frei, überlegen] intellectually; [- fit, frisch, behindert] mentally; **sich
geistig anstrengen** to make a mental effort.
geistlich ◇ *adj* [gen] religious; [Beistand]
spiritual. ◇ *adv*: **jm geistlich beistehen** to
lend sb spiritual guidance.
Geistliche (*pl* -n) *der* clergyman.
geistlos ◇ *adj* inane. ◇ *adv* inanely.
geistreich ◇ *adj* intelligent. ◇ *adv* intelligently.
Geiz *der* meanness.
geizen *vi*: **mit etw geizen** [Geld] to be mean
with sthg; [Lob] to be sparing with sthg.
Geiz|hals *der fam abw* skinflint.

geizig ◇ *adj* mean. ◇ *adv* meanly.
Geiz|kragen *der fam abw* skinflint.
Gejammer *das fam abw* moaning.
gekannt *pp* ▷ **kennen**.
Gekicher *das* giggling.
geklungen *pp* ▷ **klingen**.
gekniffen *pp* ▷ **kneifen**.
gekommen *pp* ▷ **kommen**.
gekonnt ◇ *pp* ▷ **können**. ◇ *adj* masterful. ◇ *adv* masterfully.
gekrochen *pp* ▷ **kriechen**.
gekünstelt *abw* ◇ *adj* artificial. ◇ *adv* artificially.
Gel (*pl* -e) *das* gel.
Gelächter (*pl* -) *das* laughter.
geladen ◇ *pp* ▷ **laden**. ◇ *adj* loaded;
geladen sein *fam fig* to be fuming.
gelähmt *adj* paralysed.
Gelähmte (*pl* -n) *der, die* paralysed man
(-woman *die*).
Gelände (*pl* -) *das* - 1. [Land] country; **ein ber-
giges Gelände** mountainous terrain; **auf freiem Gelände** in the open country - 2. [Gebiet]
area - 3. [Grundstück - zum Bau] site; [- um Haus]
grounds *Pl*.
Gelände|lauf *der* - 1. *SPORT* cross-country
(running) - 2. [Wettkampf] cross-country run.
Geländer (*pl* -) *das* [von Treppe] banister; [von
Brücke] parapet; [von Balkon] railing.
gelang *prät* ▷ **gelingen**.
gelangen (*perf* ist gelangt) *vi*: **an etw** (A) **gelangen** to arrive at sthg; **an die Öffentlichkeit
gelangen** to become public; **in js Besitz gelangen** to come into sb's possession; **zu etw gelangen** [Ruhm, Ansehen] to gain sthg; [Verständi-
gung] to come to sthg; **zu Geld gelangen** [durch
Erbe] to come into money; [durch Arbeit] to
make money.
gelassen ◇ *pp* ▷ **lassen**. ◇ *adj* calm.
◇ *adv* calmly.
Gelassenheit *die* composure.
gelaufen *pp* ▷ **laufen**.
geläufig *adj* [vertraut] common; **es ist mir geläufig** it is familiar to me.
gelb *adj* & *adv* yellow.
Gelb *das* yellow. ◆ **bei Gelb** *adv* on amber
UK, on yellow *US*.
Gelbe Sack *der yellow refuse bag used for
recyclable packaging*.
gelblich *adj* [Tapete, Papier] yellowish; [Haut]
sallow.
Gelbsucht *die* jaundice.
Geld (*pl* -er) *das* money; **großes Geld** notes *Pl*;
kleines Geld change, coins *Pl*; **ins Geld gehen**
to be expensive; **es ist sein Geld wert** it is
worth every penny. ◆ **Gelder** *Pl* funds.
Geld|automat *der* cash machine *ODER* dis-
penser.

Geld|börse die [Brieftasche] wallet; [für Münzen] purse.

Geld|geber, in der, die financial backer.

geldgierig adj greedy (for money).

Geld|karte die Switch card® UK, smart card which charges payments straight to one's bank account.

Geld|mittel Pl funds.

Geld|schein der banknote UK, bill US.

Geld|schrank der safe.

Geld|strafe die fine.

Geld|stück das coin.

Gelee [ʒəˈleː] (pl -s) das & der jelly.

gelegen ⬦ pp ▷ **liegen**. ⬦ adj - 1. [befindlich] situated - 2. [bedeutsam]: **mir ist an deinem Besuch viel gelegen** geh your visit means a great deal to me.

Gelegenheit (pl -en) die - 1. [geeignete Möglichkeit] opportunity - 2. [Anlass] occasion - 3. [Angebot] bargain. ➡ **bei Gelegenheit** adv when the opportunity arises.

gelegentlich ⬦ adj occasional. ⬦ adv - 1. [manchmal] occasionally - 2. [bei Gelegenheit] some time.

gelehrt ⬦ adj learned. ⬦ adv learnedly.

Gelehrte (pl -n) der, die scholar.

Gelenk (pl -e) das [beim Menschen] joint.

gelenkig adj supple.

gelernt adj trained.

gelesen pp ▷ **lesen**.

Geliebte (pl -n) der, die lover.

geliehen pp ▷ **leihen**.

gelingen (prät gelang, perf ist gelungen) vi: **die Zeichnung ist mir gut gelungen** my drawing turned out well; **es gelang mir, den Brief zu schreiben** I managed to write the letter; **es gelang ihm, das Buch zu finden** he succeeded in finding the book.

gelitten pp ▷ **leiden**.

gelockt adj: **gelocktes Haar** curly hair.

gelogen pp ▷ **lügen**.

gelöst adj relaxed.

gelten (präs gilt, prät galt, perf hat gegolten) vi - 1. [gültig sein] to be valid; **für jn/etw gelten** to apply to sb/sthg - 2. SPORT to count - 3. [anerkannt sein]: **als etw gelten** to be considered to be sthg - 4. [korrekt sein]: **das gilt nicht!** fam [gen] that doesn't count!; [schummeln] that's cheating! - 5. [akzeptieren]: **etw gelten lassen** to accept sthg - 6. [wert sein] to count; **Kreativität gilt hier nichts** creativity counts for nothing here - 7. [adressiert sein an]: **seine Bemerkung galt nicht allein dir** his remark was not only directed at you, his remark didn't only apply to you - 8. [müssen]: **in dieser Lage gilt es, einen kühlen Kopf zu bewahren** in this situation you need to ODER it is necessary to keep a cool head.

geltend adj current; **etw geltend machen** [Forderung] to make sthg; [Einwand] to raise/put forward sthg.

Geltung die - 1. [Gültigkeit] validity; **dieses Gesetz hat keine Geltung mehr** this law is no longer valid - 2. [Wirkung] prominence; **zur Geltung kommen** to be shown to its best advantage.

gelungen ⬦ pp ▷ **gelingen**. ⬦ adj successful.

gemächlich ⬦ adj leisurely. ⬦ adv: **gemächlich im Wald spazieren gehen** to go for a leisurely walk in the woods.

Gemälde (pl -) das painting.

gemäß präp: **gemäß einer Sache** (D), **einer Sache** (D) **gemäß** in accordance with sthg.

gemäßigt adj [Politiker] moderate; [Klima] temperate.

Gemecker, Gemeckere das - 1. [von Ziegen] bleating - 2. fam abw [Nörgelei] moaning.

gemein ⬦ adj - 1. [niederträchtig - Person, Verhalten] mean; [- Trick, Lüge] nasty; [- Witz] dirty - 2. fam [unfair]: **das ist gemein!** that's not fair! ⬦ adv - 1. [gemeinsam]: **etw mit jm/etw gemein haben** to have sthg in common with sb/sthg - 2. [niederträchtig] meanly - 3. fam [sehr]: **die Verletzung hat gemein wehgetan** the injury hurt like hell.

Gemeinde|zentrum das community centre.

gemeingefährlich ⬦ adj dangerous. ⬦ adv dangerously.

Gemeinheit (pl -en) die - 1. [verwerfliche Art] meanness - 2. [Handlung] mean trick - 3. fam [Ärgernis]: **so eine Gemeinheit!** it's not fair!

gemeinnützig ⬦ adj for the benefit of the community; [Verein] charitable, non-profit-making. ⬦ adv for the benefit of the community.

gemeinsam ⬦ adv - 1. [zusammen] together; **gemeinsam verantwortlich** jointly responsible - 2. [gleich]: **etw gemeinsam haben** to have sthg in common. ⬦ adj [Weg, Interessen] common; [Verantwortung] joint; **ein gemeinsamer Urlaub/Spaziergang** a holiday/walk together.

Gemeinsamkeit (pl -en) die - 1. [gleiche Eigenschaft] common feature; **sie haben viele Gemeinsamkeiten** they have a lot in common - 2. (ohne pl) [Zusammengehörigkeit]: **Gefühl der Gemeinsamkeit** sense of community.

Gemeinschaft (pl -en) die - 1. [Gruppe] community - 2. [Verbundenheit] company; **in unserer Klasse haben wir eine gute Gemeinschaft** in our class we have a good sense of community; **in js Gemeinschaft** in sb's company.

gemeinschaftlich ⬦ adj joint; [Interessen] common. ⬦ adv jointly.

Gemeinschafts|kunde die (ohne pl) SCHULE social studies Pl.

Gemeinschaft|raum der common room.

gemeint adj meant; **das war nicht so gemeint!** I didn't mean it like that!; **mein Rat war gut gemeint** my advice was well-intentioned.

Gemetzel (pl -) das bloodbath.

Gemisch (pl -e) das mixture.

gemischt adj mixed.

gemocht pp ▷ **mögen**.

gemolken pp ▷ **melken**.

Gemurmel das murmuring.

Gemüse (pl -) das vegetables Pl.

Gemüse|eintopf der vegetable stew.

Gemüse|händler, in der, die greengrocer.

gemusst pp ▷ **müssen**.

Gemüt (pl -er) das - **1.** [Wesen] disposition - **2.** (ohne pl) [Empfindungsvermögen] heart; **dieses Buch ist etwas fürs Gemüt** this is a moving book; **der Film ist ihr aufs Gemüt geschlagen** the film really got her down; [Text] **to study sthg. ◆ Gemüter** Pl feelings; **der Skandal hat die Gemüter erregt** the scandal has caused feelings to run high.

gemütlich ◇ adj - **1.** [behaglich] cosy; **es sich (D) gemütlich machen** to make o.s. at home - **2.** [Beisammensein] informal; [Abend] pleasant; [Fahrt] leisurely - **3.** [Person] friendly. ◇ adv - **1.** [behaglich] cosily - **2.** [zusammensitzen, sich unterhalten] pleasantly; [arbeiten] at a leisurely pace.

Gemütlichkeit die - **1.** [Behaglichkeit] cosiness - **2.** [Zwanglosigkeit, Ruhe] pleasant atmosphere; **in aller Gemütlichkeit** at one's leisure.

Gen (pl -e) das gene.

genannt pp ▷ **nennen**.

genau ◇ adj - **1.** [exakt] exact; [Waage, Voraussage, Arbeit] accurate - **2.** [gründlich] thorough. ◇ adv - **1.** [exakt] precisely, exactly; **genau!** precisely!, exactly!; **genau um zehn Uhr** at exactly ten o'clock; **auf die Minute/Sekunde** to the very minute/second; **die Uhr geht genau** the clock keeps perfect time - **2.** [zuhören, hinsehen] carefully; **ich kenne ihn genau** I know exactly what he's like.

genau genommen adv strictly speaking.

Genauigkeit die - **1.** [Exaktheit] exactness; [von Waage, Voraussage, Arbeit] accuracy - **2.** [Gründlichkeit] thoroughness.

genauso adv just as; **er sieht genauso aus** he looks just the same.

Gen|datei die DNA database.

genehmigen vt [Antrag, Plan] to approve; [Demonstration, Aufenthalt] to authorize; **sich (D) etw genehmigen** fam to treat o.s. to ODER allow o.s. sthg.

Genehmigung (pl -en) die - **1.** [von Antrag, Plan] approval; [von Demonstration, Aufenthalt] authorization - **2.** [Dokument] permit.

General (pl -rale ODER -räle) der general.

General|probe die eigtl & fig dress rehearsal.

generalüberholen vt to give a complete overhaul.

Generalver|sammlung die annual general meeting.

Generation (pl -en) die generation.

Generations|konflikt der conflict between the generations.

Generator (pl -toren) der generator.

generell ◇ adj general. ◇ adv generally.

Genetik die genetics (U).

Genf nt Geneva.

Genfer See der Lake Geneva.

genial ◇ adj brilliant. ◇ adv brilliantly.

Genick (pl -e) das (back of the) neck.

Genie [ʒe'ni:] (pl -s) das genius.

genieren [ʒe'ni:rən] vt to bother. ◆ **sich genieren** ref to be embarrassed; **sich vor jm genieren** to be shy of sb, to get embarrassed in sb's presence.

genießbar adj [essbar] edible; [trinkbar] drinkable.

genießen (prät genoss, perf hat genossen) vt - **1.** [gen] to enjoy - **2.** [essen] to eat; [trinken] to drink.

Genießer, in (mpl -, fpl -nen) der, die pleasure lover, bon vivant; [beim Essen] gourmet.

genießerisch ◇ adj [Mensch] appreciative; [Leben] pleasurable. ◇ adv with relish.

Genitalien Pl genitals.

Genitiv (pl -e) der GRAMM genitive.

genommen pp ▷ **nehmen**.

genormt adj standardized.

genoss prät ▷ **genießen**.

genossen pp ▷ **genießen**.

Genossenschaft (pl -en) die cooperative.

gentechnisch ◇ adj: **gentechnische Änderungen** genetic modifications. ◇ adv: **gentechnisch veränderte Lebensmittel** genetically modified foods, GM foods.

genug adv enough; **genug (von etw) haben** to have had enough (of sthg).

Genüge die: **einer Sache (D) Genüge tun** geh to satisfy sthg; **zur Genüge** abw only too well.

genügen vi - **1.** [ausreichen] to be enough; **ein Glas Wein genügt mir** a glass of wine is enough for me; **das genügt!** that's enough! - **2.** [entsprechen]: **einer Sache (D) genügen** [Anforderungen] to meet sthg; [Vorschriften] to comply with sthg.

genügend adj & adv enough.

genügsam ◇ adj [Mensch] modest. ◇ adv modestly.

Genugtuung die satisfaction; **Genugtuung für etw** satisfaction for sthg; **mit Genugtuung** with satisfaction.

Genus (pl Genera) das GRAMM gender.

Genuss (*pl* Genüsse) *der* - **1.** [Konsum] consumption; **in den Genuss von etw kommen** *fig* to receive sthg - **2.** [Befriedigung] pleasure; **das Konzert war ein Genuss** the concert was a delight.

Geografie, Geographie *die* geography.

geografisch, geographisch <> *adj* geographical. <> *adv* geographically.

Geologie *die* geology.

geologisch <> *adj* geological. <> *adv* geologically.

Geometrie *die* geometry.

geordnet *adj* orderly.

Gepäck *das* luggage.

Gepäck⎮abfertigung *die* - **1.** [Handlung] luggage check-in - **2.** [Schalter - am Flughafen] (baggage) check-in; [- am Bahnhof] luggage office.

Gepäck⎮ablage *die* luggage rack.

Gepäck⎮annahme *die* [am Flughafen] (baggage) check-in.

Gepäck⎮aufbewahrung *die* [Schalter] left-luggage office *UK*, baggage room *US*.

Gepäck⎮ausgabe *die* [am Flughafen] baggage reclaim.

Gepäck⎮schein *der* luggage ticket.

Gepäck⎮stück *das* item of luggage.

Gepäck⎮träger *der* - **1.** [von Fahrrad] carrier; [von Auto] luggage rack - **2.** [Person] porter.

Gepäck⎮wagen *der* luggage van *UK*, baggage car *US*.

gepfiffen *pp* ⊳ **pfeifen**.

gepflegt <> *adj* - **1.** [Äußeres] well-groomed; [Hände] well-cared-for; [Haare, Kleidung] neat; [Garten, Haus] well-kept - **2.** [von Qualität] quality (*vor Subst*) - **3.** [Stil, Ausdruck] refined. <> *adv* - **1.** [essen] well - **2.** [gewählt]: **sie drückt sich sehr gepflegt aus** she has a very refined way of speaking.

gepriesen *pp* ⊳ **preisen**.

gequollen *pp* ⊳ **quellen**.

gerade <> *adv* - **1.** [vor kurzem] just; **ich bin gerade gekommen** I've just arrived; **gerade erst** only just - **2.** [jetzt] at the moment; **ich bin gerade beim Saubermachen** I'm just tidying up at the moment - **3.** [in jenem Moment] just; **er wollte gerade gehen** he was just about to go - **4.** [nicht schief oder gekrümmt] straight - **5.** [besonders] exactly; **gerade deshalb** precisely for that reason; **er war nicht gerade erfreut** he wasn't exactly pleased - **6.** [ausgerechnet]: **warum gerade ich?** why me of all people?; **dass das gerade jetzt passieren musste!** why did it have to happen now of all times?; **das hat mir gerade noch gefehlt!** that's all I needed! - **7.** [knapp]: **gerade noch** only just. <> *adj* - **1.** [nicht gekrümmt] straight - **2.** [Haltung] upright.

Gerade (*pl* -n) *die* - **1.** MATH straight line - **2.** SPORT straight.

geradeaus *adv* straight ahead.

gerade⎮biegen *vt* (*unreg*) *fam* [bereinigen] to straighten out.

geradeheraus <> *adj*: **geradeheraus sein** to be frank. <> *adv* frankly.

gerade⎮stehen *vi* (*unreg*) [einstehen]: **für jn/etw geradestehen** to take responsibility for sb/sthg.

gerade stehen *vi* (*unreg*) [aufrecht stehen] to stand up straight.

geradewegs *adv* - **1.** [ohne Umweg] directly - **2.** [unmittelbar] immediately.

geradezu *adv* downright; **es wäre geradezu ein Wunder, wenn** it would be downright incredible if.

geradlinig <> *adj* straight. <> *adv* in a straight line.

Gerangel *das* - **1.** [Rauferei] scrapping - **2.** *abw* [Kampf] scramble.

Geranie (*pl* -n) *die* geranium.

gerannt *pp* ⊳ **rennen**.

gerät *präs* ⊳ **geraten**.

Gerät (*pl* -e) *das* [Apparat] device; [Werkzeug] tool; [in der Küche] utensil; **elektrisches Gerät** (electrical) appliance; **schalt das Gerät ab!** switch off the set!

geraten (*präs* gerät, *prät* geriet, *perf* ist geraten) <> *vi* - **1.** [gelangen]: **an eine unfreundliche Verkäuferin geraten** to get an unfriendly shop assistant; **in etw (A) geraten** [Schwierigkeiten, Not] to get into sthg; [Verdacht] to come under sthg; [Sturm] to be caught in sthg; **in Vergessenheit geraten** to be forgotten - **2.** [gelingen] to turn out; **das Bild ist mir gut geraten** my picture turned out well - **3.** [ähneln]: **nach jm geraten** to take after sb. <> *pp* ⊳ **raten**.

Geräteturnen *das*: **im Geräteturnen** on the apparatus.

Geratewohl *das*: **sie bewarb sich aufs Geratewohl** she applied on the off-chance; **er nahm aufs Geratewohl ein Buch aus dem Regal** he randomly selected a book from the shelf.

geräumig *adj* roomy.

Geräusch (*pl* -e) *das* noise.

geräuschempfindlich *adj* sensitive to noise.

geräuschlos <> *adj* silent. <> *adv* silently.

gerecht <> *adj* fair; [Belohnung] just; **jm/einer Sache gerecht werden** to do sb/sthg justice; **er konnte den Ansprüchen des Chefs nicht gerecht werden** he couldn't match up to the boss's expectations. <> *adv* fairly.

Gerechtigkeit *die* justice.

Gerede *das abw* - **1.** [Geschwätz] chatter - **2.** [Klatsch]: **ins Gerede kommen** to get o.s. talked about.

geregelt *adj* [Arbeit] steady; [Leben] orderly.

gereizt ◇ *adj* [Person] irritable; [Stimmung] strained. ◇ *adv* irritably.

Gericht (*pl* -e) *das* - 1. [Speise] dish - 2. [Institution] court; **vor Gericht gehen** to go to court; **vor Gericht stehen** to stand trial - 3. [Richter]: **das Gericht** the bench - 4. [Gebäude] court *UK*, courthouse *US* - 5. *(ohne pl)* [Richten] judgement; **über jn Gericht halten** to sit in judgement on sb.

gerichtlich ◇ *adj* [Verfahren, Akte] legal; [Untersuchung] judicial. ◇ *adv*: **gegen jn gerichtlich vorgehen** to start legal proceedings against sb.

Gerichts|hof *der* Court of Justice.

Gerichts|verhandlung *die* hearing.

Gerichtsvollzieher, in (*mpl* -, *fpl* -nen) *der, die* bailiff.

gerieben *pp* ▷ **reiben**.

geriet *prät* ▷ **geraten**.

gering *adj* [Gewicht, Preis, Temperatur] low; [Menge] small; [Problem, Chance] slight; [Bedeutung, Rolle] minor; [Dauer] short. ➡ **nicht im Geringsten** *adv* not in the least.

geringfügig ◇ *adj* slight, minor. ◇ *adv* slightly.

gering schätzen *vt* to have a low opinion of.

gerinnen (*prät* **gerann**, *perf* **ist geronnen**) *vi* [Milch] to curdle; [Blut] to coagulate.

Gerippe (*pl* -) *das* skeleton.

gerissen ◇ *pp* ▷ **reißen**. ◇ *adj* crafty. ◇ *adv* craftily.

geritten *pp* ▷ **reiten**.

Germane (*pl* -n) *der* Germanic man.

Germanin (*pl* -nen) *die* Germanic woman.

germanisch *adj* Germanic.

Germanistik *die (ohne pl)* German language and literature.

gern (*kompar* **lieber**, *superl* **am liebsten**), **gerne** (*kompar* **lieber**, *superl* **am liebsten**) *adv* - 1. [gen] with pleasure; **jn/etw gern haben** to like sb/sthg; **etw gern tun** to like doing sthg; **das kann ich gern machen** I'll gladly do it; **aber gern!, ja gern!** I'd love to!; **gern geschehen!** don't mention it!; **ich möchte gern wissen** I'd like to know - 2. [oft]: **der Computer stürzt gern ab** the computer tends to crash.

gerochen *pp* ▷ **riechen**.

Geröll *das (ohne pl)* [im Gebirge] scree; [im Bach] (loose) pebbles *Pl*.

geronnen *pp* ▷ **rinnen**.

Gerste *die* barley.

Gerte (*pl* -n) *die* switch.

Geruch (*pl* Gerüche) *der* smell.

geruchlos *adj* odourless.

Geruchs|sinn [gəˈrʊxzɪn] *der* sense of smell.

Gerücht (*pl* -e) *das* rumour.

gerufen *pp* ▷ **rufen**.

geruhsam ◇ *adj* leisurely. ◇ *adv*: **geruhsam durch den Garten gehen** to go for a leisurely walk round the garden.

Gerümpel *das abw* junk.

Gerundium (*pl* -dien) *das* GRAMM gerund.

gerungen *pp* ▷ **ringen**.

Gerüst (*pl* -e) *das* - 1. [beim Bauen] scaffolding - 2. [von Text] framework.

gesalzen ◇ *pp* ▷ **salzen**. ◇ *adj fam* [Preis, Miete] steep; [Beschwerde] harsh.

gesamt ◇ *adj* whole, entire; [Einkommen, Kosten] total. ◇ *adv* entirely.

Gesamtaus|gabe *die* complete edition.

gesamtdeutsch *adj* relating to both eastern and western Germany.

Gesamt|eindruck *der* overall impression.

Gesamt|schule *die* ≃ comprehensive school.

gesandt *pp* ▷ **senden**.

Gesandte, tin (*mpl* -n, *fpl* -nen) *der, die* envoy.

Gesang (*pl* Gesänge) *der* - 1. [Singen] singing - 2. [Lied, von Vogel] song.

Gesäß (*pl* -e) *das geh* buttocks *Pl*.

Geschädigte (*pl* -n) *der, die* injured party.

geschaffen *pp* ▷ **schaffen**.

Geschäft (*pl* -e) *das* - 1. [Handel] business; **die Geschäfte gehen schlecht** business is slack; **ein Geschäft abschließen** to close a deal; **du hast damit ein gutes/schlechtes Geschäft gemacht** that was a good/bad deal (for you); **mit jm Geschäfte machen** to do business with sb - 2. [Laden] shop, store; [Firma] business - 3. [Gewinn] profit - 4. [Angelegenheit] task; **sich um seine Geschäfte kümmern** to go about one's business.

geschäftig ◇ *adj* [Treiben] bustling; [Person] busy. ◇ *adv* busily.

geschäftlich ◇ *adj* - 1. [beruflich] business (*vor Subst*) - 2. [unpersönlich] businesslike. ◇ *adv* - 1. [verreisen, fliegen] on business - 2. [unpersönlich] in a businesslike manner.

Geschäfts|bedingungen *Pl* terms (and conditions).

Geschäfts|beziehungen *Pl* business contacts.

Geschäfts|frau *die* businesswoman.

Geschäfts|führer, in *der, die* - 1. [von Unternehmen] manager; [von GmbH] managing director - 2. [von Organisation] secretary.

Geschäfts|führung *die* management.

Geschäfts|lage *die* - 1. [wirtschaftlich] commercial situation - 2. [örtlich] business location.

Geschäfts|leute *Pl* businessmen.

Geschäfts|mann (*pl* -leute *ODER* -männer) *der* businessman.

Geschäfts|reise *die* business trip.

Geschäftsschluss der (ohne pl) closing time.

Geschäfts|stelle die office; [von Bank] branch.

Geschäfts|straße die high street UK, main (shopping) street US.

geschäftstüchtig adj with good business acumen.

Geschäfts|zeit die [von Laden] opening hours Pl; [von Firma] office hours Pl.

geschah prät ▷ **geschehen**.

gescheckt adj [Hund, Katze, Stoff] spotted; [Pferd - braunweiß] skewbald; [- schwarzweiß] piebald.

geschehen (präs geschieht, prät geschah, perf ist geschehen) vi - 1. [sich ereignen] to happen - 2. [widerfahren]: es kann dir nichts geschehen nothing can happen to you; ihm ist ein Unrecht geschehen he has been wronged; das geschieht dir/ihm (ganz) recht! abw that serves you/him right! - 3. [verloren sein]: es ist um seine Zukunft geschehen he has no future.

gescheit ◇ adj - 1. [klug] clever - 2. [vernünftig] sensible. ◇ adv - 1. [klug] cleverly - 2. [vernünftig] sensibly.

Geschenk (pl -e) das present.

Geschichte (pl -n) die - 1. [geschichtliche Entwicklung, Fach] history; **Geschichte machen** to make history - 2. [Erzählung, Bericht] story - 3. [Begebenheit]: es ist wieder die alte Geschichte it's the same old story; mir ist heute eine seltsame Geschichte passiert a strange thing happened to me today; du machst ja Geschichten! hum you are a one!

geschichtlich ◇ adj historical. ◇ adv historically.

Geschichts|unterricht der (ohne pl) [Schulstunden] history lessons Pl.

Geschick (pl -e) das (ohne pl) [Talent, Können] skill.

Geschicklichkeit die skilfulness.

geschickt ◇ adj - 1. [fingerfertig] skilful - 2. [raffiniert, gewandt] clever. ◇ adv - 1. [fingerfertig] skilfully - 2. [raffiniert, gewandt] cleverly.

geschieden ◇ pp ▷ **scheiden**. ◇ adj divorced.

geschieht präs ▷ **geschehen**.

geschienen pp ▷ **scheinen**.

Geschirr (pl -e) das - 1. (ohne pl) [Gefäße, Service] crockery; [benutzt] dishes Pl; ein Geschirr für sechs Personen a dinner/tea service for six people; **Geschirr spülen** ODER **abwaschen** to do the dishes, to wash up UK - 2. [für Zugtiere] harness.

Geschirrspül|maschine die dishwasher.

Geschirr|tuch das tea towel UK, dish towel US.

geschissen pp ▷ **scheißen**.

geschlafen pp ▷ **schlafen**.

Geschlecht (pl -er) das - 1. [biologische Einteilung] sex - 2. (ohne pl) [Geschlechtsteil] genitals Pl - 3. [Familie] lineage - 4. [Genus] gender.

Geschlechts|krankheit die sexually transmitted disease.

Geschlechts|organ das sexual organ.

geschlechtsreif adj sexually mature.

Geschlechtsverkehr der sexual intercourse.

geschlichen pp ▷ **schleichen**.

geschlungen pp ▷ **schlingen**.

Geschmack (pl Geschmäcke ODER Geschmäcker) der - 1. [gen] taste; **Geschmack haben** to have taste; **guten/schlechten Geschmack haben** to have good/bad taste; **an etw (D) Geschmack finden** to acquire a taste for sthg - 2. [Geschmackssinn] sense of taste.

geschmacklos ◇ adj tasteless. ◇ adv tastelessly.

Geschmack|sache = Geschmackssache.

Geschmacks|richtung die - 1. [von Nahrungsmitteln] flavour - 2. [Stilrichtung, Vorliebe] taste.

Geschmackssache, Geschmacksache die: das ist Geschmackssache that is a matter of taste.

Geschmackssinn der sense of taste.

geschmackvoll ◇ adj tasteful. ◇ adv tastefully.

geschmeidig ◇ adj [Material, Bewegung] supple. ◇ adv [gewandt] supplely.

geschmissen pp ▷ **schmeißen**.

geschmolzen pp ▷ **schmelzen**.

Geschnetzelte das (ohne pl) small, thin strips of meat cooked in a sauce.

geschnitten ◇ pp ▷ **schneiden**. ◇ adj - 1. [Fleisch] sliced - 2. [Kleid] cut; ihr Gesicht ist hübsch geschnitten she has pretty features.

geschoben pp ▷ **schieben**.

Geschöpf (pl -e) das - 1. [Lebewesen, Person] creature - 2. [Erfindung] creation.

geschoren pp ▷ **scheren**.

Geschoss (pl -e) das - 1. [Kugel] bullet; [Granate] shell - 2. [Stockwerk] floor.

geschossen pp ▷ **schießen**.

Geschrei das abw - 1. [Schreien] shouting - 2. [Gezeter] fuss.

geschrieben pp ▷ **schreiben**.

geschrien pp ▷ **schreien**.

Geschütz (pl -e) das (big) gun; **Geschütze** artillery (U).

Geschwätz das abw - 1. [Gerede] prattle - 2. [Tratsch] gossip.

geschwätzig adj abw prattling; [tratschend] gossipy.

geschweige *konj*: **geschweige denn** let alone.

geschwiegen *pp* ▷ **schweigen**.

geschwind *Süddt* ◇ *adj* quick. ◇ *adv* quickly.

Geschwindigkeit (*pl* -en) *die* speed.

Geschwister *Pl* brothers and sisters.

geschwollen ◇ *pp* ▷ **schwellen**. ◇ *adj* - 1. [Finger, Gesicht] swollen - 2. *abw* [Sätze, Ausdruck] pompous. ◇ *adv abw* [pompös] pompously.

geschwommen *pp* ▷ **schwimmen**.

geschworen *pp* ▷ **schwören**.

Geschworene (*pl* -n) *der, die* juror.

Geschwulst (*pl* Geschwülste) *die* tumour.

Geschwür (*pl* -e) *das* ulcer.

gesehen *pp* ▷ **sehen**.

Geselle (*pl* -n) *der* - 1. [Handwerker] qualified craftsman - 2. [Kerl] fellow.

gesellig *adj* - 1. [kontaktfreudig - Person] sociable; [- Tier] gregarious - 2. [anregend] convivial.

Geselligkeit *die* conviviality; **Geselligkeit brauchen** to need company.

Gesellin (*pl* -nen) *die* qualified craftswoman.

Gesellschaft (*pl* -en) *die* - 1. [Gemeinschaft] society - 2. [Anwesenheit, Umgang] company; **jm Gesellschaft leisten** to keep sb company - 3. [Fest] party; **geschlossene Gesellschaft** private party - 4. [Gruppe] group (of people) - 5. [Wirtschaftsunternehmen] company.

gesessen *pp* ▷ **sitzen**.

Gesetz (*pl* -e) *das* [staatliche Vorschrift, Regel] law.

Gesetzlbuch *das* statute book.

gesetzgebend *adj* legislative.

Gesetzlgeber *der* legislature.

Gesetzlgebung *die* legislation.

gesetzlich ◇ *adj* legal; **gesetzlicher Feiertag** public holiday; **ein gesetzlicher Anspruch** a legitimate claim. ◇ *adv* legally; **gesetzlich verankert** established in law.

gesetzmäßig *adj* - 1.: **ein gesetzmäßiger Prozess** a process governed by a natural law - 2. [Macht] legal; [Inhaber] lawful.

gesetzt *adj* sedate; **gesetzt den Fall, dass...** assuming that...

Gesicht (*pl* -er *ODER* -e) *das* face; **jm etw ins Gesicht sagen** *fig* to say sth to sb's face.

Gesichtslpunkt *der* point of view.

Gesichtslzüge *Pl* features.

Gesinnung (*pl* -en) *die* [Überzeugungen] convictions *Pl*; [Einstellung] outlook (*U*).

gesittet ◇ *adj* civilized. ◇ *adv* in a civilized manner.

gesoffen *pp* ▷ **saufen**.

gesogen *pp* ▷ **saugen**.

gesondert ◇ *adj* separate. ◇ *adv* separately.

gespannt ◇ *adj* - 1. [Stoff, Saite] taut - 2. [Person] eager; **ich bin gespannt auf seine neue Freundin** I can't wait to see his new girlfriend - 3. [Situation] tense. ◇ *adv* [erwartungsvoll, aufgeregt] eagerly.

Gespenst (*pl* -er) *das* ghost; [Bedrohung] spectre.

gespien *pp* ▷ **speien**.

gesponnen *pp* ▷ **spinnen**.

Gespött *das* mockery; **jn/sich zum Gespött der Leute machen** to make sb/o.s. a laughing stock.

Gespräch (*pl* -e) *das* - 1. [Konversation] conversation, talk; **etw ist im Gespräch** *fig* sth is under discussion - 2. [Telefonanruf] call.

gesprächig *adj* talkative.

Gesprächslpartner, in [gə'ʃprɛːçspartnɐ] *der, die*: **mein Gesprächspartner** the person I am/was talking to; **seine Gesprächspartner bei den Verhandlungen** his partners in the negotiations.

Gesprächslthema [gə'ʃprɛːçsteːma] *das* topic of conversation.

gesprochen *pp* ▷ **sprechen**.

gesprossen *pp* ▷ **sprießen**.

gesprungen *pp* ▷ **springen**.

Gespür *das* feel; **ein/kein Gespür für etw haben** to have a/no feel for sth.

Gestalt (*pl* -en) *die* - 1. [Person] figure - 2. (*ohne pl*) [Körperform] build - 3. [in Literatur] character - 4. (*ohne pl*) [Form] shape; **unser Plan nimmt Gestalt an** our plan is taking shape. ➧ **in Gestalt** *präp*: **in Gestalt einer Sache** (*G*) in the shape of sthg.

gestalten *vt* [Fest] to organize; [Schaufenster, Garten] to design. ➧ **sich gestalten** *ref* to turn out.

Gestaltung *die* [von Fest] organizing; [von Schaufenster, Garten] designing.

Geständnis (*pl* -se) *das* confession; **ein Geständnis ablegen** to make a confession.

Gestank *der* (*ohne pl*) *abw* stench.

gestatten *vt*: **jm etw gestatten** to allow sb sthg. ➧ **gestatten Sie** *interj*: **gestatten Sie?** may I?; **gestatten Sie, dass ich rauche?** do you mind if I smoke?

Geste (*pl* -n) *die* gesture.

gestehen (*prät* gestand, *perf* hat gestanden) ◇ *vt*: **ein Verbrechen/einen Mord gestehen** to confess to a crime/murder; **jm die Wahrheit gestehen** to confess the truth to sb. ◇ *vi* [aussagen] to confess.

Gestein (*pl* -e) *das* rock.

Gestell (*pl* -e) *das* stand.

gestern *adv* yesterday; **gestern Früh** first thing yesterday; **gestern Morgen/Mittag/**

Abend yesterday morning/lunchtime/evening; **von gestern sein** *fig* to be behind the times.

gestiegen *pp* ▷ **steigen**.

gestochen *pp* ▷ **stechen**.

gestohlen *pp* ▷ **stehlen**.

gestorben *pp* ▷ **sterben**.

gestoßen *pp* ▷ **stoßen**.

gestreift *adj* striped.

gestrig *adj* yesterday's; **am gestrigen Abend** yesterday evening.

gestritten *pp* ▷ **streiten**.

Gestrüpp *das* undergrowth.

gestunken *pp* ▷ **stinken**.

Gestüt (*pl* -e) *das* stud.

Gesuch (*pl* -e) *das* request.

gesund (*kompar* **gesünder** ODER **gesunder**, *superl* **gesündeste** ODER **gesundeste**) ◇ *adj* healthy; **gesunder Menschenverstand** common sense. ◇ *adv* healthily; **jn gesund schreiben** to certify sb fit; **jn gesund pflegen** to nurse sb back to health.

Gesundheit *die* health.

gesundheitlich ◇ *adj* health; **ihr gesundheitlicher Zustand** the state of her health. ◇ *adv* health-wise.

Gesundheitsamt *das* public health department.

gesundheitsschädlich *adj* damaging to one's health.

Gesundheitszustand *der* state of health.

gesungen *pp* ▷ **singen**.

gesunken *pp* ▷ **sinken**.

getan *pp* ▷ **tun**.

Getöse *das* roar.

getragen *pp* ▷ **tragen**.

Getränk (*pl* -e) *das* drink.

Getreide *das* cereals *Pl*, grain.

Getreideanbau *der* cereal growing.

getrennt ◇ *adj* separate. ◇ *adv* separately; **(von jm) getrennt leben** to be separated (from sb).

getreten *pp* ▷ **treten**.

Getriebe (*pl* -) *das* gearbox.

getrieben *pp* ▷ **treiben**.

getrogen *pp* ▷ **trügen**.

getrost *adv* without any problem.

getrunken *pp* ▷ **trinken**.

Getto (*pl* -s), **Ghetto** (*pl* -s) *das* ghetto.

Getue [gə'tu:ə] *das abw* fuss.

Getümmel *das*: **sich ins Getümmel stürzen** to throw o.s. into the fray.

Gewächs [gə'vɛks] (*pl* -e) *das* plant.

gewachsen [gə'vaksn] ◇ *pp* ▷ **wachsen**. ◇ *adj*: **jm gewachsen sein** to be a match for sb; **etw gewachsen sein** to be up to sthg.

Gewächshaus *das* greenhouse.

gewagt ◇ *adj* daring. ◇ *adv* [freizügig] daringly.

gewählt ◇ *adj* - **1.** [durch Abstimmung bestimmt] elected - **2.** [gehoben] refined. ◇ *adv* [gehoben] in a refined manner.

Gewähr *die* (*ohne pl*) guarantee; **Gewähr leisten** to guarantee. ◆ **ohne Gewähr** *adv* subject to alteration.

gewähren *vt* to give; **jm etw gewähren** to grant sb sthg; **jn gewähren lassen** to let sb do as he/she likes.

gewährleisten *vt* ▷ **Gewähr**.

Gewalt (*pl* -en) *die* - **1.** [Brutalität, Willkür] violence; **etw mit Gewalt öffnen** to force sthg open; **jn mit Gewalt zu etw zwingen** to compel sb to do sthg by (using) force; **etw mit aller Gewalt machen** to do sthg with all one's might - **2.** [Macht, Beherrschung] power; **jn/sich/etw in der Gewalt haben** to be in control of sb/o.s./sthg - **3.** [Naturgewalt] force, power.

Gewaltherrschaft *die* tyranny.

gewaltig ◇ *adj* [Kraft, Größe] enormous, huge; [Schönheit] tremendous. ◇ *adv* enormously.

gewaltsam ◇ *adj* violent; **gewaltsame Vertreibung** forcible expulsion. ◇ *adv* forcibly; [schließen] by force; **jn gewaltsam an etw hindern** to prevent sb forcibly from doing sthg.

gewalttätig ◇ *adj* violent. ◇ *adv* violently.

Gewaltverbrechen *das* violent crime.

gewandt ◇ *pp* ▷ **wenden**. ◇ *adj* - **1.** [Ausdrucksweise, Redner] skilful - **2.** [Auftreten] confident - **3.** [Bewegung] agile. ◇ *adv* - **1.** [sich ausdrücken] skilfully - **2.** [auftreten] confidently - **3.** [sich bewegen] agilely.

Gewandtheit *die* - **1.** [von Redner] skilfulness - **2.** [von Umgangsformen] confidence - **3.** [von Bewegungen] agility.

gewann *prät* ▷ **gewinnen**.

gewaschen *pp* ▷ **waschen**.

Gewässer (*pl* -) *das* stretch of water. ◆ **Gewässer** *Pl* waters.

Gewebe (*pl* -) *das* - **1.** [Stoff] fabric - **2.** [im Körper] tissue.

Gewehr (*pl* -e) *das* rifle.

Geweih (*pl* -e) *das* antlers *Pl*; [Trophäe] set of antlers.

Gewerbe (*pl* -) *das* - **1.** [Beruf] trade - **2.** (*ohne pl*) [Bereich] trade.

Gewerbeschein *der* trading licence.

gewerblich ◇ *adj* commercial. ◇ *adv* commercially.

Gewerkschaft (*pl* -en) *die* trade union *UK*, labor union *US*.

Gewerkschaft(l)er, in (*mpl* -, *fpl* -nen) *der, die* trade *UK* ODER labor *US* unionist.

Gewerkschaftsbund *der* trade union federation.

gewesen *pp* ▷ **sein**.

Gewicht (*pl* -e) *das* weight; **etw fällt ins Gewicht** *fig* sthg is of consequence.

Gewichtheben *das* weightlifting.

Gewinde (*pl* -) *das* thread.

Gewinn (*pl* -e) *der* - 1. [Profit] profit - 2. (*ohne pl*) [Nutzen] benefit - 3. [Preis] prize. ◆ **Gewinn bringend** ◇ *adj* profitable. ◇ *adv* profitably.

gewinnen (*prät* **gewann**, *perf* **hat gewonnen**) ◇ *vi* - 1. [siegen] to win - 2. (wachsen): **an etw** (*D*) **gewinnen** to gain in sthg - 3. [besser werden]: **durch etw gewinnen** to benefit from sthg. ◇ *vt* - 1. [Wettkampf, Preis] to win - 2. [Ansehen] to gain; **jn für etw gewinnen** to win sb over to sthg - 3. [Produkt] to produce.

gewinnend *adj* winning.

Gewinner, in (*mpl* -, *fpl* -nen) *der, die* winner.

Gewinnung *die* extraction.

Gewirr, Gewirre *das* [von Kabeln] tangle; [von Stimmen] confusion.

gewiss ◇ *adj* certain; **sich** (*D*) **einer Sache** (*G*) **gewiss sein** to be certain of sthg; **der Sieg ist uns gewiss** we are certain of victory. ◇ *adv* [sicherlich] certainly.

Gewissen *das* (*ohne pl*) [seelische Instanz] conscience; **gutes/schlechtes Gewissen** clear/bad conscience.

gewissenhaft ◇ *adj* conscientious. ◇ *adv* conscientiously.

Gewissens|bisse *Pl* pangs of conscience.

Gewissens|konflikt *der* moral dilemma; **in einen Gewissenskonflikt geraten** to be faced with a moral dilemma.

gewissermaßen *adv* as it were.

Gewissheit *die* (*ohne pl*) certainty; **Gewissheit erlangen** to find out for certain; **etw mit Gewissheit sagen/wissen** to say/know sthg for certain.

Gewitter (*pl* -) *das* thunderstorm.

gewittrig *adj* thundery.

gewitzt ◇ *adj* shrewd. ◇ *adv* shrewdly.

gewogen *pp* ▷ **wiegen**.

gewöhnen *vt*: **jn an jn/etw gewöhnen** to accustom sb to sb/sthg. ◆ **sich gewöhnen** *ref*: **sich an jn/etw gewöhnen** to get used to sb/sthg; **sich daran gewöhnen, etw zu tun** to get used to doing sthg.

Gewohnheit (*pl* -en) *die* habit; **jm zur Gewohnheit werden** to become a habit with sb.

gewöhnlich ◇ *adj* - 1. [normal] normal, ordinary - 2. [gewohnt] usual - 3. *abw* [primitiv] common. ◇ *adv* - 1. [normalerweise] normally, usually - 2. *abw* [primitiv] in a common way. ◆ **wie gewöhnlich** *adv* as usual.

gewohnt *adj* usual; **etw gewohnt sein** to be used to sthg.

gewöhnt *adj*: **an etw** (*A*) **gewöhnt sein** to be used to sthg.

Gewölbe (*pl* -) *das* vault.

gewonnen *pp* ▷ **gewinnen**.

geworben *pp* ▷ **werben**.

geworden *pp* ▷ **werden**.

geworfen *pp* ▷ **werfen**.

Gewühl *das* - 1. [Menschenmenge] crush - 2. [Wühlen] rummaging.

gewunden ◇ *pp* ▷ **winden**. ◇ *adj* - 1. [Weg] winding - 2. [Sätze] tortuous.

Gewürz (*pl* -e) *das* spice.

Gewürz|gurke *die* pickled gherkin.

gewusst *pp* ▷ **wissen**.

Gezeiten *Pl* tides.

Gezeter *das* *abw* scolding.

gezielt ◇ *adj* specific; **eine gezielte Frage/ Antwort** a specific question/answer. ◇ *adv*: **gezielt vorgehen** to take specific action; **jn gezielt auf etw ansprechen** to ask sb specifically about sthg.

geziert *abw* ◇ *adj* affected. ◇ *adv* affectedly.

gezogen *pp* ▷ **ziehen**.

gezwungen ◇ *pp* ▷ **zwingen**. ◇ *adj* forced. ◇ *adv* in a forced way.

gezwungenermaßen *adv*: **etw gezwungenermaßen machen** to be forced to do sthg.

ggf. *abk für* **gegebenenfalls**.

Ghetto *das* = **Getto**.

gibt *präs* ▷ **geben**.

Gicht *die* gout.

Giebel (*pl* -) *der* - 1. [auf Dach] gable - 2. [über Tor] pediment.

Gier *die* greed; **Gier nach etw** craving for sthg.

gierig ◇ *adj* greedy; **gierig nach** ODER **auf etw** (*A*) **sein** to have a craving for sthg. ◇ *adv* greedily.

gießen (*prät* **goss**, *perf* **hat gegossen**) ◇ *vt* - 1. [schütten] to pour - 2. [verschütten] to spill - 3. [Blumen] to water - 4. [Glocke, Blei] to cast; [Kerzen] to mould. ◇ *vi* [regnen]: **es gießt** it's pouring.

Gift (*pl* -e) *das* [schädliche Substanz] poison.

giftgrün *adj* lurid green.

giftig ◇ *adj* - 1. [Gift enthaltend, gesundheitsschädlich] poisonous - 2. *fam abw* [gehässig] venomous - 3. [grell] lurid. ◇ *adv* *fam abw* [gehässig] venomously.

Gift|müll *der* toxic waste.

Gigant, in (*mpl* -en, *fpl* -nen) *der, die* giant.

gilt *präs* ▷ **gelten**.

Gin [dʒɪn] *der* gin.

ging *prät* ▷ **gehen**.

Ginster (*pl* -) *der* broom *(U)*; [Stechginster] gorse *(U)*.

Gipfel (*pl* -) *der* - 1. [von Bergen] summit, peak - 2. [Höhepunkt] height - 3. [Gipfeltreffen] summit.

Gipfel|treffen *das* summit meeting.

Gips *der* - 1. [Material] plaster - 2. [Gipsverband] plaster cast.

Gips|bein *das*: **ein Gipsbein haben** to have a leg in plaster.

Gips|verband *der* plaster cast.

Giraffe (*pl* -n) *die* giraffe.

Girlande (*pl* -n) *die* garland.

Giro|konto ['ʒiːrokɔnto] *das* current account *UK*, checking account *US*.

Gischt *die* ODER *der* spray.

Gitarre (*pl* -n) *die* guitar.

Gitarrist, in (*mpl* -en, *fpl* -nen) *der, die* guitarist.

Gitter (*pl* -) *das* [aus Eisen] bars *Pl*; [gekreuzt] grille; [aus Holz] trellis; [Geländer] railings *Pl*.
hinter Gittern *adv fam* behind bars.

Glanz *der* - 1. [von Stern] brightness - 2. [von Perl] gleam - 3. [von Augen] sparkle.

glänzen *vi* - 1. [gen] to shine, to gleam; [Augen, Edelsteine] to sparkle; [Farbe] to be shiny - 2. [herausragen] to shine.

glänzend ◇ *adj* - 1. [mit Glanz] shiny; [Lack] gloss - 2. [sehr gut] brilliant. ◇ *adv* [sehr gut] brilliantly.

Glas (*pl* Gläser) *das* - 1. [Material, Trinkglas] glass; **eine Kanne aus Glas** a glass pot; **ein Glas Saft** a glass of juice; **ein Glas über den Durst trinken** *fig* to have one too many - 2. [für Marmelade] jar - 3. [Brillenglas] lens.

Glaser, in (*mpl* -, *fpl* -nen) *der, die* glazier.

glasig *adj* - 1. [Blick, Ausdruck] glazed - 2. [beim Braten] transparent.

glasklar *adj* crystal clear.

Glas|scheibe *die* pane (of glass).

Glasur (*pl* -en) *die* - 1. [für Keramik] glaze - 2. [für Speisen] icing *UK*, frosting *US*.

glatt ◇ *adj* - 1. [Oberfläche] smooth; **glatte Haare** straight hair - 2. [rutschig] slippery - 3. [reibungslos] smooth - 4. *fam* [eindeutig]: **eine glatte Lüge** a downright lie; **eine glatte Ablehnung** a flat refusal; **das ist glatter Wahnsinn!** that's utter madness! ◇ *adv* - 1.: **etw glatt streichen** to smooth sthg - 2. [verlaufen] smoothly - 3. *fam* [eindeutig]: **das haute ihn glatt um** that completely floored him.

Glätte *die* - 1. [Ebenheit] smoothness - 2. [Schlüpfrigkeit] slipperiness.

Glatteis *das (ohne pl)* black ice.

glätten *vt* [Decke] to smooth; [Falte] to smooth out. **sich glätten** *ref* [Meer] to become calm.

Glatze (*pl* -n) *die* - 1. [kahler Kopf] bald head; **eine Glatze haben** to be bald - 2. [kahle Stelle] bald patch; **eine Glatze haben** to be going bald.

Glaube *der* - 1. [Annahme] belief; **Glaube an etw** *(A)* belief in sthg; **in gutem** ODER **im guten Glauben** in good faith; **jm/einer Sache Glauben/keinen Glauben schenken** to/not to believe sb/sthg - 2. [Religion] faith.

glauben ◇ *vt* - 1. [denken] to think - 2. [für richtig halten] to believe; **jm glauben** to believe sb; **ich glaube ihm nichts mehr** I don't believe anything he says any more. ◇ *vi* - 1. [für wahr halten]: **an jn/etw glauben** to believe in sb/sthg; **jm glauben** to believe sb - 2. [gläubig sein] to believe; **dran glauben müssen** [umkommen] to bite the dust.

Glaubens|bekenntnis *das (ohne pl)* RELIG creed.

glaubhaft ◇ *adj* credible. ◇ *adv* convincingly.

gläubig ◇ *adj* - 1. [fromm] devout - 2. [vertrauensselig] trusting. ◇ *adv* - 1. [fromm] devoutly - 2. [vertrauensselig] trustingly.

Gläubige (*pl* -n) *der, die* believer.

Gläubiger, in (*mpl* -, *fpl* -nen) *der, die* creditor.

glaubwürdig ◇ *adj* credible. ◇ *adv* convincingly.

gleich ◇ *adj* - 1. [übereinstimmend] same; **den gleichen Namen haben** to have the same name; **zwei gleiche Tassen** two identical cups - 2. [egal]: **das ist mir gleich** it's all the same to me. ◇ *adv* - 1. [ebenso] equally; **gleich groß/alt sein** to be the same size/age - 2. [auf gleiche Weise] the same; **die beiden Wörter werden gleich ausgesprochen** the two words are pronounced the same - 3. [egal]: **das bleibt sich gleich, ob du nun...** it makes no difference whether you... - 4. [zeitlich] straight away, immediately; **ich komme gleich** I'm just coming; **ich komme gleich wieder** I'll be right back; **bis gleich!** see you soon! - 5. [räumlich] right; **gleich daneben** right next to it - 6. [in Fragesätzen] again; **wie hieß er doch gleich?** what's his name again? - 7. [ebensogut] just as well; **bei dem Reparaturpreis können wir doch gleich ein neues kaufen** if it's going to cost that much to repair it, we might as well buy a new one. ◇ *präp* (+ *D*) *geh* like.

gleichaltrig, gleichalterig *adj* of the same age; **gleichaltrig sein** to be the same age.

gleichberechtigt *adj* with equal rights; **gleichberechtigt sein** to have equal rights.

Gleichberechtigung *die (ohne pl)* equality, equal rights *Pl*.

gleichen (*prät* glich, *perf* hat geglichen) *vi*: **jm/einer Sache gleichen** to be like ODER resemble sb/sthg; **sich** *(D)* **gleichen** to resemble each other.

gleichfalls *adv* also, as well; **danke gleichfalls!** you too!

Gleichgewicht *das* - 1. [Balance] balance; **im Gleichgewicht** balanced; **das Gleichgewicht halten/verlieren** to keep/lose one's balance - 2. [Harmonie] equilibrium; **die Veränderungen brachten sie völlig aus dem Gleichgewicht** the changes threw her completely off balance.

gleichgültig ⟨⟩ *adj* - 1. [desinteressiert] indifferent - 2. [einerlei - Themen] trivial; **es ist gleichgültig, ob er kommt oder nicht** it's all the same whether he comes or not; **sie ist mir gleichgültig** she means nothing to me; **Politik ist ihm völlig gleichgültig** he's completely indifferent about politics. ⟨⟩ *adv* [desinteressiert] indifferently; **gleichgültig was er macht** no matter what he does.

Gleichheit *die* - 1. [Übereinstimmung] similarity - 2. [Gleichberechtigung] equality.

gleich|kommen (*perf* ist gleichgekommen) *vi* (*unreg*): **jm an etw** (*D*) **gleichkommen** to match sb for sthg.

gleich lautend *adj* identical.

gleichmäßig ⟨⟩ *adj* - 1. [Atmung, Schritte, Schichten] even - 2. [Geschwindigkeit, Rhythmus] steady - 3. [Abstände] regular. ⟨⟩ *adv* - 1. [atmen, anordnen, verteilen] evenly - 2. [sich vorwärts bewegen] steadily - 3. [wiederkehrend]: **gleichmäßig hohe Punktzahlen** consistently high scores.

Gleichnis (*pl* -se) *das* parable.

gleichschenklig, **gleichschenkelig** ['glaɪçʃɛŋk(ə)lɪç] *adj* MATH: **gleichschenkliges Dreieck** isosceles triangle.

Gleichschritt *der*: **im Gleichschritt** in step.

gleich|stellen ['glaɪçʃtɛlən] *vt* to treat equally.

Gleichstrom *der* direct current.

Gleichung (*pl* -en) *die* equation.

gleichzeitig ⟨⟩ *adj* simultaneous. ⟨⟩ *adv* at the same time.

gleich|ziehen *vi* (*unreg*): **mit jm gleichziehen** to draw level with sb, to catch up with sb.

Gleis (*pl* -e) *das* [Schienen] track; [Bahnsteig] platform.

gleiten (*prät* glitt, *perf* hat/ist geglitten) *vi* - 1. (*ist*) [sich bewegen] to glide; [rutschen] to slip - 2. (*hat*) *fam* [Arbeitnehmer] to work flexitime *UK oder* flextime *US*.

Gleit|zeit *die* flexitime *UK*, flextime *US*.

Gletscher (*pl* -) *der* glacier.

glich *prät* ⟶ **gleichen**.

Glied (*pl* -er) *das* - 1. [Gelenk] joint - 2. [Körperteil] limb - 3. [Penis] (male) member - 4. [Bindeglied - von Kette] link - 5. [Einzelteil] part; [von Satz] clause.

gliedern *vt* to organize, to structure. ◆ **sich gliedern** *ref*: **sich in etw** (*A*) **gliedern** to be divided into sthg.

Gliederung (*pl* -en) *die* - 1. [Gliedern] organization, structuring - 2. [Struktur] structure.

Gliedmaßen *Pl* limbs.

glimmen (*prät* glimmte *oder* glomm, *perf* hat geglimmt *oder* geglommen) *vi* to glow.

glimpflich ⟨⟩ *adj* [ohne Schaden]: **die Entführung nahm ein glimpfliches Ende** the kidnapping was resolved without anyone being seriously hurt. ⟨⟩ *adv* [ohne Schaden]: **glimpflich davonkommen** to get off lightly.

glitschig *adj* slippery.

glitt *prät* ⟶ **gleiten**.

glitzern *vi* [Sterne] to twinkle; [Schmuck, Augen] to sparkle; [Schnee, Tränen] to glisten; [Silber, Gold] to glitter.

global ⟨⟩ *adj* - 1. [weltumfassend] global; [Frieden] world (*vor Subst*) - 2. [vielseitig, allgemein] general. ⟨⟩ *adv* - 1. [weltumfassend] globally - 2. [vielseitig, allgemein] generally.

Globalisierung *die* globalization.

Globus (*pl* -se *oder* Globen) *der* globe.

Glocke (*pl* -n) *die* bell.

Glocken|spiel *das* - 1. [von Türmen] carillon - 2. [Musikinstrument] glockenspiel.

Glocken|turm *der* belfry, bell tower.

glomm *prät* ⟶ **glimmen**.

glorreich ⟨⟩ *adj* [Sieg, Geschichte, Ergebnis] glorious; [Einfall] brilliant. ⟨⟩ *adv* triumphantly.

Glossar (*pl* -e) *das* glossary.

glotzen *vi fam abw* to gawk, to gawp *UK*.

Glück *das* - 1. [Glücksfall] luck; **ein Glück, dass...** it's lucky that...; **Glück bringen** to bring luck, to be lucky; **Glück haben** to be lucky; **bei jm (mit etw** (*D*)**) kein Glück haben** to have no joy with sb (sthg); **er hatte mit dem Auto kein Glück** he had no luck with the car - 2. [Fortuna] fortune; **das Glück verließ ihn** *geh* fortune *oder* luck abandoned him - 3. [Segen] happiness; **das Kind war ihr ganzes Glück** the child meant everything to her. ◆ **auf gut Glück** *adv* on the off chance. ◆ **viel Glück** *interj* good luck! ◆ **zum Glück** *adv* luckily, fortunately.

glücken (*perf* ist geglückt) *vi* to be successful; **ihm glückt alles, was er in Angriff nimmt** he succeeds at everything he does.

gluckern *vi* [Wasser, Flüssigkeit] to gurgle; [Wein] to glug.

glücklich ⟨⟩ *adj* - 1. [Person, Ehe, Ende] happy - 2. [Zufall] happy, lucky; [Zeitpunkt, Reise] good - 3. [Sieger, Sieg] lucky. ⟨⟩ *adv* - 1. [verheiratet, enden] happily - 2. [letztendlich] eventually.

glücklicherweise *adv* luckily, fortunately.

Glücksbringer (*pl* -) *der* [Sache] lucky charm; [Person] lucky mascot.

Glücks|fall *der* stroke of luck.

Glücks|spiel *das* - **1.** [um Geld] game of chance - **2.** [Glückssache] lottery.

Glücks|strähne *die* lucky streak.

Glück|wunsch *der* congratulations *Pl*; **jm seine Glückwünsche aussprechen** to congratulate sb, to offer sb one's congratulations; **herzlichen Glückwunsch zum Geburtstag!** happy birthday!; **herzliche Glückwünsche!** congratulations!

Glucose = Glukose.

Glüh|birne *die* light bulb.

glühen *vi* - **1.** [brennen] to glow - **2.** *geh* [bewegt sein] to burn.

glühend <> *adj* - **1.** [brennend] glowing; [Metall, Nadel] red-hot; [Hitze] scorching - **2.** [leidenschaftlich] passionate; [Neid] deep. <> *adv* [leidenschaftlich] passionately.

Glüh|wein *der* mulled wine.

Glukose, Glucose *die* glucose.

Glut (*pl* -en) *die* - **1.** [in Feuer] embers *Pl* - **2.** *geh* [Inbrunst] ardour.

GmbH [geːɛmbeːˈhaː] (*pl* -s) (*abk für* **Gesellschaft mit beschränkter Haftung**) *die* ≃ Ltd *UK*, ≃ Inc *US*.

Gnade *die* - **1.** [Gunst] favour - **2.** [Erbarmen - menschlich] mercy; [- göttlich] grace.

gnadenlos <> *adj* merciless; [Hitze, Druck, Stress] unrelenting. <> *adv* mercilessly; [heiß] mercilessly, unrelentingly.

gnädig <> *adj* - **1.** [wohlmeinend] kind - **2.** [nachsichtig] lenient - **3.** [barmherzig] merciful. <> *adv* - **1.** [wohlmeinend] kindly - **2.** [nachsichtig] leniently. ● **gnädige Frau** *interj* Madam!

Gold *das* gold; **eine Uhr aus Gold** a gold watch.

Gold|barren *der* gold bar ODER ingot.

golden <> *adj* - **1.** [aus Gold] gold - **2.** [goldfarben] golden - **3.** [großartig - Jahre, Zeit] golden; [- Freiheit, Moment] glorious. <> *adv* [glänzen] like gold.

Gold|fisch *der* goldfish.

goldgelb *adj* & *adv* golden yellow.

Gold|medaille *die* gold medal.

Gold|schmied, in *der, die* goldsmith.

Golf (*pl* -e) <> *der* gulf. <> *das* golf.

Golf|platz *der* golf course.

Golf|strom *der* Gulf Stream.

gönnen *vt*: **jm etw gönnen** not to begrudge sb sthg; **sich** (*D*) **etw gönnen** to allow o.s. sthg.

Gönner (*pl* -) *der* patron.

gönnerhaft *abw* <> *adj* patronizing. <> *adv* patronizingly.

Gönnerin (*pl* -nen) *die* patron, patroness.

Gorilla (*pl* -s) *der* *eigtl* & *fig* gorilla.

goss *prät* ▷ **gießen**.

Gosse (*pl* -n) *die* gutter.

Gotik *die* (*ohne pl*) [Stil] Gothic (style); [Epoche] Gothic period.

gotisch *adj* Gothic.

Gott (*pl* Götter) *der* - **1.** [christlich] God; **um Gottes Willen!** [Schrecken ausdrückend] oh my God!; [flehend] for heaven's sake! - **2.** [Gottheit] god. ● **Gott sei Dank** *adv* thank goodness. ● **grüß Gott** *interj* Süddt & Österr hello!

Gottes|dienst *der* service; **zum Gottesdienst gehen** to go to church.

Göttin (*pl* -nen) *die* goddess.

göttlich <> *adj* *eigtl* & *fig* divine. <> *adv* [wunderbar] divinely.

gottlos <> *adj* - **1.** [respektlos, gottvergessen] ungodly - **2.** [ungläubig] godless. <> *adv* [respektlos, gottvergessen] in an ungodly manner.

Gouverneur, in [guvɛrˈnøːɐ, rɪn] (*mpl* -e, *fpl* -nen) *der, die* governor.

GPS [geːpeːˈʔɛs] (*abk für* **Grüne Partei der Schweiz**) *die* Swiss Green Party.

Grab (*pl* Gräber) *das* grave.

graben (*präs* gräbt, *prät* grub, *perf* hat gegraben) *vt* & *vi* to dig.

Graben (*pl* Gräben) *der* ditch; [um eine Festung] moat; [Schützengraben] trench.

Grab|stein *der* gravestone, tombstone.

gräbt *präs* ▷ **graben**.

Grabung (*pl* -en) *die* excavation.

Grad (*pl* -e) *der* - **1.** [gen] degree; **es hängt in hohem Grad davon ab, ob...** it depends to a large extent on whether...; **die Temperatur beträgt 25 Grad** the temperature is 25 degrees; **in hohem Grad verschmutzt** highly polluted - **2.** MIL rank.

gradweise *adv* gradually.

Graf (*pl* -en) *der* count.

Grafik (*pl* -en), **Graphik** (*pl* -en) *die* - **1.** [Kunst] graphic art; [Technik] graphics (*U*) - **2.** [Kunstwerk] graphic artwork - **3.** [Schema] diagram.

Gräfin (*pl* -nen) *die* countess.

grafisch, graphisch <> *adj* - **1.** [die Kunst betreffend] graphic - **2.** [schematisch] diagrammatic. <> *adv* - **1.** [künstlerisch] graphically - **2.** [schematisch] diagrammatically.

Grafschaft (*pl* -en) *die* - **1.** [von Graf] count's lands *Pl* - **2.** [Verwaltungsbezirk] county.

Gramm (*pl* -e ODER -) *das* gram; **500 Gramm** 500 grams.

Grammatik (*pl* -en) *die* grammar.

grammatikalisch, grammatisch <> *adj* grammatical. <> *adv* grammatically.

Granate (*pl* -n) *die* shell; [Handgranate] grenade.

grandios <> *adj* superb. <> *adv* superbly.

Granit *der* granite.

Grapefruit [ˈgreːpfruːt] (*pl* -s) *die* grapefruit.

Graphik = Grafik.

graphisch = grafisch.

Gras (*pl* Gräser) *das* grass; **wir sollten warten bis Gras über die Sache gewachsen ist** we should wait until the dust has settled.

grasen *vi* to graze; **Kühe grasen lassen** to graze cattle.

Gras|halm *der* blade of grass.

grassieren *vi* [Krankheit, Pest] to rage; [Mode] to be all the rage.

grässlich ⟨⟩ *adj* terrible. ⟨⟩ *adv* terribly.

Grat (*pl* -e) *der* ridge.

Gräte (*pl* -n) *die* (fish) bone.

gratis *adj* & *adv* free (of charge).

Grätsche (*pl* -n) *die*: **eine Grätsche über etw (A) machen** to hurdle sthg; **in der Grätsche stehen** to stand with one's legs astride.

gratulieren *vi* to offer one's congratulations; **jm (zu etw) gratulieren** to congratulate sb (on sthg); **jm zum Geburtstag gratulieren** to wish sb a happy birthday.

grau *adj* grey; **grau meliert** [Haar] greying; [Wolle, Stoff] flecked with grey.

Grau *das* - 1. [graue Farbe] grey - 2. [Tristheit] greyness.

Grau|brot *das* bread made from mixed wholemeal, rye and wheat flour.

Graubünden *nt* Graubünden.

grauhaarig *adj* grey-haired.

grausam ⟨⟩ *adj* - 1. [brutal] cruel - 2. [fürchterlich, schlimm] terrible. ⟨⟩ *adv* - 1. [brutal] cruelly - 2. [fürchterlich, äußerst] terribly.

Grausamkeit (*pl* -en) *die* - 1. (*ohne pl*) [grausames Wesen] cruelty - 2. [grausame Tat] atrocity.

grausig ⟨⟩ *adj* terrible. ⟨⟩ *adv* terribly.

Gravur [gra'vuːɐ̯] (*pl* -en) *die* engraving.

Graz *nt* Graz.

Grazie (*pl* -n) *die* grace; **mit Grazie** gracefully.
➤ **Grazien** *Pl* [Mythologie] Graces.

graziös ⟨⟩ *adj* graceful. ⟨⟩ *adv* gracefully.

greifbar ⟨⟩ *adj* - 1. [in Reichweite] to hand, handy - 2. [parat] available - 3. [absehbar] tangible. ⟨⟩ *adv* (*sehr*): **greifbar nahe** within reach.

greifen (*prät* griff, *perf* hat gegriffen) ⟨⟩ *vt* - 1. [fassen] to take hold of - 2. [erwischen] to catch - 3. [Akkord] to play. ⟨⟩ *vi* - 1. [fassen]: **zur Flasche/Zigarette greifen** *fig* to reach for the bottle/cigarettes; **nach etw greifen** to reach for sthg; [Macht] to strive for sthg - 2. [langen] to reach; **in etw (A) greifen** to reach into sthg - 3. [Halt finden] to grip; [Zahnrad] to catch - 4. [funktionieren] to work; **um sich greifen** to spread; **die Zahl ist zu hoch/niedrig gegriffen** the number is an overestimate/underestimate; **ihre Erwartungen sind zu hoch/niedrig gegriffen** she has set her sights too high/low.

Greif|vogel *der* bird of prey.

Greis, in (*mpl* -e, *fpl* -nen) *der, die* old man (old woman *die*).

grell ⟨⟩ *adj* - 1. [Licht, Sonne, Lampe] glaring; [Farbe, Muster] garish - 2. [Geräusch] shrill. ⟨⟩ *adv* - 1. [scheinen, leuchten] glaringly; [bunt, gefärbt] garishly - 2. [klingen, rufen] shrilly.

Grenz|bereich *der* - 1. (*ohne pl*) [von Ländern] border area - 2. [Begrenzung] limits *Pl*.

Grenze (*pl* -n) *die* - 1. [Staatsgrenze] border - 2. [Gebietsgrenze] boundary - 3. [Trennlinie] dividing line, boundary - 4. [Beschränkung] limit.
➤ **grüne Grenze** *die*: **über die grüne Grenze gehen** to cross the border at a point in the countryside where there is no border control.

grenzen *vi*: **an etw (A) grenzen** [Gebiet, Land] to border sthg; [Betrug, Tollkühnheit] to border on sthg; **aneinander grenzen** to have a common border.

grenzenlos ⟨⟩ *adj* [Landschaft, Vertrauen, Liebe] boundless; [Verlegenheit, Sorge, Ekel] extreme. ⟨⟩ *adv* [weit, lieben, begeistert] boundlessly; [verlegen, erstaunt, traurig] extremely.

Grenz|fall *der* borderline case.

Grenz|kontrolle *die* border check.

Grenz|posten *der* border guard.

Grenz|schutz *der* (*ohne pl*) border police; [in Deutschland] ➤ **Bundesgrenzschutz**.

Grenzüber|gang *der* [Grenzkontrollstelle] border crossing.

grenzüberschreitend ⟨⟩ *adj* cross-border. ⟨⟩ *adv* at a cross-border level.

Grenzverkehr *der* cross-border traffic.

Grenz|wert *der* limit.

Grieche (*pl* -n) *der* Greek.

Griechenland *nt* Greece.

Griechin (*pl* -nen) *die* Greek.

griechisch *adj* Greek.

griesgrämig ⟨⟩ *adj* grumpy. ⟨⟩ *adv* grumpily.

Grieß *der* semolina.

griff *prät* ➤ **greifen**.

Griff (*pl* -e) *der* - 1. [Greifen] grip; [von Ringer] hold; **beim Griff in die Tasche** on reaching into the pocket; **der Griff nach der Flasche** reaching for the bottle; **etw mit einem Griff tun** to do sthg in next to no time; **etw im Griff haben/bekommen** *fig* to be/get on top of sthg; **jn in den Griff bekommen** *ODER* **kriegen** *fig* to gain control of sb - 2. [Teil, Henkel] handle.

griffbereit *adj* & *adv* ready to hand.

griffig *adj* - 1. [handlich] easy to use - 2. [gut greifend] with a good grip.

Grill (*pl* -s) *der* grill.

Grille (*pl* -n) *die* - 1. [Insekt] cricket - 2. [verrückte Idee] whim.

grillen ⟨⟩ *vt* to grill. ⟨⟩ *vi* to have a barbecue.

Grimasse (*pl* -n) *die* grimace.

grimmig <> *adj* - **1.** [Gesicht, Ausdruck] grim; [Feind] fierce - **2.** [Kälte, Hunger] terrible. <> *adv* (lachen) grimly.

grinsen *vi* to grin.

Grippe (*pl* -n) *die* flu.

Grips *der* (*ohne pl*) *fam* brains *Pl*.

grob (*kompar* gröber, *superl* gröbste) <> *adj* - **1.** [Sand, Salz, Züge] coarse - **2.** [Leinen, Haut, Papier, Übersicht, Skizze] rough - **3.** [unhöflich] crude - **4.** [schlimm] serious; **aus dem Gröbsten heraus sein** [Kind] to be old enough to look after oneself. <> *adv* - **1.** [mahlen, hacken] coarsely - **2.** [planen, schätzen] roughly - **3.** [schwer wiegend]: **grob fahrlässig handeln** to be grossly negligent - **4.** [unhöflich] crudely.

Grobheit (*pl* -en) *die* - **1.** [grobe Wesensart] crudeness - **2.** [Äußerung] crude remark.

grölen *abw vi & vt* to bawl.

Grönland *nt* Greenland.

Groschen (*pl* -) *der* - **1.** [10 deutsche Pfennig] ten-pfennig coin; **bei ihm ist der Groschen gefallen** *fam fig* the penny dropped *UK*, he got it - **2.** [österreichische Münze] groschen.

groß (*kompar* größer, *superl* größte) <> *adj* - **1.** [räumlich] big, large; [Person] tall; **sie ist 1,80 groß** she's 1.80 m (tall) - **2.** [Angebot] wide; **eine große Vielfalt** a wide variety - **3.** [intensiv] great; **eine große Enttäuschung** a great disappointment; **sich große Mühe geben** to try hard - **4.** [älter] big; **mein großer Bruder** my big brother - **5.** [erwachsen] grown-up - **6.** [Buchstabe] capital - **7.** [bedeutend] great; **ein großer Dichter** a great poet; **heute kommt meine große Stunde** it's my big moment today. <> *adv* (*kompar* größer; *superl* am größten) - **1.** [räumlich]: **ein groß angelegtes Projekt** a large-scale project - **2.** [sehr] a lot; **wir haben dann nicht mehr groß gearbeitet** we didn't do a lot of work afterwards; **groß und breit** *fam* at great length - **3.** [im großen Stil] in style; **der Sänger ist groß herausgekommen** the singer became a big success - **4.** [erstaunt] great; **jn groß ansehen** to stare at sb wide-eyed - **5.** [Buchstabe]: **es wird groß geschrieben** it's written with a capital letter. ◆ **Groß und Klein** *pron*: **ein Buch für Groß und Klein** a book for young and old. ◆ **im Großen und Ganzen** *pron*: **im Großen und Ganzen** on the whole, by and large.

großartig <> *adj* - **1.** [gut] marvellous - **2.** [angeberisch] showy. <> *adv* - **1.** [gut] marvellously - **2.** [angeberisch] showily.

Großaufnahme *die* close-up.

Großbritannien *nt* Great Britain.

Großbuchstabe *der* capital (letter).

Größe (*pl* -n) *die* - **1.** [von Gegenständen, Baby, Kleidern] size - **2.** [von Personen] height - **3.** [Wichtigkeit] greatness - **4.** [Person] leading figure.

großenteils *adv* largely.

Größenwahn *der abw* megalomania.

größenwahnsinnig *adj* megalomaniac.

größer *adj* bigger, larger; **eine größere Summe** quite a large sum; **ohne größere Schwierigkeiten** without any great difficulty.

Großfamilie *die* extended family.

Großhandel *der* wholesale trade; **etw im Großhandel beziehen** to get sthg wholesale.

Großhändler, in *der, die* wholesaler.

Großmacht *die* great power.

Großmaul *das fam abw* big mouth.

großmütig <> *adj* generous. <> *adv* generously.

Großmutter *die* grandmother.

Großraum (*pl* -räume) *der* area; **im Großraum Berlin** in the Greater Berlin area.

Großrechner *der EDV* mainframe.

großschreiben *vt* (*unreg*) [mit großem Anfangsbuchstaben] to write with a capital letter, to capitalize.

Großschreibung *die* capitalization.

großspurig *abw* <> *adj* pretentious. <> *adv* pretentiously.

Großstadt *die* city (*vor Subst*).

größtenteils *adv* for the most part.

größtmöglich *adj* greatest possible.

großtun *vi* (*unreg*) *abw* to boast.

Großvater *der* grandfather.

Großverdiener, in (*mpl* **Großverdiener,** *fpl* -nen) *der, die* high earner.

großziehen *vt* (*unreg*) [Kind] to bring up; [Tier] to rear.

großzügig <> *adj* - **1.** [Person, Geste] generous - **2.** [Raum] spacious. <> *adv* - **1.** [freigebig, großmütig] generously - **2.** [weiträumig] spaciously.

Grotte (*pl* -n) *die* grotto.

grub *prät* ▷ **graben.**

Grübchen (*pl* -) *das* dimple.

Grube (*pl* -n) *die* pit.

grübeln *vi* to ponder.

Grübeln *das*: **ins Grübeln kommen** to start to ponder.

Gruft (*pl* Grüfte) *die* crypt.

grün <> *adj* [farbig, unreif, ökologisch] green. <> *adv* [ökologisch]: **grün wählen** to vote Green.

Grün (*pl* - ODER -s) *das* - **1.** green - **2.** (*ohne pl*) [Pflanzen] greenery. ◆ **bei Grün** *adv* on green.

Grünanlage *die* park.

Grund (*pl* Gründe) *der* - **1.** [Ursache] reason - **2.** (*ohne pl*) [Boden] ground; [von Meer, Bach, Glas] bottom; **auf Grund laufen** to run aground; **einer Sache (D) auf den Grund gehen** to try to get to the bottom of sthg; **jn in Grund und Boden reden** not to let sb get a word in edgeways. ➤ **im Grunde** *adv* basically. ➤ **von Grund auf** *adv* thoroughly. ➤ **zu Grunde** *adv* = zugrunde.

Grund|ausstattung *die* basic equipment.

Grund|bedürfnis *das* basic need.

Grund|begriff *der* basic principle.

Grund|besitz *der* land.

gründen <> *vt* [Partei, Unternehmen] to found; [Familie] to start; [Stiftung] to set up. <> *vi* [basieren auf]: **auf etw (D) gründen** to be based on sthg. ➤ **sich gründen** *ref*: **sich auf etw (A) gründen** to be based on sthg.

Gründer, in (*mpl* -, *fpl* -nen) *der, die* founder.

Grund|gebühr *die* standing charge.

Grund|gedanke *der* basic idea.

Grund|gesetz *das* Basic Law.

Grund|kurs *der* basic course.

Grund|lage *die* basis.

grundlegend <> *adj* fundamental. <> *adv* fundamentally.

gründlich <> *adj* thorough. <> *adv* thoroughly; **sich gründlich blamieren** to make a complete fool of o.s.

Grund|lohn *der* basic wage.

grundlos <> *adj* unfounded. <> *adv* without reason; **grundlos lachen** to laugh for no reason.

Grundnahrungs|mittel *das* basic foodstuff.

Gründonnerstag *der* Maundy Thursday.

Grund|recht *das* basic right.

Grund|riss (*pl* -se) *der* [von Gebäude] ground plan; [Schema] outline.

Grund|satz *der* principle.

grundsätzlich <> *adj* - 1. [wichtig] fundamental - 2. [allgemein] basic - 3. [bedingungslos] on principle. <> *adv* - 1. [allgemein] basically - 2. [bedingungslos] on principle - 3. [grundlegend] fundamentally; **sich grundsätzlich äußern** to state one's principles.

Grund|schule *die* primary school *UK*, elementary school *US* (for pupils aged 6 to 10).

Grund|stück *das* plot of land.

Gründung (*pl* -en) *die* [von Partei, Verein] foundation (*sg*); [von Familie] starting (*U*); [von Stiftung] setting up (*U*).

grundverschieden *adj* completely different.

Grund|wasser *das* ground water.

Grüne (*pl* -n) *das* - 1. [Farbe] green - 2. [Natur]: **im Grünen/ins Grüne** in/into the country.

Grünen *Pl*: **die Grünen** the Greens.

Grüne Punkt *der* (ohne *pl*) symbol on product packaging indicating that it is suitable for recycling.

Grün|fläche *die* green area.

Grün|kohl *der* kale.

grünlich <> *adj* greenish. <> *adv* with a greenish colour.

grunzen *vi* to grunt.

Gruppe (*pl* -n) *die* group.

Gruppen|arbeit *die* [im Unterricht] group work.

Gruppen|reise *die* group tour.

gruppieren *vt* to arrange. ➤ **sich gruppieren** *ref* to form a group/groups.

gruselig *adj* [von Film] spine-chilling; [von Erscheinung] eerie.

gruseln *vt*: **es gruselt jm** *ODER* **jn vor jm/etw** sb/sthg makes sb's flesh creep. ➤ **sich gruseln** *ref* to be frightened; **sich vor jm/etw gruseln** sb/sthg makes one's flesh creep.

Gruß (*pl* Grüße) *der* greeting; **jm Grüße von jm bestellen** *ODER* **ausrichten** to give sb sb's regards *ODER* best wishes; **herzliche Grüße!** greetings!; **viele Grüße!** best wishes!; **mit freundlichen Grüßen** yours sincerely.

grüßen <> *vt* - 1. [begrüßen] to greet - 2. [Gruß senden]: **jn von jm grüßen** to give sb sb's regards *ODER* best wishes. <> *vi* [begrüßen] to say hello. ➤ **grüß dich** *interj* hello! ➤ **grüß Gott** *interj Süddt* hello!

Grütze (*pl* -n) *die* gruel; **rote Grütze** jelly-like dessert made of red berries, fruit juice and sugar.

gucken *fam* <> *vi* to look. <> *vt* [Fotos, Zeitschriften] to look at; [Fernsehen] to watch.

Guillotine [gijo'ti:nə] (*pl* -n) *die* guillotine.

Gulasch (*pl* -e *ODER* -s) *das* & *der* goulash.

Gulasch|kanone *die* large tureen used to serve hot food at outdoor public events.

Gulden (*pl* -) *der* guilder.

Gully (*pl* -s) *der* drain.

gültig *adj* valid; **nicht mehr gültig sein** [Kreditkarte, Reisepass] to be no longer valid.

Gültigkeit *die* validity; **seine Gültigkeit verlieren** [Kreditkarte, Reisepass] to become invalid.

Gummi (*pl* -s) <> *das* & *der* - 1. [Material] rubber - 2. *fam* [Band] rubber band. <> *der* rubber.

Gummi|band (*pl* -bänder) *das* (piece of) elastic.

Gummi|knüppel *der* rubber truncheon.

Gummi|stiefel *der* rubber boot, wellington *UK*.

Gunst *die* favour; **die Gunst der Stunde nutzen** to seize the moment; siehe auch **zugunsten**.

günstig <> *adj* - 1. [Gelegenheit, Umstände] favourable - 2. [Preis] good. <> *adv* - 1. [beeinflussen] favourably - 2. [kaufen] for a good price.

Gurgel (*pl* -n) *die* throat.

gurgeln *vi* to gurgle; [mit Mundwasser] to gargle.

Gurke (*pl* -n) *die* - **1.** [Salatgurke] cucumber - **2.** [Gewürzgurke] gherkin.

Gurt (*pl* -e) *der* - **1.** [Sicherheitsgurt] belt - **2.** [Band] strap.

Gürtel (*pl* -) *der* belt.

Gürtel|linie *die*: **unter der Gürtellinie** [unfair] below the belt; [anzüglich] near the bone.

Gurtpflicht *die* obligatory use of seat belts.

Guss (*pl* Güsse) *der* - **1.** [Gießen] casting (U) - **2.** [Wasserstrahl] stream - **3.** [Regen] downpour - **4.** [Zuckerguss] icing (U) UK, frosting (U) US.

Gusseisen *das* cast iron.

gut (*kompar* besser, *superl* beste) ◇ *adj* [gen] good; **in etw gut sein** [fähig] to be good at sthg; **für etw gut sein** [günstig] to be good for sthg; **das Mittel ist gut gegen Magendrücken** this medicine is good for stomach ache; **du hast es gut!** you've got it easy!; **etw gut sein lassen** *fig* to leave ODER drop sthg. ◇ *adv* (*kompar* besser, *superl* am besten) - **1.** [gen] well; **gut kochen können** to be able to cook well, to be a good cook; **gut befreundet sein mit jm** to be good friends with sb - **2.** [schön, erfreulich]: **gut schmecken/aussehen** to taste/look good; **gut gelaunt sein** to be in a good mood; **ihr ist nicht gut** she's not well - **3.** [leicht] easily; **du hast gut reden!** it's easy for you to talk!; **so gut wie** as good as.

Gut (*pl* Güter) *das* - **1.** [Bauernhof] estate - **2.** [Ware] goods *Pl*.

Gutachten (*pl* -) *das* report.

Gutachter, in (*mpl* -, *fpl* -nen) *der, die* expert.

gutartig *adj* - **1.** [Hund, Charakter] good-natured - **2.** [Geschwulst, Tumor] benign.

gutbürgerlich *adj*: **gutbürgerliche Küche** traditional cooking.

Gute *das* good. ◆ **alles Gute** *interj* all the best! ◆ **im Guten** *adv* [versuchen] amicably; [sagen] nicely.

Güte *die* - **1.** [Milde] goodness; **(ach) du meine** ODER **liebe Güte!** (oh) my goodness! - **2.** [Qualität] quality.

Güte|klasse *die* grade.

Güter|bahnhof *der* freight depot.

Güter|verkehr *der* freight traffic.

Güter|zug *der* freight train.

Güte|zeichen *das* quality mark.

gut gehen (*perf* ist gut gegangen) *vi* (*unreg*) - **1.** [gesundheitlich]: **es geht ihr gut** she's doing well - **2.** [glücken] to turn out well - **3.** [Geschäft] to do well - **4.** [Ware] to go well.

gut gelaunt *adj* cheerful.

gut gemeint *adj* well-meant.

gutgläubig *adj* trusting.

Guthaben (*pl* -) *das* (credit) balance.

gütig ◇ *adj* kind. ◇ *adv* kindly.

gütlich *adj* amicable.

gutmütig *adj* good-natured.

Gutmütigkeit *die* (ohne pl) good nature.

Gut|schein *der* voucher.

gut|schreiben *vt* (*unreg*): **jm etw gutschreiben** to credit sthg to sb.

Gut|schrift *die* - **1.** [Handlung] crediting - **2.** [Quittung] credit slip.

gut tun *vi* (*unreg*): **ein heißes Bad wird dir gut tun** a hot bath will do you good.

gutwillig *adj* willing.

Gymnasial|lehrer, in *der, die* ≃ grammar-school teacher UK.

Gymnasiast, in (*mpl* -en, *fpl* -nen) *der, die* ≃ grammar-school pupil UK.

Gymnasium (*pl* Gymnasien) *das* ≃ grammar school UK, selective secondary school attended by 10- to 19-year-olds; **altsprachliches/neusprachliches Gymnasium** "Gymnasium" with focus on classical/modern languages.

Gymnastik *die* keep-fit.

Gynäkologe (*pl* -n) *der* gynaecologist.

Gynäkologin (*pl* -nen) *die* gynaecologist.

h (*pl* - ODER -s), **H** (*pl* - ODER -s) [haː] *das* - **1.** [Buchstabe] h, H - **2.** MUS B. ◆ **h** (*abk für* Stunde, Uhr) h, hr.

ha¹ (*abk für* Hektar) ha.

ha² *interj* ha!

Haar (*pl* -e) *das*: **graues Haar** ODER **graue Haare haben** to have grey hair; **ein paar graue Haare haben** to have a few grey hairs; **sich (D) die Haare schneiden lassen** to have one's hair cut; **jm aufs Haar gleichen** to be the spitting image of sb; **etw aufs Haar gleichen** to be an exact copy of sthg; **der Hund hat ihm kein Haar gekrümmt** the dog didn't touch a hair on his head; **sich in die Haare kriegen** ODER **geraten** *fam* to start squabbling.

Haar|bürste *die* hairbrush.

haaren *vi* to moult.

Haaresbreite *die*: **um Haaresbreite** by a hair's breadth; **um Haaresbreite hätte es einen Unfall gegeben** there was very nearly an accident.

Haar|festiger *der* setting lotion.

haargenau ◇ *adj* exact. ◇ *adv* exactly.

haarig *adj* hairy.

haarklein *adv* in minute detail.

haarscharf ◇ *adj* precise; [Beobachtung] very close. ◇ *adv* - **1.** [knapp]: **das Auto fuhr**

haarscharf an ihr vorbei the car only just missed her - **2.** [sehr genau] precisely; [beobachten] very closely.

Haar|schnitt der haircut.

Haar|spange die hairclip.

Haar|spray das & der hairspray.

haarsträubend adj - **1.** [empörend] shocking - **2.** [grauenhaft] horrifying.

Haarwasch|mittel das shampoo.

haben (präs **hat**, prät **hatte**, perf **hat gehabt**) ◇ aux to have; **sie hat gegessen** she has eaten. ◇ vt - **1.** [besitzen] to have; **ich hätte gerne** [im Restaurant, Geschäft] I'd like; **er hat zwei kleine Schwestern** he's got ODER he has two younger sisters; **das Buch hat 600 Seiten** the book has (got) 600 pages; **sie hat blaue Augen** she has (got) blue eyes - **2.** [zur Verfügung haben] to have; **hast du Geld dabei?** have you got any money on you?; **das Haus ist noch zu haben** the house is still available - **3.** [erleben] to have; **Angst/Durst/Hunger haben** to be afraid/thirsty/hungry; **sie hatte es schwer im Leben** she's had a hard life - **4.** [an etw leiden] to have; **Kopfschmerzen haben** to have a headache; **was hast du denn?** what's wrong? - **5.** [mit Zeitangaben]: **wie spät haben wir (es)?** fam what's the time?; **wir haben (jetzt) zehn Uhr** fam it's ten o'clock; **wir haben heute Dienstag** fam it's Tuesday today; **und damit hat es sich!** and that's that!; **was hast du davon?** what do you get out of it?; **der hat sie wohl nicht mehr alle!** fam he's not all there!; **haben Sie etwas dagegen, wenn ...?** do ODER would you mind if ...?; **sie scheint was gegen dich zu haben** she seems to have something against you; **sie haben hier nichts zu suchen!** they've no business here; **ich habe zu tun** I'm busy. ◆ **sich haben** ref fam to make a fuss.

Habenichts (pl -e) der abw pauper.

Habseligkeiten Pl belongings.

habsüchtig adj greedy.

Hack|braten der meat loaf.

Hacke (pl -n) die - **1.** [Ferse, Absatz] heel - **2.** [Gartengerät] hoe.

hacken ['hakən] ◇ vt - **1.** [zerkleinern] to chop - **2.** [schlagen] to hack - **3.** [bearbeiten] to hoe. ◇ vi [mit dem Schnabel]: **nach jm/etw hacken** to peck at sb/sthg.

Hackfleisch das mince UK, mincemeat US.

Hafen (pl **Häfen**) der [klein] harbour; [groß] port.

Hafen|arbeiter, in der, die docker, dock worker.

Hafen|stadt die port.

Hafer der (ohne pl) oats Pl.

Hafer|flocken Pl rolled oats.

Haft die [Gewahrsam] custody; [Strafe] imprisonment.

Haft|anstalt die prison.

haftbar adj: **für etw haftbar sein** to be liable for sthg.

Haft|befehl der warrant.

haften vi - **1.** [kleben] to stick - **2.** [bürgen]: **für jn haften** to be responsible for sb.

Häftling (pl -e) der prisoner.

Haftpflicht|versicherung die third party insurance.

Haft|strafe die prison sentence.

Haftung die [Verantwortung] liability; **Gesellschaft mit beschränkter Haftung** limited company.

Hagebutte (pl -n) die - **1.** [Frucht] rose hip - **2.** [Strauch] dog rose.

Hagel der hail.

Hagel|korn das hailstone.

hageln ◇ vi: **es hagelt** it is hailing. ◇ vt: **es hagelte Beschwerden** fig there was a stream of complaints.

Hahn (pl **Hähne**) der - **1.** [Vogel] cock - **2.** [an der Leitung] tap UK, faucet US.

Hähnchen (pl -) das - **1.** [Brathähnchen] chicken - **2.** [kleiner Hahn] cockerel.

Hai (pl -e) der shark.

Hai|fisch der shark.

häkeln vt & vi to crochet.

Häkel|nadel die crochet hook.

Haken (pl -) der - **1.** [Aufhänger] hook - **2.** [Zeichen] tick - **3.** [Problem] catch, snag.

halb ◇ adj (ohne Kompar) half; **ein halber Liter** half a litre; **der halbe Tag** half the day; **halb und halb** fam half and half; **es ist halb drei** it is half past two; **keine halben Sachen machen** not to do things by halves; **halb Düsseldorf** half of Düsseldorf. ◇ adv half; **ihre Haare sind halb lang** she has shoulder-length hair.

Halb|bruder der half-brother.

Halbdunkel das semi-darkness.

Halbe (pl -n) das & der half litre; **ein Halbes** [Bier] a half litre.

Halb|finale das semi-final.

halbherzig ◇ adj half-hearted. ◇ adv half-heartedly.

halbieren vt - **1.** [Kuchen, Apfel] to cut in half, to halve - **2.** [Linie] to bisect - **3.** [Geldsumme, Zahl] to halve. ◆ **sich halbieren** ref to halve.

Halb|insel die peninsula.

Halb|jahr das six months Pl; [Schule] ≈ term.

halbjährlich ◇ adj six-monthly, half-yearly. ◇ adv every six months, twice a year.

Halb|kreis der semi-circle.

Halb|kugel die hemisphere.

halblaut ◇ adj low. ◇ adv in a low voice.

halbmast adv: **auf halbmast** at half-mast.

Halbmond der [Mondsichel] half-moon.

halb offen *adj* half-open.

Halbpension [ˈhalppaŋzjoːn] *die* half board.

Halb|schuh *der* shoe.

Halbtags|arbeit *die* part-time work.

Halbton (*pl* -töne) *der* MUS semitone.

halbtrocken *adj* medium-dry.

halb voll *adj* half-full.

Halb|wahrheit *die* half-truth.

Halb|waise *die* child with only one living parent.

halbwegs *adv* reasonably, fairly.

Halb|zeit *die* - 1. [Hälfte] half - 2. [Pause] half-time.

Halde (*pl* -n) *die* [Kohlenhalde] slag heap.

half *prät* ⊳ **helfen**.

Hälfte (*pl* -n) *die* half; **die Hälfte der Angestellten** (of) the employees. ➟ **zur Hälfte** *adv*: **zur Hälfte gefüllt** half-full; **etw zur Hälfte tun** to half-do sthg; **der Erlös ging zur Hälfte ans Rote Kreuz** half the proceeds went to the Red Cross.

Halfter (*pl* -) ◇ *das* & *der* [für Pferde] halter. ◇ *das* [für Pistole] holster.

Halle (*pl* -n) *die* [gen] hall; [von Hotel] lobby; [zum Reiten] arena; [zum Turnen] gym; [zum Tennisspielen] covered court.

hallen *vi* to resound, to ring out.

Hallen|bad *das* indoor swimming pool.

hallo *interj* hello.

Halm (*pl* -e) *der* [von Gras] blade; [von Getreide] stalk.

Halogen|lampe *die* halogen lamp.

Hals (*pl* Hälse) *der* - 1. [Körperteil - außen] neck; [- innen] throat - 2. [von Flasche, Instrument] neck; **aus vollem Hals** at the top of one's voice; **es hängt mir zum Hals heraus** *fam abw* I'm sick of it; **etw in den falschen Hals bekommen** *fam* to take sthg the wrong way; **Hals über Kopf** in a rush ODER hurry; **jm um den Hals fallen** to fling one's arms around sb's neck.

Hals|aus|schnitt *der* neckline.

Hals|band (*pl* -bänder) *das* - 1. [für Tiere] collar - 2. [Samtband] choker.

halsbrecherisch ◇ *adj* [Geschwindigkeit] breakneck; [Fahrt] madcap. ◇ *adv* [fahren] at breakneck speed.

Hals|entzündung *die* sore throat.

Hals|kette *die* necklace.

Hals-Nasen-Ohren-|Arzt, Ärztin *der, die* ear, nose and throat specialist.

Halsschlag|ader *die* carotid artery.

Hals|schmerzen *Pl* sore throat *(sg)*; **Halsschmerzen haben** to have a sore throat.

Hals|tuch *das* scarf.

halt ◇ *interj* stop!; MIL halt!; **sag halt, wenn ich aufhören soll!** tell me when to stop. ◇ *adv* *Süddt, Österr & Schweiz* just, simply.

Halt (*pl* -e ODER -s) *der* - 1. [Stütze] hold, grip; **die Leiter hat keinen Halt** the ladder is unstable; **den Halt verlieren** to lose one's hold - 2. [Haltestelle] stop - 3. [Stopp]: **Halt machen** to stop; **vor jm/etw nicht Halt machen** *fig* to spare no one/nothing.

haltbar *adj* - 1. [konserviert]: **haltbar sein** to keep well - 2. [strapazierfähig] hard-wearing, durable - 3. [glaubhaft] tenable.

Haltbarkeit *die* [von Lebensmitteln] life; [von Material] durability.

Haltbarkeits|datum *das* best-before date.

halten (*präs* hält, *prät* hielt, *perf* hat gehalten) ◇ *vt* - 1. [fest halten] to hold - 2. [beibehalten] to keep; **die dicken Wände halten die Wärme** the thick walls keep the heat in; **Kontakt halten** to keep in touch - 3. [binden] to keep - 4. SPORT to save - 5. [behalten] to hold on to - 6. [Rede] to make; [Vortrag, Predigt] to give; [Plädoyer] to present - 7. [einhalten - Versprechen] to keep - 8. [Tier] to keep - 9. [verteidigen] to hold - 10. [ausführen, komponieren]: **die Wohnung ist ganz in Blau gehalten** the flat is decorated entirely in blue; **das Kleid ist sehr schlicht gehalten** the dress is very simple in style; **jeder, der etw auf sich hält** any self-respecting person; **jn/etw für jn/ etw halten** to take sb/sthg to be sb/sthg; **ich habe ihn für klüger gehalten** I thought he was cleverer than that; **er war nicht zu halten** there was no holding him; **viel/wenig von jm/ etw halten** to have a high/low opinion of sb/ sthg; **was hältst du von ihr?** what do you think of her? ◇ *vi* - 1. [anhalten, stoppen] to stop - 2. [ganz bleiben - Gegenstand] to hold; [- Freundschaft] to last; **jn am halten** to stand by sb. ➟ **sich halten** *ref* - 1. [in einem Zustand - Lebensmittel] to keep; **für sein Alter hält er sich gut** he's keeping well for his age; **sich fit halten** to keep fit - 2. [in einer Position] to stay, to remain - 3. [an einem Ort - sich fest halten] to hold on; [- bleiben] to stay; **sich rechts/ links halten** to keep (to the) right/left - 4. [in einer Körperhaltung]: **sich gerade halten** to stand up straight - 5. [bei einer Herausforderung] to hold one's own.

Halterung (*pl* -en) *die* holder.

Halte|stelle *die* stop.

Halteverbot *das* [Stelle] no waiting zone, clearway UK; **'hier herrscht Halteverbot'** 'this is a no waiting zone'.

haltlos ◇ *adj* [grundlos] unfounded. ◇ *adv* [unbeherrscht] uncontrollably.

halt|machen *vi* ⊳ **Halt**.

Haltung (*pl* -en) *die* - 1. [Körperhaltung] posture - 2. [Meinung, Einstellung] attitude - 3. [Beherrschung] composure; **Haltung bewahren/ verlieren** to keep/lose one's composure - 4. [von Tieren] keeping.

Halunke (*pl* -n) *der* - 1. [Gauner] scoundrel - 2. *hum* [Lausejunge] young rascal.

Hamburg *nt* Hamburg.

hämisch ⬦ *adj* gloating; [Grinsen, Lachen] malicious. ⬦ *adv* gloatingly; [grinsen, lachen] maliciously.

Hammel (*pl* -) *der* - **1.** [Tier] castrated ram - **2.** [Fleisch] mutton - **3.** *fam abw* [Schimpfwort] ass, twit *UK*.

Hammer (*pl* Hämmer) *der* [Werkzeug & SPORT] hammer.

hämmern ⬦ *vi* - **1.** [mit Hammer, Faust] to hammer - **2.** [schlagen - Herz, Puls] to pound, to throb. ⬦ *vt* - **1.** [mit Hammer] to hammer - **2.**: auf dem Klavier hämmern to pound away at the piano.

Hampelmann (*pl* -männer) *der* - **1.** [Spielzeug] jumping jack - **2.** *salopp abw* [Person] spineless person.

Hamster (*pl* -) *der* hamster.

hamstern *vt* to hoard.

Hand (*pl* Hände) *die* - **1.** [Körperteil] hand; **per Hand** manually; **Hände hoch!** hands up!; **jn an die Hand nehmen** to take sb by the hand; **etw in die Hand nehmen** [ergreifen] to take sthg in one's hand; [initiativ werden] to take sthg in hand - **2.** SPORT handball; **alle Hände voll zu tun haben** to have one's hands full; **eine Hand voll** a handful; **aus erster Hand** second-hand *(with one previous owner)*; **aus zweiter Hand** second-hand *(with two previous owners)*; **von der öffentlichen Hand bezahlt** paid for out of public funds; **etw aus der Hand geben** to give sthg up; **freie Hand haben** to have a free hand; **in festen Händen sein** to be spoken for; **in js Hand sein** to be at sb's mercy; **er ist die rechte Hand des Chefs** he's the boss's right-hand man; **linker/rechter Hand** on the left/right, on the left-hand/right-hand side; **unter der Hand** secretly. ⬦ **an Hand** *präp*.= **anhand**.

Handarbeit *die* - **1.** [Herstellung]: **in Handarbeit hergestellte Töpferwaren** handmade pottery - **2.** [Artikel] handmade article - **3.** [Textilien]: **Handarbeiten** needlework *(U)*; **eine Handarbeit** a piece of needlework - **4.** *fam* [Unterricht] needlework.

Handball *der* handball.

Handbewegung *die* gesture.

handbreit ⬦ *adj* about 10 cm, *distance of a hand's breadth.* ⬦ *adv*: **handbreit offen stehen** to be ajar.

Handbremse *die* handbrake *UK*, parking brake *US*.

Handbuch *das* [Lehrbuch] handbook.

Händedruck *der* handshake.

Handel *der* - **1.** [Handeln] trade; **mit jm Handel treiben** to do business with sb; **mit etw Handel treiben** to deal in sthg - **2.** [Geschäftsleben, Laden] business.

handeln ⬦ *vi* - **1.** [Handel treiben]: **mit etw handeln** to trade ODER deal in sthg; **mit jm han-** deln to do business with sb - **2.** [feilschen] to bargain, to haggle; **mit jm um etw handeln** to bargain ODER haggle with sb over sthg - **3.** [agieren] to act - **4.** [behandeln]: **von etw handeln** to be about sthg. ⬦ *vt* [verkaufen] to trade. ⬦ **sich handeln** *ref*: **worum handelt es sich?** what is it about?; **bei diesem Buch handelt es sich um einen Roman** this book is a novel.

Handelsbeziehungen *Pl* trade relations.

Handelskammer *die* chamber of commerce.

Handelspartner *der* trading partner.

Handelsschule *die* college attended by people who left school at 16 and wish to obtain a commercial qualification.

handelsüblich *adj* standard, customary.

Handelsvertreter, in *der, die* commercial representative, rep.

händeringend *adv* desperately.

Handfeger *der* brush.

handfest *adj* - **1.** [bodenständig] sturdy - **2.** [klar, stark] solid, firm.

Handfläche *die* palm.

Handgelenk *das* wrist.

Handgemenge *das* scuffle.

Handgepäck *das* hand luggage.

handgeschrieben *adj* handwritten.

Handgranate *die* hand grenade.

handgreiflich *adj*: **handgreiflich werden** to become violent.

Handgreiflichkeit (*pl* -en) *die* violence; **es kam zu Handgreiflichkeiten** they came to blows.

Handgriff *der* - **1.** [Handbewegung] movement (of the hand); **mit ein paar Handgriffen** in no time - **2.** [Haltegriff] handle.

Handhabe *die*: **keine Handhabe gegen jn haben** RECHT to have no evidence against sb.

handhaben *vt* - **1.** [Werkzeug] to use; [Maschine] to operate; [Gesetze, Vorschriften] to apply - **2.** [Fall] to handle.

Handicap (*pl* -s), **Handikap** (*pl* -s) ['hɛndikɛp] *das* handicap.

Handlanger (*pl* Handlanger) *der* - **1.** [Hilfsarbeiter] labourer - **2.** *abw* [Zuarbeiter] dogsbody; [von Geheimpolizei] henchman.

Händler, in (*mpl* -, *fpl* -nen) *der, die* dealer.

handlich *adj* handy.

Handlung (*pl* -en) *die* - **1.** [Tat] act - **2.** [in Texten] plot - **3.** [Laden] shop, business.

Handlungsfreiheit *die* freedom of action.

Handlungsweise *die* conduct.

Handschellen *Pl* handcuffs; **jm Handschellen anlegen** to handcuff sb.

Handschrift *die* - **1.** [Schrift] handwriting - **2.** [Text] manuscript.

handschriftlich *adj* handwritten.

Hand|schuh der glove.

Handschuh|fach das glove compartment.

Hand|stand der handstand.

Hand|tasche die handbag.

Hand|tuch das towel.

Hand|umdrehen das: **im Handumdrehen** in (next to) no time.

Hand|werk das - 1. [Beruf] trade; [künstlerisch] craft; **jm das Handwerk legen** to put an end to sb's misdemeanours - 2. (ohne pl) [Berufsstand] trade and crafts sector.

Hand|werker, in (mpl Handwerker, fpl -nen) der, die tradesman (tradeswoman die).

handwerklich <> adj [Beruf] skilled; [künstlerisch] as a craftsman/craftswoman. <> adv: **handwerklich gut gearbeitet** well-crafted; **handwerklich geschickt sein** to be good with one's hands.

Handwerkszeug das (ohne pl) tools Pl of the trade.

Handy ['hɛndi] (pl -s) das mobile (phone); **er nahm sein Handy mit** he took his mobile with him.

Hand|zeichen das signal (with one's hand); **durch Handzeichen abstimmen** to decide by a show of hands.

Hanf der hemp.

Hang (pl Hänge) der - 1. [Abhang] slope - 2. [Vorliebe]: **einen Hang zum Selbstmitleid haben** to be inclined to be self-pitying.

Hänge|brücke die suspension bridge.

hangeln (perf hat/ist gehangelt) vi (ist): **an etw (D) hangeln** to move along sthg hand over hand. ➤ **sich hangeln** ref (hat): **sich nach unten/oben hangeln** to let o.s. down/ pull o.s. up hand over hand.

Hänge|matte die hammock.

hängen (prät hing ODER hängte, perf hat gehangen ODER hat gehängt) <> vt (reg) - 1. [anbringen] to hang; **etw an etw (A) hängen** to hang sthg on sthg; **sich einen Pullover um die Schultern hängen** to drape a pullover over one's shoulders - 2. [Körperteil] to dangle - 3. [töten] to hang. <> vi (unreg) - 1. [gen] to hang - 2. [emotional]: **an jm/etw hängen** to be attached to sb/sthg - 3. [haften] to be stuck. ➤ **sich hängen** ref (reg): **sich an etw (A) hängen** to hang onto sthg.

hängen bleiben (perf ist hängen geblieben) vi (unreg) - 1. [festhängen]: **mit dem Ärmel an der Türklinke hängen bleiben** to catch one's sleeve on the doorhandle - 2. [bleiben] to stay longer than one intended - 3. [übrig bleiben]: **von dem Gelernten blieb nichts hängen** she didn't remember any of what she'd learned; **diese Arbeit bleibt immer an mir hängen** it is always me who ends up having to do this job - 4. fam [sitzen bleiben] to have to repeat the year.

hängen lassen vt (unreg) - 1. [vergessen] to leave (behind) - 2. [Person] to let down, to leave in the lurch - 3. [Körperteil]: **die Schultern hängen lassen** to let one's shoulders droop. ➤ **sich hängen lassen** ref [vernachlässigen] to let o.s. go.

Hannover nt Hanover.

Hanse die Hanseatic League.

hänseln vt: **jn (wegen etw) hänseln** to tease sb (about sthg).

Hanse|stadt die Hanseatic town.

Hantel (pl -n) die dumbbell.

Häppchen (pl -) das canapé.

happig fam <> adj [Preis] steep. <> adv greedily.

Hardware ['hɑː(r)dwɛə] die EDV hardware.

Harfe (pl -n) die harp.

Harke (pl -n) die rake.

harken vt to rake.

harmlos <> adj [Tier, Person, Bemerkung] harmless; [Eingriff, Verletzung] minor; [Vergnügen] innocent. <> adv [lachen, tun] innocently.

Harmlosigkeit (pl -en) die [von Tier, Person, Bemerkung] harmlessness; [von Krankheit] mildness; [von Verletzung] minor nature; [von Vergnügen] innocence.

Harmonie (pl -n) die harmony.

harmonieren vi: **miteinander harmonieren** [Farben] to go (well) together; [Töne] to be in harmony; [Menschen] to get on (well) with one another.

harmonisch <> adj harmonious. <> adv - 1. [passend] harmoniously - 2. MUS: **harmonisch klingen** to be harmonious.

Harn (pl -e) der urine.

Harn|blase die bladder.

Harpune (pl -n) die harpoon.

hart (kompar härter, superl härteste) <> adj - 1. [nicht weich - gen] hard; [- Ei] hard-boiled; **harte Währung** hard currency - 2. [widerstandsfähig] tough; **hart im Nehmen sein** to be tough - 3. [streng - Urteil, Strafe, Winter] harsh; [- Drogen] hard; [- Aufprall] violent - 4.: **es geht hart auf hart** fig it's a pitched battle. <> adv (kompar härter; superl am härtesten) - 1. [nicht weich] hard; **das Ei hart kochen** to hard-boil the egg - 2. [streng - bestrafen, urteilen] harshly; [- arbeiten, aufschlagen] hard - 3. [räumlich]: **hart an (+ D)** close to; **das war hart an der Grenze des Erlaubten** fig it was right on the limit of what is allowed.

Härte (pl -n) die - 1. [gen] hardness - 2. [Belastung] hardship - 3. [von Urteil, Person, Worte, Farbe, Aussprache] harshness - 4. fam abw [Zumutung]: **das ist die Härte!** that's a bit much!

hart gekocht adj hard-boiled.

hartherzig adj hard-hearted.

150

hartnäckig <> adj [Person] stubborn; [Verfolger, Krankheit] persistent. <> adv [schweigen, sich weigern] stubbornly; [verfolgen, nachfragen] persistently.

haschen vi - 1. [fangen wollen]: **nach jm/etw haschen** to snatch at sb/sthg - 2. fam [Haschisch rauchen] to smoke hash.

Haschisch das & der hashish.

Hase (pl -n) der hare; [Kaninchen] rabbit.

Haselnuss (pl -nüsse) die hazelnut.

Hass der: **Hass (auf jn/etw)** hatred (of sb/sthg).

hassen vt to hate.

hässlich <> adj - 1. [unattraktiv] ugly - 2. [gemein] nasty. <> adv - 1. [unattraktiv] tastelessly; **sich hässlich kleiden** to wear ugly clothes - 2. [gemein] nastily.

Hässlichkeit die [von Person, Einrichtung] ugliness.

hast präs > **haben**.

Hast die haste; **etw in Hast tun** to do sthg hastily.

hasten (perf ist gehastet) vi to hurry.

hastig <> adv hastily, hurriedly; **hastig laufen** to rush. <> adj hasty.

hat präs > **haben**.

hätscheln vt to pet.

hatschi interj fam atishoo!

hatte prät > **haben**.

Haube (pl -n) die - 1. [von Krankenschwester] cap; [von Nonne] veil - 2. [Motorhaube] bonnet UK, hood US - 3. [Trockenhaube] hairdryer.

Hauch der - 1. [leichter Wind] gentle breeze - 2. [Spur]: **ein Hauch von etw** a hint of sthg.

hauchdünn <> adj wafer-thin. <> adv [auftragen] very sparingly; [schneiden] into very thin slices.

hauchen vt & vi to breathe.

hauen (prät haute ODER hieb, perf hat gehauen) <> vt - 1. (prät haute) fam [Person] to hit - 2. [Gegenstand]: **einen Pfahl in den Boden hauen** to bang a post into the ground - 3. (prät haute) salopp [werfen] to chuck, to bung UK. <> vi fam [auf Tisch, gegen Wand] to bang; **jm ins Gesicht hauen** to smack sb in the mouth.

Haufen (pl -) der - 1. [Anhäufung]: **alles auf einen Haufen legen** to pile everything up - 2. fam [Menge]: **ein Haufen Freunde/Geld** loads of friends/money.

häufen vt to pile up. <> **sich häufen** ref [Briefe, Abfälle] to pile up; [Beweise] to accumulate; [Vorfall] to be on the increase.

haufenweise adv fam: **haufenweise Geld verdienen** to earn heaps ODER loads of money.

häufig <> adj [gen] frequent; [Fehler] common. <> adv often.

Häufigkeit (pl -en) die frequency.

Häufung (pl -en) die [von Gegenständen] accumulation; [von Vorfällen] mounting frequency.

Haupt|bahnhof der main station; **Leipzig Hauptbahnhof** Leipzig central (station).

hauptberuflich <> adj: **hauptberufliche Tätigkeit** main job. <> adv: **hauptberuflich ist er Landwirt** farming is his principal occupation.

Haupt|beschäftigung die main occupation.

Haupt|bestandteil der main component.

Haupt|darsteller, in der, die leading man (leading lady die).

Haupt|eingang der main entrance.

Haupt|fach das main subject; **etw im Hauptfach studieren** to study sthg as one's main subject.

Haupt|figur die central figure.

Haupt|gericht das main course.

Haupt|gewinn der first prize.

Haupt|grund der main reason.

Häuptling (pl -e) der chief.

Haupt|person die - 1. [von Buch, Film] main character - 2. [wichtigste Person]: **die Hauptperson sein** to be the star of the show.

Haupt|post die main post office.

Haupt|quartier das headquarters Pl.

Haupt|rolle die [in Film] starring role; **Tennis spielt in ihrem Leben die Hauptrolle** tennis is the most important thing in her life.

Haupt|sache die main ODER most important thing; **Hauptsache, ich bestehe** the main thing is for me to pass. <> **in der Hauptsache** adv mainly, in the main.

hauptsächlich <> adv principally, mainly. <> adj main, chief.

Haupt|saison ['haʊptzɛzõ] die high season.

Haupt|satz der main clause.

Haupt|schule die secondary school attended by less academically gifted pupils aged between 10 and 15.

Haupt|stadt die capital.

Haupt|straße die main road ODER street.

Haupt|teil der [von Text, Rede] main body; **der Hauptteil der Fracht war beschädigt** most of the cargo was damaged.

Hauptverkehrs|straße die main thoroughfare.

Hauptverkehrs|zeit die rush hour.

Haupt|wohnsitz der main place of residence.

Haupt|wort (pl -wörter) das noun.

Haus (pl Häuser) das - 1. [Wohnhaus] house - 2. [Betrieb] firm; **er ist zurzeit nicht im Haus** he is not on the premises just now; **mit den besten Empfehlungen des Hauses** with the compliments of the house - 3. [Familie] family - 4. [Theater] auditorium; **volles Haus haben** to have a full house; **Haus halten** [sparen] to budget; **mit etw Haus halten** to be careful with sthg; **mit seinen Kräften Haus halten** to conserve one's energy; **die Kinder sind von Haus aus gewöhnt mitzuhelfen** the children have been brought up to be helpful.

Haus|apotheke die - 1. [Medikamente] first-aid kit - 2. [Schränkchen] medicine cabinet.

Haus|arbeit die - 1. [im Haushalt] housework - 2. [für die Schule, für die Universität] homework.

Haus|arzt, ärztin der, die family doctor.

Haus|aufgabe die: als Hausaufgabe für morgen for tomorrow's homework; **Hausaufgaben** homework (U).

Hausbesetzer, in (mpl -, fpl -nen) der, die squatter.

Haus|bewohner, in der, die occupant.

Häuschen ['hɔʏçən] (pl -) das [Haus] cottage; **vor Freude ganz aus dem Häuschen sein** fam to be beside o.s. with joy.

Haus|eigentümer, in der, die homeowner; [Vermieter] landlord (landlady die).

hausen vi - 1. [wohnen] to live - 2. fam [toben - Sturm, Krieg] to rage; [- Eroberer, Besatzer] to rampage.

Häuserblock (pl -blöcke) der block.

Haus|flur der (entrance) hall, hallway.

Haus|frau die housewife.

hausgemacht adj home-made.

Haushalt (pl -e) der - 1. [Hausarbeit] housework; **im Haushalt helfen** to help around the house - 2. [Hausstand] estate - 3. [Familie] household; **einen Haushalt gründen** to set up home - 4. WIRTSCH budget.

haus|halten vi (unreg) ⊳ **Haus**.

Haushälter, in (mpl -, fpl -nen) der, die housekeeper.

Haushalts|artikel der household article.

Haus|herr, in der, die host (hostess die).

haushoch ⟨⟩ adj [Flammen, Wellen] towering; [Favorit, Sieg, Überlegenheit] overwhelming. ⟨⟩ adv [wachsen] as high as a house; [gewinnen] by a mile; **jm haushoch überlegen sein** to be head and shoulders above sb; **haushoch verlieren** to be hammered.

hausieren vi: **mit etw hausieren (gehen)** [verkaufen] to sell sthg from door to door; fam [sprechen über] to go on about sthg.

häuslich ⟨⟩ adj - 1. [im Haus - Arbeiten, Probleme, Frieden] domestic; [- Angelegenheit] family (vor Subst); [- Pflege] home (vor Subst) - 2. [Person]: **sie ist sehr häuslich** she's a real home bird. ⟨⟩ adv: **sich häuslich niederlassen** fam to make o.s. at home; **sich häuslich einrichten** fam to settle in.

Haus|mann der house husband.

Hausmannskost die traditional, simple fare.

Haus|marke die - 1. [Wein] house wine - 2. [von Geschäft] own-brand product - 3. [Lieblingsmarke] favourite brand.

Haus|meister, in der, die caretaker UK, janitor US.

Haus|mittel das home remedy.

Haus|nummer die house number.

Haus|ordnung die house rules Pl.

Haus|rat der (ohne pl) household contents Pl.

Haus|schuh der slipper.

Haus|tier das pet.

Haus|tür die front door.

Haus|verwaltung die property managers Pl.

Haus|wirt, in der, die landlord (landlady die).

Haut (pl Häute) die [gen] skin; [von Tier] hide; **es ging mir unter die Haut** it got under my skin; **ihm war nicht wohl in seiner Haut** he felt uncomfortable.

Haut|abschürfung (pl -en) die graze.

Haut|arzt, ärztin der, die dermatologist.

Haut|ausschlag der (skin) rash.

Haut|creme ['hautkre:m] die skin cream.

häuten vt [Früchte] to peel; [Tier] to skin. ◆ **sich häuten** ref to shed its skin.

hauteng adj skintight.

Haut|farbe die skin colour.

hautnah ⟨⟩ adj [Bild, Darstellung] graphic. ⟨⟩ adv [tanzen] very closely; **hautnah mit etw in Kontakt kommen** to come into close contact with sthg; **hautnah an etw (D) teilnehmen** to be closely involved in sthg.

Hbf. abk für **Hauptbahnhof**.

Headhunter (pl -) der headhunter.

Hebamme (pl -n) die midwife.

Hebel (pl -) der lever.

heben (prät hob, perf hat gehoben) vt - 1. [hochnehmen] to lift; [Arm, Glas] to raise; **einen heben** fam to have a drink - 2. [Niveau] to raise; [Umsatz, Selbstsicherheit] to boost, to improve; [Stimmung, Laune] to improve - 3. [Wrack] to hoist, to salvage. ◆ **sich heben** ref - 1. [hochgehen - Vorhang, Flugzeug, Ballon] to rise; [- Nebel] to lift - 2. [Niveau] to rise; [Umsatz, Laune] to improve.

hebräisch adj Hebrew.

hecheln vi [atmen] to pant.

Hecht (pl -e) der pike.

Heck (pl -e ODER -s) das [von Auto, Flugzeug] rear; [von Schiff] stern.

Hecke (pl -n) die hedge.

Hecken|schütze der sniper.

Heck|klappe die tailgate.

Heck|scheibe die rear windscreen UK ODER windshield US.

Heer (pl -e) das army.

Hefe (pl -n) die yeast.

Hefe|teig der leavened dough (U).

Heft (*pl* -e) *das* - **1.** [Schulheft] exercise book - **2.** [geheftetes Büchlein] booklet - **3.** [von Zeitschriften] issue.

heften *vt* - **1.** [befestigen]: **etw an etw** (A) **heften** [gen] to attach sthg to sthg; [mit Heftmaschine] to staple sthg to sthg - **2.** [nähen] to tack - **3.** [richten]: **die Augen auf etw** (A) **heften** to fix one's eyes on sthg. ⬤ **sich heften** *ref* [sich richten]: **sich auf etw** (A) **heften** to fix onto sthg.

Hefter (*pl* -) *der* folder.

heftig ◇ *adj* violent. ◇ *adv* violently.

Heft|klammer *die* staple.

Heft|pflaster *das* (sticking) plaster *UK*, Band-Aid® *US*.

Heft|zwecke (*pl* -n) *die* drawing pin *UK*, thumbtack *US*.

hegen *vt* - **1.** [Verdacht, Gefühle, Hoffnung] to harbour; [Abneigung, Misstrauen, Achtung] to feel - **2.** [Wald, Wild, Garten] to tend; **jn/etw hegen und pflegen** to lavish care on sb/sthg.

Hehl *das* & *der*: **kein** ODER **keinen Hehl aus etw machen** to make no secret of sthg.

Hehlerei (*pl* -en) *die* receiving (stolen goods).

Heide (*pl* -n) ◇ *die* heath. ◇ *der* heathen, pagan.

Heidekraut *das* heather.

Heidel|beere *die* bilberry.

Heiden|angst *die fam*: **eine Heidenangst haben** to be scared stiff.

Heiden|geld *das fam* fortune.

Heiden|spaß *der fam* great fun.

Heidin (*pl* -nen) *die* heathen, pagan.

heidnisch *adj* heathen, pagan.

heikel (*kompar* heikler, *superl* heikelste) *adj* - **1.** [kompliziert] awkward, tricky - **2.** [anspruchsvoll] fussy.

heil *adj* - **1.** [unzerstört] intact; [Welt] perfect - **2.** [geheilt] healed.

Heiland *der* Saviour.

Heil|bad *das* - **1.** [Kurort] spa - **2.** [Baden] medicinal bath.

heilbar *adj* [Krankheit, Patient] curable; [Wunde] healable.

heilen (*perf* hat/ist geheilt) ◇ *vt* (hat) to cure; **jn von etw heilen** [Idee] to cure sb of sthg; **jn von seinen Zweifeln heilen** to allay sb's doubts. ◇ *vi* (ist) to heal.

heilfroh *adj* relieved; **heilfroh über etw** (A) **sein** to be relieved about sthg.

heilig *adj* - **1.** [geheiligt] holy; **der heilige Christopherus** Saint Christopher; **denen ist nichts heilig** nothing is sacred to them - **2.** [Schrecken] almighty.

Heiligabend (*pl* -s) *der* Christmas Eve.

Heilige (*pl* -n) *der, die* saint.

Heiligen|schein *der* halo.

Heiligtum (*pl* -tümer) *das* - **1.** [Ort] shrine - **2.** [Gegenstand] relic.

Heil|kraft *die* healing power.

Heil|kraut *das* medicinal herb.

heillos ◇ *adj* terrible. ◇ *adv* terribly.

Heil|mittel *das* remedy, cure.

Heil|pflanze *die* medicinal plant.

Heil|praktiker, **in** *der, die* alternative therapist.

heilsam *adj* salutary.

Heilsarmee *die* Salvation Army.

Heilung (*pl* -en) *die* [von Patient, Krankheit] curing; [von Wunde] healing.

heim *adv* home.

Heim (*pl* -e) *das* home.

Heimarbeit *die*: **etw in Heimarbeit anfertigen** to make sthg at home; **Heimarbeit machen** to work from home.

Heimat *die* [von Person] home, native country/region; [von Tier] original habitat.

Heimat|anschrift *die* home address.

Heimat|hafen *der* home port, port of registration.

Heimat|kunde *die* primary school subject covering local history, natural history and geography.

Heimat|land *das* native country.

heimatlich *adj* of/from one's native country/region; **jm ein heimatliches Gefühl geben** to remind sb of home.

heimatlos *adj* [Mensch] homeless; [Tier] stray.

Heimat|museum *das* local history museum.

Heim|computer *der* home computer.

Heim|fahrt *die* journey home.

heimisch *adj* - **1.** [Bevölkerung, Industrie, Sitte] local; [Pflanze, Tier] indigenous - **2.** [zu Hause]: **heimisch werden** to become acclimatized; **sich heimisch fühlen** to feel at home.

Heimkehr *die* return journey.

heim|kehren (*perf* ist heimgekehrt) *vi* to return home.

heim|kommen (*perf* ist heimgekommen) *vi* (*unreg*) to come home.

heimlich ◇ *adj* secret. ◇ *adv* secretly.

Heimlichkeit (*pl* -en) *die* secrecy. ⬤ **Heimlichkeiten** *Pl* secrets.

Heim|reise *die* journey home.

Heim|spiel *das* home game.

heim|suchen *vt* - **1.** [Pest, Alptraum, Krankheit] to afflict; [Erdbeben] to hit - **2.** *hum* [belästigen] to descend on.

Heim|trainer [haɪmˈtrɛːnɐ] *der* exercise bike.

heimtückisch ◇ *adj* [Mensch, Verbrechen] malicious; [Krankheit] insidious. ◇ *adv* maliciously.

Heim|weg *der* way home.

Heimweh das homesickness; **(nach jm/etw)**
Heimweh haben to be homesick (for sb/sthg).

heim|zahlen vt: jm etw heimzahlen to pay
sb back for sthg.

Heirat (pl -en) die marriage.

heiraten <> vi to marry, to get married;
kirchlich heiraten to have a church wedding.
<> vt to marry.

Heirats|annonce die advertisement seeking
a marriage partner.

Heirats|antrag der proposal (of marriage).

Heirats|vermittlung die [Ort] marriage bur-
eau.

heiser <> adj hoarse. <> adv hoarsely; **sie**
hat sich heiser geschrien she shouted until she
was hoarse.

Heiserkeit (pl -en) die hoarseness.

heiß <> adj - 1. [warm] [gen] hot; **mir ist heiß**
I'm hot; **es überläuft mich heiß und kalt** I feel
hot and cold all over; **heiß auf jn sein** fam to
have the hots for sb - 2. [heftig - Diskussion,
Auseinandersetzung] heated; [- Liebe, Wunsch]
ardent, burning - 3. fam [gut] brilliant. <> adv
- 1. [warm]: **heiß baden** to have a hot bath
- 2. [heftig]: **heiß umstritten** hotly contested; **jn**
heiß lieben to love sb passionately; **es ging**
heiß her things got a bit heated.

heißblütig adj hot-blooded.

heißen (prät hieß, perf hat geheißen) vi
- 1. [mit Namen] to be called; **er heißt Tom** he's
called Tom, his name is Tom; **wie heißt du?**
what's your name? - 2. [bedeuten] to mean;
was heißt das auf Deutsch? how do you say
that in German?; **das will was heißen!** that's
quite something!; **das heißt, wenn du willst** if
you want, that is - 3. [lauten] to be; **wie heißt**
der Titel? what's the title?

Heißhunger der voracious appetite.

heiß laufen (perf hat/ist heiß gelaufen) vi
(unreg) (ist) [Motor] to overheat; [Telefon] to
buzz.

Heißluft|ballon der hot-air balloon.

heiter adj - 1. [fröhlich] cheerful - 2. [sonnig]
fine.

Heiterkeit die - 1. [Fröhlichkeit] cheerfulness
- 2. [vom Wetter] fineness.

heizen <> vi to turn on the heating; **wir hei-**
zen mit Gas/elektrisch we have gas/electric
heating. <> vt to heat.

Heizkessel der boiler.

Heiz|kissen das heated pad (for back pain
etc).

Heiz|körper der radiator.

Heiz|öl das fuel oil.

Heizung (pl -en) die - 1. [System] heating
- 2. [Heizkörper] radiator.

Heizungs|keller der boiler room.

Hektar (pl -e ODER -) das & der hectare.

Hektik die hectic pace; **bloß keine Hektik!**
fam don't panic!

hektisch <> adj - 1. [Person, Bewegung]
frantic; **hektisch werden** to panic - 2. [Ort] hectic. <> adv frantically.

Hekto|liter das & der hectolitre.

Held (pl -en) der hero.

heldenhaft <> adj heroic. <> adv heroic-
ally.

Helden|tat die heroic deed.

Heldin (pl -nen) die heroine.

helfen (präs hilft, prät half, perf hat
geholfen) vi - 1. [Hilfe leisten] to help; **jm (bei**
etw) helfen to help sb (with sthg); **sich (D) zu**
helfen wissen to know what to do - 2. [nütz-
lich sein] to help; **es hilft nichts** it's no use ODER
good; **das hilft gegen Zahnschmerzen** it's
good for toothache; **es hilft kein Weinen** it's
no good crying.

Helfer, in (mpl -, fpl -nen) der, die helper.

Helium das helium.

hell <> adj - 1. [Zimmer, Licht, Tag] bright; **es**
wird hell it's getting light - 2. [Farbe] light;
[Haar, Haut] fair - 3. [Stimme] high (esp. of child's
voice) - 4. [schlau] lucid - 5. [groß, intensiv - Freude, Begeisterung] sheer; [- Empörung, Wahn-
sinn] utter. <> adv - 1. [leuchtend] brightly
- 2. [hoch]: **hell klingen** to ring out clearly
- 3. [sehr] totally.

hellblau adj light blue.

hellblond adj very fair.

hellhörig adj - 1. [misstrauisch]: **sie wurde**
hellhörig her suspicions were aroused; **jn hell-**
hörig machen to arouse sb's suspicions
- 2. [Raum]: **die Wohnung ist sehr hellhörig** you
can hear everything through the walls in this
flat.

Helligkeit (pl -en) die [von Licht] brightness.

hell|sehen vi (unreg) to see into the future.

Hellseher, in (mpl -, fpl -nen) der, die clairvoyant.

hellwach adj - 1. [wach] wide awake - 2. fam
[rege] on the ball.

Helm (pl -e) der helmet.

Hemd (pl -en) das - 1. [Oberhemd] shirt
- 2. [Unterhemd] vest UK, undershirt US; **jn bis**
aufs Hemd ausziehen fam to have the shirt off
sb's back.

hemdsärmelig adj casual.

hemmen vt - 1. [bremsen - Bewegung, Ge-
schwindigkeit] to slow down; [Fluss] to stem
- 2. [behindern] to impede, to hinder.

Hemm|schwelle die mental block.

Hemmung (pl -en) die [Behinderung]
hindrance. ➡ **Hemmungen** Pl inhibitions;
Hemmungen haben to feel inhibited.

hemmungslos <> adj uninhibited. <> adv
uninhibitedly.

Hengst (pl -e) der [Pferd] stallion.

Henkel (pl -) der handle.

Henker (pl -) der [gen] executioner; [beim Erhängen] hangman.

Henne (pl -n) die hen.

her adv - 1. [räumlich]: **komm her!** come here!; **her damit!** give me that!; **von Norden her** from the north; **von weit her** from a long way away - 2. [zeitlich]: **das ist zehn Jahre her** that was ten years ago; **ich kenne sie von früher her** I know her from before - 3. [unter dem Aspekt]: **von der Größe her** as far as size is concerned; siehe auch **her sein**.

herab|lassen vt (unreg) to lower. ⬧ **sich herablassen** ref: **sich herablassen, etw zu tun** to condescend to do sthg.

herablassend ◇ adj condescending, patronizing. ◇ adv condescendingly, patronizingly.

herab|setzen vt - 1. [Betrag] to reduce - 2. [Person] to put down.

heran, ran adv: **nur heran!** come closer!

heran|kommen (perf ist herangekommen) vi (unreg) - 1. [kommen] to approach; **sie lässt nichts an sich (A) herankommen** she doesn't let anything bother her; **an jn herankommen** [erreichen] to get hold of sb; [entsprechen] to match up to sb; **an etw (A) herankommen** to get hold of sthg.

heran|machen ⬧ **sich heranmachen** ref: **sich an etw (A) heranmachen** to get down to sthg.

heran|treten (perf ist herangetreten) vi (unreg): **an jn herantreten** to approach sb.

heran|wachsen [hɛ'ranvaksn̩] (perf ist herangewachsen) vi (unreg) to grow up.

Heranwachsende [hɛ'ranvaksn̩də] (pl -n) der, die adolescent.

heran|ziehen (perf hat/ist herangezogen) (unreg) ◇ vt (hat) - 1. [ziehen]: **etw an etw (A) heranziehen** to pull sthg up to sthg - 2. [befragen] to consult - 3. [erziehen] to teach. ◇ vi (ist) [kommen] to draw near.

herauf, rauf adv up; **die Treppe herauf** up the stairs; **vom Tal herauf** up from the valley.

herauf|beschwören vt (unreg) - 1. [verursachen] to cause - 2. [Vergangenes] to evoke.

herauf|kommen (perf ist heraufgekommen) vi (unreg) to come up/upstairs.

heraus, raus adv out; **heraus aus dem Bett** (get) out of bed!; **heraus mit der Sprache!** spit it out!, out with it!; **aus dieser Überlegung heraus** as a result of these reflections; **es ist noch nicht heraus, wer das Rennen gewonnen hat** it's still unclear who won the race; siehe auch **heraus sein**.

heraus|bekommen vt (unreg) - 1. [Geheimnis] to find out; [Lösung] to work out - 2. [entfernen] to get out - 3. [Wechselgeld] to get back.

heraus|bringen vt (unreg) - 1. [bringen] to bring/take out - 2. [veröffentlichen, verkaufen] to bring out; **etw (ganz) groß herausbringen** to launch sthg amid a fanfare of publicity - 3. fam [entlocken]: **etw aus jm herausbringen** to get sthg out of sb - 4. [aussprechen, artikulieren] to utter.

heraus|finden (unreg) ◇ vt [entdecken] to find out. ◇ vi [herauskommen]: **aus etw herausfinden** to find a way out of sthg.

heraus|fliegen (perf hat/ist herausgeflogen) (unreg) ◇ vt (hat) [fliegen] to fly out. ◇ vi (ist) - 1. [fliegen - Tier, Gegenstand]: **aus etw herausfliegen** to fly out of sthg - 2. fam [zur Strafe] to be thrown out - 3. fam [herausfallen]: **aus etw herausfliegen** to fall out of sthg.

heraus|fordern vt - 1. SPORT [Feind] to challenge; **jn herausfordern, etw zu tun** to challenge sb to do sthg - 2. [provozieren] to provoke; **das Schicksal herausfordern** to tempt fate.

herausfordernd ◇ adj provocative; [Frage] challenging. ◇ adv provocatively.

Heraus|forderung die - 1. SPORT [Aufgabe] challenge - 2. [Provokation] provocation; [von Schicksal] tempting.

heraus|geben vt (unreg) - 1. [veröffentlichen] to publish - 2. [geben]: **jm etw herausgeben** to pass ODER hand sthg out to sb - 3. [freilassen] to return - 4. [Wechselgeld] to give back; **auf 100 Euro herausgeben** to give change from 100 euros.

Herausgeber, in (mpl -, fpl -nen) der, die - 1. [Redakteur] editor - 2. [Verleger] publisher.

heraus|gehen (perf ist herausgegangen) vi (unreg) - 1. [nach draußen] to go out; **aus sich herausgehen** fig to come out of one's shell - 2. [Fleck, Schraube] to come out.

heraus|halten (unreg) vt - 1. [nach draußen] to hold out - 2. fam [fern halten]: **jn aus etw heraushalten** to keep sb out of sthg. ⬧ **sich heraushalten** ref: **sich aus etw heraushalten** to keep out of sthg.

heraus|holen vt - 1. [holen]: **jn/etw aus etw herausholen** to get sb/sthg out of sthg - 2. [Information]: **etw aus jm herausholen** to get sthg out of sb - 3. [Leistung] to get ODER squeeze out - 4. [Geld, Gewinn] to make - 5. SPORT to make up.

heraus|hören vt: **etw aus etw heraushören** [erahnen] to detect sthg from sthg; [hören] to make out sthg amid sthg.

heraus|kommen (perf ist herausgekommen) vi (unreg) - 1. [nach draußen]: **(aus etw) herauskommen** to come out (from sthg) - 2. [Resultat]: **was kommt dabei heraus?** what's that going to achieve?; **das kommt auf dasselbe heraus** it amounts to the same thing, it makes no difference - 3. [auf den Markt kommen] to come out; **(ganz) groß herauskommen** fig to make a real splash - 4. [Verbrechen] to come to light - **5.** [entkommen]: **aus etw herauskommen** to come out ODER emerge from sthg - **6.** [deutlich werden] to stand out - **7.** [aus dem Takt kommen] to get out of time - **8.** [beim Kartenspiel] to lead - **9.** fam [sagen]: **mit etw herauskommen** to come out with sthg.

heraus|nehmen vt (unreg) - **1.** [entfernen]: **etw (aus etw) herausnehmen** to take sthg out (of sthg) - **2.** [wagen]: **sich (D) Freiheiten herausnehmen** to take liberties.

heraus|ragen vi - **1.** [hervorstechen] to stand out - **2.** [herausstehen] to jut out.

heraus|reden ⇔ **sich herausreden** ref: **sich damit herausreden, dass...** to make excuses for o.s. by saying that...

heraus|rücken (perf hat/ist herausgerückt) ⇔ vt (hat) fam [Geld] to cough up. ⇔ vi (ist) [sagen]: **mit etw herausrücken** to come out with sthg.

heraus|schlagen (perf hat/ist herausgeschlagen) (unreg) ⇔ vt (hat) - **1.** [schlagen] to knock out - **2.** [Gewinn] to make. ⇔ vi (ist) [Feuer]: **aus etw herausschlagen** to leap out of sthg.

heraus sein (perf ist heraus gewesen) vi (unreg) - **1.** [entlassen sein]: **aus etw heraus sein** to be out of sthg, to have left sthg - **2.** [entkommen sein]: **fein heraus sein** to be sitting pretty - **3.** [Produkt] to be out - **4.** [herausgegangen sein]: **aus einer Phase heraus sein** to be past a phase - **5.** [entfernt sein] to be out - **6.** [klar sein] to be known.

heraus|stellen vt - **1.** [nach draußen] to put out - **2.** [hervorheben] to highlight. ⇔ **sich herausstellen** ref [klar werden] to become clear; **wer gelogen hat, wird sich noch herausstellen** we'll soon see who has been lying; **sich als falsch/richtig herausstellen** to turn out to be wrong/right.

heraus|strecken vt to stick out.

heraus|suchen vt to pick out; **jm etw heraussuchen** to find sthg for sb.

herbei adv here; **komm herbei!** come here!

her|bitten vt (unreg) to ask to come.

her|bringen vt (unreg) to bring here.

Herbst (pl -e) der autumn UK, fall US; **im Herbst** in the autumn UK, in the fall US.

herbstlich adj autumnal.

Herd (pl -e) der - **1.** [Ofen] cooker UK, stove US - **2.** [von Revolte] seat; [von Krankheit] focus.

Herde (pl -n) die - **1.** [von Rindern, Elefanten] herd; [von Schafen] flock - **2.** abw [von Menschen] gang.

Herd|platte die hotplate.

herein, rein adv in; **herein!** come in!

herein|brechen (perf ist hereingebrochen) vi (unreg) geh - **1.** [Nacht] to fall - **2.** [Unglück]: **über jn hereinbrechen** to befall sb.

herein|fallen (perf ist hereingefallen) vi (unreg) - **1.** [getäuscht werden] to be conned; **auf**

jn/etw hereinfallen to be taken in by sb/sthg - **2.** [fallen] to fall in - **3.** [Licht] to come in, to enter.

herein|kommen (perf ist hereingekommen) vi (unreg) to come in.

herein|lassen vt (unreg) to let in.

herein|legen vt [täuschen] to take for a ride.

Her|fahrt die journey here.

her|fallen (perf ist hergefallen) vi (unreg): **über jn herfallen** [angreifen] to attack sb; **über etw (A) herfallen** [essen] to attack sthg.

Her|gang der: **der Hergang der Tat** the course of events leading to the crime.

her|geben vt (unreg) - **1.** [geben] to give; [überreichen] to hand over - **2.** [verschenken] to give away - **3.** [verzichten auf] to give up - **4.** [erbringen]: **der Text gibt für unser Thema nichts her** the text is of no use for our topic. ⇔ **sich hergeben** ref: **sich zu etw hergeben** abw to allow o.s. to get involved in sthg.

her|geholt adj: **weit hergeholt** far-fetched.

her|haben vt (unreg) fam: **wo hast du das her?** where did you get this?

her|halten (unreg) vi abw [dienen]: **als etw herhalten** to be used as sthg; **für jn herhalten** to have to take the blame for sb.

her|hören vi to listen.

Hering (pl -e) der - **1.** [Fisch] herring - **2.** [am Zelt] tent peg.

her|kommen (perf ist hergekommen) vi (unreg) - **1.** [kommen] to come here; **wo kommst du denn jetzt her?** where have you just been? - **2.** [entstehen, stammen] to come from; **wo kommen Sie her?** where do you come from?

herkömmlich adj conventional.

Herkunft die (ohne pl) [von Person] origins Pl; [von Sache] origin.

Herkunfts|land das country of origin.

her|machen vi: **viel hermachen** to look impressive; **wenig hermachen** not to look very impressive; **nichts hermachen** not to be up to much. ⇔ **sich hermachen** ref fam: **sich über etw (A) hermachen** to set about sthg.

her|nehmen vt (unreg) [nehmen, bekommen] to get.

Heroin das heroin.

Herr (pl -en) der - **1.** [Mann] gentleman; **meine Herren!** gentlemen!; **'Herren'** [WC] 'gents' - **2.** [Anrede] Mr; **an Herrn Müller** to Mr Müller; **Herr Doktor** Doctor - **3.** [Gott] Lord - **4.** [Oberhaupt, Gebieter] lord; **der Herr des Hauses** the master of the house.

herrenlos adj [Tier] stray; [Koffer] abandoned.

her|richten vt - **1.** [vorbereiten] to get ready - **2.** [reparieren] to renovate.

Herrin (pl -nen) die mistress.

herrisch ⇔ adj [Person, Worte] overbearing; [Blick] imperious. ⇔ adv in an overbearing manner.

herrlich adj wonderful.

Herrschaft (pl -en) die [über Staat, Volk] rule. ◆ **Herrschaften** Pl people; **meine Herrschaften!** ladies and gentlemen!

herrschen vi - 1. [regieren]: **(über jn/etw) herrschen** to rule (over sb/sthg) - 2. [bestehen] to prevail; **es herrschte allgemeine Unruhe** there was general unrest.

Herrscher, in (mpl -, fpl -nen) der, die ruler.

her|schieben vt (unreg) to push here; **etw vor sich (D) herschieben** [schieben] to push sthg along ahead of one; [vertagen] to put sthg off.

her sein (perf **ist her gewesen**) vi (unreg) - 1. [vergangen sein]: **es ist drei Tage her, dass wir telefoniert haben** it is three days since we phoned - 2. [herkommen] to come from; **hinter jm/etw her sein** to be after sb/sthg.

her|stellen vt - 1. [produzieren] to produce, to make; [industriell] to manufacture - 2. [Ruhe, Ordnung] to establish; **ihre Gesundheit ist wieder hergestellt** she has recovered, her health has been restored - 3. [näher rücken] to put (over) here.

Hersteller, in (mpl -, fpl -nen) der, die manufacturer.

Her|stellung die [Produktion] production; [industriell] manufacture.

herüber, rüber adv over.

herum adv - 1. [räumlich] round; **um etw herum** around sthg; **um den Tisch herum** around the table; **das Gerücht ist schon in der ganzen Nachbarschaft herum** the rumour has already got around the whole neighbourhood; **du trägst den Pullover verkehrt herum** your pullover is on the wrong way round; **was um sie herum geschieht** what's going on around her - 2. [ungefähr] around, about; **um die 50 Euro herum** around ODER about 50 euros.

herum|drehen ⟨⟩ vt [Blatt, Decke] to turn over; [Schlüssel] to turn; [Pfannkuchen] to toss. ⟨⟩ vi [drehen]: **an etw (D) herumdrehen** to turn sthg. ◆ **sich herumdrehen** ref [sich umdrehen] to turn round.

herum|fahren (perf **hat/ist herumgefahren**) (unreg) ⟨⟩ vi (ist) - 1. [im Kreis]: **um etw herumfahren** to go round sthg - 2. [umherfahren] to drive around - 3. [sich umdrehen] to turn round - 4. [wischen] ⟨⟩ vt (hat) to drive around.

herum|geben vt (unreg) to pass round.

herum|gehen (perf **ist herumgegangen**) vi (unreg) - 1. [spazieren] to walk around - 2. [zwischen Personen] to go around - 3. [im Kreis]: **um etw herumgehen** to go round sthg - 4. [Gerücht] to go around - 5. [Zeit] to pass.

herum|kommen (perf **ist herumgekommen**) vi (unreg) fam - 1. [reisen] to get around - 2. [gehen, fahren]: **um etw herumkommen** to

get round sthg - 3. [vermeiden]: **um etw herumkommen/nicht herumkommen** to get out of/not to get out of sthg.

herum|kriegen vt fam - 1. [überreden]: **sie hat mich doch noch herumgekriegt** she talked me into it in the end - 2. [verbringen]: **die Zeit herumkriegen** to kill time - 3. [räumlich]: **etw um etw herumkriegen** to get sthg round sthg.

herum|liegen vi (unreg) to lie around.

herum|lungern (perf **hat/ist herumgelungert**) vi fam [in der Stadt] to hang around; [auf dem Sofa] to lounge around.

herum|sprechen ◆ **sich herumsprechen** ref (unreg) to get around.

herum|treiben ◆ **sich herumtreiben** ref (unreg) fam to hang around.

herum|zeigen vt to show around.

herum|ziehen (perf **hat/ist herumgezogen**) (unreg) ⟨⟩ vi (ist) - 1. [herumfahren] to wander about; **in der Welt herumziehen** to roam the world - 2. [im Kreis]: **um etw herumziehen** to go round sthg. ⟨⟩ vt (hat): **etw um etw herumziehen** to put sthg round sthg.

herunter, runter adv down; **herunter vom Dach!** get down from the roof!; **auf der Fahrt von Hamburg herunter** on the journey down from Hamburg.

herunter|bekommen vt (unreg) fam - 1. [schlucken können, nach unten bekommen] to get down - 2. [entfernen können] to get off; **den Schmutz vom Teppich herunterbekommen** to get the dirt out of the carpet.

herunter|fahren vt (unreg) - 1. [reduzieren - Produktion] to scale down; [- Temperatur] to reduce - 2. EDV to shut down.

heruntergekommen adj - 1. [Haus] dilapidated - 2. [Person] down-at-heel.

herunter|holen vt to bring down.

herunter|laden vt (unreg) EDV to download.

herunter|lassen vt (unreg) - 1. [senken] to lower - 2. [gehen lassen] to let down.

herunter|machen vt: **jn/etw heruntermachen** fam to pull sb/sthg to pieces, to knock sb/sthg.

herunter|schlucken vt to swallow.

hervor adv: **hervor mit euch!** out you come!

hervor|bringen vt (unreg) - 1. [Ton] to utter - 2. [entwickeln] to produce.

hervor|gehen (perf **ist hervorgegangen**) vi (unreg): **aus etw hervorgehen** [zu entnehmen sein] to be clear from sthg; **aus dieser Familie sind mehrere Künstler hervorgegangen** this family has produced several artists; **aus etw als Sieger hervorgehen** to emerge victorious from sthg.

hervor|heben vt (unreg) to emphasize; **js Leistung hervorheben** to single out sb's performance.

hervor|holen vt to bring out.

hervorragend ⟨⟩ *adj* excellent. ⟨⟩ *adv* excellently; **hervorragend angezogen sein** to be extremely well-dressed; **hervorragend schmecken** to taste excellent.

hervor|rufen *vt (unreg)* - **1.** [verursachen] to cause - **2.** [rufen] to call out.

hervor|stechen *vi (unreg)* to stand out.

hervor|tun ▸ sich hervortun *ref (unreg)* - **1.** [auffallen] to distinguish o.s. - **2.** *abw* [angeben] to show off.

Herz *(pl -en ODER -) das* - **1.** [gen] heart - **2.** *(ohne Artikel) (ohne pl)* [Spielkartenfarbe] hearts *Pl*; **die Herzsechs** the six of hearts; **ein Herz für jn/etw haben** to be fond of sb/sthg; **es nicht übers Herz bringen, etw zu tun** not to have the heart to do sthg; **etwas auf dem Herzen haben** to have sthg on one's mind; **jm das Herz brechen** to break sb's heart; **ich möchte dir etwas ans Herz legen** allow me to give you a piece of advice; **sie/es liegt ihm am Herzen** she/it matters to him; **kein Herz haben** to be heartless. **▸ von ganzem Herzen** *adv* wholeheartedly.

Herzenslust *die*: **nach Herzenslust** to one's heart's content.

herzerfrischend ⟨⟩ *adj* refreshing. ⟨⟩ *adv* refreshingly.

herzergreifend ⟨⟩ *adj* heartrending. ⟨⟩ *adv* heartrendingly.

herzhaft ⟨⟩ *adj* - **1.** [fest] hearty - **2.** [nahrhaft] hearty and tasty. ⟨⟩ *adv* - **1.** [fest] heartily - **2.** [nahrhaft]: **herzhaft schmecken** to be hearty and tasty.

her|ziehen *(perf hat/ist hergezogen) (unreg)* ⟨⟩ *vt (hat)* [heranziehen] to pull up; **jn/etw hinter sich (D) herziehen** to drag sb/sthg along behind one. ⟨⟩ *vi* - **1.** *abw* [lästern]: **über jn herziehen** to pull sb to pieces - **2.** *(ist)* [umziehen] to move here - **3.** *(ist)* [gehen] to walk along.

Herz|infarkt *der* heart attack.

Herz|klopfen *das*: **ich habe Herzklopfen** my heart is pounding.

herzlich ⟨⟩ *adj* - **1.** [freundlich] warm - **2.** [aufrichtig] sincere. ⟨⟩ *adv* - **1.** [freundlich] warmly - **2.** [aufrichtig] sincerely - **3.** [sehr] really; **herzlich wenig** very little.

Herzog, in *(mpl Herzöge, fpl -nen) der, die* duke (duchess *die*).

Herz|schlag *der* - **1.** [Herzrhythmus] heartbeat - **2.** [Herzstillstand] heart failure (*U*).

Herz|schrittmacher *(pl -) der* pacemaker.

Herz|stillstand *der* cardiac arrest.

herzzerreißend ⟨⟩ *adj* heartrending. ⟨⟩ *adv* heartrendingly.

Hessen *nt* Hesse.

hessisch *adj* Hessian.

Hetze *die* - **1.** [Hast] (mad) rush - **2.** [Lästern] hate campaign.

hetzen *(perf hat/ist gehetzt)* ⟨⟩ *vi* - **1.** *(ist)* [rennen] to rush - **2.** *(hat)* [lästern]: **gegen jn hetzen** to stir up hatred against sb. ⟨⟩ *vt (hat)*: **jn/etw auf jn hetzen** to set sb/sthg on sb.

Heu *das* - **1.** [getrocknetes Gras] hay - **2.** *fam* [Geld] dough, dosh *UK*.

Heuchelei *(pl -en) die abw* - **1.** [Vortäuschen] hypocrisy - **2.** [Tat] piece of hypocrisy; [Äußerung] hypocritical remark.

heucheln ⟨⟩ *vt* to feign. ⟨⟩ *vi* to be a hypocrite.

Heuchler, in *(mpl -, fpl -nen) der, die* hypocrite.

heulen *vi* - **1.** [Person, Tier] to howl - **2.** [Sirene] to wail.

Heuschnupfen *der* hay fever.

heute *adv* - **1.** [als ein Tag] today; **heute Früh** early this morning; **heute Morgen/Mittag/Abend** this morning/lunchtime/evening; **heute in vierzehn Tagen/einer Woche** a fortnight/a week today; **lieber heute als morgen** sooner rather than later; **von heute auf morgen** from one day to the next, overnight - **2.** [gegenwärtig] nowadays.

heutig *adj* today's; **der heutige Tag** today.

heutzutage *adv* nowadays.

Hexe *(pl -n) die* witch.

Hexenschuss *der*: **einen Hexenschuss haben** to have lumbago.

Hexerei *(pl -en) die* witchcraft.

Hieb *(pl -e) der* [Schlag] blow. **▸ Hiebe** *Pl fam* [Prügel]: **Hiebe bekommen** to get a beating.

hiebfest *adj*: **hieb- und stichfest** watertight.

hielt *prät* ⟶ **halten**.

hier *adv* - **1.** [räumlich] here; [in der Schule]: **hier! here!, present!; der/die/das hier** this one here; **ab hier** from here; **von hier aus** from here; **hier und da** here and there; **"hier spricht Stefan"** [beim Telefon] "Stefan speaking"; **ich bin nicht von hier** I'm not from around here; **hier, nimm schon!** here, take it! - **2.** [zeitlich] now; **hier brach sie in Tränen aus** then she burst into tears; **von hier an** from now on; **hier und da** now and then - **3.** [in dieser Sache]: **hier täuschst du dich aber!** but that's where you're wrong.

hieran *adv* - **1.** [an dieser/diese Sache]: **die Erinnerung hieran fällt ihm schwer** he has difficulty remembering this - **2.** [an diesem/diesen Platz]: **hieran sind wir schon vorbeigekommen** we've already come past here.

Hierarchie *(pl -n) die* hierarchy.

hierauf *adv* - **1.** [auf dieser/diese Sache]: **hierauf beharren** to insist on this; **hierauf keine Antwort finden** to find no answer to this - **2.** [auf diesem/diesen Platz] on here - **3.** [daraufhin] hereupon.

hieraus *adv* out of this.

hier behalten *vt (unreg)* to keep here.

hierbei *adv* - **1.** [zeitlich] on this occasion - **2.** [bei dieser Sache]: **hierbei ist Konzentration nötig** you need to concentrate whilst doing this.

hier bleiben (*perf* **ist hier geblieben**) *vi* (*unreg*) to stay here.

hierdurch *adv* - **1.** [örtlich] through here - **2.** [ursächlich] as a result of this - **3.** [hiermit] hereby.

hierfür *adv* for this.

hierher *adv* here.

hierhin *adv* here.

hierin *adv* - **1.** [örtlich] in here - **2.** [in dieser Angelegenheit] in this.

hiermit *adv* - **1.** [mit diesem Gegenstand, mit dieser Angelegenheit] with this - **2.** [mit dieser Handlung] hereby.

hiernach *adv* - **1.** [zeitlich] after this - **2.** [dieser Aussage folgend] according to this.

hier sein (*perf* **ist hier gewesen**) *vi* (*unreg*) to be here.

hierüber *adv* - **1.** [räumlich] over here - **2.** [über diese Angelegenheit] about this - **3.** *geh* [zeitlich]: **hierüber vergingen mehrere Monate** this took several months.

hierum *adv* - **1.** [örtlich] around here - **2.** [um diese Sache] about this.

hierunter *adv* - **1.** [räumlich] under here - **2.** [unter dieser Sache] by this - **3.** [bei Menge] among these.

hiervon *adv* - **1.** [von diesem Gegenstand] of this - **2.** [von dieser Angelegenheit]: **hiervon hängt es ab** it depends on this; **hiervon halte ich viel** I think very highly of this - **3.** [örtlich] from here - **4.** [ursächlich] from this - **5.** [von dieser Menge] of these.

hierzu *adv* - **1.** [zu dieser Angelegenheit] to this; **ich rate dir dringend hierzu** I urge you to do this - **2.** [zu diesem Gegenstand] with this - **3.** [zu dieser Menge]: **stellen Sie sich bitte hierzu** please stand with these people here; **legen Sie die Zeitungen bitte hierzu** please add your newspapers to these.

hierzulande *adv* in this country.

hiesig *adj* local.

hieß *prät* ⊳ **heißen**.

Hilfe (*pl* **-n**) ◇ *die* - **1.** [Helfen] help; **mit js Hilfe** with sb's help; **jn/etw zu Hilfe nehmen** to use sb/sthg - **2.** [Geld - freiwillig] aid; [- rechtlich garantiert] benefit - **3.** [Haushaltshilfe] cleaner. ◇ *interj* help! ◆ **Hilfe suchend** ◇ *adj* [Blick] beseeching. ◇ *adv* beseechingly. ◆ **mit Hilfe** *adv* = **mithilfe**.

Hilfeleistung *die* aid (*U*).

Hilferuf *der* call for help.

hilflos ◇ *adj* - **1.** [hilfsbedürftig] helpless - **2.** [ratlos] clueless - **3.** [unbeholfen] awkward. ◇ *adv* - **1.** [hilfsbedürftig] helplessly - **2.** [ratlos] cluelessly - **3.** [unbeholfen] awkwardly.

hilfreich ◇ *adj* helpful; **eine hilfreiche Hand** a helping hand. ◇ *adv*: **jm hilfreich zur Seite stehen** to be a big help to sb.

Hilfsarbeiter, in *der, die* [in der Fabrik] unskilled worker; [beim Bau] labourer.

hilfsbedürftig *adj* in need (of help).

hilfsbereit *adj* helpful.

Hilfskraft *die* assistant.

Hilfsmittel *das* aid.

Hilfsverb *das* GRAMM auxiliary verb.

hilft *präs* ⊳ **helfen**.

Himalaya *der*: **der Himalaya** the Himalayas.

Himbeere *die* raspberry.

Himmel (*pl* **-**) *der* - **1.** [Firmament] sky; **am Himmel** in the sky; **unter freiem Himmel** in the open, out of doors - **2.** [Jenseits] heaven - **3.** [Vorsehung]: **der Himmel weiß, wann er endlich zurückkommt** heaven (only) knows when he will finally come back - **4.** [Baldachin] canopy; **aus heiterem Himmel** out of the blue; **im siebenten Himmel sein** to be in seventh heaven.

himmelblau *adj* sky-blue.

Himmelfahrt *die* Ascension Day.

Himmelsrichtung *die* direction; **die vier Himmelsrichtungen** the four points of the compass.

himmlisch ◇ *adj* heavenly; **eine himmlische Fügung** divine providence. ◇ *adv* [leicht, bequem, schön] wonderfully; **himmlisch schmecken/aussehen** to taste/look divine.

hin *adv* - **1.** [räumlich]: **bis zum Baum hin** up to the tree; **zur Straße hin** towards the street; **zum Norden hin** (towards the) north; **wo ist er hin?** where has he gone?; **hin und her** back and forth; **der Weg hin** the way there; **zweimal London hin und zurück** two returns *UK* ODER round-trip tickets *US* to London; **einmal London nur hin, bitte!** one for London, just a single please - **2.** [zeitlich]: **zum Abend hin** towards evening; **über viele Jahre hin** for many years; **hin und wieder** now and then - **3.** *fig*: **er brabbelte da was vor sich hin** he was mumbling something to himself; **nach außen hin** outwardly; **auf deinen Rat hin** on your advice; **auf den Verdacht hin, dass...** on the suspicion that...; **ihr Kleid/Ruf ist hin** her dress/reputation is ruined; **er war von dem Mädchen ganz hin (und weg)** he was completely taken with the girl.

hinab *adv* = **hinunter**.

hinabgehen (*perf* **ist hinabgegangen**) (*unreg*) *vt* & *vi* *geh* to go down.

hinarbeiten *vi*: **auf etw (A) hinarbeiten** to work towards sthg.

hinauf *adv* up; **den Berg hinauf** up the mountain; **von den Alpen bis an die Ostsee hinauf** from the Alps right up to the Baltic.

hinauf|gehen (*perf* ist hinaufgegangen) (*unreg*) ⟨⟩ *vi* to go up; **es geht hinauf** the road climbs. ⟨⟩ *vt* to go up.

hinauf|sehen *vi* (*unreg*): **zu jm/etw hinaufsehen** to look up at sb/sthg.

hinauf|steigen (*perf* ist hinaufgestiegen) *vi* & *vt* (*unreg*) to climb.

hinaus *adv* - 1. [räumlich] out; **das Fenster geht zur Straße hinaus** the window looks (out) onto the street; **hinaus mit dir!** get out!; **über unsere Grenzen hinaus bekannt** known beyond our borders - 2. [zeitlich]: **über das Abendbrot hinaus bleiben** to stay over dinner; **auf Monate hinaus** for months to come.

hinaus|begleiten *vt* to see out.

hinaus|gehen (*perf* ist hinausgegangen) *vi* (*unreg*) - 1. [nach draußen] to go out - 2.: **auf etw** (A) **hinausgehen** [gerichtet sein Zimmer, Fenster] to look onto sthg; [Tür, Gang] to lead into sthg; [in eine Richtung] to face sthg - 3. [überschreiten]: **über etw** (A) **hinausgehen** to go beyond sthg.

hinaus|laufen (*perf* ist hinausgelaufen) *vi* (*unreg*) - 1. [nach draußen] to run outside - 2. [abzielen]: **auf etw** (A) **hinauslaufen** to amount to sthg; **das läuft auf dasselbe hinaus** it amounts to the same thing.

hinaus|schieben *vt* (*unreg*) - 1. [nach draußen] to push outside - 2. [zeitlich] to put off, to postpone. ⬧ **sich hinausschieben** *ref* [örtlich] to push one's way out.

hinaus|werfen *vt* (*unreg*) to throw out.

hinaus|zögern *vt* to put off. ⬧ **sich hinauszögern** *ref* to be delayed.

hin|bekommen *vt* (*unreg*): **wie willst du denn das hinbekommen?** how do you intend to do ODER manage that?; **etw wieder hinbekommen** to mend sthg.

hin|bestellen *vt* to tell to come/go.

Hinblick *der*: **in** ODER **im Hinblick auf jn/etw** [in Bezug auf] with regard to sb/sthg; **in** ODER **im Hinblick auf etw** (A) [wegen] in view of sthg.

hinderlich *adj*: **jm/einer Sache hinderlich sein** to get in sb's/sthg's way.

hindern *vt* to prevent; **was hindert dich zu bleiben?** what is preventing you from staying?

Hindernis (*pl* -se) *das* obstacle; [in Leichtathletik] hurdle; [in Springreiten] jump.

hin|deuten *vi* to point; **auf jn/etw hindeuten** [zeigen] to point at sb/sthg; [in einer Menge] to point sb/sthg out; [erkennen lassen] to point to sb/sthg.

Hindi *das* Hindi; *siehe auch* **Englisch(e)**.

Hindu (*pl* -s) *der* Hindu.

hindurch *adv* - 1. [zeitlich]: **den ganzen Tag hindurch** throughout the whole day - 2. [örtlich]: **durch den Berg hindurch** through the mountain.

hinein *adv* - 1. [räumlich] in; **hinein ins Bett!** get into bed! - 2. [zeitlich]: **bis tief in die Nacht hinein arbeiten** to work late into the night.

hinein|denken ⬧ **sich hineindenken** *ref* (*unreg*): **sich in jn/etw hineindenken** to put o.s. in sb/sthg's position.

hinein|fressen *vt* (*unreg*): **etw in sich** (A) **hineinfressen** to gobble sthg up; *fam* [Sorgen] to bottle sthg up.

hinein|gehen (*perf* ist hineingegangen) *vi* (*unreg*) - 1. [nach drinnen] to go inside - 2. [hineinpassen]: **in diese Flasche geht nicht mehr als ein Liter hinein** this bottle won't hold more than a litre.

hinein|geraten (*perf* ist hineingeraten) *vi* (*unreg*): **in etw** (A) **hineingeraten** to get into sthg; **in einen einsamen Wald hineingeraten** to find o.s. in a lonely wood.

hinein|steigern ⬧ **sich hineinsteigern** *ref*: **sie hat sich in diese Sache hineingesteigert** she has become completely caught up in this affair.

hinein|versetzen ⬧ **sich hineinversetzen** *ref*: **sich in jn** ODER **in js Lage hineinversetzen** to put o.s. in sb's position.

hinein|ziehen (*perf* hat/ist hineingezogen) (*unreg*) ⟨⟩ *vt* (hat) - 1. [nach drinnen] to pull in - 2. [verwickeln]: **jn in etw** (A) **hineinziehen** to draw sb into sthg. ⟨⟩ *vi* (ist) - 1. [umziehen] to move in - 2. [gehen] to go in.

hin|fahren (*perf* hat/ist hingefahren) (*unreg*) ⟨⟩ *vi* (ist) to go there; [mit Auto] to drive there; **wo ist er hingefahren?** where did he go (to)? ⟨⟩ *vt* (hat) to take there.

Hin|fahrt *die* [mit dem Auto] journey there; [mit dem Zug] outward journey.

hin|fallen (*perf* ist hingefallen) *vi* (*unreg*) to fall (down); **sie hat die Vase hinfallen lassen** she dropped the vase.

hin|fällig *adj* - 1. [altersschwach] frail - 2. [ungültig] invalid.

Hin|flug *der* outward flight.

hin|führen ⟨⟩ *vt* to lead there. ⟨⟩ *vi* to lead there; **zu etw hinführen** to lead to sthg.

hing *prät* ⟼ **hängen**.

hin|geben *vt* (*unreg*) *geh* to give up. ⬧ **sich hingeben** *ref*: **sich einer Sache** (D) **hingeben** to devote o.s. to sthg; **sich einer Illusion hingeben** to cherish an illusion; **sich jm hingeben** to give o.s. to sb.

hingegen *konj* on the other hand.

hin|gehen (*perf* ist hingegangen) *vi* (*unreg*) [gehen] to go there; **zu etw hingehen** to go to sthg.

hin|halten *vt* (*unreg*) - 1. [reichen] to hold out - 2. [vertrösten] to keep waiting.

hin|hocken ⬧ **sich hinhocken** *ref* to crouch down.

hinken (*perf* hat/ist gehinkt) *vi* - 1. *(hat)* [humpeln] to (have a) limp - 2. *(ist)* [an einen Ort] to limp, to hobble.

hinlknien ⮞ **sich hinknien** *ref* to kneel down.

hinlkommen (*perf* ist hingekommen) *vi* (*unreg*) - 1. [ankommen] to get there; **zu etw hinkommen** to get to sthg - 2. [hingehören] to belong, to go - 3. [hingeraten]: **wenn ich wüsste, wo meine Brille hingekommen ist** if I knew where my glasses had gone - 4. [auskommen]: **mit etw hinkommen** to manage with sthg - 5. [zutreffen] to work out; **das kommt hin/nicht hin!** that is right/wrong!

hinlkriegen *vt fam* to manage; **sie hat das gut hingekriegt** she made a good job of that; **etw wieder hinkriegen** to fix sthg.

hinlänglich ⬦ *adj* sufficient. ⬦ *adv* sufficiently.

hinllegen *vt* - 1. [Gegenstand] to put down; [Zettel] to leave - 2. [ins Bett] to put to bed - 3. *fam* [bezahlen] to fork out - 4. *fam* [Darbietung] to turn in; [Prüfung] to do. ⮞ **sich hinlegen** *ref* - 1. [sich legen] to lie down - 2. *fam* [stürzen] to come a cropper.

hinlnehmen *vt* (*unreg*) - 1. [ertragen] to take - 2. *fam* [mitnehmen]: **jn/etw (zu jm) mit hinnehmen** to take sb/sthg (to sb).

hinlpflanzen ⮞ **sich hinpflanzen** *ref fam* [sich hinstellen]: **sich (vor jn) hinpflanzen** to plant o.s. (in front of sb).

hinlreichen ⬦ *vt* [zureichen]: **jm etw hinreichen** to hand sb sthg. ⬦ *vi* - 1. [sich erstrecken] to reach - 2. [ausreichen] to be enough.

Hinreise *die* journey there.

hinlreißen *vt* (*unreg*) - 1. [ziehen] to pull - 2. [begeistern] to captivate - 3. [verleiten]: **sich zu etw hinreißen lassen** [überzeugen] to let o.s. be carried away into doing sthg; [provozieren] to be driven to do sthg.

hinreißend *adj* captivating.

hinlrichten *vt* to execute.

Hinlrichtung *die* execution.

hinlschauen *vi* to look; **genau hinschauen** to look closely.

hin sein (*perf* ist hin gewesen) *vi* (*unreg*) *fam* [kaputt] to have had it; [ruiniert] to be shattered; [vor Glück] to be overjoyed.

hinlsetzen *vt* [Gegenstand] to put down; [Baby] to sit down. ⮞ **sich hinsetzen** *ref* - 1. [sich setzen] to sit down - 2. *fam* [stürzen] to land on one's backside.

Hinsicht *die* (ohne pl): **in dieser/jeder Hinsicht** in this/every respect; **in doppelter Hinsicht** in two respects.

hinlstellen *vt* - 1. [stellen] to put - 2. [absetzen] to put down - 3. [darstellen]: **jn/etw als etw hinstellen** to describe sb/sthg as sthg. ⮞ **sich**

hinlstellen *ref* - 1. [sich stellen] to stand - 2. [darstellen]: **sich als jn/etw hinstellen** to pretend to be sb/sthg.

hinten *adv* - 1. [am Ende] at the back; **da** ODER **dort hinten** back there; **sie ist hinten im Garten** she's out the back (in the garden); **im Auto hinten sitzen** to sit in the back of the car; **das dritte Haus von hinten** the third house from the end - 2. [weit entfernt]: **weit hinten** a long way behind - 3. [an der Rückseite] on the back; **das Haus hat hinten einen Balkon** the house has a balcony at the back - 4. [als Richtungsangabe] back; **von hinten** from behind.

hintenherum *adv fam* - 1. [um etw herum] round the back - 2. [indirekt] indirectly.

hinter *präp* - 1. (+ D, A) [räumlich] behind; **hinter dem Haus** behind the house, in back of the house *US*; **hinter jm herlaufen** to run after sb; **3 km hinter Köln** 3 km after Cologne - 2. [zeitlich]: **etw hinter sich** (A) **bringen** to put sthg behind one; **das hätten wir endlich hinter uns!** thank God that's behind us!

Hinterlausgang *der* rear exit.

Hinterbliebene (*pl* -n) *der, die* surviving dependant.

hintere, r, s *adj* back.

Hintere (*pl* -n) *der, die, das*: **der/die/das Hintere** the one at the back.

hintereinander *adv* - 1. [räumlich] behind each other - 2. [zeitlich] in a row.

Hinterleingang *der* rear entrance.

Hinterlgedanke *der* ulterior motive.

hintergehen (*prät* hinterging, *perf* hat hintergangen) *vt* to deceive.

Hinterlgrund *der* background; **im Hintergrund bleiben** to remain in the background; **jn/etw in den Hintergrund drängen** to push sb/sthg into the background.

Hinterhalt (*pl* -e) *der* ambush; **im Hinterhalt liegen** to lie in ambush; **in einen Hinterhalt geraten** ODER **fallen** to be ambushed.

hinterhältig ⬦ *adj* devious. ⬦ *adv* deviously.

hinterher[1] *adv* [räumlich] behind.

hinterher[2] *adv* [zeitlich] afterwards.

hinterherlfahren (*perf* ist hinterhergefahren) *vi* (*unreg*): **jm/etw hinterherfahren** to drive behind sb/sthg; [verfolgen] to drive after sb/sthg.

hinterherlgehen (*perf* ist hinterhergegangen) *vi* (*unreg*): **jm hinterhergehen** to follow sb.

Hinterlkopf *der* back of the head; **etw im Hinterkopf haben/behalten** *fig* to have/keep sthg at the back of one's mind.

hinterlassen (*präs* hinterlässt, *prät* hinterließ, *perf* hat hinterlassen) *vt* to leave; **jm etw hinterlassen** to leave sb sthg.

hinterlegen *vt*: **etw bei jm hinterlegen** to leave sthg with sb.

Hinterlist *die* cunning.

hinterlistig <> *adj* cunning. <> *adv* cunningly.

Hintern (*pl* -) *der fam* backside.

Hinterlrad *das* back wheel.

Hinterlseite *die* back.

Hinterlteil *das fam* backside.

Hintertreffen *das* (*ohne pl*): **ins Hintertreffen geraten** to fall behind.

hintertreiben (*prät* hintertrieb, *perf* hat hintertrieben) *vt* [Plan] to thwart; [Heirat] to prevent; [Gesetz, Reform] to block.

Hinterltür *die* back door.

hinterziehen (*prät* hinterzog, *perf* hat hinterzogen) *vt*: **Steuern hinterziehen** to evade tax.

hinltreten (*perf* hat/ist hingetreten) *vi* (*unreg*) - 1. (*ist*) [an einen Ort]: **zu jm/etw hintreten** to step over to sb/sthg; **vor jn hintreten** to go up to sb - 2. (*hat*) [mit Fuß] to kick.

hinüber *adv* over, across; **da hinüber** over there; **gehen Sie links/rechts hinüber** go left/right; *siehe auch* **hinüber sein**.

hinüber sein (*perf* ist hinüber gewesen) *vi* (*unreg*) *fam* - 1. [kaputt] to have had it; [erschöpft] to be done in; [betrunken] to be well away - 2. [gehen] to have gone over.

hinunter *adv* down; **die Treppe hinunter** down the stairs; **vom General bis hinunter zum einfachen Soldat** from the general down to the private.

hinunterlblicken *vi*: **in etw (A) hinunterblicken** to look down into sthg; **an sich (D) hinunterblicken** to look down at o.s.

hinunterlschlucken *vt eigtl* & *fig* to swallow.

hinunterlstürzen (*perf* hat/ist hinuntergestürzt) *vt* - 1. (*ist*) [hinunterfallen] to fall down - 2. (*hat*) [werfen] to throw down - 3. (*hat*) *fam* [schnell trinken] to gulp down. ➡ **sich hinunterstürzen** *ref* [sich hinunterwerfen]: **sich (von etw) hinunterstürzen** to throw o.s. off (sthg).

hinweg *adv geh* away; **über jn/etw hinweg** over sb/sthg; **über Jahre hinweg** for many years.

Hinweg *der* way there; **auf dem Hinweg** on the way there.

hinweglgehen (*perf* ist hinweggegangen) *vi* (*unreg*): **über etw (A) hinweggehen** to pass over sthg.

hinweglkommen (*perf* ist hinweggekommen) *vi* (*unreg*): **über etw (A) hinwegkommen** to get over sthg.

hinweglsehen *vi* (*unreg*): **über jn/etw hinwegsehen** to see over sb/sthg; **über etw (A) hinwegsehen** *fig* to overlook sthg.

hinweglsetzen ➡ **sich hinwegsetzen** *ref*: **sich über etw (A) hinwegsetzen** to disregard sthg.

Hinweis (*pl* -e) *der* [Tip, Fingerzeig] tip; [Anleitung] instruction; [Indiz] sign.

hinlweisen (*unreg*) <> *vi* - 1. [auf etw schließen lassen]: **auf etw (A) hinweisen** to point to sthg - 2. [zeigen]: **auf jn/etw hinweisen** to point to sb/sthg. <> *vt*: **jn auf etw (A) hinweisen** to point sthg out to sb.

hinlwenden *vt* to turn. ➡ **sich hinwenden** *ref* to turn.

hinlwerfen *vt* (*unreg*) - 1. [werfen] to throw down - 2. *fam* [Arbeit, Projekt] to chuck in - 3. [Skizze] to dash off - 4. [Bemerkung] to drop casually; [Frage] to ask casually - 5. *fam* [fallen lassen] to drop. ➡ **sich hinwerfen** *ref* to throw o.s. down.

hinlziehen (*perf* hat/ist hingezogen) (*unreg*) <> *vt* (*hat*) - 1. [anziehen]: **jn/etw zu sich hinziehen** to attract sb/sthg - 2. [zeitlich] to draw out. <> *vi* (*ist*) [umziehen] to move. ➡ **sich hinziehen** *ref* [lange dauern] to drag on.

hinzu *adv* in addition; **hinzu kommt noch** (and) what is more.

hinzulfügen *vt* to add; **etw zu etw hinzufügen** to add sthg to sthg.

hinzulkommen (*perf* ist hinzugekommen) *vi* (*unreg*) - 1. [ankommen]: **zu jm/etw hinzukommen** to join sb/sthg - 2. [sich ergeben] to be added on.

hinzulziehen *vt* (*unreg*) to call in.

Hirn (*pl* -e) *das* - 1. [Gehirn] brain - 2. *fam* [Denkvermögen] brains *Pl*.

Hirngespinst (*pl* -e) *das abw* figment of one's imagination.

Hirsch (*pl* -e) *der* [Tier] deer; [männlich] stag; [Fleisch] venison.

Hirse *die* millet.

Hirte (*pl* -n), **Hirt** (*pl* -en) *der* shepherd.

Hirtin (*pl* -nen) *die* shepherdess.

hissen *vt* to hoist.

Historiker, in (*mpl* -, *fpl* -nen) *der, die* historian.

historisch <> *adj* - 1. [geschichtlich] historical - 2. [entscheidend] historic. <> *adv* [geschichtlich] historically; **etw historisch betrachten** to look at sthg in historical terms.

Hit (*pl* -s) *der* hit.

Hitlparade *die* charts *Pl*.

Hitze *die* heat.

hitzebeständig *adj* heat-resistant.

hitzefrei *adj*: **hitzefrei haben** to have the day off school because of hot weather.

Hitzelwelle *die* heatwave.

hitzig <> *adj* - 1. [Person] hot-blooded; [Temperament] fiery - 2. [Diskussion, Streit] heated. <> *adv* [lebhaft] heatedly.

hitzköpfig *adj* [Person] hot-tempered.

Hitzlschlag *der* heat stroke.

HIV-positiv *adj* MED HIV-positive.

H-Milch *die* long-life milk.

hob *prät* ▷ **heben**.

Hobby ['hɔbi] (*pl* -s) *das* hobby.

Hobby|koch *der* amateur cook.

Hobby|köchin *die* amateur cook.

Hobel (*pl* -) *der* - 1. [Werkzeug] plane - 2. [Küchengerät] slicer.

Hobelbank (*pl* -bänke) *die* carpenter's bench.

hobeln ▷ *vt* [Holz] to plane; [Gemüse] to slice. ▷ *vi* to plane; **an etw** (D) **hobeln** to plane sthg.

hoch (*kompar* **höher**, *superl* **höchste**) ▷ *adj* - 1. [räumlich] high; [Baum, Gebäude] tall; [Schnee] deep; **drei Meter hoch** three metres high/tall/deep; **im hohen Norden** in the far north - 2. [bezeichnet Ausmass - Blutdruck, Tempo, Mieten, Preis *etc*] high; [- Gewicht, Strafe] heavy; [- Anzahl, Summe] large; **im hohem Grade** to a large extent; **wenn es hoch kommt** at the most - 3. [bezeichnet Qualität - Position, Ansprüche] high; [- Ehre, Begabung] great; **das ist mir zu hoch** *fam fig* that's beyond me - 4. [gesellschaftlich gehoben]: **von hoher Geburt** of high birth; **von hohem Ansehen** highly regarded; **ein hoher Beamter** a high-ranking official - 5. MUS high; **jn in den höchsten Tönen loben** *fig* to praise sb to the skies. ▷ *adv* (*kompar* **höher**; *superl* **am höchsten**) - 1. [räumlich]: **das Dorf ist hoch gelegen** the village is situated high up; **zwei Treppen hoch** two floors up; **das Flugzeug fliegt 3000 Meter hoch** the plane is flying at (a height of) 3,000 metres; **ein hoch aufgeschossener Junge** a tall boy - 2. [bezeichnet Ausmass, Qualität]: **hoch verlieren** to lose heavily; **hoch zufrieden** very content; **hoch und heilig versprechen** to promise solemnly - 3. MUS high; **du singst zu hoch!** you're singing sharp!

Hoch (*pl* -s) *das* - 1. [Jubelruf] cheer; **jm ein dreifaches Hoch ausbringen** to give three cheers for sb - 2. [Hochdruckgebiet] high.

Hochachtung *die* great respect.

hochachtungsvoll *adv* Yours faithfully (*nach Dear Sir/Madam*); Yours sincerely (*nach Dear Mr/Mrs*).

hoch|arbeiten ➤ **sich hocharbeiten** *ref* to work one's way up.

hoch begabt *adj* highly talented.

Hochbetrieb *der*: **im Büro herrscht Hochbetrieb** it's very busy in the office.

hoch bezahlt *adj* highly-paid.

Hochburg *die* stronghold.

hochdeutsch ▷ *adj* standard German. ▷ *adv* in standard German.

Hochdruck *der* - 1. [technisch, meteorologisch] high pressure; **unter Hochdruck stehen** to be under high pressure - 2. *fam fig* [Hochbetrieb]: **unter Hochdruck stehen** to be at full stretch.

Hochdruck|gebiet *das* high-pressure area.

hoch empfindlich *adj* highly sensitive.

hocherfreut ▷ *adj* highly delighted. ▷ *adv* with great delight.

hoch|fahren (*perf* hat/ist hochgefahren) (*unreg*) ▷ *vi* (ist) - 1. [nach oben] to go up; [in Auto] to drive up - 2. [erschrecken] to start; **aus dem Schlaf hochfahren** to wake up with a start - 3. [zornig] to flare up. ▷ *vt* (hat) *fam* [nach oben] to take up.

hoch|fliegen (*perf* ist hochgeflogen) *vi* (*unreg*) [Vogel, Flugzeug] to fly up.

Hoch|form *die*: **in Hochform sein** to be on top form.

Hoch|frequenz *die* PHYS high frequency.

Hoch|gebirge *das* high mountains *Pl*.

Hoch|gefühl *das*: **im Hochgefühl einer Sache** (G) elated by sthg.

hoch|gehen (*perf* ist hochgegangen) *vi* (*unreg*) - 1. [gehen, sich heben] to go up - 2. [Mine, Bombe] to go off; [Gebäude] to blow up; **etw hochgehen lassen** to blow sthg up - 3. *fam* [wütend werden] to hit the roof - 4. [aufgedeckt werden] to be uncovered; **jn hochgehen lassen** *fam* to squeal on sb.

hochgestellt *adj* [Zahl] superscript.

Hochglanz *der*: **ein Fotoabzug in Hochglanz** a gloss print; **auf Hochglanz poliert** polished until it shines; **etw auf Hochglanz bringen** *fig* to make sthg spick-and-span.

hochgradig ▷ *adj* extreme. ▷ *adv* extremely.

hoch|halten *vt* (*unreg*) [bewahren] to uphold.

hoch halten *vt* (*unreg*) [nach oben] to hold up.

Hoch|haus *das* high-rise building.

hoch|heben *vt* (*unreg*): **jn/etw hochheben** to lift sb/sthg (up).

hochkant *adv* on end.

hoch|klappen (*perf* hat/ist hochgeklappt) ▷ *vt* (hat) [Klapptisch] to fold up; [Verdeck, Armlehne] to fold back; [Kragen] to turn up; [Sitz] to tip up. ▷ *vi* (ist) [Kragen, Hutkrempe] to turn up; [Sitz] to tip up.

hoch|klettern (*perf* ist hochgeklettert) *vi*: **an etw** (D) **hochklettern** to climb (up) sthg.

hoch|kommen (*perf* ist hochgekommen) *vi* (*unreg*) - 1. [nach oben] to come up - 2. [aufstehen] to get up - 3. [beruflich] to get on - 4. [erbrechen]: **es kommt ihr bei dem Gedanken daran heute noch hoch** the thought of it still makes her feel sick today.

Hoch|konjunktur *die* boom.

hoch|krempeln *vt* to roll up.

Hoch|land *das* uplands *Pl*.

hoch|leben *vi*: **jn/etw hochleben lassen** to give three cheers for sb/sthg.

Hochleistungssport *der* top-level sport.

Hochmut *der* arrogance.

hochmütig ▷ *adj* arrogant. ▷ *adv* arrogantly.

hochnäsig *abw adj* conceited.

hoch nehmen *vt (unreg)* [Teppich] to lift up; [Baby] to pick up.

Hoch|ofen *der* blast furnace.

hochprozentig *adj* [Getränk, Spirituose] high-proof; [Lösung] highly concentrated.

Hoch|rechnung *die* projection.

hochrot *adj* bright red.

Hoch|saison *die* high season.

hoch|schlagen ['hoːxʃlaːgn̩] *(perf hat/ist hochgeschlagen) (unreg)* ◇ *vt (hat)* to turn up. ◇ *vi (ist)* to leap up.

hoch|schrecken ['hoːxʃrɛkn̩] *(prät schreckte ODER schrak hoch, perf hat/ist hochgeschreckt)* ◇ *vt (hat) (reg)* to startle. ◇ *vi (ist)* to start; **er ist aus dem Schlaf hochgeschreckt** he was startled out of sleep.

Hochschulabschluss *(pl -schlüsse) der* (university) degree.

Hoch|schule *die* college; [Universität] university.

Hochschul|lehrer, in *der, die* college lecturer; [an der Universität] university lecturer.

Hochschul|reife *die qualification required by school-leavers for university entrance.*

hochschwanger ['hoːxʃvaŋɐ] *adj* heavily pregnant.

Hoch|sommer *der* midsummer.

Hoch|spannung *die* - 1. [Strom] high voltage - 2. [Stimmung] great tension.

hoch|spielen ['hoːxʃpiːlən] *vt* to blow up.

Hoch|springer, in *der, die* SPORT high jumper.

Hochsprung *der* SPORT high jump.

höchst ['høːçst] *adv* highly.

Hochstapler, in ['hoːxʃtaːplɐ, ərɪn] *(mpl -, fpl -nen) der, die* con artist.

Höchst|belastung *die* extreme pressure; [eines Materials, einer Konstruktion] maximum load.

höchstens ['høːçstn̩s] *adv* - 1. [im äußersten Fall] at best - 2. [außer] except.

Höchstfall *der (ohne pl)*: **im Höchstfall** at (the) most.

Höchstform *die*: **in Höchstform sein** to be on top form.

Höchst|geschwindigkeit *die* speed limit.

Höchst|grenze *die* upper limit.

Hochstimmung *die* festive mood.

höchstmöglich ['høːçstmøːklɪç] *adj* highest possible.

höchstwahrscheinlich ['høːçstvaːɐ̯ʃaɪnlɪç] *adv* most probably.

Hoch|tour *die*: **auf Hochtouren laufen** [Maschine] to run at top speed; [Vorbereitungen] to be in full swing.

hochtrabend *abw* ◇ *adj* pompous. ◇ *adv* pompously.

Hochwasser *das* high water; **Hochwasser haben** to be in spate; *fam fig* to be at half-mast.

hochwertig *adj* [Produkte] high-quality; [Eiweiß] highly nutritious.

Hoch|zeit *die* wedding; **silberne/goldene Hochzeit** silver/golden wedding.

Hochzeits|kleid *das* wedding dress.

Hochzeits|nacht *die* wedding night.

Hochzeits|paar *das* bride and groom.

Hochzeits|reise *die* honeymoon.

Hochzeits|tag *der* [Tag der Hochzeit] wedding day; [Jubiläum] wedding anniversary.

hoch|ziehen *vt (unreg)* - 1. [Rollladen, Hose] to pull up; [Segel, Flagge] to hoist - 2. [heben] to raise; **die Nase hochziehen** to sniff - 3. [bauen] to put up. ◆ **sich hochziehen** *ref*: **sich an etw (D) hochziehen** to pull o.s. up by holding on to sthg; *fig* to take pleasure in sthg.

Hocke *(pl -n) die* - 1. [Haltung]: **in die Hocke gehen** to crouch down - 2. [Sprung] squat vault.

hocken *vi* - 1. [kauern] to crouch - 2. *fam* [sitzen] to sit. ◆ **sich hocken** *ref* - 1. [sich kauern] to crouch - 2. *fam* [sich setzen] to sit o.s. down.

Hocker *(pl -) der* stool.

Höcker *(pl -) der* - 1. [Ausbuchtung] bump - 2. [von Kamel] hump.

Hockey *das* hockey.

Hoden *(pl -) der* testicle.

Hof *(pl Höfe) der* - 1. [von Häusern] courtyard - 2. [Bauernhof] farm - 3. [Schulhof] playground - 4. [von Gefängnissen] yard - 5. [von Königen] court; **jm den Hof machen** *fig* to court sb.

Hofbräuhaus *das large beer hall in Munich.*

hoffen ◇ *vt* to hope; **hoffen wir das Beste!** let's hope for the best! ◇ *vi*: **auf etw hoffen** to hope for sthg; **auf jn hoffen** to pin one's hopes on sb; **auf Gott hoffen** to trust in God.

hoffentlich *adv* hopefully; **kommt er? - ja, hoffentlich!** is he coming? - I hope so!

Hoffnung *(pl -en) die* hope; **die Hoffnung aufgeben/nicht aufgeben** to give up/not to give up hope; **seine Hoffnungen auf jn/etw setzen** to pin one's hopes on sb/sthg.

hoffnungslos ◇ *adj* hopeless. ◇ *adv* hopelessly.

Hoffnungslosigkeit *die* hopelessness.

hoffnungsvoll ◇ *adj* - 1. [optimistisch] hopeful - 2. [Erfolg versprechend] promising. ◇ *adv* - 1. [optimistisch] hopefully - 2. [Erfolg versprechend] promisingly.

höflich ◇ *adj* polite. ◇ *adv* politely.

Höflichkeit *(pl -en) die* - 1. [im Auftreten] politeness - 2. [Floskel] polite remark.

Höhe *(pl -n) die* - 1. [von Schrank, Berg] height; [von Dreieck] altitude - 2. [von Preis, Temperatur] level; **ein Bußgeld in Höhe von 50 Euro** a fine of 50 euros - 3. [Richtung]: **in die Höhe** up

- 4. [Linie]: **auf der** ODER **in Höhe von etw** level with sthg; **auf gleicher Höhe** level; **das ist die Höhe!** fam that's the limit!

Hoheit (pl -en) die - **1.** [Herrschaft] sovereignty - **2.** [als Anrede] Your Highness.

Hoheits|gebiet das sovereign territory.

Höhen|lage die altitude; **in Höhenlage** at high altitude.

Höhen|sonne die sun lamp.

Höhe|punkt der high point.

hohl <> adj - **1.** [gen] hollow; [Augen] sunken; **in der hohlen Hand** in the hollow of one's hand - **2.** fam abw [dumm - Phrase] empty; [- Person] empty-headed. <> adv - **1.** [dumpf] hollowly - **2.** fam abw [geistlos] emptily.

Höhle (pl -n) die - **1.** [Grotte] cave - **2.** [von Dachs] sett; [von Löwe] den; [von Fuchs] lair.

Hohl|kreuz das (ohne pl) hollow back.

Hohl|raum der cavity.

höhnisch <> adj scornful. <> adv scornfully.

holen vt - **1.** [herbeischaffen] to fetch, to get; **sich** (D) **bei jm Rat holen** to ask sb for advice; **etw holen kommen** to come for sthg; **sich** (D) **etw holen** [gen] to get sthg; [Krankheit] to catch sthg - **2.** [kaufen] to get - **3.** [herausnehmen]: **etw aus etw holen** to take sthg out of sthg - **4.** [Arzt, Polizei, Handwerker] to call.

Holland nt Holland.

Holländer (pl -) <> der Dutchman; **die Holländer** the Dutch. <> adj (unver) Dutch.

Holländerin (pl -nen) die Dutchwoman.

holländisch adj Dutch.

Hölle die hell; **die Hölle ist los!** fam fig all hell has broken loose!; **jm die Hölle heiß machen** fam fig to give sb hell.

höllisch <> adj - **1.** [schrecklich] appalling - **2.** fam [intensiv] infernal. <> adv fam [sehr]: **die Wunde tut höllisch weh** the wound hurts like hell; **höllisch aufpassen** to be incredibly careful.

Holm (pl -e) der SPORT bar.

holpern (perf hat/ist geholpert) vi - **1.** (ist) [beim Fahren] to jolt - **2.** (hat) [beim Sprechen] to stumble.

holprig <> adj - **1.** [Weg] bumpy - **2.** [Fremdsprache] halting - **3.** [Stil] clumsy. <> adv [sprechen, lesen] haltingly.

Holunder (pl -) der - **1.** [Baum] elder - **2.** [Beere] elderberry.

Holz (pl Hölzer) das wood; [Bauholz] timber UK; **aus dem gleichen** ODER **demselben Holz (geschnitzt) sein** fig to be cast from the same mould. ◆ **Holz verarbeitend** adj timber-processing.

Holzfäller, in (mpl -, fpl -nen) der, die woodcutter UK, lumberjack US.

holzig adj woody.

Holz|kohle die charcoal.

Holz|schuh der clog.

Holz|weg der: **auf dem Holzweg sein** to be barking up the wrong tree.

Homebanking ['ho:mbɛŋkɪŋ] das home banking.

Homepage ['ho:mpeɪdʒ] (pl -s) die EDV home page.

Homeshopping das (ohne pl) home shopping.

Homöopathie die homeopathy.

Homosexualität die homosexuality.

homosexuell adj homosexual.

Honig der honey.

Honorar (pl -e) das fee.

Hopfen (pl -) der hops Pl; **bei ihm ist Hopfen und Malz verloren** he's a hopeless case.

hörbar <> adj audible. <> adv audibly.

hörbehindert adj hard of hearing.

horchen vi to listen.

Horde (pl -n) die horde.

hören <> vt - **1.** [wahrnehmen, erfahren] to hear; **er hat lange nichts von sich hören lassen** we haven't heard from him for ages; **von ihm hört man nur Gutes** you only hear good things about him - **2.** [willkürlich] to listen to. <> vi - **1.** [unwillkürlich, erfahren] to hear; **schwer hören** to be hard of hearing; **Sie werden noch von mir hören!** you haven't heard the last of this! - **2.** [zuhören, gehorchen] to listen; **hör mal!** listen!; **hören auf** (+ A) to listen to; **hätte ich doch auf ihren Rat gehört!** if only I'd listened to her advice!

Hörensagen das: **etw vom Hörensagen kennen** to know sthg from hearsay.

Hörer (pl -) der - **1.** [Zuhörer] listener - **2.** [Telefonhörer] receiver.

Hörerin (pl -nen) die listener.

Hörerschaft die listeners Pl.

Hör|fehler der hearing defect.

Hör|funk der radio.

Hör|gerät das hearing aid.

hörgeschädigt adj hard of hearing.

Horizont (pl -e) der horizon; **das geht über meinen Horizont** fig that's beyond me; **seinen Horizont erweitern** fig to broaden one's horizons.

horizontal <> adj horizontal. <> adv horizontally.

Hormon (pl -e) das hormone.

Horn (pl Hörner ODER -e) das horn.

Hörnchen (pl -) das - **1.** [Gebäck] croissant - **2.** [Horn] small horn.

Horn|haut die - **1.** [Hautschicht] patch of hard skin, callus - **2.** [des Auges] cornea.

Hornisse (pl -n) die hornet.

Horoskop (pl -e) das horoscope.

horrend adj horrendous.

Horror der - 1. [Entsetzen] horror; **einen Horror vor jm/etw haben** to be terrified of sb/sthg - 2. fam [Unangenehmes]: **das war der (reine) Horror** it was a (total) nightmare.

Hör|saal der lecture hall.

Hör|spiel das radio play.

Hort (pl -e) der - 1. [Kinderhort] day-centre where children can spend the afternoon after lessons have finished - 2. geh [Schutz] refuge.

horten vt to hoard.

Hörweite die: **in/außer Hörweite** in/out of earshot.

Hose (pl -n) die trousers Pl UK, pants Pl US; [Unterhose - von Männern] pants Pl UK, shorts Pl US; [- von Frauen] knickers Pl UK, panties Pl US; **eine neue Hose kaufen** to buy a new pair of trousers UK ODER pants US, to buy some new trousers UK ODER pants US; **sich** (D) **die Hose anziehen** to put one's trousers on; **kurze Hose** shorts Pl; **die Hosen anhaben** fam fig to wear the trousers; **die Hosen voll haben** fam fig to be crapping o.s.; **in die Hose gehen** fam to be a flop; **da ist tote Hose** fam it's totally dead there.

Hosen|bein das trouser leg.

Hosen|schlitz der fly, flies Pl UK.

Hosen|träger der braces Pl UK, suspenders Pl US.

Hospital (pl -e ODER -täler) das hospital.

Hostess (pl -en) die hostess.

Hostie (pl -n) die RELIG host.

Hotdog ['hɔt'dɔk] (pl -s) das & der hot dog.

Hotel (pl -s) das hotel; **Hotel garni** ≃ bed and breakfast.

Hotel|zimmer das hotel room.

Hotline ['hɔtlaɪn] (pl -s) die hotline.

Hr. (abk für **Herr**) Mr.

hrsg. (abk für **herausgegeben**) ed.

Hubraum der cubic capacity.

hübsch <> adj - 1. [Person, Anblick, Kleid, Blumen] pretty - 2. [Idee, Umgebung] nice - 3. fam [groß - Summe] tidy - 4. fam iron [unangenehm]: **das ist ja eine hübsche Überraschung!** what a pleasant surprise! <> adv - 1. [schön] prettily - 2. fam [sehr] jolly; **sei hübsch brav!** be really good!

Hubschrauber (pl -) der helicopter.

huckepack adv: **jn huckepack nehmen** ODER **tragen** fam to give sb a piggyback.

Huf (pl -e) der hoof.

Huf|eisen das horseshoe.

Hüfte (pl -n) die hip.

Huf|tier das hoofed animal.

Hügel (pl -) der - 1. [Berg] hill - 2. [Haufen] mound.

hügelig adj hilly.

Huhn (pl **Hühner**) das - 1. [Vogel] chicken - 2. fam [Mädchen, Frau]: **ein dummes Huhn** a silly cow; **ein verrücktes Huhn** a queer fish.

Hühnchen (pl -) das chicken.

Hühner|auge das corn.

Hühner|brühe die chicken broth.

Hühner|ei das hen's egg.

Hülle (pl -n) die cover; [Verpackung] wrapping; [von Schallplatte] sleeve; **etw in Hülle und Fülle haben** to have plenty of sthg.

hüllen vt: **jn/sich/etw in etw** (A) **hüllen** to wrap sb/o.s./sthg in sthg.

Hülse (pl -n) die - 1. [Hülle] case; [von Film, Zigarre] tube - 2. [bei Pflanzen] pod.

Hülsen|frucht die pulse.

Hummel (pl -n) die bumblebee.

Hummer (pl -) der lobster.

Humor der humour; **viel Humor haben** to have a great sense of humour; **etw mit Humor nehmen** ODER **tragen** to bear sthg with great humour.

humoristisch <> adj humorous. <> adv humorously.

humorvoll <> adj humorous. <> adv humorously.

humpeln (perf hat/ist gehumpelt) vi - 1. (hat, ist) [hinken] to walk with ODER have a limp - 2. (ist) [in eine Richtung] to limp.

Hund (pl -e) der - 1. [Tier] dog; **'Vorsicht, bissiger Hund!'** 'beware of the dog' - 2. salopp [Mann]: **er ist ein blöder Hund** he's a stupid git; **vor die Hunde gehen** fam to go to the dogs.

Hunde|hütte die kennel.

Hunde|leine die lead UK, leash US.

hundemüde adj dog-tired.

hundert num - 1. [Zahl] a ODER one hundred; **auf hundert kommen** fam to hit the roof - 2. fam [sehr viele] hundreds of; siehe auch **sechs**.

Hundert (pl -e) die ODER das hundred. ➤ **Hunderte** Pl [große Anzahl]: **Hunderte von** hundreds of. ➤ **zu Hunderten** adv: **zu Hunderten kommen** to come in their hundreds; siehe auch **Sechs**.

Hunderteuro|schein der hundred euro note UK ODER bill US.

hundertfach adv a hundred times.

Hundertjahr|feier die centenary.

hundertjährig adj hundred-year-old.

hundertprozentig <> adj - 1. [von hundert Prozent] one hundred percent - 2. [vollkommen] complete; **er ist ein hundertprozentiger Bayer** he's a Bavarian through and through. <> adv fam [völlig] completely; **etw hundertprozentig wissen** to know sthg for certain.

hundertste, r, s adj hundredth; siehe auch **sechste**.

Hundertste (pl -n) der, die, das hundredth; siehe auch **Sechste**.

hundertstel adj (unver) hundredth; **eine hundertstel Sekunde** a hundredth of a second; siehe auch **sechstel**.

Hundertstel (pl -) das hundredth; siehe auch **Sechstel**.

hunderttausend num a ODER one hundred thousand.

Hunde|steuer die dog licence fee.

Hunde|zwinger der dog cage.

Hündin (pl -nen) die bitch.

Hunger der eigtl & fig hunger; **auf etw** (A) **Hunger haben** to feel like eating sthg.

Hunger|lohn der abw starvation wage, pittance.

hungern vi - 1. [nach Nahrung] to go hungry - 2. geh [verlangen]: **nach etw hungern** to be hungry for sthg, to crave sthg.

Hungers|not die famine.

Hunger|streik der hunger strike.

hungrig <> adj hungry. <> adv hungrily.

Hupe (pl -n) die horn.

hupen vi to sound one's horn.

hüpfen (perf ist gehüpft) vi to hop.

Hürde (pl -n) die hurdle.

Hürden|lauf der: **der Hürdenlauf** the hurdles.

Hure (pl -n) die abw whore.

hurra interj hurray!

huschen (perf ist gehuscht) vi to dart; [Lächeln] to flit.

hüsteln vi to give a slight cough.

husten <> vi to cough; **auf dieses Angebot huste ich!** fam you can keep your offer! <> vt [Blut, Schleim] to cough up; **jm eins** ODER **was husten** fam to tell sb to get lost.

Husten der (ohne pl) cough; **Husten haben** to have a cough.

Husten|saft der cough mixture.

Hut (pl Hüte) <> der [Kleidungsstück] hat; **das ist ein alter Hut** fam that's old hat; **mit jm/ etw nichts am Hut haben** fam to have no time for sb/sthg; **seinen Hut nehmen** to pack one's bags; **dein Geld kannst du dir an den Hut stecken!** fam you can keep your money!; **verschiedene Interessen unter einen Hut bringen** to reconcile different interests. <> die: (vor jm) **auf der Hut sein** to be on one's guard (with sb); **beim Autofahren bin ich auf der Hut** I'm on the alert when I'm driving. ◆ **Hut ab** interj: **das hätte ich dir gar nicht zugetraut - Hut ab!** I wouldn't have thought you capable of that - hats off to you!

hüten vt [Kinder] to look after; [Geheimnis] to keep; [Tiere] to watch over. ◆ **sich hüten** ref: **sich vor jm/etw hüten** to be on one's guard against sb/sthg; **sich hüten, etw zu tun** to take care not to do sthg.

Hütte (pl -n) die - 1. [Haus] hut; [bewirtschaftete Berghütte] mountain lodge - 2. [Eisenhütte] iron and steel works (sg).

Hütten|käse der cottage cheese.

Hyäne (pl -n) die hyena.

Hyazinthe (pl -n) die hyacinth.

Hydrant (pl -en) der hydrant.

Hydraulik die hydraulics Pl.

hydraulisch <> adj hydraulic. <> adv hydraulically.

Hydrokultur die hydroponics (U).

Hygiene [hy'gie:nə] die hygiene.

hygienisch [hy'gie:nɪʃ] <> adj hygienic. <> adv hygienically.

Hymne (pl -n) die hymn.

hypnotisieren vt to hypnotize.

Hypothek (pl -en) die mortgage.

Hypothese (pl -n) die hypothesis.

Hysterie [hyste'ri:] (pl -n) die hysteria.

hysterisch <> adj hysterical; **hysterischer Anfall** (fit of) hysterics. <> adv hysterically.

i (pl - ODER -s), **I** (pl - ODER -s) [i:] das i, I.

i.A. (abk für im Auftrag) pp.

IC [i:'tse:] (pl -s) (abk für **Intercity**) der intercity train.

ICE [i:tse:'e:] (pl -s) (abk für **Intercity Express**) der intercity express train.

ich pron I; **ich bins** it's me.

ideal <> adj ideal. <> adv ideally.

Ideal (pl -e) das ideal.

Ideal|fall der ideal case.

Idealismus der idealism.

Idee (pl -n) die - 1. [gen] idea; **eine fixe Idee** an obsession - 2. [Kleinigkeit] bit.

identifizieren vt to identify; **jn/etw mit etw identifizieren** to identify sb/sthg with sthg. ◆ **sich identifizieren** ref: **sich mit jm/etw identifizieren** to identify with sb/sthg.

Identifizierung (pl -en) die identification.

identisch adj identical.

Identität die identity.

Ideologie (pl -n) die ideology.

Idiot (pl -en) der fam abw [Dummkopf] idiot.

Idiotin (pl -nen) die idiot.

idiotisch fam abw <> adj [dumm, unsinnig] idiotic. <> adv [unsinnig] idiotically.

Idol (pl -e) das idol.

Idylle (pl -n) die idyll.

idyllisch <> adj idyllic. <> adv idyllically.

Igel (pl -) der hedgehog.

ignorieren vt to ignore.

IHK [iːhaːˈkaː] (*abk für* **Industrie- und Handelskammer**) *die* chamber of commerce and industry.

ihm *pron (Dativ von er)* - **1.** [Person] (to) him; **sie sagte es ihm** she told him; **das gehört ihm** this is his, this belongs to him - **2.** [Sache] (to) it.

ihn *pron (Akkusativ von er)* - **1.** [Person] him - **2.** [Sache] it.

ihnen *pron (Dativ Plural von er/sie)* (to) them; **er ist von ihnen** it's theirs, it belongs to them; **gib ihnen den Schlüssel** give them the key.

Ihnen *pron (Von Sie)* (to) you; **gehört das Ihnen?** is this yours?, does this belong to you?; **wer hat es Ihnen gegeben?** who gave you it?, who gave it to you?; **entschuldigen Sie, meine Herren, ist der Platz neben Ihnen frei?** excuse me, gentlemen, is the seat next to you free?

ihr, e *det* - **1.** *(Singular)* her - **2.** *(Plural)* their.

ihr *pron* - **1.** [Nominativ Plural] you - **2.** [Dativ von sie - Person] (to) her; [- Sache] (to) it; **er sagte es ihr** he told her; **das gehört ihr** this is hers, this belongs to her; **mit ihr** with her.

Ihr, e *det* your.

ihre, r, s *pron* - **1.** [Singular - von Person] hers; [- von Ding] its - **2.** [Plural] theirs.

Ihre, r, s *pron* yours.

ihrer *pron (Genitiv von sie)* [Singular von Person] (of) her; [Plural] (of) them; [Singular von Ding] (of) it.

ihrerseits *adv* - **1.** [sie selbst - Singular] for her part; [- Plural] for their part - **2.** [von ihr - Person] on her part; [- Tier, Sache] on its part; [- Plural] on their part.

Ihrerseits *adv* on your part.

ihretwegen *adv* - **1.** [ihr zuliebe - von Person] for her sake; [- von Ding] for its sake; [ihnen zuliebe] for their sake - **2.** [wegen ihr - Person] because of her; [- Ding] because of it; [wegen ihnen] because of them.

Ihretwegen *adv* - **1.** [Ihnen zuliebe] for your sake - **2.** [wegen Ihnen] because of you.

ihretwillen ◆ **um ihretwillen** *adv* [Singular - Person] for her sake; [- Ding] for its sake; [Plural] for their sake.

Ihretwillen ◆ **um Ihretwillen** *adv* for your sake.

ihrige (*pl* -n) *pron geh*: **der/die/das ihrige** [Singular - von Person] hers; [- von Ding] its; [Plural] theirs.

illegal ◇ *adj* illegal. ◇ *adv* illegally.

Illusion (*pl* -en) *die* illusion.

Illustration (*pl* -en) *die* illustration.

illustrieren *vt* to illustrate.

Illustrierte (*pl* -n) *die* magazine.

im *präp* (*in + dem*) ▷ **in**.

Image [ˈɪmɪtʃ] (*pl* -s) *das* image.

Imbiss (*pl* -e) *der* - **1.** [Mahlzeit] snack - **2.** [Imbissbude] snack bar.

Imbissbudel (*pl* -n) *die fam* snack bar.

Imitation (*pl* -en) *die* imitation.

imitieren *vt* to imitate.

Immatrikulation (*pl* -en) *die* - **1.** UNI matriculation - **2.** *Schweiz* [Kfz-Zulassung] registration.

immatrikulieren *vt* - **1.** UNI to enrol - **2.** *Schweiz* [zulassen] to register. ◆ **sich immatrikulieren** *ref* UNI to matriculate.

immens ◇ *adj* immense. ◇ *adv* immensely; **immens viel** an immense amount.

immer *adv* - **1.** [zeitlich] always; **für immer und ewig** for ever and ever; **immer wieder** again and again, time and again; **immer wenn** whenever; **immer geradeaus!** keep going straight ahead!; **immer mit der Ruhe!** take it easy!; **immer noch** still - **2.** [mit Komparativ]: **immer schwieriger** more and more difficult; **immer stärker** stronger and stronger - **3.** [egal]: **was (auch) immer** whatever; **wer (auch) immer** whoever; **wie (auch) immer** however; **wo (auch) immer** wherever.

immerfort *adv* constantly.

immerhin *adv* - **1.** [wenigstens] at least - **2.** [schließlich] after all - **3.** [trotzdem] nevertheless.

immerzu *adv* constantly.

Immigrant, in (*mpl* -en, *fpl* -nen) *der, die* immigrant.

Immigration (*pl* -en) *die* immigration.

Immobilien [ɪmoˈbiːljən] *Pl* property (U).

immun *adj*: **gegen etw immun sein** to be immune to sthg.

Immunität *die* immunity.

Imperativ (*pl* -e) *der* GRAMM imperative.

Imperfekt (*pl* -e) *das* GRAMM imperfect.

impfen *vt* to vaccinate; **jn gegen etw impfen** to vaccinate sb against sthg.

Impfl**stoff** *der* vaccine.

Impfung (*pl* -en) *die* vaccination.

imponieren *vi* to impress; **jm (durch etw) imponieren** to impress sb (with sthg).

imponierend ◇ *adj* impressive. ◇ *adv* impressively.

Import (*pl* -e) *der* - **1.** [Ware] import - **2.** [Einfuhr] importation.

importieren *vt* to import.

impotent *adj* impotent.

Impotenz *die* impotence.

imprägnieren *vt* to impregnate; [gegen Wasser] to waterproof.

improvisieren [ɪmproviˈziːrən] *vt & vi* to improvise.

Impuls (*pl* -e) *der* - **1.** [Anregung] stimulus; [innere Regung] impulse; **einer Sache (D) neue Impulse geben** to breathe new life into sthg - **2.** [Stoß] impulse.

impulsiv ◇ *adj* impulsive. ◇ *adv* impuls-ively.

imstande, im Stande *adj*: zu etw imstande sein to be capable of sthg.

in ◇ *präp* - 1. (+ D) [räumlich] in; **im Bett lie-gen** to be in bed; **in der Schule** at school - 2. (+ A) [räumlich] into; **in den Fluss fallen** to fall into the river; **in die Stadt fahren** to go to ODER into town; **in die Schule gehen** to go to school; **sich in jn verlieben** to fall in love with sb - 3. (+ D) [zeitlich] in; **in dieser Woche** this week; **im Moment** at the moment; **wir fah-ren in einer Stunde** we're going in an hour - 4. (+ A) [zeitlich] into; **wir arbeiteten bis spät in die Nacht** we worked late into the night - 5. (+ D) [modal]: **in aller Eile** hurriedly; **in Betrieb sein** to be working; **ich habe mich in der Zeit geirrt** I got the time wrong - 6. (+ A) [mo-dal]: **etw in seine Einzelteile zerlegen** to take sthg to pieces - 7. (+ D) [mit Maß- oder Mengen-angaben] in; **in Millimetern** in millimetres. ◇ *adj*: **in sein** *fam* to be in.

Inbegriff *der* embodiment, epitome.

inbegriffen ◇ *adj*: **in etw (D) inbegriffen sein** to be included in sthg. ◇ *adv*: **Steuern inbegriffen** including tax.

Inbetriebnahme (*pl* -n) *die* - 1. [von Maschi-ne, Kraftwerk] commissioning; **vor Inbetrieb-nahme des Gerätes die Gebrauchsanweisung lesen** read the instructions before switching the appliance on for the first time - 2. [von Flughafen, Schwimmbad] opening.

Indefinit|pronomen *das* GRAMM indefinite pronoun.

indem *konj* - 1. [instrumental] by; **er vernichte-te die Unterlagen, indem er sie in den Reißwolf steckte** he destroyed the docu-ments by putting them through the shredder - 2. [während] while.

Inder, in (*mpl* -, *fpl* -nen) *der, die* Indian.

Indianer, in (*mpl* -, *fpl* -nen) *der, die abw* (Red) Indian.

indianisch *adj* (Red) Indian.

Indien *nt* India.

Indikativ (*pl* -e) *der* GRAMM indicative (mood).

indirekt ◇ *adj* indirect. ◇ *adv* indirectly.

indisch *adj* Indian.

Indischer Ozean *der* Indian Ocean.

indiskret ◇ *adj* indiscreet. ◇ *adv* in-discreetly.

indiskutabel *adj abw* out of the question.

Individualist, in [ɪndivi̯dua̯'lɪst, ɪn] (*mpl* -en, *fpl* -nen) *der, die* individualist.

individuell [ɪndivi̯du̯'ɛl] ◇ *adj* individual. ◇ *adv* individually; **individuell verschieden sein** to vary from case to case.

Individuum [ɪndi'vi̯:duʊm] (*pl* -viduen) *das* individual.

Indiz [ɪn'di̯:ts] (*pl* -ien) *das* - 1. RECHT piece of circumstantial evidence; **Indizien** circumstan-tial evidence - 2. [Anzeichen] indication.

Indonesien *nt* Indonesia.

Industrie (*pl* -n) *die* industry.

Industrie|gebiet *das* industrial area.

industriell ◇ *adj* industrial. ◇ *adv* indus-trially.

ineinander *adv* in/into one another; **inei-nander verliebt sein** to be in love (with one another); **ineinander verwickelt** tangled up (in each other).

ineinander fügen *vt* to fit together. ➤ **sich ineinander fügen** *ref* to fit togeth-er.

Infanterie ['ɪnfantəri̯:] *die* infantry.

Infarkt (*pl* -e) *der* heart attack.

Infekt (*pl* -e) *der* MED infection.

Infektion (*pl* -en) *die* infection.

Infektions|krankheit *die* infectious dis-ease.

Infinitiv (*pl* -e) *der* GRAMM infinitive.

infizieren *vt*: **jn (mit etw) infizieren** to infect sb (with sthg). ➤ **sich infizieren** *ref*: **sich (mit etw) infizieren** to become infected (with sthg).

Inflation (*pl* -en) *die* inflation.

Inflations|rate *die* rate of inflation.

infolge *präp*: **infolge einer Sache** (G) ODER **von etw** as a result of sthg.

infolgedessen *adv* consequently.

Informatik *die* computer science.

Informatiker, in (*mpl* -, *fpl* -nen) *der, die* computer scientist.

Information (*pl* -en) *die* - 1. information (U); **Informationen** information; **eine Information über jn/etw** (a piece of) information about sb/sthg - 2. (*ohne pl*) [in Kaufhaus, Bahnhof] in-formation desk.

Informations|material *das* information.

Informations|stand *der* information stand.

informativ *adj* informative.

informieren *vt*: **jn über jn/etw informieren** to inform sb about sb/sthg. ➤ **sich infor-mieren** *ref*: **sich (über jn/etw) informieren** to find out (about sb/sthg).

Infrarot *das* infra-red.

Infra|struktur *die* infrastructure.

Infusion (*pl* -en) *die* MED infusion.

Ingenieur, in [ɪnʒe'ni̯ø:ɐ̯, rɪn] (*mpl* -e, *fpl* -nen) *der, die* engineer.

Ingwer *der* ginger.

Inh. (*abk für* Inhaber) prop.

Inhaber, in (*mpl* -, *fpl* -nen) *der, die* - 1. [von Geschäft] owner - 2. [von Amt, Titel] holder.

inhaftieren *vt* to take into custody.

inhalieren ◇ *vt* to inhale. ◇ *vi* - **1.** MED to use an inhalant - **2.** *fam* [einen Lungenzug machen] to inhale.

Inhalt (*pl* -e) *der* - **1.** [von Gefäß, Behälter] contents *Pl* - **2.** [von Text, Gespräch] content; **Form und Inhalt** form and content - **3.** [Größe - von Fläche] area; [- von Raum] volume - **4.** [Sinn] meaning.

inhaltlich ◇ *adj*: der inhaltliche Aufbau eines Textes the way the content of a text is structured. ◇ *adv* as far as content is concerned.

Inhaltslangabe *die* - **1.** [von Text] summary - **2.** [von Paket] description of contents.

Inhaltslverzeichnis *das* [von Buch] table of contents; [von Paket] list of contents.

Initiative [initsja'ti:və] (*pl* -n) *die* - **1.** [gen] initiative; **die Initiative ergreifen** to take the initiative; **aus eigener Initiative** on one's own initiative - **2.** [Gruppe] local action group.

Injektion (*pl* -en) *die* injection.

inkl. (*abk für* inklusive) incl.

inklusive [ɪnklu'zi:və] ◇ *präp*: inklusive einer Sache (G) including sth. ◇ *adv*: bis zum 10. August inklusive until 10 August inclusive.

inkompatibel *adj* incompatible.

inkompetent ◇ *adj* incompetent. ◇ *adv* incompetently.

inkonsequent ◇ *adj* inconsistent. ◇ *adv* inconsistently.

Inland *das*: im Inland at home; **die Waren sind für das Inland bestimmt** the goods are for the domestic market; **die Reaktionen des In- und Auslandes** the reactions at home and abroad.

inländisch *adj* - **1.** [Waren, Produkte] domestic - **2.** [Presse] national.

Inlineskates ['ɪnlainskejts] *Pl* roller-blades, inline skates; **auf/mit Inlineskates fahren** to go rollerblading.

inmitten ◇ *präp*: inmitten einer Sache/Gruppe (G) in the midst of sth/a group. ◇ *adv*: inmitten von jm/etw amidst sb/sth.

innen *adv* inside; **die Schale ist innen versilbert** the bowl is silver-plated on the inside. ‣ **nach innen** *adv* inwards. ‣ **von innen** *adv* from inside; **etw von innen nach außen kehren** to turn sth inside out.

Innenlleben *das (ohne pl)* - **1.** [Seele]: sein Innenleben vor jm ausbreiten to tell sb one's innermost thoughts - **2.** [von Gerät] insides *Pl*.

Innenlminister, in *der, die* Minister of the Interior, ≃ Home Secretary *UK*, ≃ Secretary of the Interior *US*.

Innenlpolitik *die (ohne pl)* - **1.** [Handeln] domestic policy - **2.** [Bereich der Politik] home affairs *Pl*.

Innenlseite *die* inside.

Innenlstadt *die* town centre; [in Großstadt] city centre.

innere, r, s *adj* - **1.** [innen befindlich, persönlich] inner - **2.** [Struktur, Angelegenheit & MED] internal.

Innere *das (ohne pl)* - **1.** [Inhalt] inside - **2.** [von Raum] inside, interior; [von Land] interior; **Ministerium des Inneren** Ministry of the Interior - **3.** [Geist, Seele, Basis] heart; **im tiefsten Inneren** deep down (inside).

innerhalb ◇ *präp*: innerhalb einer Sache (G) within sth. ◇ *adv*: innerhalb von within.

innerlich ◇ *adj* [Erregung] inner. ◇ *adv* inwardly.

innig ◇ *adj* - **1.** [Verehrung, Wunsch, Beileid] heartfelt - **2.** [Dank] sincere - **3.** [Freundschaft] intimate. ◇ *adv* [verbunden] closely.

inoffiziell ◇ *adj* unofficial. ◇ *adv* unofficially.

Input (*pl* -s) *das & der* EDV & WIRTSCH input.

ins *präp* (in + das) [räumlich]: ins Wohnzimmer gehen to go into the living room; **ins Kino gehen** to go to the cinema; *siehe auch* **in**.

Insasse (*pl* -n) *der* - **1.** [im Fahrzeug] passenger - **2.** [von Gefängnis, psychiatrischer Anstalt] inmate.

Insassin (*pl* -nen) *die* - **1.** [im Fahrzeug] passenger - **2.** [von Gefängnis, psychiatrischer Anstalt] inmate.

insbes. (*abk für* insbesondere) esp.

insbesondere, insbesondre *adv* especially, particularly.

Inlschrift *die* inscription.

Insekt (*pl* -en) *das* insect.

Insektenschutzlmittel *das* insect repellent.

Insektenlstich *der* [von Wespe] insect sting; [von Mücke] insect bite.

Insel (*pl* -n) *die* island; **die Insel Sylt** the island of Sylt.

Inserat (*pl* -e) *das* advertisement; **ein Inserat aufgeben** to put an advertisement in the paper.

insgeheim *adv* secretly.

insgesamt *adv* - **1.** [in der Summe] in total - **2.** [im Großen und Ganzen] overall; **sie hat insgesamt einen guten Eindruck hinterlassen** she made a good overall impression.

insofern [1] *adv* in this respect.

insofern [2] *konj* provided that, so long as. ‣ **insofern als** *konj* insofar as.

in spe [ɪn'spe:] *adj* to be; **der Bürgermeister in spe** the mayor-elect.

Inspektion (*pl* -en) *die* - **1.** [von Anlage, Schule] inspection - **2.** [von Auto] service.

inspizieren *vt* to inspect.

installieren *vt* [gen & EDV] to install.

inständig ◇ *adv* urgently. ◇ *adj* urgent.

Instanz (pl -en) die - 1. [im Gerichtsverfahren] court - 2. [Dienststelle] authority.

Instinkt (pl -e) der instinct.

instinktiv ⟨⟩ adj instinctive. ⟨⟩ adv instinctively.

Institut (pl -e) das institute.

Institution (pl -en) die institution.

Instrument (pl -e) das instrument.

inszenieren vt - 1. [Theaterstück] to direct; TV & RADIO to produce - 2. [Skandal] to engineer; [Kampagne] to stage - 3. abw [vortäuschen - Protest] to stage-manage.

Inszenierung (pl -en) die - 1. [Aufführung] production - 2. [Aufführen - von Theaterstück] direction; TV & RADIO production - 3. [von Skandal] engineering; [von Kampagne] staging - 4. abw [Vortäuschung - von Protest] stage-managing.

intakt adj [Gerät, Organ] intact; [Beziehung] healthy.

Integralrechnung die integral calculus.

integrieren vt to integrate.

intellektuell [ɪntɛlɛk'tʊɛl] ⟨⟩ adj intellectual. ⟨⟩ adv intellectually.

Intellektuelle [ɪntɛlɛk'tʊɛlə] (pl -n) der, die intellectual.

intelligent ⟨⟩ adj intelligent. ⟨⟩ adv intelligently.

Intelligenz die - 1. [Verstand, Klugheit] intelligence - 2. [Intellektuelle] intelligentsia.

Intendant, in (mpl -en, fpl -nen) der, die - 1. [von Theater] artistic director and theatre manager - 2. [von Fernsehanstalt] director general.

intensiv ⟨⟩ adj - 1. [Gefühl, Farbe] strong - 2. [Licht] intense - 3. [Arbeit] intensive. ⟨⟩ adv - 1. [fühlen] strongly - 2. [leuchten] intensely - 3. [arbeiten] intensively.

Intensivkurs der crash course.

Intensivstation die intensive care unit.

interaktiv adj EDV interactive.

InterCity (pl -s) der intercity train.

interessant ⟨⟩ adj interesting. ⟨⟩ adv interestingly; **sich interessant machen** abw to attract attention (to o.s.)

Interesse (pl -n) das interest; **an jm/etw Interesse haben** to be interested in sb/sthg; **Interesse für jn/etw zeigen** to show an interest in sb/sthg; **in eigenem Interesse** in sb's own interest. ➡ **Interessen** Pl [Neigung] interests.

Interessent, in (mpl -en, fpl -nen) der, die - 1. [Interessierte] interested person - 2. [Kunde] prospective customer.

interessieren vt to interest. ➡ **sich interessieren** ref: **sich für jn/etw interessieren** to be interested in sb/sthg.

interessiert ⟨⟩ adj interested; **an jm/etw interessiert sein** to be interested in sb/sthg. ⟨⟩ adv with interest.

intern ⟨⟩ adj internal. ⟨⟩ adv internally.

Internat (pl -e) das boarding school.

international ⟨⟩ adj international. ⟨⟩ adv internationally.

Internet ['ɪntə(r)nɛt] das Internet; **im Internet** on the Internet; **im Internet surfen** to surf the Net; **etw über das Internet verkaufen** to sell sthg on ODER over the Internet.

Internetadresse (pl -n) die Internet address.

Internetcafé das Internet cafe, cybercafe.

Internetzugang (pl -zugänge) der Internet access.

Interpretation (pl -en) die - 1. [Deutung] interpretation - 2. MUS performance.

interpretieren vt - 1. [deuten] to interpret - 2. MUS to perform.

Interpunktion die punctuation.

InterRegio (pl -s) der train which covers medium distances and makes frequent stops.

Intervall [ɪntə'val] (pl -e) das [gen & MUS] interval.

Interview [ɪntə'vjuː] (pl -s) das interview.

interviewen [ɪntə'vjuːən] vt to interview.

intim adj intimate; **mit jm intim werden** amt to become intimate with sb.

Intimität (pl -en) die intimacy.

intolerant adj intolerant; **jm/etw gegenüber intolerant sein** to be intolerant of sb/sthg.

Intrige (pl -n) die intrigue, plot.

Intuition (pl -en) die intuition.

intuitiv ⟨⟩ adj intuitive. ⟨⟩ adv intuitively.

Invalide [ɪnva'liːdə] (pl -n) der, die invalid.

Invasion [ɪnva'zjoːn] (pl -en) die eigtl & fig invasion.

Inventar [ɪnvɛn'taːɐ] (pl -e) das - 1. [von Geschäft] fittings Pl and equipment; [von Haus] fixtures and fittings Pl - 2. [von Betrieb] machinery and equipment - 3. [Verzeichnis] inventory.

Inventur [ɪnvɛn'tuːɐ] (pl -en) die stocktaking; **Inventur machen** to stocktake.

investieren [ɪnvɛs'tiːrən] vt: **(in etw (A))** investieren to invest in (sthg).

Investition [ɪnvɛsti'tsjoːn] (pl -en) die investment.

inwiefern adv & konj [in welcher Hinsicht] in what way; [bis zu welchem Grad] to what extent.

inwieweit adv & konj to what extent.

Inzest (pl -e) der incest.

inzwischen adv - 1. [gleichzeitig] in the meantime - 2. [mittlerweile, jetzt] now; **inzwischen war es Winter geworden** by now winter had arrived.

Ion [joːn] (pl -en) das ion.

IQ [iː'kuː, aɪ'kjuː] (pl -s) ⟨abk für **Intelligenzquotient**⟩ der IQ.

i.R. (abk für **im Ruhestand**) retd.

Irak der Iraq.

Iran der Iran.

irdisch adj earthly, worldly.

Ire (pl -n) der Irishman.

irgend adv [irgendwie]: **wenn es irgend möglich ist** if (it's) at all possible; **wenn ich es irgend schaffe, komme ich** I'll come if I possibly can. ➡ **irgend so ein** det fam some.

irgendein, e det - **1.** [unbekannt] some - **2.** [beliebig] any.

irgendeine, r, s pron - **1.** [Person] someone, somebody; [in Fragen] anyone, anybody; **irgendeiner von uns muss es tun** one of us has to do it - **2.** [Sache] any (one); **irgendeins von den Büchern** one or other of the books.

irgendetwas pron [unbekannte Sache] something; [beliebige Sache, in Fragen] anything.

irgendjemand pron [unbekannte Person] someone, somebody; [beliebige Person, in Fragen] anyone, anybody.

irgendwann adv [zu unbekannter Zeit] sometime; [zu beliebiger Zeit] any time.

irgendwas adv [unbekannte Sache] something; [beliebige Sache, in Fragen] anything.

irgendwer pron fam - **1.** [unbekannte Person] someone, somebody - **2.** [beliebige Person, in Fragen] anyone, anybody.

irgendwie adv [auf unbekannte Weise] somehow; [auf beliebige Weise] anyhow.

irgendwo adv [an unbekanntem Ort] somewhere; [an beliebigem Ort] anywhere.

Irin (pl -nen) die Irishwoman.

Iris (pl -) die iris.

irisch adj Irish.

Irland nt Ireland.

Ironie die irony.

ironisch ⬦ adj ironic. ⬦ adv ironically.

irre (pl -n) ⬦ der, die (pl Irren) [Person] lunatic. ⬦ die (ohne pl) [Ungewissheit]: **in die Irre führen** to be misleading.

irreführen vt - **1.** [belügen] to mislead - **2.** [auf einem Weg] to cause to get lost.

irren (perf hat/ist geirrt) vi (ist) to wander. ➡ **sich irren** ref (hat): **sich (in jm/etw (D))** irren to be wrong (about sb/sthg); **wenn ich mich nicht irre** if I am not mistaken.

irritieren vt [stören] to annoy; **ihr Verhalten irritiert mich** I find her behaviour disconcerting ODER confusing.

Irrtum (pl -tümer) der mistake.

irrtümlich ⬦ adj mistaken. ⬦ adv [verwechseln, mitnehmen] by mistake.

ISDN-Anschluss (pl -Anschlüsse) der TELEKOM ISDN link.

Islam der Islam.

islamisch adj Islamic.

Island nt Iceland.

Isländer, in (mpl -, fpl -nen) der, die Icelander.

isländisch adj Icelandic.

Isolation (pl -en) die - **1.** [von Person] isolation - **2.** [Material, Abdichtung] insulation; [von Rohr, Boiler] lagging.

Isolierband (pl -bänder) das insulating tape.

isolieren vt - **1.** [Person & CHEM] to isolate - **2.** [Leitung, Wand] to insulate.

Israel nt Israel.

Israeli (pl - ODER -s) der, die Israeli.

israelisch adj Israeli.

isst präs ⬡ **essen**.

ist präs ⬡ **sein**.

Istanbul nt Istanbul.

Italien nt Italy.

Italiener, in [ita'lie:nɐ, rɪn] (mpl -, fpl -nen) der, die Italian.

italienisch [ita'lie:nɪʃ] adj Italian.

Italienisch(e) das Italian; siehe auch **Englisch(e)**.

J

j (pl - ODER -s), **J** (pl - ODER -s) [jɔt] das j, J.

ja interj - **1.** [zum Ausdruck der Zustimmung] yes - **2.** [einschränkend]: **ich würde ja gerne, aber** I'd love to, but; **ich kann es ja versuchen, aber** I can always try, but - **3.** [emphatisierend]: **da bist du ja!** there you are!; **das ist ja großartig!** that's really great!; **ich habe es dir ja gesagt!** I told you so!; **das ist es ja (eben)!** that's just it! - **4.** [als rhetorisches Element] well; **ja, wenn das so ist** well, if that's the case - **5.** [zum Ausdruck einer Drohung]: **sag ja nichts!** don't you dare say anything!; **dass du mir ja pünktlich kommst!** you'd better be on time! - **6.** [zum Ausdruck einer Bitte]: **du bleibst doch, ja?** you will stay, won't you? - **7.** [drückt Überraschung aus]: **(ach) ja?** really?

Jacht (pl -en), **Yacht** (pl -en) [jaxt] die yacht.

Jacke (pl -n) die - **1.** [Mantel, Jackett] jacket - **2.** [Strickjacke] cardigan.

Jackett [ʒa'kɛt] (pl -s) das jacket.

Jagd (pl -en) die - **1.** [auf Tiere] hunting; **auf die Jagd gehen** to go hunting - **2.** [auf Personen, Dinge]: **Jagd auf jm/etw machen** hunt for sb/sthg.

jagen (perf hat/ist gejagt) ⬦ vt (hat) to hunt; **der Dieb wurde aus der Stadt gejagt** the thief was driven out of town; **sich (D) eine**

Kugel in den Kopf jagen to shoot o.s. in the head. ⬦ *vi* - **1.** *(hat)* [als Sport] to hunt - **2.** *(ist)* [hetzen] to race.

Jäger *(pl* -*)* *der* - **1.** [von Tieren] hunter - **2.** [Flugzeug] fighter (plane).

Jägerin *(pl* -nen*)* *die* hunter.

Jägerschnitzel *(pl* -*)* *das* escalope of pork or beef with mushroom sauce.

jäh ⬦ *adj* sudden. ⬦ *adv* suddenly.

Jahr *(pl* -e*)* *das* year; im Jahr(e) 1992 in 1992; die 90er Jahre the nineties; seit Jahren for years; (ein) gutes neues Jahr! Happy New Year!; Jahr für Jahr year after year; in jungen Jahren at an early age.

jahrelang ⬦ *adj*: jahrelange Arbeit years of work. ⬦ *adv* for years.

Jahres|tag *der* anniversary.

Jahres|zeit *die* season.

Jahr|gang *der* - **1.** [Geburtsjahr]: der Jahrgang 1967 the people who were born in 1967; er ist mein Jahrgang he was born in the same year as me - **2.** [an der Schule] year - **3.** [von Wein] vintage, year - **4.** [von Zeitschrift] year's issues *Pl*.

Jahrhundert *(pl* -e*)* *das* century; im 19. Jahrhundert in the 19th century.

Jahrhundert|wende *die* turn of the century; um die Jahrhundertwende at the turn of the century.

jährlich ⬦ *adj* annual. ⬦ *adv* annually; dreimal jährlich three times a year.

Jahr|markt *der* fair.

Jahrtausend *(pl* -e*)* *das* millennium.

Jahrzehnt *(pl* -e*)* *das* decade.

jähzornig ⬦ *adj* irascible. ⬦ *adv* in a violent temper.

Jalousie [ʒalu'zi:] *(pl* -n*)* *die* Venetian blind.

Jammer *der* misery; es ist ein Jammer it's a crying shame.

jämmerlich ⬦ *adj* - **1.** [traurig] miserable - **2.** *abw* [würdelos, schlecht] pathetic. ⬦ *adv* - **1.** [traurig] miserably - **2.** *abw* [würdelos, schlecht] pathetically - **3.** [sehr]: jämmerlich frieren to be frozen stiff.

jammern *vi* to moan.

Januar *der* January; *siehe auch* **September**.

Japan *nt* Japan.

Japaner, in *(mpl* -, *fpl* -nen*)* *der, die* Japanese.

japanisch *adj* Japanese.

Japanisch(e) *das* Japanese; *siehe auch* **Englisch(e)**.

Jargon [ʒar'gõ] *(pl* -s*)* *der* jargon.

jäten *vt* [Garten] to weed; [Unkraut] to pull up.

jaulen *vi* to howl.

jawohl *interj* certainly!

Ja|wort *das*: jm sein Jawort geben to tie the knot with sb.

Jazz [dʒɛs] *der* jazz.

je ⬦ *adv* - **1.** [jeweils] each; drei Gruppen mit je fünf Personen three groups, each of five people; die drei Tore sind mit je zwei Schlössern gesichert the three gates each have two locks - **2.** [jemals] ever; seit eh und je since time immemorial; sie ist schöner denn je she is more beautiful than ever. ⬦ *präp* [pro] per; je nach depending on. ⬦ *konj*: je schneller, desto besser the quicker the better; je nachdem it depends; je nachdem, ob depending on whether. ⬦ *interj*: oh je! oh no!, oh dear!

Jeans [dʒi:nz] *(pl* -*)* *die* jeans *Pl*; eine Jeans a pair of jeans.

jede, r, s ⬦ *det* every, each; [in negativen Konstruktionen] any; ohne jeden Zweifel without any doubt; jeden zweiten Tag every second day. ⬦ *pron* - **1.** [Person] everyone, everybody; jede von ihnen each of them; jeder Zweite every second *ODER* other one; jeder kann teilnehmen anyone can take part - **2.** [Sache] each (one).

jedenfalls *adv* - **1.** [wenigstens] at least; ich jedenfalls habe keine Lust I at any rate don't want to - **2.** [auf jeden Fall] in any case.

jedermann *pron* everybody, everyone.

jederzeit *adv* at any time.

jedesmal *adv* ▷ **Mal**.

jedoch *adv & konj* however.

jegliche, r, s *pron*: hier kommt jegliche Hilfe zu spät any help will come too late; ohne jegliches Risiko with no risk.

jeher *adv*: von jeher always.

jemals *adv* ever.

jemand *pron* someone, somebody; [in Fragen] anyone, anybody.

jene, r, s ⬦ *det* that, those *Pl*. ⬦ *pron* that one, those ones *Pl*.

jenseits *präp*: jenseits einer Sache (G) *ODER* von etw [räumlich] on the other side of sthg; [ideell] beyond sthg.

Jerusalem *nt* Jerusalem.

Jet|lag ['dʒɛtlɛg] *(pl* -s*)* *der* jet lag.

jetzig *adj* current.

jetzt *adv* - **1.** [momentan, mittlerweile] now; bis jetzt so far; von jetzt an from now on; erst jetzt only just; schon jetzt already - **2.** [gegenwärtig, heute] nowadays; das gibt es jetzt nicht mehr you don't get that any more (nowadays) - **3.** [gleich, sofort] in a moment; jetzt gleich right away; von jetzt auf gleich on the spur of the moment - **4.** [damals] then - **5.** [zum Ausdruck des Ärgers]: das ist doch jetzt kein Argument! that's no argument!; jetzt mach endlich voran! get a move on, will you!

jeweilig *adj* - **1.** [zeitlich]: nach der jeweiligen Mode angezogen sein to be dressed in the fashion of the day; die Stimmung ändert sich mit der jeweiligen Laune des Chefs the atmosphere changes depending on what mood the boss happens to be in - 2. [zugehörig] respective.

jeweils *adv* - 1. [jedes Mal] each time - 2. [jeder] each; **jeweils drei Karten** three cards each - 3. [momentan] at the time.

Jh. (*abk für Jahrhundert*) C.

Jiddisch(e) *das* Yiddish; *siehe auch* **Englisch(e)**.

Job [dʒɔp] (*pl* -s) *der* - 1. [als Aushilfe] (temporary) job - 2. [Arbeit] job.

jobben [dʒɔbn̩] *vi* to work.

Jockey ['dʒɔke, 'dʒɔki] (*pl* -s) *der* jockey.

Jod *das* iodine.

jodeln *vi* to yodel.

Joga, Yoga ['joːga] = **Yoga**.

Jogging ['dʒɔgɪŋ] *das* jogging.

Joghurt, Yoghurt, Jogurt (*pl* - *ODER* -s) *das* & *der* yoghurt.

Johannisbeere *die*: **Rote Johannisbeere** redcurrant; **Schwarze Johannisbeere** blackcurrant.

Joker ['dʒoːkɐ] (*pl* -) *der* joker.

jonglieren [ʒɔŋˈliːrən] ◇ *vi* to juggle; **mit etw jonglieren** *eigtl* & *fig* to juggle sthg. ◇ *vt* [balancieren] to juggle.

Journalist, in [ʒʊrnaˈlɪst, ɪn] (*mpl* -en, *fpl* -nen) *der, die* journalist.

Jubel *der* - 1. [Freude] jubilation - 2. [Rufen] cheering.

jubeln *vi* - 1. [sich freuen] to rejoice - 2. [rufen] to cheer.

Jubiläum [jubiˈlɛːʊm] (*pl* Jubiläen) *das* anniversary; **ein Jubiläum feiern** to celebrate an anniversary.

jucken ◇ *vi* - 1. [Haut] to itch - 2. [Material] to be itchy. ◇ *vt* - 1. [kratzen]: **die Narbe juckt ihn** his scar is itchy - 2. *fam* [beeinflussen]: **es juckt mich, es zu versuchen** I'm itching to try; **das juckt mich nicht** I don't care.

Juckreiz *der* itching; **Juckreiz verspüren** to have an itch.

Jude (*pl* -n) *der* Jew.

Jüdin (*pl* -nen) *die* Jew.

jüdisch *adj* Jewish.

Judo *das* judo.

Jugend *die* (*ohne pl*) - 1. [junges Alter] youth - 2. [junge Personen] young people *Pl*; **die Jugend von heute** today's youth, young people today.

Jugendamt *das local authority service responsible for the welfare of young people.*

Jugendarbeit *die* youth work.

jugendfrei *adj*: '**nicht jugendfrei**' 'not suitable for persons under 18'.

Jugendherberge *die* youth hostel.

jugendlich ◇ *adj* - 1. [jung] young - 2. [jung wirkend] youthful. ◇ *adv*: **sich jugendlich geben/kleiden** to act/dress young.

Jugendliche (*pl* -n) *der, die* young person.

Jugendstil *der* art nouveau.

Jugoslawien *nt* Yugoslavia.

Juli *der* July; *siehe auch* **September**.

jung (*kompar* jünger, *superl* jüngste) ◇ *adj* - 1. [gen] young; [Aussehen, Stil] young, youthful; **meine jüngere Schwester** my younger sister - 2. [nicht lange zurückliegend]: **die jüngsten Ereignisse** recent events. ◇ *adv* (*kompar* jünger; *superl* am jüngsten): **jung sterben** to die young.

Junge (*pl* -n *ODER* Jungs) ◇ *der* (*pl* Jungen, Jungs) [Knabe, Mann] boy; **hallo, alter Junge** hello, my old pal; **ein schwerer Junge** *fam fig* a thug. ◇ *das* (*pl* Jungen) [Tier] young animal; **die Jungen** the young; **Junge kriegen** *ODER* **werfen** to give birth to young.

Jünger, in (*mpl* -, *fpl* -nen) *der, die* disciple.

Jungfer (*pl* -n) *die*: **alte Jungfer** *abw* old maid.

Jungfrau *die* - 1. [Frau] virgin - 2. ASTROL Virgo; **Jungfrau sein** to be a Virgo.

Junggeselle *der* bachelor; **ein eingefleischter Junggeselle** a confirmed bachelor.

jüngste *adj* ⊳ **jung**.

Jüngste (*pl* -n) *der, die, das* youngest; **er ist nicht mehr der Jüngste** he's not as young as he used to be.

Juni *der* June; *siehe auch* **September**.

Junior (*pl* Junioren) *der* - 1. [gen] junior - 2. [im Geschäft] junior partner.

Juniorin (*pl* -nen) *die* - 1. [Tochter] daughter - 2. [im Geschäft] junior partner - 3. *SPORT* junior.

Jura *der* - 1. [ohne Artikel] [Studienfach] law - 2. [Gebirge]: **der Jura** the Jura - 3. [Erdzeitalter] Jurassic period.

Jurist, in (*mpl* -en, *fpl* -nen) *der, die* lawyer.

juristisch ◇ *adj* legal. ◇ *adv* legally.

Jury [ʒyˈriː] (*pl* -s) *die* jury.

Justiz *die* - 1. [Behörde]: **jn der deutschen Justiz ausliefern** to hand sb over to the German courts; **unabhängige Justiz** independent judiciary - 2. [Rechtsprechung]: **nach irischer Justiz** under Irish law.

Justizministerium *das* Ministry of Justice.

Justizvollzugsanstalt *die amt* penal institution, penitentiary *US*.

Juwel (*pl* -en) *das* & *der* - 1. (*der*) [Schmuck] piece of jewellery - 2. [Edelstein, Prachtstück] jewel; **sie ist ein Juwel** she is a gem.

Juwelier (*pl* -e) *der* jeweller.

Juwelierin (*pl* -nen) *die* jeweller.

K

k (pl - ODER -s), **K** (pl - ODER -s) [kɑː] das k, K.

Kabarett [kaba'rɛt] (pl -s ODER -e), **Cabaret** [kaba'reː] (pl -s ODER -e) das - **1.** [Aufführung] satirical revue - **2.** [Institution] *theatre where satirical revues are performed.*

Kabarettist, in (mpl -en, fpl -nen) der, die satirical revue artist.

Kabel (pl -) das cable.

Kabelanschluss (pl -es) der: **Kabelanschluss haben** to have cable television.

Kabelfernsehen das cable television.

Kabeljau (pl -s) der cod.

Kabine (pl -n) die - **1.** [von Schiff, Flugzeug] cabin - **2.** [in Schwimmbad] cubicle; [in Kleidergeschäft] fitting room.

Kabinett (pl -e) das - **1.** [aus Ministern] cabinet - **2.** [Wein] *term designating a high-quality German wine.*

Kabrio (pl -s), **Cabrio** (pl -s) das convertible.

Kachel (pl -n) die tile.

kacheln (perf hat/ist gekachelt) ⟨⟩ vt (hat) [auslegen] to tile. ⟨⟩ vi (ist) fam [rasen] to zoom along.

Kadaver [ka'dɑːvɐ] (pl -) der carcass.

Käfer (pl -) der [Insekt, Auto] beetle.

Kaff (pl -s ODER -e) das fam dump.

Kaffee ['kafe] (pl -s), **Kaffee** [ka'feː] (pl -s) der - **1.** [gen] coffee; **eine Tasse Kaffee** a cup of coffee; **Kaffee mit Milch** white coffee; **schwarzer Kaffee** black coffee - **2.** [Mahlzeit] afternoon coffee and cake; **Kaffee trinken** [am Nachmittag] to have afternoon coffee; [in der Pause] to have a coffee break.

Kaffeefilter der filter (paper).

Kaffeekanne die coffeepot.

Kaffeeklatsch (pl -e) der: **sich zum Kaffeeklatsch treffen** to meet for a chat over a cup of coffee.

Kaffeelöffel der coffee spoon.

Kaffeemaschine die coffee machine.

Kaffeetasse die coffee cup.

Käfig (pl -e) der cage.

kahl adj - **1.** [ohne Haare] bald; **kahl werden** to go bald - **2.** [Berg, Baum] bare.

Kahn (pl Kähne) der - **1.** [Ruderboot] rowing boat UK, rowboat US - **2.** [Stechkahn] punt - **3.** [Lastkahn] barge.

Kai (pl -s ODER -e) der quay.

Kairo nt Cairo.

Kaiser (pl -) der emperor.

Kaiserin (pl -nen) die empress.

kaiserlich adj imperial.

Kaiserreich das empire.

Kaiserschmarrn (pl Kaiserschmarrn) der pancake torn into thin strips.

Kaiserschnitt der MED caesarean (section).

Kajak (pl -s) das & der kayak.

Kajüte (pl -n) die cabin.

Kakao [ka'kau] der cocoa; **jn/etw durch den Kakao ziehen** fam to take the mickey out of sb/sthg.

Kakerlake (pl -n) die cockroach.

Kaktee = Kaktus.

Kaktus (pl Kakteen ODER -se) der cactus.

Kalb (pl Kälber) das - **1.** [Tier] calf - **2.** [Fleisch] veal.

Kalbfleisch das veal.

Kalender (pl -) der - **1.** [Wandkalender] calendar - **2.** [Taschenkalender] diary; **sich** (D) **etw im Kalender rot anstreichen** fig to make sthg a red-letter day.

Kaliber (pl -) das - **1.** [von einem Geschütz] calibre - **2.** [Art, Sorte] kind, ilk.

Kalium das potassium.

Kalk der (ohne pl) - **1.** [Kalkstein] limestone - **2.** [in Wasserkessel] lime - **3.** [zum Tünchen] whitewash.

Kalkstein der limestone.

kalkulieren ⟨⟩ vt [berechnen] to calculate. ⟨⟩ vi to calculate; **genau/scharf kalkulieren** to make precise calculations.

Kalorie [kalo'riː] (pl -n) die calorie.

kalorienarm [kalo'riːənarm] ⟨⟩ adj low-calorie. ⟨⟩ adv: **kalorienarm essen** to eat low-calorie food.

kalt (kompar kälter, superl kälteste) ⟨⟩ adj cold; **es ist kalt** it's cold; **mir ist kalt** I'm cold; **kalte Füße kriegen** fig to get cold feet. ⟨⟩ adv (kompar kälter; superl am kältesten): **kalt duschen** to have a cold shower; **das Bier kaltstellen** to chill the beer; **kalt lächeln** to smile coldly.

kaltblütig ⟨⟩ adj cold-blooded. ⟨⟩ adv in cold blood.

Kälte die (ohne pl) - **1.** [gen] coldness - **2.** [Wetter] cold; **bei Kälte** in cold weather.

Kälteeinbruch der cold snap.

Kalte Krieg der cold war.

Kaltmiete die rent not including bills.

Kalzium das calcium.

kam prät ⟩ **kommen.**

Kambodscha nt Cambodia.

Kamel (pl -e) das - **1.** [Tier] camel - **2.** fig [Trottel] idiot.

Kamera (pl -s) die camera.

Kamerad, in (mpl -en, fpl -nen) der, die friend.

kameradschaftlich ⟨⟩ adj friendly. ⟨⟩ adv in a friendly way.

Kamerun *nt* Cameroon.

Kamille (*pl* -n) *die* camomile.

Kamillen|tee *der* camomile tea.

Kamin (*pl* -e) *der* - **1.** [Schornstein] chimney - **2.** [Feuerstelle] fireplace; **offener Kamin** open fireplace.

Kamm (*pl* Kämme) *der* - **1.** [Haarkamm, Hahnenkamm] comb; **alles über einen Kamm scheren** *fig* [keinen Unterschied machen] to lump everything together - **2.** [Bergkamm] ridge.

kämmen *vt* to comb.

Kammer (*pl* -n) *die* - **1.** [kleines Zimmer] cubbyhole - **2.** POL chamber.

Kammer|musik *die* chamber music.

Kampagne (*pl* -n) *die* campaign.

Kampf (*pl* Kämpfe) *der* - **1.** [Streit] fight; [politisch, sozial] struggle, fight; [in Sport] contest; [in Krieg] battle; **Kampf um etw** fight for sthg; **Kampf gegen jn/etw** fight against sb/sthg; **jm/einer Sache den Kampf ansagen** to declare war on sb/sthg - **2.** MIL fighting (U).

kämpfen *vi* to fight; **gegen jn/etw kämpfen** to fight against sb/sthg; **für jn/etw kämpfen** to fight for sb/sthg; **um jn/etw kämpfen** to fight for sb/sthg; **mit etw kämpfen** *fig* [Schlaf, Tod] to fight sthg off; [Tränen] to fight sthg back.

Kampf|gebiet *das* combat zone.

kampflos ◇ *adj* MIL peaceful. ◇ *adv* without a fight.

Kampf|richter, in *der, die* SPORT referee.

Kanada *nt* Canada.

Kanadier [ka'nɑːdjɐ] (*pl* -) *der* - **1.** [Einwohner Kanadas] Canadian - **2.** [Sportboot] Canadian canoe.

Kanadierin [ka'nɑːdjərɪn] (*pl* -nen) *die* Canadian.

kanadisch *adj* Canadian.

Kanal (*pl* Kanäle) *der* - **1.** [Wasserweg] canal - **2.** TELEKOM channel; **den Kanal voll haben** *fam* [betrunken sein] to be plastered; *fam* [es satt haben] to be fed up to the back teeth.

Kanalisation (*pl* -en) *die* - **1.** [für Abwässer] sewers *Pl* - **2.** [Ausbau eines natürlichen Wasserweges] canalization (U).

Kanal|tunnel *der* Channel Tunnel.

Kanarien|vogel *der* canary.

Kanarische Inseln *Pl* Canary Islands.

Kandidat, in (*mpl* -en, *fpl* -nen) *der, die* candidate; **jn als Kandidaten aufstellen** ODER **nominieren** to put sb forward as a candidate.

Kandis|zucker *der* sugar candy.

Känguru (*pl* -s) *das* kangaroo.

Kaninchen (*pl* -) *das* rabbit.

Kanister (*pl* -) *der* can.

kann *präs* ▷ **können**.

Kanne (*pl* -n) *die* pot.

Kannibale (*pl* -n) *der* cannibal.

Kannibalin (*pl* -nen) *die* cannibal.

kannte *prät* ▷ **kennen**.

Kanon (*pl* -s) *der* MUS canon.

Kanone (*pl* -n) *die* [Geschütz] cannon; **unter aller Kanone sein** *fam* [miserabel] to be the pits.

Kante (*pl* -n) *die* edge.

Kantine (*pl* -n) *die* canteen.

Kanton (*pl* -e) *der* canton.

Kantor (*pl* -toren) *der* choirmaster and organist.

Kantorin (*pl* -nen) *die* choirmistress and organist.

Kanu (*pl* -s) *das* canoe.

Kanzel (*pl* -n) *die* - **1.** [von Kirchen] pulpit - **2.** [von Flugzeugen] cockpit.

Kanzlei (*pl* -en) *die* office.

Kanzler (*pl* -) *der* - **1.** [Bundeskanzler] chancellor - **2.** UNI vice-chancellor *UK*, chancellor *US*.

Kanzler|amt *das* [Amtssitz des Bundeskanzlers] chancellery.

Kap (*pl* -s) *das* cape.

Kapazität (*pl* -en) *die* - **1.** [gen] capacity - **2.** [Experte] authority.

Kapelle (*pl* -n) *die* - **1.** [kleine Kirche] chapel - **2.** MUS band.

Kapell|meister, in *der, die* [Leiter - einer Musikkapelle] bandmaster; [- eines Orchesters] conductor.

Kaper (*pl* -n) *die* caper.

kapieren *vt fam* to get.

kapital [kapi'tɑːl] *adj* - **1.** [Irrtum] serious - **2.** [Hirsch] magnificent.

Kapital (*pl* -ien ODER -e) *das* [gen] capital; **aus etw Kapital schlagen** to make capital out of sthg; **geistiges Kapital** intellectual assets *Pl*; **totes Kapital** unused skills *Pl*.

Kapital|anlage *die* capital investment.

Kapitalismus *der* capitalism.

Kapitalist, in (*mpl* -en, *fpl* -nen) *der, die* capitalist.

kapitalistisch *adj* capitalist.

Kapitän (*pl* -e) *der* captain.

Kapitel (*pl* -) *das* chapter; **ein Kapitel für sich sein** *fig* to be an awkward business; **das ist ein anderes Kapitel** that's another story.

Kapitulation (*pl* -en) *die* [Aufgabe] surrender (U); **bedingungslose Kapitulation** unconditional surrender (U).

kapitulieren *vi* to surrender; **vor etw** (D) **kapitulieren** to give up in the face of sthg.

Kaplan (*pl* Kapläne) *der* curate.

Kappe (*pl* -n) *die* cap.

kappen *vt* - **1.** [beschneiden] to cut back - **2.** [durchschneiden] to cut through.

Kapsel (*pl* -n) *die* - **1.** [kleiner Behälter] box - **2.** [von Medikament, von Blüten] capsule.

kaputt *adj fam* - **1.** [Vase, Gerät] broken; [Beziehung, Gesundheit] ruined - **2.** *fig* [erschöpft]: **kaputt sein** to be done in.

kaputt|gehen (*perf* ist kaputtgegangen) *vi* (*unreg*) *fam* - **1.** [Gerät, Gegenstand] to break; [Beziehungen, Geschäfte] to be ruined - **2.** [eingehen] to die.

kaputt|lachen ◆ **sich kaputtlachen** *ref fam* to kill o.s. laughing; **sich über jn/etw kaputtlachen** to kill o.s. laughing at sb/sthg.

Kapuze (*pl* -n) *die* hood.

Karaffe (*pl* -n) *die* - **1.** [mit Stöpsel] decanter - **2.** [ohne Stöpsel] carafe.

Karamell *der* caramel.

Karamellbonbon (*pl* -s) *das* & *der* toffee.

Karat (*pl* -e ODER -) *das* - **1.** [Edelsteingewicht] carat - **2.** [Einheit]: **dieser Ring hat 20 Karat** this ring is 20 carats.

Karate *das* karate.

Karawane (*pl* -n) *die* caravan.

Kardinal (*pl* Kardinäle) *der* cardinal.

Karfreitag (*pl* -e) *der* Good Friday.

karg *adj* - **1.** [Mahlzeit, Lohn] meagre - **2.** [Raum] bare - **3.** [Boden] barren.

Karibik *die* Caribbean.

karibisch *adj* Caribbean.

kariert ⬦ *adj* - **1.** [Stoff] checked - **2.** [Papier] squared. ⬦ *adv fam* [verwirrt]: **kariert schauen** to look bewildered.

Karies ['ka:riɛs] *die* MED tooth decay.

Karikatur (*pl* -en) *die* cartoon; [Porträt] caricature.

kariös *adj* decayed.

Karlsruhe *nt* - **1.** [Stadt] Karlsruhe - **2.** [Gericht] the Federal Constitutional Court.

Karneval ['karnəval] (*pl* -e ODER -s) *der* carnival.

karnevalistisch [karnəva'lıstıʃ] *adj* carnival (*vor Subst*).

Karnevalszug *der* carnival procession.

Kärnten *nt* Carinthia.

Karo (*pl* -s) *das* - **1.** [Raute] diamond - **2.** (*ohne Artikel, ohne pl*) [Spielfarbe] diamonds *Pl* - **3.** [Spielkarte] diamond; **die Karosechs** the six of diamonds.

Karosserie (*pl* -n) *die* bodywork (*U*).

Karotte (*pl* -n) *die* carrot.

Karpfen (*pl* -) *der* carp.

Karre (*pl* -n) *die* - **1.** [Handkarre] cart - **2.** *fam* [Auto] jalopy, banger *UK*.

Karren (*pl* -) *der* [kleiner Wagen] cart.

Karriere [ka'rjeːrə] (*pl* -n) *die* career; **Karriere machen** to make a career for o.s.

Karte (*pl* -n) *die* - **1.** [Postkarte, Spielkarte] card - **2.** [Landkarte] map; **jm die gelbe/rote Karte zeigen** to show sb the yellow/red card; **mit offenen Karten spielen** to put one's cards on

the table; **alles auf eine Karte setzen** to stake everything on one chance; **schlechte Karten haben** to have been dealt a bad hand.

Kartei (*pl* -en) *die* card index.

Karteikarte *die* index card.

Karteikasten *der* index-card box.

Kartell (*pl* -e) *das* WIRTSCH cartel.

Kartenspiel *das* - **1.** [Gesellschaftsspiel] card game - **2.** [Spielkarten] pack *UK* ODER deck *US* of cards.

Kartentelefon *das* cardphone.

Kartenvorverkauf *der* advance booking.

Kartoffel (*pl* -n) *die* potato.

Kartoffelbrei *der* KÜCHE mashed potatoes *Pl*.

Kartoffelchips *Pl* crisps *UK*, chips *US*.

Kartoffelpuffer *der* KÜCHE potato pancake (*made from grated potatoes*).

Kartoffelpüree *das* KÜCHE mashed potatoes *Pl*.

Kartoffelsalat *der* KÜCHE potato salad.

Karton (*pl* -s) *der* - **1.** [Pappe] card (cardboard) - **2.** [Kiste] box.

Karussell (*pl* -s) *das* merry-go-round; **Karussell fahren** to go on the merry-go-round.

Karwoche *die* Holy Week.

Käse (*pl* -) *der* cheese; **das ist Käse!** *abw* & *fig* that's rubbish!

Käsefondue *das* KÜCHE cheese fondue.

Käsekuchen *der* KÜCHE cheesecake.

Kaserne (*pl* -n) *die* MIL barracks *Pl*.

käsig *adj* pale.

Kasino (*pl* -s) *das* - **1.** [Spielkasino] casino - **2.** MIL (officers') mess.

Kasperletheater *das* [Vorstellung] Punch and Judy show; [Gebäude] Punch and Judy theatre.

Kasse (*pl* -n) *die* - **1.** [Kassette] cashbox - **2.** [im Laden] till - **3.** [im Supermarkt] checkout - **4.** [im Theater, Kino] box office - **5.** *fam* [Krankenkasse] (health) insurance (*U*); **Kasse machen** to cash up; **knapp bei Kasse sein** *fam* to be short of cash.

Kassenarzt, ärztin *der, die* doctor who treats patients with health insurance.

Kassenbon *der* receipt.

Kassenpatient, in *der, die* patient with health insurance.

Kassenzettel *der* receipt.

Kassette (*pl* -n) *die* - **1.** [Musik- und Videokassette] cassette, tape; **etw auf Kassette aufnehmen** to record sthg on cassette ODER tape - **2.** [für Schmuck, Schallplatten, Bücher] box.

Kassettenrekorder *der* cassette recorder.

kassieren *vt* - **1.** [einziehen] to collect - **2.** *fam* [einnehmen] to pocket - **3.** *fam* [einheimsen - Lob, Kritik] to get; [- Niederlage] to suffer - **4.** *fam* [Führerschein] to take away.

Kassierer, in (*mpl* -, *fpl* -nen) *der, die* - 1. [von Geschäft, Bank] cashier - 2. [von Verein] treasurer.

Kastanie [kas'tɑ:njə] (*pl* -n) *die* chestnut.

Kasten (*pl* Kästen) *der* - 1. [Kiste] box - 2. [für Flaschen] crate - 3. [Briefkasten] postbox UK, mailbox US - 4. *fam* [Gebäude] great box of a building - 5. SPORT box - 6. *fam* [Kopf]: **etwas/viel auf dem Kasten haben** [intelligent sein] to be brainy/very brainy.

kastrieren *vt* MED to castrate.

Kasus (*pl* Kasus) *der* GRAMM case.

Kat [kat] (*pl* -s) (*abk für* **Katalysator**) *der* AUTO cat.

Katalanisch(e) *das* Catalan; *siehe auch* **Englisch(e)**.

Katalog (*pl* -e) *der* catalogue.

Katalysator (*pl* -toren) *der* [am Auto] catalytic converter; [in Chemie] catalyst.

Katamaran (*pl* -e) *der* catamaran.

katastrophal [katastro'fɑ:l] ⟨⟩ *adj* disastrous. ⟨⟩ *adv* disastrously.

Katastrophe [katas'tro:fə] (*pl* -n) *die* disaster; **eine Katastrophe sein** *fam* to be a disaster.

Katastrophengebiet [katas'tro:fəngəbi:t] *das* disaster area.

Katechismus (*pl* -men) *der* catechism.

Kategorie (*pl* -n) *die* category.

kategorisch ⟨⟩ *adj* categorical. ⟨⟩ *adv* categorically.

Kater (*pl* -) *der* - 1. [Tier] tomcat - 2. *fam* [von Alkohol] hangover; **einen Kater haben** to have a hangover.

kath. (*abk für* **katholisch**) Cath.

Kathedrale (*pl* -n) *die* cathedral.

Kathode (*pl* -n) *die* PHYS cathode.

Katholik (*pl* -en) *der* Catholic.

Katholikentag *der* biannual congress of German Catholics.

Katholikin (*pl* -nen) *die* Catholic.

katholisch *adj* Catholic.

Katholizismus *der* Catholicism.

Katz *die*: **Katz und Maus spielen** to play cat and mouse; **für die Katz sein** *fam* to be a waste of time.

Katze (*pl* -n) *die* - 1. [Tier] cat - 2. [weibliches Tier] she-cat.

Katzensprung *der*: **etw ist nur ein Katzensprung von etw entfernt** sthg is only a stone's throw away from sthg.

Kauderwelsch *das* gibberish.

kauen ⟨⟩ *vi* to chew; **an etw** (D) **kauen** [herumkauen] to chew sthg; [bewältigen] to grapple with sthg. ⟨⟩ *vt* to chew.

kauern *vi* to crouch.

Kauf (*pl* Käufe) *der* purchase; **einen Kauf abschließen** to complete a purchase; **etw in Kauf nehmen** *fig* to accept sthg.

kaufen *vt* to buy; **jm/sich etw kaufen** to buy sb/o.s. sthg.

Käufer, in (*mpl* -, *fpl* -nen) *der, die* buyer.

Kauffrau *die* businesswoman.

Kaufhaus *das* department store.

Kaufkraft *die* purchasing power.

Kaufleute *Pl* business people.

käuflich *adj* - 1. [zu erwerben]: **etw käuflich erwerben** to purchase sthg; **käuflich sein** [Ware] to be for sale; [Person] to be easily bought; **nicht käuflich sein** [Ware] not to be for sale; [Person] not to be easily bought - 2. [prostituiert]: **käufliches Mädchen** prostitute; **käufliche Liebe** prostitution.

Kaufmann (*pl* -leute) *der* businessman.

kaufmännisch *adj* commercial.

Kaufpreis *der* purchase price.

Kaugummi *das* & *der* chewing gum.

kaum *adv* - 1. [gen] hardly; **das ist kaum zu glauben** that's hard to believe; **kaum dass ich angerufen hatte, standen sie schon vor der Tür** no sooner had I rung than they were at the door - 2. [höchstens] barely.

Kaution (*pl* -en) *die* - 1. [für Wohnung] deposit - 2. [für Häftling] bail; **gegen Kaution freikommen** to be released on bail.

Kautschuk *der* (India) rubber.

Kauz (*pl* Käuze) *der*: **ein komischer Kauz** *fig* an odd bird.

Kavalier [kava'liɐ] (*pl* -e) *der* gentleman.

Kaviar [kɑ:viar] (*pl* -e) *der* caviar.

Kegel (*pl* -) *der* - 1. MATH cone - 2. [zum Spielen] skittle.

Kegelklub *der* bowling club.

kegeln *vi* to bowl.

Kehle (*pl* -n) *die* [gen] throat; **etw in die falsche Kehle bekommen** *fam* to take sthg the wrong way; **aus voller Kehle singen/schreien** to sing/shout at the top of one's voice.

Kehlkopf *der* larynx.

kehren *vt* - 1. [fegen] to sweep - 2. [wenden] to turn; **den starken Mann nach außen kehren** to act the tough guy; **in sich gekehrt** lost in one's own world. ⟐ **sich kehren** *ref* - 1. [sich kümmern]: **sich nicht an** ODER **um etw kehren** not to care about sthg - 2. [sich richten]: **sich gegen jn kehren** to turn against sb.

Kehrreim *der* refrain.

Kehrseite *die* drawback, downside; **die Kehrseite der Medaille** the downside.

kehrtmachen *vi* to turn round.

Kehrtwendung *die*: **eine Kehrtwendung machen** to turn round; [politisch] to do a U-turn.

keifen *vi abw* to nag.

Keil (*pl* -e) *der* wedge.

Keil|riemen *der* fan belt.

Keim (*pl* -e) *der* - 1. [Pflanzentrieb] shoot; **etw im Keim ersticken** *fig* to nip sthg in the bud - 2. [Bakterie] germ.

keimen *vi* [Saat] to germinate; [Kartoffeln, Zwiebeln] to sprout.

keimfrei <> *adj* [Instrumente, Milch] sterilized; [Bedingungen] sterile. <> *adv* [arbeiten] in a sterile environment.

keimtötend *adj* germicidal, antiseptic.

Keim|zelle *die* - 1. BIOL sex cell - 2. [Ausgangspunkt] germ.

kein, e *det* no, not any; **kein Mensch** no one; **es gibt keine Bananen** there are no bananas, there aren't any bananas; **ich habe kein Geld/ keine Zeit** I haven't got any money/time; **das ist doch keine Schande** it's no disgrace; **kein Wunder, dass...** it's no wonder (that...)

keine, r, s *pron* - 1. [Person] no one, nobody; **keiner weiß, dass...** no one ODER nobody knows that...; **keiner der Schüler** ODER **von den Schülern** none of the pupils - 2. [Gegenstand] none; **welchen nehmen Sie? - keinen** which do you want? - neither.

keinerlei *adj* (unver) no... at all; **keinerlei Bedenken haben** to have no scruples at all.

keinesfalls *adv* on no account; **das ist keinesfalls schwer** that's not at all difficult.

keineswegs *adv* not at all; **keineswegs besser** in no way better.

Keks (*pl* -e) *der* biscuit UK, cookie US.

Kelle (*pl* -n) *die* [Schöpflöffel] ladle.

Keller (*pl* -) *der* cellar.

Kellner, in (*mpl* -, *fpl* -nen) *der, die* waiter (waitress *die*).

Kelte (*pl* -n) *der* Celt.

keltern *vt* to press.

Keltin (*pl* -nen) *die* Celt.

keltisch *adj* Celtic.

Kenia *nt* Kenya.

kennen (*prät* **kannte**, *perf* **hat gekannt**) *vt* to know; **jn/etw gut kennen** to know sb/ sthg well; **ich kenne mich** I know what I'm like; **kennen wir uns nicht?** haven't we met somewhere before?; **da kennst du ihn aber schlecht!** you don't know what he's like!

kennen lernen *vt* - 1. [Person] to get to know, to meet; **freut mich, Sie kennen zu lernen!** pleased to meet you! - 2. [Sache] to get to know, to familiarize o.s. with. **sich kennen lernen** *ref* [sich begegnen] to meet.

Kenntnis (*pl* -nisse) *die* knowledge; **etw zur Kenntnis nehmen** to take note of sthg, to note sthg; **jn von etw in Kenntnis setzen** to inform sb of sthg; **dieser Vorfall entzieht sich meiner Kenntnis** *geh* I don't know anything about this incident. **Kenntnisse** *Pl* knowledge (U).

Kennwort (*pl* -wörter) *das* password.

Kenn|zahl *die* code number.

Kenn|zeichen *das* - 1. [Merkmal] symbol, sign; **besondere Kennzeichen** distinguishing features - 2. [an Kfz]: **amtliches Kennzeichen** registration number UK, license number US.

kennzeichnen *vt* [markieren]: **etw (mit** ODER **durch etw) kennzeichnen** to mark sthg (with sthg); **etw als etw kennzeichnen** [Produkt, Ware] to label sthg as sthg; **jn als etw kennzeichnen** to describe sb as sthg.

kennzeichnend *adj*: **für jn/etw kennzeichnend sein** to be typical ODER characteristic of sb/sthg.

Kenn|zeichnung *die* labelling.

Kenn|ziffer *die* reference number.

kentern (*perf* **ist gekentert**) *vi* to capsize.

Keramik (*pl* -en) *die* - 1. [Gefäß]: **eine Keramik** a piece of pottery - 2. (ohne *pl*) [Ton] pottery, ceramics *Pl*.

Kerbe (*pl* -n) *die* notch.

Kerbel *der* chervil.

Kerker (*pl* -) *der* dungeon.

Kerl (*pl* -e) *der* fam guy, bloke UK; **ein netter Kerl** a nice guy; **ein gemeiner Kerl** a swine.

Kern (*pl* -e) *der* - 1. [von Apfel, Birne, Zitrusfrucht] pip; [von Pfirsich, Kirsche] stone, pit US; [von Nuß] kernel - 2. [Wichtigstes] core, crux - 3. PHYS nucleus.

Kern|energie *die* nuclear power.

kerngesund *adj* as fit as a fiddle.

Kernkraft|gegner, in *der, die* opponent of nuclear power.

Kernkraft|werk *das* nuclear power station.

Kern|punkt *der* [eines Vortrags] central point; [eines Problems] crux.

Kern|stück *das* centrepiece.

Kern|waffe *die* nuclear weapon.

Kerze (*pl* -n) *die* - 1. [zur Beleuchtung] candle - 2. [Turnübung] shoulder stand.

kerzengerade *adj & adv* bolt upright.

Kerzenlicht *das* candlelight.

kess (*kompar* **kesser**, *superl* **kesseste**) <> *adj* - 1. [Person, Verhalten] cheeky - 2. [Kleidung] jaunty. <> *adv* [frech] cheekily.

Kessel (*pl* -) *der* - 1. [Topf] kettle; [groß] cauldron - 2. [Tal] basin, basin-shaped valley.

Ketchup, Ketschup ['kɛtʃap] *das & der* ketchup.

Kette (*pl* -n) *die* chain; [aus Perlen] string; [von Polizisten] cordon; [von Unfällen, Ereignissen] string, series.

ketten *vt*: **jn/etw an etw (A) ketten** to chain sb/sthg to sthg.

Ketten|fahrzeug *das* tracked vehicle.

Ketten|reaktion *die* chain reaction.

Ketten|säge *die* chain saw.

Ketzer (*pl* -) *der* heretic.

Ketzerin (*pl* -nen) *die* heretic.

keuchen (perf hat/ist gekeucht) vi to pant.

Keuchhusten der whooping cough.

Keule (pl -n) die - 1. KÜCHE leg - 2. [Waffe & SPORT] club.

keusch <> adj chaste. <> adv chastely.

Keuschheit die chastity.

Keyboard ['kiːbɔːd] (pl -s) das [Musikinstrument & EDV] keyboard.

Kfz [kaːɛf'tsɛt] (pl -) das abk für **Kraftfahrzeug**.

Kfz-Steuer die road tax.

kg (abk für **Kilogramm**) kg.

kichern vi to giggle.

kicken <> vi to play (football). <> vt to kick.

kidnappen ['kɪtnɛpn̩] vt to kidnap.

Kidnapper, in ['kɪtnɛpɐ, rɪn] (mpl -, fpl -nen) der, die kidnapper.

Kiefer (pl - ODER -n) <> der (pl Kiefer) jaw. <> die (pl Kiefern) pine.

Kiel (pl -e) der - 1. [von Schiff] keel - 2. [von Federn] quill.

Kieme (pl -n) die gill.

Kies der - 1. [auf Weg] gravel; [am Ufer] shingle - 2. salopp [Geld] cash, dosh UK.

Kieselstein der pebble.

Kiesgrube die gravel pit.

Kiew ['kiːɛf] nt Kiev.

kikeriki interj cock-a-doodle-doo!

Killer, in (mpl -, fpl -nen) der, die killer.

Kilo (pl - ODER -s) das kilo.

Kilogramm (pl -e) das kilogram.

Kilohertz (pl Kilohertz) das kilohertz.

Kilokalorie (pl -n) die kilocalorie.

Kilometer (pl -) der kilometre; **Kilometer pro Stunde** kilometres per hour.

kilometerlang adj ≈ miles long; **kilometerlange Strände** miles and miles of beaches.

Kilometerstand der ≈ mileage; **bei Kilometerstand 10.000** when there are 10,000 km on the clock.

Kilometerzähler der ≈ mileometer.

Kilowatt (pl -) das kilowatt.

Kilowattstunde (pl -n) die kilowatt hour.

Kind (pl -er) das child; **von Kind auf** ODER **an** from childhood; **ein Kind erwarten** to be expecting (a baby); **ein Kind bekommen** ODER **kriegen** to have a baby; **mit Kind und Kegel** with the whole tribe.

Kinderarzt, ärztin der, die paediatrician.

Kinderbuch das children's book.

Kindergarten der nursery school.

Kindergärtner, in der, die = **Erzieher**.

Kindergeld das (ohne Pl) child benefit UK, child allowance US.

Kinderheim das children's home.

Kinderhort der day centre where children can spend the afternoon after lessons have finished.

Kinderkrankheit die illness affecting children.

Kinderkrippe die crèche.

Kinderlähmung die polio.

kinderleicht adj fam dead easy; **es war kinderleicht** it was child's play.

kinderlieb adj fond of children.

Kinderlied das nursery rhyme.

Kindermädchen das nursemaid.

kinderreich adj: **eine kinderreiche Familie** a large family, a family with lots of children.

Kinderschutzbund der child protection league.

Kindersicherung die [an Auto] childproof lock.

Kindersitz der child seat.

Kinderspiel das children's game; **ein Kinderspiel sein** to be child's play.

Kinderstube die: **eine gute/schlechte Kinderstube haben** to have been well/badly brought up.

Kindertagesstätte die day nursery.

Kinderwagen der pram UK, baby carriage US.

Kinderzimmer das children's bedroom.

Kindesalter das childhood; **im Kindesalter** as a child, at an early age.

Kindesmisshandlung (pl -en) die child abuse.

Kindheit die childhood; **von Kindheit an** from an early age.

kindisch abw <> adj childish. <> adv childishly.

kindlich <> adj childlike. <> adv like a child.

Kinn (pl -e) das chin.

Kinnhaken der hook (to the chin).

Kino (pl -s) das cinema, movie theater US; **ins Kino gehen** to go to the movies, to go to the cinema.

Kinobesucher, in der, die moviegoer, cinemagoer.

Kinoprogramm das movie guide, cinema guide.

Kiosk (pl -e) der kiosk.

Kippe (pl -n) die - 1. fam [Zigarette] ciggy, fag UK - 2. fam [Zigarettenstummel] cigarette butt, fag end UK; **auf der Kippe stehen** [zu fallen drohen] to be precariously balanced; [gefährdet oder unsicher sein] to be in the balance; [Schüler] to be in danger of staying down a year.

kippen (perf hat/ist gekippt) <> vi (ist) to topple. <> vt (hat) - 1. [Fenster, Möbel] to tilt - 2. [Flüssigkeit] to tip - 3. fam [Schnaps] to knock back.

Kirche (pl -n) die church; **in die Kirche gehen** to go to church.

Kirchen|chor der church choir.

Kirchen|gemeinde die [Bezirk] parish; [Gottesdienstteilnehmer] congregation.

Kirchen|musik die church music.

Kirchen|schiff das ARCHIT nave.

Kirchen|steuer die church tax.

kirchlich <> adj church (vor Subst). <> adv: **sich kirchlich trauen lassen** to have a church wedding.

Kirch|turm der [mit Spitze] steeple; [ohne Spitze] church tower.

Kirmes die fair.

Kirsch|baum der cherry tree.

Kirsche (pl -n) die cherry.

Kirsch|torte die: **Schwarzwälder Kirschtorte** Black Forest gâteau.

Kissen (pl -) das [auf Stuhl, Sofa] cushion; [für Bett] pillow.

Kiste (pl -n) die - 1. [Behälter] crate, box - 2. fam [Auto] jalopy, banger UK.

kitschig adj kitschy.

Kitt der putty.

Kittchen (pl -) das fam nick UK, can US; **im Kittchen sein** ODER **sitzen** fam to be in the nick UK ODER can US.

Kittel (pl -) der [für Werkstatt] overalls Pl; [für Arzt] white coat; [für Labor] lab coat.

Kittel|schürze (pl -n) die housecoat.

kitten vt - 1. [kleben] to glue together - 2. [Ehe] to patch up.

Kitzel (pl -) der thrill.

kitzelig = kitzlig.

kitzeln vt - 1. [krabbeln] to tickle; **jn an den Füßen kitzeln** to tickle sb's feet - 2. fam [reizen - Ehrgeiz] to arouse.

kitzlig, kitzelig adj - 1. [empfindlich] ticklish - 2. [heikel] tricky.

Kiwi (pl -s) die kiwi fruit.

klaffen vi to gape.

kläffen vi abw to yap.

Klage (pl -n) die - 1. [Beschwerde] complaint - 2. RECHT action, suit; **gegen jn Klage einreichen** to bring an action against sb.

klagen <> vi - 1. [jammern] to complain; **über jn/etw klagen** to complain about sb/sthg; **über Rückenschmerzen klagen** to complain of backache - 2. [vor Gericht]: **gegen jn klagen** to take legal action against sb; **auf Schadenersatz klagen** to sue for damages. <> vt: **jm seine Not klagen** to pour out one's troubles to sb.

Kläger, in (mpl -, fpl -nen) der, die RECHT plaintiff.

klaglos adv uncomplainingly.

Klammer (pl -n) die - 1. [für Blätter] paper clip; [für Wäsche] (clothes) peg UK, clothspin US;

[für Wunde, von Heftmaschine] staple; [für Zähne] brace - 2. [Symbol] bracket; **etw in Klammern setzen** to bracket sthg; **in Klammern stehen** to be in brackets.

Klammer|affe der fam EDV at-sign.

klammern vt: **etw an etw (A) klammern** to attach sthg to sthg. **sich klammern** ref: **sich an jn/etw klammern** eigtl & fig to cling to sb/sthg.

Klamotten Pl fam gear (U), clothes.

klang prät klingen.

Klang (pl Klänge) der sound.

Klapp|bett das folding bed.

Klappe (pl -n) die - 1. [Gegenstand] flap; [bei Blasinstrument, Motor] valve; [bei Film] clapperboard; **"Klappe die Fünfte"** "take five" - 2. fam [Mund] trap.

klappen <> vt: **etw nach oben/unten klappen** [Sitz] to tip sthg forward/back. <> vi [gelingen] to work, to come off; **hat alles geklappt?** did everything go OK?; **es klappt (gut)** it works; **es klappt nicht** it doesn't work.

klapperig = klapprig.

klappern vi [Tür, Fensterladen] to rattle; [Kastagnette] to clack (together); **ich klappere mit den Zähnen** my teeth are chattering.

Klapp|rad, Klappfahrrad das folding bicycle.

klapprig, klapperig adj - 1. [Gegenstand] rickety - 2. [Person] doddery.

Klapp|sitz der folding seat.

Klaps (pl -e) der [leichter Schlag] pat.

klar <> adj - 1. [gen] clear; **mir ist nicht klar, wie das funktioniert** I'm not clear how it works; **ist dir das jetzt klar?** do you understand now?; **na klar!** of course! - 2. [bewusst]: **sich (D) über etw (A) im Klaren sein** to be aware of sthg. <> adv - 1. [deutlich] clearly - 2. [fertig]: **klar zu etw** ready for sthg. **alles klar** interj: **alles klar?** OK?; **alles klar!** OK! **klar und deutlich** <> adj perfectly clear. <> adv quite clearly.

Klär|anlage die sewage works (sg).

Klare (pl -n) der schnapps.

klären vt [Problem, Angelegenheit] to clear up.

klar|gehen (perf ist klargegangen) vi (unreg) fam to go OK.

Klarheit die [Gewissheit, Deutlichkeit] clarity; **über etw (A) Klarheit gewinnen** ODER **bekommen** to clarify sthg; **sich (D) Klarheit verschaffen** to get sthg clear.

Klarinette (pl -n) die clarinet.

klar|kommen (perf ist klargekommen) vi (unreg): **mit jm/etw klarkommen** to be able to cope with sb/sthg.

klar machen vt: **jm etw klar machen** to explain sthg to sb, to make sthg clear to sb.

Klarsicht|folie die transparent film, clingfilm UK.

Klarsicht|hülle *die* plastic cover.

klar|stellen *vt* [Problem, Frage] to clear up; **klarstellen, dass...** to make it clear that...

Klärung (*pl* -en) *die* clearing up.

klar werden (*perf* ist klar geworden) *vi* (*unreg*): **jm klar werden** to become clear to sb; **sich** (*D*) **über etw klar werden** to be able to understand sthg.

klasse *adj fam* great, neat *US*.

Klasse (*pl* -n) *die* - 1. [gen] class; **erster/zweiter Klasse** first/second class - 2. [Zimmer] classroom - 3. [Schuljahr] form *UK*, grade *US*; **eine Klasse wiederholen** to repeat a year.

Klassen|arbeit *die* class test.

Klassen|kamerad, in *der, die* classmate.

Klassen|lehrer, in *der, die* class teacher.

Klassen|zimmer *das* classroom.

Klassik *die* (*ohne pl*) - 1. [Epoche] classical period - 2. [Antike] **die Klassik** classical antiquity - 3. [Musik] classical music - 4. [Literatur] classical literature.

Klassiker, in (*mpl* -, *fpl* -nen) *der, die* - 1. [Dichter] classical author; **die Klassiker lesen** to read the classics - 2. [Referenz] classic.

klassisch *adj* - 1. [Kunst, Kultur] classical - 2. [Fehler] classic.

Klatsch *der fam* [Gerede] gossip.

klatschen (*perf* hat/ist geklatscht) ⬦ *vi* - 1. (hat) [schlagen] to slap; **in die Hände klatschen** to clap (one's hands) - 2. (hat) [Publikum] to clap - 3. (ist) [Regen] to drum; [Wellen] to slap - 4. (hat) fam [tratschen]: **über jn/etw klatschen** to gossip about sb/sthg. ⬦ *vt*: **Beifall klatschen** to applaud; **jm eine klatschen** fam to give sb a slap.

Klaue (*pl* -n) *die* - 1. [von Adler, Löwen] claw - 2. fam [Schrift] scrawl.

klauen fam ⬦ *vt* to pinch, to nick *UK*; **jm etw klauen** to pinch sthg from sb, to nick sthg off sb *UK*. ⬦ *vi* [stehlen]: **hier wird viel geklaut** a lot of stuff gets pinched ODER nicked *UK* round here.

Klausel (*pl* -n) *die* clause.

Klausur (*pl* -en) *die* UNI exam.

Klavier [kla'viːɐ̯] (*pl* -e) *das* piano; **Klavier spielen** to play the piano.

Klavier|konzert *das* - 1. [Musikstück] piano concerto - 2. [Konzert] piano recital.

kleben ⬦ *vt* [ankleben] to stick, to glue; [reparieren] to stick ODER glue together. ⬦ *vi* [halten]: **an etw** (*D*) **kleben** eigtl & fig to stick to sthg.

Kleber (*pl* -) *der* adhesive.

Klebe|streifen *der* adhesive tape.

klebrig *adj* sticky.

Kleb|stoff *der* adhesive, glue.

kleckern ⬦ *vi* [verschütten] to make a mess; **du hast gekleckert** [beim Essen] you've spilt your food. ⬦ *vt* [verschütten] to spill.

Klecks (*pl* -e) *der* [von Farbe, Senf] blob; [von Tinte] blot.

Klee *der* clover.

Klee|blatt *das* clover leaf.

Kleid (*pl* -er) *das* [Frauenkleid] dress. ➤ **Kleider** *Pl* [Kleidungsstücke] clothes.

Kleider|bügel *der* coathanger.

Kleider|schrank *der* - 1. [Möbelstück] wardrobe, closet *US* - 2. fam [Mann] man mountain.

Kleidung (*pl* -en) *die* clothes *Pl*, clothing.

Kleie (*pl* -n) *die* bran.

klein ⬦ *adj* - 1. [gen] small, little; **mein kleiner Finger** my little finger - 2. [temporal] short; **eine kleine Pause** a short break - 3. [unerheblich] little; **meine kleinste Sorge** the least of my worries; **kleine Leute** ordinary people; **aus kleinen Verhältnissen stammen** to come from a humble background. ⬦ *adv*: **ein klein wenig** a little bit; **haben Sie es nicht kleiner?** don't you have anything smaller?

Klein|anzeige *die* small ad *UK*, want ad *US*.

kleinbürgerlich *abw* ⬦ *adj* petty bourgeois. ⬦ *adv* in a petty bourgeois way.

Kleine (*pl* -n) ⬦ *der, die* - 1. [Kind] little one - 2. [als Anrede - nett] little one; [- beleidigend] shorty. ⬦ *das* [Baby] little one.

klein gedruckt *adj* in small print.

Kleingeld *das* change.

Kleinigkeit (*pl* -en) *die* - 1. [unwichtig] trifle; **für jn eine/keine Kleinigkeit sein** to be an/no easy matter for sb - 2. [klein, wenig]: **ein paar Kleinigkeiten einkaufen** to buy a few little things - 3. [zu essen] snack.

Klein|kind *das* small child.

Kleinkram *der* (*ohne pl*) fam - 1. [Gegenstände] bits and pieces *Pl* - 2. [Angelegenheiten] trifling things *Pl*.

klein|kriegen *vt* - 1. [Person]: **jn kleinkriegen** to bring sb into line; **lass dich davon nicht kleinkriegen** don't let that get you down - 2. [Gegenstand]: **etw ist nicht kleinzukriegen** sthg will last forever - 3. [zerkleinern mit Messer] to chop up.

kleinlaut ⬦ *adj* subdued. ⬦ *adv* in a subdued manner.

kleinlich *adj abw* petty.

klein machen *vt* - 1. [Holz, Pappe] to chop up - 2. fam [Geldschein] to change.

klein schneiden *vt* (*unreg*) to chop into small pieces.

klein|schreiben *vt* (*unreg*) [mit kleinem Anfangsbuchstaben] to write with a small initial letter.

Kleinschreibung *die* use of small initial letters.

Klein|stadt *die* small town.

Kleister (*pl* -) *der* paste.

Klemme (*pl* -n) *die* - 1. (*ohne pl*) fam [Bedrängnis] tight spot; **jm aus der Klemme helfen**

klemmen

to help sb out of a tight spot; **in der Klemme stecken** ODER **sitzen** ODER **sein** to be in a tight spot - 2. ELEKTR terminal.

klemmen ◇ vt - 1. [feststecken] to jam - 2. [Finger]: **sich** (D) **etw klemmen** to get sthg caught. ◇ vi [Tür, Schublade] to jam. ◆ **sich klemmen** ref fam: **sich dahinter klemmen** to get stuck in.

Klempner, in (mpl -, fpl -nen) der, die plumber.

Klerus der (ohne pl) clergy Pl.

Klette (pl -n) die - 1. fam [Mensch] limpet - 2. [Pflanze] burdock.

klettern (perf hat/ist geklettert) vi - 1. (ist) [gen] to climb - 2. (hat) SPORT to climb.

klicken vi to click.

Klient (pl -en) der client.

Klientin (pl -nen) die client.

Kliff (pl -e) das cliff.

Klima (pl -s) das climate.

Klimaanlage die air conditioning (U).

Klimaschutz (ohne Pl) der climate protection.

klimpern vi [spielen - auf Klavier] to tinkle away; [- auf Gitarre] to strum.

Klinge (pl -n) die blade.

Klingel (pl -n) die bell.

klingeln vi to ring (the bell); **es hat geklingelt** [an der Tür] there's someone at the door; [in der Schule] the bell has gone; **bei jm klingeln** to ring sb's bell; **nach jm klingeln** to ring for sb.

klingen (prät klang, perf hat geklungen) vi - 1. [gen] to sound - 2. [Glocken, Gläser] to ring.

Klinik (pl -en) die clinic.

klinisch ◇ adj clinical. ◇ adv clinically.

Klinke (pl -n) die (door) handle.

Klipp (pl -s), **Clip** (pl -s) der clip.

Klippe (pl -n) die rock; **alle Klippen umfahren** to negotiate all obstacles.

klirren vi [Scheiben] to rattle; [Gläser] to clink.

klirrend adj: **klirrende Kälte** freezing cold.

Klischee (pl -s) das cliché.

Klo (pl -s) das fam loo UK, john US; **aufs Klo gehen** to go to the loo UK ODER john US.

klobig adj - 1. [ungeschliffen] clumsy - 2. [massig - Hände] massive; [- Stuhl, Bau, Schuhe] clunky.

Klofrau die fam toilet attendant.

Klopapier das fam toilet paper.

klopfen vi - 1. [Person - an die Tür] to knock; [- auf den Tisch] to rap; **es hat geklopft** there's someone at the door - 2. [Herz] to beat. ◇ vt [Teppich, Kissen] to beat.

Klops (pl -e) der meatball.

Klosett (pl -e) das toilet.

Kloß (pl Klöße) der dumpling; **einen Kloß im Hals haben** fig to have a lump in one's throat.

Kloster (pl Klöster) das [für Nonnen] convent; [für Mönche] monastery.

Klotz (pl Klötze) der - 1. block - 2. [Scheit] log - 3. abw [Gebäude] concrete block; **einen Klotz am Bein haben** to have a millstone round one's neck.

klotzig fam ◇ adj [groß] clunky. ◇ adv: **klotzig verdienen** to earn a packet.

Klub (pl -s), **Club** (pl -s) der the club.

Kluft (pl -en ODER Klüfte) die - 1. (pl Klüfte) [zwischen Gegensätzen] gulf - 2. (pl Klüfte) [im Fels] cleft - 3. (pl Kluften) [Kleidung] outfit.

klug (kompar klüger, superl klügste) ◇ adj - 1. [schlau] clever - 2. [weise] wise; **jd wird aus jm/etw nicht klug** sb can't make sb/sthg out; **der Klügere gibt nach** discretion is the better part of valour. ◇ adv [umsichtig] wisely.

Klugheit (pl -en) die - 1. [Schläue] cleverness - 2. [Weisheit] wisdom.

Klumpen (pl -) der lump.

km (abk für Kilometer) km.

km/h (abk für Stundenkilometer) kph.

knabbern ◇ vt to nibble. ◇ vi: **an etw** (D) **knabbern** to nibble sthg.

Knabe (pl -n) der - 1. geh [Junge] boy - 2. fam [Mann] chap.

Knäckebrot das crispbread.

knacken ◇ vt - 1. [Nüsse, Finger] to crack - 2. [mit Gewalt - Schloss] to force; [- Bank] to break into - 3. [Code] to crack. ◇ vi - 1. [Holz, Finger] to crack; [Feuer, im Radio, Telefon] to crackle - 2. salopp [schlafen] to crash out - 3. [an Problemen]: **an etw** (D) **zu knacken haben** fig [sich bemühen] to have one's work cut out with sthg; [die Folgen spüren] to have a hard time getting over sthg.

knackig adj - 1. [Salat] crisp - 2. salopp [Po] sexy.

Knacks (pl -e) der fam [psychischer Schaden]: **einen Knacks haben/bekommen** to be/get screwed up.

Knall (pl -e) der [von Schuss, Tür] bang; [von Korken] pop.

knallen (perf hat/ist geknallt) ◇ vi - 1. (hat) [Schuss] to ring out; [Peitsche] to crack; [Korken] to pop - 2. (ist) fam [aufprallen] to crash; **mit dem Kopf auf den Boden knallen** to bang one's head on the floor - 3. (hat) [Sonne] to beat down. ◇ vt - 1. [werfen] to fling; **die Tür ins Schloss knallen** to slam the door - 2. [ohrfeigen]: **jm eine knallen** fam to clout sb.

knapp ◇ adj - 1. [Ergebnis, Rennen] close; [Vorsprung, Stimmenmehrheit] narrow - 2. [Kleid, Schuhe] tight - 3. [fast ganz]: **eine knappe Stunde** just under an hour; **das war knapp** that was close - 4. [wenig]: **knapp bei Kasse sein** to be short of money; **knapp werden** to be running short. ◇ adv - 1. [um weniges] narrowly - 2. [eng] tightly.

knarren vi to creak.

Knast (*pl* Knäste) *der fam* clink.

Knatsch *der* (*ohne pl*) *fam* row.

knattern *vi* [Motor] to roar; [Maschinengewehr] to rattle; [Fahne] to flap.

Knäuel (*pl* -) *das* ball.

Knauf (*pl* Knäufe) *der* knob.

knauserig *adj* stingy.

knausern *vi*: **mit etw knausern** to be stingy with sthg.

knautschen *vt* & *vi* to crumple.

Knebel (*pl* -) *der* gag.

knebeln *vt* to gag.

Knecht (*pl* -e) *der* [auf Bauernhof] farmhand; [Diener] servant.

kneifen (*prät* kniff, *perf* hat gekniffen) ◇ *vi* - 1. [Kleidung] to pinch - 2. *fam abw* [sich drücken]: **(vor etw (D)) kneifen** to duck out (of sthg). ◇ *vt* to pinch.

Kneifzange *die* pincers *Pl*.

Kneipe (*pl* -n) *die fam* bar, pub *UK*.

kneten *vt* [Teig, Muskeln] to knead; [Figur] to model.

Knick (*pl* -e ODER -s) *der* - 1. (*pl* Knicke) [Falte] crease - 2. (*pl* Knicke) [in Straße] sharp bend.

knicken *vt* - 1. [falten] to fold - 2. [Äste, Blumen] to bend.

Knicks (*pl* -e) *der* curtsey.

Knie (*pl* -) *das* [Körperteil] knee; **etw übers Knie brechen** to rush sthg.

Kniebeuge (*pl* -n) *die* knee-bend.

Kniegelenk *das* knee joint.

Kniekehle *die* hollow of the knee.

knien *vi* to kneel. ◆ **sich knien** *ref* to kneel; **sich in etw (A) knien** *fig* to buckle down to sthg.

Kniescheibe *die* kneecap.

Kniestrumpf *der* knee-length sock.

kniff *prät* ▷ kneifen.

Kniff (*pl* -e) *der* [Trick] trick.

knifflig *adj* tricky.

knipsen *fam* ◇ *vi* [fotografieren] to take snaps. ◇ *vt* - 1. [Fahrkarte] to punch - 2. [fotografieren]: **jn/etw knipsen** to snap sb/sthg.

Knirps (*pl* -e) *der* [Kind] little lad.

knirschen *vi* - 1.: **mit den Zähnen knirschen** to grind one's teeth - 2. [Schnee, Sand] to crunch.

knistern *vi* [Feuer, brennendes Holz] to crackle; [Papier] to rustle; **mit etw knistern** to rustle sthg.

knitterfrei *adj* crease-resistant.

knittern *vi* to crease.

knobeln *vi* - 1. [losen] to toss - 2. [spielen] to play dice - 3. [tüfteln]: **an etw (D) knobeln** to puzzle over sthg.

Knoblauch *der* garlic.

Knöchel (*pl* -) *der* ankle.

Knochen (*pl* -) *der* bone.

Knochenbruch *der* fracture.

Knochenmark *das* bone marrow.

knochig *adj* bony.

Knödel (*pl* -) *der* dumpling.

Knolle (*pl* -n) *die* BIOL tuber.

Knopf (*pl* Knöpfe) *der* button.

Knopfdruck *der*: **auf Knopfdruck** at the push of a button.

knöpfen *vt* to button.

Knopfloch *das* buttonhole.

Knorpel (*pl* -) *der* cartilage.

Knospe (*pl* -n) *die* bud.

knoten *vt* to tie.

Knoten (*pl* -) *der* - 1. [gen] knot - 2. MED lump.

Knotenpunkt *der* - 1. [von Straßen] junction - 2. [wichtiger Ort] centre.

Know-how ['nɔuhau] (*pl* -s) *das* know-how (*U*).

knüllen *vt* to crumple.

Knüller (*pl* -) *der fam* sensation.

knüpfen *vt* [Netz] to knot; **etw an etw (A) knüpfen** [mit Faden] to tie sthg to sthg; *fig* [Erwartungen, Bedingungen] to attach sthg to sthg.

Knüppel (*pl* -) *der* club; **jm einen Knüppel zwischen die Beine werfen** *fig* to put a spoke in sb's wheel.

knurren *vi* - 1. [Magen] to rumble - 2. [Hund] to growl - 3. [Person] to grumble.

knusprig, knusperig ◇ *adj* crisp. ◇ *adv*: **knusprig braun** crisp and brown.

knutschen *fam* ◇ *vt* to smooch with. ◇ *vi* to smooch.

K. o. (*pl* -) *der* knockout.

Kobalt *das* CHEM cobalt.

Koch [kɔx] (*pl* Köche ['kœçə]) *der* cook.

Kochbuch *das* cookbook.

kochen ◇ *vt* - 1. [Essen] to cook; [Kaffee] to make; **jm/sich etw kochen** to cook sb/o.s. sthg - 2. [Wäsche] to boil. ◇ *vi* - 1. [Wasser, Person] to boil - 2. [Koch]: **gut/schlecht kochen** to be a good/bad cook.

Kochgelegenheit *die* cooking facilities *Pl*.

Köchin [kœçɪn] (*pl* -nen) *die* cook.

Kochlöffel *der* wooden spoon.

Kochrezept *das* recipe.

Kochsalz *das* cooking salt.

Kochtopf *der* saucepan.

Kochwäsche *die* washing that needs to be boiled.

Kode (*pl* -s), **Code** (*pl* -s) ['kɔːt] *der* code.

Köder (*pl* -) *der* bait.

ködern *vt* to lure.

kodieren, codieren [ko'diːrən] *vt* to encode.

Koffein *das* caffeine.

koffeinfrei *adj* decaffeinated.

Koffer (pl -) der suitcase; **die Koffer packen** to pack one's bags.

Kofferlraum der boot UK, trunk US.

Kognak ['kɔnjak] (pl -s) der brandy.

Kohl der cabbage.

Kohle (pl -n) die - **1.** [Brennstoff] coal (U); **wie auf glühenden Kohlen sitzen** fig to be like a cat on hot bricks - **2.** fam [Geld] cash.

Kohlenhydrat (pl -e) das carbohydrate.

Kohlenlsäure die: **Mineralwasser mit/ohne Kohlensäure** sparkling/still mineral water.

Kohlelzeichnung die KUNST charcoal drawing.

Kohlrabi (pl - ODER -s) der kohlrabi.

Kohllroulade die stuffed cabbage leaves Pl.

Koje (pl -n) die - **1.** fam [Bett] bed - **2.** [Schiffsbett] bunk.

Kokain das cocaine.

Kokosnuss (pl -nüsse) die coconut.

Koks der coke.

Kolben (pl -) der - **1.** TECH piston - **2.** CHEM flask.

Kolik (pl -en), **Kolik** (pl -en) die colic (U).

Kollaps (pl -e), **Kollaps** (pl -e) der collapse (sg).

Kollege (pl -n) der colleague.

Kollegin (pl -nen) die colleague.

Kollegium [kɔ'leːgjʊm] (pl -gien) das [in Schule] teaching staff.

Kollektion (pl -en) die collection.

kollidieren (perf ist kollidiert) vi - **1.** [Fahrzeuge] to collide - **2.** [Interessen] to clash.

Kollision (pl -en) die collision.

Köln nt Cologne.

Kolonie [kolo'niː] (pl -n) die colony.

Kolonne (pl -n) die column; **(in) Kolonne fahren** to drive in convoy.

kolossal adj colossal; **ein kolossaler Irrtum** a huge mistake.

Kolumbien nt Colombia.

Koma (pl -s) das coma.

Kombination (pl -en) die - **1.** [Zusammenfügung] combination - **2.** [Schlussfolgerung] deduction - **3.** [Arbeitsanzug] overalls Pl.

kombinieren ⋄ vi to reason. ⋄ vt to combine; **etw mit etw kombinieren** to combine sthg with sthg.

Komet (pl -en) der ASTRON comet.

Komfort [kɔm'foːɐ̯] der: **mit allem Komfort** with all mod cons.

komfortabel ⋄ adj comfortable. ⋄ adv [bequem] comfortably.

Komik die comic effect.

Komiker, in (mpl -, fpl -nen) der, die comedian.

komisch adj funny.

Komitee (pl -s) das committee.

Komma (pl -s ODER -ta) das - **1.** [Satzzeichen] comma - **2.** [mathematisches Zeichen] decimal point.

Kommandeur, in [kɔman'døːɐ̯, rɪn] (mpl -e, fpl -nen) der, die commander.

kommandieren vt [Soldaten] to command.

Kommando (pl -s) das - **1.** [gen] command; **auf Kommando** on command; **das Kommando haben/übernehmen** to be in/take command - **2.** [kleine Einheit] detachment.

kommen (prät kam, perf ist gekommen) ⋄ vi - **1.** [herkommen] to come; **den Arzt kommen lassen** to call the doctor - **2.** [ein Ziel erreichen] to get; **wie komme ich zum Markt?** how do I get to the market?; **nach Hause kommen** to get home; **an die Macht kommen** to come to power - **3.** [mit Institutionen] to go; **ins/aus dem Krankenhaus kommen** to go to/leave hospital; **in die Schule kommen** to start school - **4.** [stammen] to come; **aus Deutschland kommen** to come from Germany - **5.** [folgen] to come; **rechts kommt der Bahnhof** the station's coming up on the right - **6.** [resultieren]: **von etw kommen** to result from sthg; **das kommt daher, dass...** it's because...; **das kommt davon!** see what happens!; **wie kommt es, dass...?** how is it that...? - **7.** [passieren] to happen; **das musste ja so kommen!** it had to happen!; **überraschend kommen** to come as a surprise - **8.** [Programm, Film]: **im Fernsehen kommen** to be on (the) television; **im Kino kommen** to be on at the cinema UK ODER the movies US - **9.** fam [einen Orgasmus haben] to come - **10.** [hingehören] to go, to belong; **die Kisten kommen in den Keller** the crates go ODER belong in the cellar - **11.** [anfangen]: **ins Schleudern kommen** to skid; **auf etw (A) zu sprechen kommen** to get around to talking about sthg - **12.** [mit Dativ]: **mir kam eine Idee** an idea came to me; **jm frech kommen** fam to be cheeky to sb - **13.** [figurative Verwendungen mit Präposition]: **auf eine Idee kommen** to think of an idea; **hinter etw (A) kommen** to get to the bottom of sthg; **ums Leben kommen** to lose one's life, to die; **zu sich kommen** to come round; **dazu kommen, etw zu tun** to get round to doing sthg. ⋄ vt fam: **welchen Weg bist du gekommen?** which way did you come?

kommend adj - **1.** [Woche] coming - **2.** [Generation, Mode] future.

Kommentar (pl -e) der - **1.** [in Zeitung, Buch, Radio] commentary - **2.** fam [Bemerkung] comment; **kein Kommentar** no comment.

kommentieren vt - **1.** [Ereignis] to comment on - **2.** [Text, Buch] to provide a commentary on.

kommerziell ⋄ adj commercial. ⋄ adv commercially.

Kommilitone (pl -n) der UNI fellow student.

Kommilitonin (*pl* -nen) *die* UNI fellow student.

Kommissar, in (*mpl* -e, *fpl* -nen) *der, die* [bei der Polizei] superintendent *UK*, captain *US*.

kommunal *adj* local.

Kommune (*pl* -n) *die* - 1. [Gemeinde] local authority - 2. [Wohngemeinschaft] commune.

Kommunikation (*pl* -en) *die* communication.

Kommunion (*pl* -en) *die* RELIG Communion (*U*).

Kommunismus *der* Communism.

Kommunist, in (*mpl* -en, *fpl* -nen) *der, die* Communist.

kommunistisch *adj* Communist.

Komödie [koˈmøːdjə] (*pl* -n) *die* comedy; jm eine Komödie vorspielen to put on an act for sb.

kompakt ⬦ *adj* compact. ⬦ *adv* compactly.

Kompanie [kɔmpaˈniː] (*pl* -n) *die* MIL company.

Komparativ (*pl* -e) *der* GRAMM comparative.

Kompass (*pl* -e) *der* compass.

kompatibel *adj* EDV compatible; mit etw kompatibel sein to be compatible with sthg.

kompetent ⬦ *adj* competent. ⬦ *adv* competently.

Kompetenz (*pl* -en) *die* competence (*U*).

komplett ⬦ *adj* complete. ⬦ *adv* - 1. [vollständig] fully - 2. *fam* [völlig] completely.

Komplex (*pl* -e) *der* [gen] [Psychologie] complex; Komplexe haben to have a complex.

Kompliment (*pl* -e) *das* compliment; mein Kompliment! my compliments!; jm ein Kompliment machen to pay sb a compliment.

Komplize (*pl* -n) *der* accomplice.

kompliziert ⬦ *adj* complicated. ⬦ *adv* in a complicated way.

Komplizin (*pl* -nen) *die* accomplice.

Komplott (*pl* -e) *das* plot.

komponieren *vt* [zusammenstellen & MUS] to compose.

Komponist, in (*mpl* -en, *fpl* -nen) *der, die* composer.

Komposition (*pl* -en) *die* [Zusammenstellung & MUS] composition.

Kompost (*pl* -e), **Kompost** (*pl* -e) *der* compost (*U*).

Kompott (*pl* -e) *das* stewed fruit.

Kompromiss (*pl* -e) *der* compromise.

kompromissbereit *adj* ready to compromise.

kondensieren *vt & vi* to condense.

Kondensmilch *die* condensed milk.

Kondenswasser *das* condensation.

Konditional (*pl* -e) *der* GRAMM conditional.

Konditionstraining *das* fitness training.

Konditorei (*pl* -en) *die* cake shop.

Kondom (*pl* -e) *das* condom.

Konfekt (*pl* -e) *das* confectionery (*U*).

Konfektion (*pl* -en) *die* - 1. [Kleidung] ready-to-wear clothes *Pl* - 2. [Herstellung] manufacture of ready-to-wear clothes.

Konferenz (*pl* -en) *die* - 1. [Tagung] conference - 2. [Besprechung] meeting.

Konfession (*pl* -en) *die* RELIG denomination.

Konfirmation (*pl* -en) *die* RELIG confirmation.

konfirmieren *vt* RELIG to confirm.

Konfitüre (*pl* -n) *die geh* jam.

Konflikt (*pl* -e) *der* conflict; mit etw in Konflikt geraten ODER kommen to come into conflict with sthg.

konform ⬦ *adj* concurrent; mit jm/etw konform gehen *geh* to concur with sb/sthg. ⬦ *adv*: sich konform verhalten to behave like everyone else.

Konfrontation (*pl* -en) *die* confrontation.

konfrontieren *vt*: jm mit jm/etw konfrontieren to confront sb with sb/sthg.

konfus ⬦ *adj* confused. ⬦ *adv* confusedly.

Kongo *der*: der Kongo the Congo.

Kongress (*pl* -e) *der* - 1. [Tagung] conference - 2. POL Congress.

König (*pl* -e) *der* - 1. [gen] king; die Heiligen Drei Könige the Three Wise Men - 2. [Feiertag]: Heilige Drei Könige Epiphany.

Königin (*pl* -nen) *die* queen.

königlich ⬦ *adj* - 1. [des Monarchen] royal - 2. [reichlich - Mahl] lavish; [- Trinkgeld, Geschenk] handsome; [- Vergnügen] tremendous. ⬦ *adv* - 1. [riesig] tremendously - 2. [bewirten] lavishly.

Königreich *das* kingdom.

Konjugation (*pl* -en) *die* GRAMM conjugation.

konjugieren *vt* GRAMM to conjugate.

Konjunktiv (*pl* -e) *der* GRAMM subjunctive.

Konjunktur (*pl* -en) *die* the economic situation; rückläufige Konjunktur declining economic activity; Konjunktur haben to be in demand.

konkret ⬦ *adj* concrete. ⬦ *adv* concretely.

Konkurrent, in (*mpl* -en, *fpl* -nen) *der, die* competitor.

Konkurrenz (*pl* -en) *die* competition; jm Konkurrenz machen to compete with sb. ➤ **außer Konkurrenz** *adv* as an unofficial competitor.

konkurrenzfähig ⬦ *adj* competitive. ⬦ *adv* competitively.

Konkurrenzkampf *der* competition.

Konkurs (*pl* -e) *der* - 1. [Zahlungsunfähigkeit] bankruptcy - 2. [Verfahren] bankruptcy proceedings *Pl*.

können (*präs* **kann**, *prät* **konnte**, *perf* **hat können** ODER **hat gekonnt**) ◇ *aux* - **1.** [vermögen, dürfen] can; **er kann Klavier spielen** he can play the piano; **kann ich noch ein Eis haben?** can I have another ice cream?; **könnte ich mal telefonieren?** could I use the telephone? - **2.** [zum Ausdruck der Möglichkeit] can; **es könnte verloren gegangen sein** it could ODER might have got lost; **sie kann nicht kommen** she can't come; **wir können es versuchen** we can try; **das kann schon sein** that's quite possible; **man kann nie wissen** you never know. ◇ *vi*: **fahren, so schnell man kann** to drive as fast as you can; **kann ich ins Kino?** can I go to the cinema?; **ich kann nicht mehr** *fam* I've had it, I'm exhausted. ◇ *vt* (*perf* **hat gekonnt**) [vermögen] **kannst du Deutsch?** can ODER do you speak German?; **etw auswendig können** to know sthg by heart; **der kann nichts** he's useless; **du kannst mich mal!** *vulg* piss off!

Können *das* (*ohne pl*) ability; **sein Können unter Beweis stellen** to prove one's ability.

Könner, in (*mpl* -, *fpl* -nen) *der, die* expert.

konnte *prät* ▷ **können**.

konsequent ◇ *adj* - **1.** [folgerichtig] consistent - **2.** [Gegner] resolute; [Nichtraucher, Christ] strict. ◇ *adv* - **1.** [folgerichtig] consistently - **2.** [bekämpfen] resolutely.

Konsequenz (*pl* -en) *die* - **1.** [Folge] consequence; **aus etw die Konsequenzen ziehen** to draw the obvious conclusion from sthg - **2.** [Unbeirrbarkeit] resolution.

konservativ [kɔnzɛrvaˈtiːf] ◇ *adj* conservative. ◇ *adv* conservatively.

Konservative [kɔnzɛrvaˈtiːvə] (*pl* -n) *der, die* Conservative.

Konserve [kɔnˈzɛrvə] (*pl* -n) *die* [Dose] can, tin *UK*; **sich nur von Konserven ernähren** to live only on tinned *UK* ODER canned *US* food.

Konservenidose *die* can, tin *UK*.

konservieren [kɔnzɛrˈviːrən] *vt* to preserve.

Konservierungsstoffe [kɔnzɛrˈviːrʊŋsʃtɔfə] *Pl* preservatives.

Konsonant (*pl* -en) *der* consonant.

konstant ◇ *adj* constant. ◇ *adv* constantly.

konstruieren [kɔnstruˈiːrən] *vt* - **1.** [bauen] to construct - **2.** *abw* [erfinden] to fabricate.

Konstrukteur, in [kɔnstrʊkˈtøːɐ̯, rɪn] (*mpl* -e, *fpl* -nen) *der, die* designer.

Konstruktion (*pl* -en) *die* construction.

Konsulat (*pl* -e) *das* POL consulate.

Konsum *der* [Verbrauch] consumption.

Konsument, in (*mpl* -en, *fpl* -nen) *der, die* consumer.

konsumieren *vt* to consume.

Kontakt (*pl* -e) *der* contact; **mit jm Kontakt aufnehmen** to get in touch with sb; **zu** ODER **mit jm/etw Kontakt haben** to be in contact with sb/sthg.

kontaktarm *adj*: **er ist kontaktarm** he finds it difficult to make friends.

kontaktfreudig *adj* sociable.

Kontaktlinse *die* contact lens.

Kontinent (*pl* -e), **Kontinent** (*pl* -e) *der* continent.

Konto (*pl* **Konten**) *das* [Bankkonto] account; **ein Konto eröffnen/auflösen** to open/close an account; **etw geht auf js Konto** sb is to blame for sthg.

Kontolauszug *der* bank statement.

Kontolstand *der* bank balance.

kontra, contra ◇ *präp* versus. ◇ *adv*: **kontra eingestellt sein** to be against.

Kontra (*pl* -s) *das* double; **jm Kontra geben** *fam* to contradict sb.

Kontrabass (*pl* -bässe) *der* double bass.

Kontrast (*pl* -e) *der* contrast; **einen Kontrast zu etw bilden** to contrast with sthg.

Kontrolle (*pl* -n) *die* - **1.** [Überwachung] check; **jn/etw unter Kontrolle haben** to keep a check on sb/sthg - **2.** [Beherrschung] control; **jn/etw unter Kontrolle bekommen/haben** to get/have sb/sthg under control; **die Kontrolle über sich verlieren** to lose control.

kontrollieren *vt* - **1.** [überprüfen] to check - **2.** [überwachen] to keep a check on - **3.** [beherrschen] to control.

Kontur (*pl* -en) *die* contour; [von Politiker] profile; **Kontur gewinnen/verlieren** to take/lose shape.

konventionell [kɔnvɛntsjoˈnɛl] ◇ *adj* conventional. ◇ *adv* conventionally.

Konversation [kɔnvɛrzaˈtsjoːn] (*pl* -en) *die* geh conversation.

Konzentrat (*pl* -e) *das* concentrate.

Konzentration (*pl* -en) *die* concentration.

Konzentrationslager *das* concentration camp.

konzentrieren *vt* - **1.** [richten] **etw auf etw (A) konzentrieren** to concentrate sthg on sthg - **2.** [vereinigen] to concentrate. ⇒ **sich konzentrieren** *ref* to concentrate; **sich auf etw (A) konzentrieren** to concentrate on sthg.

konzentriert ◇ *adj* concentrated. ◇ *adv* with concentration; **konzentriert nachdenken** to concentrate.

Konzept (*pl* -e) *das* - **1.** [Entwurf] draft - **2.** [Plan] plan; **jn aus dem Konzept bringen** to put sb off his/her stride.

Konzern (*pl* -e) *der* group (of companies).

Konzert (*pl* -e) *das* [Veranstaltung] concert; [Musikstück] concerto.

Konzerthaus (*pl* -häuser) *das* concert hall.

Konzession *(pl -en) die* - **1.** WIRTSCH licence - **2.** [Zugeständnis] concession.

Koordinate *(pl -n) die* coordinate.

koordinieren *vt* to coordinate.

Kopenhagen *nt* Copenhagen.

Kopf *(pl Köpfe) der* - **1.** [gen] head; **mit dem** ODER **den Kopf schütteln** to shake one's head; **jm etw an den Kopf werfen** *eigtl & fig* to hurl sthg at sb - **2.** [Anführer] leader; **den Kopf hängen lassen** to be downhearted; **jm über den Kopf wachsen** to overwhelm sb; **jm zu Kopf steigen** to go to sb's head; **etw auf den Kopf stellen** *fam* to turn sthg upside down; **und wenn du dich auf den Kopf stellst** you're wasting your breath; **sich** *(D)* **etw durch den Kopf gehen lassen** to think sthg over; **sich** *(D)* (**über etw** *(A)*) **den Kopf zerbrechen** to rack one's brains (over sthg). ◆ **aus dem Kopf** *adv* off the top of one's head. ◆ **Kopf an Kopf** *adv* neck and neck. ◆ **pro Kopf** *adv* per head. ◆ **von Kopf bis Fuß** *adv* from head to toe.

Köpfchen *(pl -) das* little head; **Köpfchen haben** *fam fig* to have brains.

köpfen ⬦ *vt* - **1.** SPORT to head - **2.** [hinrichten] to behead - **3.** *fam* [öffnen - Flasche] to crack open; [- Ei] to slice the top off. ⬦ *vi* SPORT to head.

Kopflhaut *die* scalp.

Kopflhörer *der* headphones *Pl*.

Kopflkissen *das* pillow.

kopflos ⬦ *adj* - **1.** [ohne Kopf] headless - **2.** [wirr] panicky. ⬦ *adv* in a state of panic.

Kopflrechnen *das* mental arithmetic.

Kopflsalat *der* lettuce.

Kopflschmerzen *Pl* headache *(sg)*; **Kopfschmerzen haben** to have a headache.

Kopflsprung *der* dive.

Kopflstand *der* headstand.

Kopflstütze *die* headrest.

Kopfltuch *das* headscarf.

Kopfzerbrechen *das*: **jm Kopfzerbrechen machen** ODER **bereiten** to be a real headache for sb.

Kopie [ko'piː] *(pl -n) die* copy.

kopieren *vt* to copy.

Kopierer *(pl -) der* photocopier.

Kopierlgerät *das* photocopier.

Kolpilot, in ['koːpiloːt, ɪn] *der, die* co-pilot.

koppeln *vt* - **1.** [knüpfen] to attach - **2.** [anschließen] to couple.

Koppelung *(pl -en)*, **Kopplung** *(pl -en) die* coupling.

Koralle *(pl -n) die* coral.

Koran *(pl -e) der* Koran.

Korb *(pl Körbe) der* - **1.** [Behälter & SPORT] basket - **2.** [Abfuhr] rebuff; **jm einen Korb geben** to turn sb down.

Korblstuhl *der* wicker chair.

Kord, Cord [kɔrt] *der* corduroy.

Kordel *(pl -n) die* cord.

Kork *der* cork.

Korken *(pl -) der* cork.

Korkenzieher *(pl -) der* corkscrew.

Korn *(pl Körner* ODER *-)* ⬦ *das* - **1.** [Getreide] grain, corn UK - **2.** *(pl Körner)* [Pflanzenfrucht, kleines Partikel] grain; **jn/etw aufs Korn nehmen** *fam fig* to hit out at sb/sthg. ⬦ *der (pl Korn)* [Schnaps] schnapps.

Kornlblume *die* cornflower.

Körper *(pl -) der* body.

Körperbau *der* build.

körperbehindert *adj* disabled.

Körperlgewicht *das amt* weight.

Körperlgröße *die amt* height.

körperlich ⬦ *adj* physical. ⬦ *adv* physically.

Körperpflege *die* personal hygiene.

Körperschaft *(pl -en) die* RECHT corporation.

Körperlteil *der* part of the body.

Körperlverletzung *die* bodily harm.

korpulent *adj* corpulent.

korrekt ⬦ *adj* correct. ⬦ *adv* correctly.

Korrektur *(pl -en) die* correction; **Korrektur lesen** to read the proofs.

Korrespondent, in *(mpl -en, fpl -nen) der, die* [Berichterstatter] correspondent.

Korrespondenz *die* correspondence.

Korridor *(pl -e) der* corridor.

korrigieren *vt* to correct.

korrupt *adj* corrupt.

Korruption *(pl -en) die* corruption *(U)*.

Kosmetik *(pl -ka) die* [Pflege] beauty care.

Kosmetiker, in *(mpl -, fpl -nen) der, die* beautician.

kosmetisch ⬦ *adj* cosmetic. ⬦ *adv* cosmetically.

Kosmos *der* cosmos.

Kost *die* food.

kostbar *adj* - **1.** [wertvoll, erlesen] valuable - **2.** [wichtig] precious.

Kostbarkeit *(pl -en) die* - **1.** [Wert] value - **2.** [Gegenstand] treasure.

kosten ⬦ *vi* [probieren] to have a taste; **von der Suppe kosten** to taste the soup. ⬦ *vt* - **1.** [gen] to cost; **was** ODER **wie viel kostet das?** how much is it?, how much does it cost?; **Fragen kostet nichts** there's no harm in asking - **2.** [probieren] to taste, to try.

Kosten *Pl* costs; **auf js Kosten** *(A)* at sb's expense; **auf js Kosten gehen** to be at sb's expense; **auf Kosten einer Sache** *(G)* **gehen** to be at the expense of sthg; **auf seine Kosten kommen** to get one's money's worth; [bei einer Party] to have a good time.

kostenlos ⬦ *adj* free. ⬦ *adv* free of charge.

Kosten|voranschlag *der* estimate.

köstlich ⬦ *adj* - **1.** [im Geschmack] delicious - **2.** [amüsant] delightful. ⬦ *adv* - **1.: köstlich speisen** to have a delicious meal - **2.: sich köstlich amüsieren** to enjoy o.s. enormously.

Kost|probe *die* [von Speise] taste; [von js Können] sample.

kostspielig *adj* costly.

Kostüm (*pl* -e) *das* - **1.** [Rock und Jacke] suit - **2.** [im Theater, zu Fasching] costume.

kostümieren ⬥ **sich kostümieren** *ref* to dress up (*in fancy dress*).

Kot *der* excrement.

Kotelett (*pl* -s) *das* chop, cutlet.

Koteletten *Pl* sideboards *UK*, sideburns *US*.

Kot|flügel *der* wing.

kotzen *vi salopp* to puke.

Krabbe (*pl* -n) *die* [Krebs] crab; [Garnele] shrimp.

krabbeln (*perf* hat/ist gekrabbelt) ⬦ *vi* (*ist*) to crawl. ⬦ *vt* (*hat*) *fam* [kratzen] to scratch; [kitzeln] to tickle.

Krach (*pl* Kräche) *der* - **1.** [Lärm] racket; **Krach machen** to make a racket - **2.** *fam* [Ärger] row; **er hat Krach mit seiner Freundin** he's rowing with his girlfriend - **3.** [Zusammenbruch] crash.

krachen (*perf* hat/ist gekracht) ⬦ *vi* - **1.** (*hat*) [lärmen - Donner] to crash; [- Schuss] to ring out; [- Gewehr] to bang; **dann krachts!** there'll be trouble!; **an der Ecke hat es gekracht** there's been a crash on the corner - **2.** (*ist*) *fam* [kaputtgehen - Bett, Stuhl] to collapse; [- Reißverschluss, Brett] to split; [- Eis] to crack. ⬦ *vt* (*hat*) *fam* to bang.

krächzen ⬦ *vi* [Rabe] to caw; [Person] to croak. ⬦ *vt* to croak out.

Kraft (*pl* Kräfte) *die* - **1.** [Körperkraft] strength (*U*); **am Ende seiner Kräfte sein** to be completely exhausted; **Kraft/keine Kraft haben** to be strong/weak - **2.** [Fähigkeit, Wirksamkeit] power; **aus eigener Kraft** by oneself; **mit vereinten Kräften** by joining forces - **3.** [Hilfskraft] helper. ⬥ **Kräfte** *Pl* [politisch] forces. ⬥ **außer Kraft** *adv*: **außer Kraft treten/sein** to cease to be/be no longer in force. ⬥ **in Kraft** *adv*: **in Kraft treten/setzen/sein** to come into/put into/be in force.

Kraft|fahrzeug *das amt* motor vehicle.

Kraftfahrzeug|steuer *die amt* road tax *UK*, vehicle tax *US*.

kräftig ⬦ *adj* - **1.** [stark - Person] strong; [- Schlag] powerful; [- Körperbau, Stimme]

powerful, strong - **2.** [Hunger, Farben] intense - **3.** [Mahlzeit] nourishing - **4.** [Fluch] coarse. ⬦ *adv* - **1.** [stark] hard - **2.** [fluchen] violently.

kräftigen *vt* to strengthen.

kraftlos ⬦ *adj* weak. ⬦ *adv* [wanken] weakly; [herabhängen] limply.

Kraft|probe *die* trial of strength.

Kraft|stoff *der* fuel.

kraftvoll ⬦ *adj* powerful. ⬦ *adv* powerfully.

Kraft|werk *das* power station.

Kragen (*pl* - *ODER* Krägen) *der* collar; **es geht jm an den Kragen** *fam fig* sb is in for it; **ihr platzte der Kragen** *fam fig* she blew her top.

Krähe (*pl* -n) *die* crow.

krähen *vi* to crow.

Kralle (*pl* -n) *die* claw.

Kram *der fam* - **1.** [Zeug] stuff; **jm nicht in den Kram passen** *fam fig* not to fit in with sb's plans - **2.** [Arbeit] business.

kramen *vi* to rummage about.

Krampf (*pl* Krämpfe) *der* cramp; **einen Krampf bekommen/haben** to get/have cramp.

Krampf|ader *die* varicose vein.

krampfhaft ⬦ *adj* [Husten, Verrenkungen] convulsive; [Anstrengungen] strenuous. ⬦ *adv* [zucken] convulsively; [lächeln] in a strained way; **sich krampfhaft bemühen** to make strenuous efforts; **krampfhaft nachdenken** to rack one's brains.

Kran (*pl* Kräne) *der* crane.

krank (*kompar* kränker, *superl* am kränksten) *adj* sick, ill; **er ist krank** he is ill *ODER* sick; **krank werden** to be taken ill; **diese ständigen Streitereien machen mich krank** these constant arguments are getting on my nerves.

Kranke (*pl* -n) *der, die* sick person; [im Krankenhaus] patient.

kranken *vi*: **an etw (D) kranken** to suffer from sthg.

kränken *vt* to hurt.

Kranken|geld *das (ohne pl)* sickness benefit.

Kranken|gymnastik *die* physiotherapy.

Kranken|haus *das* hospital.

Kranken|kasse *die* health insurance association.

Kranken|pfleger *der* (male) nurse.

Kranken|schwester *die* nurse.

Kranken|versicherung *die* health insurance.

Kranken|wagen *der* ambulance.

krankhaft ⬦ *adj* pathological. ⬦ *adv* [übertrieben] pathologically.

Krankheit (*pl* -en) *die* - **1.** [Zustand] illness - **2.** [bestimmte Krankheit] disease.

kränklich *adj* sickly.

krank|melden ➤ **sich krankmelden** ref to report sick.

Kränkung (pl -en) die hurt.

Kranz (pl Kränze) der - **1.** [Schmuck] wreath - **2.** [Kuchen] ring.

krass ◇ adj [Gegensatz] stark; [Verstoß, Fall] blatant. ◇ adv [ausdrücken] bluntly.

Krater (pl -) der crater.

kratzen ◇ vi - **1.** [verletzen] to scratch - **2.** [schaben] to scrape - **3.** [jucken] to itch; **es kratzt im Hals** I've got a tickle in my throat. ◇ vt - **1.** [verletzen] to scratch - **2.** [schaben] to scrape - **3.** [jucken]: **jn kratzen** to make sb itch. ➤ **sich kratzen** ref to scratch o.s.

Kratzer (pl -) der scratch.

kratzig adj - **1.** [rau] scratchy - **2.** [heiser] rough.

Kraul das SPORT crawl.

kraulen (perf hat/ist gekrault) ◇ vi (ist) SPORT to do the crawl. ◇ vt (hat) [streicheln] to tickle.

kraus adj - **1.** [lockig] frizzy - **2.** [gerunzelt] wrinkled - **3.** [wirr] confused.

kräuseln vt - **1.** [in Locken] to frizz - **2.** [in Wellen] to ripple. ➤ **sich kräuseln** ref [in Locken] to go frizzy.

Kraut (pl Kräuter) das - **1.** (ohne pl) [Kohl] cabbage - **2.** (ohne pl) [Grünes] leaves Pl - **3.** fam [Tabak] weed; **dagegen ist kein Kraut gewachsen** there is no cure for it. ➤ **Kräuter** Pl herbs.

Kräuter|tee der herbal tea.

Krawall (pl -e) der [Krach, Lärm] row; **Krawall machen** to make a row. ➤ **Krawalle** Pl [Unruhen] riots.

Krawatte (pl -n) die tie.

kreativ adj creative.

Kreativität [kreativi'tɛːt] die creativity.

Kreatur (pl -en) die creature.

Krebs (pl -e) der - **1.** [Tier] crab - **2.** (ohne pl) [Tumor] cancer; **Krebs haben** to have cancer - **3.** ASTROL Cancer; **Krebs sein** to be a Cancer.

Kredit (pl -e) der [Darlehen] credit (U); **einen Kredit aufnehmen/gewähren** to take out/grant credit.

Kredit|karte die credit card.

Kreide (pl -n) die chalk; **bei jm in der Kreide stehen** fig to be in debt to sb.

kreideweiß adj as white as a sheet.

kreieren [kre'iːrən] vt to create.

Kreis (pl -e) der - **1.** [Form, Personenkreis] circle; **im Kreis** in a circle - **2.** [Verwaltungsbezirk] district; **Kreise ziehen** to have repercussions; **sich im Kreis drehen** to go round in circles.

kreischen vi [Person] to shriek; [Tier, Säge, Bremsen] to screech.

kreisen (perf hat/ist gekreist) vi - **1.** [sich drehen] to circle; **die Erde kreist um die Sonne** the earth goes round the sun - **2.** [Gedanken]: **um etw kreisen** to revolve aroung sthg.

Kreis|lauf der - **1.** [Zyklus] cycle - **2.** [Blutkreislauf] circulation.

Kreis|laufstörungen Pl circulatory trouble (U).

Kreis|säge die - **1.** [Säge] circular saw - **2.** [Hut] boater.

Kreis|stadt die chief town of a district.

Kreis|verkehr der roundabout UK, traffic circle US.

Krem (pl -s) die = Creme.

Kreme (pl -s ODER -n) die = Creme.

kremig adj = cremig.

Krempe (pl -n) die brim.

Krempel der fam junk.

Krepppapier das crepe paper.

Kresse (pl -n) die cress (U).

Kreta nt Crete.

Kreuz (pl -e) das - **1.** [Zeichen & RELIG] cross; **über Kreuz** crosswise - **2.** [Rücken] small of the back; **mir tut das Kreuz weh** my back aches; **jn aufs Kreuz legen** fam fig to take sb for a ride - **3.** [Autobahnkreuz] intersection - **4.** (ohne pl) [Qual] burden - **5.** (ohne Artikel, ohne pl) [Spielfarbe] clubs Pl - **6.** [Spielkarte] club; **die Kreuzsechs** the six of clubs.

kreuzen (perf hat/ist gekreuzt) ◇ vt (hat) to cross. ◇ vi (hat, ist) - **1.** [Boot - hin und her fahren] to cruise - **2.** [gegen den Wind segeln] to tack. ➤ **sich kreuzen** ref - **1.** [Weg, Brief, Linie] to cross - **2.** [Ansichten] to clash.

Kreuz|fahrt die cruise.

Kreuz|gang der cloister.

kreuzigen vt to crucify.

Kreuzigung (pl -en) die crucifixion.

Kreuzung (pl -en) die - **1.** [Straßenkreuzung] crossroads (sg) - **2.** [Züchtung] cross.

Kreuzwort|rätsel das crossword (puzzle).

kriechen (prät kroch, perf ist gekrochen) vi - **1.** [Wurm, Verkehr, Kind] to crawl - **2.** [Zeit] to creep by - **3.** abw [unterwürfig sein]: **vor jm kriechen** to crawl to sb.

Kriech|spur die crawler lane.

Krieg (pl -e) der war; **jm/einer Sache den Krieg erklären** to declare war on sb/sthg.

kriegen vt fam [bekommen] to get; [Zug, Bus, Straßenbahn] to catch; [gebären - Kind] to have; **wenn wir den kriegen!** just wait till we get hold of him!

Kriegs|dienstverweigerer (pl Kriegsdienstverweigerer) der conscientious objector.

Kriegs|gefangene der, die prisoner of war.

Krimi (pl -s) der fam thriller.

Kriminal|beamte der detective.

Kriminal|beamtin die detective.

Kriminalität die crime.

Kriminalpolizei die ≃ Criminal Investigation Department UK, ≃ Federal Bureau of Investigation US.

kriminell adj criminal; **kriminell werden** to turn to crime.

Kripo (abk für Kriminalpolizei) die ≃ CID UK, ≃ FBI US.

Krippe (pl -n) die - 1. [Kinderkrippe] crèche UK, day nursery US - 2. [Futterkrippe] manger - 3. [Weihnachtskrippe] crib.

Krise (pl -n) die crisis; **in einer Krise stecken** to be in (a) crisis.

Krisen|herd der trouble spot.

Kristall (pl -e) das & der crystal.

Kriterium (pl Kriterien) das criterion.

Kritik (pl -en) die - 1. [Beurteilung] criticism; **an jm/etw Kritik üben** to criticize sb/sthg - 2. [Rezension] review.

Kritiker, in (mpl -, fpl -nen) der, die critic.

kritisch ◇ adj critical. ◇ adv - 1. [prüfend, negativ] critically - 2. [gefährlich]: **es steht kritisch um den Kranken** the patient is critical.

kritisieren vt to criticize.

kritzeln vt to scribble.

Kroatien [kro'a:tsjən] nt Croatia.

kroatisch [kro'a:tɪʃ] adj Croatian.

kroch prät ▷ **kriechen**.

Krokant der (ohne pl) praline.

Krokodil (pl -e) das crocodile.

Krokus (pl -se) der crocus.

Krone (pl -n) die - 1. [gen] crown - 2. [Herrschaft] Crown - 3. [Währung - dänische] krone; [- schwedische] krona; **einer Sache (D) die Krone aufsetzen** to cap sthg.

krönen vt to crown; **jn zum König krönen** to crown sb king.

Kron|leuchter der chandelier.

Krönung (pl -en) die - 1. [das Krönen] coronation - 2. [Höhepunkt] culmination.

Kropf (pl Kröpfe) der goitre.

Kröte (pl -n) die toad.

Krücke (pl -n) die - 1. [Stock] crutch - 2. fam abw [Person] clown.

Krug (pl Krüge) der [für Milch, Wein] jug; [für Bier] mug.

Krümel (pl -) der crumb.

krumm ◇ adj - 1. [Linie] curved; [Nagel, Rücken] bent; [Nase] hooked; [Finger, Beine] crooked - 2. fam [unehrlich] crooked; **auf eine krumme Tour** by crooked means. ◇ adv [gehen, stehen] with a stoop; [sitzen] bent over.

krümmen vt to bend. ⬥ **sich krümmen** ref to bend; [vor Schmerzen] to double up.

krumm nehmen vt (unreg) fam to take offence at; **jm etw krumm nehmen** to hold sthg against sb.

Krümmung (pl -en) die [von Horizont, Rücken] curve; [von Straße, Fluss] bend.

Krüppel (pl -) der cripple.

Kruste (pl -n) die - 1. [Rinde] crust - 2. [Schicht] scab.

Kruzifix (pl -e) das crucifix.

Kto. (abk für Konto) a/c.

Kuba nt Cuba; **auf Kuba** in Cuba.

Kübel (pl -) der [für Abfälle] bin; [für Pflanzen] tub.

Kubik|meter der cubic metre.

Küche (pl -n) die - 1. [Raum] kitchen - 2. [Kochen] cooking; **kalte/warme Küche** cold/hot food.

Kuchen (pl -) der cake.

Kuchen|blech das baking sheet.

Kuchen|form die cake tin UK ODER pan US.

Kuchen|gabel die cake fork.

Küchen|schabe die cockroach.

Kuckuck (pl -e) der cuckoo.

Kufe (pl -n) die runner.

Kugel (pl -n) die - 1. [gen & SPORT] ball; [am Weihnachtsbaum] bauble; [beim Kugelstoßen] shot - 2. [Form] sphere - 3. [Geschoss] bullet; **eine ruhige Kugel schieben** fam fig to have it easy.

Kugel|lager das ball bearing.

Kugelschreiber (pl -) der ballpoint (pen), Biro®.

kugelsicher adj bullet-proof.

Kugelstoßen das SPORT shot put.

Kuh (pl Kühe) die cow.

kühl ◇ adj cool. ◇ adv coolly; **kühl servieren** serve chilled; **kühl und trocken lagern** keep in a cool, dry place.

kühlen vt to cool.

Kühler (pl -) der - 1. AUTO radiator - 2. [für Getränke] cooler.

Kühler|haube die bonnet UK, hood US.

Kühl|schrank der fridge.

Kühl|truhe die freezer.

Kühlung (pl -en) die - 1. [Erfrischung] coolness - 2. TECH cooling.

kühn adj bold.

Küken (pl -) das - 1. [Tier] chick - 2. fam fig [Nesthäkchen] baby; [Mädchen] little girl.

kulant adj [Verkäufer, Geschäftspartner] obliging; [Preis] reasonable.

Kuli (pl -s) der - 1. [Mensch] coolie - 2. fam [Schreiber] Biro®.

Kulisse (pl -n) die - 1. [Bühnenbild] scenery (U) - 2. [Hintergrund] background.

kullern (perf ist gekullert) vi to roll.

Kult (pl -e) der cult.

kultivieren [kʊlti'viːrən] *vt* to cultivate.

kultiviert [kʊlti'viːɐ̯t] <> *adj* refined. <> *adv* in a refined manner.

Kultur (*pl* -en) *die* culture.

Kulturbeutel *der* toilet bag.

kulturell <> *adj* cultural. <> *adv* culturally.

Kulturhaus (*pl* -häuser) *das* arts centre *UK* ODER center *US*.

Kultusminister, in *der, die* minister of a German federal state responsible for education and cultural affairs.

Kümmel (*pl* -) *der* - 1. (ohne pl) [Gewürzpflanze] caraway - 2. [Schnaps] kümmel.

Kummer *der* worries *Pl*; **Kummer mit jm haben** to worry about sb; **jm Kummer machen** to worry sb.

kümmerlich *adj* miserable.

kümmern *vt* to concern; **das kümmert sie nicht** she doesn't care about that; **was kümmert es ihn?** what is it to him? **sich kümmern** *ref*: **sich um jn kümmern** [helfen] to look after sb; **sich um etw kümmern** [organisieren, zubereiten] to see to sthg; [beachten] to worry about sthg; **kümmere dich um deine eigenen Angelegenheiten!** mind your own business!

Kumpel (*pl* -) *der* - 1. [Bergarbeiter] miner - 2. *fam* [Kamerad] pal.

kündbar *adj* [Stellung, Vertrag] terminable; [Mitarbeiter] dismissible.

Kunde (*pl* -n) *der* customer.

Kundendienst *der* - 1. [Service] customer service - 2. [Servicestelle] customer service department.

Kundgebung (*pl* -en) *die* rally.

kündigen <> *vi* [Arbeitnehmer] to hand in one's notice; [Mieter] to give notice that one is leaving; **jm kündigen** [Firma] to give sb his/her notice; [Vermieter] to give sb notice to quit. <> *vt* [Vertrag, Kredit] to terminate; **seine Arbeitsstelle kündigen** to hand in one's notice; **seine Wohnung kündigen** to give notice that one is leaving; **jm die Freundschaft kündigen** to break off one's friendship with sb.

Kündigung (*pl* -en) *die* [von Vertrag] termination; [von Arbeitsstelle] notice; [von Wohnung] notice to quit; **jm die Kündigung aussprechen** to give sb his/her notice.

Kündigungsfrist *die* period of notice.

Kündigungsschutz *der* [für Mieter] protection against wrongful eviction; [für Arbeitnehmer] protection against wrongful dismissal.

Kundin (*pl* -nen) *die* customer.

Kundschaft *die* (ohne pl) customers *Pl*.

künftig <> *adj* future. <> *adv* in future.

Kunst (*pl* Künste) *die* art; **das ist keine Kunst!** there is nothing to it!

Kunstdünger *der* artificial fertilizer.

Kunsterziehung *die* (ohne pl) art lessons *Pl*.

Kunstfaser *die* synthetic fibre.

Kunstfehler *der* professional error.

kunstfertig <> *adj* skilful. <> *adv* skilfully.

Kunstgegenstand *der* objet d'art.

Kunstgeschichte *die* history of art.

Kunstgewerbe *das* (ohne pl) arts and crafts *Pl*.

Kunsthandwerk *das* craft.

Künstler, in (*mpl* -, *fpl* -nen) *der, die* - 1. [Kunstschaffende] artist - 2. [Könner] master.

künstlerisch <> *adj* artistic. <> *adv* artistically.

Künstlername *der* pseudonym.

künstlich <> *adj* - 1. [nicht natürlich] artificial - 2. [übertrieben] forced. <> *adv* - 1. [nicht natürlich] artificially - 2. [übertrieben] in a forced way.

Kunststoff *der* plastic.

Kunststück *das* - 1. [Trick] trick - 2. [Leistung] feat.

Kunstwerk *das* work of art.

kunterbunt <> *adj* varied. <> *adv* in a jumble.

Kupfer *das* copper.

Kuppe (*pl* -n) *die* - 1. [landschaftlich] (hill)top - 2. [von Fingern] tip.

Kuppel (*pl* -n) *die* dome.

Kupplung (*pl* -en) *die* - 1. [in Auto] clutch - 2. [für Anhänger] coupling.

Kur (*pl* -en) *die* health cure; **auf** ODER **zur Kur sein/gehen** to be/go on a health cure.

Kür (*pl* -en) *die* free programme.

Kurbel (*pl* -n) *die* [von Fenster, Rollo] winder; [von Drehorgel, Spieluhr] handle; [von Maschine, zum Aufziehen] crank.

Kürbis (*pl* -se) *der* pumpkin.

Kurdistan *nt* Kurdistan.

Kurgast *der* visitor to a health resort.

Kurier (*pl* -e) *der* courier.

kurieren *vt* to cure; **von etw kuriert sein** *fig* to be cured of sthg.

kurios *adj* curious.

Kuriosität (*pl* -en) *die* curiosity.

Kurort *der* health resort.

Kurs (*pl* -e) *der* - 1. [Fahrtrichtung, Lehrgang] course - 2. [Teilnehmer] course members *Pl* - 3. [Marktpreis - von Aktien] price; [- von Währung] exchange rate; **hoch im Kurs stehen** to be very popular.

Kursbuch *das* timetable.

kursieren *vi* to circulate.

Kursus (*pl* Kurse) *der* course.

Kurtaxe *die* tax paid by visitors to health resorts.

Kurve ['kʊrvə] (*pl* -n) *die* - 1. [Straßenkrümmung] bend; **die Straße macht eine Kurve** the road bends - 2. [Bogenlinie] curve.

kurvenreich *adj* [Straße] winding; [Frau] curvaceous.

kurz (*kompar* **kürzer**, *superl* **kürzeste**) ⬦ *adj*
- 1. [räumlich] short; **was ist der kürzeste Weg zum Bahnhof?** what's the quickest way to the station? - 2. [zeitlich] short, brief; **innerhalb kurzer Zeit** within a short space of time; **vor kurzem** recently; **über kurz oder lang** sooner or later. ⬦ *adv* - 1. [räumlich]: **kurz vor/hinter** just in front of/behind; **alles kurz und klein schlagen** *fam* to smash everything to pieces - 2. [zeitlich] briefly; **ich gehe mal kurz in das Geschäft dort** I'm just popping into that shop; **kurz vor dem Konzert** shortly before the concert.

kurzärmelig, kurzärmlig ⬦ *adj* short-sleeved. ⬦ *adv* in short sleeves.

Kürze *die* shortness. ⬌ **in Kürze** *adv* shortly.

kürzen *vt* - 1. [Haare, Nägel, Film, Text] to cut; [Rock, Kabel] to shorten - 2. [finanziell] to cut - 3. MATH to cancel.

kurzerhand *adv* without further ado.

kurzfristig ⬦ *adj* - 1. [unangemeldet] sudden - 2. [kurz dauernd] short-term - 3. [rasch] quick. ⬦ *adv* - 1. [unangemeldet] at short notice - 2. [kurz dauernd] for a short time - 3. [rasch] quickly.

Kurz|geschichte *die* short story.

kurzhaarig *adj* short-haired.

kürzlich *adv* recently.

kurz|schließen *vt* (*unreg*) to short-circuit. ⬌ **sich kurzschließen** *ref* to get in touch.

Kurzschluss (*pl* -schlüsse) *der* - 1. [elektrisch] short-circuit - 2. [seelisch]: **er muss es aus einem Kurzschluss heraus getan haben** something must have snapped to make him do that.

kurzsichtig ⬦ *adj eigtl* & *fig* short-sighted. ⬦ *adv* short-sightedly.

Kürzung (*pl* -en) *die* cut.

Kurzwahl|taste *die* EDV speed-dial button.

Kurzwelle *die* short wave.

kuschelig *adj* cosy.

kuscheln *vi* to cuddle up; **mit jm kuscheln** to cuddle sb. ⬌ **sich kuscheln** *ref* to cuddle up; **sich an jn kuscheln** to cuddle up to sb.

Kusine (*pl* -n) *die* cousin.

Kuss (*pl* **Küsse**) *der* kiss.

küssen *vt* & *vi* to kiss. ⬌ **sich küssen** *ref* to kiss.

Küste (*pl* -n) *die* coast.

Küster, in (*mpl* -, *fpl* -nen) *der, die* verger.

Kutsche (*pl* -n) *die* - 1. [Pferdewagen] coach - 2. *fam* [Auto] jalopy, motor UK.

Kuvert [ku'vɛːɐ] (*pl* -e) *das* envelope.

KZ [kaːˈytsɛt] (*pl* -s) *das abk für* **Konzentrationslager**.

L

l (*pl* - ODER -s), **L** (*pl* - ODER -s) [ɛl] *das* l, L. ⬌ **l** (*abk für* **Liter**) l.

labil *adj* unstable; [Kreislauf] bad; [Konstitution, Gleichgewicht] delicate.

Labor (*pl* -s ODER -e) *das* laboratory.

Laborant, in (*mpl* -en, *fpl* -nen) *der, die* laboratory technician.

Labyrinth (*pl* -e) *das* maze.

Lache (*pl* -n) *die* [von Wasser] puddle; [von Blut, Öl] pool.

lächeln *vi* to smile; **über jn/etw lächeln** to smile about sb/sth.

Lächeln *das* (*ohne pl*) smile.

lachen *vi* to laugh; **über jn/etw lachen** to laugh at sb/sth; **es** ODER **das wäre doch gelacht, wenn** *fig* it would be ridiculous if; **du hast gut lachen!** *fig* it's all right for you!

Lachen *das* laughter; **ein leises Lachen** a quiet laugh; **jn zum Lachen bringen** to make sb laugh; **etw ist zum Lachen** *fam fig* sthg is laughable; **ihm wird das Lachen schon noch vergehen** he'll soon be laughing on the other side of his face.

lächerlich *adj* [komisch] ridiculous; **jn/sich lächerlich machen** to make a fool of sb/o.s.

Lächerliche *das*: **etw ins Lächerliche ziehen** to make a joke out of sthg.

lachhaft *adj* ludicrous.

Lachs [laks] (*pl* -e) *der* salmon.

Lack (*pl* -e) *der* [farblos] varnish; [farbig] paint; [Nagellack] varnish UK, polish US.

lackieren *vt* - 1. [Holz] to varnish; [Auto] to spray - 2. [mit Nagellack] to paint.

Lackierung (*pl* -en) *die* - 1. [Lackieren - von Holz] varnishing; [- von Auto] spraying - 2. [Lack - farblos] varnish; [- farbig] paint.

Lade|fläche *die* load area.

laden (*präs* **lädt**, *prät* **lud**, *perf* **hat geladen**) ⬦ *vt* - 1. [Fracht, Waffe & EDV] to load; **der Lkw hat Kies geladen** the lorry has loaded up with gravel; **etw auf/in etw (A) laden** to load sthg onto/into sthg - 2. [mit Elektrizität] to charge - 3. *geh* [vorladen] to summon. ⬦ *vi* [mit einer Last] to load up; **der Laster hat schwer geladen** the truck is heavily laden.

Laden (*pl* **Läden**) *der* - 1. [Geschäft] shop UK, store US - 2. *fam* [Angelegenheit] business - 3. *fam* [Betrieb] outfit.

Laden|dieb, in *der, die* shoplifter.

Ladenschluss *der* (*ohne pl*) closing time.

Laden|tisch *der* counter.

Lade|rampe *die* loading platform.

lädieren *vt* to damage.

lädt *präs* ⊳ **laden**.

Ladung *(pl -en) die* - **1.** [gen] load - **2.** [zum Schießen] charge - **3.** PHYS: **positive/negative Ladung** positive/negative charge.

lag *prät* ⊳ **liegen**.

Lage *(pl -n) die* - **1.** [Stelle, Stellung] position - **2.** [Situation] situation; **zu etw in der Lage sein** to be able to do sthg; **in der Lage sein, etw zu tun** to be able to do sthg; **sich in js Lage (A) versetzen** to put o.s. in sb's position - **3.** [Schicht] layer.

Lager *(pl -) das* - **1.** *eigtl* & *fig* [Feldlager, Gesinnung] camp - **2.** [für Waren] store; **etw auf Lager haben** [als Ware] to have sthg in stock; [zur Unterhaltung] to be ready with sthg - **3.** TECH bearing.

Lagerbestand *der* stock.

Lagerfeuer *das* camp fire.

Lagerhaus *das* warehouse.

lagern ⋄ *vt* - **1.** [aufbewahren] to store - **2.**: **einen Kranken bequem lagern** to make an ill person comfortable; **den Arm hoch lagern** to put one's arm in a raised position. ⋄ *vi* [kampieren] to camp.

Lagerung *(pl -en) die* storage (U).

lahm ⋄ *adj* - **1.** [gelähmt, Ausrede] lame - **2.** [ermüdet] stiff - **3.** [matt - Mensch] dull; [- Bewegung] sluggish. ⋄ *adv fam* [sich bewegen] sluggishly; [sich entschuldigen] lamely.

lähmen *vt eigtl* & *fig* to paralyse.

lahm legen *vt* to bring to a standstill.

Lähmung *(pl -en) die eigtl* & *fig* paralysis.

Laib *(pl -e) der*: **ein Laib Brot** a loaf of bread; **ein Laib Käse** a cheese.

Laie ['laɪə] *(pl -n) der* layman (laywoman *die*); **ein medizinischer Laie** a layman when it comes to medicine.

laienhaft ['laɪənhaft] ⋄ *adj* inexpert. ⋄ *adv* inexpertly.

Laken *(pl -) das* sheet.

Lakritz *(pl -e) das* & *der* liquorice.

lallen *vt* & *vi* to babble.

Lama *(pl -s) das* llama.

Lamelle *(pl -n) die* - **1.** [von Jalousie] slat - **2.** [von Heizkörper] fin - **3.** [von Pilzen] gill.

Lamm *(pl Lämmer) das* lamb.

Lampe *(pl -n) die* light; [Bürolampe, Stehlampe] lamp.

Lampenfieber *das* stage fright.

Lampenschirm *der* lampshade.

Land *(pl Länder) das* - **1.** [Staatsgebiet, ländliche Gegend] country; **jn des Landes verweisen** to deport sb; **auf dem Land** in the country - **2.** [Gelände, Festland] land; **an Land gehen** to go ashore - **3.** [Bundesland - in Deutschland] state; [- in Österreich] province; **wieder im Land(e) sein** to be back. ➠ **hier zu Lande** *adv* = **hierzulande**.

Landbevölkerung *die* rural population.

Landebahn *die* runway.

landen *(perf hat/ist gelandet)* ⋄ *vi (ist)* - **1.** [nach einem Flug] to land - **2.** *fam* [ankommen] to land up; **bei jm (mit etw) nicht landen können** *fam* not to be able to get anywhere with sb (sthg). ⋄ *vt (hat) eigtl* & *fig* to land.

Landeplatz *der* landing strip.

Länderspiel *das* international match.

Landesebene *die*: **auf Landesebene** at state level.

Landeshauptmann *der Österr* head of a regional government in Austria.

Landesinnere *das* interior (of the country).

Landeskunde *die* study of a country and its culture.

Landesregierung *die* state government.

Landessprache *die* national language.

Landesverrat *der* treason.

Landeswährung *die* national currency.

Landhaus *das* country house.

Landkarte *die* map.

Landkreis *der* district.

landläufig *adj* popular.

Landleben *das* country life.

ländlich *adj* rural.

Landschaft *(pl -en) die* [Gelände] countryside; [Abbildung] landscape.

landschaftlich ⋄ *adj* [Schönheit, Besonderheit] of the countryside; [Sitte] regional. ⋄ *adv*: **der Schwarzwald ist landschaftlich schön** the countryside of the Black Forest is beautiful.

Landsleute *Pl* compatriots.

Landstraße *die* country road.

Landstreicher, in *(mpl Landstreicher, fpl -nen) der, die* tramp.

Landstrich *der* area.

Landtag *der* - **1.** [Volksvertretung] state parliament - **2.** [Gebäude] state parliament building.

Landung *(pl -en) die* landing.

Landweg *der* overland route.

Landwirt, in *der, die* farmer.

Landwirtschaft *die* [Agrarwesen] agriculture.

lang *(kompar länger, superl längste)* ⋄ *adj* long; [Person] tall; **drei Meter lang** three metres long; **vor langer Zeit** a long time ago; **vor nicht zu langer Zeit** not (so) long ago; **drei lange Jahre** three long years. ⋄ *adv fam* - **1.** [entlang] along; **hier/dort lang** this/that way - **2.** [zeitlich]: **drei Jahre lang** for three years; **den ganzen Tag lang** all day.

langärmelig, langärmlig *adj* long-sleeved.

langatmig ⋄ *adj* long-winded. ⋄ *adv* long-windedly.

lange (*kompar* **länger**, *superl* **am längsten**) *adv* [während langer Zeit] a long time; [seit langer Zeit] for a long time; **es dauert nicht mehr lange** it won't be long; **das mache ich nicht mehr länger** I won't be doing this for much longer; **das ist noch lange nicht alles** that's not all by any means; **ich war schon lange nicht mehr zu Hause** I haven't been home for a long time; **etw ist lange her** sthg was a long time ago.

Länge (*pl* -n) *die* - 1. [von Brett, Brief] length; **ein Stau von 5 km Länge** a 5 km-long traffic jam; **der Länge nach** [teilen] lengthways; [hinstürzen] flat on one's face - 2. (*ohne pl*) [Körpergröße] height - 3. GEOGR longitude - 4. (*ohne pl*) [Dauer] length; **in die Länge ziehen** to drag out.
 Längen *Pl* [von Film] tedious scenes; [von Buch] tedious passages.

langen *vi fam* - 1. [ausreichen] to be enough; **mir langt es!** *fam* that's enough! - 2. [greifen] to reach.

Längen|grad *der* degree of longitude.

Längen|maß *das* unit of length.

längerfristig <> *adj* longer-term. <> *adv* on a longer-term basis.

Langeweile, Langeweile *die* boredom; **aus Langeweile** out of boredom.

langfristig <> *adj* long-term. <> *adv* on a long-term basis.

Langlauf *der* SPORT cross-country skiing.

langlebig *adj* - 1. [lange lebend] long-lived - 2. [lange gebrauchsfähig] durable.

länglich *adj* oblong.

längs <> *präp*: **längs einer Sache** (G) along sthg. <> *adv* lengthways.

Längs|achse ['lɛŋsaksə] *die* longitudinal axis.

langsam <> *adj* - 1. [nicht schnell] slow - 2. [allmählich] gradual. <> *adv* - 1. [nicht schnell] slowly - 2. [nach und nach] gradually; **das wird ja langsam Zeit!** it's about time!

Langschläfer, in (*mpl* -, *fpl* -nen) *der, die* late riser.

Längs|richtung *die*: **in Längsrichtung** lengthways.

Längs|seite *die* long side.

längst *adv* for a long time; **sie war längst tot** she was long since dead, she had died a long time ago; **längst nicht** nowhere near.

längstens *adv fam* - 1. [höchstens] at (the) most - 2. [seit langem] for a long time; **es war längstens entschieden** it was long since agreed, it had been agreed a long time ago.

Langstrecken|lauf *der* [Wettbewerb] long-distance race; [Sportart] long-distance running (*U*).

Languste [laŋˈgʊstə] (*pl* -n) *die* crayfish.

langweilen *vt* to bore. 🔊 **sich langweilen** *ref* to be bored.

langweilig <> *adj* - 1. [uninteressant] boring - 2. *fam* [Zeit raubend] slow. <> *adv* boringly.

Langwelle *die* long wave.

langwierig *adj* lengthy.

Lanze (*pl* -n) *die* spear.

Lappalie [laˈpaːliə] (*pl* -n) *die* trifle.

Lappen (*pl* -) *der* cloth; **etw geht jm durch die Lappen** *fam fig* sthg slips through sb's fingers.

läppern 🔊 **sich läppern** *ref*: **das** ODER **es läppert sich** it mounts up.

läppisch *adj abw* - 1. [albern] silly - 2. [lächerlich] ridiculous.

Laptop [ˈlɛptɔp] (*pl* -s) *der* EDV laptop.

Lärche (*pl* -n) *die* larch.

Lärm *der* noise; **Lärm schlagen** *fam fig* to kick up a fuss.

lärmen *vi* to make a noise; [Radio] to blare.

Larve [ˈlarfə] (*pl* -n) *die* larva.

las *prät* ⟶ **lesen**.

lasch <> *adj* - 1. [Bewegung, Spiel] listless; [Händedruck] limp - 2. [fade] insipid - 3. [nachlässig] lax. <> *adv* - 1. [schlaff] listlessly - 2. [fade] insipidly - 3. [nachlässig] laxly.

Lasche (*pl* -n) *die* [von Umschlag] flap; [von Schuh] tongue.

Laser [ˈleːzɐ] (*pl* -) *der* laser.

Laser|drucker *der* EDV laser printer.

lassen (*präs* **lässt**, *prät* **ließ**, *perf* **hat gelassen** ODER **lassen**) <> *vt* - 1. [geschehen lassen] to let; **jn nicht ins Haus lassen** not to let sb in the house; **Wasser in die Badewanne lassen** to run a bath - 2. [unterlassen] to stop; **das Rauchen lassen** to stop smoking; **lass das!** stop it! - 3. [überlassen]: **jm etw lassen** to let sb have sthg; **eines muss man dir ja lassen** *fig* I'll say this much for you - 4. [belassen, zurücklassen] to leave; **lass mich!** let me go!; **lass es wie es ist** leave everything as it is. <> *vi* (*perf* **hat gelassen**) - 1. [belassen]: **von jm/etw lassen** to abandon sb/sthg - 2. [geschehen lassen]: **lass mal, ich mach das schon!** leave it, I'll do it. <> *aux* - 1. [veranlassen]: **etw machen** ODER **tun lassen** to have sthg done; **jn etw tun lassen** to have sb do sthg; **sich** (D) **die Haare schneiden lassen** to get ODER have one's hair cut; **sich** (D) **einen Anzug machen lassen** to have a suit made - 2. [belassen] leave; **lass die Vase auf dem Tisch stehen** leave the vase on the table - 3. [geschehen lassen]: **jn etw tun lassen** to let sb do sthg; **ich lasse mich überraschen** I want it to be a surprise; **etw mit sich/nicht mit sich machen lassen** to put up/not to put up with sthg; **die Vase fallen lassen** to drop the vase; **jn warten lassen** to keep sb waiting. 🔊 **sich lassen** *ref* (*perf* **hat lassen**): **das lässt sich machen** it can be done; **die Fenster lassen sich nicht öffnen** the windows don't open.

lässig <> *adj* casual. <> *adv* - 1. [salopp] casually - 2. *fam* [leicht] easily.

Lässigkeit *die* [Lockerheit] casualness; [Leichtigkeit] ease.

lässt *präs* ▷ **lassen**.

Last *(pl* -en) *die* - **1.** [Gewicht] load - **2.** *geh* [Bürde] burden; **jm zur Last fallen** to be a burden on sb; **jm etw zur Last legen** to accuse sb of sthg. ◆ **Lasten** *Pl* [Kosten] costs; **zu js Lasten** chargeable to sb.

lasten *vi* - **1.** [Gewicht]: **auf jm lasten** to weigh sb down; **auf etw (D) lasten** [auf Schultern] to weigh down on sthg; [auf Pfeilern] to bear down on sthg - **2.** [Verantwortung]: **auf jm lasten** to weigh on sb - **3.** [finanziell]: **auf jm/etw lasten** to be a burden on sb/sthg.

Laster *(pl* -) ◇ *das* [Untugend] vice. ◇ *der fam* [Lastwagen] truck, lorry *UK.*

lästern *vi*: **über jn/etw lästern** to make nasty remarks about sb/sthg.

lästig *adj* annoying; **jm lästig werden/sein** to become/be a nuisance to sb.

Lastkraftwagen *der amt* heavy goods vehicle.

Last-Minute-Flug [lɑːst'mɪnɪtˈfluːk] *der* last-minute flight.

Lastschrift *die* [Abbuchung] debit; [Mitteilung] debit advice.

Lastwagen *der* truck, lorry *UK.*

Latein *das* Latin; *siehe auch* **Englisch(e)**.

Lateinamerika *nt* Latin America.

lateinisch *adj* Latin.

latent ◇ *adj* latent. ◇ *adv* latently.

Laterne *(pl* -n) *die* - **1.** [Lampion] Chinese lantern - **2.** [Straßenlaterne] streetlamp.

Latinum *das*: **großes/kleines Latinum** *school examination in Latin taken after at least six/ three years.*

latschen *(perf* hat/ist gelatscht) *fam* ◇ *vi (ist)* to traipse. ◇ *vt (hat)*: **jm eine** *ODER* **ein paar latschen** to give sb a clout.

Latschen *(pl* -) *der fam* [Schuh] worn-out shoe; [Hausschuh] worn-out slipper.

Latte *(pl* -n) *die* [Brett] slat; [bei Hochsprung] bar; [von Tor] crossbar; **lange Latte** *fam* beanpole.

Lattenrost *der* slatted base.

Latz *(pl* Lätze) *der* bib.

Latzhose *die* dungarees *Pl.*

lau ◇ *adj* - **1.** [mäßig warm, zurückhaltend] lukewarm - **2.** [mild] mild - **3.** [mäßig] moderate. ◇ *adv* - **1.** [zurückhaltend] lukewarmly - **2.** [mäßig] moderately well.

Laub *das (ohne pl)* leaves *Pl.*

Laubbaum *der* deciduous tree.

Laubfrosch *der* tree frog.

Laubsäge *die* fretsaw.

Laubwald *der* deciduous forest.

Lauch *der* leek.

Lauer *die*: **auf der Lauer sitzen** *ODER* **liegen** *fam* to be on the lookout.

lauern *vi*: **auf jn/etw lauern** [warten] to lie in wait for sb/sthg.

Lauf *(pl* Läufe) *der* - **1.** *(ohne pl)* [Laufen] run - **2.** [Betrieb] running - **3.** *(ohne pl)* [Verlauf, von Fluss] course; **im Laufe des Tages** during the day; **etw nimmt seinen Lauf** sthg takes its course; **im Lauf(e) der Zeit** in the course of time; **einer Sache (D) freien Lauf lassen** [Tränen, Gefühlen] to give free rein to sthg; [Angelegenheit] to let sthg take its course - **4.** [von Gewehren] barrel.

Laufbahn *die* career.

laufen *(präs* läuft, *prät* lief, *perf* hat/ist gelaufen) ◇ *vi (ist)* - **1.** [schnell] to run - **2.** *fam* [gehen] to walk; **jn laufen lassen** to let sb go; **er läuft dauernd zum Arzt** he's always going to the doctor's - **3.** [zugange sein] to go on; **die Verhandlungen laufen noch** negotiations are still going on; **was läuft im Kino?** what's on at the cinema *ODER* movies? - **4.** [einen bestimmten Verlauf nehmen] to go; **es läuft gut** it's going well - **5.** [Motor, Maschine] to run, to be on; **ihr Radio läuft schon stundenlang** their radio has been on for hours; **bei laufender Maschine** when the machine is running *ODER* on - **6.** [funktionieren] to work - **7.** [fließen] to run; **mir läuft die Nase** my nose is running - **8.** [amtlich geführt werden]: **das Konto läuft auf ihren Namen** the account is in her name - **9.** [juristisch gültig sein] to run; **der Vertrag läuft bis zum 31.12.** the contract runs *ODER* is valid until 31 December. ◇ *vt* - **1.** *(hat, ist)* [rennen]: **er ist eine neue Bestzeit gelaufen** he set a new record; **Marathon laufen** to run the marathon - **2.** *(ist)* [gehen] to walk - **3.** *(ist)* [mit Sportgerät]: **Ski laufen** to ski; **Schlittschuh laufen** to skate. ◆ **sich laufen** *ref*: **sich warm laufen** to warm up.

laufend ◇ *adj* - **1.** [Kosten] regular; [Beschwerden, Störungen] continual - **2.** [gerade ablaufend] current - **3.** [in Betrieb] running; **auf dem Laufenden sein/bleiben** to be/keep up-to-date. ◇ *adv* [ständig] continually.

Läufer *(pl* -) *der* - **1.** *SPORT* runner - **2.** [Schachfigur] bishop.

Läuferin *(pl* -nen) *die* runner.

läufig *adj* on heat.

Laufmasche *die* ladder *UK,* run *US.*

Laufschritt *der* running step; **im Laufschritt** at a run.

läuft *präs* ▷ **laufen**.

Laufwerk *das EDV* drive.

Lauge *(pl* -n) *die* - **1.** *CHEM* alkaline solution - **2.** [Waschlauge] soapy water *(U).*

Laugenbrezel *die* pretzel.

Laune *(pl* -n) *die* - **1.** *(ohne pl)* [Stimmung] mood; **gute/schlechte Laune haben** to be in a good/bad mood - **2.** [Einfall] whim; **etw aus ei-**

ner Laune heraus tun to do sthg on a whim.
⚓ **Launen** *Pl* [von Person] moods; [von Wetter] vagaries.

launisch *adj* moody.

Laus (*pl* **Läuse**) *die* louse.

Lausbub (*pl* **-en**), **Lausbube** (*pl* **-n**) *der* little rascal.

lauschen *vi* [horchen] to listen; [heimlich] to eavesdrop.

lausig *fam* ◇ *adj* **- 1.** [schlecht, Geld] lousy **- 2.** [groß] terrible. ◇ *adv* lousily; **lausig kalt** *fam* freezing (cold).

laut ◇ *adj* loud; [lärmend] noisy; **es wurden Zweifel laut** doubts were voiced; **lauter sprechen** to speak up, to speak louder. ◇ *adv* loudly; [lärmend] noisily. ◇ *präp* **(+ G or D)** *amt* according to.

Laut (*pl* **-e**) *der* sound.

lauten *vi*: **die Anweisung lautet folgendermaßen** the instructions are as follows; **auf etw (A) lauten: die Anklage lautet auf versuchten Mord** the charge is attempted murder.

läuten *vi* to ring; **bei jm läuten** to ring sb's bell; **es läutet** there is someone at the door; **von etw läuten hören** to hear something about sthg.

lauter *adv* nothing but; **vor lauter Lärm** because of all the noise.

lauthals *adv* at the top of one's voice.

lautlos ◇ *adj* silent; [Stille] complete. ◇ *adv* silently.

Lautlschrift *die* phonetic alphabet.

Lautlsprecher *der* **- 1.** [Tonverstärker] (loud)speaker **- 2.** [Megafon] loudspeaker.

lautstark ◇ *adj* loud. ◇ *adv* loudly.

Lautlstärke *die* volume.

lauwarm ◇ *adj* lukewarm. ◇ *adv* [baden] in lukewarm water; **etw lauwarm essen/trinken** to eat/drink sthg lukewarm.

Lava ['laːva] (*pl* **Laven**) *die* lava.

Lavendel [la'vɛndl] *der* lavender.

Lawine (*pl* **-n**) *die* eigtl & fig avalanche.

lax ◇ *adj* lax. ◇ *adv* laxly.

Leasing ['liːzɪŋ] *das* leasing (U).

leben ◇ *vi* to live; **seine Mutter lebt noch** his mother is still alive; **von etw leben** to live off ODER on sthg; **vom Schreiben leben** to make one's living by ODER from writing; **es lebe der Präsident!** long live the president!; **damit kann ich leben** I can live with that. ◇ *vt* to live; **sie lebte ein erfülltes Leben** she lived a full life.

Leben (*pl* **-**) *das* **- 1.** [gen] life; **jm das Leben schwer machen** to make life difficult for sb; **sich (D) das Leben nehmen** to take one's (own) life; **ums Leben kommen** to die **- 2.** [Treiben] activity; **etw ins Leben rufen** to bring sthg into being.

lebendig ◇ *adj* **- 1.** [lebend, fortwirkend] living **- 2.** [lebhaft] lively. ◇ *adv* [lebhaft] in a lively manner.

lebensfähig *adj* capable of survival.

Lebenslgefahr *die* mortal danger; **außer Lebensgefahr sein** to be out of danger; **Vorsicht, Lebensgefahr!** danger of death!

lebensgefährlich ◇ *adj* [Situation, Handlung] extremely dangerous; [Verletzung] critical. ◇ *adv* [handeln] extremely dangerously; [sich verletzen] critically.

Lebenslgefährte *der* partner.

Lebenslgefährtin *die* partner.

Lebenslhaltungskosten *Pl* cost of living (U).

lebenslänglich *adj* & *adv* for life.

Lebenslauf *der* curriculum vitae *UK*, resumé *US*.

lebenslustig *adj* full of life.

Lebenslmittel *das* food.

Lebensmittellgeschäft *das* grocer's (shop).

lebensmüde *adj* **- 1.** [den Tod herbeisehnend] tired of life **- 2.** *fam* [leichtsinnig]: **du bist wohl lebensmüde** you're out of your mind.

Lebenslstandard *der* standard of living.

Lebenslunterhalt *der* maintenance; **seinen Lebensunterhalt verdienen** to earn one's living.

Lebenslversicherung *die* life insurance (U).

Lebenslwandel *der* (ohne pl) lifestyle.

Lebenslweise *die* way of life.

lebenswichtig *adj* essential.

Lebenslzeichen *das* eigtl & fig sign of life.

Leber (*pl* **-n**) *die* liver.

Leberlfleck *der* mole.

Leberlkäse *der* spiced meat loaf, sliced and often fried.

Leberltran *der* cod-liver oil.

Leberlwurst *die* liver sausage.

Lebelwesen *das* living being; [tierisch, pflanzlich] living thing.

lebhaft ◇ *adj* **- 1.** [gen] lively **- 2.** [Auseinandersetzung] vigorous; [Interesse] keen; [Bedauern] deep. ◇ *adv* **- 1.** [angeregt] in a lively manner **- 2.** [sich widersetzen] vigorously; [sich interessieren] keenly; [bedauern] deeply **- 3.** [gut] well.

Leblkuchen *der* gingerbread (U).

leblos ◇ *adj* lifeless. ◇ *adv* lifelessly.

leck *adj* leaky.

Leck (*pl* **-s**) *das* leak.

lecken ◇ *vt* to lick; **sich die Lippen lecken** to lick one's lips; **die Katze leckte sich das Fell** the cat licked its coat. ◇ *vi* **- 1.** [schlecken]: **an etw (D) lecken** to lick sthg **- 2.** [undicht sein] to leak. ⚓ **sich lecken** *ref* to lick o.s.

lecker *adj* delicious.

Lecker|bissen *der* - **1.** [essbar] delicacy - **2.** [Genuss] treat.

Leder (*pl* -) *das* leather *(U)*; **jm ans Leder gehen/wollen** *fam fig* to go for/want to go for sb.

Leder|hose *die* lederhosen *Pl.*

Leder|waren *Pl* leather goods.

ledig *adj* single.

lediglich *adv* only.

leer *adj* - **1.** [gen] empty; **leer ausgehen** to come away empty-handed - **2.** [unbeschrieben] blank.

Leere *die* emptiness; **sein Schlag ging ins Leere** his punch missed; **ins Leere starren** to stare into space.

leeren *vt* to empty. ◆ **sich leeren** *ref* to empty.

Leer|gut *das (ohne pl)* empties *Pl.*

Leer|lauf *der* - **1.** TECH neutral; **im Leerlauf** in neutral - **2.** [unproduktive Phase] slack period.

leer stehend *adj* empty.

Leerung (*pl* -en) *die* emptying *(U)*; [von Briefkasten] collection.

legal ◇ *adj* legal. ◇ *adv* legally.

legalisieren *vt* - **1.** [legal machen] to legalize - **2.** RECHT to authenticate.

Legalität *die* legality.

legen *vt* - **1.** [ablegen] to put; **leg den Schlüssel auf den Tisch** put the key on the table - **2.** [in horizontale Position bringen] to lay; **du musst die Flaschen ins Regal legen, nicht stellen** you should lay the bottles flat in the rack, not put them upright - **3.** [Termin] to arrange; **den Urlaub auf Juli legen** to arrange one's holidays for July - **4.** [installieren - Rohre, Kabel] to lay; **Minen legen** to lay mines; **Feuer legen** to lay a fire - **5.** [Ei] to lay. ◆ **sich legen** *ref* - **1.** [sich hinlegen] to lie down; **sich schlafen legen** to lie down to sleep - **2.** [Staub, Nebel] to settle - **3.** [Aufregung, Sturm] to die down.

Legende (*pl* -n) *die* - **1.** [gen] legend - **2.** [Irrglaube] myth.

leger [le'ʒɛːɐ̯] ◇ *adj* casual. ◇ *adv* casually.

Legierung (*pl* -en) *die* alloy.

Legislative [leɡɪslaˈtiːvə] (*pl* -n) *die* legislature.

legitim *adj* legitimate.

Lehm *der* clay.

lehmig *adj* clayey.

Lehne (*pl* -n) *die* [Rückenlehne] back; [Armlehne] arm.

lehnen ◇ *vt*: **etw gegen** ODER **an etw** *(A)* **lehnen** to lean sthg against sthg. ◇ *vi*: **an etw** *(D)* **lehnen** to lean against sthg. ◆ **sich lehnen** *ref* - **1.** [stützen]: **sich gegen** ODER **an jn/etw lehnen** to lean against sb/sthg - **2.** [sich beugen] to lean.

Lehr|amt *das amt* teaching *(U)*.

Lehr|buch *das* textbook.

Lehre (*pl* -n) *die* - **1.** [Ausbildung] apprenticeship; **in der Lehre sein** to be serving one's apprenticeship - **2.** [lehrreiche Erfahrung] lesson - **3.** [Ideologie - von Propheten, Philosophen] teachings *Pl*; [- katholisch, marxistisch] doctrine.

lehren ◇ *vi* to teach. ◇ *vt* to teach; **jn etw lehren** to teach sb sthg.

Lehrer, in (*mpl* -, *fpl* -nen) *der, die* [in Schule] teacher; [in Sportverein] instructor.

Lehr|gang *der* course.

Lehrling (*pl* -e) *der* apprentice.

Lehr|plan *der* syllabus.

lehrreich *adj* instructive.

Lehr|stelle *die* apprenticeship.

Lehr|stuhl *der amt* chair.

Lehr|zeit *die* apprenticeship.

Leib (*pl* -er) *der geh* [Körper] body; **sie ist mit Leib und Seele Krankenschwester** she is a dedicated nurse; **mit Leib und Seele dabei sein** to put one's whole heart into it; **jm etw vom Leib halten** *fam* to keep sb/sthg away from sb; **sich** *(D)* **jn/etw vom Leib halten** *fam* to keep sb/sthg at bay.

Leibeskräfte *Pl*: **aus Leibeskräften** with all one's might.

Leib|gericht *das* favourite dish.

leiblich *adj* - **1.** [körperlich] physical - **2.** [blutsverwandt] natural.

Leiche (*pl* -n) *die* corpse; **über Leichen gehen** *fam fig* to stop at nothing.

Leichen|halle *die* mortuary.

Leichnam (*pl* -e) *der geh* body.

leicht ◇ *adj* - **1.** [an Gewicht] light - **2.** [geringfügig] slight; **leichte Kopfschmerzen** a slight headache; **eine leichte Grippe** a mild attack of flu - **3.** [einfach] easy; **es leicht haben** to have it easy; **er hat es nicht leicht** he is having a hard time - **4.** [kalorienarm] diet, low-fat; [Mahlzeit] light; [Zigarette] mild. ◇ *adv* - **1.** [einfach, schnell] easily; **das ist sehr leicht möglich** that's perfectly possible; **er ist leicht beleidigt** he is quick to take offence - **2.** [geringfügig] slightly; **leicht nicken** to give a little nod; **es riecht leicht angebrannt** there's a slight smell of burning; **leicht bekleidet** scantily clad - **3.** [unbeschwert] lightly.

Leicht|athletik *die* athletics *(U)*.

leicht fallen (*perf* ist leicht gefallen) *vi* (*unreg*): **es fällt ihm leicht/nicht leicht** it comes/doesn't come easy to him.

leichtfertig *abw* ◇ *adj* rash. ◇ *adv* rashly.

leichtgläubig *adj* credulous.

Leichtigkeit *die* - **1.** [geringes Gewicht] lightness - **2.** [Mühelosigkeit] ease.

leicht machen *vt* to make easy; **jm etw leicht machen** to make sthg easy for sb.

Leicht|metall *das* light metal.

leicht nehmen vt (unreg) not to take seriously.

Leichtsinn der recklessness.

leichtsinnig <> adj reckless. <> adv recklessly.

leid adj: **jn/etw leid sein** ODER **haben** to be tired of sb/sthg.

Leid das sorrow; **sie tut mir Leid** I feel sorry for her; **es tut mir Leid** I'm sorry.

leiden (prät litt, perf hat gelitten) <> vi to suffer; **an/unter etw (D) leiden** to suffer from sthg. <> vt - 1. [erdulden] to suffer - 2. [mögen]: **jn gut/nicht leiden können** to like/not to like sb.

Leiden (pl -) das illness.

Leidenschaft (pl -en) die passion.

leidenschaftlich <> adj passionate. <> adv passionately; **leidenschaftlich gern tanzen** to adore dancing.

leider adv unfortunately.

Leidtragende (pl -n) der, die: **die Kinder sind immer die Leidtragenden** the children are always the ones to suffer.

Leih|bücherei die lending library.

leihen (prät lieh, perf hat geliehen) vt - 1. [leihweise geben]: **jm etw leihen** to lend sb sthg - 2. [ausleihen]: **sich (D) etw (von jm) leihen** to borrow sthg (from sb); [mieten] to hire UK ODER rent US sthg (from sb).

Leih|gebühr die [für Auto] hire UK ODER rental US charge; [für Buch] lending charge.

Leih|wagen der hire UK ODER rental US car.

Leim (pl -e) der glue; **aus dem Leim gehen** fam [kaputtgehen] to fall to pieces; [an Gewicht zunehmen] to put on weight.

leimen vt - 1. [zusammenfügen] to glue together - 2. [ankleben] to glue.

Leine (pl -n) die - 1. [Seil] cord; **Leine ziehen** salopp fig to scram - 2. [Wäscheleine] line - 3. [Hundeleine] lead UK, leash US.

Leinen das linen.

Lein|samen der linseed.

Lein|wand die [Projektionswand] screen.

leise <> adj - 1. [nicht laut] quiet - 2. [schwach] slight. <> adv quietly.

Leiste (pl -n) die - 1. [Latte] edging strip - 2. [Körperteil] groin.

leisten vt - 1. [vollbringen] to achieve - 2. [machen] to do - 3. [Beitrag, Anzahlung] to make.

Leistung (pl -en) die - 1. TECH [das Geleistete] performance - 2. [Ergebnis] achievement - 3. [Bezahlung] payment.

Leistungsdruck der pressure to do well.

Leistungskurs der one of two specialist subjects chosen by pupils for their "Abitur".

Leistungssport der competitive sport.

Leit|artikel der editorial.

leiten <> vt - 1. [anführen - Unternehmen, Projekt] to run; [- Gruppe, Diskussion] to lead - 2. PHYS to conduct - 3. [lenken - Bach, Verkehr] to divert; [- Antrag] to forward; **sich von etw leiten lassen** fig to let o.s. be guided by sthg. <> vi to conduct.

leitend adj - 1. [Stellung] managerial; [Direktor] managing; [Architekt] chief; **leitender Angestellter** manager - 2. [führend] guiding - 3. [weiterleitend] conductive.

Leiter (pl -n ODER -) <> die (pl Leitern) ladder. <> der (pl Leiter) [von Firma, Abteilung] manager; [von Gruppe, Projekt] leader.

Leiterin (pl -nen) die [von Firma, Abteilung] manager; [von Gruppe, Projekt] leader.

Leit|faden der introductory guide.

Leit|planke die crash barrier UK, guardrail US.

Leitung (pl -en) die - 1. [Führung] running; **unter der Leitung von jm** conducted by sb - 2. [Führungsgruppe] management (U) - 3. [Rohr] pipe - 4. [Draht] wire; [Kabel] cable - 5. [Telefonleitung] line; **eine lange Leitung haben** fam fig to be slow on the uptake.

Leitungs|rohr das pipe.

Leitungs|wasser das tap water.

Lektion (pl -en) die [das eigtl & fig lesson.

Lektor, in (mpl -toren, fpl -nen) der, die - 1. [bei Verlag] editor - 2. [an Hochschulen] language assistant.

Lektüre (pl -n) die - 1. [das Lesen] reading - 2. [Lesestoff] reading matter.

Lende (pl -n) die loin.

lenken vt - 1. [Fahrzeug, Gespräch] to steer - 2. [richten]: **die Aufmerksamkeit auf jn/etw lenken** to draw attention to sb/sthg; **er lenkte den Verdacht auf sich** he attracted suspicion - 3. [führen] to control.

Lenker (pl -) der - 1. [Lenkstange] handlebars Pl - 2. [Person] driver.

Lenkerin (pl -nen) die driver.

Lenk|rad das steering wheel.

Lenkung (pl -en) die - 1. [Steuerung] steering (U) - 2. [Beeinflussung] control.

Leopard (pl -en) der leopard.

Lepra die leprosy.

Lerche (pl -n) die lark.

lernen <> vt to learn; **Klavier spielen lernen** to learn to play the piano; **Bäcker lernen** to train to be a baker. <> vi - 1. [gen] to learn; **aus der Geschichte lernen** to learn from history - 2. [für Prüfung] to study, to revise.

Lesbierin ['lɛsbjərɪn] (pl -nen) die lesbian.

lesbisch adj lesbian.

lesen (präs liest, prät las, perf hat gelesen) <> vt - 1. [gen] to read - 2. [Früchte, Trauben] to pick. <> vi - 1. [gen] to read; **in seiner Miene war die Verzweiflung zu lesen** despair was written all over his face - 2. [einen Vortrag halten] to lecture.

Leser (pl -) der reader.

Leser|brief der reader's letter, letter to the editor.

Leserin (pl -nen) die reader.

leserlich <> adj legible. <> adv legibly.

Lese|zeichen das bookmark.

Lettland nt Latvia.

Letzt ➡ **zu guter Letzt** adv in the end.

letzte, r, s adj last; **das ist mein letztes Geld** that's the last of my money; **letztes Jahr** last year.

Letzte (pl -n) <> der, die [Person] last; **Letzter werden** to come last; **sie kam als Letzte an die Reihe** she had her turn last. <> der [Tag] last day. <> das - 1.: **er ist das Letzte** fam he's scum; **der Film ist das Letzte** fam the film is the pits - 2.: **bis ins Letzte** down to the last detail.

letztemal adv ➪ **Mal**.

letztendlich adv - 1. [am Schluss] in the end - 2. [im Grunde genommen] ultimately, in the final analysis.

letztenmal adv ➪ **Mal**.

letztens adv - 1. [an letzter Stelle] lastly - 2. [vor kurzem] recently.

letztere, r, s <> adj the latter; **in letzterem Fall** in the latter case. <> pron the latter.

Letztere der: der/die/das Letztere the latter.

letztgenannte, r, s adj: **die letztgenannte Alternative** the last alternative mentioned.

letztlich adv - 1. [am Schluss] in the end - 2. [im Grunde genommen] ultimately, in the final analysis.

leuchten vi to shine; [Feuer, Himmel] to glow.

leuchtend <> adj - 1. [Farbe] bright; **sie bekam leuchtende Augen** her eyes lit up - 2. [Vorbild, Beispiel] shining. <> adv: **leuchtend blau/rot** bright blue/red.

Leuchter (pl -) der candelabrum; [für eine Kerze] candlestick.

Leucht|farbe die luminous paint.

Leuchtstoff|röhre die fluorescent tube.

Leucht|turm der lighthouse.

leugnen <> vt to deny. <> vi to deny everything.

Leukämie die leukaemia.

Leute Pl [Menschen] people; **die jungen Leute** young people; **was die Leute sagen** what people say; **etw unter die Leute bringen** fam to spread sthg around; **unter (die) Leute gehen** fam to get out and meet people.

Leutnant (pl -s) der second lieutenant.

Lexikon (pl -ka ODER -ken) das [Enzyklopädie] encyclopaedia.

Libanon der: (der) Libanon (the) Lebanon.

Libelle (pl -n) die [Insekt] dragonfly.

liberal <> adj liberal. <> adv - 1. [tolerant]: **liberal eingestellt sein** to be liberal-minded - 2. POL: **liberal wählen** to vote Liberal.

Libyen nt Libya.

Licht (pl -er) das - 1. [Helligkeit, Lampe] light; **Licht machen** to put the light on - 2. [Kerze] candle; **ans Licht kommen** to come to light; **grünes Licht geben** to give the green light; **jetzt geht mir ein Licht auf** now I see; **jn hinters Licht führen** to pull the wool over sb's eyes.

Licht|blick der bright spot.

lichten vt to thin out. ➡ **sich lichten** ref to thin out.

lichterloh adv: **lichterloh brennen** to blaze fiercely.

Licht|hupe die AUTO: **die Lichthupe betätigen** to flash one's headlights.

Licht|maschine die AUTO alternator.

Licht|schalter der light switch.

Licht|schranke die photoelectric beam.

Lichtschutz|faktor der (protection) factor; **Lichtschutzfaktor 10** factor 10.

Licht|strahl der beam (of light).

Lichtung (pl -en) die clearing.

Lid (pl -er) das eyelid.

Lid|schatten der eye shadow.

lieb <> adj - 1. [nett] kind, nice; **wie lieb von Ihnen, dass Sie daran gedacht haben!** how kind ODER nice of you to remember! - 2. [als Anrede] dear; **Liebe Sue!** Dear Sue; **Liebe Kollegen!** colleagues! - 3. [brav] good; **sei schön lieb!** be a good boy/girl! <> adv nicely; siehe auch **lieb gewinnen**, **lieb haben**

liebäugeln vi: **mit etw liebäugeln** [Gegenstand, Kauf, Arbeitsstelle] to have one's eye on sthg; [Idee, Plan] to be thinking about sthg.

Liebe die - 1. [gen] love; **die Liebe zur Kunst** love of art; **sie war seine erste Liebe** she was his first love - 2. [Sex] sex; **käufliche Liebe** prostitution; **Liebe machen** to make love; **Liebe auf den ersten Blick** love at first sight.

lieben vt to love. ➡ **sich lieben** ref - 1. [lieb haben] to be in love - 2. [sexuell] to make love.

liebenswert adj [Art, Geste] endearing; [Person] likable.

liebenswürdig adj kind.

lieber <> ➪ **gern**. <> adv better; **das hättest du lieber nicht sagen sollen** it would have been better if you hadn't said that; **lieber nicht** maybe we shouldn't, maybe not. <> adj: **das wäre mir lieber** I'd prefer that.

Liebes|brief der love letter.

Liebes|kummer der: **Liebeskummer haben** to be lovesick.

Liebes|paar das lovers Pl.

liebevoll <> adj loving. <> adv lovingly.

lieb gewinnen vt (unreg) jn/etw lieb gewinnen to grow fond of sb/sthg.

lieb haben vt (unreg) to love; [gern haben] to be fond of. ➡ **sich lieb haben** ref to be in love.

Liebhaber (*pl* -) *der* - **1.** [gen] lover - **2.** [Sammler] collector.

Liebhaberin (*pl* -nen) *die* - **1.** [gen] lover - **2.** [Sammlerin] collector.

Liebling (*pl* -e) *der* - **1.** [als Anrede, der Oma] darling - **2.** [Bevorzugte] favourite.

Lieblings|gericht *das* favourite dish.

lieblos ◇ *adj* unaffectionate. ◇ *adv* - **1.** [ohne Liebe] unaffectionately - **2.** [nachlässig]: **sie hat das Essen lieblos zubereitet** she carelessly threw the meal together.

Liebschaft (*pl* -en) *die* abw casual affair.

liebsten ▷ **gern**. ⬧ **am liebsten** *adv*: **am liebsten würde ich jetzt nach Hause gehen** what I'd really like to do now would be to go home; **das ist mir am liebsten** I like it best of all.

Liechtenstein *nt* Liechtenstein.

Lied (*pl* -er) *das* song; RELIG hymn.

liederlich *adj* [Person] slovenly; [Arbeit] sloppy; [Lebenswandel] dissolute.

lief *prät* ▷ **laufen**.

Lieferant, in (*mpl* -en, *fpl* -nen) *der, die* supplier.

lieferbar *adj* available.

liefern ◇ *vt* - **1.** [Ware - zustellen] to deliver; [- verkaufen] to supply; **jetzt bin ich geliefert** *fam* I've had it now - **2.** [Ernte, Eier] to produce - **3.** [Beispiel, Beweis] to provide; **sie lieferten sich ein spannendes Match** they provided an exciting match. ◇ *vi* to deliver.

Lieferung (*pl* -en) *die* [Versand] delivery; [Versorgung] supply.

Liefer|wagen *der* van.

Liege (*pl* -n) *die* [für Garten] sun lounger; [zum Übernachten] camp bed *UK*, cot *US*.

liegen (*prät* lag, *perf* hat gelegen) *vi* - **1.** [gen] to lie; **das Schiff liegt im Hafen** the ship is docked; **in den Bergen liegt viel Schnee** there's a lot of snow on the hills - **2.** [angelehnt sein]: **an** *ODER* **auf etw (A) liegen** to rest on sthg - **3.** [sich befinden] to be; **Dresden liegt an der Elbe** Dresden is on the Elbe - **4.** [in Reihenfolge] to lie; **sie liegt auf dem vierten Platz** she's (lying) in fourth place; **an der Spitze liegen** to be in the lead - **5.** [mit Dativ]: **Physik liegt mir nicht** physics isn't my thing; **es liegt mir viel daran** it matters a lot to me - **6.** [mit Präpositionen]: **an mir soll es nicht liegen!** don't let me stop you!; **es liegt nicht an dir** it's not your fault; **die Entscheidung liegt bei Ihnen** it's your decision; **das liegt daran, dass...** this is because...

liegen bleiben (*perf* ist liegen geblieben) *vi* (*unreg*) - **1.** [nicht aufstehen] to remain lying down; **(im Bett) liegen bleiben** to stay in bed - **2.** [Schnee, Laub] to lie - **3.** [vergessen werden] to be left behind - **4.** [unerledigt bleiben] to be left undone - **5.** [eine Panne haben] to break down.

liegen lassen (*perf* hat liegen gelassen *ODER* liegen lassen) *vt* (*unreg*) to leave; **jn/etw links liegen lassen** *fam* fig to ignore sb/sthg.

Liege|sitz *der* reclining seat.

Liege|stuhl *der* [am Strand] deckchair; [im Garten] sun lounger.

Liege|stütz (*pl* -e) *der* press-up.

Liege|wagen *der* couchette car.

lieh *prät* ▷ **leihen**.

ließ *prät* ▷ **lassen**.

liest *präs* ▷ **lesen**.

Lifestyle ['laɪfstaɪl] *der* (ohne pl) lifestyle.

Lift (*pl* -e *ODER* -s) *der* - **1.** [Aufzug] lift *UK*, elevator *US* - **2.** (*pl* Lifte) [Skilift] ski lift.

Likör (*pl* -e) *der* liqueur.

lila *adj* (*unver*) lavender; [dunkler] mauve.

Lila *das* purple; [Zartlila] lilac; [Tieflila] mauve.

Lilie ['liːljə] (*pl* -n) *die* lily.

Limit (*pl* -s) *das* limit.

Limonade (*pl* -n) *die* fizzy drink *UK*, soda *US*; [mit Zitronengeschmack] lemonade; [mit Orangengeschmack] orangeade.

Linde (*pl* -n) *die* lime tree.

lindern *vt* [Schmerzen] to relieve; [Not] to alleviate.

Lineal (*pl* -e) *das* ruler.

Linguistik *die* linguistics (*U*).

Linie ['liːnjə] (*pl* -n) *die* - **1.** [Strich, Verwandtschaftslinie] line; **sie stammt in direkter Linie vom Kaiser Karl ab** she is directly descended from Emperor Charles - **2.** [Denkrichtung] policy - **3.** [von Verkehrsmittel] number; **die Linie 3** the number 3 - **4.** [Figur]: **auf die schlanke Linie achten** to watch one's figure; **in erster Linie** first and foremost.

Linien|bus *der* bus (*forming part of public transport network*).

Linien|flug *der* scheduled flight.

Linienverkehr *der* (ohne pl) [Flugverkehr] scheduled flights *Pl*; [Omnibusverkehr] buses (*forming part of public transport network*).

linieren, liniieren *vt* to rule (lines on).

link *adj* fam abw shady.

linke, r, s *adj* - **1.** [Seitenangabe] left - **2.** [linkspolitisch] left-wing.

Linke (*pl* -n) ◇ *die* - **1.** [Hand] left hand; **zur Linken** to the left - **2.** POL: **die Linke** the Left - **3.** [Schlag] left. ◇ *der, die* [Person] left-winger.

links ◇ *adv* - **1.** [Angabe der Seite] on the left; [Angabe der Richtung] left; **links von jm/etw** on sb's/sthg's left; **nach links fahren** to turn left; **von links** from the left; **etw mit links machen** *fam* fig to do sthg easily - **2.** [verkehrt herum] inside out; **etw von links bügeln** to iron sthg on the wrong side - **3.** [linkspolitisch] left-wing; **links wählen** to vote for the Left. ◇ *präp* (+ *G*) - **1.** [Angabe der Seite] on the left-hand side of - **2.** [politisch] to the left of.

Links|abbieger *der* car turning left.

Linksaußen (*pl* **Linksaußen**) *der* outside left.

linksextrem *adj* extreme left-wing.

Links|extremist, in *der, die* left-wing extremist.

linksgerichtet *adj* left-wing.

Linkshänder, in (*mpl* -, *fpl* **-nen**) *der, die* left-hander.

linksherum *adv* - **1.** [nach links] round to the left - **2.** [falsch herum] inside out.

Links|kurve *die* left-hand bend.

linksradikal *adj* radical left-wing.

Linksverkehr *der*: **in Großbritannien herrscht Linksverkehr** people drive on the left in Great Britain.

Linse (*pl* -n) *die* - **1.** [Nahrungsmittel] lentil - **2.** [optisch] lens.

Lippe (*pl* -n) *die* lip; **keine Klage kam über ihre Lippen** she didn't utter a word of complaint.

Lippen|stift *der* lipstick.

lispeln *vi* to lisp.

Lissabon *nt* Lisbon.

List (*pl* -en) *die* - **1.** [listiges Verhalten] cunning - **2.** [listige Handlung] cunning trick.

Liste (*pl* -n) *die* list; **auf der schwarzen Liste stehen** to be on the blacklist.

listig ⬦ *adj* cunning. ⬦ *adv* cunningly.

Litauen *nt* Lithuania.

litauisch *adj* Lithuanian.

Liter (*pl* -) *der ODER das* litre; **ein Liter Milch** a litre of milk.

literarisch ⬦ *adj* literary. ⬦ *adv* - **1.** [Literatur betreffend]: **literarisch interessiert sein** to be interested in literature; **literarisch gebildet sein** to have studied literature - **2.** [gewählt] in a literary manner.

Literatur (*pl* -en) *die* literature.

Literatur|wissenschaft *die* literary studies *Pl*.

Liter|flasche *die* litre bottle.

Litfaß|säule *die* advertising column.

litt *prät* ⊳ **leiden**.

Lizenz (*pl* -en) *die* licence.

Lkw (*pl* -s), **LKW** (*pl* -s) [ɛlkɑːˈveː] (*abk für* Lastkraftwagen) *der* truck, HGV *UK*, lorry *UK*.

Lob *das* praise; **ein hohes Lob** high praise.

loben *vt* to praise; **das lobe ich mir!** [sehr gut] that's what I like (to see)!; **da lobe ich mir doch meine alte Schreibmaschine!** give me my old typewriter any day!

lobenswert *adj* commendable, praiseworthy.

Loch (*pl* **Löcher**) *das* hole; [im Zahn] cavity.

lochen *vt* to punch a hole/holes in.

Locher (*pl* -) *der* hole punch.

löchern *vt fam* to pester.

löchrig *adj* full of holes.

Locke (*pl* -n) *die* curl; **Locken haben** to have curly hair.

locken *vt* - **1.** [anlocken] to entice; **jn in eine Falle locken** to lure sb into a trap - **2.** [wellen] to curl.

Lockenwickler (*pl* -) *der* curler.

locker ⬦ *adj* - **1.** [gen] loose; **ein lockeres Mundwerk haben** to have a loose tongue - **2.** [Beziehung] casual; [Haltung] laid-back. ⬦ *adv* - **1.** [nicht fest] loosely - **2.** [zwanglos] casually - **3.** *fam* [mit Leichtigkeit] no sweat.

locker|lassen *vi* (*unreg*): **nicht lockerlassen** not to give up.

lockern *vt* - **1.** [Schraube, Griff, Erde, Krawatte] to loosen; **die Muskeln lockern** to limber up - **2.** [Gesetze, Vorschriften] to relax. ⬥ **sich lockern** *ref* - **1.** [Schraube, Zahn] to work itself loose - **2.** [Stimmung] to become more relaxed; [Muskeln, Griff] to relax.

lockig *adj* [Haare] curly; [Mensch] curly-haired.

Lock|vogel *der* decoy.

lodern *vi* [Feuer] to blaze.

Löffel (*pl* -) *der* spoon.

löffeln *vt* to spoon.

log *prät* ⊳ **lügen**.

Logarithmus (*pl* **-men**) *der* logarithm.

Loge [ˈloːʒə] (*pl* -n) *die* - **1.** [im Theater] box - **2.** [von Freimaurern, Portier] lodge.

Logik *die* logic.

logisch ⬦ *adj* logical. ⬦ *adv* logically.

Lohn (*pl* **Löhne**) *der* - **1.** [Bezahlung] wages *Pl*, pay - **2.** [Belohnung] reward.

lohnen *vt* - **1.** [rechtfertigen] to be worth; **es lohnt eine Renovierung nicht mehr** it's no longer worth repairing - **2.** *geh* [vergelten]: **jm etw lohnen** to repay sb for sthg. ⬥ **sich lohnen** *ref* to be worth it; **es lohnt sich, etw zu tun** it's worth doing sthg.

lohnend *adj* worthwhile.

Lohn|steuer *die* income tax (*paid by employees*), ≃ PAYE *UK*.

Lohnsteuerjahres|ausgleich *der* annual adjustment of income tax.

Lohnsteuer|karte *die* form filled in by employer stating employee's annual income and tax paid.

Lok (*pl* -s) *die* [railway] engine.

lokal *adj* local.

Lokal (*pl* -e) *das* bar, pub *UK*; [Restaurant] restaurant.

Lokal|nachrichten *Pl* local news (*U*).

Lokomotive [lokomoˈtiːvə] (*pl* -n) *die* [railway] engine.

London *nt* London.

Lorbeer (*pl* -en) *der* [Gewürz] bay leaf.

Lorbeer|blatt *das* bay leaf.

los ⟨⟩ *adj* [lose] loose; **jn/etw los sein** *fam* to have got rid of sb/sthg; **es ist viel/wenig/nichts los** *fam* there is a lot/not much/nothing going on; **was ist los?** *fam* what's the matter?, what's wrong?; **was ist hier los?** *fam* what's going on here? ⟨⟩ *interj* come on!

Los (*pl* -e) *das* - 1. [Losentscheid]: **durch das Los bestimmen** to decide by drawing lots - 2. [in der Lotterie] ticket; **das große Los** the jackpot - 3. *geh* [Schicksal] lot.

lösbar *adj* solvable.

los|binden *vt* (*unreg*) to untie.

löschen *vt* - 1. [Kerze, Feuer] to extinguish, to put out - 2. [Konto] to close; [Schuld, Hypothek] to pay off - 3. [Tonträger] to erase - 4. [Schiff, Ladung] to unload - 5. EDV to delete.

Löschen *das* - 1. [von Feuer] extinguishing - 2. [von Konto] closing; [von Schuld, Hypothek] paying off - 3. [von Tonträger] erasure - 4. [von Schiff, Ladung] unloading - 5. EDV deletion.

Löschpapier *das* blotting paper.

lose ⟨⟩ *adj* loose; **ein loses Mundwerk haben** to have a loose tongue. ⟨⟩ *adv* [locker] loosely.

Löse|geld *das* ransom.

losen *vi* [mit einem Los] to draw lots; **darum losen, wer/wann/was** to draw lots to see who/when/what.

lösen *vt* - 1. [trennen - Knoten] to undo; [- Bremse] to release; [- Schraube] to unscrew; [- Haare] to let down - 2. [locker machen] to loosen - 3. [abmachen]: **etw von etw lösen** to remove sthg from sthg - 4. [rechnen] to work out - 5. [klären - Aufgabe, Rätsel] to solve - 6. [Vertrag] to cancel; [Verlobung] to break off; [Ehe] to dissolve - 7. [Fahrkarte] to buy - 8. [auflösen] to dissolve - 9. [Husten, Schleim] to loosen; [Krampf] to ease. ⇒ **sich lösen** *ref* - 1. [aus Versehen] to break free; [Schuss] to go off; [Lawine] to start; **sich aus etw lösen** to break away from sthg - 2. [Tapete, Briefmarke] to come off; [Knoten] to come undone; [Schraube] to work loose - 3. [sich auflösen] to dissolve; [Schleim] to loosen - 4. [umdenken]: **sich von etw lösen** [von Vorurteilen, Vorstellung] to rid o.s. of sthg - 5. [sich trennen]: **sich von jm lösen** to break away from sb - 6. [Muskeln] to relax; [Verkrampfung, Spannung] to ease - 7. [Problem, Rätsel] to be solved.

los|fahren (*perf* ist losgefahren) *vi* (*unreg*) to set off.

los|gehen (*perf* ist losgegangen) *vi* (*unreg*) - 1. [weggehen] to set off; **auf jn losgehen** *fig* to go for sb; **auf ein Ziel losgehen** to pursue a goal - 2. [anfangen] to start; **gleich gehts los** it's just about to start; **jetzt geht das schon wieder los!** here we go again!; **los gehts!** off we go!

los|kommen (*perf* ist losgekommen) *vi* (*unreg*) to get away; **(nicht) von jm/etw loskommen** (not) to get away from sb/sthg.

los|lassen *vt* (*unreg*) - 1. [Person, Gegenstand] to let go of; **lass mich los!** let go of me!, let me go! - 2. [Tier]: **einen Hund auf jn loslassen** to set a dog on sb; **den Hund loslassen** to let the dog off the lead UK ODER leash US - 3. [Schrei, Fluch] to let out - 4. [Subj: Gedanke, Problem]: **der Gedanke lässt mich nicht los** I can't get the thought out of my head.

los|legen *vi* *fam* to get started; **mit Fragen loslegen** to start firing questions; **na, denn mal los!** fire away, then!

löslich *adj* soluble; [Kaffeepulver, Milchpulver] instant.

los|machen *vt* to undo; [Hund] to let off the lead UK ODER leash US. ⇒ **sich losmachen** *ref* to free o.s.

Losung (*pl* -en) *die* - 1. [Motto] motto; [Spruch] slogan - 2. [Kennwort] password.

Lösung (*pl* -en) *die* - 1. [gen] solution; [von Konflikt] resolution - 2. [von Eltern, Tradition] breaking away - 3. [von Ehe, Bündnis] breakup; [von Arbeitsverhältnis] termination.

los|werden (*perf* ist losgeworden) *vt* (*unreg*) *fam* - 1. [gen] to get rid of; **ich werde das Gefühl nicht los, dass...** I can't escape the feeling that... - 2. [Vermögen] to lose.

Lot (*pl* -e) *das* - 1. [Senkblei] plumb line; **etw wieder ins Lot bringen** *fig* to put sthg right - 2. SCHIFF sounding line - 3. MATH perpendicular.

löten *vt* to solder.

Lothringen *nt* Lorraine.

Lotion [lo'tsio:n] (*pl* -en) *die* lotion.

Lotse (*pl* -n) *der* - 1. [von Schiff] pilot - 2. [Fluglotse] air traffic controller.

lotsen *vt* to guide.

Lotterie [lɔtə'ri:] (*pl* -n) *die* lottery.

Lotto *das* - 1. [Glücksspiel] (national) lottery; **im Lotto gewinnen** to win the (national) lottery - 2. [Gesellschaftsspiel] lotto.

Lotto|schein *der* (national) lottery ticket.

Loveparade ['lavpərɛjd] *die* Love Parade, annual open-air mass rave and procession in the centre of Berlin.

Löwe (*pl* -n) *der* - 1. [Tier] lion - 2. [Sternzeichen, Person] Leo; **Löwe sein** to be a Leo.

Löwenzahn *der* dandelion.

Löwin (*pl* -nen) *die* lioness.

Luchs [luks] (*pl* -e) *der* lynx; **Augen wie ein Luchs haben** to have eyes like a hawk.

Lücke (*pl* -n) *die* - 1. [gen] gap; [zum Parken] space - 2. [in Gesetz] loophole.

lückenhaft ⟨⟩ *adj* [Erinnerung, Beweisführung, Wissen] sketchy; **sein Lebenslauf ist lückenhaft** he has gaps in his CV UK ODER resumé US. ⟨⟩ *adv* [sich erinnern] sketchily.

lud *prät* ⟩ **laden**.

Luft (*pl* Lüfte) *die* - 1. [gen] air; **freie Luft** open air; **die Luft anhalten** to hold one's breath;

Luft holen [atmen] to take a breath; [eine Pause machen] to catch one's breath; **frische Luft schöpfen** to get some fresh air; **nach Luft schnappen** to gasp - 2. [Platz] room; **die Luft ist rein** *fam* the coast is clear; **in der Luft liegen** to be in the air; **jn in der Luft hängen lassen** to leave sb hanging; **in die Luft gehen** *fam* to blow one's top; **mir blieb die Luft weg** *fam* I was gobsmacked.

Luftangriff *der* air raid.

Luftballon *der* balloon.

Luftbrücke *die* airlift.

luftdicht ⟨⟩ *adj* airtight. ⟨⟩ *adv* [verschließen] hermetically.

Luftdruck *der* air pressure.

lüften ⟨⟩ *vt* - 1. [Zimmer, Wäsche] to air - 2. [Geheimnis] to reveal. ⟨⟩ *vi* to let some air in.

Luftfahrt *die* aviation.

luftig ⟨⟩ *adj* - 1. [Kleidung] light - 2. [hochgelegen]: **in luftiger Höhe** high up - 3. [Raum] airy. ⟨⟩ *adv* [leicht] lightly.

Luftlinie *die*: **600 km Luftlinie** 600 km as the crow flies.

Luftmatratze *die* airbed.

Luftpirat, in *der, die* (aircraft) hijacker.

Luftpost *die* airmail; **mit** ODER **per Luftpost** (by) airmail.

Luftpumpe *die* air pump.

Luftröhre *die* windpipe.

Luftschlange *die* streamer.

Lüftung (*pl* -en) *die* - 1. [Gerät] ventilation (system) - 2. [Lüften] ventilation.

Luftverkehr *der* air traffic.

Luftverschmutzung *die* air pollution.

Luftwaffe *die* airforce; HIST Luftwaffe.

Luftzug *der* [in Gebäude] draught; [im Freien] breath of wind.

Lüge (*pl* -n) *die* lie.

lügen (*prät* log, *perf* hat gelogen) *vi* to lie; **das ist gelogen!** that's a lie!

Lügner, in (*mpl* -, *fpl* -nen) *der, die* liar.

Lümmel (*pl* -) *der fam* - 1. [Kind] rascal - 2. *abw* [Rüpel] lout.

lümmeln ⟷ **sich lümmeln** *ref fam abw* to sprawl.

Lump (*pl* -en) *der abw* scoundrel.

Lumpen (*pl* -) *der* rag.

Lunge (*pl* -n) *die* lungs *Pl*.

Lungenentzündung *die* pneumonia.

Lunte (*pl* -n) *die* fuse.

Lupe (*pl* -n) *die* magnifying glass; **jn/etw unter die Lupe nehmen** *fam fig* to examine sb/ sthg very closely.

Lust (*pl* Lüste) *die* - 1. [Bedürfnis] desire; **die Lust am Reisen ist mir vergangen** I don't feel like travelling any more; **Lust bekommen/haben, etw zu tun** to feel like doing sthg; **ich**

habe keine Lust zum Spazierengehen I don't feel like going for a walk; **Lust/keine Lust auf etw** (A) **haben** to feel/not to feel like sthg; **ich hätte jetzt Lust auf ein Eis** I fancy an ice cream; **er arbeitet ganz nach Lust und Laune** he works as and when he feels like it - 2. [Freude] pleasure; **die Lust an etw** (D) **verlieren** no longer to take any pleasure in sthg - 3. [Begierde] desires *Pl*, lust.

lüstern ⟨⟩ *adj* lascivious. ⟨⟩ *adv*: **lüstern blicken** to leer.

lustig ⟨⟩ *adj* - 1. [komisch] funny; [unterhaltsam] entertaining; **sich über jn/etw lustig machen** to make fun of sb/sthg - 2. [fröhlich - Person, Augen] merry; [- Abend] fun, enjoyable. ⟨⟩ *adv* - 1. [komisch] funnily; [unterhaltsam] entertainingly - 2. [unbekümmert] merrily.

lustlos ⟨⟩ *adj* unenthusiastic. ⟨⟩ *adv* unenthusiastically.

lutschen ⟨⟩ *vt* to suck. ⟨⟩ *vi*: **an etw** (D) **lutschen** to suck sthg.

Lutscher (*pl* -) *der* [Süßigkeit] lollipop.

Luxemburg *nt* Luxembourg.

luxemburgisch *adj* of/from Luxembourg.

luxuriös ⟨⟩ *adj* luxurious. ⟨⟩ *adv* luxuriously.

Luxus *der* luxury.

Luzern *nt* Lucerne.

Lyrik *die* lyric poetry.

lyrisch ⟨⟩ *adj* [Dichtung] lyric; [Stil] lyrical. ⟨⟩ *adv* lyrically.

m (*pl* - ODER -s), **M** (*pl* - ODER -s) [ɛm] *das* m, M.

m. *abk für* mit.

MA *abk für* **Mittelalter**.

machbar *adj* feasible.

machen ⟨⟩ *vt* - 1. [tun] to do; **so was macht man nicht!** you can't ODER mustn't do that! - 2. [herstellen] to make; **ein Foto machen** to take a photo; **etw aus etw machen** to make sthg out of sthg; **sich** (D) **etw machen lassen** to have sthg made - 3. [Summe, Ergebnis] to be; **zwei mal drei macht sechs** two times three is six; **das macht fünf Euro** that comes to five euros - 4. [mit Substantiv]: **das Abendessen machen** to make dinner; **mach bloß keine Dummheiten!** don't do anything silly!; **eine Prüfung machen** to take an exam; **den Doktor machen** to do a doctorate; **einen Handstand machen** to do a handstand; **täglich 1000 Euro Umsatz ma-**

chen to turn over 1000 euros a day - **5.** [erledigen] to do; **Einkäufe machen** to go shopping; **(seine) Hausaufgaben machen** to do one's homework; **sich** (D) **die Haare machen** to do one's hair; **da ist nichts zu machen** there's nothing we can do about it - **6.** [durchführen]: **eine Party machen** to have a party; **eine Reise/einen Spaziergang machen** to go on a journey/for a walk; **eine Pause machen** to have a break - **7.** [verursachen]: **Licht machen** to switch on the light; **was macht das schon!** so what!; **jm Angst/Freude machen** to make sb afraid/happy; **jm Hoffnung machen** to raise sb's hopes - **8.** [mit Adjektiv] to make; **sich bemerkbar machen** to become noticeable; **mach die Musik leiser** turn the music down; **jn krank/glücklich machen** to make sb ill/happy; **machs gut!** take care! - **9.** [mit Präposition]: **sie haben aus dem alten Häuschen etwas gemacht** they've really made something out of that old cottage; **sie lässt alles mit sich machen** she is very long-suffering. ⟨⟩ *vi* - **1.** [verursachen]: **macht, dass ihr bald zurück seid!** make sure you're back soon; **mach schon** ODER **doch!** *fam* get a move on! - **2.** *fam* [Toilette verrichten]: **der Hund hat vor die Haustür gemacht** the dog made a mess outside the front door; **in die Hosen machen** to wet/dirty one's pants - **3.** [mit Adjektiv]: **Joggen macht schlank** jogging helps you lose weight; **mach schnell!** hurry up! ◆ **sich machen** *ref* - **1.** *fam* [sich entwickeln] to come on; **du machst dich!** you're coming on very well - **2.** [mit Adjektiv]: **sich beliebt/verständlich machen** to make o.s. popular/understood; **der Hut macht sich gut zu Ihrem Kleid** the hat goes well with your dress - **3.** [mit Präposition]: **sich an die Arbeit machen** to get down to work; **sich auf den Weg machen** to set off; **sich** (D) **aus etw nichts machen** not to be keen on sthg; **mach dir nichts draus!** don't let it bother you!

Machenschaft (*pl* -en) *die abw* intrigue.

Macht (*pl* Mächte) *die* power; **an die Macht kommen** to come to power; **an der Macht sein** to be in power; **die Macht der Gewohnheit** force of habit; **Macht über jn haben** to have a hold on sb; **mit aller Macht** with all one's might.

Machthaber, in (*mpl* -, *fpl* -nen) *der, die*: **die Machthaber** those in power.

mächtig ⟨⟩ *adj* - **1.** [einflussreich] powerful - **2.** [Stimme, Hieb, Stamm] mighty; [Hunger, Angst] terrible; [Gebäude] enormous. ⟨⟩ *adv* [enorm] terribly.

machtlos *adj* powerless; **gegen etw machtlos sein** to be powerless in the face of sthg.

Machtprobe *die* trial of strength.

Machtwort (*pl* -e) *das*: **ein Machtwort sprechen** to put one's foot down, to exercise one's authority.

Macke (*pl* -n) *die fam* - **1.** [Tick] quirk - **2.** [Fehler]: **mein Auto hat eine Macke** there's something up ODER wrong with my car.

Madagaskar *nt* Madagascar.

Mädchen (*pl* -) *das* - **1.** [gen] girl - **2.** [Hausangestellte] maid.

Mädchenname *der* maiden name.

Made (*pl* -n) *die* maggot.

madig *adj* maggoty, full of maggots; **jm etw madig machen** *fam fig* to spoil sthg for sb.

Madonna (*pl* Madonnen) *die* - **1.** [Muttergottes] Madonna - **2.** [Bild, Plastik] madonna.

mag *präs* ▷ **mögen**.

Magazin (*pl* -e) *das* - **1.** [Illustrierte, Behälter für Patronen] magazine - **2.** [Lager] storeroom - **3.** [Fernsehsendung] magazine (programme).

Magd (*pl* Mägde) *die* - **1.** [Dienstmagd] maid - **2.** [Landarbeiterin] farmhand.

Magen (*pl* Mägen ODER -) *der* stomach; **jm auf den Magen schlagen** *fam* to upset sb; **sich** (D) **den Magen verderben** to get an upset stomach; **mir knurrt der Magen** *fam* my stomach is rumbling.

Magenbeschwerden *Pl* stomach trouble (U).

Magengeschwür *das* stomach ulcer.

Magenschmerzen *Pl* stomachache (U).

mager ⟨⟩ *adj* - **1.** [Person, Tier, Gesicht] thin - **2.** [Fleisch] lean; [Quark] low-fat - **3.** [Ergebnis, Ernte] meagre. ⟨⟩ *adv* [fettarm]: **mager essen** to eat a low-fat diet.

Magermilch *die* skimmed milk.

magersüchtig *adj* anorexic.

Magie [ma'giː] *die* magic.

magisch ⟨⟩ *adj* magical; [Kräfte] magic. ⟨⟩ *adv* magically.

Magister (*pl* -) *der* [Titel] ≈ Master's degree.

Magnesium *das* magnesium.

Magnet (*pl* -e ODER -en) *der* magnet.

magnetisch ⟨⟩ *adj* magnetic. ⟨⟩ *adv* magnetically.

Mahagoni *das* mahogany.

mähen ⟨⟩ *vt* [Rasen] to mow; [Getreide] to reap. ⟨⟩ *vi* - **1.** [mit Mäher] to mow; [mit Sense] to reap - **2.** [blöken] to bleat.

mahlen *vt* & *vi* to grind.

Mahlzeit ⟨⟩ *die* meal. ⟨⟩ *interj* hello! *(said around lunchtime to work colleagues)*.

Mähne (*pl* -n) *die* mane.

mahnen ⟨⟩ *vt* - **1.** [ermahnen] to urge; **jn mahnen, etw zu tun** to urge sb to do sthg - **2.** [erinnern]: **jn an etw** (A) **mahnen** to remind sb of sthg. ⟨⟩ *vi* [ermahnen]: **das Ozonloch mahnt zur Vorsicht beim Sonnen** because of the hole in the ozone layer it is advisable to take care whilst sunbathing.

Mahnmal *das* memorial.

Mahnung (*pl* -en) *die* - 1. [Ermahnung] exhortation - 2. [Schreiben] reminder.

Mai *der* May; **der Erste Mai** May Day; *siehe auch* **September**.

Mai|glöckchen (*pl* Maiglöckchen) *das* lily of the valley.

Mai|käfer *der* cockchafer.

Mailand *nt* Milan.

Mailbox ['meilbɔks] (*pl* -en) *die* EDV mailbox.

mailen ◇ *vi* EDV to send an e-mail. ◇ *vt* EDV to e-mail.

Main *der*: **der Main** the (River) Main.

Mainz *nt* Mainz.

Mais *der* [als Konserve] sweetcorn; [Pflanze] maize.

Mais|kolben *der* corn on the cob.

Majestät (*pl* -en) *die* Majesty.

majestätisch ◇ *adj* majestic. ◇ *adv* majestically.

Majonäse (*pl* -n), **Mayonnaise** (*pl* -n) [majɔ'nɛːzə] *die* mayonnaise.

Major (*pl* -e) *der* major.

Majoran *der* marjoram.

makaber *adj* macabre.

makellos ◇ *adj* - 1. [tadellos] impeccable; [Figur] perfect - 2. [fehlerlos] flawless. ◇ *adv* - 1. [tadellos] impeccably - 2. [sauber] spotlessly.

Make-up [meːkˈap] (*pl* -s) *das* - 1. [Schminken] make-up - 2. [Creme] foundation.

Makler, in (*mpl* -, *fpl* -nen) *der, die* [für Immobilien] estate agent *UK*, realtor *US*; [an Börse] broker.

Makrele (*pl* -n) *die* mackerel.

mal ◇ *adv fam* - 1. [irgendwann - in Zukunft] sometime, someday; [- in Vergangenheit] once; **hier stand mal ein Gebäude** there was a building here once; **aus ihr wird mal was werden** she'll be someone some ODER one day - 2. [zum Ausdruck von Verbindlichkeit]: **ich komme um neun Uhr mal vorbei** I'll drop by at nine o'clock; **wir müssen das am Sonntag mal besprechen** we ought to discuss this on Sunday - 3. [als Aufforderung]: **hör mir mal gut zu!** now listen to me carefully!; **gib mir mal bitte den Schlüssel!** would you give me the key?; **beruhige dich mal!** calm down, will you!; **sag mal!** tell me!; **hör mal!** listen! - 4. [zur Verstärkung eines Adverbs]: **nimm schon mal Platz, ich komme gleich** just take a seat, I'll be there in a minute; **vielleicht mal** maybe; **höchstens mal** at the very most - 5. [einmal]: **er redet mal so, mal so** he says one thing one minute and another thing the next. ◇ *konj* [zur Multiplikation] times.

Mal (*pl* -e ODER Mäler) *das* - 1. (*pl* Male) [Zeitpunkt] time; **letztes/nächstes Mal** last/next time; **jedes Mal** every time; **mit einem Mal(e)** all of a sudden; **von Mal zu Mal** [immer mehr] more and more; [jedes Mal] every time; **beim ersten Mal** the first time; **beim letzten Mal** last time; **zum ersten/letzten Mal** for the first/last time - 2. (*pl* Male, Mäler) [Fleck] mark; [Muttermal] birthmark; [Pigmentmal] mole.

Mal|buch *das* colouring book.

malen *vt* & *vi* to paint.

Maler (*pl* -) *der* - 1. [Künstler] painter, artist - 2. [Handwerker] painter.

Malerei (*pl* -en) *die* painting.

Malerin (*pl* -nen) *die* - 1. [Künstlerin] painter, artist - 2. [Handwerkerin] painter.

malerisch ◇ *adj* [idyllisch] picturesque. ◇ *adv* [schön] picturesquely.

mal|nehmen *vt* (*unreg*): **etw mit etw malnehmen** to multiply sthg by sthg.

Malta *nt* Malta.

Malz *das* malt.

Malz|bier *das* malt beer.

Mama (*pl* -s) *die fam* mummy *UK*, mommy *US*.

man *pron* - 1. [jemand]: **man sagte mir** I was told; **man hat ihm eine Stelle angeboten** he was offered a job - 2. [generalisierend] you; **wie sagt man das auf Deutsch?** how do you say that in German?; **das sagt man nicht** you don't say that; **man sagt, dass...** people say that...

manche, r, s ◇ *pron* - 1. [bei Dingen - einige] some; [- viele] many (things) - 2. [bei Personen - einige] some people; [- viele] many (people); **manch einer** many a person. ◇ *det* - 1. [einige] some - 2. [viele] many. ➤ **so manche, r, s** *pron* & *det* quite a few.

manchmal *adv* sometimes.

Mandarine (*pl* -n) *die* mandarin.

Mandat (*pl* -e) *das* - 1. [gen] mandate; [von Anwalt] brief - 2. [POL - Amt] seat.

Mandel (*pl* -n) *die* almond. ➤ **Mandeln** *Pl* [im Hals] tonsils.

Mandel|entzündung *die* tonsillitis (*U*).

Manege [ma'neːʒə] (*pl* -n) *die* (circus) ring.

Mangel (*pl* Mängel) *der* ODER *die* (*pl* Mängel) - 1. [an Verantwortungsbewusstsein, Geistesgegenwart] lack; [an Lebensmitteln, Medikamenten] shortage; **aus Mangel an etw (D)** for lack of sthg; **es herrscht Mangel an etw (D)** there is a shortage of sthg - 2. [Fehler] fault; **Mängel beheben** ODER **beseitigen** to rectify faults - 3. [Not] hardship. ◇ *die* (*pl* Mangeln) mangle.

Mangel|erscheinung *die* deficiency symptom.

mangelhaft ◇ *adj* [unzureichend - Schulnote] poor. ◇ *adv* poorly.

mangeln ◇ *vi*: **es mangelt jm an etw (D)** sb lacks sthg; **es mangelt an etw (D)** [nicht genug sein] there is a shortage of sthg; [fehlen] there is a lack of sthg. ◇ *vt* to mangle.

mangelnd *adj* inadequate.

mangels *präp*: **mangels einer Sache** *(G)* for lack of sthg.

Mangelware *die*: **Mangelware sein** to be a scarce commodity; *fam fig* to be thin on the ground.

Mango *(pl -s) die* mango.

Manie *(pl -n) die* - **1.** [Tick] obsession - **2.** MED mania.

Manier *(pl -en) die* manner. ◆ **Manieren** *Pl* manners.

manisch ⟨⟩ *adj* manic. ⟨⟩ *adv* [krankhaft] manically.

Manko *(pl -s) das* - **1.** [Fehler] drawback - **2.** [Geldsumme] deficit.

Mann *(pl Männer, Leute* ODER -en) *der* - **1.** [gen] man; **von Mann zu Mann** man to man - **2.** [Ehemann] husband; **seinen Mann stehen** to hold one's own. ◆ **alle Mann** *pron* fam everyone; **alle Mann an Deck!** all hands on deck! ◆ **kleine Mann** *der* fam: **der kleine Mann** the ordinary man.

Männchen *(pl -) das* - **1.** [Tier] male - **2.** *fam* [kleiner Mann] little man.

männlich ⟨⟩ *adj* - **1.** [Lebewesen] male - **2.** [viril] manly - **3.** [zum Mann gehörig] man's - **4.** GRAMM [Substantiv] masculine. ⟨⟩ *adv* [viril] in a manly way.

Mannschaft *(pl -en) die* - **1.** [im Sport, Team] team; **vor versammelter Mannschaft** *fam* in front of everybody - **2.** [Besatzung] crew - **3.** [Soldaten] men *Pl*.

Mannschafts|geist *der* team spirit.

Mannschafts|sport *der* team sport.

Manöver [ma'nø:ve] *(pl -) das* manoeuvre.

manövrieren [manø:'vri:rən] *vt & vi eigtl & fig* to manoeuvre. ◆ **sich manövrieren** *ref* [sich bringen] to manoeuvre o.s.

Manschetten|knopf *der* cufflink.

Mantel *(pl Mäntel) der* - **1.** [Kleidungsstück] coat - **2.** *fig* [Deckmantel] cloak - **3.** TECH [von Kabel] sheath.

manuell ⟨⟩ *adj* manual. ⟨⟩ *adv* manually.

Manuskript *(pl -e) das* - **1.** [Entwurf] notes *Pl* - **2.** [Handschrift, Druckvorlage] manuscript.

Mappe *(pl -n) die* - **1.** [Hülle] folder - **2.** [Tasche] briefcase.

Marathon *(pl -s) der* ODER *das* marathon.

Marathon|läufer, in *der, die* marathon runner.

Märchen *(pl -) das* - **1.** [Erzählung] fairy tale - **2.** [Lüge] tall story.

märchenhaft ⟨⟩ *adj* - **1.** [sagenhaft] fairytale - **2.** [wunderschön] wonderful - **3.** [unglaublich] fantastic. ⟨⟩ *adv* - **1.** [wunderbar] wonderfully - **2.** [unglaublich] fantastically.

Marder *(pl -) der* marten.

Margarine *die* margarine.

Margerite *(pl -n) die* daisy.

Mariä Himmelfahrt *(ohne Artikel)* Assumption.

Marien|käfer *der* ladybird *UK*, ladybug *US*.

Marihuana *das* marijuana.

Marine *die (ohne pl)* MIL navy.

marineblau *adj* navy blue.

Marionette *(pl -n) die* - **1.** [Puppe] marionette, puppet - **2.** *fig* [Person] puppet.

Mark *(pl Mark)* ⟨⟩ *die* mark. ⟨⟩ *das (ohne pl)* - **1.** [im Knochen] marrow; **es geht mir durch Mark und Bein** *fig* it goes right through me - **2.** [Konzentrat] purée.

markant *adj* striking; [Kinn, Nase] prominent.

Marke *(pl -n) die* - **1.** [Lebensmittel, Verbrauchsgüter] brand; [Auto, Gebrauchsgegenstände] make - **2.** [Briefmarke] stamp - **3.** [Erkennungszeichen - von Hund] identity disc; [- von Polizist] badge - **4.** [Wertzeichen - für Lebensmittel] coupon; [- für Garderobe] ticket *UK*, check *US* - **5.** *fam* [Person] character.

Marken|artikel *der* branded item.

Marken|zeichen *das* trademark.

markieren ⟨⟩ *vt* - **1.** [kennzeichnen] to mark - **2.** [hervorheben] to highlight - **3.** *fam* [vortäuschen] to play. ⟨⟩ *vi fam* [vortäuschen] to fake.

Markise *(pl -n) die* awning.

Markt *(pl Märkte) der* - **1.** [gen] market; **auf den** ODER **zum Markt gehen** to go to the market; **auf den Markt bringen** to put on the market - **2.** [Platz] marketplace.

Markt|forschung *die* market research.

Markt|halle *die* covered market.

Markt|lücke *die* gap in the market.

Markt|platz *der* marketplace.

Markt|preis *der* market price.

Markt|wert *der* market value.

Markt|wirtschaft *die* market economy.

Marmelade *(pl -n) die* jam.

Marmor *der* marble.

Marokkaner, in *(mpl -, fpl -nen) der, die* Moroccan.

marokkanisch *adj* Moroccan.

Marokko *nt* Morocco.

Marone *(pl -n) die* (sweet) chestnut.

marsch *interj*: **marsch, an die Arbeit/ins Bett!** off to work/to bed!; **vorwärts marsch!** forward march!

Marsch *(pl Märsche) der* - **1.** [Gehen] walk; **sich in Marsch setzen** to set off - **2.** [beim Militär, Musikstück] march.

marschieren *(perf ist marschiert) vi* - **1.** [Soldaten] to march - **2.** [gehen] to walk.

Marschmusik *die* marching music.

Märtyrer, in *(mpl -, fpl -nen) der, die* martyr.

marxistisch ⟨⟩ *adj* Marxist. ⟨⟩ *adv* in a Marxist way.

März *der* March; *siehe auch* **September**.

Marzipan (pl -e), **Marzipan** (pl -e) das marzipan (U).

Masche (pl -n) die - 1. [beim Stricken, Häkeln] stitch - 2. [Art und Weise] trick; **die neueste Masche** fam [Marotte] the latest fad; fam [Mode] the latest thing.

Maschine (pl -n) die - 1. [Gerät, Motorrad] machine - 2. fam [Motor] engine - 3. [Flugzeug] plane - 4. [Schreibmaschine]: **Maschine schreiben** to type.

maschinell ⬦ adj [Herstellung, Bearbeitung] machine (vor Subst); [Vorgang] mechanical. ⬦ adv by machine.

Maschinenbau der mechanical engineering.

Maschinen|gewehr das machine gun.

Maschinen|pistole die submachine gun.

Maschinenschaden der engine trouble (U).

maschineschreiben, maschinenschreiben vi (unreg) ⟶ **Maschine**.

Masern Pl measles (U).

Maske (pl -n) die - 1. [zum Verkleiden & EDV] mask - 2. [beim Theater] make-up.

Masken|ball der masked ball.

maskieren vt eigtl & fig to mask. ⬥ **sich maskieren** ref - 1. [sich verdecken] to disguise o.s. - 2. [sich verkleiden] to dress up.

Maskottchen (pl -) das mascot.

maskulin, maskulin adj masculine.

Maskulinum (pl Maskulina) das GRAMM masculine noun.

maß prät ⟶ **messen**.

Maß (pl -e ODER -) ⬦ das (pl Maße) - 1. [Maßeinheit] measure - 2. [Messgerät] (tape) measure - 3. [Körpermaß]: **Maß nehmen** to take measurements - 4. [Umfang, Verhältnis] degree; **in demselben/höherem Maß als** to the same/a greater degree as/than; **Maß halten** to be moderate. ⬦ die (pl Maß) Süddt & Österr [Krug] litre (of beer). ⬥ **in Maßen** adv in moderation. ⬥ **nach Maß** adv [Anzug] made-to-measure; [Urlaub] tailor-made. ⬥ **Maße** Pl - 1. [von Räumen] dimensions - 2. [von Personen] measurements.

Massage [ma'sɑːʒə] (pl -n) die massage.

Massaker (pl -) das massacre.

Maßarbeit die: **Maßarbeit sein** to be made-to-measure.

Masse (pl -n) die mass; **die breite Masse** abw the masses Pl. ⬥ **in Massen** adv [einkaufen] in bulk; **die Leute kamen in Massen** masses of people came.

Maßeinheit die unit of measurement.

massenhaft ⬦ adj in great numbers; **die massenhaften Hinrichtungen** the great number of executions. ⬦ adv in great numbers.

Massen|medien Pl mass media.

Massen|mord der mass murder.

maßgebend, maßgeblich ⬦ adj [Person] influential; [Meinung] authoritative; [Urteil, Argument] decisive. ⬦ adv: **an etw (D) maßgebend beteiligt sein** to play a decisive role in sthg.

maßgeschneidert adj made-to-measure.

massieren vt to massage.

massig ⬦ adj massive. ⬦ adv fam: **massig zu essen** loads of eat; **massig Arbeit** loads of work.

mäßig ⬦ adj - 1. [gen] moderate - 2. [mittelmäßig - Leistung, Wetter, Schüler] average. ⬦ adv - 1. [maßvoll] in moderation - 2. [wenig] moderately.

mäßigen vt [Wut] to curb; [Worte] to moderate. ⬥ **sich mäßigen** ref [Person] to restrain o.s.; [Unwetter] to die down.

massiv ⬦ adj - 1. [Holz, Metall] solid - 2. [wuchtig] massive - 3. [heftig] strong. ⬦ adv - 1. [wuchtig] massively - 2. [heftig] strongly.

Massiv (pl -e) das massif.

Maß|krug der Süddt & Österr litre beer mug.

maßlos ⬦ adj extreme. ⬦ adv extremely.

Maßnahme (pl -n) die measure; **Maßnahmen einleiten** to introduce measures; **Maßnahmen ergreifen** ODER **treffen** to take measures.

Maßstab der - 1. [auf Landkarten] scale - 2. [Richtlinie] standard. ⬥ **im Maßstab** adv: **im Maßstab 1:25000** to a scale of 1:25,000.

maßstabgetreu, maßstabsgetreu adj & adv to scale.

Mast (pl -en ODER -e) ⬦ der (pl Maste, Masten) - 1. [auf Schiffen, für Antenne] mast - 2. [Stange - für Fahne, Leitungen] pole; [- für Hochspannungsleitungen] pylon. ⬦ die (pl Masten) [Mästen] fattening (U).

mästen vt to fatten.

masturbieren vi & vt to masturbate.

Material [mate'rjɑːl] (pl -ien) das - 1. [Werkstoff, Unterlagen] material - 2. [Gerät] equipment.

materialistisch adj materialistic.

Materie [ma'teːrjə] (pl -n) die - 1. matter - 2. geh [Themenbereich] subject matter.

materiell ⬦ adj - 1. [wirtschaftlich] financial - 2. [materialistisch] materialistic - 3. [stofflich] material. ⬦ adv - 1. [materialistisch] materialistically - 2. [wirtschaftlich] financially.

Mathematik, Mathematik die mathematics (U).

Mathematiker, in (mpl -, fpl -nen) der, die mathematician.

mathematisch ⬦ adj mathematical. ⬦ adv mathematically.

Matjes|hering der salted herring.

Matratze (pl -n) die mattress.

Matrose (pl -n) der sailor.

Matsch der - 1. [Schlamm] mud; [von Schnee] slush - 2. fam [Brei] mush.

matschen vi fam [in Pfütze] to splash around; [in Schlamm] to squelch around; **mit etw matschen** [beim Essen] to make a mush of sthg.

matt ◇ adj - 1. [kraftlos] weak; [Händedruck, Reaktion] feeble - 2. [nicht glänzend] matt - 3. [trübe - Licht] dim; [- Augen, Farbe, Glanz] dull; [- Glühbirne] pearl; [- Glas] frosted - 4. [im Schach]: **matt sein** to be checkmated. ◇ adv - 1. [im Schach]: **jn matt setzen** to checkmate sb - 2. [trübe] dimly - 3. [kraftlos] weakly; [reagieren] feebly.

Matte (pl -n) die mat.

Mauer (pl -n) die wall.

mauern ◇ vi - 1. [bauen] to build - 2. SPORT to play defensively. ◇ vt [bauen] to build.

Mauerwerk das masonry.

Maul (pl Mäuler) das - 1. [bei Tieren] mouth - 2. salopp [Mundwerk] trap; **halts Maul!** shut your trap!; **böses Maul** malicious tongue.

maulen vi fam abw to moan.

Maulkorb der muzzle.

Maulwurf der mole.

Maulwurfshügel der molehill.

Maurer, in (mpl -, fpl -nen) der, die bricklayer.

Mauritius nt Mauritius.

Maus (pl Mäuse) die - 1. EDV [Tier] mouse - 2. fam [Mädchen] cutie; **eine graue Maus** fam abw a nondescript kind of woman.

Mausefalle die mousetrap.

mausern ⇒ **sich mausern** ref - 1. [Vögel] to moult - 2. [Person] to blossom.

mausetot adj fam as dead as a doornail.

Mausklick (pl -s) der EDV mouse click; **per Mausklick die Adresse einfügen** to add the address by clicking the mouse.

Mauspad (pl -s) das mouse mat.

Mautgebühr die Österr toll.

Mautstelle die Österr tollgate.

max. (abk für maximal) max.

maximal ◇ adj maximum. ◇ adv: **das maximal zulässige Gewicht** the maximum permitted weight; **maximal 30 Personen** a maximum of 30 people.

Maximum (pl Maxima) das maximum.

Mayonnaise die = Majonäse.

Mazedonien [maze'do:njən] nt Macedonia.

MB (abk für Megabyte) MB, Mb.

MdB (abk für Mitglied des Bundestags) Member of the "Bundestag".

Mechanik (pl -en) die - 1. [Fach] mechanics (U) - 2. [Mechanismus] mechanism.

Mechaniker, in (mpl -, fpl -nen) der, die mechanic.

mechanisch ◇ adj mechanical. ◇ adv mechanically.

Mechanismus (pl Mechanismen) der mechanism.

meckern vi - 1. [Ziege] to bleat - 2. fam [nörgeln]: **über jn/etw meckern** to moan about sb/sthg.

Mecklenburg-Vorpommern nt Mecklenburg-West Pomerania.

Medaille [me'daljə] (pl -n) die medal.

Medaillon [medal'jɔŋ] (pl -s) das - 1. [Schmuck] locket - 2. [Fleisch, Fisch] medallion.

Medien Pl media.

Medikament (pl -e) das medicine; **ein Medikament gegen etw** a medicine for sthg.

Meditation (pl -en) die meditation.

meditieren vi - 1. [versunken sein] to meditate - 2. [nachdenken]: **über etw (A) meditieren** to meditate on sthg.

Medium ['me:djʊm] (pl Medien) das medium.

Medizin (pl -en) die medicine.

Mediziner, in (mpl -, fpl -nen) der, die [Arzt] doctor; [Student] medical student.

medizinisch ◇ adj - 1. [heilkundlich, ärztlich] medical - 2. [heilend] medicinal. ◇ adv medically.

Meer (pl -e) das eigtl & fig sea; **ans Meer fahren** to go to the seaside.

Meerenge die strait.

Meeresfrüchte Pl seafood (U).

Meeresgrund der seabed.

Meeresspiegel der sea level.

Meerrettich der horseradish.

Meerschweinchen (pl -) das guinea pig.

Meerwasser das seawater.

Megafon (pl -e), **Megaphon** (pl -e) [mega'fo:n] das megaphone.

Mehl das - 1. [zum Backen] flour - 2. [Pulver - von Holz] sawdust; [- von Knochen] meal; [- von Gestein] powder.

Mehlschwitze (pl -n) die roux.

mehr ◇ pron [komparativ von viel] more. ◇ adv - 1. [komparativ von viel] more; **50 Euro, mehr nicht?** 50 euros, no more than that?; **er ist mehr Gelehrter als Künstler** he is more of a scholar than an artist - 2. [übrig] more; **mehr denn je** more than ever; **es ist keiner mehr da** there is no one left; **nichts mehr** nothing more - 3. [zeitlich]: **nicht mehr** not any longer; **du bist doch kein Kind mehr!** you are not a child any more; **immer mehr, mehr und mehr** more and more; **mehr oder weniger** more or less.

Mehraufwand der extra expenditure.

mehrdeutig adj ambiguous.

mehrere det & pron several. ⇒ **mehreres** pron several things. ⇒ **zu mehreren** adv: **sie kommen zu mehreren** several (of them) are coming.

mehrfach ◇ *adj* multiple; [Olympiasieger] several times over; **ein Bericht in mehrfacher Ausfertigung** several copies of a report; **in mehrfacher Hinsicht** in more than one respect. ◇ *adv* several times.

mehrfarbig ◇ *adj* multicoloured. ◇ *adv* in many colours.

Mehrheit (*pl* -en) *die* majority; **mit großer/ knapper Mehrheit** by a large/narrow majority; **die absolute Mehrheit** an absolute majority.

mehrheitlich ◇ *adj* majority. ◇ *adv* by a majority.

mehrmalig *adj* repeated.

mehrmals *adv* several times.

mehrsprachig ◇ *adj* [Wörterbuch, Ausgabe, Person] multilingual; [Unterhaltung] in several languages. ◇ *adv*: **mehrsprachig aufwachsen** to grow up multilingual.

mehrstimmig ◇ *adj* for several voices. ◇ *adv* in harmony.

Mehrwertsteuer *die* VAT *UK*, sales tax *US*.

Mehrzahl *die* - 1. [größerer Anteil] majority - 2. [Plural] plural.

Mehrzweckhalle *die* multipurpose hall.

Meile (*pl* -n) *die* mile.

meilenweit *adv* for miles; **meilenweit entfernt** miles away.

mein, e ◇ *det* my; **meine Damen und Herren** ladies and gentlemen. ◇ *pron* mine.

meine, r, s ODER **meins** *pron* mine.

Meinleid *der* perjury (*U*).

meinen ◇ *vt* - 1. [denken, glauben] to think; **was meinst du dazu?** what do you think? - 2. [sagen] to say; **was meint er?** *fam* what did he say? - 3. [zum Ausdruck einer Intention] to mean; **etw ironisch meinen** to mean sthg ironically; **wie meinen Sie das?** what do you mean by that?; **das war nicht so gemeint** it wasn't meant like that; **gut gemeint** well-intentioned. ◇ *vi* to think; **ich meine ja nur!** it was just a suggestion; **meinen Sie?** do you think so?; **wie meinen Sie?** what did you say?; **wie Sie meinen!** as you wish!

meiner *pron* (*Genitiv von ich*) of me; **er erinnert sich meiner** he remembers me.

meinetwegen *adv* - 1. [mir zuliebe] for my sake - 2. [wegen mir] because of me - 3. [von mir aus] as far as I'm concerned; **(also) meinetwegen!** if you like.

meinetwillen ➡ **um meinetwillen** *adv* for my sake.

Meinung (*pl* -en) *die* opinion; **eine vorgefasste Meinung** a preconceived idea; **anderer Meinung sein** to be of a different opinion; **der Meinung sein, dass...** to be of the opinion that...; **einer** ODER **derselben Meinung sein** to agree; **jm die Meinung sagen** *fam fig* to give sb a piece of one's mind; **meiner Meinung nach** in my opinion.

Meinungslaustausch *der* exchange of views.

Meinungslfreiheit *die* freedom of expression.

Meinungsumlfrage *die* opinion poll.

Meinungslverschiedenheit *die* difference of opinion.

Meise (*pl* -n) *die* tit.

Meißel (*pl* -) *der* chisel.

meißeln *vi* & *vt* to chisel.

meist *adv* usually, mostly. ➡ **am meisten** *adv* most; **die am meisten besuchte Ausstellung** the most visited exhibition.

meiste ◇ *adj* (the) most; **die meisten Leute** most people; **er hat das meiste Geld** he has the most money. ◇ *pron*: **das/die meiste** (the) most. ➡ **die meisten** *pron* most people.

meistens *adv* usually, mostly.

Meister (*pl* -) *der* - 1. [Handwerker] master craftsman; **seinen Meister machen** *fam* to get one's master craftsman's certificate - 2. [Experte, Künstler] master - 3. [im Sport] champion.

Meisterin (*pl* -nen) *die* [Handwerkerin] master craftswoman; [Expertin, Künstlerin] master; [im Sport] champion.

meistern *vt* - 1. [bewältigen] to master - 2. *geh* [zügeln] to control.

Meisterschaft (*pl* -en) *die* - 1. SPORT championship - 2. [Können] mastery.

Meisterlwerk *das* masterpiece.

Mekka *nt* Mecca.

melancholisch [melaŋ'koːlɪʃ] ◇ *adj* melancholy. ◇ *adv* in a melancholy way.

melden *vt* - 1. [anzeigen, berichten] to report; [Geburt] to register; **(bei jm) nichts/nicht viel zu melden haben** *fam fig* to have no/little say (with sb) - 2. [anmelden] to announce. ➡ **sich melden** *ref* - 1. [sich bemerkbar machen - im Unterricht] to put one's hand up; [- Finder] to make o.s. known - 2. [Nachricht geben]: **melde dich mal wieder!** keep in touch!; **sich bei jm melden** [bei Freunden] to get in touch with sb; [bei Polizei] to report to sb - 3. [am Telefon] to answer; **es meldet sich niemand** there's no answer - 4. [sich anmelden] to register; **sich freiwillig zu etw melden** to volunteer for sthg.

Meldung (*pl* -en) *die* - 1. [Nachricht, Anzeige] report - 2. [Mitteilung] announcement - 3. [Anmeldung] entry.

melken (*prät* **melkte** ODER **molk**, *perf* **hat gemolken**) *vt* & *vi* to milk.

Melodie [melo'diː] (*pl* -n) *die* tune.

melodisch ◇ *adj* melodic. ◇ *adv* melodically.

Melone (*pl* -n) *die* - 1. [Frucht] melon - 2. [Hut] bowler (hat).

Membran (*pl* -en) *die* - 1. TECH diaphragm - 2. BIOL, CHEM & PHYS membrane.

Memoiren [me'moɑːrən] *Pl* memoirs.

Menge (*pl* -n) *die* - 1. [Anzahl] amount; **die doppelte/dreifache Menge** twice/three times the amount; **in rauen Mengen** *fam*: **die Leute kamen in rauen Mengen** loads of people came - 2. [Vielzahl] a lot *ODER* lots; **eine Menge Bücher** a lot *ODER* lots of books - 3. *(ohne pl)* [Menschenmasse] crowd - 4. MATH set. ➤ **eine ganze Menge** *adv* quite a lot; **eine ganze Menge Geld** quite a lot of money. ➤ **jede Menge** *adv fam* loads; **jede Menge Arbeit** loads of work.

Mengenlehre *die* MATH set theory.

mengenmäßig ⟨⟩ *adj* quantitative. ⟨⟩ *adv* quantitatively.

Mengen|rabatt *der* bulk discount.

Mensa (*pl* **Mensen**) *die* UNI university canteen.

Mensch (*pl* -en) ⟨⟩ *der* - 1. [Art, Lebewesen] human (being); **der Mensch ist ein vernunftbegabtes Tier** man is a rational animal - 2. [Person] person. ⟨⟩ *interj* [wütend] for heaven's sake!; [begeistert] wow! ➤ **kein Mensch** *pron* no one.

Menschen|kenntnis *die* knowledge of human nature.

menschenleer *adj* deserted.

Menschen|menge *die* crowd.

Menschenrechte *Pl* human rights.

Menschen|seele *die*: **keine Menschenseele** not a soul.

menschenunwürdig *adj* inhumane.

Menschenverstand *der*: **der gesunde Menschenverstand** common sense.

Menschenwürde *die* human dignity.

Menschheit *die* humanity, mankind.

menschlich ⟨⟩ *adj* - 1. [des Menschen] human - 2. [human] humane. ⟨⟩ *adv* [human] humanely.

Menstruation (*pl* -en) *die* MED menstruation.

Mentalität (*pl* -en) *die* mentality.

Menthol *das* menthol.

Menü (*pl* -s) *das* - 1. [Speisenfolge] set menu - 2. EDV menu.

merken *vt* to notice; **sich** (*D*) **etw merken** to remember sthg; **du merkst aber auch alles!** *fam iron* how observant of you!

Merkmal (*pl* -e) *das* feature.

Merk|satz *der* mnemonic.

merkwürdig ⟨⟩ *adj* strange. ⟨⟩ *adv* strangely.

Messe (*pl* -n) *die* - 1. [Gottesdienst] mass - 2. [Ausstellung] (trade) fair.

messen (*präs* **misst**, *prät* **maß**, *perf* **hat gemessen**) ⟨⟩ *vt* to measure; [Temperatur] to take. ⟨⟩ *vi* [eine bestimmte Größe haben] to measure; **er misst 1,76 m** he is 1.76m tall.

Messer (*pl* -) *das* [zum Schneiden] knife; [zum Rasieren] razor. ➤ **bis aufs Messer** *adv* to the bitter end.

messerscharf ⟨⟩ *adj* razor-sharp. ⟨⟩ *adv* [scharfsinnig] incisively.

Messe|stand *der* stand at a (trade) fair.

Messing *das* brass.

Messung (*pl* -en) *die* measurement.

Metall (*pl* -e) *das* metal.

Metall|arbeiter, in *der, die* metalworker.

Metall|industrie *die* metalworking industry.

metallisch ⟨⟩ *adj* metallic. ⟨⟩ *adv*: **metallisch schimmern** to have a metallic gleam.

Metapher [me'tafɐ] (*pl* -n) *die* metaphor.

Meteor (*pl* -e) *der* meteor.

Meteorologe (*pl* -n) *der* weather forecaster.

Meteorologin (*pl* -nen) *die* weather forecaster.

Meter (*pl* -) *das* & *der* metre; **zwei Meter breit/hoch/lang/tief sein** to be two metres wide/high/long/deep.

Meter|maß *das* tape measure.

Methan *das* methane.

Methode (*pl* -n) *die* method.

methodisch ⟨⟩ *adj* methodical. ⟨⟩ *adv* methodically.

Mett|wurst *die* soft, smoked pork or beef sausage, usually spread on bread.

Metzger (*pl* -) *der* butcher.

Metzgerei (*pl* -en) *die* butcher's.

Metzgerin (*pl* -nen) *die* butcher.

Meute (*pl* -n) *die* - 1. [Hunde] pack - 2. *fam* [Menschen] mob.

Meuterei (*pl* -en) *die* [auf Schiff] mutiny; [in Gefängnis] revolt.

meutern *vi* - 1. [sich auflehnen - Besatzung] to mutiny; [- Strafgefangene] to revolt - 2. *fam* [sich weigern] to protest.

Mexiko *nt* Mexico.

MEZ [ɛmʔɛːˈtsɛt] (*abk für* **mitteleuropäische Zeit**) *die* CET.

MFG [ɛmʔɛfˈɡeː] (*pl* -s) *die abk für* **Mitfahrgelegenheit**.

mg (*abk für* **Milligramm**) mg.

miauen *vi* to miaow.

mich *pron* (*Akkusativ von ich*) - 1. [Personalpronomen] me - 2. [Reflexivpronomen] myself; **ich entschied mich zu kündigen** I decided to hand in my notice.

Miene (*pl* -n) *die* expression; **keine Miene verziehen** not to bat an eyelid.

mies *fam abw* ⟨⟩ *adj* lousy. ⟨⟩ *adv*: **mies gelaunt sein** to be in a foul mood.

Miese *Pl fam*: **in den Miesen sein, Miese haben** to be in the red; **Miese machen** to make a loss.

Mies|muschel *die* mussel.

Miete (*pl* -n) *die* [für Wohnung, Geschäftsfläche, Garage] rent; [für Fahrzeug] hire charge *UK*, rental *US*; **zur Miete wohnen** to live in rented accommodation.

mieten *vt*: **(sich** (D)) **etw mieten** [Wohnung, Geschäftsfläche, Garage] to rent; [Fahrzeug] to hire *UK*, to rent *US*.

Mieter, in (*mpl* -, *fpl* -nen) *der, die* tenant.

Miet|preis *der* rent.

Miets|haus *das* block of flats *UK*, apartment building *US*.

Miet|vertrag *der* [für Wohnung, Geschäftsfläche] lease; [für Fahrzeug] hire *UK* ODER rental *US* agreement.

Migräne *die* migraine.

Mikro|chip *der* microchip.

Mikrofon (*pl* -e), **Mikrophon** (*pl* -e) *das* microphone.

Mikroskop (*pl* -e) *das* microscope.

mikroskopisch ◇ *adj* microscopic. ◇ *adv* - 1. [mit einem Mikroskop] under the microscope - 2. [winzig] microscopically.

Mikrowellen|herd *der* microwave (oven).

Milch *die* milk.

Milch|flasche *die* [für Säuglinge] feeding bottle; [von Molkerei] milk bottle.

milchig ◇ *adj* milky. ◇ *adv*: **milchig trüb** milky and cloudy.

Milch|produkt *das* dairy product.

Milch|pulver *das* powdered milk.

Milch|reis *der* (ohne pl) rice pudding.

Milch|straße *die* ASTRON Milky Way.

Milch|zahn *der* milk tooth.

mild, milde ◇ *adj* - 1. [gen] mild - 2. [Licht, Worte, Lächeln] gentle - 3. [Strafe, Urteil] lenient; [Herrscher] benevolent. ◇ *adv* - 1. [urteilen, strafen] leniently - 2. [scheinen, wehen, lächeln] gently - 3. [nicht scharf - würzen] lightly.

Milde *die* - 1. [von Urteil] leniency - 2. [von Licht] gentleness; [von Abend, Klima, Aroma] mildness.

mildern *vt* - 1. [abschwächen - Wut, Worte, Urteil] to moderate; [- Schärfe] to reduce; [- Aufprall] to soften - 2. [lindern] to alleviate, to relieve. ◆ **sich mildern** *ref* - 1. [Wut, Zorn] to abate - 2. [Klima] to become milder.

Milieu [mi'ljø:] (*pl* -s) *das* - 1. [Umfeld, Umwelt] environment - 2. [Unterwelt] world of prostitution.

militant ◇ *adj* militant. ◇ *adv* militantly.

Militär (*pl* -s) ◇ *das*: **das Militär** the military. ◇ *der* army officer.

Militärdienst *der* military service.

militärisch ◇ *adj* military. ◇ *adv* militarily.

Militär|regierung *die* military government.

Milliardär, in (*mpl* -e, *fpl* -nen) *der, die* billionaire.

Milliarde (*pl* -n) *die* billion.

Milligramm (*pl* -) *das* milligram.

Milliliter (*pl* -) *der* millilitre.

Millimeter (*pl* -) *der* millimetre.

Millimeterpapier *das* graph paper.

Million (*pl* -en) *die* million.

Millionär, in (*mpl* -e, *fpl* -nen) *der, die* millionaire.

Millionen|stadt *die* city with a population of over one million.

Milz (*pl* -en) *die* spleen.

Milzbrand *der* (ohne Pl) foot and mouth disease.

Mimik *die* (ohne pl) facial expressions and gestures.

Minderheit (*pl* -en) *die* minority; **in der Minderheit sein** to be in a/the minority.

minderjährig *adj* underage.

Minderjährige (*pl* -n) *der, die* minor.

mindern *vt* [Strafmaß, Preis, Wert] to reduce; [Ansehen] to diminish.

minderwertig ◇ *adj* inferior. ◇ *adv* [herstellen] poorly.

Mindestalter *das* minimum age.

mindeste *adj* slightest; **das ist das Mindeste, was man erwarten kann** that is the least you can expect. ◆ **nicht im Mindesten** *adv* not in the slightest.

mindestens *adv* at least.

Mindest|lohn *der* minimum wage.

Mine (*pl* -n) *die* - 1. [Schreibutensil - von Kugelschreiber] refill; [- von Bleistift] lead - 2. [Bergwerk, Sprengsatz] mine; [Stollen] tunnel.

Mineral (*pl* -e ODER -ien) *das* mineral.

Mineral|öl *das* mineral oil.

Mineralöl|steuer *die* tax on oil.

Mineral|wasser *das* mineral water.

mini *adv*: **mini tragen** to wear a mini.

Mini (*pl* -s) ◇ *das* - 1. (ohne pl, ohne Artikel) [Mode] miniskirts *Pl* - 2. *fam* [Kleid] mini. ◇ *der fam* [Rock] mini.

minimal ◇ *adj* minimal. ◇ *adv* minimally.

Minimum (*pl* Minima) *das* minimum (U).

Minister (*pl* -) *der* minister.

ministeriell ◇ *adj* ministerial. ◇ *adv* ministerially.

Ministerin (*pl* -nen) *die* minister.

Ministerium [mɪnɪs'te:rjʊm] (*pl* Ministerien) *das* ministry; **Ministerium des Inneren/der Finanzen** interior/finance ministry.

Minister|präsident, in *der, die* - 1. [von Bundesländern] minister president, title given to leader of government in the German federal states - 2. [Premierminister] prime minister.

Minister|rat *der* Council of Ministers.

minus ◇ *präp* minus. ◇ *adv*: minus dreizehn Grad minus thirteen degrees. ◇ *konj*: zehn minus drei ten minus three.

Minus *das (ohne pl)* - **1.** [Fehlbetrag] deficit; **im Minus stehen** to be in the red - **2.** [Zeichen] minus (sign).

Minute *(pl -n) die* minute; **auf die Minute pünktlich** on the dot.

Minze *(pl -n) die* mint.

Mio. *(abk für Million)* m.

mir *pron (Dativ von ich)* - **1.** (to) me; **er sagte es mir** he told me; **das gehört mir** this is mine, this belongs to me; **mit mir** with me - **2.** [Reflexivpronomen] myself.

Misch|brot *das* bread made from a mixture of rye and wheat flour.

mischen *vt* [Farben, Zutaten] to mix; [Karten] to shuffle; **etw mit etw mischen** to mix sthg with sthg. ► **sich mischen** *ref*: **sich unter etw (A) mischen** to mix with sthg.

Mischling *(pl -e) der* [Tier] half-breed.

Mischung *(pl -en) die* mixture.

missachten *vt* - **1.** [nicht befolgen] to disregard - **2.** [verachten] to despise.

missbilligen *vt* to disapprove of.

Miss|brauch *der* - **1.** [sexuell, von Medikamenten, von Drogen] abuse - **2.** [schlechter Gebrauch] misuse.

missbrauchen *vt* - **1.** [ausnutzen - Macht, Mittel] to misuse; [- Vertrauen] to abuse; [- Gutmütigkeit] to take advantage of - **2.** [übermäßig nutzen, sexuell] to abuse.

missen *vt* to do without; **etw nicht (mehr) missen wollen** not to want to be without sthg.

Misserfolg *(pl -e) der* failure.

missfallen *(präs* missfällt, *prät* missfiel, *perf* hat missfallen) *vi*: **es missfällt mir, wie sie...** I dislike the way she...; **der Plan missfiel ihm** he disliked the plan.

Missfallen *das* displeasure.

missgebildet *adj* deformed.

Missgeschick *(pl -e) das* mishap; **jm passiert ein Missgeschick** sb has a mishap.

missglücken *(perf* ist missglückt) *vi* to be unsuccessful; **der Versuch ist mir missglückt** my attempt was unsuccessful.

missgönnen *vt*: **jm etw missgönnen** to begrudge sb sthg.

Missgunst *die* resentment.

misshandeln *vt* to ill-treat.

Misshandlung *(pl -en) die* ill-treatment *(U)*.

Mission *(pl -en) die* mission.

Misskredit *der*: **jn in Misskredit bringen** to discredit sb; **in Misskredit geraten** ODER **kommen** to be discredited.

misslang *prät* ▷ **misslingen**.

misslingen *(prät* misslang, *perf* ist misslungen) *vi* to fail; **das Experiment ist mir misslungen** my experiment was a failure; **ein misslungener Versuch** an unsuccessful attempt.

misslungen *pp* ▷ **misslingen**.

missmutig ◇ *adj* [Person, Charakter] bad-tempered; [Gesicht, Laune] sullen; **missmutig sein** to be in a bad mood. ◇ *adv* bad-temperedly; [ansehen] sullenly.

missraten *(präs* missrät, *prät* missriet, *perf* ist missraten) ◇ *vi*: **der Braten war ihr missraten** her roast had turned out badly. ◇ *adj* which/who turned out badly.

misst *präs* ▷ **messen**.

misstrauen *vi*: **jm/etw misstrauen** to mistrust sb/sthg.

Misstrauen *das* mistrust.

misstrauisch ◇ *adj* mistrustful; **jm gegenüber misstrauisch sein** to be mistrustful of sb. ◇ *adv* mistrustfully.

Missverhältnis *(pl -se) das* discrepancy.

Missverständnis *(pl -nisse) das* misunderstanding.

missverstehen *(prät* missverstand, *perf* hat missverstanden) *vt* to misunderstand.

Misswirtschaft *die* mismanagement.

Mist *der* - **1.** [Dung] dung; [Düngemittel] manure - **2.** *fam fig & abw* [Plunder, Blödsinn] rubbish; **Mist machen** ODER **bauen** to make a mess of things - **3.** *fam* [als Ausruf]: **(so ein) Mist!** damn it!

mit ◇ *präp (+ D)* - **1.** [zusammen mit] with; **er kommt mit seiner Frau** he's coming with his wife; **Kaffee mit Zucker** coffee with sugar; **ein Haus mit Garten** a house with a garden; **eine Scheibe Brot mit Butter** a slice of bread and butter; **sich mit jm unterhalten** to talk to sb - **2.** [modal]: **mit lauter Stimme** in a loud voice; **mit Nachdruck** emphatically; **mit 100 Stundenkilometern** at 100 kilometres per hour; **mit Verspätung eintreffen** to arrive late - **3.** [mittels] with; **mit dem Hammer** with a hammer; **mit dem Zug** by train; **mit der Post** by post; **mit Scheck bezahlen** to pay by cheque - **4.** [stellt Bezug her]: **wie weit bist du mit deiner Arbeit?** how far have you got with your work?; **wie wäre es mit einer Tasse Kaffee?** how about a cup of coffee?; **er hat es mit dem Magen** he has stomach trouble - **5.** [temporal] at; **mit jedem Tag** every day; **mit 16 Jahren** at (the age of) 16; **mit der Zeit** in (the course of) time. ◇ *adv* - **1.** [auch] too; **sie war nicht mit dabei** she wasn't there - **2.** [unter anderen]: **er ist mit der beste Schüler seiner Klasse** he is one of the best pupils in his class.

Mitarbeit *die* [an Projekt] collaboration; [von Schülern, Bevölkerung] participation.

mit|arbeiten vi - **1.** [in Projekt] to collaborate; [im Haushalt] to help out; **bei/an etw (D) mitarbeiten** to collaborate on sthg - **2.** [in der Schule] to participate.

Mit|arbeiter, in der, die [Betriebsangehörige] colleague, co-worker US.

mit|bekommen vt (unreg) - **1.** [verstehen] to follow - **2.** [aufschnappen]: **etw von etw mitbekommen** to hear sthg about sthg; **(von etw) nicht viel mitbekommen** not to take much (of sthg) in - **3.** [bekommen]: **etw mitbekommen** to get sthg to take with one.

Mit|bestimmung die codetermination.

Mit|bewohner, in der, die [in Haus] other occupant; [in Wohnung] flatmate UK, roommate US.

mit|bringen vt (unreg) - **1.** [Geschenk, Personen] to bring (with one); [von Reise] to bring back; **jm etw mitbringen** to bring sthg for sb - **2.** [Fähigkeiten] to have.

Mit|bürger, in der, die fellow citizen.

miteinander adv [auskommen, streiten, flirten] with each other; [reden, verbinden] to each other; [gemeinsam] together. ◆ **alle miteinander** pron all (together).

mit|erleben vt to witness.

Mitesser (pl -) der blackhead.

mit|fahren (perf ist mitgefahren) vi (unreg) to go/come along; **mit** ODER **bei jm mitfahren** to get a lift UK ODER ride US with sb.

Mitfahr|gelegenheit die lift UK, ride US.

Mitfahr|zentrale, Mitfahrerzentrale die agency which organizes lifts, with passengers contributing to costs.

mit|fühlen vi: **mit jm mitfühlen** to sympathize with sb. ◇ vt to share.

mit|geben vt (unreg): **jm etw mitgeben** to give sb sthg.

Mitgefühl das sympathy.

mit|gehen (perf ist mitgegangen) vi (unreg) - **1.** [mitkommen] to go/come along; **mit jm mitgehen** to go/come with sb - **2.** [teilhaben] to be carried along - **3.** fam [stehlen]: **etw mitgehen lassen** to pinch sthg.

mitgenommen ◇ pp ▷ **mitnehmen**. ◇ adj worn out; **mitgenommen aussehen** to look worn out.

Mitgift (pl -en) die dowry.

Mitglied das member.

Mitglieds|beitrag der membership fee.

Mitgliedschaft (pl -en) die membership (U).

mit|halten vi (unreg): **bei etw (nicht) mithalten können** (not) to be able to keep up in sthg; **mit jm/etw (nicht) mithalten können** (not) to be able to keep up with sb/sthg.

mithilfe ◇ adv: **mithilfe von etw/** with the help of sthg/sb. ◇ präp: **mithilfe js/einer Sache** with the help of sb/sthg.

mit|hören ◇ vi [zufällig] to overhear; [heimlich] to listen in. ◇ vt [zufällig] to overhear; [heimlich] to listen in on.

mit|kommen (perf ist mitgekommen) vi (unreg) - **1.** [auch kommen] to come along; **kommst du mit?** are you coming? - **2.** [folgen können] to keep up; **da komme ich nicht (mehr) mit!** fam it's beyond me! - **3.** [eintreffen] to arrive.

Mitleid das pity; **mit jm Mitleid haben** ODER **empfinden** to feel pity for sb.

Mitleidenschaft die: **jn/etw in Mitleidenschaft ziehen** to affect sb/sthg.

mitleidig ◇ adj pitying. ◇ adv pityingly.

mit|machen ◇ vt - **1.** [Spiel, Kurs] to take part in; [Mode] to follow; **das mache ich nicht mehr länger mit** I'm not going to put up with this any longer - **2.** [erledigen]: **etw für jn mitmachen** to do sthg for sb - **3.** [aushalten] to put up with; **sie hat schon viel mitgemacht** she has been through a lot. ◇ vi [sich beteiligen] to take part; **bei etw (nicht) mitmachen** (not) to take part in sthg.

Mitmenschen Pl fellow human beings ODER men.

mit|mischen vi fam: **bei etw mitmischen** [sich einmischen] to interfere in sthg; [teilnehmen] to get involved in sthg.

mit|nehmen vt (unreg) - **1.** [mit sich nehmen] to take (with one); **ich kann dich bis zum Bahnhof mitnehmen** I can give you a lift UK ODER ride US to the station; **sich (D) etw mitnehmen** to take sthg (with one) - **2.** [strapazieren] to take it out of - **3.** [kaufen] to buy - **4.** [stehlen] to make off with - **5.** fam [wahrnehmen, besuchen] to take in.

Mit|reisende die, der fellow passenger.

mit|reißen vt (unreg) - **1.** [begeistern] to carry away - **2.** [fortreißen - bei Sturz] to pull down; [- bei Lawine] to sweep away.

mitsamt präp: **mitsamt einer Sache (D)** together with sthg.

mit|schreiben (unreg) ◇ vt - **1.** [festhalten] to take down - **2.** [Klassenarbeit, Prüfung] to do. ◇ vi [festhalten] to take notes.

Mitschuld die share of the blame.

mitschuldig adj: **(an etw (D)) mitschuldig sein** to be partly to blame (for sthg).

Mit|schüler, in der, die schoolmate.

mit|spielen ◇ vi - **1.** [auch spielen]: **bei/in etw (D) mitspielen** [Spiel] to join in sthg; [Mannschaft, Orchester] to play in sthg; [Theatergruppe, Film] to act in sthg - **2.** [wichtig sein]: **bei etw mitspielen** to play a part in sthg - **3.** [mitmachen] to play along; **bei etw mitspielen** to go along with sthg - **4.** [schaden]: **jm übel mitspielen** to give sb a hard time. ◇ vt [Spiel] to play.

Mit|spieler, in der, die [bei Spiel, in Mannschaft] other player.

Mittag (*pl* -e) *der* midday; **am Mittag** at midday; **über Mittag** at lunchtime; **zu Mittag essen** to have lunch; **gestern/heute/morgen Mittag** at midday yesterday/today/tomorrow.

Mittaglessen *das* lunch.

mittags *adv* at midday.

Mittagslpause *die* lunch break.

Mittagslschlaf *der* (*ohne pl*) afternoon nap.

Mitte (*pl* -n) *die* middle; **in der Mitte** in the middle; **Mitte vierzig** in one's mid-forties; **Mitte nächster Woche** in the middle of next week.

mitlteilen *vt*: **jm etw mitteilen** to tell sb sthg.

Mitlteilung *die* communication; [an Presse] statement; **jm eine Mitteilung machen** to inform sb; **eine schriftliche Mitteilung** a written communication.

Mittel (*pl* -) *das* - 1. [Hilfsmittel] means (*sg*); **mit allen Mitteln** by every means - 2. [Medikament] medicine; **ein Mittel gegen etw** a remedy for sthg - 3. [zur Reinigung] cleaning agent.
➥ **Mittel** *Pl* [Geldmittel] means; **öffentliche Mittel** public funds.

Mittelalter *das* (*ohne pl*) Middle Ages *Pl*.

mittelalterlich <> *adj* medieval. <> *adv* like in medieval times.

Mittelamerika *nt* Central America.

Mittelleuropa *nt* Central Europe.

Mittellfinger *der* middle finger.

Mittellgebirge *das* low-lying mountain range.

mittelgroß *adj* medium-sized; [Person] of medium height.

mittellos *adj* penniless.

mittelmäßig *abw* <> *adj* average. <> *adv* averagely.

Mittelmeer *das*: **das Mittelmeer** the Mediterranean (Sea).

Mittellpunkt *der* centre; **im Mittelpunkt stehen** to be the centre of attention.

Mittellstreifen *der* central reservation *UK*, median *US*.

Mittellweg *der* middle way.

Mittellwert *der* mean.

mitten *adv*: **mitten auf** in the middle of; **mitten durch** through the middle of; **mitten in etw** (*D*) in the middle of sthg; **mitten in etw** (*A*) into the middle of sthg; **mitten unter** among; **mitten am Tag/in der Nacht** in the middle of the day/night.

mittendrin *adv* in the middle.

mittendurch *adv* through the middle.

Mitternacht *die* midnight.

mittlere, r, s *adj* - 1. [zwischen den Extremen] average; **im mittleren Alter** middle-aged - 2. [in der Mitte liegend] middle.

Mittlere Osten *der*: **der Mittlere Osten** the Middle East.

mittlerweile *adv* [inzwischen] in the meantime; [jetzt] now.

Mittwoch (*pl* -e) *der* Wednesday; *siehe auch* **Samstag**.

mittwochs ['mɪtvɔxs] *adv* on Wednesdays; *siehe auch* **samstags**.

mitunter *adv* occasionally.

mitverantwortlich *adj* jointly responsible.

mitlverdienen *vi* to earn money as well.

mitlwirken *vi*: **(bei etw) mitwirken** [mitarbeiten] to contribute (to sthg); [mitspielen] to take part (in sthg).

mixen *vt* to mix.

MKS (*abk für* Maul- und Klauenseuche) *die* (*ohne pl*) foot-and-mouth (disease).

mobben *vt*: **jdn mobben** to bully sb at work.

Mobbing *das* workplace bullying.

Möbel (*pl* -) *das* piece of furniture; **die Möbel** the furniture.

Möbellwagen *der* removal *UK* ODER moving *US* van.

mobil *adj* - 1. [beweglich] mobile - 2. [munter] lively; **mobil machen** MIL to mobilize; **jn mobil machen** [munter machen] to liven sb up.

Mobillfunk *der* (*ohne pl*) TELEKOM mobile phone network *UK*, cellphone network *US*.

Mobilltelefon *das* mobile phone *UK*, cellphone *US*.

möblieren *vt* to furnish.

möbliert <> *adj* furnished. <> *adv*: **möbliert wohnen** to live in furnished accommodation.

mochte *prät* ▷ **mögen**.

Mode (*pl* -n) *die* [Kleidungsstil, Zeitgeschmack] fashion; **es ist jetzt groß in Mode** it is very fashionable now; **mit der Mode gehen** to follow the fashion.

Modelhaus *das* - 1. [Einzelgeschäft] fashion store - 2. [Unternehmen] fashion house.

Modell (*pl* -e) *das* model; **Modell stehen** [für Maler] to model.

modellieren *vt* to model.

Modem (*pl* -s) *das* EDV modem.

Modenlschau *die* fashion show.

Moderator (*pl* -en) *der* presenter.

Moderatorin (*pl* -nen) *die* presenter.

moderig = **modrig**.

modern[1] (*perf* hat/ist **gemodert**) *vi* to moulder.

modern[2] <> *adj* modern; [modisch] fashionable. <> *adv* - 1. [zeitgemäß] in a modern way; **modern denken** to have modern ideas - 2. [zeitgenössisch] in a modern style.

modernisieren *vt* to modernize.

Modelschmuck *der* costume jewellery.

modisch <> *adj* fashionable. <> *adv* fashionably.

modrig, moderig *adj* & *adv* musty.

Mofa (*pl* -s) *das* moped.

mogeln *vi* to cheat.

mögen (*präs* mag, *prät* mochte, *perf* hat gemocht *ODER* mögen) <> *vt* (*perf* hat gemocht) - 1. [gern haben] to like; **jn/etw (nicht) mögen** (not) to like sb/sthg - 2. [wollen]: **ich möchte bitte ein Eis** I'd like an ice-cream please; **was möchten Sie?** what would you like? <> *vi* (*perf* hat gemocht) [wollen]: **er möchte nach Hause** he wants to go home. <> *aux* (*perf* hat mögen): **ich möchte etwas trinken** I'd like something to drink; **möchtest du mitkommen?** would you like to come?; **mag sein** that may well be.

möglich *adj* & *adv* possible; **ich habe es so gut wie möglich gemacht** I did it as well as I could; **jm ist es (nicht) möglich, etw zu tun** it is (not) possible for sb to do sthg. ➡ **alles Mögliche** *pron* absolutely everything.

möglicherweise *adv* possibly.

Möglichkeit (*pl* -en) *die* - 1. [das Mögliche] possibility; **es besteht die Möglichkeit, dass...** it is possible that...; **nach Möglichkeit** if possible - 2. [Chance] opportunity. ➡ **Möglichkeiten** *Pl* [Fähigkeiten] capabilities.

möglichst ['mø:klɪçst] *adv* - 1. [wenn möglich] if possible - 2. [so viel wie möglich]: **möglichst groß/stark/viel** as big/strong/much as possible.

Mohammedaner, in (*mpl* -, *fpl* -nen) *der, die* Muslim.

mohammedanisch *adj* Muslim.

Mohn (*pl* -e) *der* - 1. [Pflanze] poppy - 2. [Samen] poppy seeds *Pl*.

Mohnblume (*pl* -n) *die* poppy.

Möhre (*pl* -n) *die* carrot.

Mokka (*pl* -s) *der* mocha.

Molekül (*pl* -e) *das* molecule.

molk *prät* ➡ **melken**.

Molke *die* whey.

Molkerei (*pl* -en) *die* dairy.

Moll *das* minor (key).

mollig *adj* plump.

Moment (*pl* -e) <> *der* moment; **im Moment** at the moment; **jeden Moment** (at) any moment; **(einen) Moment, bitte!** just a moment, please!; **Moment mal!** *fam* wait a moment! <> *das* element.

momentan <> *adj* present. <> *adv* at the moment.

Monaco *nt* Monaco.

Monarchie (*pl* -n) *die* monarchy.

Monat (*pl* -e) *der* month; **diesen/nächsten/ vorigen Monat** this/next/last month; **sie ist im fünften Monat (schwanger)** she is over four months pregnant.

monatelang <> *adj* lasting for months. <> *adv* for months.

monatlich *adj* & *adv* monthly.

Monatskarte *die* monthly season ticket.

Mönch (*pl* -e) *der* monk.

Mond (*pl* -e) *der* moon.

Mondfinsternis *die* eclipse of the moon.

Mondlandung *die* moon landing.

Mondschein *der* moonlight.

Monitor (*pl* -en *ODER* -e) *der* monitor.

Monogramm (*pl* -e) *das* monogram.

Monolog (*pl* -e) *der* monologue.

Monopol (*pl* -e) *das* monopoly; **das Monopol auf etw** (*A*) **haben** to have a monopoly on sthg.

monoton <> *adj* monotonous. <> *adv* monotonously.

Monster (*pl* -) *das* monster.

Monsun (*pl* -e) *der* monsoon.

Montag (*pl* -e) *der* Monday; *siehe auch* **Samstag**.

Montage [mɔn'tɑːʒə] (*pl* -n) *die* - 1. TECH [Zusammenbau] assembly (*U*); [Einbau] installation (*U*); **auf Montage sein** to be away on assembly/installation work - 2. [Schnitt] editing (*U*) - 3. KUNST montage.

montags *adv* on Mondays; *siehe auch* **samstags**.

Montblanc [mɔ̃'blãː] *der* Mont Blanc.

montieren *vt* - 1. TECH [zusammenbauen] to assemble; [einbauen] to install; [festmachen] to fix - 2. [schneiden] to edit.

Monument (*pl* -e) *das* monument.

monumental <> *adj* monumental. <> *adv* on a monumental scale.

Moor (*pl* -e) *das* bog.

Moos (*pl* -e) *das* - 1. [Pflanze, Pflanzengattung] moss - 2. *fam* [Geld] dough.

Moped (*pl* -s) *das* moped.

Mops (*pl* Möpse) *der* - 1. [Hund] pug (dog) - 2. *fam fig* [Mensch] roly-poly.

Moral *die* - 1. [Normen] morals *Pl* - 2. [Stimmung] morale - 3. [das Lehrreiche] moral - 4. [Ethik] morality.

moralisch <> *adj* moral. <> *adv* morally.

Morast (*pl* -e) *der* quagmire.

Morchel (*pl* -n) *die* morel.

Mord (*pl* -e) *der* murder, homicide *US*; [durch Attentat] assassination; **einen Mord begehen** to commit murder.

Mörder, in (*mpl* -, *fpl* -nen) *der, die* murderer; [durch Attentat] assassin.

mörderisch <> *adj* - 1. [lebensgefährlich] deadly; [Tempo] breakneck - 2. [Verbrechen, Absicht] murderous - 3. *fam* [groß] terrible. <> *adv* - 1. [steil, schnell] murderously - 2. *fam* [sehr] terribly.

morgen *adv* - 1. [am Tag nach heute, zukünftig] tomorrow; **bis morgen!** see you tomorrow!; **morgen früh** tomorrow morning - 2. [vormittag] morning.

Morgen (pl -) der morning; **am Morgen** in the morning; **gestern/heute Morgen** yesterday/this morning. ➡ **guten Morgen** interj good morning!

Morgen|grauen das dawn.

Morgen|rot das red dawn sky.

morgens adv in the morning; [jeden Morgen] every morning; **von morgens bis abends** from dawn till dusk.

morgig adj [Treffen] tomorrow's; **der morgige Tag** tomorrow.

Morphium das morphine.

morsch adj rotten.

morsen ◇ vt to send in Morse (code). ◇ vi to use Morse (code).

Mörtel (pl -) der mortar.

Mosaik (pl -e ODER -en) das mosaic.

Moschee [mɔ'ʃeː] (pl -n) die mosque.

Mosel die Moselle.

Moskau nt Moscow.

Moskauer (pl -) ◇ der Muscovite. ◇ adj (unver) of/from Moscow.

Moskauerin (pl -nen) die Muscovite.

Moskito (pl -s) der mosquito.

Moslem (pl -s) der Muslim.

Moslemin (pl -nen) die Muslim.

Most (pl -e) der - 1. [Fruchtsaft] (cloudy) fruit juice - 2. Süddt [Apfelwein] cider.

Motiv (pl -e) das - 1. [von Handlung] motive - 2. [von Bild] subject - 3. [Thema] motif.

motivieren [moti'viːrən] vt to motivate; **jn motivieren, etw zu tun** to motivate sb to do sthg.

Motor (pl -toren), **Motor** (pl -toren) der - 1. [von Fahrzeug] engine; [von Gerät] motor - 2. fig [Triebfeder] driving force.

Motor|rad das motorcycle, motorbike.

Motor|schaden der engine trouble (U).

Motte (pl -n) die moth.

Motto (pl -s) das motto; **unter dem Motto "keine Steuererhöhung" stehen** to have "no tax increases" as its motto.

Möwe (pl -n) die seagull.

Mrd. abk für **Milliarde**.

Mücke (pl -n) die [in Tropen] mosquito; [kleiner] midge, gnat.

Mücken|stich der mosquito bite.

müde ◇ adj tired; **einer Sache** (G) **müde sein** geh to be tired of sthg; **nicht müde werden, etw zu tun** never to tire of doing sthg. ◇ adv wearily.

Müdigkeit die tiredness.

muffig ◇ adj - 1. [modrig] musty - 2. fam [schlecht gelaunt] grumpy. ◇ adv: **muffig riechen** to smell musty.

Mühe (pl -n) die effort; **es macht mir keine Mühe** it's no trouble; **sich** (D) **Mühe machen (mit etw)** to go to some trouble (over sthg);

sich (D) **Mühe geben** to make an effort; **gib dir keine Mühe** don't bother; **mit Müh und Not** by the skin of one's teeth.

mühelos ◇ adj effortless. ◇ adv effortlessly.

mühevoll ◇ adj laborious, painstaking. ◇ adv laboriously, painstakingly.

Mühle (pl -n) die - 1. [Mahlwerk - für Getreide] mill; [- für Kaffee] grinder - 2. [Gebäude] mill - 3. [Spiel] nine men's morris - 4. fam [Fahrzeug] jalopy, banger UK.

mühsam ◇ adj laborious. ◇ adv laboriously.

mühselig ◇ adj [Arbeit, Tun] laborious; [Leben] arduous. ◇ adv laboriously.

Mulde (pl -n) die GEOGR hollow; [Griffmulde] grip.

Mull (pl -e) der [Material] muslin; [für Verband] gauze.

Müll der rubbish UK, garbage US; [radioaktiv] waste; **etw in den Müll werfen** ODER **tun** to throw sthg out ODER away.

Müll|abfuhr die - 1. [Transport] refuse UK ODER garbage US collection - 2. [Unternehmen] refuse UK ODER garbage US collection service.

Mull|binde die gauze dressing.

Müll|deponie die refuse disposal site.

Müll|eimer der dustbin UK, garbage ODER trash can US.

Müller, in (mpl -, fpl -nen) der, die miller.

Müll|schlucker der rubbish UK ODER garbage US chute.

Müll|tonne die dustbin UK, garbage ODER trash can US.

Müll|trennung die separation of household waste for recycling purposes.

Müll|wagen der dustbin lorry UK, garbage truck US.

mulmig adj uncomfortable; **mir wird mulmig** [körperlich] I feel queasy.

multikulturell adj multicultural.

multinational adj multinational.

Multiplex|kino das multiplex (cinema).

multiplizieren vt: **etw mit etw multiplizieren** to multiply sthg by sthg.

Mumie ['muːmjə] (pl -n) die mummy.

Mumm der (ohne pl) fam guts Pl; **(keinen) Mumm haben** to have (no) guts.

Mumps der MED mumps (U).

München nt Munich.

Mund (pl Münder) der mouth; **jn von Mund zu Mund beatmen** to give sb mouth-to-mouth resuscitation; **halt den Mund!** fam shut up!

Mund|art die amt dialect.

münden (perf hat/ist gemündet) vi - 1. [einmünden]: **(in etw (A)) münden** [Fluss] to flow (into sthg); [Straße] to lead (to sthg) - **2.** *geh* [enden]: **in etw** *(D)* **münden** [Vorgang] to end in sthg.

Mundlharmonika *die* harmonica, mouth-organ.

mündig *adj* - **1.** [volljährig] of age; **mündig werden** to come of age - **2.** [urteilsfähig] responsible.

mündlich ⬦ *adj* [Vereinbarung, Versprechung] verbal; [Prüfung] oral. ⬦ *adv* verbally.

mundtot *adj*: **jn mundtot machen** to silence sb.

Mündung *(pl -en) die* - **1.** [von Fluss] mouth; GEOGR estuary - **2.** [von Straße] end - **3.** [von Gewehr] muzzle.

Mundwerk *das fam*: **ein großes Mundwerk haben** to be a bigmouth; **ein loses Mundwerk haben** to be cheeky.

Munition *(pl -en) die* ammunition.

munkeln ⬦ *vi*: **es wurde schon lange darüber gemunkelt** there had already been rumours about it for some time. ⬦ *vt*: **man munkelt, dass...** it is rumoured that...

Münster *(pl -) das* cathedral, minster.

munter ⬦ *adj* - **1.** [wach]: **munter sein** to be (wide) awake - **2.** [lebhaft - Mensch, Tier, Spiel] lively - **3.** [fröhlich] cheerful. ⬦ *adv* cheerfully.

Münze *(pl -n) die* coin.

münzen *vt* [Geld] to mint; **auf jn/etw gemünzt sein** *fig* to refer to sb/sthg.

Münzfernlsprecher *der amt* pay phone *UK*, pay station *US*.

mürbe *adj* - **1.** [Kuchen, Teig] crumbly; [Fleisch] tender; [Obst] soft - **2.** [Material] rotten, crumbling - **3.** [zermürbt]: **jn mürbe machen** to wear sb down.

Mürbelteig *der* shortcrust pastry.

murmeln *vt & vi* to murmur.

murren *vi*: **(über etw** *(A)***) murren** to grumble (about sthg).

mürrisch ⬦ *adj* sullen, surly. ⬦ *adv* in a sullen ODER surly manner.

Mus *(pl -e) das* puree.

Muschel *(pl -n) die* - **1.** [Tier] mussel - **2.** [Schale] shell.

Museum [mu'ze:ʊm] *(pl Museen) das* museum.

Musical ['mju:zik(ə)l] *(pl -s) das* musical.

Musik *(pl -en) die* music.

musikalisch ⬦ *adj* musical. ⬦ *adv* musically.

Musiker, in *(mpl -, fpl -nen) der, die* musician.

Musiklunterricht *der (ohne pl)* [Schulfach] music; [Musikstunden] music lessons *Pl.*

musizieren *vi* to make music.

Muskatnuss *(pl -nüsse) die* nutmeg.

Muskel *(pl -n) der* muscle.

Muskelkater *der*: **(einen) Muskelkater haben** to be stiff.

Muskulatur *(pl -en) die* muscles *Pl.*

muskulös *adj* muscular.

Müsli *(pl -) das* muesli.

muss *präs* ⬅ **müssen**.

Muss *das (ohne pl)* necessity, must.

Muße *die* leisure; **Zeit und Muße haben, etw zu tun** to have enough time to do sthg at one's leisure.

müssen *(präs muss, prät musste, perf hat gemusst ODER müssen)* ⬦ *aux (perf hat müssen)* - **1.** [gezwungen sein] must; **etw tun müssen** to have to do sthg; **du musst aufstehen** you must get up; **sie musste lachen/niesen** she had to laugh/sneeze; **etw nicht tun müssen** not to need to do sthg - **2.** [nötig sein]: **der Brief muss noch heute weg** the letter has to go today; **muss das sein?** is that really necessary? - **3.** [wahrscheinlich sein]: **du musst Hunger haben nach der langen Reise** you must be hungry after your long journey; **das müsste alles sein** that should be all. ⬦ *vi (perf hat gemusst)* to have to; **ich muss ins Büro (gehen)** I have to go to the office; **ich muss mal** *fam* I need the toilet.

musste *prät* ⬅ **müssen**.

Muster *(pl -) das* - **1.** [Vorlage, Beispiel] model; **ein Muster an etw** *(D)* a model of sthg - **2.** [Musterung] pattern - **3.** [Warenprobe] sample.

mustern *vt* - **1.** [betrachten] to study, to scrutinize - **2.** [Wehrpflichtigen] to inspect.

Musterung *(pl -en) die* - **1.** [von Wehrpflichtigen] inspection - **2.** [Betrachtung] scrutiny.

Mut *der* courage; **jm Mut machen** to encourage sb. ➡ **nur Mut** *interj* chin up!

mutig ⬦ *adj* brave, courageous. ⬦ *adv* bravely, courageously.

mutmaßlich *adj* suspected.

Mutter *(pl Mütter ODER -n) die* - **1.** *(pl Mütter)* [gen] mother - **2.** *(pl Muttern)* [von Schraube] nut.

mütterlich ⬦ *adj* [Liebe, Frau] motherly; [Eigenschaft, Erbe] maternal. ⬦ *adv* [fürsorgend] in a motherly fashion.

mütterlicherseits *adv* on one's mother's side.

Mutterlmal *das* mole.

Mutterlsprache *die* mother tongue, native language.

Mutterltag *der* Mother's Day.

mutwillig ⬦ *adj* wilful. ⬦ *adv* wilfully.

Mütze *(pl -n) die* cap; [aus Wolle] hat.

MwSt. *(abk für Mehrwertsteuer)* VAT *UK*, sales tax *US*.

Mythos *(pl Mythen) der* myth; **er ist schon jetzt ein Mythos** he is already a legend.

N

n (pl - ODER **-s**), **N** (pl - ODER **-s**) [ɛn] das n, N.
▸ **N** (abk für Nord) N.

na interj well?; **na, wie gehts?** so how's it going, then?; **na los, mach schon!** well go on then, do it!; **na, lass das sein!** hey, leave that alone! ▸ **na also** interj there you are! ▸ **na gut** interj all right, then! ▸ **na ja** interj well! ▸ **na und** interj: **na und?** so (what)?

Nabel (pl -) der navel.

Nabel|schnur die umbilical cord.

nach präp (+ D) - 1. [zeitlich, zur Angabe einer Reihenfolge] after; **nach dem Essen** after the meal; **fünf (Minuten) nach drei** five (minutes) past three UK, five (minutes) after three US; **nach Ihnen!** after you! - 2. [räumlich] to; **nach Frankfurt** to Frankfurt; **nach Hause gehen** to go home; **nach Süden** south, southwards; **nach links/rechts abbiegen** to turn left/right - 3. [gemäß] according to; **nach Angaben der Polizei** according to the police - 4. [stellt Bezug her]: **seinem Akzent nach ist er kein Deutscher** judging by his accent, he is not German; **meiner Meinung nach** in my opinion. ▸ **nach und nach** adv little by little. ▸ **nach wie vor** adv as before.

nach|ahmen vt to imitate, to copy.

Nachbar, in (mpl -n, fpl -nen) der, die neighbour.

Nachbarschaft die neighbourhood.

nach|bessern vt [Vorschlag, Entwurf] to amend; [Preisangebot] to raise; **sie musste ihre Arbeit nachbessern** she had to redo the bits she had got wrong.

nachdem konj after. ▸ **je nachdem** konj depending on.

nach|denken vi (unreg): **(über jn/etw) nachdenken** to think (about sb/sthg).

nachdenklich ◇ adj thoughtful, pensive; **jn nachdenklich machen** to set sb thinking. ◇ adv thoughtfully, pensively.

Nachdruck (pl -e) der - 1. [Eindringlichkeit] emphasis; **einer Sache (D) Nachdruck verleihen** to reinforce sthg; **mit Nachdruck** emphatically - 2. [Nachdrucken - von Buch] reprinting; [- von Druck] reproduction - 3. [Ausgabe] reprint.

nachdrücklich ◇ adj emphatic, forceful. ◇ adv emphatically.

nach|eifern vi: **jm (in etw (D)) nacheifern** to seek to emulate sb (in sthg).

nacheinander adv - 1. [der Reihe nach] one after the other - 2. [gegenseitig] one another.

nach|empfinden vt (unreg) [nachfühlen]: **js Schmerz nachempfinden** to share sb's pain; **ich kann dir nachempfinden, wie du dich jetzt fühlst** I can understand how you feel.

Nacher|zählung die retelling (in one's own words).

Nachfolge die succession.

nach|folgen (perf ist **nachgefolgt**) vi - 1. [Nachfolge antreten]: **jm (in einem Amt) nachfolgen** to succeed sb (in an office) - 2. [nachkommen] to follow; **das nachfolgende Fahrzeug** the vehicle behind.

Nachfolger, in (mpl -, fpl -nen) der, die successor.

nach|forschen vi to make enquiries; **jm/einer Sache nachforschen** geh to investigate sb/sthg.

Nachfrage die WIRTSCH demand.

nach|fragen vi - 1. [nachhaken] to ask repeatedly - 2. [fragen] to enquire.

nach|füllen vt - 1. [füllen] to refill - 2. [nachgießen] to top up with.

nach|geben vi (unreg) - 1. [bei Streit] to give in - 2. [Brücke, Boden] to give way; [Preise, Kurse] to fall.

nach|gehen (perf ist **nachgegangen**) vi (unreg) - 1. [folgen]: **jm/einer Sache nachgehen** to follow sb/sthg - 2. [etw prüfen]: **einer Sache (D) nachgehen** to look into sthg - 3. [Uhr] to be slow; **meine Uhr geht zehn Minuten nach** my watch is ten minutes slow - 4. [nachwirken]: **jm nachgehen** to stick in sb's mind - 5. [sich widmen]: **einer Sache (D) nachgehen** to pursue sthg.

Nachgeschmack der aftertaste.

nachgiebig adj compliant; [Eltern] indulgent.

nach|haken vi to return to the same question.

nachhaltig ◇ adj lasting. ◇ adv: **nachhaltig wirken** to have a lasting effect.

nach|hängen vi (unreg) - 1. [sich erinnern]: **einer Sache (D) nachhängen** to dwell on sthg - 2. fam [zurückliegen]: **in etw (D) nachhängen** to lag behind in sthg.

Nachhause|weg der way home.

nach|helfen vi (unreg) - 1. [antreiben]: **bei jm nachhelfen müssen** to have to chivvy sb along - 2. [helfen]: **(jm) nachhelfen** to lend (sb) a hand.

nachher, nachher adv - 1. [später] later (on) - 2. [anschließend] afterwards. ▸ **bis nachher** interj see you later!

Nachhilfe die extra tuition.

Nachhinein adv: **im Nachhinein** with hindsight; **im Nachhinein zeigte sich, dass er gelogen hatte** it later turned out that he had lied.

nach|holen vt - 1. [nachträglich machen]: **etw nachholen** [Versäumtes] to catch up on sthg;

[Prüfung] to do sthg later - **2.** [nachziehen lassen]: **er holte seine Familie nach** his family joined him later.

nachljagen (*perf* ist **nachgejagt**) *vi:* **jm/einer Sache nachjagen** to chase after sb/sthg.

Nachkomme (*pl* **-n**) *der* descendant.

nachlkommen (*perf* ist **nachgekommen**) *vi* (*unreg*) - **1.** [später kommen] to come (along) later - **2.** *geh* [entsprechen]: **einer Sache** (*D*) **nachkommen** to comply with sthg.

Nachkriegslzeit *die* post-war period.

nachllassen (*unreg*) ⟷ *vi* [Schmerz, Spannung] to ease; [Regen] to ease off; [Augen, Gehör] to fail; [Geschäft, Anstrengung] to slacken; [Qualität] to drop off. ⟷ *vt* [Preis]: **jm 10% nachlassen** to give sb a 10% discount.

nachlässig ⟷ *adj* careless. ⟷ *adv* carelessly.

nachllaufen (*perf* ist **nachgelaufen**) *vi* (*unreg*): **jm/einer Sache nachlaufen** [laufen nach] to run after sb/sthg; [folgen] to follow sb/sthg; *fam* [sich bemühen um] to pursue sb/sthg.

nachlmachen *vt* - **1.** [nachahmen, kopieren] to copy; [nachäffen] to mimic; [fälschen] to forge; **jm etw nachmachen** to copy sthg off sb; **etw nachmachen lassen** to have sthg copied - **2.** [nachholen]: **etw** (*A*) **nachmachen** to catch up on sthg later.

Nachlmittag *der* afternoon; **am Nachmittag** in the afternoon; **gestern/heute/morgen Nachmittag** yesterday/this/tomorrow afternoon; **Dienstag Nachmittag** on Tuesday afternoon.

nachmittags *adv* in the afternoon.

Nachnahme (*pl* **-n**) *die:* **etw als Nachnahme versenden** to send sthg cash on delivery; **per** ODER **gegen Nachnahme** cash on delivery.

Nachlname *der* surname.

nachlprüfen *vt* - **1.** [kontrollieren] to check - **2.** [erneut prüfen] to re-examine.

nachlrechnen ⟷ *vt* - **1.** [nochmals rechnen] to check - **2.** [nachzählen] to work out. ⟷ *vi* - **1.** [nochmals rechnen] to check - **2.** [nachzählen] to work it out.

Nachlrede *die:* **üble Nachrede** slander.

Nachricht (*pl* **-en**) *die* [Neuigkeit] piece of news; [Mitteilung] message; **eine gute Nachricht haben** to have (some) good news; **die Nachricht, dass...** the news that...; **eine Nachricht von jm** [Neuigkeiten] news of sb; [Mitteilung] a message from sb. ☛ **Nachrichten** *Pl:* **die Nachrichten** the news (*sg*).

Nachrichtenlagentur *die* news agency.

Nachrichtenlsprecher, in *der, die* newsreader.

nachlrücken (*perf* ist **nachgerückt**) *vi* to move up.

Nachlruf *der* obituary.

nachlrüsten ⟷ *vt* EDV to upgrade. ⟷ *vi* MIL to rearm.

nachlsagen *vt* [behaupten]: **jm etw nachsagen** to say sthg of sb.

Nachsaison *die* low season.

nachlschicken *vt* to forward.

Nachlschlag *der* second helping.

nachlschlagen (*perf* hat/ist **nachgeschlagen**) (*unreg*) ⟷ *vi* - **1.** (*hat*) [nachlesen]: **in einem Wörterbuch nachschlagen** to consult a dictionary - **2.** (*ist*) [ähneln]: **jm nachschlagen** to take after sb. ⟷ *vt* (*hat*) [nachlesen] to look up.

Nachlschlagelwerk *das* reference work.

Nachlschlüssel *der* duplicate key.

Nachschub *der* (*ohne pl*) supplies *Pl*.

nachlsehen (*unreg*) ⟷ *vi* - **1.** [hinterhersehen]: **jm/einer Sache nachsehen** to gaze after sb/sthg - **2.** [suchen] to look - **3.** [prüfen] to check - **4.** [nachschlagen]: **in etw** (*D*) **nachsehen** to consult sthg. ⟷ *vt* - **1.** [nachschlagen]: **etw in etw** (*D*) **nachsehen** to look sthg up in sthg - **2.** [prüfen] to check - **3.** [verzeihen]: **jm seine Fehler nachsehen** to overlook sb's mistakes.

Nachsehen *das:* **das Nachsehen haben** [unterlegen sein] to come off badly; [etw nicht bekommen] to be left empty-handed.

nachlsenden *vt* (*unreg*) to forward.

nachlsitzen *vi* (*unreg*): **nachsitzen müssen** to get detention.

Nachlspeise *die* dessert.

Nachlspiel *das* [Folgen] consequences *Pl*; [Theaterstück] epilogue; **es wird ein Nachspiel haben** it will have consequences.

nachlsprechen *vt* & *vi* (*unreg*) to repeat.

nächstbeste, r, s *adj:* **bei der nächstbesten Gelegenheit** at the first available opportunity. ☛ **Nächstbeste** *der, die, das:* **der/die/das Nächstbeste** the first available one.

nächste, r, s ['nɛːçstə, ɐ, əs] *adj* - **1.** [nah] nearest, closest - **2.** [folgend] next; **der Nächste bitte!** next, please!; **wie heißt die nächste Haltestelle?** what's the next stop?; **die nächste Straße links** the next road on the left.

Nächstenlliebe ['nɛːçstənliːbə] *die* charity.

nächstens ['nɛːçstns] *adv* shortly, soon.

nächstliegend ['nɛːçstliːgnt] *adj* most obvious.

nächstmöglich ['nɛːçstmøːklɪç] *adj* next possible.

Nacht (*pl* **Nächte**) *die* night; **gestern/morgen Nacht** last/tomorrow night; **heute Nacht** tonight. ☛ **gute Nacht** *interj* good night!

Nachlteil *der* disadvantage; **zu js Nachteil** to sb's disadvantage.

nächtelang ⟷ *adj* lasting several nights. ⟷ *adv* night after night.

Nachtlfrost *der* night frost.

Nachtlhemd *das* [für Frauen] nightdress; [für Männer] nightshirt.

Nachtigall (*pl* **-en**) *die* nightingale.

Nachtisch *der (ohne pl)* dessert.

nächtlich *adj* nocturnal; [Stille] of the night.

nach|tragen *vt (unreg)* - 1. [übel nehmen]: **jm etw nachtragen** to hold sthg against sb - 2. [ergänzen] to add - 3. [hinterhertragen]: **jm etw nachtragen** to follow behind sb carrying sthg.

nachträglich ◇ *adj* [Glückwunsch] belated; [Beweis] subsequent. ◇ *adv* [beglückwünschen] belatedly; [beweisen] subsequently.

nach|trauern *vi*: **jm/einer Sache nachtrauern** to miss sb/sthg.

Nacht|ruhe *die* night's sleep.

nachts *adv* at night; **um vier Uhr nachts** at four in the morning.

Nacht|schicht *die* night shift.

Nacht|wache *die* - 1. [Dienst] night watch - 2. [Person] person on night watch.

Nacht|wächter, in *der, die* night watchman (-woman *die*).

nach|vollziehen *vt (unreg)* to comprehend.

nach|wachsen ['nɑːˈxvaksn̩] *(perf ist nachgewachsen)* *vi (unreg)* to grow again.

Nachweis *(pl -e)* *der* proof *(U)*.

nach|weisen *vt (unreg)* - 1. [Fehler] to prove - 2. [Substanz] to detect.

Nach|welt *die* posterity.

Nach|wirkung *die* aftereffect.

Nach|wuchs ['nɑːˈxvuːks] *der* - 1. [Kinder] offspring - 2. [im Beruf]: **künstlerischer/wissenschaftlicher Nachwuchs** rising generation of artists/scientists; **es fehlt an Nachwuchs** there is a lack of new blood.

nach|zahlen ◇ *vi* to pay the extra. ◇ *vt*: **drei Euro nachzahlen** to pay three euros extra.

nach|zählen *vt* to check.

Nacken *(pl -)* *der* back *ODER* nape of the neck; **ihm sitzt die Angst im Nacken** he is afraid.

nackt ◇ *adj* - 1. [ohne Kleider/Fell] naked; [Körperteil] bare - 2. [bloß] bare; **die nackte Wahrheit** the plain truth; **nackte Tatsachen** hard facts. ◇ *adv* naked.

Nadel *(pl -n)* *die* [gen] needle; [Stecknadel] pin.

Nadel|baum *der* conifer.

Nadel|öhr *das* - 1. [von Nadeln] eye - 2. *fig* [enge Stelle] bottleneck.

Nadel|wald *der* coniferous forest.

Nagel *(pl Nägel)* *der* nail; **den Nagel auf den Kopf treffen** to hit the nail on the head; **etw an den Nagel hängen** to give sthg up; **sich** *(D)* **etw unter den Nagel reißen** *fam abw* to pinch sthg for o.s.

Nagel|feile *die* nail file.

Nagel|lack *der* nail varnish.

nageln *vt* to nail; [Knochen] to pin.

nagelneu *adj* brand-new.

nagen ◇ *vi* - 1. [knabbern]: **an etw** *(D)* **nagen** to gnaw at sthg - 2. [jn beunruhigen]: **an jm nagen** [Zweifel] to prey on sb; [Hunger] to gnaw at sb. ◇ *vt* to gnaw.

Nage|tier *das* rodent.

nah *(kompar näher, superl nächste)*, **nahe** *(kompar näher, superl nächste)* ◇ *adj* near; **nah an/bei jm/etw** close to *ODER* near sb/sthg; **zu nah** too close; **in naher Zukunft** in the near future; **den Tränen/dem Wahnsinn nah sein** to be on the verge of tears/madness; **nah daran sein, etw zu tun** to be on the point *ODER* verge of doing sthg. ◇ *adv* - 1. [räumlich]: **eine nahe gelegene Stadt** a nearby town; **komm mir nicht zu nahe!** keep your distance!; **von nahem** from close up; **von nah und fern** from near and far - 2. [vertraut] closely; **nahe verwandt** closely related; **jm zu nah treten** *fig* to offend sb.

Nah|aufnahme *die* close-up.

Nähe *die* - 1. [räumlich, zeitlich] closeness; **in meiner Nähe** near me; **aus der Nähe** from close-up; **in der Nähe** nearby; **in greifbarer Nähe** within reach - 2. [emotional] closeness, intimacy; **js Nähe suchen** to seek sb's company.

nahe gehen *(perf ist nahe gegangen)* *vi (unreg)*: **jm nahe gehen** to affect sb deeply.

nahe legen *vt* - 1. [Verdacht, Vermutung] to give rise to - 2. [jn auffordern]: **jm nahe legen, etw zu tun** to advise sb to do sthg.

nahe liegen *vi (unreg)* [Idee, Plan] to suggest itself; **der Verdacht/die Vermutung liegt nahe, dass...** it seems reasonable to suspect/suppose that...

nähen ◇ *vt* - 1. [Kleid, Hose] to make - 2. [Riss] to mend - 3. [Wunde] to stitch. ◇ *vi* [schneidern] to sew.

Nahe Osten *der*: **der Nahe Osten** the Middle East.

näher ◇ *adj* - 1. [Komparativ von nahe] closer, nearer - 2. [Umstände, Angaben] more precise. ◇ *adv* - 1. [Komparativ von nahe] closer, nearer - 2. [betrachten] more closely; [erklären] more precisely.

Naherholungs|gebiet *das amt area* close to a town, offering recreational facilities.

näher kommen *(perf ist näher gekommen)* *vi (unreg)* - 1. [nahe kommen]: **jm näher kommen** to get to know sb better - 2. [entsprechen]: **einer Sache näher kommen** to get closer to sthg. ❧ **sich näher kommen** *ref* [sich nahe kommen] to get to know one another better.

nähern ❧ **sich nähern** *ref* to approach.

nahe stehen *vi (unreg)*: **sich/jm nahe stehen** to be close to one another/sb.

nahe stehend *adj* - 1.: **jm nahe stehend** [persönlich] close to sb; **einer Sache** *(D)* **nahe stehend** [politisch] sympathetic to sthg - 2. [in der Nähe] nearby.

nahezu *adv* nearly, almost.

nahm *prät* ▷ **nehmen**.
Näh|maschine *die* sewing machine.
Näh|nadel *die* (sewing) needle.
Nahost *(ohne Artikel)* the Middle East.
nahrhaft *adj* nourishing, nutritious.
Nähr|stoff *der* nutrient.
Nahrung *die* food; **feste Nahrung** solids *Pl.*
Nahrungs|mittel *das* food.
Naht *(pl Nähte) die* - **1.** [an Kleidung] seam; **aus allen Nähten platzen** *fig* to burst at the seams - **2.** [in der Medizin] suture - **3.** [in der Technik] join.
nahtlos ◇ *adj* seamless; **nahtlose Bräune** all-over tan. ◇ *adv* [ununterbrochen] seamlessly.
Nahverkehr *der* local traffic.
Nähzeug *das (ohne pl)* sewing things *Pl.*
naiv [na'i:f] ◇ *adj* naive. ◇ *adv* naively.
Naivität [naivi'tɛːt] *die* naivety.
Name *(pl -n) der* name; **im Namen von jm** in the name of sb; **jn/etw (nur) dem Namen nach kennen** to know sb/sthg (only) by name.
namhaft *adj* renowned.
Namibia *nt* Namibia.
nämlich *adv* because; **zwei von ihnen, nämlich Anna und Berthold** two of them, namely Anna and Berthold; **übermorgen, nämlich am Donnerstag** the day after tomorrow, that is, on Thursday; **wir treffen uns jetzt nämlich am Freitag** we'll now actually be meeting on Friday.
nanu *interj* well (I never)!
Napf *(pl Näpfe) der* dish, bowl.
Narbe *(pl -n) die* scar.
narbig *adj* scarred.
Narkose *(pl -n) die* anaesthetic.
närrisch ◇ *adj* - **1.** [verrückt] mad, crazy; **das närrische Treiben** [im Karneval] carnival festivities - **2.** *fam* [unglaublich] terrific. ◇ *adv* - **1.** [verrückt]: **sich närrisch gebärden** to act crazy - **2.** *fam* [unglaublich] terribly.
Narzisse *(pl -n) die* narcissus.
naschen *vt & vi* to nibble.
Nase *(pl -n) die* nose; **sich** *(D)* **die Nase putzen** to blow one's nose; **jm läuft die Nase** sb's nose is running; **über etw die Nase rümpfen** to turn one's nose up at sthg; **jn an der Nase herumführen** to pull the wool over sb's eyes.
Nasen|bluten *das (ohne pl)* nosebleed.
Nasen|loch *das* nostril.
Nashorn *(pl -hörner) das* rhinoceros.
nass ◇ *adj* wet. ◇ *adv*: **nass machen** to wet.
Nässe *die* wet; **vor Nässe triefen** to be dripping wet.
Nation *(pl -en) die* nation.
national ◇ *adj* national. ◇ *adv*: **national denken** to think in national terms.

National|feier|tag *der* national day.
National|hymne *die* national anthem.
Nationalismus *der* nationalism.
nationalistisch ◇ *adj* nationalistic. ◇ *adv*: **nationalistisch orientiert** with nationalistic leanings.
Nationalität *(pl -en) die* nationality.
Nationalsozialismus *der* National Socialism, Nazism.
NATO ['naːto] *(abk für North Atlantic Treaty Organization) die* NATO.
Natron *das* CHEM soda.
Natur *(pl -en) die* nature; **Tiere in der freien Natur** animals in the wild; **hinaus in die Natur fahren** to go out into the countryside. ⇒ **von Natur aus** *adv* by nature.
Naturalien [natuˈraːljən] *Pl*: **in Naturalien bezahlen** to pay in kind.
Naturalismus *der* naturalism.
naturbelassen *adj* natural; [Obst, Gemüse] organic.
Natur|ereignis *das* natural phenomenon.
naturgemäß ◇ *adj* natural. ◇ *adv* - **1.** [gemäß der Natur] in accordance with natural laws - **2.** [grundsätzlich] by its very nature.
naturgetreu ◇ *adj* [Abbildung] lifelike. ◇ *adv* in a lifelike manner.
Naturheilkunde *die* naturopathy.
natürlich ◇ *adj* natural. ◇ *adv* - **1.** [nicht künstlich] naturally - **2.** [selbstverständlich] of course, naturally; **natürlich war er wieder zu spät** naturally he was late again; **natürlich stimmt das, aber...** of course that's correct but... ◇ *interj* (but) of course!
naturrein *adj* pure.
Natur|schutz *der* nature conservation; **unter Naturschutz stehen** to be protected.
Naturschutz|gebiet *das* nature reserve.
Natur|wissenschaft *die* natural science.
Natur|wissenschaftler, in *der, die* scientist.
Nazi *(pl -s) der abw* Nazi.
n. Chr. *(abk für nach Christus)* AD.
NDR [ɛnydeːˈɛr] *(abk für Norddeutscher Rundfunk) der* North German Radio.
Neapel *nt* Naples.
Nebel *(pl -) der* fog; **leichter Nebel** mist.
nebelig = **neblig**.
Nebel|scheinwerfer *der* fog lamp.
Nebel|schwaden *Pl* swathes of mist.
neben *präp* - **1.** (+ D) [lokal] beside, next to - **2.** (+ D) [außer] apart from, as well as - **3.** (+ D) [verglichen mit] compared with - **4.** (+ A) [beside, next to.
nebenan *adv* next door.

nebenbei *adv* - **1.** [außerdem] in addition, as well; **etw nebenbei erledigen** to do sthg on the side - **2.** [beiläufig] in passing; **nebenbei bemerkt** by the way.

nebenberuflich ◇ *adj*: **nebenberufliche Tätigkeit** second job. ◇ *adv*: **nebenberuflich tätig sein** to have a second job.

nebeneinander *adv* - **1.** [neben jm/etw] next to each other - **2.** [gleichzeitig] simultaneously.

Neben|fach *das* SCHULE subsidiary subject.

Nebenfluss (*pl* -flüsse) *der* tributary.

Neben|geräusch *das* background noise.

nebenher *adv* in addition, as well; **nebenher arbeiten** to work on the side.

Neben|job *der* second job.

Neben|kosten *Pl* - **1.** [bei Miete] additional charges - **2.** [zusätzliche Auslagen] additional costs.

Neben|rolle *die* minor part.

Neben|sache *die* minor issue.

nebensächlich *adj* of secondary importance.

Neben|satz *der* GRAMM subordinate clause.

Neben|straße *die* side street.

neblig, nebelig *adj* foggy; **leicht neblig** misty.

necken *vt* to tease; **jn mit jm/etw necken** to tease sb about sb/sthg. ◆ **sich necken** *ref* to tease each other.

neckisch *adj* - **1.** [verschmitzt] teasing - **2.** [frech] coquettish.

Neffe (*pl* -n) *der* nephew.

negativ ◇ *adj* negative. ◇ *adv* negatively; **jm negativ beeinflussen** to have a negative influence on sb/sthg.

Negativ (*pl* -e) *das* negative.

Neger, in (*mpl* -, *fpl* -nen) *der, die abw* negro (negress *die*).

nehmen (*präs* nimmt, *prät* nahm, *perf* hat genommen) *vt* - **1.** [gen] to take; **für etw fünf Euro nehmen** to charge five euros for sthg; **ich nehme ein Omelett** I'll have an omelette; **sich (D) etw nehmen** to help o.s. with sthg; **jn/etw für voll nehmen** to take sb/sthg seriously; **es leicht/schwer nehmen** to take it lightly/hard; **wie mans nimmt** it depends (how you look at it); **etw zu sich nehmen** [Nahrung] to take sthg, to eat sthg; **etw an sich (A) nehmen** to look after sthg; **etw auf sich (A) nehmen** to take sthg on - **2.** [wegnehmen] to take away; **jm den Glauben/die Illusionen nehmen** to destroy sb's faith/illusions; **jm seine/ihre Freiheit nehmen** to deprive sb of his/her freedom - **3.** [einstellen] to take on - **4.** [verwenden] to use; **den Zug nehmen** to take the train; **sich (D) einen Anwalt nehmen** to get o.s. a lawyer.

Neid *der* envy.

neidisch ◇ *adj* envious. ◇ *adv* enviously.

neigen ◇ *vi*: **zu etw neigen** [tendieren] to have a tendency ODER be inclined to sthg; [anfällig sein] to be prone to sthg. ◇ *vt* [beugen - Körper] to bend; [- Kopf] to bow. ◆ **sich neigen** *ref* [sich beugen - Gegenstand] to bend; [- Mensch] to lean.

Neigung (*pl* -en) *die* - **1.** [Veranlagung] inclination; **künstlerische Neigungen** artistic leanings - **2.** (*ohne pl*) [Anfälligsein] susceptibility - **3.** (*ohne pl*) [Tendenz] tendency - **4.** [von Linie, Fläche] inclination.

nein *adv* no; **nein, danke!** no thank you!; **regnet es? - ich glaube nein** is it raining? - I don't think so; **aber nein!** certainly not!; **zu etw nein sagen** to say no to sthg; **nein so was!** well I never!

Nektar (*pl* -e) *der* - **1.** [Pflanzensaft] nectar (*U*) - **2.** [Getränk] fruit drink.

Nelke (*pl* -n) *die* - **1.** [Blume] carnation - **2.** [Gewürz] clove.

nennen (*prät* nannte, *perf* hat genannt) *vt* - **1.** [benennen, bezeichnen] to call - **2.** [anführen] to name; [Adresse, Name] to give. ◆ **sich nennen** *ref* - **1.** [heißen] to be called - **2.** [sich bezeichnen] to call o.s.

nennenswert ◇ *adj* significant. ◇ *adv* significantly.

Nenner (*pl* -) *der* MATH denominator.

Neon *das* CHEM neon.

Neon|licht (*pl* -er) *das* neon light.

Nerv (*pl* -en) *der* nerve. ◆ **Nerven** *Pl* nerves; **die Nerven verlieren/behalten** to lose/keep one's cool; **jm auf die Nerven gehen** ODER **fallen** to get on sb's nerves.

Nervenzusammen|bruch *der* nervous breakdown.

nervlich ◇ *adj* nervous. ◇ *adv*: **nervlich völlig am Ende sein** to be a nervous wreck.

nervös ◇ *adj* nervous; **jn nervös machen** to make sb nervous. ◇ *adv* nervously.

Nervosität *die* nervousness.

Nerz (*pl* -e) *der* - **1.** [Pelz] mink coat - **2.** [Tier] mink.

Nest (*pl* -er) *das* - **1.** [von Vögeln] nest - **2.** *fam abw* [Ortschaft] little place; **ein trostloses Nest** a miserable hole - **3.** *fam* [Bett] bed.

nett ◇ *adj* nice; **wären Sie so nett mir zu helfen?** would you mind helping me?; **eine nette Summe** a tidy sum; **das ist ja eine nette Bescherung!** what a nice mess! ◇ *adv* - **1.** [ansprechend] nicely; **sich nett unterhalten** to have a nice chat - **2.** *fam* [ziemlich]: **ganz nett verdienen** to earn pretty well.

netterweise *adv* kindly.

netto *adv* net.

Netz (*pl* -e) *das* - **1.** [zum Fischen, für Haare, im Sport] net; **jm ins Netz gehen** *fig* [gefasst werden] to fall into sb's trap - **2.** [System] network; [Strom] grid; [Internet] Web, Net; **ins Netz ge-**

hen to go on the Web - **3.** [für Akrobaten] safety net - **4.** [von Spinnen] web - **5.** [Einkaufstasche] string bag.

Netzlhaut *die* retina.

neu ◇ *adj* - **1.** [gen] new; **das ist mir neu** that's news to me; **ich bin hier neu** I'm new here - **2.** [erneuert] fresh; **eine neue Flasche holen** to fetch another bottle - **3.** [aktuell]: **die neuesten Nachrichten** the latest news; **was gibts Neues?** what's new?; **seit neuestem** just lately ODER recently. ◇ *adv* newly; **sie sind neu eingezogen** they have just (recently) moved in; **neu anfangen** to start (all over) again; **etw noch mal neu machen** to redo sthg; **neu streichen** to repaint. ➡ **aufs Neue** *adv* again. ➡ **von neuem** *adv* again.

neuartig *adj* new; **ein neuartiges Produkt** a new kind of product.

Neubau (*pl* -ten) *der* new building.

neuerdings *adv* recently, lately.

Neuerung (*pl* -en) *die* innovation; **Neuerungen einführen** to make changes.

Neugier, Neugierde *die* curiosity.

neugierig ◇ *adj* inquisitive; **sie ist neugierig, ob...** she is curious to see whether... ◇ *adv* inquisitively.

Neuheit (*pl* -en) *die* - **1.** [Produkt] innovation - **2.** [Originalität] innovativeness - **3.** [Neusein] newness.

Neuigkeit (*pl* -en) *die* news (U); **Neuigkeiten** news; **ich habe gute Neuigkeiten** I have some good news.

Neujahr (*ohne Artikel*) New Year. ➡ **prost Neujahr** *interj* Happy New Year!

neulich *adv* recently.

Neuling (*pl* -e) *der* novice.

Neulmond *der* new moon.

neun *num* nine; *siehe auch* **sechs**.

Neun (*pl* -en) *die* nine; *siehe auch* **Sechs**.

neunfach ◇ *adj* ninefold. ◇ *adv* nine times.

neunhundert *num* nine hundred.

neunmal *adv* nine times.

neuntausend *num* nine thousand.

neunte, r, s *adj* ninth; *siehe auch* **sechste**.

Neunte (*pl* -n) *der, die, das* ninth; *siehe auch* **Sechste**.

neuntel *adj* (*unver*) ninth; *siehe auch* **sechstel**.

Neuntel (*pl* -) *das* ninth; *siehe auch* **Sechstel**.

neunzehn *num* nineteen; *siehe auch* **sechs**.

Neunzehn (*pl* -en) *die* nineteen; *siehe auch* **Sechs**.

neunzig *num* ninety; *siehe auch* **sechs**.

Neunzig *die* ninety; *siehe auch* **Sechs**.

Neunzigerjahre, neunziger Jahre *Pl*: **die Neunzigerjahre** the nineties.

neureich *adj abw* nouveau riche.

Neurose (*pl* -n) *die* neurosis.

neurotisch *adj* neurotic.

Neuseeland *nt* New Zealand.

neusprachlich *adj* ▷ **Gymnasium**.

neutral ◇ *adj* neutral. ◇ *adv* neutrally.

Neutralität *die* neutrality.

Neutron (*pl* -en) *das* neutron.

Neutrum (*pl* **Neutra** ODER **Neutren**) *das* - **1.** GRAMM neuter - **2.** *abw* [Mensch] asexual creature.

neuwertig *adj* nearly new.

Neulzeit *die* (*ohne pl*) modern times *Pl*.

Newsgroup (*pl* -s) *die* EDV newsgroup.

Nicaragua *nt* Nicaragua.

nicht ◇ *adv* - **1.** [gen] not; **sie raucht nicht** she doesn't smoke; **sie mag kein Marzipan - ich auch nicht** she doesn't like marzipan - neither do I; **warum nicht?** why not? - **2.** [als Bestätigungsfrage]: **der Film war großartig, nicht wahr?** the film was great, wasn't it?; **du wusstest es schon länger, nicht (wahr)?** you've known for a while, haven't you?; **ist das nicht schön?** isn't that nice? - **3.** [verstärkend]: **was habe ich nicht alles für dich getan!** all the things I've done for you! ◇ *konj*: **nicht dass ich...** it's not that I...; **nicht nur..., sondern auch...** not only..., but also... ➡ **nicht einmal** *adv* not even; **er kann nicht einmal Englisch** he can't even speak English.

Nichte (*pl* -n) *die* niece.

Nichtlraucher *der* - **1.** [Person] non-smoker - **2.** [Abteil] no-smoking compartment.

Nichtlraucherin *die* non-smoker.

nichts *pron* nothing; **ich weiß nichts darüber** I don't know anything about it; **das macht nichts** *fig* it doesn't matter; **nichts zu danken** don't mention it; **das ist nichts für dich** it's not your kind of thing. ➡ **nichts als** *pron* nothing but. ➡ **nichts anderes** *pron* nothing else. ➡ **nichts da** *interj fam* no way!

nichts ahnend ◇ *adj* unsuspecting. ◇ *adv* unsuspectingly.

Nichtlschwimmer, in *der, die* non-swimmer.

nichts sagend *adj* [Worte, Geschwätz] empty.

Nichtstun *das* inactivity; **ich hasse dieses Nichtstun** I hate all this sitting around doing nothing.

Nickel *das* nickel.

nicken *vi* - **1.** [zustimmen] to nod; **mit dem Kopf nicken** to nod (one's head) - **2.** [dösen] to doze.

Nickerchen (*pl* -) *das*: **ein Nickerchen machen** to have a nap.

nie *adv* never; **nie im Leben!** not on your life! ➡ **nie mehr** *adv* never again. ➡ **nie und nimmer** *adv* not on your life.

nieder *adv*: **nieder mit...!** down with...!

niedere, r, s *adj* [Einkommen, Lohn, Steuerklasse] low; [Arbeit] lowly; [Motive, Triebe] base; [Adel] lesser.

Niedergang *der* decline.

niedergeschlagen <> *pp* ▷ **niederschlagen**. <> *adj* dejected. <> *adv* dejectedly.

Niederllage *die* defeat.

Niederlande *Pl*: die Niederlande the Netherlands.

Niederländer, in (*mpl* -, *fpl* -nen) *der, die* Dutchman (Dutchwoman *die*).

niederländisch *adj* Dutch.

Niederländisch(e) *das* Dutch; *siehe auch* Englisch(e).

niederllassen ◆ sich niederlassen *ref* (*unreg*) - 1. [sich setzen] to sit down - 2. [beruflich]: **sich als etw niederlassen** to set up as sthg - 3. [sich ansiedeln] to settle.

Niederlassung (*pl* -en) *die* - 1. [Unternehmen] branch - 2. [als Arzt, Rechtsanwalt] setting up in practice.

niederllegen *vt* - 1. [Amt, Mandat] to resign from - 2. *geh* [aufzeichnen] to put down - 3. *geh* [hinlegen] to lay.

Niederlösterreich *nt* Lower Austria.

Niederlsachsen ['niːdɐzaksn] *nt* Lower Saxony.

niedersächsisch ['niːdɐˈzɛksɪʃ] *adj* of/from Lower Saxony.

Niederlschlag *der* precipitation.

niederlschlagen *vt* (*unreg*) - 1. [zusammenschlagen] to knock down - 2. [Blick, Augen] to lower - 3. [Revolution] to put down. **◆ sich niederschlagen** *ref* - 1. [sich auswirken]: **sich in etw (D) ODER auf etw (A) niederschlagen** to be reflected in sthg - 2. [sich ablagern] to condense.

niederträchtig <> *adj* malicious. <> *adv* maliciously.

niedlich <> *adj* cute. <> *adv* cutely.

niedrig <> *adj* low; [Arbeit] lowly. <> *adv*: niedrig fliegen to fly low; die Preise niedrig halten to keep prices low.

niemals <> *adv* never. <> *interj* never!

niemand *pron* nobody, no one; **ich habe niemanden gesehen** I didn't see anybody; **niemand von uns spricht Französisch** none of us speaks French; **niemand anders, sonst niemand** nobody else.

Niere (*pl* -n) *die* kidney.

nieseln *vi*: es nieselt it's drizzling.

Niesellregen *der* drizzle.

niesen *vi* to sneeze.

Niete (*pl* -n) *die* - 1. [Los] losing ticket - 2. [Bolzen, Knopf] stud - 3. *fam* [Mensch] dead loss.

niet- und nagelfest *adj*: sie haben alles, was nicht niet- und nagelfest war, mitgenommen they took everything that wasn't nailed down.

Nigeria *nt* Nigeria.

Nikolaus (*pl* -läuse) *der* - 1. [Person]: **der Nikolaus** St Nicholas (*who brings children presents on 6 December*), ≃ Santa Claus - 2. [aus Schokolade] chocolate Santa Claus.

Nikolausltag *der* St Nicholas' Day (*6 December*).

Nikotin *das* nicotine.

Nil *der*: der Nil the (River) Nile.

Nillpferd *das* hippopotamus.

nimmt *präs* ▷ **nehmen**.

nirgends, nirgendwo *adv* nowhere.

Nische (*pl* -n) *die* - 1. [in der Wand - klein] niche; [- groß] recess - 2. [für Produkt, Lebewesen] niche.

nisten *vi* to nest.

Niveau [niˈvoː] (*pl* -s) *das* level; **Niveau haben** [Person] to be cultured; **der Krimi hat Niveau** the detective story is quality literature.

Nixe (*pl* -n) *die* water nymph.

nobel <> *adj* - 1. [kostspielig] luxurious - 2. *hum* [vornehm] posh - 3. *geh* [großzügig] noble. <> *adv* - 1. [kostspielig] luxuriously - 2. *geh* [großzügig] nobly - 3. *hum* [vornehm]: **sich nobel kleiden** to dress posh.

noch <> *adv* - 1. [immer noch] still; **wir haben noch Zeit** we still have time; **er hat noch nichts gesagt** he still hasn't said anything; **hast du noch Geld?** have you got any money left? - 2. [nicht später] only; **das muss noch heute gemacht werden** it has to be done today; **schafft ihr das noch bis Freitag?** do you think you'll manage it by Friday? - 3. [zur Warnung]: **du wirst noch an meine Worte denken!** mark my words! - 4. [zusätzlich]: **noch einen Kaffee, bitte!** another coffee, please!; **ich muss noch ein paar Einkäufe machen** I have to buy a few more things; **wer noch?** who else? - 5. (+ *kompar*) even; **noch schneller** even quicker; **noch komplizierter** even more complicated - 6. [rhetorisch]: **wie war noch sein Name?** what was his name again?; **man wird ja wohl noch fragen dürfen** I was only asking. <> *konj*: **weder... noch... neither... nor...** ◆ **noch einmal, noch mal** *adv* again. ◆ **noch immer, immer noch** *adv* still. ◆ **noch mehr** *adv* even more. ◆ **noch nicht** *adv* not yet. ◆ **noch und noch** *adv*: **Leute noch und noch** lots and lots of people; **es regnete noch und noch** it rained for hours on end. ◆ **noch so** *adv*: **sei es auch noch so klein** however small it may be; **es kann noch so regnen** however much it rains.

nochmals *adv* again.

Nomade (*pl* -n) *der* nomad.

Nomadin (*pl* -nen) *die* nomad.

Nominativ (*pl* -e) *der* nominative.

Nonne (*pl* -n) *die* nun.

Nordlamerika *nt* North America.

norddeutsch *adj* Northern German.

Norden der north; **nach Norden** north; **im Norden** in the north.

Nord|europa nt Northern Europe.

Nord|irland nt Northern Ireland.

nordisch adj Nordic.

Nord|kap das North Cape.

Nord|korea nt North Korea.

nördlich <> adj northern; [Wind] northerly. <> präp: **nördlich einer Sache** (G) ODER **von** etw to the north of sthg.

Nord|osten der northeast.

Nord|pol der - 1. GEOGR North Pole - 2. PHYS north pole.

Nordrhein-Westfalen nt North Rhine-Westphalia.

Nord|see die North Sea.

Nord|westen der northwest.

nörgeln vi: (über jn/etw) **nörgeln** to moan (about sb/sthg).

Norm (pl -en) die - 1. TECH [Regel] norm - 2. [Leistung] standard.

normal <> adj normal. <> adv normally.

Normal|benzin das regular petrol UK, regular gas US.

normalerweise adv normally, usually.

normalisieren vt to normalize. **sich normalisieren** ref to return to normal.

normen vt to standardize.

Norwegen nt Norway.

Norweger, in (mpl -, fpl -nen) der, die Norwegian.

norwegisch adj Norwegian.

Norwegisch(e) das Norwegian; siehe auch **Englisch(e)**.

Not (pl **Nöte**) die - 1. [Notlage, Armut] need; **in Not sein** to be in need; **Not leidend** needy - 2. [Verzweiflung] despair; **Nöte** [Sorgen] troubles; **Not tun** to be needed; **zur Not** fam if needs be.

Notar (pl -e) der notary.

notariell <> adj notarial, notary's. <> adv by a notary.

Notarin (pl -nen) die notary.

Not|arzt, ärztin der, die emergency doctor.

Not|ausgang der emergency exit.

Not|bremse die emergency brake.

notdürftig <> adj makeshift. <> adv provisionally; [bekleidet] scantily.

Note (pl -n) die - 1. [Beurteilung] mark UK, grade US - 2. MUS note; **nach Noten** with music ODER a score - 3. [Eigenschaft] touch.

Not|fall der emergency. **im Notfall** adv in an emergency.

notfalls adv if necessary.

notgedrungen adv out of necessity.

notieren <> vt - 1. [aufschreiben] to note down; **sich** (D) **etw notieren** to make a note of sthg - 2. [Aktie] to quote. <> vi WIRTSCH: **höher/niedriger notieren** to rise/fall.

nötig <> adj necessary; **etw nötig haben** to need sthg; **du hast es gerade nötig!** iron you can talk!; **sie hat es nicht nötig zu putzen** ha, she doesn't have ODER need to do the cleaning! <> adv fam urgently.

Notiz (pl -en) die note; [in der Zeitung] notice; **keine Notiz von jm/etw nehmen** to take no notice of sb/sthg. **Notizen** Pl notes.

Notiz|buch das notebook.

Not|lage die crisis.

Not|lösung die temporary solution.

Not|ruf der emergency call; [Nummer] emergency number.

Notruf|säule die emergency phone.

notwendig, notwendig <> adj - 1. [nötig] necessary - 2. [logisch] inevitable. <> adv necessarily.

Novelle [no'vɛlə] (pl -n) die - 1. [Literatur] novella - 2. RECHT amendment.

November [no'vɛmbɐ] der November; siehe auch **September**.

Nr. (abk für **Nummer**) no.

NRW abk für **Nordrhein-Westfalen**.

nüchtern <> adj - 1. [nicht betrunken] sober - 2. [sachlich] matter-of-fact - 3. [mit leerem Magen]: **nüchtern sein** to have an empty stomach; **auf nüchternen Magen** on an empty stomach. <> adv - 1. [nicht betrunken] soberly - 2. [sachlich] matter-of-factly - 3. [mit leerem Magen] on an empty stomach.

Nudel (pl -n) die noodle; **Nudeln** [italienisch] pasta; [chinesisch, in Suppe] noodles.

null <> num zero; **null Komma fünf** zero ODER nought UK point five; **eins zu null** one-zero, one-nil UK; **null und nichtig** fig null and void. <> adj (unver) fam no; siehe auch **sechs**.

Null (pl -en) die - 1. [Zahl] zero - 2. fam abw [Mensch] dead loss.

Null|punkt der - 1. [Tiefpunkt]: **auf den Nullpunkt sinken** to hit rock-bottom - 2. PHYS zero.

numerieren = **nummerieren**.

Nummer (pl -n) die - 1. [Zahl] number - 2. [Größe] size - 3. [im Zirkus] act - 4. fam [Mensch] character - 5. salopp [Geschlechtsakt] shag.

nummerieren vt to number.

Nummern|schild das numberplate UK, license plate US.

nun <> adv - 1. [gen] now; **von nun an** from now on - 2. [Ausdruck der Ungeduld]: **bist du nun zufrieden?** are you happy now?; **was denn nun?** so what happens now? <> interj now; **nun denn** right ODER well then; **nun gut** oh well. **nun mal** adv now; **das ist nun mal so!** that's just the way it is!

nur adv - 1. [lediglich] only, just; **ich bin nicht krank, nur müde** I'm not ill, just tired - 2. [jedoch] but, yet - 3. [verstärkend]: **was meint er nur?** what does he mean?; **wenn sie nur käme!** if only she would come!; **kommen Sie nur**

herein! do come in!; **nur keine Panik!** don't panic!; **hätte ich nur auf dich gehört!** if only I'd listened to you! ◆ **nur noch** adv: **ich habe nur noch 10 Euro** I've only got 10 euros left. ◆ **nur so** adv: **das sagt er nur so** fam he's just saying that; **der Putz bröckelt nur so** the plaster is crumbling really badly. ◆ **nur zu** interj go on!

nuscheln vi to mumble.

Nuss (pl Nüsse) die - 1. [Frucht] nut - 2. fam abw [Mensch]: **du dumme Nuss!** you stupid idiot!

Nussbaum (pl -bäume) der - 1. [Baum] walnut tree - 2. [Holz] walnut.

Nussknacker (pl -) der [Gerät] nut-cracker.

Nutte (pl -n) die salopp - 1. [Prostituierte] tart, hooker US - 2. abw [Frau] slut.

nutzbar adj usable; **(sich (D)) etw nutzbar machen** [Energiequelle] to harness sthg; [Boden, Land] to cultivate sthg.

nütze adj (unver.): **zu etwas/nichts nütze sein** to be of some/no use.

nutzen, nützen ⟨⟩ vt to use; **das nützt nichts/nicht viel** that's no/not much use. ⟨⟩ vi: **jm nutzen** to be of use to sb.

Nutzen der benefit.

nützlich adj useful; **sich nützlich machen** to make o.s. useful.

nutzlos ⟨⟩ adj useless. ⟨⟩ adv uselessly.

Nutzung (pl -en) die [von Bodenschätzen] exploitation; [von Energiequelle] harnessing.

NW (abk für Nordwest) NW.

Nylon® ['nailɔn] das nylon.

o (pl o ODER -s), **O** (pl O ODER -s) [o:] das o, O. ◆ **O** (abk für Ost) E.

Oase (pl -n) die oasis.

ob konj whether; **ich weiß nicht, ob er kommt** I don't know whether ODER if he'll come; **ob er wohl kommt?** I wonder if he'll come?; **und ob!** you bet! ◆ **als ob** konj as if, as though; **(so) tun als ob** to pretend (that); **er tat, als ob er sie nicht gesehen hätte** he pretended not to have seen her.

ÖBB (abk für Österreichische Bundesbahn), Austrian Railways.

Obelisk (pl -en) der obelisk.

oben adv - 1. [räumlich] up; [obenauf] at the top; **hier/dort oben** up here/there; **links/rechts oben im Bild** in the top left-hand/right-hand

corner of the picture; **bis oben hin** up to the top; **nach oben** up; [im Haus] upstairs; **mit dem Gesicht nach oben** face up; **von oben** down; **von oben bis unten** from top to bottom; **von oben herab** fig condescendingly; **weiter oben** further up; **oben ohne** fig topless - 2. [im Text] above; **siehe oben** see above; **oben erwähnt** above-mentioned.

Ober (pl -) der waiter; **Herr Ober!** waiter!

Ober|arm der upper arm.

obere, r, s adj upper.

Ober|fläche die - 1. [Außenfläche] surface - 2. MATH (surface) area.

oberflächlich ⟨⟩ adj superficial. ⟨⟩ adv superficially.

Obergeschoss (pl -e) das top floor; **im dritten Obergeschoss** on the third UK ODER fourth US floor.

Ober|haupt das head.

Ober|hemd das shirt.

Ober|körper der upper body; **den Oberkörper freimachen** to strip to the waist, to take one's top off.

Ober|lippe die upper lip.

Ober|österreich nt Upper Austria.

Ober|schenkel der thigh.

Ober|schicht die: **die Oberschicht** the upper classes Pl.

Oberst (pl -en ODER -e) der colonel.

oberste, r, s adj top; [Gericht] supreme; **die oberste Heeresleitung** the military high command.

Ober|stufe die SCHULE final three years of secondary education.

Ober|teil das top.

Ober|weite die bust (measurement).

Objekt (pl -e) das - 1. [Gegenstand, KUNST & GRAMM] object - 2. [Immobilie] property.

objektiv [ɔpjɛk'tiːf] ⟨⟩ adj objective. ⟨⟩ adv objectively.

Objektiv (pl -e) das FOTO lens.

Oboe (pl -n) die oboe.

Obst das fruit.

Obst|baum der fruit tree.

obszön ⟨⟩ adj obscene. ⟨⟩ adv obscenely.

obwohl konj although.

Ochse ['ɔksə] (pl -n) der [Rind] ox.

öde adj - 1. [trostlos] desolate - 2. fam [langweilig] dreary.

oder konj - 1. [gen] or - 2. fam [als Bestätigungsfrage]: **du kommst doch mit, oder?** you're going to come, aren't you?; **du hast doch kein Auto, oder?** you haven't got a car, have you? ◆ **oder aber** konj or (else). ◆ **oder auch** konj or. ◆ **oder so** adv or something like that.

Oder die: **die Oder** the (River) Oder.

Ofen (pl **Öfen**) der - **1.** [Wärmespender] stove; **elektrischer Ofen** (electric) heater - **2.** [Backofen] oven - **3.** fam [Motorrad] bike.

offen <> adj - **1.** [gen] open; **das Geschäft hat bis 6 Uhr offen** the shop is open until 6 o'clock; **sperrangelweit offen** wide open; **mit offenen Augen** with one's eyes open; **auf offenem Meer** on the open sea; **für etw offen sein** to have an open mind about sthg; **offen zu jm sein, jm gegenüber offen sein** to be frank ODER open with sb - **2.** [unverpackt] loose, unpacked; **offene Weine** wine by the glass/carafe - **3.** [lose] undone; **der Knopf ist offen** the button has come undone; **mit offenen Haaren** with one's hair down - **4.** [Rechnung] outstanding. <> adv openly; **etw offen zugeben** to admit sthg openly; **offen gesagt** quite honestly.

offenbar adv obviously, clearly.

offen bleiben (perf **ist offen geblieben**) vi (unreg) - **1.** [Tür, Geschäft] to stay open - **2.** [Frage, Problem] to remain unresolved.

Offenheit (pl **-en**) die - **1.** [Ehrlichkeit] frankness; **in aller Offenheit** in all honesty - **2.** [Aufgeschlossenheit] openness.

offenherzig adj - **1.** [Mensch] open-hearted - **2.** fam hum [Kleidung] revealing.

offen lassen vt (unreg) eigtl & fig to leave open.

offensichtlich <> adj [Lüge, Betrug, Bevorzugung] blatant; [Wohlstand, Begabung] obvious; **es ist offensichtlich, dass...** [eindeutig] it is clear that... <> adv obviously, clearly; [lügen] blatantly.

offen stehen vi (unreg) - **1.** [Tür, Fenster] to be open - **2.** [zugänglich sein]: **jm offen stehen** to be open to sb - **3.** [Rechnung] to be outstanding.

öffentlich <> adj public. <> adv publicly; [auftreten] in public.

Öffentlichkeit die public; **etw an die Öffentlichkeit bringen** to make sthg public; **in aller Öffentlichkeit** in front of everyone.

offiziell <> adj official. <> adv officially.

Offizier (pl **-e**) der officer.

offline ['ɔflain] adv EDV offline; **offline gehen** to go offline.

öffnen <> vt - **1.** [gen] to open - **2.** [lösen] to undo. <> vi to open; **jm öffnen** to open the door to sb. ⬧ **sich öffnen** ref to open; [neue Märkte etc] to open up.

Öffnung (pl **-en**) die opening; [von Körper] orifice; [von Flasche] mouth; [in Mauer] gap.

Öffnungszeiten Pl opening hours.

oft (kompar **öfter**, superl **am öftesten**) adv often; **wie oft?** how often?, how many times?

öfter, öfters adv quite often; **warst du schon öfter hier?** have you been here often?; **öfter als mir lieb ist** more often than I'd like.

ohne <> präp (+ A) without; **ein Ehepaar ohne Kinder** a couple with no children; **das ist ohne Weiteres möglich** it's perfectly possible. <> konj without; **sie tat es, ohne dass er merkte** she did it without him noticing; **ohne zu fragen** without asking. ⬧ **ohne mich** interj count me out!

ohnehin adv anyway.

Ohnmacht (pl **-en**) die - **1.** [Bewusstlosigkeit] unconsciousness; **in Ohnmacht fallen** to faint - **2.** [Machtlosigkeit] impotence.

ohnmächtig <> adj - **1.** [bewusstlos] unconscious; **ohnmächtig werden** to faint - **2.** [machtlos] impotent. <> adv - **1.** [bewusstlos]: **ohnmächtig daliegen** to lie there unconscious - **2.** [zusehen, ausgeliefert] helplessly.

Ohr (pl **-en**) das [von Person, Tier] ear; **halt die Ohren steif!** fam chin up!; **jn übers Ohr hauen** fam to take sb for a ride.

ohrenbetäubend <> adj deafening. <> adv deafeningly.

Ohr|feige die slap (in the face).

ohrfeigen vt to slap (in the face).

Ohr|läppchen (pl **Ohrläppchen**) das earlobe.

Ohr|ring der earring.

Ohr|wurm der catchy tune; **ein Ohrwurm sein** to be catchy.

Öko|laden der wholefood store.

ökologisch <> adj ecological. <> adv ecologically.

ökonomisch <> adj - **1.** WIRTSCH economic - **2.** [sparsam] economical. <> adv economically.

Öko|steuer die ecotax.

Öko|system das ecosystem.

Oktan (pl **-e**) das octane.

Oktave [ɔk'taːvə] (pl **-n**) die octave.

Oktober der October; **der 3. Oktober** German national holiday commemorating reunification on 3 October 1990; siehe auch **September**.

Oktober|fest das Munich beer festival.

Öl (pl **-e**) das - **1.** [gen] oil - **2.** KUNST oils Pl.

ölen vt to oil.

Öl|farbe die - **1.** KUNST oil paint; **mit Ölfarben malen** to paint in oils - **2.** [Streichmittel] oil-based paint.

Öl|gemälde das oil painting.

Öl|heizung die oil-fired central heating.

ölig <> adj oily. <> adv: **ölig glänzen** to have an oily sheen.

Olive [oˈliːvə] (pl **-n**) die olive.

Öl|pest die oil slick.

Öl|quelle die oil well.

olympisch *adj* SPORT Olympic.

Olympische Spiele *Pl* Olympic Games.

Oma (*pl* -s) *die* - 1. [Großmutter] grandma, granny - 2. *fam abw* [Frau] grandma; **die Oma vor mir** the old dear in front of me.

Omelett [ɔm(ə)'lɛt] (*pl* -e *ODER* -s) *das* omelette.

Omnibus *der* [Linienbus] bus; [Reisebus] bus, coach *UK*.

Onkel (*pl* -) *der* - 1. [Verwandter, Freund] uncle - 2. *fam* [Mann]: **gib dem Onkel die Hand** give the nice man your hand.

online ['ɔnlaɪn] ◇ *adj* EDV [angeschlossen] online; **online sein** to be online. ◇ *adv* online.

Online-Banking ['ɔnlaɪnbɛŋkɪŋ] *das* online *ODER* Internet banking.

Online-Dienst ['ɔnlaɪndiːnst] *der* EDV online service.

OP [oː'peː] (*pl* -s) (*abk für* **Operationssaal**) *der* OR *US*, operating theatre *UK*.

Opa (*pl* -s) *der* - 1. [Großvater] grandpa, grandad - 2. *fam abw* [Mann] grandpa, grandad.

Open-Air-Konzert *das* open-air concert.

Oper (*pl* -n) *die* - 1. MUS opera - 2. [Opernhaus] opera house; **in die Oper gehen** to go to the opera.

Operation (*pl* -en) *die* operation.

Operette (*pl* -n) *die* operetta.

operieren ◇ *vt* to operate on; **jn am Blinddarm operieren** to operate on sb's appendix; **sich operieren lassen** to have an operation. ◇ *vi* to operate; **behutsam operieren** to proceed carefully.

Opfer (*pl* -) *das* - 1. [Mensch - von Unglück, Leidenschaften] victim - 2. [Verzicht & RELIG] sacrifice; **jm/einer Sache zum Opfer fallen** to fall victim to sb/sthg.

opfern *vt* to sacrifice; **jm etw opfern** to sacrifice sthg for sb; **jetzt habe ich dir so viel Zeit geopfert** now I've given up so much time for you. ◆ **sich opfern** *ref* - 1. [sich aufopfern] to sacrifice o.s. - 2. *fam hum* [sich bereit erklären]: **wer opfert sich freiwillig und geht zum Chef?** who's going to volunteer to go to the boss?

Opium *das* opium.

Opposition (*pl* -en) *die* opposition; **in Opposition zu etw stehen** to be opposed to sthg.

Optik *die* - 1. PHYS optics (*U*) - 2. [Sichtweise] point of view - 3. [Erscheinungsbild] appearance.

Optiker, in (*mpl* -, *fpl* -nen) *der, die* optician.

optimal ◇ *adj* optimal. ◇ *adv* optimally.

Optimismus *der* optimism.

optimistisch ◇ *adj* optimistic. ◇ *adv* optimistically.

optisch ◇ *adj* - 1. PHYS optical - 2. [visuell] visual. ◇ *adv* [visuell] visually.

orange [o'rãːʒə] *adj* orange.

Orange[1] [o'rãŋːʒə] (*pl* -n) *die* [Frucht] orange.

Orange[2] [o'rãːʒ] (*pl* Orange) *das* [Farbe] orange.

Orangensaft *der* orange juice.

Orchester [ɔr'kɛstɐ] (*pl* -) *das* orchestra.

Orchidee [ɔrçi'deːə] (*pl* -n) *die* orchid.

Orden (*pl* -) *der* - 1. [Auszeichnung] decoration; [Medaille] medal; **jm einen Orden verleihen** to decorate sb - 2. RELIG order.

ordentlich ◇ *adj* - 1. [Person, Schreibtisch, Wohnung] tidy; [Schrift, Hausaufgabe] neat; [Leben] orderly - 2. [regelgerecht - Mitglied] full; **ordentliches Gericht** court for civil and criminal cases - 3. [Note, Ergebnis] respectable - 4. [Verdienst, Schluck] good; [Portion] good-sized; **einen ordentlichen Schreck kriegen** to get a real fright - 5. [anständig] proper. ◇ *adv* - 1. [sauber] tidily; [schreiben, gekleidet] neatly - 2. [nach Regeln] correctly, in accordance with correct procedures - 3. [viel] really well; **ordentlich verdienen** to earn good money; **sie hat mit mir ordentlich geschimpft** she gave me a real telling-off.

ordinär ◇ *adj* - 1. *abw* [vulgär - Person, Witz] crude; [- Benehmen, Kleidung] vulgar, common - 2. [normal] ordinary. ◇ *adv abw* [vulgär - lachen, fluchen] crudely; [- sich verhalten, sich kleiden] vulgarly, commonly.

ordnen *vt* - 1. [sortieren] to sort out; [Gedanken] to organize; **etw nach Datum ordnen** to arrange sthg according to date - 2. [aufräumen] to tidy up - 3. [regeln - Finanzen, Affären, Privatleben] to put in order. ◆ **sich ordnen** *ref*: **sich zu etw ordnen** to form sthg.

Ordner (*pl* -) *der* - 1. [Hefter] file - 2. [Person] steward.

Ordnerin (*pl* -nen) *die* steward.

Ordnung (*pl* -en) *die* - 1. [geordneter Zustand] tidiness; **Ordnung schaffen** to tidy up - 2. [Disziplin, Gesetzmäßigkeit] order; **für Ordnung sorgen** to keep order - 3. [Anordnung] order; **in alphabetischer Ordnung** in alphabetical order - 4. [Grad]: **eine Dummheit erster Ordnung** an extremely stupid thing to do; **etw in Ordnung bringen** [ordnen, erledigen] to sort sthg out; **in Ordnung sein** *fam* to be okay; **sie lässt ihre Tochter allein zu Hause?** das ist nicht in Ordnung she leaves her daughter alone at home? that's not right; **der Computer ist nicht in Ordnung** there's something wrong with the computer. ◆ **in Ordnung** *interj* okay!

ordnungsgemäß *adj* & *adv* in accordance with the regulations.

ordnungswidrig *amt* ◇ *adj* [Parken] illegal; **ordnungswidriges Verhalten im**

Straßenverkehr minor traffic offence. <> *adv* [parken] illegally; **sich ordnungswidrig verhalten** to contravene the regulations.

Oregano *der* oregano.

ORF (*abk für Österreichischer Rundfunk*) *Austrian radio and television corporation.*

Organ (*pl* -e) *das* - 1. [gen] organ - 2. [Stimme] voice.

Organisation (*pl* -en) *die* organization.

organisatorisch <> *adj* organizational. <> *adv* organizationally.

organisch *adj* - 1. [eines Körperteils] physical - 2. [natürlich & CHEM] organic.

organisieren *vt* - 1. [veranstalten, ordnen] to organize - 2. [gründen] to form - 3. *fam* [beschaffen] to get hold of - 4. *fam* [stehlen] to pinch. ➡ **sich organisieren** *ref* - 1. [sich zusammenschließen] to organize - 2. [sich bilden] to develop.

Organismus (*pl* -men) *der* organism.

Organizer *der* (electronic) organizer.

Organspende *die* organ donation.

Orgasmus (*pl* -men) *der* orgasm.

Orgel (*pl* -n) *die* organ.

Orient ['oːriɛnt] *der* - 1. [der Nahe Osten] Middle East - 2. [Asien] Orient.

orientalisch *adj* - 1. [vom Nahen Osten] Middle Eastern - 2. [vom Morgenland] oriental.

orientieren [oriɛn'tiːrən] *vt* - 1. [ausrichten]: etw nach ODER an etw (D) orientieren to base sthg on sthg - 2. [informieren]: **jn über etw** (A) **orientieren** to inform sb about sthg. ➡ **sich orientieren** *ref* - 1. [sich zurechtfinden] to orientate o.s., to get one's bearings - 2. [sich informieren]: **sich über etw** (A) **orientieren** to inform o.s. about sthg - 3. [sich ausrichten]: **sich nach** ODER **an etw** (D) **orientieren** to be orientated towards sthg; **sich nach der Mutter orientieren** to follow the example of one's mother.

Orientierung *die* (ohne pl) - 1. [Zurechtfinden]: **die Orientierung in der Wüste ist nicht einfach** it's not easy to get one's bearings in the desert; **dieser Stadtplan ist zu Ihrer Orientierung** this city map is to help you find your way around; **die Orientierung verlieren** to lose one's bearings - 2. [Information] information - 3. [Ausrichtung]: **Orientierung nach** ODER **an etw** (D) orientation towards sthg; [nach Vorgaben, Richtlinien] conformance to sthg; **vielen Jugendlichen fehlt die Orientierung an religiösen Werten** many young people are not guided by religious values.

Orientierungssinn *der* sense of direction.

original <> *adj* - 1. [ursprünglich] original - 2. [unverfälscht] genuine. <> *adv* - 1. [echt]: **eine original chinesische Tasse** a genuine Chinese tea cup - 2. [direkt] live.

Original (*pl* -e) *das* - 1. [Urform] original - 2. [Person] character.

Orkan (*pl* -e) *der* hurricane.

Ort (*pl* -e) *der* - 1. [gen] place; [von Verbrechen] scene; **an Ort und Stelle** on the spot - 2. [Ortschaft - Dorf] village; [- Stadt] small town. ➡ **vor Ort** *adv* on the spot.

Orthografie (*pl* -n), **Orthographie** (*pl* -n) [ɔrtogra'fiː] *die* spelling, orthography.

Orthopädie *die* orthopaedics (*U*).

orthopädisch <> *adj* orthopaedic. <> *adv* orthopaedically.

ortsansässig *adj* local.

Ortschaft (*pl* -en) *die* village.

Ortsgespräch *das* TELEKOM local call.

ortskundig *adj*: **ich bin hier ortskundig** I'm familiar with this area.

Ortsnetz *das* - 1. TELEKOM local (telephone) exchange - 2. ELEKTR local grid.

öS (*abk für österreichischer Schilling*) Sch.

Öse (*pl* -n) *die* eye; [von Schuh] eyelet.

Oslo *nt* Oslo.

Ossi (*pl* -s) *der fam* term used to describe citizen of the former GDR.

Ostblock *der* Eastern bloc.

ostdeutsch *adj* [Gebiet] Eastern German; POL East German.

Ostdeutschland *nt* [Gebiet] Eastern Germany; [DDR] East Germany.

Osten *der* - 1. [Richtung] east; **nach Osten** east - 2. [Gegend] East; **im Osten** in the East - 3. POL: **der Osten** the East.

Osterei *das* Easter egg.

Osterhase *der* Easter Bunny.

Ostern *nt* Easter; **an** ODER **zu Ostern** at Easter. ➡ **frohe Ostern** *interj* Happy Easter!

Österreich *nt* Austria.

Österreicher, in (*mpl* -, *fpl* -nen) *der, die* Austrian.

österreichisch *adj* Austrian.

Ostersonntag (*pl* -e) *der* Easter Sunday.

Osteuropa *nt* Eastern Europe.

Ostfriesland *nt* East Frisia.

Ostküste *die* east coast.

östlich <> *adj* eastern; [Wind] east. <> *adv*: **östlich einer Sache** (G) ODER **von etw** to the east of sthg.

Ostpolitik *die* Ostpolitik.

Ostpreußen *nt* East Prussia.

Ostsee *die*: **die Ostsee** the Baltic (Sea).

Otter (*pl* - ODER -n) <> *der* (*pl* Otter) otter. <> *die* (*pl* Ottern) viper.

ÖTV [øːˈteːtaʊ] (*abk für Gewerkschaft Öffentliche Dienste, Transport und Verkehr*) *die German public services and transport workers' union.*

Outdoor-Aktivitäten *Pl* outdoor pursuits.

outen *vt* to out. ➡ **sich outen** *ref* to come out.

outsourcen *vt* to outsource.

Outsourcing [ˈautsoː(r)sɪŋ] *das* out-sourcing.

oval [oˈvaːl] ◇ *adj* oval. ◇ *adv* in/into an oval.

ÖVP [øӯ:fauˈpeː] (*abk für* **Österreichische Volkspartei**) *die* Austrian People's Party, *Christian Democratic political party in Austria.*

oxidieren, oxydieren ◇ *vi* (*perf* hat/ist oxidiert *ODER* oxydiert) to oxidize. ◇ *vt* (*perf* hat oxidiert *ODER* oxydiert) to oxidize.

Ozean (*pl* -e) *der* ocean.

Ozon *der ODER das* ozone.

P

p (*pl* - *ODER* -s), **P** (*pl* - *ODER* -s) [peː] *das* p, P.

paar *adj* few. ◆ **ein paar** *det* a few; **kannst du mal ein paar Minuten rüberkommen?** can you come over here for a couple of minutes?

Paar (*pl* -e *ODER* -) *das* - 1. (*pl* Paare) [zwei Personen] couple - 2. (*pl* Paar) [zwei Dinge] pair; **ein Paar Strümpfe** a pair of socks.

paaren *vt* - 1. [Tiere] to mate - 2. [kombinieren] to combine. ◆ **sich paaren** *ref* [kopulieren] to mate.

paarmal ◆ **ein paarmal** *adv* a few times; **den Film habe ich ein paarmal gesehen** I've seen the film a couple of times.

Paarung (*pl* -en) *die* - 1. [von Tieren] mating - 2. [von Spielern, Mannschaften] pairing.

paarweise *adv* in pairs.

Pacht (*pl* -en) *die* - 1. [das Pachten, Vertrag] lease; **etw in Pacht haben** to lease sthg - 2. [Geld] rent.

Pächter, in (*mpl* -, *fpl* -nen) *der, die* - 1. [von Geschäft] leaseholder - 2. [von Grundstück] tenant.

Pack *das abw* rabble.

Päckchen (*pl* -) *das* - 1. [Paket] small parcel - 2. [Packung] packet.

packen ◇ *vt* - 1. [voll packen] to pack; **seine Sachen packen** to pack one's things - 2. [legen, stellen]: **etw auf/unter etw** (*A*) **packen** to put sthg on/under sthg; **etw aus etw packen** to take sthg out of sthg - 3. [fassen] to seize - 4. [überkommen]: **mich packt das Grauen** I am filled with horror - 5. [emotional bewegen] to grip - 6. *fam* [schaffen - Studium, Prüfung] to get through; **glaubst du, du packst es?** do you think you can manage?; **sie hat den Bus noch**

gepackt she managed to catch the bus - 7. *salopp* [begreifen] to get. ◇ *vi* [vor Reisen] to pack.

Packen (*pl* -) ◇ *der* pile; [zusammengeschnürt] bundle. ◇ *das* packing.

packend ◇ *adj* gripping. ◇ *adv* grippingly.

Pack|papier *das* brown paper.

Packung (*pl* -en) *die* - 1. [für Waren] packet - 2. MED compress; [aus Eis] ice pack - 3. [Gesichtspackung] face pack.

Pädagogik *die* education.

pädagogisch ◇ *adj* educational; **ihre pädagogischen Fähigkeiten** her teaching ability; **meine pädagogische Ausbildung** my training in education. ◇ *adv* educationally.

Paddel (*pl* -) *das* paddle.

Paddel|boot *das* canoe.

paddeln (*perf* hat/ist gepaddelt) *vi* - 1. (*hat*) [rudern] to paddle - 2. (*ist*) [Boot fahren] to canoe.

paffen *fam* ◇ *vt* [rauchen] to puff at. ◇ *vi* - 1. *abw* [rauchen] to puff away - 2. [nicht Lunge rauchen]: **du paffst ja nur!** you're not inhaling!

Page [ˈpaːʒə] (*pl* -n) *der* [im Hotel] bellboy *UK*, bellhop *US*.

Paket (*pl* -e) *das* - 1. [Postsendung] parcel - 2. [Packung] packet - 3. [Packen] bundle - 4. [Zusammenstellung] package.

Pakistan *nt* Pakistan.

Pakt (*pl* -e) *der* pact; **einen Pakt schließen** to make a pact.

Palast (*pl* Paläste) *der* palace.

Palästina *nt* Palestine.

Palästinenser, in (*mpl* -, *fpl* -nen) *der, die* Palestinian.

palästinensisch *adj* Palestinian.

Palette (*pl* -n) *die* - 1. [für Farben] palette - 2. [zum Transport] pallet - 3. [Vielfalt] range.

Palme (*pl* -n) *die* palm (tree).

Palm|sonntag (*pl* -e) *der* Palm Sunday.

Pampelmuse (*pl* -n) *die* grapefruit.

pampig *fam* ◇ *adj* - 1. [frech] insolent - 2. [breiig] mushy. ◇ *adv* [frech] insolently.

Panama|kanal *der* Panama Canal.

panieren *vt* to coat with breadcrumbs; **paniertes Schnitzel** breaded escalope of pork.

Panier|mehl *das* (*ohne pl*) breadcrumbs *Pl*.

Panik *die* panic; **in Panik geraten** to panic.

panisch ◇ *adj* [Reaktion] panic-stricken; **eine panische Angst vor etw** (*D*) **haben** to be terrified of sthg. ◇ *adv* [reagieren] with panic; **sich panisch fürchten** to be terrified.

Panne (*pl* -n) *die* - 1. [mit Auto, Maschine] breakdown; **eine Panne haben** to break down - 2. [Fehler] slip-up; [Versprecher] slip; **die Veranstaltung verlief ohne jede Panne** the event went off without a hitch.

Pannen|dienst der breakdown service.

panschen ⬦ vt [mit Chemikalien] to adulterate; [mit Wasser] to water down. ⬦ vi [mit Chemikalien] to adulterate the drinks; [mit Wasser] to water down the drinks.

Panther (pl -), **Panter** (pl -) der panther.

Pantoffel (pl -n) der slipper.

Pantomime (pl -n) ⬦ die mime. ⬦ der mime artist.

Panzer (pl -) der - 1. [Fahrzeug] tank - 2. [von Insekt, Schildkröte] shell; [von Krokodil] armour - 3. [Schutzplatte] armour plating.

Papa (pl -s) der fam dad, daddy.

Papagei (pl -en) der parrot.

Papier (pl -e) das - 1. [gen] paper - 2. [Wertpapier] security. ⬤ **Papiere** Pl [Ausweis, persönliches Dokument] documents; **Ihre Papiere bitte** your papers, please; **seine Papiere bekommen** ODER **kriegen** fam fig to be fired, to get the sack UK.

Papier|geld das paper money.

Papier|korb der wastepaper basket UK, wastebasket US.

Papier|kram der fam abw paperwork.

Papierwaren|geschäft das stationer's.

Papp|becher der paper cup.

Pappe (pl -n) die cardboard.

Papp|karton der cardboard box.

Paprika (pl - ODER -s) der - 1. [Gemüse] pepper - 2. [Gewürz] paprika.

Paprika|schote die pepper.

Papst (pl Päpste) der pope.

Parabel (pl -n) die - 1. MATH parabola - 2. [Gleichnis] parable.

Parade (pl -n) die - 1. [Aufmarsch] parade - 2. [bei Fechten] parry; [bei Ballspiel] save.

Paradies (pl -e) das paradise.

paradiesisch adj heavenly.

Paragraf (pl -en), **Paragraph** (pl -en) der - 1. [in Vertrag, Gesetz] section; [in Verfassung] article - 2. [typografisches Zeichen] paragraph.

parallel ⬦ adj parallel. ⬦ adv - 1. [gleichzeitig]: **parallel zu etw** at the same time as sthg - 2. [in gleichem Abstand]: **parallel zu etw verlaufen** to run parallel to sthg.

Parallele (pl -n) die - 1. MATH parallel line - 2. [Entsprechung] parallel; **Parallelen zu etw ziehen** to draw parallels with sthg.

Parallelogramm (pl -e) das parallelogram.

Paranuss (pl -nüsse) die brazil nut.

Parasit (pl -en) der eigtl & fig parasite.

parat ⬦ adv: **etw parat haben/halten** to have/keep sthg ready; **auf diese Frage habe ich keine passende Antwort parat** I don't have a ready answer to this question. ⬦ adj (unver): **parat sein** to be ready.

Pärchen (pl -) das couple.

Parfüm (pl -e ODER -s) das perfume.

Parfümerie [parfymə'ri:] (pl -n) die perfumery.

parfümieren vt to perfume. ⬤ **sich parfümieren** ref: **sich stark parfümieren** [Frau] to wear a lot of perfume; [Mann] to wear a lot of aftershave.

Pariser (pl -) der fam [Kondom] rubber.

Park (pl -s) der park.

Parka (pl -s) der parka.

Park|anlage die [von Stadt] park; [von Schloss] grounds Pl.

parken ⬦ vt to park. ⬦ vi - 1. [Person] to park; **falsch parken** to park illegally - 2. [Fahrzeug]: **ein parkendes Auto** a parked car.

Parken das parking.

Parkett (pl -e ODER -s) das - 1. [Fußbodenbelag] parquet - 2. [im Kino, Theater] stalls Pl UK, parquet US.

Park|gebühr die parking fee.

Park|haus das multi-storey car park UK, parking garage US.

Park|lücke die parking space.

Park|platz der - 1. [Platz] car park UK, parking lot US - 2. [Parklücke] parking space.

Park|scheibe die parking disc.

Park|schein der car park ticket UK, parking lot ticket US.

Park|uhr die parking meter.

Park|verbot das: **im Parkverbot stehen** to be in a no-parking zone.

Parlament (pl -e) das parliament.

Parlamentarier, in [parlamen'ta:rɪɐ, rɪn] (mpl -, fpl -nen) der, die Member of Parliament.

parlamentarisch ⬦ adj parliamentary. ⬦ adv in parliament.

Parmesan der Parmesan.

Parodie [paro'di:] (pl -n) die parody; **eine Parodie auf etw** a parody of sthg; **eine Parodie auf jn** a take-off of sb.

Parole (pl -n) die - 1. [Kennwort] password - 2. [Leitspruch] slogan - 3. abw [Behauptung]: **eine ausländerfeindliche Parole** a racial stereotype.

Partei (pl -en) die - 1. [gen] party; **für jn Partei ergreifen** fig to side with sb - 2. [bei Streit] side.

parteiisch ⬦ adj biased. ⬦ adv: **parteiisch urteilen** to make a biased judgement.

Parterre [par'tɛr] (pl -s) das ground floor UK, first floor US. ⬤ **im Parterre** adv on the ground floor UK ODER first floor US.

Partie [par'ti:] (pl -n) die - 1. [Teil] part - 2. [Spiel] game; **eine Partie Schach/Tennis spielen** to play a game of chess/tennis; **da bin ich mit von der Partie!** count me in!

Partitur (pl -en) die score.

Partizip (pl -ien) das participle. ⬤ **Partizip Perfekt** das past participle. ⬤ **Partizip Präsens** das present participle.

Partner, in (mpl -, fpl -nen) der, die partner; [in Film] co-star.

Partnerschaft (pl -en) die - **1.** [zwischen Personen] partnership - **2.** [zwischen Städten] twinning.

partnerschaftlich <> adj [Verhältnis] based on partnership; **partnerschaftliche Beziehung** partnership; **partnerschaftliche Zusammenarbeit** cooperation. <> adv - **1.** [freundschaftlich] in a spirit of partnership; [zusammenleben] as partners - **2.** [kollegial] in partnership.

Partnerlstadt die twin town.

partout [par'tu:] adv fam at all costs; **sie will partout nicht gehorchen!** she simply refuses to obey!

Party ['pɑːɐti] (pl -s) die party.

Pass (pl Pässe) der - **1.** [Dokument] passport - **2.** [Gebirgspass, beim Fußball] pass.

Passage [pa'saːʒə] (pl -n) die - **1.** [gen] passage - **2.** [Geschäftsstraße] arcade.

Passagier [pasa'ʒiːɐ] (pl -e) der passenger; **blinder Passagier** [auf Schiff] stowaway; [im Zug] fare dodger.

Passagierin [pasa'ʒiːrɪn] (pl -nen) die passenger.

Passant, in (mpl -en, fpl -nen) der, die passerby.

Passbild (pl -er) das passport photo.

passen vi - **1.** [die richtige Größe haben] to fit; **die Schuhe passen mir nicht** these shoes don't fit; **in etw (A) passen** to fit in sthg - **2.** [angenehm sein]: **passt es (dir) morgen besser?** does tomorrow suit you better?; **das passt mir nicht** that doesn't suit me; **das könnte dir so passen!** no way!; **das könnte ihm so passen!** he should be so lucky! - **3.** [zusammenpassen - Farben] to match; **zu jm passen** to suit sb; **sie passt in keinster Weise zu ihm** she isn't at all suited to him; **diese Schuhe passen nicht zu dem Rock** these shoes don't go with the skirt - **4.** [nicht können] to pass; **da muss ich passen!** pass!

passend <> adj - **1.** [Gelegenheit, Methode, Kleidung] suitable; [Worte] right; **der passende Schlüssel** the right key - **2.** [Farbe] matching. <> adv suitably; **passend antworten** to give a fitting reply; **haben Sie es passend?** do you have the exact amount?

Passfoto (pl -s) das passport photo.

passieren (perf hat/ist passiert) <> vt (hat) - **1.** [überschreiten, durchschreiten] to cross - **2.** [Zollkontrolle] to go through - **3.** SPORT to pass - **4.** KÜCHE to pass through a sieve. <> vi (ist) to happen; **es ist ein Unglück passiert** there's been an accident; **mir ist etwas Unglaubliches passiert** something incredible happened to me; **bei dem Unfall ist zum Glück nichts passiert** fortunately, nobody was hurt in the accident.

passiv, passiv <> adj - **1.** [untätig] passive - **2.** [Mitglied] non-active. <> adv passively.

Passiv ['pasif] (pl -e) das GRAMM passive (voice).

Passkontrolle (pl -n) die - **1.** [Kontrollieren] passport check - **2.** [Kontrollstelle] passport control.

Paste (pl -n) die paste.

Pastelllfarbe die pastel colour.

Pastete (pl -n) die - **1.** [mit Blätterteig] vol-au-vent - **2.** [ohne Blätterteig] pâté.

Pastor (pl -toren) der [katholisch] priest; [evangelisch] vicar.

Pastorin (pl -nen) die - **1.** [Pfarrerin] vicar - **2.** [Ehefrau des Pastors] vicar's wife.

Pate (pl -n) der godfather; **bei etw Pate stehen** to be the influence behind sthg.

Patenlkind das godchild.

Patenlonkel der godfather.

Patenschaft (pl -en) die: **die Patenschaft für etw übernehmen** to sponsor sthg; **die Patenschaft für jn übernehmen** to become sb's godparent.

patent <> adj - **1.** [lebenstüchtig] capable - **2.** [praktisch] neat - **3.** fam [nett] great. <> adv [tüchtig] capably.

Patent (pl -e) das patent; **auf etw (A) ein Patent anmelden** to apply for a patent for sthg.

Patenltante die godmother.

patentieren vt to patent; **sich (D) etw patentieren lassen** to take out a patent on sthg.

Pater (pl -) der father (priest).

Patient, in (mpl -en, fpl -nen) der, die patient.

Patin (pl -nen) die godmother.

Patina die patina.

Patriot, in (mpl -en, fpl -nen) der, die patriot.

patriotisch <> adj patriotic. <> adv patriotically.

Patron, in (mpl -e, fpl -nen) der, die patron saint.

Patrone (pl -n) die cartridge.

patrouillieren [patrul'(j)iːrən] (perf hat/ist patrouilliert) vi to patrol.

Patsche (pl -n) die fam - **1.** [Not]: **in der Patsche sitzen** to be in a fix; **jm aus der Patsche helfen** to help sb out of a tight spot - **2.** [Hand] paw.

patschnass adj fam soaking wet.

patzig <> adj nasty. <> adv nastily.

Pauke (pl -n) die kettledrum; **auf die Pauke hauen** fam fig to paint the town red.

pauken fam <> vi to swot UK, to grind US. <> vt to swot up on UK, to bone up on US.

pauschal <> adj - **1.** [Preis, Versicherung] all-inclusive - **2.** [Urteil] sweeping. <> adv - **1.** [beurteilen] sweepingly - **2.** [abrechnen] altogether.

Pauschale (*pl* -n) *die* flat rate.

Pauschal|reise *die* package tour.

Pauschal|urteil *das* sweeping judgement.

Päuschen ['pɔysçən] (*pl* -) *das fam* breather.

Pause (*pl* -n) *die* - 1. [Unterbrechung] break; [im Theater, Konzert] interval - 2. MUS rest.

Pausen|brot *das* snack (for the break).

pausenlos *adj* & *adv* non-stop.

Pavian ['pɑːvjɑːn] (*pl* -e) *der* baboon.

Pazifik *der:* der Pazifik the Pacific.

Pazifische Ozean *der* Pacific Ocean.

Pazifist, in (*mpl* -en, *fpl* -nen) *der, die* pacifist.

pazifistisch ⟨⟩ *adj* pacifist. ⟨⟩ *adv* in a pacifist way.

PC [peː'tseː] (*pl* - ODER -s) (*abk für* **Personal Computer**) *der* PC.

PDS [peːdeː'ɛs] (*abk für* **Partei des Demokratischen Sozialismus**) *die* Democratic Socialist Party.

Pech (*pl* -e) *das* - 1. [Unglück] bad luck; **Pech haben** to be unlucky - 2. [Erdölprodukt] pitch.

Pech|strähne *die* run of bad luck.

Pech|vogel *der* unlucky person.

Pedal (*pl* -e) *das* pedal.

pedantisch *abw* ⟨⟩ *adj* fastidious. ⟨⟩ *adv* fastidiously.

Pegel (*pl* -) *der* [von Fluss] water level; [von Lärm] level.

peilen ⟨⟩ *vt* to take a bearing on; **die Lage peilen** to see how the land lies. ⟨⟩ *vi fam:* **über den Daumen peilen** to make a rough guess.

peinlich ⟨⟩ *adj* - 1. [unangenehm] embarrassing; **das ist mir sehr peinlich** I feel very embarrassed about it - 2. [sorgfältig] scrupulous. ⟨⟩ *adv* - 1. [unangenehm] embarrassingly - 2. [sorgfältig] scrupulously.

Peitsche (*pl* -n) *die* whip.

peitschen (*perf* hat/ist gepeitscht) ⟨⟩ *vt* (hat) to whip. ⟨⟩ *vi* (ist) [Wind, Regen] to lash; [Schuss] to ring out.

Peking *nt* Peking.

Pelikan (*pl* -e) *der* pelican.

Pelle (*pl* -n) *die* Norddt [von Kartoffel] peel; [von Wurst] skin.

pellen *vt* Norddt [Kartoffel] to peel; [Wurst] to skin. ◆ **sich pellen** *ref* to peel.

Pell|kartoffel *die* unpeeled boiled potato.

Pelz (*pl* -e) *der* - 1. [Fell] fur (*U*); **jm auf den Pelz rücken** *fam fig* to pester sb - 2. [Pelzmantel] fur (coat).

pelzig *adj* - 1. [taub] numb - 2. [pelzartig] furry.

Pelz|mantel *der* fur coat.

Pendel (*pl* -) *das* pendulum.

pendeln (*perf* ist/hat gependelt) *vi* - 1. (ist) [fahren] to commute - 2. (hat) [schwingen - Glocken] to swing; [- Beine] to dangle.

Pendel|verkehr *der* [für Pendler] commuter traffic; [Hin- und Herfahren] shuttle service.

Pendler, in (*mpl* -, *fpl* -nen) *der, die* commuter.

penetrant *abw* ⟨⟩ *adj* [Mensch, Fragerei] obtrusive; [Geruch, Geklingel] penetrating. ⟨⟩ *adv* [nach etw riechen] penetratingly; [auf jn einreden] obtrusively.

Penis (*pl* -se) *der* penis.

Penizillin *das* penicillin.

pennen *vi fam* - 1. [schlafen] to sleep, to kip *UK* - 2. [nicht aufpassen] to be half-asleep - 3. [mit jm schlafen]: **mit jm pennen** *salopp* to do it with sb.

Penner, in (*mpl* -, *fpl* -nen) *der, die fam* - 1. [Stadtstreicher] tramp, bum *US* - 2. [Schlafmütze] sleepyhead.

Pension (*pl* -en) (*pl* -en) *die* - 1. [Hotel] guesthouse - 2. [Ruhestand]: **in Pension gehen** to retire; **in Pension sein** to be retired - 3. (*ohne pl*) [Bezüge] pension.

Pensionär, in [paŋzjo'ɛːɐ̯, rɪn] (*mpl* -e, *fpl* -nen) *der, die* pensioner (*retired civil servant*).

pensionieren [paŋzjo'niːrən] *vt* to pension off.

Pensum (*pl* Pensen) *das* quota.

Peperoni (*pl* -) *die* chilli (pepper).

per *präp* (+A) by.

perfekt ⟨⟩ *adj* - 1. [vollkommen] perfect - 2. [abgeschlossen]: **perfekt sein** [Vertrag, Kauf] to be finalized; [Niederlage, Sieg] to be complete; **perfekt machen** to finalize. ⟨⟩ *adv* [vollkommen] perfectly.

Perfekt (*pl* -e) *das* GRAMM perfect.

Perfektion *die* perfection.

Pergament (*pl* -e) *das* parchment.

Pergament|papier *das* greaseproof paper.

Periode (*pl* -n) *die* - 1. [Epoche, Menstruation] period - 2. MATH repetend; **1,6 Periode** 1.6 recurring.

periodisch ⟨⟩ *adj* periodic. ⟨⟩ *adv* periodically.

Perle (*pl* -n) *die* - 1. [Schmuck - aus Muschel] pearl; [- aus Holz, Glas] bead - 2. *geh* [Kostbarkeit] gem.

perlen (*perf* hat/ist geperlt) *vi* - 1. (*hat*) [sprudeln] to bubble - 2. (*ist*) *geh* [abperlen]: **Schweiß perlt ihm auf der Stirn** beads of sweat are forming on his brow.

Perlen|kette *die* pearl necklace.

Perlmutt, Perlmutt *das* mother of pearl.

Perlon ® *das* ≃ nylon.

permanent ⟨⟩ *adj* permanent. ⟨⟩ *adv* permanently.

perplex *adj:* **(ganz) perplex sein** to be stunned.

Persien *nt* Persia.

Person (*pl* -en) *die* - 1. [Mensch & GRAMM] person; **sie ist Köchin und Inhaberin in einer Person** she is chef and owner rolled into one; **etw in Person sein** *fig* to be sthg personified - 2. [Figur] character.

Personal *das* staff.

Personalabteilung *die* personnel department.

Personalausweis *der* identity card.

Personalchef, in *der, die* personnel manager.

Personalcomputer *der* EDV personal computer.

Personalien [pɛrzo'nɑːljən] *Pl* personal details.

Personalpronomen *das* GRAMM personal pronoun.

Personalrat *der* - 1. [Gremium] staff council *(for civil servants)* - 2. [Vertreter] staff council representative *(for civil servants)*.

Personalrätin *die* staff council representative *(for civil servants)*.

personell ◇ *adj* staff *(vor Subst)*. ◇ *adv* with regard to staff; **personell unterbesetzt** understaffed.

Personenwagen *der* car.

persönlich ◇ *adj* personal; **persönlich werden** to get personal. ◇ *adv* personally; **etw persönlich nehmen** to take sthg personally.

Persönlichkeit (*pl* -en) *die* personality.

Perspektive [pɛrspɛk'tiːvə] (*pl* -n) *die* - 1. [Bildaufbau, Sichtweise] perspective; **aus js Perspektive** from sb's perspective - 2. [Aussicht] prospect.

Peru *nt* Peru.

Perücke (*pl* -n) *die* wig.

Pessimismus *der* pessimism.

pessimistisch ◇ *adj* pessimistic. ◇ *adv* pessimistically.

Pest *die (ohne pl)* [Seuche] plague; **jn/etw meiden wie die Pest** *fam fig* to avoid sb/sthg like the plague; **stinken wie die Pest** *fam fig* to stink to high heaven.

Petersilie [petɐ'ziːljə] *die* parsley.

Petroleum [pe'troːleʊm] *das* paraffin UK, kerosene US.

petzen *vi fam* to tell tales.

Pf. *(abk für Pfennig)* pf.

Pfad (*pl* -e) *der* [gen & EDV] path.

Pfadfinder, in (*mpl* -, *fpl* -nen) *der, die* boy scout, girl guide UK, girl scout US.

Pfahl (*pl* Pfähle) *der* post.

Pfalz *die*: **die Pfalz** the Palatinate.

pfälzisch *adj* of/from the Palatinate.

· **Pfand** (*pl* Pfänder) *das* [von Flasche] deposit; [als Sicherheit] security; [beim Pfänderspiel] token; **etw als Pfand nehmen** to take sthg as security.

pfänden *vt* to seize.

Pfandflasche *die* returnable bottle.

Pfandhaus *das* pawnshop.

Pfändung (*pl* -en) *die* seizure *(U)*.

Pfanne (*pl* -n) *die* (frying) pan.

Pfannkuchen *der* pancake.

Pfarrei (*pl* -en) *die* parish.

Pfarrer (*pl* -) *der* [katholisch] priest; [evangelisch] minister.

Pfarrerin (*pl* -nen) *die* minister.

Pfau (*pl* -en) *der* peacock.

Pfeffer *der* pepper.

Pfefferminze, Pfefferminze *die* peppermint.

pfeffern *vt* - 1. [würzen] to put pepper on/in - 2. *fam* [werfen] to chuck - 3. *fam* [ohrfeigen]: **jm eine pfeffern** to give sb a clout.

Pfeife (*pl* -n) *die* - 1. [zum Rauchen, Musikinstrument] pipe; **nach js Pfeife tanzen** *fam fig* to dance to sb's tune; **Pfeife rauchen** to smoke a pipe - 2. [zum Pfeifen] whistle - 3. *fam abw* [Mensch] dead loss.

pfeifen (*prät* pfiff, *perf* hat gepfiffen) ◇ *vi* to whistle; **auf jn/etw pfeifen** *fam fig* not to give a damn about sb/sthg. ◇ *vt* - 1. [Lied] to whistle - 2. [Spiel] to referee.

Pfeil (*pl* -e) *der* - 1. [Waffe, Hinweiszeichen] arrow; **grüner Pfeil** filter arrow - 2. *fam* [Stichelei] barb.

Pfeiler (*pl* -) *der* pillar.

Pfennig (*pl* -e ODER -) *der* pfennig; **keinen Pfennig haben** *fam* not to have a penny.

Pferd (*pl* -e) *das* horse; **aufs falsche/richtige Pferd setzen** to back the wrong/right horse.

Pferdeäpfel *Pl* horse droppings.

Pferderennen *das* horse race.

Pferdeschwanz *der* [Frisur] ponytail.

Pferdesport *der (ohne pl)* equestrian sports *Pl*.

Pferdestall *der* stable.

Pferdestärke *die* horsepower *(U)*.

pfiff *prät* ☞ **pfeifen**.

Pfiff (*pl* -e) *der* - 1. [Ton] whistle - 2. *fig* [Reiz] style; **mit Pfiff** stylish.

Pfifferling (*pl* -e) *der* chanterelle; **nicht einen** ODER **keinen Pfifferling** *fam fig* not a thing.

pfiffig ◇ *adj* [Mensch, Idee] smart; [Gesicht] knowing. ◇ *adv* cleverly.

Pfingsten *(ohne Artikel)* Whitsun.

Pfirsich (*pl* -e) *der* peach.

Pflanze (*pl* -n) *die* plant.

pflanzen *vt* to plant.

pflanzlich ◇ *adj* [Nährstoffe, Fasern] plant *(vor Subst)*; [Öl] vegetable *(vor Subst)*; **pflanzliche Ernährung** [von Person] vegetarian diet; [von Tier] herbivorous diet. ◇ *adv*: **sich pflanzlich ernähren** [Person] to be a vegetarian; [Tier] to be a herbivore.

Pflaster (pl -) das - **1.** [Verband] plaster - **2.** (ohne pl) [Straßenbelag] (road) surface; **ein teures Pflaster sein** fig to be an expensive place.

Pflaume (pl -n) die - **1.** [Frucht] plum - **2.** fam [Mensch] drip.

Pflaumen|baum der plum tree.

Pflaumen|mus das thick plum purée, used like jam.

Pflege die - **1.** [von Lebewesen] care; **bei jm in Pflege sein** to be looked after by sb; **jn in Pflege nehmen/haben** to look after sb; **ein Kind in Pflege nehmen** to foster a child - **2.** [von Sprache, Beziehung] cultivation; [von Garten, Tradition] maintenance.

Pflege|eltern Pl foster parents.

Pflege|heim das nursing home.

Pflege|kind das foster child.

pflegeleicht adj - **1.** [Material] easy-care - **2.** fam [Person] easy to deal with.

pflegen vt - **1.** [versorgen] to look after; **jn gesund pflegen** to nurse sb back to health - **2.** [schonen] to take care of - **3.** [gewohnt sein]: **etw zu tun pflegen** geh to be in the habit of doing sthg.

Pflege|personal das nursing staff.

Pfleger, in (mpl -, fpl -nen) der, die nurse.

Pflicht (pl -en) die - **1.** [Aufgabe] duty; **etw ist Pflicht** sthg is compulsory - **2.** (ohne pl) SPORT compulsories Pl.

pflichtbewusst <> adj conscientious. <> adv conscientiously.

Pflicht|fach das compulsory subject.

Pflicht|gefühl das sense of duty.

Pflicht|versicherung die compulsory insurance.

Pflock (pl Pflöcke) der [für Tier] stake; [für Zelt] peg.

pflücken vt to pick.

Pflug (pl Pflüge) der plough.

pflügen vt & vi to plough.

Pforte (pl -n) die - **1.** [von Krankenhaus, Firma - Tor] gate; [- Eingang] entrance - **2.** geh [kleine Tür] door.

Pförtner, in (mpl -, fpl -nen) der, die porter.

Pfosten (pl -) der post.

Pfote (pl -n) die paw.

Pfropf (pl -e) der blockage; [in Ader] clot.

Pfropfen (pl -) der stopper.

pfui interj ugh!

Pfund (pl -e) das - **1.** [Gewicht] 500 grams, ≃ pound - **2.** [Währung] pound.

Pfusch der (ohne pl) fam abw botched job.

Pfuscher, in (mpl -, fpl -nen) der, die fam abw bungler.

Pfütze (pl -n) die puddle.

Phantasie = Fantasie.

phantasieren = fantasieren.

phantastisch = fantastisch.

Pharao (pl -s ODER -aonen) der Pharaoh.

Phase (pl -n) die phase.

Philharmoniker Pl Philharmonic (Orchestra) (sg).

Philippinen Pl: **die Philippinen** the Philippines.

Philosoph, in (mpl -en, fpl -nen) der, die philosopher.

Philosophie [fɪlozo'fiː] (pl -n) die philosophy.

philosophisch <> adj philosophical. <> adv philosophically.

Phonetik = Fonetik.

Phosphat (pl -e) das phosphate.

Phosphor der phosphorus.

phosphoreszieren vi to phosphoresce.

Phrase (pl -n) die cliché; **leere Phrasen** empty phrases; **Phrasen dreschen** fam fig to spout clichés.

pH-|Wert [peːˈhaːveːɐ̯t] der pH-value.

Physik die physics (U).

physikalisch <> adj - **1.** [gen] physical - **2.** [Forschung, Institut] physics (vor Subst). <> adv in terms of physics.

Physiker, in (mpl -, fpl -nen) der, die physicist.

physisch <> adj physical. <> adv physically.

Pianist, in (mpl -en, fpl -nen) der, die pianist.

Pickel (pl -) der - **1.** [Entzündung] spot - **2.** [Gerät] pickaxe; [für Eis] ice-pick.

pickelig, picklig adj spotty.

picken vt & vi to peck.

Picknick (pl -s ODER -e) das picnic; **ein Picknick machen** to have a picnic.

pieken vi to prick.

piepen vi [Vogel] to cheep; [Maus] to squeak; [Piepser] to bleep; **bei dir piepts wohl!** fam fig you're off your head!

piercen ➡ **sich piercen** ref: **sich die Nase piercen** to have one's nose pierced.

Piercing [ˈpiːrsɪŋ] (pl -s) das body piercing; **ein Piercing in der Zunge/Augenbraue haben** to have a pierced tongue/eyebrow.

piesacken vt fam to torment.

Pigment (pl -e) das pigment.

Pik (pl -) das - **1.** (ohne Artikel, ohne pl) [Spielfarbe] spades Pl - **2.** (pl Pik) [Spielkarte] spade; **die Piksechs** the six of spades.

pikant <> adj spicy. <> adv - **1.** [scharf]: **etw pikant würzen** to spice sthg well - **2.** [frivol] spicily.

Pike (pl -n) die: **etw von der Pike auf lernen** fam fig to learn sthg by working one's way up from the bottom.

Pilger (pl -) der pilgrim.

Pilger|fahrt die pilgrimage.

Pilgerin (*pl* -nen) *die* pilgrim.

pilgern (*perf* ist gepilgert) *vi* - **1.** [wallfahren] to go on a pilgrimage - **2.** *fam* [laufen] to trek.

Pille (*pl* -n) *die* - **1.** [Verhütungsmittel]: **die Pille** the pill; **die Pille nehmen** to be on the pill - **2.** *fam* [Tablette] pill.

Pilot (*pl* -en) *der* [von Flugzeug] pilot; [von Rennwagen] driver.

Pilotin (*pl* -nen) *die* [von Flugzeug] pilot; [von Rennwagen] driver.

Pils (*pl* -) *das* Pilsner.

Pilz (*pl* -e) *der* - **1.** [Pflanze - essbar] mushroom; [- giftig] toadstool - **2.** (*ohne pl*) [Hautpilz] fungal infection.

PIN (*pl* -s) (*abk für* **persönliche Identifikationsnummer**) *die* PIN (number).

pingelig *fam* <> *adj* fussy. <> *adv* fussily.

Pinguin ['pɪŋguiːn] (*pl* -e) *der* penguin.

Pinie ['piːnjə] (*pl* -n) *die* stone pine.

pink *adj* (*unver*) bright pink.

Pink *das* bright pink.

pinkeln *vi fam* to pee.

Pinsel (*pl* -) *der* brush.

pinseln *vt* & *vi* to paint.

Pinzette (*pl* -n) *die* tweezers *Pl*.

Pionier (*pl* -e) *der* - **1.** [Vorkämpfer] pioneer - **2.** [Soldat] engineer.

Pionierin (*pl* -nen) *die* pioneer.

Pipi *das fam*: **Pipi machen** to do a wee-wee.

Pirat (*pl* -en) *der* pirate.

Piratensender *der* pirate radio station.

Piratin (*pl* -nen) *die* pirate.

Pirsch *die*: **auf die Pirsch gehen** to go stalking.

Pistazie [pɪs'taːtsjə] (*pl* -n) *die* pistachio.

Piste (*pl* -n) *die* - **1.** [für Flugzeuge] runway - **2.** [Skipiste] piste - **3.** [für Fahrzeuge] track.

Pistole (*pl* -n) *die* pistol; **wie aus der Pistole geschossen** *fam fig* like a shot.

Pizza ['pɪtsa] (*pl* -s) *die* pizza.

Pizzeria [pɪtse'riːa] (*pl* **Pizzerien** ODER -s) *die* pizzeria.

Pkw ['peːkaːveː] (*pl* -s) (*abk für* **Personenkraftwagen**) *der* car, automobile *US*.

plädieren *vi* - **1.** *geh* [stimmen]: **für etw plädieren** to argue for sthg - **2.** RECHT: **für** ODER **auf etw** (*A*) **plädieren** to plead for sthg.

Plage (*pl* -n) *die* nuisance.

plagen *vt* to torment; **von etw geplagt sein** to be tormented by sthg. <> **sich plagen** *ref* to slave away; **sich mit etw plagen** to slave away at sthg.

Plakat (*pl* -e) *das* poster.

Plakette (*pl* -n) *die* [Tafel] plaque; [Abzeichen] badge.

Plan (*pl* **Pläne**) *der* - **1.** [Vorgehensweise, Vorhaben] plan; **Pläne schmieden** to make plans - **2.** [Karte] map. <> **nach Plan** *adv* according to plan.

Plane (*pl* -n) *die* tarpaulin.

planen *vt* to plan.

Planet (*pl* -en) *der* planet.

planieren *vt* to level.

Planke (*pl* -n) *die* plank.

planlos <> *adj* unsystematic. <> *adv* unsystematically.

planmäßig <> *adj* - **1.** [nach Plan] scheduled - **2.** [systematisch] systematic. <> *adv* - **1.** [nach Plan] on time - **2.** [systematisch] systematically.

planschen, plantschen *vi* to splash about.

Plantage [plan'taːʒə] (*pl* -n) *die* plantation.

Planung (*pl* -en) *die* - **1.** [Vorbereitung] planning (*U*) - **2.** [Ergebnis] plan.

plappern *vi* to prattle.

plärren *vi abw* - **1.** [weinen] to wail - **2.** [rufen] to yell - **3.** [Krach machen] to blare.

Plastik (*pl* -en) <> *das* (*ohne pl*) plastic. <> *die* sculpture.

Plastiktüte *die* plastic bag.

plastisch <> *adj* [dreidimensional] three-dimensional; **eine plastische Darstellung** a vivid description. <> *adv* - **1.** [dreidimensional] three-dimensionally - **2.** [lebendig] vividly.

Platane (*pl* -n) *die* plane tree.

Platin *das* platinum.

platonisch *adj* platonic.

plätschern (*perf* hat/ist geplätschert) *vi* - **1.** (*ist*) [fließen] to splash; [Bach] to babble - **2.** (*hat*) [Geräusch machen] to splash.

platt <> *adj* - **1.** [flach] flat (tyre); **einen Platten haben** *fam* to have a flat; **platt sein** *fam fig* to be flabbergasted - **2.** [nichts sagend] trite. <> *adv* - **1.** [flach] flat - **2.** [nichts sagend] tritely.

Platt *das* Low German, *dialect spoken in northern Germany*; **Platt sprechen** to speak Low German.

Plattdeutsch(e) *das* Low German, *dialect spoken in northern Germany*; *siehe auch* **Englisch(e)**.

Platte (*pl* -n) *die* - **1.** [Bauelement - aus Metall, Glas] sheet; [- aus Stein, Beton] slab; [- aus Holz] board - **2.** [Servierplatte] plate - **3.** [Schallplatte] record; **eine Platte auflegen** ODER **spielen** to put on ODER play a record - **4.** [Herdplatte] ring - **5.** *fam* [Glatze] bald patch. <> **kalte Platte** *die* meal of cold meats, cheese, salad etc.

Platten ▷ **platt**.

plätten *vt Norddt* [bügeln] to iron.

Plattenspieler *der* record player.

Plattfuß *der* (*ohne pl*) *fam* flat. <> **Plattfüße** *Pl*: **Plattfüße haben** to have flat feet.

Platz (*pl* **Plätze**) *der* - **1.** [Sitzplatz] seat; **Platz nehmen** *geh* to take a seat - **2.** [Freiraum] room, space; **jm/etw Platz machen** [zur Seite gehen] to make room for sb/sthg; [weichen] to make way for sb/sthg; **keinen/genug Platz haben** to have no/enough room - **3**. [Stelle, Rang] place; **auf die Plätze, fertig, los!** on your marks, get set, go! - **4**. [in Stadt] square - **5**. [bei Fußball, Hockey] pitch; [bei Tennis, Volleyball] court.   **fehl am Platz** adj out of place.   **Platz sparend** <> adj space-saving. <> adv in order to save space.

Platz|anweiser, in (mpl -, fpl -nen) der, die usher (usherette die).

Plätzchen (pl -) das - **1**. [Platz] spot - **2**. [Gebäck] biscuit UK, cookie US.

platzen (perf ist geplatzt) vi - **1**. [bersten] to burst - **2**. fam [ausfallen, scheitern - Termin, Vorstellung] to be cancelled; [- Projekt, Vertrag] to fall through; **etw platzen lassen** to cancel sthg; **vor etw (D) platzen** to be seething with sthg.

platzieren vt to place.   **sich platzieren** ref [Platz belegen] to be placed.

Platz|karte die seat reservation.

Platz|mangel der lack of space.

platzsparend adj ▷ **Platz**.

Platz|wunde die laceration.

plaudern vi to chat.

plausibel <> adj plausible; **jm etw plausibel machen** to make sthg clear to sb. <> adv plausibly.

plazieren vt = **platzieren**.

pleite adj fam: **pleite sein** to be broke.

Pleite (pl -n) die fam - **1**. [Ruin] bankruptcy; **Pleite gehen/machen** to go bust; **vor der Pleite stehen** fam to be faced with bankruptcy - **2**. [Reinfall] flop.

Plombe (pl -n) die - **1**. [Zahnfüllung] filling - **2**. [Siegel] lead seal.

plombieren vt - **1**. [füllen] to fill - **2**. [versiegeln] to put a lead seal on.

plötzlich <> adj sudden; **ganz plötzlich** all of a sudden. <> adv suddenly; **aber ein bisschen plötzlich!** fam get a move on!

plump abw <> adj clumsy. <> adv clumsily.

plumpsen (perf ist geplumpst) vi to crash; **[ins Wasser]** to splash.

Plunder der fam abw junk.

plündern <> vt - **1**. [ausrauben] to loot - **2**. [leeren] to raid. <> vi to loot.

Plural (pl -e) der GRAMM plural; **im Plural** in the plural.

plus adv, präp & konj plus.

Plus das (ohne pl) - **1**. [Mehrbetrag]: **(ein) Plus (von 100 Euro) machen** to make a profit (of 100 euros); **im Plus stehen** to be in credit - **2**. [Vorteil] advantage.

Plüsch der plush.

Plus|pol der positive pole.

Plus|punkt der - **1**. [Vorteil] plus point - **2**. [Punkt] point.

Plusquam|perfekt das GRAMM pluperfect.

Plutonium das CHEM plutonium.

PLZ abk für **Postleitzahl**.

Po (pl -s) der bottom.

pochen vi - **1**. [klopfen] to knock; **auf etw (A) pochen** fig to insist on sthg - **2**. [pulsieren - Herz] to pound; [- Blut] to throb.

Pocken Pl MED smallpox (U).

Podest (pl -e) das [für Redner] rostrum; [für Orchester, Chor] platform.

Podium ['po:diʊm] (pl Podien) das podium.

Podiums|diskussion die panel discussion.

Poesie die geh poetry.

poetisch <> adj poetic. <> adv poetically.

Pointe ['poɛ̃:tə] (pl -n) die punchline.

Pokal (pl -e) der - **1**. [Trophäe] cup - **2**. [Gefäß] goblet.

Poker der ODER das poker.

pokern vi to play poker.

Pol (pl -e) der pole; **er ist in der Familie der ruhende Pol** he is the calming influence in the family.

polar adj polar.

Polar|kreis der polar circle.

Pole (pl -n) der Pole.

polemisch <> adj polemical. <> adv polemically.

Polen nt Poland.

polieren vt to polish.

Polin (pl -nen) die Pole.

Politesse (pl -n) die traffic warden.

Politik die (ohne pl) - **1**. [des Staates] politics (U) - **2**. [Vorgehensweise] policy.

Politiker, in (mpl -, fpl -nen) der, die politician.

politisch <> adj political. <> adv politically.

Politur (pl -en) die polish.

Polizei die (ohne pl) police Pl.

Polizei|beamte der police officer.

Polizei|beamtin die police officer.

polizeilich <> adj police (vor Subst); **polizeiliches Kennzeichen** registration UK ODER license US number. <> adv by the police.

Polizei|revier das - **1**. [Polizeiwache] police station - **2**. [Bereich] police district.

Polizei|stunde die (ohne pl) closing time.

Polizei|wache die police station.

Polizist, in (mpl -en, fpl -nen) der, die policeman (policewoman die).

Pollen (pl -) der pollen (U).

polnisch adj Polish.

Polnisch(e) das Polish; siehe auch **Englisch(e)**.

Polo das polo.

Polster (pl -) das - **1.** [zum Sitzen, finanziell] cushion - **2.** [Schulterpolster] shoulder pad - **3.** fam [Fettpolster] wad of fat.

Polster|möbel Pl upholstered furniture (U).

polstern vt - **1.** [Möbel] to upholster - **2.** [Kleidung] to pad.

Polsterung (pl -en) die - **1.** [Polstern] upholstering - **2.** [Polster] upholstery (U).

Polter|abend der celebration usually held on the evening before a wedding, when crockery is broken to bring good luck.

poltern (perf hat/ist gepoltert) vi - **1.** (ist) [sich laut bewegen] to crash - **2.** (hat) [Krach machen] to make a racket; draußen hat etwas gepoltert there was a crash outside - **3.** (hat) [am Polterabend] to celebrate a "Polterabend".

Polyester [poli'ɛstɐ] das polyester.

Pommes frites [pɔm'frits] Pl chips UK, French fries US.

Pomp der pomp.

pompös ◇ adj lavish. ◇ adv lavishly.

Pony ['pɔni] (pl -s) ◇ das pony. ◇ der fringe UK, bangs US.

popelig, poplig fam abw ◇ adj - **1.** [minderwertig] lousy - **2.** [geizig] stingy - **3.** [gewöhnlich] ordinary. ◇ adv - **1.** [geizig] stingily - **2.** [billig] cheaply.

poplig = **popelig**.

Pop|musik die pop music.

Popo (pl -s) der fam bottom.

populär ◇ adj popular. ◇ adv: populär schreiben to write in an accessible way.

Popularität die popularity.

Pore (pl -n) die pore.

Porno (pl -s) der fam FILM porn film; [Pornoheft] porn mag.

Pornografie, Pornographie die pornography.

porös adj porous.

Porree der (ohne pl) leek.

Portal (pl -e) das portal.

Portier [pɔr'tje:] (pl -s) der porter.

Portion (pl -en) die - **1.** [von Essen] portion - **2.** [viel] amount.

Portmonee (pl -s), **Portemonnaie** (pl -s) [pɔrtmɔ'ne:] das purse.

Porto (pl -s) das postage (U).

portofrei adj & adv post-free UK, postpaid US.

Porträt [pɔr'trɛ:] (pl -s) das portrait.

porträtieren vt to do a portrait of.

Portugal nt Portugal.

Portugiese (pl -n) der Portuguese.

Portugiesin (pl -nen) die Portuguese.

portugiesisch adj Portuguese.

Portugiesisch(e) das Portuguese; siehe auch **Englisch(e)**.

Port|wein der port.

Porzellan (pl -e) das - **1.** [Material] porcelain - **2.** [Geschirr] china.

Posaune (pl -n) die trombone.

posieren vi to pose.

Position (pl -en) die position.

positiv ◇ adj positive. ◇ adv positively.

Possessiv|pronomen das GRAMM possessive pronoun.

Post die (ohne pl) - **1.** [Institution, Amt] post office; etw mit der Post schicken to send sthg by post UK ODER mail US; auf die ODER zur Post gehen to go to the post office - **2.** [Postsendung] post UK, mail US.

Post|amt das post office.

Post|anweisung die ≈ postal order UK, ≈ money order US.

Post|bote der postman UK, mailman US.

Post|botin die postwoman UK, mailwoman US.

Posten (pl -) der - **1.** [Ware] item - **2.** [Arbeitsstelle, Wachposten] post; auf dem Posten sein fam to be fit; nicht auf dem Posten sein fam to be under the weather.

Poster (pl -) der ODER das poster.

Postf. abk für **Postfach**.

Post|fach das PO box.

Post|karte die postcard.

postlagernd adj & adv poste restante UK, general delivery US.

Post|leit|zahl die postcode UK, zip code US.

Postspar|buch das post office savings book.

Postspar|kasse die post office savings bank.

Post|stempel der postmark.

Post|weg der: auf dem Postweg verloren gehen to get lost in the post UK ODER mail US.

postwendend adv by return (of post) UK, by return mail US.

potent adj - **1.** [Mann] potent - **2.** geh [solvent] financially strong - **3.** geh [mächtig] powerful.

Potenz (pl -en) die - **1.** [sexuelle] potency - **2.** [Kraft & MATH] power; die zweite/dritte Potenz von fünf the square/cube of five.

Potenzial (pl -e), **Potential** (pl -e) [potɛn'tsjɑ:l] das potential.

Pott (pl Pötte) der Norddt fam pot.

Pracht die magnificence; eine wahre Pracht sein fam to be magnificent.

Pracht|exemplar das [Gegenstand] magnificent example; [Person] magnificent specimen.

prächtig ◇ adj - **1.** [wunderschön] magnificent - **2.** [hervorragend] marvellous. ◇ adv - **1.** [wunderschön] magnificently - **2.** [hervorragend] marvellously.

prachtvoll ◇ adj magnificent. ◇ adv magnificently.

Prädikat (pl -e) das - **1.** [Gütezeichen] rating - **2.** GRAMM predicate.

Prag nt Prague.

prägen vt - 1. [in der Entwicklung] to influence; **von etw geprägt sein** to be influenced by sthg - 2. [von Anfang an] to shape - 3. [Wort] to coin - 4. [Münzen] to mint; [Metall, Leder] to emboss.

prägnant <> adj concise. <> adv concisely.

Prägung (pl -en) die - 1. [Muster] impression - 2. [in der Entwicklung] influence; **gesellschaftliche Prägung** social influence - 3. [von Anfang an] shaping - 4. [von Worten] coining (U).

prahlen vi to boast; **mit etw prahlen** to boast about sthg.

Praktik (pl -en) die practice. ☛ **Praktiken** Pl abw practices.

praktikabel <> adj practicable. <> adv practicably.

Praktikant, in (mpl -en, fpl -nen) der, die trainee.

Praktikum (pl Praktika) das work placement; **ein Praktikum machen** ODER **absolvieren** to be on a work placement.

praktisch <> adj practical. <> adv - 1. [gen] practically; **praktisch alles** practically everything - 2. [nicht theoretisch] in practice.

praktizieren vt & vi to practise.

Praline (pl -n) die chocolate.

prall <> adj [Po, Busen] well-rounded; [Sack] bulging; [Tomate] firm; **in der prallen Sonne** under the blazing sun. <> adv: **prall gefüllt** filled to bursting.

prallen (perf hat/ist geprallt) vi - 1. (ist) [stoßen]: **gegen/auf etw (A) prallen** to crash into sthg; **er ist mit dem Kopf auf den Boden geprallt** he banged his head on the floor - 2. (hat) [Sonne] to blaze down.

Prämie ['prɛːmiə] (pl -n) die - 1. [Beitrag] premium - 2. [Belohnung] reward - 3. [Sonderzahlung] bonus.

prämieren vt to give an award to.

Pranger (pl -) der: **jn/etw an den Pranger stellen** fig to pillory sb/sthg.

Pranke (pl -n) die paw.

Präparat (pl -e) das geh preparation.

Präposition (pl -en) die GRAMM preposition.

Prärie [prɛˈriː] (pl -n) die prairie.

Präsens ['prɛːzɛns] das GRAMM present (tense).

Präservativ [prɛzɛrvaˈtiːf] (pl -e) das condom.

Präsident, in (mpl -en, fpl -nen) der, die president.

Präsidentschaft (pl -en) die presidency.

Präsidium [prɛˈziːdjʊm] (pl -dien) das - 1. [von Verein] committee - 2. [Polizeipräsidium] headquarters Pl.

prasseln (perf hat/ist geprasselt) vi - 1. (ist) [Regen] to drum - 2. (hat) [Feuer] to crackle.

Präteritum das GRAMM preterite.

Praxis (pl Praxen) die - 1. [Wirklichkeit] practice; **etw in die Praxis umsetzen** to put sthg

into practice - 2. [Erfahrung] experience - 3. [Räumlichkeit - von Anwalt] office; [- von Arzt] surgery UK, office US. ☛ **in der Praxis** adv in practice.

präzis, präzise <> adj precise. <> adv precisely.

predigen vt & vi to preach.

Prediger, in (mpl -, fpl -nen) der, die preacher.

Predigt (pl -en) die sermon; **(jm) eine Predigt halten** to give (sb) a sermon.

Preis (pl -e) der - 1. [Geldbetrag] price - 2. [ausgesetzte Prämie] prize; **der Preis für etw** the price of sthg; **um jeden/keinen Preis** at any/not at any price. ☛ **zum halben Preis** adv at half-price.

Preisausschreiben das competition.

preisbewusst <> adj price-conscious. <> adv price-consciously.

Preiselbeere die cranberry.

preisen (prät pries, perf hat gepriesen) vt geh to praise; **sich glücklich preisen** to count o.s. lucky.

preisgünstig <> adj cheap. <> adv cheaply.

preislich <> adj price (vor Subst). <> adv with regard to price.

Preisrichter, in der, die judge.

Preisschild (pl -er) das price tag.

Preisträger, in der, die prizewinner.

Preisverleihung die prize ceremony.

preiswert <> adj cheap. <> adv cheaply.

prellen vt - 1. [betrügen] to cheat - 2. [stoßen]: **sich (D) den Schenkel/Arm prellen** to bruise one's thigh/arm - 3. [Ball] to bounce.

Prellung (pl -en) die bruise.

Premiere [prəˈmjeːrə] (pl -n) die premiere.

Premierminister, in [prəˈmjeːminɪstɐ, rɪn] der, die prime minister.

Presse (pl -n) die press.

Presseagentur die press agency.

Pressebericht der press report.

Pressefreiheit die freedom of the press.

Pressekonferenz die press conference.

Pressemeldung die press report.

pressen <> vt to press. <> vi [Schwangere] to push.

Pressesprecher, in der, die press officer.

Pressestelle die press office.

Preuße (pl -n) der HIST Prussian.

Preußin (pl -nen) die HIST Prussian.

preußisch adj HIST Prussian.

prickeln vi - 1. [kitzeln] to tingle - 2. [perlen] to sparkle.

prickelnd adj [Gefühl] thrilling; [Wein, Wasser] sparkling.

pries prät ▷ **preisen**.

Priester, in *(mpl -, fpl -nen)* der, die - **1.** [katholischer] priest - **2.** [heidnischer] priest (priestess die).

prima fam <> adj *(unver)* fantastic. <> adv fantastically.

Primel *(pl -n)* die primula.

primitiv <> adj - **1.** [gen] primitive - **2.** [Regeln, Bedürfnisse] basic. <> adv primitively.

Prinz *(pl -en)* der prince.

Prinzessin *(pl -nen)* die princess.

Prinzip *(pl -ien)* das principle. ◆ **aus Prinzip** adv on principle. ◆ **im Prinzip** adv in principle.

prinzipiell <> adj basic. <> adv - **1.** [aus Prinzip] on principle; [im Prinzip] in principle - **2.** [grundsätzlich] basically.

Priorität *(pl -en)* die priority. ◆ **Prioritäten** Pl priorities.

Prise *(pl -n)* die: eine Prise Salz/Pfeffer a pinch of salt/pepper.

pritschen vt SPORT to flick.

privat [pri'va:t] <> adj private. <> adv privately.

Privatadresse die home address.

Privatangelegenheit die private matter; das ist meine Privatangelegenheit that is a private matter.

Privateigentum das private property.

Privatinitiative die private initiative.

Privatleben das *(ohne pl)* private life.

Privatperson die private person.

Privatunterricht der private tuition.

Privileg [privi'le:k] *(pl -ien)* das privilege.

pro <> präp per; einmal pro Tag once a day. <> adv: pro und kontra argumentieren to argue for and against.

Pro *(pl -s)* das: das Pro und Kontra the pros and cons Pl.

Probe *(pl -n)* die - **1.** [Test] test; jn/etw auf die Probe stellen to put sb/sthg to the test - **2.** [Stichprobe, Warenprobe] sample - **3.** [Übung] rehearsal. ◆ **auf Probe** adv on a trial basis.

Probeexemplar das specimen copy.

proben vt & vi to rehearse.

probeweise adv on a trial basis.

probieren vt to try.

Problem *(pl -e)* das problem; Probleme mit jm/etw haben to have problems with sb/sthg. ◆ **kein Problem** interj no problem!

problematisch adj problematic.

problemlos <> adj problem-free. <> adv without any problems.

Produkt *(pl -e)* das product.

Produktion *(pl -en)* die - **1.** [Herstellung] production - **2.** [Erzeugnis] product; FILM [Sendung] production.

produktiv <> adj productive. <> adv productively.

Produktivität [produktivi'tɛ:t] die productivity.

Produzent, in *(mpl -en, fpl -nen)* der, die producer.

produzieren vt - **1.** [Ware, Film] to produce - **2.** fam abw [machen] to make.

professionell <> adj professional. <> adv professionally.

Professor *(pl --en)* der professor.

Professorin *(pl -nen)* die professor.

Profi *(pl -s)* der professional.

Profil *(pl -e)* das - **1.** [Persönlichkeit] image - **2.** [Seitenansicht] profile - **3.** [von Reifen, Sohle] tread.

Profit *(pl -e)* der profit; aus etw Profit schlagen ODER ziehen fig to profit from sthg; eigtl to make a profit out of sthg; Profit machen to make a profit.

profitieren vi: von etw profitieren to profit from sthg.

pro forma adv for form's sake.

Prognose *(pl -n)* die prognosis.

Programm *(pl -e)* das - **1.** [Programmvorschau] listings Pl - **2.** [Sendungen] programmes Pl - **3.** [Sender] channel - **4.** [Programmheft, Veranstaltungsablauf, Konzeption] programme; auf dem Programm stehen to be on the programme - **5.** [Tagesablauf] schedule; auf dem Programm stehen to be on the agenda - **6.** EDV program.

Programmheft das programme.

Programmhinweis der programme announcement.

programmieren vt - **1.** [Computer] to program - **2.** [Videorecorder] to programme.

Programmierer, in *(mpl -, fpl -nen)* der, die EDV programmer.

Programmpunkt der item *(on programme/agenda)*.

progressiv <> adj progressive. <> adv progressively.

Projekt *(pl -e)* das project.

Projektor *(pl -toren)* der projector.

projizieren vt to project.

Prolet *(pl -en)* der abw peasant.

Promenade *(pl -n)* die promenade.

Promille *(pl -)* das - **1.** MATH thousandth - **2.** [Alkoholgehalt] alcohol level; er hatte 1,5 Promille he had a blood alcohol level of 1.5 parts per thousand.

prominent adj prominent.

Prominenz die *(ohne pl)* prominent figures Pl.

Promotion [promo'tsjo:n] *(pl -en)* die UNI doctorate.

promovieren [promo'vi:rən] vi to gain a doctorate.

prompt <> adj prompt. <> adv [erwartungsgemäß] of course; [sofort] promptly.

Pronomen (*pl* - ODER **Pronomina**) *das* GRAMM pronoun.

Propaganda *die* - **1.** [Verbreitung] propaganda - **2.** [Werbung]: **für jn/etw Propaganda machen** to publicize sb/sthg.

Propan|gas *das* propane (gas).

Propeller (*pl* -) *der* propeller.

Prophet, in (*mpl* -en, *fpl* -nen) *der, die* prophet (prophetess *die*).

prophezeien *vt* to predict; [Subj: prophet] to prophesy; **jm etw prophezeien** to predict sthg for sb.

Proportion (*pl* -en) *die* proportion.

proportional <> *adj* proportional. <> *adv* proportionally.

Prosa *die* prose.

prosit, prost *interj* cheers! ➡ **prost Neujahr** *interj* Happy New Year!

Prospekt (*pl* -e) *der* brochure.

Prostituierte (*pl* -n) *die* prostitute.

Prostitution *die* prostitution.

Protest (*pl* -e) *der* protest; **gegen etw Protest einlegen** ODER **erheben** to make a protest against sthg.

Protestant, in (*mpl* -en, *fpl* -nen) *der, die* Protestant.

protestantisch *adj* Protestant.

protestieren *vi* to protest; **gegen etw protestieren** to protest against ODER about sthg.

Protest|kundgebung *die* protest rally.

Prothese (*pl* -n) *die* [für Arm, Bein] artificial limb; [für Zähne] dentures *Pl*.

Protokoll (*pl* -e) *das* - **1.** [gen] record; [Aufzeichnung - wortgetreu] transcript; [- von Sitzung] minutes *Pl*; [- polizeilich] statement; **etw zu Protokoll geben** to put sthg on the record; [- polizeilich] to say sthg in one's statement; **eine Aussage zu Protokoll nehmen** to take down a statement; **Protokoll führen** to take the minutes; [- wortgetreu] to make a transcript - **2.** [Zeremoniell] protocol.

Protokoll|führer, in *der, die* [von Sitzung] minute-taker; [im Gericht] clerk.

protokollieren <> *vt* to take down; [Sitzung] to minute. <> *vi* to keep a record; [bei Sitzung] to take the minutes.

protzig *abw adj fam* showy.

Proviant [pro'viant] *der (ohne pl)* provisions *Pl*.

Provider [pro'vaidɐ] (*pl* -) *der* EDV Internet Service Provider.

Provinz [pro'vɪnts] (*pl* -en) *die* - **1.** [Verwaltungsbezirk] province - **2.** *(ohne pl) abw* [Gegend] provinces *Pl*.

provinziell [provɪn'tsiɛl] *abw* <> *adj* provincial. <> *adv* provincially.

Provision [provi'zioːn] (*pl* -en) *die* commission.

provisorisch [provi'zoːrɪʃ] <> *adj* temporary. <> *adv* temporarily.

Provokation [provoka'tsioːn] (*pl* -en) *die* provocation.

provozieren [provo'tsiːrən] <> *vt* to provoke. <> *vi* to be provocative.

Prozent (*pl* - ODER -e) *das* percent; **Prozente bekommen** to get a discount.

Prozent|satz *der* percentage.

prozentual <> *adj* percentage *(vor Subst)*. <> *adv* in percentage terms.

Prozess (*pl* -e) *der* - **1.** [Rechtsstreit] trial; **jm den Prozess machen** to put sb on trial - **2.** [Vorgang] process.

prozessieren *vi* to go to court; **gegen jn prozessieren** to take sb to court.

Prozession (*pl* -en) *die* - **1.** [kirchliche] procession - **2.** *fam* [Schlange] line.

prüde <> *adj* prudish. <> *adv* prudishly.

prüfen <> *vt* - **1.** [Gerät, Material] to test; [bei Examen] to examine; **jn auf etw (A) prüfen** to examine sb on sthg; **jn in etw (D) prüfen** to examine sb in sthg; **etw auf etw (A) prüfen** to test sthg for sthg - **2.** [Rechnung, Aussage, Unterschrift] to check - **3.** [Angebot] to consider. <> *vi* [examinieren] to be an/the examiner.

Prüfer, in (*mpl* -, *fpl* -nen) *der, die* - **1.** [Lehrer] examiner - **2.** [Tester] tester.

Prüfling (*pl* -e) *der* candidate.

Prüfung (*pl* -en) *die* - **1.** [Kontrolle] check - **2.** [Examen] exam, examination; **eine Prüfung machen** ODER **haben** to take an exam; **eine mündliche/schriftliche Prüfung** an oral/a written exam; **eine Prüfung bestehen** to pass an exam - **3.** *geh* [Belastung] trial - **4.** [im Sport] test.

Prügel (*pl* -) *der* club. ➡ **Prügel** *Pl* thrashing *(U)*.

Prügelei (*pl* -en) *die* fight.

prügeln *vt* to beat. ➡ **sich prügeln** *ref* to fight.

Prunk *der abw* splendour.

prunkvoll <> *adj* magnificent. <> *adv* magnificently.

Psalm (*pl* -en) *der* psalm.

Psychiater, in (*mpl* -, *fpl* -nen) *der, die* psychiatrist.

psychisch <> *adj* [Wohlbefinden, Probleme] psychological; [Krankheit] mental. <> *adv* mentally.

Psycho|analyse *die* psychoanalysis.

Psychologe (*pl* -n) *der* psychologist.

Psychologie *die* psychology.

Psychologin (*pl* -nen) *die* psychologist.

psychologisch <> *adj* psychological. <> *adv* - **1.** [als Psychologe]: **jn psychologisch begutachten** to give sb a psychological examination - **2.** [mit Menschenkenntnis] psychologically.

Psycho|therapie (*pl* -n) *die* psychotherapy.

Pubertät *die* puberty.

publik *adj*: **etw publik machen** to make sthg public.

Publikation [publika'tsjo:n] (*pl* -en) *die* publication.

Publikum *das (ohne pl)* - 1. [Zuhörer, Zuschauer] audience - 2. [Gäste] clientele - 3. [Anhänger] public; [von Schriftsteller] readership.

Pudding (*pl* -e *ODER* -s) *der* blancmange.

Pudel (*pl* -) *der* poodle.

Puder (*pl* - *ODER das* powder.

Puder|dose *die* (powder) compact.

pudern *vt* to powder. ➡ **sich pudern** *ref* to powder o.s.

Puder|zucker *der* icing sugar.

Puff (*pl* -s) *der ODER das fam* brothel.

Puffer (*pl* -) *der* - 1. [von Bahnen] buffer - 2. [Kartoffelpuffer] potato pancake.

Pulli (*pl* -s) *der fam* sweater, jumper *UK*.

Pullover [pʊ'loːvɐ] (*pl* -) *der* sweater, jumper *UK*.

Puls (*pl* -e) *der* pulse; **am Puls von etw sein** to have one's finger on the pulse of sthg.

Puls|ader *die* artery; **sich (D) die Pulsadern aufschneiden** to slit one's wrists.

pulsieren *vi* to pulsate; [Blut] to pulse.

Pult (*pl* -e) *das* desk; [Stehpult] lectern.

Pulver ['pʊlfɐ, 'pʊlvɐ] (*pl* -) *das* - 1. [Stoff] powder - 2. [Schießpulver] gunpowder *(U)*.

Pulver|kaffee *der* instant coffee.

Pulver|schnee *der* powder snow.

Puma (*pl* -s) *der* puma.

pummelig *adj* chubby.

Pumpe (*pl* -n) *die* - 1. [Gerät] pump - 2. *salopp* [Herz] ticker.

pumpen ◇ *vt* - 1. [saugen] to pump - 2. *fam* [leihen]: **jm etw pumpen** to lend sb sthg; **(sich (D)) etw von jm pumpen** to borrow sthg from sb - 3. [investieren]: **Geld in etw pumpen** to pump money into sthg. ◇ *vi* [saugen] to pump.

Pumps [pœmps] (*pl* -) *der* court shoe *UK*, pump *US*.

Punker, in ['paŋkɐ, rɪn] (*mpl* -, *fpl* -nen) *der, die* punk.

Punkt (*pl* -e) *der* - 1. [gen] point - 2. [Fleck, typografisches Zeichen] dot; [am Satzende] full stop *UK*, period *US* - 3. [Zeitpunkt]: **Punkt ein Uhr** one o'clock on the dot; **der springende Punkt** the crux of the matter; **an einem toten Punkt angelangt sein** [Verhandlungen] to have reached deadlock; **ein wunder *ODER* schwacher Punkt** [Schwäche] a weak point; [heikles Thema] a sore point.

pünktlich ◇ *adj* punctual. ◇ *adv* punctually, on time.

Pünktlichkeit *die* punctuality.

Pupille (*pl* -n) *die* pupil.

Puppe (*pl* -n) *die* - 1. [Figur] doll - 2. *salopp* [Frau, Mädchen] bird *UK*, doll *US*; [als Anrede] baby.

pur *adj* - 1. [rein] pure - 2. [Whisky] neat.

Püree (*pl* -s) *das* puree.

Purzel|baum *der*: **einen Purzelbaum machen** *ODER* **schlagen** to do a somersault.

Puste *die fam* puff; **aus der *ODER* außer Puste sein** to be out of puff.

pusten *vt* & *vi* to blow.

Pute (*pl* -n) *die* - 1. [Tier] turkey (hen) - 2. *salopp abw* [Frau] cow.

Puter (*pl* -) *der* turkey (cock).

Putsch (*pl* -e) *der* putsch.

Putz *der* plaster.

putzen ◇ *vt* to clean; [Gemüse] to wash; **jm die Nase putzen** to wipe sb's nose; **sich (D) die Zähne putzen** to clean *ODER* brush one's teeth; **sich (D) die Nase putzen** to blow one's nose. ◇ *vi* to clean. ➡ **sich putzen** *ref* to wash o.s.; [Vogel] to preen o.s.

Putz|frau *die* cleaner.

Putz|lappen *der* cloth.

Putz|mittel *das* cleaning fluid.

Puzzle ['pazl] (*pl* -s) *das* jigsaw (puzzle).

Pyramide (*pl* -n) *die* pyramid.

Pyrenäen *Pl*: **die Pyrenäen** the Pyrenees.

q (*pl* - *ODER* -s), **Q** (*pl* - *ODER* -s) [ku:] *das* q, Q.

qm (*abk für* Quadratmeter) m².

Quader (*pl* -) *der* - 1. *MATH* rectangular solid - 2. [Block] stone block.

Quadrat (*pl* -e) *das* square.

quadratisch ◇ *adj* square. ◇ *adv* in squares.

Quadrat|meter *der* square metre.

quaken *vi* - 1. [Frosch] to croak; [Ente] to quack - 2. *fam abw* [reden] to squawk.

Qual (*pl* -en) *die* agony; [seelisch] torment; **jm das Leben zur Qual machen** to make sb's life a misery. ➡ **Qualen** *Pl* suffering *(sg)*, agony *(sg)*; [seelisch] torment *(sg)*; **jn von seinen/ihren Qualen erlösen** to put sb out of his/her misery.

quälen *vt* - 1. [gen] to torment; [foltern] to torture - 2. *fam* [bedrängen] to pester; **jn mit etw**

quälen to plague sb with sthg. ⟐ **sich quälen** ref - 1. [leiden] to suffer - 2. [sich abmühen] to struggle.

Quälerei (pl -en) die - 1. [Peinigung] torment; [Folter] torture; [Grausamkeit] cruelty; **Quälerei der Tiere** cruelty to animals - 2. (ohne pl) [Anstrengung] struggle.

qualifizieren vt - 1. [befähigen] to qualify - 2. [beurteilen] to classify. ⟐ **sich qualifizieren** ref [sich befähigen] to obtain qualifications; [für Wettbewerb] to qualify.

Qualität (pl -en) die quality.

Qualle (pl -n) die jellyfish.

Qualm der - 1. [von Feuer] thick smoke - 2. fam abw [von Zigaretten] fug.

qualmen ⟐ vi to smoke. ⟐ vt salopp [Zigaretten] to puff away at.

qualvoll ⟐ adj agonizing. ⟐ adv in agony.

Quantität die (ohne pl) quantity.

Quarantäne [karan'tɛːnə] (pl -n) die quarantine (U).

Quark der quark, type of soft cheese.

Quartal (pl -e) das quarter.

Quartett (pl -e) das - 1. MUS quartet - 2. (ohne pl) [Kartenspiel] children's card game where players have to collect four of a kind.

Quartier (pl -e) das accommodation (U).

Quarzluhr die quartz watch.

quasi adv virtually.

Quatsch der fam rubbish.

quatschen fam ⟐ vi - 1. [reden] to chat - 2. abw [quasseln] to chatter. ⟐ vt [reden] to talk.

Queck|silber das CHEM mercury.

Quelle (pl -n) die - 1. [Wasserquelle] spring - 2. [Informant(en), Fundstelle] source.

quellen (präs quillt, prät quoll, perf ist gequollen) vi - 1. [austreten - Flüssigkeit] to stream; [- Rauch] to billow - 2. [hervortreten] to swell; [Augen] to bulge - 3. [Feuchtigkeit aufnehmen] to soak.

quengeln vi fam to whine.

quer adv diagonally; **quer durch etw** straight through sthg; **quer über etw** (A), **quer auf etw** (D) across sthg; **quer zu etw** at right angles to sthg.

Quere die: jm in die Quere kommen fig [behindern] to get in sb's way; [Weg abschneiden] to block sb's path; [treffen] to bump into sb.

querfeldein adv cross-country.

Quer|flöte die flute.

Quer|schnitt der - 1. [Auswahl, Abbildung] cross-section - 2. [Schnitt] cut.

querschnittsgelähmt adj paraplegic.

Quer|straße die: die nächste Querstraße rechts the next turning on the right.

quetschen vt - 1. [unterbringen, drängen] to squeeze - 2. [zerdrücken] to crush - 3. [verlet-

zen]: **der Baum hat mir das Bein gequetscht** the tree crushed my leg. ⟐ **sich quetschen** ref [sich zwängen] to squeeze.

Quetschung (pl -en) die bruise.

quieken vi [Ferkel] to squeal; [Maus] to squeak.

quietschen vi - 1. [Tür, Bremse] to squeak - 2. fam [juchzen] to squeal.

quillt präs ⟹ **quellen**.

Quirl (pl -e) der whisk.

quitt adj (unver): **mit jm quitt sein** fam to be quits with sb.

quittieren ⟐ vt - 1. [bestätigen] to sign for; **etw quittieren lassen** to get a receipt for sthg - 2. [erwidern] to respond to - 3. [kündigen]: **den Dienst quittieren** to resign. ⟐ vi [Empfang bestätigen] to sign.

Quittung (pl -en) die - 1. [Beleg] receipt - 2. fig [Konsequenz]: **da hast du die Quittung!** that's the price you pay!

Quiz [kvis] (pl -) das quiz.

quoll prät ⟹ **quellen**.

Quote (pl -n) die [Anteil] proportion; [festgeschriebene Zielmenge] quota; [Einschaltquote] viewing figures Pl.

R

r (pl - ODER -s), **R** (pl - ODER -s) [ɛr] das r, R.

Rabatt (pl -e) der discount.

Rabbi (pl -s) der rabbi.

Rabe (pl -n) der raven.

rabiat ⟐ adj [gewalttätig] brutal; [wütend] furious. ⟐ adv [gewalttätig] brutally; [wütend] furiously.

Rache die revenge.

Rachen (pl -) der throat.

rächen vt to avenge. ⟐ **sich rächen** ref - 1. [Rache nehmen] to get one's revenge; **sich an jm (für** ODER **wegen etw) rächen** to take revenge on sb (for sthg) - 2. [Konsequenzen haben]: **seine Faulheit wird sich rächen** he'll pay for his laziness.

Rad (pl Räder) das - 1. [von Fahrzeug] wheel - 2. [Fahrrad] bike; **Rad fahren** to cycle - 3. [von Maschine] cog.

Radar der ODER das radar.

Radar|kontrolle die radar speed check.

Radau der racket.

radebrechen ⟨⟩ *vt*: Englisch/Deutsch radebrechen to speak broken English/German. ⟨⟩ *vi*: **er radebrechte in Englisch** he spoke broken English.

radeln (*perf* ist geradelt) *vi* to cycle.

rad|fahren *vi* (*unreg*) ⟼ **Rad**.

Rad|fahrer, in *der, die* cyclist.

Radfahr|weg *der* cycle track.

radieren *vt* & *vi* [mit Radiergummi] to erase.

Radier|gummi *der* rubber *UK*, eraser *US*.

Radieschen [ra'diːsçən] (*pl* -) *das* radish.

radikal ⟨⟩ *adj* radical. ⟨⟩ *adv* radically.

Radio (*pl* -s) *das* - **1.** (*gen*) radio; **Radio hören** to listen to the radio - **2.** (*ohne pl*) [Anstalt] radio station.

Radioaktivität (*ohne Pl*) *die* radioactivity.

Radio|rekorder (*pl* -) *der* radio cassette recorder.

Radio|sendung *die* radio programme.

Radio|wecker *der* radio alarm.

Radius (*pl* Radien) *der* radius.

Rad|rennen *das* cycle race.

Rad|sport *der* cycling.

Rad|tour *die* cycling tour.

Rad|weg *der* cycle path.

raffen *vt* - **1.** *abw* [nehmen] to stuff; **etw an sich (A) raffen** to grab sthg - **2.** [Stoff] to gather - **3.** *salopp* [begreifen] to get.

Raffinerie [rafinə'riː] (*pl* -n) *die* refinery.

raffiniert ⟨⟩ *adj* - **1.** [Person, Plan, System] ingenious; [Geschmack, Farbe] subtle; [Kleiderschnitt] sophisticated - **2.** [gerissen] cunning. ⟨⟩ *adv* - **1.** [planen, arrangieren] ingeniously; [würzen] subtly; **raffiniert kochen** to be a sophisticated cook - **2.** [gerissen] cunningly.

ragen (*perf* hat/ist geragt) *vi*: **aus etw ragen** to stick out of sthg; [Berg, Baum, Gebäude] to rise up out of sthg.

Ragout [ra'guː] (*pl* -s) *das* stew.

Rahm *der* cream.

rahmen *vt* to frame.

Rahmen (*pl* -) *der* - **1.** [von Bild, Fenster, Fahrrad] frame - **2.** [von Fahrzeugen] chassis - **3.** (*ohne pl*) [Umgebung] setting; [Kontext] context; **aus dem Rahmen fallen** to be out of place. ◆ **im Rahmen** *adv*: **im Rahmen einer Sache (G)** [Zusammenhang] in the context of sthg; [Verlauf] in the course of sthg; [innerhalb der Grenzen] within the bounds of sthg; [als Teil] as part of sthg.

räkeln, rekeln ◆ sich räkeln, sich rekeln *ref* to stretch out.

Rakete (*pl* -n) *die* rocket; MIL missile.

rammen *vt* to ram.

Rampe (*pl* -n) *die* - **1.** [Laderampe, Auffahrt] ramp - **2.** [Theater] apron.

Rampen|licht *das* (*ohne pl*) footlights *Pl*; **im Rampenlicht stehen** *fig* to be in the limelight.

ramponiert *adj fam* battered.

Ramsch *der fam abw* junk.

ran *fam* = **heran**.

Rand (*pl* Ränder) *der* - **1.** [von Stadt, Tisch, Teich] edge - **2.** [von Gefäßen] rim - **3.** [von Buchseite] margin - **4.** [Umrandung] edging (*U*); **(dunkle) Ränder um die Augen haben** to have dark rings around one's eyes; **mit jm/etw (nicht) zu Rande kommen** *fam* (not) to be able to cope with sb/sthg. ◆ **am Rande** *adv* - **1.** [nebenbei] in passing; **sich am Rande abspielen** to take place on the sidelines - **2.** [nahe]: **am Rande der Verzweiflung sein** to be close to despair.

randalieren *vi* to rampage.

Rand|bezirk *der* suburb.

Rand|gruppe *die* marginal group.

randvoll ⟨⟩ *adj* full to the brim. ⟨⟩ *adv* to the brim.

rang *prät* ⟼ **ringen**.

Rang (*pl* Ränge) *der* - **1.** [Position] rank - **2.** [Ansehen] class; **ein Wissenschaftler von Rang** a renowned scientist - **3.** [in Theater, Stadion] circle; **der erste/zweite Rang** [in Theater] the dress/upper circle; [im Wettbewerb] first/second place.

rangieren [raŋ'ʒiːrən] ⟨⟩ *vt* to shunt. ⟨⟩ *vi* to be ranked.

Rang|liste *die* (army/navy/civil service) list.

Rang|ordnung *die* order of precedence.

ran|halten ◆ sich ranhalten *ref* (*unreg*) *fam* to get on with it.

Ranke (*pl* -n) *die* tendril.

ranken (*perf* hat/ist gerankt) *vi* (*ist*) to climb. ◆ **sich ranken** *ref* to climb; **sich um etw ranken** [wachsen] to entwine itself around sthg; *fig* & *geh* [spinnen] to grow up around sthg.

rann *prät* ⟼ **rinnen**.

rannte *prät* ⟼ **rennen**.

ranzig *adj* rancid.

Raps *der* rape.

rar *adj* rare.

Rarität (*pl* -en) *die* rarity.

rasant ⟨⟩ *adj* - **1.** [schnell] rapid - **2.** *fam* [imponierend] stunning. ⟨⟩ *adv* [schnell] rapidly.

rasch ⟨⟩ *adj* quick. ⟨⟩ *adv* quickly.

rascheln *vi* to rustle.

rasen (*perf* hat/ist gerast) *vi* - **1.** (*ist*) [fahren] to race; **gegen etw rasen** to crash into sthg - **2.** (*hat*) [toben] to rage; **das Publikum raste vor Begeisterung** the audience went wild with enthusiasm.

Rasen (*pl* -) *der* [Rasenfläche] lawn; [Gras] grass.

rasend ⟨⟩ *adj* - **1.** [Entwicklung] rapid; [Geschwindigkeit] lightning (*vor Subst*); [Eile] great - **2.** [gewaltig] raging - **3.** [wütend]: **jn rasend ma-**

chen *fam* to drive sb mad. <> *adv* - 1.: **rasend schnell** incredibly quickly - 2. [enorm] terribly; **rasend verliebt sein** to be madly in love.

Rasen|mäher *der* lawnmower.

Raserei *die (ohne pl)* - 1. [Toben] rage; **jn zur Raserei bringen** to drive sb mad - 2. *abw* [Schnelligkeit] speeding.

Rasier|apparat *der* shaver.

rasieren *vt* to shave. <> **sich rasieren** *ref* to shave; **sich nass/trocken rasieren** to have a wet/dry shave.

Rasierer *(pl -)* *der fam* shaver.

Rasier|klinge *die* razor blade.

Rasier|schaum *der* shaving foam.

Rasier|wasser *das* aftershave.

raspeln *vt* [reiben] to grate.

Rasse *(pl -n)* *die* - 1. [bei Tieren] breed - 2. [bei Menschen] race.

Rassel *(pl -n)* *die* rattle.

rasseln *(perf hat/ist gerasselt)* *vi* - 1. (hat) [Geräusch erzeugen] to rattle - 2. (ist) *fam* [durchfallen]: **durch eine Prüfung rasseln** to flunk an exam.

Rassismus *der* racism.

rassistisch *adj* racist.

Rast *(pl -en)* *die* rest; **Rast machen** [beim Fahren] to stop for a break; [beim Gehen] to stop for a rest.

rasten *vi* [beim Fahren] to stop for a break; [beim Gehen] to stop for a rest.

Raster *(pl -)* *das* TECH screen; [System] framework.

Rast|hof *der* [an Autobahnen] services *Pl.*

rastlos <> *adj* tireless. <> *adv* tirelessly.

Rast|platz *der* picnic area *(with toilet facilities)*.

Rast|stätte *die* [auf Autobahnen] services *Pl.*

Rasur *(pl -en)* *die* shave.

Rat *(pl Räte)* *der* - 1. [Ratschlag] advice *(U)*; **jn einen Rat geben** to give sb a piece of advice; **jn/etw zu Rate ziehen** to consult sb/sthg; **jn um Rat fragen** ODER **bitten** to ask sb for advice; **sich (D) keinen Rat (mehr) wissen** to be at one's wits' end - 2. [Versammlung] council - 3. [Person] councillor.

rät *präs* ⊳ **raten**.

Rate *(pl -n)* *die* - 1. [Teilzahlung] instalment; **etw auf Raten kaufen** to buy sthg on hire purchase - 2. [statistische] rate.

raten *(präs rät, prät riet, perf hat geraten)* <> *vt* - 1. [erraten] to guess - 2. [empfehlen]: **jm raten, etw zu tun** to advise sb to do sthg. <> *vi* - 1. [erraten] to guess - 2. [Rat geben]: **jm zu etw raten** to advise sb to do sthg.

Raten|zahlung *die* payment by instalments.

Ratgeber *(pl -)* *der* - 1. [Mensch] adviser - 2. [Buch] guide.

Ratgeberin *(pl -nen)* *die* adviser.

Rat|haus *das* town hall.

Ration *(pl -en)* *die* ration.

rational <> *adj* rational. <> *adv* rationally.

rationalisieren *vt* to rationalize.

rationell <> *adj* efficient. <> *adv* efficiently.

rationieren *vt* to ration.

ratlos <> *adj* helpless. <> *adv* helplessly.

Rätoromanisch(e) *das* Rhaeto-Romanic; *siehe auch* **Englisch(e)**.

ratsam *adj* advisable.

Rat|schlag *der* piece of advice.

Rätsel *(pl -)* *das* - 1. [Aufgabe] puzzle; **jm ein Rätsel aufgeben** to ask sb a riddle - 2. [Geheimnis] mystery; **etw ist jm ein Rätsel** sthg is a mystery to sb; **vor einem Rätsel stehen** to be faced with a mystery.

rätselhaft *adj* mysterious; **es ist mir rätselhaft** it's a mystery to me.

rätseln *vi*: **über etw (A) rätseln** to puzzle over sthg.

Ratte *(pl -n)* *die* rat.

rau *adj* - 1. [Oberfläche, Person, Sitten] rough - 2. [Klima, Leben] harsh - 3. [angegriffen - Stimme] hoarse; [- Hals] sore.

Raub *der* robbery.

Raub|bau *der* overexploitation.

rauben *vt* - 1. [stehlen] to steal - 2. [kosten]: **jm etw rauben** to rob sb of sthg; **jm den Schlaf rauben** to deprive sb of their sleep.

Räuber, in *(mpl -, fpl -nen)* *der, die* robber.

Raub|mord *der* robbery with murder.

Raub|tier *das* predator.

Raubüber|fall *der* robbery.

Raub|vogel *der* bird of prey.

Rauch *der* smoke.

rauchen *vt & vi* to smoke.

Raucher *(pl -)* *der* smoker.

Raucherin *(pl -nen)* *die* smoker.

räuchern *vt* to smoke.

Rauch|verbot *das* ban on smoking.

rauf *fam* = **herauf**.

raufen *vi* to fight. <> **sich raufen** *ref* to fight.

Rauferei *(pl -en)* *die* fight.

rauh = **rau**.

Rauhreif = **Raureif**.

Raum *(pl Räume)* *der* - 1. [Zimmer] room - 2. [Platz & PHYS] space - 3. *(ohne pl)* GEOGR area.

räumen *vt* - 1. [Wohnung] to vacate - 2. [Platz, Posten] to clear.

Raum|fahrt *die* space travel.

Raum|inhalt *der* volume.

räumlich <> *adj* spatial. <> *adv* spatially.

Raum|schiff *das* spaceship.

Räumung *(pl -en)* *die* clearing *(U)*; [von Wohnung] vacation *(U)*; [vor Gefahr] evacuation.

Raupe (pl -n) die [Insekt] caterpillar.

Raureif der hoarfrost.

raus adv fam - **1.** = **heraus** - **2.** [hinaus] out; **raus hier!** get out!

Rausch (pl Räusche) der - **1.** [das Betrunkensein] intoxication; **einen Rausch haben** to be drunk - **2.** [Ekstase] ecstasy; **im Rausch** in ecstasy.

rauschen (perf hat/ist gerauscht) vi - **1.** (hat) [Bäume] to rustle; [Bach] to murmur; **es rauscht** [im Telefon] there's a crackle; [in den Ohren] there's a buzz - **2.** (ist) fam [gehen] to rush.

rauschend adj: **ein rauschendes Fest** a glittering party; **rauschender Beifall** loud applause.

Rauschlgift das drug.

rauschgiftsüchtig adj addicted to drugs.

rausIfliegen (perf ist rausgeflogen) vi (unreg) fam [aus Schule] to be thrown out; [aus Firma] to be fired.

rausIhalten vt (unreg) fam [nach draußen] to hold out. **sich raushalten** ref fam: **sich aus etw raushalten** to keep out of sthg.

rausIkriegen vt fam to find out.

räuspern sich räuspern ref to clear one's throat.

rausIrücken (perf hat/ist rausgerückt) fam vi (ist): **mit etw rausrücken** [ausdrücken] to come out with sthg; [herausgeben] to hand over sthg. vt (hat) [herausgeben] to hand over.

rausIschmeißen vt (unreg) fam to throw out.

Raute (pl -n) die diamond (shape).

Razzia (pl Razzien) die (police) raid.

rd. abk für **rund**.

reagieren vi to react; **auf etw** (A) **reagieren** to react to sthg.

Reaktion (pl -en) die reaction; **die Reaktion auf etw** (A) the reaction to sthg.

Reaktor (pl -toren) der (nuclear) reactor.

realistisch adj realistic. adv realistically.

Realität (pl -en) die reality.

Reallschule die secondary school for pupils up to the age of 16.

Rebe (pl -n) die vine.

rebellieren vi to rebel; **gegen jn/etw rebellieren** to rebel against sb/sthg.

Rebellion (pl -en) die rebellion.

rebellisch adj rebellious.

RebIhuhn das partridge.

RebIstock der vine.

Rechen (pl -) der rake.

RechenIaufgabe die sum.

RechenIfehler der miscalculation.

rechnen vi - **1.** [berechnen] to calculate - **2.** [schätzen] to estimate - **3.** [erwarten]: **mit jm/**

etw rechnen to expect sb/sthg - **4.** [sich verlassen]: **auf jn/etw rechnen** to count on sb/sthg; **mit jm rechnen** to rely on sb - **5.** [bedenken]: **mit jm/etw rechnen** to reckon with sb/sthg; **im Urlaub mit gutem Wetter rechnen** to reckon on having good weather on holiday. vt [berechnen] to work out. **sich rechnen** ref to be profitable.

Rechner (pl -) der EDV computer.

Rechnung (pl -en) die - **1.** WIRTSCH bill; [im Restaurant] bill UK, check US; **eine Rechnung begleichen** to pay a bill - **2.** [Rechenaufgabe] calculation; **eine Rechnung begleichen** to settle a score.

recht adj - **1.** [korrekt, passend] right; **recht und billig** fig right and proper; **zur rechten Zeit am rechten Ort** at the right place at the right time; **ist es dir recht, wenn ich morgen vorbeikomme?** is it all right with you if I come by tomorrow? - **2.** [besonders] particular; **es macht keinen rechten Spaß** it's not really much fun. adv [ziemlich] quite; **man kann ihm nichts recht machen** there's no pleasing him; **jetzt erst recht** even more.

Recht (pl -e) das - **1.** RECHT law; **Recht sprechen** to administer justice; **im Recht sein** to be in the right; **jm Recht geben** to admit sb is right - **2.** [Anrecht] right; **ein Recht auf etw** (A) **haben** to have a right to sthg. **mit** ODER **zu Recht** adv rightly.

rechte, r, s adj - **1.** [Seitenangabe] right - **2.** [rechtspolitisch] right-wing.

Rechte (pl -n) die - **1.** [rechte Hand] right hand; **zur Rechten** on the right - **2.** POL: **die Rechte** the Right. der, die right-winger. das: **nach dem Rechten sehen** to see to things.

Rechteck (pl -e) das rectangle.

rechteckig adj rectangular.

rechtfertigen vt to justify; **etw vor jm rechtfertigen** to justify sthg to sb. **sich rechtfertigen** ref: **sich (vor jm) rechtfertigen** to justify o.s. (to sb).

Rechtfertigung (pl -en) die justification.

rechthaberisch adj abw opinionated; **er ist immer so rechthaberisch** he always thinks he's right.

rechtlich adj legal. adv legally,

rechtmäßig adj lawful. adv lawfully.

rechts adv - **1.** [Angabe der Seite, Richtung] on the right; **rechts abbiegen** turn right; **nach/von rechts** to/from the right; **rechts von jm** to one's right; **rechts von etw** to the right of sthg - **2.** [Angabe der politischen Richtung] right wing; **rechts eingestellt sein** to have right-wing leanings. präp (+ G) [Angabe der Seite] to the right of.

RechtsIanwalt der lawyer.

RechtsIanwältin die lawyer.

rechtsbündig *adj* right justified.

Rechtschreibfehler *der* spelling mistake.

Recht|schreibung *die* spelling.

rechtsextrem *adj*: rechtsextreme Jugendliche young right-wing extremists.

Rechts|extremist, in *der, die abw* right-wing extremist.

rechtsgerichtet *adj* right-wing.

rechtsgültig *adj* legally valid.

Rechtshänder, in *(mpl -, fpl -nen) der, die* right-hander.

rechtsherum *adv* to the right.

rechtskräftig ◇ *adj* final; rechtskräftig sein to be legally effective. ◇ *adv*: jn rechtskräftig verurteilen to pass a final sentence on sb.

Rechts|kurve *die* right-hand bend.

Rechts|lage *die* legal situation.

Rechtsprechung *(pl -en) die* administration of justice *(U)*.

rechtsradikal *adj* extreme right-wing.

Rechts|radikale *der, die* right-wing extremist.

rechtsseitig *adj* of the right side.

Rechts|staat *der* state based upon the rule of law.

Rechts|verkehr *der* - 1. [Straßenverkehr] driving on the right - 2. RECHT law.

Rechts|weg *der* legal action; der Rechtsweg ist ausgeschlossen no legal action may be taken.

rechtwinklig, rechtwinkelig ◇ *adj* right-angled. ◇ *adv* at a right angle.

rechtzeitig ◇ *adj* timely. ◇ *adv* in time; rechtzeitig da sein/eintreffen to be/get there in time.

Reck *(pl -e ODER -s) das* horizontal bar.

recyclen [ri'saikəln] *vt* to recycle.

Recycling [ri'saiklɪŋ] *das* recycling.

Recycling|papier *das* recycled paper.

Redakteur, in [redak'tø:ɐ̯, rɪn] *(mpl -e, fpl -nen) der, die* editor.

Redaktion *(pl -en) die* - 1. [Team] editorial staff - 2. [von Texten] editing.

Rede *(pl -n) die* - 1. [Ansprache] speech; eine Rede halten to make a speech - 2. *(ohne pl)* [das Reden] talk; die Rede ist von jm/etw we are talking about sb/sthg - 3. GRAMM [gebundene] verse; [ungebundene] prose; wörtliche/indirekte Rede direct/indirect speech; jn zur Rede stellen to demand an explanation from sb.

Rede|freiheit *die* freedom of speech.

reden ◇ *vi* - 1. [gen] to talk; deutlich/langsam reden to speak clearly/slowly; (mit jm) über jn/etw reden to talk (to sb) about sb/sthg - 2. [eine Rede halten] to speak; du hast gut reden *fam* it's easy for you to talk; jn zum Reden bringen to get sb to talk; von sich reden machen to cause a stir. ◇ *vt*: Unsinn reden to talk nonsense.

Redens|art *die* saying; das ist doch nur eine Redensart it's just an expression.

Rede|wendung *die* idiom.

Redner, in *(mpl -, fpl -nen) der, die* speaker.

redselig *adj* talkative.

reduzieren *vt* - 1. [verringern] to reduce - 2. [vereinfachen]: etw auf etw *(A)* reduzieren to reduce sthg to sthg. ➡ **sich reduzieren** *ref* to decrease.

Reederei *(pl -en) die* shipping company.

Referat *(pl -e) das* - 1. [Abhandlung] paper; ein Referat halten to give a paper - 2. [Abteilung] department.

Referendar *(pl -e) der person undergoing "Referendariat"; [in Schule] student teacher.

Referendariat *(pl -e) das period of practical training in teaching or legal professions, undertaken on completion of first "Staatsexamen".*

Referendarin *(pl -nen) die person undergoing "Referendariat"; [in Schule] student teacher.*

Referenz *(pl -en) die* reference.

reflektieren ◇ *vt* - 1. [Licht] to reflect - 2. *geh* [Problem] to reflect on. ◇ *vi geh*: über etw *(A)* reflektieren to reflect on sthg.

Reflex *(pl -e) der* - 1. [Reaktion] reflex - 2. [Lichtreflex] reflection.

Reflexion *(pl -en) die* reflection.

reflexiv ◇ *adj* GRAMM reflexive. ◇ *adv* GRAMM reflexively.

Reflexiv|pronomen *das* GRAMM reflexive pronoun.

Reform *(pl -en) die* reform.

Reformations|tag *der* RELIG Reformation Day, *31 October, day on which the Reformation is celebrated.*

Reform|haus *das* health food shop.

reformieren *vt* to reform.

Reform|kost *die* health food.

Refrain [rə'frɛ̃:] *(pl -s) der* refrain.

Regal *(pl -e) das* shelves *Pl.*

Regatta *(pl Regatten) die* regatta.

rege ◇ *adj* lively; [Verkehr] busy; [Handel] brisk. ◇ *adv*: sich rege an etw *(D)* beteiligen to take a lively interest in sthg.

Regel *(pl -n) die* - 1. [Norm] rule; in aller ODER der Regel as a rule - 2. [Periode] period.

Regel|blutung *die* period.

Regel|fall *der* rule.

regelmäßig ◇ *adj* regular. ◇ *adv* regularly.

Regelmäßigkeit *(pl -en) die* regularity.

regeln *vt* [Temperatur, Geschwindigkeit] to regulate; [Angelegenheit] to settle; [Nachlass] to put in order; [Verkehr] to direct. ➡ **sich regeln** *ref* to sort itself out; **sich von selbst regeln** to sort itself out.

regelrecht *adj* - 1. *fam* [richtig] proper - 2. [ordnungsgemäß] correct.

Regelung (*pl* -en) *die* regulation.

regen *vt* to move. ➡ **sich regen** *ref* to move; [Gefühl, Hoffnung] to stir.

Regen *der* rain; **saurer Regen** acid rain.

Regen|bogen *der* rainbow.

Regen|mantel *der* raincoat.

Regen|rinne *die* gutter.

Regen|schauer *der* shower.

Regen|schirm *der* umbrella.

Regen|tropfen *der* raindrop.

Regen|wald *der* rain forest.

Regen|wurm *der* earthworm.

Regie [re'ʒi:] *die* direction; **Regie führen** to direct; **etw in eigener Regie tun** ODER **durchführen** to do sthg on one's own account.

regieren <> *vt* to rule. <> *vi* to rule; **über jn/etw regieren** to rule over sb/sthg.

Regierung (*pl* -en) *die* government.

Regierungs|chef, in *der, die* head of government.

Regierungs|sitz *der* seat of government.

Regierungs|sprecher, in *der, die* government spokesperson.

Regime [re'ʒi:m] (*pl* -) *das* regime.

Regiment (*pl* -e ODER -er) *das* - 1. (*pl* Regimenter) MIL regiment - 2. (*pl* Regimente) [Leitung] rule; **ein strenges Regiment führen** to be strict.

Region (*pl* -en) *die* region.

regional <> *adj* regional. <> *adv* regionally; **regional verschieden** different from region to region.

Regisseur, in [reʒɪ'søːɐ̯, rɪn] (*mpl* -e, *fpl* -nen) *der, die* director.

Register (*pl* -) *das* - 1. [Verzeichnis - in Buch] index; [- amtlich] register - 2. [MUS - von Orgel] stop; [- von Stimme] register.

registrieren *vt* - 1. [wahrnehmen] to notice - 2. [eintragen] to register.

reglos <> *adj* motionless. <> *adv* motionlessly.

regnen <> *vi*: **es regnet** it's raining. <> *vt*: **es regnet Konfetti** confetti is raining down.

regnerisch *adj* rainy.

regulär <> *adj* - 1. [Preis, Arbeit] normal; [Wahl, Spiel] in accordance with the rules - 2. MIL regular. <> *adv* [arbeiten] normally; [zum normalen Preis] at the normal price.

regulieren *vt* - 1. [regeln - Preis, Schaden, Verkehr] to regulate - 2. [Temperatur, Lautstärke] to adjust - 3. [Gewässer] to straighten.

Regung (*pl* -en) *die* - 1. [Bewegung] movement - 2. *geh* [Gefühl] stirring.

regungslos <> *adj* motionless. <> *adv* motionlessly.

Reh (*pl* -e) *das* deer.

Reha-|Klinik *die* rehab clinic.

Reh|bock (*pl* -böcke) *der* roebuck.

Reh|kitz (*pl* -e) *das* fawn.

Reibe (*pl* -n) *die* grater.

Reibe|kuchen *der* small pancake made from grated potatoes.

reiben (*prät* rieb, *perf* hat gerieben) <> *vt* - 1. [Körperteile] to rub; **sich** *(D)* **die Hände/die Nase/das Auge reiben** to rub one's hands/nose/eye; **jm die Hände/Wangen reiben** to rub sb's hands/cheeks - 2. [Käse, Karotten] to grate. <> *vi* to rub.

Reiberei (*pl* -en) *die* friction.

Reibung *die* - 1. PHYS friction - 2. [das Reiben] rubbing.

reibungslos <> *adj* smooth. <> *adv* smoothly.

reich <> *adj* - 1. [wohlhabend] rich; **reich an etw** *(D)* **sein** [Bodenschätzen] to be rich in sthg; [Erfahrungen] to have a wealth of sthg - 2. [Erdölvorkommen, Ernte] rich; [Erfahrung] extensive. <> *adv* [geschmückt] richly.

Reich (*pl* -e) *das* - 1. POL empire - 2. [Bereich] world.

Reiche (*pl* -n) *der, die* rich person.

reichen <> *vi* - 1. [Geld, Zeit] to be enough; [Vorrat] to last; **das reicht!** that's enough!; **mir reichts** *fam fig* I've had enough - 2.: **(von bis zu) reichen** [Grundstück, Gebiet] to extend (from to); [Kleidungsstück] to reach (from to). <> *vt*: **jm etw reichen** to pass sb sthg; **sich** *(D)* **die Hände reichen** to shake hands.

reichhaltig *adj* rich.

reichlich <> *adj* [Essen, Zeit] ample; [Trinkgeld] generous. <> *adv* - 1. [viel] amply - 2. [ziemlich] rather.

Reichs|tag ['raiçsta:k] *der* [Gebäude] Reichstag.

Reichtum (*pl* -tümer) *der* - 1. [Vermögen] wealth - 2. [Fülle]: **der Reichtum an etw** *(D)* the abundance of sthg. ➡ **Reichtümer** *Pl* riches.

Reich|weite *die* - 1. [greifbare Nähe, von Boxern] reach - 2. TECH range. ➡ **außer Reichweite** *adv* out of reach. ➡ **in Reichweite** *adv* within reach.

reif *adj* - 1. [gen] ripe; **reif fürs Irrenhaus sein** to belong in the madhouse - 2. [erwachsen] mature.

Reife *die* - 1. [von Person] maturity; **mittlere Reife** SCHULE intermediate school-leaving certificate *(for those leaving at 16)* - 2. [von Obst] ripeness.

Reifen (*pl* -) *der* - 1. [von Fahrzeugen] tyre - 2. [Ring] hoop.

Reifen|druck *der* tyre pressure.

Reifen|panne *die* flat tyre.

Reife|prüfung *die* final examination at a German "Gymnasium", required for university entrance.

Reife|zeugnis *das* certificate awarded to people who have passed the "Reifeprüfung".

reiflich ⟨⟩ *adj* very careful. ⟨⟩ *adv* very carefully.

Reihe (*pl* -n) *die* - 1. [Linie, Sitzreihe] row - 2. [Menge]: **eine Reihe von etw** a number of sthg - 3. [Reihenfolge]: **du bist an der Reihe** it's your turn; **jn außer der Reihe drannehmen** to take sb out of turn; **er kommt an die Reihe** it is his turn. ▬ **der Reihe nach** *adv* in turn.

reihen *vt* - 1. [nebeneinander stellen] to line up - 2. [auffädeln]: **etw auf etw** (A) **reihen** to string sthg on sthg - 3. [nähen] to tack.

Reihen|folge *die* order; **alphabetische Reihenfolge** alphabetical order.

Reihen|haus *das* terraced house *UK*, row house *US*.

Reiher (*pl* -) *der* heron.

Reim (*pl* -e) *der* rhyme.

reimen ⟨⟩ *vt* to rhyme. ⟨⟩ *vi* to make up rhymes. ▬ **sich reimen** *ref* to rhyme; **'Bein' reimt sich auf 'klein'** 'Bein' rhymes with 'klein'.

rein ⟨⟩ *adj* - 1. [ohne Zusätze, nicht gemischt] pure; **eine reine Arbeitergegend** a wholly working-class area - 2. [nicht als] sheer - 3. [sauber] clean; **etw ins Reine bringen** to clear sthg up; **mit jm ins Reine kommen** to sort things out with sb. ⟨⟩ *adv* - 1. [ausschließlich] purely; **rein zeitlich geht es nicht** there's simply not enough time to do it - 2. *fam* [völlig] absolutely; **er wusste auch rein gar nichts** he didn't know anything - 3. *fam* = **herein**.

Rein|fall *der fam* disaster.

rein|fallen (*perf* ist reingefallen) *vi* (unreg) *fam* - 1. [hineinfallen] to fall in - 2. [getäuscht werden] to fall for it; **auf jn/etw reinfallen** to be taken in by sb/sthg; **mit jm/etw reinfallen** to have nothing but trouble with sb/sthg.

reinigen *vt* to clean; **ein Kleidungsstück chemisch reinigen lassen** to have a garment dry-cleaned. ▬ **sich reinigen** *ref* to clean o.s.

Reinigung (*pl* -en) *die* - 1.: **die (chemische) Reinigung** the (dry) cleaner's - 2. [Säubern] cleaning.

Reinigungs|mittel *das* cleaner.

rein|legen *vt fam* - 1. [hineinlegen] to put in - 2. [übertölpeln] to take for a ride.

reinrassig *adj* purebred; [Pferd] thoroughbred.

rein|reden *vi fam* - 1. [ins Wort fallen] to butt in - 2. [sich einmischen]: **jm reinreden** to tread on sb's toes; **sich von niemandem reinreden lassen** not to take orders from anybody.

Reis *der* rice.

Reise (*pl* -n) *die* [lang] journey; [kurz] trip; **auf Reisen sein/gehen** to be/go away; **eine Reise machen** to go on a journey/trip. ▬ **gute Reise** *interj* have a good journey/trip!

Reise|apotheke *die* first-aid kit.

Reise|begleiter, in *der, die* travelling companion.

Reise|büro *das* travel agent's.

Reise|bus *der* bus, coach *UK*.

Reise|führer *der* - 1. [Mensch] guide, courier - 2. [Buch] guide book.

Reise|führerin *die* guide, courier.

Reise|gepäck *das* luggage.

Reise|gesellschaft *die* - 1. [Reisegruppe] group of tourists - 2. [Veranstalter] tour operator.

Reise|gruppe *die* group of tourists.

Reise|leiter, in *der, die* guide, courier.

reisen (*perf* ist gereist) *vi* to travel; **nach Athen/Schottland reisen** to go to Athens/Scotland.

Reisende (*pl* -n) *der, die* [Fahrgast] passenger.

Reisepass (*pl* -pässe) *der* passport.

Reise|route *die* route.

Reise|ruf *der* emergency message for a driver, broadcast over the radio.

Reise|tasche *die* travel bag.

Reise|verkehr *der* holiday traffic.

Reise|versicherung *die* travel insurance.

Reise|zeit *die* - 1. [Fahrtdauer] journey time - 2. [Saison] holiday season.

Reise|ziel *das* destination.

Reiß|brett *das* drawing board.

reißen (*prät* riss, *perf* hat/ist gerissen) ⟨⟩ *vi* - 1. (ist) [abreißen - Papier, Stoff] to tear; [- Seil, Kette] to snap - 2. (hat) [ziehen]: **an etw** (D) **reißen** to pull at sthg. ⟨⟩ *vt* (hat) - 1. [zerreißen]: **etw in Stücke reißen** to tear sthg into pieces - 2. [herunterreißen] to pull - 3. [herausreißen]: **sie wurde aus dem Schlaf gerissen** she was rudely awakened; **etw aus dem Zusammenhang reißen** to take sthg out of context - 4. [wegreißen]: **jm etw aus der Hand reißen** to snatch sthg from sb; **etw an sich** (A) **reißen** [Paket, Macht] to seize sthg; [Gespräch] to monopolize sthg; **hin und her gerissen sein** *fig* to be torn - 5. [töten] to kill. ▬ **sich reißen** *ref*: **sich um etw reißen** to fight to get sthg.

reißend *adj* - 1. [Gewässer] raging - 2. [schnell]: **reißenden Absatz finden** to sell like hot cakes - 3. [Tier] rapacious - 4. [Schmerzen] searing.

Reißverschluss (*pl* -schlüsse) *der* zip *UK*, zipper *US*.

Reiß|zwecke *die* drawing pin *UK*, thumbtack *US*.

reiten (*prät* ritt, *perf* hat/ist geritten) ⟨⟩ *vi* (ist) to ride; **im Schritt/Trab/Galopp reiten** to ride at a walk/trot/gallop. ⟨⟩ *vt* (hat) to ride.

Reiter, in (*mpl* -, *fpl* -nen) *der, die* rider.

Reit|hose *die* jodhpurs *Pl.*

Reit|pferd *das* horse *(for riding)*.

Reit|sport *der* riding.

Reit|stiefel *der* riding boot.

Reit|weg *der* bridle path.

Reiz *(pl -e) der* - 1. [Impuls] stimulus - 2. [Verlockung, Schönheit] appeal *(U)*; **die Reize einer schönen Frau** the charms of a beautiful woman.

reizbar *adj* irritable; **sie ist leicht reizbar** she is very irritable.

reizen *vt* - 1. [interessieren] to appeal to - 2. [provozieren] to provoke - 3. [Augen, Magen] to irritate - 4. [Neugier] to arouse.

reizend ⇔ *adj* charming. ⇔ *adv* charmingly.

reizlos ⇔ *adj* unattractive. ⇔ *adv* unattractively.

Reizung *(pl -en) die* irritation.

reizvoll ⇔ *adj* [verlockend] attractive; [reizend] charming. ⇔ *adv* attractively.

rekeln = **räkeln**.

Reklamation *(pl -en) die* complaint.

Reklame *die* - 1. [Werbung] advertising; **für jn/etw Reklame machen** to advertise sb/sthg; *fig* to sing sb's/sthg's praises - 2. [Werbemittel] advertisement.

reklamieren ⇔ *vt* - 1. [beanstanden] to complain about - 2. [einklagen] to claim. ⇔ *vi* [Einspruch erheben]: **gegen etw reklamieren** to object to sthg.

rekonstruieren *vt* to reconstruct.

Rekord *(pl -e) der* [Bestleistung, Spitzenwert] record; **einen Rekord aufstellen/brechen** to set/break a record.

Rekrut *(pl -en) der* MIL recruit.

rekrutieren *vt* to recruit.

Rektor *(pl -toren) der* - 1. [von Schulen] head teacher *UK*, principal *US* - 2. [von Hochschulen] vice-chancellor *UK*, president *US*.

relativ, relativ ⇔ *adj* relative. ⇔ *adv* relatively.

Relativ|pronomen *das* GRAMM relative pronoun.

Relativ|satz *der* GRAMM relative clause.

relaxen [ri'leksn] *vi fam* to take it easy.

relevant [rele'vant] *adj* relevant.

Religion *(pl -en) die* - 1. [Anschauung] religion - 2. *(ohne pl)* [Schulfach] religious education.

religiös ⇔ *adj* religious. ⇔ *adv* in a religious way; **jn religiös erziehen** to give sb a religious upbringing.

Relikt *(pl -e) das* relic.

Reling *(pl -s ODER -e) die* SCHIFF rail.

remis [rə'mi:] *adv* SPORT: **remis enden** to end in a draw.

Remoulade *(pl -n) die* remoulade.

Renaissance [rənɛ'sãːs] *die* Renaissance.

Renn|bahn *die* SPORT racetrack; [Pferdesport] racecourse.

rennen *(prät rannte, perf ist gerannt) vi* to run; **sie kommt immer zu mir gerannt, wenn sie etwas braucht** she's always running to me when she needs something; **gegen etw rennen** to run into sthg.

Rennen *(pl -) das* [Wettkampf] race; **das Rennen machen** to win.

Renner *(pl -) der fam* in-thing.

Renn|fahrer, in *der, die* racing driver.

Renn|rad *das* racing bike.

Renn|sport *der* racing.

Renn|wagen *der* racing car.

renovieren [reno'viːrən] *vt* to renovate.

Renovierung [reno'viːruŋ] *(pl -en) die* renovation.

Rente *(pl -n) die* pension; **auf** ODER **in Rente gehen** to retire.

Rentenver|sicherung *die* pension scheme.

Ren|tier, Rentier *das* reindeer.

rentieren ⬧ **sich rentieren** *ref* [rentabel sein] to be profitable; [sich lohnen] to be worthwhile.

Rentner, in *(mpl -, fpl -nen) der, die* pensioner.

Reparatur *(pl -en) die* repair; **in Reparatur sein** to be being repaired.

Reparatur|werkstatt *die* [für Autos] garage.

reparieren *vt* to repair.

Reportage [repɔr'taːʒə] *(pl -n) die* report.

Reporter, in *(mpl -, fpl -nen) der, die* reporter.

Repräsentant, in *(mpl -en, fpl -nen) der, die* representative.

repräsentativ ⇔ *adj* - 1. [ausgewogen, stellvertretend] representative - 2. [vorzeigbar] imposing. ⇔ *adv* - 1. [ausgewogen, stellvertretend] representatively - 2. [vorzeigbar] imposingly.

repräsentieren ⇔ *vt* to represent. ⇔ *vi* [öffentlich] to perform official duties.

Reproduktion *(pl -en) die* reproduction.

reproduzieren *vt* to reproduce.

Reptil *(pl -ien* ODER *-e) das* reptile.

Republik *(pl -en) die* republic.

Republikaner, in *(mpl -, fpl -en) der, die* [Anhänger der Republik] republican.

Requiem ['reːkvjɛm] *(pl -s* ODER **Requien**) *das* requiem.

Reserve [re'zɛrvə] *(pl -n) die* - 1. [Vorrat] reserve; **jn/etw in Reserve haben** ODER **halten** to have sb/sthg in reserve - 2. *(ohne pl)* [Zurückhaltung] reserve - 3. *(ohne pl)* [beim Militär] reserves *Pl.*

Reserve|kanister *der* spare can.

Reserve|rad *das* spare wheel.

Reserve|reifen *der* spare tyre.

Reserve|spieler, in der, die substitute.

reservieren [rezɛr'viːrən] vt to reserve.

reserviert [rezɛr'viːɐ̯t] adj reserved.

Reservierung [rezɛr'viːruŋ] (pl -en) die reservation.

Residenz (pl -en) die [Wohnsitz] residence; [Stadt] royal seat.

Resignation (pl -en) die resignation (U).

resignieren vi to give up.

Resonanz (pl -en) die - 1. [Widerhall] response; **die Resonanz auf etw (A)** the response to sthg - 2. [akustisch] resonance.

Respekt der respect; **Respekt vor jm haben** to have respect for sb; **Respekt!** well done!; **sich (D) Respekt verschaffen** to make o.s. respected.

respektieren vt to respect.

respektlos <> adj disrespectful. <> adv disrespectfully.

respektvoll <> adj respectful. <> adv respectfully.

Rest (pl -e) der - 1. [von Mahlzeit, Gebäude, Leichnam] remains Pl; [von Stoff] remnant - 2. [von Tag, Urlaub, Erzählung] rest; **jm/etw den Rest geben** fam fig to finish sb/sthg off.

Restaurant [rɛsto'rãː] (pl -s) das restaurant.

restaurieren vt to restore.

Restaurierung (pl -en) die restoration.

Rest|betrag der balance.

restlich adj remaining.

restlos adv totally.

Resultat (pl -e) das result.

Retorte (pl -n) die CHEM retort; **aus der Retorte** abw artificial; **ein Kind aus der Retorte** a test-tube baby.

Retorten|baby das test-tube baby.

Retrospektive [retrospɛk'tiːvə] (pl -n) die - 1. geh [Rückblick] retrospective view - 2. [Ausstellung] retrospective.

retten vt to save; [aus einer Gefahr] to rescue; **jn/etw vor jm/etw retten** to save sb/sthg from sb/sthg. ◆ **sich retten** ref to escape; **sich vor jm/etw nicht mehr retten können** fam fig to be besieged by sb/swamped with sthg.

Retter, in (mpl -, fpl -nen) der, die rescuer.

Rettich (pl -e) der radish (of large red or white variety).

Rettung die (ohne pl) rescue; **jd/etw ist js (letzte) Rettung** fig sb/sthg is sb's salvation.

Rettungs|boot das lifeboat.

Rettungs|dienst der rescue service.

Rettungs|ring der lifebelt.

Rettungs|wagen der ambulance.

Revanche [re'vãːʃ(ə)] (pl -n) die - 1. [Gegenleistung]: **als Revanche für etw** in return for sthg - 2. [Vergeltung] revenge (U) - 3. [beim Spiel] return game.

Revier [re'viːɐ̯] (pl -e) das - 1. [von Tieren] territory - 2. [Polizeirevier - Wache] (police) station; [- Bezirk] district - 3. [Bereich] domain - 4. [von Jäger, Förster] area.

Revolte [re'vɔltə] (pl -n) die revolt.

Revolution [revolu'tsjoːn] (pl -en) die revolution.

revolutionär [revolutsjo'nɛːɐ̯] adj revolutionary.

Revolutionär, in [revolutsjo'nɛːɐ̯, rɪn] (mpl -e, fpl -nen) der, die revolutionary.

Revolver [re'vɔlvɐ] (pl -) der revolver.

Revue [re'vyː] (pl -n) die - 1. [Show] revue - 2. [Zeitschrift] review.

Rezension (pl -en) die review.

Rezept (pl -e) das - 1. [ärztlich] prescription - 2. [für Speisen] recipe.

rezeptfrei adj available without a prescription.

Rezeption (pl -en) die reception.

rezeptpflichtig adj available only on prescription.

R-|Gespräch das TELEKOM reverse charge UK ODER collect US call.

Rhabarber der rhubarb.

Rhein der: **das Rhein** the (River) Rhine.

rheinisch adj Rhenish.

Rheinland das: **das Rheinland** the Rhineland.

Rheinland-Pfalz nt Rhineland-Palatinate.

Rhesus|faktor der MED rhesus factor.

rhetorisch adj rhetorical.

Rheuma das rheumatism.

Rheumatismus (pl -tismen) der rheumatism (U).

Rhododendron (pl -dendren) der rhododendron.

rhythmisch <> adj rhythmic. <> adv rhythmically.

Rhythmus (pl Rhythmen) der rhythm.

richten <> vt - 1. [hinwenden] to point; **etw auf jn/etw richten** [Waffe] to point sthg at sb/sthg; [Aufmerksamkeit] to turn sthg to sb/sthg - 2. [Brief, Appell]: **etw an jn richten** to address sthg to sb - 3. [reparieren] to fix - 4. [Essen, Zimmer] to prepare. <> vi [urteilen] to judge; **über jn/etw richten** geh to judge sb/sthg. ◆ **sich richten** ref - 1. [sich einstellen auf]: **sich nach jm/etw richten** to fit in with sb/sthg - 2. [abhängen von]: **sich nach etw richten** to depend on sthg - 3. [sich wenden]: **sich gegen jn/etw richten** to be directed at sb/sthg.

Richter, in (mpl -, fpl -nen) der, die judge.

richterlich adj judicial.

richtig <> adj - 1. [nicht falsch, passend] right; **bin ich hier richtig?** am I in the right place?; **sehr richtig!** quite right! - 2. [echt - Person] real, true; [- Sache] real - 3. [vollwertig] proper. <> adv - 1. [nicht falsch] correctly; **meine Uhr**

geht richtig my watch is right ODER accurate; **das hast du richtig gemacht!** you were right to do it! - **2.** [passend]: **er kam gerade richtig** he came at just the right moment - **3.** fam [wirklich] really.

Richtige (pl -n) ⬥ das right thing; **genau das Richtige** just the right thing; **nichts Richtiges** nothing much. ⬥ der, die right person.

richtig gehend adj [Uhr] accurate.

Richtigkeit die correctness.

rieb prät ▷ **reiben.**

riechen (prät roch, perf hat gerochen) ⬥ vi to smell. ⬥ vt [Duft] to smell.

rief prät ▷ **rufen.**

Riemen (pl -) der - **1.** [Band] strap; **sich am Riemen reißen** fam fig to pull o.s. together - **2.** [Ruder] oar.

Riese (pl -n) der giant.

rieseln (perf ist gerieselt) vi [Flüssigkeit] to trickle; [Schnee] to float down; [Putz, Kalk] to crumble.

Riesenlerfolg der huge success.

riesengroß adj enormous.

Riesenlrad das big wheel.

Riesenlslalom der giant slalom.

riesig ⬥ adj - **1.** [groß] enormous - **2.** fam [toll] fantastic. ⬥ adv fam [sehr] enormously.

riet prät ▷ **raten.**

Riff (pl -e) das reef.

Rille (pl -n) die groove.

Rind (pl -er) das - **1.** [Tier] cow - **2.** [Fleisch] beef.

Rinde (pl -n) die - **1.** [von Bäumen] bark - **2.** [von Käse] rind - **3.** [von Brot] crust.

Rinderlbraten der [roh] joint of beef; [gebraten] roast beef.

Rinderlwahnsinn, Rinderwahn der (ohne pl) mad cow disease.

Rindlfleisch das beef.

Ring (pl -e) der - **1.** [gen] ring - **2.** [Gruppe] group - **3.** [Straße] ring road. ➡ **Ringe** Pl SPORT rings.

Ringlbuch das ring binder.

Ringellnatter die grass snake.

ringen (prät rang, perf hat gerungen) ⬥ vi - **1.** SPORT to wrestle - **2.** [sich anstrengen] to struggle; **mit etw ringen geh** to wrestle with sthg. ⬥ vt: **die Hände ringen** to wring one's hands.

Ringer, in (mpl -, fpl -nen) der, die wrestler.

Ringlfinger der ring finger.

Ringlkampf der SPORT wrestling match.

Ringlrichter, in der, die referee.

rings adv: **rings um jn/etw (herum)** all around sb/sthg.

ringsherum adv all around.

ringsumher adv all around.

Rinne (pl -n) die - **1.** [Vertiefung] channel - **2.** [Abflussrinne] gutter.

Rinnlstein der gutter.

Rippchen (pl -) das KÜCHE lightly smoked pork rib.

Rippe (pl -n) die - **1.** [Knochen] rib - **2.** [von Heizkörper] fin.

Risiko (pl Risiken) das risk; **auf eigenes Risiko** at one's own risk; **ein Risiko eingehen** to take a risk.

riskant ⬥ adj risky. ⬥ adv riskily.

riskieren vt to risk.

riss prät ▷ **reißen.**

Riss (pl -e) der [in Stoff, Kleidungsstück] tear; [in Gestein, Wand] crack; [in Gesellschaft] rift.

rissig adj cracked.

ritt prät ▷ **reiten.**

Ritt (pl -e) der ride.

Ritter (pl -) der knight.

Ritual (pl -e) das ritual.

rituell adj ritual.

Ritze (pl -n) die crack.

ritzen vt [gravieren] to carve. ➡ **sich ritzen** ref [verletzen] to scratch o.s.

Rivale [ri'vaːlə] (pl -n) der rival.

Rivalin [ri'vaːlɪn] (pl -nen) die rival.

Rivalität [rivaliˈtɛːt] (pl -en) die rivalry.

Robbe (pl -n) die seal.

robben (perf ist gerobbt) vi to crawl.

Roboter (pl -) der robot.

robust adj robust.

roch prät ▷ **riechen.**

röcheln vi to breathe with a wheezing sound; [Sterbender] to give the death rattle.

Rock der rock.

Rocker, in (mpl -, fpl -nen) der, die abw rocker.

Rocklmusik die rock music.

Rodellbahn die toboggan run.

rodeln (perf hat/ist gerodelt) vi to toboggan.

roden vt to clear.

Roggen der rye.

Roggenlbrot das rye bread (U).

roh ⬥ adj - **1.** [ungekocht] raw - **2.** [grob, unbearbeitet] rough; **rohe Gewalt** brute force. ⬥ adv - **1.** [ungekocht]: **etw roh essen** to eat sthg raw - **2.** [behandeln, entwerfen] roughly.

Rohlbau (pl -ten) der shell.

Rohlkost die (ohne pl) raw fruit and vegetables Pl.

Rohlmaterial das raw material.

Rohr (pl -e) das - **1.** [Röhre] pipe - **2.** [Pflanze] reed.

Rohrlbruch der burst pipe.

Röhre (pl -n) die - **1.** TECH pipe - **2.** ELEKTR valve UK, tube US - **3.** [Backofen] oven.

Rohrlzucker der cane sugar.

Rohlstoff der raw material.

Rokoko das rococo.

Rolladen *der* = **Rollladen**.

Rollbahn *die* runway.

Rolle *(pl -n)* *die* - 1. [in Theater, in Gesellschaft] role - 2. [von Garn] reel *UK*, spool *US* - 3. [von Möbeln] castor - 4. SPORT roll; **eine/keine Rolle spielen** to/not to matter.

rollen *(perf hat/ist gerollt)* ⟨ *vi (ist)* to roll. ⟨ *vt (hat)* - 1. [Zigarette] to roll; [Teig] to roll out; [Papier, Fleisch] to roll up - 2. [fortbewegen] to roll. ⟨ **sich rollen** *ref* [Papier, Foto] to curl up; [sich wälzen] to roll around.

Roller *(pl -)* *der* scooter.

Rollerblades® *(pl -)* *Pl* roller blades, inline skates.

Rollkragen *der* polo neck.

Rollladen *(pl -läden)* *der* (rolling) shutters *Pl*.

Rollmops *der* rollmop, rolled-up pickled herring.

Rollo *(pl -s)* *das* roller blind.

Rollschuh *der* roller skate; **Rollschuh laufen** to roller-skate.

Rollsplitt *der (ohne pl)* loose chippings *Pl*.

Rollstuhl *der* wheelchair.

Rollstuhlfahrer, in *der, die* wheelchair user.

Rolltreppe *die* escalator.

Rom *nt* Rome.

Roma *Pl* Romanies.

Roman *(pl -e)* *der* - 1. [Buch] novel - 2. *fam* [lange Geschichte] long rigmarole.

romanisch *adj* - 1. [in Bezug auf Sprache] Romance - 2. [der Romanik] Romanesque.

Romanistik *die* Romance languages and literature.

Romantik *die* - 1. [Gefühl] romance - 2. [Epoche] Romantic period.

romantisch ⟨ *adj* - 1. [gefühlvoll] romantic - 2. KUNST & MUS Romantic. ⟨ *adv* romantically.

Romanze *(pl -n)* *die* romance.

Römer, in *(mpl -, fpl -nen)* *der, die* Roman.

römisch *adj* Roman.

römisch-katholisch *adj* Roman Catholic.

Rommee *(pl -s)*, **Rommé** *(pl -s)* *das* rummy *(U)*.

röntgen *vt* to X-ray.

Röntgenaufnahme *die* X-ray.

Röntgenbild *(pl -bilder)* *das* = **Röntgenaufnahme**.

Röntgenstrahlen *Pl* X-rays.

rosa *adj (unver)* pink.

Rosa *das* pink.

Rose *(pl -n)* *die* rose.

Rosenkohl *der (ohne pl)* (Brussels) sprouts *Pl*.

Rosenmontag *(pl -e)* *der* day before Shrove Tuesday which marks the height of the carnival season.

rosig *adj* rosy.

Rosine *(pl -n)* *die* raisin.

Rosmarin *der* rosemary.

Rost *(pl -e)* *der* - 1. [Eisenoxyd] rust - 2. [Gitter - zum Braten] grill; [- zum Abdecken] grating.

Rostbratwurst *die*: **Nürnberger Rostbratwurst** Nuremberg grilled sausage.

rosten *(perf hat/ist gerostet)* *vi* to rust.

rösten *vt* & *vi* to roast.

rostfrei *adj* [Stahl] stainless; [Messer] stainless steel; [Blech] rustproof.

Rösti *Pl Schweiz* potato pancake made from grated fried potatoes.

rostig *adj* rusty.

rot *(kompar* **röter** *ODER* **roter**, *superl* **röteste** *ODER* **roteste)** *adj* - 1. [Farbe] red; **rot werden** to blush - 2. *fam* POL Red.

Rot *das (ohne pl)* red. ⟨ **bei Rot** *adv* at red.

Röte *die* redness.

Rote Kreuz *das*: **das Rote Kreuz** the Red Cross.

Röteln *Pl* MED German measles *(U)*.

Rote Meer *das*: **das Rote Meer** the Red Sea.

rothaarig *adj* red-haired.

rotieren *(perf hat/ist rotiert)* *vi* - 1. *(hat)* [sich drehen, wechseln] to rotate - 2. *(hat, ist)* *fam* [durchdrehen] to be in a flap.

Rotkäppchen *das* Little Red Riding Hood.

Rotkehlchen *(pl Rotkehlchen)* *das* robin.

Rotkohl *der* red cabbage.

rötlich *adj* reddish.

Rötung *(pl -en)* *die* reddening.

Rotwein *der* red wine.

Rotwild *das* red deer *Pl*.

Roulade [ru'laːdə] *(pl -n)* *die* ≃ beef olive.

Roulette [ru'lɛːt] *(pl -s)* *das* roulette *(U)*.

Route ['ruːtə] *(pl -n)* *die* route.

Routine [ru'tiːnə] *(pl -n)* *die* - 1. [Gewohnheit] routine; **zur Routine werden** to become routine - 2. [Erfahrung]: **Routine haben** to have experience.

routiniert [ruti'niːɐt] ⟨ *adj* [Autofahrer, Redner] experienced; [Betrüger, Stil] skilful. ⟨ *adv* skilfully.

rubbeln *vt* [abrubbeln] to rub.

Rübe *(pl -n)* *die* - 1. [Pflanze] turnip - 2. *fam* [Kopf] nut.

Rubel *(pl -)* *der* rouble.

rüber *fam* = **herüber**, **hinüber**.

Rubin *(pl -e)* *der* ruby.

Rubrik *(pl -en)* *die* - 1. [Kategorie] category - 2. [von Zeitung] section.

Ruck *(pl -e)* *der* - 1. [Bewegung] jerk; **sich** *(D)* **einen Ruck geben** *fam fig* to make the effort - 2. [politisch] swing.

Rückantwort *die* reply.

Rück|blick *der* look back; **im Rückblick** looking back; **ein Rückblick auf etw** *(A)* a look back at sthg.

rücken <> *vt (perf* hat gerückt) to move. <> *vi (perf* ist gerückt) to move.

Rücken *(pl* -) *der* - **1.** [gen] back; [von Buch] spine; [von Nase] bridge - **2.** SPORT [Schwimmen] backstroke.

Rücken|lehne *die* backrest.

Rücken|mark *das (ohne pl)* spinal cord.

Rücken|schmerzen *Pl* backache *(sg).*

Rücken|schwimmen *das* backstroke.

Rücken|wind *der*: **Rückenwind haben** to have a following wind.

rück|erstatten *vt* to reimburse; **jm etw rückerstatten** to reimburse sb for sthg.

Rückfahr|karte *die* return (ticket) *UK,* round-trip ticket *US.*

Rück|fahrt *die* return journey.

rück|fällig *adj*: **rückfällig werden** to relapse.

Rück|flug *der* return flight.

Rück|frage *die* query.

Rück|gabe *die* return *(U).*

Rück|gang *der* decrease.

rück|gängig <> *adj* decreasing. <> *adv*: **etw rückgängig machen** [Geschäft] to cancel sthg; [Entschluss] to reverse sthg.

Rück|gewinnung *die* recovery.

Rück|grat *das* spine; **jm das Rückgrat brechen** *fig* [Widerstand brechen] to break sb; **Rückgrat haben** *fig* to have fight in one; **Rückgrat zeigen** to show fight.

Rück|griff *der*: **Rückgriff auf etw** *(A)* [Methode] recourse to sthg; [Mode, Musik] throwback to sthg.

Rück|kehr *die* return.

Rück|kopplung, Rückkoppelung *die* feedback *(U).*

rück|läufig <> *adj* declining; [Trend] downward; **rückläufige Entwicklung** decline. <> *adv*: **sich rückläufig entwickeln** to decline.

Rück|licht *(pl* -er) *das* rear light.

Rück|reise *die* return journey.

Rück|ruf *der* return call.

Ruck|sack *der* rucksack, pack; [für Reisen] backpack.

Rück|schlag *der* setback.

Rückschluss *(pl* -schlüsse) *der* conclusion; **aus etw Rückschlüsse ziehen** to draw conclusions from sthg.

Rück|schritt *der* backward step.

Rück|seite *die* back.

Rück|sicht *die* - **1.** [auf Person, Umstand] consideration; **aus Rücksicht auf** out of consideration for sb/sthg; **auf jn/etw Rücksicht nehmen** to show consideration for sb/sthg - **2.** [nach hinten] rear view.

rücksichtslos <> *adj* [unhöflich] inconsiderate; [verantwortungslos] reckless; [erbarmungslos] ruthless. <> *adv* [unhöflich] inconsiderately; [verantwortungslos] recklessly; [erbarmungslos] ruthlessly.

rücksichtsvoll <> *adj* considerate. <> *adv* considerately.

Rück|sitz *der* back seat.

Rück|spiegel *der* rear-view mirror.

Rück|spiel *das* SPORT return game.

Rück|stand *der* - **1.** WIRTSCH arrears *Pl*; (mit etw) **im Rückstand sein** to be in arrears (with sthg) - **2.** SPORT: **in Rückstand geraten** to fall behind; **(mit etw) im Rückstand sein** to be trailing (by sthg) - **3.** [von Gift] residue - **4.** [Abstand] gap.

rückständig *abw adj* - **1.** [Person, Politik] outdated - **2.** [Land, Technik] backward.

Rück|stau *der* [von Autos] tailback *UK,* backup *US*; [von Flüssigkeiten] backing up *(U).*

Rück|stoß *der* - **1.** PHYS thrust *(U)* - **2.** [von Gewehr] recoil.

Rück|tritt *der* - **1.** [aus Amt] resignation - **2.** *fam* [von Fahrrad] backpedal brake.

Rück|wand *die* back.

rückwärts *adv* backwards; **rückwärts einparken** to reverse into a parking space.

Rückwärts|gang *der* reverse gear; **im Rückwärtsgang** in reverse.

Rück|weg *der* way back.

rückwirkend <> *adj* [Zahlung] backdated; [Datierung, Gesetz] retrospective. <> *adv*: **die Gehaltserhöhung ist rückwirkend vom 1.1. wirksam** the salary increase is backdated to 1.1.

Rück|zahlung *die* repayment.

Rück|zug *der (ohne pl)* retreat.

Rudel *(pl* -) *das* [von Wölfen] pack; [von Hirschen] herd.

Ruder *(pl* -) *das* - **1.** [zum Rudern] oar - **2.** [zum Steuern] rudder.

Ruder|boot *das* rowing boat *UK,* rowboat *US.*

Ruderer, in *(mpl* -, *fpl* -nen) *der, die* oarsman (oarswoman *fig).*

rudern *(perf* hat/ist gerudert) <> *vi* - **1.** (hat) SPORT to row; **mit den Armen rudern** to flail one's arms - **2.** (ist) [in bestimmte Richtung] to row. <> *vt (hat)* to row.

Ruf *(pl* -e) *der* - **1.** *(ohne pl)* [Leumund] reputation - **2.** *(ohne pl)* [Aufruf] call - **3.** UNI offer of a chair - **4.** [von Tier] call.

rufen *(prät* rief, *perf* hat gerufen) <> *vi* to call; **nach jm/etw rufen** to call for sb/sthg. <> *vt* - **1.** [herbeirufen, nennen] to call; **jd/etw kommt (jm) wie gerufen** sb/sthg comes at just the right moment; **jn zu Hilfe rufen** to call on sb to help - **2.** [schreien] to shout.

Ruf|nummer *die* amt telephone number.

Rüge (pl -n) die reprimand.

rügen vt - 1. [Person] to reprimand - 2. [Mängel] to complain about.

Rügen nt Rügen.

Ruhe die - 1. [Stille] silence; **Ruhe bitte!** quiet please! - 2. [Erholung] rest - 3. [das Ungestörtsein] peace; **ich will jetzt meine Ruhe (haben)** I want a bit of peace and quiet; **in Ruhe** in peace; **jn (mit etw) in Ruhe lassen** fam to stop bothering sb (with sthg); **keine Ruhe geben** to keep pestering - 4. [Gelassenheit] calm; **sie ist durch nichts aus der Ruhe zu bringen** she won't let anything disturb her composure; **(die) Ruhe bewahren** to keep calm; **zur Ruhe kommen** to calm down.

ruhen vi - 1. [stillstehen - Verkehr, Arbeit, Maschinen] to be at a standstill; [- Waffen] to be silent - 2. geh [liegen] to lie; [schlafen] to sleep - 3. [lasten, verweilen] to rest.

Ruhe|stand der retirement; **in den Ruhestand gehen** ODER **treten** to retire; **in den Ruhestand versetzt werden** to be retired.

Ruhe|störung die: **jn wegen Ruhestörung anzeigen** to report sb for disturbing the peace; **nächtliche Ruhestörung** disturbance of the peace (at night).

Ruhe|tag der closing day; 'montags Ruhetag!' 'closed on Mondays'.

ruhig <> adj - 1. [still] quiet - 2. [unbewegt] calm - 3. [gelassen - Mensch, Stimme] calm; [- Hand] steady; [- Gewissen] clear - 4. [geruhsam] peaceful. <> adv - 1. [still - liegen] still; [- wohnen] in a quiet area; **sich ruhig verhalten** to keep quiet - 2. [gelassen] calmly - 3. fam [gerne]: **mach ruhig mit!** join in if you like!

Ruhm der fame.

Ruhr die (ohne pl) [Krankheit] dysentery.

Rühr|ei das scrambled eggs Pl.

rühren <> vt - 1. [gen] to move; **sie war gerührt** she was moved - 2. [umrühren] to stir. <> vi [ansprechen]: **an etw (A) rühren** to touch on sthg. **sich rühren** ref - 1. [sich bewegen] to move; **rührt euch!** stand at ease! - 2. fam [sich melden] to be in touch.

Ruhrgebiet das: **das Ruhrgebiet** the Ruhr.

Rühr|teig der cake mixture.

Ruin der ruin.

Ruine (pl -n) die ruin.

ruinieren vt to ruin. **sich ruinieren** ref to ruin o.s.

rülpsen vi to burp.

Rülpser (pl -) der burp.

rum fam = **herum**.

Rum (pl -s) der rum.

Rumäne (pl -n) der Romanian.

Rumänien nt Romania.

Rumänin (pl -nen) die Romanian.

rumänisch adj Romanian.

rum|gammeln vi fam to laze about.

rum|hängen vi (unreg) fam to hang around.

rum|kriegen vt fam - 1. [Person] to talk round - 2. [Zeit] to get through.

Rummel (pl -) der - 1. [Jahrmarkt] fair - 2. fam [Umstände]: **um jn/etw viel Rummel machen** to make a big fuss about sb/sthg.

Rumpf (pl Rümpfe) der - 1. [Oberkörper] trunk - 2. TECH [von Schiff] hull; [von Flugzeug] fuselage - 3. [Rest] remnant.

rümpfen vt ▷ **Nase**.

Rump|steak ['rumpste:k] das rump steak.

rund <> adj - 1. [Form, Summe] round - 2. [ungefähr]: **eine runde Woche** a good week. <> adv - 1. [ungefähr] about; **rund gerechnet** at a rough estimate - 2. [ohne Ecken] in a round shape; [laufen] smoothly - 3. [um herum]: **rund um jn/etw** [räumlich] round sb/sthg; [thematisch] all about sb/sthg.

Runde (pl -n) die - 1. [gen] round - 2. SPORT [bei Rennen] lap; [bei Boxkampf] round - 3. [Personen] group; **etw macht die Runde** sthg is doing the rounds; **über die Runden kommen** fam to get by.

Rund|fahrt die tour.

Rund|flug der sightseeing flight.

Rund|funk der - 1. [Institution] radio - 2. [Radiosender] radio station.

Rundfunk|gebühr die radio licence fee.

Rund|gang der [Spaziergang] walk; [von Wächter] round.

rund|gehen (perf ist rundgegangen) vi (unreg): **es geht rund** it's all go.

rundheraus adv straight out.

rundherum adv - 1. [ganz] completely - 2. [ringsherum] all round.

rundlich adj [Mensch] plump.

Rund|reise die tour.

rundum adv completely.

rundweg adv flatly.

runter fam = **herunter**, **hinunter**.

runter|hauen fam vt: **jm eine runterhauen** to slap sb.

runzeln vt ▷ **Stirn**.

rupfen vt [Unkraut] to pull up; [Blätter] to pull off; [Huhn] to pluck.

ruppig <> adj [unfreundlich] gruff. <> adv [unfreundlich] gruffly.

Rüsche (pl -n) die frill.

Ruß der soot.

Russe (pl -n) der Russian.

Rüssel (pl -) der [von Elefant] trunk; [von Schwein] snout; [von Fliege] proboscis.

rußig adj sooty.

Russin (pl -nen) die Russian.

russisch adj Russian.

Russisch(e) das Russian; siehe auch **Englisch(e)**.

Russland nt Russia.

rüstig *adj* sprightly.

rustikal *adj* rustic.

Rüstung *(pl -en)* die - 1. *(ohne pl)* [von Staat] armaments *Pl* - 2. [von Ritter] armour.

Rutsch *(pl -e)* der: in einem *ODER* auf einen Rutsch in one go. ➤ **guten Rutsch** *interj* Happy New Year!

Rutsch|bahn die [auf dem Spielplatz] slide; [spiralförmig] helter-skelter; [Wasserröhre] flume.

Rutsche *(pl -n)* die - 1. [Rutschbahn] slide - 2. [zum Schütten] chute.

rutschen *(perf ist gerutscht)* vi [gleiten - ausrutschen, fallen] to slip; [- mit dem Auto] to skid; auf dem Stuhl hin und her rutschen to shift around on one's chair; rutsch mal ein Stück move up a bit.

rutschfest *adj* non-slip.

rutschig *adj* slippery.

rütteln ◇ *vt* to shake. ◇ *vi*: an etw *(D)* rütteln to rattle sthg.

S

s *(pl -)*, **S** *(pl -)* [ɛs] das s, S. ➤ **S** *(abk für Süd)* S.

Saal *(pl Säle)* der hall.

Saar die: die Saar the (River) Saar.

Saarbrücken nt Saarbrücken.

Saar|land das Saarland.

saarländisch *adj* of/from Saarland.

Saat *(pl -en)* die - 1. [das Säen] sowing - 2. [Körner] seed.

Säbel *(pl -)* der sabre.

Sabotage [sabo'tɑːʒə] *(pl -n)* die sabotage *(U)*.

sabotieren *vt* to sabotage.

Sach|bearbeiter, in der, die employee in charge of a particular matter.

Sach|buch das non-fiction book.

Sache *(pl -n)* die - 1. *(ohne pl)* [Angelegenheit] matter; das ist (nicht) deine Sache that's (none of) your business; bei der Sache bleiben to keep to the point; zur Sache kommen to get to the point; nicht bei der Sache sein not to be with it; das tut nichts zur Sache fig that is beside the point - 2. *(ohne pl)* RECHT [Rechtssache] case; das ist so eine Sache fam it's a bit of a problem; mit jm gemeinsame Sache machen fam to join forces with sb; seiner Sache sicher sein to know what one is doing. ➤ **Sachen** *Pl* - 1. [gen] things - 2. fam [Stundenkilometer]:

100 Sachen draufhaben to be doing a hundred; mit 180 Sachen salopp at 180; du machst vielleicht Sachen! the things you do!; in Sachen in the matter of.

Sach|gebiet das subject area.

Sach|kenntnis die expertise *(U)*.

sachkundig ◇ *adj* knowledgeable. ◇ *adv* knowledgeably.

Sach|lage die *(ohne pl)* situation.

sachlich ◇ *adj* - 1. [Person, Diskussion] objective - 2. [Fehler, Unterschied] factual. ◇ *adv* - 1. [diskutieren, bleiben] objectively - 2. [richtig, falsch] factually.

Sach|schaden der material damage.

Sachsen ['zaksn] nt Saxony.

Sachsen-Anhalt [zaksn'anhalt] nt Saxony-Anhalt.

sächsisch ['zɛksɪʃ] *adj* Saxon.

sacht, sachte ◇ *adj* - 1. [sanft, langsam] gentle - 2. [vorsichtig] cautious. ◇ *adv* gently; sachte! fam steady on!

Sach|verstand der expertise.

Sach|verständige *(pl -n)* der, die expert.

Sack *(pl Säcke ODER -)* der - 1. *(pl Säcke, Sack)* [Behälter] sack - 2. *(pl Säcke)* salopp [Mensch] bastard - 3. *(pl Säcke)* salopp [Hodensack] balls *Pl*.

Sack|gasse die dead end; [in Wohngebiet] cul-de-sac.

Sadismus der sadism.

säen *vt* to sow.

Safe [seːf] *(pl -s)* der safe.

Saft *(pl Säfte)* der - 1. [Fruchtsaft, Strom] juice - 2. [Pflanzensaft] sap.

saftig *adj* - 1. [Obst, Fleisch] juicy - 2. fam [Rechnung, Ohrfeige] hefty.

Sage *(pl -n)* die legend.

Säge *(pl -n)* die saw.

sagen *vt* - 1. [gen] to say; jm etw sagen to tell sb sthg; sich *(D)* etw sagen to tell o.s. sthg; das kann jeder sagen! that's easy to say!; das hat nichts zu sagen that doesn't mean anything; was sagst du (denn) dazu? (so) what do you think about it? - 2. [befehlen]: etwas/nichts zu sagen haben to have a/no say in things; jm etwas/nichts zu sagen haben to have sthg/nothing to say to sb; er lässt sich nichts sagen you can't tell him anything; das Sagen haben to be in charge; das sage ich dir fam I'm telling you; das kann man wohl sagen! fam you can say that again!; dagegen ist nichts zu sagen it's perfectly all right; man sagt it is said; wem sagst du das! you're telling me! ➤ **du sagst es** *interj* you said it! ➤ **sag bloß** *interj* you don't say. ➤ **sag mal** *interj* tell me. ➤ **wie gesagt** *interj* as I've said.

sägen *vt & vi* to saw.

sagenhaft ◇ *adj* fantastic. ◇ *adv* fantastically.

Sägelspäne *Pl* wood shavings.

sah *prät* ▷ **sehen**.

Sahne *die* cream.

Sahneltorte *die* gâteau.

sahnig *adj* creamy.

Saison [sɛ'zɔŋ] (*pl* -s) *die* season.

Saite (*pl* -n) *die* string.

Saiteninstrument *das* stringed instrument.

Sakko (*pl* -s) *der ODER das* jacket.

Sakrament (*pl* -e) *das* RELIG sacrament.

Sakristei (*pl* -en) *die* sacristy.

Salamander (*pl* -) *der* salamander.

Salami (*pl* -s) *die* salami.

Salat (*pl* -e) *der* - 1. [Gericht] salad; **grüner Salat** green salad - 2. [Produkt] lettuce - 3. *fam*: **da haben wir den Salat!** *fam* I said we'd end up in this mess!

Salatlschüssel *die* salad bowl.

Salatlsoße *die* salad dressing.

Salbe (*pl* -n) *die* ointment.

Salbei *der* sage.

Salmonellenlvergiftung *die* salmonella poisoning.

Salon [sa'lɔŋ] (*pl* -s) *der* [Zimmer] drawing room.

salopp ◇ *adj* casual; [Ausdrucksweise] slangy. ◇ *adv* casually; [sich ausdrücken] slangily.

Salto (*pl* -s) *der* somersault.

Salz (*pl* -e) *das* salt.

Salzburg *nt* Salzburg.

salzen (*perf* hat gesalzen) *vt* to put salt in/on.

salzig *adj* salty.

Salzlkartoffeln *Pl* boiled potatoes.

Salzlsäure *die* hydrochloric acid.

Salzlstange *die* pretzel stick.

Salzlstreuer (*pl* Salzstreuer) *der* salt cellar.

Salzlwasser *das* - 1. [Meerwasser] saltwater - 2. [Kochwasser] salted water.

Samen (*pl* -) *der* - 1. [Sperma] sperm - 2. [Pflanzensamen] seed.

sämig *adj* thick.

Sammellband (*pl* -bände) *der* omnibus edition.

sammeln *vt* - 1. [Eindrücke, Anhänger, Kräuter] to gather - 2. [Geld, Briefmarken] to collect. ◆ **sich sammeln** *ref* [sich konzentrieren] to collect one's thoughts.

Sammellstelle *die* collection point.

Sammler, in (*mpl* -, *fpl* -nen) *der, die* collector.

Sammlung (*pl* -en) *die* - 1. [gen] collection - 2. [Ruhe] composure.

Samstag (*pl* -e) *der* Saturday; **am Samstag** on Saturday; **(am) nächsten Samstag kommt sie** she's coming next Saturday; **Samstag, den 31. Dezember** Saturday, 31 December.

Samstaglabend (*pl* -e) *der* Saturday evening; **Samstagabend muss ich nach Köln** I have to go to Cologne on Saturday evening.

Samstaglmorgen (*pl* -) *der* Saturday morning; **Samstagmorgen muss ich nach Köln** I have to go to Cologne on Saturday morning.

Samstaglnacht (*pl* -) *die* Saturday night; **Samstagnacht hat es stark geregnet** it rained hard on Saturday night.

samstags *adv* on Saturdays; **samstags morgens/abends** on Saturday mornings/evenings.

samt *präp*: **samt jm/einer Sache** (together) with sb/sthg.

Samt (*pl* -e) *der* velvet.

sämtlich ◇ *adj* all; **sämtliche Fehler verbessern** to correct all the mistakes; **er hat sämtlichen Mut verloren** he lost all his courage. ◇ *adv*: **sie waren sämtlich erschienen** they all turned up.

Sanatorium [zana'to:rjʊm] (*pl* -torien) *das* sanatorium.

Sand *der* sand; **die Straßen mit Sand streuen** to grit the roads; **im Sand verlaufen** *fig* to come to nothing.

Sandale (*pl* -n) *die* sandal.

Sandlbank (*pl* -bänke) *die* sandbank.

sandig *adj* sandy.

Sandlkasten *der* sandpit *UK*, sandbox *US*.

Sandlkorn (*pl* -körner) *das* grain of sand.

Sandlmännchen *das* sandman.

Sandlpapier *das* sandpaper.

Sandlstein *der* sandstone.

Sandlstrand *der* sandy beach.

sandte *prät* ▷ **senden**.

Sandluhr *die* hourglass.

sanft ◇ *adj* - 1. [gen] gentle - 2. [Hände, Stimme, Licht] soft - 3. [Geburt] natural; [Energie, Tourismus] sustainable; [Tod] peaceful. ◇ *adv* - 1. [gen] gently - 2. [entschlafen] peacefully.

sanftmütig ◇ *adj* gentle. ◇ *adv* gently.

sang *prät* ▷ **singen**.

Sänger, in (*mpl* -, *fpl* -nen) *der, die* singer.

sanieren *vt* - 1. [Gebäude, Viertel] to renovate - 2. [Firma] to turn around - 3. [Finanzen] to sort out. ◆ **sich sanieren** *ref* [Person] to get o.s. out of the red.

Sanierung (*pl* -en) *die* - 1. [von Gebäude, Viertel] renovation - 2. [von Firma] turning round - 3. [von Finanzen] sorting out.

sanitär *adj* sanitary; **sanitäre Anlagen** sanitation (*U*).

Sanitäter, in (*mpl* -, *fpl* -nen) *der, die* - 1. MED paramedic - 2. MIL medical orderly.

sank *prät* ▷ **sinken**.

Sankt Gallen *nt* St Gallen.

Sankt Gotthard *der* St Gotthard.

Sanktion (*pl* -en) *die* sanction; **Sanktionen verhängen** to impose sanctions.

Sankt Petersburg *nt* St Petersburg.

Saphir (*pl* -e), **Saphir** (*pl* -e) *der* sapphire.

Sardelle (*pl* -n) *die* anchovy.

Sardine (*pl* -n) *die* sardine.

Sardinien [zar'di:niən] *nt* Sardinia.

Sarg (*pl* Särge) *der* coffin, casket *US*.

Sarkasmus (*pl* -men) *der* - 1. [Spott] sarcasm - 2. [spöttische Bemerkung] sarcastic comment.

saß *prät* ⊳ **sitzen**.

Satan (*pl* -e) *der* - 1. [Teufel] Satan - 2. *abw* [Mensch] fiend.

Satellit (*pl* -en) *der* satellite.

Satelliten|schüssel *die* satellite dish.

Satire (*pl* -n) *die* satire.

satt ⟨⟩ *adj* - 1. [Mensch, Tier] full; **satt sein** to be full (up); **bist du satt?** have you had enough (to eat)?; **diese Knödel machen satt** these dumplings are filling; **davon werde ich nicht satt** I won't have enough to eat with that - 2. [Farbe, Klang] rich. ⟨⟩ *adv*: **sich satt essen** to eat one's fill; **jn/etw satt haben** *fam* to be fed up with sb/sthg.

Sattel (*pl* Sättel) *der* saddle.

satteln *vt* to saddle.

Satz (*pl* Sätze) *der* - 1. [grammatikalische Einheit] sentence - 2. [Sprung] leap - 3. [SPORT - bei Tennis] set; [- bei Badminton, Tischtennis] game - 4. [von Text - das Setzen] setting; [- das Gesetzte] type - 5. MUS movement - 6. MATH theorem - 7. [von Reifen, Unterwäsche] set - 8. [Tarif] rate.

Satz|bau *der* syntax.

Satz|teil *der* sentence part.

Satzung (*pl* -en) *die* statutes *Pl*.

Satz|zeichen *das* punctuation mark.

Sau (*pl* Säue *ODER* -en) *die* - 1. (*pl* Säue) [Schwein] sow - 2. (*pl* Sauen) [Wildschwein] female wild boar - 3. (*pl* Säue) *salopp abw* [Mensch] pig.

sauber ⟨⟩ *adj* - 1. [rein] clean - 2. *fam iron* [fein] fine - 3. [Arbeit] neat; [Darbietung] faultless. ⟨⟩ *adv* - 1. [gut] neatly - 2. [fehlerfrei] faultlessly.

Sauberkeit *die* cleanliness.

sauber machen *vt* to clean.

säubern *vt* - 1. [reinigen] to clean - 2. [Institution] to purge.

Sauce ['zo:sə] (*pl* -n) *die* sauce; [Bratensoße] gravy.

Saudi (*pl* -s) *der* Saudi.

Saudi-Arabien *nt* Saudi Arabia.

sauer ⟨⟩ *adj* - 1. [Essen] sour; **saure Gurken** (pickled) gherkins; **ein saurer Wein** an acidic wine - 2. [Stimmung] annoyed, cross; **sauer auf jn sein** *fam* to be annoyed *ODER* cross with sb; **ein saures Gesicht machen** to pull a sour face

- 3. CHEM acidic. ⟨⟩ *adv* - 1. [reagieren] crossly - 2. [nicht süß]: **sauer schmecken** to taste sour - 3. CHEM acidically.

Sauer|braten *der* sauerbraten, *braised beef marinated in vinegar*.

Sauerei (*pl* -en) *die* salopp - 1. [Schmutz] damn mess - 2. [Gemeinheit] damn disgrace.

Sauer|kirsche *die* sour cherry.

Sauer|kraut *das* sauerkraut.

säuerlich ⟨⟩ *adj* - 1. [Essen] slightly sour - 2. [Stimmung] annoyed, cross. ⟨⟩ *adv* - 1. [nicht süß]: **säuerlich schmecken** to taste slightly sour - 2. [reagieren] crossly.

Sauer|stoff *der* oxygen.

saufen (*präs* säuft, *prät* soff, *perf* hat gesoffen) ⟨⟩ *vt* - 1. [Subj: Tier] to drink - 2. *salopp* [trinken] to knock back; **sie gehen einen saufen** they're going on the booze - 3. *fam* [verbrauchen]: **mein Auto säuft zu viel** my car's a real gas-guzzler. ⟨⟩ *vi* - 1. [Tier] to drink - 2. *salopp* [Mensch] to booze.

Säufer (*pl* -) *der* salopp abw boozer.

Sauferei (*pl* -en) *die* salopp abw booze-up.

Säuferin (*pl* -nen) *die* salopp abw boozer.

säuft *präs* ⊳ **saufen**.

saugen (*prät* sog *ODER* saugte, *perf* hat gesogen *ODER* gesaugt) ⟨⟩ *vt* - 1. [heraussaugen] to suck; **etw aus etw saugen** to suck sthg out of sthg - 2. (*reg*) [mit Staubsauger] to vacuum. ⟨⟩ *vi* - 1. [ziehen] to suck; **an etw (D) saugen** to suck at sthg - 2. (*reg*) [mit Staubsauger] to vacuum.

säugen *vt* to suckle.

Säuge|tier *das* mammal.

Säugling (*pl* -e) *der* baby.

Säule (*pl* -n) *die* eigtl & *fig* pillar.

Saum (*pl* Säume) *der* hem.

säumen *vt* - 1. [Stoff] to hem - 2. *geh* [Weg] to line.

Sauna (*pl* -s *ODER* Saunen) *die* sauna.

Säure (*pl* -n) *die* - 1. CHEM acid - 2. [von Wein] acidity; [von Zitrone] sourness.

Saurier ['zauriɐ] (*pl* -) *der* dinosaur.

säuseln ⟨⟩ *vi* [Wind] to murmur. ⟨⟩ *vt* [sprechen] to purr.

sausen (*perf* hat/ist gesaust) *vi* (ist) *fam* [schnell]: **zum Bäcker sausen** to dash over to the baker's; **mit dem Fahrrad um die Ecke sausen** to hurtle round the corner on one's bike.

Saxofon (*pl* -e), **Saxophon** (*pl* -e) *das* saxophone.

SB *abk für* **Selbstbedienung**.

S-|Bahn *die* suburban railway.

S-Bahn|hof *der* suburban railway station.

SBB (*abk für* **Schweizerische Bundesbahn**), *Swiss federal railway company*.

Schabe (*pl* -n) *die* cockroach.

schaben *vt* & *vi* to scrape.

schäbig *abw* <> *adj* **- 1.** [Kleidung, Möbel] shabby **- 2.** [Bezahlung] paltry **- 3.** [Person] mean. <> *adv* **- 1.** [angezogen, eingerichtet] shabbily **- 2.** [ausnützen] shamelessly.

Schablone (*pl* **-n**) *die* **- 1.** [zum Ausmalen] stencil; [zum Rundherummalen] template **- 2.** [Schema] mould.

Schach (*pl* **-s**) *das* chess; **Schach!** check!

Schach|brett *das* chessboard.

schachmatt *adj* [beim Spiel] checkmate.

Schacht (*pl* **Schächte**) *der* shaft.

Schachtel (*pl* **-n**) *die* **- 1.** [Behälter] box; **eine Schachtel Zigaretten** a packet *UK* ODER pack *US* of cigarettes **- 2.** *salopp abw* [Frau] bag.

Schach|zug *der* eigtl & *fig* move.

schade *adj*: **es ist schade (um jn/etw)** it's a shame (about sb/sthg); **(wie) schade!** what a shame!; **zu schade für jn/etw sein** to be too good for sb/sthg.

Schädel (*pl* **-**) *der* **- 1.** [Knochen] skull **- 2.** *fam* [Kopf] nut; **mir brummt der Schädel** *fam* my head is killing me.

Schädel|bruch *der* skull fracture.

schaden *vi* [Sache] to damage; [Person] to harm; **das schadet nichts** it won't do any harm.

Schaden (*pl* **Schäden**) *der* **- 1.** [an Sachen] damage (*U*) **- 2.** [an Menschen] injury; **jm (einen) Schaden zufügen** to cause sb harm **- 3.** [Nachteil]: **es soll dein Schaden nicht sein** I'll make it worth your while.

Schaden|ersatz *der* compensation.

Schaden|freude *die* malicious pleasure.

schadenfroh *adj* gloating; **schadenfroh sein** to gloat.

Schadens|fall *der*: **einen Schadensfall melden** to make a claim; **im Schadensfall** in the event of damage.

schadhaft *adj* [mit Fabrikationsfehler] defective; [beschädigt] damaged.

schädigen *vt* to damage; [Person] to harm.

schädlich *adj* harmful; **Rauchen ist schädlich für die Gesundheit** smoking damages your health.

Schädling (*pl* **-e**) *der* pest.

Schad|stoff *der* [im Boden, in der Luft] pollutant; [im Essen] harmful substance.

Schaf (*pl* **-e**) *das* **- 1.** [Tier] sheep **- 2.** *fam abw* [Mensch] dope; **ein schwarzes Schaf** *abw* a black sheep.

Schäfer (*pl* **-**) *der* shepherd.

Schäfer|hund *der* [Hirtenhund] sheepdog.

Schäferin (*pl* **-nen**) *die* shepherdess.

schaffen¹ <> *vt* **- 1.** [beenden, bewältigen] to manage; **es schaffen, etw zu tun** to manage to do sthg; **er schafft drei Teller Spagetti zum Abendbrot** he gets through three plates of spaghetti for his dinner; **bis wann schaffst du das?** when can you have it ready by?; **du**

schaffst es! you can do it!; **das wäre geschafft!** that's that done! **- 2.** [Prüfung] to get through **- 3.** [Ärger, Unruhe] to cause **- 4.** [transportieren]: **etw an einen Ort schaffen** to take sthg somewhere; **jn ins Bett schaffen** to put sb to bed; **den Verletzten vom Spielfeld schaffen** to carry the injured player off the pitch **- 5.** [erschöpfen] to wear out; **du schaffst mich!** you'll be the death of me! **- 6.** *fam* [erreichen]: **den Bus gerade noch schaffen** only just to make it in time for the bus. <> *vi* **- 1.** [tun]: **mit jm/etw nichts zu schaffen haben** to have nothing to do with sb/sthg; **jm zu schaffen machen** to give sb trouble; **sich an etw (D) zu schaffen machen** to busy o.s. with sthg **- 2.** *Süddt* [arbeiten] to work. ◆ **geschafft** *interj* that's it!; [geglückt] done it!

schaffen² (*prät* **schuf**, *perf* **hat geschaffen**) *vt* to create; **Platz schaffen** to make room; **Ordnung schaffen** to restore order; **wie geschaffen für jn sein** to be made for sb.

Schaffner, in (*mpl* **-**, *fpl* **-nen**) *der, die* [in Bus] conductor; [in Zug] ticket collector.

Schafs|fell *das* **- 1.** [an Tier] fleece **- 2.** [Material, Teppich] sheepskin.

Schafs|käse *der* ewe's milk cheese.

Schaft (*pl* **Schäfte**) *der* **- 1.** [von Speer, Pfeil] shaft; [von Messer] handle **- 2.** [von Stiefel] leg.

Schakal (*pl* **-e**) *der* jackal.

schäkern *vi* *fam* [flirten] to flirt.

schal *adj* [Bier] flat; [Geschmack] stale.

Schal (*pl* **-s** ODER **-e**) *der* scarf.

Schale (*pl* **-n**) *die* **- 1.** [von Zwiebel, Banane, Tomate] skin; [von Apfel, Orange, Kartoffel] peel; **Kartoffelschalen** potato peelings **- 2.** [von Krebs, Ei, Kokosnuss] shell **- 3.** [Gefäß] bowl; [flach] dish.

schälen *vt* to peel; [Ei, Nüsse, Erbsen] to shell. ◆ **sich schälen** *ref* to peel.

Schall (*pl* **-e** ODER **Schälle**) *der* sound.

Schall|dämpfer *der* **- 1.** [von Auto] silencer *UK*, muffler *US* **- 2.** [von Waffe] silencer **- 3.** [von Musikinstrument] mute.

schalldicht *adj* soundproof; **etw schalldicht machen** to soundproof sthg.

schallen (*prät* **schallte** ODER **scholl**, *perf* **hat geschallt**) *vi* to resound.

schallend <> *adj* resounding. <> *adv*: **schallend lachen** to roar with laughter.

Schall|mauer *die* sound barrier.

Schall|platte *die* record.

schalten <> *vi* **- 1.** [den Gang wechseln] to change gear; **in den vierten Gang schalten** to change into fourth gear **- 2.** [umschalten]: **auf das zweite Programm schalten** to turn to channel two; **wir schalten jetzt nach Hamburg** we're now going over to Hamburg **- 3.** *fam* [reagieren] to catch on **- 4.** [tun]: **schalten und**

walten to do as one pleases. <> vt [anschließen] to connect; **etw parallel/in Serie schalten** ELEKTR to connect sthg in parallel/series.

Schalter (pl -) der - 1. [Schaltknopf] switch - 2. [für Auskunft, Verkauf] counter.

Schalt|hebel der AUTO gear lever.

Schalt|jahr das leap year.

Schaltung (pl -en) die - 1. [Gangschaltung] gear change - 2. ELEKTR circuit - 3. TV link-up.

Scham die shame; **Scham empfinden** to be ashamed.

schämen ◆ **sich schämen** ref to be ashamed; **schäm dich!** shame on you!; **sich für jn schämen** to be ashamed for sb; **ich schäme mich seinetwegen** I'm ashamed of him.

schamlos <> adj - 1. [gen] shameless - 2. [Lüge] barefaced. <> adv shamelessly.

Schande die disgrace; **zu js Schande** to sb's shame.

schändlich <> adj disgraceful. <> adv disgracefully.

Schand|tat die - 1. [Verbrechen] heinous crime - 2. fam hum [Aktion]: **zu jeder Schandtat bereit sein** to be game for anything.

Schanze (pl -n) die ski jump.

Schar (pl -en) die [von Kindern] group; [von Vögeln] flock; **Scharen von swarms of.** ◆ **in Scharen** adv [von Menschen] in droves; [von Tieren] in swarms.

scharen vt: **jn/etw um sich scharen** to gather sb/sth around o.s. ◆ **sich scharen** ref: **sich um jn scharen** to gather round sb.

scharf (kompar **schärfer**, superl **schärfste**) <> adj - 1. [gen] sharp - 2. [Geschmack] hot, spicy - 3. fam [toll] great; [erotisch] hot; **scharf auf etw sein** to be dead keen on sthg - 4. [Tempo] high; [Wind] biting - 5. [Geräusch] piercing; [Geruch] pungent - 6. [Säure] caustic - 7. [Hund, Angriff] fierce - 8. [Munition] live - 9. [Prüfer] tough. <> adv [gen] sharply; **scharf geschliffen** keenly whetted; **scharf gewürzt** hot, spicy; **scharf riechen** to be pungent; **scharf beobachten** to watch closely; **scharf nachdenken** to think hard; **jn scharf angreifen** to attack sb fiercely.

Schärfe (pl -n) die - 1. [von Messer, Sinnen] sharpness; [von Verstand] keenness - 2. [Bildschärfe] focus - 3. [von Ton, Streit] severity - 4. [von Geschmack] spiciness - 5. [von Prüfer] toughness.

scharf|machen vt fam [aggressiv machen] to rouse.

Scharf|schütze, schützin der, die marksman (markswoman die).

Scharf|sinn der astuteness.

Scharlach der scarlet fever.

Scharm der = **Charme**.

scharmant adj = **charmant**.

Scharnier (pl -e) das hinge.

scharren vi to scrape; [Hund, Pferd] to paw; **mit den Füßen scharren** to shuffle one's feet.

Schaschlik (pl -s) der ODER das shish kebab.

Schatten (pl -) der - 1. [Bereich ohne Sonne] shade; **im Schatten** in the shade - 2. [Silhouette, Fleck] shadow; **über seinen Schatten springen** to force o.s.

Schatten|seite die - 1. [von Berg, Haus] dark side - 2. [Nachteil] drawback.

Schattierung (pl -en) die - 1. [dunkle Stelle] shading - 2. [Farbe] shade.

schattig adj shady.

Schatz (pl **Schätze**) der - 1. [Reichtum] treasure - 2. fam [Liebling] darling.

schätzen vt - 1. [Wert, Alter, Schaden] to estimate - 2. [glauben, meinen] to think - 3. [mögen]: **jn/etw schätzen** to value sb/sthg; **jn/etw zu schätzen wissen** to appreciate sb/sthg.

Schatz|kammer die treasure chamber.

Schätzung (pl -en) die estimate; [das Schätzen] estimation; [von Gebäuden, Grundstücken] valuation.

schätzungsweise adv approximately.

Schätz|wert der estimated value.

Schau (pl -en) die show; **eine Schau abziehen** fam to put on a show; **jn zur Schau stellen** to exhibit sb.

Schauder (pl -) der shudder; [vor Kälte] shiver.

schauderhaft <> adj terrible. <> adv: **schauderhaft aussehen** to look terrible.

schauen vi - 1. [blicken] to look; **zu Boden schauen** to stare at the ground; **auf jn/etw schauen** to look at sb/sthg; **schau mal!** look! - 2. [sich kümmern]: **nach jm/etw schauen** to look after sb/sthg - 3. [kontrollieren] to check.

Schauer (pl -) der - 1. [Regen] shower - 2. [vor Angst] shudder; [vor Kälte] shiver.

Schaufel (pl -n) die shovel.

schaufeln vt - 1. [Erde, Kies] to shovel; [Loch] to dig - 2. fam [essen] to shovel down.

Schau|fenster das shop window.

Schaufenster|bummel der window-shopping trip.

Schaufenster|puppe die mannequin.

Schau|kasten der display case.

Schaukel (pl -n) die swing.

schaukeln <> vi - 1. [gen] to rock - 2. [auf einer Schaukel] to swing. <> vt - 1. [Baby, Wiege] to rock - 2. fam [erledigen]: **ich werde das schon schaukeln** I'll sort it out.

Schaukel|stuhl der rocking chair.

Schaulustige (pl -n) der, die onlooker.

Schaum (pl **Schäume**) der foam; [von Bier] head; **Schaum vor dem Mund haben** to be foaming at the mouth.

schäumen vi - 1. [Flüssigkeit] to foam; [Bier] to froth - 2. fam [vor Wut] to fume.

Schaum|gummi der foam rubber.

schaumig ◇ *adj* foamy. ◇ *adv*: etw schaumig rühren to beat sthg until light and fluffy.

Schaum|stoff *der* plastic foam.

Schaum|wein *der* sparkling wine.

Schau|platz *der* [von Ereignis] scene; [von Erzählung] setting.

Schau|spiel *das* - 1. [Bühnenstück] play - 2. [Gattung] drama - 3. *fam* [Spektakel] spectacle.

Schau|spieler, in *der, die* actor (actress *die*).

Schauspiel|haus *das* theatre.

Schau|steller, in (*mpl* Schausteller, *fpl* -nen) *der, die* showman (showwoman *die*).

Schau|tafel *die* wall chart (often made of plastic, wood, etc).

Scheck (*pl* -s) *der* cheque; mit Scheck bezahlen to pay by cheque; ungedeckter Scheck bad cheque.

Scheck|heft *das* chequebook.

Scheck|karte *die* cheque card.

Scheibe (*pl* -n) *die* - 1. [Glas] pane (of glass); [Fensterscheibe] window pane; [von Auto] window - 2. [von Brot, Käse, Wurst] slice.

Scheiben|wischer (*pl* Scheibenwischer) *der* windscreen *UK* ODER windshield *US* wiper.

Scheich (*pl* -s ODER -e) *der* sheikh.

Scheide (*pl* -n) *die* - 1. [Vagina] vagina - 2. [von Messer] sheath.

scheiden (*prät* schied, *perf* hat/ist geschieden) ◇ *vt* (hat) [Ehe] to dissolve; sich scheiden lassen to get divorced. ◇ *vi* (ist) geh - 1. [fortgehen] to part - 2. [entlassen werden]: aus dem Amt scheiden to resign from office.

Scheidung (*pl* -en) *die* divorce; die Scheidung einreichen to file for divorce.

Schein (*pl* -e) *der* - 1. [Lichtschein] light; im Schein einer Taschenlampe by torchlight - 2. (ohne pl) [Anschein] appearances *Pl*; der Schein trügt appearances can be deceptive - 3. UNI ≈ credit, certificate issued to students on successful completion of a course in a specific subject - 4. [Geldschein] note.

scheinbar ◇ *adj* apparent. ◇ *adv* apparently, seemingly.

scheinen (*prät* schien, *perf* hat geschienen) *vi* - 1. [leuchten] to shine - 2. [den Eindruck erwecken] to seem, to appear; es scheint, dass... it seems ODER appears that...; mir scheint, dass... it seems to me that...; das scheint dir nur so it just seems that way to you.

scheinheilig *adj* [heuchlerisch] hypocritical.

scheintot *adj* MED: scheintot sein to be apparently dead.

Scheinwerfer (*pl* -) *der* - 1. [am Auto] headlight - 2. [im Theater] spotlight; [Suchscheinwerfer] searchlight.

Scheinwerfer|licht *das* [von Autos] headlights *Pl*; [im Theater] spotlight; im Scheinwerferlicht in the spotlight.

Scheiße ◇ *die salopp* [gen] shit; nur Scheiße im Kopf haben to be a piss-artist; in der Scheiße sitzen to be in the shit. ◇ *interj salopp* shit!

scheißen (*prät* schiss, *perf* hat geschissen) *vi salopp* to shit.

Scheitel (*pl* -) *der* [Frisur] parting *UK*, part *US*.

scheitern (*perf* ist gescheitert) *vi* - 1. [Personen] to fail; [- Sport] to lose; sie sind mit ihrem Plan am Widerstand der Bewohner gescheitert their plan failed because of the opposition of the local population - 2. [Versuch, Vorhaben] to fail; an etw (D) scheitern to fail because of sthg.

Schell|fisch *der* haddock.

Schema (*pl* -s, -ta ODER Schemen) *das* - 1. [Darstellung] diagram - 2. [Muster] routine.

schematisch ◇ *adj* - 1. [grob] schematic - 2. [routiniert] mechanical. ◇ *adv* - 1. [grob] schematically - 2. [routiniert] mechanically.

schemenhaft ◇ *adj* shadowy. ◇ *adv*: etw schemenhaft erkennen to make out the silhouette of sthg.

Schenkel (*pl* -) *der* - 1. [Bein] thigh - 2. MATH side.

schenken *vt* - 1. [geben] to give (as a present); jm etw schenken to give sb sthg - 2. [erlassen]: jm etw schenken to let sb off sthg; sich etw schenken to spare o.s. sthg.

Schenkung (*pl* -en) *die* gift.

scheppern *vi* to clatter.

Scherbe (*pl* -n) *die* piece, fragment; die Scherben zusammenkehren to sweep up the broken pieces.

Schere (*pl* -n) *die* - 1. [Werkzeug] pair of scissors, scissors *Pl* - 2. [von Krebs] pincer, claw.

scheren (*prät* scherte ODER schor, *perf* hat geschert ODER geschoren) *vt* (unreg) - 1. [Schaf] to shear; [Hund] to clip - 2. [Hecke] to clip; [Haare] to crop - 3. (reg) [kümmern]: das schert mich nicht I don't care. ◆ **sich scheren** ref (reg): sich um jn/etw scheren/nicht scheren to care/not to care about sb/sthg.

Scherereien *Pl* trouble (U); das gibt Scherereien that will lead to trouble.

Scherz (*pl* -e) *der* joke.

scherzen *vi geh* to joke.

scherzhaft *adj* jokingly.

scheu ◇ *adj* shy; jm/etw scheu machen to frighten sb/sthg. ◇ *adv* shyly.

Scheu *die* shyness; ohne Scheu uninhibitedly.

scheuchen *vt* to shoo.

scheuen ◇ *vt*: keine Mühen/Kosten scheuen to spare no effort/expense. ◇ *vi* [Pferd] to shy.

Scheuerlappen der floorcloth.

scheuern ⟨⟩ vt - 1. [putzen - Boden] to scrub; [- Töpfe] to scour - 2. [reiben]: **sich** (D) **in seinen Schuhen die Fersen wund scheuern** to get sore heels because one's shoes are rubbing. ⟨⟩ vi to rub.

Scheuklappen Pl blinker.

Scheune (pl -n) die barn.

Scheusal (pl -e) das fam abw beast.

scheußlich abw ⟨⟩ adj - 1. [Verhalten, Anblick, Wetter] terrible - 2. [Aussehen, Geschmack] horrible. ⟨⟩ adv - 1. [sich verhalten, kalt] terribly - 2. [einrichten, dekorieren] horribly.

Schi = **Ski**.

Schicht (pl -en) die - 1. [Lage] layer - 2. [Gesellschaftsschicht] (social) class; **alle Schichten der Bevölkerung** all strata of society - 3. [Schichtarbeit] shift; **Schicht arbeiten** to work shifts.

schichten vt to stack.

schick adj - 1. [modisch] stylish - 2. [in] trendy - 3. [toll] great.

schicken vt to send; **jm etw schicken, etw an jn schicken** to send sb sthg, to send sthg to sb.
⟨⟩ **sich schicken** ref geh - 1. [sich gehören] to be proper - 2. [sich abfinden]: **sich in etw** (A) **schicken** to resign o.s. to sthg.

Schicksal (pl -e) das fate; **jn/etw seinem Schicksal überlassen** to leave sb/sthg to his/her/its fate.

Schiebedach das sunroof.

schieben (prät schob, perf hat geschoben) vt - 1. [wegschieben] to push; **die Schuld auf einen anderen schieben** to put the blame on sb else; **ein schlechtes Ergebnis auf etw** (A) **schieben** to blame a poor result on sthg - 2. [hineinschieben] to put - 3. fam [schmuggeln] to traffic in.
⟨⟩ **sich schieben** ref to move; **sich durch das Gewühl schieben** to push one's way through the crowd.

Schieber (pl -) der - 1. [an Gerät] slider - 2. fam [Mensch] black marketeer.

Schiebetür die sliding door.

Schiebung (pl -en) die fixing; **das ist Schiebung!** it's a fix!

schied prät ⟾ **scheiden**.

Schiedsrichter, in der, die SPORT referee; [bei Tennis] umpire.

schief ⟨⟩ adj - 1. [krumm] crooked; [geneigt] leaning; [Blick] wry; [Absatz] worn - 2. [falsch - Vergleich] false; **ein schiefes Bild abgeben** to present a lop-sided ODER distorted picture.
⟨⟩ adv: **das Sofa steht schief** the sofa is at an angle; **das Bild hängt schief** the picture isn't straight; **jn schief ansehen** to look at sb askance.

Schiefer (pl -) der slate.

schief gehen (perf ist schief gegangen) vi (unreg) to go wrong.

schiefllachen ⟾ **sich schieflachen** ref fam to kill o.s. laughing.

schief liegen vi (unreg) fam: **mit einer Meinung schief liegen** to be out in one's opinion.

schielen vi - 1. [wegen Augenfehler] to squint; **sie schielt mit einem Auge** she has a squint in one eye - 2. fam [schauen] to glance; **nach jm/etw schielen** fig to have one's eye on sb/sthg.

schien prät ⟾ **scheinen**.

Schienbein das shin.

Schiene (pl -n) die - 1. [Gleis] rail - 2. MED splint - 3. [Führungsschiene] runner.

schießen (prät schoss, perf hat/ist geschossen) ⟨⟩ vi - 1. [mit Gewehr] to shoot, to fire; **auf jn/etw schießen** to shoot ODER fire at sb/sthg - 2. (ist) [wachsen] to shoot up - 3. (ist) [sich schnell bewegen] to shoot; [Flüssigkeit] to gush - 4. (hat) SPORT to shoot. ⟨⟩ vt (hat) - 1. [gen] to shoot - 2. [Tor] to score - 3. [Foto] to take.

Schießerei (pl -en) die shoot-out.

Schiff (pl -e) das - 1. [Wasserfahrzeug] ship; **mit dem Schiff** by ship - 2. [von Kirche] nave.

Schiffahrt die = **Schifffahrt**.

Schiffbruch der shipwreck.

Schifffahrt die shipping.

Schiffsreise die voyage.

Schiffsverkehr der shipping traffic.

Schikane (pl -n) die harassment; **mit allen Schikanen** fam fig with all the extras.

schikanieren vt abw to harass.

Schikoree (pl -s) die ODER der = **Chicorée**.

Schild (pl -er ODER -e) ⟨⟩ das (pl Schilder) sign; [an Auto] numberplate UK, license plate US; [Namensschild] nameplate. ⟨⟩ der (pl Schilde) shield; **etw im Schilde führen** fig to be up to sthg.

Schilddrüse die thyroid gland.

schildern vt to describe.

Schilderung (pl -en) die description.

Schildkröte die [auf dem Land] tortoise; [im Wasser] turtle.

Schilf (pl -e) das - 1. [Pflanze] reed - 2. (ohne pl) [Gebiet] reedbed.

schillern vi to shimmer.

Schilling (pl -e ODER -) der schilling.

Schimmel (pl -) der - 1. [Pilz] mould - 2. [Pferd] white horse.

schimmelig, schimmlig adj mouldy.

schimmeln (perf hat/ist geschimmelt) vi to go mouldy.

Schimmer (pl -) geh der - 1. [Glanz] gleam - 2. [Spur] glimmer.

schimmern vi to glimmer.

schimmlig = **schimmelig**.

Schimpanse (pl -n) der chimpanzee.

schimpfen *vi* to grumble; **auf** ODER **über** jn/
etw schimpfen to grumble about sb/sthg; **mit**
jm schimpfen to tell sb off.

Schimpf|wort (*pl* -wörter ODER -e) *das*
swearword.

schinden (*prät* schund, *perf* hat geschunden)
vt - 1. [quälen] to maltreat - 2. [herausschlagen]:
Zeit schinden to play for time; **Applaus schinden** to fish for applause; **Eindruck schinden** to
try to impress. ➡ **sich schinden** *ref* to slave
away.

Schinderei (*pl* -en) *die* - 1. [Quälerei] mal-
treatment - 2. [Strapaze] struggle.

Schinken (*pl* -) *der* - 1. [Fleisch] ham - 2. *fam*
[Buch] enormous tome - 3. *fam* FILM tacky epic
saga.

Schirm (*pl* -e) *der* - 1. [Regenschirm] umbrella
- 2. [Sonnenschirm] sunshade; [zum Tragen]
parasol; [an Mütze] visor, peak.

schiss *prät* ▷ **scheißen.**

schlabberig, schlabbrig *abw adj* - 1. [wäss-
rig] watery - 2. [Pullover] baggy.

Schlacht (*pl* -en) *die* battle.

schlachten *vt* to slaughter.

Schlachter (*pl* -) *der* butcher.

Schlacht|feld *das* [Kriegsschauplatz] battle-
field.

Schlacht|hof *der* slaughterhouse.

Schlaf *der* sleep.

Schlafan|zug *der* pyjamas *Pl.*

Schläfe (*pl* -n) *die* temple.

schlafen (*präs* schläft, *prät* schlief, *perf* hat
geschlafen) *vi* - 1. [eingeschlafen sein] to sleep;
schlafen gehen, sich schlafen legen to go to
bed; **mit jm schlafen** to sleep with sb; **schlaf
schön** ODER **gut!** sleep well! - 2. [übernachten]:
bei jm schlafen to stay the night with sb
- 3. *fam* [unaufmerksam sein] to be asleep.

schlaff *adj* - 1. [nicht fest - Seil] slack; [- Penis, Händedruck] limp; [- Haut] loose; [- Mus-
keln] flabby - 2. [müde] listless; **Mensch, bist du
ein schlaffer Typ!** you're such a drip! ▷ *adv*
- 1. [lose] slackly - 2. [energielos] listlessly.

Schlaf|lied *das* lullaby.

schlaflos ▷ *adj* sleepless. ▷ *adv*
sleeplessly.

Schlaf|mittel *das* sleeping pill.

schläfrig ▷ *adj* sleepy. ▷ *adv* sleepily.

Schlaf|saal *der* dormitory.

Schlaf|sack *der* sleeping bag.

schläft *präs* ▷ **schlafen.**

Schlaf|tablette *die* sleeping pill.

schlaftrunken ▷ *adj* drowsy. ▷ *adv*
drowsily.

Schlaf|wagen *der* sleeper.

schlafwandeln (*perf* hat/ist schlafgewan-
delt) *vi* to sleepwalk.

Schlaf|zimmer *das* - 1. [Zimmer] bedroom
- 2. [Möbel] bedroom suite.

Schlag (*pl* Schläge) *der* - 1. [Stoß] blow; [leicht]
pat; [mit der Faust] punch; [mit der Hand] slap; **jm
einen Schlag versetzen** [Hieb] to hit sb; [Schock]
to be a blow to sb - 2. [Geräusch - von Uhr]
chime; *Süddt* [- Knall] crash; [- von Trommel]
bang; **Schlag zwölf** on the stroke of twelve
o'clock - 3. *fam* [Stromstoß] (electric) shock
- 4. [Hose]: **eine Hose mit Schlag** flared trousers
UK, flared pants *US*; **auf einen Schlag** in one
go; **alle erschienen auf einen Schlag** they all
turned up at once; **mich trifft der Schlag** *fam*
I'm flabbergasted. ➡ **Schläge** *Pl:* **Schläge
bekommen** to get a hiding.

Schlag|ader *die* artery.

Schlagan|fall *der* stroke.

schlagartig ▷ *adj* sudden. ▷ *adv* suddenly.

schlagen (*präs* schlägt, *prät* schlug, *perf* hat/
ist geschlagen) ▷ *vt (hat)* - 1. [prügeln] to hit;
[regelmäßig] to beat; [mit der Faust] to punch;
[mit der Hand] to slap; [leicht] to pat; **jm etw
aus der Hand schlagen** to knock sthg out of
sb's hand - 2. [besiegen] to beat; **jn eins zu null
schlagen** to beat sb one-zero - 3. [befestigen]:
jn/etw an etw (A) schlagen [mit Nägeln] to nail
sb/sthg to sthg; **einen Nagel in die Wand
schlagen** to bang a nail into the wall - 4. [Ball
- bei Fußball] to kick - 5. [Eier, Sahne, Trommel]
to beat - 6. [legen]: **die Hände vor das Gesicht
schlagen** to cover one's face with one's hands
- 7. [hinzufügen]: **etw zu etw schlagen** [Gebiet]
to annex sthg to sthg; **etw auf etw (A) schlagen** to add sthg to sthg. ▷ *vi - 1. (ist)* [aufpral-
len]: **gegen etw schlagen** [Regen] to beat
against sthg; [Wellen] to pound against sthg;
er schlug mit dem Kopf gegen die Wand he
banged his head against the wall - 2. *(hat)*
[hauen] to hit; **jm auf die Schulter schlagen** to
slap sb on the back; **nach jm schlagen** to hit
out at sb; **mit der Hand auf den Tisch schlagen**
to bang one's hand on the table; **gegen etw
schlagen** [Tür] to bang on sthg; **um sich schlagen** to lash out - 3. *(ist)* [sich auswirken]: **das
fette Essen schlägt mir auf den Magen** greasy
food affects my stomach - 4. *(hat)* [Uhr] to
strike; [mit Glocke] to chime - 5. *(ist)* [ähneln]:
nach jm schlagen to take after sb - 6. *(hat)*
[Herz, Puls] to beat - 7. *(hat, ist)* [einschlagen]:
in etw (A) schlagen to strike sthg - 8. *(ist)* [Flam-
men] to leap. ➡ **sich schlagen** *ref* - 1. [sich
prügeln]: **sich (mit jm) schlagen** to fight (sb);
sich um etw schlagen *fam* to fight for sthg; **die
Gäste schlugen sich um das kalte Büfett** the
guests fought over the cold buffet - 2. [sich be-
geben]: **sich in die Büsche schlagen** to slip off
into the bushes.

Schlager (*pl* -) *der* [Lied] hit.

Schläger (*pl* -) *der* - 1. [für Tennis, Badminton]
racquet; [für Tischtennis] bat; [für Golf] club; [für
Hockey] stick - 2. *abw* [Mensch] thug.

Schlägerei (*pl* -en) *die* fight.

schlagfertig <> adj quick-witted. <> adv: **schlagfertig antworten** to give a quick-witted reply.

Schlag|loch das pothole.

Schlag|sahne die whipped cream.

Schlag|seite die (ohne pl) list; **Schlagseite bekommen** [Schiff] to start to list; **er hatte Schlagseite** fam fig he was swaying from side to side.

schlägt präs ▷ **schlagen**.

Schlag|wort (pl -e ODER -wörter) das - 1. (pl Schlagworte) abw [Gemeinplatz] catchword - 2. (pl Schlagwörter) [Stichwort] key word.

Schlag|zeile die headline; **Schlagzeilen machen** to make the headlines.

Schlag|zeug (pl -e) das [in Band] drums Pl; [in Orchester] percussion.

Schlamassel der fam mess.

Schlamm (pl -e ODER **Schlämme**) der mud; [Ablagerung] sludge.

schlammig adj muddy.

Schlamperei (pl -en) die fam sloppiness.

schlampig abw <> adj - 1. [Person] slovenly - 2. [Arbeit] sloppy. <> adv - 1. [sich anziehen] in a slovenly way - 2. [arbeiten] sloppily.

schlang prät ▷ **schlingen**.

Schlange (pl -n) die - 1. [Tier] snake - 2. [Reihe] queue UK, line US; **Schlange stehen** to queue UK, to stand in line US.

schlängeln ⇔ sich schlängeln ref to wind one's/its way.

schlank <> adj slim; [Hals, Beine] slender. <> adv: **das macht schlank** that's good for your figure.

schlapp <> adj [müde] tired out; [energielos] listless. <> adv listlessly.

schlapp|machen vi fam: **kurz vor dem Ziel schlappmachen** to pull out just before the finishing line.

schlau <> adj clever; [listig] cunning; **aus jm/ etw nicht schlau werden** not to be able to work sb/sthg out. <> adv cleverly; [listig] cunningly.

Schlauch (pl **Schläuche**) der hose; [in Reifen] tube.

Schlauch|boot das rubber dinghy.

schlauchen vt fam to wear out.

Schlaufe (pl -n) die loop.

schlecht <> adj - 1. [gen] bad, poor; [Zeiten] hard; **ein schlechtes Gedächtnis** a bad ODER poor memory; **(das ist) nicht schlecht!** fam (that's) not bad! - 2. [gesundheitlich - Person] sick; **mir ist/wird schlecht** I feel sick; **schlecht aussehen** to look ill - 3. [Lebensmittel] off; **schlecht werden** to go off. <> adv - 1. [gen] badly, poorly; **die Geschäfte gehen schlecht** business is bad; **er sieht schlecht** he's got bad eyesight; **das Essen ist mir schlecht bekommen** the food didn't agree with me - 2. [unange-

nehm - schmecken, riechen] bad - 3. [kaum] hardly; **das kann schlecht sein** that's hardly possible.

schlecht machen vt to run down.

schlecken <> vt [lecken] to lick. <> vi fam [naschen] to eat sweet things.

schleichen (prät **schlich**, perf ist **geschlichen**) vi to creep; [Auto] to crawl. ⇔ **sich schleichen** ref to creep.

schleichend <> adj - 1. [vorsichtig] creeping - 2. [allmählich - Inflation] creeping; [- Krankheit] insidious. <> adv [langsam]: **die Autos bewegten sich schleichend vorwärts** the cars crept forwards.

Schleier (pl -) der - 1. [Stoff] veil - 2. [von Dunst, Nebel] haze; **auf dem Foto ist ein Schleier** the photo is fogged.

schleierhaft adj: **es ist mir schleierhaft, wie du das gemacht hast** it's a mystery to me how you did that.

Schleife (pl -n) die - 1. [Band] bow - 2. [Biegung] bend.

schleifen (prät **schliff** ODER **schleifte**, perf hat **geschliffen** ODER **hat/ist geschleift**) <> vt - 1. (unreg) (hat) [abschleifen - Diamanten, Glas] to cut; [- mit Sandpapier] to sand; [- optische Linsen] to grind - 2. (unreg) (hat) [schärfen] to sharpen, to grind - 3. (unreg) (hat) [drillen] to drill hard - 4. (reg) (hat) [zerren] to drag. <> vi (reg) (hat, ist) to drag.

Schleim (pl -e) der [in der Nase] mucus; [im Rachen] phlegm; [einer Schnecke] slime.

Schleim|haut die mucous membrane.

schlemmen <> vt to feast on. <> vi to feast.

schlendern (perf ist **geschlendert**) vi to stroll.

schleppen vt - 1. [tragen] to lug; [zerren] to drag - 2. [Fahrzeug] to tow - 3. fam [mitnehmen] to drag (along) - 4. fam abw [schmuggeln] to smuggle. ⇔ **sich schleppen** ref - 1. [gehen] to drag o.s. - 2. [sich hinziehen] to drag on.

Schlesien nt Silesia.

Schleswig-Holstein nt Schleswig-Holstein.

Schleuder (pl -n) die - 1. [Steinschleuder] sling; [Wurfmaschine] catapult - 2. [Wäscheschleuder] spin-dryer.

schleudern (perf **hat/ist geschleudert**) <> vt (hat) - 1. fam [werfen] to hurl - 2. [zentrifugieren - Wäsche] to spin; [- Honig] to extract. <> vi (ist) to skid.

Schleudern das: **ins Schleudern kommen** ODER **geraten** [mit dem Fahrzeug] to go into a skid; fam [unsicher werden] to be thrown.

Schleuder|sitz der ejector seat.

schleunigst adv fam - 1. [sofort] at once - 2. [schnell] hastily.

Schleuse (pl -n) die - 1. SCHIFF lock - 2. [Zwischenkammer] airlock.

schlich *prät* ⊳ **schleichen**.

schlicht ⟨⟩ *adj* simple. ⟨⟩ *adv* simply.

schlichten *vt* to settle.

schlief *prät* ⊳ **schlafen**.

schließen (*prät* **schloss**, *perf* **hat geschlossen**) ⟨⟩ *vt* - 1. [gen] to close; [Umschlag] to seal; [Stromkreis] to complete - 2. [Laden, Firma] to close down - 3. [einschließen]: **jn/etw in etw (A) schließen** to lock sb/sthg in sthg - 4. [schlussfolgern] to conclude - 5. [befestigen]: **etw an etw (A) schließen** to lock sthg to sthg - 6. [umarmen]: **er schloss sie in seine Arme** he embraced her - 7. [Vertrag] to conclude, to sign; [Bündnis] to form. ⟨⟩ *vi* - 1. [zumachen] to close - 2. [den Betrieb einstellen] to close down - 3. [schlussfolgern] to conclude - 4. [enden] to end. ◆ **sich schließen** *ref* - 1. [anschließen]: **sich an etw (A) schließen** to follow sthg - 2. [Wunde, Blüte, Kreis] to close.

Schließfach *das* [am Bahnhof] left-luggage *UK* ODER baggage *US* locker; [bei der Bank] safe-deposit box.

schließlich *adv* - 1. [endlich] finally - 2. [nun einmal] after all.

schliff *prät* ⊳ **schleifen**.

Schliff (*pl* -e) *der* - 1. [Zuschleifen - Vorgang] cutting (*U*); [- Ergebnis] cut - 2. [Schärfen - Vorgang] sharpening (*U*); [- Ergebnis] edge - 3. [Vollkommenheit]: **ihm fehlt noch der Schliff** he lacks polish - 4. [Benehmen] refinement.

schlimm *adj* - 1. [gen] bad; [Folgen] serious; **es ist schlimm, wie viele Leute jetzt arbeitslos werden** the number of people being made redundant at the moment is terrible; **halb so schlimm sein** to be not too bad; **halb so schlimm!** never mind! - 2. [böse, inakzeptabel] wicked; **es ist eine schlimme Sache, wie er mit ihr umgeht** it's terrible the way he treats her.

schlimmstenfalls *adv* at worst.

Schlinge (*pl* -n) *die* - 1. [Armschlinge] sling - 2. [in Seil] loop; [zum Aufhängen] noose - 3. [zum Jagen] snare.

Schlingel (*pl* -) *der fam* rascal.

schlingen (*prät* **schlang**, *perf* **hat geschlungen**) ⟨⟩ *vt* - 1. [binden] to tie; **etw um/in etw (A) schlingen** to tie sthg round/in sthg - 2. *fam* [essen] to gobble down - 3. [legen]: **die Arme um jn/etw schlingen** to throw one's arms around sb/sthg. ⟨⟩ *vi fam* [essen] to gobble. ◆ **sich schlingen** *ref*: **sich um etw schlingen** to wind o.s./itself around sthg.

schlingern (*perf* **hat/ist geschlingert**) *vi* to roll.

Schlips (*pl* -e) *der* tie.

Schlitten (*pl* -) *der* - 1. [Rodelschlitten] sledge *UK*, sled *US* - 2. [Pferdeschlitten] sleigh - 3. *fam* [Auto] wheels *Pl*.

schlittern (*perf* **ist geschlittert**) *vi* - 1. [Fahrzeug] to skid - 2. [Mensch] to slide - 3. [geraten]: **in den Konkurs schlittern** to slide into bankruptcy.

Schlittschuh *der* ice skate; **Schlittschuh laufen** to ice-skate.

Schlitz (*pl* -e) *der* [für Geld, Briefe] slot; [Spalte] slit.

schloss *prät* ⊳ **schließen**.

Schloss (*pl* **Schlösser**) *das* - 1. [Burg] castle; [Palast] palace - 2. [Verschluss] lock.

Schlosser, in (*mpl* -, *fpl* -nen) *der, die* metalworker; [Autoschlosser] mechanic; [für Türschlösser] locksmith.

Schlot (*pl* -e) *der* chimney.

schlottern *vi* - 1. [zittern] to tremble - 2. [zu groß sein] to hang loose.

Schlucht (*pl* -en) *die* ravine.

schluchzen *vi* to sob.

Schluck (*pl* -e) *der* - 1. [Menge] drop; **ein kleiner Schluck** a sip; **einen Schluck trinken** to have a drop (to drink); **einen Schluck nehmen** ODER **tun** to take a gulp - 2. [Schlucken] gulp.

Schluckauf *der*: **einen Schluckauf haben** to have hiccups.

schlucken ⟨⟩ *vt* - 1. [Essen, Gefühle] to swallow - 2. [übernehmen - Firma] to swallow up - 3. *fam* [Alkohol, Benzin] to guzzle. ⟨⟩ *vi* to swallow.

schlug *prät* ⊳ **schlagen**.

schlüpfen (*perf* **ist geschlüpft**) *vi* - 1. [anziehen, ausziehen]: **aus etw schlüpfen** to slip sthg off; **in etw (A) schlüpfen** to slip sthg on - 2. [sich schnell bewegen] to slip; **aus etw schlüpfen** to slip out of sthg - 3. [Küken]: **(aus etw) schlüpfen** to hatch (out of sthg).

Schlüpfer (*pl* -) *der* knickers *Pl UK*, panties *Pl US*.

Schlupfloch *das* - 1. [Öffnung] hole - 2. [Versteck] hideout.

schlüpfrig *adj* - 1. [anzüglich] lewd - 2. [rutschig] slippery.

schlurfen (*perf* **ist geschlurft**) *vi fam* to shuffle.

schlürfen *vt* & *vi* to slurp.

Schluss (*pl* **Schlüsse**) *der* - 1. [Ende] end; **zum Schluss** at the end; **mit etw Schluss machen** to stop sthg; **mit jm Schluss machen** *fam* to break up with sb; **jetzt ist aber Schluss damit!** it's over now!; **damit mache ich Schluss für heute** with that, I'll finish for today - 2. [Schlussfolgerung] conclusion; **Schlüsse aus etw ziehen** to draw conclusions from sthg - 3. [Schlussstück] ending.

Schlüssel (*pl* -) *der* - 1. [für Schloss, Auflösung] key; **der Schlüssel zu etw** *fig* the key to sthg - 2. [Schraubenschlüssel] spanner - 3. [Code] code - 4. [Verteilungsschlüssel] allocation base.

Schlüsselbein *das* collar bone.

Schlüsselbund der bunch of keys.

Schlüsselloch das keyhole.

Schlussfolgerung (pl -en) die conclusion.

schlüssig ⬦ adj conclusive. ⬦ adv conclusively.

Schlusslicht (pl -er) das - 1. [Letzter]: der Verein ist das Schlusslicht in der Tabelle the club is bottom of the table - 2. [Rücklicht] rear light, taillight.

Schlussstrich (pl -e) der: einen Schlussstrich unter etw (A) ziehen to draw a line under sthg.

Schlussverkauf (pl -käufe) der end-of-season sale.

schmächtig ⬦ adj slight. ⬦ adv [gebaut] slightly.

schmackhaft ⬦ adj tasty. ⬦ adv [kochen] appetizingly; jm etw schmackhaft machen to make sthg palatable to sb.

schmal ⬦ adj [Straße, Treppe, Hüften] narrow; [Person] thin; [Figur] slender. ⬦ adv [geschnitten] narrowly; [gebaut] slenderly; [zusammenkneifen] tightly.

schmälern vt to diminish.

Schmalz (pl -e) der - 1. [Fett - zum Kochen] lard; [- zum Essen] dripping - 2. fam [Gefühl] schmaltz.

schmalzig ⬦ adj schmaltzy. ⬦ adv schmaltzily.

schmarotzen vi - 1. abw [Person] to sponge - 2. BIOL to live as a parasite.

Schmarotzer, in (mpl -, fpl -nen) der, die abw sponger.

schmatzen vi to eat noisily; mit den Lippen schmatzen to smack one's lips.

schmecken ⬦ vi to taste; schmeckt es? does it taste good?; hat es geschmeckt? did you enjoy your meal?; es schmeckt mir I like it; nach etw schmecken to taste of sthg; es schmeckt gut/schlecht it tastes good/bad; lass es dir schmecken! enjoy your meal! ⬦ vt to taste.

Schmeichelei (pl -en) die flattery (U).

schmeicheln vi: jm schmeicheln to flatter sb.

schmeißen (prät schmiss, perf hat geschmissen) fam ⬦ vt - 1. [werfen] to chuck - 2. [spendieren]: eine Runde schmeißen to stand a round - 3. [aufgeben] to pack in - 4. [organisieren] to handle. ⬦ vi: er schmiss mit dem Geschirr nach mir he chucked the crockery at me.

schmelzen (präs schmilzt, prät schmolz, perf hat/ist geschmolzen) ⬦ vi (ist) to melt. ⬦ vt (hat) to melt; [Erz] to smelt.

Schmelzpunkt der melting point.

Schmerz (pl -en) der - 1. (meist pl) [körperlich] pain - 2. [seelisch] grief.

schmerzen vi & vt to hurt.

schmerzhaft adj painful.

schmerzlos ⬦ adj painless. ⬦ adv painlessly.

Schmerzmittel das painkiller.

Schmerztablette die painkiller.

Schmetterling (pl -e) der [Tier & SPORT] butterfly.

Schmied (pl -e) der blacksmith.

Schmiedeeisen das wrought iron.

schmieden vt - 1. [bearbeiten] to forge - 2. [befestigen]: jn an etw (A) schmieden to chain sb to sthg - 3. [Pläne] to make.

schmiegen vt to nestle. ⬦ sich schmiegen ref: sich an jn/etw schmiegen to snuggle up to sb/sthg.

Schmiere (pl -n) die - 1. [Fett] grease - 2. fam [Wache]: Schmiere stehen to act as a lookout.

schmieren ⬦ vt - 1. [mit Fett] to grease; [mit Öl] to oil - 2. TECH to lubricate; [bestechen] to bribe - 3. [streichen] to spread; ein Butterbrot schmieren ≃ to make a sandwich; wie geschmiert fam without a hitch. ⬦ vi - 1. [schreiben] to scribble - 2. [klecksen] to smudge.

Schmiergeld das fam bribe.

schmierig ⬦ adj - 1. [ölig] greasy - 2. abw [Witz, Anspielung] smutty - 3. abw [Typ] smarmy. ⬦ adv [angrinsen] smarmily; [lachen, anmachen] smuttily.

Schmiermittel das lubricant.

Schmierseife die soft soap.

schmilzt präs ▷ schmelzen.

Schminke (pl -n) die make-up.

schminken vt to make up. ⬦ sich schminken ref to put on one's make-up.

schmirgeln vt to sand.

Schmirgelpapier das sandpaper.

schmiss prät ▷ schmeißen.

Schmöker (pl -) der tome (of lightweight reading).

schmökern ⬦ vi: in einem Buch schmökern to bury o.s. in a book. ⬦ vt to bury o.s. in.

schmollen vi to sulk.

schmolz prät ▷ schmelzen.

schmoren ⬦ vt to braise. ⬦ vi - 1. [braten] to braise - 2. fam [in der Sonne] to roast - 3. fam [warten]: jn schmoren lassen to leave sb to stew (in his/her own juice).

Schmuck der - 1. [Gegenstand] jewellery - 2. [Dekoration] decoration.

schmücken vt to decorate. ⬦ sich schmücken ref to adorn o.s.

schmucklos ⬦ adj plain, unadorned. ⬦ adv plainly.

Schmuckstück das - 1. [Schmuck] piece of jewellery - 2. [aus Sammlung, Ausstellung] jewel.

Schmuggel der smuggling.

schmuggeln vt & vi to smuggle.

Schmuggler, in (mpl -, fpl -nen) der, die smuggler.

schmunzeln vi: (über etw (A)) schmunzeln to smile to o.s. (at sthg).

schmusen vi: (mit jm) schmusen to cuddle (sb); [Liebespaar] to kiss and cuddle (with sb).

Schmutz der dirt; **Schmutz abweisend** dirt-resistant.

schmutzen vi to get dirty.

Schmutzfink der fam - **1.** [schmutziger Mensch - Erwachsener] dirty pig; [- Kind] mucky pup - **2.** [unsittlicher Mensch] creep.

schmutzig adj - **1.** [gen] dirty; **sich schmutzig machen** to get dirty - **2.** [Geschäftspraktiken] shady.

Schnabel (pl Schnäbel) der beak.

Schnalle (pl -n) die buckle.

schnallen vt - **1.** [festmachen] to strap; [Gürtel] to fasten, to buckle; **den Gürtel enger schnallen** to tighten one's belt; **etw auf etw (A) schnallen** to strap sthg to sthg - **2.** fam [kapieren] to get.

schnalzen vi: **mit der Zunge/den Fingern schnalzen** to click one's tongue/fingers; **mit der Peitsche schnalzen** to crack the whip.

Schnäppchen (pl -) das snip, bargain; **mit dem Hemd habe ich ein Schnäppchen gemacht** the shirt was a real snip ODER bargain.

schnappen (perf hat/ist geschnappt) <> vt (hat) - **1.** fam [festnehmen] to catch - **2.** fam [nehmen]: **sich (D) etw schnappen** to grab sthg - **3.** [packen] to grab. <> vi - **1.** (hat) [beißen]: **nach jm/etw schnappen** to snap at sb/sthg - **2.** (ist) [federn] to spring up.

Schnappschuss (pl -schüsse) der snapshot.

Schnaps (pl Schnäpse) der schnapps.

schnarchen vi [im Schlaf] to snore.

schnattern vi - **1.** [Gänse] to gabble; [Enten] to quack - **2.** fam [reden] to chatter - **3.** [zittern]: **er schnattert vor Kälte** his teeth are chattering with cold.

schnauben vi eigtl & fig to snort; **vor Wut schnauben** to snort with anger.

schnaufen vi to wheeze.

Schnauzbart der - **1.** [Bart] moustache - **2.** fam [Mensch] guy with the 'tache.

Schnauze (pl -n) die - **1.** [Maul] muzzle; [von Schwein] snout - **2.** salopp abw [Mund] trap, gob UK; **jm eins auf die Schnauze hauen** to sock sb in the mouth; **halt die Schnauze!** salopp shut your trap!

schnäuzen sich schnäuzen ref: sich (die Nase) schnäuzen to blow one's nose.

Schnauzer (pl -) der - **1.** [Hunderasse] Schnauzer - **2.** [Schnurrbart] large moustache.

Schnecke (pl -n) die snail; [ohne Schneckenhaus] slug; **jn zur Schnecke machen** fig to give sb a dressing-down.

Schneckenhaus das snail shell.

Schnee der snow; **es liegt Schnee** there is snow (on the ground); **Schnee räumen** to clear snow.

Schneeball der snowball.

Schneebesen der whisk.

Schneefall der snowfall.

Schneeflocke die snowflake.

Schneegestöber (pl Schneegestöber) das [leicht] snow flurry; [stärker] snowstorm.

Schneeglöckchen (pl Schneeglöckchen) das snowdrop.

Schneekette die snow chain.

Schneemann (pl -männer) der snowman.

Schneepflug der snowplough.

Schneeschmelze die thaw.

Schneesturm der snowstorm.

Schneetreiben das blizzard.

Schneewittchen das Snow White.

Schneide (pl -n) die [Klinge] blade.

schneiden (prät schnitt, perf hat geschnitten) <> vt - **1.** [gen] to cut; [Hecke] to trim; [Baum] to cut back; **sich (D) die Haare schneiden lassen** to have one's hair cut - **2.** [klein schneiden - in Stücke] to chop; [- in Scheiben] to slice; [- Braten] to carve; **etw in Würfel schneiden** to cube sthg - **3.** [zurechtschneiden - Foto] to cut to size - **4.** [ausschneiden] to cut out - **5.** [beim Überholen] to cut in on; **eine Kurve schneiden** to cut a corner - **6.** [ignorieren]: **jn schneiden** to ignore sb - **7.** [überschneiden] to cut across, to cross; MATH to intersect - **8.** [hinzufügen]: **Schnittlauch in die Suppe schneiden** to chop some chives and add them to the soup - **9.** SPORT [Ball] to put spin on. <> vi - **1.** [beschädigen]: **(mit etw) in etw (A) schneiden** to cut sthg (with sthg) - **2.** [Frisör, Messer, Schere] to cut. sich schneiden ref - **1.** [sich verletzen]: to cut o.s.; **sich in den Finger schneiden** to cut one's finger - **2.** [sich überschneiden] to intersect - **3.** [sich täuschen]: **wenn du das glaubst, dann hast du dich aber geschnitten!** if you think that, you've got another think ODER thing coming!

schneidend <> adj - **1.** [Wind, Kälte] biting - **2.** [Stimme] piercing. <> adv piercingly.

Schneider (pl -) der tailor; [für Damen] dressmaker.

Schneiderin (pl -nen) die tailor; [für Damen] dressmaker.

schneidern <> vt: (sich (D)) etw schneidern to make sthg. <> vi to make clothes.

Schneidersitz der: **im Schneidersitz** cross-legged.

Schneidezahn der incisor.

schneidig adj [Bursche] dashing; [Fahrstil] daring.

schneien vi: **es schneit** it's snowing.

schnell <> adj - **1.** [gen] quick - **2.** [Tempo] fast, quick - **3.** [Person, Gefährt] fast. <> adv

- 1. [laufen] fast, quickly - 2. [zügig] quickly;
schnell machen to hurry up - 3. [bald] soon
- 4. [gleich]: **kannst du mal schnell vorbeikommen?** could you just pop round quickly?; **sag doch mal schnell** just tell me again.

Schnelle *die*: **auf die Schnelle** quickly.

Schnell|hefter *der* loose-leaf binder.

Schnelligkeit *die* speed.

Schnell|imbiss (*pl* -e) *der* snack bar.

schnellstens *adv* as quickly as possible.

Schnell|straße *die* expressway.

Schnell|zug *der* express train.

schneuzen *ref* = schnäuzen.

schnippisch ◇ *adj* pert. ◇ *adv* pertly.

Schnipsel (*pl* -) *der* scrap.

schnippen ◇ *vt* to flick. ◇ *vi* to snap.

schnitt *prät* ▷ **schneiden**.

Schnitt (*pl* -e) *der* - 1. [Öffnung] cut; [bei Operation] incision - 2. [von Haar, Kleidung] cut; [Schnittmuster] pattern - 3. [von Film] editing (*U*) - 4. [Schneiden - von Baum] cutting back; [- von Hecke] trimming - 5. *fam* [Durchschnitt] average; **im Schnitt** on average - 6. *fam* [Gewinn] profit.

Schnitte (*pl* -n) *die* - 1. [Scheibe] slice - 2. [belegtes Brot] open sandwich.

Schnitt|fläche *die* - 1. [angeschnittener Teil] cut end - 2. MATH section.

Schnitt|lauch *der* (*ohne pl*) chives *Pl*.

Schnitt|punkt *der* point of intersection.

Schnitt|wunde *die* cut.

Schnitzel (*pl* -) *das* - 1. [Fleisch] escalope - 2. [aus Papier] scrap.

schnitzen *vt* & *vi* to carve.

Schnitzer (*pl* -) *der* - 1. [Fehler] blunder - 2. [Beruf] carver.

Schnitzerei (*pl* -en) *die* carving.

Schnorchel (*pl* -) *der* snorkel.

schnorcheln *vi* to snorkel.

schnüffeln ◇ *vi* - 1. [riechen]: **an etw** (*D*) **schnüffeln** to sniff at sthg - 2. [durchsuchen] to snoop. ◇ *vt* *fam* [einatmen] to sniff.

Schnuller (*pl* -) *der* dummy *UK*, pacifier *US*.

Schnupfen (*pl* -) *der* cold; **einen Schnupfen haben/bekommen** to have/get a cold.

schnuppern ◇ *vi* - 1. [riechen]: **(an etw** (*D*)) **schnuppern** to sniff (at sthg) - 2. [testen]: **einige Stunden schnuppern** to try it out for a few classes. ◇ *vt* to sniff.

Schnur (*pl* Schnüre) *die* string; [Zugschnur] cord; [Kabel] lead.

Schnürchen *das*: **wie am Schnürchen** *fam* without a hitch.

schnüren ◇ *vt* - 1. [gen] to tie; [Mieder] to lace up - 2. [Bündel, Paket] to tie up; **etw um etw schnüren** to tie sthg around sthg. ◇ *vi*: **ins Fleisch schnüren** to bite into one's flesh.

schnurlos *Adjektiv* cordless.

Schnurr|bart *der* moustache.

schnurren (*perf* hat geschnurrt) *vi* eigtl & *fig* to purr.

Schnür|senkel (*pl* -) *der* shoelace.

schob *prät* ▷ **schieben**.

Schock (*pl* -s) *der* shock; **unter Schock stehen** to be in shock.

schockieren *vt* to shock.

schockiert ◇ *adj* shocked; **über etw** (*A*) **schockiert sein** to be shocked at sthg. ◇ *adv*: **schockiert reagieren** to react with shock.

Schokokopf *der* KÜCHE chocolate-covered marshmallow.

Schokolade (*pl* -n) *die* - 1. [Süßigkeit] chocolate - 2. [Getränk - heiß] hot chocolate; [- kalt] chocolate drink.

Scholle (*pl* -n) *die* [Fisch] plaice.

schon *adv* - 1. [bereits] already; **wir essen heute schon um elf Uhr** we're eating earlier today, at eleven o'clock; **schon damals** even then; **schon 1914** as early as 1914; **er ist schon lange hier** he's been here for a long time; **schon jetzt** already; **schon wieder** again - 2. [inzwischen] yet; **warst du schon auf der Post?** have you been to the post office yet?; **schon längst** a long time ago; **schon oft** often - 3. [zwar]: **es gefällt mir schon, aber** I do like it, but; **ja schon, aber** yes of course, but - 4. [endlich]: **komm schon!** come on!; **nun rede schon!** come on say something! - 5. [zur Beruhigung]: **du machst das schon** don't worry, I'm sure you'll manage it!; **es wird schon gehen** it will work out all right; **schon gut!, schon recht!** all right!, OK! - 6. [allein] just; **schon der Gedanke daran macht mich nervös** just thinking about it makes me nervous.

schön ◇ *adj* - 1. [Frau, Kind, Sache] beautiful; [Mann] handsome - 2. [angenehm] good; **schönes Wochenende!** have a nice weekend! - 3. [erheblich] considerable; **es ist noch ein schönes Stück** it's still quite a way; **schönen Dank!** many thanks!, thanks a lot! ◇ *adv* - 1. [gen] well; [gekleidet] beautifully - 2. [verstärkend]: **schön langsam** nice and slowly; **sei schön brav!** be a good boy/girl! ● **ganz schön** *adv fam* really. ● **na schön** *interj fam* all right!

Schöne (*pl* -n) *der, die, das*: **die Schöne** the beauty; **der Schöne** the handsome man; **das Schöne** the beautiful; **das Schöne daran** the nice thing about it; **da hast du was Schönes angerichtet!** *fam* you've gone and done it now!

schonen *vt* - 1. [pfleglich behandeln - Kleider, Auto, Möbel] to be careful with, to treat gently - 2. [schützen - Augen, Umwelt] to protect - 3. [weniger verlangen von] to go easy on; **er schont den Stürmer für das nächste Spiel** he's saving ODER resting the forward for the next game. ● **sich schonen** *ref* to take it easy.

schonend <> *adj* gentle. <> *adv* gently; **jm etw schonend beibringen** to break sthg to sb gently.

Schon|frist *die* period of grace.

Schönheit (*pl* -en) *die* - **1.** [gen] beauty - **2.** [Sehenswürdigkeit] attraction.

schön machen *vt* - **1.** [hübsch machen]: **etw schön machen** to make sthg look nice - **2.** [angenehm machen] to make agreeable; **es sich (D) schön machen** to make things nice. <> **sich schön machen** *ref* to do o.s. up.

Schonung (*pl* -en) *die* - **1.** [Baumschule] young plantation - **2.** [pflegliche Behandlung] careful ODER gentle treatment; [Schützen] protection; [verschonen] to spare; **jn um Schonung bitten** [weniger verlangen von] to ask sb to go easy on one.

schonungslos <> *adj* ruthless; [Offenheit] brutal. <> *adv* ruthlessly; [offen] brutally.

Schon|zeit *die* close season.

Schopf (*pl* Schöpfe) *der* [Haar] shock of hair; **die Gelegenheit beim Schopf packen** to grasp the opportunity with both hands.

schöpfen *vt* - **1.** [auftun] to scoop; [mit Löffel, Kelle] to ladle; **etw aus etw schöpfen** to scoop/ladle sthg out of sthg - **2.** [Mut, Kraft, Atem] to draw; **Verdacht schöpfen** to become suspicious.

Schöpfer (*pl* -) *der* [Gott] Creator.

schöpferisch <> *adj* creative. <> *adv* creatively; **schöpferisch veranlagt sein** to have creative tendencies.

Schöpf|kelle *die* ladle.

Schöpfung (*pl* -en) *die* - **1.** [Welterschaffung] Creation - **2.** *geh* [Werk] creation.

schor *prät* ▷ **scheren**.

Schorf *der* (*ohne pl*) scab.

Schorn|stein *der* chimney.

Schornstein|feger, in (*mpl* -, *fpl* -nen) *der, die* chimney sweep.

schoss *prät* ▷ **schießen**.

Schoß (*pl* Schöße) *der* - **1.** [Körperteil] lap; **auf js Schoß sitzen** to sit on sb's lap; **der Erfolg ist mir nicht in den Schoß gefallen** success wasn't handed to me on a plate - **2.** *geh* [Schutz] bosom - **3.** *geh* [Mutterleib] womb - **4.** [von Jacke] tail.

Schotte (*pl* -n) *der* Scotsman, Scot.

Schottin (*pl* -nen) *die* Scotswoman, Scot.

schottisch *adj* Scottish.

Schottland *nt* Scotland.

schraffieren *vt* to hatch.

schräg <> *adj* - **1.** [schief] sloping; [Linie] diagonal - **2.** *fam* [eigenartig] offbeat - **3.** *fam* [falsch] dodgy. <> *adv* - **1.** [schief] at an angle; [diagonal] diagonally; **jn schräg ansehen** *fam* to look askance at sb - **2.** *fam* [falsch]: **das klingt schräg** that sounds dodgy.

Schräge (*pl* -n) *die* slope; [Wand] sloping ceiling.

Schramme (*pl* -n) *die* scratch.

Schrank (*pl* Schränke) *der* [für Geschirr, Vorräte] cupboard; [für Kleider] wardrobe *UK*, closet *US*; [für Bücher] bookcase.

Schranke (*pl* -n) *die* barrier. ➠ **Schranken** *Pl* [Grenzen] limits.

schrankenlos *adj* [Freiheit] boundless.

Schrank|wand *die* wall unit.

Schraube (*pl* -n) *die* - **1.** [zum Befestigen] screw; [ohne Spitze] bolt - **2.** SPORT twist.

schrauben *vt*: **etw (auf/in etw (A)) schrauben** to screw sthg (onto/into sthg); **etw aus (A) schrauben** to screw sthg to sthg; **etw aus** ODER **von etw schrauben** to unscrew sthg from sthg; **den Deckel von der Flasche schrauben** to screw the lid off the bottle; **etw nach oben/unten schrauben** *fig* to raise/lower sthg.

Schrauben|schlüssel *der* spanner *UK*, wrench *US*.

Schrauben|zieher (*pl* Schraubenzieher) *der* screwdriver.

Schreber|garten *der* ≈ allotment.

Schreck *der* fright; **vor Schreck** in fear ODER fright; **einen Schreck kriegen** *fam* to get a fright; **jm einen Schreck einjagen** to give sb a fright.

Schrecken (*pl* -) *der* terror; **die Schrecken des Krieges** the horrors of war; **er ist der Schrecken der Nachbarschaft** he's the terror of the neighbourhood.

schreckhaft *adj* easily scared.

schrecklich <> *adj* terrible. <> *adv* terribly.

Schrei (*pl* -e) *der* shout; [von Tier, Baby] cry; [aus Angst, vor Schmerz, Lust] scream; **der letzte Schrei** *fam fig* the latest thing.

schreiben (*prät* schrieb, *perf* hat geschrieben) <> *vt* - **1.** [gen] to write; [mit Schreibmaschine] to type - **2.** [orthografisch] to spell; **wie schreibt man das?** how do you spell that?, how's that spelt? - **3.** [Klassenarbeit, Test] to do - **4.** [Rechnung] to make out; **die Firma schreibt rote Zahlen** the company is in the red. <> *vi* - **1.** [gen] to write; **an jn schreiben** to write to sb; **an etw (D) schreiben** to be writing sthg - **2.** [tippen] to type; *siehe auch* **großschreiben, kleinschreiben, krankschreiben**. ➠ **sich schreiben** *ref* - **1.** [korrespondieren] to correspond - **2.** [sich buchstabieren] to be spelt.

Schreiben (*pl* -) *das* letter.

Schreib|kraft *die* clerical assistant; [Stenotypistin] shorthand typist.

Schreib|maschine *die* typewriter.

Schreib|schrift *die* cursive script.

Schreib|tisch *der* desk.

Schreibtisch|lampe *die* desk lamp.

Schreibwaren|geschäft *das* stationery shop.

schreien (*prät* **schrie**, *perf* **hat geschrie(e)n**) *vi* [gen] to shout; [Tier, Baby] to cry; [aus Angst, vor Schmerz, Lust] to scream; **vor Schmerz schreien** to scream with pain; **schrei nicht so!** stop shouting!; **nach etw schreien** *eigtl & fig* to cry out for sthg.

Schreien *das* crying; [gellend] screaming; [Brüllen] shouting; **zum Schreien sein** *fam* to be a scream.

Schreilhals *der fam* bawler.

Schreiner, in (*mpl -, fpl -nen*) *der, die* joiner.

schrie *prät* ▷ **schreien**.

schrieb *prät* ▷ **schreiben**.

Schrift (*pl -en*) *die* - **1.** [Handschrift] handwriting *(U)* - **2.** [das Geschriebene] writing *(U)* - **3.** [Alphabet] script - **4.** type. ◆ **Schriften** *Pl* texts; [kurze Abhandlungen] papers; [Werke] works.

schriftlich ◇ *adj* written. ◇ *adv* in writing.

Schriftsteller, in (*mpl -, fpl -nen*) *der, die* writer.

schrill *adj* shrill.

Schrimp (*pl -s*), **Shrimp** (*pl -s*) [ʃrɪmp] *der* shrimp.

Schritt (*pl -e*) *der* - **1.** [gen] step; **er ist mir immer einen Schritt voraus** he's always a step ahead of me; **jn am Schritt erkennen** to recognize sb's step - **2.** [von Hose] crotch - **3.** [zur Angabe der Entfernung] pace; **drei Schritte von mir entfernt** three paces away from me - **4.** [Gangart] walk; **im Schritt reiten** to ride at a walk; **Schritt für Schritt** step by step; **mit jm/etw Schritt halten** to keep up with sb/sthg.

Schrittlmacher (*pl* **Schrittmacher**) *der* - **1.** [Vorreiter] pacesetter - **2.** [im Sport] pacemaker.

schrittweise *adv* gradually.

schroff ◇ *adj* - **1.** [Verhalten, Antwort, Wechsel] abrupt - **2.** [Felsen, Abhang] sheer - **3.** [Gegensatz] stark. ◇ *adv* [abweisen, antworten] abruptly.

schröpfen *vt fam* [ausnehmen] to rip off.

Schrot *der ODER das* - **1.** [Munition] shot - **2.** [Getreide] meal; [von Weizen] wholemeal *UK*, wholewheat *US*.

Schrott *der* - **1.** [altes Metall] scrap metal - **2.** *fam* [Plunder] junk - **3.** *fam* [Blödsinn] rubbish.

Schrottlplatz *der* scrapyard *UK*, junkyard *US*.

schrottreif *adj* fit for the scrapheap.

schrubben *vt* to scrub.

Schrubber (*pl -*) *der* hard-bristled broom (*for scrubbing floors*).

schrumpelig, schrumplig *adj* [Haut] wrinkled; [Apfel] shrivelled.

schrumpfen (*perf* **ist geschrumpft**) *vi* to shrink.

schrumplig = **schrumpelig**.

Schub (*pl* **Schübe**) *der* - **1.** [Kraft] thrust - **2.** [Anfall] bout - **3.** [Ladung, Menschengruppe] batch.

Schublkarre (*pl -n*) *die* wheelbarrow.

Schubkarren (*pl -*) *der* wheelbarrow.

Schubllade (*pl -n*) *die* drawer.

Schubs (*pl -e*) *der* push.

schubsen *vt* to push.

schüchtern ◇ *adj* [Person, Blick] shy; [Versuch, Frage] timid. ◇ *adv* [lächeln, schauen] shyly; [sich benehmen, fragen] timidly.

Schüchternheit *die* shyness.

schuf *prät* ▷ **schaffen**.

Schuft (*pl -e*) *der abw* scoundrel.

schuften *vi fam* to slave away.

Schuh (*pl -e*) *der* shoe; **jm etw in die Schuhe schieben** *fig* to pin the blame for sthg on sb.

Schuhlcreme, Schuhkrem *die* shoe polish.

Schuhlgeschäft *das* shoe shop.

Schuhlgröße *die* shoe size.

Schuhlmacher, in (*mpl* **Schuhmacher**, *fpl -nen*) *der, die* cobbler, shoemaker.

Schulabschluss (*pl -schlüsse*) *der* schoolleaving qualification.

Schullanfang *der* - **1.** [Einschulung] first day of school - **2.** [nach den Ferien] beginning of term.

Schullaufgabe *die* homework *(U)*.

Schullbesuch *der* school attendance.

Schullbildung *die* school education, schooling.

Schullbus *der* school bus.

schuld *adj*: **an etw** (*D*) **schuld sein** to be to blame for sthg; **er ist schuld daran** it's his fault.

Schuld (*pl -en*) *die* - **1.** [Verantwortung, Ursache] blame; **es war seine Schuld** it was his fault; **an etw Schuld haben** to be to blame for sthg; **jm (an etw** (*D*)**) Schuld geben** to blame sb (for sthg) - **2.** [Unrecht] guilt; **sich** (*D*) **keiner Schuld bewusst sein** to be unaware of having done anything wrong; *siehe auch* **zuschulden**. ◆ **Schulden** *Pl* debts; **Schulden haben** to be in debt; **12 Milliarden Euro Schulden haben** to have debts of 12 billion euros; **Schulden machen** to run up debts.

schuldbewusst ◇ *adj* guilty. ◇ *adv* guiltily.

schulden *vt*: **jm etw schulden** to owe sb sthg.

schuldig ◇ *adj* - **1.** [verantwortlich] guilty; **an etw** (*D*) **schuldig sein** to be to blame for sthg - **2.** [nicht bezahlt] due; **jm etw schuldig sein** *ODER* **bleiben** to owe sb sthg. ◇ *adv*: **sich schuldig bekennen** to admit one's guilt.

schuldlos *adj* innocent.

Schule (*pl -n*) *die* school; **in der Schule** at school; **zur** *ODER* **in die Schule gehen** to go to school; **Schule machen** *fig* to set a precedent.

schulen *vt* to train.

Schüler (*pl* -) *der* pupil.

Schüler|austausch *der* (school) exchange.

Schüler|ausweis *der* pupil's ID card entitling them to concessions etc.

Schülerin (*pl* -nen) *die* pupil.

Schüler|karte *die* school season ticket.

Schul|ferien *Pl* school holidays.

schulfrei *adj*: morgen ist schulfrei there's no school tomorrow; **schulfrei haben** to be off school.

Schul|hof *der* school playground.

schulisch *adj & adv* at school.

Schul|jahr *das* - 1. [Jahr] school year - 2. [Klasse] year.

Schul|klasse *die* class.

Schul|leiter, in *der, die* headmaster (headmistress *die*) *UK*, principal *US*.

schulpflichtig *adj* required to attend school; **im schulpflichtigen Alter** of school age.

Schulschluss *der*: nach Schulschluss after school.

Schul|stunde *die* period.

Schul|tasche *die* schoolbag.

Schulter (*pl* -n) *die* shoulder.

Schulter|blatt *das* shoulder blade.

Schulung (*pl* -en) *die* - 1. [gen] training - 2. [Lehrveranstaltung] training course.

Schul|zeit *die* schooldays *Pl*.

Schul|zeugnis *das* school report.

schummeln *vi* to cheat.

Schund *der abw* trash.

schunkeln (*perf* hat geschunkelt) *vi* - 1. [sich wiegen] to link arms and sway in time to the music - 2. [Schiff] to rock.

Schuppe (*pl* -n) *die* - 1. [von Fischen] scale - 2. [Hautstück] flake - 3. [Kopfschuppe] dandruff (*U*).

schuppen *vt* to scale. ➤ **sich schuppen** *ref* to flake.

schürfen ⟨⟩ *vi* [schleifen] to scrape. ⟨⟩ *vt*: sich (*D*) das Knie schürfen to graze one's knee.

Schürf|wunde *die* graze.

Schurke (*pl* -n) *der abw* villain.

Schürze (*pl* -n) *die* apron.

Schuss (*pl* Schüsse) *der* - 1. [mit Schusswaffe, beim Fußball] shot - 2. [ein wenig] dash; **ein Schuss Whisky** a dash of whisky - 3. [beim Skifahren]: **Schuss fahren** to schuss; **gut in Schuss sein** *fam* to be in good shape.

Schüssel (*pl* -n) *die* bowl.

schusselig *adj fam* scatterbrained.

Schusswaffe (*pl* -n) *die* firearm.

Schuster, in (*mpl* -, *fpl* -nen) *der, die* shoemaker.

Schutt *der* rubble.

Schuttablade|platz *der* rubbish *UK* ODER garbage *US* dump.

Schüttelfrost *der*: Schüttelfrost haben to be shivering.

schütteln *vt* to shake; **den Kopf schütteln** to shake one's head; **'vor Gebrauch schütteln'** 'shake before use'; **es schüttelte ihn bei dem Gedanken** the thought made him shudder. ➤ **sich schütteln** *ref* to shake o.s.; **sich vor etw (D) schütteln** [Lachen, Kälte] to shake with sthg; [Ekel, Entsetzen] to be filled with sthg.

schütten ⟨⟩ *vt* [Flüssigkeit] to pour; [Mehl, Kartoffeln] to tip. ⟨⟩ *vi*: es schüttet *fam* it's pouring (down).

Schutz *der* protection; **jn in Schutz nehmen** to stand up for sb.

Schutz|blech *das* mudguard.

Schutz|brief *der* travel insurance certificate.

Schütze (*pl* -n) *der* - 1. ASTROL Sagittarius; **Schütze sein** to be a Sagittarius - 2. [Sportschütze] marksman - 3. [bei Ballsport] scorer - 4. [Soldat] private.

schützen *vt*: jn/etw (vor jm/etw) schützen to protect sb/sthg (from sb/sthg). ➤ **sich schützen** *ref*: sich gegen etw ODER vor etw (D) schützen to protect o.s. against sthg ODER from sthg.

Schützen|fest *das* shooting festival.

Schutz|gebiet *das* - 1. [Naturschutzgebiet] protected area - 2. [Kolonie] protectorate.

Schutz|impfung *die* vaccination.

Schützling (*pl* -e) *der* [Kind in Obhut] charge; [Protegé] protégé (protégée *die*).

schutzlos ⟨⟩ *adj* defenceless. ⟨⟩ *adv*: jm schutzlos ausgeliefert sein to be completely at sb's mercy.

Schutz|maßnahme *die* precaution.

Schutz|patron, in *der, die* patron saint.

Schutzum|schlag *der* dust jacket.

schwabbelig *adj* [Körperteil] flabby; [Pudding] wobbly.

Schwabe (*pl* -n) *der* Swabian.

Schwaben *nt* Swabia.

Schwäbin (*pl* -nen) *die* Swabian.

schwäbisch *adj* Swabian.

schwach (*kompar* schwächer, *superl* schwächste) ⟨⟩ *adj* - 1. [gen] weak; **bei Kuchen werde ich immer schwach** I have no willpower when it comes to cakes - 2. [Konstitution] delicate - 3. [leicht - Brise, Wärme, Ahnung, Gefühl] faint; [- Druck] light; [- Versuch, Entschuldigung] feeble - 4. [Selbstbewusstsein] low - 5. FILM [Leistung, Schüler] weak, poor; [Gehör, Gedächtnis] poor; **ein schwacher Trost sein** to be cold comfort - 6. [Beteiligung] poor. ⟨⟩ *adv* - 1. [eingeschränkt, schlecht, wenig] poorly - 2. [leicht - wehen, strahlen, sich erinnern] faintly; [~ drücken] lightly; [~ protestieren] feebly - **3.** GRAMM: **das Verb wird schwach konjugiert** it is a weak verb.

Schwäche (pl -n) die - **1.** [gen] weakness; **eine Schwäche für jn/etw haben** to have a weakness for sb/sthg - **2.** [von Geräusch] faintness - **3.** [von Druck] lightness.

schwächen vt to weaken.

Schwach|kopf der fam abw dummy.

schwächlich adj delicate.

Schwächling (pl -e) der abw weakling.

Schwach|sinn der - **1.** fam [Unsinn] nonsense - **2.** MED mental deficiency.

schwachsinnig <> adj - **1.** fam [unsinnig] stupid, ridiculous - **2.** MED mentally deficient. <> adv fam stupidly.

Schwächung (pl -en) die weakening.

Schwaden Pl clouds.

schwafeln fam abw <> vi to talk drivel. <> vt to drivel on about.

Schwager (pl Schwäger) der brother-in-law.

Schwägerin (pl -nen) die sister-in-law.

Schwalbe (pl -n) die swallow.

schwamm prät $\triangleright$ **schwimmen**.

Schwamm (pl Schwämme) der - **1.** [Tier, Haushaltsschwamm] sponge - **2.** [Schimmel] dry rot.

schwammig <> adj - **1.** [Definition, Worte] woolly; [Kontur] vague, blurred - **2.** [Gesicht] pasty - **3.** [Material] spongy. <> adv [unklar] vaguely.

Schwan (pl Schwäne) der swan.

schwang prät $\triangleright$ **schwingen**.

schwanger adj pregnant; **schwanger werden** to get pregnant; **im dritten Monat schwanger sein** to be in the third month of pregnancy.

Schwangere (pl -n) die pregnant woman.

schwängern vt to make pregnant.

Schwangerschaft (pl -en) die pregnancy.

schwanken (perf hat/ist geschwankt) vi - **1.** (ist) [sich schwankend bewegen] to sway - **2.** (hat) [unentschlossen sein] to waver - **3.** (hat) [instabil sein] to fluctuate.

Schwankung (pl -en) die fluctuation.

Schwanz (pl Schwänze) der - **1.** [von Tieren] tail; **den Schwanz einziehen** fam fig to back down - **2.** vulg [männliches Glied] dick - **3.** fam [Serie] series.

schwänzen <> vi fam to skive UK, to play hookey US. <> vt [Unterricht, Stunde] to skip; **die Schule schwänzen** to skive off UK ODER play hookey US from school.

schwappen (perf hat/ist geschwappt) <> vi - **1.** (ist) [überlaufen] to spill - **2.** (hat) [sich bewegen] to slosh. <> vt (hat) to splash.

Schwarm (pl Schwärme) der - **1.** [von Kindern, Bienen] swarm; [von Fischen] shoal; [von Vögeln] flock - **2.** fam [Idol] heartthrob.

schwärmen (perf hat/ist geschwärmt) vi - **1.** (hat) [begeistert sein]: **für jn/etw schwärmen** to be mad about sb/sthg - **2.** (hat) [erzählen]: **von jm/etw schwärmen** to rave about sb/sthg - **3.** (ist) [im Schwarm fliegen] to swarm.

Schwärmer, in (mpl -, fpl -nen) der, die dreamer.

Schwarte (pl -n) die - **1.** [von Speck] rind; [von Schweinebraten] crackling (U) - **2.** fam abw [Buch] tome.

schwarz (kompar schwärzer, superl schwärzeste) <> adj - **1.** [gen] black - **2.** POL pro-CDU/CSU - **3.** [Geschäfte] illicit. <> adv: **der Stift schreibt schwarz** the pen writes in black; **schwarz auf weiß** fig in black and white; siehe auch **schwarz sehen**.

Schwarz das black.

Schwarz|afrika nt Black Africa.

Schwarz|arbeit die work on the black market; [als Nebentätigkeit] moonlighting.

Schwarz|brot das black bread.

Schwarze (pl -n) <> der, die black person. <> das (ohne pl) black; **ins Schwarze treffen** to hit the bull's-eye.

Schwärze die blackness.

Schwarze Markt der black market.

Schwarze Meer das Black Sea.

schwärzen vt to blacken.

schwarz|fahren (perf ist schwarzgefahren) vi (unreg) to travel without a ticket.

Schwarz|händler, in der, die black marketeer.

schwärzlich adj blackish.

Schwarz|markt der black market.

schwarz sehen vi (unreg): **(für jn/etw) schwarz sehen** to be pessimistic (about sb/ sthg).

Schwarz|wald der Black Forest.

schwarz-weiß <> adj black and white. <> adv in black and white.

Schwarz-Weiß-Film der black and white film.

schwatzen, schwätzen <> vi - **1.** [sich unterhalten] to chat - **2.** [in der Schule] to talk. <> vt abw: **dummes Zeug schwatzen** to talk rubbish.

Schwätzer, in (mpl -, fpl -nen) der, die abw: **ein Schwätzer sein** to talk a load of nonsense.

schwatzhaft adj abw: **ein schwatzhafter Mensch** a person who can't keep their mouth shut.

Schwebe die: **in der Schwebe** in the balance.

Schwebe|bahn die overhead monorail.

Schwebe|balken der SPORT beam.

schweben vi - **1.** [fliegen, in Wasser] to float; [Vögel] to hover; [Staubteilchen] to hang - **2.** [unentschieden sein] to hover - **3.** [Duft, Verdacht] to hang.

Schwede (pl -n) der Swede.

Schweden *nt* Sweden.

Schwedin (*pl* -nen) *die* Swede.

schwedisch *adj* Swedish.

Schwedisch(e) *das* Swedish; *siehe auch* **Englisch(e)**.

Schwefel *der* sulphur.

Schwefelsäure *die* sulphuric acid.

Schweif (*pl* -e) *der* tail.

schweigen (*prät* schwieg, *perf* hat geschwiegen) *vi* to be silent; **wenn du schweigen kannst, verrate ich dir etwas** if you can keep a secret, I'll tell you something; **von jm/etw ganz zu schweigen** to say nothing of sb/sthg.

Schweigen *das* silence; **jn zum Schweigen bringen** to silence sb.

Schweigepflicht *die* professional duty to maintain confidentiality.

schweigsam *adj* taciturn; **du bist heute schweigsam** you're rather quiet today.

Schwein (*pl* -e) *das* - 1. [Tier] pig - 2. [Schweinefleisch] pork - 3. *salopp abw* [Mensch] bastard; **armes Schwein** *salopp* póor bastard; **Schwein haben** *fam* to be jammy.

Schweinebraten *der* roast pork.

Schweinefleisch *das* pork.

Schweinerei (*pl* -en) *die fam* - 1. [schlimme Sache] goddamn scandal; **das neue Abtreibungsgesetz ist eine Schweinerei!** the new law on abortion is bloody *UK ODER* goddamn *US* disgraceful! - 2. [Schmutz] mess - 3. [Unanständiges]: **Schweinereien** filth (*U*).

Schweinestall *der eigtl* & *fig* pigsty *UK*, pigpen *US*.

Schweiß *der* sweat; **ihr brach der Schweiß aus** she broke out in a sweat.

schweißen *vt* & *vi* to weld.

schweißgebadet *adj* & *adv* bathed in sweat.

Schweißtropfen *der* drop of sweat.

Schweiz *die*: **die Schweiz** Switzerland.

Schweizer (*pl* -) *der* & *adj* (*unver*) Swiss.

Schweizerdeutsch *das* Swiss German; *siehe auch* **Englisch(e)**.

Schweizerin (*pl* -nen) *die* Swiss.

schweizerisch *adj* Swiss.

Schweizerische Eidgenossenschaft *die*: **die Schweizerische Eidgenossenschaft** the Swiss Confederation.

schwelen *vi* [Rauch entwickeln] to smoulder.

Schwelle (*pl* -n) *die* - 1. [Türschwelle] threshold; **an der Schwelle einer Sache (D)** *fig* on the threshold of sthg - 2. [der Eisenbahn] sleeper *UK*, tie *US*.

schwellen (*präs* schwillt, *prät* schwoll, *perf* ist geschwollen) *vi* to swell.

Schwellung (*pl* -en) *die* swelling.

schwenken *vt* - 1. [Kran] to swing; [Kamera] to pan - 2. [Fahne] to wave - 3. KÜCHE to toss.

schwer ◇ *adj* - 1. [Gewicht] heavy; **wie schwer bist du/ist der Koffer?** how heavy are you/is the suitcase? - 2. [schwierig] difficult; [beschwerlich] hard; **es schwer haben mit** to have a hard time with - 3. [schlimm - Krankheit, Schaden, Unfall] serious; [- Enttäuschung] huge, great - 4. [stark - Mahlzeit, Sturm] heavy. ◇ *adv* - 1. [an Gewicht] heavily - 2. [unter Mühen]: **schwer atmen** to breathe with difficulty; **schwer hören** to be hard of hearing - 3. [arbeiten] hard - 4. [schwerlich] hardly - 5. [schlimm - verletzt, krank] seriously; [- bestrafen] severely - 6. *fam* [sehr] really; **er ist schwer in Ordnung** he's all right.

Schwerarbeit *die* heavy work.

schwerbehindert, schwer behindert *adj* severely disabled.

schwer beschädigt *adj* [beschädigt] badly damaged.

schwer bewaffnet *adj* heavily armed.

Schwere ◇ *die* - 1. [gen] heaviness - 2. [von Krankheit, Schaden, Unfall] seriousness; [von Enttäuschung] enormity - 3. [Schwierigkeitsgrad] difficulty. ◇ *das*: **Schweres durchmachen** to have a difficult time (of it).

schwerelos ◇ *adj* weightless. ◇ *adv* weightlessly.

schwer erziehbar *adj* difficult.

schwer fallen (*perf* ist schwer gefallen) *vi* (*unreg*): **es fiel ihm schwer, Abschied zu nehmen** he found it difficult to say goodbye.

schwerfällig ◇ *adj* ponderous. ◇ *adv* ponderously.

schwerhörig *adj* hard of hearing.

Schwerindustrie *die* heavy industry.

Schwerkraft *die* gravity.

schwer machen *vt*: **jm etw schwer machen** to make sthg difficult for sb.

schwermütig ◇ *adj* melancholy. ◇ *adv* in a melancholy way.

schwer nehmen *vt* (*unreg*): **etw schwer nehmen** to take sthg hard.

Schwerpunkt *der* - 1. [Hauptsache] main focus - 2. PHYS centre of gravity.

Schwert (*pl* -er) *das* sword.

schwer tun ➠ **sich schwer tun** *ref* (*unreg*): **sich mit etw schwer tun** to have difficulty with sthg.

Schwerverbrecher, in *der, die* person who has committed a serious crime.

schwer verletzt *adj* seriously injured.

schwerwiegend *adj* serious.

Schwester (*pl* -n) *die* - 1. [Verwandte] sister - 2. [Krankenschwester] nurse - 3. [Ordensschwester] nun, sister.

schwieg *prät* ▷ **schweigen**.

Schwiegereltern *Pl* parents-in-law.

Schwiegermutter *die* mother-in-law.

Schwiegersohn *der* son-in-law.

Schwieger|tochter *die* daughter-in-law.

Schwieger|vater *der* father-in-law.

Schwiele (*pl* -n) *die* callus.

schwierig ◇ *adj* difficult. ◇ *adv* with difficulty.

Schwierigkeit (*pl* -en) *die* difficulty; **ohne Schwierigkeiten** without difficulty; **in Schwierigkeiten geraten/stecken** to get into/be in trouble.

schwillt *präs* ▷ **schwellen**.

Schwimm|bad *das* swimming pool.

Schwimm|becken *das* (swimming) pool.

schwimmen (*prät* schwamm, *perf* hat/ist geschwommen) *vi* & *vt* (hat, ist) to swim.

Schwimmen *das* swimming.

Schwimmer, in (*mpl* -, *fpl* -nen) *der, die* swimmer.

Schwindel *der* - 1. [Gleichgewichtsstörung] dizziness - 2. *abw* [Betrug] swindle.

schwindelig, schwindlig *adj*: **mir wird (es) schwindelig** I feel dizzy; *fig* my head is spinning.

Schwindler, in (*mpl* -, *fpl* -nen) *der, die* - 1. [Betrüger] swindler - 2. [Lügner] liar.

schwindlig = **schwindelig**.

schwingen (*prät* schwang, *perf* hat/ist geschwungen) ◇ *vi* - 1. (hat) [vibrieren] to vibrate - 2. [pendeln] to swing. ◇ *vt* (hat) to wave.

schwitzen *vi* [Person] to sweat.

schwoll *prät* ▷ **schwellen**.

schwor *prät* ▷ **schwören**.

schwören (*prät* schwor, *perf* hat geschworen) *vt* & *vi* to swear.

schwul *adj fam* gay.

schwül *adj* [Wetter] close, muggy.

Schwung (*pl* Schwünge) *der* - 1. [Bewegung] swing - 2. [Elan] zest, verve - 3. [Menge] stack.

Schwur (*pl* Schwüre) *der* oath.

scratchen *vi* to scratch.

sechs [zɛks] ◇ *num* [als Zahl, Anzahl] six; **sechs Mal** six times; **um sechs (Uhr)** at six (o'clock); **fünf vor/nach sechs** five to/past *UK* ODER after *US* six; **mit sechs kommen die Kinder in die Schule** children start school at the age of six; **sechs zu null** six-zero. ◇ *pron* six; **sie waren sechs** there were six of them; **ein Tisch für sechs** a table for six.

Sechs (*pl* -en) *die* - 1. [Zahl, Spielkarte] six - 2. [Spieler, Bus] number six - 3. [Schulnote] ≃ F, mark of 6 on a scale from 1 to 6.

sechsfach ◇ *adj*: **die sechsfache Menge** six times as much; **in sechsfacher Größe** six times as big; **die Formulare in sechsfacher Ausfertigung abgeben** to provide six copies of the forms; **der sechsfache Gewinner** the six-times winner. ◇ *adv* sixfold.

sechshundert *num* six hundred.

sechsmal *adv* six times.

sechstausend *num* six thousand.

sechste, r, s ['zɛkstə, ɐ, s] *adj* sixth; **der sechste Juni** the sixth of June, June the sixth; **auf dem sechsten Rang sein** to be sixth in the rankings.

Sechste (*pl* -n) ◇ *der, die, das* [in einer Reihenfolge] sixth; **Heinrich der Sechste** Henry the Sixth, Henry VI; **sie ist die Sechste im Weitsprung** she is sixth in the long jump. ◇ *der* [Angabe des Datums] sixth; **am Sechsten** on the sixth; **ich fahre Freitag, den Sechsten** I'm going on Friday the sixth.

sechstel *adj (unver)* sixth; **ein sechstel Liter** a sixth of a litre.

Sechstel (*pl* -) *das* sixth; **etw in Sechstel teilen** to divide sthg in six ODER into sixths.

sechzehn *num* sixteen; *siehe auch* **sechs**.

sechzehntel *adj* sixteenth.

Sechzehntel (*pl* -) *das* sixteenth.

sechzig *num* sixty; *siehe auch* **sechs**.

Sechzig *die* sixty; *siehe auch* **Sechs**.

Sechzigerjahre, sechziger Jahre *Pl*: **die Sechzigerjahre** the sixties.

See (*pl* -n) ◇ *der* lake. ◇ *die* sea; **an die See fahren** to go to the seaside; **auf hoher See** out at sea.

See|gang *der*: **leichter/hoher Seegang** calm/rough seas *Pl*.

See|hund *der* [Robbe] seal.

See|igel *der* sea urchin.

seekrank *adj* seasick.

Seele (*pl* -n) *die* [gen] soul; **etw auf der Seele haben** to have sthg on one's mind.

seelenruhig *adv* calmly.

Seeleute *Pl* ▷ **Seemann**.

seelisch ◇ *adj* psychological. ◇ *adv* mentally.

See|löwe *der* sea lion.

Seelsorge *die* pastoral care.

See|mann (*pl* -leute) *der* sailor.

See|meile *die* nautical mile.

Seenot *die*: **in Seenot geraten/sein** to get into/be in distress.

See|räuber *der* pirate.

See|rose *die* [Pflanze] water lily.

seetüchtig *adj* seaworthy.

See|weg *der*: **auf dem Seeweg** by sea.

See|zunge *die* sole.

Segel (*pl* -) *das* sail.

Segel|boot *das* sailing boat.

segelfliegen *vi* to glide.

Segel|flugzeug *das* glider.

segeln (*perf* hat/ist gesegelt) *vi* to sail.

Segel|schiff *das* sailing ship.

Segen (*pl* -) *der* blessing.

segnen *vt* to bless.

sehbehindert *adj* visually impaired.

sehen (*präs* sieht, *prät* sah, *perf* hat gesehen) ⬥ *vt* - 1. [gen] to see; [willkürlich] to watch; **etw gerne/ungerne sehen** to like/dislike sthg; **das werden wir ja gleich sehen** we'll soon see; **das kann sich sehen lassen** that's remarkable - 2. [treffen] to see, to meet. ⬥ *vi* - 1. [gen] to see; **gut/schlecht sehen** to have good/bad eyesight; **sieh mal!** look!; **jm ähnlich sehen** to look like sb - 2. [hervorstehen]: **das Wrack sieht aus dem Wasser** the wreck sticks out of the water - 3. [mit Präpositionen]: **auf jn/etw sehen** to look at sb/sthg; **nach jm/etw sehen** to look after sb/sthg. ⬥ **sich sehen** *ref* - 1. [treffen] to meet - 2. [sich fühlen]: **sich betrogen sehen** to see o.s. cheated; **sich gezwungen sehen, etw zu tun** to feel obliged to do sthg. ⬥ **mal sehen** *interj* we'll see! ⬥ **sieh mal** *interj* look! ⬥ **siehste, siehst du** *interj* there you are!

sehenswert *adj* worth seeing.

Sehenswürdigkeit (*pl* -en) *die* attraction; **Sehenswürdigkeiten** sights.

Sehkraft *die* sight.

Sehne (*pl* -n) *die* - 1. [vom Muskel] tendon - 2. [vom Bogen] string.

sehnen ⬥ **sich sehnen** *ref*: sich nach jm/etw sehnen to long for sb/sthg.

sehnig *adj* - 1. [Fleisch] stringy - 2. [Körper] sinewy.

Sehnsucht (*pl* -süchte) *die* longing; **Sehnsucht nach jm/etw haben** to long for sb/sthg.

sehnsüchtig ⬥ *adj* [Blick] longing. ⬥ *adv* longingly.

sehr *adv* very; [mit Verben] a lot, very much; **das gefällt mir sehr** I like it a lot; **zu sehr** too much; **sehr viel Geld** an awful lot of money; **bitte sehr!** you're welcome!; **danke sehr!** thank you very much!

seicht *adj* shallow.

seid *präs* ▷ **sein**.

Seide (*pl* -n) *die* silk.

seidig *adj* silky.

Seife (*pl* -n) *die* soap.

Seifen|blase *die* soap bubble.

Seil (*pl* -e) *das* rope.

Seil|bahn *die* cable railway.

sein (*präs* ist, *prät* war, *perf* ist gewesen) ⬥ *aux* - 1. [im Perfekt] to have; **sie ist gegangen** she has gone - 2. [im Konjunktiv]: **sie wäre gegangen** she would have gone. ⬥ *vi* - 1. [gen] to be; **Lehrer sein** to be a teacher; **aus etw sein** to be made of sthg; **aus Indien/Zürich sein** to be from India/Zurich; **du warst es!** it was you! - 2. [mit Infinitiv, müssen]: **mein Befehl ist sofort auszuführen** my order is to be carried out immediately - 3. [mit Infinitiv, können]: **das ist nicht zu ändern** there's nothing that can be done about it; **dieses Spiel ist noch zu gewinnen** this game can still be won - 4. [mit Dativ]: **mir ist schlecht/kalt** I'm sick/cold - 5. [mit unpersönlichem Pronomen] to be; **es**

ist zwölf Uhr it's twelve o'clock; **es ist dunkel** it's dark; **wie wäre es mit...?** what about...?; **was ist?** what's up?; **das wärs** that's all; **etw sein lassen** to give sthg up; **lass es gut sein!** leave it!; **ist was?** is there anything wrong?

sein, e *det* his.

seine, r, s *pron* [bei Personen] his; [bei Sachen, Tieren] its.

Seine [sɛːn(ə)] *die*: **die Seine** the (River) Seine.

seiner *pron* (*Genitiv von er, es*): **wir gedenken seiner** we remember him.

seinerseits *adv* - 1. [er selbst] for his part; [es selbst] for its part - 2. [von ihm - Person] on his part; [- Tier, Sache] on its part.

seinerzeit *adv* at that time.

seinesgleichen *pron abw* [Person] the likes of him; [Tier, Sache] the likes of it.

seinetwegen *adv* - 1. [ihm zuliebe - Person] for his sake; [- Tier, Sache] for its sake - 2. [wegen ihm - Person] because of him; [- Tier, Sache] because of it - 3. [von ihm aus - Person] as far as he's concerned; [- Tier] as far as it's concerned.

seinetwillen ⬥ **um seinetwillen** *adv* [Person] for his sake; [Tier] for its sake.

sein lassen *vt* (*unreg*) *fam*: **lass das sein!** stop that!; **sie kann es einfach nicht sein lassen** she just can't help herself.

seit ⬥ *präp* (+ D) - 1. [zur Angabe des Zeitpunktes] since; **seit wann?** since when? - 2. [zur Angabe der Dauer] for; **ich wohne hier seit drei Jahren** I've lived here for three years; **seit langem** for a long time. ⬥ *konj* since.

seitdem ⬥ *adv* since then. ⬥ *konj* since.

Seite (*pl* -n) *die* - 1. [gen] side; **etw zur Seite legen** to put sthg to one side; **zur Seite gehen** ODER **treten** to move aside; **auf der linken/rechten Seite** on the left-hand/right-hand side - 2. [von Buch, Heft, Zeitung] page; **auf beiden Seiten** on both sides; **jedes Ding hat seine guten und schlechten Seiten** there's a good and a bad side to everything; **jm zur Seite stehen** to stand by sb; **jn von der Seite ansehen** to look at sb askance; **jn zur Seite nehmen** to take sb aside. ⬥ **auf Seiten** *präp* (+ G) on the part of. ⬥ **Seite an Seite** *adv* side by side. ⬥ **von Seiten** *präp* (+ G) on the part of.

Seiten|sprung *der* affair; **einen Seitensprung machen** to have an affair.

Seiten|stechen *das* stitch; **Seitenstechen haben** to have a stitch.

Seiten|straße *die* side street.

seither *adv* since then.

seitlich *adj* [Fenster, Eingang] side; [Zusammenstoß] side-on; **ein seitlicher Wind** a crosswind.

seitwärts *adv* - 1. [zur Seite] sideways - 2. [auf der Seite] to one side.

Sekretär (*pl* -e) *der* - 1. [Person] secretary - 2. [Möbelstück] bureau.

Sekretariat (pl -e) das secretary's office.

Sekretärin (pl -nen) die secretary.

Sekt (pl -e) der German sparkling wine similar to champagne.

Sekte (pl -n) die sect.

Sekt|glas das champagne glass.

Sekundar|stufe die SCHULE secondary UK ODER high US school level; **Sekundarstufe I** ≃ junior high school US; **Sekundarstufe II** ≃ sixth form UK, ≃ senior high school US.

Sekunde (pl -n) die second.

selber pron (unver) = **selbst**.

selbst ⟷ pron (unver): **er selbst** himself; **sie selbst** herself, themselves Pl; **ich selbst** myself; **wir selbst** ourselves; **Sie selbst** yourself, yourselves Pl; **ich selbst** I myself; **du bist selbst schuld** it's your own fault; **das versteht sich von selbst** that goes without saying. ⟷ adv even; **selbst wenn** even if. ➠ **von selbst** adv - 1. [freiwillig] of one's own accord - 2. [automatisch] automatically, by itself.

Selbst|achtung die self-respect.

selbständig = **selbstständig**.

Selbständigkeit = **Selbstständigkeit**.

Selbst|bedienung die self-service; **Restaurant mit Selbstbedienung** self-service restaurant.

Selbst|befriedigung die masturbation.

Selbst|beherrschung die self-control.

Selbst|beteiligung die [bei Versicherungen] excess.

selbstbewusst ⟷ adj self-confident. ⟷ adv self-confidently.

Selbstbewusstsein das self-confidence.

Selbst|gespräch das: **Selbstgespräche führen** ODER halten to talk to o.s.

Selbstkosten|preis der cost price; **zum Selbstkostenpreis** at cost.

selbstlos ⟷ adj unselfish, selfless. ⟷ adv unselfishly, selflessly.

Selbst|mord der suicide; **Selbstmord begehen** to commit suicide.

selbstsicher ⟷ adj self-confident. ⟷ adv self-confidently.

selbstständig ⟷ adj - 1. [unabhängig] independent - 2. [im Beruf] self-employed; **sich selbstständig machen** to set up on one's own. ⟷ adv [unabhängig] independently.

Selbstständigkeit die independence.

selbsttätig ⟷ adj automatic. ⟷ adv automatically.

selbstverständlich ⟷ adj natural; **das ist doch selbstverständlich!** that goes without saying! ⟷ adv naturally.

Selbst|verteidigung die self-defence.

Selbst|vertrauen das self-confidence.

Selbst|zweck der end in itself.

selig ⟷ adj - 1. [glücklich - Person, Lächeln] blissfully happy; [- Schlummer] blissful - 2. [heilig gesprochen] blessed - 3. geh [tot] late. ⟷ adv [glücklich] blissfully.

Seligkeit die bliss.

Sellerie der celery.

selten ⟷ adj rare. ⟷ adv - 1. [kaum] rarely - 2. [besonders] exceptionally.

Selters (pl -) das sparkling mineral water.

seltsam ⟷ adj strange. ⟷ adv strangely.

Semester (pl -) das semester; **im achten Semester sein** to be in the second-half of one's fourth year.

Semikolon (pl -s) das semicolon.

Semmel (pl -n) die Österr & Süddt (bread) roll.

Senat (pl -e) der - 1. [gen & UNI] senate - 2. [von Berlin, Bremen, Hamburg] government of one of the three German cities that have "Land" status - 3. RECHT panel of judges.

Senator (pl -en) der [gen & UNI] senator.

Senatorin (pl -nen) die [gen & UNI] senator.

senden (prät sendete ODER sandte, perf hat gesendet ODER gesandt) ⟷ vt - 1. (reg) [ausstrahlen] to broadcast - 2. (reg) [funken] to transmit, to send - 3. (reg) (unreg) [schicken] to send; **etw an jn senden** to send sb sthg. ⟷ vi (reg) [übertragen] to broadcast.

Sende|pause die interval.

Sender (pl -) der - 1. [Station] station - 2. [Gerät] transmitter.

Sendung (pl -en) die - 1. [das Senden] dispatch - 2. [Postsendung - von Waren] consignment; [- Brief] letter; [- Paket] parcel - 3. [ausgestrahltes Programm] programme - 4. [Übertragung] broadcasting; **auf Sendung gehen** to go on (the) air.

Senegal der Senegal.

Senf (pl -e) der mustard.

sengend adj scorching.

Senior (pl Senioren) der - 1. [gen] senior - 2. [von Mannschaft, Gruppe] oldest member. ➠ **Senioren** Pl - 1. [Alte] senior citizens - 2. SPORT seniors.

Senioren|heim das old people's home.

Seniorin (pl -nen) die - 1. [gen] senior - 2. [von Mannschaft, Gruppe] oldest member.

senken vt - 1. [gen] to lower; **beschämt senkte er den Kopf** he hung his head in shame - 2. [Preis, Steuern] to cut. ➠ **sich senken** ref - 1. [Wasserspiegel] to drop; [Erdreich] to subside - 2. [Schranken, Vorhang] to come down.

senkrecht ⟷ adj vertical. ⟷ adv vertically.

Senk|rechte die - 1. [Linie] vertical line - 2. [Lot] perpendicular.

Sense (pl -n) die [Gerät] scythe.

sensibel ⟷ adj sensitive. ⟷ adv sensitively.

sentimental <> *adj* sentimental. <> *adv* sentimentally.

Seoul [se'u:l] *nt* Seoul.

separat <> *adj* separate; [Wohnung] self-contained. <> *adv* separately.

September *der* September; **am siebten September** on the seventh of September, on September the seventh; **Sonntag, den 1. September** Sunday, 1 September; **im September** in September; **Anfang/Ende September** at the beginning/end of September; **Mitte September** in mid-September.

Serbe (*pl* -n) *der* Serb.

Serbien *nt* Serbia.

Serbin (*pl* -nen) *die* Serb.

serbisch *adj* Serbian.

Serie ['ze:rjə] (*pl* -n) *die* - 1. [Reihe, Sendereihe] series - 2. [Satz] set - 3. [von Produkten] line.

serienmäßig <> *adj* standard. <> *adv* [konstruieren, anfertigen] on a mass scale; [mit etw ausgestattet] as standard.

seriös <> *adj* - 1. [vertrauenswürdig] reliable - 2. [würdevoll, solide] respectable. <> *adv* [vertrauenswürdig] reliably; [würdevoll, solide] respectably.

Serum (*pl* Seren) *das* serum.

servieren [zɛr'viːrən] *vt* [Speisen, Getränke] to serve.

Serviette [zɛr'vjɛtə] (*pl* -n) *die* serviette.

Servollenkung ['zɛrvolɛŋkʊŋ] *die* power steering (U).

Sesam *der* sesame seeds *Pl*.

Sessel (*pl* -) *der* armchair.

Sessellift *der* chairlift.

setzen (*perf* hat/ist gesetzt) <> *vt* (hat) - 1. [gen] to put; **etw in jn/etw setzen** to put sthg in sb/sthg - 2. [Denkmal, Grabmal] to put up - 3. [Frist, Belohnung, Text] to set - 4. [Pflanzen] to plant - 5. [wetten]: **etw auf etw (A) setzen** to put sthg on sthg; **es setzt was** *fam* there'll be trouble. <> *vi* - 1. (hat) [wetten] to bet; **auf jn/etw setzen** to bet on sb/sthg - 2. (hat, ist) [befördern]: **über etw (A) setzen** [Fluss] to cross sthg; [Hindernis] to get over sthg. **sich setzen** *ref* - 1. [hinsetzen] to sit down; **sich zu jm setzen** to sit with sb - 2. [Kaffeesatz] to settle.

Seuche (*pl* -n) *die* epidemic.

seufzen *vi* to sigh.

Seufzer (*pl* -) *der* sigh.

Sex *der* sex.

Sexualität *die* sexuality.

sexuell <> *adj* sexual. <> *adv* sexually.

sexy *fam* <> *adj* (unver) sexy. <> *adv* sexily.

sezieren *vt* & *vi* to dissect.

sfr. (*abk für* Schweizer Franken) Swiss francs.

Shampoo ['ʃampu] (*pl* -s) *das* shampoo.

Shareware *die* EDV shareware.

Sherry ['ʃɛri] (*pl* -s) *der* sherry.

Shorts ['ʃoːɐts] *Pl* shorts.

Show [ʃoː] (*pl* -s) *die* show.

Showmaster, in ['ʃoːmastɐ, rɪn] (*mpl* -, *fpl* -nen) *der, die* compere UK, emcee US.

Shrimp *der* = Schrimp.

Sibirien [zi'biːrjən] *nt* Siberia.

sich *pron* - 1. [Reflexivpronomen - unbestimmt] oneself; [- Person] himself (herself *die*), themselves *Pl*; [- Ding, Tier] itself, themselves *Pl*; [- bei Höflichkeitsform] yourself, yourselves *Pl*; **sich (D) etw kaufen** to buy (o.s.) sthg - 2. [reziprokes Pronomen] each other.

Sichel (*pl* -n) *die* sickle.

sicher <> *adj* - 1. [ungefährdet] safe; **in sicherem Abstand** at a safe distance; **vor jm/etw sicher sein** to be safe from sb/sthg - 2. [zuverlässig] reliable - 3. [überzeugt, gewiss] sure, certain; **sich (D) einer Sache (G) sicher sein** to be sure ODER certain about sthg - 4. [selbstbewusst] self-confident. <> *adv* - 1. [ungefährdet] safely - 2. [zuverlässig] reliably; **etw sicher wissen** to know sthg for sure; **langsam aber sicher** slowly but surely - 3. [sicherlich] certainly, definitely; **das ist sicher richtig, aber** that may be true, but; **Sie haben es sicher gemerkt** you must have noticed it - 4. [selbstbewusst] self-confidently. **aber sicher** *interj* of course!

sichergehen (*perf* ist sichergegangen) *vi* (unreg) to play safe.

Sicherheit (*pl* -en) *die* - 1. [Schutz - persönliche, öffentliche, im Straßenverkehr] safety; [- soziale, wirtschaftliche, innere] security; **in Sicherheit (vor jm/etw) sein** to be safe (from sb/sthg) - 2. [Bestimmtheit] certainty - 3. [Fundiertheit, Zuverlässigkeit] reliability - 4. [Selbstbewusstsein] confidence - 5. [Bürgschaft] surety.

Sicherheitsgurt *der* seat belt.

sicherheitshalber *adv* to be on the safe side.

Sicherheitsnadel *die* safety pin.

sicherlich *adv* certainly.

sichern *vt* to secure. **sich sichern** *ref* - 1. [sich absichern] to secure o.s.; **sich gegen etw sichern** to protect o.s. against sthg - 2. [sich verschaffen]: **sich (D) etw sichern** to secure sthg.

sicherstellen *vt* - 1. [beschlagnahmen - Geld, Fund] to seize; [- Spuren] to secure - 2. [gewährleisten] to safeguard.

Sicherung (*pl* -en) *die* - 1. [Schutz] safeguarding - 2. ELEKTR fuse - 3. [Schutzmaßnahme] safeguard.

Sicht *die* - 1. [Aussicht] visibility; **außer Sicht** out of sight - 2. [Betrachtungsweise] point of view; **aus meiner Sicht** from my point of view. **auf lange Sicht** *adv* long-term. **in Sicht** *adv* in sight; **Land in Sicht!** land ahoy!

sichtbar <> *adj* - 1. [deutlich] clear - 2. [wahrnehmbar] visible. <> *adv* [deutlich] clearly.

sichten vt - **1.** [einsehen] to sift through - **2.** geh [sehen] to sight.

sichtlich <> adj obvious. <> adv obviously.

Sicht|weite die visibility (U); außer/in Sicht-weite sein to be out of/in sight.

sickern (perf ist gesickert) vi [fließen] to seep.

sie pron - **1.** [Singular - Nominativ] she; [- Akku-sativ] her; **sie wars!** it was her! - **2.** [Plural - No-minativ] they; [- Akkusativ] them - **3.** [Tier, Ge-genstand] it.

Sie pron (Singular und Plural) you.

Sieb (pl -e) das [Küchensieb] sieve; [Teesieb] strainer.

sieben[1] <> vt - **1.** [durchsieben] to sieve - **2.** [auswählen] to weed out. <> vi [auswählen] to pick and choose.

sieben[2] num seven; siehe auch **sechs**.

Sieben (pl - ODER -en) die seven; siehe auch **Sechs**.

siebenfach adj & adv sevenfold.

siebenhundert num seven hundred.

siebenmal adv seven times.

siebentausend num seven thousand.

siebte, r, s, siebente, r, s adj seventh; sie-he auch **sechste**.

Siebte (pl -n) der, die, das seventh; siehe auch **Sechste**.

siebtel adj (unver) seventh; siehe auch **sechstel**.

Siebtel (pl -) das seventh; siehe auch **Sechs-tel**.

siebzehn num seventeen; siehe auch **sechs**.

Siebzehn (pl -en) die seventeen; siehe auch **Sechs**.

siebzig num seventy; siehe auch **sechs**.

Siebzigerjahre, siebziger Jahre Pl: die Siebzigerjahre the seventies.

sieden (prät siedete ODER sott, perf hat gesie-det ODER hat gesotten) <> vi (reg) [Flüssigkeit] to boil. <> vt to boil.

Siedler, in (mpl -, fpl -nen) der, die settler.

Siedlung (pl -en) die [Häusergruppe] housing estate UK ODER development US.

Sieg (pl -e) der victory; der Sieg über jn/etw the victory over sb/sthg.

Siegel (pl -) das seal.

siegen vi to win; über jn/etw siegen to beat sb/sthg.

Sieger (pl -) der winner.

Sieger|ehrung die medals ceremony.

Siegerin (pl -nen) die winner.

siehe vi [in Text]: **siehe oben** see above; **siehe** Seite 15 see page 15.

sieht präs ⊏> **sehen**.

siezen vt to address as "Sie". ⟳ **sich siezen** ref to address each other as "Sie".

Signal (pl -e) das signal; das Signal zu etw geben to give the signal for sthg.

Silbe (pl -n) die syllable; **jn/etw mit keiner Sil-be erwähnen** fig not to say a word about sb/sthg.

Silben|trennung die syllabification (U).

Silber das silver.

Silberhoch|zeit die silver wedding (an-niversary).

Silber|medaille die silver medal.

silbern <> adj [aus Silber] silver. <> adv [wie Silber - glänzen] with a silvery sheen.

Silo (pl -s) der ODER das silo.

Silvester [zıl'vɛstɐ] (pl -) der ODER das New Year's Eve; **Silvester feiern** to see the New Year in.

simsen vi to text.

Simulation (pl -en) die EDV simulation.

simultan <> adj simultaneous. <> adv sim-ultaneously.

sind präs ⊏> **sein**.

Sinfonie die = **Symphonie**.

Sinfoniker, in der, die = **Symphoniker**.

Singapur nt Singapore.

singen (prät sang, perf hat gesungen) <> vi - **1.** [musizieren] to sing - **2.** salopp abw [aussa-gen] to squeal. <> vt to sing; **jn in den Schlaf singen** to sing sb to sleep.

Single ['sıŋ(g)l] (pl - ODER -s) <> der single person. <> die single.

Singular der GRAMM singular.

Sing|vogel der songbird.

sinken (prät sank, perf ist gesunken) vi - **1.** [einsinken, versinken] to sink - **2.** [abnehmen, niedersinken] to fall.

Sinn (pl -e) der - **1.** [Bedeutung, Wahrneh-mungsfähigkeit] sense; **im übertragenen Sinn** figuratively - **2.** [Gefühl]: **einen/keinen Sinn für etw haben** to have a/no feeling for sthg; **er hat keinen Sinn für Humor** he has no sense of humour.

Sinn|bild das symbol.

Sinnes|organ das sense organ.

sinngemäß <> adj: **eine sinngemäße Über-setzung von etw** a translation which con-veys the general meaning of sthg. <> adv: **etw sinngemäß wiedergeben** to give the gist of sthg.

sinnig <> adj clever. <> adv cleverly.

sinnlich <> adj - **1.** [körperlichen Genuss be-treffend] sensual - **2.** [Sinneswahrnehmung be-treffend] sensory. <> adv - **1.** [körperlichen Ge-nuss betreffend] sensually - **2.** [Sin-neswahrnehmung betreffend] through the senses.

sinnlos <> adj - **1.** [unsinnig] pointless - **2.** abw [maßlos] blind (vor Subst). <> adv - **1.** [unsinnig] pointlessly - **2.** abw [maßlos - zer-stören] in a blind rage; **sich sinnlos betrinken** to get blind drunk.

Sinnlosigkeit (*pl* -en) *die* - 1. [Wesen] pointlessness - 2. [Handlung] pointless action.

sinnvoll <> *adj* - 1. [befriedigend] meaningful - 2. [zweckmäßig] sensible. <> *adv* - 1. [befriedigend] meaningfully - 2. [zweckmäßig] sensibly.

Sintflut *die* - 1. [biblisch] Flood - 2. [Übermaß - von Post, Anrufen] flood.

Sippe (*pl* -n) *die* clan.

Sirene (*pl* -n) *die* siren.

Sirup *der* - 1. [für Saft] syrup - 2. [aus Zucker] treacle UK, molasses US.

Sitte (*pl* -n) *die* - 1. [Gepflogenheit] custom; **etw ist (bei jm) Sitte** sthg is the custom (with sb) - 2. *(ohne pl) fam* [Sittenpolizei] vice squad. ➡ **Sitten** *Pl* - 1. [Benehmen] manners - 2. [Moral] morals.

sittenwidrig <> *adj* morally offensive. <> *adv* in a morally offensive way.

sittlich <> *adj* moral. <> *adv* morally.

Situation (*pl* -en) *die* situation.

Sitz (*pl* -e) *der* - 1. [in Parlament, Möbelstück] seat - 2. *(ohne pl)* [von Institution, Firma] headquarters *Pl*; [von Regierung] seat - 3. *(ohne pl)* [von Kleidung] fit.

sitzen (*prät* saß, *perf* hat gesessen) *vi* - 1. [gen] to sit; **bleiben Sie doch bitte sitzen!** please don't get up!; **auf etw** (D) **sitzen** to be sitting on sthg - 2. [Mitglied sein]: **im Vorstand sitzen** to sit on the board (of directors); **im Parlament sitzen** to have a seat in parliament - 3. [sich befinden] to be; [Firma] to be based - 4. [passen] to fit - 5. *fam* [im Gefängnis sein] to be inside - 6. *fam* [Gelerntes]: **das Gedicht sitzt** the poem has stuck; **bei dem Meister sitzt jeder Handgriff** the expert can do every move in his sleep - 7. *fam* [nicht loswerden]: **auf etw** (D) **sitzen** to be stuck with sthg.

sitzen bleiben (*perf* ist sitzen geblieben) *vi* (*unreg*) - 1. [in Schule] to have to repeat a year - 2. [auf Waren]: **auf etw** (D) **sitzen bleiben** to be stuck with sthg.

sitzen lassen *vt* (*unreg*) *fam* [Person]: **jn sitzen lassen** [versetzen] to stand sb up; [verlassen] to walk out on sb.

Sitzlgelegenheit *die* seat.

Sitzlordnung *die* seating plan.

Sitzlplatz *der* seat.

Sitzung (*pl* -en) *die* [Konferenz - von Vorstand, Abteilung] meeting; [- von Bundestag] sitting.

Sizilien [zi'tsi:ljən] *nt* Sicily.

Skala (*pl* -s ODER -len) *die* scale; [von Farben] range.

Skalpell (*pl* -e) *das* scalpel.

Skandal (*pl* -e) *der* scandal.

skandalös <> *adj* scandalous. <> *adv* scandalously.

Skandinavien [skandi'nɑ:vjən] *nt* Scandinavia.

Skandinavier, in [skandi'nɑ:vjɐ, rɪn] (*mpl* -, *fpl* -nen) *der, die* Scandinavian.

skandinavisch [skandi'nɑ:vɪʃ] *adj* Scandinavian.

Skat *der* skat; **Skat spielen** to play skat.

Skelett (*pl* -e) *das* skeleton.

Skepsis *die* scepticism.

skeptisch <> *adj* sceptical. <> *adv* sceptically.

Ski (*pl* - ODER -er), **Schi** (*pl* - ODER -er) [ʃiː] *der* ski; **auf Skiern** on skis; **Ski fahren** ODER **laufen** to ski.

Skilfahren *das* skiing.

Skifahrer, in (*mpl* -, *fpl* -innen) *der & die* skier.

Skilgebiet *das* skiing area.

Skilanglauf *der (ohne Pl)* cross-country skiing.

Skiläufer, in *der, die* skier.

Skillehrer, in *der, die* skiing instructor.

Skillift *der* ski lift.

Skilpiste *die* ski run.

Skilurlaub *der* skiing holiday UK ODER vacation US.

Skizze (*pl* -n) *die* - 1. [Zeichnung] sketch - 2. [Text] outline.

skizzieren *vt* - 1. [zeichnen] to sketch - 2. [schreiben] to outline.

Sklave ['sklɑːvə] (*pl* -n) *der* slave.

Sklavin ['sklɑːvɪn] (*pl* -nen) *die* slave.

Skorpion (*pl* -e) *der* - 1. [Tier] scorpion - 2. ASTROL [Sternzeichen, Person] Scorpio; **Skorpion sein** to be a Scorpio.

Skrupel (*pl* -) *der* scruple.

skrupellos <> *adj* unscrupulous. <> *adv* unscrupulously.

Skulptur (*pl* -en) *die* sculpture.

Slalom (*pl* -s) *der* slalom (U).

Slawe (*pl* -n) *der* Slav.

Slawin (*pl* -nen) *die* Slav.

slawisch *adj* Slavonic.

Slip (*pl* -s) *der* briefs *Pl*.

Slowakei *die* Slovakia.

Slowenien *nt* Slovenia.

Smoking (*pl* -s) *der* dinner jacket UK, tuxedo US.

SMS *die (ohne Pl) (abk für* **Short Message System**) SMS, text (message).

Snowboard (*pl* -s) *das* snowboard; **Snowboard fahren** to go snowboarding.

so <> *adv* - 1. [auf diese Art] like this; [auf jene Art] like that; **lass es so, wie es ist** leave it as it is; **so ist es!** *fam* that's right!; **weiter so!** keep it up!; **gut so!** *fam* good; **so was** something like that - 2. [mit Adjektiv, Adverb] so; **eine so schwierige Prüfung** such a difficult exam - 3. [mit Substantiv, Pronomen]: **so einer/**

eine/eins such a; **so ein Pech!** what bad luck!; **so ein Unsinn!** what nonsense!; **so eine Art Jacke** a sort of jacket; **so mancher** many (people) - **4.** [mit Geste] this; **er war so groß** he was this big - **5.** fam [etwa] about, around - **6.** [bei Zitaten]:..., **so der Minister...,** said the minister - **7.** fam [ohne etwas] as it is - **8.** fam [kostenlos] for free - **9.** fam [im Allgemeinen]: **was hast du sonst noch so gemacht?** what else did you do, then? ◇ konj as; **laufen, so schnell man kann** to run as fast as one can; **so, dass** so that. ◇ interj: **so, das wars** so, that's it; **ach so!** oh, I see! ⬥ **so dass** konj = **sodass.** ⬥ **oder so** adv fam or so.

s. o. (abk für **siehe oben**), see above.

SO (abk für **Südost**) SE.

sobald konj as soon as.

Socke (pl -n) die sock.

Sockel (pl -) der [von Denkmal] plinth; [von Haus] base.

sodass, so dass konj so that.

soeben adv just.

Sofa (pl -s) das sofa.

soff prät ⊳ **saufen.**

sofort adv - **1.** [unverzüglich] immediately, straight away - **2.** fam [gleich] in a moment.

Softwarepaket das EDV bundled software (U), software package.

sog prät ⊳ **saugen.**

sogar adv even.

Sohle (pl -n) die [Fuß-, Schuhsohle] sole.

Sohn (pl **Söhne**) der son.

solang, solange konj as long as.

solche, r, s det such.

Soldat (pl -en) der soldier.

Solidaritätszuschlag der special tax levied to help finance the reconstruction of former East Germany.

sollen (perf hat **gesollt** ODER **sollen**) ◇ aux (perf hat **sollen**) - **1.** [als Aufforderung] to be supposed to; **soll ich das Fenster aufmachen?** shall I open the window? - **2.** [als Vermutung]: **er soll 108 Jahre alt sein** he is said to be 108 years old; **was soll das heißen?** what's that supposed to mean? - **3.** [konjunktivisch] should, ought to - **4.** [als Bedingung]: **sollte sie noch kommen, sag ihr ...** if she should turn up, tell her ... ◇ vi (perf hat **gesollt**): **die Ware soll nach München** the goods are meant to go to Munich; **soll er doch!** fam let him!; **was soll das?** fam what's all this?; **was solls!** fam what the hell! ◇ vt (perf hat **gesollt**): **warum soll ich das?** why should I?

solo adv - **1.** [im Solo] solo - **2.** fam [allein] on one's own.

Somalia nt Somalia.

Sommer (pl -) der summer.

Sommerferien Pl summer holiday UK ODER vacation US.

Sommersprosse die freckle.

Sommerzeit die summertime.

Sonate (pl -n) die MUS sonata.

Sonderangebot das special offer; **im Sonderangebot** on special offer.

sonderbar ◇ adj strange. ◇ adv strangely.

Sonderfahrt die amt [Zugfahrt] special train; [Busfahrt] special bus.

Sonderfall der special case.

sondergleichen adj unparalleled.

sonderlich ◇ adj - **1.** [besondere] particular - **2.** [sonderbar] peculiar. ◇ adv: **nicht sonderlich** not particularly.

Sondermüll der hazardous waste.

sondern konj but.

Sonderschule die special school.

Sonett (pl -e) das sonnet.

Sonnabend (pl -e) der Saturday; siehe auch **Samstag.**

sonnabends adv on Saturdays; siehe auch **samstags.**

Sonne (pl -n) die sun; **die Sonne geht auf/unter** the sun rises/sets; **die Sonne scheint** the sun is shining; **in der prallen Sonne** in the blazing sun.

sonnen ⬥ **sich sonnen** ref - **1.** [sich bräunen] to sun o.s. - **2.** [in Erfolg, Ruhm]: **sich in etw (D) sonnen** fig to bask in sthg.

Sonnenaufgang der sunrise.

Sonnenblume die sunflower.

Sonnenbrand der sunburn (U).

Sonnenbrille die sunglasses Pl.

Sonnencreme die sun cream.

Sonnenenergie die solar energy.

Sonnenfinsternis die solar eclipse.

Sonnenlicht das sunlight.

Sonnenschein der sunshine.

Sonnenschirm der sunshade.

Sonnenschutz der protection against the sun.

Sonnenstich der sunstroke.

Sonnenstrahl der sunbeam.

Sonnensystem das solar system.

Sonnenuhr die sundial.

Sonnenuntergang der sunset.

Sonnenwende die solstice.

sonnig adj sunny.

Sonntag (pl -e) der Sunday; siehe auch **Samstag.**

sonntags adv on Sundays; siehe auch **samstags.**

sonst ◇ adv - **1.** [außerdem] else; **sonst nichts** nothing else; **sonst noch etwas/jemand?** fam anything/anybody else?; **sonst noch Fragen?** any more questions? - **2.** [abgesehen hiervon] otherwise, apart from that; **wer/was (denn) sonst?** who/what else? - **3.** [gewöhnlich] usually. ◇ *konj* or (else).

sonstig *adj* other.

sonst wo *adv fam* somewhere else; [in Fragen] anywhere else.

sonst woher *adv fam* somewhere else; [in Fragen] anywhere else; **die Leute kamen (von) sonst woher** people came from all over; **das könnte sonst woher stammen** that could be from anywhere.

sonst wohin *adv fam* somewhere else; [in Fragen] anywhere else.

sooft *konj* whenever.

Sopran (*pl* -e) *der* - **1.** [Stimmlage - Frau] soprano; [- Knabe] treble - **2.** (ohne *pl*) [Stimme im Chor - Frauen] sopranos *Pl*; [- Knaben] trebles *Pl* - **3.** [Sängerin] soprano; [Sänger] treble.

Sorge (*pl* -n) *die* - **1.** [Problem] worry; **sich um jn/etw Sorgen machen** to worry about sb/sthg - **2.** [Pflege] care; **Sorge dafür tragen, dass...** to make sure that... ➡ **keine Sorge** *interj* [keine Angst] don't worry!

sorgen *vi*: **für etw sorgen** to see to sthg; **für jn sorgen** to look after sb. ➡ **sich sorgen** *ref*: **sich um jn/etw sorgen** to be worried about sb/sthg.

Sorgenkind *das* problem child.

Sorgerecht *das* custody.

Sorgfalt *die* care.

sorgfältig ◇ *adj* careful. ◇ *adv* carefully.

sorglos ◇ *adj* carefree. ◇ *adv* in a carefree way.

Sorte (*pl* -n) *die* sort, type. ➡ **Sorten** *Pl* WIRTSCH foreign currency (*sg*).

sortieren *vt* to sort.

Sortiment (*pl* -e) *das* range.

sosehr *konj* however much.

Soße (*pl* -n) *die* [für Nudeln, Pudding] sauce; [für Braten] gravy; [für Salat] dressing.

Soundkarte *die* EDV sound card.

Souvenir [suvəˈniːɐ] (*pl* -s) *das* souvenir.

souverän [zuvəˈrɛːn] ◇ *adj* - **1.** POL sovereign - **2.** [überlegen] masterful. ◇ *adv* - **1.** POL: **souverän herrschen** ODER **regieren** to have sovereign power - **2.** [überlegen] masterfully.

soviel *konj* as far as; **soviel ich weiß** as far as I know.

so viel *adv* so much; **so viel du willst** as much as you want; **noch einmal so viel** as much again; **dreimal so viel** three times as much; **so viel wie** as much as; **halb so viel (wie)** half as much/many (as).

soweit *konj* as far as; **soweit ich weiß** as far as I know.

so weit ◇ *adj*: **so weit sein** to be ready; **es ist so weit** it is time. ◇ *adv* on the whole; **so weit wie möglich** as far as possible; **so weit ich weiß** as far as I know.

so wenig *adv*: **so wenig wie möglich** as little as possible.

sowie *konj* as well as.

sowieso *adv* anyway.

Sowjetunion *die*: **die ehemalige Sowjetunion** the former Soviet Union.

sowohl *konj*: **sowohl A als auch B** A as well as B, both A and B.

sozial ◇ *adj* social; [Einstellung] socially aware; **sozialer Beruf** caring profession. ◇ *adv* socially; [handeln] in a socially aware manner; **sozial eingestellt** socially aware.

Sozialabgaben *Pl* social security contributions.

Sozialamt *das* social security office.

Sozialarbeiter, in *der*, *die* social worker.

Sozialdemokrat, in *der*, *die* Social Democrat.

Sozialfall *der*: **ein Sozialfall sein** to be dependent on state benefit.

Sozialhilfe *die* ≃ income support *UK*, ≃ welfare *US*.

Sozialismus *der* socialism.

sozialkritisch *adj* socially critical.

Sozialleistungen *Pl* social security benefits.

Sozialminister, in *der*, *die* social services minister.

Sozialpädagogik *die* social education.

Sozialpolitik *die* social policy.

Sozialstaat *der* welfare state.

Sozialsystem (*pl* -e) *das* social system.

Sozialversicherung *die* social security.

Sozialwohnung *die* ≃ council flat *UK*, ≃ low-rent apartment *US*.

Soziologie *die* sociology.

sozusagen *adv* so to speak.

Spachtel (*pl* -) *die* ODER *der* spatula.

spachteln *vt* [mit Spachtelmasse] to fill.

Spagat (*pl* -e) *der* - **1.** SPORT: **einen Spagat machen** to do the splits - **2.** *fig* balancing act.

Spagetti, Spaghetti *Pl* spaghetti (*U*).

Spalt (*pl* -e) *der* crack; **etw einen Spalt weit** ODER **breit öffnen** to open sthg a crack.

Spalte (*pl* -n) *die* - **1.** [Öffnung] crack - **2.** column.

spalten *vt* [gen, CHEM & PHYS] to split; [Substanz, Verbindung] to break down.

Spaltung (*pl* -en) *die* - **1.** [Teilen - von Land, Partei] splitting up (*U*); [Teilung - von Land, Partei] split - **2.** CHEM & PHYS splitting (*U*); [von Substanz] breaking down (*U*) - **3.** MED split.

Span (*pl* Späne) *der* shaving.

Spanferkel *das* KÜCHE suckling pig.

Spange (pl -n) die - 1. [Schmuckstück] slide UK, barrette US - 2. [Zahnspange] brace.

Spanien nt Spain.

Spanier, in ['ʃpaːnɪɐ, rɪn] (mpl -, fpl -nen) der, die Spaniard.

spanisch ⟨⟩ adj Spanish. ⟨⟩ adv: **spanisch sprechen** to speak Spanish.

Spanisch(e) das Spanish; siehe auch **Englisch(e)**.

spann prät ⟾ **spinnen**.

Spannbetttuch (pl -tücher) das fitted sheet.

Spanne (pl -n) die period; **in der/einer Spanne von... bis...** between... and...

spannen ⟨⟩ vt [Bogen] to draw; [Muskeln] to tense; [Schnur] to tighten; [Netz] to stretch out: ⟨⟩ vi - 1. fam [heimlich zusehen] to take a peep - 2. [zu eng sein] to be too tight. ⟾ **sich spannen** ref: **sich über etw** (A) **spannen** to span sthg.

spannend ⟨⟩ adj exciting. ⟨⟩ adv excitingly.

Spannkraft die vigour.

Spannung (pl -en) die - 1. [gen] tension - 2. [elektrisch] voltage; **unter Spannung stehen** to be live. ⟾ **Spannungen** Pl tension (sg).

Spannungsgebiet das area of tension.

Spannweite die wingspan.

Spanplatte die chipboard (U).

Sparbuch das savings book.

Sparbüchse die money box.

sparen ⟨⟩ vt to save; **spar dir deine dummen Bemerkungen** you can keep your silly remarks. ⟨⟩ vi to save; **an etw** (D) **sparen** to save on sthg; **für** ODER **auf etw** (A) **sparen** to save (up) for sthg.

Spargel (pl -) der asparagus (U).

Sparkasse die savings bank.

spärlich ⟨⟩ adj [Haare] sparse; [Beifall, Maßnahmen] meagre. ⟨⟩ adv [bekleidet] scantily; [bewachsen, vorhanden] sparsely.

Sparprogramm das economy drive.

sparsam ⟨⟩ adj economical; **mit etw sparsam sein** to be economical with sthg. ⟨⟩ adv economically; **mit etw sparsam umgehen** to be economical with sthg.

Sparsamkeit die economy.

Sparschwein das piggy bank.

Sparte (pl -n) die - 1. WIRTSCH line of business - 2. [in Zeitungen] section.

Spaß (pl Späße) der - 1. [Vergnügen] fun; **zum Spaß** for fun; **an etw** (D) **Spaß haben** to enjoy sthg; **jdm den Spaß verderben** to spoil sb's fun; **es macht mir Spaß** I enjoy it; **Auto fahren macht mir keinen Spaß** I don't enjoy driving; **viel Spaß!** have fun!; **da hört der Spaß auf** I draw the line at that; **mir ist der Spaß vergangen** it's no fun any more - 2. [Scherz] joke; [Streich] prank; **aus** ODER **im** ODER **zum Spaß** as a joke; **Spaß machen** [nicht ernst meinen] to be joking; **Spaß/keinen Spaß verstehen** to have a/no sense of humour.

spaßen vi to joke.

spät ⟨⟩ adj late; **bis in die späte Nacht** until late at night; **wie spät ist es?** what's the time? ⟨⟩ adv late; **sie kam mal wieder zu spät** she was late again; **von früh bis spät** from dawn to dusk.

Spaten (pl -) der spade.

später adj & adv later. ⟾ **bis später** interj see you later!

spätestens adv at the latest.

Spätlese (pl -n) die [Wein] late vintage.

Spätnachmittag der late afternoon.

Spätsommer der late summer.

Spätvorstellung die late show.

Spatz (pl -en) der - 1. [Tier] sparrow - 2. fam [Anrede] pet.

Spätzle Pl Süddt small round noodles, similar to macaroni.

spazieren (perf ist spaziert) vi to stroll.

spazieren gehen (perf ist spazieren gegangen) vi (unreg) to go for a walk.

Spaziergang der walk.

Spaziergänger, in (mpl -, fpl -nen) der, die person going for a walk.

SPD [ɛspeː'deː] (abk für **Sozialdemokratische Partei Deutschlands**) die SPD.

Specht (pl -e) der woodpecker.

Speck der - 1. [tierisch - von Schwein] pork fat; [- geräuchert, durchwachsen] bacon; [- von Wal, Robbe] blubber - 2. fam [menschlich] flab.

Spediteur, in [ʃpedi'tøːɐ, rɪn] (mpl -e, fpl -nen) der, die haulier; [für Umzug] furniture mover.

Spedition [ʃpedi'tsjoːn] (pl -en) die haulage firm; [für Umzug] removal firm.

Speer (pl -e) der - 1. SPORT javelin - 2. [Waffe] spear.

Speiche (pl -n) die spoke.

Speichel der saliva.

Speicher (pl -) der - 1. [Dachboden] loft - 2. EDV memory.

speichern vt - 1. [ansammeln, abspeichern] to store - 2. EDV to save.

speien ['ʃpaɪən] (prät spie, perf hat gespie(e)n) ⟨⟩ vt [Feuer, Lava] to spew; [Wasser] to spout. ⟨⟩ vi to vomit.

Speise (pl -n) die dish; **warme Speisen** hot food; **Speisen und Getränke** meals and drinks.

speisen geh ⟨⟩ vt - 1. [essen] to dine on - 2. [zu essen geben] to feed. ⟨⟩ vi to dine.

Speiseröhre die gullet.

Speisesaal der dining room.

Speisewagen der dining car.

Spektakel (pl -) ⟨⟩ das [Aufführung, Ereignis] spectacle. ⟨⟩ der racket.

Spektrum (*pl* Spektren) *das* spectrum.

Spekulant, in (*mpl* -en, *fpl* -nen) *der, die* speculator.

Spekulation (*pl* -en) *die* speculation.

spekulieren *vi* - **1.** *fam* [hoffen]: **auf etw** (*A*) **spekulieren** to hope to get sthg - **2.** WIRTSCH: **(auf etw** (*A*)) **spekulieren** to speculate (on sthg) - **3.** [mutmaßen]: **über etw** (*A*) **spekulieren** to speculate about sthg.

spendabel *adj fam* generous.

Spende (*pl* -n) *die* donation.

spenden <> *vt* to donate; [Blut] to give. <> *vi* to give.

Spender, in (*mpl* -, *fpl* -nen) *der, die* donor; **wer war der edle Spender?** who do I/we have to thank for this?

spendieren *vt*: **(jm) etw spendieren** to buy (sb) sthg.

Sperling (*pl* -e) *der* sparrow.

Sperma (*pl* -ta ODER Spermen) *das* sperm.

Sperre (*pl* -n) *die* - **1.** [Verbot & SPORT] ban; **eine Sperre verhängen/aufheben** to impose/lift a ban - **2.** [Absperrung] barrier - **3.** TECH locking device.

sperren *vt* - **1.** [einsperren]: **jn/etw in etw** (*A*) **sperren** to shut sb/sthg in sthg - **2.** [Konto, Kredit] to freeze; [Scheck] to stop - **3.** [Straße] to close - **4.** SPORT to ban. <> **sich sperren** *ref*: **sich (gegen etw) sperren** to resist (sthg).

Sperrlholz *das* plywood.

sperrig *adj* bulky.

Sperrlmüll *der* bulky refuse (*collected separately from normal refuse*).

Sperrlsitz *der* [in Zirkus] ringside seat.

Sperrlstunde *die* closing time.

Sperrung (*pl* -en) *die* - **1.** [von Straße] closing - **2.** [von Konto, Kredit] freezing; [von Scheck] stopping.

Spesen *Pl* expenses; **auf Spesen** on expenses.

Spezi (*pl* -s) *fam* <> *der Süddt* mate. <> *das* cola and orangeade.

spezialisieren <> **sich spezialisieren** *ref*: **sich auf etw** (*A*) **spezialisieren** to specialize in sthg.

Spezialist, in (*mpl* -en, *fpl* -nen) *der, die* specialist.

Spezialität (*pl* -en) *die* speciality UK, specialty US.

speziell <> *adj* special. <> *adv* specially.

spicken <> *vt* - **1.** KÜCHE: **etw mit etw spicken** to lard sthg with sthg - **2.** [ausstatten]: **etw mit etw spicken** [Text, Rede] to pepper sthg with sthg. <> *vi* to crib.

Spicklzettel *der fam* crib (sheet).

spie *prät* ⊳ **speien**.

Spiegel (*pl* -) *der* - **1.** [Gegenstand] mirror - **2.** [von Gewässern] surface - **3.** MED level.

Spiegellbild *das* reflection.

Spiegellei *das* fried egg.

spiegelglatt *adj* very slippery.

spiegeln *vi* to shine. <> **sich spiegeln** *ref*: **sich in etw** (*D*) **spiegeln** to be reflected in sthg.

Spiegelreflexlkamera *die* reflex camera.

Spiel (*pl* -e) *das* - **1.** [Vergnügen, Wettkampf] game; **machen wir noch ein Spiel?** shall we have another game?; **ein Spiel mit jm treiben** to play games with sb - **2.** [von Musiker] playing; [von Schauspieler] acting; [von Sportler, Mannschaft] game - **3.** TECH play - **4.** [Glücksspiel] gambling; **auf dem Spiel stehen** to be at stake; **etw aufs Spiel setzen** to risk sthg; **jn/etw aus dem Spiel lassen** to leave sb/sthg out of it.

Spiellautomat *der* slot machine, fruit machine UK.

spielen <> *vi* - **1.** [gen] to play; **mit jm/etw spielen** to play with sb/sthg - **2.** [als Schauspieler] to act - **3.** [Roman, Film] to be set - **4.** [Glücksspiel machen] to gamble; **um etw spielen** to play for sthg - **5.** [einsetzen]: **seine Beziehungen spielen lassen** to pull some strings; **seinen Charme spielen lassen** to use one's charm. <> *vt* to play; **Klavier/Saxofon spielen** to play the piano/saxophone; **Lotto spielen** to do the lottery; **den Unschuldigen spielen** to act ODER play the innocent.

spielend *adv* - **1.** [einfach] easily - **2.** [beim Spielen] through play.

Spieler (*pl* -) *der* - **1.** [Mitspieler] player - **2.** [Glücksspieler] gambler.

Spielerin (*pl* -nen) *die* - **1.** [Mitspielerin] player - **2.** [Glücksspielerin] gambler.

spielerisch <> *adj* - **1.** [locker] effortless - **2.** [Fähigkeit - in Sport, Musik] as a player; [- in Theater] as an actor. <> *adv* - **1.** [locker] effortlessly - **2.** [in Sport]: **eine spielerisch enttäuschende Mannschaft** a team that gave a disappointing performance.

Spiellfeld *das* [für Fußball, Hockey] field, pitch UK; [für Tennis, Federball, Volleyball] court.

Spiellfilm *der* feature film.

Spielkonsole (*pl* -n) *die* game ODER video console.

Spiellplan *der* - **1.** [von Theatern] programme - **2.** SPORT fixture list.

Spiellplatz *der* playground.

Spiellraum *der* leeway.

Spiellregel *die* rule.

Spiellverderber, in (*mpl* -, *fpl* -nen) *der, die* spoilsport.

Spiellwaren *Pl* toys.

Spiellzeug *das* - **1.** (ohne pl) [Spielsachen] toys *Pl* - **2.** [einzelnes Spielgerät] toy.

Spieß (*pl* -e) *der* spit; **am Spieß** spit-roasted; **den Spieß umdrehen** *fig* to turn the tables.

spießen *vt*: **etw auf etw** (*A*) **spießen** to skewer sthg with sthg.

Spießer, in (*mpl* -, *fpl* -nen) *der, die abw* (petit) bourgeois.

Spinat (*pl* -e) *der* spinach.

Spind *der* locker.

Spinne (*pl* -n) *die* spider.

spinnen (*prät* spann, *perf* hat gesponnen) <> *vt* to spin. <> *vi* - 1. *fam* [verrückt sein] to be crazy; **du spinnst!, spinnst du?** are you crazy? - 2. [arbeiten] to spin.

Spinnwebe (*pl* -n) *die* cobweb.

Spion (*pl* -e) *der* - 1. [Geheimagent] spy - 2. [Türspion] peephole.

Spionage [ʃpioˈnaːʒə] *die* spying; **Spionage betreiben** to spy.

spionieren *vi* - 1. [Spionage treiben] to spy - 2. *fam abw* [neugierig sein] to snoop.

Spionin (*pl* -nen) *die* spy.

Spirale (*pl* -n) *die* - 1. [gewundene Linie] spiral - 2. MED coil.

Spirituose (*pl* -n) *die amt* spirit.

Spiritus (*pl* -se) *der* spirit.

spitz <> *adj* - 1. [Ende, Schuh, Bogen, Bemerkung] pointed; [Bleistift, Messer, Nadel] sharp - 2. [Winkel] acute - 3. *fam* [geil]: **auf jn spitz sein** to have the hots for sb; **spitz darauf sein, etw zu tun** to be dying to do sthg. <> *adv* - 1. [zulaufen] to a point - 2. [bemerken] pointedly.

Spitze (*pl* -n) *die* - 1. [von Messer, Bleistift] point; [von Kirchturm, Baum] top; [von Berg] peak - 2. [Führung]: **an der Spitze** [in Betrieb, Partei] at the top; [in Rennen] in the lead - 3. [Höchstwert] maximum; **etw auf die Spitze treiben** *fig* to take sthg too far - 4. *fam* [besonders gut]: **Spitze sein** to be great - 5. [Bemerkung] gibe.

Spitzel (*pl* -) *der* informer.

spitzen *vt* - 1. [spitz machen] to sharpen - 2. [Ohren] to prick up.

Spitzenreiter, in *der, die* leader.

spitzfindig *abw* <> *adj* hairsplitting. <> *adv*: **spitzfindig argumentieren** to split hairs.

Spitzname *der* nickname.

Splitter (*pl* -) *der* [aus Holz, Glas] splinter; [von Bombe] fragment.

Splittergruppe *die* splinter group.

splittern (*perf* hat/ist gesplittert) *vi* to splinter.

splitternackt *adj* & *adv* stark naked.

SPÖ [ɛspeːˈʔøː] (*abk für* Sozialdemokratische Partei Österreichs) *die* Austrian Social Democratic Party.

Sponsor (*pl* -soren) *der* sponsor.

Sponsorin (*pl* -nen) *die* sponsor.

spontan <> *adj* spontaneous. <> *adv* spontaneously.

Sport *der* sport; **Sport treiben** to do sport.

Sportart *die* sport.

Sporthalle *die* sports hall.

Sportlehrer, in *der, die* sports teacher.

Sportler, in (*mpl* -, *fpl* -nen) *der, die* sportsman (sportswoman *die*).

sportlich <> *adj* - 1. [Leistung, Betätigung, Verhalten] sporting; [Person, Figur] sporty - 2. [leger] casual. <> *adv* - 1. [den Sport betreffend]: **sich sportlich betätigen** to do sport - 2. [leger] casually - 3. [fair] sportingly.

Sportplatz *der* playing field.

Sportverein *der* sports club.

Sportwagen *der* - 1. [Auto] sports car - 2. [Kinderwagen] pushchair *UK*, stroller *US*.

Spott *der* mockery.

spottbillig *adj* & *adv* dirt-cheap.

spotten *vi*: (**über jn/etw**) **spotten** to mock (sb/sthg).

spöttisch <> *adj* mocking. <> *adv* mockingly.

Spottpreis *der* knockdown price.

sprach *prät* ▷ **sprechen**.

Sprache (*pl* -n) *die* [gen] language; **in deutscher Sprache** in German; **jm die Sprache verschlagen** to leave sb speechless; **raus mit der Sprache!** *fam* out with it!

Sprachkenntnisse *Pl* knowledge (*U*) of languages.

Sprachkurs *der* language course.

Sprachlabor *das* language laboratory.

sprachlich <> *adj* linguistic. <> *adv* linguistically.

sprachlos <> *adj* [Staunen] speechless; **sprachlos sein** to be speechless. <> *adv* [dastehen] speechlessly.

Sprachreise *die* language trip.

sprang *prät* ▷ **springen**.

Spray [ʃpreː, spreː] (*pl* -s) *der ODER das* spray.

Sprechanlage *die* intercom.

sprechen (*präs* spricht, *prät* sprach, *perf* hat gesprochen) <> *vi* - 1. [gen] to talk, to speak; **wer spricht da, bitte?** [am Telefon] who's speaking?; **mit jm sprechen** to talk to sb; **über jn/etw sprechen, von jm/etw sprechen** to talk about sb/sthg; **er sprach davon, dass...** he mentioned that...; **zu jm sprechen** to speak to sb; **auf jn/etw zu sprechen kommen** to discuss sb/sthg - 2. [als Redner auftreten] to speak; **frei sprechen** to speak without notes - 3. [urteilend]: **es spricht für ihn, dass...** it's in his favour that...; **alles spricht dafür, dass...** there is every reason to believe that... <> *vt* - 1. [gen] to speak; **deutsch sprechen** to speak German; **jn sprechen** to speak to sb - 2. [Gebet] to say - 3. [reden mit] to speak to.

Sprecher, in (*mpl* -, *fpl* -nen) *der, die* - 1. [von Gruppe] spokesperson - 2. [von Nachrichten] newsreader.

Sprechstunde *die* [beim Arzt] surgery.

Sprechstunden|hilfe *die* (doctor's) receptionist.

Sprech|zimmer *das* consulting room.

spreizen *vt* to spread.

sprengen *vt* - **1.** [mit Sprengstoff - Brücke, Gebäude] to blow up; [- Tür] to blow open; **etw in die Luft sprengen** to blow sth up - **2.** [mit Wasser - Rasen, Garten] to water; [- Wäsche] to sprinkle with water.

Spreng|satz *der* explosive charge.

Spreng|stoff *der* explosive.

spricht *präs* ⊏▷ **sprechen**.

Sprich|wort (*pl* -wörter) *das* proverb.

sprießen (*prät* spross, *perf* ist gesprossen) *vi* to sprout.

Spring|brunnen *der* fountain.

springen (*prät* sprang, *perf* hat/ist gesprungen) ◇ *vi* - **1.** *(ist)* [hüpfen & SPORT] to jump; **auf etw** *(A)*/**aus etw/von etw springen** to jump onto/out of/from sthg - **2.** [Ball] to bounce - **3.** *(ist)* [kaputtgehen] to crack; **mein Vater hat 20 Euro springen lassen** *fam* my dad gave me 20 euros. ◇ *vt (hat)* SPORT [Salto] to do.

Sprint (*pl* -s) *der* sprint.

Spritze (*pl* -n) *die* - **1.** [Injektion] injection - **2.** [Injektionsgerät, Küchengerät] syringe - **3.** [Wasserspritze] hose.

spritzen (*perf* hat/ist gespritzt) ◇ *vi* - **1.** *(hat)* [herumspritzen - Flüssigkeit, Person] to splash; [- Fett] to spit - **2.** *(ist)* [in bestimmte Richtung] to splash - **3.** *(hat)* [eine Spritze geben] to give an injection. ◇ *vt (hat)* - **1.** [gen] to spray; **jn nass spritzen** to splash sb - **2.** [Medikament, Droge] to inject; **sich/jm ein Schmerzmittel spritzen** to inject o.s./sb with a painkiller.

Spritzer (*pl* -) *der* splash.

spröde ◇ *adj* - **1.** [trocken] dry - **2.** [brüchig] brittle - **3.** [Mensch, Art] standoffish. ◇ *adv* [unzugänglich] standoffishly.

spross *prät* ⊏▷ **sprießen**.

Sprosse (*pl* -n) *die* rung.

Spruch (*pl* Sprüche) *der* [Redensart] saying.

Sprudel (*pl* -) *der* sparkling mineral water.

sprudeln (*perf* hat/ist gesprudelt) *vi* - **1.** [gen] to bubble - **2.** [wenn Kohlensäure entweicht] to fizz.

Sprüh|dose *die* aerosol.

sprühen (*perf* hat/ist gesprüht) ◇ *vt (hat)* to spray. ◇ *vi* - **1.** *(ist)* [fliegen] to spray - **2.** *(hat)* [glänzen]: **vor Ideen sprühen** to be bubbling over with ideas; **vor Witz sprühen** to be sparklingly witty.

Sprüh|regen *der* drizzle.

Sprung (*pl* Sprünge) *der* - **1.** [Bewegung] jump - **2.** [Riss] crack; **einen Sprung haben** to be cracked.

Sprung|brett *das* springboard.

sprunghaft ◇ *adj* - **1.** [unstet] erratic - **2.** [abrupt steigend] rapid. ◇ *adv* - **1.** [unstet] erratically - **2.** [abrupt steigend] rapidly.

SPS [ɛs peː ɛs] (*abk für* **Sozialdemokratische Partei der Schweiz**) *die* Swiss Social Democratic Party.

Spucke *die* spit.

spucken ◇ *vi* - **1.** [ausspucken] to spit - **2.** *fam* [sich übergeben] to puke. ◇ *vt* [Olivenstein, Blut] to spit.

Spuk *der* haunting; **dem Spuk ein Ende machen** *fig* to return things to normal.

spuken *vi*: **in einem Haus spuken** to haunt a house; **spukt es hier?** is this place haunted?

Spule (*pl* -n) *die* - **1.** [Rolle] spool - **2.** ELEKTR coil.

Spüle (*pl* -n) *die* sink.

spülen ◇ *vt* - **1.** [Geschirr] to wash - **2.** [Wäsche] to rinse - **3.** [hinwegtragen]: **über Bord gespült werden** to be washed overboard. ◇ *vi* - **1.** [Geschirr reinigen] to do the dishes, to wash up *UK* - **2.** [Subj: Waschmaschine] to rinse - **3.** [hinunterspülen] to flush.

Spül|maschine *die* dishwasher.

Spül|mittel *das* washing-up liquid *UK*, dishwashing liquid *US*.

Spur (*pl* -en) *die* - **1.** [Anzeichen] clue - **2.** [Abdruck] track - **3.** [Fahrstreifen] lane; **die Spur wechseln** to change lanes - **4.** [kleine Menge - von Zutat] hint; [- von Substanz] trace; **eine heiße Spur** a strong lead; **jm/einer Sache auf der Spur sein** to be on sb's/sthg's track. ◆ **keine Spur** *interj* not at all!

spürbar ◇ *adj* - **1.** [fühlbar] noticeable - **2.** [deutlich] clear. ◇ *adv* - **1.** [fühlbar] noticeably - **2.** [sichtlich] clearly.

spüren *vt* - **1.** [fühlen] to feel; **du wirst die Konsequenzen zu spüren bekommen** you'll see what the consequences are - **2.** [ahnen] to sense.

Spuren|element *das* trace element.

spurlos *adv* - **1.** [verschwinden] without a trace - **2.** [ohne negative Auswirkungen]: **die Trennung ist nicht spurlos an ihr vorübergegangen** the separation has left its mark on her.

Spurt (*pl* -s ODER -e) *der* [Endspurt] sprint for the line; [Zwischenspurt] spurt.

sputen ◆ **sich sputen** *ref* to hurry up.

Squash [skvɔʃ] *das* squash.

Sri Lanka *nt* Sri Lanka.

s. S. (*abk für* **siehe Seite**) see p.

SS [ɛsˈɛs] *die* MIL (*abk für* **Schutzstaffel**) SS.

St. - **1.** (*abk für* **Sankt**) St - **2.** *abk für* **Stück**.

Staat (*pl* -en) *der* state; **die Staaten** *fam* the States.

Staaten|bund *der* confederation.

staatenlos *adj* stateless.

staatlich <> *adj* state. <> *adv* by the state; **staatlich anerkannt** government-approved; **staatlich geprüft** government-certified.

Staats|angehörigkeit *die* nationality; **doppelte Staatsangehörigkeit** dual nationality.

Staats|anwalt, anwältin *der, die* public prosecutor *UK*, district attorney *US*.

Staats|besuch *der* state visit.

Staats|bürger, in *der, die* citizen.

Staats|dienst *der* civil service.

staatseigen *adj* state-owned.

Staats|examen *das final exam taken by law and arts students at university.*

Staats|mann (*pl* -männer) *der* statesman.

Staatsober|haupt *das* head of state.

Staats|sekretär, in *der, die* ≃ permanent secretary.

Staats|sicherheitsdienst *der security service in former GDR.*

Staats|streich *der* coup (d'état).

staatstragend *adj* pro-government.

Staats|vertrag *der* international treaty.

Stab (*pl* Stäbe) *der* rod; [von Gitter] bar; [von Dirigent] baton; MIL [von Pilger] staff; [zum Stabhochsprung] pole.

Stäbchen (*pl* -) *das* stick; [Essstäbchen] chopstick.

Stabhochsprung *der* SPORT pole vault.

stabil *adj* - 1. [Haus, Währung, Wetter] stable - 2. [Person, Gesundheit] robust; [Möbel] solid.

stabilisieren *vt* to stabilize. ⇔ **sich stabilisieren** *ref* to stabilize.

stach *prät* ⤳ **stechen**.

Stachel (*pl* -n) *der* - 1. [von Tier] sting - 2. [von Pflanze] thorn.

Stachel|beere *die* gooseberry.

Stachel|draht *der* barbed wire (*U*).

stachelig, stachlig *adj* prickly.

Stadion [ˈʃtaːdjɔn] (*pl* Stadien) *das* stadium.

Stadium [ˈʃtaːdjʊm] (*pl* Stadien) *das* stage.

Stadt (*pl* Städte) *die* - 1. [Ort] town; [Großstadt] city; **die Stadt Köln** the city of Cologne - 2. *fam* [Stadtverwaltung] town/city council.

stadtbekannt *adj* well-known throughout the town/city.

Stadt|bummel *der* stroll through town.

Städtebau *der* urban development; [Planung] town planning.

Stadt|gespräch *das:* **Stadtgespräch sein** to be the talk of the town.

städtisch *adj* - 1. [der Stadtverwaltung] municipal - 2. [der Stadt] urban.

Stadt|kern *der* town/city centre.

Stadt|plan *der* street map.

Stadt|rand *der* outskirts *Pl*.

Stadt|rat *der* - 1. [Versammlung] town/city council - 2. [Person] town/city councillor.

Stadt|rätin *die* town/city councillor.

Stadtrund|fahrt *die* city tour.

Stadt|staat *der* city state.

Stadt|teil *der* district.

Stadt|tor *das* city gate.

Stadt|viertel *das* district, quarter.

Stadt|zentrum *das* town/city centre, downtown area *US*.

Staffel (*pl* -n) *die* SPORT relay race.

Staffelei (*pl* -en) *die* easel.

staffeln *vt* to grade.

stahl *prät* ⤳ **stehlen**.

Stahl (*pl* Stähle) *der* steel (*U*).

Stahl|industrie *die* steel industry.

Stall (*pl* Ställe) *der* [gen] barn; [für Kühe] cowshed; [für Pferde] stable; [für Kaninchen] hutch; [für Schweine] sty; [für Hühner] coop.

Stamm (*pl* Stämme) *der* - 1. [von Baum] trunk - 2. [Volk] tribe - 3. [Wortstamm] stem.

Stamm|baum *der* family tree; [von Tier] pedigree.

stammeln *vt & vi* to stammer.

stammen *vi* to come; **aus etw stammen** to come from sthg; **von jm stammen** [herrühren] to come from sb; [gemacht sein] to be made by sb; **das Bild stammt von meiner Nachbarin** the picture was painted by my neighbour; **aus etw stammen** [zeitlich] to date from sthg.

Stamm|gast *der* regular.

stämmig *adj* stocky.

Stamm|platz *der* usual seat.

Stamm|tisch *der* - 1. [Personen] *group of regular customers at a pub* - 2. [Treffen] *meeting of regular customers at a pub* - 3. [Tisch] *regulars' table at a pub.*

stampfen (*perf* hat/ist gestampft) <> *vi* - 1. *(hat)* [auftreten] to stamp; **mit den Füßen stampfen** to stamp one's feet - 2. *(ist)* [gehen] to stomp. <> *vt (hat)* [Kartoffeln] to mash.

stand *prät* ⤳ **stehen**.

Stand (*pl* Stände) *der* - 1. [auf Messe, Markt] stand - 2. *(ohne pl)* [das Stehen] standing position - 3. *(ohne pl)* [Stellung - von Sonne] position; [- von Zähler] reading; [- von Entwicklung]: **der Stand der Dinge** the state of things; **auf dem neuesten Stand sein** to be right up-to-date; **einen schweren Stand (bei jm) haben** to have a tough time (with sb); ≃ **instand, imstande, zustande**.

Standard (*pl* -s) *der* standard.

Stand-by [stɛntˈbaɪ] (*pl* -s) <> *das* [bei Elektrogeräten] standby mode; **in Stand-by** in standby mode. <> *der* [bei Flugreisen] standby flight.

Ständchen (*pl* -) *das* serenade; **jm ein Ständchen bringen** to serenade sb.

Ständer (*pl* -) *der* [Gestell] stand.

Standes|amt *das* registry office.

standesamtlich ⟨> *adj* registry-office. ⟨> *adv* at the registry office.

standesgemäß ⟨> *adj* in keeping with one's social status. ⟨> *adv* according to one's social status.

standhaft ⟨> *adj* steadfast. ⟨> *adv*: **sich standhaft weigern** to refuse consistently.

stand|halten *vi (unreg)*: **einer Sache (D) standhalten** to withstand sthg.

ständig ⟨> *adj* [Schmerzen, Belästigung] constant; [Mitglied] permanent. ⟨> *adv* constantly.

Stand|ort *der* - 1. [von Firma] location; **der Standort Deutschland** Germany as an industrial location - 2. [von Person, Pflanze] position.

Stand|punkt *der* point of view.

Stand|spur *die* hard shoulder *UK*, shoulder *US*.

Stange *(pl -n) die* pole; [aus Metall] rod; **eine Stange Zigaretten** a carton of cigarettes; **ein Anzug von der Stange** an off-the-peg suit; **eine Stange Geld** *fam fig* a fortune.

Stängel *(pl -) der* stalk.

stank *prät* ⊏> **stinken**.

stanzen *vt* - 1. [Formen, Teile] to press - 2. [Löcher] to punch.

Stapel *(pl -) der* [Haufen] pile.

Stapel|lauf *der* launching (of a ship).

stapeln *vt* to pile up. ⚫ **sich stapeln** *ref* [hingestellt werden] to be piled up; [sich türmen] to be piling up.

Star [ʃtɑːɐ̯] *(pl -e ODER -s) der* - 1. *(pl Stare)* [Vogel] starling - 2. *(pl Stars)* [Person] star.

starb *prät* ⊏> **sterben**.

stark *(kompar* **stärker**, *superl* **stärkste)* ⟨> *adj* - 1. [gen] strong - 2. [Sturm, Schnupfen, Verkehr] heavy - 3. *fam* [toll] great; **stark!** great! - 4. [dick - Brille, Wände, Träger] thick; [- Figur, Beine] large - 5. [mit Maßangabe] thick - 6. [Beteiligung] good; [Interesse] strong - 7. GRAMM: **starke Verben** strong verbs; **sich für jn/etw stark machen** to stand up for sb/sthg. ⟨> *adv* - 1. [intensiv - zuschlagen, schwanken, etw vermuten] strongly; [- regnen] heavily - 2. [viel] a lot.

Stärke *(pl -n) die* - 1. [gen] strength - 2. [von Brett, Platte, Papier] thickness - 3. [für Wäsche] starch; [Speisestärke] cornflour *UK*, cornstarch *US*.

stärken *vt* - 1. [kräftigen] to strengthen - 2. [Wäsche] to starch. ⚫ **sich stärken** *ref* to fortify o.s.

Stärkung *(pl -en) die* - 1. [Mahlzeit] refreshment - 2. [Aufbau] strengthening.

starr ⟨> *adj* - 1. [unbeweglich - Glieder, Material] stiff; [- Blick] fixed - 2. [System, Regeln] fixed. ⟨> *adv* [unflexibel] doggedly.

starren *vi* - 1. [sehen] to stare; **auf jn/etw starren** to stare at sb/sthg - 2. [emporragen]: **aus etw starren** to rise up out of sthg; **vor ODER von Dreck starren** to be absolutely filthy.

starrsinnig *adj* obstinate.

Start *(pl -s ODER -e) der* - 1. [gen] start - 2. [von Flugzeug] takeoff; [von Rakete] launch.

Start|bahn *die* runway.

starten *(perf hat/ist gestartet)* ⟨> *vi (ist)* - 1. [Läufer, Pferd, Rennauto] to start - 2. [Flugzeug] to take off - 3. [abreisen] to set off. ⟨> *vt (hat)* to start.

Stasi *(abk für Staatssicherheit) die ODER der* Stasi, security service in former GDR.

Statik *die* statics *(U)*.

Station *(pl -en) die* - 1. [im Krankenhaus] ward - 2. [Haltestelle, Halt] stop - 3. [für Forschung] plant.

stationär *adv*: **stationär behandeln** to treat as an in-patient.

Statist *(pl -en) der* extra.

Statistik *(pl -en) die* statistics *Pl.*

Statistin *(pl -nen) die* extra.

Stativ *(pl -e) das* tripod.

statt ⟨> *konj* instead of; **statt früher aufzustehen,...** instead of getting up earlier,... ⟨> *präp (+ G)* instead of.

stattdessen *adv* instead.

Stätte *(pl -n) die* geh place.

statt|finden *vi (unreg)* to take place.

stattlich ⟨> *adj* - 1. [Erscheinung, Größe] imposing - 2. [Summe, Anwesen] considerable. ⟨> *adv* considerably.

Statue [ˈʃtɑːtyə, ˈstɑːtyə] *(pl -n) die* statue.

Stau *(pl -s ODER -e) der* - 1. [von Autos] traffic jam; **im Stau stehen** to be stuck in a traffic jam - 2. *(ohne pl)* [von Wasser] build-up.

Staub *der* dust; **Staub wischen** to dust; **sich aus dem Staub machen** *fam fig* to make one's getaway.

stauben *vi* to be dusty.

staubig *adj* dusty.

staubsaugen *vt & vi* to vacuum.

Staub|sauger *(pl -) der* vacuum cleaner.

Stau|damm *der* dam.

Staude *(pl -n) die* perennial.

stauen *vt* [Wasser] to dam; [Blut] to staunch. ⚫ **sich stauen** *ref* - 1. [Autos] to form a tailback - 2. [sich ansammeln - Wut, Hitze] to build up; [- Luft] to accumulate.

staunen *vi* to be amazed; **über jn/etw staunen** to be amazed at sb/sthg.

Staunen *das* amazement.

Stau|see *der* reservoir.

Stauung *(pl -en) die* [von Wasser] damming *(U)*; [von Blut] staunching *(U)*.

Std. *abk für* **Stunde**.

Steak [ʃteːk, steːk] *(pl -s) das* KÜCHE steak.

stechen (*präs* sticht, *prät* stach, *perf* hat gestochen) <> *vt* - **1.** [verletzen - mit Stachel] to sting; [- mit Nadel] to prick; [- mit Spritze] to stick; [- mit Messer] to stab - **2.** [Spargel] to cut. <> *vi* - **1.** [Nadel, Dorn, Stachel] to prick; **mit etw in etw** (*A*) **stechen** to stick sthg in sthg - **2.** [Sonne] to beat down. ⬥ **sich stechen** *ref* [sich verletzen] to prick o.s.

stechend *adj* - **1.** [Blick] piercing - **2.** [Geruch] pungent - **3.** [Schmerz] stabbing - **4.** [Sonne] burning.

Steckibrief *der* description (*of a criminal*).

Steckidose *die* socket.

stecken <> *vt* to put; **sich** (*D*) **etw in etw** (*A*) **stecken** to put sthg in sthg; **etw an etw** (*A*) **stecken** to put sthg on sthg; **die Kinder ins Bett stecken** *fam* to put the children to bed. <> *vi* [gen] to be; **wo steckst du?** where have you got to?; **hinter etw** (*D*) **stecken** *fam* to be behind sthg.

stecken bleiben (*perf* ist stecken geblieben) *vi* (*unreg*) to get stuck.

Stecker (*pl* -) *der* plug.

Steckinadel *die* pin.

Steg (*pl* -e) *der* - **1.** [über Bach, Fluss] footbridge - **2.** [zu Boot] jetty.

stehen (*prät* stand, *perf* hat gestanden) *vi* - **1.** [aufrecht sein] to stand - **2.** [sich befinden] to be; **die Vase steht auf dem Tisch** the vase is on the table; **du stehst mir im Weg** you're in the way; **vor Schwierigkeiten/einer Wahl stehen** to be faced with difficulties/a choice; **unter Alkohol stehen** to be under the influence (of alcohol); **es steht 15:3** the score is 15-3; **wie steht es mit deiner Gesundheit?** how is your health? - **3.** [geschrieben sein]: **auf dem Schild steht, dass...** the notice says that...; **in der Zeitung steht, dass...** it says in the paper that... - **4.** [Uhr, Motor, Zeiger] to have stopped - **5.** [Kleid, Farbe, Frisur]: **jm stehen** to suit sb; **jm gut/nicht stehen** to suit/not to suit sb - **6.** GRAMM: **mit Akkusativ/Dativ stehen** to take the accusative/dative; **das Substantiv steht im Plural** the noun is in the plural - **7.** *fam* [mögen]: **auf jn stehen** to fancy sb; **auf etw** (*A*) **stehen** to be into sthg - **8.** [stellvertretend]: **für etw stehen** to stand for sthg - **9.** [verantwortlich]: **zu jm/etw stehen** to stand by sb/sthg - **10.** [beurteilend]: **wie stehst du dazu?** what do you think about that?; **alles stehen und liegen lassen** to drop everything; **wie stehts?** *fam* how are things?; **die Arbeit steht mir bis hier** I've had it up to here with this job. ⬥ **sich stehen** *ref fam* [verstehen]: **sich mit jm gut stehen** to get on with sb; **sich mit jm schlecht stehen** to not get on with sb.

Stehen *das*: **im Stehen** standing up.

stehen bleiben (*perf* ist stehen geblieben) *vi* (*unreg*) - **1.** [anhalten] to stop; **wo waren wir stehen geblieben?** where were we?; **die Zeit ist stehen geblieben** time has stood still - **2.** [nach Schlag, Erschütterung] to be left standing - **3.** [Satz] to stay.

stehen lassen (*perf* hat stehen lassen ODER stehen gelassen) *vt* (*unreg*) to leave.

Stehllampe *die* standard lamp.

stehlen (*präs* stiehlt, *prät* stahl, *perf* hat gestohlen) *vt* [entwenden] to steal; **sie kann mir gestohlen bleiben** *fam* she can get lost.

Steiermark *die* Styria.

steif <> *adj* stiff; [Sahne] thick. <> *adv* stiffly; **Sahne/Eiweiß steif schlagen** to beat cream until thick/egg white until stiff; **steif und fest behaupten** *fig* to swear blind.

Steiglbügel *der* stirrup.

steigen (*prät* stieg, *perf* ist gestiegen) *vi* - **1.** [hinaufsteigen]: **auf etw** (*A*) **steigen** [auf Leiter, Berg, Baum] to climb sthg; [auf Stuhl, Pferd] to climb onto sthg; [auf Fahrrad, Motorrad] to get on sthg - **2.** [hineinsteigen]: **in etw** (*A*) **steigen** [Zug, Straßenbahn] to get on sthg; [Auto, Taxi] to get into sthg - **3.** [aussteigen]: **aus etw steigen** [Zug, Straßenbahn] to get off sthg; [Auto, Taxi] to get out of sthg - **4.** [absteigen]: **von etw steigen** to get off sthg - **5.** [Flugzeug, Preis, Temperatur, Wasser] to rise; [Nebel] to lift; **einen Drachen steigen lassen** to fly a kite - **6.** [Spannung, Misstrauen] to grow - **7.** *fam* [Fest] to take place; **ein Fest steigen lassen** to have a party.

Steigerung (*pl* -en) *die* - **1.** [von Preis, von Dosis] increase - **2.** [von Leistung] improvement - **3.** GRAMM comparison.

steil <> *adj* - **1.** [Wand, Berg, Weg] steep - **2.** [Karriere, Aufstieg] rapid. <> *adv* - **1.** [senkrecht] steeply - **2.** [schnell] rapidly.

Steillhang *der* steep slope.

Stein (*pl* -e) *der* stone; **bei jm einen Stein im Brett haben** to be in sb's good books.

Steinbock *der* - **1.** [Tier] ibex - **2.** ASTROL Capricorn; **Steinbock sein** to be a Capricorn.

Steinbruch *der* quarry.

Steingut *das* earthenware.

steinig *adj* stony.

Steinkohle *die* coal.

Steinschlag *der* falling rocks *Pl*.

Steinzeit *die* Stone Age.

steirisch *adj* Styrian.

Steiß (*pl* -e) *der* coccyx.

Stelle (*pl* -n) *die* - **1.** [Platz] place; [kleine Stelle] patch; [im Text] passage; **an vierter Stelle** in fourth place - **2.** [Arbeitsplatz] job - **3.** [Amt] office - **4.** MATH figure; **eine Zahl mit vier Stellen** a four-figure number; **zwei Stellen nach/hinter dem Komma** two decimal places; **an deiner Stelle** if I were you.

stellen *vt* - **1.** [hinstellen] to put - **2.** [aufrecht stellen] to place upright - **3.** [Gerät, Aufgabe] to set; **jm eine Frage stellen** to ask sb a question; **der Wecker auf drei Uhr stellen** to set the alarm clock for three o'clock; **das Radio lauter/leiser stellen** to turn the radio up/down - **4.** [zur Verfügung stellen]: **jm etw stellen** to provide sb with sthg - **5.** [Diagnose, Prognose, Bedingung] to make - **6.** [Forderung, Antrag] to submit - **7.** [Dieb, Täter] to catch - **8.** FOTO to pose - **9.** [konfrontieren mit]: **jn vor etw** *(A)* **stellen** to present sb with sthg; **gut/schlecht gestellt sein** to be well/badly off; **auf sich** *(A)* **(selbst) gestellt sein** to have to fend for o.s. ◆ **sich stellen** *ref* - **1.** [sich hinstellen] to go and stand; **sich auf einen Stuhl stellen** to stand on a chair - **2.** [nicht ausweichen]: **sich einer Sache** *(D)* **stellen** to face sthg - **3.** [ablehnen]: **sich gegen jn/etw stellen** to be against sb/sthg - **4.** [unterstützen]: **sich hinter jn/etw stellen** to back sb/sthg - **5.** [so tun als ob]: **sich krank/schlafend stellen** to pretend to be ill/asleep - **6.** [sich melden] to give o.s. up; **sich gut mit jm stellen** to get on good terms with sb.

Stellen|angebot *das* job offer.

Stellen|gesuch *das* 'situation wanted' advertisement.

stellenweise *adv* in places.

Stellung *(pl -en) die* position; **in seiner Stellung als Vorsitzender** in his capacity as chairman; **(zu etw) Stellung nehmen** to comment (on sthg).

Stellungnahme *(pl -n) die* statement.

Stell|vertreter, in *der, die* deputy.

stemmen *vt* - **1.** [drücken] to press - **2.** SPORT to lift; **ein Gewicht stemmen** to lift a weight above one's head; **den Körper hoch stemmen** to push one's body up. ◆ **sich stemmen** *ref* [sich drücken] to push o.s. up; **sich gegen etw stemmen** [sich abstemmen] to brace o.s. against sthg; [sich wehren] to resist sthg.

Stempel *(pl -) der* [Gerät, Abdruck] stamp; [auf Briefmarke] postmark; [in Schmuckstück] hallmark.

stempeln ◇ *vt* [Stempel anbringen] to stamp; [Briefmarke] to cancel; [Post] to postmark; [Schmuckstück] to hallmark; **jn zu etw stempeln** [klassifizieren] to brand sb sthg. ◇ *vi*: **stempeln gehen** *fam* to be on the dole *UK* ODER welfare *US*.

Stengel *der* = **Stängel**.

Stenografie *(pl -n)*, **Stenographie** *(pl -n) die* shorthand.

Stepp|decke *die* quilt.

Steppe *(pl -n) die* steppe.

steppen ◇ *vi* [tanzen] to tap dance. ◇ *vt* [nähen] to backstitch.

sterben *(präs* **stirbt**, *prät* **starb**, *perf* **ist gestorben**) *vi* to die; **an etw** *(D)* **sterben** to die of sthg; **vor etw** *(D)* **sterben** *fam fig* to die of sthg.

sterblich *adj* mortal.

stereo ◇ *adj (unver)* stereo. ◇ *adv* in stereo.

Stereoan|lage *die* stereo (system).

steril *adj* sterile.

sterilisieren *vt* to sterilize.

Stern *(pl -e) der* star.

Stern|bild *das* constellation.

Stern|schnuppe *(pl -n) die* shooting star.

Stern|warte *(pl -n) die* observatory.

Stern|zeichen *das* star sign, sign of the zodiac.

stetig ◇ *adj* steady; [Belästigungen, Wiederholung] constant. ◇ *adv* steadily; [wiederholen] constantly.

stets *adv* always.

Steuer *(pl -* ODER *-)* ◇ *die* - **1.** *(pl -n)* [Abgabe] tax; **etw von der Steuer absetzen** to claim sthg against tax; **Steuern hinterziehen** to be guilty of tax evasion - **2.** *(pl -) fam* [Steuererbehörde]: **die Steuer** the taxman. ◇ *das (pl -)* [von Fahrzeug] (steering) wheel; [von Flugzeug] controls *Pl*; [von Schiff] helm.

Steuer|bord *das* starboard.

Steuererklärung *die* tax return.

Steuer|fahndung *die* [Behörde] *body responsible for carrying out investigations into cases of suspected tax evasion.*

Steuer|mann *(pl -männer) der* helmsman.

steuern *vt* - **1.** [lenken - Schiff, Fahrzeug] to steer; [- Flugzeug] to fly; [- Spielzeugauto] to control - **2.** [beeinflussen] to guide, to steer - **3.** [organisieren] to organize - **4.** [kontrollieren & TECH] to control.

Steuer|oase *die* tax haven.

Steuer|rad *das* [von Auto] steering wheel; [von Flugzeug] wheel; [von Schiff] wheel, helm.

Steuerung *(pl -en) die* - **1.** [Lenken - von Auto, Schiff] steering; [- von Flugzeug] flying; [- von Modellflugzeug] controlling - **2.** [Steuergerät] controls *Pl*.

Steuer|zahler, in *(mpl -, fpl -nen) der, die* taxpayer.

Steward, Stewardess ['stjuːɐt ODER ʃtjuːɐt, 'stjuːɐdɛs ODER ʃtjuːɐdɛs] *(mpl -s, fpl -en) der, die* steward (stewardess *die*).

Stich *(pl -e) der* - **1.** [Einstich - von Messer] stab; [- von Biene, Wespe] sting; [- von Mücke] bite - **2.** [Färbung] tinge - **3.** [beim Nähen & MED] stitch - **4.** [Schmerz] stabbing pain; [in der Seite] stitch - **5.** [Bemerkung] gibe - **6.** [beim Kartenspiel] trick - **7.** [Bild] engraving; **einen Stich haben** *salopp* [verrückt sein] to be nuts; [ungenießbar werden] to have gone ODER be off; **jn/etw im Stich lassen** [verlassen] to leave sb/sthg; [fallen lassen] to abandon sb/sthg; **wenn mich mein Orientierungssinn nicht im Stich lässt** if my sense of direction isn't deceiving me.

sticheln ◇ *vt* to tease. ◇ *vi* to make snide remarks.

stichhaltig ◇ *adj* valid; [Beweis] conclusive. ◇ *adv* validly; [beweisen, widerlegen] conclusively.

Stich|probe *die* - 1. [Menge] (random) sample - 2. [Handlung] spot check.

sticht *präs* ▷ **stechen**.

Stich|tag *der* effective date.

Stich|wahl *die* final ballot.

Stich|wort (*pl* -e *ODER* -wörter) *das* - 1. [Notiz] note - 2. [Eintrag] headword - 3. [Schlüsselwort] keyword - 4. *fig* [im Theater]: **das Stichwort geben** to give the cue.

sticken *vt & vi* to embroider.

Stickerei (*pl* -en) *die* embroidery.

stickig *adj* stuffy.

Stick|stoff *der* nitrogen.

Stief|bruder *der* stepbrother.

Stiefel (*pl* -) *der* boot.

Stief|kind *das* stepchild.

Stief|mutter *die* stepmother.

Stief|mütterchen (*pl* Stiefmütterchen) *das* pansy.

Stief|schwester *die* stepsister.

Stief|vater *der* stepfather.

stieg *prät* ▷ **steigen**.

Stiel (*pl* -e) *der* - 1. [von Blume, Frucht, Trinkglas] stem - 2. [Griff] handle; [von Lutscher, Eis] stick.

Stier (*pl* -e) *der* - 1. [Tier] bull - 2. [Sternzeichen, Person] Taurus; **Stier sein** to be a Taurus.

stieß *prät* ▷ **stoßen**.

Stift (*pl* -e) *der* - 1. [Schreibutensil] pen; [Bleistift] pencil; [Buntstift] crayon - 2. *fam* [Lehrling] *name given to apprentices during their first year* - 3. TECH [aus Holz] peg; [aus Metall] pin.

stiften *vt* - 1. [gründen] to found - 2. [spenden] to donate; [ausgeben] to pay for - 3. [hervorrufen - Unruhe, Aufregung] to cause - 4. [spendieren] to buy.

Stiftung (*pl* -en) *die* - 1. [Institution] foundation - 2. [Schenkung] donation.

Stil (*pl* -e) *der* style; **in diesem Stil kann es nicht weitergehen!** it can't go on like this!; **im großen Stil** on a grand scale.

still ◇ *adj* - 1. [ruhig, lautlos, stressfrei] quiet; **im Stillen** secretly - 2. [bewegungslos] still - 3. [ohne Worte - Protest, Gebet, Leiden] silent - 4. [heimlich] secret. ◇ *adv* - 1. [ruhig, lautlos, stressfrei] quietly - 2. [bewegungslos] still; **sie stand still da** she was standing still - 3. [ohne Worte - protestieren, beten, leiden] silently.

Stille *die* - 1. [Ruhe] quiet - 2. [Schweigen] silence; **in aller Stille heiraten** to get married in secret.

Stilleben *das* = **Stillleben**.

stilllegen *vt* = **stilllegen**.

stillen ◇ *vt* - 1. [die Brust geben] to breastfeed - 2. [Schmerz] to stop - 3. [Hunger, Bedürfnis] to satisfy; [Durst] to quench. ◇ *vi* to breastfeed.

Stille Ozean *der*: **der Stille Ozean** the Pacific (Ocean).

stillgestanden *pp* ▷ **stillstehen**.

still|halten *vi* (*unreg*) [sich nicht wehren] to offer no resistance.

still halten *vt & vi* (*unreg*) to keep still.

Stillleben (*pl* -) *das* still life.

stilllegen *vt* to close down.

stillschweigend ◇ *adj* tacit. ◇ *adv* tacitly.

still|sitzen *vi* (*unreg*) [ruhig sein] to sit still.

Still|stand *der* stopping; [von Maschine] stoppage; [von Verhandlung] deadlock; [von Entwicklung] halt; **zum Stillstand kommen** [Verkehr, Produktion] to come to a standstill; [Verhandlungen] to reach a deadlock; [Blutungen] to stop.

still|stehen *vi* (*unreg*) - 1. [Bewegung stoppen] to stand still; **stillgestanden!** MIL attention! - 2. [Telefon]: **das Telefon stand keine Minute still** the phone never stopped ringing - 3. [stillliegen - Verkehr, Produktion] to be at a standstill; [- Uhr, Maschine] to have stopped.

Stimm|band (*pl* -bänder) *das* vocal cord.

stimmberechtigt *adj* entitled to vote.

Stimm|bruch *der*: **er ist im Stimmbruch** his voice is breaking.

Stimme (*pl* -n) *die* - 1. [gen] voice - 2. [Wählerstimme] vote; **seine Stimme abgeben** to vote; **sich der Stimme enthalten** to abstain - 3. MUS part.

stimmen ◇ *vi* - 1. [richtig sein] to be right *ODER* correct; [Gerücht, Aussage] to be true *ODER* correct; **das stimmt nicht!** that's not true! - 2. [wählen]: **für/gegen jn/etw stimmen** to vote for/against sb/sthg - 3. [übereinstimmen] to be right; **stimmt so!** keep the change! ◇ *vt* MUS to tune.

Stimm|gabel *die* tuning fork.

stimmhaft *adj* voiced.

Stimm|lage *die* voice; [beim Singen] register.

stimmlos *adj* voiceless, unvoiced.

Stimm|recht *das* right to vote.

Stimmung (*pl* -en) *die* - 1. [Laune] mood; **guter/schlechter Stimmung sein** to be in a good/bad mood - 2. [Atmosphäre] atmosphere.

Stimm|zettel *der* ballot paper.

stinken (*prät* stank, *perf* hat gestunken) *vi* - 1. *abw* [schlecht riechen]: **(nach etw) stinken** to stink (of sthg) - 2. *salopp* [reichen]: **mir stinkt es** I'm fed up to the back teeth.

Stipendium (*pl* -en) *das* [als Unterstützung] grant; [als Auszeichnung] scholarship.

stirbt *präs* ▷ **sterben**.

Stirn (*pl* -en) *die* forehead.

stöbern *vi* to rummage (around).

stochern *vi*: **(mit etw) in etw (A) stochern** to poke at sthg (with sthg); **im Essen stochern** to pick at one's food.

Stock (*pl* Stöcke *ODER* -s) *der* - **1.** (*pl* Stöcke) [Stab] stick; [von Dirigent] baton - **2.** (*pl* -s) [Stockwerk] floor, storey.

stockdunkel *adj* pitch-dark.

stocken *vi* [zum Stillstand kommen - Verkehr] to be held up; [- Gespräch] to falter; [- Produktion] to be interrupted; [- Verhandlungen] to break off.

stockend <> *adj* faltering; **es herrscht stockender Verkehr** traffic is moving slowly. <> *adv* falteringly.

Stockung (*pl* -en) *die* [Stillstand - von Verkehr] hold-up; [- von Verhandlungen] break; [- von Produktion] interruption.

Stock|werk *das* floor, storey.

Stoff (*pl* -e) *der* - **1.** [Tuch] material - **2.** [Inhalt] subject matter; [zu Roman, Film] material - **3.** [Substanz] substance.

Stoff|wechsel *der* metabolism.

stöhnen *vi* to groan.

Stollen (*pl* -) *der* - **1.** [Gang] gallery, tunnel - **2.** [Gebäck] stollen, *sweet bread loaf made with dried fruit and marzipan, eaten at Christmas.*

stolpern (*perf* ist gestolpert) *vi* to stumble; **über etw** (A) **stolpern** to trip over sthg.

stolz <> *adj* proud; **auf jn/etw stolz sein** to be proud of sb/sthg. <> *adv* proudly.

Stolz *der* pride.

stopfen <> *vt* - **1.** [ausbessern] to darn - **2.** [hineinstopfen] to stuff - **3.** [zustopfen] to plug - **4.** [füllen - Pfeife] to fill; [- Geflügel] to stuff. <> *vi* [Stuhlgang erschweren] to cause constipation.

stopp *interj* [halt] stop!

stoppen <> *vt* - **1.** [anhalten] to stop - **2.** [messen - Person, Lauf] to time. <> *vi* [anhalten] to stop.

Stopp|schild *das* stop sign.

Stopp|uhr *die* stopwatch.

Stöpsel (*pl* -) *der* [Gegenstand - von Becken] plug; [- von Flasche] stopper.

Storch (*pl* Störche) *der* stork.

stören <> *vt* - **1.** [belästigen] to disturb; [unterbrechen] to interrupt - **2.** [missfallen] to bother - **3.** [beeinträchtigen - Verhältnis] to spoil; [- Radioempfang, Fernsehempfang] to interfere with. <> *vi* [belästigend sein]: **darf ich mal kurz stören?** may I disturb you for a moment?; **'bitte nicht stören!'** 'do not disturb!'

Störung (*pl* -en) *die* - **1.** [Belästigung] disturbance; [von Zeremonie] disruption - **2.** [Funktionsstörung - von Gerät] fault; [- von Organ] disorder.

Stoß (*pl* Stöße) *der* - **1.** [Schlag] push, shove; [mit dem Fuß] kick; [in Auto, Schiff, Zug] jolt - **2.** [Stapel] pile.

stoßen (*präs* stößt, *prät* stieß, *perf* hat/ist gestoßen) <> *vt* (hat) - **1.** [schubsen] to push; [mit

der Faust] to punch; [mit dem Fuß] to kick - **2.** SPORT [Kugel] to put; [Gewichte] to press - **3.** [aufmerksam machen] **jn auf etw** (A) **stoßen** to point sthg out to sb. <> *vi* - **1.** (ist) [berühren]: **an etw** (A) **stoßen** to bang sthg; **gegen etw** (A) **stoßen** to bang into sthg; [Fahrzeug] to crash into sthg - **2.** (ist) [angrenzen]: **an etw** (A) **stoßen** [Grundstück] to border on sthg; [Zimmer] to be next to sthg - **3.** (ist) [finden]: **auf jn/ etw stoßen** to come across sb/sthg; **auf Erdöl stoßen** to strike oil - **4.** (ist) [auf Reaktion]: **auf etw** (A) **stoßen** to meet with sthg - **5.** (ist) [sich treffen mit]: **zu jm stoßen** to meet up with sb. **» sich stoßen** *ref* - **1.** [sich wehtun] to bang o.s. - **2.** [nicht mögen]: **sich an etw** (D) **stoßen** to take exception to sthg.

stößt *präs* |> **stoßen.**

stottern *vi* [sprechen] to stutter, to stammer.

Str. (*abk für* Straße) St.

Strafe (*pl* -n) *die* - **1.** [Bestrafung] punishment - **2.** [Geldbuße] fine - **3.** [in Gefängnis] sentence.

strafen *vt* to punish.

Straf|zettel *der* ticket.

Strahl (*pl* -en) *der* - **1.** [Wasserstrahl] jet - **2.** [Lichtstrahl] ray; [von Scheinwerfer, Licht, Laser] beam. **» Strahlen** *Pl* [Energiewellen] rays.

strahlen *vi* - **1.** [lachen] to beam - **2.** [leuchten] to shine - **3.** [Strahlen abgeben] to radiate - **4.** [glänzen] to sparkle.

Strähne (*pl* -n) *die* strand.

Strand (*pl* Strände) *der* beach; **am Strand** on the beach.

Straße (*pl* -n) *die* - **1.** [in Stadt] street - **2.** [Landstraße] road; **auf der Straße sitzen** *fam* [arbeitslos sein] to be out of work; [ohne Wohnung sein] to be on the streets; **auf die Straße gehen** [demonstrieren] to take to the streets; [anschaffen gehen] to walk the streets. **» auf offener Straße** *adv* in public.

Straßen|bahn *die* tram UK, streetcar US.

Straßen|karte *die* road map.

Straßen|schild *das* street sign.

Strategie (*pl* -n) *die* strategy.

sträuben **» sich sträuben** *ref* - **1.** [Federn] to become ruffled; [Fell] to bristle - **2.** [sich wehren]: **sich gegen etw sträuben** to resist sthg.

Strauch (*pl* Sträucher) *der* bush.

Strauß (*pl* Sträuße *ODER* -e) *der* - **1.** (*pl* Sträuße) [Blumen] bunch of flowers - **2.** (*pl* Strauße) [Vogel] ostrich.

streben (*perf* hat/ist gestrebt) *vi* (hat) [trachten]: **nach etw streben** to strive for sthg.

Streber, in (*mpl* -, *fpl* -nen) *der, die abw* swot UK, grind US.

Strecke (*pl* -n) *die* - **1.** [Weg] route; **diese Strecke bin ich noch nie gefahren** I've never been this way before - **2.** [Entfernung] distance

- **3.** [von Straße] stretch - **4.** [von Eisenbahn] line; [von Schienen] track; **auf offener Strecke** between stations - **5.** MATH (straight) line.

strecken vt - **1.** [ausstrecken] to stretch - **2.** [Hals] to crane - **3.** [verdünnen] to thin down; [Droge] to cut. ⟐ **sich strecken** ref - **1.** [sich recken] to stretch - **2.** [sich hinlegen] to stretch out.

streckenweise adv in places.

Streich (pl -e) der [zum Ärgern] trick; **jm einen Streich spielen** eigtl & fig to play a trick on sb.

streicheln ⟐ vt to stroke. ⟐ vi: **über etw (A) streicheln** to stroke sthg.

streichen (prät **strich**, perf **hat/ist gestrichen**) ⟐ vt (hat) - **1.** [mit Farbe] to paint; **'frisch gestrichen'** 'wet paint' - **2.** [Satz, Passage] to delete; **etw von einer Liste streichen** to cross sthg off a list - **3.** [schmieren] to spread - **4.** [Subvention, Auftrag] to cancel. ⟐ vi - **1.** (hat): **sich (D) über den Kopf streichen** to stroke one's head - **2.** (hat) [mit Farbe] to paint.

Streicher, in (mpl -, fpl -nen) der, die: **die Streicher** the strings.

Streich|holz das match.

Streich|instrument das stringed instrument.

Streichung (pl -en) die - **1.** [von Subvention, Auftrag] cancellation; **Streichungen** [an Etat] cuts - **2.** [im Text] deletion.

Streife (pl -n) die patrol.

streifen (perf **hat/ist gestreift**) vt (hat) - **1.** [berühren] to brush against - **2.** [ziehen]: **etw über etw (A) streifen** to pull sthg over sthg; **etw von etw streifen** to pull sthg off sthg - **3.** [Thema] to touch on.

Streifen (pl -) der - **1.** [Stück, Band] strip - **2.** [Strich] stripe; [auf Fahrbahn] line.

Streifen|wagen der patrol car.

Streik (pl -s) der strike; **in (den) Streik treten** to go on strike.

streiken vi - **1.** [im Streik stehen] to strike - **2.** [Motor, Maschine] to pack up.

Streit der argument; **Streit mit jm haben** to argue with sb.

streiten (prät **stritt**, perf **hat gestritten**) vi - **1.** [sich auseinander setzen]: **(über etw (A)) streiten** to argue (about sthg) - **2.** geh [kämpfen]: **gegen/für etw streiten** to fight against/ for sthg. ⟐ **sich streiten** ref: **sich (mit jm/ um etw) streiten** to argue (with sb/about sthg).

Streit|frage die contentious issue.

Streitigkeiten Pl disputes.

Streitkräfte Pl armed forces.

streitsüchtig adj quarrelsome.

streng ⟐ adj - **1.** [Eltern, Kontrolle, Diät, Regel] strict; [Blick] stern; [Maßnahme] stringent - **2.** [Geruch, Geschmack] pungent - **3.** [Gesicht, Frisur, Winter] severe. ⟐ adv - **1.** [erziehen, ver-

bieten, einhalten] strictly; [überwachen] closely; [ansehen] sternly - **2.** [durchdringend]: **streng riechen** to smell pungent.

Strenge die [von Erziehung, Kontrolle, Gesetz] strictness; [von Blick] sternness; [von Maßnahme] stringency.

streng genommen adv strictly speaking.

Stress der stress; **mach keinen Stress!** fam stay cool!

Streu die [aus Stroh] straw.

streuen ⟐ vt [Salz, Gewürze] to sprinkle; [Dünger, Stroh, Gerüchte] to spread; [Futter, Samen] to scatter. ⟐ vi [mit Sand] to grit; [mit Salz] to put down salt.

streunen (perf **hat/ist gestreunt**) vi - **1.** [irgendwo] to roam around; [Hund, Katze] to stray - **2.** (ist) [irgendwohin] to roam.

Streusel (pl -) der ODER das crumble topping.

strich prät ⟐ **streichen**.

Strich (pl -e) der - **1.** [Linie] line; [Gedankenstrich] dash; [von Pinsel] stroke - **2.** [Streichen] stroke - **3.** fam [Prostitution] prostitution; **auf den Strich gehen** fam to walk the streets; **jm einen Strich durch die Rechnung machen** to wreck sb's plans. ⟐ **unter dem Strich** adv at the end of the day.

Strick (pl -e) der rope.

stricken vt & vi to knit.

Strick|jacke die cardigan.

Strick|leiter die rope ladder.

Strick|nadel die knitting needle.

Strickzeug das (ohne pl) [Handarbeit] knitting.

striegeln vt to groom.

Striemen (pl -) der weal.

Striptease ['ʃtrɪptiːs, 'strɪptiːs] der ODER das striptease.

stritt prät ⟐ **streiten**.

strittig adj contentious.

Stroh das straw.

Stroh|dach das thatched roof.

Strolch (pl -e) der - **1.** abw [Mann] ruffian - **2.** fam hum [Schlingel] rascal.

Strom (pl Ströme) der - **1.** [elektrisch] electricity - **2.** [Fluss] river - **3.** [Strömung] current - **4.** [Menge] stream; **es regnet** ODER **gießt in Strömen** it's pouring down; **gegen den Strom schwimmen** to swim against the tide.

stromabwärts adv downstream.

stromaufwärts adv upstream.

Strom|ausfall der power failure.

strömen (perf **ist geströmt**) vi to stream.

Strom|kreis der (electrical) circuit.

Strom|stärke die current strength.

Strömung (pl -en) die - **1.** [Strom] current - **2.** [Bewegung] current of thought.

Strom|zähler der electricity meter.

Strophe (*pl -n*) *die* verse.

strotzen *vi*: **vor Gesundheit strotzen** to be bursting with health; **vor Dreck strotzen** to be filthy.

Strudel (*pl -*) *der* - **1.** [Wirbel] whirlpool - **2.** [Kuchen] strudel.

Struktur (*pl -en*) *die* - **1.** [von Systemen] structure - **2.** [von Material] texture.

Strumpf (*pl Strümpfe*) *der* - **1.** [beinlang] stocking - **2.** [Socke] sock.

Strumpf|hose *die* tights *Pl UK*, pantyhose *(U) US*.

struppig *adj* shaggy.

Stube (*pl -n*) *die* - **1.** *fam* [Wohnzimmer] living room - **2.** [Raum] room.

stubenrein *adj* house-trained.

Stück (*pl -e*) *das* [gen] piece; [von Butter, Zucker] lump.

stückeln *vi* to add patches.

Student (*pl -en*) *der* student.

Studentenwohn|heim *das* hall of residence.

Studentin (*pl -nen*) *die* student.

Studie ['ʃtuːdjə] (*pl -n*) *die* study.

Studienabschluss (*pl -schlüsse*) *der* degree.

Studien|fach *das* subject.

Studiengang (*pl -gänge*) *der* course (of study).

Studien|platz *der* university/college place.

Studien|rat *der secondary school teacher.*

Studien|rätin *die secondary school teacher.*

studieren [ʃtu'diːrən] *vt & vi* to study.

Studio (*pl -s*) *das* studio.

Studium ['ʃtuːdjʊm] (*pl Studien*) *das* - **1.** [gen] study - **2.** (*ohne pl*) [Ausbildung] studies *Pl.*

Stufe (*pl -n*) *die* - **1.** [von Treppen] step; 'Vorsicht Stufe!' 'mind the step!' - **2.** [Stand] stage - **3.** [in einer Hierarchie] level - **4.** [Schaltstufe] setting - **5.** [Abstufung] degree.

Stuhl (*pl Stühle*) *der* [Sitzmöbel] chair.

Stuhlgang *der (ohne pl)* stool.

stülpen *vt*: **etw nach außen stülpen** to turn sthg inside out; **etw auf/über etw (A) stülpen** to put sthg onto/over sthg.

stumm ◇ *adj* - **1.** [sprechunfähig] dumb - **2.** [schweigend] silent. ◇ *adv* - **1.** [sprechunfähig] dumbly - **2.** [schweigend] silently.

Stummel (*pl -*) *der* [von Arm, Bein, Schwanz] stump; [von Zigarette] butt; [von Kerze, Bleistift] stub.

Stumm|film *der* silent movie.

Stümper (*pl -*) *der abw* bungler.

Stümperin (*pl -nen*) *die abw* bungler.

stumpf ◇ *adj* - **1.** [Messer, Spitze] blunt - **2.** [Fell, Haar, Lack] dull - **3.** [Person, Ausdruck]

apathetic - **4.** MATH obtuse. ◇ *adv* - **1.** [leben, blicken] apathetically - **2.** [nicht scharf, nicht spitz] bluntly - **3.** [glanzlos] dully.

Stumpf (*pl Stümpfe*) *der* stump; [von Kerze] stub.

Stumpfsinn *der* - **1.** [Monotonie] monotony - **2.** [geistige Abwesenheit] apathy.

Stunde (*pl -n*) *die* - **1.** [Zeiteinheit] hour - **2.** [Unterrichtsstunde] lesson. ➤ **zu später Stunde** *adv geh* at a late hour.

stunden *vt*: **jm eine Zahlung stunden** to give sb longer to make a payment.

Stunden|geschwindigkeit *die*: **eine Stundengeschwindigkeit von 100 km** a speed of 100 km/h.

Stundenkilo|meter *Pl* kilometres per hour.

stundenlang ◇ *adj* lasting for hours; **nach stundenlangem Warten** after waiting for hours. ◇ *adv* for hours.

Stunden|lohn *der* hourly rate.

Stunden|plan *der* timetable.

Stunden|zeiger *der* hour hand.

stündlich ◇ *adv* - **1.** [jede Stunde] hourly, once an hour - **2.** [jeden Augenblick] at any moment. ◇ *adj* [jede Stunde] hourly.

Stups (*pl -e*) *der* nudge.

Stups|nase *die* snub nose.

stur *abw* ◇ *adj* pigheaded. ◇ *adv* pigheadedly; **stur geradeaus fahren** to drive straight on.

Sturm (*pl Stürme*) *der* - **1.** [Unwetter] storm - **2.** [von Begeisterung, Entrüstung] wave - **3.** [Andrang, Angriff] assault; **der Sturm auf die Bastille** the storming of the Bastille - **4.** [beim Fußball] forward line.

stürmen (*perf* hat/ist gestürmt) ◇ *vt (hat)* - **1.** [Geschäfte, Büfett] to besiege - **2.** [Festung, Stellung] to storm. ◇ *vi* - **1.** *(ist)* [rennen] to rush - **2.** *(hat)* [beim Fußball] to attack - **3.** *(hat)* [Sturm herrschen]: **es stürmt** it's blowing a gale.

Stürmer, in (*mpl -, fpl -nen*) *der, die* forward.

Sturm|flut *die* storm tide.

stürmisch ◇ *adj* - **1.** [windig] stormy - **2.** [Applaus] tumultuous; [Begeisterung] wild; [Protest] vehement - **3.** [leidenschaftlich] passionate. ◇ *adv* - **1.** [applaudieren] tumultuously - **2.** [leidenschaftlich] passionately - **3.** [wehen] stormily; [regnen] violently.

Sturz (*pl Stürze*) *der* fall.

stürzen (*perf* hat/ist gestürzt) ◇ *vi (ist)* - **1.** [fallen, zurückgehen] to fall - **2.** [eilen] to rush. ◇ *vt (hat)* - **1.** [Regierung, Herrscher] to bring down; [mit Gewalt] to overthrow - **2.** [Kuchen, Pudding] to turn out - **3.** [stoßen] to hurl. ➤ **sich stürzen** *ref* - **1.** [springen] to jump - **2.** [herfallen über]: **sich auf jn/etw stürzen** [bestürmen] to fall on sb/sthg; [angreifen] to pounce on sb/sthg - **3.** [sich begeben]: **sich in etw (A) stürzen** [springen] to plunge into sthg; [sich widmen] to throw o.s. into sthg.

Sturzhelm *der* crash helmet.

Stute (*pl* -n) *die* mare.

Stuttgart *nt* Stuttgart.

Stütze (*pl* -n) *die* [Vorrichtung] prop, support; [für Kopf, Rücken, Füße] rest.

stutzen ⬦ *vt* [Bart, Haare, Hecke] to trim; [Pflanze, Baum] to cut back. ⬦ *vi* [innehalten] to stop short.

stützen *vt* to support; **den Kopf in die Hände stützen** to prop one's head on one's hands; **die Ellbogen auf den Tisch stützen** to prop one's elbows on the table. ⬢ **sich stützen** *ref*: **sich auf jn/etw stützen** [auf Stock, Möbel] to lean on sb/sthg; [auf Vermutung, Beweis] to be based on sb/sthg.

stutzig *adj*: **stutzig werden** to become suspicious.

Stützpunkt *der* base.

Styropor® *das* polystyrene.

Subjekt (*pl* -e) *das* GRAMM subject.

subjektiv ⬦ *adj* subjective. ⬦ *adv* subjectively.

Substantiv (*pl* -e) *das* GRAMM noun.

Substanz (*pl* -en) *die* substance; **das geht an die Substanz** it wears you down.

subtrahieren *vt* & *vi* to subtract.

subventionieren [zʊpvɛntsjoˈniːrən] *vt* to subsidize.

Suche (*pl* -n) *die* search; **auf der Suche nach jm/etw sein** to be looking for sb/sthg; [angestrengt] to be searching for sb/sthg; **sich auf die Suche (nach jm/etw) machen** to start looking (for sb/sthg).

suchen ⬦ *vt* - **1.** [finden wollen] to look for; [angestrengt] to search for; **er/es hat hier nichts zu suchen** *fam* he/it has no business being here - **2.** [sich wünschen] to seek. ⬦ *vi*: (**nach jm/etw**) **suchen** to look (for sb/sthg); [angestrengt] to search for sb/sthg).

Suchmaschine *die* EDV search engine.

Sucht (*pl* Süchte) *die* addiction.

süchtig *adj*: (**nach etw**) **süchtig sein** to be addicted (to sthg); **süchtig machen** to be addictive.

Suchtrupp *der* search party.

Südafrika *nt* South Africa.

südafrikanisch *adj* South African.

Südamerika *nt* South America.

Südamerikaner, in *der, die* South American.

südamerikanisch *adj* South American.

süddeutsch *adj* South German.

Süden *der* south; **nach Süden** south; **im Süden** in the south.

Südeuropa *nt* Southern Europe.

Südfrucht *die* ordinary citrus fruits and certain tropical fruits, e.g. bananas.

Südkorea *nt* South Korea.

südländisch *adj* Mediterranean.

südlich ⬦ *adj* [Gegend] southern; [Richtung, Wind] southerly. ⬦ *präp*: **südlich einer Sache (G)** ODER **von etw** (to the) south of sthg.

Südosten *der* south-east.

Südpol *der* - **1.** GEOGR South Pole - **2.** PHYS south pole.

Südsee *die*: **die Südsee** the South Seas *Pl*.

Südtirol *nt* South Tyrol.

Südwesten *der* south-west.

Sueskanal [ˈzuːɛskanɑːl] *der* Suez Canal.

süffig *adj* very drinkable.

Sulfat (*pl* -e) *das* CHEM sulphate.

Sultan (*pl* -e) *der* sultan.

Sultanine (*pl* -n) *die* sultana.

Sülze (*pl* -n) *die* brawn (U) UK, headcheese (U) US.

Summe (*pl* -n) *die* sum.

summen (*perf* hat/ist gesummt) ⬦ *vi* (hat, ist) to buzz. ⬦ *vt* (hat) to hum.

summieren *vt* to add. ⬢ **sich summieren** *ref* to add up.

Sumpf (*pl* Sümpfe) *der* [Sumpfgelände] marsh; [in Tropen] swamp.

sumpfig *adj* marshy.

Sünde (*pl* -n) *die* sin.

Sündenbock *der* scapegoat.

super *fam* ⬦ *adj* (*unver*) great. ⬦ *adv* really well. ⬦ *interj* great!

Super *das* four-star (petrol) UK, premium (gas) US.

Superlativ (*pl* -e) *der* GRAMM superlative.

Supermarkt *der* supermarket.

Suppe (*pl* -n) *die* - **1.** [Essen] soup; **jm die Suppe versalzen** *fam fig* to put a spoke in sb's wheel - **2.** *fam* [Dunst, Nebel] pea souper.

Suppenschüssel *die* tureen.

Suppenteller *der* soup plate.

Suppenwürfel *der* stock cube.

Surfbrett [ˈsœːɐ̯fbrɛt] *das* - **1.** [zum Wellensurfen] surfboard - **2.** [zum Windsurfen] sailboard.

surfen [ˈsœːɐ̯fn̩] (*perf* hat/ist gesurft) *vi* - **1.** [gen & EDV] to surf - **2.** [mit Segel] to windsurf.

Surrealismus *der* surrealism.

surren (*perf* hat/ist gesurrt) *vi* - **1.** (*ist*) [Pfeil] to whizz - **2.** (*hat*) [Maschine] to whirr; [Insekt] to buzz.

suspekt *adj* suspicious; **jm suspekt sein** to make sb suspicious.

süß ◇ *adj* sweet. ◇ *adv*: **süß schmecken/aussehen** to taste/look sweet; **träume süß!** sweet dreams!

süßen *vt* to sweeten.

Süßigkeiten *Pl* sweets *UK*, candy *(U) US*.

süßlich ◇ *adj* - 1. [süß] sweetish - 2. [übertrieben freundlich] syrupy. ◇ *adv* - 1. [süß]: **süßlich schmecken** to have a sweetish taste - 2. [übertrieben freundlich] in a sickly-sweet way.

süßsauer ◇ *adj* sweet and sour. ◇ *adv*: **süßsauer schmecken** to have a sweet and sour taste.

Süß\|speise *die* dessert.

Süß\|wasser *das* fresh water.

SVP [εsfau'peː] (*abk für* Schweizer Volkspartei) *die (ohne pl)* political party in Switzerland.

SW (*abk für* Südwest) *abk für* SW.

Symbol (*pl* -e) *das* - 1. [Zeichen] symbol - 2. EDV [Icon] icon.

symbolisch ◇ *adj* symbolic. ◇ *adv* symbolically.

Symmetrie (*pl* -n) *die* symmetry.

symmetrisch ◇ *adj* symmetrical. ◇ *adv* symmetrically.

Sympathie (*pl* -n) *die* [Zuneigung] liking *(U)*; **sich** *(D)* **viele Sympathien verscherzen** to lose a lot of sympathy.

sympathisch ◇ *adj* nice; **sie ist mir sympathisch** I like her. ◇ *adv* nicely.

sympathisieren *vi*: **mit jm sympathisieren** to sympathize with sb.

Symphonie = Sinfonie.

Symphoniker = Sinfoniker.

Symptom (*pl* -e) *das* - 1. MED symptom - 2. [Anzeichen] sign.

Synagoge (*pl* -n) *die* synagogue.

synchron ◇ *adj* synchronous. ◇ *adv* synchronously.

synchronisieren *vt* FILM [Stimme] to dub; [Bewegungen, Abläufe] to synchronize.

Synonym (*pl* -e) *das* synonym.

Syntax (*pl* -en) *die* syntax.

Synthese (*pl* -n) *die*: **die Synthese aus etw** the synthesis of sthg.

synthetisch ◇ *adj* synthetic. ◇ *adv* synthetically.

Syrien *nt* Syria.

System [zys'teːm] (*pl* -e) *das* system.

systematisch ◇ *adj* systematic. ◇ *adv* systematically.

Szene (*pl* -n) *die* - 1. [im Film, Theater] scene - 2. [Vorfall] scene; **(jm) eine Szene machen** to make a scene (in front of sb) - 3. [Milieu] scene.

T

t (*pl* t ODER -s), **T** (*pl* T ODER -s) [teː] *das* t, T.
➡ **t** *abk für* **Tonne**.

Tabak (*pl* -e), **Tabak** (*pl* -e) *der* tobacco *(U)*.

Tabak\|laden *der* tobacconist's.

tabellarisch ◇ *adj* tabular. ◇ *adv* in tabular form.

Tabelle (*pl* -n) *die* - 1. [Liste] table - 2. SPORT [league] table.

Tablett (*pl* -s ODER -e) *das* tray.

Tablette (*pl* -n) *die* tablet, pill.

tabu *adj* (*unver*): **etw ist tabu** sthg is taboo.

Tabu (*pl* -s) *das* taboo.

Tachometer (*pl* -) *der* speedometer.

Tadel (*pl* -) *der geh* rebuke.

tadellos ◇ *adj* impeccable. ◇ *adv* impeccably.

tadeln *vt* to rebuke.

Tafel (*pl* -n) *die* - 1. [Schreibtafel] blackboard - 2. *geh* [Tisch] table - 3. [Stück]: **eine Tafel Schokolade** a bar of chocolate.

Tafel\|wasser (*pl* -wässer) *das* mineral water.

Tag (*pl* -e) *der* - 1. [24 Stunden] day; **in vierzehn Tagen** in a fortnight - 2. [in seinem Verlauf] day; **am helllichtenTag** in broad daylight; **über/unter Tag(e)** above/below ground.
➡ **eines Tages** *adv* [irgendwann] one day.
➡ **guten Tag** *interj* hello!; [am Morgen] good morning!; [am Nachmittag] good afternoon!
➡ **Tag für Tag** *adv* [immer] day after day.
➡ **von Tag zu Tag** *adv* [immer mehr] day by day. ➡ **Tage** *Pl* - 1. [Zeit] days; **js Tage sind gezählt** [muss sterben/weggehen] sb's days are numbered - 2. *fam* [Periode] period *(sg)*; **sie hat/bekommt ihre Tage** *fam* she's got her period; *siehe auch* **zutage**.

tagaus *adv*: **tagaus, tagein** day in, day out.

Tag der Deutschen Einheit *der* Day of German Unity.

Tage\|buch *das* diary.

tagelang ◇ *adj* lasting for days; **tagelanger Regen** days of rain. ◇ *adv* for days.

tagen *vi* - 1. [Sitzung haben - gen] to meet; [- Gericht] to be in session - 2. *geh* [hell werden]: **es tagt** day is breaking.

Tagesablauf *der* day.

Tagesan\|bruch *der* dawn.

Tages\|bedarf *der (ohne pl)* daily requirement.

Tages\|fahrt *die* day trip.

Tages\|gericht *das* dish of the day.

Tages\|geschehen *das* day's events *Pl*.

Tageslkarte *die* day ticket.

Tageslicht *das* daylight; **etw kommt ans Tageslicht** sthg comes to light.

Tageslordnung *die* agenda.

Tageslschau *die* news.

Tageslzeit *die* time of day.

Tageslzeitung *die* daily newspaper.

täglich <> *adj* daily. <> *adv* every day; **dreimal täglich** three times a day.

tagsüber *adv* during the day.

tagtäglich *adj* daily.

Tagung *(pl -en) die* conference.

Taifun *(pl -e) der* typhoon.

Taille ['taljə] *(pl -n) die* waist.

tailliert [ta'ji:ɐt] *adj* fitted.

Taiwan *nt* Taiwan.

Takt *(pl -e) der* - **1.** [musikalische Einheit] bar - **2.** *(ohne pl)* [Feingefühl] tact - **3.** *(ohne pl)* [Rhythmus] time; **jn aus dem Takt bringen** to put sb off.

Taktlgefühl *das* tact.

Taktik *(pl -en) die* tactics *Pl*.

taktisch <> *adj* [klug] tactical. <> *adv* tactically; **taktisch klug vorgehen** to use clever tactics.

taktlos <> *adj* tactless. <> *adv* tactlessly.

Taktlosigkeit *(pl -en) die* tactlessness.

Taktlstock *der* baton.

taktvoll <> *adj* tactful. <> *adv* tactfully.

Tal *(pl Täler) das* valley.

Talent *(pl -e) das* talent.

talentiert <> *adj* talented. <> *adv* with talent.

Talg *(pl -e) der* tallow; [von Menschen] sebum.

Talisman *(pl -e) der* talisman.

Talkshow ['tɔ:kʃo:] *(pl -s) die* talk show.

Tampon ['tampɔn, tam'po:n] *(pl -s) der* tampon.

Tandem *(pl -s) das* tandem.

Tang *(pl -e) der* seaweed *(U)*.

Tangente *(pl -n) die* MATH tangent.

Tango *(pl -s) der* tango.

Tank *(pl -s) der* tank.

Tankldeckel *der* fuel cap, petrol cap *UK*.

tanken <> *vi* to get some petrol *UK* ODER gas *US*. <> *vt* - **1.** [auftanken]: **Benzin tanken** to get some petrol *UK* ODER gas *US* - **2.** [genießen] to get one's fill of.

Tanker *(pl -) der* tanker.

Tanklstelle *die* petrol station *UK*, gas station *US*.

Tanklwart, in *(mpl -e, fpl -nen) der, die* petrol *UK* ODER gas *US* station attendant.

Tanne *(pl -n) die* - **1.** [Baum] fir tree - **2.** *(ohne pl)* [Holz] fir.

Tannenlbaum *der* - **1.** [Tanne] fir tree - **2.** [Weihnachtsbaum] Christmas tree.

Tannenlzapfen *der* fir cone.

Tansania *nt* Tanzania.

Tante *(pl -n) die* - **1.** [Verwandte] aunt - **2.** *fam* [als Anrede] auntie.

Tante-Emma-lLaden *der* corner shop.

Tanz *(pl Tänze) der* dance.

Tanzlbein *das (ohne pl)*: **das Tanzbein schwingen** *fam hum* to hit the floor.

tanzen *vt* & *vi* to dance; **komm, lass uns tanzen gehen** let's go dancing; **willst du mit mir tanzen?** would you like to dance?

Tänzer, in *(mpl -, fpl -nen) der, die* dancer.

Tanzlfläche *die* dance floor.

Tanzlschule *die* dancing school.

Tanzlstunde *die* - **1.** [Kurs] dancing lessons *Pl* - **2.** [Unterrichtsstunde] dancing lesson.

Tapete *(pl -n) die* wallpaper *(U)*.

Tapetenlwechsel *der fig* change of scenery.

tapezieren *vt* & *vi* to wallpaper.

tapfer <> *adj* brave. <> *adv* bravely.

Tapferkeit *die* bravery.

tappen *(perf* ist getappt*) vi*: **durch das Zimmer tappen** to patter through the room.

tapsig <> *adj* awkward. <> *adv* awkwardly.

Tarif *(pl -e) der* - **1.** WIRTSCH rate - **2.** [Gebühr] charge; [Verkehrstarif] fare.

Tariflohn *der* agreed rate of pay.

Tarifverlhandlung *die* collective bargaining.

Tariflvertrag *der* collective agreement.

tarnen *vt* to camouflage. ◆ **sich tarnen** *ref* to camouflage o.s.; **sich als etw tarnen** to disguise o.s. as sthg.

Tarnung *die* camouflage.

Tasche *(pl -n) die* - **1.** [Tragetasche, Handtasche] bag - **2.** [Hosentasche] pocket; **etw aus eigener Tasche bezahlen** to pay for sthg o.s.; **etw (schon) in der Tasche haben** *fam* to have sthg in the bag; **jm auf der Tasche liegen** *fam* to live off sb.

Taschenlbuch *das* paperback.

Taschenldieb, in *der, die* pickpocket.

Taschenlformat *das*: **im Taschenformat** pocket-sized.

Taschenlgeld *das* pocket money.

Taschenllampe *die* torch *UK*, flashlight *US*.

Taschenlmesser *das* penknife, pocketknife.

Taschenlrechner *der* pocket calculator.

Taschenltuch *(pl -tücher) das* [aus Stoff] handkerchief; [aus Papier] tissue.

Taschenluhr *die* pocket watch.

Tasse *(pl -n) die* cup; **nicht alle Tassen im Schrank haben** *fam fig* & *abw* to have a screw loose.

Tastatur *(pl -en) die* keyboard.

Taste *(pl -n) die* - **1.** [von Instrument, Computer] key - **2.** [von Geräten] button.

tasten ◇ *vi* to feel one's way; **nach etw tasten** to feel for sthg. ◇ *vt* to feel. ● **sich tasten** *ref* to feel one's way.

Tasten|instrument *das* keyboard instrument.

Tast|sinn *der* sense of touch.

tat *prät* ▷ **tun**.

Tat (*pl* -en) *die* action; **eine verbrecherische Tat** a criminal act; **eine gute Tat** a good deed; **jn auf frischer Tat ertappen** *fig* to catch sb in the act; **etw in die Tat umsetzen** to put sthg into action. ● **in der Tat** *adv* [tatsächlich] indeed.

Tatbe|stand *der* - 1. RECHT: **der Tatbestand der Bestechung** the offence of bribery; **den Tatbestand des Betrugs erfüllen** to constitute fraud - 2. [Tatsache] facts *Pl* (of the matter).

tatenlos ◇ *adj* idle. ◇ *adv* idly; **wir mussten tatenlos zusehen** we could only stand and watch.

Täter, in (*mpl* -, *fpl* -nen) *der, die* culprit.

tätig *adj* - 1. [beschäftigt]: **tätig sein** to work - 2. [aktiv] active; **tätig werden** to take action.

tätigen *vt geh* [von Geschäft] to transact.

Tätigkeit (*pl* -en) *die* [Arbeit] job; [Aktivität] activity.

tatkräftig ◇ *adj* active. ◇ *adv* actively.

tätlich ◇ *adj* physical; **tätlich werden** to become violent. ◇ *adv* physically.

Tat|ort *der* [von Verbrechen] scene of the crime.

Tätowierung (*pl* -en) *die* - 1. [Vorgang] tattooing (*U*) - 2. [Ergebnis] tattoo.

Tat|sache *die* fact; **jn vor vollendete Tatsachen stellen** *fig* to present sb with a fait accompli. ◇ *interj* it's true!

tatsächlich, tatsächlich ◇ *adj* real, actual. ◇ *adv* really; **du bist ja tatsächlich pünktlich!** you're actually on time!

tätscheln *vt* [liebkosen] to pat.

Tattoo [ta'tu:] (*pl* -s) *das* = **Tätowierung**.

Tatze (*pl* -n) *die* paw.

Tau (*pl* -e) *der* [Niederschlag] dew. ◇ *das* [Seil] rope.

taub *adj* - 1. [nichts hörend] deaf; **sich taub stellen** *fam* to turn a deaf ear - 2. [nichts fühlend] numb.

Taube (*pl* -n) ◇ *der, die* [Gehörlose] deaf person. ◇ *die* [Tier - gewöhnlich] pigeon; [- weiße] dove.

taubstumm *adj* deaf and dumb.

tauchen (*perf* hat/ist getaucht) ◇ *vi* (hat, ist) to dive. ◇ *vt* (hat) - 1. [eintauchen] to dip - 2. [drücken] to push.

Taucher, in (*mpl* -, *fpl* -nen) *der, die* diver.

Taucher|brille *die* diving goggles *Pl*.

tauen (*perf* hat/ist getaut) ◇ *vi* (hat, ist) to melt; **es taut** it's thawing. ◇ *vt* (hat) to thaw.

Taufe (*pl* -n) *die* - 1. [Vorgang] christening - 2. (*ohne pl*) [Sakrament] baptism.

taufen *vt* - 1. RELIG [Menschen] to baptize - 2. [Tiere, Gegenstände] to name.

Tauf|pate *der* godfather.

Tauf|patin *die* godmother.

taugen *vi*: **nichts/wenig taugen** to be no/not much good; **zu** ODER **für etw taugen** to be suitable for sthg.

tauglich *adj* - 1. [geeignet] suitable - 2. MIL fit (for service).

Taumel *der* (*ohne pl*) - 1. [Rausch] frenzy - 2. [Schwindel] (feeling of) dizziness.

taumeln (*perf* hat/ist getaumelt) *vi* - 1. (ist) [schwankend gehen] to stagger - 2. (hat) [schwanken] to reel.

Tausch (*pl* -e) *der* exchange.

tauschen ◇ *vt* to swap. ◇ *vi*: **mit jm tauschen** [Arbeitszeit] to swap with sb; [an js Stelle sein] to swap places with sb.

täuschen ◇ *vt* to deceive; [Gegner] to trick. ◇ *vi* to be deceptive. ● **sich täuschen** *ref* to be wrong; **sich in jm täuschen** to be wrong about sb.

täuschend ◇ *adj* deceptive. ◇ *adv* deceptively.

Täuschung (*pl* -en) *die* - 1. [Irreführung] deception - 2. [Verwechslung] illusion.

Täuschungs|manöver *das* ploy.

tausend *num* a ODER one thousand; *siehe auch* **sechs**.

Tausend (*pl* - ODER -e) *das* thousand. ● **Tausende** *Pl* [sehr viele]: **zu Tausenden** by the thousand; *siehe auch* **Sechs**.

Tausender (*pl* -) *der* MATH thousand.

Tausend|füßler (*pl* -) *der* centipede.

tausendmal *adv* a thousand times.

tausendste, r, s *adj* thousandth; *siehe auch* **sechste**.

Tausendste (*pl* -n) *der, die, das* thousandth; *siehe auch* **Sechste**.

tausendstel *adj* (*unver*) thousandth; *siehe auch* **sechstel**.

Tausendstel (*pl* -) *das* thousandth; *siehe auch* **Sechstel**.

Tau|wetter *das* thaw.

Tau|ziehen *das* tug-of-war.

Taxi (*pl* -s) *das* taxi.

Technik (*pl* -en) *die* - 1. (*ohne pl*) [Wissenschaft] technology - 2. [Methode] technique - 3. [Ausrüstung] equipment - 4. (*ohne pl*) [Funktionsweise] workings *Pl*.

Techniker, in (*mpl* -, *fpl* -nen) *der, die* engineer; [im Sport, in Musik] technician.

technisch ◇ *adj* technical; [Fortschritt] technological. ◇ *adv* technically; [fortgeschritten] technologically.

Technische Hoch|schule *die* technical college.

Technische Überwachungsverein *der amt institution charged with testing roadworthiness of cars and safety of consumer goods and installations.*

Techno *der* MUS techno.

Technologie *(pl -n) die* technology.

technologisch <> *adj* technological. <> *adv* technologically.

Teddy *(pl -s)*, **Teddybär** *(pl -en) der* teddy bear.

Tee *(pl -s) der -* 1. [gen] tea; **schwarzer Tee** black tea - 2. [Kräutertee] herbal tea.

Teelbeutel *der* teabag.

Teelkanne *die* teapot.

Teellöffel *der* teaspoon.

Teer *der* tar *(U).*

teeren *vt* to tar.

Teelsieb *das* tea strainer.

Teheran *nt* Teheran.

Teich *(pl -e) der* pond.

Teig *(pl -e) der* dough *(U).*

Teigwaren *Pl amt* pasta *(U).*

Teil *(pl -e)* <> *der* [Teilmenge] part. <> *der ODER das* [Anteil] share; **sich** *(D)* **seinen Teil denken** *fig* to keep one's thoughts to o.s. <> *das* [Bestandteil] part. ◆ **zum Teil** *adv* [teilweise] partly.

teilen <> *vt* [aufteilen] to share; [zerteilen] to divide; **etw mit jm teilen** to share sthg with sb; **sich** *(D)* **etw teilen** to share sthg. <> *vi* to share. ◆ **sich teilen** *ref* [Gruppe] to split up; [Straße] to fork; [Meinungen] to be divided.

teillhaben *vi (unreg):* **an etw** *(D)* **teilhaben** to share in sthg.

Teilhaber, in *(mpl -, fpl -nen) der, die* partner.

Teilnahme *(pl -n) die -* 1. [Aufmerksamkeit, Beteiligung] participation *(U)* - 2. [an Kurs] attendance - 3. [Mitgefühl] sympathy.

teilnahmslos <> *adj* apathetic. <> *adv* apathetically.

teillnehmen *vi (unreg) -* 1. [mitmachen]: **an etw** *(D)* **teilnehmen** to take part in sthg - 2. [mitfühlen]: **an etw** *(D)* **teilnehmen** *geh* to share in sthg.

Teilnehmer, in *(mpl -, fpl -nen) der, die* participant.

teils *adv fam* partly. ◆ **teils..., teils...** *adv* partly..., partly...

Teilung *(pl -en) die* division.

teilweise <> *adv -* 1. [zum Teil] partly - 2. [zeitweise] sometimes. <> *adj* partial.

Tel. *(abk für Telefon)* tel.

Telelarbeit *die* teleworking.

Telefon *(pl -e)*, **Telefon** *(pl -e) das -* 1. [Gerät] telephone; **am Telefon** on the telephone - 2. *fam* [Anruf]: **Telefon für dich** there's a call for you.

Telefonanlruf *der* telephone call.

Telefonat *(pl -e) das* telephone call.

Telefonlbuch *das* telephone book.

Telefonlgespräch *das* telephone conversation.

telefonieren *vi* to make a telephone call; **mit jm telefonieren** to talk to sb on the telephone.

telefonisch <> *adj* telephone *(vor Subst).* <> *adv* by telephone; **ich bin telefonisch erreichbar** you can reach me by telephone.

Telefonlkarte *die* phonecard.

Telefonlnummer *die* telephone number.

Telefonverlbindung *die* telephone line.

Telefonlzelle *die* telephone box.

Telefonlzentrale *die* switchboard.

telegrafieren *vt* to telegraph.

telegrafisch <> *adj* telegraphic. <> *adv* by telegram.

Telegramm *(pl -e) das* telegram.

Telekom® *die German telecommunications company.*

Telelobjektiv *das* FOTO telephoto lens.

Telex *(pl -e) das* telex.

Teller *(pl -) der* [Gefäß] plate; **seinen Teller leer essen** to finish what's on one's plate.

Tempel *(pl -) der* temple.

Temperament *(pl -e) das -* 1. [Energie] liveliness; **Temperament haben** to be lively - 2. [Wesen] temperament.

temperamentvoll *adj* lively.

Temperatur *(pl -en) die* temperature.

Tempo[1] *(pl -s ODER* **Tempi**) *das -* 1. *(Pl Tempos)* [Geschwindigkeit] speed; **hier gilt Tempo 30** there's a 30 km speed limit here - 2. *(Pl Tempi)* MUS tempo.

Tempo®[2] *(pl -s) das fam* [Papiertaschentuch] tissue.

Tempollimit *das* speed limit.

Tempotaschentuch® *(pl -tücher) das fam* tissue.

Tendenz *(pl -en) die -* 1. [Entwicklung] trend - 2. [Neigung] tendency.

tendieren *vi* to tend; **zu etw tendieren** to tend towards sthg.

Tennis *das* tennis.

Tennislplatz *der* tennis court.

Tennislschläger *der* tennis racquet.

Tenor *(pl* **Tenöre**) *der* tenor.

Teppich *(pl -e) der -* 1. [Einzelstück] rug - 2. [Teppichboden] carpet.

Teppichlboden *der* carpet.

Termin *(pl -e) der -* 1. [Zeitpunkt] date; [Vereinbarung] appointment; **einen Termin vereinbaren** to make an appointment - 2. RECHT hearing.

Terminal ['tø:ɡminəl] *(pl -s)* <> *der ODER das* [Gebäude] terminal. <> *das* EDV terminal.

Terminlkalender *der* diary.

Termin|plan *der* schedule.

Terpentin *(pl -e) das* turpentine *(U)*.

Terrarium [tɛˈraːrjʊm] *(pl* **Terrarien***) das* terrarium.

Terrasse *(pl -n) die* - **1.** [am Haus] patio - **2.** [am Berg] terrace.

Terrier [ˈtɛrjɐ] *(pl -) der* terrier.

Territorium [tɛriˈtoːrjʊm] *(pl* **-torien***) das* territory.

Terror *der* - **1.** [Gewalt] terrorism - **2.** [Angst] terror - **3.** *fam:* **Terror machen** *fam* to raise hell.

Terroran|schlag *der* terrorist attack.

terrorisieren *vt* to terrorize.

Terrorismus *der* terrorism.

Terrorist, in *(mpl -en, fpl -nen) der, die* terrorist.

Terz *(pl -en) die* MUS third.

Tesa® *das* Sellotape® *UK*, Scotch® tape *US*.

Tesafilm® *der* Sellotape® *UK*, Scotch® tape *US*.

Tessin *das* Ticino *(canton in south-east Switzerland)*.

Tessiner, in *(mpl -, fpl -nen) der, die* native/inhabitant of Ticino.

Test *(pl -e* ODER *-s) der* test.

Testament *(pl -e) das* - **1.** [letzter Wille] will - **2.** RELIG: **das Alte/Neue Testament** the Old/New Testament.

testamentarisch *adv:* **etw testamentarisch verfügen** to put sthg in one's will.

testen *vt* to test.

Tetanus|impfung *die* tetanus vaccination.

teuer ◇ *adj* - **1.** [Preis] expensive - **2.** geh [Freund] dear. ◇ *adv* dearly.

Teufel *(pl -) der* devil; **der Teufel ist los** *fam* all hell has broken loose; **zum Teufel mit jm/etw** *fam* [Schluss damit] to hell with sb/sthg.

Teufels|kreis *der* vicious circle.

teuflisch ◇ *adj* devilish. ◇ *adv* devilishly.

Text *(pl -e) der* - **1.** [Geschriebenes] text; [von Lied] lyrics *Pl* - **2.** [von Bild] caption.

texten *vt* to text.

Textilien *Pl* textiles.

Textil|industrie *die* textile industry.

Text|nachricht *die* text message.

Text|verarbeitung *die* EDV word processing *(U)*.

TH [teːˈhaː] *die abk für* **Technische Hochschule.**

Thailand *nt* Thailand.

Theater *(pl -) das* - **1.** theatre; **Theater spielen** to act - **2.** *fam* [Ärger] fuss; **Theater machen** to make a fuss; **so ein Theater!** such a fuss! - **3.** *fam* [Vortäuschung] play-acting; **Theater spielen** to put on an act.

Theaterauf|führung *die* performance.

Theater|kasse *die* theatre box office.

Theater|stück *das* play.

theatralisch *adj* dramatic.

Theke *(pl -n) die* - **1.** [in Kneipe] bar - **2.** [in Geschäft] counter.

Thema *(pl* **Themen***) das* subject; MUS theme; **etw ist für jn kein Thema** *fig* sthg is not important to sb; **etw ist kein Thema mehr** *fig* sthg is of no interest anymore.

Themenbe|reich *der* field.

Themse *die:* **die Themse** the (River) Thames.

Theologe *(pl -n) der* theologian.

Theologie *(pl -n) die* theology.

Theologin *(pl -nen) die* theologian.

Theoretiker, in *(mpl -, fpl -nen) der, die* theorist.

theoretisch ◇ *adj* theoretical. ◇ *adv* theoretically.

Theorie *(pl -n) die* theory.

therapeutisch ◇ *adj* therapeutic. ◇ *adv* therapeutically.

Therapie *(pl -n) die* therapy.

Thermal|bad *das* thermal bath.

Thermometer *(pl -) das* thermometer.

Thermos|flasche *die* thermos (flask).

Thermostat *(pl -e* ODER *-en) der* thermostat.

These *(pl -n) die* thesis.

Thron *(pl -e) der* throne.

thronen *vi* to sit imposingly.

Thron|folger, in *(mpl -, fpl -nen) der, die* heir to the throne.

Thunfisch, -fisch *der* tuna.

Thüringen *nt* Thuringia.

Thüringer *(pl -)* ◇ *der* native/inhabitant of Thuringia. ◇ *adj (unver)* of/from Thuringia.

Thüringerin *(pl -nen) die* native/inhabitant of Thuringia.

Thymian *(pl -e) der* thyme.

Tick *(pl -s) der* quirk; [nervös] tic.

ticken *vi* to tick.

Tide *(pl -n) die* Norddt tide.

tief ◇ *adj* - **1.** [gen] deep; **ein tiefer Fall** a long fall; **zwei Meter tief** two metres deep; **im tiefsten Winter** in the depths of winter - **2.** [niedrig] low. ◇ *adv* - **1.** [nach unten] deep - **2.** [niedrig] low; **zu tief singen** to sing flat - **3.** [zeitlich]: **bis tief in die Nacht** far into the night - **4.** [verletzt, atmen, bewegt] deeply; **tief schlafen** to be in a deep sleep.

Tief *(pl -s) das* depression.

Tiefdruck|gebiet *das* area of low pressure.

Tiefe *(pl -n) die* depth.

Tief|ebene *die* (lowland) plain.

tiefernst ◇ *adj* very serious. ◇ *adv* very seriously.

Tief|garage *die* underground car park *UK* ODER parking lot *US*.

tiefgefroren *adj* frozen.

tiefgekühlt ◇ *adj* frozen. ◇ *adv* in a freezer.

tief greifend ◇ *adj* radical. ◇ *adv* radically.

Tiefkühlfach *das* freezer compartment.

Tiefkühlkost *die* frozen food.

Tiefkühltruhe *die* freezer.

Tiefpunkt *der* low.

tief schürfend ◇ *adj* profound. ◇ *adv* profoundly.

tiefsinnig *adj* profound.

Tiefstand *der (ohne pl)* low.

Tier (*pl* -e) *das* animal; **ein großes** ODER **hohes Tier** *fam fig* a big shot.

Tierart *die* species.

Tierarzt, ärztin *der, die* vet.

Tiergarten *der* zoo.

Tierhandlung *die* pet shop.

Tierheim *das* animal home.

tierisch ◇ *adj* - **1.** [von Tieren] animal - **2.** *fam* [groß]: **ich habe tierische Angst** I'm really frightened. ◇ *adv fam* really.

Tierkreiszeichen *das* ASTROL star sign.

tierlieb *adj* animal-loving; **tierlieb sein** to be an animal lover.

Tierpark *der* zoo.

Tierquälerei *die* cruelty to animals.

Tierschutzverein *der* society for the prevention of cruelty to animals.

Tierversuch *der* animal experiment.

Tiger, in (*mpl* -, *fpl* -nen) *der, die* tiger.

Tilde (*pl* -n) *die* tilde.

tilgen *vt* to repay.

Tilsiter (*pl* -) *der* [Käse] *strong cheese with small holes in it*.

Tinktur (*pl* -en) *die* tincture.

Tinte (*pl* -n) *die* ink; **in der Tinte sitzen** *fam fig* to be in the soup.

Tintenfisch *der* octopus; [klein] squid; [Sepia] cuttlefish.

Tip = Tipp.

Tipp (*pl* -s) *der* - **1.** [Hinweis] tip - **2.** [Wette] bet.

tippen ◇ *vi* - **1.** [vorhersagen, wetten] to bet; **meistens tippe ich richtig** I'm usually right; **auf etw** (A) **tippen** to bet on sthg; **ich tippe darauf** I bet that - **2.** *fam* [Maschine schreiben] to type - **3.** [antippen] to tap; **an etw** (A) **tippen** to tap on sthg. ◇ *vt* - **1.** *fam* [Schreibmaschine schreiben] to type - **2.** [antippen] to tap.

tipptopp *fam adj (unver)* [von Person, Garten] immaculate; [von Haus] shipshape.

Tirol *nt* Tyrol.

Tiroler (*pl* -) *der* & *adj (unver)* Tyrolean.

Tirolerin (*pl* -nen) *die* Tyrolean.

tirolerisch *adj* Tyrolean.

Tisch (*pl* -e) *der* [Möbel] table; **den Tisch decken** to set the table; **unter den Tisch fallen** to fall by the wayside; **das ist vom Tisch** that's been done and dusted.

Tischdecke *die* tablecloth.

Tischler, in (*mpl* -, *fpl* -nen) *der, die* carpenter.

Tischtennis *das* table tennis.

Tischtuch (*pl* -tücher) *das* tablecloth.

Titel (*pl* -) *der* title.

Titelbild *das* cover picture.

Titelseite *die* front page.

Titelverteidiger, in *der, die* SPORT defending champion.

Toast [toːst] (*pl* -e ODER -s) *der* - **1.** [Brot] toast; [Scheibe] slice of toast - **2.** [Trinkspruch] toast.

Toastbrot *das* sliced white bread (U).

toasten [ˈtoːstn̩] *vt* to toast.

Toaster [ˈtoːstɐ] (*pl* -) *der* toaster.

toben (*perf* hat/ist getobt) *vi* - **1.** (hat) [wild werden] to go berserk - **2.** (ist) [rennen] to charge about - **3.** (hat) [wüten] to rage.

Tochter (*pl* Töchter) *die* daughter.

Tod (*pl* -e) *der* death; **jn zum Tod(e) verurteilen** to condemn sb to death; **zu Tode erschreckt** scared to death.

todernst ◇ *adj* deadly serious. ◇ *adv* in a deadly serious way.

Todesangst *die*: **eine Todesangst haben/ausstehen** to be scared to death.

Todesanzeige *die* [in Zeitung] death notice.

Todesfall *der* death.

Todeskampf *der* death throes *Pl.*

Todesopfer *das* casualty, fatality.

Todesstrafe *die* death penalty.

Todesursache *die* cause of death.

Todesurteil *das* death sentence.

todkrank *adj* terminally ill.

tödlich ◇ *adj* - **1.** [Krankheit, Unfall] fatal; [Gift, Biss] lethal - **2.** *fam* [Angst, Langeweile, Sicherheit] deadly; [Beleidigung] mortal. ◇ *adv* - **1.** [verlaufen] fatally; [wirken] lethally - **2.** *fam* [langweilig] deadly; [beleidigt] mortally.

todmüde *adj* exhausted.

todschick *fam* ◇ *adj* dead smart. ◇ *adv* dead smartly.

todsicher *fam* ◇ *adj* [Sache, Gewinn] sure-fire; **das ist todsicher** it's dead certain. ◇ *adv* definitely.

Tofu *der* tofu.

toi, toi, toi [ˈtɔy ˈtɔy ˈtɔy] *interj* - **1.** [unberufen] touch wood! - **2.** [viel Glück] best of luck!

Toilette [tɔaˈlɛtə] (*pl* -n) *die* toilet; **auf die Toilette gehen** to go to the toilet.

Toilettenpapier *das* toilet paper.

Tokio *nt* Tokyo.

tolerant ◇ *adj* tolerant. ◇ *adv* tolerantly.

Toleranz (*pl* -en) *die* tolerance.

tolerieren *vt* to tolerate.

toll *fam* ⬦ *adj* - **1.** [schön] fantastic, brilliant - **2.** [unglaublich] far-out. ⬦ *adv* - **1.** [wunderbar] fantastically, brilliantly - **2.** [sehr] like crazy; **er hat sich ganz toll gefreut** he was dead pleased.

tollen (*perf* **ist getollt**) *vi* to run around like crazy.

tollkühn ⬦ *adj* reckless; **ein tollkühner Mensch** a daredevil. ⬦ *adv* recklessly.

Tollpatsch (*pl* **-e**) *der* clumsy devil.

Tolllwut *die* rabies (*U*).

Tolpatsch = Tollpatsch.

Tomate (*pl* **-n**) *die* tomato.

Tomatenlmark *das* tomato purée.

Ton (*pl* **-e** ODER **Töne**) *der* - **1.** (*pl* Tone) [Lehm] clay - **2.** (*pl* Töne) [Laut] note - **3.** (*pl* Töne) [Tonfall] tone; **hier herrscht ein rauer Ton!** the atmosphere's terrible here!; **sich im Ton vergreifen** to adopt the wrong tone - **4.** (*pl* Töne) [Farbton] shade, tone - **5.** [von Platte, Film] sound; **den Ton angeben** to be extremely influential; **zum guten Ton gehören** to be the done thing.

Tonlart *die* - **1.** MUS key - **2.** [Tonfall] tone.

Tonauslfall *der* TV loss of sound.

Tonlband (*pl* **-bänder**) *das* - **1.** [Spule] tape - **2.** [Gerät] tape recorder.

Tonbandlgerät *das* tape recorder.

tönen ⬦ *vi* - **1.** [klingen] to sound - **2.** [prahlen] to boast. ⬦ *vt* [Haare] to tint.

Tonlfall *der* - **1.** [Tonart] tone - **2.** [Sprachmelodie] intonation.

Tonlfilm *der* sound film.

Tonllage *die* pitch.

Tonlleiter *die* scale.

Tonne (*pl* **-n**) *die* - **1.** [Behälter] barrel - **2.** [Gewicht] tonne.

top *fam* ⬦ *adj* (*unver*): **top sein** to be brilliant. ⬦ *adv* brilliantly.

TOP [tɔp] (*pl* **-**) (*abk für* **Tagesordnungspunkt**) *der* item on the agenda.

Topf (*pl* **Töpfe**) *der* - **1.** [zum Kochen] pan - **2.** [für Vorräte, Blumen] pot - **3.** *fam* [Klo] loo *UK*, john *US*.

Töpfer (*pl* **-**) *der* potter.

Töpferei (*pl* **-en**) *die* pottery.

Töpferin (*pl* **-nen**) *die* potter.

töpfern ⬦ *vt* to make (*pottery*). ⬦ *vi* to do pottery.

Topfllappen *der* oven cloth.

Tor (*pl* **-e**) *das* - **1.** SPORT goal; **ein Tor schießen** to score a goal; **im Tor stehen** to be in goal - **2.** [Tür] gate; [von Garage, Scheune] door.

Toreinlfahrt *die* entrance gate.

Torf *der* peat.

Torlhüter, in (*mpl* **-**, *fpl* **-nen**) *der, die* goalkeeper.

torkeln (*perf* **hat/ist getorkelt**) *vi* to stagger.

Torpedo (*pl* **-s**) *das* torpedo.

Torlschütze, schützin *der, die* goalscorer.

Torte (*pl* **-n**) *die* gâteau.

Tortenguss (*pl* **-güsse**) *der* glaze (in fruit flan), jelly.

Tortur (*pl* **-en**) *die* eigtl & fig torture.

Torwart, in (*mpl* **-e**, *fpl* **-nen**) *der, die* goalkeeper.

tosen (*perf* **hat/ist getost**) *vi* to roar.

Toskana *die*: **die Toskana** Tuscany.

tot ⬦ *adj* eigtl & fig dead; **ein toter Punkt** a standstill; fig a deadlock. ⬦ *adv*: **tot umfallen** to drop dead; siehe auch **tot stellen**.

total ⬦ *adj* total. ⬦ *adv* fam totally; **total gut** dead good.

Totallschaden *der* write-off.

Tote (*pl* **-n**) *der, die* dead person; **es gab mehrere Tote** several people were killed.

töten *vt* & *vi* to kill.

Totenlkopf *der* - **1.** [auf Arzneimittel, Piratenflagge] skull and crossbones - **2.** [Schädel] skull.

Totenlschädel *der* skull.

Totenlschein *der* death certificate.

Totenlsonntag *der* Sunday before Advent, day for commemoration of the dead in Protestant religion.

totenstill *adj* deathly silent.

totllachen ➠ **sich totlachen** *ref* fam to kill o.s. laughing.

Totschlag *der* RECHT manslaughter.

totlschlagen *vt* (*unreg*) [töten] to beat to death.

totlschweigen *vt* (*unreg*) to hush up.

tot stellen ➠ **sich tot stellen** *ref* to play dead.

Toupet [tuˈpeː] (*pl* **-s**) *das* toupee.

toupieren [tuˈpiːrən] *vt* to backcomb.

Tour [tuːɐ] (*pl* **-en**) *die* - **1.** [Ausflug] tour; [kürzere Fahrt] trip - **2.** fam [Verhaltensweise] ploy; **es auf die sanfte Tour versuchen** fam to use the gentle approach - **3.** [Strecke] route - **4.** TECH revolution; **auf vollen** ODER **höchsten Touren laufen** [Motor, Maschine] to run at full speed; fam [Vorbereitungen] to be in full swing; **auf Touren kommen** fam to get going.

Tourismus [tuˈrɪsmʊs] *der* tourism.

Tourist [tuˈrɪst] (*pl* **-en**) *der* tourist.

Touristin [tuˈrɪstɪn] (*pl* **-nen**) *die* tourist.

Trab *der* trot; **auf Trab sein** fig to be on the go; **jn in Trab halten** fam fig to keep sb on the go; **sich in Trab setzen** fam fig to get going.

Trabant ® (*pl* **-s**) *der* AUTO Trabant ®, small car formerly manufactured in the GDR.

traben (*perf* **ist getrabt**) *vi* to trot.

Trabi (*pl* **-s**) *der* fam colloquial name for a Trabant.

Trablrennen *das* trotting.

Tracht (pl -en) die - 1. [Kleidung] traditional costume - 2. [Schläge]: **eine Tracht Prügel** fam a beating.

trachten vi: **nach etw trachten** to strive for sthg; **jm nach dem Leben trachten** to be after sb's blood.

trächtig adj pregnant.

Trackball [tr'ɛkbɔːl] (pl -s) der EDV trackball.

Tradition (pl -en) die tradition.

traditionell <> adj traditional. <> adv traditionally.

traf prät ▷ **treffen**.

tragbar adj - 1. [Gerät] portable - 2. [Zustand, Verhalten] acceptable; **finanziell tragbar sein** to be financially viable.

träge <> adj - 1. [müde] lethargic - 2. [langsam] sluggish. <> adv - 1. [müde] lethargically - 2. [langsam] sluggishly.

tragen (präs trägt, prät trug, perf hat getragen) <> vt - 1. [schleppen] to carry - 2. [am Körper haben] to wear - 3. [bei sich haben]: **etw bei sich tragen** to carry sthg (on one) - 4. [Früchte] to produce; [Zinsen] to yield - 5. [Kosten, Schicksal, Leid] to bear; [Anteil] to pay - 6. [Einrichtung, Schule] to support - 7. [Verantwortung] to take; [Folgen] to suffer - 8. [Namen, Unterschrift] to bear. <> vi - 1. [Baum] to bear fruit - 2. [Gewicht]: **das Eis trägt noch nicht** the ice won't bear any weight yet - 3. [Reichweite haben] to carry - 4. [stützen] to support; **an etw (D) schwer tragen** to find sthg hard to bear. ▶ **sich tragen** ref fig - 1. [zu tragen sein]: **dieser Stoff trägt sich sehr angenehm** this material is very pleasant to wear; **der Koffer trägt sich schlecht** the suitcase is difficult to carry - 2. [sich selbst finanzieren] to be self-supporting - 3. geh [planen]: **sich mit etw tragen** to contemplate sthg. ▶ **Tragen** das: **zum Tragen kommen** to apply.

tragend adj load-bearing.

Träger, in (mpl -, fpl -nen) <> der, die - 1. [Lastenträger] porter - 2. [von Titel] holder - 3. [Geldgeber] sponsor. <> der - 1. ARCHIT girder - 2. [an Kleidung] strap.

Trageltasche die carrier bag.

tragfähig adj - 1. [Kompromiss, Politik] tenable - 2. [Konstruktion] solid, capable of supporting a load.

Tragifläche die wing.

Trägheit die - 1. [Faulheit] lethargy - 2. PHYS inertia.

Tragik die tragedy.

tragisch <> adj tragic. <> adv tragically.

Tragödie [tra'gøːdjə] (pl -n) die tragedy.

trägt präs ▷ **tragen**.

Tragweite die (ohne pl) consequences Pl; **von großer Tragweite** of great consequence.

Trainer, in ['trɛːnɐ, rɪn] (mpl -, fpl -nen) der, die coach.

trainieren [trɛ'niːrən] <> vt [Verein, Sportler] to coach; [Pferd] to train; [Salto, Elfmeterschießen] to practise. <> vi to train.

Training ['trɛːnɪŋ] (pl -s) das training (U).

Trainingsanlzug der tracksuit.

Traktor (pl -toren) der tractor.

trällern vt & vi to warble.

trampeln (perf hat/ist getrampelt) vi - 1. (ist) fam [gehen] to stamp - 2. (hat) [stampfen]: **mit den Füßen trampeln** to stamp one's feet.

trampen ['trɛmpn̩] (perf hat/ist getrampt) vi (hat) [an der Straße stehen] to hitchhike.

Tramper, in ['trɛmpɐ, rɪn] (mpl -, fpl -nen) der, die hitchhiker.

Trampolin (pl -e) das trampoline.

Tran (pl -e) der train oil; **im Tran sein** fam [unaufmerksam] to be out of it.

Träne (pl -n) die tear; **in Tränen ausbrechen** to burst into tears; **zu Tränen gerührt** moved to tears.

tränen vi to water.

Tränenlgas das tear gas.

trank prät ▷ **trinken**.

tränken vt to water.

Transformator (pl -toren) der transformer.

Transfusion (pl -en) die transfusion.

transitiv adj GRAMM transitive.

transparent adj transparent.

Transparent (pl -e) das banner.

Transport (pl -e) der transport.

transportabel adj portable.

transportfähig adj: **der Verletzte ist nicht transportfähig** the injured man cannot be moved.

transportieren <> vt - 1. [befördern] to transport - 2. FILM to wind on. <> vi [Kamera] to wind on; [Nähmaschine] to feed.

Transportlmittel das means (sg) of transport.

Transvestit [tansvɛs'tiːt] (pl -en) der transvestite.

Trapez (pl -e) das - 1. [im Zirkus] trapeze - 2. MATH trapezium UK, trapezoid US.

Trara das fam: **mit großem Trara** with a great hullabaloo; **Trara machen** to make a fuss.

trat prät ▷ **treten**.

Tratsch der fam abw gossip.

Traube (pl -n) die - 1. [Obst] grape - 2. BIOL raceme - 3. [Menge] cluster.

Traubenlzucker der glucose.

trauen <> vi: **jm/einer Sache trauen** to trust sb/sthg. <> vt [Brautpaar] to marry; **sich trauen lassen** to be married. ▶ **sich trauen** ref to dare.

Trauer die - 1. [Schmerz] sorrow - 2. [Staatstrauer, Trauerkleidung] mourning.

Trauerlfall der death, bereavement.

trauern vi: **(um jn) trauern** to mourn (for sb).

Trauer|spiel das: **es ist ein Trauerspiel** fam it's tragic.

Trauer|zug der funeral procession.

Traufe (pl -n) die: **vom Regen in die Traufe kommen** to jump out of the frying pan into the fire.

träufeln vt: **etw auf/in etw** (A) **träufeln** to trickle sthg onto/into sthg.

Traum (pl Träume) der dream.

Trauma (pl -ta) das trauma.

träumen ⬦ vi - 1. [gen] to dream; **schreck-lich/schön träumen** to have terrible/pleasant dreams; **von jm/etw träumen** eigtl & fig to dream about sb/sthg - 2. [abwesend sein] to dream, to daydream. ⬦ vt to dream about; **das hätte ich mir nicht träumen lassen** fig I'd never have imagined it possible.

Träumerei (pl -en) die daydream.

träumerisch ⬦ adj [Mensch] dreamy; [Gedanken] wistful. ⬦ adv dreamily.

traumhaft ⬦ adj - 1. [wunderschön] fab-ulous - 2. [souverän] amazing. ⬦ adv [wunder-schön] fabulously.

traurig ⬦ adj - 1. [betrüblich] sad - 2. [Rest, Zustand] sorry. ⬦ adv sadly.

Traurigkeit die sadness.

Trau|schein der marriage certificate.

Trauung (pl -en) die wedding; **kirchliche/ standesamtliche Trauung** church/civil wed-ding.

Trau|zeuge der witness (at a wedding).

Trau|zeugin die witness (at a wedding).

Traveller|scheck ['trɛvələ∫ɛk] der trav-eller's cheque.

treffen (präs trifft, prät traf, perf hat/ge-troffen) ⬦ vt (hat) - 1. [begegnen] to meet - 2. [Ziel] to hit; **auf dem Foto bist du gut ge-troffen** it's a good photo of you; **es gut/ schlecht getroffen haben** fig to have been lucky/unlucky - 3. [emotional verletzen] to af-fect - 4. [Verabredung, Entscheidung] to make; **eine Vereinbarung tref-fen** to come to an agreement. ⬦ vi - 1. (hat) [ins Ziel treffen] to score; **der Schuss traf nicht** the shot missed - 2. (ist) [begegnen]: **auf jn/etw treffen** to come across sb/sthg. ⬥ **sich tref-fen** ref to meet; **sich mit jm treffen** to meet sb; **es trifft sich gut/schlecht, dass...** fig it's lucky/ unlucky that...

Treffen (pl -) das meeting.

treffend ⬦ adj fitting. ⬦ adv fittingly.

Treffer (pl -) der - 1. [Tor] goal; [beim Basket-ball] basket - 2. [mit Schusswaffe] hit - 3. [Box-hieb] blow - 4. [Losgewinn] win.

Treff|punkt der meeting place.

treiben (prät trieb, perf hat/ist getrieben) ⬦ vt (hat) - 1. [gen] to drive; **jn in etw** (A)**/zu etw treiben** to drive sb to sthg; **du treibst mich noch in den Wahnsinn** you're driving me mad;

die Strömung trieb das Boot an den Strand the current carried the boat ashore; **durch Wind-kraft getrieben** wind-powered - 2. fam [anstel-len] to get up to; **was treibt ihr beiden denn da wieder?** what are you two up to now? - 3. [ansetzen] to produce - 4. [bohren - Schacht, Tunnel] to dig; **es zu bunt treiben** fam to overdo it. ⬦ vi - 1. (ist) [im Wasser] to drift; **sich treiben lassen** fig to drift - 2. (hat) [anset-zen - Blüten] to flower; [- Wurzeln] to root - 3. (hat) [Harndrang verursachen] to be a diuret-ic, to have a diuretic effect.

Treiben das (ohne pl) - 1. [Durcheinander] bustle - 2. abw [Tun] activities Pl.

Treib|haus das greenhouse.

Treibhaus|effekt der greenhouse effect.

Treib|jagd die shoot (in which game is beaten).

Treib|stoff der fuel.

Trend (pl -s) der trend; **im Trend liegen** to be in vogue.

trennen vt - 1. [gen] to separate - 2. [unter-scheiden] to distinguish. ⬥ **sich trennen** ref - 1. [Menschen] to separate; **sich von jm tren-nen** to leave sb; **sich von etw trennen** to part with sthg - 2. [Wege, Leitungen etc] to divide.

Trennung (pl -en) die - 1. [gen & CHEM] separ-ation; **in Trennung leben** to be separated - 2. [Unterscheidung] distinction - 3. GRAMM end-of-line hyphenation.

Trenn|wand die partition.

Treppe (pl -n) die [in Gebäude] stairs Pl; [im Freien] steps Pl; **eine Treppe** [in Gebäude] a stair-case; [im Freien] a flight of steps.

Treppenab|satz der half-landing.

Treppen|geländer das banister.

Treppen|haus das stairwell.

Tresen (pl -) der [Ausschank] bar; [Ladentisch] counter.

Tresor (pl -e) der safe; [Raum] strong room.

Tret|boot das pedal boat.

treten (präs tritt, prät trat, perf hat/ist getre-ten) ⬦ vt (hat) - 1. [mit dem Fuß] to kick; **jm auf den Fuß treten** to tread on sb's foot - 2. [Kupplung, Bremse] to step on, to put one's foot down on - 3. fam [antreiben]: **jn treten** to push sb. ⬦ vi - 1. (hat) [mit dem Fuß] to kick; **auf etw** (A) **treten** to step on sthg - 2. (ist) [ge-hen]: **ins Zimmer treten** to enter ODER come in-to the room; **zu jm treten** to go up to sb; **tre-ten Sie näher!** come closer! - 3. [betätigen]: **auf die Bremse treten** to step on the brake, to brake - 4. (ist) [hervor]: **aus etw treten** to issue from sthg - 5. [beginnen]: **in den Streik treten** to go on strike.

treu ⬦ adj faithful; [Anhänger, Kunde] loyal; **einer Sache** (D) **treu sein** to be true to sthg; **jm treu sein** [sexuell] to be faithful to sb; **jm/einer**

Sache treu bleiben to remain faithful to sb/ true to sthg. ⋄ *adv* [verlässlich] faithfully; [unterstützen] loyally.

Treue *die* - 1. [gen] faithfulness; [von Anhänger, Kunde] loyalty; **jm die Treue halten** to keep faith with sb - 2. [sexuell] fidelity.

treuherzig ⋄ *adj* trusting. ⋄ *adv* trustingly.

treulos ⋄ *adj* disloyal; [Liebhaber] unfaithful. ⋄ *adv* disloyally; [Liebhaber] unfaithfully.

Tribüne (*pl* -n) *die* - 1. [Sitzplätze] stand - 2. [Rednertribüne] rostrum.

Trichine (*pl* -n) *die* trichina.

Trichter (*pl* -) *der* - 1. [Gerät] funnel - 2. [nach Explosion] crater.

Trick (*pl* -s) *der* trick.

Trick|film *der* cartoon.

trieb *prät* ⊳ **treiben**.

Trieb (*pl* -e) *der* - 1. [biologisch] instinct - 2. [psychologisch] urge - 3. [pflanzlich] shoot.

triebhaft ⋄ *adj* compulsive. ⋄ *adv* compulsively.

Trieb|kraft *die* driving force; [von Handeln] motive.

Trieb|wagen *der* railcar.

Trieb|werk *das* FLUG engine.

triefen (*prät* triefte ODER troff, *perf* hat/ist getrieft) *vi* - 1. (hat) [nass sein]: **von** ODER **vor etw** (D) **triefen** eigtl & fig to drip with sthg; **eure Kleider triefen vor Nässe** your clothes are dripping wet - 2. (ist) [fließen - in Tropfen] to drip; [- in Rinnsalen] to run.

trifft *präs* ⊳ **treffen**.

triftig *adj* [Grund] good; [Argumente] valid.

Trikot (*pl* -s), **Trikot** (*pl* -s) [tri'ko:, 'trɪko] *das* [von Radrennfahrer] jersey; [von Fußballspieler] shirt; [von Tänzer] leotard.

trillern *vt* & *vi* to warble.

Triller|pfeife *die* whistle.

Trimester (*pl* -) *das* [von Studienjahr] term; WIRTSCH quarter.

trinkbar *adj* drinkable.

trinken (*prät* trank, *perf* hat getrunken) ⋄ *vt* to drink; **einen trinken** *fam* to have a drink; **einen trinken gehen** *fam* to go for a drink. ⋄ *vi* to drink; **auf jn/etw trinken** to drink to sb/sthg.

Trinker, in (*mpl* -, *fpl* -nen) *der, die* alcoholic.

Trink|geld *das* tip.

Trink|halm *der* (drinking) straw.

Trink|wasser *das* drinking water.

Trio (*pl* -s) *das* trio.

trippeln (*perf* ist getrippelt) *vi* to trip along.

Tripper (*pl* -) *der* gonorrhoea.

tritt *präs* ⊳ **treten**.

Tritt (*pl* -e) *der* - 1. [Fußtritt] kick; **jm einen Tritt (in den Bauch) versetzen** to kick sb (in the stomach) - 2. [Schritt, Gang] step; **im Tritt** in step.

Tritt|brett *das* step; [von Auto] running board.

Triumph (*pl* -e) *der* triumph.

triumphieren *vi* - 1. [siegen]: **über jn/etw triumphieren** to triumph over sb/sthg - 2. [frohlocken]: **innerlich triumphieren** to be inwardly triumphant.

trivial [tri'vja:l] *geh* ⋄ *adj* - 1. [banal] trite - 2. [unbedeutend] trivial. ⋄ *adv* - 1. [banal] tritely - 2. [unbedeutend] trivially.

trocken ⋄ *adj* - 1. [gen] dry - 2. [ohne Beilage] plain; [Brot] dry; **auf dem Trockenen sitzen** *fam* [keinen Alkohol mehr haben] to have nothing to drink; [kein Geld haben] to be broke. ⋄ *adv* drily.

Trockenheit (*pl* -en) *die* - 1. [regenlose Zeit] drought - 2. [Zustand] dryness.

trocken|legen *vt* - 1. [entwässern] to drain - 2. [Windeln wechseln] to change.

trocknen (*perf* hat/ist getrocknet) ⋄ *vt* (hat) to dry; **sich** (D) **die Tränen/Hände trocknen** to dry one's tears/hands. ⋄ *vi* (ist) to dry.

Trockner (*pl* -) *der* dryer.

Trödel *der* junk.

trödeln (*perf* hat/ist getrödelt) *vi* to dawdle.

troff *prät* ⊳ **triefen**.

trog *prät* ⊳ **trügen**.

Trog (*pl* Tröge) *der* trough.

Trommel (*pl* -n) *die* drum; [von Revolver] cylinder; [für Kabel] reel.

Trommel|fell *das* MED eardrum.

trommeln ⋄ *vi* - 1. [Musik machen, Lärm machen] to drum; **sie trommelt sehr gut** she plays the drums very well - 2. [schlagen] to beat. ⋄ *vt* - 1. [Rhythmus] to beat out - 2. [mit Lärm wecken]: **jn aus dem Bett trommeln** to get sb up by hammering on the door.

Trommler, in (*mpl* -, *fpl* -nen) *der, die* drummer.

Trompete (*pl* -n) *die* trumpet.

Trompeter, in (*mpl* -, *fpl* -nen) *der, die* trumpeter.

Tropen *Pl*: **die Tropen** the tropics.

Tropf (*pl* -e ODER Tröpfe) *der* - 1. (*pl* Tropfe) MED drip - 2. (*pl* Tröpfe) [Mensch]: **armer Tropf!** poor devil!

tröpfeln (*perf* hat/ist getröpfelt) ⋄ *vi* - 1. (ist) [tropfen] to drip - 2. (hat) *fam* [regnen]: **es tröpfelt** it's spitting. ⋄ *vt* (hat) to drip.

tropfen (*perf* hat/ist getropft) ⋄ *vi* to drip; **es tropft** it's spitting. ⋄ *vt* (hat) to drip.

Tropfen (*pl* -) *der* drop. ◆ **Tropfen** *Pl* MED drops.

Trophäe (*pl* -n) *die* [Jagdtrophäe] trophy.

tropisch <> *adj* tropical. <> *adv* tropically.

Trost *der (ohne pl)* consolation, comfort; **nicht ganz bei Trost sein** *fam* to be out of one's mind.

trösten *vt* to console, to comfort. ➡ **sich**
trösten *ref*: **sich (mit etw) trösten** to console o.s. (with sthg); **sie tröstete sich mit ihrem Liebhaber** she found consolation in her lover; **tröste dich, mir geht es doch nicht besser!** if it's any consolation, I'm not much better!

tröstlich *adj* comforting.

trostlos *adj abw* - **1.** [deprimierend] dreary - **2.** [traurig] despairing.

Trost|preis *der* consolation prize.

Trott *(pl -e) der* - **1.** [Gangart] trot - **2.** *fam* [Gewohnheit] routine.

Trottel *(pl -) der fam abw* idiot.

trotten *(perf ist getrottet) vi* to trot.

trotz *präp* (+ G) despite, in spite of.

trotzdem *adv* nevertheless.

trotzig <> *adj* [Kind] difficult; [aus gutem Grund] defiant; [Gesicht, Antwort] contrary. <> *adv* [aus gutem Grund] defiantly; [uneinsichtig] contrarily.

Trotz|kopf *der* [sturer Mensch] pigheaded so-and-so.

trüb, trübe *adj* - **1.** [Flüssigkeit] cloudy; [Augen] dull - **2.** [Wetter, Tag, Stimmung] gloomy; **mit seinen Berufschancen siehts trüb aus** it's looking bleak as far as his career prospects are concerned.

Trubel *der* hurly-burly.

trüben *vt* - **1.** [verschlechtern] to mar; [gute Laune] to dampen - **2.** [Flüssigkeit, Denken, Urteilskraft] to cloud. ➡ **sich trüben** *ref* - **1.** [Wasser] to go cloudy; [Himmel] to cloud over - **2.** [Stimmung, Laune] to be dampened.

Trübsal *die geh* [Melancholie] melancholy; [Kummer] grief; **Trübsal blasen** *fig* to mope.

trübselig <> *adj* gloomy. <> *adv* gloomily.

trudeln *(perf ist getrudelt) vi* - **1.** [fliegen] to spin - **2.** [rollen] to roll.

Trüffel *(pl -) der* truffle.

trug *prät* ⊳ **tragen**.

trügen *(prät trog, perf hat getrogen)* <> *vi* to be deceptive. <> *vt* to deceive.

trügerisch *adj* deceptive.

Trugschluss *(pl -schlüsse) der* misconception.

Truhe *(pl -n) die* chest.

Trümmer *Pl* [Ruinen] ruins; [Schutt] rubble *(U)*; [von Fahrzeug] wreckage *(U)*; **in Trümmern** *eigtl* & *fig* in ruins.

Trumpf *(pl Trümpfe) der* trump (card); **Karo ist Trumpf!** diamonds are trumps!; **Flexibilität ist Trumpf** flexibility is the order of the day.

Trunkenheit *die amt* inebriation.

Trunk|sucht *die* alcoholism.

Trupp *(pl -s) der* [von Soldaten, Polizisten] detachment, squad; [von Arbeitern] group.

Truppe *(pl -n) die* - **1.** [Einheit] unit - **2.** *(ohne pl)* [Streitkräfte] forces *Pl*; [Heer] army - **3.** [Gruppe] troupe. ➡ **Truppen** *Pl* troops.

Trut|hahn *der* turkey.

Tscheche *(pl -n) der* Czech.

Tschechien *nt* Czech Republic.

Tschechin *(pl -nen) die* Czech.

tschechisch *adj* Czech.

Tschechisch(e) *das* Czech; *siehe auch* **Englisch(e).**

Tschechische Republik *die* Czech Republic.

Tschechoslowakei *die* Czechoslovakia.

tschüs, tschüss *interj fam* bye!

Tsd. *abk für* **Tausend.**

T-Shirt ['tiːʃœːɐ̯t] *(pl -s) das* T-shirt.

TU [teːˈuː] *(pl -s) (abk für Technische Universität) die* university specializing in science and technology.

Tuba *(pl Tuben) die* tuba.

Tube *(pl -n) die* tube.

Tuberkulose *(pl -n) die* tuberculosis.

Tuch *(pl -e ODER Tücher) das* [Stoffteil, Stoff] cloth; [Halstuch] scarf; **für jn ein rotes Tuch sein** *fig* to make sb see red.

tüchtig <> *adj* - **1.** [fleißig] hardworking; [fähig] competent - **2.** [groß] big; **ein tüchtiger Schreck** a real shock. <> *adv* - **1.** [fleißig] hard; [fähig] competently - **2.** *fam* [viel]: **tüchtig kalt** really cold.

Tücke *(pl -n) die* - **1.** [Eigenschaft] deceit - **2.** [Handlung] trick, ruse.

tückisch <> *adj* - **1.** [hinterhältig - Person] deceitful; [- Plan, Idee] underhand - **2.** [schwierig] devilishly difficult - **3.** [Auto, Gerät] temperamental - **4.** [gefährlich] treacherous. <> *adv* - **1.** [hinterhältig] deceitfully - **2.** [gefährlich] treacherously.

Tugend *(pl -en) die* virtue.

tugendhaft <> *adj* virtuous. <> *adv* virtuously.

Tulpe *(pl -n) die* tulip.

tummeln ➡ **sich tummeln** *ref* to romp around.

Tumor *(pl Tumore)*, **Tumor** *(pl Tumore) der* tumour.

Tümpel *(pl -) der* pond.

Tumult *(pl -e) der* commotion.

tun *(prät tat, perf hat getan)* <> *vt* - **1.** [machen] to do; **was tust du denn da?** what are you doing?; **so etwas tut man nicht** you shouldn't do that; **was kann ich für Sie tun?** what can I do for you?; **das hat damit nichts zu tun** that's got nothing to do with it - **2.** [stellen, legen] to put - **3.** [antun]: **jm/sich etwas tun** to do something to sb/o.s. - **4.** *fam* [hinreichend sein]: **ich denke, das tut es** I think that will do; **damit ist es nicht getan** that's not enough - **5.** *fam* [funktionieren]: **das Auto tut es noch/nicht mehr** the car still works/has had it. ◇ *vi* - **1.** [machen]: **zu tun haben** to be busy; **jm gut tun** to do sb good - **2.** [vortäuschen]: **so tun, als ob** *fam* to act as if; **er tut nur so** he's only pretending - **3.** [Ausdruck einer Beziehung]: **du bekommst es mit mir zu tun, wenn...** *fam* you'll have me to answer to if...; **mit jm dienstlich zu tun haben** to know sb professionally. ◆ **sich tun** *ref*: **es tut sich etwas/nichts** something/nothing is happening.

Tun *das (ohne pl)* actions *Pl.*

tünchen *vt* to whitewash.

Tunesien *nt* Tunisia.

Tunesier, in [tu'neːzjɐ, rɪn] *(mpl -, fpl -nen)* der, die Tunisian.

tunesisch *adj* Tunisian.

Tunfisch *der* = **Thunfisch.**

tunken *vt* to dip; [Brot, Keks] to dunk.

tunlichst ['tuːnlɪçst] *adv* [unbedingt] at all costs; [möglichst] as far as possible.

Tunnel *(pl -)* der tunnel.

Tüpfelchen *(pl -)* das dot; **das Tüpfelchen auf dem i sein** to be the icing on the cake.

tupfen *vt* to dab; **etw auf etw (A) tupfen** to dab sthg onto sthg.

Tupfen *(pl -)* der spot; [kleiner] dot.

Tür *(pl -en)* die [gen] door; **Tür zu!** shut the door!; **jn vor die Tür setzen** *fam* [rauswerfen, entlassen] to kick sb out.

Turban *(pl -e)* der turban.

Turbine *(pl -n)* die turbine.

turbulent *adj* - **1.** [ereignisreich] eventful - **2.** [chaotisch] turbulent.

Türgriff *der* doorhandle.

Türke *(pl -n)* der Turk.

Türkei *die*: **die Türkei** Turkey.

Türkin *(pl -nen)* die Turk.

türkis *adj* turquoise.

Türkis *(pl -e)* der ODER das turquoise.

türkisch *adj* Turkish.

Türkisch(e) *das* Turkish; *siehe auch* **Englisch(e)**.

Türklinke *die* door handle.

Turm *(pl Türme)* der - **1.** [Bauwerk] tower - **2.** [Schachfigur] rook, castle.

türmen *(perf hat/ist getürmt)* ◇ *vi (ist)* fam to beat it, to do a runner *UK*. ◇ *vt (hat)* to pile up. ◆ **sich türmen** *ref* to be piled up.

Turmuhr *die* tower clock; [von Kirche] church clock.

turnen *(perf hat/ist geturnt)* ◇ *vt (hat)* to perform. ◇ *vi* - **1.** [an einem Sportgerät] to do gymnastics; **an den Ringen/am Barren turnen** to exercise on the rings/on the parallel bars - **2.** *(ist) fam* [klettern] to clamber about.

Turnen *das* [in der Schule] gym; [sport] gymnastics *(U)*.

Turnhalle *die* gymnasium.

Turnhose *die* (gym) shorts *Pl.*

Turnier *(pl -e)* das tournament.

Turnschuh *der* gym shoe *UK*, sneaker *US*.

Turnverein *der* sports club.

Türrahmen *der* doorframe.

Türschloss *(pl -schlösser)* das lock.

Türschwelle *die* threshold.

Tusch *(pl -e)* der fanfare.

Tusche *(pl -n)* die Indian ink.

tuscheln *vt & vi* to whisper.

tut *präs* ⊳ **tun.**

Tütchen *(pl -)* das sachet.

Tüte *(pl -n)* die bag; [mit Backpulver] packet.

tuten *vi* - **1.** [hupen] to toot; **das Schiff tutet** the ship sounds its horn - **2.** [tönen] to beep.

Tutor *(pl -en)* der tutor.

Tutorin *(pl -nen)* die tutor.

TÜV [tʏf] *(abk für* Technischer Überwachungsverein) *der (ohne pl)*: **ein Auto zum TÜV bringen** ≃ to take a car for its MOT (test) *UK*.

TV *(abk für* Fernsehen) TV.

Typ *(pl -en)* der - **1.** [Menschentyp, Art] type; **er ist der Typ eines Deutschen** he is a typical German; **(nicht) js Typ sein** *fam* (not) to be sb's type - **2.** *fam* [Kerl] guy.

Typhus *der* MED typhoid.

typisch ◇ *adj* typical; **etw ist typisch für jn** sthg is typical of sb. ◇ *adv* typically. ◇ *interj*: **typisch!** typical!

Tyrann, in *(mpl -en, fpl -nen)* der, die tyrant.

tyrannisieren *vt abw* to tyrannize.

u *(pl - ODER -s)*, **U** *(pl - ODER -s)* [uː] das u, U.

u. *abk für* **und.**

u. a. *(abk für* unter anderem), *among other things.*

u. a. m. *(abk für* und anderes mehr) etc.

U-Bahn *die* underground *UK*, subway *US*.

übel *(kompar übler, superl übelste)* ◇ *adj* - **1.** [Essen, Laune] bad; **nicht übel sein** *fam* to be not bad - **2.** [moralisch] evil; **in übler Gesellschaft** in bad company - **3.** [Zustand] nasty, bad; **übel dransein** *fam* to be in a bad way - **4.** [unwohl]: **mir ist/wird übel** I feel sick.

◇ *adv* - **1.** [schlimm] badly - **2.** [unwirsch]: **übel gelaunt (sein)** (to be) in a bad mood *ODER* temper.

Übel (*pl -*) *das* evil; **von Übel sein** to be an evil.

übel nehmen *vt (unreg)*: **jm etw übel nehmen** to hold sth against sb.

üben ◇ *vt* - **1.** [trainieren] to practise - **2.** *geh* [äußern]: **Nachsicht üben** to be lenient; **Kritik üben** to criticize. ◇ *vi* to practise.

über ◇ *präp* - **1.** (+ A) [eine Richtung anzeigend - oberhalb] over, above; [- quer über] over; [- bei Routen] via; **das Flugzeug flog über das Tal** the plane flew over the valley; **er breitete die Decke über das Bett** he spread the blanket over the bed; **über die Straße gehen** to cross the road - **2.** (+ D) [eine Position anzeigend] over, above; **die Lampe hängt über dem Tisch** the lamp hangs above *ODER* over the table - **3.** (+ A) [zeitlich] over; **über Wochen/Monate** for weeks/months; **über Nacht** overnight - **4.** (+ A) [mehr als] over; **über eine Stunde** over an hour - **5.** (+ D) [mehr als] above; **über dem Durchschnitt liegen** to be above average; **Kinder über zehn Jahren** children over ten (years of age); **seit über einem Jahr** for more than a year - **6.** (+ A) [mittels] through, via - **7.** (+ A) [stellt Bezug her] about; **ein Buch über Mozart** a book about *ODER* on Mozart - **8.** (+ A) [zur Angabe des Betrages] for; **eine Rechnung über 30 Euro** a bill for 30 euros - **9.** (+ A) *fig*: **ich bringe es nicht über mich** I can't bring myself to. ◇ *adv* - **1.** [mehr als] over - **2.** [zeitlich]: **den Winter über** all winter (long); **das ganze Jahr über** all (the) year round. ◇ *adj fam* - **1.** [überdrüssig]: **etw über haben** to have had enough of sthg - **2.** [übrig] left (over); **ich habe noch fünf Euro über** I still have five euros left.

überall, überall *adv* everywhere.

überanstrengen *vt* to overstrain. ◆ **sich überanstrengen** *ref* to overexert o.s.

überarbeiten *vt* to revise. ◆ **sich überarbeiten** *ref* to overwork.

überbacken (*präs* **überbackt** *ODER* **überbäckt**, *prät* **überbackte** *ODER* **überbuk**, *perf* **hat überbacken**) *vt* to brown; **etw mit Käse überbacken** to bake sthg with a cheese topping.

überbelichten *vt* to overexpose.

überbieten (*prät* **überbot**, *perf* **hat überboten**) *vt*: **einen Preis (um etw) überbieten** to exceed a price (by sthg); **jn (um 5.000 Euro) überbieten** to outbid sb (by 5,000 euros); **einen Rekord (um 10 cm) überbieten** to break a record (by 10 cm). ◆ **sich überbieten** *ref geh* to surpass o.s.; [Konkurrenten] to vie with each other.

Überbleibsel (*pl -*) *das* [Spur] remnant; [Ruinen, Scherben] remains *Pl*.

Überblick *der* - **1.**: **ein Überblick über etw** (A) [Übersicht] an overall perspective of sthg; [Zusammenfassung] a summary of sthg; **den Überblick verlieren** to lose perspective - **2.** [Aussicht]: **ein Überblick über etw** (A) a (panoramic) view of sthg.

überblicken *vt* - **1.** [einschätzen] to assess - **2.** [sehen] to overlook.

überbringen (*prät* **überbrachte**, *perf* **hat überbracht**) *vt*: **jm etw überbringen** to deliver sthg to sb.

überbrücken *vt* [Zeit] to fill in; [Gegensätze] to reconcile.

überdauern *vt geh* to survive.

überdehnen *vt* to strain.

überdenken (*prät* **überdachte**, *perf* **hat überdacht**) *vt* to think over.

Überdruss *der* weariness; **sie haben bis zum Überdruss Karten gespielt** *fam fig* they played cards till they got fed up with it.

übereilen *vt* to rush; **nur nichts übereilen** don't rush things, take your time.

übereilt ◇ *adj* hasty. ◇ *adv* hastily.

übereinander *adv* - **1.** [Dinge] on top of each other - **2.** [Menschen - reden, nachdenken] about each other.

übereinander schlagen *vt (unreg)*: **die Beine übereinander schlagen** to cross one's legs.

Übereinkunft (*pl -***künfte**) *die geh* agreement.

überein|stimmen *vi* - **1.** *geh* [einig sein]: **mit jm (in etw** (D)**) übereinstimmen** to agree with sb (about sthg) - **2.** [gleich sein - Zahlen, Messwerte] to tally; [- Aussagen] to correspond.

Überein|stimmung *die* - **1.** [Einigung] agreement (U) - **2.** [Gleichheit] correspondence (U); **etw (mit etw) in Übereinstimmung bringen** to bring sthg into line (with sthg).

überfahren (*präs* **überfährt**, *prät* **überfuhr**, *perf* **hat überfahren**) *vt* - **1.** [töten] to run over - **2.** [Kreuzung, Schild] to drive through.

Über|fahrt *die* crossing.

Überfall *der* attack; **Überfall auf jn/etw** attack on sb/sthg.

überfallen (*präs* **überfällt**, *prät* **überfiel**, *perf* **hat überfallen**) *vt* - **1.** [ausrauben - gen] to attack; [- Bank] to raid; [- eine Frau] to assault - **2.** *fam* [überraschen] to descend on.

überfällig *adj* overdue.

überfliegen (*prät* **überflog**, *perf* **hat überflogen**) *vt* - **1.** [fliegen] to fly over - **2.** *fig* [lesen] to glance over.

Überfluss *der* [viel] abundance; [zu viel] surplus; **im Überfluss leben** to live affluently; **etw im Überfluss haben** to have sthg in abundance.

überflüssig *adj* [überzählig] superfluous; [frei] spare; [unnötig] unnecessary.

überfordern *vt* to overtax; **jn (mit etw** (D)**) überfordern** to ask too much of sb (with sthg); **die junge Mutter war überfordert** the young mother couldn't cope.

überfragt adj: **da bin ich überfragt** I can't help you there.

Überlführung die - **1.** [Transport] transfer; [von Toten] transportation - **2.** [Brücke] bridge.

überfüllt adj overcrowded.

Übergabe die - **1.** [von Gegenstand, Besitz] handing over; **die Übergabe (einer Sache (G)) an jn** the handing over (of sthg) to sb - **2.** MIL surrender.

Übergang (pl -gänge) der - **1.** (ohne pl) [Provisorium] temporary arrangement - **2.** [Kontrast] contrast - **3.** [Weg] crossing; [Brücke] bridge - **4.** [Phase] transition.

übergeben (präs übergibt, prät übergab, perf hat übergeben) vt - **1.** [überreichen, weitergeben]: **jm etw übergeben** to hand sthg over to sb; [feierlich überreichen] to present sthg to sb - **2.** [überantworten]: **jm etw/jn übergeben** to hand sthg/sb over to sb - **3.** [freigeben] to open. ◆ **sich übergeben** ref to vomit.

übergehen[1] (prät überging, perf hat übergangen) vt - **1.**: **jn/etw übergehen** [nicht beachten] to ignore sb/sthg; [überspringen] to skip sb/sthg - **2.** [nicht berücksichtigen]: **jn bei etw übergehen** to pass sb over for sthg.

überlgehen[2] (perf ist übergegangen) vi (unreg) - **1.** [wechseln]: **zu etw übergehen** to proceed to sthg; **dazu übergehen, etw zu tun** to proceed to do sthg - **2.** [den Besitzer wechseln]: **an jn übergehen** to pass to sb.

Überlgewicht das - **1.** [von Personen]: **Übergewicht haben** to be overweight - **2.** [von Gegenständen] excess weight (U).

übergießen (prät übergoß, perf hat übergossen) vt: **jn/etw mit etw übergießen** to pour sthg over sb/sthg.

überlgreifen vi (unreg): **auf etw (A) übergreifen** to spread to sthg.

überhand nehmen vi (unreg) to get out of hand.

überhäufen vt: **jn/etw mit etw überhäufen** to inundate sb/sthg with sthg.

überhaupt ⟨⟩ adv - **1.** [verstärkend] at all; **gibt es überhaupt eine Hoffnung?** is there any hope at all?; **überhaupt nicht** not at all; **überhaupt nichts** nothing at all - **2.** [eigentlich] anyway; **wie gehts dir überhaupt?** so, how are you, anyway? - **3.** [im Allgemeinen] on the whole. ⟨⟩ interj [Ausdruck der Ungeduld, des Missfallens]: **und überhaupt** anyway.

überheblich ⟨⟩ adj arrogant. ⟨⟩ adv arrogantly.

überholen ⟨⟩ vt - **1.** [vorbeifahren] to overtake - **2.** fam [übertreffen] to leave behind - **3.** [warten] to overhaul. ⟨⟩ vi to overtake.

überholt adj outdated.

überhören vt - **1.** [nicht hören] not to hear - **2.** [ignorieren] to ignore.

überirdisch adj supernatural.

überladen (präs überlädt, prät überlud, perf hat überladen) vt to overload.

überlassen (präs überläßt, prät überließ, perf hat überlassen) vt - **1.** [leihen]: **jm etw überlassen** to let sb have sthg - **2.** [sich nicht einmischen]: **jm etw überlassen** to leave sthg to sb - **3.** [allein lassen]: **jn sich (D) selbst überlassen** to leave sb to his/her own devices.

überlastet adj - **1.** [belastet] overloaded - **2.** [überfordert]: **mit etw überlastet sein** to be overburdened with sthg.

überllaufen[1] (perf ist übergelaufen) vi (unreg) - **1.** [überfließen] to overflow - **2.** [überwechseln] to go over to the other side; **zu jm/etw überlaufen** to go over to sb/sthg.

überlaufen[2] (präs überläuft, prät überlief, perf hat überlaufen) vt - **1.** [überkommen]: **es überläuft mich** shivers run down my spine - **2.** SPORT [hinter sich lassen] to outrun; [zu weit laufen] to overshoot.

überlaufen[3] adj: **überlaufen sein** to be overcrowded; [Kurs] to be oversubscribed.

überleben ⟨⟩ vt - **1.** [lebend überstehen] to survive - **2.** [länger leben als]: **jn überleben** to outlive sb. ⟨⟩ vi to survive.

Überlebende (pl -n) der, die survivor.

überlegen[1] ⟨⟩ vt to think about, to consider; **sich (D) etw überlegen** to think sthg over [über etw nachdenken]; [sich etw ausdenken] to think of sthg. ⟨⟩ vi to think.

überlegen[2] ⟨⟩ adj [besser] superior; [arrogant] patronizing; **jm überlegen sein** to be superior to sb. ⟨⟩ adv [siegen] convincingly; [lächeln] patronizingly.

Überlegenheit die superiority.

Überlegung (pl -en) die consideration (U); **ohne Überlegung handeln** to act without thinking.

überliefern vt to hand down.

Überllieferung (pl -en) die - **1.** [das Überliefern] handing down - **2.** [das Überlieferte] tradition.

Übermacht die superior strength; **in der Übermacht sein** to be stronger.

Übermaß das excess.

übermäßig ⟨⟩ adj excessive. ⟨⟩ adv excessively; **sich übermäßig anstrengen** to overexert o.s.; **übermäßig ehrgeizig** overambitious.

übermitteln vt: **jm etw übermitteln** to pass sthg on to sb.

übermorgen adv the day after tomorrow.

übermüdet adj overtired.

Übermut der (ohne pl) high spirits Pl.

übernachten vi to stay ODER spend the night; **bei jm übernachten** to stay the night with sb.

übernächtigt adj bleary-eyed.

Übernachtung (*pl* -en) *die* overnight stay; **eine Übernachtung mit Frühstück** bed and breakfast.

Übernahme (*pl* -n) *die* - **1.** [von Firma, Betrieb] takeover; [das Übernehmen] taking over (*U*) - **2.** [Eingliederung]: **die Übernahme in ein dauerhaftes Arbeitsverhältnis** the conversion to a permanent position - **3.** [von Kosten] meeting (*U*) - **4.** [von Wort, Brauch] adoption (*U*).

übernehmen (*präs* übernimmt, *prät* übernahm, *perf* hat übernommen) *vt* - **1.** [Firma, Betrieb] to take over; **etw von jm übernehmen** to take sthg over from sb - **2.** [annehmen] to take on - **3.** [einstellen, weiterbeschäftigen] to keep on - **4.** [kopieren]: **etw von jm/etw übernehmen** [Verhaltensweise, Konzept] to adopt sthg from sb/sthg; [Text] to copy sthg from sb/sthg. ➡ **sich übernehmen** *ref* to overdo it.

überprüfen *vt* to inspect, to check; [Verdächtigen] to screen.

Überlprüfung (*pl* -en) *die* checking (*U*); [von Verdächtigern] screening (*U*).

überqueren *vt* to cross.

überragen *vt* - **1.** [größer sein] to tower above - **2.** [übertreffen] to surpass.

überragend ⬦ *adj* outstanding. ⬦ *adv* superbly.

überraschen *vt* to surprise; **jn mit etw überraschen** to surprise sb with sthg; **jn bei etw überraschen** to catch sb doing sthg; **von jm/etw überrascht werden** to be taken by surprise by sb/sthg; **vom Regen überrascht werden** to get caught in the rain.

Überraschung (*pl* -en) *die* surprise.

überreden *vt* to persuade; **jn zu etw überreden** to persuade sb to do sthg; **sich zu etw überreden lassen** to let o.s. be talked into (doing) sthg.

überreichen *vt*: **jm etw überreichen** to present sthg to sb.

überreizt ⬦ *adj* tense; [nervös] edgy, jumpy. ⬦ *adv* nervously.

Überlrest *der* remains *Pl.*

überrumpeln *vt*: **jn (mit etw) überrumpeln** to take sb by surprise (with sthg).

überrunden *vt* - **1.** SPORT to lap - **2.** [übertreffen] to outstrip.

übers *präp fam* (über + das): **der Vogel fliegt übers Haus** the bird is flying over the house; **übers Jahr verteilt** spread over the year; **übers schlechte Wetter schimpfen** to complain about the bad weather.

übersät *adj*: **mit etw übersät sein** to be strewn with sthg.

Überschallgeschwindigkeit *die* supersonic speed.

überschatten *vt* to overshadow.

überschätzen *vt* to overestimate. ➡ **sich überschätzen** *ref* to overestimate o.s.

überlschäumen (*perf* ist übergeschäumt) *vi* - **1.** [überfließen] to froth over - **2.** *fig* [emotional - vor Begeisterung, Lebenslust] to brim over; [- vor Wut, Zorn] to boil over.

überschlagen (*präs* überschlägt, *prät* überschlug, *perf* hat überschlagen) *vt* - **1.** [rechnen] to estimate (roughly) - **2.** [überblättern] to skip. ➡ **sich überschlagen** *ref* - **1.** [Auto] to overturn; [Person] to fall head over heels - **2.** [Ereignisse] to follow one another thick and fast - **3.** [Stimme] to crack.

überlschnappen (*perf* ist übergeschnappt) *vi fam* to go crazy.

überschneiden (*prät* überschnitt, *perf* hat überschnitten) ➡ **sich überschneiden** *ref* - **1.** [räumlich] to intersect - **2.** [zeitlich] to coincide - **3.** [inhaltlich] to overlap.

überschreiben (*prät* überschrieb, *perf* hat überschrieben) *vt* - **1.** [übereignen]: **jm etw überschreiben** to make sthg over to sb - **2.** [betiteln] to head.

überschreiten (*prät* überschritt, *perf* hat überschritten) *vt* - **1.** [räumlich] to cross - **2.** [inhaltlich - gen] to exceed; [- Befugnis] to overstep - **3.** [zeitlich] to pass.

Überlschrift *die* heading; [in Fettdruck] headline.

Überschuss (*pl* -schüsse) *der* - **1.** [Gewinn] profit; **Überschuss erzielen** to make a profit - **2.** [ein Zuviel] surplus.

überschüssig *adj* surplus.

überschütten *vt*: **jn/etw mit etw überschütten** to cover sb/sthg with sthg; **jn mit Lob überschütten** to shower sb with praise; **jn mit Vorwürfen überschütten** to heap criticism on sb.

überschwänglich ⬦ *adj* effusive. ⬦ *adv* effusively.

überschwemmen *vt* - **1.** [nass machen] to flood - **2.** [überreich versehen]: **jn/etw mit etw überschwemmen** to inundate sb/sthg with sthg.

Überschwemmung (*pl* -en) *die* flood.

überschwenglich = **überschwänglich**.

übersehen (*präs* übersieht, *prät* übersah, *perf* hat übersehen) *vt* - **1.** [nicht sehen, ansehen] to overlook; [absichtlich] to ignore - **2.** [einschätzen] to assess.

übersetzen[1] *vt* [in Sprache] to translate; **in etw** (*A*) **übersetzen** to translate into sthg.

überlsetzen[2] (*perf* hat/ist übergesetzt) ⬦ *vi* (ist) [überqueren] to cross. ⬦ *vt* (hat) [befördern] to take across.

Übersetzer, in (*mpl* -, *fpl* -nen) *der, die* translator.

Übersetzung (*pl* -en) *die* - **1.** [das Übersetzen] translation - **2.** TECH gear ratio.

Übersicht (*pl* -en) *die* - **1.** [Fähigkeit] overview - **2.** [Darstellung]: **eine Übersicht über etw** (*A*) an outline of sthg.

übersichtlich ⬦ adj - **1.** [gut strukturiert] clear - **2.** [gut zu sehen] open. ⬦ adv clearly.

überspitzt ⬦ adj exaggerated. ⬦ adv in an exaggerated way.

überspringen (prät übersprang, perf hat übersprungen) vt - **1.** [darüber hinwegspringen] to jump - **2.** [auslassen] to skip.

über|sprudeln (perf ist übergesprudelt) vi - **1.** [Person]: **vor etw (D) übersprudeln** to bubble over with sthg - **2.** [Flüssigkeit] to bubble over.

überstehen[1] (prät überstand, perf hat überstanden) vt [hinter sich bringen] to come through.

über|stehen[2] (perf hat/ist übergestanden) vi (unreg) [vorstehen] to jut out.

übersteigen (prät überstieg, perf hat überstiegen) vt - **1.** [zu viel sein] to exceed - **2.** [überklettern] to climb over.

überstimmen vt [Person] to outvote; [Antrag] to vote down.

Über|stunde die: **eine Überstunde** an hour's overtime.

überstürzen vt to rush into. ➤ **sich überstürzen** ref [Ereignisse] to follow in rapid succession.

übertragbar adj - **1.** [Fahrkarte, Recht] transferable; **nicht übertragbar** non-transferable - **2.** [anwendbar] applicable.

übertragen[1] (präs überträgt, prät übertrug, perf hat übertragen) vt - **1.** [anwenden]: **etw auf jn/etw übertragen** to apply sthg to sb/sthg - **2.** [senden] to broadcast - **3.** [übersetzen]: **etw in etw (A) übertragen** to translate sthg into sthg - **4.** [Krankheit] to transmit - **5.** [überantworten]: **jm etw übertragen** to assign sthg to sb. ➤ **sich übertragen** ref: **sich auf jn übertragen** fig & MED to infect sb.

übertragen[2] ⬦ adj [nicht wörtlich] figurative. ⬦ adv [nicht wörtlich] figuratively.

Übertragung (pl -en) die - **1.** [Sendung] broadcast; [das Senden] broadcasting - **2.** [von Krankheit] transmission - **3.** [Überantwortung] transfer.

übertreffen (präs übertrifft, prät übertraf, perf hat übertroffen) vt [Erwartungen] to surpass; [Rekord] to beat; **jn an Ausdauer/Schnelligkeit übertreffen** to have more stamina/be faster than sb.

übertreiben (prät übertrieb, perf hat übertrieben) ⬦ vt [bei Darstellung] to exaggerate; [Handlung] to overdo. ⬦ vi [bei Darstellung] to exaggerate; [bei Handlung] to overdo it.

Übertreibung (pl -en) die exaggeration.

übertreten[1] (präs übertritt, prät übertrat, perf hat übertreten) vt to break.

über|treten[2] (perf hat/ist übergetreten) vi (unreg) - **1.** (ist) [beitreten]: **zu etw (D) übertreten** [zu Partei] to go over to sthg; [zu Konfession] to convert to sthg - **2.** (hat) SPORT to overstep.

übertrieben ⬦ adj [Darstellung] exaggerated; [Forderung, Ehrgeiz] excessive. ⬦ adv [darstellen] in an exaggerated manner; [ernst, höflich] excessively.

überwachen vt to keep under surveillance; [Arbeit] to oversee.

überwältigen vt - **1.** [besiegen] to overpower - **2.** [überkommen] to overwhelm.

überwältigend ⬦ adj overwhelming. ⬦ adv: **überwältigend aussehen** to look stunning; **überwältigend viele Besucher** an overwhelming number of visitors.

überweisen (prät überwies, perf hat überwiesen) vt - **1.** [bezahlen] to pay; **jm etw überweisen, etw an jn überweisen** to pay sthg to sb; **Geld auf ein anderes Konto überweisen** to transfer money to another account; **Ihr Gehalt bekommen Sie überwiesen** your salary will be paid into your account - **2.** MED: **einen Patienten ins Krankenhaus überweisen** to have a patient admitted to hospital.

Überweisung (pl -en) die - **1.** [Zahlung] transfer; [Formular] money transfer form - **2.** MED referral.

überwiegen (prät überwog, perf hat überwogen) ⬦ vi - **1.** [Skepsis, Zweifel] to prevail - **2.** [zahlenmäßig] to predominate. ⬦ vt to outweigh.

überwinden (prät überwand, perf hat überwunden) vt to overcome; [Krise] to get over. ➤ **sich überwinden** ref: **sich zu etw überwinden** to force o.s. to do sthg; **sich nicht überwinden können, etw zu tun** not to be able to bring o.s. to do sthg.

Überwindung die - **1.** [gen] overcoming - **2.** [von Berg] conquering - **3.** [das Sichüberwinden]: **es ist für mich eine Überwindung** ODER **es kostet mich Überwindung, es zu tun** I have to force myself to do it.

überwintern vi - **1.** [Pflanze, Vogel] to spend the winter - **2.** [Winterschlaf halten] to hibernate - **3.** hum [Mensch] to winter.

Überzahl die majority; **in der Überzahl sein** SPORT to have a numerical advantage; [mehr sein] to be in the majority.

überzählig adj spare, surplus.

überzeugen vt to convince; **jn von etw überzeugen** to convince sb of sthg. ➤ **sich überzeugen** ref: **sich (von etw) überzeugen** to satisfy o.s. (of sthg); **überzeugen Sie sich selbst!** see for yourself!

überzeugt adj convinced; **davon überzeugt sein, dass...** to be convinced that...

Überzeugung (pl -en) die conviction; **gegen seine Überzeugung handeln** to go against one's convictions; **zur Überzeugung kommen** ODER **gelangen, dass...** to become convinced ODER come to believe that...

überziehen[1] (prät überzog, perf hat überzogen) ⬦ vi - **1.** [bei Bank] to go overdrawn

- 2. [zeitlich] to overrun. ⟨⟩ vt - 1. [Konto] to overdraw - 2. [nicht pünktlich beenden] to overrun - 3. [übertreiben] to take too far.

über|ziehen² vt (unreg) [anziehen]: **sich** (D) **etw überziehen** to pull sthg on.

überzogen ⟨⟩ adj exaggerated. ⟨⟩ adv: **überzogen reagieren** to overreact.

Über|zug der - 1. [Bezug] cover - 2. [Belag] coating.

üblich adj usual; **wie üblich** as usual.

U-|Boot das submarine.

übrig ⟨⟩ adj remaining; **ist noch etwas übrig?** is there any left?; **die übrigen Autos** the rest of the cars, the remaining cars; **die Übrigen** the rest. ⟨⟩ adv: **für jn/etw viel/nichts übrig haben** to have a lot of/no time for sb/sthg. ⟐ **im Übrigen** adv in addition.

übrig bleiben (perf **ist übrig geblieben**) vi (unreg) to be left over; **uns blieb nichts anderes** ODER **weiter übrig, als zuzustimmen** we had no alternative but to agree.

übrigens adv by the way.

Übung (pl -en) die - 1. [das Üben] practice; **aus der Übung kommen/sein** to get/be out of practice - 2. SPORT, SCHULE, MIL & MUS exercise - 3. UNI seminar.

UdSSR [uːdeːʔɛsʔɛsʔɛr] (abk für **Union der sozialistischen Sowjetrepubliken**) die HIST USSR.

UEFA-Pokal der UEFA Cup.

Ufer (pl -) das [von Fluss] bank; [von See, Meer] shore; **am Ufer** [von Fluss] on the bank; [von See, Meer] on the shore.

UFO (pl -s), **Ufo** (pl -s) [ˈyuːfoː] das UFO.

Uhr (pl -en) die - 1. [Zeitanzeiger] clock - 2. [Armbanduhr] watch - 3. [Zeit]: **es ist 3 Uhr** it is 3 o'clock; **um 3 Uhr** at 3 o'clock; **um wie viel Uhr?** (at) what time?; **wie viel Uhr ist es?** what time is it?; **rund um die Uhr** round the clock.

Uhrmacher, in (mpl -, fpl -nen) der, die [von Armbanduhren] watchmaker; [von größeren Uhren] clockmaker.

Uhr|zeiger der hand.

Uhrzeiger|sinn der: **im Uhrzeigersinn** clockwise; **gegen den Uhrzeigersinn** anticlockwise.

Uhr|zeit die time.

Uhu (pl -s) der eagle owl.

Ukraine die Ukraine.

Ukrainer, in (mpl -, fpl -nen) der, die Ukrainian.

ukrainisch adj Ukrainian.

Ukrainisch(e) das Ukrainian; siehe auch **Englisch(e)**.

UKW [uːkaːˈveː] (abk für **Ultrakurzwelle**) die FM.

ulkig adj comical, funny.

Ulme (pl -n) die elm.

Ultimatum (pl -ten) das ultimatum; **jm ein Ultimatum stellen** to give sb an ultimatum.

Ultraschall der ultrasound.

um ⟨⟩ präp (+ A) - 1. [räumlich] (a)round; **um jn/etw herum** around sb/sthg; **gleich um die Ecke** just around the corner; **um sich blicken** to look around - 2. [zur Angabe der Uhrzeit] at; **um drei Uhr** at three o'clock - 3. [zur Angabe einer Differenz] by; **die Preise steigen um 15%** prices are rising by 15% - 4. [zur Angabe von Grund]: **um etw kämpfen** to fight for sthg - 5. [zur Angabe einer Folge] after; **Tag um Tag** day after day - 6. [ungefähr] about, around; **es kostet um die 300 Euro** it costs about ODER around 300 euros. ⟨⟩ konj: **um zu** (in order) to; **zu stolz, um nachzugeben** too proud to give in. ⟨⟩ adv [vorüber] up; **die zehn Minuten sind um** the ten minutes are up. ⟐ **um so** konj = **umso**.

umarmen vt to hug. ⟐ **sich umarmen** ref to hug.

Umbau (pl -e ODER -ten) der renovation.

um|bauen ⟨⟩ vt [verändern] to renovate; **etw zu etw umbauen** to convert sthg to sthg. ⟨⟩ vi to renovate.

um|binden vt (unreg): **sich** (D) **etw umbinden** to put sthg on.

um|blättern ⟨⟩ vt to turn over. ⟨⟩ vi to turn over the page.

Umbruch der - 1. [Veränderung] radical change - 2. [von Büchern] page make-up.

um|buchen vt: **einen Flug umbuchen** to change one's flight booking.

um|denken vi (unreg) to change one's way of thinking.

um|drehen (perf **hat/ist umgedreht**) ⟨⟩ vt (hat) - 1. [Seite, Stein] to turn over; [Pulli] to turn round - 2. [Auto, Stuhl, Schlüssel] to turn. ⟨⟩ vi (ist, hat) [umkehren] to turn back. ⟐ **sich umdrehen** ref - 1. [im Stehen] to turn round; **sich nach jm/etw umdrehen** to turn round to look at sb/sthg - 2. [im Liegen] to turn over.

Um|drehung (pl -en) die - 1. [um eigene Achse] turn - 2. TECH revolution.

umeinander, umeinander adv [sich kümmern] about each other; [wickeln] around each other.

um|fahren¹ vt (unreg) [überfahren] to knock down.

umfahren² (präs **umfährt**, prät **umfuhr**, perf **hat umfahren**) vt [ausweichen] to go round.

um|fallen (perf **ist umgefallen**) vi (unreg) - 1. [umkippen] to fall over; [auf den Boden] to fall down - 2. [zusammenbrechen] to collapse - 3. fam abw [nachgeben] to give in.

Umfang (pl -fänge) der - 1. [Maß] circumference - 2. [Ausmaß von Projekt, Untersuchung] scale; [- von Buch, Zahlung] size; [- von Schaden] extent; [- von Stimme] range; **in vollem Umfang** fully.

umfangreich ⬦ adj extensive. ⬦ adv extensively, at length.

umfassen (präs umfasst, prät umfasste, perf hat umfasst) vt - 1. [beinhalten] to cover; das Buch umfasst 200 Seiten the book contains 200 pages - 2. [umschlingen]: jn umfassen to put one's arm around sb; etw umfassen to clasp sthg.

umfassend, umfassend ⬦ adj comprehensive. ⬦ adv comprehensively.

Umfeld das - 1. [Umgebung] surroundings Pl - 2. [Milieu] environment, milieu.

Umfrage die survey.

umfunktionieren vt to convert.

Umgang der contact; der Umgang mit Kindern/Tieren working with children/animals; das ist kein Umgang für dich! you shouldn't mix with people like that; mit jm Umgang haben ODER pflegen to associate with sb.

umgänglich adj [angenehm] friendly, affable; [gesellig] sociable.

Umgangsformen Pl manners.

Umgangssprache die [informelle Sprache] colloquial speech; in der Umgangssprache colloquially.

umgeben (präs umgibt, prät umgab, perf hat umgeben) vt to surround.

Umgebung (pl -en) die - 1. [Gebiet] surroundings Pl; in der Umgebung von Heilbronn in the vicinity of Heilbronn - 2. [Umfeld] environment.

umgehen[1] (präs umgeht, prät umging, perf hat umgangen) vt - 1. [Schwierigkeiten] to avoid; [Verordnung] to get round; [Antwort] to evade - 2. [Stau, Ortschaft] to bypass.

umgehen[2] (perf ist umgegangen) vi (unreg) - 1. [Grippe, Gerücht, Nachricht] to go round - 2. [behandeln]: mit jm/etw umgehen (können) [Maschine] to (know how to) handle sb/sthg; [Kind, Tier] to (know how to) treat sb/sthg; kannst du mit einem Computer umgehen? do you know how to use a computer?

umgehend ⬦ adj immediate. ⬦ adv immediately.

Umgehungsstraße die bypass.

umgekehrt ⬦ adj [Vorzeichen, Fall] opposite; [Verhältnis] inverse; [Reihenfolge] reverse; nein, es ist gerade umgekehrt! no, the opposite is true! ⬦ adv the other way round; die Sache verhält sich genau umgekehrt the opposite is true; und umgekehrt and vice versa.

umgraben vt (unreg) to dig over.

Umhang der cape.

umhängen vt - 1. [woandershin hängen] to hang somewhere else - 2. [umlegen]: jm/sich etw umhängen [Jacke, Decke] to put sthg round sb's/one's shoulders; [Kette] to hang sthg round sb's/one's neck.

umhauen vt (unreg) - 1. [fällen] to cut down - 2. fam [überraschen]: es hat mich umgehauen, als I was bowled over when - 3. salopp [Alkohol, Gestank] to knock out - 4. fam [niederschlagen] to knock for six - 5. fam [umwerfen] to knock over.

umher adv around.

umherirren (perf ist umhergeirrt) vi to wander around.

umhören ➤ sich umhören ref: sich umhören to ask around.

Umkehr die turning back.

umkehren (perf hat/ist umgekehrt) ⬦ vi (ist) to turn back. ⬦ vt (hat) [Entwicklung, Reihenfolge, Situation] to reverse. ➤ sich umkehren ref to be reversed.

umkippen (perf ist umgekippt) vi - 1. [umfallen] to fall over; [Auto] to overturn - 2. fam [bewusstlos werden] to keel over - 3. [ökologisch] to become uninhabitable - 4. [Stimmung] to take a turn for the worse.

Umkleidekabine die [in Schwimmbad] changing cubicle; [auf Sportplatz] changing room; [in Kaufhaus] fitting room.

umkommen (perf ist umgekommen) vi (unreg) to die; vor Hunger (D) umkommen fig to be dying of hunger.

Umkreis der - 1. (ohne pl) [Umgebung] vicinity; im Umkreis von 50 km within a 50 km radius - 2. MATH circumcircle.

umkrempeln vt - 1. [hochkrempeln] to roll up - 2. fam [verändern - Mensch] to reform; [- Geschäft] to reorganize completely - 3. fam [durchsuchen] to turn upside down.

Umland das surrounding area.

Umlauf der [Zirkulation] circulation.

Umlaufbahn die orbit.

Umlaut der umlaut.

umlegen vt - 1. salopp [erschießen] to bump off - 2. [verteilen - Kosten, Ausgaben]: etw auf mehrere Personen umlegen to share sthg between several people - 3. [umhängen]: sich/jm etw umlegen [Jacke, Decke] to put sthg round one's/sb's shoulders; [Kette] to put sthg round one's/sb's neck - 4. [verlegen - Termin] to change - 5. [umklappen] to fold down - 6. [Kippen] to knock down; [Baum] to fell.

umleiten vt to divert.

Umleitung die diversion.

umliegend adj surrounding.

umrechnen vt: etw (auf/in etw (A)) umrechnen to convert sthg (into sthg).

umringen vt to surround.

Umriss (pl -e) der outline; etw in groben Umrissen darstellen to give a rough outline of sthg.

umrühren vt to stir.

umrüsten ⬦ vt - 1. MIL to re-equip - 2. [ändern] to adapt. ⬦ vi to re-equip.

ums *präp (um + das)* round the; **ums Viereck gehen** to go round the block; **ihm geht es dabei weniger ums Geld, als...** for him it is not so much a question of money, as...

Um|satz *der* turnover; **wir müssen den Umsatz steigern** we have to boost our sales ODER turnover.

Um|schlag *der* - 1. [von Brief] envelope; [von Buch] dust jacket - 2. [Wechsel] sudden change - 3. MED compress - 4. [an Ärmel] cuff; [an Hose] turn-up - 5. [von Gütern] transfer - 6. [Verkauf] sale.

um|schlagen *(perf hat/ist umgeschlagen) (unreg)* <> *vi (ist)* [Wetter, Stimmung] to change suddenly. <> *vt (hat)* - 1. [umlegen - Kragen] to turn down; [- Hosenbeine] to turn up - 2. [umblättern - Seite] to turn over - 3. WIRTSCH to transfer - 4. [verkaufen] to sell - 5. [Baum] to fell.

um|schreiben¹ *(prät umschrieb, perf hat umschrieben) vt* - 1. [paraphrasieren] to paraphrase - 2. [abgrenzen] to define - 3. [schildern] to describe.

um|schreiben² *vt (unreg)* - 1. [ändern] to rewrite - 2. [übertragen]: **etw auf jn umschreiben lassen** to have sthg transferred to sb.

um|schulen <> *vt* - 1. [ausbilden] to retrain - 2. Schule wechseln lassen] to move (to another school). <> *vi* to retrain.

Um|schwung *der* sudden change.

um|sehen <> **sich umsehen** *ref (unreg)*: **sich (nach jm/etw) umsehen** [suchen] to look around (for sb/sthg); [sich umdrehen] to look round (at sb/sthg).

um sein *(perf ist um gewesen) vi (unreg) fam* to be over.

Um|sicht *die* prudence.

umso *konj (+ kompar)*: **umso schneller/mehr/wichtiger** all the faster/more/more important; **umso besser!** all the better!

umsonst <> *adj*: **umsonst sein** [erfolglos] to be in vain; [gratis] to be free (of charge). <> *adv* - 1. [erfolglos] in vain - 2. [gratis] for free, for nothing.

Um|stand *(pl -stände) der* - 1. [Mühe]: **Umstände machen** *(U)*; **wir wollen dir keine Umstände machen** we don't want to put you to any trouble; **nicht viele Umstände (mit jm/etw) machen** not to go to a great deal of trouble (over sb/sthg) - 2. [Sachlage] circumstance; **unter Umständen** in certain circumstances; **unter allen Umständen** whatever happens; **in anderen Umständen sein** *fig* to be in the family way.

umständlich <> *adj* - 1. [Methode, Arbeit] laborious - 2. [im Denken] ponderous; [beim Sprechen] long-winded. <> *adv* - 1. [mühevoll] laboriously - 2. [denken] ponderously; [sprechen] long-windedly.

Um|stands|kleid *das* maternity dress.

Um|stands|wort *(pl -wörter) das* GRAMM adverb.

umstehend *adj* - 1. [umgebend] standing round about; **die Umstehenden** the bystanders - 2. [umseitig] overleaf.

um|steigen *(perf ist umgestiegen) vi (unreg)* - 1. [beim Reisen] to change - 2. [wechseln]: **auf etw (A) umsteigen** to switch to sthg.

um|stellen¹ *vt* - 1. [anders ausrichten - Möbel] to switch round; [- Methode, Produktion, Weichen] to switch; [- Kabinett] to reshuffle; **heute Nacht werden die Uhren umgestellt** the clocks go forward/back tonight; **etw auf etw (A) umstellen** to switch sthg to sthg; **einen Betrieb auf EDV umstellen** to computerize a company - 2. [Leben, Fahrplan, Mannschaft, Programm] to change. <> **sich umstellen** *ref* to change; **sich in der Ernährung umstellen** to change one's diet; **sich auf etw (A) umstellen** [sich anpassen] to adapt to sthg.

umstellen² *vt* [einkreisen] to surround.

Um|stellung *die* - 1. [von Methode, Produktion, Weichen] switch; **Umstellung auf EDV** computerization - 2. [Veränderung] change.

um|stimmen *vt*: **jn umstimmen** to make sb change his/her mind.

um|stoßen *vt (unreg)* - 1. [Stapel, Vase, Stuhl] to knock over - 2. [Plan, Testament, Berechnungen] to wreck.

umstritten *adj* controversial; **es ist umstritten, ob** it is disputed whether.

Um|sturz *der* coup (d'état); **der Umsturz der Regierung** the overthrow of the government.

um|stürzen *(perf hat/ist umgestürzt)* <> *vi (ist)* to fall over; [Auto] to overturn. <> *vt (hat)* - 1. [umwerfen] to knock over; [Auto] to overturn - 2. [vereiteln] to upset - 3. [ablösen] to overthrow.

Um|tausch *der* exchange; 'vom Umtausch ausgeschlossen' 'no refunds or exchanges'.

um|tauschen *vt* - 1. [auswechseln] to exchange; **etw gegen etw umtauschen** to exchange sthg for sthg - 2. [Währung tauschen] to change.

um|wandeln *vt*: **etw in etw (A)/zu etw umwandeln** to convert sthg into sthg.

Um|weg *der* detour; **einen Umweg über etw (A) machen** to make a detour via sthg; **auf Umwegen** *fig* in a roundabout way.

Um|welt *die* environment.

Um|welt|belastung *die* environmental pollution ODER damage.

umweltbewusst <> *adj* environmentally aware. <> *adv* in an environmentally aware way.

umweltfreundlich <> *adj* environmentally friendly, eco-friendly. <> *adv* in an environmentally friendly ODER eco-friendly way.

Um|welt|papier *das* recycled paper.

Umwelt|schäden *Pl* ecological damage *(U)*.

Umwelt|schutz *der* environmental protection.

Umweltschützer, in *(mpl* -, *fpl* -nen) *der, die* environmentalist.

Umwelt|verschmutzung *die* pollution *(U)*.

um|werfen *vt (unreg)* - **1.** [umstürzen] to knock over - **2.** *fam*: jn umwerfen [Alkohol] to knock sb out; [Nachricht] to stun sb - **3.** [umhängen]: sich *(D)* etw umwerfen to put sthg round one's shoulders - **4.** [hinfällig machen] to upset.

um|ziehen *(perf* hat/ist umgezogen) *(unreg)* ⬦ *vi (ist)* to move; nach...umziehen to move to... ⬦ *vt (hat)* to change. ➡ **sich umziehen** *ref* to change, to get changed.

umzingeln *vt* to surround.

Um|zug *der* - **1.** [Wohnungswechsel] move - **2.** [Festzug] parade.

unabhängig ⬦ *adj* independent; von jm/ etw unabhängig sein to be independent of sb/sthg. ⬦ *adv* independently.

Unabhängigkeit *die* independence.

unabsichtlich ⬦ *adj* unintentional. ⬦ *adv* unintentionally.

unachtsam ⬦ *adj* - **1.** [unaufmerksam] inattentive - **2.** [nicht sorgsam] careless. ⬦ *adv* [nicht sorgsam] carelessly.

Unachtsamkeit *(pl* -en) *die* - **1.** [Unaufmerksamkeit] inattentiveness *(U)* - **2.** [fehlende Sorgfalt] carelessness *(U)*.

unangebracht *adj* inappropriate.

unangemessen ⬦ *adj* inappropriate. ⬦ *adv* inappropriately; unangemessen hoch disproportionately high.

unangenehm ⬦ *adj* unpleasant; etw ist jm unangenehm sb feels embarrassed about sthg. ⬦ *adv*: unangenehm berührt embarrassed; unangenehm auffallen to make a bad impression.

Unannehmlichkeiten *Pl* trouble *(U)*.

unansehnlich *adj* unattractive.

unanständig ⬦ *adj* [obszön] indecent; [Wort, Witz] rude; es ist unanständig, mit vollem Mund zu reden it's rude to talk with your mouth full. ⬦ *adv* [obszön] indecently; [unhöflich] rudely.

unauffällig ⬦ *adj* unobtrusive. ⬦ *adv* - **1.** [nicht auffällig] unobtrusively - **2.** [heimlich] without anyone noticing.

unauffindbar, unauffindbar ⬦ *adj*: unauffindbar sein to be nowhere to be found. ⬦ *adv*: etw unauffindbar verstecken to hide sthg where it cannot be found.

unaufgefordert ⬦ *adj* unasked-for. ⬦ *adv* without being asked.

unaufhaltsam, unaufhaltsam ⬦ *adj* inexorable. ⬦ *adv* inexorably.

unaufhörlich, unaufhörlich ⬦ *adj* constant. ⬦ *adv* constantly.

unaufmerksam ⬦ *adj* inattentive. ⬦ *adv* inattentively.

unaufrichtig ⬦ *adj* insincere; jm gegenüber unaufrichtig sein not to be open with sb. ⬦ *adv* insincerely.

unausstehlich, unausstehlich ⬦ *adj* unbearable. ⬦ *adv* unbearably.

unbändig *adj* [Wut, Freude, Eifersucht] unbridled; [Temperament] boisterous.

unbeabsichtigt ⬦ *adj* unintentional. ⬦ *adv* unintentionally.

unbeachtet ⬦ *adj* unnoticed. ⬦ *adv* unnoticed.

unbedenklich ⬦ *adj* safe. ⬦ *adv* [Medikament einnehmen] safely; [annehmen, zustimmen] without hesitation.

unbedeutend ⬦ *adj* - **1.** [nicht bedeutend] unimportant - **2.** [belanglos] slight. ⬦ *adv* [belanglos] slightly.

unbedingt ⬦ *adj* absolute. ⬦ *adv* - **1.** [auf jeden Fall] definitely; er will unbedingt Ski fahren he is determined to go skiing; du wolltest ja unbedingt Ski fahren it was you that wanted to go skiing - **2.** [bedingungslos] absolutely.

unbefriedigend *adj* unsatisfactory.

unbefugt ⬦ *adj* unauthorized. ⬦ *adv* without authorization.

unbegreiflich, unbegreiflich ⬦ *adj* incomprehensible. ⬦ *adv* unbelievably.

unbegrenzt ⬦ *adj* [Freiheit, Möglichkeiten] unlimited; [Vertrauen, Zustimmung] total. ⬦ *adv* [vertrauen, zustimmen] totally; [nutzen, wohnen] indefinitely.

unbegründet ⬦ *adj* unfounded. ⬦ *adv* without foundation.

unbeholfen ⬦ *adj* clumsy. ⬦ *adv* clumsily.

unbekannt ⬦ *adj* [Künstler, Substanz, Krankheit] unknown; [Flugobjekt] unidentified; er ist mir unbekannt I don't know him; diese Änderung ist mir unbekannt I don't know about this change; Anzeige gegen unbekannt RECHT charge against person or persons unknown. ⬦ *adv*: 'unbekannt verzogen' 'gone away, address unknown'.

unbekümmert, unbekümmert ⬦ *adj* [unbeschwert] carefree; [ohne Bedenken] casual. ⬦ *adv* [unbeschwert] in a carefree way; [ohne Bedenken] casually.

unbeliebt *adj* unpopular.

unbequem ⬦ *adj* - **1.** [nicht bequem] uncomfortable - **2.** [lästig] awkward. ⬦ *adv* [nicht bequem] uncomfortably.

unberechenbar, unberechenbar ⬦ *adj* unpredictable. ⬦ *adv* unpredictably.

unberechtigt ◇ *adj* [Ansprüche, Vorwürfe] unjustified; [Zutritt] unauthorized. ◇ *adv* [entlassen, bestrafen] without justification; [ohne Erlaubnis] without authorization.

unberührt *adj* - **1.** [nicht berührt - Essen, Gegenstand] untouched; [- Schnee] undisturbed; [- Natur] unspoilt - **2.** [ohne Regung] unmoved - **3.** [jungfräulich]: **unberührt sein** to be a virgin.

unbeschreiblich,   **unbeschreiblich** ◇ *adj* indescribable. ◇ *adv* indescribably; **sich unbeschreiblich freuen** to be overjoyed.

unbeschwert ◇ *adj* carefree. ◇ *adv* free from care.

unbeständig *adj* changeable.

unbestechlich, **unbestechlich** *adj* [durch Geld] incorruptible; [Kritiker] uncompromising; [Verfechter] unwavering.

unbestimmt ◇ *adj* [Zeitpunkt & GRAMM] indefinite; [Vorstellung, Äußerung] vague. ◇ *adv* vaguely.

unbeteiligt ◇ *adj* - **1.** [nicht verwickelt] uninvolved; **an etw** *(D)* **unbeteiligt sein** not to be involved in sthg - **2.** [nicht interessiert] uninterested. ◇ *adv* - **1.** [nicht verwickelt] without getting involved - **2.** [nicht interessiert] without taking an interest.

unbewacht *adj* [Haus, Gefangene] unguarded; [Gepäck, Parkplatz] unattended; **in einem unbewachten Moment** when no one was looking.

unbeweglich ◇ *adj* - **1.** [nicht beweglich, festgelegt] immovable - **2.** [unflexibel] inflexible - **3.** [steif] stiff - **4.** [unverändert] fixed. ◇ *adv* - **1.** [regungslos] motionlessly - **2.** [unverändert] fixedly.

unbewusst ◇ *adj* unconscious. ◇ *adv* unconsciously.

unbrauchbar *adj* useless.

und *konj* - **1.** [gen] and; **und wenn** even if; **und aber** even though; **eins und eins ist zwei** one and one is two; **und so weiter** and so on - **2.** [Ausdruck von Ironie]: **der und sich entschuldigen?** him, say he's sorry? ◈ **und ob** *interj* of course! ◈ **und wie** *interj* and how!

undankbar *adj* - **1.** [unhöflich] ungrateful - **2.** [schwer] thankless.

undenkbar, **undenkbar** *adj* inconceivable.

undeutlich ◇ *adj* unclear. ◇ *adv* unclearly.

undicht *adj* leaky.

undurchsichtig *adj* - **1.** [Geschichte, Mensch] shady - **2.** [Glas, Strümpfe] opaque.

uneben *adj* uneven.

unehelich ◇ *adj*: **uneheliches Kind** illegitimate child; **in einer unehelichen Beziehung leben** to live together. ◇ *adv* illegitimately.

unehrlich ◇ *adj* dishonest. ◇ *adv* dishonestly.

uneigennützig ◇ *adj* unselfish. ◇ *adv* unselfishly.

uneinig *adj* in disagreement; **sich** *(D)* **über etw** *(A)* **uneinig sein** to disagree about sthg.

unempfindlich *adj* - **1.** [robust - Stoff, Material] hardwearing *UK*, longwearing *US*; [- Gerät] sturdy; [- Pflanze] hardy - **2.** [nicht anfällig - Person] immune; [- Haut] insensitive.

unendlich ◇ *adj* [Raum, Mühe & MATH] infinite; [Weite, Arbeit, Wiederholung] endless; [Geschichte] never-ending. ◇ *adv* enormously.

Unendlichkeit *die* - **1.** [von Raum, Universum] infinity; [von Weite, Wüste] endlessness - **2.** *fam* [zeitlich] eternity.

unentbehrlich, **unentbehrlich** *adj* indispensable.

unentgeltlich, **unentgeltlich** ◇ *adj* free. ◇ *adv* [benutzen] free of charge; [arbeiten, helfen] for nothing.

unentschieden ◇ *adj* - **1.** [nicht entschieden - Spiel] drawn; [- Angelegenheit] undecided; **bei unentschiedenem Wahlausgang** if the election result is inconclusive - **2.** [vor Entscheidung] undecided; [nicht entschlussfreudig] indecisive. ◇ *adv* - **1.** [nicht entschieden]: **unentschieden spielen** to draw; **im Spiel steht es unentschieden** so far the game is a draw - **2.** [unentschlossen] undecidedly.

unentschlossen ◇ *adj* [vor Entscheidung] undecided; [nicht entschlussfreudig] indecisive. ◇ *adv* [vor Entscheidung] undecidedly; [nicht entschlussfreudig] indecisively.

unerbittlich, **unerbittlich** ◇ *adj* - **1.** [unnachgiebig] unrelenting - **2.** [gnadenlos] relentless. ◇ *adv* - **1.** [unnachgiebig] unrelentingly; **unerbittlich bleiben** to remain adamant - **2.** [gnadenlos] relentlessly.

unerfahren *adj* inexperienced.

unerfreulich *adj* unpleasant.

unerhört ◇ *adj* - **1.** [empörend] outrageous; **(das ist ja) unerhört!** that's outrageous! - **2.** [Glück, Leistung] tremendous; [Preis] exorbitant. ◇ *adv* - **1.** [ungeheuer] tremendously; **unerhört viel** a tremendous amount - **2.** [empörend] outrageously.

unerlässlich, **unerlässlich** *adj* essential.

unerlaubt ◇ *adj* unauthorized. ◇ *adv* without authorization.

unermesslich, **unermesslich** *geh* ◇ *adj* - **1.** [unendlich] immeasurable - **2.** [ungeheuer] immense. ◇ *adv* immensely.

unermüdlich, **unermüdlich** ◇ *adj* tireless. ◇ *adv* tirelessly.

unerschütterlich, **unerschütterlich** ◇ *adj* [Überzeugung, Wille] unshakeable; [Person] unflinching. ◇ *adv* unflinchingly.

unerschwinglich, **unerschwinglich** ◇ *adj* [Preis] prohibitive; [Luxusartikel] prohibitively expensive; **für jn unerschwinglich sein** to be beyond sb's means. ◇ *adv* prohibitively.

unerträglich ◇ *adj* unbearable. ◇ *adv* unbearably.

unerwartet ◇ *adj* unexpected. ◇ *adv* unexpectedly.

unerwünscht *adj* [Gast] unwelcome; [Kind] unwanted; [Benehmen] undesirable.

UNESCO [u'nɛsko] *(abk für* United Nations Educational, Scientific and Cultural Organization) *die* UNESCO.

unfähig *adj* incompetent; **unfähig sein, etw zu tun** to be incapable of doing sthg.

Unfähigkeit *die* incompetence; **die Unfähigkeit, etw zu tun** the inability to do sthg.

unfair ['ʊnfɛːɐ] ◇ *adj* unfair. ◇ *adv* unfairly.

Un|fall *der* accident.

Unfall|flucht *die* RECHT failure to stop after an accident.

Unfall|stelle *die* scene of the/an accident.

Unfall|ver|sicherung *die* accident insurance.

unfehlbar, unfehlbar *adj* infallible.

unfreiwillig ◇ *adj* - 1. [nicht freiwillig] compulsory - 2. *hum* [unabsichtlich] unintentional. ◇ *adv* - 1. [nicht freiwillig] without wanting to - 2. *hum* [unabsichtlich] unintentionally.

unfreundlich ◇ *adj* - 1. [nicht freundlich] unfriendly; **zu jm unfreundlich sein** to be unfriendly to sb - 2. [unangenehm] unpleasant. ◇ *adv* [nicht freundlich] coldly.

unfruchtbar *adj* - 1. [steril, trocken] infertile - 2. [nutzlos] fruitless.

Ungar, in *(mpl* -n, *fpl* -nen) *der, die* Hungarian.

ungarisch *adj* Hungarian.

Ungarisch(e) *das* Hungarian; *siehe auch* **Englisch(e)**.

Ungarn *nt* Hungary.

ungeahnt, ungeahnt ['ʊngəaːnt, ʊnˈgeˈaːɪnt] *adj* undreamt-of; [Schwierigkeiten] unsuspected.

ungebeten ◇ *adj* uninvited. ◇ *adv* without being invited.

ungebildet *adj* uneducated.

Ungeduld *die* impatience.

ungeduldig ◇ *adj* impatient. ◇ *adv* impatiently.

ungeeignet *adj* unsuitable.

ungefähr, ungefähr *adv* about; **wann kommst du denn ungefähr wieder?** about when will you be back?; **die Wohnung sieht ungefähr so aus** the flat looks something like this; **sowas kommt nicht von ungefähr** such a thing is no accident.

ungefährlich *adj* safe.

ungehalten ◇ *adj* indignant; **über jn/etw ungehalten sein** to be indignant about sb/sthg. ◇ *adv* indignantly.

ungeheuer, ungeheuer ◇ *adj* tremendous. ◇ *adv* tremendously.

Ungeheuer *(pl* -) *das* monster.

ungehörig *adj* [Benehmen] improper; [Antwort] impertinent. ◇ *adv* [sich benehmen] improperly.

ungehorsam *adj* disobedient.

Ungehorsam *der* disobedience.

ungeklärt *adj* - 1. [nicht entschieden - Problem, Mord] unsolved; [- Frage] unsettled - 2. [nicht gereinigt - Abwasser] untreated.

ungelegen *adj* inconvenient; **das kommt mir ungelegen** that's inconvenient for me.

ungelogen *adv fam* honestly.

ungemein, ungemein ◇ *adj* tremendous. ◇ *adv* tremendously.

ungemütlich ◇ *adj* - 1. [nicht behaglich] uncomfortable; [Mensch] unfriendly - 2. [unangenehm] unpleasant. ◇ *adv* uncomfortably.

ungenau ◇ *adj* [Ausführungen, Erklärung] imprecise; [Übersetzung, Messung] inaccurate; [Vorstellung] vague. ◇ *adv* [ausführen, erklären] imprecisely; [übersetzen, messen] inaccurately; [erkennbar] vaguely.

ungeniert, ungeniert ◇ *adj* uninhibited. ◇ *adv* without any inhibition; [sich äußern] openly.

ungenießbar, ungenießbar *adj* - 1. [Essen] inedible; [Getränk] undrinkable - 2. *fam* [schlecht gelaunt] unbearable.

ungenügend ◇ *adj* inadequate. ◇ *adv* inadequately.

ungerade *adj* MATH odd.

ungerecht ◇ *adj* unjust. ◇ *adv* unjustly.

Un|gerechtigkeit *die* injustice.

ungern *adv* reluctantly; **ich tue das nur ungern** I don't like doing this.

ungeschehen *adj*: **etw ungeschehen machen** to undo sthg.

ungeschickt ◇ *adj* - 1. [nicht geschickt] clumsy; **es wäre ungeschickt, das jetzt schon zu erwähnen** it wouldn't be wise to mention that now - 2. *Süddt fam* [ungelegen] inconvenient - 3. *Süddt fam* [unpraktisch] impractical. ◇ *adv* [nicht geschickt] clumsily.

ungeschminkt ◇ *adj* - 1. [nicht geschminkt] without make-up - 2. [unverhüllt] unvarnished. ◇ *adv* - 1. [nicht geschminkt] without make-up - 2. [unverhüllt] openly.

ungestört *adj & adv* undisturbed.

ungesund ◇ *adj* unhealthy. ◇ *adv* unhealthily.

ungetrübt *adj* - 1. [Glück] perfect; [Zeit] blissful; [Zukunft] unclouded - 2. [Glas, Wasser] clear.

ungewiss *adj* uncertain.

ungewöhnlich ◇ *adj* - **1.** [unüblich] unusual - **2.** [erstaunlich] exceptional. ◇ *adv* - **1.** [unüblich] unusually - **2.** [erstaunlich] exceptionally.

ungewohnt ◇ *adj* [fremd] unfamiliar; [Tageszeit, Großzügigkeit] unaccustomed; **etw ist für jn ungewohnt** sb is not used to sthg. ◇ *adv* unusually.

Ungeziefer *das (ohne pl)* pests *Pl*; **der Hund hat Ungeziefer** the dog has fleas.

ungezogen ◇ *adj* naughty; [Benehmen] bad; [frech] cheeky. ◇ *adv* [frech] cheekily; [sich benehmen] badly.

ungezwungen ◇ *adj* [Atmosphäre, Unterhaltung] informal; [Verhalten, Art] natural; [Lachen] easy. ◇ *adv* [sich verhalten] naturally; [sich unterhalten] informally; [sich bewegen] easily.

ungläubig ◇ *adj* - **1.** [nicht gläubig] unbelieving - **2.** [zweifelnd] disbelieving. ◇ *adv* in disbelief.

unglaublich, unglaublich ◇ *adj* - **1.** [nicht zu glauben] unbelievable - **2.** [ungeheuer] incredible. ◇ *adv* incredibly.

unglaubwürdig *adj* [Mensch] untrustworthy; [Geschichte] implausible.

ungleich ◇ *adj* unequal; [Brüder] different. ◇ *adv* - **1.** [nicht gleich] unequally; [sich verhalten] differently - **2.** [bei weitem] far.

Unglück *das* - **1.** [Vorfall] accident - **2.** [Pech] bad luck; **zu allem Unglück brach er sich auch noch den Arm** on top of everything he broke his arm as well.

unglücklich ◇ *adj* - **1.** [nicht glücklich] unhappy - **2.** [ungünstig] unfortunate - **3.** [ungeschickt] clumsy. ◇ *adv* - **1.** [nicht glücklich] unhappily - **2.** [ungeschickt] awkwardly - **3.** [ungünstig] badly.

unglücklicherweise *adv* unfortunately.

ungültig *adj* invalid.

Ungunsten *Pl*: **zu js Ungunsten** to sb's disadvantage.

ungünstig ◇ *adj* unfavourable; [Moment] inconvenient; [Witterung] bad. ◇ *adv* unfavourably.

ungut ◇ *adj* bad. ◇ *adv* badly; **nichts für ungut!** *fig* no offence!

unhaltbar, unhaltbar *adj* - **1.** [Argument, Lage, These] untenable - **2.** [Schuss] unstoppable.

Unheil *das geh* disaster.

unheimlich, unheimlich ◇ *adj* - **1.** [gruselig] eerie; **dieser Typ ist mir unheimlich** this guy makes my flesh creep; **mir wird unheimlich** I have an eerie feeling - **2.** *fam* [groß] terrible; [Menge] huge. ◇ *adv fam* [ungeheuer] dead; **unheimlich viel Geld** loads of money; **sich unheimlich freuen** to be dead pleased.

unhöflich ◇ *adj* impolite. ◇ *adv* impolitely.

Uni *(pl -s) die fam* uni.

Uniform *(pl -en)*, **Uniform** *(pl -en) die* uniform.

Union *(pl -en) die* union.

Universität [univɛrzi'tɛːt] *(pl -en) die* university.

Universum [uni'vɛrzʊm] *das* universe.

unkaputtbar *adj fam* unbreakable.

unkenntlich *adj* unrecognizable.

Unkenntnis *die*: **etw in Unkenntnis einer Sache** *(G)* **tun** to do sthg out of ignorance of sthg.

unklar ◇ *adj* unclear; **jn (über etw** *(A)*) **im Unklaren lassen** to leave sb in the dark (about sthg). ◇ *adv* - **1.** [unverständlich] unclearly - **2.** [vage] vaguely.

unklug ◇ *adj* unwise. ◇ *adv* unwisely.

Unkosten *Pl* expenses; **sich in Unkosten stürzen** *fig* to go to great expense.

Unkosten|beitrag *der* contribution towards expenses.

Unkraut *das* - **1.** *(ohne pl)* [störende Pflanzen] weeds *Pl* - **2.** [Unkrautart] weed.

unleserlich ◇ *adj* illegible. ◇ *adv* illegibly.

unlogisch ◇ *adj* illogical. ◇ *adv* illogically.

Unmenge *die* masses *Pl*; **eine Unmenge Arbeit** masses of work.

Unmensch *der abw* monster.

unmenschlich ◇ *adj* - **1.** [menschenunwürdig, brutal] inhuman - **2.** *fam* [unerträglich] terrible. ◇ *adv* - **1.** [menschenunwürdig, brutal] inhumanly - **2.** *fam* [ungeheuer] terribly.

unmerklich, unmerklich ◇ *adj* imperceptible. ◇ *adv* imperceptibly.

unmissverständlich ◇ *adj* unambiguous. ◇ *adv* unambiguously.

unmittelbar ◇ *adj* immediate; [Verbindung] direct; **in unmittelbarer Nähe** in the immediate vicinity. ◇ *adv* directly; **unmittelbar danach** immediately afterwards.

unmöglich, unmöglich ◇ *adj* [nicht möglich] impossible; **es ist mir unmöglich, das zu tun** it is impossible for me to do that; **sich unmöglich machen** to make a fool of o.s. ◇ *adv* - **1.** [nicht möglich, keinesfalls]: **das kann unmöglich stimmen** that can't possibly be right; **das kannst du unmöglich von ihm verlangen** you can't possibly ask that of him - **2.** *fam* [sich benehmen] impossibly.

unmoralisch ◇ *adj* immoral. ◇ *adv* immorally.

unnachgiebig ◇ *adj* inflexible. ◇ *adv* inflexibly.

unnahbar, unnahbar *adj* unapproachable.

unnötig ◇ *adj* unnecessary. ◇ *adv* unnecessarily.

unnütz ◇ *adj* useless. ◇ *adv* [unnötig] needlessly.

UNO ['u:no] (*abk für* United Nations Organization) *die* UN.

unordentlich ◇ *adj* untidy. ◇ *adv* untidily.

Unordnung *die* mess; **etw in Unordnung bringen** to mess sthg up; **in Unordnung geraten** to get messed up.

unparteiisch ◇ *adj* impartial. ◇ *adv* impartially.

unpassend ◇ *adj* inappropriate. ◇ *adv* inappropriately.

unpersönlich ◇ *adj* [gen & GRAMM] impersonal. ◇ *adv* [gen & GRAMM] impersonally.

unpraktisch ◇ *adj* impractical. ◇ *adv* impractically.

unpünktlich ◇ *adj* [Mensch] unpunctual; [Abfahrt, Zahlung] late. ◇ *adv* late.

unrecht ◇ *adj* - 1. [Zeit, Moment] inconvenient - 2. *geh* [Tat, Gedanke] wicked; **es ist unrecht, so etw zu denken** it is wrong to think like that. ◇ *adv* - 1. [ungelegen] inconveniently - 2. *geh* [handeln, sich benehmen] wrongly; **jm unrecht tun** to wrong sb.

Unrecht *das* wrong; **Unrecht haben, im Unrecht sein** to be wrong; **jn/sich ins Unrecht setzen** to put sb/o.s. in the wrong; **zu Unrecht** wrongly.

unrechtmäßig ◇ *adj* illegal. ◇ *adv* illegally.

unregelmäßig ◇ *adj* [gen & GRAMM] irregular. ◇ *adv* [gen & GRAMM] irregularly.

unreif *adj* - 1. [Obst] unripe - 2. [Person] immature.

Unruhe (*pl* -n) *die* (*ohne pl*) - 1. [Treiben] commotion; **er sorgt ständig für Unruhe** he's always causing a commotion; **Unruhe stiften** to stir up trouble - 2. [Ruhelosigkeit] unease; **jn in Unruhe versetzen** to make sb uneasy - 3. [Aufregung] unrest, disquiet - 4. [Bewegung]: **in Unruhe sein** to be moving restlessly. ➠ **Unruhen** *Pl* [Aufruhr] riots.

unruhig ◇ *adj* - 1. [nicht ruhig] restless - 2. [ruhelos] uneasy; **unruhig werden** to get anxious - 3. [gestört - Schlaf] fitful; [- Nacht] disturbed - 4. [Zeit] troubled - 5. [laut] noisy - 6. [Muster, Bild] busy. ◇ *adv* - 1. [nicht ruhig] restlessly - 2. [ruhelos] uneasily - 3. [schlafen] fitfully.

uns *pron* - 1. [Personalpronomen - Akkusativ, Dativ] us; **er sagte es uns** he told us; **das gehört uns** this is ours, this belongs to us; **sie hat uns gesehen** she has seen us - 2. [Reflexivpronomen] ourselves; **wir konnten uns das nicht vorstellen** we couldn't imagine that; **wir setzten uns** we sat down - 3. [einander] each other, one another.

unsachlich ◇ *adj* subjective. ◇ *adv* subjectively.

unsanft ◇ *adj* rough. ◇ *adv* roughly.

unschädlich *adj* harmless; **jn/etw unschädlich machen** to put sb/sthg out of action.

unscharf ◇ *adj* - 1. [nicht scharf] blurred - 2. [ungenau] vague. ◇ *adv*: **unscharf sehen** to have blurred vision.

unscheinbar *adj* inconspicuous.

unschlagbar, unschlagbar *adj* - 1. [nicht zu schlagen] unbeatable - 2. [nicht zu übertreffen] unsurpassable.

unschlüssig ◇ *adj* undecided; **(sich (D)) über etw (A) unschlüssig sein** to be undecided about sthg. ◇ *adv* indecisively.

Unschuld *die* - 1. [gen] innocence - 2. [Jungfräulichkeit] virginity.

unschuldig ◇ *adj* - 1. [gen] innocent; **an etw (D) unschuldig sein** not to be to blame for sthg - 2. [jungfräulich]: **ein unschuldiges Mädchen** a virgin. ◇ *adv* - 1. [gen] innocently - 2. [verurteilen] wrongly.

unselbstständig *adj* dependent.

unser, e *det* our.

unsere, r, s *ODER* **unsers** ◇ *pron* ours. ◇ *det* = **unser**.

unsereins *pron fam* the likes of us.

unsererseits, unsrerseits *adv* - 1. [wir selbst] for our part - 2. [von uns] on our part.

unseretwegen, unsertwegen *adv* - 1. [uns zuliebe] for our sake - 2. [wegen uns] because of us - 3. [von uns aus] as far as we are concerned.

unsicher ◇ *adj* - 1. [gen] uncertain - 2. [Stimme, Hand] unsteady; **ich bin mir unsicher, ob** I'm uncertain whether - 3. [unverlässlich] unreliable - 4. [gefährdet] insecure - 5. [unbeständig] unsettled - 6. [gefährlich] unsafe; **etw unsicher machen** *fam* [sich vergnügen] to hit sthg. ◇ *adv* [nicht sicher - gehen fahren] unsteadily; [- reden, auftreten] uncertainly.

Unsicherheit *die* - 1. [Ungewissheit] uncertainty; [Eigenschaft] insecurity - 2. [von Handlung] lapse.

unsichtbar ◇ *adj* invisible; **sich unsichtbar machen** to make o.s. scarce. ◇ *adv* invisibly.

Unsinn *der* nonsense.

unsinnig ◇ *adj* - 1. [blödsinnig] idiotic - 2. *fam* [ungeheuer] tremendous. ◇ *adv* tremendously.

Unsitte *die abw* bad habit.

unsportlich *adj* - 1. [Person] unsporty - 2. [Verhalten] unsporting.

unsterblich, unsterblich ◇ *adj* immortal; [Liebe] undying. ◇ *adv*: **unsterblich verliebt** madly in love; **sich unsterblich blamieren** to make an absolute fool of o.s.

unstillbar *adj* insatiable.

Unstimmigkeiten *Pl* - 1. [Differenzen] differences of opinion - 2. [Abweichungen] discrepancies.

Unsumme *die* huge amount of money.

unsympathisch *adj* unpleasant; **er/es ist mir unsympathisch** I don't like him/it.

Untat *die* evil crime.

untätig <> *adj* idle. <> *adv* idly.

untauglich *adj* unsuitable; **für den Wehrdienst untauglich** unfit for military service.

unten *adv* - 1. [räumlich - im unteren Teil] at the bottom; [- tiefer gelegen] below; [- an der Unterseite] underneath; **unten am Tisch** at the bottom of the table; **links/rechts unten im Bild** in the bottom left-hand/right-hand corner of the picture; **hier/dort unten** down here/there; **von unten** from below; **nach unten** down; [- im Haus] downstairs; **mit dem Gesicht nach unten** face down; **weiter unten** further down - 2. [im Text] below; **siehe unten** see below - 3. *fam* [im Süden]: **unten im Süden** down south - 4. *fam* [rangniedriger]: **die da unten** those at the bottom of the pile; **der ist bei mir unten durch** *fam fig* I'm finished with him.

unter <> *präp* - 1. (+ D) [räumlich] under; [an der Unterseite von] underneath; **unter dem Tisch liegen** to lie under the table; **unter uns wohnt Herr Braun** Mr Braun lives below ODER beneath us - 2. (+ A) [räumlich] under; **unter den Tisch kriechen** to crawl under the table - 3. (+ D) [weniger als] under; **Kinder unter 12 Jahren** children under the age of 12 - 4. (+ A) [weniger als] below - 5. (+ D) [zur Angabe einer Teilmenge]: **einer unter vielen** one of many; **unter uns (gesagt)** between you and me; **unter anderem** among other things - 6. (+ D) [zwischen] between; **sie haben es unter sich ausgemacht** they arranged it between themselves - 7. (+ A) [zwischen]: **sich unter die Menge mischen** to mingle ODER mix with the crowd - 8. (+ D) [zur Angabe einer Hierarchie, einer Bezeichnung] under; **unter der Aufsicht/Leitung** von under the supervision/leadership of; **unter dem Namen X bekannt sein** to be known by the name of X - 9. (+ D) [zur Angabe des Umstands] under; **unter Umständen** under ODER in certain circumstances; **unter Berücksichtigung von** taking into consideration; **unter der Bedingung, dass...** on the condition that... <> *adj* lower; **der unterste Knopf** the bottom button.

Unterarm *der* forearm.

unterbelichtet *adj* - 1. [Foto, Film] underexposed - 2. *salopp* [Mensch] dim.

Unterbewusstsein *das* subconscious.

unterbieten (*prät* unterbot, *perf* hat unterboten) *vt* - 1. [Preis, Angebot, Konkurrenz] to undercut - 2. SPORT to beat.

unterbrechen (*präs* unterbricht, *prät* unterbrach, *perf* hat unterbrochen) *vt* - 1. [stören] to interrupt - 2. [aufhören - Arbeit, Behandlung, Urlaub] to break off.

Unterbrechung (*pl* -en) *die* - 1. [Störung] interruption - 2. [Aufhören - von Arbeit, Behandlung, Urlaub] breaking off.

unterbringen *vt* (*unreg*) - 1. [an einem Platz] to fit - 2. [über Nacht] to put up - 3. [bei Firma] to get a job for - 4. [in Gedächtnis] to place.

Unterbringung *die* [Unterkunft] accommodation.

unterdessen *adv* meanwhile.

unterdrücken *vt* - 1. [Volk, Minderheit] to oppress - 2. [Gefühl, Bemerkung, Information] to suppress.

untereinander *adv* - 1. [unter sich] among ourselves/yourselves/themselves - 2. [unter das andere] one below the other.

unterentwickelt *adj* underdeveloped.

unterernährt *adj* undernourished.

Unterführung (*pl* -en) *die* underpass, subway *UK*.

Untergang (*pl* -gänge) *der* - 1. [von Volk, Kultur] decline - 2. [von Schiff] sinking - 3. [von Sonne, Mond] setting.

Untergebene (*pl* -n) *der, die* subordinate.

untergehen (*perf* ist untergegangen) *vi* (*unreg*) - 1. [Sonne, Mond] to set - 2. [Schiff, Person] to sink - 3. [Kultur, Volk] to decline.

untergeordnet *adj* - 1. [unterstellt & GRAMM] subordinate - 2. [Bedeutung, Rolle] secondary.

Untergrenze *die* lower limit.

Untergrund *der* - 1. [Boden] subsoil - 2. [Unterwelt] underground; **in den Untergrund gehen** to go underground - 3. [für Farbe, Stellfläche] surface.

Untergrundbahn *die* underground *UK*, subway *US*.

unterhaken *vt* to link arms with. ➤ **sich unterhaken** *ref*: **sich (bei jm) unterhaken** to link arms (with sb).

unterhalb <> *adv*: **unterhalb von** below. <> *präp*: **unterhalb einer Sache** (G) below sthg.

Unterhalt *der* - 1. [Zahlung] maintenance - 2. [von Familie, Kindern] keep - 3. [von Gebäude, Park] upkeep.

unterhalten (*präs* unterhält, *prät* unterhielt, *perf* hat unterhalten) *vt* - 1. [amüsieren] to entertain - 2. [Kosten übernehmen für - Familie] to support; [- Haus, Büro] to pay for the upkeep of - 3. [Kontakte] to maintain - 4. [betreiben] to run. ➤ **sich unterhalten** *ref* - 1. [reden]: **sich (mit jm/über etw** (A)**) unterhalten** to talk (with sb/about sthg) - 2. [sich amüsieren] to enjoy o.s.

unterhaltsam <> *adj* entertaining. <> *adv* entertainingly.

Unterhaltung (*pl* -en) *die* - 1. [Gespräch] conversation - 2. (*ohne Pl*) [Zeitvertreib] entertainment; **gute Unterhaltung!** enjoy yourselves! - 3. (*ohne Pl*) [von Kontakten] maintenance - 4. (*ohne Pl*) [Betreibung] running.

Unterhändler, in *der, die* negotiator.

Unterhemd *das* vest *UK*, undershirt *US*.

Unter|hose *die* [für Herren] underpants *Pl;* [für Frauen] briefs *Pl.*

unterirdisch *adj & adv* underground.

Unter|kiefer *der* lower jaw.

unter|kriegen *vt fam* to get down; **sich nicht unterkriegen lassen** *fam* not to let things get one down.

unterkühlt <> *adj* - 1. [Reaktion, Verhalten] frosty - 2. [untertemperiert] suffering from hypothermia. <> *adv* - 1. [reagieren, sich verhalten] frostily - 2. [untertemperiert] suffering from hypothermia.

Unterkunft (*pl* -künfte) *die* accommodation (*U*).

Unter|lage *die* [für Gymnastik] mat; [zum Schreiben] something to rest on. ➡ **Unterlagen** *Pl* [Urkunden] documents.

unterlassen (*präs* unterlässt, *prät* unterließ, *perf* hat unterlassen) *vt* to refrain from; **es unterlassen, etw zu tun** to refrain from doing sthg.

unterlaufen (*präs* unterläuft, *prät* unterlief, *perf* ist unterlaufen) *vt* [passieren]: **mir ist ein Fehler unterlaufen** I made a mistake.

unter|legen[1] *vt* [drunter legen] to put underneath.

unterlegen[2] *vt* - 1. [Teppich] to underlay; [Kragen, Hosenbund] to line - 2. FILM: **etw mit Musik unterlegen** to add background music to sthg.

unterlegen[3] *adj* inferior.

Unter|leib *der* abdomen.

unterliegen (*prät* unterlag, *perf* hat/ist unterlegen) *vi* - 1. *(hat)* [ausgesetzt sein]: **einer Sache (D) unterliegen** to be subject to sthg - 2. *(ist)* [verlieren] to be defeated.

Unter|lippe *die* lower lip.

Unter|miete *die*: **in** ODER **zur Untermiete wohnen** to be a subtenant.

unternehmen (*präs* unternimmt, *prät* unternahm, *perf* hat unternommen) *vt* [Versuch, Anstrengung] to make; [Reise, Ausflug] to go on; **etwas/nichts unternehmen** to do something/ nothing.

Unternehmen (*pl* -) *das* - 1. [Betrieb] business, company - 2. [Vorhaben] undertaking.

Unternehmer, in (*mpl* -, *fpl* -nen) *der, die* entrepreneur.

unternehmungslustig *adj* enterprising.

unter|ordnen *vt* to subordinate. ➡ **sich unterordnen** *ref*: **sich (jm/einer Sache) unterordnen** to subordinate o.s. (to sb/sthg).

Unterredung (*pl* -en) *die* discussion.

Unterricht (*pl* -e) *der* lessons *Pl;* **jm Unterricht geben** ODER **erteilen** to teach sb; **jm Unterricht in Englisch geben** to teach sb English; **hast du morgen Unterricht?** do you have any classes tomorrow?; **Unterricht in Deutsch nehmen** to have German lessons.

unterrichten <> *vt* - 1. [Unterricht geben] to teach; **sie unterrichtet Kinder im Zeichnen** she teaches children drawing - 2. [informieren]: **sich/jn (über etw (A)) unterrichten** to inform o.s./sb (about sthg). <> *vi* to teach.

Unterrichts|fach *das* subject.

Unter|rock *der* slip.

untersagen *vt* to forbid; **jm untersagen, etw zu tun** to forbid sb to do sthg.

unterschätzen *vt* to underestimate.

unterscheiden (*prät* unterschied ODER hat unterschieden) <> *vt* - 1. [auseinander halten, bemerken] to distinguish; **jn/etw von jm/etw unterscheiden** to tell sb/sthg from sb/sthg - 2. [abgrenzen] to distinguish between. <> *vi* - 1. [abgrenzen] to distinguish - 2. [differenzieren] to make a distinction. ➡ **sich unterscheiden** *ref*: **sich (durch etw** ODER **in etw (D)) unterscheiden** to differ (in sthg).

Unter|schenkel *der* lower leg.

Unter|schicht *die* lower classes *Pl.*

Unterschied (*pl* -e) *der* - 1. [Verschiedenheit] difference - 2. [Unterscheidung] distinction; **im Unterschied zu jm/etw** unlike sb/sthg.

unterschiedlich <> *adj* different. <> *adv* differently; **unterschiedlich groß/schnell** of varying size/speed.

Unterschlagung (*pl* -en) *die* [von Geldern] misappropriation.

Unterschlupf (*pl* -e) *der* [Obdach] shelter; [Versteck] hiding place; **Unterschlupf suchen/ finden** [Obdach] to seek/find shelter; [Versteck] to seek/find a hiding place.

unterschreiben (*prät* unterschrieb, *perf* hat unterschrieben) <> *vt* to sign. <> *vi* to sign.

Unter|schrift *die* signature.

unterschwellig <> *adj* subliminal. <> *adv* subliminally.

Untersee|boot *das* submarine.

Unter|seite *die* underside.

Untersetzer (*pl* -) *der* [für Glas] coaster; [für Topf] mat.

untersetzt *adj* stocky.

Unter|stand *der* [vor Regen, Gefahr] shelter; [für Soldaten] dugout.

unter|stellen[1] *vt* - 1. [zum Schutz] to store - 2. [unter Gegenstand] to put underneath. ➡ **sich unterstellen** *ref* [zum Schutz] to shelter.

unterstellen[2] *vt* - 1. [in Hierarchie]: **sie ist direkt dem Regierungspräsidenten unterstellt** she is directly answerable to the president - 2. [Behauptung] to assume.

unterstreichen (*prät* unterstrich, *perf* hat unterstrichen) *vt* to underline.

Unter|stufe *die* SCHULE lower school.

unterstützen *vt* to support.

Unterstützung (*pl* -en) *die* support (*U*).

untersuchen *vt* to examine; [polizeilich] to investigate; **etw auf etw (A) (hin) untersuchen** to examine sthg for sthg.

Untersuchung *(pl -en) die* - **1.** [Untersuchen - ärztlich] examination; [- polizeilich] investigation - **2.** [Studie] study.

Untersuchungsausschuss *(pl -schüsse) der* committee of inquiry.

Untersuchungslhaft *die* imprisonment whilst awaiting trial.

Untertan *(pl -en) der* subject.

Unterltasse *die* saucer; **fliegende Untertasse** *fig* flying saucer.

unterltauchen *(perf hat/ist untergetaucht)* ◇ *vi (ist)* - **1.** [tauchen] to dive; [versinken] to sink - **2.** *fig* [in der Menge] to disappear; [Verbrecher] to go to ground. ◇ *vt (hat)* to duck.

Unterteilung *(pl -en) die* division (U).

Unterltitel *der* subtitle; **mit Untertiteln** with subtitles.

Untertreibung *(pl -en) die* understatement.

unterlvermieten *vt* to sublet.

unterwandern *vt* to infiltrate.

Unterlwäsche *die* underwear.

unterwegs *adv* on the way; **unterwegs sein** to be away.

unterweisen *(prät unterwies, perf hat unterwiesen) vt geh:* **jn in etw (D) unterweisen** to instruct sb in sthg.

Unterlwelt *die* underworld.

unterwerfen *(präs unterwirft, prät unterwarf, perf hat unterworfen) vt* to subjugate. ◈ **sich unterwerfen** *ref* to submit.

unterwürfig *abw* ◇ *adj* servile. ◇ *adv* servilely.

unterzeichnen *vt* to sign.

unterziehen *(prät unterzog, perf hat unterzogen) vt* [aussetzen] to subject. ◈ **sich unterziehen** *ref* [über sich ergehen lassen]: **sich einer Sache (D) unterziehen** to undergo sthg.

Unltiefe *die* - **1.** [seichte Stelle] shallow - **2.** [sehr große Tiefe] depth.

untreu *adj* - **1.** [treulos] unfaithful; **jm untreu werden** to be unfaithful to sb - **2.** *geh* [illoyal] disloyal.

Untreue *die* [zu Liebhaber] infidelity; [Illoyalität] disloyalty.

untröstlich *adj:* **über etw (A) untröstlich sein** to be inconsolable about sthg.

untrüglich *adj* unmistakable.

unüberlegt ◇ *adj* rash. ◇ *adv* rashly.

unübersehbar ◇ *adj* [Gebiet, Weite] vast; [Schild, Hinweis, Kratzer] obvious; [Folgen] inestimable. ◇ *adv* [groß] extremely; [aufgestellt] conspicuously.

unumgänglich *adj* unavoidable.

ununterbrochen ◇ *adj* uninterrupted. ◇ *adv* nonstop.

unveränderlich *adj* unchanging.

unverantwortlich ◇ *adj* irresponsible. ◇ *adv* irresponsibly.

unverbesserlich *adj* incorrigible.

unverbindlich ◇ *adj* not binding. ◇ *adv* without obligation.

unverblümt ◇ *adj* blunt. ◇ *adv* bluntly.

unverfänglich ◇ *adj* harmless. ◇ *adv* harmlessly.

unverfroren ◇ *adj* impudent. ◇ *adv* impudently.

unvergesslich *adj* unforgettable.

unverheiratet *adj* unmarried.

unverkennbar ◇ *adj* unmistakable. ◇ *adv* unmistakably.

unvermeidlich *adj* unavoidable.

unvermittelt ◇ *adj* sudden. ◇ *adv* suddenly.

unvermutet ◇ *adj* unexpected. ◇ *adv* unexpectedly.

unvernünftig ◇ *adj* stupid. ◇ *adv* stupidly.

unverrichtet *adj:* **unverrichteter Dinge** without having achieved anything.

unverschämt ◇ *adj* - ˙**1.** [Mensch, Äußerung, Benehmen] impertinent; [Lüge] barefaced - **2.** [enorm - Glück] incredible; [- Preis] outrageous. ◇ *adv* - **1.** [taktlos] impertinently - **2.** [sehr] incredibly.

Unverschämtheit *(pl -en) die* impertinence (U).

unversehrt ◇ *adj* [Person] unscathed; [Sache] intact; **unversehrt sein/bleiben** [Person] to be/remain unscathed; [Sache] to be/remain intact. ◇ *adv* unscathed.

unverständlich *adj* - **1.** [nicht deutlich] unintelligible - **2.** [unbegreiflich]: **es ist mir unverständlich, wie...** I don't understand how...

unversucht *adj:* **nichts unversucht lassen** to try everything.

unverwüstlich *adj* [Material] durable; [Mensch, Natur] resilient; [Gesundheit] robust; [Humor] irrepressible.

unverzeihlich *adj* inexcusable.

unverzüglich ◇ *adj* immediate. ◇ *adv* immediately.

unvorbereitet *adj* unprepared; [Rede] improvised.

unvoreingenommen ◇ *adj* impartial. ◇ *adv* impartially.

unvorhergesehen ◇ *adj* [Ereignis, Problem] unforeseen; [Besuch] unexpected. ◇ *adv* unexpectedly.

unvorsichtig ◇ *adj* careless. ◇ *adv* carelessly.

unvorstellbar ◇ *adj* unimaginable. ◇ *adv* incredibly.

unvorteilhaft *adj* unflattering.

unwahrscheinlich ◇ *adj* - **1.** [nicht wahrscheinlich] unlikely - **2.** *fam* [enorm] incredible. ◇ *adv fam* [sehr] incredibly.

unweigerlich ◇ *adj* inevitable. ◇ *adv* inevitably.

Unlwetter *das* storm.

unwichtig *adj* unimportant.

unwiderruflich ◇ *adj* irrevocable. ◇ *adv* irrevocably.

unwiderstehlich, unwiderstehlich ◇ *adj* irresistible. ◇ *adv* irresistibly.

unwillig ◇ *adj* [widerwillig] reluctant; [verärgert] angry. ◇ *adv* [widerwillig] reluctantly; [verärgert] angrily.

unwillkürlich ◇ *adj* involuntary. ◇ *adv* involuntarily.

unwirsch ◇ *adj* surly. ◇ *adv* in a surly way.

Unwissenheit *die* ignorance.

unwohl *adj:* jm ist unwohl [krank] sb feels unwell; [unbehaglich] sb feels uneasy; **sich unwohl fühlen** [krank] to feel unwell; [unbehaglich] to feel uneasy.

Unwohlsein *das* indisposition.

unwürdig ◇ *adj* undignified; **einer Sache (G) unwürdig sein** to be unworthy of sthg. ◇ *adv* in an undignified manner.

unzählig, unzählig ◇ *adj* innumerable. ◇ *adv:* **unzählig viele** a huge number (of).

Unze (*pl* -n) *die* ounce.

unzertrennlich, unzertrennlich *adj* inseparable.

unzüchtig ◇ *adj* indecent. ◇ *adv* indecently.

unzufrieden *adj* dissatisfied; **mit etw unzufrieden sein** to be dissatisfied with sthg.

Unzufriedenheit *die* dissatisfaction.

unzulässig ◇ *adj* inadmissible. ◇ *adv* inadmissibly.

unzurechnungsfähig *adj* not responsible for one's actions; **jn für unzurechnungsfähig erklären** to certify sb insane.

unzureichend ◇ *adj* insufficient. ◇ *adv* insufficiently.

unzuverlässig *adj* unreliable.

üppig ◇ *adj* [Busen] full; [Frau] voluptuous; [Essen] lavish; [Haar] thick; [Vegetation] lush. ◇ *adv* [bewachsen] thickly; [speisen, leben] lavishly; **üppig geformt** voluptuous.

Urablstimmung *die* strike ballot.

Uran *das* CHEM uranium.

Urauf1führung *die* premiere.

urbar *adj:* **urbar machen** [Sumpf] to reclaim; [Stück Land] to cultivate.

Urlbevölkerung *die* original inhabitants Pl.

Urleinwohner, in *der, die* original inhabitant.

Urlenkel, in *der, die* great-grandson (great-granddaughter *die*).

Urgroßlmutter *die* great-grandmother.

Urgroßlvater *der* great-grandfather.

Urheber, in (*mpl* -, *fpl* -nen) *der, die* [von Kunstwerk] creator; [von Verbrechen] perpetrator.

Urin (*pl* -e) *der* urine (*U*).

Urkunde (*pl* -n) *die* certificate.

Urkundenlfälschung *die* forging of documents.

Urlaub (*pl* -e) *der* holiday UK, vacation US; **Urlaub machen/haben** to have a holiday UK ODER vacation US; **im** ODER **in Urlaub sein** to be on holiday UK ODER vacation US.

Urlauber, in (*mpl* -, *fpl* -nen) *der, die* holidaymaker UK, vacationer US.

Urlaubslort *der* holiday UK ODER vacation US resort.

Urlaubslzeit *die* holiday UK ODER vacation US season.

Urne (*pl* -n) *die* - **1.** [Graburne] urn - **2.** [Wahlurne] ballot box.

Urlsache *die* cause; **die Ursache für etw** the cause of sthg. ➠ **keine Ursache** *interj* don't mention it!

Urlsprung *der* origin.

ursprünglich ◇ *adj* - **1.** [anfänglich] original - **2.** [naturhaft] natural. ◇ *adv* [zunächst] originally.

Urlteil *das* - **1.** RECHT verdict - **2.** [Bewertung] opinion; **sich** (*D*) **ein Urteil bilden** to form an opinion.

urteilen *vi* to judge; **über jn/etw urteilen** to judge sb/sthg.

Urteilslkraft *die* judgement.

Urteilslspruch *der* verdict.

Uruguay *nt* Uruguay.

Urlwald *der* primeval forest; [tropisch] jungle.

urwüchsig ['uːɐ̯vyːksɪç] *adj* [Garten, Gelände] natural; [Sprache, Humor] earthy; [Stärke] elemental.

USA [uːˈɛsʔaː] (*abk für* United States of America) *die* USA.

User ['juːzɐ] (*pl* -) *der* EDV user.

usw. (*abk für* und so weiter) etc.

Utensilien [utɛnˈziːljən] *Pl* equipment (*U*).

Utopie [utoˈpiː] (*pl* -n) *die* utopia.

u. U. (*abk für* unter Umständen), possibly.

u. v. a. (*abk für* und viele(s) andere), and many others.

V

v (pl - ODER -s), **V** (pl - ODER -s) [fau] das v, V.
◆ **V** (abk für **Volt**) V.

v. abk für **von**.

vage ['vɑːgə] (kompar **vager**, superl **vagste**), **vag** [vaːk] (kompar **vager**, superl **vagste**) ◇ adj vague. ◇ adv vaguely.

Vagina [va'giːna] (pl -**nen**) die MED vagina.

Vakuum ['vaːkuʊm] (pl -**kuen**) das vacuum.

vakuumverpackt ['vaːkuʊmfɛɐpakt] adj vacuum-packed.

Vampir ['vampiːɐ] (pl -**e**) der vampire.

Vanille [va'nɪljə, va'nɪlə] die vanilla.

Vanilleeis das vanilla ice cream.

variieren [vari'iːrən] vt & vi to vary.

Vase ['vaːzə] (pl -**n**) die vase.

Vater (pl **Väter**) der father.

Vaterland das homeland.

väterlich ◇ adj - 1. [des Vaters] paternal - 2. [wohlwollend] fatherly. ◇ adv [wohlwollend] in a fatherly way.

väterlicherseits adv on one's father's side.

Vatertag der Father's Day.

Vaterunser (pl -) das RELIG: **das Vaterunser** the Lord's Prayer.

Vatikan [vati'kaːn] der: **der Vatikan** the Vatican.

V-Ausschnitt der V-neck.

v. Chr. (abk für **vor Christus**) BC.

Veganer (pl -) der vegan.

Vegetarier, in [vege'taːrjɐ, rɪn] (mpl -, fpl -**nen**) der, die vegetarian.

vegetarisch [vege'taːrɪʃ] ◇ adj vegetarian. ◇ adv: **vegetarisch leben/essen** to be a vegetarian.

vegetieren [vege'tiːrən] vi abw to live from hand to mouth.

Veilchen ['faɪlçən] (pl -) das - 1. [Blume] violet - 2. fam fig [blaues Auge] black eye.

Vene ['veːnə] (pl -**n**) die MED vein.

Venedig [ve'neːdɪç] nt Venice.

Ventil [vɛn'tiːl] (pl -**e**) das valve.

Ventilator [vɛnti'laːtɔr] (pl -**toren**) der fan.

verabreden vt to arrange; **etw mit jm verabreden** to arrange sthg with sb. ◆ **sich verabreden** ref to arrange to meet; **sich mit jm verabreden** to arrange to meet sb.

Verabredung (pl -**en**) die - 1. [Treffen - geschäftlich] appointment; [- mit Freund] date - 2. [Übereinkommen] arrangement.

verabreichen vt to administer; **jm etw verabreichen** amt to administer sthg to sb.

verabscheuen vt to detest.

verabschieden vt - 1. [zum Abschied] to say goodbye to - 2. [Gesetz] to pass. ◆ **sich verabschieden** ref [Auf Wiedersehen sagen] to say goodbye; **sich von jm verabschieden** to say goodbye to sb.

verachten vt to despise.

verächtlich ◇ adj - 1. [missbilligend] contemptuous - 2. [verachtenswert] despicable. ◇ adv - 1. [missbilligend] contemptuously - 2. [verachtenswert] despicably.

Verachtung die contempt.

verallgemeinern vt & vi to generalize.

Verallgemeinerung (pl -**en**) die generalization.

veraltet adj obsolete.

Veranda [ve'randa] (pl -**den**) die veranda.

veränderlich adj [Wetter, Stimmung] changeable; [Größe] variable.

verändern vt to change. ◆ **sich verändern** ref - 1. [anders werden] to change - 2. [eine andere Stelle annehmen] to change one's job.

Veränderung (pl -**en**) die change.

verängstigt adj frightened.

Verankerung (pl -**en**) die [das Anbringen] fixing (U); [Befestigung] fixture; [von Schiff] anchoring (U).

veranlagt adj: **melancholisch veranlagt sein** to have a melancholic disposition; **homosexuell veranlagt sein** to have homosexual tendencies Pl.

Veranlagung (pl -**en**) die disposition; [künstlerisch] bent; **homosexuelle Veranlagung** homosexual tendencies Pl.

veranlassen vt: **jn veranlassen, etw zu tun**, **jn zu etw veranlassen** to make sb do sthg; **etw veranlassen** to arrange for sthg.

Veranlassung (pl -**en**) die - 1. [Veranlassen] instigation; **auf js Veranlassung (hin)** at sb's instigation - 2. [Anlass] reason; **keine Veranlassung haben, etw zu tun** to have no reason to do sthg.

veranschaulichen vt to illustrate.

veranstalten vt - 1. [organisieren] to organize - 2. fam [machen] to make.

Veranstalter, in (mpl -, fpl -**nen**) der, die organizer.

Veranstaltung (pl -**en**) die - 1. [Ereignis] event - 2. [Organisation] organization.

verantworten vt to take responsibility for. ◆ **sich verantworten** ref: **sich vor jm/etw verantworten** to answer to sb/sthg; **sich für** ODER **wegen etw verantworten** to answer for sthg.

verantwortlich *adj* responsible; **für jn/etw verantwortlich sein** to be responsible for sb/ sthg; **jn für etw verantwortlich machen** to hold sb responsible for sthg.

Verantwortung (*pl* -en) *die* responsibility; **jn zur Verantwortung ziehen** to call sb to account; **auf eigene Verantwortung** on one's own responsibility.

verantwortungslos ◇ *adj* irresponsible. ◇ *adv* irresponsibly.

verarbeiten *vt* - **1.** [Material] to process; **etw zu etw verarbeiten** to make sthg into sthg - **2.** [Eindruck, Erlebnis] to digest; [Misserfolg] to come to terms with.

Verarbeitung (*pl* -en) *die* - **1.** [von Rohstoffen] processing (*U*) - **2.** [Qualität] quality - **3.** [psychisch] coming to terms with the past.

verärgern *vt* to annoy.

verarzten *vt* to treat.

Verb [vɛrp] (*pl* -en) *das* GRAMM verb.

Verband (*pl* -bände) *der* - **1.** [für Wunden] bandage; **einen Verband anlegen** to apply a bandage - **2.** [Organisation] association - **3.** [Gruppe] unit.

Verbandlkasten, Verbandskasten *der* first-aid box.

verbannen *vt* to exile.

verbarrikadieren *vt* to barricade. ◆ **sich verbarrikadieren** *ref* to barricade o.s. in.

verbergen (*präs* verbirgt, *prät* verbarg, *perf* hat verborgen) *vt* to hide; **etw vor jm verbergen** to hide sthg from sb. ◆ **sich verbergen** *ref* to hide.

verbessern *vt* - **1.** [Leistung] to improve - **2.** [Fehler] to correct. ◆ **sich verbessern** *ref* - **1.** [besser werden] to improve - **2.** [sich korrigieren] to correct o.s. - **3.** [sozial, finanziell] to better o.s.

Verbesserung (*pl* -en) *die* - **1.** [gen] improvement - **2.** [Korrigieren, Text] correction - **3.** [Aufstieg] betterment.

verbeugen ◆ **sich verbeugen** *ref* to bow.

Verbeugung (*pl* -en) *die* bow.

verbiegen (*prät* verbog, *perf* hat verbogen) *vt* to bend. ◆ **sich verbiegen** *ref* to bend.

verbieten (*prät* verbot, *perf* hat verboten) *vt* [Handlung] to forbid; [Partei] to ban; **jm verbieten, etw zu tun** to forbid sb to do sthg.

verbilligt ◇ *adj* reduced. ◇ *adv* at a reduced price.

verbinden (*prät* verband, *perf* hat verbunden) ◇ *vt* - **1.** [Wunde] to bandage - **2.** [Werkstücke, Material] to join - **3.** [sich korrigieren] [Orte, Punkte] to connect - **4.** [am Telefon] to put through; **jn mit jm verbinden** to put sb through to sb - **5.** [zubinden]: **jm die Augen verbinden** to blindfold sb - **6.** [kombinieren]: **etw mit etw verbinden** to combine sthg with sthg - **7.** [Freunde, Bekannte] to unite - **8.** [Gedanken]

to associate. ◇ *vi* [am Telefon]: **ich verbinde** I'll put you through; **falsch verbunden!** wrong number! ◆ **sich verbinden** *ref* - **1.** [Stoffe, Materialien] to combine - **2.** [zusammentreffen] to be combined.

verbindlich ◇ *adj* - **1.** [Person] friendly - **2.** [Zusage] binding. ◇ *adv* - **1.** [lächeln] in a friendly manner - **2.** [verpflichtend]: **er hat verbindlich zugesagt** he has firmly accepted.

Verbindung (*pl* -en) *die* - **1.** [Aneinanderfügen] joining (*U*) - **2.** [Kombination & CHEM] combination - **3.** [zwischen Orten, Punkten] link - **4.** [Zusammenhang, am Telefon, Verkehrsverbindung] connection - **5.** [mit Erinnerung] association - **6.** [zu Freund, Bekannten] contact; **sich mit jm in Verbindung setzen** to contact sb.

verbissen ◇ *adj* [Kampf, Person] dogged; [Miene] grim. ◇ *adv* [arbeiten, kämpfen] doggedly; [betrachten] grimly.

verbittert ◇ *adj* bitter. ◇ *adv* with bitterness.

verblassen (*präs* verblasst, *prät* verblasste, *perf* ist verblasst) *vi* to fade.

verbleiben (*prät* verblieb, *perf* ist verblieben) *vi* - **1.** [übereinkommen]: **wie seid ihr gestern verblieben?** what did you arrange yesterday? - **2.** [bleiben, übrig bleiben] to remain.

verbleit *adj*: **verbleites Benzin** leaded petrol; **verbleites Super** super leaded.

verblöden ◇ *vi* (*perf* ist verblödet) to turn into a moron. ◇ *vt* (*perf* hat verblödet) to turn into a moron.

verblüffen ◇ *vt* to amaze; **verblüfft sein** to be taken aback. ◇ *vi* to be amazing.

verbluten (*perf* ist verblutet) *vi* to bleed to death.

verbohrt ◇ *adj* stubborn. ◇ *adv* stubbornly.

verborgen ◇ *pp* ▷ verbergen. ◇ *adj* hidden.

Verbot (*pl* -e) *das* ban.

verboten ◇ *pp* ▷ verbieten. ◇ *adj* - **1.** [nicht erlaubt] banned; **verboten sein** to be forbidden; **'streng verboten!'** 'strictly prohibited!' - **2.** *fam* [schrecklich] horrendous; **verboten aussehen** *fam* to look a real sight.

Verbotslschild (*pl* -er) *das* sign indicating a restriction, e.g. "no parking", "no entry", etc.

Verbrauch *der* consumption; **der Verbrauch von** ODER **an etw** (*D*) the consumption of sthg.

verbrauchen *vt* to consume.

Verbraucher, in (*mpl* -, *fpl* -nen) *der, die* consumer.

Verbrechen (*pl* -) *das* crime; **ein Verbrechen begehen** to commit a crime.

Verbrecher, in (*mpl* -, *fpl* -nen) *der, die* criminal.

verbrecherisch *adj* criminal.

verbreiten vt to spread. ➤ **sich verbreiten** ref - 1. [sich ausbreiten] to spread - 2. abw [sich auslassen]: **sich über etw (A) verbreiten** to hold forth about sthg.

verbreitern vt to widen. ➤ **sich verbreitern** ref to widen.

verbrennen (prät verbrannte, perf hat/ist verbrannt) <> vt (hat) - 1. [durch Feuer] to burn - 2. [Kalorien] to convert. <> vi (ist) - 1. [durch Feuer] to burn - 2. [Kalorien] to be converted. ➤ **sich verbrennen** ref to burn o.s.

verbringen (prät verbrachte, perf hat verbracht) vt - 1. [Zeit] to spend - 2. amt [bringen] to take.

verbrüdern ➤ **sich verbrüdern** ref: **sich mit jm verbrüdern** to avow eternal brotherhood with sb; [mit Feind] to fraternize with sb.

verbrühen vt to scald. ➤ **sich verbrühen** ref to scald o.s.

verbuchen vt to enter; **einen Sieg für sich verbuchen können** to notch up a success; **der Betrag wurde auf ihrem Konto verbucht** the sum was credited to her account.

verbünden ➤ **sich verbünden** ref to form an alliance; **sich mit jm verbünden** to form an alliance with sb.

Verbündete (pl -n) der, die ally.

verbürgen vt to guarantee. ➤ **sich verbürgen** ref: **sich für jn/etw verbürgen** to vouch for sb/sthg.

verbüßen vt to serve.

Verdacht (pl -e) der suspicion; **im Verdacht stehen** to be under suspicion; **jn im** ODER **in Verdacht haben** to suspect sb.

verdächtig <> adj suspicious. <> adv suspiciously.

verdächtigen vt to suspect; **jn einer Sache (G) verdächtigen** to suspect sb of sthg.

verdammt fam adj & adv [übel] damned.

verdampfen (perf ist verdampft) vi to vaporize.

verdanken vt: **jm etw verdanken** to owe sthg to sb.

verdarb prät ▷ **verderben**.

verdauen vt to digest.

verdaulich adj: **leicht/schwer verdaulich** easy/hard to digest.

Verdauung die digestion.

Verdeck (pl -e) das [von Autos] hood.

verdecken vt [zudecken] to cover; [verbergen] to conceal; **jm die Sicht verdecken** to block sb's view.

verderben (präs verdirbt, prät verdarb, perf hat/ist verdorben) <> vi (ist) to go off. <> vt (hat) to spoil; [völlig] to ruin; **jm die Laune verderben** to put sb in a bad mood; **es sich (D) mit niemandem verderben wollen** fig not to want to fall out with anyone.

verderblich adj perishable.

verdeutlichen vt: **jm etw verdeutlichen** to explain sthg to sb.

verdienen <> vt - 1. [Gehalt, Gewinn] to earn - 2. [Lob, Strafe] to deserve. <> vi to earn; **gut/schlecht verdienen** to be well/poorly paid.

Verdienst (pl -e) <> der [Entgelt] earnings Pl. <> das [Leistung] achievement.

verdirbt präs ▷ **verderben**.

verdoppeln vt [Gewinn, Einsatz] to double; [Anstrengungen] to redouble. ➤ **sich verdoppeln** ref to double.

verdorben pp ▷ **verderben**.

verdrängen vt - 1. [räumlich] to force out - 2. [psychisch] to repress.

Verdrängung (pl -en) die - 1. [psychisch] repression (U) - 2. [Abdrängen - von Person] ousting.

verdrehen vt to twist; **die Augen verdrehen** to roll one's eyes.

verdreifachen vt to triple. ➤ **sich verdreifachen** ref to triple.

Verdruss der annoyance.

verdünnen vt to dilute; [Farbe, Soße] to thin; [Kaffee, Wein] to water down.

verdunsten (perf ist verdunstet) vi to evaporate.

verdursten (perf ist verdurstet) vi to die of thirst.

verdutzt adj nonplussed.

verehren vt - 1. [Gottheit] to worship - 2. geh [Person] to admire - 3. iron [schenken]: **jm etw verehren** to present sb with sthg.

Verehrer, in (mpl -, fpl -nen) der, die admirer.

Verehrung die - 1. [von Gottheit] worship - 2. geh [für Person] admiration.

vereidigen vt to swear in.

Verein (pl -e) der [für Sport und Hobby] club; [gemeinnützig] society.

vereinbaren vt - 1. [verabreden]: **etw mit jm vereinbaren** to agree sthg with sb; [Termin, Treffpunkt] to arrange sthg with sb - 2. [vereinen]: **etw mit etw vereinbaren** to reconcile sthg with sthg.

Vereinbarung (pl -en) die agreement; [von Termin, Treffpunkt] arrangement; **eine Vereinbarung treffen** to come to an agreement.

vereinen vt [Gruppen, Länder] to unite; [Meinungen] to reconcile; [Eigenschaften] to combine. ➤ **sich vereinen** ref [Gruppen, Länder] to unite; [Eigenschaften] to be combined.

vereinfachen vt to simplify.

vereinheitlichen vt to standardize.

vereinigen vt [Länder, Gebiete] to unite; [Firmen] to merge; **mehrere Titel auf sich vereinigen** to hold several titles. ➤ **sich vereinigen** ref [Statten, Gruppen] to unite; [Flüsse] to join up.

Vereinigte Staaten (von Amerika) *Pl* United States (of America).

Vereinigung *(pl -en) die -* 1. [Vereinigen - von Staaten] uniting *(U)*; [- von Firmen] merging *(U)* - 2. [Gruppe] organization.

vereint ◇ *adj* united. ◇ *adv* together.

Vereinte Nationen *Pl* United Nations.

vereinzelt ◇ *adj* [Regen] occasional; [Person, Überreste] odd. ◇ *adv* occasionally.

vereist *adj* icy.

vereiteln *vt* to thwart.

verenden *(perf ist verendet) vi* to perish.

vererben *vt* [Güter]: **jm etw vererben** to leave sthg to sb.

Vererbung *(pl -en) die* heredity *(U)*; **wir untersuchen die Vererbung von bestimmten Eigenschaften** we are investigating the way in which certain characteristics are passed on.

verewigen *vt* to immortalize. ◆ **sich verewigen** *ref fam hum* to immortalize o.s.

verfahren *(präs* **verfährt**, *prät* **verfuhr**, *perf* **hat/ist verfahren**) *vi (ist)* to proceed; **mit jm/etw verfahren** to deal with sb/sthg. ◆ **sich verfahren** *ref* to get lost.

Verfahren *(pl -) das -* 1. [Gerichtsverfahren] proceedings *Pl* - 2. [Methode] procedure.

Verfall *der -* 1. [Niedergang - von Gebäude] decay; [- von Person, Gesundheit] decline - 2. [von Gutschein, Garantie] expiry.

verfallen *(präs* **verfällt**, *prät* **verfiel**, *perf* **ist verfallen**) *vi -* 1. [Gebäude] to decay; [Person] to decline - 2. [Gutschein, Garantie] to expire - 3. [auf etw kommen]: **auf jn/etw verfallen** to hit on sb/sthg - 4. [geraten]: **in etw (A) verfallen** to lapse into sthg - 5. [hörig werden]: **jm/einer Sache verfallen** to become a slave to sb/sthg.

Verfallsdatum *das* sell-by date.

verfälschen *vt* [Aussage, Tatsachen] to distort; [Geschmack] to adulterate.

verfänglich *adj* awkward.

verfärben *vt* to discolour. ◆ **sich verfärben** *ref* to change colour; **sich blau/schwarz verfärben** to turn blue/black.

verfassen *vt* to write.

Verfasser, in *(mpl -, fpl -nen) der, die* author.

Verfassung *(pl -en) die -* 1. [von Staaten] constitution - 2. [von Person] condition; **in guter/schlechter Verfassung sein** in good/poor shape.

verfaulen *(perf ist verfault) vi* to rot.

verfehlen *vt* to miss.

verfeinern *vt* to refine.

verfilmen *vt*: **einen Roman verfilmen** to make a film of a novel.

verfliegen *(prät* **verflog**, *perf* **hat/ist verflogen**) *vi (ist) -* 1. [Geruch] to disappear; [Flüssigkeit] to evaporate - 2. [Zeit] to fly by.

verflixt *fam* ◇ *adj -* 1. [verdammt] damned - 2. [groß] incredible. ◇ *adv* [sehr] damned.

verfluchen *vt* to curse.

verflüchtigen ◆ **sich verflüchtigen** *ref* [Geruch] to disappear; [Gas] to disperse.

verfolgen ◇ *vt -* 1. [folgen, beobachten] to follow - 2. [Verbrecher, Ziel, Plan] to pursue - 3. [unterdrücken] to persecute.

Verfolger, in *(mpl -, fpl -nen) der, die* pursuer.

Verfolgung *(pl -en) die -* 1. [gen] pursuit *(U)* - 2. [Unterdrückung] persecution.

Verfolgungswahn *der* persecution mania.

verfrachten *vt -* 1. [verladen] to transport - 2. *fam hum* [transportieren] to cart off.

verfrüht ◇ *adj* premature. ◇ *adv* prematurely.

verfügbar *adj* available.

verfügen ◇ *vt* to order. ◇ *vi*: **über jn/etw verfügen** [haben] to have sb/sthg at one's disposal; **über etw (A) (frei) verfügen können** [bestimmen] to be able to do as one likes with sthg.

Verfügung *(pl -en) die -* 1. [Zugriff]: **jm etw zur Verfügung stellen** to put sthg at sb's disposal - 2. [Erlass] order.

verführen *vt -* 1. [verleiten]: **jn zu etw verführen** to tempt sb to do sthg; **jn zum Klauen verführen** to encourage sb to steal - 2. [zum Geschlechtsverkehr] to seduce.

verführerisch ◇ *adj -* 1. [anziehend] tempting - 2. [erotisch] seductive. ◇ *adv -* 1. [anziehend] temptingly - 2. [erotisch] seductively.

Verführung *(pl -en) die* seduction *(U)*.

vergammelt *adj fam abw -* 1. [verdorben] spoilt - 2. [heruntergekommen] scruffy.

vergangen ◇ *pp* ▷ **vergehen**. ◇ *adj* [Zeiten] past; **vergangenen Dienstag** last Tuesday.

Vergangenheit *die -* 1. [vergangene Zeit] past - 2. GRAMM past tense.

Vergaser *(pl -) der* carburettor.

vergaß *prät* ▷ **vergessen**.

vergeben *(präs* **vergibt**, *prät* **vergab**, *perf* **hat vergeben**) ◇ *vi*: **jm vergeben** to forgive sb. ◇ *vt -* 1. [verzeihen]: **jm etw vergeben** to forgive sb sthg - 2. [geben] to award - 3. [verpassen] to miss.

vergebens *adv* in vain.

vergeblich ◇ *adj* futile. ◇ *adv* in vain.

vergehen *(prät* **verging**, *perf* **hat/ist vergangen**) *vi (ist) -* 1. [Zeit] to pass - 2. [verschwinden] to disappear; **der Spaß ist mir vergangen** I'm not enjoying it any more; **vor etw (D) vergehen** *fig* to die of sthg.

Vergeltung *die* retaliation.

vergessen *(präs* **vergisst**, *prät* **vergaß**, *perf* **hat vergessen**) *vt* to forget.

Vergessenheit die: in Vergessenheit geraten to fall into oblivion.

vergesslich adj forgetful.

vergeuden vt to waste.

vergewaltigen vt [sexuell] to rape; [allgemein] to violate.

Vergewaltigung (pl -en) die rape.

vergewissern ➡ **sich vergewissern** ref to make sure.

vergießen (prät vergoss, perf hat vergossen) vt - 1. [verschütten] to spill - 2. [Blut, Tränen] to shed.

vergiften vt to poison. ➡ **sich vergiften** ref to poison o.s.

Vergiftung (pl -en) die poisoning (U).

Vergissmeinnicht (pl -e) das forget-me-not.

vergisst präs ⊳ **vergessen**.

verglasen vt to glaze.

Vergleich (pl -e) der - 1. [Gegenüberstellung] comparison; im Vergleich mit ODER zu jm/etw compared to sb/sthg - 2. RECHT settlement - 3. SPORT friendly.

vergleichbar adj comparable.

vergleichen (prät verglich, perf hat verglichen) vt to compare; jn/etw mit jm/etw vergleichen to compare sb/sthg to sb/sthg.

vergnügen ➡ **sich vergnügen** ref to enjoy o.s.

Vergnügen (pl -) das - 1. [Freude] pleasure; Tanzen macht ihr großes Vergnügen she really enjoys dancing; mit Vergnügen! with pleasure! - 2. [Unterhaltung] fun (U). ➡ **viel Vergnügen** interj have fun!

vergnügt ⬦ adj - 1. [Person] cheerful - 2. [Stunden] enjoyable. ⬦ adv cheerfully.

vergoldet adj gold-plated.

vergraben (präs vergräbt, prät vergrub, perf hat vergraben) vt to bury.

vergreifen (prät vergriff, perf hat vergriffen) ➡ **sich vergreifen** ref: sich an jm vergreifen [brutal werden] to assault sb; [sexuell] to assault sb (sexually); sich an etw (D) vergreifen [stehlen] to misappropriate sthg.

vergriffen ⬦ pp ⊳ **vergreifen**. ⬦ adj out of print.

vergrößern ⬦ vt to expand; [Foto] to enlarge; [Haus] to extend; [vermehren] to increase. ⬦ vi to magnify. ➡ **sich vergrößern** ref - 1. [größer werden] to expand; [zunehmen] to increase; [Tumor] to increase in size - 2. [mehr Raum benutzen] to get more space.

Vergrößerung (pl -en) die - 1. [Vergrößern] expansion (U); [von Haus] extension (U); [von Tumor] increase in size; [Vermehrung] increase - 2. [Foto] enlargement.

Vergrößerungs|glas das magnifying glass.

Vergünstigung (pl -en) die concession.

vergüten vt: jm etw vergüten [Unkosten] to reimburse sb for sthg; [Arbeit] to remunerate sb for sthg.

verhaften vt to arrest.

Verhaftung (pl -en) die arrest.

verhallen (perf ist verhallt) vi to die away.

verhalten (präs verhält, prät verhielt, perf hat verhalten) ➡ **sich verhalten** ref - 1. [sich benehmen] to behave - 2. [sein] to be; es verhält sich so this is how matters stand.

Verhalten das behaviour.

Verhältnis (pl -se) das - 1. [Relation] ratio; im Verhältnis zum letzten Jahr compared to last year - 2. [persönliche Beziehung] relationship; ein gutes Verhältnis zu jm haben to have a good relationship with sb - 3. [Liebesbeziehung] affair; ein Verhältnis mit jm haben to have an affair with sb. ➡ **Verhältnisse** Pl [Bedingungen] conditions; über seine Verhältnisse leben to live beyond one's means.

verhältnismäßig adv relatively.

verhandeln ⬦ vi - 1. [beraten]: mit jm verhandeln to negotiate with sb; über etw (A) verhandeln to negotiate sthg - 2. [vor Gericht] to hear a case. ⬦ vt - 1. [aushandeln] to negotiate - 2. [vor Gericht] to hear.

Verhandlung (pl -en) die - 1. [Beratung] negotiation - 2. RECHT hearing.

verhängen vt - 1. [zuhängen] to cover - 2. [Urteil, Verbot] to impose; etw über jn/etw verhängen to impose sthg on sb/sthg.

Verhängnis (pl -se) das: jn zum Verhängnis werden to be sb's downfall.

verhängnisvoll ⬦ adj [Tag, Begegnung] fateful; [Fehler] disastrous. ⬦ adv disastrously.

verharmlosen vt to play down.

verhärten (perf hat/ist verhärtet) ⬦ vi (ist) to harden. ⬦ vt (hat) to harden. ➡ **sich verhärten** ref to harden.

verheerend ⬦ adj devastating. ⬦ adv devastatingly.

verheilen (perf ist verheilt) vi to heal.

verheimlichen vt to keep secret; jm etw verheimlichen to keep sthg secret from sb.

verheiratet adj married; mit jm verheiratet sein [mit dem Ehepartner] to be married to sb; mit etw verheiratet sein fam hum [auf etw fixiert sein] to be married to sthg.

verhindern vt to prevent.

Verhör (pl -e) das interrogation.

verhören vt to interrogate. ➡ **sich verhören** ref to mishear.

verhungern (perf ist verhungert) vi to starve to death.

verhüten ⬦ vt to prevent. ⬦ vi to take precautions.

Verhütungs|mittel das contraceptive.

verirren ➡ **sich verirren** ref to get lost.

verjagen *vt* to chase away.

verjähren (*perf* ist verjährt) *vi* to come under the statute of limitations.

verjüngen *vt* [Aussehen, Haut] to rejuvenate; [Belegschaft] to introduce young blood into. ➥ **sich verjüngen** *ref* to taper.

verkalkt *adj* - 1. [verstopft] furred up - 2. *fam* [senil] senile; **verkalkt sein** to be gaga.

Ver|kauf (*pl* -käufe) *der* - 1. [das Verkaufen] sale - 2. [Abteilung] sales (U).

verkaufen *vt* - 1. [Ware] to sell; **etw an jn verkaufen** to sell sb sthg; **'zu verkaufen!'** 'for sale' - 2. *fam* [darstellen]: **(jm) etw als etw verkaufen** to sell (sb) sthg as sthg. ➥ **sich verkaufen** *ref*: sich gut/schlecht verkaufen [Ware] to sell well/poorly; [sich darstellen] to sell o.s. well/poorly.

Ver|käufer, in (*mpl* -, *fpl* -nen) *der, die* - 1. [beruflich] sales assistant UK ODER clerk US - 2. [Verkaufende] seller.

verkäuflich *adj*: verkäuflich sein to be for sale; **schwer verkäuflich sein** to be hard to sell.

Verkehr *der* - 1. [Straßenverkehr] traffic; **dichter Verkehr** heavy traffic - 2. [Gebrauch]: **etw aus dem Verkehr ziehen** [Geld] to withdraw sthg from circulation; [Produkt] to withdraw sthg from sale - 3. *geh* [Umgang] contact - 4. [Geschlechtsverkehr] intercourse.

verkehren (*perf* hat/ist verkehrt) ◇ *vi* - 1. (hat) *geh* [Person]: **mit jm verkehren** to associate with sb; **in einem Lokal verkehren** to frequent a bar - 2. [Zug, Bus] to run. ◇ *vt* (hat): **etw ins Gegenteil verkehren** to reverse sthg.

Verkehrs|ampel *die* traffic lights *Pl*.

Verkehrs|aufkommen *das*: dichtes ODER hohes Verkehrsaufkommen heavy traffic.

Verkehrs|funk *der* traffic bulletin service.

Verkehrs|kontrolle *die* traffic check.

Verkehrs|mittel *das*: die öffentlichen Verkehrsmittel public transport (U).

Verkehrs|polizei *die* (ohne pl) traffic police *Pl*.

Verkehrsun|fall *der* road accident.

Verkehrsver|bindung *die* connection.

Verkehrs|zeichen *das* road sign.

verkehrt ◇ *adj* wrong. ◇ *adv* wrongly; **verkehrt fahren** to go the wrong way. ➥ **verkehrt herum** *adv* the wrong way round.

verkennen (*prät* verkannte, *perf* hat verkannt) *vt* [Situation] to misjudge; [Absicht] to mistake.

verklagen *vt* to sue.

verkleben (*perf* hat/ist verklebt) ◇ *vi* (ist) to become sticky. ◇ *vt* (hat) - 1. [beschmieren] to make sticky - 2. [Riss] to stick something over.

verkleiden *vt* - 1. [mit Kostüm] to dress up - 2. [Innenwand] to cover; [Gebäude] to face. ➥ **sich verkleiden** *ref* to dress up.

Verkleidung (*pl* -en) *die* - 1. [Kostüm] costume - 2. [das Verkleiden] dressing up - 3. [von Innenwand] covering; [von Gebäude] facing.

verkleinern *vt* to reduce. ➥ **sich verkleinern** *ref* to decrease.

verklemmt *adj* inhibited.

verkneifen (*prät* verkniff, *perf* hat verkniffen) *vt*: sich (D) etw verkneifen to suppress sthg.

verknoten *vt* to tie together. ➥ **sich verknoten** *ref* to become knotted.

verknüpfen *vt* - 1. [verknoten] to tie together - 2. [verbinden]: etw mit etw verknüpfen to connect sthg with sthg.

verkommen (*prät* verkam, *perf* ist verkommen) *vi* - 1. [verfallen] to become rundown - 2. [verderben] to go bad - 3. [verwahrlosen]: jn verkommen lassen to let sb go to the bad.

verkrachen ➥ **sich verkrachen** *ref*: sich mit jm verkrachen to have a row with sb.

verkraften *vt* to cope with.

verkriechen (*prät* verkroch, *perf* hat verkrochen) ➥ **sich verkriechen** *ref* [kriechen] to crawl; [sich verstecken] to hide.

verkrüppelt *adj* - 1. [Mensch] crippled - 2. [Baum] twisted, gnarled.

verkümmern (*perf* ist verkümmert) *vi* to wither (away).

verkünden *vt* to announce; [Urteil] to pronounce; [Prophezeiung] to make.

verkürzen *vt* to shorten; [Leben, Urlaub] to cut short; [Arbeitszeit] to reduce; **die Zeit verkürzen** to while away the time.

Verlag (*pl* -e) *der* publishing house.

verlagern *vt* [Gewicht, Schwerpunkt] to shift; [an einen anderen Ort] to move. ➥ **sich verlagern** *ref* to shift.

verlangen ◇ *vt* - 1. [fordern] to demand; [bitten] to ask for; **viel von jm verlangen** to ask a lot of sb - 2. [erfordern] to call for - 3. [Lohn] to ask - 4. [Ausweis] to ask to see - 5. [am Telefon]: jn am Telefon verlangen to ask to speak to sb on the phone. ◇ *vi*: nach jm/etw verlangen [um etw bitten] to ask for sb/sthg; *geh* [sich sehnen] to long for sb/sthg.

Verlangen *das* - 1. [Wunsch] desire - 2. [Forderung] request. ➥ **auf Verlangen** *adv* on demand.

verlängern *vt* - 1. [zeitlich, räumlich] to extend; [Ausweis] to renew - 3. [Rock, Ärmel] to lengthen - 3. [Soße] to thin down. ➥ **sich verlängern** *ref* - 1. [zeitlich] to be extended - 2. [räumlich] to grow longer.

Verlängerung (*pl* -en) *die* - 1. [von Zeitraum, Strecke] extension - 2. [von Rock, Ärmel] lengthening; [von Ausweis] renewal - 3. SPORT extra time.

Verlängerungslschnur *die* ELEKTR extension lead *UK* ODER cord *US*.

verlangsamen *vt* to slow down; **das Tempo verlangsamen** to reduce speed. ◆ **sich verlangsamen** *ref* to slow down.

verlassen (*präs* **verlässt**, *prät* **verließ**, *perf* **hat verlassen**) *vt* to leave. ◆ **sich verlassen** *ref*: **sich auf jn/etw verlassen** to rely on sb/sthg.

verlässlich *adj* reliable.

Verllauf (*pl* -läufe) *der* course; **im Verlauf von etw/einer Sache** (*G*) in the course of sthg.

verlaufen (*präs* **verläuft**, *prät* **verlief**, *perf* **hat/ist verlaufen**) *vi* (*ist*) - 1. [Weg, Strecke, Farbe] to run - 2. [Operation, Prüfung] to go. ◆ **sich verlaufen** *ref* - 1. [sich verirren] to get lost - 2. [Menge] to disperse.

verlegen[1] *vt* - 1. [verlieren] to mislay - 2. [Termin] to postpone - 3. [an anderen Ort] to move, to transfer - 4. [Kabel, Teppichboden] to lay - 5. [Buch] to publish.

verlegen[2] ◇ *adj* embarrassed; **um etw nicht verlegen sein** not to be short of sthg. ◇ *adv* in embarrassment.

Verlegenheit (*pl* -en) *die* - 1. [Befangenheit] embarrassment; **jn in Verlegenheit bringen** to embarrass sb - 2. [Notlage] difficulty; **in finanzieller Verlegenheit** in financial difficulties.

Verleih (*pl* -e) *der* - 1. (*ohne pl*) [das Verleihen] hiring (out) - 2. [Firma - von Videos, Fahrrädern] rental shop; [- von Autos] car hire *UK* ODER rental *US* company.

verleihen (*prät* **verlieh**, *perf* **hat verliehen**) *vt* - 1. [leihen] to lend; [gegen Bezahlung] to hire out - 2. [Orden, Titel]: **jm etw verleihen** to award sb sthg - 3. [Reiz, Glanz] to give, to lend.

verleiten *vt*: **jn dazu verleiten, etw zu tun** to lead sb to do sthg.

verlernen *vt* to forget; **das Klavierspielen verlernen** to forget how to play the piano.

verletzen *vt* - 1. [Mensch, Körperteil] to injure; **sich den Fuß verletzen** to injure one's foot - 2. [Gefühle, Stolz] to hurt - 3. [Grenze] to violate; [Abkommen] to break. ◆ **sich verletzen** *ref* to hurt o.s.; [schwer] to injure o.s.

verletzlich *adj* [verletzbar] vulnerable; [empfindlich] sensitive.

verletzt ◇ *pp* ▷ **verletzen**. ◇ *adj*: **verletzt sein** [eine Wunde haben] to be injured; [gekränkt sein] to be hurt.

Verletzte (*pl* -n) *der*, *die* injured person; **ein Unfall mit vielen Verletzten** an accident in which several people were injured.

Verletzung (*pl* -en) *die* - 1. [Wunde] injury - 2. [von Grenzraum] violation; [von Gesetz, Abkommen] infringement.

verleugnen *vt* to deny; [Freund] to disown.

Verleumdung (*pl* -en) *die* [mündlich] slander; [schriftlich] libel.

verlieben ◆ **sich verlieben** *ref*: **sich (in jn/etw) verlieben** to fall in love (with sb/sthg).

verliebt ◇ *adj* [Person] in love; [Blicke] amorous; **in jn verliebt sein** to be in love with sb. ◇ *adv* amorously.

verlieren (*prät* **verlor**, *perf* **hat verloren**) ◇ *vt* to lose; **du hast hier nichts verloren** *fam* you've no business here. ◇ *vi* - 1. [nicht gewinnen] to lose; **gegen jn verlieren** to lose to sb - 2. [einbüßen] to suffer; **an etw** (*D*) **verlieren** [Reiz, Schönheit] to lose sthg. ◆ **sich verlieren** *ref* - 1. [Personen] to lose one another - 2. [Angst, Begeisterung] to evaporate.

Verlierer, in (*mpl* -, *fpl* -nen) *der*, *die* loser.

verloben ◆ **sich verloben** *ref*: **sich (mit jm) verloben** to get engaged (to sb).

Verlobte (*pl* -n) *der*, *die* fiancé (fiancée *die*).

Verlobung (*pl* -en) *die* engagement.

verlockend *adj* tempting.

verlogen *adj* false.

verlor *prät* ▷ **verlieren**.

verloren ◇ *pp* ▷ **verlieren**. ◇ *adj* lost.

verloren gehen (*perf* **ist verloren gegangen**) *vi* (*unreg*) to go missing, to disappear; **der Geschmack geht durch das Kochen verloren** it loses its taste when you boil it; **an ihm ist ein Lehrer verloren gegangen** he would have made a good teacher.

verlosen *vt* [kleine Preise] to raffle; [große Gewinne] to give away (*in a prize draw*).

Verlosung (*pl* -en) *die* [von kleinen Preisen] raffle; [von großen Gewinnen] prize draw.

Verlust (*pl* -e) *der* loss.

Vermächtnis (*pl* -se) *das* legacy.

vermasseln *vt fam*: **jm etw vermasseln** to ruin sthg for sb.

vermehren *vt* to increase. ◆ **sich vermehren** *ref* - 1. [größer werden] to increase - 2. [sich fortpflanzen] to reproduce.

vermeiden (*prät* **vermied**, *perf* **hat vermieden**) *vt* to avoid.

vermerken *vt* - 1. [notieren] to make a note of - 2. [feststellen] to note.

vermessen[1] (*präs* **vermisst**, *prät* **vermaß**, *perf* **hat vermessen**) *vt* to measure; [Land, Wand] to survey.

vermessen[2] *adj* presumptuous.

vermieten *vt*: **etw (an jn) vermieten** to rent sthg out (to sb); **'zu vermieten!'** 'to let'.

Verlmieter, in (*mpl* -, *fpl* -nen) *der*, *die* landlord (landlady *die*).

vermindern *vt* to reduce.

Verminderung (*pl* -en) *die* reduction.

vermischen *vt* to mix. ◆ **sich vermischen** *ref* to mingle.

vermissen vt - **1**. [sehnsüchtig] to miss - **2**. [suchen]: **ich vermisse meinen Regenschirm** my umbrella is missing.

vermisst adj missing.

vermitteln <> vi to mediate. <> vt - **1**. [Ehe, Kontakt] to arrange - **2**. [Job, Arbeitskraft]: **jm jn/ etw vermitteln** to find sb/sthg for sb - **3**. [Gefühl, Eindruck] to convey; [Wissen, Erfahrung] to impart, to pass on.

Vermittlung (pl -en) die - **1**. (ohne pl) [von Mitarbeitern, Jobs] finding; [von Kontakten, Ehen] arranging; **durch js Vermittlung eine Stelle bekommen** to get a job through sb - **2**. [Firma, Büro] agency - **3**. [Telefonzentrale] exchange.

Vermögen (pl -) das - **1**. [Besitz] fortune - **2**. geh [Fähigkeit] ability.

vermögend adj wealthy.

vermuten vt - **1**. [annehmen] to assume - **2**. [für wahrscheinlich halten] to suspect.

vermutlich <> adj probable. <> adv probably.

Vermutung (pl -en) die - **1**. [Annahme] supposition - **2**. [Verdacht] suspicion.

vernachlässigen vt - **1**. [gen] to neglect - **2**. [nicht beachten] to ignore.

vernehmen (präs vernimmt, prät vernahm, perf hat vernommen) vt - **1**. [verhören] to question; [vor Gericht] to examine - **2**. geh [hören] to hear.

Vernehmung (pl -en) die questioning; [vor Gericht] examination.

verneinen vt [Vorschlag] to reject; [Frage] to say no to.

vernetzen vt - **1**. to connect, to link - **2**. EDV to network, to connect to the Internet; **vernetzt sein** to be on the Internet ODER online.

vernichten vt to destroy; [Schädlinge] to exterminate.

vernichtend <> adj [Kritik, Niederlage] devastating; [Blick] withering. <> adv [kritisieren] devastatingly; **jn vernichtend ansehen** to give sb a withering look.

Vernichtung (pl -en) die destruction; [von Insekten] extermination.

Vernunft die reason; **mit/ohne Vernunft handeln** to act sensibly/foolishly; **das widerspricht jeder Vernunft** that goes against all common sense; **zur Vernunft kommen** to come to one's senses; **jn zur Vernunft bringen** to bring sb to his/her senses.

vernünftig <> adj - **1**. [klug] sensible - **2**. [ordentlich] decent; [Preis] reasonable. <> adv - **1**. [klug] sensibly - **2**. [ordentlich] decently.

veröffentlichen vt to publish.

Veröffentlichung (pl -en) die publication.

verordnen vt: **(jm) etw verordnen** to prescribe sthg (for sb).

Verordnung (pl -en) die - **1**. [von Medikament] prescription - **2**. [von Regel] regulation.

verpacken vt [Waren] to pack; [Geschenk] to wrap (up).

Verpackung (pl -en) die - **1**. [Hülle - von Ware] packaging; [- von Geschenk] wrapping paper - **2**. [Verpacken] packing.

verpassen vt - **1**. [Bus, Gelegenheit, Film] to miss - **2**. fam [Schlag, Frisur] to give.

verpesten vt abw to pollute.

verpflanzen vt to transplant; [Haut] to graft.

verpflegen vt to cater for.

Verpflegung die - **1**. [das Verpflegen] catering - **2**. [Essen] food.

verpflichten <> vt - **1**. [auf etw festlegen] to oblige; [durch Eid] to bind; **jn zu sechs Wochen gemeinnütziger Arbeit verpflichten** to give sb six weeks' community service - **2**. [Schauspieler] to engage; [Mannschaftsspieler] to sign. <> vi: **dieses Angebot verpflichtet nicht zum Kauf** no purchase necessary to take advantage of this offer. <> **sich verpflichten** ref to commit o.s.; **sich vertraglich verpflichten** to sign a contract.

Verpflichtung (pl -en) die - **1**. [Pflichten] obligation; **seine gesellschaftlichen Verpflichtungen** his social commitments - **2**. [von Schauspieler] engaging; [von Mannschaftsspieler] signing - **3**. [Schulden] commitment.

verprügeln vt to beat up.

Verrat der betrayal; [gegen Vaterland] treason.

verraten (präs verrät, prät verriet, perf hat verraten) vt - **1**. [Person, Gedanken] to betray; [Geheimnis, Versteck] to give away, to betray - **2**. [Gefühle] to show - **3**. [mitteilen]: **er hat mir den Preis nicht verraten** he didn't tell me the price. <> **sich verraten** ref to give o.s. away.

Verräter, in (mpl -, fpl -nen) der, die traitor.

verrechnen vt to include; **etw mit etw verrechnen** to offset sthg against sthg. <> **sich verrechnen** ref - **1**. [falsch rechnen] to make a mistake; **sich um fünf Euro verrechnen** to be five euros out - **2**. [sich täuschen] to miscalculate.

verregnet adj wet.

verreisen (perf ist verreist) vi to go away; **verreist sein** to be away.

verrenken vt: **sich (D) den Arm verrenken** to dislocate one's arm.

verriegeln vt to bolt.

verringern vt to reduce. <> **sich verringern** ref to decrease.

verrosten (perf ist verrostet) vi to rust.

verrücken vt to move.

verrückt <> adj - **1**. [geistesgestört] mad; **verrückt spielen** [Person] to act crazy; [Computer, Auto] to play up; **nach jm/etw verrückt sein** fam to be crazy about sb/sthg - **2**. [ausgefallen] crazy. <> adv [ausgefallen] crazily. <> **wie verrückt** adv fam like mad.

Verrückte (*pl* -n) *der, die* lunatic.

Verruf *der*: **in Verruf bringen/kommen** to bring/fall into disrepute.

verrufen *adj* disreputable.

Vers (*pl* -e) *der* line; **in Versen** in verse.

versagen *vi* to fail.

Versagen *das* failure.

Versager, in (*pl* -in) *die* failure.

versammeln *vt* to assemble, to gather. ➤ **sich versammeln** *ref* to assemble, to gather.

Versammlung (*pl* -en) *die* meeting; [im Freien] rally.

Versand *der* - 1. [Versenden] dispatch - 2. [Abteilung] dispatch department.

Versand|haus *das* mail order firm.

versäumen *vt* - 1. [Zug, Termin] to miss - 2. [Pflicht] to neglect.

verschaffen *vt*: **jm etw verschaffen** to get sb/sthg; **sich** (*D*) **etw verschaffen** to get (hold of) sthg; **sich** (*D*) **einen Vorteil verschaffen** to gain an advantage; **sich** (*D*) **Respekt verschaffen** to earn respect.

verschämt <> *adj* bashful. <> *adv* bashfully.

verschärfen *vt* [Kontrolle] to tighten up; [Lage, Krise] to aggravate. ➤ **sich verschärfen** *ref* [Gegensätze] to intensify; [Lage, Krise] to get worse.

verschätzen ➤ **sich verschätzen** *ref* to miscalculate.

verschenken *vt* - 1. [weg geben] to give away - 2. [als Geschenk] to give (*as present*) - 3. [Punkte] to throw away; [Raum] to waste.

verscherzen *vt*: **sich** (*D*) **etw verscherzen** to throw sthg away.

verscheuchen *vt* [Tier] to chase away; [Angst machen] to scare away.

verschicken *vt* to send out.

verschieben (*prät* verschob, *perf* hat verschoben) *vt* - 1. [Termin] to postpone - 2. [Möbel] to move - 3. [schmuggeln] to traffic in. ➤ **sich verschieben** *ref* - 1. [Termin] to be postponed - 2. [verrutschen] to slip.

Verschiebung (*pl* -en) *die* postponement.

verschieden <> *adj* - 1. [unterschiedlich] different - 2. [mehrere] various. <> *adv* [unterschiedlich] differently; **verschieden groß sein** to be different sizes; **die Aufgaben waren verschieden schwer** the tasks were of varying degrees of difficulty.

verschimmeln (*perf* ist verschimmelt) *vi* to go mouldy.

verschlafen (*präs* verschläft, *prät* verschlief, *perf* hat verschlafen) <> *vi* to oversleep. <> *vt* - 1. [schlafend verbringen] to sleep through - 2. *fam* [vergessen] to forget.

verschlagen *abw* <> *adj* sly. <> *adv* slyly.

verschlechtern *vt* to make worse. ➤ **sich verschlechtern** *ref* to get worse, to deteriorate.

Verschlechterung (*pl* -en) *die* deterioration.

Verschleiß *der* wear (and tear).

verschleißen (*prät* verschliss, *perf* **hat**/**ist** verschlissen) <> *vi* (**ist**) to wear out; **diese Teile sind verschlissen** these parts are worn out. <> *vt* (**hat**) to wear out.

verschleppen *vt* - 1. [Person] to take away (by force) - 2. [Gegenstand] to hide - 3. [Verhandlung] to draw out - 4. [Krankheit] to allow to drag on.

verschleudern *vt* - 1. [billig verkaufen] to give away - 2. *abw* [verschwenden] to throw away.

verschließen (*prät* verschloss, *perf* **hat** verschlossen) *vt* - 1. [Haus, Tür, Schrank] to lock - 2. [Kunststoffbehälter] to seal; [Flasche] to stop up.

verschlimmern *vt* to make worse. ➤ **sich verschlimmern** *ref* to get worse.

verschlingen (*prät* verschlang, *perf* hat verschlungen) *vt* to devour; **viel Geld verschlingen** to cost a fortune.

verschlossen *adj* [Mensch] reticent; [Raum, Tür] locked; [Umschlag] sealed.

verschlucken *vt* to swallow. ➤ **sich verschlucken** *ref* to choke.

Verschluss (*pl* -schlüsse) *der* fastener; [von Flasche] top. ➤ **unter Verschluss** *adv* under lock and key.

verschlüsseln *vt* to encode.

verschmelzen (*präs* verschmilzt, *prät* verschmolz, *perf* ist verschmolzen) *vi*: **mit etw verschmelzen** to blend with sthg.

verschmutzen (*perf* **hat**/**ist** verschmutzt) <> *vi* (**ist**) [Kleidung, Wohnung] to get dirty. <> *vt* (**hat**) [Kleidung, Wohnung] to get dirty; [Umwelt] to pollute.

verschnaufen *vi* to have a breather.

verschneit *adj* snow-covered.

verschnupft *adj*: **verschnupft sein** to have a cold.

verschollen *adj* missing.

verschonen *vt* to spare; **jn mit etw verschonen** to spare sb sthg.

verschränken *vt*: **die Arme verschränken** to fold one's arms; **die Beine verschränken** to cross one's legs.

verschreiben (*prät* verschrieb, *perf* hat verschrieben) *vt*: **jm etw verschreiben** to prescribe sb sthg. ➤ **sich verschreiben** *ref*: **ich habe mich verschrieben** I've written it down wrong.

verschreibungspflichtig *adj* available on prescription only.

verschrien *adj* notorious.

verschrotten *vt* to scrap.

verschuldet *adj* in debt.

verschütten *vt* - **1.** [Wasser, Getränk] to spill - **2.** [mit Erde] to bury.

verschweigen (*prät* **verschwieg**, *perf* hat **verschwiegen**) *vt* [Nachricht] to keep quiet about; [Wahrheit] to conceal; **jm etw verschweigen** to conceal sthg from sb.

verschwenden *vt* to waste.

verschwenderisch ◇ *adj* [mit Geld] extravagant; [mit Energie] wasteful. ◇ *adv* [mit Geld] extravagantly; [mit Energie] wastefully.

Verschwendung *die* squandering; **so eine Verschwendung!** what a waste!

verschwiegen ◇ *pp* ⊳ **verschweigen**. ◇ *adj* - **1.** [Mensch] discreet - **2.** [Winkel] secluded.

Verschwiegenheit *die* discretion.

verschwinden (*prät* **verschwand**, *perf* ist **verschwunden**) *vi* to disappear.

verschwommen ◇ *adj* blurred. ◇ *adv* vaguely; **ohne Brille sieht sie alles verschwommen** without her glasses everything looks blurred to her.

verschwören (*prät* **verschwor**, *perf* hat **verschworen**) ➺ **sich verschwören** *ref*: **sich gegen jn verschwören** to conspire against sb.

Verschwörung (*pl* **-en**) *die* conspiracy.

verschwunden ◇ *pp* ⊳ **verschwinden**. ◇ *adj* missing.

versehen (*präs* **versieht**, *prät* **versah**, *perf* hat **versehen**) *vt* - **1.** [ausrüsten]: **etw mit etw versehen** to equip sthg with sthg; **jn mit etw versehen** to provide sb with sthg - **2.** [erledigen] to perform.

Versehen (*pl* -) *das* accident. ➺ **aus Versehen** *adv* accidentally.

versehentlich ◇ *adj* accidental. ◇ *adv* accidentally.

versenden (*prät* **versandte** ODER **versendete**, *perf* hat **versandt** ODER **versendet**) *vt* to send.

versengen *vt* to scorch.

versenken *vt* [Schiff] to sink.

versetzen *vt* - **1.** [umstellen] to move; [Angestellten] to transfer, to move; [Schüler] to move up *UK*, to promote *US* - **2.** [in einen anderen Zustand]: **sich in die Lage eines anderen versetzen** to put o.s. in somebody else's position; **jn in Erstaunen/Angst versetzen** to astonish/frighten sb; **etw in Bewegung versetzen** to set sthg in motion - **3.** [verpfänden] to pawn - **4.** [bei einer Verabredung]: **jn versetzen** to stand sb up - **5.** [austeilen]: **jm einen Stoß versetzen** to give sb a push; **jm einen Schlag versetzen** to hit sb - **6.** [antworten] to retort.

Versetzung (*pl* -en) *die* - **1.** [beruflich] transfer - **2.** SCHULE moving up *UK*, promotion *US*.

verseuchen *vt* to contaminate.

versichern *vt* - **1.** [erklären] to affirm; **jm versichern, dass...** to assure sb that... - **2.** [bei Ver-**

sicherung] to insure. ➺ **sich versichern** *ref* - **1.** [bei Versicherung] to insure o.s. - **2.** [Gewissheit]: **sich einer Sache** (*G*) **versichern** to assure o.s. of sthg.

Versicherung (*pl* **-en**) *die* - **1.** [vertraglicher Schutz] insurance (*U*); [Vertrag] insurance policy; **eine Versicherung (über etw** (*A*)) **abschließen** to take out insurance ODER an insurance policy (for sthg) - **2.** [Firma] insurance company - **3.** [Angabe] assurance.

versinken (*prät* **versank**, *perf* ist **versunken**) *vi* - **1.** [in Sumpf, Sand, Schnee]: **in etw** (*A*) **versinken** to sink into sthg - **2.** [Schiff, Sonne] to sink - **3.** [in Gedanken]: **in etw** (*A*) **versinken** to become immersed in sthg.

versöhnen *vt* [Feinde] to reconcile; [besänftigen] to appease. ➺ **sich versöhnen** *ref* to become reconciled; **sich mit jm versöhnen** to make it up with sb.

versöhnlich ◇ *adj* - **1.** [Antwort, Stimmung] conciliatory - **2.** [Ende, Ausgang] optimistic. ◇ *adv* in a conciliatory way.

Versöhnung (*pl* **-en**) *die* reconciliation; [Besänftigung] appeasement.

versorgen *vt* - **1.** [versehen]: **jn/sich mit etw versorgen** to provide sb/o.s. with sthg - **2.** [beliefern - mit Strom, Wasser] to supply - **3.** [pflegen] to look after - **4.** [ernähren] to provide for.

Versorgung (*pl* **-en**) *die* - **1.** [mit Lebensmitteln] supply - **2.** [von Patienten] care.

verspäten ➺ **sich verspäten** *ref* to be late; **sich um eine halbe Stunde verspäten** to be half an hour late.

verspätet ◇ *adj* late; [Gratulation] belated. ◇ *adv* late.

Verspätung (*pl* **-en**) *die* delay; **mit Verspätung ankommen** to arrive late; **Verspätung haben** to be delayed; **eine Stunde Verspätung haben** to be an hour late.

versperren *vt* to block; **jm den Weg/die Sicht versperren** to block sb's way/view.

verspielen *vt* [Geld] to gamble away; [Glück, Chance] to throw away, to squander.

verspielt *adj* [Kind] playful; [Muster] fanciful.

versprechen (*präs* **verspricht**, *prät* **versprach**, *perf* hat **versprochen**) *vt* - **1.** [zusagen] to promise; **jm etw versprechen** to promise sb sthg - **2.** [erwarten]: **sich** (*D*) **etw von jm/ etw versprechen** to hope for sthg from sb/ sthg. ➺ **sich versprechen** *ref* [etw Falsches sagen] to trip over one's words.

Versprechen (*pl* -) *das* promise.

Verstand *der* (ohne *pl*) [Urteilsvermögen] reason; [Intellekt] mind; [Vernunft] sense; **den Verstand verlieren** *fam fig* to go out of one's mind; **jn um den Verstand bringen** *fig* to drive sb mad.

verständigen *vt*: **jn (von etw** ODER **über etw** (*A*)) **verständigen** to notify sb (of sthg).

sich verständigen *ref* - **1.** [kommunizieren] to make o.s. understood; **sich mit jm verständigen** to communicate with sb - **2.** [übereinkommen]: **sich über etw (A) verständigen** to come to an agreement on sthg.

Verständigung (*pl* -en) *die* - **1.** [Benachrichtigung] notification - **2.** [Kommunikation] communication - **3.** [Übereinkunft] agreement.

verständlich ⟨⟩ *adj* - **1.** [klar - Worte, Antwort] audible - **2.** [begreiflich - Verhalten, Angst] understandable; [- Text] comprehensible; **sich verständlich machen** to make o.s. understood. ⟨⟩ *adv* [klar] clearly.

Verständnis *das* understanding.

verständnisvoll ⟨⟩ *adj* understanding. ⟨⟩ *adv* understandingly.

verstärken *vt* - **1.** [stärker machen] to strengthen - **2.** [intensivieren] to increase; [Bemühungen] to intensify; [Strom] to boost; [Signal, Ton] to amplify - **3.** [Truppen, Team] to reinforce. **sich verstärken** *ref* [stärker werden] to intensify.

Verstärkung (*pl* -en) *die* reinforcement; **Verstärkung anfordern** to call for reinforcements.

verstauchen *vt*: **sich** (D) **den Fuß verstauchen** to sprain one's ankle.

verstauen *vt* to pack.

Versteck (*pl* -e) *das* hiding place; [von Verbrechern] hideout.

verstecken *vt* to hide. **sich verstecken** *ref*: **sich (vor jm/etw) verstecken** to hide (from sb/sthg).

verstehen (*prät* verstand, *perf* hat verstanden) ⟨⟩ *vt* - **1.** [gen] to understand; **ich konnte kein Wort verstehen** I couldn't understand ODER make out a single word; **etw unter etw** (D) **verstehen** to understand sthg by sthg; **versteh mich nicht falsch** don't get me wrong - **2.** [vermögen] to know; **etwas/nichts verstehen von** to know a bit/nothing about. ⟨⟩ *vi* to understand; **jm zu verstehen geben, dass...** to give sb to understand that... **sich verstehen** *ref* [Personen] to get on; **sich (gut) mit jm verstehen** to get on well with sb; **das versteht sich von selbst!** that goes without saying!

versteigern *vt* to auction; **etw meistbietend versteigern** to sell sthg to the highest bidder.

verstellen *vt* - **1.** [verändern] to adjust - **2.** [falsch stellen] to set wrongly; [Stimme, Schrift] to disguise - **3.** [blockieren]: **jm den Weg/die Sicht verstellen** to block sb's path/view - **4.** [an einen falschen Ort] to put in the wrong place. **sich verstellen** *ref* - **1.** [zur Täuschung - im Wesen] to play-act - **2.** [sich anders einstellen] to be moved (out of position).

verstohlen ⟨⟩ *adj* furtive. ⟨⟩ *adv* furtively.

verstopfen (*perf* hat/ist verstopft) ⟨⟩ *vt* (*hat*) to plug (up); [Abfluss] to block. ⟨⟩ *vi* (*ist*) to be blocked (up).

verstört *adj* distraught.

Ver|stoß (*pl* -stöße) *der* infringement; **ein Verstoß gegen etw** [gegen Gesetz] an infringement of sthg; [gegen Anstand] an offence against sthg.

verstoßen (*präs* verstößt, *prät* verstieß, *perf* hat verstoßen) ⟨⟩ *vi*: **gegen etw verstoßen** [Regel, Gesetz] to infringe sthg; [Anstand, Geschmack] to offend against sthg. ⟨⟩ *vt* [Kind, Ehefrau] to disown; **jn aus einer Gruppe verstoßen** to throw sb out of a group.

verstreichen (*prät* verstrich, *perf* hat/ist verstrichen) ⟨⟩ *vt* (*hat*) [Butter] to spread; [Farbe] to apply. ⟨⟩ *vi* (*ist*) [Zeit] to pass.

verstreuen *vt* - **1.** [verteilen] to scatter - **2.** [verschütten] to spill - **3.** [Creme] to spread.

verstümmeln *vt* to mutilate.

Versuch (*pl* -e) *der* - **1.** [Handlung] attempt - **2.** [wissenschaftlich] experiment.

versuchen ⟨⟩ *vt* to try; [etwas Schwieriges] to attempt. ⟨⟩ *vi* [kosten]: **von etw versuchen** to try sthg.

Versuchs|kaninchen [fɛɐ̯ˈzuːxskaniːnçən] *das* guinea pig.

Versuchung (*pl* -en) *die* temptation.

versüßen *vt* [Leben, Befinden] to make more pleasant; [schlechte Situation] to sweeten.

vertagen *vt* [verschieben] to postpone; [später fortsetzen] to adjourn.

vertauschen *vt* [verwechseln] to mix up.

verteidigen *vt* to defend. **sich verteidigen** *ref* to defend o.s.

Verteidiger, in (*mpl* -, *fpl* -nen) *der*, *die* RECHT counsel for the defence.

Verteidigung (*pl* -en) *die* defence.

Verteidigung|minister, in *der*, *die* defence minister.

verteilen *vt* - **1.** [ausgeben] to distribute; [Prospekte] to hand out - **2.** [teilen] to share out - **3.** [Creme] to spread. **sich verteilen** *ref* to spread out.

Verteilung (*pl* -en) *die* distribution.

vertiefen *vt* to deepen. **sich vertiefen** *ref* - **1.** [Graben, Loch, Falten] to become deeper - **2.** [Gefühl, Freundschaft] to become deeper - **3.** [sich konzentrieren]: **sich in etw (A) vertiefen** to become engrossed in sthg.

Vertrag (*pl* Verträge) *der* contract.

vertragen (*präs* verträgt, *prät* vertrug, *perf* hat vertragen) *vt* to stand, to bear; [Belastung, Kritik, Witz] to take; **sie verträgt keinen Kaffee** coffee doesn't agree with her. **sich vertragen** *ref*: **sich mit jm vertragen** to get on with sb.

vertraglich ⟨⟩ *adj* contractual. ⟨⟩ *adv* contractually.

verträglich *adj* [Person, Charakter] easy-going; **gut verträglich** [Essen] easily digestible; [Medikament] with few side-effects.

vertrauen *vi*: jm/einer Sache vertrauen to trust sb/sthg; **auf etw** *(A)* **vertrauen** to put one's trust in sthg; **auf sein Glück vertrauen** to trust to luck.

Vertrauen *das* trust; **zu jm Vertrauen haben** to trust sb. ◆ **im Vertrauen** *adv* in confidence. ◆ **Vertrauen erweckend** *adj*: ein Vertrauen erweckender Mensch a person who inspires confidence.

Vertrauenslehrer, **in** *der, die* teacher who represents the interests of the pupils.

Vertrauenssache *die* matter of trust.

vertrauenswürdig *adj* trustworthy.

vertraulich ⬦ *adj* - 1. [geheim] confidential - 2. [herzlich] familiar. ⬦ *adv* [geheim] confidentially.

verträumt ⬦ *adj* dreamy. ⬦ *adv* dreamily.

vertraut *adj* familiar; [Freund] close; **jm vertraut sein** to be familiar to sb; **mit etw vertraut sein** to be familiar with sthg; **sich mit etw vertraut machen** to familiarize o.s. with sthg.

vertreiben (*prät* vertrieb, *perf* hat vertrieben) *vt* - 1. [verjagen] to drive away; [aus Land] to drive out; **jn aus einem Haus vertreiben** to turn sb out of a house - 2. [verkaufen] to sell - 3. [Zeit] to pass.

vertretbar *adj* [Meinung] tenable; [Kosten, Risiko] justifiable.

vertreten (*präs* vertritt, *prät* vertrat, *perf* hat vertreten) *vt* - 1. [bei Urlaub, Krankheit] to stand in for - 2. [Interessen, Firma, Land] to represent - 3. [Standpunkt, These, Prinzip] to support - 4. [anwesend]: **vertreten sein** to be present - 5. [verletzen]: **sich** *(D)* **den Fuß vertreten** to twist one's ankle.

Vertreter, **in** (*mpl* -, *fpl* -nen) *der, die* - 1. [Stellvertreter] stand-in; [von Arzt] locum - 2. [von Firma, Gruppe] representative - 3. [von Meinung, Interessen] advocate.

Vertretung (*pl* -en) *die* - 1. [bei Urlaub, Krankheit] replacement - 2. [von Interessen, Firma, Land] representation - 3. [Person] representative - 4. [Filiale] branch; **diplomatische Vertretung** diplomatic mission.

Vertrieb *der* - 1. [Verkauf] sale - 2. [Abteilung] sales department; **im Vertrieb arbeiten** to work in sales.

vertrocknen (*perf* ist vertrocknet) *vi* [Boden] to dry out; [Pflanze, Gras] to wither.

vertrödeln *vt* to waste.

vertrösten *vt* to put off; **jn auf später vertrösten** to put sb off until later.

vertun (*prät* vertat, *perf* hat vertan) *vt* to waste. ◆ **sich vertun** *ref* to get it wrong.

vertuschen *vt* [Skandal] to hush up; [Fehler, Wahrheit] to cover up.

verübeln *vt*: **jm etw verübeln** to hold sthg against sb.

verüben *vt* to commit.

verunglücken (*perf* ist verunglückt) *vi* to have an accident; **mit dem Zug verunglücken** to be in a train crash.

verunsichern *vt* to make uneasy.

verunstalten *vt* to disfigure.

veruntreuen *vt* RECHT to embezzle.

verursachen *vt* to cause.

verurteilen *vt* - 1. [vor Gericht]: **jn zu etw verurteilen** to sentence sb to sthg - 2. [kritisieren] to condemn.

Verurteilung *die* - 1. [vor Gericht] sentencing - 2. [Missbilligung] condemnation.

vervielfachen *vt* to multiply. ◆ **sich vervielfachen** *ref* to multiply.

vervielfältigen *vt* to make copies of.

vervollkommnen *vt* to perfect.

vervollständigen *vt* to complete.

verwackelt *adj fam* blurred.

verwählen ◆ **sich verwählen** *ref* to dial the wrong number.

verwahren *vt* to keep (safe).

verwahrlosen (*perf* ist verwahrlost) *vi* to be neglected; [Garten] to run wild.

verwaist *adj* - 1. [Kind] orphaned - 2. [Ort] deserted.

verwalten *vt* [Gebäude, Besitz] to manage; [Altenheim, Geschäft] to run; [Amt] to hold; [Geld] to administer.

Verwalter, **in** (*mpl* -, *fpl* -nen) *der, die* manager; [von Geld] administrator.

Verwaltung (*pl* -en) *die* administration; [von Geschäft, Gebäude] management; **die städtische Verwaltung** the municipal authorities.

verwandeln *vt* to transform, to change; **etw in etw** *(A)* **verwandeln** to transform OR change sthg into sthg. ◆ **sich verwandeln** *ref* to change.

Verwandlung (*pl* -en) *die* transformation; [Zoologie] metamorphosis.

verwandt ⬦ *pp* ▷ **verwenden**. ⬦ *adj* related; **mit jm verwandt sein** to be related to sb.

Verwandte (*pl* -n) *der, die* relative.

Verwandtschaft (*pl* -en) *die* - 1. [alle Verwandte] family - 2. [Verwandtsein] relationship.

Verwarnung (*pl* -en) *die* caution; **eine gebührenpflichtige Verwarnung** a fine.

verwechseln [fɛrˈvɛksln] *vt* to mix up; **jn/ etw mit jm/etw verwechseln** to mistake sb/ sthg for sb/sthg.

Verwechslung (*pl* -en), **Verwechselung** (*pl* -en) [fɛrˈvɛks(ə)luŋ] *die* mixing up; **es gab eine Verwechslung** there was a mix-up.

verweigern ⋄ vt to refuse; **die Annahme von etw verweigern** to refuse to take sthg; **einen Befehl verweigern** to refuse to obey an order; **den Kriegsdienst verweigern** to be a conscientious objector; **jm etw verweigern** to refuse sb sthg. ⋄ vi fam [den Wehrdienst verweigern] to be a conscientious objector.

Verweigerung (pl -en) die refusal; **die Verweigerung eines Befehls** refusal to obey an order.

Verweis (pl -e) der [Tadel] reprimand.

verweisen (prät verwies, perf hat verwiesen) ⋄ vt - 1. [weiterleiten] : **jn/etw an jn/etw verweisen** to refer sb/sthg to sb/sthg - 2. [ausweisen - von Schule] to expel; [- aus Raum] to throw out. ⋄ vi: **auf etw (A) verweisen** to refer to sthg; **eine Tafel verweist auf den Eingang** a sign points to the entrance.

verwelken (perf ist verwelkt) vi to wilt.

verwenden (prät verwendete ODER verwandte, perf hat verwendet ODER verwandt) vt - 1. [benutzen] to use - 2. [einsetzen - Zeit, Geld] to spend; **etw für ODER zu etw verwenden** to use sthg for sthg; **Kraft auf etw verwenden** to put energy into sthg.

Verwendung (pl -en) die use.

verwerfen (präs verwirft, prät verwarf, perf hat verworfen) vt to reject.

verwerten vt - 1. [Kenntnisse] to make use of - 2. [Abfall, Altpapier] to re-use, to recycle.

verwest adj decomposed.

Verwesung die decomposition.

verwildern (perf ist verwildert) vi [Garten] to become overgrown; [Tier] to become wild.

verwirklichen vt [Traum] to realize; [Plan, Ziel] to achieve; [Idee] to put into practice. ⋆ **sich verwirklichen** ref - 1. [Hoffnung, Traum, Befürchtung] to come true - 2. [Person]: **sich selbst verwirklichen** to fulfil o.s.

Verwirklichung (pl -en) die [von Traum] realization; [von Plan, Ziel] achievement; [von Idee] putting into practice.

verwirren vt - 1. [Fäden] to tangle up - 2. [Person] to confuse.

Verwirrung (pl -en) die confusion.

verwischen vt [Spur] to cover over; [Schrift] to smudge; [Farbe] to smear; [Kontur] to blur.

verwitwet adj widowed.

verwöhnen vt to spoil.

verworren ⋄ adj confused. ⋄ adv [erzählen] in a confusing manner.

verwunden vt to wound.

Verwunderung die surprise.

Verwundete (pl -n) der, die wounded person; **die Verwundeten** the wounded.

Verwundung (pl -en) die [Wunde] wound.

verwünschen vt - 1. [verfluchen] to curse - 2. [verzaubern] to bewitch.

verwüsten vt to devastate.

Verwüstung (pl -en) die devastation (U).

verzählen ⋆ **sich verzählen** ref to miscount.

verzaubern vt to enchant; **einen Prinz in einen Frosch verzaubern** to turn a prince into a frog.

verzeichnen vt to record; [Erfolg] to notch up; **ist diese Stadt auf der Landkarte verzeichnet?** is this town (marked) on the map?

Verzeichnis (pl -se) das - 1. [Liste] list; [Katalog] catalogue; [mit Namen] index - 2. EDV directory.

verzeihen (prät verzieh, perf hat verziehen) vt to forgive; **jm etw verzeihen** to forgive sb for sthg; **verzeihen Sie bitte!** excuse me, please!; **verzeihen Sie bitte, dass ich stören muss!** please forgive the intrusion!

Verzeihung die forgiveness; **jn um Verzeihung bitten** to apologize to sb. ⋆ **Verzeihung** interj sorry!

verzerren vt - 1. [Gesicht] to contort - 2. [Bild, Klang] to distort. ⋆ **sich verzerren** ref [Gesicht] to contort.

Verzicht (pl -e) der: **der Verzicht auf Süßigkeiten fällt ihm schwer** he finds it hard to go without sweets.

verzichten vi to do without; **auf jn/etw verzichten** to do without sb/sthg; **wir werden zukünftig auf ihre Dienste verzichten** we will be dispensing with her services; **auf eine Bemerkung verzichten** to not make ODER to refrain from making a comment; **er verzichtete darauf, sich zu beschweren** he refrained from making a complaint; **zugunsten eines anderen auf eine Stelle verzichten** to let sb have a job instead of o.s.; **danke, ich verzichte** I'll pass (on that one), thanks.

verzieh prät ⊳ **verzeihen**.

verziehen (prät verzog, perf hat/ist verzogen) ⋄ pp ⊳ **verzeihen**. ⋄ vt (hat) - 1. [Miene, Mund] to screw up; **das Gesicht verziehen** to pull a face - 2. [Kind] to spoil. ⋄ vi (ist) [fortziehen] to move. ⋆ **sich verziehen** ref - 1. [Gesicht, Mund] to contort - 2. [Tür, Holz] to warp - 3. [Nebel, Rauch] to disperse; [Unwetter] to pass - 4. fam [fortgehen] to disappear; **verzieh dich** get lost!

verzieren vt to decorate.

verzögern vt - 1. [verschieben] to delay - 2. [verlangsamen] to slow down. ⋆ **sich verzögern** ref [sich verspäten] to be delayed.

Verzögerung (pl -en) die [Verspätung] delay.

verzollen vt to declare; **haben Sie etwas zu verzollen?** do you have anything to declare?

Verzug der delay. ⋆ **im Verzug** adv: **mit etw im Verzug sein** to be behind with sthg; **Gefahr ist im Verzug** danger is imminent.

verzweifeln (perf ist verzweifelt) vi to despair; **an etw (D)/über etw (A) verzweifeln** to despair of/at sthg.

verzweifelt ⟨⟩ *adj* desperate; [Blick] despairing. ⟨⟩ *adv* [kämpfen, versuchen] desperately; [sagen, anblicken] despairingly.

Verzweiflung (*pl* -en) *die* despair; **vor Verzweiflung** in despair.

Veto ['ve:to] (*pl* -s) *das* veto.

Vetter (*pl* -n) *der* cousin.

vgl. (*abk für* **vergleiche**) cf.

VHS [fauhɑː'ɛs] *die abk für* **Volkshochschule**.

vibrieren [vi'briːrən] *vi* to vibrate; [Stimme] to quiver.

Video ['viːdeo] (*pl* -s) *das* video.

Video|film *der* video.

Video|kamera *die* video camera.

Video|kassette *die* video (tape).

Video|rekorder *der* video (recorder) *UK*, VCR *US*.

Video|spiel *das* video game.

Video|text *der* videotext.

Vieh *das* - 1. [alle Tiere] livestock - 2. [Rinder] cattle.

viel (*kompar* mehr, *superl* meiste), **vieles** (*kompar* mehr, *superl* meiste) ⟨⟩ *adj*: **das viele Geld** all the money; **das Kleid mit den vielen Knöpfen** the dress with all the buttons; **vielen Dank!** thank you very much! ⟨⟩ *det* - 1. [Menge] much, a lot of; **zu viel** too much - 2. [Anzahl] many, a lot of, lots of; **zu viel** too many; **viele Menschen** many *ODER* a lot of people. ⟨⟩ *adv* - 1. [intensiv, oft] a lot; **viel arbeiten** to work a lot; **sie ist viel allein** she is alone a lot of the time - 2. [zum Ausdruck der Verstärkung] much; **viel mehr** much more; **viel zu much** too, far too; **nicht viel anders** not very different. ⟨⟩ *pron* a lot; **er sagt viel** he says a lot; **er sagt nicht viel** he doesn't say much. ⟨⟩ **nicht viel** ⟨⟩ *det* not much. ⟨⟩ *adv* not much; **er schläft nicht viel** he doesn't sleep much. ⟨⟩ **nicht viele** *det* not many. ⟨⟩ **vieles** *pron* a lot of things. ⟨⟩ **viel zu viel** *det & adv* much too much. ⟨⟩ **viel zu viele** *det* far too many; *siehe auch* **zu viel**.

vielfach ⟨⟩ *adj* [mehrfach, wiederholt] multiple; **auf vielfachen Wunsch** by popular demand; **das vielfache Gewicht** many times the weight. ⟨⟩ *adv* - 1. [mehrfach, wiederholt] several times - 2. [häufig] often.

Vielfache *das* [von Zahl] multiple; **um ein Vielfaches** many times over.

Vielfalt *die* diversity, great variety.

vielfältig *adj* diverse.

vielleicht *adv* - 1. [eventuell] perhaps - 2. *fam* [wirklich, außerordentlich] really; **der ist vielleicht gerannt!** he didn't half run! - 3. [Ausdruck der Höflichkeit]: **wären Sie vielleicht so freundlich, den Termin zu bestätigen?** could you possibly confirm the date for me? - 4. [ungefähr] about - 5. *fam* [etwa]: **hast du**

vielleicht gedacht, ich würde da mitmachen? you didn't think I would join in, did you? - 6. *fam* [Ausdruck der Ungeduld]: **vielleicht kannst du dich mal beeilen!** do you think you could possibly get a move on!

vielmals *adv*: **danke vielmals** thank you very much.

vielsagend, viel sagend ⟨⟩ *adj* meaningful. ⟨⟩ *adv* meaningfully.

vielseitig ⟨⟩ *adj* - 1. [Person] versatile - 2. [umfassend] varied. ⟨⟩ *adv*: **vielseitig begabt** multitalented; **vielseitig einsetzbar** versatile.

vielversprechend, viel sagend ⟨⟩ *adj* promising. ⟨⟩ *adv* promisingly.

vier [fiːɐ̯] *num* four; **auf allen vieren** *fam* on all fours; *siehe auch* **sechs**.

Vier (*pl* -en) *die* - 1. [Zahl] four - 2. [Schulnote] ≃ D, mark of 4 on a scale from 1 to 6; *siehe auch* **Sechs**.

Viereck (*pl* -e) *das* four-sided figure; [Rechteck] rectangle; [Quadrat] square.

viereckig *adj* four-sided; [rechteckig] rectangular; [quadratisch] square.

vierfach ⟨⟩ *adj*: **die vierfache Menge** four times as much; **in vierfacher Größe** four times as big; **der vierfache Gewinner** the four-times winner. ⟨⟩ *adv* four times.

vierhundert *num* four hundred.

viermal *adv* four times.

vierspurig *adj* four-lane.

viertausend *num* four thousand.

vierte, r, s *adj* fourth; *siehe auch* **sechste**.

Vierte (*pl* -n) *der, die, das* fourth; *siehe auch* **Sechste**.

viertel *adj* (*unver*) quarter; *siehe auch* **sechstel**.

Viertel (*pl* -) *das* - 1. [Teil] quarter; **Viertel vor/nach drei** a quarter to/past *UK ODER* after *US* three - 2. MUS crotchet *UK*; *siehe auch* **Sechstel**.

Viertel|finale *das* quarter-final.

Viertel|jahr (*pl* -e) *das* quarter.

Viertel|stunde (*pl* -n) *die* quarter of an hour.

vierzehn *num* fourteen; *siehe auch* **sechs**.

Vierzehn (*pl* -en) *die* fourteen; *siehe auch* **Sechs**.

vierzehntägig ⟨⟩ *adv* every fortnight, fortnightly. ⟨⟩ *adj* - 1. [alle zwei Wochen] fortnightly - 2. [zwei Wochen lang] two-week, fortnight-long.

vierzig *num* forty; *siehe auch* **sechs**.

Vierzigerjahre, vierziger Jahre *Pl*: **die Vierzigerjahre** the forties.

Vierzimmer|wohnung *die* four-room flat *UK ODER* apartment *US*.

Vietnam [vjɛt'nam] *nt* Vietnam.

Vikar, in [vi'kɑːɐ̯, rɪn] (*mpl* -e, *fpl* -nen) *der, die* [evangelisch] ≃ curate.

Villa ['vɪla] (pl **Villen**) die villa.

violett [vjo'lɛt] adj purple.

Violine [vjo'li:nə] (pl -n) die violin.

Violin|schlüssel der treble clef.

Viper ['vi:pɐ] (pl -n) die viper.

virtuell ◇ adj virtual; **virtuelle Realität** virtual reality. ◇ adv virtually.

Virus ['vi:rʊs] (pl **Viren**) der ODER das MED & EDV virus.

Virus|infektion die viral infection.

Visier [vi'zi:ɐ] (pl -e) das - 1. [von Helm] visor - 2. [von Gewehr] sight; **jn/etw im Visier haben** [es auf jn abgesehen haben] to have it in for sb/ sthg; [anpeilen] to have one's eye on sb/sthg.

Visite [vi'zi:tə] (pl -n) die [privat, geschäftlich] visit; [Besuch des Arztes]: **Visite machen** to do one's rounds.

Visiten|karte die visiting card.

Viskose [vɪs'ko:zə] die viscose.

Visum ['vi:zʊm] (pl **Visa** ODER **Visen**) das visa.

Vitamin [vita'mi:n] (pl -e) das vitamin.

Vitrine [vi'tri:nə] (pl -n) die - 1. [Schrank] display cabinet - 2. [Ausstellungskasten] display case.

Vize|kanzler, in der, die vice-chancellor.

Vize|präsident, in der, die vice-president.

Vogel (pl **Vögel**) der - 1. [Tier] bird - 2. fam [Person]: **ein komischer Vogel** an odd customer; **einen Vogel haben** salopp abw to be off one's head; **jm einen Vogel zeigen** fam to tap one's forehead at sb (to indicate that he/she is crazy).

Vogelscheuche (pl -n) die scarecrow.

Vokabel [vo'ka:bl] (pl -n) die word; **Vokabeln** vocabulary (U).

Vokabular [vokabu'la:ɐ] (pl -e) das vocabulary.

Vokal [vo'ka:l] (pl -e) der vowel.

Volk (pl **Völker**) das - 1. [gen] people Pl; das **deutsche Volk** the German nation ODER people - 2. (ohne pl) fam [viele Personen] crowd.

Völker|bund der HIST League of Nations.

Völker|kunde die ethnology.

Völker|recht das international law.

Völker|wanderung die HIST migration of the peoples.

Volks|ab|stimmung die referendum.

Volks|fest das festival.

Volks|hoch|schule die ≈ college of adult education.

Volks|lied das folk song.

Volks|musik die folk music.

Volks|tanz der folk dance.

volkstümlich ◇ adj - 1. [traditionell] traditional - 2. [populär] popular. ◇ adv [populär] in plain language.

Volks|wirtschaft die - 1. [Wissenschaft] economics (U) - 2. [Wirtschaft] economy.

voll ◇ adj - 1. [gen] full; **voll von** ODER **mit etw sein** to be full of sthg; **halb voll** half full; **mit vollem Recht** with every justification; **in vollem Ernst** in all seriousness - 2. fam [gesättigt]: **voll sein** to be full (up) - 3. salopp [betrunken]: **voll sein** to be plastered - 4. [vollwertig]: **in nicht für voll nehmen** fam fig not to take sb seriously. ◇ adv - 1. [völlig] totally, completely; **voll und ganz** completely - 2. salopp [verstärkend] really.

vollauf adv completely.

Voll|bart der full beard.

Voll|blut (pl -blüter) das thoroughbred.

vollenden vt to complete.

vollendet ◇ pp ▷ vollenden. ◇ adj - 1. [perfekt] perfect - 2. [fertig] completed. ◇ adv perfectly.

vollends adv completely.

Vollendung (pl -en) die - 1. [Perfektion] perfection - 2. [Vollenden] completion.

voller adj (unver) full of.

Volley|ball ['vɔlibal] der volleyball.

Voll|gas das: **mit Vollgas** at full throttle; **Vollgas geben** to put one's foot down UK, to step on the gas US.

völlig ◇ adj complete. ◇ adv completely.

volljährig adj: **volljährig sein** to be of age.

Voll|kasko|ver|sicherung die comprehensive insurance.

vollkommen ◇ adj - 1. [perfekt] perfect - 2. [absolut] complete. ◇ adv - 1. [perfekt] perfectly - 2. [absolut] completely.

Voll|korn|brot das wholemeal UK ODER whole wheat US bread.

voll machen vt fam - 1. [Bett] to wet; [Windel, Hose] to dirty - 2. [füllen] to fill - 3. [vervollständigen] to complete.

Voll|macht (pl -en) die - 1. (ohne pl) [Befugnis] authority; RECHT power of attorney; **jm (die) Vollmacht geben** ODER **erteilen** to authorize sb; RECHT to give sb power of attorney - 2. [Schreiben] letter of authorization; **schriftliche Vollmacht** written authorization.

Voll|milch die full-fat milk.

Voll|mond der full moon.

Voll|pension die full board.

vollständig ◇ adj complete. ◇ adv completely.

vollstrecken vt - 1. RECHT [Testament] to execute; [Urteil] to carry out - 2. SPORT to score from, to convert.

voll tanken vi to fill up; **bitte einmal voll tanken!** fill it up, please!

Voll|treffer der [Schuss] direct hit; **ein Volltreffer sein** to be a hit.

vollwertig adj - 1. [gleichwertig] fully-fledged - 2. [Speisen] wholefood.

Vollwertkost die wholefood.

vollzählig <> *adj* entire. <> *adv:* **sie sind vollzählig erschienen** they all turned up.

Vollzug *der* - 1. [von Urteil, Beschlagnahmung] carrying out - 2. [von Ehe] consummation - 3. *fam* [Gefängnis] clink.

Vollzugslanstalt *die* prison, penitentiary *US*.

Volt [vɔlt] (*pl* -) *das* volt.

Volumen [voˈluːmən] (*pl* -) *das* volume.

vom *präp* - 1. *(von + dem)* from the; **vom Bahnhof** from the station - 2. *(untrennbar):* **vom Fach sein** to be an expert; **müde vom Arbeiten sein** to be tired from working.

von *präp* (+ D) - 1. [räumlich] from; [von... weg] off, from; **von nach** from to; **etw vom Tisch nehmen** to take sthg from *ODER* off the table - 2. [zeitlich] from; **von Montag bis Freitag** from Monday to Friday, Monday through Friday *US*; **von heute an** from today - 3. [stellt Bezug her]: **die Zeitung von gestern** yesterday's paper; **von wem hast du das?** who gave it to you?; **ist das Buch von dir?** is the book yours?; **das war dumm/nett von dir** that was stupid/nice of you - 4. [in Passivsätzen] by; **von einem Hund gebissen werden** to be bitten by a dog; **von Hand hergestellt** made by hand - 5. [zur Angabe der Ursache] from; **müde von der Reise** tired from the journey - 6. [drückt Eigenschaften aus] of; **ein Sack von 25 kg** a 25 kg bag; **eine Fahrt von 3 Stunden** a 3-hour journey - 7. [zur Angabe einer Teilmenge] of; **ein Stück von der Torte** a piece of the cake; **neun von zehn** nine out of ten; **von mir aus** *fam* I don't mind; **von sich aus** *fam* by oneself. ◆ **von an** *präp* from; **von hier an** from here; **von jetzt an** from now on. ◆ **von aus** *präp* from; **von hier aus** from here.

voneinander *adv* from one another; **sie sind voneinander unabhängig** they are independent of one another.

vor <> *präp* - 1. (+ D) [räumlich] in front of; **vor dem Haus stehen** to stand in front of the house; **vor Gericht erscheinen** to appear before a court - 2. (+ A) [räumlich] in front of - 3. (+ D) [zeitlich - zuvor] ago; **heute vor fünf Jahren** five years ago today; **vor kurzem** recently - 4. [zur Angabe der Uhrzeit] to *UK*, before *US*; **fünf vor zwölf** five to twelve *UK*, five before twelve *US*; **fünf vor halb neun** twenty-five past eight *UK*, twenty-five after eight *US* - 5. (+ D) [wegen] with; **vor Kälte/Angst zittern** to tremble with cold/fear; **vor Freude in die Luft springen** to jump for joy; **vor Hunger sterben** to die of hunger - 6. [stellt Bezug her]: **Schutz vor etw** protection from sthg; **jn vor etw warnen** to warn sb about sthg; **vor sich hin murmeln/singen** to mutter/sing to oneself. <> *adv* forwards. ◆ **vor allem** *adv* above all.

Vorlabend *der* evening before.

voran *adv* - 1. [vorweg] at the front - 2. [vorwärts] forwards.

voranlgehen (*perf* ist vorangegangen) *vi* (*unreg*) - 1. [Arbeit, Projekt] to advance, to progress - 2. [vorne gehen] to go on ahead - 3. [vorher passieren]: **jm/etw vorangehen** to precede sb/sthg.

voranlkommen (*perf* ist vorangekommen) *vi* (*unreg*) to make progress; [Arbeit, Projekt] to advance, to progress; **gut vorankommen** to make good progress; **nicht vorankommen** not to make any progress.

vorlarbeiten *vi:* **einen Tag vorarbeiten** to work an extra day (*in order to have a day off later*). ◆ **sich vorarbeiten** *ref* to work one's way forward.

voraus *adv* in front; **jm in etw voraus sein** *fig* to be ahead of sb in sthg; **seiner Zeit voraus** ahead of one's time.

vorauslgehen (*perf* ist vorausgegangen) *vi* (*unreg*) - 1. [vorher, früher gehen] to go on ahead - 2. [vorher passieren]: **einer Sache (D) vorausgehen** to precede sthg.

vorausgesetzt <> *pp* ▷ **voraussetzen**. <> *konj* provided (that).

voraus|haben *vt* (*unreg*): **jm etw voraushaben** to have the advantage of sthg over sb.

voraus|sagen *vt* to predict.

vorauslsehen *vt* (*unreg*) to foresee; **es war vorauszusehen, dass..** it was to be expected that...

voraus|setzen *vt* - 1. [erfordern] to require - 2. [für selbstverständlich halten] to take for granted; **wir müssen voraussetzen, dass...** we must assume that...; **etw als bekannt voraussetzen** to assume that sthg is known.

Voraussetzung (*pl* -en) *die* - 1. [Erfordernis] requirement; **ihm fehlen die nötigen Voraussetzungen** he lacks the necessary qualifications; **unter der Voraussetzung, dass...** on condition that... - 2. [Annahme] assumption.

Voraussicht *die* foresight; **aller Voraussicht nach** in all probability.

voraussichtlich <> *adj* expected. <> *adv* probably.

Vorauslzahlung *die* advance payment.

Vorbehalt (*pl* -e) *der* reservation; **etw unter** *ODER* **mit Vorbehalt annehmen** to accept sthg with reservations.

vorlbehalten *vt* (*unreg*): **sich etw vorbehalten** to reserve o.s. sthg; **der Swimmingpool ist den Hotelgästen vorbehalten** the swimming pool is reserved for hotel guests only.

vorbei *adv* - 1. [räumlich] past, by; **an mir vorbei** past me - 2. [zeitlich] over; **die Schmerzen sind vorbei** the pain has gone; **mit etw ist es vorbei** *fam* sthg is over.

vorbeilgehen (*perf* ist vorbeigegangen) *vi* (*unreg*) - 1. [entlanggehen, vergehen] to pass; **an**

jm/etw vorbeigehen to pass sb/sthg - 2. [hingehen] to drop in. ➤ **im Vorbeigehen** adv in passing.

vorbei|kommen (perf ist vorbeigekommen) vi (unreg) - 1. [an etw vorüber]: **(an etw (D)) vorbeikommen** to pass (sthg) - 2. [besuchen]: **(bei jm) vorbeikommen** to drop in (on sb); **komm mal vorbei!** come round some time! - 3. [vorbeikönnen] to get past.

vorbei|reden vi: **aneinander vorbeireden** to talk at cross purposes.

vor|bereiten vt to prepare; **jn/etw auf etw (A) vorbereiten** to prepare sb/sthg for sthg. ➤ **sich vorbereiten** ref: **sich (auf etw (A)) vorbereiten** to prepare o.s. (for sthg).

Vor|bereitung die preparation; **in Vorbereitung sein** to be in preparation.

vor|bestellen vt to order in advance.

vorbestraft adj: **vorbestraft sein** to have previous convictions, to have a criminal record.

vor|beugen ◇ vi: **einer Sache (D) vorbeugen** to prevent sthg. ◇ vt to bend forward. ➤ **sich vorbeugen** ref to lean forward.

Vor|beugung die prevention.

Vor|bild das model.

vorbildlich ◇ adj exemplary. ◇ adv in exemplary fashion.

vor|bringen vt (unreg) - 1. [Wunsch, Bedenken] to express; [Bitte, Beschwerde] to make; **etw gegen etw vorbringen** to raise sthg as an objection to sthg; **etw gegen jn vorbringen** to say sthg against sb - 2. [Beweise] to produce.

vordere, r, s adj front.

Vorder|grund der foreground; **etw in den Vordergrund stellen** ODER **rücken** to place special emphasis on sthg; **im Vordergrund stehen** to be to the fore.

Vorder|mann der: **der Läufer überholte seinen Vordermann** the runner overtook the man in front of him.

Vorder|rad das front wheel.

Vorder|sitz der front seat.

vor|drängen ➤ **sich vordrängen** ref to push in.

vor|dringen (perf ist vorgedrungen) vi (unreg) to advance; [in Menschenmenge] to push forward.

Vor|druck der form.

voreilig ◇ adj rash. ◇ adv rashly.

voreinander adv - 1. [in Bezug aufeinander]: **Angst voreinander haben** to be afraid of one another - 2. [räumlich] one in front of the other.

voreingenommen ◇ adj biased; **gegen jn/etw voreingenommen sein** to be biased against sb/sthg. ◇ adv in a biased way.

vor|enthalten vt (unreg): **jm etw vorenthalten** to withhold sthg from sb; [Nachricht] to keep sthg from sb.

vorerst adv for the time being.

Vorfahr (pl -en), **Vorfahre** (pl -n) der ancestor.

vor|fahren (perf hat/ist vorgefahren) ◇ vi (ist) - 1. [nach vorn fahren] to drive forward - 2. [vorausfahren] to drive on ahead - 3. [vor Gebäude] to drive up. ◇ vt (hat) - 1. [nach vorn] to drive forward - 2. [vor Gebäude] to drive up.

Vorfahrt die right of way; **Vorfahrt haben** to have right of way.

Vorfahrts|straße die major road.

Vor|fall der [Geschehnis] occurrence, incident.

vor|fallen (perf ist vorgefallen) vi (unreg) to happen, to occur.

vor|finden vt (unreg) to find.

vor|führen vt - 1. [zeigen - FILM] to show; [- Kunststück] to perform; [- Funktionsweise] to demonstrate; **jm etw vorführen** to show sb sthg - 2. fam [blamieren] to show up.

Vor|führung die - 1. [im Theater, Kino, Zirkus] performance - 2. [von Maschine] demonstration.

Vor|gang der event, occurrence.

Vorgänger, in (mpl -, fpl -nen) der, die predecessor.

vorgefertigt adj prefabricated.

vorgegeben adj set in advance.

vor|gehen (perf ist vorgegangen) vi (unreg) - 1. [vorhergehen] to go on ahead - 2. [passieren] to go on - 3. [handeln] to proceed; **gegen jn/ etw vorgehen** to take action against sb/sthg - 4. [Uhr] to be fast - 5. [vorne gehen] to go first.

Vor|geschichte die - 1. [vorherige Entwicklung] history - 2. [Prähistorie] prehistory.

Vorgesetzte (pl -n) der, die superior.

vorgestern adv [vor zwei Tagen] the day before yesterday.

vor|haben vt (unreg) to plan; **was habt ihr am Wochenende vor?** what have you got planned for the weekend?

Vorhaben (pl -) das plan.

vor|halten (unreg) ◇ vt: **jm etw vorhalten** [halten] to hold sthg up to sb; [vorwerfen] to hold sthg against sb. ◇ vi [ausreichen] to last.

vorhanden adj existing; [Vorräte, Mittel] available; **vorhanden sein** to exist; [Vorräte, Mittel] to be available; **davon ist nichts mehr vorhanden** there's none of it left.

Vor|hang der curtain; **der eiserne Vorhang** the Iron Curtain.

Vor|hängeschloss (pl -schlösser) das padlock.

Vor|haut die foreskin.

vorher adv - 1. [früher] before; **am Tag vorher** the day before - 2. [im Voraus] before(hand).

vorherig *adj* previous.

vor|herrschen *vi* to prevail.

Vorher|sage *die* - 1. [für Wetter] forecast - 2. [des Schicksals] prediction.

vorher|sehen *vt (unreg)* [wahrsagen] to foresee; [voraussehen] to predict; [Wetter] to forecast.

vorhin, vorhin *adv* just now.

vorig *adj* last.

Vorkehrungen *Pl*: Vorkehrungen treffen to take precautions.

Vor|kenntnisse *Pl* previous experience *(U)*.

vor|kommen *(perf ist vorgekommen) vi (unreg)* - 1. [passieren] to happen - 2. [auftreten] to be found, to occur - 3. [scheinen]: **jm verdächtig vorkommen** to seem suspicious to sb; **es kommt mir vor, als sei heute Sonntag** today feels like Sunday to me; **sich überflüssig vorkommen** to feel unwanted - 4. [nach vorne kommen] to come forward.

Vorkommen *(pl -)* das - 1. [an Bodenschätzen] deposit - 2. [Existieren] presence - 3. [Auftreten] occurrence.

Vor|ladung *die* summons *(sg)*.

Vor|lage *die* - 1. [Muster] pattern - 2. [Vorlegen] presentation - 3. [Gesetzesvorlage] bill - 4. SPORT [bei Fußball] assist, pass *(leading to a goal)*.

vor|lassen *vt (unreg)*: jn vorlassen to let sb go first.

Vor|läufer, in *der, die* forerunner.

vorläufig ⬦ *adj* provisional. ⬦ *adv* provisionally; **ich wohne vorläufig bei ihm** I'm staying with him for the time being; **die Polizei nahm sie vorläufig fest** the police held them.

vorlaut ⬦ *adj*: vorlaut sein to make comments out of turn. ⬦ *adv* out of turn.

vor|legen *vt* to present; [Ausweis] to show; [Zeugnis] to submit; **jm etw vorlegen** to present sb with sthg.

vor|lesen *vt (unreg)* to read out; **jm etw vorlesen** to read sthg to sb.

Vor|lesung *die* UNI lecture.

vorletzte, r, s *adj* penultimate, last but one.

Vorliebe *(pl -n)* die preference; **eine Vorliebe für jn/etw haben** to be particularly fond of sb/sthg.

vor|liegen *vi (unreg)* [vorgelegt sein]: **der Antrag liegt vor** the application has been received; **die Ergebnisse liegen noch nicht vor** the results are not yet available; **gegen ihn liegt nichts vor** no charges have been brought against him.

vor|machen *vt* - 1. *fam* [zeigen]: **jm etw vormachen** to show sb how to do sthg - 2. [vortäuschen]: **jm etwas vormachen** to fool sb.

Vormacht|stellung *die* supremacy *(U)*.

Vor|marsch *der*: auf dem Vormarsch sein *fig* to be gaining ground.

vor|merken *vt* - 1. [Termin] to make a note of - 2. [Person]: **jn für einen Kurs vormerken** to put sb's name down for a course.

Vor|mittag *der* morning; **gestern/heute/morgen Vormittag** yesterday/this/tomorrow morning.

vormittags *adv* in the morning.

Vormund *(pl -e ODER -münder) der* guardian.

vorn, vorne *adv* in front, at the front; **da vorn** over there; **nach vorn** forwards. ➡ **von vorn** *adv* [von Anfang an] from the beginning.

Vor|name *der* first name.

vornehm ⬦ *adj* - 1. [fein - Charakter] noble; [der Oberschicht angehörend] distinguished - 2. [elegant] upmarket. ⬦ *adv* [elegant] elegantly.

vor|nehmen *vt (unreg)* - 1. [durchführen] to carry out; [Auswahl] to make - 2. [sich beschäftigen mit]: **sich (D) etw vornehmen** *fam* to tackle sthg - 3. [sich entschließen]: **sich (D) vornehmen, etw zu tun** to resolve to do sthg; **sich (D) etw fest vorgenommen haben** to have made up one's mind to do sthg.

vornherein ➡ **von vornherein** *adv* from the start.

Vor|ort *der* suburb.

Vor|platz *der* forecourt.

Vorrang *der*: vor jm Vorrang haben to take precedence over sb.

vorrangig ⬦ *adj* of prime importance. ⬦ *adv*: **etw vorrangig behandeln** to treat sthg as a matter of priority.

Vorrat *(pl -räte) der* supply; [Reserve] store; Vorräte [von Geschäft] stocks; **ein Vorrat an etw (D)** a supply/store of sthg. ➡ **auf Vorrat** *adv*: etw auf Vorrat einkaufen to stock up on sthg.

vorrätig *adj* in stock.

Vor|raum *der* anteroom.

Vor|recht *das* privilege.

Vor|richtung *die* device.

vor|rücken *(perf hat/ist vorgerückt)* ⬦ *vt (hat)* to move forward. ⬦ *vi (ist)* - 1. [räumlich] to move forward - 2. [in Hierarchie] to move up.

Vorruhe|stand *der* early retirement; **in den Vorruhestand gehen** to take early retirement.

vor|sagen ⬦ *vt*: jm etw vorsagen to tell sb sthg. ⬦ *vi*: jm vorsagen to tell sb the answer.

Vor|saison *die* low season.

Vor|satz *der* resolution; **einen Vorsatz fassen, etw zu tun** to resolve to do sthg.

vorsätzlich ⬦ *adj* RECHT premeditated. ⬦ *adv* intentionally, on purpose.

Vor|schau *die* preview.

Vor|schein *der*: zum Vorschein kommen to turn up.

vor|schieben vt (unreg) - **1.** [schieben] to push forward; [Riegel] to push across; **das Kinn vorschieben** to stick one's chin out - **2.** [Vorwand] to put forward as an excuse - **3.** [Stellvertreter] to use as a front man.

Vor|schlag der suggestion.

vor|schlagen vt (unreg) to suggest; **jm etw vorschlagen** to suggest sthg to sb; **er schlug vor, ins Kino zu gehen** he suggested going to the cinema.

vorschnell <> adj rash. <> adv rashly.

vor|schreiben vt (unreg) [Subj: Gesetz] to stipulate; **sein Vater versucht ihm alles vorzuschreiben** his father is always trying to tell him what to do.

Vor|schrift die regulation.

Vor|schule die nursery school.

Vor|schuss (pl -schüsse) der advance.

vor|sehen vt (unreg) - **1.** [planen] to plan; **die Feier ist für nächste Woche vorgesehen** the celebration is scheduled ODER planned for next week; **das ist nicht vorgesehen** there are no plans for that; **jn für etw vorsehen** to have sb in mind for sthg - **2.** [vorschreiben] to provide for. <> **sich vorsehen** ref: **sich vor jm/etw vorsehen** [achtsam sein] to beware of sb/sthg.

vor|setzen vt: **jm etw vorsetzen** to serve sb sthg.

Vorsicht <> die care. <> interj look out!; **Vorsicht, Stufe!** mind the step!

vorsichtig <> adj careful. <> adv carefully.

vorsichtshalber adv as a precaution.

Vorsichts|maßnahme die precaution; **Vorsichtsmaßnahmen treffen** to take precautions.

Vor|silbe die prefix.

Vor|sitz der chairmanship.

Vorsitzende (pl -n) der, die chairperson.

Vor|sorge die (ohne pl) [gegen Krankheit, Gefahr] precautions Pl; [für das Alter] provisions Pl; **Vorsorge treffen** to take precautions; [für das Alter] to make provisions.

vor|sorgen vi: **für etw vorsorgen** to make provisions for sthg.

vorsorglich <> adj precautionary. <> adv as a precaution.

Vor|speise die starter.

vor|spielen <> vt - **1.** [auf einem Instrument]: **jm ein Stück vorspielen** to play a piece for sb - **2.** [vortäuschen] to put on an act. <> vi [auf einem Instrument]: **jm vorspielen** to play for sb.

Vor|sprung der - **1.** [von Läufer, Auto] lead - **2.** [von Wand] ledge.

Vor|stadt die suburb.

Vor|stand der [von Firma] board of directors; [von Verein] committee; [von Partei] executive.

vor|stehen vi (unreg) - **1.** to jut out; [Backenknochen] to be prominent; [Zähne] to protrude - **2.** [einer Gruppe, Institution]: **jm/etw vorstehen** to be in charge of sthg.

vor|stellen vt - **1.** [bekannt machen] to introduce; **jn jm vorstellen** to introduce sb to sb - **2.** [sich ausdenken]: **sich** (D) **etw vorstellen** to imagine sthg - **3.** [Uhr] to put forward. <> **sich vorstellen** ref - **1.** [bekannt machen]: **sich jm vorstellen** to introduce o.s. to sb - **2.** [sich bewerben]: **sich bei jm vorstellen** to go for an interview with sb.

Vor|stellung die - **1.** [Idee] idea; **etw entspricht (nicht) js Vorstellungen** sthg is (not) as sb imagined it - **2.** [im Theater] performance - **3.** [das Vorstellen] presentation.

Vorstellungs|gespräch das interview.

Vor|strafe die RECHT previous conviction.

vor|strecken vt - **1.** [Arme, Beine] to stretch out - **2.** [Geld]: **jm etw vorstrecken** to advance sb sthg.

vor|täuschen vt to feign; **jm etw vortäuschen** to pretend sthg to sb.

Vor|teil der advantage; **zu js Vorteil** to sb's advantage; **jm gegenüber im Vorteil sein** to have an advantage over sb.

vorteilhaft adj [Geschäft, Lage] advantageous; [Haarschnitt] flattering.

Vortrag (pl -träge) der talk; **ein Vortrag über jn/etw** a talk about sb/sthg; **einen Vortrag halten** to give a talk.

vor|tragen vt (unreg) - **1.** [darbieten] to perform; [Gedicht] to recite - **2.** [darlegen] to present.

Vortritt der: **jm den Vortritt lassen** to let sb go first.

vorüber adj: **vorüber sein** to be over.

vorüber|gehen (perf ist vorübergegangen) vi (unreg) - **1.** [Person] to pass by; **an jm/etw vorübergehen** to pass by sb/sthg - **2.** [Schmerzen] to come to an end.

vorübergehend <> adj temporary. <> adv temporarily.

Vor|urteil das prejudice.

Vorver|kauf der advance booking; **Karten im Vorverkauf bekommen** to buy tickets in advance.

Vor|wahl die - **1.** [telefonisch] dialling code UK, area code US - **2.** [von Wahlen] primary US, candidate selection procedure.

Vorwand (pl -wände) der excuse; **unter dem Vorwand** under the pretext.

vorwärts adv forwards.

vorwärts gehen (perf ist vorwärts gegangen) vi (unreg) to progress; **mit dem Experiment geht es nicht vorwärts** the experiment isn't getting anywhere.

vorwärts kommen (perf ist vorwärts gekommen) vi (unreg) to make progress.

vorweg *adv* - **1.** [vorher] beforehand - **2.** [voraus] in front.

vorweg|nehmen *vt (unreg)* to anticipate.

vor|weisen *vt (unreg)* - **1.** [vorzeigen] to show - **2.** [bieten]: **etw vorweisen können** to possess sthg.

vor|werfen *vt (unreg)*: **jm etw vorwerfen** to accuse sb of sthg.

vorwiegend *adv* mainly.

Vor|wort *das* preface.

Vor|wurf *der* accusation.

vorwurfsvoll <> *adj* reproachful. <> *adv* reproachfully.

Vor|zeichen *das* - **1.** [Anzeichen] omen - **2.** MATH sign - **3.** MUS key signature.

vor|zeigen *vt*: **(jm etw) vorzeigen** to show (sb sthg).

vorzeitig <> *adj* early; [Altern, Wehen] premature. <> *adv* prematurely; **vorzeitig in Rente gehen** to take early retirement.

vor|ziehen *vt (unreg)* - **1.** [lieber mögen] to prefer; **etw einer Sache (D) vorziehen** to prefer sthg to sthg - **2.** [Termin] to bring forward - **3.** [nach vorn ziehen] to pull forward.

Vor|zug *der* - **1.** [Vorrang] advantage; **jm/etw den Vorzug geben** to give sb/sthg preference - **2.** [gute Eigenschaft] virtue.

vorzüglich <> *adj* excellent. <> *adv* excellently.

vorzugsweise *adv* mainly.

vulgär *adj* vulgar.

Vulkan *(pl -e) der* volcano.

W

w *(pl - ODER -s)*, **W** *(pl - ODER -s)* [ve:] *das* w, W. ➡ **W** *(abk für West, Watt)* W.

Waage *(pl -n) die* - **1.** [Gerät] scales *Pl* - **2.** ASTROL Libra; **Waage sein** to be Libra.

waagerecht, waagrecht <> *adj* horizontal. <> *adv* horizontally.

Wabe *(pl -n) die* honeycomb.

wach *adj* - **1.** [nicht schlafend] awake; **jn wach machen** to wake sb; **wach halten** [Person] to keep awake; [Erinnerung] to keep alive; **wach sein** to be awake; **wach werden** to wake up - **2.** [Geist] alert.

Wache *(pl -n) die* - **1.** *(ohne pl)* [Wachdienst] guard duty; **Wache halten** to be on guard - **2.** [Wächter] guard - **3.** [Polizeiwache] police station.

Wach|hund *der* guard dog.

Wacholder *(pl -) der* juniper.

Wachs [vaks] *(pl -e) das* wax *(U)*.

wachsam ['vaxzɑːm] *adj* vigilant.

wachsen [vaksn] *(präs* **wächst** *ODER* **wachst**, *prät* **wuchs** *ODER* **wachste**, *perf* **ist gewachsen** *ODER* **hat gewachst)* <> *vi (unreg) (ist)* - **1.** [größer werden] to grow - **2.** [entsprechen]: **einer Sache (D) gewachsen sein** to be up to sthg. <> *vt (reg) (hat)* [mit Wachs] to wax.

Wachsmal|stift ['vaksmɑːlʃtɪft] *der* wax crayon.

wächst [vɛkst] *präs* ▷ **wachsen**.

Wachs|tuch *das* oilcloth.

Wachstum ['vakstuːm] *das* growth.

Wachtel *(pl -n) die* quail.

Wächter, in *(mpl -, fpl -nen) der, die* guard.

Wacht|posten *der* guard.

Wachturm, Wachtturm *der* watchtower.

wackelig, wacklig *adj* - **1.** [nicht fest] wobbly - **2.** *fam* [gefährdet] shaky.

Wackel|kontakt *der* ELEKTR loose contact.

wackeln *(perf* hat/ist gewackelt) *vi* - **1.** *(hat)* [nicht fest sein] to be wobbly - **2.** *(hat)* [hin und her bewegen]: **mit etw wackeln** to shake sthg - **3.** *(ist) fam* [gehen] to totter - **4.** *(hat) fam* [Posten] to be shaky.

wacker <> *adj* - **1.** [anständig] upright - **2.** [tüchtig] hearty. <> *adv* valiantly.

Wade *(pl -n) die* calf.

Waffe *(pl -n) die* weapon.

Waffel *(pl -n) die* waffle.

Waffel|eisen *das* waffle iron.

Waffen|gewalt *die*: **mit Waffengewalt** by force of arms.

Waffen|schein *der* firearms licence.

Waffenstill|stand *der* armistice.

wagen *vt* to risk; **einen Versuch wagen** to risk an attempt; **es wagen, etw zu tun** to dare to do sthg. ➡ **sich wagen** *ref* to dare; **sich nachts nicht auf die Straße wagen** not to dare to go out on the street at night; **sich an etw (A) wagen** to attempt sthg.

Wagen *(pl -) der* - **1.** [Auto] car - **2.** [von Zug, Straßenbahn] carriage *UK*, car *US* - **3.** [mit Pferd] carriage. ➡ **der Große Wagen** *der* ASTRON the Plough. ➡ **der Kleine Wagen** *der* ASTRON the Little Bear.

Wagen|heber *(pl* Wagenheber) *der* jack.

Waggon *(pl -s)*, **Wagon** *(pl -s)* [va'gɔŋ] *der* carriage *UK*, car *US*.

waghalsig *adj* reckless.

Wagnis *(pl -se) das* risk.

Wagon = **Waggon**.

Wahl *(pl -en) die* - **1.** *(ohne pl)* [Auswahl] choice; **die Wahl haben** to have the choice; **eine Wahl treffen** to make a choice; **erste/**

zweite Wahl first/second class; **in die engere Wahl kommen** to be short-listed - **2.** [Abstimmung] election; **geheime Wahl** secret ballot; **zur Wahl gehen** to vote.

wahlberechtigt adj entitled to vote.

wählen ◇ vt - **1.** [aussuchen] to choose - **2.** [am Telefon] to dial - **3.** [politisch] to elect. ◇ vi - **1.** [aussuchen] to choose; **zwischen etw (D) und etw (D) wählen** to choose between sthg and sthg - **2.** [am Telefon] to dial - **3.** [politisch] to vote.

Wähler, in (pl -) der voter.

wählerisch adj choosy.

Wählerstimme die vote.

Wahlfach das SCHULE optional subject.

Wahlgang der ballot.

Wahlheimat die adopted home.

Wahlkabine die polling booth.

Wahlkampf der election campaign.

Wahlkreis der constituency.

Wahllokal das polling station.

wahllos adv at random.

Wahlniederlage die election defeat.

Wahlrecht das right to vote; **allgemeines Wahlrecht** universal suffrage.

Wahlrede die election speech.

Wahlsieg der election victory.

Wahlspruch der motto.

wahlweise adv: **zum Frühstück gibt es wahlweise Kaffee oder Tee** for breakfast there's a choice of coffee or tea.

Wahn der (ohne pl) delusion.

Wahnsinn der madness; **Wahnsinn!** amazing!

wahnsinnig ◇ adj - **1.** [verrückt] mad - **2.** [groß] incredible. ◇ adv fam [sehr] incredibly.

wahr adj true; **wahre Liebe/Freundschaft** true love/friendship; **das darf doch nicht wahr sein!** fam that can't be true!; **etw wahr machen** fig to carry out sthg. ◆ **nicht wahr** interj: **du warst doch gestern auch hier, nicht wahr?** you were here yesterday too, weren't you?; **das stimmt doch, nicht wahr?** that's right, isn't it?

während ◇ konj [zeitlich, gegensätzlich] while. ◇ präp during.

währenddessen adv in the meantime.

wahrhaben vt: **etw nicht wahrhaben wollen** not to want to accept sthg.

Wahrheit (pl -en) die truth (U). ◆ **in Wahrheit** adv in reality.

wahrheitsgemäß ◇ adj truthful. ◇ adv truthfully.

wahrnehmen vt (unreg) - **1.** [Veränderung, Geräusch] to notice - **2.** [Gelegenheit] to avail oneself of - **3.** [Interessen] to protect.

Wahrnehmung (pl -en) die - **1.** [Spüren] awareness (U) - **2.** [von Gelegenheit] seizing - **3.** [von Geschäft] representation.

wahrsagen vi to predict the future.

Wahrsager, in (mpl -, fpl -nen) der, die fortune-teller.

wahrscheinlich ◇ adj probable. ◇ adv probably.

Wahrscheinlichkeit (pl -en) die probability; **aller Wahrscheinlichkeit nach** in all probability.

Wahrung die protection.

Währung (pl -en) die currency; **eine harte Währung** a hard currency.

Währungseinheit die currency unit.

Währungsreform die HIST & WIRTSCH currency reform.

Währungssystem das monetary system.

Wahrzeichen das symbol.

Waise (pl -n) die orphan.

Waisenhaus das orphanage.

Waisenkind das orphan.

Wal (pl -e) der whale.

Wald (pl Wälder) der wood; [groß] forest.

Waldbrand der forest fire.

Wäldchen (pl -) das copse.

Waldgebiet das wooded area.

Waldmeister der woodruff.

Waldsterben das forest dieback.

Waldweg der forest track.

Wales ['we:ls] nt Wales.

Walkman® ['wɔ:kmɛn] (pl -men) der Walkman®.

Wall (pl Wälle) der rampart.

Wallfahrt die pilgrimage.

Wallis das Valais.

Walliser (pl -) ◇ der native/inhabitant of Valais. ◇ adj (unver) of/from Valais.

Walliserin (pl -nen) die native/inhabitant of Valais.

walliserisch adj of/from Valais.

Wallonien nt Wallonia.

wallonisch adj Walloon.

Walnuss (pl -nüsse) die walnut.

Walross (pl -rösser) das walrus.

walten vi geh to reign; **etw walten lassen** to exercise sthg.

Walze (pl -n) die roller.

walzen vt to roll.

wälzen vt - **1.** [rollen] to roll - **2.** [Buch] to pore over. ◆ **sich wälzen** ref to roll around.

Walzer (pl -) der waltz; **Walzer tanzen** to waltz.

Wälzer (pl -) der fam tome.

wand prät ▷ **winden**.

Wand (pl Wände) die - **1.** [Mauer] wall (inside) - **2.** [Felswand] rock face - **3.** [von Schrank] side;

in den eigenen vier Wänden in one's own home; jn an die Wand stellen *fam* to send sb before the firing squad.

Wandel *der* change; im Wandel begriffen to be in a state of flux.

wandeln *(perf* hat/ist gewandelt) *geh* <> *vi (ist)* to stroll. <> *vt (hat)* to change. ⮞ **sich wandeln** *ref* to change.

Wanderer *(pl -)*, **Wandrer** *(pl -)* der hiker.

Wanderin *(pl -nen)*, **Wandrerin** *(pl -nen)* die hiker.

Wander|karte *die* walking map.

wandern *(perf* ist gewandert) *vi* - 1. [als Sport] to go hiking - 2. [ziellos] to wander - 3. *fam* [gebracht werden]: ins Gefängnis wandern to end up in prison.

Wander|schuh *der* hiking ODER walking boot.

Wander|tag *der* school outing.

Wanderung *(pl -en)* die hike.

Wander|weg *der* trail.

Wand|gemälde *das* fresco.

Wandlung *(pl -en)* die change.

Wand|malerei *die* mural.

Wandrer = Wanderer.

Wandrerin = Wanderin.

Wand|schrank *der* built-in cupboard UK ODER closet US; [Kleiderschrank] built-in wardrobe UK ODER closet US.

wandte *prät* ⮞ **wenden**.

Wand|teppich *der* tapestry.

Wand|uhr *die* wall clock.

Wange *(pl -n)* die *geh* cheek.

wanken *(perf* ist/hat gewankt) *vi* - 1. *(ist)* [Betrunkener] to stagger - 2. *(hat)* [Boden, Mauer] to sway - 3. *(hat) geh* [Macht] to be under threat; [Entschluss] to waver.

wann *adv* when; bis wann? until when?, till when?; seit wann lebst du schon hier? how long have you been living here?; von wann bis wann? when?; wann du willst whenever you want.

Wanne *(pl -n)* die - 1. [Badewanne] bath - 2. [Becken] tub.

Wanze *(pl -n)* die bug.

Wappen *(pl -)* das coat of arms.

war *prät* ⮞ **sein**.

warb *prät* ⮞ **werben**.

Ware *(pl -n)* die product.

Waren|haus *das* department store.

Waren|lager *das* warehouse.

Waren|zeichen *das*: eingetragenes Warenzeichen registered trademark.

warf *prät* ⮞ **werfen**.

warm *(kompar* wärmer, *superl* wärmste) <> *adj* warm; es ist warm it's warm; mir ist/wird warm I'm warm/warming up; draußen ist es 30°C warm it's 30°C outside; mit jm

warm werden *fam fig* to get on well with sb; warme Miete *rent including heating bills*. <> *adv* warmly; warm essen to have a hot meal.

Wärme *die* warmth.

wärmedämmend *adj* insulating.

wärmen *vt & vi* to warm. ⮞ **sich wärmen** *ref* to warm o.s.

Wärm|flasche *die* hot-water bottle.

warmherzig *adj* warm-hearted.

warm laufen *(perf* hat/ist warm gelaufen) *vi (unreg) (ist)* to warm up. ⮞ **sich warm laufen** *ref* to warm up.

Warm|miete *die* rent including heating bills.

Warm|wasser *das* hot water.

Warnblinkan|lage *die* AUTO hazard lights *Pl*.

Warn|dreieck *das* AUTO warning triangle.

warnen *vt* to warn; jn vor jm/etw warnen to warn sb about sb/sthg.

Warn|schild *(pl -er)* das warning sign.

Warnung *(pl -en)* die warning.

Warschau *nt* Warsaw.

warten <> *vi* to wait; auf jn/etw warten to wait for sb/sthg; mit etw warten to put sthg on hold. <> *vt* TECH to service.

Wärter, in *(mpl -, fpl -nen)* der, die [im Zoo, Leuchtturm] keeper; [im Gefängnis] warder.

Warte|saal *der* waiting room.

Warte|zimmer *das* waiting room.

Wartung *(pl -en)* die servicing *(U)*.

warum *adv* why.

Warze *(pl -n)* die wart.

was <> *pron* - 1. [Interrogativpronomen] what; was ist? what is it?; was ist sie (von Beruf)? what does she do (for a living)? - 2. [wie viel] how much, what; was kostet das? how much is it? - 3. *fam* [warum] why; was fragst du? why do you ask? - 4. *fam* [nicht wahr]: da freust du dich, was? you're pleased, aren't you?; es ist schön, was? it's nice, isn't it?; gut, was? not bad, eh? - 5. [Relativpronomen] which, that; das, was what; alles, was everything (that); das Beste, was ich je gehört habe the best I've ever heard - 6. *fam* [etwas] something; was für what sort ODER kind of; was sind das für Tiere? what sort ODER kind of animals are those?; was für ein Lärm! what a noise!; was weiß ich! *fam* don't ask me! <> *interj fam* [wie bitte] what? ⮞ **ach, was** *interj* no it's/etc not! ⮞ **so was** *interj*: na ODER also so was! really!

Waschan|lage *die* carwash.

waschbar *adj* washable.

Wasch|becken *das* washbasin.

Wäsche *(pl -n)* die - 1. [schmutzige Wäsche] laundry - 2. [Unterwäsche] underwear - 3. [Waschen] wash.

waschecht *adj* - 1. [Stoff] colourfast - 2. [typisch] true.

Wäsche|klammer *die* clothes peg *UK*, clothespin *US*.

Wäsche|korb *der* laundry basket.

Wäsche|leine *die* washing line.

waschen (*präs* **wäscht**, *prät* **wusch**, *perf* **hat gewaschen**) *vt* to wash; **sich** *(D)* **die Haare/die Hände waschen** to wash one's hair/hands.
➡ **sich waschen** *ref* to have a wash; **er bekam eine Abreibung, die sich gewaschen hatte** he got one hell of a hiding.

Wäscherei (*pl* **-en**) *die* laundrette.

Wäsche|ständer *der* clotheshorse.

Wäsche|trockner *der* - 1. [Maschine] tumbledryer - 2. [Wäscheständer] clotheshorse.

Wasch|gelegenheit *die* washing facilities *Pl*.

Wasch|lappen *der* - 1. [Lappen] facecloth - 2. *fam abw* [Person] wimp.

Wasch|maschine *die* washing machine.

Wasch|mittel *das* detergent.

Wasch|pulver *das* washing powder.

Wasch|raum *der* washroom.

Wasch|salon *der* laundrette.

wäscht *präs* ▷ **waschen**.

Wasser (*pl* **-** *ODER* **Wässer**) *das* - 1. [gen] water; **Wasser abstoßend** water-repellent; **unter Wasser stehen** to be under water - 2. (*ohne pl*) [Körperflüssigkeit] fluid; **mir läuft das Wasser im Mund zusammen** my mouth is watering; **sich über Wasser halten** to keep one's head above water. ➡ **am Wasser** *adv* by the water.

wasserabstoßend ▷ **Wasser**.

Wasser|bad *das* KÜCHE bain-marie.

wasserdicht *adj* - 1. [Bekleidung, Uhr] waterproof - 2. *fam* [Alibi] watertight.

Wasser|farbe *die* watercolours *Pl*.

Wasser|graben *der* ditch; [Burggraben] moat.

Wasser|hahn *der* tap *UK*, faucet *US*.

Wasserkraft|werk *das* hydroelectric power station.

Wasser|leitung *die* water pipe.

wasserlöslich *adj* soluble.

Wasser|mann (*pl* **-männer**) *der* ASTROL Aquarius; **Wassermann sein** to be an Aquarius.

Wasser|melone *die* watermelon.

wässern *vt* - 1. [Pflanze, Beet] to water - 2. KÜCHE to soak.

Wasser|pflanze *die* aquatic plant.

Wasser|ratte *die* - 1. [Tier] water rat - 2. *fam* [Person] waterbaby.

wasserscheu *adj* scared of water.

Wasser|schutzpolizei *die* river police.

Wasser|ski ▷ *der* [Gerät] water ski. ▷ *nt* water-skiing.

Wasser|spiegel *der* water level.

Wasser|sport *der* water sport.

Wasser|spülung (*pl* **-en**) *die* flush.

Wasser|stand *der* water level.

Wasser|stoff *der* CHEM hydrogen.

Wasser|versorgung *die* (*ohne pl*) water supply.

Wasser|waage *die* spirit level.

Wasser|werk *das* waterworks *Pl*.

Wasser|zeichen *das* watermark.

wässrig *adj* watery.

waten (*perf* **ist gewatet**) *vi* to wade.

watscheln (*perf* **ist gewatschelt**) *vi* to waddle.

Watt (*pl* **-en** *ODER* **-**) *das* - 1. (*pl* **Watten**) [Küstengebiet] mudflats *Pl* - 2. (*pl* **Watt**) PHYS & TECH [Maßeinheit] watt.

Watte *die* cotton wool.

Watte|bausch *der* wad of cotton wool.

Watten|meer *das* mudflats *Pl*.

Watte|stäbchen *das* cotton bud.

wattiert *adj* padded.

WC [veː'tseː] (*pl* **-s**) (*abk für* water closet) *das* WC.

weben (*prät* **wob**, *perf* **hat gewoben**) *vt* to weave.

Web|seite ['websaitə] *die* EDV web page, website.

Web|stuhl *der* loom.

Wechsel ['vɛksl] (*pl* **-**) *der* - 1. [Tausch] change - 2. [Zahlungsmittel] exchange. ➡ **im Wechsel** *adv* in turns.

Wechsel|beziehung *die* correlation.

Wechsel|geld *das* change.

wechselhaft ['vɛksl̩haft] *adj* changeable.

Wechseljahre *Pl* menopause (*U*).

Wechsel|kurs *der* exchange rate.

wechseln ['vɛksl̩n] (*perf* **hat/ist gewechselt**) ◇ *vt* (**hat**) - 1. [Thema, Kleidung, Arbeitsplatz, Geld] to change; **etw gegen** *ODER* **in etw** *(A)* **wechseln** to change sthg for sthg - 2. [tauschen] to exchange. ◇ *vi* - 1. (**hat**) [sich verändern] to change - 2. (**ist**) [an anderen Ort] to move.

wechselseitig ◇ *adj* mutual. ◇ *adv* mutually.

Wechsel|strom *der* (*ohne pl*) ELEKTR alternating current.

Wechsel|stube *die* bureau de change.

Wechsel|wirkung *die* interaction.

wecken *vt* - 1. [Person] to wake - 2. [Neugier, Wunsch] to awaken.

Wecker (*pl* **-**) *der* alarm clock; **jm auf den Wecker fallen** *fam fig* to get on sb's nerves.

wedeln (*perf* **hat/ist gewedelt**) *vi*: **mit etw wedeln** to wave sthg; **mit dem Schwanz wedeln** to wag its tail.

weder ➡ **weder... noch...** *konj* neither... nor...

weg *adv* away; **er ist schon weg** he has already gone; **nichts wie weg hier!** *fam* let's get out of here!; **weg damit!** *fam* take it away!; **Hände weg!** hands off!; **weit weg** far away; **über etw** *(A)* **weg sein** *fam fig* to have got over sthg.

Weg *(pl -e)* der - **1.** [Pfad] path - **2.** [Strecke, Methode] way; **ein weiter Weg** a long way; **jm im Weg stehen** ODER **sein** to be in sb's way; **jm über den Weg laufen** to bump into sb; **(jn) nach dem Weg fragen** to ask (sb) the way; **sich auf den Weg machen** to be on one's way; **jm/ etw aus dem Weg gehen** to avoid sb/sthg; **jm nicht über den Weg trauen** not to trust sb an inch.

wegen *präp (+ G, D)* because of; **wegen Umbau geschlossen** closed for refurbishment. **von wegen** *interj fam* far from it!

weg|fahren *(perf hat/ist weggefahren) (unreg)* ◇ *vi (ist)* to leave; [verreisen] to go away; **er stieg ins Auto und fuhr weg** he got in the car and drove off. ◇ *vt (hat)* [transportieren] to move; [entsorgen] to take away.

weg|gehen *(perf ist weggegangen) vi (unreg)* - **1.** [fortgehen] to leave; [ausgehen] to go out; **geh weg!** go away! - **2.** [verschwinden] to go away - **3.** [Ware] to sell well.

weg|jagen *vt* to chase away.

weg|kommen *(perf ist weggekommen) vi (unreg)* - **1.** [fortgehen können] to get away; **von etw wegkommen** to get away from sthg; [Drogen] to get off sthg - **2.** [verschwinden] to disappear - **3.** [behandelt werden]: **gut/schlecht bei etw wegkommen** to do well/badly out of sthg.

weg|lassen *vt (unreg)* - **1.** [Person] to let go - **2.** [Abschnitt, Teil] to leave out.

weg|laufen *(perf ist weggelaufen) vi (unreg)* to run away; **vor** ODER **von jm/etw weglaufen** to run away from sb/sthg.

weg|legen *vt* to put down.

weg|machen *vt fam* to get rid of.

weg|müssen *vi (unreg)* to have to go.

weg|nehmen *vt (unreg)* to take away; **jm etw wegnehmen** to take sthg away from sb.

weg|räumen *vt* to clear away.

weg|schaffen *vt* [sich einer Sache entledigen] to get rid of; [woandershin bringen] to move.

weg|schicken *vt* [Person] to send away; [Päckchen] to send.

weg|sehen *vi (unreg)* to look away.

weg|tun *vt (unreg)* - **1.** [weglegen] to put away - **2.** [wegwerfen] to throw away.

Weg|weiser *(pl -)* der signpost.

weg|werfen *vt (unreg)* to throw away.

Wegwerf|gesellschaft die abw throwaway society.

weg|wischen *vt* to wipe away.

weg|ziehen *(perf hat/ist weggezogen) (unreg)* ◇ *vi (ist)*: **aus etw wegziehen** [Stadt] to move away from sthg; [Wohnung, Haus] to move out of sthg. ◇ *vt (hat)* to pull away; [Vorhang, Decke] to pull back.

weh *adj* painful; *siehe auch* **wehtun**. **oh weh** *interj* oh dear!

wehen *(perf hat/ist geweht)* ◇ *vi* - **1.** *(hat)* [blasen] to blow; [flattern] to flutter - **2.** *(ist)* [geweht werden - Blatt, Schneeflocken] to blow about; [- Duft, Geruch] to waft. ◇ *vt (hat)* to blow. .

Wehen *Pl* contractions.

wehleidig *adj abw* self-pitying.

wehmütig ◇ *adj* melancholy. ◇ *adv* melancholically.

Wehr *(pl -e)* ◇ *die*: **sich zur Wehr setzen** to defend o.s. ◇ *das (pl Wehre)* weir.

Wehr|dienst *der* military service.

Wehr|dienstverweigerer *(pl -) der* conscientious objector.

wehren **sich wehren** *ref* to defend o.s.

wehrlos ◇ *adj* defenceless. ◇ *adv*: **jm wehrlos ausgeliefert sein** to be defenceless against sb.

Wehr|pflicht *die* compulsory military service.

wehrpflichtig *adj* liable for military service.

weh|tun *vi*: **jm wehtun** to hurt sb; **mir tun die Füße weh** my feet hurt. **sich wehtun** *ref* to hurt o.s.

Weib *(pl -er) das fam abw* [Frau] woman.

Weibchen *(pl -) das* female.

weiblich *adj* - **1.** [Person, Tier, Geschlecht] female - **2.** [Kleidung, Verhalten & GRAMM] feminine.

weich ◇ *adj* soft; **weich werden** *fam* to soften. ◇ *adv* [landen] softly; [bremsen] gently; [liegen] comfortably; **weich gekocht** soft-boiled; **jn weich machen** to soften sb up.

Weiche *(pl -n) die* points *Pl UK*, switch *US*.

weichgekocht *adj* ▷ **weich**.

Weich|käse *der* soft cheese.

weichlich *adj abw* weak.

Weichling *(pl -e) der abw* weakling.

Weichsel *(pl -n) die*: **die Weichsel** the (River) Vistula.

Weich|spüler ['vaiçʃpyːlɐ] *(pl -) der* fabric conditioner.

Weide *(pl -n) die* - **1.** [für Vieh] meadow - **2.** [Baum] willow tree.

weiden *vi* to graze.

weigern **sich weigern** *ref*: **sich weigern, etw zu tun** to refuse to do sthg.

Weigerung *(pl -en) die* refusal.

weihen *vt* to consecrate.

Weiher *(pl -) der* pond.

Weihnachten (*pl -*) (*ohne Artikel*) Christmas; **Weihnachten feiern** to celebrate Christmas. ➤ **frohe Weihnachten** *interj* Merry Christmas!

weihnachtlich ⟨⟩ *adj* Christmassy. ⟨⟩ *adv* for Christmas.

Weihnachts|abend *der* Christmas Eve.

Weihnachts|baum *der* Christmas tree.

Weihnachts|geld *das* (*ohne pl*) Christmas bonus.

Weihnachts|geschenk *das* Christmas present.

Weihnachts|lied *das* Christmas carol.

Weihnachts|mann (*pl -männer*) *der* Father Christmas.

Weihnachts|markt *der* Christmas market.

Weihnachts|tag *der*: **erster/zweiter Weihnachtstag** Christmas/Boxing Day.

Weih|rauch *der* incense.

Weih|wasser *das* holy water.

weil *konj* because.

Weile ➤ **eine Weile** *adv* a while.

Weimarer Republik *die* Weimar Republic.

Wein (*pl -e*) *der* - **1.** [Getränk] wine - **2.** (*ohne pl*) [Pflanze] vine.

Wein|bau *der* wine-growing.

Wein|berg *der* vineyard.

Wein|brand *der* brandy.

weinen ⟨⟩ *vi* to cry; **über etw** (*A*) **weinen** to cry over sthg; **um jn weinen** to cry for sb; **vor etw** (*D*) **weinen** to cry with sthg; **wegen etw weinen** to cry because of sthg. ⟨⟩ *vt* to cry.

weinerlich *adj* tearful.

Wein|flasche *die* wine bottle.

Wein|keller *der* wine cellar.

Wein|lese (*pl -n*) *die* grape harvest.

Wein|probe *die* wine tasting.

Wein|stube *die* wine bar.

Wein|traube *die* grape.

weise ⟨⟩ *adj* wise. ⟨⟩ *adv* wisely.

Weise (*pl -n*) ⟨⟩ *die* - **1.** [Art] way - **2.** [Melodie] tune. ⟨⟩ *der, die* wise man (wise woman *die*).

weisen (*prät* **wies**, *perf* **hat gewiesen**) *geh* ⟨⟩ *vt* [zeigen]: **jm etw weisen** to show sb sthg. ⟨⟩ *vi* to point.

Weisheit (*pl -en*) *die* wisdom; **kannst du deine Weisheiten nicht für dich behalten?** can't you keep your pearls of wisdom to yourself?

Weisheits|zahn *der* wisdom tooth.

weis|machen *vt fam*: **jm etw weismachen** to make sb believe sthg.

weiß ⟨⟩ *präs* ▷ **wissen**. ⟨⟩ *adj* white.

Weiß *das* white.

Weiß|brot *das* white bread (*U*).

Weiße (*pl -n*) ⟨⟩ *der, die* [Person] white person. ⟨⟩ *das* [Farbe] white. ⟨⟩ *die*: **Berliner Weiße mit Schuss** type of wheat beer, with a shot of raspberry syrup.

Weiß|glut *die*: **jn zur Weißglut bringen** *fam fig* to send sb into a rage.

Weiß|kohl *der* white cabbage.

Weiß|wein *der* white wine.

weit ⟨⟩ *adj* [gen] wide; [Reise, Fahrt] long; **wie weit ist es bis?** how far is it to?; **ist es weit?** is it far?; **im weitesten Sinne** in the broadest sense; **mit seinen Kenntnissen ist es nicht weit her** he doesn't know enough; **bist du so weit?** are you ready?; **es ist so weit** the time has come. ⟨⟩ *adv* - **1.** [beträchtlich] far; **weit besser** far better; **weit weg** far away; **ihre Meinungen gehen weit auseinander** they differ widely in their opinions; **weit geöffnet** wide open; **weit verbreitet** widespread; **weit nach Mitternacht** long after midnight - **2.** [gehen, fahren] a long way; **zwei Kilometer weit fahren** ODER **gehen** to go two kilometres; **das geht zu weit!** that's going too far!; **so weit, so gut** so far, so good. ➤ **bei Weitem** *adv* by far; **bei Weitem nicht genug** not nearly enough. ➤ **von Weitem** *adv* from far away.

weitaus *adv* by far.

Weite (*pl -n*) *die* - **1.** (*ohne pl*) [weite Fläche] expanse; **das Weite suchen** *fig* to make o.s. scarce - **2.** SPORT distance - **3.** [von Kleidungsstücken] width.

weiter *adv* further; **was geschah weiter?** what happened then?; **immer weiter** further and further. ➤ **nicht weiter** *adv* [nicht weiter fort] no further; [nicht mehr] no longer; **es hat mich nicht weiter interessiert** I wasn't really interested in it. ➤ **und so weiter** *adv* and so on. ➤ **weiter nichts** *adv* nothing more.

weiter|arbeiten *vi* to carry on working.

weitere, r, s *adj* further.

weiter|empfehlen *vt* (*unreg*) to recommend; **jm etw weiterempfehlen** to recommend sthg to sb.

weiter|geben *vt* (*unreg*) to pass on; **etw an jn weitergeben** to pass on sthg to sb.

weiter|gehen (*perf* **ist weitergegangen**) *vi* (*unreg*) - **1.** [gehen] to go on - **2.** [sich fortsetzen] to continue.

weiterhin *adv* - **1.** [immer noch] still - **2.** [künftig] in future.

weiter|machen *vi* to carry on.

weiter|wissen *vi* (*unreg*): **nicht mehr weiterwissen** to be at one's wits' end.

weitgehend, weit gehend *adj* considerable.

weitläufig ⟨⟩ *adj* - **1.** [Haus, Grundstück] spacious - **2.** [Verwandtschaft] distant - **3.** [Schilderung] long-winded. ⟨⟩ *adv* - **1.** [angelegt] spaciously - **2.** [verwandt] distantly - **3.** [schildern] at great length.

weiträumig ◇ *adj* spacious. ◇ *adv*: **etw weiträumig umfahren** to give sthg a wide berth.

weitsichtig *adj* - 1. [sehbehindert] long-sighted - 2. [umsichtig] farsighted.

Weitsprung *der* SPORT long jump.

weitverbreitet, weit verbreitet *adj* common.

Weizen *der* wheat.

Weizenlbier *das* wheat beer.

welche, r, s ◇ *det* which. ◇ *pron* - 1. [Interrogativpronomen] which (one); **welcher von ihnen?** which (one) of them? - 2. [Relativpronomen - Person] who, that; [- Sache] which, that - 3. [Indefinitpronomen - in Aussagesätzen] some; [- in Frage- und Konditionalsätzen] any; **hast du welche?** have you got any?

welk *adj* [Blumen] wilted; [Haut] withered.

welken (*perf* **ist gewelkt**) *vi* to wilt.

Welllblech *das* corrugated iron (*U*).

Welle (*pl* -n) *die* - 1. [im Wasser] wave - 2. [beim Rundfunk] wavelength; **Wellen schlagen** to create a stir.

wellen ⬥ **sich wellen** *ref* [Papier] to wrinkle; [Haar] to become wavy; [Teppich] to ruck up.

Wellenlbelreich *der* waveband.

Wellenlgang *der*: **hoher Wellengang** heavy seas *Pl*.

Wellenlllänge *die* PHYS wavelength.

Wellenlllinie *die* wavy line.

Wellenlsittich *der* budgerigar.

wellig *adj* [Haar] wavy; [Papier] wrinkled; [Gelände] undulating.

Welllpappe *die* corrugated cardboard (*U*).

Welpe (*pl* -n) *der* [von Hund] puppy; [von Fuchs, Wolf] cub.

Welt (*pl* -en) *die* world; **auf der Welt** in the world; **die Dritte Welt** the Third World; **alle Welt** the whole world; **auf die** ODER **zur Welt kommen** to come into the world.

Weltlall *das* (*ohne pl*) universe.

Weltlanschauung *die* world view.

Weltlauslstellung *die* world fair.

weltberühmt *adj* world-famous.

weltfremd *adj* unworldly.

Weltlkrieg *der* HIST: **der Erste/Zweite Weltkrieg** the First/Second World War.

weltlich *adj* worldly.

Weltlmacht *die* world power.

Weltlmeister, in *der, die* world champion.

Weltlrang *der*: **von Weltrang** world-class.

Weltranglliste *die* SPORT world rankings *Pl*.

Weltlraum *der* space.

Weltlreise *die* round-the-world trip.

Weltlrekord *der* world record.

Weltlstadt *die* cosmopolitan city.

Weltluntergang *der* end of the world.

weltweit *adj* worldwide.

wem *pron* (*Dativ von wer*) (to) who, (to) whom; **wem gehört die Tasche?** whose bag is it?; **mit wem spreche ich?** who's speaking?; **von wem hast du das?** who did you get it from?

wen *pron* (*Akkusativ von wer*) who, whom; **für wen ist das?** who is that for?

Wende (*pl* -n) *die* - 1. [Veränderung] change - 2. SPORT turn - 3. HIST: **die Wende** the fall of the Berlin Wall.

Wendelkreis *der* - 1. [von Auto] turning circle - 2. GEOGR tropic.

Wendelltreppe *die* spiral staircase.

wenden (*prät* **wendete** ODER **wandte**, *perf* **hat gewendet** ODER **gewandt**) ◇ *vt* (*reg*) [umdrehen] to turn; [Kleidungsstück] to reverse. ◇ *vi* (*reg*) to turn around; **'bitte wenden'** 'please turn over'. ⬥ **sich wenden** *ref* - 1. (*reg*) [sich ändern]: **sich zum Besseren/ Schlechteren wenden** to take a turn for the better/worse - 2. [sich richten]: **sich an jn/etw wenden** [hilfesuchend] to turn to sb/sthg; [appellierend] to address sb/sthg; **sich gegen jn/ etw wenden** to oppose sb/sthg.

Wendelpunkt *der* turning point.

Wendung (*pl* -en) *die* - 1. [Redewendung] idiom - 2. [Drehung] turn.

wenig ◇ *det* - 1. [Anzahl] a few; **mit wenigen Worten** in few words - 2. [Menge] little. ◇ *pron* - 1. [Anzahl] a few; **es ist nur wenigen bekannt, dass...** only a few people know that... - 2. [Menge] little. ◇ *adv* a little; **wenig bekannt** little known; **wenig erfreulich** not very pleasant. ⬥ **ein wenig** *det, pron & adv* a little. ⬥ **nur wenig** ◇ *det* - 1. [Anzahl] only a few - 2. [Menge] only a little; **er hat nur wenig Zeit** he hasn't got much time. ◇ *adv* only a little. ⬥ **zu wenig** ◇ *det* - 1. [Anzahl] too few - 2. [Menge] too little. ◇ *adv & pron* too little.

weniger ◇ *adv* less. ◇ *konj*: **sieben weniger drei** seven minus three.

wenigste *adj* ▷ **wenig**. ⬥ **am wenigsten** *adv* least.

wenigstens *adv* at least.

wenn *konj* - 1. [zeitlich] when - 2. [konditional] if; **wenn ich das gewusst hätte** if I had known, had I known; **wenn er nur käme!** if only he would come! ⬥ **wenn auch** *konj* even if. ⬥ **wenn bloß** *konj* if only.

wer *pron* - 1. [Interrogativpronomen] who; **wer von euch?** which of you? - 2. [Relativpronomen] anyone ODER anybody who; **wer mitkommen will** anyone who wants to come - 3. *fam* [Indefinitpronomen - in Aussagesätzen] somebody, someone; [- in Frage- und Konditionalsätzen] anybody, anyone; **ist da wer?** is there anyone there?

Werbe|fernsehen *das* television advertising.

werben (*präs* **wirbt**, *prät* **warb**, *perf* **hat geworben**) ◇ *vi* to advertise. ◇ *vt* to attract.

Werbung (*pl* **-en**) *die* advertising.

Werde|gang *der* development; **der berufliche Werdegang** professional development.

werden (*präs* **wird**, *prät* **wurde**, *perf* **ist geworden** ODER **worden**) ◇ *aux* - 1. [zur Bildung des Futurs] will; **sie wird kommen** she will come, she'll come; **sie wird nicht kommen** she won't come; **es wird warm werden** it is going to be warm - 2. [zur Bildung des Konjunktivs] would; **würdest du/würden Sie?** would you?; **ich würde gerne** I would like to; **ich würde lieber noch bleiben** I would prefer to stay a bit longer - 3. (*perf* **ist worden**) [zur Bildung des Passivs] to be; **sie wurde kritisiert** she was criticised; **nebenan wird gelacht** there's someone laughing next door. ◇ *vi* (*perf* **ist geworden**) - 1. [gen] to become; **Vater werden** to become a father; **er will Lehrer werden** he wants to be a teacher; **alt werden** to grow ODER get old; **rot werden** to turn ODER go red; **verrückt werden** to go mad; **krank werden** to fall ill; **schlecht werden** to go off; **ich werde morgen 25** I'll be 25 tomorrow; **es wird Nacht** it's getting dark; **daraus wird nichts** nothing will come of it; **zu Stein werden** to turn to stone; **zum Mann werden** to become a man; **(na,) wirds bald!** *fam* get a move on! - 2. *fam* [gelingen, sich erholen]: **sind die Fotos was geworden?** did the photos come out?; **es wird schon wieder werden** *fam* it will be all right.

werfen (*präs* **wirft**, *prät* **warf**, *perf* **hat geworfen**) ◇ *vt* - 1. [Ball, Stein] to throw - 2. [Tor, Korb] to score. ◇ *vi* to throw; **mit etw werfen** to throw sthg. ◆ **sich werfen** *ref* to throw o.s.

Werft (*pl* **-en**) *die* shipyard.

Werk (*pl* **-e**) *das* - 1. [gen] work - 2. [Betrieb] plant.

Werk|statt (*pl* **-stätten**) *die* workshop.

Werk|tag *der* working day.

werktags *adv* on working days.

werktätig *adj* working.

Werkzeug (*pl* **-e**) *das* tool.

Werkzeug|kasten *der* tool box.

Wermut (*pl* **-s**) *der* vermouth (U).

wert *adj*: **wert sein** to be worth; **nichts wert sein** to be worthless; **viel/tausend Euro wert sein** to be worth a lot/a thousand euros; **werte Gäste!** dear guests!

Wert (*pl* **-e**) *der* value; **auf etw** (A) **Wert legen** to attach importance to sthg; **im Wert steigen/fallen** to increase/decrease in value; **das hat keinen Wert!** *fam* it's pointless.

werten *vt* [benoten] to rate; [beurteilen] to judge; [einschätzen]: **etw als Erfolg werten** to consider sthg a success.

Wertgegen|stand *der* valuable object.

wertlos *adj* worthless.

Wert|papier *das* WIRTSCH bond.

Wertung (*pl* **-en**) *die* judgement.

wertvoll *adj* valuable.

Wesen (*pl* **-**) *das* - 1. [Charakter] nature - 2. [Mensch] being - 3. [Lebewesen] creature.

wesentlich ◇ *adj* essential. ◇ *adv* considerably. ◆ **im Wesentlichen** *adv* essentially.

weshalb *adv* why.

Wespe (*pl* **-n**) *die* wasp.

wessen *pron* (Genitiv von **wer**) whose.

Wessi (*pl* **-s**) *der fam* citizen of the former West Germany.

West|deutschland *nt* western Germany; [frühere BRD] West Germany.

Weste (*pl* **-n**) *die* waistcoat UK, vest US.

Westen *der* - 1. [gen] west; **aus Westen** from the west; **nach Westen** west; **im Westen** in the west; **der Wilde Westen** the Wild West - 2. POL West.

West|europa *nt* Western Europe.

Westfalen *nt* Westphalia.

West|küste *die* West Coast.

westlich ◇ *adj* western. ◇ *präp*: **westlich einer Sache** (G) ODER **von etw** (to the) west of sthg.

weswegen *adv* why.

Wettbewerb (*pl* **-e**) *der* competition.

Wette (*pl* **-n**) *die* bet. ◆ **um die Wette** *adv*: **um die Wette laufen** to have a race; **um die Wette jodeln** to have a yodelling competition.

wetten ◇ *vi* to bet; **mit jm wetten** to bet sb; **um etw wetten** to bet sthg. ◇ *vt* to bet. ◆ **wetten, dass?** *interj* do you want to bet?

Wetter (*pl* **-**) *das* [Klima] weather; **schönes/schlechtes Wetter** good/bad weather.

Wetter|amt *das* meteorological office.

Wetter|bericht *der* weather report.

wetterfest *adj* weatherproof.

Wetter|karte *die* weather map.

Wetter|lage *die* general weather situation.

wettern *vi*: **gegen jn/etw wettern** to curse sb/sthg.

Wettervorher|sage *die* weather forecast.

Wett|kampf *der* contest.

Wett|lauf *der* race.

wett|machen *vt* to make up for.

Wett|rennen *das* race.

wetzen (*perf* **hat gewetzt**) *vt* to sharpen.

WG [veːˈɡeː] (*pl* **-s**) *die abk für* **Wohngemeinschaft**.

Whg. abk für **Wohnung**.

Whirlpool ['wœrlpu:l] der Jacuzzi®.

Whiskey (pl -s), **Whisky** (pl -s) ['vɪski] der whisky.

wichtig adj important; **etw wichtig nehmen** to take sthg seriously.

Wichtigkeit die importance.

Wichtigtuer (pl -) der fam abw bighead.

wickeln vt to wind; **etw um etw wickeln** to wrap sthg around sthg; **jn/etw in etw (A) wickeln** to wrap sb/sthg in sthg; **ein Baby wickeln** to change a baby's nappy UK ODER diaper US.

Widder (pl -) der - 1. [Tier] ram - 2. ASTROL Aries; **Widder sein** to be an Aries.

wider präp geh against.

widerlegen vt [Argument, Behauptung] to refute; **jn widerlegen** to prove sb wrong.

widerlich adj abw revolting.

widerrechtlich ⟨⟩ adj illegal. ⟨⟩ adv illegally.

Widerlruf der [von Aussage] retraction (U); [von Befehl] revocation. ◆ **bis auf Widerruf** adv until further notice.

widerrufen (prät widerrief, perf hat widerrufen) vt [von Aussage] to retract; [von Befehl] to revoke.

widerlsetzen ◆ **sich widersetzen** ref: **sich einer Sache (D) widersetzen** to oppose sthg; **sich einem Befehl widersetzen** to refuse to comply with an order.

widerspenstig ⟨⟩ adj unruly. ⟨⟩ adv in an unruly manner.

widerlspiegeln vt to reflect. ◆ **sich widerspiegeln** ref to be reflected.

widersprechen (präs widerspricht, prät widersprach, perf hat widersprochen) vi to contradict; **jm widersprechen** to contradict sb; **einer Sache/sich (D) widersprechen** to contradict sthg/o.s.

Widerlspruch der - 1. [von Personen] protest - 2. [in Aussage] contradiction.

Widerlstand der - 1. [Ablehnung & ELEKTR] resistance (U); **Widerstand gegen jn/etw** resistance against sb/sthg; **Widerstand leisten** to put up resistance; **auf Widerstand stoßen** to meet with resistance - 2. [Hindernis] obstacle.

widerstandsfähig adj resilient.

widerstehen (prät widerstand, perf hat widerstanden) vi: **jm/einer Sache widerstehen** to resist sb/sthg.

widerstrebend ⟨⟩ adj reluctant. ⟨⟩ adv reluctantly.

widerwärtig ⟨⟩ adj revolting. ⟨⟩ adv: **sich widerwärtig verhalten** to behave offensively.

Widerwille, Widerwillen der reluctance; **Widerwillen gegen jn/etw empfinden** to be disgusted by sb/sthg.

widmen vt - 1. [zueignen]: **jm etw widmen** to dedicate sthg to sb - 2. [aufwenden] to dedicate. ◆ **sich widmen** ref [sich zuwenden]: **sich jm/einer Sache widmen** to devote o.s. to sb/sthg.

Widmung (pl -en) die dedication.

wie ⟨⟩ adv how; **wie heißen Sie?** what's your name?; **sie fragte ihn, wie alt er sei** she asked him how old he was; **wie war das Wetter?** what was the weather like?; **wie gehts?** how are you?; **wie spät ist es?** what's the time?, what time is it?; **wie oft?** how often?; **wie bitte?** sorry?, excuse me?; **wie war das?** fam come again?; **wie nett von dir!** how kind of you!; **wie schade!** what a pity! ⟨⟩ interj: **er kam wohl nicht, wie?** he didn't come, did he? ⟨⟩ konj - 1. [vergleichend - vor Substantiv] like; [- vor Adjektiv, Verb, Partikel] as; **wie sein Vater** like his father; **wie... wie... as... as...; so viel, wie du willst** as much as you want; **so groß wie du** as big as you; **weiß wie Schnee** as white as snow - 2. [zum Beispiel] such as, like - 3. [dass]: **ich hörte, wie mein Nachbar Klavier spielte** I heard my neighbour playing the piano.

wieder adv - 1. [gen] again; **immer wieder, wieder und wieder** again and again; **hin und wieder** now and again; **nie wieder** never again; **was hast du denn (jetzt) wieder angestellt?** what have you done this time?; **er ist wieder da** he is back; **er ging wieder ins Haus** he went back into the house - 2. fam [wiederum] on the other hand.

wiederlbekommen vt (unreg) to get back.

wieder beleben, wiederbeleben vt to revive.

wiederlbringen vt (unreg) to bring back.

wieder erkennen, wiedererkennen vt (unreg) to recognize.

Wiederlgabe die [Bericht] account; [von Bild, Ton, Farben] reproduction; [von Musikstück, Gedicht] rendition.

wiederlgeben vt (unreg) - 1. [zurückgeben]: **jm etw wiedergeben** to give sthg back to sb - 2. [mit Worten] to give an account of - 3. [technisch] to reproduce.

wieder gutlmachen, wiedergutlmachen vt [Schaden] to compensate for; [Fehler] to put right; [Unrecht] to repair.

wiederherlstellen vt [Kontakt] to reestablish.

wiederholen vt - 1. [gen] to repeat - 2. [lernen] to revise. ◆ **sich wiederholen** ref - 1. [Sprecher] to repeat o.s. - 2. [Ereignis] to recur - 3. [Muster] to reappear.

Wiederholung (pl -en) die repetition.

Wiederhören ◆ **auf Wiederhören** interj goodbye! (on telephone).

wiedersehen vt (unreg) to see again.

Wiedersehen (pl -) das reunion. ◆ **auf Wiedersehen** interj goodbye!

wiederum *adv* - 1. [von neuem] again - 2. [andererseits] on the other hand.

Wiederver|einigung *die* HIST reunification *(U)*.

wieder verwerten, wiederverwerten *vt* to reuse.

Wiege *(pl -n)* *die* cradle.

wiegen *(prät* **wiegte** ODER **wog,** *perf* **hat gewiegt** ODER **gewogen)** *vt* - 1. *(unreg)* [abwiegen] to weigh - 2. *(reg)* [schaukeln] to rock.

Wiegen|lied *das* lullaby.

wiehern *vi* to neigh.

Wien *nt* Vienna.

Wiener *(pl -)* ◇ *der* Viennese. ◇ *adj (unver)*: **Wiener Schnitzel** Wiener schnitzel, escalope of veal coated with breadcrumbs; **Wiener Würstchen** Wiener, small sausage made of beef, pork or veal.

Wienerin *(pl -nen)* *die* Viennese.

wies *prät* ➭ **weisen**.

Wiese *(pl -n)* *die* meadow; **auf der grünen Wiese** outside town.

Wiesel *(pl -)* *das* weasel.

wieso *pron* why.

wie viel *pron* - 1. [Anzahl] how many - 2. [Menge] how much; **wie viel ist zwei mal drei?** what is two times three?; **wie viel Uhr ist es?** what's the time?, what time is it?; **wie viel älter/schneller?** how much older/faster?; **wie viel Geld das kostet!** what a lot of money it costs!

wievielt *adj* which. ➭ **zu wievielt** *adv*: **zu wievielt seid ihr in Urlaub gefahren?** how many of you went on holiday?

wieweit *konj* how far.

wild ◇ *adj* - 1. [gen] wild - 2. [unzivilisiert] savage - 3. [illegal] illegal. ◇ *adv* - 1. [gen] wildly - 2. [illegal] illegally.

Wild *das* game.

wildern ◇ *vi* [jagen - Mensch] to poach; [- Tier] to hunt. ◇ *vt* to poach.

wildfremd *adj* completely strange; **ein wildfremder Mensch** a complete stranger.

Wild|leder *das* suede *(U)*.

Wildnis *(pl -se)* *die* wilderness.

Wild|schwein *das* wild boar.

will *präs* ➭ **wollen**.

Wille *(pl -n)*, **Willen** *der* will; **beim besten Willen** with the best will in the world.

willen *präp*: **um js/einer Sache willen** for the sake of sb/sthg.

willenlos *adj* & *adv* with a total lack of will.

willensstark *adj* strong-willed.

willig ◇ *adj* willing. ◇ *adv* willingly.

willkommen *adj* welcome; **ihr seid uns jederzeit willkommen** you are always welcome. ➭ **herzlich willkommen** *interj* welcome!

Willkommen *(pl -)* *das* welcome.

willkürlich ◇ *adj* arbitrary. ◇ *adv* arbitrarily.

wimmeln *vi*: **es wimmelt von ...** it's crawling with ...

wimmern *vi* to whimper.

Wimper *(pl -n)* *die* eyelash; **ohne mit der Wimper zu zucken** *fig* without batting an eyelid.

Wimpern|tusche *die* mascara *(U)*.

Wind *(pl -e)* *der* wind; **bei Wind und Wetter** in all weathers; **Wind von etw bekommen** *fam fig* to get wind of sthg.

Winde *(pl -n)* *die* - 1. [Hebevorrichtung] winch - 2. [Pflanze] bindweed *(U)*.

Windel *(pl -n)* *die* nappy *UK*, diaper *US*.

winden *(prät* **wand,** *perf* **hat gewunden)** *vt* geh [flechten] to wind; [Kranz] to make; **etw um etw winden** to wind sthg around sthg. ➭ **sich winden** *ref* - 1. [sich schlängeln - Schlange, Aal] to slither; [- vor Schmerz] to writhe - 2. *geh* [Pflanze] to wind o.s. - 3. [Weg] to wind - 4. [vor Verlegenheit] to squirm.

windig *adj* - 1. [Wetter] windy - 2. *fam abw* [Person, Ausrede] dodgy.

Wind|mühle *die* windmill.

Wind|pocken *Pl* chickenpox *(U)*.

Windschutz|scheibe *die* windscreen *UK*, windshield *US*.

windstill *adj* [Tag] still; [Ecke] sheltered.

Wind|stoß *der* gust of wind.

Windung *(pl -en)* *die* winding.

Wink *(pl -e)* *der* - 1. [Geste] sign - 2. [Bemerkung] hint; **jm einen Wink geben** to give sb a tip.

Winkel *(pl -)* *der* - 1. MATH angle; **ein stumpfer/spitzer/rechter Winkel** an obtuse/an acute/a right angle; **toter Winkel** *fig* blind spot - 2. [Ecke] corner - 3. [Platz] spot.

winken *(perf* **hat gewinkt** ODER **gewunken)** ◇ *vi* - 1. [zur Begrüßung, zum Abschied] to wave; **jm winken** to wave to sb - 2. [als Aufforderung]: **einem Taxi winken** to hail a taxi; **dem Kellner winken** to call the waiter - 3. [Belohnung] to get. ◇ *vt*: **jn zu sich (hin) winken** to beckon sb over; **jn an einen Ort winken** to direct sb to a place.

winseln *vi* - 1. [Tier] to whine - 2. *abw* [Person] to whimper.

Winter *(pl -)* *der* winter; **den Winter über** for the winter; **im Winter** in winter.

winterlich ◇ *adj* wintery; [Kleidung, Landschaft] winter. ◇ *adv*: **winterlich kalt** cold and wintery.

Winter|reifen *der* winter tyre.

Winter|schlaf *der* hibernation.

Winterschlussverkauf *(pl -käufe)* *der* January sale.

Winter|semester *das* UNI winter semester.

Winter|spiele *Pl*: Olympische Winterspiele Winter Olympics.

Winter|sport *der* winter sport.

Winzer, in *(mpl -, fpl -nen) der, die* wine grower.

winzig *adj* tiny.

wippen *vi* to rock.

wir *pron* we; wir beide both of us; wir waren es it was us.

Wirbel *(pl -) der -* 1. [von Wasser] whirlpool; [von Wind] whirlwind - 2. [Aufregung] stir; viel Wirbel um etw machen to make a big fuss about sthg - 3. [im Haar] cowlick - 4. [im Rücken] vertebra.

wirbeln *(perf hat/ist gewirbelt)* <> *vi (ist)* to whirl; [Schneeflocken, Blätter] to swirl. <> *vt (hat)* to whirl; [Schneeflocken, Blätter] to swirl.

Wirbel|säule *die* spine.

Wirbel|tier *das* BIOL vertebrate.

wirbt *präs* ⊳ **werben**.

wird *präs* ⊳ **werden**.

wirft *präs* ⊳ **werfen**.

wirken *vi -* 1. [erscheinen] to seem; sie wirkt auf jeden sympathisch everybody finds her nice - 2. [wirksam sein] to have an effect; beruhigend wirken to have a calming effect; gegen etw wirken to be effective against sthg - 3. [beruflich, Bild, Muster] to work.

wirklich <> *adj* real. <> *adv* really.

Wirklichkeit *(pl -en) die* reality.

wirksam <> *adj* effective. <> *adv* effectively.

Wirkung *(pl -en) die* effect.

wirkungslos *adj* ineffective.

wirkungsvoll *adj* effective.

wirr <> *adj -* 1. [unordentlich] tangled - 2. [konfus] confused. <> *adv -* 1. [unordentlich] in a tangle - 2. [konfus] in a confused way.

Wirrwarr *der ODER das* confusion.

Wirt, in *(mpl -e, fpl -nen) der, die* landlord (landlady *die*).

Wirtschaft *(pl -en) die -* 1. [Ökonomie] economy; die freie Wirtschaft the private sector - 2. [Gaststätte] pub *UK*, bar *US*.

wirtschaften *vi* [leiten]: Gewinn bringend wirtschaften to run things at a profit; wer wirtschaftet auf diesem Gut? who runs this estate?; mit Geld wirtschaften to manage finances.

wirtschaftlich <> *adj -* 1. [materiell] economic - 2. [sparsam] economical. <> *adv* economically.

Wirtschafts|krise *die* economic crisis.

Wirtschafts|ministerium *das* economics ministry.

Wirtschafts|politik *die (ohne pl)* economic policy.

Wirtschafts|system *das* economic system.

Wirtschafts|zweig *der* economic sector.

Wirts|haus *das* pub, often with accommodation.

Wirts|leute *Pl* landlord and landlady.

Wirts|stube *die* bar.

wischen <> *vt* [Boden, Mund] to wipe; [Dreck] to wipe away; [putzen] to clean. <> *vi*: mit der Hand über die Stirn wischen to wipe one's hand across one's brow.

wispern *vt & vi* to whisper.

wissbegierig *adj* thirsty for knowledge.

wissen *(präs weiß, prät wusste, perf hat gewusst)* <> *vt* to know; etw über jn/etw wissen to know sthg about sb/sthg; immer alles besser wissen to always know better; weißt du was? *fam* you know what?; ich will nichts von ihm/davon wissen I don't want to have anything to do with him/it; das musst du wissen that's up to you; was weiß ich! *fam* don't ask me! <> *vi* to know; ich weiß I know!; soviel ODER soweit ich weiß as far as I know; nicht, dass ich wüsste *fam* not as far as I know; von/um etw wissen to know about sthg; man kann nie wissen you never know.

Wissen *das* knowledge; nach bestem Wissen und Gewissen to the best of one's knowledge and ability; meines Wissens to my knowledge.

Wissenschaft *(pl -en) die* science.

Wissenschaftler, in *(mpl -, fpl -nen) der, die* scientist; [in Geisteswissenschaften] academic.

wissenschaftlich <> *adj* academic; [naturwissenschaftlich] scientific. <> *adv* academically; [naturwissenschaftlich] scientifically.

wissenswert *adj* worth knowing; [Fakten] valuable.

Wissenswerte *das* useful knowledge.

wittern *vt -* 1. [riechen] to scent - 2. [vermuten] to sense.

Witterung *(pl -en) die -* 1. [Wetter] weather - 2. [Geruch] scent.

Witwe *(pl -n) die* widow.

Witwer *(pl -) der* widower.

Witz *(pl -e) der -* 1. [Scherz] joke; Witze machen ODER reißen *fam* to crack jokes; du machst wohl Witze! you can't be serious! - 2. [Humor] wit.

Witzbold *(pl -e) der fam* joker.

witzeln *vi*: über jn/etw witzeln to make fun of sb/sthg.

witzig <> *adj* funny; [Idee] original. <> *adv* [lustig] funnily.

witzlos *adj -* 1. [langweilig] dull - 2. *fam* [überflüssig] pointless.

wo <> *adv* where; von wo kam das Geräusch? where did that noise come from?

◇ *pron* where. ◇ *konj fam* - **1.** [obwohl] when - **2.** [da] since; **jetzt, wo alles vorbei ist** now that it's all over.

woanders *adv* somewhere else.

wob *prät* ▷ **weben**.

wobei *pron* - **1.** [als Frage]: **wobei ist es passiert?** how did it happen?; **wobei hast du ihn gestört?** what was he doing when you disturbed him? - **2.** [zeitlich]: **sie stürzte von der Leiter, wobei sie sich den Arm brach** she fell off the ladder and broke her arm - **3.** [allerdings] although.

Woche (*pl* -n) *die* week; **vorige** ODER **letzte Woche** last week; **diese/nächste Woche** this/next week.

Wochenende *das* weekend; **am Wochenende** at the weekend. ➠ **schönes Wochenende** *interj* have a nice weekend!

Wochenkarte *die* weekly ticket.

wochenlang ◇ *adj* lasting for weeks; **nach wochenlangem Warten** after waiting for weeks. ◇ *adv* for weeks.

Wochenmarkt *der* weekly market.

Wochentag *der* weekday.

wöchentlich *adj* & *adv* weekly.

Wodka (*pl* -s) *der* vodka.

wodurch, wodurch *pron* - **1.** [als Frage] how - **2.** [Relativpronomen] as a result of which.

wofür, wofür *pron* - **1.** [als Frage] what... for? - **2.** [Relativpronomen] for which.

wog *prät* ▷ **wiegen**.

wogegen, wogegen ◇ *pron* - **1.** [als Frage] against what - **2.** [Relativpronomen] against which. ◇ *konj* [wohingegen] whereas.

woher, woher *pron* - **1.** [als Frage] where... from; **woher kommen Sie?** where do you come from?; **woher weißt du das?** how do you know that? - **2.** [Relativpronomen] from where.

wohin, wohin *pron* - **1.** [als Frage] where; **wohin damit?** *fam* where shall I put it? - **2.** [Relativpronomen] where.

wohl (*kompar* wohler ODER **besser**, *superl* am **wohlsten** ODER **besten**) *adv* - **1.** (*kompar* wohler, *superl* am wohlsten) [zufrieden] well; **sich wohl fühlen** [gesundheitlich] to feel well; [angenehm] to feel at home; **wohl oder übel** [like it or not - **2.** [wahrscheinlich] probably; **das ist wohl möglich** quite possibly; **du bist wohl wahnsinnig!** you must be crazy! - **3.** [zum Ausdruck der Unbeantwortbarkeit]: **ob sie wohl gut angekommen sind?** I wonder if they have arrived safely - **4.** (*kompar* besser, *superl* am besten) geh [gut] well; **er weiß sehr wohl, dass...** he knows perfectly well that... ➠ **wohl aber** *konj* but.

Wohl *das* well-being; **zum Wohle der Allgemeinheit** for the common good; **zum Wohl!** cheers!

wohlbehalten *adv* safe and sound.

Wohlfahrt *die* welfare.

wohlhabend *adj* well-to-do.

wohlig ◇ *adj* [Wärme, Gefühl] pleasant; [Seufzer] contented. ◇ *adv* contentedly.

Wohlstand *der* affluence.

wohltätig *adj* charitable.

wohlverdient *adj* well-earned.

wohlwollend ◇ *adj* benevolent. ◇ *adv* benevolently.

wohnen *vi* to live; **wir wohnen vorübergehend bei Freunden** we're staying with friends at the moment; **zur Miete wohnen** to rent, to live in rented accommodation.

Wohngemeinschaft *die* shared flat/house; **in einer Wohngemeinschaft wohnen** to share a flat/house.

wohnhaft *adj amt* resident.

Wohnhaus *das* house.

Wohnheim *das* [für Studenten] hall of residence; [für Obdachlose] hostel.

wohnlich ◇ *adj* homely. ◇ *adv* in a homely way.

Wohnmobil (*pl* -e) *das* camper UK, RV US.

Wohnort *der* place of residence.

Wohnsitz *der* place of residence.

Wohnung (*pl* -en) *die* flat UK, apartment US.

Wohnungsbau *der* housebuilding.

Wohnungsnot *die* housing shortage.

Wohnungssuche *die* flat-hunting.

Wohnviertel *das* residential area.

Wohnwagen *der* caravan UK, trailer US.

Wohnzimmer *das* living room.

Wölbung (*pl* -en) *die* [von Himmel] dome; [von Oberfläche] curvature.

Wolf (*pl* Wölfe) *der* - **1.** [Tier] wolf - **2.** *fam* [Fleischwolf] mincer; **jn durch den Wolf drehen** *fig* to give sb a hard time.

Wolke (*pl* -n) *die* cloud; **aus allen Wolken fallen** *fig* to be astounded.

Wolkenbruch *der* cloudburst.

Wolkenkratzer *der* skyscraper.

wolkig *adj* cloudy.

Wolldecke *die* blanket.

Wolle *die* wool; **aus Wolle** woollen; **sich in die Wolle kriegen** *fam fig* to start arguing.

wollen (*präs* will, *prät* wollte, *perf* hat gewollt ODER wollen) ◇ *aux* (*perf* hat wollen): **er will anrufen** he wants to make a call; **wollen wir aufstehen?** shall we get up?; **ich wollte gerade gehen, da ...** I was just about to go when ...; **was willst du damit sagen?** what do you mean by that?; **diese Entscheidung will überlegt sein** this decision needs to be thought through. ◇ *vi* (*perf* hat gewollt): **das Kind will nicht** the child doesn't want to; **sie will nach Hause** she wants to go home; **ich wollte, es wäre nur schon vorbei** I wish it were over; **dann wollen wir mal!** *fam* let's do it!; **ganz wie du willst** *fam* it's up to you! ◇ *vt* *(perf hat gewollt)* - 1. [gen] to want; **ich will ein Eis** I want an ice-cream; **mach, was du willst** do as you like; **wollen, dass jd etw tut** to want sb to do sthg; **was willst du mit dem Messer?** what do you want a knife for?; **von jm etwas wollen** *fam* to fancy sb - 2. *fam* [brauchen] to need; **da ist nichts (mehr) zu wollen** *fam* there's nothing that we/etc can do about it.

Wollknäuel *das* ball of wool.

womit *pron* [Interrogativpronomen] what... with; **womit habe ich das verdient?** what did I do to deserve that?

womöglich *adv* possibly.

wonach *pron* [als Frage] for what; **wonach suchst du?** what are you looking for?; **wonach schmeckt es?** what does it taste of?

woran *pron* [Interrogativpronomen] what... on; **woran denkst du?** what are you thinking about?

worauf *pron* [Interrogativpronomen] what... on; **worauf wartest du?** what are you waiting for?

woraus *pron* [Interrogativpronomen] what... from; **woraus ist die Tasche?** what is the bag made of?

worin *pron* [Interrogativpronomen] what... in; **worin besteht der Unterschied?** what's the difference?

Workout *das* SPORT workout.

World Wide Web [wɜːld waɪd web] *das* EDV World Wide Web; **im World Wide Web** on the (World Wide) Web.

Wort *(pl* **-e** ODER **Wörter)** *das* - 1. *(pl* **Wörter)** [sprachliche Einheit] word; **Wort für Wort** word for word - 2. *(pl* **Worte)** [Äußerung] word; **etw aufs Wort glauben** to believe every word of sthg; **kein Wort sagen/glauben** not to say/believe a word; **mir fehlen die Worte!** I'm speechless!; **mit anderen Worten** in other words; **sie ließ mich nicht zu Wort kommen** she wouldn't let me speak ODER have my say - 3. *(pl* **Worte)** [Zitat] quotation - 4. *(pl* **Worte)** **geh** [Text] words *Pl* - 5. *(ohne pl)* [Zusage] word; **jm sein Wort geben** to give sb one's word; **das Wort haben/erteilen/ergreifen** to have/give/take the floor; **ein geflügeltes Wort** a well-known quotation; **für jn ein gutes Wort einlegen** to put in a good word for sb.

Wortart *die* GRAMM part of speech.

wortbrüchig *adj*: **wortbrüchig werden** to break one's word.

Wörterbuch *das* dictionary.

wortgewandt ◇ *adj* eloquent. ◇ *adv* eloquently.

wortkarg ◇ *adj* laconic. ◇ *adv* laconically.

wörtlich ◇ *adj* word-for-word. ◇ *adv* [übersetzen] word for word; **etw wörtlich nehmen** to take sthg literally.

wortlos ◇ *adj* silent. ◇ *adv* without a word.

Wortspiel *das* pun.

worüber *pron* [Interrogativpronomen] what... about; **worüber lachst du?** what are you laughing about?

worum *pron* [Interrogativpronomen] what... about; **worum geht es?** what's it about?

worunter *pron* [Interrogativpronomen] under what; **worunter hat er gelitten?** what did he suffer from?

wovor *pron* [Interrogativpronomen] what... of; **wovor hast du Angst?** what are you frightened of?

wozu *pron* [Interrogativpronomen] why; **wozu dient dieser Schalter?** what's this switch for?

Wrack *(pl* **-s** ODER **-e)** *das* wreck.

WS *abk für* **Wintersemester**.

WSV *abk für* **Winterschlussverkauf**.

Wucher *der abw* extortion; **fünf Euro für ein Sandwich? das ist Wucher!** five euros for a sandwich? that's daylight robbery!

wuchern *(perf* **hat/ist gewuchert)** *vi* - 1. *(ist)* [wild wachsen] to grow uncontrollably - 2. *(hat)* [Wucher treiben] to profiteer.

Wucherpreis *der abw* extortionate price.

wuchs [vuːks] *prät* ▷ **wachsen**.

Wuchs [vuːks] *der* - 1. [Wachstum] growth - 2. [Gestalt] stature.

Wucht *die* force; **mit voller Wucht gegen einen Baum fahren** to smash into a tree.

wuchtig *adj* - 1. [plump] massive - 2. [Schlag, Stoß] violent.

wühlen *vi* - 1. [graben] to dig - 2. [stöbern] to rummage; **in etw (D) wühlen** *fam* to rummage through sthg. ◆ **sich wühlen** *ref* [sich graben] to burrow; **sich in etw (A) wühlen** to dig into sthg.

Wulst *(pl* **Wülste)** *der* roll.

wund ◇ *adj* sore. ◇ *adv*: **sich die Füße wund laufen** to walk until one's feet are sore.

Wunde *(pl* **-n)** *die* wound.

Wunder *(pl* **-)** *das* miracle; **Wunder wirken** to work wonders; **kein Wunder!** no wonder!; **er glaubt, er sei Wunder was für ein toller Kerl** *fam* he thinks he's God's gift.

wunderbar ◇ *adj* - 1. [großartig] wonderful - 2. [übernatürlich] miraculous. ◇ *adv* [großartig] wonderfully.

Wunderkind *das* child prodigy.

wunderlich ◇ *adj* strange. ◇ *adv* strangely.

wundern *vt* to surprise. ◆ **sich wundern** *ref*: **sich (über jn/etw) wundern** to be surprised (at sb/sthg); **du wirst dich noch wundern** you're in for a nasty surprise.

wunderschön ◇ adj beautiful. ◇ adv beautifully.

Wunsch (pl Wünsche) der wish; **nach Wunsch verlaufen** to go as planned; **die besten Wünsche für etw** best wishes for sthg.

wünschen vt - **1.** [haben wollen]: **sich** (D) **etw wünschen** to want sthg; **was wünschst du dir zum Geburtstag?** what would you like for your birthday?; **wünsch dir etwas** make a wish; **(sich** (D)**) wünschen, dass...** to hope that...; **ich wünschte, das wäre schon zu Ende** I wish it was already over - **2.** [erhoffen]: **jm etw wünschen** to wish sb sthg - **3.** [verlangen] to want; **ich wünsche eine Auskunft** I would like some information; **wie viel Kilo wünschen Sie?** how many kilos would you like?; **ich wünsche das nicht, dass du so spät heimkommst** I don't want you coming home so late; **was wünschen Sie?** can I help you?; **wünschen, dass jd etw macht** to want sb to do sthg - **4.** [zu erhoffen]: **es ist zu wünschen, dass...** it is to be hoped that... - **5.** [an einen Ort]: **jn weit weg wünschen** to wish sb far away; **zu wünschen übrig lassen** to leave a lot to be desired; **ganz wie Sie wünschen!** certainly!

wünschenswert adj desirable.

Wunsch|traum der dream.

Wunsch|zettel der ≃ letter to Santa Claus (asking for presents).

wurde prät ▷ **werden**.

Würde (pl -n) die [Selbstachtung] dignity; **unter js Würde sein** to be beneath sb.

würdig ◇ adj - **1.** [würdevoll] dignified - **2.** [entsprechend] worthy; **einer Sache** (G) **würdig sein** to be worthy of sthg. ◇ adv - **1.** [würdevoll] with dignity - **2.** [entsprechend] appropriately.

würdigen vt - **1.** [mit Auszeichnung] to honour; [in Ansprache] to pay tribute to - **2.** [schätzen] to appreciate.

Wurf (pl Würfe) der - **1.** [Werfen] throw - **2.** [bei Säugetieren] litter.

Würfel (pl -) der - **1.** [Kubus] cube - **2.** [Spielwürfel] dice.

würfeln ◇ vi [Würfel werfen] to throw the dice. ◇ vt - **1.** [mit dem Würfel] to throw - **2.** [in Würfel schneiden] to dice.

Würfel|zucker der (ohne pl) sugar cubes Pl.

würgen ◇ vt [Subj: Person] to strangle; [Subj: Krawatte] to choke. ◇ vi - **1.** [schlucken]: **an etw** (D) **würgen** to choke on sthg - **2.** [Brechreiz haben] to retch.

Wurm (pl Würmer) der worm.

wurmstichig adj worm-ridden.

Wurst (pl Würste) die - **1.** [gen] sausage - **2.** [Aufschnitt] cold meats Pl; **es ist mir Wurst** fam I couldn't care less.

Würstchen (pl -) das - **1.** [kleine Wurst] frankfurter-style sausage - **2.** fam [unwichtige Person] nobody; **ein armes Würstchen** a poor thing.

Würze (pl -n) die seasoning; fig spice.

Wurzel (pl -n) die [gen & MATH] root; **Wurzeln schlagen** eigtl & fig to put down roots.

würzen vt - **1.** [Speise] to season - **2.** [Bericht] to spice up.

würzig adj [gut gewürzt] well-seasoned; [Bier] rich; [stark duftend] aromatic.

wusch prät ▷ **waschen**.

wusste prät ▷ **wissen**.

wüst ◇ adj - **1.** [vereinsamt - Gegend] desolate - **2.** [wirr - Haare] wild; [- Durcheinander] chaotic - **3.** abw [Schlägerei, Beschimpfung] savage. ◇ adv - **1.** [wirr] chaotically - **2.** abw [fluchen, schimpfen] savagely.

Wüste (pl -n) die desert.

Wut die rage; **eine Wut auf jn haben** to be furious with sb; **seine Wut an jm/etw auslassen** to vent one's anger on sb/sthg.

wüten vi to rage.

wütend ◇ adj furious; **auf** ODER **über jn wütend sein** to be furious with sb. ◇ adv furiously.

WWW abk für **World Wide Web**.

x (pl -), **X** (pl -) [ɪks] das x, X.

X-Beine Pl knock-knees.

x-beliebig adj fam any old.

x-mal adv fam countless times.

y (pl - ODER -s), **Y** (pl - ODER -s) ['ypsilɔn] das y, Y.

Yacht [jaxt] (pl -en) die = **Jacht**.

Yoga, Joga ['joːga] der ODER das yoga.

Z

z (*pl* - ODER -s), **Z** (*pl* - ODER -s) [tsɛt] *das* z, Z.
zack *interj fam* pow!
Zacke (*pl* -n) *die* [von Gabel, Harke] prong; [von Stern] point.
zackig ◇ *adj* - 1. [gezackt - Felsen, Kante, Blatt] jagged; [- Stern] pointed - 2. *fam* [forsch] brisk. ◇ *adv* - 1. [gezackt] jaggedly - 2. *fam* [forsch] briskly.
zaghaft ◇ *adj* hesitant. ◇ *adv* hesitantly.
zäh ◇ *adj* - 1. [widerstandsfähig] tough - 2. [zähflüssig] thick - 3. [hartnäckig] tenacious. ◇ *adv* - 1. [langsam] slowly - 2. [hartnäckig] firmly.
Zähigkeit *die* - 1. [von Material] toughness - 2. [von Mensch] tenacity.
Zahl (*pl* -en) *die* number; römische Zahlen Roman numerals; wir haben keine genauen Zahlen we don't have exact figures; eine gerade/ungerade Zahl an even/odd number; in den roten/schwarzen Zahlen sein *fig* to be in the red/black.
zahlbar *adj* payable; zahlbar an/in payable to/in.
zahlen ◇ *vt* - 1. [gen] to pay - 2. [Taxi, Hotelzimmer, Reparatur] to pay for. ◇ *vi* to pay; bitte zahlen! the bill, please! *UK*, the check, please! *US*
zählen ◇ *vt* - 1. [die Anzahl ermitteln] to count - 2. [rechnen]: etw zu etw zählen to count sthg as sthg - 3. [wert sein] to be worth. ◇ *vi* - 1. [gen] to count - 2. [gehören]: Monet zählt zu meinen Lieblingsmalern Monet is one of my favourite painters - 3. [vertrauen]: auf jn/etw zählen to count on sb/sthg.
zahlenmäßig ◇ *adj* numerical. ◇ *adv*: zahlenmäßig überlegen sein to have a numerical advantage.
Zähler (*pl* -) *der* - 1. [Gerät] meter - 2. MATH numerator.
Zahlgrenze *die* fare stage.
zahllos *adj* innumerable.
zahlreich ◇ *adj* numerous. ◇ *adv* in great numbers.
Zahlung (*pl* -en) *die* payment.
Zählung (*pl* -en) *die* count; [der Bevölkerung] census.
Zahlungsanweisung *die* money transfer order.
zahlungsfähig *adj* solvent.
Zahlwort (*pl* -wörter) *das* GRAMM numeral.
zahm ◇ *adj* tame. ◇ *adv* tamely.

zähmen *vt* - 1. [Tier, Natur] to tame - 2. *geh* [Neugier, Ungeduld] to curb; [Kinder] to control.
Zähmung (*pl* -en) *die* - 1. [von Tier] taming - 2. [von Neugier, Ungeduld] curbing.
Zahn (*pl* Zähne) *der* [im Mund] tooth; einen Zahn ziehen to extract a tooth; sich einen Zahn ziehen lassen to have a tooth out; sich (D) die Zähne putzen to clean ODER brush one's teeth; die dritten Zähne [Gebiss] false teeth; die Zähne zusammenbeißen *fam* to grit one's teeth; jm einen Zahn ziehen to pour cold water on sb's idea.
Zahnarzt *der* dentist.
Zahnärztin *die* dentist.
Zahnbürste *die* toothbrush.
Zahnersatz *der* (ohne *pl*) false teeth *Pl*.
Zahnfleisch *das* (ohne *pl*) gums *Pl*.
Zahnlücke *die* gap in one's teeth.
Zahnpasta (*pl* -pasten), **Zahnpaste** (*pl* -n) *die* toothpaste.
Zahnrad *das* cog.
Zahnradbahn *die* cog railway.
Zahnschmelz *der* (tooth) enamel.
Zahnschmerzen *Pl* toothache (*U*); Zahnschmerzen haben to have toothache.
Zahnseide *die* dental floss.
Zahnspange *die* brace.
Zahnstein *der* tartar.
Zahnstocher (*pl* Zahnstocher) *der* toothpick.
Zange (*pl* -n) *die* pliers *Pl*; [Beißzange, von Insekt] pincers *Pl*; [für Kohlen, Zucker] tongs *Pl*; MED forceps *Pl*; jn in die Zange nehmen *fam fig* to put the screws on sb.
zanken ◆ sich zanken *ref*: sich (mit jm um etw) zanken to quarrel (with sb about sthg).
Zäpfchen (*pl* -) *das* [Medikament] suppository.
zapfen *vt*: ein großes Bier zapfen ≈ to pull a pint.
Zapfen (*pl* -) *der* - 1. [aus Holz] tenon - 2. [von Bäumen] cone - 3. [aus Eis] icicle.
Zapfenstreich *der*: um 23 Uhr ist Zapfenstreich lights out is at eleven o'clock.
Zapfsäule *die* petrol *UK* ODER gas *US* pump.
zappeln *vi* to wriggle; auf seinem Stuhl zappeln to fidget in one's chair; jn zappeln lassen *fam fig* to let sb sweat.
zappen *vi* to channel-hop.
zart ◇ *adj* - 1. [gen] delicate - 2. [weich - Haut] soft; [- Fleisch, Gemüse, Pflänzchen] tender - 3. [Gebäck] fine - 4. [Berührung, Kuss] gentle; [Farbton] soft. ◇ *adv* [berühren, küssen, lächeln] gently.
zart besaitet *adj* very sensitive.
zartbitter *adj* [Schokolade] dark.

zärtlich <> *adj* tender, affectionate; [Fürsorge] loving; **zu jm zärtlich sein** to be tender ODER affectionate towards sb. <> *adv* tenderly, affectionately.

Zärtlichkeit *(pl -en) die* [Gefühl] tenderness. ➤ **Zärtlichkeiten** *Pl* [Liebkosungen] caresses.

Zauber *(pl -) der* magic; **das ist doch fauler Zauber!** *fam abw* that's a con!

Zauberei *(pl -en) die* magic.

Zauberer *(pl -) der* magician.

Zauber|formel *die* [Zauberspruch] (magic) spell.

zauberhaft <> *adj* enchanting. <> *adv* enchantingly.

Zauberin *(pl -nen) die* magician.

Zauber|künstler, in *der, die* magician.

Zauberkunst|stück *das* magic trick.

zaubern <> *vi* to do magic. <> *vt:* **etw aus etw zaubern** *fig* to conjure sthg from sthg.

Zauber|spruch *der* (magic) spell.

Zauber|stab *der* magic wand.

Zaum *(pl Zäume) der* bridle; **sich/etw im Zaum halten** to keep o.s./sthg in check.

zäumen *vt* to bridle.

Zaumzeug *(pl -e) das* bridle.

Zaun *(pl Zäune) der* fence.

Zaun|pfahl *der* fencepost.

z. B. *(abk für zum Beispiel)* e.g.

ZDF [tsɛtdeːˈʔɛf] *(abk für Zweites Deutsches Fernsehen) das* second German public television channel.

Zebra *(pl -s) das* zebra.

Zebra|streifen *der* zebra crossing UK, crosswalk US.

Zeder *(pl -n) die* cedar.

Zeh *(pl -en) der* toe.

Zehe *(pl -n) die* - **1.** [Fußglied] toe; **jm auf die Zehen treten** *fam fig* to tread on sb's toes - **2.** [Knoblauchzehe] clove.

Zehen|nagel *der* toenail.

Zehen|spitze *die* tip of one's toes; **auf Zehenspitzen** on tiptoe.

zehn *num* ten; *siehe auch* **sechs**.

Zehn *(pl -en) die; siehe auch* **Sechs**.

Zehner|karte *die* book of ten tickets.

Zehneuro|schein *der* ten-euro note UK ODER bill US.

zehnfach <> *adj* tenfold. <> *adv* ten times.

Zehn|kampf *der* SPORT decathlon.

zehnmal *adv* ten times.

zehntausend *num* ten thousand; *siehe auch* **sechs**.

zehnte, r, s *adj* tenth; *siehe auch* **sechste**.

Zehnte *(pl -n) der, die, das* tenth; *siehe auch* **Sechste**.

zehntel *adj (unver)* tenth; *siehe auch* **sechstel**.

Zehntel *(pl -) das* tenth; *siehe auch* **Sechstel**.

Zehntel|sekunde *die* tenth of a second.

zehren *vi:* **von etw zehren** to live on sthg.

Zeichen *(pl -) das* - **1.** [gen] sign; **jm ein Zeichen geben** to give sb a signal ODER sign; **zum Zeichen seiner Dankbarkeit** as a token of his appreciation; **zum Zeichen, dass sie ihm folgen solle** to let her know that she should follow him - **2.** [Symbol] symbol - **3.** [Tierkreiszeichen] (star) sign - **4.** EDV character.

Zeichen|block *(pl -blöcke ODER -s) der* drawing pad.

Zeichener|klärung *die* key.

Zeichen|papier *das* drawing paper.

Zeichen|setzung *die* punctuation.

Zeichen|sprache *die* sign language.

Zeichentrick|film *der* cartoon.

zeichnen <> *vt* - **1.** [darstellen] to draw - **2.** [kennzeichnen] to mark; **das Fell ist interessant gezeichnet** its coat has interesting markings - **3.** [unterzeichnen - Scheck] to sign; [- Aktien, Anleihe] to subscribe. <> *vi* to draw.

Zeichner, in *(mpl -, fpl -nen) der, die* draughtsman (draughtswoman *die*).

Zeichnung *(pl -en) die* - **1.** [Bild] drawing - **2.** [von Fell, Tier, Blüte] markings *Pl.*

Zeige|finger *der* index finger.

zeigen <> *vt* - **1.** [gen] to show; **jm etw zeigen** to show sb sthg; **den Gästen die neue Wohnung zeigen** to show the guests round the new flat; **der habe ich es gezeigt!** *fam* I showed her! - **2.** [Uhr] to say; [Waage] to read. <> *vi* to point; **nach Südost zeigen** to point south-east; **auf jn/etw zeigen** to point at sb/sthg.** ➤ **sich zeigen** *ref* - **1.** [sich verhalten] to show o.s.; **sich nachsichtig zeigen** to show lenience, to show o.s. to be lenient - **2.** [sich präsentieren]: **sich in der Öffentlichkeit zeigen** to appear in public - **3.** [erkennbar werden]: **schon zeigen sich die ersten Fehler** the first mistakes are already starting to appear; **es hat sich gezeigt, dass...** it has been shown ODER demonstrated that...; **es wird sich zeigen, ob...** time will tell whether...

Zeiger *(pl -) der* hand.

Zeile *(pl -n) die* - **1.** [von Texten] line - **2.** [Nachricht]: **jm ein paar Zeilen schreiben** to drop sb a line.

Zeit *(pl -en) die* - **1.** [gen] time; **in letzter Zeit** lately; **im Laufe der Zeit** in the course of time; **von Zeit zu Zeit** from time to time; **die Zeit stoppen** to stop the clock; **Zeit raubend** time-consuming; **Zeit sparend** time-saving; **sich (D) für jn/etw Zeit nehmen** to spend time on sb/sthg; **sich (D) die Zeit (mit Kartenspielen) vertreiben** to pass the time (playing cards); **sich (D) Zeit lassen** to take one's time - **2.** GRAMM tense - **3.** [Zeitung]: **Die Zeit** *weekly German* *newspaper.* ◆ **auf Zeit** *adv* temporarily. ◆ **eine Zeit lang** *adv* for a while. ◆ **mit der Zeit** *adv* - 1. in time - 2. = **zurzeit**.

Zeit|alter *das* age.

Zeit|ansage *die* speaking clock.

Zeit|arbeit *die* temporary work.

Zeit|bombe *die* *eigtl* & *fig* time bomb.

Zeit|druck *der:* in Zeitdruck sein, unter Zeitdruck stehen to be under time pressure.

Zeit|geist *der* spirit of the times, zeitgeist.

zeitgemäß *adj* contemporary, modern.

Zeit|genosse *der* contemporary.

Zeit|genossin *die* contemporary.

Zeit|geschehen *das (ohne pl)* current affairs *Pl*.

zeitig *adj* & *adv* early.

zeitlebens *adv* all my/his/her/*etc* life.

zeitlich ⟷ *adj* chronological. ⟷ *adv:* zeitlich begrenzt sein to be of limited duration.

Zeitliche *das:* das Zeitliche segnen to give up the ghost.

zeitlos *adj* timeless.

Zeit|lupe ◆ in Zeitlupe *adv* TV in slow motion.

Zeit|punkt *der* time; etw zum richtigen Zeitpunkt tun to do sthg at the right moment *ODER* time; zu diesem Zeitpunkt at this point in time.

Zeit|raffer *der* time-lapse photography.

Zeit|raum *der* period.

Zeit|rechnung *die:* vor unserer Zeitrechnung Before Christ; nach unserer Zeitrechnung Anno Domini.

Zeit|schrift *die* [Illustrierte] magazine; [wissenschaftlich] journal.

Zeit|soldat *der soldier who enlists for a fixed period of time.*

Zeit|spanne *die* timespan.

Zeitung *(pl -en) die* newspaper.

Zeitungs|annonce *die* newspaper advertisement.

Zeitungs|ausschnitt *der* newspaper cutting.

Zeitungs|bericht *der* newspaper report.

Zeitungs|kiosk *der* newspaper kiosk.

Zeitungs|papier *das* newspaper.

Zeit|unterschied *der* time difference.

Zeit|verlust *der* lost time.

Zeit|verschiebung *die* time difference.

Zeit|verschwendung *die* waste of time.

Zeit|vertrag *der* fixed-term *ODER* temporary contract.

Zeit|vertreib *(pl -e) der* pastime; zum Zeitvertreib to pass the time.

zeitweilig ⟷ *adj* temporary. ⟷ *adv* from time to time, on and off.

zeitweise *adv* - 1. [gelegentlich] occasionally - 2. [vorübergehend] temporarily.

Zelle *(pl -n) die* cell.

Zell|stoff *der* cellulose.

Zelt *(pl -e) das* tent; die Zelte abbrechen *fig* to up sticks; die Zelte aufschlagen *fig* to settle.

zelten *vi* to camp.

Zelt|lager *das* camp.

Zelt|platz *der* campsite.

Zelt|stange *die* tent pole.

Zement *der* cement.

zensieren ⟷ *vt* - 1. [benoten] to mark - 2. [kontrollieren] to censor. ⟷ *vi* to mark.

Zensur *(pl -en) die* - 1. [Benotung] mark - 2. [Kontrolle] censorship - 3. [Behörde] censorship board, censors *Pl*.

Zentilliter *(pl -) der* centilitre.

Zentimeter *(pl -) der* centimetre.

Zentimeter|maß *das* tape measure.

Zentner *(pl -) der unit of measurement equivalent to 50 kg in Germany and 100 kg in Austria and Switzerland.*

zentral ⟷ *adj* central. ⟷ *adv* [wohnen, gelegen] centrally.

Zentral|afrika *nt* Central Africa.

Zentrale *(pl -n) die* - 1. [zentrale Stelle] headquarters *Pl* - 2. [Telefonzentrale] switchboard.

Zentral|heizung *die* central heating.

Zentrifuge *(pl -n) die* centrifuge.

Zentrum *(pl Zentren) das* centre.

Zeppelin *(pl -e) der* zeppelin.

zerbrechen *(präs zerbricht, prät zerbrach, perf hat/ist zerbrochen)* ⟷ *vi (ist)* [Glas, Vase] to break into pieces, to smash; [Freundschaft, Ehe] to break up; an etw (D) zerbrechen *fig* to be broken by sthg. ⟷ *vt (hat)* to smash.

zerbrechlich *adj* fragile.

zerdrücken *vt* [Kartoffeln, Bananen] to mash; [Knoblauch, Insekt] to crush.

Zeremonie *(pl -n) die* ceremony.

Zerfall *der* [von Gebäude, Denkmal] decay; [von Moral, Diktatur] decline.

zerfallen *(präs zerfällt, prät zerfiel, perf ist zerfallen)* *vi* to disintegrate; [Mauer, Kuchen, Reich] to crumble; [Molekül] to decay; in etw (A) zerfallen [Molekül] to decay into sthg; [Mauer, Kuchen] to crumble into sthg.

zerfetzen *vt* to tear to pieces; [Brief] to tear up.

zerfleddern *vt* to make tatty.

zerfließen *(prät zerfloss, perf ist zerflossen)* *vi* - 1. [schmelzen] to melt - 2. [auseinander fließen] to run.

zergehen *(prät zerging, perf ist zergangen)* *vi* to melt; etw im Mund zergehen lassen to allow sthg to dissolve in one's mouth.

zerkleinern *vt* to cut up; [mit Gabel] to mash.

zerklüftet *adj* [Landschaft, Tal] rugged; [Felsen] jagged.

zerknirscht *adj* remorseful; **über etw (A) zerknirscht sein** to be full of remorse for sthg.

zerknittern *vt* to crumple.

zerkratzen *vt* to scratch.

zerlegen *vt* - **1.** [auseinander nehmen] to take apart; **etw in (seine) Einzelteile zerlegen** to dismantle sthg into its constituent parts - **2.** [Geflügel, Wild] to carve up.

zermürben *vt* to wear down.

zerquetschen *vt* to crush; [Kartoffeln] to mash.

zerreißen (*prät* zerriss, *perf* hat/ist zerrissen) ⟨⟩ *vt (hat)* - **1.** [in Stücke] to tear to pieces; [Brief] to tear up - **2.** [Strümpfe, Hose] to tear. ⟨⟩ *vi (ist)* to tear.

zerren ⟨⟩ *vt* to drag; **sich (D) einen Muskel zerren** to pull a muscle. ⟨⟩ *vi*: **an etw (D) zerren** to pull on sthg.

zerrinnen (*prät* zerronn, *perf* ist zerronnen) *vi* - **1.** [Butter] to melt - **2.** [Träume] to fade away - **3.** [Zeit] to slip by.

Zerrung (*pl* -en) *die* pulled muscle ODER ligament.

zerrüttet *adj* [Gesundheit] ruined; [Ehe] broken; **aus zerrütteten Verhältnissen** from a broken home.

zerschlagen *adj* shattered.

zerschneiden (*prät* zerschnitt, *perf* hat zerschnitten) *vt* - **1.** [in Stücke] to cut up - **2.** [verletzen] to cut.

zersetzen *vt* - **1.** [Subj: Säure, Rost] to corrode; [Subj: Fäulnis] to decompose - **2.** [untergraben] to undermine. ◆ **sich zersetzen** *ref* [durch Säure, Rost] to corrode; [durch Fäulnis] to decompose.

zersplittern (*perf* ist zersplittert) *vi* [Holz, Knochen] to splinter; [Glas, Fenster] to shatter.

zerspringen (*prät* zersprang, *perf* ist zersprungen) *vi* to shatter.

zerstäuben *vt* to spray.

Zerstäuber (*pl* -) *der* atomizer.

zerstechen (*präs* zersticht, *prät* zerstach, *perf* hat zerstochen) *vt* - **1.** [beschädigen] to puncture - **2.** [Subj: Insekten] to bite all over.

zerstören *vt* to destroy.

zerstörerisch *adj* destructive.

Zerstörung (*pl* -en) *die* destruction.

zerstreuen *vt* - **1.** [Blätter] to scatter - **2.** [Demonstranten] to disperse - **3.** [vom Alltag ablenken] to distract - **4.** [Zweifel] to dispel. ◆ **sich zerstreuen** *ref* - **1.** [Menschenmenge] to disperse - **2.** [sich vom Alltag ablenken] to distract o.s.

zerstreut ⟨⟩ *adj* absent-minded. ⟨⟩ *adv* absent-mindedly.

Zerstreuung (*pl* -en) *die* distraction.

Zertifikat (*pl* -e) *das* certificate.

zertreten (*präs* zertritt, *prät* zertrat, *perf* hat zertreten) *vt* [Insekt] to stamp on; [Zigarettenkippe] to stub out with one's foot.

zertrümmern *vt* [Schrank, Felsbrocken] to smash up; [Spiegel] to smash.

zerzaust *adj* [Haare] dishevelled.

Zettel (*pl* -) *der* piece of paper; [Nachricht] note; [Einkaufszettel] (shopping) list.

Zeug *das fam* [Sachen] stuff; [Kleidung] gear; **das Zeug zu etw haben** *fam fig* to have the makings of sthg; **wir müssen uns ins Zeug legen** we're going to have to put our backs into it. ◆ **dummes Zeug** *interj fam* rubbish!

Zeuge (*pl* -n) *der* witness.

zeugen ⟨⟩ *vi*: **von etw zeugen** *geh* to show sthg. ⟨⟩ *vt* to father.

Zeugenaussage *die* statement.

Zeugin (*pl* -nen) *die* witness.

Zeugnis (*pl* -se) *das* - **1.** [von Arbeitgeber] reference - **2.** [von Prüfung] certificate - **3.** SCHULE report.

z. H. (*abk für* zu Händen) attn.

Zickzack (*pl* -e) *der* zigzag. ◆ **im Zickzack** *adv*: **im Zickzack laufen/fahren** to zigzag.

Ziege (*pl* -n) *die* - **1.** [Tier] goat - **2.** *fam* [als Schimpfwort] cow.

Ziegel (*pl* -) *der* - **1.** [Stein] brick - **2.** [Dachziegel] tile.

Ziegelstein *der* brick.

Ziegenbock *der* billy goat.

Ziegenkäse *der* goat's cheese.

ziehen (*prät* zog, *perf* hat/ist gezogen) ⟨⟩ *vt (hat)* - **1.** [gen] to pull; [Subj: Tier - Karren] to draw; **etw durch etw ziehen** to pull sthg through sthg; **etw von etw ziehen** to pull sthg off sthg; **jn am Ärmel ziehen** to tug sb's sleeve; **jn an den Haaren ziehen** to pull sb's hair - **2.** [herausziehen - Zahn, Korken] to pull out; [- Rüben, Unkraut] to pull up - **3.** MED [Fäden] to take out - **4.** [Brieftasche, Waffe] to take out; [Hut] to doff; **etw aus etw ziehen** to take sthg out of sthg - **5.** [zeichnen] to draw - **6.** [züchten - Pflanzen] to grow; [- Tiere] to breed - **7.** [anziehen]: **Aufmerksamkeit auf sich (A) ziehen** to draw attention to o.s. - **8.** [zur Folge haben]: **etw nach sich ziehen** to lead to sthg; **Probleme nach sich ziehen** to cause problems - **9.** [aus dem Automaten] to get (*from a vending machine*) - **10.** [anlegen - Mauer, Zaun] to put up; [- Graben] to dig; [- Grenze] to draw. ⟨⟩ *vi* - **1.** *(hat)* [zerren] to pull; **an etw (D) ziehen** to pull sthg; **der Hund zog an der Leine** the dog was pulling on the lead *UK* ODER leash' *US* - **2.** *(ist)* [umziehen, sich bewegen] to move; **durch die Straßen ziehen** to wander through the streets; **eine Blaskapelle zog durchs Dorf** a brass band trooped through the village; **die Vögel ziehen nach Süden** the birds are going ODER flying south - **3.** *(hat)* [saugen]: **an etw (D) ziehen** [Pfeife, Zigarette] to take a puff on sthg

- 4. *(hat)* [Auto, Motor] to run - 5. *(ist)* [dringen]: **der Duft zog durchs ganze Haus** the scent floated throughout the house; **in etw (A) ziehen** [Flüssigkeit] to soak into sthg - 6. *(hat)* [Kaffee, Tee] to brew - 7. *(hat)* [bei Brettspiel] to move; **du musst ziehen!** it's your move! - 8. *(hat)* fam [Eindruck machen] to go down well; **das zieht bei mir nicht!** that doesn't wash with me! - 9. *(hat)* [Luftzug haben]: **es zieht** there's a draught. ◆ **sich ziehen** ref - 1. [nicht enden wollen] to drag on - 2. [sich erstrecken] to stretch.

Zieh|harmonika die concertina.

Ziehung (pl -en) die: **die Ziehung der Lottozahlen** the lottery draw; **die Ziehung der Lose** the drawing of lots.

Ziel (pl -e) das - 1. [Zielort] destination - 2. SPORT finish - 3. [Zweck] goal; **sich (D) ein Ziel setzen** to set o.s. a goal ODER target.

zielen vi to aim; **auf jn/etw zielen** to aim at sb/sthg.

Ziel|gruppe die target group.

ziellos ◇ adj aimless. ◇ adv aimlessly.

Ziel|scheibe die - 1. [beim Schießen] target - 2. [Opfer] butt.

zielstrebig ◇ adj single-minded. ◇ adv single-mindedly.

ziemlich ◇ adj fam: **mit ziemlicher Genugtuung/Sicherheit** with some satisfaction/certainty; **das war eine ziemliche Gemeinheit** that was a rather mean thing to do. ◇ adv - 1. [sehr] quite; **ziemlich viel** quite a lot - 2. fam [fast] almost.

Zierde (pl -n) die decoration.

zieren ◆ **sich zieren** ref to be coy.

zierlich ◇ adj [Person] petite; [Hände] dainty; [Porzellanfigur] delicate. ◇ adv daintily.

Zier|pflanze die ornamental plant.

Ziffer (pl -n) die figure.

Ziffer|blatt das face.

zig adj fam umpteen.

Zigarette (pl -n) die cigarette.

Zigaretten|automat der cigarette machine.

Zigaretten|schachtel die cigarette packet.

Zigarillo (pl -s) der ODER das cigarillo.

Zigarre (pl -n) die cigar.

Zigeuner, in (mpl -, fpl -nen) der, die gypsy.

zigmal adv fam umpteen times.

Zimmer (pl -) das room; **'Zimmer frei!'** 'vacancies'.

Zimmer|lautstärke die: **in Zimmerlautstärke** at low volume.

Zimmer|mädchen das chambermaid.

Zimmer|mann (pl -leute) der carpenter.

zimmern ◇ vt to make (from wood). ◇ vi to do carpentry.

Zimmer|pflanze die house plant.

Zimmer|suche die: **auf Zimmersuche sein** to be looking for a room.

Zimmer|vermittlung die accommodation service.

zimperlich abw ◇ adj: **sei nicht so zimperlich!** don't be such a wimp!; **sie ist nicht gerade zimperlich** she doesn't exactly hold back. ◇ adv: **nicht zimperlich mit jm umgehen** not to treat sb with kid gloves.

Zimt der cinnamon.

Zink das zinc.

Zinke (pl -n) die [von Gabel] prong; [von Kamm] tooth.

Zinn das - 1. [Metall] tin - 2. [Gegenstände] pewter.

Zins (pl -en) der: **Zinsen** interest (U).

zinslos adj interest-free.

Zins|satz der interest rate.

Zipfel (pl -) der corner.

Zipfel|mütze die pointed hat.

zippen vt EDV to zip.

zirka, circa ['tsɪrka] adv about, approximately; **zirka 1900** circa 1900.

Zirkel (pl -) der - 1. [Gerät] compasses Pl - 2. [Gruppe] circle.

Zirkus (pl -se) der circus.

zischen (perf hat/ist gezischt) ◇ vi - 1. *(hat)* [Geräusch] to hiss - 2. *(ist)* [Fahrzeug] to whizz. ◇ vt *(hat)* - 1. [sagen] to hiss - 2. salopp [trinken] to knock back.

Zitat (pl -e) das quotation, quote.

zitieren ◇ vt - 1. [wiedergeben] to quote - 2. [rufen]: **jn zu jm/vor etw (A) zitieren** to summon sb to sb/before sthg. ◇ vi: **aus etw zitieren** to quote from sthg.

Zitronat das KÜCHE candied lemon peel.

Zitrone (pl -n) die lemon.

Zitronen|saft der lemon juice.

zitterig, zittrig adj shaky.

zittern vi - 1. [vibrieren - Hände, Körper] to tremble; [- Stimme] to shake; **vor Kälte zittern** to shiver with cold - 2. [Angst haben]: **vor jm/etw zittern** to be terrified of sb/sthg - 3. [sich sorgen]: **um** ODER **für jn/etw zittern** to be very worried about sb/sthg.

Zivi ['tsi:vi] (pl -s) der fam man doing his "Zivildienst".

zivil [tsi'vi:l] ◇ adj - 1. [Bevölkerung, Leben] civilian - 2. fam [Preise] reasonable. ◇ adv fam [anständig] reasonably.

Zivil [tsi'vi:l] ◆ **in Zivil** adv [Soldat] in civilian clothes; [Polizist] in plain clothes.

Zivil|bevölkerung die civilian population.

Zivil|courage die courage of one's convictions.

Zivil|dienst der community service done by conscientious objectors.

Zivilisation [tsiviliza'tsjo:n] *(pl -en) die* civilization.

zivilisiert [tsivili'zi:ɐt] *adj* civilized.

Zivilist, in [tsivi'lɪst, ɪn] *(mpl -en, fpl -nen) der, die* civilian.

Zivilrecht *das* RECHT civil law.

zog *prät* ▷ **ziehen**.

zögern *vi* to hesitate; **mit etw zögern** to delay sthg.

Zölibat *das* & *der* RELIG celibacy.

Zoll *(pl Zölle ODER -) der* - 1. *(pl Zölle)* [Abgabe] duty - 2. *(ohne pl)* [Behörde] customs *Pl* - 3. *(pl Zoll)* [Maßeinheit] inch.

Zollabfertigung *die* customs clearance.

Zollamt *das* customs office.

Zollbeamte *der* customs officer.

Zollbeamtin *die* customs officer.

zollfrei *adj* duty-free.

Zollkontrolle *die* customs check.

Zöllner *(pl -) der* customs officer.

zollpflichtig *adj* liable for duty.

Zollstock *der* folding rule.

Zone *(pl -n) die* zone.

Zoo [tso:] *(pl -s) der* zoo.

Zoologie [tsoolo'gi:] *die* zoology.

Zopf *(pl Zöpfe) der* plait *UK*, braid *US*; **Zöpfe flechten** to plait *UK* ODER braid *US* one's hair.

Zorn *der* anger. ⟶ **im Zorn** *adv* in anger.

zornig ⟨⟩ *adj* angry; **auf jn/über etw (A) zornig sein** to be angry with sb/about sthg. ⟨⟩ *adv* angrily.

zottig *adj* shaggy.

z. T. *(abk für zum Teil)* partly.

zu ⟨⟩ *präp (+ D)* - 1. [räumlich - Richtung] to; [- Position] at; **zu jm/etw hin** towards sb/sthg; **zu Hause** (at) home; **zu beiden Seiten** on both sides - 2. [zeitlich] at; **zu Beginn** at the beginning; **zu Ostern/Weihnachten** at Easter/Christmas - 3. [modal]: **zu Pferd** by horse; **zu Fuß** on foot; **zu Fuß gehen** to walk; **zu meiner großen Enttäuschung** to my great disappointment - 4. [stellt Bezug her] about - 5. [in Kombination mit] with; **stell das Glas zu den anderen** put that glass with the others - 6. [für einen bestimmten Zweck] for - 7. [mit Nennung eines Endzustandes] into; **zu Eis werden** to turn into ice - 8. [aus bestimmtem Anlass] on - 9. [in Mengenangaben]: **zu viert** in fours; **wir sind zu viert** there are four of us; **zu Tausenden** in thousands; **Säcke zu 50 kg** 50 kg bags; **Orangen zu 25 Cent das Stück** oranges at 25 cents each - 10. SPORT: **3 zu 2** 3:2. ⟨⟩ *adv* - 1. [übermäßig] too; **zu alt** too old; **zu sehr** too much - 2. *fam* [zumachen]: **Tür zu!** shut the door! - 3. [zur Angabe der Richtung] towards. ⟨⟩ *konj* - 1. (+ Infinitiv) to; **etwas zu essen** something to eat; **es fängt an zu schneien** it's starting to snow; **zu verkaufen** for sale; **ohne zu fragen** without

asking - 2. *(+ pp)* to; **die zu erledigende Sache** the matter to be dealt with. ⟶ **nur zu** *interj* go ahead!; *siehe auch* **zu sein**.

zuallererst, zuallererst *adv* first of all.

zuallerletzt, zuallerletzt *adv* last of all.

Zubehör *(pl -e) das* accessories *Pl*.

zubeißen *vi (unreg)* to bite.

zubekommen *vt (unreg)* [Tür, Koffer] to get shut.

zubereiten *vt* to prepare.

zubewegen *vt*: **etw auf jn/etw zubewegen** to move sthg towards sb/sthg. ⟶ **sich zubewegen** *ref*: **sich auf jn/etw zubewegen** to make one's way towards sb/sthg.

zubinden *vt (unreg)* to tie up.

zubleiben *(perf ist zugeblieben) vi (unreg) fam* to stay shut.

zublinzeln *vi*: **jm zublinzeln** to wink at sb.

Zubringer *(pl -) der* feeder road.

Zucchini [tsu'ki:ni] *(pl -s) die* courgette *UK*, zucchini *US*.

Zucht *(pl -en) die* - 1. [Züchten - von Tieren] breeding; [- von Pflanzen] growing; [- von Perlen] cultivation - 2. *geh* [Disziplin] discipline.

züchten *vt* [Tiere] to breed; [Pflanzen] to grow; [Bakterien, Perlen] to cultivate.

Züchtung *(pl -en) die* [Züchten - von Tieren] breeding; [- von Pflanzen] growing; [- von Bakterien, Perlen] cultivation; [Zuchtergebnis - Tiere] breed; [- Pflanzen] variety.

zucken *(perf hat/ist gezuckt) vi* - 1. *(hat)* [unwillkürlich] to twitch; **mit den Schultern zucken** to shrug (one's shoulders) - 2. *(ist)* [in eine Richtung - Flamme] to leap up; [- Blitz] to flash.

zücken *vt* - 1. *geh* [Waffe] to draw - 2. *hum* [Portmonee, Notizbuch] to whip out.

Zucker *der* - 1. [Nahrungsmittel] sugar *(U)* - 2. *fam* [Krankheit] diabetes; **Zucker haben** to be diabetic.

Zuckerguss *(pl -güsse) der* icing.

zuckerkrank *adj* diabetic.

Zuckerrohr *das* sugarcane.

Zuckerrübe *die* sugar beet.

Zuckerwatte *die* candyfloss *UK*, cotton candy *US*.

zudecken *vt* to cover; **sich/jn/etw mit etw zudecken** to cover o.s./sb/sthg with sthg.

zudrehen *vt* - 1. [schließen] to turn off - 2. [zuwenden]: **jm den Rücken zudrehen** to turn one's back on sb.

zudringlich *adj* pushy.

zudrücken *vt* [Auge, Koffer] to close; [Tür] to push shut.

zueinander *adv* to each other; **zueinander passen** to go together.

zueinander halten *vi (unreg)* to stick together.

zuerst adv - 1. [als Erstes] first - 2. [am Anfang] at first - 3. [zum ersten Mal] for the first time.

zulfahren (perf ist zugefahren) vi (unreg) - 1. [sich zubewegen]: **auf jn/etw zufahren** to drive towards sb/sthg - 2. fam: **fahr zu!** get a move on!

Zulfahrt die [Zufahrtsweg] access road; [zu einem Haus] drive.

Zufahrtslstraße die access road.

Zulfall der coincidence; **etw dem Zufall überlassen** to leave sthg to chance. ➟ **durch Zufall** adv by chance.

zulfallen (perf ist zugefallen) vi (unreg) - 1. [Tür, Deckel] to slam shut; [Augen] to close - 2.: **jm zufallen** [Preis] to go to sb; [Aufgabe] to fall to sb.

zufällig ⬦ adj chance (vor Subst). ⬦ adv by chance.

zulfassen vi: **fest zufassen** to grip tightly.

Zulflucht die refuge.

zulflüstern vt: **jm etw zuflüstern** to whisper sthg to sb.

zufolge präp: **jm/einer Sache zufolge** according to sb/sthg.

zufrieden ⬦ adj contented; [mit Befriedigung] satisfied; **mit jm/etw zufrieden sein** to be satisfied with sb/sthg. ⬦ adv contentedly.

zufrieden geben ➟ **sich zufrieden geben** ref (unreg): **sich mit etw zufrieden geben** to be satisfied with sthg.

zufrieden lassen vt (unreg) to leave in peace.

zufrieden stellen vt to satisfy.

zulfügen vt: **jm Schaden/Unrecht zufügen** to do sb harm/an injustice.

Zufuhr die [von Energie] supply; [von Luft] influx.

Zug (pl Züge) der - 1. [Bahn] train; **mit dem Zug fahren** to go by train - 2. [Schar] procession - 3. [Bewegung - von Vögeln] migration; [- von Wolken] drifting - 4. [mit Spielfigur] move; **er ist am Zug** eigtl & fig it is his move - 5. [Schluck] gulp; **in einem Zug** in one go - 6. [beim Rauchen] puff - 7. [Atemzug] breath; **in vollen Zügen** in deep breaths; fig to the full - 8. (ohne pl) [Durchzug] draught - 9. [Gesichtszug]: **Züge** features - 10. [Charakterzug] characteristic - 11. [beim Schwimmen] stroke; **in groben Zügen** in broad outline; **zum Zug(e) kommen** to get a chance.

Zulgabe die - 1. [Zugeben] addition - 2. [Zugegebenes] free gift.

Zugablteil das compartment.

Zulgang der - 1. [gen & EDV] access; **Zugang zu etw haben** to have access to sthg - 2. [Zugangsweg] entrance.

zugänglich adj - 1. [Raum, Ort] accessible - 2. [Information] available; **jm etw zugänglich machen** to make sthg available to sb - 3. [Person] approachable.

Zuglbrücke die drawbridge.

zulgeben vt (unreg) - 1. [hinzugeben] to add - 2. [gestehen] to admit.

zulgehen (perf ist zugegangen) vi (unreg) - 1. [sich zubewegen]: **auf jn/etw zugehen** to approach sb/sthg - 2. [verlaufen]: **auf der Party gehts lustig zu** the party is going with a swing - 3. fam [schneller gehen]: **geh zu!** get a move on! - 4. [sich schließen - Tür, Koffer] to close; [- Knopf, Reißverschluss] to do up.

zugehörig adj that belongs with it/them; **sich jm/einer Sache zugehörig fühlen** to feel a part of sb/sthg.

Zugehörigkeit die [zu Verein, Familie] membership.

zugeknöpft adj buttoned up.

Zügel (pl -) der reins Pl.

zügellos ⬦ adj unrestrained. ⬦ adv in an unrestrained manner.

zügeln vt - 1. [Pferd] to rein in - 2. [Gefühl] to restrain.

Zulgeständnis das concession.

zulgestehen vt (unreg): **jm etw zugestehen** [gestatten] to grant sb sthg; [zugeben] to admit sthg to sb.

Zuglführer, in der, die senior guard UK ODER conductor US.

zugig adj draughty.

zügig ⬦ adj rapid. ⬦ adv rapidly.

zugleich adv at the same time.

Zuglluft die (ohne pl) draught.

Zuglpersonal das (ohne pl) train crew.

zulgreifen vi (unreg) - 1. [zufassen] to grab it/them - 2. [sich bedienen] to help o.s. - 3. [mithelfen] to do one's bit.

zugrunde, zu Grunde adv: **an etw (D) zugrunde gehen** [sterben] to perish from sthg; [ruiniert werden] to be wrecked by sthg; **einer Sache (D) zugrunde liegen** to form the basis of sthg; **jn zugrunde richten** to ruin sb.

Zuglschaffner, in der, die ticket inspector.

Zuglunglück das train accident.

zugunsten, zu Gunsten ⬦ präp: **zugunsten js/einer Sache** in favour of sb/sthg. ⬦ adv: **zugunsten von jm/etw** in favour of sb/sthg.

zugute adv: **jm/etw zugute kommen** to prove beneficial to sb/sthg.

Zugverlbindung die train connection.

Zuglverkehr der (ohne pl) train services Pl.

zulhaben vi (unreg) fam to be shut.

Zuhälter (pl -) der pimp.

zuhause adv Schweiz & Österr at home; siehe auch **Haus**.

Zuhause das home.

zu|hören *vi* to listen; **jm/einer Sache zuhören** to listen to sb/sthg.

Zu|hörer, in *der, die* listener.

zu|kehren *vt*: **jm den Rücken zukehren** to turn one's back on sb.

zu|knöpfen *vt* to button up.

zu|kommen (*perf* ist zugekommen) *vi* (*unreg*) - 1. [sich bewegen]: **auf jn/etw zukommen** to approach sb/sthg; **etw auf sich (A) zukommen lassen** *fig* to take sthg as it comes - 2. [zustehen]: **jm zukommen** to befit sb - 3. *geh* [zuteil werden]: **etw kommt jm zu** sb receives sthg; **jm etw zukommen lassen** to send sb sthg.

Zukunft *die* [künftige Zeit & GRAMM] future.
➤ **in Zukunft** *adv* in future.

zukünftig ◇ *adj* future. ◇ *adv* in future.

zu|lächeln *vi*: **jm zulächeln** to smile at sb.

Zu|lage *die* bonus.

zu|lassen *vt* (*unreg*) - 1. [erlauben] to allow - 2. [amtlich - Medikament] to license; [- Auto] to register; **jn zu einer Prüfung zulassen** to permit sb to take an examination.

zulässig *adj* permissible.

Zulassung (*pl* -en) *die* - 1. [Zulassen - von Medikament] licensing; [- von Arzt, Auto] registration; **die Zulassung zum Studium** acceptance to study at university; **die Zulassung zur Prüfung** permission to take an examination - 2. AUTO [Schein] vehicle registration document.

zu|laufen (*perf* ist zugelaufen) *vi* (*unreg*) - 1. [sich bewegen]: **auf jn/etw zulaufen** to run towards sb/sthg - 2. [Tier]: **jm zulaufen** to adopt sb - 3. [auslaufen] to taper; **spitz zulaufen** to end in a point.

zu|legen *vt* [anschaffen]: **sich (D) etw zulegen** to get o.s. sthg.

zuletzt *adv* - 1. [gen] last - 2. [am Ende] in the end.

zuliebe *präp*: **jm zuliebe** for sb's sake; **einer Sache (D) zuliebe** for the sake of sthg.

zum *präp* - 1. (zu + dem) to the; **zum Friseur gehen** to go to the hairdresser's - 2. (untrennbar): **zum Tanzen gehen** to go dancing; **zum Teil** partly; **zum Beispiel** for example; **zum Thema** on the subject of; **Fenster zum Garten** window overlooking the garden; *siehe auch* **zu.**

zu|machen *vt & vi* to close; [Mantel] to do up.

zumindest *adv* at least.

zumutbar *adj* reasonable.

zu|muten *vt*: **jm etw zumuten** to expect sthg of sb; **das kannst du ihr nicht zumuten** you can't ask her to do that.

Zumutung (*pl* -en) *die*: **etw als Zumutung empfinden** to feel that sthg is unreasonable; **eine Zumutung sein** to be unreasonable.

zunächst [tsuˈnɛːçst] *adv* - 1. [zuerst] first - 2. [einstweilen] for the moment.

zu|nähen *vt* to sew up.

Zunahme (*pl* -n) *die* increase.

zünden ◇ *vt* [Bombe, Sprengladung] to detonate; [Triebwerk] to fire. ◇ *vi* [Triebwerk] to fire; [Treibstoff] to ignite.

zündend *adj fig* [Aussprache] rousing; [Idee] exciting.

Zünder (*pl* -) *der* detonator.

Zünd|kerze *die* AUTO spark plug.

Zünd|schlüssel *der* AUTO ignition key.

Zünd|schnur *die* fuse.

Zünd|stoff *der fig* dynamite (U).

Zündung (*pl* -en) *die* - 1. [Zünden] detonation - 2. AUTO ignition.

zu|nehmen (*unreg*) ◇ *vi* - 1. [gewinnen]: **an etw (D) zunehmen** to gain in sthg - 2. [dicker werden] to put on weight. ◇ *vt*: **5 Kilo zunehmen** to put on 5 kilos.

Zuneigung *die* affection; **Zuneigung zu jm/etw** affection for sb or sthg.

Zunft (*pl* Zünfte) *die* HIST guild.

zünftig ◇ *adj* proper. ◇ *adv* properly.

Zunge (*pl* -n) *die* tongue; **auf der Zunge zergehen** to melt in the mouth; **die Zunge herausstrecken** to stick one's tongue out; **es liegt mir auf der Zunge** *fig* it's on the tip of my tongue.

Zungen|spitze *die* tip of the tongue.

zunichte *adj*: **etw zunichte machen** to ruin sthg.

zu|nicken *vi*: **jm zunicken** to nod to sb.

zunutze, zu Nutze *adj*: **sich (D) etw zunutze machen** to take advantage of sthg.

zuoberst *adv* on top.

zu|ordnen *vt*: **jn/etw jm/einer Sache zuordnen** to assign sb/sthg to sb/sthg; **Katzen werden den Raubtieren zugeordnet** cats are classified as carnivores.

zu|packen *vi* - 1. [greifen] to grab it/them - 2. [mitarbeiten] to knuckle down to it.

zupfen ◇ *vi*: **an etw (D) zupfen** to tug at sthg. ◇ *vt* - 1. [Unkraut] to pull up - 2. [Instrument, Augenbrauen, Haar] to pluck.

zur *präp* - 1. (zu + der) to the; **zur Post gehen** to go to the post office - 2. (untrennbar): **zur Zeit** at the moment; **zur Straße liegen** to face the street; **zur allgemeinen Verwunderung** to everyone's amazement; *siehe auch* **zu.**

zurechnungsfähig *adj* of sound mind.

zurecht|finden ➤ **sich zurechtfinden** *ref* (*unreg*) to find one's way around.

zurecht|kommen (*perf* ist zurechtgekommen) *vi* (*unreg*) to get on; **mit jm zurechtkommen** to get on with sb; **mit etw zurechtkommen** to cope with sthg.

zurecht|legen *vt* - 1. [Kleidung, Werkzeug] to lay out ready - 2. [Ausrede] to get ready.

zurecht|machen vt [herrichten] to get ready. ➤ **sich zurechtmachen** ref [schminken] to put one's make-up on.

zurecht|weisen vt *(unreg)* to reprimand.

Zurecht|weisung die reprimand.

zu|reden vi: jm zureden to persuade sb; jm gut zureden to talk nicely to sb.

Zürich nt Zurich.

zu|richten vt to mess up; jn übel zurichten to beat sb up.

zurück adv - 1. [gen] back; ich bin um 5 Uhr zurück I'll be back at 5 o'clock; einmal Berlin und zurück a return to Berlin *UK*, a round-trip ticket to Berlin *US* - 2. [im Rückstand] behind.

zurück|bekommen vt *(unreg)* to get back.

zurück|bleiben *(perf ist zurückgeblieben)* vi *(unreg)* - 1. [nicht folgen] to stay behind; hinter jm/etw zurückbleiben to fall behind sb/sthg - 2. [sich nicht nähern] to keep back - 3. [mit Leistung, Ergebnis] to fall behind - 4. [Erinnerung, Schaden] to be left.

zurück|blicken vi to look back; auf etw (A) zurückblicken to look back at sthg; *fig* to look back on sthg.

zurück|bringen vt *(unreg)* to bring/take back.

zurück|erhalten vt *(unreg)* to get back.

zurück|erstatten vt: jm etw zurückerstatten to refund sb sthg.

zurück|fahren *(perf hat/ist zurückgefahren)* *(unreg)* ⬦ vi *(ist)* - 1. [zurückkehren] to go back - 2. [rückwärts fahren] to drive back. ⬦ vt *(hat)* to drive back.

zurück|fallen *(perf ist zurückgefallen)* vi *(unreg)* - 1. [gen] to fall back - 2. [in Rückstand geraten] to fall behind - 3. [zurückgegeben werden]: an jn zurückfallen to revert to sb - 4. [zurückgeführt werden]: auf jn zurückfallen to reflect on sb.

zurück|fordern vt: etw zurückfordern to ask for sthg back.

zurück|führen ⬦ vt - 1. [von etwas herleiten]: etw auf etw (A) zurückführen to put sthg down to sthg - 2. [Person, Sache] to take back. ⬦ vi [Weg] to lead back.

zurück|geben vt *(unreg)* - 1. [wiedergeben - Geliehenes, Führerschein] to give back; [- Ware] to return; [- Mandat] to give up; jm etw zurückgeben to give sb sthg back - 2. [antworten] to answer - 3. [zurückspielen] to return.

zurückgeblieben adj retarded.

zurück|gehen *(perf ist zurückgegangen)* vi *(unreg)* - 1. [gen] to go back - 2. [weniger werden] to go down - 3. [zurückzuführen sein]: auf jn/etw zurückgehen to go back to sb/sthg - 4. [zurückgesandt werden]: etw zurückgehen lassen to send sthg back.

zurückgezogen ⬦ adj [Mensch] retiring; [Leben] secluded. ⬦ adv in seclusion.

zurück|greifen vi *(unreg)*: auf jn/etw zurückgreifen to fall back on sb/sthg.

zurück|halten vt *(unreg)* - 1. [Person, Meinung, Gefühl] to hold back - 2. [Nachricht, Sendung] to withhold - 3. [an etw hindern]: jn von etw zurückhalten to stop sb from doing sthg. ➤ **sich zurückhalten** ref [sich bremsen] to restrain o.s.; sich mit dem Trinken zurückhalten to watch what one drinks.

zurückhaltend ⬦ adj [Mensch] reserved; [Beifall, Äußerung] restrained. ⬦ adv with restraint.

Zurückhaltung die restraint.

zurück|holen vt to fetch back.

zurück|kehren *(perf ist zurückgekehrt)* vi *geh* to return.

zurück|kommen *(perf ist zurückgekommen)* vi *(unreg)* - 1. [zurückkehren] to come back - 2. [zurückgreifen]: auf jn/etw zurückkommen to come back to sb/sthg.

zurück|lassen vt *(unreg)* - 1. [hinterlassen] to leave behind - 2. [zurückgehen lassen] to let go back.

zurück|legen vt - 1. [wieder hinlegen] to put back - 2. [Kopf] to lean back - 3. [Geld, Ware] to put aside - 4. [Strecke] to cover. ➤ **sich zurücklegen** ref [sich zurücklehnen] to lie back.

zurück|liegen vi *(unreg)* - 1. [vergangen sein]: es liegt zwei Jahre zurück it was two years ago - 2. [im Rückstand sein] to be behind.

zurück|müssen vi *(unreg)* to have to go back.

zurück|nehmen vt *(unreg)* - 1. [Ware] to take back - 2. [widerrufen - Äußerung, Vorwurf] to take back; [- Antrag] to withdraw; [- Entscheidung, Befehl] to rescind.

zurück|rufen *(unreg)* ⬦ vt to call back; sich etw ins Bewusstsein zurückrufen to recall sthg. ⬦ vi [am Telefon] to call back.

zurück|schrecken *(perf ist zurückgeschreckt)* vi - 1. [vor Schreck] to start back in fright - 2. [sich scheuen]: vor etw (D) zurückschrecken to shy away from sthg; vor nichts zurückschrecken to stop at nothing.

zurück|stellen vt - 1. [wieder zurück] to put back - 2. [nach hinten] to move back - 3. [Heizung, Lautstärke] to turn down - 4. [verschieben - Plan, Projekt] to put off; [- Wünsche, Zweifel] to set aside.

zurück|stoßen vt *(unreg)* - 1. [wieder zurück] to push back - 2. [wegstoßen] to push away.

zurück|treten *(perf ist zurückgetreten)* vi *(unreg)* - 1. [nach hinten] to step back - 2. [von Amt] to resign.

zurück|weichen *(perf ist zurückgewichen)* vi *(unreg)* to shrink back; vor jm/etw zurückweichen to shrink away from sb/sthg; vor etw zurückweichen to shrink from sthg.

zurück|weisen vt *(unreg)* - 1. [abweisen] to reject - 2. [Vorwurf] to repudiate.

zurück|zahlen vt to pay back; jm etw zurückzahlen [Schulden] to pay sb back sthg; fam [aus Rache] to pay sb back for sthg.

zurück|ziehen (perf hat/ist zurückgezogen) (unreg) <> vt (hat) - 1. [gen] to withdraw - 2. [nach hinten] to pull back. <> vi (ist) [umziehen] to move back. ➤ **sich zurückziehen** ref [sich isolieren] to withdraw.

Zu|ruf der shout.

zu|rufen vt (unreg) to shout.

zurzeit adv at present.

Zu|sage die - 1. [zu Einladung] acceptance (U) - 2. [Versprechen] promise.

zu|sagen <> vt [versprechen] to promise; jm etw zusagen to promise sb sthg. <> vi - 1. [bei Einladung] to accept - 2. [gefallen]: jm zusagen to appeal to sb.

zusammen adv - 1. [gen] together - 2. [insgesamt] altogether; das macht zusammen 10 Euro that's 10 euros altogether.

Zusammen|arbeit die collaboration.

zusammen|arbeiten vi to work together.

zusammen|brauen vt fam to concoct. ➤ **sich zusammenbrauen** ref to be brewing.

zusammen|brechen (perf ist zusammengebrochen) vi (unreg) - 1. [gen] to collapse - 2. [Verkehr] to come to a standstill.

zusammen|bringen vt (unreg) - 1. [beschaffen] to get together - 2. [Personen] to bring together - 3. [Gelerntes] to manage.

Zusammen|bruch der collapse.

zusammen|fahren (perf ist zusammengefahren) vi (unreg) [erschrecken] to start.

zusammen|fallen (perf ist zusammengefallen) vi (unreg) - 1. [einsinken: (in sich) zusammenfallen to collapse - 2. [abmagern] to become emaciated - 3. [Termine, Flächen] to coincide.

zusammen|fassen vt to summarize.

Zusammen|fassung die summary.

zusammen|gehören vi to belong together.

zusammen|halten (unreg) <> vi - 1. [Personen] to stick together - 2. [Teile] to hold together. <> vt - 1. [verbunden halten] to hold together - 2. [beisammenhalten - Herde, Gruppe] to keep together; [- Geld] to hang on to.

Zusammen|hang der connection; etw in Zusammenhang mit etw bringen to make a connection between sthg and sthg; im Zusammenhang mit etw stehen to be connected with sthg.

zusammen|hängen vi (unreg) - 1. [befestigt sein] to be joined (together) - 2. [ursächlich]: mit etw zusammenhängen to be connected with sthg.

zusammenhängend adj coherent.

zusammenhanglos, zusammenhangslos <> adj incoherent. <> adv incoherently.

zusammen|kommen (perf ist zusammengekommen) vi (unreg) - 1. [Personen] to meet - 2. [Ereignisse, Unglück] to happen together; heute kam wirklich alles zusammen everything that could go wrong today, did go wrong - 3. [sich sammeln - Spenden] to be collected; [- Unkosten, Verluste] to mount up.

zusammen|legen <> vt - 1. [sammeln, zusammen unterbringen] to put together - 2. [falten] to fold up - 3. [Termine, Gruppen] to combine. <> vi [gemeinsam bezahlen] to club together.

zusammen|nehmen vt (unreg) to summon up. ➤ **sich zusammennehmen** ref to pull o.s. together.

zusammen|passen vi [Farben, Kleidungsstücke] to go together; [Menschen] to suit each other.

zusammen|prallen (perf ist zusammengeprallt) vi to collide.

zusammen|rechnen vt to add up.

zusammen|reißen (unreg) ➤ **sich zusammenreißen** ref fam to pull o.s. together.

zusammen|schlagen (perf hat/ist zusammengeschlagen) (unreg) <> vt (hat) - 1. [gegeneinanderschlagen - Hände] to clap; [- Absätze] to click - 2. fam [niederschlagen] to beat up. <> vi (ist): über jm/etw zusammenschlagen to engulf sb/sthg.

zusammen|schließen vt (unreg) to lock together. ➤ **sich zusammenschließen** ref to join forces.

Zusammenschluss (pl -schlüsse) der joining together (U).

Zusammensein das being together.

zusammen|setzen vt to put together. ➤ **sich zusammensetzen** ref - 1. [bestehen]: sich aus etw zusammensetzen to be composed of sthg - 2. [zusammentreffen] to get together; sich mit jm zusammensetzen to get together with sb.

Zusammensetzung (pl -en) die composition.

zusammen|stellen vt to put together.

Zusammen|stoß der [von Fahrzeugen] crash; fig [von Menschen] clash.

zusammen|stoßen (perf ist zusammengestoßen) vi (unreg) to crash.

zusammen|treffen (perf ist zusammengetroffen) vi (unreg) - 1. [Personen] to meet; mit jm zusammentreffen to meet sb - 2. [Ereignisse] to coincide.

Zusammen|treffen das [mit Freunden] meeting; [von Ereignissen] coincidence.

zusammen|tun vt (unreg) fam to put together. ➤ **sich zusammentun** ref to get together; sich mit jm zusammentun to get together with sb.

zusammen|zählen vt to count up.

zusammen|ziehen (*perf* hat/ist zusammengezogen) (*unreg*) <> *vt* (*hat*) - **1.** [enger machen - Schlinge, Netz] to pull tight; [- Augenbrauen] to knit - **2.** [sammeln] to mass. <> *vi* (*ist*) [in eine Wohnung] to move in together; **mit jm zusammenziehen** to move in with sb. <> **sich zusammenziehen** *ref* [enger, kleiner werden] to contract.

zusammen|zucken (*perf* ist zusammengezuckt) *vi* to give a start.

Zu|satz *der* addition; [in Nahrungsmittel] additive; [in Vertrag] rider.

Zusatz|gerät *das* attachment.

zusätzlich <> *adj* additional. <> *adv* in addition.

Zuschauer, in (*mpl* -, *fpl* -nen) *der, die* [im Theater, Kino] member of the audience; [im Stadion] spectator; [bei Unfall, Prügelei] onlooker. <> **Zuschauer** *Pl* [im Theater, Kino] audience (*sg*).

zu|schicken *vt*: **jm etw zuschicken** to send sthg to sb.

zu|schieben *vt* (*unreg*) - **1.** [schließen] to push shut - **2.** [hinschieben]: **jm etw zuschieben** to push sthg over to sb - **3.** [Schuld]: **jm etw zuschieben** to push sthg onto sb.

Zu|schlag *der* - **1.** [zusätzlicher Betrag - auf Lohn] additional pay (*U*); [- auf Ware] surcharge - **2.** [zur Fahrkarte] supplement - **3.** [Zusage]: **den Zuschlag erhalten** [Firma] to be awarded the contract; [Gebot] to be successful.

zu|schlagen (*perf* hat/ist zugeschlagen) (*unreg*) <> *vi* - **1.** (*ist*) [Tür, Deckel] to slam shut - **2.** (*hat*) [Person] to hit out - **3.** (*hat*) [Einsatztruppe, Terrorist] to strike - **4.** (*hat*) *fam* [kaufen] to go for it. <> *vt* (*hat*) - **1.** [Tür, Deckel] to slam shut - **2.** [zusprechen]: **jm etw zuschlagen** [einem Bieter] to knock sthg down to sb; [einer Firma] to award sthg to sb.

zu|schließen (*unreg*) <> *vt* to lock. <> *vi* to lock up.

zu|schnappen (*perf* hat/ist zugeschnappt) *vi* - **1.** (*hat*) [Hund] to snap - **2.** (*ist*) [Fälle, Tür] to click shut.

zu|schneiden *vt* (*unreg*) [Stoff, Kleidungsstück] to cut out; [Brett] to cut to size.

zu|schrauben *vt* [Flasche, Glas] to screw the top on; [Deckel] to screw on.

zu|schreiben *vt* (*unreg*): **jm etw zuschreiben** to attribute sthg to sb.

Zu|schrift *die* reply.

zuschulden, zu Schulden *adv*: **sich** (*D*) **etwas zuschulden kommen lassen** to do wrong.

Zuschuss (*pl* -schüsse) *der* [öffentlich] grant; [privat] contribution.

zu|sehen *vi* (*unreg*) - **1.** [zuschauen] to watch; **jm bei etw zusehen** to watch sb doing sthg;

bei etw zusehen to watch sthg - **2.** [veranlassen]: **zusehen, dass...** to make sure that...; **sieh zu, dass du wegkommst!** *fam* go away!

zu sein (*perf* ist zu gewesen) *vi* (*unreg*) to be closed.

zu|setzen <> *vt* - **1.** [Zutat] to add - **2.** [Geld] to pay out. <> *vi* [schaden]: **jm zusetzen** to take it out of sb.

zu|sichern *vt*: **jm etw zusichern** to assure sb of sthg.

zu|spitzen <> **sich zuspitzen** *ref* to intensify.

Zu|stand *der* state; [Gesundheitszustand] condition; **in gutem/schlechten Zustand** in good/bad condition. <> **Zustände** *Pl* situation.

zustande, zu Stande *adv*: **etw zustande bringen** to bring sthg about; **zustande kommen** to come about.

zuständig *adj* relevant.

zu|stehen *vi* (*unreg*): **etw steht jm zu** sb is entitled to sthg.

zu|steigen (*perf* ist zugestiegen) *vi* (*unreg*) to get on.

zu|stimmen *vi* to agree; **jm zustimmen** to agree with sb.

Zu|stimmung *die* agreement; **zu etw seine Zustimmung geben** to give one's consent to sthg.

zu|stoßen (*perf* hat/ist zugestoßen) (*unreg*) <> *vt* (*hat*) [schließen] to push shut. <> *vi* - **1.** (*hat*) [mit Waffe] to make a stab - **2.** (*ist*) [geschehen]: **jm zustoßen** to happen to sb.

Zu|strom *der* (*ohne pl*) stream.

zutage, zu Tage *adv*: **zutage treten** ODER **kommen** to come to the surface; *fig* to come to light.

Zutaten *Pl* ingredients.

zutiefst *adv* deeply.

zu|trauen *vt*: **jm/sich etw zutrauen** to think sb/one is capable of sthg; **ich hätte ihm mehr Geschick zugetraut** I would have expected him to show more skill.

zutraulich <> *adj* trusting. <> *adv* trustingly.

zu|treffen *vi* (*unreg*) to be correct; **auf jn/ etw zutreffen** to apply to sb/sthg.

Zu|tritt *der* entry; **Zutritt haben** to have access; **'Zutritt verboten!'** 'no entry'.

Zutun *das*: **ohne js Zutun** without sb's involvement.

zuverlässig <> *adj* reliable. <> *adv* reliably.

Zuverlässigkeit *die* reliability.

Zuversicht *die* confidence.

zuversichtlich <> *adj* confident. <> *adv* confidently.

zu viel *pron* too much.

zuvor *adv* before.

zuvor|kommen (*perf ist zuvorgekommen*) *vi (unreg):* jm zuvorkommen to beat sb to it.

zuvorkommend *adj* obliging.

Zuwachs ['tsu:vaks] *der* growth; etw auf Zuwachs kaufen to buy sthg big enough to allow room for growth.

zu|wachsen ['tsu:vaksn] (*perf ist zugewachsen*) *vi (unreg)* to become overgrown.

zuwege, zu Wege *adv:* etw zuwege bringen to bring sthg about.

zu|weisen *vt (unreg):* jm etw zuweisen to allocate sthg to sb.

zu|wenden *vt:* jm den Rücken zuwenden to turn one's back on sb. ◆ **sich zuwenden** *ref:* sich jm/etw zuwenden to turn to sb/sthg.

Zu|wendung *die* - 1. [Aufmerksamkeit] attention - 2. [Geld] contribution.

zu wenig *pron* not enough.

zuwider *adv:* mir sind Würmer zuwider I find worms revolting.

zu|winken *vi:* jm zuwinken to wave to sb.

zu|ziehen (*perf hat/ist zugezogen*) (*unreg*) ◇ *vt (hat)* - 1. [schließen - Tür, Fenster] to pull shut; [- Vorhang, Reißverschluss] to close; [- Schlinge, Knoten] to pull tight - 2. [Spezialist] to bring in - 3. [verschaffen] ◆ sich (D) etw zuziehen [Erkältung] to catch sthg; [Zorn, Neid] to incur sthg. ◇ *vi (ist)* [an einen Ort ziehen] to move into the area/town/etc.

zuzüglich *präp* (+G, D) plus.

ZVS [tsɛtfau'ɛs] (*abk für* Zentralstelle für die Vergabe von Studienplätzen) *die* ≃ UCAS *UK, German organization responsible for the allocation of student places.*

zwang *prät* ▷ **zwingen**.

Zwang (*pl* Zwänge) *der* [körperlich] force; [Druck] pressure; [gesellschaftlich] constraint; [innerer] compulsion.

zwängen *vt* to force; sich/etw in etw (A) zwängen to force o.s./sthg into sthg.

zwanglos ◇ *adj* informal. ◇ *adv* informally.

Zwangs|lage *die* predicament.

zwangsläufig ◇ *adj* inevitable. ◇ *adv* inevitably; etw zwangsläufig tun müssen to be bound to do sthg.

zwanzig *num* twenty; *siehe auch* **sechs**.

Zwanzig *die* (*ohne pl*) twenty; *siehe auch* **Sechs**.

Zwanzigeuro|schein *der* twenty-euro note *UK* ODER bill *US*.

zwanzigste, r, s *adj* twentieth; *siehe auch* **sechste**.

Zwanzigste (*pl* -n) *der, die, das* twentieth; *siehe auch* **Sechste**.

be exact; ihr geht jetzt ins Bett, und zwar sofort! go to bed right now, and I mean right now!

Zweck (*pl* -e) *der* - 1. [Ziel] purpose; für einen guten Zweck for a good cause; seinen Zweck erfüllen to serve its purpose; zu diesem Zweck for this purpose - 2. [Sinn] point.

zwecklos *adj* pointless.

zwei *num* two; für zwei essen *fig* to eat enough for two; *siehe auch* **sechs**.

Zwei (*pl* -en) *die* - 1. [Zahl] two - 2. [Schulnote] ≃ B, mark of 2 on a scale from 1 to 6; *siehe auch* **Sechs**.

Zweibett|zimmer *das* twin room.

zweideutig ◇ *adj* - 1. [mehrdeutig] ambiguous - 2. [frivol] suggestive. ◇ *adv* - 1. [mehrdeutig] ambiguously - 2. [frivol] suggestively.

Zweieuro|stück *das* two-euro piece.

zweierlei *num* - 1. [zwei verschiedene] odd - 2. [etwas anderes]: es ist zweierlei it is two different things.

zweifach ◇ *adj* double; die zweifache Menge twice as much; in zweifacher Ausfertigung in duplicate; der zweifache Gewinner the two-times winner. ◇ *adv* twice.

Zweifel (*pl* -) *der* doubt; Zweifel an etw (D) doubts *Pl* about sthg; ohne Zweifel without doubt.

zweifelhaft *adj* - 1. [unsicher] doubtful - 2. [anrüchig] dubious.

zweifellos *adv* undoubtedly.

zweifeln *vi* to doubt; an etw (D) zweifeln to doubt sthg.

Zweifels|fall *der:* im Zweifelsfall in case of doubt.

Zweig (*pl* -e) *der* branch.

Zweig|stelle *die* branch.

zweihundert *num* two hundred.

zweimal *adv* twice.

Zwei|rad *das* two-wheeler.

zweiseitig *adj* - 1. [zwei Seiten umfassend] two-page (*vor Subst*) - 2. [gegenseitig] bilateral.

zweisprachig ◇ *adj* bilingual. ◇ *adv* [aufwachsen] bilingually; [geschrieben] in two languages.

zweistellig *adj* two-figure (*vor Subst*).

zweistöckig *adj* two-storey (*vor Subst*).

zweit ◆ **zu zweit** *adv:* sie waren zu zweit there were two of them; wir sind zu zweit ins Kino gegangen two of us went to the cinema.

zweitausend *num* two thousand.

zweitbeste, r, s *adj* second best.

zweite, r, s *adj* second; *siehe auch* **sechste**.

Zweite (*pl* -n) *der, die, das* second; wie kein Zweiter like nobody else; *siehe auch* **Sechste**.

zweiteilig *adj* [Kleid, Badeanzug] two-piece (*vor Subst*); FILM two-part (*vor Subst*); [Ausgabe] two-volume (*vor Subst*).

zweitens *adv* secondly.

zweitrangig *adj* [Frage, Aufgabe] of second-ary importance; [Bedeutung] secondary.

Zweit|wagen *der* second car.

Zweizimmer|wohnung *die* two-room flat *UK ODER* apartment *US*.

Zwerch|fell *das* diaphragm.

Zwerg (*pl* -e) *der* dwarf.

Zwetsche (*pl* -n), **Zwetschge** (*pl* -n) *die* plum.

zwicken *vt* & *vi* to pinch.

Zwieback (*pl* Zwiebäcke *ODER* -e) *der* rusk.

Zwiebel (*pl* -n) *die* onion.

zwielichtig *adj* shady.

zwiespältig *adj* [Gefühle] conflicting; [Charakter] contradictory.

Zwilling (*pl* -e) *der* - **1.** [Person] twin - **2.** AST-ROL Gemini; Zwilling sein to be a Gemini. ◆ **Zwillinge** *Pl* ASTROL Gemini *(sg)*.

Zwillings|bruder *der* twin brother.

Zwillings|schwester *die* twin sister.

zwingen (*prät* zwang, *perf* hat gezwungen) *vt* to force; jn zu etw zwingen to force sb to do sthg. ◆ **sich zwingen** *ref* to force o.s.; sich zu etw zwingen to force o.s. to do sthg.

zwinkern *vi* [als Reflex] to blink; [als Zeichen] to wink.

Zwirn (*pl* -e) *der* thread.

zwischen *präp* (+D, A) - **1.** [gen] between - **2.** [inmitten] amongst.

zwischendurch *adv* - **1.** [zeitlich] in the meantime - **2.** [räumlich] here and there.

Zwischen|fall *der* incident. ◆ **Zwischen-fälle** *Pl* clashes.

Zwischen|landung *die* stopover.

Zwischen|prüfung *die* UNI intermediate examination.

Zwischen|raum *der* gap.

Zwischen|ruf *der* interjection.

Zwischenzeit *die* time in between; in der Zwischenzeit in the meantime.

zwitschern *vi* to twitter.

zwölf *num* twelve; siehe auch **sechs**.

Zwölf (*pl* -en) *die* twelve; siehe auch **Sechs**.

zwölfte, r, s *adj* twelfth; siehe auch **sechs-te**.

Zwölfte (*pl* -n) *der, die, das* twelfth; siehe auch **Sechste**.

zwölftel *adj* (unver) twelfth; siehe auch **sechstel**.

Zwölftel (*pl* -) *das* twelfth; siehe auch **Sechs-tel**.

Zyankali [tsÿaːnˈkɑːli] *das* potassium cyanide.

Zylinder [tsiˈlɪndɐ] (*pl* -) *der* - **1.** [Hut] top hat - **2.** MATH & TECH cylinder.

Zynismus [tsÿˈnɪsmʊs] *der* cynicism.

Zypern *nt* Cyprus.

Zypresse [tsÿˈprɛsə] (*pl* -n) *die* cypress.

Zyste [ˈtsÿstə] (*pl* -n) *die* MED cyst.

z. Z. = zurzeit.

a¹ (*pl* as *or* a's), **A** (*pl* As *or* A's) [eɪ] *n* [letter] a *das*, A *das*; **to get from A to B** von A nach B kommen. ◆ **A** *n* - **1.** MUS [note] A *das* - **2.** SCH [mark] ≈ eins.

a² (*stressed* [eɪ], *unstressed* [ə], *before vowel or silent 'h' an, weak form stressed* [æn], *unstressed* [ən]) *indef art* - **1.** [gen] ein(e); **a woman** eine Frau; **a restaurant** ein Restaurant; **a friend** ein Freund (eine Freundin); **an apple** ein Apfel - **2.** [referring to occupation]: **I'm a doctor** ich bin Arzt - **3.** [instead of the number one] ein(e); **a hundred** hundert; **a hundred and twenty** hundertzwanzig; **for a week** eine Woche lang - **4.** [in prices, ratios] pro; **£2 a kilo** £2 pro Kilo; **£10 a head** £10 pro Kopf; **twice a week/year** zweimal in der Woche/im *or* pro Jahr; **50 km an hour** 50 km pro Stunde - **5.**: **not a kein(e); not a soul** kein Mensch; **I haven't understood a (single) word** ich habe kein (einziges) Wort verstanden.

AA *n* (*abbr of* **Automobile Association**) ≃ ADAC *der*.

AAA *n* (*abbr of* **American Automobile Association**) ≃ ADAC *der*.

AB *n* US (*abbr of* **Bachelor of Arts**), *Hochschulabschluss in einem geisteswissenschaftlichen Fach nach drei- oder vierjährigem Studium.*

aback [ə'bæk] *adv*: **to be taken aback (by sthg)** schockiert sein (über etw (A)).

abandon [ə'bændən] ◇ *vt* - **1.** [leave, desert] verlassen - **2.** [give up] aufgeben. ◇ *n* (*U*): **with abandon** ausgelassen.

abashed [ə'bæʃt] *adj* verlegen, beschämt.

abate [ə'beɪt] *vi fml* nachlassen.

abattoir ['æbətwɑ:r] *n* Schlachthaus *das*.

abbey ['æbɪ] *n* Abtei *die*.

abbot ['æbət] *n* Abt *der*.

abbreviate [ə'bri:vɪeɪt] *vt* abkürzen.

abbreviation [ə,bri:vɪ'eɪʃn] *n* Abkürzung *die*.

ABC *n* - **1.** [alphabet] ABC *das* - **2.** *fig* [basics]: **the ABC of** das ABC (+ G).

abdicate ['æbdɪkeɪt] ◇ *vi* abdanken. ◇ *vt* [responsibility] von sich schieben.

abdomen ['æbdəmən] *n* [of person] Unterleib *der*; [of animal, insect] Hinterleib *der*.

abduct [əb'dʌkt] *vt* entführen.

aberration [,æbə'reɪʃn] *n* Abweichung *die*.

abet [ə'bet] *vt* ▷ **aid**.

abeyance [ə'beɪəns] *n fml*: **to be in abeyance** [law] außer Kraft sein.

abhor [əb'hɔ:r] *vt* verabscheuen.

abide [ə'baɪd] *vt* ausstehen. ◆ **abide by** *vt insep* sich halten an (+ A).

ability [ə'bɪlətɪ] *n* - **1.** (*U*) [capability] Fähigkeit *die* - **2.** [capability] Fähigkeit *die*, Gabe *die*; [talent] Begabung *die*.

abject ['æbdʒekt] *adj* - **1.** [poverty] bitter; **abject misery** tiefes Elend - **2.** [person] unterwürfig, demütig; **to offer an abject apology** unterwürfig um Entschuldigung bitten.

ablaze [ə'bleɪz] *adj* [on fire] in Flammen.

able ['eɪbl] *adj* - **1.** [capable] fähig; **to be able to do sthg** etw tun können; [due to circumstances] imstande *or* in der Lage sein, etw zu tun - **2.** [competent] tüchtig; [gifted] begabt.

ably ['eɪblɪ] *adv* geschickt, gekonnt.

abnormal [æb'nɔ:ml] *adj* [behaviour] abnorm; [interest] krankhaft; [workload] übermäßig.

aboard [ə'bɔ:d] ◇ *adv* [on ship, plane] an Bord; **to go aboard** an Bord gehen. ◇ *prep*: **aboard the ship/plane** an Bord des Schiffes/Flugzeugs; **aboard the bus/train** im Bus/Zug.

abode [ə'bəʊd] *n fml*: **of no fixed abode** ohne festen Wohnsitz.

abolish [ə'bɒlɪʃ] vt abschaffen.

abolition [,æbə'lɪʃn] n Abschaffung die.

abominable [ə'bɒmɪnəbl] adj [behaviour, treatment] abscheulich; [performance] furchtbar.

aborigine [,æbə'rɪdʒənɪ] n Ureinwohner der, -in die; [Australiens] Aborigine der.

abort [ə'bɔːt] vt - 1. [pregnancy] ablbrechen; [baby] abltreiben - 2. fig [plan, mission] ablbrechen - 3. COMPUT ablbrechen.

abortion [ə'bɔːʃn] n [of pregnancy] Abtreibung die; **she's going to have an abortion** sie wird eine Abtreibung vornehmen lassen.

abortive [ə'bɔːtɪv] adj misslungen.

abound [ə'baʊnd] vi - 1. [be plentiful] in großer Fülle vorhanden sein - 2. [be full]: **to abound with** OR **in sthg** reich an etw (D) sein.

about [ə'baʊt] <> adv - 1. [approximately] ungefähr, etwa; **about 50** ungefähr 50; **at about six o'clock** gegen sechs Uhr - 2. [referring to place] herum; **to walk about** herumllaufen; **is Mr Smith about?** ist Herr Smith da?; **there's a lot of flu about** die Grippe geht um - 3. [on the point of]: **to be about to do sthg** im Begriff sein, etw zu tun. <> prep - 1. [concerning] um, über (+ A); **a book about Scotland** ein Buch über Schottland; **what's it about?** worum gehts?; **to talk about sthg** über etw sprechen; **to quarrel about sthg** sich wegen etw streiten; **what about a drink?** wie wärs mit etwas zu trinken? - 2. [referring to place] herum; **to wander about the streets** in den Straßen umherschlendern.

about-turn esp UK, **about-face** esp US n - 1. MIL Kehrtwendung die - 2. fig [change of attitude] Wendung die um hundertachtzig Grad.

above [ə'bʌv] <> prep - 1. [higher than] über (+ A, D); **to fly above the clouds** über den Wolken fliegen - 2. [more than] über (+ A); **children above the age of twelve** Kinder über zwölf Jahre. <> adv - 1. [on top, higher up] oben; **the flat above** die Wohnung oben; **see above** [in text] siehe oben - 2. [more]: **children aged ten and above** Kinder ab zehn Jahren. ◆ **above all** adv vor allem.

aboveboard [ə,bʌv'bɔːd] adj ehrlich.

abrasive [ə'breɪsɪv] adj - 1. [for cleaning] Scheuer- - 2. fig [person] ungehobelt; [manner] grob.

abreast [ə'brest] adv nebeneinander. ◆ **abreast of** prep: **to keep abreast of sthg** in Bezug auf etw (A) auf dem Laufenden bleiben.

abridged [ə'brɪdʒd] adj gekürzt.

abroad [ə'brɔːd] adv [live] im Ausland; [travel, go] ins Ausland.

abrupt [ə'brʌpt] adj - 1. [sudden] abrupt - 2. [person] kurz angebunden; [manner] brüsk.

abscess ['æbsɪs] n Abszess der.

abscond [əb'skɒnd] vi [from detention centre] entfliehen; [from boarding school] wegllaufen.

abseil ['æbseɪl] vi sich ablseilen.

absence ['æbsəns] n - 1. [of person] Abwesenheit die - 2. [lack] Mangel der.

absent ['æbsənt] adj [not present]: **absent (from)** abwesend (von).

absentee [,æbsən'tiː] n Abwesende der, die.

absent-minded [-'maɪndɪd] adj zerstreut.

absolute ['æbsəluːt] adj - 1. [complete, utter] absolut, vollkommen; **it's an absolute disgrace** es ist eine ausgesprochene Schande - 2. [ruler, power] absolut.

absolutely [æbsə'luːtlɪ] <> adv [completely, utterly] vollkommen, ausgesprochen; **I'm absolutely starving** ich bin ausgesprochen hungrig. <> excl [expressing agreement] genau!

absolve [əb'zɒlv] vt: **to absolve sb (from sthg)** [from crime] jn (von etw) freilsprechen; [from sin] jn (von etw) loslsprechen; [from responsibility] jn (von etw) entbinden.

absorb [əb'zɔːb] vt - 1. [liquid] auflsaugen; [gas, heat] absorbieren - 2. fig [learn] auflnehmen - 3. [interest] fesseln; **to be absorbed in sthg** in etw (A) vertieft OR versunken sein - 4. [take over] übernehmen.

absorbent [əb'zɔːbənt] adj absorbierend.

abstain [əb'steɪn] vi - 1.: **to abstain from sthg** [drinking, smoking] sich einer Sache (G) enthalten; [sex, food] auf etw (A) verzichten - 2. [in vote] sich der Stimme enthalten.

abstention [əb'stenʃn] n [in vote] Enthaltung die.

abstract ['æbstrækt] <> adj abstrakt. <> n [summary] Abstract der.

absurd [əb'sɜːd] adj absurd.

abundant [ə'bʌndənt] adj reichlich.

abundantly [ə'bʌndəntlɪ] adv [extremely]: **it's abundantly clear** es ist mehr als klar.

abuse <> n [ə'bjuːs] - 1. (U) [offensive remarks] Beschimpfungen Pl, Schimpfworte Pl - 2. [maltreatment] Missbrauch der - 3. [of alcohol, drugs, power] Missbrauch der. <> vt [ə'bjuːz] - 1. [insult] beschimpfen - 2. [maltreat, misuse] missbrauchen.

abusive [ə'bjuːsɪv] adj ausfallend.

abysmal [ə'bɪzml] adj [behaviour, performance, weather] miserabel; [failure] erbärmlich.

abyss [ə'bɪs] n Abgrund der; fig [between people, groups] Kluft die, Abgründe Pl.

a/c (abbr of account (current)) Kto.

AC n abbr of alternating current.

academic [,ækə'demɪk] <> adj - 1. [of college, university] wissenschaftlich - 2. [studious] intellektuell - 3. [hypothetical] theoretisch. <> n Akademiker der, -in die.

academy [ə'kædəmɪ] n Akademie die.

accede [æk'siːd] vi - **1.** fml [agree]: **to accede to sthg** in etw (A) ein|willigen - **2.** [monarch]: **to accede to the throne** den Thron besteigen.

accelerate [ək'seləreɪt] ⟨⟩ vt [pace, rhythm, decline, event] beschleunigen. ⟨⟩ vi - **1.** [car, driver] beschleunigen - **2.** [inflation, growth] sich beschleunigen, zu|nehmen.

acceleration [ək,selə'reɪʃn] n Beschleunigung die.

accelerator [ək'seləreɪtər] n Gaspedal das.

accent ['æksent] n [gen] Akzent der.

accept [ək'sept] vt - **1.** [gift, advice, apology, invitation, offer] an|nehmen - **2.** [change, situation] akzeptieren, hin|nehmen - **3.** [defeat, blame] ein|gestehen; [responsibility] übernehmen - **4.** [person - as part of group] akzeptieren; [- for job] nehmen; [- as member of club] auf|nehmen - **5.** [admit]: **to accept that...** zugeben, dass...; **it is generally accepted that...** es ist allgemein anerkannt, dass... - **6.** [subj: shop, bank] akzeptieren; [subj: machine] nehmen.

acceptable [ək'septəbl] adj akzeptabel.

acceptance [ək'septəns] n - **1.** [of gift, piece of work] Annahme die - **2.** [of change, situation] Hinnahme die - **3.** [of defeat, blame] Eingeständnis das; [of responsibility] Übernehmen das - **4.** [of person - as part of group] Akzeptierung die; [- for job] Anstellung die; [- as member of group] Aufnahme die.

access ['ækses] n (U) - **1.** [entry, way in] Zutritt der, Zugang der - **2.** [opportunity to use, see]: **to have access to sthg** zu etw Zugang haben - **3.** [to Internet] Zugang der.

accessible [ək'sesəbl] adj - **1.** [place] zugänglich - **2.** [available] verfügbar.

accessory [ək'sesərɪ] n - **1.** [extra part, device] Extra das; **accessories** Zubehör das - **2.** LAW Helfershelfer der, -in die.

accident ['æksɪdənt] n - **1.** [unpleasant event] Unfall der; [more serious] Unglück das; [mishap] Missgeschick das; **to have an accident** [in car] einen Autounfall haben - **2.** [unintentional act] Versehen das - **3.** (U) [chance]: **we met by accident** wir haben uns zufällig getroffen.

accidental [,æksɪ'dentl] adj [meeting, discovery] zufällig.

accidentally [,æksɪ'dentəlɪ] adv [meet, find, discover] zufällig.

accident-prone adj: **he is accident-prone** er ist vom Pech verfolgt.

acclaim [ə'kleɪm] ⟨⟩ n Anerkennung die, Beifall der. ⟨⟩ vt feiern.

acclimatize [ə'klaɪmətaɪz], **-ise** [ə'klaɪmətaɪz], **acclimate** US ['ækləmeɪt] vi: **to acclimatize (to sthg)** sich (in etw (D)) ak|klimatisieren.

accommodate [ə'kɒmədeɪt] vt - **1.** [subj: building, car] Platz bieten für; [subj: person] unter|bringen - **2.** [oblige] entgegen|kommen (+ D), berücksichtigen.

accommodating [ə'kɒmədeɪtɪŋ] adj entgegenkommend.

accommodation UK [ə,kɒmə'deɪʃn] n [lodging] Unterkunft die.

accommodations US [ə,kɒmə'deɪʃnz] npl = **accommodation**.

accompany [ə'kʌmpənɪ] vt - **1.** [gen] begleiten - **2.** MUS: **to accompany sb (on sthg)** jn (auf etw (D)) begleiten.

accomplice [ə'kʌmplɪs] n Komplize der, -zin die.

accomplish [ə'kʌmplɪʃ] vt [achieve] erreichen, leisten; [complete] vollbringen.

accomplishment [ə'kʌmplɪʃmənt] n - **1.** [feat, deed] Leistung die - **2.** [action] Vollendung die. ⬥ **accomplishments** npl Fähigkeiten Pl.

accord [ə'kɔːd] n - **1.** [settlement] Einigung die - **2.** [agreement, harmony]: **to be in accord (with sthg)** (mit etw) im Einklang sein; **to do sthg of one's own accord** etw aus eigenem Antrieb tun, etw aus freien Stücken tun.

accordance [ə'kɔːdəns] n: **in accordance with** entsprechend (+ D), gemäß (+ D); **in accordance with your wishes** Ihren Wünschen entsprechend.

according to [ə'kɔːdɪŋ-] prep - **1.** [as stated or shown by] zufolge (+ D), laut (+ D); **to go according to plan** nach Plan gehen - **2.** [with regard to, depending on] entsprechend (+ D).

accordingly [ə'kɔːdɪŋlɪ] adv - **1.** [appropriately] (dem)entsprechend - **2.** [consequently] folglich, demgemäß.

accordion [ə'kɔːdjən] n Akkordeon das.

accost [ə'kɒst] vt belästigen.

account [ə'kaʊnt] n - **1.** [with bank, building society] Konto das - **2.** [with shop, company] Kundenkonto das - **3.** [report] Bericht der - **4.** phr: **to take account of sthg, to take sthg into account** etw berücksichtigen; **to be of no account** ohne Bedeutung sein; **on no account** auf keinen Fall. ⬥ **accounts** npl [of business] Buchführung die. ⬥ **by all accounts** adv nach allem, was man hört. ⬥ **on account of** prep aufgrund (+ G). ⬥ **account for** vt insep - **1.** [explain] erklären; **all the missing people have been accounted for** der Verbleib aller vermissten Personen ist geklärt worden - **2.** [represent] aus|machen.

accountable [ə'kaʊntəbl] adj: **accountable (for sb/sthg)** verantwortlich (für jn/etw).

accountancy [ə'kaʊntənsɪ] n Buchhaltung die, Buchführung die.

accountant [ə'kaʊntənt] n Buchhalter der, -in die.

accounts department n Buchhaltungsabteilung die, Buchführungsabteilung die.

accrue [ə'kruː] vi FIN sich an|sammeln.

accumulate [ə'kju:mjʊleɪt] <> *vt* [money, belongings] anlhäufen; [evidence] sammeln. <> *vi* [money, belongings] sich anlhäufen.

accuracy ['ækjʊrəsɪ] *n* - 1. [truth, correctness] Korrektheit *die*, Richtigkeit *die* - 2. [precision - of weapon, marksman] Präzision *die*; [- of typing, typist] Fehlerlosigkeit *die*; [- of figures, estimate] Genauigkeit *die*.

accurate ['ækjʊrət] *adj* - 1. [true] korrekt, richtig - 2. [precise - weapon, marksman] präzis(e); [- typing, typist] fehlerlos; [- figures, estimate] genau.

accurately ['ækjʊrətlɪ] *adv* - 1. [truthfully] korrekt, richtig - 2. [precisely - aim, estimate] genau; [- type] fehlerlos.

accusation [,ækju:'zeɪʃn] *n* - 1. [charge, criticism] Vorwurf *der*, Beschuldigung *die* - 2. LAW [formal charge] Anklage *die*.

accuse [ə'kju:z] *vt* - 1. [charge, criticize]: **to accuse sb of sthg** jn einer Sache (G) beschuldigen; **to accuse sb of doing sthg** jn beschuldigen, etw getan zu haben - 2. LAW: **to be accused of murder/fraud** des Mordes/Betrugs angeklagt sein OR werden; **to be accused of doing sthg** beschuldigt werden, etw getan zu haben.

accused [ə'kju:zd] *n* LAW: **the accused** der/die Angeklagte.

accustomed [ə'kʌstəmd] *adj*: **to be accustomed to sthg** etw gewohnt sein, an etw (A) gewöhnt sein; **to be accustomed to doing sthg** gewohnt sein, etw zu tun.

ace [eɪs] *n* [gen] Ass *das*.

ache [eɪk] <> *n* [dull pain] (dumpfer) Schmerz. <> *vi* - 1. [be painful] weh tun, schmerzen; **my head aches** mein Kopf tut mir weh - 2. *fig* [want]: **to be aching for sthg** sich nach etw sehnen; **to be aching to do sthg** sich danach sehnen, etw zu tun.

achieve [ə'tʃi:v] *vt* [success] erzielen; [goal] erreichen; [ambition] verwirklichen; [victory] erringen; [fame] erlangen.

achievement [ə'tʃi:vmənt] *n* [feat, deed] Leistung *die*.

acid ['æsɪd] *n* - 1. Säure *die* - 2. *inf* [LSD] Acid *das*.

acid rain *n* saurer Regen.

acknowledge [ək'nɒlɪdʒ] *vt* - 1. [accept, admit] einlgestehen, zulgeben - 2. [recognize]: **to acknowledge sb as sthg** jn als etw anlerkennen - 3. [letter]: **to acknowledge (receipt of) sthg** den Eingang OR Empfang von etw bestätigen - 4. [greet] grüßen.

acknowledg(e)ment [ək'nɒlɪdʒmənt] *n* - 1. [thanks] Anerkennung *die* - 2. [acceptance] Eingeständnis *das* - 3. [letter] Empfangsbestätigung *die*. **acknowledg(e)ments** *npl* [in book] Danksagungen *Pl*.

acne ['æknɪ] *n* Akne *die*.

acorn ['eɪkɔ:n] *n* Eichel *die*.

acoustic [ə'ku:stɪk] *adj* akustisch. **acoustics** *npl* [of room] Akustik *die*.

acquaint [ə'kweɪnt] *vt*: **to acquaint sb with sthg** [information] jn über etw (A) informieren; [method, technique] jn mit etw vertraut machen; **to be acquainted with sb** mit jm bekannt sein.

acquaintance [ə'kweɪntəns] *n* [personal associate] Bekannte *der*, *die*.

acquire [ə'kwaɪə'] *vt* - 1. [house, company, book] erwerben; [information, document] erhalten - 2. [habit] anlnehmen; [skill, knowledge] erwerben; **to acquire a taste for sthg** Gefallen an etw (D) finden.

acquisitive [ə'kwɪzɪtɪv] *adj* habgierig.

acquit [ə'kwɪt] *vt* - 1. LAW: **to acquit sb (of sthg)** jn (von etw) freilsprechen - 2. [conduct]: **to acquit o.s. well/badly** seine Sache gut/schlecht machen.

acquittal [ə'kwɪtl] *n* LAW Freispruch *der*.

acre ['eɪkə'] *n* ≃ Morgen *der*, = 4047,9 *m²*.

acrid ['ækrɪd] *adj* [smoke, smell] beißend; [taste] bitter.

acrimonious [,ækrɪ'məʊnjəs] *adj* erbittert.

acrobat ['ækrəbæt] *n* Akrobat *der*, -in *die*.

across [ə'krɒs] <> *adv* - 1. [to the other side] hinüber; [from the other side] herüber - 2. [in measurements] breit; [of circle] im Durchmesser - 3. [in crossword] waag(e)recht. <> *prep* - 1. [from one side to the other] über (+ A) - 2. [on the other side of] auf der anderen Seite (+ G). **across from** *prep* gegenüber von.

acrylic [ə'krɪlɪk] <> *adj* Acryl-, aus Acryl. <> *n* Acryl *das*.

act [ækt] <> *n* - 1. [action, deed] Tat *die*, Akt *der*; **an act of mercy** ein Gnadenakt - 2. LAW Gesetz *das* - 3. [of play, opera] Akt *der*; [in cabaret *etc*] Nummer *die* - 4. *fig* [pretence] Komödie *die*, Schau *die*; **to put on an act** Komödie spielen - 5. *phr*: **get your act together!** reiß dich mal am Riemen! <> *vi* - 1. [take action] handeln - 2. [behave] sich benehmen - 3. [in play, film] spielen - 4. *fig* [pretend] Komödie spielen; **to act innocent** unschuldig tun - 5. [take effect] wirken - 6. [fulfil function]: **to act as sthg** als etw fungieren. <> *vt* [role] spielen.

acting ['æktɪŋ] <> *adj* [interim] stellvertretend. <> *n* (U) [performance] Spiel *das*; [profession] Schauspielerei *die*.

action ['ækʃn] *n* - 1. (U) [fact of doing sthg] Handeln *das*; **to take action** etwas unternehmen; **to put sthg into action** etw in die Tat umlsetzen; **in action** [person] in Aktion; [machine] in Betrieb; **out of action** [person] nicht in Aktion; [machine] außer Betrieb - 2. [deed] Tat *die* - 3. [in battle, war] Gefecht *das* - 4. LAW [trial] Prozess *der*; [charge] Klage *die* - 5. [in play, book, film] Handlung *die* - 6. [effect] Wirkung *die*.

action replay *n* Wiederholung *die*.

activate ['æktɪveɪt] *vt* [device, machine] in Gang setzen; [alarm] auslösen.

active ['æktɪv] *adj* aktiv; [mind, interest] rege.

actively ['æktɪvlɪ] *adv* aktiv.

activity [æk'tɪvətɪ] *n* - **1.** (U) [movement, action] Geschäftigkeit *die* - **2.** [pastime, hobby] Betätigung *die*. ◆ **activities** *npl* Aktivitäten *Pl.*

actor ['æktər] *n* Schauspieler *der*.

actress ['æktrɪs] *n* Schauspielerin *die*.

actual ['æktʃʊəl] *adj* eigentlich; [cost, amount, cause] tatsächlich, wirklich.

actually ['æktʃʊəlɪ] *adv* - **1.** [really, in truth] wirklich - **2.** [by the way] übrigens.

acumen ['ækjʊmen] *n*: **business acumen** Geschäftssinn *der*.

acupuncture ['ækjʊpʌŋktʃər] *n* Akupunktur *die*.

acute [ə'kjuːt] *adj* - **1.** [pain, shortage] akut; [embarrassment, anxiety] groß - **2.** [observer, mind] scharf; [analysis, judgement, person] scharfsinnig - **3.** [sight] scharf; [hearing, sense of smell] fein - **4.** MATHS spitz.

ad [æd] (*abbr of* **advertisement**) *n inf* [in newspaper] Inserat *das*, Annonce *die*; [on TV] Werbung *die*; [in shop window] Angebot *das*.

AD (*abbr of* **Anno Domini**) A. D.

adamant ['ædəmənt] *adj*: **to be adamant (about sthg)** (in Bezug auf etw *(A)*) unnachgiebig sein; **to be adamant that...** darauf bestehen, dass...

Adam's apple ['ædəmz-] *n* Adamsapfel *der*.

adapt [ə'dæpt] <> *vt* - **1.** [adjust, modify] anlpassen; [machine, system] umlstellen; [text, materials] umlarbeiten - **2.** [book, play] adaptieren. <> *vi*: **to adapt to sthg** sich etw *(D)* anlpassen; [idea] sich mit etw anlfreunden.

adaptable [ə'dæptəbl] *adj* anpassungsfähig.

adapter, **adaptor** [ə'dæptər] *n* [for foreign plug] Adapter *der*; [for several plugs] Mehrfachstecker *der*.

add [æd] *vt* - **1.** [gen]: **to add sthg (to)** etw hinzulfügen (zu) - **2.** [total] addieren. ◆ **add on** *vt sep* - **1.** [build on, attach]: **to add sthg on (to sthg)** etw an (etw *(A)*) anlbauen - **2.** [include]: **to add sthg on (to sthg)** etw (zu etw) hinzulfügen; [number, amount] etw (zu etw) dazulrechnen. ◆ **add to** *vt insep* [increase] vergrößern, vermehren. ◆ **add up** *vt sep* [total up] zusammenlrechnen. ◆ **add up to** *vt insep* [represent] ergeben.

adder ['ædər] *n* [snake] Viper *die*.

addict ['ædɪkt] *n* - **1.** [taking drugs] Süchtige *der, die*, Abhängige *der, die* - **2.** *fig* [fan]: **to be a chocolate addict** süchtig nach Schokolade sein; **to be an exercise addict** ein Sportfanatiker sein.

addicted [ə'dɪktɪd] *adj liter & fig*: **addicted (to)** süchtig (nach).

addiction [ə'dɪkʃn] *n liter & fig*: **addiction (to)** Sucht *die* (nach).

addictive [ə'dɪktɪv] *adj*: **to be addictive** [drug] süchtig machen; *fig* [exercise, food, TV] zu einer Sucht werden können.

addition [ə'dɪʃn] *n* - **1.** MATHS Addition *die* - **2.** [extra thing] Zusatz *der*, Ergänzung *die* - **3.** [act of adding] Hinzufügen *das*; **in addition** außerdem; **in addition to** zusätzlich zu.

additional [ə'dɪʃənl] *adj* zusätzlich.

additive ['ædɪtɪv] *n* Zusatz *der*.

address [ə'dres] <> *n* - **1.** [location] Adresse *die* - **2.** [speech] Ansprache *die*. <> *vt* - **1.** [letter, parcel] adressieren - **2.** [meeting, conference] eine Ansprache halten bei - **3.** [person] anlsprechen; **to address sb as sthg** jn etw nennen.

address book *n* [gen & COMPUT] Adressbuch *das*.

adenoids ['ædɪnɔɪdz] *npl* Polypen *Pl.*

adept ['ædept] *adj*: **to be adept (at sthg)** (in etw *(D)*) geschickt sein.

adequate ['ædɪkwət] *adj* - **1.** [sufficient] ausreichend - **2.** [good enough] adäquat.

adhere [əd'hɪər] *vi* - **1.** [stick]: **to adhere (to)** kleben (an (+ *D*)) - **2.** [observe]: **to adhere to sthg** sich an etw *(A)* halten, etw befolgen - **3.** [uphold]: **to adhere to sthg** an etw *(D)* festlhalten.

adhesive [əd'hiːsɪv] <> *adj* klebend; **adhesive label** Haftetikett *das*. <> *n* Klebstoff *der*.

adhesive tape *n* Klebestreifen *der*.

adjacent [ə'dʒeɪsənt] *adj* angrenzend, Neben-; **to be adjacent to sthg** an etw *(A)* anlgrenzen.

adjective ['ædʒɪktɪv] *n* Adjektiv *das*.

adjoining [ə'dʒɔɪnɪŋ] *adj* angrenzend.

adjourn [ə'dʒɜːn] <> *vt*: **to adjourn sthg (until)** etw vertagen (auf (+ *A*)). <> *vi* sich vertagen.

adjudicate [ə'dʒuːdɪkeɪt] *vi* als Preisrichter fungieren; **to adjudicate on** OR **upon sthg** entscheiden OR urteilen bei etw.

adjust [ə'dʒʌst] <> *vt* regulieren; [settings] einlstellen; [clothing] zurechtlrücken. <> *vi*: **to adjust (to sthg)** sich (an etw *(A)*) einlstellen.

adjustable [ə'dʒʌstəbl] *adj* [machine] regulierbar; [chair] verstellbar.

adjustment [ə'dʒʌstmənt] *n* - **1.** [gen] Regulierung *die*; [of settings] Einstellung *die* - **2.** [to situation]: **adjustment (to)** Anpassung *die* (an (+ *A*)).

ad lib [,æd'lɪb] <> *adv* [freely] aus dem Stegreif. <> *n* [improvised joke] Stegreifwitz *der*. ◆ **ad-lib** *vi* improvisieren.

administer [əd'mɪnɪstər] *vt* - **1.** [company] verwalten - **2.** [punishment] verhängen; **to administer justice** Recht sprechen - **3.** [drug, medication] verabreichen.

administration [ədˌmɪnɪˈstreɪʃn] n - 1. [gen] Verwaltung die - 2. [of punishment] Verhängung die; **the administration of justice** die Rechtssprechung.

administrative [ədˈmɪnɪstrətɪv] adj Verwaltungs-, administrativ.

admirable [ˈædmərəbl] adj [worthy of admiration] bewundernswert; [excellent] großartig.

admiral [ˈædmərəl] n Admiral der.

admiration [ˌædməˈreɪʃn] n Bewunderung die.

admire [ədˈmaɪər] vt bewundern; **to admire sb for sthg** jn wegen etw (G) bewundern.

admirer [ədˈmaɪərər] n - 1. [suitor] Verehrer der, -in die - 2. [enthusiast, fan] Bewunderer der, -in die.

admission [ədˈmɪʃn] n - 1. [permission to enter] Zulassung die; [to museum etc] Eintritt der - 2. [cost of entrance] Eintrittspreis der - 3. [confession - of crime] Geständnis das; [- of guilt, mistake] Eingeständnis das.

admit [ədˈmɪt] <> vt - 1. [crime] gestehen; [mistake] einlgestehen; **to admit that** zugeben, dass; **to admit doing sthg** zugeben, etw getan zu haben; **to admit defeat** fig auflgeben - 2. [allow to enter] hereinllassen, hineinllassen; **to be admitted to hospital** UK OR **to the hospital** US ins Krankenhaus eingeliefert werden - 3. [allow to join]: **to admit sb (to sthg)** (in etw (A)) auflnehmen. <> vi: **to admit to sthg** etw zugeben.

admittance [ədˈmɪtəns] n: 'no admittance' 'kein Zutritt'.

admittedly [ədˈmɪtɪdlɪ] adv zugegebenermaßen.

admonish [ədˈmɒnɪʃ] vt fml ermahnen.

ad nauseam [ˌædˈnɔːzɪæm] adv bis zum Überdruss.

ado [əˈduː] n: **without further** OR **more ado** ohne weitere Umstände.

adolescence [ˌædəˈlesns] n Jugend die.

adolescent [ˌædəˈlesnt] <> adj - 1. [teenage] jugendlich - 2. pej [immature] unreif. <> n [teenager] Jugendliche der, Jugendliche die.

adopt [əˈdɒpt] vt - 1. [child] adoptieren - 2. [plan, method] übernehmen; [attitude, mannerism, recommendation] anlnehmen.

adoption [əˈdɒpʃn] n - 1. [of child] Adoption die - 2. (U) [of plan, method] Übernahme die; [of recommendation] Annahme die.

adore [əˈdɔːr] vt über alles lieben; **I adore these chocolate biscuits** ich esse diese Schokoladenkekse für mein Leben gern.

adorn [əˈdɔːn] vt schmücken.

adrenalin [əˈdrenəlɪn] n Adrenalin das.

Adriatic [ˌeɪdrɪˈætɪk] n: **the Adriatic (Sea)** die Adria.

adrift [əˈdrɪft] adj [boat, ship] treibend.

adult [ˈædʌlt] <> adj erwachsen; [animal] ausgewachsen; [book, film] für Erwachsene. <> n [person] Erwachsene der, die.

adultery [əˈdʌltərɪ] n (U) Ehebruch der.

advance [ədˈvɑːns] <> n - 1. [of army] Vorrücken das - 2. [improvement, progress] Fortschritt der - 3. [money] Vorschuss der. <> comp: **advance booking** Vorbestellung die; **advance payment** Vorauszahlung die; **advance warning** Vorwarnung die. <> vt - 1. [improve - cause] voranlbringen, fördern; [- interest] fördern - 2. [bring forward in time] vorlverlegen - 3.: **to advance sb sthg** [money] jm etw vorlschießen. <> vi - 1. [go forward - army] vorlrücken - 2. [improve] Fortschritte machen. ➡ **advances** npl: **to make advances to sb** [sexual] bei jm Annäherungsversuche machen. ➡ **in advance** adv im Voraus.

advanced [ədˈvɑːnst] adj - 1. [developed - plan] weit entwickelt; [- stage] vorgerückt - 2. [student, pupil] fortgeschritten.

advantage [ədˈvɑːntɪdʒ] n Vorteil der; **to one's advantage** für jn von Vorteil sein; **to have** OR **hold the advantage (over sb)** (jm gegenüber) im Vorteil sein; **to take advantage of** auslnutzen.

advent [ˈædvənt] n [of invention] Aufkommen das; [of period] Beginn der. ➡ **Advent** n RELIG Advent der.

adventure [ədˈventʃər] n Abenteuer das.

adventure playground n Abenteuerspielplatz der.

adventurous [ədˈventʃərəs] adj - 1. [person] abenteuerlustig - 2. [life, project] abenteuerlich.

adverb [ˈædvɜːb] n Adverb das.

adverse [ˈædvɜːs] adj [weather] schlecht; [conditions] ungünstig; [criticism] negativ, nachteilig; [effect] nachteilig.

advert [ˈædvɜːt] n UK = **advertisement**.

advertise [ˈædvətaɪz] vt [job, product] Reklame OR Werbung machen für; **to advertise for sb/sthg** per Anzeige suchen.

advertisement [ədˈvɜːtɪsmənt] n - 1. [in newspaper] Inserat das; [on TV] Werbung die; [in shop window] Angebot das - 2. fig [recommendation] Aushängeschild das.

advertising [ˈædvətaɪzɪŋ] n (U) - 1. [advertisements] Werbung die, Reklame die - 2. [industry] Werbebranche die.

advice [ədˈvaɪs] n (U) Rat der; **to give sb advice** jm einen Rat geben; **to take sb's advice** js Rat befolgen; **a piece of advice** ein Ratschlag.

advisable [ədˈvaɪzəbl] adj ratsam.

advise [ədˈvaɪz] <> vt - 1. [give advice to]: **advise sb to do sthg** jm raten, etw zu tun; **to advise sb against sthg** jm von etw ablraten; **to advise sb against doing sthg** jm davon ablraten, etw zu tun - **2.** [professionally]: **to advise sb on sthg** jn in etw *(D)* beraten - **3.** *fml* [inform]: **to advise sb of sthg** jn über etw *(A)* unterrichten. ◇ *vi*: **to advise against sthg** von etw ablraten; **to advise against doing sthg** davon ablraten, etw zu tun.

advisedly [ədˈvaɪzɪdlɪ] *adv* mit Bedacht.

adviser *UK*, **advisor** *US* [ədˈvaɪzəʳ] *n* Berater *der*, -in *die*.

advisory [ədˈvaɪzərɪ] *adj* [group, organization] beratend.

advocate ◇ *n* [ˈædvəkət] - **1.** *Scotland* LAW (Rechts)anwalt *der*, -wältin *die* - **2.** [supporter] Befürworter *der*, -in *die*, Verfechter *der*, -in *die*. ◇ *vt* [ˈædvəkeɪt] befürworten.

Aegean [iːˈdʒiːən] *n*: **the Aegean (Sea)** die Ägäis.

aeon *UK*, **eon** *US* [ˈiːən] *n* Äon *der*; *fig* [very long time] Ewigkeit *die*.

aerial [ˈeərɪəl] ◇ *adj* Luft-; **aerial photograph** Luftaufnahme *die*. ◇ *n* *UK* [antenna] Antenne *die*.

aerobics [eəˈrəʊbɪks] *n* (U) Aerobic *das*.

aerodynamic [ˌeərəʊdaɪˈnæmɪk] *adj* aerodynamisch. ⬣ **aerodynamics** *n* (U) [science] Aerodynamik *die*. ◇ *npl* [aerodynamic qualities] Aerodynamik *die*.

aeroplane *UK* [ˈeərəpleɪn], **airplane** *US* *n* Flugzeug *das*.

aerosol [ˈeərəsɒl] *n* Spraydose *die*.

aesthetic, esthetic *US* [iːsˈθetɪk] *adj* ästhetisch.

afar [əˈfɑːʳ] *adv*: **from afar** aus der Ferne.

affable [ˈæfəbl] *adj* umgänglich.

affair [əˈfeəʳ] *n* - **1.** [event, concern] Angelegenheit *die*, Sache *die* - **2.** [extramarital relationship] Verhältnis *das*.

affect [əˈfekt] *vt* - **1.** [influence] beeinflussen; [health] beeinträchtigen - **2.** [move emotionally] berühren - **3.** [feign] vorltäuschen.

affection [əˈfekʃn] *n* Zuneigung *die*.

affectionate [əˈfekʃnət] *adj* liebevoll.

affirm [əˈfɜːm] *vt* - **1.** [declare] versichern - **2.** [confirm] bestätigen.

affix [əˈfɪks] *vt* [stamp] kleben.

afflict [əˈflɪkt] *vt* plagen; **to be afflicted with sthg** von etw geplagt sein.

affluence [ˈæfluəns] *n* Wohlstand *der*.

affluent [ˈæfluənt] *adj* wohlhabend.

afford [əˈfɔːd] *vt* - **1.** [gen]: **to be able to afford sthg** sich *(D)* etw leisten können; **to be able to afford the time (to do sthg)** die Zeit haben (etw zu tun); **I can't afford two weeks off work** ich kann mir zwei Wochen Urlaub nicht leisten; **we can't afford to let this happen** wir können es uns nicht leisten, dies geschehen zu lassen - **2.** *fml* [provide - protection, shelter] gewähren; [- assistance] leisten.

affront [əˈfrʌnt] ◇ *n* Beleidigung *die*, Affront *der*. ◇ *vt* beleidigen.

Afghanistan [æfˈgænɪstæn] *n* Afghanistan *nt*.

afield [əˈfiːld] *adv*: **far afield** weit weg.

afloat [əˈfləʊt] *adj* - **1.** [above water] schwimmend - **2.** *fig* [out of debt]: **to stay afloat** über Wasser halten.

afoot [əˈfʊt] *adj*: **there's something afoot** da ist irgendetwas im Gange.

afraid [əˈfreɪd] *adj* - **1.** [frightened, reluctant]: **to be afraid (of sb/sthg)** (vor jm/etw) Angst haben; **to be afraid of doing** OR **to do sthg** Angst (davor) haben, etw zu tun - **2.** [in apologies]: **I'm afraid we can't come** wir können leider nicht kommen; **I'm afraid so/not** leider ja/nein.

afresh [əˈfreʃ] *adv*: **to start afresh** noch einmal von vorn anlfangen; **to look at sthg afresh** etw erneut betrachten.

Africa [ˈæfrɪkə] *n* Afrika *nt*.

African [ˈæfrɪkən] ◇ *adj* afrikanisch. ◇ *n* Afrikaner *der*, -in *die*.

aft [ɑːft] *adv* achtern; **to go aft** nach achtern gehen.

after [ˈɑːftəʳ] ◇ *prep* - **1.** [in time] nach; **day after day** Tag für Tag; **time after time** immer wieder; **the day after tomorrow** übermorgen; **the week after next** übernächste Woche - **2.** [in order] nach; **after you!** nach Ihnen!; **shut the door after you** schließe die Tür hinter dir - **3.** [in search of]: **to be after sb/sthg** jn/etw suchen - **4.** [with the name of] nach; **he is named after his father** er ist nach seinem Vater benannt - **5.** [directed at sb moving away]: **to call (sthg) after sb** jm (etw) nachlrufen - **6.** [enquiring]: **to ask after sb/sthg** sich nach jm/etw erkundigen - **7.** [telling the time] nach; **a quarter after ten** *US* Viertel nach zehn. ◇ *adv* danach. ◇ *conj* nachdem; **I came after he had gone** ich kam, nachdem er gegangen war. ⬣ **afters** *npl* UK *inf* Nachtisch *der*. ⬣ **after all** *adv* - **1.** [in spite of everything] doch - **2.** [it should be remembered] schließlich.

aftereffects [ˈɑːftərɪˌfekts] *npl* [of war, storm] Folgen *Pl*.

afterlife [ˈɑːftəlaɪf] *(pl* **-lives** [-laɪvz]) *n* Leben *das* nach dem Tode.

aftermath [ˈɑːftəmæθ] *n* Nachwirkungen *Pl*; **in the aftermath of sthg** nach etw.

afternoon [ˌɑːftəˈnuːn] *n* Nachmittag *der*; **in the afternoon** am Nachmittag; **good afternoon** guten Tag. ⬣ **afternoons** *adv* esp *US* nachmittags.

after-sales service *n* Kundendienst *der*.

aftershave [ˈɑːftəʃeɪv] *n* Rasierwasser *das*.

aftersun (lotion) [ˈɑːftəsʌn-] *n* Aftersunlotion *die*.

aftertaste ['ɑːftəteɪst] *n liter* & *fig* Nachgeschmack *der*.

afterthought ['ɑːftəθɔːt] *n* nachträgliche Idee.

afterwards ['ɑːftəwədz], **afterward** *esp US* ['ɑːftəwəd] *adv* danach; **three weeks afterwards** drei Wochen später.

again [ə'gen] *adv* - 1. [one more time] wieder; **again and again** immer wieder; **time and again** immer wieder; **never again** nie wieder; **all over again** noch einmal von vorn - 2. [once more as before] wieder; **he was ill, but he's well again now** er ist krank gewesen, aber jetzt ist er wieder gesund - 3. [asking for repetition] wieder, noch einmal; **what is his name again?** wie heißt er noch gleich? - 4. [besides] außerdem; **again, we must remember his age** außerdem müssen wir sein Alter berücksichtigen - 5. *phr*: **half as much again** noch mal halb so viel; **(twice) as much again** doppelt so viel; **come again?** *inf* wie bitte?; **then** OR **there again** andererseits.

against [ə'genst] <> *prep* - 1. [gen] gegen; **he was leaning against the wall** er stand an die Wand gelehnt; **against the law** rechtswidrig - 2. [in contrast to]: **as against** verglichen mit. <> *adv*: **are you for or against?** bist du dafür oder dagegen?

age [eɪdʒ] (*cont* **ageing** OR **aging**) <> *n* - 1. [gen] Alter *das*; **she's 20 years of age** sie ist 20 Jahre alt; **he's about my age** er ist ungefähr mein Alter; **he was still writing at the age of 80** mit 80 schrieb er immer noch; **what age are you?** wie alt sind Sie?; **to come of age** volljährig werden; **to be under age** minderjährig sein - 2. [of history] Zeitalter *das*. <> *vt* altern lassen. <> *vi* [person] altern; [wine] reifen. ◆ **ages** *npl* [a long time]: **ages ago** schon ewig her; **I haven't seen her for ages** ich habe sie eine Ewigkeit nicht gesehen.

aged <> *adj* - 1. [eɪdʒd] [of the stated age]: **a girl aged 5** ein fünfjähriges Mädchen - 2. ['eɪdʒɪd] [very old] betagt. <> *npl* ['eɪdʒɪd]: **the aged** die alten Menschen.

age group *n* Altersgruppe *die*.

agency ['eɪdʒənsɪ] *n* - 1. [business] Agentur *die* - 2. [organization] Organisation *die*.

agenda [ə'dʒendə] (*pl* -s) *n* Tagesordnung *die*; **what's on the agenda for today?** was steht heute auf dem Programm?

agent ['eɪdʒənt] *n* - 1. COMM [representative] Agent *der*, -in *die* - 2. [spy] Agent *der*, -in *die*.

aggravate ['ægrəveɪt] *vt* - 1. [make worse] verschlimmern - 2. [annoy] ärgern.

aggregate ['ægrɪgət] <> *adj* Gesamt-; **aggregate earnings** Gesamtverdienst *der*. <> *n* [total] Gesamtsumme *die*; **on aggregate** insgesamt.

aggressive [ə'gresɪv] *adj* - 1. [belligerent - person] aggressiv - 2. [forceful - person] energisch; [- campaign] aggressiv.

aggrieved [ə'griːvd] *adj* gekränkt.

aghast [ə'gɑːst] *adj*: **aghast (at)** entsetzt (über (+ A)).

agile [*UK* 'ædʒaɪl, *US* 'ædʒəl] *adj* [person] beweglich, agil; [body] gelenkig.

agitate ['ædʒɪteɪt] <> *vt* - 1. [disturb, worry] auflregen - 2. [shake] schütteln. <> *vi* [campaign actively]: **to agitate for/against sthg** für/gegen etw Propaganda machen.

AGM (*abbr of* **annual general meeting**) *n UK* JHV *die*.

agnostic [æg'nɒstɪk] <> *adj* agnostisch. <> *n* Agnostiker *der*, -in *die*.

ago [ə'gəʊ] *adv* vor; **that was a long time ago** das ist schon lange her; **three days/years ago** vor drei Tagen/Jahren.

agog [ə'gɒg] *adj* gespannt.

agonizing ['ægənaɪzɪŋ] *adj* qualvoll.

agony ['ægənɪ] *n* Qual *die*; **to be in agony** Qualen erleiden.

agony aunt *n UK inf* Kummerkastentante *die*.

agree [ə'griː] <> *vi* - 1. [concur - two or more people] einer Meinung sein; [- one person] der gleichen Meinung sein; *phrase*: **to agree with sb/sthg** jm/etw zustimmen; **to agree on sthg** sich auf etw (A) einigen - 2. [consent] einlwilligen; **to agree to sthg** sich mit etw einverstanden erklären - 3. [statements] übereinlstimmen - 4. [food]: **curries don't agree with me** Currygerichte bekommen mir nicht - 5. GRAM: **to agree (with)** übereinlstimmen (mit). <> *vt* - 1. [price, terms] vereinbaren - 2. [concur]: **I agree that...** ich bin auch der Meinung, dass...; **it was agreed that...** man einigte sich darauf, dass... - 3. [consent]: **to agree to do sthg** sich bereit OR einverstanden erklären, etw zu tun - 4. [concede]: **to agree that...** zugeben, dass...

agreeable [ə'griːəbl] *adj* - 1. [weather, experience] angenehm; [person] nett - 2. [willing]: **to be agreeable to sthg** mit etw einverstanden sein.

agreed [ə'griːd] *adj*: **to be agreed on sthg** sich über etw (A) einig sein.

agreement [ə'griːmənt] *n* - 1. [accord] Einigkeit *die*; **to be in agreement with sb/sthg** mit jm/etw übereinlstimmen - 2. [settlement] Vereinbarung *die*; [contract] Vertrag *der* - 3. [consent] Einwilligung *die* - 4. GRAM Übereinstimmung *die*.

agricultural [ˌægrɪ'kʌltʃərəl] *adj* landwirtschaftlich.

agriculture ['ægrɪkʌltʃər] *n* Landwirtschaft *die*.

aground [ə'graʊnd] *adv*: **to run aground** auf Grund laufen, stranden.

ahead [ə'hed] *adv* - 1. [in front]: **the road ahead** die Straße vor uns/ihnen/*etc*; **straight ahead** geradeaus - 2. [in competition, game]: **to**

be ahead führen - **3.** [indicating success]: **to get ahead** vorwärts kommen - **4.** [in time]: **to plan ahead** vorausIplanen; **the weeks ahead are going to be difficult** die nächsten Wochen werden schwierig sein. ◈ **ahead of** prep - **1.** [in front of] vor (+ D); **the road ahead of them** die Straße vor ihnen - **2.** [in competition, game]: **they are 10 points ahead of the other teams** sie sind den anderen Mannschaften um 10 Punkte voraus - **3.** [in time] vor; **ahead of schedule** früher als geplant.

aid [eɪd] vt - **1.** [help] unterstützen - **2.** LAW: **to aid and abet** Beihilfe leisten (+ D).

AIDS, Aids [eɪdz] (abbr of acquired immune deficiency syndrome) ◇ n Aids das. ◇ comp: **AIDS patient** Aidspatient der, -in die.

ailing ['eɪlɪŋ] adj liter & fig kränkelnd.

ailment ['eɪlmənt] n Leiden das.

aim [eɪm] ◇ n - **1.** [objective] Ziel das - **2.** [in firing gun, arrow] Zielen das; **to take aim at sthg** auf etw (A) zielen. ◇ vt - **1.**: **to aim a gun at sb/sthg** mit einem Gewehr auf jn/etw zielen; **to aim a camera at sb/sthg** eine Kamera auf jn/etw richten - **2.** [plan, programme]: **to be aimed at doing sthg** darauf ausgerichtet sein, etw zu tun - **3.** [remark, criticism]: **to be aimed at sb** gegen jn gerichtet sein. ◇ vi - **1.** [point weapon]: **to aim (at)** zielen (auf (+ A)) - **2.** [intend]: **to aim at OR for sthg** etw anIstreben; **to aim to do sthg** vorIhaben, etw zu tun.

aimless ['eɪmlɪs] adj [person, life] ziellos; [task, activity] planlos.

ain't [eɪnt] inf abbr of am not, are not, is not, have not, has not.

air [eəʳ] ◇ n - **1.** [gen] Luft die; **to throw sthg into the air** etw in die Luft werfen; **by air** [travel] mit dem Flugzeug; **to be (up) in the air** fig ungewiss sein - **2.** [look] Aussehen das; [facial expression] Miene die - **3.** RADIO & TV: **to be on the air** [programme] gesendet werden. ◇ comp Luft-. ◇ vt - **1.** [washing] nachItrocknen lassen - **2.** [room, bed] lüften - **3.** [feelings, opinions] äußern - **4.** [broadcast] senden. ◇ vi [washing] nachItrocknen.

air bag n AUT Airbag der.

airbase ['eəbeɪs] n Luftstützpunkt der.

airbed ['eəbed] n UK Luftmatratze die.

airborne ['eəbɔ:n] adj - **1.** [troops, regiment] Luftlande- - **2.** [plane] in der Luft.

air-conditioned [-kən'dɪʃnd] adj klimatisiert.

air-conditioning [-kən'dɪʃnɪŋ] n [device] Klimaanlage die; [process] Klimatisierung die.

aircraft ['eəkrɑ:ft] (pl inv) n Flugzeug das.

aircraft carrier n Flugzeugträger der.

airfield ['eəfi:ld] n Flugplatz der.

airforce ['eəfɔ:s] n Luftwaffe die.

air freshener [-,freʃnəʳ] n Raumspray das.

airgun ['eəgʌn] n Luftgewehr das.

airhostess ['eə,həustɪs] n Stewardess die.

airlift ['eəlɪft] ◇ n Luftbrücke die. ◇ vt über eine Luftbrücke befördern.

airline ['eəlaɪn] n Fluglinie die.

airliner ['eəlaɪnəʳ] n Verkehrsflugzeug das.

airmail ['eəmeɪl] n Luftpost die; **by airmail** mit OR per Luftpost.

airplane ['eəpleɪn] n US = **aeroplane**.

airport ['eəpɔ:t] n Flughafen der.

air raid n Luftangriff der.

air rifle n Luftgewehr die.

airsick ['eəsɪk] adj: **I often get airsick** im Flugzeug wird mir leicht übel.

airspace ['eəspeɪs] n Luftraum die.

air steward n Steward der.

airstrip ['eəstrɪp] n Start- und Landebahn die.

air terminal n Terminal der ODER das.

airtight ['eətaɪt] adj luftdicht.

air-traffic controller n Fluglotse der, -sin die.

airy ['eərɪ] adj - **1.** [room] luftig - **2.** [notions] abstrus; [promises] vage - **3.** [nonchalant] lässig, nonchalant.

aisle [aɪl] n - **1.** [in church - central] Mittelgang der; [- at side] Seitenschiff das - **2.** [in plane, theatre, shop] Gang der.

ajar [ə'dʒɑ:ʳ] adj angelehnt.

aka (abbr of also known as) alias.

akin [ə'kɪn] adj: **akin to** vergleichbar mit.

alacrity [ə'lækrəti] n fml [eagerness] Eifer der; **she accepted our offer with alacrity** sie nahm unser Angebot ohne zu zögern an.

alarm [ə'lɑ:m] ◇ n - **1.** [fear] Beunruhigung die - **2.** [device] Alarmanlage die; **to raise OR sound the alarm** [by activating device] Alarm geben; [by shouting] Alarm schlagen. ◇ vt [scare] beunruhigen, alarmieren.

alarm clock n Wecker der.

alarming [ə'lɑ:mɪŋ] adj beunruhigend.

alas [ə'læs] excl liter leider.

Albania [æl'beɪnjə] n Albanien nt.

Albanian [æl'beɪnjən] ◇ adj albanisch. ◇ n [person] Albaner der, -in die.

albeit [ɔ:l'bi:ɪt] conj fml wenn auch.

albino [æl'bi:nəʊ] (pl -s) n Albino der.

album ['ælbəm] n Album das.

alcohol ['ælkəhɒl] n Alkohol der.

alcoholic [,ælkə'hɒlɪk] ◇ adj [drink] alkoholisch. ◇ n Alkoholiker der, -in die.

alcove ['ælkəʊv] n [in room] Alkoven der; [in wall] Nische die.

ale [eɪl] n Ale das.

alert [ə'lɜ:t] ◇ adj - **1.** [vigilant] wachsam - **2.** [perceptive] aufmerksam; [as character trait] aufgeweckt - **3.** [aware]: **to be alert to sthg** sich (D) einer Sache (G) bewusst sein. ◇ n Alarm der; **on the alert** [watchful] auf der Hut;

MIL in Gefechtsbereitschaft. <> vt - 1. [police, fire brigade] alarmieren; [to imminent danger] warnen - 2. [make aware]: **to alert sb to sthg** jm etw bewusst machen.

A level (abbr of Advanced level) n einzelne Prüfung des Schulabschlusses weiterführender Schulen in England, Wales und Nordirland.

alfresco [æl'freskəʊ] adj & adv im Freien.

algae ['ældʒi:] npl Algen Pl.

algebra ['ældʒɪbrə] n Algebra die.

Algeria [æl'dʒɪərɪə] n Algerien nt.

alias ['eɪlɪəs] (pl -es) <> adv alias. <> n Deckname der.

alibi ['ælɪbaɪ] n Alibi das.

alien ['eɪljən] <> adj - 1. [foreign] ausländisch - 2. [from outer space] außerirdisch - 3. [unfamiliar] fremd. <> n - 1. [from outer space] Außerirdische der, die - 2. LAW [foreigner] Ausländer der, -in die.

alienate ['eɪljəneɪt] vt [voters, supporters] verärgern, entfremden.

alight [ə'laɪt] (pt & pp -ed OR alit) <> adj: **to be alight** brennen; **to set sthg alight** etw anlzünden. <> vi fml - 1. [bird, insect] sich niederlassen - 2. [from train, bus] auslsteigen.

align [ə'laɪn] vt [line up] auslrichten.

alike [ə'laɪk] adj & adv [similar] ähnlich; [identical] gleich; **to look alike** [similar] ähnlich auslsehen; [identical] gleich auslsehen.

alimony ['ælɪmənɪ] n Unterhaltszahlung die.

alive [ə'laɪv] adj [living, lively] lebendig; **is he still alive?** lebt er noch?; **to keep a tradition alive** eine Tradition aufrechtlerhalten.

alkali ['ælkəlaɪ] (pl -s OR -es) n Alkali das.

all [ɔ:l] <> adj - 1. [the whole of with sg noun] ganze; **all the money** das ganze Geld; **all the time** immer; **all day/evening** den ganzen Tag/Abend; **all his life** sein ganzes Leben lang - 2. [every one of with pl noun] alle(r) (s); **all the people** alle Menschen; **all three died** alle drei starben; **at all hours** zu jeder Tages- und Nachtzeit. <> pron - 1. [everything]: **all of the cake** der ganze Kuchen; **is that all?** [in shop] ist das alles?; **she ate it all, she ate all of it** sie aß alles auf; **it's all gone** es ist nichts mehr da - 2. [everybody]: **all of us went, we all went** wir sind alle gegangen - 3. (with superl): **the best of all** der/die/das Allerbeste; **the biggest of all** der/die/das Allergrößte; **he is the cleverest of all** er ist der Klügste von allen; **and, best of all,...** und (was) das Beste ist,... <> adv - 1. [completely] ganz; **all alone** ganz allein; **dressed all in red** ganz in rot gekleidet; **the water spilled all over the carpet** das Wasser ergoss sich über den Teppichboden; **I'd forgotten all about that** das hatte ich völlig vergessen; **all told** [in total] insgesamt - 2. [in scores] beide; **it's two all** es steht zwei beide - 3. (with compar): **you'll feel all the bet-**

ter for it du wirst dich danach umso besser fühlen; **to run all the faster** noch schneller laufen - 4. phr: **all over** [finished] alles vorbei. ⟹ **above all** adv = above. ⟹ **after all** adv = after. ⟹ **all but** adv fast; **all but empty** fast leer. ⟹ **all in all** adv alles in allem. ⟹ **at all** adv = at. ⟹ **in all** adv [in total] zusammen; [in summary] alles in allem.

Allah ['ælə] n Allah.

all-around adj US = all-round.

allay [ə'leɪ] vt fml [fears, doubts] weitgehend zerstreuen; [anger] vermindern.

all clear n - 1. [signal] Entwarnung die - 2. fig [go-ahead] Bewilligung die.

allegation [,ælɪ'geɪʃn] n Behauptung die.

allege [ə'ledʒ] vt behaupten; **he is alleged to have passed on the information** er soll die Informationen weitergegeben haben.

allegedly [ə'ledʒɪdlɪ] adv angeblich.

allergic [ə'lɜ:dʒɪk] adj: **allergic (to)** allergisch (gegen).

allergy ['ælədʒɪ] n Allergie die; **to have an allergy to sthg** eine Allergie gegen etw haben.

alleviate [ə'li:vɪeɪt] vt mildern.

alley(way) ['ælɪ(weɪ)] n [street] (enge) Gasse die; [in garden] Weg der.

alliance [ə'laɪəns] n Bündnis das.

allied ['ælaɪd] adj - 1. MIL verbündet, alliiert - 2. [related] verwandt.

alligator ['ælɪgeɪtə] (pl inv OR -s) n Alligator der.

all-important adj [crucial] entscheidend.

all-in adj UK [price] Pauschal-. ⟹ **all in** <> adj [tired] völlig OR total erledigt. <> adv UK [inclusive] alles inklusive.

all-night adj [party, session] die ganze Nacht dauernd; [shop] nachts durchgehend geöffnet.

allocate ['æləkeɪt] vt: **to allocate sthg to sb** [money, resources] jm etw zur Verfügung stellen; [task, seats] jm etw zulweisen; [tickets] etw an jn verteilen.

allot [ə'lɒt] vt [task] zulweisen; [money, resources] zur Verfügung stellen; [time] vorlsehen.

allotment [ə'lɒtmənt] n - 1. UK [garden] Schrebergarten der - 2. [sharing out - of task] Zuweisung die; [- of money, resources] Verteilung die; [- of time] Vorsehen das - 3. [share - of money, resources] Anteil der; [- of time] Zeitrahmen der.

all-out adj [effort] äußerst; [war] total; [attack] massiv.

allow [ə'laʊ] vt - 1. [permit] erlauben; **to allow sb to do sthg** jm erlauben, etw zu tun; **to be allowed to do sthg** etw tun dürfen - 2. [allocate - money] einlrechnen; [- time] einlplanen - 3. [admit]: **to allow that...** einlräumen, dass... ⟹ **allow for** vt insep einlkalkulieren.

allowance [ə'lauəns] *n* - 1. [grant] finanzielle Unterstützung; **travel allowance** Reisekostenzuschuss *der*; **clothing allowance** Kleidungsgeld *das* - 2. US [pocket money] Taschengeld *das* - 3. [excuse]: **to make allowances for sb** mit jm Nachsicht haben; **to make allowances for sthg** etw berücksichtigen.

alloy ['ælɔɪ] *n* Legierung *die*.

all right <> *adv* - 1. [healthy, unharmed]: **to feel all right** sich ganz gut fühlen; **did you get home all right?** bist du gut nach Hause gekommen? - 2. *inf* [acceptably] ganz gut - 3. *inf* [indicating agreement] okay - 4. *inf* [certainly]: **it's pneumonia all right** es ist sicher Lungenentzündung - 5. [do you understand?]: **all right?** okay? - 6. [now then]: **all right, let's go** okay, auf gehts. <> *adj* - 1. [healthy, unharmed]: **are you all right?** bist du in Ordnung? - 2. *inf* [acceptable]: **it was all right** es war ganz ordentlich; **that's all right** [never mind] das ist schon in Ordnung - 3. [permitted]: **is it all right if I make a phone call?** haben Sie etwas dagegen, wenn ich (kurz) telefoniere?

all-round UK, **all-around** US *adj* [athlete] Allround-; [worker] vielseitig begabt.

all-time *adj* [record, best] absolut.

allude [ə'luːd] *vi*: **to allude to sthg** auf etw (A) an|spielen.

alluring [ə'ljuərɪŋ] *adj* verführerisch.

allusion [ə'luːʒn] *n* Anspielung *die*.

ally *n* ['ælaɪ] Verbündete *der, die*.

almighty [ɔːl'maɪtɪ] *adj inf* [noise, fuss] Riesen-.

almond ['ɑːmənd] *n* Mandel *die*.

almost ['ɔːlməust] *adv* fast, beinahe; **I almost missed the bus** ich hätte beinahe den Bus verpasst.

alms [ɑːmz] *npl dated* Almosen *Pl*.

aloft [ə'lɒft] *adv* [in the air]: **to hold sthg aloft** etw in die Höhe halten.

alone [ə'ləun] <> *adj* allein(e). <> *adv* - 1. [without others] allein(e) - 2. [only] nur, allein; **you alone can help me** nur du *OR* du allein kannst mir helfen - 3. [untouched, unchanged]: **to leave sthg alone** etw in Ruhe lassen; **leave me alone!** lass mich in Ruhe! ◆ **let alone** *conj* geschweige denn.

along [ə'lɒŋ] <> *adv* - 1. [indicating movement]: **to stroll along** dahin|schlendern; **they went along to the demonstration** sie gingen zu der Vorführung - 2. [with others]: **to take sb/sthg along** jn/etw mit|nehmen; **to come along** mit|kommen. <> *prep* entlang (+ A); **they walked along the river** sie liefen den Fluss entlang; **they walked along the forest path** wie folgten dem Waldweg; **the trees along the path** die Bäume neben dem Weg. ◆ **all along** *adv* die ganze Zeit. ◆ **along with** *prep* zusammen mit.

alongside [ə,lɒŋ'saɪd] <> *prep* neben (+ D); [with verbs of motion] neben (+ A). <> *adv* daneben.

aloof [ə'luːf] <> *adj* unnahbar. <> *adv*: **to remain aloof (from)** sich fern halten (von).

aloud [ə'laud] *adv* laut.

alphabet ['ælfəbet] *n* Alphabet *das*.

alphabetical [,ælfə'betɪkl] *adj* alphabetisch.

Alps [ælps] *npl*: **the Alps** die Alpen *Pl*.

already [ɔːl'redɪ] *adv* schon.

alright [,ɔːl'raɪt] *adv* & *adj* = **all right**.

Alsatian [æl'seɪʃn] *n* [dog] (deutscher) Schäferhund.

also ['ɔːlsəu] *adv* auch.

altar ['ɔːltər] *n* Altar *der*.

alter ['ɔːltər] <> *vt* ändern; [appearance] verändern; [text] ab|ändern. <> *vi* sich ändern; [appearance] sich verändern.

alteration [,ɔːltə'reɪʃn] *n* Änderung *die*; [of appearance] Veränderung *die*; [of text] Abänderung *die*.

alternate <> *adj* [UK ɔːl'tɜːnət, US 'ɔːltərnət] - 1. [by turns] abwechselnd - 2. [every other]: **on alternate days** jeden zweiten Tag. <> *vt* ['ɔːltərneɪt] ab|wechseln. <> *vi* ['ɔːltərneɪt]: **to alternate (with)** sich ab|wechseln (mit); **to alternate between sthg and sthg** zwischen etw (D) und etw (D) (ab)|wechseln.

alternately [ɔːl'tɜːnətlɪ] *adv* abwechselnd.

alternating current ['ɔːltəneɪtɪŋ-] *n* ELEC Wechselstrom *der*.

alternative [ɔːl'tɜːnətɪv] <> *adj* - 1. [different, other] andere(r) (s) - 2. [nontraditional] alternativ. <> *n* Alternative *die*; **an alternative to sb/sthg** eine Alternative zu jm/etw; **to have no alternative (but to do sthg)** keine (andere) Wahl haben (als etw zu tun).

alternatively [ɔːl'tɜːnətɪvlɪ] *adv* oder aber, aber auch.

alternative medicine *n* (U) alternative Heilmethoden *Pl*.

alternator ['ɔːltəneɪtər] *n* ELEC Wechselstromgenerator *der*; [in car] Lichtmaschine *die*.

although [ɔːl'ðəu] *conj* obwohl.

altitude ['æltɪtjuːd] *n* Höhe *die*.

altogether [,ɔːltə'geðər] *adv* - 1. [completely] vollkommen - 2. [in general, in total] insgesamt.

aluminium UK [,æljʊ'mɪnɪəm], **aluminum** US [ə'luːmɪnəm] <> *n* Aluminium *das*. <> *comp* Aluminium-.

always ['ɔːlweɪz] *adv* immer; **you can always stay at my place** du kannst auch bei mir übernachten.

am [æm] *vb* ▷ **be**.

a.m. (*abbr of* **ante meridiem**) vormittags; **at 3 a.m.** um 3 Uhr morgens *OR* früh; **12 a.m.** 12 Uhr.

amalgamate [əˈmælgəmeɪt] ◇ *vt* mischen. ◇ *vi* sich verbinden.

amass [əˈmæs] *vt* [fortune, power, information] anhäufen.

amateur [ˈæmətər] ◇ *adj* - **1.** [nonprofessional] Amateur- - **2.** *pej* [unprofessional] dilettantisch.. ◇ *n* [nonprofessional] Amateur *der*, -in *die*.

amateurish [ˈæmətə:rɪʃ] *adj pej* [unprofessional] dilettantisch.

amaze [əˈmeɪz] *vt* erstaunen, verblüffen.

amazed [əˈmeɪzd] *adj* erstaunt, verblüfft.

amazement [əˈmeɪzmənt] *n* Erstaunen *das*.

amazing [əˈmeɪzɪŋ] *adj* erstaunlich.

Amazon [ˈæməzn] *n* - **1.** [river]: **the Amazon** der Amazonas - **2.** [region]: **the Amazon (Basin)** das Amazonasbecken; **the Amazon rainforest** der Regenwald am Amazonas.

ambassador [æmˈbæsədər] *n* Botschafter *der*, -in *die*.

amber [ˈæmbər] *n* - **1.** [substance] Bernstein *der* - **2.** *UK* [colour of traffic light] Gelb *das*.

ambiguous [æmˈbɪgjuəs] *adj* [two possible meanings] zweideutig; [many possible meanings] mehrdeutig.

ambition [æmˈbɪʃn] *n* - **1.** Ehrgeiz *der* - **2.** [objective, goal] Ambition *die*.

ambitious [æmˈbɪʃəs] *adj* ehrgeizig.

amble [ˈæmbl] *vi* schlendern.

ambulance [ˈæmbjʊləns] *n* Krankenwagen *der*, Ambulanz *die*.

ambush [ˈæmbʊʃ] ◇ *n* Hinterhalt *der*. ◇ *vt* [attack] aus dem Hinterhalt überfallen.

amenable [əˈmi:nəbl] *adj*: **amenable (to sthg)** (etw (D)) zugänglich.

amend [əˈmend] *vt* [change] abländern. ◆ **amends** *npl*: **to make amends (for sthg)** Entschädigungen (für etw) bieten.

amendment [əˈmendmənt] *n* Änderung *die*.

amenities [əˈmi:nətɪz] *npl* Einrichtungen *Pl*.

America [əˈmerɪkə] *n* Amerika *nt*.

American [əˈmerɪkn] ◇ *adj* amerikanisch. ◇ *n* Amerikaner *der*, -in *die*.

American football *n UK* American Football *der*.

American Indian *n* Indianer *der*, -in *die*.

amiable [ˈeɪmjəbl] *adj* freundlich.

amicable [ˈæmɪkəbl] *adj* freundschaftlich; [agreement] gütlich.

amid(st) [əˈmɪd(st)] *prep fml* inmitten (+ G).

amiss [əˈmɪs] ◇ *adj*: **is there anything amiss?** stimmt etwas nicht? ◇ *adv*: **to take sthg amiss** etw übel nehmen.

ammonia [əˈməʊnjə] *n* Ammoniak *der*.

ammunition [ˌæmjʊˈnɪʃn] *n* Munition *die*.

amnesia [æmˈni:zjə] *n* Amnesie *die*.

amnesty [ˈæmnəstɪ] *n* Amnestie *die*.

amok [əˈmɒk] *adv*: **to run amok** Amok laufen.

among(st) [əˈmʌŋ(st)] *prep* unter (+ D); **amongst other things** unter anderem; **I count him amongst my friends** ich zähle ihn zu meinen Freunden; **they were talking amongst themselves** sie unterhielten sich.

amoral [ˌeɪˈmɒrəl] *adj* amoralisch.

amorous [ˈæmərəs] *adj* amourös.

amount [əˈmaʊnt] *n* - **1.** [quantity] Menge *die* - **2.** [sum of money] Betrag *der*. ◆ **amount to** *vt insep* - **1.** [total] sich belaufen auf (+ A) - **2.** [be equivalent to] hinauslaufen auf (+ A).

amp [æmp] *n abbr of* **ampere**.

ampere [ˈæmpeə:r] *n* Ampere *das*.

amphibious [æmˈfɪbɪəs] *adj* amphibisch.

ample [ˈæmpl] *adj* - **1.** [enough] reichlich - **2.** [large] großzügig.

amplifier [ˈæmplɪfaɪər] *n* Verstärker *der*.

amputate [ˈæmpjʊteɪt] *vt & vi* amputieren.

Amsterdam [ˌæmstəˈdæm] *n* Amsterdam *nt*.

amuck [əˈmʌk] *adv* = **amok**.

amuse [əˈmju:z] *vt* - **1.** [make laugh] amüsieren - **2.** [entertain] unterhalten; **to amuse o.s. (with sthg)** sich *(D)* (mit etw) die Zeit vertreiben.

amused [əˈmju:zd] *adj* amüsiert; **to be amused at** *OR* **by sthg** von etw erheitert sein; **to keep o.s. amused** sich die Zeit vertreiben.

amusement [əˈmju:zmənt] *n* - **1.** [enjoyment] Vergnügen *das* - **2.** [diversion, game] Unterhaltungsmöglichkeit *die*.

amusement arcade *n* Spielhalle *die*.

amusement park *n* Vergnügungspark *der*.

amusing [əˈmju:zɪŋ] *adj* [funny] amüsant.

an (*stressed* [æn], *unstressed* [ən]) *indef art* ⊳ **a²**.

anaemic *UK*, **anemic** *US* [əˈni:mɪk] *adj* [suffering from anaemia] anämisch.

anaesthetic *UK*, **anesthetic** *US* [ˌænɪsˈθetɪk] *n* Anästhetikum *das*, Narkosemittel *das*; **under anaesthetic** unter Narkose, in der Narkose.

analogue *UK*, **analog** *US* [ˈænəlɒg] *adj* analog.

analogy [əˈnælədʒɪ] *n* Analogie *die*; **by analogy** analog dazu.

analyse *UK*, **-lyze** *US* [ˈænəlaɪz] *vt* analysieren.

analysis [əˈnæləsɪs] (*pl* **-ses** [əˈnæləsi:z]) *n* [gen] Analyse *die*.

analyst [ˈænəlɪst] *n* - **1.** [political, computer, statistics] Analytiker *der*, -in *die* - **2.** [psychoanalyst] Psychoanalytiker *der*, -in *die*.

analytic(al) [ˌænəˈlɪtɪk(l)] *adj* analytisch.

analyze *vt US* = **analyse**.

anarchist [ˈænəkɪst] *n* Anarchist *der*, -in *die*.

anarchy [ˈænəkɪ] *n* Anarchie *die*.

anathema [əˈnæθəmə] *n* Anathema *das*.

anatomy [əˈnætəmɪ] *n* Anatomie *die*.

ancestor [ˈænsestər] *n* [person] Vorfahr *der*.

anchor [ˈæŋkər] <> *n* - **1.** NAUT Anker *der*; **to drop/weigh anchor** Anker werfen/lichten - **2.** TV Moderator *der*, -in *die*. <> *vt* - **1.** [secure] sichern - **2.** TV moderieren. <> *vi* NAUT ankern.

anchovy [ˈæntʃəvɪ] (*pl inv OR* -**ies**) *n* Sardelle *die*.

ancient [ˈeɪnʃənt] *adj* - **1.** [dating from distant past] alt - **2.** *hum* [very old] alt, uralt.

ancillary [ænˈsɪlərɪ] *adj* [staff, device] Hilfs-.

and (*stressed* [ænd], *unstressed* [ənd] [ən]) *conj* - **1.** [gen] und; **and you?** und du/Sie?; **my wife and I** meine Frau und ich; **nice and warm** schön warm - **2.** [in numbers]: **a hundred and one** hunderteins; **an hour and a quarter** eineinviertel Stunden - **3.** [with repetition]: **more and more** immer mehr; **for days and days** tagelang - **4.** (*with infinitive*) [in order to]: **to try and do sthg** versuchen, etw zu tun; **wait and see!** warte es ab!, warten Sie es ab! ➣ **and all that** *adv* und dergleichen. ➣ **and so on, and so forth** *adv* und so weiter, und so fort.

Andes [ˈændiːz] *n*: **the Andes** die Anden *Pl*.

anecdote [ˈænɪkdəʊt] *n* Anekdote *die*.

anemic *adj US* = **anaemic**.

anesthetic *etc US* = **anaesthetic** *etc* .

anew [əˈnjuː] *adv* von neuem.

angel [ˈeɪndʒəl] *n liter* & *fig* Engel *der*.

anger [ˈæŋgər] <> *n* Zorn *der*. <> *vt* ärgern.

angina [ænˈdʒaɪnə] *n* Angina pectoris *die*.

angle [ˈæŋgl] *n* - **1.** MATHS [corner] Winkel *der* - **2.** [point of view] Standpunkt *der* - **3.** [slope] Schräge *die*; **at an angle** im schrägen Winkel.

angler [ˈæŋglər] *n* Angler *der*, -in *die*.

Anglican [ˈæŋglɪkən] <> *adj* anglikanisch. <> *n* Anglikaner *der*, -in *die*.

angling [ˈæŋglɪŋ] *n* Angeln *das*.

angry [ˈæŋgrɪ] *adj* böse; **to be angry (with sb)** (jm) böse sein; **to get angry (with sb)** böse werden (auf jn).

anguish [ˈæŋgwɪʃ] *n* Qual *die*.

angular [ˈæŋgjʊlər] *adj* [face, jaw, body] kantig; [furniture, car] eckig.

animal [ˈænɪml] <> *adj* - **1.** [gen] Tier- - **2.** [physical] animalisch. <> *n* - **1.** [living creature] Tier *das* - **2.** *inf pej* [brutal person] Bestie *die*.

animate [ˈænɪmət] *adj* [alive] lebend.

animated [ˈænɪmeɪtɪd] *adj* [lively] lebhaft.

aniseed [ˈænɪsiːd] *n* Anis *der*.

ankle [ˈæŋkl] <> *n* Knöchel *der*. <> *comp* Knöchel-; **ankle socks** Söckchen *Pl*.

annex [ˈæneks] *vt* annektieren.

annexe [ˈæneks] *n* [building] Anbau *der*.

annihilate [əˈnaɪəleɪt] *vt* vernichten.

anniversary [ˌænɪˈvɜːsərɪ] *n* Jahrestag *der*.

announce [əˈnaʊns] *vt* - **1.** [make public] ankündigen - **2.** [state, declare] verkünden.

announcement [əˈnaʊnsmənt] *n* [public statement] Bekanntmachung *die*; **government announcement** Regierungserklärung *die*.

announcer [əˈnaʊnsər] *n* Ansager *der*, -in *die*; **television announcer** Fernsehansager *der*, -in *die*; **radio announcer** Radioansager *der*, -in *die*.

annoy [əˈnɔɪ] *vt* ärgern.

annoyance [əˈnɔɪəns] *n* Ärgernis *das*.

annoyed [əˈnɔɪd] *adj* verärgert; **to be annoyed at sthg/with sb** über etw/jn verärgert sein; **to get annoyed** sich ärgern.

annoying [əˈnɔɪɪŋ] *adj* ärgerlich.

annual [ˈænjʊəl] <> *adj* jährlich, Jahres-. <> *n* - **1.** [plant] einjährige Pflanze - **2.** [book] Jahrbuch *das*.

annual general meeting *n* Jahreshauptversammlung *die*.

annul [əˈnʌl] *vt* annullieren.

annulment [əˈnʌlmənt] *n* Annullierung *die*.

annum [ˈænəm] *n*: **per annum** pro Jahr.

anomaly [əˈnɒməlɪ] *n* Anomalie *die*.

anonymous [əˈnɒnɪməs] *adj* anonym.

anorak [ˈænəræk] *n esp UK* Anorak *der*.

anorexia (nervosa) [ˌænəˈreksɪə(nɜːˈvəʊsə)] *n* Anorexie *die*, Magersucht *die*.

anorexic [ˌænəˈreksɪk] <> *adj* magersüchtig. <> *n* Magersüchtige *der, die*.

another [əˈnʌðər] <> *adj* - **1.** [additional] noch eine(r) (s); **in another few minutes** in einigen Minuten - **2.** [different] ein anderer, eine andere, ein anderes. <> *pron* - **1.** [an additional one] noch eine(r) (s); **one after another** einer/eine/eines nach dem/der anderen - **2.** [a different one] etwas anderes; **they love one another** sie lieben einander, sie lieben sich; **they are always arguing with one another** sie streiten immer miteinander, sie streiten (sich) immer.

answer [ˈɑːnsər] <> *n* - **1.** [reply] Antwort *die*; **in answer to** als Antwort auf (+ A) - **2.** [solution] Lösung *die*. <> *vt* - **1.** [reply to - question, letter, advertisement] beantworten - **2.** [respond to]: **to answer the door** die Tür öffnen; **to answer the phone** den Hörer abnehmen. <> *vi* [reply] antworten. ➣ **answer back** *vt sep* & *vi* widersprechen (+ D). ➣ **answer for** *vt insep* verantworten.

answerable [ˈɑːnsərəbl] *adj* [accountable] verantwortlich; **answerable to sb/for sthg** jm gegenüber/für etw verantwortlich.

answering machine [ˈɑːnsərɪŋ-] *n* Anrufbeantworter *der*.

ant [ænt] *n* Ameise *die*.

antagonism [ænˈtægənɪzm] *n* Feindlichkeit *die*, Feindseligkeit *die*.

antagonize, -ise [ænˈtægənaɪz] *vt*: to antagonize sb jn gegen sich auflbringen.

Antarctic [ænˈtɑːktɪk] ◇ *n*: the Antarctic die Antarktis. ◇ *adj* antarktisch.

antelope [ˈæntɪləʊp] (*pl inv OR* -s) *n* Antilope *die*.

antenatal [ˌæntɪˈneɪtl] *adj* Schwangerschafts-.

antenatal clinic *n* Sprechstunde *die* für Schwangere.

antenna [ænˈtenə] *n* - 1. (*pl -nae* [-niː]) [of insect, lobster] Fühler *der* - 2. (*pl -s*) *US* [aerial] Antenne *die*.

anthem [ˈænθəm] *n* Hymne *die*.

anthology [ænˈθɒlədʒɪ] *n* Anthologie *die*.

anthrax [ˈænθræks] *n* Milzbrand *der*.

antibiotic [ˌæntɪbaɪˈɒtɪk] *n* Antibiotikum *das*.

antibody [ˈæntɪˌbɒdɪ] *n* Antikörper *der*.

anticipate [ænˈtɪsɪpeɪt] *vt* - 1. [expect] erwarten, vorauslsehen - 2. [preempt]: to anticipate sb jm zuvorlkommen.

anticipation [ænˌtɪsɪˈpeɪʃn] *n* Erwartung *die*; in anticipation of in Erwartung von.

anticlimax [ˌæntɪˈklaɪmæks] *n* Enttäuschung *die*.

anticlockwise *UK* [ˌæntɪˈklɒkwaɪz] ◇ *adj* [direction] Links-. ◇ *adv* gegen den Uhrzeigersinn, nach links.

antics [ˈæntɪks] *npl* - 1. [of children, animals] Possen *Pl* - 2. *pej* [of politician *etc*] Eskapaden *Pl*.

anticyclone [ˌæntɪˈsaɪkləʊn] *n* Hoch *das*.

antidepressant [ˌæntɪdɪˈpresnt] *n* Antidepressivum *das*.

antidote [ˈæntɪdəʊt] *n liter & fig*: antidote (to) Gegenmittel *das* (gegen).

antifreeze [ˈæntɪfriːz] *n* Frostschutzmittel *das*.

antihistamine [ˌæntɪˈhɪstəmɪn] *n* Antihistamin *das*.

antiperspirant [ˌæntɪˈpɜːspərənt] *n* Deodorant *das*.

antiquated [ˈæntɪkweɪtɪd] *adj* antiquiert.

antique [ænˈtiːk] ◇ *adj* antik. ◇ *n* Antiquität *die*.

antique shop *n* Antiquitätenhandlung *die*.

anti-Semitism [ˌæntɪˈsemɪtɪzəm] *n* Antisemitismus *der*.

antiseptic [ˌæntɪˈseptɪk] ◇ *adj* steril, desinfiziert. ◇ *n* Antiseptikum *das*.

antisocial [ˌæntɪˈsəʊʃl] *adj* - 1. [damaging to society] unsozial - 2. [unsociable] ungesellig; [working hours] unsozial.

antlers [ˈæntləz] *npl* Geweih *das*.

anus [ˈeɪnəs] *n* After *der*.

anvil [ˈænvɪl] *n* Amboss *der*.

anxiety [æŋˈzaɪətɪ] *n* - 1. [worry, cause of worry] Sorge *die* - 2. [keenness] Ungeduld *die*.

anxious [ˈæŋkʃəs] *adj* - 1. [worried] besorgt; to be anxious about sb/sthg sich um jn/etw sorgen - 2. [keen]: to be anxious to do sthg darauf brennen, etw zu tun.

any [ˈenɪ] ◇ *adj* - 1. (*in questions*): have you got any money? hast du Geld?; have you got any postcards? haben Sie Postkarten?; can I be of any help? kann ich Ihnen irgendwie behilflich sein? - 2. (*with negatives*): I haven't got any money ich habe kein Geld; we don't have any rooms wir haben keine Zimmer frei; he never does any housework er tut nie etwas im Haushalt - 3. [no matter which] irgendein(e); take any one you like nimm, welches du willst; any beer will do jedes Bier ist recht; at any time jederzeit. ◇ *pron* - 1. (*in questions*) welche; I'm looking for a hotel – are there any nearby? ich suche ein Hotel – gibts hier welche in der Nähe?; can any of you change a tyre? kann jemand von euch einen Reifen wechseln? - 2. (*with if*): if any wenn überhaupt; few foreign films, if any, are successful here nur wenige ausländische Filme haben hier Erfolg - 3. (*with negatives*): I don't want any (of them) ich möchte keinen/keines/keine (von denen) - 4. [no matter which one] jede(r) (s); take any you like nimm, welches du willst; you can sit at any of the tables Sie können sich an jeden beliebigen Tisch setzen. ◇ *adv* - 1. (*in questions*): is there any more ice cream? ist noch Eis da?; is that any better? ist das besser? - 2. (*with negatives*): we can't wait any longer wir können nicht mehr länger warten; I can't see it any more ich kann es nicht mehr sehen.

anybody [ˈenɪˌbɒdɪ] *pron* = anyone.

anyhow [ˈenɪhaʊ] *adv* - 1. [in spite of that] trotzdem - 2. [carelessly] durcheinander, wahllos - 3. [returning to topic] jedenfalls.

anyone [ˈenɪwʌn] *pron* - 1. [any person] jeder; anyone can tell you that (ein) jeder kann dir das sagen; anyone else would have given up jeder andere hätte es aufgegeben; if anyone asks, you haven't seen me wenn jemand fragt, du hast mich nicht gesehen - 2. (*in questions*) irgendjemand; has anyone seen my book? hat irgendjemand mein Buch gesehen?; do you know anyone else? kennst du sonst noch jemanden? - 3. (*in negative statements*): there wasn't anyone in niemand war zu Hause; I didn't see anyone else ich habe sonst niemanden gesehen; there was hardly anyone there es war kaum jemand dort.

anyplace [ˈenɪpleɪs] *adv US* = anywhere.

anything [ˈenɪθɪŋ] *pron* - 1. [no matter what] alles; he eats anything er isst alles; if anything should happen to him falls ihm irgendetwas zustoßen sollte - 2. *(in questions)* irgendetwas; **would you like anything else?** darf es noch etwas sein? - 3. *(in negative statements)*: **I don't want anything at all** ich möchte überhaupt nichts (haben); **he didn't tell me anything** er hat mir nichts gesagt; **hardly anything** kaum etwas; **not for anything** um keinen Preis.

anyway ['enɪweɪ] *adv* - 1. [in any case] sowieso - 2. [in spite of that] trotzdem - 3. [in conversation] jedenfalls; **anyway, there we were** nun ja, jedenfalls standen wir da.

anywhere ['enɪweə] *adv* - 1. [any place] überall; **sit anywhere you like** setz dich einfach irgendwohin; **anywhere else** woanders, anderswo - 2. *(in questions)* irgendwo; **have you seen my jacket anywhere?** hast du meine Jacke irgendwo gesehen?; **did you go anywhere else?** bist du/seid Ihr noch irgendwo anders hingegangen? - 3. *(in negative statements)*: **I can't find it anywhere** ich kann es nirgends finden; **we didn't see anywhere interesting** wir haben nichts Interessantes gesehen.

apart [ə'pɑːt] *adv* - 1. [separated in space] getrennt; **she stood apart from the group** sie hielt sich abseits der Gruppe - 2. [in several pieces] auseinander; **to fall apart** auseinander fallen; **to take sthg apart** etw auseinander nehmen - 3. [aside, excepted] beiseite; **joking apart** Spaß beiseite. ◆ **apart from** *prep* [except for] mit Ausnahme von. ◇ *conj* [in addition to] abgesehen von.

apartheid [ə'pɑːtheɪt] *n* Apartheid *die*.

apartment [ə'pɑːtmənt] *n esp US* Wohnung *die*.

apartment building *n US* Wohnblock *der*.

apathy ['æpəθɪ] *n* Teilnahmslosigkeit *die*.

ape [eɪp] ◇ *n* [animal] Menschenaffe *der*. ◇ *vt pej* [imitate] nachäffen.

aperitif [əperə'tiːf] *n* Aperitif *der*.

aperture ['æpə,tjʊə] *n* - 1. [hole, opening] Öffnung *die* - 2. PHOT Blende *die*.

apex ['eɪpeks] (*pl* -es *OR* apices) *n liter* [top] Spitze *der*; *fig* Gipfel *der*.

APEX ['eɪpeks] (*abbr of* advance purchase excursion) *n UK* zeitlich reglementierter Vorverkauf verbilligter Flugtickets und Bahnfahrkarten.

apices ['eɪpɪsiːz] *Pl* ▷ **apex**.

apiece [ə'piːs] *adv* [object] pro Stück.

apocalypse [ə'pɒkəlɪps] *n* Apokalypse *die*.

apologetic [ə,pɒlə'dʒetɪk] *adj* entschuldigend; **to be apologetic (about sthg)** sich (für etw *OR* wegen etw (*G*)) entschuldigen.

apologize, -ise [ə'pɒlədʒaɪz] *vi* sich entschuldigen; **to apologize to sb for sthg** sich bei jm für etw entschuldigen.

apology [ə'pɒlədʒɪ] *n* Entschuldigung *die*.

apostle [ə'pɒsl] *n* RELIG Apostel *der*.

apostrophe [ə'pɒstrəfɪ] *n* GRAM Apostroph *der*.

appal *UK*, **appall** *US* [ə'pɔːl] *vt* entsetzen.

appalling [ə'pɔːlɪŋ] *adj* entsetzlich.

apparatus [,æpə'reɪtəs] (*pl inv OR* -es) *n* Apparat *der*; [device] Gerät *das*; [in gym] Geräte *Pl*.

apparel [ə'pærəl] *n US* Kleidung *die*.

apparent [ə'pærənt] *adj* - 1. [evident] offensichtlich - 2. [seeming] scheinbar.

apparently [ə'pærəntlɪ] *adv* - 1. [according to rumour] anscheinend - 2. [seemingly] scheinbar.

appeal [ə'piːl] ◇ *vi* - 1. [request] (dringend) bitten; **to appeal to sb for sthg** jn (dringend) um etw bitten; **to appeal to the public to do sthg** die Öffentlichkeit dazu aufrufen, etw zu tun - 2. [to sb's honour, common sense]: **to appeal to** appellieren an (+ *A*) - 3. LAW: **to appeal (against)** Berufung einlegen (gegen) - 4. [attract, interest]: **to appeal to sb** jm gefallen, jm zulsagen. ◇ *n* - 1. [for help, money] Aufruf *der*, Appell *der*; [for mercy] Gesuch *das* - 2. LAW Berufung *die* - 3. [charm, interest] Reiz *der*.

appealing [ə'piːlɪŋ] *adj* [person] ansprechend; [baby] süß; [idea] reizvoll.

appear [ə'pɪə] ◇ *vi* - 1. [gen] erscheinen - 2. [in play] aufltreten. ◇ *vt* [seem] scheinen; **it would appear that...** es hat den Anschein,... *OR* es scheint, als ob...

appearance [ə'pɪərəns] *n* - 1. [gen] Erscheinen *das*; [of symptoms] Auftreten *das* - 2. [outward aspect] äußere Erscheinung; [facial features] Aussehen *das* - 3. [in play, film, on TV] Auftritt *der*.

appease [ə'piːz] *vt* [person, anger] (durch Zugeständnisse) beschwichtigen.

append [ə'pend] *vt fml*: **to append sthg (to)** [add] etw hinzulfügen (zu); [enclose] etw beilfügen (+ *D*).

appendices [ə'pendɪsiːz] *Pl* ▷ **appendix**.

appendicitis [ə,pendɪ'saɪtɪs] *n (U)* Blinddarmentzündung *die*.

appendix [ə'pendɪks] (*pl* -dixes *OR* -dices) *n* - 1. MED Blinddarm *der*; **to have one's appendix out** *OR* **removed** sich (*D*) den Blinddarm herauslnehmen lassen - 2. [in book] Anhang *der*.

appetite ['æpɪtaɪt] *n*: **appetite (for)** Appetit *der* (auf (+ *A*)).

appetizer, -iser ['æpɪtaɪzə] *n* [appetitanregendes] Häppchen; [starter] Vorspeise *die*.

appetizing, -ising ['æpɪtaɪzɪŋ] *adj* appetitlich.

applaud [ə'plɔːd] ◇ *vt* - 1. [person] applaudieren (+ *D*) - 2. *fig* [effort] loben; [decision] begrüßen. ◇ *vi* applaudieren.

applause [ə'plɔːz] *n* Applaus *der*.

apple ['æpl] *n* Apfel *der*.

apple tree *n* Apfelbaum *der*.

appliance [ə'plaɪəns] *n* Gerät *das*.

applicable [ə'plɪkəbl] *adj* zutreffend; **delete where not applicable** Nichtzutreffendes streichen; **to be applicable to sb/sthg** auf jn/etw zutreffen.

applicant ['æplɪkənt] *n*: **applicant (for)** [for job] Bewerber *der*, -in *die* (um OR für); [for state benefit] Antragsteller *der*, -in *die* (für).

application [,æplɪ'keɪʃn] *n* - 1. [for job, college]: **application (for)** Bewerbung *die* (um OR für) - 2. [for club]: **application (for)** Antrag *der* (auf (+ A)) - 3. [of knowledge, rule] Anwendung *die*; [of invention] Einsatz *der* - 4. [use] Verwendung *die* - 5. [diligence] Fleiß *der* - 6. COMPUT: **application (program)** Anwendungsprogramm *das*.

application form *n* [for job] Bewerbungsformular *das*; [for state benefit, club] Antragsformular *das*.

applied [ə'plaɪd] *adj* [science] angewandt.

apply [ə'plaɪ] <> *vt* - 1. [rule, skill] anlwenden - 2. [paint, ointment] aufltragen; **to apply the brakes** bremsen. <> *vi* - 1. [for work, grant]: **to apply (for)** sich bewerben (um OR für); **to apply to sb for sthg** sich bei jm um OR für etw bewerben - 2. [be relevant]: **to apply (to)** zutreffen (auf (+ A)).

appoint [ə'pɔɪnt] *vt* [to job, position] einlstellen; [to office] ernennen.

appointment [ə'pɔɪntmənt] *n* - 1. (U) [to job, position] Einstellung *die*; [to office] Ernennung *die* - 2. [job, position] Stelle *die* - 3. [with doctor, hairdresser, in business] Termin *der*; **to have an appointment** einen Termin haben; **to make an appointment** einen Termin vereinbaren.

apportion [ə'pɔ:ʃn] *vt* [money] auflteilen; [blame] zulweisen.

appraisal [ə'preɪzl] *n* Beurteilung *die*.

appreciable [ə'pri:ʃəbl] *adj* [difference] merklich; [amount] beträchtlich.

appreciate [ə'pri:ʃɪeɪt] <> *vt* - 1. [value] schätzen; **her books were not appreciated at the time** ihre Bücher wurden damals nicht gewürdigt - 2. [recognize, understand] sich (D) bewusst sein (+ G) - 3. [help, advice] dankbar sein für; **thanks, I really appreciate it!** danke schön, sehr nett von dir/Ihnen! <> *vi* FIN im Wert steigen.

appreciation [ə,pri:ʃɪ'eɪʃn] *n* - 1. [liking] Anerkennung *die* - 2. [understanding] Verständnis *das* - 3. [gratitude] Dankbarkeit *die*.

appreciative [ə'pri:ʃjətɪv] *adj* [person; audience] dankbar; **to be appreciative of sthg** etw zu schätzen wissen.

apprehensive [,æprɪ'hensɪv] *adj*: **apprehensive (about)** besorgt (wegen (+ G)).

apprentice [ə'prentɪs] *n* Lehrling *der*; **an apprentice mechanic** ein Mechanikerlehrling.

apprenticeship [ə'prentɪsʃɪp] *n* Lehre *die*.

approach [ə'prəʊtʃ] <> *n* - 1. [arrival] (Heran)nahen *das* - 2. [access] Zugang *der*; [road] Zufahrt *die* - 3. [method] Ansatz *der* - 4. [proposal]: **to make an approach to sb** an jn heranltreten. <> *vt* - 1. [come near to] sich nähern (+ D); **temperatures approaching 35°C** Temperaturen von bis zu 35°C - 2. [speak to]: **to approach sb about sthg** wegen etw an jn heranltreten (G) - 3. [problem, task] anlgehen. <> *vi* sich nähern.

approachable [ə'prəʊtʃəbl] *adj* - 1. [person] umgänglich - 2. [place] erreichbar.

appropriate <> *adj* [ə'prəʊprɪət] angemessen; [clothing, moment] passend. <> *vt* [ə'prəʊprɪeɪt] - 1. LAW [steal] sich anleignen - 2. [allocate] bestimmen.

approval [ə'pru:vl] *n* - 1. [liking, admiration] Anerkennung *die* - 2. [official agreement] Genehmigung *die* - 3. COMM: **on approval** zur Probe.

approve [ə'pru:v] <> *vi*: **to approve of sb** von jm etwas halten; **to approve of sthg** mit etw einverstanden sein; **I don't approve of him** ich halte nichts von ihm. <> *vt* genehmigen.

approx. [ə'prɒks] *abbr of* **approximately**.

approximate *adj* [ə'prɒksɪmət] ungefähr.

approximately [ə'prɒksɪmətlɪ] *adv* ungefähr, circa.

apricot ['eɪprɪkɒt] *n* [fruit] Aprikose *die*.

April ['eɪprəl] *n* April *der*; *see also* **September**.

April Fools' Day *n* der erste April.

apron ['eɪprən] *n* [clothing] Schürze *die*.

apt [æpt] *adj* - 1. [pertinent] treffend - 2. [likely]: **to be apt to do sthg** dazu neigen, etw zu tun.

aptitude ['æptɪtju:d] *n* Begabung *die*; **to have an aptitude for sthg** eine Begabung für etw haben.

aptly ['æptlɪ] *adv* treffend.

aqualung ['ækwəlʌŋ] *n* Presslufttauchgerät *das*.

aquarium [ə'kweərɪəm] (*pl* -riums OR -ria [-rɪə]) *n* Aquarium *das*.

Aquarius [ə'kweərɪəs] *n* Wassermann *der*.

aquatic [ə'kwætɪk] *adj* Wasser-.

aqueduct ['ækwɪdʌkt] *n* Aquädukt *der* ODER *das*.

Arab ['ærəb] <> *adj* arabisch. <> *n* [person] Araber *der*, -in *die*.

Arabian [ə'reɪbjən] *adj* arabisch.

Arabic ['ærəbɪk] <> *adj* arabisch. <> *n* [language] Arabisch(e) *das*.

Arabic numeral *n* arabische Ziffer.

arable ['ærəbl] *adj*: **arable land** Ackerland *das*.

arbitrary ['ɑ:bɪtrərɪ] *adj* willkürlich.

arbitration [,ɑ:bɪ'treɪʃn] *n* Schlichtungsverfahren *das*; **to go to arbitration** vor eine Schlichtungskommission gehen.

arcade [ɑ:'keɪd] *n* - 1. [for shopping] Passage *die* - 2. ARCHIT [covered passage] Arkade *die*.

arch [ɑ:tʃ] <> *adj* [knowing] schelmisch. <> *n* - 1. ARCHIT [knowing] Bogen *der*; [arched entrance] Torbogen *der* - 2. [of foot] Wölbung *die*. <> *vt* [back] krümmen. <> *vi* sich wölben.

archaeologist [,ɑ:kɪ'ɒlədʒɪst] *n* Archäologe *der*, -in *die*.

archaeology [,ɑ:kɪ'ɒlədʒɪ] *n* Archäologie *die*.

archaic [ɑ:'keɪɪk] *adj* [language] veraltet.

archbishop [,ɑ:tʃ'bɪʃəp] *n* Erzbischof *der*.

archenemy [,ɑ:tʃ'enɪmɪ] *n* Erzfeind *der*, -in *die*.

archeology etc [,ɑ:kɪ'ɒlədʒɪ] = **archaeology** etc .

archer ['ɑ:tʃər] *n* Bogenschütze *der*.

archery ['ɑ:tʃərɪ] *n* Bogenschießen *das*.

archetypal [,ɑ:kɪ'taɪpl] *adj* typisch.

architect ['ɑ:kɪtekt] *n* - 1. [of buildings] Architekt *der*, -in *die* - 2. *fig* [of plan, event] Urheber *der*, -in *die*.

architecture ['ɑ:kɪtektʃər] *n* - 1. [gen & COMPUT] Architektur *die* - 2. [style of building] Baustil *der*.

archives ['ɑ:kaɪvz] *npl* [of documents] Archiv *das*.

archway ['ɑ:tʃweɪ] *n* Torbogen *der*.

Arctic ['ɑ:ktɪk] <> *adj* - 1. GEOG arktisch - 2. *inf* [cold] eiskalt. <> *n*: **the Arctic** die Arktis.

ardent ['ɑ:dənt] *adj* leidenschaftlich; [desire] brennend.

arduous ['ɑ:djʊəs] *adj* [task] mühselig; [climb, journey] anstrengend.

are (weak form [ər], strong form [ɑ:r]) *vb* ⊳ **be**.

area ['eərɪə] *n* - 1. [region] Gegend *die*; [in town] Viertel *das*; **in the Bristol area** im Raum Bristol - 2. *fig* [approximate size, number]: **in the area of** im Bereich von - 3. [surface size] Fläche *die* - 4. [space] Bereich *der*; **a parking area** ein Parkplatz - 5. [of knowledge, interest, subject] Gebiet *das*.

area code *n* US Vorwahl *die*.

arena [ə'ri:nə] *n* liter & *fig* Arena *die*.

aren't [ɑ:nt] abbr of **are not**.

Argentina [,ɑ:dʒən'ti:nə] *n* Argentinien *nt*.

Argentine ['ɑ:dʒəntaɪn], **Argentinian** [,ɑ:dʒən'tɪnɪən] <> *adj* argentinisch. <> *n* Argentinier *der*, -in *die*.

arguably ['ɑ:gjʊəblɪ] *adv* möglicherweise.

argue ['ɑ:gju:] <> *vi* - 1. [quarrel]: **to argue (with sb about sthg)** sich (mit jm über etw (A)) streiten - 2. [reason] argumentieren; **to argue for/against sthg** für/gegen etw einltreten. <> *vt*: **to argue the case for sthg** für etw einltreten; **to argue that** die Meinung vertreten, dass.

argument ['ɑ:gjʊmənt] *n* - 1. [quarrel] Streit *der*; **to have an argument (with sb)** sich (mit jm) streiten - 2. [reason] Argument *das* - 3. (U) [reasoning] Diskussion *die*.

argumentative [,ɑ:gjʊ'mentətɪv] *adj* streitsüchtig.

arise [ə'raɪz] (*pt* arose, *pp* arisen [ə'rɪzn]) *vi* [problems, difficulties] aufltreten; [opportunities] sich ergeben; **to arise from sthg** sich aus etw ergeben; **if the need arises** falls sich die Notwendigkeit ergibt.

aristocrat [UK 'ærɪstəkræt, US ə'rɪstəkræt] *n* Aristokrat *der*, -in *die*, Adlige *der*, *die*.

arithmetic [ə'rɪθmətɪk] *n* Arithmetik *die*, Rechnen *das*; [calculation] Rechnung *die*.

ark [ɑ:k] *n* [ship] Arche *die*.

arm [ɑ:m] <> *n* - 1. [of person] Arm *der*; **arm in arm** Arm in Arm; **to keep sb at arm's length** *fig* jn auf Distanz halten - 2. [of garment] Ärmel *der* - 3. [of chair] Armlehne *die*. <> *vt* [with weapons] bewaffnen. ◆ **arms** *npl* [weapons] Waffen *Pl*; **to take up arms** zu den Waffen greifen; **to be up in arms (about sthg)** (wegen etw (G)) aufgebracht sein.

armaments ['ɑ:məmənts] *npl* Waffen *Pl*.

armband ['ɑ:m,bænd] *n* Armbinde *die*; [for swimming] Schwimmflügel *der*.

armchair ['ɑ:mtʃeər] *n* Sessel *der*.

armed [ɑ:md] *adj* - 1. [police, thieves] bewaffnet - 2. *fig* [with information]: **armed with sthg** mit etw ausgestattet.

armed forces *npl* Streitkräfte *Pl*.

armhole ['ɑ:mhəʊl] *n* Armloch *das*.

armour UK, **armor** US ['ɑ:mər] *n* - 1. [for person] Rüstung *die* - 2. [for military vehicle] Panzerung *die*.

armoured car *n* MIL Panzerwagen *der*.

armoury UK, **armory** US ['ɑ:mərɪ] *n* Arsenal *das*.

armpit ['ɑ:mpɪt] *n* Achselhöhle *die*.

armrest ['ɑ:mrest] *n* Armlehne *die*.

arms control ['ɑ:mz-] *n* Rüstungskontrolle *die*.

army ['ɑ:mɪ] *n* - 1. MIL Heer *das*, Armee *die*; **to be in the army** beim Militär sein - 2. *fig* [large group] Heer *das*.

A road *n* UK ≃ Bundesstraße *die*.

aroma [ə'rəʊmə] *n* Duft *der*.

arose [ə'rəʊz] *pt* ⊳ **arise**.

around [ə'raʊnd] <> *adv* - 1. [here and there] herum; **to travel around** herumlreisen; **to sit around doing nothing** untätig herumlsitzen - 2. [on all sides] herum; **all around** auf allen Seiten - 3. [present, nearby]: **is she around?** ist sie da?; **around here** [in the area] hier in der

Gegend; **cars have been around for over a century** Autos gibt es schon seit über hundert Jahren - **4.** [in a circle]: **to go around** sich drehen; **to spin around (and around)** sich im Kreis drehen - **5.** [to the other side]: **to go around** herumgehen; **to turn around** sich umdrehen; **to look around** sich umsehen - **6.** *phr*: **to have been around** *inf* [travelled a lot] (viel) herumgekommen sein. ⟨> *prep* - **1.** [surrounding] um herum - **2.** [near]: **around here/there** hier/dort in der Nähe; **is there a bank anywhere around here?** gibt es hier irgendwo eine Bank? - **3.** [all over]: **150 offices around the world** 150 Büros in der ganzen Welt; **all around the country** im ganzen Land; **we walked around the town** wir spazierten durch die Stadt - **4.** [in a circle]: **we walked around the lake** wir gingen um den See herum; **to go/drive around sthg** etw herumgehen/herumfahren; **around the clock** *fig* rund um die Uhr - **5.** [approximately] ungefähr - **6.** [in circumference]: **she measures 30 inches around the waist** um die Taille misst sie 75 cm - **7.** [so as to avoid] um herum; **to get around an obstacle** um ein Hindernis herumgehen; **to find a way around a problem** einen Ausweg für ein Problem finden.

arouse [əˈrauz] *vt* - **1.** [excite] erregen; [interest, suspicion] erwecken - **2.** [wake] (auf)lwecken.

arrange [əˈreɪndʒ] *vt* - **1.** [flowers] arrangieren; [books, objects] (an)lordnen; [furniture] (um)lstellen - **2.** [event] planen; [meeting] vereinbaren; [party] arrangieren; **to arrange to do sthg** vereinbaren, etw zu tun - **3.** MUS bearbeiten, arrangieren.

arrangement [əˈreɪndʒmənt] *n* - **1.** [agreement] Vereinbarung *die*; **to come to an arrangement** eine Einigung erzielen - **2.** [of objects] Anordnung *die* - **3.** MUS Bearbeitung *die*, Arrangement *das*. ⬥ **arrangements** *npl* [preparations] Vorbereitungen *Pl*; **please make your own arrangements for accommodation** bitte arrangieren Sie Ihre Unterkunft selbst.

array [əˈreɪ] ⟨> *n* [of objects, people, ornaments] Aufgebot *das*. ⟨> *vt* [ornaments] auflstellen.

arrears [əˈrɪəz] *npl* [money owed] Rückstände *Pl*; **to be paid in arrears** rückwirkend bezahlt werden; **to be in arrears** im Rückstand sein.

arrest [əˈrest] ⟨> *n* [by police] Verhaftung *die*; **to be under arrest** verhaftet sein. ⟨> *vt* - **1.** [subj: police] verhaften - **2.** *fml* [sb's attention] erregen - **3.** *fml* [stop - development] hemmen; [- spread of disease] auflhalten.

arrival [əˈraɪvl] *n* - **1.** [at place] Ankunft *die*; **on arrival** bei der Ankunft; **late arrival** [of train, bus, mail] verspätete Ankunft - **2.** [of new system, technology] Aufkommen *das* - **3.** [person] Ankömmling *der*; **new arrival** [person] Neuankömmling *der*.

arrive [əˈraɪv] *vi* - **1.** [gen] anlkommen; **to arrive at a conclusion/decision** zu einem Schluss/einer Entscheidung kommen - **2.** [moment, event] kommen.

arrogant [ˈærəgənt] *adj* arrogant.

arrow [ˈærəʊ] *n* Pfeil *der*.

arse UK [ɑːs], **ass** US [æs] *n vulg* [buttocks] Arsch *der*.

arsenic [ˈɑːsnɪk] *n* Arsen *das*.

arson [ˈɑːsn] *n* Brandstiftung *die*.

art [ɑːt] ⟨> *n* Kunst *die*. ⟨> *comp* Kunst-. ⬥ **arts** *npl* - **1.** SCH & UNIV [humanities] Geisteswissenschaften *Pl* - **2.** [fine arts]: **the arts** die schönen Künste *Pl*.

artefact [ˈɑːtɪfækt] *n* = **artifact**.

artery [ˈɑːtərɪ] *n* Arterie *die*.

art gallery *n* Kunstgalerie *die*.

arthritis [ɑːˈθraɪtɪs] *n* Arthritis *die*.

artichoke [ˈɑːtɪtʃəʊk] *n* Artischocke *die*.

article [ˈɑːtɪkl] *n* - **1.** [item] Gegenstand *der*; COMM Ware *die*, Artikel *der*; **article of clothing** Kleidungsstück *das* - **2.** [in newspaper, magazine] Artikel *der* - **3.** [in agreement, contract] Paragraph *der*; [in constitution] Artikel *der* - **4.** GRAM Artikel *der*.

articulate ⟨> *adj* [ɑːˈtɪkjʊlət] [speech] leichtverständlich; **to be articulate** [person] sich gut ausldrücken können. ⟨> *vt* [ɑːˈtɪkjʊleɪt] [thought, wish] zum Ausdruck bringen, artikulieren.

articulated lorry [ɑːˈtɪkjʊleɪtɪd-] *n* UK Sattelschlepper *der*.

artifact [ˈɑːtɪfækt] *n* Artefakt *das*.

artificial [ˌɑːtɪˈfɪʃl] *adj* - **1.** [non-natural] künstlich - **2.** [insincere] gekünstelt.

artillery [ɑːˈtɪlərɪ] *n* Artillerie *die*.

artist [ˈɑːtɪst] *n* Künstler *der*, -in *die*.

artistic [ɑːˈtɪstɪk] *adj* - **1.** [gen] künstlerisch; [person] künstlerisch begabt - **2.** [attractive] kunstvoll.

artistry [ˈɑːtɪstrɪ] *n* Kunstwertigkeit *die*.

as (unstressed [əz], stressed [æz]) ⟨> *conj* - **1.** [referring to time] als - **2.** [referring to manner] wie; **as expected** wie erwartet; **do as I say** tu, was ich dir sage; **it's hard enough as it is** es ist ohnehin schon schwierig genug - **3.** [introducing a statement] wie; **as I told you** wie ich dir bereits gesagt habe; **as you know** wie du weißt - **4.** [because] weil, da. ⟨> *adv* (in comparisons): **as ... as so ... wie; **he's as tall as I am** er ist so groß wie ich; **as many as** so viele wie; **as much as** so viel wie. ⟨> *prep* als; **she works as a nurse** sie arbeitet als Krankenschwester; **to consider sb as a friend** jn als Freund betrachten. ⬥ **as for** *prep*: **as for me** was mich betrifft. ⬥ **as from, as of** *prep* ab; **as from** OR **of Monday** ab Montag. ⬥ **as if, as though** *conj* als ob, als wenn; **he looked at me as if I were mad** er sah mich an, als ob ich verrückt wäre; **as if by chance** wie durch Zufall. **as to** prep UK: **she questioned him as to his motives** sie fragte ihn nach seinen Beweggründen.

a.s.a.p. (abbr of **as soon as possible**) baldmöglichst.

asbestos [æs'bestəs] n Asbest der.

ASBO ['æzbə] n (abbr of **antisocial behaviour order**) Verwarnung gegen asoziales Verhalten.

ascend [ə'send] ⟨⟩ vt [hill] besteigen; [staircase] hinauflgehen; [ladder] hinauflsteigen. ⟨⟩ vi [climb] auflsteigen; [subj: path, road etc] anlsteigen.

ascendant [ə'sendənt] n: **to be in the ascendant** im Aufstieg begriffen sein.

ascent [ə'sent] n - 1. [gen] Aufstieg der - 2. [upward slope] Steigung die.

ascertain [,æsə'teɪn] vt ermitteln.

ascribe [ə'skraɪb] vt: **to ascribe sthg to sthg** einer Sache (D) etw zulschreiben; **to ascribe sthg to sb** jm etw zulschreiben.

ash [æʃ] n - 1. [from cigarette, fire] Asche die - 2. [tree] Esche die.

ashamed [ə'ʃeɪmd] adj beschämt; **to be ashamed of sb/sthg** sich js/etw (G) schämen; **to be ashamed to do sthg** sich schämen, etw zu tun.

ashore [ə'ʃɔːr] adv [go, swim] an Land.

ashtray ['æʃtreɪ] n Aschenbecher der.

Ash Wednesday n Aschermittwoch der.

Asia [UK 'eɪʃə, US 'eɪʒə] n Asien nt.

Asian [UK 'eɪʃn, US 'eɪʒn] ⟨⟩ adj asiatisch. ⟨⟩ n [from Far East] Asiat der, -in die.

aside [ə'saɪd] ⟨⟩ adv - 1. [to one side] beiseite, zur Seite; **step aside!** treten Sie zur Seite!; **to take sb aside** jn beiseite nehmen - 2. [apart]: **joking aside** Spaß beiseite; **aside from** abgesehen von. ⟨⟩ n - 1. [in play] Apart das - 2. [remark] beiläufige Bemerkung.

ask [ɑːsk] ⟨⟩ vt - 1. [gen] fragen; **to ask a question** eine Frage stellen; **to ask sb sthg** jn etw fragen - 2. [request - permission, forgiveness] bitten um; (phrase): **to ask sb for sthg** jn um etw bitten; **to ask sb for advice** jn um Rat fragen; **to ask sb to do sthg** jn (darum) bitten, etw zu tun - 3. [invite] einlladen; **to ask sb (round) to dinner** jn zum Abendessen einlladen - 4. [price] verlangen. ⟨⟩ vi - 1. [enquire] fragen - 2. [request] bitten. **ask after** vt insep sich erkundigen nach. **ask for** vt insep - 1. [ask to talk to] verlangen; **he's asking for you** er will Sie sprechen - 2. [request] bitten um.

askance [ə'skæns] adv: **to look askance at sb** jn missbilligend anlschauen; **to look askance at sthg** etw (D) ablehnend gegenüberlstehen.

askew [ə'skjuː] adj schief.

asking price ['ɑːskɪŋ-] n Verkaufspreis der.

asleep [ə'sliːp] adj schlafend; **to fall asleep** einlschlafen.

asparagus [ə'spærəgəs] n Spargel der.

aspect ['æspekt] n - 1. [facet] Aspekt der - 2. [appearance] Aussehen das.

aspersions [ə'spɜːʃnz] npl: **to cast aspersions (on sthg)** abfällige Bemerkungen (über etw (A)) machen.

asphalt ['æsfælt] n (U) Asphalt der.

asphyxiate [əs'fɪksɪeɪt] vt ersticken.

aspiration [,æspə'reɪʃn] n [desire, ambition] Bestrebung die.

aspire [ə'spaɪər] vi: **to aspire to sthg** nach etw streben; **to aspire to do sthg** danach streben, etw zu tun.

aspirin ['æsprɪn] n Aspirin® das.

ass [æs] n - 1. [animal] Esel der - 2. US vulg = **arse**.

assailant [ə'seɪlənt] n Angreifer der, -in die.

assassin [ə'sæsɪn] n Attentäter der, -in die (dessen Mordanschlag glückt).

assassinate [ə'sæsɪneɪt] vt ermorden; **to be assassinated** einem Attentat zum Opfer fallen.

assassination [ə,sæsɪ'neɪʃn] n (geglücktes) Attentat, (politischer) Mord.

assault [ə'sɔːlt] ⟨⟩ n - 1. MIL: **assault (on sthg)** Sturmangriff der (auf etw (A)) - 2. [physical attack]: **assault (on sb)** (tätlicher) Angriff (auf jn). ⟨⟩ vt [attack - physically] (tätlich) anlgreifen; [- sexually] belästigen.

assemble [ə'sembl] ⟨⟩ vt - 1. [gather - people] zusammenlrufen; [- evidence, material] zusammenltragen; [- Parliament] einlberufen - 2. [fit together] zusammenlbauen. ⟨⟩ vi [people] sich versammeln; [Parliament] zusammenltreten.

assembly [ə'semblɪ] n - 1. [gen] Versammlung die; [at school] Morgenandacht die - 2. (U) [fitting together] Zusammenbau der; [of device, machine] Montage die.

assembly line n Fließband das.

assent [ə'sent] ⟨⟩ n Zustimmung die. ⟨⟩ vi zulstimmen; **to assent to sthg** etw (D) zulstimmen.

assert [ə'sɜːt] vt - 1. [conviction, belief] behaupten; [innocence] beteuern - 2. [authority] geltend machen.

assertive [ə'sɜːtɪv] adj [person, tone] energisch; [attitude] selbstbewusst.

assess [ə'ses] vt - 1. [judge] einlschätzen, beurteilen - 2. [estimate - value] schätzen; [- damages] festlsetzen.

assessment [ə'sesmənt] n - 1. [judgement] Einschätzung die - 2. [estimate - of value] Schätzung die; [- of damages] Festsetzung die.

asset ['æset] n - 1. [valuable quality] Vorteil der - 2. [valuable person] Stütze die. **assets** npl COMM Vermögen das.

assign [ə'saɪn] vt - 1. [allot]: **to assign sthg (to sb/sthg)** (jm/etw) etw zulteilen OR zulweisen

- 2. [appoint]: **to assign sb (to sthg)** jn (etw *(D)*) zuteilen OR zuweisen; **to assign sb to do sthg** jn damit beauftragen, etw zu tun.

assignment [ə'saɪnmənt] *n* - **1.** [task] Aufgabe *die*; [at school] Projekt *das*; [job] Auftrag *der* - **2.** [act of appointing] Zuteilung *die*; [to task] Betrauung *die*; [to post] Berufung *die*.

assimilate [ə'sɪmɪleɪt] *vt* - **1.** [gen] aufl-nehmen - **2.** [people]: **to assimilate sb (into sthg)** jn (in etw *(A)*) integrieren.

assist [ə'sɪst] *vt* helfen *(+ D)*; **to assist sb with sthg** jm bei etw helfen; **to assist sb in doing sthg** jm helfen, etw zu tun.

assistance [ə'sɪstəns] *n (U)* Hilfe *die*; **to be of assistance (to sb)** (jm) helfen OR behilflich sein.

assistant [ə'sɪstənt] <> *n* - **1.** [helper] Assistent *der*, -in *die* - **2.** [in shop] Verkäufer *der*, -in *die*. <> *comp* stellvertretend; **assistant editor** Redaktionsassistent *der*, -in *die*.

associate <> *adj* [ə'səʊʃɪət] [member] außerordentlich. <> *n* [ə'səʊʃɪət] [business partner] Partner *der*, -in *die*. <> *vt* [ə'səʊʃɪeɪt] [connect] in Verbindung bringen, assoziieren; **to associate sb/sthg with sb/sthg** jn/etw mit jm/etw in Verbindung bringen; **to be associated with sb/sthg** mit jm/etw in Verbindung gebracht werden. <> *vi* [ə'səʊʃɪeɪt]: **to associate with sb** mit jm verkehren.

association [ə,səʊsɪ'eɪʃn] *n* - **1.** [organization] Verband *der* - **2.** *(U)* [relationship] Verkehr *der*, Umgang *der*; **in association with sb/sthg** in Zusammenarbeit mit jm/etw.

assorted [ə'sɔːtɪd] *adj* [colours, sizes] verschieden; [sweets] gemischt.

assortment [ə'sɔːtmənt] *n* [mixture - of people] Mischung *die*; [- of goods] Auswahl *die*.

assume [ə'sjuːm] *vt* - **1.** [suppose, adopt] anl-nehmen - **2.** [undertake] übernehmen.

assumed name [ə'sjuːmd-] *n* falscher Name.

assuming [ə'sjuːmɪŋ] *conj*: **assuming (that)...** vorausgesetzt(, dass)...

assumption [ə'sʌmpʃn] *n* [supposition] Annahme *die*.

assurance [ə'ʃʊərəns] *n* - **1.** [promise] Zusicherung *die* - **2.** [confidence] Selbstsicherheit *die* - **3.** *(U)* FIN [insurance] Versicherung *die*.

assure [ə'ʃʊə] *vt* [reassure] versichern *(+ D)*; **to assure sb of sthg** jn einer Sache *(G)* versichern; **to be assured of sthg** [be certain] sich *(D)* einer Sache *(G)* sicher sein.

assured [ə'ʃʊəd] *adj* selbstsicher.

asterisk ['æstərɪsk] *n* Sternchen *das*.

asthma ['æsmə] *n* Asthma *das*.

astonish [ə'stɒnɪʃ] *vt* erstaunen.

astonished [ə'stɒnɪʃd] *adj* erstaunt.

astonishment [ə'stɒnɪʃmənt] *n* Erstaunen *das*.

astound [ə'staʊnd] *vt* verblüffen.

astray [ə'streɪ] *adv*: **to go astray** [object] verloren gehen; [animal] sich verirren; **to lead sb astray** *fig* jn vom rechten Weg abl-bringen.

astride [ə'straɪd] <> *adv* rittlings. <> *prep* rittlings auf *(+ D)*.

astrology [ə'strɒlədʒɪ] *n* Astrologie *die*.

astronaut ['æstrənɔːt] *n* Astronaut *der*, -in *die*.

astronomical [,æstrə'nɒmɪkl] *adj liter* & *fig* astronomisch.

astronomy [ə'strɒnəmɪ] *n* Astronomie *die*.

astute [ə'stjuːt] *adj* clever.

asylum [ə'saɪləm] *n* - **1.** *dated* [mental hospital] psychiatrische Anstalt - **2.** *(U)* [protection] Asyl *das*.

at (*unstressed* [ət], *stressed* [æt]) *prep* - **1.** [indicating place, position]: **there was a knock at the door** es klopfte an der Tür; **he studies at Cambridge** er studiert in Cambridge; **at the bottom of the hill** am Fuß(el) des Hügels; **at my father's** bei meinem Vater; **at home** zu Hause; **at school** in der Schule; **at work** bei der Arbeit - **2.** [indicating direction]: **to aim at sb/sthg** auf jn/etw zielen; **to smile at sb** jn anllächeln; **to look at sb/sthg** jn/etw anlsehen - **3.** [indicating particular time]: **at midnight/noon/eleven o'clock** um Mitternacht/zwölf Uhr mittags/elf Uhr; **at Christmas/Easter** zu OR an Weihnachten/Ostern; **at night** bei Nacht, nachts - **4.** [indicating age, speed, rate]: **at your age** in deinem Alter; **at 52 (years of age)** mit 52 (Jahren); **at 100 miles per hour** mit 100 Meilen pro Stunde; **at high speed** mit hoher Geschwindigkeit - **5.** [indicating price]: **at £50 (a pair)** für 50 Pfund (das Paar) - **6.** [indicating particular state, condition]: **at peace/war** im Frieden/Krieg; **at lunch** beim Mittagessen - **7.** *(after adjectives)*: **amused/appalled/puzzled at sthg** über etw *(A)* belustigt/entsetzt/verblüfft; **to be bad/good at sthg** in etw *(D)* schlecht/gut sein. ◆ **at all** *adv* - **1.** *(with negative)*: **not at all** [when thanked] keine Ursache; [when answering a question] überhaupt nicht; **she's not at all happy** sie ist überhaupt nicht glücklich - **2.** [in the slightest]: **have you done anything at all today?** hast du heute überhaupt irgendetwas gemacht?; **do you know her at all?** kennst du sie überhaupt?

ate [*UK* et, *US* eɪt] *pt* ⊳ **eat**.

atheist ['eɪθɪɪst] *n* Atheist *der*, -in *die*.

Athens ['æθɪnz] *n* Athen *nt*.

athlete ['æθliːt] *n* Leichtathlet *der*, -in *die*.

athletic [æθ'letɪk] *adj* - **1.** [relating to athletics] athletisch - **2.** [sporty] sportlich. ◆ **athletics** *npl* Leichtathletik *die*.

Atlantic [ət'læntɪk] <> *adj* atlantisch. <> *n*: **the Atlantic (Ocean)** der Atlantik.

atlas ['ætləs] *n* Atlas *der*.

atmosphere ['ætmə‚sfɪər] n - 1. [gen] Atmosphäre die - 2. [in room] Luft die.

atmospheric [‚ætməs'ferɪk] adj - 1. [pressure, pollution] atmosphärisch - 2. [music, place, film] stimmungsvoll.

atom ['ætəm] n TECH Atom das.

atom bomb n Atombombe die.

atomic [ə'tɒmɪk] adj Atom-.

atone [ə'təʊn] vi: to atone for sthg [crime, sin] (für) etw büßen; [mistake, behaviour] etw wieder gutmachen.

A to Z n Stadtplan der (im Buchformat).

atrocious [ə'trəʊʃəs] adj grauenhaft.

atrocity [ə'trɒsətɪ] n Gräueltat die.

attach [ə'tætʃ] vt - 1. [fasten] befestigen; [document] beilheften; to attach sthg to sthg einer Sache an etw (D) befestigen; [document] einer Sache (D) etw beilheften - 2. [attribute]: to attach sthg to sthg [importance] etw (D) etw beilmessen; [blame] etw (D) etw zulschreiben - 3. COMPUT anlheften, anlhängen.

attaché case n Aktenkoffer der.

attached [ə'tætʃt] adj [fond]: to be attached to sb/sthg an jm/etw hängen.

attachment [ə'tætʃmənt] n - 1. [device] Zusatzgerät das - 2. COMPUT Attachment das, Anhang der.

attack [ə'tæk] <> n - 1. [physical]: attack (on sb) [on person] Überfall der (auf jn); [on enemy] Angriff der (auf jn) - 2. [verbal]: attack (on sthg) Angriff der (auf etw (A)) - 3. [of illness] Anfall der. <> vt - 1. [physically - person] überfallen; [- enemy] angreifen - 2. [verbally] anlgreifen - 3. [affect] befallen - 4. [deal with] in Angriff nehmen. <> vi anlgreifen.

attacker [ə'tækər] n Angreifer der, -in die.

attain [ə'teɪn] vt [rank, objectives] erreichen; [success, happiness] erlangen.

attainment [ə'teɪnmənt] n [skill] Fertigkeit die.

attempt [ə'tempt] <> n Versuch der; an attempt at a smile ein Versuch, zu lächeln; to make an attempt on sb's life einen Mordanschlag auf jn verüben. <> vt [try] versuchen; to attempt to do sthg versuchen, etw zu tun.

attend [ə'tend] <> vt - 1. [meeting] teillnehmen an (+ D); [party] gehen zu - 2. [school, church] besuchen. <> vi - 1. [be present] anwesend sein - 2. [pay attention]: to attend (to sthg) auflpassen (bei etw). ◆ **attend to** vt insep - 1. [deal with] sich kümmern um - 2. [look after - customer] bedienen; [- patient] behandeln.

attendance [ə'tendəns] n - 1. [number present - at meeting] Teilnehmerzahl die; [- at concert, cinema] Besucherzahl die - 2. [presence] Anwesenheit die, Teilnahme die; to have a poor attendance record oft fehlen.

attendant [ə'tendənt] n [at museum] Aufseher der, -in die; [at petrol station] Tankwart der; car park attendant Parkplatzwächter der, -in die.

attention [ə'tenʃn] <> n (U) - 1. [awareness, interest] Aufmerksamkeit die; to attract sb's attention jn auf sich (A) aufmerksam machen; to bring sthg to sb's attention, to draw sb's attention to sthg jn auf etw (A) aufmerksam machen; to pay attention to sb/sthg jm/etw Aufmerksamkeit schenken; to pay attention auflpassen - 2. [care] Fürsorge die - 3. COMM: for the attention of zu Händen (von). <> excl MIL stillgestanden!

attentive [ə'tentɪv] adj aufmerksam.

attic ['ætɪk] n Dachboden der.

attitude ['ætɪtjuːd] n - 1. [way of thinking]: attitude (to OR towards sb/sthg) Einstellung die (gegenüber jm/zu etw) - 2. [behaviour, posture] Haltung die.

attn (abbr of for the attention of) z. Hd.

attorney [ə'tɜːnɪ] n US [lawyer] (Rechts)anwalt der, -wältin die.

attorney general (pl attorneys general) n ≃ Generalbundesanwalt der.

attract [ə'trækt] vt - 1. [draw, cause to come near] anlziehen, anllocken - 2. [be attractive to] anziehend wirken auf (+ A) - 3. [support] gewinnen; [criticism] auf sich (A) ziehen - 4. [magnetically] anlziehen.

attraction [ə'trækʃn] n - 1. [liking] Anziehungskraft die; to feel an attraction to sb sich zu jm hingezogen fühlen - 2. (U) [appeal, charm] Reiz der - 3. [attractive feature, event] Attraktion die.

attractive [ə'træktɪv] adj - 1. [person] anziehend - 2. [thing, idea] attraktiv.

attribute <> vt [ə'trɪbjuːt] - 1. [ascribe]: to attribute sthg to sb/sthg etw jm/etw zulschreiben - 2. [work of art, remark]: to attribute sthg to sb jm etw zulschreiben. <> n ['ætrɪbjuːt] [quality] Eigenschaft die.

aubergine ['əʊbəʒiːn] n UK Aubergine die.

auburn ['ɔːbən] adj [hair] rotbraun.

auction ['ɔːkʃn] <> n Auktion die, Versteigerung die; at OR by auction bei einer Auktion OR Versteigerung; to put sthg up for auction etw zur Versteigerung anlbieten. <> vt versteigern. ◆ **auction off** vt sep versteigern.

auctioneer [‚ɔːkʃə'nɪər] n Auktionator der.

audacious [ɔː'deɪʃəs] adj [daring] kühn; [impudent] dreist.

audible ['ɔːdəbl] adj hörbar.

audience ['ɔːdjəns] n [gen] Publikum das; [of TV programme] Zuschauer Pl; [of radio programme] Zuhörer Pl.

audio-visual adj audiovisuell.

audit ['ɔːdɪt] <> n Buchprüfung die. <> vt prüfen.

audition [ɔːˈdɪʃn] n [of actor] Vorsprechen das; [of singer] Probesingen das; [of musician] Probespiel das.

auditor [ˈɔːdɪtəʳ] n Buchprüfer der, -in die.

auditorium [ˌɔːdɪˈtɔːrɪəm] (pl -riums OR -ria [-rɪə]) n Zuschauerraum der.

augur [ˈɔːgəʳ] vi: to augur well/badly etwas Gutes/nichts Gutes verheißen.

August [ˈɔːgəst] n August der; see also **September**.

aunt [ɑːnt] n Tante die.

auntie, aunty [ˈɑːntɪ] n inf Tantchen das.

au pair [ˌəʊˈpeəʳ] n Aupairmädchen das.

aura [ˈɔːrə] n Aura die.

aural [ˈɔːrəl] adj SCH: aural comprehension Hörverständnis die.

auspices [ˈɔːspɪsɪz] npl: under the auspices of unter der Schirmherrschaft (+ G).

auspicious [ɔːˈspɪʃəs] adj [start] vielversprechend; [day, occasion] günstig.

Aussie [ˈɒzɪ] inf <> adj australisch. <> n Australier der, -in die.

austere [ɒˈstɪəʳ] adj - 1. [person] streng; [life] asketisch - 2. [room, building] karg.

austerity [ɒˈsterətɪ] n - 1. [of person] Strenge die; [of life - for religious reasons] Entsagung die; [- for economic reasons] Entbehrung die - 2. [of room, building] Kargheit die.

Australia [ɒˈstreɪljə] n Australien nt.

Australian [ɒˈstreɪljən] <> adj australisch. <> n Australier der, -in die.

Austria [ˈɒstrɪə] n Österreich nt.

Austrian [ˈɒstrɪən] <> adj österreichisch. <> n Österreicher der, -in die.

authentic [ɔːˈθentɪk] adj authentisch.

author [ˈɔːθəʳ] n Autor der, -in die; [by profession] Schriftsteller der, -in die.

authoritarian [ɔːˌθɒrɪˈteərɪən] adj autoritär.

authoritative [ɔːˈθɒrɪtətɪv] adj - 1. [person, voice] Respekt einflößend - 2. [report] verlässlich.

authority [ɔːˈθɒrətɪ] n - 1. [official organization] Behörde die, Amt das - 2. (U) [power] Autorität die; to have authority over sb Weisungsbefugnis gegenüber jm haben; in authority verantwortlich - 3. [permission] Erlaubnis die - 4. [expert] Autorität die. **authorities** npl: the authorities die Behörden.

authorize, -ise [ˈɔːθəraɪz] vt genehmigen; [biography] autorisieren; [money] bewilligen; to authorize sb to do sthg jn ermächtigen, etw zu tun.

autistic [ɔːˈtɪstɪk] adj autistisch.

auto [ˈɔːtəʊ] (pl -s) n US Auto das.

autobiography [ˌɔːtəbaɪˈɒgrəfɪ] n Autobiografie die.

autocratic [ˌɔːtəˈkrætɪk] adj autokratisch.

autograph [ˈɔːtəgrɑːf] <> n Autogramm das. <> vt signieren.

automate [ˈɔːtəmeɪt] vt automatisieren.

automatic [ˌɔːtəˈmætɪk] <> adj automatisch. <> n - 1. [car] Wagen der mit Automatikgetriebe - 2. [gun] automatische Waffe - 3. [washing machine] Waschautomat der.

automatically [ˌɔːtəˈmætɪklɪ] adv automatisch.

automobile [ˈɔːtəməbiːl] n US Auto(mobil) das.

autonomy [ɔːˈtɒnəmɪ] n (U) Autonomie die.

autopsy [ˈɔːtɒpsɪ] n Autopsie die.

autumn [ˈɔːtəm] n Herbst der.

auxiliary [ɔːgˈzɪljərɪ] adj - 1. [providing assistance] Hilfs-; auxiliary nurse Schwesternhelferin die - 2. GRAM [verb] Hilfs-. <> n [in hospital] Hilfskraft die.

Av. abbr of avenue.

avail [əˈveɪl] <> n: to no avail vergeblich, ohne Erfolg. <> vt: to avail o.s. of sthg von etw Gebrauch machen.

available [əˈveɪləbl] adj verfügbar; [product] lieferbar; (phrase): to be available [person] zur Verfügung stehen.

avalanche [ˈævəlɑːnʃ] n liter & fig Lawine die.

avarice [ˈævərɪs] n Habgier die.

Ave. abbr of avenue.

avenge [əˈvendʒ] vt rächen.

avenue [ˈævənjuː] n Allee die (in der Stadt).

average [ˈævərɪdʒ] <> adj - 1. [mean] durchschnittlich - 2. [typical]: the average Englishman der Durchschnittsengländer - 3. pej [mediocre] durchschnittlich, mittelmäßig. <> n Durchschnitt der; on average im Durchschnitt. <> vt: we averaged 80 miles per hour wir sind durchschnittlich 80 Meilen pro Stunde gefahren. **average out** vi: to average out at durchschnittlich betragen.

aversion [əˈvɜːʃn] n [dislike]: aversion (to) Abneigung die (gegen).

avert [əˈvɜːt] vt - 1. [problem] vermeiden; [accident, disaster] verhindern - 2. [eyes, glance] ablwenden.

aviary [ˈeɪvjərɪ] n Vogelhaus das.

avid [ˈævɪd] adj begeistert, passioniert; avid for sthg begierig auf etw (A).

avocado [ˌævəˈkɑːdəʊ] (pl -s OR -es) n: avocado (pear) Avocado die.

avoid [əˈvɔɪd] vt - 1. [problem, accident, mistake] vermeiden; to avoid doing sthg vermeiden, etw zu tun - 2. [keep away from] meiden.

await [əˈweɪt] vt erwarten.

awake [əˈweɪk] (pt awoke OR awaked, pp awoken) <> adj [not sleeping] wach. <> vt - 1. [person] wecken - 2. fig [memories, feelings] erwecken. <> vi auflwachen.

awakening [əˈweɪknɪŋ] n Erwachen das.

award [əˈwɔːd] <> n [prize] Preis der; [for bravery] Auszeichnung die. <> vt: to award sb sthg, to award sthg to sb [prize] jm etw verleihen; [free kick, penalty] jm etw geben; [damages, compensation] jm etw zulsprechen.

aware [əˈweəʳ] adj - **1.** [conscious]: **to be aware of sthg** sich (D) einer Sache (G) bewusst sein; **to be aware that...** sich (D) bewusst sein, dass... - **2.** [informed, sensitive] (gut) informiert sein; **to be aware of sthg** über etw (A) informiert sein.

awareness [əˈweənɪs] n Bewusstsein das.

away [əˈweɪ] ⇔ adv - **1.** [indicating movement] weg; **to walk away (from)** weglgehen (von); **to run away (from)** weglaufen (von); **to look away (from)** weglsehen (von); **to turn away (from)** sich ablwenden (von) - **2.** [at a distance]: **far away** weit entfernt; **10 miles away (from here)** 10 Meilen (von hier) entfernt; **it's still two weeks away** bis dahin sind es noch zwei Wochen - **3.** [absent] weg; [not at home or in the office] nicht da; **Mr Stone is away on a business trip** Herr Stone ist auf Geschäftsreise - **4.** [in a safe place]: **to put sthg away** etw weglräumen - **5.** [indicating removal or disappearance]: **to fade away** verblassen; **to take sthg away (from sb)** (jm) etw weglnehmen; **to give sthg away** [as a present] etw verschenken - **6.** [continuously]: **to work away** in einem fort arbeiten - **7.** phr: **straight** OR **right away** sofort. ⇔ adj SPORT: **away game** Auswärtsspiel das.

awe [ɔ:] n Ehrfurcht die; **to be in awe of sb** Ehrfurcht vor jm haben.

awesome [ˈɔ:səm] adj - **1.** [impressive] Ehrfurcht gebietend - **2.** inf [fantastic] irre.

awful [ˈɔ:fʊl] adj - **1.** [terrible] furchtbar, schrecklich - **2.** inf [very great]: **an awful lot** sehr viel; **an awful lot of time/money/books** eine Menge Zeit/Geld/Bücher.

awfully [ˈɔ:flɪ] adv inf [very] furchtbar.

awkward [ˈɔ:kwəd] adj - **1.** [clumsy - movement] ungeschickt, unbeholfen; [- position] ungünstig; [- person] unbeholfen - **2.** [embarrassed - person] verlegen; [- silence] betreten; [- situation, questions] peinlich - **3.** [uncooperative] unkooperativ - **4.** [inconvenient] ungünstig - **5.** [difficult, delicate] schwierig.

awning [ˈɔ:nɪŋ] n - **1.** [of tent] Vordach das - **2.** [of shop] Markise die.

awoke [əˈwəʊk] pt ⇨ **awake**.

awoken [əˈwəʊkn] pp ⇨ **awake**.

awry [əˈraɪ] ⇔ adj schief. ⇔ adv: **to go awry** schief gehen.

axe UK, **ax** US [æks] ⇔ n Axt die. ⇔ vt [project] auflgeben; [jobs] streichen, kürzen.

axes [ˈæksi:z] Pl ⇨ **axis**.

axis [ˈæksɪs] (pl axes) n Achse die.

axle [ˈæksl] n Achse die.

aye [aɪ] ⇔ adv - **1.** Scotland [yes] ja - **2.** NAUT [yes] zu Befehl, jawohl. ⇔ n [vote] Jastimme die.

Azores [əˈzɔ:z] npl: **the Azores** die Azoren Pl.

B

b (pl b's OR bs), **B** (pl B's OR Bs) [bi:] n [letter] b das, B das. ◆ **B** n - **1.** MUS H das - **2.** SCH [mark] ≈ zwei.

BA n abbr of **Bachelor of Arts**.

babble [ˈbæbl] ⇔ n [noise] Gemurmel das. ⇔ vi plappern.

baboon [bəˈbu:n] n Pavian der.

baby [ˈbeɪbɪ] n Baby das; **don't be such a baby!** benimm dich nicht wie ein Baby!

baby buggy n - **1.** UK [pushchair] Sportwagen der - **2.** US = **baby carriage**.

baby carriage n US Kinderwagen der.

baby food n Babynahrung die.

baby-sit vi babysitten.

baby-sitter [-ˌsɪtəʳ] n Babysitter der, -in die.

bachelor [ˈbætʃələʳ] n Junggeselle der.

Bachelor of Arts n [degree] erster akademischer Grad der Geisteswissenschaften an Universitäten in englischsprachigen Ländern.

Bachelor of Science n [degree] erster akademischer Grad der Naturwissenschaften an Universitäten in englischsprachigen Ländern.

back [bæk] ⇔ adv - **1.** [backwards] zurück; **stand back (please)!** (bitte) zurücktreten!; **to tie back** zurücklbinden; **to push back** [shove] zurücklschieben - **2.** [to former position or state] zurück; **when will you be back?** wann bist du wieder da?; **back and forth** hin und her; **to give sthg back** etw zurücklgeben; **we went back to sleep** wir sind wieder eingeschlafen; **back home** bei uns zu Hause - **3.** [earlier]: **two weeks back** vor zwei Wochen; **it dates back to 1960** es stammt aus dem Jahr(e) 1960; **I found out back in January** ich habe es schon im Januar erfahren; **to think back to sthg** an etw (A) zurückldenken - **4.** [in reply, in return]: **to write/phone/pay back** zurücklschreiben/-rufen/-zahlen - **5.** [in fashion again]: **to be back (in fashion)** wieder modern sein. ⇔ n - **1.** [of person, animal, hand] Rücken der; [of chair] Lehne die; **to do sthg behind sb's back** etw hinter js Rücken tun; **to put one's back into sthg** sich bei etw anlstrengen; **get off my back!** inf lass mich in Ruhe! - **2.** [opposite or reverse side - of bank note, page] Rückseite die; **back of the head** Hinterkopf der - **3.** [not front - inside car] Rücksitz der; [- of room] hinterer Teil; **at the back of, in back of** US hinter (+ D); **at the back of the cupboard** hinten im Schrank - **4.** SPORT [player] Verteidiger der; [in rugby] Spieler der der Hintermannschaft. ⇔ adj (in compounds) - **1.** [at the back - wheels, legs, door] Hinter- - **2.** [overdue - rent] überfällig.

◇ *vt* - **1.** [reverse] zurücklsetzen - **2.** [support] unterstützen - **3.** [bet on]: **to back a horse** (Geld) auf jn Pferd setzen. ◇ *vi* [car, driver] rückwärts fahren. ◆ **back to back** *adv* [stand] Rücken an Rücken. ◆ **back to front** *adv* [the wrong way round] verkehrt herum. ◆ **back down** *vi* nachlgeben. ◆ **back out** *vi* [of arrangement] auslsteigen. ◆ **back up** ◇ *vt sep* - **1.** [support] unterstützen - **2.** [confirm] bestätigen - **3.** [reverse] zurücklsetzen - **4.** COMPUT ein Backup machen von. ◇ *vi* [car, driver] zurücklsetzen.

backache ['bækeɪk] *n (U)* Rückenschmerzen *Pl*.

backbencher [ˌbæk'bentʃər] *n UK* POL parlamentarischer Hinterbänkler.

backbone ['bækbəʊn] *n liter & fig* Rückgrat *das*.

backcloth ['bækklɒθ] *n UK* = **backdrop**.

backdate [ˌbæk'deɪt] *vt* zurückldatieren.

back door *n* Hintertür *die*.

backdrop ['bækdrɒp] *n liter & fig* Hintergrund *der*.

backfire [ˌbæk'faɪər] *vi* - **1.** [motor vehicle] Fehlzündungen haben - **2.** [plan] fehllschlagen; **to backfire on sb** auf jn zurücklfallen.

backgammon ['bækˌgæmən] *n* Backgammon *das*.

background ['bækgraʊnd] *n* - **1.** [gen] Hintergrund *der*; **in the background** *liter & fig* im Hintergrund - **2.** [upbringing] Herkunft *die*.

backhand ['bækhænd] *n* Rückhand *die*.

backhanded ['bækhændɪd] *adj fig* [compliment] zweifelhaft.

backhander ['bækhændər] *n UK inf* [bribe] Schmiergeld *das*.

backing ['bækɪŋ] *n* - **1.** *(U)* [support] Unterstützung *die* - **2.** [lining] Verstärkung *die*.

backing group *n* MUS Begleitband *die*.

backlash ['bæklæʃ] *n* Gegenschlag *der*.

backlog ['bæklɒg] *n* Rückstände *Pl*; **to have a backlog of work** mit der Arbeit im Rückstand sein.

back number *n* alte Ausgabe.

backpack ['bækpæk] *n* Rucksack *der*.

back pay *n* ausstehender Lohn.

back seat *n* [in car] Rücksitz *der*; **to take a back seat** *fig* sich im Hintergrund halten.

backside [ˌbæk'saɪd] *n inf* Hintern *der*.

backstage [ˌbæk'steɪdʒ] *adv* hinter den Kulissen.

back street *n UK* kleine Seitenstraße.

backstroke ['bækstrəʊk] *n* Rückenschwimmen *das*.

backup ['bækʌp] *n* - **1.** *(U)* [support] Unterstützung *die* - **2.** COMPUT Sicherungskopie *die*.

backward ['bækwəd] ◇ *adj* - **1.** [gen] rückwärts gerichtet; **a backward glance** ein Blick über die Schulter - **2.** *pej* [child, country] zurückgeblieben. ◇ *adv US* = **backwards**.

backwards ['bækwədz], **backward** US ['bækwəd] *adv* [towards the rear] rückwärts; **to fall backwards** nach hinten fallen; **backwards and forwards** hin und her; **to look backwards** zurücklblicken.

backwater [ˌbækˌwɔːtər] *n* [place] Kaff *das*.

backyard [ˌbæk'jɑːd] *n* - **1.** *UK* [yard] Hinterhof *der* - **2.** *US* [garden] Garten *der* hinter dem Haus.

bacon ['beɪkən] *n (U)* Schinkenspeck *der*.

bacteria [bæk'tɪərɪə] *npl* Bakterien *Pl*.

bad [bæd] (*comp* **worse**, *superl* **worst**) ◇ *adj* - **1.** [unpleasant, unfavourable - gen] schlecht; [- smell] übel; **bad breath** Mundgeruch *der*; **he is in a bad way** es geht ihm gar nicht gut; **smoking is bad for you** Rauchen ist schädlich; **too bad!** Pech! - **2.** [serious] schwer; **to have a bad cold** einen starken Schnupfen haben - **3.** [inadequate - eyesight, excuse] schwach; **to be bad at sthg** etw schlecht können; **he's bad at English** er ist schlecht in Englisch; **not bad** nicht schlecht - **4.** [injured, unhealthy] schlimm; **my bad leg** mein schlimmes Bein; **he has a bad heart** er hat ein schwaches Herz - **5.** [naughty] ungezogen; [wicked] böse, übel; **he's a bad lot** er ist ein übler Bursche - **6.** [food - rotten, off] verdorben; **to go bad** verderben - **7.** [guilty]: **he really feels bad about it** es tut ihm wirklich leid. ◇ *adv US* = **badly**.

baddy ['bædɪ] (*pl* -**ies**) *n inf* Böse *der*.

badge [bædʒ] *n* - **1.** [for fun] Button *der* - **2.** [for employee, visitor] Schild(chen) *das* - **3.** [sewn-on] Abzeichen *das* - **4.** [on car] Emblem *das*.

badger ['bædʒər] ◇ *n* Dachs *der*. ◇ *vt* [pester]: **to badger sb** jm keine Ruhe lassen.

badly ['bædlɪ] (*comp* **worse**, *superl* **worst**) *adv* - **1.** [poorly] schlecht; **to treat sb badly** jn schlecht behandeln - **2.** [wounded, beaten, affected] schwer - **3.** [very much]: **to be badly in need of sthg** etw dringend benötigen.

badly-off *adj* [poor] nicht gut gestellt.

badminton ['bædmɪntən] *n (U)* Federball *das*; SPORT Badminton *das*.

bad-tempered [-'tempəd] *adj* - **1.** [by nature] übellaunig - **2.** [in a bad mood] schlecht gelaunt.

baffled [bæfld] *adj* ratlos.

bag [bæg] ◇ *n* - **1.** [container] Tasche *die*; [for shopping] Tüte *die*; [large, for coal, cement] Sack *der*; [of tea, rice] Beutel *der*; **to pack one's bags** *fig* [leave] seine Sachen packen - **2.** [handbag] Handtasche *die*; [when travelling] Reisetasche *die* - **3.** [bagful]: **a bag of crisps** *UK* eine Tüte Chips; **a bag of potatoes** ein Sack Kartoffeln - **4.** *v inf pej* [nasty woman] Ziege *die*.

◇ *vt* - **1.** *UK inf* [get] sich *(D)* schnappen - **2.** *UK inf* [reserve] belegen, besetzen. ◆ **bags** *npl* - **1.** [under eyes] Tränensäcke *Pl* - **2.** [lots]: **bags of time/room** *inf* eine Menge OR jede Menge Zeit/Platz.

bagel ['beɪɡəl] *n kleines ringförmiges Brötchen.*

baggage ['bæɡɪdʒ] *n* Gepäck *das.*

baggage reclaim *n* Gepäckausgabe *die.*

baggy ['bæɡɪ] *adj* weit (geschnitten).

bagpipes ['bæɡpaɪps] *npl* Dudelsack *der.*

Bahamas [bə'hɑːməz] *npl*: **the Bahamas** die Bahamas.

bail [beɪl] *n (U)* LAW Kaution *die*; **on bail** gegen Kaution. ◆ **bail out** ◇ *vt sep* - **1.** LAW [pay bail for] (die) Kaution stellen für - **2.** [rescue] aus der Klemme helfen (+ *D*) - **3.** [boat] ausl-schöpfen. ◇ *vi* [from plane] ab|springen.

bailiff ['beɪlɪf] *n* [in charge of repossession] Gerichtsvollzieher *der*; [in court] Gerichtsdiener *der.*

bait [beɪt] ◇ *n (U)* Köder *der.* ◇ *vt* - **1.** [hook, trap] mit einem Köder versehen - **2.** [torment - person] piesacken; [- bear, badger] quälen.

bake [beɪk] ◇ *vt* - **1.** [bread, cake *etc*] backen - **2.** [ground] ausl|dörren; [clay, brick] brennen. ◇ *vi* backen.

baked beans [beɪkt-] *npl* weiße Bohnen *Pl* in Tomatensoße.

baked potato *n* in der Schale gebackene Kartoffel.

baker ['beɪkə'] *n* Bäcker *der*, -in *die*; **baker's (shop)** Bäckerei *die*, Bäckerladen *der.*

bakery ['beɪkərɪ] *n* Bäckerei *die.*

baking ['beɪkɪŋ] *n* [cooking] Backen *das.*

balaclava [mbælə'klɑːvə] *n UK eng anliegende Kopfbedeckung, die nur das Gesicht frei lässt.*

balance ['bæləns] ◇ *n* - **1.** [equilibrium] Gleichgewicht *das*; **to keep/lose one's balance** das Gleichgewicht halten/verlieren; **off balance** aus dem Gleichgewicht. *fig* [counterweight] Ausgleich *der* - **3.** *fig* [weight, force]: **balance of power** Gleichgewicht *das* der Kräfte - **4.** [scales] Waage *die* - **5.** [remainder] Rest *der* - **6.** [of bank account] Kontostand *der.* ◇ *vt* - **1.** [keep in balance] im Gleichgewicht halten - **2.** [compare]: **to balance sthg against sthg** etw gegen etw ab|wägen - **3.** [in accounting]: **to balance the books/the budget** die Bilanz machen. ◇ *vi* - **1.** [maintain equilibrium] das Gleichgewicht halten - **2.** [in accounting] sich ausl|gleichen. ◆ **on balance** *adv* alles in allem.

balanced diet [,bælənst-] *n* ausgewogene Ernährung.

balance of payments *n* Zahlungsbilanz *die.*

balance of trade *n* Handelsbilanz *die.*

balance sheet *n* Bilanz *die.*

balcony ['bælkənɪ] *n* - **1.** [on building] Balkon *der* - **2.** [in theatre] oberster Rang.

bald [bɔːld] *adj* - **1.** [head, man] glatzköpfig, kahl(köpfig) - **2.** [tyre] völlig abgenutzt - **3.** *fig* [unadorned] nüchtern, unverblümt.

bale [beɪl] *n* Ballen *der.* ◆ **bale out** *UK* ◇ *vt sep* [boat] ausl|schöpfen. ◇ *vi* [from plane] ab|springen.

Balearic Islands [,bælɪ'ærɪk-], **Balearics** [,bælɪ'ærɪks] *npl*: **the Balearic Islands** die Balearen.

balk [bɔːk] *vi*: **to balk (at)** zurück|schrecken (vor (+ *D*)).

Balkans ['bɔːlkənz], **Balkan States** *npl*: **the Balkans** der Balkan.

ball [bɔːl] *n* - **1.** [in game] Ball *der*; [in snooker, bowling] Kugel *die*; **to be on the ball** auf Draht sein; **to play ball** *fig* mitl|machen - **2.** [of wool] Knäuel *das* - **3.** [of foot] Ballen *der* - **4.** [dance] Ball *der.* ◆ **balls** *v inf* ◇ *n (U)* [nonsense] Schwachsinn *der.* ◇ *npl* [testicles] Eier *Pl.* ◇ *excl* Scheiße!

ballad ['bæləd] *n* Ballade *die.*

ballast ['bæləst] *n* Ballast *der.*

ball bearing *n* Kugellager *das.*

ball boy *n* Balljunge *der.*

ballerina [,bælə'riːnə] *n* Ballerina *die.*

ballet ['bæleɪ] *n* Ballett *das.*

ballet dancer *n* Balletttänzer *der*, -in *die.*

ball game *n* - **1.** *US* [baseball match] Baseballspiel *das* - **2.** *fig* [situation]: **it's a whole new ball game** *inf* das ist eine ganz neue Lage.

balloon [bə'luːn] *n* - **1.** [toy] Luftballon *der* - **2.** [hot-air balloon] Heißluftballon *der.*

ballot ['bælət] ◇ *n* - **1.** [voting process] Abstimmung *die.* ◇ *vt* [members] abstimmen lassen.

ballot box *n* Wahlurne *die.*

ballot paper *n* Stimmzettel *der.*

ball park *n US* Baseballstadion *das.*

ballpoint (pen) ['bɔːlpɔɪnt-] *n* Kugelschreiber *der.*

ballroom ['bɔːlrum] *n* Ballsaal *der.*

ballroom dancing *n (U)* Gesellschaftstanz *der.*

balmy ['bɑːmɪ] *adj* [evening] mild.

balsawood ['bɒlsəwʊd] *n* Balsaholz *das.*

Baltic ['bɔːltɪk] ◇ *adj* [port, coast] Ostsee-, baltisch. ◇ *n*: **the Baltic (Sea)** die Ostsee.

Baltic State *n*: **the Baltic States** die Baltischen Staaten.

bamboo [bæm'buː] *n* Bambus *der.*

bamboozle [bæm'buːzl] *vt inf* verwirren.

ban [bæn] ◇ *n* Verbot *das*; **ban on smoking** Rauchverbot *das.* ◇ *vt* verbieten; **to ban sb from doing sthg** jm etw verbieten.

banal [bə'nɑːl] *adj pej* banal.

banana [bə'nɑːnə] *n* Banane *die.*

band [bænd] n - **1.** [musical - pop] Gruppe die; [- traditional, classical] Kapelle die; [- jazz] Band die - **2.** [gang] Bande die - **3.** [of colour, metal] Streifen der - **4.** [range] Klasse die. ◆ **band together** vi sich zusammenschließen.

bandage ['bændɪdʒ] ◇ n Verband der. ◇ vt verbinden.

Band-Aid ® n Heftpflaster das.

bandit ['bændɪt] n Bandit der.

bandstand ['bændstænd] n Musikpavillon der.

bandwagon ['bændwægən] n: to jump on the bandwagon auf den fahrenden Zug aufspringen.

bandy ['bændɪ] adj [bandy-legged] krummbeinig. ◆ **bandy about, bandy around** vt sep [words] um sich werfen mit.

bang [bæŋ] ◇ adv [right]: **bang in the middle** genau in der Mitte; **his description was bang on** seine Beschreibung passte aufs Haar; **bang on time** auf die Minute pünktlich. ◇ n - **1.** [blow] Schlag der - **2.** [loud noise] Knall der. ◇ vt - **1.** [hit] anschlagen - **2.** [door] zuschlagen. ◇ vi - **1.** [knock]: **to bang on the door/wall** [once] gegen die Tür/die Wand schlagen; [more than once] gegen die Tür/die Wand hämmern - **2.** [make a loud noise] (herum)|poltern - **3.** [crash]: **to bang into sb/sthg** gegen jn/etw stoßen. ◇ excl peng! ◆ **bangs** npl US Pony der.

banger ['bæŋəʳ] n UK - **1.** inf [sausage] Würstchen das - **2.** inf [old car] alte Kiste - **3.** [firework] Knallkörper der.

bangle ['bæŋgl] n Armreif der.

banish ['bænɪʃ] vt liter & fig verbannen.

banister ['bænɪstəʳ] n Geländer das.

banisters ['bænɪstəz] npl = banister.

bank [bæŋk] ◇ n - **1.** FIN Bank die - **2.** [of data, blood etc] Bank die - **3.** [of river, lake] Ufer das - **4.** [slope] Böschung die - **5.** [of fog, cloud] Bank die; **a bank of snow** eine Schneeverwehung. ◇ vt FIN einzahlen. ◇ vi - **1.** FIN: **who do you bank with?** bei welcher Bank sind Sie? - **2.** [plane] sich in die Kurve legen. ◆ **bank on** vt insep sich verlassen auf (+ A).

bank account n Bankkonto das.

bank balance n Kontostand der.

bank card n = banker's card.

bank charges npl Bankgebühren Pl.

bank draft n Banküberweisung die.

banker ['bæŋkəʳ] n FIN Bankier der.

banker's card n UK Scheckkarte die.

bank holiday n UK Feiertag der.

banking ['bæŋkɪŋ] n Bankwesen das.

bank manager n Filialleiter der, -in die.

bank note n Banknote die, Geldschein der.

bank rate n Diskontsatz der.

bankrupt ['bæŋkrʌpt] adj bankrott; **to go bankrupt** bankrott machen, in Konkurs gehen.

bankruptcy ['bæŋkrəptsɪ] n Bankrott der.

bank statement n Kontoauszug der.

banner ['bænəʳ] n Transparent das.

bannister n = banister.

bannisters npl = banister.

banquet ['bæŋkwɪt] n Festessen das.

banter ['bæntəʳ] n (U) Frotzeleien Pl.

bap [bæp] n UK weiches Brötchen das.

baptism ['bæptɪzm] n Taufe die.

Baptist ['bæptɪst] n Baptist der, -in die.

baptize, -ise [UK bæp'taɪz, US 'bæptaɪz] vt taufen.

bar [bɑːʳ] ◇ n - **1.** [of wood, metal] Stange die; [of gold] Barren der; [of soap] Stück das; [of chocolate - slab] Tafel die; [- long and thin] Riegel der; (phrase): **to be behind bars** hinter Gittern sitzen; **the bar** [in gymnastics] der Balken - **2.** fig [obstacle] Hindernis das - **3.** [in hotel] Bar die; [pub] Kneipe die - **4.** [counter] Theke die - **5.** MUS Takt der. ◇ vt - **1.** [door, window] verriegeln - **2.** [block] (ver)sperren; **to bar sb's way** jm den Weg versperren. ◇ prep [except] ausgenommen, außer (+ D); **bar none** ohne Ausnahme. ◆ **Bar** n: **to be called to the Bar** UK als Anwalt zugelassen werden.

barbaric [bɑː'bærɪk] adj barbarisch.

barbecue ['bɑːbɪkjuː] n - **1.** [grill] Grill der - **2.** [party] Barbecue das, Grillparty die.

barbed wire [bɑːbd-] n Stacheldraht der.

barber ['bɑːbəʳ] n (Herren)friseur der; **barber's (shop)** (Herren)friseursalon der.

barbiturate [bɑː'bɪtjʊrət] n Barbiturat das.

bar code n Strichkodierung die.

bare [beəʳ] ◇ adj - **1.** [feet, legs, body] nackt, bloß; [rock, branches, landscape] kahl - **2.** [basic]: **the bare facts** die reinen Tatsachen; **the bare minimum** das strikte Minimum - **3.** [room, cupboard] leer. ◇ vt entblößen; **to bare one's teeth** die Zähne fletschen.

barefaced ['beəfeɪst] adj schamlos, frech.

barefoot(ed) [,beə'fʊt(ɪd)] ◇ adj barfüßig. ◇ adv barfuß.

barely ['beəlɪ] adv [scarcely] kaum, knapp.

bargain ['bɑːgɪn] ◇ n - **1.** [agreement] Geschäft das; **into the bargain** obendrein - **2.** [good buy] Schnäppchen das. ◇ vi (ver)handeln; **to bargain with sb for sthg** mit jm um etw handeln OR feilschen. ◆ **bargain for, bargain on** vt insep erwarten, rechnen mit.

barge [bɑːdʒ] ◇ n Schleppkahn der, Lastkahn der. ◇ vi inf: **to barge into a room** in ein Zimmer herein|platzen; **to barge past sb/sthg** an jm/etw vorbei|stürmen. ◆ **barge in** vi: **to barge in (on sb)** herein|platzen (bei jm).

baritone ['bærɪtəʊn] n Bariton der.

bark [bɑːk] ◇ n - 1. [of dog] Bellen das - 2. [on tree] Rinde die, Borke die. ◇ vi [dog] bellen; **to bark at sb/sthg** jn/etw an|bellen.

barley ['bɑːlɪ] n Gerste die.

barley sugar n UK Malzbonbon der ODER das.

barmaid ['bɑːmeɪd] n Bardame die.

barman ['bɑːmən] (pl -men [-mən]) n Barkeeper der.

barn [bɑːn] n Scheune die.

barometer [bə'rɒmɪtər] n liter & fig Barometer das.

baron ['bærən] n Baron der; **oil baron** Ölmagnat der; **press baron** Pressezar der.

baroness ['bærənɪs] n Baronin die; [not married] Baronesse die.

barrack ['bærək] vt UK aus|pfeifen, aus|buhen. ◆ **barracks** npl Kaserne die.

barrage ['bærɑːʒ] n - 1. [of firing] Sperrfeuer das; **a barrage of complaints/questions** eine Flut von Beschwerden/Fragen - 2. UK [dam] Staudamm der.

barrel ['bærəl] n - 1. [for beer, wine] Fass das - 2. [for oil] Tonne die; [as measure] Barrel das - 3. [of gun] Lauf der.

barren ['bærən] adj [woman, land, soil] unfruchtbar.

barricade [ˌbærɪ'keɪd] n Barrikade die.

barrier ['bærɪər] n Barriere die; [at car park, level crossing] Schranke die.

barring ['bɑːrɪŋ] prep: **barring accidents** falls nichts passiert.

barrister ['bærɪstər] n UK Rechtsanwalt der, -wältin die.

barrow ['bærəʊ] n [market stall] Karren der.

bartender ['bɑːtendər] n US Barkeeper der.

barter ['bɑːtər] ◇ n Tauschhandel der. ◇ vt & vi tauschen.

base [beɪs] ◇ n - 1. [of post, lamp, mountain] Fuß der; [of triangle] Basis die; [of box] Boden der - 2. [of food, paint] Basis die - 3. [centre of activities - gen] Standort der; [- military, in mountaineering] Stützpunkt der - 4. [in baseball] Mal das. ◇ vt - 1. [locate - MIL] stationieren; (phrase): **he's based in Paris** sein Büro ist in Paris - 2. [use as starting point]: **to base sthg (up)on sthg** etw auf etw (A) gründen OR basieren. ◇ adj pej [dishonourable] niederträchtig.

baseball ['beɪsbɔːl] n (U) Baseball der.

baseball cap n Baseballkappe die.

basement ['beɪsmənt] n [of house] Keller der; [of department store] Untergeschoss das.

base rate n Leitzins der.

bases ['beɪsiːz] Pl ▷ **basis**.

bash [bæʃ] inf ◇ n - 1. [blow] (heftiger) Schlag - 2. [attempt]: **to have a bash (at sthg)** (etw) mal probieren. ◇ vt [hit] schlagen; **to bash one's head** sich (D) den Kopf an|hauen.

bashful ['bæʃfʊl] adj schüchtern.

basic ['beɪsɪk] adj grundlegend, wesentlich; [vocabulary, principle] Grund-; [meal, accommodation] einfach. ◆ **basics** npl: **the basics** die Grundlagen Pl.

basically ['beɪsɪklɪ] adv grundsätzlich.

basil ['bæzl] n Basilikum das.

basin ['beɪsn] n - 1. [sink] Waschbecken das - 2. UK [bowl] Schüssel die.

basis ['beɪsɪs] (pl -ses) n - 1. [reason] Grundlage die, Basis die; **on the basis that...** in der Annahme, dass... - 2. [foundation, arrangement] Basis die; **on a weekly basis** wöchentlich; **on the basis of** auf der Grundlage (+ G).

bask [bɑːsk] vi sich aalen.

basket ['bɑːskɪt] n Korb der.

basketball ['bɑːskɪtbɔːl] n Basketball der.

bass [beɪs] adj [part, singer] Bass-.

bass drum [beɪs-] n große Trommel.

bass guitar [beɪs-] n Bassgitarre die.

bassoon [bə'suːn] n Fagott das.

bastard ['bɑːstəd] n - 1. [illegitimate child] Bastard der - 2. v inf pej [unpleasant person] Scheißkerl der; phrase: **the poor bastard** die arme Sau.

bastion ['bæstɪən] n fig Bastion die.

bat [bæt] n - 1. [animal] Fledermaus die - 2. [cricket, baseball] Schlagholz das; [for table tennis] Schläger der - 3. phr: **to do sthg off one's own bat** etw auf eigene Faust tun.

batch [bætʃ] n - 1. [of papers, letters, work] Stapel der - 2. [of products] Ladung die - 3. [of people] Schwung der.

bated ['beɪtɪd] adj: **with bated breath** mit angehaltenem Atem.

bath [bɑːθ] ◇ n Bad das; [bathtub] (Bade)wanne die; **to have** OR **take a bath** ein Bad nehmen, baden. ◇ vt baden. ◆ **baths** npl UK Bad das.

bathe [beɪð] ◇ vt - 1. [wound] (aus)|waschen, baden - 2. [in light, sweat] baden. ◇ vi baden.

bathing ['beɪðɪŋ] n Baden das.

bathing cap n Badekappe die.

bathing costume, bathing suit n Badeanzug der.

bathrobe ['bɑːθrəʊb] n Bademantel der.

bathroom ['bɑːθrʊm] n - 1. UK [room with bath] Badezimmer das - 2. US [toilet] Toilette die.

bath towel n Badetuch das.

bathtub ['bɑːθtʌb] n Badewanne die.

baton ['bætən] n - 1. [of conductor] Taktstock der - 2. [in relay race] Staffelstab der - 3. UK [of policeman] Schlagstock der.

batsman ['bætsmən] (pl -men [-mən]) n Schlagmann der.

battalion [bə'tæljən] n Bataillon das.

batter ['bætə'] ◇ n CULIN Teig der. ◇ vt [person] schlagen, verprügeln. ◇ vi [on door, wall] hämmern, trommeln.

battered ['bætəd] adj - 1. [person] verprügelt - 2. [car, hat, suitcase] verbeult - 3. CULIN im Teigmantel.

battery ['bætərɪ] N Batterie die.

battle ['bætl] ◇ n - 1. [in war] Schlacht die - 2. [struggle]: battle (for/against) Kampf der (für/gegen); that's half the battle damit ist schon eine Menge gewonnen. ◇ vi: to battle (for/against) kämpfen (für/gegen).

battlefield ['bætlfiːld], **battleground** [-graʊnd] n liter & fig Schlachtfeld das.

battlements ['bætlmənts] npl Zinnen Pl.

battleship ['bætlʃɪp] n Schlachtschiff das.

bauble ['bɔːbl] n Christbaumkugel die.

baulk [bɔːk] vi = balk.

bawdy ['bɔːdɪ] adj derb.

bawl [bɔːl] ◇ vt [shout] brüllen. ◇ vi - 1. [shout] brüllen - 2. [weep] heulen.

bay [beɪ] n - 1. GEOG Bucht die - 2. [for loading] Ladeplatz der - 3. [for parking] Parkbucht die - 4. phr: to keep sb at bay jn auf Abstand halten.

bay leaf n Lorbeerblatt das.

bay window n Erkerfenster das.

bazaar [bə'zɑː'] n - 1. [market] Basar der - 2. UK [charity sale] Wohltätigkeitsbasar der.

B & B n abbr of bed and breakfast.

BBC (abbr of British Broadcasting Corporation) n BBC die.

BC (abbr of before Christ) v. Chr.

Bcc [,biːsiː'siː] n (abbr of blind carbon copy) Bcc.

be [biː] (pt was OR were, pp been) ◇ vi - 1. [exist] sein; there is/are es ist/sind da, es gibt; are there any shops near here? gibt es hier in der Nähe irgendwelche Geschäfte?; there is someone in the room es ist jemand im Zimmer; be that as it may wie dem auch sei - 2. [referring to location] sein; the hotel is near the airport das Hotel befindet sich in der Nähe des Flughafens; he will be here tomorrow er kommt morgen - 3. [referring to movement] sein; have you ever been to California? warst du schon mal in Kalifornien?; I'll be there in ten minutes ich komme in zehn Minuten; where have you been? wo bist du gewesen? - 4. [occur] sein; my birthday is in June mein Geburtstag ist im Juni - 5. [identifying, describing] sein; he's a doctor er ist Arzt; I'm British ich bin Brite/Britin; I'm hot/cold mir ist heiß/kalt; you are right du hast Recht; be quiet! sei still!, seid still!; one and one are two eins und eins ist zwei - 6. [referring to health]: how are you? wie geht es Ihnen?; I'm fine mir geht es gut; she is ill sie ist krank - 7. [referring to age]: how old are you? wie alt bist du?; I am 14 (years old) ich bin 14 (Jahre alt) - 8. [refer-

ring to cost] kosten; how much is it? wie viel kostet es?; it's £10 es kostet 10 Pfund - 9. [referring to time, dates] sein; what time is it? wie viel Uhr ist es?, wie spät ist es?; it's ten o'clock es ist zehn Uhr; today is February 17th heute haben wir den 17. Februar - 10. [referring to measurement] sein; it's ten metres long/high ist zehn Meter lang/hoch; I'm 8 stone ich wiege 50 Kilo - 11. [referring to the weather] sein; it's hot/cold es ist heiß/kalt - 12. [for emphasis] sein; is that you? bist du das?; yes, it's me ja, ich bins. ◇ aux vb - 1. (in combination with present participle to form continuous tense): I'm learning German ich lerne Deutsch; what is he doing? was macht er?; it's snowing es schneit; we've been visiting the museum wir waren im Museum; I've been living in London for 10 years ich wohne seit 10 Jahren in London; he is going on holiday next week nächste Woche fährt er in Urlaub - 2. (forming passive) werden; they were defeated sie wurden geschlagen; the flight was delayed das Flugzeug hatte Verspätung; it is said man sagt - 3. (with infinitive to express an order): all rooms are to be vacated by 10.00 a.m. alle Zimmer müssen bis 10 Uhr geräumt sein; you are not to tell anyone das darfst du niemandem erzählen - 4. (with infinitive to express future tense): the race is to start at noon das Rennen ist für 12 Uhr angesetzt - 5. (in tag questions): it's cold, isn't it? es ist kalt, nicht wahr?; you're not going now, are you? willst du schon gehen?

beach [biːtʃ] n Strand der.

beacon ['biːkən] n - 1. [fire, lighthouse] Leuchtfeuer das - 2. [radio beacon] Funkfeuer das.

bead [biːd] n [of glass, wood, sweat] Perle die.

beak [biːk] n [of bird] Schnabel der.

beaker ['biːkə'] n Becher der.

beam [biːm] ◇ n - 1. [of wood] Balken der; [of steel] Träger der - 2. [of light] Strahl der - 3. US AUT: high/low beams Fern-/Abblendlicht das. ◇ vt [signal, news] ausstrahlen. ◇ vi strahlen.

bean [biːn] n Bohne die; to be full of beans inf voller Tatendrang sein; to spill the beans inf [confess] singen.

beanbag ['biːnbæg] n [seat] Sitzsack die.

beanshoot ['biːnʃuːt], **beansprout** [-spraʊt] n (Soja)bohnensprosse die.

bear [beə'] (pt bore, pp borne) ◇ n [animal] Bär der. ◇ vt - 1. [gen] tragen - 2. [tolerate] ertragen, aushalten - 3. [ill will, hatred] hegen. ◇ vi - 1. [turn]: to bear left/right sich links/rechts halten - 2. [have effect]: to bring pressure/influence to bear on sb bei jm Druck/Einfluss geltend machen. ◆ **bear down** vi: to bear down on sb/sthg auf jn/etw zulsteuern. ◆ **bear out** vt sep bestätigen. ◆ **bear up** vi: to bear up well sich tapfer halten. **bear with** vt insep: **bear with me for a minute, will you?** einen Moment Geduld, bitte.

beard [bɪəd] n Bart der.

bearer ['beərər] n - 1. [of stretcher, coffin] Träger der - 2. [of news, letter] Überbringer der, -in die - 3. [of cheque, passport] Inhaber der, -in die - 4. [of name, title] Träger der, -in die.

bearing ['beərɪŋ] n - 1. [relevance] Bedeutung die; **to have a bearing on sthg** bei etw eine Rolle spielen - 2. [deportment] (Körper)haltung die - 3. TECH Lager das - 4. [on compass]: **to take a bearing** die Richtung bestimmen; **to get one's bearings** fig sich orientieren; **to lose one's bearings** fig die Orientierung verlieren.

beast [biːst] n - 1. [animal] Tier das - 2. inf pej [person - unpleasant] Ekel das; [- evil] Bestie die.

beat [biːt] (pt beat, pp beaten) <> n - 1. [of drum, heart, pulse] Schlag der - 2. [MUS - rhythm] Rhythmus der; [- measure] Takt der - 3. [of policeman] Runde die. <> vt - 1. [gen] schlagen; **to beat a record** einen Rekord brechen; **it beats me** inf ich habe keine Ahnung - 2. MUS: **to beat time** (den) Takt schlagen OR anlgeben - 3. phr: **beat it!** inf [go away] verschwinde!, hau ab! <> vi - 1. [rain - on roof] trommeln - 2. [heart, pulse] schlagen. **beat off** vt sep [resist] ablwehren. **beat up** vt sep inf [person] zusammenlschlagen.

beating ['biːtɪŋ] n - 1. [punishment] Prügel Pl; **to give sb a beating** jm eine Tracht Prügel verabreichen - 2. [defeat] Niederlage die.

beautiful ['bjuːtɪful] adj - 1. [person] schön - 2. [picture, music, weather] wundervoll, herrlich - 3. inf [goal, player] herrlich, toll.

beautifully ['bjuːtəflɪ] adv - 1. [dressed, decorated] wunderschön - 2. inf [cook, sing, play] wunderbar.

beauty ['bjuːtɪ] n Schönheit die.

beauty parlour n Schönheitssalon der.

beauty salon n = **beauty parlour**.

beauty spot n - 1. [place] schönes Fleckchen - 2. [on skin] Schönheitsfleck der.

beaver ['biːvər] n Biber der.

became [bɪ'keɪm] pt ▷ **become**.

because [bɪ'kɒz] conj weil. **because of** prep wegen (+ G, D).

beck [bek] n: **to be at sb's beck and call** nach js Pfeife tanzen.

beckon ['bekən] <> vt [make a signal to] zulwinken (+ D). <> vi: **to beckon to sb** jm zulwinken.

become [bɪ'kʌm] (pt became, pp become) vt werden; **to become old/rich/famous** alt/reich/berühmt werden; **to become accustomed to sthg** sich an etw (A) gewöhnen.

becoming [bɪ'kʌmɪŋ] adj - 1. [attractive]: **it's very becoming** es steht ihr/dir/etc gut - 2. [appropriate] schicklich.

bed [bed] n - 1. [to sleep on] Bett das; **to go to bed** zu OR ins Bett gehen; **to get out of bed** auflstehen; **to go to bed with sb** euph mit jm ins Bett gehen - 2. [flowerbed] Beet das - 3. [of sea] Meeresgrund der; [of river] Flussbett das.

bed and breakfast n Zimmer das mit Frühstück.

bedclothes ['bedkləʊðz] npl Bettzeug das.

bedlam ['bedləm] n Chaos das.

bed linen n Bettwäsche die.

bedraggled [bɪ'drægld] adj schmutzig und nass.

bedridden ['bed,rɪdn] adj bettlägerig.

bedroom ['bedrum] n Schlafzimmer das.

bedside ['bedsaɪd] n: **at sb's bedside** an js Bett.

bedside table n Nachttisch der.

bed-sit(ter) n UK Wohnschlafzimmer das.

bedsore ['bedsɔːr] n wund gelegene Stelle.

bedspread ['bedspred] n Tagesdecke die.

bedtime ['bedtaɪm] n Schlafenszeit die.

bee [biː] n Biene die.

beech [biːtʃ] n - 1. [tree] Buche die - 2. [wood] Buchenholz das.

beef [biːf] n Rindfleisch das.

beefburger ['biːf,bɜːgər] n Hamburger der.

beefsteak ['biːf,steɪk] n Beefsteak das.

beehive ['biːhaɪv] n Bienenstock der.

beeline ['biːlaɪn] n: **to make a beeline for sb/sthg** inf geradewegs auf jn/etw zulsteuern.

been [biːn] pp ▷ **be**.

beer [bɪər] n Bier das.

beer garden n Biergarten der.

beermat ['bɪə,mæt] n Bierdeckel der.

beet [biːt] n - 1. [sugar beet] Zuckerrübe die - 2. US [beetroot] rote Rübe, Rote Bete.

beetle ['biːtl] n Käfer der.

beetroot ['biːtruːt] n rote Rübe, Rote Bete.

before [bɪ'fɔːr] <> prep - 1. [in time] vor (+ D); **they arrived before us** sie sind vor uns angekommen; **the week before last** vorletzte Woche; **the day before yesterday** vorgestern; **the day before** der Tag zuvor; **before long** bald - 2. [in front of, facing] vor (+ D); **before my (very) eyes** vor meinen Augen; **we have a difficult task before us** wir haben eine schwierige Aufgabe vor uns. <> adv [previously] schon einmal; **never before** noch nie. <> conj bevor.

beforehand [bɪ'fɔːhænd] adv vorher.

befriend [bɪ'frend] vt sich anlfreunden mit.

beg [beg] <> vt - 1. [money, food] betteln um - 2. [favour, forgiveness] bitten um; **to beg sb for sthg** jm um etw bitten; **to beg sb to do sthg** jn bitten, etw zu tun. <> vi - 1. [for money, food]: **to beg (for)** betteln (um) - 2. [for favour, forgiveness]: **to beg (for)** bitten (um).

began [bɪ'gæn] pt ▷ **begin**.

beggar ['begə'] *n* Bettler *der,* -in *die.*

begin [bɪ'gɪn] (*pt* **began,** *pp* **begun,** *cont* **-ning**) ⟨⟩ *vt* beginnen, anlfangen; **to begin doing** OR **to do sthg** beginnen OR anlfangen, etw zu tun. ⟨⟩ *vi* beginnen, anlfangen; **to begin with** zunächst, zu Anfang.

beginner [bɪ'gɪnə'] *n* Anfänger *der,* -in *die.*

beginning [bɪ'gɪnɪŋ] *n* Anfang *der;* **from the beginning** von Anfang an.

begrudge [bɪ'grʌdʒ] *vt* - 1. [envy]: **to begrudge sb sthg** jm etw missgönnen - 2. [do unwillingly]: **to begrudge doing sthg** etw widerwillig tun.

begun [bɪ'gʌn] *pp* ▷ **begin.**

behalf [bɪ'hɑːf] *n:* **on** UK OR **in** US **behalf of** im Namen (+ G), im Auftrag (+ G).

behave [bɪ'heɪv] *vt:* **to behave o.s.** sich benehmen. ⟨⟩ *vi* sich verhalten; [with good manners] sich benehmen.

behaviour UK**, behavior** US [bɪ'heɪvjə'] *n* Benehmen *das.*

behead [bɪ'hed] *vt* enthaupten, köpfen.

beheld [bɪ'held] *pt & pp* ▷ **behold.**

behind [bɪ'haɪnd] ⟨⟩ *prep* - 1. [at the back of] hinter (+ D); [with verbs of motion] hinter (+ A) - 2. [causing, responsible for] hinter (+ D); **what's behind this campaign?** was hat es mit dieser Kampagne auf sich?; **what's behind it?** was steckt dahinter? - 3. [supporting]: **to be behind sb** *fig* jn unterstützen - 4. [indicating deficiency, delay]: **behind schedule** im Rückstand. ⟨⟩ *adv* - 1. [at, in the back] hinten; **the others followed behind** die anderen kamen hinterher; **to leave sthg behind** etw zurücklassen; **to stay behind** (da)bleiben - 2. [late]: **to be behind (with sthg)** (mit etw) im Verzug sein. ⟨⟩ *n inf* Hintern *der.*

behold [bɪ'həʊld] (*pt & pp* **beheld**) *vt liter* erblicken.

beige [beɪʒ] ⟨⟩ *adj* beige. ⟨⟩ *n* Beige *das.*

being ['biːɪŋ] *n* - 1. [creature] Wesen *das,* Geschöpf *das* - 2. [existence]: **in being** existierend, vorhanden; **to come into being** entstehen.

belated [bɪ'leɪtɪd] *adj* verspätet.

belch [beltʃ] ⟨⟩ *n* Rülpser *der.* ⟨⟩ *vt* [smoke, fire] (aus)lspeien. ⟨⟩ *vi* [person] rülpsen.

beleaguered [bɪ'liːgəd] *adj liter & fig* belagert.

Belgian ['beldʒən] ⟨⟩ *adj* belgisch. ⟨⟩ *n* Belgier *der,* -in *die.*

Belgium ['beldʒəm] *n* Belgien *nt.*

Belgrade [,bel'greɪd] *n* Belgrad *nt.*

belief [bɪ'liːf] *n* - 1. [gen]: **belief (in)** Glaube *der* (an (+ A)) - 2. [opinion] Meinung *die;* **it's my belief that...** ich bin davon überzeugt, dass...

believe [bɪ'liːv] ⟨⟩ *vt* glauben; **to believe sb** jm glauben; **I believe so** ich glaube ja; **I don't believe it!** das darf (ja wohl) nicht wahr sein!;

believe it or not ob du/Sie es glaubst/glauben oder nicht. ⟨⟩ *vi* glauben; **to believe in sb/ sthg** an jn/etw glauben.

believer [bɪ'liːvə'] *n* RELIG Gläubige *der, die;* **I'm a great believer in corporal punishment** ich halte viel von der Prügelstrafe.

belittle [bɪ'lɪtl] *vt* schmälern.

bell [bel] *n* Glocke *die;* [of phone, door, bike] Klingel *die.*

belligerent [bɪ'lɪdʒərənt] *adj* - 1. [at war] kriegführend - 2. [aggressive] angriffslustig.

bellows ['beləʊz] *npl* Blasebalg *der.*

belly ['belɪ] *n* Bauch *der.*

bellyache ['belɪeɪk] *n* Bauchschmerzen *Pl.*

belly button *n inf* Bauchnabel *der.*

belong [bɪ'lɒŋ] *vi* gehören; **to belong to sb** jm gehören; **to belong to a party/club** einer Partei/einem Verein anlgehören.

belongings [bɪ'lɒŋɪŋz] *npl* Sachen *Pl.*

beloved [bɪ'lʌvd] *adj* geliebt.

below [bɪ'ləʊ] ⟨⟩ *adv* - 1. [in a lower position] unten; **they live on the floor below** sie wohnen ein Stockwerk tiefer; **see below** [in text] siehe unten - 2. [with numbers, quantities]: **children of 5 and below** Kinder bis zu 5 Jahre - 3. NAUT: **to go below** unter Deck gehen. ⟨⟩ *prep* - 1. [lower than] unter (+ D); [with verbs of motion] unter (+ A) - 2. [in rank, status] unter (+ D); **a sergeant is below a captain** ein Feldwebel steht unter einem Hauptmann - 3. [less than] unter (+ D); **10 degrees below (zero)** 10 Grad unter Null; **below average** unter dem Durchschnitt.

belt [belt] ⟨⟩ *n* - 1. [for clothing] Gürtel *der* - 2. TECH Riemen *der.* ⟨⟩ *vt inf* [hit] verprügeln.

beltway ['belt,weɪ] *n* US Umgehungsstraße *die.*

bemused [bɪ'mjuːzd] *adj* verwirrt.

bench [bentʃ] *n* - 1. POL [seat] Bank *die* - 2. [in workshop] Werkbank *die;* [in laboratory] Labortisch *der.*

benchmark ['bentʃmɑːk] *n* [standard] Standard *der;* [standard & COMPUT] Benchmark *die.*

bend [bend] (*pt & pp* **bent**) ⟨⟩ *n* - 1. [in river, pipe] Biegung *die;* [in road] Kurve *die* - 2. AUT: **round the bend** *inf* verrückt. ⟨⟩ *vt* [arm, leg, knee] beugen; [back] krümmen; [head] neigen; [wire, fork, tube] (ver)biegen. ⟨⟩ *vi* - 1. [arm, leg] beugen; [branch, tree] biegen - 2. [person] sich bücken - 3. [road] eine Kurve machen; [river] eine Biegung machen. ◈ **bend down** *vi* sich bücken. ◈ **bend over** *vi* sich bücken; **to bend over backwards for sb** alles für jn tun.

beneath [bɪ'niːθ] ⟨⟩ *adv* [below] unten. ⟨⟩ *prep* - 1. [under] unter (+ D); [with verbs of motion] unter (+ A); **she shoved it beneath the bed** sie schob es unter das Bett - 2. [unworthy of]: **that is beneath him** das ist unter seiner Würde.

benefactor ['benɪfæktəʳ] n Wohltäter *der*, -in *die*.

beneficial [ˌbenɪˈfɪʃl] adj nützlich; **to be beneficial to sb/sthg** jm/etw zugute kommen.

beneficiary [ˌbenɪˈfɪʃərɪ] n LAW [of will] Begünstigte *der*, *die*.

benefit ['benɪfɪt] ◇ n - **1.** (U) [advantage] Nutzen *der*; **to be to sb's benefit, to be of benefit to sb** zu js Nutzen sein; **for the benefit of** zum Nutzen von; **to give sb the benefit of the doubt** jm trotz Zweifels Glauben schenken - **2.** [good point] Vorteil *der* - **3.** [allowance of money] Unterstützung *die*. ◇ vt nützen (+ D). ◇ vi: **to benefit from sthg** von etw profitieren.

Benelux ['benɪlʌks] n: **the Benelux countries** die Beneluxstaaten, die Beneluxländer.

benevolent [bɪˈnevələnt] adj wohlwollend.

benign [bɪˈnaɪn] adj - **1.** [influence] gut; [climate] mild - **2.** MED gutartig.

bent [bent] ◇ pt & pp ▷ **bend**. ◇ adj - **1.** [wire, bar] gebogen, verbogen - **2.** [person, body] gebeugt - **3.** UK inf [dishonest] korrupt - **4.** [determined]: **to be bent on sthg** etw unbedingt wollen/haben wollen; **to be bent on doing sthg** etw unbedingt tun wollen. ◇ n [natural aptitude]: **bent (for)** Neigung *die* (zu).

bequeath [bɪˈkwiːð] vt liter & fig hinterlassen.

bequest [bɪˈkwest] n Nachlass *der*.

berate [bɪˈreɪt] vt schelten.

bereaved [bɪˈriːvd] (pl inv) ◇ adj: **to be bereaved** trauern. ◇ npl: **the bereaved** die Hinterbliebenen Pl.

beret ['bereɪ] n Baskenmütze *die*.

berk [bɜːk] n UK inf Dussel *der*.

Berlin [bɜːˈlɪn] n Berlin nt.

berm [bɜːm] n US Grünstreifen *der*.

Bermuda [bəˈmjuːdə] n Bermudainseln Pl.

Bern [bɜːn] n Bern nt.

berry ['berɪ] n Beere *die*.

berserk [bəˈzɜːk] adj: **to go berserk** wild werden.

berth [bɜːθ] ◇ n - **1.** [in harbour] Liegeplatz *der* - **2.** [on ship] Koje *die*; [on train] Schlafwagenplatz *der*. ◇ vi [ship] anllegen.

beseech [bɪˈsiːtʃ] (pt & pp **besought** OR **beseeched**) vt liter [implore]: **to beseech sb (to do sthg)** jn anlflehen (, etw zu tun).

beset [bɪˈset] (pt & pp inv) ◇ adj: **beset with** OR **by sthg** von etw heimgesucht. ◇ vt heimlsuchen.

beside [bɪˈsaɪd] prep - **1.** [next to] neben (+ A, D) - **2.** [compared with] verglichen mit - **3.** phr: **to be beside o.s. with joy/anger** vor Freude/Wut außer sich sein.

besides [bɪˈsaɪdz] ◇ adv außerdem. ◇ prep außer (+ D); **besides being expensive, it's also ugly** es ist nicht nur teuer, sondern auch hässlich.

besiege [bɪˈsiːdʒ] vt liter & fig belagern.

besotted [bɪˈsɒtɪd] adj: **besotted (with)** vernarrt (in jn).

besought [bɪˈsɔːt] pt & pp ▷ **beseech**.

best [best] ◇ adj beste(r) (s); **my best friend** mein bester Freund/meine beste Freundin. ◇ adv am besten; **which car do you like best?** welches Auto gefällt dir am besten?; **what type of beer do you like best?** welches Bier magst du am liebsten? ◇ n - **1.** Beste *der*, *die*, *das*; **to do one's best** sein Bestes tun - **2.** phr: **to make the best of sthg** das Beste aus etw machen; **for the best** nur zum Guten; **all the best!** alles Gute! ▸ **at best** adv bestenfalls.

best man n Trauzeuge *der*.

bestow [bɪˈstəʊ] vt fml: **to bestow sthg on sb** jm etw gewähren.

best-seller n [book] Bestseller *der*.

bet [bet] (pt & pp inv OR -ted) ◇ n - **1.** [wager] Wette *die*; **to have a bet on sthg** auf etw (A) wetten - **2.** fig [prediction]: **it's a safe bet that...** man kann sicher sein, dass... ◇ vt wetten. ◇ vi - **1.** [gamble]: **to bet (on sthg)** (auf etw (A)) wetten - **2.** fig [predict]: **to bet on sthg** sich auf etw (A) verlassen.

betray [bɪˈtreɪ] vt verraten; [trust] missbrauchen.

betrayal [bɪˈtreɪəl] n Verrat *der*.

better ['betəʳ] ◇ adj (compar of good, well) besser; **to get better** besser werden; **I hope you get better soon** ich hoffe, es geht dir bald besser; **to get better and better** immer besser werden. ◇ adv besser; [like] lieber. ◇ n [best one] Bessere *der*, *die*, *das*; **to get the better of sb** die Oberhand über jn gewinnen; **my curiosity got the better of me** meine Neugier war stärker. ◇ vt [improve] verbessern; **to better o.s.** sich verbessern.

better off adj besser dran.

betting ['betɪŋ] n (U) - **1.** [bets] Wetten *das* - **2.** [odds] Wetten Pl.

betting shop n UK Wettannahmestelle *die*.

between [bɪˈtwiːn] ◇ prep zwischen (+ D); [with verbs of motion] zwischen (+ A); **between now and next month** bis nächsten Monat; **we had only twenty pounds between us** wir hatten (zusammen) nur zwanzig Pfund. ◇ adv: **(in)between** zwischen.

beverage ['bevərɪdʒ] n fml Getränk *das*.

beware [bɪˈweəʳ] vi sich in Acht nehmen; **to beware of sthg** sich vor etw in Acht nehmen; **'beware of the dog'** 'Vorsicht bissiger Hund'.

bewildered [bɪˈwɪldəd] adj verwirrt.

beyond [bɪˈjɒnd] ◇ prep - **1.** [in space] jenseits (+ G), über (+ A) hinaus; **it's just beyond**

the park es ist direkt auf der anderen Seite des Parks - **2.** [in time]: **beyond the year 2010** über das Jahr 2010 hinaus; **beyond midnight** bis nach Mitternacht; **beyond the age of five** ab dem fünften Lebensjahr - **3.** [outside the range of] über (+ A, D); **the town has changed beyond all recognition** die Stadt hat sich bis zur Unkenntlichkeit verändert. <> adv - **1.** [in space] jenseits (davon) - **2.** [in time] darüber hinaus, danach.

bias ['baɪəs] n - **1.** [prejudice] Voreingenommenheit die - **2.** [tendency] Tendenz die.

biased ['baɪəst] adj - **1.** [person]: **to be biased (against)** voreingenommen sein (gegenüber) - **2.** [system]: **to be biased against/towards sb** jn benachteiligen/bevorteilen.

bib [bɪb] n [for baby] Latz der, Lätzchen das.

Bible ['baɪbl] n Bibel die.

bicarbonate of soda [baɪ'kɑːbənət-] n Natron das.

biceps ['baɪseps] (pl inv) n Bizeps der.

bicker ['bɪkər] vi sich zanken.

bicycle ['baɪsɪkl] n Fahrrad das.

bicycle path n Fahrradweg der.

bicycle pump n Luftpumpe die.

bid [bɪd] <> n - **1.** [attempt] Versuch der - **2.** [at auction] Gebot das - **3.** COMM Angebot das. <> vt (pt **bid**) [at auction] bieten. <> vi (pt **bid**) [at auction]: **to bid (for)** bieten (für).

bidder ['bɪdər] n Bietende der, die.

bidding ['bɪdɪŋ] n [at auction] Bieten das.

bide [baɪd] vt: **to bide one's time** (eine Gelegenheit) abwarten.

bifocals [baɪ'fəʊklz] npl Brille die mit Bifokalgläsern.

big [bɪg] adj - **1.** [gen] groß; **how big is it?** wie groß ist es?; **my big brother** mein großer Bruder; **big ideas** hochfliegende Ideen - **2.** [important] bedeutend; **the big day** der große Tag - **3.** [conceited]: **to have a big head** eingebildet sein - **4.** inf [phr]: **he's into motorbikes in a big way** er ist vernarrt in Motorräder.

bigamy ['bɪgəmɪ] n Bigamie die.

big deal inf <> n: **it's no big deal** das ist kein Problem; **what's the big deal?** was ist schon dabei? <> excl und wenn schon!

Big Dipper [-'dɪpər] n - **1.** UK [rollercoaster] Achterbahn die - **2.** US ASTRON: **the Big Dipper** der Große Bär.

bigheaded [,bɪg'hedɪd] adj inf eingebildet.

bigot ['bɪgət] n bigotter Mensch.

bigoted ['bɪgətɪd] adj bigott.

bigotry ['bɪgətrɪ] n Bigotterie die.

big time n inf: **to make** OR **hit the big time** ganz groß rauskommen.

big toe n großer Zeh.

big top n Zirkuszelt das.

big wheel n UK [at fairground] Riesenrad das.

bike [baɪk] n inf - **1.** [cycle] Rad - **2.** [motorcycle] Motorrad das.

bikeway ['baɪkweɪ] n US Radweg der.

bikini [bɪ'kiːnɪ] n Bikini der.

bile [baɪl] n Galle die.

bilingual [baɪ'lɪŋgwəl] adj zweisprachig.

bill [bɪl] <> n - **1.** [statement of cost] Rechnung die - **2.** [in parliament] Gesetzentwurf der - **3.** [of show, concert] Programm das - **4.** US [bank note] Geldschein der, Banknote die - **5.** [poster]: **'post** OR **stick no bills'** 'Plakate ankleben verboten' - **6.** [of bird] Schnabel der. <> vt: **to bill sb (for sthg)** jm eine Rechnung (für etw) schicken.

billboard ['bɪlbɔːd] n Plakatwand die.

billet ['bɪlɪt] n Quartier das.

billfold ['bɪlfəʊld] n US Brieftasche die.

billiards ['bɪljədz] n (U) Billard das.

billion ['bɪljən] num - **1.** [thousand million] Milliarde die - **2.** UK dated [million million] Billion die.

bimbo ['bɪmbəʊ] (pl **-s** OR **-es**) n inf pej Tussi die.

bin [bɪn] n UK [for rubbish] Abfalleimer der.

bind [baɪnd] (pt & pp **bound**) vt - **1.** [gen] binden - **2.** [bandage] verbinden - **3.** [constrain] verpflichten.

binder ['baɪndər] n [cover] Ordner der.

binding ['baɪndɪŋ] <> adj verbindlich, bindend. <> n [of book] Einband der.

binge [bɪndʒ] inf <> n: **to go on a binge** [on drink] auf Sauftour gehen; [on food] eine Fresstour machen. <> vi: **to binge on sthg** [drink] etw saufen; [food] etw fressen.

bingo ['bɪŋgəʊ] n Bingo das.

binoculars [bɪ'nɒkjʊləz] npl Fernglas das.

biochemistry [,baɪəʊ'kemɪstrɪ] n Biochemie die.

biodegradable [,baɪəʊdɪ'greɪdəbl] adj biologisch abbaubar.

biography [baɪ'ɒgrəfɪ] n Biografie die.

biological [,baɪə'lɒdʒɪkl] adj biologisch.

biological weapon n biologische Waffe die.

biology [baɪ'ɒlədʒɪ] n Biologie die.

biotechnology [,baɪəʊtek'nɒlədʒɪ] n Biotechnologie die.

bioterrorism [,baɪəʊ'terərɪzm] n Bioterrorismus der.

birch [bɜːtʃ] n [tree] Birke die.

bird [bɜːd] n - **1.** [creature] Vogel der - **2.** inf [woman] Braut die.

birdie ['bɜːdɪ] n [in golf] Birdie das.

bird's-eye view n Vogelperspektive die.

bird-watcher [-,wɒtʃər] n Vogelbeobachter der, -in die.

Biro® ['baɪərəʊ] n Kugelschreiber der.

birth [bɜːθ] n - **1.** [of baby] Geburt die; **to give birth (to)** gebären - **2.** fig [of idea, system, country] Geburtsstunde die.

birth certificate n Geburtsurkunde die.

birth control n (U) Geburtenregelung die; **to use birth control** verhüten.

birthday ['bɜːdeɪ] n Geburtstag der.

birthmark ['bɜːθmɑːk] n Muttermal das.

birthrate ['bɜːreɪt] n Geburtenrate die.

biscuit ['bɪskɪt] n - **1.** UK [thin dry cake] Keks der - **2.** US [bread-like cake] Hefebrötchen, das üblicherweise mit Bratensaft gegessen wird.

bisect [baɪ'sekt] vt - **1.** GEOM halbieren - **2.** [cut in two] durchschneiden.

bishop ['bɪʃəp] n - **1.** [in church] Bischof der - **2.** [in chess] Läufer der.

bison ['baɪsn] (pl inv OR -s) n Bison der.

bit [bɪt] ⇔ pt ⊳ **bite**. ⇔ n - **1.** [small piece] Stück das; **bits and pieces** UK [objects] Krimskrams der; **to fall to bits** kaputtgehen, auseinander fallen - **2.** [unspecified amount]: **a bit of** ein bisschen; **quite a bit of** eine ganze Menge - **3.** [short time]: **for a bit** für ein Weilchen - **4.** [of drill] Bohrer der - **5.** [of bridle] Trensengebiss das - **6.** COMPUT Bit das. ⬥ **a bit** adv [tired, late, confused] ein bisschen. ⬥ **bit by bit** adv Stück für Stück.

bitch [bɪtʃ] n - **1.** [female dog] Hündin die - **2.** v inf pej [woman] Miststück das.

bitchy [bɪtʃɪ] adj inf gehässig, gemein.

bite [baɪt] (pt bit, pp bitten) ⇔ n Biss der; **to have a bite (to eat)** etwas Essen essen. ⇔ vt beißen. ⇔ vi - **1.** [animal, person, insect] beißen; **to bite into sthg** in etw (hinein)lbeißen - **2.** [tyres, clutch] greifen - **3.** fig [sanction, law] greifen.

biting ['baɪtɪŋ] adj - **1.** [wind, cold] schneidend, beißend - **2.** [caustic - comment] bissig.

bitmap ['bɪtmæp] n COMPUT Bitmap das.

bitten ['bɪtn] pp ⊳ **bite**.

bitter ['bɪtər] ⇔ adj - **1.** [gen] bitter; **it's bitter (weather) today** es ist heute bitterkalt - **2.** [argument, war] erbittert - **3.** [resentful] verbittert. ⇔ n UK [beer] dem Altbier ähnliches Bier.

bitterness ['bɪtənɪs] n Bitterkeit die.

bizarre [bɪ'zɑːr] adj exzentrisch; [house, landscape] bizarr.

blab [blæb] vi inf quatschen.

black [blæk] ⇔ adj - **1.** [gen] schwarz - **2.** [future] finster, düster. ⇔ n - **1.** [colour] Schwarz das; **in black and white** [in writing] schwarz auf weiß; **in the black** [solvent] in den schwarzen Zahlen - **2.** [person] Schwarze der, die. ⇔ vt UK [boycott] boykottieren. ⬥ **black out** vi [faint] ohnmächtig werden.

blackberry ['blækbərɪ] n Brombeere die.

blackbird ['blækbɜːd] n Amsel die.

blackboard ['blækbɔːd] n Tafel die.

blackcurrant [ˌblæk'kʌrənt] n schwarze Johannisbeere.

blacken ['blækn] ⇔ vt [in colour] schwärzen. ⇔ vi [sky] sich verdunkeln.

black eye n schwarzes Auge.

Black Forest n Schwarzwald der.

blackhead ['blækhed] n Mitesser der.

black ice n (U) Glatteis das.

blackleg ['blækleg] n pej Streikbrecher der, -in die.

blacklist ['blæklɪst] ⇔ n schwarze Liste. ⇔ vt auf die schwarze Liste setzen.

blackmail ['blækmeɪl] ⇔ n Erpressung die. ⇔ vt erpressen.

black market n Schwarzmarkt der.

blackout ['blækaʊt] n - **1.** [in wartime] Verdunkelung die - **2.** [power cut] Stromausfall der - **3.** [suppression of news] Nachrichtensperre die - **4.** [fainting] Ohnmachtsanfall der.

black pudding n UK Blutwurst die.

Black Sea n: **the Black Sea** das Schwarze Meer.

black sheep n schwarzes Schaf.

blacksmith ['blæksmɪθ] n Schmied der, -in die.

black spot n [for road accidents] Gefahrenstelle die.

bladder ['blædər] n ANAT Blase die.

blade [bleɪd] n - **1.** [of knife, razor] Klinge die - **2.** [of propeller, saw, oar] Blatt das - **3.** [of grass] Halm der.

blame [bleɪm] ⇔ n Schuld die; **to take the blame for sthg** die Schuld für etw auf sich (A) nehmen. ⇔ vt beschuldigen; **to blame sthg on sb/sthg** jm/etw die Schuld an etw (D) geben; **they blamed her for the defeat** sie gaben ihr die Schuld an der Niederlage; **to be to blame for sthg** an etw (D) schuld sein.

bland [blænd] adj - **1.** [person] farblos - **2.** [food] fad - **3.** [music, style] nichtssagend.

blank [blæŋk] ⇔ adj leer. ⇔ n - **1.** [empty space] Leere die, leere Stelle - **2.** MIL [cartridge] Platzpatrone die.

blank cheque n Blankoscheck der; **to give sb a blank cheque to do sthg** fig jm freie Hand lassen, etw zu tun.

blanket ['blæŋkɪt] n - **1.** [bed cover] Decke die - **2.** [layer] Schicht die.

blare [bleər] vi plärren.

blasphemy ['blæsfəmɪ] n Blasphemie die.

blast [blɑːst] ⇔ n - **1.** [of bomb] Explosion die - **2.** [of air] Windstoß der. ⇔ vt [hole, tunnel] sprengen. ⇔ excl UK inf verdammt. ⬥ **(at) full blast** adv - **1.** [maximum volume] auf höchster Lautstärke - **2.** [maximum effort, speed] auf Hochtouren.

blasted ['blɑːstɪd] adj inf verdammt.

blast-off n [space] Start der.

blatant ['bleɪtənt] *adj* [shameless] unverhohlen.

blaze [bleɪz] ⟨⟩ *n* - 1. [fire] Brand *der* - 2. fig [of colour, light] Pracht *die*. ⟨⟩ *vi* - 1. [fire] lodern - 2. fig [with colour, emotion] brennen.

blazer ['bleɪzər] *n* Blazer *der*.

bleach [bliːtʃ] ⟨⟩ *n* (U) [for clothes] Bleichmittel *das*; [for cleaning] Reinigungsmittel *das*. ⟨⟩ *vt* [hair, clothes] bleichen.

bleachers ['bliːtʃəz] *npl US* SPORT *nicht überdachte Zuschauertribüne*.

bleak [bliːk] *adj* - 1. [weather] trüb, trostlos; [place] trostlos - 2. [future, face, person] trüb.

bleary-eyed [,blɪərɪ'aɪd] *adj* verschlafen.

bleat [bliːt] *vi* - 1. [sheep] blöken; [goat] meckern - 2. fig [person] meckern.

bleed [bliːd] (*pt & pp* bled [bled]) ⟨⟩ *vt* [drain] entlüften. ⟨⟩ *vi* bluten.

bleeper ['bliːpər] *n* Piepser *der*.

blemish ['blemɪʃ] *n liter & fig* Makel *der*.

blend [blend] ⟨⟩ *n liter & fig* Mischung *die*. ⟨⟩ *vt* (ver)mischen; **to blend sthg with sthg** etw mit etw mischen. ⟨⟩ *vi* [colours, sounds] sich (ver)mischen.

blender ['blendər] *n* [food mixer] Mixer *der*.

bless [bles] (*pt & pp* -ed OR blest) *vt* - 1. RELIG segnen - 2. phr: **bless you!** [after sneezing] Gesundheit!; [thank you] du bist ein Engel!

blessing ['blesɪŋ] *n liter & fig* Segen *der*.

blest [blest] *pt & pp* ⊳ **bless**.

blew [bluː] *pt* ▷ **blow**.

blight [blaɪt] *vt* beeinträchtigen.

blimey ['blaɪmɪ] *excl UK inf* herrje!

blind [blaɪnd] ⟨⟩ *adj* [gen] blind; **to be blind to sthg** gegenüber einer Sache (D) OR für etw blind sein. ⟨⟩ *n* [for window] Jalousie *die*. ⟨⟩ *npl*: **the blind** die Blinden *Pl*. ⟨⟩ *vt* blenden; **to blind sb to sthg** fig jn für etw blind machen.

blind alley *n liter & fig* Sackgasse *die*.

blind date *n* Rendezvous mit einem oder einer Unbekannten.

blinders ['blaɪndəz] *npl US* Scheuklappen *Pl*.

blindfold ['blaɪndfəʊld] ⟨⟩ *adv* mit verbundenen Augen. ⟨⟩ *n* Augenbinde *die*. ⟨⟩ *vt*: **to blindfold sb** jm die Augen verbinden.

blindingly ['blaɪndɪŋlɪ] *adv* [obvious] völlig.

blindly ['blaɪndlɪ] *adv liter & fig* blindlings.

blindness ['blaɪndnɪs] *n* Blindheit *die*.

blind spot *n* - 1. [when driving] toter Winkel - 2. fig [inability to understand]: **to have a blind spot about sthg** (überhaupt) keine Begabung für etw haben.

blink [blɪŋk] ⟨⟩ *n phr*: **to be on the blink** inf [machine] eine Macke haben. ⟨⟩ *vt* [eyes] anblinzeln. ⟨⟩ *vi* [light] aufscheinen.

blinkered ['blɪŋkəd] *adj* fig [view, attitude] engstirnig.

blinkers ['blɪŋkəz] *npl UK* [for horse] Scheuklappen *Pl*.

bliss [blɪs] *n* Glück *das*, (Glück)seligkeit *die*; **it was sheer bliss** es war die reinste Wonne.

blissful ['blɪsfʊl] *adj* herrlich; **in blissful ignorance** in völliger Ahnungslosigkeit.

blister ['blɪstər] ⟨⟩ *n* Blase *die*. ⟨⟩ *vi* - 1. [skin] Blasen bekommen - 2. [paint] Blasen werfen.

blithely ['blaɪðlɪ] *adv* unbekümmert.

blitz [blɪts] *n* MIL Luftangriff *der*.

blizzard ['blɪzəd] *n* Schneesturm *der*.

bloated ['bləʊtɪd] *adj* - 1. [body, face] aufgedunsen - 2. [with food] übersatt.

blob [blɒb] *n* - 1. [of paint] Klecks *der*; [of cream] Klacks *der* - 2. [indistinct form] Fleck *der*.

block [blɒk] ⟨⟩ *n* - 1. [building]: **block (of flats)** Wohnhaus *das*; **office block** Bürohaus *das* - 2. [of ice, wood, stone] Klotz *der* - 3. *US* [of buildings] Block *der* - 4. [mental] geistige Sperre. ⟨⟩ *vt* - 1. [road, path, law] blockieren; [pipe] verstopfen - 2. [view] versperren.

blockade [blɒ'keɪd] ⟨⟩ *n* Blockade *die*. ⟨⟩ *vt* blockieren, sperren.

blockage ['blɒkɪdʒ] *n* Verstopfung *die*.

blockbuster ['blɒkbʌstər] *n* inf Kassenschlager *der*.

block capitals *npl* Blockschrift *die*.

block letters *npl* Blockschrift *die*.

blog [blɒg] *n* Blog *der*.

bloke [bləʊk] *n UK* inf Typ *der*.

blond [blɒnd] *adj* blond.

blonde [blɒnd] ⟨⟩ *adj* blond. ⟨⟩ *n* [woman] Blondine *die*.

blood [blʌd] *n* Blut *das*; **in cold blood** kaltblütig.

bloodbath ['blʌdbɑːθ] *n* Blutbad *das*.

blood cell *n* Blutzelle *die*.

blood donor *n* Blutspender *der*.

blood group *n* Blutgruppe *die*.

bloodhound ['blʌdhaʊnd] *n* Bluthund *der*.

blood poisoning *n* Blutvergiftung *die*.

blood pressure *n* Blutdruck *der*.

bloodshed ['blʌdʃed] *n* Blutvergießen *das*.

bloodshot ['blʌdʃɒt] *adj* [eyes] blutunterlaufen.

bloodstream ['blʌdstriːm] *n* Blutstrom *der*.

blood test *n* Blutprobe *die*.

bloodthirsty ['blʌd,θɜːstɪ] *adj* blutrünstig.

blood transfusion *n* Transfusion *die*.

bloody ['blʌdɪ] ⟨⟩ *adj* - 1. [gen] blutig - 2. *UK* v inf [for emphasis] verdammt; **bloody hell!** verdammt noch mal! ⟨⟩ *adv UK* v inf verdammt.

bloody-minded [-'maɪndɪd] *adj UK* inf stur.

bloom [bluːm] ⟨⟩ *n* Blüte *die*. ⟨⟩ *vi* blühen.

blooming ['bluːmɪŋ] ⟨⟩ *adj UK* inf [for emphasis] verflixt. ⟨⟩ *adv UK* inf verflixt.

blossom ['blɒsəm] ◇ n Blüte die; **in blossom** in Blüte. ◇ vi - 1. [tree] blühen - 2. fig [person] aufblühen.

blot [blɒt] ◇ n - 1. [of ink etc] (Tinten)klecks der - 2. fig [blemish] Makel der; **a blot on the landscape** ein Schandfleck in der Landschaft. ◇ vt - 1. [dry] abllöschen - 2. [spot with ink] beklecksen. ◆ **blot out** vt sep [memory] ausllöschen.

blotchy ['blɒtʃɪ] adj fleckig.

blotting paper ['blɒtɪŋ-] n (U) Löschpapier das.

blouse [blauz] n Bluse die.

blow [bləʊ] (pt **blew**, pp **blown**) ◇ vi - 1. [wind] wehen; [stronger] blasen - 2. [move in the wind] wehen; **the door blew open/shut** die Tür flog auf/zu - 3. [person] blasen - 4. [fuse] durchlbrennen - 5. [whistle] ertönen. ◇ vt - 1. [subj: wind] wehen; [stronger] blasen - 2. [clear]: **to blow one's nose** sich (D) die Nase putzen - 3. [whistle, horn, trumpet] blasen. ◇ n Schlag der. ◆ **blow away** vi weglfliegen. ◆ **blow out** vt sep auslblasen. ◇ vi - 1. [candle] auslgehen - 2. [tyre] platzen. ◆ **blow over** vi - 1. [storm] sich legen - 2. [argument] in Vergessenheit geraten. ◆ **blow up** ◇ vt sep - 1. [inflate] auflblasen; [with pump] auflpumpen - 2. [with bomb] in die Luft jagen - 3. [photograph] vergrößern. ◇ vi [explode] explodieren.

blow-dry ◇ n Fönen das; **a cut and blow-dry** Schneiden und Fönen. ◇ vt fönen.

blowlamp UK ['bləʊlæmp], **blowtorch** esp US ['bləʊtɔːtʃ] n Lötlampe die.

blown [bləʊn] pp ▷ **blow**.

blowout ['bləʊaʊt] n [of tyre]: **he had a blowout** ihm platzte ein Reifen.

blowtorch n esp US = **blowlamp**.

blubber ['blʌbə'] ◇ n Walfischspeck der. ◇ vi pej flennen, heulen.

bludgeon ['blʌdʒən] vt prügeln.

blue [bluː] ◇ adj - 1. [in colour] blau - 2. inf [sad] trübsinnig - 3. [film] Porno-; [joke] unanständig. ◇ n Blau das; **out of the blue** aus heiterem Himmel. ◆ **blues** npl - 1. MUS: **the blues** der Blues - 2. inf [sad feeling]: **the blues** ein Anfall von Melancholie.

bluebell ['bluːbel] n Glockenblume die.

blueberry ['bluːbərɪ] n Heidelbeere die.

blue cheese n Blauschimmelkäse der.

blue-collar adj: **blue-collar worker** Arbeiter der, -in die.

blue jeans npl US (Blue) Jeans die.

blueprint ['bluːprɪnt] n - 1. CONSTR Blaupause die - 2. fig [plan, programme] Entwurf der.

bluff [blʌf] ◇ adj [person, manner] raubeinig. ◇ n - 1. [deception] Bluff der; **to call sb's bluff** jn dazu aufllordern, seine Drohung wahr zu machen - 2. [cliff] Steilhang der. ◇ vi bluffen.

blunder ['blʌndə'] ◇ n Schnitzer der. ◇ vi [make mistake] einen Schnitzer machen; [socially] sich blamieren.

blunt [blʌnt] ◇ adj - 1. [knife, pencil, instrument] stumpf - 2. [person] geradeheraus; [manner, question] unverblümt. ◇ vt fig [enthusiasm] dämpfen; [impact] ablschwächen.

blur [blɜːʳ] ◇ n verschwommener Fleck; **he couldn't remember anything about the accident, it was all a blur** er konnte sich an nichts bezüglich des Unfalls erinnern, alles war verschwommen. ◇ vt - 1. [outline, photograph] unscharf machen - 2. [distinction] undeutlich machen.

blurb [blɜːb] n inf [on book] Klappentext der.

blurt [blɜːt] ◆ **blurt out** vt sep herauslplatzen mit.

blush [blʌʃ] ◇ n Röte die. ◇ vi rot werden.

blusher ['blʌʃə'] n Rouge das.

blustery ['blʌstərɪ] adj stürmisch.

BMX (abbr of **bicycle motorcross**) n: **BMX bike** BMX-Rad das.

BO n abbr of **body odour**.

boar [bɔːʳ] n - 1. [male pig] Eber der - 2. [wild pig] Keiler der.

board [bɔːd] ◇ n - 1. [plank] Brett das - 2. [for notices - large] schwarzes Brett; [- small] Pinnwand die - 3. [for games] Spielbrett das - 4. [blackboard] Tafel die - 5. ADMIN: **board (of directors)** Vorstand der; **board of examiners** Prüfungskommission die; **board of enquiry** Untersuchungsausschuss der - 6. UK [at hotel, guesthouse] Verpflegung die; **board and lodging** Unterkunft und Verpflegung; **full/half board** Voll-/Halbpension die - 7. phr: **above board** offen. ◇ vt [train, bus] einlsteigen in (+ A); **to board a ship/aircraft** an Bord eines Schiffes/Flugzeugs gehen. ◆ **across the board** ◇ adj [increase] generell. ◇ adv [apply] überall. ◆ **on board** ◇ prep [ship, plane] an Bord (+ G); [bus, train] in (+ D). ◇ adv: **to be on board** [on ship, plane] an Bord sein; [on train] im Zug sein; **to take sthg on board** [knowledge] etw berücksichtigen; [advice] etw anlnehmen. ◆ **board up** vt sep mit Brettern vernageln.

boarder ['bɔːdə'] n - 1. [lodger] Pensionsgast der - 2. [at school] Internatsschüler der, -in die.

boarding card ['bɔːdɪŋ-] n Bordkarte die.

boarding house ['bɔːdɪŋhaʊs] (pl [-haʊzɪz]) n Pension die.

boarding school ['bɔːdɪŋ-] n Internat das.

Board of Trade n UK: **the Board of Trade** das Handelsministerium.

boardroom ['bɔːdrʊm] n Sitzungssaal der.

boast [bəʊst] ◇ n Prahlerei die. ◇ vi prahlen; **to boast about sthg** mit etw prahlen.

boastful ['bəʊstfʊl] adj prahlerisch.

boat [bəʊt] n Boot das; [large] Schiff das; (phrase): **by boat** mit dem Boot; [large] mit dem Schiff.

boater ['bəʊtər] n [hat] steifer Strohhut.

boatswain ['bəʊsn] n NAUT Bootsmann der.

bob [bɒb] <> n - 1. [hairstyle] Bubikopf der - 2. UK inf dated [shilling] Schilling der - 3. [bobsleigh] Bob der. <> vi [boat, ship] auf und ab schaukeln.

bobbin ['bɒbɪn] n Spule die.

bobby ['bɒbɪ] n UK inf [policeman] Polizist der.

bobsleigh ['bɒbsleɪ] n Bob der.

bode [bəʊd] vi liter: **to bode well/ill (for sb/ sthg)** ein gutes/schlechtes Zeichen (für jn/ etw) sein.

bodily ['bɒdɪlɪ] <> adj körperlich; **bodily functions** Körperfunktionen Pl. <> adv [carry, lift] mit dem ganzen Körper.

body ['bɒdɪ] n - 1. [of human, animal] Körper der - 2. [corpse] Leiche die - 3. [organization] Organisation die - 4. [of car] Karosserie die; [of plane] Rumpf der - 5. [group] Gruppe die - 6. [of wine] Körper der - 7. [of hair] Volumen das - 8. [garment] Body der.

body building n Bodybuilding das.

bodyguard ['bɒdɪgɑːd] n [one person] Leibwächter der; [group of people] Leibwache die.

body odour n Körpergeruch der.

bodywork ['bɒdɪwɜːk] n Karosserie die.

bog [bɒg] n - 1. [marsh] Sumpf der - 2. UK inf [toilet] Klo das.

bogged down [,bɒgd-] adj: **bogged down (in sthg)** liter & fig (in etw (D)) festgefahren.

boggle ['bɒgl] vi: **the mind boggles!** es übersteigt den Verstand!

bog-standard adj inf stinknormal.

bogus ['bəʊgəs] adj [identity] falsch; [emotion] geheuchelt.

boil [bɔɪl] <> n - 1. [on skin] Furunkel der ODER das - 2. [boiling point]: **to bring sthg to the boil** etw zum Kochen bringen; **to come to the boil** zu kochen beginnen. <> vt kochen; **to boil the kettle** Wasser aufsetzen. <> vi kochen; **the kettle is boiling** das Wasser im Kessel kocht. ◆ **boil down to** vt insep fig hinauslaufen auf (+ A). ◆ **boil over** vi - 1. [liquid] überkochen - 2. fig [feelings] ihren Höhepunkt erreichen.

boiled ['bɔɪld] adj gekocht; **boiled potatoes** Salzkartoffeln Pl; **boiled sweets** Bonbons Pl; **boiled egg** gekochtes Ei.

boiler ['bɔɪlər] n Boiler der.

boiler suit n UK Overall der, Blaumann der.

boiling ['bɔɪlɪŋ] adj [hot liquid] kochend heiß; [weather] wahnsinnig heiß; **I'm boiling (hot)!** mir ist fürchterlich heiß!

boiling point n Siedepunkt der.

boisterous ['bɔɪstərəs] adj ungestüm.

bold [bəʊld] adj - 1. [person, plan] kühn, mutig - 2. ART [lines, colour] kräftig; [design] kühn - 3. TYPO: **bold type** OR **print** Fettdruck der.

bollard ['bɒlɑːd] n Poller der.

bollocks ['bɒlɒks] UK v inf <> npl Eier Pl. <> excl Scheiße!

bolster ['bəʊlstər] <> n Nackenrolle die. <> vt [confidence] stärken.

bolt [bəʊlt] <> n - 1. [on door, window] Riegel der - 2. [type of screw] Bolzen der. <> adv: **bolt upright** kerzengerade. <> vt - 1. [fasten together] verschrauben - 2. [close] verriegeln - 3. [food] hinunterschlingen. <> vi [run-horse] durchgehen; [- person] flüchten.

bomb [bɒm] <> n Bombe die. <> vt [from the air] bombardieren; [on the ground] einen Bombenanschlag verüben auf (+ A).

bombard [bɒm'bɑːd] vt [from the air] bombardieren; [from gun] beschießen; **to bombard sb with sthg** fig jn mit etw bombardieren.

bomb disposal squad n Bombenräumkommando das.

bomber ['bɒmər] n - 1. [plane] Bomberflugzeug das - 2. [person] Bombenleger der, -in die.

bombing ['bɒmɪŋ] n [from the air] Bombardierung die; [on the ground] Bombenanschlag der.

bombshell ['bɒmʃel] n fig schwerer Schlag.

bona fide [,bəʊnə'faɪdɪ] adj [genuine] echt.

bond [bɒnd] <> n - 1. [emotional link] enge Beziehung; **bonds of friendship** freundschaftliche Bande Pl - 2. [binding promise]: **my word is my bond** was ich verspreche, halte ich auch - 3. FIN Obligation die. <> vt - 1. [glue]: **to bond sthg to sthg** etw an etw (A) kleben - 2. fig [people]: **the experience bonded them together** die Erfahrung band sie aneinander.

bone [bəʊn] <> n Knochen der; [of fish] Gräte die; **bones** [of skeleton] Gebeine Pl. <> vt [meat] von den Knochen lösen; [fish] entgräten.

bone-dry adj knochentrocken.

bone-idle adj inf stinkfaul.

bonfire ['bɒn,faɪər] n großes Feuer (im Freien).

bonfire night n UK 5. November, Jahrestag der Pulververschwörung.

bonk vt & vi UK v inf bumsen.

Bonn [bɒn] n Bonn nt.

bonnet ['bɒnɪt] n - 1. UK [of car] Kühlerhaube die; Motorhaube die - 2. [hat - for woman] Haube die; [- for baby] Häubchen das.

bonny ['bɒnɪ] adj Scotland [baby] prächtig; [girl] hübsch.

bonus ['bəʊnəs] (pl -es) n - 1. [extra money] Prämie die; **Christmas bonus** Weihnachtsgratifikation die - 2. fig [added advantage] Pluspunkt der.

bony ['bəʊnɪ] adj [person, hand, face] knochig.

boo [buː] (pl -s) <> excl buh! <> n Buhruf der. <> vt auslbuhen, auslpfeifen. <> vi buhen.

boob [buːb] n inf [mistake] Schnitzer der. ➤ **boobs** npl UK v inf [breasts] Möpse Pl.

booby trap ['buːbɪ-] n - 1. [bomb] getarnte Bombe - 2. [prank] Falle die (mit deren Hilfe ein Streich gespielt wird).

book [bʊk] <> n - 1. [for reading] Buch das - 2. [of stamps, matches, tickets] Heftchen das; [of cheques] Heft das. <> vt - 1. [table, room] reservieren lassen; [ticket] bestellen; [performer] engagieren; [plane seat] buchen; **to be fully booked** [restaurant, hotel] ausgebucht sein; [performance] ausverkauft sein - 2. inf [subj: police] auflschreiben - 3. UK FTBL verwarnen. <> vi [book table, room] reservieren lassen; [book ticket] vorlbestellen; [book plane seat] buchen. ➤ **books** npl COMM Bücher die. ➤ **book up** vt sep buchen; **to be booked up** [restaurant, hotel] ausgebucht sein; [performance] ausverkauft sein.

bookcase ['bʊkkeɪs] n Bücherregal das.

bookie ['bʊkɪ] n inf Buchmacher der.

booking ['bʊkɪŋ] n - 1. esp UK [of seat, room] Reservierung die; [of ticket] Bestellung die - 2. FTBL Verwarnung die.

booking office n esp UK [in station] Fahrkartenschalter der.

bookkeeping ['bʊkˌkiːpɪŋ] n COMM Buchhaltung die.

booklet ['bʊklɪt] n Broschüre die.

bookmaker ['bʊkˌmeɪkər] n Buchmacher der.

bookmark ['bʊkmɑːk] <> n [gen & COMPUT] Lesezeichen das. <> vt COMPUT [web page] Bookmark die ODER das.

bookseller ['bʊkˌselər] n Buchhändler der, -in die.

bookshelf ['bʊkʃelf] (pl -shelves [-ʃelvz]) n Bücherbord das.

bookshop UK ['bʊkʃɒp], **bookstore** US ['bʊkstɔːr] n Buchhandlung die.

book token n esp UK Büchergutschein der.

boom [buːm] <> n - 1. [of cannons, guns] Donnern das; [of voice] Dröhnen das - 2. [in business, economy] Boom der, Aufschwung der - 3. NAUT Baum der - 4. [for TV camera, microphone] Galgen der. <> vi - 1. [cannons, guns] donnern; [voice] dröhnen - 2. [business, economy] einen Aufschwung nehmen.

boon [buːn] n Segen der.

boost [buːst] <> n - 1. [in profits, production] Zunahme die - 2. [in popularity] Steigerung die; [in spirits, morale] Verbesserung die; **to give sb a boost** [encourage] jm Auftrieb geben. <> vt - 1. [profits, production] anlkurbeln - 2. [popularity] steigern; [morale, spirits] heben.

booster ['buːstər] n [vaccine] Auffrischimpfung die.

boot [buːt] <> n - 1. [footwear] Stiefel der; [for football, rugby] Schuh der - 2. UK [of car] Kofferraum der. <> vt - 1. inf [kick] einen Tritt geben (+ D); [ball] kicken - 2. COMPUT booten, hochfahren. ➤ **to boot** adv noch dazu. ➤ **boot up** vi COMPUT booten.

booth [buːð] n - 1. [at fair] (Markt)bude die - 2. [for telephone] Telefonzelle die - 3. [for voting] Kabine die.

booty ['buːtɪ] n liter Beute die.

booze [buːz] inf <> n [alcohol] Alkohol der. <> vi saufen.

bop [bɒp] inf <> n [dance]: **to have a bop** rocken. <> vi [dance] rocken.

border ['bɔːdər] <> n - 1. [between countries] Grenze die - 2. [of dress, handkerchief] Bordüre die; [of plate] Rand der - 3. [outer limit] Rand der - 4. [in garden] Rabatte die. <> vt - 1. [country] grenzen an (+ A) - 2. [field, garden] umschließen; [path] säumen. ➤ **border on** vt insep [verge on] grenzen an (+ A).

borderline ['bɔːdəlaɪn] <> adj: **borderline case** Grenzfall der. <> n fig Grenze die.

bore [bɔːr] <> pt ▷ **bear**. <> n - 1. [person] Langweiler der; [situation, event] Plage die - 2. [of gun] Kaliber das; **a 12-bore shotgun** eine Flinte vom Kaliber 12. <> vt - 1. [not interest] langweilen; **to bore sb stiff** OR **to tears** OR **to death** jn zu Tode langweilen - 2. [drill] bohren.

bored [bɔːd] adj gelangweilt; **she is bored with always staying in** es langweilt sie, immer zu Hause zu bleiben.

boredom ['bɔːdəm] n Langeweile die.

boring ['bɔːrɪŋ] adj langweilig.

born [bɔːn] adj: **to be born** geboren werden; **I was born in London/1968** ich bin OR wurde in London/1968 geboren; **a born entertainer** ein geborener Entertainer.

borne [bɔːn] pp ▷ **bear**.

borough ['bʌrə] n Regierungsbezirk, der entweder eine Stadt oder einen Stadtteil umfasst.

borrow ['bɒrəʊ] vt sich (D) leihen; [book from library] auslleihen; **to borrow sthg from sb** sich (D) etw von jm leihen OR borgen.

Bosnia ['bɒznɪə] n Bosnien nt.

Bosnian ['bɒznɪən] <> adj bosnisch. <> n Bosnier der, -in die.

bosom ['bʊzəm] n - 1. [breasts] Busen der; [of dress] Brustteil der - 2. fig [of family] Schoß der; **bosom friend** Busenfreund der, -in die.

boss [bɒs] n - 1. [gen] Chef der, -in die - 2. fig [of gang] Boss der. ➤ **boss about, boss around** vt sep pej herumlkommandieren.

bossy ['bɒsɪ] adj herrisch.

bosun ['bəʊsn] n = **boatswain**.

botany ['bɒtənɪ] n Botanik die.

botch [bɒtʃ] ➤ **botch up** vt sep inf mehr schlecht als recht machen.

both [bəʊθ] <> *pron* beide; **both of us** wir beide; **both of them speak German** sie sprechen beide Deutsch; **do you prefer music or painting? – I like them both** bevorzugst du Musik oder Malerei? – ich mag beides. <> *adj* beide. <> *adv*: **both my sister and I** sowohl meine Schwester als auch ich.

bother ['bɒðər] <> *vt* - 1. [worry, hurt] stören; **what you told me yesterday has been bothering me** was du mir gestern gesagt hast, hat mich beschäftigt; **she can't be bothered to do it** sie hat keine Lust, das zu tun - 2. [annoy] ärgern; [pester] belästigen; **I'm sorry to bother you** entschuldigen Sie die Störung. <> *vi* sich bemühen; **no, don't bother!** nein, das ist nicht nötig!; **to bother about sthg** sich um etw kümmern; **don't bother to phone me** Sie brauchen mich nicht anzurufen; **I didn't bother to lock up** ich habe mir nicht die Mühe gemacht abzuschließen; **don't bother getting up** bleiben Sie doch sitzen. <> *n* Mühe *die*; **no bother at all** überhaupt kein Problem; **if it isn't too much of a bother** wenn es Ihnen nichts ausmacht. <> *excl* verflixt!

bothered ['bɒðəd] *adj* [annoyed] verärgert.

Botox® ['bəʊtɒks] *n* Botox *das*.

bottle ['bɒtl] <> *n* - 1. [container, quantity] Flasche *die* - 2. [for baby] Fläschchen *das*, Flasche *die* - 3. (U) UK *inf* [courage] Mumm *der*. <> *vt* - 1. [wine] in Flaschen abfüllen - 2. [fruit] einlmachen. ◆ **bottle up** *vt sep* [feelings] in sich (D) auflstauen.

bottle bank *n* Altglascontainer *der*.

bottleneck ['bɒtlnek] *n* Engpass *der*.

bottle-opener *n* Flaschenöffner *der*.

bottom ['bɒtəm] <> *adj* - 1. [lowest] unterste(r) (s) - 2. [least successful] schlechteste(r) (s); **to be bottom in sthg** [subject] der Schlechteste in etw (D) sein. <> *n* - 1. [of glass, bottle, bag] Boden *der*; [of page, list, ladder] unteres Ende; [of sea, lake] Grund *der*; [of hill, mountain] Fuß *der*; *(phrase)*: **at the bottom unten** - 2. [of street, garden] **at the bottom of** am Ende (+ G) - 3. [of organization] unteres Ende; **he worked his way up from the bottom** er hat sich hoch gearbeitet - 4. [buttocks] Hintern *der* - 5. [cause] **to get to the bottom of sthg** einer Sache (D) auf den Grund gehen. ◆ **bottom out** *vi* den Tiefstand erreichen.

bottom line *n fig* [result]: **the bottom line** das Endergebnis.

bough [baʊ] *n* Ast *der*.

bought [bɔːt] *pt & pp* ▷ **buy**.

boulder ['bəʊldər] *n* (gerundeter) Felsbrocken *der*.

bounce [baʊns] <> *vi* - 1. [ball] springen; **the ball bounced onto the car** der Ball prallte auf das Auto - 2. [person - with energy, enthusiasm] hüpfen; **to bounce on sthg** [jump up and down]

auf etw (D) springen - 3. *inf* [cheque] platzen. <> *vt* [ball] aufprallen lassen. <> *n* [rebound] Aufprall *der*.

bouncer ['baʊnsər] *n inf* Rausschmeißer *der*.

bound [baʊnd] <> *pt & pp* ▷ **bind**. <> *adj* - 1. [certain]: **to be bound to do sthg** etw bestimmt tun; **it was bound to happen** das musste so kommen; **he's bound to win** er gewinnt hundertprozentig - 2. [forced, morally obliged]: **bound by sthg** durch etw gebunden; **bound to do sthg** gezwungen, etw zu tun; **I'm bound to say** OR admit ich muss sagen OR zugeben - 3. [en route]: **to be bound for** unterwegs sein nach. <> *n* [leap] Sprung *der*. <> *vt* [border]: **to be bounded by** begrenzt sein von. ◆ **bounds** *npl* Grenzen *Pl*; **out of bounds** verboten.

boundary ['baʊndrɪ] *n* Grenze *die*.

bourbon ['bɜːbən] *n* Bourbon *der*.

bout [baʊt] *n* - 1. [attack, session] Anfall *der* - 2. [boxing match] Kampf *der*.

bow¹ [baʊ] <> *n* - 1. [act of bowing] Verbeugung *die* - 2. [of ship] Bug *der*. <> *vt* [lower] beugen. <> *vi* - 1. [make a bow] sich verbeugen - 2. [defer]: **to bow to sthg** sich einer Sache (D) beugen.

bow² [bəʊ] *n* - 1. [weapon, for musical instrument] Bogen *der* - 2. [knot] Schleife *die*.

bowels ['baʊəlz] *npl liter & fig* Eingeweide *Pl*.

bowl [bəʊl] <> *n* Schüssel *die*; [of pipe] Kopf *der*. <> *vi* [in cricket] den Ball werfen. ◆ **bowls** *n* britische Variante des französischen Boulespiels, bei der die Spielkugeln gerollt werden. ◆ **bowl over** *vt sep* umlwerfen.

bow-legged [,bəʊ'legɪd] *adj* o-beinig.

bowler ['bəʊlər] *n* - 1. [in cricket] Werfer *der*, -in *die* - 2. [headgear]: **bowler (hat)** Melone *die*.

bowling ['bəʊlɪŋ] *n*: (tenpin) bowling Bowling *das*.

bowling alley *n* Bowlingbahn *die*.

bowling green *n* Rasen- oder Kunstrasenfläche, auf der "bowls" gespielt wird.

bow tie [bəʊ-] *n* Fliege *die*.

box [bɒks] <> *n* - 1. [made of wood or metal] Kiste *die*; [smaller] Kasten *der*; [made of cardboard] Karton *der*; [smaller] Schachtel *die*; **a box of chocolates** eine Schachtel Pralinen - 2. [in theatre] Loge *die* - 3. [on form] Kästchen *das* - 4. UK *inf* [television]: **the box** die Glotze. <> *vi* [fight] boxen.

boxer ['bɒksər] *n* - 1. [fighter] Boxer *der* - 2. [dog] Boxer *der*, -hündin *die*.

boxer shorts *npl* Boxershorts *Pl*.

boxing ['bɒksɪŋ] *n* Boxen *das*.

Boxing Day *n* Zweiter Weihnachtsfeiertag.

boxing glove *n* Boxhandschuh *der*.

box office n Kasse die (von Kino, Theater, bei Konzert).

boy [bɔɪ] ◇ n [young male, son] Junge der. ◇ excl: **(oh) boy!** inf oh, Mann!

boycott ['bɔɪkɒt] ◇ n Boykott der. ◇ vt boykottieren.

boyfriend ['bɔɪfrend] n Freund der.

boyish ['bɔɪɪʃ] adj jungenhaft.

bra [brɑː] n Büstenhalter der, BH der.

brace [breɪs] ◇ n - 1. [on teeth] Klammer die - 2. [on leg] Stützapparat der. ◇ vt - 1. [steady, support]: **to brace o.s.** sich festlhalten - 2. fig [mentally prepare]: **to brace o.s. (for sthg)** sich (auf etw (A)) gefasst machen. ◈ **braces** npl UK [for trousers] Hosenträger der.

bracelet ['breɪslɪt] n Armband das.

bracken ['brækn] n (U) Farnkraut das.

bracket ['brækɪt] ◇ n - 1. [support] Halterung die; **(angle) bracket** Winkelträger der - 2. [parenthesis] Klammer die; **in brackets** in Klammern - 3. [group] Klasse die. ◇ vt [enclose in brackets] einlklammern, in Klammern setzen.

brag [bræg] vi prahlen.

braid [breɪd] ◇ n - 1. (U) [on uniform] Tresse die - 2. esp US [hairstyle] Zopf der. ◇ vt esp US flechten.

brain [breɪn] n - 1. [organ] Gehirn das - 2. [mind, person] Kopf der. ◈ **brains** npl [intelligence] Grips der, Intelligenz die.

brainchild ['breɪntʃaɪld] n Geistesprodukt das.

brainwash ['breɪnwɒʃ] vt: **to brainwash sb** jn einer Gehirnwäsche unterziehen.

brainwave ['breɪnweɪv] n Geistesblitz der.

brainy ['breɪnɪ] adj inf gescheit.

brake [breɪk] ◇ n - 1. [on vehicle] Bremse die - 2. fig [restraint] Zurückhaltung die. ◇ vi bremsen.

brake light n Bremslicht das.

bramble ['bræmbl] n [bush] Brombeerbusch der; [fruit] Brombeere die.

bran [bræn] n (U) Kleie die.

branch [brɑːntʃ] ◇ n - 1. [of tree] Zweig der, Ast der - 2. [of river] Arm der; [of railway] Nebenstrecke die - 3. [of company, bank, organization] Zweigstelle die - 4. [of subject] Zweig der. ◇ vi [road] sich teilen. ◈ **branch out** vi sein Tätigkeitsfeld erweitern.

brand [brænd] ◇ n - 1. COMM [make] Marke die ‧ 2. fig [type, style] Sorte die, Art die. ◇ vt - 1. [cattle] mit einem Brandzeichen versehen - 2. fig [classify]: **to brand sb (as) sthg** jn als etw brandmarken.

brandish ['brændɪʃ] vt schwingen.

brand name n Markenname der.

brand-new adj nagelneu, brandneu.

brandy ['brændɪ] n Brandy der.

brash [bræʃ] adj pej [person, manner] laut.

brass [brɑːs] n - 1. [metal] Messing das - 2. MUS: **the brass** die Blechbläser Pl.

brass band n Blaskapelle die.

brat [bræt] n inf pej Balg das.

bravado [brəˈvɑːdəʊ] n Wagemut der.

brave [breɪv] ◇ adj mutig, tapfer. ◇ n [warrior] Krieger der. ◇ vt [weather] trotzen (+ D); [anger, displeasure, punishment] über sich (A) ergehen lassen.

bravery ['breɪvərɪ] n Mut die.

brawl [brɔːl] n Handgemenge das.

brawn [brɔːn] n (U) - 1. [muscle] Muskelkraft die - 2. UK [meat] Schweinskopfsülze die.

bray [breɪ] vi [donkey] schreien.

brazen ['breɪzn] adj unverschämt, frech. ◈ **brazen out** vt sep: **to brazen it out** sich (D) nichts anmerken lassen.

brazier ['breɪzjər] n Kohlenbecken das.

Brazil [brəˈzɪl] n Brasilien nt.

Brazilian [brəˈzɪljən] ◇ adj brasilianisch. ◇ n Brasilianer der, -in die.

brazil nut n Paranuss die.

breach [briːtʃ] ◇ n - 1. [of law, agreement] Bruch der; **to be in breach of sthg** gegen etw verstoßen; **breach of contract** Vertragsbruch der - 2. [opening, gap] Bresche die. ◇ vt - 1. [disobey] verletzen - 2. [make hole in] durchbrechen.

breach of the peace n öffentliche Ruhestörung.

bread [bred] n (U) [food] Brot das; **bread and butter** [food] Butterbrot das; fig [main income] Lebensunterhalt der.

bread bin UK, **bread box** US n Brotkasten der.

breadcrumbs ['bredkrʌmz] npl Brotkrümel Pl; [for coating food] Paniermehl das.

breadline ['bredlaɪn] n: **to be on the breadline** am Existenzminimum leben.

breadth [bretθ] n - 1. [in measurements] Breite die - 2. fig [scope] Spektrum das.

breadwinner ['bred,wɪnər] n Ernährer der, -in die.

break [breɪk] (pt **broke**, pp **broken**) ◇ n - 1. [gap, interruption] Unterbrechung die; **break in sthg** Unterbrechung in etw (D) - 2. [fracture, rupture, change] Bruch der; **break with sthg** Bruch der mit etw - 3. [pause, rest] Unterbrechung die; SCH Pause die; **weekend break** Urlaubswochenende das; **to take** OR **have a break** eine (kurze) Pause machen; **to have a break from sthg** mit etw pausieren; **without a break** ohne Unterbrechung - 4. inf [luck, chance] Chance die. ◇ vt - 1. [gen] brechen; [smash] zerbrechen; [windows] einlschlagen - 2. [cause to stop working] kaputtlmachen - 3. [interrupt - journey, silence] unterbrechen; (phrase): **to break sb's fall** js

Fall bremsen - **4.** [tell]: **to break the news of sth to sb** jm etw mitteilen. ⬦ *vi* - **1.** [gen] brechen - **2.** [stop working] kaputtlgehen - **3.** [pause] eine Pause machen - **4.** [weather] umlschlagen - **5.** [escape]: **to break loose** OR **free** loslbrechen - **6.** [voice] brechen - **7.** [news] bekannt werden - **8.** *phr*: **to break even** seine Kosten decken. ⬦ **break away** *vi* [escape] weglaufen. ⬦ **break down** ⬦ *vt sep* - **1.** [destroy] einlschlagen - **2.** [analyse] auflschlüsseln. ⬦ *vi* [gen] zusammenlbrechen; **the car has broken down** das Auto hat eine Panne. ⬦ **break in** ⬦ *vi* - **1.** [enter by force] einlbrechen - **2.** [interrupt]: **to break in (on sb/sth)** (jn/etw) unterbrechen. ⬦ *vt sep* - **1.** [horse] zulreiten - **2.** [person] einlarbeiten. ⬦ **break into** *vt insep* - **1.** [enter by force] einlbrechen in (+ A) - **2.** [begin suddenly] auslbrechen in (+ A). ⬦ **break off** *vt sep & vi* ablbrechen. ⬦ **break out** *vi* - **1.** [begin suddenly] auslbrechen - **2.** [escape]: **to break out (of)** auslbrechen (aus). ⬦ **break up** ⬦ *vt sep* - **1.** [object] zerbrechen; [ice, soil] auflbrechen - **2.** [bring to an end]: **the police broke up the party** die Polizei sprengte die Party; **she broke up the fight** sie trennte die Kämpfenden. ⬦ *vi* - **1.** [object] auseinander brechen - **2.** [relationship] in die Brüche gehen; [fight, party] enden; **to break up with sb** sich von jm trennen - **3.** [crowd] auseinander treiben - **4.** [school] enden; [pupils, teachers] in die Ferien gehen.

breakage ['breɪkɪdʒ] *n* Bruchschaden *der*.

breakdown ['breɪkdaʊn] *n* - **1.** [of system] Zusammenbruch *der*; [of car] Panne *die*; [of machine] Störung *die*; [in talks] Scheitern *das* - **2.** [analysis] Aufschlüsselung *die*.

breakfast ['brekfəst] *n* Frühstück *das*; **to have breakfast** frühstücken.

break-in *n* Einbruch *der*.

breakneck ['breɪknek] *adj*: **at breakneck speed** in halsbrecherischem Tempo.

breakthrough ['breɪkθru:] *n* Durchbruch *der*.

breakup ['breɪkʌp] *n* [of relationship] Scheitern *das*.

breast [brest] *n* Brust *die*.

breast-feed *vt & vi* stillen.

breaststroke ['breststrəʊk] *n* Brustschwimmen *das*.

breath [breθ] *n* Atem *der*; **bad breath** Mundgeruch *der*; **he took a deep breath** er holte tief Atem; **out of breath** außer Atem; **to get one's breath back** Luft holen.

breathalyse UK, **-yze** US ['breθəlaɪz] *vt* (ins Röhrchen) blasen lassen.

breathe [bri:ð] ⬦ *vi* atmen. ⬦ *vt* [inhale] einlatmen. ⬦ **breathe in** *vt sep & vi* einlatmen. ⬦ **breathe out** *vi* auslatmen.

breather ['bri:ðər] *n inf* Atempause *die*.

breathing ['bri:ðɪŋ] *n* Atmen *das*.

breathless ['breθlɪs] *adj* atemlos.

breathtaking ['breθ,teɪkɪŋ] *adj* atemberaubend.

breed [bri:d] (*pt & pp* **bred** [bred]) ⬦ *n* - **1.** [of animal] Rasse *die* - **2.** *fig* [sort, style] Art *die*. ⬦ *vt* - **1.** [animals, plants] züchten - **2.** *fig* [suspicion] säen. ⬦ *vi* züchten.

breeding ['bri:dɪŋ] *n (U)* - **1.** [of animals] Aufzucht *die*; [of plants] Züchtung *die* - **2.** [manners] Erziehung *die*.

breeze [bri:z] *n* Brise *die*.

breezy ['bri:zɪ] *adj* - **1.** [windy] windig - **2.** [cheerful] leichtherzig, fröhlich.

brevity ['brevɪtɪ] *n* Kürze *die*.

brew [bru:] ⬦ *vt* [beer] brauen; [tea, coffee] auflgießen. ⬦ *vi* - **1.** [tea, coffee] ziehen - **2.** *fig* [trouble, storm] sich zusammenlbrauen.

brewery ['bru:ərɪ] *n* Brauerei *die*.

bribe [braɪb] ⬦ *n* Bestechung *die*. ⬦ *vt*: **to bribe sb (to do sth)** jn bestechen(, etw zu tun).

bribery ['braɪbərɪ] *n (U)* Bestechung *die*.

brick [brɪk] *n* Ziegelstein *der*, Backstein *der*.

bricklayer ['brɪk,leɪər] *n* Maurer *der*.

bridal ['braɪdl] *adj* Braut-.

bride [braɪd] *n* Braut *die*.

bridegroom ['braɪdgrʊm] *n* Bräutigam *der*.

bridesmaid ['braɪdzmeɪd] *n* Brautjungfer *die*.

bridge [brɪdʒ] ⬦ *n* - **1.** [gen] Brücke *die* - **2.** [card game] Bridge *das*. ⬦ *vt fig* [gap] überbrücken.

bridle ['braɪdl] *n* Zaum *der*.

bridle path *n* Reitweg *der*.

brief [bri:f] ⬦ *adj* - **1.** [short] kurz - **2.** [skimpy, concise] knapp; **please be brief** fassen Sie sich kurz; **in brief** kurz (gesagt). ⬦ *n* - **1.** LAW [statement] Unterlagen *Pl* - **2.** UK [instructions] Auftrag *der*. ⬦ *vt*: **to brief sb (on sth)** jn (über etw (A)) unterrichten. ⬦ **briefs** *npl* [underwear] Slip *der*; **a pair of briefs** ein Slip.

briefcase ['bri:fkeɪs] *n* Aktentasche *die*.

briefing ['bri:fɪŋ] *n* Einsatzbesprechung *die*.

briefly ['bri:flɪ] *adv* kurz.

brigade [brɪ'geɪd] *n* - **1.** MIL Brigade *die* - **2.** [organization] Truppe *die*.

brigadier [,brɪgə'dɪər] *n* UK Brigadegeneral *der*.

bright [braɪt] *adj* - **1.** [room, light] hell - **2.** [colour] leuchtend - **3.** [lively, cheerful] strahlend - **4.** [intelligent] klug, gescheit; **a bright girl** ein aufgewecktes Mädchen - **5.** [future, prospects] glänzend. ⬦ **brights** *npl* US *inf* AUT Fernlicht *das*.

brighten ['braɪtn] *vi* sich auflhellen. ⬦ **brighten up** ⬦ *vt sep* - **1.** [room, house] auflhellen - **2.** [situation, prospects] auflheitern.

◇ *vi* - **1.** [become more cheerful] fröhlicher werden; [face] sich auf|hellen - **2.** [weather] sich auf|hellen.

brilliance ['brɪljəns] *n* - **1.** [cleverness] Großartigkeit *die* - **2.** [of colour, light] Strahlen *das*.

brilliant ['brɪljənt] *adj* - **1.** [gen] glänzend, brilliant - **2.** [colour, light] strahlend - **3.** *inf* [wonderful, enjoyable] toll; **oh brilliant!** *iro* na toll!

brim [brɪm] ◇ *n* - **1.** [edge] Rand *der* - **2.** [of hat] Krempe *die*. ◇ *vi* - **1.** [with liquid]: **to brim with sthg** randvoll mit etw sein - **2.** [with feeling]: **to brim with ideas** vor Ideen über|sprudeln; **to brim with self-confidence** vor Selbstbewusstsein strotzen.

brine [braɪn] *n* (U) Sole *die*, Lake *die*.

bring [brɪŋ] (*pt & pp* brought) *vt* - **1.** [take along] mit|bringen; [move] bringen; **to bring sb good luck** jm Glück bringen - **2.** [cause] führen zu; **to bring sthg to an end** etw zu Ende bringen; **to bring sthg into being** etw ins Leben rufen. ⬧ **bring about** *vt sep* verursachen. ⬧ **bring around** *vt sep* [make conscious] zu Bewusstsein bringen. ⬧ **bring back** *vt sep* - **1.** [return] zurück|bringen - **2.** [shopping, gift] mit|bringen - **3.** [reinstate - custom] wieder ein|führen; [- government] wieder an die Macht bringen - **4.** [cause to remember]: **to bring back memories** Erinnerungen wach|rufen. ⬧ **bring down** *vt sep* - **1.** [shoot down - plane] ab|schießen - **2.** [government, tyrant] stürzen - **3.** [prices] senken - **4.** THEAT: **to bring the house down** stürmischen Beifall ernten. ⬧ **bring forward** *vt sep* - **1.** [meeting, election] vor|verlegen - **2.** [in bookkeeping] übertragen. ⬧ **bring in** *vt sep* - **1.** [introduce] ein|führen - **2.** [earn] ein|bringen - **3.** [involve] ein|schalten. ⬧ **bring off** *vt sep* [plan] in die Tat um|setzen; [deal] zustande bringen; **you'll never bring it off** das schaffst du nie. ⬧ **bring out** *vt sep* - **1.** [new product, book] heraus|bringen - **2.** [reveal - flavour] betonen; **to bring sthg out in sb** [characteristic] etw in jm wach|rufen. ⬧ **bring round, bring to** *vt sep* = **bring around**. ⬧ **bring up** *vt sep* - **1.** [child] erziehen; **I was brought up in Liverpool** ich bin in Liverpool aufgewachsen - **2.** [subject] an|sprechen - **3.** [food] erbrechen.

brink [brɪŋk] *n*: **on the brink of** am Rand(e) (+ G).

brisk [brɪsk] *adj* - **1.** [walk, swim] flott - **2.** [manner, tone] forsch.

bristle ['brɪsl] ◇ *n* Borste *die*. ◇ *vi* - **1.** [hair] sich sträuben - **2.** [person]: **to bristle (at sthg)** zornig reagieren (auf etw (A)).

Britain ['brɪtn] *n* Großbritannien *nt*.

British ['brɪtɪʃ] ◇ *adj* britisch. ◇ *npl*: **the British** die Briten *Pl*.

British Isles *npl*: **the British Isles** die Britischen Inseln.

Briton ['brɪtn] *n* Brite *der*, -tin *die*.

brittle ['brɪtl] *adj* [china] zerbrechlich; [material] spröde; [bones] schwach.

broach [brəʊtʃ] *vt* [subject] an|schneiden.

broad [brɔːd] ◇ *adj* - **1.** [wide] breit - **2.** [wide-ranging, extensive] weit - **3.** [introduction, description] umfassend - **4.** [hint] deutlich - **5.** [accent] stark. ◇ *n* US *inf* [woman] Braut *die*. ⬧ **in broad daylight** *adv* am helllichten Tag.

B road *n* UK ≃ Landstraße *die*.

broadband ['brɔːdbænd] *n* COMPUT Breitband *das*.

broad bean *n* dicke Bohne, Saubohne *die*.

broadcast ['brɔːdkɑːst] (*pt & pp inv*) ◇ *n* RADIO & TV Sendung *die*, Übertragung *die*. ◇ *vt* RADIO & TV senden, übertragen.

broaden ['brɔːdn] ◇ *vt* - **1.** [make wider] verbreitern, erweitern - **2.** [make more wide-ranging] vergrößern; **to broaden one's mind** seinen Horizont erweitern. ◇ *vi* [become wider] sich verbreitern.

broadly ['brɔːdlɪ] *adv* [generally] allgemein.

broadminded [ˌbrɔːd'maɪndɪd] *adj* tolerant.

broccoli ['brɒkəlɪ] *n* Brokkoli *der*.

brochure ['brəʊʃər] *n* Prospekt *der*.

broil [brɔɪl] *vt* US grillen.

broke [brəʊk] ◇ *pt* ⬡ **break**. ◇ *adj inf* [penniless] pleite.

broken ['brəʊkn] ◇ *pp* ⬡ **break**. ◇ *adj* - **1.** [damaged, in pieces] zerbrochen - **2.** [fractured] gebrochen - **3.** [not working] kaputt - **4.** [interrupted] unterbrochen - **5.** [marriage, home] kaputt, zerrüttet - **6.** [hesitant, inaccurate] gebrochen.

broker ['brəʊkər] *n* [of shares, commodities] Broker *der*, -in *die*; **(insurance) broker** Versicherungsmakler *der*, -in *die*.

brolly ['brɒlɪ] *n* UK *inf* (Regen)schirm *der*.

bronchitis [brɒŋ'kaɪtɪs] *n* (U) Bronchitis *die*.

bronze [brɒnz] *n* Bronze *die*.

brooch [brəʊtʃ] *n* Brosche *die*.

brood [bruːd] ◇ *n* Brut *die*. ◇ *vi*: **to brood (over OR about sthg)** (über etw (D)) brüten.

brook [brʊk] *n* Bach *der*.

broom [bruːm] *n* [brush] Besen *der*.

broomstick ['bruːmstɪk] *n* Besenstiel *der*.

Bros, bros (*abbr of* brothers) Gebr.

broth [brɒθ] *n* Brühe *die*.

brothel ['brɒθl] *n* Bordell *das*.

brother ['brʌðər] *n* Bruder *der*.

brother-in-law (*pl* brothers-in-law) *n* Schwager *der*.

brought [brɔːt] *pt & pp* ⬡ **bring**.

brow [braʊ] *n* - **1.** [forehead] Stirn *die* - **2.** [eyebrow] Braue *die* - **3.** [of hill] Bergkuppe *die*.

brown [braʊn] ◇ *adj* - **1.** [colour] braun; **brown bread** Graubrot *das* - **2.** [tanned] braun. ◇ *n* [colour] Braun *das*. ◇ *vt* [food] bräunen.

Brownie (Guide) ['braʊnɪ] *n* Pfadfinderin *die*.

brown paper *n (U)* Packpapier *das*.

brown rice *n* brauner Reis.

brown sugar *n* brauner Zucker.

browse [braʊz] ◇ *vt* COMPUT: **to browse the Web** im Web surfen. ◇ *vi* - **1.** [in shop] sich umsehen - **2.** [read]: **to browse through sthg** in etw *(D)* blättern - **3.** [graze] weiden.

browser ['braʊzər] *n* COMPUT Browser *der*.

bruise [bruːz] ◇ *n* Bluterguss *der*, blauer Fleck. ◇ *vt* - **1.** [part of body] sich prellen; [fruit] beschädigen; **she bruised her arm** sie holte sich einen blauen Fleck am Arm - **2.** *fig* [pride, feelings] verletzen.

brunch [brʌntʃ] *n* Brunch *der*.

brunette [bruːˈnet] *n* Brünette *die*.

brunt [brʌnt] *n*: **to bear** OR **take the brunt of sthg** die Hauptlast von etw tragen.

brush [brʌʃ] ◇ *n* - **1.** [with bristles] Bürste *die*; [for painting] Pinsel *der* - **2.** [encounter]: **to have a brush with the law** mit dem Gesetz in Konflikt kommen. ◇ *vt* - **1.** [clean with brush - hair] bürsten; [- teeth] putzen - **2.** [touch lightly] berühren. ◆ **brush aside** *vt sep* [disregard] vom Tisch wischen. ◆ **brush off** *vt sep* [dismiss] zurückweisen; **to brush sb off** jn abblitzen lassen. ◆ **brush up** ◇ *vt sep* *fig* [revise] auffrischen. ◇ *vi*: **to brush up (on sthg)** (etw) auffrischen.

brush-off *n inf*: **to give sb the brush-off** jm eine Abfuhr erteilen.

brusque [bruːsk] *adj* brüsk.

Brussels ['brʌslz] *n* Brüssel *nt*.

brussels sprouts *npl* Rosenkohl *der*.

brutal ['bruːtl] *adj* brutal.

brute [bruːt] ◇ *adj*: **brute force** rohe Gewalt. ◇ *n* Tier *das*, Vieh *das*.

BSc *n abbr of* **Bachelor of Science**.

BSE *(abbr of* bovine spongiform encephalopathy) *n* BSE *das*.

bubble ['bʌbl] ◇ *n* (Luft)bläschen *das*. ◇ *vi* - **1.** [produce bubbles] Bläschen bilden - **2.** [make a bubbling sound] blubbern - **3.** *fig* [person]: **to bubble with sthg** vor etw *(D)* sprühen.

bubble bath *n (U)* Schaumbad *das*.

bubble gum *n (U)* Kaugummi *der* ODER *das*.

bubblejet printer ['bʌbldʒet-] *n* Tintenstrahldrucker *der*.

Bucharest [ˌbjuːkəˈrest] *n* Bukarest *nt*.

buck [bʌk] ◇ *n* - **1.** *(pl inv)* [male animal - rabbit, hare] Rammler *der*; [- deer] Bock *der* - **2.** *(pl* -s) *esp US inf* [dollar] Dollar *der* - **3.** *(pl* -s) *inf* [responsibility]: **to pass the buck** die Verant-

wortung weiterlreichen. ◇ *vi* [horse] bocken. ◆ **buck up** *inf vi* - **1.** [hurry up] sich beeilen - **2.** [cheer up] aufleben.

bucket ['bʌkɪt] *n* Eimer *der*.

buckle ['bʌkl] ◇ *n* Schnalle *die*, Spange *die*. ◇ *vt* - **1.** [fasten] zulschnallen - **2.** [bend] einldellen, verbeulen. ◇ *vi* [wheel] sich verbiegen; [knees, legs] nachlgeben.

bud [bʌd] ◇ *n* Knospe *die*. ◇ *vi* Knospen treiben, auslschlagen.

Budapest [ˌbjuːdəˈpest] *n* Budapest *nt*.

Buddha ['bʊdə] *n* Buddha *der*.

Buddhism ['bʊdɪzm] *n* Buddhismus *der*.

budding ['bʌdɪŋ] *adj* [aspiring] angehend.

buddy ['bʌdɪ] *n esp US inf* [friend] Kumpel *der*.

budge [bʌdʒ] ◇ *vt* - **1.** [move] bewegen - **2.** [change mind of] beeinflussen. ◇ *vi* - **1.** [move] sich rühren - **2.** [change mind] nachlgeben.

budgerigar ['bʌdʒərɪgɑːr] *n* Wellensittich *der*.

budget ['bʌdʒɪt] ◇ *adj* [cheap - travel, holiday] kostengünstig; [- prices] niedrig. ◇ *n* Budget *das*. ◆ **budget for** *vt insep* einlplanen.

budgie ['bʌdʒɪ] *n inf* Wellensittich *der*.

buff [bʌf] ◇ *adj* [brown] braun. ◇ *n inf* [expert] Kenner *der*, -in *die*.

buffalo ['bʌfələʊ] *(pl inv,* -es OR -s) *n* Büffel *der*, Buffalo *der*.

buffer ['bʌfər] *n* - **1.** [gen] Puffer *der* - **2.** [for trains] Prellbock *der*.

buffet[1]['bʊfeɪ] *n* - **1.** [meal] Buffet *das* - **2.** [cafeteria] Stehimbiss *der*.

buffet[2]['bʌfɪt] *vt* [physically] rütteln.

buffet car ['bʊfeɪ-] *n* Speisewagen *der*.

bug [bʌg] ◇ *n* - **1.** *esp US* [small insect] Insekt *das*; [beetle] Käfer *der* - **2.** *inf* [germ] Bazillus *der* - **3.** *inf* [listening device] Wanze *die* - **4.** COMPUT Programmfehler *der*. ◇ *vt inf* - **1.** [room, phone] verwanzen - **2.** [annoy] nerven.

bugger ['bʌgər] *UK v inf* ◇ *n* [unpleasant person] Scheißkerl *der*; **he's a lazy bugger!** er ist ein fauler Sack!; **the poor bugger!** der arme Kerl! ◇ *excl* Scheiße! ◆ **bugger off** *vi*: **bugger off!** hau ab!

buggy ['bʌgɪ] *n* Kinderwagen *der*.

bugle ['bjuːgl] *n* Signalhorn *das*.

build [bɪld] *(pt & pp* built) ◇ *vt* - **1.** [construct] bauen - **2.** *fig* [form, create] auflbauen. ◇ *n (U)* Statur *die*. ◆ **build on** ◇ *vt insep* [further] auflbauen. ◇ *vt sep* [base on]: **to build sthg on sthg** etw auf etw *(D)* auflbauen. ◆ **build up** ◇ *vt sep* [strengthen] auflbauen. ◇ *vi* [increase] zulnehmen. ◆ **build upon** *vt insep* & *vt sep* = **build on**.

builder ['bɪldər] n Bauarbeiter der, -in die.

building ['bɪldɪŋ] n - **1.** [structure] Gebäude das - **2.** (U) [profession] Bau der.

building and loan association n US Bausparkasse die.

building site n Baustelle die.

building society n UK Bausparkasse die.

buildup ['bɪldʌp] n [increase] Steigerung die, Zunahme die.

built [bɪlt] pt & pp ⊏▷ **build**.

built-in adj - **1.** CONSTR eingebaut - **2.** [inherent] automatisch.

built-up adj: built-up area bebautes Gebiet.

bulb [bʌlb] n - **1.** [for lamp] (Glüh)birne die - **2.** [of plant] Zwiebel die.

Bulgaria [bʌl'geərɪə] n Bulgarien nt.

Bulgarian [bʌl'geərɪən] ◇ adj bulgarisch. ◇ n - **1.** [person] Bulgare der, -rin die - **2.** [language] Bulgarisch(e) das.

bulge [bʌldʒ] ◇ n [lump] Beule die. ◇ vi: to bulge (with sthg) (mit etw) voll gestopft sein.

bulk [bʌlk] ◇ n - **1.** [mass] Ausmaß das - **2.** [of person] Masse die - **3.** COMM: in bulk en gros - **4.** [majority]: the bulk of der Großteil (+ G). ◇ adj en gros, Groß-.

bulky ['bʌlkɪ] adj sperrig, unhandlich; [garment] unhandlich.

bull [bʊl] n [male cow] Stier der, Bulle der.

bulldog ['bʊldɒg] n Bulldogge die.

bulldozer ['bʊldəʊzər] n Bulldozer der.

bullet ['bʊlɪt] n [for gun] Kugel die.

bulletin ['bʊlətɪn] n - **1.** [brief report] Bericht der - **2.** [regular publication] Bulletin das.

bullet-proof adj kugelsicher.

bullfight ['bʊlfaɪt] n Stierkampf der.

bullfighter ['bʊl,faɪtər] n Torero der.

bullfighting ['bʊl,faɪtɪŋ] n (U) Stierkampf der.

bullion ['bʊljən] n (U) Barren der.

bullock ['bʊlək] n Ochse der.

bullring ['bʊlrɪŋ] n Stierkampfarena die.

bull's-eye n Schwarze das, Zentrum das.

bully ['bʊlɪ] ◇ n Tyrann der. ◇ vt drangsalieren, tyrannisieren; to bully sb into doing sthg jn so drangsalieren, dass er/sie etw tut.

bum [bʌm] n - **1.** esp UK v inf [bottom] Hintern der - **2.** US inf pej [tramp] Gammler der, -in die.

bum bag n inf Gürteltasche die.

bumblebee ['bʌmblbiː] n Hummel die.

bump [bʌmp] ◇ n - **1.** [lump] Beule die; [in road] Unebenheit die, Hubbel der - **2.** [knock, blow] Delle die - **3.** [noise] Bums der. ◇ vt [knock, damage] anschlagen. ◈ **bump into** vt insep [meet by chance] treffen.

bumper ['bʌmpər] ◇ adj Riesen-; bumper harvest Rekordernte die. ◇ n - **1.** [on car] Stoßstange die - **2.** US RAIL Rammbohle die.

bumpy ['bʌmpɪ] adj holp(e)rig.

bun [bʌn] n - **1.** [cake] süße Stückchen das - **2.** [bread roll] Milchbrötchen das - **3.** [hairstyle] Knoten der.

bunch [bʌntʃ] ◇ n [group - of people] Traube die, Haufen der; [- of flowers] Strauß der; [- of grapes] Traube die; [- of parsley, asparagus, keys] Bund der. ◇ vi sich bauschen. ◈ **bunches** npl [hairstyle] Zöpfe Pl.

bundle ['bʌndl] ◇ n Bündel das. ◇ vt stopfen.

bung [bʌŋ] ◇ n Stöpsel der, Zapfen der. ◇ vt UK inf [put] schmeißen.

bungalow ['bʌŋgələʊ] n Bungalow der.

bungle ['bʌŋgl] vt verpfuschen.

bunion ['bʌnjən] n Ballen der.

bunk [bʌŋk] n - **1.** [bed] Koje die; [in dorm] Bett das - **2.** = bunk bed.

bunk bed n Etagenbett das.

bunker ['bʌŋkər] n Bunker der.

bunny ['bʌnɪ] n: bunny (rabbit) Häschen das.

bunting ['bʌntɪŋ] n (U) Wimpel Pl.

buoy [UK bɔɪ, US 'buːɪ] n Boje die. ◈ **buoy up** vt sep [encourage] beleben, stärken.

buoyant ['bɔɪənt] adj - **1.** [able to float] schwimmfähig - **2.** [optimistic] beschwingt.

burden ['bɜːdn] ◇ n Bürde die, Last die; to be a burden on sb eine Last für jn sein. ◇ vt: to burden sb with sthg jn mit etw belasten.

bureau ['bjʊərəʊ] (pl -x) n - **1.** [office, branch] Büro das - **2.** UK [desk] Sekretär der - **3.** US [chest of drawers] Kommode die.

bureaucracy [bjʊə'rɒkrəsɪ] n Bürokratie die.

bureau de change (pl bureaux de change) n Wechselstube die.

bureaux ['bjʊərəʊz] Pl ⊏▷ **bureau**.

burger ['bɜːgər] n Hamburger der.

burglar ['bɜːglər] n Einbrecher der, -in die.

burglar alarm n Alarmanlage die.

burglarize vt US = burgle.

burglary ['bɜːglərɪ] n Einbruch der.

burgle ['bɜːgl], **burglarize** US ['bɜːgləraɪz] vt einbrechen in (+ A).

burial ['berɪəl] n Begräbnis das.

burly ['bɜːlɪ] adj stämmig, kräftig.

Burma ['bɜːmə] n Birma nt.

burn [bɜːn] (pt & pp burnt OR -ed) ◇ vt - **1.** [gen] verbrennen; [house] abbrennen - **2.** [overcook] anbrennen lassen - **3.** [use as fuel] verbrauchen - **4.** [with chemical] verätzen - **5.** [CD] brennen. ◇ vi - **1.** [gen] brennen - **2.** [food] anbrennen - **3.** [face, cheeks] glühen - **4.** [get sunburned] einen Sonnenbrand bekommen. <> *n* - **1.** [wound, injury] Brandwunde *die* - **2.** [mark - on carpet, sofa] Brandfleck *der*. ➧ **burn down** <> *vt sep* niederlbrennen. <> *vi* [building, town] ablbrennen.

burner ['bɜːnɔʳ] *n* [on cooker] Brenner *der*.

burnt [bɜːnt] *pt & pp* ▷ **burn**.

burp [bɜːp] *inf* <> *n* Rülpser *der*. <> *vi* auflstoßen.

burrow ['bʌrəʊ] <> *n* Bau *der*. <> *vi* - **1.** [dig] graben - **2.** *fig* [search] wühlen.

bursar ['bɜːsəʳ] *n* Schatzmeister *der*.

bursary ['bɜːsərɪ] *n* UK Stipendium *das*.

burst [bɜːst] (*pt & pp inv*) <> *vi* - **1.** [break open] platzen - **2.** [explode] explodieren - **3.** [go suddenly]: **to burst in** hineinlplatzen. <> *vt* [tyre, balloon, bubble] platzen lassen; [dam, river bank] durchlbrechen. <> *n* [bout] Explosion *die*. ➧ **burst into** *vt insep* auslbrechen in (+ A); *(phrase)*: **the house burst into flames** im Haus brach Feuer aus. ➧ **burst out** *vt insep* - **1.** [say suddenly] loslplatzen - **2.** [begin suddenly]: **to burst out laughing/crying** in Gelächter/Tränen auslbrechen.

bursting ['bɜːstɪŋ] *adj* [eager]: **to be bursting to do sthg** darauf brennen, etw zu tun.

bury ['berɪ] *vt* - **1.** [in ground - person] begraben; [- thing] vergraben - **2.** [hide] vergraben.

bus [bʌs] *n* Bus *der*; **by bus** mit dem Bus.

bush [bʊʃ] *n* - **1.** [gen] Busch *der* - **2.** *phr*: **to beat about the bush** um den heißen Brei herumlreden.

bushy ['bʊʃɪ] *adj* buschig.

business ['bɪznɪs] *n* - **1.** *(U)* [commerce] Geschäft *das*; **on business** geschäftlich; **to mean business** *inf* es ernst meinen; **to go out of business** zulmachen, schließen - **2.** [company] Firma *die* - **3.** *(U)* [concern] Angelegenheit *die*; **mind your own business!** *inf* kümmere dich um deine eigenen Sachen! - **4.** [affair, matter] Sache *die*.

businesslike ['bɪznɪslaɪk] *adj* sachlich.

businessman ['bɪznɪsmæn] (*pl* -men [-men]) *n* Geschäftsmann *der*.

business trip *n* Geschäftsreise *die*.

businesswoman ['bɪznɪs,wʊmən] (*pl* -women [-,wɪmɪn]) *n* Geschäftsfrau *die*.

busker ['bʌskəʳ] *n* UK Straßenmusikant *der*, -in *die*.

bus shelter *n* Wartehäuschen *das*.

bus station *n* Busbahnhof *der*.

bus stop *n* Bushaltestelle *die*.

bust [bʌst] (*pt & pp inv or* -ed) <> *adj inf* - **1.** [broken] kaputt - **2.** [bankrupt]: **to go bust** pleite gehen. <> *n* - **1.** [bosom] Busen *der* - **2.** [statue] Büste *die*. <> *vt inf* [break] kaputt machen. <> *vi inf* kaputt gehen.

bustle ['bʌsl] <> *n* [activity] reges Treiben. <> *vi*: **to bustle about** OR **around** hin und her eilen.

busy ['bɪzɪ] <> *adj* - **1.** [active] (viel) beschäftigt - **2.** [hectic - life] bewegt; [- week] hektisch; [- place] belebt; [- office] geschäftig; *(phrase)*: **to be busy doing sthg** damit beschäftigt sein, etw zu tun - **3.** *esp US* TELEC [engaged] besetzt. <> *vt*: **to busy o.s. doing sthg** sich damit beschäftigen, etw zu tun.

busybody ['bɪzɪ,bɒdɪ] *n pej* Wichtigtuer *der*, -in *die*.

busy signal *n* US TELEC Besetztzeichen *das*.

but [bʌt] <> *conj* aber; [with negatives] sondern; **we were poor but happy** wir waren arm, aber glücklich; **she owns not one but two houses** sie hat nicht nur eins, sondern zwei Häuser. <> *prep* [except] außer; **he has no one but himself to blame** das hat er sich (D) selbst zuzuschreiben; **the last but one** der/die/das Vorletzte; **anyone but him would have helped** jeder andere hätte geholfen. <> *adv fml* [only] nur. ➧ **but for** *prep* ohne.

butcher ['bʊtʃəʳ] <> *n* - **1.** [shopkeeper] Fleischer *der*, Metzger *der*; **butcher's (shop)** Fleischerei *die*, Metzgerei *die* - **2.** *fig* [killer] Schlächter *der*. <> *vt* - **1.** [kill for meat] schlachten - **2.** *fig* [massacre] ablschlachten.

butler ['bʌtləʳ] *n* Butler *der*.

butt [bʌt] <> *n* - **1.** [of cigarette] Kippe *die*; [of cigar] Stummel *der* - **2.** [of rifle] Kolben *der* - **3.** [for water] Fass *das* - **4.** [target] Zielscheibe *die* - **5.** *esp US inf* [bottom] Hintern *der*. <> *vt* [hit with head] mit dem Kopf stoßen. ➧ **butt in** *vi* [interrupt] sich einlmischen, dazwischenlplatzen; **to butt in on sb/sthg** sich bei jm/etw einlmischen.

butter ['bʌtəʳ] <> *n* Butter *die*. <> *vt* buttern, mit Butter bestreichen.

buttercup ['bʌtəkʌp] *n* Butterblume *die*.

butter dish *n* Butterdose *die*.

butterfly ['bʌtəflaɪ] *n* - **1.** [insect] Schmetterling *der* - **2.** *(U)* [swimming style] Schmetterlingsstil *der*.

buttocks ['bʌtəks] *npl* Hintern *der*.

button ['bʌtn] <> *n* - **1.** [on clothes, machine] Knopf *der* - **2.** *US* [badge] Anstecker *der*. <> *vt* = **button up**. ➧ **button up** *vt sep* zulknöpfen.

button mushroom *n* junger Champignon.

buttress ['bʌtrɪs] *n* Stützpfeiler *der*.

buxom ['bʌksəm] *adj* vollbusig.

buy [baɪ] (*pt & pp bought*) <> *vt* - **1.** [purchase] kaufen; [company] auflkaufen; **to buy sthg from sb** etw von jm kaufen - **2.** *fig* [bribe] kaufen, bestechen. <> *n* Kauf *der*. ➧ **buy out** *vt sep* - **1.** [in business] auslzahlen - **2.** [from army]: **to buy o.s. out** sich freilkaufen. ➧ **buy up** *vt sep* auflkaufen.

buyer *n* - 1. [purchaser] Käufer *der*, -in *die* - 2. [profession] Einkäufer *der*, -in *die*.

buyout ['baɪaʊt] *n* Aufkauf *der*.

buzz [bʌz] ◇ *n* [noise - of insect, machinery] Summen *das*; [- of conversation] Gemurmel *das*; **to give sb a buzz** *inf* TELEC jn anlrufen. ◇ *vi* - 1. [insect, machinery] summen - 2. *fig* [place]: **the office was buzzing with excitement** im Büro herrschte große Aufregung - 3. *fig*: **my head was buzzing** mir schwirrte der Kopf. ◇ *vt* [on intercom] rufen.

buzzer ['bʌzər] *n* Summer *der*.

buzzword ['bʌzwɜːd] *n inf* Modewort *das*.

by [baɪ] ◇ *prep* - 1. [expressing cause, agent] von; **he was hit by a car** er ist von einem Auto angefahren worden; **by Mozart** von Mozart - 2. [indicating method, means, manner] mit; **by car/train** mit dem Auto/Zug; **to pay by credit card** mit Kreditkarte bezahlen; **to take sb by the hand** jn an der Hand nehmen; **made by hand** handgemacht; **he got rich by buying land** er wurde durch Grundstückskäufe reich - 3. [near to, beside] an *(+ D)*; **by the sea** am Meer; **by my side** an meiner Seite, neben mir - 4. [past] an *(+ D)* vorbei; **a car went by the house** ein Auto fuhr am Haus vorbei - 5. [via] durch; **exit by the door on the left** Ausgang durch die Tür auf der linken Seite; **we came by way of Paris** wir kamen über Paris - 6. [with time]: **it will be ready by tomorrow** bis morgen wird es fertig sein; **be there by nine** sei spätestens um neun da; **she should be there by now** sie müsste inzwischen da sein; **by then it was too late** zu diesem Zeitpunkt war es bereits zu spät; **by day** tagsüber; **by night** nachts - 7. [expressing quantity]: **sold by the dozen** im Dutzend verkauft; **prices fell by 20%** die Preise fielen um 20%; **by the day/week/month/hour** pro Tag/Woche/Monat/Stunde - 8. [expressing meaning]: **what do you mean by that?** was meinst du damit? - 9. [in division] durch; [in multiplication] mit; **two metres by five** zwei mal fünf Meter - 10. [according to] nach; **by law** nach dem Gesetz; **it's fine by me** ich bin damit einverstanden; **by nature** von Natur aus; **by profession** von Beruf - 11. [expressing gradual process]: **day by day** Tag für Tag; **they came out one by one** sie kamen einer nach dem anderen heraus; **little by little** nach und nach - 12. *phr*: **by mistake** versehentlich; **by chance** durch Zufall; **by the way** übrigens. ◇ *adv* ▷ **go, pass** etc. ◆ **by and large** *adv* im Großen und Ganzen. ◆ **(all) by oneself** ◇ *adv* allein; **did you do it all by yourself?** hast du das ganz allein gemacht? ◇ *adj* allein; **I'm all by myself today** ich bin heute ganz allein.

bye(-bye) [baɪ(baɪ)] *excl inf* tschüs!

byelaw ['baɪlɔː] *n* = **bylaw**.

by-election *n* Nachwahl *die*.

bygone ['baɪɡɒn] *adj* vergangen. ◆ **bygones** *npl*: **to let bygones be bygones** die Vergangenheit ruhen lassen.

bylaw ['baɪlɔː] *n* Verordnung *die*.

bypass ['baɪpɑːs] ◇ *n* - 1. [road] Umgehungsstraße *die* - 2. MED: **bypass (operation)** Bypassoperation *die*. ◇ *vt* - 1. [place] umlfahren, umgehen - 2. [issue, person] umgehen.

by-product *n liter* & *fig* Nebenprodukt *das*.

bystanders ['baɪˌstændərz] *npl*: **the bystanders** die Umstehenden *Pl*.

byte [baɪt] *n* COMPUT Byte *das*.

byword ['baɪwɜːd] *n* [symbol]: **to be a byword for sthg** ein Synonym für etw sein.

C

c (*pl* **c's** OR **cs**), **C** (*pl* **C's** OR **Cs**) [siː] *n* [letter] c *das*, C *das*. ◆ **C** *n* - 1. MUS C *das*; **C major** C-Dur - 2. SCH [mark] ≈ drei - 3. (*abbr of* celsius, centigrade) C.

c., ca. (*abbr of* circa) ca.

cab [kæb] *n* - 1. [taxi] Taxi *das* - 2. [of lorry] Führerhaus *das*.

cabaret ['kæbəreɪ] *n* Varieté *das*.

cabbage ['kæbɪdʒ] *n* [vegetable] Kohl *der*.

cabin ['kæbɪn] *n* - 1. [on ship, in aircraft] Kabine *die* - 2. [house] Hütte *die*.

cabin crew *n* Begleitpersonal *das*.

cabinet ['kæbɪnɪt] *n* - 1. [cupboard] Vitrine *die* - 2. POL Kabinett *das*.

cable ['keɪbl] ◇ *n* - 1. [rope] Seil *das* - 2. [telegram] Telegramm *das* - 3. ELEC Kabel *das* - 4. TV = **cable television**. ◇ *vt* [telegraph] telegrafieren.

cable car *n* Drahtseilbahn *die*.

cable television, cable TV *n* Kabelfernsehen *das*.

cache [kæʃ] *n* - 1. [store] geheimes Lager, Versteck *das* - 2. COMPUT Zwischenspeicher *der*.

cackle ['kækl] *vi* [person] kichern.

cactus ['kæktəs] (*pl* **-tuses** OR **-ti** [-taɪ]) *n* Kaktus *der*.

cadet [kə'det] *n* [in police] Kadett *der*, -in *die*.

cadge [kædʒ] UK *inf* ◇ *vt*: **to cadge sthg (off** OR **from sb)** etw (von jm) schnorren. ◇ *vi*: **to cadge off** OR **from sb** von jm schnorren.

caesarean (section) [sə'zeərɪən-] *n* UK Kaiserschnitt *der*.

cafe, café ['kæfeɪ] *n* Café *das*.

cafeteria [ˌkæfɪ'tɪərɪə] *n* Cafeteria *die*.

caffeine ['kæfi:n] n Koffein das.

cage [keɪdʒ] n Käfig der.

cagey ['keɪdʒɪ] (comp -ier, superl -iest) adj inf zugeknöpft, verschlossen.

cagoule [kə'gu:l] n UK Regenjacke die.

cajole [kə'dʒəʊl] vt zulreden; **to cajole sb into doing sthg** jn überreden, etw zu tun.

cake [keɪk] n - 1. [sweet food] Kuchen der; **a piece of cake** inf fig ein Kinderspiel - 2. [of soap] Stück das.

caked [keɪkt] adj: **caked with sthg** verkrustet mit etw.

calcium ['kælsɪəm] n Kalzium das.

calculate ['kælkjʊleɪt] vt - 1. [work out] auslrechnen - 2. [plan, intend]: **to be calculated to do sthg** darauf ausgelegt sein, etw zu tun.

calculating ['kælkjʊleɪtɪŋ] adj pej berechnend.

calculation [ˌkælkjʊ'leɪʃn] n [sum] Berechnung die.

calculator ['kælkjʊleɪtər] n Taschenrechner der, Rechenmaschine die.

calendar ['kælɪndər] n - 1. [gen] Kalender der - 2. [list of events] Veranstaltungskalender der.

calf [kɑ:f] (pl calves) n - 1. [young animal] Kalb das - 2. [of leg] Wade die.

calibre, caliber US ['kælɪbər] n Kaliber das.

California [ˌkælɪ'fɔ:njə] n Kalifornien nt.

calipers npl US = callipers.

call [kɔ:l] ⟨> n - 1. [shout - of person, animal] Ruf der; **a call for help** Hilferuf der - 2. [visit] Besuch der; **to pay sb a call** bei jm vorbeilgehen - 3. [demand]: **she has a lot of calls on her time** ihre Zeit ist stark beansprucht; **there are calls for a referendum** verschiedentlich wird nach einem Referendum verlangt; **there's no call for that sort of behaviour!** das gehört sich nicht! - 4. [telephone call] Anruf der - 5. [for flight] Aufruf der. ⟨> vt - 1. [name, describe] nennen; **to be called** heißen; **what's he called?** wie heißt er?; **to call sb names** jn beschimpfen; **let's call it £10** sagen wir 10 Pfund - 2. [shout] rufen - 3. [telephone] anlrufen; [doctor] rufen - 4. [meeting] einlberufen; [election] anlsetzen; [flight] auflrufen; [strike] auslrufen. ⟨> vi - 1. [shout] rufen - 2. [telephone] anlrufen; **who's calling?** wie war der Name? - 3. [visit] vorbeilkommen; **this train calls at...** dieser Zug hält in... ⟪ **on call** adj: **to be on call** [doctor, nurse] Bereitschaftsdienst haben. ⟪ **call back** ⟨> vt sep zurücklrufen. ⟨> vi - 1. [phone again] zurücklrufen - 2. [visit again] wiederlkommen. ⟪ **call for** vt insep - 1. [come to fetch] ablholen - 2. [demand] verlangen; [require] erfordern. ⟪ **call in** ⟨> vt sep - 1. [send for - army, riot police] einlsetzen - 2. FIN [loan] einlfordern. ⟨> vi: **to call in (on sb)** (bei jm) vorbeilschauen. ⟪ **call off** vt sep - 1. [cancel] ablsagen - 2. [dog, attacker] zurücklrufen. ⟪ **call on** vt insep - 1. [visit] be-

suchen - 2. [ask]: **to call on sb to do sthg** jn aufllfordern, etw zu tun. ⟪ **call out** ⟨> vt sep - 1. [shout out] auslrufen - 2. [doctor, fire brigade] rufen. ⟨> vi [shout out] rufen. ⟪ **call round** vi vorbeilkommen. ⟪ **call up** vt sep - 1. MIL einlberufen - 2. [on telephone] anlrufen - 3. COMPUT auflrufen.

call box n UK Telefonzelle die.

caller ['kɔ:lər] n - 1. [visitor] Besucher der, -in die - 2. [on telephone] Anrufer der, -in die.

calling ['kɔ:lɪŋ] n - 1. [profession, trade] Beruf der - 2. [vocation] Berufung die.

calling card n US Visitenkarte die.

callipers UK, **calipers** US ['kælɪpəz] npl - 1. MATHS Taster der, Zirkel der - 2. MED Beinschienen die.

callous ['kæləs] adj gefühllos, herzlos.

callus ['kæləs] (pl -es) n Schwiele die.

calm [kɑ:m] ⟨> adj - 1. [person, voice] ruhig - 2. [weather, day] windstill - 3. [water] still. ⟨> n Ruhe die. ⟨> vt beruhigen. ⟪ **calm down** ⟨> vt sep beruhigen. ⟨> vi sich beruhigen.

Calor gas® ['kælə-] n UK britische Handelsmarke für Butangas.

calorie ['kælərɪ] n Kalorie die.

calves [kɑ:vz] Pl ⟫ calf.

Cambodia [kæm'bəʊdjə] n Kambodscha nt.

camcorder ['kæmˌkɔːdər] n Camcorder der.

came [keɪm] pt ⟫ come.

camel ['kæml] n [animal] Kamel das.

cameo ['kæmɪəʊ] (pl -s) n - 1. [piece of jewellery] Kamee die - 2. [in film] kleine Nebenrolle, in der ein berühmter Schauspieler zu sehen ist.

camera ['kæmərə] n Kamera die. ⟪ **in camera** adv LAW unter Ausschluss der Öffentlichkeit.

cameraman ['kæmərəmæn] (pl -men [-men]) n Kameramann der.

cameraphone ['kæmərəfəʊn] n Fotohandy das.

camouflage ['kæməflɑːʒ] ⟨> n - 1. MIL Tarnung die - 2. [of bird] Tarngefieder das; [of animal] Tarnkleid das. ⟨> vt MIL tarnen.

camp [kæmp] ⟨> n - 1. [for tents] Lagerplatz der - 2. MIL Feldlager das - 3. [for refugees, faction] Lager das. ⟨> vi MIL lagern; [holiday] campen. ⟪ **camp out** vi campen.

campaign [kæm'peɪn] ⟨> n - 1. [project, crusade] Kampagne die - 2. [in war] Feldzug der. ⟨> vi: **to campaign for sthg** sich für etw einlsetzen; **to campaign against sthg** gegen etw anlgehen.

camp bed n Feldbett das.

camper ['kæmpər] n - 1. [person] Camper der, -in die - 2. [vehicle]: **camper (van)** Wohnmobil das.

campground ['kæmpgraʊnd] n US Campingplatz der, Zeltplatz der.

camping ['kæmpɪŋ] n Camping das; **to go camping** zelten gehen.

camping site, campsite ['kæmpsaɪt] n Campingplatz der, Zeltplatz der.

campus ['kæmpəs] (pl -es) n Universitätsgelände das, Campus der.

can¹ (pt & pp -ned, cont -ning) (weak form [kən], strong form [kæn]) <> n [container] Dose die. <> vt konservieren, eindosen.

can² (weak form [kən], strong form [kæn], conditional and preterite form could; negative form cannot and can't) aux vb - **1.** [be able to] können; **can you help me?** können Sie mir helfen?; **I can see you** ich kann dich sehen, ich sehe dich; **can you see/hear anything?** sehen/hören Sie etwas?, können Sie etwas sehen/hören? - **2.** [know how to] können; **can you drive?** kannst du Auto fahren?; **I can speak German/play the piano** ich spreche Deutsch/spiele Klavier - **3.** [be allowed to] können, dürfen; **you can't smoke here** Sie können OR dürfen hier nicht rauchen; **you can use my car if you like** du kannst mein Auto nehmen - **4.** [in polite requests] können; **can you tell me the time?** können Sie mir sagen, wie viel Uhr es ist? - **5.** [indicating disbelief, puzzlement] können; **what can she have done with it?** was hat sie bloß damit gemacht?; **you can't be serious!** das ist doch wohl nicht dein Ernst! - **6.** [indicating possibility] können; **they could be lost** sie könnten sich verlaufen haben.

Canada ['kænədə] n Kanada nt.

Canadian [kə'neɪdjən] <> adj kanadisch. <> n Kanadier der, -in die.

canal [kə'næl] n Kanal der.

Canaries [kə'neərɪz] npl: **the Canaries** die Kanaren Pl.

canary [kə'neərɪ] n Kanarienvogel der.

cancel ['kænsl] (UK) (US pt & pp -ed, cont -ing) <> vt - **1.** [call off - event, party] ausfallen lassen; [- appointment, meeting] absagen; [- order, booking] stornieren; (phrase): **the concert has been cancelled** das Konzert fällt aus; **the flight has been cancelled** der Flug ist gestrichen worden - **2.** [invalidate - stamp] entwerten; [- cheque] stornieren; [- debt] streichen; [- subscription] abbestellen. <> vi: **we had to cancel** wir mussten absagen.

➠ **cancel out** vt sep: **to cancel each other out** einander ausgleichen.

cancellation [,kænsə'leɪʃn] n Stornierung die; [of meeting, visit] Absage die; [of subscription] Abbestellung die.

cancer ['kænsər] n Krebs der. ➠ **Cancer** n Krebs der.

candelabra [,kændɪ'lɑːbrə] n Leuchter der.

candid ['kændɪd] adj offen, ehrlich.

candidate ['kændɪdət] n - **1.** [for job] Kandidat der, -in die - **2.** [for exam] Prüfling der.

candle ['kændl] n Kerze die.

candlelight ['kændllaɪt] n Kerzenlicht das.

candlelit ['kændllɪt] adj im Kerzenschein.

candlestick ['kændlstɪk] n Kerzenständer der.

candour UK, **candor** US ['kændər] n Offenheit die.

candy ['kændɪ] n esp US - **1.** (U) [confectionery] Süßigkeiten Pl - **2.** [sweet] Bonbon das.

candy bar n US Schokoriegel der.

candyfloss UK ['kændɪflɒs], **cotton candy** US n (U) Zuckerwatte die.

cane [keɪn] <> n - **1.** (U) [for making furniture] Rohr das - **2.** [walking stick] Spazierstock der - **3.** [for punishment]: **the cane** der Rohrstock - **4.** [for supporting plant] Stock der. <> vt mit den Rohrstock züchtigen.

canine ['keɪnaɪn] <> adj Hunde-. <> n: **canine (tooth)** Eckzahn der.

canister ['kænɪstər] n Kanister der, Behälter der; [for tea, film] Dose die.

cannabis ['kænəbɪs] n Cannabis der.

canned [kænd] adj [food] Konserven-; [drink] Dosen-.

cannibal ['kænɪbl] n Kannibale der, -lin die.

cannon ['kænən] (pl inv OR -s) n - **1.** [on ground] Kanone die - **2.** [on aircraft] Bordkanone die.

cannonball ['kænənbɔːl] n Kanonenkugel die.

cannot ['kænɒt] vb = **can²**.

canny ['kænɪ] adj umsichtig, sparsam.

canoe [kə'nuː] n Paddelboot das, Kanu das.

canoeing [kə'nuːɪŋ] n Kanufahren das.

canon ['kænən] n - **1.** [clergyman] Domherr der - **2.** [general principle] Grundregel die.

can opener n Dosenöffner der.

canopy ['kænəpɪ] n [over bed, seat] Baldachin der.

can't [kɑːnt] abbr of **cannot**.

cantankerous [kæn'tæŋkərəs] adj streitsüchtig.

canteen [kæn'tiːn] n - **1.** [restaurant - in workplace] Kantine die; [- in university] Mensa die - **2.** [box of cutlery] Besteckkasten der.

canter ['kæntər] <> n Kanter der. <> vi im Handgalopp reiten.

canvas ['kænvəs] n - **1.** (U) [cloth] Segeltuch das - **2.** [art - for painting] Leinwand die; [- finished painting] Gemälde das.

canvass ['kænvəs] vt - **1.** POL: **to canvass voters** um Wählerstimmen werben - **2.** COMM: **to canvass opinion** eine Meinungsumfrage durchführen.

canyon ['kænjən] n Cañon der.

cap [kæp] vt [outdo]: **to cap it all** als Krönung des Ganzen.

capability [,keɪpə'bɪlətɪ] n - **1.** [ability] Fähigkeit die - **2.** MIL Potenzial das.

capable ['keɪpəbl] *adj* - 1. [able, having capacity]: **to be capable of sthg** zu etw fähig sein; **to be capable of doing sthg** fähig sein, etw zu tun - 2. [competent, skilful] kompetent.

capacity [kə'pæsɪtɪ] *n* - 1. (U) [limit] Fassungsvermögen *das*; [of room, hall] Sitzplätze *Pl*; **the theatre has a capacity of 200** das Theater fasst 200 Personen - 2. [ability] Fähigkeit *die*; **capacity for sthg** die Fähigkeit zu etw; **capacity for doing** OR **to do sthg** die Fähigkeit, etw zu tun - 3. [position] Stellung *die*; **in a capacity** in der Funktion (+ G).

cape [keɪp] *n* - 1. GEOG Kap *das* - 2. [cloak] Cape *das*, Umhang *der*.

caper ['keɪpər] *n* - 1. [food] Kaper *die* - 2. inf [escapade] Eskapade *die*.

capital ['kæpɪtl] <> *adj* - 1.: **capital letter** Großbuchstabe *der* - 2. [offence] Kapital-. <> *n* - 1. [of country]: **capital (city)** Hauptstadt *die* - 2. [letter] Großbuchstabe *der* - 3. (U) [money] Kapital *das*; **to make capital out of sthg** fig aus etw Kapital schlagen.

capital expenditure *n* Kapitalaufwand *der*.

capital gains tax *n* Kapitalertragssteuer *die*.

capitalism ['kæpɪtəlɪzm] *n* Kapitalismus *der*.

capitalist ['kæpɪtəlɪst] <> *adj* kapitalistisch. <> *n* Kapitalist *der*, -in *die*.

capitalize, -ise ['kæpɪtəlaɪz] *vi*: **to capitalize on sthg** aus etw Nutzen ziehen.

capital punishment *n* (U) Todesstrafe *die*.

capitulate [kə'pɪtjʊleɪt] *vi*: **to capitulate (to sthg)** kapitulieren (vor etw (D)).

Capricorn ['kæprɪkɔːn] *n* Steinbock *der*.

capsize [kæp'saɪz] <> *vt* zum Kentern bringen. <> *vi* kentern.

capsule ['kæpsjuːl] *n* - 1. [gen] Kapsel *die* - 2. [on spacecraft] Raumkapsel *die*.

captain ['kæptɪn] *n* Kapitän *der*; [in army] Hauptmann *der*.

caption ['kæpʃn] *n* Bildunterschrift *die*.

captivate ['kæptɪveɪt] *vt* bezaubern.

captive ['kæptɪv] <> *adj* - 1. [imprisoned] gefangen - 2. fig [unable to leave]: **captive audience** unfreiwilliges Publikum. <> *n* Gefangene *der*, *die*.

captor ['kæptər] *n* Person, die jemanden gefangen nimmt.

capture ['kæptʃər] <> *vt* - 1. [take prisoner - person] gefangen nehmen; [- animal] einfangen - 2. [city, market, audience] erobern; [interest, imagination, votes] gewinnen - 3. COMPUT erfassen. <> *n* Gefangennahme *die*; [of city] Eroberung *die*.

car [kɑːr] <> *n* - 1. [motor car] Auto *das*, Wagen *der* - 2. [on train] Wagen *der*. <> *comp* Automobil-, Auto-.

carafe [kə'ræf] *n* Karaffe *die*.

car alarm *n* Autoalarm *der*.

caramel ['kærəmel] *n* - 1. [burnt sugar] Karamell *der* - 2. [sweet] Karamellbonbon *das*.

carat ['kærət] *n* UK Karat *das*.

caravan ['kærəvæn] *n* - 1. UK [vehicle - towed by car] Wohnwagen *der*, Caravan *der*; [- towed by horse] Pferdewagen *der* - 2. [traveling group] Karawane *die*.

caravan site *n* UK Wohnwagenplatz *der*.

carbohydrate [,kɑːbəʊ'haɪdreɪt] *n* (U) Kohle(n)hydrat *das*. ◆ **carbohydrates** *npl* [food] Kohle(n)hydrate *Pl*.

carbon ['kɑːbən] *n* [element] Kohlenstoff *der*.

carbonated ['kɑːbəneɪtɪd] *adj* mit Kohlensäure versetzt.

carbon copy *n* - 1. [document] Durchschlag *der* - 2. fig [exact copy]: **she's a carbon copy of her mother** sie ist ihrer Mutter wie aus dem Gesicht geschnitten.

carbon dioxide [-daɪ'ɒksaɪd] *n* Kohlendioxyd *das*.

carbon monoxide *n* Kohlenmonoxid *das*.

carbon paper *n* (U) Kohlepapier *das*.

car-boot sale *n* UK auf einem (Park)platz oder in einem Parkhaus stattfindender Trödelmarkt.

carburettor UK, **carburetor** US [,kɑːbə'retər] *n* Vergaser *der*.

carcass ['kɑːkəs] *n* [of animal] Kadaver *der*.

card [kɑːd] *n* - 1. [playing card] Spielkarte *die* - 2. [for identification] Karte *die* - 3. [greetings card] Grußkarte *die* - 4. [postcard] Postkarte *die* - 5. (U) [cardboard] Pappe *die*. ◆ **cards** *npl* [game] Kartenspiel *das*; **to play cards** Karten spielen. ◆ **on the cards** UK, **in the cards** US *adv* inf durchaus möglich.

cardboard ['kɑːdbɔːd] <> *n* (U) Pappe *die*. <> *comp* Papp-.

cardboard box *n* Pappkarton *der*.

cardiac ['kɑːdɪæk] *adj* Herz-.

cardigan ['kɑːdɪgən] *n* Strickjacke *die*.

cardinal ['kɑːdɪnl] <> *adj* äußerste(r) (s); **cardinal sin** Todsünde *die*. <> *n* RELIG Kardinal *der*.

card index *n* UK Kartei *die*.

card table *n* Kartentisch *der*.

care [keər] *vi* - 1. [be concerned]: **you really don't care, do you?** dir ist das wohl ganz egal, wie?; **to care about sb/sthg** an jn/an etw denken - 2. [mind] sich kümmern; **I don't care if/that/how** es ist mir egal, ob/dass/wie; **who cares?** wen interessiert das schon?; **I don't honestly care what I look like** es kümmert OR interessiert mich ehrlich gesagt nicht, wie ich aussehe. ◆ **care of** *prep* bei. ◆ **care for** *vt insep* [like] Interesse haben für; **I don't much care for opera** ich mache mir nichts aus Oper;

does she still care for him? bedeutet er ihr noch immer viel?; **would you care for a drink?** möchtest du etwas trinken?

career [kə'rɪə'] ◇ n - 1. [job] Beruf der; **to make a career out of sth** etw zum Beruf machen - 2. [working life] Laufbahn die; [in retrospect] Werdegang der - 3. [very successful] Karriere die; **to make a career for o.s.** Karriere machen. ◇ vi rasen.

careers adviser n Berufsberater der, -in die.

carefree ['keəfri:] adj sorglos, sorgenfrei.

careful ['keəful] adj - 1. [cautious] vorsichtig; **to be careful with sth** vorsichtig mit etw um|gehen; **to be careful to do sth** darauf achten, etw zu tun - 2. [thorough] gründlich.

carefully ['keəflɪ] adv - 1. [cautiously] vorsichtig - 2. [thoroughly] gründlich.

careless ['keəlɪs] adj - 1. [inattentive] unaufmerksam - 2. [unconcerned] nachlässig.

caress [kə'res] ◇ n Liebkosung die. ◇ vt liebkosen.

caretaker ['keə,teɪkə'] n UK Hausmeister der, -in die.

car ferry n Autofähre die.

cargo ['kɑ:gəʊ] (pl -es OR -s) n Ladung die.

car hire n (U) UK Autovermietung die.

Caribbean [UK kærɪ'bi:ən, US kə'rɪbɪən] n - 1. [sea]: **the Caribbean (Sea)** das Karibische Meer, die Karibische See - 2. [region]: **the Caribbean** die Karibik.

caring ['keərɪŋ] adj mitfühlend.

carnage ['kɑ:nɪdʒ] n (U) Gemetzel das.

carnal ['kɑ:nl] adj liter fleischlich.

carnation [kɑ:'neɪʃn] n Nelke die.

carnival ['kɑ:nɪvl] n - 1. [festive occasion] Karneval der - 2. [fair] Volksfest das.

carnivorous [kɑ:'nɪvərəs] adj Fleisch fressend.

carol ['kærəl] n: **(Christmas) carol** Weihnachtslied das.

carousel [,kærə'sel] n - 1. esp US [at fair] Karussell das - 2. [at airport] Gepäckband das.

carp [kɑ:p] (pl inv OR -s) ◇ n Karpfen der. ◇ vi nörgeln; **to carp about sb** über jn meckern.

car park n UK Parkplatz der.

carpenter ['kɑ:pəntə'] n [working on buildings] Zimmermann der; [making furniture] Tischler der.

carpentry ['kɑ:pəntrɪ] n [working on buildings] Zimmerhandwerk das; [making furniture] Tischlerhandwerk das.

carpet ['kɑ:pɪt] ◇ n [floor covering] Teppich(boden) der. ◇ vt [floor] mit Teppich(boden) aus|legen.

carpet sweeper [-,swi:pə'] n Teppichkehrmaschine die.

car phone n Autotelefon das.

car radio n Autoradio das.

car rental n (U) US Autovermietung die.

carriage ['kærɪdʒ] n - 1. [horsedrawn vehicle] Kutsche die - 2. UK [railway coach] Wagen der - 3. [transport of goods] Transport der; **carriage paid** OR **free** UK frachtfrei, frei Haus.

carriageway ['kærɪdʒweɪ] n UK Fahrbahn die.

carrier ['kærɪə'] n - 1. COMM Spediteur der - 2. [of disease] Überträger der, -in die - 3. = **carrier bag**.

carrier bag n Tragetasche die.

carrot ['kærət] n - 1. [vegetable] Möhre die, Karotte die - 2. inf [incentive] Köder der.

carry ['kærɪ] ◇ vt - 1. [transport] tragen - 2. [be equipped with] dabeilhaben, mit sich führen - 3. [disease] übertragen - 4. [involve] mit sich bringen - 5. [motion, proposal] an|nehmen - 6. [be pregnant with] tragen - 7. MATHS: **5 carry 1** 5 Rest 1. ◇ vi [sound] tragen. ◆ **carry away** vt insep: **to get carried away** sich hin|reißen lassen. ◆ **carry forward** vt sep übertragen. ◆ **carry off** vt sep - 1. [plan, performance] schaffen - 2. [prize] gewinnen. ◆ **carry on** ◇ vt insep [continue] fortlführen; **to carry on doing sth** etw weiterhin tun. ◇ vi - 1. [continue] weiterlmachen; **to carry on with sth** mit etw weiterlmachen - 2. inf [make a fuss] sich auflführen. ◆ **carry out** vt insep [task, plan, order] auslführen; [experiment, investigation] durchlführen; [promise, threat] wahr machen. ◆ **carry through** vt sep [accomplish] durchlführen.

carryall ['kærɔ:l] n US Reisetasche die.

carrycot ['kærɪkɒt] n esp UK Babytragetasche die.

carry-out n US Essen oder Getränke zum Mitnehmen.

carsick ['kɑ:,sɪk] adj reisekrank.

cart [kɑ:t] ◇ n - 1. [vehicle] Wagen der - 2. US [for shopping]: **(shopping** OR **grocery) cart** Einkaufswagen der. ◇ vt inf schleppen.

carton ['kɑ:tn] n Karton der; [of cream, yoghurt] Becher der; [of milk] Tüte die.

cartoon [kɑ:'tu:n] n - 1. [satirical drawing] Karikatur die - 2. [comic strip] Comic(strip) der - 3. [film] Zeichentrickfilm der.

cartridge ['kɑ:trɪdʒ] n - 1. [for gun, pen] Patrone die - 2. [for camera] Film der.

cartwheel ['kɑ:twi:l] n Rad das; **to do cartwheels** Rad schlagen.

carve [kɑ:v] ◇ vt - 1. [wood] schnitzen; [stone] hauen - 2. [meat] auflschneiden - 3. [cut] ritzen. ◇ vi den Braten/das Fleisch auflschneiden. ◆ **carve out** vt sep: **to carve out a career** sich eine Karriere auflbauen. ◆ **carve up** vt sep [divide] aufteilen.

carving ['kɑ:vɪŋ] n [object] Skulptur die.

carving knife n Tranchiermesser das.

car wash n [place] Autowaschanlage die.

case [keɪs] *n* - **1.** [gen] Fall *der*; **in that case** in dem Fall; **as** *or* **whatever the case may be** je nachdem; **in case of emergency/doubt** im Notfall/Zweifelsfall - **2.** [argument] Angelegenheit *die*; **the case for the defence** die Verteidigung - **3.** [packing case] Kiste *die*; [small box] Kästchen *das*; [for glasses, cigarettes] Etui *das*; [for musical instrument] Kasten *der* - **4.** UK [suitcase] Koffer *der*. ➤ **in any case** *adv* wie dem auch sei. ➤ **in case** ⬦ *conj* falls. ⬦ *adv*: **(just) in case** für alle Fälle.

cash [kæʃ] ⬦ *n* (U) - **1.** [notes and coins] Bargeld *das*; **to pay (in) cash** bar bezahlen - **2.** *inf* [money] Geld *das*; **I'm a bit short of cash** ich bin etwas knapp mit Kasse - **3.** [payment]: **cash in advance** Vorkasse *die*; **cash on delivery** zahlbar bei Empfang. ⬦ *vt* einlösen.

cash and carry *n* [for retailers] Großhandelsmarkt *der*; [for public] Verbrauchermarkt *der*.

cash box *n* Geldkassette *die*.

cash card *n* Kontokarte *die*.

cash desk *n* UK Kasse *die*.

cash dispenser [-dɪˌspensə'] *n* Geldautomat *der*.

cashew (nut) ['kæʃuː-] *n* Cashewnuss *die*.

cashier [kæˈʃɪə'] *n* Kassierer *der*, -in *die*.

cash machine *n* = **cash dispenser**.

cashmere [kæʃˈmɪə'] *n* Kaschmir *der*.

cashpoint (machine) ['kæʃpɔɪnt-] *n* Geldautomat *der*.

cash register *n* Registrierkasse *die*.

casing ['keɪsɪŋ] *n* Gehäuse *das*; [of cable] Hülle *die*; [of tyre] Mantel *der*.

casino [kəˈsiːnəʊ] (*pl* -s) *n* Kasino *das*.

cask [kɑːsk] *n* Fass *das*.

casket ['kɑːskɪt] *n* - **1.** [for jewels] (Schmuck)kästchen *das* - **2.** US [coffin] Sarg *der*.

casserole ['kæsərəʊl] *n* - **1.** [stew] Fleischeintopf *der* - **2.** [pan] Schmortopf *der*.

cassette [kæˈset] *n* Kassette *die*.

cassette player *n* Kassettenspieler *der*.

cassette recorder *n* Kassettenrekorder *der*.

cast [kɑːst] (*pt & pp inv*) ⬦ *n* - **1.** [of play, film] Besetzung *die* - **2.** MED Gipsverband *der*. ⬦ *vt* - **1.** [gen] werfen; **to cast one's eye over sthg** einen Blick auf etw (A) werfen; **to cast doubt on sthg** etw in Zweifel ziehen - **2.** [choose for play, film]: **she cast him in the role of Hamlet** sie gab ihm die Rolle des Hamlet - **3.** POL: **to cast one's vote** seine Stimme abgeben - **4.** [metal, statue] gießen. ➤ **cast aside** *vt sep* fallen lassen. ➤ **cast off** *vi* - **1.** NAUT ablegen - **2.** [in knitting] Maschen abnehmen. ➤ **cast on** *vi* [in knitting] Maschen anschlagen.

castaway ['kɑːstəweɪ] *n* Schiffbrüchige *der*, *die*.

caster ['kɑːstə'] *n* Rolle *die*.

caster sugar *n* UK Feinkristallzucker *der*.

casting vote *n* entscheidende Stimme.

cast iron *n* (U) Gusseisen *das*.

castle ['kɑːsl] *n* - **1.** [fortress] Burg *die*; [mansion] Schloss *das* - **2.** [in chess] Turm *der*.

castor ['kɑːstə'] *n* = **caster**.

castrate [kæˈstreɪt] *vt* kastrieren.

casual ['kæʒʊəl] *adj* - **1.** [relaxed] gleichgültig - **2.** *pej* [offhand] nachlässig - **3.** [chance] zufällig - **4.** [clothes]: **casual clothes** zwanglose Kleidung - **5.** [work, worker] Gelegenheits-.

casually ['kæʒʊəlɪ] *adv* - **1.** [in a relaxed manner] gleichgültig - **2.** [dress] leger.

casualty ['kæʒjʊəltɪ] *n* - **1.** [dead person] Todesopfer *das*; [injured person] Unfallopfer *das* - **2.** = **casualty department**.

casualty department *n* Ambulanz *die*.

cat [kæt] *n* - **1.** [domestic] Katze *die* - **2.** [wild] Raubkatze *die*.

catalogue UK, **catalog** US ['kætəlɒg] ⬦ *n* [of items] Katalog *der*. ⬦ *vt* katalogisieren.

catalyst ['kætəlɪst] *n* - **1.** CHEM Katalysator *der* - **2.** *fig* [cause] Auslöser *der*.

catalytic converter [ˌkætəˈkɪtɪk-] *n* Katalysator *der*.

catapult UK ['kætəpʊlt] ⬦ *n* - **1.** [handheld] Katapult *das* - **2.** HIST [machine] Katapult *das*. ⬦ *vt* schleudern; **she was catapulted to fame** *fig* sie wurde über Nacht berühmt.

cataract ['kætərækt] *n* MED grauer Star.

catarrh [kəˈtɑːr] *n* Katarrh *der*.

catastrophe [kəˈtæstrəfɪ] *n* Katastrophe *die*.

catch [kætʃ] (*pt & pp caught*) ⬦ *vt* - **1.** [ball, fish, animal] fangen - **2.** [criminal] fassen - **3.** [discover] überraschen; **to catch sb doing sthg** jn bei etw ertappen - **4.** [train, plane] erreichen - **5.** [hear clearly] hören - **6.** [interest] wecken; [imagination] anlregen; **I tried to catch his attention** ich versuchte, ihn auf mich aufmerksam zu machen - **7.** [sight]: **to catch sight of sb/sthg, to catch a glimpse of sb/sthg** jn/etw flüchtig zu Gesicht bekommen - **8.** [illness, disease]: **to catch malaria/measles** an Malaria/Masern erkranken; **to catch a cold** sich erkälten - **9.** [trap]: **to catch one's finger in the door** sich den Finger in der Tür (ein)klemmen - **10.** [strike] treffen. ⬦ *vi* - **1.** [clothing] hängen bleiben; [foot, limb] stecken bleiben - **2.** [fire] anlgehen. ⬦ *n* - **1.** [of ball *etc*]: **good catch!** sehr gut gefangen! - **2.** [of fish] Fang *der* - **3.** [fastener] Verschluss *der* - **4.** [snag] Haken *der*. ➤ **catch on** *vi* - **1.** [become popular] Anklang finden - **2.** *inf* [understand] begreifen; **to catch on to sthg** etw (A) kommen. ➤ **catch out** *vt sep* [trick] hereinlegen. ➤ **catch up** ⬦ *vt sep* - **1.** [come level with] einholen - **2.** [involve]: **to get caught up in sthg** in etw (A) verwickelt werden. ⬦ *vi* auflholen; **to catch up on sthg** etw nachlholen. **catch up with** vt insep - 1. [in race, work] einlholen - 2. [criminal] ausfindig machen.

catching ['kætʃɪŋ] adj ansteckend.

catchment area ['kætʃmənt-] n Einzugsgebiet das.

catchphrase ['kætʃfreɪz] n [of performer] Lieblingsspruch der.

catchy ['kætʃɪ] adj: **a catchy tune** ein Ohrwurm.

categorically [ˌkætɪ'gɒrɪklɪ] adv kategorisch.

category ['kætəgərɪ] n Kategorie die.

cater ['keɪtər] vi [provide food]: **to cater for sb** jn mit Lebensmitteln versorgen. **cater for** vt insep UK [tastes, needs] befriedigen.

caterer ['keɪtərər] n Lebensmittellieferant der, -in die.

catering ['keɪtərɪŋ] n (U) [industry] Gaststättengewerbe das; [at wedding, party] Essen das.

caterpillar ['kætəpɪlər] n Raupe die.

cathedral [kə'θiːdrəl] n Kathedrale die.

Catholic ['kæθlɪk] adj katholisch. n Katholik der, -in die. **catholic** adj: **to have very catholic tastes** vielseitig interessiert sein.

cat litter n Katzenstreu das.

Catseyes ['kætsaɪz] npl UK Katzenaugen Pl.

cattle ['kætl] npl Vieh das.

catty ['kætɪ] adj inf pej [spiteful] gehässig.

catwalk ['kætwɔːk] n Laufsteg der.

caucus ['kɔːkəs] n - 1. US POL Sitzung die, Versammlung die - 2. UK POL Gremium das.

caught [kɔːt] pt & pp catch.

cauliflower ['kɒlɪˌflaʊər] n Blumenkohl der.

cause [kɔːz] n - 1. [reason why sthg happens] Ursache die - 2. [grounds]: **cause (for)** Grund der (zu); **to have no cause to do sthg** keinen Grund haben, etw zu tun; **I have no cause for complaint** ich habe keinen Grund zur Klage - 3. [movement, aim] Sache die; **for a good cause** für eine gute Sache. vt verursachen; **to cause sb to do sthg** jn veranlassen, etw zu tun.

caustic ['kɔːstɪk] adj - 1. CHEM ätzend - 2. fig [comment] bissig.

caution ['kɔːʃn] n - 1. [care] Vorsicht die; [prudence] Umsicht die; 'proceed with caution' 'vorsichtig vorgehen' - 2. [warning] Warnung die - 3. UK LAW Verwarnung die. vt - 1. [warn]: **to caution sb against doing sthg** jn davor warnen, etw zu tun - 2. UK LAW verwarnen.

cautious ['kɔːʃəs] adj [careful] vorsichtig; [prudent] umsichtig.

cavalry ['kævlrɪ] n (U) - 1. [on horseback] Kavallerie die - 2. [in armoured vehicles] motorisierte Truppen Pl.

cave [keɪv] n Höhle die. **cave in** vi [physically collapse] einlstürzen.

caveman ['keɪvmæn] (pl -men [-men]) n Höhlenmensch der.

cavernous ['kævənəs] adj [room, building] höhlenartig.

caviar(e) ['kævɪɑːr] n Kaviar der.

cavity ['kævətɪ] n - 1. [in object, structure] Hohlraum der; [in body] Höhle die - 2. [in tooth] Loch das.

cavort [kə'vɔːt] vi herumltollen.

CB n (abbr of Citizens' Band) CB.

CBI (abbr of Confederation of British Industry) n britischer Unternehmerverband.

cc n (abbr of cubic centimetre) cm³. abbr of **carbon copy**.

CD n (abbr of compact disc) CD die.

CD player n CD-Player der, CD-Spieler der.

CD-ROM [ˌsiːdiː'rɒm] (abbr of compact disc read-only memory) n CD-ROM die.

CD-RW n (abbr of compact disc rewriteable) CD-RW die.

cease [siːs] fml vt beenden, einlstellen; **to cease doing** OR **to do sthg** auflhören, etw zu tun. vi auflhören, enden.

cease-fire n Waffenruhe die.

ceaseless ['siːslɪs] adj fml unaufhörlich.

cedar (tree) ['siːdər-] n Zeder die.

ceiling ['siːlɪŋ] n - 1. [of room] Decke die - 2. [limit] oberste Grenze.

celebrate ['selɪbreɪt] vt [victory, anniversary] feiern. vi feiern.

celebrated ['selɪbreɪtɪd] adj berühmt.

celebration [ˌselɪ'breɪʃn] n - 1. (U) [activity] Feiern das - 2. [event] Feier die.

celebrity [sɪ'lebrətɪ] n [star] Star der.

celery ['selərɪ] n Stangensellerie die ODER der.

celibate ['selɪbət] adj RELIG zölibatär; fig enthaltsam.

cell [sel] n - 1. [gen] Zelle die - 2. COMPUT Feld das.

cellar ['selər] n - 1. [basement] Keller der - 2. [stock of wine] Weinkeller der.

cello ['tʃeləʊ] (pl -s) n Cello das.

Cellophane ['seləfeɪn] n Zellophan das.

Celsius ['selsɪəs] adj Celsius-, Celsius; **20 degrees Celsius** 20 Grad Celsius.

Celt [kelt] n Kelte der, -tin die.

Celtic ['keltɪk] adj keltisch.

cement [sɪ'ment] n (U) [for concrete] Zement der. vt - 1. [cover with cement] betonieren - 2. fig [friendship] festigen.

cement mixer n Betonmischmaschine die.

cemetery ['semɪtrɪ] n Friedhof der.

censor ['sensər] n Zensor der. vt zensieren.

censorship ['sensəʃɪp] n Zensur die.

censure ['senʃər] ⟨⟩ n Tadel der. ⟨⟩ vt tadeln.

census ['sensəs] (pl censuses) n Volkszählung die.

cent [sent] n Cent der.

centenary UK [sen'ti:nəri], **centennial** US [sen'tenjəl] n Hundertjahrfeier die.

center n, adj & vt US = centre.

centigrade ['sentigreid] adj Celsius-; **16 degrees centigrade** 16 Grad Celsius.

centilitre UK, **centiliter** US ['senti,li:tər] n Zentiliter der.

centimetre UK, **centimeter** US ['senti,mi:tər] n Zentimeter der.

centipede ['sentipi:d] n Tausendfüßler der.

central ['sentrəl] adj zentral.

Central America n Mittelamerika nt.

central heating n Zentralheizung die.

centralize, -ise ['sentrəlaiz] vt zentralisieren.

central locking [-'lɒkɪŋ] n Zentralverriegelung die.

central reservation n UK Mittelstreifen der.

centre UK, **center** US ['sentər] ⟨⟩ n - 1. [gen] Mitte die, Zentrum das; [of circle] Mittelpunkt der - 2. [building, place] Zentrum das - 3. [of event, activity] Zentrum das, Mittelpunkt der; **she always wants to be the centre of attention** sie will immer im Mittelpunkt stehen; **centre of gravity** Schwerpunkt der - 4. POL Mitte die - 5. [in basketball, netball] Center der. ⟨⟩ adj - 1. [middle] Mittel-, mittlere(r) (s) - 2. POL: **centre party** Partei der Mitte. ⟨⟩ vt [text, image] zentrieren.

centre forward n Mittelstürmer der, -in die.

century ['sentʃuri] n Jahrhundert das.

ceramic [sɪ'ræmɪk] adj keramisch. ⟶ **ceramics** npl [objects] Keramik die.

cereal ['sɪərɪəl] n - 1. [crop] Getreide das - 2. (U) [breakfast food] Frühstücksflocken Pl.

ceremonial [,serɪ'məunjəl] adj feierlich.

ceremony ['serɪmənɪ] n - 1. [event] Zeremonie die - 2. [formality] Förmlichkeit die; **to stand on ceremony** sehr förmlich sein.

certain ['sɜ:tn] adj - 1. [gen] sicher; **he is certain to be late** er kommt bestimmt zu spät; **to make certain** nachprüfen; **I always make certain of being on time** ich achte immer darauf, pünktlich zu sein; **for certain** sicher - 2. [particular, individual] gewiss; **to a certain extent** bis zu einem gewissen Grad.

certainly ['sɜ:tnlɪ] adv sicher(lich); **can I bring a friend along? – certainly!** kann ich einen Bekannten/eine Bekannte mitbringen? – na klar!; **do you dye your hair? – certainly not!** färbst du dir die Haare? – natürlich nicht!

certainty ['sɜ:tntɪ] n Sicherheit die; **it's a certainty that he will win the race** es steht fest, dass er das Rennen gewinnen wird.

certificate [sə'tɪfɪkət] n Bescheinigung die; [from school, college] Zeugnis das; [of birth] Urkunde die.

certified ['sɜ:tɪfaɪd] adj - 1. [teacher, accountant] geprüft - 2. [document] beglaubigt.

certified mail n US Einschreiben das.

certified public accountant n US Buchhalter der, -in die.

certify ['sɜ:tɪfaɪ] vt - 1. [declare true] bescheinigen; **this is to certify that...** hiermit wird bescheinigt, dass... - 2. [declare insane] für unzurechnungsfähig erklären.

cervical [sə'vaɪkl] adj Gebärmutter-.

cervical smear n Abstrich der.

cervix ['sɜ:vɪks] (pl -ices [-ɪsi:z]) n Gebärmutterhals der.

cesarean (section) n US = caesarean section.

cesspit ['sespɪt], **cesspool** ['sespu:l] n Senkgrube die.

cf. (abbr of confer) vgl.

CFC (abbr of chlorofluorocarbon) n FCKW das.

ch. (abbr of chapter) Kap.

chafe [tʃeɪf] vt [rub] scheuern.

chaffinch ['tʃæfɪntʃ] n Buchfink der.

chain [tʃeɪn] ⟨⟩ n Kette die; **a chain of events** eine Kette von Ereignissen. ⟨⟩ vt anketten.

chain reaction n Kettenreaktion die.

chain saw n Kettensäge die.

chain smoker n Kettenraucher der, -in die.

chain store n Filiale die einer Ladenkette.

chair [tʃeər] ⟨⟩ n - 1. [gen] Stuhl der - 2. [university post] Lehrstuhl der. ⟨⟩ vt [meeting, discussion] den Vorsitz führen bei, leiten.

chair lift n Sessellift der.

chairman ['tʃeəmən] (pl -men [-mən]) n Vorsitzende der.

chairperson ['tʃeə,pɜ:sn] (pl -s) n Vorsitzende der, die.

chalet ['ʃæleɪ] n [in mountains] Chalet das.

chalk [tʃɔ:k] n - 1. [for drawing] Kreide die - 2. (U) [type of rock] Kalkstein der.

chalkboard ['tʃɔ:kbɔ:d] n US Tafel die.

challenge ['tʃælɪndʒ] ⟨⟩ n - 1. [gen] Herausforderung die - 2. [to authority] Infragestellung die. ⟨⟩ vt - 1. [to fight, competition]: **to challenge sb (to sthg)** jn (zu etw) herausfordern - 2. [question] in Frage stellen.

challenging ['tʃælɪndʒɪŋ] adj herausfordernd.

chamber ['tʃeɪmbər] n Kammer die.

chambermaid ['tʃeɪmbəmeɪd] n Zimmermädchen das.

chamber music n Kammermusik die.

chamber of commerce n Handelskammer die.

chameleon [kə'miːljən] n Chamäleon das.

champagne [ˌʃæm'peɪn] n Champagner der.

champion ['tʃæmpjən] n - 1. [of competition] Meister der, -in die, Champion der - 2. [of cause] Verfechter der, -in die.

championship ['tʃæmpjənʃɪp] n Meisterschaft die.

chance [tʃɑːns] <> n - 1. (U) [luck] Glück das; **by chance** zufällig; **by any chance** vielleicht - 2. [likelihood] Chance die, Möglichkeit die; **she doesn't stand a chance of winning the match** sie hat keine Chance, das Spiel zu gewinnen; **on the off chance** auf gut Glück - 3. [opportunity] Gelegenheit die, Chance die - 4. [risk]: **to take a chance** es riskieren. <> adj [meeting] zufällig. <> vt [risk] riskieren; **he's chancing his luck a bit** er fordert sein Glück heraus.

chancellor ['tʃɑːnsələr] n Kanzler der.

Chancellor of the Exchequer n UK Schatzkanzler der.

chandelier [ˌʃændə'lɪər] n Kronleuchter der.

change [tʃeɪndʒ] <> n - 1. [alteration] Änderung die; [difference] Veränderung die; **change in sb/sthg** Veränderung in jm/etw; **a change for the better** eine Verbesserung; **a change for the worse** eine Verschlechterung - 2. [contrast, for variety] Abwechslung die; **for a change** zur Abwechslung - 3. [switch, replacement] Wechsel der; **a change of clothes** Kleidung zum Wechseln - 4. (U) [money returned after payment] Wechselgeld das - 5. (U) [coins] Kleingeld das; **have you got change for a £5 note?** können Sie mir einen Fünfpfundschein wechseln? <> vt - 1. [alter, make different] ändern; **to change sthg into sthg** etw in etw (A) umlwandeln; **to change one's mind** seine Meinung ändern - 2. [replace] auslwechseln; [product purchased] umltauschen - 3. [switch] wechseln; **to change clothes, to get changed** sich umlziehen; **to change trains/planes** umlsteigen - 4. [money] wechseln - 5. [bed] wechseln; [baby] trockenllegen. <> vi - 1. [alter, become different] sich ändern, sich verändern; **to change into sthg** sich in etw (A) verwandeln - 2. [put on different clothes] sich umlziehen - 3. [on train, bus] umlsteigen; **all change!** alles auslsteigen! ➤ **change over** vi: **to change over to sthg** auf etw (A) umlstellen.

changeable ['tʃeɪndʒəbl] adj - 1. [mood] wechselnd - 2. [weather] wechselhaft.

change machine n Geldwechselautomat der.

changeover ['tʃeɪndʒˌəʊvər] n: **changeover (to sthg)** Umstellung die (auf etw (A)).

changing ['tʃeɪndʒɪŋ] adj sich (ver)ändernd, wechselnd.

changing room n [in sports] Umkleideraum der; [in shop] Umkleidekabine die.

channel ['tʃænl] (UK) (US) <> n - 1. [gen] Kanal der - 2. [route] Fahrrinne die, [water] leiten. ➤ **Channel** n: **the (English) Channel** der Ärmelkanal. ➤ **channels** npl: **to go through the proper channels** sich an die richtigen Stellen wenden.

Channel Islands npl: **the Channel Islands** die Kanalinseln Pl.

Channel Tunnel n: **the Channel Tunnel** der Kanaltunnel.

chant [tʃɑːnt] n - 1. RELIG [song] Gesang der - 2. [repeated words] Sprechchor der.

chaos ['keɪɒs] n Chaos das.

chaotic [keɪ'ɒtɪk] adj chaotisch.

chap [tʃæp] n UK inf [man] Kerl der.

chapel ['tʃæpl] n [part of church, small church] Kapelle die.

chaplain ['tʃæplɪn] n Hausgeistliche der.

chapped [tʃæpt] adj aufgesprungen.

chapter ['tʃæptər] n Kapitel das.

char [tʃɑːr] vt [burn] verkohlen.

character ['kærəktər] n - 1. [nature - of place] Charakter der; [- of person] Wesen das; **in character** typisch - 2. [unusual quality, style] Originalität die - 3. [in film, book, play] Gestalt die - 4. inf [unusual person] Original das - 5. [letter, symbol] Schriftzeichen das.

characteristic [ˌkærəktə'rɪstɪk] <> adj charakteristisch. <> n Kennzeichen das.

characterize, -ise ['kærəktəraɪz] vt - 1. [typify] kennzeichnen - 2. [portray]: **to characterize sthg as sthg** etw als etw beschreiben.

charade [ʃə'rɑːd] n Farce die. ➤ **charades** n (U) Scharade die.

charcoal ['tʃɑːkəʊl] n (U) [for drawing] Kohle die; [for barbecue] Holzkohle die.

charge [tʃɑːdʒ] <> n - 1. [cost] Gebühr die; **free of charge** gebührenfrei - 2. LAW Anklage die - 3. [command, control] Verantwortung die; **to take charge (of sthg)** [of organization, group of people] die Leitung (einer Sache (G)) übernehmen; **in charge** zuständig; **in charge of** verantwortlich für - 4. ELEC Ladung die - 5. MIL Sturmangriff der. <> vt - 1. [customer] berechnen (+ D); **to charge £10 for sthg** für etw 10 Pfund verlangen; **to charge sthg to sb** jm etw in Rechnung stellen - 2. [suspect, criminal] anlklagen; **to charge sb with sthg** jn wegen etw anlklagen - 3. [attack] anlgreifen - 4. ELEC auflladen. <> vi - 1. [rush] stürmen - 2. [attack] anlgreifen.

charge card n Kundenkreditkarte die.

chargé d'affaires ['ʃɑːˌʒeɪdæ'feər] (pl **chargés d'affaires**) n Diplomat, der anstelle eines Botschafters ein Land vertritt.

charger ['tʃɑːdʒər] n [for batteries] Ladegerät das.

chariot ['tʃærɪət] n Streitwagen der.

charisma [kə'rɪzmə] n Charisma das.

charity ['tʃærətɪ] n - 1. (U) [gifts, money] Spenden Pl - 2. [organization] Wohltätigkeitsorganisation die, karitative Einrichtung - 3. [kindness] Nächstenliebe die.

charm [tʃɑːm] <> n - 1. (U) [appeal, attractiveness] Charme der - 2. [spell] Bann der - 3. [on bracelet] Anhänger der; **lucky charm** Glücksbringer der. <> vt bezaubern.

charming ['tʃɑːmɪŋ] adj bezaubernd; [person] charmant.

chart [tʃɑːt] <> n - 1. [diagram] Diagramm das; [for weather forecast] Wetterkarte die - 2. [map] Karte die. <> vt - 1. [map - seas, skies] kartieren; [- movements] auf einer Karte erfassen - 2. fig [record] aufzeichnen.
➤ **charts** npl: **the charts** die Hitparade.

charter ['tʃɑːtər] <> n [document - of organization] Charta die; [- of town] Gründungsurkunde die. <> vt [plane, boat] chartern.

chartered accountant [,tʃɑːtəd-] n UK Wirtschaftsprüfer der, -in die.

charter flight n Charterflug der.

charter plane n Charterflugzeug das.

chase [tʃeɪs] <> n Verfolgungsjagd die; [hunt] Jagd die. <> vt - 1. [pursue] jagen; [criminal] verfolgen - 2. [drive away] fortjagen. <> vi: **to chase after sb/sthg** jm/etw nachljagen.

chasm ['kæzm] n - 1. [deep crack] tiefe Felsspalte - 2. fig [divide] Kluft die.

chassis ['ʃæsɪ] (pl inv) n [of vehicle] Fahrgestell das.

chat [tʃæt] <> n Plauderei die; **to have a chat** plaudern. <> vi - 1. plaudern - 2. [on Internet] chatten. ➤ **chat up** vt sep UK inf sich heranlmachen an (+ A).

chat room n COMPUT Diskussionsforum das, Chatroom der.

chat show n UK Talkshow die.

chatter ['tʃætər] <> n [of person] Geplapper das. <> vi - 1. [person] plappern - 2. [animal, bird] zwitschern - 3. [teeth] klappern.

chatterbox ['tʃætəbɒks] n inf [child] Plappermäulchen das.

chatty ['tʃætɪ] adj - 1. [person] gesprächig - 2. [letter] im Plauderton geschrieben.

chauffeur ['ʃəʊfər] n Chauffeur der.

chauvinist ['ʃəʊvɪnɪst] n Chauvinist der.

cheap [tʃiːp] <> adj - 1. [inexpensive] billig - 2. [reduced in price] preiswert - 3. [poor-quality] billig - 4. [vulgar] billig; **to feel cheap** sich schäbig fühlen. <> adv billig.

cheapen ['tʃiːpn] vt [degrade - thing or place] herablsetzen; [- person] erniedrigen.

cheaply ['tʃiːplɪ] adv billig.

cheat [tʃiːt] <> n - 1. [person] Betrüger der, -in die; [in exam, game] Mogler der, -in die - 2. [act] Betrug der. <> vt betrügen; **to cheat sb out of sthg** jn um etw betrügen. <> vi [in exam, game] mogeln. ➤ **cheat on** vt insep inf [be unfaithful to] betrügen.

check [tʃek] <> n - 1. [inspection, test]: **check (on sthg)** Überprüfung die (von etw); **to keep a check on sthg** etw (regelmäßig) überprüfen - 2. [restraint]: **to put a check on sthg** etw unter Kontrolle halten; **in check** unter Kontrolle - 3. US [bill] Rechnung die - 4. [pattern] Karomuster das - 5. US = **cheque**. <> vt - 1. [test, verify] kontrollieren - 2. [restrain] unter Kontrolle halten; [advance] auflhalten; **to check o.s.** innelhalten. <> vi [have a look] nachlsehen; [ask sb] nachlfragen; **to check on sthg** etw überprüfen. ➤ **check in** <> vt sep [luggage] abfertigen lassen; [coat] ablgeben. <> vi - 1. [at hotel] sich anlmelden - 2. [at airport] einlchecken. ➤ **check out** <> vt sep [investigate] überprüfen. <> vi [from hotel] sich ablmelden. ➤ **check up** vi: **to check up on sb** [supervise] jn kontrollieren; [investigate] über jn Nachforschungen anlstellen; **to check up on sthg** etw überprüfen.

checkbook n US = **chequebook**.

checked [tʃekt] adj [patterned] kariert.

checkered adj US = **chequered**.

checkers ['tʃekəz] n (U) US Damespiel das.

check-in n Abfertigung die; [check-in desk] Abfertigungsschalter der.

checking account ['tʃekɪŋ-] n US Girokonto das.

checkmate ['tʃekmeɪt] n Schachmatt das.

checkout ['tʃekaʊt] n [in supermarket] Kasse die.

checkpoint ['tʃekpɔɪnt] n Kontrollpunkt der.

checkup ['tʃekʌp] n Kontrolluntersuchung die, Vorsorgeuntersuchung die.

Cheddar (cheese) ['tʃedər-] n Cheddar(käse) der.

cheek [tʃiːk] n - 1. [of face] Backe die, Wange die - 2. inf [impudence] Frechheit die.

cheekbone ['tʃiːkbəʊn] n Wangenknochen der, Backenknochen der.

cheeky ['tʃiːkɪ] adj frech.

cheer [tʃɪər] <> n [shout] Hurraruf der; [cheering] Jubelgeschrei das; **three cheers for Linda!** ein dreifaches Hurra für Linda! <> vt - 1. [shout approval, encouragement at] zuljubeln (+ D) - 2. [gladden] auflmuntern. <> vi jubeln. ➤ **cheers** excl - 1. [said before drinking] prost! - 2. UK inf [goodbye] tschüs! - 3. UK inf [thank you] danke! ➤ **cheer up** <> vt sep auflmuntern. <> vi vergnügter werden; **cheer up!** Kopf hoch!

cheerful ['tʃɪəfʊl] adj heiter; [music, colour] fröhlich.

cheerio [ˌtʃɪərɪ'əʊ] *excl UK inf* tschüs!

cheese [tʃiːz] *n* Käse *der*.

cheeseboard ['tʃiːzbɔːd] *n* - 1. [board] Käsebrett *das* - 2. [on menu] Käseplatte *die*.

cheeseburger ['tʃiːz,bɜːgər] *n* Cheeseburger *der*.

cheesecake ['tʃiːzkeɪk] *n* Käsekuchen *der*.

cheetah ['tʃiːtə] *n* Gepard *der*.

chef [ʃef] *n* [cook] Koch *der*, Köchin *die*; [head cook] Chefkoch *der*, -köchin *die*.

chemical ['kemɪkl] <> *adj* chemisch. <> *n* Chemikalie *die*.

chemist ['kemɪst] *n* - 1. *UK* [pharmacist] Apotheker *der*, -in *die*; **chemist's (shop)** [dispensing] Apotheke *die*; [non-dispensing] Drogerie *die* - 2. [scientist] Chemiker *der*, -in *die*.

chemistry ['kemɪstrɪ] *n* [science] Chemie *die*.

cheque *UK*, **check** *US* [tʃek] *n* Scheck *der*.

chequebook *UK*, **checkbook** *US* ['tʃekbʊk] *n* Scheckheft *das*.

cheque (guarantee) card *n UK* Scheckkarte *die*.

chequered *UK* ['tʃekəd], **checkered** *US* ['tʃekərd] *adj* [varied] bewegt.

cherish ['tʃerɪʃ] *vt* [person] liebevoll sorgen für; [thing] hegen und pflegen; [hope] hegen.

cherry ['tʃerɪ] *n* - 1. [fruit] Kirsche *die* - 2.: **cherry (tree)** Kirschbaum *der*.

chess [tʃes] *n* Schach *das*.

chessboard ['tʃesbɔːd] *n* Schachbrett *das*.

chest [tʃest] *n* - 1. ANAT Brust *die* - 2. [trunk] Truhe *die*.

chestnut ['tʃesnʌt] <> *adj* [colour] kastanienbraun. <> *n* - 1. [nut] Kastanie *die* - 2.: **chestnut (tree)** Kastanienbaum *der*.

chest of drawers (*pl* **chests of drawers**) *n* Kommode *die*.

chew [tʃuː] <> *n* [sweet] Kaubonbon *der* ODER *das*. <> *vt* - 1. [food] kauen - 2. [nails, pencil] kauen an (+ *D*). ◆ **chew up** *vt sep* zerkauen, zerbeißen.

chewing gum ['tʃuːɪŋ-] *n* (*U*) Kaugummi *der*.

chic [ʃiːk] *adj* schick.

chick [tʃɪk] *n* - 1. [baby bird] Junge *das*, Küken *das* - 2. *inf* [girl] Braut *die*.

chicken ['tʃɪkɪn] *n* - 1. [bird] Huhn *das* - 2. (*U*) [food] Hähnchen *das* - 3. *inf* [coward] Feigling *der*. ◆ **chicken out** *vi inf*: **to chicken out of sthg** vor etw (*D*) kneifen; **to chicken out of doing sthg** sich (aus Angst) davor drücken, etw zu tun.

chickenpox ['tʃɪkɪnpɒks] *n* Windpocken *Pl*.

chickpea ['tʃɪkpiː] *n* Kichererbse *die*.

chicory ['tʃɪkərɪ] *n* [vegetable] Chicorée *die* ODER *der*.

chief [tʃiːf] <> *adj* - 1. [most important] Haupt- - 2. [head] leitend. <> *n* - 1. [of organ-

ization] Leiter *der*, -in *die*, Chef *der*, -in *die*; **chief of police** Polizeipräsident *der*, -in *die* - 2. [of tribe] Häuptling *der*.

chief executive *n* [of company] Direktor *der*, -in *die*.

chiefly ['tʃiːflɪ] *adv* hauptsächlich.

chiffon ['ʃɪfɒn] *n* Chiffon *der*.

chilblain ['tʃɪlbleɪn] *n* Frostbeule *die*.

child [tʃaɪld] (*pl* **children**) *n* Kind *das*.

child benefit *n UK* Kindergeld *das*.

childhood ['tʃaɪldhʊd] *n* Kindheit *die*.

childish ['tʃaɪldɪʃ] *adj pej* kindisch.

childlike ['tʃaɪldlaɪk] *adj* kindlich.

childminder ['tʃaɪld,maɪndər] *n UK* Tagesmutter *die*.

childproof ['tʃaɪldpruːf] *adj* kindersicher.

children ['tʃɪldrən] *Pl* ▷ **child**.

children's home *n* Kinderheim *das*.

Chile *n* Chile *nt*.

chili ['tʃɪlɪ] *n* = **chilli**.

chill [tʃɪl] <> *adj* kühl. <> *n* - 1. [illness] Erkältung *die* mit leichtem Fieber - 2. [in temperature]: **there's a chill in the air** es ist kühl draußen - 3. [feeling of fear] Schauder *der*. <> *vt* - 1. [drink] kühlen; [food] kalt stellen - 2. [person - with cold]: **I'm chilled to the bone** ich bin bis auf die Knochen durchgefroren. <> *vi* [drink, food] kühl werden.

chilli ['tʃɪlɪ] (*pl* **-ies**) *n* [vegetable] Chili *der*; **chilli con carne** Chili con Carne.

chilling ['tʃɪlɪŋ] *adj* - 1. [very cold] eisig - 2. [frightening] schaudererregend.

chilly ['tʃɪlɪ] *adj* kühl.

chime [tʃaɪm] <> *n* [of bells] Geläut *das*; [of clock] Schlagen *das*; [of door bell] Läuten *das*. <> *vt* [time] schlagen. <> *vi* [bell] läuten; [clock] schlagen. ◆ **chime in** *vi* sich einschalten.

chimney ['tʃɪmnɪ] *n* Schornstein *der*.

chimneypot ['tʃɪmnɪpɒt] *n* Schornsteinaufsatz *der*.

chimneysweep ['tʃɪmnɪswiːp] *n* Schornsteinfeger *der*.

chimp [tʃɪmp] *n inf* Schimpanse *der*.

chimpanzee [tʃɪmpən'ziː] *n* Schimpanse *der*.

chin [tʃɪn] *n* Kinn *das*.

china ['tʃaɪnə] *n* Porzellan *das*.

China ['tʃaɪnə] *n* China *nt*.

Chinese [ˌtʃaɪ'niːz] <> *adj* chinesisch. <> *n* [language] Chinesisch(e) *das*. <> *npl*: **the Chinese** die Chinesen *Pl*.

chink [tʃɪŋk] *n* [narrow opening] Ritze *die*; **a chink of light** ein dünner Lichtstrahl.

chip [tʃɪp] <> *n* - 1. *UK* [fried potato]: **chips** Pommes frites *Pl* - 2. *US* [potato crisp] Chip *der* - 3. [fragment - of wood] Span *der*; [- of stone, metal] Splitter *der* - 4. [flaw] angeschlagene

Stelle - 5. [microchip, token] Chip der. <> vt [damage] anlschlagen. **chip in** inf vi - 1. [contribute] etwas beilsteuern - 2. [interrupt] sich einlschalten. **chip off** vt sep ablkratzen.

chipboard ['tʃɪpbɔːd] n (U) Spanplatte die.

chip shop n UK Imbissbude die.

chiropodist [kɪ'rɒpədɪst] n Fußpfleger der, -in die.

chirp [tʃɜːp] vi [bird] zwitschern.

chirpy ['tʃɜːpɪ] adj esp UK inf munter.

chisel ['tʃɪzl] (UK) (US) <> n [for stone] Meißel der; [for wood] Beitel der. <> vt [in stone] meißeln; [in wood] stemmen.

chit [tʃɪt] n Zettel der.

chitchat ['tʃɪttʃæt] n inf Geplauder das.

chivalry ['ʃɪvlrɪ] n - 1. liter [of knights] Rittertum das - 2. [courtesy] Ritterlichkeit die.

chives [tʃaɪvz] npl Schnittlauch der.

chlorine ['klɔːriːn] n Chlor das.

choc-ice ['tʃɒkaɪs] n UK Eis mit Schokoladenüberzug.

chock [tʃɒk] n Keil der.

chock-a-block, chock-full adj inf überfüllt.

chocolate ['tʃɒkələt] <> n - 1. (U) [food] Schokolade die - 2. [sweet] Praline die - 3. [drink]: **(hot) chocolate** heiße Schokolade. <> comp [made of chocolate] Schokoladen-.

choice [tʃɔɪs] <> n - 1. [gen] Wahl die - 2. [variety, selection] Auswahl die. <> adj erlesen, ausgesucht.

choir ['kwaɪə'] n Chor der.

choirboy ['kwaɪəbɔɪ] n Chorknabe der.

choke [tʃəʊk] <> n AUT Choke der. <> vt - 1. [strangle] würgen; **to choke sb to death** jn erwürgen; **the fumes choked her** durch den Rauch bekam sie keine Luft mehr - 2. [block] verstopfen. <> vi keine Luft mehr kriegen; [on fishbone] sich verschlucken; **to choke to death** ersticken.

cholera ['kɒlərə] n Cholera die.

choose [tʃuːz] (pt chose, pp chosen) <> vt - 1. [select - career] wählen; [- cake, dress] auslwählen - 2. [opt]: **to choose to do sthg** beschließen, etw zu tun. <> vi [select]: **to choose (from sthg)** eine Wahl treffen (zwischen etw (D)).

choos(e)y ['tʃuːzɪ] (comp -ier, superl -iest) adj wählerisch.

chop [tʃɒp] <> n [meat] Kotelett das. <> vt - 1. [wood] hacken; [food] schneiden - 2. inf [funding, budget] kürzen - 3. phr: **to chop and change** es sich (D) dauernd anders überlegen. **chop down** vt sep fällen. **chop up** vt sep [wood] klein hacken; [food] klein schneiden.

chopper ['tʃɒpə'] n - 1. [axe] Hackbeil das - 2. inf [helicopter] Hubschrauber der.

choppy ['tʃɒpɪ] adj kabbelig.

chopsticks ['tʃɒpstɪks] npl Stäbchen Pl.

chord [kɔːd] n MUS Akkord der.

chore [tʃɔːr] n lästige Pflicht; **household chores** Hausarbeit die.

chorus ['kɔːrəs] n - 1. [part of song] Refrain der - 2. [singers] Chor der.

chose [tʃəʊz] pt ⊳ choose.

chosen ['tʃəʊzn] pp ⊳ choose.

Christ [kraɪst] <> n Christus der. <> excl oh Gott!

christen ['krɪsn] vt taufen.

christening ['krɪsnɪŋ] n Taufe die.

Christian ['krɪstʃən] <> adj christlich. <> n Christ der, -in die.

Christianity [ˌkrɪstɪ'ænətɪ] n Christentum das.

Christian name n Vorname der.

Christmas ['krɪsməs] n Weihnachten das; **Happy OR Merry Christmas!** Frohe Weihnachten!

Christmas card n Weihnachtskarte die.

Christmas Day n erster Weihnachtstag.

Christmas Eve n Heiligabend der.

Christmas pudding n UK schwere Süßspeise mit Trockenfrüchten, die an Weihnachten gegessen wird.

Christmas tree n Weihnachtsbaum der.

chrome [krəʊm], **chromium** ['krəʊmɪəm] <> n Chrom das. <> comp Chrom-.

chronic ['krɒnɪk] adj - 1. [illness, unemployment] chronisch - 2. [alcoholic] Gewohnheits-; [liar] chronisch.

chronicle ['krɒnɪkl] n Chronik die.

chronological [ˌkrɒnə'lɒdʒɪkl] adj chronologisch.

chrysanthemum [krɪ'sænθəməm] (pl -s) n Chrysantheme die.

chubby ['tʃʌbɪ] adj mollig.

chuck [tʃʌk] vt inf - 1. [throw] schmeißen - 2. [job] hinlschmeißen; [girlfriend, boyfriend] Schluss machen mit. **chuck away, chuck out** vt sep inf weglschmeißen.

chuckle ['tʃʌkl] vi in sich (A) hineinllachen.

chug [tʃʌg] vi tuckern.

chum [tʃʌm] n inf [friend] Kumpel der.

chunk [tʃʌŋk] n - 1. [of bread, cheese] Stück das - 2. inf [large amount] großer Teil.

church [tʃɜːtʃ] n Kirche die; **to go to church** in die Kirche gehen.

Church of England n: **the Church of England** die Anglikanische Kirche.

churchyard ['tʃɜːtʃjɑːd] n Friedhof der.

churlish ['tʃɜːlɪʃ] adj [impolite] unhöflich; [loutish] ungehobelt.

churn [tʃɜːn] <> n - 1. [for making butter] Butterfass das - 2. [for milk] Milchkanne die. <> vt [stir up] auflwühlen. **churn out** vt sep inf am laufenden Band produzieren.

chute [ʃuːt] *n* Rutsche *die*; [for rubbish] Müllschlucker *der*.

chutney ['tʃʌtnɪ] *n* Chutney *das*.

CIA (*abbr of* **Central Intelligence Agency**) *n* CIA *die ODER der*.

CID (*abbr of* **Criminal Investigation Department**) *n* ≃ Kripo *die*.

cider ['saɪdər] *n* Cidre *der*, Apfelwein *der*.

cigar [sɪ'gɑːr] *n* Zigarre *die*.

cigarette [ˌsɪgə'ret] *n* Zigarette *die*.

cinder ['sɪndər] *n* Asche *die*.

Cinderella [ˌsɪndə'relə] *n* Aschenputtel *das*.

cinecamera [ˌsɪnɪˈkæmərə] *n* Filmkamera *die*.

cinema ['sɪnəmə] *n* Kino *das*.

cinnamon ['sɪnəmən] *n* Zimt *der*.

cipher ['saɪfər] *n* [secret writing system] Chiffre *die*, Kode *der*.

circa ['sɜːkə] *prep* etwa, zirka.

circle ['sɜːkl] <> *n* - **1.** [gen] Kreis *der*; **to go round in circles** sich im Kreis bewegen - **2.** [in theatre, cinema] Balkon *der*. <> *vt* - **1.** [draw a circle round] einJkreisen - **2.** [move round] umkreisen. <> *vi* kreisen.

circuit ['sɜːkɪt] *n* - **1.** ELEC Stromkreis *der* - **2.** [lap] Runde *die* - **3.** [motor racing track] Rennstrecke *die* - **4.** [series of venues] Tour *die*.

circuitous [sə'kjuːɪtəs] *adj* umständlich.

circular ['sɜːkjʊlər] <> *adj* - **1.** [in shape] rund, kreisförmig - **2.** [route] Rund-. <> *n* - **1.** [letter, memo] Rundschreiben *das* - **2.** [advertisement] Wurfsendung *die*.

circulate ['sɜːkjʊleɪt] <> *vi* - **1.** [gen] zirkulieren - **2.** [rumour, story] umlgehen, kursieren - **3.** [socialize] sich unter die Leute mischen. <> *vt* - **1.** [document] zirkulieren lassen - **2.** [rumour, story] in Umlauf setzen.

circulation [ˌsɜːkjʊ'leɪʃn] *n* - **1.** [of blood] Zirkulation *die*, Kreislauf *der* - **2.** [of money, document] Umlauf *der*; **in circulation** im Umlauf - **3.** [of magazine, newspaper] Auflage *die* - **4.** [of heat, air] Zirkulation *die*.

circumcision [ˌsɜːkəm'sɪʒn] *n* Beschneidung *die*.

circumference [sə'kʌmfərəns] *n* Umfang *der*.

circumflex ['sɜːkəmfleks] *n*: **circumflex (accent)** Zirkumflex *der*.

circumspect ['sɜːkəmspekt] *adj* umsichtig.

circumstances ['sɜːkəmstənsɪz] *npl* Umstände *Pl*; **under** OR **in no circumstances** unter keinen Umständen, auf keinen Fall; **under** OR **in the circumstances** unter diesen Umständen.

circumvent [ˌsɜːkəm'vent] *vt fml* umlgehen.

circus ['sɜːkəs] *n* Zirkus *der*.

cistern ['sɪstən] *n* - **1.** UK [in roof] Wassertank *der* - **2.** [in toilet] Spülkasten *der*.

cite [saɪt] *vt* - **1.** [mention, quote] zitieren - **2.** LAW vorladen.

citizen ['sɪtɪzn] *n* - **1.** [of country] Staatsbürger *der*, -in *die* - **2.** [of town] Bürger *der*, -in *die*.

Citizens' Advice Bureau *n* Bürgerberatungsstelle *die*.

Citizens' Band *n* CB-Funk *der*.

citizenship ['sɪtɪznʃɪp] *n* [nationality] Staatsangehörigkeit *die*.

citrus fruit ['sɪtrəs-] *n* Zitrusfrucht *die*.

city ['sɪtɪ] *n* Stadt *die*; [large] Großstadt *die*.
➤ **City** *n* UK: **the City** Londoner Finanzviertel.

city centre *n* Innenstadt *die*.

city hall *n* US Rathaus *das*.

civic ['sɪvɪk] *adj* - **1.** [leader, event] Stadt- - **2.** [duty, pride] bürgerlich, Bürger-.

civil ['sɪvl] *adj* - **1.** [disorder, marriage] zivil - **2.** [polite] höflich.

civil engineering *n* Hoch- und Tiefbau *der*.

civilian [sɪ'vɪljən] <> *n* Zivilist *der*, -in *die*. <> *comp* [government] Zivil-; [organization] zivil; **in civilian clothes** in Zivil.

civilization [ˌsɪvəlaɪ'zeɪʃn] *n* - **1.** [advanced world] Zivilisation *die* - **2.** [society, culture] Kultur *die*.

civilized ['sɪvəlaɪzd] *adj* zivilisiert.

civil law *n* bürgerliches Recht.

civil liberties *npl* Freiheitsrechte *Pl*.

civil rights *npl* Bürgerrechte *Pl*.

civil servant *n* Beamte *der*, -in *die* (im Staatsdienst).

civil service *n* Staatsdienst *der*.

civil war *n* Bürgerkrieg *der*.

CJD (*abbr of* **Creutzfeldt-Jakob disease**) *n* CJK *die*.

cl (*abbr of* **centilitre**) *n* cl.

clad [klæd] *adj liter* [dressed]: **clad in sthg** in etw (D) gekleidet.

claim [kleɪm] <> *n* - **1.** [for territory, expenses, refund] Anspruch *der*; [demand] Forderung *die*; **to lay claim to sthg** etw für sich beanspruchen - **2.** [assertion] Behauptung *die*. <> *vt* - **1.** [money] beantragen; [lost property] beanspruchen; [expenses] einlreichen; [credit] für sich in Anspruch nehmen; **he claimed responsibility for it** er bekannte, dafür verantwortlich zu sein - **2.** [assert] behaupten. <> *vi*: **to claim for sthg** Ansprüche auf etw (A) geltend machen.

claimant ['kleɪmənt] *n* Antragsteller *der*, -in *die*; LAW Kläger *der*, -in *die*.

clairvoyant [kleə'vɔɪənt] *n* Hellseher *der*, -in *die*.

clam [klæm] *n* Klaffmuschel *die*.

clamber ['klæmbər] *vi* klettern.

clammy ['klæmɪ] *adj inf* [skin] feucht und klamm; [weather] schwül.

clamour *UK*, **clamor** *US* ['klæmər] *vi*: to clamour for sthg etw lautstark fordern.

clamp [klæmp] <> *n* - **1.** [fastener] Schraubzwinge *die* - **2.** MED & TECH Klemme *die*. <> *vt* - **1.** [with fastener] festklemmen - **2.** [parked car] Parkkralle anlegen (+ *D*). ❧ **clamp down** *vi*: to clamp down (on) durchgreifen (gegen).

clan [klæn] *n* Clan *der*.

clandestine [klæn'destɪn] *adj* geheim.

clang [klæŋ] *n* [of bell] lautes Tönen.

clap [klæp] <> *vt* Beifall klatschen (+ *D*); to clap one's hands in die Hände klatschen; to clap eyes on sb/sthg jn/etw zu Gesicht bekommen. <> *vi* Beifall klatschen.

clapping ['klæpɪŋ] *n* Beifall *der*.

claret ['klærət] *n* [wine] roter Bordeaux.

clarify ['klærɪfaɪ] *vt* (näher) erläutern.

clarinet [,klærə'net] *n* Klarinette *die*.

clarity ['klærətɪ] *n* Klarheit *die*.

clash [klæʃ] <> *n* - **1.** [incompatibility]: a clash of interests ein Interessenkonflikt; a clash of personalities ein Zusammenprall verschiedener Persönlichkeiten - **2.** [fight] Zusammenstoß *der* - **3.** [disagreement] Meinungsverschiedenheit *die*. <> *vi* - **1.** [ideas, beliefs] aufeinander prallen; [colours] sich beißen - **2.** [fight]: to clash (with sb) (mit jm) zusammenstoßen - **3.** [disagree]: to clash (with sb) (mit jm) aneinander geraten.

clasp [klɑːsp] <> *n* [on necklace, bracelet] Verschluss *der*; [on belt] Schnalle *die*. <> *vt* ergreifen.

class [klɑːs] <> *n* - **1.** [gen] Klasse *die* - **2.** [lesson] Stunde *die*; an evening class ein Abendkurs - **3.** [social group] Schicht *die*; upper class Oberschicht *die*; the working class die Arbeiterklasse. <> *vt* einstufen; to class sb as sthg jn als etw einstufen.

classic ['klæsɪk] <> *adj* [gen] klassisch. <> *n* Klassiker *der*.

classical ['klæsɪkl] *adj* - **1.** klassisch - **2.** [sculpture, architecture] klassizistisch.

classified ['klæsɪfaɪd] *adj* [secret]: classified information Verschlusssache *die*.

classified ad *n* Annonce *die*.

classify ['klæsɪfaɪ] *vt* klassifizieren.

classmate ['klɑːsmeɪt] *n* Klassenkamerad *der*, -in *die*.

classroom ['klɑːsrʊm] *n* Klassenzimmer *das*.

classy ['klɑːsɪ] *adj inf* [clothes, restaurant] nobel; [car] edel; [person] vornehm.

clatter ['klætər] *n* Geklapper *das*.

clause [klɔːz] *n* - **1.** [in legal document] Klausel *die* - **2.** GRAM Satz *der*.

claw [klɔː] <> *n* [of animal, bird] Kralle *die*. <> *vt* kratzen. <> *vi*: to claw at sthg sich an etw (*A*) krallen.

clay [kleɪ] *n* [soil] Lehm *der*; [for pottery] Ton *der*.

clean [kliːn] <> *adj* - **1.** [gen] sauber - **2.** [reputation, driving licence] tadellos - **3.** [joke] harmlos - **4.** [line, movement] klar - **5.** [break] glatt. <> *vt* sauber machen; to clean one's teeth *UK* sich (*D*) die Zähne putzen. <> *vi* putzen. ❧ **clean out** *vt sep* [room, cupboard] gründlich aufräumen. ❧ **clean up** *vt sep* [mess] aufräumen; [with cloth] sauber machen; to clean o.s. up sich waschen.

cleaner ['kliːnər] *n* - **1.** [person] Putzfrau *die* - **2.** [substance] Reiniger *der*.

cleaning ['kliːnɪŋ] *n*: to do the cleaning sauber machen.

cleanliness ['klenlɪnɪs] *n* Reinlichkeit *die*.

cleanse [klenz] *vt* [skin, wound] säubern.

cleanser ['klenzər] *n* - **1.** [for skin] Reinigungsmilch *die* - **2.** [detergent] Reinigungsmittel *das*.

clean-shaven [-'ʃeɪvn] *adj* glatt rasiert.

clear [klɪər] <> *adj* - **1.** [gen] klar; to make sthg clear (to sb) (jm) etw klar machen; to make it clear that... deutlich machen, dass...; to make o.s. clear sich klar ausdrücken - **2.** [obvious] eindeutig - **3.** [sound] deutlich; [speaker] deutlich hörbar - **4.** [skin, complexion, conscience] rein - **5.** [road, view] frei; try and keep Friday clear versuch dir Freitag freizuhalten. <> *adv*: stand clear! zurücktreten!; to be clear of sthg etw nicht berühren; to stay clear of sb, to steer clear of sb jm aus dem Wege gehen; to stay clear of sthg, to steer clear of sthg etw meiden. <> *vt* - **1.** [path, road] räumen; [pipe] reinigen; to clear the table den Tisch abräumen - **2.** [take out of the way] aus dem Weg räumen - **3.** [jump over] überspringen - **4.** [debt] begleichen - **5.** [authorize] genehmigen - **6.** [prove not guilty] freisprechen; to clear one's name seinen Namen reinlwaschen; to be cleared of sthg von etw freigesprochen werden. <> *vi* [fog, smoke] sich verziehen; [weather] sich aufklären. ❧ **clear away** *vt sep* wegräumen. ❧ **clear off** *vi UK inf* ablhauen. ❧ **clear out** <> *vt sep* [room, cupboard] gründlich aufräumen. <> *vi inf* [leave] verschwinden. ❧ **clear up** <> *vt sep* - **1.** [tidy] aufräumen; [toys, litter] wegräumen - **2.** [mystery] aufklären; [problem, confusion] klären. <> *vi* - **1.** [weather] sich aufklären - **2.** [tidy up] aufräumen.

clearance ['klɪərəns] *n* (*U*) [permission] Genehmigung *die*; [for takeoff] Starterlaubnis *die*.

clear-cut *adj* klar umrissen.

clearing ['klɪərɪŋ] *n* [in forest] Lichtung *die*.

clearly ['klɪəlɪ] *adv* - **1.** [speak, write] deutlich - **2.** [think, explain] klar - **3.** [obviously] eindeutig.

cleavage ['kliːvɪdʒ] *n* [between breasts] Dekolletee *das*.

cleaver ['kliːvər] *n* Hackbeil *das*.

clef [klef] *n* Notenschlüssel *der*.

cleft [kleft] *n* [in rock] Spalt *der*.

clench [klentʃ] *vt* umklammern; [fist] ballen; [teeth] zusammenlbeißen.

clergy ['klɜːdʒɪ] *npl*: **the clergy** die Geistlichkeit.

clergyman ['klɜːdʒɪmən] (*pl* -**men** [-mən]) *n* Geistliche *der*.

clerical ['klerɪkl] *adj* - **1.** [in office] Büro- - **2.** [in church] geistlich.

clerk [UK klɑːk, US klɜːrk] *n* - **1.** [in office] Büroangestellte *der*, *die* - **2.** [in court] Gerichtsschreiber *der*, -**in** *die* - **3.** US [shop assistant] Verkäufer *der*, -**in** *die*.

clever ['klevər] *adj* - **1.** [person] klug; **to be clever with one's hands** geschickte Hände haben - **2.** [idea, device] raffiniert.

click [klɪk] ⬥ *n* Klicken *das*. ⬥ *vt* [fingers] schnippen mit; [tongue] schnalzen mit. ⬥ *vi* [gen & COMPUT] klicken; **to click on sthg** COMPUT etw anlklicken; **suddenly it all clicked** plötzlich wurde alles klar.

client ['klaɪənt] *n* Kunde *der*, -**din** *die*; [of lawyer] Klient *der*, -**in** *die*.

cliff [klɪf] *n* [by sea] Klippe *die*.

climate ['klaɪmɪt] *n liter & fig* Klima *das*.

climax ['klaɪmæks] *n* [culmination] Höhepunkt *der*.

climb [klaɪm] ⬥ *n* [of mountain] Aufstieg *der*. ⬥ *vt* [tree, wall] hochlklettern; [rope] hochlklettern an (+ D); [ladder, stairs] hinauflsteigen; [hill] steigen auf (+ A); [mountain] besteigen. ⬥ *vi* - **1.** [person, plant] klettern - **2.** [road, prices, costs] anlsteigen; [plane] (auf)lsteigen.

climber ['klaɪmər] *n* [person] Kletterer *der*, -**rin** *die*; [mountaineer] Bergsteiger *der*, -**in** *die*.

climbing ['klaɪmɪŋ] *n* Klettern *das*; [mountaineering] Bergsteigen *das*; **to go climbing** bergsteigen gehen.

clinch [klɪntʃ] *vt* [deal] ablschließen.

cling [klɪŋ] (*pt & pp* clung) *vi* - **1.** [hold tightly]: **to cling to** sich klammern an (+ A) - **2.** [clothes]: **to cling (to sb)** sich (an jn) anlschmiegen.

clingfilm ['klɪŋfɪlm] *n (U)* UK Frischhaltefolie *die*.

clinic ['klɪnɪk] *n* Klinik *die*.

clinical ['klɪnɪkl] *adj* - **1.** MED klinisch - **2.** [coldly rational] nüchtern.

clink [klɪŋk] *vi* klirren.

clip [klɪp] ⬥ *n* - **1.** [fastener] Klammer *die*; [on earring] Klipp *der* - **2.** [of film, video] Ausschnitt *der*, Clip *der*. ⬥ *vt* - **1.** [fasten]: **to clip sthg onto sthg** [papers] etw an etw (A) heften - **2.** [cut] schneiden.

clipboard ['klɪpbɔːd] *n* - **1.** [for hair] Klemmbrett *das* - **2.** COMPUT Zwischenablage *die*.

clippers ['klɪpəz] *npl* - **1.** [for hair] Haarschneidemaschine *die* - **2.** [for nails] Nagelknipser *der*, Nagelzange *die*.

clipping ['klɪpɪŋ] *n* [newspaper cutting] Zeitungsausschnitt *der*.

cloak [kləʊk] *n* [garment] Umhang *der*.

cloakroom ['kləʊkrʊm] *n* - **1.** [for clothes] Garderobe *die* - **2.** UK [toilets] Waschraum *der*.

clock [klɒk] *n* - **1.** [gen] Uhr *die*; **round the clock** rund um die Uhr - **2.** [mileometer] Tachometer *der*. ⬥ **clock in** *vi* UK [at work] (den Arbeitsbeginn) stechen. ⬥ **clock off** *vi* UK [at work] (das Arbeitsende) stechen.

clockwise ['klɒkwaɪz] *adj & adv* im Uhrzeigersinn.

clockwork ['klɒkwɜːk] ⬥ *n*: **like clockwork** wie am Schnürchen. ⬥ *comp* [toy, train] zum Aufziehen.

clog [klɒg] *vt* verstopfen. ⬥ **clogs** *npl* Clogs *Pl*. ⬥ **clog up** *vt sep & vi* verstopfen.

close¹ [kləʊs] ⬥ *adj* - **1.** [near] nahe; **close to** nahe an (+ D); [with verbs of motion] nahe an (+ A); **the house is close to the river** das Haus steht nahe am Fluss; **she sat down close to me** sie setzte sich in meine Nähe; **don't get too close to the edge** geh nicht zu nahe an den Abgrund; **that was a close shave** OR **thing** OR **call** das war knapp; **when seen from close up** OR **to** aus der Nähe betrachtet - **2.** [friend, contact, link] eng; **to be close to sb** jm nahe stehen - **3.** [resemblance] stark - **4.** [examination, inspection] genau; **on closer examination** bei näherer Betrachtung - **5.** [weather] schwül - **6.** [race, contest] knapp. ⬥ *adv* nah; **close by, close at hand** in der Nähe; **close behind** dicht dahinter; **to stand close together** nahe beieinander stehen. ⬥ **close on, close to** *prep* [almost] beinahe.

close² [kləʊz] ⬥ *vt* - **1.** [gen] schließen - **2.** [road] sperren - **3.** [meeting, event] beenden; [speech, novel] beschließen - **4.** [bank account] aufllösen - **5.** [deal] ablschließen. ⬥ *vi* - **1.** [door, eyes, wound] sich schließen - **2.** [shop, office, book, share price] schließen - **3.** [deadline, offer] enden. ⬥ *n* [end] Schluss *der*; **to draw to a close** zu Ende gehen. ⬥ **close down** ⬥ *vt sep* [shut] schließen. ⬥ *vi* [shut down] stillgelegt werden.

closed [kləʊzd] *adj* geschlossen.

close-knit [,kləʊs-] *adj* eng verbunden.

closely ['kləʊslɪ] *adv* - **1.** [gen] eng; [resemble] stark - **2.** [watch, guard, listen] genau; [follow] dicht.

closet ['klɒzɪt] ⬥ *adj inf* heimlich; **he's a closet socialist** er ist ein verkappter Sozialist. ⬥ *n* US Schrank *der*.

close-up ['kləʊs-] *n* Nahaufnahme *die*.

closing time *n* [for pubs] Sperrstunde *die*; [for shops] Ladenschlusszeit *die*.

closure ['kləʊʒəʳ] n - 1. [of business, company] Schließung die - 2. [of road, railway line] Sperrung die.

clot [klɒt] ◇ n - 1. [lump] Klumpen der; [of blood] Blutgerinnsel das - 2. UK inf [fool] Hornochse der. ◇ vi [blood] gerinnen.

cloth [klɒθ] n - 1. (U) [material] Stoff der - 2. [for cleaning] Lappen der - 3. [tablecloth] Tischtuch das.

clothe [kləʊð] vt fml [dress] kleiden.

clothes [kləʊðz] npl Kleider Pl; to put one's clothes on sich anlziehen; to take one's clothes off sich auslziehen.

clothes brush n Kleiderbürste die.

clothesline ['kləʊðzlaɪn] n Wäscheleine die.

clothes peg UK, **clothespin** US ['kləʊðzpɪn] n Wäscheklammer die.

clothing ['kləʊðɪŋ] n Kleidung die; a piece of clothing ein Kleidungsstück.

cloud [klaʊd] n Wolke die. ◆ **cloud over** vi [sky] sich bewölken.

cloudy ['klaʊdɪ] adj - 1. [day, sky] bedeckt - 2. [beer, water] trüb.

clout [klaʊt] inf ◇ n (U) [influence] Schlagkraft die. ◇ vt [hit] schlagen.

clove [kləʊv] n: a clove of garlic eine Knoblauchzehe. ◆ **cloves** npl [spice] Gewürznelken Pl.

clover ['kləʊvəʳ] n Klee der.

clown [klaʊn] ◇ n - 1. [performer] Clown der - 2. [fool] Idiot der. ◇ vi herumlalbern.

cloying ['klɔɪɪŋ] adj - 1. [scent] süßlich - 2. [sentimentality] kitschig.

club [klʌb] ◇ n - 1. [association] Klub der - 2. [nightclub] Nachtklub der - 3. [weapon] Knüppel der, Prügel der - 4. SPORT [equipment]: (golf) club (Golf)schläger der. ◇ vt [hit] prügeln. ◆ **clubs** npl [playing cards] Kreuz das; the six of clubs die Kreuzsechs. ◆ **club together** vi UK zusammenllegen.

clubhouse ['klʌbhaʊs] (pl [-haʊzɪz]) n Klubhaus das.

cluck [klʌk] vi [hen] gackern.

clue [klu:] n [hint] Hinweis der; [in crime] Spur die; [in crossword] Frage die; I haven't (got) a clue (about) ich habe keine Ahnung (von).

clued-up [klu:d-] adj UK inf gut informiert.

clump [klʌmp] n [of trees, flowers] Gruppe die.

clumsy ['klʌmzɪ] adj [person] tollpatschig; [movement, remark] ungeschickt.

clung [klʌŋ] pt & pp ⊏ **cling**.

cluster ['klʌstəʳ] ◇ n Gruppe die; [of grapes] Traube die. ◇ vi - 1. [people] sich scharen - 2. [things] sich drängen.

clutch [klʌtʃ] ◇ n AUT Kupplung die. ◇ vt festlhalten. ◇ vi: to clutch at sb/sthg nach jm/etw greifen.

clutter ['klʌtəʳ] n Unordnung die.

cm (abbr of centimetre) n cm.

c/o (abbr of care of) = **care**.

Co. abbr of **Company**, **County**.

coach [kəʊtʃ] ◇ n - 1. [bus] (Reise)bus der - 2. RAIL Wagen der - 3. [horsedrawn] Kutsche die - 4. SPORT Trainer der, -in die - 5. [tutor] Nachhilfelehrer der, -in die. ◇ vt - 1. SPORT trainieren - 2. [tutor]: to coach sb (in sthg) jm Nachhilfestunden (in etw (D)) geben.

coach station n Busbahnhof der.

coal [kəʊl] n (U) [mineral] Kohle die.

coalfield ['kəʊlfi:ld] n Kohlenrevier das.

coalition [,kəʊə'lɪʃn] n POL Koalition die; **coalition government** Koalitionsregierung die.

coalmine ['kəʊlmaɪn] n Kohlenbergwerk das.

coarse [kɔ:s] adj - 1. [rough - hair] dick; [- skin] derb; [- sandpaper, fabric] grob - 2. [vulgar - remark, laugh] ordinär; [- joke] derb; [- person] ordinär.

coast [kəʊst] ◇ n Küste die. ◇ vi [car] im Leerlauf fahren.

coastal ['kəʊstl] adj Küsten-.

coaster ['kəʊstəʳ] n Untersetzer der.

coastguard ['kəʊstgɑ:d] n - 1. [person] Mitglied das der Küstenwache - 2. [organization]: the coastguard die Küstenwache.

coastline ['kəʊstlaɪn] n Küste die.

coat [kəʊt] ◇ n - 1. [garment] Mantel der - 2. [of animal] Fell das - 3. [of paint, varnish] Schicht die. ◇ vt: to coat sthg (with sthg) etw (mit etw) überziehen.

coat hanger n Kleiderbügel der.

coating ['kəʊtɪŋ] n [of chocolate] Überzug der; [of dust] Schicht die.

coat of arms (pl coats of arms) n Wappen das.

coax [kəʊks] vt: to coax sb (to do OR into doing sthg) jn überreden(, etw zu tun).

cob [kɒb] n ⊏ **corn on the cob**.

cobbles ['kɒblz], **cobblestones** ['kɒblstəʊnz] npl Kopfsteinpflaster das.

cobweb ['kɒbweb] n Spinnennetz das.

cocaine [kəʊ'keɪn] n Kokain das.

cock [kɒk] ◇ n - 1. [male chicken] Hahn der - 2. [male bird] Männchen das - 3. vulg [penis] Schwanz der. ◇ vt - 1.: to cock a gun den Hahn einer Schusswaffe spannen - 2. [head]: to cock one's head (to one side) den Kopf auf die Seite legen. ◆ **cock up** vt sep UK v inf versauen.

cockerel ['kɒkrəl] n junger Hahn.

cockle ['kɒkl] n Herzmuschel die.

Cockney ['kɒknɪ] (pl -ies) n - 1. [person] Cockney der - 2. [dialect, accent] Cockney das.

cockpit ['kɒkpɪt] n Cockpit das.

cockroach ['kɒkrəʊtʃ] n Küchenschabe die.

cocktail ['kɒkteɪl] n Cocktail der.

cocktail party n Cocktailparty die.

cock-up n v inf: **to make a cock-up** Scheiße bauen; **to make a cock-up of sthg** etw versauen.

cocky ['kɒkɪ] adj inf überheblich.

cocoa ['kəʊkəʊ] n Kakao der.

coconut ['kəʊkənʌt] n Kokosnuss die.

cod [kɒd] (pl inv OR -s) n Kabeljau der.

COD abbr of **cash on delivery**.

code [kəʊd] ⟨⟩ n - 1. [cipher] Kode der - 2. [set of rules] Kodex der; **code of behaviour** Verhaltenskodex der - 3. TELEC Vorwahl die. ⟨⟩ vt - 1. [encode] verschlüsseln, chiffrieren - 2. [give identifier to] kennzeichnen.

cod-liver oil n Lebertran der.

coerce [kəʊ'ɜːs] vt zwingen; **to coerce sb into doing sthg** jn dazu zwingen, etw zu tun.

C of E n abbr of **Church of England**.

coffee ['kɒfɪ] n Kaffee der.

coffee bar n UK Café das.

coffee break n Kaffeepause die.

coffee morning n UK morgendliches Kaffeetrinken, das zu Wohltätigkeitszwecken organisiert wird.

coffeepot ['kɒfɪpɒt] n Kaffeekanne die.

coffee shop n - 1. UK [café] Café das - 2. US [restaurant] Café das - 3. [shop selling coffee] Kaffeegeschäft das.

coffee table n Couchtisch der.

coffin ['kɒfɪn] n Sarg der.

cog [kɒg] n [tooth on wheel] Zahn der; [wheel] Zahnrad das.

coherent [kəʊ'hɪərənt] adj [answer] folgerichtig; [theory, ideas, story, speech] schlüssig; [account] zusammenhängend.

cohesive [kəʊ'hiːsɪv] adj [united - group] einheitlich; [- image] stimmig.

coil [kɔɪl] ⟨⟩ n - 1. [of rope, wire] Rolle die; [of hair] Locke die; [of smoke] Kringel der - 2. ELEC Spule die - 3. UK [contraceptive device] Spirale die. ⟨⟩ vt auflrollen; **to coil sthg around sb/sthg** etw um jn/etw wickeln. ⟨⟩ vi sich ringeln. ⇨ **coil up** vt sep auflrollen.

coin [kɔɪn] ⟨⟩ n Münze die. ⟨⟩ vt [invent] prägen.

coincide [ˌkəʊɪn'saɪd] vi - 1. [occur simultaneously]: **to coincide (with sthg)** (mit etw) zusammenlfallen - 2. [be in agreement] übereinlstimmen.

coincidence [kəʊ'ɪnsɪdəns] n Zufall der.

coincidental [kəʊˌɪnsɪ'dentl] adj zufällig.

coke [kəʊk] n - 1. [fuel] Koks der - 2. drug sl [cocaine] Koks der.

cola ['kəʊlə] n Cola die ODER das.

colander ['kʌləndəʳ] n Sieb das.

cold [kəʊld] ⟨⟩ adj - 1. [gen] kalt; **I'm cold** mir ist kalt - 2. [unfriendly - eyes, smile, voice] kalt; [- person] gefühlskalt. ⟨⟩ n - 1. [illness] Erkältung die; **to catch (a) cold** sich erkälten - 2. [low temperature] Kälte die.

cold-blooded [-'blʌdɪd] adj - 1. [unfeeling - person] gefühllos; [- attitude] herzlos - 2. [ruthless] kaltblütig.

cold calling n unaufgeforderte Telefonwerbung die.

cold sore n Bläschenausschlag der.

cold war n: **the cold war** der Kalte Krieg.

coleslaw ['kəʊlslɔː] n (U) Krautsalat der.

collaborate [kə'læbəreɪt] vi - 1. [work together]: **to collaborate (with sb)** (mit jm) zusammenlarbeiten - 2. pej [with enemy]: **to collaborate (with sb)** (mit jm) kollaborieren.

collapse [kə'læps] ⟨⟩ n - 1. [destruction] Einsturz der - 2. [failure - of marriage, government] Scheitern das; [- of empire] Untergang der; [- of system, business, company] Zusammenbruch der - 3. MED Kollaps der. ⟨⟩ vi - 1. [fall down, fall in - house, building, roof] einlstürzen; [- stage, bridge] zusammenlbrechen; [- lung] zusammenlfallen; (phrase): **I collapsed into bed** ich ließ mich aufs Bett fallen - 2. [fail - marriage, government] scheitern; [- system, business, company] zusammenlbrechen - 3. MED kollabieren - 4. [folding table, chair] sich zusammenlklappen lassen.

collapsible [kə'læpsəbl] adj zusammenklappbar.

collar ['kɒləʳ] ⟨⟩ n - 1. [on clothes] Kragen der - 2. [for dog] Halsband das - 3. TECH Bund der. ⟨⟩ vt inf [detain] fassen.

collarbone ['kɒləbəʊn] n Schlüsselbein das.

collate [kə'leɪt] vt - 1. [information, evidence] sammeln - 2. [pages, photocopies] sortieren.

collateral [kə'lætərəl] n Sicherheit die.

colleague ['kɒliːg] n Kollege der, -gin die.

collect [kə'lekt] ⟨⟩ vt - 1. [gen] sammeln; [empty glasses, bottles] einlsammeln; [dust] anlziehen; [one's belongings] zusammenlsuchen; [taxes] einlziehen; **to collect o.s.** sich sammeln - 2. [go to get, fetch] ablholen. ⟨⟩ vi - 1. [dust, dirt] sich anlsammeln - 2. [for charity, gift] sammeln. ⟨⟩ adv US TELEC: **to call (sb) collect** ein R-Gespräch (mit jm) führen.

collection [kə'lekʃn] n - 1. [gen] Sammlung die - 2. (U) [of taxes] Einziehen das; [of rubbish] Abfuhr die; [of mail] Leerung die.

collective [kə'lektɪv] ⟨⟩ adj kollektiv. ⟨⟩ n Produktionsgenossenschaft die.

collector [kə'lektəʳ] n [as a hobby] Sammler der, -in die.

college ['kɒlɪdʒ] n - 1. [for further education] ≃ Fachhochschule die; **college of technology** technische Hochschule - 2. [of university] College das.

college of education n pädagogische Hochschule.

collide [kə'laɪd] vi: to collide (with sb/sthg) (mit jm/etw) zusammenlstoßen.

colliery ['kɒljərɪ] n Kohlengrube die.

collision [kə'lɪʒn] n [crash]: collision (with sb/sthg) Zusammenstoß der (mit jm/etw), Kollision die (mit jm/etw); to be on a collision course with sb/sthg fig mit jm/etw auf Kollisionskurs sein.

colloquial [kə'ləʊkwɪəl] adj umgangssprachlich.

collude [kə'luːd] vi: to collude with sb mit jm gemeinsame Sache machen.

Colombia [kə'lɒmbɪə] n Kolumbien nt.

colon ['kəʊlən] n - 1. ANAT Dickdarm der - 2. [punctuation mark] Doppelpunkt der.

colonel ['kɜːnl] n Oberst der.

colonial [kə'ləʊnjəl] adj kolonial-.

colonize, -ise ['kɒlənaɪz] vt kolonisieren.

colony ['kɒlənɪ] n Kolonie die.

color etc n, adj, vt & vi US = **colour** etc.

colossal [kə'lɒsl] adj gewaltig.

colour UK, **color** US ['kʌlər] <> n Farbe die; in colour in Farbe. <> adj [not black and white] Farb-. <> vt - 1. [give colour to] färben; [with pen, crayon] kolorieren - 2. fig [affect] beeinflussen. <> vi [blush] erröten.

colour bar n Rassenschranke die.

colour-blind adj farbenblind.

coloured UK, **colored** US ['kʌləd] adj farbig.

colourful UK, **colorful** US ['kʌləfʊl] adj - 1. [brightly coloured] farbenfroh - 2. [story] ereignisreich; [description] farbig - 3. [person] schillernd.

colouring UK, **coloring** US ['kʌlərɪŋ] n - 1. [dye] Farbstoff der - 2. [complexion] Gesichtsfarbe die; [of hair] Farbe die - 3. [colours] Farben Pl.

colour scheme n Farbzusammenstellung die.

colt [kəʊlt] n Hengstfohlen das.

column ['kɒləm] n - 1. [structure, of smoke] Säule die - 2. [of people, vehicles, numbers] Kolonne die - 3. [of text] Spalte die - 4. [article] Kolumne die.

columnist ['kɒləmnɪst] n Kolumnist der, -in die.

coma ['kəʊmə] n Koma das.

comb [kəʊm] <> n Kamm der. <> vt - 1. [hair] kämmen - 2. [search] durchkämmen.

combat ['kɒmbæt] <> n Kampf der. <> vt bekämpfen.

combination [ˌkɒmbɪ'neɪʃn] n - 1. (U) [act of combining] Verbindung die - 2. [mixture, for safe] Kombination die.

combine <> vt [kəm'baɪn] vereinigen; to combine sthg with sthg [two substances, activities] etw mit etw verbinden; [two qualities] etw mit etw vereinigen. <> vi [kəm'baɪn] [businesses, political parties]: to combine (with sb/sthg) sich (mit jm/etw) zusammenlschließen. <> n ['kɒmbaɪn] [group] Firmengruppe die.

combined adj: combined with sb/sthg zusammen mit jm/etw; combined efforts vereinte Anstrengungen Pl; combined attack gemeinsamer Angriff.

come [kʌm] (pt came, pp come) vi - 1. [move] kommen; come here! komm her!; coming! ich komme schon! - 2. [arrive] kommen; to come home nach Hause kommen; the news came as a shock (to him) die Nachricht war ein Schock (für ihn) - 3. [in competition, in order]: to come first/last Erster/Letzter werden; P comes before Q P kommt vor Q - 4. [become] werden; to come true wahr werden; to come undone auflgehen - 5. [be sold]: they come in packs of six es gibt sie im Sechserpack - 6. [happen]: come what may was auch geschieht - 7. [begin gradually]: we have come to think that wir sind zu der Ansicht gekommen, dass; he has come to like Baltimore inzwischen gefällt ihm Baltimore recht gut - 8. inf [have orgasm] kommen - 9. phr: come to think of it wenn es mir recht überlege. <> to come adv: for generations to come auf Generationen hin; in years to come we will look back on today with pride wir werden später mit Stolz auf diesen Tag zurückblicken. <> **come about** vi [happen] geschehen; [come into being] entstehen; how did it come about? wie ist es dazu gekommen? <> **come across** vt insep [find] stoßen auf (+ A). <> **come along** vi - 1. [arrive] kommen - 2. [progress] voranlkommen. <> **come apart** vi auseinanderlfallen. <> **come at** vt insep [attack] loslgehen auf (+ A). <> **come back** vi - 1. [gen] zurücklkommen; to come back to sthg auf etw (A) zurücklkommen - 2. [memory]: it will come back to me in a minute es wird mir gleich einfallen. <> **come by** vt insep [get, obtain]: to come by sthg an etw (A) kommen; they are hard to come by sie sind schwer zu finden. <> **come down** vi - 1. [price, rain] fallen - 2. [descend] herunterlkommen. <> **come down to** vt insep: it comes down to a choice between money and happiness es läuft auf eine Entscheidung zwischen Geld und Glück hinaus; it all comes down to profitability letztlich ist die Rentabilität entscheidend. <> **come down with** vt insep [illness] bekommen. <> **come forward** vi sich melden. <> **come from** vt insep - 1. [person]: I come from Ireland ich komme aus Irland; my family comes from Belgium meine Familie stammt aus Belgien - 2. [originate from]: caviar comes from sturgeon Kaviar stammt vom Stör; where is that noise coming from? woher kommt dieses Geräusch? <> **come in** vi - 1. [enter] hereinlkommen; come in! herein! - 2. [finish race] anlkommen; to come in first

Erste/Erster werden. ➡ **come in for** vt insep [criticism] einstecken müssen. ➡ **come into** vt insep - 1. [inherit] erben - 2. [begin to be]: to come into being eintreten. ➡ **come off** vi - 1. [button, top] abgehen - 2. [succeed] klappen - 3. [dirt, mud] abgehen - 4. phr: come off it! inf hör doch auf! ➡ **come on** vi - 1. [start] anlfangen; the rain came on es fing an zu regnen - 2. [start working - light, machine] anlgehen - 3. [progress] voranlkommen - 4. phr: come on! [as encouragement, hurry up] komm!; [in disbelief] hör doch auf! ➡ **come out** vi - 1. [become known] herauslkommen - 2. [appear - book, record] erscheinen; [- stars] zu sehen sein - 3. [go on strike] streiken - 4. [declare publicly]: to come out for/against sthg sich für/gegen etw auslsprechen - 5. [stain] herauslgehen. ➡ **come out with** vt insep [idea] anlkommen mit; [remark] machen. ➡ **come round** vi - 1. [visit] vorbeilkommen - 2. [regain consciousness] zu sich kommen. ➡ **come through** ◇ vt insep [war, illness, difficult situation] überstehen. ◇ vi [survive] durchlkommen. ➡ **come to** ◇ vt insep - 1. [reach]: to come to an end zu Ende gehen; to come to a decision zu einer Entscheidung kommen - 2. [amount to]: the bill comes to £20 das macht 20 Pfund. ◇ vi [regain consciousness] zu sich kommen. ➡ **come under** vt insep - 1. [be governed by - jurisdiction, rules] fallen unter (+ A); to come under sb's influence unter js Einfluss geraten - 2. [suffer]: to come under attack (from) angegriffen werden (von). ➡ **come up** vi - 1. [go upstairs] heraufkommen - 2. [be mentioned] erwähnt werden; to come up for discussion zur Diskussion kommen - 3. [happen] passieren - 4. [job] frei werden - 5. [sun, moon] auflgehen - 6. [be imminent] bevorlstehen; my birthday is coming up ich habe bald Geburtstag. ➡ **come up against** vt insep [difficulties, obstacles] stoßen auf (+ A); [opponent] treffen auf (+ A). ➡ **come up to** vt insep - 1. [approach - person, object] kommen zu; it's coming up to Christmas/six o'clock es ist bald Weihnachten/gleich sechs Uhr - 2. [reach]: the water comes up to my waist das Wasser reicht mir bis zur Taille. ➡ **come up with** vt insep [answer, idea, solution] sich (D) ausldenken.

comeback ['kʌmbæk] n [of person] Comeback das; to make a comeback [person] ein Come-back schaffen; [activity, style] wieder in Mode kommen.

comedian [kə'miːdjən] n Komiker der, -in die.

comedown ['kʌmdaʊn] n inf Abstieg der.

comedy ['kɒmədɪ] n - 1. [play, film] Komödie die - 2. [humour] Komik die.

comet ['kɒmɪt] n Komet der.

come-uppance [,kʌm'ʌpəns] n inf: to get one's come-uppance die Quittung kriegen.

comfort ['kʌmfət] ◇ n - 1. [ease] Behaglichkeit die - 2. [luxury] Komfort der - 3. [solace] Trost der; to take comfort from sthg Trost in etw (D) finden. ◇ vt trösten.

comfortable ['kʌmftəbl] adj - 1. [chair, shoes, sofa, life] bequem; [house, hotel, coach] komfortabel - 2. [at ease]: to be comfortable sich wohl fühlen; make yourself comfortable machen Sie es sich bequem - 3. [financially secure - income] ausreichend; to be comfortable keine finanziellen Sorgen haben - 4. [after operation, accident]: his condition is comfortable ihm geht es (den Umständen entsprechend) gut - 5. [lead] sicher; [victory] leicht.

comfortably ['kʌmftəblɪ] adv - 1. [sit] bequem; [sleep] gut - 2. [without financial difficulty] bequem - 3. [win] mühelos.

comfort station n US euph Bedürfnisanstalt die.

comic ['kɒmɪk] ◇ adj komisch. ◇ n - 1. [comedian] Komiker der, -in die - 2. [magazine] Comicheft das.

comical ['kɒmɪkl] adj ulkig, komisch.

comic strip n Comicstrip der.

coming ['kʌmɪŋ] ◇ adj [future] kommend. ◇ n: comings and goings Kommen und Gehen das.

comma ['kɒmə] n Komma das.

command [kə'mɑːnd] ◇ n - 1. [order] Befehl der; MIL Kommando das - 2. (U) [control] Kommando das - 3. [mastery] Beherrschung die; to have sthg at one's command etw zur Verfügung haben - 4. COMPUT Befehl der. ◇ vt - 1. [order]: to command sb (to do sthg) jm befehlen(, etw zu tun) - 2. MIL [control] befehligen - 3. [deserve - respect, attention, admiration] verdienen.

commandeer [,kɒmən'dɪər] vt MIL beschlagnahmen.

commander [kə'mɑːndər] n - 1. [in army] Kommandant der, Befehlshaber der - 2. [in navy] Fregattenkapitän der.

commando [kə'mɑːndəʊ] (pl -s OR -es) n - 1. [unit] Kommandotrupp der - 2. [soldier] Angehörige der, die eines Kommandotrupps.

commemorate [kə'meməreɪt] vt - 1. [honour] gedenken (+ G) - 2. [subj: statue, plaque] erinnern an (+ A).

commemoration [kə,memə'reɪʃn] n: in commemoration of zum Gedenken an (+ A).

commence [kə'mens] fml ◇ vt beginnen; to commence doing sthg (damit) beginnen, etw zu tun. ◇ vi beginnen.

commend [kə'mend] vt - 1. [praise]: to commend sb (on OR for sthg) jn (wegen etw) loben - 2. [recommend]: to commend sthg (to sb) (jm) etw empfehlen.

commensurate [kə'menʃərət] adj fml: to be commensurate with sthg etw (D) entsprechen.

comment ['kɒment] <> n Bemerkung die; **no comment** kein Kommentar. <> vt: **to comment that...** bemerken OR äußern, dass... <> vi: **to comment (on sthg)** sich (über etw (A)) äußern.

commentary ['kɒmentrɪ] n - **1.** RADIO & TV Livereportage die - **2.** [written] Kommentar der.

commentator ['kɒmenteɪtǝʳ] n RADIO & TV Reporter der, -in die.

commerce ['kɒmɜ:s] n Handel der.

commercial [kǝ'mɜ:ʃl] <> adj - **1.** [regarding business - law, organization] Handels-; [- premises] Geschäfts- - **2.** [profit-making] kommerziell. <> n [advert] Werbespot der.

commercial break n Werbepause die.

commiserate [kǝ'mɪzǝreɪt] vi: **to commiserate (with sb)** (jm) sein Mitgefühl ausprechen.

commission [kǝ'mɪʃn] <> n - **1.** (U) [money] Provision die - **2.** [piece of work] Auftrag der - **3.** [investigative body] Kommission die. <> vt [work] in Auftrag geben; **to commission sb to do sthg** jn damit beauftragen(, etw zu tun).

commissionaire [kǝ,mɪʃǝ'neǝʳ] n UK Portier der.

commissioner [kǝ'mɪʃnǝʳ] n [of police] Präsident der, -in die.

commit [kǝ'mɪt] vt - **1.** [crime, sin] begehen - **2.** [money, resources]: **to commit sthg to sthg** etw für etw bestimmen; **to commit o.s. (to sthg)** sich (auf etw (A)) festlegen; **to commit o.s. to doing sthg** sich verpflichten, etw zu tun - **3.** [consign] einlweisen; **to commit sthg to memory** sich (D) etw merken.

commitment [kǝ'mɪtmǝnt] n - **1.** [dedication] Engagement das - **2.** [responsibility] Verpflichtung die.

committee [kǝ'mɪtɪ] n Ausschuss der.

commodity [kǝ'mɒdǝtɪ] n [product] Produkt das.

common ['kɒmǝn] <> adj - **1.** [ordinary, widespread] häufig; [practice] weit verbreitet; **the common cold** die Erkältung; **the common man** der Normalbürger - **2.** [shared] gemeinsam; **it's common to us all** es ist uns allen gemein - **3.** UK pej [vulgar] gewöhnlich. <> n [land] Gemeinde die. ▪ **in common** adv gemein; **we've got a lot in common** wir haben viel gemein.

common-law adj: **she is his common-law wife** sie lebt mit ihm in eheähnlicher Gemeinschaft.

commonly ['kɒmǝnlɪ] adv [generally] allgemein.

Common Market n: **the Common Market** der Gemeinsame Markt.

commonplace ['kɒmǝnpleɪs] adj alltäglich.

common room n Aufenthaltsraum der.

Commons ['kɒmǝnz] npl UK: **the Commons** das (britische) Unterhaus.

common sense n gesunder Menschenverstand.

Commonwealth ['kɒmǝnwelθ] n: **the Commonwealth** das Commonwealth.

commotion [kǝ'mǝʊʃn] n [activity] Aufregung die; [noise] Lärm der; **to cause a commotion** für Aufregung sorgen.

communal ['kɒmjʊnl] adj [kitchen] Gemeinschafts-; [garden, ownership] gemeinsam.

commune n ['kɒmju:n] Kommune die.

communicate [kǝ'mju:nɪkeɪt] <> vt mitlteilen. <> vi sich verständigen; **to communicate with** kommunizieren mit.

communication [kǝ,mju:nɪ'keɪʃn] n - **1.** (U) [contact] Kommunikation die; **to be in communication with sb** Kontakt mit jm haben - **2.** [letter, phone call] Mitteilung die.

communication cord n UK Notbremse die.

Communion [kǝ'mju:njǝn] n [Protestant] Abendmahl das; [Catholic] Kommunion die.

Communism ['kɒmjʊnɪzm] n Kommunismus der.

Communist ['kɒmjʊnɪst] <> adj kommunistisch. <> n Kommunist der, -in die.

community [kǝ'mju:nǝtɪ] n - **1.** [group] Gemeinschaft die; [local] Gemeinde die; [ethnic] Bevölkerungsgruppe die - **2.** [people in general]: **the community** die Gesellschaft.

community centre n Gemeindezentrum das.

commutation ticket [,kɒmju:'teɪʃn] n US Zeitnetzkarte die.

commute [kǝ'mju:t] <> vt LAW umlwandeln. <> vi [to work] pendeln.

commuter [kǝ'mju:tǝʳ] n Pendler der, -in die.

compact <> adj [kǝm'pækt] kompakt; [style, text] gedrängt. <> n ['kɒmpækt] - **1.** [for face powder] Puderdose die - **2.** US AUT: **compact (car)** Kompaktauto das.

compact disc n Compactdisc die.

compact disc player n CD-Player der.

companion [kǝm'pænjǝn] n [person] Gefährte der, -tin die.

companionship [kǝm'pænjǝnʃɪp] n (U) Gesellschaft die.

company ['kʌmpǝnɪ] n - **1.** [business] Firma die; **insurance company** Versicherung die - **2.** [of actors] Schauspieltruppe die - **3.** (U) [companionship] Gesellschaft die; **she's good company** es ist schön, mit ihr zusammen zu sein; **to keep sb company** jm Gesellschaft leisten - **4.** [guests] Besuch der - **5.** MIL Kompanie die - **6.** NAUT Besatzung die.

comparable ['kɒmprǝbl] adj: **comparable (to OR with)** vergleichbar (mit).

comparative [kǝm'pærǝtɪv] adj - **1.** [relative] relativ - **2.** [study, literature] vergleichend - **3.** GRAM: **comparative form** Komparativ der.

comparatively [kəm'pærətıvlı] *adv* [relatively] relativ, verhältnismäßig.

compare [kəm'peəʳ] <> *vt* vergleichen; to compare sb/sthg with OR to jn/etw vergleichen mit; compared with OR to verglichen mit, im Vergleich zu. <> *vi*: to compare (with sb/sthg) sich (mit jm/etw) vergleichen lassen.

comparison [kəm'pærɪsn] *n* Vergleich *der*; in comparison (with OR to) im Vergleich (zu).

compartment [kəm'pɑːtmənt] *n* - 1. [in fridge, desk, drawer] Fach *das* - 2. RAIL Abteil *das*.

compass ['kʌmpəs] *n* [for finding direction] Kompass *der*. ➡ **compasses** *npl*: (a pair of) compasses ein Zirkel.

compassion [kəm'pæʃn] *n* Mitgefühl *das*.

compassionate [kəm'pæʃənət] *adj* mitfühlend.

compatible [kəm'pætəbl] *adj* - 1. [people]: to be compatible zueinander passen - 2. COMPUT kompatibel.

compel [kəm'pel] *vt* [force] zwingen; to compel sb to do sthg jn (dazu) zwingen, etw zu tun.

compelling [kəm'pelɪŋ] *adj* zwingend.

compensate ['kɒmpenseɪt] <> *vt*: to compensate sb for sthg [financially] jn für etw entschädigen. <> *vi*: to compensate for sthg etw gutmachen.

compensation [,kɒmpen'seɪʃn] *n*: compensation (for sthg) Entschädigung *die* (für etw).

compete [kəm'piːt] *vi* - 1. [vie]: to compete (for sthg) (um etw) kämpfen - 2. COMM: to compete (with sb/sthg) (mit jm/etw) konkurrieren; to compete for sthg [contract, business] um etw kämpfen - 3. [take part] teilnehmen.

competence ['kɒmpɪtəns] *n* Fähigkeit *die*.

competent ['kɒmpɪtənt] *adj* fähig.

competition [,kɒmpɪ'tɪʃn] *n* - 1. [rivalry & COMM] Konkurrenz *die* - 2. [race, contest] Wettbewerb *der*.

competitive [kəm'petətɪv] *adj* - 1. [person] vom Konkurrenzdenken geprägt - 2. [exam] Auswahl-; [sport] Wettkampf- - 3. COMM [goods, prices, company] konkurrenzfähig.

competitor [kəm'petɪtəʳ] *n* - 1. COMM Konkurrent *der*, -in *die* - 2. [in race, contest] Teilnehmer *der*, -in *die*.

compile [kəm'paɪl] *vt* [programme, album] zusammenstellen; [book, report] abfassen.

complacency [kəm'pleɪsnsɪ] *n* Selbstzufriedenheit *die*.

complain [kəm'pleɪn] *vi* - 1. [moan]: to complain (about) sich beschweren (über (+ A)) - 2. MED: to complain of sthg über etw (A) klagen.

complaint [kəm'pleɪnt] *n* - 1. [gen] Beschwerde *die*; to have no complaints [be satisfied] sich nicht beklagen können - 2. MED Leiden *das*.

complement <> *vt* ['kɒmplɪment] gut ergänzen; [food] vervollkommnen. <> *n* ['kɒmplɪmənt] [accompaniment & GRAM] Ergänzung *die*.

complementary [,kɒmplɪ'mentərɪ] *adj* [colour] (einander) ergänzend.

complete [kəm'pliːt] <> *adj* - 1. [entire] vollständig; complete with komplett mit - 2. [finished] abgeschlossen, fertig - 3. [total - disaster, surprise] völlig; she was a complete stranger to me sie war mir völlig fremd. <> *vt* - 1. [make whole] vervollständigen - 2. [finish] beenden - 3. [questionnaire, form] ausfüllen.

completely [kəm'pliːtlɪ] *adv* vollkommen.

completion [kəm'pliːʃn] *n* [finishing] Beendigung *die*.

complex ['kɒmpleks] <> *adj* [complicated] kompliziert. <> *n* - 1. [of buildings] (Gebäude)komplex *der* - 2. PSYCHOL Komplex *der*.

complexion [kəm'plekʃn] *n* - 1. [of face] Teint *der* - 2. [aspect] Aspekt *der*.

compliance [kəm'plaɪəns] *n* Einverständnis *das*; compliance with sthg [with rules] Einhalten *das* einer Sache (G).

complicate ['kɒmplɪkeɪt] *vt* komplizieren.

complicated ['kɒmplɪkeɪtɪd] *adj* kompliziert.

complication [,kɒmplɪ'keɪʃn] *n* - 1. [complexity] Kompliziertheit *die* - 2. MED Komplikation *die*.

compliment <> *n* ['kɒmplɪmənt] Kompliment *das*. <> *vt* ['kɒmplɪ,ment]: to compliment sb (on sthg) jm ein Kompliment/Komplimente (wegen etw (G)) machen. ➡ **compliments** *npl fml*: with compliments mit den besten Empfehlungen; my compliments to the chef! mein Kompliment an den Küchenchef!

complimentary [,kɒmplɪ'mentərɪ] *adj* - 1. [admiring] schmeichelhaft; to be complimentary [person] sich bewundernd äußern - 2. [drink] Frei-.

complimentary ticket *n* Freikarte *die*.

comply [kəm'plaɪ] *vi*: to comply with sthg [contract] etw erfüllen; [request] etw nachkommen; [law, standards] etw einhalten.

component [kəm'pəʊnənt] *n* Teil *das*.

compose [kəm'pəʊz] *vt* - 1. [constitute] bilden; to be composed of sthg sich aus etw zusammensetzen - 2. [poem] verfassen; [music] komponieren; [letter] abfassen - 3. [make calm]: to compose o.s. sich fassen.

composed [kəm'pəʊzd] *adj* [calm] beherrscht, gelassen.

composer [kəm'pəʊzəʳ] *n* Komponist *der*, -in *die*.

composition [ˌkɒmpəˈzɪʃn] n - **1.** [piece of music] Komposition die - **2.** [contents] Zusammensetzung die - **3.** [essay] Aufsatz der.

compost [UK 'kɒmpɒst, US 'kɒmpəʊst] n Kompost der.

composure [kəm'pəʊʒər] n Beherrschung die, Fassung die.

compound n ['kɒmpaʊnd] - **1.** CHEM Verbindung die - **2.** [mixture] Mischung die - **3.** [enclosed area] umzäuntes Gelände - **4.** GRAM zusammengesetztes Wort.

comprehend [ˌkɒmprɪ'hend] vt [understand] begreifen, verstehen.

comprehension [ˌkɒmprɪ'henʃn] n Verständnis das; **it's beyond my comprehension** es ist mir unbegreiflich.

comprehensive [ˌkɒmprɪ'hensɪv] adj - **1.** [wide-ranging] umfassend - **2.** [insurance] Vollkasko-.

comprehensive (school) n UK Gesamtschule die.

compress ⟨⟩ n [ˌkɒmpres] MED Kompresse die. ⟨⟩ vt [kəm'pres] - **1.** [squeeze] zusammenpressen; **compressed air** Pressluft die - **2.** [text] kürzen.

comprise [kəm'praɪz] vt - **1.** [consist of]: **to be comprised of** bestehen aus - **2.** [constitute] bilden.

compromise ['kɒmprəmaɪz] ⟨⟩ n Kompromiss der. ⟨⟩ vt kompromittieren. ⟨⟩ vi einen Kompromiss schließen.

compulsion [kəm'pʌlʃn] n Zwang der.

compulsive [kəm'pʌlsɪv] adj [behaviour, gambler, liar] zwanghaft.

compulsory [kəm'pʌlsərɪ] adj [retirement] Zwangs-; **it is compulsory to do sthg** es ist Pflicht, etw zu tun; **attendance is compulsory** die Teilnahme ist verpflichtend.

computer [kəm'pju:tər] ⟨⟩ n Computer der. ⟨⟩ comp Computer-.

computer game n Computerspiel das.

computerized [kəm'pju:təraɪzd] adj computerisiert.

computer science n Informatik die.

computing [kəm'pju:tɪŋ] n elektronische Datenverarbeitung; [subject] Informatik die.

comrade ['kɒmreɪd] n - **1.** POL Genosse der, -sin die - **2.** [companion] Kamerad der, -in die.

con [kɒn] inf ⟨⟩ n [trick] Schwindel der. ⟨⟩ vt [trick] reinlegen; **to con sb out of sthg** jn um etw bringen; **to con sb into doing sthg** jn durch einen Trick dazu bringen, etw zu tun.

concave [ˌkɒn'keɪv] adj konkav.

conceal [kən'si:l] vt (phrase): **to conceal sthg (from sb)** [object] etw (vor jm) verstecken; [feelings, information] etw (vor jm) verbergen.

concede [kən'si:d] vt [a point] zulegeben; [defeat] einlgestehen.

conceit [kən'si:t] n Arroganz die.

conceited [kən'si:tɪd] adj eingebildet.

conceive [kən'si:v] ⟨⟩ vt - **1.** [plan, idea] sich (D) ausldenken - **2.** MED [child] empfangen. ⟨⟩ vi - **1.** MED empfangen - **2.** [imagine]: **to conceive of sthg** sich (D) etw vorlstellen.

concentrate ['kɒnsəntreɪt] ⟨⟩ vt konzentrieren. ⟨⟩ vi: **to concentrate (on)** sich konzentrieren (auf (+ A)).

concentration [ˌkɒnsən'treɪʃn] n Konzentration die.

concentration camp n Konzentrationslager das, KZ das.

concept ['kɒnsept] n [idea] Vorstellung die; [principle] Konzept das.

concern [kən'sɜ:n] ⟨⟩ n - **1.** [worry] Besorgnis die; [cause of worry] Sorge die; **to show concern for sb/sthg** sich um jn/etw Gedanken machen - **2.** COMM [company] Unternehmen das. ⟨⟩ vt - **1.** [worry] beunruhigen; **to be concerned (about)** besorgt sein (um) - **2.** [involve] anlgehen; **to be concerned with sthg** [subj: person] mit etw zu tun haben; **to concern o.s. with sthg** sich mit etw befassen; **as far as I'm concerned** was mich betrifft - **3.** [subj: book, film] handeln von.

concerning [kən'sɜ:nɪŋ] prep bezüglich (+ G).

concert ['kɒnsət] n Konzert das.

concerted [kən'sɜ:tɪd] adj [effort] vereint.

concert hall n Konzerthalle die.

concertina [ˌkɒnsə'ti:nə] n Konzertina die.

concerto [kən'tʃɜ:təʊ] (pl -s) n Konzert das.

concession [kən'seʃn] n - **1.** [allowance] Zugeständnis das - **2.** COMM [franchise] Konzession die - **3.** [special price] Preisermäßigung die.

concise [kən'saɪs] adj präzis(e), exakt.

conclude [kən'klu:d] ⟨⟩ vt - **1.** [end] beenden - **2.** [deduce]: **to conclude (that)...** schließen(, dass)..., folgern(, dass)... - **3.** [agreement, deal] ablschließen. ⟨⟩ vi [finish] enden, schließen.

conclusion [kən'klu:ʒn] n - **1.** [opinion] Schlussfolgerung die - **2.** [ending] Abschluss der - **3.** [of agreement, deal] Abschluss der.

conclusive [kən'klu:sɪv] adj eindeutig.

concoct [kən'kɒkt] vt - **1.** [story, excuse, alibi] sich (D) ausldenken - **2.** [meal] kreieren; [drink] zusammenlbrauen.

concoction [kən'kɒkʃn] n [meal] selbst kreiertes Gericht; [drink] Gebräu das.

concourse ['kɒŋkɔ:s] n [hall] Eingangshalle die.

concrete ['kɒŋkri:t] ⟨⟩ adj liter & fig konkret. ⟨⟩ n Beton der. ⟨⟩ comp [made of concrete] Beton-.

concur [kən'kɜ:r] vi [agree]: **to concur (with sthg)** (etw (D)) zulstimmen.

concurrently [kən'kʌrəntlɪ] *adv* gleichzei-tig.

concussion [kən'kʌʃn] *n* Gehirnerschütte-rung *die*.

condemn [kən'dem] *vt* - 1. [disapprove of]: **to condemn sb (for sthg)** jn (wegen etw (G)) ver-urteilen - 2. [force] verdammen - 3. LAW [sen-tence]: **to condemn sb to sthg** jn zu etw verur-teilen - 4. [building] für unbewohnbar erklären.

condensation [ˌkɒndenˈseɪʃn] *n* [on win-dows etc] Kondenswasser *das*.

condense [kən'dens] *vt* [text] zusammenl-fassen.

condensed milk [kən'denst-] *n* Kondens-milch *die*.

condescending [ˌkɒndɪˈsendɪŋ] *adj* he-rablassend.

condition [kən'dɪʃn] ◇ *n* - 1. [of object, building] Zustand *der* - 2. [of person, patient] Ver-fassung *die*; **out of condition** schlecht in Form - 2. MED [illness] Leiden *das* - 3. [requirement] Be-dingung *die*, Voraussetzung *die*; **on condition that** unter der Bedingung, dass. ◇ *vt* - 1. PSY-CHOL konditionieren - 2. [determine] bestim-men - 3. [hair] pflegen.

conditional [kən'dɪʃənl] ◇ *adj* [provisional] vorbehaltlich. ◇ *n* GRAM Konditional *der*.

conditioner [kən'dɪʃnər] *n* - 1. [for hair] Pfle-gespülung *die* - 2. [for clothes] Weichspü-ler *der*.

condolences [kən'dəʊlənsɪz] *npl* Bei-leid *das*.

condom ['kɒndəm] *n* Kon-dom *der* ODER *das*.

condominium [ˌkɒndəˈmɪnɪəm] *n* US - 1. [apartment] Eigentumswohnung *die* - 2. [building] Apartmenthaus *das*.

condone [kən'dəʊn] *vt* hinwegsehen über (+ A).

conducive [kən'djuːsɪv] *adj*: **to be condu-cive to sthg** einer Sache (D) förderlich sein.

conduct ◇ *n* ['kɒndʌkt] - 1. [behaviour] Ver-halten *das* - 2. [of business, talks] Durchfüh-rung *die*. ◇ *vt* [kən'dʌkt] - 1. [carry out] durchführen - 2. [behave]: **to conduct o.s. well/badly** sich gut/schlecht benehmen - 3. MUS di-rigieren - 4. PHYS [heat, electricity] leiten.

conducted tour [kən'dʌktɪd-] *n* Füh-rung *die*.

conductor [kən'dʌktər] *n* - 1. MUS Diri-gent *der*, -in *die* - 2. [on bus] Schaffner *der*, -in *die* - 3. US [on train] Zugführer *der*.

cone [kəʊn] *n* - 1. [shape] Kegel *der* - 2. [for ice cream] Eistüte *die* - 3. [from tree] Zapfen *der* - 4. [on roads] Pylon *der*, Pylone *die*.

confectionery [kən'fekʃnərɪ] *n* (U) Süßwa-ren *Pl*.

confederation [kənˌfedəˈreɪʃn] *n* Bund *der*.

confer [kən'fɜːr] ◇ *vt fml*: **to confer sthg (on sb)** [title, degree] (jm) etw verleihen. ◇ *vi*: **to confer (with sb on** OR **about sthg)** sich (mit jm über etw (A)) beraten.

conference ['kɒnfərəns] *n* Konferenz *die*.

confess [kən'fes] ◇ *vt* - 1. RELIG beichten - 2. [admit] gestehen. ◇ *vi* [admit]: **to confess (to sthg)** (etw) gestehen.

confession [kən'feʃn] *n* - 1. [of guilt] Ge-ständnis *das* - 2. (U) RELIG Beichte *die*.

confetti [kən'fetɪ] *n* (U) Konfetti *Pl*.

confide [kən'faɪd] *vi*: **to confide in sb** sich jm anvertrauen.

confidence ['kɒnfɪdəns] *n* - 1. (U) [self-assur-ance] Selbstvertrauen *das* - 2. (U) [trust] Ver-trauen *das*; **to have confidence in sb** Vertrau-en zu jm haben - 3. [secrecy]: **in confidence** im Vertrauen - 4. [secret] vertrauliche Informati-on.

confidence trick *n* Schwindel *der*.

confident ['kɒnfɪdənt] *adj* - 1. [self-assured] selbstbewusst - 2. [sure] überzeugt; **to be con-fident of sthg** von etw überzeugt sein.

confidential [ˌkɒnfɪˈdenʃl] *adj* vertraulich.

confine *vt* [kən'faɪn] beschränken; **to be confined to** beschränkt sein auf (+ A); **to con-fine o.s. to sthg** sich auf etw (A) beschrän-ken; **to confine o.s. to doing sthg** sich darauf beschränken, etw zu tun. ➡ **confines** *npl* Grenzen *Pl*.

confined [kən'faɪnd] *adj* [space, area] be-schränkt.

confinement [kən'faɪnmənt] *n* [state of im-prisonment] Haft *die*.

confirm [kən'fɜːm] *vt* - 1. [gen] bestätigen - 2. RELIG konfirmieren; [Roman Catholic] fir-men.

confirmation [ˌkɒnfəˈmeɪʃn] *n* (U) - 1. [rati-fication] Bestätigung *die* - 2. RELIG Konfirmati-on *die*; [of Roman Catholic] Firmung *die*.

confirmed [kən'fɜːmd] *adj* [bachelor, spinster] überzeugt.

confiscate ['kɒnfɪskeɪt] *vt* beschlagnah-men, konfiszieren.

conflict ◇ *n* ['kɒnflɪkt] Konflikt *der*. ◇ *vi* [kən'flɪkt] [clash] sich (D) widersprechen; **to conflict with sb/sthg** im Widerspruch zu jm/etw stehen.

conflicting [kən'flɪktɪŋ] *adj* widersprüch-lich.

conform [kən'fɔːm] *vi* - 1. [behave as expected] sich anpassen - 2. [be in accordance]: **to con-form (to** OR **with sthg)** (nach etw (D)) rich-ten.

confound [kən'faʊnd] *vt* [confuse] verblüf-fen.

confront [kən'frʌnt] *vt* - 1. [opponent, enemy, problem] sich stellen (+ D); **to be confronted with a problem** mit einem Problem konfron-tiert werden; **the problem that confronts us**

das Problem, das sich uns stellt - **2.** [present]: **to confront sb (with sthg)** jn (mit etw) konfrontieren.

confrontation [ˌkɒnfrʌn'teɪʃn] n Konfrontation *die*, Auseinandersetzung *die*.

confuse [kən'fju:z] vt - **1.** [bewilder] verwirren - **2.** [mix up]: **to confuse sb/sthg (with)** jn/etw verwechseln (mit) - **3.** [complicate - situation] verworren machen.

confused [kən'fju:zd] adj [person] verwirrt; [ideas, thoughts, situation] verworren; **to get confused** konfus werden.

confusing [kən'fju:zɪŋ] adj verwirrend.

confusion [kən'fju:ʒn] n - **1.** [perplexity] Verwirrung *die* - **2.** [mixing up] Verwechslung *die* - **3.** [bewilderment] Verlegenheit *die* - **4.** [disorder] Durcheinander *das*.

congeal [kən'dʒi:l] vi [blood] gerinnen; [food] fest werden.

congenial [kən'dʒi:njəl] adj angenehm.

congested [kən'dʒestɪd] adj [roads, nose] verstopft.

congestion [kən'dʒestʃn] n (U) - **1.** [overcrowding] Stau *der* - **2.** MED Blutandrang *der*.

conglomerate [ˌkən'glɒmərət] n COMM Großkonzern *der (aus mehreren Firmen bestehend)*.

congratulate [kən'grætʃʊleɪt] vt: **to congratulate sb (on sthg)** jm (zu etw) gratulieren.

congratulations [kənˌgrætʃʊ'leɪʃənz] ⬦ npl Glückwunsch *der*, Glückwünsche *Pl.* ⬦ excl herzlichen Glückwunsch!

congregate ['kɒŋgrɪgeɪt] vi [people] sich versammeln; [animals] sich sammeln.

congregation [ˌkɒŋgrɪ'geɪʃn] n RELIG Gemeinde *die*.

congress ['kɒŋgres] n [meeting] Kongress *der*. ➡ **Congress** n US POL der Kongress.

congressman ['kɒŋgresmən] (pl -men [-mən]) n US POL Kongressabgeordnete *der*.

conifer ['kɒnɪfə'] n Nadelbaum *der*.

conjugation [ˌkɒndʒʊ'geɪʃn] n GRAM Konjugation *die*.

conjunction [kən'dʒʌŋkʃn] n - **1.** GRAM Konjunktion *die* - **2.** [combination] Verbindung *die*; [of events] Zusammentreffen *das*.

conjunctivitis [kənˌdʒʌŋktɪ'vaɪtɪs] n (U) Bindehautentzündung *die*.

conjure ['kʌndʒə'] vt & vi zaubern. ➡ **conjure up** vt sep [evoke] heraufbeschwören.

conjurer ['kʌndʒərə'] n Zauberer *der*, -rin *die*.

conjuror ['kʌndʒərə'] n = **conjurer**.

conker ['kɒŋkə'] n UK (Ross)kastanie *die*.

conman ['kɒnmæn] (pl -men [-men]) n Betrüger *der*.

connect [kə'nekt] ⬦ vt - **1.** [join]: **to connect sthg (to sthg)** etw (mit etw) verbinden - **2.** [on telephone] verbinden - **3.** [associate] in Verbindung OR Zusammenhang bringen; **to connect sb/sthg to, to connect sb/sthg with** jn/etw in Verbindung bringen mit; **to be connected** [two things] miteinander zu tun haben - **4.** ELEC [to power supply]: **to connect sthg (to sthg)** etw (an etw *(A)*) anschließen. ⬦ vi [train, plane, bus]: **to connect with** Anschluss haben an (+ *A*).

connected [kə'nektɪd] adj [related]: **to be connected with sthg** mit etw in Zusammenhang stehen.

connection [kə'nekʃn] n - **1.** [relationship]: **to have a connection with** in Zusammenhang stehen mit; **connection between** Zusammenhang zwischen; **in connection with** im Zusammenhang mit - **2.** ELEC [between wires] Schaltung *die* - **3.** [on telephone] Verbindung *die* - **4.** [plane, train, bus] Anschluss *der* - **5.** [professional acquaintance]: **connections** Beziehungen *Pl.*

connive [kə'naɪv] vi - **1.** [plot]: **to connive (with sb)** sich (mit jm) verschwören - **2.** [allow to happen]: **to connive at sthg** etw dulden.

connoisseur [ˌkɒnə'sɜ:'] n Kenner *der*, -in *die*; **a connoisseur of wine** ein Weinkenner.

conquer ['kɒŋkə'] vt - **1.** [take by force - land, city] erobern; [- people] besiegen - **2.** fig [overcome] besiegen.

conqueror ['kɒŋkərə'] n [of land, city] Eroberer *der*, -in *die*; [of people] Sieger *der*, -in *die*.

conquest ['kɒŋkwest] n - **1.** [act of land, city] Eroberung *die*; [- of people] Sieg *der* - **2.** [thing conquered] Eroberung *die*.

cons [kɒnz] npl - **1.** UK inf (abbr of **conveniences**): **all mod cons** mit allem modernen Komfort - **2.** ➡ **pro**.

conscience ['kɒnʃəns] n Gewissen *das*.

conscientious [ˌkɒnʃɪ'enʃəs] adj gewissenhaft.

conscious ['kɒnʃəs] adj - **1.** [awake] bei Bewusstsein - **2.** [aware]: **to be conscious of sthg** sich einer Sache *(G)* bewusst sein; **fashion-conscious** modebewusst; **to be money-conscious** sehr auf Geld achten - **3.** [intentional - effort, decision] bewusst; [- insult] absichtlich.

consciousness ['kɒnʃəsnɪs] n Bewusstsein *das*.

conscript n MIL Wehrpflichtige *der*.

conscription [kən'skrɪpʃn] n Wehrpflicht *die*.

consecutive [kən'sekjʊtɪv] adj aufeinanderfolgend; [numbers] fortlaufend; **for four consecutive days** vier Tage hintereinander.

consent [kən'sent] ⬦ n (U) - **1.** [permission] Zustimmung *die* - **2.** [agreement]: **he is, by common consent, a good minister** man hält ihn allgemein für einen guten Minister. ⬦ vi: **to consent (to sthg)** (einer Sache *(D)*) zulstimmen.

consequence ['kɒnsɪkwəns] n - 1. [result] Folge die; **to take the consequences** die Konsequenzen tragen; **in consequence** folglich - 2. (U) [importance] Bedeutung die; **a person of consequence** eine bedeutende Person.

consequently ['kɒnsɪkwəntlɪ] adv folglich.

conservation [ˌkɒnsə'veɪʃn] n [of buildings] Schutz der, Erhaltung die; **nature conservation** Naturschutz der; **conservation of energy/ water** sorgsamer Umgang mit Energie/Wasser.

conservative [kən'sɜːvətɪv] ◇ adj - 1. [traditional] konservativ - 2. [cautious] vorsichtig. ◇ n Konservative der, die. ◆ **Conservative** ◇ adj POL konservativ. ◇ n POL Konservative der, die.

Conservative Party n: **the Conservative Party** die Konservative Partei.

conservatory [kən'sɜːvətrɪ] n Wintergarten der.

conserve ◇ n ['kɒnsɜːv] Marmelade die. ◇ vt [kən'sɜːv] [energy, supplies, electricity] sorgsam umlgehen mit; [nature, wildlife] schützen.

consider [kən'sɪdər] vt - 1. [think about] erwägen - 2. [take into account] berücksichtigen; **all things considered** alles in allem - 3. [believe]: **I consider him (to be) an expert** ich halte ihn für einen Experten.

considerable [kən'sɪdrəbl] adj beträchtlich.

considerably [kən'sɪdrəblɪ] adv beträchtlich.

considerate [kən'sɪdərət] adj rücksichtsvoll.

consideration [kənˌsɪdə'reɪʃn] n - 1. [thought] Überlegung die; **to take sthg into consideration** etw berücksichtigen - 2. [thoughtfulness] Rücksichtnahme die - 3. [factor] Gesichtspunkt der - 4. [discussion]: **the matter is under consideration** die Angelegenheit wird zur Zeit geprüft.

considering [kən'sɪdərɪŋ] ◇ prep in Anbetracht (+ G). ◇ conj wenn man bedenkt, dass. ◇ adv eigentlich; **the play was quite good, considering** das Stück war eigentlich ganz gut.

consign [kən'saɪn] vt: **to consign sthg to the attic/shed/etc** etw auf den Dachboden/in den Schuppen/etc verbannen; **to consign sthg to the scrapheap** fig etw rauslwerfen.

consignment [ˌkən'saɪnmənt] n Sendung die; [bigger] Ladung die.

consist [kən'sɪst] ◆ **consist in** vt insep: **to consist in sthg** in etw (D) bestehen; **to consist in doing sthg** darin bestehen, etw zu tun. ◆ **consist of** vt insep bestehen aus.

consistency [kən'sɪstənsɪ] n - 1. [coherence] Beständigkeit die; [of several things] Einheitlichkeit die - 2. [texture] Konsistenz die.

consistent [kən'sɪstənt] adj - 1. [constant] beständig - 2. [steady] stetig - 3. [coherent]: **to be consistent (with)** im Einklang stehen (mit).

consolation [ˌkɒnsə'leɪʃn] n Trost der.

console ◇ n ['kɒnsəʊl] [control panel] Bedienungsfeld das; [of computer game] Spielkonsole die. ◇ vt [kən'səʊl] trösten.

consonant ['kɒnsənənt] n Konsonant der.

consortium [kən'sɔːtjəm] (pl -tiums OR -tia [-tjə]) n Konsortium das.

conspicuous [kən'spɪkjʊəs] adj auffällig.

conspiracy [kən'spɪrəsɪ] n Verschwörung die.

conspire [kən'spaɪər] vt: **to conspire to do sthg** heimlich planen, etw zu tun.

constable ['kʌnstəbl] n UK Wachtmeister der, -in die.

constant ['kɒnstənt] adj - 1. [unvarying] konstant, beständig - 2. [recurring] ständig.

constantly ['kɒnstəntlɪ] adv [always] dauernd, ständig.

consternation [ˌkɒnstə'neɪʃn] n Bestürzung die.

constipated ['kɒnstɪpeɪtɪd] adj verstopft.

constipation [ˌkɒnstɪ'peɪʃn] n (U) Verstopfung die.

constituency [kən'stɪtjʊənsɪ] n Wahlkreis der.

constituent [kən'stɪtjʊənt] n - 1. [voter] Wähler der, -in die - 2. [element] Bestandteil der.

constitute ['kɒnstɪtjuːt] vt - 1. [represent] darlstellen - 2. [form] bilden - 3. [set up] einlrichten.

constitution [ˌkɒnstɪ'tjuːʃn] n - 1. [health] Konstitution die - 2. [composition] Zusammensetzung die.

constraint [kən'streɪnt] n - 1. [restriction] Beschränkung die - 2. [coercion]: **under constraint** unter Zwang.

construct vt [kən'strʌkt] [build] bauen.

construction [kən'strʌkʃn] n - 1. [act of building] Bau der; **under construction** im Bau - 2. [building industry] Bauindustrie die - 3. [structure] Konstruktion die.

constructive [kən'strʌktɪv] adj konstruktiv.

construe [kən'struː] vt fml [interpret]: **to construe sthg as** etw auflfassen als.

consul ['kɒnsəl] n Konsul der.

consulate ['kɒnsjʊlət] n Konsulat das.

consult [kən'sʌlt] ◇ vt - 1. [ask advice of - doctor, lawyer] konsultieren; [- friend] um Rat fragen - 2. [refer to - dictionary] nachlschlagen in (+ D); [- map] nachlsehen auf (+ D). ◇ vi: **to consult with sb** sich mit jm beraten.

consultant [kən'sʌltənt] n - 1. [expert] Berater der, -in die - 2. UK [hospital doctor] Facharzt der, -ärztin die.

consultation [,kɒnsəl'teɪʃn] n [meeting, discussion] Beratung *die*.

consulting room [kən'sʌltɪŋ-] n Sprechzimmer *das*.

consume [kən'sjuːm] vt - 1. [food, drink] zu sich nehmen - 2. [fuel, energy] verbrauchen.

consumer [kən'sjuːmər] n Verbraucher *der*, -in *die*.

consumer goods npl Konsumgüter *Pl*.

consumer society n Konsumgesellschaft *die*.

consummate vt ['kɒnsəmeɪt] [marriage] vollziehen.

consumption [kən'sʌmpʃn] n (U) - 1. [of food, drink] Konsum *der* - 2. [of fuel, energy] Verbrauch *der*.

cont. (abbr of **continued**) Forts.

contact ['kɒntækt] ⟷ n Kontakt *der*; **to be in contact with sthg** [touching] etw berühren; **to lose contact with sb** den Kontakt zu jm verlieren; **to make contact with sb** mit jm Kontakt auf|nehmen; **in contact (with sb)** in Kontakt (mit jm). ⟷ vt sich in Verbindung setzen mit.

contact lens n Kontaktlinse *die*.

contagious [kən'teɪdʒəs] adj liter & fig ansteckend.

contain [kən'teɪn] vt - 1. [hold, include] enthalten - 2. fml [control - enthusiasm, anger, excitement] unter Kontrolle halten; [- epidemic, riot] unter Kontrolle bringen; [- enemy troops] in Schach halten; [- population growth] in Grenzen halten.

container [kən'teɪnər] n - 1. [box, bottle etc] Behälter *der* - 2. COMM [for transporting goods] Container *der*.

contaminate [kən'tæmɪneɪt] vt [make impure] verunreinigen; [make poisonous] verseuchen.

cont'd (abbr of **continued**) Forts.

contemplate ['kɒntempleɪt] vt - 1. [consider] erwägen - 2. liter [look at] betrachten.

contemporary [kən'tempərərɪ] ⟷ adj [life] zeitgenössisch. ⟷ n Zeitgenosse *der*, -sin *die*.

contempt [kən'tempt] n (U) - 1. [scorn]: **contempt (for)** Verachtung *die* (für) - 2. LAW: **contempt (of court)** Missachtung *die* des Gerichts.

contemptuous [kən'temptʃʊəs] adj verächtlich; **to be contemptuous of sthg** etw verachten.

contend [kən'tend] ⟷ vi - 1. [deal]: **to contend with sthg** mit etw zu kämpfen haben - 2. [compete]: **to contend for sthg** um etw kämpfen. ⟷ vt fml [claim]: **to contend that...** behaupten, dass...

contender [kən'tendər] n - 1. [in fight, race] Konkurrent *der*, -in *die* - 2. [in election] Kandidat *der*, -in *die*.

content ⟷ adj [kən'tent]: **content (with)** zufrieden (mit); **to be content to do sthg** etw gerne tun. ⟷ n ['kɒntent] - 1. [amount contained] Gehalt *der* - 2. [subject matter] Inhalt *der*. ⟷ vt [kən'tent]: **to content o.s. with sthg** sich mit etw zufrieden geben. ⬥ **contents** npl - 1. [of container, document] Inhalt *der* - 2. [at front of book] Inhaltsverzeichnis *das*.

contented [kən'tentɪd] adj zufrieden.

contention [kən'tenʃn] n - 1. [assertion] Behauptung *die* - 2. (U) [disagreement]: **to be a source of contention** ein Streitpunkt sein.

contest ⟷ n ['kɒntest] - 1. [competition] Wettkampf *der*; **a beauty contest** ein Schönheitswettbewerb - 2. [for power, control] Kampf *der*. ⟷ vt [kən'test] - 1. [compete for] kämpfen um - 2. [dispute - statement] bestreiten; [- decision] Einspruch erheben gegen; [- will] an|fechten.

contestant [kən'testənt] n [in sports] Wettkampfteilnehmer *der*, -in *die*; [in quiz, election] Kandidat *der*, -in *die*.

context ['kɒntekst] n - 1. [of word, phrase] Kontext *der* - 2. [of event, idea] Zusammenhang *der*.

continent ['kɒntɪnənt] n Kontinent *der*. ⬥ **Continent** n UK: **the Continent** Kontinentaleuropa *das*.

continental [,kɒntɪ'nentl] adj kontinental.

continental breakfast n Frühstück mit Kaffee oder Tee, Brötchen und Marmelade.

continental quilt n UK Steppdecke *die*.

contingency [kən'tɪndʒənsɪ] n Eventualität *die*.

contingency plan n Ausweichplan *der*.

continual [kən'tɪnjʊəl] adj - 1. [without interruption - noise] pausenlos; [- growth] ununterbrochen; [- jealousy] dauernd - 2. [frequently repeated] ständig, dauernd.

continually [kən'tɪnjʊəlɪ] adv - 1. [without interruption] ununterbrochen - 2. [frequently] ständig.

continuation [kən,tɪnjʊ'eɪʃn] n Fortsetzung *die*.

continue [kən'tɪnjuː] ⟷ vt [carry on] fort|setzen; **to continue singing/working/etc** OR **to sing/work/etc** weiter|singen/weiter|arbeiten/etc; **"And now," he continued** "Und nun," fuhr er fort. ⟷ vi - 1. [carry on] an|dauern; **to continue with sthg** etw fortsetzen - 2. [begin again - gen] weiter|gehen; [- people] weiter|machen - 3. [resume speaking] fort|fahren - 4. [resume travelling] weiter|fahren; [on foot] weiter|gehen.

continuous [kən'tɪnjʊəs] adj ununterbrochen.

continuously [kən'tɪnjʊəslɪ] adv ununterbrochen.

contort [kən'tɔːt] *vt* [face, image] verzerren; [one's body] verrenken.

contortion [kən'tɔːʃn] *n* [position] Verrenkung *die*.

contour ['kɒn,tʊər] *n* - **1.** [outline] Kontur *die* - **2.** [on map] Höhenlinie *die*.

contraband ['kɒntrəbænd] ⟨⟩ *adj* geschmuggelt. ⟨⟩ *n (U)* Schmuggelware *die*.

contraception [,kɒntrə'sepʃn] *n* Empfängnisverhütung *die*.

contraceptive [,kɒntrə'septɪv] ⟨⟩ *adj* Verhütungs-; [advice] zur Empfängnisverhütung. ⟨⟩ *n* Verhütungsmittel *das*.

contract ⟨⟩ *n* ['kɒntrækt] Vertrag *der*; a contract of employment ein Arbeitsvertrag. ⟨⟩ *vt* [kən'trækt] - **1.** [through legal agreement]: to contract to do sthg sich vertraglich verpflichten, etw zu tun - **2.** *fml* [disease] sich *(D)* zuziehen. ⟨⟩ *vi* [kən'trækt] [decrease in size, length] sich zusammenlziehen.

contraction [kən'trækʃn] *n* [short form] Kontraktion *die*.

contractor [kən'træktər] *n* [person] Auftragnehmer *der*, -in *die*; [company] beauftragte Firma.

contradict [,kɒntrə'dɪkt] *vt* widersprechen *(+ D)*.

contradiction [,kɒntrə'dɪkʃn] *n* Widerspruch *der*.

contraflow ['kɒntrəfləʊ] *n* Umleitung auf die Gegenfahrbahn (bei Baustellen auf der Fahrbahn).

contraption [kən'træpʃn] *n* Apparat *der*.

contrary ['kɒntrəri] ⟨⟩ *adj* - **1.** [opposing] gegensätzlich; to be contrary to sthg im Gegensatz zu etw stehen - **2.** [kən'treəri] [stubborn] widerspenstig. ⟨⟩ *n* Gegenteil *das*; on the contrary im Gegenteil. ◆ **contrary to** *prep* im Gegensatz zu.

contrast ⟨⟩ *n* ['kɒntrɑːst]: contrast (with OR to) Gegensatz *der* (zu); the contrast between der Unterschied zwischen; by OR in contrast im Gegensatz dazu; in contrast with OR to sthg im Gegensatz zu etw. ⟨⟩ *vt* [kən'trɑːst]: to contrast sthg with sthg etw einer Sache *(D)* gegenüberstellen. ⟨⟩ *vi* [kən'trɑːst]: to contrast (with sthg) im Gegensatz (zu etw) stehen; [colours] sich (gegen etw) abheben.

contravene [,kɒntrə'viːn] *vt* verstoßen gegen.

contribute [kən'trɪbjuːt] ⟨⟩ *vt* [ideas] beitragen; [money] beisteuern; [help, advice] zur Verfügung stellen. ⟨⟩ *vi* - **1.** [donate]: to contribute (to sthg) (für etw) spenden - **2.** [be part of cause]: to contribute to sthg zu etw beitragen - **3.** [write material]: to contribute to sthg für etw einen Beitrag/Beiträge schreiben.

contribution [,kɒntrɪ'bjuːʃn] *n*: contribution (to sthg) Beitrag *der* (zu etw).

contributor [kən'trɪbjutər] *n* - **1.** [of money] Spender *der*, -in *die* - **2.** [to magazine, newspaper] freier Mitarbeiter, freie Mitarbeiterin; [regular] Mitarbeiter *der*, -in *die*.

contrive [kən'traɪv] *vt fml* - **1.** [engineer] entwickeln; [meeting] arrangieren - **2.** [manage]: to contrive to do sthg es zu Wege bringen, etw zu tun.

contrived [kən'traɪvd] *adj* gewollt.

control [kən'trəʊl] ⟨⟩ *n* - **1.** *(U)* [power to manage - of situation, language] Beherrschung *die*; [- of traffic] Regelung *die*; [- of disease, crowd, fire] Kontrolle *die*; [- of budget] Aufsicht *die*; *(phrase)*: to be in control of [situation, place] unter Kontrolle haben; under control unter Kontrolle; to get a situation under control eine Situation in den Griff bekommen - **2.** [of emotions] Beherrschung *die*; to lose control die Beherrschung verlieren - **3.** [limit] Beschränkung *die* - **4.** COMPUT Control *die*. ⟨⟩ *vt* - **1.** [have power to manage - company] leiten; [- government] unter sich *(D)* haben; [- country] beherrschen; [- traffic] regulieren; [- crowds, rioters] unter Kontrolle haben - **2.** [operate - car, plane] steuern; [- machine] bedienen - **3.** [curb] unter Kontrolle bringen - **4.** [emotions] beherrschen; to control o.s. sich beherrschen. ◆ **controls** *npl* [of machine, plane] Bedienung *das*.

control panel *n* [of car] Armaturenbrett *das*; [of plane, machine] Bedienungsfeld *das*.

control tower *n* Kontrollturm *der*.

controversial [,kɒntrə'vɜːʃl] *adj* umstritten.

controversy ['kɒntrəvɜːsɪ, *UK* kən'trɒvəsɪ] *n* Streit *der*.

convalesce [,kɒnvə'les] *vi* genesen.

convene [kən'viːn] ⟨⟩ *vt* [meeting, conference] einlberufen. ⟨⟩ *vi* sich versammeln; [court, parliament] zusammenltreten.

convenience [kən'viːnjəns] *n* - **1.** [ease of use]: I like the convenience of it ich finde es so praktisch; for convenience aus praktischen Gründen - **2.** [benefit]: please reply at your earliest convenience *fml* wir bitten um baldmöglichste Antwort; a telephone is provided for your convenience ein Telefon wird Ihnen zur Verfügung gestellt.

convenient [kən'viːnjənt] *adj* - **1.** [suitable] günstig; to be convenient for sb jm passen - **2.** [handy] praktisch; to be convenient for the shops günstig in der Nähe von Geschäften gelegen sein.

convent ['kɒnvənt] *n* Kloster *das* (für Frauen).

convention [kən'venʃn] *n* - **1.** [practice] Brauch *der*; [social rule] Konvention *die* - **2.** [agreement] Abkommen *das* - **3.** [assembly] Tagung *die*.

conventional [kən'venʃənl] *adj* - 1. *pej* [dull] konventionell; [person] konventionsgebunden - 2. [traditional] üblich - 3. [weapon, war] konventionell.

converge [kən'vɜ:dʒ] *vi* - 1. [come together] zusammenllaufen; **to converge on sb/sthg** von überall her zu jm/etw strömen - 2. [become similar] sich einander annlähern.

conversant [kən'vɜ:sənt] *adj fml*: **conversant with sthg** mit etw vertraut.

conversation [ˌkɒnvə'seɪʃn] *n* Gespräch *das*; **to have a conversation** sich unterhalten.

converse *vi* [kən'vɜ:s] *fml* [talk]: **to converse (with sb)** sich (mit jm) unterhalten.

conversely [kən'vɜ:slɪ] *adv fml* umgekehrt.

conversion [kən'vɜ:ʃn] *n* - 1. [process] Umwandlung *die* - 2. [converted building, room] Umbau *der* - 3. RELIG [change in belief] Bekehrung *die* - 4. [in rugby] Verwandlung *die*.

convert ⟨⟩ *vt* [kən'vɜ:t] - 1. [change]: **to convert sthg (in)to sthg** [miles, pounds] etw in etw (A) umlrechnen; [energy] etw in etw (A) umlwandeln - 2. *fig* & RELIG: **to convert sb (to sthg)** jn (zu etw) bekehren - 3. [building, room, ship]: **to convert sthg (in)to sthg** etw zu etw umlbauen. ⟨⟩ *vi* [kən'vɜ:t]: **to convert from sthg to sthg** [gas, electricity] sich von etw auf etw (A) umlstellen; [religion] von etw zu etw konvertieren. ⟨⟩ *n* ['kɒnvɜ:t] Bekehrte *der*, *die*.

convertible [kən'vɜ:təbl] *n* [car] Kabrio *das*.

convex [kɒn'veks] *adj* konvex.

convey [kən'veɪ] *vt* - 1. *fml* [people, cargo] belfördern - 2. [feelings, thoughts] vermitteln; **to convey sthg to sb** jm etw vermitteln.

conveyor belt [kən'veɪə-] *n* [in factory] Fließband *das*; [at airport] Förderband *das*.

convict ⟨⟩ *n* ['kɒnvɪkt] Strafgefangene *der*, *die*. ⟨⟩ *vt* [kən'vɪkt]: **to convict sb of sthg** jn wegen etw verurteilen.

conviction [kən'vɪkʃn] *n* - 1. [gen] Überzeugung *die* - 2. LAW [of criminal] Verurteilung *die*; **previous convictions** Vorstrafen *Pl*.

convince [kən'vɪns] *vt* [persuade] überzeugen; **to convince sb of sthg** jn von etw überzeugen; **to convince sb to do sthg** jn überreden, etw zu tun.

convincing [kən'vɪnsɪŋ] *adj* - 1. [person, argument, speech] überzeugend - 2. [win, victory] klar.

convoluted ['kɒnvəlu:tɪd] *adj* [plot, reasoning] verwickelt; [sentence] gewunden.

convoy ['kɒnvɔɪ] *n* Konvoi *der*.

convulse [kən'vʌls] *vt*: **to be convulsed with laughter** sich vor Lachen schütteln; **to be convulsed with pain** sich vor Schmerzen krümmen.

convulsion [kən'vʌlʃn] *n* MED Konvulsion *die*.

cook [kʊk] ⟨⟩ *n* Koch *der*, Köchin *die*. ⟨⟩ *vt* - 1. [food, meal] machen; [boil] kochen; [roast, fry] braten; **to cook sthg (in the oven)** etw im Ofen garen lassen - 2. *inf* [falsify] frisieren. ⟨⟩ *vi* [boil] kochen; [roast, fry] braten.

cookbook ['kʊkˌbʊk] *n* = **cookery book**.

cooker ['kʊkə-] *n esp UK* [stove] Herd *der*.

cookery ['kʊkərɪ] *n* Kochen *das*.

cookery book *n* Kochbuch *das*.

cookie ['kʊkɪ] *n* - 1. Keks *der*, Plätzchen *das* - 2. COMPUT Cookie *das*.

cooking ['kʊkɪŋ] *n* (U) - 1. [activity] Kochen *das* - 2. [food] Küche *die*; **her cooking's awful** ihre Kochkünste sind grauenvoll.

cool [ku:l] ⟨⟩ *adj* - 1. [gen] kühl; [dress] leicht - 2. [person] ruhig; **to keep a cool head** einen kühlen Kopf behalten - 3. *inf* [excellent, fashionable] cool. ⟨⟩ *vt* kühlen. ⟨⟩ *vi* ablkühlen. ⟨⟩ *n inf* [calm]: **to keep one's cool** die Ruhe bewahren; **to lose one's cool** die Nerven verlieren. **cool down** *vi* [become less warm] ablkühlen; [person] kühler werden.

cool bag *n* Kühltasche *die*.

cool box *UK*, **cooler** *US* ['ku:lə-] *n* Kühlbox *die*.

coop [ku:p] *n* Käfig *der*. **coop up** *vt sep inf* einlpferchen.

co-op ['kəʊˌɒp] *n abbr of* **cooperative**.

cooperate [kəʊ'ɒpəreɪt] *vi*: **to cooperate (with sb)** (mit jm) zusammenlarbeiten.

cooperation [kəʊˌɒpə'reɪʃn] *n* (U) - 1. [collaboration] Zusammenarbeit *die* - 2. [assistance] Mitarbeit *die*, Kooperation *die*.

cooperative [kəʊ'ɒpərətɪv] ⟨⟩ *adj* - 1. [helpful] kooperativ - 2. [collective] auf Genossenschaftsbasis. ⟨⟩ *n* [enterprise] Genossenschaft *die*, Kooperative *die*.

coordinate ⟨⟩ *n* [kəʊ'ɔ:dɪnət] [on map, graph] Koordinate *die*. ⟨⟩ *vt* [kəʊ'ɔ:dɪneɪt] koordinieren. **coordinates** *npl* [clothes] Kleidung *die* zum Kombinieren.

coordination [kəʊˌɔ:dɪ'neɪʃn] *n* Koordination *die*.

cop [kɒp] *n inf* Polizist *der*, -in *die*.

cope [kəʊp] *vi* zurechtlkommen; **to cope with sthg** etw schaffen.

Copenhagen [ˌkəʊpən'heɪgən] *n* Kopenhagen *nt*.

copier ['kɒpɪə-] *n* [photocopier] Kopierer *der*.

cop-out *n inf* Rückzieher *der*.

copper ['kɒpə-] *n* - 1. [metal] Kupfer *das* - 2. *UK inf* [policeman] Polizist *der*, -in *die*.

copse [kɒps] *n* Wäldchen *das*.

copy ['kɒpɪ] ⟨⟩ *n* - 1. [gen] Kopie *die* - 2. [of book, magazine] Exemplar *das*. ⟨⟩ *vt* - 1. [imitate] nachlahmen - 2. [photocopy] kopieren.

copyright ['kɒpɪraɪt] *n* Copyright *das*.

coral ['kɒrəl] *n* (U) Koralle *die*.

cord [kɔːd] *n* - 1. [string] Schnur *die* - 2. [wire] Kabel *das* - 3. *(U)* [fabric] Kord *der*. ◆ **cords** *npl inf* Kordhose *die*.

cordial ['kɔːdjəl] ◇ *adj* freundlich. ◇ *n* Fruchtsirup *der*.

cordon ['kɔːdn] *n* Kette *die*. ◆ **cordon off** *vt sep* absperren.

corduroy ['kɔːdərɔɪ] *n (U)* Kord *der*.

core [kɔːʳ] *vt* entkernen.

coriander [ˌkɒrɪˈændəʳ] *n* Koriander *der*.

cork [kɔːk] *n* - 1. [material] Kork *der* - 2. [stopper] Korken *der*.

corkscrew ['kɔːkskruː] *n* Korkenzieher *der*.

corn [kɔːn] *n* - 1. *(U) UK* [cereal] Korn *das*, Getreide *das* - 2. *(U) esp US* [maize] Mais *der* - 3. [callus] Hühnerauge *das*.

corned beef [kɔːnd-] *n* Cornedbeef *das*.

corner ['kɔːnəʳ] ◇ *n* Ecke *die*; **to cut corners** oberflächlich arbeiten. ◇ *vt* - 1. *fig* [person, animal] in die Enge treiben - 2. [market] monopolisieren.

corner shop *n* Laden *der* an der Ecke.

cornerstone ['kɔːnəstəʊn] *n fig* Grundstein *der*.

cornet ['kɔːnɪt] *n* - 1. [instrument] Kornett *das* - 2. *UK* [ice-cream cone] Hörnchen *das*.

cornflakes ['kɔːnfleɪks] *npl* Cornflakes *Pl*.

cornflour *UK* ['kɔːnflaʊəʳ], **cornstarch** *US* [-stɑːtʃ] *n (U)* Stärkemehl *das*.

corn on the cob *n* Maiskolben *der*.

corny ['kɔːnɪ] *adj inf* abgedroschen.

coronary ['kɒrənrɪ], **coronary thrombosis** [-θrɒmˈbəʊsɪs] (*pl* coronary thromboses [-siːz]) *n* Herzinfarkt *der*.

coronation [ˌkɒrəˈneɪʃn] *n* Krönung *die*.

coroner ['kɒrənəʳ] *n* für die Untersuchung ungeklärter Todesfälle zuständiger Beamter.

corporal ['kɔːpərəl] *n* Hauptgefreite *der*.

corporal punishment *n (U)* körperliche Züchtigung *die*, Prügelstrafe *die*.

corporate ['kɔːpərət] *adj* - 1. [business] körperschaftlich - 2. [collective] gemeinsam.

corporation [ˌkɔːpəˈreɪʃn] *n* - 1. [council] Gemeindeverwaltung *die* - 2. [large company] Handelsgesellschaft *die*.

corps [kɔːʳ] (*pl inv*) *n* Korps *das*.

corpse [kɔːps] *n* Leiche *die*.

correct [kəˈrekt] ◇ *adj* - 1. [right, accurate] korrekt, richtig; **you're quite correct** du hast ganz Recht - 2. [appropriate, suitable] angemessen. ◇ *vt* korrigieren.

correction [kəˈrekʃn] *n* - 1. *(U)* [act of correcting] Korrigieren *das* - 2. [change] Korrektur *die*, Berichtigung *die*.

correlation [ˌkɒrəˈleɪʃn] *n (U)*: **correlation (between)** Wechselbeziehung *die* (zwischen).

correspond [ˌkɒrɪˈspɒnd] *vi* - 1. [be equivalent]: **to correspond with** OR **to sthg** etw *(D)* entsprechen - 2. [tally]: **to correspond (with** OR **to sthg)** (mit etw) übereinstimmen - 3. [write letters]: **to correspond (with sb)** (mit jm) korrespondieren.

correspondence [ˌkɒrɪˈspɒndəns] *n* - 1. [letters] Briefe *Pl* - 2. *(U)* [letter-writing]: **correspondence with/between** Briefwechsel *der* mit/zwischen *(D)*.

correspondence course *n* Fernkurs *der*.

correspondent [ˌkɒrɪˈspɒndənt] *n* Korrespondent *der*, -in *die*.

corridor ['kɒrɪdɔːʳ] *n* Gang *der*.

corroborate [kəˈrɒbəreɪt] *vt* bestätigen.

corrode [kəˈrəʊd] ◇ *vt* zerfressen. ◇ *vi* korrodieren.

corrosion [kəˈrəʊʒn] *n (U)* Korrosion *die*.

corrugated iron *n* Wellblech *das*.

corrupt [kəˈrʌpt] ◇ *adj* - 1. [gen] korrupt - 2. [depraved] verdorben. ◇ *vt* - 1. [deprave] verderben - 2. COMPUT [damage] beschädigen.

corruption [kəˈrʌpʃn] *n (U)* - 1. [dishonesty] Korruption *die* - 2. [depravity] Verdorbenheit *die* - 3. [debasement] Verführung *die*.

corset ['kɔːsɪt] *n* Korsett *das*.

cosh [kɒʃ] *n* Knüppel *der*.

cosmetic [kɒzˈmetɪk] ◇ *adj fig* [superficial] kosmetisch. ◇ *n* Kosmetikum *das*. ◆ **cosmetics** *n* Kosmetik *die*.

cosmopolitan [ˌkɒzməˈpɒlɪtn] *adj* [place] kosmopolitisch; [person] welterfahren.

cosset ['kɒsɪt] *vt* verhätscheln.

cost [kɒst] ◇ *n* - 1. [price] Kosten *Pl* - 2. *fig* [loss, damage] Preis *der*; **at the cost of his health** auf Kosten seiner Gesundheit; **at all costs** um jeden Preis. ◇ *vt* - 1. (*pt & pp inv*) [gen] kosten - 2. (*pt & pp* -ed) COMM [estimate price of] die Kosten kalkulieren (+ G). ◆ **costs** *npl* LAW Kosten *Pl*.

co-star *n*: **to be the co-star in a film** eine der Hauptrollen in einem Film spielen.

Costa Rica [ˌkɒstəˈriːkə] *n* Costa Rica *nt*.

cost-effective *adj* kosteneffektiv.

costing ['kɒstɪŋ] *n* Kalkulation *die*.

costly ['kɒstlɪ] *adj* kostspielig, teuer.

cost of living *n*: **the cost of living** die Lebenshaltungskosten *Pl*.

cost price *n* Selbstkostenpreis *der*.

costume ['kɒstjuːm] *n* - 1. THEAT Kostüm *das* - 2. *(U)* [dress] Tracht *die* - 3. [swimming costume] Badeanzug *der*.

costume jewellery *n* Modeschmuck *der*.

cosy *UK*, **cozy** *US* ['kəʊzɪ] *adj* [warm and comfortable] gemütlich.

cot [kɒt] *n* - 1. *UK* [for child] Kinderbett *das* - 2. *US* [folding bed] Feldbett *das*.

cottage ['kɒtɪdʒ] *n* Häuschen *das*.

cottage cheese *n (U)* Hüttenkäse *der*.

cottage pie n UK Hackfleisch mit einer Lage Kartoffelbrei, im Ofen überbacken.

cotton ['kɒtn] ⬦ n (U) - 1. [fabric] Baumwolle die - 2. [thread] Faden der. ⬦ comp [fabric] Baumwoll-. ◆ **cotton on** vi inf: **to cotton on (to sthg)** (etw) kapieren.

cotton candy n US = candyfloss.

cotton wool n Watte die.

couch [kaʊtʃ] n - 1. [sofa] Sofa das, Couch die - 2. [in doctor's surgery] Liege die.

cough [kɒf] n Husten der.

cough mixture n UK Hustensaft der.

cough sweet n UK Hustenpastille die.

cough syrup n = cough mixture.

could [kʊd] pt ▷ can².

couldn't ['kʊdnt] abbr of **could not**.

could've ['kʊdəv] abbr of **could have**.

council ['kaʊnsl] n - 1. [local authority] Stadtverwaltung die - 2. [group, organization] Rat der - 3. [meeting] Beratung die.

council estate n Sozialsiedlung die.

council house n UK ≃ Sozialwohnung die, mit öffentlichen Mitteln gebautes Einfamilienhaus für eine Familie mit niedrigem Einkommen.

councillor ['kaʊnsələr] n Stadtrat der, -rätin die.

council tax n UK Gemeindesteuer die.

counsel ['kaʊnsəl] (US) (US) n - 1. (U) fml [advice] Rat der - 2. [lawyer] Rechtsanwalt der, -wältin die; **counsel for the defence** Verteidiger der, -in die; **counsel for the prosecution** Anklagevertreter der, -in die.

counsellor UK, **counselor** US ['kaʊnsələr] n - 1. [adviser] Berater der, -in die - 2. US [lawyer] Rechtsanwalt der, -wältin die.

count [kaʊnt] ⬦ n - 1. [total] Zählung die; **to keep count of sthg** etw mitzählen; **to lose count of sthg** den Überblick über etw (A) verlieren - 2. [aristocrat] Graf der. ⬦ vt - 1. [add up] zählen - 2. [consider, include]: **to count sb/sthg as sthg** jn/etw als etw ansehen; **there are six, not counting the broken ones** es sind sechs, die zerbrochenen nicht mitgezählt. ⬦ vi zählen; **to count (up) to** zählen bis; **to count for nothing** umsonst gewesen sein; **to count as sthg** als etw zählen. ◆ **count against** vt insep sprechen gegen. ◆ **count on** vt insep - 1. [rely on] zählen auf (+ A) - 2. [expect] rechnen mit. ◆ **count up** vt insep zusammenzählen. ◆ **count upon** vt insep = **count on**.

countdown ['kaʊntdaʊn] n Countdown der.

counter ['kaʊntər] ⬦ n - 1. [in shop] Ladentisch der - 2. [in board game] Spielmarke die - 3. US [in kitchen] Theke die. ⬦ vt: **to counter sthg with sthg** etw (D) mit etw begegnen.

⬦ vi: **to counter with sthg** mit etw reagieren. ◆ **counter to** adv entgegen (+ D); **to run counter to sthg** etw (D) zuwiderlaufen.

counteract [,kaʊntə'rækt] vt entgegenwirken (+ D).

counterattack ['kaʊntərə,tæk] vi einen Gegenangriff führen.

counterclockwise [,kaʊntə'klɒkwaɪz] adj & adv US gegen den Uhrzeigersinn.

counterfeit ['kaʊntəfɪt] adj gefälscht.

counterfoil ['kaʊntəfɔɪl] n Kontrollabschnitt der.

counterpart ['kaʊntəpɑːt] n Gegenstück das.

counterproductive [,kaʊntəprə'dʌktɪv] adj die entgegengesetzte Wirkung habend.

countess ['kaʊntɪs] n Gräfin die.

countless ['kaʊntlɪs] adj unzählig.

country ['kʌntrɪ] n - 1. [nation] Land das; **the country** [countryside] das Land; **they live in the country** sie leben auf dem Land - 2. [area of land, region] Gebiet das.

country house n Landhaus das.

countryman ['kʌntrɪmən] (pl -men [-mən]) n Landsmann der.

countryside ['kʌntrɪsaɪd] n (U) Landschaft die.

county ['kaʊntɪ] n Grafschaft die.

county council n UK Grafschaftsrat der.

coup [kuː] n - 1. [rebellion]: **coup (d'état)** Staatsstreich der - 2. [masterstroke] Coup der.

couple ['kʌpl] ⬦ n - 1. [in relationship] Paar das - 2. [small number]: **a couple (of)** [two] zwei; [a few] ein paar. ⬦ vt [join]: **to couple sthg (to sthg)** etw (an etw (A)) koppeln.

coupon ['kuːpɒn] n Gutschein der.

courage ['kʌrɪdʒ] n Mut der; **to take courage (from sthg)** sich (durch etw) ermutigt fühlen.

courgette [kɔː'ʒet] n UK Zucchini die.

courier ['kʊrɪər] n - 1. [on holiday tour] Reiseleiter der, -in die - 2. [to deliver letters, packages] Kurier der.

course [kɔːs] n - 1. [of study - for student] Kurs(us) der; [- for employee] Lehrgang der; (phrase): **a course of lectures** eine Vorlesungsreihe - 2. MED [of treatment] Reihe die - 3. [path, route] Kurs der; **in the course of time** im Laufe der Zeit; **during the course of the negotiations** im Verlauf der Verhandlungen; **on course** liter & fig auf Kurs; **off course** vom Kurs abgewichen - 4. [plan]: **course (of action)** Vorgehensweise die - 5. [of time]: **in due course** zu gegebener Zeit; **in the course of** im Laufe (+ G) - 6. [in meal] Gang der - 7. SPORT [for horseracing] Bahn die, Strecke die; [for golf] Platz der. ◆ **of course** adv natürlich; **of course not** natürlich nicht.

coursebook ['kɔːsbʊk] n Lehrbuch das.

coursework ['kɔːswɜːk] *n (U)* Mitarbeit *die* im Unterricht.

court [kɔːt] *n* - **1.** [for trial] Gericht *das*; *(phrase):* **to take sb to court** jn verklagen - **2.** SPORT Platz *der* - **3.** [courtyard, of monarch] Hof *der*.

courteous ['kɜːtjəs] *adj* höflich.

courtesy ['kɜːtɪsɪ] *n* Höflichkeit *die*. ⏹ **courtesy of** *prep* [thanks to] dank (+ *G*).

courthouse ['kɔːthaʊs] (*pl* [-haʊzɪz]) *n US* Gerichtsgebäude *das*.

court-martial (*pl* -s OR courts-martial) (UK) (US) *n* [trial] Kriegsgerichtsverhandlung *die*.

courtroom ['kɔːtrʊm] *n* Gerichtssaal *der*.

courtyard ['kɔːtjɑːd] *n* Hof *der*.

cousin ['kʌzn] *n* Cousin *der*, Kusine *die*.

cove [kəʊv] *n* Bucht *die*.

covenant ['kʌvənənt] *n* [of money] Zahlungsverpflichtung *die*.

cover ['kʌvər] ⟨⟩ *n* - **1.** [of machine, typewriter] Abdeckung *die*; [of seat, cushion] Überzug *der* - **2.** [lid] Deckel *der* - **3.** [of book, magazine] Einband *der* - **4.** [blanket] Decke *die* - **5.** (U) [protection, shelter, insurance] Schutz *der*; **to take cover** [from weather] sich unterlstellen; [from gunfire] in Deckung gehen; **under cover** [from weather] geschützt - **6.** [disguise] Tarnung *die*. ⟨⟩ *vt* - **1.** [gen] beldecken; **to be covered in blood** blutüberströmt sein - **2.** [insure]: **to cover sb (against sthg)** [subj: policy] jn (gegen etw) versichern - **3.** [report on] berichten über (+ *A*) - **4.** [deal with] behandeln - **5.** [pay for - damage] decken. ⏹ **cover up** *vt sep fig* [to conceal] vertuschen.

coverage ['kʌvərɪdʒ] *n (U)* [of news] Berichterstattung *die*.

cover charge *n* Gedeckgebühr *die*.

covering ['kʌvərɪŋ] *n* Belag *der*.

covering letter *UK*, **cover letter** *US n* Begleitbrief *der*.

cover note *n UK* vorläufiger Versicherungsschein.

covert ['kʌvət] *adj* verdeckt, versteckt; [look, glance] verstohlen.

cover-up *n* Vertuschung *die*.

covet ['kʌvɪt] *vt fml* begehren.

cow [kaʊ] ⟨⟩ *n* Kuh *die*. ⟨⟩ *vt* einlschüchtern.

coward ['kaʊəd] *n* Feigling *der*.

cowardly ['kaʊədlɪ] *adj* feige.

cowboy ['kaʊbɔɪ] *n* [cattlehand] Cowboy *der*.

cower ['kaʊər] *vi* sich ducken; [squat] kauern.

cox [kɒks], **coxswain** ['kɒksən] *n* Steuermann *der*.

coy [kɔɪ] *adj* kokett, neckisch.

cozy *adj & n US* = **cosy.**

crab [kræb] *n* Krabbe *die*, Krebs *der*.

crack [kræk] ⟨⟩ *n* - **1.** [fault] Riss *der*; [in cup, glass, mirror] Sprung *der* - **2.** [in curtains, door] Spalt *der*; [in wall] Ritze *die* - **3.** [sharp noise] Knall *der* - **4.** *inf* [attempt]: **to have a crack at sthg** sich an etw (*D*) versuchen - **5.** [cocaine] Crack *das*. ⟨⟩ *adj* toll, erstklassig. ⟨⟩ *vt* - **1.** [damage] einen Riss machen in (+ *D*); [cup, glass, mirror] anlschlagen; [skin] rissig machen - **2.** [whip] knallen mit - **3.** [bang, hit] anlschlagen; **I cracked my head on the doorpost** ich habe mir den Kopf am Türrahmen gestoßen - **4.** [solve] lösen; [code] knacken - **5.** *inf* [make]: **to crack a joke** einen Witz reißen. ⟨⟩ *vi* - **1.** [be damaged] einen Riss bekommen; [cup, glass, mirror] springen; [skin] auflspringen - **2.** [person] zusammenlbrechen. ⏹ **crack down** *vi*: **to crack down (on sb/sthg)** (bei jm/ etw) hart durchlgreifen. ⏹ **crack up** *vi* durchldrehen.

cracker ['krækər] *n* - **1.** [biscuit] Keks *der* - **2.** *UK* [for Christmas] Knallbonbon *das*.

crackers ['krækəz] *adj UK inf* [mad] verrückt.

crackle ['krækl] *vi* knacken.

cradle ['kreɪdl] ⟨⟩ *n* [bed, birthplace] Wiege *die*. ⟨⟩ *vt* an sich (*A*) drücken.

craft [krɑːft] *n* - **1.** [trade, skill] Handwerk *das* - **2.** (*pl inv*) [boat] Boot *das*.

craftsman ['krɑːftsmən] (*pl* -men [-mən]) *n* Handwerker *der*.

craftsmanship ['krɑːftsmənʃɪp] *n (U)* Handwerkskunst *die*.

crafty ['krɑːftɪ] *adj* schlau.

crag [kræg] *n* Felszacken *der*.

cram [kræm] ⟨⟩ *vt* - **1.** [stuff]: **to cram sthg into sthg** etw in etw (*A*) stopfen - **2.** [overfill]: **to be crammed (with sthg)** (mit etw) vollgestopft sein. ⟨⟩ *vi* [study] pauken, büffeln.

cramp [kræmp] ⟨⟩ *n* Krampf *der*; **I've got cramp** ich habe einen Krampf; **stomach cramps** Magenkrämpfe. ⟨⟩ *vt* [hinder] hemmen, behindern.

cranberry ['krænbərɪ] *n* Preiselbeere *die*.

crane [kreɪn] *n* [machine] Kran *der*.

crank [kræŋk] ⟨⟩ *n* - **1.** TECH Kurbel *die* - **2.** *inf* [eccentric] Spinner *der*, -in *die*. ⟨⟩ *vt* [handle, mechanism] kurbeln.

crankshaft ['kræŋkʃɑːft] *n* Kurbelwelle *die*.

cranny ['krænɪ] *n* ⟾ **nook.**

crap [kræp] *n v inf* Scheiße *die*.

crash [kræʃ] ⟨⟩ *n* - **1.** [of car] Unfall *der*; [of plane] Absturz *der*; [of train] Unglück *das*; [collision] Zusammenstoß *der*; **to have a crash** verunglücken; [collide] zusammenlstoßen - **2.** [loud noise] Krachen *das*. ⟨⟩ *vt* [car] einen Unfall haben mit; **she crashed her car into a tree** sie krachte mit dem Auto gegen einen Baum. ⟨⟩ *vi* - **1.** [car driver] verunglücken; [plane] ablstürzen; [collide] zusammenlstoßen;

to crash into sthg [in car] mit dem Auto gegen etw krachen - **2.** FIN [business, company] bankrott gehen; [stock market] zusammen|brechen.

crash course n Intensivkurs der.

crash helmet n Sturzhelm der.

crash-land vi eine Bruchlandung machen.

crass [kræs] adj dumm und geschmacklos.

crate [kreɪt] n Kiste die; [of milk bottles, beer] Kasten der.

crater ['kreɪtər] n Krater der.

cravat [krə'væt] n Halstuch das.

crave [kreɪv] <> vt sich sehnen nach. <> vi: **to crave for sthg** sich nach etw sehnen; [subj: pregnant woman] Gelüste auf etw (A) haben.

crawl [krɔːl] <> vi - **1.** [gen] kriechen; [baby, insect] krabbeln; **to crawl along** [traffic] im Schneckentempo vorwärts|kommen - **2.** inf [be covered]: **to be crawling with** wimmeln von. <> n [swimming stroke]: **the crawl** das Kraulen; **to do the crawl** kraulen.

crayfish ['kreɪfɪʃ] (pl inv OR -es) n [saltwater] Languste die.

crayon ['kreɪɒn] n [pencil] Buntstift der; [of wax] Wachsmalstift der.

craze [kreɪz] n Mode die (die gerade "in" ist); **the latest craze** der letzte Schrei.

crazy ['kreɪzɪ] adj inf - **1.** [mad] verrückt - **2.** [enthusiastic]: **to be crazy about sthg/sb** auf etw (A) /nach jm verrückt sein.

creak [kriːk] vi [door, floorboard] knarren; [bed, hinge, handle] quietschen.

cream [kriːm] <> adj [in colour] creme(farben). <> n - **1.** [food] Sahne die; [filling for chocolates, biscuits] Creme die - **2.** (U) [cosmetic] Creme die.

cream cake n UK Sahnetorte die; [bun] Sahnetörtchen das.

cream cheese n Frischkäse der.

cream cracker n UK Kräcker der.

cream tea n UK Nachmittagstee mit Gebäck, Marmelade und Sahne.

crease [kriːs] <> n [in fabric - deliberate] Bügelfalte die; [- accidental] Falte die. <> vt [deliberately] falten; [accidentally] zerknittern. <> vi [fabric] knittern.

create [kriː'eɪt] vt - **1.** [gen] schaffen; [the world] erschaffen - **2.** [noise, fuss] verursachen; [impression] machen; [difficulties] bereiten.

creation [kriː'eɪʃn] n - **1.** [gen] Schaffung die; [of the world] Erschaffung die - **2.** [work of art] Werk das; [dress, hat, hairstyle] Kreation die.

creative [kriː'eɪtɪv] adj kreativ.

creature ['kriːtʃər] n [animal] Lebewesen das, Geschöpf das.

crèche [kreʃ] n UK (Kinder)hort der.

credence ['kriːdns] n: **to give** OR **lend credence to sthg** etw glaubwürdig machen.

credentials [krɪ'denʃlz] npl - **1.** [papers] (Ausweis)papiere pl - **2.** fig [qualifications] Qualifikationen pl.

credibility [,kredə'bɪlətɪ] n Glaubwürdigkeit die.

credit ['kredɪt] <> n - **1.** [financial aid] Kredit der; **to be in credit** im Plus sein; **on credit** auf Kredit - **2.** (U) [honour] Ehre die; [approval] Anerkennung die; **he was never given any credit for it** man hat ihm nie Anerkennung dafür gezollt - **3.** SCH & UNIV [mark] Auszeichnung die; [unit of work] Schein der - **4.** FIN [money credited] Guthaben das. <> vt - **1.** FIN gut|schreiben - **2.** inf [believe] glauben - **3.** [attribute]: **to credit sb with sthg** jm etw zu|schreiben. ◆ **credits** npl CIN Nachspann der.

credit card n Kreditkarte die.

credit note n COMM & FIN Gutschrift die.

creditor ['kredɪtər] n Gläubiger der, -in die.

creed [kriːd] n - **1.** [political] Kredo das - **2.** RELIG Konfession die.

creek [kriːk] n - **1.** [of sea] Meeresarm der - **2.** US [stream] Bach der.

creep [kriːp] (pt & pp crept) <> vi [gen] kriechen; [person] schleichen. <> n inf [loathsome person] widerlicher Typ; [groveller] Schleimer der. ◆ **creeps** npl: **to give sb the creeps** inf jm nicht geheuer sein.

creeper ['kriːpər] n [plant - growing along ground] Kriechpflanze die; [- growing upwards] Kletterpflanze die.

creeping adj [gradual] schleichend.

creepy ['kriːpɪ] adj inf unheimlich.

creepy-crawly [-'krɔːlɪ] (pl creepy-crawlies) n inf Krabbeltier das.

cremate [krɪ'meɪt] vt einläschern.

cremation [krɪ'meɪʃn] n Einäscherung die.

crematorium UK [,kremə'tɔːrɪəm] (pl -riums OR -ria [-rɪə]), **crematory** US ['kremətrɪ] n Krematorium das.

crepe [kreɪp] n - **1.** [cloth] Krepp der - **2.** [rubber] Kreppgummi der - **3.** [thin pancake] Crêpe die.

crepe bandage n UK elastische Binde.

crepe paper n Krepppapier das.

crept [krept] pt & pp ⊳ **creep.**

crescent ['kresnt] n - **1.** [shape] Halbmond der - **2.** [street] halbkreisförmig verlaufende Straße.

cress [kres] n Kresse die.

crest [krest] n - **1.** [of bird] Haube die; [of cock, hill, wave] Kamm der - **2.** [of school, noble family] Wappen das.

crestfallen ['krest,fɔːln] adj geknickt.

Crete [kriːt] n Kreta nt.

cretin ['kretɪn] n inf pej Idiot der, -in die.

crevice ['krevɪs] n Spalte die.

crew [kruː] n - **1.** [of ship, plane] Besatzung die, Crew die - **2.** CIN & TV Crew die.

crew cut n Bürstenschnitt der.

crew-neck n runder Halsausschnitt.

crib [krɪb] ◇ n - 1. [cradle] Krippe die - 2. US [cot] Kinderbett das. ◇ vt inf [copy]: **to crib sthg off** OR **from sb** etw von jm abschreiben.

crick [krɪk] n: **I've got a crick in my neck** ich habe einen steifen Hals.

cricket ['krɪkɪt] n - 1. [game] Kricket das - 2. [insect] Grille die.

crime [kraɪm] n - 1. [gen] Verbrechen das; **crime is on the decrease** die Zahl der Verbrechen nimmt ab - 2. fig [shameful act] Schande die.

criminal ['krɪmɪnl] ◇ adj kriminell; [act, offence] strafbar. ◇ n Kriminelle der, die.

crimson ['krɪmzn] adj - 1. [in colour] purpurrot - 2. [with embarrassment] knallrot.

cringe [krɪndʒ] vi - 1. [out of fear] zurücklweichen - 2. inf [with embarrassment] schaudern; **to cringe at sthg** vor etw (D) zurücklschrecken.

crinkle ['krɪŋkl] vt [paper, clothes] zerknittern.

cripple ['krɪpl] ◇ n offens Krüppel der. ◇ vt - 1. MED [disable] zum Krüppel machen - 2. [ship, plane] aktionsunfähig machen - 3. fig [country, industry] lähmen.

crisis ['kraɪsɪs] (pl crises ['kraɪsiːz]) n Krise die.

crisp [krɪsp] adj - 1. [pastry, bacon] knusprig; [apple, vegetables] frisch und knackig - 2. [weather] frisch. ◆ **crisps** npl UK Chips Pl.

crisscross ['krɪskrɒs] ◇ adj [pattern] gitterartig. ◇ vt [subj: roads] kreuz und quer führen durch.

criterion [kraɪˈtɪərɪən] (pl -rions OR -ria [-rɪə]) n Kriterium das.

critic ['krɪtɪk] n Kritiker der, -in die.

critical ['krɪtɪkl] adj kritisch; [illness] schwer; [crucial] entscheidend; **to be critical of sb/sthg** jn/etw kritisieren.

critically ['krɪtɪklɪ] adv kritisch; [ill] schwer; **to be critically important** von entscheidender Bedeutung sein.

criticism ['krɪtɪsɪzm] n - 1. [gen] Kritik die - 2. [unfavourable comment] Kritikpunkt der.

criticize, -ise ['krɪtɪsaɪz] vt & vi kritisieren.

croak [krəʊk] vi [frog] quaken; [raven, person] krächzen.

Croat ['krəʊæt] ◇ adj kroatisch. ◇ n [person] Kroate der, -tin die.

Croatia [krəʊˈeɪʃə] n Kroatien nt.

Croatian [krəʊˈeɪʃn] adj & n = **Croat**.

crochet ['krəʊʃeɪ] n Häkeln das.

crockery ['krɒkərɪ] n Geschirr das.

crocodile ['krɒkədaɪl] (pl inv OR -s) n Krokodil das.

crocus ['krəʊkəs] (pl -cuses) n Krokus der.

crony ['krəʊnɪ] n inf [friend] Kumpel der.

crook [krʊk] n [criminal] Gauner der.

crooked ['krʊkɪd] adj - 1. [picture, tie, teeth] schief; [path] gewunden - 2. inf [dishonest - person] unehrlich; [- deal] krumm.

crop [krɒp] n - 1. [kind of plant] Feldfrucht die - 2. [harvest] Ernte die - 3. [whip] Reitpeitsche die - 4. [haircut] Kurzhaarschnitt der. ◆ **crop up** vi [problem] auftauchen.

croquette [krɒˈket] n Krokette die.

cross [krɒs] ◇ adj [angry] böse; **to be cross with sb** böse auf jn sein. ◇ n - 1. [gen] Kreuz das - 2. [hybrid] Kreuzung die. ◇ vt - 1. [street, road, river] überqueren; [room, desert] durchqueren; **it crossed my mind that...** der Gedanke ging mir durch den Kopf, dass... - 2. [place one across the other] (über)kreuzen; [arms] verschränken; [legs] übereinander schlagen - 3. UK [cheque] als Verrechnungsscheck kennzeichnen. ◇ vi [intersect] sich kreuzen. ◆ **cross off** vt sep streichen. ◆ **cross out** vt sep auslstreichen.

crossbar ['krɒsbɑːr] n - 1. [of goal] Querlatte die - 2. [of bicycle] Stange die.

cross-Channel ferry n Fähre die über den Ärmelkanal.

cross-country ◇ adj [run] Querfeldein-; [skiing] Langlauf-. ◇ n Querfeldeinlauf der.

cross-examine vt liter & fig ins Kreuzverhör nehmen.

cross-eyed [-aɪd] adj: **to be cross-eyed** schielen.

crossfire ['krɒs,faɪər] n Kreuzfeuer das.

crossing ['krɒsɪŋ] n - 1. [place] Übergang der - 2. [sea journey] Überfahrt die.

cross-legged [-legd] adv im Schneidersitz.

cross-purposes npl: **to talk at cross-purposes** aneinander vorbeilreden.

cross-reference n Querverweis der.

crossroads ['krɒsrəʊdz] (pl inv) n Kreuzung die.

cross-section n Querschnitt der.

crosswalk ['krɒswɔːk] n US Fußgängerüberweg der.

crossword (puzzle) ['krɒswɜːd-] n Kreuzworträtsel das.

crotch [krɒtʃ] n - 1. [of man] Hodengegend die; [of woman] Schamgegend die - 2. [of clothes] Schritt der.

crotchet ['krɒtʃɪt] n Viertel(note) die.

crotchety ['krɒtʃɪtɪ] adj UK inf griesgrämig.

crouch [kraʊtʃ] vi kauern.

crow [krəʊ] ◇ n Krähe die; **10 miles as the crow flies** 10 Meilen Luftlinie. ◇ vi - 1. [cock] krähen - 2. inf [gloat]: **to crow over sthg** sich mit etw brüsten.

crowbar ['krəʊbɑːr] n Brecheisen das.

crowd [kraʊd] ◇ n [mass of people] Menschenmenge die; **crowds of people** große

Menschenmengen. <> *vi* sich drängen. <> *vt* [streets, town] bevölkern; **we were crowded into a small room** wir wurden in ein kleines Zimmer gedrängt.

crowded ['kraʊdɪd] *adj* voll; [train, shop, bar] überfüllt; [timetable, flat] eng; **to be crowded with people** voller Menschen sein.

crown [kraʊn] <> *n* - **1.** [of monarch, tooth] Krone *die* - **2.** [top - of hat] oberes Ende; [- of head] Scheitel *der*; [- of hill] Kuppe *die*. <> *vt* - **1.** [king, queen] krönen - **2.** [tooth] überkronen - **3.** [top] bedecken. ➡ **Crown** *n*: **the Crown** [monarchy] die Krone.

crown jewels *npl* Kronjuwelen *Pl.*

crow's feet *npl* Krähenfüße *Pl.*

crucial ['kruːʃl] *adj* entscheidend.

crucifix ['kruːsɪfɪks] *n* Kruzifix *das*.

Crucifixion [,kruːsɪ'fɪkʃn] *n*: **the Crucifixion** die Kreuzigung.

crude [kruːd] *adj* - **1.** [raw] Roh-, roh - **2.** [vulgar] derb, ordinär - **3.** [drawing] grob; [method, shelter] primitiv.

crude oil *n* Rohöl *das*.

cruel [kruəl] *adj* grausam.

cruelty ['kruəltɪ] *n* Grausamkeit *die*; **cruelty to children** Kindesmisshandlung *die*; **cruelty to animals** Tierquälerei *die*.

cruet ['kruːɪt] *n* Menage *die*.

cruise [kruːz] <> *n* Kreuzfahrt *die*. <> *vi* [ship] kreuzen; [plane] fliegen.

cruiser ['kruːzə'] *n* - **1.** [warship] Kreuzer *der* - **2.** [cabin cruiser] Vergnügungsjacht *die*.

crumb [krʌm] *n* [of food] Krümel *der*.

crumble ['krʌmbl] <> *n* mit Streuseln bedeckte überbackene Obstnachspeise. <> *vt* zerkrümeln; [into larger pieces] zerbröckeln. <> *vi* - **1.** [plaster] bröckeln; [bread] krümeln; [building, wall] zerbröckeln - **2.** *fig* [society, empire] verfallen; [hopes] dahinlschwinden.

crumbly ['krʌmblɪ] *adj* [plaster] bröckelig; [bread, cake] krümelig.

crumpet ['krʌmpɪt] *n* kleines rundes Hefeteigbrot zum Toasten.

crumple ['krʌmpl] *vt* [clothes] zerknittern; [paper] zerknüllen.

crunch [krʌntʃ] <> *n (phrase)*: **if** OR **when it comes to the crunch** *inf* wenn es darauf anlkommt. <> *vt* [with teeth] (krachend) kauen.

crunchy ['krʌntʃɪ] *adj* [apple, vegetables] frisch und knackig; [chocolate bar] knusprig.

crusade [kruː'seɪd] *n* liter & *fig* Kreuzzug *der*.

crush [krʌʃ] <> *n* - **1.** [crowd] Gedränge *das* - **2.** *inf* [infatuation]: **to have a crush on sb** für jn schwärmen. <> *vt* - **1.** [squeeze - limb] quetschen; [- clothes, garlic] zerdrücken - **2.** [ice, tablet] zerstoßen - **3.** [destroy] zerquetschen; **to be**

crushed to death zu Tode gequetscht werden - **4.** *fig* [army, hopes] vernichten; [opposition] niederlschlagen.

crust [krʌst] *n* Kruste *die*.

crutch [krʌtʃ] *n* [stick] Krücke *die*.

crux [krʌks] *n* Kern *der*; **the crux of the matter** der springende Punkt.

cry [kraɪ] *n* - **1.** [shout] Ruf *der*; [louder] Schrei *der*; **a cry of pain** ein Schmerzensschrei; **a cry for help** ein Hilferuf - **2.** [of bird] Schrei *der*. ➡ **cry off** *vi* einen Rückzieher machen. ➡ **cry out** *vt sep* & *vi* schreien.

cryptic ['krɪptɪk] *adj* rätselhaft.

crystal ['krɪstl] *n* Kristall *der*.

cub [kʌb] *n* - **1.** [young animal] Junge *das* - **2.** [boy scout] Wölfling *der*.

Cuba ['kjuːbə] *n* Kuba *nt*.

Cuban ['kjuːbən] <> *adj* kubanisch. <> *n* Kubaner *der*, -in *die*.

cubbyhole ['kʌbɪhəʊl] *n* [room] Kabäuschen *das*; [compartment] Fach *das*.

cube [kjuːb] <> *n* - **1.** [object, shape] Würfel *der* - **2.** MATHS dritte Potenz. <> *vt* MATHS in die dritte Potenz erheben; **3 cubed** 3 hoch 3.

cubic ['kjuːbɪk] *adj* Kubik-.

cubicle ['kjuːbɪkl] *n* Kabine *die*.

Cub Scout *n* Wölfling *der*.

cuckoo ['kʊkuː] *n* Kuckuck *der*.

cuckoo clock *n* Kuckucksuhr *die*.

cucumber ['kjuːkʌmbə'] *n* Gurke *die*.

cuddle ['kʌdl] <> *n*: **to give sb a cuddle** jn in den Arm nehmen. <> *vt* an sich *(A)* drücken; [doll, dog] knuddeln. <> *vi* schmusen.

cuddly toy *n* Knuddeltier *das*.

cue [kjuː] *n* - **1.** RADIO, THEAT & TV Stichwort *das*; **on cue** wie gerufen - **2.** [in snooker, pool] Queue *das*.

cuff [kʌf] *n* - **1.** [of sleeve] Manschette *die* - **2.** US [of trouser] Aufschlag *der*.

cuff link *n* Manschettenknopf *der*.

cul-de-sac ['kʌldəsæk] *n* Sackgasse *die*.

cull [kʌl] <> *n* Kontrolle der Größe eines Viehbestands durch das Töten der schwächsten Tiere. <> *vt* - **1.** [kill]: **to cull seals** Robbenschlag betreiben - **2.** *fml* [gather] sammeln.

culminate ['kʌlmɪneɪt] *vi*: **to culminate in sthg** in etw *(D)* gipfeln.

culmination [,kʌlmɪ'neɪʃn] *n* Höhepunkt *der*.

culottes [kjuː'lɒts] *npl* Hosenrock *der*.

culpable ['kʌlpəbl] *adj fml* [person] schuldig.

culprit ['kʌlprɪt] *n* Schuldige *der*, *die*; [guilty of a crime] Täter *der*, -in *die*.

cult [kʌlt] <> *n* - **1.** RELIG Kult *der* - **2.** [book, film] Kultsymbol *das*. <> *comp* [book, film] Kult-.

cultivate ['kʌltɪveɪt] vt - 1. [farm - land] bebauen; [- crops] anlbauen - 2. [develop - interest, taste] entwickeln; [- friendship] pflegen; [- image] kultivieren.

cultural ['kʌltʃərəl] adj kulturell.

culture ['kʌltʃər] n Kultur die.

cultured ['kʌltʃəd] adj kultiviert.

cumbersome ['kʌmbəsəm] adj [object] unhandlich; [parcel] sperrig.

cunning ['kʌnɪŋ] <> adj [plan] schlau; [person] gerissen; [device] schlau ausgedacht. <> n [of plan] Schlauheit die; [of person] Gerissenheit die.

cup [kʌp] n - 1. [gen] Tasse die; **a cup of tea** eine Tasse Tee - 2. [trophy, competition] Pokal der - 3. [of bra] Körbchen das.

cupboard ['kʌbəd] n Schrank der.

Cup Final n: the Cup Final das Pokalendspiel.

curate ['kjʊərət] n Vikar der.

curator [,kjʊə'reɪtər] n [of museum] Kustos der.

curb [kɜːb] <> n - 1. [control]: **to put a curb on sthg** etw im Zaum halten - 2. US [of road] Bordstein der. <> vt zügeln.

curdle ['kɜːdl] vi gerinnen.

cure [kjʊər] <> n - 1. MED: cure (for) Heilmittel das (für) - 2. [solution]: cure (for sthg) Mittel das (gegen etw). <> vt - 1. MED [illness, person] heilen - 2. [solve] beheben - 3. [rid]: **to cure sb of sthg** fig jn von etw heilen - 4. [preserve - smoke] räuchern; [- salt] pökeln; [- dry] trocknen.

cure-all n Allheilmittel das.

curfew ['kɜːfjuː] n Ausgangssperre die.

curio ['kjʊərɪəʊ] (pl -s) n Kuriosität die.

curiosity [,kjʊərɪ'ɒsətɪ] n - 1. [inquisitiveness] Neugier die - 2. [rarity] Kuriosität die.

curious ['kjʊərɪəs] adj - 1. [inquisitive]: curious (about) neugierig (auf (+ A)) - 2. [strange] merkwürdig, seltsam.

curl [kɜːl] <> n [of hair] Locke die. <> vt - 1. [hair] in Locken legen - 2. [tail, ribbon] (ein)rollen. <> vi - 1. [hair] sich locken - 2. [paper, leaf] sich zusammenlrollen - 3. [smoke, snake] sich schlängeln. ◆ **curl up** vi [person, animal] sich zusammenlrollen; **to curl up in bed** sich ins Bett kuscheln.

curler ['kɜːlər] n Lockenwickler der.

curling tongs npl Lockenstab der.

curly ['kɜːlɪ] adj [hair] lockig.

currant ['kʌrənt] n Korinthe die.

currency ['kʌrənsɪ] n - 1. [money] Währung die - 2. fml [acceptability]: **to gain currency** sich verbreiten, Verbreitung finden.

current ['kʌrənt] <> adj gegenwärtig. <> n [flow - of water] Strömung die; [- of air] Luftströmung die; [- of electricity] Strom der.

current account n UK Girokonto das.

current affairs npl aktuelle Fragen Pl.

currently ['kʌrəntlɪ] adv gegenwärtig.

curriculum [kə'rɪkjələm] (pl -lums OR -la [-lə]) n Lehrplan der.

curriculum vitae [-'viːtaɪ] (pl curricula vitae) n Lebenslauf der.

curry ['kʌrɪ] n Currygericht das; **chicken curry** Huhn mit Curry(sauce).

curse [kɜːs] <> n - 1. [evil spell, swearword] Fluch der - 2. [source of problems] Plage die. <> vt verfluchen. <> vi [swear] fluchen.

cursor ['kɜːsər] n COMPUT Cursor der.

cursory ['kɜːsərɪ] adj flüchtig.

curt [kɜːt] adj barsch.

curtail [kɜː'teɪl] vt [visit] ablkürzen.

curtain ['kɜːtn] n [gen] Vorhang der.

curts(e)y ['kɜːtsɪ] (pt & pp curtsied) <> n Knicks der. <> vi knicksen.

curve [kɜːv] <> n Kurve die. <> vi [road, river] einen Bogen machen; [surface] sich wölben.

cushion ['kʊʃn] <> n [for sitting on] Kissen das. <> vt dämpfen, ablfangen.

cushy ['kʊʃɪ] adj inf bequem, lässig.

custard ['kʌstəd] n ≈ Vanillesoße die.

custody ['kʌstədɪ] n - 1. [of child] Sorgerecht das - 2. [of suspect]: **in custody** in Untersuchungshaft.

custom ['kʌstəm] n - 1. [tradition] Brauch der; [habit] Gepflogenheit die - 2. COMM [trade] Einkauf der. ◆ **customs** n (U) [place] Zoll der.

customary ['kʌstəmrɪ] adj üblich.

customer ['kʌstəmər] n Kunde der, -din die.

customize, -ise ['kʌstəmaɪz] vt - 1. [make] individuell herlrichten - 2. [modify] anlpassen, modifizieren.

Customs and Excise n (U) UK britische Finanzbehörde, die indirekte Steuern (Ex- und Importsteuer, Mehrwertsteuer und Verbrauchssteuer) einzieht und verwaltet.

customs duty n (U) Zoll der.

customs officer n Zollbeamte der, -tin die.

cut [kʌt] (pt & pp inv) <> n - 1. [slit] Schnitt der - 2. [wound] Schnittwunde die - 3. [of meat] Fleischstück das - 4. [in salary, film, article] Kürzung die - 5. [style - of clothes, hair] Schnitt der. <> vt - 1. [gen] schneiden; **to cut one's finger** sich (D) in den Finger schneiden - 2. [salary, costs, expenditure] reduzieren - 3. [grass] mähen - 4. [cards] ablheben - 5. inf [lecture, class] schwänzen. <> vi - 1. [gen] schneiden - 2. [intersect] sich kreuzen. ◆ **cut back** <> vt sep - 1. [prune] zurücklschneiden - 2. [reduce] reduzieren. <> vi: **to cut back on sthg** etw einlschränken. ◆ **cut down** <> vt sep - 1. [chop down] fällen - 2. [reduce] reduzieren. <> vi: **to cut down on sthg** etw einlschränken. ◆ **cut in** vi - 1. [interrupt]: **to cut in (on sb)** (jn) unterbrechen - 2. [in car]: **to cut in on** OR **in front of sb** jn schneiden. ◆ **cut**

off vt sep - **1.** [sever] ablschneiden - **2.** [disconnect - electricity, gas, telephone] ablstellen; **I got cut off** [on telephone] das Gespräch wurde unterbrochen - **3.** [isolate]: **to be cut off (from sb/ sthg)** (von jm/etw) abgeschnitten sein - **4.** [discontinue] stoppen. ◆ **cut out** vt sep - **1.** [article, photo] auslschneiden; [tumour] herauslschneiden - **2.** [sewing] zulschneiden - **3.** [stop] auflhören mit; **cut it out!** lass das sein! - **4.** [exclude] auslschließen. ◆ **cut up** vt sep [vegetables] schneiden; [wood] hacken; [meat] auflschneiden.

cutback ['kʌtbæk] n: cutback (in) Kürzung die (von).

cute [kju:t] adj süß.

cuticle ['kju:tɪkl] n Nagelhaut die.

cutlery ['kʌtlərɪ] n (U) Besteck das.

cutlet ['kʌtlɪt] n Kotelett das.

cutout ['kʌtaut] n - **1.** [on machine] Stoppschalter der - **2.** [shape] Ausschneidemodell das.

cut-price, cut-rate US adj Billig-.

cut-throat adj [ruthless] gnadenlos.

cutting ['kʌtɪŋ] ◇ adj [wit] scharf; [remark] spitz, verletzend; [person] sarkastisch. ◇ n - **1.** [of plant] Ableger der - **2.** [from newspaper] Ausschnitt der - **3.** UK [for road, railway] Durchstich der.

CV n abbr of **curriculum vitae**.

cwt. abbr of **hundredweight**.

cyanide ['saɪənaɪd] n Cyanid das.

cycle ['saɪkl] ◇ n - **1.** [series of events] Kreislauf der, Zyklus der - **2.** [of machine] Durchlauf der, Durchgang der - **3.** [bicycle] Fahrrad das - **4.** [of poems, songs] Zyklus der. ◇ comp Fahrrad-. ◇ vi Fahrrad fahren.

cycling ['saɪklɪŋ] n Fahrradfahren das.

cyclist ['saɪklɪst] n Fahrradfahrer der, -in die.

cylinder ['sɪlɪndər] n - **1.** [gen] Zylinder der - **2.** [for gas, oxygen] Flasche die.

cymbals ['sɪmblz] npl Becken das.

cynic ['sɪnɪk] n Zyniker der, -in die.

cynical ['sɪnɪkl] adj zynisch.

cynicism ['sɪnɪsɪzm] n Zynismus der.

Cypriot ['sɪprɪət] n Zypriot der, -in die.

Cyprus ['saɪprəs] n Zypern nt.

cyst [sɪst] n Zyste die.

czar [zɑːr] n Zar der.

Czech [tʃek] ◇ adj tschechisch. ◇ n - **1.** [person] Tscheche der, -chin die - **2.** [language] Tschechisch(e) das.

Czechoslovakia [ˌtʃekəslə'vækɪə] n Tschechoslowakei die.

Czech Republic n: the Czech Republic die Tschechische Republik.

D

d (pl **d's** OR **ds**), **D** (pl **D's** OR **Ds**) [diː] n [letter] d das, D das. ◆ **D** n - **1.** MUS D das; (phrase): **D flat** Des das - **2.** SCH [mark] ≃ vier.

DA n abbr of **district attorney**.

dab [dæb] ◇ n [small amount] Klecks der. ◇ vt - **1.** [skin, wound] abltupfen - **2.** [cream, ointment]: **to dab sthg on(to) sthg** etw auf etw (A) tupfen.

dabble ['dæbl] vi: **to dabble (in sthg)** [in politics etc] (mit etw (D)) sich nebenbei beschäftigen.

dachshund ['dækshʊnd] n Dackel der.

dad [dæd], **daddy** ['dædɪ] n inf Vati der.

daddy longlegs [-'lɒŋlegz] (pl inv) n Schnake die.

daffodil ['dæfədɪl] n Osterglocke die.

daft [dɑːft] adj UK inf doof, blöd.

dagger ['dægər] n Dolch der.

daily ['deɪlɪ] ◇ adj täglich. ◇ adv täglich. ◇ n [newspaper] Tageszeitung die.

dainty ['deɪntɪ] adj zierlich.

dairy ['deərɪ] n - **1.** [on farm] Molkerei die - **2.** [shop] Milchgeschäft das.

dairy products npl Molkereiprodukte Pl.

dais ['deɪɪs] n Podium das.

daisy ['deɪzɪ] n Gänseblümchen das.

dam [dæm] ◇ n (Stau)damm der. ◇ vt (auf)stauen.

damage ['dæmɪdʒ] ◇ n: damage (to sthg) Schaden der (an etw (D)). ◇ vt - **1.** [physically] beschädigen - **2.** fig [chances, reputation] schaden (+ D). ◆ **damages** npl LAW Schaden(s)ersatz der.

damn [dæm] ◇ adj & adv inf verdammt. ◇ n inf: **not to give OR care a damn (about sthg)** sich einen Dreck scheren (um etw). ◇ vt RELIG [condemn] verdammen. ◇ excl inf verdammt!, Mist!

damned [dæmd] inf ◇ adj verdammt; **well I'll be OR I'm damned!** Donnerwetter! ◇ adv verdammt.

damning ['dæmɪŋ] adj vernichtend.

damp [dæmp] ◇ adj feucht. ◇ n Feuchtigkeit die. ◇ vt anlfeuchten.

dampen ['dæmpən] vt - **1.** [make wet] anlfeuchten - **2.** fig [emotion] dämpfen.

damson ['dæmzn] n Damaszenerpflaume die.

dance [dɑːns] ◇ n - **1.** [gen] Tanz der - **2.** [social event] Tanzabend der - **3.** [art form] Tanzen das. ◇ vi tanzen.

dancer ['dɑːnsəʳ] n Tänzer der, -in die.

dancing ['dɑːnsɪŋ] n Tanzen das.

dandelion ['dændɪlaɪən] n Löwenzahn der.

dandruff ['dændrʌf] n Schuppen Pl.

Dane [deɪn] n Däne der, -nin die.

danger ['deɪndʒəʳ] n Gefahr die; **in danger** in Gefahr; **out of danger** außer Gefahr; **danger to sb/sthg** Gefahr für jn/etw; **to be in danger of doing sthg** Gefahr laufen, etw zu tun.

dangerous ['deɪndʒərəs] adj gefährlich.

dangle ['dæŋgl] <> vt baumeln lassen; **to dangle sthg in front of sb** fig jn mit etw locken. <> vi baumeln.

Danish ['deɪnɪʃ] <> adj dänisch. <> n [language] Dänisch(e) das.

Danish (pastry) n Hefeteilchen das.

dank [dæŋk] adj naßkalt.

dapper ['dæpəʳ] adj adrett.

dappled ['dæpld] adj scheckig.

dare [deəʳ] <> vt - 1. [be brave enough]: **to dare to do sthg** sich trauen, etw zu tun - 2. [challenge]: **to dare sb to do sthg** jn herausfordern, etw zu tun - 3. phr: **I dare say** ich glaube schon. <> vi es wagen, sich trauen; **how dare you!** was fällt dir ein! <> n Mutprobe die.

daredevil ['deə,devl] n Draufgänger der, -in die.

daring ['deərɪŋ] <> adj [person, action] kühn, verwegen; [comment, clothes] gewagt. <> n Wagemut der, Kühnheit die.

dark [dɑːk] <> adj dunkel. <> n - 1. [darkness]: **the dark** die Dunkelheit; **to be in the dark about sthg** fig keine Ahnung von etw haben - 2. [night]: **before/after dark** vor/nach Einbruch der Dunkelheit.

darken ['dɑːkn] <> vt verdunkeln. <> vi [gen] sich verdunkeln.

dark glasses npl Sonnenbrille die.

darkness ['dɑːknɪs] n Dunkelheit die.

darkroom ['dɑːkrum] n Dunkelkammer die.

darling ['dɑːlɪŋ] <> adj [dear] lieb. <> n - 1. [loved person, term of address] Schatz der - 2. [favourite] Liebling der.

darn [dɑːn] <> adj & adv inf verdammt, verflixt. <> vt [repair] stopfen.

dart [dɑːt] <> n [arrow] (Wurf)pfeil der. <> vi [move quickly] flitzen. **darts** n (U) [game] Darts Pl.

dartboard ['dɑːtbɔːd] n Dartscheibe die.

dash [dæʃ] <> n - 1. [of liquid] Schuss der - 2. [in punctuation] Gedankenstrich der - 3. [rush]: **to make a dash for sthg** sich auf etw (A) stürzen. <> vt - 1. liter [throw] schleudern - 2. [hopes] zerstören. <> vi stürzen.

dashboard ['dæʃbɔːd] n Armaturenbrett das.

dashing ['dæʃɪŋ] adj [man] schneidig, flott.

data ['deɪtə] n Daten Pl.

database ['deɪtəbeɪs] n Datenbank die.

data processing n Datenverarbeitung die.

date [deɪt] <> n - 1. [in time] Datum das; **to bring sb up to date** jn über den Stand der Dinge informieren; **to bring sthg up to date** etw auf den neuesten Stand bringen; **out of date** [fashion, dictionary] veraltet; [passport] abgelaufen; **to keep sb/sthg up to date** jn/etw auf dem Laufenden halten; **to date** bis heute - 2. [appointment, person] Verabredung die - 3. [fruit] Dattel die. <> vt - 1. [gen] datieren - 2. [go out with] ausgehen mit. <> vi [go out of fashion] altmodisch werden.

dated ['deɪtɪd] adj altmodisch.

date of birth n Geburtsdatum das.

daub [dɔːb] vt: **to daub sthg with sthg** etw mit etw beschmieren; **to daub sthg on sthg** etw auf etw (A) schmieren.

daughter ['dɔːtəʳ] n Tochter die.

daughter-in-law (pl **daughters-in-law**) n Schwiegertochter die.

daunting ['dɔːntɪŋ] adj überwältigend.

dawdle ['dɔːdl] vi trödeln.

dawn [dɔːn] <> n - 1. [of day] Morgengrauen das, Tagesanbruch der - 2. fig [of era, period] Beginn der. <> vi liter & fig an|brechen; **the day is dawning** es dämmert. **dawn (up)on** vt insep: **it finally dawned on me that...** mir dämmerte schließlich, dass...

day [deɪ] n - 1. [gen] Tag der; **the day before/after** am Tag zuvor/danach; **the day before yesterday** vorgestern; **the day after tomorrow** übermorgen; **any day now** jeden Tag (in Kürze); **one day, some day, one of these days** irgendwann, eines Tages; **to make sb's day** jn sehr erfreuen - 2. [period]: **in those days** damals; **in my day** zu meiner Zeit. **days** adv [work] tagsüber.

daybreak ['deɪbreɪk] n Tagesanbruch der; **at daybreak** bei Tagesanbruch.

daycentre ['deɪsentəʳ] n UK [for old people] Altentagesstätte die; [for children] Kindertagesstätte die.

daydream ['deɪdriːm] vi [not concentrate] vor sich hin träumen; [be idealistic] Luftschlösser bauen.

daylight ['deɪlaɪt] n - 1. [light] Tageslicht das - 2. [dawn] Tagesanbruch der.

day off (pl **days off**) n arbeitsfreier Tag.

day return n UK Tagesrückfahrkarte die.

daytime ['deɪtaɪm] <> n Tag der. <> comp: **daytime job** Arbeit am Tage oder über Tag; **daytime television** tagsüber ausgestrahlte Fernsehprogramme.

day-to-day adj [routine, life] (all)täglich; **on a day-to-day basis** tageweise.

day trip n Tagesausflug der.

daze [deɪz] <> n: **in a daze** benommen, betäubt. <> vt benommen machen.

dazzle ['dæzl] vt blenden.

DC n abbr of **direct current**.

deacon ['di:kn] n Diakon der.

deactivate [,di:'æktɪveɪt] vt entschärfen.

dead [ded] <> adj - 1. [person, animal, flower] tot; **the dead man/woman** der/die Tote; **to shoot sb dead** jn erschießen - 2. [battery] leer; [telephone line, radio] tot - 3. [numb - arm, fingers] wie abgestorben, taub - 4. [lifeless - town] wie ausgestorben; [- party] öde. <> adv - 1. [precisely] genau; **it's dead ahead** es ist genau geradeaus; **dead on time** auf die Minute pünktlich - 2. inf [very] total; **'dead slow'** 'Schrittgeschwindigkeit'; **dead tired** todmüde - 3. [suddenly]: **to stop dead** [in car] plötzlich stehen bleiben. <> npl: **the dead** die Toten Pl.

deaden ['dedn] vt - 1. [noise] dämpfen - 2. [feeling] betäuben.

dead end n liter & fig Sackgasse die.

dead heat n totes Rennen.

deadline ['dedlaɪn] n letztmöglicher Termin.

deadlock ['dedlɒk] n Stillstand der.

dead loss n inf Reinfall der; **dead loss at sthg** Niete die in etw (D).

deadly ['dedlɪ] <> adj tödlich; [enemy, sin] Tod-. <> adv tödlich.

deadpan ['dedpæn] adj [delivery, manner] ausdruckslos; [humour] trocken.

deaf [def] <> adj taub; **to be deaf to sthg** fig sich in Bezug auf etw (A) taub stellen. <> npl: **the deaf** die Gehörlosen Pl.

deaf-aid n UK Hörgerät das.

deaf-and-dumb adj taubstumm.

deafen ['defn] vt taub machen.

deafness ['defnɪs] n Taubheit die.

deal [di:l] (pt & pp dealt) <> n - 1. [quantity]: **a good OR great deal** (sehr) viel; **a good OR great deal of** eine Menge - 2. [business agreement] Geschäft das; **to do OR strike a deal with sb** ein Geschäft mit jm abschließen - 3. inf [treatment]: **to give sb a fair/rough deal** jn fair/unfair behandeln. <> vt - 1. [strike]: **to deal sb/ sthg a blow, to deal a blow to sb/sthg** jm/etw einen Schlag versetzen - 2. [cards] austeilen. <> vi - 1. [in cards] geben - 2. [in drugs, arms] handeln. ▸ **deal in** vt insep COMM handeln mit. ▸ **deal out** vt sep - 1. [cards] austeilen - 2. [share out] verteilen. ▸ **deal with** vt insep - 1. [handle, cope with] sich kümmern um - 2. [be concerned with] handeln von - 3. [be faced with] es zu tun haben mit.

dealer ['di:lər] n - 1. [trader] Händler der, -in die - 2. [in cards] Kartengeber der, -in die.

dealing ['di:lɪŋ] n [trading] Handel der. ▸ **dealings** npl [relations] Umgang der; **to have dealings with sb** mit jm (geschäftlich) zu tun haben.

dealt [delt] pt & pp ▷ **deal**.

dean [di:n] n UNIV & RELIG Dekan der.

dear [dɪər] <> adj - 1. [loved] lieb; **to be dear to sb** jm lieb und teuer sein - 2. esp UK [expensive] teuer - 3. [in letter]: **Dear Tony** Lieber Tony; **Dear Mr Blair** Sehr geehrter Herr Blair; **Dear Sir or Madam** Sehr geehrte Damen und Herren. <> n: **my dear** mein Lieber, meine Liebe. <> excl: **oh dear!** ach je!; **dear me!** du meine Güte!

dearly ['dɪəlɪ] adv [love] von ganzem Herzen; [hope, wish] sehr.

death [deθ] n Tod der; **to frighten/worry sb to death** jn zu Tode erschrecken; **to be sick to death of sthg** etw gründlich satt haben.

death certificate n Totenschein der.

death duty UK, **death tax** US n Erbschaftssteuer die.

deathly ['deθlɪ] adj [silence] tödlich.

death penalty n Todesstrafe die.

death rate n Sterblichkeitsrate die.

death tax n US = **death duty**.

death trap n inf Todesfalle die.

debar [di:'bɑ:r] vt ausschließen.

debase [dɪ'beɪs] vt [quality, value, concept] entwerten; **to debase o.s.** sich erniedrigen.

debate [dɪ'beɪt] <> n Debatte die; **to be open to debate** zur Debatte stehen. <> vt debattieren, diskutieren; **to debate whether to do sthg** darüber diskutieren, ob etw getan werden soll. <> vi debattieren, diskutieren.

debauchery [dɪ'bɔ:tʃərɪ] n Ausschweifung die.

debit ['debɪt] <> n Soll das, Debet das. <> vt debitieren, belasten.

debris ['deɪbri:] n (U) Trümmer Pl.

debt [det] n Schuld die; **to be in debt** Schulden haben; **to be in sb's debt** in js Schuld stehen.

debt collector n Schuldeneintreiber der.

debtor ['detər] n Schuldner der, -in die.

debug [,di:'bʌg] vt COMPUT [program] Fehler beseitigen in.

debunk [,di:'bʌŋk] vt entlarven.

debut ['deɪbju:] n Debüt das.

decade ['dekeɪd] n Jahrzehnt das.

decadence ['dekədəns] n Dekadenz die.

decadent ['dekədənt] adj dekadent.

decaffeinated [dɪ'kæfɪneɪtɪd] adj entkoffeiniert.

decanter [dɪ'kæntər] n Karaffe die.

decathlon [dɪ'kæθlɒn] n Zehnkampf der.

decay [dɪ'keɪ] <> n - 1. [of body] Verwesung die; [of plant, wood] Verrotten das; (tooth) decay Karies die - 2. fig [of building] Zerfall der; [of society] Untergang der. <> vi - 1. [tooth] faulen; [body] verwesen; [plant, wood] verrotten - 2. fig [building] zerfallen; [society] untergehen.

deceased [dɪ'si:st] (pl inv) fml <> adj verstorben. <> n: **the deceased** der/die Verstorbene.

deceit [dɪ'si:t] n Betrug der.

deceitful [dɪ'si:tful] adj betrügerisch.

deceive [dɪ'si:v] vt [trick] betrügen; [subj: memory, eyes] täuschen; **to deceive o.s.** sich (D) selbst etwas vormachen.

December [dɪ'sembər] n Dezember der; see also **September**.

decency ['di:snsɪ] n [respectability] Anstand der; **he didn't have the decency to thank me** er hat es nicht für nötig gehalten, sich bei mir zu bedanken.

decent ['di:snt] adj anständig; **are you decent?** [dressed] hast du was an?

deception [dɪ'sepʃn] n Täuschung die.

deceptive [dɪ'septɪv] adj irreführend.

decide [dɪ'saɪd] <> vt - 1. [resolve] (sich) entscheiden, beschließen; **to decide to do sthg** (sich) entscheiden etw zu tun; **to decide that...** entscheiden, dass..., beschließen, dass... - 2. [issue, case, match] entscheiden; **what finally decided you?** was hat dich schließlich dazu gebracht? <> vi [make up one's mind] (sich) entscheiden, (sich) entschließen. ◆ **decide (up)on** vt insep sich entscheiden für.

decided [dɪ'saɪdɪd] adj - 1. [distinct] entschieden - 2. [resolute] bestimmt.

decidedly [dɪ'saɪdɪdlɪ] adv - 1. [distinctly] entschieden - 2. [resolutely] bestimmt.

deciduous [dɪ'sɪdjʊəs] adj Laub-.

decimal ['desɪml] <> adj dezimal.·<> n Dezimalzahl die.

decimal point n Dezimalpunkt der.

decimate ['desɪmeɪt] vt dezimieren.

decipher [dɪ'saɪfər] vt entziffern.

decision [dɪ'sɪʒn] n [choice, judgement] Entscheidung die.

decisive [dɪ'saɪsɪv] adj - 1. [person] entschlossen - 2. [factor, event] entscheidend.

deck [dek] n - 1. [of ship, bus, plane] Deck das - 2. [of cards] Spiel das - 3. US [of house] Terrasse die.

deckchair ['dektʃeər] n Liegestuhl der.

declaration [,deklə'reɪʃn] n - 1. [statement, proclamation] Erklärung die - 2. [to customs] Zollerklärung die.

Declaration of Independence n: the Declaration of Independence die (amerikanische) Unabhängigkeitserklärung.

declare [dɪ'kleər] vt - 1. [state, proclaim] erklären - 2. [goods at customs, taxes] deklarieren.

decline [dɪ'klaɪn] <> n Niedergang der; **to be in decline** sich verschlechtern; **to be on the decline** (ab)sinken. <> vt [offer, request] ablehnen; **to decline to do sthg** ablehnen, etw zu tun. <> vi - 1. [deteriorate] sich verschlechtern - 2. [refuse] ablehnen.

decode [,di:'kəʊd] vt entschlüsseln.

decompose [,di:kəm'pəʊz] vi [vegetable matter] verfaulen; [flesh] verwesen.

decongestant [,di:kən'dʒestənt] n schleimlösendes Mittel.

decorate ['dekəreɪt] vt - 1. [make pretty - cake, dessert] verzieren; [- with balloons, streamers, flags] dekorieren, schmücken - 2. [with paint] streichen; [with wallpaper] tapezieren - 3. [with medal] auslzeichnen.

decoration [,dekə'reɪʃn] n - 1. [ornament] Dekoration die; [on cake] Verzierung die; **Christmas tree decorations** Christbaumschmuck der - 2. [appearance of room, building] Dekor das - 3. [medal] Auszeichnung die.

decorator ['dekəreɪtər] n Maler der, -in die.

decoy <> n [dɪ'kɔɪ] - 1. [for hunting] Köder der - 2. [person] Lockvogel der. <> vt [dɪ'kɔɪ] anlocken.

decrease <> n ['di:kri:s]: **decrease (in sthg)** [crime, unemployment] Rückgang der (an etw (D)); [size, spending] Abnahme die (einer Sache (G)). <> vt [dɪ'kri:s] verringern; [price] herablsetzen. <> vi [dɪ'kri:s] [in size] ablnehmen; [of numbers] zurücklgehen, sinken.

decree [dɪ'kri:] <> n - 1. [order, decision] Erlass der - 2. US [judgment] Urteil das. <> vt verordnen.

decree nisi [-'naɪsaɪ] (pl decrees nisi) n UK LAW vorläufiges Scheidungsurteil.

decrepit [dɪ'krepɪt] adj [person] altersschwach; [house, car] heruntergekommen.

dedicate ['dedɪkeɪt] vt - 1. [book, song, poem]: **to dedicate sthg to sb** jm etw widmen - 2. [devote]: **to dedicate one's life to sthg** sein Leben etw (D) widmen.

dedication [,dedɪ'keɪʃn] n - 1. [commitment] Hingabe die - 2. [in book] Widmung die.

deduce [dɪ'dju:s] vt schließen; **to deduce sthg from sthg** etw aus etw schließen.

deduct [dɪ'dʌkt] vt: **to deduct sthg (from)** etw ablziehen (von).

deduction [dɪ'dʌkʃn] n - 1. [conclusion] Folgerung die - 2. [of money, number] Abzug der.

deed [di:d] n - 1. [action] Tat die - 2. LAW Urkunde die; **deed of sale** Kaufvertrag der.

deem [di:m] vt fml erachten; **to deem it wise to do sthg** es für sinnvoll erachten, etw zu tun.

deep [di:p] <> adj - 1. [gen] tief - 2. [colour] dunkel - 3. [thoughts, feelings] stark - 4. [sigh, breath] schwer. <> adv tief; **deep down** fig innerlich.

deepen ['di:pn] vi - 1. [river, sea] tiefer werden - 2. [crisis, recession, feeling] sich verstärken.

deep freeze n Tiefkühltruhe die.

deep-fry *vt* frittieren.

deeply ['di:plɪ] *adv* - **1.** [gen] tief - **2.** [grateful, sorry, regret, moving] zutiefst.

deep-sea *adj* Tiefsee-.

deer [dɪər] (*pl inv*) *n* [male] Hirsch *der*; [female] Reh *das*.

deface [dɪ'feɪs] *vt* [poster] verunstalten.

defamatory [dɪ'fæmətrɪ] *adj fml* verleumderisch.

default [dɪ'fɔ:lt] <> *n* - **1.** [failure]: **to win by default** durch Nichtantreten des Gegners gewinnen - **2.** COMPUT Voreinstellung *die*. <> *vi* [in sports] nicht anltreten.

defeat [dɪ'fi:t] <> *n* Niederlage *die*; [of motion] Ablehnung *die*; **to admit defeat** sich geschlagen geben. <> *vt* - **1.** [team, opponent] schlagen - **2.** [motion, proposal] ablehnen.

defeatist [dɪ'fi:tɪst] <> *adj* defätistisch. <> *n* Defätist *der*.

defect <> *n* ['di:fekt] Mangel *der*, Fehler *der*. <> *vi* [dɪ'fekt] POL überllaufen.

defective [dɪ'fektɪv] *adj* defekt.

defence UK, **defense** US [dɪ'fens] *n* - **1.** [gen] Verteidigung *die*; **in my defence** zu meiner Verteidigung - **2.** [protective device, system] Abwehr *die*.

defenceless UK, **defenseless** US [dɪ'fenslɪs] *adj* schutzlos.

defend [dɪ'fend] *vt* verteidigen; **to defend sb against sb/sthg** jn gegen jn/etw verteidigen.

defendant [dɪ'fendənt] *n* Angeklagte *der, die*, Beklagte *der, die*.

defender [dɪ'fendər] *n* Verteidiger *der*, -in *die*.

defense *n US* = **defence.**

defenseless *adj US* = **defenceless.**

defensive [dɪ'fensɪv] <> *adj* - **1.** [weapons, tactics] Verteidigungs- - **2.** [person] defensiv. <> *n*: **on the defensive** in der Defensive.

defer [dɪ'fɜ:r] <> *vt* verschieben. <> *vi*: **to defer to sb** sich jm beugen, sich jm fügen.

deferential [ˌdefə'renʃl] *adj* respektvoll.

defiance [dɪ'faɪəns] *n* Trotz *der*; **in defiance of sb/sthg** jm/etw zum Trotz.

defiant [dɪ'faɪənt] *adj* trotzig.

deficiency [dɪ'fɪʃnsɪ] *n* - **1.** [lack] Mangel *der* - **2.** [inadequacy] Mangelhaftigkeit *die*.

deficient [dɪ'fɪʃnt] *adj* - **1.** [lacking]: **he is deficient in sthg** es mangelt ihm an etw (D) - **2.** [inadequate] ungenügend.

deficit ['defɪsɪt] *n* Defizit *das*.

defile [dɪ'faɪl] *vt* besudeln.

define [dɪ'faɪn] *vt* - **1.** [give meaning of] definieren - **2.** [describe] bestimmen, festlegen.

definite ['defɪnɪt] *adj* - **1.** [plan, date] bestimmt, definitiv - **2.** [answer] eindeutig; [improvement, difference] deutlich - **3.** [confident - person] bestimmt.

definitely ['defɪnɪtlɪ] *adv* definitiv.

definition [defɪ'nɪʃn] *n* - **1.** [of word, expression, concept] Definition *die* - **2.** [of image] Bildschärfe *die*.

deflate [dɪ'fleɪt] <> *vt* [balloon, tyre] die Luft ablassen aus. <> *vi* [balloon, tyre] Luft verlieren.

deflation [dɪ'fleɪʃn] *n* ECON Deflation *die*.

deflect [dɪ'flekt] *vt* ablenken.

defogger [ˌdi:'fɒgər] *n US* AUT Scheibenbelüftung *die*.

deformed [dɪ'fɔ:md] *adj* deformiert.

defraud [dɪ'frɔ:d] *vt* betrügen.

defrost [ˌdi:'frɒst] <> *vt* - **1.** [fridge] abltauen; [frozen food] aufltauen - **2.** US AUT [de-ice] enteisen; [demist] belüften. <> *vi* - **1.** [fridge] abltauen - **2.** [frozen food] aufltauen.

deft [deft] *adj* geschickt.

defunct [dɪ'fʌŋkt] *adj* [organization] nicht mehr bestehend.

defuse [ˌdi:'fju:z] *vt UK liter & fig* entschärfen.

defy [dɪ'faɪ] *vt* - **1.** [disobey] trotzen (+ D) - **2.** [challenge]: **to defy sb to do sthg** jn herauslfordern, etw zu tun - **3.** *fig*: **that defies description** das spottet jeder Beschreibung.

degenerate <> *adj* [dɪ'dʒenərət] degeneriert, entartet. <> *vi* [dɪ'dʒenəreɪt]: **to degenerate (into)** auslarten (zu).

degrading [dɪ'greɪdɪŋ] *adj* entwürdigend.

degree [dɪ'gri:] *n* - **1.** [unit of measurement] Grad *der* - **2.** [qualification] akademischer Grad; **to have/take a degree (in sthg)** einen akademischen Abschluss (in etw (D)) haben/machen - **3.** [amount - of risk, truth] Maß *das*; *(phrase)*: **to a (certain) degree** bis zu einem gewissen Grad; **by degrees** allmählich, nach und nach.

dehydrated [ˌdi:haɪ'dreɪtɪd] *adj* [person] ausgetrocknet.

de-ice [di:'aɪs] *vt* enteisen.

deign [deɪn] *vi*: **to deign to do sthg** sich herablassen, etw zu tun.

deity ['di:ɪtɪ] *n* Gottheit *die*.

dejected [dɪ'dʒektɪd] *adj* niedergeschlagen.

delay [dɪ'leɪ] <> *n* Verspätung *die*. <> *vt* - **1.** [plane, train, traveller] auflhalten; [start, operation, recovery] verzögern - **2.** [postpone - meeting, journey, decision] verschieben; *(phrase)*: **to delay doing sthg** es auflschieben, etw zu tun. <> *vi* zögern.

delayed [dɪ'leɪd] *adj* verspätet.

delectable [dɪ'lektəbl] *adj* - **1.** [food] köstlich - **2.** [person] reizend.

delegate <> *n* ['delɪgət] Delegierte *der, die*. <> *vt* ['delɪgeɪt] delegieren; **to delegate sb to do sthg** jn beauftragen, etw zu tun; **to delegate sthg to sb** jm mit etw beauftragen.

delegation [,delɪ'geɪʃn] n - **1.** [group of people] Delegation die - **2.** (U) [act of delegating] Delegieren das.

delete [dɪ'liːt] vt [word, line, name] streichen; COMPUT löschen, entfernen.

deli ['delɪ] n abbr of **delicatessen**.

deliberate <> adj [dɪ'lɪbərət] - **1.** [intentional] absichtlich - **2.** [slow] bedächtig. <> vi [dɪ'lɪbəreɪt] fml beraten.

deliberately [dɪ'lɪbərətlɪ] adv [on purpose] absichtlich.

delicacy ['delɪkəsɪ] n - **1.** [of lace, china] Feinheit die; [of health, instrument] Empfindlichkeit die - **2.** (U) [tact] Feingefühl das - **3.** [food] Delikatesse die.

delicate ['delɪkət] adj - **1.** [lace, china, flavour] fein; [fingers, colour] zart - **2.** [child, person, health, instrument] empfindlich - **3.** [situation, subject] heikel.

delicatessen [,delɪkə'tesn] n Delikatessengeschäft das.

delicious [dɪ'lɪʃəs] adj [tasty] köstlich.

delight [dɪ'laɪt] <> n Freude die; **to take delight in doing sthg** Freude daran haben, etw zu tun. <> vt erfreuen. <> vi: **to delight in doing sthg** sich damit vergnügen, etw zu tun.

delighted [dɪ'laɪtɪd] adj sehr erfreut; **delighted by** OR **with sthg** hocherfreut über etw (A); **to be delighted to do sthg** etw mit Vergnügen tun.

delightful [dɪ'laɪtfʊl] adj reizend; [meal] köstlich.

delinquent [dɪ'lɪŋkwənt] <> adj straffällig. <> n Straftäter der, -in die.

delirious [dɪ'lɪrɪəs] adj - **1.** MED im Delirium - **2.** [ecstatic] ekstatisch.

deliver [dɪ'lɪvər] vt - **1.** [distribute]: **to deliver sthg (to sb)** [mail, newspaper] (jm) etw zustellen; COMM (jm) etw liefern - **2.** [give - speech, lecture] halten; [- message, warning] überbringen - **3.** [a blow, kick] versetzen - **4.**: **to deliver a woman's baby** eine Frau von ihrem Baby entbinden - **5.** fml [liberate]: **to deliver sb (from sthg)** jn (von etw) erlösen - **6.** US POL [votes] stellen.

delivery [dɪ'lɪvərɪ] n - **1.** [of goods] Lieferung die; [of letters] Zustellung die - **2.** (U) [way of speaking] Vortragsweise die - **3.** [birth] Entbindung die.

delude [dɪ'luːd] vt täuschen; **to delude o.s.** sich etwas vormachen.

delusion [dɪ'luːʒn] n Täuschung die.

delve [delv] vi - **1.** [into mystery]: **to delve into sthg** sich in etw (A) vertiefen - **2.** [in bag, cupboard] greifen.

demand [dɪ'mɑːnd] <> n - **1.** [claim, firm request] Forderung die; **it makes great demands on my time** es nimmt viel von meiner Zeit in Anspruch; **on demand** bei Bedarf - **2.** (U) COMM: **demand (for)** Nachfrage die (nach); in

demand [product, person] gefragt. <> vt - **1.** [request forcefully] fordern, verlangen; **to demand to do sthg** verlangen, etw zu tun - **2.** [enquire forcefully] zu wissen verlangen - **3.** [require] erfordern.

demanding [dɪ'mɑːndɪŋ] adj - **1.** [job] anstrengend - **2.** [person, public] anspruchsvoll.

demean [dɪ'miːn] vt erniedrigen.

demeaning [dɪ'miːnɪŋ] adj erniedrigend.

demeanour UK, **demeanor** US [dəmiːnər] n (U) fml Verhalten das.

demented [dɪ'mentɪd] adj wahnsinnig.

demise [dɪ'maɪz] n (U) fml - **1.** [death] Ableben das - **2.** fig [of company, custom] Ende das.

demister [,diː'mɪstər] n UK AUT Scheibenbelüftung die.

demo ['deməʊ] (pl -s) n inf abbr of **demonstration**.

democracy [dɪ'mɒkrəsɪ] n Demokratie die.

democrat ['deməkræt] n Demokrat der, -in die. ▸ **Democrat** n US Wähler bzw. Angehöriger der Demokratischen Partei der USA.

democratic [,demə'krætɪk] adj demokratisch. ▸ **Democratic** adj US die Demokratische Partei der USA betreffend.

Democratic Party n US: **the Democratic Party** die Demokraten.

demolish [dɪ'mɒlɪʃ] vt - **1.** [building] abreißen - **2.** [idea, argument] zunichte machen.

demonstrate ['demənstreɪt] <> vt - **1.** [prove] beweisen - **2.** [appliance, machine] vorführen - **3.** [ability, talent] zeigen. <> vi: **to demonstrate (for/against)** demonstrieren (für/gegen).

demonstration [demən'streɪʃn] n - **1.** [public meeting] Demonstration die - **2.** [of new appliance, machine] Vorführung die - **3.** fml [of feelings] Ausdruck der.

demonstrator ['demənstreɪtər] n [protester] Demonstrant der, -in die.

demoralized [dɪ'mɒrəlaɪzd] adj demoralisiert, entmutigt.

demote [,diː'məʊt] vt degradieren.

demure [dɪ'mjʊər] adj sittsam.

den [den] n [of animal] Höhle die.

denial [dɪ'naɪəl] n - **1.** [refutation] Leugnung die - **2.** (U) [refusal] Verweigerung die.

denier ['denɪər] n Denier das.

denigrate ['denɪgreɪt] vt fml verunglimpfen.

denim ['denɪm] n (U) Jeansstoff der. ▸ **denims** npl Jeans Pl.

denim jacket n Jeansjacke die.

Denmark ['denmɑːk] n Dänemark nt.

denomination [dɪ,nɒmɪ'neɪʃn] n - **1.** RELIG Konfession die - **2.** FIN Nennwert der.

denounce [dɪ'naʊns] vt [person] anlgreifen; [actions] anlprangern.

dense [dens] *adj* - **1.** [thick] dicht - **2.** *inf* [stupid] schwer von Begriff.

dent [dent] <> *n* Beule *die*. <> *vt* einlbeulen.

dental ['dentl] *adj* Zahn-; **dental appointment** Termin *der* beim Zahnarzt.

dental floss *n* Zahnseide *die*.

dental surgeon *n* Zahnarzt *der*, -ärztin *die*.

dentist ['dentɪst] *n* Zahnarzt *der*, -ärztin *die*; **to go to the dentist('s)** zum Zahnarzt gehen.

dentures ['dentʃəz] *npl* Gebiss *das*.

deny [dɪ'naɪ] *vt* - **1.** [refute] bestreiten; [publicly] dementieren - **2.** *fml* [refuse] verweigern; **to deny sb sthg** jm etw verweigern.

deodorant [diː'əudərənt] *n* Deodorant *das*.

depart [dɪ'paːt] *vi fml* - **1.** [leave] weglgehen; [by car, bus *etc*] weglfahren; [on journey] ablreisen; **to depart from** [train] ablfahren von; [plane] ablfliegen von - **2.** [differ]: **to depart from sthg** von etw ablweichen.

department [dɪ'paːtmənt] *n* - **1.** [in organization, shop] Abteilung *die* - **2.** SCH & UNIV Fachbereich *der* - **3.** [in government] Ministerium *das*.

department store *n* Kaufhaus *das*.

departure [dɪ'paːtʃər] *n* - **1.** [leaving - on journey] Abreise *die*; [- of train] Abfahrt *die*; [- of plane] Abflug *der*; **'departures'** [in airport] 'Abflug' - **2.** [variation]: **departure (from sthg)** Abweichung *die* (von etw).

departure lounge *n* Abflughalle *die*.

depend [dɪ'pend] *vi* - **1.**: **to depend on sb/sthg** [financially] von jm/etw ablhängen; [to rely on] auf jn/etw angewiesen sein; **I can depend on you** ich kann mich auf dich verlassen - **2.** [be determined]: **to depend on sb/sthg** von jm/etw ablhängen; **it depends on what happens/who is there** das hängt davon ab, was passiert/wer da ist; **depending on the weather** je nachdem, wie das Wetter wird.

dependable [dɪ'pendəbl] *adj* verlässlich.

dependant [dɪ'pendənt] *n* versorgungsabhängige Angehörige *der*, *die*.

dependent [dɪ'pendənt] *adj* - **1.** [reliant]: **to be dependent (on sb/sthg)** [financially] abhängig sein (von jm/etw); [rely on] angewiesen sein (auf jn/etw) - **2.** [addicted] abhängig - **3.** [determined by]: **to be dependent on sb/sthg** von jm/etw abhängig sein.

depict [dɪ'pɪkt] *vt* - **1.** [show in picture] darstellen - **2.** [describe]: **to depict sb/sthg as sthg** jn/etw als etw beschreiben.

deplete [dɪ'pliːt] *vt* vermindern.

deplorable [dɪ'plɔːrəbl] *adj* beklagenswert.

deplore [dɪ'plɔːr] *vt* verurteilen.

deploy [dɪ'plɔɪ] *vt* einlsetzen.

deport [dɪ'pɔːt] *vt* auslweisen.

depose [dɪ'pəuz] *vt* [king, ruler] ablsetzen.

deposit [dɪ'pɒzɪt] <> *n* - **1.** GEOL [of gold, oil] Ablagerung *die* - **2.** [in wine] Bodensatz *der* - **3.** [payment into bank] Einzahlung *die* - **4.** [down payment] Anzahlung *die* - **5.** [returnable payment - on bottle] Pfand *das*; [- on hired goods] Kaution *die*. <> *vt* - **1.** [in bank] deponieren - **2.** [bag, case, shopping] abllegen.

deposit account *n* UK Sparkonto *das*.

depot ['depəu] *n* - **1.** [storage area - for buses] Depot *das*; [- for goods] Lagerhaus *das* - **2.** US [terminus - for trains] Bahnhof *der*; [- for buses] Busbahnhof *der*.

depreciate [dɪ'priːʃɪeɪt] *vi* an Wert verlieren.

depress [dɪ'pres] *vt* - **1.** [sadden] deprimieren - **2.** ECON [economy, market] sich hemmend auswirken auf (+ A); [prices, share values] verringern.

depressed [dɪ'prest] *adj* - **1.** [person] deprimiert, niedergeschlagen - **2.** [area] unterentwickelt *(in wirtschaftlicher Hinsicht)*.

depressing [dɪ'presɪŋ] *adj* deprimierend.

depression [dɪ'preʃn] *n* - **1.** [sadness] Niedergeschlagenheit *die*; MED Depression *die* - **2.** ECON Depression *die* - **3.** *fml* [hollow] Vertiefung *die*.

deprivation [,deprɪ'veɪʃn] *n* Entbehrung *die*; **sleep deprivation** Schlafentzug *der*.

deprive [dɪ'praɪv] *vt*: **to deprive sb of sthg** [to take sthg away] jn einer Sache (*G*) berauben; [to prevent sb from having sthg] jm etw vorlenthalten.

depth [depθ] *n* Tiefe *die*; **to be out of one's depth** [in water] nicht mehr stehen können; *fig* [unable to cope] überfordert sein; **in depth** eingehend. ◆ **depths** *npl*: **the depths of the sea** die Tiefen des Meeres; **in the depths of winter** im tiefsten Winter; **to be in the depths of despair** in tiefster Verzweiflung sein.

deputize, -ise ['depjutaɪz] *vi*: **to deputize for sb** jn vertreten *(eine Person höheren Rangs)*.

deputy ['depjutɪ] <> *adj* stellvertretend. <> *n* - **1.** [second-in-command] Stellvertreter *der*, -in *die* - **2.** US [deputy sheriff] Hilfssheriff *der*.

derail [dɪ'reɪl] *vt* [train] entgleisen lassen.

deranged [dɪ'reɪndʒd] *adj* geistesgestört.

derby [UK 'daːbɪ, US 'dɜːbɪ] *n* - **1.** [sports event] Derby *das* - **2.** US [hat] Melone *die*.

derelict ['derəlɪkt] *adj* verfallen.

deride [dɪ'raɪd] *vt* verhöhnen.

derisory [də'raɪzərɪ] *adj* - **1.** [ridiculous] lächerlich - **2.** [scornful] höhnisch.

derivative [dɪ'rɪvətɪv] <> *adj pej* nachgeahmt. <> *n* Derivat *das*.

derive [dɪ'raɪv] <> *vt* - **1.**: **to derive pleasure from sthg** Freude an etw (*D*) haben; **to derive satisfaction from sthg** Befriedigung aus etw ziehen - 2.: to be derived from sthg [from language] aus etw stammen; [from word] von etw abgeleitet sein. ⟨⟩ vi: to derive from sthg [from language] aus etw stammen; [from word] von etw abgeleitet sein.

derogatory [dɪˈrɒgətrɪ] adj abfällig.

derv [dɜːv] n UK Diesel der.

descend [dɪˈsend] ⟨⟩ vi - 1. fml [go down - person] herunter|gehen/hinunter|gehen; [- in vehicle] herunter|fahren/hinunter|fahren; [- from carriage, ladder etc] herunter|steigen/hinunter|steigen; [- plane] die Flughöhe verringern - 2. [fall]: to descend on sb/sthg [silence] sich über jn/etw legen; [gloom] jn/etw befallen. ⟨⟩ vt fml [go down] hinunter|gehen.

descendant [dɪˈsendənt] n Nachkomme der.

descended [dɪˈsendɪd] adj: to be descended from sb von jm ab|stammen.

descent [dɪˈsent] n - 1. [downwards movement]: a steep descent ein steiler Abstieg - 2. (U) [origin] Abstammung die.

describe [dɪˈskraɪb] vt beschreiben.

description [dɪˈskrɪpʃn] n - 1. [account] Beschreibung die - 2. [type] Art die.

desecrate [ˈdesɪkreɪt] vt entweihen.

desert ⟨⟩ n [ˈdezət] GEOG Wüste die. ⟨⟩ vt [dɪˈzɜːt] [abandon - place] verlassen; [- person] im Stich lassen. ⟨⟩ vi [dɪˈzɜːt] MIL desertieren. ⟨⟩ **deserts** npl [dɪˈzɜːts]: to get one's just deserts bekommen, was man verdient hat.

deserted [dɪˈzɜːtɪd] adj verlassen, öde.

deserter [dɪˈzɜːtər] n Deserteur der.

desert island [ˈdezət-] n einsame Insel.

deserve [dɪˈzɜːv] vt verdienen; to deserve to do sthg verdienen, etw zu tun.

deserving [dɪˈzɜːvɪŋ] adj verdienstvoll.

design [dɪˈzaɪn] ⟨⟩ n - 1. [plan, drawing] Entwurf der - 2. [art] Design das - 3. [pattern] Muster das - 4. [shape] Konstruktion die; [of dress] Schnitt der - 5. [intention] Absicht die; by design absichtlich; to have designs on sb/sthg es auf jn/etw abgesehen haben. ⟨⟩ vt entwerfen; to be designed to do sthg dafür vorgesehen sein, etw zu tun.

designate [ˈdezɪgneɪt] [appoint - area] bestimmen; [- person] ernennen; (phrase): to designate sb to do sthg bestimmen, dass jd etw tut.

designer [dɪˈzaɪnər] ⟨⟩ adj [jeans, glasses] Designer-. ⟨⟩ n [in industry] Konstrukteur der; [in theatre] Bühnenbildner der, -in die; [of clothes] Modedesigner der, -in die.

desirable [dɪˈzaɪərəbl] adj - 1. fml [appropriate] wünschenswert - 2. [attractive] reizvoll - 3. [sexually attractive] begehrenswert.

desire [dɪˈzaɪər] ⟨⟩ n - 1. [wish]: desire (for sthg/to do sthg) der Wunsch (nach etw/etw

zu tun) - 2. (U) [sexual longing] Begierde die. ⟨⟩ vt - 1. [want] wünschen - 2. [feel sexual longing for] begehren.

desist [dɪˈzɪst] vi fml: to desist (from doing sthg) davon ab|lsehen (etw zu tun).

desk [desk] n - 1. [piece of furniture] Schreibtisch der; [in school] Pult das - 2. [service point] Schalter der; [in hotel] Empfang der.

desk diary n Tischkalender der.

desktop [ˈdesktɒp] n COMPUT Desktop das.

desktop publishing n Desktop-Publishing das.

desolate [ˈdesələt] adj - 1. [place] trostlos - 2. [person] tieftraurig.

despair [dɪˈspeər] ⟨⟩ n Verzweiflung die. ⟨⟩ vi verzweifeln; to despair of sb/sthg an jm/etw verzweifeln; to despair of doing sthg die Hoffnung aufgeben, etw zu tun.

despairing [dɪˈspeərɪŋ] adj verzweifelt.

despatch [dɪˈspætʃ] n & vt = dispatch.

desperate [ˈdespərət] adj - 1. [reckless - criminal, person] zum Äußersten entschlossen; [- attempt, measures] verzweifelt - 2. [serious, hopeless] hoffnungslos - 3. [despairing] verzweifelt - 4. [in great need]: to be desperate for sthg etw dringend benötigen.

desperately [ˈdespərətlɪ] adv - 1. [seriously, hopelessly] hoffnungslos - 2. [very - busy, sorry] äußerst; (phrase): she desperately wants to travel sie wünscht sich nichts mehr als zu reisen.

desperation [ˌdespəˈreɪʃn] n Verzweiflung die; in desperation aus Verzweiflung.

despicable [dɪˈspɪkəbl] adj [person] verachtenswert; [behaviour, act] verabscheuungswürdig.

despise [dɪˈspaɪz] vt [person] verachten; [racism] verabscheuen.

despite [dɪˈspaɪt] prep trotz (+ G).

despondent [dɪˈspɒndənt] adj verzagt.

dessert [dɪˈzɜːt] n Dessert das.

dessertspoon [dɪˈzɜːtspuːn] n Dessertlöffel der.

destination [ˌdestɪˈneɪʃn] n [of means of transport] Bestimmungsort der; [of traveller] Reiseziel das.

destined [ˈdestɪnd] adj [intended]: to be destined for sthg zu etw bestimmt sein; to be destined to do sthg dazu bestimmt sein, etw zu tun.

destiny [ˈdestɪnɪ] n Schicksal das.

destitute [ˈdestɪtjuːt] adj notleidend; to be destitute Not leiden.

destroy [dɪˈstrɔɪ] vt [ruin] zerstören.

destruction [dɪˈstrʌkʃn] n (U) Zerstörung die, Vernichtung die.

detach [dɪ'tætʃ] *vt* [remove] ablnehmen; [tear off] abltrennen; **to detach sthg from sthg** etw von etw ablnehmen/abltrennen.

detached [dɪ'tætʃt] *adj* [unemotional] distanziert, unbeteiligt.

detached house *n* Einfamilienhaus *das*.

detachment [dɪ'tætʃmənt] *n* [aloofness] Distanziertheit *die*.

detail ['diːteɪl] <> *n* - 1. [small point] Detail *das*; [specific] Einzelheit *die* - 2. *(U)* [collection of facts, points] Details *Pl*; **to go into detail** ins Detail gehen; **in detail** im Detail. <> *vt* [list] auflisten. ◆ **details** *npl* [information] Informationen *Pl*; [personal information] Personalien *Pl*.

detailed ['diːteɪld] *adj* detailliert.

detain [dɪ'teɪn] *vt* - 1. [in police station] in polizeilichem Gewahrsam behalten; [in hospital] zur stationären Behandlung behalten - 2. [delay] auflhalten.

detect [dɪ'tekt] *vt* - 1. [subj: person] bemerken - 2. [subj: machine] ausfindig machen.

detection [dɪ'tekʃn] *n* - 1. *(U)* [discovery] Entdeckung *die* - 2. [investigation] Ermittlungsarbeit *die*.

detective [dɪ'tektɪv] *n* [private] Detektiv *der*, -in *die*; [police officer] Kriminalbeamte *der*, -tin *die*.

detective novel *n* Kriminalroman *der*.

detention [dɪ'tenʃn] *n* - 1. [of suspect] Untersuchungshaft *die* - 2. [at school] Nachsitzen *das*.

deter [dɪ'tɜːr] *vt* ablhalten; **to deter sb from doing sthg** jn ablhalten, etw zu tun.

detergent [dɪ'tɜːdʒənt] *n* [for clothes] Waschmittel *das*; [for dishes] Spülmittel *das*.

deteriorate [dɪ'tɪərɪəreɪt] *vi* sich verschlechtern.

determination [dɪ,tɜːmɪ'neɪʃn] *n* [resolve] Entschlossenheit *die*.

determine [dɪ'tɜːmɪn] *vt* - 1. [establish, find out] bestimmen, ermitteln - 2. [control] entscheiden - 3. *fml* [resolve]: **to determine to do sthg** sich dazu entschließen, etw zu tun - 4. [fix, establish] festlegen.

determined [dɪ'tɜːmɪnd] *adj* - 1. [person] resolut; **to be determined to do sthg** fest entschlossen sein, etw zu tun - 2. [effort] angestrengt.

deterrent [dɪ'terənt] *n* Abschreckungsmittel *das*.

detest [dɪ'test] *vt* verabscheuen.

detonate ['detəneɪt] <> *vt* zur Detonation bringen. <> *vi* detonieren.

detour ['diː,tʊər] *n* Umweg *der*.

detract [dɪ'trækt] *vi*: **to detract from** [quality] beeinträchtigen; [enjoyment, achievement] schmälern.

detriment ['detrɪmənt] *n*: **to the detriment of sb/sthg** zum Schaden von jm/etw.

detrimental [,detrɪ'mentl] *adj* [effect] schädlich; [consequences] nachteilig.

deuce [djuːs] *n* TENNIS Einstand *der*.

devaluation [,diːvæljʊ'eɪʃn] *n* FIN Abwertung *die*.

devastated ['devəsteɪtɪd] *adj* - 1. [area, city] verwüstet - 2. *fig* [person] am Boden zerstört.

devastating ['devəsteɪtɪŋ] *adj* - 1. [disastrous - hurricane, storm] verheerend; [- news, experience] niederschmetternd - 2. [very effective - charm, wit] umwerfend; [- remark, argument] vernichtend; [- player, speaker] überragend.

develop [dɪ'veləp] <> *vt* - 1. [land, area, resources] erschließen - 2. [illness] bekommen; [habit] anlnehmen; **the machine developed a fault** an der Maschine ist ein Fehler aufgetreten - 3. [industry, sector] fördern - 4. [machine, weapon, product] weiterlentwickeln - 5. [business, company] auslbauen; [idea, argument, plot] entfalten - 6. PHOT entwickeln. <> *vi* - 1. [gen] sich entwickeln; [plot] sich entfalten - 2. [fault, problem] aufltauchen; [illness] sich entwickeln.

developing country [dɪ'veləpɪŋ-] *n* Entwicklungsland *das*.

development [dɪ'veləpmənt] *n* - 1. [gen] Entwicklung *die*; [of business, company] Ausbau *der*; [of idea, argument, plot] Entfaltung *die* - 2. *(U)* [of land, area, resources] Erschließung *die* - 3. [developed land] Neubausiedlung *die*.

deviate ['diːvɪeɪt] *vi*: **to deviate (from sthg)** (von etw) ablweichen.

device [dɪ'vaɪs] *n* - 1. [apparatus] Gerät *das* - 2. [plan, method] Mittel *das* - 3. [bomb] Sprengkörper *der*.

devil ['devl] *n* - 1. [evil spirit] Teufel *der* - 2. *inf* [person] Teufel *der*; **poor devil!** armer Teufel!; **you silly devil!** du Trottel!; **you lucky devil!** du Glückspilz! - 3. [for emphasis]: **who/where/why the devil?** wer/wo/warum zum Teufel? ◆ **Devil** *n* [Satan]: **the Devil** der Teufel.

devious ['diːvjəs] *adj* [plan, means] fragwürdig; [person] verschlagen.

devise [dɪ'vaɪz] *vt* entwerfen.

devoid [dɪ'vɔɪd] *adj fml*: **devoid of** bar (+ G).

devolution [,diːvə'luːʃn] *n* POL Dezentralisierung *die*.

devote [dɪ'vəʊt] *vt*: **to devote sthg to sthg** etw für etw verwenden.

devoted [dɪ'vəʊtɪd] *adj* [mother] hingebungsvoll; [husband, wife] liebevoll und treu; **to be devoted to sb/sthg** jn/etw innig lieben.

devotion [dɪ'vəʊʃn] *n*: **devotion (to sb/sthg)** Hingabe *die* (an jn/etw).

devour [dɪ'vaʊər] *vt liter* & *fig* verschlingen.

devout [dɪ'vaʊt] *adj* RELIG fromm.

dew [djuː] *n* Tau *der*.

diabetes [,daɪə'biːtiːz] n Diabetes der.

diabetic [,daɪə'betɪk] ⬦ adj [person] zuckerkrank. ⬦ n Diabetiker der, -in die.

diabolic(al) [,daɪə'bɒlɪk(l)] adj - **1.** [evil] teuflisch - **2.** inf [very bad] sauschlecht.

diagnose ['daɪəgnəʊz] vt [illness] diagnostizieren.

diagnosis [,daɪəg'nəʊsɪs] (pl -oses [-əʊsiːz]) n [of illness] Diagnose die.

diagonal [daɪ'ægənl] ⬦ adj diagonal. ⬦ n Diagonale die.

diagram ['daɪəgræm] n Schaubild das.

dial ['daɪəl] (UK) (US) ⬦ n - **1.** [of watch, clock] Zifferblatt das; [of meter] Skala die - **2.** [of radio] Skala die - **3.** [of telephone] Wählscheibe die. ⬦ vt [number] wählen.

dialect ['daɪəlekt] n Dialekt der.

dialling code ['daɪəlɪŋ-] n UK Vorwahl die.

dialling tone UK ['daɪəlɪŋ-], **dial tone** US n Amtszeichen das.

dialogue UK, **dialog** US ['daɪəlɒg] n Dialog der.

dial tone n US = **dialling tone.**

dialysis [daɪ'ælɪsɪs] n Dialyse die.

diameter [daɪ'æmɪtər] n Durchmesser der.

diamond ['daɪəmənd] n - **1.** [gem] Diamant der - **2.** [shape] Raute die. ⬟ **diamonds** npl Karo das; **the six of diamonds** die Karosechs.

diaper ['daɪəpər] n US Windel die.

diaphragm ['daɪəfræm] n [contraceptive] Diaphragma das.

diarrh(o)ea [,daɪə'rɪə] n Durchfall der.

diary ['daɪərɪ] n - **1.** [appointment book] (Termin)kalender der - **2.** [personal record] Tagebuch das.

dice [daɪs] (pl inv) ⬦ n [for games] Würfel der. ⬦ vt würfeln.

dictate [dɪk'teɪt] vt - **1.** [read out] diktieren - **2.** [impose] vorschreiben.

dictation [dɪk'teɪʃn] n Diktat das; **to take** OR **do dictation** ein Diktat aufnehmen.

dictator [dɪk'teɪtər] n POL Diktator der, -in die.

dictatorship [dɪk'teɪtəʃɪp] n Diktatur die.

dictionary ['dɪkʃənrɪ] n Wörterbuch das; [for a particular subject] Lexikon das.

did [dɪd] pt ⊳ **do.**

diddle ['dɪdl] vt inf übers Ohr hauen.

didn't ['dɪdnt] abbr of **did not.**

die [daɪ] ⬦ vi (pt & pp **died**, cont **dying**) - **1.** [person] sterben; [animal, plant] eingehen; **to be dying** im Sterben liegen; **to be dying for sthg** inf sich nach etw sehnen; **to be dying to do sthg** inf darauf brennen, etw zu tun - **2.** fig [love, anger] vergehen; [memory] schwinden. ⬦ n (pl **dice** [daɪs] esp US [dice] Würfel der. ⬟ **die away** vi [sound] leiser

werden. ⬟ **die down** vi [wind] sich legen; [sound] leiser werden; [fire] herunter|brennen. ⬟ **die out** vi aus|sterben.

diehard ['daɪhɑːd] n Ewiggestrige der, die.

diesel ['diːzl] n - **1.** [vehicle] Diesel der - **2.** [fuel] Dieselöl das.

diesel engine n - **1.** [of car] Dieselmotor der - **2.** RAIL Diesellokomotive die.

diesel fuel, diesel oil n Dieselkraftstoff der, Dieselöl das.

diet ['daɪət] ⬦ n - **1.** [eating pattern] Ernährung die - **2.** [to lose weight, for medical reasons] Diät die; **to be/go on a diet** eine Diät machen. ⬦ comp [low-calorie] Diät-. ⬦ vi [to lose weight] eine Diät machen.

differ ['dɪfər] vi - **1.** [be different] verschieden sein; **to differ from sb/sthg** sich von jm/etw unterscheiden - **2.** [disagree]: **to differ with sb (about sthg)** mit jm (über etw (D)) verschiedener Meinung sein.

difference ['dɪfrəns] n Unterschied der; **it doesn't make any difference** es ist egal; **difference of opinion** Meinungsverschiedenheit die.

different ['dɪfrənt] adj - **1.** [not like before] anders; [not identical] verschieden, unterschiedlich; [various] verschieden; **to be different from** UK OR **than** US **sb/sthg** anders sein als jd/etw - **2.** [unusual] außergewöhnlich.

differentiate [,dɪfə'renʃɪeɪt] ⬦ vt: **to differentiate sthg from sthg** etw von etw unterscheiden. ⬦ vi: **to differentiate (between)** unterscheiden (zwischen (+ D)).

difficult ['dɪfɪkəlt] adj - **1.** [hard] schwierig; **to make life difficult for sb** jm das Leben schwer machen - **2.** [awkward] schwierig.

difficulty ['dɪfɪkəltɪ] n Schwierigkeit die; **to have difficulty (in) doing sthg** Schwierigkeiten haben, etw zu tun.

diffident ['dɪfɪdənt] adj schüchtern.

diffuse vt [dɪ'fjuːz] - **1.** [light] aus|strahlen - **2.** [information] verbreiten.

dig [dɪg] (pt & pp **dug**) ⬦ n - **1.** fig [unkind remark] Seitenhieb der - **2.** ARCHAEOL Ausgrabung die. ⬦ vt [hole] graben; [garden] um|graben. ⬦ vi [in ground] graben. ⬟ **dig up** vt sep [liter & fig] aus|graben.

digest vt [dɪ'dʒest] [liter & fig] verdauen.

digestion [dɪ'dʒestʃn] n Verdauung die.

digestive biscuit n UK mürber Keks aus Vollkornmehl.

digestive system n Verdauungsapparat der.

digger ['dɪgər] n [machine] Bagger der.

digit ['dɪdʒɪt] n - **1.** [figure] Ziffer die - **2.** [finger] Finger der; [toe] Zehe die.

digital ['dɪdʒɪtl] adj digital.

digital camera n Digitalkamera die.

digital radio n Digitalradio das.

digital television n digitales Fernsehen.

digital watch n Digitaluhr die.

dignified ['dɪɡnɪfaɪd] adj würdevoll.

dignity ['dɪɡnətɪ] n Würde die.

digress [daɪ'ɡres] vi: **to digress (from sth)** (von etw) abschweifen.

digs [dɪɡz] npl UK inf Bude die.

dike [daɪk] n - 1. [wall, bank] Damm der - 2. inf pej [lesbian] Lesbe die.

dilapidated [dɪ'læpɪdeɪtɪd] adj baufällig.

dilemma [dɪ'lemə] n Dilemma das.

diligent ['dɪlɪdʒənt] adj sorgfältig.

dilute [daɪ'luːt] <> adj verdünnt. <> vt: **to dilute sth (with sth)** etw (mit etw) verdünnen.

dim [dɪm] <> adj - 1. [room] halbdunkel; [light] trüb - 2. [indistinct - shape, sight] undeutlich; [- sound, memory] schwach - 3. [eyes] schwach - 4. inf [stupid] beschränkt. <> vt dämpfen. <> vi [light, hope] schwinden.

dime [daɪm] n US Zehncentstück das.

dimension [dɪ'menʃn] n Dimension die. ⮞ **dimensions** pl [of room, object] Abmessungen pl; **in three dimensions** dreidimensional.

diminish [dɪ'mɪnɪʃ] <> vt [subj: person] herabsetzen; [subj: thing] verringern. <> vi [importance, popularity] abnehmen.

diminutive [dɪ'mɪnjʊtɪv] <> adj fml winzig. <> n GRAM Verkleinerungsform die.

dimmer n Dimmer der. ⮞ **dimmers** npl US - 1. [dipped headlights] Abblendlicht das - 2. [parking lights] Begrenzungsleuchten pl.

dimmer switch ['dɪmə-] n = **dimmer**.

dimple ['dɪmpl] n Grübchen das.

din [dɪn] n inf Getöse das.

dine [daɪn] vi fml speisen. ⮞ **dine out** vi auswärts speisen.

diner ['daɪnə] n - 1. [person] Gast der (in einem Restaurant) - 2. US [restaurant] Lokal das.

dinghy ['dɪŋɡɪ] n [for sailing] kleines Segelboot; **(rubber) dinghy** Schlauchboot das.

dingy ['dɪndʒɪ] adj schmuddelig.

dining car ['daɪnɪŋ-] n Speisewagen der.

dining room ['daɪnɪŋ-] n - 1. [in house] Esszimmer das - 2. [in hotel] Speisesaal der.

dinner ['dɪnə] n - 1. [meal - in the evening] (warmes) Abendessen; [- at noon] Mittagessen das - 2. [formal event] (Abend)essen das.

dinner jacket n [jacket] Smokingjacke die; [suit] Smoking der.

dinner party n Abendgesellschaft die (mit Essen).

dinnertime ['dɪnətaɪm] n Essenszeit die.

dinosaur ['daɪnəsɔː] n Dinosaurier der.

dint [dɪnt] n fml: **by dint of** mittels (+ G).

dip [dɪp] <> n - 1. [in road, ground] Senke die - 2. [sauce] Dip der - 3. [swim]: **to go for a dip** (kurz) schwimmen gehen. <> vt - 1. [into liquid]: **to dip sth in(to) sth** etw in etw (A) (ein)tauchen - 2. UK [headlights] ab|blenden. <> vi [wing, road, ground] sich senken.

diploma [dɪ'pləʊmə] (pl -s) n Diplom das.

diplomacy [dɪ'pləʊməsɪ] n Diplomatie die.

diplomat ['dɪpləmæt] n [official] Diplomat der, -in die.

diplomatic [,dɪplə'mætɪk] adj diplomatisch.

dipstick ['dɪpstɪk] n AUT Ölmessstab der.

dire ['daɪə] adj [serious - warning] dringend; [- consequences] schwerwiegend; (phrase): **to be in dire need of sth** etw dringend brauchen.

direct [dɪ'rekt] <> adj - 1. [gen] direkt - 2. [exact] genau. <> vt - 1. [aim]: **to direct sth at sb** [question, remark] etw an jn richten; **the campaign is directed at teenagers** die Kampagne zielt auf Teenager ab - 2. [person to place] den Weg erklären (+ D) - 3. [manage, be in charge of] leiten - 4. [TV programme] leiten; [film, play] Regie führen bei - 5. [order]: **to direct sb to do sth** jn an|weisen, etw zu tun. <> adv direkt.

direct current n Gleichstrom der.

direct debit n UK Dauerauftrag der.

direction [dɪ'rekʃn] n - 1. [orientation] Richtung die - 2. [of play, film] Regie die; [of TV programme] Leitung die. ⮞ **directions** npl - 1. [to place] Wegbeschreibung die; **to ask (sb) for directions** (jn) nach dem Weg fragen - 2. [for use] Gebrauchsanweisung die.

directly [dɪ'rektlɪ] adv - 1. [gen] direkt - 2. [exactly] genau - 3. [very soon] sofort.

director [dɪ'rektə] n - 1. [of company] Direktor der, -in die - 2. [of film, play] Regisseur der, -in die; [of TV programme] Leiter der, -in die.

directory [dɪ'rektərɪ] n - 1. [book, list] Verzeichnis das; **(telephone) directory** Telefonbuch das - 2. COMPUT Directory das.

directory enquiries n UK Fernsprechauskunft die.

dire straits npl: **in dire straits** in großen Nöten.

dirt [dɜːt] n - 1. [mud, dust] Schmutz der - 2. [earth] Erde die.

dirt cheap inf adj spottbillig.

dirty ['dɜːtɪ] <> adj - 1. [not clean] schmutzig - 2. [unfair] gemein; **to play a dirty trick on sb** jm übel mitspielen - 3. [smutty] schmutzig, unanständig. <> vt beschmutzen.

disability [,dɪsə'bɪlətɪ] n Behinderung die.

disabled [dɪs'eɪbld] <> adj behindert. <> npl: **the disabled** die Behinderten pl.

disadvantage [,dɪsəd'vɑːntɪdʒ] n Nachteil der; **to be at a disadvantage** im Nachteil sein.

disagree [,dɪsə'ɡriː] vi - 1. [with another person] nicht übereinstimmen; [two people] sich nicht einig sein; **to disagree with sb** mit jm nicht übereinlstimmen; **to disagree with sthg** mit etw nicht einverstanden sein - **2.** [statements, accounts] nicht übereinlstimmen - **3.** [subj: food, drink]: **to disagree with sb** jm nicht bekommen.

disagreeable [,dɪsə'griːəbl] *adj* - **1.** [smell, job] unangenehm - **2.** [person] unfreundlich.

disagreement [,dɪsə'griːmənt] *n* - **1.** [of opinions] Uneinigkeit *die* - [of records] Diskrepanz *die* - **2.** [argument] Meinungsverschiedenheit *die*; **to be in disagreement about sthg** [people] verschiedener Ansicht in Bezug auf etw *(A)* sein.

disallow [,dɪsə'laʊ] *vt* - **1.** *fml* [appeal, claim] zurücklweisen - **2.** [goal] nicht anlerkennen.

disappear [,dɪsə'pɪəʳ] *vi* verschwinden.

disappearance [,dɪsə'pɪərəns] *n* Verschwinden *das*.

disappoint [,dɪsə'pɔɪnt] *vt* enttäuschen.

disappointed [,dɪsə'pɔɪntɪd] *adj*: **disappointed (in** OR **with sthg)** (von etw) enttäuscht.

disappointing [,dɪsə'pɔɪntɪŋ] *adj* enttäuschend.

disappointment [,dɪsə'pɔɪntmənt] *n* Enttäuschung *die*.

disapproval [,dɪsə'pruːvl] *n* Missfallen *das*.

disapprove [,dɪsə'pruːv] *vi*: **to disapprove of sthg** etw missbilligen; **to disapprove of sb** etwas gegen jn haben.

disarm [dɪs'ɑːm] *vi* ablrüsten.

disarmament [dɪs'ɑːməmənt] *n* Abrüstung *die*.

disarray [,dɪsə'reɪ] *n*: **to be in disarray** *fml* [clothes, hair, room] in Unordnung sein; [group] schlecht organisiert sein.

disaster [dɪ'zɑːstəʳ] *n* Katastrophe *die*.

disastrous [dɪ'zɑːstrəs] *adj* katastrophal.

disband [dɪs'bænd] <> *vt* aufllösen. <> *vi* sich aufllösen.

disbelief [,dɪsbɪ'liːf] *n*: **in** OR **with disbelief** ungläubig.

disc UK, **disk** US [dɪsk] *n* - **1.** [shape] Scheibe *die* - **2.** MED Bandscheibe *die* - **3.** [record] Platte *die*.

discard [dɪ'skɑːd] *vt* weglwerfen.

discern [dɪ'sɜːn] *vt* - **1.** [see] wahrlnehmen - **2.** [detect] erkennen.

discerning [dɪ'sɜːnɪŋ] *adj* kritisch.

discharge <> *n* ['dɪstʃɑːdʒ] - **1.** [of patient, prisoner, soldier] Entlassung *die* - **2.** [toxic emission] Ausstoß *der* - **3.** MED [from wound] Ausfluss *der*. <> *vt* [dɪs'tʃɑːdʒ] - **1.** [patient, prisoner, soldier] entlassen - **2.** *fml* [fulfil] erfüllen - **3.** [emit] auslstoßen.

disciple [dɪ'saɪpl] *n* - **1.** RELIG Jünger *der* - **2.** *fig* [follower] Anhänger *der*, -in *die*.

discipline ['dɪsɪplɪn] <> *n* Disziplin *die*. <> *vt* - **1.** [train] disziplinieren - **2.** [punish] belstrafen.

disc jockey *n* Diskjockei *der*.

disclose [dɪs'kləʊz] *vt* enthüllen.

disclosure [dɪs'kləʊʒəʳ] *n* Enthüllung *die*.

disco ['dɪskəʊ] *(pl* **-s)** *n abbr of* **discotheque**.

discomfort [dɪs'kʌmfət] *n* - **1.** *(U)* [physical pain] Beschwerden *Pl*; **to be in discomfort** Beschwerden haben - **2.** [anxiety, embarrassment] Unbehagen *das*.

disconcert [,dɪskən'sɜːt] *vt* verunsichern.

disconnect [,dɪskə'nekt] *vt* - **1.** [detach] trennen - **2.** [remove plug of] den Stecker herauslziehen von; [from water/gas supply] von der Wasserzufuhr/Gaszufuhr trennen; **to disconnect sb's telephone** jm das Telefon ablstellen; **we've been disconnected** man hat uns das Telefon/das Gas/das Wasser/den Strom abgestellt - **3.** [when talking]: **we've been disconnected** die Verbindung wurde unterbrochen.

disconsolate [dɪs'kɒnsələt] *adj* untröstlich.

discontent [,dɪskən'tent] *n*: **discontent (with sthg)** Unzufriedenheit *die* (mit etw).

discontented [,dɪskən'tentɪd] *adj*: **to be discontented (with sthg)** (mit etw) unzufrieden sein.

discontinue [,dɪskən'tɪnjuː] *vt* [service, supply] einlstellen; [visits] beenden; [production] auslaufen lassen.

discord ['dɪskɔːd] *n* - **1.** *fml* [conflict] Uneinigkeit *die* - **2.** MUS Disharmonie *die*.

discotheque ['dɪskəʊtek] *n* Diskothek *die*.

discount <> *n* ['dɪskaʊnt] Rabatt *der*. <> *vt* [UK dɪs'kaʊnt, US 'dɪskaʊnt] - **1.** [disregard] verwerfen - **2.** COMM [product] zu einem geringeren Preis anlbieten.

discourage [dɪs'kʌrɪdʒ] *vt* - **1.** [dishearten] entmutigen - **2.** [dissuade]: **to discourage sb from doing sthg** jn davon ablbringen, etw zu tun.

discover [dɪ'skʌvəʳ] *vt* - **1.** [find] entdecken; [cause of sthg] herauslfinden - **2.** [realize] festlstellen.

discovery [dɪ'skʌvərɪ] *n* Entdeckung *die*.

discredit [dɪs'kredɪt] *vt* diskreditieren.

discreet [dɪ'skriːt] *adj* diskret.

discrepancy [dɪ'skrepənsɪ] *n*: **discrepancy (in/between)** Diskrepanz *die* (zwischen *(+ D)*).

discretion [dɪ'skreʃn] *n* - **1.** [tact] Diskretion *die* - **2.** [judgment]: **use your own discretion** handeln Sie nach eigenem Ermessen; **at the discretion of** nach Ermessen *(+ G)*.

discriminate [dɪ'skrɪmɪneɪt] *vi* - **1.** [distinguish]: **to discriminate (between)** unterscheiden (zwischen *(+ D)*) - **2.** [treat unfairly]: **to discriminate against sb** jn diskriminieren.

discriminating [dɪˈskrɪmɪneɪtɪŋ] *adj* [person, eye, audience] kritisch; [taste] fein.

discrimination [dɪˌskrɪmɪˈneɪʃn] *n* - 1. [prejudice] Diskriminierung *die* - 2. [good judgment] Urteilsvermögen *das*.

discus [ˈdɪskəs] (*pl* -es) *n* Diskus *der*.

discuss [dɪˈskʌs] *vt* besprechen; [in political, academic context] diskutieren; **to discuss sthg with sb** etw mit jm besprechen.

discussion [dɪˈskʌʃn] *n* - 1. (U) [act of discussing] Besprechen *das*; [in political, academic context] Diskussion *die*; **to be under discussion** zur Diskussion stehen - 2. [talk] Gespräch *das*; [in political, academic context] Diskussion *die*.

disdain [dɪsˈdeɪn] *fml n*: **disdain (for sb/sthg)** Verachtung *die* (für jn/etw).

disease [dɪˈziːz] *n liter* & *fig* Krankheit *die*.

disembark [ˌdɪsɪmˈbɑːk] *vi* von Bord gehen.

disenchanted [ˌdɪsɪnˈtʃɑːntɪd] *adj*: **disenchanted (with sthg)** (von etw) ernüchtert.

disengage [ˌdɪsɪnˈgeɪdʒ] *vt* - 1. [release]: **to disengage o.s./sthg (from sthg)** sich/etw (von etw) loslmachen - 2. TECH [gears, mechanism] auslrücken.

disfigure [dɪsˈfɪgər] *vt* verunstalten.

disgrace [dɪsˈgreɪs] <> *n* Schande *die*; **to be in disgrace** in Ungnade gefallen sein. <> *vt*: **to disgrace sb** jm Schande machen; **to disgrace o.s.** sich blamieren.

disgraceful [dɪsˈgreɪsful] *adj* skandalös.

disgruntled [dɪsˈgrʌntld] *adj* verstimmt.

disguise [dɪsˈgaɪz] <> *n* Verkleidung *die*; **in disguise** verkleidet. <> *vt* - 1. [dress up] verkleiden - 2. [voice, handwriting] verstellen - 3. [disappointment, surprise] verbergen; [fact] verschleiern; [taste of sthg] überdecken.

disgust [dɪsˈgʌst] <> *n*: **disgust (at sthg)** Abscheu *der* (vor etw (D)). <> *vt* anlekeln.

disgusting [dɪsˈgʌstɪŋ] *adj* ekelhaft.

dish [dɪʃ] *n* - 1. [bowl] Schüssel *die*; [shallow] Schale *die* - 2. US [plate] Teller *der* - 3. [food] Gericht *das*. **dishes** *npl* Geschirr *das*; **to do OR wash the dishes** Geschirr spülen OR ablwaschen. **dish out** *vt sep inf* auslteilen. **dish up** *vt sep inf* [food] aufltun.

dish aerial UK, **dish antenna** US *n* Parabolantenne *die*, Satellitenschüssel *die*.

dishcloth [ˈdɪʃklɒθ] *n* Spültuch *das*.

disheartened [dɪsˈhɑːtnd] *adj* entmutigt.

dishevelled UK, **disheveled** US [dɪˈʃevəld] *adj* [hair] zerzaust; [person] unordentlich.

dishonest [dɪsˈɒnɪst] *adj* - 1. [person] unehrlich; [trader] unredlich - 2. [action] unredlich, unlauter.

dishonor *n* & *vt* US = **dishonour**.

dishonorable *adj* US = **dishonourable**.

dishonour UK, **dishonor** US [dɪsˈɒnər] <> *n* Unehre *die*. <> *vt* entehren.

dishonourable UK, **dishonorable** US [dɪsˈɒnərəbl] *adj* unehrenhaft.

dish towel *n* US Geschirrtuch *das*.

dishwasher [ˈdɪʃˌwɒʃər] *n* [machine] Geschirrspülmaschine *die*.

disillusioned [ˌdɪsɪˈluːʒnd] *adj* desillusioniert; **disillusioned with sb/sthg** von jm/etw enttäuscht.

disincentive [ˌdɪsɪnˈsentɪv] *n* Abschreckungsmittel *das*.

disinclined [ˌdɪsɪnˈklaɪnd] *adj*: **to be disinclined to do sthg** abgeneigt sein, etw zu tun.

disinfect [ˌdɪsɪnˈfekt] *vt* desinfizieren.

disinfectant [ˌdɪsɪnˈfektənt] *n* Desinfektionsmittel *das*.

disintegrate [dɪsˈɪntɪgreɪt] *vi* [object] zerfallen.

disinterested [ˌdɪsˈɪntrəstɪd] *adj* - 1. [objective] unparteiisch - 2. *inf* [uninterested]: **disinterested (in sb/sthg)** nicht interessiert (an jm/etw).

disjointed [dɪsˈdʒɔɪntɪd] *adj* zusammenhanglos.

disk [dɪsk] *n* - 1. COMPUT: **(floppy) disk** Diskette *die*; **(hard) disk** Festplatte *die* - 2. US = **disc**.

disk drive UK, **diskette drive** US *n* COMPUT [for floppy disk] Diskettenlaufwerk *das*.

diskette [dɪsˈket] *n* COMPUT Diskette *die*.

diskette drive *n* US = **disk drive**.

dislike [dɪsˈlaɪk] <> *n*: **dislike (of)** Abneigung *die* (gegen); **to take a dislike to sb/sthg** eine Abneigung gegen jn/etw empfinden. <> *vt* nicht mögen.

dislocate [ˈdɪsləkeɪt] *vt* MED auslrenken.

dislodge [dɪsˈlɒdʒ] *vt*: **to dislodge sb/sthg (from)** jn/etw entfernen (von OR aus).

disloyal [ˌdɪsˈlɔɪəl] *adj*: **disloyal (to sb)** illoyal (gegenüber jm).

dismal [ˈdɪzml] *adj* - 1. [gloomy, depressing] trist - 2. [attempt, failure] kläglich.

dismantle [dɪsˈmæntl] *vt* auseinander nehmen.

dismay [dɪsˈmeɪ] <> *n* Bestürzung *die*. <> *vt* bestürzen.

dismiss [dɪsˈmɪs] *vt* - 1. [employee, class, troops]: **to dismiss sb (from sthg)** jn (aus etw) entlassen - 2. [refuse to take seriously] abltun - 3. LAW [case] ablweisen.

dismissal [dɪsˈmɪsl] *n* [from job] Entlassung *die*.

dismount [ˌdɪsˈmaʊnt] *vi*: **to dismount (from sthg)** ablsteigen (von etw).

disobedience [ˌdɪsəˈbiːdjəns] *n* Ungehorsam *der*.

disobedient [ˌdɪsəˈbiːdjənt] *adj* ungehorsam.

disobey [ˌdɪsəˈbeɪ] *vt* [rule] übertreten; [person] nicht gehorchen (+ D).

disorder [dɪs'ɔːdə] *n* - 1. [disarray]: **in disorder** in Unordnung - 2. [rioting] Unruhen *Pl* - 3. MED Funktionsstörung *die*.

disorderly [dɪs'ɔːdəlɪ] *adj* - 1. [untidy] unordentlich - 2. [unruly - behaviour] ungehörig.

disorganized, -ised [dɪs'ɔːgənaɪzd] *adj* [person] unorganisiert; [system] unstrukturiert.

disorientated *UK* [dɪs'ɔːrɪənteɪtɪd], **disoriented** *US* [dɪs'ɔːrɪəntɪd] *adj* desorientiert.

disown [dɪs'əʊn] *vt* [son, daughter] verstoßen; [friend] verleugnen.

disparaging [dɪ'spærɪdʒɪŋ] *adj* geringschätzig.

dispassionate [dɪ'spæʃnət] *adj* objektiv.

dispatch [dɪ'spætʃ] <> *n* Bericht *der*. <> *vt* [person, troops, submarine] entsenden; [message, letter, parcel] senden.

dispel [dɪ'spel] *vt* [doubts, fears] zerstreuen; [illusions] nehmen.

dispense [dɪ'spens] *vt* - 1. [advice] erteilen; **to dispense justice** Recht sprechen - 2. [drugs, medicine] abgeben. ◆ **dispense with** *vt insep* - 1. [do without] verzichten auf (+ A) - 2. [make unnecessary] unnötig machen.

dispensing chemist *UK*, **dispensing pharmacist** *US* [dɪ'spensɪŋ-] *n* Apotheker *der*, -in *die*.

disperse [dɪ'spɜːs] <> *vt* [crowd] zerstreuen. <> *vi* [crowd] sich zerstreuen.

dispirited [dɪ'spɪrɪtɪd] *adj* entmutigt.

displace [dɪs'pleɪs] *vt* [supplant] ablösen.

display [dɪ'spleɪ] <> *n* - 1. [of goods, merchandise] Auslage *die*; [in museum] Ausstellung *die* - 2.: **it was a fine display of courage/skill from him** er zeigte viel Mut/Geschick - 3. [performance] Vorführung *die* - 4. COMPUT Display *das*. <> *vt* - 1. [goods, merchandise] ausstellen - 2. [courage, skill, self-control] zeigen.

displease [dɪs'pliːz] *vt* verärgern; **to be displeased with sthg** mit etw unzufrieden sein.

displeasure [dɪs'pleʒə] *n* Missfallen *das*.

disposable [dɪ'spəʊzəbl] *adj* - 1. [to be thrown away after use] Wegwerf-; **disposable nappy** *UK*, **disposable diaper** *US* Wegwerfwindel *die* - 2. [available] verfügbar.

diposable camera *n* Einmalkamera *die*.

disposal [dɪ'spəʊzl] *n* (U) - 1. [removal] Beseitigung *die* - 2. [availability]: **to be at sb's disposal** jm zur Verfügung stehen; **to put sthg at sb's disposal** jm etw zur Verfügung stellen.

disposed [dɪ'spəʊzd] *adj* - 1. [willing]: **to be disposed to do sthg** geneigt sein, etw zu tun - 2. [friendly]: **to be well disposed to** OR **towards sb** jm wohlwollend gegenüber stehen.

dispose ◆ **dispose of** *vt insep* [rubbish, problem] beseitigen.

disposition [ˌdɪspə'zɪʃn] *n* [temperament] Naturell *das*; **he has a cheerful disposition** er ist ein fröhlicher Mensch.

disprove [ˌdɪs'pruːv] *vt* widerlegen.

dispute [dɪ'spjuːt] <> *n* - 1. [quarrel] Streit *der* - 2. (U) [disagreement] Meinungsverschiedenheit *die*; **they are in dispute** zwischen ihnen herrschen Unstimmigkeiten - 3. INDUST Auseinandersetzung *die*. <> *vt* - 1. [question, challenge] bestreiten - 2. [fight for - championship] jm streitig machen; [- territory] beanspruchen.

disqualify [ˌdɪs'kwɒlɪfaɪ] *vt* - 1. [subj: illness, criminal record]: **to disqualify sb from doing sthg** jn dafür ungeeignet machen, etw zu tun - 2. SPORT disqualifizieren - 3. *UK*: **to disqualify sb from driving** jm den Führerschein entziehen.

disquiet [dɪs'kwaɪət] *n* Unruhe *die*.

disregard [ˌdɪsrɪ'gɑːd] <> *n*: **disregard (for sthg)** Geringschätzung *die* (für etw). <> *vt* ignorieren.

disrepair [ˌdɪsrɪ'peə] *n* Baufälligkeit *die*; **to fall into disrepair** verfallen.

disreputable [dɪs'repjʊtəbl] *adj* in einem schlechten Ruf stehend.

disrepute [ˌdɪsrɪ'pjuːt] *n*: **to bring sthg into disrepute** etw in Verruf bringen.

disrupt [dɪs'rʌpt] *vt* [meeting, lesson] stören; [transport system] behindern.

dissatisfaction ['dɪsˌsætɪs'fækʃn] *n* Unzufriedenheit *die*.

dissatisfied [ˌdɪs'sætɪsfaɪd] *adj*: **dissatisfied (with sthg)** unzufrieden (mit etw).

dissect [dɪ'sekt] *vt* MED [animal] sezieren; [plant] präparieren.

dissent [dɪ'sent] <> *n* (U) Nichtübereinstimmung *die*. <> *vi*: **to dissent from sthg** in Bezug auf etw anderer Meinung sein.

dissertation [ˌdɪsə'teɪʃn] *n* [for degree] schriftliche Abschlussarbeit; [for PhD] Dissertation *die*.

disservice [ˌdɪs'sɜːvɪs] *n*: **to do sb a disservice** jm einen schlechten Dienst erweisen.

dissimilar [ˌdɪ'sɪmɪlə] *adj*: **dissimilar (to)** verschieden (von); **to be not dissimilar to sthg** etw (D) nicht unähnlich sein.

dissipate ['dɪsɪpeɪt] *vt* [efforts, money] verschwenden, vergeuden.

dissociate [dɪ'səʊʃɪeɪt] *vt*: **to dissociate o.s. from sthg** sich von etw distanzieren.

dissolute ['dɪsəluːt] *adj* [way of life] ausschweifend; [person, behaviour] zügellos.

dissolve [dɪ'zɒlv] <> *vt* auflösen. <> *vi* [substance] sich auflösen.

dissuade [dɪ'sweɪd] *vt*: **to dissuade sb from doing sthg** jn davon abbringen, etw zu tun.

distance ['dɪstəns] n - **1.** [between two places] Entfernung die; [distance covered] Strecke die - **2.** [distant point]: **at a distance of five metres** in 5 Metern Entfernung; **to follow sb at a distance** jm in einiger Entfernung folgen; **from a distance** aus der Entfernung; **in the distance** in der Ferne.

distant ['dɪstənt] adj - **1.** [place]: **distant (from)** weit entfernt (von) - **2.** [future] fern; **it's all in the distant past** das ist alles schon lange her - **3.** [relative] entfernt - **4.** [manner] kühl.

distaste [dɪs'teɪst] n (U): **distaste (for sthg)** Widerwille der (gegen etw).

distasteful [dɪs'teɪstful] adj sehr unangenehm.

distended [dɪ'stendɪd] adj aufgebläht.

distil UK, **distill** US [dɪ'stɪl] vt - **1.** [water] destillieren; [whisky] brennen - **2.** fig [information] herausdestillieren.

distillery [dɪ'stɪlərɪ] n Brennerei die.

distinct [dɪ'stɪŋkt] adj - **1.** [different]: **distinct (from)** verschieden (von); **as distinct from** im Unterschied zu - **2.** [clear] deutlich, klar.

distinction [dɪ'stɪŋkʃn] n - **1.** [difference] Unterschied der; **to draw** OR **make a distinction between** einen Unterschied machen zwischen (+ D) - **2.** (U) [excellence] Rang der - **3.** [in exam result] Auszeichnung die.

distinctive [dɪ'stɪŋktɪv] adj unverkennbar.

distinguish [dɪ'stɪŋgwɪʃ] <> vt - **1.** [tell apart]: **to distinguish sthg from sthg** etw von etw unterscheiden - **2.** [discern, perceive] erkennen - **3.** [make different] unterscheiden. <> vi: **to distinguish between** unterscheiden zwischen (+ D).

distinguished [dɪ'stɪŋgwɪʃt] adj [visitor, politician] bedeutend; [career] glänzend.

distinguishing [dɪ'stɪŋgwɪʃɪŋ] adj charakteristisch.

distort [dɪ'stɔːt] vt - **1.** [shape, face, sound] verzerren - **2.** [truth, facts] verzerrt darstellen.

distract [dɪ'strækt] vt: **to distract sb (from sthg)** jn (von etw) ablenken.

distracted [dɪ'stræktɪd] adj geistesabwesend.

distraction [dɪ'strækʃn] n [interruption, diversion] Ablenkung die.

distraught [dɪ'strɔːt] adj verzweifelt.

distress [dɪ'stres] <> n (U) [suffering - mental] Kummer der; [- physical] Leiden das. <> vt [upset] Kummer machen (+ D).

distressing [dɪ'stresɪŋ] adj bestürzend.

distribute [dɪ'strɪbjuːt] vt - **1.** [gen] verteilen; [prizes] verleihen - **2.** COMM [goods] vertreiben.

distribution [ˌdɪstrɪ'bjuːʃn] n - **1.** [gen] Verteilung die; [of prizes] Verleihung die - **2.** COMM [of goods] Vertrieb der.

distributor [dɪ'strɪbjʊtər] n COMM & AUT Verteiler der.

district ['dɪstrɪkt] n - **1.** [of country] Gebiet das; [of city] Stadtteil der - **2.** [administrative area] Bezirk der.

district attorney n US LAW Bezirksstaatsanwalt der, -anwältin die.

district nurse n UK Gemeindeschwester die.

distrust [dɪs'trʌst] <> n Misstrauen das. <> vt misstrauen (+ D).

disturb [dɪ'stɜːb] vt - **1.** [interrupt] stören - **2.** [upset, worry] beunruhigen - **3.** [alter - surface of water] bewegen; [- papers] durcheinanderbringen.

disturbance [dɪ'stɜːbəns] n - **1.** [fight] Krawall der - **2.** (U) [interruption, disruption] Störung die.

disturbed [dɪ'stɜːbd] adj - **1.** [upset, ill] gestört - **2.** [worried] beunruhigt.

disturbing [dɪ'stɜːbɪŋ] adj beunruhigend.

disuse [ˌdɪs'juːs] n: **to fall into disuse** [regulation] außer Gebrauch kommen; [building, mine] nicht mehr genutzt werden.

disused [ˌdɪs'juːzd] adj stillgelegt.

ditch [dɪtʃ] <> n Graben der. <> vt inf - **1.** [boyfriend, girlfriend] abservieren - **2.** [plan] fallen lassen - **3.** [old car] (einfach) zurücklassen.

dither ['dɪðər] vi zaudern.

ditto ['dɪtəʊ] adv dito.

dive [daɪv] <> vi (UK pt & pp **-d**; US pt & pp **-d** OR **dove**) - **1.** [goalkeeper] hechten; [bird, aircraft] einen Sturzflug machen; [submarine] abtauchen - **2.** [as sport - from board] einen Kopfsprung machen; [- underwater] tauchen; **he dived into the water** er sprang kopfüber ins Wasser - **3.** [rush] stürzen. <> n - **1.** [of swimmer] Kopfsprung der; **to go into a dive** [bird, aircraft] einen Sturzflug machen; [submarine] abtauchen - **2.** inf pej [bar, restaurant] Kaschemme die.

diver ['daɪvər] n [from board] Springer der, -in die; [underwater] Taucher der, -in die.

diverge [daɪ'vɜːdʒ] vi - **1.** [opinions, interests] voneinander abweichen; **to diverge from sthg** von etw abweichen - **2.** [roads, paths] sich trennen.

diversify [daɪ'vɜːsɪfaɪ] vt & vi diversifizieren.

diversion [daɪ'vɜːʃn] n - **1.** [distraction] Ablenkung die - **2.** [of traffic, river] Umleitung die - **3.** [of funds] Umverteilung die.

diversity [daɪ'vɜːsətɪ] n Mannigfaltigkeit die.

divert [daɪ'vɜːt] vt - **1.** [traffic, river] umleiten - **2.** [funds] umverteilen - **3.** [person, attention] ablenken.

divide [dɪ'vaɪd] <> vt - **1.** [form barrier between] trennen - **2.** [share out, distribute] auflteilen - 3. [split up]: **to divide sthg into** etw auf|teilen in (+ A) - 4. MATHS: **to divide 9 by 3, to divide 3 into 9** 9 durch 3 teilen OR dividieren - 5. [disunite] spalten. ◇ vi [split into two] sich teilen.

dividend ['dɪvɪdend] n Dividende die.

divine [dɪ'vaɪn] adj liter & fig göttlich.

diving ['daɪvɪŋ] n [from board] Springen das; [underwater] Tauchen das.

divingboard ['daɪvɪŋbɔːd] n Sprungbrett das.

divinity [dɪ'vɪnətɪ] n - 1. [godliness] Göttlichkeit die - 2. [study] Theologie die.

division [dɪ'vɪʒn] n - 1. [barrier] Trennung die; [of country, group] Teilung die; **division between** Trennung zwischen (+ D) - 2. [sharing out, distribution] Teilung die - 3. MATHS Division die - 4. [disagreement] Uneinigkeit die - 5. [department] Abteilung die - 6. UK [in sports league] Liga die.

divorce [dɪ'vɔːs] ◇ n LAW Scheidung die. ◇ vt LAW [husband, wife] sich scheiden lassen von.

divorced [dɪ'vɔːst] adj - 1. LAW geschieden; **to get divorced** sich scheiden lassen - 2. fig [separated]: **to be divorced from sthg** keine Beziehung haben zu etw.

divorcee [dɪvɔː'siː] n geschiedener Mann (geschiedene Frau).

divulge [daɪ'vʌldʒ] vt preis|geben.

DIY n UK abbr of **do-it-yourself**.

dizzy ['dɪzɪ] adj [person] schwind(e)lig.

DJ n abbr of disc jockey.

DNA (abbr of deoxyribonucleic acid) n DNS die.

do [duː] (pt did, pp done, pl dos OR do's) ◇ aux vb - 1. (in negatives): **don't do that!** tu das nicht!; **she didn't listen** sie hat nicht zugehört; **don't park your car there** stell dein Auto nicht dort ab - 2. (in questions): **did he like it?** hat es ihm gefallen?; **how do you do it?** wie macht du das?; **what did he want?** was wollte er? - 3. (referring back to previous verb): **I eat more than you do** ich esse mehr als du; **no I didn't** nein, habe ich nicht!; **so do I** ich auch - 4. (in question tags): **so, you like Denver, do you?** Sie mögen Denver also, nicht wahr?; **you come from Ireland, don't you?** Sie kommen aus Irland, oder?; **I like coffee – do you?** ich mag Kaffee – du auch? - 5. (for emphasis): **I do like this bedroom** das Schlafzimmer gefällt mir wirklich; **do come in!** kommen Sie doch herein! ◇ vt - 1. [perform] machen, tun; **I've a lot to do** ich habe viel zu tun; **to do one's homework** seine Hausaufgaben machen; **what is she doing?** was macht sie?; **what can I do for you?** was kann ich für Sie tun?; **to do aerobics/gymnastics** Aerobik/Gymnastik machen; **to do

the cooking** kochen; **well done!** bravo! - 2. [clean, brush, cook etc]: **to do one's make-up** sich schminken; **to do one's teeth** sich (D) die Zähne putzen; **how would you like the steak done?** wie möchten Sie Ihr Steak (haben)? - 3. [take action] tun, machen; **he couldn't do anything about it** er konnte nichts dagegen tun OR machen; **I'll do my best to help** ich helfe, so gut ich kann - 4. [cause]: **the storm did a lot of damage** der Sturm hat viel Schaden angerichtet - 5. [have as job]: **what do you do?** was machen Sie beruflich?; **what do you want to do when you leave school?** was willst du machen, wenn du mit der Schule fertig bist? - 6. [provide, offer]: **do you do vegetarian food?** haben Sie vegetarisches Essen?; **we do pizzas for under £4** wir bieten Pizzas für weniger als 4 Pfund an - 7. [study] studieren, machen; **I did physics at school** ich habe Physik in der Schule gehabt OR gemacht - 8. [subj: vehicle] fahren; **the car can do 110 mph** das Auto schafft 175 km/h - 9. inf [visit]: **we did Switzerland in a week** wir haben uns in einer Woche die Schweiz angesehen - 10. [be good enough for] genügen (+ D); **that'll do me nicely** das genügt mir - 11. inf [cheat]: **to do sb** jn übers Ohr hauen. ◇ vi - 1. [behave, act] tun; **do as I say** tu, was ich sage; **you would do well to reconsider** Sie sollten es sich lieber noch einmal überlegen - 2. [progress, get on]: **to do well/badly** gut/schlecht voran|kommen; [in exam] gut/schlecht ab|schneiden; **he will do well** er wird Erfolg haben - 3. [be sufficient] reichen, genügen; **will £5 do?** genügen 5 Pfund OR sind 5 Pfund genug?; **that will do (nicely)** das genügt OR reicht; **that will do!** [showing annoyance] das reicht! - 4. phr: **how do you do?** Guten Tag!; **how are you doing?** wie gehts? ◇ n [party] Party die. ◆ **dos** npl: **dos and don'ts** was man tun und lassen sollte. ◆ **do away with** vt insep [law, practice] ab|schaffen. ◆ **do down** vt sep: **to do sb/o.s. down** jn/sich schlecht machen. ◆ **do out of** vt sep: **to do sb out of £10** jn um 10 Pfund betrügen. ◆ **do up** vt sep - 1. [fasten] zu|machen; **do your shoes up** binde dir die Schuhe - 2. [decorate] renovieren - 3. [wrap up] ein|packen. ◆ **do with** vt insep - 1. [need]: **I could do with a drink** ich könnte einen Drink gebrauchen; **the floor could do with a wash** der Boden könnte mal (wieder) geputzt werden - 2. [have connection with]: **what has that got to do with it?** was hat das damit zu tun?; **that has nothing to do with you** das geht dich gar nichts an. ◆ **do without** ◇ vt insep: **to do without sthg** ohne etw auskommen; **I can do without your sarcasm** [expressing annoyance] Sie können sich Ihren Sarkasmus sparen. ◇ vi: **we'll just have to do without then** dann müssen wir eben so auskommen.

docile [UK 'dəʊsaɪl, US 'dɒsəl] adj fügsam.

dock [dɒk] ◇ n - **1.** [in harbour] Dock das - **2.** [in court] Anklagebank die. ◇ vi [ship] anlegen.

docker ['dɒkə*ʳ*] n Hafenarbeiter der, -in die.

dockyard ['dɒkjɑːd] n Werft die.

doctor ['dɒktə*ʳ*] ◇ n - **1.** [of medicine] Arzt der, Ärztin die; **to go to the doctor's** zum Arzt gehen - **2.** [holder of PhD] Doktor der. ◇ vt [tamper with - results] fälschen; [- text] verfälschen.

doctorate ['dɒktərət], **doctor's degree** n Doktorwürde die.

doctrine ['dɒktrɪn] n Doktrin die, Lehre die.

document n ['dɒkjumənt] Dokument das.

documentary [,dɒkjʊ'mentərɪ] ◇ adj dokumentarisch. ◇ n Dokumentarfilm der.

dodge [dɒdʒ] ◇ n inf Trick der. ◇ vt [avoid] ausIweichen. ◇ vi: **to dodge out of the way/to one side** zur Seite springen.

dodgy ['dɒdʒɪ] adj UK inf [business, deal] windig; [plan] dubios.

doe [dəʊ] n [female deer - roe deer] Ricke die; [- red deer] Hirschkuh die.

does (weak form [dəz], strong form [dʌz]) vb ⊳ **do**.

doesn't ['dʌznt] abbr of **does not**.

dog [dɒg] ◇ n [animal] Hund der. ◇ vt [subj: problems, bad luck]: **dogged by problems** von Problemen geplagt; **dogged by bad luck** von Pech verfolgt.

dog collar n - **1.** [of dog] Halsband das - **2.** [of clergyman] steifer weißer Kragen.

dog-eared [-ɪəd] adj mit Eselsohren.

dog food n Hundefutter das.

dogged ['dɒgɪd] adj beharrlich.

dogsbody ['dɒgz,bɒdɪ] n UK inf Mädchen das für alles.

doing ['duːɪŋ] n: **is this your doing?** ist das dein Werk? ◆ **doings** npl [activities] Taten Pl.

do-it-yourself n Heimwerken das.

doldrums ['dɒldrəmz] npl: **to be in the doldrums** fig [industry] in einer Flaute stecken; [person] Trübsal blasen.

dole [dəʊl] n UK [unemployment benefit] Arbeitslosenunterstützung die; **to be on the dole** Arbeitslosenunterstützung beziehen. ◆ **dole out** vt sep austeilen.

doll [dɒl] n Puppe die.

dollar ['dɒlə*ʳ*] n Dollar der.

dollop ['dɒləp] n inf Klacks der.

dolphin ['dɒlfɪn] n Delfin der.

domain [də'meɪn] n [sphere of interest] Gebiet das.

dome [dəʊm] n ARCHIT Kuppel die.

domestic [də'mestɪk] ◇ adj - **1.** [internal - flight] Inland-; [- policy] Innen- - **2.** [household, home-loving] häuslich - **3.** [not wild] Haus-. ◇ n Hausangestellte der, die.

domestic science n Hauswirtschaftslehre die.

dominant ['dɒmɪnənt] adj [personality] dominant; [nation, group, colour] dominierend.

dominate ['dɒmɪneɪt] vt dominieren.

domineering [,dɒmɪ'nɪərɪŋ] adj herrisch.

domino ['dɒmɪnəʊ] (pl -es) n Dominostein der. ◆ **dominoes** npl [game] Domino das.

don [dɒn] n UK UNIV Universitätsdozent der, -in die.

donate [də'neɪt] vt spenden.

done [dʌn] ◇ pp ⊳ **do**. ◇ adj - **1.** [finished] erledigt; **I'm nearly done** ich bin fast fertig - **2.** [cooked] gar. ◇ excl [to conclude deal] abgemacht!

donkey ['dɒŋkɪ] (pl -s) n Esel der.

donor ['dəʊnə*ʳ*] n Spender der, -in die.

donor card n Organspenderausweis der.

don't [dəʊnt] abbr of **do not**.

doodle ['duːdl] ◇ n Kritzelei die. ◇ vi vor sich hin kritzeln.

doom [duːm] n (U) Verhängnis das.

doomed [duːmd] adj zum Scheitern verurteilt; **to be doomed to sthg** zu etw verurteilt sein.

door [dɔː*ʳ*] n Tür die.

doorbell ['dɔːbel] n Türklingel die.

doorknob ['dɔːnɒb] n Türknauf der.

doorman ['dɔːmən] (pl -men [-mən]) n Portier der.

doormat ['dɔːmæt] n liter & fig Fußabtreter der.

doorstep ['dɔːstep] n Eingangsstufe die; **the supermarket's right on her doorstep** sie hat den Supermarkt direkt vor der Tür.

doorway ['dɔːweɪ] n Eingang der.

dope [dəʊp] ◇ n - **1.** drug sl [cannabis] Hasch der - **2.** [for athlete, horse] Aufputschmittel das - **3.** inf [fool] Trottel der. ◇ vt dopen.

dopey ['dəʊpɪ] (comp -ier, superl -iest) adj inf - **1.** [groggy] benommen - **2.** [stupid] blöd.

dormant ['dɔːmənt] adj - **1.** [volcano] untätig - **2.** (phrase): **to lie dormant** [talents] schlummern.

dormitory ['dɔːmətrɪ] n - **1.** [room] Schlafsaal der - **2.** US [in university] Wohnheim das.

DOS [dɒs] (abbr of disk operating system) n DOS das.

dose [dəʊs] n - **1.** [of medicine, drug] Dosis die - **2.** [of illness] Anfall der.

dot [dɒt] ◇ n Punkt der. ◇ vt verstreuen. ◆ **on the dot** adv: **at four on the dot** Punkt vier Uhr; **to arrive on the dot** auf die Minute pünktlich (an)Ikommen.

dote ◆ **dote upon** vt insep vernarrt sein in (+ A).

dotted line ['dɒtɪd-] n punktierte Linie.

double ['dʌbl] ⟨⟩ adj doppelt; [row, door] Doppel-; **to have a double meaning** doppeldeutig sein; **two double one** zwei eins eins; **Susanne with a double "n"** Susanne mit zwei "n". ⟨⟩ adv - 1. [twice]: **double the amount/number** doppelt so viel/viele - 2. [two of the same] doppelt; **to see double** doppelt sehen - 3. [in two - fold] einmal; (phrase): **to bend double** sich zusammenlkrümmen. ⟨⟩ n - 1. [twice the amount] Doppelte das - 2. [of alcohol] Doppelter der - 3. [look-alike] Ebenbild das - 4. CIN Double das. ⟨⟩ vt [increase twofold] verdoppeln. ⟨⟩ vi [increase twofold] verdoppeln. ◆ **doubles** npl TENNIS Doppel das.

double-barrelled UK, **double-barreled** US [-'bærəld] adj - 1. [shotgun] doppelläufig - 2. [name] Doppel-.

double bass [-beɪs] n Kontrabass der.

double bed n Doppelbett das.

double-breasted [-'brestɪd] adj zweireihig.

double-check vt noch einmal überprüfen.

double chin n Doppelkinn das.

double-click ⟨⟩ vt & vi COMPUT doppelklicken. ⟨⟩ n COMPUT Doppelklick der.

double cream n UK Schlagsahne die.

double-cross vt doppeltes Spiel treiben mit.

double-decker [-'dekər] n Doppeldecker der.

double-dutch n UK hum Kauderwelsch das.

double fault n TENNIS Doppelfehler der.

double-glazing [-'gleɪzɪŋ] n Doppelverglasung die.

double-park vi AUT in der zweiten Reihe parken.

double room n Doppelzimmer das.

double vision n doppeltes Sehen.

doubly ['dʌblɪ] adv: **doubly difficult/important/etc** umso schwieriger/wichtiger/etc.

doubt [daʊt] ⟨⟩ n Zweifel der; **there is no doubt that...** es besteht kein Zweifel, dass...; **to cast doubt on sthg** etw in Zweifel ziehen; **no doubt** ohne Zweifel; without (a) **doubt/beyond (all) doubt** ohne Zweifel; **to be in doubt** ungewiss sein. ⟨⟩ vt - 1. [distrust] zweifeln an (+ D) - 2. [consider unlikely] bezweifeln.

doubtful ['daʊtful] adj - 1. [unlikely, dubious] zweifelhaft - 2. [uncertain] ungewiss.

doubtless ['daʊtlɪs] adv ohne Zweifel.

dough [dəʊ] n (U) - 1. [for baking] Teig der - 2. v inf [money] Knete die.

doughnut ['dəʊnʌt] n ≃ Berliner der.

douse [daʊs] vt - 1. [fire, light] löschen - 2. [person] übergießen.

dove[1] [dʌv] n [bird] Taube die.

dove[2] [dəʊv] pt US ▷ **dive**.

dowdy ['daʊdɪ] adj ohne jeden Schick.

down [daʊn] ⟨⟩ adv - 1. [towards the bottom] nach unten, hinunter/herunter; **to fall down** [person] hinlfallen; [thing] herunterlfallen; **to bend down** sich bücken; **head down** mit gesenktem Kopf - 2. [along]: **I'm going down to the shops** ich gehe einkaufen - 3. [downstairs] herunter; **I'll come down later** ich komme später herunter - 4. [southwards] hinunter/herunter; **we're going down to London** wir fahren hinunter nach London - 5. [reduced]: **prices are coming down** die Preise fallen - 6. [as far as]: **down to the last detail** bis ins letzte Detail; **down to the present** bis in die heutige Zeit. ⟨⟩ prep - 1. [towards the bottom of]: **they ran down the hill** sie liefen den Hügel hinunter; **to fall down the stairs** die Treppe hinunterlfallen - 2. [along] entlang; **I was walking down the street when** ich lief gerade die Straße entlang, als. ⟨⟩ adj - 1. inf [depressed] down - 2. [not in operation]: **the computers are down again** die Computer tun es wieder (mal) nicht. ⟨⟩ n (U) [feathers] Daunen Pl. ⟨⟩ vt - 1. [knock over] niederlschlagen - 2. [swallow] hastig trinken - 3. phr: **to down tools** die Arbeit niederllegen. ◆ **downs** npl UK Hügelland das. ◆ **down with** excl: **down with the King!** nieder mit dem König!

down-and-out ⟨⟩ adj heruntergekommen. ⟨⟩ n Landstreicher der, -in die.

down-at-heel adj esp UK heruntergekommen.

downbeat ['daʊnbiːt] adj inf [ending] undramatisch.

downcast ['daʊnkɑːst] adj fml niedergeschlagen.

downfall ['daʊnfɔːl] n - 1. (U) [ruin - of dictator] Sturz der; [- of business] Ruin der - 2. [cause of ruin] Ruin der.

downhearted [,daʊn'hɑːtɪd] adj niedergeschlagen.

downhill [,daʊn'hɪl] ⟨⟩ adj [path] bergab führend. ⟨⟩ adv - 1. [downwards] bergab, abwärts - 2. fig: **her career went downhill after that** mit ihrer Karriere ging es danach bergab. ⟨⟩ n [skiing] Abfahrtslauf der.

Downing Street ['daʊnɪŋ-] n Straße, in der sich der offizielle Wohnsitz des britischen Premierministers und des Schatzkanzlers befindet.

down payment n Anzahlung die.

downpour ['daʊnpɔːr] n Platzregen der.

downright ['daʊnraɪt] ⟨⟩ adj [fool, cheat, cheek] ausgesprochen; [lie] glatt; [insult] grob. ⟨⟩ adv ausgesprochen.

downstairs [,daʊn'steəz] ⟨⟩ adj: **a downstairs flat** eine Parterre- OR Erdgeschosswohnung. ⟨⟩ adv [be, live] unten; **to go downstairs** (die Treppe) hinunterlgehen; **to come downstairs** (die Treppe) herunterlkommen.

downstream [,daʊn'striːm] adv flussabwärts, stromabwärts.

down-to-earth adj sachlich, nüchtern.

downtown [ˌdaʊnˈtaʊn] esp US ◇ adj: **downtown New York** im Stadtzentrum von New York. ◇ adv [go] ins Stadtzentrum; [live] im Stadtzentrum.

downturn [ˈdaʊntɜːn] n: **downturn (in sthg)** Abnahme die (von etw).

down under adv UK [live] in Australien/Neuseeland; [go] nach Australien/Neuseeland.

downward [ˈdaʊnwəd] ◇ adj - 1. [towards ground] abwärts gerichtet; **downward glance** Blick nach unten; **downward movement** Abwärtsbewegung die - 2. [decreasing] abnehmend, fallend. ◇ adv US = **downwards**.

downwards [ˈdaʊnwədz] adv [look, move] nach unten.

dowry [ˈdaʊərɪ] n Mitgift die.

doz. abbr of **dozen**.

doze [dəʊz] ◇ n Nickerchen das. ◇ vi dösen. ➡ **doze off** vi einlnicken.

dozen [ˈdʌzn] n Dutzend das; **a dozen eggs** ein Dutzend Eier. ➡ **dozens** npl inf: **dozens of** Dutzende (von); **dozens of times** x-mal.

dozy [ˈdəʊzɪ] adj - 1. [sleepy] schläfrig - 2. UK inf [stupid] blöd.

Dr. abbr of **Drive, Doctor**.

drab [dræb] adj - 1. [colour, buildings] trist; [clothes] langweilig; [place] trostlos - 2. [life] eintönig, farblos.

draft [drɑːft] ◇ n - 1. [early version] Entwurf der; [picture, plan] Skizze die - 2. [money order] Zahlungsanweisung die - 3. US MIL: **the draft** die Einberufung - 4. US = **draught**. ◇ vt - 1. [write] entwerfen - 2. US MIL einlberufen, einlziehen - 3. [recruit] rekrutieren.

draftsman n US = **draughtsman**.

drafty adj US = **draughty**.

drag [dræg] ◇ vt - 1. [pull] ziehen - 2. [lake, river] (mit dem Schleppnetz) ablsuchen. ◇ vi - 1. [trail]: **to drag on the ground** auf dem Boden schleifen - 2. [pass slowly] sich in die Länge ziehen. ◇ n - 1. inf [slow] langweilige Sache/Person; **what a drag!** wie öde! - 2. inf [on cigarette] Zug der - 3. [cross-dressing]: **in drag** in Frauenkleidern. ➡ **drag on** vi sich in die Länge ziehen.

dragon [ˈdrægən] n liter & fig Drache der.

dragonfly [ˈdrægnflaɪ] n Libelle die.

drain [dreɪn] ◇ n - 1. [pipe] Abflussrohr das; [grating in street] Gully der; **that's £50 down the drain** fig die 50 Pfund sind zum Fenster rausgeworfen - 2. [depletion]: **drain on sthg** [resources, funds] Belastung die für etw; [energy, time] Verlust der von etw. ◇ vt - 1. [remove water from - vegetables] ablgießen; [- marsh, field] entwässern - 2. [deplete - funds, resources] erschöpfen; [- strength, energy] entziehen; (phrase): **to feel drained** sich ausgelaugt fühlen - 3. [drink, glass] ausltrinken. ◇ vi [dry] abltropfen.

drainage [ˈdreɪnɪdʒ] n [ditches, channels] Entwässerungssystem das; [in city] Kanalisation die.

draining board UK [ˈdreɪnɪŋ-], **drainboard** US [ˈdreɪnbɔːrd] n Abtropfbrett das.

drainpipe [ˈdreɪnpaɪp] n Abflussrohr das.

drama [ˈdrɑːmə] n - 1. [play, genre, event] Drama das - 2. [dramatic quality] Dramatik die.

dramatic [drəˈmætɪk] adj dramatisch.

dramatist [ˈdræmətɪst] n Dramatiker der, -in die.

dramatize, -ise [ˈdræmətaɪz] vt dramatisieren.

drank [dræŋk] pt ▷ **drink**.

drape [dreɪp] vt drapieren; **to be draped with** OR **in sthg** mit etw drapiert sein. ➡ **drapes** npl US Vorhänge Pl.

drastic [ˈdræstɪk] adj drastisch.

draught UK, **draft** US [drɑːft] n - 1. [air current] Luftzug der; **there's a draught in here** hier zieht es - 2. [from barrel]: **on draught** [beer] vom Fass. ➡ **draughts** n UK Damespiel das; **to play draughts** Dame spielen.

draught beer n UK Fassbier das.

draughtsman UK (pl -men [-mən]), **draftsman** US (pl -men [-mən]) [ˈdrɑːftsmən] n technischer Zeichner.

draughty UK, **drafty** US [ˈdrɑːftɪ] adj zugig.

draw [drɔː] ◇ (pt drew, pp drawn) ◇ vt - 1. [sketch] zeichnen - 2. [pull, pull out] ziehen - 3. [conclusion, comparison, distinction] ziehen - 4. [criticism, support] hervorlrufen; **to draw sb's attention to sthg** js Aufmerksamkeit auf etw (A) lenken. ◇ vi - 1. [sketch] zeichnen - 2. [move]: **to draw away** weglziehen; **to draw near** heranlziehen - 3. SPORT unentschieden spielen; **to draw with sb** gegen jn unentschieden spielen. ◇ n - 1. SPORT [result] Unentschieden das - 2. [lottery] Ziehung die - 3. [attraction] Anziehungspunkt der. ➡ **draw out** vt sep - 1. [encourage] aus der Reserve locken - 2. [prolong] in die Länge ziehen - 3. [withdraw] ablheben. ➡ **draw up** ◇ vt sep [draft] auflsetzen; [list] auflstellen. ◇ vi [stop] anlhalten.

drawback [ˈdrɔːbæk] n Nachteil der.

drawbridge [ˈdrɔːbrɪdʒ] n Zugbrücke die.

drawer [drɔːr] n Schublade die.

drawing [ˈdrɔːɪŋ] n - 1. [picture] Zeichnung die - 2. [skill, act] Zeichnen das.

drawing pin n UK Reißzwecke die.

drawing room n Salon der.

drawl [drɔːl] n gedehntes Sprechen.

drawn [drɔːn] pp ▷ **draw**.

dread [dred] ◇ n Furcht die. ◇ vt fürchten; **to dread doing sthg** es schrecklich finden, etw tun zu müssen.

dreadful [ˈdredfʊl] adj schrecklich, furchtbar; (phrase): **I feel dreadful** [guilty] es ist mir sehr peinlich.

dreadfully ['drɛdfʊlɪ] adv - 1. [badly] furchtbar - 2. [extremely] schrecklich.

dream [driːm] (pt & pp -ed OR dreamt) <> n Traum der. <> adj Traum-. <> vt [during sleep] träumen. <> vi: to dream (of OR about sthg) (von etw) träumen; I wouldn't dream of it fig das würde mir nicht im Traum einfallen; to dream of doing sthg davon träumen, etw zu tun. ◆ dream up vt sep sich (D) einfallen lassen OR ausldenken.

dreamt [drɛmt] pt & pp ▷ dream.

dreamy ['driːmɪ] adj - 1. [distracted] verträumt - 2. [languorous] traumhaft.

dreary ['drɪərɪ] adj - 1. [gloomy, depressing] trostlos - 2. [dull, boring] langweilig, öde.

dredge [drɛdʒ] vt auslbaggern. ◆ dredge up vt sep - 1. [from lake, river] heraufholen, herauslholen - 2. fig [from past] auslgraben.

dregs [drɛgz] npl - 1. [of liquid] (Boden)satz der - 2. fig [of society] Abschaum der.

drench [drɛntʃ] vt durchlnässen; to be drenched in OR with sweat in Schweiß gebadet sein.

dress [drɛs] <> n - 1. [frock] Kleid das - 2. [type of clothing] Kleidung die. <> vt - 1. [clothe] anlziehen; to be dressed angezogen sein; to be dressed in gekleidet sein in (+ D); to get dressed sich anlziehen - 2. [wound] verbinden - 3. [salad] anlmachen. <> vi sich anlziehen, sich kleiden. ◆ dress up vi - 1. [in costume] sich verkleiden - 2. [in best clothes] sich festlich anlziehen.

dress circle n THEAT erster Rang.

dresser ['drɛsər] n - 1. [for dishes] Küchenbüffet das (mit Tellerbord) - 2. US [chest of drawers] Frisiertisch der, Frisierkommode die.

dressing ['drɛsɪŋ] n - 1. [bandage] Verband der - 2. [for salad] Dressing das, Salatsoße die - 3. US [for turkey etc] Füllung die.

dressing gown n Bademantel der.

dressing room n - 1. SPORT Umkleidekabine die - 2. THEAT Garderobe die.

dressing table n Frisiertisch der.

dressmaker ['drɛs,meɪkər] n Schneider der, -in die.

dress rehearsal n Generalprobe die.

dressy ['drɛsɪ] adj elegant.

drew [druː] pt ▷ draw.

dribble ['drɪbl] <> n [trickle] Rinnsal das. <> vt SPORT [footballer] dribbeln. <> vi - 1. [drool] sabbern - 2. [spill] tropfen - 3. SPORT [ball] dribbeln.

dried [draɪd] <> pt & pp ▷ dry. <> adj getrocknet; dried milk Trockenmilch die.

drier ['draɪər] n = dryer.

drift [drɪft] <> n - 1. [mass - of snow, leaves, sand] Verwehung die - 2. [meaning]: I get her general drift ich verstehe, worauf sie hinauswill. <> vi [boat, snow, sand, leaves] treiben.

drill [drɪl] <> n - 1. [tool] Bohrer der - 2. [exercise, training] Übung die (für den Ernstfall). <> vt - 1. [metal, wood, hole] bohren - 2. [instruct] drillen; to drill sthg into sb jm etw einlbläuen.

drink [drɪŋk] (pt drank, pp drunk) <> n - 1. [gen] Getränk das; a drink of water ein Glas Wasser - 2. [alcoholic beverage] Drink der; to have a drink etwas trinken - 3. [alcohol] Alkohol der. <> vt trinken. <> vi trinken.

drink-driving UK, **drunk-driving** US n Trunkenheit am Steuer.

drinker ['drɪŋkər] n Trinker der, -in die.

drinking water n Trinkwasser das.

drip [drɪp] <> n - 1. [drop] Tropfen der - 2. MED Tropf der, Infusion die; to be on a drip am Tropf hängen. <> vi tropfen.

drip-dry adj bügelfrei.

drive [draɪv] (pt drove, pp driven) <> n - 1. [journey] Fahrt die; an hour's drive eine Stunde Fahrt; to go for a drive spazieren fahren - 2. [urge] Trieb der - 3. [campaign] Aktion die - 4. (U) [energy] Energie die - 5. [in front of house] Einfahrt die - 6. [stroke - in golf] Treibschlag der; [- in tennis] Drive der - 7. AUT: left-/right-hand drive Links-/Rechtslenkung die - 8. COMPUT Laufwerk das. <> vt - 1. [vehicle, passenger] fahren; to drive sb home jn nach Hause fahren - 2. TECH [operate] anltreiben; driven by electricity mit elektrischem Antrieb - 3. [chase - cattle, clouds, people] treiben; they were driven from their homeland sie wurden aus ihrer Heimat vertrieben - 4. [motivate]: driven by greed/ambition von Gier/Ehrgeiz getrieben - 5. [force]: to drive sb to do sthg jn dazu treiben, etw zu tun; to drive sb hard jn schinden; to drive sb mad OR crazy jn verrückt machen - 6. [hammer] schlagen. <> vi fahren; can you drive? kannst du Auto fahren?

drivel ['drɪvl] n inf Quatsch der.

driven ['drɪvn] pp ▷ drive.

driver ['draɪvər] n [of vehicle] Fahrer der, -in die.

driver's license n US = driving licence.

driveway ['draɪvweɪ] n Auffahrt die.

driving ['draɪvɪŋ] <> adj [rain] strömend; [wind] stürmisch. <> n Fahren das.

driving instructor n Fahrlehrer der, -in die.

driving lesson n Fahrstunde die.

driving licence UK, **driver's license** US n Führerschein der.

driving school n Fahrschule die.

driving test n Fahrprüfung die.

drizzle ['drɪzl] <> n Sprühregen der. <> impers vb: it's drizzling es nieselt.

drone [drəʊn] n - 1. [sound - of machine, engine, loudspeaker] Dröhnen das; [- of insect] Summen das - 2. [male bee] Drohne die.

drool [druːl] *vi* - **1.** [dribble] sabbern - **2.** *fig* [admire]: **he stood there drooling over the sports car** er konnte sich an dem Sportwagen nicht satt sehen.

droop [druːp] *vi* [hang down] herunterhängen; [flower] den Kopf hängen lassen.

drop [drɒp] <> *n* - **1.** [of liquid] Tropfen *der* - **2.** [sweet] Drops *der* ODER *das* - **3.** [decrease]: **drop (in sthg)** Rückgang *der* (von etw); [in salary] Minderung *die* (von etw) - **4.** [vertical distance] Höhenunterschied *der*; **there's a 50 m drop** hier geht es 50 m (senkrecht) hinunter. <> *vt* - **1.** [gen] fallen lassen; **to drop (sb) a hint** (jm gegenüber) eine Anspielung machen - **2.** [decrease, lower] senken - **3.** [leave out] weglassen - **4.** [let out of car] absetzen - **5.** [write]: **to drop sb a line** OR **note** jm ein paar Zeilen schreiben. <> *vi* - **1.** [fall] fallen; [with exhaustion] umlfallen - **2.** [decrease] sinken - **3.** [voice] leiser werden. ◆ **drops** *npl* MED Tropfen *Pl.* ◆ **drop in** *vi inf*: **to drop in (on sb)** vorbeilkommen (bei jm). ◆ **drop off** <> *vt sep* [person] absetzen; [letter, package] ablschicken. <> *vi* - **1.** [fall asleep] einlnicken - **2.** [grow less] zurücklgehen. ◆ **drop out** *vi*: **to drop out (of** OR **from sthg)** auslsteigen (aus etw).

dropout ['drɒpaʊt] *n* - **1.** [from society] Aussteiger *der*, -in *die* - **2.** [from university] Studienabbrecher *der*, -in *die*.

droppings ['drɒpɪŋz] *npl* Kot *der*; [of horses] Äpfel *Pl.*

drought [draʊt] *n* Dürre *die*.

drove [drəʊv] *pt* ⊳ **drive**.

drown [draʊn] <> *vt* [person, animal] ertränken. <> *vi* ertrinken.

drowsy ['draʊzɪ] *adj* schläfrig.

drudgery ['drʌdʒərɪ] *n* Schinderei *die*.

drug [drʌg] <> *n* - **1.** [medication] Arzneimittel *das* - **2.** [illegal substance] Droge *die*; **to be on drugs** drogen- OR rauschgiftabhängig sein. <> *vt* [person, animal] verabreichen (+ D); [food, drink] mit Drogen versetzen.

drug abuse *n* Drogenmissbrauch *der*.

drug addict *n* Drogensüchtige *der, die*.

druggist ['drʌgɪst] *n* US Apotheker *der*, -in *die*.

drugstore ['drʌgstɔːr] *n* US Drugstore *der*.

drum [drʌm] <> *n* - **1.** [instrument, cylinder] Trommel *die* - **2.** [container] Tonne *die*. <> *vt* & *vi* trommeln. ◆ **drums** *npl* Schlagzeug *das*. ◆ **drum up** *vt sep* [business] anlkurbeln.

drummer ['drʌmər] *n* Schlagzeuger *der*, -in *die*.

drumstick ['drʌmstɪk] *n* - **1.** [for drum] Trommelschlägel *der* - **2.** [of chicken] Keule *die*.

drunk [drʌŋk] <> *pp* ⊳ **drink**. <> *adj* [on alcohol] betrunken. <> *n* [on one occasion] Betrunkene *der, die*; [habitual] Trinker *der*, -in *die*.

drunkard ['drʌŋkəd] *n* Trinker *der*, -in *die*.

drunk-driving *n* US = **drink-driving**.

drunken ['drʌŋkn] *adj* [person] betrunken; **a drunken evening** ein feuchtfröhlicher Abend; **in a drunken stupor** sinnlos betrunken.

dry [draɪ] <> *adj* - **1.** [gen] trocken - **2.** [river, lake] ausgetrocknet - **3.** [thirsty] durstig; **to feel** OR **be dry** durstig sein, Durst haben. <> *vt* & *vi* trocknen. ◆ **dry up** <> *vt sep* [dishes] abltrocknen. <> *vi* - **1.** [river, lake, well] ausltrocknen - **2.** [supplies, inspiration] zur Neige gehen - **3.** [actor, speaker] stecken bleiben - **4.** [dry dishes] abltrocknen.

dry cleaner *n*: **dry cleaner's** chemische Reinigung.

dryer ['draɪər] *n* [for clothes] Trockner *der*.

dry land *n* Festland *das*.

dry rot *n* Trockenfäule *die*.

dry ski slope *n* Sommerskihang *der*.

DSS (*abbr of* **Department of Social Security**) *n* britisches Sozialamt.

DTI (*abbr of* **Department of Trade and Industry**) *n* Handels- und Industrieministerium *das*.

DTP (*abbr of* **desktop publishing**) *n* DTP *das*.

dual ['djuːəl] *adj* doppelt, Doppel-.

dual carriageway *n* UK vierspurige Straße.

dubbed [dʌbd] *adj* - **1.** CIN synchronisiert - **2.** [nicknamed] genannt.

dubious ['djuːbjəs] *adj* - **1.** [suspect, questionable] dubios, zweifelhaft - **2.** [uncertain, undecided]: **to be dubious about doing sthg** nicht wissen, ob man etw tun soll.

Dublin ['dʌblɪn] *n* Dublin *nt*.

duchess ['dʌtʃɪs] *n* Herzogin *die*.

duck [dʌk] <> *n* Ente *die*. <> *vt* - **1.** [head] ducken, einlziehen - **2.** [responsibility, duty] auslweichen (+ D). <> *vi* sich ducken.

duckling ['dʌklɪŋ] *n* - **1.** [animal] Entenküken *das* - **2.** (U) [food] junge Ente.

duct [dʌkt] *n* - **1.** [pipe] Leitung *die*, Rohr *das* - **2.** ANAT Kanal *der*.

dud [dʌd] <> *adj* - **1.** [false] falsch - **2.** [useless] wertlos. <> *n* [bomb, shell] Blindgänger *der*.

dude [duːd] *n* US inf Typ *der*.

due [djuː] <> *adj* - **1.** [expected] fällig; **the book's due (out) in May** das Buch soll im Mai erscheinen - **2.** [proper] ordnungsgemäß, nötig; **in due course** zu gegebener Zeit - **3.** [owed, owing] fällig. <> *adv*: **due west** genau nach Westen. <> *dues* *npl* Abgaben *Pl*, Gebühren *Pl.* ◆ **due to** *prep* wegen (+ G, D).

duel ['djuːəl] *n* Duell *das*.

duet [djuːˈet] *n* Duett *das*.

duffel bag ['dʌfl-] *n* Seesack *der*.

duffel coat ['dʌfl-] n Dufflecoat der.

dug [dʌg] pt & pp ⊳ **dig**.

duke [djuːk] n Herzog der.

dull [dʌl] ◇ adj - **1.** [boring] langweilig - **2.** [colour, light] matt - **3.** [day, weather] trüb - **4.** [noise, pain] dumpf. ◇ vt - **1.** [senses] abstumpfen; [pain] dämpfen - **2.** [make less bright - metal] stumpf werden lassen.

duly ['djuːlɪ] adv - **1.** [properly] ordnungsgemäß - **2.** [as expected] erwartungsgemäß.

dumb [dʌm] adj - **1.** [unable to speak] stumm; **to be struck dumb** sprachlos sein - **2.** esp US inf [stupid] dumm.

dumbfound [dʌm'faund] vt verblüffen; **to be dumbfounded** verblüfft sein, sprachlos sein.

dummy ['dʌmɪ] ◇ adj unecht; **a dummy gun** eine Spielzeugpistole. ◇ n - **1.** [model of human figure - for tailoring] Schneiderpuppe die; [- for crash testing] Dummy der; [- in shop] Schaufensterpuppe die - **2.** [copy, fake object] Attrappe die - **3.** UK [for baby] Schnuller der.

dump [dʌmp] ◇ n - **1.** [for rubbish] Müllhalde die - **2.** [for ammunition] Munitionslager das. ◇ vt - **1.** inf [put down] abladen - **2.** [dispose of - waste, rubbish] wegwerfen; [- car] zurücklassen - **3.** inf [jilt] in die Wüste schicken.

dumper (truck) UK ['dʌmpər-], **dump truck** US n Kipper der, Kipplaster der.

dumping ['dʌmpɪŋ] n [of waste] Abladen das; 'no dumping' 'Schutt abladen verboten'.

dumpling ['dʌmplɪŋ] n CULIN Kloß der.

dump truck n US = **dumper truck**.

dumpy ['dʌmpɪ] adj inf dicklich, untersetzt.

dunce [dʌns] n Ignorant der.

dune [djuːn] n Düne die.

dung [dʌŋ] n Dung der, Mist der.

dungarees [ˌdʌŋgə'riːz] npl UK [for work] Arbeitshose die; [fashion garment] Segeltuch das.

dungeon ['dʌndʒən] n Verlies das.

duo ['djuːəu] n - **1.** [of singers, musicians] Duett das; [on stage] Duo das - **2.** [couple] Duo das.

duplex ['djuːpleks] n US - **1.** [apartment] Doppelapartment die - **2.** [house] Zweifamilienhaus das.

duplicate ◇ adj ['djuːplɪkət] [document] kopiert; **a duplicate key** ein Nachschlüssel. ◇ n ['djuːplɪkət] Kopie die; **in duplicate** in doppelter Ausfertigung. ◇ vt ['djuːplɪkeɪt] [copy - document] kopieren; [- key] nachlmachen.

durable ['djuərəbl] adj strapazierfähig.

duration [dju'reɪʃn] n Dauer die; **for the duration of** für die Dauer von.

duress [dju'res] n: **under duress** unter Zwang.

during ['djuərɪŋ] prep während (+ G).

dusk [dʌsk] n Abenddämmerung die.

dust [dʌst] ◇ n Staub der. ◇ vt - **1.** [clean] ablstauben - **2.** [cover]: **to dust sthg with sthg** etw mit etw bestäuben.

dustbin ['dʌstbɪn] n UK Mülltonne die.

dustbin lorry n UK Müllwagen der.

duster ['dʌstər] n [cloth] Staubtuch das.

dust jacket n [on book] Schutzumschlag der.

dust(bin)man ['dʌst,bɪn,mən] (pl -men [-mən]) n UK Müllmann der.

dustpan ['dʌstpæn] n Kehrschaufel die.

dusty ['dʌstɪ] adj staubig, verstaubt.

Dutch [dʌtʃ] ◇ adj niederländisch, holländisch. ◇ n [language] Niederländisch(e) das. ◇ adv: **to go Dutch** getrennt bezahlen.

dutiful ['djuːtɪful] adj pflichtbewusst.

duty ['djuːtɪ] n - **1.** (U) [responsibility] Pflicht die; **to do one's duty** seine Pflicht tun - **2.** (U) [work] Dienst der; **to be on duty** Dienst haben; **to be off duty** dienstfrei haben - **3.** [tax] Zoll der. ⬥ **duties** npl [tasks] Aufgaben Pl.

duty-free adj (U) zollfrei.

duvet ['duːveɪ] n UK Daunendecke die.

duvet cover n UK Bettbezug der (für eine Daunendecke).

DVD (abbr of Digital Versatile Disk) n DVD die.

DVD player n DVD-Player der.

dwarf [dwɔːf] (pl -s OR **dwarves** [dwɔːvz]) ◇ n Zwerg der, -in die. ◇ vt [tower over] winzig erscheinen lassen.

dwell [dwel] (pt & pp **dwelt** OR **-ed**) vi liter [live] wohnen. ⬥ **dwell on** vt insep [talk about] sich lange befassen mit; [think about] lange nachldenken über (+ A).

dwelling ['dwelɪŋ] n liter Wohnung die.

dwelt [dwelt] pt & pp ⊳ **dwell**.

dwindle ['dwɪndl] vi dahinlschwinden.

dye [daɪ] ◇ n Farbstoff der. ◇ vt färben.

dying ['daɪɪŋ] ◇ cont ⊳ **die**. ◇ adj - **1.** [person, animal] sterbend - **2.** fig [tradition, language] aussterbend.

dyke [daɪk] n = **dike**.

dynamic [daɪ'næmɪk] adj dynamisch.

dynamite ['daɪnəmaɪt] n (U) - **1.** [explosive] Dynamit das - **2.** inf fig [story, news]: **to be dynamite** viel Zündstoff enthalten - **3.** inf fig [excellent]: **to be dynamite** eine Wucht sein.

dynamo ['daɪnəməu] (pl -s) n TECH Dynamo der; AUT Lichtmaschine die.

dynasty [UK 'dɪnəstɪ, US 'daɪnəstɪ] n Dynastie die.

dyslexia [dɪs'leksɪə] n (U) Legasthenie die.

dyslexic [dɪs'leksɪk] adj legasthenisch; **to be dyslexic** Legastheniker/Legasthenikerin sein.

E

e (pl **e's** OR **es**), **E** (pl **E's** OR **Es**) [i:] n [letter] e das, E das. ◆ **E** n - 1. MUS E das - 2. abbr of **east** - 3. inf (abbr of **ecstasy**) E das.

each [i:tʃ] ⟨⟩ adj jede(r) (s). ⟨⟩ pron: **each (one)** jede(r) (s); **each other** einander; **separated from each other** voneinander getrennt; **they know each other** sie kennen sich; **they kissed each other on the cheek** sie küssten sich auf die Wange; **there's one each** es ist für jeden eins da; **I'd like one of each** ich möchte von jedem/jeder eins; **they cost £10 each** sie kosten je 10 Pfund.

eager ['i:gər] adj [person] eifrig; (phrase): **to be eager for sthg** auf etw (A) erpicht sein; **to be eager to do sthg** etw unbedingt tun wollen.

eagle ['i:gl] n Adler der.

ear [ɪər] n - 1. [of person, animal] Ohr das; **I'll play it by ear** ich werde es auf mich zukommen lassen - 2. [of corn] Ähre die.

earache ['ɪəreɪk] n Ohrenschmerzen Pl.

eardrum ['ɪədrʌm] n Trommelfell das.

earl [ɜ:l] n Graf der.

earlier ['ɜ:lɪər] adj & adv früher; **earlier on** früher.

earliest ['ɜ:lɪəst] ⟨⟩ adj - 1. [first] frühstmöglich; **at the earliest opportunity** so bald wie möglich - 2. [most early] frühest. ⟨⟩ adv: **she'll not be back till four o'clock at the earliest** sie wird frühestens um vier Uhr wieder hier sein.

earlobe ['ɪələʊb] n Ohrläppchen das.

early ['ɜ:lɪ] ⟨⟩ adj früh; **early death** vorzeitiger Tod; **at an early hour** zu früher Stunde; **at an early age** [early in life] schon früh; [as a child] im Kindesalter; **in the early afternoon** am frühen Nachmittag; **to have an early breakfast/night** früh frühstücken/zu Bett gehen. ⟨⟩ adv früh; **to leave early** [person] früher gehen; [bus, train] zu früh abfahren; **as early as next week** schon nächste Woche; **early on** früh.

early closing n: **today is early closing** heute schließen die Geschäfte früher.

early retirement n: **to take early retirement** in den vorzeitigen Ruhestand gehen.

earmark ['ɪəmɑ:k] vt: **to be earmarked for sthg** für etw vorgesehen sein.

earn [ɜ:n] vt - 1. [gen] verdienen - 2. COMM erwirtschaften.

earnest ['ɜ:nɪst] adj ernsthaft. ◆ **in earnest** ⟨⟩ adj: **I'm in earnest** ich meine es ernst. ⟨⟩ adv ernsthaft; **to begin in earnest** richtig anfangen.

earnings ['ɜ:nɪŋz] npl [of person] Einkommen das; [of business] Ertrag der.

earphones ['ɪəfəʊnz] npl Kopfhörer der.

earpiece n [of telephone] Hörmuschel die; [of radio, mobile phone] ≈ Kopfhörer der.

earplugs ['ɪəplʌgz] npl Ohropax® Pl.

earring ['ɪərɪŋ] n Ohrring der.

earshot ['ɪəʃɒt] n: **within/out of earshot** in/außer Hörweite.

earth [ɜ:θ] ⟨⟩ n Erde die; **how/what/where/why on earth ?** wie/was/wo/warum um Himmels willen ?; **to cost the earth** UK ein Vermögen kosten. ⟨⟩ vt UK: **to be earthed** geerdet sein.

earthenware ['ɜ:θnweər] n (U) Töpferwaren Pl.

earthquake ['ɜ:θkweɪk] n Erdbeben das.

earthy ['ɜ:θɪ] adj [humour, person] derb.

ease [i:z] ⟨⟩ n - 1. [in doing sthg] Leichtigkeit die; **to do sthg with ease** mit Leichtigkeit tun - 2. [comfort]: **a life of ease** ein komfortables Leben; **to put sb at ease** jm die Befangenheit nehmen; **I feel at ease (with him)** ich fühle mich (in seiner Gegenwart) wohl; **ill at ease** unbehaglich. ⟨⟩ vt - 1. [make less severe - pain] lindern; [- restriction, problem] verringern - 2. [move carefully]: **she eased herself out of the armchair** sie erhob sich behutsam aus dem Sessel; **she eased the window open** sie öffnete behutsam das Fenster. ⟨⟩ vi [pain, rain] nachlassen; [grip] sich lockern. ◆ **ease off** vi [pain, rain] nachlassen. ◆ **ease up** vi - 1. [rain] nachlassen - 2. [relax] sich (D) mehr Ruhe gönnen.

easel ['i:zl] n Staffelei die.

easily ['i:zɪlɪ] adv - 1. [without difficulty] leicht - 2. [undoubtedly] zweifellos - 3. [in a relaxed manner] entspannt.

east [i:st] ⟨⟩ adj Ost-, östlich; **east wind** Ostwind der. ⟨⟩ adv [travel, face] ostwärts, nach Osten; [be] east of östlich von. ⟨⟩ n - 1. [direction] Osten der - 2. [region]: **the east** der Osten. ◆ **East** n: **the East** [Asia & POL] der Osten.

East End n: **the East End** der Londoner Osten nördlich der Themse.

Easter ['i:stər] n Ostern Pl.

Easter egg n Osterei das.

easterly ['i:stəlɪ] adj östlich; **easterly wind** Ostwind der; **in an easterly direction** in östlicher Richtung.

eastern ['i:stən] adj Ost-. ◆ **Eastern** adj - 1. [from Asia] östlich - 2. POL Ost-.

East German ⟨⟩ adj ostdeutsch. ⟨⟩ n Ostdeutsche der, die.

East Germany n: **(the former) East Germany** Ostdeutschland nt.

eastward ['i:stwəd] <> *adj* (in) Richtung Osten. <> *adv* = **eastwards**.

eastwards ['i:stwədz] *adv* ostwärts.

easy ['i:zı] <> *adj* - 1. [not difficult] leicht; [route] einfach - 2. [comfortable] leicht; **an easy life** ein bequemes Leben - 3. [relaxed] ungezwungen. <> *adv*: **to take it** OR **things easy** *inf* [ease up] sich *(D)* mehr Ruhe gönnen; [have a rest] eine ruhige Kugel schieben.

easy chair *n* [armchair] Sessel *der*.

easygoing [,ɪzɪ'gəʊɪŋ] *adj* [person] unbekümmert; [manner] lässig.

eat [i:t] (*pt* **ate**, *pp* **eaten**) *vt* [subj: person] essen; [subj: animal] fressen. **eat away, eat into** *vt insep* - 1. [subj: rust, acid] zerfressen - 2. [savings] auflzehren.

eaten ['i:tn] *pp* **eat**.

eaves ['i:vz] *npl* [of house] Dachvorsprung *der*.

eavesdrop ['i:vzdrɒp] *vi* lauschen; **to eavesdrop on sb** jn belauschen.

ebb [eb] <> *n* Ebbe *die*. <> *vi* [tide, sea] zurücklgehen.

ebony ['ebənı] *n* Ebenholz *das*.

EC (*abbr of* **European Community**) *n* EG *die*.

ECB (*abbr of* **Eurpean Central Bank**) *n* EZB *die*.

e-cash *n* COMPUT elektronisches Geld.

eccentric [ɪk'sentrɪk] <> *adj* exzentrisch. <> *n* Exzentriker *der*, -in *die*.

echo ['ekəʊ] (*pl* -es) <> *n* - 1. [sound] Echo *das* - 2. [reminder] Reminiszenz *die*. <> *vt* [repeat-opinion] wiederlgeben. <> *vi* widerlhallen.

eclipse [ɪ'klɪps] <> *n* - 1. [of sun, moon] Eklipse *die*, Finsternis *die* - 2. *fig* [decline] Niedergang *der*. <> *vt fig* [overshadow] in den Schatten stellen.

eco-friendly *adj* umweltfreundlich.

ecological [,i:kə'lɒdʒɪkl] *adj* ökologisch; **an ecological group** eine Gruppe von Umweltschützern.

ecology [ɪ'kɒlədʒɪ] *n* Ökologie *die*.

economic [,i:kə'nɒmɪk] *adj* - 1. [growth, system, policy] Wirtschafts- - 2. [business] wirtschaftlich.

economical [,i:kə'nɒmɪkl] *adj* wirtschaftlich; [person] sparsam.

economics [,i:kə'nɒmɪks] <> *n (U)* [study] Wirtschaftswissenschaften *Pl.* <> *npl* [of plan, business, trade] Wirtschaftlichkeit *die*.

economize, -ise [ɪ'kɒnəmaɪz] *vi* sparen; **to economize on sthg** an etw *(D)* sparen.

economy [ɪ'kɒnəmɪ] *n* - 1. [system] Wirtschaft *die* - 2. [saving]: **it is a false economy** es hilft nicht zu sparen; **to make economies** Sparmaßnahmen treffen; **economy measure** Sparmaßnahme *die*.

economy class *n* Touristenklasse *die*.

ecstasy ['ekstəsɪ] *n* - 1. [great happiness] Ekstase *die*; **to go into ecstasies about sthg** etw *(A)* in Verzückung geraten - 2. *(U)* [drug] Ecstasy *das*.

ecstatic [ek'stætɪk] *adj* ekstatisch.

eczema ['eksɪmə] *n (U)* Ekzem *das*.

edge [edʒ] <> *n* - 1. [of cliff, path, forest] Rand *der*; [of table, coin, book] Kante *die* - 2. [of blade] Schneide *die* - 3. [advantage]: **to have an edge over sb, to have the edge on sb** jm gegenüber einen Vorteil haben; **to have an edge over sthg, to have the edge on sthg** etw *(D)* überlegen sein. <> *vi* [move slowly]: **to edge forwards** sich Stück für Stück vorwärtslbewegen; **to edge away** sich langsam zurücklziehen. **on edge** *adj*: **to be on edge** [person] nervös sein; [nerves] gereizt sein.

edgeways ['edʒweɪz], **edgewise** ['edʒwaɪz] *adv* seitwärts.

edgy ['edʒɪ] *adj* nervös.

edible ['edɪbl] *adj* essbar.

Edinburgh ['edɪnbrə] *n* Edinburgh *nt*.

edit ['edɪt] *vt* - 1. [correct, select material for] redigieren - 2. CIN, RADIO & TV schneiden - 3. [newspaper, magazine] herauslgeben - 4. COMPUT editieren.

edition [ɪ'dɪʃn] *n* - 1. [of book, newspaper] Ausgabe *die* - 2. [broadcast] Sendung *die*.

editor ['edɪtə'] *n* - 1. [of newspaper, magazine, book] Herausgeber *der*, -in *die* - 2. [of section of newspaper, programme] Redakteur *der*, -in *die* - 3. [copy editor] Lektor *der*, -in *die* - 4. CIN, RADIO & TV Cutter *der*, -in *die* - 5. COMPUT Editor *der*.

editorial [,edɪ'tɔ:rɪəl] <> *adj* redaktionell; **editorial department/staff** Redaktion *die*. <> *n* Leitartikel *der*.

educate ['edʒʊkeɪt] *vt* - 1. SCH & UNIV auslbilden; [subj: parents] erziehen - 2. [inform] informieren.

education [,edʒʊ'keɪʃn] *n* Ausbildung *die*; [by parents] Erziehung *die*.

educational [,edʒʊ'keɪʃənl] *adj* - 1. [establishment, policy] Bildungs-; **educational background** Ausbildung *die* - 2. [toy] didaktisch; [experience] lehrreich.

EEC (*abbr of* **European Economic Community**) *n* EWG *die*.

eel [i:l] *n* Aal *der*.

eerie ['ɪərɪ] *adj* unheimlich.

efface [ɪ'feɪs] *vt* [mark, inscription] entfernen; [memory] ausllöschen.

effect [ɪ'fekt] <> *n* - 1. [result] Wirkung *die*; **to have an effect on sb/sthg** eine Wirkung auf jn/etw haben; **to take effect** [law, rule] in Kraft treten; [drug] wirken; **to put sthg into effect** etw in Kraft setzen - 2. [impression] Wirkung *die*, Effekt *der*; **for effect** aus Effekthascherei. <> *vt* bewirken. **effects** *npl* - 1.:

(special) effects (Spezial)effekte *Pl* - 2. [property] Habe *die*. ➤ **in effect** *adv* in Wirklichkeit.

effective [ɪ'fektɪv] *adj* - 1. [successful] effektiv - 2. [actual] eigentlich - 3. [in operation] wirksam.

effectively [ɪ'fektɪvlɪ] *adv* - 1. [successfully] effektiv - 2. [in fact] in Wirklichkeit.

effectiveness [ɪ'fektɪvnɪs] *n* [success] Effektivität *die*.

effeminate [ɪ'femɪnət] *adj pej* weibisch.

effervescent [ˌefə'vesənt] *adj* sprudelnd.

efficiency [ɪ'fɪʃənsɪ] *n* [of person] Tüchtigkeit *die*; [of machine] Leistungsfähigkeit *die*; [of system] Effizienz *die*.

efficient [ɪ'fɪʃnt] *adj* [person] tüchtig; [machine] leistungsfähig; [method] effizient.

effluent ['efluənt] *n* Abwasser *das*.

effort ['efət] *n* - 1. [exertion] Anstrengung *die*; **it's not worth the effort** es ist nicht der Mühe wert; **to make the effort to do sthg** sich bemühen, etw zu tun; **with effort** mit Mühe - 2. [attempt] Versuch *der*; **to make an/no effort to do sthg** sich anstrengen/sich nicht anstrengen, etw zu tun.

effortless ['efətlɪs] *adj* mühelos.

effusive [ɪ'fjuːsɪv] *adj* überschwänglich.

e.g. (*abbr of exempli gratia*) *adv* z. B.

egg [eg] *n* Ei *das*. ➤ **egg on** *vt sep* anstacheln.

eggcup ['egkʌp] *n* Eierbecher *der*.

eggplant ['egplɑːnt] *n US* Aubergine *die*.

eggshell ['egʃel] *n* Eierschale *die*.

egg white *n* Eiweiß *das*.

egg yolk *n* Eigelb *das*.

ego ['iːgəʊ] (*pl* -s) *n* [opinion of self] Selbstbewusstsein *das*; PSYCHOL Ego *das*.

egoism ['iːgəʊɪzm] *n* Egoismus *der*.

egoistic [ˌiːgəʊ'ɪstɪk] *adj* egoistisch.

egotistic(al) [ˌiːgə'tɪstɪk(l)] *adj* egoistisch.

Egypt ['iːdʒɪpt] *n* Ägypten *nt*.

Egyptian [ɪ'dʒɪpʃn] ◇ *adj* ägyptisch. ◇ *n* Ägypter *der*, -in *die*.

eiderdown ['aɪdədaʊn] *n esp UK* [bed cover] Daunendecke *die*.

eight [eɪt] *num* acht; *see also* **six**.

eighteen [ˌeɪ'tiːn] *num* achtzehn; *see also* **six**.

eighth [eɪtθ] *num* achte(r) (s); *see also* **sixth**.

eighty ['eɪtɪ] *num* achtzig; *see also* **sixty**.

Eire ['eərə] *n* Irland *nt*.

either ['aɪðər, 'iːðər] ◇ *adj* - 1. [one or the other]: **either will do** es ist egal, welches (von beiden); **either way I will lose** wie ich es auch mache, ich werde dabei verlieren - 2. [each] beide; **on either side** auf beiden Seiten. ◇ *pron*: **I'll take either (of them)** ich nehme einen/eine/eins (von beiden); **I don't like**

either (of them) ich mag keinen/keine/keins (von beiden). ◇ *adv* (*in negatives*): **I can't either** ich auch nicht. ◇ *conj*: **either...or...** entweder...oder...; **I don't like either him or her** ich mag weder ihn noch sie; **without either writing or phoning** ohne zu schreiben oder anzurufen.

eject [ɪ'dʒekt] *vt* - 1. [object] ausßtoßen - 2. [person]: **to eject sb (from)** jn hinausßwerfen (aus).

eke ➤ **eke out** *vt sep* strecken.

elaborate ◇ *adj* [ɪ'læbrət] [explanation] ausführlich; [plan] ausgefeilt; [carving] kunstvoll; [ceremony] kompliziert. ◇ *vi* [ɪ'læbəreɪt]: **to elaborate (on sthg)** (etw) näher erläutern.

elapse [ɪ'læps] *vi* [time] verstreichen.

elastic [ɪ'læstɪk] ◇ *adj* - 1. [stretchy] elastisch - 2. *fig* [flexible] flexibel. ◇ *n (U)* [material] Gummiband *das*.

elasticated [ɪ'læstɪkeɪtɪd] *adj* [waistband] mit Gummizug.

elastic band *n UK* Gummiband *das*.

elated [ɪ'leɪtɪd] *adj* in Hochstimmung.

elbow ['elbəʊ] *n* Ellbogen *der*.

elder ['eldər] ◇ *adj* ältere(r) (s). ◇ *n* - 1. [older person]: **show respect to your elders** zeige Respekt gegenüber älteren Menschen - 2. [of church] Presbyter *der*.

elderly ['eldəlɪ] ◇ *adj* ältere(r) (s). ◇ *npl*: **the elderly** ältere Menschen *Pl*.

eldest ['eldɪst] *adj* älteste(r) (s).

elect [ɪ'lekt] ◇ *adj*: **president elect** designierter Präsident. ◇ *vt* [by voting] wählen; **he was elected (as) party leader** er wurde zum Parteivorsitzenden gewählt.

election [ɪ'lekʃn] *n* Wahl *die*; **to have** OR **hold an election** eine Wahl abhalten.

elector [ɪ'lektər] *n* [voter] Wähler *der*, -in *die*.

electorate [ɪ'lektərət] *n*: **the electorate** die Wählerschaft.

electric [ɪ'lektrɪk] *adj* - 1. [gen] elektrisch - 2. *fig* [atmosphere] elektrisiert. ➤ **electrics** *npl UK inf* [in car, machine] Elektrik *die*.

electrical [ɪ'lektrɪkl] *adj* elektrisch; **electrical goods** Elektrowaren *Pl*.

electrical shock *n US* = **electric shock**.

electric blanket *n* Heizdecke *die*.

electric cooker *n* Elektroherd *der*.

electric fire *n* Heizstrahler *der*.

electrician [ˌɪlek'trɪʃn] *n* Elektriker *der*, -in *die*.

electricity [ˌɪlek'trɪsətɪ] *n* [current] Strom *der*; [in physics] Elektrizität *die*.

electric shock *UK*, **electrical shock** *US n* Stromschlag *der*.

electrify [ɪ'lektrɪfaɪ] *vt* - 1. [railway line] elektrifizieren - 2. *fig* [excite] elektrisieren.

electrocute [ɪ'lektrəkjuːt] *vt*: **to electrocute o.s.**, **to be electrocuted** sich durch Stromschlag töten; **to be electrocuted** [executed] auf dem elektrischen Stuhl hingerichtet werden.

electrolysis [ˌɪlek'trɒləsɪs] *n* Elektrolyse *die*.

electron [ɪ'lektrɒn] *n* Elektron *das*.

electronic [ˌɪlek'trɒnɪk] *adj* elektronisch. ◆ **electronics** ◇ *n* (U) [technology] Elektronik *die*. ◇ *npl* [of car, machine] Elektronik *die*.

electronic data processing *n* elektronische Datenverarbeitung.

elegant [ˈelɪgənt] *adj* elegant.

element [ˈelɪmənt] *n* - 1. [gen] Element *das*; [component] Bestandteil *der*; **an element of truth** ein Körnchen Wahrheit - 2. [of heater, kettle] Heizelement *das*. ◆ **elements** *npl* - 1. [basics] Grundlagen *Pl* - 2. [weather]: **the elements** die Elemente *Pl*.

elementary [ˌelɪ'mentərɪ] *adj* [precautions, mistake, question] simpel; [education, maths] Elementar-.

elementary school *n US* Grundschule *die*.

elephant [ˈelɪfənt] (*pl inv OR* -s) *n* Elefant *der*.

elevate [ˈelɪveɪt] *vt* - 1. [raise] heben - 2. [give importance to] erheben; [promote] befördern.

elevator [ˈelɪveɪtə^r] *n US* Fahrstuhl *der*.

eleven [ɪ'levn] *num* elf; *see also* **six**.

elevenses [ɪ'levnzɪz] *n UK* zweites Frühstück.

eleventh [ɪ'levnθ] *num* elfte(r) (s); *see also* **sixth**.

elicit [ɪ'lɪsɪt] *vt fml*: **to elicit sthg (from sb)** (jm) etw entlocken.

eligible [ˈelɪdʒəbl] *adj* [suitable, qualified] geeignet; **to be eligible for sthg** für etw in Frage kommen.

eliminate [ɪ'lɪmɪneɪt] *vt* - 1. [remove] ausschließen; [disease, poverty] eliminieren - 2. [from competition]: **to be eliminated from sthg** aus etw ausscheiden.

elite [ɪ'liːt] ◇ *adj* Elite-. ◇ *n* Elite *die*.

elitist [ɪ'liːtɪst] *adj* elitär.

elk [elk] (*pl inv OR* -s) *n* Elch *der*; [Canadian] Elk *der*.

elm [elm] *n*: **elm (tree)** Ulme *die*.

elongated [ˈiːlɒŋgeɪtɪd] *adj* [face, shape] lang gezogen.

elope [ɪ'ləʊp] *vi* durchbrennen.

eloquent [ˈeləkwənt] *adj* - 1. [speaker] wortgewandt - 2. [speech, words] wohlgesetzt.

else [els] *adv*: **I don't want anything else** ich will nichts mehr; **anything else?** sonst noch etwas?; **everyone else** alle anderen; **nobody else** niemand anders; **nothing else** sonst nichts; **somebody else** [additional person] noch jemand anders; [different person] jemand anders; **anybody else (but you) would have giv-** en up jeder andere (außer dir) hätte aufgegeben; **something else** [additional thing] noch etwas; [different thing] etwas anderes; **somewhere else** woanders; **to go somewhere else** woandershin gehen; **what else?** [in addition] was (sonst) noch?; [instead] was sonst?; **who else?** [in addition] wer (sonst) noch?; [instead] wer sonst? ◆ **or else** *conj* [or if not] sonst, oder; **come in or else go out** komm entweder herein oder geh hinaus.

elsewhere [els'weə^r] *adv* woanders.

elude [ɪ'luːd] *vt* - 1. [police, pursuers] entwischen - 2. [subj: fact, name] entfallen sein (+ D).

elusive [ɪ'luːsɪv] *adj* [quality] schwer fassbar; [success] schwer erreichbar; **he is very elusive** er ist selten anzutreffen.

emaciated [ɪ'meɪʃɪeɪtɪd] *adj* stark abgemagert.

e-mail ◇ *n* E-Mail *die ODER das*; **by e-mail** per E-Mail. ◇ *vt*: **to e-mail sb** jm ein(e) E-Mail schicken.

e-mail address *n* COMPUT E-Mail-Adresse *die*.

emanate [ˈeməneɪt] *fml vi*: **to emanate from** [idea] stammen von; [smell] kommen von/aus.

emancipate [ɪ'mænsɪpeɪt] *vt* befreien; [women] emanzipieren.

embankment [ɪm'bæŋkmənt] *n* - 1. [along road, path] Böschung *die* - 2. [along river] Damm *der*; [along railway] Bahndamm *der*.

embark [ɪm'bɑːk] *vi* - 1. [board ship] sich einschiffen - 2. [start]: **to embark (up)on sthg** mit etw beginnen.

embarrass [ɪm'bærəs] *vt* in Verlegenheit bringen.

embarrassed [ɪm'bærəst] *adj* verlegen.

embarrassing [ɪm'bærəsɪŋ] *adj* peinlich.

embarrassment [ɪm'bærəsmənt] *n* Verlegenheit *die*; **to be an embarrassment to sb** jn in Verlegenheit bringen.

embassy [ˈembəsɪ] *n* Botschaft *die*.

embedded [ɪm'bedɪd] *adj* - 1. [in rock, wood, mud]: **to be embedded in sthg** in etw (D) feststecken - 2. *fig* [feeling] fest verwurzelt.

embellish [ɪm'belɪʃ] *vt* - 1. [decorate]: **to embellish sthg with sthg** etw mit etw schmücken - 2. *fig* [story] ausschmücken.

embers [ˈembəz] *npl* Glut *die*.

embezzle [ɪm'bezl] *vt* unterschlagen.

embittered [ɪm'bɪtəd] *adj* verbittert.

emblem [ˈembləm] *n* Emblem *das*.

embody [ɪm'bɒdɪ] *vt* - 1. [epitomize] verkörpern - 2. [include] enthalten.

embossed [ɪm'bɒst] *adj* geprägt.

embrace [ɪm'breɪs] ◇ *n* Umarmung *die*. ◇ *vt* [hug] umarmen. ◇ *vi* sich umarmen.

embroider [ɪm'brɔɪdə^r] *vt* - 1. [design] sticken; [tablecloth, blouse] besticken - 2. [story] ausschmücken.

embroidery [ɪm'brɔɪdərɪ] n - 1. [skill] Sticken das - 2. [designs] Stickerei die.

embroil [ɪm'brɔɪl] vt: **to get embroiled (in sthg)** (in etw (A)) verwickelt werden.

embryo ['embrɪəʊ] (pl -s) n Embryo der.

emerald ['emərəld] n Smaragd der.

emerge [ɪ'mɜːdʒ] ◇ vi - 1. [come out] auftauchen; **to emerge from sthg** aus etw herauslkommen - 2. [facts, truth] herauslkommen. ◇ vt: **it emerged that...** es stellte sich heraus, dass...

emergency [ɪ'mɜːdʒənsɪ] ◇ adj Not-. ◇ n Notfall der; **in an emergency** im Notfall.

emergency brake n US Notbremse die.

emergency exit n Notausgang der.

emergency landing n Notlandung die.

emergency room n US Unfallstation die.

emergency services npl Hilfsdienste Pl.

emigrant ['emɪɡrənt] n Auswanderer der.

emigrate ['emɪɡreɪt] vi auslwandern.

eminent ['emɪnənt] adj berühmt und anerkannt.

emit [ɪ'mɪt] vt fml [light] auslstrahlen; [radiation, smoke] emittieren; [sound, heat] ablgeben.

emotion [ɪ'məʊʃn] n - 1. [particular feeling] Gefühl das, Emotion die - 2. (U) [strength of feeling] Gemütsbewegung die; **she showed no emotion** sie blieb vollkommen unbewegt; **to speak with emotion** ergriffen sprechen.

emotional [ɪ'məʊʃənl] adj - 1. [person - by nature] gefühlsbetont; [- temporarily] emotional; (phrase): **to get emotional** emotional werden - 2. [scene, farewell] emotionsgeladen; [music] gefühlvoll; [appeal, speech] gefühlsbetont - 3. [problems, needs, reaction] emotional.

emperor ['empərər] n Kaiser der.

emphasis ['emfəsɪs] (pl -ases [-əsiːz]) n Betonung die; **to lay** OR **place emphasis on sthg** großen Wert auf etw (A) legen.

emphasize, -ise ['emfəsaɪz] vt betonen; [point, feature] hervorlheben.

emphatic [ɪm'fætɪk] adj [forceful] entschieden.

emphatically [ɪm'fætɪklɪ] adv - 1. [with emphasis] mit Nachdruck - 2. [deny] entschieden.

empire ['empaɪər] n POL Reich das.

employ [ɪm'plɔɪ] vt - 1. [give work to] beschäftigen; [recruit] anlstellen; **to be employed as a secretary** als Sekretär(in) arbeiten - 2. fml [use] anlwenden.

employee [ɪm'plɔɪiː] n Angestellte der, die.

employer [ɪm'plɔɪər] n Arbeitgeber der, -in die.

employment [ɪm'plɔɪmənt] n (U) Arbeit die; [recruitment] Anstellung die; **to be in employment** eine Stelle haben.

employment agency n Stellenvermittlung die.

empower [ɪm'paʊər] vt fml: **to be empowered to do sthg** ermächtigt sein, etw zu tun.

empress ['emprɪs] n Kaiserin die.

empty ['emptɪ] ◇ adj leer; **on an empty stomach** MED auf nüchternen Magen. ◇ vt leeren; [bin] ausleeren; [room] ausräumen; **to empty sthg into/out of sthg** [pour] etw in etw (A)/aus etw schütten. ◇ vi [room, theatre] sich leeren. ◇ n inf [bottle] leere Flasche; [glass] leeres Glas.

empty-handed [-'hændɪd] adv unverrichteter Dinge.

EMU (abbr of European Monetary Union) n WWU die.

emulate ['emjʊleɪt] vt [person, example] nachleifern (+ D); [system] nachlahmen.

emulsion [ɪ'mʌlʃn] n: **emulsion (paint)** Dispersionsfarbe die.

enable [ɪ'neɪbl] vt: **to enable sb to do sthg** es jm möglich machen, etw zu tun.

enact [ɪ'nækt] vt - 1. LAW erlassen - 2. [scene, play] auflführen.

enamel [ɪ'næml] n - 1. [on metal, glass] Email das - 2. [on tooth] Zahnschmelz der - 3. [paint] Emaillack der.

encapsulate [ɪn'kæpsjʊleɪt] vt fig zusammenlfassen.

enchanting [ɪn'tʃɑːntɪŋ] adj bezaubernd.

encircle [ɪn'sɜːkl] vt umgeben; [subj: troops] umringen.

enclose [ɪn'kləʊz] vt - 1. [surround] umgeben; **enclosed space** abgeschlossener Raum; **to be enclosed by** OR **with sthg** von etw umgeben sein - 2. [put in envelope] beillegen; **please find enclosed** als Anlage senden wir Ihnen.

enclosure [ɪn'kləʊʒər] n - 1. [place] eingezäuntes Grundstück; [for animals] Gehege das - 2. [in letter] Anlage die.

encompass [ɪn'kʌmpəs] vt fml umfassen.

encore ['ɒŋkɔːr] ◇ n Zugabe die. ◇ excl Zugabe!

encounter [ɪn'kaʊntər] ◇ n Begegnung die; [battle] Kampf der. ◇ vt fml - 1. [meet] begegnen (+ D) - 2. [experience] stoßen auf (+ A).

encourage [ɪn'kʌrɪdʒ] vt - 1. [person] ermutigen; **to encourage sb to do sthg** jn ermutigen OR ermuntern, etw zu tun - 2. [foster] fördern.

encouragement [ɪn'kʌrɪdʒmənt] n Ermutigung die; [support] Förderung die.

encroach [ɪn'krəʊtʃ] vi: **to encroach (up)on sthg** [on territory] in etw (A) vorldringen; [on rights, privacy] in etw (A) einlgreifen.

encyclop(a)edic [ɪnˌsaɪkləʊ'piːdɪk] adj enzyklopädisch.

end [end] <> n - 1. [finish] Ende *das*; **from beginning to end** von vorn bis hinten; **at the end of May** Ende Mai; **at an end** zu Ende; **to come to an end** enden; **to put an end to sthg** etw *(D)* ein Ende setzen; **at the end of the day** *fig* schließlich und endlich; **in the end** [finally] schließlich - 2. [extremity] Ende *das*; [of box] Seite *die*; [of finger, stick] Spitze *die*; **to make ends meet** [financially] zurechtkommen - 3. [leftover part] Rest *der*; [of candle] Stummel *der* - 4. *fml* [purpose] Ziel *das* - 5. *liter* [death] Ende *das*. <> vt beenden. <> vi enden; **to end in failure** in einem Misserfolg enden. ☞ **on end** adv - 1. [upright] hochkant - 2. [continuously]: **for days on end** tagelang. ☞ **end up** vi: **to end up in prison** im Gefängnis landen; **to end up doing sthg** schließlich etw tun.

endanger [ɪnˈdeɪndʒəʳ] vt gefährden.

endearing [ɪnˈdɪərɪŋ] adj liebenswert.

endeavour *UK*, **endeavor** *US fml* [ɪnˈdevəʳ] <> n Bemühung *die*. <> vi: **to endeavour to do sthg** sich bemühen, etw zu tun.

ending [ˈendɪŋ] n - 1. [of story, film] Ende *das*, Schluss *der* - 2. GRAM Endung *die*.

endive [ˈendaɪv] n - 1. [salad vegetable] Endivie *die* - 2. [chicory] Chicorée *die* ODER *der*.

endless [ˈendlɪs] adj endlos; [possibilities, desert] unendlich.

endorse [ɪnˈdɔːs] vt - 1. [approve] billigen - 2. [cheque] auf der Rückseite unterschreiben, indossieren.

endorsement [ɪnˈdɔːsmənt] n - 1. [approval] Billigung *die* - 2. *UK* [on driving licence] Strafvermerk *der* (auf dem Führerschein).

endow [ɪnˈdaʊ] vt [equip]: **to be endowed with sthg** mit etw ausgestattet sein; **to be endowed with charm/talent** Charme/Talent haben.

endurance [ɪnˈdjʊərəns] n Durchhaltevermögen *das*; **it was beyond endurance** es war nicht auszuhalten.

endure [ɪnˈdjʊəʳ] <> vt ertragen. <> vi *fml* Bestand haben.

endways *UK* [ˈendweɪz], **endwise** *US* [ˈendwaɪz] adv - 1. [lengthways] mit dem Ende nach vorn - 2. [end to end] mit den Enden aneinander.

enemy [ˈenɪmɪ] <> n Feind *der*. <> comp feindlich.

energetic [ˌenəˈdʒetɪk] adj - 1. [lively] energiegeladen; **to feel/be energetic** viel Energie haben - 2. [game, activity] viel Energie erfordernd - 3. [supporter, campaigner] tatkräftig.

energy [ˈenədʒɪ] n [gen] Energie *die*.

enforce [ɪnˈfɔːs] vt [high standards, discipline] sorgen für; **to enforce a law** für die Einhaltung eines Gesetzes sorgen.

enforced [ɪnˈfɔːst] adj aufgezwungen.

engage [ɪnˈgeɪdʒ] <> vt - 1. [attract - attention] in Anspruch nehmen; [- interest] fesseln - 2. TECH [gear] einlegen; **to engage the clutch** kuppeln - 3. *fml* [employ] anstellen; **to be engaged in OR on sthg** mit etw beschäftigt sein. <> vi: **to engage in sthg** sich mit etw befassen.

engaged [ɪnˈgeɪdʒd] adj - 1. [couple]: **engaged (to sb)** (mit jm) verlobt; **to get engaged** sich verloben - 2. [busy] beschäftigt - 3. [toilet, telephone number] besetzt.

engaged tone n *UK* Besetztzeichen *das*.

engagement [ɪnˈgeɪdʒmənt] n - 1. [of couple] Verlobung *die* - 2. [appointment - gen] Verpflichtung *die*; [- business] Termin *der*.

engagement ring n Verlobungsring *der*.

engaging [ɪnˈgeɪdʒɪŋ] adj [manner, personality] einnehmend; [smile] gewinnend.

engender [ɪnˈdʒendəʳ] vt *fml* erzeugen.

engine [ˈendʒɪn] n - 1. [of car, plane] Motor *der*; [of ship] Maschine *die* - 2. RAIL Lokomotive *die*.

engine driver n *UK* Lokomotivführer *der*.

engineer [ˌendʒɪˈnɪəʳ] n - 1. [of roads, machines, bridges] Techniker *der*, -in *die*; [with degree] Ingenieur *der*, -in *die* - 2. *US* [engine driver] Lokomotivführer *der*.

engineering [ˌendʒɪˈnɪərɪŋ] n (U) Technik *die*; [mechanical] Maschinenbau *der*.

England [ˈɪŋglənd] n England *nt*.

English [ˈɪŋglɪʃ] <> adj englisch. <> n Englisch(e) *das*. <> npl: **the English** die Engländer *Pl*.

English breakfast n englisches Frühstück.

English Channel n: **the English Channel** der Ärmelkanal.

Englishman [ˈɪŋglɪʃmən] (pl -men [-mən]) n Engländer *der*.

Englishwoman [ˈɪŋglɪʃˌwʊmən] (pl -women [-wɪmɪn]) n Engländerin *die*.

engrave [ɪnˈgreɪv] vt [metal, glass] gravieren; [design] eingravieren.

engraving [ɪnˈgreɪvɪŋ] n [design] Gravierung *die*; [print] Stich *der*.

engrossed [ɪnˈgrəʊst] adj: **to be engrossed (in sthg)** (in etw *(A)*) vertieft sein.

engulf [ɪnˈgʌlf] vt [subj: fire, water] verschlingen; [subj: panic, fear] überwältigen.

enhance [ɪnˈhɑːns] vt verbessern; [value, chances] steigern, erhöhen; [beauty] betonen.

enjoy [ɪnˈdʒɔɪ] vt - 1. [like] genießen; **she enjoyed the film/book** der Film/das Buch hat ihr gefallen; **did you enjoy it?** hast du es genossen?, hat es dir gefallen?; **to enjoy doing sthg** etw gern(e) tun; **to enjoy o.s.** sich amüsieren; **enjoy yourself!** viel Spaß! - 2. *fml* [possess] genießen; **to enjoy good health** sich guter Gesundheit erfreuen.

enjoyable [ɪnˈdʒɔɪəbl] *adj* [job, work, experience] angenehm; [holiday, day] schön; [film, book] unterhaltsam.

enjoyment [ɪnˈdʒɔɪmənt] *n* [gen] Vergnügen *das*.

enlarge [ɪnˈlɑːdʒ] *vt* vergrößern; [scope, interest, circle of friends] erweitern. ► **enlarge (up)on** *vt insep* sich genauer äußern über (+ A).

enlargement [ɪnˈlɑːdʒmənt] *n* Vergrößerung *die*.

enlighten [ɪnˈlaɪtn] *vt fml* aufklären.

enlightened [ɪnˈlaɪtnd] *adj* [person] aufgeklärt; [approach] fortschrittlich.

enlist [ɪnˈlɪst] ◇ *vt* - 1. MIL [recruit] einlziehen - 2. [support, help] in Anspruch nehmen. ◇ *vi* MIL: **to enlist (in)** sich melden (zu).

enmity [ˈenmətɪ] *n* Feindschaft *die*.

enormity [ɪˈnɔːmətɪ] *n* ungeheures Ausmaß.

enormous [ɪˈnɔːməs] *adj* ungeheuer groß.

enough [ɪˈnʌf] ◇ *adj* genug; **enough time** Zeit genug; **have you got enough money?** hast du genügend Geld? ◇ *pron* genug; **is that enough?** reicht das?; **to have had enough (of sthg)** genug (von etw) haben; **I've had enough!** [expressing annoyance] jetzt reichts mir aber!; **more than enough** mehr als genug; **it's enough to drive you crazy!** es ist zum Verrücktwerden! ◇ *adv* - 1. [sufficiently] genug; **good enough** gut genug; **would you be good enough to open the door for me?** *fml* wärst du so gut und öffnest mir die Tür? - 2. [rather]: **he seems a nice enough chap** er scheint ganz nett zu sein; **strangely enough** merkwürdigerweise; **sure enough** tatsächlich.

enquire [ɪnˈkwaɪər] *vt & vi* = **inquire**.

enquiry [ɪnˈkwaɪrɪ] *n* = **inquiry**.

enraged [ɪnˈreɪdʒd] *adj* wütend.

enrol, enroll US [ɪnˈrəʊl] ◇ *vt* einlschreiben; SCH anlmelden. ◇ *vi*: **to enrol (on** OR **in)** sich einschreiben (für).

ensue [ɪnˈsjuː] *vi fml* folgen.

ensure [ɪnˈʃʊər] *vt* sicherlstellen; [safety, privacy] gewährleisten; **to ensure (that)** dafür sorgen, dass.

ENT (*abbr of* Ear, Nose & Throat) HNO.

entail [ɪnˈteɪl] *vt* mit sich bringen.

enter [ˈentər] ◇ *vt* - 1. [house, room] einltreten in (+ A), betreten; [car, bus, train] einlsteigen in (+ A); [subj: vehicle] fahren in (+ A); [subj: ship] einllaufen in (+ A); [country] einlreisen in (+ A) - 2. [army] einltreten in (+ A); [competition, race] teillnehmen an (+ D) - 3. [horse, competitor] anlmelden; [poem, story] einlreichen - 4. [write down] einltragen - 5. COMPUT einlgeben. ◇ *vi* - 1. [come or go in] einltreten; [enter bus, train] einlsteigen; [enter country] einlreisen - 2. [register]: **to enter**

(for sthg) sich (für etw) anlmelden. ► **enter into** *vt insep* [negotiations] treten in (+ A); **to enter into an agreement with sb** mit jm ein Abkommen schließen.

enter key *n* COMPUT Eingabetaste *die*.

enterprise [ˈentəpraɪz] *n* - 1. [company, project] Unternehmen *das*; **private enterprise** Privatwirtschaft *die* - 2. (*U*) [initiative] Initiative *die*.

enterprising [ˈentəpraɪzɪŋ] *adj* [person] einfallsreich; [plan, idea] innovativ.

entertain [ˌentəˈteɪn] *vt* - 1. [amuse] unterhalten - 2. [dinner guest] bewirten - 3. *fml* [idea, proposal] erwägen; [hopes] nähren; [suspicion, ambition] hegen.

entertainer [ˌentəˈteɪnər] *n* Unterhalter *der*, -in *die*, Entertainer *der*, -in *die*.

entertaining [ˌentəˈteɪnɪŋ] *adj* unterhaltsam.

entertainment [ˌentəˈteɪnmənt] *n* - 1. [amusement] Unterhaltung *die* - 2. [show] Darbietung *die*.

enthral UK, **enthrall** US [ɪnˈθrɔːl] *vt* fesseln.

enthusiasm [ɪnˈθjuːzɪæzm] *n* - 1. [eagerness] Begeisterung *die*, Enthusiasmus *der* - 2. [hobby] Leidenschaft *die*.

enthusiast [ɪnˈθjuːzɪæst] *n* Enthusiast *der*, -in *die*.

enthusiastic [ɪnˌθjuːzɪˈæstɪk] *adj* begeistert, enthusiastisch.

entice [ɪnˈtaɪs] *vt* locken; **to entice sb away from sthg** jn von etw wegllocken.

entire [ɪnˈtaɪər] *adj* ganz; [amount, population] gesamt; [confidence, attention] voll.

entirely [ɪnˈtaɪəlɪ] *adv* ganz; **I agree entirely** ich stimme voll und ganz zu.

entirety [ɪnˈtaɪrətɪ] *n fml*: **in its entirety** in seiner Gesamtheit.

entitle [ɪnˈtaɪtl] *vt* [allow]: **to entitle sb to sthg** jn zu etw berechtigen; **to entitle sb to do sthg** jn dazu berechtigen, etw zu tun.

entitled [ɪnˈtaɪtld] *adj* - 1. [allowed] berechtigt; **to be entitled to sthg** das Recht auf etw (A) haben - 2. [called]: **to be entitled** den Titel haben.

entitlement [ɪnˈtaɪtlmənt] *n* Berechtigung *die*; [to compensation, holiday] Anspruch *der*.

entrance ◇ *n* [ˈentrəns] - 1. [way in]: **entrance (to)** Eingang *der* (zu) - 2. [arrival] Eintritt *der*; [of actor] Auftritt *der* - 3. [admission] Eintritt *der*; **to gain entrance to sthg** *fml* [building] Zutritt zu etw erhalten; [society, university] die Zulassung zu etw erhalten; **'no entrance'** 'Zutritt verboten'. ◇ *vt* [ɪnˈtrɑːns] [delight] bezaubern.

entrance examination *n* Aufnahmeprüfung *die*.

entrance fee *n* Eintrittsgeld *das*; [for club] Aufnahmegebühr *die*.

entrant ['entrənt] *n* [in competition, exam, race] Teilnehmer *der*, -in *die*.

entreat [ɪn'triːt] *vt*: to entreat sb to do sthg jn inständig bitten, etw zu tun; [plead with] jn anflehen, etw zu tun.

entrenched [ɪn'trentʃt] *adj* (fest) verwurzelt.

entrepreneur [ˌɒntrəprə'nɜːr] *n* Unternehmer *der*, -in *die*.

entrust [ɪn'trʌst] *vt*: to entrust sthg to sb jm etw anvertrauen; to entrust sb with sthg jn mit etw betrauen.

entry ['entrɪ] *n* - 1. [entrance, arrival]: entry (into) Eingang *der* (in (+ A)) - 2. *(U)* [admission]: entry (to) [to country] Einreise *die* (in (+ A)); [to building] Zutritt *der* (zu); [to event] Einlass *der* (in (+ A)); to gain entry to [house] gelangen in (+ A); [organization] beitreten (+ D); 'no entry' 'Zutritt verboten', AUT 'Durchfahrt verboten' - 3. [for race] Nennung *die*; [for competition] Einsendung *die* - 4. [in diary, dictionary, ledger] Eintragung *die*.

entry form *n* Anmeldeformular *das*.

entry phone *n* Türsprechanlage *die*.

envelop [ɪn'veləp] *vt*: to envelop sb/sthg in sthg jn/etw in etw (A) (ein)hüllen.

envelope ['envələup] *n* Briefumschlag *der*.

envious ['enviəs] *adj*: envious (of sb/sthg) neidisch (auf jn/etw).

environment [ɪn'vaɪərənmənt] *n* - 1. [surroundings] Umgebung *die* - 2. [natural world]: the environment die Umwelt.

environmental [ɪn,vaɪərən'mentl] *adj* Umwelt-.

environmentally [ɪn,vaɪərən'mentəlɪ] *adv* umwelt-; environmentally friendly umweltfreundlich.

envisage [ɪn'vɪzɪdʒ], **envision** *US* [ɪn'vɪʒn] *vt* sich vorstellen.

envoy ['envɔɪ] *n* Gesandte *der, die*.

envy ['envɪ] *n* Neid *der*. *vt* beneiden; to envy sb sthg jn um etw beneiden.

eon *n US* = aeon.

epic ['epɪk] *adj* [poetry] episch; [journey] lang und abenteuerlich; [story] monumental. *n* [book, film] Epos *das*.

epidemic [ˌepɪ'demɪk] *n* Epidemie *die*.

epileptic [ˌepɪ'leptɪk] *adj* epileptisch. *n* Epileptiker *der*, -in *die*.

episode ['epɪsəud] *n* - 1. [event] Episode *die* - 2. [broadcast] Folge *die*.

epitaph ['epɪtɑːf] *n* Epitaph *das*.

epitome [ɪ'pɪtəmɪ] *n*: the epitome of der Inbegriff (+ G).

epitomize, -ise [ɪ'pɪtəmaɪz] *vt* beispielhaft zeigen.

epoch ['iːpɒk] *n* Epoche *die*.

equal ['iːkwəl] *(UK) (US)* *adj* - 1. [of the same quantity, size, shape, degree] gleich; they're of equal size sie sind gleich groß; to be equal to sthg [sum] etw (D) entsprechen - 2. [in status] gleich(berechtigt); equal rights Gleichberechtigung *die* - 3. [capable]: to be equal to sthg etw (D) gewachsen sein. *n* [person] Gleichgestellte *der, die*. *vt* - 1. MATHS gleichen - 2. [in standard] gleichlkommen (+ D).

equality [iː'kwɒlətɪ] *n* Gleichheit *die*.

equalize, -ise ['iːkwəlaɪz] *vt & vi* SPORT auslgleichen.

equalizer, -iser ['iːkwəlaɪzər] *n* SPORT Ausgleich *der*.

equally ['iːkwəlɪ] *adv* - 1. [to the same extent] ebenso - 2. [divide, share] in gleiche Teile - 3. [by the same token] gleichzeitig.

equal opportunities *npl* Chancengleichheit *die*.

equate [ɪ'kweɪt] *vt*: to equate sthg with sthg etw mit etw gleichlsetzen.

equation [ɪ'kweɪʒn] *n* MATHS Gleichung *die*.

equator [ɪ'kweɪtər] *n*: the equator der Äquator.

equilibrium [ˌiːkwɪ'lɪbrɪəm] *n* Gleichgewicht *das*.

equip [ɪ'kwɪp] *vt* - 1. [provide with equipment] auslstatten; to equip sb/sthg with sthg jn/etw mit etw auslrüsten - 2. [prepare mentally]: to equip sb for sthg jn für etw vorlbereiten.

equipment [ɪ'kwɪpmənt] *n (U)* Ausrüstung *die*; electrical equipment Elektrogeräte *Pl*.

equity *n (U)* FIN [market value] Eigenkapital *das*. ◆ **equities** *npl* [stock exchange] Stammaktien *Pl*.

equivalent [ɪ'kwɪvələnt] *adj* entsprechend, äquivalent; to be equivalent to sthg etw (D) entsprechen. *n* Gegenstück *das*.

equivocal [ɪ'kwɪvəkl] *adj* [statement, remark] zweideutig.

er [ɜːr] *excl* äh.

era ['ɪərə] *(pl -s)* *n* Ära *die*.

eradicate [ɪ'rædɪkeɪt] *vt* auslrotten.

erase [ɪ'reɪz] *vt* - 1. [rub out] auslradieren; [tape, recording] löschen - 2. *fig* [memory] (aus dem Gedächtnis) tilgen.

eraser [ɪ'reɪzər] *n esp US* Radiergummi *der*.

erect [ɪ'rekt] *adj* - 1. [person, posture] aufrecht - 2. [penis] erigiert. *vt* - 1. [building, statue] errichten, bauen - 2. [tent] auflbauen; [roadblock, sign] auflstellen.

erection [ɪ'rekʃn] *n* - 1. *(U)* [of building, statue] Errichtung *die*, Bau *der* - 2. [erect penis] Erektion *die*.

ERM *(abbr of Exchange Rate Mechanism)* *n* WUM *der*.

erode [ɪ'rəud] *vt* - 1. GEOL erodieren - 2. *fig* [destroy] unterlgraben.

erosion [ɪ'rəuʒn] *n* GEOL Erosion *die*.

erotic [ɪ'rɒtɪk] *adj* erotisch.

err [ɜːʳ] *vi* sich irren.

errand ['erənd] *n* Besorgung *die*; **to go on** OR **run an errand (for sb)** (für jn) eine Besorgung OR einen Botengang machen.

erratic [ɪ'rætɪk] *adj* wechselhaft; [movement, bus service] unregelmäßig; [performance] variabel; [player] unberechenbar.

error ['erəʳ] *n* - **1.** [mistake] Fehler *der* - **2.** (U) [making mistakes]: **in error** aus Versehen.

erupt [ɪ'rʌpt] *vi* aus!brechen.

eruption [ɪ'rʌpʃn] *n* Ausbruch *der*.

escalate ['eskəleɪt] *vi* eskalieren.

escalator ['eskəleɪtəʳ] *n* Rolltreppe *die*.

escapade [,eskə'peɪd] *n* Eskapade *die*.

escape [ɪ'skeɪp] ◇ *n* - **1.** [from person, place, situation]: **escape (from sb/sthg)** Flucht *die* (vor jn/vor OR aus etw); **there was no escape** es gab kein Entkommen; **to make an** OR **one's escape (from)** flüchten (aus) - **2.** [from danger]: **to have a narrow escape** mit knapper Not entkommen - **3.** [leakage] Ausströmen *das* - **4.** COMPUT Escape *das*. ◇ *vi* - **1.** [avoid] entkommen (+ D) - **2.** [subj: fact, name] entfallen; **her name escapes me just now** ihr Name fällt mir momentan nicht ein. ◇ *vt* - **1.** [from person, place, situation]: **to escape (from sb/sthg)** fliehen OR flüchten (vor jm/vor OR aus etw); **to escape from prison** aus dem Gefängnis fliehen - **2.** [from danger] davon!kommen - **3.** [leak] aus!strömen.

escapism [ɪ'skeɪpɪzm] *n* Realitätsflucht *die*.

escort ◇ *n* ['eskɔːt] - **1.** [guard] Geleitschutz *der*, Eskorte *die*; **under escort** unter Bewachung - **2.** [companion] Begleiter *der*, -in *die*. ◇ *vt* [ɪ'skɔːt] [accompany] begleiten; [for protection] eskortieren.

Eskimo ['eskɪməʊ] (*pl* -s) *n* [person] Eskimo *der*, -frau *die*.

especially [ɪ'speʃəlɪ] *adv* - **1.** [in particular, more than usually] besonders - **2.** [specifically] speziell.

espionage ['espɪə,nɑːʒ] *n* Spionage *die*.

Esquire [ɪ'skwaɪəʳ] *n* ≃ Herr/Herrn, *britische Höflichkeitsanrede in der Postanschrift*.

essay ['eseɪ] *n* - **1.** SCH Aufsatz *der* - **2.** LIT & UNIV Essay *der*.

essence ['esns] *n* - **1.** [nature] Wesentliche *das*, Kern *der*; **in essence** im Wesentlichen - **2.** (U) CULIN Essenz *die*.

essential [ɪ'senʃl] *adj* - **1.** [necessary]: **essential (to** OR **for sthg)** (unbedingt) notwendig (für etw) - **2.** [basic] wesentlich. ◆ **essentials** *npl* - **1.** [basic commodities] Notwendigste *das* - **2.** [most important elements] Grundlagen *Pl*.

essentially [ɪ'senʃəlɪ] *adv* im Grunde.

establish [ɪ'stæblɪʃ] *vt* - **1.** [create - company, organization] gründen; [- system, law, post] schaffen - **2.** [initiate]: **to establish contact with** sb Kontakt mit jm auf!nehmen - **3.** [ascertain] fest!stellen, ermitteln - **4.** [cause to be accepted] bestätigen.

establishment [ɪ'stæblɪʃmənt] *n* - **1.** (U) [creation, foundation] Gründung *die*, Errichtung *die* - **2.** [shop, business] Unternehmen *das*. ◆ **Establishment** *n*: **the Establishment** das Establishment.

estate [ɪ'steɪt] *n* - **1.** [land, property] Gut *das* - **2.** [for housing] Wohnsiedlung *die*; [for industry] Industriegebiet *das* - **3.** LAW [inheritance] Besitz *der*, Besitztümer *Pl*.

estate agent *n* UK Grundstücksmakler *der*, -in *die*; **estate agent's** Immobilienbüro *das*.

estate car *n* UK Kombiwagen *der*.

esteem ◇ *n* Achtung *die*, Wertschätzung *die*. ◇ *vt* schätzen, achten.

esthetic *etc adj* US = **aesthetic** *etc* .

estimate ◇ *n* ['estɪmət] - **1.** [calculation, reckoning] Schätzung *die* - **2.** COMM Kostenvoranschlag *der*. ◇ *vt* ['estɪmeɪt] schätzen, ein!schätzen.

estimation [,estɪ'meɪʃn] *n* (U) - **1.** [opinion] Urteil *das*, Einschätzung *die*; **to go up/down in one's estimation** in js Achtung steigen/sinken - **2.** [calculation] Schätzung *die*.

Estonia [e'stəʊnɪə] *n* Estland *nt*.

estranged [ɪ'streɪndʒd] *adj* getrennt lebend.

estuary ['estjʊərɪ] *n* Flußmündung *die*.

etc. (*abbr of* etcetera) usw.

etching ['etʃɪŋ] *n* Radierung *die*.

eternal [ɪ'tɜːnl] *adj* ewig.

eternity [ɪ'tɜːnətɪ] *n* Ewigkeit *die*.

ethic ['eθɪk] *n* Ethik *die*. ◆ **ethics** ◇ *n* [study] Ethik *die*. ◇ *npl* [morals] Moral *die*.

ethical ['eθɪkl] *adj* ethisch.

Ethiopia [,iːθɪ'əʊpɪə] *n* Äthiopien *nt*.

ethnic cleansing [,eθnɪk'klenzɪŋ] *n* ethnische Säuberung.

etiquette ['etɪket] *n* Etikette *die*.

EU (*abbr of* European Union) *n* EU *die*.

euphemism ['juːfəmɪzm] *n* Euphemismus *der*.

euphoria [juː'fɔːrɪə] *n* Euphorie *die*.

euro ['jʊərəʊ] *n* Euro *der*.

Eurocheque ['jʊərəʊ,tʃek] *n* Euroscheck *der*.

euro cent *n* Eurocent *der*.

Euroland *n* Euroland *das*.

Euro MP *n* Europaabgeordnete *der*, *die*.

Europe ['jʊərəp] *n* Europa *nt*.

European [,jʊərə'piːən] ◇ *adj* europäisch. ◇ *n* Europäer *der*, -in *die*.

European Community *n*: **the European Community** die Europäische Gemeinschaft.

European Monetary System n: the European Monetary System das Europäische Währungssystem.

European Parliament n: the European Parliament das Europäische Parlament.

European Union n: the European Union die Europäische Union.

euro zone n Eurozone die.

euthanasia [ˌjuːθəˈneɪzjə] n Euthanasie die.

evacuate [ɪˈvækjʊeɪt] vt evakuieren.

evade [ɪˈveɪd] vt - 1. [pursuers, capture] sich entziehen (+ D) - 2. [issue, question] ausweichen (+ D) - 3. [subj: love, success]: love/success has always evaded him ihm ist die Liebe/der Erfolg immer versagt geblieben.

evaluate [ɪˈvæljʊeɪt] vt bewerten.

evaporate [ɪˈvæpəreɪt] vi - 1. [liquid] verdunsten - 2. fig [feeling] schwinden.

evaporated milk [ɪˈvæpəreɪtɪd-] n Kondensmilch die.

evasion [ɪˈveɪʒn] n - 1. [of responsibility, payment etc] Ausweichen das, Umgehen das - 2. [lie] Ausflucht die.

evasive [ɪˈveɪsɪv] adj - 1. [to avoid question, subject] ausweichend - 2. [to avoid being hit]: to take evasive action ein Ausweichmanöver machen.

eve [iːv] n [day before] Vortag der.

even [ˈiːvn] ◇ adj - 1. [rate, speed] gleichmäßig - 2. [calm] ausgeglichen - 3. [level, flat] eben - 4. [teams] gleich stark; the scores were even es herrschte Gleichstand; to get even with sb es jm heimzahlen - 5. [number] gerade. ◇ adv - 1. [for emphasis] sogar; not even nicht einmal; without even thinking ohne auch nur einen Moment nachzudenken; even now sogar jetzt; even then selbst dann - 2. [in comparisons] noch; even better noch besser; even more stupid (sogar) noch dümmer. ◆ **even if** conj selbst OR auch wenn. ◆ **even out** ◇ vt sep - 1. [gen] ausgleichen; to even things out das Kräfteverhältnis ausgleichen - 2. [surface] ebnen. ◇ vi sich ausgleichen. ◆ **even so** adv trotzdem. ◆ **even though** conj obwohl.

evening [ˈiːvnɪŋ] n Abend der; in the evenings am Abend. ◆ **evenings** adv US am Abend.

evening class n Abendkurs der.

evening dress n - 1. [formal clothes] Abendkleidung die - 2. [woman's garment] Abendkleid das.

event [ɪˈvent] n - 1. [happening] Ereignis das - 2. SPORT Wettkampf der - 3. [case] Fall der; in the event of im Falle (+ G); in the event of rain bei Regen; in the event that falls. ◆ **in any event** adv [all the same] wie dem auch sei, wie auch immer. ◆ **in the event** adv UK letztlich.

eventful [ɪˈventfʊl] adj ereignisreich; [life] bewegt.

eventual [ɪˈventʃʊəl] adj: the eventual winner/outcome was... der Sieger/das Resultat war schließlich...

eventuality [ɪˌventʃʊˈælətɪ] n (möglicher) Fall, Eventualität die.

eventually [ɪˈventʃʊəlɪ] adv schließlich.

ever [ˈevər] adv - 1. [at any time] je, jemals; the worst film I've ever seen der schlechteste Film, den ich je gesehen habe; have you ever been to Chicago? sind Sie jemals in Chicago gewesen?; don't ever speak to me like that again! so redest du nicht noch einmal mit mir!; hardly ever fast nie - 2. [all the time] immer; for ever [eternally] für immer; [for a long time] seit Ewigkeiten; I'll love you for ever ich werde dich immer lieben; as ever wie immer; ever larger immer größer - 3. [for emphasis]: why/how ever did you do it? warum/wie hast du das bloß gemacht?; what ever is the matter with you? was ist denn mit dir los?; he was ever so angry er war sehr verärgert; ever such a mess ein fürchterliches Durcheinander. ◆ **ever since** ◇ adv seitdem. ◇ prep & conj seit.

evergreen [ˈevəgriːn] n [plant] immergrüne Pflanze; [tree] immergrüner Baum.

everlasting [ˌevəˈlɑːstɪŋ] adj ewig; [peace] immer während.

every [ˈevrɪ] adj [each] jede(r) (s); every day jeden Tag; every few days alle paar Tage; one in every ten eine(r) (s) von zehn. ◆ **every now and then, every so often** adv dann und wann, ab und zu. ◆ **every other** adj: every other day/car jeden zweiten Tag/Wagen. ◆ **every which way** adv US überallhin.

everybody [ˈevrɪˌbɒdɪ] pron = everyone.

everyday [ˈevrɪdeɪ] adj (all)täglich.

everyone pron alle; [each person] jeder; as everyone knows wie jeder weiß.

everyplace adv US = everywhere.

everything pron alles; money isn't everything Geld ist nicht alles.

everywhere, everyplace US adv überall; [go] überallhin.

evict [ɪˈvɪkt] vt: to evict sb (from a house) jn zur Räumung zwingen (eines Hauses).

evidence [ˈevɪdəns] n (U) - 1. [proof] Beweis der - 2. LAW Beweismaterial das; piece of evidence Beweisstück das; to give evidence (als Zeuge/Zeugin) aussagen.

evident [ˈevɪdənt] adj offensichtlich.

evidently [ˈevɪdəntlɪ] adv offensichtlich.

evil [ˈiːvl] ◇ adj [morally bad] böse, schlecht; [practice] übel. ◇ n - 1. [wickedness] Böse das - 2. [wicked thing] Übel das.

evoke [ɪˈvəʊk] vt hervorrufen.

evolution [ˌiːvəˈluːʃn] n - 1. BIOL Evolution die - 2. [development] Entwicklung die.

evolve [ɪˈvɒlv] ◇ vt entwickeln. ◇ vi - 1. BIOL: **to evolve (into/from)** sich entwickeln (in (+ D)/aus) - 2. [develop] sich entwickeln.

ewe [juː] n Mutterschaf das.

ex- [eks] prefix Ex-, ehemalige(r) (s).

exacerbate [ɪgˈzæsəbeɪt] vt verschlimmern.

exact [ɪgˈzækt] ◇ adj genau; **to be exact** um genau zu sein. ◇ vt: **to exact sthg (from sb)** etw (von jm) erzwingen OR erpressen.

exacting [ɪgˈzæktɪŋ] adj - 1. [demanding, tiring] anspruchsvoll - 2. [rigorous] streng.

exactly [ɪgˈzæktlɪ] ◇ adv genau, exakt; **not exactly** [not really] nicht gerade; [as reply] nicht wirklich. ◇ excl genau!

exaggerate [ɪgˈzædʒəreɪt] vt & vi übertreiben.

exaggeration [ɪgˌzædʒəˈreɪʃn] n Übertreibung die.

exalted [ɪgˈzɔːltɪd] adj [important - person] hoch gestellt; [- position] hoch.

exam [ɪgˈzæm] (abbr of **examination**) n Prüfung die; **to take** OR **sit an exam** eine Prüfung machen OR ablegen.

examination [ɪgˌzæmɪˈneɪʃn] n - 1. [test, inspection, consideration] Prüfung die - 2. MED Untersuchung die - 3. LAW [of witness, suspect] Vernehmung die, Verhör das.

examine [ɪgˈzæmɪn] vt - 1. [look at, inspect] überprüfen - 2. MED untersuchen - 3. [consider, test knowledge of] prüfen - 4. LAW vernehmen.

examiner [ɪgˈzæmɪnər] n Prüfer der, -in die.

example [ɪgˈzɑːmpl] n - 1. [instance] Beispiel das; **for example** zum Beispiel - 2. [model] Vorbild das.

exasperate [ɪgˈzæspəreɪt] vt zum Verzweifeln bringen.

exasperation [ɪgˌzæspəˈreɪʃn] n Verzweiflung die.

excavate ['ekskəveɪt] vt - 1. ARCHAEOL ausgraben - 2. CONSTR ausheben.

exceed [ɪkˈsiːd] vt - 1. [be bigger than] übersteigen - 2. [go beyond, go over] übersteigen; [limit] überschreiten; [expectations] übertreffen.

exceedingly [ɪkˈsiːdɪŋlɪ] adv äußerst.

excel [ɪkˈsel] ◇ vi: **to excel (in** OR **at sthg)** sich hervortun (in etw (D)). ◇ vt: **to excel o.s.** UK sich selbst übertreffen.

excellence ['eksələns] n [high quality] hervorragende Qualität; [high performance] hervorragende Leistung.

excellent ['eksələnt] adj ausgezeichnet.

except [ɪkˈsept] ◇ prep außer; **everyone except her** alle außer ihr. ◇ conj: **he does nothing except sleep** er tut nichts anderes als schlafen; **I'll do anything except typing** ich mache alles, nur nicht Maschine schreiben.

◇ vt: **present company excepted** Anwesende ausgenommen. ◆ **except for** prep & conj abgesehen von.

excepting [ɪkˈseptɪŋ] prep & conj = **except**.

exception [ɪkˈsepʃn] n - 1. [exclusion] Ausnahme die; **an exception to the rule** die Ausnahme von der Regel; **with the exception of** mit Ausnahme von; **to take exception to sthg** an etw (D) Anstoß nehmen.

exceptional [ɪkˈsepʃənl] adj außergewöhnlich.

excerpt ['eksɜːpt] n: **excerpt (from)** [from text] Auszug der (aus); [from film, play, piece of music] Ausschnitt der (aus).

excess [ɪkˈses] ◇ adj (before nouns ['ekses]) [fat in diet] überschüssig; [weight] über-. ◇ n Übermaß das.

excess baggage n Übergewicht das.

excess fare n UK Nachlösegebühr die.

excessive [ɪkˈsesɪv] adj übermäßig; [price] überhöht.

exchange [ɪksˈtʃeɪndʒ] ◇ n - 1. [of information, students] Austausch der; **to be on an exchange** [student] Austauschstudent(in) sein - 2. [swap] Tausch der; **in exchange** dafür; **in exchange for** im Tausch gegen - 3. TELEC: **(telephone) exchange** Fernmeldeamt das. ◇ vt [houses, seats, jobs] tauschen; [addresses] austauschen; [in shop] umtauschen; **to exchange sthg for sthg** etw gegen etw eintauschen; [foreign currency] etw in etw (A) umtauschen; [in shop] etw gegen etw umtauschen; **to exchange sthg with sb** etw mit jm (aus)ltauschen.

exchange rate n FIN Wechselkurs der.

Exchequer [ɪksˈtʃekər] n UK: **the Exchequer** das Schatzamt.

excise ['eksaɪz] n (U) Verbrauchssteuer die.

excite [ɪkˈsaɪt] vt - 1. [person] begeistern - 2. [interest, curiosity, feeling] erregen.

excited [ɪkˈsaɪtɪd] adj aufgeregt.

excitement [ɪkˈsaɪtmənt] n Aufregung die.

exciting [ɪkˈsaɪtɪŋ] adj aufregend; [story, race, film] spannend.

exclaim [ɪkˈskleɪm] ◇ vt ausrufen. ◇ vi: **to exclaim in delight/horror** vor Freude/Entsetzen aufschreien.

exclamation mark UK, **exclamation point** US n Ausrufezeichen das.

exclude [ɪkˈskluːd] vt - 1. [not include]: **to exclude sb/sthg (from sthg)** jn/etw (von etw) ausnehmen - 2. [prevent from entering]: **to exclude sb (from)** jm den Zutritt verweigern (zu) - 3. [reject, rule out] ausschließen.

excluding [ɪkˈskluːdɪŋ] prep außer (+ D).

exclusive [ɪkˈskluːsɪv] ◇ adj - 1. [high-class] exklusiv - 2. [sole] ausschließlich - 3. PRESS Exklusiv-. ◇ n [interview] Exklusivinterview das; [report] Exklusivbericht der. ◆ **exclusive of** prep exklusive (+ G).

excrement ['ekskrımənt] n (U) fml Exkremente Pl.

excruciating [ık'skru:ʃıeıtıŋ] adj - **1.** [pain, headache] schrecklich - **2.** [embarrassment, experience] unerträglich.

excursion [ık'skɜ:ʃn] n Ausflug der.

excuse ◇ n [ık'skju:s]: **excuse (for)** Entschuldigung die (für); **that's just an excuse** das ist nur eine Ausrede. ◇ vt [ık'skju:z] - **1.** [justify] entschuldigen - **2.** [forgive] verzeihen; **to excuse sb for sthg** jm etw verzeihen - **3.** [let off]: **to excuse sb (from sthg)** jn (von etw) befreien - **4.** phr: **excuse me!** [to attract attention] entschuldigen Sie bitte!; [forgive me] Entschuldigung!; US [sorry] Verzeihung!

ex-directory adj UK: **to be ex-directory** nicht im Telefonbuch stehen.

execute ['eksıkju:t] vt - **1.** [kill] hinrichten - **2.** fml [order, plan, movement] ausführen.

execution [,eksı'kju:ʃn] n [killing] Hinrichtung die.

executive [ıg'zekjutıv] ◇ adj: **executive position** leitende Position. ◇ n COMM leitende Angestellte der, die.

executor [ıg'zekjutər] n Testamentsvollstrecker der.

exemplify [ıg'zemplıfaı] vt [typify] ein typisches Beispiel sein für.

exempt [ıg'zempt] ◇ adj: **exempt (from)** befreit (von). ◇ vt: **to exempt sb/sthg from** jn/etw befreien von.

exercise ['eksəsaız] ◇ n - **1.** (U) [physical movement] Bewegung die - **2.** [series of movements] gymnastische Übung - **3.** [activity]: **it's a pointless exercise** das ist eine sinnlose Übung. ◇ vt - **1.** [horse] bewegen; [dog] auslführen - **2.** fml [power] ausüben; [right] wahrlnehmen; [caution] walten lassen. ◇ vi sich bewegen.

exercise book n Heft das.

exert [ıg'zɜ:t] vt ausüben; **to exert o.s.** sich anstrengen.

exertion [ıg'zɜ:ʃn] n - **1.** [of influence, power] Ausübung die - **2.** [effort] Anstrengung die.

exhale [eks'heıl] vt & vi ausatmen.

exhaust [ıg'zɔ:st] ◇ n - **1.** (U) [fumes] Abgase Pl - **2.** [on car]: **exhaust (pipe)** Auspuff der. ◇ vt - **1.** [tire] erschöpfen - **2.** [use up] auflbrauchen; [subject] erschöpfen; **my patience is exhausted** meine Geduld ist zu Ende.

exhausted [ıg'zɔ:stıd] adj erschöpft.

exhausting [ıg'zɔ:stıŋ] adj anstrengend.

exhaustion [ıg'zɔ:stʃn] n Erschöpfung die.

exhaustive [ıg'zɔ:stıv] adj [search, study] eingehend; [list] erschöpfend.

exhibit [ıg'zıbıt] ◇ n - **1.** ART Ausstellungsstück das - **2.** LAW Beweisstück das. ◇ vt - **1.** fml [demonstrate] zeigen - **2.** ART ausstellen.

exhibition [,eksı'bıʃn] n - **1.** ART Ausstellung die - **2.** [demonstration]: **it was a fine exhibition of skill** er/sie zeigte viel Geschick - **3.** phr: **to make an exhibition of o.s.** UK sich lächerlich machen.

exhilarating [ıg'zıləreıtıŋ] adj aufregend.

exile ['eksaıl] ◇ n - **1.** [condition] Exil das; **in exile** im Exil - **2.** [person] Person die, die im Exil lebt. ◇ vt: **to exile sb (to)** jn auslweisen OR verbannen (nach).

exist [ıg'zıst] vi existieren.

existence [ıg'zıstəns] n - **1.** [state of being] Existenz die; **to be in existence** existieren; **to come into existence** entstehen - **2.** [life] Dasein die.

existing [ıg'zıstıŋ] adj bestehend; [government] gegenwärtig.

exit ['eksıt] ◇ n - **1.** [way out] Ausgang der; [from motorway] Ausfahrt die - **2.** [departure]: **to make an exit** hinausgehen. ◇ vi [from building] hinausgehen; [from stage] abgehen; [from motorway] abfahren.

exodus ['eksədəs] n Auszug der.

exonerate [ıg'zɒnəreıt] vt: **to exonerate sb (from)** jn entlasten (von).

exorbitant [ıg'zɔ:bıtənt] adj [cost, price] übertrieben hoch; [demands] übertrieben.

exotic [ıg'zɒtık] adj exotisch.

expand [ık'spænd] ◇ vt [department, influence, area] vergrößern; [business, production, knowledge] erweitern. ◇ vi sich vergrößern; [business] erweitern; [metal] sich ausdehnen. ◆ **expand (up)on** vt insep weiter auslführen.

expanse [ık'spæns] n: **an expanse of water/ sand** eine Wasserfläche/Sandfläche.

expansion [ık'spænʃn] n [of business, production, knowledge] Erweiterung die; [of department, influence, area] Vergrößerung die.

expect [ık'spekt] ◇ vt - **1.** [anticipate] erwarten; [count on] rechnen mit; **to expect sthg from sb** etw von jm erwarten; **to expect to do sthg** damit rechnen, etw zu tun; **to expect sb to do sthg** erwarten, dass jd etw tut; **what do you expect?** was willst du denn? - **2.** [suppose]: **to expect (that)** glauben, dass...; **I expect so** ich denke schon - **3.** [be pregnant with]: **to be expecting a baby** ein Kind erwarten. ◇ vi [be pregnant]: **to be expecting** in anderen Umständen sein.

expectancy n ▷ **life expectancy**.

expectant [ık'spektənt] adj [crowd, person] erwartungsvoll.

expectant mother n werdende Mutter.

expectation [,ekspek'teıʃn] n: **they have no expectation of winning** sie erwarten nicht, dass sie gewinnen; **against** OR **contrary to all expectation(s)** wider Erwarten.

expedient [ɪk'spiːdjənt] *adj fml* angebracht.

expedition [ˌekspɪ'dɪʃn] *n* - **1.** [organized journey] Expedition *die* - **2.** [short trip] Tour *die*.

expel [ɪk'spel] *vt* - **1.** [person]: **to expel sb (from)** [country] jn auslweisen (aus); [school] jn verweisen (von) - **2.** [liquid, gas] auslstoßen.

expend [ɪk'spend] *vt*: **to expend sthg (on)** etw auflwenden (auf (+ A)).

expendable [ɪk'spendəbl] *adj* [person] entbehrlich.

expenditure [ɪk'spendɪtʃər] *n (U)* [of money] Ausgaben *Pl*.

expense [ɪk'spens] *n* - **1.** [amount spent] Ausgabe *die* - **2.** *(U)* [cost] Kosten *Pl*; **at the expense of** auf Kosten *(+ G)*; **at his expense** auf seine Kosten. ➡ **expenses** *npl* COMM Spesen *Pl*.

expense account *n* Spesenkonto *das*.

expensive [ɪk'spensɪv] *adj* - **1.** [financially] teuer - **2.** *fig* [mistake] schwerwiegend.

experience [ɪk'spɪərɪəns] ◇ *n* - **1.** *(U)* [knowledge, practice] Erfahrung *die* - **2.** [event] Erlebnis *das*. ◇ *vt* erfahren; [change] erleben.

experienced [ɪk'spɪərɪənst] *adj*: **experienced (at *or* in)** erfahren (in *(+ D)*).

experiment [ɪk'sperɪmənt] ◇ *n* - **1.** [science] Experiment *das* - **2.** [exploratory attempt] Versuch *der*. ◇ *vi liter & fig*: **to experiment (with)** experimentieren (mit).

expert ['ekspɜːt] ◇ *adj* [player] ausgezeichnet; [advice] fachmännisch. ◇ *n* Fachmann *der*, -frau *die*.

expertise [ˌekspɜː'tiːz] *n* Sachkenntnis *die*.

expire [ɪk'spaɪər] *vi* [licence, passport] abllaufen.

expiry [ɪk'spaɪərɪ] *n* Ablauf *der*.

explain [ɪk'spleɪn] ◇ *vt* erklären; **"my car broke down", she explained** "mein Auto ist kaputtgegangen", sagte sie; **to explain o.s.** [justify o.s.] sich rechtfertigen; [clarify one's meaning] sich klar ausldrücken; **to explain sthg to sb** jm etw erklären. ◇ *vi* erklären.

explanation [ˌeksplə'neɪʃn] *n*: **explanation (for)** Erklärung *die* (für).

explicit [ɪk'splɪsɪt] *adj* - **1.** [clearly expressed] explizit - **2.** [graphic] eindeutig.

explode [ɪk'spləʊd] ◇ *vt* [bomb] explodieren. ◇ *vi* - **1.** [bomb] explodieren - **2.** *fig* [with feeling]: **to explode in anger** (vor Wut) explodieren.

exploit ◇ *n* ['eksplɔɪt] Heldentat *die*. ◇ *vt* [ɪk'splɔɪt] - **1.** [workers] auslbeuten; [friend] auslnutzen - **2.** [resources] auslschöpfen; [opportunity] nutzen.

exploitation [ˌeksplɔɪ'teɪʃn] *n* - **1.** [of workers] Ausbeutung *die*; [of friend] Ausnutzung *die* - **2.** [of resources] Ausschöpfung *die*.

exploration [ˌeksplə'reɪʃn] *n* - **1.** [of place] Erforschung *die* - **2.** [of idea, theory] Untersuchung *die*.

explore [ɪk'splɔːr] ◇ *vt* - **1.** [place] erforschen - **2.** [idea, theory] untersuchen. ◇ *vi* auf Erkundungstour gehen.

explorer [ɪk'splɔːrər] *n* Erforscher *der*, -in *die*.

explosion [ɪk'spləʊʒn] *n liter & fig* Explosion *die*.

explosive [ɪk'spləʊsɪv] ◇ *adj* [material, situation] explosiv; [question] heikel; [temper] explosiv. ◇ *n* Sprengstoff *der*.

export ◇ *n* ['ekspɔːt] Export *der*, Ausfuhr *die*. ◇ *comp* ['ekspɔːt] Export-. ◇ *vt* [ɪk'spɔːt] *liter & fig* exportieren.

exporter [ek'spɔːtər] *n* Exporteur *der*; [country] Exportland *das*.

expose [ɪk'spəʊz] *vt* - **1.** [uncover - skin] entblößen; [- underlying layer] freillegen; **to be exposed to sthg** einer Sache *(D)* ausgesetzt sein - **2.** [crime] aufldecken; [criminal] entlarven - **3.** PHOT belichten.

exposed [ɪk'spəʊzd] *adj* [place] ungeschützt.

exposure [ɪk'spəʊʒər] *n* - **1.** [to light, sun, radiation]: **exposure (to)** Ausgesetztsein *das (+ D)* - **2.**: **to die from exposure** [hypothermia] erfrieren - **3.** [PHOT - time] Belichtung *die*; [- photograph] Aufnahme *die* - **4.** [publicity] Publicity *die*.

exposure meter *n* Belichtungsmesser *der*.

expound [ɪk'spaʊnd] *fml vt* darllegen.

express [ɪk'spres] ◇ *adj* - **1.** UK [letter, delivery] Eil- - **2.** *fml* [request] ausdrücklich; [purpose] bestimmt. ◇ *adv* [send] per Express. ◇ *n*: **express (train)** D-Zug *der*. ◇ *vt* [feeling, opinion] ausldrücken.

expression [ɪk'spreʃn] *n* - **1.** [gen] Ausdruck *der* - **2.** [of feeling, opinion] Äußerung *die* - **3.** [look on face] Gesichtsausdruck *der*.

expressive [ɪk'spresɪv] *adj* ausdrucksvoll.

expressly [ɪk'spreslɪ] *adv* ausdrücklich.

expressway [ɪk'spreswei] *n* US Schnellstraße *die*.

exquisite [ɪk'skwɪzɪt] *adj* [object, jewellery] exquisit; [food] köstlich; [painting, manners] ausgezeichnet; [taste] erlesen.

ext., extn. *(abbr of extension)* App.

extend [ɪk'stend] ◇ *vt* - **1.** [road, building] auslbauen - **2.** [visit, visa, deadline] verlängern - **3.** [authority, law] ausldehnen - **4.** *fml* [head, arm] auslstrecken - **5.** [offer - credit, help] gewähren; *(phrase)*: **to extend a welcome to sb** jn willkommen heißen. ◇ *vi* - **1.** [stretch - in space] sich erstrecken; [- in time] anldauern - **2.** [rule, law]: **to extend to sb/sthg** sich auf jn/ etw erstrecken.

extension [ɪk'stenʃn] *n* - **1.** [new room, building] Anbau *der* - **2.** [of visit, visa, deadline] Verlängerung *die* - **3.** TELEC Nebenanschluss *der* - **4.** ELEC Verlängerungskabel *das*.

extension lead n [lead] Verlängerungsschnur die.

extensive [ɪkˈstensɪv] adj - **1.** [damage] beträchtlich - **2.** [land, area] ausgedehnt - **3.** [discussions, tests] ausgedehnt; [use] häufig.

extensively [ɪkˈstensɪvlɪ] adv - **1.** [modify, damage] beträchtlich - **2.** [discuss] ausführlich; [read] viel.

extent [ɪkˈstent] n - **1.** [of land, area] Ausdehnung die - **2.** [of knowledge, damage] Umfang der; [of problem] Größe die - **3.** [degree]: **to what extent?** inwieweit ?; **to the extent that** [in that, in so far as] insofern dass; [to the point where] derart, dass; **to a certain extent** in gewissem Maße; **to a large** OR **great extent** in hohem Maße; **to some extent** bis zu einem gewissen Grade.

extenuating circumstances [ɪkˈstenjʊeɪtɪŋ-] npl mildernde Umstände Pl.

exterior [ɪkˈstɪərɪər] <> adj [wall, lights] Außen-. <> n [of house, car, person] Äußere das.

exterminate [ɪkˈstɜːmɪneɪt] vt ausrotten.

external [ɪkˈstɜːnl] adj - **1.** [outside] äußere(r) (s); **for external use only** nur äußerlich anzuwenden - **2.** [foreign - debt] Auslands-; [- affairs] auswärtig.

extinct [ɪkˈstɪŋkt] adj - **1.** [species] ausgestorben - **2.** [volcano] erloschen.

extinguish [ɪkˈstɪŋgwɪʃ] vt fml [fire] löschen; [cigarette] ausdrücken.

extinguisher [ɪkˈstɪŋgwɪʃər] n: **(fire) extinguisher** Feuerlöscher der.

extol, extoll US [ɪkˈstəʊl] vt rühmen.

extort [ɪkˈstɔːt] vt: **to extort sthg from sb** etw von jm erpressen.

extortionate [ɪkˈstɔːʃnət] adj [price] Wucher-; [demand] ungeheuer.

extra [ˈekstrə] <> adj [additional] zusätzlich; **extra charge** Zuschlag der. <> n - **1.** [addition] Extra das - **2.** CIN & THEAT Statist der, -in die. <> adv [to pay, charge] extra. ⬢ **extras** npl [in price] zusätzliche Kosten Pl.

extra- [ˈekstrə] prefix besonders; **an extra-special present** ein ganz besonderes Geschenk.

extract <> n [ˈekstrækt] - **1.** [from book] Auszug der; [from film, piece of music] Ausschnitt der - **2.** [substance] Extrakt der. <> vt [ɪkˈstrækt] - **1.** [pull out]: **to extract sthg (from)** etw ziehen (aus) - **2.** [information, confession]: **to extract sthg (from sb)** etw (aus jm) herausholen - **3.** [coal, oil]: **to extract sthg (from)** etw gewinnen (aus).

extradite [ˈekstrədaɪt] vt: **to extradite sb (from/to)** jn ausliefern (von/an).

extramural [ˌekstrəˈmjʊərəl] adj UNIV: **extramural studies** Studium für Teilzeitstudenten.

extraordinary [ɪkˈstrɔːdnrɪ] adj - **1.** [very special] außergewöhnlich - **2.** [strange] merkwürdig.

extraordinary general meeting n außerordentliche Hauptversammlung.

extravagance [ɪkˈstrævəgəns] n - **1.** [excessive spending] Verschwendung die - **2.** [luxury] Extravaganz die.

extravagant [ɪkˈstrævəgənt] adj - **1.** [wasteful - person, use] verschwenderisch; [- tastes] kostspielig - **2.** [gift, party, behaviour] extravagant - **3.** [claim] übertrieben.

extreme [ɪkˈstriːm] <> adj - **1.** [gen] äußerste(r) (s); **extreme heat** extreme Hitze - **2.** [conditions, views, politician] extrem. <> n [furthest limit] Extrem das.

extremely [ɪkˈstriːmlɪ] adv [very] äußerst.

extremist [ɪkˈstriːmɪst] <> adj extremistisch. <> n Extremist der, -in die.

extricate [ˈekstrɪkeɪt] vt: **to extricate sthg (from)** etw befreien (aus); **to extricate o.s. (from)** sich herauswinden (aus); fig sich befreien (aus).

extrovert [ˈekstrəvɜːt] <> adj extrovertiert. <> n extrovertierter Mensch.

exuberance [ɪgˈzjuːbərəns] n Ausgelassenheit die.

exultant [ɪgˈzʌltənt] adj [person, crowd] jubelnd; [smile] triumphierend.

eye [aɪ] (cont **eyeing** OR **eying**) <> n - **1.** [gen] Auge das; **to cast** OR **run one's eye over sthg** etw überfliegen; **to catch the waiter's eye** den Kellner auf sich (A) aufmerksam machen; **to have one's eye on sb/sthg** ein Auge auf jn/etw haben; **to keep one's eyes open for, to keep an eye out for** Ausschau halten nach (+ D); **to keep an eye on** aufpassen auf (+ A) - **2.** [of needle] Öhr das. <> vt [suspiciously] beäugen; [with desire] sehnsüchtig anschauen.

eyeball [ˈaɪbɔːl] n Augapfel der.

eyebath [ˈaɪbɑːθ] n Augenbad das.

eyebrow [ˈaɪbraʊ] n Augenbraue die.

eyebrow pencil n Augenbrauenstift der.

eyedrops [ˈaɪdrɒps] npl Augentropfen Pl.

eyeglasses [ˈaɪˌglɑːsɪz] npl US Brille die.

eyelash [ˈaɪlæʃ] n Augenwimper die.

eyelid [ˈaɪlɪd] n Augenlid das.

eyeliner [ˈaɪˌlaɪnər] n Eyeliner der.

eye-opener n inf: **it was an eye-opener for me** das hat mir die Augen geöffnet.

eye shadow n Lidschatten der.

eyesight [ˈaɪsaɪt] n (U) Sehkraft die; **to have good/bad eyesight** gute/schlechte Augen haben.

eyesore [ˈaɪsɔːr] n Schandfleck der.

eyestrain [ˈaɪstreɪn] n Überanstrengung die der Augen.

eyewitness [ˌaɪˈwɪtnɪs] n Augenzeuge der, -gin die.

F

f (pl **f's** OR **fs**), **F** (pl **F's** OR **Fs**) [ef] n [letter] f das, F das. ➡ **F** n - 1. MUS F das - 2. (abbr of **Fahrenheit**) F.

fable ['feɪbl] n Fabel die.

fabric ['fæbrɪk] n - 1. [cloth] Stoff der - 2. [of building] Bausubstanz die - 3. [of society] Gefüge das.

fabrication [,fæbrɪ'keɪʃn] n [lie] Lüge die.

fabulous ['fæbjʊləs] adj inf [excellent] toll.

facade [fə'sɑːd] n liter & fig Fassade die.

face [feɪs] ◇ n - 1. [of person] Gesicht das; **face to face** [with person] von Angesicht zu Angesicht; **to come face to face with** sthg mit etw konfrontiert werden; **to say** sthg **to** sb's **face** jm etw offen ins Gesicht sagen - 2. [expression] Gesicht das; **to make** OR **pull a face** ein Gesicht ziehen - 3. [of cliff] Wand die; [of coin] Vorderseite die; [of building] Fassade die; **on the face of it** auf den ersten Blick - 4. [of clock, watch] Zifferblatt das - 5. [respect]: **to lose face** das Gesicht verlieren; **to save face** das Gesicht wahren. ◇ vt - 1. [look towards] gegenüberlstehen (+ D); **my house faces south** mein Haus liegt nach Süden; **the hotel faces the harbour** das Hotel liegt gegenüber vom Hafen - 2. [confront] sich stellen (+ D); **to be faced with** sthg [problem, decision] mit etw konfrontiert werden - 3. [facts, truth] ins Auge sehen (+ D); **let's face it!** machen wir uns nichts vor! - 4. inf [cope with]: **I can't face another omelette** ich kann kein Omelett mehr sehen!; **I can't face it!** ich bringe es einfach nicht über mich. ➡ **face down** adv [person] mit dem Gesicht nach unten; [playing card] mit der Bildseite nach unten. ➡ **face up** adv [person] mit dem Gesicht nach oben; [playing card] mit der Bildseite nach oben. ➡ **in the face of** prep [in spite of] trotz (+ G). ➡ **face up to** vt insep [responsibility] sich auf (A) nehmen; [problem] sich stellen (+ D).

facecloth ['feɪsklɒθ] n UK Waschlappen der.

face cream n Gesichtscreme die.

face-lift n - 1. [on face] Gesichtsstraffung die - 2. fig [on building]: **to give** sthg **a face-lift** etw verschönern.

face-saving [-,seɪvɪŋ] adj: **a face-saving agreement/measure** eine Vereinbarung/Maßnahme, um das Gesicht zu wahren.

facet ['fæsɪt] n - 1. [aspect] Seite die - 2. [of jewel] Facette die.

facetious [fə'siːʃəs] adj leicht spöttisch.

face value n [of coin, stamp] Nennwert der; **to take** sthg **at face value** fig etw für bare Münze nehmen.

facility [fə'sɪlətɪ] n [feature] Einrichtung die. ➡ **facilities** npl [amenities] Ausstattung die; **cooking facilities** Kochgelegenheiten Pl.

facsimile [fæk'sɪmɪlɪ] n - 1. [message] Fax das - 2. [exact copy] Faksimile das.

fact [fækt] n Tatsache die; **it is a fact that...** es steht fest, dass...; **to know** sthg **for a fact** etw genau wissen. ➡ **in fact** adv [in reality] tatsächlich; [moreover] sogar.

fact of life n Tatsache die (mit der man sich abfinden muss). ➡ **facts of life** npl euph: **to tell** sb **the fact of lifes of life** jn aufklären.

factor ['fæktər] n Faktor der.

factory ['fæktərɪ] n Fabrik die.

fact sheet n UK Informationsblatt das.

factual ['fæktʃʊəl] adj [account] auf Tatsachen beruhend.

faculty ['fækltɪ] n - 1. [ability] Fähigkeit die - 2. UNIV [section] Fakultät die; [staff] Lehrkörper der.

fad [fæd] n Tick der.

fade [feɪd] ◇ vi - 1. [material, colour] verbleichen; [flower] verwelken - 2. [light] nachllassen - 3. [sound] verklingen - 4. [feeling, interest, smile] schwinden; [memory] verblassen. ◇ vt [material, colour] auslbleichen.

faeces UK, **feces** US ['fiːsiːz] npl Fäkalien Pl.

fag [fæg] n - 1. UK inf [cigarette] Glimmstengel der - 2. US pej [homosexual] Schwuler der.

Fahrenheit ['færənhaɪt] adj Fahrenheit.

fail [feɪl] ◇ vt - 1. [not succeed in]: **to fail to do** sthg etw nicht tun können; **you can't fail to notice it** du kannst es nicht übersehen; **he failed to persuade them** es gelang ihm nicht, sie zu überreden - 2. [exam, test] durchlfallen; [candidate] durchlfallen lassen. ◇ vi - 1. [not succeed] scheitern - 2. [in exam, test] durchlfallen - 3. [brakes, engine, heart] versagen; [lights] auslfallen - 4. [eyesight] nachllassen; [health] sich verschlechtern.

failing ['feɪlɪŋ] ◇ n [weakness] Schwäche die. ◇ prep wenn nicht; **failing any renewed fighting** wenn es keine neuen Kampfhandlungen gibt; **failing that** andernfalls.

failure ['feɪljər] n - 1. [gen] Misserfolg der - 2. [person] Versager der - 3. [of engine, brakes, heart] Versagen das; [of lights] Ausfall der.

faint [feɪnt] ◇ adj - 1. [slight] schwach; [image] kaum sichtbar; [chance] gering; **I haven't the faintest idea** ich habe keinen blassen Schimmer - 2. [dizzy] schwindelig. ◇ vi ohnmächtig werden.

fair [feər] ◇ adj - 1. [just - judge, person] gerecht; [- result, decision, trial] fair; (phrase): **it's not fair!** das ist ungerecht! - 2. [quite large] ziemlich groß - 3. [quite good] ziemlich gut - 4. [hair, person] blond - 5. [skin, complexion] hell - 6. [weather] schön. <> n - 1. UK [funfair] Jahrmarkt der - 2. [trade fair] Messe die. <> adv [play, fight] fair. ☞ **fair enough** excl UK inf na gut!

fair-haired [-'heəd] adj blond.

fairly ['feəlɪ] adv - 1. [rather] ziemlich - 2. [treat, distribute] gerecht; [describe, fight, play] fair.

fairy ['feərɪ] n Fee die.

fairy tale n Märchen das.

faith [feɪθ] n - 1. [trust]: **faith (in)** Vertrauen das (zu); **in bad faith** mit böser Absicht; **I told you that in good faith** ich habe dir das im Vertrauen gesagt - 2. [particular religion] Religion die - 3. (U) [religious belief] Glaube der.

faithful ['feɪθfʊl] adj - 1. [friend, dog, lover] treu - 2. [account, translation] getreu, genau.

faithfully ['feɪθfʊlɪ] adv (phrase): **Yours faithfully** UK [in letter] hochachtungsvoll.

fake [feɪk] <> adj [painting, passport] gefälscht; [gun, jewellery] unecht. <> n - 1. [object, painting] [of painting, passport] Fälschung die; [of gun, jewellery] Imitation die - 2. [person] Schwindler der, -in die. <> vt - 1. [signature, results] fälschen - 2. [simulate] vortäuschen; [illness] simulieren. <> vi: he's faking er tut nur so.

falcon ['fɔ:lkən] n Falke der.

fall [fɔ:l] (pt fell, pp fallen) <> vi - 1. [gen] fallen; [person] hinfallen; [from great height, heavily, in sport] stürzen; [thing to ground] herunter-/hinunterlfallen; **the city fell to the enemy troops** die Stadt fiel in die Hände der feindlichen Truppen; **to fall flat** [joke] daneben gehen - 2. [decrease - temperature] fallen; [- number] ablnehmen; [- demand, wind] nachlassen - 3. [become - ill, silent, vacant] werden; (phrase): **to fall asleep** einlschlafen; **to fall in love** sich verlieben; **to fall open** sich öffnen; **to fall to bits** OR **pieces** auseinander fallen - 4. [occur]: **to fall (on)** fallen (auf (+ D)); **they fall into two groups** sie lassen sich in zwei Gruppen zuordnen. <> n - 1. [accident, from power] Sturz der; **to have a fall** stürzen - 2.: **fall of snow** Schneefall der - 3. [of city, country] Eroberung die - 4. [decrease]: **fall (in)** Abnahme die (+ G) - 5. US [autumn] Herbst der. ☞ **falls** npl [waterfall] Wasserfall der. ☞ **fall apart** vi - 1. [book, chair] auseinander fallen - 2. fig [country, person] zusammenlbrechen. ☞ **fall back** vi - 1. [retreat] zurücklweichen - 2. [lag behind] zurücklfallen. ☞ **fall back on** vt insep [resort to] zurücklgreifen auf (+ A). ☞ **fall behind** vi - 1. [in race] zurücklfallen - 2. [with rent, work] in Rückstand geraten. ☞ **fall for** vt insep - 1. inf [fall in love with] sich verlieben in (+ A) - 2. [trick] hereinlfallen auf (+ A). ☞ **fall in** vi [roof, ceiling] einlstürzen. ☞ **fall off** vi - 1. [drop off]

herunter-/hinunterlfallen - 2. [diminish] zurücklgehen. ☞ **fall out** vi - 1. [hair, tooth] auslfallen - 2. [quarrel]: **to fall out (with sb)** sich (mit jm) zerstreiten. ☞ **fall over** <> vt insep [step, obstacle] fallen über (+ A). <> vi [lose balance - person] hinlfallen; [- chair, jug] umlkippen. ☞ **fall through** vi [plan, deal] fehllschlagen.

fallacy ['fæləsɪ] n Irrtum der.

fallen ['fɔ:ln] pp ▷ **fall**.

fallible ['fæləbl] adj [person] fehlbar; [method, plan] nicht unfehlbar.

fallout ['fɔ:laʊt] n [radiation] radioaktiver Niederschlag.

fallow ['fæləʊ] adj [land] brach; **to lie fallow** brachlliegen.

false [fɔ:ls] adj - 1. [gen] falsch - 2. [fake - nose, eyelashes] künstlich; [- passport] gefälscht; phrase: **false ceiling** Einschubdecke die.

false alarm n falscher Alarm.

falsely ['fɔ:lslɪ] adv - 1. [accused, imprisoned] zu Unrecht - 2. [laugh] gekünstelt.

false teeth npl künstliches Gebiss.

falsify ['fɔ:lsɪfaɪ] vt [facts, accounts] verfälschen.

falter ['fɔ:ltər] vi - 1. [move unsteadily] wankend - 2. [voice] stocken - 3. [hesitate] zögern.

fame [feɪm] n Ruhm der.

familiar [fə'mɪljər] adj - 1. [known] vertraut - 2. [conversant]: **to be familiar with sthg** sich mit etw auslkennen - 3. pej [overly informal] vertraulich.

familiarity [fə,mɪlɪ'ærətɪ] n [gen] Vertrautheit die.

familiarize, -ise [fə'mɪljəraɪz] vt: **to familiarize o.s. with sthg** sich mit etw vertraut machen; **to familiarize sb with sthg** jn mit etw vertraut machen.

family ['fæmlɪ] n Familie die.

family credit n (U) UK staatlicher Zuschuss an einkommensschwache Familien.

family planning n Familienplanung die.

famine ['fæmɪn] n Hungersnot die.

famished ['fæmɪʃt] adj inf [very hungry]: **I'm famished** ich sterbe vor Hunger.

famous ['feɪməs] adj: **famous (for)** berühmt (für).

fan [fæn] <> n - 1. [held in hand] Fächer der - 2. [electric] Ventilator der - 3. [enthusiast] Fan der. <> vt - 1. [cool]: **to fan one's face** sich (D) das Gesicht fächeln - 2. [stimulate - fire, flames] anlfachen; [- feelings] entfachen; [- fears] schüren. ☞ **fan out** vi [army, search party] auslschwärmen.

fanatic [fə'nætɪk] n Fanatiker der, -in die.

fan belt n Keilriemen der.

fanciful ['fænsɪfʊl] adj - 1. [odd] abstrus - 2. [elaborate] fantastisch.

fancy ['fænsɪ] <> adj - 1. [elaborate - clothes, design, restaurant, hotel] ausgefallen; [- food, cakes] fein - 2. [expensive] exklusiv. <> n - 1. [liking] Lust die; to take a fancy to angetan sein von; to take sb's fancy jm gefallen, jn ansprechen - 2. [whim] Laune die. <> vt - 1. inf [want] Lust haben auf (+ A); to fancy doing sthg Lust dazu haben, etw zu tun - 2. [person] scharf sein auf (+ A).

fancy dress n (Masken)kostüm das.

fancy-dress party n Kostümfest das.

fanfare ['fænfeər] n MUS Fanfare die.

fang [fæŋ] n - 1. [of snake] Giftzahn der - 2. [of wolf] Reißzahn der.

fan heater n Heizlüfter der.

fanny ['fænɪ] n US inf [buttocks] Po der.

fantasize, -ise ['fæntəsaɪz] vi fantasieren; to fantasize about doing sthg sich vorstellen, etw zu tun.

fantastic [fæn'tæstɪk] adj inf [gen] fantastisch.

fantasy ['fæntəsɪ] n Fantasie die.

fao (abbr of for the attention of) z. H. (von).

far [fɑːr] (comp farther OR further, superl farthest OR furthest) <> adv - 1. [in distance, time] weit; have you come far? sind Sie von weit her gekommen?; how far is it (to London)? wie weit ist es (bis London)?; as far as [town, country] bis nach; [station, school] bis zu; so far [until now] bisher; far and wide überall; he will go far fig er wird es weit bringen - 2. [in degree]: far better/quicker weitaus besser/schneller; as far as I'm concerned was mich betrifft; as far as I know so weit ich weiß; far and away, by far bei weitem; far from it keineswegs. <> adj: at the far end am anderen Ende; the far right/left [in politics] die extreme Rechte/Linke.

faraway ['fɑːrəweɪ] adj - 1. [place, country] weit entfernt - 2. [look] abwesend.

farce [fɑːs] n fig & THEAT Farce die.

farcical ['fɑːsɪkl] adj lächerlich.

fare [feər] n - 1. [payment] Fahrpreis der; [for flight] Flugpreis der - 2. fml [food] Kost die.

Far East n: the Far East der Ferne Osten.

farewell [,feə'wel] n Lebewohl das; they said their farewells sie verabschiedeten sich.

farm [fɑːm] <> n Bauernhof der. <> vt bewirtschaften.

farmer ['fɑːmər] n Bauer der, Bäuerin die.

farmhouse ['fɑːmhaus] (pl [-hauzɪz]) n Bauernhaus das.

farming ['fɑːmɪŋ] n Landwirtschaft die.

farmland ['fɑːmlænd] n (U) Ackerland das.

farmstead ['fɑːmsted] n US Gehöft das.

farmyard ['fɑːmjɑːd] n Hof der.

far-reaching [-'riːtʃɪŋ] adj weitreichend.

farsighted [,fɑː'saɪtɪd] adj - 1. [person] weitblickend; [plan] auf weite Sicht konzipiert - 2. US [longsighted] weitsichtig.

fart [fɑːt] inf <> n [wind] Furz der. <> vi furzen.

farther ['fɑːðər] compar ⮕ far.

farthest ['fɑːðəst] superl ⮕ far.

fascinate ['fæsɪneɪt] vt faszinieren.

fascinating ['fæsɪneɪtɪŋ] adj faszinierend.

fascination [,fæsɪ'neɪʃn] n Faszination die.

fascism ['fæʃɪzm] n Faschismus der.

fashion ['fæʃn] <> n - 1. [current style] Mode die; to be in/out of fashion modern/unmodern sein - 2. [manner] Art die; after a fashion so einiger maßen. <> vt fml [shape] formen.

fashionable ['fæʃnəbl] adj [clothes, hairstyle] modisch.

fashion show n Mode(n)schau die.

fast [fɑːst] <> adj - 1. [rapid] schnell; [journey] kurz - 2. [clock, watch]: to be fast vorgehen - 3. [dye] farbecht. <> adv - 1. [rapidly] schnell - 2. [firmly] fest; to hold fast to sthg [grip firmly] an etw (D) festhalten; to be fast asleep fest schlafen. <> n [act] Fasten das; [period] Fastenzeit die. <> vi fasten.

fasten ['fɑːsn] <> vt - 1. [coat, door, bag, window] zumachen; to fasten one's seat belt sich anschnallen - 2. [attach]: to fasten sthg to sthg etw an etw (D) befestigen. <> vi: to fasten on to sthg an etw (D) befestigt werden.

fastener ['fɑːsnər] n Verschluss der.

fastening ['fɑːsnɪŋ] n Verschluss der.

fast food n Fastfood das.

fastidious [fə'stɪdɪəs] adj sehr genau.

fat [fæt] <> adj [gen] dick. <> n Fett das.

fatal ['feɪtl] adj - 1. [mistake, decision] fatal - 2. [accident, illness] tödlich.

fatality [fə'tælətɪ] n [accident victim] Todesopfer das.

fate [feɪt] n Schicksal das.

fateful ['feɪtfʊl] adj verhängnisvoll.

father ['fɑːðər] n Vater der.

Father Christmas n UK Weihnachtsmann der.

father-in-law (pl father-in-laws OR fathersin-law) n Schwiegervater der.

fathom ['fæðəm] <> n Faden der. <> vt: to fathom sb/sthg (out) jn/etw ergründen.

fatigue [fə'tiːg] n - 1. [exhaustion] Erschöpfung die - 2. [in metal] Ermüdung die.

fatten ['fætn] vt mästen.

fattening ['fætnɪŋ] adj dick machend; to be fattening dick machen.

fatty ['fætɪ] adj - 1. [food, meat] fett - 2. BIOL [tissue, acid] Fett-.

fatuous ['fætjʊəs] adj albern.

faucet ['fɔːsɪt] n US Wasserhahn der.

fault ['fɔ:lt] ⬦ n - **1.** [responsibility] Schuld die; **it's my fault** es ist meine Schuld; **whose fault is it?** wer ist schuld daran? - **2.** [error, defect, in tennis] Fehler der; **to find fault with sb/sthg** etwas an jm/etw auszusetzen haben; **at fault** im Unrecht - **3.** GEOL Verwerfung die. ⬦ vt: **to fault sb (on sthg)** jm widerlegen (in Bezug auf etw (A)).

faultless ['fɔ:ltlıs] adj fehlerfrei.

faulty ['fɔ:ltı] adj fehlerhaft.

fauna ['fɔ:nə] n Fauna die.

favorites ['feıvrıts] n COMPUT Favoriten Pl.

favour UK, **favor** US ['feıvər] ⬦ n - **1.** (U) [approval] Gunst die; **in sb's favour** zu js Gunsten; **to be in/out of favour (with sb)** (bei jm) beliebt/unbeliebt sein; **to curry favour with sb** sich bei jm einlschmeicheln - **2.** [kind act] Gefallen der, Gefälligkeit die; **to do sb a favour** jm einen Gefallen tun. ⬦ vt - **1.** [prefer] bevorzugen - **2.** [benefit] begünstigen. ⬥ **in favour** adv [in agreement]: **to be in favour** dafür sein. ⬥ **in favour of** prep - **1.** [in preference to] zugunsten (+ G) - **2.** [in agreement with]: **to be in favour of sthg** für etw sein; **to be in favour of doing sthg** dafür sein, etw zu tun.

favourable UK, **favorable** US ['feıvrəbl] adj - **1.** [conditions, weather] günstig - **2.** [review, impression] positiv.

favourite UK, **favorite** US ['feıvrıt] ⬦ adj Lieblings-. ⬦ n - **1.** [person] Liebling der; **this jacket is my favourite** das ist meine Lieblingsjacke - **2.** [in race, contest] Favorit der, -in die.

favouritism UK, **favoritism** US ['feıvrıtızm] n Günstlingswirtschaft die.

fawn [fɔ:n] ⬦ adj rehbraun. ⬦ vi: **to fawn on sb** sich bei jm einlschmeicheln.

fax [fæks] ⬦ n - **1.** [device] Faxgerät das - **2.** [message] Fax das. ⬦ vt [document] faxen; **to fax sb sthg** jm etw faxen.

fax machine n Faxgerät das.

FBI (abbr of **Federal Bureau of Investigation**) n FBI das.

fear [fıər] ⬦ n - **1.** [gen] Angst die, Furcht die - **2.** [risk] Gefahr die; **for fear of waking him** aus Angst, dass er aufwachen könnte; **no fear!** inf auf keinen Fall! ⬦ vt Angst haben vor (+ D); **to fear the worst** das Schlimmste befürchten.

fearful ['fıəful] adj - **1.** fml: **to be fearful of sthg** vor etw (D) Angst haben - **2.** [noise, temper] furchterregend.

fearless ['fıəlıs] adj furchtlos.

feasible ['fi:zəbl] adj [plan] durchführbar.

feast [fi:st] n Festessen das.

feat [fi:t] n Meisterleistung die.

feather ['feðər] n Feder die.

feature ['fi:tʃər] ⬦ n - **1.** [characteristic - gen] Merkmal das; [- of personality] Charakterzug der - **2.** [facial] Gesichtszug der - **3.** [article] Reportage die - **4.** RADIO & TV [programme] Feature das - **5.** CIN Kinofilm der. ⬦ vt: **the film**

features Brad Pitt Brad Pitt spielt in dem Film mit; **the exhibition features the work of two young artists** die Ausstellung zeigt das Werk zweier junger Künstler. ⬦ vi: **to feature (in)** vorlkommen (in (+ D)).

feature film n Spielfilm der.

February ['februərı] n Februar der; see also **September**.

feces npl US = **faeces**.

fed [fed] pt & pp ⬤ **feed**.

federal ['fedrəl] adj Bundes-.

federation [,fedə'reıʃn] n - **1.** [country] Föderation die - **2.** [association] Zusammenschluss der.

fed up adj: **to be fed up with sb/sthg** jn/etw satt haben; **I'm (feeling) fed up** ich habe keine Lust mehr.

fee [fi:] n [for service] Gebühr die; [for membership] Beitrag der; [for doctor] Honorar das; **school fees** Schulgeld das.

feeble ['fi:bəl] adj - **1.** [weak] schwach - **2.** [excuse, joke] lahm.

feed [fi:d] (pt & pp fed) ⬦ vt - **1.** [baby, animal] füttern - **2.** [insert]: **to feed sthg into sthg** etw in etw (A) einlführen; [coins] etw in etw (A) einlwerfen. ⬦ vi [baby] essen; [animal] fressen. ⬦ n - **1.** [for baby] Mahlzeit die - **2.** [for animal] Futter das.

feedback ['fi:dbæk] n (U) - **1.** [reaction] Feedback das - **2.** ELEC Rückkoppelung die.

feeding bottle ['fi:dıŋ-] n UK Saugflasche die.

feel [fi:l] (pt & pp felt) ⬦ vt - **1.** [touch] fühlen; [examine] befühlen - **2.** [be aware of - tension, presence] spüren - **3.** [think]: **to feel that** glauben, dass; **he felt it (to be) his duty** er hielt es für seine Pflicht - **4.** [experience - sensation] spüren, fühlen; [- emotion] empfinden; **I feel the cold a lot** ich leide sehr unter der Kälte; **I felt myself blushing** ich fühlte, wie ich rot wurde - **5.** phr: **I'm not feeling myself today** ich bin heute nicht ich selbst. ⬦ vi - **1.** [happy, angry, sleepy] sein; [lonely, fit, uncomfortable] sich fühlen; **I feel cold** mir ist kalt; **I feel stupid** ich komme mir blöd vor; **I feel ill** ich fühle mich nicht gut; **to feel like sthg** Lust haben auf etw (A); **I don't feel like it** ich habe keine Lust dazu - **2.** [seem - light, heavy, soft etc] sich anlfühlen - **3.** [by touch]: **to feel for sthg** nach etw (D) tasten. ⬦ n - **1.** [of material]: **it has a soft feel** es fühlt sich weich an - **2.** [atmosphere] Atmosphäre die.

feeler ['fi:lər] n [of insect, snail] Fühler der.

feeling ['fi:lıŋ] n - **1.** [gen] Gefühl das - **2.** [impression] Eindruck der; [opinion] Meinung die. ⬥ **feelings** npl Gefühle Pl; **to hurt sb's feelings** jn verletzen.

feet [fi:t] Pl ⬤ **foot**.

feign [feın] vt fml vorltäuschen.

fell [fel] ⬦ pt ▷ **fall**. ⬦ vt - **1.** [tree] fällen - **2.** [person] niederlstrecken.

fellow ['feləʊ] ⬦ adj Mit-; **fellow passenger** Mitreisende der, die; **fellow sufferer** Leidensgenosse der, -sin die; **fellow student** Kommilitone der, -nin die. ⬦ n - **1.** dated [man] Kerl der - **2.** [comrade] Kamerad der - **3.** [of society] Mitglied das; [of college] Fellow der.

fellowship ['feləʊʃɪp] n - **1.** [organization] Vereinigung die - **2.** [UNIV - scholarship] Stipendium das; [- post] Stellung die eines Fellows.

felt [felt] ⬦ pt & pp ▷ **feel**. ⬦ n Filz der.

felt-tip pen n Filzstift der.

female ['fiːmeɪl] ⬦ adj weiblich; **female worker** Arbeiterin die; **female student** Studentin die. ⬦ n - **1.** [animal] Weibchen das - **2.** inf pej [woman] Weib das.

feminine ['femɪnɪn] ⬦ adj feminin. ⬦ n GRAM Femininum das.

feminist ['femɪnɪst] n Feminist der, -in die.

fence [fens] ⬦ n Zaun der; **to sit on the fence** fig nicht Partei ergreifen. ⬦ vt einlzäunen.

fencing ['fensɪŋ] n - **1.** SPORT Fechten das - **2.** [fences] Zäune Pl.

fend [fend] vi: **to fend for o.s.** für sich selbst sorgen. ➡ **fend off** vt sep ablwehren.

fender ['fendər] n - **1.** [round fireplace] Kamingitter das - **2.** [on boat] Fender der - **3.** US [over car wheel] Kotflügel der.

ferment ⬦ n ['fɜːment] [unrest] Aufruhr der. ⬦ vi [fə'ment] [beer, wine] gären.

fern [fɜːn] n Farn der.

ferocious [fə'rəʊʃəs] adj [animal] wild; [attack, criticism] heftig.

ferret ['ferɪt] n Frettchen das. ➡ **ferret about, ferret around** vi inf herumlstöbern.

ferry ['ferɪ] ⬦ n Fähre die. ⬦ vt transportieren.

fertile ['fɜːtaɪl] adj - **1.** [gen] fruchtbar - **2.** [imagination] reich.

fertilizer ['fɜːtɪlaɪzər] n Dünger der.

fervent ['fɜːvənt] adj leidenschaftlich.

fester ['festər] vi [wound, sore] eitern.

festival ['festəvl] n - **1.** [series of organized events] Festival das - **2.** [holiday] Feiertag der.

festive ['festɪv] adj festlich.

festive season n: **the festive season** die Weihnachtszeit.

festivities [fes'tɪvətɪz] npl Feierlichkeiten Pl.

festoon [fe'stuːn] vt schmücken.

fetch [fetʃ] vt - **1.** [go and get] holen; [person from station, school etc] ablholen - **2.** [sell for] einlbringen; **to fetch a high price** einen hohen Preis erzielen.

fetching ['fetʃɪŋ] adj attraktiv.

fete, fête [feɪt] ⬦ n Wohltätigkeitsbasar der. ⬦ vt durch Feiern ehren.

fetish ['fetɪʃ] n - **1.** [sexual obsession] Fetisch der - **2.** [mania] Manie die.

fetus ['fiːtəs] n = **foetus**.

feud [fjuːd] ⬦ n Fehde die. ⬦ vi in Fehde liegen.

feudal ['fjuːdl] adj feudal; [system, lord] Feudal-.

fever ['fiːvər] n liter & fig Fieber das.

feverish ['fiːvərɪʃ] adj - **1.** MED fiebrig - **2.** [frenzied] fieberhaft.

few [fjuː] ⬦ adj wenige; **the first few times** die ersten paar Male; **in a few minutes** in einigen Minuten. ⬦ pron: **a few** ein paar; **a few more** noch ein paar; **quite a few, a good few** eine ganze Menge; **few and far between** dünn gesät.

fewer ['fjuːər] ⬦ adj weniger. ⬦ pron weniger; **there are far fewer (of them) now** heute gibt es weit weniger.

fewest ['fjuːəst] adj: **(the) fewest** die wenigsten.

fiancé [fɪ'ɒnseɪ] n Verlobte der.

fiancée [fɪ'ɒnseɪ] n Verlobte die.

fiasco [fɪ'æskəʊ] (UK pl -s) (US pl -s OR -es) n Fiasko das.

fib [fɪb] inf ⬦ n Schwindelei die; **to tell fibs** schwindeln. ⬦ vi schwindeln.

fibre UK, **fiber** US ['faɪbər] n - **1.** [gen] Faser die - **2.** (U) [roughage] Ballaststoffe Pl - **3.** [strength]: **moral fibre** Charakterstärke die.

fibreglass UK, **fiberglass** US ['faɪbəɡlɑːs] n Fiberglas das.

fickle ['fɪkl] adj wankelmütig.

fiction ['fɪkʃn] n - **1.** (U) [literature] Belletristik die - **2.** [lie] Fiktion die.

fictional ['fɪkʃənl] adj [work] erzählend; [character] fiktiv; [event] erfunden.

fictitious [fɪk'tɪʃəs] adj frei erfunden.

fiddle ['fɪdl] ⬦ n - **1.** [violin] Geige die - **2.** UK inf [fraud] Schiebung die; **tax fiddle** Steuermanipulation die. ⬦ vt UK inf frisieren. ⬦ vi - **1.** [fidget]: **to fiddle (about OR around)** (herum)lzappeln; **to fiddle (about OR around) with sthg** an etw (D) OR mit etw (herum)lspielen - **2.** [waste time]: **to fiddle about OR around** herumltrödeln.

fiddly ['fɪdlɪ] adj UK inf knifflig.

fidget ['fɪdʒɪt] vi zappeln.

field [fiːld] ⬦ n - **1.** [gen] Feld das; **in the field** in der Praxis - **2.** [for sports] Spielfeld das - **3.** [of knowledge] Gebiet das - **4.** COMPUT Datenfeld das. ⬦ vt [question] parieren.

field day n: **to have a field day** fig seinen großen Tag haben.

field marshal n Feldmarschall der.

field trip n Exkursion die.

fieldwork ['fi:ldwɜ:k] n Arbeit die im Gelände.

fiend [fi:nd] n - **1.** [cruel person] Teufel der - **2.** inf [fanatic] Fanatiker der, -in die.

fiendish ['fi:ndɪʃ] adj - **1.** [evil] teuflisch - **2.** inf [very difficult, complex] verteufelt schwer.

fierce [fɪəs] adj [dog] bissig; [lion, warrior] aggressiv; [storm, temper] heftig; [competition] hart; [criticism] scharf; [heat] glühend.

fiery ['faɪərɪ] adj - **1.** [burning] brennend - **2.** [speech] feurig; [temper] hitzig.

fifteen [fɪf'ti:n] num fünfzehn; see also **six**.

fifth [fɪfθ] num fünfte(r) (s); see also **sixth**.

Fifth Amendment n US: to take the Fifth Amendment die Aussage verweigern.

fifty ['fɪftɪ] (pl -ies) num fünfzig; see also **sixty**.

fifty-fifty adj & adv fifty-fifty.

fig [fɪg] n Feige die.

fight [faɪt] (pt & pp fought) ⇔ n - **1.** [brawl] Schlägerei die; [between boxers] Kampf der; **to have a fight with sb** sich mit jm schlagen; **to put up a fight** sich heftig zur Wehr setzen - **2.** fig [struggle] Kampf der - **3.** [argument] Streit der; **to have a fight (with sb)** Streit (mit jm) haben - **4.** [fighting spirit]: **there was no fight left in him** er war kampfmüde. ⇔ vt - **1.** [physically] sich schlagen mit; [in battle, war] kämpfen mit OR gegen - **2.** [battle] austragen; [war] führen - **3.** [prejudice, racism] bekämpfen. ⇔ vi - **1.** [physically] sich schlagen; [in war] kämpfen - **2.** fig [struggle]: **to fight for/against sthg** für/gegen etw kämpfen - **3.** [argue]: **to fight about** OR **over sthg** sich um OR über etw (A) streiten. ◆ **fight back** ⇔ vt insep [tears, anger] zurückhalten. ⇔ vi sich zur Wehr setzen.

fighter ['faɪtər] n - **1.** [plane] Jagdflugzeug das - **2.** [soldier] Kämpfer der - **3.** [combative person] Kämpfernatur die.

fighting ['faɪtɪŋ] n (U) [in war] Kämpfe Pl; [brawling] Schlägereien Pl.

figment ['fɪgmənt] n: **a figment of your/his imagination** ein Hirngespinst von dir/ihm.

figurative ['fɪgərətɪv] adj - **1.** [language] bildlich - **2.** ART gegenständlich.

figure [UK 'fɪgə, US 'fɪgjər] ⇔ n - **1.** [number] Zahl die; [digit] Ziffer die; **in single/double figures** in ein-/zweistelligen Zahlen - **2.** [outline of person] Gestalt die - **3.** [personality] Persönlichkeit die; **a father figure** eine Vaterfigur - **4.** [shape of body] Figur die - **5.** [diagram] Abbildung die. ⇔ vt esp US [suppose] schätzen. ⇔ vi [feature] auftauchen; **to figure prominently** eine wichtige Rolle spielen. ◆ **figure out** vt sep [answer] herausbekommen; [puzzle, problem] lösen.

figurehead ['fɪgəhed] n liter & fig Galionsfigur die.

figure of speech n Redensart die.

file [faɪl] ⇔ n - **1.** [folder] Aktenordner der - **2.** [report] Akte die; **on file, on the files** in der Akte, in den Akten - **3.** COMPUT Datei die - **4.** [tool] Feile die - **5.** [line]: **in single file** hintereinander. ⇔ vt - **1.** [put in folder] abheften - **2.** [complaint, petition, lawsuit] einlreichen - **3.** [wood, metal] feilen; **to file one's fingernails** sich (D) die Fingernägel feilen. ⇔ vi - **1.** [walk in single file]: **to file in/out** nacheinander hinein-/hinauslgehen - **2.** LAW: **to file for divorce** die Scheidung einlreichen.

filet n US = fillet.

filing cabinet ['faɪlɪŋ-] n Aktenschrank der.

fill [fɪl] ⇔ vt - **1.** [gen] füllen - **2.** [repair - crack] zulspachteln; [- hole in ground] zulschütten - **3.** [fulfil - role] spielen; [- vacancy] besetzen; [- need] befriedigen. ⇔ vi sich füllen. ⇔ n: **to eat one's fill** sich satt essen. ◆ **fill in** ⇔ vt sep - **1.** [form, questionnaire] auslfüllen; [name, address] einlsetzen - **2.** [inform]: **to fill sb in (on sthg)** jn (über etw (A)) ins Bild setzen. ⇔ vi: **to fill in for sb** für jn einlspringen. ◆ **fill out** ⇔ vt sep [form, questionnaire] auslfüllen. ⇔ vi [get fatter] fülliger werden. ◆ **fill up** ⇔ vt sep voll füllen. ⇔ vi sich füllen.

fillet UK, **filet** US ['fɪlɪt] n Filet das.

fillet steak n Filetsteak das.

filling ['fɪlɪŋ] ⇔ adj [food] sättigend. ⇔ n Füllung die.

filling station n Tankstelle die.

film [fɪlm] ⇔ n - **1.** [movie, for camera] Film der - **2.** [layer] Schicht die. ⇔ vt filmen; [book, play] verfilmen. ⇔ vi drehen.

film star n Filmstar der.

Filofax® ['faɪləʊfæks] n Filofax® der.

filter ['fɪltər] ⇔ n Filter der. ⇔ vt filtern.

filter coffee n Filterkaffee der.

filter lane n UK Abbiegespur die.

filter-tipped [-'tɪpt] adj mit Filter.

filth [fɪlθ] n - **1.** [dirt] Dreck der - **2.** [obscenity] Obszönitäten Pl.

filthy ['fɪlθɪ] adj - **1.** [very dirty] dreckig - **2.** [obscene] obszön.

fin [fɪn] n - **1.** [on fish] Flosse die - **2.** US [for swimmer] Schwimmflosse die.

final ['faɪnl] ⇔ adj - **1.** [last] letzte(r) (s) - **2.** [at end]: **the final score** der Schlussstand - **3.** [decision, version, defeat] endgültig; **I said no, and that's final!** ich sagte nein, und damit basta! ⇔ n [of ball games] Endspiel das; [of races] Endrunde die. ◆ **finals** npl UNIV Examen das.

finale [fɪ'nɑ:lɪ] n Finale das.

finalize, -ise ['faɪnəlaɪz] vt [arrangements, details, dates] endgültig festlegen; [deal] zum Abschluss bringen.

finally ['faɪnəlɪ] *adv* - **1.** [at last] schließlich; [with relief] endlich - **2.** [lastly] zum Schluss.

finance ◇ *n* ['faɪnæns] *(U)* - **1.** [money] Geldmittel *Pl* - **2.** [money management] Finanzwesen *das*. ◇ *vt* ['faɪ'næns] finanzieren. ◆ **finances** *npl* Finanzen *Pl*.

financial [fɪ'nænʃl] *adj* finanziell.

find [faɪnd] *(pt & pp found)* ◇ *vt* - **1.** [gen] finden - **2.** [discover]: **to find that** feststellen, dass; **I found myself back where I started** ich stellte fest, dass ich wieder da angekommen war, wo ich angefangen hatte - **3.** LAW: **to be found guilty/not guilty** für schuldig/nicht schuldig befunden werden. ◇ *n* Fund *der*. ◆ **find out** ◇ *vi* herausfinden. ◇ *vt insep* [information, truth] herausfinden. ◇ *vt sep* [person] auf die Schliche kommen (+ D).

findings ['faɪndɪŋz] *npl* Ergebnis *das*.

fine [faɪn] ◇ *adj* - **1.** [good - food, work] ausgezeichnet; [- building] prächtig; [- weather, day] schön; *(phrase)*: **how are you? – fine, thanks we ate?** danke - gut, danke - **2.** [satisfactory] in Ordnung, gut; **everything OK? – yes, fine!** ist alles OK? – ja, alles in Ordnung!; **more tea? – no, I'm fine, thanks** noch mehr Tee? – danke, ich habe genug; **it's fine by me** ich habe nichts dagegen - **3.** [hair] fein; [thread, wire] dünn - **4.** [sand, powder, sandpaper] fein - **5.** [small, exact - detail] klein - **6.** [grand - clothes, people] vornehm. ◇ *adv* - **1.** [quite well] gut; **that suits me fine** das passt mir gut - **2.** [thinly] fein. ◇ *n* Geldstrafe *die*. ◇ *vt* zu einer Geldstrafe verurteilen.

fine arts *npl* schöne Künste *Pl*.

fine-tune *vt liter* & *fig* fein abstimmen.

finger ['fɪŋɡə'] ◇ *n* Finger *der*. ◇ *vt* [feel] anfassen.

fingernail ['fɪŋɡəneɪl] *n* Fingernagel *der*.

fingerprint ['fɪŋɡəprɪnt] *n* Fingerabdruck *der*.

fingertip ['fɪŋɡətɪp] *n* Fingerspitze *die*; **to have sthg at one's fingertips** etw parat haben.

finicky ['fɪnɪkɪ] *adj pej* [eater] wählerisch; [person] pingelig; [task] knifflig.

finish ['fɪnɪʃ] ◇ *n* - **1.** [end] Ende *das*; [of race] Finish *das* - **2.** [on furniture, pottery] Oberfläche *die*. ◇ *vt* - **1.** [complete] beenden; **to finish doing the ironing/eating breakfast/etc** mit dem Bügeln/dem Frühstück/etc fertig sein; **to finish writing a letter** einen Brief zu Ende schreiben - **2.** [food] auflessen; [drink] austrinken; [supplies] aufbrauchen; [cigarette] zu Ende rauchen; [book] auslesen - **3.** [work, school]: **I finish work at half past five** ich mache um halb sechs Feierabend; **I finish school at half past three** ich habe um halb vier Schule aus. ◇ *vi* - **1.** [end] zu Ende sein; **when do you finish?** [stop work] wann machst du Feierabend? - **2.** [complete task] fertig werden; **I haven't finished yet** ich bin noch nicht fertig - **3.** [in race, competition]: **to finish top of the**

league Tabellenführer werden; **to finish fifth** Fünfter werden. ◆ **finish off** *vt sep* - **1.** [complete] beenden - **2.** [food] auflessen; [drink] austrinken. ◆ **finish up** *vi*: **we finished up in a pub** wir sind schließlich in einer Kneipe gelandet; **she finished up running her own company** zum Schluss leitete sie ihre eigene Firma.

finishing line ['fɪnɪʃɪŋ-] *n* Ziellinie *die*.

finite ['faɪnaɪt] *adj* - **1.** [limited] begrenzt - **2.** GRAM finit.

Finland ['fɪnlənd] *n* Finnland *nt*.

Finn [fɪn] *n* Finne *der*, -nin *die*.

Finnish ['fɪnɪʃ] ◇ *adj* finnisch. ◇ *n* [language] Finnisch(e) *das*.

fir [fɜː'] *n* Tanne *die*.

fire ['faɪə'] ◇ *n* - **1.** [gen] Feuer *das*; **to be on fire** brennen; **to catch fire** Feuer fangen; [forest, building] in Brand geraten; **to set fire to sthg** etw anzünden; [deliberately] etw in Brand setzen - **2.** [in forest, of building] Brand *der* - **3.** *UK* [heater] Ofen *der* - **4.** *(U)* [shooting]: **under fire** unter Beschuss; **to open fire (on sb)** das Feuer eröffnen (auf jn). ◇ *vt* - **1.** [shoot - bullet, missile] abfeuern; [- gun] abschießen - **2.** [from job] feuern - **3.** [imagination] beflügeln - **4.** [pottery] brennen. ◇ *vi*: **to fire (on OR at sb/sthg)** (auf jn/etw) schießen OR feuern.

fire alarm *n* Feueralarm *der*.

firearm ['faɪərɑːm] *n* Schusswaffe *die*.

firebomb ['faɪəbɒm] *n* Brandbombe *die*.

fire brigade *UK*, **fire department** *US n* Feuerwehr *die*.

fire engine *n* Feuerwehrauto *das*.

fire escape *n* [stairs] Feuertreppe *die*; [ladder] Feuerleiter *die*.

fire extinguisher *n* Feuerlöscher *der*.

fireguard ['faɪəɡɑːd] *n* Kamingitter *das*.

firelighter ['faɪəlaɪtə'] *n* Feueranzünder *der*.

fireman ['faɪəmən] *(pl* -men [-mən]*) n* Feuerwehrmann *der*.

fireplace ['faɪəpleɪs] *n* Kamin *der*.

fireproof ['faɪəpruːf] *adj* feuerfest.

fireside ['faɪəsaɪd] *n*: **by the fireside** am Kamin.

fire station *n* Feuerwache *die*.

firewall ['faɪəwɔːl] *n* COMPUT Firewall *die*.

firewood ['faɪəwʊd] *n* Brennholz *das*.

firework ['faɪəwɜːk] *n* Feuerwerkskörper *der*; *(phrase)*: **fireworks** Feuerwerk *das*.

firing squad *n* Exekutionskommando *das*.

firm [fɜːm] ◇ *adj* - **1.** [in texture] fest - **2.** [structure, shelf] stabil - **3.** [forceful, strong - pressure, hold, control] fest; [- leader, voice] energisch; *(phrase)*: **you must be firm with him** sie müssen ihm gegenüber bestimmt auftreten;

to stand firm standhaft bleiben - **4.** [belief] unerschütterlich; [answer] entschieden; [evidence] sicher. ◇ *n* Firma *die*.

first [fɜːst] ◇ *adj* erste(r) (s); **for the first time** zum ersten Mal; **I'll do it first thing (in the morning)** das ist das Erste, was ich morgen tun werde; **at first sight** auf den ersten Blick; **in the first place** zunächst einmal. ◇ *adv* - **1.** [firstly] zuerst; [arrive, speak *etc*] als erste(r) (s); **first of all** zuallererst; **what should I do first?** was soll ich zuerst tun? - **2.** [for the first time] zum ersten Mal. ◇ *pron* erste *der*, *die*, *das*; **the first of January** der erste Januar. ◇ *n* - **1.** [event]: **the balloon race was a world first** der Ballonwettflug war der erste seiner Art auf der Welt - **2.** *UK* UNIV Abschluss mit "sehr gut" - **3.** AUT: **first (gear)** erster Gang. ➡ **at first** *adv* zuerst. ➡ **at first hand** *adv* aus erster Hand.

first aid *n* Erste Hilfe.

first-aid kit *n* Verbandskasten *der*.

first-class *adj* - **1.** [excellent] erstklassig - **2.** [ticket] erster Klasse; **first-class compartment** Erste-Klasse-Abteil *das*; [stamp] *für Briefe, die innerhalb Großbritanniens schneller befördert werden sollen*.

first course *n* erster Gang.

first floor *n* - **1.** *UK* [above ground level] erster Stock - **2.** *US* [at ground level] Erdgeschoss *das*.

firsthand [fɜːstˈhænd] *adj & adv* aus erster Hand.

first lady *n* POL First Lady *die*, *Frau des US-Präsidenten*.

firstly [ˈfɜːstlɪ] *adv* zuerst; [followed by "secondly"] erstens.

first name *n* Vorname *der*.

first-rate *adj* erstklassig.

fish [fɪʃ] (*pl inv OR* -**es**) ◇ *n* Fisch *der*. ◇ *vi*: **to fish (for)** fischen; [with rod] angeln; **to fish for compliments** *fig* auf Komplimente aus sein.

fish and chips *npl UK* frittierter Fisch mit Pommes frites.

fish and chip shop *n UK* Imbissstube, die hauptsächlich frittierten Fisch mit Pommes frites verkauft.

fishcake [ˈfɪʃkeɪk] *n* Fischfrikadelle *die*.

fisherman [ˈfɪʃəmən] (*pl* -**men** [-mən]) *n* Fischer *der*; [angler] Angler *der*, -in *die*.

fish fingers *UK*, **fish sticks** *US npl* Fischstäbchen *das*.

fishing [ˈfɪʃɪŋ] *n* Fischen *das*; [with rod] Angeln *das*; [industry] Fischerei *die*; **to go fishing** auf Fischfang gehen; [with rod] angeln gehen.

fishing boat *n* Fischerboot *das*.

fishing rod *n* Angelrute *die*.

fishmonger [ˈfɪʃˌmʌŋɡəʳ] *n esp UK* Fischhändler *der*, -in *die*; **fishmonger's (shop)** Fischgeschäft *das*.

fish shop *n* Fischgeschäft *das*.

fish sticks *npl US* = **fish fingers**.

fish tank *n* [in house] Aquarium *das*.

fishy [ˈfɪʃɪ] *adj* - **1.** [smell, taste] Fisch- - **2.** *fig* [suspicious]: **there's something fishy about it** daran ist etwas faul.

fist [fɪst] *n* Faust *die*.

fit [fɪt] ◇ *adj* - **1.** [suitable]: **fit (for)** geeignet (für); **to be fit to do sthg** die richtige Person sein, um etw zu tun; **he's not fit to drive** [drunk] er ist nicht mehr in der Lage, Auto zu fahren; **fit to eat** essbar - **2.** [healthy] fit; **to keep/get fit** fit bleiben/werden. ◇ *n* - **1.** [of clothes, shoes *etc*]: **to be a good fit** gut passen - **2.** [epileptic, of anger, coughing] Anfall *der*; **to have a fit** MED einen Anfall haben OR erleiden; *fig* [be angry] einen Wutanfall kriegen; **to work in fits and starts** die Arbeit mehrmals unterbrechen. ◇ *vt* - **1.** [subj: clothes, shoes] passen (+ *D*); [subj: key] passen in (+ *A*) - **2.** [insert]: **to fit sthg into sthg** etw in etw (*A*) stecken - **3.** [install] einbauen; **to fit sthg with sthg** etw mit etw ausstatten - **4.** [correspond to] entsprechen (+ *D*); **he fits the description** die Beschreibung passt auf ihn. ◇ *vi* passen. ➡ **fit in** ◇ *vt sep* [find time for - person] dazwischenschieben; [- task] zusätzlich erledigen. ◇ *vi* [belong]: **he's never fitted in here** er hat hier nie hingepasst.

fitness [ˈfɪtnɪs] *n* - **1.** [health] Fitness *die*, Kondition *die* - **2.** [suitability - for job]: **fitness (for)** Eignung *die* (für).

fitted carpet *n* Teppichboden *der*.

fitted kitchen *n UK* Einbauküche *die*.

fitter [ˈfɪtəʳ] *n* [mechanic] Monteur *der*, -in *die*, Installateur *der*, -in *die*.

fitting [ˈfɪtɪŋ] ◇ *adj fml* angemessen. ◇ *n* - **1.** [part] Zubehörteil *das* - **2.** [for clothing] Anprobe *die*. ➡ **fittings** *npl* Ausstattung *die*; [electrical, pipes] Installation *die*.

fitting room *n* Umkleidekabine *die*.

five [faɪv] *num* fünf; *see also* **six**.

fiver [ˈfaɪvəʳ] *n inf* - **1.** *UK* [amount] fünf britische Pfund *Pl*; [note] Fünfpfundschein *der* - **2.** *US* [amount] fünf Dollar *Pl*; [note] Fünfdollarschein *der*.

fix [fɪks] ◇ *vt* - **1.** [attach] befestigen; **to fix sthg to sthg** etw an etw (*D*) befestigen; **to fix one's eyes on sthg** seine Augen auf etw (*A*) heften - **2.** [decide - date, amount, price] festsetzen; *(phrase)*: **I've fixed it with him** ich habe es mit ihm abgemacht; **how are you fixed for money?** wie sieht es bei dir mit dem Geld aus? - **3.** [repair] reparieren - **4.** *inf* [rig - race, fight] manipulieren - **5.** *esp US* [food, drink] machen. ◇ *n* - **1.** *inf* [difficult situation]: **to be in a fix** in der Patsche sitzen - **2.** *drug sl* Fix *der*. ➡ **fix up** *vt sep* - **1.** [provide]: **to fix sb up with sthg** jm etw besorgen - **2.** [arrange] arrangieren.

fixation [fɪk'seɪʃn] *n* Fixierung *die*.

fixed [fɪkst] *adj* - 1. [attached] fest - 2. [charge, rate] festgesetzt - 3. [smile, stare, belief] starr.

fixture ['fɪkstʃər] *n* - 1. [in building] festes Inventar; **fixtures and fittings** *zu einer Wohnung gehörende Ausstattung und Installationen* - 2. [sports event] Spiel *das*.

fizz [fɪz] *vi* [drink] sprudeln.

fizzle ['fɪzl] ⇔ **fizzle out** *vi* [fire, enthusiasm] verpuffen.

fizzy ['fɪzɪ] *adj* kohlensäurehaltig.

flabbergasted ['flæbəgɑːstɪd] *adj* platt.

flabby ['flæbɪ] *adj* wabbelig.

flag [flæg] ⇔ *n* Fahne *die*; [of country] Flagge *die*, Fahne *die*. ⇔ *vi* [person] ermüden; [enthusiasm, energy] nachlassen. ⇔ **flag down** *vt sep* anhalten.

flagpole ['flægpəʊl] *n* Fahnenstange *die*.

flagrant ['fleɪɡrənt] *adj* himmelschreiend.

flagstone ['flæɡstəʊn] *n* Steinplatte *die*; [on floors] Fliese *die*.

flair [fleər] *n* - 1. [talent]: **flair (for)** Talent *das* (für) - 2. [stylishness - of person] Ausstrahlung *die*.

flak [flæk] *n inf* [criticism]: **to get a lot of flak** unter schweren Beschuss geraten.

flake [fleɪk] ⇔ *n* [of snow] Flocke *die*; [of skin] Schuppe *die*. ⇔ *vi* [paint] ablblättern; [skin] sich schuppen.

flamboyant [flæm'bɔɪənt] *adj* extravagant; [design, decoration] üppig.

flame [fleɪm] *n* Flamme *die*; **to be in flames** in Flammen stehen; **to burst into flames** in Brand geraten.

flamingo [flə'mɪŋɡəʊ] (*pl* -s *OR* -es) *n* Flamingo *der*.

flammable ['flæməbl] *adj* leicht entflammbar.

flan [flæn] *n* [sweet] Torte *die*; [savoury] Quiche *die*.

flank [flæŋk] ⇔ *n* Flanke *die*. ⇔ *vt*: **to be flanked by sb/sthg** von jm/etw flankiert sein.

flannel ['flænl] *n* - 1. [fabric] Flannel *der* - 2. *UK* [facecloth] Waschlappen *der*.

flap [flæp] ⇔ *n* - 1. [of pocket] Klappe *die*; [of envelope] Lasche *die*; [of table] hochklappbarer Teil - 2. *inf* [panic]: **in a flap** in Panik. ⇔ *vt* [wings] schlagen mit; [arms] wedeln mit. ⇔ *vi* [sail, flag, clothes] flattern.

flapjack ['flæpdʒæk] *n* - 1. *UK* [biscuit] Haferflockenkeks *der* - 2. *US* [pancake] Pfannkuchen *der*.

flare [fleər] ⇔ *n* [distress signal] Leuchtsignal *das*. ⇔ *vi* - 1. [fire]: **to flare (up)** (auf)lodern - 2.: **to flare (up)** [war, violence, disease] auslbrechen - 3. [trousers, skirt] ausgestellt sein - 4. [nostrils] sich blähen. ⇔ **flares** *npl UK* [trousers] Hose *die* mit Schlag.

flash [flæʃ] ⇔ *n* - 1. [of light - bright] Aufblitzen *das*; *(phrase)*: **a flash of lightning** ein Blitz; **a flash of inspiration** *fig* ein Geistesblitz; **in a flash** blitzartig - 2. PHOT Blitz *der*. ⇔ *vt* - 1. [torch]: **to flash a torch on sthg** etw anleuchten; **to flash one's headlights** die Lichthupe benutzen; **to flash sb a look/smile** jn plötzlich (kurz) anlschauen/anllächeln - 2. [show briefly - passport, image] kurz zeigen. ⇔ *vi* [light] auflblinken; **to flash by** *OR* **past** vorbeilsausen.

flashback ['flæʃbæk] *n* [in film] Rückblende *die*.

flashbulb ['flæʃbʌlb] *n* Blitzlicht *das*.

flashgun ['flæʃɡʌn] *n* Blitzgerät *das*.

flashlight ['flæʃlaɪt] *n* [torch] Taschenlampe *die*.

flashy ['flæʃɪ] *adj inf* protzig.

flask [flɑːsk] *n* - 1. [Thermos] Thermosflasche *die* - 2. [hip flask] Flachmann *der*.

flat [flæt] ⇔ *adj* - 1. [gen] flach; [feet, tyre] platt; **flat roof** Flachdach *das* - 2. [refusal, denial] glatt - 3. [voice] monoton - 4. MUS - singer, instrument] zu tief; *(phrase)*: **C flat** Ces *das*; **D flat** Des *das*; **A flat** As *das*; **B flat** B *das* - 5. COMM [fare, fee] Pauschal- - 6. [drink] abgestanden - 7. [battery] leer. ⇔ *adv* - 1. [level] flach - 2. [exactly]: **in five minutes flat** in ganzen fünf Minuten. ⇔ *n* - 1. *UK* [apartment] Wohnung *die* - 2. [MUS - note] erniedrigter Ton; [- symbol] Erniedrigungszeichen *das*. ⇔ **flat out** *adv* [work] auf Hochtouren.

flatly ['flætlɪ] *adv* [refuse, deny] rundweg.

flatmate ['flætmeɪt] *n UK* Mitbewohner *der*, -in *die*.

flat rate *n* Pauschalpreis *der*.

flat screen *n* [TV, monitor] Flachbildschirm *der*.

flatten ['flætn] *vt* - 1. [surface] glätten; [paper] glatt streichen - 2. [destroy] dem Erdboden gleichmachen. ⇔ **flatten out** ⇔ *vi* eben(er) werden. ⇔ *vt sep* [surface] glätten; [paper] glatt streichen.

flatter ['flætər] *vt* schmeicheln (+ *D*).

flattering ['flætərɪŋ] *adj* schmeichelhaft.

flattery ['flætərɪ] *n (U)* Schmeicheleien *Pl*.

flaunt [flɔːnt] *vt* zur Schau stellen.

flavour *UK*, **flavor** *US* ['fleɪvər] ⇔ *n* - 1. [taste] Geschmack *der* - 2. *fig* [atmosphere] Touch *der*. ⇔ *vt* [food, drink] Geschmack verleihen (+ *D*).

flavouring *UK*, **flavoring** *US* ['fleɪvərɪŋ] *n* Aroma *das*.

flaw [flɔː] *n* Fehler *der*.

flawless ['flɔːlɪs] *adj* fehlerlos.

flax [flæks] *n* [plant] Flachs *der*.

flea [fliː] *n* Floh *der*.

flea market *n* Flohmarkt *der*.

fleck [flek] ⇔ n Tupfen der. ⇔ vt: **flecked (with)** besprenkelt (mit).

fled [fled] pt & pp ▷ **flee**.

flee [fli:] (pt & pp **fled**) ⇔ vt [country] fliehen aus; [enemy] fliehen vor (+ D). ⇔ vi fliehen.

fleece [fli:s] ⇔ n - 1. [of sheep] Schaffell das - 2. [material] Fleece das; [jacket] Fleecejacke die. ⇔ vt inf [cheat] ab|zocken.

fleet [fli:t] n - 1. [of ships] Flotte die - 2. [of cars, buses] Fuhrpark der.

fleeting ['fli:tɪŋ] adj flüchtig.

Flemish ['flemɪʃ] ⇔ adj flämisch. ⇔ n [language] Flämisch(e) das.

flesh [fleʃ] n [of person] Fleisch das; [of fruit] Fruchtfleisch das; [of vegetable] Mark das; **flesh and blood** [family] Fleisch und Blut.

flesh wound n Fleischwunde die.

flew [flu:] pt ▷ **fly**.

flex [fleks] ⇔ n ELEC Kabel das. ⇔ vt [arm, knee] beugen.

flexible ['fleksəbl] adj - 1. [material, bar] biegsam - 2. [person, system] flexibel.

flexitime ['fleksɪtaɪm] n Gleitzeit die.

flick [flɪk] ⇔ n [with finger] Schnippen das. ⇔ vt [switch - turn on] an|knipsen; [- turn off] aus|knipsen. ➠ **flick through** vt insep durch|blättern.

flicker ['flɪkər] vi [light, candle] flackern; [TV, screen] flimmern; [shadow, eyelids] zucken.

flick knife n UK Klappmesser das.

flight [flaɪt] n - 1. [of plane, bird] Flug der - 2.: **a flight of steps/stairs** eine Treppe - 3. [escape] Flucht die.

flight attendant n Flugbegleiter der, -in die.

flight deck n - 1. [of aircraft carrier] Flugdeck das - 2. [of aircraft] Cockpit das.

flight recorder n Flugschreiber der.

flimsy ['flɪmzɪ] adj - 1. [material, clothes, shoes] dünn; [paper] hauchdünn; [structure] nicht sehr stabil - 2. [excuse] schwach; [argument] fadenscheinig.

flinch [flɪntʃ] vi zurück|zucken.

fling [flɪŋ] (pt & pp **flung**) ⇔ n [affair] Affäre die. ⇔ vt [throw] schleudern.

flint [flɪnt] n Feuerstein der.

flip [flɪp] ⇔ vt - 1. [omelette, steak etc] wenden; **to flip a coin** eine Münze werfen; **to flip open** auf|klappen; **to flip over** um|drehen; **to flip through** [magazine] durch|blättern - 2. [switch - turn on] an|knipsen; [- turn off] aus|knipsen. ⇔ vi inf [become angry] aus|flippen. ⇔ n [of coin]: **it was decided on the flip of a coin** wir haben eine Münze geworfen, um zu entscheiden.

flip-flops npl UK [shoe] Badelatschen Pl.

flippant ['flɪpənt] adj leichtfertig.

flipper ['flɪpər] n - 1. [of animal] Flosse die - 2. [for swimmer, diver] Schwimmflosse die.

flirt [flɜːt] ⇔ n: **he's a terrible flirt** er flirtet mit allen. ⇔ vi [with person]: **to flirt (with)** flirten (mit).

flirtatious [flɜː'teɪʃəs] adj kokett.

flit [flɪt] vi [bird] flattern.

float [fləʊt] ⇔ n - 1. [for fishing] Schwimmer der; [for swimming] Schwimmbrett das - 2. [in procession] Festwagen der - 3. [money] Wechselgeld das. ⇔ vi - 1. [on water - not sink] schwimmen; [- move] treiben - 2. [through air] schweben.

flock [flɒk] n [of birds] Schwarm der; [of sheep] Herde die; [of people] Schar die.

flog [flɒg] vt - 1. [whip] aus|peitschen - 2. UK inf [sell] verkloppen.

flood [flʌd] ⇔ n Flut die. ⇔ vt - 1. [gen] überschwemmen; [kitchen] unter Wasser setzen - 2. [with light] durchfluten.

flooding ['flʌdɪŋ] n Überschwemmung die.

floodlight ['flʌdlaɪt] n Scheinwerfer der.

floor [flɔː] ⇔ n - 1. [of room] Fußboden der - 2. [storey] Stock der - 3. [at meeting, debate] Publikum das - 4. [for dancing] Tanzfläche die. ⇔ vt - 1. [knock down] zu Boden schlagen - 2. [subj: comment, question]: **to floor sb** jm die Sprache verschlagen.

floorboard ['flɔːbɔːd] n Diele die.

flop [flɒp] n inf [failure] Flop der.

floppy ['flɒpɪ] adj schlaff herunterhängend.

floppy (disk) n Diskette die.

flora ['flɔːrə] n Flora die.

florid ['flɒrɪd] adj - 1. [face, complexion] gerötet - 2. [style] blumig.

florist ['flɒrɪst] n Florist der, -in die; **florist's (shop)** Blumengeschäft das.

flotsam ['flɒtsəm] n: **flotsam and jetsam** Treibgut und Strandgut.

flounder ['flaʊndər] vi - 1. [in water] sich ab|strampeln - 2. [in conversation, speech] ins Schwimmen kommen.

flour ['flaʊər] n Mehl das.

flourish ['flʌrɪʃ] ⇔ vi - 1. [plant, flower] prächtig gedeihen - 2. [company, business] florieren. ⇔ vt schwenken.

flout [flaʊt] vt missachten.

flow [fləʊ] ⇔ n - 1. [river, of liquid] Fluss der; [of words] Redefluss der; **flow of information/traffic** Informations-/Verkehrsfluss - 2. [of tide] Flut die. ⇔ vi - 1. [gen] fließen; [air, people] strömen - 2. [hair, dress] wallen.

flowchart ['fləʊtʃɑːt], **flow diagram** n Flussdiagramm das.

flower ['flaʊər] ⇔ n [plant] Blume die; [blossom] Blüte die; **in flower** in Blüte. ⇔ vi blühen.

flowerbed ['flaʊəbed] n Blumenbeet das.

flowerpot ['flaʊəpɒt] n Blumentopf der.

flowery ['flaʊərɪ] adj - 1. [dress, material] geblümt - 2. pej [language] blumig.

flown [fləʊn] pp ▷ **fly**.

flu [fluː] n (U) Grippe die.

fluctuate ['flʌktʃʊeɪt] vi schwanken.

fluency ['fluːənsɪ] n - 1. [in a foreign language] Gewandtheit die - 2. [in speaking, writing] Flüssigkeit die.

fluent ['fluːənt] adj - 1. [in a foreign language] fließend - 2. [writing] flüssig; [speaker] gewandt.

fluffy ['flʌfɪ] adj [animal] flaumweich; [jumper] flauschig.

fluid ['fluːɪd] ◇ n Flüssigkeit die. ◇ adj - 1. [movement] fließend; [style] flüssig - 2. [situation] Veränderungen unterworfen.

fluid ounce n = 28,41 cm³.

fluke [fluːk] n inf [chance]: **it was a fluke** das war reiner Dusel.

flummox ['flʌməks] vt esp UK inf durcheinander bringen.

flung [flʌŋ] pt & pp ▷ **fling**.

flunk [flʌŋk] US inf vt SCH & UNIV [- exam, test] fallen durch; [- student] durchfallen lassen.

fluorescent [flʊə'resənt] adj fluoreszierend.

fluoride ['flʊəraɪd] n Fluorid das.

flurry ['flʌrɪ] n [of snow] Gestöber das; (phrase): **there was a flurry of activity** es herrschte eine rege Betriebsamkeit.

flush [flʌʃ] ◇ adj [level]: **to be flush with sthg** bündig mit etw abschließen. ◇ n - 1. [in toilet] Spülung die - 2. [blush] Röte die. ◇ vt [with water]: **to flush the toilet** spülen. ◇ vi - 1. [toilet] spülen - 2. [blush] erröten.

flushed [flʌʃt] adj - 1. [face] gerötet - 2. [excited]: **to be flushed with sthg** über etw (A) aufgeregt und glücklich sein.

flustered ['flʌstəd] adj konfus.

flute [fluːt] n MUS Querflöte die.

flutter ['flʌtər] vi flattern.

flux [flʌks] n: **to be in a state of flux** im Fluss sein.

fly [flaɪ] ◇ n - 1. [insect] Fliege die - 2. [of trousers] Hosenschlitz der. ◇ vt - 1. [plane] fliegen; [kite] steigen lassen; [model aircraft] fliegen lassen; [passengers, goods] fliegen; [airline] fliegen mit - 2. [flag] gehisst haben. ◇ vi - 1. [gen] fliegen; **the days flew by** OR **past** die Tage sind schnell verflogen - 2. [flag] wehen. ◆ **fly away** vi wegfliegen.

fly-fishing n Fliegenfischen das.

flying ['flaɪɪŋ] ◇ adj [animal] Flug-; **flying leap** großer Sprung. ◇ n Fliegen das.

flying colours npl: **to pass (sthg) with flying colours** (etw) glänzend bestehen.

flying saucer n fliegende Untertasse.

flying start n: **to get off to a flying start** einen glänzenden Start haben.

flying visit n Stippvisite die.

flyover ['flaɪˌəʊvər] n UK Überführung die.

flysheet ['flaɪʃiːt] n Überzelt das.

FM (abbr of **frequency modulation**) UKW.

foal [fəʊl] n Fohlen das.

foam [fəʊm] ◇ n - 1. [bubbles] Schaum der - 2. [material]: **foam (rubber)** Schaumgummi der. ◇ vi schäumen.

fob [fɒb] ◆ **fob off** vt sep: **to fob sthg off on sb** jm etw andrehen; **to fob sb off with sthg** jn mit etw abspeisen.

focal point ['fəʊkl-] n fig Mittelpunkt der.

focus ['fəʊkəs] (pl -cuses OR -ci [-kaɪ]) ◇ n PHOT Fokus der; [of rays] Brennpunkt der; [of discussion] Mittelpunkt der; **in focus** [image] scharf; **out of focus** [image] unscharf. ◇ vt - 1. [lens, camera]: **to focus sthg (on)** etw einstellen (auf (+ A)) - 2. [mentally]: **to focus one's attention on sb/sthg** seine Aufmerksamkeit auf jn/etw richten. ◇ vi: **to focus on** [with eyes] den Blick richten auf (+ A); [with camera] mit der Kamera scharf stellen auf (+ A); fig [mentally] konzentrieren auf (+ A).

focused, focussed ['fəʊkəst] adj [mentally] konzentriert.

fodder ['fɒdər] n Futter das.

foe [fəʊ] n liter Feind der.

foetus ['fiːtəs] n Fötus der.

fog [fɒg] n Nebel der.

foggy ['fɒgɪ] adj neblig.

foghorn ['fɒghɔːn] n Nebelhorn das.

fog lamp n Nebelscheinwerfer der.

foible ['fɔɪbl] n Eigenheit die.

foil [fɔɪl] ◇ n (U) [material] Folie die. ◇ vt [criminal] einen Strich durch die Rechnung machen (+ D); [plot, plan] vereiteln.

fold [fəʊld] ◇ vt - 1. [sheet, blanket, paper] falten; **to fold one's arms** die Arme verschränken - 2. [wrap] einlwickeln. ◇ vi - 1. [bed, chair, bicycle] sich zusammenklappen lassen - 2. inf [business] einlgehen. ◇ n [in material, paper] Falte die. ◆ **fold up** vt sep - 1. [sheet, blanket, paper] zusammenlfalten - 2. [chair, bed, bicycle] zusammenlklappen. ◇ vi [chair, bed, bicycle] sich zusammenklappen lassen.

folder ['fəʊldər] n [for papers] Mappe die.

folding ['fəʊldɪŋ] adj [chair, table] Klapp-.

foliage ['fəʊlɪɪdʒ] n (U) Blätter Pl.

folk [fəʊk] ◇ adj Volks-. ◇ npl [people] Leute Pl. ◆ **folks** npl inf [relatives]: **my folks** meine Leute.

folklore ['fəʊklɔː] n Folklore die.

folk music n [popular] Folk der; [traditional] Volksmusik die.

folk song n [popular] Folksong der; [traditional] Volkslied das.

folksy ['fəʊksɪ] adj US inf gemütlich.

follow ['fɒləʊ] ◇ vt - 1. [gen] folgen (+ D); **a presentation, followed by a discussion** ein Vortrag, gefolgt von einer Diskussion

- **2.** [pursue] verfolgen - **3.** [advice, instructions] befolgen - **4.** [news, sb's career] verfolgen; [fashion] sich interessieren für. ◇ *vi* folgen; **it follows that...** daraus folgt, dass...; **I don't quite follow** [understand] da komm ich nicht ganz mit. ◈ **follow up** *vt sep* - **1.** [complaint] nachlgehen (+ D); [suggestion] auflgreifen - **2.** [supplement]: **to follow sthg up with sthg** etw auf etw (A) folgen lassen.

follower ['fɒləʊəʳ] *n* [disciple, believer] Anhänger *der*, -in *die*.

following ['fɒləʊɪŋ] ◇ *adj* folgend; **the following day** am nächsten Tag. ◇ *n* [supporters] Anhängerschaft *die*. ◇ *prep* [after] nach.

folly ['fɒlɪ] *n* [foolishness] Torheit *die*.

fond [fɒnd] *adj* [affectionate] liebevoll; **to be fond of sb** jn gerne haben; **to be fond of sthg/ of doing sthg** etw gerne haben/tun.

fondle ['fɒndl] *vt* streicheln.

font [fɒnt] *n* - **1.** [in church] Taufstein *der* - **2.** COMPUT & TYPO Schrift *die*.

food [fuːd] *n* Essen *das*; [for animals] Futter *das*; **health foods** Reformkost *die*.

food poisoning [-,pɔɪznɪŋ] *n* Lebensmittelvergiftung *die*.

food processor [-,prəʊsesəʳ] *n* Küchenmaschine *die*.

foodstuffs ['fuːdstʌfs] *npl* Nahrungsmittel *Pl*.

fool [fuːl] ◇ *n* [idiot] Narr *der*. ◇ *vt* täuschen; **to fool sb into doing sthg** jn durch Tricks dazu bringen, etw zu tun. ◈ **fool about, fool around** *vi* - **1.** [behave foolishly]: **to fool about (with sthg)** (mit etw) herumlalbern - **2.** [be unfaithful]: **to fool about (with sb)** (mit jm) eine Affäre haben - **3.** *US* [tamper]: **to fool around with sthg** mit etw Blödsinn machen.

foolhardy ['fuːl,hɑːdɪ] *adj* tollkühn.

foolish ['fuːlɪʃ] *adj* - **1.** [unwise, silly] töricht - **2.** [laughable, undignified] dumm; **to look foolish** albern auslsehen; **to feel foolish** sich (D) albern vorlkommen.

foolproof ['fuːlpruːf] *adj* absolut sicher.

foot [fʊt] ◇ *n* - **1.** (*pl* feet) [gen] Fuß *der*; [of sheep, cow] Huf *der*; [of bed] Fußende *das*; [of page] Ende *das*; **to be on one's feet** auf den Beinen sein; **to get to one's feet** auflstehen; **on** *OR* **by foot** zu Fuß; **to find one's feet** Fuß fassen; **to have/get cold feet** kalte Füße bekommen; **to put one's foot in it** ins Fettnäpfchen treten; **to put one's feet up** die Beine hochlegen - **2.** (*pl inv* *OR* feet) [measurement] Fuß *der*, = 30,48 cm. ◇ *vt inf*: **to foot the bill (for sthg)** die Rechnung (für etw) bezahlen.

foot-and-mouth disease *n* Maul- und Klauenseuche *die*.

football ['fʊtbɔːl] *n* - **1.** *UK* [soccer] Fußball *der* - **2.** *US* [American football] Football *der* - **3.** [ball - in soccer] Fußball *der*; [- in American football] Ball *der*.

footballer ['fʊtbɔːləʳ] *n* *UK* Fußballspieler *der*, -in *die*.

football player *n* Fußballspieler *der*, -in *die*.

footbridge ['fʊtbrɪdʒ] *n* Fußgängerbrücke *die*.

foothills ['fʊthɪlz] *npl* Gebirgsausläufer *Pl*.

foothold ['fʊthəʊld] *n* Halt *der*.

footing ['fʊtɪŋ] *n* - **1.** [foothold] Halt *der*; **to lose one's footing** den Halt verlieren - **2.** [basis] Basis *die*; **to be on a war footing** auf einen Krieg vorbereitet sein.

footlights ['fʊtlaɪts] *npl* Rampenlicht *das*.

footnote ['fʊtnəʊt] *n* Fußnote *die*.

footpath ['fʊtpɑːθ] (*pl* [-pɑːðz]) *n* Fußweg *der*.

footprint ['fʊtprɪnt] *n* Fußabdruck *der*.

footstep ['fʊtstep] *n* [sound] Schritt *der*.

footwear ['fʊtweəʳ] *n* Schuhwerk *das*.

for [fɔːʳ] ◇ *prep* - **1.** [expressing purpose, reason, destination] für; **this is for you** dieses Buch ist für dich; **a ticket for Manchester** eine Fahrkarte nach Manchester; **for this reason** aus diesem Grund; **a cure for sore throats** ein Mittel gegen Halsschmerzen; **what did you do that for?** wozu *OR* warum hast du das getan?; **to jump for joy** vor Freude an die Decke springen; **what's it for?** wofür ist das?; **to go for a walk** spazieren gehen; **it's time for bed** es ist Zeit schlafen *OR* ins Bett zu gehen; **'for sale'** 'zu verkaufen' - **2.** [during] seit; **I've lived here for ten years** ich lebe seit zehn Jahren hier; **we talked for hours** wir redeten stundenlang - **3.** [by, before] für; **be there for 8 p.m.** sei um acht Uhr abends da; **I'll do it for tomorrow** ich mache es bis morgen; **be there at 7.30 for 8 o'clock** versucht um 19.30 Uhr da zu sein, damit wir um 20.00 Uhr anfangen können - **4.** [on the occasion of]: **I got socks for Christmas** ich habe Socken zu Weihnachten bekommen; **what's for dinner?** was gibt's zum Abendessen? - **5.** [on behalf of] für; **to do sthg for sb** etw für jn tun - **6.** [with time and space] für; **there's no room for it** dafür ist kein Platz; **to have time for sthg** für etw Zeit haben - **7.** [expressing distance]: **we drove for miles** wir fuhren meilenweit; **road works for 20 miles** Straßenarbeiten auf 20 Meilen - **8.** [expressing price]: **I bought it for five pounds** ich habe es für fünf Pfund gekauft; **for free** gratis - **9.** [expressing meaning]: **what's the German for "boy"?** wie heißt "boy" auf Deutsch?; **P for Peter** P wie Peter - **10.** [with regard to] für; **it's warm for November** es ist warm für November; **it's too far for him to walk** zum Gehen ist es für ihn zu weit; **to feel sorry for sb** jn bemitleiden; **to be glad for sb** sich für jn freuen - **11.** [in favour of] für; **is she for or against it?** ist sie dafür oder dagegen?; **to vote for sthg** für etw stimmen; **I'm all for doing it** ich bin sehr dafür, dass wir das tun - **12.** [in ratios] für; **for every person who passes the test there are five who fail** auf jede Person, die die Prüfung besteht, kommen fünf, die durchfallen - **13.** phr: **you'll be for it when...** du kannst dich auf etwas gefasst machen, wenn... ◇ conj liter denn. ◆ **for all** ◇ prep - **1.** [in spite of] trotz; **for all that** trotzdem - **2.** [considering how little]: **for all the good it's done me** so wenig, wie es mir genützt hat. ◇ conj: **for all I care** meinetwegen; **for all I know** so viel ich weiß.

forage ['fɒrɪdʒ] vi [search] herumlstöbern; **to forage for sthg** nach etw stöbern.

foray ['fɒreɪ] n (Raub)überfall der.

forbad [fə'bæd], **forbade** [fə'beɪd] pt ▷ **forbid**.

forbid [fə'bɪd] (pt **-bade** OR **-bad**, pp **forbid** OR **-bidden**) vt verbieten; **to forbid sb to do sthg** jm verbieten, etw zu tun.

forbidden [fə'bɪdn] ◇ pp ▷ **forbid**. ◇ adj [activity] verboten; **forbidden subject** Tabuthema das.

forbidding [fə'bɪdɪŋ] adj [person] abweisend; [landscape] unwirtlich.

force [fɔːs] ◇ n - **1.** [strength, magnitude] Stärke die; [of explosion, blow] Wucht die; **a force ten gale** ein Sturm mit Windstärke zehn - **2.** [violence] Gewalt die; **by force** mit Gewalt - **3.** PHYS Kraft die - **4.** [powerful person, influence] Macht die - **5.** [effect]: **to be in/come into force** in Kraft sein/treten. ◇ vt - **1.** [compel] zwingen; **to force sb to do sthg** jn zwingen, etw zu tun; **to force sthg on sb** jm etw auflzwingen - **2.** [lock, door] auflbrechen - **3.** [push] pressen. ◆ **forces** npl: **the forces** die Streitkräfte Pl; **to join forces (with sb)** sich (mit jm) zusammenltun.

force-feed vt zwangsernähren.

forceful ['fɔːsful] adj [person] energisch; [words] eindringlich; [speech] überzeugend.

forceps ['fɔːseps] npl Zange die.

forcibly ['fɔːsəblɪ] adv [seize, enter, remove] gewaltsam.

ford [fɔːd] n Furt die.

fore [fɔːr] ◇ adj NAUT vordere(r) (s); **fore deck** Vordeck das. ◇ n: **to come to the fore** fig [become well-known] bekannt werden; [become important] bedeutend werden.

forearm ['fɔːrɑːm] n Unterarm der.

foreboding [fɔː'bəudɪŋ] n Vorahnung die.

forecast ['fɔːkɑːst] (pt & pp inv OR **-ed**) ◇ n Prognose die; **(weather) forecast** (Wetter)vorhersage die. ◇ vt vorherlsagen.

foreclose [fɔː'kləuz] vt & vi: **to foreclose (on)** a mortgage eine (durch eine Hypothek gesicherte) Schuldforderung geltend machen.

forecourt ['fɔːkɔːt] n Vorhof der.

forefront ['fɔːfrʌnt] n: **to be in** OR **at the forefront of sthg** [campaign, movement] an der Spitze einer Sache (G) stehen.

forego [fɔː'gəu] vt = **forgo**.

foregone conclusion ['fɔːgɒn-] n: **it's a foregone conclusion** es stand von vornherein fest.

foreground ['fɔːgraund] n Vordergrund der.

forehand ['fɔːhænd] n Vorhand die.

forehead ['fɔːhed] n Stirn die.

foreign ['fɒrən] adj [gen] ausländisch; [correspondent, debt] Auslands-; [policy] Außen-; (phrase): **foreign person** Ausländer der, -in die; **foreign holiday** Urlaub der im Ausland; **foreign country** fremdes Land; **foreign countries** das Ausland.

foreign affairs npl Außenpolitik die.

foreign currency n (U) Devisen Pl.

foreigner ['fɒrənər] n Ausländer der, -in die.

foreign language n Fremdsprache die.

foreign minister n Außenminister der, -in die.

Foreign Office n UK: **the Foreign Office** das Außenministerium.

Foreign Secretary n UK Außenminister der, -in die.

foreman ['fɔːmən] (pl **-men** [-mən]) n - **1.** [of workers] Vorarbeiter der - **2.** [of jury] Obmann der, -männin die.

foremost ['fɔːməust] ◇ adj führend. ◇ adv: **first and foremost** vor allem.

forensic [fə'rensɪk] adj [examination] gerichtsmedizinisch.

forerunner ['fɔː,rʌnər] n [precursor] Vorläufer der, -in die.

foresee [fɔː'siː] (pt **-saw** [-'sɔː]) (pp **-seen**) vt vorherlsehen, vorauslsehen.

foreseeable [fɔː'siːəbl] adj vorhersehbar; **for the foreseeable future** in absehbarer Zeit.

foreseen [fɔː'siːn] pp ▷ **foresee**.

foreshadow [fɔː'ʃædəu] vt ahnen lassen.

foresight ['fɔːsaɪt] n (U) Weitsicht die.

forest ['fɒrɪst] n Wald der.

forestall [fɔː'stɔːl] vt zuvorlkommen (+ D).

forestry ['fɒrɪstrɪ] n Forstwirtschaft die; [science] Forstwissenschaft die.

foretaste ['fɔːteɪst] n Vorgeschmack der.

foretell [fɔː'tel] (pt & pp **-told**) vt vorherlsagen.

foretold [fɔː'təuld] pt & pp ▷ **foretell**.

forever [fə'revər] adv [eternally] ewig; [disappear, exile] für immer.

forewarn [fɔː'wɔːn] vt vorlwarnen.

foreword ['fɔːwɜːd] n Vorwort das.

forfeit ['fɔːfɪt] <> n Strafe die. <> vt [deposit, chance] einlbüßen; [right] verwirken.

forgave [fə'geɪv] pt ⊳ **forgive**.

forge [fɔːdʒ] <> n [place] Schmiede die. <> vt - 1. [metal] schmieden - 2. [friendship, alliance] schließen; [relationship] knüpfen - 3. [signature, passport, banknotes] fälschen.
forge ahead vi voranlkommen.

forger ['fɔːdʒər] n Fälscher der, -in die.

forgery ['fɔːdʒərɪ] n Fälschung die.

forget [fə'get] (pt -got, pp -gotten) <> vt vergessen; **to forget to do sthg** vergessen, etw zu tun; **to forget how to dance** das Tanzen verlernen; **forget it!** vergiss es! <> vi es vergessen; **to forget about sthg** etw vergessen.

forgetful [fə'getful] adj vergesslich.

forgive [fə'gɪv] (pt -gave) (pp -given [-'gɪvən]) vt [person] verzeihen (+ D); [sins] vergeben; **to forgive sb for sthg** jm etw verzeihen.

forgiveness [fə'gɪvnɪs] n Verzeihung die.

forgo [fɔː'gəʊ] (pt -went) (pp -gone [-'gɒn]) vt verzichten auf (+ A).

forgot [fə'gɒt] pt ⊳ **forget**.

forgotten [fə'gɒtn] pp ⊳ **forget**.

fork [fɔːk] <> n - 1. [for food, gardening] Gabel die - 2. [in road, path, river] Gabelung die. <> vi [road, river] sich gabeln; **to fork left/right** [driver] nach links/rechts abbiegen. **fork out** inf <> vt insep blechen. <> vi: **to fork out (for sthg)** (für etw) blechen.

forklift truck ['fɔːklɪft-] n Gabelstapler der.

forlorn [fə'lɔːn] adj - 1. [expression] betrübt; [cry] verzweifelt - 2. [desolate - person] einsam und unglücklich; [- place] trostlos - 3. [hope] schwach; [attempt] verzweifelt.

form [fɔːm] <> n - 1. [shape, type] Form die; [shape of person] Gestalt die; **in the form of** in Form von - 2. [health & SPORT] Form die; **on form** UK, **in form** US in Form; **off form** nicht in Form; **according to form, true to form** wie erwartet - 3. [piece of paper] Formular das; [application form] Bewerbungsbogen der - 4. UK SCH [class] Klasse die - 5. [etiquette]: **it is bad form to arrive late** es ist schlechtes Benehmen, zu spät zu kommen; **for form's sake** der Form halber. <> vt - 1. [plan] entwerfen; [friendship] schließen; [character] formen; **to form an idea of sthg** sich (D) eine Vorstellung von etw machen - 2. [circle, sentence, plural, government] bilden - 3. [constitute] sein; **to form part of sthg** ein Teil von etw sein. <> vi sich bilden.

formal ['fɔːml] adj - 1. [language] formell; [person] förmlich - 2. [event] feierlich; **formal clothes** Gesellschaftskleidung die - 3. [offer, decision] offiziell; **formal education** Ausbildung die in einer Institution.

formality [fɔː'mælətɪ] n - 1. (U) [correctness] Förmlichkeit die - 2. [convention] Formalität die.

format ['fɔːmæt] <> n - 1. [size & COMPUT] Format das - 2. [structure, arrangement] Struktur die. <> vt COMPUT formatieren.

formation [fɔː'meɪʃn] n - 1. (U) [of company] Gründung die; [of government] Bildung die - 2. [arrangement] Formation die.

formative ['fɔːmətɪv] adj prägend; **formative years** entscheidende Jahre.

former ['fɔːmər] <> adj - 1. [previous] früher, ehemalig; **in former times** früher - 2. [first] erstere(r) (s). <> n: **the former** der/die/das Erstere.

formerly ['fɔːməlɪ] adv früher.

formidable ['fɔːmɪdəbl] adj [task] Respekt einflößend; [task] gewaltig.

formula ['fɔːmjʊlə] (pl -as OR -ae [-iː]) n [gen] Formel die.

formulate ['fɔːmjʊleɪt] vt - 1. [express] formulieren - 2. [plan] auslarbeiten.

forsake [fə'seɪk] (pt -sook, pp -saken) vt liter [person] verlassen; [habit] auflgeben.

forsook [fə'sʊk] pt ⊳ **forsake**.

fort [fɔːt] n Fort das.

forth [fɔːθ] adv liter [outwards, onwards]: **to go/send forth** fortlgehen/-schicken; **to bring forth** hervorlbringen.

forthcoming [fɔːθ'kʌmɪŋ] adj - 1. [future - election, events] bevorstehend; [- book] in Kürze erscheinend - 2. [willing to talk] mitteilsam.

forthright ['fɔːθraɪt] adj [person, manner] direkt; [opinions] unverblümt.

forthwith [,fɔːθ'wɪθ] adv fml unverzüglich.

fortified wine ['fɔːtɪfaɪd-] n mit zusätzlichem Alkohol angereicherter Wein.

fortify ['fɔːtɪfaɪ] vt - 1. [place] befestigen - 2. fig [person, resolve] bestärken.

fortnight ['fɔːtnaɪt] n vierzehn Tage Pl.

fortnightly ['fɔːt,naɪtlɪ] <> adj [visit, meeting] alle zwei Wochen stattfindend; [magazine] alle zwei Wochen erscheinend. <> adv alle vierzehn Tage, alle zwei Wochen.

fortress ['fɔːtrɪs] n Festung die.

fortunate ['fɔːtʃʊnət] adj glücklich; **to be fortunate** Glück haben; **it's fortunate that...** es ist ein Glück, dass...

fortunately ['fɔːtʃnətlɪ] adv zum Glück.

fortune ['fɔːtʃuːn] n - 1. [money] Vermögen das; **it costs a fortune** inf es kostet ein Vermögen - 2. [luck] Glück das - 3. [fate] Schicksal das - 4. [future]: **to tell sb's fortune** jm die Zukunft voraussagen.

fortune-teller [-,telər] n Wahrsager der, -in die.

forty ['fɔːtɪ] num vierzig; see also **sixty**.

forward ['fɔːwəd] ⬦ adj - 1. [movement] vorwärts- - 2. [planning] Voraus-; **we're no further forward now than we were last year** wir sind jetzt nicht weiter als letztes Jahr - 3. [impudent] dreist. ⬦ adv - 1. [in space - go, move] vorwärts; [- look, lean] nach vorn; [- fall] vornüber - 2. [in time]: **to bring a meeting forward** ein Treffen vorverlegen; **from this time forward** [now] von jetzt an; [then] seitdem; **to put a clock forward** eine Uhr vorstellen. ⬦ n SPORT Stürmer der, -in die. ⬦ vt [letter, parcel] nachsenden; **'please forward'** 'bitte nachsenden'.

forwarding address ['fɔːwədɪŋ-] n Nachsendeadresse die.

forwards ['fɔːwədz] adv = forward.

forwent [fɔː'went] pt ⬅ forgo.

fossil ['fɒsl] n Fossil das.

forward slash n Schrägstrich der.

foster ['fɒstər] ⬦ adj [family, mother] Pflege-. ⬦ vt - 1. [child] in Pflege nehmen - 2. [idea, hope] hegen; [relations] fördern.

foster child n Pflegekind das.

foster parents npl Pflegeeltern Pl.

fought [fɔːt] pt & pp ⬅ fight.

foul [faul] ⬦ adj - 1. [water] faulig; [air] verpestet; [food] verdorben; [smell, taste] übel - 2. [very unpleasant] schrecklich; **she's in a foul mood today** sie ist heute in sehr schlechter Stimmung - 3. [language] unflätig. ⬦ n SPORT Foul das. ⬦ vt - 1. [make dirty] verunreinigen - 2. SPORT foulen.

found [faund] ⬦ pt & pp ⬅ find. ⬦ vt - 1. [organization, town] gründen; [hospital, school] errichten - 2. [base]: **to be founded on** sthg auf etw (D) basieren.

foundation [faun'deɪʃn] n - 1. [basis] Grundlage die; **without foundation** unbegründet - 2. [organization] Stiftung die - 3. [cosmetic]: **foundation (cream)** Grundierungscreme die. ⬩ **foundations** npl CONSTR Fundament das.

founder ['faundər] ⬦ n [person] Gründer der, -in die. ⬦ vi [sink] sinken.

foundry ['faundrɪ] n Gießerei die.

fountain ['fauntɪn] n [man-made] Springbrunnen der.

fountain pen n Füllfederhalter der.

four [fɔːr] num vier; **on all fours** auf allen vieren; see also **six**.

four-letter word n Vulgärausdruck der.

four-poster (bed) n Himmelbett das.

foursome ['fɔːsəm] n Quartett das.

fourteen [ˌfɔː'tiːn] num vierzehn; see also **six**.

fourth [fɔːθ] num vierte(r) (s); see also **sixth**.

Fourth of July n: **the Fourth of July** der vierte Juli, Nationalfeiertag (Unabhängigkeitstag) in den USA.

four-wheel drive n - 1. [vehicle] Fahrzeug das mit Allradantrieb - 2. [system] Allradantrieb der.

fowl [faul] (pl inv or -s) n [chicken] Huhn das; [turkey] Truthahn der; [duck] Ente die.

fox [fɒks] ⬦ n Fuchs der. ⬦ vt - 1. [outwit] täuschen - 2. [baffle] vor ein Rätsel stellen.

foxcub ['fɒkskʌb] n Fuchswelpe der.

foyer ['fɔɪeɪ] n - 1. [of hotel, theatre] Foyer das - 2. US [of house] Diele die.

fracas ['frækɑː, US 'freɪkəs] (UK pl inv) (US pl fracases) n Tumult der.

fraction ['frækʃn] n - 1. MATHS Bruch der - 2. [small part] Bruchteil der.

fractionally ['frækʃnəlɪ] adv geringfügig.

fracture ['fræktʃər] ⬦ n Bruch der. ⬦ vt brechen; **to fracture one's arm** sich (D) den Arm brechen.

fragile ['frædʒaɪl] adj zerbrechlich; [health] anfällig.

fragment n ['frægmənt] - 1. [of china, glass] Scherbe die - 2. [of text] Fragment das; [of conversation] Fetzen der.

fragrance ['freɪgrəns] n Duft der.

fragrant ['freɪgrənt] adj duftend.

frail [freɪl] adj - 1. [person, health] zart - 2. [structure] brüchig.

frame [freɪm] ⬦ n - 1. [gen] Rahmen der; [of glasses, bed] Gestell das; [of house, boat] Gerippe das - 2. [physique] Körper der - 3. phr: **frame of mind** Gemütsverfassung die. ⬦ vt - 1. [painting, photograph] rahmen - 2. fig [surround] umrahmen - 3. [thoughts, answer] formulieren - 4. inf [falsely incriminate]: **to frame sb** jm eine Sache anhängen.

framework ['freɪmwɜːk] n - 1. [of boat, house] Gerippe das - 2. [of society, democracy] (Grund)struktur die; [of essay] Gliederung die; **within the framework of** im Rahmen (+ G).

France [frɑːns] n Frankreich nt.

franchise ['fræntʃaɪz] n - 1. POL Wahlrecht das - 2. COMM Lizenz die.

frank [fræŋk] ⬦ adj offen; **to be frank, ...** offen gestanden, ... ⬦ vt [letter] (frei)lstempeln.

frankly ['fræŋklɪ] adv - 1. [talk] offen - 2. [to be honest] offen gestanden.

frantic ['fræntɪk] adj - 1. [person] außer sich - 2. [activity, day, pace] hektisch.

fraternity [frə'tɜːnətɪ] n - 1. [community]: **the medical/banking fraternity** die Mediziner/Bankfachleute - 2. US [of students] Studentenverbindung die.

fraternize, -ise ['frætənaɪz] vi: **to fraternize (with sb)** sich (mit jm) verbrüdern; **to fraternize with the enemy** mit dem Feind fraternisieren.

fraud [frɔːd] *n* - **1.** *(U)* [crime] Betrug *der* - **2.** [deceitful act] Schwindel *der* - **3.** *pej* [impostor] Betrüger *der*, -in *die*.

fraught [frɔːt] *adj* - **1.** [full]: **fraught with danger** gefährlich; **fraught with problems** voller Probleme - **2.** *UK* [frantic - person] gestresst.

fray [freɪ] <> *vi* [clothing, fabric] auslfransen; [rope] sich durchlscheuern. <> *n liter*: **to join in the fray** sich in den Kampf/Streit einlmischen.

frayed [freɪd] *adj* - **1.** [clothing, fabric] ausgefranst; [rope] durchgescheuert - **2.** *fig* [nerves] strapaziert; **tempers were frayed** Gemüter waren erhitzt.

freak [friːk] <> *adj* außergewöhnlich. <> *n* - **1.** [strange creature - in appearance] Missgeburt *die*; [- in behaviour] Irre *der*, *die* - **2.** [unusual event] außergewöhnliche Begebenheit - **3.** *inf* [fanatic]: **a fitness freak** ein Fitnessfanatiker; **a computer freak** ein Computerfreak.
➠ **freak out** *inf vi* - **1.** [get angry] auslflippen - **2.** [panic] durchldrehen.

freckle [frekl] *n* Sommersprosse *die*.

free [friː] *(comp* **freer**, *superl* **freest**, *pt & pp* **freed**) <> *adj* - **1.** [gen] frei; **free period** SCH Freistunde *die*; **she is free to leave** es steht ihr frei, zu gehen; **feel free to disagree** sie sind nicht gezwungen, zuzustimmen; **feel free!** nur zu!; **to set sb/an animal free** jn/ein Tier freillassen; **if you have a free moment** wenn Sie einen Moment Zeit haben - **2.** [costing nothing] kostenlos; **'admission free'** 'Eintritt frei'; **free of charge** umsonst. <> *adv* - **1.** [without payment] kostenlos; **for free** umsonst - **2.** [without restraint]: **to cut free** los1schneiden; [from wrecked vehicle] befreien; **to work free** sich lockern. <> *vt* - **1.** [prisoner, animal] freillassen; [country, city] befreien - **2.** [make available] zur Verfügung stellen - **3.** [extricate - person] befreien; [- object] herauslkriegen.

freedom [friːdəm] *n* Freiheit *die*; **freedom of speech** Redefreiheit *die*.

freefone [friːfəʊn] *adj UK*: **a freefone number** eine gebührenfreie Telefonnummer.

free-for-all *n* - **1.** [brawl] allgemeine Schlägerei - **2.** [argument] allgemeine lautstarke Auseinandersetzung.

free gift *n* Gratisgabe *die*.

freehand [friːhænd] <> *adj* [drawing] Freihand-. <> *adv* aus der Hand.

free house *n* Wirtshaus, das keiner bestimmten Brauerei gehört und daher Bier verschiedener Marken ausschenken darf.

free kick *n* Freistoß *der*.

freelance [friːlɑːns] <> *adj* [work] freiberuflich; [translator, journalist] freiberuflich tätig. <> *n* Freiberufler *der*, -in *die*.

freely [friːlɪ] *adv* - **1.** [available, move] frei; [admit, talk] offen; [travel] ungehindert - **2.** [generously] großzügig.

Freemason [friːˌmeɪsn] *n* Freimaurer *der*.

freepost [friːpəʊst] *adv* [send] portofrei.

free-range *adj UK* [eggs] von frei laufenden Hühnern; [hens] frei laufend.

freestyle [friːstaɪl] *n* [in swimming] Freistil *der*.

free time *n* Freizeit *die*.

free trade *n* Freihandel *der*.

freeware [friːweəʳ] *n* COMPUT Freeware *die*.

freeway [friːweɪ] *n US* Autobahn *die*.

freewheel [ˌfriːwiːl] *vi* [cyclist] (mit dem Fahrrad) rollen; [motorist] im Leerlauf fahren.

free will *n* freier Wille; **to do sthg of one's own free will** etw aus freien Stücken tun.

freeze [friːz] *(pt* **froze**, *pp* **frozen)** <> *vt* einlfrieren; [pond, river] zufrieren lassen; [lock, pipes] einfrieren lassen. <> *vi* - **1.** [pond, river] zulfrieren; [pipes] einlfrieren - **2.** METEOR frieren - **3.** [stop moving] in der Bewegung erstarren; **freeze!** keine Bewegung! <> *n* - **1.** [cold weather] Frost *der* - **2.**: **wage/price freeze** Lohn-/Preisstopp *der*.

freezer [friːzəʳ] *n* [upright] Tiefkühlschrank *der*; [chest] Tiefkühltruhe *die*; [part of fridge] Gefrierfach *das*.

freezing [friːzɪŋ] <> *adj* eiskalt; **I'm freezing** mir ist eiskalt. <> *n inf*: **above/below freezing** über/unter dem Gefrierpunkt.

freezing point *n* Gefrierpunkt *der*.

freight [freɪt] *n* [goods] Fracht *die*.

freight train *n* Güterzug *der*.

French [frentʃ] <> *adj* französisch. <> *n* [language] Französisch(e) *das*. <> *npl*: **the French** die Franzosen *Pl*.

French bean *n* grüne Bohne.

French doors *npl* = **French windows**.

French dressing *n* - **1.** [in UK] Vinaigrette *die* - **2.** [in US] Salatsoße mit Majonäse und Ketschup.

French fries *npl esp US* Pommes frites *pl*.

Frenchman [frentʃmən] *(pl* **-men** [-mən]) *n* Franzose *der*.

French stick *n UK* Baguette *das*.

French windows *npl* große zweiflügelige Glastür.

Frenchwoman [frentʃˌwʊmən] *(pl* **-women** [-ˌwɪmɪn]) *n* Französin *die*.

frenetic [frəˈnetɪk] *adj* [activity] hektisch; [pace] rasend.

frenzy [frenzɪ] *n*: **in a frenzy** hektisch.

frequency [friːkwənsɪ] *n* - **1.** [rate] Häufigkeit *die* - **2.** [radio wave] Frequenz *die*.

frequent <> *adj* [friːkwənt] häufig; **she is a frequent visitor** sie kommt häufig zu Besuch. <> *vt* [frɪˈkwent] häufig besuchen.

frequently ['fri:kwəntlı] *adv* häufig.

fresh [freʃ] *adj* - **1.** [gen] frisch; [information] neu; **fresh water** Süßwasser *das* - **2.** [new] neu; **to make a fresh pot of tea** noch einmal eine Kanne Tee machen; **to give sth a fresh coat of paint** etw neu streichen - **3.** [refreshing] erfrischend; **to get some fresh air** an die frische Luft gehen - **4.** [original] originell.

freshen ['freʃn] *vi* [wind] auflfrischen. ◆ **freshen up** *vi* [person] sich frisch machen.

fresher ['freʃər] *n UK inf* Erstsemester *das*.

freshly ['freʃlı] *adv* frisch.

freshman ['freʃmən] (*pl* **-men** [-mən]) *n* Erstsemester *das*.

freshness ['freʃnıs] *n* - **1.** [of food, air, taste] Frische *die* - **2.** [originality] Originalität *die*.

freshwater ['freʃ,wɔ:tər] *adj* Süßwasser-.

fret [fret] *vi* [worry] sich (*D*) Sorgen machen.

friction ['frıkʃn] *n* (*U*) - **1.** [force] Reibung *die* - **2.** [rubbing] Reiben *das* - **3.** [conflict] Reibereien *Pl*.

Friday ['fraıdı] *n* Freitag *der*; *see also* **Saturday**.

fridge [frıdʒ] *n esp UK* Kühlschrank *der*.

fridge-freezer *n UK* Kühlgefrierkombination *die*.

fried [fraıd] ⬦ *pt & pp* ⊳ **fry**. ⬦ *adj* gebraten; **fried egg** Spiegelei *das*.

friend [frend] *n* [gen] Freund *der*, -in *die*; **to be friends (with sb)** (mit jm) befreundet sein; **to make friends (with sb)** sich (mit jm) anlfreunden.

friendly ['frendlı] *adj* freundlich; [country] befreundet; **to be friendly with sb** mit jm befreundet sein.

friendship ['frendʃıp] *n* Freundschaft *die*.

fries [fraız] *npl* = **French fries**.

frieze [fri:z] *n* ARCHIT Fries *der*; [on wallpaper] Bordüre *die*.

fright [fraıt] *n* - **1.** (*U*) [fear] Angst *die*; **to take fright** es mit der Angst zu tun bekommen - **2.** [shock] Schreck *der*; **to give sb a fright** jn erschrecken, jm einen Schreck einjagen.

frighten ['fraıtn] *vt* Angst machen (+ *D*).

frightened ['fraıtnd] *adj* [person] verängstigt; [voice, expression] angsterfüllt; **to be frightened (of)** Angst haben (vor (+ *D*)).

frightening ['fraıtnıŋ] *adj* beängstigend.

frightful ['fraıtfʊl] *adj* schrecklich.

frigid ['frıdʒıd] *adj* [sexually] frigide.

frill [frıl] *n* - **1.** [on clothes] Rüsche *die* - **2.** *inf* [extra]: **with no frills** ohne Extras.

fringe [frındʒ] *n* - **1.** [on clothes, curtain] Fransen *Pl* - **2.** *UK* [of hair] Pony *der* - **3.** [edge] Rand *der*.

frisk [frısk] *vt* [search] durchsuchen.

frisky ['frıskı] *adj inf* quicklebendig.

fritter ['frıtər] *n* CULIN *in Pfannkuchenteig getauchtes und gebratenes Obst-, Gemüse- oder Fleischstück.* ◆ **fritter away** *vt sep* vergeuden.

frivolous ['frıvələs] *adj* frivol.

frizzy ['frızı] *adj* kraus.

fro [frəʊ] ⊳ **to**.

frock [frɒk] *n dated* Kleid *das*.

frog [frɒg] *n* [animal] Frosch *der*; **to have a frog in one's throat** einen Frosch im Hals haben.

frolic ['frɒlık] (*pt & pp* **-ked**, *cont* **-king**) *vi* herumltollen.

from (*weak form* [frəm], *strong form* [frɒm]) *prep* - **1.** [expressing origin, source] von; **where did you get that from?** woher hast du das?; **I'm from England** ich bin aus England; **I bought it from a supermarket** ich habe es in einem Supermarkt gekauft; **the train from Manchester** der Zug aus Manchester; **we moved from Boston to Denver** wir sind von Boston nach Denver umgezogen - **2.** [expressing removal, deduction] von; **away from home** weg von zu Hause; **to take sth away from sb** jm etw weglnehmen; **take 5 (away) from 9** ziehe 5 von 9 ab; **he took a notebook from his pocket** er nahm ein Notizbuch aus der Tasche; **to drink from a cup** aus einer Tasse trinken - **3.** [expressing distance] von; **five miles from London** fünf Meilen von London entfernt; **it's not far from here** es ist nicht weit von hier - **4.** [expressing position] von; **from here you can see the valley** von hier aus kann man das Tal sehen - **5.** [expressing starting time] von an; **open from nine to five** von neun bis fünf geöffnet; **from next year** ab nächstem Jahr; **from now on** von nun an - **6.** [expressing change] von; **the price has gone up from one to two pounds** der Preis ist von einem Pfund auf zwei Pfund gestiegen - **7.** [expressing range]: **tickets cost from $10** Karten gibt es ab 10 Dollar; **it could take from two to six months** es könnte zwischen zwei und sechs Monaten dauern - **8.** [as a result of] von; **I'm tired from walking** ich bin vom Gehen müde; **to suffer from asthma** an Asthma leiden - **9.** [expressing protection] vor (+ *D*); **sheltered from the wind** windgeschützt - **10.** [in comparisons]: **different from** anders als; **to distinguish good from bad** gut und böse auseinander halten - **11.** [indicating material]: **made from wood/plastic** aus Holz/Kunststoff (gemacht) - **12.** [on the evidence of]: **to speak from experience** aus Erfahrung sprechen; **from what I can see** so wie ich es verstehe; **to judge from appearances** nach dem Äußeren urteilen.

front [frʌnt] ⬦ *n* - **1.** [most forward part] Vorderseite *die*; [of house] Vorderfront *die*; **at the front** vorne; **at the front of the train** vorne im Zug; **on the front of her dress** vorn auf ihrem Kleid; **to lie on one's front** auf dem Bauch liegen - 2. MIL & METEOR Front die - 3. [by the sea] (Strand)promenade die - 4. [outward appearance]: **it's all a front** es ist alles nur Fassade. <> erste(r) (s); Vorder-, vordere(r) (s); [row, page] erste(r) (s); **front garden** Vorgarten der. ➡ **in front** adv vorne; **the people front** die vorne sitzenden/stehenden Leute. ➡ **in front of** prep vor (+ D).

frontbench [ˌfrʌntˈbentʃ] n POL führende Mitglieder der Regierung oder der Opposition.

front door n [of house] Haustür die.

frontier [ˈfrʌnˌtɪər, US frʌnˈtɪər] n liter & fig Grenze die.

front room n Wohnzimmer das.

front-runner n SPORT Läufer der, -in die an der Spitze; fig Spitzenkandidat der, -in die.

frost [frɒst] n - 1. (U) [layer of ice] Frost der, Reif der - 2. [weather] Frost der.

frostbite [ˈfrɒstbaɪt] n (U) Erfrierungen Pl.

frosted [ˈfrɒstɪd] adj - 1. [opaque]: **frosted glass** Milchglas das - 2. US CULIN mit Zuckerguss überzogen.

frosting [ˈfrɒstɪŋ] n US CULIN Zuckerguss der.

frosty [ˈfrɒstɪ] adj - 1. liter & fig [cold] frostig - 2. [field] bereift; [ground] gefroren.

froth [frɒθ] n Schaum der.

frown [fraʊn] vi die Stirn runzeln. ➡ **frown (up)on** vt insep missbilligen.

froze [frəʊz] pt ⊏⊐ **freeze**.

frozen [ˈfrəʊzn] <> pp ⊏⊐ **freeze**. <> adj - 1. [ground] gefroren; [pipes] eingefroren; [lake] zugefroren - 2. [food] tiefgefroren - 3. [very cold] eiskalt; **I'm frozen** mir ist eiskalt.

frugal [ˈfruːgl] adj - 1. [meal] einfach - 2. [person] sparsam.

fruit [fruːt] (pl inv OR -s) n - 1. [food] Obst das; [variety of fruit] Frucht die - 2. fig [result] Frucht die.

fruitcake [ˈfruːtkeɪk] n Kuchen mit Trockenfrüchten.

fruiterer [ˈfruːtərər] n UK Obsthändler der, -in die.

fruitful [ˈfruːtfʊl] adj fruchtbar.

fruition [fruːˈɪʃn] n: **to come to fruition** [plans] Wirklichkeit werden; [hopes] in Erfüllung gehen.

fruit juice n Fruchtsaft der.

fruitless [ˈfruːtlɪs] adj fruchtlos.

fruit machine n UK Spielautomat der.

fruit salad n Obstsalat der.

frumpy [ˈfrʌmpɪ] adj inf [clothes] unmodisch; [person] unmodisch gekleidet.

frustrate [frʌˈstreɪt] vt - 1. [person] frustrieren - 2. [plan, attempt] vereiteln.

frustrated [frʌˈstreɪtɪd] adj - 1. [person] frustriert - 2. [poet, artist] gescheitert.

frustration [frʌˈstreɪʃn] n Frustration die.

fry [fraɪ] <> vt [food] braten; **to fry an egg** ein Spiegelei machen. <> vi [food] braten.

frying pan [ˈfraɪɪŋ-] n Bratpfanne die.

ft. (abbr of foot) & (abbr of feet) ft.

fuck [fʌk] vt & vi vulg ficken. ➡ **fuck off** excl vulg verpiss dich!

fudge [fʌdʒ] n (U) [sweet] weiches Bonbon aus Milch, Zucker und Butter.

fuel [fjʊəl] (UK) (US) <> n [for fire] Brennmaterial das; [for aircraft, ship] Treibstoff der; [for vehicle] Benzin das. <> vt [argument, violence] anheizen.

fuel tank n Benzintank der.

fugitive [ˈfjuːdʒɪtɪv] n: **to be a fugitive from justice** vor der Justiz auf der Flucht sein.

fulfil UK, **fulfill** US [fʊlˈfɪl] vt - 1. [carry out - duty] erfüllen; [- promise] halten; [- role] ausläfüllen - 2. [satisfy - need] befriedigen; [- requirement] entsprechen (+ D); [- hope, ambition] erfüllen.

fulfilment UK, **fulfillment** US [fʊlˈfɪlmənt] n (U) - 1. [satisfaction] Befriedigung die - 2. [carrying through - of ambition, dream] Erfüllung die; [- of need] Befriedigung die.

full [fʊl] <> adj - 1. [filled] voll; **I'm full (up)** [after meal] ich bin satt; **the bus is full** der Bus ist voll besetzt; **the room was full of furniture** das Zimmer war voll mit Möbeln; **his pockets were full of sweets** er hatte die Taschen voller Süßigkeiten - 2. [complete - day, amount] ganz; [- details] genau; [- report] ausführlich - 3. [plump - face] voll; [- figure] mollig - 4. [skirt, sleeve] weit - 5. [flavour] voll. <> adv [very]: **he knows full well that...** er weiß ganz genau, dass... <> n: **in full** vollständig.

full-blown [-ˈbləʊn] adj [heart attack] groß; [war] richtig; **full-blown Aids** Vollbild-Aids das.

full board n (U) Vollpension die.

full-fledged adj US = **fully-fledged**.

full moon n Vollmond der.

full-scale adj - 1. [life-size] in Originalgröße - 2. [thorough - inquiry] umfassend; [- war] total.

full stop n Punkt der.

full time n UK SPORT Spielende das. ➡ **fulltime** <> adj [job, employment] Ganztags-; [worker] Vollzeit-. <> adv ganztags.

full up adj - 1. [after meal] satt - 2. [bus, train] voll.

fully [ˈfʊlɪ] adv - 1. [completely] vollkommen; **fully trained/automatic** vollausgebildet/-automatisch - 2. [in detail - answer] ausführlich; [- describe] detailliert.

fully-fledged UK, **full-fledged** US [-ˈfledʒd] adj fig [doctor, lawyer] vollausgebildet.

fumble [ˈfʌmbl] vi [in bag, pocket] wühlen; **to fumble for sthg** [for light switch] nach etw tasten; [for words] nach etw suchen.

fume [fjuːm] vi [with anger] kochen. ➡ **fumes** npl Dämpfe Pl; [from car] Abgase Pl; [from fire] Rauch der.

fumigate ['fju:mɪgeɪt] *vt* [room, building] auslräuchern.

fun [fʌn] *n* - 1. [gen] Spaß *der*; **it's good fun** es macht viel Spaß; **to have fun** sich amüsieren; **for fun, for the fun of it** aus *or* zum Spaß - 2. [ridicule]: **to make fun of sb, to poke fun at sb** sich über jn lustig machen.

function ['fʌŋkʃn] ⟩ *n* - 1. [gen] Funktion *die* - 2. [social event] Veranstaltung *die*. ⟩ *vi* - 1. [work] funktionieren - 2. [serve]: **to function as** dienen als.

functional ['fʌŋkʃnəl] *adj* - 1. [practical] funktionell - 2. [operational] funktionsfähig.

fund [fʌnd] ⟩ *n* - 1. [amount of money] Fonds *der* - 2. *fig* [of knowledge, experience] Fundus *der*. ⟩ *vt* finanzieren. **funds** *npl* Gelder *Pl*; **public funds** öffentliche Mittel *Pl*.

fundamental [,fʌndə'mentl] *adj* - 1. [basic - idea] grundlegend; [- principle, change, error] fundamental - 2. [vital]: **to be fundamental (to)** von fundamentaler Bedeutung sein (für).

funding ['fʌndɪŋ] *n* Gelder *Pl*.

funeral ['fju:nərəl] *n* Beerdigung *die*.

funeral parlour *n* Beerdigungsinstitut *das*.

funfair ['fʌnfeə'] *n* Kirmes *die*.

fungus ['fʌŋgəs] (*pl* **-gi** [-gaɪ] *or* **-guses**) *n* BOT Pilz *der*.

funnel ['fʌnl] (*UK*) (*US*) *n* - 1. [tube] Trichter *der* - 2. [on ship] Schornstein *der*.

funny ['fʌnɪ] *adj* - 1. [amusing] lustig - 2. [odd] komisch - 3. [ill]: **I feel funny** mir ist komisch. **funnies** *npl US* Cartoons *Pl*.

fur [fɜ:'] *n* - 1. [on animal] Fell *das* - 2. [garment] Pelz *der*.

fur coat *n* Pelzmantel *der*.

furious ['fjʊərɪəs] *adj* - 1. [very angry] wütend - 2. [violent] heftig; **at a furious pace/speed** mit rasender Geschwindigkeit.

furlong ['fɜ:lɒŋ] *n* Achtelmeile *die*.

furnace ['fɜ:nɪs] *n* [for melting metal] Schmelzofen *der*.

furnish ['fɜ:nɪʃ] *vt* - 1. [room, house] einlrichten - 2. *fml* [provide - proof, explanation] liefern; **to furnish sb with sthg** jm etw liefern.

furnished ['fɜ:nɪʃt] *adj* möbliert.

furnishings ['fɜ:nɪʃɪŋz] *npl* Einrichtungsgegenstände *Pl*.

furniture ['fɜ:nɪtʃə'] *n* (U) Möbel *Pl*; **a piece of furniture** ein Möbelstück.

furrow ['fʌrəʊ] *n* - 1. [in field] Furche *die* - 2. [on forehead] Runzel *die*.

furry ['fɜ:rɪ] *adj* - 1. [animal] mit dichtem Fell - 2. [material] flauschig; **furry toy** Plüschtier *das*.

further ['fɜ:ðə'] ⟩ *compar* ▷ **far**. ⟩ *adv* - 1. [gen] weiter; **further back** weiter hinten; [in time] weiter zurück; **further on** weiter; **the police decided not to take the matter any further** die Polizei entschied, die Angelegenheit nicht weiterzuverfolgen - 2. [in addi-

tion] darüber hinaus. ⟩ *adj* [additional] weitere(r) (s); **until further notice** bis auf Weiteres. ⟩ *vt* [career] voranlbringen; [aim] unterstützen.

further education *n UK* Erwachsenenbildung *die*.

furthermore [,fɜ:ðə'mɔ:'] *adv* außerdem.

furthest ['fɜ:ðɪst] ⟩ *superl* ▷ **far**. ⟩ *adj* am weitesten entfernt. ⟩ *adv* am weitesten.

furtive ['fɜ:tɪv] *adj* [glance] verstohlen; [behaviour] heimlichtuerisch.

fury ['fjʊərɪ] *n* Wut *die*.

fuse *UK*, **fuze** *US* [fju:z] ⟩ *n* - 1. [of plug] Sicherung *die* - 2. [of bomb, firework] Zünder *der*. ⟩ *vt* [ideas, styles] verbinden. ⟩ *vi* ELEC: **the lights have fused** die Sicherung (für das Licht) ist durchgebrannt.

fusebox ['fju:zbɒks] *n* Sicherungskasten *der*.

fused [fju:zd] *adj* [plug] gesichert.

fuselage ['fju:zəlɑ:ʒ] *n* (Flugzeug)rumpf *der*.

fuss [fʌs] ⟩ *n* Theater *das*; **to make a fuss** Aufhebens machen. ⟩ *vi* sich aufregen.

fussy ['fʌsɪ] *adj* - 1. [person] pingelig - 2. [design, dress] verspielt.

futile ['fju:taɪl] *adj* zwecklos.

futon ['fu:tɒn] *n* Futon *der*.

future ['fju:tʃə'] ⟩ *n* - 1. [time ahead] Zukunft *die*; **in future** in Zukunft; **in the future** in der Zukunft - 2. GRAM: **future (tense)** Futur *das*. ⟩ *adj* künftig; **at a future date** zu einem späteren Zeitpunkt.

fuze *n*, *vt* & *vi US* = **fuse**.

fuzzy ['fʌzɪ] *adj* - 1. [hair] kraus - 2. [image, photo] unscharf - 3. [ideas] wirr.

G

g[1] (*pl* **g's** *or* **gs**), **G** (*pl* **G's** *or* **Gs**) [dʒi:] *n* [letter] g *das*, G *das*. **G** ⟩ *n* MUS G *das*. ⟩ *abbr of* **good**.

g[2] [dʒi:] (*abbr of* **gram**) g.

gab [gæb] *n* ▷ **gift**.

gabble ['gæbl] ⟩ *vt* herunterlrasseln. ⟩ *vi* brabbeln. ⟩ *n* Gebrabbel *das*.

gable ['geɪbl] *n* Giebel *der*.

gadget ['gædʒɪt] *n* Gerät *das*.

Gaelic ['geɪlɪk] ⟩ *adj* gälisch. ⟩ *n* Gälisch(e) *das*.

gag [gæg] <> n - **1.** [for mouth] Knebel der - **2.** inf [joke] Gag der. <> vt knebeln.

gage n & vt US = **gauge**.

gaiety ['geɪətɪ] n Fröhlichkeit die.

gaily ['geɪlɪ] adv [cheerfully] fröhlich; [dressed] in leuchtenden Farben; **gaily coloured** farbenfroh.

gain [geɪn] <> n - **1.** [profit] Gewinn der; [advantage] Vorteil der - **2.** [increase] Zunahme die. <> vt - **1.** [support] gewinnen; [advantage] sich verschaffen; [reputation] erwerben; [victory] erringen - **2.** [increase]: **to gain weight** zulnehmen; **to gain speed** schneller werden; **to gain strength/popularity** an Stärke/Beliebtheit gewinnen. <> vi - **1.** [increase]: **to gain in sthg** an etw (D) gewinnen - **2.** [profit]: **to gain (from/by sthg)** (von/durch etw) profitieren - **3.** [watch, clock] vorlgehen. ✎ **gain on** vt insep: **to gain on sb** jm (immer) näher kommen.

gait [geɪt] n Gang der.

gala ['gɑːlə] n [celebration] Festveranstaltung die.

galaxy ['gæləksɪ] n Galaxis die.

gale [geɪl] n Sturm der.

gall [gɔːl] n: **to have the gall to do sthg** die Frechheit haben, etw zu tun.

gallant adj - **1.** ['gælənt] [courageous] mutig - **2.** [gə'lænt, 'gælənt] [polite to women] galant.

gall bladder n Gallenblase die.

gallery ['gælərɪ] n - **1.** [gen] Galerie die - **2.** THEAT dritter Rang.

galley ['gælɪ] (pl -s) n [kitchen - of ship] Kombüse die; [- of aircraft] Bordküche die.

Gallic ['gælɪk] adj gallisch.

galling ['gɔːlɪŋ] adj ärgerlich.

gallivant [ˌgælɪ'vænt] vi inf sich herumltreiben.

gallon ['gælən] n Gallone die.

gallop ['gæləp] <> n - **1.** [pace of horse] Galopp der - **2.** [horse ride] Galoppritt der. <> vi [horse] galoppieren.

gallows ['gæləʊz] (pl inv) n Galgen der.

gallstone ['gɔːlstəʊn] n Gallenstein der.

galore [gə'lɔːr] adv in Hülle und Fülle.

galvanize, -ise ['gælvənaɪz] vt - **1.** TECH galvanisieren - **2.** [impel]: **to galvanize sb into action** jn dazu veranlassen, aktiv zu werden.

gamble ['gæmbl] <> n [risk] Risiko das. <> vi - **1.** [bet] (um Geld) spielen - **2.** [take risk]: **to gamble on sthg** sich auf etw (A) verlassen.

gambler ['gæmblər] n Spieler der, -in die.

gambling ['gæmblɪŋ] n Spielen das (um Geld).

game [geɪm] <> n - **1.** [gen] Spiel das; **fancy a game of chess/cards?** hast du Lust auf eine Partie Schach/Karten? - **2.** [hunted animals, meat] Wild das - **3.** phr: **the game's up** das Spiel ist aus; **to give the game away** alles verderben; **to play games with sb** sein Spiel mit jm treiben. <> adj - **1.** [brave] mutig - **2.** [willing]: **to be game for sthg** für etw bereit sein; **to be game to do sthg** bereit sein, etw zu tun. ✎ **games** <> n SCH Sport der. <> npl [sporting event] Spiele Pl.

gamekeeper ['geɪmˌkiːpər] n Wildhüter der.

game reserve n Wildreservat das.

gammon ['gæmən] n geräucherter und gekochter Vorderschinken.

gamut ['gæmət] n Skala die.

gang [gæŋ] n [of criminals] Bande die, Gang die; [of young people] Clique die. ✎ **gang up** vi inf sich zusammenlltun; **to gang up on sb** sich gegen jn verbünden.

gangrene ['gæŋgriːn] n Wundbrand der.

gangster ['gæŋstər] n Gangster der.

gangway ['gæŋweɪ] n - **1.** UK [aisle] Gang der - **2.** [gangplank] Gangway die.

gaol [dʒeɪl] n & vt UK = **jail**.

gap [gæp] n - **1.** [empty space, omission] Lücke die - **2.** [in time] Abstand der - **3.** fig [disparity] Kluft die.

gape [geɪp] vi - **1.** [person] gaffen; **to gape at sb/sthg** jn/etw begaffen - **2.** [hole, shirt, wound] klaffen.

gaping ['geɪpɪŋ] adj - **1.** [person] gaffend - **2.** [hole, shirt, wound] klaffend.

gap year n einjährige Pause zwischen Schule und Studium.

garage [UK 'gærɑːʒ, 'gærɪdʒ, US gə'rɑːʒ] n - **1.** [for keeping car] Garage die - **2.** UK [for fuel] Tankstelle die - **3.** [for car repair] Werkstatt die - **4.** [for selling cars] Autohändler der.

garbage ['gɑːbɪdʒ] n esp US - **1.** [refuse] Müll der - **2.** inf [nonsense] Unsinn der.

garbage can n US Mülltonne die.

garbage truck n US Müllauto das.

garbled ['gɑːbld] adj entstellt.

garden ['gɑːdn] <> n - **1.** [private] Garten der - **2.** [public] Grünanlage die. <> vi gärtnern.

garden centre n Gartencenter das.

gardener ['gɑːdnər] n - **1.** [professional] Gärtner der, -in die - **2.** [amateur] Hobbygärtner der, -in die.

gardening ['gɑːdnɪŋ] n Gartenarbeit die.

gargle ['gɑːgl] vi gurgeln.

gargoyle ['gɑːgɔɪl] n Wasserspeier der.

garish ['geərɪʃ] adj grell.

garland ['gɑːlənd] n Girlande die.

garlic ['gɑːlɪk] n Knoblauch der.

garlic bread n (U) Knoblauchbrot das.

garment ['gɑːmənt] n Kleidungsstück das.

garnish ['gɑːnɪʃ] <> n CULIN Garnierung die. <> vt CULIN garnieren.

garrison ['gærɪsn] n Garnison die.

garter ['gɑːtər] n - **1.** [around leg] Strumpfband das - **2.** US [suspender] Strumpfhalter der.

gas [gæs] (pl **gases** OR **gasses**) ⬦ n - 1. [gen] Gas das - 2. US [fuel for vehicle] Benzin das; **to step on the gas** inf aufs Gas treten OR steigen. ⬦ vt [poison] vergasen.

gas cooker n UK Gasherd der.

gas fire n UK Gasofen der.

gas gauge n US Benzinuhr die.

gash [gæʃ] ⬦ n tiefe Schnittwunde. ⬦ vt: **to gash one's hand/arm** sich in die Hand/den Arm schneiden.

gasket ['gæskɪt] n Dichtung die.

gas mask n Gasmaske die.

gas meter n Gaszähler der, Gasuhr die.

gasoline ['gæsəliːn] n US Benzin das.

gasp [gɑːsp] ⬦ n Keuchen das. ⬦ vi - 1. [breathe quickly] keuchen - 2. [in shock, surprise] nach Luft schnappen.

gas pedal n US Gaspedal das.

gas station n US Tankstelle die.

gas stove n = **gas cooker**.

gas tank n US Benzintank der.

gastroenteritis ['gæstrəʊ,entə'raɪtɪs] n Magen-Darm-Katarr der.

gastronomy [gæs'trɒnəmɪ] n Gastronomie die.

gasworks ['gæswɜːks] (pl inv) n Gaswerk das.

gate [geɪt] n - 1. [in wall, fence] Tor das - 2. [at airport] Flugsteig der.

gatecrash ['geɪtkræʃ] vt inf hereinlplatzen.

gateway ['geɪtweɪ] n Tor das.

gather ['gæðər] ⬦ vt - 1. [collect] sammeln; **to gather together** sich versammeln - 2. [speed]: **to gather speed** schneller werden - 3. [understand]: **to gather that** annehmen, dass; **as far as I can gather** soweit ich weiß - 4. [into folds] raffen, kräuseln. ⬦ vi [come together - people] sich versammeln; [- crowd] sich anlsammeln; [- clouds] sich zusammenlziehen.

gathering ['gæðərɪŋ] n Versammlung die.

gaudy ['gɔːdɪ] adj grell.

gauge, gage US [geɪdʒ] ⬦ n - 1. [measuring instrument] Messinstrument das - 2. [calibre] Kaliber das - 3. RAIL Spurweite die. ⬦ vt - 1. [measure, calculate] messen - 2. [judge, predict] beurteilen.

gaunt [gɔːnt] adj hager.

gauntlet ['gɔːntlɪt] n (phrase): **to run the gauntlet** Spießruten laufen; **to throw down the gauntlet (to sb)** (jm) den Fehdehandschuh hinlwerfen.

gauze [gɔːz] n Gaze die.

gave [geɪv] pt ▷ **give**.

gawky ['gɔːkɪ] adj unbeholfen.

gawp [gɔːp] vi gaffen; **to gawp at sb/sthg** jn/etw anlgaffen.

gay [geɪ] ⬦ adj - 1. [homosexual] schwul - 2. [cheerful, lively] fröhlich - 3. [brightly coloured] bunt. ⬦ n [homosexual] Schwule der.

gay rights npl Rechte Pl von Homosexuellen.

gaze [geɪz] ⬦ n Blick der. ⬦ vi: **to gaze (at sb/sthg)** (jn/etw) anlstarren.

GB (abbr of **Great Britain**) n GB.

GCSE (abbr of **General Certificate of Secondary Education**) n Abschlussprüfung an weiterführenden Schulen in England, Wales und Nordirland.

GDP (abbr of **gross domestic product**) n BIP das.

gear [gɪər] ⬦ n - 1. TECH [mechanism] Zahnrad das - 2. [on car, bicycle] Gang der; **out of gear** im Leerlauf; **in gear** mit eingelegtem Gang - 3. (U) [equipment, clothes] Ausrüstung die. ⬦ vt: **to gear sthg to sb/sthg** etw auf jn/etw auslrichten. ◈ **gear up** vi: **to gear up for sthg** sich für etw rüsten; **to gear up to do sthg** sich dafür rüsten, etw zu tun.

gearbox ['gɪəbɒks] n Getriebegehäuse das; **six-speed gearbox** Sechsganggetriebe das.

gear lever, gear stick UK, **gear shift** US n Schaltknüppel der.

geese [giːs] Pl ▷ **goose**.

gel [dʒel] ⬦ n Gel das. ⬦ vi fig [idea, plan] Gestalt anlnehmen.

gelatin ['dʒelətɪn], **gelatine** [,dʒelə'tiːn] n Gelatine die.

gelignite ['dʒelɪgnaɪt] n Plastiksprengstoff der.

gem [dʒem] n - 1. [jewel] (geschliffener) Edelstein - 2. fig [person] Juwel das.

Gemini ['dʒemɪnaɪ] n [sign] Zwillinge Pl.

gender ['dʒendər] n Geschlecht das.

gene [dʒiːn] n Gen das.

general ['dʒenərəl] ⬦ adj [gen] allgemein. ⬦ n MIL General der. ◈ **in general** adv - 1. [as a whole] im Allgemeinen - 2. [usually] gewöhnlich.

general anaesthetic n Vollnarkose die.

general delivery adv US postlagernd.

general election n Parlamentswahlen Pl.

generalization [,dʒenərəlaɪ'zeɪʃn] n Verallgemeinerung die.

general knowledge n Allgemeinbildung die.

generally ['dʒenərəlɪ] adv - 1. [usually] im Allgemeinen - 2. [in a general way] allgemein.

general practitioner n Arzt der, Ärztin die für Allgemeinmedizin.

general public n: **the general public** die breite Öffentlichkeit.

general store n Gemischtwarenhandlung die.

general strike n Generalstreik der.

generate ['dʒenəreɪt] *vt* - **1.** [energy, power, heat] erzeugen - **2.** [interest, excitement] hervorrufen; [jobs, employment] schaffen.

generation [ˌdʒenə'reɪʃn] *n* - **1.** [gen] Generation *die* - **2.** [of energy, power, heat] Erzeugung *die*.

generator ['dʒenəreɪtər] *n* Generator *der*.

generosity [ˌdʒenə'rɒsətɪ] *n* Freigebigkeit *die*, Großzügigkeit *die*.

generous ['dʒenərəs] *adj* großzügig.

genetic [dʒɪ'netɪk] *adj* genetisch. ◆ **genetics** *n* Genetik *die*, Vererbungslehre *die*.

genetically modified *adj* genmanipuliert, gentechnisch verändert.

Geneva [dʒɪ'niːvə] *n* Genf *nt*.

genial ['dʒiːnjəl] *adj* jovial.

genitals ['dʒenɪtlz] *npl* Genitalien *Pl*.

genius ['dʒiːnjəs] (*pl* **-es**) *n* Genie *das*.

gent [dʒent] *n UK inf* Gentleman *der*. ◆ **gents** *n UK* [toilets] Herrentoilette *die*.

genteel [dʒen'tiːl] *adj* - **1.** [refined] vornehm - **2.** [affected] geziert.

gentle ['dʒentl] *adj* - **1.** [person] sanftmütig - **2.** [rain, breeze, movement] sanft, leicht - **3.** [slope, curve] sanft - **4.** [hint] zart.

gentleman ['dʒentlmən] (*pl* **-men** [-mən]) *n* - **1.** [well-bred man] Gentleman *der* - **2.** [man] Herr *der*.

gently ['dʒentlɪ] *adv* - **1.** [speak] sanft - **2.** [blow] leicht; [move, heat] behutsam - **3.** [slope, curve] allmählich.

genuine ['dʒenjuɪn] *adj* - **1.** [real] echt - **2.** [sincere] aufrichtig.

geography [dʒɪ'ɒɡrəfɪ] *n* [science] Geografie *die*; [in school] Erdkunde *die*.

geology [dʒɪ'ɒlədʒɪ] *n* Geologie *die*.

geometric(al) [ˌdʒɪə'metrɪk(l)] *adj* geometrisch.

geometry [dʒɪ'ɒmətrɪ] *n* Geometrie *die*.

geranium [dʒɪ'reɪnjəm] (*pl* **-s**) *n* Geranie *die*.

geriatric [ˌdʒerɪ'ætrɪk] *adj* - **1.** [of old people] geriatrisch - **2.** *pej* [very old, inefficient] veraltet, altersschwach.

germ [dʒɜːm] *n liter* & *fig* Keim *der*.

German ['dʒɜːmən] <> *adj* deutsch. <> *n* - **1.** [person] Deutsche *der*, *die* - **2.** [language] Deutsch(e) *das*.

German measles *n* Röteln *die*.

Germany ['dʒɜːmənɪ] *n* Deutschland *nt*.

germinate ['dʒɜːmɪneɪt] *vi liter* & *fig* keimen.

gesticulate [dʒes'tɪkjuleɪt] *vi* gestikulieren.

gesture ['dʒestʃər] <> *n* Geste *die*. <> *vi*: **to gesture to** OR **towards sb** auf jn deuten.

get [get] (*UK pt & pp* got; *US pt* got, *pp* gotten) <> *vt* - **1.** [obtain] bekommen; [buy] kaufen; **she got a job** sie hat eine Stelle gefunden;

he got us two tickets er hat uns zwei Karten besorgt - **2.** [receive] bekommen; **I got a book for Christmas** ich habe zu Weihnachten ein Buch bekommen; **when did you get the news?** wann haben Sie die Nachricht bekommen? - **3.** [train, plane, bus] nehmen; **let's get a taxi** lass uns ein Taxi nehmen - **4.** [fetch] holen; **could you get me the manager?** [on phone] könnten Sie mir den Geschäftsführer geben?; **can I get you something to eat/drink?** möchtest du etwas essen/trinken? - **5.** [illness] bekommen; **I got this cold while I was on holiday** ich habe mir diese Erkältung im Urlaub zugezogen - **6.** [catch] fangen; **the police have got the killer** die Polizei hat den Mörder gefasst - **7.** [cause to be done]: **to get sthg done** etw machen lassen; **can I get my car repaired here?** kann ich mein Auto hier reparieren lassen? - **8.** [cause to become]: **she got the children ready for school** sie machte die Kinder für die Schule fertig; **I can't get the car started** ich kriege das Auto nicht an; **to get lunch** das Mittagessen zubereiten - **9.** [ask, tell]: **to get sb to do sthg** jn bitten, etw zu tun - **10.** [move]: **I can't get it through the door** ich bekomme es nicht durch die Tür - **11.** [understand] verstehen; **I don't get it** das verstehe ich nicht - **12.** [time, chance] haben; **we didn't get the chance to see everything** wir hatten nicht die Gelegenheit, uns alles anzuschauen; **I haven't got (the) time** ich habe keine Zeit - **13.** [idea, feeling] haben; **I get a lot of enjoyment from it** ich habe viel Spaß daran - **14.** [answer - phone]: **could you get the phone?** könntest du ans Telefon gehen? - **15.** *phr*: **we get a lot of German tourists here** zu uns kommen viele deutsche Touristen; **we get a lot of rain here in winter** hier regnet es viel im Winter. <> *vi* - **1.** [become] werden; **it's getting late** es wird spät; **to get lost** sich verirren; **get lost!** *inf* hau ab!; **to get ready** sich fertig machen - **2.** [into particular state, position]: **to get into trouble** in Schwierigkeiten geraten; **how do you get to the river from here?** wie kommt man von hier zum Fluss?; **to get dressed** sich anziehen; **to get married** heiraten - **3.** [arrive] ankommen; **when does the train get here?** wann kommt der Zug hier an? - **4.** [eventually succeed]: **I finally got to meet him last week** letzte Woche habe ich ihn endlich getroffen; **she got to like the class** allmählich gefiel ihr ihr Kurs; **to get to know sb** jn kennen lernen - **5.** [progress]: **how far have you got?** wie weit bist du gekommen?; **we're getting nowhere** so kommen wir nicht weiter. <> *aux vb* werden; **to get delayed** aufgehalten werden; **to get killed** getötet werden; **to get excited** aufgeregt werden; **let's get going** OR **moving !** also los! ◆ **get about** *vi* - **1.** [move from place to place] herumlkommen; **he gets about a lot** er kommt viel herum - **2.** [news, rumour] sich verbreiten. ◆ **get along** *vi* - **1.** [manage]: **to get along (without sb/sthg)** (ohne jn/etw) zurechtlkommen - 2. [progress]: **how are you getting along?** wie kommst du voran? - 3. [in relationship]: **to get along (with sb)** (mit jm) auslkommen - 4. [leave] gehen; **I must be getting along** ich muss jetzt gehen. ◆ **get around, get round** ⟨⟩ vt insep [problem] umlgehen. ⟨⟩ vi - 1. [move from place to place] herumlkommen - 2. [circulate - news] sich verbreiten - 3. [eventually do]: **to get around to sthg/to doing sthg** dazu kommen, etw zu tun. ◆ **get at** vt insep - 1. [reach] heranlkommen an (+ A); [truth] herauslbekommen - 2. [imply]: **what are you getting at?** worauf willst du hinaus? - 3. inf [nag]: **stop getting at me!** nörgel nicht dauernd an mir rum! ◆ **get away** ⟨⟩ vt sep: **get him away from here** bring ihn von hier weg. ⟨⟩ vi - 1. [leave] weglkommen; **I need to get away by five** ich muss um fünf Uhr gehen OR weg - 2. [escape] entkommen. ◆ **get away with** vt insep durchlkommen mit. ◆ **get back** ⟨⟩ vt sep - 1. [recover, regain] zurücklbekommen - 2. [take revenge on]: **to get sb back for sthg** jm etw heimlzahlen. ⟨⟩ vi - 1. [return] zurücklkommen - 2. [move away] zurückltreten. ◆ **get back to** vt insep - 1. [return to previous state, activity]: **to get back to sleep** wieder einlschlafen; **to get back to work** zur Arbeit zurücklkehren - 2. [phone back]: **I'll get back to you later** ich rufe Sie später zurück. ◆ **get by** vi [manage, survive] zurechtlkommen; **to get by on sthg** mit etw auslkommen. ◆ **get down** vt sep - 1. [depress] deprimieren; **don't let it get you down** lass dich davon nicht unterkriegen - 2. [fetch from higher level] herunterlholen - 3. [write] auflschreiben. ◆ **get down to** vt insep: **to get down to doing sthg** sich daran machen, etw zu tun; **to get down to sthg** sich an etw (A) machen. ◆ **get in** vi - 1. [arrive] anlkommen - 2. [into car, bus] einlsteigen. ◆ **get into** vt insep - 1. [car] einlsteigen in (+ A) - 2. [become involved in] geraten in (+ A); **to get into an argument with sb** mit jm in Streit geraten - 3. [enter into a particular situation, state] geraten in (+ A); **to get into a panic** in Panik geraten; **to get into trouble** in Schwierigkeiten geraten. ◆ **get off** ⟨⟩ vt sep [remove - clothes, shoes] auslziehen; [- stain] herauslbekommen; [- lid] ablbekommen; **to get sb/sthg off one's hands** jn/etw loslwerden. ⟨⟩ vt insep [bus, train] auslsteigen aus; [bicycle] ablsteigen von. ⟨⟩ vi - 1. [from train, bus] auslsteigen; [from bicycle] ablsteigen - 2. [leave] loslgehen; [in car] loslfahren - 3. [escape punishment] davonlkommen. ◆ **get on** ⟨⟩ vt insep [bus, train] einlsteigen in (+ A); [bicycle] steigen auf (+ A). ⟨⟩ vi - 1. [on train, bus] einlsteigen; [on bicycle] auflsteigen - 2. [in relationship] sich verstehen; **how do you get on with his family?** wie kommst du mit seiner Familie aus? - 3. [progress]: **how are you getting on?** wie kommst du voran? - 4. [proceed]:

to get on (with sthg) (mit etw) weiterlmachen - 5. [have success] Erfolg haben. ◆ **get out** ⟨⟩ vt sep - 1. [take out] herauslnehmen - 2. [remove]: **how do you get wine stains out?** wie bekommst man Weinflecken heraus? ⟨⟩ vi - 1. [from car, bus] auslsteigen - 2. [become known - news] herauslkommen. ◆ **get out of** vt insep - 1. [car, bus, train] auslsteigen aus - 2. [escape from] herauslkommen aus; **to get out of a difficult situation** sich aus einer schwierigen Lage befreien - 3. [avoid]: **to get out of sthg** um etw herumlkommen; **to get out of doing sthg** darum herumlkommen, etw zu tun. ◆ **get over** ⟨⟩ vt insep - 1. [recover from] hinweglkommen über (+ A) - 2. [overcome] überwinden. ⟨⟩ vt sep [communicate] verständlich machen. ◆ **get round** vt insep & vi = **get around**. ◆ **get through** ⟨⟩ vt insep - 1. [work, task] erledigen - 2. [exam] bestehen - 3. [food, drink] verbrauchen - 4. [survive] überstehen. ⟨⟩ vi - 1. [on phone] durchlkommen; **I couldn't get through to her** ich konnte sie nicht erreichen - 2. [make oneself understood]: **I can't get through to her** ich konnte es ihr nicht verständlich machen. ◆ **get to** vt insep inf [annoy] auf die Nerven gehen; **don't let him get to you** lass dich von ihm nicht ärgern. ◆ **get together** ⟨⟩ vt sep - 1. [organize - team, report] zusammenlstellen; [- demonstration] organisieren - 2. [gather - people] zusammenlbringen; [- belongings] zusammenlpacken. ⟨⟩ vi zusammenlkommen. ◆ **get up** ⟨⟩ vi auflstehen. ⟨⟩ vt insep - 1. [organize - petition etc] organisieren - 2. [gather]: **to get up speed** in Fahrt kommen. ◆ **get up to** vt insep inf anlstellen; **I wonder what they're getting up to** ich frage mich, was die da treiben.

get-together n inf Zusammenkunft die.

ghastly ['gɑːstlɪ] adj - 1. inf [very bad, unpleasant] scheußlich, grässlich - 2. [horrifying, macabre] schrecklich, schauerlich.

gherkin ['gɜːkɪn] n Gewürzgurke die.

ghetto ['getəʊ] (pl -s OR -es) n Getto das.

ghetto blaster [-ˌblɑːstə] n inf Gettoblaster der.

ghost [gəʊst] n Geist der, Gespenst das.

giant ['dʒaɪənt] ⟨⟩ adj riesig. ⟨⟩ n [very tall man] Riese der.

gibberish ['dʒɪbərɪʃ] n [meaningless] Unsinn der, Quatsch der; [hard to understand] Kauderwelsch das.

gibe [dʒaɪb] n Seitenhieb der.

Gibraltar [dʒɪˈbrɔːltə] n Gibraltar nt.

giddy ['gɪdɪ] adj [dizzy] schwindelig.

gift [gɪft] n - 1. [present] Geschenk das - 2. [talent] Talent das, Begabung die; **to have a gift for sthg** ein Talent OR eine Begabung für etw haben; **to have a gift for doing sthg** ein Talent OR eine Begabung haben, etw zu tun; **the gift of the gab** die Überzeugungsgabe.

gift certificate n US = **gift token**.

gifted ['gɪftɪd] adj talentiert, begabt.

gift token, gift voucher UK, **gift certificate** US n Geschenkgutschein der.

gift wrap n Geschenkpapier das.

gig [gɪg] n inf Gig der, Konzert das.

gigabyte [ˈgɪgəˈbaɪt] n Gigabyte das.

gigantic [dʒaɪˈgæntɪk] adj gigantisch.

giggle [ˈgɪgl] vi [laugh] kichern.

gilded [ˈgɪldɪd] adj = **gilt**.

gills [gɪlz] npl Kiemen Pl.

gilt [gɪlt] ◇ adj vergoldet. ◇ n [gold layer] Vergoldung die.

gimmick [ˈgɪmɪk] n pej Spielerei die.

gin [dʒɪn] n Gin der; **gin and tonic** Gin Tonic der.

ginger [ˈdʒɪndʒər] ◇ adj UK [colour - hair] rotblond; [- cat] rötlichbraun. ◇ n Ingwer der.

ginger ale n Ginger Ale das.

ginger beer n Ingwerbier das.

gingerbread [ˈdʒɪndʒəbred] n (U) [biscuit] Pfefferkuchen mit Ingwergeschmack.

gingerly [ˈdʒɪndʒəlɪ] adv vorsichtig.

gipsy [ˈdʒɪpsɪ] ◇ adj Zigeuner-. ◇ n Zigeuner der, -in die.

giraffe [dʒɪˈrɑːf] (pl inv OR -s) n Giraffe die.

girder [ˈgɜːdər] n Träger der.

girdle [ˈgɜːdl] n [corset] Mieder das.

girl [gɜːl] n Mädchen das; [daughter] Tochter die, Mädchen das.

girlfriend [ˈgɜːlfrend] n Freundin die.

girl guide UK, **girl scout** US n Pfadfinderin die.

giro [ˈdʒaɪrəʊ] (pl -s) n UK [system] Giro das; **giro (cheque)** Giroscheck für Sozialhilfeempfänger.

gist [dʒɪst] n Wesentliche das; **to get the gist (of sthg)** das Wesentliche (einer Sache (G)) mitbekommen.

give [gɪv] (pt gave, pp given) ◇ vt - 1. [gen] geben; **to give sb sthg** jm etw geben; **to give sb a push/kiss** jm einen Schubs/Kuss geben; **to give sb a look/smile** in anlsehen/anllächeln; **to give a cry** auflschreien - 2. [as present]: **to give sb sthg** jm etw schenken; [as donation] jm etw spenden - 3. [speech] halten - 4. [attention, time]: **he gives the issue a lot of attention** er widmet der Sache viel Aufmerksamkeit - 5. [communicate] geben; **when will you give me your decision?** wann werden Sie mir Ihre Entscheidung mitteilen?; **give her my regards** grüß sie schön von mir - 6. [produce] machen; **to give sb a surprise** jm eine Überraschung bereiten; **to give sb pleasure/trouble** jm Freude/Probleme bereiten OR machen; **to give sb a fright** jn erschrecken; **what gave you that idea?** wie bist du auf diese Idee gekom-

men? ◇ vi [yield] nachlgeben. ◇ n [elasticity] Nachgiebigkeit die. ◆ **give or take** prep: **5,000 people, give or take a few hundred** schätzungsweise 5000 Leute. ◆ **give away** vt sep - 1. [hand over] weglgeben - 2. [reveal] verraten; **to give the game away** alles verraten. ◆ **give back** vt sep zurücklgeben. ◆ **give in** vi - 1. [agree unwillingly] nachlgeben; **to give in to sb/sthg** jm/etw nachlgeben - 2. [admit defeat] sich geschlagen geben. ◆ **give off** vt insep ablgeben. ◆ **give out** ◇ vt sep [distribute] auslteilen. ◇ vi [fail - legs, machine] versagen; [- strength, supply] zu Ende gehen. ◆ **give up** ◇ vt sep - 1. [stop, abandon] auflgeben; **to give up doing sthg** auflhören, etw zu tun - 2. [surrender]: **to give o.s. up (to sb)** sich (jm) ergeben. ◇ vi [admit defeat] auflgeben.

given [ˈgɪvn] ◇ adj - 1. [fixed] bestimmt - 2. [prone]: **to be given to sthg** zu etw neigen; **to be given to doing sthg** die Angewohnheit haben, etw zu tun. ◇ prep [taking into account] angesichts (+ G); **given that...** angesichts der Tatsache, dass...

given name n US Vorname der.

glacier [ˈglæsjər] n Gletscher der.

glad [glæd] adj - 1. [happy] froh; **to be glad about sthg** sich über etw (A) freuen - 2. [grateful]: **to be glad of sthg** dankbar für etw sein.

gladly [ˈglædlɪ] adv [willingly, eagerly] gern(e).

glamor n US = **glamour**.

glamorous [ˈglæmərəs] adj [film star, lifestyle] glamourös; [job] Traum-.

glamour UK, **glamor** US [ˈglæmər] n [of film star, lifestyle] Glamour der; [of job] Reiz der.

glance [glɑːns] ◇ n Blick der; **at a glance** auf einen Blick; **at first glance** auf den ersten Blick. ◇ vi: **to glance at sb** jn kurz anlsehen; **to glance at sthg** einen Blick auf etw (A) werfen. ◆ **glance off** vt insep [subj: ball, bullet] ablprallen an (+ D); [subj: light] reflektiert werden von.

gland [glænd] n Drüse die.

glandular fever [ˌglændjʊlər-] n Drüsenfieber das.

glare [gleər] ◇ n - 1. [scowl] langer wütender Blick - 2. (U) [of light, sun] greller Schein; **the glare of publicity** das Rampenlicht der Öffentlichkeit. ◇ vi - 1. [scowl] böse blicken; **to glare at sb/sthg** jn/etw böse anlstarren - 2. [light, sun] grell scheinen.

glaring [ˈgleərɪŋ] adj - 1. [error, example] eklatant - 2. [light, sun] grell.

glass [glɑːs] ◇ n - 1. [gen] Glas das; **a glass of wine** ein Glas Wein - 2. (U) [glassware] Glaswaren Pl. ◇ comp Glas-. ◆ **glasses** npl [spectacles] Brille die; [binoculars] Fernglas das; **a pair of glasses** eine Brille.

glaze [gleɪz] ◇ n Glasur die. ◇ vt [pottery & CULIN] glasieren.

glazier ['gleɪzjə'] *n* Glaser *der*, -in *die*.

gleam [gli:m] ⟨⟩ *n* [of surface] Schimmer *der*; [of light, sunset] Schein *der*. ⟨⟩ *vi* [surface, object] schimmern; [gold, brass] glänzen; [light] scheinen; [eyes] funkeln.

gleaming ['gli:mɪŋ] *adj* [surface, object] schimmernd; [gold, brass] glänzend; [light] scheinend; [eyes] funkelnd.

glean [gli:n] *vt* [gather] zusammenⅼtragen.

glee [gli:] *n* [joy] Freude *die*; [gloating] Schadenfreude *die*.

glen [glen] *n Ireland & Scotland* enges Tal.

glib [glɪb] *adj pej* - 1. [answer, excuse] leichthin gesagt - 2. [person] aalglatt.

glide [glaɪd] *vi* - 1. [move smoothly - boat] gleiten; [- dancer] schweben - 2. [fly] schweben.

glider ['glaɪdə'] *n* Segelflugzeug *das*.

gliding ['glaɪdɪŋ] *n* Segelfliegen *das*.

glimmer ['glɪmə'] *n* - 1. [faint light] schwacher Schein - 2. *fig*: **she didn't show a glimmer of interest/understanding** sie zeigte nicht die leiseste Spur von Interesse/Verständnis.

glimpse [glɪmps] ⟨⟩ *n* [look] flüchtiger Blick. ⟨⟩ *vt* - 1. [catch sight of] flüchtig OR kurz sehen - 2. [perceive]: **to glimpse sb's true feelings** einen Eindruck von js wahren Gefühlen bekommen.

glint [glɪnt] ⟨⟩ *n* - 1. [of metal, sunlight] Glitzern *das* - 2. [in eyes]: **there was a glint of anger in his eyes** seine Augen funkelten böse. ⟨⟩ *vi* - 1. [metal, sunlight] glitzern - 2. [eyes] funkeln.

glisten ['glɪsn] *vi* [gold, lips] glänzen; [lake, raindrops] glitzern.

glitter ['glɪtə'] ⟨⟩ *n* - 1. [of object, light] Glitzern *das* - 2. [decoration, make-up] Glitzerstaub *der*. ⟨⟩ *vi* glitzern; [diamonds, stars] funkeln.

gloat [gləʊt] *vi*: **to gloat (over sthg)** [over sb's misfortune] sich hämisch (über etw *(A)*) freuen; [over one's own success] sich selbstzufrieden (über etw *(A)*) freuen.

global ['gləʊbl] *adj* global; [economy, peace] Welt-.

global warming [-'wɔ:mɪŋ] *n* Erwärmung *die* der Erdatmosphäre.

globe [gləʊb] *n* - 1. [Earth]: **the globe** die Erde - 2. [sphere representing world] Globus *der*.

gloom [glu:m] *n* - 1. [darkness] Düsterkeit *die* - 2. [unhappiness] Trübsinn *der*.

gloomy ['glu:mɪ] *adj* - 1. [place, landscape, weather] düster - 2. [person, atmosphere] trübsinnig - 3. [outlook] düster; [news] bedrückend.

glorious ['glɔ:rɪəs] *adj* - 1. [illustrious] glorreich - 2. [wonderful] herrlich.

glory ['glɔ:rɪ] *n* - 1. [fame, honour] Ruhm *der* - 2. [splendour] Herrlichkeit *die*.

gloss [glɒs] *n* - 1. [shine] Glanz *der* - 2.: **gloss (paint)** Lackfarbe *die*. ◆ **gloss over** *vt insep* [treat briefly] nur ganz kurz erwähnen; [hide] unter den Teppich kehren.

glossary ['glɒsərɪ] *n* Glossar *das*.

glossy ['glɒsɪ] *adj* glänzend; [photo, paper] Glanz-.

glove [glʌv] *n* Handschuh *der*; **to fit like a glove** [garment] wie angegossen passen.

glove compartment *n* Handschuhfach *das*.

glow [gləʊ] ⟨⟩ *n* [of fire, light, sunset] Schein *der*. ⟨⟩ *vi* [light] scheinen; [fire, sky] glühen.

glower ['glaʊə'] *vi* wütend dreinⅼblicken; **to glower at sb/sthg** jn/etw wütend anⅼblicken.

glucose ['glu:kəʊs] *n* Glukose *die*.

glue [glu:] (*cont* glueing OR gluing) ⟨⟩ *n* Klebstoff *der*. ⟨⟩ *vt* kleben; **to glue sthg to sthg** etw an etw *(A)* kleben.

glum [glʌm] *adj* trübsinnig.

glut [glʌt] *n*: **glut (of sthg)** Überangebot *das* (an etw *(D)*).

glutton ['glʌtn] *n* Vielfraß *der*; **to be a glutton for punishment** ein Masochist sein.

GM *adj abbr of* **genetically modified**.

GMO (*abbr of* **genetically modified organism**) *n* GVO *der*.

gnarled [nɑ:ld] *adj* knorrig.

gnat [næt] *n* Mücke *die*.

gnaw [nɔ:] *vt* nagen an (+ *D*); [fingernails] kauen an (+ *D*); **to gnaw a hole in sthg** ein Loch in etw *(A)* nagen.

gnome [nəʊm] *n* Gnom *der*; [in garden] Gartenzwerg *der*.

GNP (*abbr of* **gross national product**) *n* BSP *das*.

go [gəʊ] (*pt* went, *pp* gone, *pl* goes) ⟨⟩ *vi* - 1. [move] gehen; [by vehicle, travel] fahren; [by plane] fliegen; **to go shopping/for a walk** einkaufen/spazieren gehen; **I'll go and collect the cases** ich gehe die Koffer abholen; **to go home/to school** nach Hause/in die Schule gehen; **to go to Austria** nach Österreich fahren; **to go by bus** mit dem Bus fahren; **to go by plane** fliegen; **to go to work** zur Arbeit gehen - 2. [leave] gehen; [in vehicle] fahren; **it's time we went** es wird Zeit, dass wir gehen; **let's go!** gehen wir!; **when does the bus go?** wann fährt der Bus ab?; **go away!** geh weg! - 3. [lead]: **where does this path go?** wohin führt dieser Weg? - 4. [time] vergehen - 5. [progress - negotiations, preparations, business] laufen; **how are your studies going?** wie läuft es mit deinem Studium?; **how did the party go?** wie war die Party?; **to go well** gut gehen; **how's it going?** wie gehts? - 6. [become] werden; **she went pale** sie wurde bleich; **to go bankrupt** Bankrott machen - 7. [be]: **our cries went unheard** unsere Rufe blieben ungehört;

to go hungry hungern - **8.** [expressing future tense]: **to be going to do sthg** etw tun werden; **it's going to rain tomorrow** morgen wird es regnen; **we're going to go to Switzerland** wir fahren in die Schweiz; **she's going to have a baby** sie bekommt ein Baby - **9.** [function - gen] laufen; [- watch, clock] gehen - **10.** [become damaged] kaputtgehen; **the fuse has gone** die Sicherung ist herausgesprungen - **11.** [bell, alarm] losgehen; **the bell went es klingelte** - **12.** [match] zusammenpassen; **to go with** passen zu; **red wine doesn't go with fish** Rotwein passt nicht zu Fisch - **13.** [fit] passen, gehen; **it won't go into my case** es passt OR passt nicht in meinen Koffer - **14.** [belong] kommen; **the plates go in the cupboard** die Teller kommen in den Schrank - **15.** [in division] gehen; **three into two won't go** zwei durch drei geht nicht - **16.** inf [with negative - giving advice]: **now, don't go catching cold** erkälte dich bloß nicht - **17.** inf [expressing irritation]: **he's gone and broken my computer!** er hat doch tatsächlich meinen Computer kaputtgemacht!; **now what's he gone and done?** was hat er jetzt wieder gemacht?; **you've gone and done it now!** jetzt hast du es geschafft! ◇ **n** - **1.** [turn]: **it's your go** du bist dran - **2.** inf [attempt] Versuch der; **to have a go at sthg** etw versuchen; **to have a go on sthg** etw ausprobieren; **'50p a go'** 'jede Runde 50 Pence' - **3.** phr: **to have a go at sb** inf [criticize] jn zur Schnecke machen. ◆ **to go** adv [remaining]: **how long is there to go until Christmas?** wie lange ist es noch bis Weihnachten? ◆ **go about** ◇ **vt insep** [perform]: **to go about one's business** seinen Geschäften nachgehen. ◇ **vi** ◆ **go around**. ◆ **go ahead** vi - **1.**: **to go ahead (with sthg)** (mit etw) anfangen OR beginnen; **go ahead!** bitte! - **2.** [take place] stattfinden. ◆ **go along** vi: **he was making it up as he went along** er sagte einfach, was ihm gerade in den Sinn kam. ◆ **go along with** vt insep [idea, plan] zustimmen (+ D). ◆ **go around** vi - **1.** [associate]: **to go around with sb** mit jm herumziehen - **2.** [joke, illness, story] herumgehen; [rumour] umgehen. ◆ **go away** vi weggehen; [by vehicle] wegfahren; **go away!** geh weg! ◆ **go back** vi - **1.** [return] zurückgehen; [by vehicle] zurückfahren - **2.** [to activity]: **to go back to work** [after interruption] die Arbeit wieder aufnehmen; [after holiday] wieder arbeiten gehen; **to go back to sleep** wieder einlschlafen - **3.** [date from]: **their friendship goes back to 1955** sie sind schon seit 1955 befreundet. ◆ **go back on** vt insep: **to go back on one's word** sein Wort nicht halten. ◆ **go by** ◇ **vi** [time] vergehen. ◇ **vt insep** - **1.** [be guided by - instincts] folgen (+ D); [- instructions] befolgen - **2.** [judge by - appearances] gehen nach; **going by her accent, I'd say she was French** ihrem Akzent nach ist sie Französin. ◆ **go down** ◇ **vi** - **1.** [decrease - prices, value,

temperature] sinken - **2.** [sun] untergehen - **3.** [tyre] platt werden - **4.** [be accepted]: **to go down well/badly** gut/schlecht ankommen. ◇ **vt insep** [stairs, road] hinuntergehen. ◆ **go for** vt insep - **1.** [choose] wählen; [buy] nehmen - **2.** [be attracted to]: **to go for sb/sthg** jn/etw bevorzugen - **3.** [attack]: **to go for sb** auf jn losgehen - **4.** [try to obtain] aus sein auf (+ A); **just go for it and ask her out!** frag sie einfach, ob sie mit dir ausgehen will! ◆ **go in** vi hineingehen. ◆ **go in for** vt insep - **1.** [enter - competition] mitmachen bei; [- exam] machen - **2.** inf [activity]: **he goes in for sports in a big way** er ist ein großer Sportfan. ◆ **go into** vt insep - **1.** [investigate] sich befassen mit - **2.** [take up as a profession]: **to go into teaching** Lehrer werden. ◆ **go off** ◇ **vi** - **1.** [alarm] losgehen; [bomb] explodieren - **2.** [food] schlecht werden - **3.** [light, heating] ausgehen. ◇ **vt insep** inf [lose interest in] nicht mehr mögen. ◆ **go on** ◇ **vi** - **1.** [happen] los sein; **what's going on next door?** was ist nebenan los? - **2.** [light, heating] angehen - **3.** [continue]: **to go on doing sthg** etw weiter tun - **4.** [pass - time] vergehen - **5.** [talk for too long]: **to go on (and on) about sthg** auf etw (D) herumlreiten; **don't go on about it!** hör doch mal (damit) auf! ◇ **vt insep** [be guided by]: **I've got nothing to go on** ich habe keine Anhaltspunkte. ◆ **go on at** vt insep [nag]: **to go on at sb** an jm herumnörgeln. ◆ **go out** vi - **1.** [light, heating] ausgehen - **2.** [move outside] hinausgehen; **to go out for a meal** essen gehen; **to go out for a walk** einen Spaziergang machen - **3.** [have relationship]: **to go out with sb** mit jm zusammen sein; **we've been going out for six years** wir sind seit sechs Jahren zusammen - **4.** [tide]: **the tide is going out** die Ebbe hat eingesetzt. ◆ **go over** vt insep - **1.** [check] überprüfen - **2.** [repeat]: **to go over sthg again** etw wiederholen. ◆ **go round** vi [revolve] sich drehen; see also **go around**. ◆ **go through** vt insep - **1.** [experience] durchlmachen - **2.** [search] durchsuchen. ◆ **go through with** vt insep: **the government is going through with the plan** die Regierung setzt den Plan in die Tat um; **she couldn't go through with it** sie brachte es nicht fertig. ◆ **go towards** vt insep [contribute to] bestimmt sein für. ◆ **go under** vi liter & fig untergehen. ◆ **go up** ◇ **vi** - **1.** [increase] steigen - **2.** [move upwards - balloon] auflsteigen; [- person] auflsteigen. ◇ **vt insep** [stairs, hill] hinauflsteigen. ◆ **go without** vt insep: **to go without sthg** ohne etw auslkommen.

goad [gəʊd] vt [provoke] provozieren.

go-ahead ◇ **adj** fortschrittlich. ◇ **n** Erlaubnis die.

goal [gəʊl] n - **1.** SPORT Tor das; **to score a goal** ein Tor erzielen - **2.** [aim] Ziel das.

goalkeeper ['gəʊl,ki:pər] n Torwart der.

goalpost ['gəʊlpəʊst] *n* Torpfosten der.

goat [gəʊt] *n* Ziege die.

goat's cheese *n* Ziegenkäse der.

gob [gɒb] *n UK inf* [mouth] Maul das.

gobble ['gɒbl] *vt* hinunter‖schlingen.

go-between *n* Vermittler der, -in die.

gobsmacked ['gɒbsmækt] *adj UK inf* platt.

go-cart *n* = **go-kart**.

god [gɒd] *n* Gott der. ⊳ **God** ⊳ *n* Gott der; God knows keine Ahnung; for God's sake! um Gottes willen!; thank God! Gott sei Dank! ⊳ *excl:* (my) God! (mein) Gott!

godchild ['gɒdtʃaɪld] (*pl* -children [-,tʃɪl-drən]) *n* Patenkind das.

goddaughter ['gɒd,dɔːtər] *n* Patentochter die.

goddess ['gɒdɪs] *n* Göttin die.

godfather ['gɒd,fɑːðər] *n* Pate der.

godforsaken ['gɒdfə,seɪkn] *adj* gottverlassen.

godmother ['gɒd,mʌðər] *n* Patin die.

godsend ['gɒdsend] *n* Geschenk das des Himmels.

godson ['gɒdsʌn] *n* Patensohn der.

goes [gəʊz] *vb* ⊳ **go**.

goggles ['gɒglz] *npl* [in industry] Schutzbrille die; [for diving] Taucherbrille die; [for skiing] Skibrille die.

going ['gəʊɪŋ] ⊳ *adj* - 1. [rate, salary] üblich - 2. UK [available]: any jobs going? gibt es freie Stellen? ⊳ *n* - 1. [progress]: have you finished already? – that's good going bist du schon fertig? – du bist gut OR schnell vorangekommen; it was slow going es ging nur langsam voran - 2. [in horse racing] Geläuf das; the going is good die Bahn ist gut; this novel is heavy going dieser Roman liest sich schwer.

go-kart [-kɑːt] *n UK* Go-Kart der.

gold [gəʊld] ⊳ *adj* [gold-coloured] golden. ⊳ *n* [gen] Gold das. ⊳ *comp* [made of gold] Gold-.

golden ['gəʊldən] *adj* - 1. [made of gold] Gold- - 2. [gold-coloured] golden.

goldfish ['gəʊldfɪʃ] (*pl inv*) *n* Goldfisch der.

gold leaf *n* Blattgold das.

gold medal *n* Goldmedaille die.

goldmine ['gəʊldmaɪn] *n* - 1. [mine] Goldmine die - 2. [profitable business] Goldgrube die.

gold-plated [-'pleɪtɪd] *adj* vergoldet.

goldsmith ['gəʊldsmɪθ] *n* Goldschmied der, -in die.

golf [gɒlf] *n* Golf das.

golf ball *n* [for golf] Golfball der.

golf club *n* - 1. [place, society] Golfklub der - 2. [equipment] Golfschläger der.

golf course *n* Golfplatz der.

golfer ['gɒlfər] *n* Golfspieler der, -in die.

gone [gɒn] ⊳ *pp* ⊳ **go**. ⊳ *adj* [no longer here] weg. ⊳ *prep* [past] nach; it's gone twelve (o'clock) es ist zwölf Uhr vorbei.

gong [gɒŋ] *n* Gong der.

good [gʊd] (*comp* better, *superl* best) ⊳ *adj* - 1. [gen] gut; it's good to see you again schön, Sie wieder zu sehen; to have a good time sich gut amüsieren; to feel good sich wohl fühlen; it tastes/smells good es schmeckt/riecht gut; is this meat still good? kann man das Fleisch noch essen?; it's good for you [beneficial] das wird dir gut tun; [food] das ist gesund; a good opportunity eine günstige Gelegenheit; to be good at sthg etw gut können; good at French gut in Französisch; she's good with her hands sie ist geschickt mit den Händen - 2. [suitable] geeignet; he would make a good president er eignet sich zum Präsidenten - 3. [kind] lieb; that's very good of you das ist sehr nett von Ihnen; to be good to sb gut zu jm sein; would you be good enough to open the door? wären Sie so liebenswürdig, mir die Tür zu öffnen? - 4. [well-behaved] artig, brav; be good! sei brav! - 5. [thorough] gründlich - 6. [considerable]: a good while/deal ziemlich lange/viel; a good ten minutes gute zehn Minuten. ⊳ *n* - 1. [moral correctness] Gute das; to be up to no good nichts Gutes im Schilde führen - 2. [use]: it's no good [there's no point] es hat keinen Zweck - 3. [benefit]: it will do him good es wird ihm gut tun. ⊳ **goods** *npl* Waren Pl. ⊳ **as good as** *adv* so gut wie; as good as new so gut wie neu. ⊳ **for good** *adv* für immer. ⊳ **good afternoon** *excl* guten Tag! ⊳ **good evening** *excl* guten Abend! ⊳ **good morning** *excl* guten Morgen! ⊳ **good night** *excl* gute Nacht!

goodbye [,gʊd'baɪ] ⊳ *excl* auf Wiedersehen!; [on phone] auf Wiederhören! ⊳ *n*: to say goodbye auf Wiedersehen sagen; to wave goodbye zum Abschied winken.

good deed *n* gute Tat.

good fortune *n* Glück das.

Good Friday *n* Karfreitag der.

good-humoured [-'hjuːməd] *adj* [person - temporarily] gut gelaunt; [- by nature] gutmütig; [rivalry] freundschaftlich.

good-looking [-'lʊkɪŋ] *adj* gut aussehend.

good-natured [-'neɪtʃəd] *adj* [person] gutmütig; [rivalry] freundschaftlich; [argument] friedlich.

goodness ['gʊdnɪs] ⊳ *n* - 1. [kindness] Güte die - 2. [of food] Nährgehalt der. ⊳ *excl:* (my) goodness! meine Güte!; for goodness' sake! um Himmels willen!; thank goodness! Gott sei Dank!

goods train *n UK* Güterzug der.

goodwill [,gʊd'wɪl] *n* (U) guter Wille; [between countries & COMM] Goodwill der.

goody ['gʊdɪ] <> n inf [in story] Gute der, Gute die. <> excl toll!, prima! **goodies** npl inf - **1.** [delicious food] Leckerbissen Pl - **2.** [desirable objects] schöne Dinge Pl.

goose [guːs] (pl geese) n Gans die.

gooseberry ['gʊzbərɪ] n Stachelbeere die.

goosebumps US ['guːsbʌmps] npl = **gooseflesh**.

gooseflesh ['guːsfleʃ] n Gänsehaut die.

goose pimples UK, **goosebumps** US ['guːsbʌmps] npl = **gooseflesh**.

gore [gɔːr] <> n (U) liter [blood] Blut das. <> vt [subj: bull] mit den Hörnern verletzen.

gorge [gɔːdʒ] <> n Schlucht die. <> vt: to gorge o.s. on OR with sthg sich mit etw voll stopfen.

gorgeous ['gɔːdʒəs] adj - **1.** [place, present, weather] herrlich, wunderschön - **2.** inf [person] toll aussehend; **to be gorgeous** toll auslsehen.

gorilla [gə'rɪlə] n Gorilla der.

gormless ['gɔːmlɪs] adj UK inf dämlich.

gory ['gɔːrɪ] adj [story, film] blutrünstig.

gosh [gɒʃ] excl inf mein Gott!, Mensch!

go-slow n UK Bummelstreik der.

gospel ['gɒspl] n [doctrine] Lehre die. **Gospel** n [in Bible] Evangelium das.

gossip ['gɒsɪp] <> n - **1.** [conversation] Klatsch der; **to have a gossip** klatschen - **2.** [person] Klatschbase die. <> vi klatschen.

gossip column n Klatschspalte die.

got [gɒt] pt & pp ⊳ **get**.

gotten ['gɒtn] pp US ⊳ **get**.

goulash ['guːlæʃ] n Gulasch das.

gourmet ['gʊəmeɪ] n Feinschmecker der, -in die.

gout [gaʊt] n Gicht die.

govern ['gʌvn] <> vt - **1.** POL regieren - **2.** [determine] bestimmen. <> vi POL regieren.

governess ['gʌvənɪs] n Gouvernante die.

government ['gʌvnmənt] n Regierung die.

governor ['gʌvənər] n - **1.** POL Gouverneur der, -in die - **2.** [of school] Mitglied das des Schulbeirats; [of bank] Mitglied das des Direktoriums - **3.** [of prison] Direktor der, -in die.

gown [gaʊn] n - **1.** [dress] Kleid das; [evening gown] Abendkleid das - **2.** UNIV & LAW Talar der - **3.** MED Kittel der.

GP n abbr of **general practitioner**.

grab [græb] <> vt - **1.** [with hands]: **to grab (hold of)** [person] packen; [object] schnappen; **to grab (hold of) sb's arm** jn am Arm packen - **2.** fig [opportunity] (beim Schopf) ergreifen; [sandwich, lunch] schnell essen - **3.** inf [appeal to]: **how does that grab you?** wie findest du das? <> vi: **to grab at sthg** [with hands] nach etw greifen.

grace [greɪs] <> n - **1.** (U) [elegance] Grazie die, Anmut die - **2.** [extra time]: **ten days' grace** zehn Tage Aufschub - **3.** [prayer] Tischgebet das. <> vt [adorn] schmücken.

graceful ['greɪsfʊl] adj [beautiful] graziös, anmutig; [line, curve] gefällig.

gracious ['greɪʃəs] <> adj [polite] höflich. <> excl: **(good) gracious!** ach du meine Güte!

grade [greɪd] <> n - **1.** [quality] Güteklasse die; **high-grade** hochwertig - **2.** [in company, organization]: **(salary) grade** Gehaltsstufe die - **3.** US [class] Klasse die - **4.** [in exam, test] Note die - **5.** US [gradient] Gefälle das. <> vt - **1.** [classify] klassifizieren - **2.** [test, exam] benoten.

grade crossing n US Bahnübergang der.

grade school n US Grundschule die.

gradient ['greɪdjənt] n [of road - upward] Steigung die; [- downward] Gefälle das.

gradual ['grædʒʊəl] adj allmählich.

gradually ['grædʒʊəlɪ] adv allmählich.

graduate <> n ['grædʒʊət] - **1.** [person with a degree] Graduierte der, die - **2.** US [of high school] ≃ Abiturient der (mit bestandenem Abitur). <> vi ['grædʒʊeɪt] - **1.** [with a degree]: **to graduate (from)** seinen Hochschulabschluss machen (an (+ D)) - **2.** US [from high school]: **to graduate (from)** ≃ das Abitur machen (an (+ D)).

graduation [,grædʒʊ'eɪʃn] n [university or school ceremony] Abschlussfeier die.

graffiti [grə'fiːtɪ] n (U) Graffiti Pl.

graft [grɑːft] <> n - **1.** [from plant] Pfropfreis das - **2.** MED Transplantat das - **3.** UK inf [hard work] Plackerei die - **4.** US inf [corruption] Schiebung die. <> vt - **1.** [to graft sthg (onto)** etw pfropfen (auf (+ A)) - **2.** MED: **to graft sthg (onto)** etw transplantieren (in (+ A)).

grain [greɪn] n - **1.** [of corn, rice, salt, sand] Korn das - **2.** (U) [crops] Getreide das, Korn das - **3.** [in wood] Maserung die.

gram [græm] n Gramm das.

grammar ['græmər] n Grammatik die.

grammar school n - **1.** [in UK] ≃ Gymnasium das - **2.** [in US] ≃ Grundschule die.

grammatical [grə'mætɪkl] adj grammatisch; **it's not grammatical** es ist nicht grammatikalisch richtig.

gramme [græm] n UK = **gram**.

gramophone ['græməfəʊn] n dated Grammofon das.

gran [græn] n UK inf Oma die, Omi die.

grand [grænd] (pl inv) <> adj [house, style] prachtvoll; [design, plan] ehrgeizig; [person, job] bedeutend. <> n inf [thousand pounds] tausend Pfund Pl; [thousand dollars] tausend Dollar Pl.

grandad ['grændæd] n inf Opa der, Opi der.

grandchild ['græntʃaɪld] (*pl* -children [-,tʃɪl-drən]) *n* Enkelkind *das*.

granddad ['grændæd] *n inf* = **grandad**.

granddaughter ['græn,dɔ:tər] *n* Enkelin *die*.

grandeur ['grændʒər] *n* [of building] Pracht *die*; [of scenery] Herrlichkeit *die*.

grandfather ['grænd,fɑ:ðər] *n* Großvater *der*.

grandma ['grænmɑ:] *n inf* Oma *die*, Omi *die*.

grandmother ['græn,mʌðər] *n* Großmutter *die*.

grandpa ['grænpɑ:] *n inf* Opa *der*, Opi *der*.

grandparents ['græn,peərənts] *npl* Großeltern *Pl*.

grand piano *n* Flügel *der*.

grand slam *n* SPORT Grandslam *der*.

grandson ['grænsʌn] *n* Enkel *der*.

grandstand ['grændstænd] *n* (überdachte) Tribüne.

grand total *n* Endsumme *die*.

granite ['grænɪt] *n* Granit *der*.

granny ['grænɪ] *n inf* Oma *die*, Omi *die*.

grant [grɑ:nt] ◇ *n* [money] Zuschuss *der*; [money] [for study] Stipendium *das*. ◇ *vt fml* - **1.** [request, right] gewähren; [appeal] nachlkommen (+ *D*); [wish] erfüllen - **2.** [admit] zulgeben - **3.** *phr*: **to take sthg for granted** etw als selbstverständlich betrachten.

granule ['grænju:l] *n* Körnchen *das*.

grape [greɪp] *n* (Wein)traube *die*.

grapefruit ['greɪpfru:t] (*pl inv OR* -s) *n* Grapefruit *die*, Pampelmuse *die*.

grapevine ['greɪpvaɪn] *n* Weinstock *der*; **we heard on the grapevine that...** *fig* wir haben gehört, dass...

graph [grɑ:f] *n* Diagramm *das*.

graphic ['græfɪk] *adj* - **1.** [vivid] anschaulich - **2.** ART grafisch. ◆ **graphics** *npl* [pictures] grafische Darstellungen *Pl*.

graphic artist *n* Grafiker *der*, -in *die*.

graphite ['græfaɪt] *n* Graphit *das*.

graph paper *n* Millimeterpapier *das*.

grapple ['græpl] ◆ **grapple with** *vt insep* liter & *fig* ringen mit.

grasp [grɑ:sp] ◇ *n* - **1.** [grip] Griff *der* - **2.** [understanding]: **to have a good grasp of sthg** [language] etw gut beherrschen; [situation] etw verstehen. ◇ *vt* - **1.** [with hands] ergreifen - **2.** [understand] begreifen.

grasping ['grɑ:spɪŋ] *adj pej* [greedy] habgierig.

grass [grɑ:s] *n* - **1.** [on ground] Gras *das*; [lawn] Rasen *der* - **2.** *drug sl* [marijuana] Gras *das*.

grasshopper ['grɑ:s,hɒpər] *n* Heuschrecke *die*.

grass roots ◇ *npl* [ordinary people] Basis *die*. ◇ *comp*: **grass roots opinion/support** Meinung/Unterstützung der Basis; **at grass roots level** an der Basis.

grass snake *n* Ringelnatter *die*.

grate [greɪt] ◇ *n* [in fireplace] (Kamin)rost *der*. ◇ *vt* [cheese, carrots] reiben. ◇ *vi* [irritate] auf die Nerven gehen.

grateful ['greɪtful] *adj*: **to be grateful to sb (for sthg)** jm (für etw) dankbar sein.

grater ['greɪtər] *n* Reibe *die*.

gratify ['grætɪfaɪ] *vt* [please]: **to be gratified to hear/discover that...** mit Genugtuung hören/entdecken, dass...

grating ['greɪtɪŋ] ◇ *adj* nervend. ◇ *n* [grille] Gitter *das*.

gratitude ['grætɪtju:d] *n*: **gratitude (to sb)** Dankbarkeit *die* (gegenüber jm).

gratuitous [grə'tju:ɪtəs] *adj fml* unnötig.

grave [greɪv] ◇ *adj* - **1.** [solemn] ernst - **2.** [serious - situation, threat, illness] ernst; [- news] schlimm. ◇ *n* Grab *das*.

gravel ['grævl] *n* Kies *der*.

gravestone ['greɪvstəʊn] *n* Grabstein *der*.

graveyard ['greɪvjɑ:d] *n* Friedhof *der*.

gravity ['grævətɪ] *n* (U) - **1.** [force] Schwerkraft *die* - **2.** *fml* [seriousness] Ernst *der*.

gravy ['greɪvɪ] *n* (U) [meat juice] Bratensaft *der*; [sauce] Soße *die*.

gray *adj* & *n US* = **grey**.

graze [greɪz] ◇ *vt* - **1.** [cattle] grasen OR weiden lassen - **2.** [knee, elbow] auflschürfen - **3.** [touch lightly] streifen. ◇ *vi* [animals] grasen, weiden. ◇ *n* [wound] Schürfwunde *die*.

grease [gri:s] ◇ *n* (U) - **1.** [animal fat] Fett *das* - **2.** [lubricant] Schmiere *die*. ◇ *vt* [engine, machine] schmieren; [baking tray] einlfetten.

greaseproof paper [,gri:spru:f-] *n UK* Pergamentpapier *das*.

greasy ['gri:sɪ] *adj* - **1.** [food, hair, hands] fettig - **2.** [clothes] schmierig.

great [greɪt] ◇ *adj* - **1.** [large] groß; **to a great extent** in hohem Maße; **the great majority** die überwiegende Mehrheit; **a great deal of money** eine Menge OR sehr viel Geld - **2.** [very good] großartig; **we had a great time** wir haben uns toll amüsiert. ◇ *excl*: **(that's) great!** (das ist) toll!

Great Britain *n* Großbritannien *nt*.

greatcoat ['greɪtkəʊt] *n* langer schwerer Mantel.

great-grandchild *n* Urenkel *der*, -in *die*.

great-grandfather *n* Urgroßvater *der*.

great-grandmother *n* Urgroßmutter *die*.

greatly ['greɪtlɪ] *adv* sehr.

greatness ['greɪtnɪs] *n* [importance] Bedeutung *die*; [size] Größe *die*.

Greece [gri:s] *n* Griechenland *nt*.

greed [griːd] *n* - 1. [for food] Gefräßigkeit *die* - 2. *fig* [for money, power] Gier *die*.

greedy ['griːdɪ] *adj* - 1. [for food] gefräßig - 2. *fig*: **greedy for money/power** geld-/machtgierig.

Greek [griːk] <> *adj* griechisch. <> *n* - 1. [person] Grieche *der*, -chin *die* - 2. [language] Griechisch(e) *das*.

green [griːn] <> *adj* grün; **green (with envy)** blass *or* grün (vor Neid). <> *n* - 1. [colour] Grün *das* - 2. [in village]: **(village) green** (Dorf)wiese *die* - 3. GOLF Grün *das*. ◆ **Green** *n* POL Grüne *der*, *die*; **the Greens** die Grünen. ◆ **greens** *npl* [vegetables] Grüngemüse *das*.

greenback ['griːnbæk] *n* US *inf* [banknote] Dollarschein *der*.

green belt *n* UK Grüngürtel *der*.

green card *n* - 1. UK [for insuring vehicle] grüne Versicherungskarte - 2. US [resident's permit] Aufenthaltserlaubnis *die*.

greenfly ['griːnflaɪ] (*pl inv or* -ies) *n* (grüne) Blattlaus.

greengrocer ['griːnˌɡrəʊsər] *n* Obst- und Gemüsehändler *der*, -in *die*; **greengrocer's (shop)** Obst- und Gemüsegeschäft *das*.

greenhouse ['griːnhaʊs] (*pl* [-haʊzɪz]) *n* Gewächshaus *das*, Treibhaus *das*.

greenhouse effect *n*: **the greenhouse effect** der Treibhauseffekt.

Greenland ['griːnlənd] *n* Grönland *nt*.

green salad *n* grüner Salat.

greet [griːt] *vt liter* & *fig* begrüßen; [say hello to in passing] grüßen.

greeting ['griːtɪŋ] *n* Gruß *der*; **to exchange greetings** sich grüßen. ◆ **greetings** *npl* [on card]: **Christmas greetings** Weihnachtsgrüße; **birthday greetings** Glückwünsche zum Geburtstag.

greetings card UK, **greeting card** US *n* Glückwunschkarte *die*.

grenade [ɡrəˈneɪd] *n*: **(hand) grenade** (Hand)granate *die*.

grew [ɡruː] *pt* ▷ **grow**.

grey UK, **gray** US [ɡreɪ] <> *adj* grau; [life] trostlos; **to go grey** grau werden. <> *n* Grau *das*.

grey-haired [-ˈheəd] *adj* grauhaarig.

greyhound ['ɡreɪhaʊnd] *n* Windhund *der*.

grid [ɡrɪd] *n* - 1. [grating] Gitter *das* - 2. [for maps] Gitternetz *das*; ELEC Überlandleitungsnetz *das*.

griddle ['ɡrɪdl] *n* gusseiserne Platte zum Backen von Pfannkuchen.

gridlock ['ɡrɪdlɒk] *n* [in traffic] Zusammenbruch *der* des Verkehrs.

grief [ɡriːf] *n* - 1. [sorrow] Trauer *die* - 2. *inf* [trouble] Ärger *der* - 3. *phr*: **to come to grief** [in an accident] verunglücken; [plan] scheitern; **good grief!** ach du lieber Himmel!

grievance ['ɡriːvns] *n* [complaint] Beschwerde *die*.

grieve [ɡriːv] *vi*: **to grieve (for sb/sthg)** (um jn/etw) trauern.

grievous ['ɡriːvəs] *adj fml* [wound] schlimm; [mistake] schwer wiegend.

grill [ɡrɪl] <> *n* [of cooker] Grill *der*; [over fire] Bratrost *der*. <> *vt* - 1. [cook] grillen - 2. *inf* [interrogate - interviewee] ausquetschen; [- prisoner, suspect] ins Verhör nehmen.

grille [ɡrɪl] *n* Gitter *das*; **radiator grille** AUT Kühlergrill *der*.

grim [ɡrɪm] *adj* - 1. [face, smile] grimmig; [determination] eisern - 2. [place, situation] trostlos; [prospect] düster; [news] grauenvoll.

grimace ['ɡrɪməs] <> *n* Grimasse *die*. <> *vi* Grimassen schneiden; **to grimace with pain** vor Schmerz das Gesicht verziehen.

grime [ɡraɪm] *n* Schmutz *der*; [soot] Ruß *der*.

grimy ['ɡraɪmɪ] *adj* schmutzig; [sooty] verrußt.

grin [ɡrɪn] <> *n* Grinsen *das*. <> *vi* grinsen; **to grin at sb/sthg** jn/etw anlgrinsen.

grind [ɡraɪnd] (*pt & pp* ground) <> *vt* [coffee, pepper, flour] mahlen. <> *vi* [car, gears] knirschen. <> *n* [hard, boring work] Schinderei *die*; **the daily grind** der tägliche Trott. ◆ **grind down** *vt sep* [oppress] unterdrücken. ◆ **grind up** *vt sep* zermahlen.

grinder ['ɡraɪndər] *n* [for coffee, pepper] Mühle *die*.

grip [ɡrɪp] <> *n* - 1. [physical hold]: **to release one's grip on sb/sthg** jn/etw loslassen - 2. [control]: **to have a (good) grip on a situation** eine Situation im Griff haben; **to get to grips with sthg** etw in den Griff bekommen; **to get a grip on o.s.** sich zusammenreißen - 3. [of tyres] Haftung *die*; [of shoes] Halt *der* - 4. [handle] Griff *der*. <> *vt* - 1. [grasp] festhalten - 2. [subj: tyres] haften auf (+ *D*) - 3. [imagination, attention, audience] fesseln.

gripe [ɡraɪp] *inf* <> *n* [complaint] Gemecker *das*. <> *vi*: **to gripe (about sthg)** (über etw (*A*)) meckern.

gripping ['ɡrɪpɪŋ] *adj* [story, film] fesselnd.

grisly ['ɡrɪzlɪ] *adj* grausig.

gristle ['ɡrɪsl] *n* Knorpel *der*.

grit [ɡrɪt] <> *n* (*U*) - 1. [for roads, in winter] Streusand *der* - 2. *inf* [courage] Schneid *der*. <> *vt* [road, steps] streuen.

groan [ɡrəʊn] <> *n* Stöhnen *das*. <> *vi* - 1. [moan] stöhnen - 2. [door, table] ächzen - 3. [complain] sich beklagen.

grocer ['ɡrəʊsər] *n* Lebensmittelhändler *der*, -in *die*; **grocer's (shop)** Lebensmittelgeschäft *das*.

groceries ['ɡrəʊsərɪz] *npl* Lebensmittel *Pl*.

groggy ['ɡrɒɡɪ] *adj* geschwächt.

groin [ɡrɔɪn] *n* Leiste *die*.

groom [gru:m] ⟨⟩ n - **1.** [of horses] Stallbursche der, Stallgehilfin die - **2.** [bridegroom] Bräutigam der. ⟨⟩ vt - **1.** [horse] striegeln; [dog] bürsten - **2.** [candidate]: **to groom sb (for)** jn vorbereiten (auf (+ A)).

groomed [gru:md] adj: **well groomed** gepflegt.

groove [gru:v] n Rille die.

grope [grəʊp] vi: **to grope (about) for sthg** [object] nach etw tasten.

gross [grəʊs] (pl inv OR -es) ⟨⟩ adj - **1.** [weight, income] Brutto- - **2.** fml [error, misconduct] grob; [exaggeration] krass - **3.** inf [coarse, vulgar - person, behaviour] ordinär - **4.** inf [obese] fett. ⟨⟩ n Gros das.

grossly ['grəʊslɪ] adv [for emphasis] äußerst.

grotesque [grəʊ'tesk] adj grotesk.

grotto ['grɒtəʊ] (pl -es OR -s) n Grotte die.

grotty ['grɒtɪ] adj UK inf mies.

ground [graʊnd] ⟨⟩ pt & pp ▷ **grind**. ⟨⟩ n - **1.** [gen] Boden der; **above ground** über der Erde; **below ground** unter der Erde; **on the ground** auf dem Boden; fig vor Ort; **to gain/lose ground** an Boden gewinnen/verlieren; **to cut the ground from under sb's feet** jm den Boden unter den Füßen wegziehen; **to stand one's ground** nicht von der Stelle weichen; fig auf seinem Standpunkt beharren - **2.** SPORT Sportplatz der; [stadium] Stadion das; **football ground** Fußballplatz der; [stadium] Fußballstadion das. ⟨⟩ vt - **1.** [base]: **to be grounded on** OR **in sthg** basieren auf etw (D) - **2.** inf [aircraft, pilot] nicht fliegen lassen - **3.** esp US [child]: **to be grounded** Hausarrest haben - **4.** US ELEC: **to be grounded** geerdet sein. **grounds** npl - **1.** [reason] Grund der; **to have grounds for doing sthg** einen Grund dafür haben, etw zu tun; **on health grounds** aus gesundheitlichen Gründen - **2.** [of building] Gelände das - **3.**: **coffee grounds** Kaffeesatz der.

ground crew n Bodenpersonal das.

ground floor n Erdgeschoss das.

grounding ['graʊndɪŋ] n: **to have a grounding in sthg** Grundkenntnisse in etw (D) haben.

groundless ['graʊndlɪs] adj grundlos.

groundsheet ['graʊndʃi:t] n Bodenplane die.

ground staff n UK [at airport] Bodenpersonal das.

groundwork ['graʊndwɜ:k] n (U) Vorarbeit Pl.

group [gru:p] ⟨⟩ n [gen] Gruppe die. ⟨⟩ vt gruppieren; [classify] klassifizieren. ⟨⟩ vi: **to group (together)** sich zusammenltun.

groupie ['gru:pɪ] n inf Groupie das.

grouse [graʊs] (pl inv OR -s) ⟨⟩ n [bird] Schottisches Moorschneehuhn. ⟨⟩ vi inf meckern.

grove [grəʊv] n Hain der.

grovel ['grɒvl] (UK) (US) vi kriechen; **to grovel to sb** vor jm kriechen.

grow [grəʊ] (pt grew, pp grown) ⟨⟩ vi - **1.** [gen] wachsen; [problem] sich vergrößern; [love] stärker werden; [idea] Formen annehmen; **to grow in popularity** an Beliebtheit gewinnen - **2.** [become] werden; **to grow old** alt werden; **to grow to do sthg** allmählich etw tun. ⟨⟩ vt [crops, vegetables] anbauen; [flowers] züchten; **to grow one's hair/a beard** sich (D) die Haare/einen Bart wachsen lassen. **grow on** vt insep inf [subj: music, idea]: **it'll grow on you** es wird dir mit der Zeit immer besser gefallen. **grow out of** vt insep vt inf - **1.** [clothes, shoes] herauswachsen aus - **2.** [habit] ablegen. **grow up** vi [person] auflwachsen; [become adult] erwachsen werden; **grow up!** werd endlich erwachsen!

grower ['grəʊəʳ] n [of flowers] Züchter der, -in die; [of crops, vegetables] Anbauer der, -in die.

growl [graʊl] vi knurren; [bear, engine] brummen.

grown [grəʊn] ⟨⟩ pp ▷ **grow**. ⟨⟩ adj erwachsen.

grown-up ⟨⟩ adj [fully grown] ausgewachsen; [mature] erwachsen. ⟨⟩ n Erwachsene der, die.

growth [grəʊθ] n - **1.** [increase - of economy, company, population] Wachstum das; [- of research, opposition, nationalism] Zunahme die - **2.** [development - of person] Entwicklung die - **3.** MED Geschwulst die.

grub [grʌb] n - **1.** [insect] Larve die - **2.** inf [food] Futter das.

grubby ['grʌbɪ] adj [clothes] schmuddelig; [hands, child] schmutzig.

grudge [grʌdʒ] ⟨⟩ n Groll der; **to bear sb a grudge, to have a grudge against sb** einen Groll gegen jn hegen. ⟨⟩ vt: **to grudge sb sthg** jm etw missgönnen.

gruelling UK, **grueling** US ['grʊəlɪŋ] adj strapaziös.

gruesome ['gru:səm] adj grausig.

gruff [grʌf] adj - **1.** [voice] rau - **2.** [person, manner] barsch.

grumble ['grʌmbl] vi [complain]: **to grumble (about)** murren (über (+ A)).

grumpy ['grʌmpɪ] adj inf mürrisch.

grunt [grʌnt] ⟨⟩ n Grunzen das. ⟨⟩ vi grunzen.

G-string n - **1.** MUS G-Saite die - **2.** [clothing] Tangaslip der.

guarantee [ˌgærən'ti:] ⟨⟩ n Garantie die; [document] Garantieschein der; **to give sb a guarantee that...** jm garantieren, dass... ⟨⟩ vt - **1.** COMM Garantie geben auf (+ A) - **2.** [promise] garantieren.

guard [gɑːd] ◇ n - **1.** [person] Wachposten der; [for prisoner] Gefängniswärter der, -in die; [group of guards] Wache die - **2.** [supervision] Überwachung die; **to be on guard** Wache haben; **to catch sb off guard** jn überrumpeln - **3.** UK RAIL Schaffner der, -in die - **4.** [protective device] Schutz der; [for machine] Schutzvorrichtung die; [for fire] Schutzgitter das - **5.** [in boxing] Deckung die. ◇ vt bewachen.

guard dog n Wachhund der.

guarded ['gɑːdɪd] adj [reply, statement] vorsichtig.

guardian ['gɑːdjən] n - **1.** LAW [of child] Vormund der - **2.** [protector] Wächter der, -in die.

guardrail ['gɑːdreɪl] n Geländer das.

guard's van n UK Schaffnerabteil das.

guerila [gə'rɪlə] n = guerrilla.

Guernsey ['gɜːnzɪ] n [place] Guernsey nt.

guerrilla [gə'rɪlə] n Guerillakämpfer der, -in die.

guerrilla warfare n (U) Guerillakrieg der.

guess [ges] ◇ n - **1.** [at facts, figures] Schätzung die; **at a guess** schätzungsweise - **2.** [hypothesis] Vermutung die. ◇ vt [answer, name] raten; [correctly] erraten, richtig schätzen; [figure, weight] schätzen; **guess what!** stell dir vor! ◇ vi - **1.** [gen] raten; **to guess at sthg** etw zu erraten versuchen - **2.** [suppose] glauben, denken; **I guess (so)** ich glaube (schon).

guesswork ['gesw3ːk] n (U) (reine) Vermutung.

guest [gest] n Gast der; **be my guest!** nur zu!

guesthouse ['gesthaʊs] (pl [-haʊzɪz]) n Pension die.

guestroom ['gestrʊm] n Gästezimmer das.

guffaw [gʌ'fɔː] vi schallend lachen.

guidance ['gaɪdəns] n (U) - **1.** [help from teacher, parents] Anleitung die; [counselling] Beratung die - **2.** [leadership] Führung die.

guide [gaɪd] ◇ n - **1.** [for tourists] Fremdenführer der, -in die; **tour guide** Reiseleiter der, -in die - **2.** [guide book] Führer der; [manual] Handbuch das - **3.** [indication] Orientierungshilfe die; **to use sthg as a guide** etw als Vorbild nehmen - **4.** = girl guide. ◇ vt - **1.** [lead] führen; (phrase): **to be guided by sb/sthg** [influenced] sich von jm/etw leiten lassen - **2.** [plane, missile] lenken.

guide book n Führer der.

guide dog n Blindenhund der.

guided tour ['gaɪdɪd-] n Führung die.

guideline ['gaɪdlaɪn] n Richtlinie die.

guild [gɪld] n [association] Vereinigung die.

guile [gaɪl] n liter List die.

guillotine ['gɪlə,tiːn] ◇ n - **1.** [for executions] Guillotine die - **2.** [for paper] Papierschneidemaschine die. ◇ vt [execute] guillotinieren.

guilt [gɪlt] n Schuld die.

guilty ['gɪltɪ] adj - **1.** [gen] schuldig; [smile, look] schuldbewusst - **2.:** **to be found guilty/not guilty** LAW für schuldig/nicht schuldig befunden werden.

guinea pig n - **1.** [animal] Meerschweinchen das - **2.** [subject of experiment] Versuchskaninchen das.

guise [gaɪz] n fml: **to present sthg in a new guise** etw anders darstellen; **under the guise of friendship** unter dem Deckmantel der Freundschaft.

guitar [gɪ'tɑːr] n Gitarre die.

guitarist [gɪ'tɑːrɪst] n Gitarrist der, -in die.

gulf [gʌlf] n - **1.** [sea] Golf der - **2.** liter & fig [gap] Kluft die. ⇒ **Gulf** n: **the Gulf** der Golf.

gull [gʌl] n Möwe die.

gullet [gʌlɪt] n Speiseröhre die.

gullible ['gʌləbl] adj leichtgläubig.

gully ['gʌlɪ] n - **1.** [valley] Schlucht die - **2.** [ditch] Graben der.

gulp [gʌlp] ◇ n Schluck der. ◇ vt hinunterschlucken. ◇ vi schlucken. ⇒ **gulp down** vt sep hinunterschlucken.

gum [gʌm] ◇ n - **1.** [chewing gum] Kaugummi der - **2.** [adhesive] Klebstoff der - **3.** ANAT Zahnfleisch das. ◇ vt [stick] kleben.

gummed adj gummiert.

gun [gʌn] n - **1.** [weapon - revolver] Pistole die, Revolver der; [- rifle, shotgun] Gewehr das; [- cannon] Kanone die - **2.** SPORT [starting pistol] Startpistole die - **3.** [for paint, spraying] Pistole die. ⇒ **gun down** vt sep [person, animal] niederschießen.

gunfire ['gʌnfaɪər] n (U) MIL Geschützfeuer das; [of small arms] Schießerei die.

gunman ['gʌnmən] (pl -men [-mən]) n (mit einer Schußwaffe) bewaffneter Mann.

gunpoint ['gʌnpɔɪnt] n: **to hold sb at gunpoint** jn mit einer Pistole/einem Gewehr bedrohen.

gunpowder ['gʌn,paʊdər] n Schießpulver das.

gunshot ['gʌnʃɒt] n Schuss der.

gurgle ['gɜːgl] vi - **1.** [water] gluckern - **2.** [baby] glucksen.

guru ['gʊruː] n Guru der.

gush [gʌʃ] ◇ n Strahl der. ◇ vi - **1.** [flow out] herausschießen - **2.** pej [enthuse] schwärmen.

gust [gʌst] n Windstoß der, Böe die.

gusto ['gʌstəʊ] n: **with gusto** mit Genuss.

gut [gʌt] ◇ n - **1.** MED Darm der - **2.** inf [stomach] Bauch der. ◇ vt - **1.** [animal, fish] ausnehmen - **2.** [building]: **the fire gutted the house** das Haus brannte völlig aus. ⇒ **guts** npl inf - **1.** [intestines] Eingeweide Pl; **to hate sb's guts** jn absolut nicht ausstehen können - **2.** [courage] Mumm der.

gutter ['gʌtər] n - 1. [beside road] Rinnstein der - 2. [on roof] Dachrinne die.

guy [gaɪ] n - 1. inf [man] Typ der - 2. esp US [person]: **are you ready, guys?** seid ihr fertig? - 3. UK [dummy] Puppe, die Guy Fawkes darstellt und in der "Guy Fawkes' Night" verbrannt wird.

Guy Fawkes' Night n Nacht des 5. November, Jahrestag der Pulververschwörung gegen König James I und das Parlament 1605.

guzzle ['gʌzl] ⟨⟩ vt [food] hinunterlschlingen; [drink] hinunterlkippen. ⟨⟩ vi [eat] sich voll fressen.

gym [dʒɪm] n inf - 1. [gymnasium - in school] Turnhalle die; [- in hotel] Fitnessraum der; [- health club] Fitnessstudio das - 2. [exercises] Turnen das.

gymnasium [dʒɪm'neɪzjəm] (pl -iums OR -ia [-jə]) n [in school] Turnhalle die; [in hotel] Fitnessraum der; [health club] Fitnessstudio das.

gymnast ['dʒɪmnæst] n Turner der, -in die.

gymnastics [dʒɪm'næstɪks] n (U) [exercises] Gymnastik die; [discipline] Turnen das.

gym shoes npl Turnschuhe Pl.

gynaecologist UK, **gynecologist** US [,gaɪnə'kɒlədʒɪst] n Gynäkologe der, -gin die.

gynaecology, **gynecology** US [,gaɪnə'kɒlədʒɪ] n Gynäkologie die.

gypsy ['dʒɪpsɪ] adj & n = gipsy.

gyrate [dʒaɪ'reɪt] vi sich schnell drehen; [disco dancer] ausgelassen tanzen.

h (pl h's OR hs), **H** (pl H's OR Hs) [eɪtʃ] n [letter] h das, H das.

haberdashery ['hæbədæʃərɪ] n (U) [goods] Kurzwaren Pl.

habit ['hæbɪt] n - 1. [usual practice] Gewohnheit die; **to get into the habit of doing sthg** sich (D) daran gewöhnen, etw zu tun - 2. [drug addiction] Abhängigkeit die - 3. [garment] Habit das.

habitat ['hæbɪtæt] n Lebensraum der.

habitual [hə'bɪtjʊəl] adj - 1. [customary] gewohnt - 2. [offender, smoker, drinker] Gewohnheits-.

hack [hæk] ⟨⟩ n pej [writer] Schreiberling der. ⟨⟩ vt [cut] hacken; **to hack sthg to pieces** etw zerhacken. ◆ **hack into** vt insep COMPUT eindringen in (+ A).

hacker ['hækər] n COMPUT Hacker der.

hackneyed ['hæknɪd] adj pej abgedroschen.

hacksaw ['hæksɔː] n Metallsäge die.

had (weak form [həd], strong form [hæd]) pt & pp ▷ **have**.

haddock ['hædək] (pl inv) n Schellfisch der.

hadn't ['hædnt] abbr of **had not**.

haemorrhage ['hemərɪdʒ] n & vi = **hemorrhage**.

haemorrhoids ['hemərɔɪdz] npl = **hemorrhoids**.

haggard ['hægəd] adj verhärmt.

haggis ['hægɪs] n schottische Spezialität aus Schafsinnereien, im Schafsmagen gekocht.

haggle ['hægl] vi: **to haggle (over OR about)** feilschen (um).

Hague [heɪg] n: **The Hague** Den Haag nt.

hail [heɪl] ⟨⟩ n liter & fig Hagel der; **a hail of bullets** ein Kugelhagel. ⟨⟩ vt - 1. [call] rufen; [taxi] heranlwinken, anlhalten - 2. [acclaim]: **to hail sb/sthg as sthg** jn/etw als etw feiern. ⟨⟩ impers vb METEOR hageln.

hailstone ['heɪlstəʊn] n Hagelkorn das.

hailstorm ['heɪlstɔːm] n Hagelsturm der.

hair [heər] ⟨⟩ n - 1. (U) [on human head] Haare Pl, Haar das; [single hair] Haar das; **to have one's hair cut** sich (D) die Haare schneiden lassen; **to do one's hair** sich (D) die Haare machen - 2. [on animal, insect, plant] Haar das - 3. [on human skin] Haar das. ⟨⟩ comp Haar-.

hairbrush ['heəbrʌʃ] n Haarbürste die.

haircut ['heəkʌt] n Haarschnitt der; **to get a haircut** sich (D) die Haare schneiden lassen.

hairdo ['heəduː] (pl -s) n inf Frisur die.

hairdresser ['heə,dresər] n Friseur der, -seuse die; **hairdresser's (salon)** Friseur der.

hairdryer ['heə,draɪər] n [handheld] Föhn der; [with hood] Trockenhaube die.

hair gel n Haargel das.

hairgrip ['heəgrɪp] n UK Haarklammer die.

hairpin ['heəpɪn] n Haarnadel die.

hairpin bend n Haarnadelkurve die.

hair-raising [-,reɪzɪŋ] adj haarsträubend.

hair remover [-rɪ,muːvər] n Enthaarungscreme die.

hairspray ['heəspreɪ] n Haarspray das.

hairstyle ['heəstaɪl] n Frisur die.

hairy ['heərɪ] adj - 1. [animal, person, body] behaart - 2. inf [dangerous] haarig.

half [UK hɑːf, US hæf] ⟨⟩ adj halb(e) (er) (es); **half my life** mein halbes Leben (lang); **half a dozen** ein halbes Dutzend; **half an hour** eine halbe Stunde. ⟨⟩ adv halb; **half as big** halb so groß; **half as much again** noch einmal halb so viel; **half past ten** UK, **half after ten** US halb elf; **it's half past** es ist halb; **it isn't half cold** UK inf es ist unheimlich kalt; **half-and-half** halb und halb. ⟨⟩ n - 1. (pl halves) [50%]

Hälfte *die*; **half of it** die Hälfte davon; **in half** [cut, tear] in zwei Hälften; **to go halves (with sb)** (mit jm) halbe-halbe machen - **2.** (*pl* **halves**) [fraction] Halbe(s) *das*; **four and a half** viereinhalb - **3.** (*pl* **halves**) SPORT [of sports match] Spielhälfte *die* - **4.** (*pl* **halves** OR **halfs**) [of beer] kleines Bier - **5.** (*pl* **halves** OR **halfs**) [child's ticket] Fahrkarte *die* zum halben Preis; **one and a half** ein Erwachsener und ein Kind.

half board *n* (U) *esp UK* Halbpension *die*.

half-caste [-kɑːst] *pej* ◇ *adj* Halbblut-. ◇ *n* Mischling *der*.

half-fare *n* halber Fahrpreis.

half-hearted [-ˈhɑːtɪd] *adj* halbherzig.

half hour *n* halbe Stunde.

half-mast *n UK*: **at half-mast** [flag] auf halbmast.

half moon *n* Halbmond *der*.

half note *n US* MUS halbe Note.

halfpenny [ˈheɪpnɪ] (*pl* **-pennies** OR **-pence**) *n* halber Penny.

half-price *adj* & *adv* zum halben Preis.

half term *n UK* kurze Schulferien in der Mitte des Trimesters.

half time *n* Halbzeit *die*.

halfway [hɑːfˈweɪ] ◇ *adj*: **at the halfway stage** OR **point of sthg** in der Mitte von etw. ◇ *adv*: **to go halfway** die Hälfte des Weges zurücklegen; **halfway through the holidays** mitten im Urlaub.

hall [hɔːl] *n* - **1.** [in house] Diele *die*, Flur *der* - **2.** [meeting room] Saal *der* - **3.** [public building] Halle *die* - **4.** *UK* UNIV [hall of residence] Studentenwohnheim *das* - **5.** [country house] Herrensitz *der*.

hallmark [ˈhɔːlmɑːk] *n* - **1.** [typical feature] Kennzeichen *das* - **2.** [on metal] Feingehaltsstempel *der*.

hallo [hʌˈləʊ] *excl* = **hello**.

hall of residence (*pl* **halls of residence**) *n UK* UNIV Studentenwohnheim *das*.

Hallowe'en, Halloween [ˌhæləʊˈiːn] *n* Abend vor Allerheiligen, an dem sich Kinder oft als Gespenster verkleiden.

hallucinate [həˈluːsɪneɪt] *vi* halluzinieren.

hallway [ˈhɔːlweɪ] *n* Diele *die*, Flur *der*.

halo [ˈheɪləʊ] (*pl* **-es** OR **-s**) *n* [of saint, angel] Heiligenschein *der*.

halt [hɔːlt] ◇ *n*: **to come to a halt** *liter* & *fig* zum Stillstand kommen; **to call a halt to sthg** etw (D) Einhalt gebieten. ◇ *vt* [person] anhalten; [development, activity] zum Stillstand bringen. ◇ *vi* [vehicle] anhalten, halten; [person] stehen bleiben; [development, activity] stillstehen.

halve [*UK* hɑːv, *US* hæv] *vt* - **1.** [reduce by half] halbieren - **2.** [divide] teilen.

halves [*UK* hɑːvz, *US* hævz] *Pl* ▷ **half**.

ham [hæm] ◇ *n* [meat] Schinken *der*. ◇ *comp* [salad, sandwich] Schinken-.

hamburger [ˈhæmbɜːgə^r] *n* - **1.** [burger] Hamburger *der* - **2.** (U) *US* [mince] Hackfleisch *das*.

hamlet [ˈhæmlɪt] *n* kleines Dorf.

hammer [ˈhæmə^r] ◇ *n* Hammer *der*. ◇ *vt* - **1.** [with tool - nail] einschlagen; [- panel] hämmern - **2.** *inf fig* [fact, order]: **to hammer sthg into sb** jm etw einbläuen - **3.** *inf fig* [team, player] ablservieren. ◇ *vi*: **to hammer (on)** hämmern (an (+ A)). ◆ **hammer out** *vt insep* [agreement, solution] auslarbeiten. ◇ *vt sep* [metal] auslhämmern; [dent] auslbeulen.

hammock [ˈhæmək] *n* Hängematte *die*.

hamper [ˈhæmpə^r] ◇ *n* - **1.** [for picnic] Picknickkorb *der* - **2.** *US* [for laundry] Wäschekorb *der*. ◇ *vt* [impede] behindern.

hamster [ˈhæmstə^r] *n* Hamster *der*.

hand [hænd] ◇ *n* - **1.** [part of body] Hand *die*; **to hold hands** Händchen halten; **by hand** von Hand; **to get** OR **lay one's hands on sb/sthg** an jn/etw heranlkommen; **to have one's hands full** alle Hände voll zu tun haben; **to try one's hand at sthg** sich in etw (D) versuchen - **2.** [help] Hilfe *die*; **can I give you a hand?** kann ich dir helfen?; **to give** OR **lend sb a hand** jm helfen - **3.** [worker] Arbeiter *der*, -in *die*; [on ship] Besatzungsmitglied *das* - **4.** [of clock, watch] Zeiger *der* - **5.** [handwriting] Handschrift *die* - **6.** [of cards] Blatt *das*. ◇ *vt*: **to hand sthg to sb, to hand sb sthg** jm etw geben OR reichen. ◆ **(close) at hand** *adv* nah in Reichweite. ◆ **in hand** *adv* - **1.** [time, money]: **I have ten pounds in hand** ich habe zehn Pfund übrig; **we have an hour in hand** es bleibt uns noch eine Stunde - **2.** [problem, situation]: **to have sthg in hand** etw in Bearbeitung haben. ◆ **on hand** *adv* zur Stelle. ◆ **on the one hand** *adv* einerseits. ◆ **on the other hand** *adv* andererseits. ◆ **out of hand** ◇ *adj* [situation]: **to get out of hand** außer Kontrolle geraten. ◇ *adv* [completely] rundweg. ◆ **to hand** *adv* zur Hand. ◆ **hand down** *vt sep* [heirloom] hinterlassen; [knowledge] weiterlgeben. ◆ **hand in** *vt sep* [lost property] ablgeben; [essay, application] einlreichen. ◆ **hand out** *vt sep* austeilen. ◆ **hand over** ◇ *vt sep* - **1.** [gen] übergeben - **2.** TELEC: **I'll hand you over to the manager** ich gebe Ihnen (mal) den Manager. ◇ *vi*: **to hand over (to sb)** (an jn) übergeben.

handbag [ˈhændbæg] *n* Handtasche *die*.

handball [ˈhændbɔːl] *n* [game] Handball *der*.

handbook [ˈhændbʊk] *n* Handbuch *das*.

handbrake [ˈhændbreɪk] *n* Handbremse *die*.

handcuffs [ˈhændkʌfs] *npl* Handschellen *Pl*.

handful [ˈhændfʊl] *n* [gen] Hand *die* voll; [of grass, hair] Büschel *das*.

handgun ['hændgʌn] n Handfeuerwaffe die.

handheld PC ['hændheld-] n Palmtop der.

handicap ['hændɪkæp] ◇ n - 1. [disability] Behinderung die - 2. fig [disadvantage] Nachteil der - 3. SPORT Handicap das. ◇ vt [hinder] behindern.

handicapped ['hændɪkæpt] adj [disabled] behindert.

handicraft ['hændɪkrɑːft] n [skill] Handwerk das.

handiwork ['hændɪwɜːk] n (U) Handarbeit die.

handkerchief ['hæŋkətʃɪf] (pl -chiefs OR -chieves [-tʃiːvz]) n Taschentuch das.

handle ['hændl] ◇ n Griff der; [of door] Klinke die; [of broom, spade, frying pan] Stiel der; [of jug, cup] Henkel der. ◇ vt - 1. [with hands] anfassen - 2. [control - tool, machine, words] handhaben; [- car, ship] steuern - 3. [process - orders, complaints] bearbeiten; [- stolen goods] verschieben - 4. [cope with - situation, crisis, death] umgehen mit.

handlebars ['hændlbɑːz] npl Lenker der.

handler ['hændlər] n: (baggage) handler Gepäckabfertiger der, -in die.

hand luggage n (U) UK Handgepäck das.

handmade [,hænd'meɪd] adj in Handarbeit hergestellt.

handout ['hændaʊt] n - 1. [of money, food] Almosen das - 2. [leaflet] Flugblatt das - 3. [for lecture, discussion] Handout das.

handrail ['hændreɪl] n Geländer das.

handset ['hændset] n TELEC Hörer der.

handshake ['hændʃeɪk] n Händedruck der.

handsome ['hænsəm] adj - 1. [man] gut aussehend - 2. [reward] großzügig; [profit] groß.

handstand ['hændstænd] n Handstand der.

hand towel n Händehandtuch das.

handwriting ['hænd,raɪtɪŋ] n Handschrift die.

handy ['hændɪ] adj inf - 1. [useful] praktisch; **to come in handy** nützlich sein - 2. [person] geschickt - 3. [near]: **the newsagent's is very handy** der Zeitungshändler ist gleich um die Ecke.

handyman ['hændɪmæn] (pl -men [-men]) n Heimwerker der.

hang [hæŋ] ◇ vt - 1. (pt & pp hung) [suspend] aufhängen; **to hang sthg on sthg** etw an etw (A) hängen - 2. (pt & pp hung OR hanged) [execute] hängen. ◇ vi hängen. ◇ n: **to get the hang of sthg** inf kapieren, wie etw funktioniert. ➤ **hang about, hang around** vi - 1. [loiter] herumlhängen - 2. [wait] warten. ➤ **hang down** vi herunterhängen. ➤ **hang on** vi - 1. [keep hold]: **to hang on (to)** sich festlhalten (an (+ D)) - 2. inf [continue waiting] warten; **hang on!** Moment mal!; [on tele-

phone] bleiben Sie am Apparat! - 3. [persevere] auslhalten. ➤ **hang out** vi inf [spend time] herumlhängen. ➤ **hang round** vi = **hang about**. ➤ **hang up** ◇ vt sep [suspend] aufhängen. ◇ vi [on telephone] aufhängen. ➤ **hang up on** vt insep TELEC: **he hung up on me** er hat einfach aufgelegt.

hangar ['hæŋər] n Hangar der.

hanger ['hæŋər] n [coat hanger] Kleiderbügel der.

hangers-on npl Gefolgsleute Pl.

hang gliding n Drachenfliegen das.

hangover ['hæŋ,əʊvər] n [from drinking] Kater der.

hang-up n inf PSYCHOL Komplex der.

hanker ['hæŋkər] ➤ **hanker after, hanker for** vt insep sich sehnen nach.

hankie, hanky ['hæŋkɪ] n inf abbr of **handkerchief**.

haphazard [,hæp'hæzəd] adj willkürlich.

happen ['hæpən] vi - 1. [occur] geschehen, passieren; **to happen to sb** jm passieren - 2. [chance]: **to happen to do sthg** zufällig etw (A) tun; **as it happens** zufälligerweise.

happening ['hæpənɪŋ] n Ereignis das.

happily ['hæpɪlɪ] adv - 1. [contentedly]: **the children were playing happily** die Kinder spielten vergnügt - 2. [fortunately] glücklicherweise - 3. [willingly] gern.

happiness ['hæpɪnɪs] n Glück das.

happy ['hæpɪ] adj - 1. [contented] glücklich - 2. [causing contentment - life, day] glücklich; [- story] erfreulich; **Happy Christmas!** OR fröhliche Weihnachten!; **Happy New Year!** frohes neues Jahr!; **Happy Birthday!** herzlichen Glückwunsch zum Geburtstag! - 3. [satisfied] zufrieden; **to be happy with** OR **about sthg** glücklich OR zufrieden mit etw sein - 4. [willing]: **to be happy to do sthg** etw gerne tun.

happy-go-lucky adj inf unbeschwert.

harangue [hə'ræŋ] ◇ n Standpauke die. ◇ vt: **to harangue sb** jm eine Standpauke halten.

harass ['hærəs] vt belästigen.

harbour UK, **harbor** US ['hɑːbər] ◇ n Hafen der. ◇ vt - 1. [feeling] hegen - 2. [person] versteckt halten.

hard [hɑːd] ◇ adj - 1. [gen] hart; **to be hard on sb** streng mit jm sein - 2. [difficult, strenuous] schwer; **it is hard to believe that...** es ist kaum zu glauben, dass...; **hard of hearing** schwerhörig - 3. [kick, push] heftig - 4. [fact] nackt - 5. UK POL: **the hard left/right** der linke/rechte Flügel der Partei. ◇ adv - 1. [work, hit] hart; **to try hard** sich (D) viel Mühe geben; **to listen hard** genau hinlhören - 2. [rain] heftig - 3. phr: **to be hard pushed** OR **put** OR **pressed**

to do sthg Schwierigkeiten haben, etw zu tun; **to feel hard done by** sich benachteiligt fühlen.

hardback ['hɑːdbæk] ⬦ adj gebunden. ⬦ n [book] gebundene Ausgabe.

hardboard ['hɑːdbɔːd] n Pressspanplatte die.

hard-boiled adj [egg] hart gekocht.

hard cash n Bargeld das.

hard copy n COMPUT Papierausdruck der.

hard disk n Festplatte die.

harden ['hɑːdn] ⬦ vt - **1.** fig [person] abl-härten - **2.**: **to harden sb's opinion/attitude** jn in seiner Meinung/Einstellung bestärken. ⬦ vi - **1.** [glue, concrete] härten - **2.** [attitude, ideas, opinion] sich verhärten.

hardheaded adj nüchtern.

hard-hearted [-'hɑːtɪd] adj hartherzig.

hard labour n Zwangsarbeit die.

hard-liner n Hardliner der, -in die.

hardly ['hɑːdlɪ] adv - **1.** [scarcely, not really] kaum; **hardly ever** fast nie; **hardly anything** fast nichts - **2.** [only just] gerade erst.

hardship ['hɑːdʃɪp] n Entbehrung die.

hard shoulder n UK AUT Standspur die.

hard up adj inf knapp bei Kasse.

hardware ['hɑːdweəʳ] n (U) - **1.** [tools, equipment] Eisenwaren Pl - **2.** COMPUT Hardware die.

hardware shop n Eisenwarenhandlung die.

hardwearing [ˌhɑːd'weərɪŋ] adj UK strapazierfähig.

hardworking [ˌhɑːd'wɜːkɪŋ] adj fleißig.

hardy ['hɑːdɪ] adj - **1.** [person, animal] abgehärtet - **2.** [plant] mehrjährig.

hare [heəʳ] n Hase der, Feldhase der.

haricot (bean) ['hærɪkəʊ-] n weiße Bohne.

harm [hɑːm] ⬦ n [physical] Verletzung die; [psychological] Schaden der; **to do harm to sb/ sthg, to do sb/sthg harm** jm/etw Schaden zufügen, jm/etw schaden; **she means no harm by it** sie meint es nicht böse; **to be out of harm's way** [person] in Sicherheit sein; [thing] aus dem Weg sein. ⬦ vt [physically] verletzen; [psychologically] schädigen.

harmful ['hɑːmfʊl] adj schädlich.

harmless ['hɑːmlɪs] adj harmlos; [substance] unschädlich.

harmonica [hɑːˈmɒnɪkə] n Mundharmonika die.

harmonize, -ise ['hɑːmənaɪz] ⬦ vt [views, policies] in Einklang bringen. ⬦ vi - **1.** [sounds, colours]: **to harmonize (with sthg)** harmonieren (mit etw) - **2.** MUS harmonisieren.

harmony ['hɑːmənɪ] n Harmonie die.

harness ['hɑːnɪs] ⬦ n - **1.** [for horse] Geschirr das - **2.** [for person, child] Gurt der. ⬦ vt - **1.** [horse] anlschirren - **2.** [energy, solar power] nutzbar machen.

harp [hɑːp] n MUS Harfe die. ◆ **harp on** vi: **to harp on (about sthg)** immer wieder anlfangen (von etw).

harpoon [hɑːˈpuːn] ⬦ n Harpune die. ⬦ vt harpunieren.

harpsichord ['hɑːpsɪkɔːd] n Cembalo das.

harrowing ['hærəʊɪŋ] adj grauenvoll.

harsh [hɑːʃ] adj - **1.** [person, criticism, treatment, words] hart, streng - **2.** [conditions, weather] rau - **3.** [voice] barsch; [cry] schrill - **4.** [colour, contrast, light] grell - **5.** [landscape] trostlos - **6.** [taste] streng.

harvest ['hɑːvɪst] ⬦ n Ernte die. ⬦ vt ernten.

has (weak form [həz], strong form [hæz]) vb ▷ **have**.

has-been n inf pej vergessene Größe.

hash [hæʃ] n - **1.** [meat] Haschee das - **2.** inf [mess]: **to make a hash of sthg** etw vermasseln.

hashish ['hæʃɪʃ] n Haschisch das.

hasn't ['hæznt] abbr of **has not**.

hassle ['hæsl] inf ⬦ n Ärger der. ⬦ vt ärgern.

haste [heɪst] n - **1.** [rush] Eile die; **to do sthg in haste** etw in Eile tun - **2.** [speed] Eile die.

hasten ['heɪsn] ⬦ vt beschleunigen. ⬦ vi: **to hasten (to do sthg)** sich beeilen(, etw zu tun).

hastily ['heɪstɪlɪ] adv - **1.** [rashly] übereilt - **2.** [quickly] hastig.

hasty ['heɪstɪ] adj - **1.** [rash] übereilt - **2.** [quick] hastig.

hat [hæt] n Hut der.

hatch [hætʃ] ⬦ vt - **1.** [egg] auslbrüten - **2.** fig [scheme, plot] auslhecken. ⬦ vi [chick] auslschlüpfen. ⬦ n [for serving food] Durchreiche die.

hatchback ['hætʃˌbæk] n Schräghecklimousine die.

hatchet ['hætʃɪt] n Beil das.

hate [heɪt] ⬦ n [emotion] Hass der. ⬦ vt hassen, verabscheuen; **to hate doing sthg** es hassen, etw zu tun.

hateful ['heɪtfʊl] adj abscheulich.

hatred ['heɪtrɪd] n Hass der.

hat trick n SPORT Hattrick der.

haughty ['hɔːtɪ] adj hochmütig.

haul [hɔːl] ⬦ n - **1.** [of drugs, stolen goods] Beute die - **2.** [distance]: **a long haul** ein langer Weg. ⬦ vt [pull] ziehen.

haulage ['hɔːlɪdʒ] n (U) [business] Transportunternehmen das.

haulier UK ['hɔːlɪəʳ], **hauler** US ['hɔːlər] n [business] Spedition die.

haunch [hɔːntʃ] n - **1.** [of person] Gesäß das - **2.** [of animal] Keule die.

haunt [hɔ:nt] ⬦ n [place] Lieblingsort der; [pub] Stammlokal das. ⬦ vt - 1. [subj: ghost] spuken in (+ D), umlgehen in (+ D) - 2. [subj: memory, fear, problem] verfolgen.

have [hæv] (pt & pp had) ⬦ aux vb (to form perfect tenses) haben/sein; **I have burnt it** ich habe es verbrannt; **he has come** er ist gekommen; **I have finished** ich bin fertig; **I have lived here for three years** ich wohne hier seit drei Jahren; **have you seen the film?** hast du den Film gesehen?; **have you been there? – no, I haven't/yes, I have** warst du schon mal dort? – nein, noch nie/ja; **she hasn't gone yet, has she?** sie ist noch nicht gegangen, oder?; **we had already left** wir waren schon gegangen; **I would never have gone if I'd known** ich wäre nie gegangen, wenn ich das gewusst hätte. ⬦ modal vb [be obliged]: **to have (got) to do sthg** etw tun müssen; **do you have to go, have you got to go?** musst du wirklich gehen?; **I've got to go to work** ich muss arbeiten gehen; **do you have to pay?** muss man bezahlen? ⬦ vt - 1. [possess]: **to have (got) haben; I have no money, I haven't got any money** ich habe kein Geld; **she has (got) brown hair** sie hat braunes Haar - 2. [illness] haben; **to have a cold** eine Erkältung haben - 3. [need to deal with]: **to have (got) haben; I've got things to do** ich habe einiges zu erledigen - 4. [receive - news, letter] bekommen; **we don't have many visitors** wir haben OR bekommen wenig Besuch - 5. [instead of another verb] haben; **to have a read of sthg** etw lesen; **to have a bath** ein Bad nehmen; **to have breakfast** frühstücken; **to have a cigarette** eine Zigarette rauchen; **to have a game of chess** eine Partie Schach spielen; **to have lunch/dinner** zu Mittag/zu Abend essen; **to have a shower** duschen; **to have a swim** schwimmen; **I've had a bad day** heute ist alles schief gegangen - 6. [give birth to]: **to have a baby** ein Kind bekommen - 7. [cause to be done]: **to have sb do sthg** jn etw tun lassen; **to have sthg done** etw machen lassen; **I'm having the house decorated** ich lasse das Haus tapezieren; **to have one's hair cut** sich (D) die Haare schneiden lassen - 8. [experience, suffer - accident] haben - 9. [organize - party] malchen; [- meeting] ablhalten - 10. inf [cheat]: **you've been had!** du bist reingelegt worden! - 11. phr: **to have it in for sb** es auf jn abgesehen haben; **to have had it** [car, machine, clothes] hinüber sein; **I've had it** [be tired] ich kann nicht mehr; [be in trouble] ich bin geliefert. ➤ **have on** vt sep - 1. [be wearing] anlhaben - 2. [tease] anlführen; **you're having me on!** du willst mich wohl auf den Arm nehmen! ➤ **have out** vt sep - 1. [appendix, tonsils] helrausgenommen bekommen; **to have a tooth out** einen Zahn gezogen bekommen - 2. [discuss frankly]: **to have it out with sb** sich mit jm auslsprechen.

haven ['heɪvn] n Zufluchtsort der.

haven't ['hævnt] abbr of **have not**.

havoc ['hævək] n Chaos das, Verwüstung die; **to play havoc with sthg** [health] etw ruinieren; [plans] etw über den Haufen werfen.

Hawaii [hə'waɪi:] n Hawaii nt.

hawk [hɔ:k] n liter & fig Falke der.

hawker ['hɔ:kər] n - 1. [street vendor] Straßenhändler der, -in die - 2. [door-to-door] Hausierer der, -in die.

hay [heɪ] n Heu das.

hay fever n Heuschnupfen der.

haystack ['heɪˌstæk] n Heuschober der.

haywire ['heɪˌwaɪər] adj inf: **to go haywire** [person] durchldrehen; [machine] verrückt spielen.

hazard ['hæzəd] ⬦ n [danger] Gefahr die; [risk] Risiko das. ⬦ vt - 1. [life, reputation] riskieren - 2. [guess, suggestion] wagen.

hazardous ['hæzədəs] adj [risky] riskant; [dangerous] gefährlich.

hazard warning lights npl UK Warnblinkanlage die.

haze [heɪz] n - 1. [mist] Dunst der - 2. [state of confusion] Verwirrtheit die.

hazelnut ['heɪzlˌnʌt] n Haselnuss die.

hazy ['heɪzɪ] adj - 1. [misty] dunstig - 2. [vague, confused] verwirrt.

he [hi:] pers pron er; **he's tall** er ist groß; **he doesn't care** ihm ist es egal; **there he is** dort ist er; **HE can't do it** DER kann das nicht tun.

head [hed] ⬦ n - 1. [part of body] Kopf der; **a** OR **per head** pro Kopf; **to laugh one's head off** sich totllachen; **to sing/shout one's head off** aus vollem Halse singen/schreien - 2. [mind, brain] Verstand der; **to have a head for figures** eine Begabung für Zahlen haben; **to be off one's head** UK, **to be out of one's head** US [mad] verrückt OR durchgedreht sein; inf [drunk] besoffen sein; **to go to sb's head** [alcohol, success, praise] jm zu Kopf steigen; **to keep one's head** den Kopf nicht verlieren; **to lose one's head** den Kopf verlieren - 3. [top, extremity - of stairs] oberer Absatz; [- of queue] Anfang der; [- of table, bed] Kopfende das; [- of procession, arrow] Spitze die - 4. [of flower, cabbage] Kopf der - 5. [leader - gen] Leiter der, -in die; [- of family] Oberhaupt das - 6. [head teacher] Schulleiter der, -in die. ⬦ vt - 1. [procession, queue, list] anlführen - 2. [organization, delegation] leiten - 3. FTBL köpfen. ⬦ vi [gen] gehen; [by car, bus, train] fahren; **where are you heading?** wohin gehst/fährst du? ➤ **heads** npl [on coin] Kopf der; **heads or tails?** Kopf oder Zahl? ➤ **head for** vt insep - 1. [place]: **to head for Glasgow** Richtung Glasgow fahren - 2. fig [trouble, disaster] zulsteuern auf (+ A).

headache ['hedeɪk] n Kopfschmerzen Pl; **to have a headache** Kopfschmerzen haben.

headband ['hedbænd] n Stirnband das.

headdress ['hed,dres] n Kopfschmuck der.

header ['hedər] n - 1. FTBL Kopfball der - 2. [at top of page] Kopfzeile die.

headfirst [,hed'fɜːst] adv kopfüber.

heading ['hedɪŋ] n Überschrift die.

headlamp ['hedlæmp] n UK Scheinwerfer der.

headland ['hedlənd] n Landspitze die.

headlight ['hedlaɪt] n Scheinwerfer der.

headline ['hedlaɪn] n - 1. [in newspaper] Schlagzeile die - 2. [of news broadcast]: **the news headlines** die Kurznachrichten Pl.

headlong ['hedlɒŋ] adv - 1. [at great speed] halsbrecherisch - 2. [impetuously] blindlings - 3. [dive, fall] kopfüber.

headmaster [,hed'mɑːstər] n Schulleiter der.

headmistress [,hed'mɪstrɪs] n Schulleiterin die.

head office n Hauptsitz der.

head-on <> adj [collision] frontal; [confrontation] direkt. <> adv frontal; [meet] direkt.

headphones ['hedfəʊnz] npl Kopfhörer der.

headquarters [,hed'kwɔːtəz] npl [of business, organization] Hauptniederlassung die; [of armed forces] Hauptquartier das.

headrest ['hedrest] n Kopfstütze die.

headroom ['hedrʊm] n [in car] Kopfraum der; [below bridge] lichte Höhe.

headscarf ['hedskɑːf] (pl -s OR -scarves [-skɑːvz]) n Kopftuch das.

headset ['hedset] n Kopfhörer der.

head start n: **head start (on OR over sb)** Vorsprung der (vor OR gegenüber jm).

headstrong ['hedstrɒŋ] adj eigenwillig.

head waiter n Oberkellner der.

headway ['hedweɪ] n: **to make headway** voranǀkommen.

headword ['hedwɜːd] n Stichwort das.

heady ['hedɪ] adj [exciting] aufregend.

heal [hiːl] <> vt - 1. [person, wound] heilen - 2. fig [breach, division] schlichten, beilegen. <> vi heilen.

healing ['hiːlɪŋ] <> adj heilend. <> n (U) Heilung die.

health [helθ] n Gesundheit die.

health centre n Ärztezentrum das.

health food n Reformkost die.

health food shop n Reformhaus das.

health service n Gesundheitsdienst der.

healthy ['helθɪ] adj - 1. [gen] gesund - 2. [profit, sum] ordentlich - 3. [attitude] vernünftig; [respect] angebracht.

heap [hiːp] <> n Haufen der. <> vt [pile up] aufǀhäufen; **to heap sthg on(to) sthg** etw auf etw (A) häufen. ➡ **heaps** npl inf: **heaps of money/people/books** ein Haufen Geld/Leute/Bücher; **heaps of time** eine Menge Zeit.

hear [hɪər] (pt & pp heard [hɜːd]) <> vt - 1. [perceive] hören - 2. [learn of] hören; **to hear (that) ...** hören, dass ... - 3. LAW [listen to] anǀhören. <> vi - 1. [gen] hören; **to hear from sb** von jm hören - 2. [know]: **to hear about sthg** etw erfahren - 3. phr: **to have heard of sb/sthg** von jm/etw gehört haben; **I won't hear of it!** ich möchte nichts davon hören!

hearing ['hɪərɪŋ] n - 1. [sense] Gehör das - 2. LAW [trial] Verhandlung die.

hearing aid n Hörgerät das.

hearsay ['hɪəseɪ] n Hörensagen das.

hearse [hɜːs] n Leichenwagen der.

heart [hɑːt] n - 1. [gen] Herz das; **from the heart** von Herzen; **to break sb's heart** jm das OR js Herz brechen - 2. (U) [courage] Mut der; **to lose heart** den Mut verlieren - 3. [core - of city] Herz das; [- of problem] Kern der. ➡ **hearts** npl [playing cards] Herz das; **the six of hearts** die Herzsechs. ➡ **at heart** adv im Grunde. ➡ **by heart** adv auswendig.

heartache ['hɑːteɪk] n Kummer der.

heart attack n Herzanfall der.

heartbeat ['hɑːtbiːt] n Herzschlag der.

heartbroken ['hɑːt,brəʊkn] adj untröstlich.

heartburn ['hɑːtbɜːn] n Sodbrennen das.

heart failure n Herzversagen das.

heartfelt ['hɑːtfelt] adj tief empfunden.

hearth [hɑːθ] n Kamin der.

heartless ['hɑːtlɪs] adj herzlos.

heartwarming ['hɑːt,wɔːmɪŋ] adj herzerfreuend.

hearty ['hɑːtɪ] adj - 1. [laughter, praise, welcome] herzlich - 2. [meal, appetite] herzhaft.

heat [hiːt] <> n - 1. [warmth] Wärme die - 2. (U) [specific temperature] Temperatur die - 3. (U) [fire, source of heat] Feuer das - 4. (U) [hot weather] Hitze die - 5. fig [pressure]: **in the heat of the moment** in der Hitze des Gefechts - 6. [eliminating round - in race] Vorlauf der; [- in competition] Vorrunde die - 7. ZOOL: **on heat** UK, **in heat** US brünstig; [dog, cat] läufig; [horse] rossig. <> vt heiß machen, erhitzen; [house, pool] heizen. ➡ **heat up** <> vt sep heiß machen. <> vi sich erwärmen.

heated ['hiːtɪd] adj - 1. [room, swimming pool] beheizt - 2. [argument, discussion, person] hitzig.

heater ['hiːtər] n [in car] Heizung die; [in room, water tank] Heizgerät das.

heath [hiːθ] n Heide die.

heathen ['hiːðn] <> adj heidnisch. <> n Heide der, -din die.

heather ['heðər] n Heidekraut das.

heating ['hiːtɪŋ] n Heizung die.

heatstroke ['hiːtstrəʊk] n Hitzschlag der.

heat wave n Hitzewelle die.

heave [hi:v] ⟨⟩ vt - **1.** [pull] hieven; [push] schieben - **2.** inf [throw] schmeißen - **3.** [give out]: **to heave a sigh** einen Seufzer auslstoßen. ⟨⟩ vi - **1.** [pull] ziehen - **2.** [rise and fall] sich heben und senken - **3.** [retch] brechen.

heaven ['hevn] n [Paradise] Himmel der.
heavens ⟨⟩ npl: **the heavens** liter der Himmel. ⟨⟩ excl: **(good) heavens!** du lieber Himmel!

heavenly ['hevnlɪ] adj inf [delightful] himmlisch, herrlich.

heavily ['hevɪlɪ] adv - **1.** [smoke, drink] stark; [rain] heftig - **2.** [built] solide - **3.** [breathe, sigh] schwer, laut - **4.** [fall, land] schwerfällig - **5.** [sleep] tief.

heavy ['hevɪ] adj - **1.** [in weight] schwer - **2.** [fighting, losses] schwer; [rain] heftig; [traffic, smoker, drinker] stark; **to be a heavy sleeper** immer tief und fest schlafen - **3.** [person - fat] dick; [- solidly built] untersetzt - **4.** [coat, sweater] dick - **5.** [food, responsibility] schwer - **6.** [breathing, step, fall] schwerfällig - **7.** [schedule, week] arbeitsreich - **8.** [work, job] anstrengend.

heavy cream n US Schlagsahne die.

heavy goods vehicle n UK Schwertransporter der.

heavyweight ['hevɪweɪt] ⟨⟩ adj SPORT Schwergewichts-. ⟨⟩ n - **1.** [boxer] Schwergewichtler der - **2.** [intellectual] Größe die.

Hebrew ['hi:bru:] ⟨⟩ adj hebräisch. ⟨⟩ n [language] Hebräisch(e) das.

heck [hek] excl: **what/where/why the heck ... ?** was/wo/warum zum Teufel ... ?; **a heck of a nice guy** ein wahnsinnig netter Kerl; **a heck of a lot of people** wahnsinnig viele Leute.

heckle ['hekl] ⟨⟩ vt (durch Zwischenrufe) unterbrechen. ⟨⟩ vi zwischenlrufen.

hectic ['hektɪk] adj hektisch.

he'd [hi:d] abbr of **he had, he would**.

hedge [hedʒ] ⟨⟩ n [shrub] Hecke die. ⟨⟩ vi [prevaricate] Ausflüchte machen.

hedgehog ['hedʒhɒg] n Igel der.

heed [hi:d] ⟨⟩ n: **to take heed of sthg** etw (D) Beachtung schenken. ⟨⟩ vt fml beachten.

heedless ['hi:dlɪs] adj: **to be heedless of sthg** etw nicht beachten.

heel [hi:l] n - **1.** [of foot] Ferse die - **2.** [of shoe] Absatz der.

hefty ['heftɪ] adj inf - **1.** [person] kräftig - **2.** [fee, fine] saftig; [salary] dick.

heifer ['hefər] n Färse die.

height [haɪt] n - **1.** [gen] Höhe die; [of person] Größe die; **5 metres in height** 5 Meter hoch; **what height are you?** wie groß sind Sie? - **2.** [zenith] Höhepunkt der.

heighten ['haɪtn] ⟨⟩ vt [feeling, awareness] verstärken; [anxiety] steigern. ⟨⟩ vi sich verstärken.

heir [eər] n Erbe der, -bin die.

heiress ['eərɪs] n Erbin die.

heirloom ['eəlu:m] n Erbstück das.

heist [haɪst] n inf Raubüberfall der.

held [held] pt & pp ⟶ **hold**.

helicopter ['helɪkɒptər] n Hubschrauber der.

hell [hel] ⟨⟩ n - **1.** [gen] Hölle die - **2.** inf [for emphasis]: **what/where/why the hell ... ?** was/wo/warum zum Teufel ... ?; **one** OR **a hell of a mess** ein wahnsinniges Durcheinander; **one** OR **a hell of a nice guy** ein wahnsinnig netter Kerl - **3.** phr: **to hell with the expense!** (es ist mir) egal, was es kostet!; **to do sthg for the hell of it** inf etw aus Jux machen; **to give sb hell** inf jm die Hölle heißmachen; **go to hell!** v inf hau ab! ⟨⟩ excl inf verdammt!

he'll [hi:l] abbr of **he will**.

hellish ['helɪʃ] adj inf höllisch, schrecklich.

hello [hə'ləʊ] excl hallo.

helm [helm] n liter & fig Ruder das.

helmet ['helmɪt] n Helm der.

help [help] ⟨⟩ n Hilfe die; **to be of help** behilflich sein; **to be a help** eine Hilfe sein; **with sb's help** mit js Hilfe; **with the help of sthg** mit Hilfe einer Sache (G). ⟨⟩ vt - **1.** [assist] helfen (+ D); **to help sb (to) do sthg** jm helfen, etw zu tun; **to help sb with sthg** jm bei etw helfen - **2.** [make easier for] erleichtern; **to help sb (to) do sthg** es jm erleichtern, etw zu tun - **3.** [contribute to]: **to help (to) do sthg** helfen, etw zu tun - **4.** [avoid]: **I can't help it** ich kann nichts dafür; **I couldn't help laughing** ich mußte einfach lachen - **5.** phr: **to help o.s.** sich bedienen; **to help o.s. to sthg** sich (D) etw nehmen. ⟨⟩ vi helfen; **to help sb with sthg** bei etw helfen. ⟨⟩ excl Hilfe! **help out** ⟨⟩ vt sep auslhelfen (+ D). ⟨⟩ vi auslhelfen.

helper ['helpər] n - **1.** [on any task] Helfer der, -in die - **2.** US [to do housework] Hausgehilfe der, -fin die.

helpful ['helpful] adj - **1.** [willing to help] hilfsbereit - **2.** [useful] nützlich, hilfreich.

helping ['helpɪŋ] n Portion die.

helpless ['helplɪs] adj hilflos.

helpline ['helplaɪn] n Servicenummer die; COMPUT Hotline die.

Helsinki ['helsɪŋkɪ] n Helsinki nt.

hem [hem] ⟨⟩ n Saum der. ⟨⟩ vt säumen. **hem in** vt sep einlengen.

hemisphere ['hemɪˌsfɪər] n Hemisphäre die.

hemline ['hemlaɪn] n Saum der.

hemorrhage ['hemərɪdʒ] n Blutung die.

hemorrhoids ['hemərɔɪdz] npl Hämorriden Pl.

hen [hen] *n* [female chicken] Huhn *das*.

hence [hens] *adv fml* - **1.** [therefore] folglich - **2.** [from now]: **ten years hence** in zehn Jahren.

henceforth [,hens'fɔ:θ] *adv fml* fortan.

henchman ['hentʃmən] (*pl* -**men** [-mən]) *n pej* Helfershelfer *der*.

henna ['henə] *n* Henna *die ODER das*.

henpecked ['henpekt] *adj pej*: **to be henpecked** unter dem Pantoffel stehen; **a henpecked husband** ein Pantoffelheld.

her [hɜːr] <> *pers pron (accusative)* sie; *(dative)* ihr; **I know her** ich kenne sie; **it's her** sie ist es; **send it to her** schick es ihr; **tell her ...** sag ihr ...; **he's worse than her** er ist schlimmer als sie; **she took her luggage with her** sie nahm ihr Gepäck mit. <> *poss adj* ihr; **her friend** ihr Freund/ihre Freundin; **her children** ihre Kinder; **she washed her hair** sie hat sich die Haare gewaschen.

herald ['herəld] *vt fml* an|künd(ig)en.

herb [hɜːb] *n* Kraut *das*.

herd [hɜːd] <> *n liter & fig* Herde *die*. <> *vt* treiben.

here [hɪər] *adv* hier; **come here!** komm her!; **here you are!** [when giving sthg] bitte!; [greeting sb] da bist du ja!; **here we are** da sind wir; **here and there** hier und da; **here and now** sofort; **here's to you!** [in toast] auf Ihr Wohl!

hereabouts *UK* [,hɪərə'baʊts], **hereabout** *US* [,hɪərə'baʊt] *adv* in dieser Gegend.

hereafter [,hɪər'ɑːftər] <> *adv fml* im Folgenden. <> *n*: **the hereafter** das Jenseits.

hereby [,hɪə'baɪ] *adv fml* hiermit.

hereditary [hɪ'redɪtrɪ] *adj* erblich, Erb-.

heresy ['herəsɪ] *n* Ketzerei *die*, Häresie *die*.

herewith [,hɪə'wɪð] *adv fml* anbei.

heritage ['herɪtɪdʒ] *n* Erbe *das*.

hermit ['hɜːmɪt] *n* Einsiedler *der*, -in *die*.

hernia ['hɜːnɪə] *n* Bruch *der*, Hernie *die*.

hero ['hɪərəʊ] (*pl* -**es**) *n* [gen] Held *der*.

heroic [hɪ'rəʊɪk] *adj* [person, deed] heldenhaft. **heroics** *npl pej* Heldenstücke *Pl*.

heroin ['herəʊɪn] *n* Heroin *das*.

heroine ['herəʊɪn] *n* Heldin *die*.

heron ['herən] (*pl inv OR* -**s**) *n* Reiher *der*.

herring ['herɪŋ] (*pl inv OR* -**s**) *n* Hering *der*.

hers [hɜːz] *poss pron* ihre (r) (s); **a friend of hers** ein Freund von ihr; **these shoes are hers** diese Schuhe gehören ihr; **she ate my portion and hers** sie aß meine und ihre Portion.

herself [hɜː'self] *pron* - **1.** *(reflexive)* sich; **she hurt herself** sie hat sich verletzt - **2.** *(after prep)* sich selbst; **she did it herself** [stressed] sie hat es selbst getan; **by herself** allein.

he's [hiːz] *abbr of* **he is**, **he has**.

hesitant ['hezɪtənt] *adj* [person] unentschlossen, zögerlich.

hesitate ['hezɪteɪt] *vi* zögern; **to hesitate to do sthg** Bedenken haben, etw zu tun.

hesitation [,hezɪ'teɪʃn] *n* Zögern *das*.

heterosexual [,hetərəʊ'sekʃʊəl] <> *adj* heterosexuell. <> *n* Heterosexuelle *der, die*.

het up [,het-] *adj inf* aufgeregt.

hexagon ['heksəgən] *n* Sechseck *das*.

hey [heɪ] *excl* he!

heyday ['heɪdeɪ] *n* Glanzzeit *die*.

HGV (*abbr of* **heavy goods vehicle**) *n* Lkw *der*.

hi [haɪ] *excl inf* hallo!

hiatus [haɪ'eɪtəs] (*pl* -**es**) *n fml* Unterbrechung *die*.

hibernate ['haɪbəneɪt] *vi* Winterschlaf halten.

hiccough, hiccup ['hɪkʌp] <> *n* - **1.** [sound] Schluckauf *der*; **to have hiccoughs** (den) Schluckauf haben - **2.** *fig* [difficulty] kleines Problem. <> *vi* schlucksen.

hid [hɪd] *pt* ▷ **hide**.

hidden ['hɪdn] <> *pp* ▷ **hide**. <> *adj* versteckt; **hidden costs** verdeckte Unkosten.

hide [haɪd] (*pt* **hid**, *pp* **hidden**) <> *vt* - **1.** [conceal - person, item] verstecken; [- emotions, facts] verbergen; *(phrase)*: **to hide sthg (from sb)** etw (vor jm) verstecken/verbergen - **2.** [cover] verdecken. <> *vi* sich verstecken. <> *n* [animal skin] Haut *die*.

hide-and-seek *n* Versteckspiel *das*.

hideaway ['haɪdəweɪ] *n inf* Versteck *das*.

hideous ['hɪdɪəs] *adj* grässlich.

hiding ['haɪdɪŋ] *n* - **1.** [concealment]: **to be in hiding** sich verstecken - **2.** *inf* [beating]: **to give sb a (good) hiding** jm eine (ordentliche) Abreibung verpassen.

hiding place *n* Versteck *das*.

hierarchy ['haɪərɑːkɪ] *n* Hierarchie *die*.

hi-fi ['haɪfaɪ] *n* Hi-Fi *das*.

high [haɪ] <> *adj* - **1.** [gen] hoch; *(before noun)* hohe (r) (s); **how high is it?** wie hoch ist es?; **it's 10 metres high** es ist 10 Meter hoch; **high winds** starker Wind - **2.** *inf* [from drugs] high. <> *n* - **1.** [weather front] Hoch *das* - **2.** [highest point] Höchststand *der*. <> *adv* hoch; **to aim high** hoch hinaus|wollen.

highbrow ['haɪbraʊ] *adj* intellektuell; [literature, tastes] anspruchsvoll.

high chair *n* (Kinder)hochstuhl *der*.

high-class *adj* [superior - hotel, restaurant] vornehm; [- performance] hochwertig.

High Court *n UK* LAW oberster Gerichtshof.

higher ['haɪər] *adj* [exam, qualification] höher. **Higher** *n* SCH: **Higher (Grade)** schottischer Abiturabschluss in einem Fach.

higher education *n* Hochschulbildung *die*.

high jump *n* SPORT Hochsprung *der*.

Highlands ['haɪləndz] *npl*: **the Highlands** [of Scotland] das schottische Hochland.

highlight ['haɪlaɪt] ◇ n [of event, occasion] Höhepunkt der. ◇ vt hervorheben. ➣ **highlights** npl [in hair] Strähnchen Pl.

highlighter (pen) ['haɪlaɪtər-] n Textmarker der.

highly ['haɪlɪ] adv - 1. [very, extremely] höchst - 2. [very well] sehr gut - 3. [at an important level]: **highly placed** hoch plaziert - 4. [favourably] sehr gut; **I highly recommend it** ich kann es sehr empfehlen.

highly-strung [-'strʌŋ] adj nervös.

Highness ['haɪnɪs] n: **His/Her/Your (Royal) Highness** Seine/Ihre/Eure (Königliche) Hoheit.

high-pitched [-'pɪtʃt] adj [voice] hoch; [shout, scream] schrill.

high point n Höhepunkt der.

high-powered [-'paʊəd] adj [dynamic - activity, place] anspruchsvoll, leistungsorientiert; [- person] dynamisch.

high-ranking [-'ræŋkɪŋ] adj ranghoch.

high-rise adj: **high-rise building** Hochhaus das.

high school n höhere Schule.

high season n Hochsaison die.

high spot n Höhepunkt der.

high street n UK Hauptstraße die.

high-tech [-'tek] adj Hightech-.

high tide n Flut die.

highway ['haɪweɪ] n - 1. US [main road between cities] Schnellstraße die - 2. UK [any main road] Landstraße die.

Highway Code n UK: **the Highway Code** die Straßenverkehrsordnung.

hijack ['haɪdʒæk] ◇ n Entführung die. ◇ vt entführen.

hijacker ['haɪdʒækər] n [of aircraft] Flugzeugentführer der, -in die; [of vehicle] Entführer der, -in die.

hike [haɪk] ◇ n Wanderung die. ◇ vi wandern.

hiker ['haɪkər] n Wanderer der, -rin die.

hiking ['haɪkɪŋ] n Wandern das; **to go hiking** wandern gehen.

hilarious [hɪ'leərɪəs] adj urkomisch.

hill [hɪl] n - 1. [mound] Hügel der - 2. [slope] Hang der.

hillside ['hɪlsaɪd] n Hang der.

hilly ['hɪlɪ] adj hügelig.

hilt [hɪlt] n Heft das; **to support/defend sb to the hilt** jn voll und ganz unterstützen/verteidigen.

him [hɪm] pers pron (accusative) ihn; (dative) ihm; **I know him** ich kenne ihn; **it's him** er ist es; **send it to him** schick es ihm; **tell him** sag ihm; **she's worse than him** sie ist schlimmer als er; **he took his luggage with him** er nahm sein Gepäck mit.

Himalayas [ˌhɪmə'leɪəz] npl: **the Himalayas** der Himalaja.

himself [hɪm'self] pron - 1. (reflexive) sich; **he hurt himself** er hat sich verletzt - 2. (after prep) sich selbst; **he did it himself** [stressed] er hat es selbst getan; **by himself** allein.

hind [haɪnd] (pl inv OR -s) ◇ adj: **hind legs** Hinterbeine Pl. ◇ n Hirschkuh die.

hinder ['hɪndər] vt behindern.

hindrance ['hɪndrəns] n - 1. [obstacle] Hindernis das - 2. (U) [delay] Behinderung die.

hindsight ['haɪndsaɪt] n (U): **with the benefit of hindsight** im Nachhinein.

Hindu ['hɪnduː] (pl -s) ◇ adj Hindu-, hinduistisch. ◇ n Hindu der.

hinge [hɪndʒ] n [on door, window] Angel die; [on lid] Scharnier das. ➣ **hinge (up)on** vt insep [depend on] abhängen von.

hint [hɪnt] ◇ n - 1. [indirect suggestion] Andeutung die; **to drop a hint** eine Andeutung machen - 2. [useful suggestion, tip] Tipp der - 3. [small amount, trace] Spur die. ◇ vi: **to hint at sthg** etw andeuten. ◇ vt: **to hint that...** andeuten, dass...

hip [hɪp] n [part of body] Hüfte die.

hippie ['hɪpɪ] n Hippie der.

hippo ['hɪpəʊ] (pl -s) ◇ n Nilpferd das.

hippopotamus [ˌhɪpə'pɒtəməs] (pl -muses OR -mi [-maɪ]) n Nilpferd das.

hippy ['hɪpɪ] n = **hippie**.

hire ['haɪər] ◇ n (U) [of car, television, venue] Mieten das; [of suit] Leihen das; **'for hire'** 'zu vermieten'; [taxi sign] 'frei'. ◇ vt - 1. [rent - car, television, venue] mieten; [- suit] leihen - 2. [employ] anstellen. ➣ **hire out** vt sep [car, television, venue] vermieten; [suit] verleihen.

hire car n UK Mietwagen der.

hire purchase n Ratenkauf der.

his [hɪz] ◇ poss adj sein; **his friend** sein Freund/seine Freundin; **his children** seine Kinder; **he has washed his hair** er hat sich die Haare gewaschen. ◇ poss pron seine (r) (s); **a friend of his** ein Freund von ihm; **these shoes are his** diese Schuhe gehören ihm; **he ate my portion and his** er aß meine und seine Portion.

hiss [hɪs] vi zischen; [cat] fauchen.

historic [hɪ'stɒrɪk] adj historisch.

historical [hɪ'stɒrɪkəl] adj historisch.

history ['hɪstərɪ] n - 1. [gen] Geschichte die - 2. [past record] Vorgeschichte die.

hit [hɪt] (pt & pp inv) ◇ n - 1. [blow] Schlag der - 2. [successful strike] Treffer der - 3. [success] Erfolg der; [record] Hit der - 4. COMPUT [of website] Treffer der. ◇ comp Erfolgs-; [record] Hit-. ◇ vt - 1. [strike] schlagen - 2. [subj: stones, bullet] treffen; [subj: vehicle -

tree, wall] fahren gegen; [- person] erwischen - **3**. [reach] erreichen - **4**. *phr*: **to hit it off (with sb)** sich gut (mit jm) verstehen.

hit-and-miss *adj* = **hit-or-miss**.

hit-and-run ◇ *n*: **hit-and-run (accident)** Unfall *der* mit Fahrerflucht. ◇ *adj* [driver] unfallflüchtig.

hitch [hɪtʃ] ◇ *n* [problem, snag] Problem *das*. ◇ *vt* - **1**. [solicit]: **to hitch a lift** trampen - **2**. [fasten]: **to hitch sthg on(to) sthg** etw an etw (D) befestigen. ◇ *vi* [hitchhike] trampen. ◆ **hitch up** *vt sep* [skirt, trousers] hochlziehen.

hitchhike ['hɪtʃhaɪk] *vi* trampen.

hitchhiker ['hɪtʃhaɪkə^r] *n* Anhalter *der*, -in *die*, Tramper *der*, -in *die*.

hi-tech [,haɪ'tek] *adj* = **high-tech**.

hitherto [,hɪðə'tuː] *adv fml* bisher.

hit-or-miss *adj* willkürlich.

HIV (*abbr of* **human immunodeficiency virus**) *n* HIV; **to be HIV-positive** HIV-positiv sein.

hive [haɪv] *n* [for bees] Bienenstock *der*; **to be a hive of activity** *fig* der reinste Bienenstock sein. ◆ **hive off** *vt sep* [separate] ablspalten, auslgliedern.

HNC (*abbr of* **Higher National Certificate**) *n* britische Qualifikation in technischen Fächern.

HND (*abbr of* **Higher National Diploma**) *n* britische Hochschulqualifikation in technischen Fächern.

hoard [hɔːd] ◇ *n* Vorrat *der*. ◇ *vt* horten.

hoarding ['hɔːdɪŋ] *n UK* Plakatwand *die*.

hoarse [hɔːs] *adj* heiser.

hoax [həʊks] *n* [joke] Streich *der*; [threat, alarm] blinder Alarm.

hob [hɒb] *n UK* [on cooker] Kochfläche *die*.

hobble ['hɒbl] *vi* humpeln.

hobby ['hɒbɪ] *n* Hobby *das*.

hobbyhorse ['hɒbɪhɔːs] *n* [favourite topic] Lieblingsthema *das*.

hobo ['həʊbəʊ] (*pl* **-es** *OR* **-s**) *n US* Landstreicher *der*, Penner *der*.

hockey ['hɒkɪ] *n* - **1**. [on grass] Hockey *das* - **2**. *US* [ice hockey] Eishockey *das*.

hockey stick *n* Hockeyschläger *der*.

hoe [həʊ] ◇ *n* Hacke *die*. ◇ *vt* hacken.

hog [hɒg] ◇ *n* - **1**. *US* [pig] Schwein *das* - **2**. *inf* [greedy person] Vielfraß *der* - **3**. *phr*: **to go the whole hog** aufs Ganze gehen. ◇ *vt inf* [monopolize - road] in Beschlag nehmen; [- attention] mit Beschlag belegen.

Hogmanay ['hɒgm[ə]neɪ] *n Scotland* Silvester *der ODER das*.

hoist [hɔɪst] ◇ *n* [device for lifting] Lastenaufzug *der*. ◇ *vt* - **1**. [load, person] heben, hieven - **2**. [sail, flag] hissen.

hold [həʊld] (*pt & pp* **held**) ◇ *vt* - **1**. [gen] halten; **to hold sb prisoner/hostage** jn gefangen halten/als Geisel festlhalten - **2**. [position,

responsibility, title, driving licence] haben; [belief, principle] vertreten - **3**. [meeting, talks] abllhalten; [conversation] führen - **4**. *fml* [consider]: **to hold sthg to be necessary/important** etw für notwendig/wichtig erachten *OR* halten; **to hold (that)** der Meinung sein, dass; **to hold sb responsible for sthg** jn für etw verantwortlich machen - **5**. [on telephone]: **please hold the line** bitte bleiben Sie am Apparat - **6**. [attention, interest] fesseln - **7**. [support] tragen - **8**. [contain] enthalten; **what does the future hold for him?** was birgt die Zukunft für ihn? - **9**. [have space for] Platz haben für - **10**. *phr*: **hold it!, hold everything!** halt!; **to hold one's own** sich behaupten können. ◇ *vi* - **1**. [promise, objection] gelten; [weather] sich halten; **his luck held** das Glück blieb ihm treu; **to hold still** *OR* **steady** stillhalten - **2**. [on phone] am Apparat bleiben. ◇ *n* - **1**. [grip] Griff *der*; **to keep hold of sthg** [with hand] etw festlhalten; [save] etw behalten; **to take** *OR* **lay hold of sthg** etw fassen *OR* packen; **to get hold of sthg** [obtain] etw belkommen; **to get hold of sb** [find] jn erreichen - **2**. [of ship, aircraft] Laderaum *der*, Frachtraum *der* - **3**. [control, influence]: **to have a hold over sb** [person] jn in der Hand haben; [feeling, idea] von jm Besitz ergreifen. ◆ **hold back** *vt sep* [gen] zurücklhalten. ◆ **hold down** *vt sep*: **to hold down a job** sich in einer Stelle halten. ◆ **hold off** *vt sep* [fend off] ablwehren. ◆ **hold on** *vi* - **1**. [wait, on phone] warten; **hold on!** [on phone] einen Moment, bitte! - **2**. [grip]: **to hold on (to sthg)** sich (an etw (D)) festlhalten. ◆ **hold out** ◇ *vt sep* [hand] auslstrecken; [arms] auslbreiten. ◇ *vi* - **1**. [last] reichen - **2**. [resist]: **to hold out (against sb/sthg)** sich (gegen jn/etw) behaupten. ◆ **hold up** *vt sep* - **1**. [raise] hochlheben - **2**. [delay - traffic, production] auflhalten; [- plans] verzögern.

holdall ['həʊldɔːl] *n UK* Reisetasche *die*.

holder ['həʊldə^r] *n* - **1**. [container] Halter *der*; [for cigarette] Spitze *die* - **2**. [owner] Inhaber *der*, -in *die*.

holding ['həʊldɪŋ] *n* - **1**. [investment] Aktienbesitz *der* - **2**. [farm] Gut *das*.

holdup ['həʊldʌp] *n* - **1**. [robbery] bewaffneter Raubüberfall - **2**. [delay] Verzögerung *die*; [of traffic] stockender Verkehr.

hole [həʊl] *n* - **1**. [gen] Loch *das*; **hole in one** [in golf] Ass *das* - **2**. *inf* [horrible place] Loch *das*; [town] Kaff *das* - **3**. *inf* [predicament]: **to get o.s. into a hole** in die Bredouille kommen; **to be in a hole** in der Bredouille sein.

holiday ['hɒlɪdeɪ] *n* - **1**. [vacation] Urlaub *der*; **holidays** Urlaub *der*; *SCH* Ferien *Pl*; **to be on holiday** im Urlaub sein; **to go on holiday** in Urlaub fahren - **2**. [public holiday] Feiertag *der*.

holiday camp *n UK* ≃ Feriendorf *das*.

holidaymaker ['hɒlɪdɪ,meɪkə^r] *n UK* Urlauber *der*, -in *die*.

holiday pay n UK Urlaubsgeld das.

holiday resort n UK Ferienort der.

holistic [həʊˈlɪstɪk] adj holistisch.

Holland [ˈhɒlənd] n Holland nt.

holler [ˈhɒlə*] vt & vi inf brüllen.

hollow [ˈhɒləʊ] ◇ adj hohl; [cheeks] eingefallen; [victory, success] wertlos; [promise] leer. ◇ n - 1. [in tree] Höhlung die - 2. [in ground, pillow] Mulde die; **the hollow of one's hand/back** die hohle Hand/das Kreuz. ◆ **hollow out** vt sep aushöhlen.

holly [ˈhɒlɪ] n Stechpalme die.

holocaust [ˈhɒləkɔːst] n: **a nuclear holocaust** ein atomarer Holocaust. ◆ **Holocaust** n: **the Holocaust** der Holocaust.

holster [ˈhəʊlstə*] n Pistolenhalfter das.

holy [ˈhəʊlɪ] adj heilig; [ground] geweiht.

Holy Ghost n: **the Holy Ghost** der Heilige Geist.

Holy Land n: **the Holy Land** das Heilige Land.

Holy Spirit n: **the Holy Spirit** der Heilige Geist.

home [həʊm] ◇ n - 1. [place of residence, institution] Heim das - 2. [place of origin] Heimat die - 3. [family unit] Zuhause das; **to leave home** von zu Hause weglaufen. ◇ adj - 1. [market, product] inländisch - 2. SPORT Heim-. ◇ adv: **to go home** nach Hause gehen; [from abroad] zurückfahren/zurückfliegen; **to be home** zu Hause sein. ◆ **at home** adv - 1. [in one's house, flat] daheim, zu Hause - 2. [comfortable]: **to feel at home somewhere** sich irgendwo wohl fühlen; **to make o.s. at home** es sich (D) bequem machen - 3. [in one's own country]: **at home the shops close at five** bei uns machen die Geschäfte um fünf zu.

home address n Privatadresse die.

home brew n (U) selbst gebrautes Bier.

home computer n Heimcomputer der.

home cooking n bürgerliche Küche.

Home Counties npl UK: **the Home Counties** die London umgebenden Grafschaften.

home economics n (U) Hauswirtschaft(slehre) die.

home help n UK Haushaltshilfe die.

homeland [ˈhəʊmlænd] n [country of birth] Heimatland das.

homeless [ˈhəʊmlɪs] ◇ adj obdachlos. ◇ npl: **the homeless** die Obdachlosen.

homely [ˈhəʊmlɪ] adj - 1. [simple, unpretentious - place] schlicht; (phrase): **homely fare** Hausmannskost die - 2. [ugly] unattraktiv.

homemade [ˌhəʊmˈmeɪd] adj selbst gemacht; [bread] selbst gebacken; [food] hausgemacht.

Home Office n UK: **the Home Office** das Innenministerium.

homeopathy [ˌhəʊmɪˈɒpəθɪ] n Homöopathie die.

home page n COMPUT Homepage die.

Home Secretary n UK Innenminister der, -in die.

homesick [ˈhəʊmsɪk] adj heimwehkrank; **to be/feel homesick** Heimweh haben.

hometown [ˈhəʊmtaʊn] n Heimatstadt die.

homework [ˈhəʊmwɜːk] n (U) - 1. SCH Hausaufgaben Pl - 2. inf [preparation]: **he's really done his homework** er hat sich gut vorbereitet.

homey, homy [ˈhəʊmɪ] adj US [place, atmosphere] heimelig.

homicide [ˈhɒmɪsaɪd] n Mord der.

homogeneous [ˌhɒməˈdʒiːnɪəs] adj homogen.

homophobic [ˌhɒməˈfəʊbɪk] adj homosexuellenfeindlich, homophob.

homosexual [ˌhɒməˈsekʃʊəl] ◇ adj homosexuell. ◇ n Homosexuelle der, die.

homy adj US = homey.

hone [həʊn] vt - 1. [knife, sword] schleifen, wetzen - 2. [intellect, wit] schärfen.

honest [ˈɒnɪst] ◇ adj - 1. [trustworthy, legal] redlich - 2. [truthful] ehrlich; **to be honest**, ehrlich gesagt,.. ◇ adv inf ehrlich.

honestly [ˈɒnɪstlɪ] ◇ adv - 1. [in a trustworthy manner] redlich - 2. [truthfully] ehrlich. ◇ excl also wirklich!

honesty [ˈɒnɪstɪ] n - 1. [trustworthiness] Redlichkeit die - 2. [truthfulness] Ehrlichkeit die.

honey [ˈhʌnɪ] n - 1. [food] Honig der - 2. esp US [dear] Liebling die.

honeycomb [ˈhʌnɪkəʊm] n - 1. [in wax] Bienenwabe die - 2. [pattern] Wabenmuster das.

honeymoon [ˈhʌnɪmuːn] ◇ n - 1. [after wedding] Flitterwochen Pl; [trip] Hochzeitsreise die - 2. fig [initial trouble-free period] Schonzeit die. ◇ vi Hochzeitsreise machen.

Hong Kong [ˌhɒŋˈkɒŋ] n Hongkong nt.

honk [hɒŋk] ◇ vi [motorist] hupen. ◇ vt: **to honk one's horn** auf die Hupe drücken.

honor etc US = honour etc.

honorary [UK ˈɒnərərɪ, US ɒnəˈreərɪ] adj - 1. [given as an honour] Ehren-; **honorary degree** ehrenhalber verliehener akademischer Grad - 2. [unpaid] ehrenamtlich.

honour UK, **honor** US [ˈɒnə*] ◇ n Ehre die; **a man of honour** ein Ehrenmann; **in her honour** zu ihren Ehren. ◇ vt - 1. [fulfil - debt] begleichen; [- promise, agreement] erfüllen; [- cheque] akzeptieren - 2. fml [bring honour to] ehren. ◆ **honours** npl - 1. [tokens of respect] Ehren Pl - 2. UNIV der erste erreichbare akademische Grad, der in ein oder zwei Fächern erlangt wird.

honourable UK, **honorable** US [ˈɒnrəbl] adj ehrenhaft.

hood [hʊd] n - 1. [on cloak, jacket] Kapuze die; [of robber] Maske die - 2. [of cooker] Abzugshaube die; [of pram, convertible car] Verdeck das - 3. US [car bonnet] Motorhaube die.

hoodlum ['hu:dləm] n US inf [youth] Rowdy der; [gangster] Gangster der.

hoof [hu:f] (pl -s OR hooves) n Huf der.

hook [hʊk] ◇ n Haken der. ◇ vt - 1. [fasten with hook]: **to hook sthg on to sthg** etw an etw (D) festhaken - 2. [fish] an die Angel bekommen. ◆ **off the hook** adv - 1. TELEC: **the telephone is off the hook** der Hörer ist abgenommen; **to leave the phone off the hook** den Hörer nicht auflegen - 2. [out of trouble]: **to be off the hook** aus dem Schneider sein. ◆ **hook up** vt sep: **to hook sthg up to sthg** COMPUT & TELEC etw an etw (A) anschließen.

hooked [hʊkt] adj - 1. [shaped like a hook] gebogen; **hooked nose** Hakennase die - 2. inf [addicted]: **to be hooked on sthg** [on drugs] von etw abhängig sein; [on music, money, art] auf etw (A) ganz versessen sein.

hook(e)y ['hʊkɪ] n US inf: **to play hookey** (die Schule) schwänzen.

hooligan ['hu:lɪgən] n Rowdy der.

hoop [hu:p] n Reifen der.

hooray [hʊ'reɪ] excl = **hurray**.

hoot [hu:t] ◇ n - 1. [of owl] Schrei der - 2. [of horn] Hupen das - 3. UK inf [amusing thing, person]: **to be a hoot** zum Schießen sein. ◇ vi - 1. [owl] schreien - 2. [horn] hupen. ◇ vt [horn]: **to hoot one's horn** hupen.

hooter ['hu:tər] n [horn - of car] Hupe die; [- of factory] Sirene die.

Hoover® ['hu:vər] n UK Staubsauger der. ◆ **hoover** vt & vi (staub)saugen.

hooves [hu:vz] Pl ▷ **hoof**.

hop [hɒp] ◇ n [of person, animal, bird] Hüpfer der. ◇ vi - 1. [jump] hüpfen - 2. inf [move nimbly] springen; **to hop on a bus/train/plane** kurz entschlossen den Bus/den Zug/das Flugzeug nehmen. ◇ vt inf phr: **hop it!** verschwinde! ◆ **hops** npl [for making beer] Hopfen der.

hope [həʊp] ◇ vi hoffen; **to hope for sthg** auf etw (A) hoffen; **I hope so** hoffentlich; **I hope not** hoffentlich nicht. ◇ vt: **to hope (that)...** hoffen, dass...; **to hope to do sthg** hoffen, etw zu tun. ◇ n - 1. (U) [belief, optimism] Hoffnung die; **to be beyond hope** [situation] aussichtslos OR hoffnungslos sein - 2. [expectation, chance] Hoffnung die; **in the hope of doing sthg** in der Hoffnung, etw zu tun.

hopeful ['həʊpfʊl] adj - 1. [person] hoffnungsvoll; **to be hopeful that...** zuversichtlich sein, dass...; **to be hopeful of doing sthg** zuversichtlich sein, etw zu tun - 2. [sign, future] vielversprechend.

hopefully ['həʊpfəlɪ] adv - 1. [in a hopeful way] hoffnungsvoll - 2. [with luck] hoffentlich.

hopeless ['həʊplɪs] adj - 1. [despairing, impossible] hoffnungslos - 2. inf [useless] miserabel.

hopelessly ['həʊplɪslɪ] adv hoffnungslos.

horizon [hə'raɪzn] n [of sky] Horizont der; **on the horizon** liter & fig am Horizont.

horizontal [ˌhɒrɪ'zɒntl] ◇ adj horizontal. ◇ n: **the horizontal** die Horizontale.

hormone ['hɔ:məʊn] n Hormon das.

horn [hɔ:n] n - 1. [gen] Horn das - 2. [on car] Hupe die; [on ship] Signalhorn das.

hornet ['hɔ:nɪt] n Hornisse die.

horny ['hɔ:nɪ] adj - 1. [scale, body] hornig; [hand] schwielig - 2. v inf [sexually excited] geil.

horoscope ['hɒrəskəʊp] n Horoskop das.

horrendous [hɒ'rendəs] adj - 1. [horrific] entsetzlich - 2. inf [unpleasant - bill, amount] horrend; [- weather] scheußlich.

horrible ['hɒrəbl] adj schrecklich.

horrid ['hɒrɪd] adj esp UK fürchterlich; **don't be so horrid** sei nicht so gemein.

horrific [hɒ'rɪfɪk] adj entsetzlich.

horrify ['hɒrɪfaɪ] vt entsetzen.

horror ['hɒrər] n - 1. [alarm, fear] Entsetzen das - 2. [horrifying thing] Schrecken der; **the horrors of war** die Gräuel des Krieges.

horror film n Horrorfilm der.

horse [hɔ:s] n Pferd das.

horseback ['hɔ:sbæk] ◇ adj: **horseback riding** US Reiten das. ◇ n: **on horseback** zu Pferd.

horse chestnut n [tree, nut] Rosskastanie die.

horseman ['hɔ:smən] (pl -men [-mən]) n Reiter der.

horsepower ['hɔ:sˌpaʊər] n (U) Pferdestärke die.

horse racing n Pferderennen das.

horseradish ['hɔ:sˌrædɪʃ] n (U) [plant] Meerrettich der.

horse riding n Reiten das.

horseshoe ['hɔ:sʃu:] n Hufeisen das.

horsewoman ['hɔ:sˌwʊmən] (pl -women [-ˌwɪmɪn]) n Reiterin die.

horticulture ['hɔ:tɪˌkʌltʃər] n Gartenbau der.

hose [həʊz] ◇ n [hosepipe] Schlauch der. ◇ vt [garden] sprengen.

hosepipe ['həʊzpaɪp] n Schlauch der.

hosiery ['həʊzɪərɪ] n (U) Strumpfwaren Pl.

hospitable [hɒ'spɪtəbl] adj gastfreundlich.

hospital ['hɒspɪtl] n Krankenhaus das.

hospitality [ˌhɒspɪ'tælətɪ] n Gastfreundschaft die.

host [həʊst] <> n - **1.** [gen] Gastgeber der; **host country** Gastland das - **2.** [compere] Moderator der - **3.** liter [large number]: **a host of sthg** eine Schar von etw. <> vt moderieren.

hostage ['hɒstɪdʒ] n Geisel die.

hostel ['hɒstl] n Wohnheim das; **(youth) hostel** Jugendherberge die.

hostess ['həʊstes] n [at party] Gastgeberin die.

hostile [UK 'hɒstaɪl, US 'hɒstl] adj - **1.** [antagonistic, unfriendly]: **hostile (to sb/sthg)** feindselig (gegenüber jm/etw) - **2.** [weather conditions] widrig; [climate] unwirtlich - **3.** MIL [territory, forces] feindlich.

hostility [hɒ'stɪlətɪ] n (U) Feindseligkeit die.
◆ **hostilities** npl Feindseligkeiten Pl.

hot [hɒt] adj - **1.** heiß; **I'm hot** mir ist heiß - **2.** [cooked] warm - **3.** [spicy] scharf - **4.** inf [expert] stark; **to be hot on** OR **at sthg** super in etw (D) sein - **5.** [recent]: **a hot piece of news** das Neueste vom Neuesten - **6.** [temper] hitzig.

hot-air balloon n Heißluftballon der.

hotbed ['hɒtbed] n Brutstätte die.

hot-cross bun n Rosinenbrötchen mit kleinem Teigkreuz, das zum Ostern gegessen wird.

hot dog n Hotdog der ODER das.

hotel [həʊ'tel] n Hotel das.

hot flush UK, **hot flash** US n Hitzewallung die; **hot flushes** fliegende Hitze.

hotheaded [,hɒt'hedɪd] adj hitzköpfig.

hothouse ['hɒthaʊs] n (pl [-haʊzɪz]) [greenhouse] Treibhaus das.

hot line n - **1.** [between government heads] heißer Draht - **2.** [for crisis, disaster] Hotline die.

hotly ['hɒtlɪ] adv - **1.** [argue, debate, deny] heftig - **2.** [pursue]: **they were hotly pursued by a policeman** ein Polizist war ihnen dicht auf den Fersen.

hotplate ['hɒtpleɪt] n Kochplatte die.

hot-tempered [-'tempəd] adj jähzornig.

hot-water bottle n Wärmflasche die.

hound [haʊnd] <> n Jagdhund der. <> vt verfolgen.

hour ['aʊər] n Stunde die; **half an hour** eine halbe Stunde; **per** OR **an hour** pro OR die Stunde; **on the hour** zur vollen Stunde; **every hour, on the hour** jede volle Stunde. ◆ **hours** npl [of business] Geschäftszeiten Pl; [of pub, museum etc] Öffnungszeiten Pl; [of doctor] Sprechstunde die.

hourly ['aʊəlɪ] <> adj - **1.** [happening every hour] stündlich - **2.** [per hour] Stunden-. <> adv - **1.** [every hour] stündlich - **2.** [per hour] pro Stunde.

house <> n [haʊs] (pl ['haʊzɪz]) - **1.** [gen] Haus das; **to move house** umziehen; **on the house** auf Kosten des Hauses; **to bring the house down** das Publikum zum Toben bringen - **2.** SCH eine der traditionellen Schülerge-

meinschaften innerhalb einer Schule, die untereinander Wettbewerbe veranstalten. <> vt [haʊz] [subj: person] unterbringen; **the building houses three families/offices** im Gebäude sind drei Familien/Büros untergebracht. <> adj [haʊs] Haus-; **house style** hauseigener Stil; **house red/white** [wine] Hausmarke die (Rot-/Weißwein).

houseboat ['haʊsbəʊt] n Hausboot das.

household ['haʊshəʊld] <> adj - **1.** [domestic] Haushalts- - **2.** [familiar]: **to be a household name** ein Begriff sein. <> n Haushalt der.

housekeeper ['haʊs,ki:pər] n Haushälterin die.

housekeeping ['haʊs,ki:pɪŋ] n - **1.** [work] Haushaltsführung die - **2.** [budget]: **housekeeping (money)** Haushaltsgeld das.

house music n Hausmusik die.

House of Commons n UK: **the House of Commons** das britische Unterhaus.

House of Lords n UK: **the House of Lords** das britische Oberhaus.

House of Representatives n US: **the House of Representatives** das Repräsentantenhaus.

houseplant ['haʊsplɑ:nt] n Zimmerpflanze die.

Houses of Parliament npl UK: **the Houses of Parliament** Sitz des britischen Parlaments.

housewarming (party) ['haʊs,wɔ:mɪŋ-] n Einzugsparty die.

housewife ['haʊswaɪf] (pl -wives [-waɪvz]) n Hausfrau die.

housework ['haʊswɜ:k] n Hausarbeit die.

housing ['haʊzɪŋ] n (U) [accommodation] Wohnungen Pl; [act] Unterbringung die.

housing association n UK Wohnungsbaugesellschaft die.

housing benefit n (U) UK Wohngeld das.

housing estate UK, **housing project** US n Wohnsiedlung die.

hovel ['hɒvl] n armselige Hütte.

hover ['hɒvər] vi [fly] schweben.

hovercraft ['hɒvəkrɑ:ft] (pl inv OR -s) n Luftkissenfahrzeug das.

how [haʊ] adv - **1.** [referring to way, manner] wie; **how do you get there?** wie kommt man dahin?; **tell me how to do it** sag mir, wie man das macht - **2.** [referring to health, general state] wie; **how are you?** wie gehts dir?; **how are you doing?, how are things?** wie gehts dir?; **how is your room?** wie ist dein Zimmer?; **how do you do?** guten Tag! - **3.** [referring to degree, amount] wie; **how far?** wie weit?; **how long?** wie lang?; **how many?** wie viele?; **how much?** wie viel?; **how much is it?** wie viel kostet es?; **how old are you?** wie alt bist du? - **4.** [in exclamations] wie; **how nice/awful!** wie schön/schrecklich!; **how I wish I could!** wenn ich doch nur könnte! ◆ **how about** adv: **how about a drink?** wie wäre es mit einem Drink?;

I could do with a night off, how about you? ich könnte mir einen freien Abend gebrauchen, du auch?

however [haʊˈevər] ⟨⟩ conj [in whatever way] wie (immer). ⟨⟩ adv - **1.** [nevertheless] jedoch; **however, it was not to be** es sollte jedoch nicht sein - **2.** [no matter how] wie auch; **however difficult/good it is** wie schwierig/gut es auch ist; **however many/much you have** wie viele/viel du auch hast - **3.** [how] wie bloß; **however did you know?** woher hast du das bloß gewusst?

howl [haʊl] vi - **1.** [animal, wind] heulen - **2.** [person] schreien; **to howl with laughter** brüllen vor Lachen.

hp (abbr of horsepower) n PS.

HP n - **1.** (abbr of hire purchase); **to buy sthg on HP** etw auf Raten kaufen - **2.** = **hp**.

HQ (abbr of headquarters) n HQ das.

hr (abbr of hour) Std.

hrs (abbr of hour) Std.

hub [hʌb] n - **1.** [of wheel] (Rad)nabe die - **2.** [of activity] Zentrum das.

hubbub [ˈhʌbʌb] n Lärm der.

hubcap [ˈhʌbkæp] n Radkappe die.

huddle [ˈhʌdl] vi - **1.** [crouch, curl up] kauern - **2.** [crowd together]: **to huddle (together)** sich (zusammen)|drängen.

hue [hjuː] n [colour] Farbton der.

huff [hʌf] n: **in a huff** beleidigt.

hug [hʌg] ⟨⟩ n Umarmung die; **to give sb a hug** jn umarmen. ⟨⟩ vt - **1.** [embrace] umarmen - **2.** [hold - one's knees] umfassen - **3.** [stay close to]: **to hug the coast/kerb** dicht an der Küste/am Straßenrand entlang|fahren.

huge [hjuːdʒ] adj riesig; [subject] vielfältig.

hulk [hʌlk] n - **1.** [of ship] (Schiffs)rumpf der - **2.** [person] Koloss der.

hull [hʌl] n [of ship] Schiffskörper der.

hullo [həˈləʊ] excl = **hello**.

hum [hʌm] ⟨⟩ vi - **1.** [bee] summen; [car, machine] brummen - **2.** [sing] summen - **3.** [be busy - place] voller Leben sein; [- office] voller Aktivität sein. ⟨⟩ vt [tune] summen.

human [ˈhjuːmən] ⟨⟩ adj menschlich. ⟨⟩ n: **human (being)** Mensch der.

humane [hjuːˈmeɪn] adj [compassionate] human.

humanitarian [hjuːˌmænɪˈteərɪən] adj humanitär.

humanity [hjuːˈmænətɪ] n - **1.** [kindness, sympathy] Humanität die - **2.** [mankind] Menschheit die. ⟐ **humanities** npl: **the humanities** die Geisteswissenschaften.

human race n: **the human race** die menschliche Rasse.

human resources npl Humankapital das.

human rights npl Menschenrechte Pl.

humble [ˈhʌmbl] ⟨⟩ adj [position, job, origins] niedrig; [clerk] einfach; [home, room, opinion] bescheiden; [person] demütig. ⟨⟩ vt demütigen.

humbug [ˈhʌmbʌg] n UK [sweet] Pfefferminzbonbon der ODER das.

humdrum [ˈhʌmdrʌm] adj [life] eintönig.

humid [ˈhjuːmɪd] adj feucht.

humidity [hjuːˈmɪdətɪ] n (Luft)feuchtigkeit die.

humiliate [hjuːˈmɪlɪeɪt] vt demütigen.

humiliation [hjuːˌmɪlɪˈeɪʃn] n Demütigung die.

humility [hjuːˈmɪlətɪ] n Demut die.

humor n & vt US = **humour**.

humorous [ˈhjuːmərəs] adj [remark, story] lustig; [person] humorvoll.

humour UK, **humor** US [ˈhjuːmər] ⟨⟩ n [comedy] Humor der; [of situation, remark] Komik die. ⟨⟩ vt: **to humour sb** jm seinen Willen lassen.

hump [hʌmp] n - **1.** [hill] Hügel der - **2.** [of camel] Höcker der; [of person] Buckel der.

hunch [hʌntʃ] n inf Gefühl das, Ahnung die.

hunchback [ˈhʌntʃbæk] n Bucklige der, die.

hundred [ˈhʌndrəd] num hundert; **a** OR **one hundred** (ein)hundert; see also **six**. ⟐ **hundreds** npl Hunderte Pl.

hundredth [ˈhʌndrəθ] num hundertste(r) (s); see also **sixth**.

hundredweight [ˈhʌndrədweɪt] n - **1.** [in UK] ≃ Zentner der, = 50,8 kg - **2.** [in US] ≃ Zentner der, = 45,36 kg.

hung [hʌŋ] pt & pp ⟩ **hang**.

Hungarian [hʌŋˈgeərɪən] ⟨⟩ adj ungarisch. ⟨⟩ n - **1.** [person] Ungar der, -in die - **2.** [language] Ungarisch(e) das.

Hungary [ˈhʌŋgərɪ] n Ungarn nt.

hunger [ˈhʌŋgər] n liter & fig Hunger der.

hunger strike n Hungerstreik der.

hung over adj inf verkatert.

hungry [ˈhʌŋgrɪ] adj hungrig; **to be hungry** Hunger haben; **to be hungry for sthg** fig sich nach etw sehnen.

hung up adj inf: **to be hung up (on** OR **about)** sich verrückt machen (wegen **(+ G)**).

hunk [hʌŋk] n - **1.** [of bread, cheese] Stück das - **2.** inf [attractive man]: **he's a real hunk** er ist ein richtiger Mann.

hunt [hʌnt] ⟨⟩ n - **1.** SPORT Jagd die; UK [for foxes] Fuchsjagd die; [hunters] Jagdgesellschaft die - **2.** [search] Suche die. ⟨⟩ vi - **1.** [for food, sport] jagen - **2.** UK [for foxes] auf die Fuchsjagd gehen - **3.** [search]: **to hunt (for)** suchen (nach). ⟨⟩ vt - **1.** [animals, birds] jagen - **2.** [criminal] fahnden nach.

hunter [ˈhʌntər] n [of animals, birds] Jäger der.

hunting [ˈhʌntɪŋ] n (U) - **1.** SPORT Jagd die - **2.** UK [foxhunting] Fuchsjagd die.

hurdle ['hɜːdl] n liter & fig Hürde die. ◆ **hurdles** npl SPORT Hürdenlauf der.

hurl [hɜːl] vt schleudern; **to hurl abuse at sb** jm Beschimpfungen an den Kopf werfen.

hurray [hʊ'reɪ] excl hurra!

hurricane ['hʌrɪkən] n Orkan der; [tropical] Hurrikan der.

hurried ['hʌrɪd] adj [meal] hastig; [departure] überstürzt; [glance] flüchtig; [note] eilig geschrieben.

hurriedly ['hʌrɪdlɪ] adv [eat] hastig; [leave, write] eilig.

hurry ['hʌrɪ] ◇ vt [person] (zur Eile) antreiben; [process] beschleunigen; **don't hurry me** hetz mich nicht; **to hurry to do sthg** sich beeilen, etw zu tun. ◇ vi sich beeilen. ◇ n Eile die; **to be in a hurry** in Eile sein; **to do sthg in a hurry** etw in Eile tun. ◆ **hurry up** vi sich beeilen.

hurt [hɜːt] (pt & pp inv) ◇ vt - 1. [cause physical pain to] wehltun (+ D); **to hurt one's leg/arm** sich (D) am Bein/Arm wehltun; **to hurt o.s.** sich (D) wehltun - 2. [injure, upset] verletzen; **to hurt sb's feelings** js Gefühle verletzen - 3. [harm] schaden (+ D). ◇ vi - 1. [gen] wehltun - 2. [harm] schaden (+ D). ◇ adj [leg, arm, feelings] verletzt; [look, voice] gekränkt.

hurtful ['hɜːtfʊl] adj verletzend.

hurtle ['hɜːtl] vi sausen.

husband ['hʌzbənd] n Ehemann der; **my husband** mein Mann.

hush [hʌʃ] ◇ n Schweigen das. ◇ excl still! ◆ **hush up** vt sep [affair] vertuschen.

husk [hʌsk] n [of seed] Hülse die; [of grain] Spelze die.

husky ['hʌskɪ] ◇ adj [voice] rau. ◇ n [dog] Husky der, Eskimohund der.

hustle ['hʌsl] ◇ vt [hurry]: **he hustled her out of the room** er drängte sie schnell aus dem Raum. ◇ n: **hustle and bustle** geschäftiges Treiben.

hut [hʌt] n Hütte die; [temporary building] Baracke die.

hutch [hʌtʃ] n Stall der.

hyacinth ['haɪəsɪnθ] n Hyazinthe die.

hydrant ['haɪdrənt] n Hydrant der.

hydraulic [haɪ'drɔːlɪk] adj hydraulisch.

hydroelectric [ˌhaɪdrəʊɪ'lektrɪk] adj hydroelektrisch; **hydroelectric power** durch Wasserkraft erzeugte Energie.

hydrofoil ['haɪdrəfɔɪl] n Tragflächenboot das.

hydrogen ['haɪdrədʒən] n Wasserstoff der.

hyena [haɪ'iːnə] n Hyäne die.

hygiene ['haɪdʒiːn] n Hygiene die; **personal hygiene** Körperpflege die.

hygienic [haɪ'dʒiːnɪk] adj hygienisch.

hymn [hɪm] n Kirchenlied das.

hype [haɪp] inf ◇ n Publicity die. ◇ vt Publicity machen für.

hyperactive [ˌhaɪpər'æktɪv] adj überaktiv.

hypermarket ['haɪpəˌmɑːkɪt] n Großmarkt der.

hyphen ['haɪfn] n Bindestrich der; [at end of line] Trennungsstrich der.

hypnosis [hɪp'nəʊsɪs] n Hypnose die.

hypnotic [hɪp'nɒtɪk] adj hypnotisch.

hypnotize, -ise ['hɪpnətaɪz] vt hypnotisieren.

hypocrisy [hɪ'pɒkrəsɪ] n Heuchelei die.

hypocrite ['hɪpəkrɪt] n Heuchler der, -in die.

hypocritical [ˌhɪpə'krɪtɪkl] adj heuchlerisch.

hypothesis [haɪ'pɒθɪsɪs] (pl **-theses** [-θɪsiːz]) n Hypothese die.

hypothetical [ˌhaɪpə'θetɪkl] adj hypothetisch.

hysteria [hɪs'tɪərɪə] n Hysterie die.

hysterical [hɪs'terɪkl] adj - 1. [gen] hysterisch - 2. inf [very funny] urkomisch.

hysterics [hɪs'terɪks] npl [panic] hysterischer Anfall; **to be in hysterics** inf [with laughter] sich auslschütten vor Lachen.

i (pl **i's** OR **is**), **I** (pl **I's** OR **Is**) [aɪ] n [letter] i das, I das.

I [aɪ] pers pron ich; **I'm tall** ich bin groß; **she and I were at college together** ich war mit ihr zusammen im College.

ice [aɪs] ◇ n - 1. (U) [gen] Eis das; [on pond] Eisschicht die; [on road] Glatteis das - 2. UK [ice cream] (Speise)eis das, Eiscreme die. ◇ vt UK [cake] glasieren. ◆ **ice over, ice up** vi [windscreen] vereisen; [lake] zulfrieren.

iceberg ['aɪsbɜːg] n Eisberg der.

iceberg lettuce n Eisbergsalat der.

icebox ['aɪsbɒks] n - 1. UK [in refrigerator] Eisfach das - 2. US [refrigerator] Eisschrank der.

ice cream n Eis das, Eiscreme die.

ice cube n Eiswürfel der.

ice hockey n Eishockey das.

Iceland ['aɪslənd] n Island nt.

Icelandic [aɪs'lændɪk] ◇ adj isländisch. ◇ n [language] Isländisch(e) das.

ice lolly n UK Eis das am Stiel.

ice pick n Eispickel der.

ice rink n Schlittschuhbahn *die*.

ice skate n Schlittschuh *der*. ➤ **ice-skate** vi Schlittschuh laufen, Eis laufen.

ice-skating n Schlittschuhlaufen *das*, Eislaufen *das*; [sport] Eiskunstlauf *der*; **to go ice-skating** Schlittschuh laufen gehen.

icicle ['aisikl] n Eiszapfen *der*.

icing ['aisiŋ] n [of cake] Zuckerguss *der*.

icing sugar n UK Puderzucker *der*.

icon ['aikɒn] n - 1. RELIG Ikone *die* - 2. COMPUT Icon *das*.

icy ['aisi] adj - 1. [wind, cold, weather] eisig; **it's icy cold** es ist eiskalt - 2. [road, pavement] vereist - 3. fig [welcome, atmosphere] eisig.

I'd [aid] abbr of **I would, I had**.

ID n (abbr of identification) Ausweis *der*.

idea [ai'diə] n - 1. [plan, suggestion] Idee *die* - 2. [notion] Vorstellung *die*; **you have no idea how difficult it is** du kannst dir nicht vorstellen, wie schwer es ist; **can you give me an idea of the price?** können Sie mir einen ungefähren Preis nennen?; **to have an idea that...** glauben, dass...; **to have no idea** keine Ahnung haben - 3. [intention] Absicht *die*; **what's the big idea?** inf was soll das (heißen)?

ideal [ai'diəl] ◇ adj ideal. ◇ n Ideal *das*.

ideally [ai'diəli] adv - 1. [located] ideal; **he was ideally suited to the job** er war perfekt geeignet für die Stelle - 2. [preferably] idealerweise, im Idealfall.

identical [ai'dentikl] adj identisch.

identification [ai,dentifi'keiʃn] n - 1. [gen] Identifizierung *die* - 2. (U) [documentation] Ausweispapiere Pl; **do you have any identification?** können Sie sich ausweisen?

identify [ai'dentifai] ◇ vt - 1. [gen] identifizieren; [cause, need] erkennen; **to identify o.s.** sich ausweisen - 2. [connect]: **to identify sb with sthg** jn mit etw in Verbindung bringen. ◇ vi [empathize]: **to identify with sb/sthg** sich mit jm/etw identifizieren.

identity [ai'dentəti] n Identität *die*.

identity card n Personalausweis *der*.

ideology [,aidi'ɒlədʒi] n Weltanschauung *die*; pej Ideologie *die*.

idiom ['idiəm] n - 1. [phrase] Redewendung *die* - 2. fml [style] Idiom *das*.

idiomatic [,idiə'mætik] adj idiomatisch.

idiosyncrasy [,idiə'siŋkrəsi] n [of person] Eigenheit *die*; [of thing] Besonderheit *die*.

idiot ['idiət] n Idiot *der*.

idiotic [,idi'ɒtik] adj idiotisch.

idle ['aidl] ◇ adj - 1. [person - inactive] untätig, müßig; [- lazy] faul - 2. [machine, factory] stillstehend; [workers] unbeschäftigt - 3. [threat] leer - 4. [glance] flüchtig - 5. [futile] sinnlos. ◇ vi [engine] im Leerlauf sein. ➤ **idle away** vt sep [time] vertrödeln.

idol ['aidl] n - 1. [hero] Idol *das* - 2. RELIG Götze *der*.

idolize, -ise ['aidəlaiz] vt vergöttern.

idyllic [i'dilik] adj idyllisch.

i.e. (abbr of id est) d. h.

if [if] conj wenn, falls; (in indirect questions after "know", "wonder") ob; **if I were you** wenn ich du wäre; **pleasant weather, if rather cold** schönes Wetter, wenn auch ziemlich kalt; **as if** als ob. ➤ **if not** conj wenn nicht, falls nicht. ➤ **if only** ◇ conj - 1. [expressing regret] wenn nur; **if only I had known** wenn ich das nur vor bloß gewusst hätte - 2. [providing a reason] (und) sei es nur; **go and see him, if only to please me** geh ihn besuchen, und sei es nur mir zuliebe. ◇ excl: **if only!** das wäre schön!

igloo ['iglu:] (pl -s) n Iglu *der ODER das*.

ignite [ig'nait] ◇ vt entzünden; AUT zünden. ◇ vi sich entzünden; AUT zünden.

ignition [ig'niʃn] n [in car] Zündung *die*.

ignition key n Zündschlüssel *der*.

ignorance ['ignərəns] n Unwissenheit *die*; [of particular subject, information etc] Unkenntnis *die*.

ignorant ['ignərənt] adj - 1. [uneducated] ungebildet; [lacking information] unwissend - 2. fml [unaware]: **to be ignorant of sthg** von etw nichts wissen - 3. inf [rude] ungehobelt.

ignore [ig'nɔ:r] vt ignorieren.

ilk [ilk] n: **people of that ilk** solche Leute; **and others of that ilk** und seines-/ihresgleichen.

ill [il] ◇ adj - 1. [sick] krank; **to feel ill** sich unwohl OR krank fühlen; **to be taken ill, to fall ill** krank werden - 2. [bad - omen, treatment] schlecht; [- effects] nachteilig; (phrase): **ill at ease** unbehaglich. ◇ adv schlecht; **to speak/ think ill of sb** schlecht über jn reden/denken.

I'll [ail] abbr of **I will, I shall**.

ill-advised [-əd'vaizd] adj unklug.

illegal [i'li:gl] adj [action] gesetzwidrig; [organization] illegal.

illegible [i'ledʒəbl] adj unleserlich.

illegitimate [,ili'dʒitimət] adj - 1. [child] unehelich - 2. [activity] unzulässig.

ill-equipped [-i'kwipt] adj: **to be ill-equipped to do sthg** [unsuited] nicht dafür geeignet sein, etw zu tun.

ill-fated [-'feitid] adj unglückselig.

ill feeling n Feindseligkeit *die*.

ill health n schwache Gesundheit.

illicit [i'lisit] adj illegal.

illiteracy [i'litərəsi] n Analphabetentum *das*.

illiterate [i'litərət] ◇ adj - 1. [unable to read] des Lesens und Schreibens unkundig; **to be illiterate** Analphabet(in) sein - 2. [uneducated] ungebildet. ◇ n Analphabet *der*, -in *die*.

illness ['ilnis] n Krankheit *die*.

illogical [ɪˈlɒdʒɪkl] *adj* unlogisch.

ill-suited *adj* nicht zusammenpassend; **to be ill-suited to sthg** für etw ungeeignet sein.

ill-treat *vt* misshandeln; [worker] schlecht behandeln.

illuminate [ɪˈluːmɪneɪt] *vt* - **1.** [light up] beleuchten - **2.** [problem, subject] erhellen.

illumination [ɪˌluːmɪˈneɪʃn] *n* [lighting] Beleuchtung *die*. ➡ **illuminations** *npl UK* festliche Beleuchtung.

illusion [ɪˈluːʒn] *n* Illusion *die*; **to be under the illusion that...** sich einlbilden, dass...; **optical illusion** optische Täuschung.

illustrate [ˈɪləstreɪt] *vt* illustrieren.

illustration [ˌɪləˈstreɪʃn] *n* - **1.** [picture] Illustration *die* - **2.** [example] Beispiel *das*.

illustrious [ɪˈlʌstrɪəs] *adj fml* berühmt; [career] glanzvoll.

ill will *n* böses Blut; **he didn't bear anyone any ill will** er war niemandem feindlich gesinnt.

I'm [aɪm] *abbr of* **I am**.

image [ˈɪmɪdʒ] *n* - **1.** [gen] Bild *das*; [in mirror] Spiegelbild *das* - **2.** [in mind] Vorstellung *die* - **3.** [of company, public figure] Image *das*.

imagery [ˈɪmɪdʒrɪ] *n* [in writing] Metaphorik *die*; [in visual arts] Bildersymbolik *die*.

imaginary [ɪˈmædʒɪnrɪ] *adj* imaginär.

imagination [ɪˌmædʒɪˈneɪʃn] *n* - **1.** [ability, fantasy] Fantasie *die* - **2.** [mind] Einbildung *die*; **it's all in her imagination** das bildet sie sich nur ein.

imaginative [ɪˈmædʒɪnətɪv] *adj* fantasievoll; [concerning new ideas] einfallsreich.

imagine [ɪˈmædʒɪn] *vt* - **1.** [visualize] sich (D) vorstellen, sich (D) denken; **to imagine doing sthg** sich (D) vorstellen, etw zu tun; **imagine (that)!** stell dir das mal vor! - **2.** [dream] sich (D) einbilden; **you imagined it** du hast es dir (nur) eingebildet - **3.** [suppose] anlnehmen, vermuten.

imbalance [ˌɪmˈbæləns] *n* Ungleichgewicht *das*.

imbecile [ˈɪmbɪsiːl] *n* Idiot *der*.

IMF (*abbr of* **International Monetary Fund**) *n* IWF *der*.

imitate [ˈɪmɪteɪt] *vt* nachlahmen.

imitation [ˌɪmɪˈteɪʃn] ◇ *n* - **1.** [gen] Nachahmung *die* - **2.** [copy] Kopie *die*. ◇ *adj* unecht, imitiert; **imitation leather** Kunstleder *das*.

immaculate [ɪˈmækjʊlət] *adj* - **1.** [clean and tidy] makellos - **2.** [behaviour] tadellos.

immaterial [ˌɪməˈtɪərɪəl] *adj* [irrelevant] unwichtig.

immature [ˌɪməˈtjʊəʳ] *adj* - **1.** [person, behaviour] unreif - **2.** BOT & ZOOL noch nicht voll entwickelt.

immediate [ɪˈmiːdjət] *adj* - **1.** [response, attention] unverzüglich; [need, problem] dringend; **to take immediate action** sofort OR unverzüglich handeln - **2.** [future, neighbourhood] unmittelbar; **the immediate area** das Gebiet in unmittelbarer Nähe; **the immediate family** die engste Familie.

immediately [ɪˈmiːdjətlɪ] ◇ *adv* - **1.** [at once] sofort - **2.** [directly] unmittelbar, direkt. ◇ *conj* [as soon as] sobald.

immense [ɪˈmens] *adj* enorm.

immerse [ɪˈmɜːs] *vt* - **1.** [in liquid]: **to immerse sthg in sthg** etw in etw (A) eintauchen - **2.** *fig* [involve]: **to immerse o.s. in sthg** sich in etw (A) stürzen.

immersion heater [ɪˈmɜːʃn-] *n* Heißwasserbereiter *der*.

immigrant [ˈɪmɪgrənt] *n* Einwanderer *der*, -derin *die*.

immigration [ˌɪmɪˈgreɪʃn] *n* Einwanderung *die*.

imminent [ˈɪmɪnənt] *adj* [danger] drohend; [death, disaster] unmittelbar bevorstehend.

immobilize, -ise [ɪˈməʊbɪlaɪz] *vt* [machine, lift] lahm legen; [vehicle] gegen Wegfahren sichern.

immoral [ɪˈmɒrəl] *adj* unmoralisch.

immortal [ɪˈmɔːtl] *adj* unsterblich.

immortalize, -ise [ɪˈmɔːtəlaɪz] *vt* unsterblich machen.

immovable [ɪˈmuːvəbl] *adj* - **1.** [fixed] unbeweglich - **2.** [obstinate] unnachgiebig.

immune [ɪˈmjuːn] *adj* - **1.** MED: **immune (to)** immun (gegen) - **2.** *fig*: **to be immune to criticism** gegen Kritik unempfindlich sein.

immunity [ɪˈmjuːnətɪ] *n* MED: **immunity (to)** Immunität *die* (gegen).

immunize, -ise [ˈɪmjuːnaɪz] *vt*: **to immunize sb (against)** MED jn immunisieren (gegen).

impact *n* [ˈɪmpækt] - **1.** [force of contact] Aufprall *der*; [of two moving objects] Zusammenprall *der* - **2.** [effect] Auswirkung *die*; **to make an impact on sb** Eindruck auf jn machen; **to make an impact on sthg** einen Einfluss auf etw (A) haben.

impair [ɪmˈpeəʳ] *vt* beeinträchtigen.

impart [ɪmˈpɑːt] *vt fml* - **1.** [knowledge, skills]: **to impart sthg to sb** jm etw vermitteln - **2.** [feeling, quality]: **to impart sthg to sthg** etw (D) etw verleihen.

impartial [ɪmˈpɑːʃl] *adj* [person] unparteiisch; [news report] objektiv.

impassable [ɪmˈpɑːsəbl] *adj* unpassierbar.

impassive [ɪmˈpæsɪv] *adj* unbewegt.

impatience [ɪmˈpeɪʃns] *n* Ungeduld *die*.

impatient [ɪmˈpeɪʃnt] *adj* ungeduldig; **to be impatient to do sthg** es nicht erwarten können, etw zu tun.

impeccable [ɪmˈpekəbl] *adj* untadelig.

impede [ɪmˈpiːd] *vt* [person] hindern; [progress, activity] behindern.

impediment [ɪmˈpedɪmənt] *n* - **1.** [obstacle] Hindernis *das* - **2.** [disability] Behinderung *die*.

impel [ɪmˈpel] *vt*: **to impel sb to do sthg** jn (dazu) nötigen, etw zu tun.

impending [ɪmˈpendɪŋ] *adj* [doom, disaster] drohend; [interview, test] bevorstehend.

imperative [ɪmˈperətɪv] ◇ *adj* dringend notwendig. ◇ *n* - **1.** [necessity] dringende Notwendigkeit - **2.** GRAM Imperativ *der*.

imperfect [ɪmˈpɜːfɪkt] ◇ *adj* [work, copy] fehlerhaft; [knowledge] mangelhaft. ◇ *n* GRAM: **imperfect (tense)** Imperfekt *das*.

imperial [ɪmˈpɪərɪəl] *adj* - **1.** [of an empire] imperial; [of an emperor] kaiserlich - **2.** [measurement] britisch.

imperil [ɪmˈperɪl] (*UK*) (*US*) *vt fml* gefährden.

impersonal [ɪmˈpɜːsnl] *adj* - **1.** [unemotional] unpersönlich - **2.** GRAM: **impersonal verb** unpersönlich gebrauchtes Verb.

impersonate [ɪmˈpɜːsəneɪt] *vt* - **1.** [mimic] imitieren, nachlahmen - **2.** [pretend to be] sich ausgeben als.

impersonation [ɪm,pɜːsəˈneɪʃn] *n* [by mimic] Imitation *die*, Nachahmung *die*.

impertinent [ɪmˈpɜːtɪnənt] *adj* unverschämt.

impervious [ɪmˈpɜːvɪəs] *adj*: **to be impervious to charm** für Charme unempfänglich sein; **to be impervious to criticism** von Kritik unberührt sein.

impetuous [ɪmˈpetʃʊəs] *adj* impulsiv.

impetus [ˈɪmpɪtəs] *n* - **1.** (*U*) [momentum] Schwung *der* - **2.** [stimulus] Impuls *der*.

impinge [ɪmˈpɪndʒ] *vi*: **to impinge on sb/sthg** sich auf jn/etw auswirken.

implant ◇ *n* [ˈɪmplɑːnt] Implantat *das*. ◇ *vt* [ɪmˈplɑːnt] - **1.** [instil]: **to implant sthg in sb** jm etw einimpfen - **2.** MED: **to implant sthg in(to) sb** jm etw implantieren.

implausible [ɪmˈplɔːzəbl] *adj* [story] unglaubwürdig.

implement ◇ *n* [ˈɪmplɪmənt] [tool] Werkzeug *das*; [piece of equipment] Gerät *das*. ◇ *vt* [ˈɪmplɪment] [plan] ausführen; [law] vollziehen; [policy] in die Praxis umlsetzen.

implication [,ɪmplɪˈkeɪʃn] *n* - **1.** (*U*) [involvement] Verwicklung *die* - **2.** [inference] Auswirkung *die*; **by implication** implizit.

implicit [ɪmˈplɪsɪt] *adj* - **1.** [inferred] implizit; [acknowledgement] stillschweigend; [criticism] unausgesprochen - **2.** [faith, belief] blind.

implore [ɪmˈplɔːr] *vt*: **to implore sb (to do sthg)** jn inständig bitten(, etw zu tun).

imply [ɪmˈplaɪ] *vt* - **1.** [suggest]: **I'm not implying that...** ich will damit nicht sagen, dass... - **2.** [responsibility] mit einlschließen.

impolite [ˈɪmpəˈlaɪt] *adj* unhöflich.

import ◇ *n* [ˈɪmpɔːt] - **1.** [product] Importware *die* - **2.** (*U*) [act of importing] Import *der*. ◇ *vt* [ɪmˈpɔːt] - **1.** [goods] importieren - **2.** COMPUT importieren.

importance [ɪmˈpɔːtns] *n* (*U*) Wichtigkeit *die*; [significance] Bedeutung *die*.

important [ɪmˈpɔːtnt] *adj* wichtig; [significant] bedeutend; [person] einflussreich; **to be important to sb** für jn wichtig sein.

importer [ɪmˈpɔːtər] *n* [person, firm] Importeur *der*; [country] Importland *das*.

impose [ɪmˈpəʊz] ◇ *vt*: **to impose sthg (on sb/sthg)** (jm/etw) etw auflerlegen; **to impose a tax on sb** jn besteuern. ◇ *vi*: **to impose (on sb)** (jm) zur Last fallen.

imposing [ɪmˈpəʊzɪŋ] *adj* beeindruckend.

imposition [,ɪmpəˈzɪʃn] *n* - **1.** [enforcement - gen] Auferlegung *die*; [- of tax] Erhebung *die* - **2.** [burden] Zumutung *die*.

impossible [ɪmˈpɒsəbl] *adj* unmöglich.

impostor, imposter *US* [ɪmˈpɒstər] *n* Hochstapler *der*, -in *die*.

impotent [ˈɪmpətənt] *adj* - **1.** [sexually] impotent - **2.** [powerless] machtlos.

impound [ɪmˈpaʊnd] *vt* beschlagnahmen.

impoverished [ɪmˈpɒvərɪʃt] *adj liter & fig* verarmt.

impractical [ɪmˈpræktɪkl] *adj* praxisfern.

impregnable [ɪmˈpregnəbl] *adj* [fortress, defences] uneinnehmbar; *fig* [person] unangreifbar; [position, argument] unanfechtbar.

impregnate [ˈɪmpregneɪt] *vt* - **1.** [saturate]: **to impregnate sthg with sthg** etw mit etw tränken; [to protect material] etw mit etw imprägnieren - **2.** *fml* [fertilize] befruchten.

impress [ɪmˈpres] *vt* - **1.** [make impression on] beeindrucken; [deliberately] imponieren (+ *D*); **to be favourably/unfavourably impressed** einen guten/schlechten Eindruck haben - **2.** [make clear]: **to impress sthg on sb** jm etw einlschärfen. .

impression [ɪmˈpreʃn] *n* - **1.** [gen] Eindruck *der*; **to make an impression** Eindruck machen; **to be under the impression (that)...** den Eindruck haben, dass... - **2.** [impersonation] Nachahmung *die*, Imitation *die*; **to do an impression of sb** jn imitieren OR nachlahmen - **3.** [of book] Nachdruck *der*.

impressive [ɪmˈpresɪv] *adj* beeindruckend.

imprint *n* [ˈɪmprɪnt] [mark] Abdruck *der*.

imprison [ɪmˈprɪzn] *vt* inhaftieren.

improbable [ɪmˈprɒbəbl] *adj* [unlikely] unwahrscheinlich.

impromptu [ɪmˈprɒmptjuː] *adj* improvisiert.

improper [ɪmˈprɒpər] *adj* - **1.** [unsuitable - treatment] unangebracht; [- behaviour] unpassend - **2.** [dishonest - actions] unehrenhaft; [- dealings] unlauter - **3.** [rude] unanständig.

improve [ɪm'pruːv] ⬦ *vi* [weather, work, student] besser werden; [delinquent, health] sich bessern; [productivity] sich steigern; **to improve (up)on** übertreffen; [offer] überbieten. ⬦ *vt* - **1.** [make better] verbessern - **2.** [increase - vocabulary, knowledge] erweitern; [- productivity] erhöhen, steigern - **3.** [cultivate]: **to improve one's mind** sich (weiter)|bilden; **to improve o.s.** an sich (*D*) arbeiten.

improvement [ɪm'pruːvmənt] *n* Verbesserung *die*; [in health, sb's behaviour, weather] Besserung *die*; [in productivity, sports] Steigerung *die*.

improvise ['ɪmprəvaɪz] ⬦ *vt* improvisieren; [shelter] notdürftig erstellen. ⬦ *vi* improvisieren.

impudence ['ɪmpjʊdəns] *n* Unverschämtheit *die*.

impudent ['ɪmpjʊdənt] *adj* unverschämt.

impulse ['ɪmpʌls] *n* Impuls *der*; **to do sthg on impulse** etw aus einem Impuls heraus tun.

impulsive [ɪm'pʌlsɪv] *adj* impulsiv.

impunity [ɪm'pjuːnətɪ] *n*: **with impunity** ungestraft.

impurity [ɪm'pjʊərətɪ] *n* Unreinheit *die*.

in [ɪn] ⬦ *prep* - **1.** [indicating place, position] in (*+ D*); (with verbs of motion) in (*+ A*); **it's in the box/garden** es ist in der Schachtel/im Garten; **put it in the box/garden** leg es in die Schachtel/in den Garten; **in the street/world** auf der Straße/Welt; **in the country** auf dem Lande; **in the sky** am Himmel; **in Paris/Belgium** in Paris/Belgien; **to be in hospital/prison** im Krankenhaus/Gefängnis sein; **in here/there** hier/dort drinnen - **2.** [wearing] in (*+ D*); **she was still in her nightclothes** sie war noch im Nachthemd; **(dressed) in red** rot gekleidet - **3.** [at a particular time, during] in (*+ D*); **in April** im April; **she was born in 1999** sie wurde 1999 geboren; **in (the) spring/winter** im Frühling/Winter; **in the afternoon/morning** am Nachmittag/Morgen; **ten o'clock in the morning** zehn Uhr morgens - **4.** [within, after] in (*+ D*); **he learned to type in two weeks** er lernte in zwei Wochen Maschine schreiben; **it'll be ready in an hour** es ist in einer Stunde fertig - **5.** [expressing time passed] seit; **it's my first decent meal in weeks** das ist meine erste anständige Mahlzeit seit Wochen - **6.** [indicating situation, circumstances] in (*+ D*); **in the sun/rain** in der Sonne/im Regen; **to be in pain** Schmerzen haben; **in danger/difficulty** in Gefahr/Schwierigkeiten; **in these circumstances** unter diesen Umständen - **7.** [indicating manner]: **to write in ink** mit Tinte schreiben; **in a soft voice** mit sanfter Stimme; **they were talking in English** sie sprachen Englisch; **in writing** schriftlich - **8.** [indicating emotional state]: **in anger/delight/amazement/despair** wütend/entzückt/erstaunt/verzweifelt; **in my excitement** in meiner Aufregung - **9.** [specifying area of activity]: **advances in medi-**

cine Fortschritte in der Medizin; **he's in computers** er ist in der Computerbranche - **10.** [referring to quantity]: **to buy sthg in large/small quantities** etw in großen/kleinen Mengen kaufen; **in (their) thousands** zu Tausenden - **11.** [referring to age]: **she's in her twenties** sie ist in den Zwanzigern - **12.** [describing arrangement] in (*+ D*); **in a circle/line** im Kreis/in einer Reihe; **to stand in twos** zu zweit dastehen - **13.** [indicating colour] in (*+ D*); **it comes in green or blue** es gibt es in grün oder blau - **14.** [as regards]: **a rise in prices** ein Preisanstieg; **to be 3 metres in length** 3 Meter lang sein; **a change in direction** ein Richtungswechsel - **15.** [in ratios]: **one in ten** jeder Zehnte; **an increase of five pence in the pound** eine Preiserhöhung von fünf Prozent - **16.** (after superl) in (*+ D*): **the best in the world** der/die/das Beste in der Welt - **17.** (+ present participle): **she made a mistake in accepting the offer** sie machte einen Fehler, indem sie das Angebot annahm. ⬦ *adv* - **1.** [inside] herein/hinein; **you can go in now** du kannst jetzt hineingehen - **2.** [at home, work] da; **is Judith in?** ist Judith da?; **to stay in** zu Hause bleiben - **3.** [of train, boat, plane]: **to get in** an|kommen; **the train isn't in yet** der Zug ist noch nicht angekommen - **4.** [in shop]: **is my new TV in yet?** ist mein neuer Fernseher schon da? - **5.** [of tide]: **the tide is in** es ist Flut - **6.** *phr*: **you're in for a surprise** du wirst eine Überraschung erleben; **he's in for it** *inf* der kann sich auf etwas gefasst machen; **my luck is in** das Glück ist auf meiner Seite. ⬦ *adj inf* [in]; **short skirts are in this year** kurze Röcke sind dieses Jahr in.
⬥ **ins** *npl*: **she knows the ins and outs of the matter** sie ist mit allen Feinheiten der Sache vertraut.

in. *abbr of* **inch.**

inability [ˌɪnə'bɪlətɪ] *n* Unfähigkeit *die*.

inaccessible [ˌɪnək'sesəbl] *adj* - **1.** [place] unzugänglich - **2.** [book, film, music] schwer verständlich.

inaccurate [ɪn'ækjʊrət] *adj* [imprecise] ungenau; [incorrect] inkorrekt.

inadequate [ɪn'ædɪkwət] *adj* unzureichend.

inadvertently [ˌɪnəd'vɜːtəntlɪ] *adv* [forget, break] aus Versehen; [discover] zufällig.

inadvisable [ˌɪnəd'vaɪzəbl] *adj* nicht ratsam.

inane [ɪ'neɪn] *adj* dumm.

inanimate [ɪn'ænɪmət] *adj* leblos.

inappropriate [ɪnə'prəʊprɪət] *adj* unpassend.

inarticulate [ˌɪnɑː'tɪkjʊlət] *adj* [person]: **to be inarticulate** sich nicht gut ausdrücken können.

inasmuch [ˌɪnəz'mʌtʃ] ⬥ **inasmuch as** *conj fml* [because] da; [to the extent that] insofern als.

inaudible [ɪ'nɔːdɪbl] *adj* unhörbar.

inaugural [ɪ'nɔːgjʊrəl] *adj* [meeting] Eröffnungs-; [speech] Antritts-.

inauguration [ɪ,nɔːgjʊ'reɪʃn] *n* - 1. [of leader, president] Amtseinführung *die* - 2. [of building] Einweihung *die*.

inborn [,ɪn'bɔːn] *adj* angeboren.

inbound ['ɪnbaʊnd] *adj* ankommend.

inbox ['ɪnbɒks] *n* COMPUT Posteingang *der*.

inbred [,ɪn'bred] *adj* [characteristic, quality] angeboren.

inbuilt [,ɪn'bɪlt] *adj* [quality, defect] angeboren.

inc. *(abbr of* inclusive*)* inkl.

Inc. [ɪŋk] *abbr of* **incorporated**.

incapable [ɪn'keɪpəbl] *adj* - 1. [unable]: **to be incapable of sthg** zu etw nicht fähig sein; **to be incapable of doing sthg** nicht fähig sein, etw zu tun - 2. [incompetent] unfähig.

incapacitated [,ɪnkə'pæsɪteɪtɪd] *adj* [for work] arbeitsunfähig.

incarcerate [ɪn'kɑːsəreɪt] *vt fml* einkerkern.

incendiary device [ɪn'sendjərɪ-] *n* Brandsatz *der*.

incense ⟨⟩ *n* ['ɪnsens] Weihrauch *der*. ⟨⟩ *vt* [ɪn'sens] [anger] erbosen, erzürnen.

incentive [ɪn'sentɪv] *n* Anreiz *der*.

incentive scheme *n* Anreizsystem *das*.

inception [ɪn'sepʃn] *n fml* Beginn *der*; [of institution] Gründung *die*.

incessant [ɪn'sesnt] *adj* unaufhörlich.

incessantly [ɪn'sesntlɪ] *adv* unaufhörlich.

incest ['ɪnsest] *n* Inzest *der*.

inch [ɪntʃ] ⟨⟩ *n* Zoll *der*, = 2,54 cm. ⟨⟩ *vi*: **to inch forward/through** sich zentimeterweise vorwärts bewegen/hindurchlbewegen.

incidence ['ɪnsɪdəns] *n* Häufigkeit *die*.

incident ['ɪnsɪdənt] *n* - 1. [event] Vorfall *der*; **the meeting went off without incident** das Treffen verlief ohne Zwischenfälle - 2. POL Zwischenfall *der*.

incidental [,ɪnsɪ'dentl] *adj* [minor] nebensächlich; **incidental expenses** Nebenausgaben *Pl*.

incidentally [,ɪnsɪ'dentəlɪ] *adv* [by the way] übrigens.

incinerate [ɪn'sɪnəreɪt] *vt* verbrennen.

incipient [ɪn'sɪpɪənt] *adj fml* beginnend.

incisive [ɪn'saɪsɪv] *adj* [person] scharfsinnig; [comment, writing] pointiert.

incite [ɪn'saɪt] *vt* aufhetzen; **to incite sb to do sthg** jn dazu aufstacheln, etw zu tun.

incl. *(abbr of* inclusive*)* inkl.

inclination [,ɪnklɪ'neɪʃn] *n* - 1. [desire, slope] Neigung *die* - 2. [tendency]: **to have an inclination to do sthg** die Neigung (dazu) haben, etw zu tun.

incline ⟨⟩ *n* ['ɪnklaɪn] [slope] Hang *der*; [angle] Neigung *die*. ⟨⟩ *vt* [ɪn'klaɪn] [head, body] neigen.

inclined [ɪn'klaɪnd] *adj* - 1. [tending] geneigt; **to be inclined to do sthg** dazu neigen, etw zu tun - 2. [wanting]: **to be inclined to do sthg** Lust haben, etw zu tun - 3. [sloping] geneigt.

include [ɪn'kluːd] *vt* - 1. [gen] (mit) einlschließen; [contain] enthalten - 2. [add, count] mitlrechnen.

included [ɪn'kluːdɪd] *adj* eingeschlossen; **service is not included** die Bedienung ist nicht inbegriffen.

including [ɪn'kluːdɪŋ] *prep* einschließlich (+ G); **up to and including last month** bis einschließlich des letzten Monats.

inclusive [ɪn'kluːsɪv] *adj* einschließlich, inklusive; **inclusive price** Pauschalpreis *der*; **from the 8th to the 16th inclusive** vom 8. bis einschließlich 16.; **inclusive of** einschließlich (+ G).

incoherent [,ɪnkəʊ'hɪərənt] *adj* [speech] zusammenhanglos; **he was incoherent** er drückte sich unklar aus.

income ['ɪnkʌm] *n* Einkommen *das*.

income support *n UK* Sozialhilfe *die*.

income tax *n* Einkommensteuer *die*.

incompatible [,ɪnkəm'pætɪbl] *adj* [ideas, jobs, characters] unvereinbar; [computers] inkompatibel; **to be incompatible with sb** nicht zu jm passen.

incompetent [ɪn'kɒmpɪtənt] *adj* unfähig, inkompetent; [work] unzulänglich.

incomplete [,ɪnkəm'pliːt] *adj* unvollständig; [story] nicht abgeschlossen.

incomprehensible [ɪn,kɒmprɪ'hensəbl] *adj* unverständlich.

inconceivable [,ɪnkən'siːvəbl] *adj* undenkbar, unvorstellbar.

inconclusive [,ɪnkən'kluːsɪv] *adj* [meeting, debate] ergebnislos; [evidence, argument] nicht schlüssig.

incongruous [ɪn'kɒŋgrʊəs] *adj* [clothes, behaviour] unpassend.

inconsequential [,ɪnkɒnsɪ'kwenʃl] *adj* [insignificant] unbedeutend.

inconsiderate [,ɪnkən'sɪdərət] *adj* rücksichtslos.

inconsistency [,ɪnkən'sɪstənsɪ] *n* Widersprüchlichkeit *die*.

inconsistent [,ɪnkən'sɪstənt] *adj* widersprüchlich; [performance] schwankend; [work] unbeständig; [behaviour] inkonsequent; **to be inconsistent with sthg** mit etw nicht übereinlstimmen.

inconspicuous [,ɪnkən'spɪkjʊəs] *adj* unauffällig.

inconvenience [,ɪnkən'viːnjəns] ◇ n Unannehmlichkeit die. ◇ vt Unannehmlichkeiten OR Umstände bereiten.

inconvenient [,ɪnkən'viːnjənt] adj ungünstig; **to be inconvenient for sb** jm ungelegen kommen.

incorporate [ɪn'kɔːpəreɪt] vt einlschließen; **to incorporate sb/sthg in(to) sthg** jn/etw in etw (A) auflnehmen.

incorporated company n COMM (im Handelsregister) eingetragene Gesellschaft.

incorrect [,ɪnkə'rekt] adj falsch; [behaviour] inkorrekt.

incorrigible [ɪn'kɒrɪdʒəbl] adj unverbesserlich.

increase ◇ n ['ɪnkriːs]: **increase (in)** [number, unemployment] Zunahme die (+ G); [price, demand, speed] Erhöhung die (+ G); [output] Steigerung die (+ G); **to be on the increase** (ständig) zulnehmen. ◇ vt [ɪn'kriːs] [price, wages, speed] erhöhen; [output] steigern; [fear, efforts] verstärken. ◇ vi [ɪn'kriːs] steigen; [unemployment, pain] zulnehmen; [anxiety] wachsen.

increasing [ɪn'kriːsɪŋ] adj [number, use, frequency] zunehmend; [anxiety, demand] wachsend.

increasingly [ɪn'kriːsɪŋlɪ] adv zunehmend.

incredible [ɪn'kredəbl] adj - 1. [wonderful] sagenhaft - 2. [very large, unbelievable] unglaublich.

incredulous [ɪn'kredjʊləs] adj ungläubig.

increment ['ɪnkrɪmənt] n Zuwachs der; [of salary] Gehaltserhöhung die.

incriminating [ɪn'krɪmɪneɪtɪŋ] adj belastend.

incubator ['ɪnkjʊbeɪtər] n [for baby] Brutkasten der.

incur [ɪn'kɜːr] vt [loss] erleiden; [expenses] haben; [debts] machen.

indebted [ɪn'detɪd] adj [grateful]: **to be indebted to sb** jm zu Dank verpflichtet sein.

indecent [ɪn'diːsnt] adj unanständig.

indecisive [,ɪndɪ'saɪsɪv] adj - 1. [person] unentschlossen - 2. [result] unklar.

indeed [ɪn'diːd] adv wirklich, tatsächlich; [certainly] natürlich; **very big indeed** wirklich sehr groß; **thank you very much indeed** vielen herzlichen Dank; **indeed?** [in surprise] wirklich?, so?

indefinite [ɪn'defɪnɪt] adj - 1. [period, number] unbestimmt - 2. [answer] unklar.

indefinitely [ɪn'defɪnətlɪ] adv [wait] unbegrenzt lange; [closed] bis auf weiteres; [postpone] auf unbestimmte Zeit.

indent [ɪn'dent] vt [text] einlrücken.

independence [,ɪndɪ'pendəns] n - 1. [gen] Unabhängigkeit die - 2. [in character] Selbstständigkeit die.

Independence Day n (amerikanischer) Unabhängigkeitstag (4. Juli).

independent [,ɪndɪ'pendənt] adj - 1. [gen]: **independent (of)** unabhängig (von) - 2. [person - in character] selbstständig.

independent school n UK nicht staatliche Schule.

in-depth adj eingehend.

indescribable [,ɪndɪ'skraɪbəbl] adj unbeschreiblich.

indestructible [,ɪndɪ'strʌktəbl] adj unzerstörbar.

index ['ɪndeks] n - 1. (pl -es) [of book] Register das - 2. (pl -es) [in library] Kartei die - 3. (pl -es OR indices) ECON Index der.

index card n Karteikarte die.

index finger n Zeigefinger der.

index-linked [-,lɪŋkt] adj der Inflationsrate angepasst.

India ['ɪndɪə] n Indien nt.

Indian ['ɪndɪən] ◇ adj - 1. [from India] indisch - 2. [from the Americas] indianisch, Indianer-. ◇ n - 1. [from India] Inder der, -in die - 2. [from the Americas] Indianer der, -in die.

Indian Ocean n: **the Indian Ocean** der Indische Ozean.

indicate ['ɪndɪkeɪt] ◇ vt - 1. [with finger, pointer] zeigen auf (+ A); [subj: dial, arrow, gauge] anlzeigen - 2. [intention, fact] anldeuten - 3. [mention - desire, preference] zum Ausdruck bringen - 4. [suggest] hinldeuten auf (+ A). ◇ vi [when driving] blinken.

indication [,ɪndɪ'keɪʃn] n - 1. [suggestion]: **can you give me an indication of when you will arrive?** können Sie mir ungefähr sagen, wann Sie ankommen? - 2. [sign] (An)zeichen das; [hint] Hinweis der.

indicative [ɪn'dɪkətɪv] ◇ adj: **to be indicative of sthg** auf etw (A) hindeuten, auf etw (A) schließen lassen. ◇ n GRAM Indikativ der.

indicator ['ɪndɪkeɪtər] n - 1. [sign] Indikator der - 2. [on car] Blinker der.

indices ['ɪndɪsiːz] Pl ⊳ **index**.

indict [ɪn'daɪt] vt: **to indict sb (for)** jn anlklagen (wegen (+ G)).

indictment [ɪn'daɪtmənt] n - 1. LAW Anklageerhebung die - 2. [criticism]: **an indictment of** ein Armutszeugnis für.

indifference [ɪn'dɪfrəns] n Gleichgültigkeit die.

indifferent [ɪn'dɪfrənt] adj - 1. [uninterested] gleichgültig; **to be indifferent to sthg** sich für etw nicht interessieren - 2. [mediocre] mittelmäßig.

indigenous [ɪn'dɪdʒɪnəs] adj [culture, traditions] einheimisch, landeseigen.

indigestion [,ɪndɪ'dʒestʃn] n (U) Magenverstimmung die.

indignant [ɪnˈdɪɡnənt] *adj*: **to be indignant (at)** empört sein (über *(+ A)*).

indignity [ɪnˈdɪɡnətɪ] *n* Demütigung *die*.

indigo [ˈɪndɪɡəʊ] *adj* indigoblau.

indirect [ˌɪndɪˈrekt] *adj* indirekt; **an indirect route** ein Umweg.

indiscreet [ˌɪndɪˈskriːt] *adj* indiskret; [tactless] taktlos.

indiscriminate [ˌɪndɪˈskrɪmɪnət] *adj* wahllos; [treatment] willkürlich; [person] unkritisch.

indispensable [ˌɪndɪˈspensəbl] *adj* unentbehrlich.

indisputable [ˌɪndɪˈspjuːtəbl] *adj* unbestreitbar; [evidence] unanfechtbar.

indistinguishable [ˌɪndɪˈstɪŋɡwɪʃəbl] *adj*: **to be indistinguishable (from sb/sthg)** (von jm/etw) nicht zu unterscheiden sein.

individual [ˌɪndɪˈvɪdʒʊəl] <> *adj* - 1. [single] einzeln; [tuition] Einzel-; **individual case** Einzelfall *der* - 2. [distinctive] individuell. <> *n* Einzelne *die*, Individuum *das*.

individually [ˌɪndɪˈvɪdʒʊəlɪ] *adv* einzeln.

Indonesia [ˌɪndəˈniːzɪə] *n* Indonesien *nt*.

indoor [ˈɪndɔːr] *adj* [swimming pool, sports] Hallen-; [plant] Zimmer-.

indoors [ˌɪnˈdɔːz] *adv* [stay] drinnen; [go] nach drinnen.

induce [ɪnˈdjuːs] *vt* [persuade]: **to induce sb to do sthg** jn dazu bringen, etw zu tun.

inducement [ɪnˈdjuːsmənt] *n* [incentive] Anreiz *der*.

induction course *n* Einführungskurs *der*.

indulge [ɪnˈdʌldʒ] <> *vt* - 1. [whim] nachgeben *(+ D)*; [passion] frönen *(+ D)* - 2. [child, person] verwöhnen. <> *vi*: **to indulge in sthg** etw *(D)* frönen.

indulgence [ɪnˈdʌldʒəns] *n* - 1. *(U)* [tolerance, kindness] Nachsicht *die* - 2. [special treat] Luxus *der*.

indulgent [ɪnˈdʌldʒənt] *adj* nachsichtig; [giving way] nachgiebig.

industrial [ɪnˈdʌstrɪəl] *adj* industriell; [city, area, society] Industrie-.

industrial action *n*: **to take industrial action** in den Ausstand treten.

industrial estate *UK*, **industrial park** *US n* Industriegebiet *das*.

industrialist [ɪnˈdʌstrɪəlɪst] *n* Industrielle *der, die*.

industrial park *n US* = **industrial estate**.

industrial relations *npl* Beziehungen *Pl* zwischen Arbeitgebern und Gewerkschaften.

industrial revolution *n* industrielle Revolution.

industrious [ɪnˈdʌstrɪəs] *adj* fleißig.

industry [ˈɪndəstrɪ] *n* - 1. [gen] Industrie *die*; **the tourist industry** die Tourismusbranche - 2. [hard work] Fleiß *der*.

inebriated [ɪˈniːbrɪeɪtɪd] *adj fml* betrunken.

inedible [ɪnˈedɪbl] *adj* - 1. [unpleasant to eat] ungenießbar - 2. [poisonous] nicht essbar.

ineffective [ˌɪnɪˈfektɪv] *adj* unwirksam.

ineffectual [ˌɪnɪˈfektʃʊəl] *adj* [person] unfähig; [plan] ineffizient.

inefficiency [ˌɪnɪˈfɪʃnsɪ] *n* [of person] Unfähigkeit *die*; [of process] Unproduktivität *die*; [of machine] Unwirtschaftlichkeit *die*.

inefficient [ˌɪnɪˈfɪʃnt] *adj* [person] unfähig, ineffizient; [process] unproduktiv; [machine] unwirtschaftlich.

ineligible [ɪnˈelɪdʒəbl] *adj*: **to be ineligible for sthg** [promotion] für etw nicht infrage kommen; [benefits] auf etw *(A)* keinen Anspruch haben.

inept [ɪˈnept] *adj* [person] unfähig; [comment] unpassend; [performance, attempt] ungeschickt.

inequality [ˌɪnɪˈkwɒlətɪ] *n* - 1. [gen] Ungleichheit *die* - 2. [difference] Unterschied *der*.

inert [ɪˈnɜːt] *adj* [person] reglos.

inertia [ɪˈnɜːʃə] *n* [gen] Trägheit *die*.

inescapable [ˌɪnɪˈskeɪpəbl] *adj* unausweichlich.

inevitable [ɪnˈevɪtəbl] <> *adj* unvermeidlich. <> *n*: **the inevitable** das Unvermeidliche.

inevitably [ɪnˈevɪtəblɪ] *adv* zwangsläufig.

inexcusable [ˌɪnɪkˈskjuːzəbl] *adj* unverzeihlich, unentschuldbar.

inexhaustible [ˌɪnɪɡˈzɔːstəbl] *adj* unerschöpflich.

inexpensive [ˌɪnɪkˈspensɪv] *adj* preiswert.

inexperienced [ˌɪnɪkˈspɪərɪənst] *adj* unerfahren; **to be inexperienced in sthg** mit etw wenig vertraut sein.

inexplicable [ˌɪnɪkˈsplɪkəbl] *adj* unerklärlich.

infallible [ɪnˈfæləbl] *adj* unfehlbar.

infamous [ˈɪnfəməs] *adj* berüchtigt.

infancy [ˈɪnfənsɪ] *n* frühe Kindheit; **to be in its infancy** *fig* (noch) in den Kinderschuhen stecken.

infant [ˈɪnfənt] *n* - 1. [baby] Säugling *der* - 2. [young child] Kleinkind *das*.

infantry [ˈɪnfəntrɪ] *n* Infanterie *die*.

infant school *n UK* Vorschule *die* (für 5- bis 7-Jährige).

infatuated [ɪnˈfætjʊeɪtɪd] *adj*: **to be infatuated (with sb/sthg)** (in jn/etw) vernarrt sein.

infatuation [ɪnˌfætjʊˈeɪʃn] *n*: **infatuation (with sb/sthg)** Vernarrtheit *die* (in jn/etw).

infect [ɪnˈfekt] *vt* MED infizieren.

infection [ɪnˈfekʃn] *n* MED Infektion *die*; **ear infection** Ohrenentzündung *die*.

infectious [ɪn'fekʃəs] *adj liter* & *fig* ansteckend.

infer [ɪn'fɜːr] *vt* - 1. [deduce]: **to infer that...** folgern, dass...; **to infer sthg (from sthg)** etw (aus etw) folgern - 2. *inf* [imply] anldeuten.

inferior [ɪn'fɪərɪər] ⟨⟩ *adj* - 1. [lower in status] untergeordnet; **to be inferior (to sb/sthg)** (jm/etw) untergeordnet sein - 2. [lower in quality] minderwertig; **to feel inferior** sich unterlegen fühlen; **to be inferior to sthg** von geringerer Qualität als etw sein. ⟨⟩ *n* [in status] Untergebene *der*, *die*.

inferiority [ɪn,fɪərɪ'ɒrətɪ] *n* - 1. [in status] untergeordnete Stellung - 2. [in quality] Minderwertigkeit *die*.

inferiority complex *n* Minderwertigkeitskomplex *der*.

inferno [ɪn'fɜːnəʊ] (*pl* -s) *n* Flammenmeer *das*.

infertile [ɪn'fɜːtaɪl] *adj* unfruchtbar.

infested [ɪn'festɪd] *adj*: **infested with sthg** [vermin, insects] von etw befallen; [weeds] von etw überwuchert.

infighting ['ɪn,faɪtɪŋ] *n (U)* [rivalry] interne Machtkämpfe *Pl*; [quarrelling] interne Querelen *Pl*.

infiltrate ['ɪnfɪltreɪt] *vt* [territory] infiltrieren; [party, organization] unterwandern.

infinite ['ɪnfɪnət] *adj* unendlich.

infinitive [ɪn'fɪnɪtɪv] *n* Infinitiv *der*.

infinity [ɪn'fɪnətɪ] *n* - 1. [unreachable point] Unendlichkeit *die*. MATHS Unendliche *das*.

infirm [ɪn'fɜːm] *adj* gebrechlich.

infirmary [ɪn'fɜːmərɪ] *n* - 1. [hospital] Krankenhaus *das* - 2. [room] Krankenzimmer *das*.

infirmity [ɪn'fɜːmətɪ] *n* - 1. [individual weakness or illness] Gebrechen *das* - 2. [state of being weak or ill] Gebrechlichkeit *die*.

inflamed [ɪn'fleɪmd] *adj* MED entzündet.

inflammable [ɪn'flæməbl] *adj* leicht entzündlich.

inflammation [,ɪnflə'meɪʃn] *n* MED Entzündung *die*.

inflatable [ɪn'fleɪtəbl] *adj* aufblasbar.

inflate [ɪn'fleɪt] *vt* - 1. [fill with air - tyre] auflpumpen; [- life-jacket, balloon] aufblasen - 2. ECON [increase] in die Höhe treiben.

inflation [ɪn'fleɪʃn] *n* ECON Inflation *die*.

inflationary [ɪn'fleɪʃnrɪ] *adj* ECON [policy, spiral] Inflations-; [trend, wage rise] inflationär.

inflation rate *n* ECON Inflationsrate *die*.

inflict [ɪn'flɪkt] *vt*: **to inflict sthg on sb** [pain] jm etw zufügen; [problem] jm mit etw belasten; [punishment] jn mit etw belegen; [responsibility] jm etw übertragen.

influence ['ɪnfluəns] ⟨⟩ *n*: **influence (on sb/sthg), influence (over sb/sthg)** Einfluss *der* (auf jn/etw); **under the influence of** unter dem Einfluss von. ⟨⟩ *vt* beeinflussen.

influential [,ɪnflu'enʃl] *adj* einflussreich.

influenza [,ɪnflu'enzə] *n fml* Grippe *die*.

influx ['ɪnflʌks] *n* Zustrom *der*.

inform [ɪn'fɔːm] *vt* benachrichtigen; [police] verständigen; **to inform sb of/about sthg** jm etw mitteilen. ⟨⟩ **inform on** *vt insep* anlzeigen.

informal [ɪn'fɔːml] *adj* - 1. [casual, relaxed - party, clothes] zwanglos; [- language] informell - 2. [non-official] inoffiziell.

informant [ɪn'fɔːmənt] *n* Informant *der*, -in *die*.

information [,ɪnfə'meɪʃn] *n (U)*: information (on OR about sthg) Informationen *Pl* (über etw (A)); **to get information** sich informieren; **a piece of information** eine Auskunft, eine Information; **'Information'** 'Information', 'Auskunft'; **for your information** COMM zu Ihrer Kenntnisnahme OR Information.

information desk *n* Auskunftsschalter *der*.

information technology *n* Informationstechnologie *die*.

informative [ɪn'fɔːmətɪv] *adj* [person] auskunftsfreudig; [book, film] informativ.

informer [ɪn'fɔːmər] *n* [denouncer] Informant *der*, -in *die*.

infrared [,ɪnfrə'red] *adj* Infrarot-.

infrastructure ['ɪnfrə,strʌktʃər] *n* Infrastruktur *die*.

infringe [ɪn'frɪndʒ] ⟨⟩ *vt* - 1. [right] verletzen - 2. [law, agreement] verstoßen gegen. ⟨⟩ *vi*: **to infringe on sb's rights** js Rechte verletzen.

infringement [ɪn'frɪndʒmənt] *n* - 1. [of right] Verletzung *die* - 2. [of law, agreement] Verstoß *der*.

infuriating [ɪn'fjʊərɪeɪtɪŋ] *adj*: **he/his behaviour is infuriating!** er/sein Benehmen macht mich rasend!

ingenious [ɪn'dʒiːnɪəs] *adj* genial; [device, method] raffiniert; [person] einfallsreich.

ingenuity [,ɪndʒɪ'njuːətɪ] *n* [of person] Genialität *die*, Einfallsreichtum *der*; [of device, method] Raffiniertheit *die*.

ingot ['ɪŋgət] *n* [of gold, silver] Barren *der*.

ingrained [,ɪn'greɪnd] *adj* - 1. [dirt] tief sitzend - 2. [belief] unerschütterlich; [hatred] tief.

ingratiating [ɪn'greɪʃɪeɪtɪŋ] *adj* [smile] zuckersüß; [person, manner] schmeichlerisch.

ingredient [ɪn'griːdɪənt] *n* - 1. [in cooking] Zutat *die* - 2. [element] Element *das*.

inhabit [ɪn'hæbɪt] *vt* bewohnen.

inhabitant [ɪn'hæbɪtənt] *n* [of country, city] Einwohner *der*, -in *die*; [of house] Bewohner *der*, -in *die*.

inhale [ɪn'heɪl] ⟨⟩ *vt* einlatmen. ⟨⟩ *vi* [breathe in] einlatmen; [smoker] Lungenzüge machen.

inhaler [ɪn'heɪləʳ] n MED Inhalationsapparat der.

inherent [ɪn'hɪərənt, ɪn'herənt] adj: her inherent laziness die ihr eigene Faulheit; the dangers inherent in this sport die mit diesem Sport verbundenen Gefahren.

inherently [ɪn'hɪərəntlɪ, ɪn'herəntlɪ] adv von Natur aus.

inherit [ɪn'herɪt] <> vt: to inherit sthg (from sb) etw (von jm) erben. <> vi erben.

inheritance [ɪn'herɪtəns] n Erbe das.

inhibit [ɪn'hɪbɪt] vt hemmen.

inhibition [ˌɪnhɪ'bɪʃn] n Hemmung die.

inhospitable [ˌɪnhɒ'spɪtəbl] adj - 1. [person] ungastlich - 2. [climate, area] unwirtlich.

in-house <> adj hausintern; in-house staff fest angestellte Mitarbeiter. <> adv im Hause.

inhuman [ɪn'hju:mən] adj [cruel] unmenschlich.

initial [ɪ'nɪʃl] (UK) (US) <> adj - 1. [early] anfänglich - 2.: initial letter Initiale die. <> vt mit seinen Initialen unterschreiben; [as authorization] ablzeichnen. ⏩ **initials** npl Initialen Pl.

initially [ɪ'nɪʃəlɪ] adv anfangs.

initiate vt [ɪ'nɪʃɪeɪt] - 1. [start] initiieren; [talks, scheme] in die Wege leiten - 2. [teach]: to initiate sb (into sthg) [into mystery, secret] jn (in etw (A)) einweihen; [into group] jn (in etw (A)) feierlich aufnehmen; [into skill] jn (in etw (A)) einlführen.

initiative [ɪ'nɪʃətɪv] n Initiative die.

inject [ɪn'dʒekt] vt - 1. MED: to inject sb with sthg, to inject sthg into sb jm etw spritzen OR injizieren - 2. fig [add]: to inject sthg into sthg [fun, excitement] etw in etw (A) bringen; [money, funds] etw in etw (A) pumpen; [resources] etw zu etw beilsteuern.

injection [ɪn'dʒekʃn] n - 1. MED Spritze die, Injektion die - 2. [of funds] Zuschuss der.

injure ['ɪndʒəʳ] vt [hurt physically, offend] verletzen.

injured [ɪn'dʒəd] <> adj [physically hurt, offended] verletzt. <> npl: the injured die Verletzten.

injury ['ɪndʒərɪ] n (U) - 1. [physical harm] Verletzungen Pl - 2. [wound, to one's feelings] Verletzung die; to do o.s. an injury sich verletzen.

injury time n (U) Nachspielzeit die.

injustice [ɪn'dʒʌstɪs] n Ungerechtigkeit die; to do sb an injustice jm unrecht tun.

ink [ɪŋk] n (U) [for writing] Tinte die; [for drawing] Tusche die; [for printing] Druckfarbe die.

ink-jet printer n Tintenstrahldrucker der.

inkling ['ɪŋklɪŋ] n: to have an inkling of sthg etw ahnen.

inlaid [ˌɪn'leɪd] adj: inlaid (with sthg) (mit etw) eingelegt.

inland <> adj ['ɪnlənd] Binnen-. <> adv [ɪn'lænd] landeinwärts.

Inland Revenue n UK: the Inland Revenue ≃ das Finanzamt.

in-laws npl inf angeheiratete Verwandte Pl; [parents-in-law] Schwiegereltern Pl.

inlet ['ɪnlet] n - 1. [stretch of water - from lake] (schmale) Bucht; [- from sea] Meeresarm der - 2. [way in] Zuleitung die.

inmate ['ɪnmeɪt] n Insasse der, -sin die.

inn [ɪn] n Wirtshaus das.

innate [ɪ'neɪt] adj angeboren.

inner ['ɪnəʳ] adj - 1. [most central] innere(r) (s); [room] innen liegend; [courtyard] Innen-; inner ear Innenohr das; Inner London Innenstadt die Londons - 2. [unexpressed, secret] innere.

inner city n: the inner city die Innenstadt, die Innenbezirke einer Stadt, in denen es oft soziale Probleme gibt.

inner tube n Schlauch der.

innings ['ɪnɪŋz] (pl inv) n UK [in cricket] Durchgang der.

innocence ['ɪnəsəns] n (U) Unschuld die.

innocent ['ɪnəsənt] adj unschuldig; to be innocent of sthg an etw (D) unschuldig sein.

innocuous [ɪ'nɒkjʊəs] adj harmlos.

innovation [ˌɪnə'veɪʃn] n Innovation die.

innovative ['ɪnəvətɪv] adj innovativ.

innuendo [ˌɪnju:'endəʊ] (pl -es OR -s) n - 1. [individual remark] versteckte Andeutung, Anspielung die - 2. (U) [style of speaking] Anspielungen Pl.

innumerable [ɪ'nju:mərəbl] adj unzählig.

inoculate [ɪ'nɒkjʊleɪt] vt impfen.

inordinately [ɪ'nɔ:dɪnətlɪ] adv fml außerordentlich.

in-patient n stationärer Patient, stationäre Patientin.

input ['ɪnpʊt] (pt & pp inv OR -ted) <> n (U) - 1. [contribution - money, resources] Investition die; [- labour, effort] Beitrag der - 2. COMPUT Eingabe die - 3. ELEC Energiezufuhr die. <> vt COMPUT einlgeben.

inquest ['ɪnkwest] n LAW gerichtliche Untersuchung der Todesursache.

inquire [ɪn'kwaɪəʳ] <> vt: to inquire when/whether OR if/how sich erkundigen wann/ob/wie. <> vi [ask for information] sich erkundigen; to inquire about sthg sich nach etw erkundigen, nach etw fragen. ⏩ **inquire after** vt insep sich erkundigen nach. ⏩ **inquire into** vt insep untersuchen.

inquiry [ɪn'kwaɪərɪ] n - 1. [question] Anfrage die; to make inquiries Erkundigungen einlziehen; [police] Nachforschungen anlstellen - 2. [investigation] Untersuchung die.

inquisitive [ɪn'kwɪzətɪv] adj [curious] neugierig; [for knowledge] wissbegierig.

inroads ['ɪnrəʊdz] npl: **to make inroads into sthg** [savings, supplies] etw anlgreifen; [field of knowledge] in etw (A) vorldringen.

insane [ɪn'seɪn] adj - **1.** MED [mad] geisteskrank - **2.** fig [person, idea, jealousy] verrückt.

insanity [ɪn'sænətɪ] n (U) MED [madness] Geisteskrankheit die.

insatiable [ɪn'seɪʃəbl] adj unersättlich.

inscription [ɪn'skrɪpʃn] n - **1.** [on wall, headstone, plaque - written] Aufschrift die; [- cut] Inschrift die - **2.** [in book] Widmung die.

inscrutable [ɪn'skruːtəbl] adj unergründlich; [look] undurchdringlich.

insect ['ɪnsekt] n Insekt das.

insecticide [ɪn'sektɪsaɪd] n (U) Insektizid das.

insect repellent n (U) Insektenschutzmittel das.

insecure [ˌɪnsɪ'kjʊəʳ] adj unsicher.

insensitive [ɪn'sensətɪv] adj - **1.** [unkind, thoughtless] unsensibel - **2.** [unresponsive]: **insensitive to sthg** unempfänglich für etw - **3.** [to pain, cold]: **insensitive to sthg** unempfindlich gegen etw.

inseparable [ɪn'seprəbl] adj - **1.** [subjects, facts]: **to be inseparable (from sthg)** (mit etw) untrennbar verbunden sein - **2.** [people] unzertrennlich.

insert vt [ɪn'sɜːt] - **1.** [put inside]: **to insert sthg (in** OR **into sthg)** etw (in etw (A)) einlführen - **2.** [include, add]: **to insert sthg (in** OR **into sthg)** etw (in etw (A)) einlfügen. ◇ n ['ɪnsɜːt] Einlage die.

insertion [ɪn'sɜːʃn] n - **1.** [act of inserting] Einführen das - **2.** [thing inserted - in text] Einfügung die.

in-service training n UK (berufsbegleitende) Fortbildung.

inshore ◇ adj ['ɪnʃɔːʳ] Küsten-. ◇ adv [ɪn'ʃɔːʳ] [be situated] in Küstennähe.

inside [ɪn'saɪd] ◇ prep - **1.** [indicating place, position] in (+ D); (with verbs of motion) in (+ A); **it's inside the box** es ist in der Schachtel; **put it inside the box** leg es in die Schachtel; **come inside the house!** komm ins Haus! - **2.** [indicating time, limit]: **inside three weeks** in weniger als drei Wochen; **he was just inside the record** er lag knapp unter der Rekordzeit. ◇ adv - **1.** [referring to place, object, building] innen; **to be inside** drinnen sein; **to come inside** hereinlkommen; **to go inside** hineinlgehen; **there was something inside** es war etwas drin - **2.** [referring to body, mind] innerlich - **3.** inf prison sl im Kittchen OR Knast; **to be inside** sitzen. ◇ adj Innen-; **an inside toilet** eine Toilette im Haus; **inside information** vertrauliche Information. ◇ n [interior, inner part]: **the inside** das Innere; **lock the door from the inside** schließ die Tür von innen ab; **on the inside** innen; **inside out** [clothes] links (he-

rum); **to turn sthg inside out** etw auf links drehen; **to know sthg inside out** fig etw in- und auswendig kennen. ◆ **insides** npl inf [intestines] Eingeweide Pl. ◆ **inside of** prep US [building, object] in.

inside lane n AUT [in UK] linke Fahrspur; AUT [in Europe, US etc] rechte Fahrspur.

insight ['ɪnsaɪt] n - **1.** (U) [wisdom]: **insight (into sthg)** Verständnis das (für etw) - **2.** [glimpse]: **insight (into sthg)** Einblick das (in etw (A)).

insignificant [ˌɪnsɪg'nɪfɪkənt] adj unbedeutend.

insincere [ˌɪnsɪn'sɪəʳ] adj [person, remark] unaufrichtig; [smile] falsch.

insinuate [ɪn'sɪnjʊeɪt] vt pej [imply]: **to insinuate (that)** anldeuten (dass).

insipid [ɪn'sɪpɪd] adj pej - **1.** [taste, colour, music] fade; [person, character] geistlos - **2.** [food, drink] fade, geschmacklos.

insist [ɪn'sɪst] ◇ vt - **1.** [state firmly]: **to insist that** darauf beharren, dass - **2.** [demand]: **to insist that** darauf bestehen, dass. ◇ vi: **to insist on sthg** auf etw (D) bestehen; **to insist on doing sthg** darauf bestehen, etw zu tun.

insistent [ɪn'sɪstənt] adj - **1.** [determined] beharrlich; **to be insistent on sthg** auf etw (D) beharren OR bestehen - **2.** [continual] anhaltend.

insofar [ˌɪnsəʊ'fɑːʳ] ◆ **insofar as** conj insofern als.

insole ['ɪnsəʊl] n Einlegesohle die.

insolent ['ɪnsələnt] adj frech.

insolvent [ɪn'sɒlvənt] adj zahlungsunfähig, insolvent.

insomnia [ɪn'sɒmnɪə] n Schlaflosigkeit die.

inspect [ɪn'spekt] vt - **1.** [letter, person] genau betrachten - **2.** [factory, troops, premises] inspizieren; [machine] prüfen.

inspection [ɪn'spekʃn] n - **1.** [examination] Prüfung die - **2.** [of factory, troops, premises] Inspektion die; [of machine] Prüfung die.

inspector [ɪn'spektəʳ] n - **1.** [official] Inspektor der, -in die; [on bus, train] Kontrolleur der, -in die - **2.** [of police] ≈ Kommissar der.

inspiration [ˌɪnspə'reɪʃn] n - **1.** (U) [source of ideas] Inspiration die - **2.** [brilliant idea] Eingebung die.

inspire [ɪn'spaɪəʳ] vt inspirieren; **to inspire sb with sthg, to inspire sthg in sb** [confidence, passion, enthusiasm] in jm etw wecken; [respect] jm etw einlflößen.

install UK, **instal** US [ɪn'stɔːl] vt [machinery, equipment] installieren.

installation [ˌɪnstə'leɪʃn] n - **1.** [base, site] Anlage die - **2.** (U) [act of fitting] Installation die.

instalment UK, **installment** US [ɪn'stɔːlmənt] n - **1.** [payment] Rate die; **to pay**

in instalments in Raten zahlen - **2.** [episode - of story] Fortsetzung *die*; [- of TV, radio programme] Folge *die*.

instance ['ɪnstəns] *n* Fall *der*; **for instance** zum Beispiel.

instant ['ɪnstənt] ◇ *adj* - **1.** [immediate] sofort, unmittelbar - **2.** [food]: **instant coffee** Instant- OR Pulverkaffee *der*; **instant mashed potato** fertiges Kartoffelpüree. ◇ *n* [moment] Augenblick *der*, Moment *der*; **the instant (that)...** in dem Augenblick, in dem...; **this instant** sofort.

instantly ['ɪnstəntlɪ] *adv* sofort.

instead [ɪn'sted] *adv* stattdessen; **instead of** statt (+ G); **instead of him** an seiner Stelle.

instep ['ɪnstep] *n* Spann *der*, Fußrücken *der*.

instigate ['ɪnstɪgeɪt] *vt* [discussions] den Anstoß geben zu; [meeting] in die Wege leiten; [investigation] einleiten; [strike, revolt] anlstiften zu.

instil UK, **instill** US [ɪn'stɪl] *vt*: **to instil sth in(to) sb** jm etw beilbringen.

instinct ['ɪnstɪŋkt] *n* - **1.** (U) [natural ability] Instinkt *der*; **by instinct** instinktiv - **2.** [impulse] Impuls *der*.

instinctive [ɪn'stɪŋktɪv] *adj* instinktiv.

institute ['ɪnstɪtjuːt] ◇ *n* Institut *das*. ◇ *vt* - **1.** [establish] einlführen - **2.** [proceedings] anlstrengen.

institution [ˌɪnstɪ'tjuːʃn] *n* - **1.** [tradition, system, organization] Institution *die* - **2.** [home] Heim *das*, Anstalt *die*.

instruct [ɪn'strʌkt] *vt* - **1.** [tell, order]: **to instruct sb to do sthg** jn anlweisen, etw zu tun - **2.** [teach] unterrichten; **to instruct sb in sthg** jn in etw (D) unterrichten.

instruction [ɪn'strʌkʃn] *n* - **1.** [order] Anweisung *die* - **2.** (U) [teaching] Unterricht *der*. ◆ **instructions** *npl* [for use] Gebrauchsanleitung *die*.

instructor [ɪn'strʌktər] *n* Lehrer *der*, -in *die*.

instrument ['ɪnstrʊmənt] *n* - **1.** [gen] Instrument *das* - **2.** liter [means] Mittel *das*.

instrumental [ˌɪnstrʊ'mentl] *adj* [important, helpful]: **to be instrumental in sthg** eine entscheidende Rolle bei etw spielen.

instrument panel *n* Armaturenbrett *das*.

insubordinate [ˌɪnsə'bɔːdɪnət] *adj fml* aufsässig; MIL ungehorsam.

insubstantial [ˌɪnsəb'stænʃl] *adj* - **1.** [fragile] zerbrechlich - **2.** [unsatisfying - meal] dürftig; [- book] ohne Substanz.

insufficient [ˌɪnsə'fɪʃnt] *adj fml*: **insufficient (for sthg)** unzureichend (für etw); **to be insufficient to do sthg** nicht dafür auslreichen, um etw zu tun.

insular ['ɪnsjʊlər] *adj* [narrow-minded] engstirnig.

insulate ['ɪnsjʊleɪt] *vt* - **1.** [house, tank & ELEC] isolieren - **2.** [protect] schützen; **to insulate sb against** OR **from sthg** jn gegen etw ablschirmen.

insulating tape ['ɪnsjʊleɪtɪŋ-] *n* (U) UK Isolierband *das*.

insulation [ˌɪnsjʊ'leɪʃn] *n* (U) [material] Isolierung *die*.

insulin ['ɪnsjʊlɪn] *n* Insulin *das*.

insult ◇ *vt* [ɪn'sʌlt] beleidigen. ◇ *n* ['ɪnsʌlt] Beleidigung *die*.

insuperable [ɪn'suːprəbl] *adj fml* unüberwindlich.

insurance [ɪn'ʃʊərəns] *n* liter & fig: insurance **(against sthg)** Versicherung (gegen etw).

insurance policy *n* Versicherungspolice *die*.

insure [ɪn'ʃʊər] ◇ *vt* - **1.** [against fire, accident, theft]: **to insure sb/sthg against sthg** jn/ etw gegen etw versichern - **2.** US [make certain] sicher stellen. ◇ *vi* [protect]: **to insure against sthg** sich gegen etw ablsichern.

insurer [ɪn'ʃʊərər] *n* Versicherungsgeber *der*, -in *die*.

insurmountable [ˌɪnsə'maʊntəbl] *adj* unüberwindlich.

intact [ɪn'tækt] *adj* unversehrt, intakt.

intake ['ɪnteɪk] *n* - **1.** [amount consumed] Aufnahme *die* - **2.** [people recruited]: **this year's intake includes several overseas students** dieses Jahr wurden einige ausländische Studenten aufgenommen - **3.** [inlet] Einlass *der*.

integral ['ɪntɪgrəl] *adj* [part, feature] wesentlich; **to be integral to sthg** für etw wesentlich sein.

integrate ['ɪntɪgreɪt] *vt* - **1.** [include in a larger unit, combine] integrieren - **2.** [minorities, marginalized people] integrieren, einlgliedern.

integrity [ɪn'tegrətɪ] *n* - **1.** [honour] Integrität *die* - **2.** fml [wholeness] Einheit *die*.

intellect ['ɪntəlekt] *n* - **1.** [ability to reason] Verstand *der* - **2.** [mind, intelligence] Intellekt *der*.

intellectual [ˌɪntə'lektjʊəl] ◇ *adj* intellektuell. ◇ *n* Intellektuelle *der, die*.

intelligence [ɪn'telɪdʒəns] *n* (U) - **1.** [ability to reason] Intelligenz *die* - **2.** [information service] Nachrichtendienst *der* - **3.** [information] Information *die*.

intelligent [ɪn'telɪdʒənt] *adj* intelligent.

intend [ɪn'tend] *vt* beabsichtigen; **to be intended as sthg** als etw gemeint sein; **it was intended to be a surprise** es sollte eine Überraschung sein; **to intend doing** OR **to do sthg** beabsichtigen, etw zu tun.

intended [ɪn'tendɪd] *adj* [result] beabsichtigt.

intense [ɪn'tens] *adj* - **1.** [competition, pain, emotion] heftig; [concentration] äußerst; [colour, light] intensiv; [heat] stark - **2.** [person - serious] ernsthaft; [- emotional] heftig.

intensely [ɪn'tenslɪ] *adv* äußerst.

intensify [ɪn'tensɪfaɪ] ◇ *vt* intensivieren. ◇ *vi* [cold, heat] zulnehmen; [pressure, problem] sich verschärfen.

intensity [ɪn'tensətɪ] *n* - **1.** [of competition, pain, emotion] Heftigkeit *die*; [of colour, light, concentration] Intensität *die*; [of heat] Stärke *die* - **2.** [of person - seriousness] Ernsthaftigkeit *die*; [- of emotional nature] Heftigkeit *die*.

intensive [ɪn'tensɪv] *adj* intensiv.

intensive care *n*: **to be in intensive care** auf der Intensivstation sein.

intent [ɪn'tent] ◇ *adj* - **1.** [expression] gespannt - **2.** [determined]: **to be intent (up)on doing sthg** fest entschlossen sein, etw zu tun. ◇ *n fml* Absicht *die*; **to all intents and purposes** im Grunde, so gut wie.

intention [ɪn'tenʃn] *n* Absicht *die*.

intentional [ɪn'tenʃənl] *adj* absichtlich.

intently [ɪn'tentlɪ] *adv* konzentriert.

interact [ˌɪntər'ækt] *vi* - **1.** [people]: **to interact (with sb) (mit jm)** Kontakt haben - **2.** [forces, ideas]: **to interact (with sthg) (mit etw)** in Wechselwirkung stehen.

intercede [ˌɪntə'siːd] *vi fml*: **to intercede (with sb)** sich einlsetzen (bei jm).

intercept [ˌɪntə'sept] *vt* ablfangen.

interchange *n* ['ɪntətʃeɪndʒ] [road junction] Kreuzung *die*.

interchangeable [ˌɪntə'tʃeɪndʒəbl] *adj*: **interchangeable (with sb/sthg)** austauschbar (mit jm/etw).

intercom ['ɪntəkɒm] *n* Gegensprechanlage *die*.

intercourse ['ɪntəkɔːs] *n*: **(sexual) intercourse** (Geschlechts)verkehr *der*.

interest ['ɪntrəst] ◇ *n* - **1.** [enthusiasm, appeal, advantage] Interesse *das*; **interest in sb/sthg** Interesse an jm/etw - **2.** [hobby] Hobby *das* - **3.** *(U)* [financial charge] Zinsen *Pl* - **4.** [share in company] Anteil *der*. ◇ *vt* interessieren; **can I interest you in buying my car?** wären Sie interessiert, mein Auto zu kaufen?

interested ['ɪntrəstɪd] *adj* - **1.** [enthusiastic, curious] interessiert; *(phrase)*: **to be interested in sthg** [in job] Interesse haben an etw (+ *D*); [in butterflies, films] sich für etw (*A*) interessieren; **to be interested in doing sthg** interessiert sein, etw zu tun - **2.** [concerned] beteiligt.

interesting ['ɪntrəstɪŋ] *adj* interessant.

interest rate *n* Zinssatz *der*.

interface *n* ['ɪntəfeɪs] COMPUT Schnittstelle *die*.

interfere [ˌɪntə'fɪər] *vi* - **1.** [meddle]: **to interfere (in sthg)** sich (in etw (*A*)) einlmischen - **2.** [cause disruption]: **to interfere with sthg** etw stören.

interference [ˌɪntə'fɪərəns] *n (U)* - **1.** [meddling]: **interference (with** OR **in sthg)** Einmischung *die* (in etw (*A*)) - **2.** RADIO & TV Störung *die*.

interim ['ɪntərɪm] ◇ *adj* [measure] Übergangs-; [report] Zwischen-. ◇ *n*: **in the interim** in der Zwischenzeit.

interior [ɪn'tɪərɪər] ◇ *adj* Innen-. ◇ *n* [inside] Innere *das*.

interlock [ˌɪntə'lɒk] *vi* TECH ineinander greifen; **to interlock with sthg** in etw (*A*) greifen.

interlude ['ɪntəluːd] *n* [period of time] Zwischenzeit *die*.

intermediary [ˌɪntə'miːdjərɪ] *n* Mittelsmann *der*, -person *die*.

intermediate [ˌɪntə'miːdjət] *adj* - **1.** [transitional] Zwischen- - **2.** [post-beginner — course] für fortgeschrittene Anfänger.

interminable [ɪn'tɜːmɪnəbl] *adj* endlos.

intermission [ˌɪntə'mɪʃn] *n* Pause *die*.

intermittent [ˌɪntə'mɪtənt] *adj* in Abständen auftretend.

intern ◇ *vt* [ɪn'tɜːn] internieren. ◇ *n* ['ɪntɜːn] *esp US* [trainee - teacher] Assistent *der*, -in *die*; [- doctor] Assistenzarzt *der*, -ärztin *die*.

internal [ɪn'tɜːnl] *adj* - **1.** [within the body] innere(r) (s) - **2.** [within a country - flight] Inlands-; [- trade] Binnen- - **3.** [within an organization] intern.

internally [ɪn'tɜːnəlɪ] *adv* - **1.** [within the body] innerlich - **2.** [within a country] landesintern - **3.** [within an organization] intern.

Internal Revenue *n US*: **the Internal Revenue** das Finanzamt.

international [ˌɪntə'næʃənl] ◇ *adj* international. ◇ *n UK* - **1.** SPORT [match] Länderspiel *das* - **2.** SPORT [player] Nationalspieler *der*, -in *die*.

Internet ['ɪntənet] *n*: **the Internet** das Internet.

Internet service provider *n* COMPUT Internetprovider *der*.

interpret [ɪn'tɜːprɪt] ◇ *vt* [understand] ausllegen, interpretieren; **to interpret sthg as** etw interpretieren als. ◇ *vi* dolmetschen.

interpreter [ɪn'tɜːprɪtər] *n* [person] Dolmetscher *der*, -in *die*.

interpreting [ɪn'tɜːprɪtɪŋ] *n* [occupation] Dolmetschen *das*.

interrelate [ˌɪntərɪ'leɪt] *vi*: **to interrelate (with sthg)** (mit etw) in Beziehung stehen.

interrogate [ɪn'terəgeɪt] *vt* [question] verhören.

interrogation [ɪnˌterə'geɪʃn] *n* Verhör *das*.

interrogation mark n US Fragezeichen das.

interrogative [,ɪntə'rɒgətɪv] <> adj GRAM Frage-. <> n - 1. GRAM [form]: **the interrogative** die Frageform - 2. GRAM [word] Fragefürwort das.

interrupt [,ɪntə'rʌpt] vt & vi unterbrechen.

interruption [,ɪntə'rʌpʃn] n Unterbrechung die.

intersect [,ɪntə'sekt] <> vi sich kreuzen. <> vt kreuzen.

intersection [,ɪntə'sekʃn] n [junction] Kreuzung die.

intersperse [,ɪntə'spɜ:s] vt: **to be interspersed with sthg** von etw unterbrochen OR durchsetzt sein.

interstate (highway) ['ɪntəsteɪt-] n US Interstate-Highway der, Autobahn zwischen den US-Bundesstaaten.

interval ['ɪntəvl] n - 1. [period of time]: **interval (between)** Abstand der (zwischen (+ D)); **at intervals of** in Abständen von - 2. UK [at play, concert] Pause die.

intervene [,ɪntə'vi:n] vi - 1. [person, government] einlgreifen; **to intervene in sthg** in etw (A) einlgreifen - 2. [event] dazwischenlkommen.

intervention [,ɪntə'venʃn] n Eingreifen das.

interview ['ɪntəvju:] <> n - 1. [for job] Vorstellungsgespräch das - 2. PRESS Interview das. <> vt - 1. [for job] ein Vorstellungsgespräch führen mit - 2. PRESS interviewen.

interviewer ['ɪntəvju:ə'] n - 1. [for job] Leiter der, -in die des Vorstellungsgesprächs - 2. PRESS Interviewer der, -in die.

intestine [ɪn'testɪn] n Darm der.

intimacy ['ɪntɪməsɪ] n [closeness]: **intimacy (between/with)** Vertrautheit die (zwischen (+D)/mit). **intimacies** npl Vertraulichkeiten Pl.

intimate adj ['ɪntɪmət] - 1. [friend, relationship] vertraut; **to be on intimate terms with sb** mit jm auf vertrautem Fuße stehen - 2. [place, atmosphere, dinner] intim - 3. [thoughts, details] persönlich - 4. [thorough - knowledge] gründlich.

intimately ['ɪntɪmətlɪ] adv - 1. [directly] direkt - 2. [as close friends] vertraulich; **to know sb intimately** jn gut kennen - 3. [thoroughly] gründlich.

intimidate [ɪn'tɪmɪdeɪt] vt einlschüchtern.

into ['ɪntʊ] prep - 1. [inside] in (+ A); **to put sthg into sthg** [lying down] etw in etw (A) legen; [upright] etw etw (A) stellen; **to put sthg into one's pocket** etw in die Tasche stecken; **to go into the house** ins Haus hineinlgehen - 2. [against]: **to bump/crash into sthg** gegen etw stoßen/knallen - 3. [indicating transformation, change] in (+ A); **to change into sthg** [become] zu etw werden; [clothes] sich (D) etw anlziehen; **to translate into German** ins Deut-

sche übersetzen - 4. [concerning, about] über (+ A) - 5. MATHS: **4 into 20 goes 5 (times)** 20 (geteilt) durch 4 ist 5 - 6. [indicating elapsed time]: **I was a week into my holiday when...** in meiner zweiten Urlaubswoche...; **late into the night** bis tief in die Nacht hinein - 7. inf [interested in]: **to be into sthg** etw mögen; **she's into jazz** sie ist ein Jazzfan.

intolerable [ɪn'tɒlrəbl] adj unerträglich.

intolerance [ɪn'tɒlərəns] n Intoleranz die.

intolerant [ɪn'tɒlərənt] adj intolerant.

intoxicated [ɪn'tɒksɪkeɪtɪd] adj - 1. [drunk]: **to be intoxicated** berauscht sein - 2. fig [excited]: **to be intoxicated by** OR **with sthg** von etw berauscht sein.

intractable [ɪn'træktəbl] adj fml [insoluble] hartnäckig.

intramural [,ɪntrə'mjʊərəl] adj innerhalb der Universität.

intransitive [ɪn'trænzətɪv] adj intransitiv.

intravenous [,ɪntrə'vi:nəs] adj intravenös.

in-tray n Eingangsablage die.

intricate ['ɪntrɪkət] adj knifflig.

intrigue <> n ['ɪntri:g] Intrige die. <> vt [ɪn'tri:g] faszinieren.

intriguing [ɪn'tri:gɪŋ] adj faszinierend.

intrinsic [ɪn'trɪnsɪk] adj immanent.

introduce [,ɪntrə'dju:s] vt - 1. [one person to another] vorlstellen; **to introduce sb to sb** jm in vorlstellen - 3. RADIO & TV [programme] moderieren - 3. [animal, plant, method]: **to introduce sthg (to** OR **into)** etw einlführen (in (+ D)) - 4. [to new experience]: **to introduce sb to sthg** jn in etw (A) einlführen - 5. [signal start of] einlleiten.

introduction [,ɪntrə'dʌkʃn] n - 1. [of method, technology] Einführung die - 2. [preface]: **introduction to sthg** Einleitung zu etw.

introductory [,ɪntrə'dʌktrɪ] adj einleitend; **an introductory offer** ein Eröffnungsangebot.

introvert ['ɪntrəvɜ:t] n introvertierter Mensch.

introverted ['ɪntrəvɜ:tɪd] adj introvertiert.

intrude [ɪn'tru:d] vi stören; **to intrude (up)on sb/sthg** jn/etw stören.

intruder [ɪn'tru:də'] n Eindringling der.

intrusive [ɪn'tru:sɪv] adj aufdringlich.

intuition [,ɪntju:'ɪʃn] n - 1. (U) [sense] Intuition die - 2. [hunch] Vorahnung die.

inundate ['ɪnʌndeɪt] vt - 1. fml [flood] überschwemmen - 2. [overwhelm]: **to be inundated with sthg** von etw überschwemmt werden.

invade [ɪn'veɪd] vt - 1. MIL einlmarschieren in (+ A) - 2. [subj: shoppers, fans] einlfallen - 3. [privacy, calm] stören.

invalid <> adj [ɪn'vælɪd] - 1. [ticket, contract, vote] ungültig - 2. [argument, theory] nicht schlüssig. <> n ['ɪnvəlɪd] Invalide der, -din die.

invaluable [ɪnˈvæljʊəbl] *adj*: invaluable (to sb/sthg) unschätzbar (für jn/etw).

invariably [ɪnˈveərɪəblɪ] *adv* stets.

invasion [ɪnˈveɪʒn] *n* - 1. MIL Invasion *die* - 2. *fig* [intrusion] Eingriff *der*.

invent [ɪnˈvent] *vt* erfinden.

invention [ɪnˈvenʃn] *n* - 1. [creation, untruth] Erfindung *die* - 2. (U) [inventiveness] Vorstellungsgabe *die*.

inventive [ɪnˈventɪv] *adj* einfallsreich.

inventor [ɪnˈventər] *n* Erfinder *der*, -in *die*.

inventory [ˈɪnvəntrɪ] *n* - 1. [list] Inventar *das* - 2. US [goods] Bestand *der*.

invert [ɪnˈvɜːt] *vt fml* umldrehen.

inverted commas [ɪn,vɜːtɪd-] *npl* UK Anführungszeichen *die*.

invest [ɪnˈvest] ⟨⟩ *vt* - 1. [money]: to invest sthg (in sthg) etw (in etw (A)) investieren - 2. [time, energy]: to invest sthg in sthg etw in etw (A) investieren. ⟨⟩ *vi* - 1. [financially]: to invest (in sthg) (in etw (A)) investieren - 2. *fig* [in sthg useful]: to invest in sthg in etw (A) investieren.

investigate [ɪnˈvestɪgeɪt] *vt* untersuchen.

investigation [ɪn,vestɪˈgeɪʃn] *n* Untersuchung *die*; an investigation into sthg eine Untersuchung von etw.

investment [ɪnˈvestmənt] *n* - 1. [gen] Investition *die* - 2. [financial product, purchase] Anlage *die*.

investor [ɪnˈvestər] *n* Anleger *der*, -in *die*.

inveterate [ɪnˈvetərət] *adj* [liar, gambler] unverbesserlich.

invidious [ɪnˈvɪdɪəs] *adj* - 1. [unfair] ungerecht - 2. [unpleasant] unangenehm.

invigilate [ɪnˈvɪdʒɪleɪt] UK ⟨⟩ *vt* Aufsicht führen bei. ⟨⟩ *vi* Aufsicht führen.

invigorating [ɪnˈvɪgəreɪtɪŋ] *adj* erfrischend, belebend.

invincible [ɪnˈvɪnsɪbl] *adj* unschlagbar.

invisible [ɪnˈvɪzɪbl] *adj* unsichtbar.

invitation [,ɪnvɪˈteɪʃn] *n* [request to attend] Einladung *die*.

invite [ɪnˈvaɪt] *vt* - 1. [request to attend] einlladen; to invite sb to sthg jn zu etw einladen - 2. [ask politely]: to invite sb to do sthg jn ersuchen, etw zu tun - 3. [trouble, criticism] herauslfordern.

inviting [ɪnˈvaɪtɪŋ] *adj* einladend.

invoice [ˈɪnvɔɪs] ⟨⟩ *n* Rechnung *die*. ⟨⟩ *vt* - 1. [customer] eine Rechnung schicken an (+ A) - 2. [goods] in Rechnung stellen.

invoke [ɪnˈvəʊk] *vt* [feeling] hervorlrufen.

involuntary [ɪnˈvɒləntrɪ] *adj* [movement] unwillkürlich.

involve [ɪnˈvɒlv] *vt* - 1. [entail, require - work, travelling] mit sich bringen; [- special equipment,

knowledge] erfordern - 2. [concern, affect] betreffen - 3. [make part of sthg]: to involve sb in sthg jn in etw (A) hineinlziehen.

involved [ɪnˈvɒlvd] *adj* - 1. [complex] kompliziert - 2. [participating]: to be involved in sthg an etw (D) beteiligt sein - 3. [in a relationship]: to be/get involved with sb mit jm eine enge Beziehung haben/einlgehen - 4. [entailed]: what is involved (in it)? worum geht es (dabei)?

involvement [ɪnˈvɒlvmənt] *n* - 1. [participation]: involvement (in sthg) Beteiligung (an etw (D)) - 2. [commitment]: involvement (in sthg) Engagement (für etw).

inward [ˈɪnwəd] ⟨⟩ *adj* - 1. [feelings, satisfaction] innerlich - 2. [flow, movement] nach innen gehend. ⟨⟩ *adv* US = inwards.

inwards [ˈɪnwədz], **inward** US *adv* nach innen.

iodine [UK ˈaɪədiːn, US ˈaɪədaɪn] *n* (U) Jod *das*.

iota [aɪˈəʊtə] *n* Jota *das*.

IOU (*abbr of* I owe you) *n* Schuldschein *der*.

IQ (*abbr of* intelligence quotient) *n* IQ *der*.

IRA *n* (*abbr of* Irish Republican Army) IRA *die*.

Iran [ɪˈrɑːn] *n* Iran *der*.

Iranian [ɪˈreɪnɪən] ⟨⟩ *adj* iranisch. ⟨⟩ *n* [person] Iraner *der*, -in *die*.

Iraq [ɪˈrɑːk] *n* Irak *der*.

Iraqi [ɪˈrɑːkɪ] ⟨⟩ *adj* irakisch. ⟨⟩ *n* [person] Iraker *der*, -in *die*.

irate [aɪˈreɪt] *adj* zornig.

Ireland [ˈaɪələnd] *n* Irland *nt*.

iris [ˈaɪərɪs] (*pl* -es) *n* - 1. [flower] Schwertlilie *die*, Iris *die* - 2. [of eye] Iris *die*.

Irish [ˈaɪrɪʃ] ⟨⟩ *adj* irisch. ⟨⟩ *n* [language] Irisch(e) *das*. ⟨⟩ *npl*: the Irish die Iren.

Irishman [ˈaɪrɪʃmən] (*pl* -men [-mən]) *n* Ire *der*.

Irish Sea *n*: the Irish Sea die Irische See.

Irishwoman [ˈaɪrɪʃ,wʊmən] (*pl* -women [-,wɪmɪn]) *n* Irin *die*.

iron [ˈaɪən] ⟨⟩ *adj* - 1. [made of iron] eisern; iron bar Eisenstange *die* - 2. *fig* [very strict] eisern. ⟨⟩ *n* - 1. [metal, golf club] Eisen *das* - 2. [for clothes] Bügeleisen *das*. ⟨⟩ *vt* bügeln.
➡ **iron out** *vt sep* [problems] auslbügeln.

ironic(al) [aɪˈrɒnɪk(l)] *adj* - 1. [using irony] ironisch - 2. [paradoxical] paradox.

ironing [ˈaɪənɪŋ] *n* - 1. [work] Bügeln *das* - 2. [clothes] Bügelwäsche *die*.

ironing board *n* Bügelbrett *das*.

ironmonger [ˈaɪən,mʌŋgər] *n* UK Eisenwarenhändler *der*, -in *die*; ironmonger's (shop) Eisenwarenhandlung *die*.

irony [ˈaɪrənɪ] *n* Ironie *die*.

irrational [ɪˈræʃənl] *adj* irrational.

irreconcilable [ɪ,rekənˈsaɪləbl] *adj* [views, differences] unvereinbar.

irregular [ɪˈregjʊləʳ] adj [gen & GRAM] unregelmäßig; [surface] uneben.

irrelevant [ɪˈreləvənt] adj unwichtig.

irreparable [ɪˈrepərəbl] adj irreparabel.

irreplaceable [ˌɪrɪˈpleɪsəbl] adj unersetzlich.

irrepressible [ˌɪrɪˈpresəbl] adj unerschütterlich; **he's irrepressible** er ist nicht unterzukriegen.

irresistible [ˌɪrɪˈzɪstəbl] adj unwiderstehlich.

irrespective [ˌɪrɪˈspektɪv] ➠ **irrespective of** prep ungeachtet (+ G).

irresponsible [ˌɪrɪˈspɒnsəbl] adj unverantwortlich.

irrigation [ˌɪrɪˈgeɪʃn] ⟨⟩ n [of land] Bewässerung die. ⟨⟩ comp Bewässerungs-.

irritable [ˈɪrɪtəbl] adj [person, mood] reizbar; [voice, reply] gereizt.

irritate [ˈɪrɪteɪt] vt - 1. [make angry] ärgern - 2. [make sore] reizen.

irritated [ˈɪrɪteɪtɪd] adj [angry, sore] gereizt.

irritating [ˈɪrɪteɪtɪŋ] adj - 1. [person, noise] ärgerlich - 2. [substance, material] reizend.

irritation [ɪrɪˈteɪʃn] n - 1. [anger] Ärger der - 2. [cause of anger] Ärgernis das - 3. [soreness] Reizung die.

IRS (abbr of Internal Revenue Service) n US: **the IRS** das Finanzamt.

is [ɪz] vb ⟼ be.

Islam [ˈɪzlɑːm] n [religion] Islam der.

island [ˈaɪlənd] n liter & fig Insel die.

islander [ˈaɪləndəʳ] n Inselbewohner der, -in die.

isle [aɪl] n Insel die.

Isle of Man n: **the Isle of Man** die Insel Man.

Isle of Wight [-waɪt] n: **the Isle of Wight** Wight.

isn't [ˈɪznt] abbr of is not.

isobar [ˈaɪsəbɑːʳ] n METEOR Isobare die.

isolate [ˈaɪsəleɪt] vt isolieren.

isolated [ˈaɪsəleɪtɪd] adj - 1. [place] abgelegen - 2. [person] isoliert - 3. [example, incident] einzeln.

Israel [ˈɪzreɪəl] n Israel nt.

Israeli [ɪzˈreɪlɪ] ⟨⟩ adj israelisch. ⟨⟩ n Israeli der, die.

issue [ˈɪʃuː] ⟨⟩ n - 1. [important subject] Frage die; **to make an issue of sthg** ein Problem aus etw machen - 2. [edition] Ausgabe die - 3. [of stamps, bank notes, shares] Ausgabe die. ⟨⟩ vt - 1. [statement] ab|geben; [decree] erlassen; [warning] aus|sprechen - 2. [stamps, bank notes, shares] aus|geben - 3. [passport, documents] aus|stellen; [uniforms] aus|geben.

it [ɪt] pron - 1. (subj) [referring to specific person or thing] er/sie/es; (direct object) ihn/sie/es; (indirect object) ihm/ihr; **it's big** er/sie/es ist groß; **she hit it** sie hat ihn/sie/es getroffen; **get the cat/dog and give it a drink** hole die Katze/den Hund und gib ihr/ihm etwas zu trinken - 2. (with prepositions): **tell me about it** erzähl mir davon; **you're good at it** du kannst das gut; **a table with a chair beside it** ein Tisch mit einem Stuhl daneben; **what did you learn from it?** was hast du daraus gelernt?; **put your hand in it** steck deine Hand hinein; **stand on top of it** stell dich darauf; **put the books on it** leg die Bücher darauf; **it had a sheet over it** darüber lag ein Tuch; **shall we go to it?** sollen wir hin|gehen?; **put the box under it** stell die Schachtel darunter; **a free book came with it** es war ein kostenloses Buch dabei - 3. (impersonal use) es; **it's hot** es ist heiß; **it's raining** es regnet; **it's Sunday** es ist Sonntag; **it's six o'clock** es ist sechs Uhr; **it's the children that worry me most** am meisten mache ich mir um die Kinder sorgen; **it's said that...** man sagt, dass... - 4. (nonspecific) es; **it's easy** es ist einfach; **it's a difficult question** das ist eine schwierige Frage; **who is it? – it's Mary/me** wer ist da? – Mary/ich bins.

IT n abbr of information technology.

Italian [ɪˈtæljən] ⟨⟩ adj italienisch. ⟨⟩ n - 1. [person] Italiener der, -in die - 2. [language] Italienisch(e) das.

italic [ɪˈtælɪk] adj kursiv. ➠ **italics** npl Kursivschrift die.

Italy [ˈɪtəlɪ] n Italien nt.

itch [ɪtʃ] ⟨⟩ n Juckreiz der. ⟨⟩ vi [part of body] jucken; **I'm itching** es juckt mich; **I'm itching to do it** es juckt mich, das zu tun.

itchy [ˈɪtʃɪ] adj juckend; **to be itchy** [part of body] jucken; **I feel itchy** es juckt mich.

it'd [ˈɪtəd] abbr of it would, it had.

item [ˈaɪtəm] n - 1. [object] Gegenstand der; [in shop] Artikel der; [on agenda] Punkt der; COMM Posten der; **item of clothing** Kleidungsstück das - 2. [of news] Meldung die.

itemize, -ise [ˈaɪtəmaɪz] vt auf einer Liste einzeln auf|führen.

itinerary [aɪˈtɪnərərɪ] n Reiseroute die.

it'll [ɪtl] abbr of it will.

its [ɪts] poss adj [masculine, neuter subject] sein; [feminine subject] ihr; **the dog wagged its tail** der Hund wedelte mit dem Schwanz.

it's [ɪts] abbr of it is, it has.

itself [ɪtˈself] pron - 1. (reflexive) sich - 2. (after prep) sich selbst; **by itself** allein; **in itself** an sich - 3. (stressed) selbst; **the house itself is fine** das Haus selbst ist in Ordnung.

I've [aɪv] abbr of I have.

ivory [ˈaɪvərɪ] n Elfenbein das.

ivy [ˈaɪvɪ] n Efeu der.

Ivy League n US Gruppe von alten, angesehenen Universitäten im Osten der USA.

J

j (*pl* **j's** OR **js**), **J** (*pl* **J's** OR **Js**) [dʒeɪ] *n* [letter] j *das*, J *das*.

jab [dʒæb] ◇ *n* - 1. [push] Stoß *der*; [with needle, knife] Stich *der* - 2. *UK inf* [injection] Spritze *die*. ◇ *vt* [with sthg] stechen; **to jab sthg into sb/sthg** etw in jn/etw (hinein)lstoßen.

jabber ['dʒæbəʳ] *vi* plappern.

jack [dʒæk] *n* - 1. [for car] Wagenheber *der* - 2. [playing card] Bube *der*. ◈ **jack up** *vt sep* [car] aufbocken.

jackal ['dʒækəl] *n* Schakal *der*.

jackdaw ['dʒækdɔː] *n* Dohle *die*.

jacket ['dʒækɪt] *n* - 1. [garment] Jacke *die*; [of suit] Jacket *das* - 2. [of book] Schutzumschlag *der* - 3. *US* [of record] Plattenhülle *die*.

jacket potato *n* in der Schale gebackene Kartoffel.

jack knife *n* Klappmesser *das*. ◈ **jackknife** *vi* [lorry] sich querlstellen.

jack plug *n* Bananenstecker *der*.

jackpot ['dʒækpɒt] *n* Jackpot *der*.

jaded ['dʒeɪdɪd] *adj* abgestumpft.

jagged ['dʒægɪd] *adj* [metal] schartig; [edge] ausgezackt; [rocks] zerklüftet.

jail [dʒeɪl] ◇ *n* Gefängnis *das*; **in jail** im Gefängnis; **to go to jail** ins Gefängnis kommen. ◇ *vt* einlsperren.

jailer ['dʒeɪləʳ] *n* Gefängniswärter *der*, -in *die*.

jam [dʒæm] ◇ *n* - 1. [preserve] Marmelade *die* - 2. [of traffic] Stau *der* - 3. *inf* [difficult situation] Klemme *die*. ◇ *vt* - 1. [mechanism, brakes] blockieren; **to get one's finger jammed** sich (*D*) den Finger einlquetschen - 2. [cram]: **to jam sthg into sthg** etw in etw (*A*) stopfen - 3. [streets, town] verstopfen - 4. TELEC: **thousands of callers jammed the switchboard** Tausende von Anrufern blockierten die Leitungen der (Telefon)zentrale - 5. RADIO stören. ◇ *vi* [stick - window, door] klemmen; [- brakes, lever] sich verklemmen. ◈ **jam on** *vt sep*: **to jam the brakes on** eine Vollbremsung machen.

Jamaica [dʒə'meɪkə] *n* Jamaika *nt*; **in Jamaica** auf Jamaika.

jam-packed [-'pækt] *adj inf* proppenvoll.

jangle ['dʒæŋgl] *vt* [keys] klimpern mit.

janitor ['dʒænɪtəʳ] *n US & Scotland* [caretaker] Hausmeister *der*.

January ['dʒænjʊərɪ] *n* Januar *der*; *see also* **September**.

Japan [dʒə'pæn] *n* Japan *nt*.

Japanese [,dʒæpə'niːz] (*pl inv*) ◇ *adj* japanisch. ◇ *n* [language] Japanisch(e) *das*. ◇ *npl* [people]: **the Japanese** die Japaner *Pl*.

jar [dʒɑːʳ] ◇ *n* Glas *das*. ◇ *vt* [shake] durchlschütteln. ◇ *vi* - 1. [noise, voice]: **to jar (on sb)** unangenehm sein (für jn) - 2. [colours] sich beißen.

jargon ['dʒɑːgən] *n* Fachsprache *die*.

jaundice ['dʒɔːndɪs] *n* Gelbsucht *die*.

jaundiced ['dʒɔːndɪst] *adj fig* [attitude, view] verbittert.

jaunt [dʒɔːnt] *n* Ausflug *der*.

jaunty ['dʒɔːntɪ] *adj* [hat, wave] flott; [person] munter.

javelin ['dʒævlɪn] *n* Speer *der*.

jaw [dʒɔː] *n* [of person, animal] Kiefer *der*.

jawbone ['dʒɔːbəʊn] *n* Kieferknochen *der*.

jay [dʒeɪ] *n* Eichelhäher *der*.

jaywalker ['dʒeɪwɔːkəʳ] *n* im Straßenverkehr unachtsamer Fußgänger.

jazz [dʒæz] *n* MUS Jazz *der*. ◈ **jazz up** *vt sep inf* auflpeppen.

jazzy ['dʒæzɪ] *adj* [colour, clothes] poppig.

jealous ['dʒeləs] *adj* [envious]: **to be jealous (of)** neidisch sein (auf (+ *A*)).

jealousy ['dʒeləsɪ] *n* - 1. [envy] Neid *der* - 2. [possessiveness] Eifersucht *die*.

jeans [dʒiːnz] *npl* Jeans *Pl*.

Jeep® [dʒiːp] *n* Jeep® *der*.

jeer [dʒɪəʳ] ◇ *vt* verhöhnen. ◇ *vi* [crowd, fans] höhnisch johlen; **to jeer at sb** jn verhöhnen.

Jello® ['dʒeləʊ] *n US* Wackelpudding *der*.

jelly ['dʒelɪ] *n* - 1. *UK* [dessert] Wackelpudding *der* - 2. *US* [jam] Gelee *das*.

jellyfish ['dʒelɪfɪʃ] (*pl inv* OR **-es**) *n* Qualle *die*.

jeopardize, -ise ['dʒepədaɪz] *vt* gefährden.

jerk [dʒɜːk] ◇ *n* - 1. [movement] Ruck *der* - 2. *inf pej* [fool] Trottel *der*. ◇ *vi* einen Satz machen.

jersey ['dʒɜːzɪ] (*pl* **-s**) *n* - 1. [sweater] Pullover *der* - 2. (*U*) [cloth] Jersey *der*.

Jersey ['dʒɜːzɪ] *n* Jersey *nt*; **in Jersey** auf Jersey.

jest [dʒest] *n* Scherz *der*; **in jest** im Spaß.

Jesus (Christ) ['dʒiːzəs-] ◇ *n* Jesus (Christus). ◇ *excl inf* Menschenskind!

jet [dʒet] *n* - 1. [aircraft] Jet *der*, Düsenflugzeug *das* - 2. [of liquid, gas, steam] Strahl *der*.

jet-black *adj* pechschwarz.

jet engine *n* Düsentriebwerk *das*.

jetfoil ['dʒetfɔɪl] *n* Tragflügelboot *das*.

jet lag *n* Jetlag *der*.

jetsam ['dʒetsəm] *n* ▷ **flotsam**.

jettison ['dʒetɪsən] *vt* - **1.** [cargo, bombs - from plane] abwerfen; [- from ship] über Bord werfen - **2.** *fig* [discard - ideas, hope] über Bord werfen; [- unwanted possession] wegwerfen.

jetty ['dʒetɪ] *n* Landungssteg *der*.

Jew [dʒu:] *n* Jude *der*, Jüdin *die*.

jewel ['dʒu:əl] *n* Edelstein *der*; [in watch] Stein *der*; **jewels** [jewellery] Schmuck *der*.

jeweller UK, **jeweler** US ['dʒu:ələr] *n* Juwelier *der*; **jeweller's (shop)** Juweliergeschäft *das*.

jewellery UK, **jewelry** US ['dʒu:əlrɪ] *n* Schmuck *der*; **piece of jewellery** Schmuckstück *das*.

Jewish ['dʒu:ɪʃ] *adj* jüdisch.

jibe [dʒaɪb] *n* spöttische Bemerkung.

jiffy ['dʒɪfɪ] *n inf*: **in a jiffy** sofort.

Jiffy bag® *n* Versandtasche *die*.

jig [dʒɪg] *n* [dance] lebhafter Schreittanz, vor allem auf dem Land früher beliebt.

jigsaw (puzzle) ['dʒɪgsɔ:-] *n* Puzzle(spiel) *das*.

jilt [dʒɪlt] *vt* sitzen lassen.

jingle ['dʒɪŋgl] ⇔ *n* [in advertising] Jingle *der*. ⇔ *vi* [bells] bimmeln; [keys] klimpern.

jinx [dʒɪŋks] *n*: **there's a jinx on it** es ist verhext.

jitters ['dʒɪtəz] *npl inf*: **the jitters** das große Zittern.

job [dʒɒb] *n* - **1.** [paid work] Stelle *die*; **to lose one's job** entlassen werden - **2.** [task] Arbeit *die*; **on the job** bei der Arbeit - **3.** [difficult time]: **to have a job doing sthg** (große) Mühe haben, etw zu tun - **4.** *phr*: **that's just the job** UK *inf* das ist genau das Richtige.

job centre *n* UK Arbeitsamt *das*.

jobless ['dʒɒblɪs] *adj* arbeitslos.

jobsharing ['dʒɒbʃeərɪŋ] *n* Jobsharing *das*.

jockey ['dʒɒkɪ] *(pl* -s) ⇔ *n* Jockey *der*. ⇔ *vi*: **to jockey for position** um eine gute Position kämpfen.

jocular ['dʒɒkjʊlər] *adj* witzig, lustig.

jodhpurs ['dʒɒdpəz] *npl* Reithose *die*.

jog [dʒɒg] ⇔ *n* [run]: **to go for a jog** joggen gehen. ⇔ *vt* [nudge - person] anstoßen; [- table, sb's arm, elbow] stoßen gegen; **to jog sb's memory** js Gedächtnis nachhelfen. ⇔ *vi* [run] joggen.

jogging ['dʒɒgɪŋ] *n* Joggen *das*; **to go jogging** joggen gehen.

john [dʒɒn] *n* US *inf* [toilet] Klo *das*.

join [dʒɔɪn] ⇔ *n* Naht(stelle) *die*. ⇔ *vt* - **1.** [connect] verbinden; **to join sthg to sthg** etw mit etw verbinden - **2.** [other people] sich anschließen (+ D); **I'll join you in a moment** [follow you] ich komme gleich nach - **3.** [club, organization] beitreten (+ D); [company] anfangen bei; [army] gehen zu - **4.** [take part in] teilnehmen an (+ D); **to join the queue** UK, **to join the line** US sich in die Schlange einlreihen. ⇔ *vi* - **1.** [connect - rivers] ineinander fließen; [- edges, pieces] miteinander verbunden sein - **2.** [become a member] Mitglied werden. ⇔ *vi* mitlmachen bei. ⇔ **join up** *vi* MIL zum Militär gehen.

joiner ['dʒɔɪnər] *n* Tischler *der*, -in *die*.

joint [dʒɔɪnt] ⇔ *adj* [effort] vereint; [responsibility] gemeinsam; [owner] Mit-. ⇔ *n* - **1.** ANAT Gelenk *das* - **2.** [in structure] Verbindungsstelle *die*; [in carpentry] Fuge *die* - **3.** UK [of meat] Braten *der* - **4.** *inf pej* [place] Laden *der* - **5.** *drug sl* [cannabis cigarette] Joint *der*.

joint account *n* gemeinsames Konto.

jointly ['dʒɔɪntlɪ] *adv* gemeinsam.

joke [dʒəʊk] ⇔ *n* Witz *der*; **to play a joke on sb** jm einen Streich spielen; **it's no joke** [not easy] das ist keine Kleinigkeit; **to be a joke** [person] eine Witzfigur sein. ⇔ *vi* Witze machen; **to joke about sthg** über etw (A) Witze machen; **you must be joking!** das meinst du doch nicht im Ernst!

joker ['dʒəʊkər] *n* - **1.** [person] Spaßvogel *der* - **2.** [playing card] Joker *der*.

jolly ['dʒɒlɪ] ⇔ *adj* lustig, fröhlich. ⇔ *adv* UK [very] super.

jolt [dʒəʊlt] ⇔ *n* - **1.** [jerk] Ruck *der* - **2.** [shock]: **to give sb a jolt** jm einen Schock versetzen. ⇔ *vt* - **1.** [jerk] durchlschütteln - **2.** [shock]: **to jolt sb into doing sthg** jn so auflrütteln, dass er etw tut.

jostle ['dʒɒsl] ⇔ *vt* anlrempeln. ⇔ *vi* drängeln.

jot [dʒɒt] *n*: **there isn't a jot of truth in it** es ist kein Funken Wahrheit darin. ⇔ **jot down** *vt sep* sich (D) notieren.

journal ['dʒɜ:nl] *n* - **1.** [magazine] Zeitschrift *die* - **2.** [diary] Tagebuch *das*.

journalism ['dʒɜ:nəlɪzm] *n* Journalismus *der*.

journalist ['dʒɜ:nəlɪst] *n* Journalist *der*, -in *die*.

journey ['dʒɜ:nɪ] *(pl* -s) *n* Reise *die*; **to go on a journey** verreisen; **an hour's journey** eine Stunde Fahrt.

jovial ['dʒəʊvɪəl] *adj* fröhlich.

joy [dʒɔɪ] *n* Freude *die*.

joyful ['dʒɔɪfʊl] *adj* [person] froh; [shout] freudig; [scene, news] erfreulich.

joystick ['dʒɔɪstɪk] *n* - **1.** [in aircraft] Steuerknüppel *der* - **2.** [for computers] Joystick *der*.

Jr. *(abbr of Junior)* jun.

jubilant ['dʒu:bɪlənt] *adj* [person, fans] überglücklich; [shout] Jubel-.

jubilee ['dʒu:bɪli:] *n* Jubiläum *das*.

judge [dʒʌdʒ] ⬦ n - 1. LAW Richter der, -in die - 2. SPORT Schiedsrichter der, -in die; [of competition] Preisrichter der, -in die. ⬦ vt - 1. LAW [case] verhandeln - 2. [competition] beurteilen - 3. [estimate] (ein)schätzen. ⬦ vi [decide] (be)urteilen; **to judge from** OR **by sthg, judging from** OR **by sthg** nach etw zu urteilen.

judg(e)ment ['dʒʌdʒmənt] n - 1. LAW Urteil das - 2. [opinion] Urteil das - 3. [ability to form opinion] Urteilsvermögen das.

judicial [dʒuː'dɪʃl] adj Gerichts-.

judiciary [dʒuː'dɪʃərɪ] n: **the judiciary** das Gerichtswesen.

judicious [dʒuː'dɪʃəs] adj klug.

judo ['dʒuːdəʊ] n Judo das.

jug [dʒʌg] n Krug der.

juggernaut ['dʒʌgənɔːt] n [truck] Laster der.

juggle ['dʒʌgl] vt & vi - 1. [throw] jonglieren - 2.: **to juggle (with) figures** die Zahlen so hindrehen, wie man sie haben will.

juggler ['dʒʌglər] n Jongleur der, -in die.

juice [dʒuːs] n Saft der.

juicy ['dʒuːsɪ] adj [fruit] saftig.

jukebox ['dʒuːkbɒks] n Musikbox die.

July [dʒuː'laɪ] n Juli der; see also **September**.

jumble ['dʒʌmbl] ⬦ n [mixture] Durcheinander das. ⬦ vt: **to jumble (up)** [objects] durcheinander werfen; [words] durcheinander bringen.

jumble sale n UK in Gemeinde- und Stadthallen abgehaltener Trödelmarkt, dessen Erlös wohltätigen Vereinen zugute kommt.

jumbo jet ['dʒʌmbəʊ-] n Jumbojet der.

jumbo-sized [-saɪzd] adj Riesen-.

jump [dʒʌmp] ⬦ n - 1. [leap] Sprung der - 2. [rapid increase] Sprung der. ⬦ vt - 1. [fence, stream] überspringen; **to jump the queue** sich vordrängen - 2. inf [attack] überfallen. ⬦ vi - 1. [gen] springen; **to jump over sthg** über etw (A) springen - 2. [with fright, surprise] einen Satz machen; **you made me jump!** du hast mich erschreckt! - 3. [increase] sprunghaft ansteigen. ➠ **jump at** vt insep fig [opportunity] ergreifen. ➠ **jump in** vi hereinspringen; **jump in!** [get in car] spring rein! ➠ **jump out** vi heraus|springen; **to jump out (of) the window** aus dem Fenster springen. ➠ **jump up** vi [get up quickly] auf|springen.

jumper ['dʒʌmpər] n - 1. UK [pullover] Pullover der - 2. US [dress] Trägerkleid das.

jump leads npl Starthilfekabel Pl.

jump-start vt mit Starthilfe zünden.

jumpsuit ['dʒʌmpsuːt] n Overall der.

jumpy ['dʒʌmpɪ] adj nervös.

junction ['dʒʌŋkʃn] n [of roads] Kreuzung die; [of railway lines, pipes] Knotenpunkt der; [on motorway] Anschlussstelle die.

June [dʒuːn] n Juni der; see also **September**.

jungle ['dʒʌŋgl] n liter & fig Dschungel der.

junior ['dʒuːnɪər] ⬦ adj - 1. [younger] jünger - 2. [lower in rank] untergeordnet; **junior partner** Juniorpartner der - 3. US [after name] junior. ⬦ n - 1. [person of lower rank] Person niedrigeren Ranges - 2. [younger person] Jüngere der, die; **he is two years my junior** er ist zwei Jahre jünger als ich - 3. US SCH & UNIV Schüler/Student im vorletzten Jahr.

junior high school n US Schule zwischen Grund- und Oberschule.

junior school n UK Grundschule die (für 7- bis 11-Jährige).

junk [dʒʌŋk] n - 1. inf [unwanted things] Ramsch der - 2. [boat] Dschunke die.

junk food n pej ungesundes Essen wie Fast Food, Chips, Süßigkeiten.

junkie ['dʒʌŋkɪ] n drug sl Junkie der, Fixer der, -in die.

junk mail n (U) pej Reklamemüll der (der mit der Post kommt).

junk shop n Trödelladen der.

Jupiter ['dʒuːpɪtər] n [planet] Jupiter der.

jurisdiction [ˌdʒʊərɪs'dɪkʃn] n [of court] Zuständigkeitsbereich der.

juror ['dʒʊərər] n Geschworene der, die.

jury ['dʒʊərɪ] n - 1. [in court of law]: **the jury** die Geschworenen Pl - 2. [in contest] Jury die.

just [dʒʌst] ⬦ adv - 1. [recently] gerade; **to have just done sthg** gerade etw getan haben - 2. [at this or that moment] gerade; **I was just about to pick up the phone, when...** ich wollte gerade den Hörer abnehmen, als...; **we were just leaving, when...** wir wollten gerade gehen, als...; **I'm just coming** ich komme schon - 3. [exactly] genau; **just what I need** genau das, was ich brauche; **it's just as good** es ist genauso gut - 4. [only] nur; **just a bit** nur ein bisschen; **just over an hour** etwas über eine Stunde; **just a minute!** einen Moment! - 5. [simply] einfach; **'just add water'** 'nur Wasser zugeben' - 6. [almost not]: **(only) just** gerade (noch) - 7. [for emphasis]: **just look what you've done!** sieh nur, was du gemacht hast! - 8. [in requests]: **could you just open your mouth?** können Sie mal den Mund auf|machen? ⬦ adj [fair] gerecht; **it's only just** es ist nur recht und billig. ➠ **just about** adv [almost] fast. ➠ **just now** adv - 1. [a short time ago] gerade; **I was speaking to her just now** ich habe gerade mit ihr gesprochen - 2. [at this moment] im Moment.

justice ['dʒʌstɪs] n (U) - 1. [fairness] Gerechtigkeit die - 2. LAW [power of law] Justiz die - 3. [of cause, claim] Rechtmäßigkeit die.

justify ['dʒʌstɪfaɪ] *vt* - **1.** [gen] rechtfertigen - **2.** TYPO justieren; COMPUT auslrichten.

justly ['dʒʌstlɪ] *adv* zu Recht, mit Recht.

jut [dʒʌt] *vi*: to jut (out) (her)vorlragen.

juvenile ['dʒuːvənaɪl] ◇ *adj* - **1.** LAW jugendlich; **juvenile crime** die Jugendkriminalität - **2.** *pej* [childish] infantil. ◇ *n* LAW Jugendliche *der, die*.

juxtapose [,dʒʌkstə'pəʊz] *vt*: to juxtapose sthg with sthg etw neben etw *(A)* stellen.

K

k (*pl* k's OR ks), **K** (*pl* K's OR Ks) [keɪ] *n* [letter] k *das*, K *das*. ◆ **K** *n* - **1.** (*abbr of* kilobyte) Kb *das* - **2.** (*abbr of* thousand) Tsd.

kaleidoscope [kə'laɪdəskəʊp] *n* Kaleidoskop *das*.

kangaroo [,kæŋgə'ruː] *n* Känguru *das*.

kaput [kə'pʊt] *adj inf* kaputt.

karaoke [kærɪ'əʊkiː] *n* Karaoke *das*.

karat ['kærət] *n* US Karat *das*.

karate [kə'rɑːtɪ] *n* Karate *das*.

kayak ['kaɪæk] *n* Kajak *der ODER das*.

KB (*abbr of* kilobyte(s)) *n* COMPUT Kb *das*.

kcal (*abbr of* kilocalorie) kcal.

kebab [kɪ'bæb] *n*: (shish) kebab Kebab *der*; (doner) kebab Gyros *der*.

keel [kiːl] *n* Kiel *der*; to get sthg back on an even keel etw wieder auf die Beine bringen. ◆ **keel over** *vi* [ship] kentern; [person] umlkippen.

keen [kiːn] *adj* - **1.** [enthusiastic] begeistert; to be keen on sthg etw sehr mögen; to be keen to do OR on doing sthg etw unbedingt tun wollen; she wasn't keen on the idea sie war von der Sache nicht angetan - **2.** [interest, desire, competition] stark - **3.** [edge] scharf; [eyesight, hearing] gut - **4.** [wind] scharf.

keep [kiːp] (*pt & pp* kept) ◇ *vt* - **1.** [retain] behalten; please keep the change bitte behalten Sie das Wechselgeld; to keep a seat for sb einen Platz für jn frei halten - **2.** [store] auflbewahren - **3.** [maintain] halten; to keep sb waiting jn warten lassen; to keep sb awake jn wach halten - **4.** [promise, appointment] einlhalten - **5.** [secret] für sich behalten; to keep sthg from sb etw vor jm geheim halten - **6.** [delay]: what kept you? wo bist du denn so lang gewesen? - **7.** [record, diary] führen; to keep a note of sthg etw auflschreiben - **8.** [prevent]: to keep sb from doing sthg jn davon ablhalten, etw zu tun; the noise kept me from sleeping der Lärm ließ mich nicht schlafen - **9.** [own - farm animals] halten - **10.** *phr*: they keep themselves to themselves sie bleiben für sich. ◇ *vi* - **1.** [remain] bleiben; to keep fit fit bleiben; to keep silent schweigen; to keep warm sich warm halten; to keep clear of sthg sich von etw fern halten - **2.** [continue]: to keep doing sthg [continuously] etw weiter tun; [repeatedly] etw dauernd tun; to keep going [walking] weitergehen; [driving] weiterlfahren; [working] weiterlmachen; 'keep left' 'links halten'; keep straight on [walking] gehen Sie immer geradeaus; [driving] fahren Sie immer geradeaus - **3.** [food] sich halten - **4.** UK [in health]: how are you keeping? wie geht es dir? ◇ *n* [food, lodging] Unterhalt *der*; to earn one's keep sein eigenes Brot verdienen. ◆ **for keeps** *adv* für immer. ◆ **keep back** ◇ *vt sep* - **1.** [information] verschweigen - **2.** [money] zurücklbehalten. ◇ *vi* [stand back] zurücklbleiben. ◆ **keep off** *vt insep* [subject, food, drink] vermeiden; 'keep off the grass' 'Rasen betreten verboten'. ◆ **keep on** *vi* - **1.** [continue]: to keep on doing sthg [continuously] etw weiter tun; [repeatedly] etw dauernd tun - **2.** [talk incessantly]: to keep on (about sthg) dauernd (über etw *(A)*) reden. ◆ **keep out** ◇ *vt sep* nicht hereinllassen. ◇ *vi*: 'keep out!' 'Betreten verboten!' ◆ **keep to** *vt insep* - **1.** [rule, promise, plan]: to keep sich an etw *(A)* halten - **2.** [not deviate from]: to keep to the point bei der Sache bleiben; keep to the path! auf dem Weg bleiben! ◆ **keep up** ◇ *vt sep* - **1.** [prevent from falling] halten - **2.** [maintain - standards, friendship] aufrechtlerhalten; [- house, garden] instand halten; keep it up! weiter so! - **3.** [prevent from going to bed]: to keep sb up jn vom Schlafen ablhalten. ◇ *vi* [maintain pace, level] mitlhalten; to keep up with sb/sthg mit jm/etw mithalten können; to keep up with the news sich auf dem Laufenden halten.

keeper ['kiːpər] *n* - **1.** [in zoo] Wärter *der*, -in *die* - **2.** [of museum] Kustos *der*.

keep-fit UK *n* Fitness *die*.

keeping ['kiːpɪŋ] *n* - **1.** [care]: in safe keeping sicher verwahrt; for safe keeping zur Verwahrung - **2.** [conformity]: to be in keeping with sthg [regulations, decision] etw *(D)* entsprechen; [clothes, furniture, style] zu etw passen.

keepsake ['kiːpseɪk] *n* Andenken *das*.

kennel ['kenl] *n* - **1.** [for dog] Hundehütte *die*; [for many dogs] Zwinger *der* - **2.** US = **kennels**. ◆ **kennels** *npl* UK [for boarding pets] Tierpension *die*.

Kenya ['kenjə] *n* Kenia *nt*.

kept [kept] *pt & pp* ▷ **keep**.

kerb [kɜːb] *n* UK Bordsteinkante *die*.

kernel ['kɜːnl] *n* [of nut] Kern *der*.

kerosene ['kerəsi:n] *n* Petroleum *das*.

ketchup ['ketʃəp] *n* Ketschup *der ODER das*.

kettle ['ketl] *n* Kessel *der*; **to put the kettle on** Wasser aufsetzen.

key [ki:] <> *n* - **1.** [gen] Schlüssel *der* - **2.** [of typewriter, computer, piano] Taste *die* - **3.** MUS Tonart *die*. <> *adj* [main] Schlüssel-.

keyboard ['ki:bɔ:d] *n* - **1.** [of typewriter, computer] Tastatur *die*, Keyboard *das* - **2.** [of piano] Klaviatur *die*; [of organ] Manual *das*.

keyed up [,ki:d-] *adj* aufgeregt, nervös.

keyhole ['ki:həʊl] *n* Schlüsselloch *das*.

keynote ['ki:nəʊt] *n* [main point] Hauptgedanke *der*.

keypad ['ki:pæd] *n* COMPUT Tastenfeld *das*.

key ring *n* Schlüsselring *der*.

kg (*abbr of* **kilogram**) kg.

khaki ['kɑːkɪ] <> *adj* kakifarben. <> *n* [colour] Kaki *das*.

kHz (*abbr of* **kilohertz**) *n* kHz.

kick [kɪk] <> *n* - **1.** [with foot] (Fuß)tritt *der* - **2.** *inf* [excitement]: **to do sthg for kicks** etw aus Spaß tun; **to get a kick from sthg** an etw (D) Spaß haben. <> *vt* - **1.** [with foot - gen] treten; [- ball] kicken; **I could have kicked myself!** ich hätte mich ohrfeigen können! - **2.** *inf* [habit] auflgeben. <> *vi* [person] treten; [baby] strampeln; [animal] auslschlagen, treten. ◆ **kick off** *vi* - **1.** FTBL anlstoßen - **2.** *inf fig* [start] anlfangen. ◆ **kick out** *vt sep inf* rauslschmeißen.

kid [kɪd] <> *n* - **1.** *inf* [child] Kind *das* - **2.** [young goat] Zicklein *das*. <> *comp inf* [brother, sister] kleine(r). <> *vt inf* - **1.** [tease] veralbern - **2.** [delude]: **to kid o.s.** sich (D) etwas vorlmachen. <> *vi inf*: **to be kidding** Spaß machen; **you're kidding!** das ist nicht dein Ernst!

kidnap ['kɪdnæp] (*UK*) (*US* *pt* & *pp* **-ed**, *cont* **-ing**) *vt* entführen, kidnappen.

kidnapper *UK*, **kidnaper** *US* ['kɪdnæpə'] *n* Kidnapper *der*, **-in** *die*, Entführer *der*, **-in** *die*.

kidnapping *UK*, **kidnaping** *US* ['kɪdnæpɪŋ] *n* Kidnapping *das*.

kidney ['kɪdnɪ] (*pl* **kidneys**) *n* Niere *die*.

kidney bean *n* Kidneybohne *die*.

kill [kɪl] <> *vt* - **1.** [person, animal] töten; [murder] umlbringen; [plant] eingehen lassen; **to kill o.s.** sich umlbringen - **2.** *fig* [hope] zerstören; [conversation, desire] zum Erliegen bringen; [pain] abltöten. <> *vi* töten.

killer ['kɪlə'] *n* [person] Mörder *der*, **-in** *die*.

killing ['kɪlɪŋ] *n* - **1.** [murder] Tötung *die* - **2.** *inf* [profit]: **to make a killing** ein Riesengeschäft machen.

killjoy ['kɪldʒɔɪ] *n* Spielverderber *der*.

kiln [kɪln] *n* [for bricks, pottery] Brennofen *der*; [for hops] Darrofen *der*.

kilo ['ki:ləʊ] (*pl* **-s**) (*abbr of* **kilogram**) *n* Kilo *das*.

kilobyte ['kɪləbaɪt] *n* Kilobyte *das*.

kilogram(me) ['kɪləgræm] *n* Kilogramm *das*.

kilohertz ['kɪləhɜːts] (*pl inv*) *n* Kilohertz *das*.

kilometre *UK* ['kɪlə,miːtə'], **kilometer** *US* [kɪ'lɒmɪtər] *n* Kilometer *der*.

kilowatt ['kɪləwɒt] *n* Kilowatt *das*.

kilt [kɪlt] *n* Kilt *der*, Schottenrock *der*.

kin [kɪn] *n* ⊳ **kith**.

kind [kaɪnd] <> *adj* nett; **that's very kind of you** das ist sehr nett von dir. <> *n* Art *die*; [of cheese, wine *etc*] Sorte *die*; **what kind of music do you like?** welche Musik magst du?; **what kind of car do you drive?** was für ein Auto hast du?; **kind of** *inf* irgendwie; **they're two of a kind** sie sind vom gleichen Schlag; **all kinds of animals** allerlei Tiere; **in kind** [payment] in Naturalien.

kindergarten ['kɪndə,gɑːtn] *n* Kindergarten *der*.

kind-hearted [-'hɑːtɪd] *adj* gutherzig.

kindle ['kɪndl] *vt fig* [idea, feeling] entfachen.

kindly ['kaɪndlɪ] <> *adj* gütig, wohltätig. <> *adv* - **1.** [speak, smile] freundlich - **2.** [please] freundlicherweise.

kindness ['kaɪndnɪs] *n* - **1.** [gentleness] Freundlichkeit *die* - **2.** [helpful act] Gefälligkeit *die*.

kindred ['kɪndrɪd] *adj* ähnlich; **kindred spirit** verwandte Seele.

king [kɪŋ] *n* König *der*.

kingdom ['kɪŋdəm] *n* - **1.** [country] Königreich *das* - **2.** [of animals, plants] Reich *das*.

kingfisher ['kɪŋ,fɪʃə'] *n* Eisvogel *der*.

king-size(d) [-saɪz(d)] *adj* Kingsize-.

kinky ['kɪŋkɪ] *adj inf* abartig.

kiosk ['ki:ɒsk] *n* - **1.** [small shop] Kiosk *der* - **2.** *UK* [telephone box] Telefonzelle *die*.

kip [kɪp] *UK inf* <> *n*: **to have a kip** eine Runde schlafen. <> *vi* eine Runde schlafen.

kipper ['kɪpə'] *n* Räucherhering *der*.

kiss [kɪs] <> *n* Kuss *der*; **to give sb a kiss** jm einen Kuss geben. <> *vt* küssen. <> *vi* küssen.

kiss of life *n*: **the kiss of life** die Mund-zu-Mund-Beatmung.

kit [kɪt] *n* - **1.** [set] Ausrüstung *die*, Satz *der*; **repair kit** Flickzeug *das* - **2.** (*U*) [sports clothes] Sportsachen *Pl* - **3.** [to be assembled] Bausatz *der*.

kitchen ['kɪtʃɪn] *n* Küche *die*.

kitchen roll *n* Küchenrolle *die*.

kitchen sink *n* Spülbecken *das*.

kitchen unit *n* Küchenelement *das*.

kite [kaɪt] *n* [toy] Drachen *der*.

kitesurfing ['kaɪtsɜːfɪŋ] *n* Drachenfliegen *das*.

kith [kɪθ] *n*: **kith and kin** Kind und Kegel.

kitten ['kɪtn] *n* Kätzchen *das*.

kitty ['kɪtɪ] *n* [for bills, drinks] Gemeinschaftskasse *die*; [in card games] Bank *die*.

kiwi ['kiːwiː] *n* [bird] Kiwi *der*.

kiwi fruit *n* Kiwi *die*.

km (*abbr of* kilometre) km.

km/h (*abbr of* kilometres per hour) km/h.

knack [næk] *n* Trick *der*; **to have a** OR **the knack of doing sthg** [ability] den Dreh raushaben, etw zu tun; **he has a** OR **the knack of turning up late** er hat das Talent, (immer) zu spät zu kommen.

knackered ['nækəd] *adj* UK *inf* kaputt.

knapsack ['næpsæk] *n* Rucksack *der*.

knead [niːd] *vt* [dough, clay] kneten.

knee [niː] *n* Knie *das*.

kneecap ['niːkæp] *n* Kniescheibe *die*.

kneel [niːl] (*UK pt* & *pp* **knelt**) (*US pt* & *pp* **knelt** OR **-ed**) *vi* knien. ◆ **kneel down** *vi* niederlknien.

knelt [nelt] *pt* & *pp* ⊳ **kneel**.

knew [njuː] *pt* ⊳ **know**.

knickers ['nɪkəz] *npl* **- 1.** UK [underwear] Schlüpfer *der* **- 2.** US [knickerbockers] Knickerbockers *Pl*.

knick-knacks ['nɪknæks] *npl* Nippes *Pl*.

knife [naɪf] (*pl* **knives**) <> *n* Messer *das*. <> *vt* einlstechen auf (+ A).

knight [naɪt] <> *n* **- 1.** [gen] Ritter *der* **- 2.** [in chess] Springer *der*. <> *vt* in den Adelsstand erheben.

knighthood ['naɪthʊd] *n*: **to get** OR **be given a knighthood** in den Adelsstand erhoben werden.

knit [nɪt] (*pt* & *pp inv* OR **-ted**) <> *adj*: **closely** OR **tightly knit** *fig* eng verbunden. <> *vt* stricken. <> *vi* **- 1.** [with wool] stricken **- 2.** [join] zusammenlwachsen.

knitting ['nɪtɪŋ] *n* (U) **- 1.** [activity] Stricken *das* **- 2.** [thing being knitted] Strickzeug *das*.

knitting needle *n* Stricknadel *die*.

knitwear ['nɪtweə'] *n* (U) Strickwaren *Pl*.

knives [naɪvz] *Pl* ⊳ **knife**.

knob [nɒb] *n* **- 1.** [handle] Griff *der*, Knauf *der* **- 2.** [on TV, radio] Knopf *der*.

knock [nɒk] <> *n* **- 1.** [hit - on body] Schlag *der*; [- on door] Klopfen *das* **- 2.** *inf* [piece of bad luck] Schlag *der*. <> *vt* **- 1.** [hit] (an)lschlagen, (an)lstoßen **- 2.** *inf* [criticize] stark kritisieren. <> *vi* **- 1.** [on door]: **to knock (at** OR **on)** klopfen (auf OR an (+ A)) **- 2.** [car engine] klopfen. ◆ **knock down** *vt sep* **- 1.** [pedestrian] anlfahren **- 2.** [building] niederlreißen. ◆ **knock off** *vi inf* [stop working] Feierabend machen. ◆ **knock out** *vt sep*

- 1. [make unconscious - subj: person, punch] k.o. schlagen; [- subj: drug] bewusstlos werden lassen **- 2.** [from competition] auslscheiden. ◆ **knock over** *vt sep* **- 1.** [push over] umlstoßen; [person] umlwerfen **- 2.** [pedestrian] überfahren.

knocker ['nɒkə'] *n* [on door] Türklopfer *der*.

knock-on effect *n* UK Auswirkung *die*.

knockout ['nɒkaʊt] *n* **- 1.** [in boxing] Knockout *der*, K.o. *der* **- 2.** *inf* [sensation]: **she's a knockout** sie ist toll.

knot [nɒt] <> *n* **- 1.** [in rope, string] Knoten *der*; **to tie/untie a knot** einen Knoten machen/lösen **- 2.** [in wood] Ast *der* **- 3.** [ship's speed] Knoten *der*. <> *vt* [rope, string] knoten.

know [nəʊ] (*pt* **knew**, *pp* **known**) <> *vt* **- 1.** [fact, information] wissen; **as far as I know** so viel ich weiß; **to let sb know sthg** jn etw wissen lassen **- 2.** [person, place] kennen; **to get to know sb** jn kennen lernen **- 3.** [language, skill] können; **to know how to do sthg** etw tun können **- 4.** [recognize] erkennen **- 5.** [call]: **to be known as** bekannt sein als **- 6.** [distinguish] unterscheiden können; **to know right from wrong** Gut und Böse unterscheiden können. <> *vi*: **I know** das weiß ich; **to know about sthg** [understand] sich mit etw auslkennen; [have heard about] etw wissen; **to know of** kennen, wissen von; **you know** [for emphasis] weißt du. <> *n*: **to be in the know** im Bilde sein.

know-all *n* UK Besserwisser *der*, -in *die*.

know-how *n* Know-how *das*.

knowing ['nəʊɪŋ] *adj* [look, smile] wissend.

knowingly ['nəʊɪŋlɪ] *adv* **- 1.** [look, smile] wissend **- 2.** [act] wissentlich.

know-it-all *n* = **know-all**.

knowledge ['nɒlɪdʒ] *n* (U) **- 1.** [learning] Kenntnisse *Pl* **- 2.** [awareness] Wissen *das*; **I had no knowledge of it** ich wusste nichts davon; **to the best of my knowledge** soweit OR soviel ich weiß.

knowledgeable ['nɒlɪdʒəbl] *adj* sachkundig.

known [nəʊn] *pp* ⊳ **know**.

knuckle ['nʌkl] *n* ANAT (Finger)knöchel *der*.

koala (bear) [kəʊˈɑːlə-] *n* Koala(bär) *der*.

Koran [kɒˈrɑːn] *n*: **the Koran** der Koran.

Korea [kəˈrɪə] *n* Korea *nt*.

Korean [kəˈrɪən] <> *adj* koreanisch. <> *n* **- 1.** [person] Koreaner *der*, -in *die* **- 2.** [language] Koreanisch(e) *das*.

kosher ['kəʊʃə'] *adj* koscher.

kung fu [ˌkʌŋˈfuː] *n* Kung-Fu *das*.

Kurd [kɜːd] *n* Kurde *der*, -din *die*.

Kuwait [kʊˈweɪt] *n* **- 1.** [country] Kuwait *nt* **- 2.** [city] Kuwait-City *nt*.

L

l¹ (pl **l's** OR **ls**), **L** (pl **L's** OR **Ls**) [el] n [letter] l das, L das.

l² [el] (abbr of litre) l.

lab [læb] n inf Labor das.

label ['leɪbl] (UK) (US) ◇ n - 1. [on bottle, clothing] Etikett das; [tied on] Anhänger der; [stuck on] Aufkleber der - 2. [of record] Label das. ◇ vt - 1. [fix label to - bottle, clothing] etikettieren; [- with tied-on label] mit Anhänger versehen; [- with stuck-on label] mit Aufkleber versehen - 2. [describe]: **to label sb (as) sthg** jn als etw einlstufen.

labor etc n US = **labour** etc .

laboratory [UK lə'bɒrətrɪ, US 'læbrə,tɔ:rɪ] n Labor(atorium) das.

laborious [lə'bɔ:rɪəs] adj mühsam.

labor union n US (Arbeiter)gewerkschaft die.

labour UK, **labor** US ['leɪbər] ◇ n - 1. [work] Arbeit die - 2. (U) [workers] Arbeiterschaft die, Arbeiter Pl - 3. MED (Geburts)wehen Pl. ◇ vi - 1. [work] arbeiten - 2. [struggle]: **to labour at** OR **over sthg** sich mit etw plagen. **Labour** UK ◇ adj POL Labour-. ◇ n POL Labour Party die.

laboured UK, **labored** US ['leɪbəd] adj [breathing] schwer; [style] schwerfällig.

labourer UK, **laborer** US ['leɪbərər] n Arbeiter der, -in die.

Labour Party n UK: **the Labour Party** die Labour Party.

Labrador ['læbrədɔ:r] n [dog] Labrador der.

labyrinth ['læbərɪnθ] n Labyrinth das.

lace [leɪs] ◇ n - 1. (U) [material] Spitze die - 2. [for shoe] Schnürsenkel der. ◇ vt - 1. [shoe, boot] (zu)lschnüren - 2. [drink] mit einem Schuss Alkohol versetzen. **lace up** vt sep zulschnüren.

lack [læk] ◇ n: **lack (of)** Mangel der (an (+ D)); **for lack of money** aus Geldmangel; **there is no lack of** es mangelt nicht an (+ D). ◇ vt: **he lacks confidence/intelligence** es mangelt ihm an Selbstvertrauen/Intelligenz. ◇ vi: **to be lacking** fehlen; **he is lacking in confidence/intelligence** es mangelt ihm an Selbstvertrauen/Intelligenz.

lackadaisical [,lækə'deɪzɪkl] adj pej lustlos.

lacklustre UK, **lackluster** US ['læk,lʌstər] adj [performance] glanzlos; [person, party] langweilig.

laconic [lə'kɒnɪk] adj lakonisch.

lacquer ['lækər] n - 1. [for wood, metal] Lack der - 2. [for hair] Haarspray das.

lacrosse [lə'krɒs] n Lacrosse das.

lad [læd] n inf - 1. [young boy] Junge der - 2. [male friend] Kumpel der.

ladder ['lædər] ◇ n - 1. [for climbing] Leiter die - 2. UK [in tights] Laufmasche die. ◇ vt UK: **I've laddered my tights** ich habe eine Laufmasche.

laden ['leɪdn] adj: **laden (with)** beladen (mit).

ladies UK ['leɪdɪz], **ladies room** US n Damentoilette die.

ladle ['leɪdl] n (Schöpf)kelle die.

lady ['leɪdɪ] ◇ n - 1. [woman] Dame die - 2. [by birth or upbringing] Lady die. ◇ comp: **lady doctor** Ärztin; **lady dentist** Zahnärztin. **Lady** n [member of nobility] Lady die.

ladybird UK ['leɪdɪbɜ:d], **ladybug** US ['leɪdɪbʌg] n Marienkäfer der.

ladylike ['leɪdɪlaɪk] adj damenhaft.

lag [læg] ◇ vi: **to lag (behind)** zurücklbleiben. ◇ vt isolieren. ◇ n [time lag] zeitliche Verzögerung.

lager ['lɑ:gər] n helles Bier.

lagoon [lə'gu:n] n Lagune die.

laid [leɪd] pt & pp ▷ **lay**.

laid-back adj inf gelassen.

lain [leɪn] pp ▷ **lie**.

lair [leər] n Lager das.

lake [leɪk] n See der.

Lake District n: **the Lake District** der Lake District, Seenlandschaft in Nordwestengland.

lamb [læm] n Lamm das.

lambswool ['læmzwʊl] n Lambswool die.

lame [leɪm] adj liter & fig lahm.

lament [lə'ment] ◇ n Klage die; [song] Klagelied das. ◇ vt beklagen.

lamentable ['læməntəbl] adj beklagenswert.

laminated ['læmɪneɪtɪd] adj geschichtet.

lamp [læmp] n Lampe die; [on street] Laterne die.

lampoon [læm'pu:n] vt verspotten.

lamppost ['læmppəʊst] n Laternenpfahl der.

lampshade ['læmpʃeɪd] n Lampenschirm der.

lance [lɑ:ns] ◇ n [spear] Lanze die. ◇ vt MED auflschneiden.

land [lænd] ◇ n - 1. [gen] Land das - 2. [property] Land das. ◇ vt - 1. [plane] landen - 2. [cargo] löschen - 3. [fish] an Land ziehen - 4. inf [job, contract] kriegen - 5. inf [put]: **to land sb in trouble/jail** jn in Schwierigkeiten/ins Gefängnis bringen - 6. inf [encumber]: **to land sb with sb/sthg** jm etw auflhalsen. ◇ vi - 1. [plane, passenger] landen; [from ship] an Land gehen - 2. [fall] fallen. **land up** vi inf [in place] landen; [in situation] enden.

landing ['lændɪŋ] n - 1. [between stairs] Treppenabsatz der - 2. [of aeroplane] Landung die.

landing card n Einreisekarte die.

landlady ['lænd,leɪdɪ] n - 1. [of pub] Wirtin die - 2. [of lodgings] Vermieterin die.

landlord ['lændlɔːd] n - 1. [of pub] Wirt der - 2. [of lodgings] Vermieter der.

landmark ['lændmɑːk] n - 1. [prominent feature] Wahrzeichen das - 2. fig [in history] Meilenstein der.

landowner ['lænd,əʊnər] n Grundbesitzer der, -in die.

landscape ['lændskeɪp] n [scenery] Landschaft die.

landslide ['lændslaɪd] n liter & fig Erdrutsch der.

lane [leɪn] n - 1. [country road] (enge) Landstraße - 2. [division of road] Fahrspur die, Fahrstreifen der; 'get in lane' 'Bitte einordnen'; 'keep in lane' 'Auf der Fahrspur bleiben' - 3. [in swimming pool, on racetrack] Bahn die - 4. [for shipping] Schifffahrtsweg der; [for aircraft] Flugroute die.

language ['læŋgwɪdʒ] n Sprache die; bad language Kraftausdrücke Pl.

language laboratory n Sprachlabor das.

languid ['læŋgwɪd] adj [gesture] lässig; [person] träge.

languish ['læŋgwɪʃ] vi - 1. [suffer] schmachten - 2. [become weak - person, plant] verkümmern.

lank [læŋk] adj [hair] strähnig.

lanky ['læŋkɪ] adj schlaksig.

lantern ['læntən] n Laterne die.

lap [læp] ⋄ n - 1. [knees] Schoß der - 2. SPORT Runde die. ⋄ vt - 1. [subj: animal] (auf)lschlecken - 2. SPORT [runner, car] überrunden. ⋄ vi [water, waves] plätschern.

lapel [lə'pel] n Revers das.

lapse [læps] ⋄ n - 1. [failing]: **lapse of concentration** Konzentrationsschwäche die; **memory lapse** Gedächtnislücke die - 2. [in behaviour] Lapsus der - 3. [of time]: **after a lapse of three years** nach drei Jahren. ⋄ vi - 1. [licence, passport] ablaufen; [law] nicht mehr gelten; [custom] aussterben - 2. [standards] verfallen; [quality] sich verschlechtern - 3. [subj: person]: **to lapse into sthg** in etw (A) verfallen; [coma] in etw (A) fallen.

lap-top (computer) n Laptop der.

lard [lɑːd] n Schweineschmalz das.

larder ['lɑːdər] n [room] Vorratsraum der; [cupboard] Vorratsschrank der.

large [lɑːdʒ] adj groß; [person] korpulent. ➡ **at large** ⋄ adj: **to be at large** [prisoner] auf freiem Fuß sein; [animal] frei herumllaufen. ⋄ adv [as a whole]: **society/the world at large** die ganze Gesellschaft/Welt.

largely ['lɑːdʒlɪ] adv zum größten Teil.

lark [lɑːk] n - 1. [bird] Lerche die - 2. inf [joke] Jux der. ➡ **lark about** vi herumlalbern.

laryngitis [,lærɪn'dʒaɪtɪs] n (U) Kehlkopfentzündung die.

lasagna, lasagne [lə'zænjə] n (U) Lasagne Pl.

laser ['leɪzər] n Laser der.

laser printer n Laserdrucker der.

lash [læʃ] ⋄ n - 1. [eyelash] Wimper die - 2. [blow with whip] Peitschenhieb der. ⋄ vt - 1. [whip as punishment] auslpeitschen - 2. [subj: wind, rain, waves] peitschen gegen - 3. [tie]: **to lash sthg to sthg** etw an etw (D) festlbinden. ➡ **lash out** vi - 1. [physically] um sich schlagen; **to lash out at** OR **against sb** (auf jn) einlschlagen OR loslschlagen - 2. [verbally]: **to lash out at** OR **against sb** Schimpftiraden auf jn losllassen; jn beschimpfen.

lass [læs] n Mädel das.

lasso [læ'suː] (pl -s) ⋄ n Lasso das. ⋄ vt mit dem Lasso einlfangen.

last [lɑːst] ⋄ adj letzte(r) (s); **last Tuesday** letzten Dienstag; **last but one** vorletzte(r) (s); **that's the last thing I want** das ist das Letzte, was ich will. ⋄ adv zuletzt. ⋄ pron: **to be the last to arrive/sit down/**etc als Letzte(r) anlkommen/sich hinlsetzen/etc; **I'm always the last to be told** ich bin immer der Letzte, der etwas erfährt; **to leave sthg till last** etw bis zuletzt auflschieben; **the Saturday before last** vorletzten Samstag; **the last but one** der/die/das Vorletzte. ⋄ n [final thing]: **the last I saw/heard of him** das Letzte, was ich von ihm sah/hörte. ⋄ vi - 1. [continue to exist or function] dauern; [shoes] halten; [luck, feeling] anlhalten - 2. [keep fresh] sich halten - 3. [be enough for]: **this will last a week** das wird für eine Woche reichen. ➡ **at (long) last** adv endlich.

last-ditch adj allerletzte(r) (s).

lasting ['lɑːstɪŋ] adj [peace] dauerhaft; [effect, mistrust] anhaltend.

lastly ['lɑːstlɪ] adv zum Schluss.

last-minute adj in letzter Minute; [flight, ticket] Last-Minute-.

last name n Familienname der.

latch [lætʃ] n Riegel der. ➡ **latch onto** vt insep inf [idea] ablfahren auf; [person] sich hängen an.

late [leɪt] ⋄ adj - 1. [not on time]: **to be late** [person] zu spät dran sein; [train, bus] Verspätung haben; **to be late for sthg** zu etw zu spät kommen - 2. [near end of]: **in the late evening/afternoon/morning** am späten Abend/Nachmittag/Vormittag; **he arrived in late December** er kam Ende Dezember - 3. [later than normal] spät - 4. [dead] verstorben - 5. [former] vorige. ⋄ adv - 1. [not on time]: **to arrive (20 minutes) late** [bus, train] (20 Minuten) Verspätung haben; [person] (20 Minuten) zu spät kommen - 2. [later than normal, near end of period] spät; **late in the afternoon** am späten Nachmittag; **late in August** Ende August; **I worked late** ich habe lange gearbeitet. ◆ **of late** adv in letzter Zeit.

latecomer ['leɪt,kʌməʳ] n Zuspätkommende der, die.

lately ['leɪtlɪ] adv in letzter Zeit.

latent ['leɪtənt] adj latent vorhanden.

later ['leɪtəʳ] ◇ adj später. ◇ adv: later (on) später.

lateral ['lætərəl] adj seitlich.

latest ['leɪtɪst] ◇ adj [most recent] neueste(r) (s). ◇ n: **at the latest** spätestens.

lather ['lɑːðəʳ] ◇ n (Seifen)schaum der. ◇ vt einseifen.

Latin ['lætɪn] ◇ adj [studies, student] Latein-. ◇ n [language] Latein(ische) das.

Latin America n Lateinamerika nt.

Latin American adj lateinamerikanisch.

latitude ['lætɪtjuːd] n GEOG Breite die.

latter ['lætəʳ] ◇ adj - **1.** [later - years] spätere; **in the latter part of the century** in der zweiten Hälfte des Jahrhunderts - **2.** [second] zweite(r) (s); [opposed to former] letzte(r) (s). ◇ n: **the latter** der/die/das Letztere.

lattice ['lætɪs] n Gitter das.

Latvia ['lætvɪə] n Lettland nt.

laudable ['lɔːdəbl] adj lobenswert.

laugh [lɑːf] ◇ n - **1.** [sound] Lachen das - **2.** inf [fun, joke] Spaß der; **to do sthg for laughs** OR **a laugh** etw aus OR zum Spaß machen. ◇ vi lachen. ◆ **laugh at** vt insep [mock] sich lustig machen über (+ A). ◆ **laugh off** vt sep [dismiss] mit einem Lachen abtun.

laughable ['lɑːfəbl] adj pej lächerlich.

laughing stock ['lɑːfɪŋstɒk] n Zielscheibe die des Spotts.

laughter ['lɑːftəʳ] n Gelächter das.

launch [lɔːntʃ] ◇ n - **1.** [of new ship] Stapellauf der - **2.** [into air - of missile] Abschuss der - **3.** [start] Beginn der - **4.** COMM [of new book, product] Lancieren das - **5.** [boat] Barkasse die. ◇ vt - **1.** [into water - boat] zu Wasser lassen; [- new ship] vom Stapel lassen - **2.** [into air - space rocket, satellite] in den Weltraum schießen; [- missile] abschießen - **3.** [start - campaign] beginnen; (phrase): **to launch an attack** einen Angriff durchführen - **4.** COMM [new book, product] lancieren.

launch(ing) pad ['lɔːntʃ(ɪŋ)-] n for rocket, missile, satellite] Abschussrampe die.

launder ['lɔːndəʳ] vt - **1.** [clothes] waschen und bügeln - **2.** inf [money] waschen.

laund(e)rette [lɔːn'dret], **Laundromat®** US ['lɔːndrəmæt] n Waschsalon der.

laundry ['lɔːndrɪ] n - **1.** (U) [clothes] Wäsche die - **2.** [business] Wäscherei die.

laurel ['lɒrəl] n Lorbeer der.

lava ['lɑːvə] n Lava die.

lavatory ['lævətrɪ] n Toilette die.

lavender ['lævəndəʳ] n [plant] Lavendel der.

lavish ['lævɪʃ] ◇ adj - **1.** [generous] großzügig; **to be lavish with sthg** [with money, time] mit etw großzügig sein - **2.** [sumptuous - decoration] aufwendig; [- banquet] üppig. ◇ vt: **to lavish sthg on sb** [praise, attention, money] jn mit etw förmlich überhäufen.

law [lɔː] n - **1.** [legislation, rule, natural or scientific principle] Gesetz das; **to become law** rechtskräftig werden; **to break the law** das Gesetz brechen; **against the law** gesetzeswidrig; **law and order** Recht und Ordnung - **2.** (U) [legal system]: **(the) law** das Recht - **3.** [subject studied] Jura.

law-abiding [-ə,baɪdɪŋ] adj gesetzestreu.

law court n Gericht das.

lawful ['lɔːfʊl] adj fml rechtmäßig.

lawn [lɔːn] n Rasen der.

lawnmower ['lɔːn,məʊəʳ] n Rasenmäher der.

lawn tennis n Rasentennis das.

law school n juristische Fakultät.

lawsuit ['lɔːsuːt] n Klage die.

lawyer ['lɔːjəʳ] n (Rechts)anwalt der, -anwältin die.

lax [læks] adj lax; [discipline] lasch; [behaviour] locker.

laxative ['læksətɪv] n Abführmittel das.

lay [leɪ] (pt & pp laid) ◇ pt ▷ **lie**. ◇ vt - **1.** [in specified position] legen - **2.** [prepare - trap, snare] auflstellen; **to lay the table** den Tisch decken - **3.** [carpet, cable, pipes] verlegen; [bricks, foundations] legen - **4.** [egg] legen - **5.**: **to lay the blame (for sthg) on sb** jm die Schuld (für etw) geben; **to lay emphasis on sthg** Wert auf etw (A) legen. ◇ adj - **1.** RELIG Laien- - **2.** [untrained, unqualified] laienhaft; **lay person** Laie der. ◆ **lay aside** vt sep - **1.** [save - food, money] zur Seite legen - **2.** [knitting, book] weglegen. ◆ **lay down** vt sep - **1.** [regulations] auflstellen - **2.** [arms, tools] niederlegen. ◆ **lay off** ◇ vt sep [workers] entlassen. ◇ vt insep inf - **1.** [leave alone] in Ruhe lassen - **2.** [stop, give up]: **to lay off alcohol/cigarettes** mit dem Trinken/Rauchen aufhören. ◆ **lay on** vt sep UK [provide, supply] sorgen für. ◆ **lay out** vt sep - **1.** [clothes, tools, ingredients] bereitlegen - **2.** [garden, house, town] planen.

layabout ['leɪəbaʊt] n UK inf Faulenzer der.

lay-by (pl -s) n UK [small] Parkbucht die; [large] Rastplatz der.

layer ['leɪəʳ] n - **1.** [of substance, material] Schicht die - **2.** fig [level] Ebene die.

layman ['leɪmən] (pl -men [-mən]) n fig & RELIG Laie der.

layout ['leɪaʊt] *n* [of house] Raumaufteilung *die*; [of garden] Anlage *die*; [of text] Layout *das*.

laze [leɪz] *vi*: **to laze (about OR around)** faulenzen.

lazy ['leɪzɪ] *adj* - 1. [person] faul - 2. [action] träge.

lazybones ['leɪzɪbəʊnz] (*pl inv*) *n* Faulpelz *der*.

lb *abbr of* **pound**.

LCD (*abbr of* **liquid crystal display**) *n* LCD; **LCD display** LCD-Anzeige *die*.

lead¹ [liːd] (*pt & pp* **led**) <> *n* - 1. (U) [winning position] Führung *die*; **to be in OR have the lead** in Führung liegen - 2. [amount ahead] Vorsprung *der* - 3. (U) [initiative, example]: **to take the lead** [do sthg first] mit gutem Beispiel voranlgehen; **I followed his lead** ich folgte seinem Beispiel - 4. (U) [stage or film role]: **the lead** die Hauptrolle - 5. [clue] Anhaltspunkt *der* - 6. [for dog] Leine *die* - 7. [wire, cable] Kabel *das*. <> *adj* [most important]: **lead singer** Leadsänger *der*, -in *die*; **lead actor** Hauptdarsteller *der*; **lead story** Leitartikel *der*. <> *vt* - 1. [procession, parade] anlführen - 2. [person, existence] führen - 3. [team, investigation] leiten; [political party] führen - 4. [strike, campaign] organisieren - 5. [cause, influence]: **to lead sb to do sthg** jn veranlassen, etw zu tun. <> *vi* - 1. [go] führen - 2. [give access to]: **to lead to/ into sthg** zu etw/in etw (A) führen - 3. [be winning] führen - 4. [result in]: **to lead to sthg** zu etw führen. **lead up to** *vt insep* - 1. [precede]: **the events that led up to the disaster** die Ereignisse, die der Katastrophe vorausgingen - 2. [in conversation - topic] zulsteuern auf (+ A); (*phrase*): **what are you leading up to?** worauf willst du hinaus?

lead² [led] <> *n* - 1. [metal] Blei *das* - 2. [in pencil] Mine *die*. <> *comp* Blei-.

leaded ['ledɪd] *adj* [petrol] verbleit.

leader ['liːdər] *n* - 1. [head - of organization] Leiter *der*, -in *die*; [- of political party] Vorsitzende *der*, *die*; [- of gang] Anführer *der*, -in *die* - 2. [in race, competition] Führende *der*, *die*; **to be the leader** in Führung liegen - 3. *UK* [in newspaper] Leitartikel *der*.

leadership ['liːdəʃɪp] *n* [position, people in charge] Führung *die*; [quality] Führungsqualitäten *Pl*.

lead-free [led-] *adj* bleifrei.

leading ['liːdɪŋ] *adj* [prominent] führend.

leading light *n* herausragende Persönlichkeit.

leaf [liːf] (*pl* **leaves**) *n* - 1. [of tree, plant, book] Blatt *das* - 2. [of table] Platte *die* (*zur Vergrößerung eines Tisches*). **leaf through** *vt insep* durchlblättern.

leaflet ['liːflɪt] *n* Broschüre *die*; [commercial] Prospekt *der*; [political] Flugblatt *das*.

league [liːg] *n* - 1. [group - of people, countries] Bündnis *das*; (*phrase*): **to be in league with sb** mit jm verbündet sein - 2. *SPORT* Liga *die*.

leak [liːk] <> *n* - 1. [in pipe, tank, roof] undichte Stelle; [in boat] Leck *das* - 2. [disclosure]: **there has been a leak** es ist etwas durchgesickert. <> *vt* [make known] durchlsickern lassen. <> *vi* [pipe, tank, roof, shoe] undicht sein; [boat] lecken; [gas] auslströmen; [liquid] auslaufen; **to leak (out) from sthg** aus etw auslströmen/auslaufen. **leak out** *vi* [news, secret] durchlsickern.

lean [liːn] (*pt & pp* **leant OR -ed**) <> *adj* - 1. [person - thin] dünn; [- slim] schlank - 2. [meat, harvest, year] mager. <> *vt*: **to lean sthg against sthg** etw gegen OR an etw (A) lehnen. <> *vi* - 1. [bend, slope - person] sich beugen; [- wall] sich neigen; (*phrase*): **to lean forward** sich vorlbeugen - 2. [rest]: **to lean on/ against sthg** sich an etw (A)/gegen etw lehnen. **lean back** *vi* sich zurücklehnen.

leaning ['liːnɪŋ] *n*: **leaning (towards sthg)** Neigung *die* (zu etw).

leant [lent] *pt & pp* ▷ **lean**.

lean-to (*pl* **-s**) *n* angebauter Schuppen.

leap [liːp] (*pt & pp* **leapt OR -ed**) <> *n* - 1. [jump] Sprung *der* - 2. [increase] sprunghafter Anstieg. <> *vi* [jump] springen.

leapfrog ['liːpfrɒg] <> *n* (U) Bockspringen *das*. <> *vt fig* überlspringen.

leapt [lept] *pt & pp* ▷ **leap**.

leap year *n* Schaltjahr *das*.

learn [lɜːn] (*pt & pp* **-ed OR learnt**) <> *vt* - 1. [acquire knowledge, skill of] (er)lernen; **to learn (how) to cook/read/etc** kochen/lesen/ *etc* lernen - 2. [memorize] (auswendig) lernen - 3. [hear] erfahren; **to learn that...** erfahren, dass... <> *vi* - 1. [acquire knowledge, skill] lernen - 2. [hear]: **to learn of OR about sthg** von etw erfahren.

learned ['lɜːnɪd] *adj* - 1. [person] gelehrt - 2. [journal, paper, book] wissenschaftlich.

learner ['lɜːnər] *n*: **she's a quick learner** sie lernt schnell; **learners of English** Englischlerner *Pl*.

learner (driver) *n* Fahrschüler *der*, -in *die*.

learning ['lɜːnɪŋ] *n* (U) [process] Lernen *das*; [knowledge] Wissen *das*; [result] Gelehrsamkeit *die*.

learnt [lɜːnt] *pt & pp* ▷ **learn**.

lease [liːs] <> *n* *LAW* [of premises] Pacht *die*; [contract] Pachtvertrag *der*; [of car] Leasing *das*; [contract] Leasingvertrag *der*. <> *vt* [premises - to sb] verpachten; [- from sb] pachten; [- car] leasen.

leasehold ['liːshəʊld] *adj* [property] Pacht-.

leash [liːʃ] *n* (Hunde)leine *die*.

least [liːst] (*superl of* **little**) <> *adj* wenigste(r) (s); **he earns the least money** er verdient am wenigsten. <> *pron*: **(the) least** das Wenigste; **it's the least I can do** das ist das Mindeste, was ich tun kann; **not in the least** nicht im Geringsten; **to say the least** gelinde gesagt. ◇ adv am wenigsten. ● **at least** adv wenigstens. ● **least of all** adv am allerwenigsten.

leather ['leðə'] ◇ n Leder das. ◇ comp Leder-.

leave [li:v] (pt & pp left) ◇ vt - 1. [gen] verlassen; **leave the door open** lass die Tür offen; **let's leave it at that** lassen wir es dabei - 2. [not take away] lassen - 3. [not use, not eat] übrig lassen - 4. [a mark, scar, message, in will] hinterlassen; **to leave one's money to sb** jm sein Geld hinterlassen - 5. [space, gap] lassen - 6. [entrust] überlassen; **he left it to her to decide** er hat ihr die Entscheidung überlassen. ◇ vi gehen; [train, bus] abfahren. ◇ n (U) - 1. [time off work] Urlaub der; **on leave** auf Urlaub - 2. fml [permission] Erlaubnis die. ● **leave behind** vt sep zurücklassen. ● **leave out** vt sep auslassen.

leave of absence n Urlaub der.

leaves [li:vz] Pl ⊳ **leaf**.

Lebanon ['lebənən] n Libanon der.

lecherous ['letʃərəs] adj lüstern.

lecture ['lektʃə'] ◇ n - 1. [talk - at university] Vorlesung die; [- at conference] Vortrag der - 2. [criticism, reprimand] Strafpredigt die. ◇ vt [scold]: **to lecture sb** jm eine Strafpredigt halten. ◇ vi [give talk]: **to lecture (on/in sthg)** eine Vorlesung/einen Vortrag (über etw (A)) halten.

lecturer ['lektʃərə'] n - 1. [teacher] Dozent der, -in die - 2. [speaker] Redner der, -in die.

led [led] pt & pp ⊳ **lead¹**.

ledge [ledʒ] n [of window - outside] Fenstersims der; [- inside] Fensterbrett das.

ledger ['ledʒə'] n Hauptbuch das.

leek [li:k] n: **a leek** eine Stange Lauch.

leer [lıə'] ◇ n lüsterner Blick. ◇ vi: **to leer at sb** jm einen lüsternen Blick zuwerfen.

leeway ['li:weı] n [room to manoeuvre] Spielraum der.

left [left] ◇ pt & pp ⊳ **leave**. ◇ adj - 1. [remaining] übrig; **to be left** übrig geblieben sein - 2. [side, hand, foot] linke(r) (s). ◇ adv links. ◇ n [direction]: **on the left** auf der linken Seite; **to the left** [position] auf der linken Seite; [movement] auf die linke Seite; **keep to the left!** sich links halten! ● **Left** n POL: **the Left** die Linke.

left-hand adj linke(r) (s); **the left-hand side** die linke Seite.

left-hand drive adj mit Linkssteuer.

left-handed [-'hændıd] adj [person] linkshändig.

left luggage (office) n UK Gepäckaufbewahrung die.

leftover ['leftəuvə'] adj übrig geblieben. ● **leftovers** npl Reste Pl.

left wing n POL linker Flügel. ● **left-wing** adj POL linke(r) (s).

leg [leg] n - 1. [gen] Bein das; phrase: **to pull sb's leg** jn auf den Arm nehmen - 2. CULIN [of chicken] Schenkel der; [of lamb, pork] Keule die - 3. [of journey] Etappe die; [of tournament] Runde die.

legacy ['legəsı] n - 1. [gift of money] Erbschaft die - 2. fig [consequence] Erbe das.

legal ['li:gl] adj - 1. [concerning the law - system] Rechts-; [- advice] juristisch; **the legal profession** die Juristenschaft - 2. [lawful] legal.

legalize, -ise ['li:gəlaız] vt legalisieren.

legal tender n (U) legales Zahlungsmittel.

legend ['ledʒənd] n - 1. [myth] Sage die - 2. fig [person] Legende die.

leggings ['legınz] npl Leggings Pl.

legible ['ledʒəbl] adj lesbar.

legislation [,ledʒıs'leıʃn] n (U) [laws] Gesetze Pl.

legislature ['ledʒısleıtʃə'] n Legislative die.

legitimate [lı'dʒıtımət] adj - 1. [government] rechtmäßig; [business, action] legal - 2. [argument] stichhaltig; [complaint, question] berechtigt - 3. [child] ehelich.

legroom ['legrom] n Beinfreiheit die.

leg-warmers [-,wɔ:məz] npl Legwarmer Pl.

leisure [UK 'leʒə', US 'li:ʒə'] n Freizeit die; **do it at (your) leisure** machen Sie es, wenn Sie Zeit haben.

leisure centre n Freizeitzentrum das.

leisurely [UK 'leʒəlı, US 'li:ʒərlı] adj & adv gemächlich.

leisure time n Freizeit die.

lemon ['lemən] n [fruit] Zitrone die.

lemonade [,lemə'neıd] n - 1. UK [fizzy] Limonade die - 2. [made with fresh lemons] Zitronensaftgetränk (aus Zitronen, Zucker und Wasser bestehend).

lemon juice n (U) Zitronensaft der.

lemon sole n Seezunge die.

lemon squash n (U) UK Zitronengetränk das.

lemon squeezer [-,skwi:zə'] n Zitronenpresse die.

lemon tea n Zitronentee der.

lend [lend] (pt & pp lent) vt - 1. [money, book]: **to lend sb sthg, to lend sthg to sb** jm etw leihen; **I don't like lending money** ich verleihe nicht gerne Geld - 2. [support, assistance]: **to lend one's support to sb** jn unterstützen; **to lend one's assistance to sb** jm helfen - 3. [credibility, quality]: **to lend sthg to sb/sthg** jm/einer Sache etw verleihen.

lending rate ['lendıŋ-] n Darlehenszinssatz der.

length [leŋθ] *n* - **1.** [gen] Länge *die*; **in length** in der Länge, lang - **2.** [whole distance]: **we walked the length of the street** wir gingen die ganze Straße entlang - **3.** [of swimming pool] Länge *die* - **4.** [of string, wood, cloth] Stück *das* - **5.** *phr*: **he went to great lengths to achieve his goal** er tat alles Mögliche, um sein Ziel zu erreichen. ◆ **at length** *adv* - **1.** [eventually] endlich - **2.** [in detail] ausführlich.

lengthen ['leŋθən] ◇ *vt* verlängern. ◇ *vi* länger werden.

lengthways ['leŋθweɪz] *adv* der Länge nach, längs.

lengthy ['leŋθɪ] *adj* lang, langwierig; [stay, visit] ausgedehnt; [discussions] langwierig.

lenient ['liːnɪənt] *adj* [person] nachsichtig; [verdict, sentence] mild.

lens [lenz] *n* - **1.** PHOT & ANAT Linse *die*; [of glasses] Glas *das* - **2.** [contact lens] Kontaktlinse *die*.

lent [lent] *pt* & *pp* ▷ **lend**.

Lent [lent] *n* Fastenzeit *die*.

lentil ['lentɪl] *n* Linse *die*.

Leo ['liːəʊ] *n* Löwe *der*.

leopard ['lepəd] *n* Leopard *der*.

leotard ['liːətɑːd] *n* - **1.** [in ballet, circus] Trikot *das* - **2.** [in gymnastics] Gymnastikanzug *der*.

leper ['lepər] *n* Leprakranke *der, die*.

leprosy ['leprəsɪ] *n* Lepra *die*.

lesbian ['lezbɪən] *n* Lesbe *die*, Lesbierin *die*.

less [les] (*compar of* **little**) ◇ *adj* weniger; **less than** weniger als; **of less value** von geringerem Wert. ◇ *pron* weniger; **less than 20** weniger als 20. ◇ *adv* weniger; **less and less** immer weniger. ◇ *prep* [minus] weniger; **purchase price less 10%** Kaufpreis abzüglich 10%.

lessen ['lesn] ◇ *vt* [risk, chances, effect] verringern; [pain] lindern. ◇ *vi* nachlassen.

lesser ['lesər] *adj* geringer; **to a lesser extent** OR **degree** in geringerem Umfang.

lesson ['lesn] *n* - **1.** [class] (Unterrichts)stunde *die* - **2.** [example]: **to teach sb a lesson** jm eine Lektion erteilen.

let [let] (*pt* & *pp inv*) *vt* - **1.** [allow] lassen; **to let sb do sthg** jn etw tun lassen; **she let her hair grow** sie ließ sich (D) die Haare wachsen; **to let go of sthg** etw loslassen; **to let sb go** [release] jn loslassen; **to let o.s. go** [neglect] sich gehen lassen; **to let sb have sthg** [permanently] jm etw überlassen; **he wouldn't let me have the book** er wollte mir das Buch nicht geben; **to let sb know sthg** jn etw wissen lassen; **let me know as soon as possible** sagen Sie mir so bald wie möglich Bescheid - **2.** [in verb forms]: **let's go!** gehen wir!; **let me see** lass mich überlegen - **3.** [rent out] vermieten; **'to let'** 'zu vermieten'. ◆ **let alone** *conj* geschweige denn. ◆ **let down** *vt sep* - **1.** [per-son - disappoint] enttäuschen; [- not help] im Stich lassen - **2.** [let air out of]: **to let sb's tyres down** jm die Luft aus den Reifen lassen. ◆ **let in** *vt sep* hereinlassen; **to let o.s. in for sthg** sich auf etw (A) einlassen; **to let sb in on sthg** [secret, plan] jn in etw (A) einlweihen. ◆ **let off** *vt sep* - **1.** [excuse] davonkommen lassen - **2.** [from vehicle] aussteigen lassen - **3.** [cannon, missile] ablfeuern; [firework] loslassen. ◆ **let on** *vi*: **to let on about sthg** etw verraten. ◆ **let out** *vt sep* heraus-/hinauslassen; **let me out!** lass mich heraus!; **to let out a scream** einen Schrei auslstoßen. ◆ **let up** *vi* nachlassen.

letdown ['letdaʊn] *n inf* Enttäuschung *die*.

lethal ['liːθl] *adj* tödlich.

lethargic [ləˈθɑːdʒɪk] *adj* träge, lethargisch.

let's [lets] *abbr of* **let us**.

letter ['letər] *n* - **1.** [written message] Brief *der* - **2.** [of alphabet] Buchstabe *der*.

letter bomb *n* Briefbombe *die*.

letterbox ['letəbɒks] *n* UK Briefkasten *der*.

lettuce ['letɪs] *n* Kopfsalat *der*.

letup ['letʌp] *n* Pause *die*.

leuk(a)emia [luːˈkiːmɪə] *n* Leukämie *die*.

level ['levl] (*UK*) (*US*) ◇ *adj* - **1.** [equal in height]: **to be level (with sthg)** (mit etw) auf gleicher Höhe sein - **2.** [equal in standard] ebenbürtig - **3.** [flat] waagerecht; [teaspoon] gestrichen. ◇ *n* - **1.** [amount - gen] Niveau *das*; [- of noise] Pegel *der*; [- of temperature] Höhe *die* - **2.** [of liquid] Stand *der* - **3.** [standard] Niveau *das* - **4.** US [spirit level] Wasserwaage *die* - **5.** [storey] Geschoss *das*; [of multistorey car park] Ebene *die* - **6.** *phr*: **to be on the level** *inf* ehrlich sein. ◇ *vt* - **1.** [make flat] ebnen - **2.** [demolish] dem Erdboden gleichlmachen. ◆ **level off, level out** *vi* - **1.** [unemployment, inflation] aufhören zu steigen - **2.** AERON [aircraft] ablfangen. ◆ **level with** *vt insep inf* ehrlich sein mit.

level crossing *n* UK ebener Bahnübergang.

level-headed [-ˈhedɪd] *adj* vernünftig.

lever [UK 'liːvər, US 'levər] *n* [handle, bar] Hebel *der*.

leverage [UK 'liːvərɪdʒ, US 'levərɪdʒ] *n* (U) - **1.** *fig* [influence] Einfluss *der* - **2.** [principle] Hebelwirkung *die*; [force] Hebelkraft *die*.

levy ['levɪ] (*pl* **levies**) ◇ *n*: **levy (on sthg)** Steuer *die* (auf etw (A)). ◇ *vt* erheben.

lewd [ljuːd] *adj* [joke, song] unanständig; [remark] anzüglich.

liability [ˌlaɪəˈbɪlətɪ] *n* - **1.** [hindrance] Belastung *die* - **2.** LAW [legal responsibility]: **liability (for sthg)** Haftung *die* (für etw). ◆ **liabilities** *npl* FIN Verbindlichkeiten *Pl*, Schulden *Pl*.

liable ['laɪəbl] *adj* - **1.** [likely]: **to be liable to do sthg** die Neigung haben, etw zu tun - **2.** [prone]: **to be liable to sthg** für etw anfällig OR empfänglich sein - **3.** LAW: **to be liable (for**

sthg) [debt, accident, damage] (für etw) verantwortlich sein; **to be liable to sthg** [fine, arrest, imprisonment] für etw haftbar sein.

liaise [lɪ'eɪz] *vi*: **to liaise with** Kontakt aufnehmen mit; **to liaise between** als Verbindungsperson agieren zwischen *(+ D)*.

liar ['laɪə*r*] *n* Lügner *der*, -in *die*.

libel ['laɪbl] *(UK)* *(US)* ⟨⟩ *n* (schriftliche) Verleumdung. ⟨⟩ *vt* (schriftlich) verleumden.

liberal ['lɪbərəl] *adj* - **1.** [tolerant] liberal - **2.** [generous] großzügig. ◆ **Liberal** ⟨⟩ *adj* POL liberal. ⟨⟩ *n* POL Liberale *der*, *die*.

Liberal Democrat ⟨⟩ *adj* liberaldemokratisch. ⟨⟩ *n* Liberaldemokrat *der*, -in *die*.

liberate ['lɪbəreɪt] *vt* befreien.

liberation [ˌlɪbə'reɪʃn] *n* Befreiung *die*.

liberty ['lɪbətɪ] *n* Freiheit *die*; **at liberty** auf freiem Fuß; **you are at liberty to leave** es steht dir frei zu gehen; **to take liberties (with sb)** sich *(D)* (jm gegenüber) Freiheiten herausnehmen.

Libra ['liːbrə] *n* Waage *die*.

librarian [laɪ'breərɪən] *n* Bibliothekar *der*, -in *die*.

library ['laɪbrərɪ] *n* Bibliothek *die*.

library book *n* Leihbuch *das*.

libretto [lɪ'bretəʊ] *(pl* **-s)** *n* Libretto *das*.

Libya ['lɪbɪə] *n* Libyen *nt*.

lice [laɪs] *Pl* ▷ **louse**.

licence ['laɪsəns] ⟨⟩ *n* - **1.** [permit - for dog] Genehmigung *die*; [- for TV] Anmeldung *die*; [- for driver] Führerschein *der*; [- for marriage] Erlaubnis *die*, Lizenz *die*; [- for bar, pub] Konzession *die*; [- for pilot] Pilotenschein *der* - **2.** COMM Lizenz *die*. ⟨⟩ *vt US* = **license**.

license ['laɪsəns] ⟨⟩ *vt* COMM: **to license sb to do sthg** jm eine Lizenz erteilen, etw zu tun; **to license sthg** eine Lizenz OR Konzession für etw erteilen. ⟨⟩ *n US* = **licence**.

licensed ['laɪsənst] *adj* - **1.** [person]: **to be licensed to do sthg** die Genehmigung haben, etw zu tun - **2.** [object] zugelassen - **3.** *UK* [premises] mit Schankerlaubnis OR Schankkonzession.

license plate *n US* Nummernschild *das*.

lick [lɪk] *vt* [with tongue] lecken.

licorice ['lɪkərɪʃ, 'lɪkərɪs] *n* = **liquorice**.

lid [lɪd] *n* - **1.** [cover] Deckel *der* - **2.** [eyelid] Augenlid *das*.

lie [laɪ] ⟨⟩ *n* Lüge *die*; **to tell lies** lügen. ⟨⟩ *vi* - **1.** *(pt* lied, *pp* lied, *cont* lying) [tell lie] lügen; **to lie to sb** jn anlügen; **to lie about sthg** über etw *(A)* nicht die Wahrheit sagen - **2.** *(pt* lay, *pp* lain, *cont* lying) [be horizontal, be situated] liegen; **to lie in wait for sb** jm auflauern; **to lie idle** [machine] stillstehen - **3.** *(pt* lay, *pp* lain, *cont* lying) [lie down] sich legen - **4.** *(pt* lay, *pp* lain, *cont* lying) [difficulty, answer, responsibility *etc*] liegen - **5.** *(pt* lay, *pp* lain, *cont* lying)

phr: **to lie low** sich versteckt halten. ◆ **lie about, lie around** *vi* herumliegen. ◆ **lie down** *vi* sich hinlegen. ◆ **lie in** *vi UK* im Bett bleiben.

lie-down *n UK* Nickerchen *das*; **to have a lie-down** sich (kurz) hinlegen.

lie-in *n UK*: **to have a lie-in** richtig ausschlafen.

lieutenant [*UK* lef'tenənt, *US* luː'tenənt] *n* [in army] Oberleutnant *der*; [in navy] Kapitänleutnant *der*.

life [laɪf] *(pl* lives) *n* - **1.** [gen] Leben *das*; **to come to life** zum Leben erwachen; **that's life!** so ist das Leben!; **he was sent to prison for life** er wurde zu einer lebenslänglichen Haftstrafe verurteilt; **to scare the life out of sb** jn zu Tode erschrecken - **2.** *inf* [life imprisonment] lebenslängliche Freiheitsstrafe; **to get life** *inf* lebenslängliche Freiheitsstrafe kriegen.

life assurance *n* = **life insurance**.

life belt *n* Rettungsring *der*.

lifeboat ['laɪfbəʊt] *n* Rettungsboot *das*.

life buoy *n* Rettungsboje *die*.

life cycle *n* Lebenszyklus *der*.

life expectancy [-ɪk'spektənsɪ] *n* Lebenserwartung *die*.

lifeguard ['laɪfgɑːd] *n* Rettungsschwimmer *der*, -in *die*.

life insurance *n* Lebensversicherung *die*.

life jacket *n* Schwimmweste *die*.

lifeless ['laɪflɪs] *adj* leblos.

lifelike ['laɪflaɪk] *adj* lebensecht.

lifeline ['laɪflaɪn] *n* - **1.** [rope] Rettungsleine *die* - **2.** *fig* [with outside] Verbindung *die* mit der Außenwelt.

life preserver [-prɪˌzɜː'və*r*] *n US* - **1.** [belt] Rettungsring *der* - **2.** [jacket] Schwimmweste *die*, Rettungsweste *die*.

life raft *n* Rettungsfloß *das*.

lifesaver ['laɪfˌseɪvə*r*] *n* Lebensretter *der*.

life sentence *n* lebenslange Freiheitsstrafe.

life-size(d) [-saɪz(d)] *adj* lebensgroß.

lifespan ['laɪfspæn] *n* - **1.** [of person, animal] Lebenserwartung *die* - **2.** [of product, machine] Lebensdauer *die*.

lifestyle ['laɪfstaɪl] *n* Lebensstil *der*.

lifetime ['laɪftaɪm] *n* Lebenszeit *die*.

lift [lɪft] ⟨⟩ *n* - **1.** [ride]: **to give sb a lift** jn (im Auto) mitnehmen - **2.** *UK* [elevator] Fahrstuhl *der*. ⟨⟩ *vt* - **1.** [hand, arm, leg] heben - **2.** [object] hochheben - **3.** [ban, embargo] aufheben - **4.** [plagiarize - idea] stehlen; [- writing] abschreiben - **5.** *inf* [steal] klauen. ⟨⟩ *vi* - **1.** [lid, top] sich heben - **2.** [mist, fog, clouds] sich lichten.

lift-off *n* Abheben *das*.

light [laɪt] *(pt & pp* lit OR **-ed)** ⟨⟩ *adj* - **1.** [gen] leicht - **2.** [pale, bright] hell; **light blue** hellblau. ⟨⟩ *n* - **1.** *(U)* [brightness] Licht *das* - **2.** [device -

lamp] Lampe *die*; [- on car] Scheinwerfer *der*; [- in street] Laterne *die*; **to put** OR **turn the light on** das Licht einlschalten - **3.** [for cigarette, pipe] Feuer *das*; **to set light to sthg** etw anlzünden - **4.** [perspective]: **in the light of** UK, **in light of** US angesichts (+ G) - **5.** phr: **to come to light** ans Licht kommen. ⬥ vt - **1.** [ignite] anlzünden - **2.** [illuminate] erleuchten. ⬥ adv: **to travel light** mit wenig Gepäck reisen. ⬤ **light up** ⬥ vt sep - **1.** [sky, room, stage] erleuchten - **2.** [cigarette, cigar, pipe] anlzünden. ⬥ vi - **1.** [face, eyes] auflleuchten - **2.** inf [start smoking] sich *(D)* eine anlzünden.

light bulb *n* Glühbirne *die*.

lighten ['laɪtn] ⬥ vt - **1.** [make brighter - gen] heller machen; [- hair] auflhellen - **2.** [make less heavy - load] leichter machen; [- workload] erleichtern. ⬥ vi [mood, atmosphere] lockerer OR entspannter werden.

lighter ['laɪtər] *n* Feuerzeug *das*.

light-headed [-'hedɪd] *adj* schwindlig.

light-hearted [-'hɑːtɪd] *adj* - **1.** [cheerful] heiter, unbeschwert - **2.** [amusing] fröhlich.

lighthouse ['laɪthaʊs] *(pl* [-haʊzɪz]*) n* Leuchtturm *der*.

lighting ['laɪtɪŋ] *n* Beleuchtung *die*.

light meter *n* PHOT Belichtungsmesser *der*.

lightning ['laɪtnɪŋ] *n (U)* Blitz *der*.

lightweight ['laɪtweɪt] ⬥ adj [object] leicht. ⬥ n Leichtgewicht *das*; **political lightweights** Schmalspurpolitiker *Pl*.

likable ['laɪkəbl] *adj* sympathisch.

like [laɪk] ⬥ prep wie; **like this/that** so; **what's it like?** wie ist es?; **to look like sb/ sthg** jm/etw ähnlich sehen; **it looks like rain** es sieht nach Regen aus. ⬥ vt mögen; **to like doing sthg** etw gern tun; **do you like it?** gefällt es dir?; **as you like** wie Sie wollen/wie du willst; **I don't like to bother her** ich will sie nicht stören; **I'd like to sit down** ich würde mich gern hinsetzen; **I'd like a drink** ich würde gern etwas trinken; **we'd like you to come for dinner** wir möchten Sie zum Essen einladen. ⬥ n: **and the like** und dergleichen.

likeable ['laɪkəbl] *adj* = **likable**.

likelihood ['laɪklɪhʊd] *n* Wahrscheinlichkeit *die*.

likely ['laɪklɪ] *adj* - **1.** [probable] wahrscheinlich; **they're likely to win** sie werden wahrscheinlich gewinnen; **a likely story!** iro na klar! - **2.** [suitable] geeignet.

liken ['laɪkn] *vt*: **to liken sb/sthg to** jn/etw vergleichen mit.

likeness ['laɪknɪs] *n* - **1.** [resemblance]: **likeness (to sb/sthg)** Ähnlichkeit *die* (mit jm/etw) - **2.** [portrait] Bildnis *das*, Porträt *das*.

likewise ['laɪkwaɪz] *adv* gleichfalls, ebenfalls; **to do likewise** das Gleiche tun.

liking ['laɪkɪŋ] *n*: **liking for sb/sthg** Vorliebe *die* für jn/etw; **to have a liking for sb/sthg** für jn/etw eine Vorliebe haben; **that's not to my liking** das ist nicht nach meinem Geschmack.

lilac ['laɪlək] ⬥ adj [colour] lila. ⬥ n - **1.** [tree] Flieder *der* - **2.** [colour] Lila *das*.

Lilo® ['laɪləʊ] *(pl* -s*) n* UK Luftmatratze *die*.

lily ['lɪlɪ] *n* Lilie *die*.

limb [lɪm] *n* - **1.** [of body] Glied *das*; **limbs** Glieder *Pl*, Gliedmaßen *Pl* - **2.** [of tree] Ast *der*.

limber ['lɪmbər] ⬤ **limber up** *vi* sich auflockern, Lockerungsübungen machen.

limbo ['lɪmbəʊ] *(pl* -s*) n* [uncertain state]: **to be in limbo** in der Schwebe sein.

lime [laɪm] *n* - **1.** [fruit] Limone *die*; **lime juice** Limonensaft *der* - **2.** [linden tree] Linde *die*.

limelight ['laɪmlaɪt] *n*: **the limelight** das Rampenlicht.

limerick ['lɪmərɪk] *n* Limerick *der*.

limestone ['laɪmstəʊn] *n* Kalkstein *der*.

limit ['lɪmɪt] ⬥ n - **1.** [restriction] Begrenzung *die* - **2.** [boundary, greatest extent] Grenze *die*; **'off limits'** esp US 'Zutritt verboten'; **that subject is off limits** das Thema ist tabu; **within limits** [to a certain extent] innerhalb bestimmter Grenzen. ⬥ vt begrenzen.

limitation [ˌlɪmɪ'teɪʃn] *n* - **1.** [restriction, control] Begrenzung *die* - **2.** [shortcoming]: **limitations** Grenzen *Pl*.

limited ['lɪmɪtɪd] *adj* begrenzt.

limited company, limited liability company *n* Gesellschaft *die* mit beschränkter Haftung.

limousine ['lɪməziːn] *n* luxuriöse Limousine.

limp [lɪmp] ⬥ adj schlaff; [lettuce, flowers] welk. ⬥ n Hinken *das*; **to walk with a limp** hinken. ⬥ vi hinken.

line [laɪn] ⬥ n - **1.** [mark] Linie *die*; **to draw the line at sthg** fig bei etw den Schlussstrich ziehen - **2.** [row] Reihe *die* - **3.** [queue] Schlange *die*; **to stand** OR **wait in line** Schlange stehen OR anlstehen - **4.** [direction of movement] Gerade *die*; **he can't walk in a straight line** er kann nicht (mehr) geradeaus gehen - **5.** [alignment]: **in line (with)** in einer Linie (mit); **to step out of line** [misbehave] aus der Reihe tanzen - **6.** [RAIL - railway track] Gleise *Pl*; [- route] Bahnlinie *die*; **the line was blocked** die Strecke war blockiert - **7.** [of poem, song, text] Zeile *die* - **8.** [wrinkle] Falte *die* - **9.** [rope] Leine *die*; [wire] Kabel *das*; [string] Schnur *die* - **10.** TELEC [telephone connection] Leitung *die*; **hold the line** bleiben Sie am Apparat - **11.** inf [short letter] kurze Nachricht; **to drop sb a line** jm ein paar Zeilen schreiben - **12.** inf [field of activity] Branche *die* - **13.** MIL: **enemy lines** feindliche Linien - **14.** [limit, borderline] Grenze *die* - **15.** COMM [type of product] Modell *das*; [group of products] Kollektion *die*. ⬥ *vt* [cover inside surface of - drawer] auslschlagen; [- garment, curtains] füttern. ⬥ **out of line** *adj* fehl am Platz. ⬥ **line up** ⬥ *vt sep* - **1.** [in rows] auflstellen - **2.** *inf* [organize] arrangieren. ⬥ *vi* - **1.** [in a row] sich auflstellen - **2.** [in a queue] sich anlstellen.

lined [laɪnd] *adj* - **1.** [paper] liniert - **2.** [face] faltig.

linen ['lɪnɪn] *(U) n (U)* - **1.** [cloth] Leinen *das* - **2.** [tablecloths etc] Wäsche *die*.

liner ['laɪnər] *n* [ship] Linienschiff *das*.

linesman ['laɪnzmən] *(pl* **-men** [-mən]) *n* SPORT Linienrichter *der*.

linger ['lɪŋɡər] *vi* - **1.** [dawdle]: **we lingered over our meal** wir aßen in aller Gemütlichkeit; **she lingered behind after school** sie blieb nach Schulschluss noch da - **2.** [persist] zurücklbleiben.

lingo ['lɪŋɡəʊ] *(pl* **-es**) *n inf* - **1.** [language] Sprache *die* - **2.** [specialist jargon] (Fach)jargon *der*.

linguist ['lɪŋɡwɪst] *n* - **1.** [person good at languages] Sprachkundige *der*, *die* - **2.** [student or teacher of linguistics] Linguist *der*, -in *die*.

lining ['laɪnɪŋ] *n* - **1.** [of garment, curtains, box] Futter *das* - **2.** [of stomach, nose] Schleimhaut *die* - **3.** *(U)* AUT [of brakes] Belag *der*.

link [lɪŋk] ⬥ *n* - **1.** [of chain] Glied *das* - **2.** [connection]: **link (between/with)** Verbindung *die* (zwischen (+ D)/mit OR zu). ⬥ *vt* verbinden; **to link arms with sb** sich bei jm unterhaken. ⬥ **link up** *vt sep* verbinden; *(phrase)*: **to link sthg up with sthg** etw mit etw verbinden.

lino ['laɪnəʊ], **linoleum** [lɪ'nəʊlɪəm] *n* Linoleum *das*.

lion ['laɪən] *n* Löwe *der*.

lip [lɪp] *n* - **1.** [of mouth] Lippe *die* - **2.** [of container] Rand *der*.

lip-read *vi* von den Lippen lesen.

lip salve [-sælv] *n UK* Lippenbalsam *der*.

lip service *n*: **to pay lip service to sthg** ein Lippenbekenntnis zu etw ablegen.

lipstick ['lɪpstɪk] *n* Lippenstift *der*.

liqueur [lɪ'kjʊər] *n* Likör *der*.

liquid ['lɪkwɪd] ⬥ *adj* flüssig. ⬥ *n* Flüssigkeit *die*.

liquidation [,lɪkwɪ'deɪʃn] *n* Liquidation *die*.

liquidize, -ise ['lɪkwɪdaɪz] *vt UK* CULIN mit dem Mixer pürieren.

liquidizer, -iser ['lɪkwɪdaɪzər] *n UK* (elektrischer) Mixer.

liquor ['lɪkər] *n esp US* [alcoholic drink] Alkohol *der*; [spirits] Spirituosen *Pl*.

liquorice ['lɪkərɪʃ, 'lɪkərɪs] *n* Lakritze *die*.

liquor store *n US* Wein- und Spirituosenhandlung *die*.

Lisbon ['lɪzbən] *n* Lissabon *nt*.

lisp [lɪsp] ⬥ *n* Lispeln *das*. ⬥ *vi* lispeln.

list [lɪst] ⬥ *n* Liste *die*. ⬥ *vt* - **1.** [in writing] aufllisten - **2.** [in speech] auflführen.

listed building [,lɪstɪd-] *n UK* unter Denkmalschutz stehendes Gebäude.

listen ['lɪsn] *vi* - **1.** [give attention] zulhören; **to listen to sb/sthg** jm/etw zulhören; **to listen for sthg** auf etw (A) horchen - **2.** [heed advice] hören; **to listen to sb/sthg** auf jn/etw hören.

listener ['lɪsnər] *n* Zuhörer *der*, -in *die*; [radio] Hörer *der*, -in *die*.

listless ['lɪstlɪs] *adj* apathisch.

lit [lɪt] *pt & pp* ⯈ **light**.

liter *n US* = **litre**.

literacy ['lɪtərəsɪ] *n (U)* Lese- und Schreibfähigkeit *die*.

literal ['lɪtərəl] *adj* wörtlich.

literally ['lɪtərəlɪ] *adv* - **1.** [for emphasis] im wahrsten Sinne des Wortes, buchstäblich - **2.** [not figuratively] wörtlich.

literary ['lɪtərərɪ] *adj* literarisch; **a literary critic** ein Literaturkritiker *der*.

literate ['lɪtərət] *adj* - **1.** [able to read and write] des Lesens und Schreibens kundig - **2.** [well-read] gebildet.

literature ['lɪtrətʃər] *n* - **1.** [novels, plays, poetry] Literatur *die* - **2.** [printed information] Informationsmaterial *das*.

lithe [laɪð] *adj* geschmeidig.

Lithuania [,lɪθjʊ'eɪnɪə] *n* Litauen *nt*.

litigation [,lɪtɪ'ɡeɪʃn] *n (U) fml* Prozess *der*.

litre *UK*, **liter** *US* ['liːtər] *n* Liter *der*.

litter ['lɪtər] ⬥ *n* - **1.** [waste material] Abfall *der* - **2.** [newborn animals] Wurf *der* - **3.** [for litter tray]: **(cat) litter** (Katzen)streu *die*. ⬥ *vt*: **to be littered with sthg** mit etw übersät sein.

litterbin ['lɪtə,bɪn] *n UK* Mülleimer *der*.

little ['lɪtl] ⬥ *adj* - **1.** [small, younger] klein; **the little ones** die Kleinen *Pl* - **2.** [in distance, time] kurz - **3.** (*comp* **less**, *superl* **least**) [not much] wenig; **he speaks little English** er spricht wenig Englisch; **he speaks a little English** er spricht ein bisschen Englisch. ⬥ *pron* wenig; **a little** ein bisschen. ⬥ *adv* wenig; **little by little** nach und nach; **as little as possible** so wenig wie möglich.

little finger *n* kleiner Finger.

live¹ [lɪv] *vi* - **1.** [have home] wohnen - **2.** [be alive] leben; **to live to a great age** ein hohes Alter erreichen - **3.** [survive] überleben. ⬥ *vt* führen; **to live a happy life** ein glückliches Leben führen; **to live it up** *inf* in Saus und Braus leben. ⬥ **live down** *vt sep*: **she'll never live this down** das wird ihr auf ewig anhängen. ⬥ **live off** *vt insep* [savings, land] leben

von. ◆ **live on** ◇ *vt insep* [savings] leben von; [food] sich ernähren von; **I have enough to live on** ich habe genug zum Leben. ◇ *vi* [continue] weiterlleben. ◆ **live together** *vi* zusammenlwohnen. ◆ **live up to** *vt insep* [reputation] gerecht werden (+ D); [expectations] entsprechen (+ D). ◆ **live with** *vt insep* - 1. [in same house] zusammenlwohnen mit - 2. *inf* [problem, situation] sich ablfinden mit.

live² [laɪv] *adj* - 1. [alive] lebendig - 2. [programme, performance] Live-; ELEC [wire] geladen - 3. [ammunition] scharf.

livelihood ['laɪvlɪhʊd] *n* Lebensunterhalt *der*.

lively ['laɪvlɪ] *adj* lebhaft.

liven ['laɪvn] ◆ **liven up** ◇ *vt sep* beleben. ◇ *vi* [person] auflleben.

liver ['lɪvə'] *n* Leber *die*.

lives [laɪvz] *Pl* ⊏> **life**.

livestock ['laɪvstɒk] *n* Nutzvieh *das*.

livid ['lɪvɪd] *adj inf* [angry] wütend.

living ['lɪvɪŋ] ◇ *adj* - 1. [person] lebend - 2. [language] lebendig. ◇ *n* - 1. [means of earning money] Lebensunterhalt *der*; **what do you do for a living?** was machen Sie beruflich? - 2. [lifestyle] Leben *das*.

living conditions *npl* Lebensbedingungen *Pl*.

living room *n* Wohnzimmer *das*.

living standards *npl* Lebensstandard *der*.

living wage *n* zum Leben ausreichender Lohn.

lizard ['lɪzəd] *n* Eidechse *die*.

llama ['lɑːmə] *n* (*pl inv OR* -s) Lama *das*.

load [ləʊd] ◇ *n* - 1. [something carried] Ladung *die* - 2. [large amount] **loads of, a load of** *inf* eine Menge; **what a load of rubbish!** *inf* was für ein Blödsinn! ◇ *vt* - 1. [container, vehicle] beladen; **to load sthg with sthg** etw mit etw beladen - 2. [gun, cannon]: **to load (with sthg)** etw (mit etw) laden - 3. [camera]: **to load a camera with a film** einen Film in eine Kamera einllegen - 4. COMPUT [program] laden. ◆ **load up** ◇ *vt sep* beladen. ◇ *vi* auflladen.

loaded ['ləʊdɪd] *adj* - 1. [question, statement] gewichtig - 2. [gun] geladen; [camera] mit eingelegtem Film - 3. *inf* [rich] stinkreich.

loaf [ləʊf] *n* (*pl* loaves) Laib *der*.

loan [ləʊn] ◇ *n* - 1. [money lent] Darlehen *das*, Kredit *der* - 2. [act of lending] Ausleihen *das*; **on loan** ausgeliehen. ◇ *vt*: **to loan sthg (to sb), to loan (sb) sthg** etw (an jn) verleihen.

loath [ləʊθ] *adj*: **to be loath to do sthg** etw nur ungern tun.

loathe [ləʊð] *vt* verabscheuen; **to loathe doing sthg** es verabscheuen, etw zu tun.

loaves [ləʊvz] *Pl* ⊏> **loaf**.

lob [lɒb] ◇ *n* TENNIS Lob *der*. ◇ *vt* - 1. [throw] (in hohem Bogen) werfen - 2. TENNIS lobben.

lobby ['lɒbɪ] ◇ *n* - 1. [anteroom] Vorraum *der*; [in hotel] Empfangshalle *die*; [in theatre] Foyer *das* - 2. [pressure group] Lobby *die*. ◇ *vt* Einfluss nehmen auf (+ A).

lobe [ləʊb] *n* [of ear] Ohrläppchen *das*.

lobster ['lɒbstə'] *n* Hummer *der*.

local ['ləʊkl] ◇ *adj* - 1. [of the immediate area - tradition] örtlich; [- phone call] Orts-; [- hospital, shop, inhabitants] örtlich - 2. ADMIN & POL [services, council] Kommunal-. ◇ *n inf* - 1. [person]: **the locals** die Einheimischen *Pl* - 2. *UK* [pub] Stammkneipe *die*.

local authority *n UK* Kommunalverwaltung *die*.

local call *n* Ortsgespräch *das*.

local government *n* Kommunalverwaltung *die*.

locality [ləʊ'kælətɪ] *n* Gegend *die*.

localized, -ised ['ləʊkəlaɪzd] *adj* örtlich begrenzt.

locally ['ləʊkəlɪ] *adv* [in region] am Ort; [in neighbourhood] in der Nachbarschaft.

locate [*UK* ləʊ'keɪt, *US* 'ləʊkeɪt] *vt* - 1. [find] ausfindig machen, lokalisieren - 2. [situate]: **to be located** sich befinden.

location [ləʊ'keɪʃn] *n* - 1. [place] Ort *der* - 2. CIN: **the film was shot on location in China** die Außenaufnahmen zu diesem Film wurden in China gemacht.

loch [lɒk, lɒx] *n Scotland* See *der*.

lock [lɒk] ◇ *n* - 1. [of door, window, box] Schloss *das* - 2. [on canal] Schleuse *die* - 3. AUT [steering lock] Einschlag *der* - 4. [of hair] Locke *die*. ◇ *vt* - 1. [fasten securely] ablschließen; [bicycle] anlschließen - 2. [keep safely]: **to lock sthg in** etw in etw (A) einlschließen - 3. [immobilize] sperren. ◇ *vi* - 1. [fasten securely] verschließen - 2. [become immobilized] blockieren. ◆ **lock away** *vt sep* weglschließen. ◆ **lock in** *vt sep* einlschließen. ◆ **lock out** *vt sep* auslsperren. ◆ **lock up** *vt sep* - 1. [person] einlsperren - 2. [house] ablschließen - 3. [valuables] weglschließen.

locker ['lɒkə'] *n* [at gym, work] Spind *der*; [at station] Schließfach *das*.

locker room *n US* Umkleideraum *der*.

locket ['lɒkɪt] *n* Medaillon *das*.

locomotive [ˌləʊkə'məʊtɪv] *n* Lokomotive *die*.

locust ['ləʊkəst] *n* Heuschrecke *die*.

lodge [lɒdʒ] ◇ *n* - 1. [caretaker's room, of Freemasons] Loge *die* - 2. [of manor house] Pförtnerhaus *das* - 3. [for hunting] Jagdhütte *die*. ◇ *vi* - 1. [stay, live]: **to lodge with sb** bei jm (zur Untermiete) wohnen - 2. [become stuck] steckenlbleiben - 3. *fig* [in mind] sich festlsetzen. <> *vt fml* [register] einlreichen.

lodger ['lɒdʒər] *n* Untermieter *der*, -in *die*.

lodging ['lɒdʒɪŋ] *n* ▷ **board**.
➤ **lodgings** *npl* möblierte Zimmer *Pl*.

loft [lɒft] *n* Dachboden *der*.

lofty ['lɒftɪ] *adj* - 1. [noble] hoch; [feelings] erhaben; [aims] hoch gesteckt - 2. *pej* [haughty] hochmütig - 3. *liter* [high] hoch.

log [lɒg] <> *n* - 1. [of wood] Holzscheit *das* - 2. [written record - of ship] Logbuch *das*; [- of plane] Bordbuch *das*. <> *vt* - 1. [information - on paper] einltragen; [- in computer] einlgeben - 2. [speed, distance, time] zurückllegen. ➤ **log in** *vi* COMPUT (sich) einlloggen. ➤ **log out** *vi* COMPUT (sich) auslloggen.

logbook ['lɒgbʊk] *n* [of car] Fahrtenbuch *das*.

loggerheads ['lɒgəhedz] *n*: **to be at loggerheads** sich *(D)* in den Haaren liegen.

logic ['lɒdʒɪk] *n* Logik *die*.

logical ['lɒdʒɪkl] *adj* logisch.

logistics [lə'dʒɪstɪks] *n (U)* Logistik *die*.

logo ['ləugəu] *(pl* -s*) n* Logo *das*.

loin [lɔɪn] *n* Lende *die*.

loiter ['lɔɪtər] *vi* - 1. [hang about] herumllungern - 2. [dawdle] trödeln, bummeln.

loll [lɒl] *vi* [sit, lie about] (sich) lümmeln, herumllümmeln.

lollipop ['lɒlɪpɒp] *n* Lutscher *der*, Lolli *der*.

lollipop lady *n* UK meist ältere Dame in der Funktion eines Schülerlotsen.

lollipop man *n* UK meist älterer Herr in der Funktion eines Schülerlotsen.

lolly ['lɒlɪ] *n* [lollipop] Lutscher *der*, Lolli *der*.

London ['lʌndən] *n* London *nt*.

Londoner ['lʌndənər] *n* Londoner *der*, -in *die*.

lone [ləun] *adj* [lonely] einsam; [only] einzig.

loneliness ['ləunlɪnɪs] *n* Einsamkeit *die*.

lonely ['ləunlɪ] *adj* einsam.

loner ['ləunər] *n* Einzelgänger *der*, -in *die*.

lonesome ['ləunsəm] *adj* US inf einsam.

long [lɒŋ] <> *adj* lang; **it's 2 metres long** es ist 2 Meter lang; **it's two hours long** es dauert zwei Stunden; **the book is 500 pages long** das Buch hat 500 Seiten; **how long is it?** [in distance] wie lang ist es?; [in time] wie lange dauert es?; **a long time** lange. <> *adv* lange; **I won't be long** ich komme gleich wieder; **how long will it take?** wie lange dauert es?; **all day long** den ganzen Tag; **before long** bald; **no longer** nicht mehr; **so long!** *inf* tschüs! <> *vt*: **to long to do sthg** sich danach sehnen, etw zu tun. ➤ **as long as, so long as** *conj* [if] solange. ➤ **long for** *vt insep* sich sehnen nach.

long-distance *adj*: **a long-distance race** ein Langstreckenrennen; **he's a long-distance lorry driver** er ist Fernfahrer.

long-distance call *n* Ferngespräch *das*.

longhand ['lɒŋhænd] *n* Langschrift *die*.

long-haul *adj*: **long-haul flight** Langstreckenflug *der*.

longing ['lɒŋɪŋ] <> *adj* sehnsüchtig. <> *n*: **longing (for sthg)** Sehnsucht *die* (nach etw).

longitude ['lɒndʒɪtjuːd] *n* GEOG (geografische) Länge.

long jump *n* Weitsprung *der*.

long-life *adj* [battery] mit langer Lebensdauer; **long-life milk** H-Milch *die*.

long-range *adj* - 1. [missile, bomber] Langstrecken- - 2. [plan, forecast] langfristig.

long shot *n fig*: **it's a long shot, but it might work** es ist ein gewagtes Unternehmen, aber es könnte klappen.

longsighted [,lɒŋ'saɪtɪd] *adj* weitsichtig.

long-standing *adj* (schon) lange bestehend.

longsuffering [,lɒŋ'sʌfərɪŋ] *adj* geduldig.

long term *n*: **in the long term** auf lange Sicht.

long wave *n* Langwelle *die*.

longwinded [,lɒŋ'wɪndɪd] *adj* langatmig.

loo [luː] *(pl* -s*) n* UK inf Klo *das*.

look [lʊk] <> *n* - 1. [with eyes] Blick *der*; **to give sb a look** jm einen Blick zuwerfen; **to have a look at sthg** sich *(D)* etw anlsehen; **let me have a look!** lass mich mal sehen! - 2. [search]: **to have a look (for sthg)** (etw) suchen - 3. [appearance] Aussehen *das*; **by the look** OR **looks of it** allem Anschein nach. <> *vi* - 1. [with eyes] sehen; **to look at sb/sthg** jn/ etw anlsehen; **I'm just looking** [in shop] ich wollte mich nur umsehen - 2. [search] suchen - 3. [building, room]: **to look onto** gehen auf *(+ A)* - 4. [seem] auslsehen; **he looks as if he hasn't slept** er sieht aus, als hätte er nicht geschlafen; **it looks like rain** es sieht nach Regen aus; **she looks like her mother** sie sieht ihrer Mutter ähnlich. ➤ **looks** *npl*: **(good) looks** gutes Aussehen. ➤ **look after** *vt insep* [take care of] sich kümmern um. ➤ **look at** *vt insep* anlsehen; **he looked at his watch** er sah OR schaute auf seine Uhr. ➤ **look down on** *vt insep* [condescend to] herablsehen auf *(+ A)*. ➤ **look for** *vt insep* suchen. ➤ **look forward to** *vt insep* sich freuen auf *(+ A)*. ➤ **look into** *vt insep* [examine] untersuchen. ➤ **look on** *vi* [watch] zulsehen. ➤ **look out** *vi* auflpassen; **look out!** Vorsicht! ➤ **look out for** *vt insep* [person, place] Ausschau halten nach; [opportunity] suchen nach. ➤ **look round** <> *vt insep* [city, museum] besichtigen; **to look round the shops** einen Einkaufsbummel machen. <> *vi* - 1. [look at surroundings] sich umlsehen - 2. [turn] sich umldrehen. ➤ **look to** *vt insep* - 1. [depend on] sich verlassen auf *(+ A)*; **they looked to her**

for help sie verließen sich darauf, dass sie ihnen helfen würde - 2. [think about] planen. **look up** <> vt sep - 1. [in dictionary] nachlschlagen; [in phone book] herauslsuchen - 2. [visit]: **to look sb up in** aufsuchen. <> vi sich bessern. **look up to** vt insep [admire]: **to look up to sb** zu jm aufsehen.

lookout ['lukaut] n - 1. [place] Ausguck der - 2. [person] Wachposten der - 3. [search]: **to be on the lookout for sthg** nach etw Ausschau halten.

loom [lu:m] vi - 1. [rise up] (plötzlich) aufltauchen - 2. fig [be imminent - date] bevorlstehen; [- threat, difficulties] sich ablzeichnen.

loony ['lu:ni] inf <> adj bekloppt, verrückt. <> n Bekloppte der, die, Verrückte der, die.

loop [lu:p] n - 1. [shape] Schleife die, Schlinge die - 2. [contraceptive] Spirale die.

loophole ['lu:phəul] n fig Schlupfloch das.

loose [lu:s] adj - 1. [not firmly fixed - joint, tooth, handle] lose, locker - 2. [unpackaged - sweets, nails, paper] lose - 3. [not tight-fitting - clothes, fit] locker sitzend, leger - 4. [animal - free, not restrained] frei laufend; [- which has escaped] entlaufen; [hair] offen - 5. [translation, definition] frei.

loose change n Kleingeld das.

loose end n: **to be at a loose end** UK, **to be at loose ends** US nichts zu tun haben.

loosely ['lu:slı] adv - 1. [hold, connect, tie] locker - 2. [translate, define] frei.

loosen ['lu:sn] vt lockern. **loosen up** vi - 1. [before game, race] sich aufwärmen - 2. inf [relax] sich entspannen.

loot [lu:t] <> n Beute die. <> vt auslplündern, auslrauben.

looting ['lu:tıŋ] n Plündern das.

lop [lɒp] vt stutzen, beschneiden. **lop off** vt sep abschneiden.

lop-sided [-'saıdıd] adj [uneven] schief.

lord [lɔ:d] n UK Lord der. **Lord** n - 1. RELIG: **the Lord** [God] der Herr; **good Lord!** UK Grundgütiger!, oh mein Gott! - 2. [in titles] Lord der. **Lords** npl UK POL: **the (House of) Lords** das Oberhaus.

lorry ['lɒrı] n UK Lastkraftwagen der.

lorry driver n UK Lastkraftwagenfahrer der.

lose [lu:z] (pt & pp lost) <> vt - 1. [gen] verlieren; **to lose sight of sb/sthg** jn/etw aus den Augen verlieren; **to lose one's way** sich verirren - 2. [waste - time] verschwenden; [- opportunity] versäumen - 3. [subj: clock, watch] nachlgehen - 4. [pursuers] abschütteln. <> vi verlieren. **lose out** vi: **to lose out (on sthg)** (bei etw) den Kürzeren ziehen.

loser ['lu:zər] n - 1. [of competition] Verlierer der, -in die - 2. pej [unsuccessful person] Loser der.

loss [lɒs] n - 1. [gen] Verlust der; **to make a loss** Verlust machen - 2. [of match, competition]

Niederlage die - 3. phr: **I'm at a loss to explain it** ich weiß nicht, wie ich es erklären soll; **he was at a loss for words** ihm fehlten die Worte.

lost [lɒst] <> pt & pp > **lose**. <> adj - 1. [unable to find way] verirrt; **to get lost** sich verirren, sich verlieren; **get lost!** inf verschwinde!, hau ab! - 2. [keys, wallet] verloren.

lost-and-found office n US Fundbüro das.

lost property office n UK Fundbüro das.

lot [lɒt] n - 1. [large amount]: **a lot of, lots of** eine Menge - 2. inf [group of things]: **put this lot in my office** bring das hier in mein Büro - 3. [destiny] Los das - 4. [at auction] Posten der - 5. [entire amount]: **the lot** alles, das Ganze - 6. US [of land] Parzelle die; [car park] Stellfläche die, Parkplatz der - 7. phr: **to draw lots** losen. **a lot** adv (sehr) viel.

lotion ['ləuʃn] n Lotion die.

lottery ['lɒtərı] n - 1. [raffle] Lotterie die - 2. [risky venture] Glücksspiel das.

loud [laud] <> adj - 1. [not quiet, noisy] laut - 2. [garish] grell. <> adv laut; **out loud** laut.

loudhailer [,laud'heılər] n UK Megafon das.

loudly ['laudlı] adv [noisily] laut.

loudspeaker [,laud'spi:kər] n Lautsprecher der.

lounge [laundʒ] <> n - 1. [in house] Wohnzimmer das - 2. [in airport, hotel] Lounge die - 3. UK = **lounge bar**. <> vi sich lümmeln.

lounge bar n UK abgetrennter, meist gemütlicherer Teil eines Pubs, in dem die Getränke teurer sind.

louse [laus] n - 1. (pl lice) [insect] Laus die - 2. (pl -s) fig [person] Laus die.

lousy ['lauzı] adj inf [poor-quality] lausig.

lout [laut] n Flegel der, Lümmel der.

lovable ['lʌvəbl] adj liebenswert.

love [lʌv] <> n - 1. [gen] Liebe die; **a love of** OR **for sthg** eine Liebe zu OR für etw; **give her my love** grüße sie herzlich von mir; **love from** [at end of letter] alles Liebe von; **to be in love** verliebt sein; **to fall in love (with sb)** sich (in jn) verlieben; **to make love** miteinander schlafen - 2. inf [term of address] Schatz der - 3. TENNIS Null. <> vt lieben; **to love to do sthg** OR **doing sthg** etw sehr OR wahnsinnig gern tun.

love affair n Affäre die.

love life n Liebesleben das.

lovely ['lʌvlı] adj - 1. [in looks - child] reizend; [- person] sehr hübsch; [in character] reizend - 2. [good, nice] wunderschön; **it was lovely to meet you** es war sehr nett, Sie kennen zu lernen.

lover ['lʌvər] n - 1. [sexual partner] Geliebte der, die - 2. [enthusiast]: **a lover of** ein Liebhaber, eine Liebhaberin (+ G).

loving ['lʌvıŋ] adj liebevoll.

low [ləu] <> adj - 1. [gen] niedrig; **to keep a low profile** sich unauffällig benehmen

- 2. [standard, quality, opinion] schlecht - **3.** [level, sound, note, neckline] tief - **4.** [light, heat] schwach - **5.** [supplies] knapp - **6.** [voice] leise - **7.** [depressed] niedergeschlagen. <> *adv* [fly, bend, sink] tief. <> *n* - **1.** [low point] Tiefstand *der* - **2.** [area of low pressure] Tief *das*.

low-calorie *adj* kalorienarm.

low-cut *adj* tief ausgeschnitten.

lower ['ləʊəʳ] *vi* - **1.** [sky] dunkel sein - **2.** [frown]: **to lower at sb** jn finster anlblicken.

low-fat *adj* fettarm.

low-key *adj* [negotiations] informell; [approach] zurückhaltend.

low-lying *adj* tief gelegen.

loyal ['lɔɪəl] *adj*: **to be loyal to sb** [friend, supporter] jm treu sein; [king, boss] gegenüber jm loyal sein.

loyalty ['lɔɪəltɪ] *n* [of friend, supporter] Treue *die*; [to government] Loyalität *die*.

lozenge ['lɒzɪndʒ] *n* [tablet] Pastille *die*.

LP (*abbr of long-playing record*) *n* LP *die*.

L-plate *n* UK Schild mit einem L, welches anzeigt, das der Fahrer des Wagens Fahrschüler ist.

Ltd, ltd (*abbr of limited*) GmbH.

lubricant ['luːbrɪkənt] *n* Schmiermittel *das*.

lubricate ['luːbrɪkeɪt] *vt* schmieren.

luck [lʌk] *n*: **(good)luck** Glück *das*; **good luck!** viel Glück!; **bad luck** Pech *das*; **bad luck!, hard luck!** so ein Pech!; **to be in luck** Glück haben; **with (any) luck** mit (ein bisschen) Glück.

luckily ['lʌkɪlɪ] *adv* glücklicherweise.

lucky ['lʌkɪ] *adj* - **1.** [fortunate] glücklich; **to be lucky** Glück haben; **it was a lucky guess** das war gut geraten - **2.** [bringing good luck] Glück bringend; [number] Glücks-.

lucrative ['luːkrətɪv] *adj* lukrativ.

ludicrous ['luːdɪkrəs] *adj* lächerlich.

lug [lʌg] *vt inf* schleppen.

luggage ['lʌgɪdʒ] *n* UK Gepäck *das*.

luggage rack *n* UK [in train] Gepäckablage *die*; [on car] Dachgepäckträger *der*.

lukewarm ['luːkwɔːm] *adj* - **1.** [tepid] lauwarm - **2.** [unenthusiastic] lau.

lull [lʌl] <> *n* Pause *die*; **a lull in the fighting** eine Kampfpause. <> *vt* - **1.** [make sleepy]: **to lull sb to sleep** jn in den Schlaf lullen - **2.** [reassure]: **to lull sb into a false sense of security** jn in Sicherheit wiegen.

lullaby ['lʌləbaɪ] *n* Schlaflied *das*.

lumber ['lʌmbəʳ] *n* (U) - **1.** US [timber] Bauholz *das* - **2.** UK [bric-a-brac] Gerümpel *das*. ◆ **lumber with** *vt sep* UK *inf*: **to lumber sb with sthg** jm etw aufhalsen.

lumberjack ['lʌmbədʒæk] *n* Holzfäller *der*.

luminous ['luːmɪnəs] *adj* [armband] leuchtend; [dial, paint] Leucht-.

lump [lʌmp] <> *n* - **1.** [piece - of earth, in sauce] Klumpen *der*; [- of coal, cheese] Stück *das*

- 2. [MED - bump] Beule *die*; [- tumour] Knoten *der* - **3.** [of sugar] Stück *das*. <> *vt*: **to lump together** [not differentiate between] in einen Topf werfen; **you'll just have to lump it** *inf* du musst dich damit abfinden.

lump sum *n* Pauschalbetrag *der*.

lunacy ['luːnəsɪ] *n* Wahnsinn *der*.

lunar ['luːnəʳ] *adj* Mond-.

lunatic ['luːnətɪk] *pej* <> *adj* wahnwitzig. <> *n* Wahnsinnige *der, die*, Irre *der, die*.

lunch [lʌntʃ] <> *n* Mittagessen *das*; **to have lunch** zu Mittag essen. <> *vi* zu Mittag essen.

luncheon meat *n* Frühstücksfleisch *das*.

luncheon voucher *n* UK Essensbon *der*.

lunch hour *n* Mittagspause *die*.

lunchtime ['lʌntʃtaɪm] *n* Mittagszeit *die*.

lung [lʌŋ] *n* Lunge *die*.

lunge [lʌndʒ] *vi*: **to lunge forward** nach vorn springen; **to lunge at sb** sich auf jn stürzen.

lurch [lɜːtʃ] <> *n*: **to leave sb in the lurch** jn im Stich lassen. <> *vi* [person] taumeln; [drunkard] torkeln; [ship] schlingern; [car] sich ruckartig bewegen.

lure [ljʊəʳ] <> *n* [attraction] Reiz *der*. <> *vt* [tempt] locken.

lurid ['ljʊərɪd] *adj* - **1.** [brightly coloured] grell; [clothes] in grellen Farben - **2.** [sensational] reißerisch.

lurk [lɜːk] *vi* [person, danger] lauern.

luscious ['lʌʃəs] *adj* [fruit] saftig.

lush [lʌʃ] *adj* - **1.** [grass] saftig; [vegetation] üppig - **2.** *inf* [decorations] üppig.

lust [lʌst] *n* - **1.** (U) [sexual desire] (sexuelle) Begierde - **2.** [greed]: **lust for sthg** Gier *die* nach etw. ◆ **lust after, lust for** *vt insep* - **1.** [money, power] gieren nach - **2.** [person] begehren.

Luxembourg ['lʌksəmbɜːg] *n* Luxemburg *nt*.

luxurious [lʌg'ʒʊərɪəs] *adj* - **1.** [expensive] luxuriös - **2.** [voluptuous] üppig.

luxury ['lʌkʃərɪ] <> *n* Luxus *der*; [expensive item] Luxusartikel *der*. <> *comp* Luxus-.

LW (*abbr of long wave*) LW.

Lycra® ['laɪkrə] <> *n* (U) Lycra® *das*. <> *comp* aus Lycra®.

lying ['laɪɪŋ] <> *adj* lügnerisch, verlogen. <> *n* [dishonesty] Lügen *das*.

lynch [lɪntʃ] *vt* lynchen.

lyric ['lɪrɪk] *adj*: **lyric poetry** Lyrik *die*. ◆ **lyrics** *npl* [of song] Text *der*.

lyrical ['lɪrɪkl] *adj* - **1.** [poetic] lyrisch - **2.** [enthusiastic]: **to wax lyrical about sthg** von etw schwärmen.

M

m¹ *(pl* **m's** OR **ms)**, **M** *(pl* **M's** OR **Ms)** [em] *n* [letter] m *das*, M *das*. **M** UK *abbr of* **motorway**.

m² *abbr of* **metre**, **million**, **mile**.

MA *n abbr of* **Master of Arts**.

mac [mæk] *n* UK inf abbr of **mackintosh**.

macaroni [ˌmækəˈrəʊnɪ] *n (U)* Makkaroni *Pl*.

machine [məˈʃiːn] *n* - **1**. [device] Maschine *die* - **2**. [organization] Apparat *der*.

machine gun [məˈʃiːngʌn] *n* Maschinengewehr *das*.

machinery [məˈʃiːnərɪ] *n (U)* - **1**. [machines] Maschinen *Pl* - **2**. fig [system] Maschinerie *die*.

macho [ˈmætʃəʊ] *adj* inf machohaft.

mackerel [ˈmækrəl] *(pl inv* OR **-s)** *n* Makrele *die*.

mackintosh [ˈmækɪntɒʃ] *n* UK Regenmantel *der*.

mad [mæd] *adj* - **1**. [insane, foolish] verrückt; **to go mad** verrückt werden - **2**. [furious] wütend; **to go mad at sb** auf jn sehr wütend werden - **3**. [very enthusiastic]: **to be mad about sb/sthg** ganz verrückt nach jm/auf etw *(A)* sein.

madam [ˈmædəm] *n* fml [form of address] gnädige Frau.

mad cow disease *n* Rinderwahnsinn *der*.

madden [ˈmædn] *vt* wahnsinnig machen.

made [meɪd] *pt* & *pp* ⊳ **make**.

made-to-measure *adj* maßgeschneidert.

made-up *adj* - **1**. [face, eyes] geschminkt - **2**. [story, excuse] erfunden.

madly [ˈmædlɪ] *adv* [frantically] wie verrückt; **to be madly in love (with sb)** bis über beide Ohren (in jn) verliebt sein.

madman [ˈmædmən] *(pl* **-men** [-mən]) *n* Verrückte *der*, Irre *der*.

madness [ˈmædnɪs] *n* Wahnsinn *der*.

Mafia [ˈmæfɪə] *n*: **the Mafia** die Mafia.

magazine [ˌmægəˈziːn] *n* - **1**. [periodical] Zeitschrift *die*, Magazin *das* - **2**. [news programme, of gun] Magazin *das*.

maggot [ˈmægət] *n* Made *die*.

magic [ˈmædʒɪk] ⟨⟩ *adj* - **1**. [potion, spell, trick] Zauber- - **2**. inf [moment, feeling] wundervoll. ⟨⟩ *n* - **1**. [sorcery] Magie *die* - **2**. [conjuring] Zauberei *die* - **3**. [special quality] Zauber *der*.

magical [ˈmædʒɪkl] *adj* magisch.

magician [məˈdʒɪʃn] *n* Zauberer *der*.

magistrate [ˈmædʒɪstreɪt] *n* Friedensrichter *der*, -in *die*.

magnanimous [mægˈnænɪməs] *adj* großmütig.

magnate [ˈmægneɪt] *n* Magnat *der*.

magnesium [mægˈniːzɪəm] *n* Magnesium *das*.

magnet [ˈmægnɪt] *n* liter & fig Magnet *der*.

magnetic [mægˈnetɪk] *adj* - **1**. [force, object] magnetisch - **2**. fig: **to have a magnetic personality** ein sehr anziehendes Wesen haben.

magnificent [mægˈnɪfɪsənt] *adj* [building, gown] prächtig; [idea, book] großartig.

magnify [ˈmægnɪfaɪ] *vt* [TECH - image] vergrößern; [- sound] verstärken.

magnifying glass [ˈmægnɪfaɪɪŋ-] *n* Lupe *die*.

magnitude [ˈmægnɪtjuːd] *n (U)* - **1**. [size] Größe *die* - **2**. [importance] Bedeutung *die*.

magpie [ˈmægpaɪ] *n* Elster *die*.

mahogany [məˈhɒgənɪ] *n* [wood] Mahagoni *das*.

maid [meɪd] *n* [servant] Dienstmädchen *das*; [in hotel] Zimmermädchen *das*.

maiden [ˈmeɪdn] ⟨⟩ *adj* [voyage, flight] Jungfern-. ⟨⟩ *n* liter [young girl] Maid *die*.

maiden name *n* Mädchenname *der*.

mail [meɪl] ⟨⟩ *n (U)* Post *die*; **by mail** mit der Post. ⟨⟩ *vt* esp US (mit der Post) (ver)schicken OR senden.

mailbox [ˈmeɪlbɒks] *n* US - **1**. [for letters] Briefkasten *der* - **2**. COMPUT Mailbox *die*.

mailing list [ˈmeɪlɪŋ-] *n* Mailingliste *die*.

mailman [ˈmeɪlmən] *(pl* **-men** [-mən]) *n* US Postbote *der*, Briefträger *der*.

mail order *n* Versandhandel *der*.

mailshot [ˈmeɪlʃɒt] *n* - **1**. [material] Postwurfsendung *die* - **2**. [activity]: **to do a mailshot** Postwurfsendungen verschicken.

maim [meɪm] *vt* verstümmeln.

main [meɪn] ⟨⟩ *adj* Haupt-. ⟨⟩ *n* Hauptleitung *die*; **a gas main** eine Hauptgasleitung. **mains** *npl*: **to turn the water/gas off at the mains** den Haupthahn für das Wasser/Gas abdrehen. **in the main** *adv* im Allgemeinen.

main course *n* Hauptgericht *das*.

mainframe (computer) [ˈmeɪnfreɪm-] *n* Großrechner *der*.

mainland [ˈmeɪnlənd] ⟨⟩ *adj*: **mainland Britain** das britische Festland. ⟨⟩ *n*: **the mainland** das Festland.

mainly [ˈmeɪnlɪ] *adv* hauptsächlich.

main road *n* Hauptstraße *die*.

mainstay [ˈmeɪnsteɪ] *n* [person] wichtigste Stütze; **tourism is the mainstay of the economy** der Tourismus ist der Hauptpfeiler der Wirtschaft.

mainstream [ˈmeɪnstriːm] *adj* vorherrschend; [music] Mainstream-.

maintain [meɪn'teɪn] *vt* - **1.** [friendship, order, image] aufrechterhalten - **2.** [speed, temperature] beibehalten - **3.** [family, children] unterhalten - **4.** [vehicle, building] instand halten - **5.** [assert - one's innocence] beteuern; **to maintain (that)** behaupten, dass.

maintenance ['meɪntənəns] *n (U)* - **1.** [of vehicle, building] Instandhaltung *die* - **2.** [paid to ex-wife] Unterhalt *der* - **3.** [of law and order] Aufrechterhaltung *die*.

maize [meɪz] *n* Mais *der*.

majestic [mə'dʒestɪk] *adj* majestätisch.

majesty ['mædʒəstɪ] *n* Erhabenheit *die*.
➤ **Majesty** *n*: His/Her/Your Majesty Seine/Ihre/Eure Majestät.

major ['meɪdʒər] ◇ *adj* - **1.** [important] bedeutend; [problem]: **a major operation** eine größere Operation - **2.** [main] Haupt- - **3.** MUS [key, scale] Dur-; **C major** C-Dur. ◇ *n* Major *der*.

majority [mə'dʒɒrətɪ] *n* Mehrheit *die*; **in a** OR **the majority** in der Mehrzahl.

make [meɪk] *(pt & pp made)* ◇ *vt* - **1.** [produce] machen; [manufacture] herstellen; **it's made of wood** es ist aus Holz - **2.** [prepare] machen; **to make lunch** das Mittagessen machen - **3.** [perform, do] machen; **to make a decision** eine Entscheidung treffen; **to make an effort** sich anstrengen; **to make a phone call** telefonieren; **to make a speech** eine Rede halten - **4.** [cause to be] machen; **to make sb happy/sad** jn glücklich/traurig machen; **to make sthg into sthg** etw zu etw machen - **5.** [cause to do]: **to make sb/sthg do sthg** jn/etw dazu|bringen OR veranlassen, etw zu tun - **6.** [force] zwingen; **to make sb do sthg** jn zwingen, etw zu tun - **7.** [add up to] machen; **that makes £5** das macht 5 Pfund - **8.** [calculate]: **I make it 50** ich komme auf 50; **what time do you make it?** wie spät hast du? - **9.** [earn] verdienen; **to make a profit/loss** einen Gewinn/Verlust machen - **10.** [reach, be able to attend]: **we didn't make the train** wir haben den Zug nicht geschafft - **11.** [gain - friend, enemy] machen; **to make friends with sb** mit jm Freundschaft schließen - **12.** *phr*: **to make it** es schaffen; **I won't be able to make it tonight** ich schaffe es heute Abend nicht; **to make do with sthg** mit etw aus|kommen. ◇ *n* [brand] Marke *die*. ➤ **make for** *vt insep* - **1.** [move towards] zu|halten auf (+ A) - **2.** [contribute to, enable] fördern. ➤ **make of** *vt sep* halten von. ➤ **make off** *vi* sich davon|machen. ➤ **make out** ◇ *vt sep* - **1.** *inf* [see] aus|machen; [hear, understand] verstehen - **2.** [cheque, receipt] aus|stellen; [application form] aus|füllen; [list] auf|stellen. ◇ *vt insep* [pretend, claim]: **to make out (that)...** vor|geben, dass... ➤ **make up** ◇ *vt sep* - **1.** [compose, constitute] bilden; **to be made up of sthg** aus etw bestehen - **2.** [invent] erfinden, sich *(D)* aus|denken; **she made it up** sie hat es

erfunden - **3.** [face] schminken. ◇ *vi* [become friends again]: **to make up with sb** sich mit jm versöhnen.

make-up *n (U)* - **1.** [cosmetics] Make-up *das* - **2.** [composition] Beschaffenheit *die*; [of team] Zusammensetzung *die*.

making ['meɪkɪŋ] *n* [of product] Herstellung *die*; [of cake] Backen *das*.

malaria [mə'leərɪə] *n* Malaria *die*.

Malaysia [mə'leɪzɪə] *n* Malaysia *nt*.

male [meɪl] ◇ *adj* - **1.** [staff, members] männlich; **male cat** Kater *der* - **2.** [concerning men - problems] Männer-; [- hormone] männlich. ◇ *n* - **1.** [animal] Männchen *das* - **2.** [human] Mann *der*.

malevolent [mə'levələnt] *adj* boshaft; [intention, action] böswillig.

malfunction [mæl'fʌŋkʃn] ◇ *n* Fehlfunktion *die*. ◇ *vi* nicht richtig funktionieren.

malice ['mælɪs] *n* Boshaftigkeit *die*.

malicious [mə'lɪʃəs] *adj* boshaft; [act, intention] böswillig.

malign [mə'laɪn] ◇ *adj* [influence] schädlich; [behaviour] Unheil bringend. ◇ *vt* verleumden.

malignant [mə'lɪgnənt] *adj* MED bösartig.

mall [mɔːl] *n esp* US: **(shopping) mall** Einkaufszentrum *das*.

mallet ['mælɪt] *n* [tool] Holzhammer *der*.

malnutrition [,mælnjuː'trɪʃn] *n* Unterernährung *die*.

malpractice [,mæl'præktɪs] *n* LAW Amtsmissbrauch *der*.

malt [mɔːlt] *n* [grain] Malz *das*.

mammal ['mæml] *n* Säugetier *das*.

mammoth ['mæməθ] ◇ *adj* ungeheuer groß. ◇ *n* Mammut *das*.

man [mæn] *(pl* men [men]*)* ◇ *n* - **1.** [gen] Mann *der* - **2.** [type]: **he's not a betting man** er macht sich nicht viel aus Wetten - **3.** *(U)* [human beings] Mensch *der*. ◇ *vt* [ship, spaceship] bemannen.

manage ['mænɪdʒ] ◇ *vi* zurecht|kommen; **thanks, I can manage!** danke, ich komme schon zurecht! ◇ *vt* - **1.** [succeed]: **to manage to do sthg** es schaffen, etw zu tun - **2.** [control - company, organization] leiten; [- popstar, boxer, football team] managen - **3.** [be available for]: **I could manage a few hours on Friday** Freitag hätte ich ein paar Stunden Zeit; **I can't manage four o'clock** vier Uhr schaffe ich nicht.

management ['mænɪdʒmənt] *n* - **1.** *(U)* [control - of company, organization] Leitung *die* - **2.** [people in control - of business] Geschäftsführung *die*; [- of operation] Leitung *die*.

manager ['mænɪdʒər] *n* [of company, shop] Geschäftsführer *der*, -in *die*; [of organization] Leiter *der*, -in *die*; [of popstar, boxer, football team] Manager *der*, -in *die*.

managerial [,mænɪ'dʒɪərɪəl] *adj* [post] leitend.

mandate ['mændeɪt] *n* - **1.** [elected right or authority] Mandat *das* - **2.** [task] Auftrag *der*.

mane [meɪn] *n* Mähne *die*.

mangle ['mæŋgl] *vt* [body, car] (übel) zulrichten.

mango ['mæŋgəʊ] (*pl* -es OR -s) *n* Mango *die*.

manhandle ['mæn,hændl] *vt* [person] grob behandeln.

manhole ['mænhəʊl] *n* Kanalschacht *der*.

mania ['meɪnɪə] *n* [excessive liking]: **mania (for)** Leidenschaft *die* (für).

maniac ['meɪnɪæk] *n* - **1.** [madman] Wahnsinnige *der, die* - **2.** [fanatic]: **a TV/sex maniac** ein Fernseh-/Sexbesessener, eine Fernseh-/Sexbesessene.

manic ['mænɪk] *adj* [overexcited - person] aufgedreht.

manicure ['mænɪ,kjʊər] *n* Maniküre *die*.

manifest ['mænɪfest] *fml vt* bekunden, zum Ausdruck bringen; **to manifest itself** sich zeigen.

manifesto [,mænɪ'festəʊ] (*pl* -s OR -es) *n* Manifest *das*.

manipulate [mə'nɪpjʊleɪt] *vt* - **1.** [people] manipulieren - **2.** [machine, controls] bedienen.

manipulative [mə'nɪpjʊlətɪv] *adj* manipulativ.

mankind [mæn'kaɪnd] *n* Menschheit *die*.

manly ['mænlɪ] *adj* [voice, bearing] männlich; [behaviour] mannhaft.

man-made *adj* [fibre] Kunst-; [environment] von Menschen geschaffen.

manner ['mænər] *n* - **1.** [method] Art *die*, Weise *die*; **in this manner** auf diese Art und Weise - **2.** [attitude] Auftreten *das*; **I don't like your manner!** mir gefällt nicht, wie Sie mit mir reden! ➠ **manners** *npl* Manieren *Pl*.

manoeuvre UK, **maneuver** US [mə'nuːvər] ⬦ *n* [movement] Manöver *das*. ⬦ *vt* [car, ship] manövrieren.

manor ['mænər] *n* Herrenhaus *das*.

manpower ['mæn,paʊər] *n* (U) Arbeitskräfte *Pl*.

mansion ['mænʃn] *n* Villa *die*.

manslaughter ['mæn,slɔːtər] *n* (U) Totschlag *der*.

manual ['mænjʊəl] ⬦ *adj* [work, system] manuell. ⬦ *n* [handbook] Handbuch *das*.

manufacture [,mænjʊ'fæktʃər] *vt* [make] herlstellen.

manufacturer [,mænjʊ'fæktʃərər] *n* Hersteller *der*.

manure [mə'njʊər] *n* Dung *der*.

manuscript ['mænjʊskrɪpt] *n* [untyped copy] Manuskript *das*.

many ['menɪ] (*comp* **more**, *superl* **most**) ⬦ *adj* viele; **many people** viele Leute. ⬦ *pron* viele; **how many?** wie viele?

map [mæp] *n* (Land)karte *die*; [of town] Stadtplan *der*.

maple ['meɪpl] *n* Ahorn *der*.

marathon ['mærəθn] *n* Marathon(lauf) *der*.

marble ['mɑːbl] *n* [stone] Marmor *der*.

march [mɑːtʃ] ⬦ *n* MIL Marsch *der*. ⬦ *vi* - **1.** [soldiers, protesters] marschieren - **2.** [walk briskly]: **to march up to sb** schnurstracks auf jn zulmarschieren.

March [mɑːtʃ] *n* März *der*; *see also* **September**.

marcher ['mɑːtʃər] *n* [protester] Demonstrant *der*, -in *die*.

mare [meər] *n* Stute *die*.

margarine [,mɑːdʒə'riːn, ,mɑːgə'riːn] *n* Margarine *die*.

margin ['mɑːdʒɪn] *n* - **1.** [in contest] Spielraum *der* - **2.** COMM: **profit margin** Gewinnspanne *die* - **3.** [edge - of page, wood] Rand *der*.

marginal ['mɑːdʒɪnl] *adj* [unimportant] von geringer Bedeutung; [effect, adjustment] geringfügig.

marigold ['mærɪgəʊld] *n* Ringelblume *die*.

marihuana, marijuana [,mærɪ'wɑːnə] *n* Marihuana *das*.

marine [mə'riːn] ⬦ *adj* [plant] im Meer lebend. ⬦ *n* Marineinfanterist *der*.

marital ['mærɪtl] *adj* [happiness, crisis] Ehe-; [sex, rights] ehelich.

marital status *n* Familienstand *der*.

maritime ['mærɪtaɪm] *adj* See-.

mark [mɑːk] ⬦ *n* - **1.** [stain] Fleck *der*; [on person's skin] Mal *das* - **2.** [sign] Zeichen *das* - **3.** SCH & UNIV Note *die* - **4.** [stage, level]: **we've reached the halfway mark** wir haben die Hälfte hinter uns - **5.** [currency] Mark *die*. ⬦ *vt* - **1.** [stain] fleckig machen; [scratch] zerkratzen - **2.** [label] kennzeichnen - **3.** SCH & UNIV korrigieren - **4.** [identify] markieren - **5.** [commemorate] begehen.

marked [mɑːkt] *adj* [noticeable] merklich.

market ['mɑːkɪt] ⬦ *n* Markt *der*. ⬦ *vt* verlmarkten.

marketing ['mɑːkɪtɪŋ] *n* COMM Marketing *das*.

marketplace ['mɑːkɪtpleɪs] *n* [in a town] Marktplatz *der*.

marmalade ['mɑːməleɪd] *n* (U): **(orange) marmalade** Orangenmarmelade *die*.

marriage ['mærɪdʒ] *n* - **1.** [wedding] Hochzeit *die*, Heirat *die*; [ceremony] Trauung *die* - **2.** [state] Ehe *die*.

marrow ['mærəʊ] *n* - **1.** UK [vegetable] Speisekürbis *der* - **2.** (U) [in bones] (Knochen)mark *das*.

marry ['mærɪ] ⬦ *vt* - **1.** [become spouse of] heiraten; **to get married** heiraten - **2.** [subj: priest, minister, registrar] trauen. ⬦ *vi* heiraten.

Mars [mɑːz] *n* [planet] Mars *der*.

marsh [mɑːʃ] n Sumpf der.

marshal ['mɑːʃl] (UK) (US) <> n MIL Marschall der. <> vt [support] sichern.

martial arts [,mɑːʃl-] npl Kampfsportarten Pl.

martial law [,mɑːʃl-] n Kriegsrecht das.

martyr ['mɑːtər] n Märtyrer der, -in die.

marvel ['mɑːvl] (UK) (US) <> n Wunder das; you're a marvel! du bist ja unglaublich! <> vi: to marvel (at sthg) staunen (über etw (A)).

marvellous UK, **marvelous** US ['mɑːvələs] adj wunderbar.

Marxism ['mɑːksɪzm] n Marxismus der.

Marxist ['mɑːksɪst] <> adj marxistisch. <> n Marxist der, -in die.

masculine ['mæskjʊlɪn] adj - 1. [typically male] männlich - 2. GRAM [woman] maskulin.

mash [mæʃ] vt (zu Brei) zerdrücken.

mashed potatoes [mæʃt-] npl Kartoffelbrei der.

mask [mɑːsk] <> n Maske die. <> vt - 1. [truth, feelings] verbergen - 2. [smell, flavour] überdecken.

masochist ['mæsəkɪst] n Masochist der, -in die.

mason ['meɪsn] n - 1. [stonemason] Steinmetz der - 2. [Freemason] Freimaurer der.

mass [mæs] <> n - 1. [gen & PHYS] Masse die - 2. [large quantity] Unmenge die; a mass of people eine große Menschenmenge. <> adj [unemployment, protest etc] Massen-. ◆ **Mass** n RELIG Messe die.

massacre ['mæsəkər] n Massaker das.

massage [UK 'mæsɑːʒ, US məˈsɑːʒ] <> n Massage die. <> vt massieren.

massive ['mæsɪv] adj riesig; [dose] sehr groß.

mass media n & npl: the mass media die Massenmedien.

mast [mɑːst] n - 1. [on boat] Mast der - 2. RADIO & TV Sendemast der.

master ['mɑːstər] <> n - 1. [gen] Herr der - 2. UK [teacher] Lehrer der. <> vt [job, skill, language] beherrschen.

Master of Arts (pl Masters of Arts) n - 1. [degree] ≃ Magister Artium der - 2. [person] Inhaber des "Master of Arts".

Master of Science (pl Masters of Science) n - 1. [degree] ≃ Magister rerum naturalium der - 2. [person] Inhaber des "Master of Science".

masterpiece ['mɑːstəpiːs] n liter & fig Meisterwerk das.

master's degree n Magister(titel) der.

mat [mæt] n [on table] Untersetzer der; [on floor] (Fuß)matte die; [in sport] Matte die.

match [mætʃ] <> n - 1. [game] Spiel das; [in boxing, wrestling] Kampf der - 2. [for lighting] Streichholz das - 3. [equal]: to be no match for sb jm nicht gewachsen sein; to meet one's match seinen Meister finden. <> vt - 1. [views,

feelings, ideas] übereinstimmen mit - 2. [in colour, design] passen zu (+ D) - 3. [be as good as] gleichkommen (+ D). <> vi - 1. [views, ideas] übereinstimmen - 2. [in colour, design] zusammenpassen.

matchbox ['mætʃbɒks] n Streichholzschachtel die.

matching ['mætʃɪŋ] adj (dazu) passend.

mate [meɪt] <> n - 1. inf [friend] Kumpel der - 2. UK inf [term of address] Kumpel der - 3. [of animal - male] Männchen das; [- female] Weibchen das - 4. NAUT: (first) mate Maat der. <> vi [animals]: to mate (with) sich paaren (mit).

material [məˈtɪərɪəl] <> adj - 1. [physical] materiell - 2. [important] wesentlich. <> n - 1. [substance] Material das - 2. [fabric] Stoff der - 3. (U) [ideas, information] Stoff der, Material das. ◆ **materials** npl: building materials Baumaterialien Pl; writing materials Schreibzeug das; cleaning materials Putzzeug das.

materialistic [mə,tɪərɪəˈlɪstɪk] adj materialistisch.

materialize, -ise [məˈtɪərɪəlaɪz] vi - 1. [happen - crisis] eintreten; [- threat] in die Tat umgesetzt werden - 2. [appear] auftauchen.

maternal [məˈtɜːnl] adj - 1. [instinct] Mutter-; [person] mütterlich - 2. [on mother's side]: maternal grandparents Großeltern mütterlicherseits.

maternity [məˈtɜːnətɪ] n Mutterschaft die.

maternity dress n Umstandskleid das.

maternity leave n (U) Mutterschaftsurlaub der.

maternity ward n Entbindungsstation die.

math n US = **maths**.

mathematical [,mæθəˈmætɪkl] adj mathematisch.

mathematics [,mæθəˈmætɪks] n (U) Mathematik die.

maths UK [mæθs], **math** US [mæθ] (abbr of mathematics) inf n (U) Mathe die.

matinée ['mætɪneɪ] n Nachmittagsvorstellung die.

matriculation [mə,trɪkjʊˈleɪʃn] n UNIV Immatrikulation die.

matrimonial [,mætrɪˈməʊnɪəl] adj [problems, dispute] Ehe-; [harmony] ehelich.

matrimony ['mætrɪmənɪ] n Ehestand der.

matron ['meɪtrən] n UK [in hospital] Oberschwester die.

matt UK, **matte** US [mæt] adj matt.

matted ['mætɪd] adj verfilzt.

matter ['mætər] <> n - 1. [question, situation] Angelegenheit die; that's quite another OR a different matter das ist etwas ganz anderes; that's a matter of opinion das ist Ansichtssache; to make matters worse die Sache noch schlimmer machen; and to make matters worse zu allem Unglück, und obendrein; as a

matter of course selbstverständlich - **2.** [trouble]: **there's something the matter with my radio** etwas stimmt nicht mit dem Radio; **what's the matter?** was ist (denn) los?; **what's the matter with it/her?** was ist (los) damit/mit ihr? - **3.** [substance] Materie *die* - **4.** *(U)* [material] Stoff *der*; **reading matter** Lesestoff *der*. ⟨⟩ *vi* von Bedeutung sein; **it doesn't matter** das macht nichts; **it doesn't matter what I do** ganz gleich was ich tue. ➤ **as a matter of fact** *adv* sogar. ➤ **for that matter** *adv* eigentlich. ➤ **no matter** *adv*: **no matter how** ganz gleich wie; **no matter what** ganz egal was.

matter-of-fact *adj* sachlich, nüchtern.

mattress ['mætrɪs] *n* Matratze *die*.

mature [mə'tjʊər] ⟨⟩ *adj* - **1.** [person] reif - **2.** [cheese] reif; [wine] ausgereift. ⟨⟩ *vi* - **1.** [child] erwachsen werden; [animal] zur vollen Größe heran|wachsen; [plant] die volle Größe erreichen - **2.** *fig* [grow up] reifer werden - **3.** [cheese] reifen; [wine] aus|reifen - **4.** [insurance policy] fällig werden.

mature student *n* UK UNIV Person, *die* erst einige Jahre nach dem Schulabschluss ein Studium aufnimmt.

maul [mɔ:l] *vt* übel zurichten.

mauve [məʊv] *adj* mauve.

max. [mæks] *abbr of* **maximum**.

maxim ['mæksɪm] *(pl* -s) *n* Maxime *die*.

maxima ['mæksɪmə] *pl* ⊳ **maximum**.

maximum ['mæksɪməm] *(pl* **maxima** OR -s) ⟨⟩ *adj* maximal; [speed, weight, temperature] Höchst-. ⟨⟩ *n* Maximum *das*.

may [meɪ] *aux vb* - **1.** [expressing possibility] können; **it may be done as follows** man kann wie folgt vorgehen; **it may rain** es könnte regnen; **they may have got lost** sie haben sich vielleicht verirrt; **be that as it may** wie dem auch sei; **come what may** komme, was wolle - **2.** [expressing permission] können; **may I smoke?** darf ich rauchen?; **you may sit, if you wish** Sie dürfen sich setzen, wenn Sie wollen - **3.** [when conceding a point]: **it may be a long walk, but it's worth it** es ist vielleicht ein langer Weg, aber es lohnt sich - **4.** *fml* [expressing wish, hope]: **may you be very happy!** ich wünsche dir, dass du glücklich wirst!

May [meɪ] *n* Mai *der; see also* **September**.

maybe ['meɪbi:] *adv* vielleicht.

May Day *n* der 1. Mai.

mayhem ['meɪhem] *n* Chaos *das*.

mayonnaise [,meɪə'neɪz] *n* Majonäse *die*.

mayor [meər] *n* Bürgermeister *der*.

mayoress ['meərɪs] *n* [female mayor] Bürgermeisterin *die*; [mayor's wife] Frau *die* des Bürgermeisters.

maze [meɪz] *n* - **1.** [system of paths] Irrgarten *der* - **2.** *fig* [of ideas] Wirrwarr *der*; [of streets] Labyrinth *das*.

MB *(abbr of* **megabyte)** Mb *das*.

MD *n* (*abbr of* **Doctor of Medicine**) Dr. med.

me [mi:] *pers pron* (*accusative*) mich; (*dative*) mir; **she knows me** sie kennt mich; **it's me** ich bins; **send it to me** schick es mir; **tell me** sagen Sie mal, sag mal; **he's worse than me** er ist schlechter als ich.

meadow ['medəʊ] *n* Wiese *die*.

meagre *UK*, **meager** *US* ['mi:gər] *adj* dürftig.

meal [mi:l] *n* - **1.** [occasion] Mahlzeit *die*; **to go out for a meal** essen gehen - **2.** [food] Essen *das*, Gericht *das*.

mealtime ['mi:ltaɪm] *n* Essenszeit *die*.

mean [mi:n] (*pt & pp* **meant**) ⟨⟩ *vt* - **1.** [signify] bedeuten; **the name means nothing to me** der Name sagt mir nichts - **2.** [intend] beabsichtigen; **to mean to do sthg** vorhaben, etw zu tun; **the bus was meant to leave at eight** der Bus hätte eigentlich um acht Uhr abfahren sollen; **it's meant to be good** das soll gut sein; **he means well** er meint es gut - **3.** [with remark] meinen; **what do you mean by that?** was meinst du damit? - **4.** [be serious about] ernst meinen; **I didn't mean it!** ich habe es nicht so gemeint!; **I mean it!** es ist mein Ernst!, ich meine es ernst! - **5.** *phr*: **Paul, I mean Peter** [when correcting o.s.] Paul, ich meine (natürlich) Peter. ⟨⟩ *adj* - **1.** [miserly] geizig - **2.** [unkind] gemein; **to be mean to sb** gemein zu jm sein - **3.** [average] durchschnittlich. ⟨⟩ *n* [average] Durchschnitt *der*.

meander [mɪ'ændər] *vi* - **1.** [river, road] sich schlängeln - **2.** [person] schlendern.

meaning ['mi:nɪŋ] *n* Bedeutung *die*; [of film, work of art, life] Sinn *der*; **what's the meaning of this?** was soll denn das?

meaningful ['mi:nɪŋfʊl] *adj* - **1.** [look, comment] vielsagend - **2.** [discussion, relationship] ernsthaft.

meaningless ['mi:nɪŋlɪs] *adj* - **1.** [word, lyrics] ohne Sinn - **2.** [futile] sinnlos.

means [mi:nz] (*pl inv*) ⟨⟩ *n* [method] Mittel *das*; **means of transport** Verkehrsmittel *das*; **by means of** mittels (+ *G*), durch. ⟨⟩ *npl* [money] Mittel *Pl*; **it is beyond my means** das kann ich mir nicht leisten; **can I have one? by all means!** darf ich eins haben? (aber) selbstverständlich! ➤ **by no means** *adv* keineswegs.

meant [ment] *pt & pp* ⊳ **mean**.

meantime ['mi:n,taɪm] *n*: **in the meantime** in der Zwischenzeit.

meanwhile ['mi:n,waɪl] *adv* inzwischen.

measles ['mi:zlz] *n*: **(the) measles** Masern *Pl*.

measly ['mi:zlɪ] *adj inf* mick(e)rig.

measure ['meʒər] ⟨⟩ *n* - **1.** [step, action] Maßnahme *die* - **2.** [of alcohol] ausgeschenkte Menge - **3.** [indication]: **to be a measure of sthg**

ein Zeichen für etw sein. ⬦ *vt* messen; [room] auslmessen; [damage, harm] ablschätzen.

measurement ['meʒəmənt] *n* - **1.** [figure] Maß *das* - **2.** (U) [act of measuring] Messung *die*. ⬥ **measurements** *npl* [of sb's body] Maße *Pl*; **to take sb's measurements** bei jm Maß nehmen.

meat [mi:t] *n* Fleisch *das*.

meatball ['mi:tbɔ:l] *n* Fleischklößchen *das*.

meat pie *n* UK Fleischpastete *die*.

meaty ['mi:tɪ] *adj fig* [full of ideas] aussagehaltig.

Mecca ['mekə] *n* GEOG Mekka *nt*.

mechanic [mɪ'kænɪk] *n* Mechaniker *der*, -in *die*. ⬥ **mechanics** ⬦ *n* (U) [study] Mechanik *die*. ⬦ *npl* [way sthg works] Funktionsweise *die*.

mechanical [mɪ'kænɪkl] *adj* [device, action, smile] mechanisch.

mechanism ['mekənɪzm] *n* - **1.** [of machine, behaviour] Mechanismus *der* - **2.** [procedure] Verfahren *das*.

medal ['medl] *n* Medaille *die*.

medallion [mɪ'dæljən] *n* Medaillon *das*.

meddle ['medl] *vi*: **to meddle (in/with sthg)** sich (in etw (A)) einlmischen; **to meddle with sb** sich mit jm einllassen.

media ['mi:dɪə] ⬦ *Pl* ⊳ **medium**. ⬦ *n & npl*: **the media** die Medien *Pl*.

mediaeval [,medɪ'i:vl] *adj* = **medieval**.

median ['mi:dɪən] *n* US [of road] Mittelstreifen *der*.

mediate ['mi:dɪeɪt] *vi*: **to mediate (for/between)** vermitteln (für/zwischen (+ D)).

mediator ['mi:dɪeɪtə*r*] *n* Vermittler *der*, -in *die*.

Medicaid ['medɪkeɪd] *n* US *staatliche Gesundheitsfürsorge für einkommensschwache US-Bürger*.

medical ['medɪkl] ⬦ *adj* medizinisch. ⬦ *n* ärztliche Untersuchung.

Medicare ['medɪkeə*r*] *n* US *staatliche Gesundheitsfürsorge für ältere US-Bürger*.

medicated ['medɪkeɪtɪd] *adj* medizinisch.

medicine ['medsɪn] *n* - **1.** [treatment of illness] Medizin *die* - **2.** [substance] Medikament *das*.

medieval [,medɪ'i:vl] *adj* mittelalterlich.

mediocre [,mi:dɪ'əʊkə*r*] *adj* mittelmäßig.

meditate ['medɪteɪt] *vi* - **1.** [reflect, ponder]: **to meditate (on OR upon)** nachdenken (über (+ A)) - **2.** [practise meditation] meditieren.

Mediterranean [,medɪtə'reɪnɪən] ⬦ *n* - **1.** [sea]: **the Mediterranean (Sea)** das Mittelmeer - **2.** [area around sea]: **the Mediterranean** der Mittelmeerraum. ⬦ *adj* Mittelmeer-, mediterran.

medium ['mi:dɪəm] ⬦ *adj* mittlere(r) (s). ⬦ *n* Medium *das*.

medium-size(d) [-saɪz(d)] *adj* mittelgroß.

medium wave *n* Mittelwelle *die*.

medley ['medlɪ] (*pl* **medleys**) *n* - **1.** [mixture] Gemisch *das* - **2.** [selection of music] Medley *das*, Potpourri *das*.

meek [mi:k] *adj* sanftmütig; [voice] sanft.

meet [mi:t] (*pt & pp* **met**) ⬦ *vt* - **1.** [by arrangement] sich treffen mit; [by chance] treffen; [get to know] kennen lernen; **to arrange to meet sb** sich mit jm verabreden; **pleased to meet you!** sehr erfreut! - **2.** [go to collect] ablholen - **3.** [need, requirement] erfüllen - **4.** [cost, expense] begleichen - **5.** [join - subj: road, river] treffen auf (+ A). ⬦ *vi* - **1.** [by arrangement, by chance] sich treffen; [committee *etc*] zusammenlkommen - **2.** [get to know each other] sich kennen lernen - **3.** [intersect] aufeinander treffen - **4.** [join] zusammenlkommen. ⬦ *n* US [sports meeting] Sportfest *das*. ⬥ **meet up** *vi*: **to meet up (with sb)** sich (mit jm) treffen. ⬥ **meet with** *vt insep* - **1.** [problems, resistance] stoßen auf (+ A) - **2.** [by arrangement] sich treffen mit.

meeting ['mi:tɪŋ] *n* - **1.** [for discussions, business] Meeting *das*, Sitzung *die* - **2.** [coming together - by chance] Begegnung *die*; [- by arrangement] Treffen *das*.

megabyte ['megəbaɪt] *n* COMPUT Megabyte *das*.

megaphone ['megəfəʊn] *n* Megafon *das*.

melancholy ['melənkəlɪ] *adj* melancholisch; [facts, news] traurig.

mellow ['meləʊ] ⬦ *adj* - **1.** [light] warm - **2.** [smooth, pleasant] angenehm; [sound, tones] lieblich, sanft; [wine] ausgereift; [whisky] mild - **3.** [gentle, relaxed] milde, sanft. ⬦ *vi* [person] abgeklärt werden.

melody ['melədɪ] *n* Melodie *die*.

melon ['melən] *n* Melone *die*.

melt [melt] ⬦ *vt* [make liquid - chocolate, snow] schmelzen; [butter] zerlassen. ⬦ *vi* - **1.** [become liquid] schmelzen - **2.** *fig* [soften - person] dahinlschmelzen; [- heart] überlgehen - **3.** *fig* [disappear]: **to melt away** [savings, anger] dahinlschmelzen, weglschmelzen. ⬥ **melt down** *vt sep* einlschmelzen.

meltdown ['meltdaʊn] *n* Kernschmelze *die*.

melting pot ['meltɪŋ-] *n fig* Schmelztiegel *der*.

member ['membə*r*] *n* Mitglied *das*; **a member of staff** ein Firmenangehöriger, eine Firmenangehörige.

Member of Congress (*pl* **Members of Congress**) *n* US Kongressmitglied *das*.

Member of Parliament (*pl* **Members of Parliament**) *n* Parlamentsabgeordnete *der*, *die*.

membership ['membəʃɪp] *n (U)* - **1.** [fact of belonging] Mitgliedschaft *die* - **2.** [number of members] Mitgliederzahl *die* - **3.** [people]: **the membership** die Mitglieder.

membership card *n* Mitgliedskarte *die*.

memento [mɪ'mentəʊ] *(pl -s)* n Andenken *das*.

memo ['meməʊ] *(pl -s)* n Mitteilung *die*.

memoirs ['memwɑːz] *npl* Memoiren *Pl*.

memorandum [,memə'rændəm] *(pl -da* [-də] *OR* **-dums)** *n fml* Memorandum *das*.

memorial [mɪ'mɔːrɪəl] <> *adj* Gedenk-. <> *n* Denkmal *das*.

memorize, -ise ['meməraɪz] *vt* auswendig lernen.

memory ['meməri] *n* - **1.** [ability to remember] Gedächtnis *das* - **2.** *(U)* [things remembered] Erinnerung *die*; **I have no memory of** it ich kann mich nicht daran erinnern; **from memory** auswendig - **3.** [event, experience remembered] Erinnerung *die* - **4.** *(U)* [of dead person] Andenken *das* - **5.** COMPUT Speicher *der*.

men [men] *Pl* ⊳ **man**.

menace ['menəs] <> *n* - **1.** [threat] Drohung *die*; [danger] drohende Gefahr - **2.** *(U)* [threatening quality] Bedrohung *die* - **3.** *inf* [nuisance, pest] Plage *die*. <> *vt* bedrohen.

menacing ['menəsɪŋ] *adj* bedrohlich.

mend [mend] <> *n inf*: **to be on the mend** auf dem Weg der Besserung sein. <> *vt* [repair] reparieren; [clothes] flicken.

menial ['miːnɪəl] *adj* niedrig.

meningitis [,menɪn'dʒaɪtɪs] *n* MED Hirnhautentzündung *die*, Meningitis *die*.

menopause ['menəpɔːz] *n (U)*: **the menopause** die Wechseljahre, die Menopause.

men's room *n US*: **the men's room** die Herrentoilette.

menstruation [,menstru'eɪʃn] *n (U)* Menstruation *die*, Periode *die*.

menswear ['menzweə'] *n (U)* Herrenbekleidung *die*.

mental ['mentl] *adj* - **1.** [intellectual] geistig - **2.** [psychiatric] psychiatrisch; **mental illness** Geisteskrankheit *die*; **her mental health** ihr Geisteszustand - **3.** [performed in the mind] im Kopf; **mental arithmetic** Kopfrechnen *das*.

mental hospital *n* Nervenklinik *die*.

mentality [men'tælətɪ] *n (U)* Mentalität *die*.

mentally handicapped *npl*: **the mentally handicapped** die geistig Behinderten *Pl*.

mention ['menʃn] <> *vt* erwähnen; **to mention sthg to sb** etw jm gegenüber erwähnen; **not to mention** ganz zu schweigen von; **don't mention it!** gern geschehen! <> *n* Erwähnung *die*; **to get a mention** erwähnt werden.

menu ['menjuː] *n* - **1.** [in restaurant - card] Speisekarte *die*; [- dishes] Menü *das* - **2.** COMPUT Menü *das*.

meow *n* & *vi US* = **miaow**.

MEP (*abbr of* Member of the European Parliament) *n* MdEP *das*.

mercenary ['mɜːsɪnrɪ] <> *adj* - **1.** [only interested in money] gewinnsüchtig - **2.** MIL Söldner-. <> *n* [soldier] Söldner *der*.

merchandise ['mɜːtʃəndaɪz] *n (U)* Ware *die*.

merchant ['mɜːtʃənt] *n* Händler *der*, -in *die*.

merchant bank *n UK* Handelsbank *die*.

merchant navy *UK*, **merchant marine** *US* *n* Handelsmarine *die*.

merciful ['mɜːsɪfʊl] *adj* [person] barmherzig.

merciless ['mɜːsɪlɪs] *adj* gnadenlos.

mercury ['mɜːkjʊrɪ] *n* Quecksilber *das*.

Mercury ['mɜːkjʊrɪ] *n* [planet] Merkur *der*.

mercy ['mɜːsɪ] *n* - **1.** [kindness, pity] Gnade *die*; **to be at the mercy of sb/sthg** *fig* jm/etw ausgeliefert sein - **2.** [blessing] Segen *der*.

mere [mɪə'] *adj*: **a mere £10 is all it costs** es kostet bloß *OR* nur 10 Pfund; **it took him a mere two hours** er brauchte bloß *OR* nur zwei Stunden; **she's a mere child!** sie ist ja noch ein Kind!

merely ['mɪəlɪ] *adv* bloß, nur.

merge [mɜːdʒ] <> *vt* - **1.** COMM fusionieren - **2.** COMPUT mischen. <> *vi* - **1.** COMM: **to merge (with)** fusionieren (mit) - **2.** [roads, lines] zusammenlaufen - **3.** [blend] ineinander überlgehen; **to merge into the landscape/background** mit der Landschaft/dem Hintergrund verschmelzen.

merger ['mɜːdʒə'] *n* COMM Fusion *die*.

meringue [mə'ræŋ] *n* Baiser *das*.

merit ['merɪt] <> *n (U)* [value] Wert *der*; **she was chosen for the post on merit** sie bekam die Stelle aufgrund ihrer guten Leistungen. <> *vt* verdienen. ◆ **merits** *npl* Vorteile *Pl*.

mermaid ['mɜːmeɪd] *n* Meerjungfrau *die*.

merry ['merɪ] *adj* - **1.** [party] fröhlich; **Merry Christmas!** frohe *OR* fröhliche Weihnachten! - **2.** *inf* [tipsy] angeheitert.

merry-go-round *n* Karussell *das*.

mesh [meʃ] *n (U)* [netting]: **(wire) mesh** Maschendraht *der*.

mesmerize, -ise ['mezməraɪz] *vt*: **to be mesmerized by sb/sthg** fasziniert *OR* gebannt sein von jm/etw.

mess [mes] *n* - **1.** [untidy state] Durcheinander *das* - **2.** [sthg spilt, knocked over] Schweinerei *die* - **3.** [muddle] Durcheinander *das*; [problematic situation] Schlamassel *der* - **4.** MIL Messe *die*. ◆ **mess about, mess around** *inf* <> *vt sep* an der Nase herumlführen. <> *vi* - **1.** [fool around, waste time] herumlgammeln - **2.** [interfere]: **to mess about with** [machine] herumlbasteln an (+ D); [sb's papers] durcheinander bringen. ◆ **mess up** *vt sep*

inf - 1. [make dirty] verdrecken; [make untidy] in Unordnung bringen **- 2.** [plan, evening] verderben.

message ['mesɪdʒ] *n* **- 1.** [piece of information] Nachricht *die* **- 2.** [idea, moral] Botschaft *die*.

messenger ['mesɪndʒəʳ] *n* Bote *der*.

messy ['mesɪ] *adj* **- 1.** [untidy] unordentlich; [dirty] dreckig **- 2.** *inf* [complicated, confused] kompliziert.

met [met] *pt & pp* ⊳ **meet**.

metal ['metl] ◇ *n* Metall *das*. ◇ *adj* Metall-, metallen.

metallic [mɪ'tælɪk] *adj* **- 1.** [sound] metallisch **- 2.** [shiny]: **metallic paint** Metalliclackierung *die*; **metallic blue** metallicblau.

metalwork ['metəlwɜːk] *n (U)* [craft] Metallarbeit *die*.

metaphor ['metəfəʳ] *n* [symbol, image] Metapher *die*.

mete [miːt] ◆ **mete out** *vt sep*: **to mete sthg out to sb** jm etw zulmessen.

meteor ['miːtɪəʳ] *n* Meteor *der*.

meteorology [miːtɪə'rɒlədʒɪ] *n* Meteorologie *die*.

meter ['miːtəʳ] ◇ *n* **- 1.** [device - for gas, electricity] Zähler *der*; [- in taxi] Uhr *die*; [- for parking] Parkuhr *die* **- 2.** *US* = **metre**. ◇ *vt* messen.

method ['meθəd] *n* Methode *die*.

methodical [mɪ'θɒdɪkl] *adj* methodisch.

Methodist ['meθədɪst] ◇ *adj* Methodisten-. ◇ *n* Methodist *der*, -in *die*.

meths [meθs] *n (U) UK inf* Brennspiritus *der*.

methylated spirits [,meθɪleɪtɪd-] *n (U)* Brennspiritus *der*.

meticulous [mɪ'tɪkjʊləs] *adj* genau.

metre *UK*, **meter** *US* ['miːtəʳ] *n* [unit of measurement] Meter *der*.

metric ['metrɪk] *adj* metrisch.

metronome ['metrənəʊm] *n* Metronom *das*.

metropolitan [,metrə'pɒlɪtn] *adj* Stadt-.

mettle ['metl] *n (U)*: **to be on one's mettle** sein Bestes geben; **to show one's mettle** zeigen, was man kann.

mew [mjuː] *n & vi* = **miaow**.

mews [mjuːz] *(pl inv) n UK* [stables] Stallungen *Pl*; [street] Gasse mit ehemaligen Stallungen.

Mexican ['meksɪkn] ◇ *adj* mexikanisch. ◇ *n* Mexikaner *der*, -in *die*.

Mexico ['meksɪkəʊ] *n* Mexiko *nt*.

MI5 (*abbr of* Military Intelligence 5) *n* MI5 *der*, britische Spionageabwehr.

miaow *UK* [miːˈaʊ], **meow** *US* [mɪ'aʊ] ◇ *n* Miau *das*. ◇ *vi* miauen.

mice [maɪs] *Pl* ⊳ **mouse**.

mickey ['mɪkɪ] *n*: **to take the mickey out of sb** *UK inf* jn auf den Arm nehmen.

microchip ['maɪkrəʊtʃɪp] *n* Mikrochip *der*.

microcomputer [,maɪkrəʊkəm'pjuːtəʳ] *n* Mikrocomputer *der*.

microfilm ['maɪkrəʊfɪlm] *n* Mikrofilm *der*.

microphone ['maɪkrəfəʊn] *n* Mikrofon *das*.

microscope ['maɪkrəskəʊp] *n* Mikroskop *das*.

microscopic [,maɪkrə'skɒpɪk] *adj* [very small] mikroskopisch.

microwave (oven) [,maɪkrəweɪv-] *n* Mikrowellenherd *der*.

mid- [mɪd] *prefix*: **in mid-June** Mitte Juni; **a mid-morning snack** ein zweites Frühstück; **he is in his mid-fifties** er ist Mitte fünfzig; **in the mid-20th century** Mitte des 20. Jahrhunderts.

midair [,mɪd'eəʳ] ◇ *adj*: **midair collision** Zusammenstoß in der Luft. ◇ *n*: **in midair** in der Luft.

midday [mɪd'deɪ] *n* Mittag *der*; **at midday** mittags.

middle ['mɪdl] ◇ *adj* [central] Mittel-, mittlere(r) (s). ◇ *n* **- 1.** [gen] Mitte *die*; **in the middle (of sthg)** in der Mitte (von etw); **in the middle of the night** mitten in der Nacht; **to be in the middle of doing sthg** gerade dabei sein, etw zu tun **- 2.** [waist] Taille *die*.

middle-aged [-'eɪdʒd] *adj* im mittleren Alter, mittleren Alters.

Middle Ages *npl*: **the Middle Ages** das Mittelalter.

middle-class *adj* Mittelklasse-.

middle classes *npl*: **the middle classes** die Mittelklasse.

Middle East *n*: **the Middle East** der Nahe Osten.

middleman ['mɪdlmæn] *(pl -men [-men]) n* **- 1.** COMM Zwischenhändler *der* **- 2.** [in negotiations] Vermittler *der*.

middle name *n* zweiter Vorname.

midfield [,mɪd'fiːld] *n* FTBL Mittelfeld *das*.

midge [mɪdʒ] *n* Mücke *die*.

midget ['mɪdʒɪt] *n* Zwerg *der*.

Midlands ['mɪdləndz] *npl*: **the Midlands** Region im Zentrum von England.

midnight ['mɪdnaɪt] *n* Mitternacht *die*; **at midnight** um Mitternacht.

midriff ['mɪdrɪf] *n* Bauch *der*.

midst [mɪdst] *n*: **in the midst of** mitten in (+ D); **to be in the midst of doing sthg** gerade dabei sein, etw zu tun.

midsummer ['mɪd,sʌməʳ] *n (U)* Hochsommer *der*.

midway [,mɪd'weɪ] *adv* **- 1.** [in space]: **midway (between)** auf halbem Wege (zwischen) **- 2.** [in time] in der Mitte; **midway through** mitten in (+ D).

midweek ◇ *adj* ['mɪdwiːk]: **a midweek meeting/match** ein Mitte der Woche stattfindendes Treffen/Spiel. ◇ *adv* [,mɪd'wiːk] Mitte der Woche.

midwife ['mɪdwaɪf] (*pl* **-wives** [-waɪvz]) *n* Hebamme *die*.

might [maɪt] ◇ *modal vb* - **1.** [expressing possibility] können; **they might still come** sie könnten noch kommen; **they might have been killed** sie sind vielleicht umgekommen - **2.** [expressing suggestion]: **you might have told me!** das hättest du mir doch sagen können!; **it might be better to wait** sie sollten vielleicht lieber warten - **3.** *fml* [asking permission]: **might I have a few words?** könnte ich Sie mal sprechen?; **he asked if he might leave the room** er fragte, ob er das Zimmer verlassen dürfte - **4.** [when conceding a point]: **it might be expensive, but it's good quality** es ist zwar teuer, aber es ist eine gute Qualität - **5.** [would]: **I'd hoped you might come too** ich hatte gehofft, du würdest auch mitkommen - **6.** *phr*: **I might have known/guessed** das hätte ich eigentlich wissen/mir eigentlich denken können. ◇ *n* (U) Macht *die*; **with all one's might** mit aller Macht OR Kraft.

mighty ['maɪtɪ] ◇ *adj* [powerful] mächtig. ◇ *adv* US *inf* mächtig.

migraine ['miːgreɪn, 'maɪgreɪn] *n* Migräne *die*.

migrant ['maɪgrənt] *n* - **1.** [bird] Zugvogel *der* - **2.** [worker] Wanderarbeiter *der*, -in *die*.

migrate [UK maɪ'greɪt, US 'maɪgreɪt] *vi* - **1.** [bird] in den Süden ziehen - **2.** [person] ablwandern.

mike [maɪk] (*abbr of* **microphone**) *n* *inf* Mikro *das*.

mild [maɪld] *adj* - **1.** [gen] mild; [sedative, illness] leicht - **2.** [person, manner] sanft.

mildew ['mɪldjuː] *n* [on books, walls] Schimmel *der*.

mildly ['maɪldlɪ] *adv* milde; **to put it mildly** gelinde gesagt.

mile [maɪl] *n* Meile *die*; **to be miles away** [distracted] (mit seinen Gedanken) ganz woanders sein. ◆ **miles** *adv* (*in comparisons*) weit; **miles better** weit besser.

mileage ['maɪlɪdʒ] *n* - **1.** [recorded] Meilenzahl *die* - **2.** (U) *inf* [advantage] Vorteil *der*.

mileometer [maɪ'lɒmɪtər] *n* ≃ Kilometerzähler *der*.

milestone ['maɪlstəʊn] *n* liter & fig Meilenstein *der*.

militant ['mɪlɪtənt] ◇ *adj* militant. ◇ *n* militanter Student/Arbeiter/*etc*.

military ['mɪlɪtrɪ] ◇ *adj* Militär-, militärisch. ◇ *n*: **the military** das Militär.

militia [mɪ'lɪʃə] *n* Miliz *die*.

milk [mɪlk] ◇ *n* Milch *die*. ◇ *vt* - **1.** [cow, goat] melken - **2.** [company] schröpfen; fig [situation, scandal] ausilnutzen.

milk chocolate *n* Milchschokolade *die*.

milkman ['mɪlkmən] (*pl* **-men** [-mən]) *n* Milchmann *der*.

milk shake *n* Milchshake *der*.

milky ['mɪlkɪ] *adj* - **1.** UK [coffee] Milch-; [tea] mit Milch - **2.** [complexion] milchig.

Milky Way *n*: **the Milky Way** die Milchstraße.

mill [mɪl] *n* - **1.** [flour mill, grinder] Mühle *die* - **2.** [cloth factory] Weberei *die*. ◆ **mill about, mill around** *vi* umherllaufen.

millennium [mɪ'lenɪəm] (*pl* **-nnia** [-nɪə]) *n* Millennium *das*.

millet ['mɪlɪt] *n* (U) Hirse *die*.

milligram(me) ['mɪlɪgræm] *n* Milligramm *das*.

millimetre UK, **millimeter** US ['mɪlɪ,miːtər] *n* Millimeter *der*.

million ['mɪljən] *n* - **1.** [1,000,000] Million *die* - **2.** [enormous number]: **a million, millions** of zig.

millionaire [,mɪljə'neər] *n* Millionär *der*, -in *die*.

milometer [maɪ'lɒmɪtər] *n* = **mileometer**.

mime [maɪm] ◇ *n* - **1.** [acting, act] Pantomime *die* - **2.** [actor]: **mime (artist)** Pantomime *der*, -min *die*. ◇ *vt* mimen.

mimic ['mɪmɪk] (*pt* & *pp* **-ked**, *cont* **-king**) ◇ *n* Imitator *der*, -in *die*. ◇ *vt* nachlahmen.

min. *abbr of* **minute, minimum**.

mince [mɪns] ◇ *n* (U) UK Hackfleisch *das*. ◇ *vt* - **1.** [meat] durchldrehen - **2.**: **not to mince one's words** kein Blatt vor den Mund nehmen. ◇ *vi* [walk] trippeln.

mincemeat ['mɪnsmiːt] *n* (U) - **1.** [fruit] Mischung aus Äpfeln, Rosinen, Fett und Gewürzen, die im Teigmantel gebacken wird - **2.** US [minced meat] Hackfleisch *das*.

mince pie *n* mit Mincemeat gefüllte Pastete.

mincer ['mɪnsər] *n* Fleischwolf *der*.

mind [maɪnd] ◇ *n* - **1.** [reason] Verstand *der*; **to be out of one's mind** nicht bei Sinnen OR verrückt sein; **no one in their right mind would do that** das kein vernünftiger Mensch würde das tun; **state of mind** Geisteszustand *der* - **2.** [thoughts] Gedanken *Pl*; **I can't get her out of my mind** sie geht mir nicht aus dem Kopf; **to come into/cross sb's mind** jm in den Sinn kommen; **to have sthg on one's mind** etw auf dem Herzen haben - **3.** [intellect] Geist *der* - **4.** [attention]: **to keep one's mind on sthg** sich auf etw (A) konzentrieren; **if you put your mind to it** wenn du dich anstrengst - **5.** [opinion]: **to my mind** meiner Ansicht OR Meinung nach; **to change one's mind** seine Meinung ändern; **to keep an open mind** sich nicht festlegen; **to make one's mind up**

sich entschließen; **to speak one's mind** seine Meinung frei äußern; **to be in two minds about sthg** hinsichtlich einer Sache (G) unentschlossen sein - **6.** [memory] Gedächtnis das; **to bear sthg in mind** etw nicht vergessen - **7.** [intention]: **to have sthg in mind** an etw (A) denken; **to have a mind to do sthg** die Absicht haben, etw zu tun - **8.** [intelligent person, thinker] Geist der; **he is one of the greatest minds of the 19th century** er ist einer der größten Köpfe des 19. Jahrhunderts. ◇ vi - **1.** [object]: **I don't mind** ich habe nichts dagegen; **do you mind if ...?** macht es Ihnen etwas aus, wenn ...?, stört es Sie, wenn ...? - **2.** [care, worry]: **I don't mind if... es macht mir nichts aus, wenn...; **never mind** [don't worry] mach dir nichts draus; [it's not important] es macht nichts. ◇ vt - **1.** [object to]: **I don't mind it/him** ich habe nichts dagegen/gegen ihn; **do you mind waiting?** macht es dir etwas aus, zu warten? - **2.** [bother about]: **I don't mind what he says** es ist mir gleichgültig, was er sagt - **3.** [pay attention to] achten auf (+ A) - **4.** [take care of] sich kümmern um. ◆ **mind you** adv allerdings.

minder ['maɪndər] n UK [bodyguard] Leibwächter der, -in die.

mindful ['maɪndful] adj: **to be mindful of sthg** sich (D) einer Sache (G) bewusst sein.

mindless ['maɪndlɪs] adj - **1.** [stupid] sinnlos - **2.** [not requiring thought] geistlos.

mine [maɪn] ◇ n - **1.** [for excavating minerals] Bergwerk das; [for gold, diamond] Mine die - **2.** [bomb] Mine die. ◇ vt - **1.** [coal, gold] fördern - **2.** [lay mines in] verminen.

mine [maɪn] poss pron meine(r) (s) (meine); **it's mine** es gehört mir; **a friend of mine** ein Freund von mir.

minefield ['maɪnfiːld] n liter & fig Minenfeld das.

miner ['maɪnər] n Bergarbeiter der, -in die.

mineral ['mɪnərəl] ◇ adj GEOL mineralisch. ◇ n GEOL Mineral das.

mineral water n (U) Mineralwasser das.

mingle ['mɪŋgl] vi - **1.** [combine]: **to mingle (with)** sich mischen (mit) - **2.** [at party]: **to mingle (with the guests)** sich unter die Gäste mischen.

miniature ['mɪnətʃər] ◇ adj Miniatur-. ◇ n - **1.** [painting] Miniatur die - **2.** [of alcohol] Miniflasche die - **3.** [small scale]: **in miniature** im Kleinen, Miniatur-.

minibus ['mɪnɪbʌs] (pl -es) n Kleinbus der.

minicab ['mɪnɪkæb] n UK Kleintaxi das.

minima ['mɪnɪmə] Pl ⊳ **minimum**.

minimal ['mɪnɪml] adj minimal.

minimum ['mɪnɪməm] (pl -mums OR -ma) ◇ adj Mindest-. ◇ n Minimum das.

mining ['maɪnɪŋ] ◇ n Bergbau der. ◇ adj Bergbau-; [accident] Gruben-.

miniskirt ['mɪnɪskɜːt] n Minirock der.

minister ['mɪnɪstər] n - **1.** POL: **minister (of** OR **for sthg)** Minister der, -in die (für etw) - **2.** RELIG Pastor der, -in die. ◆ **minister to** vt insep sich kümmern um; **to minister to sb's needs** js Bedürfnisse befriedigen.

ministerial [,mɪnɪ'stɪərɪəl] adj POL Ministerial-, ministeriell.

minister of state n: **minister of state (for sthg)** Staatsminister der, -in die (für etw).

ministry ['mɪnɪstrɪ] n - **1.** POL Ministerium das - **2.** RELIG: **the ministry** das geistliche Amt.

mink [mɪŋk] (pl inv) n [fur, animal] Nerz der.

minor ['maɪnər] ◇ adj - **1.** [unimportant] unbedeutend - **2.** MUS [key] Moll-; **in B minor** in H-Moll. ◇ n [in age] Minderjährige der, die.

minority [maɪ'nɒrɪtɪ] n Minderheit die.

mint [mɪnt] ◇ n - **1.** (U) [herb] Minze die - **2.** [sweet] Pfefferminzbonbon das ODER der - **3.** [for coins]: **the Mint** die Münze; **in mint condition** in neuwertigem OR tadellosem Zustand. ◇ vt [coins] prägen.

minus ['maɪnəs] (pl -es) ◇ prep - **1.** MATHS minus, weniger - **2.** [in temperatures] minus. ◇ adj - **1.** MATHS negativ - **2.** SCH [in grades] minus. ◇ n - **1.** MATHS Minus das - **2.** [disadvantage] Nachteil der.

minus sign n Minuszeichen das.

minute [mɪnɪt] n - **1.** [period of 60 seconds] Minute die - **2.** [moment] Moment der; **at any minute** jederzeit; **this minute** sofort, auf der Stelle. ◆ **minutes** npl [of meeting] Protokoll das.

minute [maɪ'njuːt] adj [tiny] winzig.

miracle ['mɪrəkl] n Wunder das.

miraculous [mɪ'rækjuləs] adj - **1.** RELIG wundersam - **2.** fig [recovery, escape] wunderbar.

mirage [mɪ'rɑːʒ] n [in desert] Fata Morgana die.

mire [maɪər] n [U] Morast der, Schlamm der.

mirror ['mɪrər] ◇ n Spiegel der. ◇ vt [copy] widerlspiegeln.

misadventure [,mɪsəd'ventʃər] n [unfortunate accident] Missgeschick das.

misapprehension [,mɪsæprɪ'henʃn] n Missverständnis das.

misbehave [,mɪsbɪ'heɪv] vi sich schlecht benehmen.

miscalculate [,mɪs'kælkjuleɪt] ◇ vt - **1.** [amount, time, distance] falsch berechnen - **2.** fig [misjudge] falsch einlschätzen. ◇ vi - **1.** MATHS sich verrechnen - **2.** fig [misjudge] sich verschätzen.

miscarriage [,mɪs'kærɪdʒ] n Fehlgeburt die.

miscarriage of justice n Justizirrtum der.

miscellaneous [,mɪsə'leɪnɪəs] adj verschieden.

mischief ['mɪstʃɪf] *n (U)* - **1.** [naughty behaviour] Unfug *der* - **2.** [harm] Schaden *der*.

mischievous ['mɪstʃɪvəs] *adj* - **1.** [playful] schelmisch - **2.** [naughty] unartig.

misconception [,mɪskən'sepʃn] *n* falsche Vorstellung, falsche Auffassung.

misconduct [,mɪs'kɒndʌkt] *n* [bad behaviour] schlechtes Benehmen.

miscount [,mɪs'kaʊnt] *vt* falsch zählen. *vi* sich verzählen.

misdemeanour *UK*, **misdemeanor** *US* [,mɪsdɪ'miːnəʳ] *n* LAW Vergehen *das*.

miser ['maɪzəʳ] *n* Geizhals *der*.

miserable ['mɪzrəbl] *adj* - **1.** [person, life] elend; **don't look so miserable** guck nicht so jämmerlich - **2.** [conditions, pay, weather] miserabel; [evening, holiday] schrecklich - **3.** [failure] kläglich.

miserly ['maɪzəlɪ] *adj* geizig.

misery ['mɪzərɪ] *n* - **1.** [unhappiness] Kummer *der* - **2.** [poverty] Elend *das*, Armut *die*.

misfire [,mɪs'faɪəʳ] *vi* - **1.** [gun, car engine] fehlzünden - **2.** [plan] fehlschlagen.

misfit ['mɪsfɪt] *n* Außenseiter *der*, -in *die*.

misfortune [mɪs'fɔːtʃuːn] *n* - **1.** [bad luck] Pech *das* - **2.** [piece of bad luck] Unglück *das*.

misgivings [mɪs'gɪvɪŋz] *npl* Bedenken *Pl*.

misguided [,mɪs'gaɪdɪd] *adj* [opinion] töricht.

mishandle [,mɪs'hændl] *vt* - **1.** [person, animal] schlecht behandeln - **2.** [negotiations, business] falsch handhaben.

mishap ['mɪshæp] *n* [unfortunate event] Missgeschick *das*.

misinterpret [,mɪsɪn'tɜːprɪt] *vt* falsch auslegen OR deuten.

misjudge [,mɪs'dʒʌdʒ] *vt* - **1.** [calculate wrongly] falsch einschätzen - **2.** [appraise wrongly] falsch beurteilen.

mislay [,mɪs'leɪ] *(pt & pp* **-laid** [-'leɪd]) *vt* verlegen.

mislead [,mɪs'liːd] *(pt & pp* **-led**) *vt* irreführen.

misleading [,mɪs'liːdɪŋ] *adj* irreführend.

misled [,mɪs'led] *pt & pp* ▷ **mislead**.

misplace [,mɪs'pleɪs] *vt* verlegen.

misprint ['mɪsprɪnt] *n* Druckfehler *der*.

miss [mɪs] *vt* - **1.** [person in crowd, film, turning, opportunity, train, flight] verpassen - **2.** [subj: bullet, ball, footballer] verfehlen - **3.** [wife, family, home] vermissen; **I miss reading English newspapers** ich vermisse es, englische Zeitungen zu lesen - **4.** [meeting, appointment, school] versäumen - **5.** [disaster] entkommen *(+ D)*; **I just missed being run over** ich wäre beinahe überfahren worden. *vi* [fail to hit] nicht treffen. *n*: **to give sthg a miss** *inf* sich *(D)* etw verkneifen. ▰ **miss out** *vt sep* [omit - by accident] übersehen; [- deliberately] auslassen. *vi*: **to miss out on sthg** etw verpassen.

Miss [mɪs] *n* Fräulein *nt*.

misshapen [,mɪs'ʃeɪpn] *adj* [hands, fingers, toes] missgebildet; [biscuits, cake] missraten.

missile [*UK* 'mɪsaɪl, *US* 'mɪsəl] *n* - **1.** [weapon] Rakete *die*, Flugkörper *der* - **2.** [thrown object] Wurfgeschoss *das*.

missing ['mɪsɪŋ] *adj* - **1.** [lost] verschwunden; **missing in action** vermisst; **sixty people are still missing** sechzig Personen werden immer noch vermisst - **2.** [not present] fehlend; **who's missing?** wer fehlt?

mission ['mɪʃn] *n* - **1.** [task, duty] Auftrag *der* - **2.** [delegation] Delegation *die*, Gesandtschaft *die* - **3.** ASTRON & MIL Mission *die* - **4.** [RELIG - building, teaching] Mission *die*.

missionary ['mɪʃənrɪ] *n* Missionar *der*, -in *die*.

misspend [,mɪs'spend] *(pt & pp* **-spent** [-'spent]) *vt* [money, talent, youth] vergeuden.

mist [mɪst] *n* Nebel *der*. ▰ **mist over, mist up** *vi* beschlagen.

mistake [mɪ'steɪk] *(pt* **-took**, *pp* **-taken**) *n* Fehler *der*; **to make a mistake** [in writing, work] einen Fehler machen; [be mistaken] sich irren; **by mistake** irrtümlich. *vt* - **1.** [misunderstand] falsch verstehen, missverstehen - **2.** [fail to distinguish]: **to mistake sb/sthg for** jn/etw verwechseln mit.

mistaken [mɪ'steɪkn] *pp* ▷ **mistake**. *adj* - **1.** [person]: **to be mistaken** sich irren; **to be mistaken about sb/sthg** sich in jm/etw irren - **2.** [belief, idea] irrig, falsch.

mistletoe ['mɪsltəʊ] *n (U)* Mistel *die*.

mistook [mɪ'stʊk] *pt* ▷ **mistake**.

mistreat [,mɪs'triːt] *vt* schlecht behandeln.

mistress ['mɪstrɪs] *n* - **1.** [of house, situation] Herrin *die* - **2.** [female lover] Geliebte *die*.

mistrust [,mɪs'trʌst] *n* Misstrauen *das*. *vt* misstrauen *(+ D)*.

misty ['mɪstɪ] *adj* neblig.

misunderstand [,mɪsʌndə'stænd] *(pt & pp* **-stood**) *vt* missverstehen. *vi* falsch verstehen.

misunderstanding [,mɪsʌndə'stændɪŋ] *n* - **1.** [lack of understanding, wrong interpretation] Missverständnis *das* - **2.** [disagreement] Meinungsverschiedenheit *die*.

misunderstood [,mɪsʌndə'stʊd] *pt & pp* ▷ **misunderstand**.

misuse *n* [,mɪs'juːs] Missbrauch *der*; [of funds] Zweckentfremdung *die*. *vt* [,mɪs'juːz] [abuse] missbrauchen; [funds] zweckentfremden.

mitigate ['mɪtɪgeɪt] *vt fml* lindern.

mitten ['mɪtn] *n* Fausthandschuh *der*.

mix [mɪks] ⬦ vt - **1.** [substances] mischen; [activities] miteinander verbinden; **to mix sthg with sthg** etw mit etw vermischen - **2.** [drink, song] mixen; [cement] mischen. ⬦ vi - **1.** [substances] sich vermischen - **2.** [socially]: **to mix with sb** mit jm verkehren, Umgang pflegen mit jm. ⬦ n - **1.** [combination] Mischung die - **2.** MUS Mix der. ⬥ **mix up** vt sep - **1.** [confuse] verwechseln - **2.** [disorder] durcheinander bringen.

mixed [mɪkst] adj gemischt.

mixed grill n gemischter Grillteller.

mixed up adj - **1.** [confused] verwirrt - **2.** [involved]: **to be mixed up in sthg** in etw (A) verwickelt sein.

mixer ['mɪksə'] n - **1.** [device] Mixer der; [cement] Mischer der - **2.** [soft drink] alkoholfreies Getränk, wie z. B. Fruchtsaft, das zum Mischen mit Spirituosen verwendet wird.

mixture ['mɪkstʃə'] n Mischung die.

mix-up n inf Verwechslung die.

ml (abbr of millilitre) ml.

mm (abbr of millimetre) mm.

MMR [ˌemem'ɑːr] n MED (abbr of **measles, mumps & rubella**) MMR.

moan [məʊn] ⬦ n [of pain] Stöhnen das; [of sadness] Seufzer der. ⬦ vi - **1.** [in pain] stöhnen; [in sadness] seufzen - **2.** inf [complain] jammern; **to moan about sb/sthg** jammern OR sich beklagen über jn/etw.

moat [məʊt] n [around castle] Burggraben der; [in zoo] Wassergraben der.

mob [mɒb] ⬦ n Mob der. ⬦ vt belagern.

mobile ['məʊbaɪl] ⬦ adj - **1.** [able to move] beweglich - **2.** inf [having transport] motorisiert. ⬦ n [phone] Handy das.

mobile home n Wohnmobil das.

mobile phone n Handy das.

mobilize, -ise ['məʊbɪlaɪz] ⬦ vt - **1.** [support, workforce] mobilisieren - **2.** MIL mobil machen. ⬦ vi MIL mobil machen.

mock [mɒk] ⬦ adj [surprise] gespielt; [Georgian house] Pseudo-; [exam] Übungs-. ⬦ vt [deride] verspotten.

mockery ['mɒkərɪ] n - **1.** [scorn] Spott der - **2.** [travesty] Farce die.

mode [məʊd] n [manner] Art (und Weise) die; **mode of transport** Transportmittel das.

model ['mɒdl] (UK) (US) ⬦ n - **1.** [gen] Modell das - **2.** [basis for imitation] Vorlage die; [person, society] Vorbild das - **3.** [best example] Musterbeispiel das. ⬦ adj - **1.** [miniature] Modell- - **2.** [exemplary] Muster-, musterhaft. ⬦ vt - **1.** [shape] modellieren - **2.** [in fashion show] vorführen - **3.** [copy]: **to model o.s. on sb** sich (D) jn zum Vorbild nehmen. ⬦ vi [in fashion show] als Modell arbeiten, modeln.

modem ['məʊdem] n COMPUT Modem das.

moderate ⬦ adj ['mɒdərət] - **1.** [views, habits] gemäßigt; [demands] bescheiden - **2.** [heat] mäßig; [quantity] angemessen; **of moderate height/size** mittelgroß - **3.** [success, ability] mittelmäßig. ⬦ n ['mɒdərət] POL Gemäßigte der, die. ⬦ vt ['mɒdəreɪt] mäßigen.

moderation [ˌmɒdə'reɪʃn] n Mäßigung die; **in moderation** in Maßen.

modern ['mɒdən] adj modern.

modernize, -ise ['mɒdənaɪz] vt & vi modernisieren.

modern languages npl neue Sprachen Pl.

modest ['mɒdɪst] adj bescheiden.

modesty ['mɒdɪstɪ] n Bescheidenheit die.

modicum ['mɒdɪkəm] n fml: **a modicum of** ein bisschen; **a modicum of truth** ein Körnchen Wahrheit.

modify ['mɒdɪfaɪ] vt - **1.** [alter] ändern, abländern - **2.** [tone down] mäßigen.

module ['mɒdjuːl] n - **1.** [unit] Modul das; SCH & UNIV zu einem Kurs gehörende Unterrichtseinheit - **2.** [of spacecraft] Raumkapsel die.

mogul ['məʊgl] n [magnate] Mogul der.

mohair ['məʊheə'] n (U) Mohair der.

moist [mɔɪst] adj feucht.

moisten ['mɔɪsn] vt befeuchten.

moisture ['mɔɪstʃə'] n Feuchtigkeit die.

moisturizer, -iser ['mɔɪstʃəraɪzə'] n Feuchtigkeitscreme die.

molar ['məʊlə'] n Backenzahn der.

molasses [mə'læsɪz] n (U) Melasse die.

mold etc n & vt US = **mould**.

mole [məʊl] n - **1.** [animal] Maulwurf der - **2.** [on skin] Muttermal das, Leberfleck der - **3.** [spy] Spion der.

molecule ['mɒlɪkjuːl] n Molekül das.

molest [mə'lest] vt - **1.** [attack sexually] sexuell belästigen - **2.** [bother] belästigen.

mollusc, mollusk US ['mɒləsk] n Weichtier das.

mollycoddle ['mɒlɪˌkɒdl] vt inf verhätscheln, verzärteln.

molt vt & vi US = **moult**.

molten ['məʊltn] adj geschmolzen.

mom [mɒm] n US inf Mutter die; [within speaker's family] Mutti die.

moment ['məʊmənt] n - **1.** [very short period of time] Moment der, Augenblick der - **2.** [particular point in time] Zeitpunkt der; **at any moment** jeden Moment; **at the moment** im Moment; **for the moment** vorerst.

momentarily ['məʊməntərɪlɪ] adv - **1.** [for a short time] momentan - **2.** US [immediately] jeden Moment OR Augenblick.

momentary ['məʊməntrɪ] adj kurz.

momentous [mə'mentəs] adj bedeutsam.

momentum [mə'mentəm] n [speed] Schwung der; **to gain** OR **gather momentum** [object, campaign] in Fahrt kommen.

momma ['mɒmə], **mommy** ['mɒmɪ] n US Mama die, Mami die.

Monaco ['mɒnəkəʊ] n Monaco nt.

monarch ['mɒnək] n Monarch der, -in die.

monarchy ['mɒnəkɪ] n Monarchie die.

monastery ['mɒnəstrɪ] n Kloster das.

Monday ['mʌndɪ] n Montag der; see also **Saturday**.

monetary ['mʌnɪtrɪ] adj Währungs-.

money ['mʌnɪ] n (U) Geld das; **to make money** Geld machen; **to get one's money's worth** für sein Geld gebotten bekommen.

moneybox ['mʌnɪbɒks] n Sparbüchse die.

money order n Zahlungsanweisung die.

mongrel ['mʌŋgrəl] n [dog] Mischling der.

monitor ['mɒnɪtər] ◇ n Monitor der. ◇ vt - 1. [check] überwachen, kontrollieren - 2. [listen to] abhören, mithören.

monk [mʌŋk] n Mönch der.

monkey ['mʌŋkɪ] (pl monkeys) n [animal] Affe der.

mono ['mɒnəʊ] ◇ adj [with noun] Mono-; [with adj] mono-. ◇ n inf [sound] Mono das.

monochrome ['mɒnəkrəʊm] adj monochrom, schwarz-weiß.

monocle ['mɒnəkl] n Monokel das.

monologue, monolog US ['mɒnəlɒg] n Monolog der.

monopolize, -ise [mə'nɒpəlaɪz] vt monopolisieren; [conversation] beherrschen; [person] in Beschlag nehmen.

monopoly [mə'nɒpəlɪ] n: **monopoly (on** OR **of)** Monopol das (auf (+ A)).

monotonous [mə'nɒtənəs] adj monoton.

monotony [mə'nɒtənɪ] n Monotonie die.

monsoon [mɒn'suːn] n Monsun der.

monster ['mɒnstər] n Monster das.

monstrosity [mɒn'strɒsətɪ] n Monstrosität die, Ungeheuerlichkeit die.

monstrous ['mɒnstrəs] adj - 1. [appalling] abscheulich - 2. [hideous] scheußlich - 3. [very large] riesig.

month [mʌnθ] n Monat der.

monthly ['mʌnθlɪ] ◇ adj monatlich; [magazine] Monats-. ◇ adv monatlich. ◇ n [magazine] Monatsmagazin das.

monument ['mɒnjumənt] n - 1. [memorial] Monument das - 2. [historic building] Denkmal das.

monumental [,mɒnju'mentl] adj - 1. [very large] monumental - 2. [important] bedeutend - 3. [extremely bad] ungeheuerlich.

moo [muː] (pl -s) vi muhen.

mood [muːd] n Stimmung die; [of person] Laune die; **to be in a (bad) mood** schlechte Laune haben; **to be in a good mood** gute Laune haben.

moody ['muːdɪ] adj pej - 1. [changeable] launisch - 2. [bad-tempered] schlecht gelaunt.

moon [muːn] n Mond der.

moonlight ['muːnlaɪt] (pt & pp -ed) n Mondlicht das.

moonlighting ['muːnlaɪtɪŋ] n [illegal work] Schwarzarbeit die.

moonlit ['muːnlɪt] adj [place] mondbeschienen; [night] mondhell.

moor [mɔːr] ◇ vt vertäuen. ◇ vi anlegen.

moorland ['mɔːlənd] n esp UK Heideland das.

moose [muːs] (pl inv) n Elch der.

mop [mɒp] ◇ n - 1. [for cleaning] Mopp der - 2. inf [of hair]: **mop of hair** (Haar)mähne die. ◇ vt wischen. ◆ **mop up** vt sep [liquid, dirt] aufwischen.

mope [məʊp] vi pej Trübsal blasen.

moped ['məʊped] n Moped das.

moral ['mɒrəl] ◇ adj - 1. [relating to morals] moralisch - 2. [behaving correctly] moralisch einwandfrei. ◇ n [lesson] Moral die. ◆ **morals** npl [principles] Moral die.

morale [mə'rɑːl] n Moral die.

morality [mə'rælətɪ] n Moralität die.

morbid ['mɔːbɪd] adj morbid.

more [mɔːr] ◇ adv - 1. (in comparatives): **more difficult (than)** schwieriger (als); **speak more clearly, please** sprich bitte deutlicher; **much more quickly** viel schneller - 2. [to a greater degree] mehr; **we ought to go to the cinema more** wir sollten öfters ins Kino gehen; **I couldn't agree more** ich stimme dem völlig zu; **she's more like a mother to me than a sister** sie ist mehr wie eine Mutter als wie eine Schwester; **we were more hurt than angry** wir waren eher verletzt als zornig; **we'd be more than happy to help** wir würden sehr gerne helfen; **more than ever** mehr denn je - 3. [referring to time]: **once/twice more** noch einmal/zweimal; **I don't go there any more** ich gehe da nicht mehr hin. ◇ adj - 1. [larger number, amount of] mehr; **there are more tourists than usual** es sind mehr Touristen als gewöhnlich; **more than ten men** mehr als zehn Männer - 2. [additional] mehr; **we need more money/time** wir brauchen mehr Geld/Zeit; **two more bottles** noch zwei Flaschen; **is there any more cake?** ist noch mehr Kuchen da?; **there's no more wine** es ist kein Wein mehr da; **have some more tea** nehmen Sie noch etwas Tee. ◇ pron - 1. [larger number, amount] mehr; **I've got more than you** ich habe mehr als du; **more than 20** mehr als 20 - 2. [additional amount] mehr; **we need more**

wir brauchen mehr; **I'd like two more** ich möchte noch zwei; **to see more of sb** jn öfter sehen; **is there any more?** ist noch mehr da?; **there's no more** es ist nichts mehr da; **I have no more (of them)** ich habe keine mehr; **have some more** nimm dir noch; **(and) what's more** außerdem; **the more he has, the more he wants** je mehr er hat, desto mehr will er haben. ➡ **more and more** ◇ adv - 1. [increasingly] immer mehr; **more and more depressed/difficult** immer deprimierter/schwieriger - 2. [increasingly often] immer mehr OR öfter. ◇ adj immer mehr; **there are more and more cars on the roads** es gibt immer mehr Autos auf den Straßen. ◇ pron immer mehr; **we are spending more and more on petrol** wir geben immer mehr für Benzin aus. ➡ **more or less** adv [almost] mehr oder weniger; **she more or less suggested I had stolen it** sie hat mehr oder weniger behauptet, dass ich es gestohlen hätte; **it cost $500, more or less** es kostete um die $500.

moreover [mɔːˈrəʊvə] adv fml außerdem.

morgue [mɔːg] n Leichenhalle die.

morning [ˈmɔːnɪŋ] n - 1. [first part of day] Morgen der, Vormittag der; **in the morning** [before lunch] morgens; [tomorrow morning] morgen - 2. [between midnight and noon] Morgen der. ➡ **mornings** adv US morgens.

Morocco [məˈrɒkəʊ] n Marokko nt.

moron [ˈmɔːrɒn] n inf Bekloppte der, die.

morose [məˈrəʊs] adj griesgrämig.

morphine [ˈmɔːfiːn] n Morphium das.

Morse (code) [mɔːs-] n (U) Morsezeichen Pl.

morsel [ˈmɔːsl] n Bissen der, Happen der.

mortal [ˈmɔːtl] ◇ adj - 1. [not eternal] sterblich - 2. [causing death] tödlich - 3. [danger, fear] Todes-; **mortal enemy** Todfeind der; **mortal combat** Kampf der um Leben und Tod. ◇ n Sterbliche der, die.

mortality [mɔːˈtælətɪ] n Sterblichkeit die.

mortar [ˈmɔːtə] n - 1. [cement mixture] Mörtel der - 2. [gun, bowl] Mörser der.

mortgage [ˈmɔːgɪdʒ] ◇ n Hypothek die. ◇ vt mit einer Hypothek belasten.

mortified [ˈmɔːtɪfaɪd] adj beschämt.

mortuary [ˈmɔːtʃʊərɪ] n Leichenhalle die.

mosaic [məˈzeɪɪk] n Mosaik das.

Moscow [ˈmɒskəʊ] n Moskau nt.

Moslem [ˈmɒzləm] adj & n = **Muslim**.

mosque [mɒsk] n Moschee die.

mosquito [məˈskiːtəʊ] (pl -es OR -s) n Moskito der.

moss [mɒs] n (U) Moos das.

most [məʊst] (superl of **many** & **much**) ◇ adj - 1. [the majority of] die meisten; **most people agree** die meisten Leute sind dieser Meinung - 2. [the largest amount of] der/die/das

meiste; **I drank (the) most beer** ich habe das meiste Bier getrunken. ◇ adv - 1. [in superlatives]: **she spoke (the) most clearly** sie sprach am deutlichsten; **the most expensive hotel in town** das teuerste Hotel in der Stadt - 2. [to the greatest degree] am meisten; **I like this one most** mir gefällt dieses am besten - 3. fml [very] äußerst, höchst; **it was a most pleasant evening** es war ein äußerst angenehmer Abend. ◇ pron - 1. [the majority] die meisten Pl; **most of the villages** die meisten Dörfer; **most of the time** die meiste Zeit; **most of the work** der größte Teil der Arbeit - 2. [the largest amount] das meiste; **she earns (the) most** sie verdient am meisten - 3. phr: **at most** höchstens; **to make the most of sthg** das Beste aus etw machen; **to make the most of an opportunity** eine Gelegenheit voll ausnutzen.

mostly [ˈməʊstlɪ] adv hauptsächlich.

MOT n (abbr of **Ministry of Transport (test)**) ≃ TÜV der.

motel [məʊˈtel] n Motel das.

moth [mɒθ] n Nachtfalter der; [eating clothes] Motte die.

mothball [ˈmɒθbɔːl] n Mottenkugel die.

mother [ˈmʌðə] ◇ n Mutter die. ◇ vt pej [spoil] bemuttern.

motherhood [ˈmʌðəhʊd] n Mutterschaft die.

mother-in-law (pl mothers-in-law OR mother-in-laws) n Schwiegermutter die.

motherly [ˈmʌðəlɪ] adj mütterlich.

mother-of-pearl n Perlmutt das.

mother-to-be (pl mothers-to-be) n werdende Mutter.

mother tongue n Muttersprache die.

motif [məʊˈtiːf] n [pattern] Muster das.

motion [ˈməʊʃn] ◇ n - 1. [movement] Bewegung die; **to set sthg in motion** etw in Bewegung setzen - 2. [proposal] Antrag der. ◇ vt & vi: **to motion (to) sb to do sthg** jm durch Zeichen zu verstehen geben, etw zu tun.

motionless [ˈməʊʃənlɪs] adj bewegungslos.

motion picture n US Film der.

motivated [ˈməʊtɪveɪtɪd] adj motiviert.

motivation [ˌməʊtɪˈveɪʃn] n Motivation die.

motive [ˈməʊtɪv] n Motiv das.

motor [ˈməʊtə] ◇ adj UK [relating to cars] Auto-. ◇ n [engine] Motor der.

motorbike [ˈməʊtəbaɪk] n inf Motorrad das.

motorboat [ˈməʊtəbəʊt] n Motorboot das.

motorcar [ˈməʊtəkɑː] n UK fml Automobil das.

motorcycle [ˈməʊtəsaɪkl] n Motorrad das.

motorcyclist [ˈməʊtəsaɪklɪst] n Motorradfahrer der, -in die.

motoring ['məʊtərɪŋ] *adj* UK [offence] Verkehrs-; [magazine] Auto-.

motorist ['məʊtərɪst] *n* Autofahrer *der*, -in *die*.

motor racing *n* Autorennen *das*.

motor scooter *n* Motorroller *der*.

motor vehicle *n* Kraftfahrzeug *das*.

motorway ['məʊtəweɪ] *n* UK Autobahn *die*.

mottled ['mɒtld] *adj* [leaf] gesprenkelt; [skin, face] fleckig.

motto ['mɒtəʊ] (*pl* -s *OR* -es) *n* [maxim] Motto *das*.

mould, mold US [məʊld] ◇ *n* - 1. [growth] Schimmel *der* - 2. [shape] Form *die*. ◇ *vt* formen.

mouldy, moldy US ['məʊldɪ] *adj* schimmelig.

moult, molt US [məʊlt] *vi* [bird] sich mausern; [animal] im Fellwechsel *OR* Haarwechsel sein.

mound [maʊnd] *n* - 1. [small hill] Hügel *der* - 2. [untidy pile] Haufen *der*; [of papers, blankets] Stapel *der*.

mount [maʊnt] ◇ *n* - 1. [support, frame - for photograph] Rahmen *der*; [- for jewel] Fassung *die*; [- for machine] Sockel *der* - 2. [horse, pony] Reittier *das* - 3. [mountain]: **Mount Everest** Mount Everest; **Mount Etna** Etna. ◇ *vt* - 1. [climb onto] besteigen - 2. *fml* [climb up - stairs] hochlsteigen - 3. [organize] organisieren - 4. [fix in place - jewel] einlfassen; [- photographic slide] rahmen; **to mount sthg on the wall** etw an die Wand hängen. ◇ *vi* [increase] sich erhöhen.

mountain ['maʊntɪn] *n liter & fig* Berg *der*.

mountain bike *n* Mountainbike *das*.

mountaineer [,maʊntɪ'nɪəʳ] *n* Bergsteiger *der*, -in *die*.

mountaineering [,maʊntɪ'nɪərɪŋ] *n* Bergsteigen *das*.

mountainous ['maʊntɪnəs] *adj* [full of mountains] bergig.

mourn [mɔːn] ◇ *vt* trauern um. ◇ *vi* trauern; **to mourn for sb** um jn trauern.

mourner ['mɔːnəʳ] *n* Trauernde *der*, *die*.

mournful ['mɔːnfʊl] *adj* traurig.

mourning ['mɔːnɪŋ] *n (phrase)*: **to be in mourning** [mourn] trauern; [wear mourning clothes] Trauerkleidung tragen.

mouse [maʊs] (*pl* mice) *n* [animal & COMPUT] Maus *die*.

mouse mat, mouse pad *n* COMPUT Mauspad *das*.

mousetrap ['maʊstræp] *n* Mausefalle *die*.

mousse [muːs] *n* - 1. [food] Mousse *die* - 2. [for hair] Schaumfestiger *der*.

moustache UK [mə'stɑːʃ], **mustache** US ['mʌstæʃ] *n* Schnurrbart *der*.

mouth *n* [maʊθ] - 1. [of person] Mund *der* - 2. [entrance - of cave, tunnel] Eingang *der*; [- of river] Mündung *die*.

mouthful ['maʊθfʊl] *n* [amount - of food] Bissen *der*; [- of drink] Schluck *der*.

mouthorgan ['maʊθ,ɔːgən] *n* Mundharmonika *die*.

mouthpiece ['maʊθpiːs] *n* - 1. [of telephone] Sprechmuschel *die* - 2. [of musical instrument] Mundstück *das* - 3. [spokesperson] Sprachrohr *das*.

mouthwash ['maʊθwɒʃ] *n (U)* Mundwasser *das*.

mouth-watering [-,wɔːtərɪŋ] *adj* appetitlich, appetitanregend.

movable ['muːvəbl] *adj* beweglich.

move [muːv] ◇ *n* - 1. [movement] Bewegung *die*; **to get a move on** *inf* sich beeilen - 2. [to new house] Umzug *der*; [to higher position in company] Aufstieg *der* - 3. [in board game] Zug *der*; **it's your move** du bist am Zug - 4. [course of action]: **it would be a good move** es wäre klug. ◇ *vt* - 1. [arm, head] bewegen; [piece of furniture] rücken; [car] weglfahren; [piece in board game] einen Zug machen mit - 2. [change]: **to move house** umlziehen; **to move sb to another job** jn versetzen - 3. [affect emotionally] bewegen, rühren - 4. [in debate]: **to move that...** beantragen, dass... - 5. *fml* [cause]: **to move sb to do sthg** jn dazu bewegen, etw zu tun. ◇ *vi* - 1. [shift] sich bewegen - 2. [act] handeln - 3. [to new house] umlziehen. ◆ **move about** *vi* - 1. [fidget] sich unruhig (hin und her) bewegen - 2. [travel] unterwegs sein. ◆ **move along** ◇ *vt sep* [person, crowds] zum Weitergehen veranlassen. ◇ *vi* weiterlgehen; [in car] weiterlfahren. ◆ **move around** *vi* = **move about**. ◆ **move away** *vi* [go in opposite direction] weglgehen; [car] weglfahren. ◆ **move in** *vi* - 1. [to new house] umlziehen - 2. [troops] einlrücken; [competitors] auf den Plan treten. ◆ **move on** *vi* - 1. [after stopping] weiterlgehen; [in car] weiterlfahren - 2. [in discussion] fortlfahren. ◆ **move out** *vi* [from house] auslziehen. ◆ **move over** *vi* zur Seite rutschen *OR* rücken. ◆ **move up** *vi* [on seat] auflrutschen, auflrücken.

moveable ['muːvəbl] *adj* = **movable**.

movement ['muːvmənt] *n* - 1. [motion, gesture, group] Bewegung *die* - 2. [transportation] Beförderung *die* - 3. [trend] Trend *der* - 4. MUS Satz *der*.

movie ['muːvɪ] *n esp* US Film *der*; **to go to the movies** zum Kino gehen.

movie camera *n* Filmkamera *die*.

moving ['muːvɪŋ] *adj* - 1. [touching] bewegend - 2. [not fixed] beweglich.

mow [məʊ] (*pt* -ed, *pp* -ed *OR* mown) *vt* mähen. ◆ **mow down** *vt sep* niederlmähen.

mower ['məʊəʳ] n [lawnmower] Rasenmäher der.

mown [məʊn] pp ▷ **mow**.

MP n UK abbr of **Member of Parliament**.

MP3 [ˌempiː'θriː] n (abbr of MPEG-1 Audio Layer-3) MP3.

MP3 player n MP3-Spieler der.

mpg (abbr of miles per gallon) n: **31 mpg** 9,1 l auf 100 km.

mph (abbr of miles per hour) n: **he was doing 50 mph** er fuhr 80 km/h (schnell).

Mr ['mɪstəʳ] n Herr.

Mrs ['mɪsɪz] n Frau, Fr.

MRSA [ˌemɑːres'eɪ] n MED (abbr of **methicillin resistant Staphylococcus aureus**) MRSA der.

Ms [mɪz] n Frau, Fr.

MS n (abbr of multiple sclerosis) MS.

MSc n abbr of **Master of Science**.

much [mʌtʃ] (comp **more**, superl **most**) ◇ adj viel; **I haven't got much money** ich habe nicht viel Geld; **as much food as you can eat** so viel du essen kannst; **how much is left?** wie viel ist übrig?; **we have too much work** wir haben zu viel Arbeit. ◇ adv - 1. [to a great extent] viel; **it's much better** es ist viel besser; **I like it very much** es gefällt mir sehr gut; **it's not much good** inf es ist nicht besonders; **nothing much** nichts Besonderes; **thank you very much** vielen Dank; **much as I like him** so gern ich ihn auch mag; **much to my surprise** sehr zu meiner Überraschung; **much the same** ziemlich das Gleiche; **he's not so much stupid as lazy** er ist weniger dumm als faul; **he left without so much as a goodbye** er hat sich nicht einmal verabschiedet - 2. [often] oft; **we don't go there much** wir gehen da nicht oft hin. ◇ pron viel; **I haven't got much** ich habe nicht viel; **as much as you like** so viel Sie wollen; **how much is it?** wie viel kostet es?; **you've got too much** du hast zu viel; **I don't think much of him** ich halte nicht viel von ihm; **I thought as much** das habe ich mir gedacht; **I'm not much of a cook** ich bin kein großer Koch; **so much for his friendship!** und das nennt sich Freundschaft!

muck [mʌk] n (U) inf - 1. [dirt] Dreck der - 2. [manure] Mist der. ◆ **muck about, muck around** UK inf ◇ vt sep an der Nase herumführen. ◇ vi herumalbern. ◆ **muck up** vt sep UK inf vermasseln.

mucky ['mʌkɪ] adj inf dreckig.

mucus ['mjuːkəs] n (U) Schleim der.

mud [mʌd] n Schlamm der.

muddle ['mʌdl] ◇ n [disorder] Durcheinander das. ◇ vt - 1. [put into disorder] durcheinander bringen - 2. [confuse - person] verwirren. ◆ **muddle along** vi vor sich (A) hin wursteln. ◆ **muddle through** vi sich

durch|wursteln OR durch|schlagen. ◆ **muddle up** vt sep durcheinander bringen.

muddy ['mʌdɪ] ◇ adj [floor, boots] schmutzig; [river] schlammig. ◇ vt fig [issue, situation] verworren machen.

mudguard ['mʌdgɑːd] n [on car] Kotflügel der; [on motorcycle] Schutzblech das.

muesli ['mjuːzlɪ] n UK Müsli das.

muff [mʌf] ◇ n [for hands] Muff der; [for ears] Ohrenwärmer der. ◇ vt inf verpatzen.

muffin ['mʌfɪn] n - 1. UK [bread roll] kleines flaches Milchbrötchen, das warm und mit Butter gegessen wird - 2. US [cake] kleiner Kuchen.

muffle ['mʌfl] vt [quieten] dämpfen.

muffler ['mʌfləʳ] n US [for car] Auspuff der.

mug [mʌg] ◇ n - 1. [cup, mugful] Tasse die - 2. inf [fool] Trottel der. ◇ vt [attack and rob] überfallen und berauben.

mugging ['mʌgɪŋ] n Straßenraub der.

muggy ['mʌgɪ] adj schwül.

mule [mjuːl] n - 1. [animal] Maultier das - 2. [slipper] Schlappen der.

mull [mʌl] ◆ **mull over** vt sep gründlich durch|denken.

mulled [mʌld] adj: **mulled wine** Glühwein der.

multicoloured UK, **multicolored** US ['mʌltɪˌkʌləd] adj bunt, mehrfarbig.

multilateral [ˌmʌltɪ'lætərəl] adj multilateral.

multilingual [ˌmʌltɪ'lɪŋgwəl] adj mehrsprachig.

multinational [ˌmʌltɪ'næʃənl] n multinationales Unternehmen.

multiple ['mʌltɪpl] ◇ adj vielfach. ◇ n MATHS Vielfache das.

multiple sclerosis [-sklɪ'rəʊsɪs] n (U) multiple Sklerose.

multiplex (cinema) ['mʌltɪpleks-] n großes Kino mit mehreren Vorführsälen.

multiplication [ˌmʌltɪplɪ'keɪʃn] n (U) - 1. MATHS Multiplikation die - 2. [increase] Vervielfachung die, Vermehrung die.

multiply ['mʌltɪplaɪ] ◇ vt - 1. MATHS multiplizieren - 2. [increase] vermehren. ◇ vi - 1. MATHS multiplizieren - 2. [increase] sich vervielfältigen - 3. [breed] sich vermehren.

multistorey UK, **multistory** US [ˌmʌltɪ'stɔːrɪ] adj mehrstöckig; **multistorey car park** Parkhaus das.

multitude ['mʌltɪtjuːd] n [large number] Vielzahl die.

mum [mʌm] UK inf ◇ n Mutter die; [within speaker's family] Mutti die. ◇ adj: **to keep mum** den Mund halten.

mumble ['mʌmbl] ⬦ vt [response] murmeln; [words] nuscheln. ⬦ vi vor sich (A) hin murmeln; **stop mumbling** hör auf zu nuscheln.

mummy ['mʌmɪ] n - 1. UK inf [mother] Mami die - 2. [preserved body] Mumie die.

mumps [mʌmps] n (U) Mumps der.

munch [mʌntʃ] vt & vi mampfen.

mundane [mʌn'deɪn] adj [ordinary] alltäglich.

municipal [mjuː'nɪsɪpl] adj städtisch; [park, administration] Stadt-.

municipality [mjuːˌnɪsɪ'pælətɪ] n Stadt die.

mural ['mjuːərəl] n Wandgemälde das.

murder ['mɜːdər] ⬦ n Mord der. ⬦ vt ermorden.

murderer ['mɜːdərər] n Mörder der, -in die.

murderous ['mɜːdərəs] adj [thugs] mordgierig; [attack] mörderisch.

murky ['mɜːkɪ] adj - 1. [dark - place] düster; [- water] trüb - 2. [shameful] dunkel, finster.

murmur ['mɜːmər] ⬦ n - 1. [low sound - of voices] Gemurmel das; [- of disapproving voices] Murmeln das - 2. MED [of heart] Herzgeräusch das. ⬦ vt & vi murmeln.

muscle ['mʌsl] n - 1. [organ] Muskel der - 2. (U) MED [tissue] Muskelgewebe das - 3. (U) fig [power] Macht die. ➤ **muscle in** vi mitlmischen.

muscular ['mʌskjʊlər] adj - 1. [of muscles] Muskel- - 2. [strong] muskulös.

muse [mjuːz] ⬦ n Muse die. ⬦ vi sinnieren.

museum [mjuː'zɪəm] n Museum das.

mushroom ['mʌʃrʊm] ⬦ n [cultivated] Pilz der, Champignon der. ⬦ vi [grow quickly - organization, movement] sehr schnell wachsen; [- houses] wie Pilze aus dem Boden schießen.

music ['mjuːzɪk] n - 1. [gen] Musik die; **a piece of music** ein Musikstück - 2. [subject studied] Musik die - 3. [written] Noten Pl.

musical ['mjuːzɪkl] ⬦ adj - 1. [education, director] Musik- - 2. [talented in music] musikalisch - 3. [voice, sound] melodiös. ⬦ n Musical das.

musical instrument n Musikinstrument das.

music centre n Kompaktanlage die.

music hall n UK Varieté das.

musician [mjuː'zɪʃn] n Musiker der, -in die.

Muslim ['mʊzlɪm] ⬦ adj moslemisch. ⬦ n Moslem der, Moslemin die.

mussel ['mʌsl] n Miesmuschel die.

must [mʌst] ⬦ aux vb müssen; [with negative] dürfen; **I must go** ich muss gehen; **you mustn't be late** du darfst nicht zu spät kommen; **do it, if you must** tu es, wenn es sein muss; **the room must be vacated by ten** das

Zimmer ist bis zehn Uhr zu räumen; **you must have seen it** du musst es doch gesehen haben; **you must see that film** du musst dir diesen Film ansehen; **you must be joking!** das kann doch nicht dein Ernst sein! ⬦ n: **it's a must** inf das ist ein Muss.

mustache n US = **moustache**.

mustard ['mʌstəd] n Senf der.

muster ['mʌstər] ⬦ vt - 1. [summon - strength, courage] zusammenlnehmen; [- support] zusammenlbekommen - 2. [assemble - volunteers, helpers] versammeln; [- troops] zusammenlziehen. ⬦ vi [troops] sich sammeln.

mustn't ['mʌsnt] abbr of **must not**.

must've ['mʌstəv] abbr of **must have**.

musty ['mʌstɪ] adj [smell, room, air] muffig; [books] moderig.

mute [mjuːt] adj [person] stumm.

muted ['mjuːtɪd] adj - 1. [sound, colour] gedämpft - 2. [protest] verhalten.

mutilate ['mjuːtɪleɪt] vt - 1. [maim] verstümmeln - 2. [damage, spoil] ruinieren.

mutiny ['mjuːtɪnɪ] ⬦ n Meuterei die. ⬦ vi meutern.

mutter ['mʌtər] ⬦ vt murmeln. ⬦ vi murmeln; [grumble] murren.

mutton ['mʌtn] n Hammelfleisch das.

mutual ['mjuːtʃʊəl] adj - 1. [aid] gegenseitig; **by mutual consent** in gegenseitigem Einverständnis - 2. [friend, interest] gemeinsam.

mutually ['mjuːtʃʊəlɪ] adv [reciprocally - beneficial, convenient] für beide Seiten; [- agreed] von beiden Seiten.

muzzle ['mʌzl] ⬦ n - 1. [dog's nose and jaws] Schnauze die - 2. [for dog] Maulkorb der - 3. [of gun] Mündung die. ⬦ vt - 1. [dog] einen Maulkorb anlegen (+ D) - 2. fig [press, opposition] knebeln.

MW (abbr of medium wave) MW.

my [maɪ] ⬦ poss adj mein; **my friend** mein Freund, meine Freundin; **my children** meine Kinder; **I washed my hair** ich habe mir die Haare gewaschen. ⬦ excl: **(oh) my!** meine Güte!

myself [maɪ'self] pron - 1. (reflexive: accusative) mich; (reflexive: dative) mir; **I have hurt myself** ich habe mich verletzt; **I bought myself some new clothes** ich habe mir neue Kleider gekauft - 2. (after prep: accusative) mich selbst; (after prep: dative) mir selbst; **I did it myself** ich habe es selbst gemacht; **by myself** allein.

mysterious [mɪ'stɪərɪəs] adj - 1. [puzzling - illness, sound] rätselhaft; [- disappearance] mysteriös - 2. [secretive] geheimnisvoll.

mystery ['mɪstərɪ] n - 1. [puzzle] Rätsel das - 2. [secret] Geheimnis das.

mystical ['mɪstɪkl] adj mystisch.

mystified ['mɪstɪfaɪd] *adj* verwirrt.

mystifying ['mɪstɪfaɪɪŋ] *adj* [action] rätsel-haft; [decision] unerklärlich.

mystique [mɪ'stiːk] *n* (U) geheimnisvoller Nimbus.

myth [mɪθ] *n* - 1. [legend] Mythos *der* - 2. [false belief] Irrglauben *der*.

mythical ['mɪθɪkl] *adj* - 1. [legendary] my-thisch - 2. [imaginary - place, time] fiktiv.

mythology [mɪ'θɒlədʒɪ] *n* Mythologie *die*.

N

n (*pl* n's OR ns), **N** (*pl* N's OR Ns) [en] *n* [letter] n *das*, N *das*. ➤ **N** (*abbr of* north) N.

n/a, N/A - 1. (*abbr of* not applicable) entf. - 2. (*abbr of* not available) n. bez.

nab [næb] *vt inf* - 1. [arrest] schnappen - 2. [claim quickly] sich (D) schnappen.

nag [næg] ◇ *vt* [pester] keine Ruhe lassen (+ D); [find fault with] herumlnörgeln an (+ D); **to nag sb to do sthg** jm zulsetzen, damit er/sie etw tut. ◇ *n UK inf* [horse] Klepper *der*.

nagging ['nægɪŋ] *adj* [thought, doubt, pain] quälend.

nail [neɪl] ◇ *n* [gen] Nagel *der*. ◇ *vt*: **to nail sthg to sthg** etw an etw (A) nageln. ➤ **nail down** *vt sep liter & fig* festlnageln.

nailbrush ['neɪlbrʌʃ] *n* Nagelbürste *die*.

nail clippers [-,klɪpəz] *npl* Nagelknip-ser *der*.

nail file *n* Nagelfeile *die*.

nail polish *n* Nagellack *der*.

nail scissors *npl* Nagelschere *die*.

nail varnish *n* Nagellack *der*.

nail varnish remover [-rɪ'muːvər] *n* Na-gellackentferner *der*.

naive, naïve [naɪ'iːv] *adj* naiv.

naked ['neɪkɪd] *adj* - 1. [nude] nackt - 2. [flame] offen; [light bulb] nackt; **with the na-ked eye** mit bloßem Auge - 3. [truth, aggres-sion] nackt.

name [neɪm] ◇ *n* - 1. [gen] Name *der*; **what's your name?** wie heißen Sie?; **my name is** ich heiße; **to know sb by name** jn mit Na-men kennen; **to know sb only by name** jn nur dem Namen nach kennen; **in the name of** im Namen (+ G); **the account is in her name** das Konto läuft auf ihren Namen; **to call sb names** jn beschimpfen - 2. [reputation] Name *der*, Ruf *der*; **to clear one's name** seine Unschuld beweisen. ◇ *vt* - 1. [baby, place, ship] einen

Namen geben (+ D); **they named their daugh-ter Kate** sie nannten ihre Tochter Kate; **I name this ship "Bounty"** ich taufe das Schiff auf den Namen "Bounty"; **to name sb after sb** *UK*, **to name sb for sb** *US* jn nach jm nen-nen; **to name sthg after sthg** *UK*, **to name sthg for sthg** *US* etw nach etw benennen - 2. [re-veal identity of]: **to name sb** js Namen nennen - 3. [choose - price, date] nennen; [- successor] ernennen.

namely ['neɪmlɪ] *adv* nämlich.

namesake ['neɪmseɪk] *n* Namensvetter *der*, -in *die*.

nanny ['nænɪ] *n* [childminder] Kindermäd-chen *das*.

nap [næp] ◇ *n* [sleep] Nickerchen *das*; **to take** OR **have a nap** ein Nickerchen machen. ◇ *vi* [sleep] ein Nickerchen machen; **to be caught napping** *inf* überrumpelt werden.

nape [neɪp] *n*: **nape (of the neck)** Nacken *der*.

napkin ['næpkɪn] *n* [serviette] Serviette *die*.

nappy ['næpɪ] *n UK* Windel *die*.

narcotic [nɑː'kɒtɪk] *n* Betäubungsmit-tel *das*. ➤ **narcotics** *npl* Rauschgift *das*.

narrative ['nærətɪv] ◇ *adj* [ability, skill] er-zählerisch; [poem] narrativ. ◇ *n* [account] Schilderung *die*.

narrator [*UK* nə'reɪtər, *US* 'næreɪtər] *n* [in book] Erzähler *der*, -in *die*; [of documentary] Kommentator *der*, -in *die*.

narrow ['nærəʊ] ◇ *adj* - 1. [not wide] schmal; [valley, lane] eng - 2. [attitude, beliefs] engstirnig - 3. [victory, defeat, majority] knapp. ◇ *vt* - 1. [almost shut]: **to narrow one's eyes** die Augen zu Schlitzen verengen - 2. [differ-ence, gap] verringern. ◇ *vi* - 1. [become less wide] sich verengen - 2. [eyes] zu Schlitzen werden - 3. [difference, gap] sich verringern. ➤ **narrow down** *vt sep* [restrict - choice] einl-schränken; [- possibilities] beschränken.

narrowly ['nærəʊlɪ] *adv* [just] knapp; [escape] mit knapper Not.

narrow-minded [-'maɪndɪd] *adj* engstirnig.

nasal ['neɪzl] *adj* - 1. [sound] näselnd - 2. ANAT Nasen-.

nasty ['nɑːstɪ] *adj* - 1. [unkind - person, beha-viour] gemein; [- remark] gehässig - 2. [smell, taste, weather] scheußlich - 3. [problem, ques-tion] schwierig - 4. [injury, accident, fall] schlimm.

nation ['neɪʃn] *n* Nation *die*; [people] Volk *das*.

national ['næʃənl] ◇ *adj* - 1. [nationwide - strike] national, landesweit; [- newspaper] überregional; [- library, debt] Staats- - 2. [typical of nation] landestypisch; [custom] Volks-. ◇ *n* Staatsbürger *der*, -in *die*.

national anthem *n* Nationalhymne *die*.

national curriculum n Programm, das die Fächer und zu erreichenden Standards in den staatlichen Schulen in England und Wales festlegt.

national dress n Landestracht die.

National Health Service n staatlicher britischer Gesundheitsdienst.

National Insurance n (U) UK - 1. [system] Sozialversicherung die - 2. [payments] Sozialversicherungsbeiträge Pl.

nationalism ['næʃnəlɪzm] n Nationalismus der.

nationalist ['næʃnəlɪst] <> adj nationalistisch. <> n Nationalist der, -in die.

nationality [ˌnæʃə'nælətɪ] n Nationalität die.

nationalize, -ise ['næʃnəlaɪz] vt verstaatlichen.

national service n Wehrdienst der.

National Trust n britische Organisation, die im Besitz historischer Bauwerke ist und diese unterhält.

nationwide ['neɪʃənwaɪd] adj & adv landesweit.

native ['neɪtɪv] <> adj [customs, population, plant] einheimisch; **native country** Heimatland das; **a native Italian** ein gebürtiger Italiener; **native speaker** Muttersprachler der; **native language** Muttersprache die; (phrase): **native to** [plant, animal] beheimatet in (+ D). <> n [person] Einheimische der, die; offens [of colony] Eingeborene der, die.

Native American n Indianer der, -in die.

Nativity [nə'tɪvətɪ] n: **the Nativity** die Geburt Christi.

NATO ['neɪtəʊ] (abbr of North Atlantic Treaty Organization) n NATO die.

natural ['nætʃrəl] adj - 1. [gen] natürlich - 2. [inborn - instinct, skill] angeboren; [- footballer, musician etc] geboren - 3. [disaster, phenomenon] Natur-.

natural gas n Erdgas das.

naturalize, -ise ['nætʃrəlaɪz] vt [make citizen] einbürgern.

naturally ['nætʃrəlɪ] adv - 1. [of course] natürlich - 2. [behave, speak] natürlich - 3. [cheerful, talented] von Natur aus.

natural yoghurt n Naturjogurt der ODER das ODER die.

nature ['neɪtʃər] n - 1. [gen] Natur die - 2. [temperament] Wesen das; **by nature** von Natur aus - 3. [type] Art die.

nature reserve n Naturschutzgebiet das.

naughty ['nɔːtɪ] adj - 1. [child] ungezogen - 2. [word, story] unanständig.

nausea ['nɔːsɪə] n Übelkeit die.

nauseating ['nɔːzɪeɪtɪŋ] adj fig [disgusting] abscheulich.

nautical ['nɔːtɪkl] adj nautisch; [map] See-; [term] seemännisch.

naval ['neɪvl] adj Marine-; [battle, forces] See-.

nave [neɪv] n Kirchenschiff das.

navel ['neɪvl] n Nabel der.

navigate ['nævɪgeɪt] <> vt [steer - plane, ship] navigieren. <> vi [in plane, ship] navigieren; **I'll drive, and you navigate** ich fahre, und du dirigierst mich.

navigation [ˌnævɪ'geɪʃn] n Navigation die.

navigator ['nævɪgeɪtər] n Navigator der.

navy ['neɪvɪ] n [armed force] (Kriegs)marine die.

navy (blue) <> adj marineblau. <> n Marineblau das.

Nazi ['nɑːtsɪ] (pl -s) n Nazi der.

NB (abbr of nota bene) NB.

near [nɪər] <> adj nahe; **in the near future** demnächst; **the nearest hospital** das nächste Krankenhaus; **a near disaster** beinahe ein Unglück; **it was a near thing (for us)** wir sind gerade noch davongekommen. <> adv nahe; **near at hand** (ganz) in der Nähe; **to come** OR **draw near to sb/sthg** sich jm/etw nähern; **a near impossible task** eine nahezu unmögliche Aufgabe. <> prep: **near (to)** nahe an (+ D); **near the door** bei der Tür; **near to death/despair** dem Tode/der Verzweiflung nahe. <> vt sich nähern (+ D); **the road is nearing completion** die Straße ist fast fertig. <> vi sich nähern.

nearby [nɪə'baɪ] <> adj nahe gelegen. <> adv in der Nähe.

nearly ['nɪəlɪ] adv [almost] fast, beinahe; **I nearly fell** ich bin fast OR beinahe gefallen; **not nearly** bei weitem nicht.

near miss n [between aircraft] Beinahezusammenstoß der.

nearside ['nɪəsaɪd] n Beifahrerseite die.

nearsighted [ˌnɪə'saɪtɪd] adj US kurzsichtig.

neat [niːt] adj - 1. [tidy] ordentlich; [sb's appearance] adrett - 2. [skilful - solution] elegant; [- manoeuvre] geschickt - 3. [whisky, vodka etc] pur - 4. US inf [very good] super.

neatly ['niːtlɪ] adv - 1. [tidily] ordentlich; [dress] adrett - 2. [skilfully] geschickt.

necessarily [ˌnesə'serɪlɪ, UK 'nesəsrəlɪ] adv notwendigerweise; **not necessarily** nicht unbedingt.

necessary ['nesəsrɪ] adj - 1. [required] notwendig, nötig; **to make it necessary for sb to do sthg** es erforderlich machen, dass jd etw tut - 2. [inevitable] unausweichlich.

necessity [nɪ'sesətɪ] n - 1. [need] Notwendigkeit die; **of necessity** notwendigerweise - 2. [necessary thing] Notwendigkeit die.

neck [nek] n - 1. [gen] Hals der - 2. [of shirt] Kragen der; [of dress] Ausschnitt der. ◆ **neck**

and neck adj gleichauf; **the two horses are neck and neck** zwischen den beiden Pferden gibt es ein Kopf-an-Kopf-Rennen.

necklace ['neklɪs] n (Hals)kette die.

neckline ['neklaɪn] n Ausschnitt der.

necktie ['nektaɪ] n US Krawatte die.

nectarine ['nektərɪn] n Nektarine die.

need [niːd] ⬦ n - **1.** [requirement, necessity] Bedürfnis das; **to be in** OR **have need of sthg** etw brauchen; **in need of repair** reparaturbedürftig; **there is no need (for you) to cry** du brauchst nicht zu weinen; **if need be** notfalls - **2.** [distress, poverty] Not die. ⬦ vt brauchen; **to need to do sthg** etw tun müssen; **you don't need to wait for me** du brauchst nicht auf mich zu warten; **that's all I need!** fig das hat mir gerade noch gefehlt! ⬦ aux vb: **need we go?** müssen wir gehen?; **it need not happen** es muss nicht dazu kommen.

needle ['niːdl] n Nadel die.

needless ['niːdlɪs] adj unnötig; **needless to say** selbstverständlich.

needlework ['niːdlwɜːk] n (U) Handarbeit die.

needn't ['niːdnt] abbr of need not.

needy ['niːdɪ] adj bedürftig.

negative ['negətɪv] ⬦ adj - **1.** [not affirmative] negativ - **2.** [pessimistic] pessimistisch. ⬦ n - **1.** PHOT Negativ das - **2.** LING Verneinung die; [word] Verneinungswort das; **to answer in the negative** mit "Nein" antworten.

neglect [nɪ'glekt] ⬦ n Vernachlässigung die. ⬦ vt - **1.** [not take care of] vernachlässigen - **2.** [not do - duty] versäumen; [- task, work] unerledigt lassen; **to neglect to do sthg** es versäumen, etw zu tun.

negligee ['neglɪʒeɪ] n Negligee das.

negligence ['neglɪdʒəns] n Nachlässigkeit die; [causing danger & LAW] Fahrlässigkeit die.

negligible ['neglɪdʒəbl] adj unerheblich.

negotiate [nɪ'gəʊʃɪeɪt] ⬦ vt - **1.** [agreement, deal] aushandeln - **2.** [obstacle] überwinden; [bend] nehmen; [hill, rapids] passieren. ⬦ vi verhandeln; **to negotiate with sb for sthg** mit jm über etw (A) verhandeln.

negotiation [nɪˌgəʊʃɪ'eɪʃn] n Verhandlung die.

neigh [neɪ] vi wiehern.

neighbor etc n US = **neighbour** etc .

neighbour UK, **neighbor** US ['neɪbə] n Nachbar der, -in die; [at table] Tischnachbar der, -in die; [country] Nachbarland das.

neighbourhood UK, **neighborhood** US ['neɪbəhʊd] n [small area of town] Gegend die; [people] Nachbarschaft die; (phrase): **it costs in the neighbourhood of £3,000** [approximately] es kostet so um die 3000 Pfund.

neighbouring UK, **neighboring** US ['neɪbərɪŋ] adj angrenzend.

neighbourly UK, **neighborly** US ['neɪbəlɪ] adj [relations, deed] gutnachbarlich.

neither ['naɪðə, 'niːðə] ⬦ adj: **neither bag is big enough** keine der beiden Taschen ist groß genug. ⬦ pron: **neither of us** keiner von uns beiden. ⬦ conj: **neither do I** ich auch nicht; **neither nor** weder noch; **that's neither here nor there** fig das hat nichts mit der Sache zu tun.

neon light n Neonlicht das.

nephew ['nefjuː] n Neffe der.

Neptune ['neptjuːn] n [planet] Neptun der.

nerd [nɜːd] n inf: **computer nerd** Computerfreak der.

nerve [nɜːv] n - **1.** ANAT Nerv der - **2.** [courage] Mut der; **to lose/keep one's nerve** seine Nerven verlieren/behalten - **3.** [cheek] Frechheit die. ⬦ **nerves** npl Nerven pl; **to get on sb's nerves** jm auf die Nerven gehen.

nerve-racking [-ˌrækɪŋ] adj nervenaufreibend.

nervous ['nɜːvəs] adj [condition, twitch] nervös; [tissue, illness] Nerven-; **to be nervous of** Angst haben vor (+ D); **to be nervous about sthg** nervös wegen etw sein.

nervous breakdown n Nervenzusammenbruch der.

nest [nest] ⬦ n - **1.** [gen] Nest das - **2.** [of tables] Satz der. ⬦ vi [bird] nisten.

nest egg n [money] Notgroschen der.

nestle ['nesl] vi [make o.s. comfortable] es sich bequem machen.

net [net] ⬦ adj - **1.** [profit, weight] Netto-, netto - **2.** [final] End-. ⬦ n [gen] Netz das. ⬦ vt - **1.** [catch] mit dem Netz fangen - **2.** fig [husband] sich (D) angeln; [criminal] fangen; [fortune] verdienen - **3.** [profit, sum - subj: deal] netto einbringen; [- subj: person] netto einnehmen. ⬦ **Net** n COMPUT: **the Net** das Internet.

netball ['netbɔːl] n Korbball der.

net curtains npl Tüllgardinen pl.

Netherlands ['neðələndz] npl: **the Netherlands** die Niederlande pl.

nett [net] adj = **net**.

netting ['netɪŋ] n (U) - **1.** [gen] Netz das; [metal] Maschendraht der - **2.** [fabric] Tüll der.

nettle ['netl] n Nessel die.

network ['netwɜːk] n - **1.** [gen] Netz das - **2.** RADIO & TV [station] Sendenetz das - **3.** COMPUT Netzwerk das.

neurosis [ˌnjʊə'rəʊsɪs] (pl -ses [siːz]) n Neurose die.

neurotic [ˌnjʊə'rɒtɪk] ⬦ adj neurotisch. ⬦ n Neurotiker der, -in die.

neuter ['njuːtə] ⬦ adj GRAM sächlich. ⬦ vt [animal] kastrieren.

neutral ['nju:trəl] <> adj - **1.** POL & ELEC neutral - **2.** [inexpressive] ausdruckslos - **3.** [pale grey-brown] naturfarben - **4.** [colourless] farblos. <> n (U) AUT Leerlauf der; **in neutral** im Leerlauf.

neutrality [nju:'trælətɪ] n POL Neutralität die.

neutralize, -ise ['nju:trəlaɪz] vt [effects] neutralisieren.

never ['nevər] adv nie; (simple negative) nicht; **she's never late** sie kommt nie zu spät; **he never said a word about it** er hat gar nichts davon gesagt; **never mind!** macht nichts!; **you've never asked him to dinner!** [in disbelief] hast du ihn wirklich zum Essen eingeladen?; **well I never!** na so was!

never-ending adj endlos.

nevertheless [,nevəðə'les] adv trotzdem.

new adj [nju:] neu; **as good as new** so gut wie neu. <> **news** n [nju:z] (U) - **1.** [information] Nachricht die; **that's news to me** das ist mir neu - **2.** RADIO & TV Nachrichten Pl.

newborn ['nju:bɔ:n] adj neugeboren.

newcomer ['nju:,kʌmər] n: **newcomer (to sthg)** Neuling der (in etw (D)).

newfangled [,nju:'fæŋgld] adj inf pej neumodisch.

new-found adj [confidence, strength] neu gefunden.

newly ['nju:lɪ] adv neu; **newly painted** frisch gestrichen.

newlyweds ['nju:lɪwedz] npl Frischvermählte Pl.

new moon n Neumond der.

news agency n Nachrichtenagentur die.

newsagent UK ['nju:zeɪdʒənt], **newsdealer** US ['nju:zdi:lər] n Zeitungshändler der, -in die; **newsagent's (shop)** Zeitungshändler der.

newsflash ['nju:zflæʃ] n Kurzmeldung die.

newsletter ['nju:z,letər] n Rundschreiben das, Mitteilungsblatt das.

newspaper ['nju:z,peɪpər] n - **1.** [publication, company] Zeitung die - **2.** [paper] Zeitungspapier das.

newsreader ['nju:z,ri:dər] n Nachrichtensprecher der, -in die.

newsstand ['nju:zstænd] n Zeitungskiosk der.

newt [nju:t] n Wassermolch der.

New Year n Neujahr das; **Happy New Year!** frohes neues Jahr!

New Year's Day n Neujahrstag der.

New Year's Eve n Silvester der ODER das.

New York [-'jɔ:k] n New York nt.

New Zealand [-'zi:lənd] n Neuseeland nt.

New Zealander [-'zi:ləndər] n Neuseeländer der, -in die.

next [nekst] <> adj nächste(r) (s); **when does the next bus leave?** wann fährt der nächste Bus ab? <> adv - **1.** [afterwards] als nächstes, danach - **2.** [on next occasion] das nächste Mal; **the week after next** übernächste Woche - **3.** (with superlatives): **the next most expensive** der/die/das nächstteuerste; **the next best thing to do would be to...** das nächstbeste wäre, zu... <> pron: **next please!** der Nächste bitte! ⏩ **next to** prep - **1.** [near] neben - **2.** [in comparisons]: **next to music I like the theatre best** nach Musik mag ich Theater am liebsten - **3.** [almost] fast; **next to nothing** fast nichts; **I got it for next to nothing** ich habe es fast umsonst bekommen.

next door adv nebenan. ⏩ **next-door** adj: **next-door neighbour** direkter Nachbar, direkte Nachbarin.

next of kin n nächste Angehörige der, die.

NHS n abbr of **National Health Service**.

NI n abbr of **National Insurance**.

nib [nɪb] n Feder die.

nibble ['nɪbl] vt knabbern.

nice [naɪs] adj - **1.** [car, picture, weather] schön; [dress] hübsch; [food] gut; **to have a nice time** Spaß haben; **it's nice and warm** es ist schön warm - **2.** [kind, pleasant] nett, sympathisch; **to be nice to sb** nett zu jm sein.

nice-looking [-'lʊkɪŋ] adj [person] gut aussehend; [car, house] schön.

nicely ['naɪslɪ] adv - **1.** [well, attractively - dressed, decorated] hübsch; [- made] schön - **2.** [politely - ask] höflich; [- behave] gut - **3.** [satisfactorily] gut; **that will do nicely** das ist genau richtig.

niche [ni:ʃ] n [in wall] Nische die.

nick [nɪk] <> n - **1.** [cut] Kerbe die, Einkerbung die - **2.** UK inf [condition]: **to be in good/bad nick** [object] gut/schlecht erhalten sein; [person] in guter/schlechter Verfassung sein - **3.** phr: **in the nick of time** in letzter Minute. <> vt - **1.** [cut - wood] einkerben - **2.** UK inf [steal] klauen - **3.** UK inf [arrest] schnappen.

nickel ['nɪkl] n - **1.** [metal] Nickel das - **2.** US [coin] Fünfcentstück die.

nickname ['nɪkneɪm] n Spitzname der.

nicotine ['nɪkəti:n] n Nikotin das.

niece [ni:s] n Nichte die.

niggle ['nɪgl] vt [worry] zu schaffen machen (+ D).

night [naɪt] n - **1.** [not day] Nacht die; **at night** nachts - **2.** [evening] Abend der; **at night** abends - **3.** phr: **to have an early/a late night** früh/spät ins Bett gehen. ⏩ **nights** adv - **1.** US [at night] nachts - **2.** UK [night shift]: **to work nights** Nachtschicht arbeiten.

nightcap ['naɪtkæp] n [drink] Schlummertrunk der.

nightclub ['naɪtklʌb] n Nightclub der.

nightdress ['naɪtdres] n Nachthemd das.

nightfall ['naɪtfɔːl] n: at nightfall bei Einbruch der Dunkelheit.

nightgown ['naɪtgaʊn] n Nachthemd das.

nightie ['naɪtɪ] n inf Nachthemd das.

nightingale ['naɪtɪŋgeɪl] n Nachtigall die.

nightlife ['naɪtlaɪf] n Nachtleben das.

nightly ['naɪtlɪ] <> adj nächtlich. <> adv [every evening] jeden Abend; [every night] jede Nacht.

nightmare ['naɪtmeəʳ] n liter & fig Albtraum der.

night porter n Nachtportier der.

night school n (U) Abendschule die.

night shift n Nachtschicht die.

nightshirt ['naɪtʃɜːt] n Nachthemd das (für Herren).

nighttime ['naɪttaɪm] n (U) Nacht die.

nil [nɪl] n - 1. [nothing] null - 2. UK SPORT: two nil zwei zu null.

Nile [naɪl] n: the Nile der Nil.

nimble ['nɪmbl] adj - 1. [person] wendig; [fingers] geschickt - 2. [mind] beweglich.

nine [naɪn] num neun; see also six.

nineteen [,naɪn'tiːn] num neunzehn; see also six.

ninety ['naɪntɪ] num neunzig; see also sixty.

ninth [naɪnθ] num neunte(r) (s); see also sixth.

nip [nɪp] <> n - 1. [bite] leichter Biss; [pinch] Kniff der - 2. [of drink] Schluck der. <> vt [bite] beißen; [pinch] kneifen.

nipple ['nɪpl] n - 1. [of breast] Brustwarze die - 2. [of baby's bottle] Schnuller der.

nit [nɪt] n - 1. [in hair] Nisse die - 2. UK inf [idiot] Blödmann der.

nitpicking ['nɪtpɪkɪŋ] n inf (U) Spitzfindigkeit die.

nitrogen ['naɪtrədʒən] n Stickstoff der.

nitty-gritty [,nɪtɪ'grɪtɪ] n inf: to get down to the nitty-gritty zur Sache kommen.

no [nəʊ] (pl -es) <> adv nein; to answer no mit einem Nein antworten; I am no richer than he is ich bin nicht reicher als er. <> adj kein; I have no money left ich habe kein Geld übrig; it's no easy job es ist keine leichte Aufgabe; it's no good OR use es nützt nichts; in no time im Nu; 'no smoking' 'Rauchen verboten'; no way! inf auf keinen Fall! <> n Nein das; she won't take no for an answer sie lässt sich nicht davon abbringen.

No., no. (abbr of number) Nr.

nobility [nə'bɪlətɪ] n - 1. [aristocracy]: the nobility der Adel - 2. [nobleness] Vornehmheit die.

noble ['nəʊbl] adj - 1. [aristocratic] adlig - 2. [fine, distinguished] edel, nobel.

nobody ['nəʊbədɪ] <> pron niemand; nobody else can do it das kann sonst keiner. <> n pej Niemand der.

no-claim(s) bonus n Schadenfreiheitsrabatt der.

nocturnal [nɒk'tɜːnl] adj - 1. [at night] nächtlich - 2. [animal] Nacht-.

nod [nɒd] <> vt: to nod one's head mit dem Kopf nicken. <> vi nicken; to nod to sb jm zulnicken. ◆ nod off vi einlnicken.

noise [nɔɪz] n - 1. [sound] Geräusch das - 2. (U) [unpleasant sound] Krach der.

noisy ['nɔɪzɪ] adj laut.

nominal ['nɒmɪnl] adj - 1. [in name only] nominell - 2. [very small] gering.

nominate ['nɒmɪneɪt] vt - 1. [propose]: to nominate sb (for/as sthg) jn (für/als etw) nominieren - 2. [appoint]: to nominate sb to sthg jn zu etw ernennen.

nominee [,nɒmɪ'niː] n Kandidat der, -in die.

non- [nɒn] prefix [with noun] Nicht-; [with adj] nicht-.

nonalcoholic [,nɒnælkə'hɒlɪk] adj nicht alkoholisch, ohne Alkohol.

nonaligned [,nɒnə'laɪnd] adj blockfrei.

nonchalant [UK 'nɒnʃələnt, US ,nɒnʃə'lɑːnt] adj nonchalant, lässig.

noncommittal [,nɒnkə'mɪtl] adj [reply, attitude] unverbindlich; he was noncommittal er legte sich nicht fest.

nonconformist [,nɒnkən'fɔːmɪst] <> adj nonkonformistisch. <> n Nonkonformist der, -in die.

nondescript [UK 'nɒndɪskrɪpt, US ,nɒndɪ'skrɪpt] adj unscheinbar.

none [nʌn] <> pron [not any] keine(r) (s); none of us keiner von uns; none of the money nichts von dem Geld; I'll have none of your nonsense ich will nichts von dem Unsinn hören; it is none of his business es geht ihn gar nichts an. <> adv: I'm none the wiser ich bin um nichts schlauer geworden; like him none the worse for it ich mag ihn deshalb nicht weniger. ◆ none too adv: none too soon keine Minute zu früh.

nonentity [nɒ'nentətɪ] n Null die.

nonetheless [,nʌnðə'les] adv nichtsdestoweniger.

non-event n Reinfall der.

nonexistent [,nɒnɪg'zɪstənt] adj nicht existierend; to be nonexistent nicht existieren.

nonfiction [,nɒn'fɪkʃn] n (U) Sachliteratur die.

no-nonsense adj sachlich.

nonpayment [,nɒn'peɪmənt] n (U) Nichtzahlung die.

nonplussed, nonplused US [,nɒn'plʌst] adj verblüfft.

nonreturnable [,nɒnrɪ'tɜːnəbl] adj [bottle] Einweg-.

nonsense ['nɒnsəns] <> *n (U)* - **1.** [meaningless words, foolish idea] Unsinn *der* - **2.** [foolish behaviour] Dummheiten *Pl.* <> *excl* Unsinn!

nonsensical [nɒn'sensɪkl] *adj* unsinnig.

nonsmoker [ˌnɒn'sməʊkəʳ] *n* Nichtraucher *der*, -in *die*.

nonstick [ˌnɒn'stɪk] *adj* antihaftbeschichtet.

nonstop [ˌnɒn'stɒp] <> *adj* [flight, race] Nonstop-; [activity, rain] ohne Unterbrechung. <> *adv* ununterbrochen.

noodles ['nuːdlz] *npl* Nudeln *Pl.*

nook [nʊk] *n* [of room] Winkel *der*; **in every nook and cranny** in allen Ecken OR Winkeln.

noon [nuːn] *n* Mittag *der*.

no one *pron* = **nobody**.

noose [nuːs] *n* Schlinge *die*.

no-place *adv* US = **nowhere**.

nor [nɔːʳ] *conj* auch nicht; **nor do I** ich auch nicht; **I don't know, nor do I care** das weiß ich nicht, und es ist mir auch egal.

norm [nɔːm] *n* Norm *die*.

normal ['nɔːml] *adj* normal.

normality [nɔː'mælɪtɪ] *n* Normalität *die*.

normally ['nɔːməlɪ] *adv* - **1.** [usually] normalerweise - **2.** [in a normal way] normal.

north [nɔːθ] <> *adj* Nord-. <> *adv* nach Norden; **north of** nördlich von. <> *n* Norden *der*.

North Africa *n* Nordafrika *nt*.

North America *n* Nordamerika *nt*.

North American <> *adj* nordamerikanisch. <> *n* Nordamerikaner *der*, -in *die*.

northeast [ˌnɔːθ'iːst] <> *n* Nordosten *der*. <> *adj* nordöstlich, Nordost-. <> *adv* nordostwärts; **northeast of** nordöstlich von.

northerly ['nɔːðəlɪ] *adj* [direction] nördlich; [area] im Norden; [wind] Nord-.

northern ['nɔːðən] *adj* [region, dialect] nördlich; [Europe] Nord-.

Northern Ireland *n* Nordirland *nt*.

northernmost ['nɔːðənməʊst] *adj* nördlichste(r) (s).

North Pole *n*: **the North Pole** der Nordpol.

North Sea *n*: **the North Sea** die Nordsee.

northward ['nɔːθwəd] <> *adj* [migration] nördlich. <> *adv* = **northwards**.

northwards ['nɔːθwədz] *adv* nach Norden.

northwest [ˌnɔːθ'west] <> *n* Nordwesten *der*. <> *adj* nordwestlich, Nordwest-. <> *adv* nordwestwärts; **northwest of** nordwestlich von.

Norway ['nɔːweɪ] *n* Norwegen *nt*.

Norwegian [nɔː'wiːdʒən] <> *adj* norwegisch. <> *n* - **1.** [person] Norweger *der*, -in *die* - **2.** [language] Norwegisch(e) *das*.

nose [nəʊz] *n* [of person] Nase *die*; **it's under your nose** es ist vor deiner Nase; **to keep one's nose out of sthg** sich aus etw heraushalten;

to look down one's nose at sb/sthg *fig* von oben auf jn/etw herabschauen; **to poke** OR **stick one's nose into sthg** *inf* seine Nase in etw (A) stecken; **to turn up one's nose at sthg** seine Nase über etw (A) rümpfen. ◆ **nose about, nose around** *vi* herumschnüffeln.

nosebleed ['nəʊzbliːd] *n* Nasenbluten *das*.

nosey ['nəʊzɪ] *adj* = **nosy**.

nostalgia [nɒ'stældʒə] *n (U)* Nostalgie *die*; **nostalgia for sthg** Sehnsucht *die* nach etw.

nostril ['nɒstrəl] *n* Nasenloch *das*.

nosy ['nəʊzɪ] *adj* neugierig.

not [nɒt] *adv* nicht; **she's not there** sie ist nicht da; **not any** kein; **not yet** noch nicht; **not at all** [pleased, interested] überhaupt nicht; [in reply to thanks] gern geschehen; **not that I'm afraid of him** nicht etwa, dass ich Angst vor ihm habe; **not to worry!** keine Sorge!

notable ['nəʊtəbl] *adj* [person] bedeutend; [success] bemerkenswert; [improvement] beachtlich, beträchtlich; **to be notable for sthg** durch etw auffallen; **with the notable exception of** mit Ausnahme von.

notably ['nəʊtəblɪ] *adv* - **1.** [in particular] vor allem - **2.** [noticeably] deutlich.

notary ['nəʊtərɪ] *n*: **notary (public)** Notar *der*, -in *die*.

notch [nɒtʃ] *n* [cut] Kerbe *die*.

note [nəʊt] <> *n* - **1.** [short letter] Zettel *der* - **2.** [written reminder, record] Notiz *die*; **to take note of sthg** etw bemerken - **3.** [paper money] Geldschein *der*; **a £5 note** eine Fünfpfundnote - **4.** [MUS - symbol] Note *die*; [- sound] Klang *der* - **5.** [tone] Ton *der*. <> *vt* - **1.** [observe] bemerken - **2.** [mention] erwähnen. ◆ **notes** *npl* [in book] Anmerkungen *Pl.* ◆ **note down** *vt sep* aufschreiben.

notebook ['nəʊtbʊk] *n* - **1.** [for writing in] Notizbuch *das* - **2.** COMPUT Notebook *das*.

noted ['nəʊtɪd] *adj*: **noted (for sthg)** bekannt (für etw).

notepad ['nəʊtpæd] *n* Notizblock *der*.

notepaper ['nəʊtpeɪpəʳ] *n* Briefpapier *das*.

noteworthy ['nəʊtˌwɜːðɪ] *adj* bemerkenswert.

nothing ['nʌθɪŋ] <> *pron* nichts; **nothing new/interesting** nichts Neues/Interessantes; **for nothing** [for free] umsonst; [in vain] vergeblich; **she is nothing if not discreet** diskret ist sie auf jeden Fall; **nothing but** nichts als; **he does nothing but complain** er beschwert sich dauernd; **he thinks nothing of walking ten miles** es macht ihm nichts aus, zehn Meilen zu gehen. <> *adv*: **nothing like** [very unlike] ganz anders als; **nothing like enough** lange nicht genug; **nothing like as good** längst nicht so gut.

notice ['nəʊtɪs] <> *n* - **1.** [piece of paper - announcing sthg] Ankündigung *die*; [- informing of sthg] Mitteilung *die* - **2.** [attention]: **it es-**

caped her notice es entging ihrer Aufmerksamkeit; **to take notice/no notice of sb/sthg** jn/etw beachten/nicht beachten - **3.** (U) [warning] Bescheid der; **at short notice** kurzfristig; **until further notice** bis auf Weiteres - **4.** [at work]: **to be given one's notice** gekündigt werden; **to hand in one's notice** seine Kündigung einlreichen. <> vt bemerken.

noticeable ['nəʊtɪsəbl] adj deutlich.

notice board n Anschlagbrett das.

notify ['nəʊtɪfaɪ] vt: **to notify sb (of sthg)** jn benachrichtigen (über etw (A)).

notion ['nəʊʃn] n [concept, idea] Idee die, Vorstellung die. ⬢ **notions** npl US [haberdashery] Kurzwaren Pl.

notorious [nəʊ'tɔːrɪəs] adj [person] berühmt; [criminal, event] berühmt-berüchtigt; [place] verrufen.

notwithstanding [ˌnɒtwɪθ'stændɪŋ] fml <> prep trotz (+ G). <> adv trotzdem.

nought [nɔːt] num Null die; **noughts and crosses** Kreuzchen- und Kringelspiel das.

noun [naʊn] n Substantiv das.

nourish ['nʌrɪʃ] vt [feed] ernähren.

nourishing ['nʌrɪʃɪŋ] adj nahrhaft.

nourishment ['nʌrɪʃmənt] n Nahrung die.

novel ['nɒvl] <> adj neuartig. <> n Roman der.

novelist ['nɒvəlɪst] n Romanschriftsteller der, -in die.

novelty ['nɒvltɪ] n - **1.** [quality] Neuartigkeit die - **2.** [unusual object, event] Neuheit die - **3.** [cheap object] Krimskrams der.

November [nə'vembər] n November der; see also **September**.

novice ['nɒvɪs] n - **1.** [inexperienced person] Neuling der - **2.** RELIG Novize der, -zin die.

now [naʊ] <> adv - **1.** [gen] jetzt; **just now** gerade eben; **right now** [at the moment] im Moment; [immediately] sofort; **by now** inzwischen; **from now on** von jetzt an; **three days from now** heute in drei Tagen; **any day/time now** jeden Tag/Moment; **(every) now and then** OR **again** hin und wieder; **for now** erst einmal - **2.** [introducing statement]: **now (then)** also. <> conj: **now (that)...** jetzt, wo...

nowadays ['naʊədeɪz] adv heutzutage.

nowhere UK ['nəʊweər], **no-place** US adv nirgendwo, nirgends; **nowhere near** nicht annähernd; **dinner is nowhere near ready** das Abendessen ist noch lange nicht fertig; **to be getting nowhere** [achieve nothing] nichts erreichen; [make no progress] nicht voranlkommen.

nozzle ['nɒzl] n Düse die.

nuance ['njuːɑːns] n Nuance die.

nuclear ['njuːklɪər] adj nuklear, Nuklear-.

nuclear bomb n Atombombe die.

nuclear disarmament n nukleare Abrüstung.

nuclear energy n Atomenergie die.

nuclear power n Atomkraft die, Kernkraft die; **nuclear power station** Atomkraftwerk das.

nuclear reactor n Atomreaktor der.

nuclear war n Atomkrieg der.

nucleus ['njuːklɪəs] (pl -lei [-lɪaɪ]) n Kern der; **atomic nucleus** Atomkern der.

nude [njuːd] <> adj nackt. <> n [figure, painting] Akt der; **in the nude** nackt.

nudge [nʌdʒ] vt [with elbow] anlstupsen.

nudist ['njuːdɪst] <> adj Nudisten-; **nudist beach** Nacktbadestrand der. <> n Nudist der, -in die.

nugget ['nʌgɪt] n - **1.** [of gold] Nugget das, Goldklümpchen das - **2.** fig: **a nugget of information** ein wertvolles Stück Information.

nuisance ['njuːsns] n - **1.** [annoying thing, situation] Ärgernis das; **what a nuisance!** wie ärgerlich! - **2.** [annoying person] Nervensäge die; **to make a nuisance of o.s.** lästig werden.

null [nʌl] adj: **null and void** null und nichtig.

numb [nʌm] adj [shoulder, hand] taub, gefühllos; [person] benommen; **to be numb with sthg** [with cold, fear, shock] starr vor etw (D) sein; [with grief] benommen vor etw (D) sein.

number ['nʌmbər] <> n - **1.** [numeral] Zahl die, Ziffer die - **2.** [of telephone, house, car] Nummer die - **3.** [quantity] Anzahl die, Zahl die; **a number of** mehrere; **any number of** unzählig - **4.** [song] Nummer die. <> vt - **1.** [amount to] zählen - **2.** [give a number to] nummerieren - **3.** [include]: **he is numbered among the greatest politicians of this century** er zählt zu den größten Politikern dieses Jahrhunderts.

number one <> adj [main] vorrangig. <> n inf [oneself] Nummer eins.

numberplate ['nʌmbəpleɪt] n Nummernschild das.

Number Ten n: **Number Ten (Downing Street)** Sitz des britischen Premierministers.

numeral ['njuːmərəl] n Ziffer die.

numerate ['njuːmərət] adj UK rechenkundig.

numerical [njuː'merɪkl] adj numerisch.

numerous ['njuːmərəs] adj zahlreich.

nun [nʌn] n Nonne die.

nurse [nɜːs] <> n Krankenschwester die; [male] Krankenpfleger der. <> vt - **1.** MED [person] pflegen - **2.** [desire, dream, hope] hegen, nähren - **3.** [breast-feed] stillen.

nursery ['nɜːsərɪ] n - **1.** [for children] Kinderzimmer das - **2.** [for plants] Gärtnerei die.

nursery rhyme n Kinderreim der.

nursery school n Kindergarten der.

nursing ['nɜːsɪŋ] n (U) - **1.** [profession] Krankenpflege die - **2.** [care] Pflege die.

nursing home *n* [for old people] Pflege-heim *das*.

nurture ['nɜːtʃər] *vt* - **1.** [children] nähren; [plants] hegen - **2.** [hope, desire, plan] hegen.

nut [nʌt] *n* - **1.** [to eat] Nuss *die* - **2.** TECH Schraubenmutter *die* - **3.** *inf* [mad person] Spinner *der*, -in *die*. ➠ **nuts** *inf* ◇ *adj*: to be nuts verrückt sein. ◇ *excl US* verdammt!

nutcrackers ['nʌtˌkrækəz] *npl* Nussknacker *der*.

nutmeg ['nʌtmeg] *n* Muskatnuss *die*.

nutritious [njuːˈtrɪʃəs] *adj* nahrhaft.

nutshell ['nʌtʃel] *n*: in a nutshell kurz gefasst.

nuzzle ['nʌzl] *vi*: to nuzzle (up) against sb/sthg sich an jn/etw anschmiegen *OR* drücken.

nylon ['naɪlɒn] ◇ *n* [fabric] Nylon *das*. ◇ *comp* Nylon-.

o (*pl* o's *OR* os), **O** (*pl* O's *OR* Os) [əʊ] *n* - **1.** [letter] o *das*, O *das* - **2.** [zero] Null *die*.

oak [əʊk] ◇ *n* - **1.** [tree] Eiche *die* - **2.** (U) [wood] Eichenholz *das*. ◇ *comp* Eichenholz-.

OAP *n* abbr of **old age pensioner**.

oar [ɔːr] *n* Ruder *das*.

oasis [əʊˈeɪsɪs] (*pl* oases [əʊˈeɪsiːz]) *n liter* & *fig* Oase *die*.

oath [əʊθ] *n* - **1.** [promise] Eid *der*; on *OR* under oath unter Eid - **2.** [swearword] Fluch *der*.

oatmeal ['əʊtmiːl] *n* [food] Hafermehl *das*.

oats [əʊts] *npl* Hafer *der*.

obedience [əˈbiːdɪəns] *n*: obedience (to sb) Gehorsam *der* (gegenüber jm).

obedient [əˈbiːdɪənt] *adj* gehorsam.

obese [əʊˈbiːs] *adj* fettleibig.

obey [əˈbeɪ] ◇ *vt* [person] gehorchen (+ D); [orders, command, law] befolgen. ◇ *vi* gehorchen.

obituary [əˈbɪtʃʊərɪ] *n* Nachruf *der*.

object ◇ *n* ['ɒbdʒɪkt] - **1.** [thing] Gegenstand *der* - **2.** [aim] Ziel *das*; the object of the exercise der Zweck der Übung - **3.** GRAM Objekt *das*. ◇ *vt* [ɒbˈdʒekt]: to object that... einlwenden, dass... ◇ *vi* [ɒbˈdʒekt] dagegen sein; to object to sthg gegen etw sein; to object to doing sthg etwas dagegen haben, etw zu tun.

objection [əbˈdʒekʃn] *n* Einwand *der*; to have no objection to sthg keinen Einwand gegen etw haben; to have no objection to doing sthg nichts dagegen haben, etw zu tun.

objectionable [əbˈdʒekʃənəbl] *adj* [behaviour, language] anstößig; [person] unausstehlich, widerwärtig.

objective [əbˈdʒektɪv] ◇ *adj* objektiv. ◇ *n* Ziel *das*.

obligation [ˌɒblɪˈɡeɪʃn] *n* - **1.** [compulsion] Zwang *der* - **2.** [duty] Verpflichtung *die*.

obligatory [əˈblɪɡətrɪ] *adj* obligatorisch; to be obligatory Pflicht sein.

oblige [əˈblaɪdʒ] *vt* - **1.** [force]: to oblige sb to do sthg jn zwingen, etw zu tun - **2.** *fml* [do a favour for]: to oblige sb jm einen Gefallen tun.

obliging [əˈblaɪdʒɪŋ] *adj* zuvorkommend.

oblique [əˈbliːk] ◇ *adj* - **1.** [look, compliment] indirekt; [hint] versteckt - **2.** [line] Schräg-, schräg. ◇ *n* TYPO Schrägstrich *der*.

obliterate [əˈblɪtəreɪt] *vt* ausllöschen.

oblivion [əˈblɪvɪən] *n* - **1.** [unconsciousness] Bewusstlosigkeit *die* - **2.** [state of being forgotten] Vergessenheit *die*, Vergessen *das*.

oblivious [əˈblɪvɪəs] *adj*: to be oblivious to sthg sich (D) einer Sache (G) nicht bewusst sein.

oblong ['ɒblɒŋ] ◇ *adj* rechteckig. ◇ *n* Rechteck *das*.

obnoxious [əbˈnɒkʃəs] *adj* [smell] widerlich; [remark] gemein; [person] unausstehlich.

oboe ['əʊbəʊ] *n* Oboe *die*.

obscene [əbˈsiːn] *adj* obszön.

obscure [əbˈskjʊər] ◇ *adj* - **1.** [not well-known] unbekannt - **2.** [difficult to understand, see] unklar. ◇ *vt* - **1.** [make difficult to understand] unklar machen - **2.** [hide] verdecken.

observance [əbˈzɜːvəns] *n* (U) Einhaltung *die*.

observant [əbˈzɜːvnt] *adj* aufmerksam.

observation [ˌɒbzəˈveɪʃn] *n* - **1.** (U) [action of watching] Beobachtung *die* - **2.** [remark] Bemerkung *die*, Äußerung *die*.

observatory [əbˈzɜːvətrɪ] *n* Observatorium *das*, Sternwarte *die*.

observe [əbˈzɜːv] *vt* - **1.** *fml* [notice] bemerken - **2.** [watch carefully] beobachten - **3.** [obey] einlhalten - **4.** [remark] bemerken.

observer [əbˈzɜːvər] *n* - **1.** [watcher] Zuschauer *der*, -in *die* - **2.** [commentator] Beobachter *der*, -in *die*.

obsess [əbˈses] *vt*: to be obsessed by *OR* with sb/sthg von jm/etw besessen sein.

obsessive [əbˈsesɪv] *adj* obsessiv, zwanghaft.

obsolete ['ɒbsəliːt] *adj* veraltet, überholt.

obstacle ['ɒbstəkl] *n* Hindernis *das*.

obstetrics [ɒbˈstetrɪks] *n* Geburtshilfe *die*.

obstinate ['ɒbstənət] *adj* - **1.** [person] verbohrt - **2.** [cough, resistance] hartnäckig.

obstruct [əb'strʌkt] *vt* - **1.** [road, path] blockieren, versperren - **2.** [progress, justice, traffic] behindern.

obstruction [əb'strʌkʃn] *n* - **1.** [in road, pipe] Blockierung *die* - **2.** [of justice] Behinderung *die* - **3.** SPORT Behinderung *die*.

obtain [əb'teɪn] *vt* erhalten.

obtainable [əb'teɪnəbl] *adj* erhältlich.

obtrusive [əb'truːsɪv] *adj* [person, behaviour] aufdringlich; [colour] auffällig; [smell] penetrant.

obtuse [əb'tjuːs] *adj* - **1.** *fml* [person] begriffsstutzig - **2.** GEOM [angle] stumpf.

obvious ['ɒbvɪəs] *adj* offensichtlich.

obviously ['ɒbvɪəslɪ] *adv* - **1.** [of course] selbstverständlich - **2.** [clearly] eindeutig.

occasion [ə'keɪʒn] *n* - **1.** [circumstance, time] Gelegenheit *die*; **on one occasion** einmal - **2.** [important event] Anlass *der*; **to rise to the occasion** sich der Lage gewachsen zeigen - **3.** *fml* [reason, motive] Grund *der*.

occasional [ə'keɪʒənl] *adj* gelegentlich.

occasionally [ə'keɪʒnəlɪ] *adv* gelegentlich.

occult [ɒ'kʌlt] *adj* okkult.

occupant ['ɒkjʊpənt] *n* - **1.** [of building, room] Bewohner *der*, -in *die* - **2.** [of chair] Inhaber *der*, -in *die*; [of vehicle] Insasse *der*, -sin *die*.

occupation [ˌɒkjʊ'peɪʃn] *n* - **1.** [job] Beruf *der* - **2.** [pastime] Beschäftigung *die* - **3.** MIL Besetzung *die*, Okkupation *die*.

occupational hazard *n* Berufsrisiko *das*.

occupier ['ɒkjʊpaɪə'] *n* Bewohner *der*, -in *die*.

occupy ['ɒkjʊpaɪ] *vt* - **1.** [house, room] bewohnen; [seat] belegen - **2.** MIL besetzen, okkupieren - **3.** [keep busy]: **to occupy o.s.** sich beschäftigen - **4.** [time, space] in Anspruch nehmen; **how do you occupy your evenings?** wie füllst du deine Abende aus?

occur [ə'kɜːr] *vi* - **1.** [happen] sich ereignen; [change] stattfinden; [difficulty] auftreten - **2.** [exist, be found] vorkommen - **3.** [come to mind]: **to occur to sb** jm in den Sinn kommen.

occurrence [ə'kʌrəns] *n* [event] Vorkommnis *das*, Ereignis *das*.

ocean ['əʊʃn] *n* - **1.** [in names] Ozean *der* - **2.** *US* [sea] Meer *das*.

ochre *UK*, **ocher** *US* ['əʊkər] *adj* ockerfarben.

o'clock [ə'klɒk] *adv* Uhr; **five o'clock** fünf Uhr.

octave ['ɒktɪv] *n* MUS Oktave *die*.

October [ɒk'təʊbər] *n* Oktober *der*; *see also* **September**.

octopus ['ɒktəpəs] *(pl* -**puses** *OR* -**pi** [-paɪ]*) n* Tintenfisch *der*.

OD *abbr of* **overdose**.

odd [ɒd] *adj* - **1.** [strange] seltsam - **2.** [not part of pair] einzeln - **3.** [number] ungerade - **4.** [leftover] überzählig - **5.** [occasional] gelegentlich - **6.** *inf* [approximately] ungefähr; **twenty odd years** mehr als zwanzig Jahre.

➡ **odds** *npl* - **1.** [probability] Wahrscheinlichkeit *die*; **the odds are that** aller Wahrscheinlichkeit nach; **against all** *OR* **the odds** wider Erwarten - **2.** [bits]: **odds and ends** Krimskrams *der* - **3.** *phr*: **to be at odds with sb/sthg** sich mit jm/etw uneinig sein.

oddity ['ɒdɪtɪ] *n* - **1.** [strange person] Sonderling *der*; [strange thing] Kuriosität *die* - **2.** [strangeness] Eigenartigkeit *die*.

odd jobs *npl* Gelegenheitsarbeiten *Pl*.

oddly ['ɒdlɪ] *adv* seltsam.

oddments ['ɒdmənts] *npl* Einzelstücke *Pl*.

odds-on ['ɒdz-] *adj inf*: **the odds-on favourite** der klare Favorit; **it's odds-on that...** es ist sehr wahrscheinlich, dass...

odometer [əʊ'dɒmɪtər] *n* Kilometerzähler *der*.

odour *UK*, **odor** *US* ['əʊdər] *n* Geruch *der*.

of (unstressed [əv], stressed [ɒv]) *prep* - **1.** [gen] von *(the genitive case is often used instead of "von")*; **the cover of the book** der Umschlag des Buches; **the handle of the door** der Türgriff; **a friend of mine** ein Freund von mir; **the works of Shakespeare** die Werke Shakespeares *OR* von Shakespeare; **the Queen of England** die Königin von England; **the University of Leeds** die Universität Leeds; **south of Boston** südlich von Boston/des Flusses - **2.** [expressing quantity, contents, age]: **a pound of sweets** ein Pfund Bonbons; **a piece of cake** ein Stück Kuchen; **a cup of coffee** eine Tasse Kaffee; **a rise of 20%** ein Anstieg um 20%; **a town of 50,000 people** eine Stadt mit 50 000 Einwohnern; **thousands of people** Tausende von Leuten; **a girl of six** ein sechsjähriges Mädchen; **both/one of us** beide/einer von uns; **a man of courage** ein mutiger Mann - **3.** [made from] aus; **a house of stone** ein Haus aus Stein; **it's made of wood** es ist aus Holz - **4.** [with emotions]: **a love of France** eine Liebe zu Frankreich; **a fear of flying** Angst vor dem Fliegen - **5.** [on the part of] von; **that was very kind of you** das war so nett von Ihnen - **6.** [referring to place names]: **the city of Birmingham** die Stadt Birmingham - **7.** [indicating resemblance] von; **it was the size of a pea** es war so groß wie eine Erbse, es hatte die Größe einer Erbse - **8.** [with dates, periods of time]: **the 26th of April** der 26. April; **the summer of 1969** der Sommer 1969; **in September of last year** im September letzten Jahres - **9.** [indicating cause of death]: **to die of sthg** an etw (D) sterben - **10.** *US* [in telling the time] vor; **it's ten of four** es ist zehn vor vier.

off [ɒf] ⬦ adv - **1.** [away] weg; **to get off** [from bus, train, plane] auslsteigen; **we're off to Austria next week** wir fahren nächste Woche nach Österreich; **to go** OR **drop off to sleep** einlschlafen - **2.** [expressing removal] ab; **to take sthg off** [clothes, shoes] etw auslziehen; [lid, wrapper] etw ablnehmen; **with his shoes off** ohne Schuhe - **3.** [not working]: **to turn sthg off** [TV, radio, engine] etw auslschalten; [tap] etw zuldrehen - **4.** [expressing distance or time away]: **it's 10 miles off** es sind noch 10 Meilen bis dahin; **it's a long way off** [in distance] es ist noch ein weiter Weg bis dahin; [in time] bis dahin ist es noch lange hin - **5.** [not at work]: **I'm taking a week off** ich nehme mir eine Woche frei. ⬦ prep - **1.** [away from] von; **to get off sthg** [bed, chair] von etw auflstehen; [bus, train, plane] aus etw auslsteigen; [ship] etw verlassen; **off the coast** vor der Küste; **it's just off the main road** es ist gleich in der Nähe der Hauptstraße - **2.** [absent from]: **to be off work** frei haben - **3.** inf [from] von; **I bought it off her** ich habe es von ihr gekauft - **4.** inf [no longer liking or needing]: **I'm off my food at the moment** ich habe zur Zeit keinen Appetit; **she's off drugs now** sie nimmt keine Drogen mehr. ⬦ adj - **1.** [meat, cheese, milk, beer] schlecht - **2.** [not working] aus; [tap] zu - **3.** [cancelled] abgesagt; **the deal is off** die Sache ist abgeblasen - **4.** [not available]: **the soup's off** es ist keine Suppe mehr da.

offal [ˈɒfl] n Innereien Pl.

off-chance n: **on the off-chance** auf gut Glück.

off colour adj kränklich.

off duty adv außer Dienst, dienstfrei. ⬦ **off-duty** adj außer Dienst.

offence UK, **offense** US [əˈfens] n - **1.** [crime] Verbrechen das - **2.** [displeasure, hurt] Beleidigung die; **to take offence** beleidigt sein.

offend [əˈfend] vt beleidigen.

offender [əˈfendər] n - **1.** [criminal] Straftäter der, -in die - **2.** [culprit] Schuldige der, die.

offense n US = **offence**.

offensive [əˈfensɪv] ⬦ adj - **1.** [causing offence] beleidigend; [behaviour] anstößig - **2.** [aggressive] Angriffs-, aggressiv. ⬦ n - **1.** MIL Offensive die, Angriff der - **2.** fig [attack]: **to go on** OR **take the offensive** in die Offensive gehen.

offer [ˈɒfər] ⬦ n Angebot das; **on offer** [available] verkäuflich; [at a special price] im Angebot. ⬦ vt anlbieten; **to offer sthg to sb**, **to offer sb sthg** jm etw anlbieten; **to offer to do sthg** anlbieten, etw zu tun. ⬦ vi sich anlbieten.

offering [ˈɒfərɪŋ] n - **1.** [something offered] Gabe die - **2.** RELIG [sacrifice] Opfer das.

off guard adv unvorbereitet.

offhand [ˌɒfˈhænd] ⬦ adj lässig. ⬦ adv auf Anhieb.

office [ˈɒfɪs] n - **1.** [gen] Büro das - **2.** [government department] Behörde die - **3.** [position of authority] Amt das; **in office** im Amt.

office block n Bürogebäude das.

office hours npl Bürostunden Pl.

officer [ˈɒfɪsər] n - **1.** MIL Offizier der - **2.** [in organization] Vertreter der, -in die - **3.** [in police force] Polizeibeamte der, -tin die.

office worker n Büroangestellte der, die.

official [əˈfɪʃl] ⬦ adj offiziell. ⬦ n Beamte der, -tin die; SPORT Funktionär der, -in die.

offing [ˈɒfɪŋ] n: **in the offing** in Sicht.

off-licence n UK Wein- und Spirituosenhandlung die.

off-line adj COMPUT offline.

off-peak adj: **off-peak electricity** Nachtstrom der; **off-peak fares** verbilligter Tarif; **during off-peak hours** außerhalb der Stoßzeiten.

off-putting [-ˌpʊtɪŋ] adj abstoßend.

off season n: **the off season** die Nebensaison.

offset [ˈɒfset] (pt & pp inv) vt auslgleichen.

offshore [ˌɒfˈʃɔːr] ⬦ adj - **1.** [in or on the sea] Offshore- - **2.** [near coast] in Küstennähe; **offshore waters** Küstengewässer Pl. ⬦ adv - **1.** [out at sea] offshore, im offenen Meer - **2.** [near coast] in Küstennähe.

offside ⬦ adv [ˌɒfˈsaɪd] SPORT im Abseits. ⬦ n [ˈɒfsaɪd] [of vehicle] Fahrerseite die.

offspring [ˈɒfsprɪŋ] (pl inv) n - **1.** fml & hum [of people] Nachwuchs der - **2.** [of animals] Junge(s) das.

offstage [ˌɒfˈsteɪdʒ] adj & adv hinter der Bühne, hinter den Kulissen.

off-the-cuff adj & adv unüberlegt.

off-the-peg adj UK: **off-the-peg suit** Anzug der von der Stange.

off-the-record adj & adv inoffiziell.

off-white adj gebrochen weiß.

often [ˈɒfn, ˈɒftn] adv oft; **how often do the buses run?** wie oft fährt der Bus?; **every so often** gelegentlich; **as often as not**, **more often than not** meistens.

ogle [ˈəʊgl] vt pej begaffen.

oh [əʊ] excl - **1.** [to introduce comment] ach! - **2.** [expressing hesitation, joy, surprise, fear] oh!; **oh no!** oh nein!

oil [ɔɪl] ⬦ n Öl das. ⬦ vt ölen, schmieren.

oilcan [ˈɔɪlkæn] n Ölkanne die.

oilfield [ˈɔɪlfiːld] n Ölfeld das.

oil filter n Ölfilter der.

oil-fired [-ˌfaɪəd] adj ölbefeuert; **oil-fired central heating** Ölheizung die.

oil painting n - **1.** [picture] Ölgemälde das - **2.** [art] Ölmalerei die.

oilrig [ˈɔɪlrɪg] n Ölbohrinsel die.

oil slick *n* Ölteppich *der.*

oil tanker *n* - 1. [ship] Öltanker *der* - 2. [lorry] Tankwagen *der.*

oil well *n* Ölquelle *die.*

oily ['ɔɪlɪ] *adj* [rag, clothes] ölig; [food] fettig.

ointment ['ɔɪntmənt] *n* Salbe *die.*

OK (*pt & pp* OKed, *cont* OKing), **okay** [,əʊ'keɪ] *inf* <> *adj* in Ordnung; **are you OK?** ist alles in Ordnung?; **is that OK with you?** ist dir das recht? <> *adv* [well] gut. <> *excl* - 1. [expressing agreement] okay! - 2. [to introduce new topic]: **OK, let's get started** Okay, fangen wir an. <> *vt* sein Okay geben zu.

old [əʊld] <> *adj* - 1. [gen] alt; **how old are you?** wie alt bist du?; **I'm 36 years old** ich bin 36 (Jahre alt); **to get old** alt werden; **in the old days** früher - 2. [for emphasis]: **any old thing** das Erstbeste; **good old George!** der gute alte Georg! <> *npl*: **the old** ältere Leute.

old age *n* (U) Alter *das.*

old age pensioner *n UK* Rentner *der,* -in *die.*

old-fashioned [-'fæʃnd] *adj* [person, clothes] altmodisch; [ideas] überholt.

old people's home *n* Altersheim *das.*

O level (*abbr of* ordinary level) *n UK* ≃ mittlere Reife, *früherer Schulabschluss in England und Wales, 1988 durch das GCSE ersetzt.*

olive ['ɒlɪv] *n* Olive *die.*

olive green *adj* olivgrün.

olive oil *n* Olivenöl *das.*

Olympic [ə'lɪmpɪk] *adj* olympisch.
Olympics *npl*: **the Olympics** die Olympischen Spiele.

Olympic Games *npl*: **the Olympic Games** die Olympischen Spiele.

omelet(te) ['ɒmlɪt] *n* Omelett *das.*

omen ['əʊmən] *n* Omen *das.*

ominous ['ɒmɪnəs] *adj* ominös.

omission [ə'mɪʃn] *n* Auslassung *die.*

omit [ə'mɪt] *vt* auslassen; **to omit to do sthg** es unterlassen, etw zu tun; [unintentionally] es versäumen, etw zu tun.

on [ɒn] <> *prep* - 1. [indicating position, location] auf (+ D); (with verbs of motion) auf (+ A); **it's on the table** es ist auf dem Tisch; **put it on the table** leg es auf den Tisch; **on the wall/ceiling** an der Wand/der Decke; **on page four** auf Seite vier; **on my left/right** zu meiner Linken/Rechten; **on the left/right** auf der linken/rechten Seite; **we stayed on a farm** wir übernachteten auf einem Bauernhof; **on the Rhine** am Rhein; **on the main road** an der Hauptstraße; **he had a scar on his face** er hatte eine Narbe im Gesicht; **do you have any money on you?** hast du Geld bei dir? - 2. [indicating means] auf (+ D); **recorded on tape** auf Band; **on TV/the radio** im Radio/Fernsehen; **it runs on unleaded petrol** es fährt mit

bleifreiem Benzin; **he lives on fruit and yoghurt** er lebt von Obst und Joghurt; **to cut o.s. on sthg** sich an etw (D) schneiden - 3. [indicating mode of transport]: **to be on the train/plane** im Zug/Flugzeug sein; **to travel on the bus/train** mit dem Bus/Zug fahren; **to get on a bus** in einen Bus einsteigen; **on foot** zu Fuß - 4. [using, supported by]: **to stand on one leg** auf einem Bein stehen; **he was lying on his back** er lag auf dem Rücken; **to be on medication** Medikamente nehmen; **to be on drugs** [addicted] drogensüchtig sein; **to be on social security** Sozialhilfe bekommen - 5. [about] über (+ A); **a book on Germany** ein Buch über Deutschland - 6. [indicating time] an (+ D): **on Tuesday** am Dienstag; **on Tuesdays** dienstags; **on 25 August** am 25. August; **on arrival** bei Ankunft; **on my return, on returning** bei meiner Rückkehr - 7. [indicating activity]: **to work on sthg** an etw (D) arbeiten; **he's here on business** er ist geschäftlich hier; **on holiday** im Urlaub; **she's on the telephone** [talking] sie telefoniert gerade; **to be on fire** brennen - 8. [according to]: **on good authority** aus guter Quelle; **on this evidence** aufgrund dieser Beweise - 9. [indicating influence, effect] auf (+ A); **the effect on Britain** die Auswirkungen auf Großbritannien; **a tax on imports** eine Steuer auf Importe - 10. [earning]: **she's on £25,000 a year** sie ist verdient £25.000 pro Jahr; **to be on a low income** ein niedriges Einkommen haben - 11. [referring to musical instrument] auf (+ D); **on the violin/flute** auf der Geige/Flöte - 12.: **on the cheap** billig; **on the sly** hintenherum - 13. *inf* [paid by]: **the drinks are on me** die Drinks gehen auf mich. <> *adv* - 1. [in place, covering]: **to have sthg on** [clothes, hat] etw anhaben; **put the lid on** mach den Deckel drauf; **to put one's clothes on** sich (D) (seine Kleider) anziehen - 2. [film, play, programme]: **the news is on** die Nachrichten laufen; **what's on at the cinema?** was läuft im Kino?; **there's nothing on tonight** heute Abend kommt nichts - 3. [working] an; **you left the heater on** du hast das Heizgerät angelassen; **to turn sthg on** [TV, radio, engine] etw einschalten; [tap] etw aufdrehen - 4. [indicating continuing action] weiter; **to work on** weiterarbeiten; **we talked on into the night** wir redeten noch bis in die Nacht hinein; **he kept on walking** er ging immer weiter - 5. [forward]: **send my mail on (to me)** senden Sie mir die Post nach - 6. [with transport]: **to get on** einsteigen; **is everyone on?** sind alle eingestiegen? - 7. *phr*: **earlier on** früher; **later on** später; **it's just not on!** *inf* das geht einfach nicht!; **to be** OR **go on at sb (to do sthg)** [pester] jm zulsetzen (, etw zu tun). **from on** *adv*: **from that moment on** von dem Moment an; **from now on** von jetzt an, ab jetzt; **from then on** von da an. **on and off** *adv* ab und zu. **on to, onto** *prep* (written as onto for senses 4 and 5 only) - 1. [to a position on top of] auf (+ A); **she**

jumped on to the chair sie sprang auf den Stuhl - 2. [into a vehicle] in *(+ A)*; **she got on to the bus** sie stieg in den Bus ein - 3. [wall, door] an *(+ A)*; **stick the photo on to the page** kleb das Foto auf die Seite - 4. [aware of]: **to be onto sb** [subj: police] jm auf der Spur sein; **she's onto something** sie hat etwas entdeckt - 5. [into contact with]: **to get onto sb** sich an jn wenden.

once [wʌns] ⬦ *adv* einmal; **not once** kein einziges Mal; **for once** ausnahmsweise; **once more** [one more time] noch einmal; [again] wieder; **once and for all** ein für allemal; **once (upon a time)** there was es war einmal. ⬦ *conj* wenn. ⬟ **at once** *adv* - 1. [immediately] sofort - 2. [at the same time] gleichzeitig; **all at once** auf einmal.

oncoming ['ɒn,kʌmɪŋ] *adj*: **oncoming traffic** Gegenverkehr *der*.

one [wʌn] ⬦ *num* - 1. [the number 1] eins; **thirty-one** einunddreißig; **at one/one thirty** [time] um eins/halb zwei; **in ones and twos** vereinzelt - 2. *(with masculine and neuter nouns)* ein; *(with feminine nouns)* eine; **one brother and one sister** ein Bruder und eine Schwester; **one hundred/thousand** (ein)hundert/(ein)tausend; **page one** Seite eins; **one-fifth** ein Fünftel; **one or two** einige. ⬦ *adj* - 1. [only] einzige(r) (s); **it's her one ambition** das ist ihr einziger Ehrgeiz - 2. [indefinite]: **one day** [in past, future] eines Tages; **one of these days** irgendwann einmal; **one afternoon/night** an einem Nachmittag/Abend - 3. *fml* [a certain] ein gewisser (eine gewisse); **one James Smith** ein gewisser James Smith. ⬦ *pron* - 1. [referring to a particular thing or person]: **the red/blue one** der/die/das Rote/Blaue; **the best ones** die besten; **the one on the table** der/die/das auf dem Tisch; **the one I told you about** der/die/das, von dem/der/dem ich dir erzählt habe; **the ones you want** die OR diejenigen, die du willst; **I like that one** ich mag den/die/das (da); **which one?** welche(r) (s) ?; **a red dot and a blue one** ein roter Punkt und ein blauer - 2. [indefinite]: **there's only one left** es ist nur eine/einer/eins übrig; **have you got one?** hast du eine/einen/eins?; **one of my friends** einer meiner Freunde; **not one (of them)** keiner (von ihnen); **one by one** einer nach dem anderen - 3. [referring to money]: **one fifty, please** eins fünfzig, bitte - 4. *fml* [you, anyone] man; **one never knows** man weiß nie; **to give one's opinion** seine Meinung sagen; **to cut one's finger** sich *(D)* in den Finger schneiden. ⬟ **for one** *adv*: **I for one will come** ich jedenfalls werde kommen.

one-armed bandit [-ɑːmd] *n* einarmiger Bandit.

one-man *adj* Einmann-.

one-off *inf* ⬦ *adj* [event, offer, concert] einmalig; **one-off object/product** Einzel-

stück *das*. ⬦ *n* - 1. [unique event] einmalige Sache - 2. [unique object, product] Einzelstück *das*.

one-on-one *adj US* = **one-to-one**.

one-parent family *n* Einelternfamilie *die*.

oneself [wʌn'self] *pron fml* - 1. *(reflexive)* sich; **to make oneself comfortable** es sich *(D)* bequem machen - 2. *(after prep)* sich selbst; **to look at oneself in the mirror** sich (selbst) im Spiegel betrachten - 3. *(stressed)* selbst; **to do sthg oneself** etw selbst tun.

one-sided [-'saɪdɪd] *adj* einseitig.

one-to-one *UK*, **one-on-one** *US adj*: **one-to-one discussion** Diskussion *die* unter vier Augen; **one-to-one tuition** Einzelunterricht *der*.

one-way *adj*: **one-way street** Einbahnstraße *die*; **one-way traffic** Einbahnverkehr *der*; **one-way ticket** einfache Fahrkarte.

ongoing ['ɒn,ɡəʊɪŋ] *adj* [situation] andauernd; [project] laufend; [discussions] im Gang befindlich.

onion ['ʌnjən] *n* Zwiebel *die*.

online ⬦ *adj* ['ɒnlaɪn] COMPUT Online-. ⬦ *adv* [,ɒn'laɪn] COMPUT online.

online banking *n* COMPUT Onlinebanking *das*.

online shopping *n* COMPUT Onlineshopping *das*.

onlooker ['ɒn,lʊkər] *n* Zuschauer *der*, -in *die*; [at accident scene] Schaulustige *der, die*.

only ['əʊnlɪ] ⬦ *adj* einzige(r) (s); **an only child** ein Einzelkind. ⬦ *adv* nur; **I only want one** ich möchte nur einen/eine/eines; **I only wish I could** ich würde es wirklich gern tun; **only yesterday** erst gestern; **we've only just arrived** wir sind gerade erst angekommen; **there's only just enough** es ist gerade noch genug da; **not only** nicht nur. ⬦ *conj* aber; **I would go, only I'm too tired** ich würde gehen, aber ich bin zu müde.

onset ['ɒnset] *n* Beginn *der*; [of war, illness] Ausbruch *der*.

onshore [,ɒn'ʃɔːr] *adv* an Land.

onslaught ['ɒnslɔːt] *n* - 1. [physical] (heftiger) Angriff - 2. [verbal] (verbale) Attacke.

onto (*stressed* ['ɒntuː], *unstressed before consonant* ['ɒntə], *unstressed before vowel* ['ɒntʊ]) *prep* ⬳ **on**.

onus ['əʊnəs] *n*: **the onus is on him to convince us** es liegt an ihm, uns zu überzeugen.

onward ['ɒnwəd] ⬦ *adj*: **onward journey** Weiterreise *die*. ⬦ *adv* = **onwards**.

onwards ['ɒnwədz] *adv* [forwards] vorwärts; **to travel onwards** weiterreisen; **from now onwards** von jetzt an; **from October onwards** ab Oktober.

ooze [uːz] ⬦ *vt fig* [charm] aus|strahlen; [confidence] strotzen vor *(+ D)*. ⬦ *vi* [liquid, blood] triefen; [mud] (heraus)|quellen.

opaque [əʊ'peɪk] *adj* - 1. [not transparent] undurchsichtig - 2. *fig* [text, meaning] unverständlich.

open ['əʊpn] ◇ *adj* - 1. [gen] offen; **wide open** weit offen - 2. [receptive - mind, person]: **to be open to sthg** [ready to accept] für etw offen sein; **open to question** fraglich; **two options are open to us** zwei Möglichkeiten stehen uns offen - 3. [shop, office, library] geöffnet; **open to the public** der Öffentlichkeit zugänglich - 4. [inaugurated] eröffnet - 5. [unobstructed - road, passage] frei; [- view] weit - 6. [not enclosed]: **open country** freies Land; **in the open air** im Freien. ◇ *n*: **in the open** [in the fresh air] im Freien; **to bring sthg out into the open** etw ans Licht bringen. ◇ *vt* - 1. [gen] öffnen; **to open fire** das Feuer eröffnen - 2. [bank account, meeting, event, new building] eröffnen. ◇ *vi* - 1. [door, window, eyes, flower] sich öffnen - 2. [begin business] öffnen - 3. [commence] beginnen. ◆ **open on to** *vt insep* [subj: door] führen auf (+ A). ◆ **open up** ◇ *vt sep* - 1. [gen] öffnen - 2. [for development - country, market] erschließen. ◇ *vi* - 1. [unlock door] aufschließen - 2. [for business] öffnen - 3. [become available - possibilities, chances] sich eröffnen - 4. [become less reserved] offener werden.

opener ['əʊpnə'] *n* Öffner *der*.

opening ['əʊpnɪŋ] ◇ *adj* [speech, scene] Eröffnungs-. ◇ *n* - 1. [beginning] Anfang *der* - 2. [gap] Öffnung *die* - 3. [opportunity] Möglichkeit *die* - 4. [job vacancy] freie Stelle.

opening hours *npl* Öffnungszeiten *Pl.*

openly ['əʊpənlɪ] *adv* [frankly] offen; [publicly] öffentlich.

open-minded [-'maɪndɪd] *adj* aufgeschlossen.

open-plan *adj* [office] Großraum-.

Open University *n UK*: **the Open University** britische Fernuniversität.

opera ['ɒpərə] *n* Oper *die*.

opera house *n* Opernhaus *das*.

operate ['ɒpəreɪt] ◇ *vt* - 1. [machine] bedienen - 2. COMM [business] leiten, führen. ◇ *vi* - 1. [law] sich auswirken; [system] funktionieren; [system] funktionieren; [machine - function]·funktionieren; [- be in operation] in Betrieb sein - 2. COMM [business] arbeiten - 3. MED: **to operate (on sb/sthg)** (jn/etw) operieren.

operating theatre *UK*, **operating room** *US* ['ɒpəreɪtɪŋ-] *n* Operationssaal *der*.

operation [,ɒpə'reɪʃn] *n* - 1. [planned activity - MIL] Operation *die*; [- of police force] Einsatz *der*; **rescue operation** Rettungsaktion *die*; **relief operation** Hilfsaktion *die* - 2. (U) [COMM - management] Leitung *die*; [- company, business] Unternehmen *das* - 3. (U) [of machine - running] Betrieb *der*; [- control] Bedienung *die*; **to be in operation** [- machine] in Be-

trieb sein; [- law] in Kraft sein; [- system] angewendet werden - 4. MED Operation *die*; **to have an operation** operiert werden.

operational [,ɒpə'reɪʃənl] *adj* [machine]: **to be operational** [ready for use] betriebsbereit sein; [in use] in Betrieb sein.

operator ['ɒpəreɪtə'] *n* - 1. [TELEC - at telephone exchange] Vermittlung *die*; [- at switchboard] Telefonist *der*, -in *die* - 2. [of machine] Maschinenarbeiter *der*, -in *die*; [of computer] Operator *der*, -in *die* - 3. COMM [person in charge] Unternehmer *der*, -in *die*.

opinion [ə'pɪnjən] *n* Meinung *die*, Ansicht *die*; MED Gutachten *das*; **what's your opinion of him?** was halten Sie von ihm?; **to be of the opinion that** der Meinung *OR* Ansicht sein, dass; **to have a high/low opinion of sb** eine hohe/schlechte Meinung von jm haben; **in my opinion** meiner Meinung *OR* Ansicht nach.

opinionated [ə'pɪnjəneɪtɪd] *adj pej* rechthaberisch.

opinion poll *n* Meinungsumfrage *die*.

opponent [ə'pəʊnənt] *n* Gegner *der*, -in *die*.

opportune ['ɒpətjuːn] *adj* [moment] günstig.

opportunist [,ɒpə'tjuːnɪst] *n* Opportunist *der*, -in *die*.

opportunity [,ɒpə'tjuːnətɪ] *n* Gelegenheit *die*; **to take the opportunity to do** *OR* **of doing sthg** die Gelegenheit ergreifen, um etw zu tun.

oppose [ə'pəʊz] *vt* [resist] sich widersetzen (+ D); [ideas, views] ablehnen.

opposed [ə'pəʊzd] *adj*: **to be opposed to sthg** gegen etw sein; **as opposed to** im Gegensatz zu.

opposing [ə'pəʊzɪŋ] *adj* [points of view] entgegengesetzt; [teams] gegnerisch.

opposite ['ɒpəzɪt] ◇ *adj* - 1. [facing] gegenüberliegend; **the houses opposite** die Häuser gegenüber - 2. [very different] entgegengesetzt. ◇ *adv* gegenüber. ◇ *prep* [facing] gegenüber (+ D). ◇ *n* Gegenteil *das*.

opposite number *n* Pendant *das*.

opposition [,ɒpə'zɪʃn] *n* - 1. [disapproval] Widerstand *der*, Opposition *die* - 2. [opposing team] Gegner *Pl*. ◆ **Opposition** *n UK* POL: **the Opposition** die Opposition.

oppress [ə'pres] *vt* - 1. [persecute] unterdrücken - 2. [subj: worries] bedrücken.

oppressive [ə'presɪv] *adj* - 1. [regime, government, society] repressiv - 2. [heat, weather] drückend - 3. [situation, silence] bedrückend.

opt [ɒpt] ◇ *vt*: **to opt to do sthg** sich dafür entscheiden, etw zu tun. ◇ *vi*: **to opt for sthg** sich für etw entscheiden. ◆ **opt in** *vi*: **to opt in to sthg** einer *(D)* beitreten. ◆ **opt out** *vi*: **to opt out (of)** [scheme, system] austreten (aus).

optical ['ɒptɪkl] *adj* optisch.

optician [ɒp'tɪʃn] *n* Optiker *der*, -in *die*; **to go to the optician's** zum Optiker gehen.

optimist ['ɒptɪmɪst] *n* Optimist *der*, -in *die*.

optimistic [ˌɒptɪ'mɪstɪk] *adj*: **she's optimistic about passing her driving test** sie ist optimistisch, dass sie die Fahrprüfung bestehen wird.

optimum ['ɒptɪməm] *adj* optimal.

option ['ɒpʃn] *n* [choice] Wahl *die*; [alternative to be chosen] (Wahl)möglichkeit *die*; **to have the option to do** OR **of doing sthg** die Möglichkeit haben, etw zu tun.

optional ['ɒpʃənl] *adj* [subject] Wahl-; [course] fakultativ; **optional extra** Extra *das*.

or [ɔːr] *conj* - 1. [linking alternatives] oder; **either one or the other** entweder das eine oder das andere; **or (else)** [otherwise] sonst; **ten kilometres or so** [approximately] ungefähr zehn Kilometer - 2. *(after negatives)* noch; **he cannot read or write** er kann weder lesen noch schreiben.

oral ['ɔːrəl] ◇ *adj* - 1. [exam] mündlich - 2. MED [medicine] zum Einnehmen; [hygiene] Mund-; **oral vaccine** Schluckimpfung *die*. ◇ *n* mündliche Prüfung.

orally ['ɔːrəlɪ] *adv* MED oral; **to take sthg orally** etw einlnehmen.

orange ['ɒrɪndʒ] ◇ *adj* [colour] orange. ◇ *n* - 1. [fruit] Orange *die*, Apfelsine *die* - 2. (U) [colour] Orange *das*.

orator ['ɒrətər] *n* Redner *der*, -in *die*.

orbit ['ɔːbɪt] ◇ *n* [in space] Umlaufbahn *die*. ◇ *vt* umkreisen.

orchard ['ɔːtʃəd] *n* Obstgarten *der*.

orchestra ['ɔːkɪstrə] *n* Orchester *das*.

orchid ['ɔːkɪd] *n* Orchidee *die*.

ordain [ɔː'deɪn] *vt* RELIG: **to be ordained** (zum Priester) geweiht werden.

ordeal [ɔː'diːl] *n* Tortur *die*.

order ['ɔːdər] ◇ *n* - 1. [instruction] Anweisung *die*; MIL Befehl *der*; **until further orders** bis auf weiteren Befehl; **to be under orders to do sthg** MIL den Befehl haben, etw zu tun - 2. COMM [request, in restaurant] Bestellung *die*; **to place an order with sb for sthg** bei jm eine Bestellung für etw auflgeben; [contract to manufacture or supply goods] Auftrag *der*; **to place an order with sb for sthg** jm für etw einen Auftrag erteilen; **to order on Bestellung** - 3. (U) [sequence] Reihenfolge *die*; **arranged in order of importance** nach Wichtigkeit geordnet; **in alphabetical order** in alphabetischer Reihenfolge - 4. (U) [neatness, discipline, system] Ordnung *die* - 5. [fitness for use]: **in order** [valid] in Ordnung; **in working order** funktionstüchtig; **out of order** [machine, lift] außer Betrieb; **you're out of order!** *inf* pass auf, was du sagst/machst! - 6. RELIG Orden *der* - 7. US [portion] Portion *die*. ◇ *vt* - 1. [command] anlordnen; MIL befehlen (+ D);

[subj: court] verfügen; **to order sb to do sthg** jn anlweisen, etw zu tun; MIL jm befehlen, etw zu tun; **to order that...** anlordnen, dass...; MIL befehlen, dass... - 2. COMM [request] bestellen; [to be manufactured: suit, aircraft, ship] in Auftrag geben. ◈ **in the order of** UK, **on the order of** US *prep* etwa. ◈ **in order that** *conj* damit. ◈ **in order to** *conj* um zu; **in order to get a better view** um eine bessere Sicht zu bekommen. ◈ **order about, order around** *vt sep* herumlkommandieren.

order form *n* Bestellschein *der*.

orderly ['ɔːdəlɪ] ◇ *adj* ordentlich. ◇ *n* [in hospital] Pfleger *der*, -in *die*.

ordinarily ['ɔːdənrəlɪ] *adv* [normally] gewöhnlich, normalerweise.

ordinary ['ɔːdənrɪ] ◇ *adj* - 1. [normal] gewöhnlich, normal; **ordinary people** einfache Leute - 2. *pej* [unexceptional] gewöhnlich. ◇ *n*: **out of the ordinary** außergewöhnlich.

ore [ɔːr] *n* Erz *das*.

oregano [ˌɒrɪ'gɑːnəʊ] *n* Oregano *der*.

organ ['ɔːgən] *n* - 1. ANAT Organ *das* - 2. MUS Orgel *die*.

organic [ɔː'gænɪk] *adj* - 1. [of animals, plants] organisch - 2. [food] biodynamisch.

organization [ˌɔːgənaɪ'zeɪʃn] *n* - 1. [gen] Organisation *die* - 2. (U) [arrangement] Ordnung *die*.

organize, -ise ['ɔːgənaɪz] *vt* organisieren; [affairs, thoughts] ordnen.

organizer, -iser ['ɔːgənaɪzər] *n* [person] Organisator *der*, -in *die*.

orgasm ['ɔːgæzm] *n* Orgasmus *der*.

orgy ['ɔːdʒɪ] *n* Orgie *die*.

oriental [ˌɔːrɪ'entl] *adj* orientalisch.

origami [ˌɒrɪ'gɑːmɪ] *n* Origami *das*.

origin ['ɒrɪdʒɪn] *n* - 1. [starting point] Ursprung *der* - 2. (U) [birth] Herkunft *die*; **country of origin** Herkunftsland *das*. ◈ **origins** *npl* Herkunft *die*.

original [ə'rɪdʒənl] ◇ *adj* - 1. [first] ursprünglich - 2. [document] Original-; **original painting** Original *das* - 3. [new, unusual] originell. ◇ *n* Original *das*.

originally [ə'rɪdʒənəlɪ] *adv* [initially] ursprünglich.

originate [ə'rɪdʒəneɪt] ◇ *vt* [scheme, policy] ins Leben rufen; [new style] begründen. ◇ *vi*: **to originate in/from** seinen Ursprung haben in *(+ D)*.

ornament ['ɔːnəmənt] *n* - 1. [object] Ziergenstand *der* - 2. (U) [decoration] Verzierungen *Pl*.

ornamental [ˌɔːnə'mentl] *adj* dekorativ; **ornamental garden** Ziergarten *der*.

ornate [ɔː'neɪt] *adj* reich verziert; [language] blumig.

ornithology [ˌɔːnɪˈθɒlədʒɪ] n Ornithologie die.

orphan [ˈɔːfn] ◇ n Waise die, Waisenkind das. ◇ vt: **to be orphaned** (zur) Waise werden.

orphanage [ˈɔːfənɪdʒ] n Waisenhaus das.

orthodox [ˈɔːθədɒks] adj - **1.** [conventional] konventionell - **2.** RELIG orthodox.

orthopaedic [ˌɔːθəˈpiːdɪk] adj orthopädisch.

Oslo [ˈɒzləʊ] n Oslo nt.

ostensible [ɒˈstensəbl] adj angeblich.

ostentatious [ˌɒstənˈteɪʃəs] adj [person] protzenhaft; [behaviour] betont auffällig.

osteopath [ˈɒstɪəpæθ] n Osteopath der, -in die.

ostracize, -ise [ˈɒstrəsaɪz] vt ächten.

ostrich [ˈɒstrɪtʃ] n Strauß der.

other [ˈʌðər] ◇ adj andere(r) (s); **the other one** der/die/das andere; **the other day** neulich; **every other day** jeden zweiten Tag; **any other questions?** sonst noch Fragen? ◇ pron andere(r) (s); **one or other (of us)** der eine oder andere (von uns); **one after the other** hintereinander. ◇ adv: **other than** außer; **it was none other than the king** es war kein anderer als der König.

otherwise [ˈʌðəwaɪz] ◇ adv - **1.** [apart from that] ansonsten, sonst - **2.** [differently] anders; **to be otherwise engaged** anderweitig beschäftigt sein; **otherwise known as** auch bekannt als. ◇ conj [or else] sonst, andernfalls.

otter [ˈɒtər] n Otter der.

ouch [aʊtʃ] excl au!, aua!

ought [ɔːt] aux vb: **I ought to go now** ich sollte jetzt gehen; **you ought not to have said that du** hättest das nicht sagen sollen; **you ought to see a doctor** du solltest zum Arzt gehen; **the car ought to be ready by Friday** das Auto sollte Freitag fertig sein; **that ought to be enough for three** das dürfte für drei Personen genügen.

ounce [aʊns] n - **1.** [unit of measurement] Unze die (= 28,35 g) - **2.** fig [of truth, intelligence] Funken der.

our [aʊər] poss adj unser; **our children** unsere Kinder; **we washed our hair** wir haben uns die Haare gewaschen; **a home of our own** ein eigenes Haus.

ours [aʊəz] poss pron unsere(r) (s); **this suitcase is ours** dieser Koffer gehört uns; **a friend of ours** ein Freund von uns.

ourselves [aʊəˈselvz] pron (reflexive, after prep) uns; **we did it ourselves** wir haben es selbst gemacht; **(all) by ourselves** (ganz) allein.

oust [aʊst] vt fml: **to oust sb from sthg** [position, job] jn aus etw verdrängen.

out [aʊt] ◇ adj [light, cigarette] aus. ◇ adv - **1.** [outside] draußen; **to come out (of)** herauskommen (aus); **to get out (of)** aussteigen (aus); **it's cold out today** es ist heute kalt draußen; **out you go!** raus mit dir!; **out here/there** hier/dort draußen - **2.** [not at home, work]: **she's out** sie ist nicht da; **to go out** ausgehen; **to go out for a walk** einen Spaziergang machen - **3.** [so as to be extinguished] aus; **put your cigarette out!** mach deine Zigarette aus! - **4.** [of tides]: **the tide is out** es ist Ebbe - **5.** [expressing removal]: **to take sthg out (of)** etw herausnehmen (aus); [money] etw abheben (von); **he poured the water out** er schüttete das Wasser aus - **6.** [expressing distribution]: **to hand sthg out** etw austeilen - **7.** [wrong]: **the bill's £10 out** die Rechnung stimmt um 10 Pfund nicht - **8.** [published, known]: **the book is just out** das Buch ist soeben erschienen; **the secret is out** das Geheimnis ist gelüftet - **9.** [in flower] aufgeblüht; **the roses are out** die Rosen blühen - **10.** [visible]: **the moon is out** der Mond scheint - **11.** [out of fashion] aus der Mode - **12.** inf [on strike]: **they've been out for months now** sie streiken schon seit Monaten - **13.** [determined]: **to be out for revenge** auf Rache aus sein; **I'm not out to make money** ich bin nicht darauf aus, Geld zu verdienen. ◆ **out of** prep - **1.** [away from, outside]: **stay out of the sun** bleib aus der Sonne; **I was out of the country** ich war im Ausland - **2.** [indicating cause, origin] aus (+ D); **out of respect/curiosity** aus Respekt/Neugierde; **made out of wood** aus Holz (gemacht) - **3.** [without]: **I'm out of** OR **I've run out of cigarettes** ich habe keine Zigaretten mehr - **4.** [to indicate proportion]: **five out of ten** fünf von zehn - **5.** phr: **out of danger/control** außer Gefahr/Kontrolle. ◆ **out of doors** adv im Freien.

out-and-out adj [liar, fool, crook] ausgemacht.

outback [ˈaʊtbæk] n: **the outback** weit abseits der Städte gelegener Teil Australiens.

outboard (motor) [ˈaʊtbɔːd-] n Außenbordmotor der.

outbreak [ˈaʊtbreɪk] n [of war, disease] Ausbruch der.

outburst [ˈaʊtbɜːst] n [of emotion, violence] Ausbruch der.

outcast [ˈaʊtkɑːst] n [socially] Außenseiter der, -in die; [from family, group] Verstoßene der, die.

outcome [ˈaʊtkʌm] n Ergebnis das.

outcry [ˈaʊtkraɪ] n Aufschrei der der Empörung.

outdated [ˌaʊtˈdeɪtɪd] adj [belief, concept, method] überholt; [language] antiquiert.

outdid [ˌaʊtˈdɪd] pt ▷ **outdo**.

outdo [ˌaʊtˈduː] (pt -did, pp -done [-ˈdʌn]) vt übertreffen.

outdoor ['aʊtdɔːr] *adj* [life, activity] im Freien; **outdoor swimming pool** Freibad *das*; **outdoor clothes** Straßenkleidung *die*.

outdoors [aʊt'dɔːz] *adv* draußen, im Freien; [go] nach draußen.

outer ['aʊtər] *adj* [wall] Außen-; [layer] äußere(r) (s).

outer space *n* Weltraum *der*.

outfit ['aʊtfɪt] *n* - 1. [clothes] Kleider *Pl*; [fancy dress] Kostüm *das* - 2. *inf* [organization] Laden *der*, Verein *der*.

outgoing ['aʊt,gəʊɪŋ] *adj* - 1. [from job] (aus dem Amt) scheidend - 2. [friendly, sociable] kontaktfreudig. **outgoings** *npl* UK Ausgaben *Pl*.

outgrow [,aʊt'grəʊ] (*pt* **-grew** [-'gruː], *pp* **-grown** [-'grəʊn]) *vt* - 1. [grow too big for] herauswachsen aus - 2. [habit] ablegen.

outhouse ['aʊthaʊs] (*pl* [-haʊzɪz]) *n* Nebengebäude *das*.

outing ['aʊtɪŋ] *n* [trip] Ausflug *der*.

outlandish [aʊt'lændɪʃ] *adj* sonderbar.

outlaw ['aʊtlɔː] <> *n* Geächtete *der*, *die*; [in the Wild West] Bandit *der*. <> *vt* [make illegal] verbieten.

outlay ['aʊtleɪ] *n* Kostenaufwand *der*.

outlet ['aʊtlet] *n* - 1. [for feelings] Ventil *das* - 2. [hole, pipe] Auslass *der* - 3. [shop] Verkaufsstelle *die* - 4. *US* ELEC Steckdose *die*.

outline ['aʊtlaɪn] <> *n* - 1. [brief description] Abriss *der*; **in outline** in Grundzügen - 2. [silhouette] Umriss *der*. <> *vt* [describe briefly] umreißen, skizzieren.

outlive [,aʊt'lɪv] *vt* [subj: person] überleben.

outlook ['aʊtlʊk] *n* - 1. [attitude, disposition] Einstellung *die* - 2. [prospect] Aussichten *Pl*.

outlying ['aʊt,laɪɪŋ] *adj* [villages] abgelegen; **outlying district** Außenbezirk *der*.

outmoded [,aʊt'məʊdɪd] *adj* überholt.

outnumber [,aʊt'nʌmbər] *vt* zahlenmäßig überlegen sein (+ *D*).

out-of-date *adj* [passport, season ticket] abgelaufen; [clothes] altmodisch; [belief] überholt.

out of doors *adv* draußen, im Freien; [go] nach draußen.

out-of-the-way *adj* [isolated] abgelegen.

outpatient ['aʊt,peɪʃnt] *n* ambulanter Patient, ambulante Patientin; **outpatients (department)** Ambulanz *die*.

output ['aʊtpʊt] *n* (*U*) - 1. [production - of factory, writer] Produktion *die*; [- in agriculture] Ertrag *der* - 2. [COMPUT - printing out] Ausdrucken; [- printout] Ausdruck *der*.

outrage ['aʊtreɪdʒ] <> *n* - 1. (*U*) [anger, shock] Empörung *die* - 2. [atrocity] Verbrechen *das*. <> *vt* empören; [sense of morality] zuwiderlaufen (+ *D*).

outrageous [aʊt'reɪdʒəs] *adj* - 1. [offensive, shocking - crime] verabscheuungswürdig; [- language] unflätig; [- behaviour] unerhört - 2. [extravagant, wild - outfit, idea] exzentrisch.

outright <> *adj* ['aʊtraɪt] [refusal, denial] kategorisch; [disaster] total; [winner, victory] klar; [lie] glatt. <> *adv* [,aʊt'raɪt] [ask] ohne Umschweife; [deny] kategorisch; [win, fail] klar.

outset ['aʊtset] *n*: **at the outset** zu OR am Anfang; **from the outset** von Anfang an.

outside <> *adv* [,aʊt'saɪd] draußen; **to go outside** nach draußen gehen. <> *prep* ['aʊt'saɪd] - 1. [gen] außerhalb (+ *G*); **we live just outside London** wir wohnen gleich außerhalb Londons; **outside (office) hours** außerhalb der Dienststunden - 2. [in front of] vor (+ *A*, *D*); **outside the door** vor der Tür. <> *adj* ['aʊt'saɪd] - 1. [exterior] Außen- - 2. [help, advice] von außen; **outside influence** äußere Einflüsse - 3. [unlikely]: **there's an outside chance** es besteht eine geringe Chance. <> *n* ['aʊtsaɪd] [of building, car, container] Außenseite *die*; **to open the door from the outside** die Tür von außen öffnen. **outside of** *prep* - 1. *US* [on the outside of] außerhalb (+ *G*) - 2. [apart from] außer.

outside lane *n* Überholspur *die*.

outside line *n* Amtsleitung *die*.

outsider [,aʊt'saɪdər] *n* Außenseiter *der*, -in *die*.

outsize ['aʊtsaɪz] *adj* - 1. [book, portion] überdimensional - 2.: **outsize clothes** Kleidung *die* in Übergröße.

outskirts ['aʊtskɜːts] *npl*: **the outskirts** die Außenbezirke *Pl*; **on the outskirts** am Stadtrand.

outsource ['aʊtsɔːs] *vt* outsourcen.

outsourcing ['aʊtsɔːsɪŋ] *n* Outsourcing *das*.

outspoken [,aʊt'spəʊkn] *adj* freimütig.

outstanding [,aʊt'stændɪŋ] *adj* - 1. [excellent - person] außergewöhnlich; [- performance, achievement] hervorragend - 2. [very obvious, important] bemerkenswert - 3. [not paid - money] ausstehend; [- bill] unbezahlt - 4. [still to be done - work] unerledigt; [- problem] ungeklärt.

outstay [,aʊt'steɪ] *vt*: **to outstay one's welcome** länger bleiben als erwünscht.

outstretched [,aʊt'stretʃt] *adj* ausgestreckt.

outstrip [,aʊt'strɪp] *vt* - 1. [do better than] übertreffen - 2. [run faster than] überholen.

out-tray *n* Ablage *die* für Ausgänge.

outward ['aʊtwəd] <> *adj* - 1. [going away]: **outward journey** Hinreise *die* - 2. [external, visible]: **she maintained her outward composure** sie blieb äußerlich ruhig; **he shows no outward sign of his grief** nach außen hin zeigt er nichts von seinem Kummer. <> *adv US* = **outwards**.

outwardly ['aʊtwədlɪ] *adv* nach außen hin.

outwards UK ['aʊtwədz], **outward** US adv
nach außen.

outweigh [,aʊt'weɪ] vt überwiegen.

outwit [,aʊt'wɪt] vt überlisten.

oval ['əʊvl] <> adj oval. <> n Oval das.

Oval Office n: the Oval Office Büro des US-
Präsidenten im Weißen Haus.

ovary ['əʊvərɪ] n ANAT Eierstock der.

ovation [əʊ'veɪʃn] n Ovation die, begeister-
ter Beifall; **to give sb a standing ovation** jm
stehende Ovationen darlbringen.

oven ['ʌvn] n [for cooking] Backofen der.

ovenproof ['ʌvnpruːf] adj feuerfest.

over ['əʊvəʳ] <> prep - 1. [directly above] über
(+ D); **a bridge over the road** eine Brücke über
der Straße - 2. [indicating place, position] über
(+ D); [indicating direction] über (+ A); **she wore
a veil over her face** sie trug einen Schleier vor
dem Gesicht; **put your coat over the chair** leg
deinen Mantel über den Stuhl - 3. [across] über
(+ A); **to walk over sthg** über etw laufen; **he
threw it over the wall** er warf es über die
Mauer; **it's just over the road** es ist gleich gegenüber; **it's over the river** es ist auf der anderen Seite des Flusses; **with a view over the
gardens** mit Blick auf die Gärten - 4. [more
than] über (+ A); **it cost over $1,000** es hat über
1000 Dollar gekostet; **over and above this
amount** über den Betrag hinaus - 5. [about]
über (+ A); **an argument over the price** ein
Streit über den Preis - 6. [during]: **over the
weekend** übers Wochenende; **over the past
two years** in den letzten zwei Jahren; **to discuss sthg over lunch/a cup of coffee** etw beim
Essen/bei einer Tasse Kaffee besprechen
- 7. [to do]: **he took a long time over it** er hat
lange dazu gebraucht - 8. [recovered from] über
(+ A); **to be over sthg** über etw (A) hinweg
sein - 9. [by means of] über (+ A); **over the
phone** am Telefon; **over the radio** im Radio.
<> adv - 1. [referring to distance away]: **over by
the gate** drüben beim Tor; **over here/there**
hier/da drüben - 2. [across] herüber/hinüber;
to drive over herüberlfahren/hinüberlfahren
- 3. [round to other side]: **to turn sthg over** etw
umldrehen; **to roll over** sich umldrehen
- 4. [more]: **children aged 12 and over** Kinder
ab 12; **sums of £100 and over** Summen von
100 Pfund und mehr - 5. [remaining] übrig; **to
be (left) over** übrig bleiben - 6. [at/to sb's
house]: **to invite sb over for dinner** jn zu sich
zum Essen einlladen; **I was over at my mum's
yesterday** ich war gestern bei meiner Mutter - 7. RADIO over; **over and out!** over and out!
- 8. [involving repetitions]: **(all) over again** wieder von vorne; **over and over (again)** immer
wieder. <> adj [finished]: **to be over** zu Ende
sein.

overall <> adj ['əʊvərɔːl] - 1. [total] Gesamt-
- 2. [general] allgemein. <> adv [,əʊvər'ɔːl]
- 1. [in total] insgesamt - 2. [in general] im

Großen und Ganzen. <> n ['əʊvərɔːl]
- 1. [coat] Kittel der - 2. US [with trousers] Overall der. ◈ **overalls** npl - 1. [with long sleeves]
Overall der - 2. US [with bib] Latzhose die.

overawe [,əʊvər'ɔː] vt [subj: person - make feel
fear] einlschüchtern; [- make feel respect] Ehrfurcht einlflößen (+ D); [subj: surroundings]
überwältigen.

overbalance [,əʊvə'bæləns] vi das Gleichgewicht verlieren.

overbearing [,əʊvə'beərɪŋ] adj pej herrisch.

overboard ['əʊvəbɔːd] adv NAUT: **to fall overboard** über Bord gehen.

overcame [,əʊvə'keɪm] pt ▷─ **overcome**.

overcast [,əʊvə'kɑːst] adj bedeckt.

overcharge [,əʊvə'tʃɑːdʒ] vt: **to overcharge
sb (for sthg)** jm zu viel berechnen (für etw).

overcoat ['əʊvəkəʊt] n Mantel der.

overcome [,əʊvə'kʌm] (pt -came, pp -come)
vt - 1. [control, deal with] überwinden - 2. [over-
whelm]: **to be overcome with emotion** gerührt sein; **to be overcome by fear** von Furcht
ergriffen werden; **he was overcome by the
fumes** die Dämpfe machten ihn bewusstlos.

overcrowded [,əʊvə'kraʊdɪd] adj [room,
pub, prison] überfüllt; [town] übervölkert.

overcrowding [,əʊvə'kraʊdɪŋ] n [of room,
pub, prison] Überfüllung die; [of town] Über-
völkerung die.

overdo [,əʊvə'duː] (pt -did [-'dɪd], pp -done
[-'dʌn]) vt - 1. [exaggerate, do too much] es
übertreiben mit; **to overdo it** es übertreiben;
[work too hard] sich übernehmen - 2. [overcook
- vegetables] verkochen; [- steak] verbraten.

overdose n ['əʊvədəʊs] Überdosis die.

overdraft ['əʊvədrɑːft] n Kontoüberzie-
hung die.

overdrawn [,əʊvə'drɔːn] adj [account] überzogen; **I'm (£200) overdrawn** mein Konto ist
(um 200 Pfund) überzogen.

overdue [,əʊvə'djuː] adj - 1. [late - library
book] überfällig; **the train is 20 minutes overdue** der Zug hat 20 Minuten Verspätung
- 2. [reform, rent, bill] überfällig.

overestimate [,əʊvər'estɪmeɪt] vt - 1. [guess
too high a value for] zu hoch einlschätzen
- 2. [overrate] überschätzen.

overflow <> vi [,əʊvə'fləʊ] - 1. [bath] überlaufen; [river] über die Ufer treten - 2. [place,
container]: **to be overflowing (with sthg)** [room]
überfüllt sein (mit etw); [drawer, box] über-
quellen (vor etw). <> n ['əʊvəfləʊ] [pipe, hole]
Überlauf der.

overgrown [,əʊvə'grəʊn] adj [garden, path]
überwuchert.

overhaul <> n ['əʊvəhɔːl] - 1. [service] Über-
holung die - 2. [revision] Überarbeitung die.
<> vt [,əʊvə'hɔːl] - 1. [service] überholen
- 2. [revise] überarbeiten.

overhead ◇ *adj* ['əʊvəhed]: **overhead cable** ELEC Hochspannungsleitung *die*; **overhead lighting** Deckenbeleuchtung *die*. ◇ *adv* [,əʊvə'hed] über uns/ihm/*etc*; the clouds overhead die Wolken am Himmel. ◇ *n* ['əʊvəhed] *(U)* US Gemeinkosten *Pl*. **♣ overheads** *npl* UK Gemeinkosten *Pl*.

overhead projector *n* Overheadprojektor *der*.

overhear [,əʊvə'hɪər] *(pt & pp* -heard [-'hɜːd]) *vt* [remark] zufällig hören; [conversation] zufällig mithören.

overheat [,əʊvə'hiːt] ◇ *vt* [room] überheizen. ◇ *vi* [engine, car] heiß laufen; [photocopier, toaster] zu heiß werden.

overjoyed [,əʊvə'dʒɔɪd] *adj*: to be overjoyed (at sthg) (über etw *(A))* überglücklich sein.

overkill ['əʊvəkɪl] *n* [excess]: to be overkill zu viel des Guten sein.

overladen [,əʊvə'leɪdn] ◇ *pp* ▷ **overload**. ◇ *adj* zu schwer beladen.

overland ['əʊvəlænd] *adj & adv* auf dem Landweg.

overlap *vi* [,əʊvə'læp] - **1.** [cover each other] einander teilweise überdecken - **2.** [be similar]: to overlap (with sthg) [ideas, systems] sich teilweise decken (mit etw); [timetable, holiday] sich überschneiden (mit etw).

overleaf [,əʊvə'liːf] *adv* auf der Rückseite.

overload [,əʊvə'ləʊd] *(pp* -loaded OR -laden) *vt* - **1.** [put too much in] überladen - **2.** ELEC überlasten - **3.** [with work, problems]: to be overloaded (with sthg) überlastet sein (mit etw).

overlook [,əʊvə'lʊk] *vt* - **1.** [look over] eine Aussicht haben auf *(+ A)*; a room overlooking the square ein Zimmer mit Blick auf den Platz - **2.** [disregard, miss] übersehen - **3.** [excuse] hinwegsehen über *(+ A)*.

overnight ◇ *adj* ['əʊvənaɪt]: **overnight stay** Übernachtung *die*; **overnight bag** kleine Reisetasche; to be an overnight success [person] über Nacht großen Erfolg haben; [play] über Nacht ein großer Erfolg sein. ◇ *adv* [,əʊvə'naɪt] über Nacht.

overpass ['əʊvəpɑːs] *n* US Überführung *die*.

overpower [,əʊvə'paʊər] *vt* überwältigen.

overpowering [,əʊvə'paʊərɪŋ] *adj* [feeling] überwältigend; [heat] unerträglich; [smell] penetrant; [person] einschüchternd.

overran [,əʊvə'ræn] *pt* ▷ **overrun**.

overrated [,əʊvə'reɪtɪd] *adj*: to be overrated überschätzt werden.

override [,əʊvə'raɪd] *(pt* -rode, *pp* -ridden [-'rɪdn]) *vt* - **1.** [be more important than] Vorrang haben vor *(+ D)* - **2.** [overrule - decision] auflheben.

overriding [,əʊvə'raɪdɪŋ] *adj* vorrangig.

overrode [,əʊvə'rəʊd] *pt* ▷ **override**.

overrule [,əʊvə'ruːl] *vt* [person] überstimmen; [decision] auflheben; [objection] ablweisen.

overrun [,əʊvə'rʌn] *(pt* -ran, *pp* -run) ◇ *vt* - **1.** MIL [occupy] einfallen in *(+ A)* - **2.** *fig*: to be overrun with [insects, rats] wimmeln von; [weeds] überwuchert sein von; [tourists] überlaufen sein von. ◇ *vi* [last too long] länger als vorgesehen dauern.

oversaw [,əʊvə'sɔː] *pt* ▷ **oversee**.

overseas ◇ *adj* ['əʊvəsiːz] - **1.** [in or to foreign countries] Auslands-; **overseas aid** Entwicklungshilfe *die* - **2.** [from abroad] aus dem Ausland. ◇ *adv* [,əʊvə'siːz] [travel] nach Übersee; [study, live] in Übersee.

oversee [,əʊvə'siː] *(pt* -saw, *pp* -seen [-'siːn]) *vt* beaufsichtigen.

overshadow [,əʊvə'ʃædəʊ] *vt* - **1.** *fig* [outweigh, eclipse]: to be overshadowed by sb/sthg von jm/etw in den Schatten gestellt werden - **2.** *fig* [mar, cloud]: to be overshadowed by sthg [subj: party, victory] von etw überschattet werden; [subj: happiness, peace of mind] durch etw stark beeinträchtigt werden.

overshoot [,əʊvə'ʃuːt] *(pt & pp* -shot [-ʃɒt]) *vt* [go past - turning] vorbeifahren an *(+ D)*; [- runway] hinauslrollen über *(+ A)*.

oversight ['əʊvəsaɪt] *n* Versehen *das*.

oversleep [,əʊvə'sliːp] *(pt & pp* -slept [-'slept]) *vi* verschlafen.

overstep [,əʊvə'step] *vt* überschreiten; to overstep the mark zu weit gehen.

overt ['əʊvɜːt] *adj* unverhohlen.

overtake [,əʊvə'teɪk] *(pt* -took, *pp* -taken [-'teɪkn]) ◇ *vt* - **1.** AUT überholen - **2.** [subj: disaster, misfortune] ereilen. ◇ *vi* überholen.

overthrow *(pt* -threw [-'θruː], *pp* -thrown [-'θrəʊn]) ◇ *n* ['əʊvəθrəʊ] [of government] Sturz *der*. ◇ *vt* [,əʊvə'θrəʊ] [government, president] stürzen.

overtime ['əʊvətaɪm] ◇ *n (U)* - **1.** [extra time worked] Überstunden *Pl* - **2.** US SPORT Verlängerung *die*. ◇ *adv*: to work overtime Überstunden machen.

overtones ['əʊvətəʊnz] *npl* Untertöne *Pl*.

overtook [,əʊvə'tʊk] *pt* ▷ **overtake**.

overture ['əʊvə,tjʊər] *n* MUS Ouvertüre *die*.

overturn [,əʊvə'tɜːn] ◇ *vt* - **1.** [turn over] umlwerfen - **2.** [overrule] auflheben - **3.** [overthrow] stürzen. ◇ *vi* [boat] kentern; [lorry] umlstürzen.

overweight [,əʊvə'weɪt] *adj* [person] übergewichtig.

overwhelm [,əʊvə'welm] *vt* überwältigen.

overwhelming [,əʊvə'welmɪŋ] *adj* - **1.** [feeling, quality] überwältigend - **2.** [victory, majority] überwältigend; [defeat] vernichtend.

overwork [,əʊvə'wɜːk] ◇ *n (U)* Überlastung *die*. ◇ *vt* [give too much work to] mit Arbeit überlasten.

owe [əʊ] *vt*: to owe sthg to sb, to owe sb sthg [money, respect, gratitude] jm etw schulden; [good looks, success] jm etw verdanken.

owing ['əʊɪŋ] *adj*: the amount owing der ausstehende Betrag; to be owing ausl stehen.
➡ **owing to** *prep* wegen (+ G).

owl [aʊl] *n* Eule *die*.

own [əʊn] ◇ *adj* eigen; I have my own bedroom ich habe ein eigenes Zimmer; she makes her own clothes sie näht ihre Kleider selbst. ◇ *pron*: it has a taste all of its own es hat einen ganz eigenen Geschmack; on my own allein; to get one's own back *inf* sich revanchieren; he can hold his own er kann sich behaupten. ◇ *vt* [possess] besitzen; who owns this car? wem gehört dieses Auto?
➡ **own up** *vi*: to own up (to sthg) (etw) zugeben.

owner ['əʊnə**r**] *n* Besitzer *der*, -in *die*; [of firm, shop] Inhaber *der*, -in *die*.

ownership ['əʊnə**ʃ**ɪp] *n* Besitz *der*.

ox [ɒks] (*pl* oxen) *n* Ochse *der*.

Oxbridge ['ɒksbrɪdʒ] *n* die Universitäten Oxford und Cambridge.

oxen ['ɒksn] *Pl* ▷ **ox**.

oxtail soup [ˌɒksteɪl-] *n* Ochsenschwanzsuppe *die*.

oxygen ['ɒksɪdʒən] *n* Sauerstoff *der*.

oxygen mask *n* Sauerstoffmaske *die*.

oyster ['ɔɪstə**r**] *n* Auster *die*.

oz. *abbr of* **ounce**.

ozone ['əʊzəʊn] *n* Ozon *das*.

ozone-friendly *adj* FCKW-frei.

ozone layer *n* Ozonschicht *die*.

P

p[1] (*pl* p's OR ps), **P** (*pl* P's OR Ps) [piː] *n* [letter] p *das*, P *das*.

p[2] [piː] *abbr of* **page, penny, pence**.

P45 [ˌpiːfɔːtɪˈfaɪv] *n UK* ≃ Lohnsteuerkarte *die*, Steuerbescheinigung, die bei einem Arbeitsplatzwechsel dem neuen Arbeitgeber vorgelegt werden muss.

pa [pɑː] *n esp US inf* Papa *der*, Vati *der*.

p.a. (*abbr of* per annum) p. a.

PA *n* - 1. *UK abbr of* **personal assistant** - 2. (*abbr of* public address system) Lautsprecheranlage *die*.

pace [peɪs] ◇ *n* - 1. [speed, rate] Tempo *das*; to keep pace (with sb/sthg) (mit jm/ etw) Schritt halten - 2. [step] Schritt *der*. ◇ *vi* [walk up and down] auf und ab gehen.

pacemaker ['peɪsˌmeɪkə**r**] *n* MED Herzschrittmacher *der*.

Pacific [pəˈsɪfɪk] ◇ *adj* pazifisch; [coast] Pazifik-. ◇ *n*: the Pacific (Ocean) der Pazifik.

pacifier ['pæsɪfaɪə**r**] *n US* [for child] Schnuller *der*.

pacifist ['pæsɪfɪst] *n* Pazifist *der*, -in *die*.

pacify ['pæsɪfaɪ] *vt* - 1. [person] beruhigen - 2. [country, region] befriedigen.

pack [pæk] ◇ *n* - 1. [bag - on back] Rucksack *der*; [- carried by animal] Last *die* - 2. [packet - of cigarettes, tissues] Packung *die*; [- of washing powder] Paket *das* - 3. [of cards] (Karten)spiel *das* - 4. [group - of wolves] Rudel *das*; [- of hounds] Meute *die*; [- of thieves] Bande *die*. ◇ *vt* - 1. [for journey, holiday - bag, suitcase] packen; [- clothes, toothbrush] einl packen - 2. [put in container, parcel] einl packen; [product] verpacken - 3. [crowd into] füllen; to be packed into sthg in etw (A) gezwängt sein. ◇ *vi* [for journey, holiday] packen. ➡ **pack in** ◇ *vt sep UK inf* [job] hinl schmeißen; [boyfriend] sausen lassen; [smoking] aufl hören mit; pack it in! [stop annoying me, shut up] hör (doch) auf damit! ◇ *vi inf* [break down] den Geist aufl geben. ➡ **pack off** *vt sep inf* fortl schicken.

package ['pækɪdʒ] ◇ *n* - 1. [gen & COMPUT] Paket *das* - 2. *esp US* [packet - of cigarettes, tissues] Packung *die*; [- of washing powder] Paket *das*. ◇ *vt* [wrap up, pack up] verpacken.

package deal *n* Paket *das*.

package tour *n* Pauschalreise *die*.

packaging ['pækɪdʒɪŋ] *n* (U) [wrapping] Verpackung *die*.

packed [pækt] *adj* - 1. [place]: packed (with) (über)voll (mit) - 2. [magazine, information pack]: packed with voll mit.

packed lunch *n UK* Lunchpaket *das*.

packet ['pækɪt] *n* - 1. [box, bag, contents - of biscuits, cigarettes] Packung *die*; [- of washing powder] Paket *das* - 2. [parcel] Päckchen *das*.

packing ['pækɪŋ] *n* (U) - 1. [protective material] Verpackungsmaterial *das* - 2. [for journey, holiday] Packen *das*.

packing case *n* Kiste *die*.

pact [pækt] *n* Pakt *der*.

pad [pæd] ◇ *n* - 1. [for garment] Polster *das* - 2. [for protection] Schützer *der* - 3. [notepad] Block *der* - 4. [for absorbing liquid]: pad of cotton wool Wattebausch *der*; sanitary pad Damenbinde *die* - 5. [space]: (launch) pad Abschussrampe *die* - 6. *inf dated* [home] Bude *die*. ◇ *vt* [furniture] polstern; [clothing] wattieren.

padding ['pædɪŋ] n (U) - **1.** [protective material] Polsterung die - **2.** [in speech, essay, letter] Füllwerk das.

paddle ['pædl] ◇ n - **1.** [for canoe, dinghy] Paddel das - **2.** [wade]: **to have a paddle** durchs Wasser waten. ◇ vi - **1.** [in canoe, dinghy] paddeln - **2.** [wade] waten.

paddle boat, paddle steamer n Raddampfer der.

paddling pool ['pædlɪŋ-] n - **1.** [in park] Planschbad das - **2.** [inflatable] Planschbecken das.

paddock ['pædək] n - **1.** [small field] Koppel die - **2.** [at racecourse] Sattelplatz der.

paddy field ['pædɪ-] n Reisfeld das.

padlock ['pædlɒk] ◇ n Vorhängeschloss das. ◇ vt (mit einem Vorhängeschloss) verschließen.

paediatrics [,piːdɪ'ætrɪks] n = **pediatrics**.

pagan ['peɪɡən] ◇ adj heidnisch. ◇ n Heide der, -din die.

page [peɪdʒ] ◇ n - **1.** [side of paper] Seite die - **2.** [leaf, sheet of paper] Blatt das. ◇ vt [call out name of] ausrufen lassen; **paging Miss Smith!** Miss Smith, bitte!

pageant ['pædʒənt] n [show] historisches Schauspiel; [parade] Festumzug der.

pageantry ['pædʒəntrɪ] n Prunk der.

page break n COMPUT Seitenumbruch der.

paid [peɪd] ◇ pt & pp ▷ **pay**. ◇ adj bezahlt.

pail [peɪl] n Eimer der.

pain [peɪn] n - **1.** [ache] Schmerz der - **2.** (U) [physical suffering] Schmerzen Pl; **to be in pain** Schmerzen haben - **3.** (U) [mental suffering] Qualen Pl. ◆ **pains** npl [effort] Mühe die; **to be at pains to do sthg** sich (D) große Mühe geben, etw zu tun; **to take pains to do sthg** sich (D) Mühe geben, etw zu tun.

pained [peɪnd] adj [expression] gequält.

painful ['peɪnfʊl] adj - **1.** [physically] schmerzhaft; **to be painful** wehtun, schmerzen - **2.** [distressing] schmerzlich.

painfully ['peɪnfʊlɪ] adv - **1.** [physically] unter Schmerzen - **2.** [distressingly] schmerzlich.

painkiller ['peɪn,kɪlər] n schmerzstillendes Mittel.

painless ['peɪnlɪs] adj - **1.** [physically] schmerzlos - **2.** [unproblematic] unproblematisch; [exam, decision] leicht.

painstaking ['peɪnz,teɪkɪŋ] adj sorgfältig.

paint [peɪnt] ◇ n Farbe die; [on car, furniture] Lack der. ◇ vt - **1.** [picture, portrait] malen - **2.** [wall, room] streichen; [car, fingernails] lackieren; [lips, face] schminken. ◇ vi ART malen.

paintbrush ['peɪntbrʌʃ] n Pinsel der.

painter ['peɪntər] n Maler der, -in die.

painting ['peɪntɪŋ] n - **1.** [picture] Gemälde das - **2.** [artistic] Malen das; [activity] Malerei die - **3.** [by decorator] Anstreichen das.

paintwork ['peɪntwɜːk] n (U) [on wall] Anstrich der; [on car] Lack der.

pair [peər] n Paar das; **in pairs** paarweise; **a pair of pliers** eine Zange; **a pair of scissors** eine Schere; **a pair of shorts** Shorts Pl; **a pair of spectacles** eine Brille; **a pair of tights** eine Strumpfhose; **a pair of trousers** eine Hose.

pajamas [pə'dʒɑːməz] npl US = **pyjamas**.

Pakistan [UK ,pɑːkɪ'stɑːn, US ,pækɪ'stæn] n Pakistan nt.

Pakistani [UK ,pɑːkɪ'stɑːnɪ, US ,pækɪstænɪ] ◇ adj pakistanisch. ◇ n Pakistaner der, -in die.

pal [pæl] n inf Kumpel der; **be a pal!** sei so nett!

palace ['pælɪs] n Palast der; [of bishop, aristocracy] Palais das; [grand house] Schloss das.

palatable ['pælətəbl] adj - **1.** [food] wohlschmeckend - **2.** [suggestion, idea] annehmbar.

palate ['pælət] n Gaumen der.

palaver [pə'lɑːvər] n inf [fuss] Theater das.

pale [peɪl] adj [colour, face] blass; [clothes] hell; [light] fahl.

Palestine ['pælə,staɪn] n Palästina nt.

Palestinian [,pælə'stɪnɪən] ◇ adj palästinensisch. ◇ n [person] Palästinenser der, -in die.

palette ['pælət] n ART Palette die.

pall [pɔːl] ◇ n - **1.: a pall of smoke** eine Rauchglocke - **2.** US [over coffin] Sargtuch das. ◇ vi an Reiz verlieren.

pallet ['pælɪt] n Palette die.

palm [pɑːm] n - **1.** [tree] Palme die - **2.** [of hand] Handfläche die; **to read sb's palm** jm aus der Hand lesen. ◆ **palm off** vt sep inf: **to palm sthg off on sb** jm etw anldrehen; **to palm sb off with sthg** jn mit etw ablspeisen.

Palm Sunday n Palmsonntag der.

palmtop [-'pɑːmtɒp] n COMPUT Palmtopcomputer der.

palm tree n Palme die.

palpable ['pælpəbl] adj [obvious] offensichtlich.

paltry ['pɔːltrɪ] adj armselig.

pamper ['pæmpər] vt verhätscheln.

pamphlet ['pæmflɪt] n [for information] Broschüre die; [for publicity] (Werbe)prospekt der; [political] Pamphlet das.

pan [pæn] ◇ n - **1.** [for frying] Pfanne die; [saucepan] Topf der - **2.** US [for baking] Backform die. ◇ vt inf [criticize] verreißen. ◇ vi CIN schwenken.

panacea [,pænə'sɪə] n Allheilmittel das.

panama [,pænə'mɑː] n: **panama (hat)** Panamahut der.

Panama Canal *n*: the Panama Canal der Panamakanal.

pancake ['pænkeɪk] *n* Pfannkuchen *der*.

Pancake Day *n UK* Fastnachtsdienstag *der*.

panda ['pændə] (*pl inv OR* -s) *n* Panda *der*.

pandemonium [,pændɪ'məʊnɪəm] *n* Chaos *das*.

pander ['pændə^r] *vi*: **to pander to sb/sthg** jm/etw nachlgeben.

pane [peɪn] *n* Scheibe *die*.

panel ['pænl] *n* - **1**. [of experts, interviewers] Gremium *das*; [on TV and radio programmes] Diskussionsrunde *die* - **2**. [of wood] Platte *die* - **3**. [of machine] Schalttafel *die*.

panelling *UK*, **paneling** *US* ['pænəlɪŋ] *n* Täfelung *die*.

pang [pæŋ] *n* [of guilt, fear, regret] Anfall *der*; **pangs of conscience** Gewissensbisse *Pl*.

panic ['pænɪk] (*pt & pp* -ked, *cont* -king) <> *n* Panik *die*. <> *vi* in Panik geraten; **don't panic!** keine Panik!

panicky ['pænɪkɪ] *adj* [feeling] panisch; **to feel panicky** Angst bekommen.

panic-stricken *adj* von Panik erfasst *OR* ergriffen.

panorama [,pænə'rɑːmə] *n* Panorama *das*.

pansy ['pænzɪ] *n* - **1**. [flower] Stiefmütterchen *das* - **2**. *inf pej* [man] Tunte *die*.

pant [pænt] *vi* keuchen; [dog] hecheln. ● **pants** *npl* - **1**. *UK* [underpants - for men] Unterhose *die*; [- for women] Schlüpfer *der* - **2**. *US* [trousers] Hose *die*.

panther ['pænθə^r] (*pl inv OR* -s) *n* Panther *der*.

panties ['pæntɪz] *npl inf* Schlüpfer *der*.

pantihose ['pæntɪhəʊz] *npl US* = **panty hose**.

pantomime ['pæntəmaɪm] *n UK* meist um die Weihnachtszeit aufgeführtes Märchenspiel.

pantry ['pæntrɪ] *n* Speisekammer *die*.

panty hose ['pæntɪhəʊz] *npl US* Strumpfhose *die*.

papa [*UK* pə'pɑː, *US* 'pæpə] *n dated* [father] Papa *der*.

paper ['peɪpə^r] <> *n* - **1**. [for writing on] Papier *das*; **a piece of paper** [scrap] ein Stück Papier; [sheet] ein Blatt Papier; **on paper** [written down] schriftlich; [in theory] auf dem Papier - **2**. [newspaper] Zeitung *die* - **3**. [exam] Klausur *die* - **4**. [essay] Arbeit *die* - **5**. [at conference] Referat *das*. <> *adj* - **1**. [cup, napkin, hat] Papier-, aus Papier - **2**. [qualifications] auf dem Papier; [profits] nominell. <> *vt* [with wallpaper] tapezieren. ● **papers** *npl* - **1**. [identity papers] Papiere *Pl* - **2**. [documents] Dokumente *Pl*, Unterlagen *Pl*.

paperback ['peɪpəbæk] *n*: **paperback (book)** Taschenbuch *das*.

paper bag *n* Papiertüte *die*.

paper clip *n* Büroklammer *die*.

paper handkerchief *n* Papiertaschentuch *das*.

paper shop *n UK* Zeitungsgeschäft *das*.

paperweight ['peɪpəweɪt] *n* Briefbeschwerer *der*.

paperwork ['peɪpəwɜːk] *n (U)* Schreibarbeit *die*.

paprika ['pæprɪkə] *n* Paprika *der*.

par [pɑː^r] *n* - **1**.: **to be on a par with sb/sthg** [person] sich mit jm/etw messen können; [company, country] mit jm/etw vergleichbar sein - **2**. [in golf] Par *das*; **above/below par** *fig* über/unter dem Durchschnitt - **3**. [good health]: **to feel below** *OR* **under par** nicht ganz auf dem Posten *OR* Damm sein.

parable ['pærəbl] *n RELIG* Gleichnis *das*; [moral story] Parabel *die*.

parachute ['pærəʃuːt] <> *n* Fallschirm *der*. <> *vi* mit dem Fallschirm ablspringen.

parade [pə'reɪd] <> *n* - **1**. [procession] Umzug *der* - **2**. *MIL* Parade *die*. <> *vt* - **1**. [people - soldiers] marschieren lassen; [- captives] zur Schau stellen - **2**. [object] vor sich (D) herltragen - **3**. *fig* [flaunt] zur Schau stellen. <> *vi* paradieren; [soldiers] marschieren.

paradise ['pærədaɪs] *n* Paradies *das*.

paradox ['pærədɒks] *n* Paradox(on) *das*.

paradoxically [,pærə'dɒksɪklɪ] *adv* paradoxerweise.

paraffin ['pærəfɪn] *n* Paraffin *das*.

paragon ['pærəgən] *n* Muster *das*.

paragraph ['pærəgrɑːf] *n* Absatz *der*.

parallel ['pærəlel] (*UK*) (*US*) <> *adj liter & fig*: **parallel (to** *OR* **with)** parallel (zu). <> *n* - **1**. [gen] Parallele *die* - **2**. *GEOG* Breitenkreis *der*; **the 38th parallel** der 38. Breitengrad.

paralyse *UK*, **paralyze** *US* ['pærəlaɪz] *vt* - **1**. *MED* lähmen - **2**. *fig* [immobilize] lahm legen.

paralysis [pə'rælɪsɪs] (*pl* -lyses [-lɪsiːz]) *n MED* Lähmung *die*.

paralyze *vt US* = **paralyse**.

paramedic [,pærə'medɪk] *n* Sanitäter *der*, -in *die*.

parameter [pə'ræmɪtə^r] *n* Parameter *der*.

paramount ['pærəmaʊnt] *adj*: **to be paramount** Vorrang *OR* Priorität haben; **of paramount importance** von äußerster Wichtigkeit.

paranoid ['pærənɔɪd] *adj* - **1**. *MED* paranoid - **2**. [worried, suspicious]: **she's paranoid about being on time** sie hat ständig Angst, zu spät zu kommen; **you're getting paranoid!** dein Misstrauen ist ja krankhaft!

paraphernalia [,pærəfə'neɪlɪə] *n* Drum und Dran *das*.

parasite ['pærəsaɪt] n liter & fig Schmarotzer der, Parasit der.

parasol ['pærəsɒl] n Sonnenschirm der.

paratrooper ['pærətru:pə'] n Fallschirmjäger der.

parcel ['pɑ:sl] (UK) (US) n Paket das. ➡ **parcel up** vt sep als Paket verpacken.

parched [pɑ:tʃt] adj - 1. [very dry - grass, plain] ausgetrocknet, verdorrt; [- throat, lips] trocken - 2. inf [very thirsty]: **I'm parched** ich habe riesigen Durst.

parchment ['pɑ:tʃmənt] n Pergament das.

pardon ['pɑ:dn] ◇ n - 1. LAW Begnadigung die - 2. [forgiveness]: **I beg your pardon?** [showing surprise or offence] erlauben Sie mal!; [what did you say?] (wie) bitte?; **I beg your pardon!** [apologizing] Entschuldigung! ◇ vt - 1. LAW begnadigen - 2. [forgive] verzeihen, vergeben; **to pardon sb for sthg** jm etw verzeihen; **pardon?** [what did you say?] wie bitte?; **pardon me!** Entschuldigung!, Verzeihung!

parent ['peərənt] n [father] Vater der; [mother] Mutter die; **parents** Eltern Pl.

parental [pə'rentl] adj elterlich.

parenthesis [pə'renθɪsɪs] (pl -theses [-θɪsi:z]) n: **in parentheses** in Klammern.

Paris ['pærɪs] n Paris nt.

parish ['pærɪʃ] n Gemeinde die.

parity ['pærətɪ] n [state] Gleichheit die.

park [pɑ:k] ◇ n Park der. ◇ vt parken; [bicycle] abstellen. ◇ vi parken.

parking ['pɑ:kɪŋ] n (U) - 1. [act] Parken das; **'no parking'** 'Parken verboten' - 2. [space] Parkplätze Pl.

parking lot n US Parkplatz der.

parking meter n Parkuhr die.

parking ticket n Strafzettel der.

parlance ['pɑ:ləns] n: **in common/legal parlance** im allgemeinen/juristischen Sprachgebrauch.

parliament ['pɑ:ləmənt] n Parlament das.

parliamentary [,pɑ:lə'mentərɪ] adj parlamentarisch.

parlour UK, **parlor** US ['pɑ:lə'] n [cafe]: **ice cream parlour** Eisdiele die.

parochial [pə'rəʊkɪəl] adj pej [person] engstirnig; [view, approach] eng, beschränkt.

parody ['pærədɪ] ◇ n Parodie die; **a parody of** eine Parodie auf (+ A). ◇ vt parodieren.

parole [pə'rəʊl] n (U) Bewährung die; **on parole** auf Bewährung.

parrot ['pærət] n Papagei der.

parry ['pærɪ] vt liter & fig abwehren.

parsley ['pɑ:slɪ] n Petersilie die.

parsnip ['pɑ:snɪp] n Pastinak der.

parson ['pɑ:sn] n Pfarrer der, -in die.

part [pɑ:t] ◇ n - 1. [gen] Teil der; **in this part of Germany** in dieser Gegend Deutschlands; **for the better part of two hours** fast zwei Stunden; **for the most part** zum größten Teil - 2. [of TV serial] Fortsetzung die - 3. [component] Teil das; **to form part of sthg** Teil von etw sein - 4. [acting role] Rolle die; fig [involvement] Anteil der; **his part in the crime** seine Rolle bei dem Verbrechen; **to play an important part in sthg** eine wichtige Rolle bei etw spielen; **to take part in sthg** an etw (D) teilnehmen; **for my/his/etc part** was mich/ihn/etc anbetrifft; **on the part of** vonseiten (+ G) - 5. US [hair parting] Scheitel der. ◇ adv teils. ◇ vt - 1. [separate] trennen - 2. [curtains] öffnen; [branches] zur Seite schieben; [legs] auflmachen; [hair] scheiteln. ◇ vi - 1. [people] sich trennen - 2. [curtains, lips, legs] sich öffnen; [crowd, branches] sich teilen. ➡ **parts** npl: **in these parts** in dieser Gegend; **in foreign parts** in fremden Ländern. ➡ **part with** vt insep sich trennen von.

part exchange n: **in part exchange (for)** in Zahlung (für).

partial ['pɑ:ʃl] adj - 1. [incomplete] Teil-, teilweise - 2. [biased] parteiisch - 3. [fond]: **to be partial to sthg** eine Schwäche für etw haben.

participant [pɑ:'tɪsɪpənt] n Teilnehmer der, -in die.

participate [pɑ:'tɪsɪpeɪt] vi: **to participate (in)** teillnehmen (an (+ D)).

participation [pɑ:,tɪsɪ'peɪʃn] n Teilnahme die.

participle ['pɑ:tɪsɪpl] n Partizip das.

particle ['pɑ:tɪkl] n - 1. [tiny piece] Teilchen das - 2. GRAM Partikel die.

particular [pə'tɪkjʊlə'] adj - 1. [specific] bestimmt - 2. [special] besondere(r) (s) - 3. [fussy] eigen. ➡ **particulars** npl Einzelheiten Pl. ➡ **in particular** adv besonders; **nothing in particular** nichts Besonderes.

particularly [pə'tɪkjʊləlɪ] adv [very] besonders.

parting ['pɑ:tɪŋ] n - 1. [farewell] Abschied der - 2. UK [in hair] Scheitel der.

partisan [,pɑ:tɪ'zæn] ◇ adj parteiisch. ◇ n [freedom fighter] Partisan der, -in die.

partition [pɑ:'tɪʃn] ◇ n [wall, screen] Trennwand die. ◇ vt teilen.

partly ['pɑ:tlɪ] adv zum Teil, teilweise.

partner ['pɑ:tnə'] ◇ n - 1. [gen] Partner der, -in die - 2. [in a business] Geschäftspartner der, -in die - 3. [in crime] Komplize der, -zin die. ◇ vt: **to partner sb** js Partner sein.

partnership ['pɑ:tnəʃɪp] n - 1. [relationship] Partnerschaft die - 2. [business] (Personen)gesellschaft die.

partridge ['pɑ:trɪdʒ] (pl inv OR -s) n Rebhuhn das.

part-time ◇ adj Teilzeit-. ◇ adv: **to work part-time** Teilzeit arbeiten.

party ['pɑːtɪ] ⬦ n - 1. POL & LAW Partei die - 2. [social gathering] Party die; **to have a party** eine Party geben - 3. [group of people] Gruppe die. ⬦ vi inf feiern.

party line n - 1. POL Parteilinie die - 2. TELEC Gemeinschaftsanschluss der.

pass [pɑːs] ⬦ vt - 1. [walk past] vorbeigehen an (+ D); [drive past] vorbeifahren an (+ D) - 2. AUT [overtake] überholen - 3. [hand over] reichen; **to pass sthg to sb, to pass sb sthg** jm etw reichen - 4. [in football, hockey etc]: **to pass sb the ball, to pass the ball to sb** jm den Ball zuspielen OR passen - 5. [exam, test] bestehen - 6. [candidate] bestehen lassen - 7. [approve - law] verabschieden; [- motion] annehmen; **this product has been passed as fit for sale** dieses Produkt ist für den Verkauf freigegeben worden - 8. [life, time] verbringen - 9. [exceed] überschreiten - 10. [judgement] fällen; [sentence] verhängen. ⬦ vi - 1. [walk past] vorbeigehen; [drive past] vorbeifahren; **to let sb pass** jn vorbeilassen; **if you're passing this way** falls Sie hier vorbeikommen - 2. AUT [overtake] überholen - 3. [road, river, path] führen; [pipe, cable] verlaufen - 4. [time, holiday, lesson] vergehen - 5. [in test, exam] bestehen - 6. [in football, hockey etc] einen Pass spielen. ⬦ n - 1. [document] Ausweis der - 2. UK [in exam] Bestehen das; **to get a pass** bestehen - 3. [between mountains] Pass der - 4. [in football, hockey etc] Pass der; [in tennis] Passierschlag der - 5. phr: **to make a pass at sb** inf bei jm Annäherungsversuche machen. ⬦ **pass as** vt insep durchgehen für. ⬦ **pass away** vi entschlafen. ⬦ **pass by** ⬦ vt insep [walk past] vorbeigehen an (+ D); [drive past] vorbeifahren an (+ D). ⬦ vt sep fig [subj: news, events] vorbeigehen an (+ D). ⬦ vi [walk past] vorbeigehen; [drive past] vorbeifahren. ⬦ **pass for** vt insep = **pass as**. ⬦ **pass on** ⬦ vt sep liter & fig: **to pass sthg on (to sb)** etw (an jn) weitergeben. ⬦ vi - 1. [move on] weitermachen; **let's pass on to the next question** gehen wir zur nächsten Frage über - 2. = **pass away**. ⬦ **pass out** vi - 1. [faint] ohnmächtig werden - 2. UK MIL ernannt werden. ⬦ **pass over** vt insep [subject, problem] übergehen; **to be passed over for promotion** bei der Beförderung übergangen werden. ⬦ **pass through** vi durchkommen; **we're just passing through** wir sind nur auf der Durchreise. ⬦ **pass up** vt sep [opportunity] vorübergehen lassen; [invitation, offer] ablehnen.

passable ['pɑːsəbl] adj - 1. [satisfactory] passabel - 2. [road, path] passierbar.

passage ['pæsɪdʒ] n - 1. [corridor] Gang der; [between houses] Durchgang der - 2. [through crowd] Weg der - 3. ANAT Gang der - 4. (U) fml [transition] Übergang der; **the passage of time** der Strom der Zeit - 5. [sea journey] Überfahrt die.

passageway ['pæsɪdʒweɪ] n Gang der; [between houses] Durchgang der.

passbook ['pɑːsbʊk] n Sparbuch das.

passenger ['pæsɪndʒəʳ] n [gen] Passagier der; [in taxi] Fahrgast der; [in car] Insasse der, -sin die.

passerby [,pɑːsə'baɪ] (pl **passersby** [,pɑːsəz'baɪ]) n Passant der, -in die.

passing ['pɑːsɪŋ] adj [remark] beiläufig; [fashion, mood] vorübergehend. ⬦ **in passing** adv [mention] beiläufig.

passion ['pæʃn] n Leidenschaft die.

passionate ['pæʃənət] adj leidenschaftlich.

passive ['pæsɪv] adj - 1. [person] passiv - 2. GRAM passivisch, Passiv-.

Passover ['pɑːs,əʊvəʳ] n Passah das.

passport ['pɑːspɔːt] n (Reise)pass der.

passport control n Passkontrolle die.

password ['pɑːswɜːd] n Passwort das.

past [pɑːst] ⬦ adj - 1. [former] ehemalig - 2. [earlier] vergangene(r) (s); **in past times** in früheren Zeiten - 3. [most recent, last] letzte(r) (s); **the past month** der letzte Monat - 4. [finished] vorbei. ⬦ n - 1. [time]: **the past** die Vergangenheit; **in the past** früher - 2. [personal history] Vergangenheit die - 3. GRAM Vergangenheit die. ⬦ adv - 1. [telling the time] nach; [by] vorbei; **to run past** vorbeilaufen nach - 2. [by] vorbei; **to run past** vorbeilaufen. ⬦ prep - 1. [telling the time] nach; **twenty past four** zwanzig nach vier; **at half/a quarter past** eight um halb/viertel neun - 2. [by] an (+ D) vorbei; **he drove past the house** er fuhr am Haus vorbei - 3. [beyond] hinter (+ D).

pasta ['pæstə] n (U) Nudeln Pl.

paste [peɪst] ⬦ n - 1. [smooth mixture] Brei der - 2. (U) CULIN Brotaufstrich der - 3. [glue] Kleister der. ⬦ vt kleben; COMPUT einfügen.

pastel ['pæstl] adj pastellfarben.

pasteurize, -ise ['pɑːstʃəraɪz] vt pasteurisieren.

pastille ['pæstɪl] n Pastille die.

pastime ['pɑːstaɪm] n Hobby das.

pastor ['pɑːstəʳ] n Pfarrer der, -in die.

past participle n Partizip Perfekt das.

pastry ['peɪstrɪ] n - 1. [mixture] Teig der - 2. [cake] Teilchen das.

past tense n Vergangenheit die.

pasture ['pɑːstʃəʳ] n [field] Weide die.

pasty ['pæstɪ] n UK CULIN Pastete die.

pat [pæt] ⬦ adv: **to have sthg off pat** etw parat haben. ⬦ n - 1. [light stroke] Klaps der - 2. [of butter] Portion die. ⬦ vt [dog, hand] tätscheln; [back, shoulder] (leicht) klopfen auf (+ A).

patch [pætʃ] ⬦ n - 1. [piece of material] Flicken der - 2. [over eye] Augenklappe die - 3. [small area] Fleck der; **there were still**

patches of snow es lag vereinzelt OR stellenweise noch Schnee; **a bald patch** eine kahle Stelle - **4.** [of land] Stück (Land) das; **vegetable patch** Gemüsebeet das - **5.** [period of time]: **to be going through a difficult patch** eine schwierige Zeit durchlmachen. <> vt flicken.
🔷 **patch up** vt sep - **1.** [mend] zusammenlflicken - **2.** fig [quarrel] beillegen; [marriage] kitten.

patchy ['pætʃɪ] adj - **1.** [fog, sunshine] vereinzelt; [colour] fleckig - **2.** [knowledge] lückenhaft - **3.** [performance, game] unterschiedlich (in der Qualität).

pâté ['pæteɪ] n (U) Pastete die.

patent [UK 'peɪtənt, US 'pætənt] <> adj [obvious] offensichtlich. <> n Patent das. <> vt patentieren lassen.

patent leather n Lackleder das.

paternal [pə'tɜːnl] adj - **1.** [love, attitude] väterlich - **2.** [on father's side]: **paternal grandmother/grandfather** Großmutter die/Großvater der väterlicherseits.

path [pɑːθ] (pl [pɑːðz]) n - **1.** [track] Weg der; [narrower] Pfad der - **2.** [way ahead, course of action] Weg der - **3.** [trajectory] Bahn die.

pathetic [pə'θetɪk] adj - **1.** [causing pity] Mitleid erregend; **to be a pathetic sight** ein Bild des Jammers bieten - **2.** [useless - attempt, effort] erbärmlich; **she's pathetic** sie ist ein hoffnungsloser Fall.

pathological [ˌpæθə'lɒdʒɪkl] adj - **1.** MED pathologisch - **2.** [uncontrollable] krankhaft.

pathology [pə'θɒlədʒɪ] n Pathologie die.

pathos ['peɪθɒs] n Pathos das.

pathway ['pɑːθweɪ] n Weg der; [narrower] Pfad der.

patience ['peɪʃns] n - **1.** [quality] Geduld die - **2.** [card game] Patience die.

patient ['peɪʃnt] <> adj geduldig. <> n Patient der, -in die.

patio ['pætɪəʊ] (pl -s) n Terrasse die.

patriotic [UK ˌpætrɪ'ɒtɪk, US ˌpeɪtrɪ'ɒtɪk] adj patriotisch.

patrol [pə'trəʊl] <> n [of police] Streife die; [of soldiers] Patrouille die. <> vt [subj: police - in vehicle] Streife fahren in (+ D); [- on foot] seine Runden machen in (+ D); [subj: soldiers] patrouillieren.

patrol car n Streifenwagen der.

patrolman [pə'trəʊlmən] (pl -men [-mən]) n US (Streifen)polizist der.

patron ['peɪtrən] n - **1.** [sponsor] Förderer der, -derin die - **2.** UK [of charity, campaign] Schirmherr der, -in die.

patronize, -ise ['pætrənaɪz] vt pej [talk down to] von oben herab behandeln.

patronizing, -ising ['pætrənaɪzɪŋ] adj pej gönnerhaft.

patter ['pætər] <> n - **1.** [of feet] Getrappel das; [of raindrops] Platschen das - **2.** [talk] Sprüche Pl. <> vi [dog, feet] trappeln; [rain] platschen.

pattern ['pætən] n - **1.** [design] Muster das - **2.** [of life, work] Ablauf der - **3.** [of distribution] Schema das - **4.** [for sewing] Schnittmuster das; [for knitting] Strickanleitung die - **5.** [model] Vorbild das.

paunch [pɔːntʃ] n Bauch der.

pauper ['pɔːpər] n Arme der, die.

pause [pɔːz] <> n Pause die; **without a pause** ohne Unterbrechung. <> vi - **1.** [stop speaking] innelhalten - **2.** [stop doing sthg] eine Pause machen OR einlegen.

pave [peɪv] vt pflastern; **to pave the way for sb/sthg** jm/etw den Weg ebnen.

pavement ['peɪvmənt] n - **1.** UK [at side of road] Bürgersteig der - **2.** US [road surface] Fahrbahnbelag der.

pavilion [pə'vɪljən] n - **1.** [at sports field] Klubhaus das - **2.** [at exhibition] Pavillon der.

paving stone n Pflasterstein der.

paw [pɔː] n [of dog] Pfote die; [of lion, bear] Tatze die.

pawn [pɔːn] <> n - **1.** [chesspiece] Bauer der - **2.** [unimportant person] Schachfigur die. <> vt verpfänden.

pawnbroker ['pɔːnˌbrəʊkər] n Pfandleiher der, -in die.

pawnshop ['pɔːnʃɒp] n Pfandhaus das.

pay [peɪ] (pt & pp paid) <> vt - **1.** [bill, debt, person] bezahlen; [fine, taxes, fare, sum of money] zahlen; **to pay sb for sthg** jm das Geld für etw geben; **how much did you pay for it?** wie viel hast du dafür gezahlt? - **2.** [be profitable, advantageous to]: **it won't pay you to sell the house just now** es wird sich für dich nicht lohnen, das Haus jetzt zu verkaufen; **it will pay you to keep quiet** es wird für dich von Vorteil sein, wenn du schweigst - **3.**: **to pay sb a compliment** jm ein Kompliment machen; **to pay a visit to sb/a place** jn/einen Ort besuchen. <> vi - **1.** [for services, work, goods] (be)zahlen; **to pay for sthg** etw bezahlen - **2.** [be profitable - crime] sich lohnen; [- work] sich rentieren - **3.** fig [suffer] bezahlen; **to pay dearly for sthg** teuer für etw bezahlen. <> n [wages] Lohn der; [salary] Gehalt das. 🔷 **pay back** vt sep - **1.** [return money to]: **I'll pay you back (the money) tomorrow** ich zahle dir morgen das Geld zurück - **2.** [revenge o.s. on]: **I'll pay you back for that!** das werde ich dir heimlzahlen! 🔷 **pay off** <> vt sep - **1.** [debt] ablbezahlen; [loan] tilgen - **2.** [employee] auslzahlen - **3.** [informer, blackmailer] Schweigegeld zahlen (+ D). <> vi [be successful] sich auslzahlen. 🔷 **pay up** vi zahlen.

payable ['peɪəbl] adj - **1.** [debt, loan]: **to be payable** fällig sein - **2.** [cheque]: **to be payable to sb** an jn zu zahlen sein; **to make a cheque payable to sb** einen Scheck auf jn auslstellen.

paycheck ['peɪtʃek] n US [cheque] Lohnscheck der; [money] Lohn der.

payday ['peɪdeɪ] n Zahltag der.

payee [peɪ'i:] n Zahlungsempfänger der, -in die.

pay envelope n US Lohntüte die.

payment ['peɪmənt] n - 1. [act of paying] Bezahlung die - 2. [amount of money] Zahlung die.

pay packet n UK - 1. [envelope] Lohntüte die - 2. [wages] Lohn der.

pay-per-view adj Pay-per-View-.

pay phone, pay station US n Münzfernsprecher der.

payroll ['peɪrəʊl] n: to be on the payroll angestellt sein.

payslip UK ['peɪslɪp], **paystub** US ['peɪstʌb] n [for wages] Lohnstreifen der; [for salary] Gehaltsstreifen der.

pay station n US = pay phone.

paystub n US = payslip.

PC n - 1. (abbr of personal computer) PC der - 2. abbr of police constable.

PDA [ˌpiːdiː'eɪ] n (abbr of personal digital assistant) PDA der.

PE n abbr of physical education.

pea [piː] n Erbse die.

peace [piːs] n - 1. [tranquillity] Ruhe die; peace of mind Seelenfrieden der; to be at peace with o.s. mit sich selbst im Reinen sein - 2. [no war] Frieden der; to make (one's) peace with sb/sthg mit jm/etw Frieden schließen - 3. [law and order] Ruhe die und Ordnung.

peaceful ['piːsfʊl] adj friedlich.

peacetime ['piːstaɪm] n (U) Friedenszeiten Pl.

peach [piːtʃ] <> adj [in colour] pfirsichfarben. <> n [fruit] Pfirsich der.

peacock ['piːkɒk] n Pfau der.

peak [piːk] <> n - 1. [mountain top] Gipfel der - 2. [highest point] Höhepunkt der; to be at one's peak auf dem Höhepunkt seiner Leistungen sein - 3. [of cap] Schirm der. <> adj: in peak condition in Höchstform. <> vi den Höchststand erreichen.

peaked [piːkt] adj: peaked cap Schirmmütze die.

peak hour n TELEC & ELEC Hauptbelastungszeit die; [for traffic] Hauptverkehrszeit die.

peak period n Hochsaison die.

peak rate n Höchsttarif der.

peal [piːl] <> n - 1. [of bells] Glockenläuten das - 2.: peals of laughter schallendes Gelächter; peal of thunder Donnerschlag der. <> vi [bells] läuten.

peanut ['piːnʌt] n Erdnuss die.

peanut butter n Erdnussbutter die.

pear [peər] n Birne die.

pearl [pɜːl] n Perle die.

peasant ['peznt] n [in countryside] (armer) Bauer, (arme) Bäuerin.

peat [piːt] n Torf der.

pebble ['pebl] n Kiesel(stein) der.

peck [pek] <> n [kiss] Küsschen das. <> vt - 1. [with beak - hand] picken nach - 2. [kiss] ein Küsschen geben (+ D).

peckish ['pekɪʃ] adj UK inf (etwas) hungrig.

peculiar [pɪ'kjuːljər] adj - 1. [odd] seltsam, eigenartig - 2. [slightly ill]: to feel peculiar sich komisch fühlen - 3. [characteristic]: to be peculiar to sb/sthg jm/etw eigentümlich sein.

peculiarity [pɪˌkjuːlɪ'ærətɪ] n - 1. [strange habit] Eigenheit die - 2. [individual characteristic] Charakteristikum das - 3. [oddness] Eigenartigkeit die.

pedal ['pedl] (UK) (US) n Pedal das.

pedal bin n Treteimer der.

pedantic [pɪ'dæntɪk] adj pej pedantisch.

peddle ['pedl] vt - 1. [drugs] handeln mit - 2. [rumour, gossip] verbreiten.

pedestal ['pedɪstl] n Sockel der.

pedestrian [pɪ'destrɪən] <> adj pej langweilig. <> n Fußgänger der, -in die.

pedestrian crossing n UK Fußgängerüberweg der.

pedestrian precinct UK, **pedestrian zone** US n Fußgängerzone die.

pediatrics [ˌpiːdɪ'ætrɪks] n Kinderheilkunde die, Pädiatrie die.

pedigree ['pedɪgriː] <> adj mit einem Stammbaum. <> n Stammbaum der.

pedlar UK, **peddler** US ['pedlər] n: (drug) pedlar Drogenhändler der, -in die.

pee [piː] inf <> n - 1. [act of urinating]: to have a pee pinkeln; to go for a pee pinkeln gehen - 2. [urine] Urin der. <> vi pinkeln.

peek [piːk] inf <> n (phrase): to have OR take a peek at sthg einen kurzen Blick auf etw (A) werfen. <> vi gucken.

peel [piːl] <> n (U) Schale die. <> vt schälen. <> vi [walls, paint] abblättern; [wallpaper] sich lösen; [skin, nose, back] sich schälen.

peelings ['piːlɪŋz] npl Schalen Pl.

peep [piːp] <> n - 1. [look]: to have OR take a peep at sthg einen kurzen Blick auf etw (A) werfen - 2. inf [sound] Piep(s) der; I haven't heard a peep from them ich habe keinen Pieps von ihnen gehört. <> vi [look] gucken.

peephole ['piːphəʊl] n [in door] Spion der.

peer [pɪər] <> n - 1. [noble] Angehöriger des hohen Adels in Großbritannien - 2. [equal]: he is respected by his peers er ist sehr anerkannt bei seinesgleichen. <> vi angestrengt schauen.

peer group n Peergroup die.

peeved [piːvd] adj inf eingeschnappt.

peevish ['pi:vɪʃ] adj [remark, mood] gereizt; [person - as characteristic] reizbar; [- temporarily] gereizt.

peg [peg] ◇ n - 1. [hook] Haken der - 2. [for washing line] (Wäsche)klammer die - 3. [for tent] Hering der. ◇ vt [price] festlsetzen.

pejorative [pɪ'dʒɒrətɪv] adj abwertend.

pekinese [,pi:kə'ni:z] (pl inv OR -s) n Pekinese der.

Peking [pi:'kɪŋ] n Peking nt.

pelican ['pelɪkən] (pl inv OR -s) n Pelikan der.

pelican crossing n UK Ampelübergang der.

pellet ['pelɪt] n [for gun] Schrotkugel die.

pelt [pelt] ◇ vt: **to pelt sb (with sthg)** jn (mit etw) bewerfen. ◇ vi - 1. [rain]: **it's pelting (with rain)** es schüttet - 2. [run very fast] rasen.

pelvis ['pelvɪs] (pl -vises) n Becken das.

pen [pen] n - 1. [for writing]: **(ballpoint) pen** Kugelschreiber der; **(fountain) pen** Füllfederhalter der; **(felt-tipped) pen** Filzstift der - 2. [enclosure] Pferch der.

penal ['pi:nl] adj LAW: **penal system** Strafrecht das; **penal reform** Strafrechtsreform die.

penalize, -ise ['pi:nəlaɪz] vt - 1. [punish & SPORT] bestrafen - 2. [put at a disadvantage] benachteiligen.

penalty ['penltɪ] n - 1. [punishment] Strafe die; **to pay the penalty (for sthg)** fig (für etw) büßen müssen - 2. [fine] Geldstrafe die - 3. SPORT: **penalty (kick)** FTBL Strafstoß der; RUGBY Straftritt der.

penance ['penəns] n (U) - 1. RELIG Buße die - 2. fig [punishment] Strafe die.

pence [pens] UK Pl ▷ **penny**.

penchant [UK pãʃã, US 'pentʃənt] n: **to have a penchant for sthg** eine Schwäche OR Vorliebe für etw haben.

pencil ['pensl] (UK) (US) n Bleistift der; **in pencil** mit Bleistift. ◆ **pencil in** vt sep [person] vorlmerken; [date] vorläufig festlhalten.

pencil case n Federmäppchen das.

pencil sharpener [-'ʃɑ:pnər] n (Blei-stift)spitzer der.

pendant ['pendənt] n [jewel on chain] Anhänger der.

pending ['pendɪŋ] fml ◇ adj: **to be pending** [about to happen] bevorlstehen; LAW [waiting to be dealt with] noch anhängig sein. ◇ prep bis zu; **pending further inquiries** bis weitere Untersuchungen durchgeführt worden sind.

pendulum ['pendjʊləm] (pl -s) n Pendel das.

penetrate ['penɪtreɪt] vt - 1. [get into - subj: person] vorldringen in (+ A); [- subj: wind, rain, light] durchldringen; [- subj: sharp object, bullet] einldringen in (+ A) - 2. [infiltrate] sich einlschleusen in (+ A).

pen friend n Brieffreund der, -in die.

penguin ['peŋgwɪn] n Pinguin der.

penicillin [,penɪ'sɪlɪn] n Penizillin das.

peninsula [pə'nɪnsjʊlə] (pl -s) n Halbinsel die.

penis ['pi:nɪs] (pl penises ['pi:nɪsɪz]) n Penis der.

penitentiary [,penɪ'tenʃərɪ] n US Gefängnis das.

penknife ['pennaɪf] (pl -knives [-naɪvz]) n Taschenmesser das.

pen name n Pseudonym das.

pennant ['penənt] n Wimpel der.

penniless ['penɪlɪs] adj mittellos.

penny ['penɪ] n - 1. (pl -ies) UK [coin] Penny der - 2. (pl -ies) US [coin] Centstück das - 3. (pl pence) UK [value]: **30 pence** 30 Pence.

pen pal n inf Brieffreund der, -in die.

pension ['penʃn] n - 1. Rente die - 2. [disability pension] Erwerbsunfähigkeitsrente die.

pensioner ['penʃənər] n UK: **(old-age) pensioner** Rentner der, -in die.

pensive ['pensɪv] adj nachdenklich.

pentagon ['pentəgən] n Fünfeck das. ◆ **Pentagon** n US: **the Pentagon** das Pentagon.

Pentecost ['pentɪkɒst] n - 1. [Christian] Pfingsten das - 2. [Jewish] Ernte(dank)fest das.

penthouse ['penthaʊs] (pl [-haʊzɪz]) n Penthouse das.

pent up ['pent-] adj [emotions] unterdrückt; [energy] angestaut.

penultimate [pe'nʌltɪmət] adj vorletzte(r) (s).

people ['pi:pl] ◇ n [nation, race] Volk das. ◇ npl - 1. [persons] Menschen Pl, Leute Pl; **a lot of people** viele Menschen OR Leute; **five people** fünf Personen OR Leute - 2. [in indefinite uses] Leute die; **people say that** man sagt OR es heißt, dass - 3. [inhabitants - of country] Bevölkerung die; [- of town, city] Einwohner Pl - 4. POL: **the people** das Volk. ◇ vt: **to be peopled by** OR **with** bevölkert sein von.

pep [pep] n inf Schwung der. ◆ **pep up** vt sep inf - 1. [person] munter machen - 2. [party, event] in Schwung bringen.

pepper ['pepər] n - 1. [spice] Pfeffer der - 2. [vegetable] Paprika der.

pepperbox n US ▷ **pepper pot**.

peppermint ['pepəmɪnt] n - 1. [sweet] Pfefferminz(bonbon) das - 2. [herb] Pfefferminze die.

pepper pot UK, **pepperbox** US ['pepəbɒks] n Pfefferstreuer der.

pep talk n inf: **to give sb a pep talk** jm ein paar aufmunternde Worte sagen.

per [pɜ:r] prep [expressing rate, ratio] pro; **as per instructions** gemäß Anweisung.

per annum [pər'ænəm] adv pro Jahr.

per capita [pə'kæpɪtə] adv pro Kopf.

perceive [pə'si:v] *vt* - **1.** [see] wahr|nehmen - **2.** [notice, realize] erkennen - **3.** [conceive, consider]: **to perceive sb/sthg as** jn/etw betrachten als.

per cent [pə'sent] *n* Prozent *das.*

percentage [pə'sentɪdʒ] *n* Prozentsatz *der.*

perception [pə'sepʃn] *n* - **1.** [of colour, sound, time] Wahrnehmung *die* - **2.** [insight] Auffassungsvermögen *das.*

perceptive [pə'septɪv] *adj* scharfsinnig.

perch [pɜ:tʃ] <> *n* [for bird] (Sitz)stange *die.* <> *vi* - **1.** [bird]: **to perch (on sthg)** sich (auf etw (D)) nieder|lassen - **2.** [person]: **to perch on (the edge of)** a desk sich auf die Kante eines Schreibtisches setzen.

percolator ['pɜ:kəleɪtər] *n* Kaffeemaschine *die.*

percussion [pə'kʌʃn] *n* MUS: **percussion instrument** Schlaginstrument *das.*

perennial [pə'renɪəl] <> *adj* - **1.** [continual] immer wieder auftretend - **2.** BOT perennierend. <> *n* BOT perennierende Pflanze.

perfect <> *adj* ['pɜ:fɪkt] - **1.** [ideal, faultless] perfekt, vollkommen - **2.** [for emphasis - nuisance] ausgesprochen; **perfect strangers** wildfremde Leute. <> *n* ['pɜ:fɪkt] GRAM: **perfect (tense)** Perfekt *das.* <> *vt* [pə'fekt] vervollkommnen.

perfection [pə'fekʃn] *n* [faultlessness] Perfektion *die*; **to do sthg to perfection** etw perfekt machen.

perfectionist [pə'fekʃənɪst] *n* Perfektionist *der*, -in *die.*

perfectly ['pɜ:fɪktlɪ] *adv* - **1.** [for emphasis - honest, frank, ridiculous] absolut; **you know perfectly well** du weißt ganz genau - **2.** [to perfection] exakt, genau.

perforate ['pɜ:fəreɪt] *vt* [paper - with one hole] lochen; [- with row of holes] perforieren; [lung, eardrum] durchstechen.

perform [pə'fɔ:m] <> *vt* - **1.** [carry out - operation] durch|führen; [- miracle] vollbringen; [- service, function] erfüllen - **2.** [play, concert] auf|führen; [part] spielen; [dance] vor|tanzen. <> *vi* - **1.** [car, machine] laufen; [in exam] ab|schneiden; **he is performing well** [employee] er leistet gute Arbeit; [sportsman] er ist in Hochform - **2.** [actor, singer] auf|treten.

performance [pə'fɔ:məns] *n* - **1.** [of task, duty] Erfüllung *die*; [of operation] Durchführung *die* - **2.** [at cinema] Vorstellung *die*; [of play, concert] Aufführung *die* - **3.** [by actor, singer, of car, engine] Leistung *die.*

performer [pə'fɔ:mər] *n* Künstler *der*, -in *die.*

perfume ['pɜ:fju:m] *n* - **1.** [for woman] Parfüm *das* - **2.** [pleasant smell] Duft *der.*

perfunctory [pə'fʌŋktərɪ] *adj* [search, read] oberflächlich; [kiss, glance] flüchtig; [explanation, apology] der Form halber.

perhaps [pə'hæps] *adv* vielleicht; **perhaps so** (das) mag sein; **perhaps not** vielleicht nicht.

peril ['perɪl] *n* (U) *liter* Gefahr *die.*

perimeter [pə'rɪmɪtər] *n* Begrenzung *die*; **perimeter fence** Umzäunung *die.*

period ['pɪərɪəd] <> *n* - **1.** [of time] Zeit *die*; **over a period of several years** über einen Zeitraum von mehreren Jahren - **2.** HIST Zeitalter *das*, Epoche *die*; **the Elizabethan period** die elisabethanische Zeit - **3.** SCH (Schul)stunde *die*; **free period** Freistunde *die* - **4.** [menstruation] Periode *die* - **5.** *US* [full stop] Punkt *der.* <> *comp* [dress, furniture] zeitgenössisch.

periodic [,pɪərɪ'ɒdɪk] *adj* [events] regelmäßig wiederkehrend; [visits] regelmäßig.

periodical [,pɪərɪ'ɒdɪkl] <> *adj* = **periodic.** <> *n* [magazine] Zeitschrift *die.*

peripheral [pə'rɪfərəl] <> *adj* - **1.** [of little importance] nebensächlich - **2.** [vision] peripher; [region, group] Rand-. <> *n* COMPUT Peripheriegerät *das.*

perish ['perɪʃ] *vi* - **1.** [die] um|kommen - **2.** [food] verderben; [rubber] verschleißen.

perishable ['perɪʃəbl] *adj* verderblich. **perishables** *npl* verderbliche Waren *Pl.*

perjury ['pɜ:dʒərɪ] *n* (U) LAW Meineid *der.*

perk [pɜ:k] *n inf* Vergünstigung *die.* **perk up** *vi* [become more energetic] munter werden; [become more cheerful] auf|leben.

perky ['pɜ:kɪ] *adj inf* munter.

perm [pɜ:m] *n* Dauerwelle *die.*

permanent ['pɜ:mənənt] <> *adj* - **1.** [not temporary] dauerhaft; [job] fest - **2.** [continuous] ständig; [constant] konstant. <> *n US* [perm] Dauerwelle *die.*

permeate ['pɜ:mɪeɪt] *vt liter & fig* durch|dringen.

permissible [pə'mɪsəbl] *adj* erlaubt.

permission [pə'mɪʃn] *n* (U) Erlaubnis *die*; [official] Genehmigung *die.*

permit <> *vt* [pə'mɪt] - **1.** [allow] erlauben; **to permit sb to do sthg** jm erlauben, etw zu tun; **to permit sb sthg** jm etw gestatten - **2.** [enable] zul|assen. <> *n* ['pɜ:mɪt] Genehmigung *die.*

perpendicular [,pɜ:pən'dɪkjʊlər] <> *adj*: **perpendicular (to)** senkrecht (zu). <> *n* MATHS Senkrechte *die.*

perpetrate ['pɜ:pɪtreɪt] *vt fml* [crime, murder] begehen.

perpetual [pə'petʃʊəl] *adj* - **1.** *pej* [continuous] ständig - **2.** [everlasting] ewig.

perplexing [pə'pleksɪŋ] *adj* verblüffend.

persecute ['pɜ:sɪkju:t] *vt* verfolgen.

persevere [,pɜ:sɪ'vɪər] *vi* - **1.** [with difficulty] durch|halten; **to persevere with sthg** [studies, job] mit etw weiter|machen; [search] etw nicht auf|geben - **2.** [with determination]: **to persevere in doing sthg** darauf beharren, etw zu tun.

Persian ['pɜ:ʃn] *adj* persisch.

persist [pə'sɪst] vi - **1.** [problem, situation, rain] anlhalten, fortldauern - **2.** [person]: **to persist in doing sthg** etw unaufhörlich tun.

persistence [pə'sɪstəns] n - **1.** [continuation] Fortdauer die, Anhalten das - **2.** [determination] Beharrlichkeit die.

persistent [pə'sɪstənt] adj - **1.** [constant] fortdauernd - **2.** [determined] hartnäckig.

person ['pɜːsn] (pl **people** OR **persons**) fml n - **1.** [man or woman] Mensch der; **in person** persönlich - **2.** GRAM Person die.

personable ['pɜːsnəbl] adj von angenehmem Äußeren.

personal ['pɜːsənl] adj - **1.** [gen] persönlich - **2.** [letter, message] privat.

personal assistant n persönlicher Assistent, persönliche Assistentin.

personal column n Privatanzeigen Pl.

personal computer n Personal Computer der.

personality [ˌpɜːsə'nælətɪ] n Persönlichkeit die.

personally ['pɜːsnəlɪ] adv persönlich.

personal organizer, -iser n Terminplaner der.

personal property n (U) LAW Privateigentum das.

personal stereo n Walkman® der.

personify [pə'sɒnɪfaɪ] vt [represent] verkörpern; **she's evil personified** sie ist das Böse in Person.

personnel [ˌpɜːsə'nel] ⬦ n (U) [department] Personalabteilung die. ⬦ npl [staff] Personal das.

perspective [pə'spektɪv] n Perspektive die.

Perspex® ['pɜːspeks] n UK Plexiglas® das.

perspiration [ˌpɜːspə'reɪʃn] n - **1.** [sweat] Schweiß der - **2.** [sweating] Schwitzen das.

persuade [pə'sweɪd] vt [convince] überzeugen; **to persuade sb to do sthg** jn überreden, etw zu tun; **to persuade sb that...**; **to persuade sb of sthg** jn von etw überzeugen.

persuasion [pə'sweɪʒn] n - **1.** (U) [act of persuading] Überredung die - **2.** [belief] Überzeugung die.

persuasive [pə'sweɪsɪv] adj überzeugend.

pertain [pə'teɪn] vi fml: **to pertain to** gehören zu.

pertinent ['pɜːtɪnənt] adj relevant.

perturb [pə'tɜːb] vt fml beunruhigen.

peruse [pə'ruːz] vt [read - thoroughly] sorgfältig durchllesen; [- quickly] überfliegen.

pervade [pə'veɪd] vt durchdringen.

perverse [pə'vɜːs] adj pervers.

perversion [UK pə'vɜːʃn, US pər'vɜːrʒn] n [sexual deviation] Perversion die.

pervert ⬦ n ['pɜːvɜːt] Perverse der, die. ⬦ vt [pə'vɜːt] - **1.** [distort - truth] verzerren; [- course of justice] behindern - **2.** [corrupt morally - person, mind] verderben.

pessimist ['pesɪmɪst] n Pessimist der, -in die.

pessimistic [ˌpesɪ'mɪstɪk] adj pessimistisch.

pest [pest] n - **1.** [in garden, on farm] Schädling der - **2.** inf [annoying person, thing] Pest die, Plage die.

pester ['pestə'] vt belästigen.

pet [pet] ⬦ adj [favourite] Lieblings-. ⬦ n - **1.** [animal] Haustier das - **2.** [favourite person] Liebling der. ⬦ vt [stroke] streicheln. ⬦ vi [sexually] Petting machen.

petal ['petl] n Blütenblatt das.

peter ['piːtə'] ⬥ **peter out** vi [supply] versiegen; [path] auslaufen.

petite [pə'tiːt] adj zierlich.

petition [pɪ'tɪʃn] ⬦ n - **1.** [supporting campaign] Petition die - **2.** LAW: **petition for divorce** Scheidungsantrag der. ⬦ vt [lobby]: **to petition sb** eine Petition bei jm einlreichen.

petrified ['petrɪfaɪd] adj [terrified] verängstigt, gelähmt vor Angst.

petrol ['petrəl] n UK Benzin das.

petrol bomb n UK Benzinbombe die.

petrol can n UK Benzinkanister der.

petrol pump n UK Zapfsäule die.

petrol station n UK Tankstelle die.

petrol tank n UK Benzintank der.

petticoat ['petɪkəʊt] n Unterrock der.

petty ['petɪ] adj - **1.** [small-minded] kleinlich - **2.** [trivial] geringfügig.

petty cash n Portokasse die.

petulant ['petjʊlənt] adj mürrisch; [child] bockig.

pew [pjuː] n Kirchenbank die.

pewter ['pjuːtə'] n Zinn das.

phantom ['fæntəm] ⬦ adj [imaginary] Phantom-. ⬦ n [ghost] Phantom das.

pharmaceutical [ˌfɑːmə'sjuːtɪkl] adj pharmazeutisch.

pharmacist ['fɑːməsɪst] n [in shop] Apotheker der, -in die.

pharmacy ['fɑːməsɪ] n [shop] Apotheke die.

phase [feɪz] n Phase die. ⬥ **phase in** vt sep schrittweise OR allmählich einlführen. ⬥ **phase out** vt sep auslaufen lassen.

PhD (abbr of Doctor of Philosophy) n Dr. phil.

pheasant ['feznt] (pl inv OR -s) n Fasan der.

phenomena [fɪ'nɒmɪnə] Pl ⬡ **phenomenon**.

phenomenal [fɪ'nɒmɪnl] adj [remarkable] phänomenal.

phenomenon [fɪ'nɒmɪnən] (pl -**mena**) n Phänomen das.

philanthropist [fɪˈlænθrəpɪst] *n* Philanthrop *der*, Menschenfreund *der*.

philosopher [fɪˈlɒsəfəʳ] *n* Philosoph *der*, -in *die*.

philosophical [ˌfɪləˈsɒfɪkl] *adj* - 1. [gen] philosophisch - 2. [stoical] gelassen.

philosophy [fɪˈlɒsəfɪ] *n* Philosophie *die*.

phlegm [flem] *n (U)* [mucus] Schleim *der*.

phobia [ˈfəʊbɪə] *n* Phobie *die*.

phone [fəʊn] <> *n* Telefon *das*; **to be on the phone** [speaking] telefonieren, am Telefon sein; *UK* [connected to network] Telefon haben. <> *comp* Telefon-. <> *vt & vi* anlrufen. ← **phone back** *vt sep & vi* zurücklrufen. ← **phone up** *vt sep & vi* anlrufen.

phone book *n* Telefonbuch *das*.

phone booth *n UK* Telefonkabine *die*.

phone box *n UK* Telefonzelle *die*.

phone call *n* Telefonanruf *der*, Telefongespräch *das*; **to make a phone call** telefonieren.

phonecard [ˈfəʊnkɑːd] *n* Telefonkarte *die*.

phone-in *n* Radio- oder TV-Programm, *bei dem Zuhörer bzw. Zuschauer anrufen können, um ihre Meinung zu äußern.*

phone number *n* Telefonnummer *die*.

phonetics [fəˈnetɪks] *n (U)* Fonetik *die*.

phoney *UK*, **phony** *US inf* [ˈfəʊnɪ] <> *adj* - 1. [false] falsch - 2. [insincere] unaufrichtig. <> *n* [person] Hochstapler *der*, -in *die*.

photo [ˈfəʊtəʊ] *n* Foto *das*; **to take a photo (of)** ein Foto machen (von).

photocopier [ˈfəʊtəʊˌkɒpɪəʳ] *n* Fotokopierer *der*.

photocopy [ˈfəʊtəʊˌkɒpɪ] <> *n* Fotokopie *die*. <> *vt* fotokopieren.

photograph [ˈfəʊtəgrɑːf] <> *n* Fotografie *die*, Aufnahme *die*; **to take a photograph (of sb/sthg)** jn/etw fotografieren. <> *vt* fotografieren.

photographer [fəˈtɒgrəfəʳ] *n* Fotograf *der*, -in *die*.

photography [fəˈtɒgrəfɪ] *n (U)* Fotografie *die*.

phrasal verb [ˌfreɪzl-] *n* Verb *das* mit Präposition.

phrase [freɪz] <> *n* - 1. [part of sentence] Satzglied *das* - 2. [expression] Wendung *die*. <> *vt* [express] ausldrücken.

phrasebook [ˈfreɪzbʊk] *n* Sprachführer *der*.

physical [ˈfɪzɪkl] <> *adj* - 1. [relating to the body] körperlich - 2. [world, object] fassbar, materiell - 3. [relating to physics] physikalisch. <> *n* ärztliche Untersuchung.

physical education *n* Sportunterricht *der*.

physically [ˈfɪzɪklɪ] *adv* - 1. [bodily] körperlich - 2. [materially] materiell, physisch.

physically handicapped <> *adj* körperbehindert. <> *npl*: **the physically handicapped** die Körperbehinderten *Pl*.

physician [fɪˈzɪʃn] *n* Arzt *der*, Ärztin *die*.

physicist [ˈfɪzɪsɪst] *n* Physiker *der*, -in *die*.

physics [ˈfɪzɪks] *n (U)* Physik *die*.

physiotherapy [ˌfɪzɪəʊˈθerəpɪ] *n* Physiotherapie *die*.

physique [fɪˈziːk] *n* Körperbau *der*.

pianist [ˈpɪənɪst] *n* Pianist *der*, -in *die*.

piano [pɪˈænəʊ] *(pl -s)* *n* Klavier *das*.

pick [pɪk] <> *n* - 1. [tool] Spitzhacke *die* - 2. [selection]: **take your pick** such dir einen/eine/eins aus - 3. [best]: **the pick of** das Beste von. <> *vt* - 1. [choose] auslsuchen; [winner] auslwählen - 2. [fruit, flowers] pflücken - 3. [remove] entfernen - 4. [nose, teeth]: **to pick one's nose** in der Nase bohren; **to pick one's teeth** in seinen Zähnen stochern - 5. [provoke]: **to pick a fight (with sb)** (mit jm) einen Streit anlfangen - 6. [lock] knacken. ← **pick on** *vt insep* auf dem Kieker haben. ← **pick out** *vt sep* - 1. [recognize] erkennen - 2. [select] auslsuchen; [winner] auslwählen. ← **pick up** <> *vt sep* - 1. [lift up] hochlheben; [after dropping] auflheben - 2. [collect - gen] ablholen; [- hitchhiker] mitlnehmen - 3. [acquire - habit] anlnehmen; [- tips] bekommen; [- skill, language] lernen; **to pick up speed** schneller werden - 4. *inf* [man, woman] anlmachen - 5. RADIO & TELEC [signal] emplfangen - 6. [conversation, work] wieder auflnehmen. <> *vi* - 1. [improve] sich verbessern - 2. [resume] weiterlmachen.

pickaxe *UK*, **pickax** *US* [ˈpɪkæks] *n* Spitzhacke *die*.

picket [ˈpɪkɪt] <> *n* [at place of work] Streikposten *der*. <> *vt* [place of work] Streikposten auflstellen vor (+ D).

picket line *n* Streikpostenkette *die*.

pickle [ˈpɪkl] <> *n* - 1. *(U)* [food] Pickles *Pl* - 2. *inf* [difficult situation]: **to be in a pickle** in der Tinte sitzen. <> *vt* einllegen.

pickpocket [ˈpɪkˌpɒkɪt] *n* Taschendieb *der*, -in *die*.

pick-up *n* - 1. [of record player] Tonabnehmer *der* - 2. [truck] Pick-up *der*.

picnic [ˈpɪknɪk] *(pt & pp -ked, cont -king)* <> *n* Picknick *das*. <> *vi* picknicken.

pictorial [pɪkˈtɔːrɪəl] *adj* [illustrated] bebildert.

picture [ˈpɪktʃəʳ] <> *n* - 1. [gen] Bild *das*; [painting] Gemälde *das*; **as pretty as a picture** bildhübsch - 2. [movie] Film *der* - 3. [in one's mind] Vorstellung *die* - 4. [prospect] Aussicht *die* - 5. *phr*: **to get the picture** *inf* kapieren; **to put sb in the picture** jn ins Bild setzen. <> *vt* - 1. [in mind] sich *(D)* vorlstellen - 2. [in photo] fotografieren; [in painting, drawing] darlstellen. ← **pictures** *npl UK*: **the pictures** [cinema] das Kino.

picture book *n* Bilderbuch *das*.

picturesque [ˌpɪktʃəˈresk] *adj* malerisch.

pie [paɪ] n - **1.** [sweet] Obstkuchen der - **2.** [savoury] Pastete die.

piece [piːs] n - **1.** [gen] Stück das; [component] Teil das; **a piece of news** eine Neuigkeit; **a piece of advice** ein Rat; **a piece of furniture** ein Möbelstück; **a fifty pence piece** ein Fünfzigpencestück; **to fall to pieces** auseinanderlfallen; **to take sthg to pieces** etw auseinander nehmen; **in one piece** [intact, unharmed] heil - **2.** [in chess] Figur die; [in backgammon, draughts] Stein der - **3.** [of journalism] Artikel der. ◆ **piece together** vt sep [facts] zusammenlfügen.

piecemeal ['piːsmiːl] adj & adv stückweise.

piecework ['piːswɜːk] n (U) Akkordarbeit die.

pier [pɪəʳ] n [at seaside] Pier der.

pierce [pɪəs] vt [subj: bullet, noise, light] durchldringen; [subj: needle] durchlstechen; **to have one's ears pierced** sich (D) Ohrlöcher stechen lassen.

piercing ['pɪəsɪŋ] ◇ adj [sound, voice] durchdringend; [wind] schneidend; [look, eyes] stechend. ◇ n Piercing das.

pig [pɪg] n - **1.** [animal] Schwein das - **2.** inf pej [greedy eater] Vielfraß der - **3.** inf pej [unkind person] Schwein das.

pigeon ['pɪdʒɪn] (pl inv or -s) n Taube die.

pigeonhole ['pɪdʒɪnhəʊl] ◇ n [compartment] Fach das. ◇ vt fig [classify] in eine Kategorie einlordnen.

piggybank ['pɪgɪbæŋk] n Sparschwein das.

pigheaded [ˌpɪg'hedɪd] adj stur.

pigment ['pɪgmənt] n Pigment das.

pigpen n US = **pigsty**.

pigskin ['pɪgskɪn] n Schweinsleder das.

pigsty ['pɪgstaɪ], **pigpen** US ['pɪgpen] n liter & fig Schweinestall der.

pigtail ['pɪgteɪl] n Zopf der.

pilchard ['pɪltʃəd] n Sardine die.

pile [paɪl] ◇ n - **1.** [heap] Haufen der; **a pile or piles of money/work** inf ein Haufen Geld/Arbeit - **2.** [neat stack] Stapel der, Stoß der - **3.** [of carpet, fabric] Flor der. ◇ vt stapeln; **to be piled high with sthg** mit etw voll gestapelt sein. ◆ **piles** npl MED Hämorriden Pl. ◆ **pile into** vt insep inf [car] sich zwängen in (+ A); [room] drängen in (+ A). ◆ **pile up** ◇ vt sep [books, boxes] auflstapeln. ◇ vi [accumulate] sich anlhäufen.

pileup ['paɪlʌp] n Massenkarambolage die.

pilfer ['pɪlfəʳ] vt & vi stehlen.

pilgrim ['pɪlgrɪm] n Pilger der, -in die.

pilgrimage ['pɪlgrɪmɪdʒ] n Pilgerfahrt die.

pill [pɪl] n Pille die; [contraceptive]: **the pill** die Pille; **to be on the pill** die Pille nehmen.

pillage ['pɪlɪdʒ] vt plündern.

pillar ['pɪləʳ] n Pfeiler der.

pillar box n UK Briefkasten der.

pillion ['pɪljən] n Soziussitz der; **to ride pillion** auf dem Soziussitz mitlfahren.

pillow ['pɪləʊ] n - **1.** [for bed] Kopfkissen das - **2.** US [on sofa, chair] Kissen das.

pillowcase ['pɪləʊkeɪs], **pillowslip** ['pɪləʊslɪp] n Kopfkissenbezug der.

pilot ['paɪlət] ◇ n - **1.** [of plane] Pilot der, -in die - **2.** NAUT Lotse der - **3.** TV Pilotfilm der. ◇ comp [trial] Pilot-. ◇ vt - **1.** [plane] führen, fliegen - **2.** NAUT lotsen - **3.** [scheme] testen.

pilot light n Zündflamme die.

pimp [pɪmp] n inf Zuhälter der.

pimple ['pɪmpl] n Pickel der.

pin [pɪn] ◇ n - **1.** [for sewing] Nadel die; **I've got pins and needles in my feet** inf meine Füße sind eingeschlafen - **2.** [drawing pin] Reißzwecke die; [safety pin] Sicherheitsnadel die - **3.** [of plug] Kontaktstift der - **4.** TECH Bolzen der, Stift der - **5.** US [brooch] Brosche die; [badge] Anstecknadel die. ◇ vt: **to pin sthg to** or **on etw** (A) heften an (+ A); **to pin sb to the wall/ground** jn gegen die Wand/auf den Boden drücken; **to pin the blame for sthg on sb** jm die Schuld an etw zulschieben. ◆ **pin down** vt sep - **1.** [identify] bestimmen - **2.** [force to make a decision] festlegen.

pinafore ['pɪnəfɔːʳ] n - **1.** [apron] Schürze die - **2.** UK [dress] Trägerkleid das.

pinball ['pɪnbɔːl] n (U) Flipper der.

pincers ['pɪnsəz] npl - **1.** [tool] Kneifzange die - **2.** [of crab, lobster] Schere die.

pinch [pɪntʃ] ◇ n - **1.** [nip] Kneifen das - **2.** [of salt, herbs etc] Prise die. ◇ vt - **1.** [nip] kneifen - **2.** inf [steal] klauen. ◆ **at a pinch** UK, **in a pinch** US adv zur Not.

pincushion ['pɪnˌkʊʃn] n Nadelkissen das.

pine [paɪn] ◇ n - **1.** [tree] Kiefer die - **2.** [wood] Kiefernholz das. ◇ vi: **to pine for** sich sehnen nach.

pineapple ['paɪnæpl] n Ananas die.

ping [pɪŋ] n [sound] Ping das.

pink [pɪŋk] ◇ adj rosa; **to go pink** erröten. ◇ n [colour] Rosa das.

pinnacle ['pɪnəkl] n fig [of career, success] Höhepunkt der.

pinpoint ['pɪnpɔɪnt] vt bestimmen.

pin-striped [-ˌstraɪpt] adj Nadelstreifen-.

pint [paɪnt] n - **1.** UK [unit of measurement] Pint das, = 0,568 l. - **2.** US [unit of measurement] Pint das, = 0,473 l. - **3.** UK [beer]: **let's go for a pint** lass uns ein Bier trinken gehen; **a pint of Guinness** ein großes (Glas) Guinness.

pioneer [ˌpaɪə'nɪəʳ] n Pionier der.

pious ['paɪəs] adj - **1.** [religious] fromm - **2.** pej [sanctimonious] scheinheilig.

pip [pɪp] n - **1.** [seed] Kern der - **2.** UK: **the pips** [on radio] Zeitzeichen das; [on public telephone] Warnton, der ertönt, wenn Geld nachgeworfen werden muss.

pipe [paɪp] ⟨> n - **1.** [for gas, water] Rohr das, Leitung die - **2.** [for smoking] Pfeife die. ⟨> vt [liquid, gas] leiten. ◆ **pipes** npl MUS [bagpipes] Dudelsack der. ◆ **pipe down** vi inf still sein. ◆ **pipe up** vi inf sich (spontan) zu Wort melden.

pipe cleaner n Pfeifenreiniger der.

pipeline ['paɪplaɪn] n Pipeline die.

piper ['paɪpə'] n MUS [on bagpipes] Dudelsackspieler der, -in die.

piping hot [,paɪpɪŋ-] adj siedend heiß.

pirate ['paɪrət] ⟨> adj [video, copy etc] Piraten-, Raub-. ⟨> n [sailor] Pirat der. ⟨> vt [copy illegally] Raubkopien machen von.

pirouette [,pɪru'et] ⟨> n Pirouette die. ⟨> vi Pirouetten drehen.

Pisces ['paɪsiːz] n Fische Pl; **I'm (a) Pisces** ich bin Fisch.

piss [pɪs] v inf ⟨> n [urine] Pisse die; **to have a piss** pissen gehen. ⟨> vi pissen.

pissed [pɪst] adj v inf - **1.** UK [drunk] voll, besoffen - **2.** US [annoyed] stocksauer.

pissed off adj v inf stocksauer.

pistol ['pɪstl] n Pistole die.

piston ['pɪstən] n Kolben der.

pit [pɪt] ⟨> n - **1.** [large hole, coalmine] Grube die - **2.** [for orchestra] Orchestergraben der - **3.** US [of fruit] Kern der. ⟨> vt: **to be pitted against sb** [in game] gegen jn spielen (müssen); [in fight] gegen jn kämpfen (müssen). ◆ **pits** npl [in motor racing]: **the pits** die Boxen Pl.

pitch [pɪtʃ] ⟨> n - **1.** SPORT Feld das, Platz der - **2.** MUS Tonhöhe die; [of voice] Stimmlage die; [of instrument] Tonlage die - **3.** [level, degree] Ausmaß das - **4.** [in market, on street] Standplatz der - **5.** inf [sales talk] Verkaufsvortrag der - **6.** [of roof] Neigung die. ⟨> vt - **1.** [throw] werfen - **2.** [set level of] anlsetzen - **3.** [camp, tent] auflschlagen. ⟨> vi - **1.** [fall] fallen; **to pitch forward** nach vorne fallen - **2.** [ship] stampfen; [plane] ablsacken.

pitch-black adj stockfinster.

pitcher ['pɪtʃər] n US - **1.** [jug] Krug der - **2.** [in baseball] Pitcher der.

pitchfork ['pɪtʃfɔːk] n Mistgabel die.

pitfall ['pɪtfɔːl] n [hazard] Falle die.

pith [pɪθ] n [of fruit] weiße Haut.

pithy ['pɪθɪ] adj prägnant.

pitiful ['pɪtɪful] adj - **1.** [arousing pity] Mitleid erregend - **2.** [arousing contempt] jämmerlich.

pitiless ['pɪtɪlɪs] adj erbarmungslos.

pit stop n Boxenstopp der.

pittance ['pɪtəns] n Hungerlohn der.

pity ['pɪtɪ] ⟨> n - **1.** [compassion] Mitleid das; **to take** OR **have pity on sb** Mitleid mit jm haben - **2.** [shame]: **it's a pity (that)...** (es ist) schade(, dass)...; **what a pity!** wie schade! ⟨> vt bemitleiden.

pivot ['pɪvət] n - **1.** TECH [joint] Drehgelenk das - **2.** fig [crux] Dreh- und Angelpunkt der.

pizza ['piːtsə] n Pizza die.

placard ['plækɑːd] n Plakat das.

placate [plə'keɪt] vt beschwichtigen.

place [pleɪs] ⟨> n - **1.** [location] Ort der; [spot, place in text & MATHS] Stelle die; **place of birth** Geburtsort; **to two decimal places** bis auf zwei Stellen nach dem Komma - **2.** [home] Zuhause das; **let's go to my place** gehen wir zu mir - **3.** [post, vacancy] Stelle die - **4.** [role, function] Rolle die - **5.** [table setting] Gedeck das - **6.** [instance]: **in the first place** am Anfang; **why didn't you say so in the first place?** warum hast du das nicht gleich OR direkt gesagt?; **in the first place..., and in the second place...** erstens..., zweitens... - **7.** phr: **to take place** stattlfinden; **to take sb's place** js Platz einlnehmen. ⟨> vt - **1.** [put] stellen; [put flat] legen; **to place the blame on sb** jm die Schuld zulschieben; **to place an ad in the paper** eine Anzeige in die Zeitung setzen - **2.** [identify] einlordnen - **3.** [make]: **to place an order** COMM eine Bestellung auflgeben; **to place a bet on sthg** auf etw (D) wetten - **4.** [be situated]: **the house is well placed for the tube** das Haus liegt ganz in der Nähe der U-Bahn; **how are we placed for money/time?** wie viel Geld/Zeit haben wir? - **5.** [in race]: **to be placed** sich platzieren. ◆ **all over the place** adv überall. ◆ **in place** adv - **1.** [in proper position] an seinem Platz - **2.** [established, set up] eingerichtet. ◆ **in place of** prep anstatt (+ G). ◆ **out of place** adv - **1.** [in wrong position] nicht an seinem Platz - **2.** [unsuitable] unpassend.

place mat n Platzset das.

placement ['pleɪsmənt] n [work experience] Praktikum das.

placid ['plæsɪd] adj - **1.** [person, child, animal] ausgeglichen - **2.** [place] ruhig.

plagiarize, -ise ['pleɪdʒəraɪz] vt plagiieren.

plague [pleɪg] ⟨> n - **1.** MED Seuche die; (U) [specific disease] Pest die - **2.** [nuisance] Plage die. ⟨> vt plagen; **to be plagued by bad luck** vom Pech verfolgt sein.

plaice [pleɪs] (pl inv) n Scholle die.

plain [pleɪn] ⟨> adj - **1.** [simple] einfach, schlicht; [paper] unliniert; [in colour] einfarbig; [unpatterned] uni; [yoghurt] Natur-; **in plain clothes** in Zivil - **2.** [clear] klar - **3.** [blunt - statement, answer] unverblümt; **the plain truth** die reine Wahrheit - **4.** [absolute - madness, stupidity] absolut, schier - **5.** [not pretty] unattraktiv. ⟨> adv inf [completely] einfach. ⟨> n GEOG Ebene die.

plain chocolate n UK Bitterschokolade die.

plain-clothes adj in Zivil.

plainly ['pleɪnlɪ] adv - **1.** [upset, angry] sichtlich; [remember, hear] deutlich - **2.** [frankly] offen - **3.** [simply] einfach, schlicht.

plaintiff ['pleɪntɪf] *n* Kläger *der*, -in *die*.

plait [plæt] ⇔ *n* Zopf *der*. ⇔ *vt* flechten.

plan [plæn] ⇔ *n* - **1.** [gen] Plan *der*; **to make plans** Pläne machen; **have you got any plans for tonight?** hast du heute Abend etwas vor?; **to go according to plan** nach Plan verlaufen - **2.** [of story, project] Konzept *das*, Entwurf *der*. ⇔ *vt* - **1.** [organize] planen - **2.** [intend]: **to plan to do sthg** vorhaben, etw zu tun - **3.** [design] entwerfen. ⇔ *vi* planen; **to plan for sthg** Pläne für etw machen. ⬥ **plan on** *vt insep*: **to plan on doing sthg** vorlhaben, etw zu tun.

plane [pleɪn] *n* - **1.** [aircraft] Flugzeug *das* - **2.** GEOM Ebene *die* - **3.** *fig* [level] Niveau *das* - **4.** [tool] Hobel *der* - **5.** [tree] Platane *die*.

planet ['plænɪt] *n* Planet *der*.

plank [plæŋk] *n* [piece of wood] (langes) Brett.

planning ['plænɪŋ] *n* Planung *die*.

planning permission *n (U)* Baugenehmigung *die*.

plant [plɑːnt] ⇔ *n* - **1.** BOT Pflanze *die* - **2.** [factory] Werk *das*, Fabrik *die* - **3.** *(U)* [heavy machinery] Maschinen *Pl*. ⇔ *vt* - **1.** [tree, vegetable] pflanzen; [seed] säen; [field, garden] bepflanzen - **2.** [place firmly] auflstellen; **he planted a kiss on her cheek** er gab ihr einen Kuss auf die Wange - **3.** [bomb, microphone, spy] platzieren, anlbringen; [thought, idea] pflanzen, setzen.

plantation [plæn'teɪʃn] *n* - **1.** [piece of land] Plantage *die* - **2.** [of trees] Anpflanzung *die*.

plaque [plɑːk] *n* - **1.** [plate] Gedenktafel *die* - **2.** *(U)* [on teeth] Zahnbelag *der*.

plaster ['plɑːstə^r] ⇔ *n* - **1.** [for wall, ceiling] Putz *der* - **2.** [for broken bones] Gips *der* - **3.** *UK* [for cut]: **(sticking) plaster** Pflaster *das*. ⇔ *vt* - **1.** [wall, ceiling] verputzen - **2.** [cover] pflastern.

plaster cast *n* - **1.** [for broken bones] Gipsverband *der* - **2.** [model, statue] Gipsform *die*.

plastered ['plɑːstəd] *adj inf* [drunk] besoffen.

plasterer ['plɑːstərə^r] *n* Putzer *der*, -in *die*.

plaster of paris *n* Gips *der*.

plastic ['plæstɪk] ⇔ *adj* Plastik-. ⇔ *n* [material] Plastik *das*.

Plasticine® UK ['plæstɪsiːn], **play dough** US *n* Plastilin *das*.

plastic surgery *n* plastische Chirurgie *die*.

plate [pleɪt] ⇔ *n* [dish] Teller *der*; **to have a lot on one's plate** *fig* viel um die Ohren haben. ⇔ *vt*: **to be plated with silver/gold** versilbert/vergoldet sein.

plateau ['plætəʊ] *(pl* **-s** *OR* **-x** [-z]) *n* - **1.** GEOG Plateau *das* - **2.** *fig* [steady level]: **prices have reached a plateau** die Preise haben sich stabilisiert.

plate-glass *adj* Spiegelglas-.

platform ['plætfɔːm] *n* - **1.** [gen & COMPUT] Plattform *die*; [for speaker, performer] Podium *das* - **2.** [at railway station] Bahnsteig *der*; **platform 12** Gleis 12.

platinum ['plætɪnəm] *n* Platin *das*.

platoon [plə'tuːn] *n* Zug *der*.

platter ['plætə^r] *n* [dish] Platte *die*.

plausible ['plɔːzəbl] *adj* [reason, excuse] plausibel; [person] überzeugend.

play [pleɪ] ⇔ *n* - **1.** [gen] Spiel *das*; **in play** SPORT im Spiel; **out of play** SPORT im Aus; **to come into play** *fig* eine Rolle spielen; **play on words** Wortspiel *das* - **2.** [in theatre] Schauspiel *das*, Stück *das*; [on radio] Hörspiel *das*; [on television] Fernsehspiel *das*. ⇔ *vt* spielen; [opposing player or team] spielen gegen; **to play the piano** Klavier spielen; **to play a trick on sb** jm einen Streich spielen; **to play a part** OR **role in sthg** *fig* eine Rolle in etw *(D)* spielen; **to play it cool** so tun, als sei nichts gewesen. ⇔ *vi* spielen; **to play for time** versuchen, Zeit zu gewinnen; **to play safe** auf Nummer sicher gehen. ⬥ **play along** *vi*: **to play along (with sb)** (jm) vorübergehend fügen. ⬥ **play down** *vt sep* herunterlspielen. ⬥ **play up** ⇔ *vt sep* [emphasize] betonen. ⇔ *vi* [machine, part of body] Schwierigkeiten machen; [children] sich wie wild gebärden.

play-act *vi* schauspielern.

playboy ['pleɪbɔɪ] *n* Playboy *der*.

play dough *n US* = **Plasticine®**.

player ['pleɪə^r] *n* [gen] Spieler *der*, -in *die*.

playful ['pleɪfʊl] *adj* [comment] neckisch; [person, animal] verspielt.

playground ['pleɪgraʊnd] *n* [at school] Schulhof *der*; [in park] Spielplatz *der*.

playgroup ['pleɪgruːp] *n* Krabbelgruppe *die*.

playing card ['pleɪɪŋ-] *n* Spielkarte *die*.

playing field ['pleɪɪŋ-] *n* Sportplatz *der*.

playmate ['pleɪmeɪt] *n* Spielkamerad *der*, -in *die*.

play-off *n* Entscheidungsspiel *das*.

playpen ['pleɪpen] *n* Laufstall *der*.

playschool ['pleɪskuːl] *n* Krabbelgruppe *die*.

plaything ['pleɪθɪŋ] *n* *liter* & *fig* Spielzeug *das*.

playtime ['pleɪtaɪm] *n (U)* [at school]: **at playtime** in der großen Pause.

playwright ['pleɪraɪt] *n* Dramatiker *der*, -in *die*.

plc *(abbr of public limited company)* AG *die*.

plea [pliː] *n* - **1.** [appeal] Appell *der* - **2.** LAW Plädoyer *das*; **what's your plea?** wie plädieren Sie?

plead [pliːd] *(pt & pp* **-ed** *OR* **pled)** ⇔ *vt* - **1.** LAW plädieren; **to plead guilty/not guilty** sich schuldig/nicht schuldig bekennen

- 2. sich berufen auf (+ A). ⟨⟩ vi - 1. [beg] flehen; **to plead with sb to do sthg** jn an|flehen, etw zu tun; **to plead for sthg** um etw flehen - 2. LAW: **to plead sb's case** jn in einer Sache vertreten.

pleasant ['pleznt] adj angenehm; [smile] freundlich; [day] schön.

pleasantry ['plezntrı] n: **to exchange pleasantries** Nettigkeiten aus|tauschen.

please [pli:z] ⟨⟩ vt gefallen (+ D); **there's no pleasing him** man kann ihm nichts recht machen; **he's hard to please** er ist nicht leicht zufriedenzustellen; **please yourself!** wie du willst! ⟨⟩ vi gefallen; **may I? – please do!** darf ich? – bitte sehr!; **he does as he pleases** er macht, was ihm gefällt. ⟨⟩ adv bitte; **yes, please!** ja, bitte!

pleased [pli:zd] adj [happy] erfreut; [satisfied] zufrieden; **to be pleased about sthg** sich über etw (A) freuen; **to be pleased with sb/sthg** mit jm/etw zufrieden sein; **pleased to meet you!** angenehm!

pleasing ['pli:zɪŋ] adj erfreulich.

pleasure ['pleʒə'] n - 1. [gen] Freude die; **with pleasure** gern(e); **it's a pleasure!, my pleasure !** gern geschehen! - 2. (U) [enjoyment] Vergnügen das.

pleat [pli:t] ⟨⟩ n Falte die. ⟨⟩ vt fälteln.

pled [pled] pt & pp ▷ **plead**.

pledge [pledʒ] ⟨⟩ n - 1. [promise] Versprechen das - 2. [token] Pfand das. ⟨⟩ vt - 1. [promise] versprechen - 2. [commit]: **to be pledged to sthg** zu etw verpflichtet werden; **to pledge o.s. to sthg** sich zu etw verpflichten - 3. [pawn] verpfänden.

plentiful ['plentɪfʊl] adj reichlich.

plenty ['plentɪ] ⟨⟩ n (U) Überfluss der. ⟨⟩ pron: **we've got plenty** wir haben mehr als genug; **five will be plenty** fünf sind mehr als genug; **plenty of** viel, eine Menge. ⟨⟩ adv US [very] sehr.

pliable ['plaɪəbl], **pliant** ['plaɪənt] adj - 1. [metal] biegsam; [material] geschmeidig - 2. [person] anpassungsfähig.

pliers ['plaɪəz] npl Zange die.

plight [plaɪt] n Elend das.

plimsoll ['plɪmsəl] n UK Turnschuh der.

plinth [plɪnθ] n Plinthe die.

plod [plɒd] vi - 1. [walk slowly] schwerfällig gehen - 2. [work slowly] sich ab|mühen.

plonk [plɒŋk] n (U) UK inf [wine] billiger Wein. ▰ **plonk down** vt sep inf hin|knallen.

plot [plɒt] ⟨⟩ n - 1. [conspiracy] Komplott das - 2. [of story, film, play] Handlung die - 3. [of land] Stück das Land; [allotment] Parzelle die. ⟨⟩ vt - 1. [conspire] planen; **to plot to do sthg** gemeinsam planen, etw zu tun - 2. [chart] ein|zeichnen; MATHS auf|zeichnen. ⟨⟩ vi: **to plot (against)** sich verschwören (gegen).

plough UK, **plow** US [plaʊ] ⟨⟩ n Pflug der. ⟨⟩ vt pflügen; **to plough money into sthg** Geld in etw (A) stecken. ⟨⟩ vi [crash]: **to plough into sthg** in etw (A) rasen.

ploughman's ['plaʊmənz] (pl inv) n UK: **ploughman's (lunch)** Pubmahlzeit aus Käse, Brot und Pickles.

plow etc n & vb US = **plough** etc .

ploy [plɔɪ] n Trick der.

pluck [plʌk] ⟨⟩ vt - 1. [flower, fruit] pflücken - 2. [pull] ziehen - 3. [chicken] rupfen - 4. [eyebrows, guitar, harp] zupfen. ⟨⟩ n (U) dated Mut der. ▰ **pluck up** vt sep: **to pluck up the courage to do sthg** den Mut auf|bringen, etw zu tun.

plug [plʌg] ⟨⟩ n - 1. ELEC Stecker der; [socket] Steckdose die - 2. [for bath, sink] Stöpsel der. ⟨⟩ vt - 1. [hole, ears] verstopfen - 2. inf [advertise] Schleichwerbung für etw machen. ▰ **plug in** vt sep ELEC ein|stecken.

plughole ['plʌghəʊl] n Abfluss der.

plum [plʌm] n [fruit] Pflaume die.

plumb [plʌm] ⟨⟩ adv - 1. UK [exactly] genau; **plumb in the middle** genau in der/die Mitte - 2. US [completely] völlig, komplett. ⟨⟩ vt: **to plumb the depths of sthg** den Tiefpunkt von etw erreichen.

plumber ['plʌmə'] n Klempner der.

plumbing ['plʌmɪŋ] n (U) - 1. [fittings] Leitungen Pl - 2. [work] Installieren das von Sanitäranlagen.

plume [plu:m] n - 1. [on bird, hat] Feder die; [on helmet] Federbusch der - 2. [column]: **a plume of smoke** eine Rauchfahne.

plummet ['plʌmɪt] vi - 1. [plane, bird] (senkrecht) hinunter|stürzen - 2. [prices, value, shares] rapide fallen.

plump [plʌmp] ⟨⟩ adj rundlich, mollig. ⟨⟩ vi: **to plump for sthg** sich für etw entscheiden. ▰ **plump up** vt sep auf|schütteln.

plunder ['plʌndə'] vt plündern.

plunge [plʌndʒ] ⟨⟩ n - 1. [rapid decrease] Sturz der - 2. [dive] Sprung der; [head-on] Kopfsprung der; **to take the plunge** den Schritt wagen. ⟨⟩ vt - 1. [immerse]: **to plunge sthg into sthg** etw in etw (A) werfen - 2. [thrust]: **to plunge sthg into sthg** etw in etw (A) treiben; **plunged into darkness** in Dunkelheit getaucht. ⟨⟩ vi - 1. [dive] springen; [out of control] stürzen - 2. [prices, value] fallen.

plunger ['plʌndʒə'] n [for sinks, drains] Saugglocke die.

pluperfect [,plu:'pɜ:fɪkt] n: **pluperfect (tense)** Plusquamperfekt das.

plural ['plʊərəl] ⟨⟩ adj GRAM im Plural. ⟨⟩ n Plural der; **in the plural** im Plural.

plus [plʌs] (pl -es OR -ses) ⟨⟩ adj - 1. [over, more than]: **30 plus** mehr als 30, über 30 - 2. [in school marks] plus. ⟨⟩ n - 1. MATHS [sign] Pluszeichen *das* - **2.** *inf* [bonus] Plus *das.* <> *prep* - **1.** MATHS plus, und - **2.** [as well as] und. <> *conj* [moreover] und (außerdem).

plush [plʌʃ] *adj* luxuriös.

plus sign *n* Pluszeichen *das.*

Pluto ['pluːtəʊ] *n* [planet] Pluto *der.*

plutonium [pluːˈtəʊnɪəm] *n* Plutonium *das.*

ply [plaɪ] *vt* - **1.** [work at]: **to ply a trade** ein Gewerbe betreiben - **2.**: **to ply sb with drink** jm Alkohol aufdrängen; **to ply sb with questions** jn mit Fragen bedrängen.

-ply [plaɪ] *adj*: **four-ply** [wood] vierschichtig; [wool] vierfädig.

plywood ['plaɪwʊd] *n* Sperrholz *das.*

p.m., pm *(abbr of post meridiem)* nachmittags; **at 9 p.m.** um 21 Uhr OR 9 Uhr abends.

PM *n abbr of* **prime minister.**

PMT *n abbr of* **premenstrual tension.**

pneumatic [njuːˈmætɪk] *adj* pneumatisch.

pneumatic drill *n* Pressluftbohrer *der.*

pneumonia [njuːˈməʊnɪə] *n (U)* Lungenentzündung *die.*

poach [pəʊtʃ] <> *vt* - **1.** [hunt illegally] wildern - **2.** [idea] kopieren - **3.** [egg] pochieren. <> *vi* wildern.

poacher ['pəʊtʃəʳ] *n* [person] Wilderer *der.*

poaching ['pəʊtʃɪŋ] *n* Wildern *das.*

PO Box *n abbr of* **Post Office Box.**

pocket ['pɒkɪt] <> *n* - **1.** [in clothes] Tasche *die*; **to be out of pocket** draufzahlen; **to pick sb's pocket** jm etwas (aus der Tasche) stehlen - **2.** [of warm air, mineral] Einschluss *der*; **pocket of resistance** Widerstandsnest *das* - **3.** [of snooker, pool table] Loch *das.* <> *adj* Taschen-. <> *vt* einlstecken.

pocketbook ['pɒkɪtbʊk] *n* - **1.** [notebook] Notizbuch *das* - **2.** US [handbag] Handtasche *die.*

pocketknife ['pɒkɪtnaɪf] *(pl* **-knives** [-naɪvz]*) n* Taschenmesser *das.*

pocket money *n* Taschengeld *das.*

pod [pɒd] *n* [of plants] Hülse *die.*

podcast ['pɒdkɑːst] *n* Podcast *der.*

podgy ['pɒdʒɪ] *adj inf* pummelig.

podia ['pəʊdɪə] *npl* ⊳ **podium.**

podiatrist [pəˈdaɪətrɪst] *n* US Fußpfleger *der*, -in *die.*

podium ['pəʊdɪəm] *(pl* **-diums** OR **-dia**) *n* Podium *das.*

poem ['pəʊɪm] *n* Gedicht *das.*

poet ['pəʊɪt] *n* Dichter *der*, -in *die.*

poetic [pəʊˈetɪk] *adj* poetisch.

poetry ['pəʊɪtrɪ] *n (U)* [poems] Dichtung *die.*

poignant ['pɔɪnjənt] *adj* [moving] ergreifend.

point [pɔɪnt] <> *n* - **1.** [tip] Spitze *die* - **2.** [in discussion, debate] Punkt *der*; **to make a point** eine Anmerkung machen; **to make one's**

point seinen Standpunkt deutlich machen - **3.** [meaning] Sinn *der*; **you've missed the point of what he is trying to say** du hast nicht verstanden, worauf er hinauswill; **to get** OR **come to the point** zur Sache kommen; **that's beside the point** das tut hier nichts zur Sache - **4.** [feature]: **good** OR **strong point** Stärke *die*; **bad** OR **weak point** Schwäche *die* - **5.** [purpose] Zweck *der*; **there's no point** es hat keinen Sinn - **6.** MATHS Komma *das*; **five point seven** fünf Komma sieben - **7.** [in scores] Punkt *der* - **8.** UK ELEC Steckdose *die* - **9.** US [full stop] Punkt *der* - **10.** *phr*: **to make a point of doing sthg** etw bewusst tun. <> *vt*: **to point sthg (at)** etw richten (auf (+ A)). <> *vi* - **1.** [person]: **to point at** OR **to** zeigen auf (+ A) - **2.** *fig* [evidence, facts]: **to point to sb/sthg** auf jn/etw hinlweisen. ◆ **points** *npl* UK RAIL Weiche *die.* ◆ **on the point of** *prep*: **to be on the point of doing sthg** im Begriff sein, etw zu tun; **I was on the point of going** ich wollte gerade gehen. ◆ **up to a point** *adv* bis zu einem gewissen Punkt. ◆ **point out** *vt sep* - **1.** [indicate] zeigen - **2.** [call attention to] hinlweisen auf (+ A).

point-blank *adv* - **1.** [directly] direkt; [ask] geradeheraus; [refuse] rundweg - **2.** [shoot] aus nächster Nähe.

pointed ['pɔɪntɪd] *adj* - **1.** [sharp] spitz - **2.** [meaningful] betont; [remark] spitz.

pointer ['pɔɪntəʳ] *n* - **1.** [tip] Hinweis *der* - **2.** [needle on dial] Zeiger *der* - **3.** [stick] Zeigestock *der* - **4.** COMPUT Mauszeiger *der.*

pointless ['pɔɪntlɪs] *adj* zwecklos, sinnlos.

point of view *(pl* **points of view)** *n* [attitude] Standpunkt *der.*

poise [pɔɪz] *n (U)* [composure] Selbstsicherheit *die.*

poised [pɔɪzd] *adj* - **1.** [ready] bereit; **to be poised to do sthg** bereit sein, etw zu tun; **to be poised for sthg** bereit sein für etw OR zu etw - **2.** [composed] gefasst.

poison ['pɔɪzn] <> *n* Gift *das.* <> *vt* - **1.** [gen] vergiften - **2.** *fig* [corrupt] verschmutzen - **3.** [atmosphere, water] verderben.

poisoning ['pɔɪznɪŋ] *n* Vergiftung *die.*

poisonous ['pɔɪznəs] *adj* [gen] giftig.

poke [pəʊk] <> *vt* - **1.** [with finger, stick] stoßen; **to poke sb in the ribs** jm einen Stoß in die Rippen geben - **2.** [thrust] stecken; **he poked his head round the door** er steckte den Kopf zur Tür herein - **3.** [fire] schüren. <> *vi*: **to poke out of** hervorlschauen aus (+ D). ◆ **poke about, poke around** *vi inf* herumlstochern.

poker ['pəʊkəʳ] *n* - **1.** [game] Poker *das* - **2.** [for fire] Schürhaken *der.*

poker-faced [-ˌfeɪst] *adj* mit einem Poker-face.

poky ['pəʊkɪ] *adj pej* eng.

Poland ['pəʊlənd] *n* Polen *nt*.

polar ['pəʊlə'] *adj* GEOG polar.

Polaroid® ['pəʊlərɔɪd] *n* - **1.** [camera] Polaroidkamera® *die* - **2.** [photograph] Polaroidfoto *das*.

pole [pəʊl] *n* - **1.** Stange *die*; [for electricity] Pfahl *der*; [for flag] Mast *der*; [for skiing] Stock *der* - **2.** GEOG & ELEC Pol *der*.

Pole [pəʊl] *n* Pole *der*, -lin *die*.

pole vault *n*: the pole vault der Stabhochsprung.

police [pə'liːs] ◇ *npl* - **1.** [police force]: **the police** die Polizei - **2.** [policemen] Polizisten *Pl*. ◇ *vt* [area] kontrollieren.

police car *n* Streifenwagen *der*.

police constable *n* UK Wachtmeister *der*, -in *die*.

police force *n* Polizei *die*.

policeman [pə'liːsmən] (*pl* -men [-mən]) *n* Polizist *der*.

police officer *n* Polizeibeamte *der*, -tin *die*.

police station *n* UK Polizeiwache *die*.

policewoman [pə'liːs,wʊmən] (*pl* -women [-,wɪmɪn]) *n* Polizistin *die*.

policy ['pɒləsɪ] *n* - **1.** [plan] Politik *die* - **2.** [for insurance] Police *die*.

polio ['pəʊlɪəʊ] *n* (U) Kinderlähmung *die*.

polish ['pɒlɪʃ] ◇ *n* - **1.** [cleaning material] Politur *die*; window polish Glasreiniger *der* - **2.** [shine] Glanz *der*; [of furniture] Politur *die* - **3.** *fig* [of performance] Brillianz *die*; [of style, manners] Schliff *der*. ◇ *vt* - **1.** [shine] polieren - **2.** *fig* [perfect]: **to polish sthg (up)** etw verfeinern. ◆ **polish off** *vt sep inf* - **1.** [meal] verputzen - **2.** [job] schnell erledigen; [book] verschlingen.

Polish ['pəʊlɪʃ] ◇ *adj* polnisch. ◇ *n* [language] Polnisch(e) *das*.

polished ['pɒlɪʃt] *adj* - **1.** [surface] poliert - **2.** [person, manners] geschliffen - **3.** [performance] brilliant.

polite [pə'laɪt] *adj* höflich.

political [pə'lɪtɪkl] *adj* politisch.

politically correct *adj* politisch korrekt.

politician [,pɒlɪ'tɪʃn] *n* Politiker *der*, -in *die*.

politics ['pɒlətɪks] ◇ *n* (U) Politik *die*. ◇ *npl* - **1.** [personal beliefs] politische Ansichten - **2.** [of a group, area] Politik *die*.

poll [pəʊl] ◇ *n* - **1.** [election] Wahl *die* - **2.** [survey] Umfrage *die*. ◇ *vt* - **1.** [people] befragen - **2.** [votes] erhalten. ◆ **polls** *npl*: **to go to the polls** wählen gehen.

pollen ['pɒlən] *n* Blütenstaub *der*.

polling booth *n* Wahlkabine *die*.

polling day *n* UK Wahltag *der*.

polling station *n* Wahllokal *das*.

pollute [pə'luːt] *vt* verschmutzen.

pollution [pə'luːʃn] *n* Verschmutzung *die*.

polo ['pəʊləʊ] *n* Polo *das*.

polo neck *n* UK - **1.** [collar] Rollkragen *der* - **2.** [jumper] Rollkragenpullover *der*.

polo shirt *n* Polohemd *das*.

polyethylene *n* US = **polythene**.

polystyrene [,pɒlɪ'staɪriːn] *n* Styropor® *das*.

polytechnic [,pɒlɪ'teknɪk] *n* UK Polytechnikum *das*, ≈ technische Hochschule.

polythene UK ['pɒlɪθiːn], **polyethylene** US [,pɒlɪ'eθɪliːn] *n* Polyethylen *das*.

polythene bag *n* UK Plastiktüte *die*.

pomegranate ['pɒmɪ,grænɪt] *n* Granatapfel *der*.

pomp [pɒmp] *n* Pomp *der*.

pompom ['pɒmpɒm] *n* Pompon *der*.

pompous ['pɒmpəs] *adj* [pretentious] aufgeblasen; [speech] geschwollen.

pond [pɒnd] *n* Teich *der*.

ponder ['pɒndə'] *vt* & *vi* nachdenken; **to ponder on** OR **over sthg** über etw (A) nachldenken.

ponderous ['pɒndərəs] *adj* schwerfällig.

pong [pɒŋ] UK *inf n* Gestank *der*, Mief *der*.

pontoon [pɒn'tuːn] *n* - **1.** [bridge] Ponton *der* - **2.** UK [game] Siebzehnundvier *das*.

pony ['pəʊnɪ] *n* Pony *das*.

ponytail ['pəʊnɪteɪl] *n* Pferdeschwanz *der*.

poodle ['puːdl] *n* Pudel *der*.

pool [puːl] ◇ *n* - **1.** [of water, blood] Lache *die*; [of light] Lichtkegel *der*; [of rain] Pfütze *die* - **2.** [swimming pool] Swimmingpool *der*; [small pond] Teich *der* - **3.** [game] Poolbillard *das*. ◇ *vt* zusammenlegen. ◆ **pools** *npl* UK: **the pools** das Fußballtoto.

poor [pɔː'] ◇ *adj* - **1.** [impoverished, unfortunate] arm - **2.** [not very good] schlecht. ◇ *npl*: **the poor** die Armen *Pl*.

poorly ['pɔːlɪ] ◇ *adj* UK *inf* krank. ◇ *adv* [badly] schlecht.

pop [pɒp] ◇ *n* - **1.** [music] Pop *der* - **2.** UK *inf* [fizzy drink] Brause *die* - **3.** *esp* US *inf* [father] Papa *der* - **4.** [noise] Knall *der*. ◇ *vt* - **1.** [balloon, bubble] platzen, zerplatzen - **2.** [put] stecken. ◇ *vi* [balloon] platzen; [cork] knallen; **my ears are popping** ich habe Druck auf den Ohren. ◆ **pop in** *vi* [visit] vorbeischauen. ◆ **pop up** *vi* auftauchen.

pop concert *n* Popkonzert *das*.

popcorn ['pɒpkɔːn] *n* Popcorn *das*.

pope [pəʊp] *n* Papst *der*.

pop group *n* Popgruppe *die*.

poplar ['pɒplə'] *n* Pappel *die*.

poppy ['pɒpɪ] *n* Mohn *der*.

Popsicle® ['pɒpsɪkl] *n* US Eis *das* am Stiel.

popular ['pɒpjʊlər] *adj* - **1.** [well-liked] populär, beliebt - **2.** [common] weit verbreitet - **3.** [newspaper, politics] volksnah; [entertainment] volkstümlich; [debate] öffentlich.

popularize, -ise ['pɒpjʊləraɪz] *vt* - **1.** [make popular] popularisieren - **2.** [simplify] vereinfachen.

population [,pɒpjʊ'leɪʃn] *n* [gen] Bevölkerung *die*.

porcelain ['pɔːsəlɪn] *n* Porzellan *das*.

porch [pɔːtʃ] *n* - **1.** [entrance] Windfang *der* - **2.** US [veranda] Veranda *die*.

porcupine ['pɔːkjʊpaɪn] *n* Stachelschwein *das*.

pore [pɔːr] *n* Pore *die*. **◆ pore over** *vt insep* brüten über.

pork [pɔːk] *n* Schweinefleisch *das*.

pork pie *n* Schweinefleischpastete *die*.

pornography [pɔː'nɒɡrəfɪ] *n* Pornografie *die*.

porous ['pɔːrəs] *adj* porös.

porridge ['pɒrɪdʒ] *n* Haferbrei *der*.

port [pɔːt] *n* - **1.** [coastal town] Hafenstadt *die*; [harbour] Hafen *der* - **2.** NAUT Backbord *das* - **3.** [drink] Portwein *der* - **4.** COMPUT Anschluss *der*.

portable ['pɔːtəbl] *adj* tragbar.

porter ['pɔːtər] *n* - **1.** UK [at hotel, museum] Pförtner *der*, Portier *der* - **2.** [at station, airport] Gepäckträger *der* - **3.** US [on train] Schlafwagenschaffner *der*.

portfolio [,pɔːt'fəʊlɪəʊ] *(pl -s) n* - **1.** [case] Aktentasche *die* - **2.** [sample of work] Mappe *die* - **3.** FIN Portefeuille *das*.

porthole ['pɔːthəʊl] *n* Bullauge *das*.

portion ['pɔːʃn] *n* - **1.** [part, share] Teil *der* - **2.** [of food] Portion *die*.

portrait ['pɔːtreɪt] *n* liter & fig Porträt *das*.

portray [pɔː'treɪ] *vt* - **1.** [gen] darstellen - **2.** [subj: artist] porträtieren.

Portugal ['pɔːtʃʊɡl] *n* Portugal *nt*.

Portuguese [,pɔːtʃʊ'ɡiːz] *(pl inv)* ◇ *adj* portugiesisch. ◇ *n* - **1.** [person] Portugiese *der*, -sin *die* - **2.** [language] Portugiesisch(e) *das*. ◇ *npl*: **the Portuguese** die Portugiesen *Pl*.

pose [pəʊz] ◇ *n* - **1.** [position] Haltung *die* - **2.** pej [pretence] Pose *die*. ◇ *vt* - **1.** [problem, danger, threat] darstellen - **2.** [a question] stellen. ◇ *vi* - **1.** [for photo] posieren; [for painting] Modell stehen - **2.** pej [behave affectedly] posieren - **3.** [pretend to be]: **to pose as a tourist** sich als Tourist ausgeben.

posh [pɒʃ] *adj inf* nobel.

position [pə'zɪʃn] ◇ *n* - **1.** [place, situation] Lage *die* - **2.** [of plane, ship] Position *die* - **3.** [of body] Haltung *die* - **4.** [setting, rank] Stellung *die* - **5.** [in race, combat] Platz *der*

- **6.** [job] Stelle *die* - **7.** [stance, opinion]: **position on sthg** Haltung gegenüber etw *(D)*. ◇ *vt* positionieren.

positive ['pɒzətɪv] *adj* - **1.** [gen] positiv - **2.** [sure, certain] sicher; **to be positive about sthg** sich einer Sache *(G)* sicher sein - **3.** [evidence, fact] definitiv - **4.** [for emphasis] total.

possess [pə'zes] *vt* besitzen; **what possessed you to do that?** was ist in Sie gefahren, dass Sie das gemacht haben?

possession [pə'zeʃn] *n* Besitz *der*. **◆ possessions** *npl* Habe *die*; **his personal possessions** all seine Sachen.

possessive [pə'zesɪv] ◇ *adj* - **1.** pej [person] besitzergreifend - **2.** GRAM Possessiv-. ◇ *n* GRAM Possessivfunktion *die*.

possibility [,pɒsə'bɪlətɪ] *n* Möglichkeit *die*.

possible ['pɒsəbl] *adj* möglich; **would it be possible for me to see him?** könnte ich ihn vielleicht sehen?; **as soon as possible** so bald wie möglich; **as much as possible** so viel wie möglich; **if possible** wenn möglich.

possibly ['pɒsəblɪ] *adv* - **1.** [perhaps] möglicherweise - **2.** [conceivably] möglich; **I'll do all I possibly can** ich werde mein Möglichstes tun; **I can't possibly do that** das kann ich unmöglich tun.

post [pəʊst] ◇ *n* - **1.** [service, letters, delivery] Post *die*; **by post** per Post - **2.** [pole] Pfosten *der*; **to pip sb at the post** [in race] jn knapp schlagen; *fig* jm etw vor der Nase wegschnappen - **3.** [job & MIL] Posten *der*. ◇ *vt* - **1.** [by mail] per OR mit der Post schicken - **2.** [employee] versetzen.

postage ['pəʊstɪdʒ] *n* Porto *das*; **postage and packing** Porto und Verpackung *die*.

postal ['pəʊstl] *adj* Post-, postalisch.

postal order *n* Postanweisung *die*.

postbox ['pəʊstbɒks] *n* UK Briefkasten *der*.

postcard ['pəʊstkɑːd] *n* Postkarte *die*.

postcode ['pəʊstkəʊd] *n* UK Postleitzahl *die*.

postdate [,pəʊst'deɪt] *vt* vorldatieren.

poster ['pəʊstər] *n* Poster *das*, Plakat *das*.

poste restante [,pəʊst'restɑːnt] *n (U)* *esp UK*: **to send sthg poste restante** etw postlagernd schicken.

posterior [pɒ'stɪərɪər] ◇ *adj* [rear] hintere(r) (s). ◇ *n hum* Hinterteil *das*.

postgraduate [,pəʊst'ɡrædʊət] ◇ *adj* [studies, course] Aufbau-. ◇ *n*: **postgraduate (student)** Student, der ein Aufbaustudium absolviert.

posthumous ['pɒstjʊməs] *adj* postum.

postman ['pəʊstmən] *(pl -men* [-mən]*) n* Briefträger *der*, Postbote *der*.

postmark ['pəʊstmɑːk] ◇ *n* Poststempel *der*. ◇ *vt* stempeln.

postmortem [ˌpəʊstˈmɔːtəm] n
- 1. [autopsy]: **postmortem (examination)** Obduktion die - 2. fig [analysis] Analyse die.

post office n Post die.

post office box n Postfach das.

postpone [ˌpəʊstˈpəʊn] vt verschieben; [decision] aufschieben.

postscript [ˈpəʊstskrɪpt] n [to letter] Postskriptum das.

posture [ˈpɒstʃəʳ] n liter & fig Haltung die.

postwar [ˌpəʊstˈwɔːʳ] adj Nachkriegs-.

posy [ˈpəʊzɪ] n Blumensträußchen das.

pot [pɒt] ◇ n - 1. [for cooking, flowers] Topf der - 2. [for tea, coffee] Kanne die - 3. [for paint] Büchse die; [for jam] Glas das - 4. (U) drug sl [cannabis] Hasch das. ◇ vt [plant] eintopfen.

potassium [pəˈtæsɪəm] n Kalium das.

potato [pəˈteɪtəʊ] (pl -es) n Kartoffel die.

potato peeler [-ˌpiːləʳ] n Kartoffelschäler der.

potent [ˈpəʊtənt] adj - 1. [argument] stichhaltig - 2. [drink, drug] stark.

potential [pəˈtenʃl] ◇ adj potenziell. ◇ n (U) [of person] Potenzial das; **to have potential** [person] das Potenzial haben; [scheme, plan, company, business] entwicklungsfähig sein.

potentially [pəˈtenʃəlɪ] adv potenziell.

pothole [ˈpɒthəʊl] n - 1. [in road] Schlagloch das - 2. [underground] Höhle die.

potholing [ˈpɒtˌhəʊlɪŋ] n UK Höhlenforschung die; **to go potholing** eine Höhle erforschen (gehen).

potion [ˈpəʊʃn] n Trank der.

potluck [ˌpɒtˈlʌk] n: **to take potluck** aufs Geratewohl auswählen; [at meal] mit dem vorlieb nehmen, was gerade da ist.

potshot [ˈpɒtˌʃɒt] n: **to take a potshot at sthg** aufs Geratewohl auf etw (A) schießen.

potted [ˈpɒtɪd] adj - 1. [grown in pot] Topf- - 2. [meat] eingemacht.

potter [ˈpɒtəʳ] n [craftsperson] Töpfer der, -in die. ◆ **potter about, potter around** vi UK [do minor work] herumwerkeln; [work slowly] herumtrödeln.

pottery [ˈpɒtərɪ] n - 1. (U) [clay objects] Töpferwaren Pl - 2. [craft] Töpfern das.

potty [ˈpɒtɪ] UK inf ◇ adj verrückt; **to be potty about sb/sthg** nach jm/etw verrückt sein. ◇ n Töpfchen das.

pouch [paʊtʃ] n Beutel der.

poultry [ˈpəʊltrɪ] ◇ n [meat] Geflügel das. ◇ npl [birds] Geflügel das.

pounce [paʊns] vi: **to pounce on** OR **upon** sich stürzen auf (+ A).

pound [paʊnd] ◇ n - 1. UK [unit of money, currency system] Pfund das - 2. [unit of weight] ≃ Pfund das (= 454g) - 3. [for cars] Abstellplatz der (für abgeschleppte Fahrzeuge); [for dogs] Asyl das. ◇ vt [pulverize] pulverisieren. ◇ vi - 1. [strike loudly]: **to pound on sthg** [wall, door] an OR gegen etw (A) hämmern; [table] auf etw (A) hämmern - 2. [beat, throb - heart] pochen; [- head] brummen.

pound coin n Einpfundmünze die.

pound sterling n Pfund das Sterling.

pour [pɔːʳ] ◇ vt [cause to flow]: **to pour sthg (into sthg)** [liquid] etw (in etw (A)) gießen; [grain, sugar] etw (in etw (A)) schütten; **to pour sb a drink, to pour a drink for sb** jm einen Drink eingießen. ◇ vi liter & fig strömen; **sweat was pouring off him** ihm lief der Schweiß herunter. ◇ impers vb [rain hard] (wie aus Eimern) gießen. ◆ **pour in** vi (in großen Mengen) eintreffen. ◆ **pour out** vt sep - 1. [from container] ausschütten - 2. [drink] einschenken.

pouring [ˈpɔːrɪŋ] adj [rain] strömend.

pout [paʊt] vi schmollen.

poverty [ˈpɒvətɪ] n (U) [hardship] Armut die.

poverty-stricken [-ˌstrɪkən] adj verarmt.

powder [ˈpaʊdəʳ] ◇ n [for baking, washing] Pulver das; [for face, body] Puder der. ◇ vt [face, body] pudern.

powder compact n Puderdose die.

powdered [ˈpaʊdəd] adj - 1. [in powder form]: **powdered milk** Trockenmilch die; **powdered eggs** Trockenei das - 2. [covered in powder] gepudert.

powder puff n Puderquaste die.

powder room n Damentoilette die.

power [ˈpaʊəʳ] ◇ n - 1. (U) [control, influence] Macht die; **to be in power** an der Macht sein; **to come to power** an die Macht kommen; **to take power** die Macht übernehmen - 2. [ability, capacity] Vermögen das, Fähigkeit die; **to be (with)in one's power to do sthg** in js Macht liegen, etw zu tun - 3. [legal authority] Macht die; **to have the power to do sthg** das Recht haben, etw zu tun - 4. (U) [strength] Stärke die - 5. (U) TECH [energy] Energie die - 6. (U) [electricity] Strom der - 7. [powerful person, group] Macht die. ◇ vt [machine] antreiben.

powerboat [ˈpaʊəbəʊt] n Rennboot das.

power cut n Stromsperre die.

power failure n Stromausfall der.

powerful [ˈpaʊəfʊl] adj - 1. [influential] mächtig - 2. [strong] kräftig; [drug, smell] stark; [blow, kick] kraftvoll; [machine] leistungsstark - 3. [very convincing, very moving - piece of writing, speech] überzeugend; [- work of art] überwältigend.

powerless [ˈpaʊəlɪs] adj machtlos; **he was powerless to help** es stand nicht in seiner Macht zu helfen.

power point n UK Steckdose die.

power station n Kraftwerk das.

power steering n Servolenkung die.

pp (*abbr of* per procurationem) pp.

p & p (*abbr of* postage and packing) *n* Post- und Verpackungsgebühr.

PR *n* - **1.** *abbr of* **proportional representation** - **2.** *abbr of* **public relations**.

practicable ['præktɪkəbl] *adj* durchführbar.

practical ['præktɪkl] *adj* - **1.** [gen] praktisch - **2.** [practicable] durchführbar, umsetzbar. ◇ *n* Praktikum *das*.

practicality [,præktɪ'kælətɪ] *n* Praxisbezogenheit *die*.

practical joke *n* Streich *der*.

practically ['præktɪklɪ] *adv* - **1.** [sensibly] praktisch - **2.** [almost] fast.

practice, practise *US* ['præktɪs] *n* - **1.** *(U)* [training] Übung *die*; [for sport] Training *das*; [for music] Üben *das*; **to be out of practice** aus der Übung sein - **2.** [training session - of choir] Probe *die*; [- of sport] Training *das* - **3.** [implementation]: **to put sthg into practice** etw in die Praxis umsetzen; **in practice** [in fact] in Wirklichkeit, tatsächlich - **4.** [habit, regular activity - of group] Brauch *der*; [- of person] Gewohnheit *die* - **5.** [business] Praxis *die*.

practicing *adj US* = **practising**.

practise, practice *US* ['præktɪs] ◇ *vt* - **1.** [musical instrument, movement in sport] üben; [foreign language] sprechen - **2.** [customs, beliefs] auslüben - **3.** [do as profession] praktizieren. ◇ *vi* - **1.** [train] üben - **2.** [doctor, lawyer] praktizieren.

practising, practicing *US* ['præktɪsɪŋ] *adj* praktizierend.

Prague [prɑːg] *n* Prag *nt*.

prairie ['preərɪ] *n* Prärie *die*.

praise [preɪz] ◇ *n* Lob *das*; **to sing sb's praises** ein Loblied auf jn singen. ◇ *vt* loben.

praiseworthy ['preɪz,wɜːðɪ] *adj* lobenswert.

pram [præm] *n UK* Kinderwagen *der*.

prance [prɑːns] *vi* - **1.** [vain person] (herum)lstolzieren; [child] herumlhüpfen - **2.** [horse] tänzeln.

prank [præŋk] *n* Streich *der*.

prawn [prɔːn] *n* Garnele *die*.

pray [preɪ] *vi* RELIG beten; **to pray to God** zu Gott beten.

prayer [preə^r] *n* - **1.** *(U)* [act of praying] Beten *das*, Gebet *das* - **2.** [set of words] Gebet *das* - **3.** *fig* [strong hope] starke Hoffnung.

prayer book *n* Gebetsbuch *das*.

preach [priːtʃ] ◇ *vt liter* & *fig* predigen. ◇ *vi* - **1.** RELIG predigen - **2.** *pej* [pontificate]: **to preach (at sb)** (jm) eine Predigt halten.

preacher ['priːtʃə^r] *n* Prediger *der*, -in *die*.

precarious [prɪ'keərɪəs] *adj* wackelig; [situation] prekär.

precaution [prɪ'kɔːʃn] *n* Vorsichtsmaßnahme *die*.

precede [prɪ'siːd] *vt* vorauslgehen (*+ D*).

precedence ['presɪdəns] *n*: **to take precedence over sb/sthg** den Vorrang vor jm/gegenüber etw haben.

precedent ['presɪdənt] *n* Präzedenzfall *der*.

precinct ['priːsɪŋkt] *n* - **1.** *UK* [for pedestrians] Fußgängerzone *die*; [for shopping] verkehrsfreies Einkaufsviertel - **2.** *US* [district] Bezirk *der*; **police precinct** Polizeirevier *das*. ➭ **precincts** *npl* [around building] Umgebung *die*, Bereich *der*.

precious ['preʃəs] *adj* - **1.** [gen] kostbar - **2.** *inf iro* [damned] verflixt, verdammt - **3.** [affected] affektiert.

precipice ['presɪpɪs] *n* Steilwand *die*.

precise [prɪ'saɪs] *adj* genau.

precisely [prɪ'saɪslɪ] *adv* genau.

precision [prɪ'sɪʒn] *n* *(U)* Genauigkeit *die*.

preclude [prɪ'kluːd] *vt fml* [possibility, misunderstanding] auslschließen; [event, action] unmöglich machen; **to preclude sb from doing sthg** es jm unmöglich machen, etw zu tun.

precocious [prɪ'kəʊʃəs] *adj* frühreif.

preconceived [,priːkən'siːvd] *adj* vorgefasst.

precondition [,priːkən'dɪʃn] *n fml* (Vor)bedingung *die*.

predator ['predətə^r] *n* [animal] Raubtier *das*; [bird] Raubvogel *der*.

predecessor ['priːdɪsesə^r] *n* - **1.** [person] Vorgänger *der*, -in *die* - **2.** [thing] Vorläufer *der*.

predicament [prɪ'dɪkəmənt] *n* missliche Lage.

predict [prɪ'dɪkt] *vt* vorherlsagen.

predictable [prɪ'dɪktəbl] *adj* [result, reaction] vorhersehbar; [person, behaviour] berechenbar.

prediction [prɪ'dɪkʃn] *n* [something foretold] Voraussage *die*.

predispose [,priːdɪs'pəʊz] *vt*: **to be predisposed to do sthg** dazu neigen, etw zu tun; **to be predisposed to sthg** zu etw neigen.

predominant [prɪ'dɒmɪnənt] *adj* vorherrschend.

predominantly [prɪ'dɒmɪnəntlɪ] *adv* überwiegend.

preempt [,priː'empt] *vt* zuvorlkommen (*+ D*).

preen [priːn] *vt* - **1.** [subj: bird] putzen - **2.** *fig* [subj: person]: **to preen o.s.** sich zurechtlmachen.

prefab ['priːfæb] *n inf* Fertighaus *das*.

preface ['prefɪs] *n* [in book] Vorwort *das*; **preface to sthg** [to text] Vorwort einer Sache (*G*); [to speech] Einleitung der einer Sache (*G*).

prefect ['priːfekt] *n UK* [pupil] Aufsichtsschüler *der*, -in *die*.

prefer [prɪ'fɜːr] *vt* vorziehen, bevorzugen; **to prefer sthg to sthg** etw etw *(D)* vorziehen; **to prefer to do sthg** es vorziehen, etw zu tun.

preferable ['prefrəbl] *adj*: **to be preferable (to sthg)** (etw *(D)*) vorzuziehen sein.

preferably ['prefrəblɪ] *adv* vorzugsweise.

preference ['prefərəns] *n* - **1.** [liking]: **preference (for sthg)** Vorliebe *die* (für etw) - **2.** [precedence]: **to give sb/sthg preference, to give preference to sb/sthg** jm/etw den Vorzug geben.

preferential [,prefə'renʃl] *adj* [treatment] bevorzugt.

prefix ['priːfɪks] *n* GRAM Präfix *das*.

pregnancy ['pregnənsɪ] *n* Schwangerschaft *die*.

pregnant ['pregnənt] *adj* [woman] schwanger; [animal] trächtig.

prehistoric [,priːhɪ'stɒrɪk] *adj* prähistorisch, vorgeschichtlich.

prejudice ['predʒʊdɪs] <> *n* [bias]: **prejudice (against)** Vorurteil *das* (gegen). <> *vt* [jeopardize] schaden (+ *D*).

prejudiced ['predʒʊdɪst] *adj* voreingenommen.

prejudicial [,predʒʊ'dɪʃl] *adj*: **to be prejudicial to sb** für jn schädlich sein; **to be prejudicial to sthg** einer Sache *(D)* abträglich sein.

preliminary [prɪ'lɪmɪnərɪ] *adj* [activity] vorbereitend; [talks, investigation] Vor-; [report, results] vorläufig.

prelude ['preljuːd] *n* [event]: **prelude to sthg** Auftakt *der* zu etw.

premarital [,priː'mærɪtl] *adj* vor der Ehe.

premature ['premə,tjʊər] *adj* - **1.** [death, baldness] vorzeitig - **2.**: **premature birth/child** Frühgeburt *die* - **3.** *pej* [decision, action] übereilt.

premeditated [,priː'medɪteɪtɪd] *adj* vorsätzlich.

premenstrual syndrome, premenstrual tension [priː,menstrʊəl-] *n* prämenstruelles Syndrom.

premier ['premjər] <> *adj* führend. <> *n* Premierminister *der*, -in *die*.

premiere ['premɪeər] *n* Premiere *die*.

premise ['premɪs] *n* Voraussetzung *die*. **premises** *npl* Räumlichkeiten *Pl*; **on the premises** im Hause.

premium ['priːmɪəm] *n* - **1.**: **to sell sthg at a premium** [above usual value] etw über Wert verkaufen; **to be at a premium** [in great demand] sehr gefragt sein - **2.** [insurance payment] Prämie *die*.

premium bond *n* UK Prämienanleihe *die*, britische Staatsanleihe, die eine monatliche Verlosungsteilnahme beinhaltet.

premonition [,premə'nɪʃn] *n* Vorahnung *die*.

preoccupied [priː'ɒkjʊpaɪd] *adj* in Gedanken vertieft OR versunken; **to be preoccupied with sthg** mit etw beschäftigt sein.

prepaid ['priːpeɪd] *adj* [envelope] portofrei; [items] im Voraus bezahlt.

preparation [,prepə'reɪʃn] *n* - **1.** *(U)* [act of preparing] Vorbereitung *die* - **2.** [prepared mixture - food] Fertigmischung *die*; [- medicine, cosmetics] Präparat *das*. **preparations** *npl* [plans] Vorbereitungen *Pl*.

preparatory [prɪ'pærətrɪ] *adj* vorbereitend.

preparatory school *n* - **1.** [in UK] *private Grundschule, die auf die Aufnahme in eine Public School vorbereitet* - **2.** [in US] *private höhere Schule, die auf die Aufnahme in eine Hochschule vorbereitet.*

prepare [prɪ'peər] <> *vt* - **1.** [make ready] vorbereiten; **to prepare to do sthg** sich anschicken, etw zu tun - **2.** [make, assemble] zubereiten. <> *vi*: **to prepare for sthg** sich auf etw *(A)* vorbereiten.

prepared [prɪ'peəd] *adj* - **1.** [organized, done beforehand] vorbereitet - **2.** [willing]: **to be prepared to do sthg** bereit sein, etw zu tun - **3.** [ready]: **to be prepared for sthg** auf etw *(A)* vorbereitet sein.

preposition [,prepə'zɪʃn] *n* Präposition *die*.

preposterous [prɪ'pɒstərəs] *adj* absurd.

prep school *n abbr of* **preparatory school**.

prerequisite [,priː'rekwɪzɪt] *n*: **prerequisite (of OR for)** Voraussetzung *die* (für).

prerogative [prɪ'rɒgətɪv] *n* Vorrecht *das*.

preschool [,priː'skuːl] *adj* Vorschul-.

prescribe [prɪ'skraɪb] *vt* - **1.** MED verschreiben - **2.** [order] vorschreiben.

prescription [prɪ'skrɪpʃn] *n* MED Rezept *das*.

presence ['prezns] *n* - **1.** [being present] Anwesenheit *die*, Gegenwart *die*; **in his presence** in seiner Gegenwart - **2.** *(U)* [personality, charisma] Ausstrahlung *die*.

presence of mind *n* Geistesgegenwart *die*.

present <> *adj* ['preznt] - **1.** [current] gegenwärtig, derzeitig - **2.** [in attendance] anwesend; **to be present at sthg** bei etw anwesend sein. <> *n* ['preznt] - **1.** [current time]: **the present** die Gegenwart; **at present** zur Zeit - **2.** [gift] Geschenk *das* - **3.** GRAM: **present (tense)** Präsens *das*, Gegenwart *die*. <> *vt* [prɪ'zent] - **1.** [gift, award] überreichen; **to present sb with sthg, to present sthg to sb** jm etw überreichen - **2.** [opportunity] bieten; [problem] aufwerfen - **3.** [introduce - person] vorstellen; *(phrase)*: **to present sb to sb** jn vorstellen - **4.** [TV, radio programme] moderieren - **5.** [facts, figures, report] vorlegen - **6.** [portray] darstellen - **7.** [arrive, go]: **to present o.s.** [at reception] sich melden; [for interview] erscheinen - **8.** [perform] darbieten.

presentable [prɪ'zentəbl] *adj* präsentabel.

presentation [,prezn'teɪʃn] *n* - **1.** *(U)* [publication, broadcasting] Präsentation *die* - **2.** *(U)* [of product] Aufmachung *die*; [of policy, text] Präsentation *die* - **3.** [ceremony] Verleihung *die* - **4.** [talk] Präsentation *die* - **5.** [performance] Darbietung *die*.

present day *n*: the present day der heutige Tag, jetzt. ➡ **present-day** *adj* heutig.

presenter [prɪ'zentər] *n* UK Moderator *der*, -in *die*.

presently ['prezəntlɪ] *adv* - **1.** [soon] bald - **2.** [now] gegenwärtig, jetzt.

preservation [,prezə'veɪʃn] *n* *(U)* - **1.** [of democracy, law and order] Aufrechterhaltung *die*; [of building, wildlife, countryside] Erhaltung *die* - **2.** [of food] Konservierung *die*.

preservative [prɪ'zɜːvətɪv] *n* [in food] Konservierungsmittel *das*; [for wood] Schutzmittel *das*.

preserve [prɪ'zɜːv] ◇ *vt* - **1.** [democracy, peace, situation] aufrechterhalten; [building, wildlife, way of life] erhalten - **2.** [food] konservieren; [fruit] einlwecken. ◇ *n* [jam] Konfitüre *die*.

preset [,priː'set] (*pt & pp inv*) *vt* [oven] vorlheizen; [VCR] programmieren.

president ['prezɪdənt] *n* Präsident *der*, -in *die*.

presidential [,prezɪ'denʃl] *adj* [decision] des Präsidenten; [campaign, election] Präsidentschafts-; [staff, limousine] Präsidenten-.

press [pres] ◇ *n* - **1.** [push]: to give sthg a press etw drücken; at the press of a button auf Knopfdruck - **2.** [journalism]: the press die Presse - **3.** [printing machine, pressing machine] Presse *die*. ◇ *vt* - **1.** [push firmly] drücken; to press sthg against sthg etw gegen etw pressen - **2.** [squeeze] drücken; [grapes] keltern; [flowers] pressen - **3.** [iron] bügeln - **4.** [urge, force] drängen; to press sb to do sthg OR into doing sthg jn drängen OR zwingen, etw zu tun - **5.** [pursue - claim, point] beharren auf. ◇ *vi* - **1.** [push hard]: to press (on) drücken (auf (+ A)) - **2.** [surge] drängen. ➡ **press on** *vi* [continue]: to press on with weiterlmachen (mit).

press agency *n* Presseagentur *die*.

press conference *n* Pressekonferenz *die*.

pressed [prest] *adj*: to be pressed for time/money unter Zeitdruck/finanziellem Druck stehen.

pressing ['presɪŋ] *adj* [urgent] dringend.

press officer *n* Pressesprecher *der*, -in *die*.

press release *n* Pressemitteilung *die*.

press-stud *n* UK Druckknopf *der*.

press-up *n* UK Liegestütz *der*.

pressure ['preʃər] *n* *(U)* liter & fig Druck *der*; to put pressure on sb (to do sthg) auf jn Druck auslüben (, etw zu tun).

pressure cooker *n* Schnellkochtopf *der*.

pressure gauge *n* Druckmesser *der*.

pressure group *n* Interessengruppe *die*.

pressurize, -ise ['preʃəraɪz] *vt* - **1.** TECH unter Druck setzen - **2.** UK [force]: to pressurize sb to do OR into doing sthg jn (dazu) drängen, etw zu tun.

prestige [pre'stiːʒ] *n* Prestige *das*.

presumably [prɪ'zjuːməblɪ] *adv* vermutlich.

presume [prɪ'zjuːm] *vt* [assume] anlnehmen; to presume (that)... anlnehmen, dass...; he is presumed dead es wird davon ausgegangen, dass er tot ist.

presumption [prɪ'zʌmpʃn] *n* - **1.** [assumption] Annahme *die* - **2.** *(U)* [audacity] Vermessenheit *die*.

presumptuous [prɪ'zʌmptʃʊəs] *adj* anmaßend.

pretence, pretense US [prɪ'tens] *n*: he made no pretence of being interested er gab nicht vor, interessiert zu sein; under false pretences unter Vortäuschung falscher Tatsachen.

pretend [prɪ'tend] ◇ *vt* - **1.** [make believe]: to pretend to do sthg vorgeben, etw zu tun; to pretend (that)... tun, als ob... - **2.** [claim]: to pretend to do sthg behaupten, dass man etw tut. ◇ *vi* [feign] so tun.

pretense *n* US = pretence.

pretension [prɪ'tenʃn] *n* [claim] Anspruch *der*.

pretentious [prɪ'tenʃəs] *adj* [person] wichtigtuerisch; [film, book] prätentiös.

pretext ['priːtekst] *n* Vorwand *der*; on OR under the pretext that... unter dem Vorwand, dass...; on OR under the pretext of doing sthg unter dem Vorwand, etw zu tun wollen.

pretty ['prɪtɪ] ◇ *adj* hübsch. ◇ *adv* [quite, rather] ziemlich; pretty much OR well so ziemlich.

prevail [prɪ'veɪl] *vi* - **1.** [be widespread] vorlherrschen; [custom] weit verbreitet sein - **2.** [triumph] sich durchlsetzen; to prevail over sb/sthg sich gegen jn/etw durchlsetzen - **3.** [persuade]: to prevail (up)on sb to do sthg jn dazu bringen, etw zu tun.

prevailing [prɪ'veɪlɪŋ] *adj* - **1.** [belief, opinion] vorlherrschend; [fashion] aktuell - **2.** [wind] vorlherrschend.

prevalent ['prevələnt] *adj* vorlherrschend; [illness] weitverbreitet.

prevent [prɪ'vent] *vt* verhindern; [illness] vorlbeugen (+ D); to prevent sb (from) doing sthg jn daran hindern, etw zu tun.

preventive [prɪ'ventɪv] *adj* vorbeugend; [measures, medicine] Präventiv-.

preview ['priːvjuː] *n* - **1.** [early showing - of film, play] Vorauffführung *die*; [- of exhibition] Vorbesichtigung *die* - **2.** [trailer for films] Vorschau *die*.

previous ['priːvɪəs] *adj* - **1.** [earlier, prior] früher; **previous conviction** Vorstrafe *die* - **2.** [with days and dates] vorhergehend; **in previous years** in früheren Jahren - **3.** [former] vorherig.

previously ['priːvɪəslɪ] *adv* - **1.** [formerly] vorher - **2.** [with days and dates] zuvor.

prewar [ˌpriːˈwɔːʳ] *adj* Vorkriegs-.

prey [preɪ] *n (U)* Beute *die*. ◆ **prey on** *vt insep* - **1.** [subj: animal, bird] Beute machen auf (+ A) - **2.** [trouble]: **to prey on sb's mind** jn bedrücken.

price [praɪs] ◇ *n* - **1.** [cost] Preis *der* - **2.** [value] Wert *der*; **to be without price** (mit Geld) nicht zu bezahlen sein. ◇ *vt* [set cost of] den Preis festlegen von; **it was priced at £100** es sollte 100 Pfund kosten.

priceless ['praɪslɪs] *adj* - **1.** [very valuable] von unschätzbarem Wert - **2.** *inf* [funny] wahnsinnig komisch.

price list *n* Preisliste *die*.

price tag *n* [label] Preisschild *das*.

pricey ['praɪsɪ] (*comp* -**ier**, *superl* -**iest**) *adj inf* teuer.

prick [prɪk] ◇ *n* - **1.** [scratch, wound] Stich *der* - **2.** *vulg* [penis] Schwanz *der* - **3.** *vulg* [stupid person] Arschloch *das*. ◇ *vt* [jab, pierce] stechen in (+ A); **to prick one's finger** sich (D) in den Finger stechen. ◆ **prick up** *vt sep*: **to prick up one's ears** *liter* & *fig* seine Ohren spitzen.

prickle ['prɪkl] ◇ *n* - **1.** [thorn] Stachel *der* - **2.** [sensation] Prickeln *das*. ◇ *vi* prickeln.

prickly ['prɪklɪ] *adj* - **1.** [thorny] stachelig - **2.** *fig* [touchy] reizbar.

pride [praɪd] ◇ *n* Stolz *der*; **to take pride in sthg** auf etw (A) stolz sein. ◇ *vt*: **to pride o.s. on sthg** auf etw (A) stolz sein.

priest [priːst] *n* Priester *der*.

priestess ['priːstɪs] *n* Priesterin *die*.

priesthood ['priːsthʊd] *n (U)* - **1.** [position, office]: **the priesthood** das Priesteramt - **2.** [priests collectively]: **the priesthood** die Priesterschaft.

prig [prɪg] *n* Tugendbold *der*.

prim [prɪm] *adj* [person, behaviour] sittsam.

primarily ['praɪmərɪlɪ] *adv* in erster Linie.

primary ['praɪmərɪ] ◇ *adj* [main - concern, aim, reason] Haupt-. ◇ *n US POL* Vorwahl *die* (zur Bestimmung der Präsidentschaftskandidaten einer Partei).

primary school *n* Grundschule *die*.

primary teacher *n* [in UK] Grundschullehrer *der*, -in *die*.

primate ['praɪmeɪt] *n* - **1.** ZOOL Primat *der* - **2.** RELIG Primas *der*.

prime [praɪm] ◇ *adj* - **1.** [main - concern, aim, reason] Haupt- - **2.** [excellent] erstklassig. ◇ *n* [peak]: **to be in one's prime** in den besten Jahren sein. ◇ *vt* [paint] grundieren.

prime minister *n* Premierminister *der*, -in *die*.

primer ['praɪməʳ] *n* - **1.** [paint] Grundierung *die* - **2.** [textbook] Fibel *die*.

primitive ['prɪmɪtɪv] *adj* primitiv.

primrose ['prɪmrəʊz] *n* Himmelsschlüssel *der*.

Primus stove® ['praɪməs-] *n* Campingkocher *der*.

prince [prɪns] *n* - **1.** [son of king, queen] Prinz *der* - **2.** [ruler] Fürst *der*.

princess [prɪnˈses] *n* Prinzessin *die*.

principal ['prɪnsəpl] ◇ *adj* Haupt-. ◇ *n* [of school, college] Direktor *der*, -in *die*.

principle ['prɪnsəpl] *n* - **1.** [gen] Prinzip *das* - **2.** [integrity] Prinzipien *Pl*; **to do sthg on principle** OR **as a matter of principle** etw aus Prinzip tun. ◆ **in principle** *adv* im Prinzip.

print [prɪnt] ◇ *n* - **1.** *(U)* [printed characters] Schrift *die*; [printed matter] Gedruckte *das*; **in large/small print** groß/klein gedruckt; **in print** [available] erhältlich; [in newspaper] gedruckt; **to be out of print** vergriffen sein - **2.** ART Druck *der* - **3.** [photograph] Abzug *der* - **4.** [fabric] bedruckter Stoff - **5.** [footprint, fingerprint] Abdruck *der*. ◇ *vt* - **1.** [gen] drucken - **2.** [write clearly] in Druckschrift schreiben. ◇ *vi* [printer] drucken. ◆ **print out** *vt sep* COMPUT ausIdrucken.

printed matter ['prɪntɪd-] *n (U)* Drucksache *die*.

printer ['prɪntəʳ] *n* [person & COMPUT] Drucker *der*; [firm] Druckerei *die*.

printing ['prɪntɪŋ] *n (U)* - **1.** [act] Drucken *das* - **2.** [trade] Druckereigewerbe *das*.

printout ['prɪntaʊt] *n* Ausdruck *der*.

prior ['praɪəʳ] ◇ *adj* - **1.** [previous - agreement] vorherig; [- warning] Vor-; **a prior engagement** eine anderweitige Verpflichtung - **2.** [more important] vorrangig. ◇ *n* [monk] Prior *der*. ◆ **prior to** *prep* vor (+ D); **prior to leaving** bevor ich/er/etc ging.

priority [praɪˈɒrətɪ] *n* - **1.** [matter] vordringliche Sache - **2.** [urgency] Vorrang *der*; **to have** OR **take priority (over sthg)** Vorrang (vor etw (D)) haben.

prise [praɪz] *vt*: **to prise sthg open** etw aufbrechen.

prison ['prɪzn] *n* Gefängnis *das*.

prisoner ['prɪznəʳ] *n* Gefangene *der*, *die*.

prisoner of war (*pl* **prisoners of war**) *n* Kriegsgefangene *der*, *die*.

privacy [*UK* 'prɪvəsɪ, *US* 'praɪvəsɪ] *n (U)* Privatsphäre *die*.

private ['praɪvɪt] ◇ *adj* - **1.** [gen] privat; [hospital, house, industry, life] Privat- - **2.** [confidential] vertraulich - **3.** [personal - belongings, plans] persönlich - **4.** [secluded] abgelegen

- **5.** [reserved] in sich zurückgezogen. ⬦ *n* - **1.** [soldier] einfacher Soldat; **Private Smith** Soldat Smith - **2.** [secrecy]: **in private** [of conversation between two people] unter vier Augen; [of meeting] hinter geschlossenen Türen.

private enterprise *n (U)* freies Unternehmertum.

private eye *n* Privatdetektiv *der*, -in *die*.

privately ['praɪvtlɪ] *adv* - **1.** [not by the state] privat; **privately owned** in Privatbesitz - **2.** [confidentially - discuss between two people] unter vier Augen; [- discuss in meeting] hinter verschlossenen Türen; [- meet, agree] insgeheim - **3.** [personally] persönlich.

private property *n (U)* Privatgrundstück *das*.

private school *n* Privatschule *die*.

privatize, -ise ['praɪvɪtaɪz] *vt* privatisieren.

privet ['prɪvɪt] *n (U)* Liguster *der*.

privilege ['prɪvɪlɪdʒ] *n* - **1.** [special advantage] Privileg *das* - **2.** [honour] Ehre *die*.

privy ['prɪvɪ] *adj*: **to be privy to sthg** *fml* in etw *(A)* eingeweiht sein.

prize [praɪz] ⬦ *adj* - **1.** [prizewinning] preisgekrönt - **2.** [perfect]: **prize idiot** Vollidiot. ⬦ *n* Preis *der*. ⬦ *vt* [value] (hoch)lschätzen.

prize-giving [-,gɪvɪŋ] *n UK* Preisverleihung *die*.

prizewinner ['praɪz,wɪnəʳ] *n* Preisträger *der*, -in *die*.

pro [prəʊ] *n* - **1.** *inf* [professional] Profi *der* - **2.** [advantage]: **the pros and cons** das Für und Wider.

probability [,prɒbə'bɪlətɪ] *n* [gen] Wahrscheinlichkeit *die*.

probable ['prɒbəbl] *adj* wahrscheinlich.

probably ['prɒbəblɪ] *adv* wahrscheinlich.

probation [prə'beɪʃn] *n (U)* - **1.** [of prisoner] Bewährung *die*; **to put sb on probation** jm Bewährung geben - **2.** [trial period] Probezeit *die*; **I'm on probation** ich bin in der Probezeit.

probe [prəʊb] ⬦ *n* - **1.** [investigation]: **probe (into)** Untersuchung *die* (+ G) - **2.** MED & TECH Sonde *die*. ⬦ *vt* - **1.** [investigate] sondieren; [mystery] erforschen - **2.** [prod - with stick] suchend herumlstochern in (+ D).

problem ['prɒbləm] ⬦ *n* Problem *das*; **no problem!** *inf* kein Problem! ⬦ *comp* Problem-.

procedure [prə'siːdʒəʳ] *n* Verfahren *das*.

proceed ⬦ *vt* [prə'siːd]: **to proceed to do sthg** dazu übergehen, etw zu tun. ⬦ *vi* [prə'siːd] - **1.** [continue] fortlfahren; [activity] fortgesetzt werden; [event] weiterlgehen; **to proceed with sthg** mit etw fortlfahren - **2.** *fml* [go, advance - on foot] gehen; [- in vehicle] fah-

ren; **to proceed somewhere** sich irgendwohin begeben. ⬦ **proceeds** *npl* ['prəʊsiːdz] Erlös *der*.

proceedings [prə'siːdɪŋz] *npl* - **1.** [series of actions] Vorgänge *Pl*; [event] Veranstaltung *die* - **2.** [legal action] Verfahren *das*.

process ['prəʊses] ⬦ *n* - **1.** [series of actions] Prozess *der*; **electoral process** Wahlverfahren *das*; **in the process** dabei; **to be in the process of doing sthg** dabei sein, etw zu tun - **2.** [method] Verfahren *das*. ⬦ *vt* - **1.** [treat - materials] verarbeiten; [- food] behandeln - **2.** [examine, deal with - application] bearbeiten; [- information, data] verarbeiten.

processing ['prəʊsesɪŋ] *n (U)* - **1.** [treating - of materials] Verarbeitung *die*; [- of food] Behandeln *das* - **2.** [examining - of applications] Bearbeitung *die*; [- of information, data] Verarbeitung *die*.

procession [prə'seʃn] *n* Zug *der*; **in procession** in einem langen Zug.

proclaim [prə'kleɪm] *vt* [independence] proklamieren; [innocence, loyalty] beteuern; **to proclaim sb king** jn zum König ernennen.

procure [prə'kjʊəʳ] *vt* [tickets, supplies] beschaffen; [somebody's release] bewirken.

prod [prɒd] *vt* [push, poke - person] anlstupsen; [- ground, food] herumlstochern in (+ D).

prodigy ['prɒdɪdʒɪ] *n* Wunderkind *das*.

produce ⬦ *n* ['prɒdjuːs] *(U)* - **1.** [goods] Erzeugnisse *Pl* - **2.** [fruit and vegetables] Obst und Gemüse *das*. ⬦ *vt* [prə'djuːs] - **1.** [manufacture, make] produzieren; [work of art] schaffen - **2.** [yield - raw materials] liefern; [- heat, crop, gas] erzeugen; [- interest, profit] einlbringen - **3.** [cause - results, agreements] erzielen; [- disaster] hervorlrufen - **4.** [give birth to - subj: woman] gebären; [- subj: animal] werfen - **5.** [leaves, flowers] hervorlbringen - **6.** [present, show - evidence, argument] liefern; [- passport, letter] vorlzeigen - **7.** [gen] produzieren.

producer [prə'djuːsəʳ] *n* - **1.** [gen] Produzent *der*, -in *die* - **2.** [manufacturer] Hersteller *der*, -in *die*.

product ['prɒdʌkt] *n* [thing manufactured or grown] Produkt *das*.

production [prə'dʌkʃn] *n* - **1.** *(U)* [process - of goods] Produktion *die*; [- of electricity, heat] Erzeugung *die*; [- of blood cells] Bildung *die* - **2.** *(U)* [output] Produktion *die* - **3.** CIN, THEAT & TV Produktion *die*.

production line *n* Fertigungsstraße *die*.

productive [prə'dʌktɪv] *adj* - **1.** [worker] produktiv; [land] ertragreich; [business] leistungsfähig - **2.** [meeting, relationship, experience] Gewinn bringend.

productivity [,prɒdʌk'tɪvətɪ] *n* Produktivität *die*.

profane [prəˈfeɪn] *adj* [vulgar] gottesläster-lich.

profession [prəˈfeʃn] *n* - **1.** [career] Be-ruf *der*; **by profession** von Beruf - **2.** [body of people] Berufsstand *der*; **the medical/teaching profession** die Ärzteschaft/Lehrerschaft.

professional [prəˈfeʃənl] ◇ *adj* - **1.** [relat-ing to a profession - qualifications] beruflich; [- advice, help, opinion] fachmännisch; **profes-sional people** hochqualifizierte Personen - **2.** [full-time, of high standard] professionell; [army, actor] Berufs-; [footballer] Profi-. ◇ *n* - **1.** [full-time sportsperson] Profi *der*; [full-time actor] Berufsschauspieler *der* - **2.** [skilled per-son]: **he's a real professional** er ist ein echter Profi.

professor [prəˈfesər] *n* - **1.** *UK* [head of depart-ment] Professor *der*, -in *die* - **2.** *US & Canada* [teacher, lecturer] Dozent *der*, -in *die*.

proficiency [prəˈfɪʃənsɪ] *n (U)*: **proficiency (in)** Kompetenz *die* (in (+ D)).

profile [ˈprəʊfaɪl] *n* - **1.** [outline of face] Pro-fil *das*; **to keep a low profile** *fig* sich unauf-fällig verhalten - **2.** [biography] Porträt *das*.

profit [ˈprɒfɪt] ◇ *n* - **1.** [financial gain] Ge-winn *der*, Profit *der* - **2.** [advantage]: **you may learn something to your profit** du könntest et-was lernen, was nützlich für dich ist. ◇ *vi*: **to profit (from** OR **by sthg)** (von etw) profitie-ren.

profitability [ˌprɒfɪtəˈbɪlətɪ] *n* Rentabili-tät *die*.

profitable [ˈprɒfɪtəbl] *adj* Gewinn brin-gend.

profound [prəˈfaʊnd] *adj* - **1.** [intense - feel-ing, silence] tief; [- change] tief greifend; [- ef-fect] nachhaltig - **2.** [penetrating, wise - idea, book] tiefgründig.

profusely [prəˈfjuːslɪ] *adv* - **1.** [bleed, sweat] sehr stark - **2.** [thank] überschwänglich; **to apologize profusely** sich vielmals entschuldi-gen.

profusion [prəˈfjuːʒn] *n*: **profusion (of)** (Über)fülle *die* (von).

prognosis [prɒgˈnəʊsɪs] (*pl* **-noses** [-ˈnəʊsiːz]) *n* Prognose *die*.

program [ˈprəʊgræm] (*pt & pp* **-med** OR **-ed**, *cont* **-ming** OR **-ing**) ◇ *n* - **1.** COMPUT Pro-gramm *das* - **2.** *US* = **programme**. ◇ *vt* - **1.** COMPUT programmieren - **2.** *US* = **pro-gramme**.

programer *n US* = **programmer**.

programme *UK*, **program** *US* [ˈprəʊgræm] ◇ *n* - **1.** [gen] Programm *das* - **2.** RADIO & TV Sendung *die*. ◇ *vt* programmieren.

programmer *UK*, **programer** *US* [ˈprəʊgræmər] *n* COMPUT Programmierer *der*, -in *die*.

programming [ˈprəʊgræmɪŋ] *n* COMPUT Pro-grammieren *das*.

progress ◇ *n* [ˈprəʊgres] - **1.** [physical move-ment] Vorwärtskommen *das* - **2.** [headway] Vo-ranschreiten *das*; **to make progress (in sthg)** (bei etw) Fortschritte machen; **in progress** im Gange - **3.** [evolution] Fortschritt *der*. ◇ *vi* [prəˈgres] - **1.** [improve - science, technology, work] vorankommen; [- patient, student] Fort-schritte machen - **2.** [continue]: **as the journey/meeting progressed** im Laufe der Reise/des Treffens.

progressive [prəˈgresɪv] *adj* - **1.** [forward-looking] fortschrittlich - **2.** [gradual] fortschrei-tend.

prohibit [prəˈhɪbɪt] *vt* verbieten; **to prohibit sb from doing sthg** jm verbieten, etw zu tun.

project ◇ *n* [ˈprɒdʒekt] - **1.** [plan, idea] Vor-haben *das*, Projekt *das* - **2.** SCH [study] Pro-jekt *das*. ◇ *vt* [prəˈdʒekt] - **1.** [plan] planen - **2.** [estimate] voraussagen; [costs] überschla-gen - **3.** [film, light] projizieren - **4.** [present] dar[l]stellen; [image] vermitteln. ◇ *vi* [prəˈdʒekt] [jut out] hervor[l]ragen.

projectile [prəˈdʒektaɪl] *n* Geschoss *das*.

projection [prəˈdʒekʃn] *n* - **1.** [estimate] Vo-raussage *die*; [of costs] Überschlagen *das* - **2.** *(U)* [of film, light] Projektion *die*.

projector [prəˈdʒektər] *n* Projektor *der*.

proletariat [ˌprəʊlɪˈteərɪət] *n* Proletari-at *das*.

prolific [prəˈlɪfɪk] *adj* sehr produktiv.

prologue, prolog *US* [ˈprəʊlɒg] *n* - **1.** [intro-duction] Prolog *der* - **2.** *fig* [preceding event]: **to be the prologue to sthg** die Vorstufe für etw sein.

prolong [prəˈlɒŋ] *vt* verlängern.

prom [prɒm] *n* - **1.** *UK inf* [at seaside] (*abbr of* **promenade**) Strandpromenade *die* - **2.** *US* [ball - at high school] Schulball *der*; [- at college] Stu-dentenball *der*.

promenade [ˌprɒməˈnɑːd] *n UK* [at seaside] Strandpromenade *die*.

prominent [ˈprɒmɪnənt] *adj* - **1.** [important - person] prominent; [- ideas, issues] wichtig - **2.** [noticeable - building, landmark] exponiert; [- features] markant.

promiscuous [prɒˈmɪskjʊəs] *adj* promisku-itiv.

promise [ˈprɒmɪs] ◇ *n* - **1.** [vow] Verspre-chen *das* - **2.** *(U)* [hope, prospect]: **promise (of)** Aussicht *die* (auf (+ A)). ◇ *vt* versprechen; **to promise sb sthg** jm etw versprechen; **to prom-ise (sb) to do sthg** (jm) versprechen, etw zu tun. ◇ *vi* versprechen.

promising [ˈprɒmɪsɪŋ] *adj* vielverspre-chend.

promontory [ˈprɒməntrɪ] *n* Kap *das*.

promote [prə'məʊt] vt - 1. [foster] fördern - 2. [push, advertise] Werbung machen für - 3. [in job] befördern - 4. SPORT: **to be promoted** aufsteigen.

promoter [prə'məʊtər] n - 1. [of event, concert] Veranstalter der, -in die - 2. [of cause, idea] Förderer der.

promotion [prə'məʊʃn] n - 1. [in job] Beförderung die - 2. [advertising] Werbung die - 3. [campaign] Werbekampagne die.

prompt [prɒmpt] <> adj - 1. [quick] prompt; [action] sofortig - 2. [punctual] pünktlich. <> adv: **at nine o'clock prompt** Punkt 9 Uhr. <> vt - 1. [provoke, persuade]: **to prompt sb to do sthg** jn dazu veranlassen, etw zu tun - 2. THEAT soufflieren (+ D).

promptly ['prɒmptlɪ] adv - 1. [quickly] prompt - 2. [punctually] pünktlich.

prone [prəʊn] adj [susceptible]: **to be prone to sthg** zu etw neigen; **to be prone to do sthg** dazu neigen, etw zu tun.

prong [prɒŋ] n Zinke die.

pronoun ['prəʊnaʊn] n Pronomen das.

pronounce [prə'naʊns] vt - 1. [say aloud] auslsprechen - 2. [declare, state - verdict, opinion] verkünden; **to pronounce sb fit for work/dead** jn für arbeitsfähig/tot erklären.

pronounced [prə'naʊnst] adj [accent] stark; [improvement, deterioration] deutlich.

pronouncement [prə'naʊnsmənt] n Erklärung die.

pronunciation [prə,nʌnsɪ'eɪʃn] n Aussprache die.

proof [pru:f] n - 1. [evidence] Beweis der - 2. PRESS [first copy] Korrekturfahne die - 3. [of alcohol] Alkoholgehalt der.

prop [prɒp] <> n liter & fig Stütze die. <> vt: **to prop sthg against sthg** etw gegen etw lehnen. ◆ **props** npl [in film, play] Requisiten Pl. ◆ **prop up** vt sep - 1. [support physically - wall] ablstützen; [- ladder] anllehnen - 2. fig [sustain - regime] stützen; [- organization] unterstützen; [- company] vor dem Konkurs bewahren.

propel [prə'pel] vt anltreiben.

propeller [prə'pelər] n [of plane] Propeller der; [of ship] Schraube die.

propensity [prə'pensətɪ] n fml: **propensity for** OR **to sthg** Hang zu etw; **to have a propensity to do sthg** dazu neigen, etw zu tun.

proper ['prɒpər] adj - 1. [real] richtig - 2. [correct] korrekt - 3. [decent] anständig.

properly ['prɒpəlɪ] adv - 1. [satisfactorily, correctly] richtig - 2. [decently] anständig.

proper noun n Eigenname der.

property ['prɒpətɪ] n - 1. [possession] Eigentum das - 2. [specific building] Haus das; [piece of land] Grundstück das - 3. (U) [buildings, land] Immobilien Pl - 4. [quality] Eigenschaft die.

property owner n [of house] Hausbesitzer der, -in die; [of land] Grundbesitzer der, -in die.

prophecy ['prɒfɪsɪ] n Prophezeiung die.

prophesy ['prɒfɪsaɪ] vt prophezeien.

prophet ['prɒfɪt] n RELIG Prophet der.

proportion [prə'pɔːʃn] n - 1. [part] Teil der, Anteil der - 2. [ratio, comparison] Verhältnis das - 3. (U) ART: **in proportion** in den richtigen Proportionen; **out of proportion** mit verschobenen Proportionen; **a sense of proportion** fig ein vernünftiger Maßstab.

proportional [prə'pɔːʃənl] adj im Verhältnis stehend; MATHS proportional; **to be proportional to sthg** zu etw im Verhältnis stehen; MATHS zu etw proportional sein.

proportional representation n (U) Verhältniswahlsystem das.

proportionate [prə'pɔːʃnət] adj: **proportionate (to sthg)** im Verhältnis (zu etw).

proposal [prə'pəʊzl] n - 1. [plan, suggestion] Vorschlag der - 2. [offer of marriage] Heiratsantrag der.

propose [prə'pəʊz] <> vt - 1. [plan, solution, person] vorlschlagen; [toast] auslbringen - 2. [motion] einlbringen, stellen - 3. [intend]: **to propose doing** OR **to do sthg** vorlhaben OR beabsichtigen, etw zu tun. <> vi: **to propose (to sb)** (jm) einen Heiratsantrag machen.

proposition [,prɒpə'zɪʃn] n - 1. [statement of theory] These die - 2. [suggestion] Vorschlag der.

proprietor [prə'praɪətər] n Besitzer der, -in die.

propriety [prə'praɪətɪ] n fml [moral correctness] Anstand der.

pro rata [-'rɑːtə] adj & adv anteilig.

prose [prəʊz] n Prosa die.

prosecute ['prɒsɪkjuːt] vt LAW strafrechtlich verfolgen.

prosecution [,prɒsɪ'kjuːʃn] n - 1. [criminal charge] strafrechtliche Verfolgung - 2. [lawyers]: **the prosecution** die Anklage(vertretung).

prosecutor ['prɒsɪkjuːtər] n esp US Ankläger der, -in die.

prospect <> n ['prɒspekt] Aussicht die. <> vi [prə'spekt]: **to prospect (for sthg)** [gold] schürfen (nach etw); [oil] bohren (nach etw). ◆ **prospects** npl: **prospects (for sthg)** Aussichten Pl (auf etw (A)); **he has good prospects** er hat gute Erfolgsaussichten.

prospective [prə'spektɪv] adj voraussichtlich.

prospectus [prə'spektəs] (pl -es) n (Werbe)prospekt der.

prosper ['prɒspər] vi [business, country] blühen; [person] Erfolg haben.

prosperity [prɒ'sperətɪ] n Wohlstand der.

prosperous ['prɒspərəs] *adj* [person] wohlhabend; [business, place] blühend.

prostitute ['prɒstɪtjuːt] *n* Prostituierte *die*; **(male) prostitute** Stricher *der*, Strichjunge *der*.

prostrate *adj* ['prɒstreɪt] [lying flat] (auf dem Bauch) ausgestreckt.

protagonist [prə'tægənɪst] *n* Hauptfigur *die*, Protagonist *der*, -in *die*.

protect [prə'tekt] *vt* schützen; **to protect sb/sthg from/against** jn/etw schützen vor (+ D)/gegen.

protection [prə'tekʃn] *n*: **protection (from/against)** Schutz *der* (vor (+ D)/gegen).

protective [prə'tektɪv] *adj* - 1. [layer, clothing] Schutz-, schützend - 2. [feelings, instinct] Beschützer-.

protein ['prəutiːn] *n* Protein *das*.

protest <> *n* ['prəutest] - 1. [complaint] Protest *der* - 2. [demonstration] Protestkundgebung *die*. <> *vt* [prə'test] - 1. [one's innocence] beteuern - 2. *US* [protest against] protestieren gegen. <> *vi* [prə'test] [complain]: **to protest (about/against sthg)** protestieren (gegen etw).

Protestant ['prɒtɪstənt] <> *adj* protestantisch. <> *n* Protestant *der*, -in *die*.

protester [prə'testər] *n* [demonstrator] Protestierende *der*, *die*.

protest march *n* Protestmarsch *der*.

protocol ['prəutəkɒl] *n* (U) Protokoll *das*.

prototype ['prəutətaɪp] *n* Prototyp *der*.

protracted [prə'træktɪd] *adj* langwierig.

protrude [prə'truːd] *vi*: **to protrude (from sthg)** (aus etw) hervorlstehen.

protuberance [prə'tjuːbərəns] *n* Auswuchs *der*.

proud [praud] *adj* stolz; **to be proud of sb/sthg** auf jn/etw stolz sein.

prove [pruːv] (*pp* -d *OR* proven) *vt* - 1. [show to be true] beweisen - 2. [show o.s. to be]: **to prove (to be) sthg** sich als etw erweisen; **to prove o.s. to be sthg** sich als etw erweisen.

proven ['pruːvn, 'prəuvn] <> *pp* ▷ **prove**. <> *adj* [fact] erwiesen, bewiesen; [liar] ausgewiesen.

proverb ['prɒvɜːb] *n* Sprichwort *das*.

provide [prə'vaɪd] *vt* [food, money, information] zur Verfügung stellen; [opportunity] bieten; **to provide sb with sthg, to provide sthg for sb** jm etw zur Verfügung stellen. **◆ provide for** *vt insep* - 1. [support] sorgen für - 2. *fml* [make arrangements for] vorlsorgen für.

provided [prə'vaɪdɪd] **◆ provided (that)** *conj* vorausgesetzt, dass.

providing [prə'vaɪdɪŋ] **◆ providing (that)** *conj* vorausgesetzt, dass.

province ['prɒvɪns] *n* - 1. [part of country] Provinz *die* - 2. [specialist subject] Fachgebiet *das*; [area of responsibility] Aufgabenbereich *der*.

provincial [prə'vɪnʃl] *adj* - 1. [of a province] Provinz- - 2. *pej* [narrow-minded] provinziell.

provision [prə'vɪʒn] *n* - 1. [act of supplying] Bereitstellung *die* - 2. (U) [arrangement] Vorkehrung *die* - 3. [in agreement, law] Bestimmung *die*. **◆ provisions** *npl* [supplies] Vorräte *Pl*.

provisional [prə'vɪʒənl] *adj* provisorisch.

proviso [prə'vaɪzəu] (*pl* -s) *n* Vorbehalt *der*; **with the proviso that...** unter dem Vorbehalt, dass...

provocative [prə'vɒkətɪv] *adj* - 1. [controversial] provokativ - 2. [sexy] aufreizend.

provoke [prə'vəuk] *vt* - 1. [annoy] provozieren - 2. [cause - criticism, reaction] hervorlrufen, erregen; [- argument] provozieren.

prow [prau] *n* Bug *der*.

prowess ['prauɪs] *n* (U) *fml* Erfahrenheit *die*.

prowl [praul] <> *n*: **to be on the prowl** (auf Beutezug) herumlstreifen. <> *vt* durchstreifen. <> *vi* herumlstreifen, umherlstreifen.

prowler ['praulər] *n* Herumtreiber *der*, -in *die*.

proxy ['prɒksɪ] *n*: **by proxy** in Vertretung.

prudent ['pruːdnt] *adj* [person] umsichtig; [action] überlegt.

prudish ['pruːdɪʃ] *adj* prüde.

prune [pruːn] <> *n* [fruit] Backpflaume *die*. <> *vt* [hedge, tree] beschneiden.

pry [praɪ] *vi* neugierig sein; **to pry into sthg** seine Nase in etw stecken.

PS *n abbr of* postscript.

psalm [sɑːm] *n* Psalm *der*.

pseudonym ['sjuːdənɪm] *n* Pseudonym *das*.

psyche ['saɪkɪ] *n* Psyche *die*.

psychiatric [ˌsaɪkɪ'ætrɪk] *adj* [hospital, department] psychiatrisch; [illness, problem] psychisch.

psychiatrist [saɪ'kaɪətrɪst] *n* Psychiater *der*, -in *die*.

psychiatry [saɪ'kaɪətrɪ] *n* (U) Psychiatrie *die*.

psychic ['saɪkɪk] <> *adj* - 1. [clairvoyant - powers] übersinnlich; (phrase): **she is psychic** sie hat übersinnliche Kräfte - 2. [mental] psychisch. <> *n* Person *die* mit übersinnlichen Kräften.

psychoanalysis [ˌsaɪkəuə'næləsɪs] *n* Psychoanalyse *die*.

psychoanalyst [ˌsaɪkəu'ænəlɪst] *n* Psychoanalytiker *der*, -in *die*.

psychological [ˌsaɪkə'lɒdʒɪkl] *adj* psychologisch.

psychologist [saɪ'kɒlədʒɪst] *n* Psychologe *der*, -gin *die*.

psychology [saɪ'kɒlədʒɪ] *n* Psychologie *die*.

psychopath ['saɪkəpæθ] n Psychopath der, -in die.

psychotic [saɪ'kɒtɪk] ◇ adj psychotisch. ◇ n Psychotiker der, -in die.

pt - 1. abbr of pint - 2. (abbr of point) Pkt.

PTO (abbr of please turn over) b.w.

pub [pʌb] n Pub der, Bierlokal das.

puberty ['pjuːbətɪ] n Pubertät die.

pubic ['pjuːbɪk] adj Scham-.

public ['pʌblɪk] ◇ adj - 1. [of people in general, open to all] öffentlich - 2. [of, by the state] staatlich, Staats- - 3. [known to everyone]: **public figure** bekannte Persönlichkeit; **it's public knowledge that...** es ist allgemein bekannt, dass... ◇ n: **the public** die Öffentlichkeit; **in public** in der Öffentlichkeit.

public-address system n Lautsprecheranlage die.

publican ['pʌblɪkən] n UK Wirt der, -in die.

publication [ˌpʌblɪ'keɪʃn] n - 1. (U) [act of publishing] Veröffentlichung die - 2. [book, article] Publikation die.

public bar n UK schlicht eingerichteter Teil eines Pubs, in dem die Getränke billiger als in der "Lounge Bar" sind.

public company n Aktiengesellschaft die.

public convenience n UK öffentliche Toilette.

public holiday n gesetzlicher Feiertag.

public house n UK fml Gaststätte die.

publicity [pʌb'lɪsɪtɪ] n (U) - 1. [media attention] Publicity die - 2. [information] Werbung die, Reklame die.

publicize, -ise ['pʌblɪsaɪz] vt bekannt machen.

public limited company n ≃ Aktiengesellschaft die.

public opinion n (U) öffentliche Meinung.

public relations ◇ n (U) [work] Öffentlichkeitsarbeit die, Public Relations Pl. ◇ npl: **it would be good for public relations** es wäre gut für unser öffentliches Ansehen.

public school n - 1. UK [private school] höhere Privatschule - 2. US & Scotland [state school] staatliche Schule.

public transport n (U) öffentliche Verkehrsmittel Pl.

publish ['pʌblɪʃ] vt veröffentlichen.

publisher ['pʌblɪʃər] n - 1. [company] Verlag der - 2. [person] Verleger der, -in die.

publishing ['pʌblɪʃɪŋ] n Verlagswesen das.

pub lunch n Mittagessen das im Pub.

pucker ['pʌkər] vt [lips for kissing] spitzen.

pudding ['pʊdɪŋ] n - 1. [sweet food] Nachspeise die - 2. (U) UK [part of meal] Nachtisch der, Dessert das.

puddle ['pʌdl] n Pfütze die.

puff [pʌf] ◇ n - 1. [of cigarette, pipe] Zug der - 2.: **puff of wind** Windhauch der; **puff of smoke** Rauchwölkchen das. ◇ vt paffen. ◇ vi - 1. [smoke]: **to puff at** OR **on sthg** an etw (D) paffen - 2. [pant] keuchen, schnaufen. ◆ **puff out** vt sep [cheeks] auflblasen; [chest] anschwellen lassen; [feathers] auflplustern.

puffed [pʌft] adj [swollen]: **puffed up** angeschwollen.

puff pastry, puff paste US n (U) Blätterteig der.

puffy ['pʌfɪ] adj aufgedunsen.

pull [pʊl] ◇ vt - 1. [rope, hair] ziehen an (+ D); [curtains - open] auflziehen; fig etw scharf kritisieren - 2. [curtains - open] auflziehen; [- close] zulziehen - 3. [trigger] drücken; [lever] ziehen - 4. [take out - cork] herauslziehen; [- gun, tooth] ziehen - 5. [muscle, hamstring] sich (D) zerren - 6. [crowd, voters] anlziehen. ◇ vi [tug with hand] ziehen. ◇ n - 1. [tug with hand] Ziehen das, Zug der; **to give the rope a pull** am Seil ziehen - 2. (U) [influence] Einfluss der. ◆ **pull apart** vt sep [separate] auseinander ziehen. ◆ **pull at** vt insep ziehen an (+ D). ◆ **pull away** vi - 1. [from roadside]: **to pull away (from)** weglfahren - 2. [in race]: **to pull away (from)** sich ablsetzen (von). ◆ **pull down** vt sep [demolish] ablreißen. ◆ **pull in** vi [car, bus] anlhalten; [train] einlfahren. ◆ **pull off** vt sep - 1. [take off] auslziehen - 2. [succeed in - coup, robbery] landen; [- deal] an Land ziehen. ◆ **pull out** ◇ vt sep [withdraw] zurücklziehen. ◇ vi - 1. [train] ablfahren - 2. [vehicle - from kerb] ablfahren; [- from lane] auslscheren - 3. [withdraw] sich zurücklziehen. ◆ **pull over** vi [vehicle, driver] an den Straßenrand fahren. ◆ **pull through** vi [patient] durchlkommen. ◆ **pull together** vt sep: **to pull o.s. together** sich zusammenlreißen. ◆ **pull up** ◇ vt sep - 1. [raise] hochlziehen - 2. [move closer] heranlziehen. ◇ vi anlhalten.

pulley ['pʊlɪ] (pl -s) n [wheel] Rolle die; [whole system] Flaschenzug der.

pullover ['pʊlˌəʊvər] n Pullover der.

pulp [pʌlp] ◇ adj: **pulp novel** Schundroman der; **pulp fiction** Schundliteratur die. ◇ n [soft mass] Brei die.

pulpit ['pʊlpɪt] n Kanzel die.

pulsate [pʌl'seɪt] vi pulsieren; [air, sound] vibrieren.

pulse [pʌls] ◇ n - 1. [in body] Puls der - 2. TECH Impuls der. ◇ vi [blood, music] pulsieren. ◆ **pulses** npl [food] Hülsenfrüchte Pl.

puma ['pjuːmə] (pl inv OR -s) n Puma der.

pummel ['pʌml] (UK) (US) vt mit den Fäusten bearbeiten, einlschlagen auf (+ A).

pump [pʌmp] ◇ n - 1. [machine] Pumpe die - 2. [for petrol] Zapfsäule die, Tanksäule die.

◇ *vt* [convey by pumping] pumpen. ◇ *vi* [machine, person, heart] pumpen. ➡ **pumps** *npl* [shoes] Pumps *Pl.*

pumpkin ['pʌmpkɪn] *n* Kürbis *der.*

pun [pʌn] *n* Wortspiel *das.*

punch [pʌntʃ] ◇ *n* - **1.** [blow] (Faust)schlag *der* - **2.** [for making holes in paper] Locher *der* - **3.** *(U)* [drink - cold] Bowle *die*; [- hot] Punsch *der.* ◇ *vt* - **1.** [hit] (mit der Faust) schlagen - **2.** [perforate - ticket] lochen; *(phrase):* **to punch a hole in sthg** ein Loch in etw machen.

Punch-and-Judy show [,pʌntʃən'dʒuːdɪ-] *n* Kasperletheater *das.*

punch ball *n* Punchingball *der.*

punch line *n* Pointe *die.*

punch-up *n UK inf* Schlägerei *die.*

punchy ['pʌntʃɪ] *adj inf* [style] prägnant; [slogan] durchschlagend.

punctual ['pʌŋktʃʊəl] *adj* pünktlich.

punctuation [,pʌŋktʃʊ'eɪʃn] *n* Zeichensetzung *die*, Interpunktion *die.*

punctuation mark *n* Satzzeichen *das.*

puncture ['pʌŋktʃər] ◇ *n* [in tyre, ball] (kleines) Loch; **I had a puncture** ich hatte einen Platten. ◇ *vt* - **1.** [tyre, ball] ein Loch machen in (+ A) - **2.** [lung, skin] punktieren.

pundit ['pʌndɪt] *n* Experte *der*, -tin *die.*

pungent ['pʌndʒənt] *adj* - **1.** [smell] stechend, beißend; [taste] scharf - **2.** *fig* [criticism, remark] scharf.

punish ['pʌnɪʃ] *vt* bestrafen; **to punish sb for sthg** jn für etw bestrafen.

punishing ['pʌnɪʃɪŋ] *adj* [work, schedule] strapaziös.

punishment ['pʌnɪʃmənt] *n* - **1.** *(U)* [act of punishing] Bestrafung *die* - **2.** [means of punishment] Strafe *die.*

punk [pʌŋk] ◇ *adj* Punker-. ◇ *n* - **1.** [music]: **punk (rock)** Punk(rock) *der* - **2.** [person]: **punk (rocker)** Punker *der*, -in *die* - **3.** *US inf* [lout] Rowdy *der*, Randalierer *der.*

punt [pʌnt] *n* - **1.** [boat] Stechkahn *der* - **2.** [Irish currency] Punt *das.*

punter ['pʌntər] *n UK inf* [customer] Kunde *der*, -din *die.*

puny ['pjuːnɪ] *adj* [person] kümmerlich; [limbs] schwächlich; [effort] erbärmlich.

pup [pʌp] *n* - **1.** [young dog] Hundejunge *das* - **2.**: **seal pup** Robbenjunge *das.*

pupil ['pjuːpɪl] *n* - **1.** [student, follower] Schüler *der*, -in *die* - **2.** [of eye] Pupille *die.*

puppet ['pʌpɪt] *n* - **1.** *fig* [string puppet] Marionette *die* - **2.** [glove puppet] Handpuppe *die.*

puppy ['pʌpɪ] *n* Hundejunge *das.*

purchase ['pɜːtʃəs] *fml* ◇ *n* - **1.** *(U)* [act of buying] Kauf *der* - **2.** [thing bought]: **purchases** Einkäufe *Pl*; **this was a good purchase** das war ein guter Kauf - **3.** *(U)* [grip] Halt *der.* ◇ *vt* kaufen.

purchaser ['pɜːtʃəsər] *n* Käufer *der*, -in *die.*

pure [pjʊər] *adj* - **1.** [unadulterated, untainted] rein - **2.** [voice, sound] klar - **3.** *liter* [chaste] rein - **4.** [science, maths] theoretisch - **5.** [for emphasis] pur.

puree ['pjʊəreɪ] *n* Püree *das.*

purely ['pjʊəlɪ] *adv* rein.

purge [pɜːdʒ] ◇ *n* POL Säuberungsaktion *die.* ◇ *vt* - **1.** POL säubern - **2.** [rid]: **to purge sthg/o.s. of sthg** etw/sich von etw befreien.

purify ['pjʊərɪfaɪ] *vt* [air, water] reinigen.

purist ['pjʊərɪst] *n* Purist *der*, -in *die.*

purity ['pjʊərətɪ] *n (U)* - **1.** [of air, water] Reinheit *die* - **2.** [of sound, voice] Klarheit *die.*

purple ['pɜːpl] ◇ *adj* violett, lila. ◇ *n* Violett *das*, Lila *das.*

purport [pə'pɔːt] *vi fml*: **to purport to do/be sthg** vorgeben, etw zu tun/sein.

purpose ['pɜːpəs] *n* - **1.** [objective, reason] Zweck *der* - **2.** [use]: **to no purpose** umsonst - **3.** [determination] Entschlossenheit *die.* ➡ **on purpose** *adv* absichtlich, mit Absicht.

purposeful ['pɜːpəsfʊl] *adj* zielbewusst.

purr [pɜːr] *vi* - **1.** [cat, person] schnurren - **2.** [engine, machine] summen.

purse [pɜːs] ◇ *n* - **1.** [for money] Portmonee *das* - **2.** *US* [handbag] Handtasche *die.* ◇ *vt* [lips] aufwerfen, schürzen.

purser ['pɜːsər] *n* Zahlmeister *der*, -in *die.*

pursue [pə'sjuː] *vt* - **1.** [criminal, car] verfolgen - **2.** [hobby, interest] nachgehen (+ D); [aim] verfolgen - **3.** [matter] weiterverfolgen.

pursuer [pə'sjuːər] *n* Verfolger *der*, -in *die.*

pursuit [pə'sjuːt] *n* - **1.** *(U) fml* [attempt to obtain, achieve]: **the pursuit of sthg** das Streben nach etw - **2.** [chase] Verfolgung *die* - **3.** [occupation, activity] Beschäftigung *die.*

pus [pʌs] *n* Eiter *der.*

push [pʊʃ] ◇ *vt* - **1.** [press, move - button] drücken; [- bicycle, person] schieben; *(phrase):* **to push the door open/to** die Tür aufl-/zulmachen - **2.** [encourage] (nachdrücklich) ermutigen; **to push sb to do sthg** jn (nachdrücklich) ermutigen, etw zu tun - **3.** [force] drängen; **to push sb into doing sthg** jn drängen, etw zu tun - **4.** *inf* [promote] Werbung machen für. ◇ *vi* - **1.** [shove] schieben; [in crowd] drängen - **2.** [on button, bell] drücken - **3.** [campaign]: **to push for sthg** auf etw (A) drängen. ◇ *n* - **1.** [shove] Stoß *der*, Schubs *der* - **2.** [on button, bell]: **to give sthg a push** etw drücken - **3.** [campaign] (groß angelegte) Aktion. ➡ **push around** *vt sep inf fig* [bully] herumlschubsen. ➤ **push in** vi [in queue] (sich) vorldrängen. ➤ **push off** vi inf [go away] verschwinden. ➤ **push on** vi [continue] weiterlmachen. ➤ **push through** vt sep [new law, reform] durchlbringen.

pushchair ['puʃtʃeəʳ] n UK Sportwagen der.

pushed [puʃt] adj inf: **to be pushed for time** unter Zeitdruck stehen; **to be pushed for money** in Geldnöten sein; **to be hard pushed to do sthg** es schwer finden, etw zu tun.

pusher ['puʃəʳ] n drug sl Dealer der, -in die.

pushover ['puʃ,əuvəʳ] n inf [sucker]: **he's a pushover** er lässt sich leicht reinlegen.

push-up n esp US Liegestütz der.

pushy ['puʃɪ] adj pej aufdringlich, aggressiv.

puss [pus], **pussy (cat)** ['pusɪ-] n inf Mieze(katze) die.

put [put] (pt & pp inv) vt - **1.** [place] tun; [place upright] stellen; [lay flat] legen; **to put sthg into sthg** etw in etw (A) hineinltun/hineinlstellen/hineinllegen; **he put his arm round her shoulder** er legte ihr den Arm um die Schulter; **I put the children first** bei mir kommen die Kinder zuerst; **he put his hand in his pocket** er steckte die Hand in die Tasche; **that puts me in a difficult position** das bringt mich in eine schwierige Lage - **2.** [send]: **to put sb in prison/hospital** jn ins Gefängnis stecken/ins Krankenhaus schicken; **to put a child to bed** ein Kind ins Bett bringen - **3.** [express] sagen - **4.** [ask]: **to put a question (to sb)** (jm) eine Frage stellen - **5.** [make]: **to put a proposal to sb** einen Vorschlag machen - **6.** [write] schreiben - **7.** [cause]: **to put sb to a lot of trouble** jm viel Mühe machen - **8.** [estimate]: **to put sthg at** etw schätzen auf (+ A) - **9.** [invest - money, time, energy]: **to put sthg into sthg** etw in etw (A) investieren - **10.** [apply]: **to put the blame on sb** jm die Schuld geben. ➤ **put across** vt sep [ideas] verständlich machen. ➤ **put away** vt sep - **1.** [tidy away] weglräumen - **2.** inf [lock up] einlsperren - **3.** inf [eat] verdrücken; [drink] schlucken. ➤ **put back** vt sep - **1.** [replace] zurückllegen; [upright] zurücklstellen; **put it back in the bag** stecke es wieder in die Tasche - **2.** [postpone] verschieben - **3.** [clock, watch] zurücklstellen. ➤ **put by** vt sep [money] zurückllegen. ➤ **put down** vt sep - **1.** [place] setzen; [place upright] (hin)lstellen; [lay flat] (hin)llegen - **2.** [passenger] ablsetzen - **3.** [deposit] anlzahlen - **4.** [riot, rebellion] niederlschlagen - **5.** [write down] auflschreiben; **to put sthg down in writing** etw schriftlich niederllegen - **6.** UK [animal] einlschläfern. ➤ **put down to** vt sep: **to put sthg down to sthg** etw einer Sache (D) zulschreiben. ➤ **put forward** vt sep - **1.** [plan, theory, name] vorlschlagen; [proposal] machen - **2.** [meeting, date] vorlverlegen - **3.** [clock, watch] vorlstellen. ➤ **put in** vt sep - **1.** [spend - time] verwenden auf (+ A) - **2.** [submit] einlreichen - **3.** [install] einlbauen. ➤ **put in for** vt insep [request] sich bewerben um. ➤ **put off** vt sep - **1.** [postpone] verschieben; **to put off doing sthg** es verschieben, etw zu tun - **2.** [switch off] auslschalten, auslmachen - **3.** [cause to wait] hinlhalten - **4.** [discourage]: **to put sb off doing sthg** jn davon ablbringen, etw zu tun - **5.** [distract] ablenken - **6.** [cause to dislike]: **to put sb off doing sthg** es jm verleiden, etw zu tun - **7.** [passenger] ablsetzen. ➤ **put on** vt sep - **1.** [clothes] anlziehen; [hat, glasses] auflsetzen; [make-up] auflegen; **put your clothes on!** zieh dich an! - **2.** [play, show] auflführen; [exhibition] veranstalten - **3.** [gain in weight]: **to put on weight** zulnehmen; **I've put on two kilos** ich habe zwei Kilo zugenommen - **4.** [TV, radio, light] anlschalten; [handbrake] anlziehen - **5.** [CD, record] auflegen; [tape] einllegen; [music] anlstellen - **6.** [start cooking] auflstellen; **to put the kettle on** Wasser aufllsetzen - **7.** [feign] vorltäuschen - **8.** [add] auflschlagen - **9.** [provide - bus, train] einlsetzen. ➤ **put out** vt sep - **1.** [place outside - milk bottles] hinauslstellen; [- rubbish] hinausllbringen; [- cat] hinauslsetzen - **2.** [issue - book, record] veröffentlichen; [- statement] ablgeben - **3.** [cigarette, fire, light] auslmachen - **4.** [hand, arm, leg] auslstrecken - **5.** [annoy]: **to be put out** verärgert sein - **6.** [inconvenience]: **to put sb out** jm Umstände machen. ➤ **put through** vt sep [phonecall] durchlstellen; **to put sb through to sb** jn mit jm verbinden. ➤ **put up** ◇ vt sep - **1.** [tent, statue, building] auflstellen - **2.** [umbrella] auflspannen; [flag] hochlziehen - **3.** [notice] anlschlagen; [sign] anlbringen; [curtains] auflhängen - **4.** [provide - money] stellen - **5.** [propose - candidate] auflstellen - **6.** [increase - price, cost] hochltreiben - **7.** [provide accommodation for] unterlbringen. ◇ vt insep [resistance] leisten; **to put up a fight** sich wehren. ◇ vi UK [in hotel] unterlkommen. ➤ **put up with** vt insep dulden.

putrid ['pju:trɪd] adj fml [decayed] faulig.

putt [pʌt] ◇ n Schlag der. ◇ vt & vi putten, einllochen.

putty ['pʌtɪ] n Kitt der.

puzzle ['pʌzl] ◇ n - **1.** [game] Rätsel das; [toy] Geduldsspiel das; **(jigsaw) puzzle** Puzzle das - **2.** [mystery] Rätsel das. ◇ vt verblüffen. ◇ vi: **to puzzle over sthg** sich (D) über etw (A) den Kopf zerbrechen. ➤ **puzzle out** vt sep herauslfinden.

puzzling ['pʌzlɪŋ] adj verblüffend.

pyjamas [pə'dʒɑ:məz] npl Schlafanzug der.

pylon ['paɪlən] n ELEC Mast der.

pyramid ['pɪrəmɪd] n Pyramide die.

Pyrex® ['paɪreks] n (U) ≃ Jenaer Glas® das.

python ['paɪθn] (pl inv OR -s) n Pythonschlange die.

Q

q (*pl* **q's** *OR* **qs**), **Q** (*pl* **Q's** *OR* **Qs**) [kjuː] *n* q *das*, Q *das*.

quack [kwæk] *n* - **1.** [noise] Quaken *das* - **2.** *inf pej* [doctor] Quacksalber *der*.

quadrangle ['kwɒdræŋgl] *n* - **1.** [figure] Viereck *das* - **2.** [courtyard] (viereckiger) Hof.

quadruple [kwɒ'druːpl] <> *adj* vierfach. <> *vt* vervierfachen. <> *vi* sich vervierfachen.

quadruplets ['kwɒdrʊplɪts] *npl* Vierlinge *Pl*.

quail [kweɪl] (*pl inv OR* -**s**) *n* Wachtel *die*.

quaint [kweɪnt] *adj* [cottage] urig; [tradition] kurios.

quake [kweɪk] <> *n inf* (*abbr of* **earthquake**) Beben *das*. <> *vi* beben, zittern.

qualification [ˌkwɒlɪfɪ'keɪʃn] *n* - **1.** [examination, certificate, skill] Qualifikation *die* - **2.** [qualifying statement] Einschränkung *die*.

qualified ['kwɒlɪfaɪd] *adj* - **1.** [trained] ausgebildet - **2.** [able]: **to be qualified to do sthg** qualifiziert sein, etw zu tun - **3.** [limited] eingeschränkt.

qualify ['kwɒlɪfaɪ] <> *vt* - **1.** [statement] einlschränken - **2.** [entitle]: **to qualify sb to do sthg** jn berechtigen, etw zu tun. <> *vi* - **1.** [pass exams & SPORT] sich qualifizieren - **2.** [be entitled]: **to qualify for sthg** zu etw berechtigt sein.

quality ['kwɒlətɪ] <> *n* - **1.** [gen] Qualität *die* - **2.** [characteristic] Eigenschaft *die*. <> *comp* Qualitäts-.

qualms [kwɑːmz] *npl* Skrupel *Pl*.

quandary ['kwɒndərɪ] *n* (*phrase*): **to be in a quandary about** *OR* **over sthg** in einer Zwickmühle stecken wegen etw *OR* in Bezug auf etw (*A*).

quantify ['kwɒntɪfaɪ] *vt* in Zahlen auslldrücken.

quantity ['kwɒntətɪ] *n* Menge *die*; **to be an unknown quantity** eine unbekannte Größe sein.

quarantine ['kwɒrəntiːn] <> *n* Quarantäne *die*. <> *vt* unter Quarantäne stellen.

quarrel ['kwɒrəl] (*UK*) (*US*) <> *n* Streit *der*. <> *vi* sich streiten; **to quarrel with sb** sich mit jm streiten; **to quarrel with sthg** an etw (*D*) etwas auszusetzen haben.

quarrelsome ['kwɒrəlsəm] *adj* streitsüchtig.

quarry ['kwɒrɪ] *n* - **1.** [place] Steinbruch *der* - **2.** [prey] Beute *die*.

quart [kwɔːt] *n UK* [unit of measurement] Quart *das* (= 1,14 l); *US* Quart *das* (= 0,95 l).

quarter ['kwɔːtər] *n* - **1.** [fraction, area in town] Viertel *das* - **2.** [in telling time]: **a quarter past (two)** *UK*, **a quarter after (two)** *US* Viertel nach (zwei); **a quarter to (two)** *UK*, **a quarter of (two)** *US* Viertel vor (zwei) - **3.** [of year] Vierteljahr *das*, Quartal *das* - **4.** *US* [coin] Vierteldollar *der* - **5.** [four ounces] ≃ Viertelpfund *das* - **6.** [direction] Richtung *die*; **from an unexpected quarter** von unerwarteter Seite. ◆ **quarters** *npl* [rooms] Quartier *das*. ◆ **at close quarters** *adv* aus der Nähe.

quarterfinal [ˌkwɔːtə'faɪnl] *n* Viertelfinalspiel *das*.

quarterly ['kwɔːtəlɪ] <> *adj & adv* vierteljährlich. <> *n* Vierteljahresschrift *die*.

quartet [kwɔː'tet] *n* Quartett *das*.

quartz [kwɔːts] *n* (*U*) Quarz *der*.

quartz watch *n* Quarzuhr *die*.

quash [kwɒʃ] *vt* - **1.** [decision, sentence] auflheben - **2.** [rebellion] unterdrücken.

quasi- ['kweɪzaɪ] *prefix* quasi-.

quaver ['kweɪvər] *n* MUS Achtelnote *die*.

quay [kiː] *n* Kai *der*.

quayside ['kiːsaɪd] *n* Kai *der*.

queasy ['kwiːzɪ] *adj* unwohl.

queen [kwiːn] *n* - **1.** [royalty, bee] Königin *die* - **2.** [in chess, playing card] Dame *die*.

queen mother *n*: **the queen mother** die Königinmutter.

queer [kwɪər] <> *adj* [odd] seltsam, eigenartig; **I'm feeling a bit queer** mir ist nicht ganz wohl. <> *n inf pej* [homosexual] Schwule *der*.

quell [kwel] *vt* unterdrücken.

quench [kwentʃ] *vt* stillen.

query ['kwɪərɪ] <> *n* Frage *die*. <> *vt* [decision] in Frage stellen; [invoice] beanstanden.

quest [kwest] *n liter*: **quest (for sthg)** Suche *die* (nach etw).

question ['kwestʃn] <> *n* Frage *die*; **to ask (sb) a question** (jm) eine Frage stellen; **to bring** *OR* **call sthg into question** etw in Frage stellen; **to be beyond question** außer Zweifel *OR* Frage stehen; **without question** ohne Zweifel; (*phrase*): **there's no question of doing it** es kommt nicht in Frage, es zu tun. <> *vt* - **1.** [interrogate] befragen - **2.** [express doubt about] bezweifeln. ◆ **in question** *adv*: **the thing in question** der/die/das Betreffende. ◆ **out of the question** *adj* ausgeschlossen.

questionable ['kwestʃənəbl] *adj* - **1.** [uncertain] fraglich - **2.** [not right, not honest] fragwürdig.

question mark *n* Fragezeichen *das*.

questionnaire [ˌkwestʃə'neər] *n* Fragebogen *der*.

queue [kju:] *UK* <> *n* Schlange *die*. <> *vi* Schlange stehen; **to queue (up) for sthg** für etw anstehen.

quibble ['kwɪbl] *pej* <> *n* Spitzfindig-keit *die*. <> *vi* spitzfindig sein; **to quibble over** OR **about sthg** über etw (A) streiten.

quiche [ki:ʃ] *n* Quiche *die*.

quick [kwɪk] *adj* & *adv* schnell.

quicken ['kwɪkn] <> *vt* [make faster] be-schleunigen. <> *vi* [get faster] schneller wer-den.

quickly ['kwɪklɪ] *adv* schnell.

quicksand ['kwɪksænd] *n* Treibsand *der*.

quick-witted [-'wɪtɪd] *adj* [person] geistes-gegenwärtig; [response] schlagkräftig.

quid [kwɪd] (*pl inv*) *n UK inf* Pfund *das*.

quiet ['kwaɪət] <> *adj* - **1.** [not noisy, calm] ruhig - **2.** [not talkative, silent] still; **to keep quiet about sthg** über etw (A) nichts sagen; **be quiet!** sei/seid still! - **3.** [discreet - clothes, col-ours] dezent; **to have a quiet word with sb** mit jm unter vier Augen reden - **4.** [wedding] im kleinen Kreis. <> *n* Ruhe *die*; **on the quiet** *inf* heimlich. <> *vt US* zum Schweigen brin-gen. ◆ **quiet down** *US* <> *vt sep* beruhi-gen. <> *vi* sich beruhigen.

quieten ['kwaɪətn] *vt* beruhigen. ◆ **quieten down** <> *vt sep* beruhigen. <> *vi* sich beruhigen.

quietly ['kwaɪətlɪ] *adv* - **1.** [without noise] lei-se - **2.** [without excitement] ruhig - **3.** [without fuss] in aller Stille.

quilt [kwɪlt] *n* Steppdecke *die*.

quintet [kwɪn'tet] *n* Quintett *das*.

quintuplets [kwɪn'tju:plɪts] *npl* Fünflin-ge *Pl*.

quip [kwɪp] <> *n* geistreiche Bemerkung. <> *vt* witzeln.

quirk [kwɜ:k] *n* - **1.** [habit] Marotte *die* - **2.** [strange event]: **a quirk of fate** eine Laune des Schicksals.

quit [kwɪt] (*UK pt & pp inv* OR **-ted**) (*US pt & pp inv*) <> *vt* - **1.** [resign from - job] aufgeben, kündigen; [- army] verlassen - **2.** [stop] aufhören mit. <> *vi* - **1.** [resign] kün-digen - **2.** [stop] aufhören.

quite [kwaɪt] *adv* - **1.** [fairly] ziemlich; **quite a lot** ziemlich viel; **quite a few** ziemlich vie-le - **2.** [completely] ganz; **I quite agree** das fin-de ich auch - **3.** [after negative]: **not quite big enough** nicht groß genug; **I don't quite under-stand** ich verstehe nicht ganz - **4.** [for em-phasis]: **it was quite a surprise** es war eine ziemliche Überraschung; **she's quite a singer** sie singt ganz gut - **5.** [to express agreement]: **quite (so)!** richtig!

quits [kwɪts] *adj inf*: **to be quits (with sb)** (mit jm) quitt sein; **we'll call it quits** [forget the debt] es ist schon in Ordnung; [stop doing sthg] las-sen Sie uns jetzt aufhören.

quiver ['kwɪvər] *vi* zittern.

quiz [kwɪz] (*pl* **-zes**) <> *n* - **1.** [competition, game] Quiz *das* - **2.** *US* SCH Prüfung *die*. <> *vt*: **to quiz sb (about sthg)** jn (über etw (A)) ausl-fragen.

quizzical ['kwɪzɪkl] *adj* fragend.

quota ['kwəʊtə] *n* Quote *die*.

quotation [kwəʊ'teɪʃn] *n* - **1.** [citation] Zi-tat *das* - **2.** COMM Kostenvoranschlag *der*.

quotation marks *npl* Anführungszei-chen *Pl*; **in quotation marks** in Anführungszei-chen.

quote [kwəʊt] <> *n* - **1.** [citation] Zitat *das* - **2.** COMM Kostenvoranschlag *der*. <> *vt* [cite] zitieren. <> *vi* [cite] zitieren; **to quote from sthg** zitieren aus etw.

quotient ['kwəʊʃnt] *n* Quotient *der*.

R

r (*pl* **r's** OR **rs**), **R** (*pl* **R's** OR **Rs**) [ɑːr] *n* r *das*, R *das*.

rabbi ['ræbaɪ] *n* Rabbiner *der*.

rabbit ['ræbɪt] *n* Kaninchen *das*.

rabbit hutch *n* Kaninchenstall *der*.

rabble ['ræbl] *n* - **1.** [disorderly crowd] auf-wieglerische Menge - **2.** [riffraff]: **the rabble** der Pöbel.

rabies ['reɪbiːz] *n* Tollwut *die*.

RAC (*abbr of* **Royal Automobile Club**) *n* ≃ ADAC *der*.

race [reɪs] <> *n* - **1.** [competition] Rennen *das* - **2.** *fig* [for power, control] Wettlauf *der*; **arms race** Wettrüsten *das* - **3.** [people, ethnic back-ground] Rasse *die*. <> *vt* - **1.** [compete against]: **to race sb** mit jm um die Wette laufen/fahren/ *etc* - **2.** [animal, vehicle] antreten lassen. <> *vi* - **1.** [compete]: **to race against sb** gegen jn an-treten - **2.** [rush] rennen - **3.** [heart, pulse] rasen - **4.** [engine] durchdrehen.

race car *n US* = **racing car**.

racecourse ['reɪskɔ:s] *n* Rennbahn *die*.

race driver *n US* = **racing driver**.

racehorse ['reɪshɔ:s] *n* Rennpferd *das*.

racetrack ['reɪstræk] *n* Rennbahn *die*.

racial ['reɪʃəl] *adj* Rassen-.

racial discrimination *n* Rassendiskrimi-nierung *die*.

racing ['reɪsɪŋ] *n* [motor racing] Renn-sport *der*; [horse racing] Pferderennsport *der*.

racing car *UK*, **race car** *US* n Rennwagen *der*.

racing driver *UK*, **race driver** *US* n Rennfahrer *der*, -in *die*.

racism ['reɪsɪzm] n Rassismus *der*.

racist ['reɪsɪst] <> adj rassistisch. <> n Rassist *der*, -in *die*.

rack [ræk] n - **1.** [frame] Ständer *der* - **2.** [for luggage] Ablage *die*.

racket ['rækɪt] n - **1.** [noise] Krach *der* - **2.** [illegal activity] Gaunerei *die* - **3.** SPORT Schläger *der*.

racquet ['rækɪt] n Schläger *der*.

racy ['reɪsɪ] adj feurig.

radar ['reɪdɑːr] n Radar *der*.

radiant ['reɪdɪənt] adj strahlend.

radiate ['reɪdɪeɪt] vt auslstrahlen.

radiation [,reɪdɪ'eɪʃn] n (U) [radioactive] radioaktive Strahlung.

radiator ['reɪdɪeɪtər] n - **1.** [in house] Heizkörper *der* - **2.** AUT Kühler *der*.

radical ['rædɪkl] <> adj - **1.** POL radikal - **2.** [fundamental] fundamental. <> n POL Radikale *der, die*.

radically ['rædɪklɪ] adv radikal.

radii ['reɪdɪaɪ] Pl [> **radius**.

radio ['reɪdɪəʊ] (pl -s) <> n - **1.** [system of communication] Rundfunk *der* - **2.** [broadcasting, equipment] Radio *das*. <> comp Radio-. <> vt [message] funken; [person] anlfunken.

radioactive [,reɪdɪəʊ'æktɪv] adj radioaktiv.

radio alarm n Radiowecker *der*.

radio-controlled [-kən'trəʊld] adj ferngesteuert.

radiology [,reɪdɪ'ɒlədʒɪ] n Radiologie *die*.

radish ['rædɪʃ] n Radieschen *das*.

radius ['reɪdɪəs] (pl radii) n - **1.** MATHS Radius *der* - **2.** ANAT Speiche *die*.

RAF [ɑːreɪ'ef, ræf] n abbr of **Royal Air Force**.

raffle ['ræfl] <> n Tombola *die*. <> vt verlosen.

raffle ticket n Los *das*.

raft [rɑːft] n Floß *das*.

rafter ['rɑːftər] n Dachsparren *der*.

rag [ræg] n - **1.** [piece of cloth] Lumpen *der* - **2.** pej [newspaper] Käseblatt *das*. ◆ **rags** npl [clothes] Lumpen *Pl*.

rag-and-bone man n Lumpensammler *der*.

rag doll n Flickenpuppe *die*.

rage [reɪdʒ] <> n - **1.** [fury] Wut *die*; **to fly into a rage** in Rage geraten - **2.** inf [fashion]: **to be all the rage** der letzte Schrei sein. <> vi toben; [disease] wüten.

ragged ['rægɪd] adj - **1.** [person, clothes] zerlumpt - **2.** [coastline] zerklüftet - **3.** [performance] stümperhaft.

raid [reɪd] <> n - **1.** MIL [attack] Angriff *der* - **2.** [forced entry - by thieves] Überfall *der*; [- by police] Razzia *die*. <> vt - **1.** MIL [attack] anlgreifen - **2.** [enter by force - subj: thieves] einlbrechen in (+ A); [- subj: police] eine Razzia machen in (+ D).

raider ['reɪdər] n - **1.** [attacker] Angreifer *der*, -in *die* - **2.** [thief] Einbrecher *der*, -in *die*.

rail [reɪl] n - **1.** [fence] Geländer *das*; [on ship] Reling *die* - **2.** [bar, of railway] Schiene *die* - **3.** (U) [form of transport] (Eisen)bahn *die*. <> comp Eisenbahn-, Bahn-.

railcard ['reɪlkɑːd] n UK ≃ Bahncard *die*.

railing ['reɪlɪŋ] n Geländer *das*; [on ship] Reling *die*.

railway *UK* ['reɪlweɪ], **railroad** *US* ['reɪlrəʊd] n - **1.** [track] Gleis *das* - **2.** [company, system] (Eisen)bahn *die*.

railway line n - **1.** [route] (Eisen)bahnlinie *die* - **2.** [track] Gleis *das*.

railwayman ['reɪlweɪmən] (pl -men [-mən]) n UK Eisenbahner *der*.

railway station n Bahnhof *der*.

railway track n Gleis *das*.

rain [reɪn] <> n Regen *der*. <> impers vb & vi regnen; **it's raining** es regnet.

rainbow ['reɪnbəʊ] n Regenbogen *der*.

rain check n US: **to take a rain check on sthg** etw auf ein andermal verschieben.

raincoat ['reɪnkəʊt] n Regenmantel *der*.

raindrop ['reɪndrɒp] n Regentropfen *der*.

rainfall ['reɪnfɔːl] n (U) Niederschlag *der*.

rain forest n Regenwald *der*.

rainy ['reɪnɪ] adj regnerisch.

raise [reɪz] <> vt - **1.** [lift up] heben; [window] hochlziehen; **to raise o.s.** sich auflrichten - **2.** [increase, improve] anlheben; **to raise one's voice** [make louder] seine Stimme heben; [in protest] seine Stimme erheben - **3.** [obtain - from donations] auflbringen; [- by selling, borrowing] auftreiben - **4.** [evoke] (herauf)lbeschwören - **5.** [child, animal] auflziehen - **6.** [crop] anlbauen - **7.** [mention] auflwerfen. <> n US Erhöhung *die*.

raisin ['reɪzn] n Rosine *die*.

rake [reɪk] <> n [implement] Harke *die*, Rechen *der*. <> vt - **1.** [smooth] harken, rechen - **2.** [gather] zusammenlrechen.

rally ['rælɪ] <> n - **1.** [meeting] Versammlung *die* - **2.** [car race] Rallye *die* - **3.** SPORT [exchange of shots] Ballwechsel *der*. <> vt sammeln. <> vi - **1.** [come together] sich sammeln - **2.** [recover] sich erholen. ◆ **rally round** <> vt insep sich scharen um. <> vi sich seiner/ihrer/etc anlnehmen.

ram [ræm] <> n [animal] Widder *der*. <> vt rammen.

RAM [ræm] n (abbr of random access memory) n RAM.

ramble ['ræmbl] ⟨⟩ n Wanderung die. ⟨⟩ vi - 1. [walk] wandern - 2. [talk] schwafeln.

rambler ['ræmblər] n [walker] Spaziergänger der, -in die.

rambling ['ræmblɪŋ] adj - 1. [building] weitläufig - 2. [conversation, book] weitschweifig.

ramp [ræmp] n Rampe die.

rampage [ræm'peɪdʒ] n: **to go on the rampage** randalieren.

rampant ['ræmpənt] adj - 1. [unrestrained] wuchernd; **to be rampant** wüten - 2. [widespread] weit verbreitet.

ramparts ['ræmpɑːts] npl Schutzwall der.

ramshackle ['ræm,ʃækl] adj heruntergekommen.

ran [ræn] pt ⟶ **run**.

ranch [rɑːntʃ] n Ranch die.

rancher ['rɑːntʃər] n Viehzüchter der, -in die.

rancid ['rænsɪd] adj ranzig.

rancour UK, **rancor** US ['ræŋkər] n Bitterkeit die.

random ['rændəm] ⟨⟩ adj willkürlich; **random sample** Stichprobe die. ⟨⟩ n: **at random** [choose, sample] willkürlich; [fire, hit out] ziellos.

random access memory n (U) COMPUT Arbeitsspeicher der.

randy ['rændɪ] adj UK inf scharf.

rang [ræŋ] pt ⟶ **ring**.

range [reɪndʒ] ⟨⟩ n - 1. [distance covered] Reichweite die; **at close range** auf kurze Entfernung - 2. [variety] Auswahl die; **there was a wide range of people there** es waren ganz unterschiedliche Leute da - 3. [bracket] Klasse die - 4. [of mountains, hills] Kette die - 5. [shooting area] Platz der - 6. MUS [of voice] Stimmumfang der. ⟨⟩ vt [place in row] aufstellen. ⟨⟩ vi - 1. [vary]: **to range from ... to ...** reichen von ... bis ...; **to range between ... and ...** liegen zwischen ... und ... - 2. [deal with, include]: **to range over sthg** sich erstrecken auf etw (A).

ranger ['reɪndʒər] n [of park] Aufseher der, -in die; [of forest] Förster der, -in die.

rank [ræŋk] ⟨⟩ adj - 1. [utter, absolute] ausgesprochen - 2. [offensive] übel. ⟨⟩ n - 1. [in army, police] Rang der; **the rank and file** MIL die Mannschaft; [of political party, organization] die Basis - 2. [social class] Stand der - 3. [row, line] Reihe die; **taxi rank** Taxistand der. ⟨⟩ vt [classify]: **to rank sb among the great writers** jn zu den großen Schriftstellern zählen; **he is ranked fourth in the world** er steht an vierter Stelle in der Weltrangliste. ⟨⟩ vi: **to rank as** gelten als; **to rank among** zählen zu. ⟶ **ranks** npl - 1. MIL: **the ranks** die einfachen Soldaten - 2. fig [members] Reihen Pl.

rankle ['ræŋkl] vi: **it still rankles with me** es wurmt mich noch immer.

ransack ['rænsæk] vt - 1. [plunder] plündern - 2. [search] durchwühlen.

ransom ['rænsəm] n Lösegeld das; **to hold sb to ransom** [keep prisoner] jn als Geisel halten; fig [put in impossible position] jn erpressen.

rant [rænt] vi schwadronieren.

rap [ræp] ⟨⟩ n - 1. [knock] Klopfen das - 2. MUS Rap der. ⟨⟩ vt [on table] klopfen auf (+ A); **to rap sb on the knuckles** jm auf die Finger klopfen.

rape [reɪp] ⟨⟩ n - 1. [crime, attack] Vergewaltigung die - 2. fig [destruction]: **the rape of the countryside** der Raubbau an der Landschaft - 3. [plant] Raps der. ⟨⟩ vt vergewaltigen.

rapid ['ræpɪd] adj rapide, schnell. ⟶ **rapids** npl Stromschnelle die.

rapidly ['ræpɪdlɪ] adv schnell.

rapist ['reɪpɪst] n Vergewaltiger der.

rapport [ræ'pɔːr] n: **a (good) rapport with/between** ein gutes Verhältnis mit/zwischen (+ D).

rapture ['ræptʃər] n: **to go into raptures over** OR **about sb/sthg** über jn/etw in Verzückung geraten.

rapturous ['ræptʃərəs] adj begeistert.

rare [reər] adj - 1. [scarce, infrequent] selten - 2. [exceptional] rar - 3. CULIN [underdone] blutig.

rarely ['reəlɪ] adv selten.

raring ['reərɪŋ] adj: **to be raring to go** in den Startlöchern sein.

rarity ['reərətɪ] n - 1. [unusual object, person] Rarität die - 2. (U) [scarcity] Seltenheit die.

rascal ['rɑːskl] n [mischievous child] Frechdachs der.

rash [ræʃ] ⟨⟩ adj [person] unbesonnen; [action, decision, promise] voreilig. ⟨⟩ n - 1. MED Ausschlag der - 2. [spate] Serie die.

rasher ['ræʃər] n Streifen der.

raspberry ['rɑːzbərɪ] n [fruit] Himbeere die.

rat [ræt] n - 1. [animal] Ratte die - 2. pej [person] Schwein das.

rate [reɪt] ⟨⟩ n - 1. [speed] Tempo das; **at this rate** bei diesem Tempo - 2. [ratio, proportion] Rate die - 3. [of taxation, interest] Satz der. ⟨⟩ vt - 1. [consider]: **to rate sb/sthg (as)** jn/etw einschätzen (als); **to rate sb/sthg among** jn/etw zählen zu - 2. [deserve] verdienen. ⟶ **at any rate** adv auf jeden Fall.

ratepayer ['reɪt,peɪər] n UK Steuerzahler der, -in die.

rather ['rɑːðər] adv - 1. [slightly, a bit] ziemlich; **he's had rather too much to drink** er hat ziemlich viel getrunken - 2. [for emphasis] recht; **I rather thought so** das habe ich mir fast gedacht; **I rather like him** ich mag ihn recht gern - 3. [expressing a preference] lieber; **would you rather leave?** möchtest du lieber gehen?;

I'd rather not lieber nicht - **4.** [more exactly]: **or rather** vielmehr - **5.** [on the contrary]: **(but) rather** vielmehr. ◆ **rather than** conj statt.

ratify ['rætɪfaɪ] vt ratifizieren.

rating ['reɪtɪŋ] n [standing]: **popularity rating** Beliebtheitsgrad der; **what is her rating in the polls?** wie hoch ist ihr Beliebtheitsgrad?

ratio ['reɪʃɪəʊ] (pl -s) n Verhältnis das.

ration ['ræʃn] ⟨⟩ n Ration die. ⟨⟩ vt [goods] rationieren. ◆ **rations** npl Rationen Pl.

rational ['ræʃənl] adj - **1.** [reasonable] rational - **2.** [capable of reason] vernünftig.

rationale [ˌræʃəˈnɑːl] n Gründe Pl.

rationalize, -ise ['ræʃənəlaɪz] vt rationalisieren.

rat race n ständiger Konkurrenzkampf.

rattle ['rætl] ⟨⟩ n [toy] Klapper die. ⟨⟩ vt - **1.** [make rattling noise with - keys] klimpern mit; [subj: wind - windows] rütteln an (+ D) - **2.** [unsettle] durcheinander bringen. ⟨⟩ vi [make rattling noise] klappern; [bottles] klirren.

rattlesnake ['rætlsneɪk], **rattler** US ['rætlər] n Klapperschlange die.

raucous ['rɔːkəs] adj [voice, laughter] rau; [behaviour] wüst.

ravage ['rævɪdʒ] vt verheeren, verwüsten. ◆ **ravages** npl Verheerung die.

rave [reɪv] ⟨⟩ adj glänzend. ⟨⟩ n UK inf [event] Rave der ODER das. ⟨⟩ vi - **1.** [talk angrily]: **to rave about/against sthg** über etw (A)/gegen etw wettern - **2.** [talk enthusiastically]: **to rave about sthg** von etw schwärmen.

raven ['reɪvn] n Rabe der.

ravenous ['rævənəs] adj ausgehungert; (phrase): **I'm ravenous!** ich habe einen Bärenhunger!

ravine [rəˈviːn] n Schlucht die.

raving ['reɪvɪŋ] adj: **he's a raving lunatic** er ist total verrückt.

ravioli [ˌrævɪˈəʊlɪ] n (U) Ravioli Pl.

ravishing ['rævɪʃɪŋ] adj hinreißend.

raw [rɔː] adj - **1.** [uncooked] roh - **2.** [untreated] roh, Roh- - **3.** [painful - wound] offen; [- skin] wund - **4.** [inexperienced] unerfahren.

raw deal n: **to get a raw deal** schlecht wegkommen.

raw material n - **1.** [natural substance] Rohstoff der - **2.** (U) fig [basis] Grundlage die.

ray [reɪ] n - **1.** [beam] Strahl der - **2.** fig [glimmer] Schimmer der.

rayon ['reɪɒn] n Reyon das.

raze [reɪz] vt (phrase): **the house was razed to the ground** das Haus wurde dem Erdboden gleichgemacht.

razor ['reɪzər] n Rasierapparat der.

razor blade n Rasierklinge die.

RC (abbr of **Roman Catholic**) adj röm.-kath.

Rd (abbr of **Road**) Str.

R & D (abbr of **research and development**) n F & E.

re [riː] prep betreffs (+ G).

RE n (abbr of **religious education**) Religionsunterricht der.

reach [riːtʃ] ⟨⟩ vt - **1.** [arrive at] an|kommen in (+ D) - **2.** [be able to touch] heran|kommen an (+ A) - **3.** [contact, extend as far as, attain, achieve] erreichen. ⟨⟩ vi - **1.** [person, arm, hand] greifen; **to reach (out) for sthg** nach etw greifen - **2.** [land] reichen. ⟨⟩ n [of boxer] Reichweite die; **within sb's reach** [easily touched] innerhalb js Reichweite; **within easy reach of the station** vom Bahnhof leicht zu erreichen; **out of** OR **beyond sb's reach** [not easily touched] außerhalb js Reichweite.

react [rɪˈækt] vi - **1.** [rebel]: **to react against sthg** sich gegen etw auflehnen - **2.** CHEM: **to react with sthg** auf etw (A) reagieren.

reaction [rɪˈækʃn] n - **1.** [response & MED]: **reaction (to sthg)** Reaktion die (auf etw (A)) - **2.** [rebellion]: **reaction (against sthg)** Gegenreaktion die (auf etw (A)) - **3.** [reflex] Reaktionsfähigkeit die; **she's got very quick reactions** sie hat sehr gute Reflexe.

reactionary [rɪˈækʃənrɪ] ⟨⟩ adj reaktionär. ⟨⟩ n Reaktionär der, -in die.

reactor [rɪˈæktər] n [nuclear reactor] Reaktor der.

read [riːd] (pt & pp inv) ⟨⟩ vt - **1.** [book, magazine, music] lesen; **read music** Noten lesen - **2.** [say aloud]: **to read sb sthg** jm etw vorlesen - **3.** [subj: sign, notice] besagen; [subj: gauge, meter, barometer] an|zeigen - **4.** [take reading from - meter, gauge] ablesen - **5.** [interpret] verstehen; [sb's thoughts] lesen - **6.** UK UNIV studieren. ⟨⟩ vi - **1.** [in book, magazine] lesen; **to read about sthg** von etw lesen - **2.** [read aloud]: **to read to sb (from)** jm vorlesen (aus). ◆ **read out** vt sep vorlesen. ◆ **read over, read through** vt sep durch|lesen. ◆ **read up on** vt insep nachlesen über (+ A).

readable ['riːdəbl] adj [book] lesenswert.

reader ['riːdər] n [person who reads] Leser der, -in die.

readership ['riːdəʃɪp] n [total number of readers] Leser Pl.

readily ['redɪlɪ] adv - **1.** [willingly] bereitwillig - **2.** [easily] leicht.

reading ['riːdɪŋ] n - **1.** [act of reading] Lesen das - **2.** [reading material] Lektüre die - **3.** [recital] Lesung die - **4.** [taken from meter] Zählerstand der; [taken from thermometer] Thermometerstand der - **5.** [POL - of bill] Lesung die.

readjust [ˌriːəˈdʒʌst] ⟨⟩ vt [mechanism, instrument] nach|stellen; [mirror] ein|stellen; [policy] neu an|passen. ⟨⟩ vi: **to readjust to sthg** sich wieder an etw (A) gewöhnen.

readout ['riːdaʊt] n COMPUT Anzeige die.

ready ['redɪ] <> adj - 1. [prepared] fertig; **to be ready to do sthg** bereit sein, etw zu tun; **to be ready for sthg** für etw bereit sein; **to get ready** sich fertig machen; **to get sthg ready** etw fertig machen - 2. [willing]: **to be ready to do sthg** bereit sein, etw zu tun - 3. [in need of]: **to be ready for sthg** etw gebrauchen können; **I'm ready for bed** ich bin bettreif - 4. [likely]: **to be ready to collapse** zum Umfallen müde sein; **she was ready to cry** sie war den Tränen nahe. <> vt vor|bereiten.

ready cash n Bargeld das.

ready-made adj - 1. [product] Fertig- - 2. fig [reply, excuse] vorgefertigt.

ready money n Bargeld das.

ready-to-wear adj: **ready-to-wear clothes** Konfektionskleidung die, Kleidung die von der Stange.

real ['rɪəl] <> adj - 1. [authentic, for emphasis] echt; **this is the real thing!** [marvellous] das ist unglaublich toll!; **this time it's for real** diesmal ist es echt - 2. [actually existing] real - 3. [cost, value] tatsächlich; **in real terms** real. <> adv US wirklich.

real estate n (U) Immobilien Pl.

realign [,riːə'laɪn] vt [brakes] nach|stellen.

realism ['rɪəlɪzm] n Realismus der.

realistic [,rɪə'lɪstɪk] adj realistisch.

reality [rɪ'ælətɪ] n Realität die.

reality TV n Reality-TV das.

realization [,rɪəlaɪ'zeɪʃn] n (U) - 1. [awareness, recognition] Realisation die - 2. [achievement] Realisierung die.

realize, -ise [ˈrɪəlaɪz] vt - 1. [become aware of, understand] begreifen - 2. [achieve] verwirklichen - 3. COMM erzielen.

really ['rɪəlɪ] <> adv - 1. [for emphasis] wirklich; **really good/bad** wirklich gut/schlecht; **you really ought to see this film** du solltest dir den Film unbedingt ansehen - 2. [actually] eigentlich; **not really** eigentlich nicht - 3. [honestly] wirklich - 4. [to sound less negative] eigentlich. <> excl - 1. [expressing doubt, surprise]: **really?** wirklich? - 2. [expressing disapproval]: **really! also wirklich!**

realm [relm] n - 1. [field] Bereich der - 2. [kingdom] Reich das.

realtor ['rɪəltər] n US Grundstücksmakler der, -in die.

reap [riːp] vt liter & fig ernten.

reappear [,riːə'pɪər] vi wieder erscheinen.

rear [rɪər] <> adj [wheel] Hinter-; **rear window** [of car] Heckscheibe die. <> n - 1. [back] Rückseite die; **to bring up the rear** die Nachhut bilden - 2. inf [buttocks] Hintern der. <> vt [children, animals, plants] auf|ziehen. <> vi: **to rear (up)** sich auf|bäumen.

rearm [riː'ɑːm] <> vt wieder bewaffnen. <> vi wieder auf|rüsten.

rearrange [,riːə'reɪndʒ] vt - 1. [arrange differently] um|stellen - 2. [reschedule] verlegen.

rearview mirror ['rɪəvjuː-] n Rückspiegel der.

reason ['riːzn] <> n - 1. [cause]: **reason (for sthg)** Grund der (für etw); **for some reason** aus irgendeinem Grund - 2. [justification]: **to have reason to do sthg** Grund haben, etw zu tun - 3. [common sense] Vernunft die; **to listen to reason** auf die Stimme der Vernunft hören; **it stands to reason** es ist logisch. <> vt [conclude]: **to reason that...** folgern, dass... <> vi vernünftig denken. ⬛ **reason with** vt insep vernünftig reden mit.

reasonable ['riːznəbl] adj - 1. [sensible] vernünftig - 2. [acceptable - decision, explanation] angemessen; [- work] ganz gut; [- offer] akzeptabel; [- price] vernünftig - 3. [fairly large]: **a reasonable amount/number** ziemlich viel/viele.

reasonably ['riːznəblɪ] adv - 1. [quite] ziemlich - 2. [sensibly] vernünftig.

reasoned ['riːznd] adj durchdacht.

reasoning ['riːznɪŋ] n (U) Argumentation die.

reassess [,riːə'ses] vt [position, opinion] neu ein|schätzen.

reassurance [,riːə'ʃʊərəns] n - 1. [comfort] Beruhigung die - 2. [promise] Versicherung die.

reassure [,riːə'ʃʊər] vt beruhigen.

reassuring [,riːə'ʃʊərɪŋ] adj beruhigend.

rebate ['riːbeɪt] n Nachlass der.

rebel <> n ['rebl] Rebell der, -in die. <> vi [rɪ'bel]: **to rebel (against)** rebellieren (gegen).

rebellion [rɪ'beljən] n Rebellion die.

rebellious [rɪ'beljəs] adj rebellisch.

rebound vi [rɪ'baʊnd] [ball] ab|prallen.

rebuff [rɪ'bʌf] n Abfuhr die.

rebuild [,riː'bɪld] (pt & pp -built [,riː'bɪlt]) vt wieder auf|bauen.

rebuke [rɪ'bjuːk] <> n Tadel der. <> vt: **to rebuke sb (for sthg)** jn (für etw) tadeln.

recall [rɪ'kɔːl] <> n (U) [memory] Erinnerung die. <> vt - 1. [remember] sich erinnern an (+ A) - 2. [summon back] zurück|rufen.

recap inf vt & vi [,riː'kæp] [summarize] zusammen|fassen.

recapitulate [,riːkə'pɪtjʊleɪt] vt & vi zusammen|fassen.

recd, rec'd abbr of **received**.

recede [rɪ'siːd] vi - 1. [move away] zurück|weichen; **his hair is receding** er bekommt eine leichte Stirnglatze - 2. fig [disappear, fade] schwinden.

receding [rɪ'siːdɪŋ] adj [chin] fliehend; [hairline] zurück|weichend.

receipt [rɪ'siːt] n - 1. [piece of paper] Quittung die - 2. (U) [act of receiving] Empfang der. ⬛ **receipts** npl [money taken] Einnahmen Pl.

receive [rɪ'siːv] *vt* - **1.** [gift, letter] erhalten - **2.** [news] erfahren - **3.** [setback] erfahren; **to receive an injury** verletzt werden - **4.** [visitor, guest] empfangen - **5.** [greet]: **to be well/badly received** gut/schlecht aufgenommen werden.

receiver [rɪ'siːvər] *n* - **1.** [of telephone] Hörer *der* - **2.** [radio, TV set] Empfänger *der* - **3.** FIN [official] Konkursverwalter *der*, -in *die*.

recent ['riːsnt] *adj* neueste(r) (s).

recently ['riːsntlɪ] *adv* kürzlich.

receptacle [rɪ'septəkl] *n* Behälter *der*.

reception [rɪ'sepʃn] *n* Empfang *der*.

reception desk *n* Empfang *der*.

receptionist [rɪ'sepʃənɪst] *n* Empfangschef *der*, Empfangsdame *die*.

recess ['riːses, UK rɪ'ses] *n* - **1.** [vacation] Ferien *Pl*; **to be in/go into recess** eine Sitzungspause haben/beginnen - **2.** [alcove] Nische *die* - **3.** [of mind, memory] Winkel *der* - **4.** US SCH Pause *die*.

recession [rɪ'seʃn] *n* Rezession *die*.

recharge [,riː'tʃɑːdʒ] *vt* (auf)laden.

recipe ['resɪpɪ] *n liter* & *fig* Rezept *das*.

recipient [rɪ'sɪpɪənt] *n* Empfänger *der*, -in *die*.

reciprocal [rɪ'sɪprəkl] *adj* wechselseitig.

recital [rɪ'saɪtl] *n* [of poetry] Vortrag *der*; [of music] Konzert *das*.

recite [rɪ'saɪt] *vt* - **1.** [perform aloud] vortragen - **2.** [list] aufzählen.

reckless ['rekləs] *adj* leichtsinnig.

reckon ['rekn] *vt* - **1.** *inf* [think]: **to reckon (that)** schätzen, dass - **2.** [consider, judge]: **to be reckoned to be sthg** als etw eingeschätzt werden - **3.** [calculate] schätzen. ◆ **reckon on** *vt insep* zählen auf (+ A). ◆ **reckon with** *vt insep* [expect] rechnen mit.

reckoning ['rekənɪŋ] *n* (U) [calculation] Schätzung *die*.

reclaim [rɪ'kleɪm] *vt* - **1.** [claim back - lost item, luggage] abholen; [- tax, expenses] zurückerlangen - **2.** [make fit for use] gewinnen.

recline [rɪ'klaɪn] *vi* [lie back] sich zurücklehnen.

reclining [rɪ'klaɪnɪŋ] *adj* verstellbar.

recluse [rɪ'kluːs] *n* Einsiedler *der*, -in *die*.

recognition [,rekəg'nɪʃn] *n* (U) - **1.** [identification] Erkennen *das*; **to have changed beyond OR out of all recognition** nicht wiederzuerkennen sein - **2.** [acknowledgement] Anerkennung *die*; **in recognition of** in Anerkennung (+ G).

recognizable ['rekəgnaɪzəbl] *adj* erkennbar.

recognize, -ise ['rekəgnaɪz] *vt* - **1.** [gen] erkennen - **2.** [officially accept, approve] anerkennen.

recoil ◇ *vi* [rɪ'kɔɪl] - **1.** [draw back] zurückweichen - **2.** *fig* [shrink from]: **to recoil from/at sthg** vor etw (D) zurückschrecken. ◇ *n* ['riːkɔɪl] [of gun] Rückstoß *der*.

recollect [,rekə'lekt] *vt* sich erinnern an (+ A).

recollection [,rekə'lekʃn] *n* Erinnerung *die*.

recommend [,rekə'mend] *vt* - **1.** [commend, speak in favour of]: **to recommend sb/sthg (to sb)** (jm) jn/etw empfehlen - **2.** [advise] raten zu.

recompense ['rekəmpens] ◇ *n*: **recompense (for sthg)** Entschädigung *die* (für etw). ◇ *vt*: **to recompense sb (for sthg)** jn (für etw) entschädigen.

reconcile ['rekənsaɪl] *vt* - **1.** [beliefs, ideas] (miteinander) vereinbaren; **to reconcile sthg with sthg** etw mit etw vereinbaren - **2.** [people] versöhnen - **3.** [resign]: **to reconcile o.s. to sthg** sich mit etw aussöhnen.

reconditioned [,riːkən'dɪʃnd] *adj* überholt.

reconnaissance [rɪ'kɒnɪsəns] *n* (U) Erkundung *die*.

reconsider [,riːkən'sɪdər] ◇ *vt* neu überdenken. ◇ *vi*: **it's not too late to reconsider** Sie können es sich noch einmal überlegen.

reconstruct [,riːkən'strʌkt] *vt* - **1.** [building, bridge, country] wieder aufbauen - **2.** [event, crime] rekonstruieren.

record ◇ *n* ['rekɔːd] - **1.** [written account] Aufzeichnung *die*; **off the record** inoffiziell - **2.** [vinyl disc] (Schall)platte *die* - **3.** [best achievement] Rekord *der* - **4.** [history]: **to have a good record** gute Leistungen aufweisen können; **to have a criminal record** vorbestraft sein. ◇ *adj* ['rekɔːd] Rekord-. ◇ *vt* [rɪ'kɔːd] - **1.** [write down] aufzeichnen - **2.** [put on tape *etc*] aufnehmen.

recorded delivery [rɪ'kɔːdɪd-] *n*: **to send sthg by recorded delivery** etw per Einschreiben schicken.

recorder [rɪ'kɔːdər] *n* - **1.** [machine]: **(tape) recorder** Tonbandgerät *das*; **(cassette) recorder** Kassettenrekorder *der*; **(video) recorder** Videorekorder *der* - **2.** [musical instrument] Blockflöte *die*.

record holder *n* Rekordinhaber *der*, -in *die*.

recording [rɪ'kɔːdɪŋ] *n* - **1.** [individual recording] Aufnahme *die* - **2.** (U) [process of recording] Aufzeichnung *die*.

record player *n* Plattenspieler *der*.

recount ◇ *n* ['riːkaʊnt] Nachzählung *die*. ◇ *vt* - **1.** [rɪ'kaʊnt] [narrate] erzählen - **2.** [,riː'kaʊnt] [count again] nachzählen.

recoup [rɪ'kuːp] *vt* [recover] wieder einlbringen.

recourse [rɪ'kɔːs] *n fml*: **to have recourse to sthg** Zuflucht zu etw nehmen.

recover [rɪ'kʌvər] ◇ *vt* - **1.** [stolen goods, money] zurücklbekommen; **to recover sthg**

from sb/somewhere etw von jm/irgendwo zurücklbekommen - **2.** [one's strength, balance, senses] wiederlgewinnen. ◇ *vi* [from illness]: **to recover (from)** genesen (von etw.).

recovery [rɪ'kʌvərɪ] *n* - **1.** [from illness]: **recovery (from)** Genesung *die* (von) - **2.** *fig* [of currency, economy] Erholung *die* - **3.** [of stolen goods, money] Wiedererlangung *die*.

recreation [,rekrɪ'eɪʃn] *n* [leisure] Erholung *die*.

recrimination [rɪ,krɪmɪ'neɪʃn] *n (U)* Gegenbeschuldigung *die*. ◆ **recriminations** *npl* gegenseitige Beschuldigungen *Pl.*

recruit [rɪ'kru:t] ◇ *n* [in armed forces] Rekrut *der*, -in *die*; [in company, organization] neues Mitglied. ◇ *vt* - **1.** [find, employ - in armed forces] rekrutieren; [- in company, organization] einstellen - **2.** [persuade to join] werben; **they recruited her to help out** sie haben sie zur Hilfe herangezogen. ◇ *vi* [look for new staff] einlstellen.

recruitment [rɪ'kru:tmənt] *n (U)* [of staff] Einstellung *die*; [of soldiers] Rekrutierung *die*.

rectangle ['rek,tæŋgl] *n* Rechteck *das*.

rectangular [rek'tæŋgjulər] *adj* rechteckig.

rectify ['rektɪfaɪ] *vt fml* berichtigen.

rector ['rektər] *n* - **1.** [priest] Pfarrer *der* - **2.** *Scotland* [head - of school] Direktor *der*, -in *die*; [- of college, university] Rektor *der*, -in *die*.

rectory ['rektərɪ] *n* Pfarrhaus *das*.

recuperate [rɪ'ku:pəreɪt] *vi fml*: **to recuperate (from)** genesen (von).

recur [rɪ'kɜ:r] *vi* wiederlkehren; [problem, error] wieder aufltreten.

recurrence [rɪ'kʌrəns] *n fml* Wiederkehr *die*; [of problem, error] Wiederaufltreten *das*.

recurrent [rɪ'kʌrənt] *adj* immer wiederkehrend; [problem, error] immer wieder auftretend.

recycle [,ri:'saɪkl] *vt* recyceln.

recycle bin *n* COMPUT Papierkorb *der*.

red [red] ◇ *adj* rot. ◇ *n* [colour] Rot *das*; **to be in the red** *inf* in den roten Zahlen sein.

red card *n* FTBL: **to be shown the red card, to get a red card** die rote Karte gezeigt bekommen.

red carpet *n*: **to roll out the red carpet for sb** für jn den roten Teppich auslrollen.

Red Cross *n*: **the Red Cross** das Rote Kreuz.

redcurrant ['redkʌrənt] *n* (rote) Johannisbeere.

redden ['redn] *vi* [person, face] erröten.

redecorate [,ri:'dekəreɪt] *vt & vi* renovieren.

redeem [rɪ'di:m] *vt* - **1.** [save, rescue] retten - **2.** [from pawnbroker] einlösen.

redeeming [rɪ'di:mɪŋ] *adj*: **her one redeeming feature is...** ihre einzige positive Eigenschaft ist...

redeploy [,ri:dɪ'plɔɪ] *vt* [troops] umverlegen; [workers, staff] an anderer Stelle einlsetzen.

red-faced [-'feɪst] *adj* [with embarrassment] mit rotem Kopf.

red-haired [-'heəd] *adj* rothaarig.

red-handed [-'hændɪd] *adj*: **to catch sb red-handed** jn auf frischer Tat ertappen.

redhead ['redhed] *n* Rotkopf *der*.

red herring *n fig* falsche Spur.

red-hot *adj* - **1.** [extremely hot] rot glühend - **2.** *inf* [very good] klasse, super.

redid [,ri:'dɪd] *pt* ▷ **redo**.

redirect [,ri:dɪ'rekt] *vt* - **1.** [mail] nachlsenden - **2.** [aircraft, aid] umlleiten; [one's energies] anders einlsetzen.

rediscover [,ri:dɪs'kʌvər] *vt* - **1.** [re-experience] wieder entdecken - **2.** [make popular, famous again]: **to be rediscovered** wieder entdeckt werden.

red light *n* [traffic signal] rote Ampel.

red-light district *n* Rotlichtviertel *das*.

redo [,ri:'du:] (*pt* -**did**, *pp* -**done**) *vt* [do again] noch einmal machen; [letter, essay] noch einmal schreiben.

redolent ['redələnt] *adj*: **to be redolent of sthg** *liter* [reminiscent] an etw (A) erinnern.

redone [,ri:'dʌn] *pp* ▷ **redo**.

redouble [,ri:'dʌbl] *vt*: **to redouble one's efforts (to do sthg)** seine Anstrengungen verdoppeln (etw zu tun).

redraft [,ri:'drɑːft] *vt* neu ablfassen.

red tape *n fig* Bürokratie *die*.

reduce [rɪ'dju:s] ◇ *vt* - **1.** [make smaller, less] reduzieren - **2.** [force, bring]: **to be reduced to doing sthg** dazu gezwungen sein, etw zu tun; **to be reduced to tears** zum Weinen gebracht werden. ◇ *vi US* [lose weight] ablnehmen.

reduction [rɪ'dʌkʃn] *n* - **1.** [decrease]: **reduction (in sthg)** Reduzierung (einer Sache (G)) - **2.** [amount of decrease]: **reduction (of)** Ermäßigung *die* (um).

redundancy [rɪ'dʌndənsɪ] *n UK* - **1.** [job loss]: redundancies Entlassungen *Pl* - **2.** [jobless state] Arbeitslosigkeit *die*.

redundant [rɪ'dʌndənt] *adj* - **1.** *UK* [jobless]: **to be made redundant** den Arbeitsplatz verlieren - **2.** [superfluous] überflüssig.

reed [ri:d] *n* - **1.** [plant] Schilfrohr *das* - **2.** [of musical instrument] Rohrblatt *das*.

reef [ri:f] *n* [in sea] Riff *das*.

reek [ri:k] ◇ *n* Gestank *der*. ◇ *vi*: **to reek (of sthg)** (nach etw) stinken.

reel [ri:l] ◇ *n* - **1.** [roll] Spule *die* - **2.** [on fishing rod] Rolle *die*. ◇ *vi* [stagger] torkeln. ◆ **reel in** *vt sep* [fishing line] einlrollen; [fish] einlholen. ◆ **reel off** *vt sep* [list] ablspulen.

reenact [ˌriːɪˈnækt] *vt* nachlspielen.

ref *n* - 1. *inf* SPORT (*abbr of* referee) Schiri *der* - 2. ADMIN *abbr of* **reference**.

refectory [rɪˈfektərɪ] *n* [in school, college] Speisesaal *der*.

refer [rɪˈfɜːʳ] *vt* - 1. [person]: **to refer sb to sb** jn an jn verweisen; **to refer sb to sthg** [document, article] jn auf etw (A) verweisen - 2. [report, case, decision]: **to refer sthg to sb/sthg** etw an jn/etw weiterlleiten. ➠ **refer to** *vt insep* - 1. [mention] erwähnen; [as support for argument] sich beziehen auf (+ A) - 2. [apply to, concern] betreffen - 3. [consult] zu Rate ziehen.

referee [ˌrefəˈriː] *n* - 1. SPORT Schiedsrichter *der*, -in *die* - 2. UK [for job application] Referenz *die*. ⬦ *vt* SPORT leiten. ⬦ *vi* SPORT Schiedsrichter sein.

reference [ˈrefrəns] *n* - 1. [act of mentioning]: **to make reference to sb/sthg** jn/etw erwähnen; **with reference to** *fml* mit Bezug auf (+ A) - 2. [mention]: **reference (to)** Anspielung *die* (auf (+ A)) - 3. [in catalogue, on map] Verweis *der* - 4. COMM [in letter, for job application] Referenz *die*.

reference book *n* Nachschlagewerk *das*.

reference number *n* [for customer] Kundennummer *die*; [for member] Mitgliedsnummer *die*; [on file] Aktenzeichen *das*.

referendum [ˌrefəˈrendəm] (*pl* -s OR -da [-də]) *n* POL Referendum *das*.

refill ⬦ *n* [ˈriːfɪl] - 1. [for pen, lighter] Nachfüllpatrone *die* - 2. *inf* [drink]: **would you like a refill?** möchten Sie nachgeschenkt haben? ⬦ *vt* [ˌriːˈfɪl] nachlfüllen.

refine [rɪˈfaɪn] *vt* - 1. [oil, food] raffinieren - 2. [details, speech] verfeinern.

refined [rɪˈfaɪnd] *adj* - 1. [genteel] fein - 2. [highly developed, purified] raffiniert.

refinement [rɪˈfaɪnmənt] *n* - 1. [improvement]: **refinement (on sthg)** Verfeinerung *die* (von etw) - 2. (*U*) [gentility] Feinheit *die*.

reflect [rɪˈflekt] ⬦ *vt* - 1. [show, be a sign of] widerlspiegeln - 2. [throw back - light, heat] reflektieren; [- image] spiegeln - 3. [think, consider]: **to reflect that...** daran denken, dass... ⬦ *vi* [think, consider]: **to reflect (on** OR **upon sthg)** reflektieren (über etw (A)).

reflection [rɪˈflekʃn] *n* - 1. [sign, consequence] Widerspiegelung *die* - 2. [criticism]: **this is no reflection on your judgement** das ist keine Kritik an Ihrem Urteil - 3. [image] Spiegelung *die* - 4. (*U*) *liter* [thinking] Reflexion *die*; **on reflection** bei näherer Überlegung.

reflector [rɪˈflektəʳ] *n* Rückstrahler *der*.

reflex [ˈriːfleks] *n*: **reflex (action)** Reflex *der*.

reflexive [rɪˈfleksɪv] *adj* GRAM reflexiv.

reform [rɪˈfɔːm] ⬦ *n* Reform *die*. ⬦ *vt* - 1. [change] reformieren - 2. [improve behaviour of] bessern. ⬦ *vi* [behave better] sich bessern.

Reformation [ˌrefəˈmeɪʃn] *n*: **the Reformation** die Reformation.

reformatory [rɪˈfɔːmətrɪ] *n* US Besserungsanstalt *die*.

reformer [rɪˈfɔːməʳ] *n* Reformer *der*, -in *die*.

refrain [rɪˈfreɪn] ⬦ *n* Refrain *der*. ⬦ *vi fml*: **to refrain from doing sthg** es unterlassen, etw zu tun.

refresh [rɪˈfreʃ] *vt* erfrischen.

refresher course [rɪˈfreʃəʳ-] *n* Auffrischungskurs *der*.

refreshing [rɪˈfreʃɪŋ] *adj* erfrischend.

refreshments [rɪˈfreʃmənts] *npl* Erfrischungen *Pl*.

refrigerator [rɪˈfrɪdʒəreɪtəʳ] *n* Kühlschrank *der*.

refuel [ˌriːˈfjuəl] (*UK*) (*US*) *vt* & *vi* aufltanken.

refuge [ˈrefjuːdʒ] *n* - 1. [place of safety] Zuflucht *die* - 2. [safety]: **to seek** OR **take refuge** [hide] Zuflucht suchen; **to seek** OR **take refuge in sthg** *fig* in etw (D) Zuflucht suchen.

refugee [ˌrefjuˈdʒiː] *n* Flüchtling *der*.

refund ⬦ *n* [ˈriːfʌnd] Rückzahlung *die*. ⬦ *vt* [rɪˈfʌnd]: **to refund sthg to sb, to refund sb sthg** etw an jn zurücklzahlen.

refurbish [ˌriːˈfɜːbɪʃ] *vt* renovieren.

refusal [rɪˈfjuːzl] *n*: **refusal (to do sthg)** Weigerung *die* (etw zu tun).

refuse[1] [rɪˈfjuːz] ⬦ *vt* - 1. [withhold, deny]: **to refuse sb sthg, to refuse sthg to sb** jm etw verweigern - 2. [decline] abllehnen; **to refuse to do sthg** sich weigern, etw zu tun. ⬦ *vi* sich weigern.

refuse[2] [ˈrefjuːs] *n* Müll *der*.

refuse collection [ˈrefjuːs-] *n* Müllabfuhr *die*.

refute [rɪˈfjuːt] *vt fml* widerlegen.

regain [rɪˈgeɪn] *vt* [recover] wiedergewinnen; **to regain consciousness** wieder zu Bewusstsein kommen.

regal [ˈriːgl] *adj* majestätisch.

regard [rɪˈgɑːd] ⬦ *n* - 1. (*U*) *fml* [respect, esteem]: **to hold sb/sthg in high/low regard** jn/etw hoch/gering achten - 2. [aspect]: **in this/that regard** in dieser/jener Hinsicht. ⬦ *vt*: **to regard o.s./sb/sthg as** sich/jn/etw halten für; **to be highly regarded** hoch geachtet sein. ➠ **regards** *npl* [in greetings] Grüße *Pl*; **send her my regards** grüße sie von mir. ➠ **as regards** *prep* in Bezug auf (+ A). ➠ **in regard to, with regard to** *prep* bezüglich (+ G).

regarding [rɪˈgɑːdɪŋ] *prep* in Bezug auf (+ A).

regardless [rɪˈgɑːdlɪs] *adv* trotzdem. ➠ **regardless of** *prep* ohne Rücksicht auf (+ A).

regime [reɪˈʒiːm] *n pej* Regime *das*.

regiment [ˈredʒɪmənt] *n* MIL Regiment *das*.

region ['riːdʒən] n - 1. [of country] Gebiet das, Region die - 2. [of body] Bereich der - 3. [range]: **in the region of** ungefähr.

regional ['riːdʒənl] adj regional.

register ['redʒɪstər] ◇ n [of school class] Klassenbuch das. ◇ vt - 1. [record officially, show, measure] registrieren - 2. [express] zeigen. ◇ vi - 1. [enrol]: **to register as/for sthg** sich als/für etw (an)melden - 2. [book in] sich eintragen - 3. inf [be properly understood]: **it didn't register (with her)** sie registrierte es gar nicht.

registered ['redʒɪstəd] adj - 1. [officially listed - company, charity] eingetragen - 2. [letter, parcel] eingeschrieben.

registered trademark n eingetragenes Warenzeichen.

registrar [ˌredʒɪ'strɑːr] n [keeper of records] Standesbeamte der, -tin die.

registration [ˌredʒɪ'streɪʃn] n - 1. [in records] Eintragung die - 2. [on course] Anmeldung die - 3. AUT = **registration number**.

registration number n AUT Kennzeichen das.

registry ['redʒɪstrɪ] n Registratur die.

registry office n Standesamt das.

regret [rɪ'gret] ◇ n Bedauern das; **I have no regrets about it** ich bedauere es nicht. ◇ vt bedauern; **to regret doing sthg** bedauern, etw getan zu haben.

regretfully [rɪ'gretfʊlɪ] adv mit Bedauern.

regrettable [rɪ'gretəbl] adj bedauerlich.

regroup [ˌriː'gruːp] vi sich neu gruppieren; [soldiers] sich neu formieren.

regular ['regjʊlər] ◇ adj - 1. [gen & GRAM] regelmäßig - 2. [usual] üblich - 3. US [in size] klein - 4. US [pleasant]: **he's a regular guy** er ist O.K. - 5. US [normal] normal. ◇ n [customer, client] Stammkunde der, -din die.

regularly ['regjʊləlɪ] adv regelmäßig.

regulate ['regjʊleɪt] vt - 1. [control] regulieren - 2. [adjust] regeln.

regulation [ˌregjʊ'leɪʃn] ◇ adj [standard] vorgeschrieben. ◇ n - 1. [rule] Vorschrift die - 2. (U) [control] Regulierung die.

rehabilitate [ˌriːə'bɪlɪteɪt] vt rehabilitieren.

rehearsal [rɪ'hɜːsl] n Probe die.

rehearse [rɪ'hɜːs] vt & vi proben.

reheat [ˌriː'hiːt] vt aufwärmen.

reign [reɪn] ◇ n liter & fig Herrschaft die. ◇ vi - 1. [rule]: **to reign (over)** herrschen (über (+ A)) - 2. [prevail]: **to reign over** sich ausbreiten über (+ D).

reimburse [ˌriːɪm'bɜːs] vt [person] entschädigen; [expenses] zurückerstatten; **to reimburse sb for sthg** jm etw zurückerstatten.

rein [reɪn] n fig: **to give sb (a) free rein** jm freie Hand lassen. ◆ **reins** npl [for horse] Zügel Pl.

reindeer ['reɪnˌdɪər] n (pl inv) Rentier das.

reinforce [ˌriːɪn'fɔːs] vt - 1. [ceiling, frame, cover]: **to reinforce sthg (with sthg)** etw (mit etw) verstärken - 2. [dislike, prejudice] bestärken - 3. [argument, claim] stützen.

reinforced concrete [ˌriːɪn'fɔːst-] n Stahlbeton der.

reinforcement [ˌriːɪn'fɔːsmənt] n [in construction] Verstärkung die. ◆ **reinforcements** npl MIL Verstärkung die.

reinstate [ˌriːɪn'steɪt] vt - 1. [employee] wieder einstellen - 2. [payment, policy] wieder aufnehmen.

reissue [riː'ɪʃuː] ◇ n Neuausgabe die; [of book] Neuauflage die. ◇ vt neu herausgeben; [book] neu auflegen.

reiterate [riː'ɪtəreɪt] vt fml wiederholen.

reject ◇ n ['riːdʒekt]: **rejects** [from factory] Ausschuss der. ◇ vt [rɪ'dʒekt] ablehnen.

rejection [rɪ'dʒekʃn] n - 1. [of offer, values, religion] Ablehnung die - 2. [for job] Absage die.

rejoice [rɪ'dʒɔɪs] vi: **to rejoice (at OR in sthg)** sich freuen (über etw (A)).

rejuvenate [rɪ'dʒuːvəneɪt] vt verjüngen.

rekindle [ˌriː'kɪndl] vt fig wieder entflammen.

relapse [rɪ'læps] n Rückfall der.

relate [rɪ'leɪt] ◇ vt - 1. [connect]: **to relate sthg to sthg** etw zu etw in Beziehung bringen OR setzen - 2. [tell] erzählen. ◇ vi - 1. [connect]: **to relate to sthg** mit etw zusammenhängen - 2. [concern]: **to relate to sb/sthg** jn/etw betreffen - 3. [empathize]: **to relate to sb/sthg** einen Bezug zu jm/etw haben. ◆ **relating to** prep im Zusammenhang mit.

related [rɪ'leɪtɪd] adj - 1. [in same family] verwandt; **to be related to sb** mit jm verwandt sein - 2. [connected] zusammenhängend; **to be related to sthg** mit etw zusammenhängen.

relation [rɪ'leɪʃn] n - 1. (U) [connection]: **relation to/between** Beziehung die zu/zwischen (+ D) - 2. [family member] Verwandte der, die. ◆ **relations** npl [relationship]: **relations (between/with)** Beziehungen Pl (zwischen (+ D)/mit).

relationship [rɪ'leɪʃnʃɪp] n Beziehung die.

relative ['relətɪv] ◇ adj - 1. [gen] relativ - 2. [respective] jeweilig. ◇ n Verwandte der, die. ◆ **relative to** prep fml - 1. [compared to] im Vergleich zu - 2. [connected with] sich beziehend auf (+ A).

relatively ['relətɪvlɪ] adv relativ.

relax [rɪ'læks] ◇ vt - 1. [mind, muscle, person] entspannen - 2. [grip, discipline, regulation] lockern. ◇ vi - 1. [person, body, muscle] sich entspannen - 2. [grip] sich lockern.

relaxation [ˌriːlæk'seɪʃn] n (U) [rest] Entspannung die.

relaxed [rɪ'lækst] adj entspannt.

relaxing [rɪ'læksɪŋ] adj entspannend.

relay <> n ['riːleɪ] - 1. SPORT: **relay (race)** Staffellauf *der*; **to work in relays** fig sich (bei der Arbeit) ablösen - 2. RADIO & TV Relais *das*. <> vt - 1. ['riːleɪ] RADIO & TV [broadcast] übertragen - 2. ['riːleɪ] [message, news]: **to relay sthg (to sb)** (jm) etw ausrichten.

release [rɪ'liːs] <> n - 1. (U) [from captivity] Freilassung *die* - 2. (U) [from pain, suffering] Erlösung *die* - 3. [statement] Verlautbarung *die* - 4. [of gas, fumes] Freisetzen *das* - 5. [of film, video, CD] Freigabe *die*; **the movie is on release from Friday** der Film ist von Freitag an im Kino (zu sehen) - 6. [video, CD] **new release** Neuerscheinung *die*; [film] neuer Film. <> vt - 1. [set free] freilassen; **to release sb from prison/captivity** jn aus dem Gefängnis/ der Gefangenschaft entlassen; **to release sb from sthg** [promise, contract] jn von etw befreien - 2. [make available] freisetzen - 3. [from control, grasp] loslassen - 4. [brake, lever, handle] lösen - 5. [let out, emit]: **to be released (from/into sthg)** freigesetzt werden (aus etw/in etw (A)) - 6. [film, video, CD] herausbringen; [statement, news story] veröffentlichen.

relegate ['relɪgeɪt] vt - 1. [lower status of]: **to relegate sthg/sb (to)** jn/etw verbannen (in (+ A)) - 2. UK SPORT: **to be relegated** absteigen.

relent [rɪ'lent] vi [person] nachlgeben.

relentless [rɪ'lentlɪs] adj erbarmungslos.

relevant ['reləvənt] adj - 1. [connected]: **relevant (to)** relevant (für) - 2. [important]: **relevant (to)** wichtig (für) - 3. [appropriate] entsprechend.

reliable [rɪ'laɪəbl] adj zuverlässig.

reliably [rɪ'laɪəblɪ] adv zuverlässig.

reliant [rɪ'laɪənt] adj: **reliant on** abhängig von (+ D).

relic ['relɪk] n - 1. [old object, custom - still in use] Überbleibsel *das*; [- no longer in use] Relikt *das* - 2. RELIG Reliquie *die*.

relief [rɪ'liːf] n - 1. [comfort] Erleichterung *die* - 2. (U) [for poor, refugees] Hilfe *die* - 3. US [social security] Fürsorge *die*.

relieve [rɪ'liːv] vt - 1. [ease, lessen] lindern; **to relieve sb of sthg** jn von etw befreien - 2. [take over from]: **to relieve sb of sthg** jn einer Sache (G) entheben - 3. [give help to] helfen (+ D).

religion [rɪ'lɪdʒn] n - 1. [belief in a god] Glaube *der* - 2. [system of belief] Religion *die*.

religious [rɪ'lɪdʒəs] adj religiös.

relinquish [rɪ'lɪŋkwɪʃ] vt aufgeben.

relish ['relɪʃ] <> n - 1. [enjoyment]: **with (great) relish** genüsslich - 2. [pickle] Soße *die*. <> vt [enjoy] genießen; **to relish the idea** OR **thought of doing sthg** sich darauf freuen, etw zu tun.

relocate [ˌriːləʊ'keɪt] <> vt verlegen. <> vi den Standort wechseln.

reluctance [rɪ'lʌktəns] n Widerwille *der*.

reluctant [rɪ'lʌktənt] adj widerwillig; **to be reluctant to do sthg** abgeneigt sein, etw zu tun.

reluctantly [rɪ'lʌktəntlɪ] adv widerwillig.

rely [rɪ'laɪ] ► **rely on** vt insep - 1. [count on] sich verlassen auf (+ A) - 2. [be dependent on]: **to rely on sb/sthg for sthg** wegen etw auf jn/ etw angewiesen sein.

remain [rɪ'meɪn] <> vt: **that remains to be done** das bleibt (noch) zu tun. <> vi bleiben. ► **remains** npl - 1. [of meal, ancient civilization, building] Überreste Pl - 2. [corpse] menschliche Überreste Pl.

remainder [rɪ'meɪndər] n Rest *der*.

remaining [rɪ'meɪnɪŋ] adj verbleibend.

remand [rɪ'mɑːnd] <> n LAW: **on remand** in Untersuchungshaft. <> vt (phrase): **to be remanded in custody** in Untersuchungshaft bleiben.

remark [rɪ'mɑːk] <> n Bemerkung *die*. <> vt: **to remark that...** bemerken, dass...

remarkable [rɪ'mɑːkəbl] adj bemerkenswert.

remarry [ˌriː'mærɪ] vi wieder heiraten.

remedial [rɪ'miːdjəl] adj - 1. SCH Förder- - 2. [corrective - action] abhelfend.

remedy ['remədɪ] <> n: **remedy (for sthg)** [for ill health] Heilmittel *das* (für OR gegen etw); [solution] Lösung *die* (für etw). <> vt abhelfen (+ D).

remember [rɪ'membər] <> vt - 1. [recollect] sich erinnern an (+ A); **to remember doing sthg** sich daran erinnern, etw getan zu haben - 2. [not forget] denken an (+ A); **to remember to do sthg** daran denken, etw zu tun. <> vi sich erinnern.

remembrance [rɪ'membrəns] n fml: **in remembrance of** zur Erinnerung an (+ A).

Remembrance Day n nationaler britischer Trauertag zum Gedenken an die in den beiden Weltkriegen gefallenen Soldaten. Er wird an dem 11. November nächstliegenden Sonntag begangen.

remind [rɪ'maɪnd] vt - 1. [tell]: **to remind sb about sthg** jn an etw (A) erinnern; **to remind sb to do sthg** jn daran erinnern, etw zu tun - 2. [be reminiscent of]: **to remind sb of sb/sthg** jn an jn/etw erinnern.

reminder [rɪ'maɪndər] n - 1. [to jog memory]: **to give sb a reminder to do sthg** jn daran erinnern, etw zu tun - 2. [for bill, membership, licence] Mahnung *die*.

reminisce [ˌremɪ'nɪs] vi: **to reminisce (about sthg)** in Erinnerungen (an etw (A)) schwelgen.

reminiscent [ˌremɪ'nɪsnt] adj: **to be reminiscent of sb/sthg** an jn/etw erinnern.

remiss [rɪ'mɪs] adj nachlässig.

remit <> n ['riːmɪt] UK Aufgabenbereich *der*. <> vt [rɪ'mɪt] [send] überweisen.

remittance [rɪ'mɪtns] n Überweisung *die*.

remnant ['remnənt] n Rest *der*.

remorse [rɪ'mɔ:s] n Reue *die*.

remorseful [rɪ'mɔːsfʊl] adj reuig.

remorseless [rɪ'mɔːslɪs] adj - 1. [pitiless] unbarmherzig - 2. [unstoppable] unaufhaltsam.

remote [rɪ'məʊt] adj - 1. [distant - place] abgelegen; [- time] entfernt - 2. [aloof] unnahbar - 3. [unconnected, irrelevant]: **remote from** entfernt von - 4. [slight - resemblance] entfernt; [- chance, possibility] gering.

remote control n - 1. (U) [system] Fernsteuerung *die* - 2. [machine, device] Fernbedienung *die*.

remotely [rɪ'məʊtlɪ] adv - 1. [slightly]: **not remotely** nicht im Entferntesten, nicht im Geringsten - 2. [distantly] entfernt.

removable [rɪ'muːvəbl] adj [detachable] abnehmbar.

removal [rɪ'muːvl] n - 1. *UK* [change of house] Umzug *der* - 2. [act of removing] Entfernen *das*.

removal van n *UK* Möbelwagen *der*.

remove [rɪ'muːv] vt - 1. [take away, clean]: **to remove sthg (from)** etw entfernen (aus/von) - 2. [clothes, hat] ablegen - 3. [from a job]: **to remove sb (from)** jn entfernen (von) - 4. [problem] beseitigen; [suspicion] zerstreuen.

remuneration [rɪ,mjuːnə'reɪʃn] n *fml* - 1. [pay] Bezahlung *die* - 2. [amount of money] Vergütung *die*.

render ['rendər] vt - 1. [make] machen - 2. [give - help, service] leisten.

rendezvous ['rɒndɪvuː] (pl inv) n - 1. [meeting] Rendezvous *das* - 2. [place] Treffpunkt *der*.

renegade ['renɪgeɪd] n Abtrünnige *der*, *die*.

renew [rɪ'njuː] vt - 1. [repeat, restart] wieder aufnehmen - 2. [extend validity of] verlängern - 3. [increase]: **with renewed enthusiasm/interest** mit neuem Enthusiasmus/Interesse.

renewable [rɪ'njuːəbl] adj - 1. [resources] erneuerbar - 2. [contract, licence, membership] verlängerbar.

renewal [rɪ'njuːəl] n (U) [of contract, licence, membership] Verlängerung *die*.

renounce [rɪ'naʊns] vt - 1. [reject] abschwören (+ D) - 2. *fml* [relinquish] verzichten auf (+ A).

renovate ['renəveɪt] vt renovieren.

renown [rɪ'naʊn] n Ruf *der*.

renowned [rɪ'naʊnd] adj: **renowned (for sthg)** berühmt (für etw).

rent [rent] <> n Miete *die*. <> vt - 1. [subj: tenant, hirer] mieten - 2. [subj: owner] vermieten.

rental ['rentl] <> adj Miet-. <> n [money] Leihgebühr *die*; [for house] Miete *die*.

rental car n Mietwagen *der*.

renunciation [rɪ,nʌnsɪ'eɪʃn] n (U) - 1. [relinquishing]: **renunciation of sthg** Verzicht *der* auf etw (A) - 2. [rejection]: **renunciation of sthg** Abschwörung *die* von etw.

reorganize, -ise [,riː'ɔːgənaɪz] vt neu organisieren.

rep [rep] n abbr of **representative**, **repertory company**.

repaid [,riː'peɪd] pt & pp ▷ **repay**.

repair [rɪ'peər] <> n Reparatur *die*; **in good/bad repair** in gutem/schlechtem Zustand. <> vt - 1. [fix, mend] reparieren; [puncture, crack] ausļbessern - 2. [make amends for] wieder gutļmachen.

repair kit n Flickzeug *das*.

repartee [,repɑː'tiː] n (U) Schlagabtausch *der*.

repatriate [,riː'pætrɪeɪt] vt repatriieren.

repay [,riː'peɪ] (pt & pp repaid) vt - 1. [money] zurückļzahlen; **to repay sb sthg, to repay sthg to sb** jm etw zurückļzahlen - 2. [kindness] vergelten.

repayment [riː'peɪmənt] n Rückzahlung *die*.

repeal [rɪ'piːl] vt aufļheben.

repeat [rɪ'piːt] <> vt wiederholen. <> n [broadcast] Wiederholung *die*.

repeatedly [rɪ'piːtɪdlɪ] adv wiederholt.

repel [rɪ'pel] vt - 1. [disgust] ablstoßen - 2. [drive away] abļwehren.

repellent [rɪ'pelənt] <> adj abstoßend. <> n: **(insect) repellent** Insektenabwehrmittel *das*.

repent [rɪ'pent] <> vt bereuen. <> vi: **to repent of sthg** über etw (A) Reue empfinden.

repentance [rɪ'pentəns] n Reue *die*.

repercussions [,riːpə'kʌʃnz] npl Auswirkungen *Pl*.

repertoire ['repətwɑːr] n Repertoire *das*.

repertory ['repətrɪ] n [repertoire] Repertoire *das*.

repetition [,repɪ'tɪʃn] n Wiederholung *die*.

repetitious [,repɪ'tɪʃəs], **repetitive** [rɪ'petɪtɪv] adj monoton.

replace [rɪ'pleɪs] vt - 1. [gen] ersetzen; **to replace sb/sthg with sb/sthg** jn/etw durch jn/etw ersetzen - 2. [put back - upright] zurückļstellen; [- lying flat] zurückļlegen.

replacement [rɪ'pleɪsmənt] n - 1. [act of replacing] Ersetzen *das* - 2. [new person, object]: **replacement (for sthg)** Ersatz *der* (für etw); **replacement (for sb)** [in job - temporary] Vertretung *die* (von jm); [- permanent] Nachfolger *der*, -in *die* (von jm).

replay <> n ['riːpleɪ] - 1. [recording]: **(action) replay** Wiederholung *die* - 2. [game] Wiederholungsspiel *das*. <> vt [,riː'pleɪ] - 1. [match, game] wiederholen - 2. [film, tape] nochmals abļspielen.

replenish [rɪ'plenɪʃ] *vt fml*: to replenish sthg **(with sthg)** etw (mit etw) wieder auflfüllen.

replica ['replɪkə] *n* Kopie *die*.

reply [rɪ'plaɪ] ◇ *n*: **in reply (to sthg)** Antwort *die* (auf etw *(A)*). ◇ *vt* antworten. ◇ *vi* antworten; **to reply to sb/sthg** jm/auf etw *(A)* antworten.

reply coupon *n* Antwortschein *der*.

report [rɪ'pɔːt] ◇ *n* - **1.** [description, account] Bericht *der* - **2.** PRESS Reportage *die* - **3.** UK SCH Zeugnis *das*. ◇ *vt* - **1.** [news, crime] melden - **2.** [make known]: **to report that...** berichten, dass...; **to report sthg (to sb)** (jm) etw berichten - **3.** [complain about]: **to report sb (to sb)** jn (bei jm) anzeigen; **to report sb for sthg** jn wegen etw anlzeigen. ◇ *vi* - **1.** [give account]: **to report (on sthg)** (über etw *(A)*) berichten - **2.** PRESS: **this is John Smith, reporting from Moscow** John Smith (mit einem Bericht) aus Moskau; **to report on sthg** über etw berichten - **3.** [present o.s.]: **to report to...** sich melden bei...; **to report for duty** sich zum Dienst melden.

report card *n* US SCH Zeugnis *das*.

reportedly [rɪ'pɔːtɪdlɪ] *adv* angeblich.

reporter [rɪ'pɔːtər] *n* [in TV, radio, press] Reporter *der*, -in *die*, Berichterstatter *der*, -in *die*.

repossess [ˌriːpə'zes] *vt* wieder in Besitz nehmen.

reprehensible [ˌreprɪ'hensəbl] *adj fml* verwerflich.

represent [ˌreprɪ'zent] *vt* - **1.** [act for] vertreten - **2.** [constitute, symbolize] darstellen.

representation [ˌreprɪzen'teɪʃn] *n* [depiction] Darstellung *die*. ◆ **representations** *npl fml*: **to make representations to sb** sich mit einem Anliegen an jn wenden.

representative [ˌreprɪ'zentətɪv] ◇ *adj* - **1.** [acting for main group] stellvertretend - **2.** [typical]: **representative (of)** repräsentativ (für). ◇ *n* - **1.** [of company, organization, group] Vertreter *der*, -in *die* - **2.** US POL Abgeordnete *der*, *die*.

repress [rɪ'pres] *vt* unterdrücken.

repression [rɪ'preʃn] *n* (U) Unterdrückung *die*.

reprieve [rɪ'priːv] ◇ *n* - **1.** [of death sentence] Begnadigung *die* - **2.** [respite] Gnadenfrist *die*. ◇ *vt* begnadigen.

reprimand ['reprɪmɑːnd] ◇ *n* Tadel *der*. ◇ *vt* tadeln.

reprisal [rɪ'praɪzl] *n* - **1.** [counterblow] Vergeltungsmaßnahme *die* - **2.** [revenge]: **in reprisal (for)** als Vergeltung (für).

reproach [rɪ'prəʊtʃ] ◇ *n* Vorwurf *der*; **to be beyond reproach** über jeden Vorwurf erhaben sein. ◇ *vt*: **to reproach sb (for OR with sthg)** jm (wegen etw) Vorwürfe machen.

reproduce [ˌriːprə'djuːs] ◇ *vt* [copy] reproduzieren. ◇ *vi* BIOL sich fortlpflanzen.

reproduction [ˌriːprə'dʌkʃn] *n* - **1.** [replica] Reproduktion *die*; **reproduction furniture** Stilmöbel *Pl* - **2.** (U) [copying, simulation] Reproduktion *die*; **sound reproduction** Tonwiedergabe *die* - **3.** BIOL Fortpflanzung *die*.

reprove [rɪ'pruːv] *vt*: **to reprove sb (for sthg)** jn (wegen etw) tadeln.

reptile ['reptaɪl] *n* Reptil *das*.

republic [rɪ'pʌblɪk] *n* Republik *die*.

republican [rɪ'pʌblɪkən] ◇ *adj* republikanisch. ◇ *n* Republikaner *der*, -in *die*. ◆ **Republican** ◇ *adj* - **1.** [in USA] republikanisch; **the Republican Party** die Republikanische Partei - **2.** [in Northern Ireland] *bezeichnet einen Befürworter einer vereinten unabhängigen Republik Irland bzw. dessen Ideen*. ◇ *n* - **1.** [in USA] Republikaner *der*, -in *die* - **2.** [in Northern Ireland] *Befürworter einer vereinten unabhängigen Republik Irland*.

repulse [rɪ'pʌls] *vt* - **1.** [refuse] zurücklweisen; [person] verstoßen - **2.** MIL [drive back] ablwehren.

repulsive [rɪ'pʌlsɪv] *adj* abstoßend.

reputable ['repjʊtəbl] *adj* seriös.

reputation [ˌrepjʊ'teɪʃn] *n* Ruf *der*.

repute [rɪ'pjuːt] *n fml* [reputation]: **of good/ill repute** von gutem/schlechtem Ruf.

reputed [rɪ'pjuːtɪd] *adj*: **he is a reputed expert/millionaire** er soll ein Fachmann/Millionär sein; **to be reputed to be sthg** als etw gelten.

reputedly [rɪ'pjuːtɪdlɪ] *adv*: **he is reputedly the best surgeon** er gilt als der beste Chirurg.

request [rɪ'kwest] ◇ *n*: **request (for sthg)** Bitte *die* (um etw); **on request** auf Wunsch. ◇ *vt* bitten um; **to request sb to do sthg** jn bitten, etw zu tun.

require [rɪ'kwaɪər] *vt* erfordern; **to be required to do sthg** aufgefordert werden, etw zu tun.

requirement [rɪ'kwaɪəmənt] *n* - **1.** [condition] Erfordernis *das* - **2.** [need] Bedarf *der*.

reran [ˌriː'ræn] *pt* ▷ **rerun**.

rerun (*pt* **reran**, *pp* **rerun**) ◇ *n* ['riːrʌn] Wiederholung *die*. ◇ *vt* [ˌriː'rʌn] [gen] wiederholen.

resat [ˌriː'sæt] *pt* & *pp* ▷ **resit**.

rescind [rɪ'sɪnd] *vt* LAW annulieren.

rescue ['reskjuː] ◇ *n* Rettung *die*. ◇ *vt* retten; **to rescue sb/sthg from sb/sthg** jn/etw vor jm/aus etw retten.

rescuer ['reskjʊər] *n* Retter *der*, -in *die*.

research [rɪ'sɜːtʃ] ◇ *n* (U): **research (on OR into sthg)** Forschung *die* (über etw *(A)*); **research and development** Forschung und Entwicklung *die*. ◇ *vt* erforschen; [article, book] recherchieren.

researcher [rɪ'sɜːtʃər] n Forscher der, -in die.

resemblance [rɪ'zembləns] n: resemblance (to/between) Ähnlichkeit die (mit/zwischen (+ D)).

resemble [rɪ'zembl] vt ähneln.

resent [rɪ'zent] vt sich ärgern über (+ A); I resent that! das ärgert mich!

resentful [rɪ'zentfʊl] adj verärgert.

resentment [rɪ'zentmənt] n Groll der.

reservation [ˌrezə'veɪʃn] n - 1. [booking] Reservierung die - 2. [doubt]: without reservation ohne Vorbehalt - 3. US [for Native Americans] Reservat das. ◆ reservations npl [doubts] Vorbehalte Pl.

reserve [rɪ'zɜːv] <> n - 1. [supply] Reserve die; in reserve in Reserve - 2. SPORT [substitute] Reservespieler der, -in die - 3. [sanctuary] Reservat das - 4. (U) [restraint, shyness] Reserve die. <> vt - 1. [keep for particular purpose]: to reserve sthg for sb/sthg etw für jn/etw reservieren - 2. [book] reservieren - 3. [retain]: to reserve the right to do sthg sich das Recht vorbehalten, etw zu tun.

reserved [rɪ'zɜːvd] adj reserviert.

reservoir ['rezəvwɑːr] n [lake] Reservoir das.

reset [ˌriː'set] (pt & pp inv) vt - 1. [clock] neu stellen; [meter] zurückstellen - 2. COMPUT rücksetzen.

reshape [ˌriː'ʃeɪp] vt [policy, thinking] umformen.

reshuffle [ˌriː'ʃʌfl] <> n POL Umbildung die. <> vt POL umbilden.

reside [rɪ'zaɪd] vi fml - 1. [live] seinen Wohnsitz haben - 2. [be located, found]: to reside in sthg in etw (D) liegen.

residence ['rezɪdəns] n [house] Wohnsitz der.

residence permit n Aufenthaltserlaubnis die.

resident ['rezɪdənt] <> adj - 1. [settled, living] wohnhaft - 2. [on-site, live-in] Haus-. <> n [of town, street] Bewohner der, -in die; [in hotel] Gast der.

residential [ˌrezɪ'denʃl] adj: residential course Kurs, bei dem die Teilnehmer auf dem Schulgelände untergebracht werden; residential care Pflege die im Haus.

residential area n Wohngebiet das.

residue ['rezɪdjuː] n CHEM Rückstand der.

resign [rɪ'zaɪn] <> vt - 1. [give up - job] kündigen; [- post] zurücktreten von - 2. [accept calmly]: to resign o.s. to sthg sich mit etw abfinden. <> vi [from job] kündigen; [from post] zurücktreten.

resignation [ˌrezɪg'neɪʃn] n - 1. [from job] Kündigung die; [from post] Rücktritt der - 2. [calm acceptance] Resignation die.

resigned [rɪ'zaɪnd] adj: to be resigned to sthg sich mit etw abgefunden haben.

resilient [rɪ'zɪliənt] adj - 1. [material] elastisch - 2. [person] unverwüstlich.

resist [rɪ'zɪst] vt Widerstand leisten gegen; [temptation, offer] widerstehen (+ D).

resistance [rɪ'zɪstəns] n (U): resistance (to sthg) Widerstand der (gegen etw).

resit (pt & pp resat) UK <> n ['riːsɪt] Wiederholungsprüfung die. <> vt [ˌriː'sɪt] wiederholen.

resolute ['rezəluːt] adj energisch.

resolution [ˌrezə'luːʃn] n - 1. [motion, decision] Resolution die - 2. [vow, promise] Vorsatz der - 3. [determination] Entschlossenheit die - 4. (U) [solution - of problem] Lösung die; [- of dispute, argument] Beilegung die.

resolve [rɪ'zɒlv] <> n [determination] Entschlossenheit die. <> vt - 1. [vow, promise]: to resolve that... beschließen, dass...; to resolve to do sthg sich entschließen, etw zu tun - 2. [solve - problem] lösen; [- dispute, argument] beilegen.

resort [rɪ'zɔːt] n - 1. [for holidays] Urlaubsort der - 2. [solution]: as a last resort als letzte Möglichkeit; in the last resort im schlimmsten Fall. ◆ resort to vt insep [lying, begging] sich verlegen auf (+ A); [violence] anwenden.

resound [rɪ'zaʊnd] vi - 1. [noise] schallen - 2. [place]: to resound with widerhallen von.

resounding [rɪ'zaʊndɪŋ] adj - 1. [noise, voice] schallend - 2. [success, victory] gewaltig.

resource [rɪ'zɔːs] n [asset] Ressourcen Pl; natural resources Naturschätze Pl.

resourceful [rɪ'zɔːsfʊl] adj einfallsreich.

respect [rɪ'spekt] <> n - 1. (U) [admiration]: respect (for) Respekt der (vor); with respect, bei allem Respekt, - 2. (U) [observance]: respect for sthg Achtung die vor etw - 3. [aspect] Hinsicht die; in this/that respect in dieser/jener Hinsicht. <> vt - 1. [admire] anerkennen; to respect sb for sthg jn für etw respektieren - 2. [observe] achten. ◆ respects npl Grüße Pl; give my respects to your wife grüßen Sie Ihre Frau von mir. ◆ with respect to prep in Bezug auf (+ A).

respectable [rɪ'spektəbl] adj - 1. [morally correct] ehrbar - 2. [adequate, quite good] ansehnlich.

respectful [rɪ'spektfʊl] adj respektvoll.

respective [rɪ'spektɪv] adj jeweilig.

respectively [rɪ'spektɪvlɪ] adv beziehungsweise; Jill and John are four and six years old respectively Jill and John sind vier beziehungsweise sechs Jahre alt.

respite ['respaɪt] n - 1. [pause] Atempause die; without respite ohne Unterbrechung - 2. [delay] Aufschub der.

resplendent [rɪˈsplendənt] *adj liter* pracht-voll.

respond [rɪˈspɒnd] *vi*: to respond (to sthg) antworten (auf etw (A)).

response [rɪˈspɒns] *n* Antwort *die*.

responsibility [rɪˌspɒnsəˈbɪlətɪ] *n* - 1. [charge, blame]: responsibility (for sthg) Verantwortung *die* (für etw) - 2. [duty - of job, position] Aufgabe *die*; *phrase*: responsibility (to sb) Verantwortung *die* (jm gegenüber).

responsible [rɪˈspɒnsəbl] *adj* - 1. [in charge, to blame]: responsible (for sthg) verantwort-lich (für etw) - 2. [answerable]: responsible to sb jm (gegenüber) verantwortlich - 3. [sens-ible] vernünftig - 4. [position, task] verantwor-tungsvoll.

responsibly [rɪˈspɒnsəblɪ] *adv* verantwor-tungsbewusst.

responsive [rɪˈspɒnsɪv] *adj*: to be respons-ive [audience] mitgehen; [class] mitlmachen.

rest [rest] <> *n* - 1. [remainder]: the rest der Rest; the rest of the cake/customers der Rest des Kuchens/der Kunden - 2. [relaxation] Ru-he *die* - 3. [break] Pause *die* - 4. [support] Stüt-ze *die*. <> *vt* - 1. [relax] auslruhen - 2. [sup-port, lean]: to rest sthg on/against sthg etw auf (+ A)/gegen etw lehnen - 3. *phr*: rest assured (that)... seien Sie versichert, dass... <> *vi* - 1. [relax, be still] sich auslruhen - 2. [depend]: to rest (up)on sb/sthg von jm/etw ablhängen - 3. [be supported]: to rest on sthg auf etw (D) ruhen; to rest against sthg an etw (D) lehnen.

restaurant [ˈrestərɒnt] *n* Restaurant *das*.

restful [ˈrestful] *adj* ruhig.

rest home *n* Pflegeheim *das*.

restive [ˈrestɪv] *adj* unruhig.

restless [ˈrestlɪs] *adj* - 1. [bored, fidgety] rast-los - 2. [sleepless] schlaflos.

restoration [ˌrestəˈreɪʃn] *n* (U) - 1. [reestab-lishment] Wiederherstellung *die* - 2. [renova-tion] Restaurierung *die*.

restore [rɪˈstɔːr] *vt* - 1. [reestablish] wieder herlstellen; the palace has been restored to its former glory dem Palast ist seine alte Pracht wiedergegeben worden - 2. [renovate] restau-rieren - 3. [give back] zurücklgeben.

restrain [rɪˈstreɪn] *vt* - 1. [hold back] zurückl-halten; to restrain o.s. from doing sthg sich zurücklhalten (davon), etw zu tun - 2. [dog, attacker] bändigen - 3. [repress] unterdrücken.

restrained [rɪˈstreɪnd] *adj* - 1. [person] be-herrscht - 2. [tone] verhalten.

restraint [rɪˈstreɪnt] *n* - 1. [rule, check] Be-schränkung *die* - 2. [self-control] Selbstbeherr-schung *die*.

restrict [rɪˈstrɪkt] *vt* [limit] einlschränken; to restrict sb/sthg to sb/sthg jn/etw auf jn/etw beschränken.

restriction [rɪˈstrɪkʃn] *n* [limitation, regula-tion] Einschränkung *die*.

restrictive [rɪˈstrɪktɪv] *adj* einschränkend.

rest room *n US* Toilette *die*.

result [rɪˈzʌlt] <> *n* - 1. [gen] Ergebnis *das* - 2. [consequence] Folge *die*; as a result folglich; as a result of sthg als Folge von etw. <> *vi*: to result in sthg zu etw führen; to result from sthg aus etw folgen.

resume [rɪˈzjuːm] <> *vt* [activity] wieder auflnehmen. <> *vi* wieder beginnen.

résumé [ˈrezjuːmeɪ] *n* - 1. [summary] Resü-mee *das*, Zusammenfassung *die* - 2. *US* [of ca-reer, qualifications] Lebenslauf *der*.

resumption [rɪˈzʌmpʃn] *n* Wiederaufnah-me *die*.

resurgence [rɪˈsɜːdʒəns] *n* Wiederaufle-ben *das*.

resurrection [ˌrezəˈrekʃn] *n* [of policy, festiv-al, legal case] Wiederbelebung *die*.

resuscitation [rɪˌsʌsɪˈteɪʃn] *n* Wiederbele-bung *die*.

retail [ˈriːteɪl] <> *n* Einzelhandel *der*. <> *adv* im Einzelhandel. <> *vi*: it retails at £10 es kostet im Einzelhandel 10 Pfund.

retailer [ˈriːteɪlər] *n* Einzelhändler *der*, -in *die*.

retail price *n* Einzelhandelspreis *der*.

retain [rɪˈteɪn] *vt* - 1. [pride, power, independ-ence] behalten - 2. [heat] speichern.

retainer [rɪˈteɪnər] *n* [fee] Vorschuss *der*.

retaliate [rɪˈtælɪeɪt] *vi* zurücklschlagen.

retaliation [rɪˌtælɪˈeɪʃn] *n* Vergeltung *die*.

retarded [rɪˈtɑːdɪd] *adj offens* [child] zurück-geblieben.

retch [retʃ] *vi* würgen.

reticent [ˈretɪsənt] *adj* zurückhaltend.

retina [ˈretɪnə] (*pl* -nas *OR* -nae [-niː]) *n* Netz-haut *die*, Retina *die*.

retinue [ˈretɪnjuː] *n* Gefolge *das*.

retire [rɪˈtaɪər] *vi* - 1. [from work] in den Ru-hestand treten - 2. *fml* [to another place, to bed] sich zurücklziehen.

retired [rɪˈtaɪəd] *adj* pensioniert; to be re-tired im Ruhestand sein.

retirement [rɪˈtaɪəmənt] *n* (U) - 1. [act of re-tiring] Pensionierung *die* - 2. [life after work] Ru-hestand *der*.

retiring [rɪˈtaɪərɪŋ] *adj* [shy] zurückhaltend.

retort [rɪˈtɔːt] <> *n* [sharp reply] (scharfe) Er-widerung. <> *vt*: to retort that... erwidern, dass...

retrace [rɪˈtreɪs] *vt*: to retrace one's steps denselben Weg zurücklgehen.

retract [rɪˈtrækt] <> *vt* - 1. [take back] zurücklnehmen - 2. [draw in] einlziehen. <> *vi* [be drawn in] eingezogen werden.

retrain [ˌriːˈtreɪn] *vt* umlschulen.

retreat [rɪˈtriːt] <> *n* - 1. MIL [withdrawal]: re-treat (from) Rückzug *der* (aus) - 2. [refuge] Zu-flucht *die*. <> *vi* - 1. [withdraw]: to retreat (to) sich zurück|ziehen (in (+ A)); **she retreated hastily** sie wich hastig zurück **- 2.** MIL: **to retreat (from)** den Rückzug an|treten (aus) **- 3.** [from principle, policy, lifestyle]: **to retreat from sthg** etw auf|geben.

retribution [,retrɪ'bjuːʃn] n Vergeltung die.

retrieval [rɪ'triːvl] n COMPUT Wiederauffinden das.

retrieve [rɪ'triːv] vt **- 1.** [get back] zurück|bekommen **- 2.** COMPUT wiederauffinden **- 3.** [situation] retten.

retriever [rɪ'triːvər] n [dog] Apportierhund der; [of specific breed] Retriever der.

retrospect ['retrəspekt] n: **in retrospect** im Nachhinein.

retrospective [,retrə'spektɪv] adj **- 1.** [mood] (zu)rückblickend **- 2.** [law, pay rise] rückwirkend.

return [rɪ'tɜːn] ◇ n **- 1.** [arrival back]: **return (to)** Rückkehr die (nach); **return to sthg** fig Rückkehr die zu etw **- 2.** [giving back] Rückgabe die **- 3.** TENNIS Return der **- 4.** UK [ticket] Rückfahrkarte die; [for plane] Rückflugticket das **- 5.** [profit] Ertrag der **- 6.** COMPUT [on keyboard] Eingabetaste die. ◇ vt **- 1.** [give back] zurück|geben; [loan] zurück|zahlen **- 2.** [visit, compliment, love] erwidern **- 3.** [replace] zurück|stellen **- 4.** LAW [verdict] fällen **- 5.** POL [candidate] wählen. ◇ vi [come back] zurück|kommen; [go back] zurück|gehen; [pain] wieder|kehren; **to return from Germany** aus Deutschland zurück|kehren or zurück|kommen; **to return to London** nach London zurück|kehren or zurück|kommen; **to return to work** wieder arbeiten; **to return to a subject** auf ein Thema zurück|kommen. ◆ **returns** npl **- 1.** COMM Gewinn der **- 2.** [on birthday]: **many happy returns (of the day)!** herzlichen Glückwunsch (zum Geburtstag)! ◆ **in return** adv dafür. ◆ **in return for** prep für.

return ticket n UK Rückfahrkarte die.

reunification [,riːjuːnɪfɪ'keɪʃn] n Wiedervereinigung die.

reunion [,riː'juːnjən] n **- 1.** [party] Treffen das **- 2.** (U) [meeting again] Wiedersehen das.

reunite [,riːjuː'naɪt] vt wieder vereinigen; **to be reunited with sb/sthg** mit jm/etw wieder vereint sein.

rev [rev] inf ◇ n (abbr of **revolution**) Umdrehung die. ◇ vt: **to rev the engine (up)** den Motor hoch drehen lassen.

revamp [,riː'væmp] vt inf **- 1.** [reorganize] auf Vordermann bringen **- 2.** [redecorate] auf|möbeln.

reveal [rɪ'viːl] vt enthüllen.

revealing [rɪ'viːlɪŋ] adj **- 1.** [dress, blouse] offenherzig **- 2.** [comment] aufschlussreich.

revel ['revl] (UK) (US) vi: **to revel in sthg** [freedom, success] etw in vollen Zügen genießen; [gossip] in etw (D) schwelgen.

revelation [,revə'leɪʃn] n **- 1.** [surprising fact] Enthüllung die **- 2.** [surprising experience] Offenbarung die; **to be a revelation to sb** jm die Augen öffnen.

revenge [rɪ'vendʒ] ◇ n Rache die; [in game] Revanche die; **to take revenge (on sb)** sich (an jm) rächen. ◇ vt rächen; **to revenge o.s. on sb/sthg** sich an jm/etw rächen.

revenue ['revənjuː] n [income] Einnahmen Pl; [of State] Staatseinnahmen Pl.

reverberate [rɪ'vɜːbəreɪt] vi **- 1.** [re-echo] widerhallen; [shock wave] sich fortsetzen **- 2.** [have repercussions] Auswirkungen haben.

reverberations [rɪ,vɜːbə'reɪʃnz] npl **- 1.** [echoes] Widerhall der **- 2.** [repercussions] Auswirkungen Pl.

revere [rɪ'vɪər] vt fml verehren.

Reverend ['revərənd] n: **(the) Reverend Peter James** Pfarrer Peter James.

reversal [rɪ'vɜːsl] n **- 1.** [of order, position, trend] Umkehrung die; [of decision] Umstoßung die; [of roles] Vertauschung die **- 2.** [piece of ill luck] Rückschlag der.

reverse [rɪ'vɜːs] ◇ adj umgekehrt; [side] Rück-. ◇ n **- 1.** AUT: **reverse (gear)** Rückwärtsgang der **- 2.** [opposite]: **the reverse** das Gegenteil **- 3.** [back]: **the reverse** die Rückseite; [of coin] die Kehrseite. ◇ vt **- 1.** AUT rückwärts fahren mit **- 2.** [order, position, trend] um|kehren; [decision] um|stoßen; [roles] tauschen **- 3.** [turn over] um|drehen **- 4.** UK TELEC: **to reverse the charges** ein R-Gespräch führen. ◇ vi AUT rückwärts fahren.

reverse-charge call n UK R-Gespräch das.

reversing light [rɪ'vɜːsɪŋ-] n UK Rückfahrscheinwerfer der.

revert [rɪ'vɜːt] vi: **to revert to sthg** zu etw zurück|kehren; **to revert to type** fig wieder in die alten Gewohnheiten verfallen.

review [rɪ'vjuː] ◇ n **- 1.** [examination] Überprüfung die **- 2.** [critique] Besprechung die, Rezension die. ◇ vt **- 1.** [reassess] überprüfen **- 2.** [write critique of] besprechen **- 3.** [troops] inspizieren, mustern **- 4.** US [study] wiederholen.

reviewer [rɪ'vjuːər] n Rezensent der, -in die.

revile [rɪ'vaɪl] vt liter schmähen.

revise [rɪ'vaɪz] ◇ vt **- 1.** [alter] revidieren **- 2.** [rewrite] überarbeiten **- 3.** UK [study] wiederholen. ◇ vi UK: **to revise (for sthg)** (für etw) den Stoff wiederholen.

revision [rɪ'vɪʒn] n **- 1.** [alteration] Revision die **- 2.** UK [study]: **to do some revision** den Stoff wiederholen.

revitalize, -ise [,riː'vaɪtəlaɪz] vt wieder beleben.

revival [rɪ'vaɪvl] *n* [of economy, interest] Wiederbelebung *die*.

revive [rɪ'vaɪv] ◇ *vt* wieder beleben; [tradition, memories] wieder aufleben lassen; [play] wieder auflführen. ◇ *vi* - **1.** [regain consciousness] wieder zu sich kommen - **2.** [plant, economy, interest] wieder aufleben, wieder erblühen.

revolt [rɪ'vəolt] ◇ *n* Aufstand *der*, Revolte *die*. ◇ *vt* anlwidern. ◇ *vi*: **to revolt (against)** revoltieren (gegen).

revolting [rɪ'vəoltɪŋ] *adj* widerlich.

revolution [,revə'luːʃn] *n* - **1.** fig & POL Revolution *die* - **2.** TECH [circular movement] Umdrehung *die*.

revolutionary [,revə'luːʃnərɪ] ◇ *adj* liter & fig revolutionär. ◇ *n* POL Revolutionär *der*, -in *die*.

revolve [rɪ'vɒlv] *vi* sich drehen; **to revolve (a)round** liter & fig sich drehen um.

revolver [rɪ'vɒlvə'] *n* Revolver *der*.

revolving [rɪ'vɒlvɪŋ] *adj* Dreh-.

revolving door *n* Drehtür *die*.

revue [rɪ'vjuː] *n* Revue *die*.

revulsion [rɪ'vʌlʃn] *n* Ekel *der*.

reward [rɪ'wɔːd] ◇ *n* Belohnung *die*. ◇ *vt* belohnen; **to reward sb for/with sthg** jn für/mit etw belohnen.

rewarding [rɪ'wɔːdɪŋ] *adj* lohnend; **it is a rewarding book** es lohnt sich, das Buch zu lesen.

rewind [,riː'waɪnd] (*pt & pp* rewound) *vt* [tape] zurücklspulen.

rewire [,riː'waɪə'] *vt* [house] neu verkabeln; [plug] neu anlschließen.

reword [,riː'wɜːd] *vt* neu formulieren.

rewound [,riː'waʊnd] *pt & pp* ▷ **rewind**.

rewrite [,riː'raɪt] (*pt* rewrote [,riː'rəʊt], *pp* rewritten [,riː'rɪtn]) *vt* neu schreiben.

Reykjavik ['rekjəvɪk] *n* Reykjavik *nt*.

rhapsody ['ræpsədɪ] *n* - **1.** MUS Rhapsodie *die* - **2.** [strong approval]: **to go into rhapsodies over sthg** von etw zu schwärmen beginnen.

rhetoric ['retərɪk] *n* (U) Rhetorik *die*.

rhetorical question [rɪ'tɒrɪkl-] *n* rhetorische Frage.

rheumatism ['ruːmətɪzm] *n* Rheuma *das*.

Rhine [raɪn] *n*: **the Rhine** der Rhein.

rhino ['raɪnəʊ] (*pl inv OR* -s) *n* = **rhinoceros**.

rhinoceros [raɪ'nɒsərəs] (*pl inv OR* -es) *n* Nashorn *das*, Rhinozeros *das*.

rhododendron [,rəʊdə'dendrən] *n* Rhododendron *der ODER das*.

rhubarb ['ruːbɑːb] *n* Rhabarber *der*.

rhyme [raɪm] ◇ *n* Reim *der*. ◇ *vi*: **to rhyme (with sthg)** sich (mit etw) reimen.

rhythm ['rɪðm] *n* Rhythmus *der*.

rib [rɪb] *n* [of body, framework] Rippe *die*.

ribbon ['rɪbən] *n* - **1.** [for decoration] Band *das* - **2.** [for typewriter] Farbband *das*.

rice [raɪs] *n* Reis *der*.

rice pudding *n* Milchreis *der*.

rich [rɪtʃ] ◇ *adj* - **1.** [gen] reich; **to be rich in sthg** reich an etw (D) sein - **2.** [soil] fruchtbar - **3.** [food, cake] schwer. ◇ *npl*: **the rich** die Reichen *Pl*. ➝ **riches** *npl* Reichtümer *Pl*.

richly ['rɪtʃlɪ] *adv* - **1.** [well - rewarded] reich - **2.** [abundantly] reichlich - **3.** [sumptuously, expensively] reich.

richness ['rɪtʃnɪs] *n* (U) - **1.** [of deposit] Reichtum *der* - **2.** [of soil] Fruchtbarkeit *die* - **3.** [of food] Schwere *die*.

rickety ['rɪkətɪ] *adj* wackelig.

ricochet ['rɪkəʃeɪ] (*pt & pp* -ed OR -ted, *cont* -ing OR -ting) ◇ *n* Abprall *der*. ◇ *vi*: **to ricochet (off sthg)** (von etw) ablprallen.

rid [rɪd] (*pt* rid OR -ded, *pp* rid) *vt*: **to rid sb/ sthg of sthg** jn/etw von etw befreien; **to rid o.s. of sthg** sich von etw befreien.

ridden ['rɪdn] *pp* ▷ **ride**.

riddle ['rɪdl] *n* Rätsel *das*.

riddled ['rɪdld] *adj*: **to be riddled with holes** ganz durchlöchert sein; **to be riddled with errors** voller Fehler sein.

ride [raɪd] (*pt* rode, *pp* ridden) ◇ *n* - **1.** [on horseback] Ritt *der*; **to go for a ride** reiten gehen - **2.** [on bicycle, motorbike, in car] Fahrt *die*; **to go for a ride** eine Fahrt/Tour machen - **3.** *phr*: **to take sb for a ride** *inf* [trick] jn reinlegen. ◇ *vt* - **1.** [horse] reiten - **2.** [bicycle, motorbike] fahren; **to ride a bicycle/motorbike** Rad/Motorrad fahren - **3.** [distance - on horse] reiten; [- on bicycle, motorbike] fahren - **4.** US [train, bus, elevator] fahren mit. ◇ *vi* - **1.** [on horseback] reiten - **2.** [on bicycle, motorbike] fahren - **3.** [in car, bus]: **to ride in sthg** mit etw fahren.

rider ['raɪdə'] *n* - **1.** [on horseback] Reiter *der*, -in *die* - **2.** [on bicycle, motorbike] Fahrer *der*, -in *die*.

ridge [rɪdʒ] *n* - **1.** [on mountain] Kamm *der*, Rücken *der* - **2.** [on flat surface] Riffel *die*.

ridicule ['rɪdɪkjuːl] ◇ *n* Spott *der*. ◇ *vt* lächerlich machen, verspotten.

ridiculous [rɪ'dɪkjuləs] *adj* lächerlich.

riding ['raɪdɪŋ] *n* Reiten *das*.

riding school *n* Reitschule *die*.

rife [raɪf] *adj*: **to be rife** grassieren.

riffraff ['rɪfræf] *n* Gesindel *das*.

rifle ['raɪfl] *n* Gewehr *das*.

rifle range *n* Schießstand *der*.

rift [rɪft] *n* - **1.** GEOL Spalt *der* - **2.** [quarrel]: **a rift between** eine Kluft zwischen (+ D).

rig [rɪg] ◇ *n*: (oil) **rig** Bohrinsel *die*. ◇ *vt* [fix outcome of] manipulieren. ➝ **rig up** *vt sep* aufstellen, montieren.

rigging ['rɪgɪŋ] n (U) [on ship] Takelung die.

right [raɪt] <> adj - 1. [gen] richtig; **have you got the right time?** haben Sie die genaue Zeit?; **to be right (about sthg)** (bezüglich etw) Recht haben; **to get the answer right** die richtige Antwort geben - 2. [going well]: **things aren't right between them** sie kommen nicht gut miteinander aus - 3. [not left] rechte(r) (s) - 4. UK inf [idiot, mess] richtig, total. <> n - 1. [moral correctness, entitlement] Recht das; **to be in the right** im Recht sein; **human rights** Menschenrechte Pl; **by rights** rechtmäßig, von Rechts wegen - 2. [right-hand side] rechte Seite; **on your right** zu Ihrer Rechten; **on the right** rechts. <> adv - 1. [correctly] richtig - 2. [not left] rechts - 3. [emphatic use]: **stay right here** bleib hier; **to turn right round** sich ganz herumldrehen - 4. [immediately] gleich; **right now** [immediately] (jetzt); (jetzt) - [at this very moment] (jetzt) gerade; **right away** sofort. <> vt - 1. [correct] wiedergutmachen - 2. [make upright] aufrichten. <> excl gut!, O. K.! ➠ **Right** n POL: **the Right** die Rechte.

right angle n rechter Winkel; **at right angles to sthg** im rechten Winkel zu etw.

righteous ['raɪtʃəs] adj [person] rechtschaffen; [anger] selbstgerecht.

rightful ['raɪtful] adj rechtmäßig.

right-hand adj [on the right] rechte(r) (s).

right-hand drive adj rechts gesteuert.

right-handed [-'hændɪd] adj rechtshändig.

right-hand man n rechte Hand.

rightly ['raɪtlɪ] adv - 1. [correctly, without error] ganz richtig - 2. [appropriately, aptly] korrekt, richtig - 3. [justifiably] mit Recht.

right of way n - 1. AUT Vorfahrt die - 2. [access] Durchgangsrecht das.

right wing n: **the right wing** der rechte Flügel. ➠ **right-wing** adj rechtsgerichtet.

rigid ['rɪdʒɪd] adj - 1. [hard, stiff, inflexible] starr - 2. [strict] strikt.

rigor n US = **rigour**.

rigorous ['rɪgərəs] adj streng.

rigour UK, **rigor** US ['rɪgər] n Strenge die. ➠ **rigours** npl Unbilden Pl.

rile [raɪl] vt ärgern.

rim [rɪm] n [of glass] Rand der; [of spectacles] Fassung die; [of wheel] Felge die.

rind [raɪnd] n [of fruit] Schale die; [of cheese] Rinde die; [of bacon] Schwarte die.

ring [rɪŋ] <> n - 1. [telephone call]: **to give sb a ring** jn anlrufen - 2. [sound of bell] Klingeln das - 3. [quality, tone]: **her excuse had a familiar ring (about it)** ihre Ausrede kam mir bekannt vor; **there's a ring of truth about it** es klingt sehr wahrscheinlich - 4. [object, jewellery, for boxing] Ring der - 5. [of people, trees] Kreis der - 6. [people working together] Ring der; **crime ring** Verbrecherring der. <> vt (pt rang, pp rung) - 1. UK [phone] anl-

rufen - 2. [bell] läuten; **to ring the doorbell** (an der Tür) klingeln OR läuten - 3. (pt & pp -ed) [draw a circle round] einlkreisen - 4. (pt & pp -ed) [surround] umringen; **to be ringed with sthg** von etw umringt sein. <> vi (pt rang, pp rung) - 1. UK [phone] klingeln - 2. [doorbell, person at door] klingeln, läuten - 3. [to attract attention]: **to ring (for sb)** (nach jm) läuten. ➠ **ring back** vt sep & vi UK zurücklrufen. ➠ **ring off** vi UK auflhängen. ➠ **ring up** vt sep UK anlrufen.

ring binder n Ringbuch das.

ringing ['rɪŋɪŋ] n [of bell] Läuten das; [of telephone] Klingeln das; [in ears] Klingen das.

ringing tone n UK TELEC Freizeichen das.

ringleader ['rɪŋˌliːdər] n Anführer der, -in die.

ringlet ['rɪŋlɪt] n Ringellocke die.

ring road n UK Umgehungsstraße die.

ring tone n [on mobile phone] Klingelton der.

rink [rɪŋk] n [for ice-skating] Eisbahn die; [for roller-skating] Rollschuhbahn die.

rinse [rɪns] vt [clothes] spülen; [vegetables] waschen; **to rinse one's hands** die Hände ablspülen; **to rinse one's mouth out** sich (D) den Mund auslspülen.

riot ['raɪət] <> n Aufruhr der; **to run riot** [hooligans] randalieren; [children] außer Rand und Band sein; [plants] wuchern. <> vi einen Aufruhr machen.

rioter ['raɪətər] n Aufrührer der, -in die.

riotous ['raɪətəs] adj [mob] randalierend; [party, behaviour] ausgelassen, wild.

riot police npl Bereitschaftspolizei die.

rip [rɪp] <> n Riss der. <> vt - 1. [tear, shred] zerreißen - 2. [remove]: **to rip sthg from** OR **off sthg** etw von etw ablreißen. <> vi reißen.

RIP (abbr of rest in peace) R. I. P.

ripe [raɪp] adj [ready to eat] reif; **to be ripe for sthg** fig für etw reif sein.

ripen ['raɪpn] <> vt reifen lassen. <> vi reifen.

rip-off n inf [excessive charge] Wucher der.

ripple ['rɪpl] <> n - 1. [in water] kleine Welle - 2. [sound]: **a ripple of laughter** sanftes Gelächter; **a ripple of applause** kurzer Applaus. <> vt kräuseln.

rise [raɪz] (pt rose, pp risen ['rɪzn]) <> n - 1. UK [increase in amount]: **rise (in sthg)** Anstieg der (einer Sache (G)) - 2. UK [increase in salary] Gehaltserhöhung die - 3. [to power, fame] Aufstieg der - 4. [slope] Steigung die - 5. phr: **to give rise to sthg** zu etw führen. <> vi - 1. [go upwards, become higher, increase] steigen - 2. [sun, bread] aufgehen - 3. [stand up, get out of bed] auflstehen - 4. [slope upwards] (an)lsteigen - 5. [become louder - voice] lauter werden - 6. [become higher in pitch] höher werden - 7. [prove o.s.]: **to rise to the occasion** der Lage gewachsen sein; **to rise to the challenge**

die Herausforderung annehmen - **8.** [rebel] sich erheben - **9.** [in status] aufsteigen; **to rise to power** an die Macht kommen.

rising ['raɪzɪŋ] ◇ *adj* - **1.** [sloping upwards] (an)steigend - **2.** [increasing, tide] steigend - **3.** [increasingly successful] aufsteigend. ◇ *n* [rebellion] Aufstand *der*, Erhebung *die*.

risk [rɪsk] ◇ *n* Risiko *das*; **to run the risk of doing sthg** Gefahr laufen, etw zu tun; **to take a risk** ein Risiko einlgehen; **at one's own risk** auf eigenes Risiko; **at risk** in Gefahr; **to put at risk** gefährden. ◇ *vt* - **1.** [put in danger] riskielreh - **2.** [take the chance of]: **to risk doing sthg** riskieren, etw zu tun.

risky ['rɪskɪ] *adj* riskant.

risqué [rɪ'skeɪ] *adj* gewagt, schlüpfrig.

rite [raɪt] *n* Ritus *der*.

ritual ['rɪtʃʊəl] ◇ *adj* rituell. ◇ *n* Ritual *das*.

rival ['raɪvl] (*UK*) (*US*) ◇ *adj* Konkurrenz-, konkurrierend. ◇ *n* Rivale *der*, -lin *die*; COMM Konkurrent *der*, -in *die*. ◇ *vt* sich messen mit, konkurrieren mit.

rivalry ['raɪvlrɪ] *n* Rivalität *die*.

river ['rɪvə^r] *n* Fluss *der*; **the River Thames** *UK*, **the Thames River** *US* die Themse.

river bank *n* Flussufer *das*.

riverbed ['rɪvəbed] *n* Flussbett *das*.

riverside ['rɪvəsaɪd] *n*: **the riverside** das Flussufer.

rivet ['rɪvɪt] ◇ *n* Niete *die*. ◇ *vt* - **1.** [fasten with rivets] nieten - **2.** *fig* [fascinate]: **to be riveted by sthg** von etw gefesselt sein.

road [rəʊd] *n* Straße *die*; **by road** [send] per Spedition; [travel] mit dem Auto/Bus/*etc*; **on the road to victory/success/recovery** auf dem Weg zum Sieg/zum Erfolg/der Besserung.

roadblock ['rəʊdblɒk] *n* Straßensperre *die*.

road map *n* Straßenkarte *die*.

road safety *n* Verkehrssicherheit *die*.

roadside ['rəʊdsaɪd] *n*: **by the roadside** am Straßenrand.

road sign *n* Verkehrszeichen *das*.

road tax *n* Kraftfahrzeugsteuer *die*.

roadway ['rəʊdweɪ] *n* Fahrbahn *die*.

road works *npl* (Straßen)bauarbeiten *Pl*.

roam [rəʊm] ◇ *vt* [countryside] durchstreifen; [streets] herumlziehen in (*+ D*). ◇ *vi* [in countryside] wandern; [in streets] herumlziehen.

roar [rɔː^r] ◇ *vi* - **1.** [lion, person] brüllen; **to roar with laughter** vor Lachen brüllen - **2.** [wind, engine] heulen. ◇ *vt* brüllen. ◇ *n* - **1.** [of lion, person] Brüllen *das* - **2.** [of wind, engine] Heulen *das*; [of traffic] Lärm *der*.

roaring ['rɔːrɪŋ] ◇ *adj* - **1.** [traffic] lärmend; [wind, engine] heulend - **2.** [fire] prasselnd - **3.** [for emphasis]: **a roaring success** ein Riesenerfolg; **to do a roaring trade** ein Riesengeschäft machen. ◇ *adv*: **roaring drunk** sternhagelvoll.

roast [rəʊst] ◇ *adj*: **roast beef** Rinderbraten *der*, Roastbeef *das*; **roast chicken** Brathähnchen *das*; **roast pork** Schweinebraten *der*. ◇ *n* Braten *der*. ◇ *vt* - **1.** [meat] braten; [potatoes] im Ofen in Fett backen - **2.** [coffee beans, nuts] rösten.

rob [rɒb] *vt* [person] bestehlen; [bank, house] auslrauben; **to rob sb of sthg** [of money, goods] jm etw stehlen; *fig* [of opportunity, glory] jn einer Sache (*G*) berauben.

robber ['rɒbə^r] *n* Räuber *der*, -in *die*.

robbery ['rɒbərɪ] *n* Raub *der*.

robe [rəʊb] *n* - **1.** [of priest, judge, monarch] Robe *die* - **2.** *US* [dressing gown] Morgenrock *der*.

robin ['rɒbɪn] *n* Rotkehlchen *das*.

robot ['rəʊbɒt] *n* Roboter *der*.

robust [rəʊ'bʌst] *adj* [person, health] robust; [economy] stabil; [criticism, defence] stark.

rock [rɒk] ◇ *n* - **1.** (*U*) [substance] Stein *der* - **2.** [boulder] Fels(en) *der* - **3.** *US* [pebble] Stein *der* - **4.** [music] Rock *der* - **5.** *UK* [sweet]: **stick of rock** Zuckerstange *die*. ◇ *comp* [band, concert, singer] Rock-. ◇ *vt* - **1.** [cause to move] schaukeln; [baby] wiegen - **2.** [shock] erschüttern. ◇ *vi* [boat, cradle, in chair] schaukeln. ➥ **on the rocks** *adv* - **1.** [drink] mit Eis - **2.** [marriage, relationship] kaputt.

rock bottom *n*: **to be at rock bottom** auf dem Tiefpunkt sein; **to hit rock bottom** den Tiefpunkt erreichen. ➥ **rock-bottom** *adj* [prices] Schleuder-.

rockery ['rɒkərɪ] *n* Steingarten *der*.

rocket ['rɒkɪt] ◇ *n* Rakete *die*. ◇ *vi* hoch schießen.

rocket launcher [-ˌlɔːntʃə^r] *n* Raketenwerfer *der*.

rocking chair ['rɒkɪŋ-] *n* Schaukelstuhl *der*.

rocking horse ['rɒkɪŋ-] *n* Schaukelpferd *das*.

rocky ['rɒkɪ] *adj* - **1.** [full of rocks] steinig - **2.** [unsteady] wackelig.

Rocky Mountains *npl*: **the Rocky Mountains** die Rocky Mountains.

rod [rɒd] *n* Stange *die*; [for fishing] Angel *die*.

rode [rəʊd] *pt* ▷ **ride**.

rodent ['rəʊdənt] *n* Nagetier *das*.

roe [rəʊ] *n* [of fish] Rogen *der*.

rogue [rəʊg] *n* - **1.** [likable rascal] Frechdachs *der* - **2.** *dated* [dishonest person] Schurke *der*.

role [rəʊl] *n* Rolle *die*.

roll [rəʊl] ◇ *n* - **1.** [of material, paper, film] Rolle *die* - **2.** [of bread] Brötchen *das*; **a cheese roll** ein Käsebrötchen - **3.** [list] Liste *die*; **electoral roll** Wählerverzeichnis *das* - **4.** [sound - of thunder] Rollen *das*; [- of drums] Wirbel *der*.

◇ *vt* - 1. [turn over] rollen - 2. [make into cylinder] auf|rollen; [umbrella] zusammen|rollen; **rolled into one** *fig* in einem. ◇ *vi* - 1. [gen] rollen - 2. [make loud noise - thunder] rollen; [- drums] wirbeln. **roll about, roll around** *vi* herum|rollen; [person] sich wälzen. **roll over** *vi* [person] sich um|drehen. **roll up** ◇ *vt sep* - 1. [make into cylinder] auf|rollen, zusammen|rollen - 2. [sleeves] hoch|krempeln. ◇ *vi* - 1. [vehicle] vor|fahren - 2. *inf* [person] auf|kreuzen.

roll call *n* Namensaufruf *der*; MIL Appell *der*.

roller ['rəʊlə^r] *n* - 1. [cylinder] Walze *die* - 2. [curler] (Locken)wickler *der*.

roller blades *npl* Rollerblades *Pl*.

roller coaster *n* Achterbahn *die*.

roller skate *n* Rollschuh *der*.

rolling ['rəʊlɪŋ] *adj* - 1. [hills] wellig - 2. *phr*: **to be rolling in it** *inf* im Geld schwimmen.

rolling pin *n* Nudelholz *das*.

roll-on *adj* & *n*: **roll-on (deodorant)** Deoroller *der*.

ROM [rɒm] (*abbr of* read only memory) *n* ROM.

Roman ['rəʊmən] ◇ *adj* römisch. ◇ *n* Römer *der*, -in *die*.

Roman Catholic ◇ *adj* römisch-katholisch. ◇ *n* Katholik *der*, -in *die*.

romance [rəʊˈmæns] *n* - 1. [romantic quality] Romantik *die* - 2. [love affair] Romanze *die* - 3. [novel] Liebesroman *der*.

Romania [ru:ˈmeɪnjə] *n* Rumänien *nt*.

Romanian [ru:ˈmeɪnjən] ◇ *adj* rumänisch. ◇ *n* - 1. [person] Rumäne *der*, -nin *die* - 2. [language] Rumänisch(e) *das*.

romantic [rəʊˈmæntɪk] *adj* - 1. [gen] romantisch - 2. [novel, film, play] Liebes-.

Rome [rəʊm] *n* Rom *nt*.

romp [rɒmp] ◇ *n*: **to have a romp** herum|toben, herum|tollen. ◇ *vi* [play noisily] herum|toben, herum|tollen.

rompers ['rɒmpəz] *npl* Strampelhose *die*.

romper suit ['rɒmpə^r-] *n* = **rompers**.

roof [ru:f] *n* - 1. [of building, vehicle] Dach *das*; **to go through** OR **hit the roof** an die Decke gehen - 2. [upper part - of cave] Gewölbe *das*; **roof of the mouth** Gaumen *der*.

roofing ['ru:fɪŋ] *n* (U) [material] Deckung *die*.

roof rack *n* Dachträger *der*.

rooftop ['ru:ftɒp] *n* Dach *das*.

rook [rʊk] *n* - 1. [bird] Krähe *die* - 2. [chess piece] Turm *der*.

rookie ['rʊkɪ] *n* US *inf* Grünschnabel *der*.

room [ru:m, rʊm] *n* - 1. [in house, hotel] Zimmer *das*; [in office, public building *etc*] Raum *der* - 2. (U) [space] Platz *der*; **to make room for sb/ sthg** für jn/etw Platz machen - 3. (U) [oppor-

tunity, possibility]: **there is still room for improvement** es könnte besser sein; **there is no room for sentimentality in politics** Sentimentalität hat in der Politik nichts zu suchen.

roommate ['ru:mmeɪt] *n* Zimmergenosse *der*, -sin *die*.

room service *n* (U) Zimmerservice *der*.

roomy ['ru:mɪ] *adj* [house, car] geräumig; [garment] weit.

roost [ru:st] ◇ *n* Hühnerstange *die*. ◇ *vi* [hens] auf der Stange sitzen.

rooster ['ru:stə^r] *n* Hahn *der*.

root [ru:t] ◇ *n* *liter* & *fig* Wurzel *die*; **to take root** [plant] Wurzel fassen; [idea] Fuß fassen; **the root of the problem** die Ursache des Problems. ◇ *vi* [search] wühlen. **roots** *npl* [origins] Wurzeln *Pl*. **root for** *vt insep* *esp US inf* an|feuern. **root out** *vt sep* [eradicate] aus|rotten.

rope [rəʊp] ◇ *n* Seil *das*; **to know the ropes** sich aus|kennen. ◇ *vt*: **to rope together** zusammen|binden; [climbers] an|seilen. **rope in** *vt sep* *inf* [involve] ran|kriegen.

rosary ['rəʊzərɪ] *n* Rosenkranz *der*.

rose [rəʊz] ◇ *pt* ⊳ **rise**. ◇ *adj* [pink] rosa. ◇ *n* [flower] Rose *die*.

rosé ['rəʊzeɪ] *n* Rosé *der*.

rose bush *n* Rosenstrauch *der*.

rosemary ['rəʊzmərɪ] *n* Rosmarin *der*.

rosette [rəʊˈzet] *n* Rosette *die*.

roster ['rɒstə^r] *n* Dienstplan *der*.

rostrum ['rɒstrəm] (*pl* -trums OR -tra [-trə]) *n* [for speaker, conductor] Pult *das*.

rosy ['rəʊzɪ] *adj* *liter* & *fig* rosig.

rot [rɒt] ◇ *n* - 1. (U) [decay - of wood, food] Fäulnis *die*; [- in society, organization] Verfall *der*; **dry rot** Trockenfäule *die*; **to stop the rot** den Verfall auf|halten; **the rot set in** es ging abwärts - 2. *UK dated* [nonsense] Quatsch *der*. ◇ *vt* faulen lassen. ◇ *vi* faulen.

rota ['rəʊtə] *n* Dienstplan *der*.

rotary ['rəʊtərɪ] ◇ *adj* rotierend, Rotations-. ◇ *n* US [roundabout] Kreisverkehr *der*.

rotate [rəʊˈteɪt] ◇ *vt* [turn] drehen. ◇ *vi* [turn] sich drehen, rotieren.

rotation [rəʊˈteɪʃn] *n* [turning movement] Drehung *die*, Rotation *die*.

rote [rəʊt] *n*: **by rote** auswendig.

rotten ['rɒtn] *adj* - 1. [decayed] verfault - 2. *inf* [poor-quality, unskilled] lausig - 3. *inf* [mean] gemein - 4. *inf* [unpleasant, unenjoyable] mies - 5. *inf* [unwell]: **to feel rotten** sich mies fühlen.

rouge [ru:ʒ] *n* Rouge *das*.

rough [rʌf] ◇ *adj* - 1. [not smooth - surface] rau; [- road] uneben, holprig - 2. [violent] grob, rau - 3. [crude, basic - shelter, conditions] primitiv; [- people, manners] **rau - 4.** [not detailed, not exact] grob; **rough draft** Rohentwurf *der*; **at a rough guess** grob geschätzt; **can you give me a rough idea of the cost?** können Sie mir sagen, wie viel es ungefähr kostet? **- 5.** [unpleasant, tough - life, time] hart; [- journey] anstrengend; [- area] rau; **to be rough on sb** hart für jn sein **- 6.** [stormy] stürmisch **- 7.** [harsh - voice] rau; [- wine] sauer. ⟨⟩ *adv*: **to sleep rough** im Freien übernachten. ⟨⟩ *n* **- 1.** GOLF: **the rough** das Rough **- 2.** [draft]: **to write sthg in rough** ein Konzept für etw machen. ⟨⟩ *vt phr*: **to rough it** primitiv leben.

rough and ready *adj* primitiv; [person] rau(beinig).

roughen ['rʌfn] *vt* [surface] auflrauen.

roughly ['rʌfli] *adv* **- 1.** [gen] grob **- 2.** [approximately] etwa.

roulette [ruːˈlet] *n* Roulette *das*.

round [raʊnd] ⟨⟩ *adj* rund. ⟨⟩ *prep* **- 1.** [surrounding] um herum; **there were soldiers all round the building** rund um das Gebäude waren Soldaten **- 2.** [near]: **round here/there** hier/dort in der Nähe; **is there a bank anywhere round here?** gibt es hier irgendwo eine Bank? **- 3.** [all over]: **150 offices round the world** 150 Büros in der ganzen Welt; **all round the country** im ganzen Land; **to go round a museum** ein Museum besuchen; **to show sb round sthg** jn in etw *(D)* herumlführen **- 4.** [in a circle]: **we walked round the lake** wir gingen um den See herum; **to go/drive round sthg** um etw herumlgehen/herumlfahren; **round the clock** *fig* rund um die Uhr **- 5.** [in circumference]: **she measures 30 inches round the waist** um die Taille misst sie 75 cm **- 6.** [on or to the other side of]: **to go round the corner** um die Ecke sein/gehen **- 7.** [so as to avoid] um herum; **to get round an obstacle** um ein Hindernis herumlgehen; **to find a way round a problem** einen Ausweg für ein Problem finden. ⟨⟩ *adv* **- 1.** [on all sides] herum; **all round** auf allen Seiten, rundherum **- 2.** [near]: **round about** [in distance] in der Nähe; [approximately] rund; **round about ten o'clock** gegen zehn Uhr **- 3.** [here and there] herum; **to travel round** herumlreisen **- 4.** [in a circle]: **to go round** sich drehen; **to spin round (and round)** sich im Kreis drehen **- 5.** [to the other side]: **to go round** herumlgehen; **to turn round** sich umldrehen; **to look round** sich umlsehen; **it's a long way round** das ist ein Umweg **- 6.** [on a visit]: **why don't you come round?** warum kommst du nicht vorbei?; **I spent the day round at her house** ich war den ganzen Tag bei ihr (zu Hause) **- 7.** [when sharing]: **to hand sthg round** etw herumlreichen **- 8.** [continuously]: **all year round** das ganze Jahr über. ⟨⟩ *n* **- 1.** [gen & SPORT] Runde *die*; **a round of applause** eine Runde Applaus **- 2.** [of ammunition] Schuss *der* **- 3.** [of drinks] Runde *die*; **it's my round** es ist meine Runde **- 4.**: **a round of sandwiches** ein

Sandwich **- 5.** [of toast] Scheibe *die*. ⟨⟩ *vt* [turn]: **to round a bend** um eine Kurve fahren. ⬥ **round off** *vt sep* ablrunden. ⬥ **round up** *vt sep* **- 1.** [animals] zusammenltreiben **- 2.** [number] auflrunden.

roundabout ['raʊndəbaʊt] ⟨⟩ *adj* umständlich. ⟨⟩ *n UK* **- 1.** [on road] Kreisverkehr *der* **- 2.** [at fairground, playground] Karussell *das*.

rounders ['raʊndəz] *n (U) UK* Schlagball *der*.

roundly ['raʊndli] *adv* [criticize] scharf; [defeated] vernichtend.

round trip *n* Rundreise *die*.

roundup ['raʊndʌp] *n* [summary] Zusammenfassung *die*.

rouse [raʊz] *vt* **- 1.** [wake up] wecken **- 2.** [impel]: **to rouse o.s. to do sthg** sich dazu auflraffen, etw zu tun; **to rouse sb to action** jn zum Handeln bewegen **- 3.** [subj: orator] in Erregung versetzen **- 4.** [give rise to] hervorlrufen; [emotions, interest] wecken, wachlrufen.

rousing ['raʊzɪŋ] *adj* [speech] mitreißend; [cheer] stürmisch.

rout [raʊt] ⟨⟩ *n* Niederlage *die*. ⟨⟩ *vt* in die Flucht schlagen.

route [ruːt] ⟨⟩ *n* **- 1.** [line of travel] Strecke *die*, Route *die* **- 2.** [fixed itinerary]: **air/bus/shipping route** Flug-/Bus-/Schifffahrtslinie *die* **- 3.** *fig* [to achievement] Weg *der*. ⟨⟩ *vt* [flight, traffic] legen; [goods] schicken.

route map *n* [for public transport] Streckenkarte *die*; [for holiday route] Tourenplan *der*.

routine [ruːˈtiːn] ⟨⟩ *adj* routinemäßig, Routine-. ⟨⟩ *n* Routine *die*.

row¹ [raʊ] ⟨⟩ *n* Reihe *die*; **in a row** nacheinander. ⟨⟩ *vt & vi* rudern.

row² [raʊ] ⟨⟩ *n* **- 1.** [quarrel] Streit *der*, Krach *der* **- 2.** *inf* [noise] Krach *der*, Krawall *der*. ⟨⟩ *vi* [quarrel] sich streiten.

rowboat ['raʊbaʊt] *n US* Ruderboot *das*.

rowdy ['raʊdi] *adj* [person] wild, randalierend; [party, atmosphere] laut.

row house [raʊ-] *n US* Reihenhaus *das*.

rowing ['raʊɪŋ] *n* Rudern *das*.

rowing boat *n UK* Ruderboot *das*.

royal ['rɔɪəl] ⟨⟩ *adj* [regal] königlich. ⟨⟩ *n inf* Angehörige *der, die* der königlichen Familie.

Royal Air Force *n*: **the Royal Air Force** die Königliche Luftwaffe.

royal family *n* königliche Familie.

Royal Mail *n UK*: **the Royal Mail** die Königliche Post.

Royal Navy *n*: **the Royal Navy** die Königliche Marine.

royalty ['rɔɪəlti] *n (U)* [persons] Königshaus *das*. ⬥ **royalties** *npl* Tantiemen *Pl*.

rpm (*abbr of* **revolutions per minute**) *npl* U/min.

RSPCA (*abbr of* **Royal Society for the Prevention of Cruelty to Animals**) *n* britischer Tierschutzverein.

RSVP (*abbr of* **répondez s'il vous plaît**) u.A.w.g.

rub [rʌb] ◇ *vt* reiben; **to rub one's hands together** sich (D) die Hände reiben; **he rubbed sun cream into her back** er rieb ihren Rücken mit Sonnencreme ein; **to rub sb up the wrong way** *UK*, **to rub sb the wrong way** *US fig* in verstimmen. ◇ *vi*: **to rub against** *OR* **on sthg** an etw (D) reiben; [person, animal] sich an etw (D) reiben; **to rub together** sich reiben. ➤ **rub off on** *vt insep* [subj: quality] abfärben auf (+ A). ➤ **rub out** *vt sep* [erase] ausradieren.

rubber ['rʌbər] ◇ *adj* [made of rubber] Gummi-. ◇ *n* - **1.** [substance] Gummi *der* - **2.** *UK* [eraser] Radiergummi *der* - **3.** [in cards] Robber *der* - **4.** *US inf* [condom] Gummi *der*.

rubber band *n* Gummiband *das*.

rubber plant *n* Gummibaum *der*.

rubber stamp *n* Stempel *der*. ➤ **rubber-stamp** *vt* stempeln.

rubbish ['rʌbɪʃ] ◇ *n* (U) - **1.** [refuse] Abfall *der*, Müll *der* - **2.** *inf fig* [worthless thing] Mist *der* - **3.** *inf* [nonsense] Quatsch *der*, Blödsinn *der*. ◇ *vt inf* [person, opinion] lächerlich machen; [play, book] verreißen. ◇ *excl inf* Quatsch!

rubbish bag *n UK* Müllsack *der*.

rubbish bin *n UK* Mülleimer *der*.

rubbish dump, rubbish tip *n UK* Müllabladeplatz *der*.

rubble ['rʌbl] *n* Schutt *der*.

ruby ['ru:bɪ] *n* [gem] Rubin *der*.

rucksack ['rʌksæk] *n* Rucksack *der*.

rudder ['rʌdər] *n* Ruder *das*.

ruddy ['rʌdɪ] *adj* - **1.** [reddish] rot; [complexion] gesund - **2.** *UK dated* [for emphasis] verdammt.

rude [ru:d] *adj* - **1.** [impolite] unhöflich - **2.** [dirty, naughty] unanständig - **3.** [unexpected]: **rude awakening** böses Erwachen.

rudimentary [,ru:dɪ'mentərɪ] *adj* [basic] elementar.

rueful ['ru:fʊl] *adj* reumütig; [smile] wehmütig.

ruffian ['rʌfjən] *n* Grobian *der*.

ruffle ['rʌfl] *vt* - **1.** [hair, fur] zersausen; [water] kräuseln - **2.** [pride] verletzen; **to ruffle sb's composure** jn aus der Ruhe bringen.

rug [rʌg] *n* - **1.** [carpet] kleiner Teppich; [by bed] Bettvorleger *der* - **2.** [blanket] Decke *die*.

rugby ['rʌgbɪ] *n* Rugby *das*.

rugged ['rʌgɪd] *adj* - **1.** [rocky, uneven - landscape] wild; [- cliffs] zerklüftet - **2.** [sturdy] stabil.

rugger ['rʌgər] *n UK inf* Rugby *das*.

ruin ['ru:ɪn] ◇ *n* - **1.** [financial downfall] Ruin *der* - **2.** [ruined building] Ruine *die*. ◇ *vt* ruinieren; [chances, atmosphere] verderben. ➤ **in ruins** *adv*: **to be in ruins** [town, country] in Ruinen liegen; [building] eine Ruine sein; [marriage, career, plans] ruiniert sein.

rule [ru:l] ◇ *n* - **1.** [regulation, guideline] Regel *die* - **2.** [norm]: **the rule** die Regel; **as a rule** in der Regel - **3.** (U) [control] Herrschaft *die*. ◇ *vt* - **1.** [control, guide] beherrschen - **2.** [govern] regieren - **3.** [decide]: **to rule that...** entscheiden, dass... ◇ *vi* - **1.** [give decision] entscheiden - **2.** *fml* [be paramount] herrschen - **3.** [govern] regieren. ➤ **rule out** *vt sep* ausschließen.

ruled [ru:ld] *adj* [lined] liniert.

ruler ['ru:lər] *n* - **1.** [for measurement] Lineal *das* - **2.** [leader] Herrscher *der*, -in *die*.

ruling ['ru:lɪŋ] ◇ *adj* [in control] herrschend. ◇ *n* [decision] Entscheidung *die*.

rum [rʌm] *n* Rum *der*.

Rumania [ru:'meɪnjə] *n* = **Romania**.

Rumanian [ru:'meɪnjən] *adj & n* = **Romanian**.

rumble ['rʌmbl] ◇ *n* [of thunder] Grollen *das*; [of lorry, train] Rumpeln *das*; [of stomach] Knurren *das*. ◇ *vi* [thunder] grollen; [train] rumpeln; [stomach] knurren.

rummage ['rʌmɪdʒ] *vi* wühlen, stöbern.

rumour *UK*, **rumor** *US* ['ru:mər] *n* Gerücht *das*.

rumoured *UK*, **rumored** *US* ['ru:məd] *adj*: **he is rumoured to be married already** er soll angeblich schon verheiratet sein.

rump [rʌmp] *n* - **1.** [of animal] Hinterteil *das* - **2.** *inf* [of person] Hinterteil *das*.

rump steak *n* Rumpsteak *das*.

rumpus ['rʌmpəs] *n inf* Spektakel *das*, Krach *der*.

run [rʌn] (*pt* **ran**, *pp* **run**) ◇ *n* - **1.** [on foot] Lauf *der*; **to go for a run** laufen gehen; **at a run** im Lauf; **on the run** auf der Flucht - **2.** [in car] Fahrt *die*; **to go for a run** einen Ausflug im Auto machen - **3.** [series] Reihe *die*; **a run of bad luck** eine Pechsträhne - **4.** THEAT: **it had an eight-week run on Broadway** es wurde für acht Wochen am Broadway gespielt - **5.** [great demand]: **a run on sthg** ein Ansturm auf etw (A) - **6.** [in tights] Laufmasche *die* - **7.** [in cricket, baseball] Lauf *der* - **8.** [for skiing] Abfahrt *die*; [for bobsleigh] Bahn *die* - **9.** [term, period]: **in the long/short run** auf lange/kurze Sicht (gesehen). ◇ *vt* - **1.** [on foot] rennen, laufen; **to run a race** ein Rennen laufen - **2.** [business, hotel] führen; [course, event] leiten - **3.** [operate - machine, film, computer program] laufen lassen; [- experiment] durchführen - **4.** [have and use - car] halten - **5.** [water, tap] laufen lassen; **to run a bath** ein Bad einlassen - **6.** [article, headline] veröffentlichen - **7.** *inf* [drive] fahren; **I'll run you home** ich fahre dich nach Hause - **8.** [move, pass]: **to run one's hand along sthg/over sthg** mit der Hand an etw (D) entlang/über etw (A) fahren. <> *vi* - **1.** [on foot, in race] laufen; [fast] rennen; **we had to run for the bus** wir mussten rennen, um den Bus zu erwischen - **2.** [road, track] führen, verlaufen; [river] fließen; [pipe, cable] verlaufen; **the path runs along the coast** der Weg verläuft entlang der Küste - **3.** [in election]: **to run (for)** kandidieren (für) - **4.** [progress, develop] laufen; **to run smoothly** gut laufen - **5.** [operate - machine, engine] laufen; [- factory] arbeiten; **to run on unleaded petrol** mit bleifreiem Benzin fahren; **to run off mains electricity** mit Netzstrom laufen - **6.** [bus, train] fahren; **the bus runs every hour** der Bus fährt jede Stunde - **7.** [liquid, tears, tap] laufen - **8.** [eyes] tränen; **my nose is running** mir läuft die Nase - **9.** [colour] auslaufen; [clothes] abfärben - **10.** [continue - contract] gültig sein, laufen; [- play] laufen. ◆ **run about** *vi* herumlaufen. ◆ **run across** *vt insep* [meet] zufällig treffen. ◆ **run around** *vi* = **run about**. ◆ **run away** *vi* [flee]: **to run away (from)** weglaufen (von); [fast] weglrennen (von). ◆ **run down** <> *vt sep* - **1.** [in vehicle] überfahren - **2.** [criticize] heruntermachen - **3.** [allow to decline] abbauen. <> *vi* [battery] leer werden; [clock] abllaufen. ◆ **run into** *vt insep* - **1.** [meet - person] zufällig treffen - **2.** [encounter - problem] stoßen auf (+ A); **to run into debt** in Schulden geraten - **3.** [in vehicle] laufen *OR* fahren gegen. ◆ **run off** <> *vt sep* [copy] drucken. <> *vi*: **to run off (with sthg)** sich (mit etw) davonmachen; **to run off with sb** mit jm durchlbrennen. ◆ **run out** *vi* - **1.** [supply, fuel] auslgehen; **time is running out** die Zeit wird knapp - **2.** [licence, contract] abllaufen. ◆ **run out of** *vt insep*: **we've run out of petrol/money** wir haben kein Benzin/Geld mehr. ◆ **run over** *vt sep* [knock down] überfahren. ◆ **run through** *vt insep* - **1.** [practise] durchlgehen - **2.** [read through] schnell durchllesen. ◆ **run to** *vt insep* [amount to] sich belaufen auf (+ A). ◆ **run up** *vt sep* [debt] machen; [bill] zusammenkommen lassen. ◆ **run up against** *vt insep* stoßen auf (+ A).

runaway ['rʌnəweɪ] <> *adj* [child] ausgerissen; [horse] durchgegangen; [inflation] galoppierend; [victory] sehr überzeugend. <> *n* [escapee] Ausreißer *der*, -in *die*.

rundown ['rʌndaʊn] *n* - **1.** [report] Bericht *der* - **2.** [decline] Abbau *der*. ◆ **rundown** *adj* - **1.** [dilapidated] heruntergekommen - **2.** [tired] erschöpft.

rung [rʌŋ] <> *pp* ▷ **ring**. <> *n liter & fig* Sprosse *die*.

runner ['rʌnər] *n* - **1.** [athlete] Läufer *der*, -in *die* - **2.** [of sledge, skate] Kufe *die*; [of drawer] Schiene *die*.

runner bean *n UK* Stangenbohne *die*.

runner-up (*pl* runners-up) *n* Zweite *der, die*.

running ['rʌnɪŋ] <> *adj* - **1.** [continuous] ständig - **2.** [consecutive] hintereinander; **three weeks running** drei Wochen hintereinander - **3.** [water] fließend. <> *n* - **1.** SPORT Laufen *das* - **2.** [management, control] Leitung *die* - **3.** [of machine] Betrieb *der* - **4.** *phr*: **to be in the running (for sthg)** im Rennen (für etw) liegen; **to be out of the running (for sthg)** aus dem Rennen (für etw) sein.

runny ['rʌnɪ] *adj* - **1.** [food] flüssig - **2.** [nose] laufend; [eyes] wässerig; **he had a runny nose** ihm lief die Nase.

run-of-the-mill *adj* durchschnittlich, nullachtfünfzehn.

runt [rʌnt] *n* - **1.** [animal] *kleinstes Tier eines Wurfs* - **2.** *pej* [person] mickriger Kerl.

run-up *n* - **1.** [preceding time]: **in the run-up to** in der Zeit vor (+ D) - **2.** SPORT Anlauf *der*.

runway ['rʌnweɪ] *n* Start- und Landebahn *die*; [for takeoff] Startbahn *die*; [for landing] Landebahn *die*.

rupture ['rʌptʃər] *n* - **1.** MED Bruch *der* - **2.** [of relationship] (Ab)bruch *der*.

rural ['rʊərəl] *adj* ländlich.

ruse [ruːz] *n* List *die*.

rush [rʌʃ] <> *n* - **1.** [hurry] Eile *die*; **to be in a rush** es sehr eilig haben; **to make a rush for sthg** auf etw (A) zulstürzen *OR* zuleilen - **2.** [demand]: **rush (for** *OR* **on sthg)** Ansturm *der* (auf etw (A)) - **3.** [busiest period] Stoßzeit *die* - **4.** [surge of blood] Andrang *der*; [- of water] Schwall *der*. <> *vt* - **1.** [hurry - work] hastig erlledigen; [- meal] hastig essen; [- person] drängen - **2.** [send quickly - people] schnell bringen; [- supplies, troops] schnell schicken; **to rush sb to hospital** jn schnell ins Krankenhaus bringen - **3.** [attack suddenly] zulstürmen auf (+ A); [enemy, position] stürmen. <> *vi* - **1.** [hurry] sich beeilen - **2.** [crowd] stürzen; [air, blood, water] schießen. ◆ **rushes** *npl* BOT Binsen *Pl*.

rush hour *n* Hauptverkehrszeit *die*, Stoßzeit *die*.

rusk [rʌsk] *n* Zwieback *der*.

Russia ['rʌʃə] *n* Russland *nt*.

Russian ['rʌʃn] <> *adj* russisch. <> *n* - **1.** [person] Russe *der*, -sin *die* - **2.** [language] Russisch(e) *das*.

rust [rʌst] <> *n* [on metal] Rost *der*. <> *vi* rosten.

rustle ['rʌsl] <> *vt* - **1.** [paper] rascheln mit; [subj: wind - leaves] rascheln lassen - **2.** *US* [cattle] stehlen. <> *vi* [paper, leaves] rascheln.

rusty ['rʌstɪ] adj - 1. [metal] rostig - 2. fig [skill] eingerostet; **I'm rusty** ich bin aus der Übung.

rut [rʌt] n [furrow] Furche die; **to get into a rut** in einen Trott kommen.

ruthless ['ruːθlɪs] adj [person] rücksichtslos; [investigation, destruction] schonungslos; [murder] brutal.

RV n US (abbr of **recreational vehicle**) Wohnmobil das.

rye [raɪ] n [grain] Roggen der.

rye bread n (U) Roggenbrot das.

S

s (pl **ss** OR **s's**), **S** (pl **Ss** OR **S's**) [es] n [letter] s das, S das. ► **S** (abbr of **south**) S.

Sabbath ['sæbəθ] n: **the Sabbath** der Sabbat.

sabotage ['sæbətɑːʒ] ⬦ n Sabotage die. ⬦ vt sabotieren.

sachet ['sæʃeɪ] n [of shampoo, cream] Einzelpackung die; [of sugar, coffee] Portionspackung die.

sack [sæk] ⬦ n - 1. [bag] Sack der - 2. UK inf [dismissal]: **to get** OR **be given the sack** rausgeschmissen werden. ⬦ vt UK inf [dismiss] rausschmeißen.

sacred ['seɪkrɪd] adj liter & fig heilig.

sacrifice ['sækrɪfaɪs] ⬦ n liter & fig Opfer das. ⬦ vt liter & fig opfern.

sacrilege ['sækrɪlɪdʒ] n liter & fig Sakrileg das.

sad [sæd] adj traurig.

sadden ['sædn] vt traurig machen; **I was saddened to hear of her death** die Nachricht von ihrem Tod machte mich sehr traurig.

saddle ['sædl] ⬦ n Sattel der. ⬦ vt - 1. [put saddle on] satteln - 2. fig [burden]: **to saddle sb with sthg** jm etw aufhalsen; **to be saddled with sthg** etw am Hals haben.

saddlebag ['sædlbæg] n Satteltasche die.

sadistic [sə'dɪstɪk] adj sadistisch.

sadly ['sædlɪ] adv - 1. [sorrowfully] traurig - 2. [regrettably] leider.

sadness ['sædnɪs] n - 1. [sorrow] Trauer die - 2. [distressing nature] Traurigkeit die.

s.a.e., sae n abbr of **stamped addressed envelope.**

safari [sə'fɑːrɪ] n Safari die.

safe [seɪf] ⬦ adj sicher; [product] ungefährlich; **it's not safe for young children** es ist gefährlich für kleine Kinder; **have a safe jour-**

ney! gute Reise!; safe and sound wohlbehalten; phrase: **it's safe to say that...** man kann mit Sicherheit sagen, dass...; **to be on the safe side** um sicher zu gehen. ⬦ n Safe der.

safe-conduct n - 1. [document giving protection] Geleitbrief der - 2. [protection] sicheres Geleit.

safe-deposit box n Banksafe der.

safeguard ['seɪfgɑːd] ⬦ n: **safeguard (against sthg)** Schutz der (gegen etw). ⬦ vt: **to safeguard sb/sthg (against sthg)** jn/etw (vor etw (D)) schützen.

safekeeping [ˌseɪf'kiːpɪŋ] n (sichere) Aufbewahrung.

safely ['seɪflɪ] adv sicher; [arrive] wohlbehalten; **I can safely say (that)** ich kann mit Sicherheit sagen, dass.

safe sex n Safersex der.

safety ['seɪftɪ] n Sicherheit die.

safety belt n Sicherheitsgurt der.

safety pin n Sicherheitsnadel die.

sag [sæg] vi [sink downwards] durchhängen.

sage [seɪdʒ] ⬦ adj [wise] weise. ⬦ n - 1. [herb] Salbei die - 2. [wise man] Weise der.

Sagittarius [ˌsædʒɪ'teərɪəs] n Schütze der.

Sahara [sə'hɑːrə] n: **the Sahara (Desert)** die (Wüste) Sahara.

said [sed] pt & pp ▷ **say.**

sail [seɪl] ⬦ n - 1. [of boat] Segel das; **to set sail** losfahren - 2. [journey by boat]: **to go for a sail** segeln gehen. ⬦ vt - 1. [ship] steuern; [sailing boat] segeln mit - 2. [sea] befahren. ⬦ vi - 1. [person - travel] mit dem Schiff fahren; [- leave] ablfahren; SPORT segeln - 2. [ship - move] fahren; [- leave] ablfahren - 3. [sailing boat] segeln - 4. fig [through air] segeln. ► **sail through** vt insep [exam] spielend bestehen.

sailboat n US = **sailing boat.**

sailing ['seɪlɪŋ] n - 1. SPORT Segeln das; **plain sailing** ganz einfach - 2. [trip by ship]: **there are ten sailings a day** das Schiff fährt zehnmal am Tag.

sailing boat UK, **sailboat** US ['seɪlbəʊt] n Segelboot das.

sailing ship n Segelschiff das.

sailor ['seɪlə'] n Seemann der; [in navy] Matrose der; SPORT Segler der, -in die.

saint [seɪnt] n RELIG Heilige der, die.

saintly ['seɪntlɪ] adj [person] gütig.

sake [seɪk] n - 1. [benefit, advantage]: **for the sake of sb** jm zuliebe; **for my/your sake** mir/ dir zuliebe - 2. [purpose]: **for the sake of peace/ your health** um des Friedens/deiner Gesundheit willen; **let us say, for the sake of argument, that...** sagen wir spaßeshalber, dass... - 3. phr: **for God's** OR **Heaven's sake!** um Gottes willen!

salad ['sæləd] n Salat der.

salad bowl n Salatschüssel *die*.

salad cream n UK majonäseartige Salatsoße.

salad dressing n Salatsoße *die*, Dressing *das*.

salami [sə'lɑːmɪ] n Salami *die*.

salary ['sælərɪ] n Gehalt *das*.

sale [seɪl] n - **1.** [instance of selling] Verkauf *der*; **to make a sale** etwas verkaufen - **2.** (U) [selling] Verkauf *der*; **to be on sale** verkauft werden; **to be for sale** zu verkaufen sein - **3.** [at reduced prices] Ausverkauf *der* - **4.** [auction] Auktion *die*. ◆ **sales** npl - **1.** [quantity sold] Absatz *der* - **2.** [at reduced prices]: **the sales** der Schlussverkauf.

saleroom UK ['seɪlrʊm], **salesroom** US ['seɪlzrʊm] n [for auction] Auktionsraum *der*.

sales assistant ['seɪlz-], **salesclerk** ['seɪlzklɜːrk] US n Verkäufer *der*, -in *die*.

salesman ['seɪlzmən] (pl -**men** [-mən]) n Verkäufer *der*; [representative] Vertreter *der*.

sales rep n inf Vertreter *der*, -in *die*.

salesroom n US = **saleroom**.

saleswoman ['seɪlz,wʊmən] (pl -**women** [-,wɪmɪn]) n Verkäuferin *die*; [representative] Vertreterin *die*.

saliva [sə'laɪvə] n Speichel *der*.

salmon ['sæmən] (pl inv OR -**s**) n Lachs *der*.

salmonella [,sælmə'nelə] n (U): **salmonella (poisoning)** Salmonellenvergiftung *die*.

salon [sæ'lɒn] n Salon *der*.

saloon [sə'luːn] n - **1.** UK [car] Limousine *die* - **2.** US [bar] Wirtschaft *die*; [in the Wild West] Saloon *der* - **3.** [on ship] Salon *der*.

salt [sɔːlt, sɒlt] ◇ n Salz *das*; **to take sth with a pinch of salt** etw nicht wörtlich nehmen. ◇ vt - **1.** [food] salzen - **2.** [roads] streuen. ◆ **salt away** vt sep inf [money] auf die hohe Kante legen.

saltcellar UK ['sɔːlt,selər], **salt shaker** US [-,ʃeɪkər] n Salzstreuer *der*.

saltwater ['sɔːlt,wɔːtər] ◇ n Salzwasser *das*. ◇ adj Meeres-.

salty ['sɔːltɪ] adj [tasting of salt] salzig.

salute [sə'luːt] ◇ n - **1.** MIL [with hand] Gruß *der*; **to give a salute** salutieren - **2.** MIL [firing of guns] Salut *der* - **3.** [formal acknowledgement]: **salute (to sth)** Würdigung *die* (von etw). ◇ vt - **1.** MIL salutieren vor (+ D) - **2.** [acknowledge formally, honour] würdigen; [person] ehren. ◇ vi MIL salutieren.

salvage ['sælvɪdʒ] ◇ n (U) - **1.** [rescue of ship] Bergung *die* - **2.** [property rescued] Bergungsgut *das*. ◇ vt - **1.** [rescue]: **to salvage sth (from)** etw bergen (aus) - **2.** fig: **to salvage one's reputation** seinen Ruf retten.

salvation [sæl'veɪʃn] n (U) - **1.** [saviour] Rettung *die* - **2.** RELIG Erlösung *die*.

Salvation Army n: **the Salvation Army** die Heilsarmee.

same [seɪm] ◇ adj - **1.** [identical]: **the same** derselbe/dieselbe/dasselbe, dieselben Pl; **you've got the same book as me** du hast das gleiche Buch wie ich; **the same thing** dasselbe; **the same ones** dieselben; **at the same time** [simultaneously] zur gleichen Zeit; [nevertheless] andererseits; **one and the same** ein und derselbe/dieselbe/dasselbe - **2.** [unchanged]: **the same der/die/das Gleiche, die Gleichen** Pl; **the same ones** die Gleichen. ◇ pron - **1.** [identical]: **the same** derselbe/dieselbe/dasselbe, dieselben Pl; **I'll have the same as her** ich möchte das Gleiche wie sie; **all** OR **just the same** [nevertheless] trotzdem; **it's all the same to me** es ist mir gleich; **they are all the same** sie sind alle gleich; **the same to you** gleichfalls; **(the) same again, please** noch einen/eine/eins, bitte; **it's not the same** es ist nicht dasselbe - **2.** [unchanged]: **the same** der/die/das Gleiche, die Gleichen Pl; **her views are still the same** sie hat immer noch die gleichen Ansichten. ◇ adv [identically]: **to dress/feel the same** sich gleich anziehen/fühlen; **they look the same** sie sehen gleich aus.

sample ['sɑːmpl] ◇ n - **1.** [of product] Probe *die*; [of fabric] Muster *das* - **2.** [for analysis] Probe *die* - **3.** [representative portion - of work] Musterbeispiel *das*; [- of people in survey] Auswahl *die*. ◇ vt - **1.** [taste] kosten - **2.** [try out, test] ausprobieren.

sanatorium, sanitorium US (pl -**riums** OR -**ria** [-rɪə]), [,sænə'tɔːrɪəm] n Sanatorium *das*.

sanctimonious [,sæŋktɪ'məʊnjəs] adj pej frömmlerisch.

sanction ['sæŋkʃn] ◇ n - **1.** [formal approval] Billigung *die* - **2.** [punishment] Strafe *die*. ◇ vt [authorize] billigen.

sanctuary ['sæŋktʃʊərɪ] n - **1.** [for birds, wildlife] Schutzgebiet *das* - **2.** [safety, place of safety] Zufluchtsort *der*.

sand [sænd] ◇ n Sand *der*. ◇ vt [make smooth] schmirgeln.

sandal ['sændl] n Sandale *die*.

sandalwood ['sændlwʊd] n Sandelholz *das*.

sandbox n US = **sandpit**.

sandcastle ['sænd,kɑːsl] n Sandburg *die*.

sand dune n Sanddüne *die*.

sandpaper ['sænd,peɪpər] ◇ n Sandpapier *das*. ◇ vt mit Sandpapier abschmirgeln.

sandpit UK ['sændpɪt], **sandbox** US ['sændbɒks] n Sandkasten *der*.

sandwich ['sænwɪdʒ] ◇ n Sandwich *das*; **ham/cheese sandwich** Schinken-/Käsebrot *das*. ◇ vt fig: **to be sandwiched between** eingeklemmt sein zwischen (+ D).

sandwich board n zweiteilige Reklametafel zum Umhängen.

sandwich course n UK Kurs, bei dem sich Studium und Praktikum abwechseln.

sandy ['sændɪ] *adj* - **1.** [beach] sandig - **2.** [sand-coloured] sandfarben.

sane [seɪn] *adj* - **1.** [not mad] normal, bei Verstand - **2.** [sensible] vernünftig.

sang [sæŋ] *pt* ▷ **sing**.

sanitary ['sænɪtrɪ] *adj* - **1.** [connected with health - officer, system] Gesundheits-; [- procedures] sanitär - **2.** [clean, hygienic] hygienisch.

sanitary towel, sanitary napkin *US n* Damenbinde *die*.

sanitation [,sænɪ'teɪʃn] *n (U)* sanitäre Einrichtungen *Pl*.

sanitorium *n US* = **sanatorium**.

sanity ['sænɪtɪ] *n (U)* - **1.** [saneness] Verstand *der* - **2.** [good sense] Vernunft *die*.

sank [sæŋk] *pt* ▷ **sink**.

Santa (Claus) ['sæntə (,klɔːz)] *n* der Weihnachtsmann.

sap [sæp] ◇ *n (U)* [of plant] Saft *der*. ◇ *vt* [weaken] schwächen.

sapling ['sæplɪŋ] *n* junger Baum.

sapphire ['sæfaɪə*r*] *n* Saphir *der*.

sarcastic [sɑː'kæstɪk] *adj* sarkastisch.

sardine [sɑː'diːn] *n* Sardine *die*.

Sardinia [sɑː'dɪnjə] *n* Sardinien *nt*.

sardonic [sɑː'dɒnɪk] *adj* [smile, look] hämisch.

SAS *(abbr of Special Air Service) n* Spezialeinheit der britischen Armee.

SASE *n US abbr of* **self-addressed stamped envelope**.

sash [sæʃ] *n* [strip of cloth] Schärpe *die*.

sat [sæt] *pt & pp* ▷ **sit**.

SAT [sæt] *n* - **1.** *(abbr of Standard Assessment Task)*, *Eignungstest für Schulkinder in England und Wales* - **2.** *(abbr of Scholastic Aptitude Test)*, *Zulassungsprüfung an US-Universitäten*.

Satan ['seɪtn] *n* Satan *der*.

satchel ['sætʃəl] *n* Schultasche *die*.

satellite ['sætəlaɪt] ◇ *n* liter & *fig* Satellit *der*. ◇ *comp* Satelliten-.

satellite TV *n* Satellitenfernsehen *das*.

satin ['sætɪn] ◇ *n* Satin *der*. ◇ *comp* - **1.** [made of satin] Satin- - **2.** [wallpaper, paint, finish] seidenmatt.

satire ['sætaɪə*r*] *n* Satire *die*.

satisfaction [,sætɪs'fækʃn] *n* - **1.** [pleasure] Befriedigung *die* - **2.** [something that pleases]: **the job has few satisfactions** die Arbeit ist nicht sehr befriedigend - **3.** [fulfilment - of need, demand] Befriedigung *die*; [- of criteria] Erfüllung *die*.

satisfactory [,sætɪs'fæktərɪ] *adj* befriedigend.

satisfied ['sætɪsfaɪd] *adj* [happy] zufrieden; **to be satisfied with sthg** mit etw zufrieden sein.

satisfy ['sætɪsfaɪ] *vt* - **1.** [make happy] zufrieden stellen - **2.** [convince] überzeugen; **to satisfy sb/o.s. that...** jn/sich davon überzeugen, dass... - **3.** [fulfil - need, demand] befriedigen; [- requirements] genügen *(+ D)*.

satisfying ['sætɪsfaɪɪŋ] *adj* befriedigend.

satsuma [,sæt'suːmə] *n* Satsuma *die*.

saturate ['sætʃəreɪt] *vt* - **1.** [drench] tränken; [subj: rain] durchnässen - **2.** [fill completely, swamp - area, town] überschwemmen; [- market] sättigen.

saturated *adj* - **1.** [drenched] getränkt; [with rain] durchnässt - **2.** [fat] gesättigt.

Saturday ['sætədɪ] ◇ *n* Samstag *der*; **what day is it? – it's Saturday** was ist heute? – es ist Samstag; **on Saturday** am Samstag; **on Saturdays** samstags; **last/this/next Saturday** letzten/diesen/nächsten Samstag; **every Saturday** jeden Samstag; **every other Saturday** jeden zweiten Samstag; **the Saturday before** den Samstag davor, am vorhergehenden Samstag; **the Saturday before last** vorletzten Samstag; **the Saturday after next, Saturday week, a week on Saturday** übernächsten Samstag, Samstag in einer Woche. ◇ *comp* Samstags-; **Saturday morning/afternoon/evening/night** Samstagmorgen *der*/-nachmittag *der*/-abend *der*/-nacht *die*.

sauce [sɔːs] *n* CULIN Soße *die*, Sauce *die*.

saucepan ['sɔːspən] *n* Kochtopf *der*.

saucer ['sɔːsə*r*] *n* Untertasse *die*.

saucy ['sɔːsɪ] *adj inf* frech.

Saudi Arabia ['saʊdɪ-] *n* Saudi-Arabien *nt*.

sauna ['sɔːnə] *n* Sauna *die*; **to have a sauna** in die Sauna gehen.

saunter ['sɔːntə*r*] *vi* schlendern.

sausage ['sɒsɪdʒ] *n* Wurst *die*.

sausage roll *n UK* Würstchen in Blätterteig.

sauté [*UK* 'səʊteɪ, *US* sɔːˈteɪ] *(pt & pp* **sautéed** *OR* **sautéd)* ◇ *adj* [potatoes] Röst-, Brat-. ◇ *vt* [potatoes] rösten, braten; [meat] sautieren.

savage ['sævɪdʒ] ◇ *adj* [attack, criticism, person] brutal; [dog] bissig. ◇ *n* Wilde *der, die*. ◇ *vt* [attack physically] anfallen.

save [seɪv] ◇ *vt* - **1.** [rescue] retten; **to save sb from sthg** jn vor etw *(D)* retten; **to save sb's life** jm das Leben retten - **2.** [money, time, space] sparen - **3.** [reserve] aufheben; **to save a seat for sb** jm einen Platz freihalten; **to save one's strength/voice** seine Kräfte/Stimme schonen - **4.** [make unnecessary - trouble, work] ersparen; [- expense] vermeiden; **to save sb from doing sthg** es jm ersparen, etw zu tun - **5.** SPORT abwehren - **6.** COMPUT speichern. ◇ *vi* [save money] sparen. ◇ *n* SPORT Parade *die*. ◇ *prep fml:* **save (for)** außer *(+ D)*. ◆ **save on** *vt insep* sparen. ◆ **save up** *vi:* **to save up (for sthg)** (auf etw *(A)*) sparen.

savings ['seɪvɪŋz] *npl* Ersparnisse *Pl*.

savings account n US Sparkonto das.

savings and loan association n US Bausparkasse die.

savings bank n Sparkasse die.

saviour UK, **savior** US ['seɪvjər] n Retter der, -in die.

savour UK, **savor** US ['seɪvər] vt genießen.

savoury UK, **savory** US ['seɪvərɪ] ⟨⟩ adj - 1. [not sweet] pikant - 2. [respectable, pleasant] angenehm. ⟨⟩ n (pikantes) Häppchen.

saw [sɔː] (UK pt -ed, pp sawn) (US pt & pp -ed) ⟨⟩ pt ▷ **see**. ⟨⟩ n Säge die. ⟨⟩ vt sägen.

sawdust ['sɔːdʌst] n Sägemehl das.

sawed-off shotgun n US = **sawn-off shotgun**.

sawmill ['sɔːmɪl] n Sägewerk das.

sawn [sɔːn] pp UK ▷ **saw**.

sawn-off shotgun UK, **sawed-off shotgun** ['sɔːd-] US n Gewehr mit abgesägtem Lauf.

saxophone ['sæksəfəʊn] n Saxofon das.

say [seɪ] (pt & pp said) ⟨⟩ vt - 1. [gen] sagen; **to say sthg again** etw nochmal sagen, etw wiederholen; **who should I say it is?** wen darf ich melden?; **he's said to be good** er soll gut sein - 2. [subj: clock, meter] anlzeigen; [subj: sign] besagen; **the letter says...** in dem Brief steht...; **it says here that...** hier heißt es, dass... - 3. [assume]: **I'd say he's lying** meiner Meinung nach lügt er; **(let's) say you were to lose** nehmen wir an, du verlierst; **shall we say nine (o'clock)?** sagen wir um neun? - 4. phr: **that goes without saying** das versteht sich von selbst; **that's not saying much** das will nicht viel heißen; **it has a lot to be said for it** es spricht vieles dafür. ⟨⟩ n: **to have a/no say (in sthg)** etw/nichts (bei etw) zu sagen haben; **to have one's say** seine Meinung äußern. ⟪ **that is to say** adv das heißt.

saying ['seɪɪŋ] n Redensart die.

scab [skæb] n - 1. [of wound] Schorf der - 2. pej [non-striker] Streikbrecher der, -in die.

scaffold ['skæfəʊld] n - 1. [frame] Gerüst das - 2. [for executions] Schafott das.

scaffolding ['skæfəldɪŋ] n (U) Gerüst das.

scald [skɔːld] ⟨⟩ n Verbrühung die. ⟨⟩ vt [burn] verbrühen.

scale [skeɪl] ⟨⟩ n - 1. [set of numbers] Skala die; [of pay] Tarif der - 2. [of ruler, thermometer] Einteilung die - 3. [size] Größe die; [extent] Ausmaß das; **on a small/large scale** im Kleinen/Großen; **the project is on a large scale** das Projekt ist groß angelegt - 4. [size ratio] Maßstab der; **to scale** maßstab(s)getreu - 5. MUS Tonleiter die - 6. [of fish, snake] Schuppe die - 7. US = **scales**. ⟨⟩ vt - 1. [climb] erklimmen - 2. [remove scales from] schuppen. ⟪ **scales** npl Waage die. ⟪ **scale down** vt sep [industry] ablbauen; [investment] reduzieren; [production] drosseln.

scallop ['skɒləp] ⟨⟩ n [shellfish] Kammmuschel die; CULIN Jakobsmuschel die. ⟨⟩ vt [decorate] mit einem Bogenrand verzieren.

scalp [skælp] ⟨⟩ n - .1. ANAT Kopfhaut die - 2. [removed from head] Skalp der. ⟨⟩ vt skalpieren.

scalpel ['skælpəl] n Skalpell das.

scamper ['skæmpər] vi [children, dog] flitzen; [mouse] huschen; **to scamper around** [children] herumltollen.

scampi ['skæmpɪ] n (U) Scampi Pl.

scan [skæn] ⟨⟩ n MED & TECH Scan der; [on pregnant woman] Ultraschalluntersuchung die. ⟨⟩ vt - 1. [examine carefully - map] studieren; [- area] ablsuchen; [- crowd] mit den Augen ablsuchen - 2. [glance at] überfliegen - 3. MED computertomografisch untersuchen - 4. COMPUT & TECH scannen.

scandal ['skændl] n - 1. [scandalous event, outrage] Skandal der - 2. (U) [rumours] Skandalgeschichten Pl.

scandalize, -ise ['skændəlaɪz] vt schockieren.

Scandinavia [ˌskændɪ'neɪvjə] n Skandinavien nt.

Scandinavian [ˌskændɪ'neɪvjən] ⟨⟩ adj skandinavisch. ⟨⟩ n [person] Skandinavier der, -in die.

scant [skænt] adj wenig.

scanty ['skæntɪ] adj [amount, resources] dürftig, spärlich; [dress] knapp.

scapegoat ['skeɪpgəʊt] n Sündenbock der.

scar [skɑːr] n liter & fig Narbe die.

scarce ['skeəs] adj knapp.

scarcely ['skeəslɪ] adv kaum.

scare [skeər] ⟨⟩ n - 1. [sudden fright] Schreck(en) der; **to give sb a scare** jn erschrecken - 2. [public panic] Panik die; **a bomb scare** ein Bombenalarm. ⟨⟩ vt [frighten] erschrecken. ⟪ **scare away, scare off** vt sep verscheuchen.

scarecrow ['skeəkrəʊ] n Vogelscheuche die.

scared ['skeəd] adj - 1. [very frightened] verängstigt; **to be scared** Angst haben; **to be scared stiff** OR **to death** fürchterliche Angst haben - 2. [nervous, worried]: **to be scared that...** befürchten, dass...

scarf [skɑːf] (pl -s OR scarves) n Schal der; [headscarf] Kopftuch das.

scarlet ['skɑːlət] adj scharlachrot.

scarves [skɑːvz] Pl ▷ **scarf**.

scathing ['skeɪðɪŋ] adj [remark, criticism] scharf.

scatter ['skætər] ⟨⟩ vt [spread out] verstreuen; [seed] streuen. ⟨⟩ vi [crowd] sich zerstreuen; [birds] auflfliegen.

scatterbrained ['skætəbreɪnd] adj inf zerstreut.

scenario [sɪ'nɑːrɪəʊ] (pl -s) n Szenario das.

scene [siːn] *n* Szene *die*; [location] Ort *der*; **behind the scenes** hinter den Kulissen; **it's not my scene** das ist nicht mein Fall; **to set the scene** [give background information] Hintergrundinformationen geben; **to set the scene for sthg** den Nährboden für etw bilden.

scenery ['siːnəri] *n* (U) - 1. [of countryside] Landschaft *die* - 2. [in theatre] Kulissen *Pl.*

scenic ['siːnik] *adj* [view] schön.

scent [sent] *n* - 1. [smell - of flowers] Duft *der*; [- of animal] Witterung *die* - 2. [perfume] Parfüm *das.*

scepter *n US* = **sceptre**.

sceptic *UK*, **skeptic** *US* ['skeptik] *n* Skeptiker *der*, -in *die.*

sceptical *UK*, **skeptical** *US* ['skeptikl] *adj* skeptisch; **to be sceptical about sthg** bezüglich etw (G) skeptisch sein.

sceptre *UK*, **scepter** *US* ['septər] *n* Zepter *das.*

schedule [*UK* 'ʃedjuːl, *US* 'skedʒʊl] ⋄ *n* - 1. [plan] Plan *der*, Programm *das*; **ahead of/behind schedule** früher/später als geplant; **on schedule** pünktlich, planmäßig - 2. [written list] Verzeichnis *das.* ⋄ *vt*: **to schedule sthg (for)** etw planen *OR* anlsetzen (für).

scheduled flight [*UK* 'ʃedjuːld, *US* 'skedʒʊld-] *n* Linienflug *der.*

scheme [skiːm] ⋄ *n* - 1. [plan] Programm *das*; **pension scheme** Altersversorgung *die* - 2. *pej* [dishonest plan] raffinierter Plan - 3. [arrangement, decoration - of room] Einrichtung *die*; **colour scheme** Farbzusammenstellung *die.* ⋄ *vi pej* Pläne schmieden.

scheming ['skiːmɪŋ] *adj* raffiniert; [politician] intrigant.

schizophrenic [,skɪtsə'frenɪk] ⋄ *adj* schizophren. ⋄ *n* Schizophrene *der*, *die.*

scholar ['skɒlər] *n* - 1. [expert] Gelehrte *der*, *die* - 2. *dated* [school student] Schüler *der*, -in *die* - 3. [holder of scholarship] Stipendiat *der*, -in *die.*

scholarship ['skɒləʃɪp] *n* - 1. [grant] Stipendium *das* - 2. [learning] Gelehrsamkeit *die.*

school [skuːl] *n* - 1. [gen] Schule *die*; **to go to school** in die Schule gehen; **at school** in der Schule - 2. UNIV [department] Fachbereich *der*; **school of medicine/law** medizinische/juristische Fakultät - 3. *US* [university] Universität *die* - 4. [group of fish, dolphins] Schwarm *der.*

schoolbook ['skuːlbʊk] *n* Schulbuch *das.*

schoolboy ['skuːlbɔɪ] *n* Schuljunge *der*, Schüler *der.*

schoolchild ['skuːltʃaɪld] (*pl* -children [-tʃɪldrən]) *n* Schulkind *das.*

schooldays ['skuːldeɪz] *npl* Schulzeit *die.*

schoolgirl ['skuːlgɜːl] *n* Schulmädchen *das*, Schülerin *die.*

schooling ['skuːlɪŋ] *n* [education] Ausbildung *die.*

school-leaver [-,liːvər] *n UK* Schulabgänger *der*, -in *die.*

schoolmaster ['skuːl,mɑːstər] *n dated* Schulmeister *der.*

schoolmistress ['skuːl,mɪstrɪs] *n dated* Schulmeisterin *die.*

schoolteacher ['skuːl,tiːtʃər] *n* Lehrer *der*, -in *die.*

school year *n* Schuljahr *das.*

sciatica [saɪ'ætɪkə] *n* Ischias *die.*

science ['saɪəns] *n* - 1. (U) [system of knowledge] Wissenschaft *die* - 2. [branch of knowledge] Naturwissenschaft *die.*

science fiction *n* Science-Fiction *die.*

scientific [,saɪən'tɪfɪk] *adj* wissenschaftlich.

scientist ['saɪəntɪst] *n* Wissenschaftler *der*, -in *die*; [of physical or natural sciences] Naturwissenschaftler *der*, -in *die.*

scintillating ['sɪntɪleɪtɪŋ] *adj* [conversation, speaker] vor Geist sprühend.

scissors ['sɪzəz] *npl* Schere *die*; **a pair of scissors** eine Schere.

scoff [skɒf] ⋄ *vt UK inf* verputzen. ⋄ *vi* [mock] spotten; **to scoff at sb/sthg** über jn/etw spotten.

scold [skəʊld] *vt* auslschimpfen.

scone [skɒn, skəʊn] *n* kleiner brötchenartiger Kuchen, der mit Butter oder Marmelade und Schlagsahne bestrichen gegessen wird.

scoop [skuːp] ⋄ *n* - 1. [kitchen implement] Schaufel *die*; [for potato, ice-cream] Portionierer *der* - 2. [scoopful] Kugel *die* - 3. [news report] Exklusivbericht *der.* ⋄ *vt* schaufeln; [liquid] schöpfen. ◆ **scoop out** *vt sep* [remove] herauslöffeln.

scooter ['skuːtər] *n* - 1. [toy] (Tret)roller *der* - 2. [motorcycle] (Motor)roller *der.*

scope [skəʊp] *n* (U) - 1. [opportunity] Möglichkeit *die* - 2. [range] Umfang *der.*

scorch [skɔːtʃ] *vt* - 1. [clothes] versengen; [food] anlbrennen; [skin] verbrennen - 2. [grass, fields] versengen.

scorching ['skɔːtʃɪŋ] *adj inf*: **scorching (hot)** [day, weather] knallheiß; [sun] sengend.

score [skɔːr] ⋄ *n* - 1. SPORT Spielstand *der*; [at end of game] Ergebnis *das*; **the score is 4-3** es steht 4 zu 3 - 2. [in test, competition] Punkte *Pl* - 3. *dated* [twenty] zwanzig - 4. MUS Noten *Pl* - 5. [subject]: **on that score** in dieser Hinsicht. ⋄ *vt* - 1. SPORT erzielen; [goal] schießen - 2. [achieve - success] erzielen; [- victory] erringen; [- hit] landen - 3. [win in an argument]: **to score a point over sb** jn auslstechen - 4. [cut - surface] einlkerben; [- line] einlritzen. ⋄ *vi* SPORT Punkte erzielen; **to score a goal** [in football] ein Tor schießen; [in handball] ein Tor werfen. ◆ **score out** *vt sep UK* durchlstreichen.

scoreboard ['skɔːbɔːd] *n* Anzeigetafel *die.*

scorer ['skɔːrəʳ] *n* - **1.** [official] Anschreiber *der*, -in *die* - **2.** [player]: **(goal)scorer** Torschütze *der*, -zin *die*.

scorn [skɔːn] <> *n (U)* Verachtung *die*. <> *vt* - **1.** [despise] verachten - **2.** *fml* [refuse to accept] verschmähen.

scornful ['skɔːnfʊl] *adj* [laugh, remark] verächtlich; **to be scornful of sthg** etw verachten.

Scorpio ['skɔːpɪəʊ] (*pl* -s) *n* Skorpion *der*.

scorpion ['skɔːpjən] *n* Skorpion *der*.

Scot [skɒt] *n* Schotte *der*, -tin *die*.

scotch [skɒtʃ] *vt* [idea, rumour] ein Ende setzen *(+ D)*.

Scotch [skɒtʃ] <> *adj* schottisch. <> *n* [whisky] Scotch *der*.

Scotch (tape)® *n US* Tesafilm® *der*.

scot-free *adj inf*: **to get off scot-free** ungeschoren davonkommen.

Scotland ['skɒtlənd] *n* Schottland *nt*.

Scots [skɒts] <> *adj* schottisch. <> *n* [dialect] Schottisch *das*.

Scotsman ['skɒtsmən] (*pl* -men [-mən]) *n* Schotte *der*.

Scotswoman ['skɒtswʊmən] (*pl* -women [-,wɪmɪn]) *n* Schottin *die*.

Scottish ['skɒtɪʃ] *adj* schottisch.

scoundrel ['skaʊndrəl] *n dated* Schurke *der*.

scour [skaʊəʳ] *vt* - **1.** [clean] scheuern - **2.** [search] durchkämmen.

scourge [skɜːdʒ] *n* Geißel *die*.

scout [skaʊt] *n* MIL Kundschafter *der*, -in *die*.
◆ **Scout** *n* [boy scout] Pfadfinder *der*.
◆ **scout around** *vi*: **to scout around (for sthg)** (nach etw) herumsuchen.

scowl [skaʊl] <> *n* finsterer OR böser Blick. <> *vi* ein finsteres OR böses Gesicht machen; **to scowl at sb** jn finster OR böse ansehen.

scrabble ['skræbl] *vi* - **1.** [scramble] klettern - **2.** [feel around] herumwühlen; **to scrabble around for sthg** nach etw wühlen.

scramble ['skræmbl] <> *n* [rush] Gedrängel *das*. <> *vi* - **1.** [climb] klettern - **2.** [struggle]: **to scramble for sthg** um etw kämpfen.

scrambled eggs ['skræmbld-] *npl* Rührei *das*.

scrap [skræp] <> *n* - **1.** [small piece] Stückchen *das*; [of paper, material, conversation] Fetzen *der*; **not a scrap of evidence** kein einziger Beweis - **2.** [metal] Schrott *der* - **3.** *inf* [fight] Rauferei *die*; [quarrel] Streit *der*. <> *vt* [plan, system] aufgeben; [car, ship] verschrotten.
◆ **scraps** *npl* [food] (Essens)reste *Pl*.

scrapbook ['skræpbʊk] *n* Erinnerungsalbum *das*.

scrape [skreɪp] <> *n* - **1.** [scraping noise] Kratzen *das* - **2.** *dated* [difficult situation]: **to get into a scrape** in die Klemme geraten. <> *vt* - **1.** [remove]: **to scrape sthg off sthg** etw von etw abschaben - **2.** [peel] schaben - **3.** [rub

against - car, bumper] schrammen; [- glass] verkratzen; [- knee, skin] aufschürfen. <> *vi* [rub]: **to scrape against sthg** etw streifen.
◆ **scrape through** *vt insep* [exam, test] mit knapper Not bestehen.

scraper ['skreɪpəʳ] *n* [for paint] Spachtel *der*.

scrap merchant *n UK* Schrotthändler *der*, -in *die*.

scrap paper *UK*, **scratch paper** *US n* Schmierpapier *das*.

scrapyard ['skræpjɑːd] *n* Schrottplatz *der*.

scratch [skrætʃ] <> *n* - **1.** [on skin, surface] Kratzer *der* - **2.** *phr*: **to start sthg from scratch** etw ganz von vorne anfangen; **to be up to scratch** den Erwartungen entsprechen. <> *vt* - **1.** [skin] kratzen; **to scratch o.s.** sich kratzen - **2.** [surface] verkratzen. <> *vi* - **1.** [branch, knife, thorn]: **to scratch at/against sthg** an etw *(D)*/gegen etw kratzen - **2.** [person, animal] sich kratzen.

scratch card *n* Rubbellos *das*.

scratch paper *n US* = scrap paper.

scrawl [skrɔːl] <> *n* [scribble] Kritzelei *die*. <> *vt* [scribble] hinkritzeln.

scrawny ['skrɔːnɪ] *adj* [person, legs, arms] dürr; [animal] mager.

scream [skriːm] <> *n* [of person] Schrei *der*. <> *vt* schreien. <> *vi* [person] schreien.

scree [skriː] *n* Geröll *das*.

screech [skriːtʃ] <> *n* - **1.** [of person, bird] Kreischen *das* - **2.** [of tyres, brakes] Quietschen *das*. <> *vt* kreischen. <> *vi* - **1.** [person, bird] kreischen - **2.** [tyres] quietschen.

screen [skriːn] <> *n* - **1.** [viewing surface] Bildschirm *der*; [in cinema] Leinwand *die* - **2.** [films]: **the (big) screen** der Film - **3.** [protective panel] Wandschirm *der*. <> *vt* - **1.** [in cinema] zeigen - **2.** [on TV] ausstrahlen - **3.** [hide] abschirmen - **4.** [shield]: **to screen sthg (from sb/sthg)** etw (gegen jn/etw) abschirmen - **5.** [candidate, luggage] überprüfen.

screening ['skriːnɪŋ] *n* - **1.** [in cinema] Vorführung *die* - **2.** [on TV] Ausstrahlung *die* - **3.** *(U)* [for security] Überprüfung *die* - **4.** *(U)* MED [examination] Untersuchung *die*.

screenplay ['skriːnpleɪ] *n* Drehbuch *das*.

screw [skruː] <> *n* [nail] Schraube *die*. <> *vt* - **1.** [fix with screws]: **to screw sthg to sthg** etw an etw *(A)* schrauben - **2.** [lid]: **to screw on/off** etw zu-/aufschrauben - **3.** *vulg* [have sex with] bumsen, vögeln. <> *vi* [lid]: **to screw on/off** sich zu-/aufschrauben lassen; **to screw together** sich zusammenschrauben lassen.
◆ **screw up** *vt sep* - **1.** [crumple up] zusammenknüllen - **2.** [contort, twist - eyes] zusammenkneifen; [- face] verziehen - **3.** *v inf* [ruin] vermasseln.

screwdriver ['skruː,draɪvəʳ] *n* [tool] Schraubenzieher *der*.

scribble ['skrɪbl] ◇ n Gekritzel das. ◇ vt hinǀkritzeln. ◇ vi [write] (vor sich hin)ǀschreiben; [messily] kritzeln.

script [skrɪpt] n - 1. [of film] Skript das - 2. [system of writing] Schrift die - 3. [handwriting] Handschrift die.

scriptwriter ['skrɪpt,raɪtər] n Textautor der, -in die; [of film] Filmautor der, -in die.

scroll [skrəʊl] n [roll of paper] Schriftrolle die. ◆ **scroll down** vi COMPUT hinunterǀscrollen. ◆ **scroll up** vi COMPUT hinaufǀscrollen.

scrounge [skraʊndʒ] inf vt: to scrounge sthg (off sb) etw (bei jm) abǀstauben OR schnorren.

scrounger ['skraʊndʒər] n inf Schnorrer der, -in die.

scrub [skrʌb] ◇ n - 1. [rub]: to give sthg a (good) scrub etw (gründlich) schrubben - 2. [undergrowth] Gestrüpp das. ◇ vt schrubben.

scruff [skrʌf] n: by the scruff of the neck am Genick.

scruffy ['skrʌfɪ] adj [person, clothes] ungepflegt; [part of town] heruntergekommen.

scrum(mage) ['skrʌm(ɪdʒ)] n RUGBY Gedränge das.

scrunchy ['skrʌntʃɪ] n Zopfband das.

scruples ['skruːplz] npl Skrupel Pl.

scrutinize, -ise ['skruːtɪnaɪz] vt [genau] untersuchen; [face] prüfend anǀsehen.

scrutiny ['skruːtɪnɪ] n (U) (genaue) Untersuchung OR Prüfung.

scuff [skʌf] vt - 1. [drag]: to scuff one's feet schlurfen - 2. [damage - shoes, floor] abǀwetzen; [- furniture] abǀnutzen.

scuffle ['skʌfl] n Rauferei die.

scullery ['skʌlərɪ] n Spülküche die.

sculptor ['skʌlptər] n Bildhauer der, -in die.

sculpture ['skʌlptʃər] ◇ n - 1. [work of art] Skulptur die, Plastik die - 2. (U) [art] Bildhauerei die, Skulptur die. ◇ vt formen; [in stone, wood] hauen.

scum [skʌm] n - 1. [froth] Schaum der - 2. v inf pej [worthless people] Abschaum der.

scupper ['skʌpər] vt - 1. NAUT [sink] versenken - 2. UK fig [plan] zerschlagen; [chance] ruinieren.

scurrilous ['skʌrələs] adj fml verleumderisch.

scurry ['skʌrɪ] vi hasten; [mouse] huschen.

scuttle ['skʌtl] ◇ n: (coal) scuttle Kohleneimer der. ◇ vi [rush] hasten; [mouse] huschen.

scythe [saɪð] n Sense die.

SDLP (abbr of Social Democratic and Labour Party) n gemäßigte pro-irische Partei Nordirlands.

sea [siː] ◇ n [ocean] Meer das, See die; to be at sea [ship, sailor] auf See sein; to be all at sea fig [person] verwirrt sein; by sea [send] auf dem Seeweg; [travel] mit dem Schiff fahren; by the sea am Meer; out to sea aufs Meer hinaus. ◇ comp See-.

seabed ['siːbed] n: the seabed der Meeresgrund.

seafood ['siːfuːd] n (U) Meeresfrüchte Pl.

seafront ['siːfrʌnt] n Strandpromenade die.

seagull ['siːgʌl] n Möwe die.

seal [siːl] ◇ n - 1. (pl inv) [animal] Robbe die - 2. (pl -s) [official mark] Siegel das - 3. (pl -s) [official fastening] Versiegelung die; [on letter] Siegel das; [of metal] Plombe die. ◇ vt - 1. [stick down] zuǀkleben - 2. [block up] abǀdichten. ◆ **seal off** vt sep abǀriegeln.

sea level n Meeresspiegel der.

sea lion (pl inv OR -s) n Seelöwe der.

seam [siːm] n - 1. SEW Naht die - 2. [of coal] Flöz das.

seaman ['siːmən] (pl -men [-mən]) n Seemann der.

seamy ['siːmɪ] adj anrüchig.

séance ['seɪɒns] n spiritistische Sitzung.

seaplane ['siːpleɪn] n Wasserflugzeug das.

seaport ['siːpɔːt] n Seehafen der.

search [sɜːtʃ] ◇ n - 1. [for lost person, object]: search (for) Suche die (nach); in search of auf der Suche nach - 2. [of person, luggage, house] Durchsuchung die. ◇ vt durchsuchen; [city] abǀsuchen; [one's mind, memory] durchǀforschen. ◇ vi: to search (for) suchen (nach).

search engine n COMPUT Suchmaschine die.

searching ['sɜːtʃɪŋ] adj [look] prüfend, forschend; [question] tiefschürfend; [examination] gründlich.

searchlight ['sɜːtʃlaɪt] n Suchscheinwerfer der.

search party n Suchmannschaft die.

search warrant n Durchsuchungsbefehl der.

seashell ['siːʃel] n Muschel die.

seashore ['siːʃɔːr] n: the seashore der Strand.

seasick ['siːsɪk] adj seekrank.·

seaside ['siːsaɪd] n: the seaside das Meer.

season ['siːzn] ◇ n - 1. [time of year] Jahreszeit die - 2. [for particular activity] Zeit die - 3. [of holiday] Saison die; out of season außerhalb der Saison - 4. [of food]: strawberries are out of season zu dieser Jahreszeit gibt es keine Erdbeeren - 5. [series - of films] Saison die; [- of lectures] Reihe die. ◇ vt [food] würzen.

seasonal ['siːzənl] adj [change] saisonal; [work] Saison-.

seasoned ['siːznd] adj [experienced] erfahren.

seasoning ['siːznɪŋ] n [for food] Gewürz das.

season ticket n Dauerkarte die; [for train] Zeitkarte die; [for theatre] Abonnement das.

seat [siːt] ◇ n - 1. [chair, part of chair, in parliament] Sitz der - 2. [place to sit] (Sitz)platz der;

take OR **have a seat** nehmen Sie Platz - 3. [of skirt] Sitz der; [of trousers] Hosenboden der. <> vt [person, guests] setzen.

seat belt n Sicherheitsgurt der.

seawater ['si:,wɔ:tər] n Meerwasser das, Seewasser das.

seaweed ['si:wi:d] n Seetang der.

seaworthy ['si:,wɜ:ði] adj seetüchtig.

sec. (abbr of **second**) n sek.

secede [sɪ'si:d] vi fml: **to secede (from sthg)** sich (von etw) ab| spalten.

secluded [sɪ'klu:dɪd] adj abgelegen.

seclusion [sɪ'klu:ʒn] n Abgeschiedenheit die.

second ['sekənd] <> n - 1. [of time, of angle] Sekunde die - 2. UK UNIV Note an britischen Universitäten, die dem deutschen "Gut" entspricht - 3. [moment] Moment der; **wait a second!** einen Moment! - 4. AUT: **second (gear)** zweiter Gang. <> num zweite(r) (s); **the second** der/die/das Zweite; **on the second (of March)** am zweiten (März); **she's second only to him** nur er ist besser als sie; **to come second** den zweiten Platz belegen; see also **sixth**.
➤ **seconds** npl - 1. COMM Waren Pl zweiter Wahl - 2. [of food] zweite Portion.

secondary ['sekəndrɪ] adj - 1. SCH: **secondary education** höhere Schulbildung - 2. [less important - road, cause] Neben-; [- issue] nebensächlich; **to be secondary to sthg** weniger wichtig als etw sein.

secondary school n höhere Schule.

second-class ['sekənd-] adj - 1. pej [less important] zweitklassig; [citizen] zweiter Klasse - 2. [ticket, seat] Zweite-Klasse- - 3. [postage]: **second-class stamp** billigere Briefmarke für Post, die weniger schnell befördert wird - 4. UK UNIV Note an britischen Universitäten, die dem deutschen "Gut" entspricht.

second-hand ['sekənd-] <> adj - 1. [goods] gebraucht; [clothes] Secondhand- - 2. [shop] Gebrauchtwaren-; [selling clothes] Secondhand- - 3. fig [indirect] aus zweiter Hand. <> adv [not new] gebraucht.

second hand ['sekənd-] n [of clock] Sekundenzeiger der.

secondly ['sekəndlɪ] adv zweitens.

secondment [sɪ'kɒndmənt] n UK einstweilige Versetzung.

second-rate ['sekənd-] adj pej zweitklassig, zweitrangig.

second thought ['sekənd-] n: **to have second thoughts about sthg** sich (D) etw anders überlegen; **on second thoughts** UK, **on second thought** US nach nochmaligem Überlegen.

secrecy ['si:krəsɪ] n (U) - 1. [being kept secret] Geheimhaltung die - 2. [secretiveness] Heimlichtuerei die.

secret ['si:krɪt] <> adj geheim; [admirer] heimlich. <> n Geheimnis das; **in secret** im Geheimen.

secretarial [,sekrə'teərɪəl] adj: **secretarial staff** Büroangestellte Pl.

secretary [UK 'sekrətrɪ, US 'sekrə,terɪ] n - 1. [clerical worker] Sekretär der, -in die - 2. [head of organization] Geschäftsführer der, -in die - 3. POL [minister] Minister der, -in die.

Secretary of State n - 1. UK [minister]: **Secretary of State (for sthg)** Minister der, -in die (für etw) - 2. US [in charge of foreign affairs] Außenminister der, -in die.

secretive ['si:krətɪv] adj [person] heimlichtuerisch.

secretly ['si:krɪtlɪ] adv [privately] heimlich.

sect [sekt] n Sekte die.

sectarian [sek'teərɪən] adj konfessionsbedingt; [war, quarrel] Konfessions-.

section ['sekʃn] n - 1. [portion] Teil der; [of book, road] Abschnitt der; [of law] Absatz der; [of community] Gruppe die; [of fruit] Stück das; **the sports section of the newspaper** der Sportteil der Zeitung - 2. GEOM Schnitt der.

sector ['sektər] n Sektor der.

secular ['sekjʊlər] adj säkular, weltlich; [music] profan.

secure [sɪ'kjʊər] <> adj - 1. [gen] sicher - 2. [building] einbruchsicher, sicher OR fest verschlossen. <> vt - 1. [obtain] sich (D) sichern; [agreement] erzielen - 2. [make safe] sichern - 3. [fasten] fest | machen; [door, window, lid] sicher verschließen.

security [sɪ'kjʊərətɪ] n Sicherheit die.
➤ **securities** npl FIN Wertpapiere Pl.

security guard n Wache die.

sedan [sɪ'dæn] n US Limousine die.

sedate [sɪ'deɪt] <> adj ruhig. <> vt Beruhigungsmittel geben (+ D).

sedation [sɪ'deɪʃn] n: **they've got him under sedation** er hat Beruhigungsmittel bekommen.

sedative ['sedətɪv] n Beruhigungsmittel das.

sediment ['sedɪmənt] n (Boden)satz der; CHEM & GEOL Sediment das.

seduce [sɪ'dju:s] vt verführen; **to seduce sb into doing sthg** jn dazu verleiten, etw zu tun.

seductive [sɪ'dʌktɪv] adj verführerisch.

see [si:] (pt **saw**, pp **seen**) <> vt - 1. [gen] sehen; **as I see it** wie ich es sehe; **what do you see in him?** was findest du bloß an ihm?; see p. 10 siehe S. 10; **do you see what I mean?** verstehst du, was ich meine? - 2. [visit] besuchen; [doctor, solicitor] gehen zu; **to see sb about sthg** jn wegen etw sprechen; **see you!** tschüs!; **see you soon/later!** bis bald!; **see you tomorrow/on Thursday!** bis morgen/Donnerstag! - 3. [accompany] begleiten - 4. [make sure]: **to see that...** dafür sorgen, dass... ◇ *vi* - **1.** [with eyes] sehen; **let me see** [have a look] lass mich mal sehen - **2.** [understand] verstehen; **I see** ich verstehe; **you see, it's not that far at all** du siehst ja, es ist gar nicht weit - **3.** [find out]: **I'll go and see** ich sehe mal nach; **let's see, let me see** [when thinking] warten Sie mal, also - **4.** [decide]: **I'll (have to) see** ich muss es mir überlegen. ◆ **seeing as, seeing that** *conj inf* da. ◆ **see about** *vt insep* - **1.** [organize] sich kümmern um - **2.** [expressing doubt]: **we'll see about that** das werden wir sehen. ◆ **see off** *vt sep* - **1.** [say goodbye to] verabschieden - **2.** *UK* [chase away] verjagen. ◆ **see through** ◇ *vt insep* [person, scheme] durchschauen. ◇ *vt sep* - **1.** [not abandon - deal, project] zu Ende bringen - **2.** [help to survive] durchlbringen. ◆ **see to** *vt insep* [deal with] sich kümmern um; [repair] reparieren; **I'll see to it that he gets it** ich sorge dafür, dass er es bekommt.

seed [si:d] *n* - **1.** [of plant] Samen *der*; [pip] Kern *der* - **2.** SPORT: **to be the top/fourth seed** als Nummer eins/vier gesetzt sein. ◆ **seeds** *npl fig* [beginnings] Keim *der*.

seedling ['si:dlɪŋ] *n* Sämling *der*.

seedy ['si:dɪ] *adj* [shabby] schäbig; [disreputable] zwielichtig.

seek [si:k] (*pt & pp* sought) *vt fml* suchen; **to seek sb's advice/help** jn um Rat fragen/Hilfe bitten; **to seek to do sthg** danach streben, etw zu tun.

seem [si:m] ◇ *vi* scheinen; **he seems better** es scheint ihm besser zu gehen; **they seem to believe that...** sie glauben anscheinend, dass...; **I seem to remember his name was John** ich glaube, er hieß John. ◇ *impers vb* scheinen; **it seems (that)...** anscheinend...; **it seems to me (that) you're right** mir scheint, du hast Recht; **so it would seem** so scheint es wenigstens.

seemingly ['si:mɪŋlɪ] *adv* scheinbar.

seen [si:n] *pp* ▷ **see**.

seep [si:p] *vi* sickern.

seesaw ['si:sɔ:] *n* Wippe *die*.

seethe [si:ð] *vi* - **1.** [person] vor Wut schäumen - **2.** [place]: **to be seething with sthg** von etw wimmeln.

see-through *adj* durchsichtig.

segment ['segmənt] *n* - **1.** [of report, audience] Teil *der*; [of market] Segment *das* - **2.** [of fruit] Stück *das*.

segregate ['segrɪgeɪt] *vt* trennen.

seize [si:z] *vt* - **1.** [grab] packen, greifen - **2.** [win - control, power] übernehmen; [- town] einlnehmen - **3.** [arrest] festlnehmen - **4.** [chance, opportunity] ergreifen. ◆ **seize (up)on** *vt insep* [suggestion, idea] sich stützen auf (+ *A*). ◆ **seize up** *vi* - **1.** [body] versagen - **2.** [engine] sich festlfressen.

seizure ['si:ʒər] *n* - **1.** MED Anfall *der* - **2.** *(U)* [taking - of town] Einnahme *die*; [- of control, power] Übernahme *die*; [- of goods by customs] Beschlagnahme *die*.

seldom ['seldəm] *adv* selten.

select [sɪ'lekt] ◇ *adj* - **1.** [carefully chosen] auserlesen - **2.** [exclusive] exklusiv. ◇ *vt* auslwählen.

selection [sɪ'lekʃn] *n* [choice, assortment, range] Auswahl *die*.

selective [sɪ'lektɪv] *adj* - **1.** [not general, limited] selektiv - **2.** [choosy] wählerisch.

self [self] (*pl* selves) *n* Selbst *das*; **she's her old self again** sie ist wieder ganz die Alte.

self-addressed stamped envelope [-ə'drest-] *n US* adressierter und frankierter Rückumschlag.

self-assured *adj* selbstbewusst.

self-catering *adj* mit Selbstversorgung.

self-centred [-'sentəd] *adj* egozentrisch.

self-confessed [-kən'fest] *adj* erklärt.

self-confidence *n* Selbstbewusstsein *das*.

self-confident *adj* selbstbewusst.

self-conscious *adj* verlegen, befangen.

self-contained [-kən'teɪnd] *adj* - **1.** [person - independent] unabhängig; [- reserved] reserviert - **2.** [flat] abgeschlossen.

self-control *n* Selbstbeherrschung *die*.

self-defence *n* Selbstverteidigung *die*.

self-discipline *n* Selbstdisziplin *die*.

self-employed [-ɪm'plɔɪd] *adj* selbstständig.

self-esteem *n* Selbstachtung *die*.

self-explanatory *adj* aus sich heraus verständlich.

self-important *adj pej* überheblich.

self-indulgent *adj pej* [person] genusssüchtig.

self-interest *n pej* Eigennutz *der*.

selfish ['selfɪʃ] *adj* selbstsüchtig, egoistisch.

selfishness ['selfɪʃnɪs] *n* Selbstsucht *die*, Egoismus *der*.

selfless ['selflɪs] *adj* selbstlos.

self-made *adj* [man] Selfmade-.

self-opinionated *adj pej* rechthaberisch.

self-pity *n pej* Selbstmitleid *das*.

self-portrait *n* Selbstporträt *das*.

self-possessed *adj* beherrscht.

self-preservation *n* Selbsterhaltung *die*; **instinct for self-preservation** Selbsterhaltungstrieb *der*.

self-raising flour *UK* [-ˌreɪzɪŋ-], **self-rising flour** *US n (U)* Mehl *das* mit Backpulverzusatz.

self-reliant *adj* selbstständig.

self-respect *n* Selbstachtung *die*.

self-respecting [-rɪs'pektɪŋ] *adj*: no self-respecting parent would dress their child so badly Eltern, die etwas auf sich halten, würden ihr Kind nicht so furchtbar anziehen.

self-restraint *n* Selbstbeherrschung *die*.

self-righteous *adj pej* selbstgerecht.

self-rising flour *n US* = **self-raising flour**.

self-satisfied *adj pej* selbstzufrieden.

self-service *n* Selbstbedienung *die*.

self-sufficient *adj* [person, community]: **to be self-sufficient (in sthg)** sich selbst (mit etw) versorgen.

self-taught *adj* autodidaktisch.

sell [sel] (*pt & pp* **sold**) ⟨⟩ *vt* - **1.** [goods] verkaufen; **to sell sthg to sb, to sell sb sthg** etw an jn verkaufen, jm etw verkaufen; **I sold it for fifty pounds** ich habe es für fünfzig Pfund verkauft - **2.** [promote sale of]: **such a cover will sell the magazine** mit so einem Titelbild verkauft sich die Zeitschrift garantiert gut - **3.** *fig* [make enthusiastic about]: **to sell sthg to sb, to sell sb sthg** jm etw schmackhaft machen; **I'm not sold on the idea** ich bin von der Idee nicht begeistert ⟨⟩ *vi* - **1.** [person] verkaufen - **2.** [product] sich verkaufen; **to sell for** OR **at** verkauft werden für OR zu. ⬥ **sell off** *vt sep* verkaufen. ⬥ **sell out** ⟨⟩ *vt sep* [performance]: **to be sold out** ausverkauft sein. ⟨⟩ *vi* - **1.** [shop, ticket office]: **we've sold out** wir sind ausverkauft; **we've sold out of bread** wir haben kein Brot mehr - **2.** [betray one's principles] sich verkaufen.

sell-by date *n UK* Verfallsdatum *das*.

seller ['selər] *n* [vendor] Verkäufer *der*, -in *die*.

selling price *n* Verkaufspreis *der*.

Sellotape® ['seləteɪp] *n UK* Tesafilm® *der*, Klebeband *das*.

sell-out *n* [performance, match]: **to be a sellout** ausverkauft sein.

selves [selvz] *Pl* ⟦⟩ **self**.

semaphore ['seməfɔːr] *n* (*U*) Flaggenzeichen *Pl*.

semblance ['sembləns] *n fml* Anschein *der*.

semen ['siːmen] *n* (*U*) Samen *der*.

semester [sɪ'mestər] *n* Semester *das*.

semicircle ['semɪ,sɜːkl] *n* Halbkreis *der*.

semicolon [,semɪ'kəʊlən] *n* Semikolon *das*.

semidetached [,semɪdɪ'tætʃt] *adj & n UK*: **semidetached (house)** Doppelhaushälfte *die*.

semifinal [,semɪ'faɪnl] *n* Halbfinale *das*.

seminar ['semɪnɑːr] *n* Seminar *das*.

seminary ['semɪnəri] *n* RELIG Priesterseminar *das*.

semiskilled [,semɪ'skɪld] *adj* angelernt.

semolina [,semə'liːnə] *n* Grieß *der*.

Senate ['senɪt] *n* POL: **the Senate** der Senat.

senator ['senətər] *n* Senator *der*, -in *die*.

send [send] (*pt & pp* **sent**) *vt* - **1.** [letter, message, money] schicken; [signal] senden; **to send sb sthg, to send sthg to sb** jm etw schicken, etw an jn schicken - **2.** [tell to go]: **to send sb (to)** jn schicken (zu); **to send sb for sthg** jn nach etw schicken - **3.** [into a specific state]: **to send sb to sleep** jn zum Einschlafen bringen; **to send sb into a rage** jn wütend machen. ⬥ **send back** *vt sep* zurückschicken. ⬥ **send for** *vt insep* - **1.** [person] holen lassen - **2.** [by post] anfordern. ⬥ **send in** *vt sep* - **1.** [visitor] hereinschicken - **2.** [troops, police] entsenden, schicken - **3.** [submit] einreichen. ⬥ **send off** *vt sep* - **1.** [by post] abschicken - **2.** SPORT [player] vom Platz verweisen. ⬥ **send off for** *vt insep* [by post] schriftlich anfordern. ⬥ **send up** *vt sep inf UK* [imitate] parodieren.

sender ['sendər] *n* Absender *der*, -in *die*.

send-off *n* Verabschiedung *die*.

senile ['siːnaɪl] *adj* senil.

senior ['siːnjər] ⟨⟩ *adj* - **1.** [high-ranking - position, manager] leitend; [- official] höher; [- nurse, doctor] Ober-; [- police officer] ranghoch - **2.** [higher-ranking]: **to be senior to sb** höher als jd gestellt sein - **3.** SCH [classes] höher; [pupils] älter. ⟨⟩ *n* - **1.** [older person]: **I'm five years his senior, I'm his senior by five years** ich bin fünf Jahre älter als er - **2.** SCH Schüler/Student im letzten Schul-/Studienjahr.

senior citizen *n* Senior *der*, -in *die*.

sensation [sen'seɪʃn] *n* - **1.** [feeling] Gefühl *das* - **2.** [cause of excitement] Sensation *die*.

sensational [sen'seɪʃənl] *adj* [news, victory, show] sensationell; [person, appearance] toll.

sense [sens] ⟨⟩ *n* - **1.** [faculty] Sinn *der* - **2.** [feeling, sensation] Gefühl *das*; **sense of guilt** Schuldgefühl *das*; **sense of justice** Gerechtigkeitssinn *der* - **3.** [natural ability] Gefühl *das*; **business sense** Geschäftssinn *der*; **a sense of humour** Humor *der* - **4.** [wisdom, reason] Vernunft *die* - **5.** [meaning] Bedeutung *die*; **to make sense** [have clear meaning] Sinn haben; [be logical] sinnvoll sein; **to make no sense** keinen Sinn machen - **6.** *phr*: **to come to one's senses** [be sensible again] (wieder) zur Vernunft kommen; [regain consciousness] (wieder) zu Bewusstsein kommen. ⟨⟩ *vt* [feel] spüren; **to sense (that)...** spüren, dass... ⬥ **in a sense** *adv* in gewissem Sinne.

senseless ['senslɪs] *adj* - **1.** [stupid] sinnlos - **2.** [unconscious] bewusstlos.

sensibilities [,sensɪ'bɪlətɪz] *npl* [delicate feelings] Empfindlichkeit *die*.

sensible ['sensəbl] *adj* vernünftig.

sensitive ['sensɪtɪv] *adj* - **1.** [eyes, skin] empfindlich; **sensitive to heat/light** hitze-/lichtempfindlich - **2.** [understanding, aware]: **to be sensitive (to sthg)** (gegenüber etw) aufmerksam sein - **3.** [easily hurt, touchy]: **to be sensitive to sthg** gegenüber etw empfindlich sein; **to**

be sensitive about sthg wegen etw empfindlich sein - **4.** [controversial] heikel - **5.** [instrument] empfindlich.

sensual ['sensjʊəl] *adj* sinnlich.

sensuous ['sensjʊəs] *adj* sinnlich.

sent [sent] *pt* & *pp* ⊏> **send**.

sentence ['sentəns] <> *n* - **1.** [group of words] Satz *der* - **2.** LAW [decision] Urteil *das*; **a sentence of five years** eine fünfjährige Haftstrafe. <> *vt*: **to sentence sb (to sthg)** jn (zu etw) verurteilen.

sentiment ['sentɪmənt] *n* [feeling] Gefühl *das*; [opinion] Meinung *die*.

sentimental [ˌsentɪˈmentl] *adj* sentimental.

sentry ['sentrɪ] *n* Wache *die*.

separate <> *adj* ['seprət] - **1.** [not joined, apart]: **separate (from sthg)** getrennt (von etw) - **2.** [individual, distinct] verschieden; **write on a separate piece of paper** schreiben Sie auf ein neues Blatt. <> *vt* ['sepəreɪt] - **1.** [keep or set apart]: **to separate (from)** trennen (von); **to separate sb/sthg into** jn/etw einteilen in (+ A) - **2.** [distinguish] unterscheiden; **to separate sb/sthg from** jn/etw unterscheiden von. <> *vi* ['sepəreɪt] - **1.** [go different ways]: **to separate (from)** sich trennen (von) - **2.** [come apart, divide] auseinander gehen - **3.** [couple] sich trennen.

separately ['seprətlɪ] *adv* getrennt.

separation [ˌsepəˈreɪʃn] *n* Trennung *die*; [division] Einteilung *die*.

September [sepˈtembər] *n* September *der*; **in September** im September; **last/this/next September** letzten/diesen/nächsten September; **by September** bis September; **every September** jeden September, jedes Jahr im September; **during September** im September; **at the beginning/end of September** Anfang/Ende September; **in the middle of September** Mitte September.

septic ['septɪk] *adj* eitrig; MED septisch.

septic tank *n* Klärgrube *die*.

sequel ['siːkwəl] *n* - **1.** [book, film]: **sequel (to sthg)** Fortsetzung *die* (von etw) - **2.** [consequence]: **sequel to sthg** Folge *die* von etw.

sequence ['siːkwəns] *n* - **1.** [series] Reihe *die* - **2.** *(U)* [order] Reihenfolge *die* - **3.** [of film] Sequenz *die*.

Serbia ['sɜːbjə] *n* Serbien *nt*.

serene [sɪˈriːn] *adj* [person] gelassen.

sergeant ['sɑːdʒənt] *n* - **1.** [in the army] Feldwebel *der* - **2.** [in the police] Wachtmeister *der*, -in *die*.

sergeant major *n* Hauptfeldwebel *der*.

serial ['sɪərɪəl] *n* [on TV] Serie *die*; [on radio] Sendereihe *die*; [in newspaper] Fortsetzungsroman *der*.

series ['sɪəriːz] *(pl inv)* *n* - **1.** [sequence] Reihe *die* - **2.** RADIO & TV Serie *die*.

serious ['sɪərɪəs] *adj* - **1.** [gen] ernst; [situation, problem, illness, loss] schwer; [shortage] groß - **2.** [newspaper] seriös; **are you serious?** ist das dein Ernst?

seriously ['sɪərɪəslɪ] *adv* - **1.** [earnestly] ernsthaft; **to take sb/sthg seriously** jn/etw ernst nehmen - **2.** [very badly - ill] schwer; [- lacking] sehr.

seriousness ['sɪərɪəsnɪs] *n* - **1.** [of person, expression, situation] Ernst *der* - **2.** [of illness, loss] Schwere *die*.

sermon ['sɜːmən] *n* - **1.** [in church] Predigt *die* - **2.** *fig* & *pej* [lecture] Moralpredigt *die*.

serrated [sɪˈreɪtɪd] *adj* gezackt.

servant ['sɜːvənt] *n* [in household] Diener *der*, -in *die*.

serve [sɜːv] <> *vt* - **1.** [work for] dienen (+ D) - **2.** [have effect]: **this only served to make him more angry** das führte nur dazu, dass er noch ärgerlicher wurde; **to serve a purpose** einem Zweck dienen - **3.** [provide - with gas, electricity, water] versorgen; **which motorways serve Birmingham?** welche Autobahnen führen nach Birmingham? - **4.** [food or drink]: **to serve sthg to sb, to serve sb sthg** jm etw servieren - **5.** [customer] bedienen - **6.** LAW: **to serve sb with a writ** jn vor Gericht laden - **7.** [complete, carry out - prison sentence] verbüßen; [- apprenticeship] absolvieren; **to serve a term of office** im Amt sein - **8.** SPORT aufschlagen - **9.** *phr*: **it serves you right** das geschieht dir recht. <> *vi* - **1.** [be employed - as soldier] dienen; [- in profession] arbeiten; **to serve on** [committee] angehören (+ D) - **2.** [function]: **to serve as sthg** als etw dienen - **3.** [with food, drink] servieren - **4.** [in shop, bar *etc*] bedienen - **5.** SPORT aufschlagen. <> *n* SPORT Aufschlag *der*. ◈ **serve out, serve up** *vt sep* [food] servieren.

service ['sɜːvɪs] <> *n* - **1.** [organization, system] Dienst *der*; **bus/train service** Bus-/Zugverbindung *die* - **2.** [amenity] Dienstleistung *die*, Service *der* - **3.** [employment - length of time] Dienstzeit *die* - **4.** *(U)* [in shop, bar *etc*] Bedienung *die*, Service *der*; **'service not included'** 'Trinkgeld nicht inbegriffen' - **5.** MIL Militärdienst *der* - **6.** [mechanical check - of car] Durchsicht *die*; [- of machine] Wartung *die* - **7.** RELIG Gottesdienst *der* - **8.** [set of tableware] Service *das* - **9.** [operation] Betrieb *der*; **in/out of service** in/außer Betrieb - **10.** SPORT Aufschlag *der* - **11.** [help]: **to be of service to sb** [person] jm behilflich sein; [thing] jm von Nutzen sein. <> *vt* [car, machine] warten. ◈ **services** *npl* - **1.** [on motorway] Raststätte *die* (mit Tankstelle) - **2.** [armed forces]: **the services** das Militär - **3.** [help] Hilfe *die*, Dienste *Pl*.

serviceable ['sɜːvɪsəbl] *adj* praktisch.

service area *n* Raststätte *die* (mit Tankstelle).

service charge *n* Bedienungszuschlag *der*, Service *der*.

serviceman ['sɜːvɪsmən] (pl -men [-mən]) n MIL Militärangehörige der.

service provider n COMPUT Provider der.

service station n Raststätte die (mit Tankstelle).

serviette [,sɜːvɪ'et] n Serviette die.

session ['seʃn] n - 1. [of court, parliament] Sitzung die - 2. [meeting] Treffen das; recording session Aufnahme die - 3. US [school term] Semester das.

set [set] (pt & pp inv) <> adj - 1. [specified, prescribed] festgelegt, festgesetzt; [book, text] vorgeschrieben - 2. [fixed - phrase, expression] fest; [- ideas, routine] starr - 3. [ready]: to be (all) set (to do sthg) startbereit sein(, etw zu tun) - 4. [determined]: to be set on doing sthg entschlossen sein, etw zu tun; to be dead set against sthg völlig gegen etw sein. <> n - 1. [collection, group] Satz der; set of teeth Gebiss das; chess set Schachspiel das - 2. [television, radio] Apparat der - 3. [of film] Filmkulisse die; [of play] Kulisse die - 4. TENNIS Satz der. <> vt - 1. [put in specified position, place] stellen; [lying down] legen - 2. [fix, insert]: to set sthg in(to) sthg etw in etw (A) einlassen - 3. [indicating change of state or activity]: to set sb free jn befreien; to set sb's mind at rest jn beruhigen; to set sthg on fire etw anlzünden; her remark set me thinking ihre Bemerkung brachte mich zum Nachdenken - 4. [prepare in advance - trap] auflstellen; [- table] decken - 5. [clock, meter] stellen - 6. [time, deadline, minimum wage] festlsetzen, festllegen - 7. [create - trend] setzen; [- example] geben; [- precedent] schaffen; [- record] auflstellen - 8. [assign - target] setzen; [- essay, homework] auflgeben; [- exam] auslarbeiten - 9. MED [bone, broken leg] richten - 10. [story, film] spielen - 11. [hair] legen. <> vi - 1. [sun] unterlgehen - 2. [jelly, cement] fest werden. ◆ **set about** vt insep [start]: to set about sthg etw in Angriff nehmen; to set about doing sthg sich daranlmachen, etw zu tun. ◆ **set aside** vt sep - 1. [keep, save - food] auflheben; [- money] beiseite legen; [- time] einlplanen - 2. [not consider] außer Acht lassen. ◆ **set back** vt sep [delay] zurücklwerfen. ◆ **set off** <> vt sep - 1. [initiate, cause] auslösen - 2. [trigger - bomb] zünden; [- alarm] auslösen. <> vi [on journey] auflbrechen. ◆ **set out** <> vt sep - 1. [arrange, spread out] zurechtlegen; [chairs] auflstellen; [food] anlrichten - 2. [clarify, explain] darllegen. <> vt insep [intend]: to set out to do sthg sich (D) vorlnehmen, etw zu tun. <> vi [on journey] auflbrechen. ◆ **set up** vt sep - 1. [establish, arrange - fund, organization] gründen; [- interview, meeting] anlsetzen; [- erect - roadblock] errichten; to set up camp Zelte aufschlagen - 3. [install] auflstellen - 4. inf [incriminate] als Schuldigen hinlstellen.

setback ['setbæk] n Rückschlag der.

settee [se'tiː] n Sofa das, Couch die.

setting ['setɪŋ] n - 1. [surroundings] Umgebung die - 2. [of dial, control] Einstellung die.

settle ['setl] <> vt - 1. [argument, differences] beillegen - 2. [pay - bill, debt] begleichen; [- account] auslgleichen - 3. [nerves, stomach] beruhigen. <> vi - 1. [go to live] sich niederllassen - 2. [make o.s. comfortable] es sich (D) bequem machen - 3. [come to rest - dust] sich legen; [- sediment] sich setzen. ◆ **settle down** vi - 1. [give one's attention]: to settle down to work sich an die Arbeit machen; to settle down to doing sthg sich daranlmachen, etw zu tun - 2. [assume stable lifestyle] sesshaft werden - 3. [make o.s. comfortable] es sich (D) bequem machen - 4. [become calm] sich beruhigen. ◆ **settle for** vt insep sich zufriedenlgeben mit. ◆ **settle in** vi [in house] sich einlleben; [in job] sich einlgewöhnen. ◆ **settle on** vt insep [choose] sich entscheiden für. ◆ **settle up** vi [financially]: to settle up (with sb) ablrechnen (mit jm).

settlement ['setlmənt] n - 1. [agreement] Übereinkunft die, Einigung die - 2. [village] (An)siedlung die - 3. [payment] Begleichung die, Bezahlung die.

settler ['setlər] n Siedler der, -in die.

set-up n inf - 1. [system] System das; [organization] Organisation die - 2. [deception to incriminate] Falle die.

seven ['sevn] num sieben; see also **six**.

seventeen [,sevn'tiːn] num siebzehn; see also **six**.

seventeenth [,sevn'tiːnθ] num siebzehnte (r) (s); see also **sixth**.

seventh ['sevnθ] num siebte (r) (s); see also **sixth**.

seventy ['sevntɪ] num siebzig; see also **sixty**.

sever ['sevər] vt - 1. [limb] abltrennen; [rope] durchlschneiden; [ligament] reißen - 2. [relationship, ties] ablbrechen.

several ['sevrəl] <> adj [some] mehrere, einige. <> pron mehrere, einige.

severe [sɪ'vɪər] adj - 1. [shock, pain, gale] stark; [illness, injury] schwer; [problem] ernst - 2. [stern - person] streng; [- criticism] heftig.

severity [sɪ'verətɪ] n (U) - 1. [of storm] Stärke die; [of illness] Schwere die; [of problem] Ernst der - 2. [sternness - of person] Strenge die; [- of criticism] Heftigkeit die.

sew [səʊ] (UK pp sewn) (US pp sewed OR sewn) vt & vi nähen. ◆ **sew up** vt sep [join] zusammenlnähen.

sewage ['suːɪdʒ] n Abwasser das.

sewer ['suːər] n Abwasserkanal der.

sewing ['səʊɪŋ] n (U) - 1. [activity] Nähen das - 2. [items] Näharbeit die.

sewing machine n Nähmaschine die.

sewn [səʊn] pp ▷ **sew**.

sex [seks] *n* - **1.** [gender] Geschlecht *das* - **2.** [sexual intercourse] Sex *der*; **to have sex (with sb)** (mit jm) Sex haben.

sexist ['seksɪst] <> *adj* sexistisch. <> *n* Sexist *der*, -in *die*.

sexual ['sekʃʊəl] *adj* - **1.** [of sexuality, sexual intercourse] sexuell; [disease, organ] Geschlechts- - **2.** [of gender]: **sexual equality/rivalry** Gleichheit/Rivalität zwischen den Geschlechtern.

sexual discrimination *n* Diskriminierung *die* aufgrund des Geschlechts.

sexual harassment *n (U)* sexuelle Belästigung.

sexual intercourse *n (U)* Geschlechtsverkehr *der*.

sexually transmitted disease *n* sexuell übertragbare Krankheit.

sexy ['seksɪ] *adj inf* sexy.

shabby ['ʃæbɪ] *adj* schäbig; [street] heruntergekommen.

shack [ʃæk] *n* Hütte *die*.

shackle ['ʃækl] *vt* - **1.** [chain] fesseln - **2.** *liter* [restrict] (be)hindern.

shade [ʃeɪd] <> *n* - **1.** *(U)* [shadow] Schatten *der* - **2.** [lampshade] Lampenschirm *der* - **3.** [colour] Farbton *der* - **4.** [nuance] Schattierung *die*. <> *vt* - **1.** [from light] beschatten - **2.** [drawing] schattieren. ◆ **shades** *npl inf* [sunglasses] Sonnenbrille *die*.

shadow ['ʃædəʊ] *n* Schatten *der*; **there's not a** OR **the shadow of a doubt** es gibt nicht den geringsten Zweifel.

shadow cabinet *n* Schattenkabinett *das*.

shadowy ['ʃædəʊɪ] *adj* - **1.** [dark] dunkel - **2.** [unknown, sinister] mysteriös.

shady ['ʃeɪdɪ] *adj* - **1.** [place] schattig - **2.** [tree] Schatten spendend - **3.** *inf* [dishonest, sinister] zweifelhaft.

shaft [ʃɑːft] *n* - **1.** [vertical passage] Schacht *der* - **2.** [rod - of tool] Stiel *der*; [- of column] Schaft *der*; [- of propeller] Welle *die* - **3.** [of light] Strahl *der*.

shaggy ['ʃægɪ] *adj* [hair, beard, dog] struppig; [carpet] verfilzt.

shake [ʃeɪk] *(pt* shook, *pp* shaken) <> *vt* - **1.** [move vigorously] schütteln; **to shake hands** sich *(D)* die Hände schütteln; **to shake sb's hand, to shake hands with sb** jm die Hand schütteln, js Hand schütteln; **to shake one's head** den Kopf schütteln - **2.** [upset, undermine] erschüttern. <> *vi* zittern. <> *n*: **to give sthg a shake** etw schütteln. ◆ **shake off** *vt sep* [police, pursuer] abschütteln; [illness] loslwerden. ◆ **shake up** *vt sep* [upset] stark mitlnehmen.

shaken ['ʃeɪkn] *pp* ▷ **shake**.

shaky ['ʃeɪkɪ] *adj* - **1.** [unsteady - chair, table] wackelig; [- hand, writing, voice] zitternd; [- person] zitterig - **2.** [weak, uncertain] schwach; [finances] unsicher.

shall *(weak form* [ʃəl], *strong form* [ʃæl]) *aux vb* - **1.** *(1st person sg & 1st person pl)* [to express future tense] werden; **I shall be late tomorrow** morgen werde ich später kommen; **I shall be ready soon** ich bin bald fertig; **will you be there? – we shall** werdet ihr dort sein? – da sind wir hin?; **I'll tell her too, shall I?** ich sag es ihr auch, okay? - **2.** *(esp 1st person sg & 1st person pl)* [in questions] sollen; **shall I buy some wine?** soll ich Wein kaufen?; **where shall we go?** wo gehen wir hin?; **I'll tell her too, shall I?** ich sag es ihr auch, okay? - **3.** [in orders] sollen; **you shall tell me what happened!** du wirst mir erzählen, was passiert ist!; **payment shall be made within a week** die Zahlung muss innerhalb einer Woche erfolgen.

shallow ['ʃæləʊ] *adj* - **1.** [in size] flach - **2.** *pej* [superficial] seicht.

sham [ʃæm] <> *adj* [feeling] vorgetäuscht. <> *n* [piece of deceit] Schein *der*.

shambles ['ʃæmblz] *n* - **1.** [disorder] Chaos *das* - **2.** [fiasco] Disaster *das*.

shame [ʃeɪm] <> *n* - **1.** [remorse] Scham *die* - **2.** [dishonour]: **to bring shame (up)on sb** Schande über jn bringen - **3.** [pity]: **it's a shame (that)...** schade, dass...; **what a shame!** (wie) schade! <> *vt* beschämen; **to shame sb into doing sthg** jn moralisch zwingen, etw zu tun.

shameful ['ʃeɪmfʊl] *adj* schändlich.

shameless ['ʃeɪmlɪs] *adj* schamlos.

shampoo [ʃæm'puː] *(pl -s, pt & pp -ed, cont -ing)* <> *n* - **1.** [liquid] Shampoo *das* - **2.** [act of shampooing]: **to give one's hair a shampoo** sich *(D)* das Haar schampunieren. <> *vt* [hair] schampunieren; [carpet] reinigen.

shamrock ['ʃæmrɒk] *n* Klee *der*.

shandy ['ʃændɪ] *n* [in Northern Germany] Alsterwasser *das*; [in Southern Germany] Radler *das*.

shan't [ʃɑːnt] *abbr of* **shall not**.

shantytown ['ʃæntɪtaʊn] *n* Slum *der*.

shape [ʃeɪp] <> *n* - **1.** [outer form] Form *die* - **2.** [figure, abstract structure] Gestalt *die*; **to take shape** Gestalt anlnehmen - **3.** [form, health]: **to be in good/bad shape** [person] in guter/schlechter Form sein; **his business is in bad shape** seine Geschäfte laufen schlecht. <> *vt* - **1.** [mould physically]: **to shape sthg (into)** etw formen (in (+ A)) - **2.** [influence - person, character] formen; [- ideas, life, future] beeinflussen. ◆ **shape up** *vi* [develop] sich entwickeln.

-shaped ['ʃeɪpt] *suffix* -förmig; **egg-shaped** eiförmig.

shapeless ['ʃeɪplɪs] *adj* formlos.

shapely ['ʃeɪplɪ] *adj* [legs] wohlproportioniert; [woman] wohlgeformt.

share [ʃeəʳ] <> *n*: **to do one's share of sthg** seinen Beitrag zu etw leisten. <> *vt* teilen. <> *vi* [share book] zusammen hineinlschauen; **there's only one room left – we'll have to share** es gibt nur noch ein Zimmer –

wir müssen es teilen; **to share in** sthg sich an etw (D) beteiligen. ◆ **shares** npl FIN Aktien Pl. ◆ **share out** vt sep verteilen.

shareholder ['ʃeə,həʊldər] n Aktionär der, -in die.

shark [ʃɑːk] (pl inv OR -s) n [fish] Hai der.

sharp [ʃɑːp] ◇ adj - 1. [not blunt] scharf; [needle, pencil] spitz - 2. [well-defined] scharf - 3. [intelligent, keen - person, mind] scharfsinnig; [- eyesight, hearing] scharf - 4. [sudden - increase, fall] abrupt; [- turn] scharf; [- slope] steil - 5. [angry, severe] scharf; **she was rather sharp with me** sie war recht schroff zu mir - 6. [piercing, loud] schrill - 7. [painful] schneidend - 8. [bitter] herb - 9. [MUS - raised a semitone] um einen Halbton erhöht; **C sharp** Cis das; **D sharp** Dis das; **A sharp** Ais das. ◇ adv - 1. [punctually] pünktlich; **at eight o'clock sharp** Punkt acht Uhr - 2. [quickly, suddenly]: **to turn sharp right/left** scharf nach rechts/links abbiegen. ◇ n [MUS - note] erhöhter Ton; [- symbol] Kreuz das.

sharpen ['ʃɑːpn] vt [make sharp] schärfen; [pencil] (an)lspitzen.

sharpener ['ʃɑːpnər] n [for pencil] Spitzer der; [for knife] Messerschärfer der.

sharply ['ʃɑːplɪ] adv - 1. [distinctly] scharf - 2. [suddenly - increase, fall] abrupt; [- turn] scharf; [- slope] steil - 3. [harshly] scharf.

shatter ['ʃætər] ◇ vt - 1. [glass, window] zerschmettern - 2. fig [beliefs, hopes, dreams] zerschlagen. ◇ vi [glass, window] zerspringen.

shattered ['ʃætəd] adj - 1. [shocked, upset] niedergeschmettert - 2. UK inf [very tired] völlig fertig.

shave [ʃeɪv] ◇ n [with razor] Rasur die; **to have a shave** sich rasieren. ◇ vt - 1. [with razor] rasieren - 2. [wood] ablhobeln. ◇ vi sich rasieren.

shaver ['ʃeɪvər] n Rasierapparat der.

shaving brush ['ʃeɪvɪŋ-] n Rasierpinsel der.

shaving cream ['ʃeɪvɪŋ-] n Rasiercreme die.

shaving foam ['ʃeɪvɪŋ-] n Rasierschaum der.

shawl [ʃɔːl] n Schultertuch das.

she [ʃiː] ◇ pers pron - 1. [referring to woman, girl, animal] sie; **she's tall** sie ist groß; **there she is** da ist sie; **she can't do it** sie kann es nicht tun; **if I were** OR **was she** fml wenn ich sie wäre - 2. [referring to boat, car, country] es; **she sails tomorrow** es fährt morgen ab. ◇ comp: **she-bear** Bärin die.

sheaf [ʃiːf] (pl sheaves) n - 1. [of papers, letters] Bündel das - 2. [of corn, grain] Garbe die.

shear [ʃɪər] (pt -ed, pp -ed OR shorn) vt scheren. ◆ **shears** npl - 1. [for garden] Heckenschere die - 2. [for dressmaking] große Schere.

sheath [ʃiːθ] (pl -s [ʃiːðz]) n - 1. [for knife] Scheide die - 2. [for cable] Umhüllung die, Ummantelung die - 3. UK [condom] Kondom das.

sheaves [ʃiːvz] Pl ▷ **sheaf**.

shed [ʃed] (pt & pp inv) ◇ n Schuppen der. ◇ vt - 1. [gen] verlieren - 2. [employees] entlassen; [inhibitions] überwinden - 3. [tears, blood] vergießen.

she'd (weak form [ʃɪd], strong form [ʃiːd]) abbr of **she had**, **she would**.

sheen [ʃiːn] n Glanz der.

sheep [ʃiːp] (pl inv) n Schaf das.

sheepdog ['ʃiːpdɒg] n Hütehund der.

sheepish ['ʃiːpɪʃ] adj verlegen.

sheepskin ['ʃiːpskɪn] n Schaffell das.

sheer [ʃɪər] adj - 1. [absolute] rein - 2. [very steep] senkrecht - 3. [delicate] hauchdünn.

sheet [ʃiːt] n - 1. [for bed] Bettuch das, Laken das - 2. [of paper] Blatt das - 3. [of glass] Scheibe die; [of metal] Blech das; [of wood] Platte die.

shelf [ʃelf] (pl shelves) n Regal das.

shell [ʃel] ◇ n - 1. [of egg, nut] Schale die - 2. [of tortoise] Panzer der; [of snail] Haus das - 3. [on beach] Muschel die - 4. [of building] Rohbau der; [of car] Karosserie die; [of boat] Rumpf der - 5. MIL Granate die. ◇ vt - 1. [remove covering from] schälen; [peas] enthülsen - 2. MIL beschießen.

she'll [ʃiːl] abbr of **she will**, **she shall**.

shellfish ['ʃelfɪʃ] (pl inv) n - 1. [creature] Schalentier das - 2. (U) [food] Meeresfrüchte Pl.

shell suit n UK Jogginganzug der (aus Nylon).

shelter ['ʃeltər] ◇ n - 1. [building, structure] Unterstand der; [against air raids] (Luftschutz)bunker der; [in mountains] Berghütte die - 2. [cover, protection] Schutz der - 3. [accommodation] Obdach das. ◇ vt - 1. [from rain, sun, bombs]: **to be sheltered by/from** sthg von/vor etw (D) geschützt sein - 2. [give asylum to - refugee] Obdach geben (+ D); [- fugitive, criminal] Unterschlupf gewähren (+ D). ◇ vi: **to shelter from/in** sthg vor/in etw (D) Schutz suchen.

sheltered ['ʃeltəd] adj - 1. [place] geschützt - 2. [life, childhood] behütet - 3. [accommodation, housing] betreut.

shelve [ʃelv] vt [plan] auflschieben.

shelves [ʃelvz] Pl ▷ **shelf**.

shepherd ['ʃepəd] ◇ n Schäfer der. ◇ vt fig führen.

shepherd's pie ['ʃepədz-] n mit Kartoffelbrei überbackenes Hackfleisch.

sheriff ['ʃerɪf] n US [law officer] Sheriff der.

sherry ['ʃerɪ] n Sherry der.

she's [ʃiːz] abbr of **she is**, **she has**.

shield [ʃiːld] ◇ n - 1. [armour] Schild der - 2. UK [sports trophy] Trophäe die - 3. [protection]: **shield against** sthg Schutz der gegen etw. ◇ vt: **to shield sb/o.s. (from** sthg) jn/sich (vor etw (D)) schützen.

shift [ʃɪft] ⬦ n - **1.** [slight change] Veränderung die - **2.** [period of work, workers] Schicht die. ⬦ vt - **1.** [move, put elsewhere] verschieben - **2.** [change slightly] ändern - **3.** US AUT: **to shift gear** schalten. ⬦ vi - **1.** [move] sich bewegen; [move up - person] rutschen; [- thing] verrutschen - **2.** [change slightly - attitude, opinion] sich ändern; [- wind] umlschlagen - **3.** US AUT schalten.

shifty [ʃɪftɪ] adj inf verschlagen.

shilling [ʃɪlɪŋ] n UK Shilling der.

shimmer [ʃɪmər] ⬦ n Schimmer der; [in heat] Flimmern das. ⬦ vi schimmern; [in heat] flimmern.

shin [ʃɪn] n Schienbein das.

shinbone [ʃɪnbəʊn] n Schienbein das.

shine [ʃaɪn] (pt & pp shone) ⬦ n Glanz der. ⬦ vt - **1.** [torch, lamp]: **to shine sthg on sthg** mit etw auf etw leuchten - **2.** [polish] polieren. ⬦ vi [moon, sun] scheinen; [stars, light] leuchten; [eyes, metal, shoes] glänzen.

shingle [ʃɪŋgl] n [on beach] Strandkies der. ➡ **shingles** (U) n MED Gürtelrose die.

shiny [ʃaɪnɪ] adj glänzend.

ship [ʃɪp] ⬦ n Schiff das. ⬦ vt [send] versenden; [send by ship - people] befördern; [- goods] verschiffen.

shipbuilding [ʃɪpbɪldɪŋ] n Schiffbau der.

shipment [ʃɪpmənt] n - **1.** [cargo] Sendung die; [in ship] Ladung die - **2.** [act of shipping] Versand der; [by ship] Verschiffung die.

shipping [ʃɪpɪŋ] n (U) - **1.** [transport] Versand der; [by ship] Verschiffung die - **2.** [ships] Schiffe Pl.

shipshape [ʃɪpʃeɪp] adj tipptopp in Ordnung.

shipwreck [ʃɪprek] ⬦ n - **1.** [destruction of ship] Schiffbruch der - **2.** [wrecked ship] Schiffswrack das. ⬦ vt: **to be shipwrecked** Schiffbruch erleiden.

shipyard [ʃɪpjɑːd] n (Schiffs)werft die.

shirk [ʃɜːk] vt sich drücken vor (+ D).

shirt [ʃɜːt] n Hemd das.

shirtsleeves [ʃɜːtsliːvz] npl: **to be in (one's) shirtsleeves** in Hemdsärmeln sein.

shit [ʃɪt] (pt & pp inv, -ted OR shat) vulg ⬦ n [excrement, nonsense] Scheiße die. ⬦ vi scheißen. ⬦ excl Scheiße!

shiver [ʃɪvər] ⬦ n Schauder der. ⬦ vi: **to shiver (with sthg)** (vor etw (D)) zittern.

shoal [ʃəʊl] n [of fish] Schwarm der.

shock [ʃɒk] ⬦ n - **1.** [surprise, reaction] Schock der - **2.** MED: **to be suffering from shock, to be in (a state of) shock** unter Schock stehen - **3.** [impact] Wucht die - **4.** ELEC Schlag der. ⬦ vt & vi [upset] schockieren.

shock absorber [-əb‚zɔːbər] n Stoßdämpfer der.

shocking [ʃɒkɪŋ] adj - **1.** [very bad] miserabel - **2.** [scandalous, horrifying] schockierend.

shod [ʃɒd] ⬦ pt & pp ⬦ **shoe.** ⬦ adj: **well/poorly shod** gut/schlecht beschuht.

shoddy [ʃɒdɪ] adj schäbig.

shoe [ʃuː] (pt & pp -d OR shod) ⬦ n [for person] Schuh der. ⬦ vt [horse] beschlagen.

shoebrush [ʃuːbrʌʃ] n Schuhbürste die.

shoehorn [ʃuːhɔːn] n Schuhanzieher der.

shoelace [ʃuːleɪs] n Schnürsenkel der.

shoe polish n (U) Schuh(putz)creme die.

shoe shop n Schuhgeschäft das.

shoestring [ʃuːstrɪŋ] n fig: **on a shoestring** mit minimalen (finanziellen) Mitteln.

shone [ʃɒn] pt & pp ⬦ **shine.**

shoo [ʃuː] ⬦ vt verscheuchen. ⬦ excl husch!

shook [ʃʊk] pt ⬦ **shake.**

shoot [ʃuːt] (pt & pp shot) ⬦ vt - **1.** [fire gun at - killing] erschießen; [- wounding] anlschießen; **to shoot o.s.** [kill o.s.] sich erschießen - **2.** UK [hunt] jagen - **3.** [arrow] ablschießen - **4.** CIN drehen. ⬦ vi - **1.** [fire gun]: **to shoot (at sb/sthg)** (auf jn/etw) schießen - **2.** UK [hunt] jagen - **3.** [move quickly]: **to shoot in/out/past** herein-/heraus-/vorbeischießen - **4.** CIN drehen - **5.** SPORT schießen. ⬦ n - **1.** UK [hunting expedition] Jagd die - **2.** [of plant] Trieb der. ➡ **shoot down** vt sep [plane, helicopter] ablschießen; [person] niederlschießen. ➡ **shoot up** vi - **1.** [grow quickly] schnell wachsen - **2.** [increase quickly] in die Höhe schießen.

shooting [ʃuːtɪŋ] n - **1.** [killing] Schießerei die - **2.** [hunting] Jagd die.

shooting star n Sternschnuppe die.

shop [ʃɒp] ⬦ n - **1.** [store] Geschäft das, Laden der - **2.** [workshop] Werkstatt die. ⬦ vi einlkaufen; **to go shopping** einkaufen gehen.

shop assistant n UK Verkäufer der, -in die.

shop floor n: **the shop floor** [workers] die Arbeiter Pl; **on the shop floor** bei den Arbeitern.

shopkeeper [ʃɒp‚kiːpər] n Ladenbesitzer der, -in die.

shoplifting [ʃɒp‚lɪftɪŋ] n (U) Ladendiebstahl der.

shopper [ʃɒpər] n Käufer der, -in die.

shopping [ʃɒpɪŋ] n (U) - **1.** [purchases] Einkäufe Pl - **2.** [act of shopping] Einkaufen das; **to do the shopping** einkaufen (gehen).

shopping bag n Einkaufstasche die.

shopping centre UK, **shopping mall** US, **shopping plaza** US [-‚plɑːzə] n Einkaufszentrum das.

shop steward n gewerkschaftliche Vertrauensperson.

shopwindow [‚ʃɒpwɪndəʊ] n Schaufenster das.

shore [ʃɔːr] n Ufer das; **on shore** [not at sea] an Land. ◆ **shore up** vt sep - 1. [prop up] ablstützen - 2. fig [sustain] stützen.

shorn [ʃɔːn] ◇ pp ▷ **shear**. ◇ adj [head, sheep] geschoren; [hair] kurz geschoren.

short [ʃɔːt] ◇ adj - 1. [gen] kurz - 2. [in height] klein - 3. [curt]: **to be short (with sb)** (zu jm) schroff OR barsch sein - 4. [lacking] knapp; **we're £10 short** uns fehlen 10 Pfund; **he is short on intelligence/money** es mangelt ihm an Intelligenz/Geld - 5. [abbreviated]: **to be short for sthg** die Kurzform von etw sein. ◇ adv - 1. [lacking]: **we're running short of food** unsere Lebensmittelvorräte gehen langsam zur Neige - 2. [suddenly, abruptly]: **to cut sthg short** etw vorzeitig ablbrechen; **to stop short** plötzlich stehenlbleiben. ◇ n - 1. UK [alcoholic drink] Schnaps der - 2. CIN Kurzfilm der. ◆ **shorts** npl - 1. [short trousers] Shorts Pl - 2. US [underwear] Boxershorts Pl. ◆ **for short** adv: he's called Bob for short er wird kurz Bob genannt. ◆ **in short** adv kurz gesagt. ◆ **nothing short of** prep nichts anderes als. ◆ **short of** prep [apart from]: **short of ringing up, I don't see how I can find out** ich kann es nur herauslfinden, wenn ich anrufe.

shortage [ʃɔːtɪdʒ] n Mangel der, Knappheit die.

shortbread [ʃɔːtbred] n (U) Buttergebäck das.

short-change vt - 1. [in shop, restaurant] zu wenig herauslgeben (+ D) - 2. fig [reward unfairly] übers Ohr gehauen werden.

short circuit n Kurzschluss der.

shortcomings [ʃɔːtˌkʌmɪŋz] npl Unzulänglichkeiten Pl.

short cut n - 1. [quick route] Abkürzung die - 2. [quick method] schneller Weg.

shorten [ʃɔːtn] ◇ vt - 1. [in time] verkürzen - 2. [in length] kürzen. ◇ vi [days, nights] kürzer werden.

shortfall [ʃɔːtfɔːl] n: **shortfall (in/of sthg)** Defizit das (bei/von etw).

shorthand [ʃɔːthænd] n (U) [writing system] Stenografie die, Kurzschrift die.

shorthand typist n UK Stenotypist der, -in die.

short list n UK engere Wahl.

shortly [ʃɔːtlɪ] adv [soon] bald; **shortly before/after our arrival** kurz vor/nach unserer Ankunft.

shortsighted [ˌʃɔːtsaɪtɪd] adj liter & fig kurzsichtig.

short-staffed [-ˈstɑːft] adj: **to be short-staffed** an Personalmangel leiden.

short story n Kurzgeschichte die.

short-tempered [-ˈtempəd] adj reizbar.

short-term adj kurzfristig.

short wave n Kurzwelle die.

shot [ʃɒt] ◇ pt & pp ▷ **shoot**. ◇ n - 1. [gunshot, injection, drink] Schuss der; **like a shot** [quickly] wie der Blitz - 2. [marksman] Schütze der, -zin die - 3. [SPORT - in football] Schuss der; [- in golf, tennis] Schlag der - 4. [photograph] Aufnahme die - 5. CIN Einstellung die - 6. inf [try, go] Versuch der.

shotgun [ʃɒtgʌn] n Schrotflinte die.

should [ʃʊd] aux vb - 1. [expressing obligation]: **we should leave now** wir sollten jetzt gehen; **you should have seen her!** du hättest sie sehen sollen! - 2. [asking for advice, permission]: **should I go too?** soll ich auch gehen?; **should I do it now?** soll ich es jetzt tun? - 3. [as suggestion]: **I should deny everything** ich würde alles abstreiten; **I shouldn't take too much notice** kümmern Sie sich nicht zu sehr darum - 4. [expressing probability]: **she should be home soon** sie müsste bald zu Hause sein - 5. [ought to]: **they should have won the match** sie hätten das Spiel gewinnen müssen; **that should do** das dürfte genügen - 6. fml [expressing wish]: **I should like to come with you** ich würde gerne mit dir kommen - 7. (as conditional): **should you need anything, call reception** fml sollten Sie irgendetwas brauchen, rufen Sie die Rezeption an; **how should I know?** wie soll ich das wissen? - 8. (in subordinate clauses): **we decided that you should meet him** wir beschlossen, dass du ihn kennenlernen solltest - 9. [expressing uncertain opinion]: **I should imagine he's about 50** meiner Meinung nach ist er etwa 50.

shoulder [ʃəʊldər] ◇ n Schulter die. ◇ vt - 1. [load] auf die Schulter(n) nehmen - 2. [responsibility] übernehmen.

shoulder blade n Schulterblatt das.

shoulder strap n - 1. [on dress] Träger der - 2. [on bag] Schulterriemen der.

shouldn't [ʃʊdnt] abbr of **should not**.

should've [ʃʊdəv] abbr of **should have**.

shout [ʃaʊt] ◇ n Schrei der. ◇ vt schreien. ◇ vi schreien; **to shout at sb** jn anlschreien. ◆ **shout down** vt sep niederlschreien.

shouting [ʃaʊtɪŋ] n Geschrei das.

shove [ʃʌv] inf ◇ n: **to give sb a shove** jm einen Schubs geben; **to give sthg a shove** etw rücken; [car] etw anlschieben. ◇ vt [push - person] schubsen; [- thing] schieben; [stuff] stopfen. ◆ **shove off** vi - 1. [in boat] (vom Ufer) ablstoßen - 2. inf [go away] verschwinden.

shovel [ʃʌvl] (UK) (US) ◇ n Schaufel die. ◇ vt [with a shovel] schaufeln.

show [ʃəʊ] (pt -ed, pp shown OR -ed) ◇ n - 1. [entertainment] Show die - 2. CIN Vorstellung die - 3. [exhibition] Ausstellung die - 4. [display - of strength] Zurschaustellen das; [- of temper] Anfall der, Ausbruch der. ◇ vt zeigen; [subj: thermometer, dial] anlzeigen; [profit, loss] auflweisen; [work of art] ausl stellen; **to show sb sthg, to show sthg to sb** jm etw zeigen; **to show sb to the door/his table** jn zur Tür bringen/zu seinem Tisch führen. ◇ *vi* - **1.** [indicate, make clear] zeigen - **2.** [be visible] zu sehen sein - **3.** CIN: **what's showing tonight?** welcher Film läuft heute Abend? ◆ **show off** ◇ *vt sep* vorführen. ◇ *vi* anlgeben. ◆ **show up** ◇ *vt sep* [embarrass] blamieren. ◇ *vi* - **1.** [stand out] hervorlstehen, hervorltreten - **2.** [arrive] aufltauchen.

show business *n* Showbusiness *das*, Showgeschäft *das*.

showdown ['ʃəʊdaʊn] *n*: **to have a showdown with sb** mit jm eine klärende Auseinandersetzung haben.

shower ['ʃaʊər] ◇ *n* - **1.** [device] Dusche *die* - **2.** [wash]: **to have** OR **take a shower** duschen - **3.** [of rain] Schauer *der* - **4.** [of confetti, sparks] Regen *der*; [of insults, abuse] Flut *der*. ◇ *vt*: **to shower sb with sthg** jn mit etw überschütten. ◇ *vi* [wash] duschen.

shower cap *n* Duschhaube *die*.

showing ['ʃəʊɪŋ] *n* CIN Vorstellung *die*.

show jumping [-,dʒʌmpɪŋ] *n* Springreiten *das*.

shown [ʃəʊn] *pp* ▷ **show**.

show-off *n inf* Angeber *der*, -in *die*.

showpiece ['ʃəʊpiːs] *n* [main attraction] Paradestück *das*.

showroom ['ʃəʊrʊm] *n* Ausstellungsraum *der*.

shrank [ʃræŋk] *pt* ▷ **shrink**.

shrapnel ['ʃræpnl] *n (U)* Granatsplitter *Pl*.

shred [ʃred] ◇ *n* - **1.** [of paper] Schnitzel *der*; [of fabric] Fetzen *der* - **2.** *fig* [of truth] Funken *der*; [of evidence] Hauch *der*. ◇ *vt* - **1.** CULIN [cabbage, lettuce] in Streifen schneiden - **2.** [paper in shredder] in den Reißwolf stecken.

shredder ['ʃredər] *n* - **1.** CULIN [in food processor] Zerkleinerer *der* - **2.** [for documents] Aktenvernichter *der*.

shrewd [ʃruːd] *adj* scharfsinnig; [person] klug; [action, judgement, move] klug.

shriek [ʃriːk] ◇ *n* Schrei *der*. ◇ *vi*: **to shriek (with/in)** aufschreien (vor *(+ D)*).

shrill [ʃrɪl] *adj* [high-pitched] schrill.

shrimp [ʃrɪmp] *n* Garnele *die*.

shrine [ʃraɪn] *n* Schrein *der*.

shrink [ʃrɪŋk] *(pt* shrank, *pp* shrunk) ◇ *vt* eingehen lassen. ◇ *vi* - **1.** [become smaller] schrumpfen; [person] kleiner werden; [clothing] einlgehen - **2.** *fig* [contract, diminish] zusammenlschrumpfen; [of trade] zurücklgehen - **3.** [recoil]: **to shrink away from sb/sthg** vor jm/etw zurücklweichen. ◇ *n inf* [psychoanalyst] Nervenklempner *der*.

shrink-wrap *vt* einlschweißen.

shrivel ['ʃrɪvl] *(UK) (US)* ◇ *vt*: **to shrivel (up)** [plant] welken lassen; [skin] runzelig werden lassen. ◇ *vi*: **to shrivel (up)** [plant] welken; [skin] runzelig werden.

shroud [ʃraʊd] ◇ *n* [cloth] Leichentuch *das*. ◇ *vt*: **to be shrouded in sthg** in etw *(A)* eingehüllt sein.

Shrove Tuesday ['ʃrəʊv-] *n* Faschingsdienstag *der*, Fastnachtsdienstag *der*.

shrub [ʃrʌb] *n* Strauch *der*, Busch *der*.

shrubbery ['ʃrʌbərɪ] *n* Gebüsch *das*.

shrug [ʃrʌg] ◇ *vt*: **to shrug one's shoulders** mit den Achseln zucken. ◇ *vi* mit den Achseln zucken. ◆ **shrug off** *vt sep* beiseite schieben.

shrunk [ʃrʌŋk] *pp* ▷ **shrink**.

shudder ['ʃʌdər] *vi* - **1.** [person]: **to shudder (with sthg)** (vor etw *(D)*) schauern OR schaudern - **2.** [machine, vehicle] beben.

shuffle ['ʃʌfl] *vt* - **1.**: **to shuffle one's feet** mit den Füßen scharren; [when walking] schlurfen - **2.** [cards] mischen - **3.** [papers] durchlsortieren.

shun [ʃʌn] *vt* meiden *(+ D)*.

shunt [ʃʌnt] *vt* RAIL rangieren.

shut [ʃʌt] *(pt & pp inv)* ◇ *adj* geschlossen. ◇ *vt* schließen, zulmachen. ◇ *vi* schließen; [eyes] zulfallen. ◆ **shut away** *vt sep* - **1.** [criminal] einlsperren - **2.** [valuables] einlschließen. ◆ **shut down** *vt sep & vi* [factory, business] schließen. ◆ **shut out** *vt sep* [person, cat] auslsperren; [light, noise] am Eindringen hindern. ◆ **shut up** ◇ *vt sep* - **1.** [lock up] ablschließen - **2.** [silence] zum Schweigen bringen. ◇ *vi* - **1.** *inf* [be quiet] den Mund halten; **shut up!** halt den Mund! - **2.** [close] schließen.

shutter ['ʃʌtər] *n* - **1.** [on window] Fensterladen *der* - **2.** [in camera] Blende *die*.

shuttle ['ʃʌtl] ◇ *adj*: **shuttle service** Shuttle-Service *der*, Pendelverkehr *der*. ◇ *n* [plane] Pendelflugzeug *das*; [train] Pendelzug *der*; [bus] Pendelbus *der*.

shuttlecock ['ʃʌtlkɒk] *n* Federball *der*.

shy [ʃaɪ] ◇ *adj* [timid] schüchtern. ◇ *vi* scheuen.

Siberia [saɪ'bɪərɪə] *n* Sibirien *nt*.

siblings ['sɪblɪŋz] *npl* Geschwister *Pl*.

Sicily ['sɪsɪlɪ] *n* Sizilien *nt*.

sick [sɪk] *adj* - **1.** [unwell] krank; **she's off sick this week** sie fehlt diese Woche wegen Krankheit - **2.** [nauseous]: **she felt sick** ihr war schlecht OR übel - **3.** [vomiting]: **to be sick** UK sich übergeben (müssen) - **4.** [fed up]: **to be sick of sthg** etw satt haben; **to be sick of doing sthg** es satt haben, etw zu tun - **5.** [offensive - joke] makaber; [- humour] schwarz.

sicken ['sɪkn] ◇ *vt* [disgust] krank machen. ◇ *vi* UK: **to be sickening for sthg** etw auslbrüten.

sickening ['sɪkənɪŋ] adj - **1.** [disgusting] widerlich - **2.** hum [infuriating] unerträglich.

sickle ['sɪkl] n Sichel die.

sick leave n: to be on sick leave krankgeschrieben sein.

sickly ['sɪklɪ] adj - **1.** [unhealthy] kränklich - **2.** [nauseating] widerlich.

sickness ['sɪknɪs] n - **1.** [illness] Krankheit die - **2.** UK [nausea] Übelkeit die; [vomiting] Erbrechen das.

sick pay n (U) Lohnfortzahlung die im Krankheitsfall.

side [saɪd] ⬦ n - **1.** [gen] Seite die; on every side, on all sides auf allen Seiten; from side to side von einer Seite auf die andere, hin und her; at or by sb's side an js Seite; side by side Seite an Seite; on one's mother's side mütterlicherseits; on one's father's side väterlicherseits - **2.** [inner surface - of cave, crate, bathtub] Wand die - **3.** [of river, lake] Ufer das; [of road] Rand der - **4.** [team] Mannschaft die - **5.** [of argument] Standpunkt der; to take sb's side für jn Partei ergreifen - **6.** [aspect of character, personality] Seite die; [- of situation] Aspekt der; to be on the safe side um sicherzugehen. ⬦ adj [situated on side] Seiten-. ➣ side with vt insep Partei ergreifen für.

sideboard ['saɪdbɔːd] n Anrichte die, Büfett das.

sideboards UK ['saɪdbɔːdz], **sideburns** US ['saɪdbɜːnz] npl Koteletten Pl.

side effect n - **1.** MED [secondary effect] Nebenwirkung die - **2.** [unplanned result] Nebeneffekt der.

sidelight ['saɪdlaɪt] n Seitenlicht das.

sideline ['saɪdlaɪn] n - **1.** [extra business] Nebenbeschäftigung die - **2.** SPORT [painted line] Seitenlinie die.

sidelong ['saɪdlɒŋ] ⬦ adj Seiten-. ⬦ adv: to look sidelong at sb/sthg jn/etw aus dem Augenwinkel anlschauen.

sidesaddle ['saɪd,sædl] adv: to ride sidesaddle im Damensitz reiten.

sideshow ['saɪdʃəʊ] n Nebenattraktion die.

sidestep ['saɪdstep] vt liter & fig auslweichen (+ D).

side street n Nebenstraße die, Seitenstraße die.

sidetrack ['saɪdtræk] vt: to be sidetracked abgelenkt werden.

sidewalk ['saɪdwɔːk] n US Bürgersteig der.

sideways ['saɪdweɪz] ⬦ adj [movement] zur Seite; [look] Seiten-. ⬦ adv seitwärts.

siding ['saɪdɪŋ] n Abstellgleis das.

siege [siːdʒ] n - **1.** [by army] Belagerung die - **2.** [by police] Umstellen das.

sieve [sɪv] ⬦ n Sieb das. ⬦ vt sieben.

sift [sɪft] ⬦ vt - **1.** [sieve] sieben - **2.** fig [examine carefully] sichten, durchlsehen. ⬦ vi: to sift through sthg etw durchlsehen or durchlgehen.

sigh [saɪ] ⬦ n Seufzer der. ⬦ vi seufzen.

sight [saɪt] ⬦ n - **1.** [vision] Sehvermögen das; he has good/poor sight er sieht gut/schlecht - **2.** [act of seeing]: it was their first sight of their grandchild sie haben ihr Enkelkind zum ersten Mal gesehen; in sight in Sicht; out of sight außer Sicht; at first sight auf den ersten Blick - **3.** [spectacle] Anblick der - **4.** [on gun] Visier das. ⬦ vt [see] erspähen; [land] sichten. ➣ sights npl [on tour] Sehenswürdigkeiten Pl.

sightseeing ['saɪt,siːɪŋ] n Sightseeing das; to do some or go sightseeing Sehenswürdigkeiten besichtigen.

sightseer ['saɪt,siːər] n Tourist der, -in die.

sign [saɪn] ⬦ n - **1.** [written symbol, gesture] Zeichen das - **2.** [notice] Schild das - **3.** [indication] Anzeichen das; there's no sign of him yet von ihm ist noch nichts zu sehen. ⬦ vt [letter] unterschreiben; [document] unterzeichnen; [painting] signieren; to sign one's name unterschreiben. ➣ sign on vi - **1.** [enrol - for course] sich einlschreiben; MIL sich verpflichten - **2.** [register as unemployed] sich beim Arbeitsamt melden. ➣ sign up ⬦ vt sep [employee] einlstellen; [recruit] verpflichten. ⬦ vi [enrol - for course] sich einlschreiben; MIL sich verpflichten.

signal ['sɪgnl] (UK) (US) ⬦ n Signal das. ⬦ vt: to signal sb to do sthg jm ein Zeichen geben, etw zu tun. ⬦ vi - **1.** AUT blinken - **2.** [indicate]: to signal to sb to do sthg jm ein Zeichen geben, etw zu tun.

signature ['sɪgnətʃər] n [name] Unterschrift die.

significance [sɪg'nɪfɪkəns] n (U) Bedeutung die.

significant [sɪg'nɪfɪkənt] adj - **1.** [large, important] bedeutend - **2.** [full of hidden meaning] bedeutsam.

signify ['sɪgnɪfaɪ] vt bedeuten.

signpost ['saɪnpəʊst] n Wegweiser der.

Sikh [siːk] ⬦ adj Sikh-. ⬦ n Sikh der, die.

silence ['saɪləns] ⬦ n - **1.** [of person, on topic] Schweigen das - **2.** [of place] Stille die, Ruhe die. ⬦ vt zum Schweigen bringen.

silencer ['saɪlənsər] n Schalldämpfer der.

silent ['saɪlənt] adj - **1.** [speechless] still - **2.** [taciturn] schweigsam - **3.** [noiseless] ruhig, leise - **4.** CIN Stumm- - **5.** LING stumm.

silhouette [,sɪluː'et] n Silhouette die.

silicon chip n Siliziumchip der.

silk [sɪlk] ⬦ n Seide die. ⬦ comp Seiden-.

silky ['sɪlkɪ] adj seidig; [voice] samtig.

sill [sɪl] n [of window] (Fenster)sims der.

silly ['sɪlɪ] *adj* - **1.** [foolish] dumm - **2.** [comical] komisch - **3.** [childish, ridiculous]: **don't be so silly!** sei nicht so albern!

silo ['saɪləʊ] (*pl* **-s**) *n* Silo *das*.

silt [sɪlt] *n* Schlick *der*, Schlamm *der*.

silver ['sɪlvər] <> *adj* [greyish-white] silbern. <> *n* (U) - **1.** [metal, silverware] Silber *das* - **2.** [coins] Silbermünzen *Pl*. <> *comp* [made of silver] Silber-.

silver foil, silver paper *n* (U) Alufolie *die*.

silver-plated [-'pleɪtɪd] *adj* versilbert.

silverware ['sɪlvəweər] *n* - **1.** [objects made of silver] Silber *das* - **2.** US [cutlery] Besteck *das*.

similar ['sɪmɪlər] *adj* ähnlich; **to be similar to sthg** so ähnlich wie etw sein.

similarly ['sɪmɪləlɪ] *adv* ebenso.

simmer ['sɪmər] *vt & vi* auf kleiner Flamme kochen.

simple ['sɪmpl] *adj* - **1.** [easy] einfach - **2.** [plain - clothing, furniture, style] schlicht; [- fact, truth] rein; [- way of life] einfach - **3.** [mentally retarded] einfältig.

simple-minded [-'maɪndɪd] *adj* [person] einfältig; [view] vereinfacht.

simplicity [sɪm'plɪsətɪ] *n* [ease] Einfachheit *die*; [plainness - of clothing, furniture, style] Schlichtheit *die*.

simplify ['sɪmplɪfaɪ] *vt* vereinfachen.

simply ['sɪmplɪ] *adv* - **1.** [merely] einfach - **2.** [for emphasis]: **you simply must go** du musst unbedingt gehen; **the weather is simply dreadful** das Wetter ist einfach scheußlich - **3.** [in an uncomplicated way - live] einfach; [- dress] schlicht.

simulate ['sɪmjʊleɪt] *vt* - **1.** [feign - gen] vortäuschen; [- illness] simulieren - **2.** [produce effect, appearance of] simulieren.

simultaneous [UK ,sɪmʊl'teɪnjəs, US ,saɪmʊl'teɪnjəs] *adj* gleichzeitig; [broadcast] direkt; [interpreting] Simultan-.

sin [sɪn] <> *n* Sünde *die*. <> *vi*: **to sin (against)** sündigen (gegen).

since [sɪns] <> *adv* seitdem; **I haven't seen them since** ich habe sie seitdem nicht mehr gesehen; **she has since moved to London** inzwischen ist sie nach London umgezogen; **since then** seitdem. <> *prep* seit; **I've been here since six o'clock** ich bin hier seit sechs Uhr. <> *conj* - **1.** [in time] seit; **it's ages since I saw her** ich habe sie schon seit langem nicht mehr gesehen - **2.** [because] da.

sincere [sɪn'sɪər] *adj* aufrichtig.

sincerely [sɪn'sɪəlɪ] *adv* aufrichtig; **Yours sincerely** [at end of letter] mit freundlichen Grüßen.

sincerity [sɪn'serətɪ] *n* Aufrichtigkeit *die*.

sinew ['sɪnjuː] *n* Sehne *die*.

sinful ['sɪnfʊl] *adj* sündig.

sing [sɪŋ] (*pt* **sang**, *pp* **sung**) <> *vt* singen. <> *vi* singen.

Singapore [,sɪŋə'pɔːr] *n* Singapur *nt*.

singe [sɪndʒ] *vt* versengen.

singer ['sɪŋər] *n* Sänger *der*, -in *die*.

singing ['sɪŋɪŋ] *n* (U) Gesang *der*.

single ['sɪŋgl] <> *adj* - **1.** [sole] einzig; **every single** jede/jeder/jedes einzelne - **2.** [unmarried] ledig - **3.** UK [one-way] einfach. <> *n* - **1.** UK [one-way ticket] einfache Fahrkarte - **2.** MUS Single *die*. ➤ **singles** *npl* TENNIS Einzel *das*. ➤ **single out** *vt sep*: **to single sb out (for sthg)** jn (für etw) auslsuchen OR auslwählen.

single bed *n* Einzelbett *das*.

single-breasted [-'brestɪd] *adj* einreihig.

single cream *n* (U) UK Sahne mit niedrigem Fettgehalt.

single file *n*: **in single file** im Gänsemarsch.

single-handed [-'hændɪd] *adv* eigenhändig.

single-minded [-'maɪndɪd] *adj* zielstrebig.

single parent *n* [mother] alleinerziehende Mutter; [father] alleinerziehender Vater.

single-parent family *n* Familie *die* mit nur einem Elternteil.

single room *n* Einzelzimmer *das*.

singlet ['sɪŋglɪt] *n* - **1.** UK [underwear] Unterhemd *das* - **2.** SPORT ärmelloses Trikot.

singular ['sɪŋgjʊlər] <> *adj* - **1.** GRAM im Singular, in der Einzahl - **2.** [unusual] eigentümlich; [unique] einzigartig. <> *n* Singular *der*, Einzahl *die*.

sinister ['sɪnɪstər] *adj* finster, unheimlich.

sink [sɪŋk] (*pt* **sank**, *pp* **sunk**) <> *n* - **1.** [in kitchen] Spülbecken *das* - **2.** [in bathroom] Waschbecken *das*. <> *vt* - **1.** [in water] versenken - **2.** [teeth, claws]: **to sink sthg into sthg** etw in etw (A) graben. <> *vi* - **1.** [gen] sinken; [person - in water] unterlgehen; **to sink to one's knees** auf die Knie sinken - **2.** *fig* [heart, spirits]: **my heart sank when I heard the news** meine Stimmung sank, als ich die Nachricht hörte - **3.** [building, ground] sich senken. ➤ **sink in** *vi*: **it hasn't sunk in yet** ich habe/er hat/etc es noch nicht realisiert.

sink unit *n* Spüle *die*.

sinner ['sɪnər] *n* Sünder *der*, -in *die*.

sinus ['saɪnəs] (*pl* **-es**) *n* Stirnhöhle *die*.

sip [sɪp] <> *n* kleiner Schluck. <> *vt* nippen an (+ D), in kleinen Schlucken trinken.

siphon ['saɪfn] <> *n*: **(soda) siphon** Siphon *der*. <> *vt* - **1.** : **to siphon (off)** ablsaugen - **2.** *fig* [transfer] verlagern.

sir [sɜːr] *n* - **1.** [form of address] mein Herr - **2.** [in titles] Sir *der*.

siren ['saɪərən] *n* Sirene *die*.

sirloin (steak) ['sɜːlɔɪn-] *n* Lendensteak *das*.

sissy ['sɪsɪ] *n inf* Waschlappen *der*.

sister ['sɪstə^r] n - 1. [gen] Schwester die
- 2. UK [senior nurse] Oberschwester die.

sister-in-law (pl sisters-in-law OR sister-in-laws) n Schwägerin die.

sit [sɪt] (pt & pp sat) <> vt - 1. [place] setzen
- 2. UK [examination] ablegen. <> vi - 1. [be in seated position] sitzen - 2. [sit down] sich hinsetzen - 3. [be member]: **to sit on sthg** in etw (D) sitzen - 4. [be in session] tagen. **sit about, sit around** vi herumlsitzen. **sit down** vi sich setzen. **sit in on** vt insep beiwohnen (+ D). **sit through** vt insep bis zum Ende durchlhalten. **sit up** vi - 1. [be sitting upright] aufrecht sitzen; [move into upright position] sich auflsetzen - 2. [stay up] auflbleiben.

sitcom ['sɪtkɒm] n inf Situationskomödie die.

site [saɪt] <> n - 1.: **archaeological site** Ausgrabungsstätte die; **building site** Baustelle die
- 2. [location, place] Ort der, Stelle die - 3. [website] Website die. <> vt: **to be sited** gelegen sein.

sit-in n Sit-in das.

sitting ['sɪtɪŋ] n - 1.: **dinner is served in two sittings** das Abendessen wird in zwei Schichten serviert - 2. [session] Sitzung die.

sitting room n Wohnzimmer das.

situated ['sɪtjueɪtɪd] adj [located]: **to be situated** sich befinden.

situation [,sɪtju'eɪʃn] n - 1. [circumstances] Lage die, Situation die - 2. [location] Lage die
- 3. [job] Stelle die; **'Situations Vacant'** UK 'Stellenangebote'.

six [sɪks] <> num adj - 1. [numbering six] sechs
- 2. [referring to age]: **she's six (years old)** sie ist sechs (Jahre alt). <> num pron sechs; **I want six** ich möchte sechs (Stück); **there were six of us** wir waren zu sechst; **groups of six** [people] Sechsergruppen; [objects] Gruppen von jeweils sechs. <> num n - 1. [the number six] Sechs die; **two hundred and six** zweihundertsechs - 2. [six o'clock]: **at six** um sechs (Uhr)
- 3. [in addresses]: **six Peyton Place** Peyton Place sechs - 4. [group of six]: **the batteries come in sixes** die Batterien werden im Sechserpack verkauft; **we need one more person to make a six** wir brauchen noch eine Person, um eine Sechsergruppe zu bilden - 5. [in scores] sechs; **six-zero** sechs zu null - 6. [in cards] Sechs die; **the six of hearts** die Herzsechs.

sixteen [sɪks'tiːn] num sechzehn; see also **six**.

sixteenth [sɪks'tiːnθ] num sechzehnte(r) (s); see also **sixth**.

sixth [sɪksθ] <> num adj sechste(r) (s).
<> num adv [on list] an sechster Stelle; **he came sixth** er wurde Sechster. <> num pron [in series] Sechste(r) (s). <> n - 1. [fraction] Sechstel das - 2. [in dates] Sechste der; **the sixth of March** der sechste März.

sixth form n UK SCH ≃ Oberstufe die.

sixth form college n UK zu den A-Levels führende Schule für Schüler ab 16 Jahren.

sixty ['sɪkstɪ] num sechzig; see also **six**.
sixties npl - 1. [decade]: **the sixties** die Sechzigerjahre - 2. [in ages]: **to be in one's sixties** in den Sechzigern sein.

size [saɪz] n Größe die; **to cut sb down to size** jn zurechtlstutzen. **size up** vt sep sich (D) eine Meinung bilden über (+ A).

sizeable ['saɪzəbl] adj ziemlich groß.

sizzle ['sɪzl] vi brutzeln.

skate [skeɪt] <> n - 1. [ice skate] Schlittschuh der - 2. [roller skate] Rollschuh der
- 3. (pl inv OR -s) [fish] Rochen der. <> vi - 1. [on ice skates] Schlittschuh laufen - 2. [on roller skates] Rollschuh laufen.

skateboard ['skeɪtbɔːd] n Skateboard das.

skater ['skeɪtə^r] n - 1. [on ice] Schlittschuhläufer der, -in die - 2. [on roller skates] Rollschuhläufer der, -in die.

skating ['skeɪtɪŋ] n - 1. [on ice] Schlittschuhlaufen das - 2. [on roller skates] Rollschuhlaufen das.

skeleton ['skelɪtn] n Skelett das.

skeleton key n Dietrich der.

skeptic etc n US = **sceptic** etc.

sketch [sketʃ] <> n - 1. [drawing] Skizze die
- 2. [brief description] kurze Darstellung - 3. [on TV, radio, stage] Sketch der. <> vt - 1. [draw] skizzieren - 2. [describe] kurz darllegen.

sketchbook ['sketʃbʊk] n Skizzenbuch das.

sketchpad ['sketʃpæd] n Skizzenblock der.

sketchy ['sketʃɪ] adj oberflächlich.

skewer ['skjuə^r] <> n Spieß der. <> vt auflspießen.

ski [skiː] (pt & pp skied, cont skiing) <> n Ski der. <> vi Ski fahren.

ski boots npl Skistiefel Pl.

skid [skɪd] <> n Schleudern das; **to go into a skid** ins Schleudern geraten. <> vi schleudern.

skier ['skiːə^r] n Skiläufer der, -in die.

skiing ['skiːɪŋ] n Skifahren das.

ski jump n - 1. [slope] Sprungschanze die
- 2. [sporting event] Skispringen das.

skilful, skillful US ['skɪlful] adj geschickt.

ski lift n Skilift der.

skill [skɪl] n - 1. [expertise] Geschicklichkeit die - 2. [craft, technique] Fertigkeit die.

skilled [skɪld] adj - 1. [skilful] geschickt; **skilled in** OR **at doing sthg** geschickt darin sein, etw zu tun - 2. [trained - worker] ausgebildet; [- work, labour] fachmännisch.

skillful etc US = **skilful** etc.

skim [skɪm] <> vt [remove] ablschöpfen.
<> vi - 1. [bird]: **to skim over sthg** hinweglgleiten über (+ A) - 2. [read]: **to skim through sthg** etw überfliegen.

skim(med) milk [skɪm(d)-] *n* Magermilch *die*.

skimp [skɪmp] ⟨⟩ *vt* sparen an *(+ D)*. ⟨⟩ *vi*: **to skimp on sthg** an etw *(D)* sparen.

skimpy ['skɪmpɪ] *adj* dürftig; [clothes] knapp.

skin [skɪn] ⟨⟩ *n* - **1.** [of person, on liquid] Haut *die* - **2.** [of animal] Fell *das* - **3.** [of fruit, vegetable] Schale *die*. ⟨⟩ *vt* - **1.** [animal] häuten - **2.** [graze] aufl schürfen.

skin-deep *adj* oberflächlich.

skinny ['skɪnɪ] *adj inf* dürr.

skin-tight *adj* hauteng.

skip [skɪp] ⟨⟩ *n* - **1.** [little jump] Hüpfer *der* - **2.** *UK* [large container] Sperrmüllcontainer *der*. ⟨⟩ *vt* [miss - page] überspringen; [- meal] auslassen; **to skip school** die Schule schwänzen. ⟨⟩ *vi* - **1.** [move in little jumps] hüpfen - **2.** *UK* [jump over rope] seil springen.

ski pants *npl* Skihosen *Pl.*

ski pole *n* Skistock *der*.

skipper ['skɪpər] *n* Kapitän *der*.

skipping rope *n UK* Springseil *das*.

skirmish ['skɜːmɪʃ] *n* - **1.** MIL Gefecht *das* - **2.** *fig* [disagreement] Auseinandersetzung *die*.

skirt [skɜːt] ⟨⟩ *n* [garment] Rock *der*. ⟨⟩ *vt liter & fig* umgehen.

ski tow *n* Skilift *der*.

skittle ['skɪtl] *n UK* Kegel *der*; **to have a game of skittles** kegeln (gehen).

skive [skaɪv] *vi UK inf*: **to skive (off)** [from school] schwänzen; [from work] blau machen.

skulk [skʌlk] *vi* - **1.** [hide] sich verstecken - **2.** [prowl] herum schleichen.

skull [skʌl] *n* Schädel *der*.

skunk [skʌŋk] *n* Stinktier *das*.

sky [skaɪ] *n* Himmel *der*.

skylight ['skaɪlaɪt] *n* Dachfenster *das*.

skyscraper ['skaɪ,skreɪpər] *n* Wolkenkratzer *der*.

slab [slæb] *n* - **1.** [of concrete, stone] Platte *die*; [of wood] Tafel *die* - **2.** [of meat, chocolate, cake] großes Stück.

slack [slæk] ⟨⟩ *adj* - **1.** [not taut] locker - **2.** [not busy] flau - **3.** [careless] nachlässig. ⟨⟩ *n*: **there is too much slack in the rope** das Seil ist nicht straff genug.

slacken ['slækn] ⟨⟩ *vt* - **1.** [make slower] verlangsamen - **2.** [make looser] lockern. ⟨⟩ *vi* [become slower] langsamer reißen.

slagheap ['slæghiːp] *n* Halde *die*.

slam [slæm] ⟨⟩ *vt* - **1.** [shut] zul knallen - **2.** [place roughly]: **to slam sthg on(to) sthg** etw auf etw *(A)* knallen. ⟨⟩ *vi* [shut] zul knallen.

slander ['slɑːndər] ⟨⟩ *n (U)* Verleumdung *die*. ⟨⟩ *vt* verleumden.

slang [slæŋ] *n* Slang *der*.

slant [slɑːnt] ⟨⟩ *n* - **1.** [diagonal angle] Schräge *die* - **2.** [point of view] Blickwinkel *der*. ⟨⟩ *vt* [bias] zurecht l biegen. ⟨⟩ *vi* schräg sein.

slanting ['slɑːntɪŋ] *adj* schräg.

slap [slæp] ⟨⟩ *n* Schlag *der*; [in face] Ohrfeige *die*; [on back] Klaps *der*. ⟨⟩ *vt* - **1.** [person] schlagen; **to slap sb's face** jm eine Ohrfeige geben; **to slap sb on the back** jm auf den Rücken klopfen - **2.** [put]: **to slap sthg on(to) sthg** etw auf etw *(A)* knallen. ⟨⟩ *adv inf* [directly] direkt.

slapdash ['slæpdæʃ], **slaphappy** ['slæp,hæpɪ] *adj inf* schlampig.

slapstick ['slæpstɪk] *n* Slapstick *der*.

slap-up *adj UK inf* Super-.

slash [slæʃ] ⟨⟩ *n* - **1.** [long cut] Schnitt *der* - **2.** *esp US* [oblique stroke] Schrägstrich *der*. ⟨⟩ *vt* - **1.** [cut - material] (zer)schneiden; [- tyres] zerschlitzen, aufl schlitzen; **to slash one's wrists** sich die Pulsadern aufl schneiden - **2.** *inf* [reduce drastically] stark reduzieren.

slat [slæt] *n* [in blind] Lamelle *die*; [in bench] Latte *die*.

slate [sleɪt] ⟨⟩ *n* - **1.** *(U)* [rock] Schiefer *der* - **2.** [on roof] Schieferplatte *die*. ⟨⟩ *vt* [criticize] verreißen.

slaughter ['slɔːtər] ⟨⟩ *n* - **1.** [of animals] Schlachten *das* - **2.** [of people] Abschlachten *das*. ⟨⟩ *vt* - **1.** [animals] schlachten - **2.** [people] abl schlachten.

slaughterhouse ['slɔːtəhaus] *(pl* [-haʊzɪz]) *n* Schlachthof *der*.

slave [sleɪv] ⟨⟩ *n* [servant] Sklave *der*, -vin *die*. ⟨⟩ *vi*: **to slave (over sthg)** sich (mit etw) abl plagen.

slavery ['sleɪvərɪ] *n* Sklaverei *die*.

sleaze [sliːz] *n* Korruption *die*.

sleazy ['sliːzɪ] *adj* [area, bar] schäbig; [behaviour] korrupt.

sledge [sledʒ], **sled** *US* [sled] *n* Schlitten *der*.

sledgehammer ['sledʒ,hæmər] *n* Vorschlaghammer *der*.

sleek [sliːk] *adj* - **1.** [hair, fur] seidig glänzend - **2.** [car, plane] schnittig.

sleep [sliːp] *(pt & pp* slept) ⟨⟩ *n* Schlaf *der*; **to go to sleep** [doze off, go numb] einl schlafen. ⟨⟩ *vi* schlafen. ◆ **sleep in** *vi* [oversleep] verschlafen. ◆ **sleep with** *vt insep euph* schlafen mit.

sleeper ['sliːpər] *n* - **1.** [person]: **to be a heavy/light sleeper** einen tiefen/leichten Schlaf haben - **2.** [sleeping compartment] Schlafwagenabteil *das* - **3.** [train] Schlafwagenzug *der* - **4.** *UK* [on railway track] Schwelle *die*.

sleeping bag ['sliːpɪŋ-] *n* Schlafsack *der*.

sleeping car ['sliːpɪŋ-] *n* Schlafwagen *der*.

sleeping pill ['sliːpɪŋ-] *n* Schlaftablette *die*.

sleepless ['sliːplɪs] *adj* schlaflos.

sleepwalk ['sli:pwɔ:k] *vi* schlafwandeln.

sleepy ['sli:pɪ] *adj* [person] schläfrig.

sleet [sli:t] <> *n* Schneeregen *der*. <> *impers vb*: **it's sleeting** es fällt Schneeregen.

sleeve [sli:v] *n* - **1.** [of garment] Ärmel *der* - **2.** [for record] Hülle *die*.

sleigh [sleɪ] *n* Schlitten *der*.

slender ['slendər] *adj* - **1.** [thin] schlank - **2.** [scarce - resources] knapp; [- hope, chance] gering.

slept [slept] *pt & pp* ⊳ **sleep**.

S-level *n UK* SCH S-Level *das (ergänzendes Fortgeschrittenenniveau).*

slice [slaɪs] <> *n* - **1.** [thin piece] Scheibe *die*; [of pizza] Stück *das* - **2.** [proportion] Teil *der* - **3.** SPORT Slice *der*. <> *vt* - **1.** [cut into slices] in Scheiben schneiden - **2.** SPORT slicen. ➡ **slice off** *vt sep* [sever] abltrennen.

slick [slɪk] <> *adj* - **1.** [smoothly efficient] geschickt gemacht - **2.** *pej* [person] aalglatt; [answer, argument] glatt. <> *n*: **(oil) slick** Ölteppich *der*.

slide [slaɪd] (*pt & pp* slid [slɪd]) <> *n* - **1.** PHOT Dia(positiv) *das* - **2.** [in playground] Rutsche *die* - **3.** *UK* [for hair] Haarspange *die* - **4.** [decline - of person] Abrutschen *das*. <> *vt* gleiten lassen. <> *vi* - **1.** [on ice, slippery surface] schlittern - **2.** [move quietly] gleiten - **3.** [decline - person] ablrutschen; [- prices, standards] ablsinken.

sliding door [,slaɪdɪŋ-] *n* Schiebetür *die*.

slight [slaɪt] <> *adj* - **1.** [minor] leicht; **not the slightest interest** nicht das geringste Interesse; **not in the slightest** nicht im Geringsten - **2.** [slender] schmal. <> *n* [insult] Kränkung *die*. <> *vt* [offend] kränken.

slightly ['slaɪtlɪ] *adv* [to small extent] etwas.

slim [slɪm] <> *adj* - **1.** [person] schlank - **2.** [object] schmal - **3.** [chance, possibility] gering. <> *vi* [lose weight] ablnehmen; [diet] eine Diät machen.

slime [slaɪm] *n* Schleim *der*.

slimming ['slɪmɪŋ] *n* Abnehmen *das*.

sling [slɪŋ] (*pt & pp* slung) <> *n* - **1.** [for injured arm] Armschlinge *die* - **2.** [for carrying things] Trageriemen *der*. <> *vt* - **1.** [hang roughly]: **she slung the bag over her shoulder** sie hängte sich die Tasche über die Schulter - **2.** *inf* [throw] schleudern - **3.** [hang by both ends] spannen.

slip [slɪp] <> *n* - **1.** [mistake] Versehen *das*; **a slip of the tongue** ein Versprecher - **2.** [form] Abschnitt *der* - **3.** [of paper]: **slip (of paper)** Zettel *der* - **4.** [underwear] Unterrock *der* - **5.** *phr*: **to give sb the slip** *inf* jm entkommen. <> *vt* - **1.** [put, slide] stecken - **2.** [clothes]: **to slip sthg on/off** etw überlziehen/auslziehen - **3.** [escape]: **it slipped my mind** ich habe es vergessen. <> *vi* - **1.** [lose balance] auslrutschen - **2.** [move unexpectedly - hand, foot]

rutschen; **it slipped out of my hand** es rutschte mir aus der Hand; **I let it slip** [revealed it] es ist mir herausgerutscht - **3.** [decline] sinken - **4.** [move discreetly] schlüpfen; **to slip into/out of sthg** [clothes] in etw *(A)*/aus etw schlüpfen. ➡ **slip away** *vi* [leave] sich davonlschleichen. ➡ **slip on** *vt sep* [clothes] überlziehen; [shoes] anlziehen. ➡ **slip up** *vi* sich vertun.

slipped disc [,slɪpt-] *n* Bandscheibenvorfall *der*.

slipper ['slɪpər] *n* Hausschuh *der*.

slippery ['slɪpərɪ] *adj* - **1.** [surface, soap] rutschig - **2.** [person] windig.

slip road *n UK* [onto motorway] Auffahrt *die*; [leaving motorway] Ausfahrt *die*.

slip-up *n inf* Versehen *das*.

slit [slɪt] (*pt & pp inv*) <> *n* Schlitz *der*. <> *vt* auflschlitzen.

slither ['slɪðər] *vi* - **1.** [car, person] rutschen - **2.** [snake] gleiten.

sliver ['slɪvər] *n* - **1.** [splinter] Splitter *der* - **2.** [slice] hauchdünne Scheibe.

slob [slɒb] *n inf* Dreckschwein *das*.

slog [slɒg] *inf* <> *n* [tiring work] Schinderei *die*. <> *vi* [work]: **to slog (away) at sthg** sich mit etw ablplagen.

slogan ['sləʊgən] *n* Slogan *der*.

slop [slɒp] <> *vt* verschütten. <> *vi* überlschwappen.

slope [sləʊp] <> *n* - **1.** [of roof, ground] Neigung *die* - **2.** [hill] Hang *der*. <> *vi* [shelf, table] schräg sein.

sloping ['sləʊpɪŋ] *adj* schräg; [land] abfallend.

sloppy ['slɒpɪ] *adj* [careless] schlampig.

slot [slɒt] *n* - **1.** [opening] Schlitz *der* - **2.** [groove] Nut *die* - **3.** [place in broadcasting schedule] Sendezeit *die*.

slot machine *n* - **1.** [vending machine] Münzautomat *der* - **2.** [arcade machine] Spielautomat *der*.

slouch [slaʊtʃ] *vi* [when sitting] sich hinllümmeln; [when standing] schlaff dalstehen.

Slovakia [slə'vækɪə] *n* Slowakei *die*.

slovenly ['slʌvnlɪ] *adj* schlampig.

slow [sləʊ] <> *adj* - **1.** [not fast] langsam - **2.** [clock, watch]: **to be slow** nachlgehen - **3.** [not intelligent] langsam. <> *adv*: **to go slow** [driver] langsam fahren; [workers] Bummelstreik machen. <> *vt* verlangsamen. <> *vi* [person] langsam werden; [car] langsamer fahren; [increase, progress] sich verlangsamen. ➡ **slow down, slow up** <> *vt sep* verlangsamen. <> *vi* langsamer werden; [car] langsamer fahren; [walker] langsamer gehen.

slowdown ['sləʊdaʊn] *n* Verlangsamung *die*.

slowly ['sləʊlɪ] *adv* langsam.

slow motion n Zeitlupe *die*.

sludge [slʌdʒ] n Schlamm *der*.

slug [slʌg] n - **1.** ZOOL Nacktschnecke *die* - **2.** *inf* [of alcohol] Schluck *der* - **3.** *US inf* [bullet] Kugel *die*.

sluggish ['slʌgɪʃ] adj träge; [business] flau.

sluice [sluːs] n Schleuse *die*.

slum [slʌm] n [area] Slum *der*.

slumber ['slʌmbər] *liter* ◇ n Schlummer *der*. ◇ vi schlummern.

slump [slʌmp] ◇ n - **1.** [decline] slump (in sthg) Abfall *der* (einer Sache (G)) - **2.** [period of economic depression] Konjunkturabschwung *der*. ◇ vi - **1.** [business, market] plötzlich zurückgehen; [prices] stürzen - **2.** [person] sich fallen lassen.

slung [slʌŋ] pt & pp ▷ **sling**.

slur [slɜːr] ◇ n [insult]: **slur (on sb/sthg)** Schande *die* (für jn/etw). ◇ vt [speech]: **to slur one's words** mit schwerer Zunge sprechen.

slush [slʌʃ] n Schneematsch *der*.

slut [slʌt] n *inf* Schlampe *die*.

sly [slaɪ] (*comp* **slyer** OR **slier**, *superl* **slyest** OR **sliest**) adj - **1.** [look, smile, grin] wissend - **2.** [cunning] listig.

smack [smæk] ◇ n [slap] Klaps *der*; [on face] Ohrfeige *die*. ◇ vt - **1.** [slap] einen Klaps geben (+ D); [in the face] ohrfeigen - **2.** [put] knallen.

small [smɔːl] ◇ adj klein; **a small number** eine geringe Anzahl; **a small matter** eine Kleinigkeit; **a small business** ein Kleinbetrieb; **to feel small** sich schämen. ◇ adv: **to chop sthg up small** etw klein schneiden.

small ads [-ædz] npl *UK* Kleinanzeigen *Pl*.

small change n Kleingeld *das*.

smallholder ['smɔːl,həʊldər] n *UK* Kleinbauer *der*, -bäuerin *die*.

small hours npl frühe Morgenstunden *Pl*.

smallpox ['smɔːlpɒks] n (U) Pocken *Pl*.

small print n: **the small print** das Kleingedruckte.

small talk n Small Talk *der*.

smarmy ['smɑːmɪ] adj schleimig.

smart [smɑːt] ◇ adj - **1.** [elegant] elegant - **2.** *esp US* [clever] klug - **3.** [fashionable, exclusive] exklusiv - **4.** [rapid] flott. ◇ vi - **1.** [sting] brennen - **2.** [feel anger and humiliation] verletzt sein.

smarten ['smɑːtn] ✦ **smarten up** vt sep [room] aufräumen; **to smarten up one's appearance** sich herrichten.

smash [smæʃ] ◇ n - **1.** [sound] Krach *der* - **2.** *inf* [car crash] Unfall *der* - **3.** TENNIS Schmetterball *der*. ◇ vt - **1.** [break into pieces] zerschlagen - **2.** *fig* [defeat] zerschlagen. ◇ vi - **1.** [break into pieces] zerbrechen - **2.** [crash, col-

lide]: **to smash through sthg** durch etw rasen; **the car smashed into the tree** das Auto krachte gegen den Baum.

smashing ['smæʃɪŋ] adj *inf* klasse, toll.

smattering ['smætərɪŋ] n: **to have a smattering of sthg** Grundkenntnisse in etw (D) haben; **I have a smattering of German** ich kann ein bisschen Deutsch.

smear [smɪər] ◇ n - **1.** [dirty mark] Fleck *der* - **2.** MED Abstrich *der* - **3.** [slander] Verleumdung *die*. ◇ vt - **1.** [smudge - page, painting] verschmieren; [- paint, ink] verwischen - **2.** [spread]: **to smear sthg onto sthg** etw auf etw (A) schmieren - **3.** [slander] verleumden.

smell [smel] (pt & pp **-ed** OR **smelt**) ◇ n - **1.** [odour] Geruch *der*; [unpleasant] Gestank *der* - **2.** (U) [sense of smell] Geruchssinn *der* - **3.** [sniff]: **to have a smell of sthg** an etw (D) riechen. ◇ vt - **1.** [notice an odour of, sense] riechen - **2.** [sniff at] riechen an (+ D); [subj: dog] schnuppern an (+ D). ◇ vi - **1.** [have sense of smell] riechen - **2.** [have particular smell]: **to smell of sthg** nach etw riechen; **to smell like sthg** wie etw riechen; **to smell good/bad** gut/schlecht riechen - **3.** [smell unpleasantly] übel riechen.

smelly ['smelɪ] adj übel riechend.

smelt [smelt] pt & pp ▷ **smell**.

smile [smaɪl] ◇ n Lächeln *das*. ◇ vi lächeln.

smiley ['smaɪlɪ] n COMPUT Smiley *der*.

smirk [smɜːk] n Grinsen *das*.

smock [smɒk] n Kittel *der*.

smog [smɒg] n Smog *der*.

smoke [sməʊk] ◇ n [from fire] Rauch *der*. ◇ vt - **1.** [cigarette, cigar] rauchen - **2.** [fish, meat, cheese] räuchern. ◇ vi rauchen.

smoked [sməʊkt] adj [food] geräuchert.

smoker ['sməʊkər] n - **1.** [person who smokes] Raucher *der* - **2.** RAIL [compartment] Raucherabteil *das*.

smoke shop n *US* Tabakladen *der*.

smoking ['sməʊkɪŋ] n Rauchen *das*; **'no smoking'** 'Rauchen verboten'.

smoky ['sməʊkɪ] adj rauchig.

smolder vi *US* = **smoulder**.

smooth [smuːð] ◇ adj - **1.** [surface] glatt - **2.** [sauce, paste] sämig - **3.** [flow, pace, supply] gleichmäßig - **4.** [taste] weich - **5.** [flight, ride] ruhig; [takeoff, landing] weich; [engine] ruhig laufend - **6.** *pej* [person, manner] aalglatt - **7.** [trouble-free] glatt verlaufend; [transition] reibungslos. ◇ vt - **1.** [hair, skirt, tablecloth] glatt streichen - **2.** [rub]: **smooth the oil into your skin** reiben Sie ihre Haut mit dem Öl ein. ✦ **smooth out** vt sep - **1.** [skirt, sheet, crease] glatt streichen - **2.** [difficulties] aus dem Weg räumen.

smother ['smʌðər] vt - **1.** [cover thickly]: **to smother sthg in** OR **with sthg** etw mit etw be-

decken - **2.** [suffocate, extinguish] ersticken
- **3.** fig [repress] unterdrücken - **4.** [suffocate
with love] (mit Liebe) erdrücken.

smoulder UK, **smolder** US ['sməʊldər] vi
liter & fig schwelen.

SMS [,esem'es] n (abbr of short message system) SMS die.

smudge [smʌdʒ] ◇ n [dirty mark] Fleck der;
[of ink] verwischte Stelle. ◇ vt [spoil - by blur-
ring] verschmieren; [- outline, ink] verwischen;
[- by dirtying] beschmutzen.

smug [smʌg] adj pej selbstzufrieden.

smuggle ['smʌgl] vt schmuggeln.

smuggler ['smʌglər] n Schmuggler der,
-in die.

smuggling ['smʌglɪŋ] n Schmuggel der.

smutty ['smʌtɪ] adj inf pej [lewd] schmutzig.

snack [snæk] n Snack der, Imbiss der.

snack bar n Snackbar die, Imbissstube die.

snag [snæg] ◇ n [problem] Haken der.
◇ vi: to snag on sthg an etw (D) hängenl
bleiben.

snail [sneɪl] n Schnecke die.

snake [sneɪk] n Schlange die.

snap [snæp] ◇ adj spontan; [election] Spon-
tan-. ◇ n - **1.** [of twig, branch] Knacken das;
[of whip] Knallen das - **2.** inf [photograph]
Schnappschuss der - **3.** [card game] Schnipp-
schnappschnurr das. ◇ vt - **1.** [break - rope]
zerreißen; to snap one's fingers mit den Fingern schnippen - **2.** [say sharply] hervorl
stoßen. ◇ vi - **1.** [break] (zer)brechen; [rope]
(zer)reißen - **2.** [attempt to bite]: to snap (at sb/
sthg) (nach jm/etw) schnappen - **3.** [speak
sharply]: to snap at sb jn anlfahren. ◆ **snap
up** vt sep zulschlagen bei (+ D).

snappy ['snæpɪ] adj inf [stylish, quick] flott;
make it snappy! mach hin!

snapshot ['snæpʃɒt] n Schnappschuss der.

snare [sneər] ◇ n Falle die. ◇ vt in einer
Falle fangen.

snarl [snɑːl] ◇ n Knurren das. ◇ vi
knurren.

snatch [snætʃ] ◇ n [of song, conversation]
Bruchstück das. ◇ vt [grab] schnappen.

sneak [sniːk] (US pt snuck) ◇ n UK inf Pet-
ze die. ◇ vt [bring secretly] schmuggeln; to
sneak a look at sb/sthg jn/etw heimlich ansehen. ◇ vi [move quietly] schleichen; to
sneak up on sb sich an jn heranlschleichen.

sneakers ['sniːkəz] npl US Sportschuhe Pl.

sneaky ['sniːkɪ] adj inf hinterhältig.

sneer [snɪər] ◇ n spöttisches Lächeln.
◇ vi [smile unpleasantly] spöttisch lächeln.

sneeze [sniːz] ◇ n Niesen das. ◇ vi niesen.

snide [snaɪd] adj abfällig.

sniff [snɪf] ◇ vt - **1.** [smell] riechen an (+ D)
- **2.** [drug] schnüffeln. ◇ vi schniefen.

snigger ['snɪgər] ◇ n hämisches Kichern.
◇ vi hämisch kichern.

snip [snɪp] ◇ n inf [bargain] Schnäppchen das. ◇ vt [cut] schnippeln.

sniper ['snaɪpər] n Heckenschütze der.

snippet ['snɪpɪt] n Bruchstück das.

snob [snɒb] n Snob der.

snobbish ['snɒbɪʃ], **snobby** ['snɒbɪ] adj
snobistisch.

snooker ['snuːkər] n Snooker das.

snoop [snuːp] vi inf (herum)lschnüffeln.

snooty ['snuːtɪ] adj hochnäsig.

snore [snɔːr] ◇ n Schnarchen das. ◇ vi
schnarchen.

snoring ['snɔːrɪŋ] n Schnarchen das.

snorkel ['snɔːkl] n Schnorchel der.

snort [snɔːt] ◇ n Schnauben das. ◇ vi
schnauben.

snout [snaʊt] n Schnauze die.

snow [snəʊ] ◇ n Schnee der. ◇ impers vb:
it's snowing es schneit.

snowball ['snəʊbɔːl] ◇ n Schneeball der.
◇ vi fig lawinenartig anlwachsen.

snowdrift ['snəʊdrɪft] n Schneewehe die.

snowdrop ['snəʊdrɒp] n Schneeglöckchen das.

snowfall ['snəʊfɔːl] n Schneefall der.

snowflake ['snəʊfleɪk] n Schneeflocke die.

snowman ['snəʊmæn] (pl -men [-men]) n
Schneemann der.

snowplough UK, **snowplow** US ['snəʊp-
laʊ] n [vehicle] Schneepflug der.

snowstorm ['snəʊstɔːm] n Schneesturm der.

SNP (abbr of Scottish National Party) n natio-
nalistische Partei in Schottland.

Snr, snr (abbr of senior) sen.

snub [snʌb] ◇ n Abfuhr die. ◇ vt: to snub
sb jm eine Abfuhr erteilen.

snuck [snʌk] pt US ▷ sneak.

snug [snʌg] adj - **1.** [person, feeling, place] gemütlich - **2.** [close-fitting] gut sitzend.

snuggle ['snʌgl] vi: to snuggle up to sb sich
an jm kuscheln; to snuggle down in bed sich
ins Bett kuscheln.

so [səʊ] ◇ adv - **1.** [to such a degree] so; it's so
difficult that es ist so schwierig, dass; don't
be so stupid! sei nicht so dumm!; I (do) so
hope you can come ich hoffe so sehr, dass
du kommen kannst; so much money/many
cars so viel Geld/viele Autos; I liked it so much
that... es gefiel mir so sehr or gut, dass...; so
much so that... dermaßen, dass... - **2.** [referring
back]: so what's the point then? was soll das
also?; so you knew already? du hast es also

schon gewusst?; **I think so** ich glaube (schon); **I don't think so** ich glaube nicht; **I'm afraid so** leider ja; **I told you so** das habe ich dir gleich gesagt; **if so** falls ja; **is that so?** tatsächlich? - **3.** [also] auch; **so can I** ich auch; **so do I** ich auch; **he is clever and so is she** er ist intelligent und sie auch - **4.** [in this way] so - **5.** [in expressing agreement]: **so there is** ja, stimmt; **that's her car - so it is!** das ist ihr Auto - tatsächlich!; **so I see** das sehe ich - **6.** [referring to unspecified amount, limit]: **they pay us so much a week** sie zahlen uns so viel die Woche; **or so** oder so. ◇ *conj* - **1.** [consequently] also; **he said yes and so we got married** er sagte ja, also heirateten wir; **I'm away next week so I won't be there** ich bin nächste Woche weg, also werde ich nicht kommen - **2.** [to introduce a statement] also; **so what have you been up to?** na, was treibst du so?; **so that's who she is!** das ist sie also!; **so what?** *inf* na und?; **so there!** *inf* das wars! **◆ and so on, and so forth** *adv* und so weiter. **◆ so as** *conj* um; **we didn't knock so as not to disturb them** wir klopften nicht an, um sie nicht zu stören. **◆ so that** *conj* damit.

soak [səʊk] ◇ *vt* - **1.** [leave immersed] einlweichen - **2.** [wet thoroughly] durchnässen; **to be soaked with sthg** mit etw durchtränkt sein. ◇ *vi* - **1.** [become thoroughly wet]: **to leave sthg to soak, to let sthg soak** etw einlweichen - **2.** [spread]: **to soak into sthg** in etw *(A)* einlsickern; **to soak through sthg** durch etw (hindurch)lsickern. **◆ soak up** *vt sep* [liquid] auflsaugen.

soaking ['səʊkɪŋ] *adj*: **soaking (wet)** durchnässt.

so-and-so *n inf* - **1.** [to replace a name]: **Mr So-and-so** Herr Soundso - **2.** [annoying person]: **you little so-and-so!** du Biest!

soap [səʊp] *n* - **1.** (U) [for washing] Seife *die* - **2.** TV Seifenoper *die*.

soap dish *n* Seifenschale *die*.

soap opera *n* Seifenoper *die*.

soap powder *n* Seifenpulver *das*.

soapy ['səʊpɪ] *adj* seifig.

soar [sɔːʳ] *vi* - **1.** [bird, kite, rocket] auflsteigen - **2.** [increase rapidly] rapide anlsteigen.

sob [sɒb] *n* Schluchzer *der*.

sober ['səʊbəʳ] *adj* - **1.** [not drunk] nüchtern - **2.** [serious] ernsthaft - **3.** [plain] einfach. **◆ sober up** *vi* nüchtern werden.

sobering ['səʊbərɪŋ] *adj* ernüchternd.

so-called [-kɔːld] *adj* so genannt.

soccer ['sɒkəʳ] *n (U)* Fußball *der*.

sociable ['səʊʃəbl] *adj* gesellig.

social ['səʊʃl] *adj* - **1.** [behaviour, background, conditions] sozial, gesellschaftlich - **2.** [gathering, drinking] gesellig.

socialism ['səʊʃəlɪzm] *n* Sozialismus *der*.

socialist ['səʊʃəlɪst] ◇ *adj* sozialistisch. ◇ *n* Sozialist *der*, -in *die*.

socialize, -ise ['səʊʃəlaɪz] *vi*: **to socialize with sb** mit jm gesellschaftlich verkehren; **she socializes a lot** sie geht viel aus.

social security *n (U)* Sozialversicherung *die*.

social services *npl* Sozialeinrichtungen *Pl*.

social worker *n* Sozialarbeiter *der*, -in *die*.

society [sə'saɪətɪ] *n* - **1.** [mankind, community] Gesellschaft *die* - **2.** [club, organization] Verein *der*, Klub *der*.

sociology [ˌsəʊsɪ'ɒlədʒɪ] *n* Soziologie *die*.

sock [sɒk] *n* Socke *die*, Socken *der*.

socket ['sɒkɪt] *n* - **1.** ELEC Steckdose *die* - **2.** ANAT [of joint] Gelenkpfanne *die*; [of eye] Augenhöhle *die*.

sod [sɒd] *n* - **1.** [of turf] Sode *die* - **2.** *v inf* [man] Scheißkerl *der*; [woman] Miststück *das*.

soda ['səʊdə] *n* - **1.** CHEM Soda *das*, Natron *das* - **2.** [soda water] Soda *das* - **3.** *US* [fizzy drink] Limonade *die*.

soda water *n* Sodawasser *das*.

sodden ['sɒdn] *adj* durchnässt.

sodium ['səʊdɪəm] *n* Natrium *das*.

sofa ['səʊfə] *n* Sofa *das*.

Sofia ['səʊfjə] *n* Sofia *nt*.

soft [sɒft] *adj* - **1.** [gen] weich - **2.** [breeze, sound, knock, nature] sanft - **3.** [light, colour, music] gedämpft - **4.** [not strict] mild.

softball ['sɒftbɔːl] *n* Softball *der*.

soft drink *n* alkoholfreies Getränk.

soften ['sɒfn] ◇ *vt* - **1.** [substance] weich machen; [water] enthärten - **2.** [punch, impact, effect, light] dämpfen; [blow, attitude] mildern. ◇ *vi* - **1.** [substance] weich werden - **2.** [eyes, voice, expression] sanft werden.

softhearted [ˌsɒft'hɑːtɪd] *adj* weichherzig.

softly ['sɒftlɪ] *adv* - **1.** [move, touch] sanft - **2.** [speak, sing, shine] leise - **3.** [smile, look] sanft.

soft return *n* COMPUT weicher Zeilenumbruch.

software ['sɒftweəʳ] *n* COMPUT Software *die*.

soggy ['sɒgɪ] *adj* durchnässt; [ground] matschig.

soil [sɔɪl] ◇ *n* - **1.** [earth] Erde *die*; [ground & GEOG] Boden *der* - **2.** *fig* [territory] Boden *der*. ◇ *vt* [dirty] beschmutzen.

soiled [sɔɪld] *adj* schmutzig.

solar ['səʊləʳ] *adj* Sonnen-.

solar energy *n* Solarenergie *die*.

sold [səʊld] *pt & pp* ▷ **sell**.

solder ['səʊldəʳ] ◇ *n (U)* TECH Lot *das*. ◇ *vt* löten.

soldier ['səʊldʒəʳ] *n* Soldat *der*.

sold out *adj* ausverkauft.

sole [səʊl] <> *adj* - 1. [only] einzig - 2. [exclusive] alleinig. <> *n* - 1. [of foot] Sohle *die* - 2. (*pl inv or* -s) [fish] Seezunge *die*.

solemn ['sɒləm] *adj* - 1. [person, face, voice] ernst - 2. [agreement, promise, occasion, music] feierlich.

solicit [sə'lɪsɪt] <> *vt fml* [request] werben um. <> *vi* [prostitute] sich anbieten.

solicitor [sə'lɪsɪtər] *n UK* Rechtsanwalt *der*, -anwältin *die*.

solid ['sɒlɪd] <> *adj* - 1. [not liquid or gas] fest - 2. [gold, silver, wood] massiv - 3. [building, base, relationship, person] solide - 4. [support] einmütig; [evidence] handfest; [majority] solide - 5. [line] ununterbrochen, durchgängig; **two hours solid, two solid hours** zwei volle Stunden. <> *adv*: **to be packed solid** brechend voll sein. <> *n* [not liquid or gas] fester Stoff. ◆ **solids** *npl* [food] feste Nahrung.

solidarity [,sɒlɪ'dærətɪ] *n* Solidarität *die*.

solitaire [,sɒlɪ'teər] *n* - 1. [jewel] Solitär *der* - 2. [board game] Solitaire *das* - 3. *US* [card game] Patience *die*.

solitary ['sɒlɪtrɪ] *adj* - 1. [involving one person, single] einzeln - 2. [enjoying solitude] einsam.

solitary confinement *n* Einzelhaft *die*.

solitude ['sɒlɪtjuːd] *n* Einsamkeit *die*.

solo ['səʊləʊ] (*pl* -s) <> *adj* - 1. MUS Solo- - 2. [attempt, flight] Allein-. <> *n* MUS Solo *das*. <> *adv* - 1. MUS solo - 2. [fly, climb] allein.

soloist ['səʊləʊɪst] *n* Solist *der*, -in *die*.

soluble ['sɒljʊbl] *adj* - 1. [substance] löslich - 2. [problem] lösbar.

solution [sə'luːʃn] *n* Lösung *die*; **a solution to sthg** eine Lösung für etw.

solve [sɒlv] *vt* lösen.

solvent ['sɒlvənt] <> *adj* FIN solvent. <> *n* [substance] Lösungsmittel *das*.

Somalia [sə'mɑːlɪə] *n* Somalia *nt*.

sombre *UK*, **somber** *US* ['sɒmbər] *adj* düster.

some [sʌm] <> *adj* - 1. [a certain amount of] etwas; **some money** etwas Geld; **some meat** ein bisschen Fleisch; **would you like some (more) tea?** möchtest du (noch) Tee? - 2. [a certain number of] einige; **some people** einige Leute; **I bought some sweets** ich habe Bonbons gekauft; **can I have some sweets?** kann ich Bonbons haben?; **I've known her for some years** ich kenne sie schon seit einigen Jahren - 3. *(contrastive use)* [certain] manche; **some jobs are better paid than others** manche Jobs sind besser bezahlt als andere - 4. [in imprecise statements] irgendein(e); **she married some Italian (or other)** sie hat irgend so einen Italiener geheiratet; **there must be some mistake** das muss ein Irrtum sein - 5. *inf iro* [not very good]: **some welcome that was!** das war vielleicht ein enttäuschender Empfang; **some friend you are!** du bist mir vielleicht ein

Freund! <> *pron* - 1. [a certain amount] etwas; **I've read some of the article** ich habe einen Teil des Artikels gelesen; **some of it is mine** ein Teil davon gehört mir; **take some bread - I've already got some** nimm dir Brot - ich habe schon - 2. [a certain number] einige; **have some strawberries - I've already got some** nimm dir Erdbeeren - ich habe schon welche; **some (of them) left early** einige (von ihnen) gingen vorher - 3. [some people] manche; **some say he lied** manche sagen, dass er gelogen hat. <> *adv* [in approximations]: **there were some 7,000 people there** es waren ungefähr or um die 7000 Leute da.

somebody ['sʌmbədɪ] *pron* jemand; **ask somebody else** frag jemand anders; **somebody or other** irgend jemand; **he really thinks he's somebody** [important person] er glaubt wirklich, er ist wer.

someday ['sʌmdeɪ] *adv* eines Tages.

somehow ['sʌmhaʊ], **someway** *US* ['sʌmweɪ] *adv* irgendwie.

someone ['sʌmwʌn] *pron* = **somebody**.

someplace *adv US* = **somewhere**.

somersault ['sʌməsɔːlt] <> *n* Purzelbaum *der*; SPORT Salto *der*. <> *vi* einen Purzelbaum schlagen; SPORT einen Salto machen.

something ['sʌmθɪŋ] <> *pron* etwas; **I saw something moving** ich sah, wie sich etwas bewegte; **something nice** etwas Schönes; **there's something about him I don't like** er hat etwas an sich, das mir nicht gefällt; **something else** sonst etwas; **something or other** irgend etwas; **or something** *inf* oder so etwas; **well, at least that's something** nun, das ist immerhin etwas; **there's something in what you say** es ist schon etwas Wahres an dem, was du sagst; **it's really something!** es ist ganz toll!; **it came as something of a surprise to me** es war schon irgendwie eine Überraschung für mich. <> *adv* [in approximations]: **something like/in the region of** ungefähr; **it looks something like a rose** es sieht so ähnlich wie eine Rose aus.

sometime ['sʌmtaɪm] <> *adj* ehemalig. <> *adv* irgendwann.

sometimes ['sʌmtaɪmz] *adv* manchmal.

someway *adv US* = **somehow**.

somewhat ['sʌmwɒt] *adv* ziemlich.

somewhere *UK* ['sʌmweər], **someplace** *US* ['sʌmpleɪs] *adv* - 1. [gen - with verbs of position] irgendwo; [- with verbs of motion] irgendwohin; **somewhere else** irgendwo anders/irgendwo andershin; **somewhere or other** irgendwo/irgendwohin - 2. [in approximations] ungefähr; **somewhere around or in the region of 50** ungefähr 50.

son [sʌn] *n* Sohn *der*.

song [sɒŋ] *n* Lied *das*; [of bird] Gesang *der*.

sonic ['sɒnɪk] *adj* Schall-.

son-in-law (*pl* sons-in-law *OR* son-in-laws) *n* Schwiegersohn *der*.

soon [su:n] *adv* - **1.** [in a short time] bald; **soon after** *OR* **afterwards** kurz danach - **2.** [early]: **how soon can you be ready?** wie schnell kannst du fertig sein?; **too soon** zu früh; **not a minute too soon** keine Minute zu früh; **as soon as** sobald; **as soon as possible** so bald wie möglich.

sooner ['su:nər] *adv* - **1.** [earlier] früher; **no sooner than** kaum als (auch schon); **sooner or later** früher oder später; **the sooner the better** je früher, desto besser - **2.** [expressing preference] lieber.

soot [sʊt] *n* Ruß *der*.

soothe [su:ð] *vt* - **1.** [pain] lindern - **2.** [person, fear] beruhigen.

sophisticated [sə'fɪstɪkeɪtɪd] *adj* - **1.** [stylish] hochelegant - **2.** [intelligent] kultiviert - **3.** [complicated] hoch entwickelt.

sophomore ['sɒfəmɔːr] *n* US Student *der*, -in *die* im zweiten Studienjahr.

soporific [ˌsɒpə'rɪfɪk] *adj* einschläfernd.

sopping ['sɒpɪŋ] *adj*: **sopping (wet)** klatschnass.

soppy ['sɒpɪ] *adj inf pej* rührselig.

soprano [sə'prɑːnəʊ] (*pl* -s) *n* - **1.** [person] Sopranistin *die* - **2.** [voice] Sopran *der*.

sorbet ['sɔːbeɪ] *n* Sorbet *das*.

sordid ['sɔːdɪd] *adj* [desires, thoughts, past] schmutzig.

sore [sɔːr] <> *adj* - **1.** [painful] wund, entzündet; **to have a sore throat/head** Halsschmerzen/Kopfschmerzen haben - **2.** US inf [angry] sauer. <> *n* MED wunde *OR* entzündete Stelle.

sorrow ['sɒrəʊ] *n* - **1.** [feeling of sadness] Kummer *der* - **2.** [cause of sadness] Leid *das*.

sorry ['sɒrɪ] <> *adj* - **1.** [expressing apology]: **I'm sorry** es tut mir leid; **I'm sorry about the mess** entschuldige bitte die Unordnung; **I'm sorry for what I did** was ich getan habe, tut mir leid; **I'm sorry to bother you, but could you ...** Verzeihung, könnten Sie ... - **2.** [expressing disappointment]: **I'm sorry you couldn't come** schade, dass du nicht kommen konntest; **we were sorry about his resignation** wir bedauern seinen Rücktritt; **we're sorry to see you go** wir finden es schade, dass du gehst - **3.** [expressing regret]: **I'm sorry I ever came here** ich bereue, jemals hierhergekommen zu sein; **I'm sorry to have to announce ...** ich muss Ihnen leider mitteilen ... - **4.** [expressing sympathy]: **to be** *OR* **feel sorry for sb** jn bedauern *OR* bemitleiden - **5.** [expressing polite disagreement]: **I'm sorry, but ...** Entschuldigung *OR* Verzeihung, aber ... - **6.** [poor, pitiable] bedauernswert. <> *excl* - **1.** [expressing apology] Entschuldigung!, Verzeihung! - **2.** [asking for repetition] wie bitte? - **3.** [to correct o.s.] ich meine (natürlich).

sort [sɔːt] <> *n* [kind, type] Sorte *die*; **what sort of car have you got?** was für ein Auto hast du?; **a sort of** eine Art (von). <> *vt* [classify, separate] sortieren. ◆ **sort of** *adv* [rather] irgendwie. ◆ **sort out** *vt sep* - **1.** [into groups] sortieren - **2.** [tidy up - papers, clothes] wegräumen; [- room] aufräumen; [- affairs, finances] regeln - **3.** [work out, arrange] sich (D) überlegen.

SOS (*abbr of* save our souls) *n* SOS *das*.

so-so *adj* & *adv inf* so la la.

sought [sɔːt] *pt* & *pp* ▷ **seek**.

soul [səʊl] *n* - **1.** [gen] Seele *die* - **2.** [perfect example] Inbegriff *der*; **I'm the soul of discretion** ich bin die Verschwiegenheit in Person - **3.** [music] Soul *der*.

soul-destroying [-dɪˌstrɔɪɪŋ] *adj* [boring] geisttötend; [discouraging] sehr entmutigend.

sound [saʊnd] <> *adj* - **1.** [mind, body] gesund - **2.** [building, structure] intakt - **3.** [advice, investment] vernünftig - **4.** [thorough] ordentlich. <> *adv*: **to be sound asleep** tief *OR* fest schlafen. <> *n* - **1.** [noise] Geräusch *das*; [of music, voice, instrument] Klang *der*; [of person, animal] Laut *der* - **2.** (U) PHYS Schall *der* - **3.** [volume] Lautstärke *die* - **4.** [impression, idea] Gedanke *der*; **I don't like the sound of this new plan** der neue Plan behagt mir nicht; **by the sound of it** allem Anschein nach. <> *vt* ertönen lassen; [alarm] auslösen; [bell] läuten; [horn] hupen. <> *vi* - **1.** [make a noise] ertönen; **to sound like sthg** wie etw klingen - **2.** [seem] klingen, zu sein scheinen; **she sounds nice** sie scheint nett zu sein; **it sounds like a good investment** das hört sich nach einer guten Investition an. ◆ **sound out** *vt sep*: **to sound sb out** bei jm vorfühlen; [furtively] jn aushorchen.

sound barrier *n* Schallmauer *die*.

sound effects *npl* Klangeffekte *Pl*.

soundly ['saʊndlɪ] *adv* - **1.** [beat, defeat] vernichtend - **2.** [sleep] tief, fest.

soundproof ['saʊndpruːf] *adj* schalldicht.

soundtrack ['saʊndtræk] *n* Soundtrack *der*.

soup [su:p] *n* Suppe *die*.

soup plate *n* Suppenteller *der*.

soup spoon *n* Suppenlöffel *der*.

sour ['saʊər] <> *adj* sauer; [relationship] erkalten. <> *vt* [person] verbittern; [relationship] erkalten lassen.

source [sɔːs] *n* Quelle *die*.

south [saʊθ] <> *adj* Süd-, südlich. <> *adv* nach Süden, südwärts; **south of** südlich von; **in the south of England** im Süden Englands. <> *n* - **1.** [direction] Süden *der* - **2.** [region]: **the south** der Süden.

South Africa *n* Südafrika *nt*.

South America *n* Südamerika *nt*.

southeast [,saʊθ'i:st] ⬦ adj südöstlich, Südost-. ⬦ adv südostwärts, nach Südosten; **southeast of** südöstlich von. ⬦ n [direction] Südosten der.

southerly ['sʌðəlɪ] adj - 1. [direction] südlich; [area] im Süden - 2. [wind] Süd-.

southern ['sʌðən] adj [region, dialect] südlich; [Europe] Süd-.

South Korea n Südkorea nt.

South Pole n: the South Pole der Südpol.

southward ['saʊθwəd] ⬦ adj südlich, nach Süden. ⬦ adv = southwards.

southwards ['saʊθwədz] adv nach Süden.

southwest [,saʊθ'west] ⬦ adj südwestlich, Südwest-. ⬦ adv südwestwärts, nach Südwesten; **southwest of** südwestlich von. ⬦ n Südwesten der.

souvenir [,su:və'nɪər] n Souvenir das, Andenken das.

sovereign ['sɒvrɪn] n - 1. [ruler] Herrscher der, -in die - 2. [coin] Sovereign der.

soviet ['saʊvɪət] n Sowjet der. ◆ **Soviet** ⬦ adj sowjetisch. ⬦ n [person] Sowjetbürger der, -in die.

Soviet Union n: the (former) Soviet Union die (ehemalige) Sowjetunion.

sow¹ [saʊ] (pt -ed, pp sown OR -ed) vt - 1. [seeds] säen, auslsäen - 2. fig [doubt] säen.

sow² [saʊ] n [pig] Sau die.

sown [saʊn] pp ➣ sow¹.

soya ['sɔɪə] n Soja das.

soy(a) bean ['sɔɪ(ə)-] n Sojabohne die.

spa [spɑː] n [spring] Mineralquelle die; [place] Bad das.

space [speɪs] ⬦ n - 1. (U) [room] Raum der; there isn't enough space in here hier ist nicht genug Platz - 2. [outer space] Weltraum der - 3. [gap] Zwischenraum der - 4. [area] Fläche die, Raum der - 5. TYPO Leerzeichen das - 6. [period of time] Zeitraum der; within the space of ten minutes innerhalb von zehn Minuten; in a short space of time [in future] in Kürze; [in past] nach kurzer Zeit - 7. [seat, place] Platz der. ⬦ comp Weltraum-. ⬦ vt in regelmäßigen Abständen anlordnen. ◆ **space out** vt sep [arrange] in regelmäßigen Abständen anlordnen.

spacecraft ['speɪskrɑːft] (pl inv) n Raumschiff das.

spaceman ['speɪsmæn] (pl -men [-men]) n [astronaut] Raumfahrer der.

spaceship ['speɪsʃɪp] n Raumschiff das.

space shuttle n Spaceshuttle das.

spacesuit ['speɪssuːt] n Raumanzug der.

spacious ['speɪʃəs] adj geräumig.

spade [speɪd] n - 1. [tool] Spaten der - 2. [playing card] Pik das. ◆ **spades** npl Pik das; the six of spades die Piksechs.

spaghetti [spə'getɪ] n (U) Spaghetti Pl.

Spain [speɪn] n Spanien nt.

spam [spæm] n COMPUT Spam der.

span [spæn] ⬦ pt ➣ spin. ⬦ n - 1. [in time] Zeitraum der, Zeitspanne die - 2. [range] Reihe die - 3. [of hands, arms, wings, bridge] Spannweite die. ⬦ vt - 1. [encompass] umfassen - 2. [cross] überspannen.

Spaniard ['spænjəd] n Spanier der, -in die.

spaniel ['spænjəl] n Spaniel der.

Spanish ['spænɪʃ] ⬦ adj spanisch. ⬦ n [language] Spanisch(e) das.

spank [spæŋk] vt: to spank sb [once] jm einen Klaps auf den Hintern geben; [several times] jm den Hintern versohlen.

spanner ['spænər] n Schraubenschlüssel der.

spar [spɑːr] vi [boxing] sparren.

spare [speər] ⬦ adj - 1. [surplus] zusätzlich, Ersatz-; **have you got a spare pencil?** hast du einen Bleistift übrig? - 2. [free] frei. ⬦ n inf [part] Ersatzteil das. ⬦ vt - 1. [make available] entbehren können, übrig haben; **can you spare five minutes?** hast du (mal) fünf Minuten Zeit?; to spare [extra] übrig, zur Verfügung; **we had an hour to spare** wir hatten (noch) eine Stunde Zeit - 2. [not harm] verschonen - 3. [effort, trouble] scheuen; to spare no expense keine Kosten scheuen - 4. [save, protect from]: to spare sb sthg jm etw ersparen.

spare part n AUT Ersatzteil das.

spare time n Freizeit die.

spare wheel n Ersatzrad das.

sparing ['speərɪŋ] adj: to be sparing with sthg mit etw sparsam sein.

sparingly ['speərɪŋlɪ] adv sparsam.

spark [spɑːk] n - 1. [from fire, electricity] Funke der - 2. fig [of understanding, interest, humour] Funken der.

sparkle ['spɑːkl] ⬦ n [of jewel, frost, stars, sea] Glitzern das; [of eyes] Funkeln das. ⬦ vi [jewel, frost, stars, sea] glitzern; [eyes] funkeln.

sparkling ['spɑːklɪŋ] adj - 1. [mineral water] sprudelnd - 2. [wit] sprühend.

sparkling wine n Schaumwein der, Sekt der.

spark plug n Zündkerze die.

sparrow ['spærəʊ] n Spatz der, Sperling der.

sparse [spɑːs] adj spärlich; [hair] schütter, dünn.

spasm ['spæzm] n - 1. MED [muscular contraction] Krampf der - 2. [fit] Anfall der.

spastic ['spæstɪk] n MED Spastiker der, -in die.

spat [spæt] pt & pp ➣ spit.

spate [speɪt] n Flut die.

spatter ['spætər] vt bespritzen.

spawn [spɔːn] ⬦ n Laich der. ⬦ vt fig [produce] erzeugen. ⬦ vi ZOOL laichen.

speak [spi:k] (*pt* **spoke**, *pp* **spoken**) <> *vt* sprechen. <> *vi* - **1.** [say words] sprechen; **to speak to** OR **with sb** mit jm sprechen OR reden; **to speak to sb about sthg** mit jm über etw (A) sprechen OR reden; **to speak about sb/sthg** über jn/etw sprechen OR reden - **2.** [make a speech] sprechen, reden; **to speak on sthg** über etw (A) sprechen - **3.** [in giving an opinion]: **generally speaking** im Allgemeinen, im Großen und Ganzen; **personally speaking** meiner Ansicht nach; **so to speak** *adv* sozusagen. **speak for** *vt insep* [represent] sprechen für. **speak up** *vi* - **1.** [say something] sprechen; **to speak up for sb/sthg** für jn/etw eintreten - **2.** [speak louder] lauter sprechen.

speaker ['spi:kər] *n* - **1.** [person talking] Sprecher *der*, -in *die* - **2.** [in lecture] Redner *der*, -in *die* - **3.** [of a language]: **a German speaker** ein Sprecher/eine Sprecherin des Deutschen - **4.** [loudspeaker, in hi-fi] Lautsprecher *der*. **Speaker** *n* UK [in House of Commons] Präsident *der*, -in *die* des Unterhauses.

spear [spɪər] *n* Speer *der*.

spearhead ['spɪəhed] *vt* anführen.

spec [spek] *n* UK inf: **on spec** aufs Geratewohl.

special ['speʃl] *adj* - **1.** [specific, out of the ordinary] besondere (r) (s), spezielle (r) (s) - **2.** [valued]: **to be special to sb** jm viel bedeuten.

special delivery *n* Eilzustellung *die*.

specialist ['speʃəlɪst] <> *adj* Fach-. <> *n* [expert] Spezialist *der*, -in *die*; [doctor] Facharzt *der*, -ärztin *die*.

speciality [,speʃɪ'ælətɪ], **specialty** US ['speʃltɪ] *n* - **1.** [field of knowledge] Spezialgebiet *das* - **2.** [service, product] Spezialität *die*.

specialize, -ise ['speʃəlaɪz] *vi*: **to specialize (in sthg)** sich (auf etw (A)) spezialisieren; [have special qualifications] (auf etw (A)) spezialisiert sein.

specially ['speʃəlɪ] *adv* - **1.** [on purpose, specifically] speziell - **2.** [really] besonders.

specialty *n* US = **speciality**.

species ['spi:ʃi:z] (*pl inv*) *n* Spezies *die*, Art *die*.

specific [spə'sɪfɪk] *adj* bestimmt, spezifisch; **to be specific to sb/sthg** jn/etw eigen sein.

specifically [spə'sɪfɪklɪ] *adv* - **1.** [explicitly] ausdrücklich - **2.** [particularly, precisely] im Besonderen.

specify ['spesɪfaɪ] *vt* spezifizieren, herausstellen; **to specify that...** deutlich machen, dass..., herausstellen, dass...

specimen ['spesɪmən] *n* - **1.** [example] Exemplar *das* - **2.** [sample] Probe *die*.

speck [spek] *n* - **1.** [small stain] Fleck *der*; [of paint, mud] Spritzer *der* - **2.** [small particle - of dust] Körnchen *das*; [- of soot] Flocke *die*.

speckled ['spekld] *adj*: **speckled (with sthg)** gesprenkelt (mit etw).

specs [speks] *npl* inf Brille *die*.

spectacle ['spektəkl] *n* - **1.** [sight] Anblick *der*; **to make a spectacle of o.s.** sich unmöglich benehmen - **2.** [event] Spektakel *das*. **spectacles** *npl* UK [glasses] Brille *die*.

spectacular [spek'tækjʊlər] *adj* spektakulär.

spectator [spek'teɪtər] *n* Zuschauer *der*, -in *die*.

spectre UK, **specter** US ['spektər] *n* - **1.** fml [ghost] Gespenst *das* - **2.** fig [frightening prospect] Schreckgespenst *das*.

speculation [,spekjʊ'leɪʃn] *n* Spekulation *die*.

sped [sped] *pt* & *pp* ▷ **speed**.

speech [spi:tʃ] *n* - **1.** (U) [ability to speak, dialect] Sprache *die* - **2.** [formal talk] Rede *die* - **3.** THEAT Text *der* - **4.** [manner of speaking] Sprechweise *die*; **his speech is clear and precise** er spricht klar und deutlich - **5.** GRAM: **direct/indirect speech** direkte/indirekte Rede.

speechless ['spi:tʃlɪs] *adj*: **to be speechless (with sthg)** (vor etw (D)) sprachlos sein.

speed [spi:d] (*pt* & *pp* **-ed** OR **sped**) <> *n* - **1.** [pace, rapid rate] Geschwindigkeit *die*, Tempo *das*; **speed of light/sound** Licht-/Schallgeschwindigkeit *die*; **at high/low speed** mit hoher/niedriger Geschwindigkeit; **at top** OR **full speed** mit Höchstgeschwindigkeit - **2.** [gear] Gang *der* - **3.** PHOT [of film] Lichtempfindlichkeit *die*. <> *vi* - **1.** [move fast]: **to speed along/away/by** entlang-/davon-/vorbeijagen - **2.** AUT [go too fast] zu schnell fahren. **speed up** <> *vt sep* beschleunigen; [person] auf Trab bringen. <> *vi* [worker] sich beeilen; [driver, vehicle] beschleunigen; [production] sich erhöhen.

speedboat ['spi:dbəʊt] *n* Rennboot *das*.

speed dating *n* Speed-Dating *das*.

speeding ['spi:dɪŋ] *n* zu schnelles Fahren; LAW Geschwindigkeitsüberschreitung *die*.

speed limit *n* Geschwindigkeitsbeschränkung *die*.

speedometer [spɪ'dɒmɪtər] *n* Tachometer *der* ODER *das*.

speedway ['spi:dweɪ] *n* - **1.** SPORT Speedway-Rennen *das* - **2.** US [road] Schnellstraße *die*.

speedy ['spi:dɪ] *adj* schnell.

spell [spel] (UK *pt* & *pp* **spelt** OR **-ed**) (US *pt* & *pp* **-ed**) <> *n* - **1.** [period of time] Weile *die*; **with some sunny spells** mit sonnigen Abschnitten; **for a spell** eine Weile - **2.** [enchantment] Zauber *der*; **to cast** OR **put a spell on sb** jn verzaubern - **3.** [magic word] Zauberspruch *der*. <> *vt* - **1.** [word, name] schreiben; [aloud] buchstabieren - **2.** fig [signify] bedeuten; [aloud] buchstabieren; **it spells disaster**

das bedeutet Unglück. ⟨⟩ *vi*: **to be able to spell** fehlerfrei schreiben können. ◆ **spell out** *vt sep* - **1.** [read aloud] buchstabieren - **2.** [explain]: **to spell sthg out (for** OR **to sb)** (jm) etw klarmachen.

spellbound ['spelbaυnd] *adj* gebannt.

spelling ['spelɪŋ] *n* - **1.** [of a particular word] Schreibweise *die* - **2.** [ability to spell] Rechtschreibung *die*.

spelt [spelt] *pt & pp UK* ▷ **spell**.

spend [spend] (*pt & pp* **spent**) *vt* - **1.** [pay out] ausgeben; **she spends a lot of money on clothes** sie gibt viel Geld für Kleidung aus - **2.** [time, life] verbringen; **he spent two hours shopping** er ist zwei Stunden lang einkaufen gewesen.

spent [spent] ⟨⟩ *pt & pp* ▷ **spend**. ⟨⟩ *adj* [fuel, matches] verbraucht; [ammunition] verschossen; [patience, energy] erschöpft.

sperm [spɜːm] (*pl inv* OR **-s**) *n* - **1.** [cell] Spermium *das* - **2.** (*U*) [fluid] Sperma *das*.

spew [spjuː] ⟨⟩ *vt* [flames, lava] speien. ⟨⟩ *vi*: **to spew (out) from sthg** aus etw hervorschießen.

sphere [sfɪəʳ] *n* - **1.** [globe] Kugel *die* - **2.** [of interest, activity] Bereich *der*; **sphere of influence** Einflussbereich *der*.

spice [spaɪs] *n* - **1.** CULIN Gewürz *das* - **2.** (*U*) *fig* [excitement] Würze *die*.

spick-and-span [ˌspɪkən'spæn] *adj* blitzblank.

spicy ['spaɪsɪ] *adj* pikant.

spider ['spaɪdəʳ] *n* Spinne *die*.

spike [spaɪk] ⟨⟩ *n* - **1.** [on railings] Spitze *die*; [on shoe] Spike *der* - **2.** [on plant] Stachel *der*. ⟨⟩ *vt* [drink] einen Schuss (Alkohol) zulgeben.

spill [spɪl] (*UK pt & pp* **spilt** OR **-ed**) (*US pt & pp* **-ed**) ⟨⟩ *vt* - **1.** [liquid, salt] verschütten - **2.** [blood] vergießen. ⟨⟩ *vi* [liquid, salt] sich ergießen.

spilt [spɪlt] *pt & pp UK* ▷ **spill**.

spin [spɪn] (*pt* **span** OR **spun**, *pp* **spun**) ⟨⟩ *n* - **1.** [turn] Drehung *die* - **2.** AERON Trudeln *das*; **the plane went into a spin** das Flugzeug begann zu trudeln - **3.** *inf* [in car] Spritztour *die*; **to go for a spin** eine Spritztour machen - **4.** SPORT [on ball] Effet *der*. ⟨⟩ *vt* - **1.** [gen] schnell drehen - **2.** [in spin-dryer] schleudern; [coin in the air] hochwerfen - **3.** [thread, cloth, wool] spinnen - **4.** SPORT [ball] einen Effet geben (+ *D*). ⟨⟩ *vi* - **1.** [gen] sich schnell drehen; [plane] trudeln - **2.** [spinner of thread] spinnen - **3.** [in spin-dryer] schleudern. ◆ **spin out** *vt sep* [story, explanation] in die Länge ziehen; [money, food] strecken.

spinach ['spɪnɪdʒ] *n* Spinat *der*.

spinal column ['spaɪnl-] *n* Wirbelsäule *die*.

spinal cord ['spaɪnl-] *n* Rückenmark *das*.

spindly ['spɪndlɪ] *adj* [arms, legs] spindeldürr; [plant] zierlich.

spin-dryer *n UK* Wäscheschleuder *die*.

spine [spaɪn] *n* - **1.** ANAT Wirbelsäule *die* - **2.** [of book] Rücken *der* - **3.** [of hedgehog, plant] Stachel *der*.

spin-off *n* [by-product] Nebenprodukt *das*.

spinster ['spɪnstəʳ] *n* Unverheiratete *die*.

spiral ['spaɪərəl] (*UK*) (*US*) ⟨⟩ *adj* spiralförmig. ⟨⟩ *n liter & fig* Spirale *die*. ⟨⟩ *vi* [move in spiral curve - staircase, path] sich (hoch)lwinden; [- smoke] spiralförmig aufsteigen.

spiral staircase *n* Wendeltreppe *die*.

spire ['spaɪəʳ] *n* Turmspitze *die*.

spirit ['spɪrɪt] *n* - **1.** [soul, ghost] Geist *der*; **to be with sb in spirit** in Gedanken bei jm sein - **2.** (*U*) [courage] Mut *der* - **3.** (*U*) [attitude] Geist *der*; [mood] Stimmung *die*; **fighting spirit** Kampfgeist *der* - **4.** [essence] Geist *der*, Sinn *der*. ◆ **spirits** *npl* - **1.** [mood] Stimmung *die*, Laune *die*; **to be in high/low spirits** guter/schlechter Laune sein - **2.** [alcohol] Spirituosen *Pl*.

spirited ['spɪrɪtɪd] *adj* [action, defence] beherzt; [performance] lebendig; [debate] lebhaft.

spirit level *n* Wasserwaage *die*.

spiritual ['spɪrɪtʃʊəl] *adj* - **1.** [of the spirit] geistig, spirituell - **2.** [religious] geistlich.

spit [spɪt] (*UK pt & pp* **spat**) (*US pt & pp* **spit**) ⟨⟩ *n* - **1.** [saliva] Spucke *die* - **2.** [skewer] Spieß *der*. ⟨⟩ *vi* [from mouth] spucken. ⟨⟩ *impers vb UK* [rain lightly] tröpfeln.

spite [spaɪt] ⟨⟩ *n* (*U*) Bosheit *die*. ⟨⟩ *vt* ärgern. ◆ **in spite of** *prep* trotz (+ *G*).

spiteful ['spaɪtfʊl] *adj* boshaft.

spittle ['spɪtl] *n* Spucke *die*.

splash [splæʃ] ⟨⟩ *n* - **1.** [sound] Platschen *das* - **2.** [patch - of colour] Tupfen *der*; [- of light] Fleck *der*. ⟨⟩ *vt* - **1.** [subj: person] bespritzen - **2.** [subj: water] spritzen auf (+ *A*) - **3.** [apply haphazardly] klatschen. ⟨⟩ *vi* - **1.** [person]: **to splash about** OR **around** herumlspritzen - **2.** [water, liquid]: **to splash on/against sthg** klatschen an etw (*A*)/gegen etw.

spleen [spliːn] *n* - **1.** ANAT Milz *die* - **2.** (*U*) *fig* [anger]: **to vent one's spleen on sb** seine Wut OR schlechte Laune an jm auslassen.

splendid ['splendɪd] *adj* - **1.** [very good] großartig - **2.** [magnificent, beautiful] prachtvoll.

splint [splɪnt] *n* Schiene *die*.

splinter ['splɪntəʳ] ⟨⟩ *n* Splitter *der*. ⟨⟩ *vi* [glass, bone, wood] splittern.

split [splɪt] (*pt & pp inv*, *cont* **-ting**) ⟨⟩ *n* - **1.** [crack] Spalt *der* - **2.** [tear] Riss *der* - **3.** [division, schism] Spaltung *die*, Riss *der*. ⟨⟩ *vt* - **1.** [crack, divide] spalten; **the collision split the ship in two** bei dem Zusammenstoß zerbrach das Schiff in zwei Teile - **2.** [tear] zerreißen - **3.** [share] teilen; **we'll split the costs** wir werⴻ

den uns die Kosten teilen; **to split the difference** sich in der Mitte treffen. ◇ *vi* - **1.** [crack - wood, stone] sich spalten; [- ship] auseinanderlbrechen - **2.** [tear - fabric] reißen; [- seam, trousers] platzen; **the bag split open** die Tasche platzte auf - **3.** [divide] sich teilen. ➤ **split up** *vi* sich trennen; **to split up with sb** sich von jm trennen.

split second *n* Bruchteil *der* einer Sekunde.

splutter ['splʌtəʳ] *vi* - **1.** [person speaking, engine] stottern - **2.** [fire, flames] zischen.

spoil [spɔɪl] (*pt & pp* **-ed** OR **spoilt**) *vt* - **1.** [ruin] verderben; **to spoil sb's fun** jm den Spaß verderben - **2.** [pamper] verwöhnen; **to be spoilt for** .**choice** die Qual der Wahl haben. ➤ **spoils** *npl* Beute *die*.

spoiled [spɔɪld] *adj* = **spoilt**.

spoilsport ['spɔɪlspɔːt] *n* Spielverderber *der*, -in *die*.

spoilt [spɔɪlt] ◇ *pt & pp* ▷ **spoil**. ◇ *adj* - **1.** [child] verzogen - **2.** [food, dinner] verdorben.

spoke [spəʊk] ◇ *pt* ▷ **speak**. ◇ *n* Speiche *die*.

spoken ['spəʊkn] *pp* ▷ **speak**.

spokesman ['spəʊksmən] (*pl* -**men** [-mən]) *n* Sprecher *der*.

spokeswoman ['spəʊks,wʊmən] (*pl* -**women** [-,wɪmɪn]) *n* Sprecherin *die*.

sponge [spʌndʒ] (*UK cont* **spongeing**) (*US cont* **sponging**) ◇ *n* - **1.** [for cleaning, washing] Schwamm *der* - **2.** [cake] Biskuitkuchen *der* - ◇ *vt* [face] ablwaschen; [wall, car] mit einem Schwamm ablwaschen. ◇ *vi inf*: **to sponge off sb** jm auf der Tasche liegen.

sponge bag *n UK* Kulturbeutel *der*.

sponge cake *n* Biskuitkuchen *der*.

sponsor ['spɒnsəʳ] ◇ *n* - **1.** [of team, film, TV programme] Sponsor *der* - **2.** [of student, museum, for charity] Förderer *der*, -in *die*. ◇ *vt* - **1.** [team, film, TV programme] sponsern - **2.** [student, museum, for charity] finanziell unterstützen - **3.** [bill, appeal, proposal] unterstützen.

sponsored walk [,spɒnsəd-] *n* Wohltätigkeitsmarsch *der*.

sponsorship ['spɒnsəʃɪp] *n* (*U*) finanzielle Unterstützung.

spontaneous [spɒn'teɪnjəs] *adj* spontan.

spooky ['spuːkɪ] *adj inf* unheimlich.

spool [spuːl] *n* Spule *die*.

spoon [spuːn] *n* Löffel *der*.

spoon-feed *vt* - **1.** [feed with spoon] füttern - **2.** *fig* [students, pupils] gängeln.

spoonful ['spuːnfʊl] (*pl* -**s** OR **spoonsful**) *n* Löffel *der*; **a spoonful of salt** ein Löffel Salz.

sporadic [spə'rædɪk] *adj* sporadisch; [showers, shooting] vereinzelt.

sport [spɔːt] *n* - **1.** [games] Sport *der*; [type of sport] Sportart *die*; **she's good at sport** sie ist sportlich - **2.** *dated* [cheerful person]: **he's a (good) sport** er ist in Ordnung.

sporting ['spɔːtɪŋ] *adj* - **1.** [relating to sport] sportlich; **sporting event** Wettkampf *der* - **2.** [generous, fair] anständig, fair.

sports car ['spɔːts-] *n* Sportwagen *der*.

sportsman ['spɔːtsmən] (*pl* -**men** [-mən]) *n* Sportler *der*.

sportsmanship ['spɔːtsmənʃɪp] *n* sportliche Fairness.

sportswear ['spɔːtsweəʳ] *n* (*U*) [in sport] Sportbekleidung *die*; [for leisure] Freizeitkleidung *die*.

sportswoman ['spɔːts,wʊmən] (*pl* -**women** [-,wɪmɪn]) *n* Sportlerin *die*.

sporty ['spɔːtɪ] *adj inf* sportlich.

spot [spɒt] ◇ *n* - **1.** [of blood, ink, paint] Fleck *der* - **2.** [pimple] Pickel *der* - **3.** *inf* [small amount]: **a few spots of rain** ein paar Regentropfen; **a spot of** ein bisschen, etwas; **to have a spot of lunch** eine Kleinigkeit zu Mittag essen; **to do a spot of work** ein bisschen arbeiten - **4.** [place] Stelle *die*; **what a lovely spot!** was für ein schönes Plätzchen!; **to do sthg on the spot** etw an der Stelle tun. ◇ *vt* [notice] sehen; [mistake] finden.

spot check *n* Stichprobe *die*.

spotless ['spɒtlɪs] *adj* [clean] blitzsauber.

spotlight ['spɒtlaɪt] *n* [in theatre, TV] Scheinwerfer *der*; [at home] Spot *der*; **to be in the spotlight** *fig* im Rampenlicht stehen.

spotted ['spɒtɪd] *adj* [material, garment] gepunktet.

spotty ['spɒtɪ] *adj UK* [skin] pick(e)lig.

spouse [spaʊs] *n* Gatte *der*, -tin *die*.

spout [spaʊt] ◇ *n* - **1.** [of kettle, watering can] Schnabel *der* - **2.** [of water - from fountain, geyser] Strahl *der*. ◇ *vi*: **to spout from** OR **out of sthg** [liquid] aus etw hervorlspritzen; [flames] aus etw hervorlschießen.

sprain [spreɪn] ◇ *n* Verstauchung *die*. ◇ *vt*: **to sprain one's ankle/wrist** sich (*D*) den Knöchel/das Handgelenk verstauchen.

sprang [spræŋ] *pt* ▷ **spring**.

sprawl [sprɔːl] *vi* - **1.** [person] sich auslstrecken - **2.** [city, suburbs] sich unkontrolliert auslbreiten.

spray [spreɪ] ◇ *n* - **1.** [droplets] Sprühnebel *der*; [of sea] Gischt *die* - **2.** [pressurized liquid] Spray *das* - **3.** [can, container] Sprühdose *die*. ◇ *vt* - **1.** [plant, field] besprühen; [crops] spritzen; **to spray one's hair** sich das Haar mit Haarspray stylen - **2.** [paint, perfume] sprühen.

spread [spred] (*pt & pp inv*) ◇ *n* - **1.** CULIN [paste] Brotaufstrich *der*; **cheese spread** Streichkäse *der* - **2.** [diffusion, growth] Ausbreitung *die* - **3.** [range] Umfang *der* - **4.** *US* [bedspread] Decke *die*. ◇ *vt* - **1.** [open out - map, tablecloth, arms] auslbreiten; [- fingers, legs] spreizen - 2. [apply]: **to spread sthg with butter** etw mit Butter bestreichen; **to spread butter/ jam on one's bread** Butter/Marmelade aufs Brot streichen - 3. [diffuse, disseminate] verbreiten - 4. [over a surface, share evenly] verteilen. ◇ vi - 1. [disease, fire, rumour, news] sich auslbreiten - 2. [water, cloud] sich ausldehnen. ◆ **spread out** vi [disperse] sich verteilen.

spread-eagled [-,i:gld] adj: **to be** OR **lie spread-eagled** ausgestreckt dalliegen.

spreadsheet ['spredʃi:t] n COMPUT Tabelle die.

spree [spri:] n: **to go on a spending/shopping spree** groß einkaufen gehen.

sprightly ['spraɪtlɪ] adj [old person] rüstig.

spring [sprɪŋ] (pt sprang, pp sprung) ◇ n - 1. [season] Frühling der, Frühjahr das; **in (the) spring** im Frühling, im Frühjahr - 2. [coil] Feder die - 3. [water source] Quelle die. ◇ vi - 1. [leap] springen; **to spring to one's feet** auflspringen - 2. [be released]: **the branch sprang back** der Zweig schnellte zurück; **to spring shut** zulfallen; **to spring open** auflspringen - 3. [originate]: **to spring from sthg** aus etw entstehen. ◆ **spring up** vi - 1. [get up] auflspringen - 2. [grow in size, height] wachsen - 3. [appear - building] aus dem Boden schießen; [- wind] auflkommen; [- problem] auflauchen.

springboard ['sprɪŋbɔ:d] n liter & fig Sprungbrett das.

spring-clean vt: **to spring-clean the house** Frühjahrsputz machen.

spring onion n UK Frühlingszwiebel die.

springtime ['sprɪŋtaɪm] n: **in (the) springtime** im Frühling.

springy ['sprɪŋɪ] adj [carpet, mattress, step] federnd; [ground, rubber] elastisch.

sprinkle ['sprɪŋkl] vt [liquid] sprenkeln, sprengen; [powder, salt] streuen; **to sprinkle sthg with sthg** [liquid] etw mit etw (be)sprengen; [powder, salt] etw mit etw bestreuen.

sprinkler ['sprɪŋklər] n - 1. [for gardens] Rasensprenger der - 2. [for extinguishing fires]: **a sprinkler system** Sprinkleranlage die.

sprint [sprɪnt] ◇ n SPORT [race] Lauf der, Sprint der; **to break into** OR **put on a sprint** loslspurten. ◇ vi rennen; SPORT sprinten.

sprout [spraʊt] ◇ n - 1. CULIN: **(brussels) sprouts** Rosenkohl der - 2. [shoot] Trieb der. ◇ vt - 1. [germinate] keimen lassen - 2. [grow - leaves, shoots] (aus)ltreiben; [- beard, moustache] sich (D) wachsen lassen. ◇ vi - 1. [germinate] keimen - 2. [grow] wachsen, sprießen.

spruce [spru:s] ◇ adj gepflegt. ◇ n [tree] Fichte die. ◆ **spruce up** vt sep [room, house] auf Vordermann bringen.

sprung [sprʌŋ] pp ▷ **spring.**

spry [spraɪ] adj rüstig.

spun [spʌn] pt & pp ▷ **spin.**

spur [spɜ:r] ◇ n - 1. [incentive]: **spur (to sthg)** Ansporn der OR Antrieb der (für etw) - 2. [on rider's boot] Sporn der. ◇ vt - 1. [horse] die Sporen geben (+ D) - 2. [encourage]: **to spur sb to do sthg** jn anspornen, etw zu tun. ◆ **on the spur of the moment** adv ganz spontan. ◆ **spur on** vt sep [encourage] anlspornen.

spurn [spɜ:n] vt verschmähen.

spurt [spɜ:t] ◇ n - 1. [of water, steam] Strahl der - 2. [of energy] Anfall der - 3. [burst of speed] Spurt der. ◇ vi: **to spurt (out of** OR **from sthg)** [water, steam, flames] (heraus)l-schießen (aus etw).

spy [spaɪ] ◇ n Spion der, -in die. ◇ vt sichten. ◇ vi - 1. [work as spy] spionieren - 2. [watch secretly]: **to spy on sb** jm nachl-spionieren.

spying ['spaɪɪŋ] n Spionage die.

Sq., sq. abbr of **square.**

squabble ['skwɒbl] ◇ n Zank der. ◇ vi: **to squabble (about** OR **over sthg)** sich (wegen etw) zanken.

squad [skwɒd] n - 1. [police department] Dezernat das - 2. MIL Trupp der - 3. SPORT Mannschaft die.

squadron ['skwɒdrən] n [of fighter planes] Staffel die; [of warships] Geschwader das.

squalid ['skwɒlɪd] adj - 1. [filthy - place] dreckig und verkommen; [- conditions] erbärmlich - 2. [base, dishonest] schmutzig.

squall [skwɔ:l] n [storm] Bö(e) die.

squalor ['skwɒlər] n Schmutz der.

squander ['skwɒndər] vt [money] verschwenden; [opportunity] vertun.

square [skweər] ◇ adj - 1. [in shape] quadratisch; [face, brackets] eckig - 2. UK [MATHS - referring to area] Quadrat-; [- when each side is of same length] im Quadrat - 3. [not owing money]: **to be square** quitt sein. ◇ n - 1. [shape] Quadrat das - 2. [in town, city] Platz der - 3. inf [unfashionable person] Spießer der, -in die. ◇ vt - 1. MATHS [multiply by itself] quadrieren; **4 squared is 16** 4 hoch 2 ist 16, 4 (zum) Quadrat ist 16 - 2. [balance, reconcile]: **to square sthg with sthg** etw mit etw in Einklang bringen. ◆ **square up** vi [settle up]: **to square up with sb** mit jm ablrechnen.

squarely ['skweəlɪ] adv - 1. [directly] genau - 2. [honestly] offen und ehrlich.

squash [skwɒʃ] ◇ n - 1. SPORT Squash das - 2. UK [drink]: **lemon/orange squash** Fruchtsaftgetränk mit Zitronen-/Orangengeschmack - 3. US [vegetable] Kürbis der. ◇ vt [hat] zerdrücken; [box] zusammenldrücken; [fruit] zerquetschen.

squat [skwɒt] ◇ adj gedrungen. ◇ vi [crouch]: **to squat (down)** sich (hin)lhocken; **he was squatting** er hockte.

squatter ['skwɒtər] *n UK* [in empty building] Hausbesetzer *der*, -in *die*.

squawk [skwɔ:k] *n* [of bird] Kreischen *das*.

squeak [skwi:k] *n* - 1. [of animal] Quieken *das* - 2. [of door, hinge] Quietschen *das*.

squeal [skwi:l] *vi* [person] kreischen; [animal] quieken.

squeamish ['skwi:mɪʃ] *adj* zart besaitet.

squeeze [skwi:z] <> *n* [pressure]: **to give sthg a squeeze** etw drücken. <> *vt* - 1. [press firmly] drücken; [orange, lemon] auslpressen - 2. [extract, press out - juice] herauslpressen; [ex-tract, press out - juice] herauslpressen; **to squeeze sthg out of sthg** etw aus etw drü-cken - 3. [cram]: **to squeeze sthg into sthg** etw in etw (A) hineinlpressen OR zwängen.

squelch [skweltʃ] *vi* [through mud] patschen.

squid [skwɪd] (*pl inv* OR **-s**) *n* Tintenfisch *der*.

squiggle ['skwɪgl] *n* Schnörkel *der*.

squint [skwɪnt] <> *n* MED: **to have a squint** schielen. <> *vi* - 1. MED schielen - 2. [half-close one's eyes]: **to squint at sthg** etw blinzelnd anl-sehen.

squirm [skwɜ:m] *vi liter & fig* sich winden.

squirrel [*UK* 'skwɪrəl, *US* 'skwɜ:rəl] *n* Eich-hörnchen *das*.

squirt [skwɜ:t] <> *vt* [force out] spritzen. <> *vi*: **to squirt (out of sthg)** (heraus)lspritzen (aus etw).

Sr *abbr of* **senior**.

Sri Lanka [ˌsri:'læŋkə] *n* Sri Lanka *nt*.

St *abbr of* **saint**, **street**.

stab [stæb] <> *n* - 1. [with knife] Stich *der* - 2. *inf* [attempt]: **to have a stab at sthg** etw probieren - 3. [twinge]: **a stab of pain** ein stech-ender Schmerz. <> *vt* - 1. [with knife] einl-stechen (auf (+ A)); **to stab sb to death** jn er-stechen; **to stab sb in the back** *fig* jm in den Rücken fallen - 2. [with fork] auflspießen.

stable ['steɪbl] <> *adj* - 1. [steady, unchang-ing] stabil; [job] sicher - 2. [solid, anchored - lad-der, shelf] stabil; [- ship, aircraft] sicher - 3. [per-son, personality]: **(mentally) stable** innerlich gefestigt. <> *n* [building] Reitstall *der*; [horses] Rennstall *der*.

stack [stæk] <> *n* [pile] Stoß *der*, Stapel *der*. <> *vt* [pile up] stapeln.

stadium ['steɪdjəm] (*pl* **-diums** OR **-dia** [-djə]) *n* Stadion *das*.

staff [stɑ:f] <> *n* [employees] Personal *das*. <> *vt* mit Personal ausllstatten.

stag [stæg] (*pl inv* OR **-s**) *n* [deer] Hirsch *der*.

stage [steɪdʒ] <> *n* - 1. [period, phase] Stadi-um *das*, Phase *die*; **at this stage** zu diesem Zeitpunkt - 2. [platform] Bühne *die*. <> *vt* - 1. THEAT auflführen, inszenieren - 2. [organize] veranstalten.

stagecoach ['steɪdʒkəʊtʃ] *n* Postkut-sche *die*.

stage fright *n* Lampenfieber *das*.

stagger ['stægər] <> *vt* - 1. [astound] die Sprache verschlagen (+ D) - 2. [arrange at differ-ent times] staffeln. <> *vi* [totter] schwanken.

stagnant ['stægnənt] *adj* - 1. [water] ste-hend; [air] verbraucht - 2. [business, career, eco-nomy] stagnierend.

stagnate [stæg'neɪt] *vi* - 1. [water] stehen; [air] verbraucht werden - 2. [business, career, economy] stagnieren.

stag night, stag party *n* feucht-fröhlicher Männerabend, mit dem ein Bräutigam am Abend vor der Hochzeit sein Jungesellenda-sein beschließt.

staid [steɪd] *adj* [person] seriös, gesetzt; [ap-pearance, attitude] bieder.

stain [steɪn] <> *n* [mark] Fleck *der*. <> *vt* [dis-colour] Flecken hinterlassen auf (+ D).

stained glass *n* farbiges Glas.

stainless steel ['steɪnlɪs-] *n* Edelstahl *der*.

stain remover [-ˌrɪmu:vər] *n* Fleckenentfer-ner *der*.

stair [steər] *n* [step] Stufe *die*. ◆ **stairs** *npl* Treppe *die*.

staircase ['steəkeɪs] *n* Treppe *die*.

stairway ['steəweɪ] *n* Treppenaufgang *der*, Treppe *die*.

stairwell ['steəwel] *n* Treppenhaus *das*.

stake [steɪk] <> *n* - 1. [share]: **to have a stake in sthg** einen Anteil an etw (D) haben - 2. [wooden post] Pfahl *der* - 3. [in gambling] Einsatz *der*. <> *vt* - 1. [risk]: **to stake sthg on sthg** etw auf etw (A) setzen - 2. [in gambling] setzen. ◆ **to be at stake** *adv* auf dem Spiel stehen.

stale [steɪl] *adj* [bread] altbacken; [cake] tro-cken; [water, beer, air] abgestanden.

stalemate ['steɪlmeɪt] *n* - 1. [deadlock] Sack-gasse *die* - 2. CHESS Patt *das*.

stalk [stɔ:k] <> *n* [i] Stiel *der*; [of cabbage] Strunk *der*. <> *vt* [animal] sich heranlpirschen an (+ A); [person] nachllstellen (+ D).

stall [stɔ:l] <> *n* - 1. [table] Stand *der* - 2. [in stable] Box *die*. <> *vt* AUT ablwürgen. <> *vi* - 1. AUT ablsterben - 2. [delay]: **to stall for time** versuchen, Zeit zu schinden. ◆ **stalls** *npl UK* [in theatre, cinema] Parkett *das*.

stallion ['stæljən] *n* Hengst *der*.

stamina ['stæmɪnə] *n* Ausdauer *die*.

stammer ['stæmər] <> *n* Stottern *das*; **to have a stammer** stottern. <> *vi* stottern.

stamp [stæmp] <> *n* - 1. [postage stamp] Briefmarke *die* - 2. [rubber stamp] Stempel *der*. <> *vt* - 1. [produce by stamping] auflstempeln - 2. [stomp]: **to stamp one's foot** auflstampfen (mit dem Fuß). <> *vi* - 1. [walk] stampfen, trampeln - 2. [with one foot]: **to stamp on sthg** auf etw (A) treten.

stamp album *n* Briefmarkenalbum *das*.

stamp-collecting [-kə,lektɪŋ] n Briefmarkensammeln das.

stamped addressed envelope ['stæmptə,drest-] n UK frankierter Rückumschlag.

stampede [stæm'pi:d] n - 1. [of animals] panische Flucht - 2. [of people] Massenandrang der.

stance [stæns] n - 1. [posture] Haltung die - 2. [attitude]: **stance (on)** Einstellung die (zu).

stand [stænd] (pt & pp **stood**) <> n - 1. [stall] Stand der - 2. [for umbrellas, coats, bicycle] Ständer der - 3. [at sports stadium] Tribüne die - 4. fig & MIL: **to make a stand** Widerstand leisten - 5. [position] Standpunkt der - 6. US LAW Zeugenstand der. <> vt - 1. [place] stellen - 2. [withstand - pressure, heat] ertragen; **I can't stand him** ich kann ihn nicht ausstehen - 3. [put up with] aushalten. <> vi - 1. [gen] stehen; **to be standing** stehen - 2. [rise to one's feet] aufstehen - 3. UK POL [be a candidate] kandidieren. ◆ **stand back** vi zurücktreten. ◆ **stand by** <> vt insep - 1. [person] halten zu - 2. [promise] halten; [decision, offer] bleiben bei. <> vi - 1. [in readiness] sich bereithalten - 2. [not intervene] danebenstehen. ◆ **stand down** vi [resign] zurücktreten. ◆ **stand for** vt insep - 1. [signify] stehen für - 2. [tolerate] hinnehmen. ◆ **stand in** vi: **to stand in for sb** für jn einspringen. ◆ **stand out** vi - 1. [be clearly visible] herausstechen - 2. [be superior] sich abheben. ◆ **stand up** <> vt sep [boyfriend, girlfriend etc] versetzen. <> vi - 1. [on one's feet] stehen - 2. [rise to one's feet] aufstehen - 3. [be upright] aufrecht stehen. ◆ **stand up for** vt insep eintreten für. ◆ **stand up to** vt insep - 1. [bad treatment] sich wehren gegen; [weather, heat] trotzen (+ D) - 2. [person, boss] sich behaupten gegenüber.

standard ['stændəd] <> adj Standard-; [spelling, pronunciation] korrekt. <> n - 1. [level] Niveau das; **up to standard** der Norm entsprechend - 2. [point of reference] Maßstab der - 3. [flag] Fahne die. ◆ **standards** npl [principles] Wertvorstellungen Pl.

standard lamp n UK Stehlampe die.

standard of living (pl **standards of living**) n Lebensstandard der.

standby ['stændbaɪ] (pl **standbys**) <> n [substitute] Ersatz der; **on standby** in Bereitschaft. <> comp [ticket] Stand-by-.

stand-in n - 1. [replacement] Vertretung die - 2. [stunt person] Double das.

standing ['stændɪŋ] <> adj [permanent] ständig; [army] stehend. <> n - 1. [reputation] Ruf der - 2. [duration] Dauer die.

standing order n Dauerauftrag der.

standing room n (U) Stehplätze Pl.

standoffish [,stænd'ɒfɪʃ] adj kühl.

standpoint ['stændpɔɪnt] n Standpunkt der.

standstill ['stændstɪl] n: **to come to a standstill** [stop moving] stehen bleiben; fig zum Erliegen kommen.

stand-up adj: **stand-up comedian** Komiker der, -in die; **stand-up comedy** Comedyshow die.

stank [stæŋk] pt ▷ **stink**.

staple ['steɪpl] <> adj [principal] Haupt-. <> n - 1. [for paper] (Heft)klammer die - 2. [principal commodity] Grundnahrungsmittel das. <> vt zusammenheften.

stapler ['steɪplər] n Hefter der.

star [stɑ:r] <> n - 1. [gen] Stern der - 2. [celebrity] Star der. <> comp [performer] Star-; **star attraction** Spitzenattraktion die. <> vi [actor]: **to star (in)** die Hauptrolle spielen (in (+ D)). ◆ **stars** npl [horoscope] Sterne Pl.

starboard ['stɑ:bəd] <> adj Steuerbord-. <> n: **to starboard** nach Steuerbord.

starch [stɑ:tʃ] n Stärke die.

stardom ['stɑ:dəm] n Ruhm der.

stare [steər] <> n starrer Blick. <> vi starren; **to stare at sb/sthg** jn/etw anstarren.

stark [stɑ:k] <> adj - 1. [landscape, room] kahl - 2. [fact, truth] nackt; [contrast] scharf. <> adv: **stark naked** splitternackt.

starling ['stɑ:lɪŋ] n Star der.

starry ['stɑ:rɪ] adj sternenklar.

Stars and Stripes n: **the Stars and Stripes** das Sternenbanner.

start [stɑ:t] <> n - 1. [beginning] Anfang der, Beginn der - 2. [jump] Schreck(en) der - 3. SPORT Start der - 4. [lead, advantage] Vorsprung der. <> vt - 1. [begin] anfangen, beginnen; **to start work** anfangen zu arbeiten; **to start a race** ein Rennen starten; **to start doing** OR **to do sthg** anfangen, etw zu tun; **it started me thinking** es gab mir zu denken - 2. [engine, car] starten; [cassette player] einschalten; **to start a fire** [arson] Feuer legen; [for warmth] Feuer machen - 3. [business] gründen; [shop] aufmachen; [society] ins Leben rufen. <> vi - 1. [begin] beginnen, anfangen; **to start with sb/sthg** mit jm/etw beginnen; **starting from next week** ab nächster Woche; **to start with** [at first] zuerst; [in the first place] erstens; [when ordering meal] als Vorspeise - 2. [car, engine] starten; [tape] laufen - 3. [on journey] aufbrechen - 4. [jump] zusammenschrecken. ◆ **start off** <> vt sep [meeting, discussion] beginnen; [rumour] in Umlauf bringen; **this should be enough to start you off** das sollte für den Anfang reichen. <> vi - 1. [begin] beginnen, anfangen - 2. [on journey] aufbrechen. ◆ **start out** vi - 1. [in life, career] anfangen; **to start out as sthg** ursprünglich etw sein - 2. [on journey] aufbrechen. ◆ **start up** <> vt sep - 1. [business] gründen; [shop] aufmachen; [society] ins

Leben rufen - **2.** [car, engine] starten. ◇ *vi* - **1.** [guns, music, noise] losgehen - **2.** [car, engine] starten - **3.** [set up business] anfangen.

starter ['stɑːtə*r*] *n* - **1.** *UK* [of meal] Vorspeise *die* - **2.** AUT Anlasser *der* - **3.** SPORT [official] Starter *der*, -in *die*; [competitor] Teilnehmer *der*, -in *die*.

starting point ['stɑːtɪŋ-] *n* Ausgangspunkt *der*.

startle ['stɑːtl] *vt* erschrecken.

startling ['stɑːtlɪŋ] *adj* überraschend.

starvation [stɑːˈveɪʃn] *n* Hunger *der*; **to die of starvation** verhungern.

starve [stɑːv] ◇ *vt* [deprive of food] aushungern. ◇ *vi* [have no food] hungern; [die of hunger] verhungern; **I'm starving!** ich habe einen Mordshunger.

state [steɪt] ◇ *n* - **1.** [condition] Zustand *der* - **2.**: **to get into a state** sich aufregen - **3.** [country, region] Staat *der*. ◇ *comp* Staats-. ◇ *vt* [declare] erklären; [specify] angeben. ◆ **State** *n* [government]: **the State** der Staat. ◆ **States** *npl* [USA]: **the States** die Vereinigten Staaten *Pl*.

State Department *n* US Außenministerium *das*.

stately ['steɪtlɪ] *adj* [building] stattlich; [person] würdevoll.

statement ['steɪtmənt] *n* - **1.** [declaration & LAW] Aussage *die* - **2.** [from bank] Kontoauszug *der*.

state of mind (*pl* states of mind) *n* [mood] Verfassung *die*.

statesman ['steɪtsmən] (*pl* -men [-mən]) *n* Staatsmann *der*.

static ['stætɪk] ◇ *adj* [unchanging] konstant. ◇ *n* [on TV, radio] Empfangsstörung *die*.

static electricity *n* Reibungselektrizität *die*.

station ['steɪʃn] ◇ *n* - **1.** [for trains] Bahnhof *der*; [for buses] Busbahnhof *der* - **2.** RADIO Sender *der* - **3.** [police or fire station] Wache *die* - **4.** [position] Platz *der*. ◇ *vt* - **1.** [position] aufstellen - **2.** MIL stationieren.

stationary ['steɪʃnərɪ] *adj* stehend.

stationer ['steɪʃnə*r*] *n*: **stationer's (shop)** Schreibwarenhandlung *die*.

stationery ['steɪʃnərɪ] *n* (U) Schreibwaren *Pl*.

stationmaster ['steɪʃn,mɑːstə*r*] *n* Bahnhofsvorsteher *der*, -in *die*.

station wagon *n* US Kombiwagen *der*.

statistic [stəˈtɪstɪk] *n* [number] statistisches Ergebnis; **statistics** Statistik *die*. ◆ **statistics** *n* (U) [science] Statistik *die*.

statistical [stəˈtɪstɪkl] *adj* statistisch.

statue ['stætjuː] *n* Statue *die*.

stature ['stætʃə*r*] *n* - **1.** [height, size] Statur *die* - **2.** [importance] Format *das*.

status ['steɪtəs] *n* - **1.** [legal or social position] Status *der* - **2.** [prestige] Prestige *das*.

status symbol *n* Statussymbol *das*.

statute ['stætjuːt] *n* - **1.** [law] Gesetz *das* - **2.** [of organization] Statut *das*.

statutory ['stætjutrɪ] *adj* gesetzlich.

staunch [stɔːntʃ] ◇ *adj* treu. ◇ *vt* [blood] stillen; [flow] stauen.

stave [steɪv] (*pt & pp* -d OR stove) *n* MUS Notenlinien *Pl*. ◆ **stave off** *vt sep* [danger, disaster] abwenden; [hunger] lindern.

stay [steɪ] ◇ *vi* bleiben; [as guest] übernachten; **I'm staying at the hotel/with friends** ich wohne im Hotel/bei Freunden; **to stay for dinner** zum Abendessen bleiben; **to stay the night** übernachten. ◇ *n* [visit] Aufenthalt *der*. ◆ **stay in** *vi* [stay at home] zu Hause bleiben. ◆ **stay on** *vi* bleiben. ◆ **stay out** *vi* - **1.** [not come home]: **he stayed out last night** er ist letzte Nacht nicht nach Hause gekommen - **2.** [not get involved]: **to stay out of sth** sich aus etw raushalten. ◆ **stay up** *vi* - **1.** [not go to bed] aufbleiben - **2.** [shelf, picture] hängen bleiben; [socks] oben bleiben.

stead [sted] *n*: **to stand sb in good stead** jm zustattenkommen.

steadfast ['stedfɑːst] *adj* - **1.** [supporter] treu - **2.** [resolve] unerschütterlich - **3.** [gaze] unverwandt.

steadily ['stedɪlɪ] *adv* - **1.** [improve, increase] stetig - **2.** [breathe, move] gleichmäßig - **3.** [look, say] ruhig.

steady ['stedɪ] ◇ *adj* - **1.** [gradual] stetig - **2.** [regular, constant] konstant - **3.** [not shaking, calm] ruhig - **4.** [boyfriend, job] fest - **5.** [worker] zuverlässig. ◇ *vt* - **1.** [boat, camera] ins Gleichgewicht bringen - **2.** [voice, nerves] beruhigen.

steak [steɪk] *n* - **1.** [meat] Steak *das* - **2.** [fish] Fischsteak *das*.

steal [stiːl] (*pt* stole, *pp* stolen) ◇ *vt liter & fig* stehlen; **to steal sthg from sb** jm etw stehlen. ◇ *vi* [move stealthily] schleichen.

stealthy ['stelθɪ] *adj* verstohlen.

steam [stiːm] ◇ *n* Dampf *der*. ◇ *vt* CULIN dämpfen. ◇ *vi* dampfen. ◆ **steam up** ◇ *vt sep* [window] beschlagen lassen. ◇ *vi* [window, glasses] beschlagen.

steamboat ['stiːmbəʊt] *n* Dampfer *der*.

steam engine *n* Dampflok *die*.

steamroller ['stiːm,rəʊlə*r*] *n* Dampfwalze *die*.

steamy ['stiːmɪ] *adj* - **1.** [room] voll Dampf - **2.** *inf* [erotic] heiß.

steel [stiːl] ◇ *n* Stahl *der*. ◇ *comp* Stahl-.

steelworks ['stiːlwɜːks] (*pl inv*) *n* Stahlwerk *das*.

steep [stiːp] ◇ *adj* - **1.** [gen] steil - **2.** *inf* [expensive] gesalzen. ◇ *vt* [soak] einweichen.

steeple ['sti:pl] *n* Kirchturm *der*.

steer ['stɪər] <> *n* [bullock] junger Ochse. <> *vt* - 1. [boat] steuern; [car] lenken - 2. [person] lotsen. <> *vi* steuern; **to steer clear of sb/ sthg** *fig* einen großen Bogen um jn/etw machen.

steering ['stɪərɪŋ] *n* Lenkung *die*.

steering wheel *n* Lenkrad *das*.

stem [stem] <> *n* - 1. [of plant, glass] Stiel *der* - 2. [of pipe] Hals *der* - 3. GRAM Stamm *der*. <> *vt* [stop] eindämmen. **stem from** *vt insep* herrühren von.

stench [stentʃ] *n* Gestank *der*.

stencil ['stensl] (*UK*) (*US*) <> *n* Schablone *die*. <> *vt* [design, pattern] mit einer Schablone zeichnen; [words] mit einer Schablone schreiben.

step [step] <> *n* - 1. [pace, stage] Schritt *der*; **to be in step/out of step with public opinion** *fig* im Einklang/nicht im Einklang mit der öffentlichen Meinung sein; **to keep in step with sthg** mit etw Schritt halten; **step by step** Schritt für Schritt - 2. [measure] Maßnahme *die*; **it's a step in the right direction** das ist immerhin ein Anfang - 3. [of staircase, ladder] Stufe *die*. <> *vi* treten; **step this way** folgen Sie mir bitte; **she stepped off the bus** sie stieg aus dem Bus; **to step on/in sthg** auf/in etw (A) treten; **to step on it** *inf* [drive fast] aufs Gas drücken; **to step up** *inf* einen Zahn zulegen. **steps** *npl* - 1. [stairs] Stufen *Pl* - 2. *UK* [stepladder] Trittleiter *die*. **step down** *vi* [resign] zurücktreten. **step in** *vi* [intervene] einschreiten. **step up** *vt sep* [increase] steigern.

stepbrother ['step,brʌðər] *n* Stiefbruder *der*.

stepdaughter ['step,dɔ:tər] *n* Stieftochter *die*.

stepfather ['step,fɑ:ðər] *n* Stiefvater *der*.

stepladder ['step,lædər] *n* Trittleiter *die*.

stepmother ['step,mʌðər] *n* Stiefmutter *die*.

stepping-stone ['stepɪŋ-] *n* - 1. [in river] Trittstein *der* - 2. *fig* [way to success] Sprungbrett *das*.

stepsister ['step,sɪstər] *n* Stiefschwester *die*.

stepson ['stepsʌn] *n* Stiefsohn *der*.

stereo ['sterɪəu] (*pl* -s) <> *adj* Stereo-. <> *n* - 1. [stereo system] Stereoanlage *die* - 2. [stereo sound] Stereo *das*.

stereotype ['sterɪətaɪp] *n* Klischee *das*.

sterile ['steraɪl] *adj* - 1. [germ-free] steril - 2. [man, woman, animal] unfruchtbar.

sterilize, -ise ['sterəlaɪz] *vt* sterilisieren.

sterling ['stɜ:lɪŋ] <> *adj* - 1. [pound]: **£100 sterling** 100 Pfund Sterling - 2. [excellent] gediegen. <> *n* (*U*) Pfund *das* Sterling.

sterling silver *n* Sterlingsilber *das*.

stern [stɜ:n] <> *adj* streng. <> *n* Heck *das*.

steroid ['stɪərɔɪd] *n* Steroid *das*.

stethoscope ['steθəskəup] *n* Stethoskop *das*.

stew [stju:] <> *n* Eintopf *der*. <> *vt* schmoren.

steward ['stjuəd] *n* - 1. *UK* [on plane, ship] Steward *der* - 2. *UK* [at public event] Ordner *der*, -in *die*.

stewardess ['stjuədɪs] *n* Stewardess *die*.

stick [stɪk] (*pt & pp* stuck) <> *n* - 1. [piece of wood] Stock *der* - 2. [of dynamite, celery, cinnamon, rhubarb] Stange *die*; [of chewing gum, chalk] Stück *das* - 3. SPORT Schläger *der*. <> *vt* - 1. [with adhesive] kleben; **to stick sthg on** OR **to sthg** etw an etw (A) kleben - 2. [into pocket etc] stecken; **to stick sthg in(to) sthg** etw in etw (A) stecken - 3. *inf* [put] tun - 4. *UK inf* [tolerate] ertragen. <> *vi* - 1. [arrow, dart, spear] stecken - 2. [adhere]: **to stick (to)** kleben (an OR auf (+ D)) - 3. [become jammed] klemmen. **stick out** <> *vt sep* - 1. [extend - tongue, head] herausstrecken; [- hand] ausstrecken - 2. *inf* [endure]: **to stick it out** es durchhalten. <> *vi* - 1. [protrude] vorstehen; [ears] abstehen - 2. *inf* [be noticeable] auffallen. **stick to** *vt insep* [person, decision] bleiben bei; [path] bleiben auf (+ D); [promise] halten. **stick up** *vi* vorstehen; [hair] hochstehen. **stick up for** *vt insep* eintreten für.

sticker ['stɪkər] *n* Aufkleber *der*.

sticking plaster ['stɪkɪŋ-] *n* Heftpflaster *das*.

stick shift *n* *US* - 1. [gear lever] Schalthebel *der* - 2. [car] Auto *das* mit Gangschaltung.

sticky ['stɪkɪ] *adj* - 1. [hands] klebrig; **sticky tape** Klebeband *das*; **sticky label** Aufkleber *der* - 2. *inf* [awkward] heikel.

stiff [stɪf] <> *adj* - 1. [gen] steif; [rod, brush] hart; [shoes] fest; [drawer, door] widerspenstig - 2. [resistance, drink] stark; [penalty] hart - 3. [difficult] schwer. <> *adv inf*: **to be bored stiff** sich zu Tode langweilen; **to be scared stiff** starr vor Angst sein.

stiffen ['stɪfn] <> *vt* - 1. [material] steif machen - 2. [resistance, resolve] verstärken. <> *vi* - 1. [gen] steif werden; [with horror] erstarren - 2. [resistance, resolve] sich verstärken.

stifle ['staɪfl] <> *vt* - 1. [suffocate] ersticken - 2. [suppress] unterdrücken. <> *vi* [suffocate] ersticken.

stifling ['staɪflɪŋ] *adj* drückend.

stigma ['stɪgmə] *n* - 1. [social disgrace] Schande *die* - 2. BOT Stigma *das*.

stile [staɪl] *n* Zaunübertritt *der*.

stiletto [stɪ'letəu] *n* *UK* [shoe] Stöckelschuh *der*.

still [stɪl] <> *adv* - 1. [gen] noch; **we've still got ten minutes** wir haben noch zehn Minuten; **I still haven't seen it** ich habe es noch nicht gesehen; **still bigger/more important** noch größer/wichtiger; **still more money** noch mehr Geld - **2.** [even now] immer noch; **she could still change her mind** sie könnte es sich immer noch anders überlegen - **3.** [nevertheless] trotzdem; **you still have to pay** Sie müssen trotzdem zahlen - **4.** [motionless]: **to stand still** stillstehen; **sit still!** sitz still! $\diamond$ *adj* - **1.** [motionless] bewegungslos; **please be still!** sitz/steh bitte still! - **2.** [calm, quiet] ruhig - **3.** [not windy] windstill - **4.** [not fizzy] ohne Kohlensäure. $\diamond$ *n* - **1.** PHOT Standfoto *das* - **2.** [for making alcohol] Destillierapparat *der*.

stillborn ['stɪlbɔːn] *adj* tot geboren.

still life (*pl* -s) *n* Stillleben *das*.

stilted ['stɪltɪd] *adj* gespreizt.

stilts [stɪlts] *npl* - **1.** [for person] Stelzen *Pl* - **2.** [for building] Pfähle *Pl*.

stimulate ['stɪmjʊleɪt] *vt* - **1.** [interest] anregen; [growth, economy] ankurbeln - **2.** [person - physically] erregen; [- mentally] stimulieren.

stimulating ['stɪmjʊleɪtɪŋ] *adj* - **1.** [physically] belebend - **2.** [mentally] stimulierend.

stimulus ['stɪmjʊləs] (*pl* -li [-laɪ]) *n* - **1.** [gen] Anreiz *der* - **2.** BIOL Reiz *der*.

sting [stɪŋ] (*pt & pp* stung) $\diamond$ *n* - **1.** [wound, pain, mark] Stich *der* - **2.** [part of bee, wasp, scorpion] Stachel *der*. $\diamond$ *vt* - **1.** [subj: bee, wasp, scorpion] stechen; **I was stung by the nettles** ich habe mich an den Brennnesseln verbrannt - **2.** *fig* [subj: remark, criticism] schmerzen. $\diamond$ *vi* [bee, wasp, scorpion] stechen; [nettle, smoke, eyes, skin] brennen.

stingy ['stɪndʒɪ] *adj inf* geizig.

stink [stɪŋk] (*pt* stank OR stunk, *pp* stunk) $\diamond$ *n* Gestank *der*. $\diamond$ *vi* [smell] stinken.

stint [stɪnt] $\diamond$ *n* [period of time] Zeit *die*; **he did a two-year stint as editor** er arbeitete zwei Jahre lang als Redakteur. $\diamond$ *vi*: **to stint on sthg** mit etw sparen.

stipulate ['stɪpjʊleɪt] *vt* festlegen.

stir [stɜːr] $\diamond$ *n* [excitement] Aufsehen *das*. $\diamond$ *vt* - **1.** [mix] umrühren - **2.** [subj: wind] spielen mit - **3.** [excite] bewegen. $\diamond$ *vi* - **1.** [move] sich bewegen - **2.** [emotion] wach werden. $\spadesuit$ **stir up** *vt sep* - **1.** [dust, mud] aufwühlen - **2.** [trouble, feelings, memories] wachrufen.

stirrup ['stɪrəp] *n* Steigbügel *der*.

stitch [stɪtʃ] $\diamond$ *n* - **1.** [in sewing, for wound] Stich *der*; [in knitting] Masche *die* - **2.** [pain]: **to have a stitch** Seitenstechen haben. $\diamond$ *vt* nähen.

stoat [stəʊt] *n* Hermelin *das*.

stock [stɒk] $\diamond$ *n* - **1.** [supply] Vorrat *der* - **2.** (U) COMM [of shop] Lagerbestand *der*; **in stock** vorrätig; **out of stock** nicht vorrätig - **3.** FIN: **stocks and shares** Wertpapiere und Aktien - **4.** (U) [ancestry] Herkunft *die* - **5.** CULIN Brühe *die* - **6.** [livestock] Nutzvieh *das* - **7.** *phr:*

to take stock (of) Bilanz ziehen (über (+ A)). $\diamond$ *adj* [typical] stereotyp. $\diamond$ *vt* - **1.** [have in stock] auf Lager haben - **2.** [shelves] auffüllen; [lake with fish] bestücken. $\spadesuit$ **stock up** *vi*: **to stock up (on** OR **with)** sich eindecken (mit).

stockbroker ['stɒkˌbrəʊkər] *n* Börsenmakler *der*, -in *die*.

stock cube *n UK* Brühwürfel *der*.

stock exchange *n* Börse *die*.

stockholder ['stɒkˌhəʊldər] *n US* Aktionär *der*, -in *die*.

Stockholm ['stɒkhəʊm] *n* Stockholm *nt*.

stocking ['stɒkɪŋ] *n* Strumpf *der*.

stock market *n* Börse *die*.

stockpile ['stɒkpaɪl] $\diamond$ *n* Lager *das*. $\diamond$ *vt* horten.

stocktaking ['stɒkˌteɪkɪŋ] *n (U)* Inventur *die*.

stocky ['stɒkɪ] *adj* stämmig.

stodgy ['stɒdʒɪ] *adj* [food] schwer.

stoical ['stəʊɪkl] *adj* stoisch.

stoke [stəʊk] *vt* [fire] schüren.

stole [stəʊl] *pt* $\Box\!\!\!\Box$ **steal**.

stolen ['stəʊln] *pp* $\Box\!\!\!\Box$ **steal**.

stolid ['stɒlɪd] *adj* stur.

stomach ['stʌmək] $\diamond$ *n* - **1.** [organ] Magen *der* - **2.** [belly] Bauch *der*. $\diamond$ *vt* [tolerate] ertragen.

stomachache ['stʌməkeɪk] *n* Magenschmerzen *Pl*.

stomach upset *n* Magenverstimmung *die*.

stone [stəʊn] $\diamond$ *n* - **1.** [gen] Stein *der* - **2.** (*pl inv* OR -s) [unit of measurement] = *6,35 kg*. $\diamond$ *comp* aus Stein; [bridge, wall] Stein-. $\diamond$ *vt* mit Steinen bewerfen.

stone-cold *adj* eiskalt.

stonework ['stəʊnwɜːk] *n* Mauerwerk *das*,

stood [stʊd] *pt & pp* $\Box\!\!\!\Box$ **stand**.

stool [stuːl] *n* [seat] Hocker *der*.

stoop [stuːp] $\diamond$ *n* [bent back]: **to walk with a stoop** gebeugt gehen. $\diamond$ *vi* - **1.** [bend forwards] sich bücken - **2.** [have a stoop] gebeugt gehen.

stop [stɒp] $\diamond$ *n* - **1.** [of bus] Haltestelle *die*; [of train] Station *die* - **2.** [in journey] Halt *der*; [longer] Aufenthalt *der* - **3.** [standstill]: **to put a stop to sthg** einer Sache (D) ein Ende machen - **4.** [in punctuation] Punkt *der*. $\diamond$ *vt* - **1.** [halt - person, car] anhalten; [- machine, engine] abstellen; [- ball] stoppen; **to stop doing sthg** aufhören, etw zu tun; **to stop smoking** mit dem Rauchen aufhören - **2.** [prevent] verhindern; **to stop sb from doing sthg** jn daran hindern, etw zu tun; **to stop sthg from happening** verhindern, dass etw geschieht - **3.** [hole, gap] stopfen. $\diamond$ *vi* - **1.** [come to an end] aufhören - **2.** [halt] anhalten; [walker, machine, watch] stehen bleiben; [on journey] Halt machen - **3**. [stay] bleiben. ◆ **stop off** *vi* Halt machen. ◆ **stop up** *vt sep* [block] zulstopfen.

stopgap ['stɒpgæp] *n* Notlösung *die*.

stopover ['stɒp,əʊvər] *n* Zwischenstation *die*.

stoppage ['stɒpɪdʒ] *n* - **1**. [strike] Streik *der* - **2**. *UK* [deduction] Abzug *der*.

stopper ['stɒpər] *n* Pfropfen *der*.

stopwatch ['stɒpwɒtʃ] *n* Stoppuhr *die*.

storage ['stɔːrɪdʒ] *n* - **1**. [act of storing] Lagerung *die* - **2**. COMPUT Speichern *das*.

store [stɔːr] ◇ *n* - **1**. *esp US* [shop] Laden *der*, Geschäft *das*; [department store] Kaufhaus *das* - **2**. [supply]: **store of sthg** Vorrat *der* an etw (D) - **3**. [storage place] Lager *das*. ◇ *vt* - **1**. [keep, save - address, details] aufbewahren; [- goods, provisions] lagern; [- furniture] einlstellen - **2**. COMPUT speichern. ◆ **store up** *vt sep* [information] anlsammeln; **to store food** Lebensmittelvorräte anllegen.

storekeeper ['stɔː,kiːpər] *n US* Ladenbesitzer *der*, -in *die*.

storeroom ['stɔːrʊm] *n* Lagerraum *der*.

storey *UK* (*pl* -s), **story** *US* (*pl* -ies) ['stɔːrɪ] *n* Stockwerk *das*.

stork [stɔːk] *n* Storch *der*.

storm [stɔːm] ◇ *n* - **1**. [bad weather] Sturm *der* - **2**. [violent reaction - of abuse, tears] Flut *die*; [- of protest] Sturm *der*. ◇ *vt* stürmen - **2**. [say angrily] toben. ◇ *vi* [go angrily] stürmen.

stormy ['stɔːmɪ] *adj liter* & *fig* stürmisch.

story ['stɔːrɪ] *n* - **1**. [tale, history] Geschichte *die* - **2**. [article - in newspaper] Artikel *der*; [- on TV/radio news] Bericht *der* - **3**. *euph* [lie] Märchen *das* - **4**. *US* = **storey**.

stout [staʊt] ◇ *adj* - **1**. [corpulent] korpulent - **2**. [strong] kräftig; [boots] fest - **3**. [brave] tapfer. ◇ *n* Starkbier *das*.

stove [stəʊv] ◇ *pt* & *pp* ⊏⊐ **stave**. ◇ *n* - **1**. [for cooking] Herd *der* - **2**. [for heating] Ofen *der*.

stow [stəʊ] *vt*: **to stow sthg (away)** etw verstauen.

stowaway ['stəʊəweɪ] *n* blinder Passagier.

straddle ['strædl] *vt* - **1**. [subj: person - chair] rittlings sitzen auf (+ D); [- gap] breitbeinig stehen über (+ D) - **2**. [subj: bridge] überspannen; **the town straddles the border** der Ort erstreckt sich zu beiden Seiten der Grenze.

straggle ['strægl] *vi* - **1**. [buildings] verstreut liegen; [plant] wuchern - **2**. [person, group] zurücklbleiben.

straggler ['stræglər] *n* Nachzügler *der*, -in *die*.

straight [streɪt] ◇ *adj* - **1**. [not curved, level, upright] gerade - **2**. [not curly] glatt - **3**. [honest, frank] ehrlich, offen - **4**. [tidy] ordentlich; **to put**

a room straight ein Zimmer auflräumen - **5**. [simple - exchange] einfach; [- choice] klar - **6**. [undiluted] pur - **7**. *phr*: **to get sthg straight** etw klarlstellen. ◇ *adv* - **1**. [in a straight line, upright] gerade - **2**. [directly, immediately] direkt - **3**. [honestly, frankly] offen - **4**. [undiluted] pur. ◆ **straight off** *adv* sofort. ◆ **straight out** *adv* rundheraus.

straightaway [,streɪtə'weɪ] *adv* sofort.

straighten ['streɪtn] *vt* - **1**. [tidy - dress] gerade ziehen; [- room, desk] auflräumen - **2**. [make straight] begradigen - **3**. [make level] auslrichten. ◆ **straighten out** *vt sep* [sort out] klären.

straightforward [,streɪt'fɔːwəd] *adj* - **1**. [easy] einfach - **2**. [honest, frank] offen, ehrlich.

strain [streɪn] ◇ *n* - **1**. [gen] Belastung *die* - **2**. MED [of muscle] Zerrung *die*; [of back] Überanstrengung *die*. ◇ *vt* - **1**. [work hard - eyes] überanstrengen - **2**. MED [injure]: **to strain a muscle/one's back** sich einen Muskel zerren/ seinen Rücken überanstrengen - **3**. [overtax - resources] überbeanspruchen; [- patience] auf die Probe stellen - **4**. [drain] durch ein Sieb gießen - **5**. TECH [rope, girder, ceiling] belasten. ◇ *vi*: **to strain to do sthg** sich anlstrengen, etw zu tun. ◆ **strains** *npl liter* [of music] Klänge *Pl*.

strained [streɪnd] *adj* - **1**. [forced] angestrengt - **2**. [tense] angespannt - **3**. MED [sprained] gezerrt.

strainer ['streɪnər] *n* Sieb *das*.

strait [streɪt] *n* GEOG Meerenge *die*. ◆ **straits** *npl*: **in dire** *OR* **desperate straits** in einer Notlage.

straitjacket ['streɪt,dʒækɪt] *n* Zwangsjacke *die*.

straitlaced [,streɪt'leɪst] *adj pej* spießig.

strand [strænd] *n* Faden *der*; [of hair] Strähne *die*.

stranded ['strændɪd] *adj* [person, car] festsitzend.

strange [streɪndʒ] *adj* - **1**. [unusual, unexpected] seltsam - **2**. [unfamiliar] fremd.

stranger ['streɪndʒər] *n* - **1**. [unknown person] Unbekannte *der*, *die*; **she's a complete stranger to me** ich kenne sie überhaupt nicht - **2**. [person from elsewhere] Fremde *der*, *die*.

strangle ['stræŋgl] *vt* - **1**. [kill] erwürgen - **2**. *fig* [stifle] ersticken.

strap [stræp] ◇ *n* - **1**. [for carrying] Riemen *der* - **2**. [for fastening - of dress, bra] Träger *der*; [- of watch] Armband *das*. ◇ *vt* [fasten]: **to strap sthg (on)to sthg** etw auf etw (A) schnallen.

strapping ['stræpɪŋ] *adj* stramm.

strategic [strə'tiːdʒɪk] *adj* strategisch.

strategy ['strætɪdʒɪ] *n* Strategie *die*.

straw [strɔː] *n* - **1.** [dried corn] Stroh *das* - **2.** [for drinking] Strohhalm *der*.

strawberry ['strɔːbərɪ] <> *n* Erdbeere *die*. <> *comp* Erdbeer-.

stray [streɪ] <> *adj* - **1.** [cat, dog] streunend - **2.** [bullet] verirrt. <> *vi* - **1.** [person, animal] herumlstreunen; **to stray from the path** vom Weg ablweichen - **2.** [thoughts, mind] ablschweifen.

streak [striːk] <> *n* - **1.** [mark, line] Streifen *der*; **a streak of lightning** ein Blitz(strahl) - **2.** [in character] Zug *der*. <> *vi* [move quickly] sausen.

stream [striːm] <> *n* - **1.** [gen] Strom *der* - **2.** [brook] Bach *der* - **3.** [of abuse, complaints] Flut *die* - **4.** UK SCH Leistungsgruppe *die*. <> *vt* UK SCH in Leistungsgruppen einlteilen. <> *vi* strömen.

streamer ['striːmər] *n* [for party] Luftschlange *die*.

streamlined ['striːmlaɪnd] *adj* - **1.** [aerodynamic] stromlinienförmig - **2.** [efficient] rationalisiert.

street [striːt] *n* Straße *die*.

streetcar ['striːtkɑːr] *n* US Straßenbahn *die*.

street lamp, street light *n* Straßenlaterne *die*.

street plan *n* Stadtplan *der*.

strength [streŋθ] *n* - **1.** [gen] Stärke *die* - **2.** (U) [confidence, courage] Kraft *die* - **3.** [solidity] Stabilität *die*.

strengthen ['streŋθn] *vt* - **1.** [gen] stärken - **2.** [team, structure, resolve] verstärken - **3.** [friendship, ties, bond] festigen - **4.** [make braver, more confident] bestärken.

strenuous ['strenjʊəs] *adj* [exercise] anstrengend; [effort] gewaltig.

stress [stres] <> *n* - **1.** [emphasis]: **to lay** OR **put stress on sthg** etw besonders betonen - **2.** [tension, anxiety] Stress *der* - **3.** TECH [physical pressure]: **stress (on sthg)** Druck *der* (auf etw (A)) - **4.** LING [on word, syllable] Betonung *die*. <> *vt* [emphasize & LING] betonen.

stressful ['stresfʊl] *adj* stressig.

stretch [stretʃ] <> *n* - **1.** [area] Stück *das* - **2.** [period of time] Zeitspanne *die*; **for a five-year stretch** für fünf Jahre. <> *vt* - **1.** [pull longer or wider] dehnen - **2.** [pull taut] spannen - **3.** [extend to full length] auslstrecken - **4.** [rules, meaning, truth]: **to stretch the rules** eine Ausnahme machen; **to stretch the truth** übertreiben - **5.** [budget, resources] strecken - **6.** [provide challenge for] fordern. <> *vi* - **1.** [area]: **to stretch over** sich auslldehnen über (+ A); **to stretch from ... to** reichen von bis - **2.** [person, animal] sich strecken - **3.** [material, elastic] sich dehnen. **stretch out** <> *vt sep* [hold out] auslstrecken. <> *vi* [lie down] sich auslstrecken.

stretcher ['stretʃər] *n* Trage *die*.

strew [struː] (*pt* -ed, *pp* strewn [struːn] OR -ed) *vt* [scatter untidily]: **to be strewn with sthg** [freckles, confetti] mit etw übersät sein; **the streets were strewn with litter** die Straßen waren voller Müll.

stricken ['strɪkn] *adj*: **to be stricken by** OR **with sthg** [doubt, horror, panic] von etw erfüllt sein; [illness] an etw (D) leiden.

strict [strɪkt] *adj* - **1.** [severe] streng - **2.** [exact, precise] genau; **in the strictest sense of a word** im engsten Sinne des Wortes.

strictly ['strɪktlɪ] *adv* - **1.** [severely, rigidly, absolutely] streng - **2.** [precisely, exactly] genau; **strictly speaking** genau genommen - **3.** [exclusively] ausschließlich.

stride [straɪd] (*pt* strode, *pp* stridden ['strɪdn]) <> *n* [step] Schritt *der*; **to take sthg in one's stride** *fig* mit etw leicht fertig werden. <> *vi* schreiten.

strident ['straɪdnt] *adj* - **1.** [voice, sound] durchdringend - **2.** [demand] lautstark.

strike [straɪk] (*pt & pp* struck) <> *n* - **1.** [refusal to work, do sthg] Streik *der*; **to be (out) on strike** streiken; **to go on strike** in Streik treten - **2.** MIL [attack] Angriff *der* - **3.** [find] Fund *der*. <> *vt* - **1.** [hit deliberately] schlagen; [hit accidentally - car] fahren gegen; [- boat] auflaufen auf (+ A) - **2.** [subj: hurricane, disaster, lightning] treffen - **3.** [subj: thought]: **it strikes me that ...** mir fällt auf, dass ...; **he strikes me as very capable** er scheint mir sehr fähig zu sein - **4.** [bargain] auslhandeln - **5.** [match] anlzünden - **6.** [chime] schlagen. <> *vi* - **1.** [stop working] streiken - **2.** [happen suddenly - disaster, hurricane] loslbrechen; [- lightning] einlschlagen - **3.** [attack] anlgreifen - **4.** [chime] schlagen. **strike down** *vt sep* niederlschlagen. **strike out** <> *vt sep* durchlstreichen. <> *vi* - **1.** [head out] loslziehen - **2.** [do sthg different]: **to strike out on one's own** eigene Wege gehen. **strike up** *vt insep* - **1.** [friendship, conversation] anlfangen - **2.** [music] anlfangen zu spielen.

striker ['straɪkər] *n* - **1.** [person on strike] Streikende *der, die* - **2.** FTBL Stürmer *der*, -in *die*.

striking ['straɪkɪŋ] *adj* - **1.** [noticeable, unusual] auffallend - **2.** [attractive] unwerfend.

string [strɪŋ] (*pt & pp* strung) *n* - **1.** [gen] Schnur *die*; **to pull strings** Beziehungen spielen lassen - **2.** [of onions] Zopf *der*; **string of pearls** [necklace] Perlenkette *die* - **3.** [series] Reihe *die* - **4.** [for musical instrument, tennis racket] Saite *die*; [for bow] Sehne *die*. **strings** *npl* MUS: **the strings** die Streicher *Pl*. **string out** *vt sep* [disperse]: **to be strung out** verteilt sein. **string together** *vt sep fig* [words, sentences] aneinanderlfügen.

string bean *n* Stangenbohne *die*.

stringent ['strɪndʒənt] *adj* streng.

strip [strɪp] <> *n* - **1.** [of fabric, paper, land, water] Streifen *der* - **2.** UK SPORT [clothes] Tri-

kot *das*. ⬦ *vt* - **1.** [undress] auslziehen - **2.** [remove - paint] ablkratzen; [- wallpaper] ablziehen. ⬦ *vi* [undress] sich auslziehen.
⬛ **strip off** *vi* sich auslziehen.

strip cartoon *n* UK Comic *der*.

stripe [straɪp] *n* - **1.** [band of colour] Streifen *der* - **2.** [sign of rank] Ärmelstreifen *der*.

striped [straɪpt] *adj* gestreift.

stripper ['strɪpər] *n* - **1.** [performer of striptease] Stripper *der*, -in *die* - **2.** [liquid] Entferner *der*; [tool] Spachtel *der*.

striptease ['strɪptiːz] *n* Striptease *der*.

strive [straɪv] (*pt* strove, *pp* striven ['strɪvn]) *vi fml*: **to strive for sthg** nach etw streben; **to strive to do sthg** bemüht sein, etw zu tun.

strode [strəʊd] *pt* ⟼ **stride**.

stroke [strəʊk] ⬦ *n* - **1.** MED Schlaganfall *der* - **2.** [of pen, brush] Strich *der* - **3.** [in swimming - movement] Zug *der*; [- style] Stil *der* - **4.** [in rowing, in ball game, of clock] Schlag *der* - **5.** UK TYPO [oblique] Schrägstrich *der* - **6.** [piece]: **a stroke of genius** ein Geniestreich; **a stroke of luck** ein Glücksfall; **at a stroke** mit einem Streich. ⬦ *vt* streicheln.

stroll [strəʊl] ⬦ *n* Spaziergang *der*. ⬦ *vi* spazieren gehen.

stroller ['strəʊlər] *n* US [for baby] Sportwagen *der*.

strong [strɒŋ] *adj* - **1.** [gen] stark; **strong point** Stärke *die* - **2.** [physically powerful, healthy] kräftig - **3.** [solid, sturdy] stabil; [measures] energisch - **4.** [argument, case, evidence] überzeugend.

stronghold ['strɒŋhəʊld] *n fig* Hochburg *die*.

strongly ['strɒŋlɪ] *adv* - **1.** [sturdily, solidly] solide - **2.** [in degree or intensity] stark - **3.** [support] energisch; **do you feel strongly about it?** ist es Ihnen wichtig?

strong room *n* Tresorraum *der*.

strove [strəʊv] *pt* ⟼ **strive**.

struck [strʌk] *pt* & *pp* ⟼ **strike**.

structure ['strʌktʃər] *n* - **1.** [organization, arrangement] Struktur *die* - **2.** [building, construction] Konstruktion *die*.

struggle ['strʌgl] ⬦ *n* Kampf *der*; **a struggle for sthg** ein Kampf um etw; **it will be a struggle to finish on time** wir werden uns sehr anstrengen müssen, um rechtzeitig fertig zu werden. ⬦ *vi* - **1.** [try hard, strive] kämpfen; **to struggle for sthg** um etw kämpfen; **she struggled to reach the switch** sie hatte Mühe, an den Schalter zu kommen - **2.** [fight]: **to struggle (with sb)** (mit jm) kämpfen.

strum [strʌm] *vt* klimpern; [guitar] klimpern auf (+ D).

strung [strʌŋ] *pt* & *pp* ⟼ **string**.

strut [strʌt] ⬦ *n* CONSTR Strebe *die*. ⬦ *vi* stolzieren.

stub [stʌb] ⬦ *n* - **1.** [of cigarette, pencil] Stummel *der* - **2.** [of ticket, cheque] Abschnitt *der*. ⬦ *vt*: **to stub one's toe** sich den Zeh stoßen.
⬛ **stub out** *vt sep* ausldrücken.

stubble ['stʌbl] *n* (U) Stoppeln *Pl*.

stubborn ['stʌbən] *adj* - **1.** [person - resolute] hartnäckig; [- unreasonable] dickköpfig, stur - **2.** [stain] hartnäckig.

stuck [stʌk] ⬦ *pt* & *pp* ⟼ **stick**. ⬦ *adj* - **1.** [fixed tightly, jammed - window, lid] verklemmt; [- finger, toe, garment] eingeklemmt - **2.** [stumped]: **I'm stuck** ich komme nicht weiter - **3.** [stranded]: **he got stuck in Birmingham** er saß in Birmingham fest - **4.** [in an unpleasant situation, trapped]: **to be stuck** festlsitzen.

stuck-up *adj inf pej* hochnäsig.

stud [stʌd] *n* - **1.** [metal decoration] Niete *die* - **2.** [earring] Ohrstecker *der* - **3.** UK [on boot, shoe] Stollen *der* - **4.** [place for breeding horses] Gestüt *das*.

studded ['stʌdɪd] *adj*: **studded with sthg** mit etw besetzt.

student ['stjuːdnt] ⬦ *n* - **1.** [at college, university] Student *der*, -in *die* - **2.** [scholar]: **to be a student of history/human nature** sich für Geschichte/die menschliche Natur interessieren. ⬦ *comp* Studenten-.

student loan *n* UK Studentendarlehen *das*.

studio ['stjuːdɪəʊ] (*pl* -s) *n* - **1.** [artist's workroom] Atelier *das* - **2.** CIN, RADIO & TV Studio *das*.

studio flat UK, **studio apartment** US *n* Atelierwohnung *die*.

studious ['stjuːdjəs] *adj* fleißig.

study ['stʌdɪ] ⬦ *n* - **1.** (U) [learning] Studium *das* - **2.** [piece of research] Untersuchung *die* - **3.** [room] Arbeitszimmer *das*. ⬦ *vt* & *vi* studieren.

stuff [stʌf] ⬦ *n* (U) *inf* - **1.** [matter, things, substance] Zeug *das* - **2.** [belongings] Sachen *Pl*. ⬦ *vt* - **1.** [push, put] stopfen - **2.** [fill, cram]: **to stuff sthg (with sthg)** etw (mit etw) vollstopfen - **3.** CULIN füllen.

stuffed [stʌft] *adj* - **1.** [filled, crammed]: **stuffed with sthg** mit etw vollgestopft - **2.** *inf* [with food] voll - **3.** CULIN gefüllt - **4.** [animal] ausgestopft.

stuffing ['stʌfɪŋ] *n* (U) - **1.** [for furniture] Polsterung *die* - **2.** [for toys & CULIN] Füllung *die*.

stuffy ['stʌfɪ] *adj* - **1.** [room] stickig - **2.** [formal, old-fashioned] spießig.

stumble ['stʌmbl] *vi* - **1.** [trip] stolpern - **2.** [hesitate, make mistake] stocken.
⬛ **stumble across**, **stumble on** *vt insep* stoßen auf (+ A); [person] stolpern über (+ A).

stumbling block ['stʌmblɪŋ-] *n* Hindernis *das*.

stump [stʌmp] ⬦ *n* [remaining part] Stumpf *der*. ⬦ *vt* [subj: question, problem]: **to be stumped by a problem/question** keine Lösung/Antwort wissen.

stun [stʌn] *vt* - **1.** [knock unconscious] bewusstlos schlagen - **2.** [shock, surprise] verblüffen.

stung [stʌŋ] *pt & pp* ⊳ **sting**.

stunk [stʌŋk] *pt & pp* ⊳ **stink**.

stunning ['stʌnɪŋ] *adj* - **1.** [beautiful] atemberaubend - **2.** [shocking] schrecklich; [surprising] sensationell.

stunt [stʌnt] ⟨⟩ *n* - **1.** [for publicity] Werbetrick *der* - **2.** CIN Stunt *der*. ⟨⟩ *vt* hemmen.

stunt man *n* Stuntman *der*.

stupefy ['stju:pɪfaɪ] *vt* - **1.** [tire, bore] abstumpfen lassen - **2.** [surprise] verblüffen.

stupendous [stju:'pendəs] *adj inf* - **1.** [wonderful] toll - **2.** [very large] enorm.

stupid ['stju:pɪd] *adj* - **1.** [foolish] dumm - **2.** *inf* [wretched, damned] blöd.

stupidity [stju:'pɪdətɪ] *n* Dummheit *die*.

sturdy ['stɜ:dɪ] *adj* kräftig; [furniture, bridge] stabil.

stutter ['stʌtər] *vi* [in speaking] stottern.

sty [staɪ] *n* Schweinestall *der*.

stye [staɪ] *n* Gerstenkorn *das*.

style [staɪl] ⟨⟩ *n* - **1.** [gen] Stil *der*; **in style** im großen Stil; **that's not my style** das ist nicht meine Art - **2.** [fashion, design] Mode *die*. ⟨⟩ *vt* [hair] stylen.

stylish ['staɪlɪʃ] *adj* elegant.

stylist ['staɪlɪst] *n* [hairdresser] Stylist *der*, -in *die*.

stylus ['staɪləs] (*pl* -es) *n* [on record player] Nadel *die*.

suave [swɑ:v] *adj* gewandt; *pej* glatt.

sub [sʌb] *n inf* - **1.** SPORT (*abbr of* substitute) Ersatz *der* - **2.** *abbr of* **submarine** - **3.** *UK abbr of* subscription.

subconscious [,sʌb'kɒnʃəs] ⟨⟩ *adj* unterbewusst. ⟨⟩ *n*: **the subconscious** das Unterbewusstsein.

subcontract [,sʌbkən'trækt] *vt* an (ein) Subunternehmen vergeben.

subdue [səb'dju:] *vt* - **1.** [enemy, rioters, crowds] unterwerfen - **2.** [feelings, passions] unterdrücken.

subdued [səb'dju:d] *adj* - **1.** [person] ruhig - **2.** [sound, feelings, lighting, colour] gedämpft.

subject ⟨⟩ *adj* ['sʌbdʒekt] - **1.** [subordinate]: **subject to sthg** etw (*D*) unterworfen - **2.** [liable]: **subject to sthg** [disease] anfällig für etw; **subject to tax** steuerpflichtig; **prices subject to change** COMM Preisänderungen vorbehalten. ⟨⟩ *n* ['sʌbdʒekt] - **1.** [topic under consideration] Thema *das*; **he is the subject of an inquiry** es wird eine Untersuchung über ihn durchgeführt - **2.** GRAM Subjekt *das* - **3.** SCH & UNIV Fach *das* - **4.** [citizen] Staatsbürger *der*, -in *die*. ⟨⟩ *vt* [səb'dʒekt] - **1.** [subjugate] unterwerfen - **2.** [force to experience]: **to subject sb**

to sthg [punishment, inquiry] jn einer Sache (*D*) unterziehen. ⟨⟩ **subject to** *prep* ['sʌbdʒekt] [depending on] abhängig von.

subjective [səb'dʒektɪv] *adj* subjektiv.

subject matter *n* Stoff *der*.

subjunctive [səb'dʒʌŋktɪv] *n* GRAM: **subjunctive (mood)** Konjunktiv *der*.

sublet [,sʌb'let] (*pt & pp inv*) *vt* untervermieten.

sublime [sə'blaɪm] *adj* [wonderful] erhaben.

submachine gun [,sʌbmə'ʃi:n-] *n* Maschinenpistole *die*.

submarine [,sʌbmə'ri:n] *n* U-Boot *das*.

submerge [səb'mɜ:dʒ] ⟨⟩ *vt* - **1.** [flood] überschwemmen - **2.** [plunge into liquid] eintauchen. ⟨⟩ *vi* tauchen.

submission [səb'mɪʃn] *n* - **1.** [obedience, capitulation] Unterwerfung *die* - **2.** [presentation] Einreichen *das*.

submissive [səb'mɪsɪv] *adj* unterwürfig.

submit [səb'mɪt] ⟨⟩ *vt* [present] einreichen. ⟨⟩ *vi* [admit defeat] sich ergeben; *(phrase)*: **to submit to sb/sthg** sich jm/etw unterwerfen.

subordinate ⟨⟩ *adj* [sə'bɔ:dɪnət] *fml* [less important]: **subordinate (to sthg)** (einer Sache (*D*)) untergeordnet. ⟨⟩ *n* [sə'bɔ:dɪnət] Untergebene *der*, *die*.

subpoena [sə'pi:nə] (*pt & pp* -ed) ⟨⟩ *n* LAW Vorladung *die*. ⟨⟩ *vt* LAW vorladen.

subscribe [səb'skraɪb] *vi* - **1.** [to magazine, newspaper]: **to subscribe to sthg** etw abonnieren - **2.** [to view, belief]: **to subscribe to sthg** sich einer Sache (*D*) anschließen.

subscriber [səb'skraɪbər] *n* - **1.** [to magazine, newspaper] Abonnent *der*, -in *die* - **2.** [to service] Teilnehmer *der*, -in *die*.

subscription [səb'skrɪpʃn] *n* [to newspaper, magazine] Abonnement *das*; [to club, organization] Mitgliedsbeitrag *der*.

subsequent ['sʌbsɪkwənt] *adj* nachfolgend.

subsequently ['sʌbsɪkwəntlɪ] *adv* anschließend.

subservient [səb'sɜ:vjənt] *adj* [servile]: **subservient (to sb)** (jm gegenüber) unterwürfig.

subside [səb'saɪd] *vi* - **1.** [grow less intense] nachlassen - **2.** [grow quieter] leiser werden - **3.** [sink - building, ground] sich senken; [- river] sinken.

subsidence [səb'saɪdns, 'sʌbsɪdns] *n* (*U*) CONSTR Bodensenkung *die*.

subsidiary [səb'sɪdjərɪ] ⟨⟩ *adj* untergeordnet. ⟨⟩ *n*: **subsidiary (company)** Tochter(gesellschaft) *die*.

subsidize, -ise ['sʌbsɪdaɪz] *vt* subventionieren.

subsidy ['sʌbsɪdɪ] *n* Subvention *die*.

substance ['sʌbstəns] *n* - **1.** [material, tangibility] Substanz *die* - **2.** [essence, gist] Kern *der* - **3.** (*U*) [importance] Gewicht *das*.

substantial [səb'stæn∫l] *adj* - **1.** [large, considerable] beträchtlich - **2.** [solid, well-built] solide.

substantially [səb'stænʃəlɪ] *adv* - **1.** [quite a lot] beträchtlich - **2.** [mainly] im Wesentlichen.

substitute ['sʌbstɪtjuːt] ⋄ *n* - **1.** [replacement]: **substitute (für)** Ersatz *der* (für) - **2.** SPORT Ersatzspieler *der*, -in *die*. ⋄ *vt*: **to substitute sb/sthg for sb/sthg** jn/etw durch jn/etw ersetzen.

subtitle ['sʌb,taɪtl] *n* [of book] Untertitel *der*. ◆ **subtitles** *npl* CIN Untertitel *Pl*.

subtle ['sʌtl] *adj* - **1.** [nuance, difference] fein; [colour, music] zart - **2.** [comment, method] subtil.

subtlety ['sʌtltɪ] *n* - **1.** [of difference] Feinheit *die*; [of colour, music] Zartheit *die* - **2.** [of comment, method] Subtilität *die*.

subtotal ['sʌb,təʊtl] *n* Zwischensumme *die*.

subtract [səb'trækt] *vt*: **to subtract sthg (from sthg)** etw (von etw) subtrahieren OR abziehen.

subtraction [səb'trækʃn] *n* Subtraktion *die*.

suburb ['sʌbɜːb] *n* Vorort *der*. ◆ **suburbs** *npl* Vororte *Pl*.

suburban [sə'bɜːbn] *adj* - **1.** [of suburbs] Vorort- - **2.** *pej* [boring] spießig.

suburbia [sə'bɜːbɪə] *n (U)* die Vororte *Pl*.

subversive [səb'vɜːsɪv] *adj* subversiv.

subway ['sʌbweɪ] *n* - **1.** UK [underground walkway] Unterführung *die* - **2.** US [underground railway] U-Bahn *die*.

succeed [sək'siːd] ⋄ *vt* nachfolgen (+ D); [thing, event] folgen (+ D). ⋄ *vi* [be successful] erfolgreich sein; **he succeeded in persuading her** es gelang ihm, sie zu überreden.

succeeding [sək'siːdɪŋ] *adj fml* nachfolgend.

success [sək'ses] *n* Erfolg *der*.

successful [sək'sesful] *adj* erfolgreich.

succession [sək'seʃn] *n* [series] Folge *die*.

successive [sək'sesɪv] *adj* aufeinander folgend.

succinct [sək'sɪŋkt] *adj* prägnant.

succumb [sə'kʌm] *vi* [to a bad influence]: **to succumb to sthg** einer Sache *(D)* erliegen.

such [sʌtʃ] ⋄ *adj* - **1.** [gen] solche(r) (s); **such people** solche Leute; **I've never heard such nonsense** ich habe noch nie so einen Unsinn gehört!; **shoplifting and such crimes** Ladendiebstahl und derartige Delikte; **there's no such thing** so etwas gibt es nicht; **countries such as Spain and France** Länder wie Spanien und Frankreich - **2.** [whatever]: **I've spent such money as I had** ich habe mein weniges Geld ausgegeben - **3.** [so great]: **there are such differences that...** die Unterschiede sind so groß, dass...; **such was their skill that...** sie waren so

geschickt, dass... ⋄ *adv*: **such big houses** so große Häuser, solche großen Häuser; **such a man** ein solcher Mann, so ein Mann; **it's such a lovely day** es ist so ein schöner Tag; **such a thing should never have happened** so etwas hätte nie passieren dürfen; **such a lot** so viel; **such a long time** so lange; **in such a way that...** auf solche Weise, dass... ⋄ *pron*: **and such (like)** und dergleichen. ◆ **as such** *adv* als solche(r) (s). ◆ **such and such** *adj* das und das; **on such and such a day** an dem und dem Tag.

suck [sʌk] *vt* - **1.** [by mouth] saugen; [lollipop, thumb] lutschen - **2.** [draw in] einlsaugen.

sucker ['sʌkər] *n* - **1.** [suction pad] Saugnapf *der* - **2.** *inf* [gullible person] Depp *der*.

suction ['sʌkʃn] *n* - **1.** [drawing in] Sogwirkung *die* - **2.** [adhesion] Saugwirkung *die*.

Sudan [suː'dɑːn] *n* Sudan *der*.

sudden ['sʌdn] *adj* plötzlich; **all of a sudden** plötzlich.

suddenly ['sʌdnlɪ] *adv* plötzlich.

sue [suː] *vt* verklagen; **to sue sb for sthg** [libel etc] jn wegen etw verklagen; [sum of money] jn auf etw *(A)* verklagen.

suede [sweɪd] *n* Wildleder *das*.

suet ['sʊɪt] *n* Nierenfett *das*.

suffer ['sʌfər] ⋄ *vt* erleiden. ⋄ *vi* leiden; **to suffer from sthg** MED an etw *(D)* leiden.

sufferer ['sʌfrər] *n*: **rheumatism sufferer** Rheumakranke *der*, *die*; **hay fever sufferer** an Heuschnupfen Leidende *der*, *die*.

suffering ['sʌfrɪŋ] *n* Leiden *das*.

suffice [sə'faɪs] *vi fml* genügen.

sufficient [sə'fɪʃnt] *adj* genügend.

sufficiently [sə'fɪʃntlɪ] *adv* genug.

suffocate ['sʌfəkeɪt] *vt* & *vi* ersticken.

suffuse [sə'fjuːz] *vt*: **suffused with sthg** von etw durchdrungen.

sugar ['ʃʊɡər] ⋄ *n* Zucker *der*. ⋄ *vt* zuckern.

sugar beet *n (U)* Zuckerrübe *die*.

sugarcane ['ʃʊɡəkeɪn] *n* Zuckerrohr *das*.

sugary ['ʃʊɡərɪ] *adj* [high in sugar] süß.

suggest [sə'dʒest] *vt* - **1.** [propose] vorlschlagen - **2.** [imply] anldeuten.

suggestion [sə'dʒestʃn] *n* - **1.** [proposal, idea] Vorschlag *der* - **2.** *(U)* [implication]: **there was no suggestion of corruption** nichts deutete auf Korruption hin.

suggestive [sə'dʒestɪv] *adj* - **1.** [implying sexual connotation] anzüglich - **2.** [implying a certain conclusion]: **to be suggestive of sthg** auf etw *(A)* hindeuten - **3.** [reminiscent]: **to be suggestive of sthg** an etw *(A)* denken lassen.

suicide ['sʊɪsaɪd] *n liter* & *fig* Selbstmord *der*; **to commit suicide** Selbstmord begehen.

suit [suːt] ⬦ n - **1.** [matching clothes] Anzug der; [for woman] Kostüm das - **2.** [in cards] Farbe die - **3.** LAW Prozess der. ⬦ vt - **1.** [look attractive on] stehen (+ D) - **2.** [be convenient or appropriate to] passen (+ D); **suit yourself!** mach, was du willst! ⬦ vi: **does that suit?** passt dir das?

suitable ['suːtəbl] adj: **suitable (for)** geeignet (für).

suitably ['suːtəbli] adv [dressed] passend; [impressed] gehörig.

suitcase ['suːtkeɪs] n Koffer der.

suite [swiːt] n - **1.** [of rooms] Suite die - **2.** [of furniture] Garnitur die.

suited ['suːtɪd] adj - **1.** [suitable]: **to be suited to/for sthg** für etw geeignet sein - **2.** [compatible]: **to be well/ideally suited** gut/ideal zusammenpassen.

sulfur n US = **sulphur**.

sulk [sʌlk] vi schmollen.

sulky ['sʌlkɪ] adj [remark] beleidigt; [child] schmollend; **to be in a sulky mood** schmollen.

sullen ['sʌlən] adj missmutig.

sulphur UK, **sulfur** US ['sʌlfər] n Schwefel der.

sultana [səl'tɑːnə] n UK [dried grape] Sultanine die.

sultry ['sʌltrɪ] adj - **1.** [weather, day] schwül - **2.** [woman] sinnlich.

sum [sʌm] n Summe die. ⬟ **sum up** vt sep & vi [summarize] zusammenlfassen.

summarize, -ise ['sʌməraɪz] vt & vi zusammenlfassen.

summary ['sʌmərɪ] n Zusammenfassung die.

summer ['sʌmər] ⬦ n Sommer der; **in (the) summer** im Sommer. ⬦ comp Sommer-.

summerhouse ['sʌməhaʊs] (pl [-haʊzɪz]) n Gartenhaus das.

summer school n Ferienkurs der.

summertime ['sʌmətaɪm] n: **in (the) summertime** im Sommer.

summit ['sʌmɪt] n [mountain top, meeting] Gipfel der.

summon ['sʌmən] vt [to sb's office] herbeizitieren; [doctor, fire brigade] rufen. ⬟ **summon up** vt sep [courage, energy] auflbringen.

summons ['sʌmənz] (pl summonses) ⬦ n LAW Vorladung die. ⬦ vt LAW vorlladen.

sumptuous ['sʌmptʃʊəs] adj [decor, fittings] prächtig; [meal] üppig; [hotel] luxuriös.

sun [sʌn] n Sonne die.

sunbathe ['sʌnbeɪð] vi sich sonnen.

sunbed ['sʌnbed] n Sonnenbank die.

sunburn ['sʌnbɜːn] n (U) Sonnenbrand der.

sunburned ['sʌnbɜːnd], **sunburnt** ['sʌnbɜːnt] adj sonnengebräunt; [excessively] sonnenverbrannt.

Sunday ['sʌndɪ] n Sonntag der; **Sunday lunch** Sonntagsessen das; see also **Saturday**.

Sunday school n Sonntagsschule die.

sundial ['sʌndaɪəl] n Sonnenuhr die.

sundown ['sʌndaʊn] n Sonnenuntergang der.

sundry ['sʌndrɪ] adj fml verschiedene; **all and sundry** jedermann. ⬟ **sundries** npl fml Verschiedenes nt.

sunflower ['sʌnˌflaʊər] n Sonnenblume die.

sung [sʌŋ] pp ⬅ **sing**.

sunglasses ['sʌnˌglɑːsɪz] npl Sonnenbrille die.

sunk [sʌŋk] pp ⬅ **sink**.

sunlight ['sʌnlaɪt] n Sonnenlicht das.

sunny ['sʌnɪ] adj liter & fig sonnig; **sunny side up** US [fried egg] einseitig gebraten.

sunrise ['sʌnraɪz] n Sonnenaufgang der.

sunroof ['sʌnruːf] n [of car] Schiebedach das.

sunset ['sʌnset] n Sonnenuntergang der.

sunshade ['sʌnʃeɪd] n Sonnenschirm der.

sunshine ['sʌnʃaɪn] n Sonnenschein der.

sunstroke ['sʌnstrəʊk] n Sonnenstich der.

suntan ['sʌntæn] n Sonnenbräune die.

super ['suːpər] adj inf toll.

superb [suː'pɜːb] adj erstklassig.

supercilious [ˌsuːpə'sɪlɪəs] adj hochnäsig.

superficial [ˌsuːpə'fɪʃl] adj oberflächlich.

superfluous [suː'pɜːflʊəs] adj überflüssig.

superhuman [ˌsuːpə'hjuːmən] adj übermenschlich.

superimpose [ˌsuːpərɪm'pəʊz] vt: **to superimpose sthg on sthg** etw mit etw überlagern.

superintendent [ˌsuːpərɪn'tendənt] n - **1.** UK [of police] Polizeikommissar der, -in die - **2.** fml [of department] Direktor der, -in die.

superior [suː'pɪərɪər] ⬦ adj - **1.** [better]: **superior (to)** besser (als) - **2.** [of high quality - goods] besonders hochwertig; **a person of superior intelligence** ein Mensch von überragender Intelligenz - **3.** [of higher rank]: **superior (to sb)** höher (als jd) - **4.** pej [arrogant] überheblich. ⬦ n [senior] Vorgesetzte der, die.

superlative [suː'pɜːlətɪv] ⬦ adj [of the highest quality - performance] unübertrefflich; [- player] überragend. ⬦ n GRAM Superlativ der.

supermarket ['suːpəˌmɑːkɪt] n Supermarkt der.

supernatural [ˌsuːpə'nætʃrəl] adj übernatürlich.

superpower ['suːpəˌpaʊər] n Supermacht die.

supersede [ˌsuːpə'siːd] vt ablösen.

supersonic [ˌsuːpə'sɒnɪk] adj Überschall-.

superstitious [ˌsuːpə'stɪʃəs] adj abergläubisch.

superstore ['su:pəstɔ:ʳ] n Verbraucher-markt der; **DIY superstore** Heimwerker-markt der.

supervise ['su:pəvaɪz] vt beaufsichtigen.

supervisor ['su:pəvaɪzəʳ] n Aufsicht die; [of university students] Tutor der, -in die.

supper ['sʌpəʳ] n - 1. [main evening meal] Abendessen das - 2. [light evening meal] Abend-brot das.

supple ['sʌpl] adj - 1. [person] beweglich - 2. [material] geschmeidig.

supplement <> n ['sʌplɪmənt] - 1. [addi-tion - to charge] Zuschlag der; [- to diet] Ergän-zung die - 2. [of newspaper] Beilage die; [in book] Nachtrag der. <> vt ['sʌplɪment] ergän-zen.

supplementary [ˌsʌplɪ'mentərɪ] adj [addi-tional] zusätzlich.

supplier [sə'plaɪəʳ] n Lieferant der, -in die.

supply [sə'plaɪ] <> n - 1. [store, reserve] Vorrat der - 2. [network]: **the water/electricity supply** die Wasser-/Stromversorgung - 3. (U) ECON Angebot das. <> vt: **to supply sthg (to sb)** [deliver] etw liefern (an jn); **to supply sb (with sthg)** [deliver] jn (mit etw) beliefern; **he sup-plied the police with the necessary informa-tion** er lieferte der Polizei die nötigen Infor-mationen; **to supply sthg with sthg** etw mit etw versorgen. **supplies** npl Vorräte Pl; [for office] Bürobedarf der; [for army] Nach-schub der.

support [sə'pɔ:t] <> n - 1. [gen] Unterstüt-zung die - 2. [object, person] Stütze die. <> vt - 1. [gen] unterstützen - 2. [physically] stützen - 3. [theory] untermauern.

supporter [sə'pɔ:təʳ] n - 1. [of person, plan] Anhänger der, -in die - 2. SPORT Fan der.

suppose [sə'pəʊz] <> vt [assume] anl-nehmen. <> vi - 1. [assume]: **I suppose (so)** das nehme ich an; **I suppose not** wahrscheinlich nicht - 2. [agree]: **I suppose so** ja, gut; **I suppose not** wahrscheinlich nicht.

supposed [sə'pəʊzd] adj - 1. [doubtful] an-geblich - 2. [intended]: **to be supposed to do sthg** etw tun sollen - 3. [reputed]: **it is sup-posed to be good** es soll gut sein.

supposedly [sə'pəʊzɪdlɪ] adv angeblich.

supposing [sə'pəʊzɪŋ] conj: **supposing you are right** angenommen, dass Sie Recht ha-ben; **supposing he came back?** wenn er nun zurückkäme?

suppress [sə'pres] vt unterdrücken.

supreme [sʊ'pri:m] adj - 1. [highest in rank] Ober- - 2. [great] größte(r) (s).

surcharge ['sɜ:tʃɑ:dʒ] n: **surcharge (on sthg)** Zuschlag der (auf etw (A)).

sure [ʃʊəʳ] <> adj sicher; **to be sure of sthg** sich einer Sache (G) sicher sein; **with such qualifications she can be sure of getting a job** mit so einer Qualifikation findet sie mit Si-cherheit eine Stelle; **be sure to lock the door** denke daran, die Tür abzuschließen; **to make sure (that)...** sicherstellen, dass...; **I'm sure (that)...** ich bin (mir) sicher, dass...; **to be sure of o.s.** selbstsicher sein; [about specific matter] sich (D) seiner Sache sicher sein. <> adv - 1. esp US inf [yes] sicher - 2. US [really] wirk-lich. **for sure** adv: **I don't know for sure** da bin ich nicht ganz sicher; **she'll come for sure** sie kommt bestimmt. **sure enough** adv tatsächlich.

surely ['ʃʊəlɪ] adv [expressing surprise] sicher-lich; **surely you can't be serious?** das ist doch nicht dein Ernst?

surf [sɜ:f] <> n Brandung die. <> vt: **to surf the Internet** im Internet surfen.

surface ['sɜ:fɪs] <> n liter & fig Oberflä-che die; **on the surface** [of person] äußerlich; **to scratch the surface of sthg** fig etw oberfläch-lich behandeln. <> vi liter & fig auftauchen.

surface mail n Post, die auf dem Land-/See-weg befördert wird.

surfboard ['sɜ:fbɔ:d] n Surfbrett das.

surfeit ['sɜ:fɪt] n fml: **surfeit of sthg** Über-maß das an etw (D).

surfing ['sɜ:fɪŋ] n Surfen das.

surge [sɜ:dʒ] <> n [of water] Schwall der; [of electricity] Stoß der; [of interest, support] Wo-ge die. <> vi strömen; [interest, support] anl-schwellen; [sales, applications] in die Höhe schießen.

surgeon ['sɜ:dʒən] n Chirurg der, -in die.

surgery ['sɜ:dʒərɪ] n - 1. MED [performing oper-ations] Chirurgie die; **to have surgery** operiert werden - 2. UK MED [place] Praxis die.

surgical ['sɜ:dʒɪkl] adj - 1. [connected with sur-gery] chirurgisch - 2. [worn as treatment] ortho-pädisch.

surgical spirit n UK Wunddesinfektions-mittel das.

surly ['sɜ:lɪ] adj mürrisch.

surmount [sɜ:'maʊnt] vt [overcome] über-winden.

surname ['sɜ:neɪm] n Nachname der.

surpass [sə'pɑ:s] vt fml [exceed] übertreffen.

surplus ['sɜ:pləs] <> adj überschüssig. <> n: **surplus (of sthg)** Überschuss der (an etw (D)).

surprise [sə'praɪz] <> n Überraschung die. <> vt überraschen.

surprised [sə'praɪzd] adj überrascht.

surprising [sə'praɪzɪŋ] adj überraschend.

surprisingly [sə'praɪzɪŋlɪ] adv überraschen-derweise.

surrender [sə'rendəʳ] <> n Kapitulati-on die. <> vi - 1. [stop fighting]: **to surrender (to sb)** sich (jm) ergeben - 2. fig [give in]: **to sur-render (to sthg)** (etw (D)) nachgeben.

surreptitious [ˌsʌrəp'tɪʃəs] adj heimlich.

surrogate ['sʌrəgeɪt] ⬦ *adj* Ersatz-. ⬦ *n* Ersatz *der*.

surrogate mother *n* Leihmutter *die*.

surround [sə'raʊnd] *vt* - **1.** [gen] umlgeben - **2.** [trap] umzingeln.

surrounding [sə'raʊndɪŋ] *adj* [area, countryside] umliegend. ⬦ **surroundings** *npl* Umgebung *die*.

surveillance [sɜː'veɪləns] *n (U)* Überwachung *die*; **to keep sb under surveillance** jn überwachen.

survey ⬦ *n* ['sɜːveɪ] - **1.** [statistical investigation] Untersuchung *die*; [of public opinion] Umfrage *die* - **2.** [physical examination - of land] Vermessung *die*; [- of building] Begutachtung *die*. ⬦ *vt* [sə'veɪ] - **1.** [contemplate] betrachten - **2.** [investigate statistically] untersuchen - **3.** [examine, assess - land] vermessen; [- building] begutachten.

surveyor [sə'veɪər] *n* [of land] Landvermesser *der*, -in *die*; [of building] Baugutachter *der*, -in *die*.

survival [sə'vaɪvl] *n* [continuing to live] Überleben *das*.

survive [sə'vaɪv] ⬦ *vt* überleben. ⬦ *vi* - **1.** [continue to exist] überleben - **2.** *inf* [cope successfully] es auslhalten.

survivor [sə'vaɪvər] *n* - **1.** [person who escapes death] Überlebende *der, die* - **2.** *fig* [fighter] Kämpfernatur *die*.

susceptible [sə'septəbl] *adj* - **1.** [likely to be influenced]: **susceptible to sthg** empfänglich für etw - **2.** MED: **susceptible to sthg** anfällig für etw.

suspect ⬦ *adj* ['sʌspekt] verdächtig. ⬦ *n* ['sʌspekt] Verdächtige *der, die*. ⬦ *vt* [sə'spekt] - **1.** [distrust] zweifeln an (+ *D*) - **2.** [think likely] vermuten - **3.** [consider guilty]: **to suspect sb (of sthg)** jn (einer Sache *(G)*) verdächtigen.

suspend [sə'spend] *vt* - **1.** [hang] auflhängen - **2.** [temporarily discontinue] zeitweilig einlstellen - **3.** [temporarily remove - from job] suspendieren; [- from school] zeitweilig von der Schule verweisen.

suspender belt [sə'spendər-] *n UK* Strumpfhaltergürtel *der*.

suspenders [sə'spendəz] *npl* - **1.** *UK* [for stockings] Strumpfhalter *Pl*, Strapse *Pl* - **2.** *US* [for trousers] Hosenträger *Pl*.

suspense [sə'spens] *n (U)* Spannung *die*.

suspension [sə'spenʃn] *n* - **1.** [temporary discontinuation] Einstellung *die* - **2.** [removal - from job] Suspendierung *die*; [- from school] zeitweiliger Schulverweis - **3.** AUT Federung *die*.

suspension bridge *n* Hängebrücke *die*.

suspicion [sə'spɪʃn] *n* - **1.** *(U)* [distrust] Misstrauen *das* - **2.** [idea, theory] Verdacht *der*.

suspicious [sə'spɪʃəs] *adj* - **1.** [having suspicions] misstrauisch - **2.** [causing suspicion] verdächtig.

sustain [sə'steɪn] *vt* - **1.** [maintain - interest, opposition, activity] aufrechtlerhalten; [- hope] bewahren; [- rate, speed] beilbehalten - **2.** [nourish physically] ernähren - **3.** [injury, damage] davonltragen - **4.** [withstand - weight] auslhalten.

sustenance ['sʌstɪnəns] *n (U) fml* Nahrung *die*.

SW (*abbr of* **short wave**) UW.

swab [swɒb] *n* [cotton wool] Tupfer *der*.

swagger ['swægər] *vi* stolzieren.

swallow ['swɒləʊ] ⬦ *n* [bird] Schwalbe *die*. ⬦ *vt* - **1.** [food, drink] schlucken - **2.** *fig* [accept] schlucken - **3.** *fig* [anger, tears] hinunterlschlucken. ⬦ *vi* schlucken.

swam [swæm] *pt* ▷ **swim**.

swamp [swɒmp] ⬦ *n* Sumpf *der*. ⬦ *vt* - **1.** [flood] unter Wasser setzen - **2.** [overwhelm]: **to swamp sb/sthg (with sthg)** jn/etw (mit etw) überfluten.

swan [swɒn] *n* [bird] Schwan *der*.

swap [swɒp] *vt* - **1.** [exchange]: **to swap sthg (with sb)** etw (mit jm) tauschen; **to swap sthg (over OR round)** etw (aus)ltauschen - **2.** [replace]: **to swap sthg for sthg** etw gegen etw einltauschen.

swarm [swɔːm] *n* Schwarm *der*.

swarthy ['swɔːðɪ] *adj* dunkel.

swastika ['swɒstɪkə] *n* Hakenkreuz *das*.

swat [swɒt] *vt* totlschlagen.

sway [sweɪ] ⬦ *vt* [influence] beeinflussen. ⬦ *vi* sich wiegen; [drunk person] schwanken.

swear [sweər] (*pt* swore, *pp* sworn) ⬦ *vt* schwören; **to swear to do sthg** schwören, etw zu tun. ⬦ *vi* - **1.** [state emphatically] schwören - **2.** [use swearwords] fluchen.

swearword ['sweəwɜːd] *n* Kraftausdruck *der*.

sweat [swet] ⬦ *n* [perspiration] Schweiß *der*. ⬦ *vi liter & fig* schwitzen.

sweater ['swetər] *n* Pullover *der*.

sweatshirt ['swetʃɜːt] *n* Sweatshirt *das*.

sweaty ['swetɪ] *adj* [clothes] verschwitzt; [skin] schweißnass.

swede [swiːd] *n UK* Steckrübe *die*.

Swede [swiːd] *n* Schwede *der*, -din *die*.

Sweden ['swiːdn] *n* Schweden *nt*.

Swedish ['swiːdɪʃ] ⬦ *adj* schwedisch. ⬦ *n* [language] Schwedisch(e) *das*.

sweep [swiːp] (*pt & pp* swept) ⬦ *n* - **1.** [of arm, hand] Schwung *der* - **2.** [with brush]: **to give sthg a sweep** etw kehren OR fegen - **3.** [chimneysweep] Schornsteinfeger *der*, -in *die*. ⬦ *vt* - **1.** [with brush] fegen, kehren

- 2. [scan] ablsuchen **- 3.** [spread through] überlrollen. **sweep up** vt sep & vi [with brush] zusammenlkehren OR l-fegen.

sweeping ['swi:pɪŋ] adj **- 1.** [effect, change] tief greifend **- 2.** [statement] pauschal.

sweet [swi:t] ⇔ adj **- 1.** [gen] süß **- 2.** [gentle, kind] lieb. ⇔ n UK **- 1.** [candy] Bonbon das **- 2.** [dessert] Nachtisch der, Dessert das.

sweet corn n Mais der.

sweeten ['swi:tn] vt [add sugar to] süßen.

sweetheart ['swi:thɑ:t] n **- 1.** [term of endearment] Liebling der **- 2.** [boyfriend or girlfriend] Freund der, -in die.

sweetness ['swi:tnɪs] n **- 1.** [gen] Süße die **- 2.** [of character, voice] Liebenswürdigkeit die.

sweet pea n Wicke die.

swell [swel] (pt -ed, pp swollen OR -ed) ⇔ vi **- 1.** [become larger]: **to swell (up)** anlschwellen **- 2.** [fill with air - lungs, balloons] sich füllen; [- sails] sich blähen **- 3.** [increase in number] anlwachsen **- 4.** [become louder] anlschwellen. ⇔ vt [increase] steigern. ⇔ n [of sea]: **there is a heavy swell** es herrscht starker Seegang. ⇔ adj US inf klasse, prima.

swelling ['swelɪŋ] n [on body] Schwellung die.

sweltering ['sweltərɪŋ] adj [heat] drückend; [weather, day] drückend heiß.

swept [swept] pt & pp ⊳ **sweep**.

swerve [swɜ:v] vi [vehicle, driver] auslschwenken.

swift [swɪft] ⇔ adj **- 1.** [fast] schnell **- 2.** [prompt] prompt. ⇔ n [bird] Mauersegler der.

swig [swɪg] inf n inf Schluck der.

swill [swɪl] ⇔ n (U) [pig food] Schweinefutter das. ⇔ vt UK [wash] waschen; [glass, cup] auslspülen.

swim [swɪm] (pt swam, pp swum) ⇔ n: **to have a swim** schwimmen; **to go for a swim** schwimmen gehen. ⇔ vi **- 1.** [move through water] schwimmen **- 2.** [feel dizzy]: **my head was swimming** mir war ganz schwindlig.

swimmer ['swɪmər] n Schwimmer der, -in die.

swimming ['swɪmɪŋ] n Schwimmen das; **to go swimming** schwimmen gehen.

swimming cap n Badekappe die.

swimming costume n UK Badeanzug der.

swimming pool n Schwimmbad das.

swimming trunks npl Badehose die.

swimsuit ['swɪmsu:t] n Badeanzug der.

swindle ['swɪndl] ⇔ n Betrug der. ⇔ vt betrügen; **to swindle sb out of sthg** jn um etw betrügen.

swine [swaɪn] n inf pej [person] Schwein das.

swing [swɪŋ] (pt & pp swung) ⇔ n **- 1.** [child's toy] Schaukel die **- 2.** [change - in opinion, mood] Umschwung der **- 3.** [swaying movement] Schwingen das **- 4.** inf [blow]: **to take a swing at sb** nach jm schlagen **- 5.** phr: **to be in full swing** in vollem Gange sein. ⇔ vt **- 1.** [move back and forth] hin und her schwingen; [arms] schwingen mit **- 2.** [turn] schwenken. ⇔ vi **- 1.** [move back and forth] hin und her schwingen; [dangle - legs] baumeln **- 2.** [turn]: **the door swung open** die Tür schwang auf; **he swung round** er drehte sich um **- 3.** [change] umlschwenken; **the party has swung to the left** die Partei hat einen Linksschwenk gemacht.

swing bridge n Drehbrücke die.

swing door n Pendeltür die.

swingeing ['swɪndʒɪŋ] adj esp UK [cuts] drastisch; [criticism] scharf.

swipe [swaɪp] ⇔ vt **- 1.** inf [steal] klauen **- 2.** [plastic card] durchlziehen. ⇔ vi: **to swipe at sb** nach jm schlagen.

swirl [swɜ:l] ⇔ n Wirbel der. ⇔ vi wirbeln.

swish [swɪʃ] ⇔ adj inf [posh] schick. ⇔ vt [tail] schlagen mit.

Swiss [swɪs] ⇔ adj Schweizer, schweizerisch. ⇔ n Schweizer der, -in die. ⇔ npl: **the Swiss** die Schweizer Pl.

switch [swɪtʃ] ⇔ n **- 1.** [control device] Schalter der **- 2.** [change - of policy] Änderung die; **the switch to a different system** die Umstellung auf ein anderes System. ⇔ vt **- 1.** [transfer] wechseln; **to switch sthg to sthg** [conversation, attention] etw auf etw (A) lenken; [allegiance] etw auf etw (A) übertragen **- 2.** [swap, exchange] vertauschen; **to switch jobs** den Arbeitsplatz wechseln. **switch off** vt sep [device] auslschalten. **switch on** vt sep [device] anlschalten.

switchboard ['swɪtʃbɔ:d] n Zentrale die.

Switzerland ['swɪtsələnd] n Schweiz die.

swivel ['swɪvl] (UK) (US) ⇔ vt drehen. ⇔ vi sich drehen.

swivel chair n Drehstuhl der.

swollen ['swəʊln] ⇔ pp ⊳ **swell**. ⇔ adj [part of body] geschwollen; [river] angeschwollen; **swollen with pride** stolzgeschwellt.

swoop [swu:p] ⇔ n [raid] Razzia die. ⇔ vi [plane] einen Sturzflug machen; [bird] herablstoßen.

swop [swɒp] n, vt & vi = **swap**.

sword [sɔ:d] n Schwert das.

swordfish ['sɔ:dfɪʃ] (pl inv OR -es) n Schwertfisch der.

swore [swɔ:r] pt ⊳ **swear**.

sworn [swɔ:n] pp ⊳ **swear**.

swot [swɒt] UK inf ⇔ n pej Streber der, -in die. ⇔ vi: **to swot (for sthg)** büffeln (für etw).

swum [swʌm] pp ⊳ **swim**.

swung [swʌŋ] pt & pp ⊳ **swing**.

sycamore ['sɪkəmɔːʳ] n Bergahorn der.

syllable ['sɪləbl] n Silbe die.

syllabus ['sɪləbəs] (pl -buses OR -bi [-baɪ]) n Lehrplan der.

symbol ['sɪmbl] n Symbol das.

symbolize, -ise ['sɪmbəlaɪz] vt symbolisieren.

symmetry ['sɪmətrɪ] n (U) Symmetrie die.

sympathetic [ˌsɪmpə'θetɪk] adj - 1. [understanding] verständnisvoll - 2. [willing to support] wohlgesinnt; **to be sympathetic to sthg** einer Sache (D) wohlwollend gegenüberstehen; [new ideas] für etw zugänglich sein.

sympathize, -ise ['sɪmpəθaɪz] vi - 1. [feel sorry] mitfühlen, Mitleid haben; **to sympathize with sb** mit jm mitfühlen - 2. [understand]: **to sympathize with sthg** für etw Verständnis haben - 3. [support]: **to sympathize with sthg** mit etw sympathisieren.

sympathizer, -iser ['sɪmpəθaɪzəʳ] n [supporter] Sympathisant der, -in die.

sympathy ['sɪmpəθɪ] n [compassion] Mitgefühl das, Mitleid das; (phrase): **to have sympathy for sb** Mitleid mit jm haben.

symphony ['sɪmfənɪ] n Sinfonie die.

symposium [sɪm'pəʊzjəm] (pl -siums OR -sia [-zjə]) n fml Symposium das.

symptom ['sɪmptəm] n liter & fig Symptom das.

synagogue ['sɪnəgɒg] n Synagoge die.

syndicate n ['sɪndɪkət] Syndikat das.

syndrome ['sɪndrəʊm] n MED [set of symptoms] Syndrom das.

synonym ['sɪnənɪm] n: **synonym (for OR of sthg)** Synonym das (für OR von etw).

synopsis [sɪ'nɒpsɪs] (pl -ses [-siːz]) n Zusammenfassung die.

syntax ['sɪntæks] n LING Syntax die.

synthetic [sɪn'θetɪk] adj - 1. [man-made] synthetisch; **synthetic fibre** Kunstfaser die - 2. pej [insincere] künstlich.

syphilis ['sɪfɪlɪs] n Syphilis die.

syphon ['saɪfn] n & vt = **siphon**.

Syria ['sɪrɪə] n Syrien nt.

syringe [sɪ'rɪndʒ] n Spritze die.

syrup ['sɪrəp] n (U) - 1. [sugar and water] Sirup der - 2. UK: **(golden) syrup** Sirup der (Brotaufstrich) - 3. [medicine]: **cough syrup** Hustensaft der.

system ['sɪstəm] n System das; **road/railway/transport system** Straßen-/Bahn-/Transportnetz das; **stereo system** Stereoanlage die; **to get sthg out of one's system** inf etw loslwerden.

systematic [ˌsɪstə'mætɪk] adj systematisch.

systems analyst ['sɪstəmz-] n COMPUT Systemanalytiker der, -in die.

T

t (pl t's OR ts), **T** (pl T's OR Ts) [tiː] n t das, T das.

ta [tɑː] excl UK inf danke.

tab [tæb] n - 1. [of maker] Etikett das; [bearing owner's name] Namensschild das - 2. [for opening can] Verschluss der - 3. US [bill] Rechnung die; **to pick up the tab** die Rechnung übernehmen - 4. phr: **to keep tabs on sb** jn genau beobachten.

tabby ['tæbɪ] n: **tabby (cat)** getigerte Katze.

table ['teɪbl] ⬦ n - 1. [piece of furniture] Tisch der - 2. [diagram] Tabelle die. ⬦ vt UK [propose] einlbringen.

tablecloth ['teɪblklɒθ] n Tischdecke die, Tischtuch das.

table football n Tischfußball der.

table lamp n Tischlampe die.

tablemat ['teɪblmæt] n Set das.

tablespoon ['teɪblspuːn] n Servierlöffel der.

tablet ['tæblɪt] n - 1. [pill] Tablette die - 2. [piece of stone] Tafel die - 3. [of soap] Stück das.

table tennis n Tischtennis das.

tabloid ['tæblɔɪd] n: **tabloid (newspaper)** Boulevardzeitung die; **the tabloid press** die Boulevardpresse.

tacit ['tæsɪt] adj stillschweigend.

taciturn ['tæsɪtɜːn] adj schweigsam.

tack [tæk] ⬦ n - 1. [nail] kleiner Nagel - 2. NAUT Kurs der - 3. fig [course of action] Weg der. ⬦ vt - 1. [fasten with nail]: **to tack sthg to sthg** etw an etw (A) nageln - 2. [in sewing] heften. ⬦ vi NAUT kreuzen.

tackle ['tækl] ⬦ n - 1. FTBL Tackling das - 2. RUGBY Fassen das - 3. [equipment, gear] Ausrüstung die - 4. [for lifting] Flaschenzug der. ⬦ vt - 1. [deal with] anlgehen - 2. [attack & FTBL] anlgreifen - 3. RUGBY fassen.

tacky ['tækɪ] adj - 1. inf [cheap] billig; [tasteless] geschmacklos - 2. [sticky] klebrig.

tact [tækt] n Takt der; **he has no tact** er hat kein Taktgefühl.

tactful ['tæktfʊl] adj taktvoll.

tactic ['tæktɪk] n Taktik die. ⬦ **tactics** n (U) MIL Taktik die.

tactical ['tæktɪkl] adj taktisch.

tactile adj: **a tactile person** eine Person, die Körperkontakt mag.

tactless ['tæktlɪs] adj taktlos.

tadpole ['tædpəʊl] n Kaulquappe die.

tag [tæg] *n* - **1.** [on clothing - of maker] Etikett *das*; [- bearing owner's name] Namensschild *das* - **2.** [of paper] Schild *das*; **price tag** Preisschild *das*; **luggage tag** Gepäckanhänger *der*. ◆ **tag along** *vi inf* mitlkommen.

tail [teɪl] ◇ *n* - **1.** [of animal, bird, fish] Schwanz *der* - **2.** [of coat] Schoß *der*; [of shirt] Zipfel *der*. ◇ *vt inf* [follow - person] beschatten; [- car] folgen (+ *D*). ◆ **tails** ◇ *adv* [side of coin] Zahl *die*; **heads or tails?** Kopf oder Zahl? ◇ *npl* [formal dress] Frack *der*. ◆ **tail off** *vi* [decrease in volume] leiser werden.

tailback ['teɪlbæk] *n* UK Rückstau *der*.

tailcoat ['teɪlkəʊt] *n* Frack *der*.

tail end *n* Ende *das*.

tailgate ['teɪlgeɪt] *n* [of hatchback car] Heckklappe *die*.

tailor ['teɪlə'] ◇ *n* Schneider *der*, -in *die*. ◇ *vt* [adjust]: **to tailor sthg to sthg** [plans, policy] etw auf etw (*A*) zulschneiden; [product] etw auf etw (*A*) ablstimmen.

tailor-made *adj fig*: **to be tailor-made for sb** [role, job] genau auf jn zugeschnitten sein.

tailwind ['teɪlwind] *n* Rückenwind *der*.

tainted ['teɪntɪd] *adj* - **1.** [reputation] beschmutzt; [money] schmutzig - **2.** US [food] verdorben.

Taiwan [ˌtaɪ'wɑːn] *n* Taiwan *nt*.

take [teɪk] (*pt* took, *pp* taken) ◇ *vt* - **1.** [gen] nehmen; **she took my arm** sie nahm mich beim Arm; **to take the train/bus** den Zug/Bus nehmen; **to take a bath** ein Bad nehmen; **to take an exam/a photo/a walk** eine Prüfung/ein Foto/einen Spaziergang machen; **to take risks** Risiken einlgehen; **to take a decision** eine Entscheidung treffen; **to take an interest in sthg** sich für etw interessieren; **to take pity on sb** Mitleid mit jm haben; **I take the view that...** ich bin der Meinung, dass...; **to take a seat** Platz nehmen; **to be taken ill** krank werden - **2.** [bring, accompany] bringen; [take along] mitlnehmen; **to take sthg to sb** jm etw bringen; **to take sb to the station** jn zum Bahnhof bringen; **he took her to the theatre** er ging mit ihr ins Theater - **3.** [remove, steal] (mit)lnehmen; **to take sthg from sb** jm etw (ab)lnehmen; [steal] jm etw weglnehmen - **4.** [capture - city] einlnehmen, erobern; [- prisoner] machen - **5.** [control, power] übernehmen; **to take charge** die Leitung übernehmen - **6.** [accept] anlnehmen; [subj: machine] nehmen; [opportunity] wahrlnehmen; [responsibility] übernehmen; **do you take travellers' cheques?** nehmen Sie Travellerschecks?; **to take sb's advice** js Rat (*D*) folgen - **7.** [receive - prize, praise] bekommen; **to take criticism** kritisiert werden - **8.** [contain] fassen; **the car can take six people** in dem Auto haben sechs Leute Platz - **9.** [size in clothes, shoes] haben; **what size do you take?** welche Größe haben Sie?; **I take a (size) 34** ich habe Größe 34 - **10.** [bear] ertra-

gen; **I can't take any more** mir reichts - **11.** [require] erfordern; **how long will it take?** wie lange wird es dauern?, wie lange braucht es? - **12.** [react to] auflnehmen; **to take sthg seriously** etw ernst nehmen; **to take sthg badly** etw schlecht auflnehmen; **to take sthg the wrong way** etw falsch aufllfassen - **13.** [temperature, pulse] messen - **14.** [rent] mieten - **15.** [make - sum of money] einlnehmen - **16.** GRAM: **this verb takes the dative** dieses Verb wird mit dem Dativ konstruiert - **17.** [assume]: **I take it (that)...** ich gehe davon aus, dass... ◇ *n* CIN Einstellung *die*. ◆ **take after** *vt insep* nachlschlagen (+ *D*); **he takes after his mother/father** er schlägt nach seiner Mutter/seinem Vater. ◆ **take apart** *vt sep* [dismantle] auseinanderlnehmen. ◆ **take away** *vt sep* - **1.** [remove]: **to take sthg away (from sb)** (jm) etw weglnehmen; **is it to take away?** zum Mitnehmen? - **2.** [deduct] ablziehen. ◆ **take back** *vt sep* - **1.** [return] zurücklbringen - **2.** [faulty goods, statement] zurücklnehmen. ◆ **take down** *vt sep* - **1.** [pictures, curtains] ablnehmen; [scaffolding, tent] ablbauen - **2.** [from shelf] herunterlnehmen - **3.** [write down] auflschreiben - **4.** [lower] herunterllassen. ◆ **take in** *vt sep* - **1.** [bring inside - washing] hereinlbringen - **2.** [deceive] hereinllegen; **to be taken in (by sb/sthg)** (auf jn/etw) hereinlfallen - **3.** [understand] auflnehmen - **4.** [include] einlschließen - **5.** [provide accommodation for] auflnehmen - **6.** [clothes] enger machen. ◆ **take off** ◇ *vt sep* - **1.** [remove] ablnehmen; [clothing] auslziehen; **to take one's clothes off** sich auslziehen - **2.** [have as holiday]: **to take time off** sich (*D*) freilnehmen; **to take a week off** sich (*D*) eine Woche freilnehmen - **3.** UK *inf* [imitate] nachlläffen. ◇ *vi* - **1.** [plane] ablheben - **2.** [go away suddenly] verschwinden. ◆ **take on** *vt sep* - **1.** [job, responsibility] anlnehmen - **2.** [employ] anlstellen, einlstellen - **3.** [confront] sich anllegen mit; [competitor, sports team] anltreten gegen. ◆ **take out** *vt sep* - **1.** [remove - from container] herauslnehmen; [- tooth] ziehen; [- money from bank] ablheben - **2.** [library book] auslleihen - **3.** [loan] auflnehmen; [insurance policy] ablschließen; [patent] anlmelden - **4.** [go out with] auslgehen mit. ◆ **take over** ◇ *vt sep* [company, job] übernehmen. ◇ *vi* - **1.** [take control] die Kontrolle übernehmen - **2.** [in job]: **to take over from sb** jn abllösen. ◆ **take to** *vt insep* - **1.** [come to like] mögen - **2.** [begin]: **to take to doing sthg** anlfangen, etw zu tun; **she's taken to getting up earlier** sie steht nun früher auf; **to take to drink** zu trinken anlfangen. ◆ **take up** *vt sep* - **1.** [begin - post] anltreten; [- job] auflnehmen; **to take up the clarinet** anlfangen, Klarinette zu spielen - **2.** [time, effort, space] in Anspruch nehmen - **3.** [trousers, dress] kürzen. ◆ **take up on** *vt sep* [accept]: **to take sb up on an offer** js Angebot anlnehmen.

takeaway UK ['teɪkə,weɪ], **takeout** US ['teɪkaʊt] <> n [food] Essen das zum Mitnehmen. <> comp [food] zum Mitnehmen.

taken ['teɪkn] pp ▷ **take**.

takeoff ['teɪkɒf] n [of plane] Start der.

takeout n US = **takeaway**.

takeover ['teɪk,əʊvər] n Übernahme die.

takings ['teɪkɪŋz] npl Einnahmen Pl.

talc [tælk], **talcum (powder)** ['tælkəm-] n Talk der.

tale [teɪl] n Geschichte die.

talent ['tælənt] n Talent das.

talented ['tæləntɪd] adj talentiert.

talk [tɔːk] <> n - **1.** [conversation] Gespräch das, Unterhaltung die; **to have a talk** sich unterhalten; [more formal] ein Gespräch führen - **2.** [gossip] Gerede das - **3.** [lecture] Vortrag der. <> vi - **1.** [speak] sprechen, reden; **to talk to sb** mit jm reden OR sprechen; **to talk to o.s.** Selbstgespräche führen; **to talk about sb/ sthg** über jn/etw sprechen OR reden; **talking of him/that, …** da wir gerade von ihm/davon sprechen …; **he's talking of buying a car** er redet davon, dass er sich ein neues Auto kaufen will - **2.** [gossip] klatschen - **3.** [make a speech] eine Rede halten; **to talk on** OR **about sthg** über etw (A) sprechen. <> vt - **1.** [politics, sport, business] reden über (+ A) OR von - **2.** [nonsense] reden. ▸ **talks** npl Gespräche Pl. ▸ **talk into** vt sep: **to talk sb into doing sthg** jn dazu überreden, etw zu tun. ▸ **talk out of** vt sep: **to talk sb out of doing sthg** jm ausreden, etw zu tun. ▸ **talk over** vt sep [discuss] bereden, besprechen.

talkative ['tɔːkətɪv] adj gesprächig.

talk show n US Talkshow die.

tall [tɔːl] adj - **1.** [person] groß; **I'm 5 feet tall** ich bin 1,50 m groß; **how tall are you?** wie groß bist du? - **2.** [building, tree] hoch.

tally ['tælɪ] <> n [record]: **to keep a tally of sthg** über etw (A) Buch führen. <> vi übereinstimmen.

talon ['tælən] n Kralle die.

tambourine [,tæmbə'riːn] n Tamburin das.

tame [teɪm] <> adj - **1.** [animal, bird] zahm - **2.** pej [dull] lahm. <> vt - **1.** [animal, bird] zähmen; [lion] bändigen - **2.** [person] bändigen.

tamper ['tæmpər] ▸ **tamper with** vt insep sich (D) zu schaffen machen an (+ D).

tampon ['tæmpɒn] n Tampon der.

tan [tæn] <> adj [light brown] hellbraun. <> n [from sun] Bräune die; **to get a tan** braun werden. <> vi braun werden.

tangent ['tændʒənt] n GEOM Tangente die; **to go off at a tangent** fig plötzlich vom Thema abschweifen.

tangerine [,tændʒə'riːn] n Mandarine die.

tangible ['tændʒəbl] adj [difference, benefit] merklich; [results] greifbar.

tangle ['tæŋgl] n - **1.** [mass] Gewirr das - **2.** fig [mess] Durcheinander das; **to get (o.s.) into a tangle** sich verstricken.

tank [tæŋk] n - **1.** [container] Tank der; **(fish) tank** Aquarium das - **2.** MIL Panzer der.

tanker ['tæŋkər] n - **1.** [ship] Tanker der - **2.** [truck] Tankwagen der.

tanned [tænd] adj [suntanned] braun (gebrannt).

Tannoy® ['tænɔɪ] n Lautsprecheranlage die.

tantalizing ['tæntəlaɪzɪŋ] adj verlockend.

tantamount ['tæntəmaʊnt] adj: **to be tantamount to sthg** einer Sache (D) gleichkommen.

tantrum ['tæntrəm] (pl -s) n Wutanfall der.

Tanzania [,tænzə'nɪə] n Tansania nt.

tap [tæp] <> n - **1.** [device] Hahn der; **the hot(-water)/cold(-water) tap** der Warmwasser-/Kaltwasserhahn - **2.** [light blow] Klaps der; **she gave him a tap on the shoulder** sie klopfte ihm auf die Schulter; [on door] Klopfen das. <> vt - **1.** [knock] klopfen - **2.** [make use of] erschließen - **3.** [listen secretly to] abhören.

tap dance n Stepptanz der.

tape [teɪp] <> n - **1.** [magnetic tape] Magnetband das - **2.** [cassette] Kassette die - **3.** [adhesive material] Klebeband das. <> vt - **1.** [record] aufnehmen - **2.** [fasten with adhesive tape] (mit Klebeband) verkleben OR zukleben; **to tape together** zusammenkleben.

tape measure n Maßband das.

taper ['teɪpər] vi [corridor] sich verengen; [trousers] nach unten enger werden.

tape recorder n Tonbandgerät das; [cassette recorder] Kassettenrekorder der.

tapestry ['tæpɪstrɪ] n [piece of work] Wandteppich der.

tar [tɑːr] n Teer der.

target ['tɑːgɪt] <> n - **1.** [of missile, bomb] Ziel das - **2.** [for archery, shooting] Zielscheibe die - **3.** fig [butt of criticism] Zielscheibe die - **4.** fig [goal] Ziel das. <> vt - **1.** [aim weapon at] zielen auf (+ A) - **2.** [channel resources towards] sich (D) zum Ziel setzen; **to target the young** die Jugendlichen als Zielgruppe haben.

tariff ['tærɪf] n - **1.** [tax] Zoll der - **2.** UK [price list] Preisliste die.

Tarmac® ['tɑːmæk] n [material] Makadam der. ▸ **tarmac** n AERON: **the tarmac** die Rollbahn.

tarnish ['tɑːnɪʃ] vt - **1.** [make dull] stumpf werden lassen - **2.** fig [reputation] beflecken.

tarpaulin [tɑː'pɔːlɪn] n [sheet] Plane die.

tart [tɑːt] <> adj - **1.** [bitter-tasting] herb; [fruit] sauer - **2.** [sarcastic] scharf. <> n - **1.** [sweet pastry] Kuchen der; [small] Törtchen das; **fruit tart** Obstkuchen/-törtchen - **2.** UK v inf [prostitute] Nutte *die*. ◆ **tart up** *vt sep UK inf pej* [building, room] auflmotzen; **to tart o.s. up** sich aufltakeln.

tartan ['tɑːtn] ◇ *n* - 1. *(U)* [cloth] Schottenstoff *der* - 2. [pattern] Schottenkaro *das*. ◇ *comp* im Schottenkaro.

task [tɑːsk] *n* Aufgabe *die*.

task force *n* - 1. MIL Spezialeinheit *die* - 2. [group of helpers] Kommando *das*.

tassel ['tæsl] *n* Quaste *die*.

taste [teɪst] ◇ *n* - 1. [sense of taste] Geschmackssinn *der* - 2. [flavour] Geschmack *der*; **to have a funny taste** komisch schmecken - 3. [try] Kostprobe *die*; **to have a taste** probieren - 4. *fig* [liking, preference]: **taste (for sthg)** Vorliebe *die* (für etw) - 5. *fig* [experience]: **his first taste of success** sein erstes Erfolgserlebnis; **I've had a taste of power** ich habe erfahren, wie es ist, Macht zu haben - 6. *(U)* [discernment] Geschmack *der*; **she has (good) taste** sie hat (guten) Geschmack; **in bad taste** geschmacklos; **in good taste** geschmackvoll. ◇ *vt* - 1. [food - experience flavour of] schmecken; [- test, try] probieren, kosten - 2. *fig*: **to taste success** ein Erfolgserlebnis haben. ◇ *vi* schmecken; **to taste of/like sthg** nach/wie etw schmecken.

tasteful ['teɪstful] *adj* geschmackvoll.

tasteless ['teɪstlɪs] *adj liter* & *fig* geschmacklos.

tasty ['teɪstɪ] *adj* schmackhaft.

tatters ['tætəz] *npl*: **to be in tatters** [clothes] in Fetzen sein; *fig* [confidence, reputation] sehr angeschlagen sein.

tattoo [tə'tuː] *(pl -s)* ◇ *n* [design] Tätowierung *die*. ◇ *vt* tätowieren.

tatty ['tætɪ] *adj UK inf pej* schäbig.

taught [tɔːt] *pt* & *pp* ▷ **teach**.

taunt [tɔːnt] ◇ *vt* verspotten. ◇ *n* spöttische Bemerkung.

Taurus ['tɔːrəs] *n* Stier *der*; **I'm a Taurus** ich bin Stier.

taut [tɔːt] *adj* straff.

tawdry ['tɔːdrɪ] *adj pej* geschmacklos.

tax [tæks] ◇ *n* [money paid to government] Steuer *die*. ◇ *vt* - 1. [gen] besteuern - 2. [patience, ingenuity] strapazieren.

taxable ['tæksəbl] *adj* steuerpflichtig.

tax allowance *n* Steuerfreibetrag *der*.

taxation [tæk'seɪʃn] *n* - 1. [system] Besteuerung *die* - 2. [amount] Steuer *die*.

tax collector *n* Finanzbeamte *der*, -tin *die*.

tax disc *n UK* Steuermarke *die*.

tax-free *UK*, **tax-exempt** *US adj* steuerfrei.

taxi ['tæksɪ] ◇ *n* Taxi *das*. ◇ *vi* [plane] rollen.

taxi driver *n* Taxifahrer *der*, -in *die*.

tax inspector *n* Steuerprüfer *der*, -in *die*.

taxi rank *UK*, **taxi stand** *n* Taxistand *der*.

taxpayer ['tæks,peɪər] *n* Steuerzahler *der*, -in *die*.

tax return *n* Steuererklärung *die*.

TB *(abbr of tuberculosis)* *n* TB *die*.

tea [tiː] *n* - 1. [drink] Tee *der* - 2. *UK* [afternoon meal] Nachmittagstee *der* - 3. *UK* [evening meal] Abendessen *das*.

teabag ['tiːbæg] *n* Teebeutel *der*.

tea break *n UK* Teepause *die*.

teach [tiːtʃ] *(pt* & *pp* **taught)** ◇ *vt* - 1. [gen] unterrichten; **to teach sb sthg** jm Unterricht geben in etw *(D)*, jn in etw *(D)* unterrichten; **to teach sb to swim** jm das Schwimmen beibringen; **to teach (sb) that...** (jn)(be)lehren, dass... - 2. [advocate] lehren; **to teach sb sthg**, **to teach sb to do sthg** jn etw lehren; **to teach sb to do sthg** jn lehren, etw zu tun. ◇ *vi* unterrichten.

teacher ['tiːtʃər] *n* Lehrer *der*, -in *die*.

teaching ['tiːtʃɪŋ] *n* - 1. [profession, work] Unterrichten *das* - 2. [thing taught] Lehre *die*.

tea cloth *n* - 1. [tablecloth] (kleine) Tischdecke *die* - 2. [tea towel] Geschirrtuch *das*.

tea cosy *UK*, **tea cozy** *US n* Teewärmer *der*.

teacup ['tiːkʌp] *n* Teetasse *die*.

teak [tiːk] *n* Teakholz *das*.

team [tiːm] *n* - 1. SPORT Team *das*, Mannschaft *die* - 2. [group] Team *das*.

teammate ['tiːmmeɪt] *n* Mannschaftsmitglied *das*.

teamwork ['tiːmwɜːk] *n (U)* Teamarbeit *die*.

teapot ['tiːpɒt] *n* Teekanne *die*.

tear[1] [tɪər] *n* [when crying] Träne *die*.

tear[2] [teər] *(pt* **tore**, *pp* **torn)** ◇ *vt* - 1. [rip] zerreißen - 2. [remove roughly] reißen. ◇ *vi* - 1. [rip] (zer)reißen - 2. *inf* [move quickly] rasen. ◇ *n* [rip] Riss *der*. ◆ **tear apart** *vt sep* - 1. [rip up] zerreißen - 2. [upset greatly] fertig machen. ◆ **tear down** *vt sep* [building, poster] ablreißen. ◆ **tear up** *vt sep* zerreißen.

teardrop ['tɪədrɒp] *n* Träne *die*.

tearful ['tɪəful] *adj* [person] tränenüberströmt.

tear gas [tɪər-] *n* Tränengas *das*.

tearoom ['tiːrʊm] *n* Teestube *die*.

tease [tiːz] ◇ *n inf* - 1. [joker] Witzbold *der* - 2. [sexually] Schäker *der*, -in *die*. ◇ *vt*: **to tease sb (about sthg)** jn (wegen etw) auflziehen.

tea service, **tea set** *n* Teeservice *das*.

teaspoon ['tiːspuːn] *n* Teelöffel *der*.

teat [tiːt] *n* - 1. [of animal] Zitze *die* - 2. [of bottle] Sauger *der*.

teatime ['tiːtaɪm] *n (U) UK* [in evening] Abendessenszeit *die*; [in afternoon] Teezeit *die*.

tea towel *n* Geschirrtuch *das*.

technical ['teknɪkl] *adj* technisch; **technical term** Fachbegriff *der*.

technical college n UK ≃ Fachhochschule die.

technicality [ˌteknɪˈkælətɪ] n - **1.** [intricacy] technische Einzelheit - **2.** [petty rule] Formsache die.

technically [ˈteknɪklɪ] adv - **1.** [theoretically] theoretisch - **2.** [scientifically] technisch.

technician [tekˈnɪʃn] n [worker] Techniker der, -in die.

technique [tekˈniːk] n Technik die.

technological [ˌteknəˈlɒdʒɪkl] adj technologisch.

technology [tekˈnɒlədʒɪ] n Technologie die.

teddy [ˈtedɪ] n: **teddy (bear)** Teddy(bär) der.

tedious [ˈtiːdjəs] adj langweilig.

tee [tiː] n GOLF Tee das, Abschlag der.

teem [tiːm] vi - **1.** [rain] gießen - **2.** [be busy]: **to be teeming with** wimmeln von.

teenage [ˈtiːneɪdʒ] adj Teenager-; [children] halbwüchsig.

teenager [ˈtiːnˌeɪdʒər] n Teenager der.

teens [tiːnz] npl: **to be in one's teens** im Teenageralter sein.

tee shirt n T-Shirt das.

teeter [ˈtiːtər] vi - **1.** [wobble] schwanken - **2.** fig [be in danger]: **to be teetering on the brink of disaster** am Rande einer Katastrophe stehen.

teeth [tiːθ] Pl ⊏▷ **tooth**.

teethe [tiːð] vi [baby] zahnen.

teething troubles npl fig Anfangsschwierigkeiten Pl.

teetotaller UK, **teetotaler** US [tiːˈtəʊtlər] n Abstinenzler der, -in die.

tel. (abbr of telephone) Tel.

telecommunications [ˈtelɪkəˌmjuːnɪˈkeɪʃnz] npl Telekommunikationswesen das.

telegram [ˈtelɪɡræm] n Telegramm das.

telegraph [ˈtelɪɡrɑːf] <> n Telegraf der. <> vt telegrafieren.

telegraph pole, telegraph post UK n Telegrafenmast der.

telepathy [tɪˈlepəθɪ] n Telepathie die.

telephone [ˈtelɪfəʊn] <> n Telefon das; **to be on the telephone** UK [connected] Telefon haben; [speaking] am Telefon sein. <> vt anrufen. <> vi telefonieren.

telephone book n Telefonbuch das.

telephone booth n UK Telefonkabine die.

telephone box n UK Telefonzelle die.

telephone call n Telfonanruf der, Telefongespräch das; **to make a telephone call** telefonieren.

telephone directory n Telefonbuch das.

telephone number n Telefonnummer die.

telephonist [tɪˈlefənɪst] n UK Telefonist der, -in die.

telescope [ˈtelɪskəʊp] n Teleskop das.

teletext [ˈtelɪtekst] n Videotext der.

televise [ˈtelɪvaɪz] vt im Fernsehen übertragen.

television [ˈtelɪˌvɪʒn] n - **1.** [medium, industry] Fernsehen das; **on television** im Fernsehen - **2.** [apparatus] Fernseher der.

television set n Fernseher der.

telex [ˈteleks] <> n Telex das. <> vt (ein) Telex schicken (+ D); [message] telexen.

tell [tel] (pt & pp **told**) <> vt - **1.** [fact] sagen; [story, joke, lie] erzählen; **to tell sb (that)** jm sagen, dass; **to tell sb sthg, to tell sthg to sb** jm etw erzählen; **to tell the truth** die Wahrheit sagen; **to tell sb the time** im sagen, wie spät es ist - **2.** [instruct, reveal] sagen; **to tell sb to do sthg** jm sagen, dass er/sie etw tun soll; **to tell sb (that)** jm sagen, dass - **3.** [judge, recognize] wissen; **to tell the time** die Uhr lesen können. <> vi - **1.** [reveal secret]: **he won't tell** er wird nichts sagen - **2.** [judge] beurteilen - **3.** [have effect] sich zeigen. ▭▶ **tell apart** vt sep unterscheiden. ▭▶ **tell off** vt sep ausschimpfen.

telling [ˈtelɪŋ] adj - **1.** [effective] wirkungsvoll - **2.** [revealing] aufschlussreich.

telly [ˈtelɪ] n UK inf - **1.** [medium] Fernsehen das; **on telly** im Fernsehen - **2.** [apparatus] Flimmerkiste die.

temp [temp] UK inf <> n (abbr of **temporary (employee)**) Zeitarbeitskraft die. <> vi als Zeitarbeitskraft arbeiten.

temper [ˈtempər] <> n - **1.** [state of mind, mood] Laune die; **to lose one's temper** die Beherrschung verlieren - **2.** [angry state]: **to be in a temper** wütend sein - **3.** [temperament] Temperament das. <> vt fml [moderate] mäßigen.

temperament [ˈtemprəmənt] n Temperament das.

temperamental [ˌtemprəˈmentl] adj launisch, launenhaft.

temperature [ˈtemprətʃər] n Temperatur die; **to have a temperature** Fieber haben.

tempestuous [temˈpestjʊəs] adj liter & fig stürmisch.

template [ˈtemplɪt] n [of shape, letter] Schablone die.

temple [ˈtempl] n - **1.** RELIG Tempel der - **2.** ANAT Schläfe die.

temporarily [ˌtempəˈrerəlɪ] adv vorübergehend.

temporary [ˈtempərərɪ] adj vorübergehend; [job] befristet.

tempt [tempt] vt [entice]: **to tempt sb to do sthg** jn dazu verlocken, etw zu tun.

temptation [tempˈteɪʃn] n - **1.** [state] Versuchung die - **2.** [tempting thing] Verlockung die.

tempting [ˈtemptɪŋ] adj verlockend.

ten [ten] num zehn; see also **six**.

tenable ['tenəbl] *adj* [reasonable, credible] haltbar.

tenacious [tɪ'neɪʃəs] *adj* hartnäckig.

tenancy ['tenənsɪ] *n* - **1.** [period - of building] Mietdauer *die*; [- of land] Pachtzeit *die* - **2.** [possession - of building] Mieten *das*; [- of land] Pachten *das*.

tenant ['tenənt] *n* Mieter *der*, -in *die*.

tend [tend] *vt* - **1.** [have tendency]: **to tend to do sthg** [person] dazu neigen, etw zu tun - **2.** [look after] sich kümmern um.

tendency ['tendənsɪ] *n* - **1.** [trend]: **tendency towards sthg** Tendenz *die* zu etw - **2.** [leaning, habit] Neigung *die*; **to have the tendency to do sthg** die Neigung haben, etw zu tun.

tender ['tendər] ⟨⟩ *adj* - **1.** [caring, gentle] zärtlich - **2.** [meat] zart - **3.** [sore] empfindlich. ⟨⟩ *n* COMM Angebot *das.* ⟨⟩ *vt fml* [offer - money] an⎮bieten; [- resignation] ein⎮reichen.

tendon ['tendən] *n* Sehne *die.*

tenement ['tenəmənt] *n* Mietshaus *das.*

tennis ['tenɪs] *n* Tennis *das.*

tennis ball *n* Tennisball *der.*

tennis court *n* Tennisplatz *der.*

tennis racket *n* Tennisschläger *der.*

tenor ['tenər] *n* Tenor *der.*

tense [tens] ⟨⟩ *adj* angespannt. ⟨⟩ *n* GRAM Zeit(form) *die.* ⟨⟩ *vt* [muscles] an⎮spannen.

tension ['tenʃn] *n (U)* - **1.** [anxiety] Anspannung *die*; [between people] Spannung *die* - **2.** TECH [tightness] Spannung *die.*

tent [tent] *n* Zelt *das.*

tentacle ['tentəkl] *n* Fangarm *der*, Tentakel *der* ODER *das.*

tentative ['tentətɪv] *adj* - **1.** [person, step, smile] zögernd - **2.** [agreement, plan] vorläufig.

tenterhooks ['tentəhʊks] *npl*: **to be on tenterhooks** auf glühenden Kohlen sitzen.

tenth [tenθ] *num* zehnte(r) (s); *see also* **sixth**.

tent peg *n* Hering *der*, Zeltpflock *der.*

tent pole *n* Zeltstange *die.*

tenuous ['tenjʊəs] *adj* schwach.

tepid ['tepɪd] *adj liter & fig* lauwarm.

term [tɜːm] ⟨⟩ *n* - **1.** [word, expression] Begriff *der*, Ausdruck *der* - **2.** SCH & UNIV Trimester *das* - **3.** [period of time]: **a prison term** eine Haftstrafe; **in the long/short term** auf lange/kurze Sicht. ⟨⟩ *vt* bezeichnen; **to term sb/sthg sthg** jn/etw als etw bezeichnen. ➠ **terms** *npl* - **1.** [of contract, agreement] Konditionen *Pl* - **2.** [conditions]: **in international terms** im internationalen Vergleich; **in real terms** effektiv - **3.** [of relationship]: **to be on good terms (with sb)** (mit jm) gut aus⎮kommen - **4.** *phr*: **to come to terms with sthg** sich mit etw ab⎮finden. ➠ **in terms of** *prep* in Bezug auf (+ A).

terminal ['tɜːmɪnl] ⟨⟩ *adj* MED unheilbar. ⟨⟩ *n* - **1.** RAIL Endbahnhof *der*; AERON Terminal *der* - **2.** COMPUT Terminal *das* - **3.** ELEC Pol *der.*

terminate ['tɜːmɪneɪt] ⟨⟩ *vt fml* beenden; [contract] auf⎮lösen; [pregnancy] ab⎮brechen. ⟨⟩ *vi* [bus, train] enden.

terminus ['tɜːmɪnəs] (*pl* -**ni** OR -**nuses**) *n* Endstation *die.*

terrace ['terəs] *n* - **1.** UK [of houses] Häuserreihe *die* - **2.** [patio] Terrasse *die.* ➠ **terraces** *npl* FTBL: **the terraces** die Ränge *Pl.*

terraced house *n* UK Reihenhaus *das.*

terrain [te'reɪn] *n* Gelände *das.*

terrible ['terəbl] *adj* furchtbar, schrecklich.

terribly ['terəblɪ] *adv* [extremely] furchtbar, schrecklich.

terrier ['terɪər] *n* Terrier *der.*

terrific [tə'rɪfɪk] *adj* - **1.** [wonderful] großartig - **2.** [enormous] enorm.

terrified ['terɪfaɪd] *adj*: **to be terrified (of sb/ sthg)** wahnsinnige Angst haben (vor jm/ etw).

terrifying ['terɪfaɪɪŋ] *adj* fürchterlich.

territory ['terɪtrɪ] *n* - **1.** [political area] Territorium *das* - **2.** [terrain] Gelände *das.*

terror ['terər] *n* - **1.** [fear] panische Angst - **2.** *inf* [rascal] Teufel *der.*

terrorism ['terərɪzm] *n* Terrorismus *der.*

terrorist ['terərɪst] *n* Terrorist *der*, -in *die.*

terrorize, -ise ['terəraɪz] *vt* terrorisieren.

terse [tɜːs] *adj* - **1.** [reply, remark] knapp - **2.** [person] kurz angebunden.

Terylene® ['terəliːn] *n* Trevira® *das.*

test [test] ⟨⟩ *n* - **1.** [trial] Test *der*; [of friendship, courage] Probe *die* - **2.** [examination of knowledge, skill - SCH] Klassenarbeit *die*; UNIV Klausur *die*; **driving test** Fahrprüfung *die* - **3.** MED [medical check] Test *der.* ⟨⟩ *vt* - **1.** [car, method] testen; [friendship, courage] auf die Probe stellen; **to have one's eyes tested** seine Augen testen lassen - **2.** [pupil] prüfen; **to test sb on sthg** jn in etw (D) prüfen.

test-drive *vt* Probe fahren.

testicles ['testɪklz] *npl* Hoden *Pl.*

testify ['testɪfaɪ] ⟨⟩ *vt*: **to testify that...** bezeugen, dass... ⟨⟩ *vi* - **1.** LAW aus⎮sagen - **2.** [be proof]: **to testify to sthg** von etw zeugen.

testimony [UK 'testɪmənɪ, US 'testəməʊnɪ] *n (U)* LAW Aussage *die.*

testing ['testɪŋ] *adj* [difficult] schwer.

test match *n* UK internationales Cricket- oder Rugbyspiel.

test tube *n* Reagenzglas *das.*

test-tube baby *n* Retortenbaby *das.*

tetanus ['tetənəs] *n* Tetanus *der*, Wundstarrkrampf *der.*

tether ['teðər] ⟨⟩ *vt* an⎮binden. ⟨⟩ *n*: **to be at the end of one's tether** am Ende sein.

text [tekst] ⟨⟩ n - 1. [gen] Text der - 2. [of speech, interview] Wortlaut der - 3. [on mobile phone] Textnachricht die. ⟨⟩ vt [with mobile phone] simsen.

textbook ['tekstbʊk] n Lehrbuch das.

textile ['tekstaɪl] n Textilie die.

text message n Textnachricht die.

texture ['tekstʃər] n Beschaffenheit die.

Thai [taɪ] ⟨⟩ adj thailändisch. ⟨⟩ n - 1. [person] Thailänder der, -in die - 2. [language] Thai das.

Thailand ['taɪlænd] n Thailand nt.

Thames [temz] n: the Thames die Themse.

than (weak form [ðən], strong form [ðæn]) ⟨⟩ prep als; you're better than me du bist besser als ich; more than ten mehr als zehn. ⟨⟩ conj als; I'd rather stay in than go out ich bleibe lieber zu Hause als auszugehen; no sooner had we arrived than the music began kaum waren wir angekommen, da begann die Musik zu spielen.

thank [θæŋk] vt: to thank sb (for sthg) jm (für etw) danken; thank God OR goodness OR heavens! Gott sei Dank! ⬥ **thanks** ⟨⟩ npl Dank der. ⟨⟩ excl danke. ⬥ **thanks to** prep dank (+ D).

thankful ['θæŋkfʊl] adj - 1. [grateful]: thankful (for sthg) dankbar (für etw) - 2. [relieved] erleichtert.

thankless ['θæŋklɪs] adj undankbar.

thanksgiving ['θæŋks,gɪvɪŋ] n Danksagung die. ⬥ **Thanksgiving (Day)** n amerikanisches Erntedankfest.

thank you excl danke schön!; thank you for ... danke für ...

that [ðæt] (pl those) ⟨⟩ pron - 1. (demonstrative use) das, die Pl; who's/what's that? wer/was ist das?; that's interesting das ist interessant; is that Lucy? [on phone] bist du das, Lucy?; [pointing] ist das Lucy?; how much are those? wieviel kosten die (da)?; all those I saw all die, die ich sah; after that danach; what do you mean by that? was willst du damit sagen? - 2. (referring to thing or person further away) jene(r) (s), jene Pl; this is new, that is old dies ist neu, jenes ist alt; I want those there ich möchte die da - 3. (weak form [ðət]) (introducing relative clause: subject) der/die/das, die Pl; a shop that sells antiques ein Geschäft, das Antiquitäten verkauft - 4. (weak form [ðət]) (introducing relative clause: object) den/die/das, die Pl; the film that I saw ich the film, den ich gesehen habe; everything that I have done alles, was ich gemacht habe; the best that he could do das Beste, was er machen konnte - 5. (weak form [ðət]) (introducing relative clause: after prep + D) dem/der/ dem, denen Pl; (introducing relative clause: after prep + A) den/die/das, die Pl; the place that I'm looking for der Ort, nach dem ich suche; the envelope that I put it in der Umschlag, in den ich es steckte; the night that we went to the theatre der Abend, an dem wir ins Theater gingen. ⟨⟩ adj - 1. (demonstrative use) der/die/das, die Pl; that film was good der Film war gut; who's that man? wer ist der Mann?; what's that noise? was ist das für ein Lärm?; those chocolates are delicious die Pralinen da schmecken köstlich - 2. (referring to thing or person further away) jene(r) (s), jene Pl; I prefer that book ich bevorzuge das Buch da; I'll have that one ich nehme das da. ⟨⟩ adv so; it wasn't that bad/good es war nicht so schlecht/gut. ⟨⟩ conj (weak form [ðət]) dass; he recommended that I phone you er empfahl mir, dich anzurufen. ⬥ **that is (to say)** adv das heißt.

thatched [θætʃt] adj: thatched roof Reetdach das.

that's [ðæts] abbr of that is.

thaw [θɔ:] ⟨⟩ vt auftauen. ⟨⟩ vi - 1. [ice, frozen food] tauen - 2. fig [atmosphere] sich entspannen. ⟨⟩ n Tauwetter das.

the (weak form [ðə], before vowel [ðɪ], strong form [ði:]) def art - 1. [gen] der/die/das, die Pl; the man der Mann; the woman die Frau; the book das Buch; the girls die Mädchen; the Wilsons die Wilsons; to play the piano Klavier spielen; ten pence in the pound zehn Pence pro Pfund; you're not the Jack Straw, are you? Sie sind nicht der Jack Straw, oder?; it's the place to go to in Paris da geht man in Paris hin - 2. (with an adj to form a noun): the British/ poor die Briten/Armen; the impossible das Unmögliche - 3. [in dates] der; the twelfth (of May) der Zwölfte (Mai); the forties die Vierziger - 4. [in comparisons]: the more I see of her, the less I like her je mehr ich sie sehe, desto weniger mag ich sie; the sooner the better je eher, desto besser - 5. [in titles]: Elizabeth the Second Elisabeth die Zweite.

theatre UK, **theater** US ['θɪətər] n - 1. [building] Theater das - 2. [art, industry]: the theatre das Theater - 3. [in hospital] Operationssaal der - 4. US [cinema] Kino das.

theatregoer UK, **theatergoer** US ['θɪətə,gəʊə/] n Theaterbesucher der, -in die.

theatrical [θɪ'ætrɪkl] adj - 1. [of the theatre] Theater- - 2. fig [for effect] theatralisch.

theft [θeft] n Diebstahl der.

their [ðeə/] poss adj ihr; their house ihr Haus; their children ihre Kinder; they brushed their teeth sie putzten sich (D) die Zähne; it wasn't their fault das war nicht ihre Schuld.

theirs [ðeəz] poss pron ihre(r) (s); that is theirs das ist ihres; this house is theirs dieses Haus gehört ihnen; a friend of theirs ein Freund von ihnen; it wasn't our fault, it was theirs das war nicht unsere Schuld, es war ihre.

them *(weak form* [ðəm]*, strong form* [ðem]*) pers pron & Pl (accusative)* sie; *(dative)* ihnen; **I know them** ich kenne sie; **I like them** sie gefallen mir; **it's them** sie sind es; **send it to them** schicke es ihnen; **tell them** sage ihnen; **he's worse than them** er ist schlimmer als sie; **if I were** OR **was them** wenn ich sie wäre; **you can't expect them to do it** du kannst nicht erwarten, dass **sie** das tun; **all of them** sie alle; **none of them** keiner von ihnen; **some/a few of them** einige von ihnen; **most of them** die meisten; **both of them** alle beide; **there are three of them** es gibt drei davon; [people] sie sind zu dritt; **neither of them** keiner/keine/keines von beiden.

theme [θiːm] *n* [gen] Thema *das.*

theme tune *n* [of film] Titelmelodie *die;* [of TV, radio programme] Erkennungsmelodie *die.*

themselves [ðemˈselvz] *pron* sich; **they washed themselves** sie wuschen sich; **by themselves** [alone] allein; **they did it (by) themselves** sie machten es selbst; **they have the garden (all) to themselves** sie haben den Garten (ganz) für sich allein.

then [ðen] ◇ *adv* - **1.** [not now, next, afterwards] dann; [in the past] damals; **the film starts at eight – I'll see you then** der Film fängt um acht an – bis dann; **I had breakfast, then I went to work** ich frühstückte und ging dann zur Arbeit; **we were much younger then** wir waren damals viel jünger; **before then** vorher; **by/until then** bis dahin; **from then on** von da an; **since then** seitdem **- 2.** [in that case] also; **go on, then** also machs!; **you knew all along, then?** du hast es also die ganze Zeit gewusst? **- 3.** [therefore] also; **these, then, were the reasons for our failure** das waren also die Gründe für unser Versagen **- 4.** [with "if" clauses] dann; **if you help me now, then I'll help you later** wenn Sie mir jetzt helfen, dann helfe ich Ihnen später **- 5.** [furthermore, also] außerdem; **(and) then there are the children to consider** und dann müssen wir an die Kinder denken. ◇ *adj* damalig; **the then president** der damalige Präsident.

theoretical [θɪəˈretɪkl] *adj* theoretisch.

theorize, -ise [ˈθɪəraɪz] *vi:* **to theorize (about sthg)** theoretisieren (über etw (A)).

theory [ˈθɪərɪ] *n* Theorie *die;* **in theory** theoretisch, in der Theorie.

therapist [ˈθerəpɪst] *n* Therapeut *der,* -in *die.*

therapy [ˈθerəpɪ] *n* Therapie *die.*

there [ðeəʳ] ◇ *pron* [indicating existence]: **there is/are** es gibt; **are there any left?** sind noch welche übrig?; **there are three of us** wir sind zu dritt; **there's a page missing** es fehlt eine Seite; **there must be some mistake** das muss ein Irrtum sein. ◇ *adv* - **1.** [in existence, present] da; **is anyone there?** ist da jemand?; **is**

John there, please? [on phone] ist John da? - **2.** [at/in that place] dort; [to that place] dorthin; **that man there** der Mann dort; **I'm going there next week** ich gehe nächste Woche hin; **we're there at last!** endlich sind wir da!; **it's 6 kilometres there and back** es sind 6 Kilometer hin und zurück; **there it/he is** da ist es/er; **in/ over there** da drinnen/drüben; **up there** dort oben. ◇ *excl:* **there, I told you so!** ich habe es dir doch gleich gesagt!; **there, there (don't cry)** na, na (weine nicht). ➠ **there and then, then and there** *adv* auf der Stelle.

thereabouts [ðeərəˈbauts], **thereabout** US [ðeərəˈbaut] *adv:* **at eight o'clock or thereabouts** so um acht Uhr herum; **fifty or thereabouts** so ungefähr fünfzig; **somewhere thereabouts** da irgendwo.

thereafter [ˌðeərˈɑːftəʳ] *adv fml* danach.

thereby [ˌðeəʳˈbaɪ] *adv fml* damit.

therefore [ˈðeəfɔːʳ] *adv* deshalb, deswegen.

there's [ðeəz] *abbr of* **there is.**

thermal [ˈθɜːml] *adj* [clothes] Thermo-.

thermometer [θəˈmɒmɪtəʳ] *n* Thermometer *das.*

Thermos (flask) ® [ˈθɜːməs-] *n* Thermosflasche ® *die.*

thermostat [ˈθɜːməstæt] *n* Thermostat *der.*

thesaurus [θɪˈsɔːrəs] *n* (*pl* **-es**) Thesaurus *der.*

these [ðiːz] *Pl* ▷ **this.**

thesis [ˈθiːsɪs] *n* (*pl* **theses** [ˈθiːsiːz]) *n* - **1.** [argument] These *die* - **2.** [doctoral dissertation] Dissertation *die,* Doktorarbeit *die.*

they [ðeɪ] *pers pron & Pl* - **1.** [gen] sie; **they're happy** sie sind glücklich; **they're pretty earrings** das sind hübsche Ohrringe; **it's they who are responsible** sie sind es, die verantwortlich sind; **they can't do it** die können es nicht tun - **2.** [unspecified people] man; **they still haven't repaired the road** sie haben immer noch nicht die Straße repariert; **they say that...** man sagt, dass...

they'd [ðeɪd] *abbr of* **they had, they would.**

they'll [ðeɪl] *abbr of* **they shall, they will.**

they're [ðeəʳ] *abbr of* **they are.**

they've [ðeɪv] *abbr of* **they have.**

thick [θɪk] ◇ *adj* - **1.** [gen] dick; **it is one metre thick** es ist einen Meter dick - **2.** [dense] dicht; **thick with smoke** voller Rauch - **3.** *inf* [stupid] dumm - **4.** [accent] stark. ◇ *n:* **to be in the thick of it** mittendrin sein.

thicken [ˈθɪkn] ◇ *vt* [soup, sauce] eindicken. ◇ *vi* [forest, crowd, fog] dichter werden; [soup, sauce] dicker werden.

thickness [ˈθɪknɪs] *n* - **1.** [width, depth] Dicke *die* - **2.** [density] Dichte *die* - **3.** [viscosity] Dickflüssigkeit *die.*

thickset [ˌθɪkˈset] *adj* gedrungen.

thick-skinned [-'skɪnd] *adj* dickfellig.

thief [θiːf] (*pl* thieves) *n* Dieb *der*, -in *die*.

thieve [θiːv] *vt* & *vi* stehlen.

thieves [θiːvz] *Pl* ▷ **thief**.

thigh [θaɪ] *n* Oberschenkel *der*.

thimble ['θɪmbl] *n* Fingerhut *der*.

thin [θɪn] *adj* - 1. [gen] dünn - 2. [sparse] gering; [mist] leicht; [hair] dünn, schütter - 3. [poor - excuse] fadenscheinig. ◆ **thin down** *vt sep* verdünnen.

thing [θɪŋ] *n* - 1. [affair, item, subject] Sache *die*, Ding *das*; **the (best) thing to do would be...** das Beste wäre (es)...; **the thing is ...** die Sache ist die, dass ...; **not a thing** gar nichts - 3. [object, creature] Ding *das*; **the lucky thing!** der/die Glückliche!; **you poor thing!** du Armer/Arme! ◆ **things** *npl* - 1. [clothes, possessions] Sachen *Pl* - 2. *inf* [life] Dinge *Pl*.

think [θɪŋk] (*pt* & *pp* thought) ◇ *vt* - 1. [believe] **to think (that)...** denken(, dass)..., glauben(, dass)...; **I think so** ich glaube schon; **I don't think so** ich glaube nicht - 2. [have in mind]: **to think (that)...** denken(, dass)...; **what are you thinking?** woran denkst du? - 3. [imagine] sich (D) denken, sich (D) vor|stellen - 4. [in polite requests]: **do you think you could help me?** könnten Sie mir vielleicht helfen? ◇ *vi* - 1. [use mind] denken; **I thought for a long time** ich dachte lange nach - 2. [have stated opinion]: **what do you think of OR about his new film?** was hältst du von seinem neuen Film?; **I don't think much of them/it** ich halte nicht viel von ihnen/davon; **to think a lot of sb/sthg** viel von jm/etw halten - 3. *phr*: **to think twice before doing sthg** es sich (D) genau überlegen, bevor man etw tut. ◆ **think about** *vt insep* [consider] nachdenken über (+ *A*); **to think about doing sthg** daran denken, etw zu tun. ◆ **think of** *vt insep* - 1. [consider, remember, show consideration for] denken an (+ *A*); **to think of doing sthg** daran denken, etw zu tun; **I can't think of her name** ich kann mich nicht an ihren Namen erinnern, ich komme nicht auf ihren Namen - 2. [conceive] sich (D) aus|denken; **to think of doing sthg** die Idee haben, etw zu tun; **we'll think of sthg** wir werden uns (D) etwas einfallen lassen. ◆ **think over** *vt sep* überdenken. ◆ **think up** *vt sep* sich (D) aus|denken.

think tank *n* Expertenkommission *die*.

third [θɜːd] ◇ *num* dritte(r) (s). ◇ *n* - 1. [fraction] Drittel *das* - 2. *UK* UNIV Abschluss mit "Befriedigend"; *see also* **sixth**.

thirdly ['θɜːdlɪ] *adv* drittens.

third-rate *adj pej* drittklassig.

Third World *n*: the Third World die Dritte Welt.

thirst [θɜːst] *n* Durst *der*; **a thirst for sthg** *fig* ein Durst nach etw; **thirst for adventure** Abenteuerlust *die*.

thirsty ['θɜːstɪ] *adj*: **to be OR feel thirsty** Durst haben, durstig sein; **this is thirsty work** diese Arbeit macht durstig.

thirteen [,θɜː'tiːn] *num* dreizehn; *see also* **six**.

thirty ['θɜːtɪ] *num* dreißig; *see also* **sixty**.

this [ðɪs] (*pl* these) ◇ *pron* - 1. (*referring to thing, person mentioned*) this is for you das ist für dich; **who's/what's this?** wer/was ist das?; **what are these?** was ist das?; **this is Daphne Logan** [introducing someone] das ist Daphne Logan; [introducing o.s. on phone] hier ist Daphne Logan; **before this** früher - 2. (*referring to thing, person nearer speaker*) diese(r) (s), diese *Pl*; **which shoes do you want, these or those?** welche Schuhe wollen Sie, die hier oder die da?; **I want these here** ich möchte die hier. ◇ *adj* - 1. (*referring to thing, person*) diese(r) (s), diese *Pl*; **I prefer this book** ich bevorzuge dieses Buch; **these chocolates are delicious** diese Pralinen schmecken köstlich; **I'll have this one/these ones** ich nehme dieses/diese; **this morning/evening** heute Morgen/Abend; **this week** diese Woche; **this Sunday/summer** diesen Sonntag/Sommer - 2. *inf* [a certain]: **there was this man** da war dieser Mann; **this woman came over to my table** diese Frau kam an meinen Tisch. ◇ *adv* so; **it was this big** es war so groß; **this far** bis hier.

thistle ['θɪsl] *n* Distel *die*.

thorn [θɔːn] *n* [prickle] Dorn *der*.

thorny ['θɔːnɪ] *adj* - 1. [prickly] dornig - 2. *fig* [tricky, complicated] heikel.

thorough ['θʌrə] *adj* - 1. [exhaustive, meticulous] gründlich; [worker] sorgfältig, gewissenhaft - 2. [complete, utter] völlig; **that's a thorough nuisance** das ist wirklich lästig.

thoroughbred ['θʌrəbred] *n* [horse] Vollblut *das*.

thoroughfare ['θʌrəfeər] *n fml* Durchgangsstraße *die*.

thoroughly ['θʌrəlɪ] *adv* - 1. [fully, in detail] gründlich - 2. [completely, utterly] durch und durch.

those [ðəʊz] *Pl* ▷ **that**.

though [ðəʊ] ◇ *conj* - 1. [in spite of the fact that] obwohl, obgleich - 2. [even if] wenn auch. ◇ *adv* [nevertheless] aber; **he's quite intelligent, though** er ist aber ziemlich intelligent.

thought [θɔːt] ◇ *pt* & *pp* ▷ **think**. ◇ *n* - 1. [notion] Gedanke *der* - 2. (*U*) [act of thinking] Nachdenken *das*; **to give some thought to sthg** über etw (*A*) nachdenken; **after much thought** nach langem Überlegen - 3. [philosophy] Denken *das* - 4. [gesture]: **it's the thought that counts** der gute Wille zählt. ◆ **thoughts** *npl* Gedanken *Pl*.

thoughtful ['θɔːtful] *adj* - 1. [pensive - person, mood] nachdenklich - 2. [considerate - person] rücksichtsvoll; [- action, remark] wohl überlegt.

thoughtless ['θɔːtlıs] *adj* [person, behaviour] rücksichtslos; [remark] unüberlegt.

thousand ['θaʊznd] *num* - 1. [number] tausend; a/one thousand (ein)tausend; five thousand and forty-two fünftausend(und)zweiundvierzig; thousands of Tausende von - 2. *fig* [umpteen]: a thousand tausend; I have a thousand things to do ich habe tausend Dinge zu tun; *see also* six.

thousandth ['θaʊzntθ] <> *num* tausendste(r) (s). <> *n* [fraction] Tausendstel *das; see also* sixth.

thrash [θræʃ] *vt* - 1. [beat, hit] prügeln - 2. *inf* [trounce] fertig machen. ● **thrash about, thrash around** *vi* sich hin und her werfen. ● **thrash out** *vt sep* durchldiskutieren.

thread [θred] <> *n* - 1. [of cotton, wool] Faden *der* - 2. [of screw] Gewinde *das* - 3. *fig* [theme]: to follow the thread of sb's argument js Gedankengang *(D)* folgen; she lost the thread of what she was saying) sie hat den Faden verloren. <> *vt* [needle] einlfädeln; [beads] auflziehen.

threadbare ['θredbeər] *adj* [garment] abgetragen; [carpet] abgewetzt.

threat [θret] *n* - 1. [warning] Drohung *die* - 2. [menace]: threat (to sb/sthg) Bedrohung *die* OR Gefahr *die* (für jn/etw) - 3. [risk]: the threat of war/inflation die Gefahr eines Krieges/einer Inflation; there is a threat of storms es kann Stürme geben.

threaten ['θretn] <> *vt* - 1. [issue threat]: to threaten sb (with sthg) jm (mit etw) drohen; to threaten to do sthg drohen, etw zu tun - 2. [be likely]: to threaten to do sthg drohen, etw zu tun - 3. [endanger] bedrohen, gefährden. <> *vi* drohen.

three [θriː] *num* drei; *see also* six.

three-dimensional [-dı'menʃənl] *adj* dreidimensional.

threefold ['θriːfəʊld] *adj & adv* dreifach.

three-piece *adj* dreiteilig.

three-ply *adj* [wool] dreifädig; [wood] dreischichtig.

thresh [θreʃ] *vt* dreschen.

threshold ['θreʃhəʊld] *n* - 1. [doorway] Türschwelle *die* - 2. [level] Schwelle *die*.

threw [θruː] *pt* ▷ **throw**.

thrift shop *n* US Secondhandladen, dessen Erlöse einem wohltätigen Zweck zugute kommen.

thrifty ['θrıftı] *adj* [person] sparsam.

thrill [θrıl] <> *n* - 1. [sudden feeling] Erregung *die*; a thrill of horror ein Schauder des

Entsetzens; I felt a thrill of joy ich war freudig erregt - 2. [exciting experience] (aufregendes) Erlebnis. <> *vt* begeistern, mitlreißen.

thrilled [θrıld] *adj*: to be thrilled (with sthg) (von etw) begeistert sein; I was thrilled to meet her ich fand es sehr aufregend, sie zu treffen.

thriller ['θrılər] *n* Thriller *der*.

thrilling ['θrılıŋ] *adj* [match, book, film] spannend; [news] umwerfend.

thrive [θraıv] (*pt* -d OR throve, *pp* -d) *vi* [person - be successful] erfolgreich sein; [plant] prächtig gedeihen, [business] blühen.

thriving ['θraıvıŋ] *adj* [person - successful] erfolgreich; [plant] prächtig gedeihend; [business] blühend.

throat [θrəʊt] *n* - 1. [inside mouth] Hals *der* - 2. [front of neck] Kehle *die*.

throb [θrɒb] *vi* - 1. [beat - pulse, heart] pochen; [- blood] pulsieren; [- engine, machine, music] dröhnen - 2. [be painful]: my head is throbbing ich habe pochende Kopfschmerzen.

throes [θrəʊz] *npl*: to be in the throes of sthg mitten in etw *(D)* stecken.

throne [θrəʊn] *n* Thron *der*.

throng [θrɒŋ] <> *n* [crowd] Menschenmenge *die*; a throng of Scharen *Pl* von. <> *vt* [place] belagern; [streets] sich drängen in (+ *D*).

throttle ['θrɒtl] <> *n* - 1. [valve] Drosselklappe *die* - 2. [lever] Gashebel *der*; [Pedal] Gaspedal *das*; at full throttle mit Vollgas. <> *vt* [strangle] erwürgen.

through [θruː] <> *adj* - 1. [finished]: to be through (with sthg) (mit etw) fertig sein - 2. [referring to transport]: through traffic Durchgangsverkehr *der*; a through train ein durchgehender Zug. <> *adv* - 1. [from one end to another] durch; to let sb through jn durchllassen; wet through völlig durchnässt - 2. [until]: I slept through till ten ich schlief bis zehn durch; we stayed through till Friday wir blieben bis Freitag. <> *prep* - 1. [from one side to another] durch; he went through the park er ging durch den Park; to drill through sthg etw durchlbohren; I'm halfway through this book ich habe das Buch schon halb gelesen - 2. [during, throughout] während (+ *G*); all through his life sein ganzes Leben hindurch - 3. [because of] wegen (+ *G*); absent through illness wegen Krankheit abwesend; through fear aus Furcht - 4. [by means of] durch; I got the job through a friend ich bekam die Stelle durch einen Freund - 5. US [up until and including]: Monday through Thursday Montag bis Donnerstag. ● **through and through** *adv* - 1. [completely] durch und durch - 2. [thoroughly - know] gründlich.

throughout [θruː'aʊt] <> *prep* - 1. [during]: throughout the day/morning den ganzen Tag/Morgen (über); throughout the year das ganze Jahr (hindurch); throughout her life ihr ganzes Leben lang - 2. [everywhere in] überall in (+ D); throughout the country im ganzen Land. <> adv - 1. [all the time] die ganze Zeit (über) - 2. [everywhere] überall; [completely] ganz.

throve [θrəʊv] pt ⊳ **thrive**.

throw [θrəʊ] (pt **threw**, pp **thrown**) <> vt - 1. [propel, put] werfen - 2. [move suddenly]: **he threw himself to the floor/onto the bed** er warf sich auf den Boden/das Bett - 3. [rider] ablwerfen - 4. fig [force]: **to throw sb into confusion** jn durcheinander bringen - 5. fig [confuse] aus dem Konzept bringen. <> n [toss, pitch] Wurf der. **throw away** vt sep - 1. [discard] weglwerfen - 2. fig [money, time] vergeuden; [opportunity] nicht nutzen. **throw out** vt sep - 1. [discard] weglwerfen - 2. fig [reject] abllehnen - 3. [force to leave] hinauslwerfen. **throw up** vi inf [vomit] sich übergeben.

throwaway ['θrəʊə,weɪ] adj - 1. [product, bottle] Wegwerf- - 2. [remark] beiläufig.

throw-in n UK FTBL Einwurf der.

thrown [θrəʊn] pp ⊳ **throw**.

thru [θruː] adj, adv & prep US inf = **through**.

thrush [θrʌʃ] n [bird] Drossel die.

thrust [θrʌst] (pt & pp inv) <> n - 1. [forward movement - of knife, sword] Stoß der; MIL Vorstoß der - 2. [main aspect] Tenor der. <> vt [jab, shove]: **to thrust sthg into sthg** [knife, stick] etw in etw (A) stoßen; **she thrust the money into her pocket** sie stopfte das Geld in ihre Tasche.

thud [θʌd] <> n dumpfer Aufschlag. <> vi dumpf auflschlagen; [feet] stampfen.

thug [θʌg] n Schläger der.

thumb [θʌm] <> n [of hand] Daumen der. <> vt inf [hitch]: **to thumb a lift** per Anhalter fahren. **thumb through** vt insep durchlblättern.

thumbs down [,θʌmz-] n: **to get** OR **be given the thumbs down** abgelehnt werden.

thumbs up n [go-ahead]: **to get** OR **be given the thumbs up** grünes Licht bekommen.

thumbtack ['θʌmtæk] n US Reißzwecke die.

thump [θʌmp] <> n - 1. [blow] Schlag der - 2. [thud] Bums der. <> vt [punch] schlagen. <> vi [heart] heftig pochen.

thunder ['θʌndər] <> n (U) - 1. METEOR Donner der - 2. fig [loud sound] Donnern · das. <> impers vb METEOR: **it is thundering** es donnert.

thunderbolt ['θʌndəbəʊlt] n - 1. METEOR Blitz der - 2. fig [shock]: **the news was a thunderbolt** die Nachricht schlug wie ein Blitz ein.

thunderclap ['θʌndəklæp] n Donnerschlag der.

thunderstorm ['θʌndəstɔːm] n Gewitter das.

Thursday ['θɜːzdɪ] n Donnerstag der; see also **Saturday**.

thus [ðʌs] adv fml - 1. [as a consequence] daher - 2. [in this way] auf diese Weise - 3. [as follows] folgendermaßen.

thwart [θwɔːt] vt vereiteln; [person] einen Strich durch die Rechnung machen (+ D).

thyme [taɪm] n Thymian der.

tiara [tɪˈɑːrə] n [piece of jewellery] Diadem das.

Tibet [tɪˈbet] n Tibet nt.

tic [tɪk] n Zucken das.

tick [tɪk] <> n - 1. [written mark] Häkchen das - 2. [sound] Ticken das - 3. [insect] Zecke die. <> vt [name] ablhaken; [answer, box on form] anlkreuzen. <> vi [make ticking sound] ticken. **tick off** vt sep - 1. [mark off] ablhaken - 2. inf [tell off]: **to tick sb off (for sthg)** jn (wegen etw) rüffeln. **tick over** vi - 1. [engine] im Leerlauf sein - 2. [business, organization] ganz gut laufen.

ticket ['tɪkɪt] n - 1. [for match, concert] Eintrittskarte die; [for bus, train, tram] Fahrkarte die, Fahrschein der; [for plane] Ticket das; [for lottery, raffle] Los das; [for library] Ausweis der; [for car park] Parkschein der - 2. [on product]: **(price) ticket** Preisschild das - 3. [notice of traffic offence] Strafzettel der.

ticket collector n UK [on train] Schaffner der, -in die; [in station] Fahrkartenkontrolleur der, -in die.

ticket inspector n UK [on bus, tram] Fahrkartenkontrolleur der, -in die; [on train] Schaffner der, -in die.

ticket machine n [for public transport] Fahrscheinautomat der; [in car park] Parkscheinautomat der.

ticket office n [at railway station] Fahrkartenschalter der; [at theatre] Theaterkasse die.

tickle ['tɪkl] <> vt [touch lightly] kitzeln; [subj: beard, wool] kratzen. <> vi [foot, back] jucken; [beard, wool] kratzen.

ticklish ['tɪklɪʃ] adj [sensitive to touch] kitzlig.

tidal ['taɪdl] adj Gezeiten-.

tidal wave n Flutwelle die.

tidbit ['tɪdbɪt] n US = **titbit**.

tiddlywinks ['tɪdlɪwɪŋks], **tiddledywinks** US ['tɪdldɪwɪŋks] n (U) [game] Flohhüpfspiel das.

tide [taɪd] n - 1. [of sea] Gezeiten Pl; **high tide** Flut die; **low tide** Ebbe die; **the tide is in/out** es ist Flut/Ebbe - 2. fig [trend]: **the tide of (public) opinion** der Trend der öffentlichen Meinung; **to swim with/against the tide** mit dem/gegen den Strom schwimmen - 3. fig [large quantity]: **a tide of protest** eine Flut von Protesten.

tidy ['taɪdɪ] <> adj [gen] ordentlich; [appearance] gepflegt. <> vt auflräumen. **tidy up** vt sep & vi auflräumen.

tie [taɪ] (*pt & pp* **tied,** *cont* **tying**) ⟨⟩ *n* - 1. [necktie] Krawatte *die* - 2. [in game, competition] Unentschieden *das*. ⟨⟩ *vt* - 1. [attach]: **to tie sthg (on)to sthg** etw an etw (A) binden; **to tie sthg round sthg** etw um etw binden; **my hands are tied** *fig* mir sind die Hände gebunden; **to tie sthg with sthg** etw mit etw zusammenbinden - 2. [do up, fasten] binden; [knot] machen - 3. *fig* [link]: **to be tied to sb/sthg** an jn/etw gebunden sein. ⟨⟩ *vi* [in sport] unentschieden spielen. ⟐ **tie down** *vt sep* *fig* [restrict]: **to be tied down by sthg** durch etw eingeschränkt sein. ⟐ **tie in with** *vt insep* passen zu. ⟐ **tie up** *vt sep* - 1. [parcel, papers] verschnüren; [person] fesseln; [animal] anbinden - 2. [shoelaces] binden - 3. *fig* [savings] fest anlegen - 4. *fig* [link]: **to be tied up with sthg** mit etw zusammenhängen.

tiebreak(er) ['taɪbreɪk(ər)] *n* - 1. TENNIS Tiebreak *das* - 2. [extra question] Entscheidungsfrage *die*.

tiepin ['taɪpɪn] *n* Krawattennadel *die*.

tier [tɪər] *n* [of seats] Rang *der*; [of cake] Etage *die*.

tiff [tɪf] *n* Krach *der*.

tiger ['taɪgər] *n* Tiger *der*.

tight [taɪt] ⟨⟩ *adj* - 1. [close-fitting] eng; **the dress was a very tight fit** das Kleid war sehr eng - 2. [secure - lid] fest sitzend; [- screw] fest angezogen; [- knot] fest - 3. [taut] straff - 4. [close together - bundle] fest zusammengebunden; **they stood in a tight group** sie standen eng zusammen - 5. [schedule] eng; [money, match, finish] knapp - 6. [rule, control] streng - 7. [bend] scharf, eng - 8. *inf* [drunk] voll - 9. *inf* [miserly] knauserig. ⟨⟩ *adv* - 1. [firmly, securely] fest; **to hold tight** festhalten; **to shut** OR **close sthg tight** [eyes] etw fest schließen; [lid] etw fest verschließen - 2. [tautly] straff. ⟐ **tights** *npl* Strumpfhose *die*.

tighten ['taɪtn] ⟨⟩ *vt* - 1. [knot, belt, screw] anziehen - 2. [make tauter] straffen, spannen - 3. [strengthen]: **to tighten one's hold** OR **grip on sthg** etw fester halten; fig [on party, country] seine Macht in etw (D) ausbauen - 4. [rule, control, security] verschärfen. ⟨⟩ *vi* [grip, hold] fester werden; [rope, chain] sich spannen.

tightfisted [,taɪt'fɪstɪd] *adj* *inf* *pej* knauserig.

tightly ['taɪtlɪ] *adv* [firmly, securely] fest.

tightrope ['taɪtrəʊp] *n* Drahtseil *das*.

tile [taɪl] *n* - 1. [on roof] Dachziegel *der* - 2. [on floor, wall] Fliese *die*, Kachel *die*.

tiled [taɪld] *adj* [floor, wall, bath] gefliest.

till [tɪl] ⟨⟩ *prep & conj* bis. ⟨⟩ *n* Kasse *die*.

tilt [tɪlt] ⟨⟩ *vt* [object, chair] kippen; [head] neigen. ⟨⟩ *vi* [person, chair] kippen; [head] sich neigen.

timber ['tɪmbər] *n* - 1. (U) [wood] Holz *das* - 2. [beam] Balken *der*.

time [taɪm] ⟨⟩ *n* - 1. [gen] Zeit *die*; **at that time** zu der Zeit, damals; **now is the time to do it** jetzt ist der richtige Zeitpunkt OR die richtige Zeit, es zu tun; **it will take time** es wird einige Zeit dauern; **to have no time for sb/sthg** keine Zeit für jn/etw haben; **to pass the time** sich (D) die Zeit vertreiben; **to play for time** versuchen, Zeit zu gewinnen. 2. [as measured by clock] Uhrzeit *die*; **what time is it?**, **what's the time?** wie spät ist es?, wie viel Uhr ist es?; **at this time of the day** zu dieser Tageszeit; **in a week's/year's time** in einer Woche/einem Jahr; **could you tell me the time?** können Sie mir sagen, wie spät es ist?; **can she tell the time?** kann sie schon die Uhr lesen? - 3. [while, spell]: **it was a long time before...** es dauerte lange, bevor...; **in a short time** bald; **for a time** einige Zeit(lang) - 4. [era] Zeit *die*; **in ancient times** zur Zeit der Antike; **in modern times** heutzutage - 5. [occasion] Mal *das*; **this time** diesmal, dieses Mal; **(the) last time** letztes Mal, das letzte Mal; **three times a week** dreimal pro OR in der Woche; **from time to time** von Zeit zu Zeit; **time after time, time and again** immer wieder - 6. [experience]: **we had a good time** es war schön; **to have a hard time** viel durchmachen; **to have a hard time doing sthg** Schwierigkeiten haben, etw zu tun - 7. [degree of lateness]: **to be in good time** OR **ahead of time** früh dran sein; **on time** pünktlich; **did you get there in time?** warst du rechtzeitig dort? - 8. MUS Takt *der*; **to beat time** den Takt anlegen; **in 4/4 time** im Viervierteltakt. ⟨⟩ *vt* - 1. [schedule]: **the meeting was timed to start at nine o'clock** der Beginn der Sitzung war auf neun Uhr angesetzt - 2. [measure - race, runner] die Zeit stoppen von; **I timed how long it took him** ich habe gestoppt, wie lange er gebraucht hat - 3. [choose appropriate moment for] zeitlich abstimmen. ⟐ **times** ⟨⟩ *npl*: **four times as much/many** viermal so viel/viele; **three times as big** dreimal so groß. ⟨⟩ *prep* MATHS mal; **10 times 4 is 40** 10 mal 4 ist 40. ⟐ **about time** *adv*: **it's about time (that)...** es wird (langsam) Zeit, dass... ⟐ **at a time** *adv*: **three/four at a time** drei/vier auf einmal; **one at a time** eine(r) (s) nach dem anderen; **for months at a time** monatelang. ⟐ **at times** *adv* manchmal. ⟐ **at the same time** *adv* - 1. [simultaneously] gleichzeitig, zur gleichen Zeit - 2. [equally] trotzdem, dennoch. ⟐ **for the time being** *adv* vorläufig. ⟐ **in time** *adv* - 1. [not late] rechtzeitig; **to be in time for sthg** rechtzeitig für etw kommen - 2. [eventually] schließlich; [over a long period] mit der Zeit.

time bomb *n* *liter* & *fig* Zeitbombe *die*.

time lag *n* Zeitabstand *der*.

timeless ['taɪmlɪs] *adj* zeitlos.

time limit *n* Frist *die*.

timely ['taɪmlɪ] *adj* rechtzeitig.

time off *n* (U) freie Zeit.

time-out (*pl* **time-outs**) *n* SPORT Auszeit *die*.

timer ['taɪmə^r] *n* [time switch] Schaltuhr *die*.

time scale *n* [for project] Zeitspanne *die*.

time-share *n* UK Ferienwohnung, an der man einen Besitzanteil hat.

time switch *n* Schaltuhr *die*.

timetable ['taɪm,teɪbl] *n* - **1.** SCH Stundenplan *der* - **2.** [of buses, trains] Fahrplan *der* - **3.** [schedule] Programm *das*.

time zone *n* Zeitzone *die*.

timid ['tɪmɪd] *adj* schüchtern.

timing ['taɪmɪŋ] *n* (U) - **1.** [of actor, musician, tennis player] Timing *das* - **2.** [chosen moment]: **the timing of the remark/election was unfortunate** der Zeitpunkt der Bemerkung/Wahlen war unglücklich gewählt - **3.** SPORT [measuring] Stoppen *das*.

tin [tɪn] *n* - **1.** (U) [metal] Blech *das* - **2.** UK [can] Dose *die* - **3.** [for storing] Dose *die*.

tin can *n* Blechdose *die*.

tinfoil ['tɪnfɔɪl] *n* (U) Alufolie *die*.

tinge [tɪndʒ] *n* Spur *die*.

tinged [tɪndʒd] *adj*: **tinged with sthg** mit einer Spur von etw.

tingle ['tɪŋgl] *vi* kribbeln.

tinker ['tɪŋkə^r] <> *n* Frechdachs *der*. <> *vi*: **to tinker (with sthg)** (an etw (D)) herumbasteln.

tinned [tɪnd] *adj* UK Dosen-.

tin opener *n* UK Dosenöffner *der*.

tinsel ['tɪnsl] *n* ≃ Lametta *das*.

tint [tɪnt] *n* Ton *der*.

tinted ['tɪntɪd] *adj* getönt.

tiny ['taɪnɪ] *adj* winzig.

tip [tɪp] <> *n* - **1.** [end] Spitze *die* - **2.** UK [dump] Müllkippe *die* - **3.** [gratuity] Trinkgeld *das* - **4.** [piece of advice] Tipp *der*. <> *vt* - **1.** [tilt] kippen - **2.** [spill] schütten - **3.** [give a gratuity to] Trinkgeld geben (+ D). <> *vi* - **1.** [tilt] kippen - **2.** [spill] herausfallen; [liquid] sich ergießen. ◆ **tip over** *vt sep* & *vi* umlkippen.

tip-off *n* Tipp *der*.

tipped ['tɪpt] *adj* [cigarette] mit Filter.

tipsy ['tɪpsɪ] *adj inf* beschwipst.

tiptoe ['tɪptəʊ] <> *n*: **on tiptoe** auf Zehenspitzen. <> *vi* auf Zehenspitzen gehen.

tire ['taɪə^r] <> *n* US = **tyre**. <> *vt* ermüden. <> *vi* - **1.** [get tired] müde werden - **2.** [get fed up]: **to tire of sb/sthg** von jm/etw genug haben.

tired ['taɪəd] *adj* - **1.** [sleepy] müde - **2.** [fed up]: **to be tired of sthg** etw leid sein; **to be tired of doing sthg** es leid sein, etw zu tun.

tireless ['taɪəlɪs] *adj* unermüdlich.

tiresome ['taɪəsəm] *adj* lästig.

tiring ['taɪərɪŋ] *adj* ermüdend.

tissue ['tɪʃuː] *n* - **1.** [paper handkerchief] Tempo® *das*, Papiertaschentuch *das* - **2.** (U) BIOL Gewebe *das*.

tissue paper *n* (U) Seidenpapier *das*.

tit [tɪt] *n* - **1.** [bird] Meise *die* - **2.** *vulg* [breast] Titte *die*.

titbit UK ['tɪtbɪt], **tidbit** US ['tɪdbɪt] *n liter* & *fig* Leckerbissen *der*.

tit for tat [-'tæt] *n* wie du mir, so ich dir.

titillate ['tɪtɪleɪt] *vt* [person] anlregen.

title ['taɪtl] *n* Titel *der*.

titter ['tɪtə^r] *vi* kichern.

TM *abbr of* **trademark**.

to (*unstressed before consonant* [tə], *unstressed before vowel* [tʊ], *stressed* [tuː]) <> *prep* - **1.** [indicating direction] nach; **to go to Liverpool/Spain** nach Liverpool/Spanien fahren; **to go to the USA** in die USA fahren; **to go to school/the cinema** in die Schule/ins Kino gehen; **to go to university** auf die Universität gehen; **to go to work/the doctor's** zur Arbeit/zum Arzt gehen; **the road to Bakersfield** die Straße nach Bakersfield - **2.** [indicating position]: **I nailed it to the wall** ich habe es an die Wand genagelt; **to the left** links; **to the right** rechts; **the east/west (of the river)** östlich/westlich (des Flusses) - **3.** (*to express indirect object*): **to give sthg to sb** jm etw geben; **to talk to sb** mit jm sprechen; **to listen to the radio** Radio hören; **we added milk to the mixture** wir fügten Milch zu der Mischung hinzu - **4.** [as far as] bis; **from here to London** von hier bis London; **to count to ten** bis zehn zählen; **we work from nine to five** wir arbeiten von 9 bis 5; **a year to the day** ein Jahr auf den Tag genau - **5.** UK [in telling the time] vor; **it's ten to three** es ist zehn vor drei - **6.** [per] pro; **10 kilometres to the litre** 10 Kilometer pro Liter - **7.** [in ratios]: **six votes to four** sechs Stimmen gegen vier; **he's ten to one to win** es steht zehn zu eins, dass er gewinnt - **8.** [of, for]: **the key to the car** der Schlüssel für das Auto; **a letter to my daughter** ein Brief an meine Tochter - **9.** [indicating reaction, effect] zu; **to my surprise** zu meiner Überraschung; **it would be to your advantage** es wäre zu Ihrem Vorteil - **10.** [in stating opinion]: **to me, he's lying** meiner Meinung nach, lügt er; **it seemed quite unnecessary to me/him/***etc* mir/ihm/*etc* erschien dies recht unnötig - **11.** [indicating process, change of state]: **to turn to ice** zu Eis werden; **it could lead to trouble** das könnte Ärger geben. <> *with inf* - **1.** (*forming simple infinitive*): **to walk** gehen; **to laugh** lachen - **2.** (*following another vb*): **to begin/try to do sthg** anlfangen/versuchen, etw zu tun; **to want to do sthg** etw tun wollen - **3.** (*following an adj*) zu; **difficult to do** schwer zu tun; **ready to go** bereit zu gehen - **4.** (*indicating purpose*) um zu; **we came here to look at the castle** wir sind hierher gekommen, um das Schloss anzuschauen - **5.** *(replacing a relative clause)*: **he is the first to complain** er ist der Erste, der sich beschwert; **to have a lot to do** viel zu tun haben; **he told me to leave** er sagte, ich solle gehen - **6.** *(to avoid repetition of infinitive)*: **I meant to call him, but I forgot to** ich wollte ihn eigentlich anrufen, vergaß es aber; **you ought to** du solltest es tun - **7.** [in contexts]: **to be honest** um ehrlich zu sein; **to sum up** zusammenzufassen, <> *adv* [shut]: **push the door to** druck die Tür zu. <> **to and fro** *adv* hin und her; **to go to and fro** kommen und gehen.

toad [təʊd] *n* Kröte *die*.

toadstool ['təʊdstuːl] *n* Giftpilz *der*.

toast [təʊst] <> *n (U)* [bread, drink] Toast *der*. <> *vt* - **1.** [bread] toasten - **2.** [person] trinken auf *(+ A)*.

toasted sandwich [,təʊstɪd-] *n* getoastetes Sandwich.

toaster ['təʊstə'] *n* Toaster *der*.

tobacco [tə'bækəʊ] *n* Tabak *der*.

tobacconist [tə'bækənɪst] *n*: **tobacconist's (shop)** Tabakwarenhandlung *die*.

toboggan [tə'bɒgən] *n* Schlitten *der*.

today [tə'deɪ] *n & adv (U)* heute.

toddler ['tɒdlə'] *n* Kleinkind *das*.

to-do *(pl* -s) *n inf dated* Getue *das*.

toe [təʊ] <> *n* - **1.** [of foot] Zeh *der*, Zehe *die* - **2.** [of sock, shoe] Spitze *die*. <> *vt*: **to toe the line** sich an die Regeln halten; [in political party] sich an die Parteilinie halten.

toenail ['təʊneɪl] *n* Zehennagel *der*.

toffee ['tɒfɪ] *n* - **1.** [sweet] Karamellbonbon *das* - **2.** [substance] Karamell *das*.

together [tə'geðə'] *adv* - **1.** [gen] zusammen; **to go together** [belong together] zusammengehören - **2.** [at the same time] zur gleichen Zeit. <> **together with** *prep* zusammen mit.

toil [tɔɪl] *fml* <> *n* Mühe *die*. <> *vi* sich abmühen.

toilet ['tɔɪlɪt] *n* Toilette *die*; **to go to the toilet** zur Toilette gehen.

toilet bag *n* Kulturbeutel *der*.

toilet paper *n* Toilettenpapier *das*.

toiletries ['tɔɪlɪtrɪz] *npl* Toilettenartikel *Pl*.

toilet roll *n* Rolle *die* Toilettenpapier.

token ['təʊkn] <> *adj* symbolisch. <> *n* - **1.** [voucher, disc] Gutschein *der* - **2.** [symbol] Zeichen *das*. <> **by the same token** *adv* ebenso.

told [təʊld] *pt & pp* ⊳ **tell**.

tolerable ['tɒlərəbl] *adj* [reasonable] annehmbar.

tolerance ['tɒlərəns] *n* Toleranz *die*.

tolerant ['tɒlərənt] *adj* - **1.** [not bigoted]: **tolerant of sb/sthg** tolerant gegenüber jm/etw - **2.** [resistant]: **tolerant to sthg** unempfindlich gegen etw.

tolerate ['tɒləreɪt] *vt* - **1.** [put up with - noise, heat, behaviour] ertragen - **2.** [permit] dulden, tolerieren.

toll [təʊl] *n* - **1.** [number] Zahl *die*; **the death toll** die Zahl der Toten - **2.** [fee] Gebühr *die* - **3.** *phr*: **to take its toll** seinen Tribut fordern.

tomato [*UK* tə'mɑːtəʊ, *US* tə'meɪtəʊ] *(pl* -es) *n* Tomate *die*.

tomb [tuːm] *n* Grab *das*.

tomboy ['tɒmbɔɪ] *n*: **she was a bit of a tomboy** sie war wie ein Junge.

tombstone ['tuːmstəʊn] *n* Grabstein *der*.

tomcat ['tɒmkæt] *n* Kater *der*.

tomorrow [tə'mɒrəʊ] *n & adv* morgen.

ton [tʌn] *(pl inv OR* -s) *n* - **1.** *UK* [imperial unit of measurement] ≃ Tonne *die* (= 1016 kg) - **2.** *US* [unit of measurement] ≃ Tonne *die* (= 907 kg) - **3.** [metric unit of measurement] Tonne *die* (= 1000 kg). <> **tons** *npl UK inf*: **tons of** ein Haufen *(+ G)*.

tone [təʊn] *n* [gen] Ton *der*; **to lower the tone** das Niveau senken. <> **tone down** *vt sep* mäßigen. <> **tone up** *vt sep* in Form bringen.

tone-deaf *adj*: **to be tone-deaf** kein musikalisches Gehör haben.

tongs [tɒŋz] *npl* - **1.** [for sugar] Zange *die* - **2.** [for hair] Lockenstab *der*.

tongue [tʌŋ] *n* - **1.** [gen] Zunge *die*; **to hold one's tongue** *fig* den Mund halten; **to have a sharp tongue** eine scharfe Zunge haben - **2.** *fml* [language] Sprache *die*.

tongue-in-cheek *adj* ironisch.

tongue-tied *adj*: **to be tongue-tied** kein Wort herausbringen.

tonic ['tɒnɪk] *n* - **1.** [tonic water] Tonic *das* - **2.** [medicine] Tonikum *das*.

tonic water *n* Tonic *das*.

tonight [tə'naɪt] *n & adv* heute Abend; [during night] heute Nacht.

tonne [tʌn] *(pl inv OR* -s) *n* Tonne *die*.

tonsil ['tɒnsl] *n* Mandel *die*.

tonsil(l)itis [,tɒnsɪ'laɪtɪs] *n (U)* Mandelentzündung *die*.

too [tuː] *adv* - **1.** [also] auch - **2.** [excessively] zu; **too many** zu viel; **it's too late to go out** es ist zu spät zum Ausgehen; **I know her all OR only too well** ich kenne sie nur zu gut; **it was none too comfortable** es war nicht gerade bequem; **not too good** nicht besonders gut; **how do you feel? not too bad** wie fühlst du dich? ganz gut; **I'd be only too happy to help** ich würde wirklich OR nur zu gerne helfen.

took [tʊk] *pt* ⊳ **take**.

tool [tu:l] *n* - 1. [implement] Werkzeug *das* - 2. *fig* [means] Hilfsmittel *das*.

tool box *n* Werkzeugkasten *der*.

tool kit *n* Werkzeugsatz *der*.

toot [tu:t] <> *n*: **to give a toot** hupen. <> *vi* hupen.

tooth [tu:θ] (*pl* **teeth**) *n* Zahn *der*.

toothache ['tu:θeɪk] *n* (*U*) Zahnschmerzen *Pl*.

toothbrush ['tu:θbrʌʃ] *n* Zahnbürste *die*.

toothpaste ['tu:θpeɪst] *n* Zahnpasta *die*.

toothpick ['tu:θpɪk] *n* Zahnstocher *der*.

top [tɒp] <> *adj* - 1. [highest] oberste(r) (s) - 2. [most important, successful] Spitzen-; **she was top in the exam** sie war die Beste in der Prüfung - 3. [maximum] Höchst-. <> *n* - 1. [highest point - of road] Ende *das*; [- of stairs] oberste Stufe; [- of hill] Gipfel *der*; [- of tree] Krone *die*; **at the top of the page** oben auf der Seite; **from top to bottom** von oben bis unten; **on top** oben; **at the top of one's voice** aus vollem Halse - 2. [lid, cap - of bottle, jar] Deckel *der*; [- of pen, tube] Kappe *die* - 3. [upper side - of table] Platte *die*; [- of box] Oberseite *die* - 4. [clothing] Oberteil *das* - 5. [toy] Kreisel *der* - 6. [in organization, league, table] Spitze *die*; **to be top of the class** Klassenbeste(r) sein. <> *vt* - 1. [be first in - table, chart] anführen; [- poll, league] an erster Stelle liegen in (+ D) - 2. [better] übertreffen; [offer] überbieten - 3. [exceed] übersteigen - 4. [cover]: **to top with cream** Sahne geben auf (+ A); **topped with** mit. ◆ **on top of** *prep* - 1. [indicating position] auf (+ D); [indicating direction] auf (+ A) - 2. [in addition to] zusätzlich zu. ◆ **top up** *UK*, **top off** *US vt sep* nachfüllen.

top floor *n* oberstes Stockwerk.

top hat *n* Zylinder *der*.

top-heavy *adj* kopflastig.

topic ['tɒpɪk] *n* Thema *das*.

topical ['tɒpɪkl] *adj* aktuell.

topless ['tɒplɪs] *adj* [barebreasted] oben ohne.

topmost ['tɒpməust] *adj* oberste(r) (s).

topping ['tɒpɪŋ] *n* Garnierung *die*.

topple ['tɒpl] <> *vt* [government, leader] stürzen. <> *vi* fallen.

top-secret *adj* streng geheim.

topspin ['tɒpspɪn] *n* (*U*) Topspin *der*.

topsy-turvy [,tɒpsɪ'tɜ:vɪ] *adj* - 1. [messy] durcheinander - 2. [haywire] verkehrt.

torch [tɔ:tʃ] *n* - 1. *UK* [electric] Taschenlampe *die* - 2. [flaming stick] Fackel *die*.

tore [tɔ:ʳ] *pt* ▷ **tear²**.

torment <> *n* ['tɔ:ment] Qual *die*. <> *vt* [tɔ:'ment] [worry, annoy] quälen.

torn [tɔ:n] *pp* ▷ **tear²**.

tornado [tɔ:'neɪdəu] (*pl* **-es** *OR* **-s**) *n* Tornado *das*.

torpedo [tɔ:'pi:dəu] (*pl* **-es**) *n* Torpedo *der*.

torrent ['tɒrənt] *n* - 1. [rushing water] reißender Strom - 2. [of words] Schwall *der*.

torrid ['tɒrɪd] *adj* liter & *fig* heiß.

tortoise ['tɔ:təs] *n* Schildkröte *die*.

tortoiseshell ['tɔ:təʃel] <> *adj* [cat] Schildpatt-. <> *n* [material] Schildpatt *das*.

torture ['tɔ:tʃəʳ] <> *n* - 1. (*U*) [punishment] Folter *die* - 2. *fig* [cruel treatment] Qual *die*. <> *vt* foltern.

Tory ['tɔ:rɪ] <> *adj* Tory-, konservativ. <> *n* Tory *der, die*, Konservative *der, die*.

toss [tɒs] <> *vt* - 1. [throw carelessly] werfen; **she tossed back her head** sie warf ihren Kopf zurück - 2. [food] schwenken; [salad] mischen; [pancake] wenden - 3. [coin] werfen; **I'll toss you for it** lass uns eine Münze werfen - 4. [boat, passengers] hin und her werfen. <> *vi* [move about]: **to toss and turn** sich hin und her werfen. ◆ **toss up** *vi* eine Münze werfen.

tot [tɒt] *n* - 1. *inf* [small child] kleines Kind - 2. [of drink] Schluck *der*.

total ['təutl] (*UK*) (*US*) <> *adj* - 1. [complete - dedication, despair, darkness] völlig; [- eclipse, failure] total; **total fool** Volldiot *der* - 2. [amount, number] Gesamt-. <> *n* Gesamtsumme *die*; **a total of 50 people** insgesamt 50 Leute. <> *vt* - 1. [add up] zusammenzählen - 2. [amount to] sich belaufen auf (+ A).

totally ['təutəlɪ] *adv* völlig.

totter ['tɒtəʳ] *vi* - 1. [walk unsteadily] taumeln - 2. *fig* [government] schwanken.

touch [tʌtʃ] <> *n* - 1. (*U*) [act of touching] Berührung *die*; **to be soft to the touch** sich weich anfühlen - 2. [detail] Detail *das* - 3. (*U*) [style] Note *die* - 4. [contact]: **to get in touch with sb** sich mit jm in Verbindung setzen; **to keep in touch (with sb)** (mit jm) in Kontakt bleiben; **to lose touch with sb** jn aus den Augen verlieren; **to be out of touch with sthg** in Bezug auf etw (*A*) nicht auf dem Laufenden sein - 5. [small amount]: **a touch (of sthg)** eine Spur (von etw) - 6. SPORT: **in touch** im Aus. <> *vt* - 1. [make contact with] anfassen - 2. [move emotionally] rühren - 3. [eat, drink] anrühren. <> *vi* - 1. [make contact - people, things] sich berühren; **don't touch!** nicht anfassen! - 2. [be in contact] aneinander stoßen. ◆ **touch down** *vi* [plane] aufsetzen. ◆ **touch on** *vt insep* rühren an (+ A).

touch-and-go *adj* ungewiss.

touchdown ['tʌtʃdaun] *n* - 1. [of plane] Aufsetzen *das* - 2. [in American football] Touchdown *der*.

touched [tʌtʃt] *adj* - 1. [moved] bewegt - 2. *inf* [slightly mad] nicht ganz richtig im Kopf.

touching ['tʌtʃɪŋ] *adj* rührend.

touchline ['tʌtʃlaɪn] *n* Auslinie *die*.

touchy ['tʌtʃı] adj - **1.** [person] empfindlich - **2.** [subject, question] heikel.

tough [tʌf] adj - **1.** [gen] hart - **2.** [meat] zäh - **3.** [decision, life] schwer - **4.** [criminal, neighbourhood] rau.

toughen ['tʌfn] vt - **1.** [character] hart machen - **2.** [material] härten.

toupee ['tu:peı] n Toupet das.

tour [tʊər] ⟨> n - **1.** [trip] Tour die - **2.** [of building, town, museum] Rundgang der - **3.** [of pop group etc] Tournee die; **to be on tour** auf Tournee sein. ⟨> vt - **1.** [visit - city, museum] besichtigen; [- country] reisen durch - **2.** SPORT & THEAT eine Tournee machen durch.

touring ['tʊərıŋ] n Herumreisen das.

tourism ['tʊərızm] n Tourismus der, Fremdenverkehr der.

tourist ['tʊərıst] n Tourist der, -in die.

tourist (information) office n Touristeninformation die, Fremdenverkehrsbüro das.

tournament ['tɔ:nəmənt] n Turnier das.

tour operator n Reiseveranstalter der.

tout [taʊt] ⟨> n Schwarzhändler der, -in die. ⟨> vt [tickets, goods] anbieten. ⟨> vi: **to tout for custom** auf Kundenfang sein.

tow [təʊ] ⟨> n: **to give sb a tow** jn ablschleppen; **to be on tow** UK abgeschleppt werden. ⟨> vt ablschleppen.

towards UK [tə'wɔ:dz], **toward** US [tə'wɔ:d] prep - **1.** [in the direction of] zu; **to run towards sb** auf jn zullaufen; **efforts towards his release** Bemühungen um seine Freilassung - **2.** [facing] nach - **3.** [with regard to] gegenüber; **his feelings towards me** seine Gefühle mir gegenüber OR für mich - **4.** [in time] gegen; **towards nine o'clock** gegen neun Uhr - **5.** [in space]: **to sit towards the back/front** hinten/vorne sitzen - **6.** [as contribution] für; **he gave £20 towards the disaster relief fund** er spendete £20 für Katastrophenhilfsfonds.

towel ['taʊəl] n Handtuch das.

towelling UK, **toweling** US ['taʊəlıŋ] n (U) Frotteestoff der.

towel rail n Handtuchhalter der.

tower ['taʊər] ⟨> n Turm der. ⟨> vi hochlragen; **to tower over sb/sthg** jn/etw überragen.

tower block n UK Hochhaus das.

town [taʊn] n Stadt die; **to go out on the town** einen drauflmachen; **to go to town** fig [spend a lot] es sich (D) was kosten lassen; [take trouble] sich ins Zeug legen.

town centre n Stadtmitte die.

town council n Stadtrat der.

town hall n - **1.** [building] Rathaus das - **2.** (U) fig [council] Stadtrat der.

town plan n Stadtplan der.

town planning n (U) Stadtplanung die.

towpath ['təʊpɑ:θ] (pl [-pɑ:ðz]) n Leinpfad der.

towrope ['təʊrəʊp] n Abschleppseil das.

tow truck n US Abschleppwagen der.

toxic ['tɒksık] adj giftig.

toy [tɔı] n Spielzeug das. ➤ **toy with** vt insep spielen mit.

toy shop n Spielwarenladen der.

trace [treıs] ⟨> n Spur die. ⟨> vt - **1.** [find] auflspüren - **2.** [follow progress of] verfolgen - **3.** [mark outline of] nachlzeichnen; [with tracing paper] durchlpausen.

tracing paper n (U) Transparentpapier das.

track [træk] ⟨> n - **1.** [path] Pfad der - **2.** SPORT Bahn die - **3.** RAIL Gleis das - **4.** [mark, trace] Spur die - **5.** [on record, tape, CD] Stück das - **6.** phr: **to lose track of sb/sthg** jn/etw aus den Augen verlieren; **to be on the right/wrong track** auf der richtigen/falschen Spur sein. ⟨> vt [follow] nachlspüren (+ D). ➤ **track down** vt sep [person, animal] auflspüren; [book, address] auflstöbern.

track record n: **to have a good track record** gute Erfolge aufzuweisen haben.

tracksuit ['træksu:t] n Trainingsanzug der.

traction ['trækʃn] n (U) PHYS Zugkraft die; **in traction** im Streckverband.

tractor ['træktər] n Traktor der.

trade [treıd] ⟨> n - **1.** [commerce] Handel der - **2.** [job] Handwerk das; **by trade** von Beruf. ⟨> vt [exchange] tauschen; **to trade sthg for sthg** etw gegen etw einltauschen. ⟨> vi COMM [do business]: **to trade (with sb)** (mit jm) Handel treiben. ➤ **trade in** vt sep [exchange] in Zahlung geben.

trade fair n Messe die.

trade-in n: **they gave her a trade-in on her old cooker** sie nahmen ihren alten Herd in Zahlung.

trademark ['treıdmɑ:k] n - **1.** COMM Warenzeichen das - **2.** fig [characteristic]: **honesty is his trademark** er ist für seine Ehrlichkeit bekannt.

trade name n COMM Handelsname der.

trader ['treıdər] n Händler der, -in die.

tradesman ['treıdzmən] (pl -men [-mən]) n [shopkeeper, trader] Händler der.

trades union n UK = **trade union**.

Trades Union Congress n UK: **the Trades Union Congress** der Gewerkschaftsbund.

trade union n Gewerkschaft die.

trading ['treıdıŋ] n Handel der.

trading estate n UK Industriegebiet das.

tradition [trə'dıʃn] n - **1.** (U) [system of customs] Tradition die - **2.** [established practice] Brauch der.

traditional [trə'dıʃənl] adj traditionell.

traffic ['træfık] (pt & pp -ked, cont -king) ⟨> n - **1.** [vehicles] Verkehr der - **2.** [illegal trade]

Handel *der*; **the traffic in drugs/arms** der Drogen-/Waffenhandel. ⋄ *vi*: **to traffic in sthg** mit etw handeln.

traffic circle *n* US Kreisverkehr *der*.

traffic jam *n* Stau *der*.

trafficker ['træfɪkəʳ] *n* Händler *der*, -in *die*.

traffic lights *npl* Ampel *die*.

traffic warden *n* UK Hilfspolizist *der*, Politesse *die*.

tragedy ['trædʒədɪ] *n* Tragödie *die*.

tragic ['trædʒɪk] *adj* tragisch.

trail [treɪl] ⋄ *n* - 1. [path] Weg *der* - 2. [traces] Spur *die*. ⋄ *vt* - 1. [drag behind, tow] hinter sich (D) herlschleifen - 2. [lag behind] zurücklliegen hinter (+ D). ⋄ *vi* - 1. [drag behind] schleifen - 2. [move slowly] trotten - 3. SPORT [lose] zurücklliegen. ✦ **trail away, trail off** *vi*: **his voice trailed away** seine Stimme wurde leiser und verstummte schließlich.

trailer ['treɪləʳ] *n* - 1. [vehicle for luggage] Anhänger *der* - 2. *esp* US [for living in] Wohnwagen *der* - 3. CIN Trailer *der*.

train [treɪn] ⋄ *n* - 1. RAIL Zug *der*; **by train** mit dem Zug - 2. [of dress] Schleppe *die* - 3. [connected sequence]: **train of thought** Gedankengang *der*. ⋄ *vt* - 1. [teach - animal] dressieren; **to train sb to do sthg** jm beilbringen, etw zu tun - 2. [for job] auslbilden; **to train sb as sthg** jn zu etw auslbilden - 3. SPORT trainieren - 4. [gun, camera]: **to train sthg on sb/sthg** etw auf jn/etw richten. ⋄ *vi* - 1. [for job]: **to train (as)** eine Ausbildung machen (als) - 2. SPORT: **to train (for sthg)** (für etw) trainieren.

train driver *n* Zugführer *der*, -in *die*.

trained [treɪnd] *adj* ausgebildet.

trainee [treɪ'niː] *n* Auszubildende *der*, *die*; [academic, technical] Praktikant *der*, -in *die*.

trainer ['treɪnəʳ] *n* - 1. [of dogs] Dresseur *der*, -euse *die*; [of horses] Trainer *der*, -in *die* - 2. SPORT Trainer *der*, -in *die*. ✦ **trainers** *npl* UK [shoes] Turnschuhe *Pl*.

training ['treɪnɪŋ] *n* - 1. [for job] Ausbildung *die* - 2. SPORT Training *das*.

training shoes *npl* UK Turnschuhe *Pl*.

traipse [treɪps] *vi* latschen.

trait [treɪt] *n* Charakterzug *der*.

traitor ['treɪtəʳ] *n*: **traitor (to sthg)** Verräter *der*, -in *die* (an etw (D)).

trajectory [trə'dʒektərɪ] *n* TECH Flugbahn *die*.

tram [træm] *n* UK Straßenbahn *die*.

tramp [træmp] ⋄ *n* [homeless person] Landstreicher *der*, -in *die*. ⋄ *vi* [trudge] trotten.

trample ['træmpl] *vt* niederltrampeln.

trampoline ['træmpəliːn] *n* Trampolin *das*.

trance [trɑːns] *n* [hypnotic state] Trance *die*.

tranquil ['træŋkwɪl] *adj liter* friedlich.

tranquillizer UK, **tranquilizer** US ['træŋkwɪlaɪzəʳ] *n* Beruhigungsmittel *das*.

transaction [træn'zækʃn] *n* [piece of business] Transaktion *die*.

transcend [træn'send] *vt fml* [go beyond] hinauslgehen über (+ A).

transcript ['trænskrɪpt] *n* [of speech, conversation] Mitschrift *die*.

transfer ⋄ *n* ['trænsfɜːʳ] - 1. (U) [from one place to another - of money] Überweisung *die*; [- of prisoner] Überführung *die*; [- of patient] Verlegung *die* - 2. (U) [from one person to another] Übertragung *die* - 3. [for job] Versetzung *die* - 4. SPORT Wechsel *der*, Transfer *der* - 5. [design] Abziehbild *das*. ⋄ *vt* [træns'fɜːʳ] - 1. (U) [from one place to another - money] überweisen; [- prisoner] überführen; [- patient] verlegen - 2. [from one person to another]: **to transfer sthg to sb** jm etw übertragen - 3. [for job] versetzen - 4. SPORT transferieren. ⋄ *vi* [træns'fɜːʳ] [to different job *etc* & SPORT] wechseln.

transfix [træns'fɪks] *vt* [immobilize] erstarren lassen.

transform [træns'fɔːm] *vt*: **to transform sb/sthg (into)** jn/etw verwandeln (in (+ A)).

transfusion [træns'fjuːʒn] *n* Transfusion *die*.

transistor [træn'zɪstəʳ] *n* ELECTRON Transistor *der*.

transit ['trænsɪt] *n*: **in transit** [goods] auf dem Transport.

transition [træn'zɪʃn] *n*: **transition from sthg to sthg** Übergang *der* von etw zu etw.

transitive ['trænzɪtɪv] *adj* GRAM transitiv.

transitory ['trænzɪtrɪ] *adj* vergänglich.

translate [træns'leɪt] *vt* - 1. [languages] übersetzen - 2. *fig* [transform]: **to translate a plan into action** einen Plan in die Tat umlsetzen.

translation [træns'leɪʃn] *n* Übersetzung *die*.

translator [træns'leɪtəʳ] *n* Übersetzer *der*, -in *die*.

transmission [trænz'mɪʃn] *n* - 1. [passing on & ELECTRON] Übertragung *die* - 2. RADIO & TV [programme] Sendung *die*.

transmit [trænz'mɪt] *vt* übertragen.

transmitter [trænz'mɪtəʳ] *n* ELECTRON Sender *der*.

transparency [trans'pærənsɪ] *n* - 1. PHOT Dia(positiv) *das* - 2. [for overhead projector] Folie *die*.

transparent [træns'pærənt] *adj* - 1. [seethrough] durchsichtig - 2. [obvious] offensichtlich.

transpire [træn'spaɪəʳ] *fml* ⋄ *vt*: **it transpires that ...** es stellt sich heraus, dass ... ⋄ *vi* [happen] passieren.

transplant <> n ['trænspla:nt] [MED - operation] Transplantation die; [- organ, tissue] Transplantat das. <> vt [træns'pla:nt] - 1. MED transplantieren - 2. BOT [seedlings] umlpflanzen.

transport <> n ['trænspɔ:t] - 1. [system] Verkehrsmittel Pl - 2. [of goods, people] Beförderung die, Transport der. <> vt [træn'spɔ:t] [goods, people] befördern, transportieren.

transportation [ˌtrænspɔ:'teɪʃn] n esp US = transport.

transpose [træns'pəʊz] vt [change round] umlstellen.

trap [træp] <> n Falle die. <> vt - 1. [animal, bird] fangen - 2. fig [trick] eine Falle stellen (+ D) - 3. [immobilize, catch]: **to be trapped in a relationship** in einer Beziehung gefangen sein - 4. [energy] speichern.

trapdoor ['træp'dɔ:'] n Falltür die.

trapeze [trə'pi:z] n Trapez die.

trappings ['træpɪŋz] npl äußere Zeichen Pl.

trash [træʃ] n - 1. US [refuse] Abfall der - 2. inf pej [sthg of poor quality] Ramsch der; [book, film] Schund der.

trashcan ['træʃkæn] n US Abfalleimer der.

traumatic [trɔ:'mætɪk] adj traumatisch.

travel ['trævl] (UK) (US) <> n (U) Reisen das. <> vt [distance] fahren; **to travel the world/country** durch die Welt/das Land reisen. <> vi - 1. [journey] reisen - 2. [go, move - train] fahren; [- light] sich fortlbewegen; [- current] fließen; [- news] sich verbreiten.

travel agency n Reisebüro das.

travel agent n Reiseveranstalter der, -in die; **travel agent's** Reisebüro das.

travelcard ['trævlka:d] n Zeitkarte die.

traveller UK, **traveler** US ['trævlə'] n - 1. [person on journey] Reisende der, die - 2. [itinerant] Herumreisende der, die.

traveller's cheque n Travellerscheck der.

travelling UK, **traveling** US ['trævlɪŋ] adj - 1. [itinerant] Wander- - 2. [for taking on journeys, of travel] Reise-.

travelsick ['trævəlsɪk] adj reisekrank.

travesty ['trævəstɪ] n: **it was a travesty of justice** es war eine Verhöhnung der Gerechtigkeit.

trawler ['trɔ:lə'] n Trawler der.

tray [treɪ] n - 1. [for carrying] Tablett das - 2. [for papers, mail] Korb der.

treacherous ['tretʃərəs] adj - 1. [person, behaviour] verräterisch - 2. [rock, tides] tückisch.

treachery ['tretʃərɪ] n Verrat der.

treacle ['tri:kl] n UK Sirup der.

tread [tred] (pt trod, pp trodden) <> n - 1. [on tyre, shoe] Profil das - 2. [sound or way of walking] Schritt der, Tritt der. <> vi [place foot]: **to tread on sthg** auf etw (A) treten.

treason ['tri:zn] n Verrat der.

treasure ['treʒə'] <> n Schatz der. <> vt [memory] bewahren; [object] sorgfältig auflbewahren.

treasurer ['treʒərə'] n Schatzmeister der, -in die.

treasury ['treʒərɪ] n [room] Schatzkammer die. ➡ **Treasury** n: **the Treasury** das Finanzministerium.

treat [tri:t] <> vt - 1. [gen] behandeln; **to treat sthg as a joke** etw als Witz anlsehen - 2. [give sthg special]: **to treat sb (to sthg)** jn (zu etw) einlladen. <> n [sthg special]: **what a treat!** was für ein Genuss!; **to give sb a treat** jm eine Freude bereiten; **this is my treat** ich lade dich ein.

treatment ['tri:tmənt] n [gen] Behandlung die; [specific method of medical care] Behandlungsmethode die.

treaty ['tri:tɪ] n Vertrag der.

treble ['trebl] <> adj [with numbers]: **treble 4** dreimal 4. <> n - 1. (U) MUS [musical range] Oberstimme die - 2. MUS [boy singer] Knabensopran der. <> vt verdreifachen. <> vi sich verdreifachen.

treble clef n Violinschlüssel der.

tree [tri:] n [plant & COMPUT] Baum der.

treetop ['tri:tɒp] n Baumkrone die.

tree-trunk n Baumstamm der.

trek [trek] <> n anstrengender Marsch. <> vi - 1. [go on long journey]: **to trek through the jungle** durch den Urwald ziehen - 2. inf [walk laboriously]: **I had to trek all the way home** ich musste den ganzen Weg nach Hause laufen.

tremble ['trembl] vi zittern.

tremendous [trɪ'mendəs] adj - 1. [impressive, large] enorm - 2. inf [really good] sagenhaft.

tremor ['tremə'] n - 1. [of body, voice] Zittern das - 2. [small earthquake] Beben das.

trench [trentʃ] n - 1. [channel] Graben der - 2. MIL Schützengraben der.

trend [trend] n [tendency] Trend der, Tendenz die.

trendy ['trendɪ] adj inf in, angesagt.

trepidation [ˌtrepɪ'deɪʃn] n (U) fml: **in or with trepidation** mit einem beklommenen Gefühl.

trespass ['trespəs] vi: **to trespass (on sb's land)** ein Grundstück unbefugt betreten; **'no trespassing'** 'Betreten verboten'.

trespasser ['trespəsə'] n Unbefugte der, Unbefugte die.

trial ['traɪəl] n - 1. LAW Prozess der; **to be on trial (for sthg)** (wegen etw) vor Gericht stehen - 2. [test, experiment] Versuch der; **on trial** zur Probe; **by trial and error** durch Ausprobieren - 3. [unpleasant experience] Qual die.

triangle ['traɪæŋgl] n - 1. [shape] Dreieck das - 2. MUS Triangel der.

tribe [traɪb] n [social group] Stamm der.

tribunal [traɪˈbjuːnl] n Tribunal das.

tributary [ˈtrɪbjʊtrɪ] n GEOG Nebenfluss der.

tribute [ˈtrɪbjuːt] n - 1. [respect] Tribut der; **to pay tribute to sb/sthg** jm/etw Tribut zollen - 2. [evidence]: **it's a tribute to his strength of character that...** es ist ein Beweis für seine Charakterstärke, dass...

trice [traɪs] n: **in a trice** im Nu.

trick [trɪk] ⬦ n - 1. [to deceive] Streich der; **to play a trick on sb** jm einen Streich spielen - 2. [to entertain] Trick der - 3. [ability, knack] Trick der; **that will do the trick** damit ist das Problem gelöst. ⬦ vt austricksen; **to trick sb into doing sthg** jn durch List dazu bringen, etw zu tun.

trickery [ˈtrɪkərɪ] n Betrug der.

trickle [ˈtrɪkl] ⬦ n [of liquid] Rinnsal das; [drip] Tröpfeln das. ⬦ vi - 1. [liquid] rinnen - 2. [people]: **to trickle in/out** nach und nach herein-/herauskommen. ·

tricky [ˈtrɪkɪ] adj [difficult] verzwickt.

tricycle [ˈtraɪsɪkl] n Dreirad das.

tried [traɪd] adj: **tried and tested** erprobt, bewährt.

trifle [ˈtraɪfl] n - 1. CULIN Dessert aus Biskuit, Früchten, Vanillecreme und Sahne in Schichten - 2. [unimportant thing] Kleinigkeit die. ⬥ **a trifle** adv fml eine Spur.

trifling [ˈtraɪflɪŋ] adj pej unbedeutend.

trigger [ˈtrɪgər] ⬦ n [on gun] Abzug der. ⬦ vt auslösen. ⬥ **trigger off** vt sep = trigger.

trill [trɪl] n - 1. MUS Triller der - 2. [of birds] Trällern das.

trim [trɪm] ⬦ adj - 1. [neat and tidy] gepflegt - 2. [slim] schlank. ⬦ n [cut]: **to give sb OR sb's hair a trim** jm die Haare nachlschneiden. ⬦ vt - 1. [cut - hedge] zurücklschneiden; [- hair] nachlschneiden; [- lawn] mähen; [- nails] schneiden - 2. [decorate]: **to trim sthg (with sthg)** etw (mit etw) verzieren.

trinket [ˈtrɪŋkɪt] n Schmuckstück das.

trio [ˈtriːəʊ] (pl -s) n Trio das.

trip [trɪp] ⬦ n - 1. [journey] Ausflug der - 2. drug sl [experience] Trip der. ⬦ vt [make stumble] ein Bein stellen (+ D). ⬦ vi [stumble]: **to trip (over sthg)** (über etw (A)) stolpern. ⬥ **trip up** vt sep [make stumble] ein Bein stellen (+ D).

tripe [traɪp] n (U) - 1. CULIN Kaldaunen Pl - 2. inf [nonsense] Quatsch der.

triple [ˈtrɪpl] ⬦ adj dreifach. ⬦ vt verdreifachen. ⬦ vi sich verdreifachen.

triple jump n: **the triple jump** der Dreisprung.

triplets [ˈtrɪplɪts] npl Drillinge Pl.

tripod [ˈtraɪpɒd] n Stativ das.

trite [traɪt] adj pej banal.

triumph [ˈtraɪəmf] ⬦ n Triumph der. ⬦ vi: **to triumph (over)** triumphieren (über (+ A)).

trivia [ˈtrɪvɪə] n (U) Belanglosigkeiten Pl.

trivial [ˈtrɪvɪəl] adj pej trivial.

trod [trɒd] pt ⬤ **tread**.

trolley [ˈtrɒlɪ] (pl trolleys) n - 1. UK [for shopping] Einkaufswagen der; [for luggage] Gepäckwagen der - 2. UK [for food, drinks] Servierwagen der - 3. US [vehicle] Straßenbahn die.

trombone [trɒmˈbəʊn] n Posaune die.

troop [truːp] ⬦ n [large group] Schar die. ⬦ vi strömen. ⬥ **troops** npl MIL Truppen Pl.

trophy [ˈtrəʊfɪ] n SPORT Trophäe die.

tropical [ˈtrɒpɪkl] adj tropisch.

tropics [ˈtrɒpɪks] npl: **the tropics** die Tropen.

trot [trɒt] ⬦ n Trab der. ⬦ vi traben. ⬥ **on the trot** adv inf hintereinander.

trouble [ˈtrʌbl] ⬦ n - 1. [difficulty] Problem das; **to be in trouble** [having problems] in Schwierigkeiten stecken - 2. [bother]: **it's no trouble** es macht mir keine Mühe; **to take the trouble to do sthg** sich (D) die Mühe machen, etw zu tun - 3. (U) [pain, illness] Beschwerden Pl; **to have heart/kidney trouble** es mit dem Herzen/den Nieren haben - 4. [fighting & POL] Unruhen Pl. ⬦ vt - 1. [worry, upset] beunruhigen - 2. [interrupt, disturb] stören - 3. [cause pain to] zu schaffen machen (+ D). ⬥ **troubles** npl - 1. [worries] Sorgen Pl - 2. POL [unrest] Unruhen Pl.

troubled [ˈtrʌbld] adj - 1. [worried, upset] besorgt - 2. [disturbed - sleep] unruhig; [- place] von Unruhen geschüttelt; **troubled times** turbulente Zeiten.

troublemaker [ˈtrʌbl,meɪkər] n Unruhestifter der, -in die.

troublesome [ˈtrʌblsəm] adj lästig.

trough [trɒf] n - 1. [for animals] Trog der - 2. [low point] Tal das.

troupe [truːp] n Truppe die.

trousers [ˈtraʊzəz] npl Hose die; **a pair of trousers** eine Hose.

trout [traʊt] (pl inv OR -s) n Forelle die.

trowel [ˈtraʊəl] n - 1. [for the garden] Pflanzkelle die - 2. [for cement, plaster] Kelle die.

truant [ˈtruːənt] n [child] Schwänzer der, -in die; **to play truant** (die Schule) schwänzen.

truck [trʌk] n - 1. esp US [lorry] Lastwagen der - 2. RAIL Güterwagon der.

truck driver n esp US Lastwagenfahrer der, -in die.

trucker [ˈtrʌkər] n US Lastwagenfahrer der, -in die.

truck farm n US Gemüsegärtnerei die.

trudge [trʌdʒ] vi sich schleppen; [through snow, mud] stapfen.

true [tru:] *adj* - **1.** [factual] wahr; **to come true** wahr werden - **2.** [genuine] echt, wahr - **3.** [faithful] getreu - **4.** [precise, exact] gerade.

truffle ['trʌfl] *n* Trüffel *die*.

truly ['tru:lɪ] *adv* - **1.** wirklich - **2.** *phr*: **yours truly** [at end of letter] mit freundlichen Grüßen; [me] ich.

trump [trʌmp] *n* [card] Trumpf *der*.

trumped-up ['trʌmpt-] *adj pej* konstruiert.

trumpet ['trʌmpɪt] *n* MUS Trompete *die*.

truncheon ['trʌntʃən] *n* Knüppel *der*.

trundle ['trʌndl] *vi* entlanglzockeln; [downhill] hinunterlzockeln.

trunk [trʌŋk] *n* - **1.** [of tree] Stamm *der* - **2.** ANAT Rumpf *der* - **3.** [of elephant] Rüssel *der* - **4.** [luggage] Schrankkoffer *der* - **5.** US [of car] Kofferraum *der*. **trunks** *npl* [for swimming] Badehose *die*.

trunk road *n* UK Fernstraße *die*.

truss [trʌs] *n* MED Bruchband *das*.

trust [trʌst] ◇ *vt* - **1.** [have confidence in] trauen (+ D), vertrauen (+ D); **to trust sb to do sthg** jm zultrauen, etw zu tun - **2.** [entrust]: **to trust sb with sthg** jm mit etw vertrauen - **3.** *fml* [hope]: **I trust (that)** ich hoffe(, dass). ◇ *n* - **1.** (U) [faith] Vertrauen *das*; **trust in sb/ sthg** Vertrauen zu jm/etw - **2.** (U) [responsibility] Verantwortung *die* - **3.** FIN Treuhandschaft *die* - **4.** COMM Trust *der*.

trusted ['trʌstɪd] *adj* bewährt.

trustee [trʌs'ti:] *n* - **1.** FIN & LAW Treuhänder *der*, -in *die* - **2.** [manager of institution] Verwalter *der*, -in *die*.

trust fund *n* Treuhandvermögen *das*.

trusting ['trʌstɪŋ] *adj* vertrauensvoll.

trustworthy ['trʌst,wɜ:ðɪ] *adj* vertrauenswürdig.

truth [tru:θ] *n* Wahrheit *die*; **to tell the truth,...** um die Wahrheit zu sagen,...; **in (all) truth** in aller Aufrichtigkeit.

truthful ['tru:θful] *n* ehrlich.

try [traɪ] ◇ *vt* - **1.** [attempt] versuchen; **to try to do sthg** versuchen, etw zu tun - **2.** [sample] probieren; [test] auslprobieren - **3.** LAW [case] gerichtlich verhandeln; [criminal] vor Gericht stellen - **4.** [tax, strain] auf die Probe stellen. ◇ *vi* versuchen; **to try for sthg** sich um etw bemühen. ◇ *n* [attempt & SPORT] Versuch *der*; **to give sthg a try** etw mal versuchen. **try on** *vt sep* [clothes] anlprobieren. **try out** *vt sep* auslprobieren.

trying ['traɪɪŋ] *adj* schwierig.

T-shirt *n* T-Shirt *das*.

tub [tʌb] *n* - **1.** [of margarine, ice cream] Becher *der* - **2.** *inf* [bath] Wanne *die*.

tubby ['tʌbɪ] *adj inf* rundlich.

tube [tju:b] *n* - **1.** [hollow cylinder - inflexible] Röhrchen *das*, Rohr *das*; [- flexible]

Schlauch *der* - **2.** [of toothpaste, glue] Tube *die* - **3.** UK [underground train] U-Bahn *die*; *(phrase)*: **by tube** mit der U-Bahn.

tuberculosis [tju:,bɜ:kjʊ'ləʊsɪs] *n* Tuberkulose *die*.

tubular ['tju:bjʊləʳ] *adj* Röhren-.

TUC *n abbr of* **Trades Union Congress**.

tuck [tʌk] *vt* [place neatly] stecken. **tuck away** *vt sep* [store] verstecken. **tuck in** ◇ *vt sep* - **1.** [child, patient] zuldecken - **2.** [clothes] hineinlstecken. ◇ *vi inf* zullangen. **tuck up** *vt sep* zuldecken.

tuck shop *n* UK Schulkiosk *der*.

Tuesday ['tju:zdɪ] *n* Dienstag *der*; *see also* **Saturday**.

tuft [tʌft] *n* Büschel *das*.

tug [tʌg] ◇ *n* - **1.** [pull] Ruck *der* - **2.** [boat] Schleppkahn *der*. ◇ *vt* (ruckartig) ziehen; **she tugged his sleeve** sie zupfte ihn am Ärmel. ◇ *vi*: **to tug at sthg** (ruckartig) an etw (D) ziehen.

tug-of-war *n* Tauziehen *das*.

tuition [tju:'ɪʃn] *n* (U) Unterricht *der*.

tulip ['tju:lɪp] *n* Tulpe *die*.

tumble ['tʌmbl] ◇ *vi* - **1.** [person, prices] fallen - **2.** [water] stürzen. ◇ *n* Sturz *der*.

tumbledown ['tʌmbldaʊn] *adj* baufällig.

tumble-dryer [-,draɪəʳ] *n* Wäschetrockner *der*.

tumbler ['tʌmbləʳ] *n* [glass - short] Whiskyglas *das*; [- tall] Becherglas *das*.

tummy ['tʌmɪ] *n inf* - **1.** [outside of stomach] Bauch *der* - **2.** [inside of stomach] Magen *der*.

tumour UK, **tumor** US ['tju:məʳ] *n* Tumor *der*.

tuna [UK 'tju:nə, US 'tu:nə] (*pl inv OR* -s), **tuna fish** (*pl* **tuna fish**) *n* Tunfisch *der*.

tune [tju:n] ◇ *n* [song, melody] Melodie *die*. ◇ *vt* - **1.** MUS stimmen - **2.** [engine, RADIO & TV] einlstellen. **tune in** *vi* RADIO & TV einlschalten; **to tune in to sthg** etw einlschalten. **tune up** *vi* MUS stimmen. **in tune** ◇ *adj* MUS (richtig) gestimmt. ◇ *adv* - **1.** MUS richtig - **2.** [in agreement]: **to be in tune with sb/sthg** mit jm/etw im Einklang stehen. **out of tune** ◇ *adj* MUS verstimmt. ◇ *adv* - **1.** MUS falsch - **2.** [not in agreement]: **out of tune with sb/sthg** mit jm/etw nicht im Einklang stehen.

tuneful ['tju:nful] *adj* melodisch.

tuner ['tju:nəʳ] *n* - **1.** RADIO & TV Tuner *der* - **2.** MUS Stimmer *der*, -in *die*.

tunic ['tju:nɪk] *n* [clothing] Hemdbluse *die*; [of uniform] Uniformjacke *die*.

tuning fork ['tju:nɪŋ-] *n* Stimmgabel *die*.

Tunisia [tju:'nɪzɪə] *n* Tunesien *das*.

tunnel ['tʌnl] (UK) (US) ◇ *n* Tunnel *der*. ◇ *vi* graben.

turban ['tɜːbən] *n* [man's headdress] Turban *der*.

turbine ['tɜːbaɪn] *n* Turbine *die*.

turbocharged ['tɜːbəʊtʃɑːdʒd] *adj* mit Turboaufladung.

turbulence ['tɜːbjʊləns] *n (U) liter & fig* Turbulenz *die*.

turbulent ['tɜːbjʊlənt] *adj* - 1. [period of time & PHYS] turbulent - 2. [winds, weather] stürmisch - 3. [crowd] ungestüm.

tureen [təˈriːn] *n* Suppenterrine *die*.

turf [tɜːf] *(pl* -s OR turves) ◇ *n* - 1. *(U)* [grass surface] Rasen *der* - 2. [clod] Grassode *die*. ◇ *vt* [with grass] mit Rollrasen bedecken. ◆ **turf out** *vt sep UK inf* [evict] rausschmeißen.

Turk [tɜːk] *n* Türke *der*, -kin *die*.

turkey ['tɜːkɪ] *(pl* turkeys) *n* Truthahn *der*.

Turkey ['tɜːkɪ] *n* Türkei *die*; **in Turkey** in der Türkei.

Turkish ['tɜːkɪʃ] ◇ *adj* türkisch. ◇ *n* [language] Türkisch(e) *das*.

Turkish delight *n (U)* türkischer Honig.

turmoil ['tɜːmɔɪl] *n (U)* Aufruhr *der*.

turn [tɜːn] ◇ *n* - 1. [in road, river] Kurve *die* - 2. [of knob, key, switch] Drehung *die* - 3. [change] Wendung *die* - 4. [in game, order]: **it's my turn** ich bin an der Reihe, ich bin dran; **in turn** der Reihe nach - 5. [performance] Nummer *die* - 6. MED Anfall *der* - 7. *phr*: **to do sb a good turn** jm etwas Gutes tun. ◇ *vt* - 1. [key, head, wheel, chair] drehen - 2. [corner] biegen um - 3. [page, omelette] wenden - 4. [direct]: **to turn one's attention to sb/sthg** jm/etw seine Aufmerksamkeit zuwenden - 5. [transform]: **to turn sthg into sthg** etw in etw *(A)* verwandeln - 6. [make]: **to turn sthg red** etw rot werden lassen; **to turn sthg inside out** das Innere von etw nach außen drehen. ◇ *vi* - 1. [change direction] wenden; **his thoughts turned to his family** er dachte an seine Familie - 2. [wheel, knob, head, person] sich drehen - 3. [in book]: **to turn to sthg** etw aufschlagen - 4. [for consolation, advice]: **to turn to sb/sthg** sich an jm/etw wenden - 5. [become] werden; **to turn into sthg** sich in etw *(A)* verwandeln. ◆ **turn around** *vt sep & vi* = **turn round**. ◆ **turn away** ◇ *vt sep* [refuse entry to] abweisen. ◇ *vi* sich abwenden. ◆ **turn back** ◇ *vt sep* - 1. [force to return] zurückschicken - 2. [fold back] aufschlagen. ◇ *vi* [return] umlkehren. ◆ **turn down** *vt sep* - 1. [reject] abweisen, ablehnen - 2. [heating, lighting, sound] herunterldrehen. ◆ **turn in** *vi inf* [go to bed] sich aufs Ohr legen. ◆ **turn off** ◇ *vt insep* [leave - road, path] ablbiegen von. ◇ *vt sep* [switch off] ablschalten. ◇ *vi* [leave path, road] ablbiegen. ◆ **turn on** ◇ *vt sep* - 1. [make work] einlschalten - 2. *inf* [excite sexually] anlmachen. ◇ *vt insep* [attack] loslgehen auf *(+ A)*. ◆ **turn out** ◇ *vt sep* - 1. [switch off]

auslschalten - 2. [empty] leeren. ◇ *vt insep*: **to turn out to be sthg** sich als etw erweisen; **it turns out that...** es stellt sich heraus, dass... ◇ *vi* - 1. [end up]: **it will turn out all right** es wird (schon) alles in Ordnung kommen - 2. [attend]: **to turn out (for sthg)** (zu etw) erscheinen. ◆ **turn over** ◇ *vt sep* - 1. [playing card, stone, page] umldrehen - 2. [consider] überdenken - 3. [hand over]: **to turn sthg over to sb** jn/etw überlgeben. ◇ *vi* - 1. [roll over] sich umldrehen - 2. *UK* TV umlschalten. ◆ **turn round** ◇ *vt sep* - 1. [rotate] umldrehen - 2. [words, sentence] umldrehen - 3. [quantity of work] bearbeiten. ◇ *vi* [person] sich umldrehen. ◆ **turn up** ◇ *vt sep* [heat, lighting, radio, TV] aufldrehen. ◇ *vi inf* - 1. [appear, arrive, be found] aufltauchen - 2. [happen] sich ergeben.

turning ['tɜːnɪŋ] *n* [side road] Abzweigung *die*.

turning point *n* Wendepunkt *der*.

turnip ['tɜːnɪp] *n* Rübe *die*.

turnout ['tɜːnaʊt] *n* [attendance] Teilnahme *die*.

turnover ['tɜːn‚əʊvər] *n (U)* - 1. [of personnel] Fluktuation *die* - 2. FIN Umsatz *der*.

turnpike ['tɜːnpaɪk] *n US* gebührenpflichtige Autobahn.

turnstile ['tɜːnstaɪl] *n* Drehkreuz *das*.

turntable ['tɜːn‚teɪbl] *n* [on record player] Plattenteller *der*.

turn-up *n UK* - 1. [on trousers] Aufschlag *der* - 2. *inf* [surprise]: **a turn-up for the books** eine echte Überraschung.

turpentine ['tɜːpəntaɪn] *n (U)* Terpentin *das*.

turquoise ['tɜːkwɔɪz] ◇ *adj* türkis. ◇ *n* - 1. [mineral, gem] Türkis *der* - 2. [colour] Türkis *das*.

turret ['tʌrɪt] *n* [on castle] Eckturm *der*.

turtle ['tɜːtl] *(pl inv* OR -s) *n* Schildkröte *die*.

turtleneck ['tɜːtlnek] *n* - 1. [garment] Rollkragenpullover *der* - 2. [neck] Rollkragen *der*.

turves [tɜːvz] *Pl* ▷ **turf**.

tusk [tʌsk] *n* Stoßzahn *der*.

tussle ['tʌsl] ◇ *n* Gerangel *das*. ◇ *vi*: **to tussle over sthg** *liter* (sich) um etw *(A)* raufen; *fig* eine Auseinandersetzung wegen etw haben.

tutor ['tjuːtər] *n* - 1. [private] Privatlehrer *der*, -in *die* - 2. UNIV Tutor *der*, -in *die*.

tutorial [tjuːˈtɔːrɪəl] *n* Tutorium *das*.

tuxedo [tʌkˈsiːdəʊ] *(pl* -s) *n US* Smoking *der*.

TV *(abbr of* television) *n* - 1. *(U)* [medium, industry] Fernsehen *das* - 2. [apparatus] Fernseher *der*.

twang [twæŋ] *n* - 1. [of spring, guitar string] vibrierender Ton; [of rubber band] schnappender Ton - 2. [accent] Tonfall *der*.

tweed [twiːd] *n* Tweed *der*.

tweezers ['twiːzəz] *npl* Pinzette *die*.

twelfth [twelfθ] *num* zwölfte (r) (s); *see also* **sixth**.

twelve [twelv] *num* zwölf; *see also* **six**.

twentieth ['twentiəθ] *num* zwanzigste (r) (s); *see also* **sixth**.

twenty ['twenti] *num* zwanzig; *see also* **sixty**.

twice [twaɪs] *adv* zweimal.

twiddle ['twɪdl] *vt* [knob, button] herumldrehen an (+ D).

twig [twɪg] *n* Zweig *der*.

twilight ['twaɪlaɪt] *n* [in evening] Dämmerung *die*.

twin [twɪn] ⬦ *adj* - **1.** [child, sibling] Zwillings-; **twin girls** Zwillingsschwestern - **2.** [towns] Partner-; *(phrase):* **twin beds** zwei Einzelbetten. ⬦ *n* [sibling] Zwilling *der*.

twine [twaɪn] ⬦ *n* (U) Schnur *die*. ⬦ *vt*: **to twine sthg round sthg** etw um etw wickeln.

twinge [twɪndʒ] *n* Stich *der*.

twinkle ['twɪŋkl] *vi* funkeln.

twin room *n* Zweibettzimmer *das*.

twin town *n* Partnerstadt *die*.

twirl [twɜːl] ⬦ *vt* - **1.** [spin] herumlwirbeln - **2.** [twist, moustache] zwirbeln. ⬦ *vi* wirbeln.

twist [twɪst] ⬦ *n* - **1.** [in road, staircase, river] Biegung *die* - **2.** *fig* [in plot] Wendung *die*. ⬦ *vt* - **1.** [gen] verdrehen - **2.** [lid, knob, dial] drehen - **3.** MED [sprain]: **to twist one's ankle** sich (D) den Fuß verrenken. ⬦ *vi* - **1.** [road, river] sich schlängeln - **2.** [body] sich winden; [face] sich verziehen.

twit [twɪt] *n UK inf* Trottel *der*.

twitch [twɪtʃ] ⬦ *n* Zucken *das*. ⬦ *vi* zucken.

two [tuː] *num* zwei; **in two** in zwei Teile; *see also* **six**.

twofaced [ˌtuːˈfeɪst] *adj pej* falsch.

twofold ['tuːfəʊld] *adj & adv* zweifach.

two-piece *adj* [suit, swimsuit] zweiteilig.

twosome ['tuːsəm] *n inf* Paar *das*.

two-way *adj* [in both directions] in beiden Richtungen.

tycoon [taɪˈkuːn] *n* Magnat *der*.

type [taɪp] ⬦ *n* - **1.** [sort, kind] Art *die*; **what type of car are you looking for?** was für ein Auto suchen Sie denn? - **2.** [in classification] Gruppe *die* - **3.** (U) TYPO Schrift *die*. ⬦ *vt & vi* tippen.

typecast ['taɪpkɑːst] (*pt & pp inv*) *vt* festllegen (auf eine bestimmte Rolle).

typeface ['taɪpfeɪs] *n* TYPO Schrift *die*.

typescript ['taɪpskrɪpt] *n* Manuskript *das*.

typewriter ['taɪpˌraɪtər] *n* Schreibmaschine *die*.

typhoid (fever) ['taɪfɔɪd-] *n* (U) Typhus *der*.

typhoon [taɪˈfuːn] *n* Taifun *der*.

typical ['tɪpɪkl] *adj* typisch; **typical of sb/ sthg** typisch für jn/etw.

typing ['taɪpɪŋ] *n* Tippen *das*, Maschineschreiben *das*.

typist ['taɪpɪst] *n* Schreibkraft *die*.

typography [taɪˈpɒgrəfɪ] *n* Typografie *die*.

tyranny ['tɪrənɪ] *n* (U) [of person, government] Tyrannei *die*.

tyrant ['taɪrənt] *n* Tyrann *der*, -in *die*.

tyre *UK*, **tire** *US* ['taɪər] *n* Reifen *der*.

tyre pressure *n* (U) Reifendruck *der*.

U

u (*pl* **u's** OR **us**), **U** (*pl* **U's** OR **Us**) [juː] *n* [letter] u *das*, U *das*.

U-bend *n* U-Bogen *der*.

udder ['ʌdər] *n* Euter *das*.

UFO (*abbr of* **unidentified flying object**) *n* UFO *das*.

Uganda [juːˈgændə] *n* Uganda *nt*.

ugly ['ʌglɪ] *adj* - **1.** [unattractive] hässlich - **2.** *fig* [unpleasant] unerfreulich.

UHF (*abbr of* **ultra-high frequency**) *n* UHF.

UK *n abbr of* **United Kingdom**.

Ukraine [juːˈkreɪn] *n*: **the Ukraine** die Ukraine.

ulcer ['ʌlsər] *n* - **1.** [in stomach] Geschwür *das* - **2.** [in mouth, stomach] Aphthe *die*.

Ulster ['ʌlstər] *n* Ulster *nt*.

ulterior [ʌlˈtɪərɪər] *adj*: **an ulterior motive** Hintergedanke *der*.

ultimata [ˌʌltɪˈmeɪtə] *pl* ➲ **ultimatum**.

ultimate ['ʌltɪmət] ⬦ *adj* - **1.** [final, longterm] letzte(r) (s) - **2.** [most powerful] absolut. ⬦ *n*: **the ultimate in sthg** das Höchste an etw (D).

ultimately ['ʌltɪmətlɪ] *adv* [finally, in the long term] letztlich.

ultimatum [ˌʌltɪˈmeɪtəm] (*pl* **-tums** OR **-ta** [-tə]) *n* Ultimatum *das*.

ultrasound ['ʌltrəsaʊnd] *n* Ultraschall *der*.

ultraviolet [ˌʌltrə'vaɪələt] *adj* ultraviolett.

umbilical cord [ʌm'bɪlɪkl-] *n* Nabelschnur *die*.

umbrella [ʌm'brelə] ⟨⟩ *n* - 1. [portable] Regenschirm *der* - 2. [fixed] Sonnenschirm *der*. ⟨⟩ *adj* Schirm-.

umpire ['ʌmpaɪəʳ] ⟨⟩ *n* Schiedsrichter *der*, -in *die*. ⟨⟩ *vt* Schiedsrichter sein bei.

umpteen [ˌʌmp'tiːn] *num adj inf* zigmal.

umpteenth [ˌʌmp'tiːnθ] *num adj inf*: **for the umpteenth time** zum x-ten Mal.

UN (*abbr of* United Nations) *n* UNO *die*, UN *die*.

unabated [ˌʌnə'beɪtɪd] *adj* unvermindert.

unable [ʌn'eɪbl] *adj*: **to be unable to do sthg** außer Stande sein, etw zu tun.

unacceptable [ˌʌnək'septəbl] *adj* unannehmbar.

unaccompanied [ˌʌnə'kʌmpənɪd] *adj* [luggage] aufgegeben; [child, song] ohne Begleitung.

unaccountably [ˌʌnə'kaʊntəblɪ] *adv* [inexplicably] unerklärlicherweise.

unaccounted [ˌʌnə'kaʊntɪd] *adj*: **unaccounted for** unauffindbar.

unaccustomed [ˌʌnə'kʌstəmd] *adj* [unused]: **to be unaccustomed to sthg** an etw (A) nicht gewöhnt sein; **to be unaccustomed to doing sthg** nicht daran gewöhnt sein, etw zu tun.

unadulterated [ˌʌnə'dʌltəreɪtɪd] *adj* rein.

unanimous [juː'nænɪməs] *adj* einstimmig.

unanimously [juː'nænɪməslɪ] *adv* einstimmig.

unanswered [ˌʌn'ɑːnsəd] *adj* unbeantwortet.

unappetizing, -ising [ˌʌn'æpɪtaɪzɪŋ] *adj* unappetitlich.

unarmed [ˌʌn'ɑːmd] *adj* unbewaffnet.

unashamed [ˌʌnə'ʃeɪmd] *adj* schamlos.

unassuming [ˌʌnə'sjuːmɪŋ] *adj* bescheiden.

unattached [ˌʌnə'tætʃt] *adj* - 1. [not fastened, linked]: **unattached to sthg** unabhängig von etw - 2. [without partner] ungebunden.

unattended [ˌʌnə'tendɪd] *adj* unbeaufsichtigt.

unattractive [ˌʌnə'træktɪv] *adj* unattraktiv.

unauthorized, -ised [ˌʌn'ɔːθəraɪzd] *adj* unrechtmäßig; [biography] nicht autorisiert.

unavailable [ˌʌnə'veɪləbl] *adj* nicht verfügbar; [person] nicht zu erreichen.

unavoidable [ˌʌnə'vɔɪdəbl] *adj* unvermeidlich.

unaware [ˌʌnə'weəʳ] *adj*: **to be unaware of sthg** sich (D) einer Sache (G) nicht bewusst sein; **she was unaware of my presence** sie bemerkte mich nicht.

unawares [ˌʌnə'weəz] *adv*: **to catch** OR **take sb unawares** jn überraschen.

unbalanced [ˌʌn'bælənst] *adj* - 1. [biased] unausgewogen - 2. [deranged] psychisch labil.

unbearable [ʌn'beərəbl] *adj* unerträglich.

unbeatable [ˌʌn'biːtəbl] *adj* unschlagbar.

unbeknown(st) [ˌʌnbɪ'nəʊn(st)] *adv*: **unbeknownst to him** ohne sein Wissen.

unbelievable [ˌʌnbɪ'liːvəbl] *adj* unglaublich.

unbia(s)sed [ˌʌn'baɪəst] *adj* unvoreingenommen.

unborn [ˌʌn'bɔːn] *adj* [child] ungeboren.

unbreakable [ˌʌn'breɪkəbl] *adj* unzerbrechlich.

unbridled [ˌʌn'braɪdld] *adj* ungezügelt.

unbutton [ˌʌn'bʌtn] *vt* aufknöpfen.

uncalled-for [ˌʌn'kɔːld-] *adj* unnötig.

uncanny [ʌn'kænɪ] *adj* unheimlich.

unceasing [ˌʌn'siːsɪŋ] *adj fml* beständig.

unceremonious ['ʌnˌserɪ'məʊnjəs] *adj* [abrupt] brüsk.

uncertain [ʌn'sɜːtn] *adj* - 1. [person, plans] unsicher; **in no uncertain terms** unmissverständlich - 2. [weather] unvorhersehbar; [future] ungewiss - 3. [cause, motive] unklar.

unchanged [ˌʌn'tʃeɪndʒd] *adj* unverändert.

unchecked [ˌʌn'tʃekt] *adj & adv* [unrestrained] uneingeschränkt.

uncivilized, -ised [ˌʌn'sɪvɪlaɪzd] *adj* [barbaric] unzivilisiert.

uncle ['ʌŋkl] *n* Onkel *der*.

unclear [ˌʌn'klɪəʳ] *adj* - 1. [meaning, instructions] unklar - 2. [future, person] unsicher - 3. [motives, details] undurchsichtig.

uncomfortable [ˌʌn'kʌmftəbl] *adj* - 1. [shoes, chair, clothes] unbequem - 2. *fig* [fact, truth] unbequem - 3. [person]: **to feel uncomfortable** [in physical discomfort] sich nicht wohl fühlen; [ill at ease] sich unbehaglich fühlen.

uncommon [ʌn'kɒmən] *adj* - 1. [rare] selten - 2. *fml* [extreme] außergewöhnlich.

uncompromising [ˌʌn'kɒmprəmaɪzɪŋ] *adj* unnachgiebig.

unconcerned [ˌʌnkən'sɜːnd] *adj* [not anxious] unbesorgt.

unconditional [ˌʌnkən'dɪʃənl] *adj* bedingungslos.

unconscious [ʌn'kɒnʃəs] ⟨⟩ *adj* - 1. [having lost consciousness] bewusstlos - 2. *fig* [unaware]: **to be unconscious of sthg** sich (D) einer Sache (G) nicht bewusst sein - 3. PSYCHOL unbewusst. ⟨⟩ *n* PSYCHOL: **the unconscious** das Unbewusste.

unconsciously [ʌn'kɒnʃəslɪ] *adv* unbewusst.

uncontrollable [ˌʌnkən'trəʊləbl] *adj* - **1.** [irrepressible] unbezwingbar - **2.** [inflation, growth, epidemic] unkontrollierbar - **3.** [child, animal] nicht zu bändigen.

unconventional [ˌʌnkən'venʃənl] *adj* unkonventionell.

unconvinced [ˌʌnkən'vɪnst] *adj* nicht überzeugt.

uncouth [ʌn'kuːθ] *adj* ungehobelt.

uncover [ʌn'kʌvər] *vt liter* & *fig* aufdecken.

undecided [ˌʌndɪ'saɪdɪd] *adj* - **1.** [person] unentschlossen - **2.** [issue] unentschieden.

undeniable [ˌʌndɪ'naɪəbl] *adj* unbestreitbar.

under ['ʌndər] <> *prep* - **1.** [beneath, below] unter (+ D); (with verbs of motion) unter (+ A); it's under the table es ist unter dem Tisch; put it under the table leg es unter den Tisch - **2.** [less than] unter (+ D); children under ten Kinder unter zehn; in under two hours in weniger als zwei Stunden - **3.** [indicating conditions or circumstances]: under the circumstances unter diesen Umständen; to be under pressure unter Druck sein - **4.** [undergoing]: to be under review/discussion revidiert/diskutiert werden; under construction im Bau - **5.** [directed, governed by] unter (+ D); Britain under Blair Großbritannien unter Blair - **6.** [according to] nach; under the terms of the will nach dem Testament - **7.** [in classification, name, title] unter (+ D). <> *adv* - **1.** [beneath] unten; how long can you stay under? [underwater] wie lange kannst du unter Wasser bleiben?; she lifted the blanket and crawled under sie hob die Decke hoch und kroch darunter - **2.** [less]: children of 12 and under Kinder bis zu 12 Jahren.

underage [ʌndər'eɪdʒ] *adj* minderjährig.

undercarriage ['ʌndə,kærɪdʒ] *n* Fahrgestell *das*.

undercharge [ˌʌndə'tʃɑːdʒ] *vt* zu wenig berechnen (+ D).

underclothes ['ʌndəkləʊðz] *npl* Unterwäsche *die*.

undercoat ['ʌndəkəʊt] *n* [of paint] Grundierung *die*.

undercover ['ʌndə,kʌvər] *adj* [agent] Geheim-.

undercurrent ['ʌndə,kʌrənt] *n fig* [tendency] Unterton *der*.

undercut [ˌʌndə'kʌt] (*pt & pp inv*) *vt* [in price] unterbieten.

underdeveloped [ˌʌndədɪ'veləpt] *adj* unterentwickelt.

underdog ['ʌndədɒg] *n*: the underdog der/die Schwächere.

underdone [ˌʌndə'dʌn] *adj* nicht gar.

underestimate *vt* [ˌʌndər'estɪmeɪt] - **1.** [time, money, amount] zu niedrig schätzen - **2.** [strength, abilities] unterschätzen.

underfoot [ˌʌndə'fʊt] *adv* unter den Füßen.

undergo [ˌʌndə'gəʊ] (*pt* -went, *pp* -gone [-'gɒn]) *vt* [operation, examination] sich unterziehen (+ D); [training] teilnehmen an (+ D); [difficulties] durchlmachen.

undergraduate [ˌʌndə'grædjʊət] *n* Student *der*, -in *die*.

underground <> *adj* ['ʌndəgraʊnd] - **1.** [below ground] unterirdisch - **2.** *fig* [secret, illegal] Untergrund-. <> *adv* [ˌʌndə'graʊnd]: to go/be forced underground in den Untergrund gehen/gedrängt werden. <> *n* ['ʌndəgraʊnd] - **1.** *UK* [transport system] U-Bahn *die* - **2.** [activist movement] Untergrund *der*.

undergrowth ['ʌndəgrəʊθ] *n* (U) Unterholz *das*.

underhand [ˌʌndə'hænd] *adj* hinterhältig.

underline [ˌʌndə'laɪn] *vt liter* & *fig* unterstreichen.

underlying [ˌʌndə'laɪɪŋ] *adj* zugrunde liegend.

undermine [ˌʌndə'maɪn] *vt fig* [weaken] untergraben.

underneath [ˌʌndə'niːθ] <> *prep* [indicating location] unter (+ D); [indicating movement] unter (+ A); from underneath sthg unter etw (D) hervor. <> *adv* darunter. <> *n* [underside]: the underneath die Unterseite.

underpaid *adj* ['ʌndəpeɪd] unterbezahlt.

underpants ['ʌndəpænts] *npl* Unterhose *die*.

underpass ['ʌndəpɑːs] *n* Unterführung *die*.

underprivileged [ˌʌndə'prɪvɪlɪdʒd] *adj* unterprivilegiert.

underrated [ˌʌndə'reɪtɪd] *adj* unterschätzt.

undershirt ['ʌndəʃɜːt] *n US* Unterhemd *das*.

underside ['ʌndəsaɪd] *n*: the underside die Unterseite.

understand [ˌʌndə'stænd] (*pt & pp* -stood) <> *vt* - **1.** [gen] verstehen - **2.** *fml* [have heard]: to understand that... glauben, dass... <> *vi* verstehen.

understandable [ˌʌndə'stændəbl] *adj* verständlich.

understanding [ˌʌndə'stændɪŋ] <> *n* - **1.** [knowledge, insight] Kenntnis *die* - **2.** (U) [sympathy] Verständnis *das* - **3.** [interpretation, conception] Auffassung *die*; it was my understanding that ... ich dachte, dass ... - **4.** [informal agreement] Übereinkunft *die*. <> *adj* [sympathetic] verständnisvoll.

understated [ˌʌndə'steɪtɪd] *adj* untertrieben.

understatement [ˌʌndə'steɪtmənt] *n* - **1.** [inadequate statement] Untertreibung *die* - **2.** (U) [quality of understating] Understatement *das*.

understood [ˌʌndə'stʊd] *pt* & *pp* ➪ **understand**.

understudy ['ʌndəˌstʌdɪ] *n* zweite Besetzung.

undertake [ˌʌndə'teɪk] (*pt* **-took**, *pp* **-taken** [-'teɪkn]) *vt* - **1.** [take on] auf sich (A) nehmen - **2.** [promise]: **to undertake to do sthg** sich verpflichten, etw zu tun.

undertaker ['ʌndəˌteɪkəʳ] *n* Leichenbestatter *der*, -in *die*.

undertaking [ˌʌndə'teɪkɪŋ] *n* - **1.** [task] Aufgabe *die* - **2.** [promise] Versprechen *das*.

undertone ['ʌndətəʊn] *n* - **1.** [quiet voice] leise Stimme - **2.** [underlying feeling] Unterton *der*.

undertook [ˌʌndə'tʊk] *pt* ➪ **undertake**.

underwater [ˌʌndə'wɔːtəʳ] <> *adj* Unterwasser-. <> *adv* unter Wasser.

underwear ['ʌndəweəʳ] *n* Unterwäsche *die*.

underwent [ˌʌndə'went] *pt* ➪ **undergo**.

underwriter ['ʌndəˌraɪtəʳ] *n* Versicherer *der*.

undid [ˌʌn'dɪd] *pt* ➪ **undo**.

undies ['ʌndɪz] *npl inf* Unterwäsche *die*.

undisputed [ˌʌndɪ'spjuːtɪd] *adj* unbestritten.

undistinguished [ˌʌndɪ'stɪŋgwɪʃt] *adj* mittelmäßig.

undo [ˌʌn'duː] (*pt* **-did**, *pp* **-done**) *vt* - **1.** [unfasten] auflmachen - **2.** [nullify] zunichte machen.

undoing [ˌʌn'duːɪŋ] *n* (U) *fml* Verderben *das*.

undone [ˌʌn'dʌn] <> *pp* ➪ **undo**. <> *adj* - **1.** [unfastened] offen - **2.** *fml* [not done] ungetan.

undoubted [ʌn'daʊtɪd] *adj* unbestritten.

undoubtedly [ʌn'daʊtɪdlɪ] *adv fml* zweifellos.

undress [ˌʌn'dres] <> *vt* auslziehen. <> *vi* sich auslziehen.

undue [ˌʌn'djuː] *adj fml* unangemessen.

undulate ['ʌndjʊleɪt] *vi fml* - **1.** [in movement - snake, road] sich schlängeln - **2.** [in shape - landscape] sich wellenförmig erstrecken.

unduly [ˌʌn'djuːlɪ] *adv fml* unnötig.

unearth [ˌʌn'ɜːθ] *vt* - **1.** [dig up] auslgraben - **2.** *fig* [discover] auflstöbern.

unease [ʌn'iːz] *n* (U) Unbehagen *das*.

uneasy [ʌn'iːzɪ] *adj* - **1.** [person, feeling] unbehaglich - **2.** [silence] verlegen - **3.** [peace] unsicher.

uneconomic ['ʌnˌiːkə'nɒmɪk] *adj* unökonomisch.

uneducated [ˌʌn'edjʊkeɪtɪd] *adj* - **1.** [person] ungebildet - **2.** [behaviour, manners, speech] unkultiviert.

unemployed [ˌʌnɪm'plɔɪd] <> *adj* [out-of-work] arbeitslos. <> *npl*: **the unemployed** die Arbeitslosen *Pl*.

unemployment [ˌʌnɪm'plɔɪmənt] *n* Arbeitslosigkeit *die*.

unemployment benefit *UK n* (U) Arbeitslosenunterstützung *die*.

unerring [ˌʌn'ɜːrɪŋ] *adj* untrüglich.

uneven [ˌʌn'iːvn] *adj* - **1.** [not flat] uneben - **2.** [inconsistent] ungleichmäßig - **3.** [unfair] ungleich.

unexpected [ˌʌnɪk'spektɪd] *adj* unerwartet.

unexpectedly [ˌʌnɪk'spektɪdlɪ] *adv* unerwartet.

unfailing [ʌn'feɪlɪŋ] *adj* [loyalty, support, good humour] unerschöpflich.

unfair [ˌʌn'feəʳ] *adj* ungerecht.

unfaithful [ˌʌn'feɪθfʊl] *adj* [sexually] untreu.

unfamiliar [ˌʌnfə'mɪljəʳ] *adj* - **1.** [not well-known] unbekannt - **2.** [not acquainted]: **to be unfamiliar with sb/sthg** jn/etw nicht kennen.

unfashionable [ˌʌn'fæʃnəbl] *adj* unmodisch.

unfasten [ˌʌn'fɑːsn] *vt* auflmachen; [rope] auflknoten.

unfavourable *UK*, **unfavorable** *US* [ˌʌn'feɪvrəbl] *adj* - **1.** [not conducive] ungünstig - **2.** [negative] unvorteilhaft.

unfeeling [ʌn'fiːlɪŋ] *adj* herzlos.

unfinished [ˌʌn'fɪnɪʃt] *adj* unerledigt.

unfit [ˌʌn'fɪt] *adj* - **1.** [not in good shape] nicht fit - **2.** [not suitable]: **unfit (for sthg)** ungeeignet (für etw).

unfold [ʌn'fəʊld] <> *vt* [open out] auseinanderlfalten. <> *vi* [story, truth] an den Tag kommen.

unforeseen [ˌʌnfɔː'siːn] *adj* unvorhergesehen.

unforgettable [ˌʌnfə'getəbl] *adj* unvergesslich.

unforgivable [ˌʌnfə'gɪvəbl] *adj* unverzeihlich.

unfortunate [ʌn'fɔːtʃnət] *adj* - **1.** [unlucky] unglücklich - **2.** [regrettable] bedauernswert.

unfortunately [ʌn'fɔːtʃnətlɪ] *adv* leider.

unfounded [ˌʌn'faʊndɪd] *adj* unbegründet.

unfriendly [ˌʌn'frendlɪ] *adj* unfreundlich.

unfurnished [ˌʌn'fɜːnɪʃt] *adj* unmöbliert.

ungainly [ʌn'geɪnlɪ] *adj* unbeholfen.

ungrateful [ʌn'greɪtfʊl] *adj* undankbar.

unhappy [ʌn'hæpɪ] *adj* - **1.** [sad] unglücklich - **2.** [not pleased]: **to be unhappy (about** OR **with sthg)** nicht glücklich (über etw (A) OR mit etw) sein - **3.** *fml* [unfortunate] unglückselig.

unharmed [ˌʌn'hɑːmd] *adj* unverletzt.

unhealthy [ʌn'helθɪ] *adj* ungesund.

unheard-of [ʌn'hɜːdɒv] *adj* - 1. [unknown] unbekannt - 2. [unprecedented] unerhört.

unhook [ˌʌn'hʊk] *vt* - 1. [unfasten hooks of] aufhaken - 2. [remove from hook] ablhaken, vom Haken nehmen.

unhurt [ˌʌn'hɜːt] *adj* unverletzt.

unhygienic [ˌʌnhaɪ'dʒiːnɪk] *adj* unhygienisch.

unidentified flying object *n* unbekanntes Flugobjekt.

unification [ˌjuːnɪfɪ'keɪʃn] *n (U)* Vereinigung *die*.

uniform ['juːnɪfɔːm] ◇ *adj* gleichförmig. ◇ *n* Uniform *die*.

unify ['juːnɪfaɪ] *vt* vereinen.

unilateral [ˌjuːnɪ'lætərəl] *adj* einseitig.

unimportant [ˌʌnɪm'pɔːtənt] *adj* unwichtig.

uninhabited [ˌʌnɪn'hæbɪtɪd] *adj* unbewohnt.

uninjured [ˌʌn'ɪndʒəd] *adj* unverletzt.

unintelligent [ˌʌnɪn'telɪdʒənt] *adj* nicht intelligent.

unintentional [ˌʌnɪn'tenʃənl] *adj* unabsichtlich.

union ['juːnjən] ◇ *n* - 1. [trade union] Gewerkschaft *die* - 2. [alliance] Union *die*. ◇ *comp* Gewerkschafts-.

Union Jack *n*: **the Union Jack** der Union Jack, *britische Nationalflagge*.

unique [juː'niːk] *adj* - 1. [unparalleled] einzigartig - 2. *fml* [peculiar, exclusive]: **this custom is unique to our country** diesen Brauch gibt es nur in unserem Land.

unison ['juːnɪzn] *n (U)* [agreement] Einklang *der*; **in unison** [simultaneously] unisono.

unit ['juːnɪt] *n* - 1. [gen] Einheit *die* - 2. [part of machine or system, piece of furniture] Element *das* - 3. [department] Abteilung *die*.

unite [juː'naɪt] ◇ *vt* vereinigen. ◇ *vi* sich vereinigen.

united [juː'naɪtɪd] *adj* - 1. [in harmony] vereint - 2. [unified] vereinigt.

United Kingdom *n*: **the United Kingdom** das Vereinigte Königreich.

United Nations *n*: **the United Nations** die Vereinten Nationen *Pl.*

United States *n*: **the United States (of America)** die Vereinigten Staaten (von Amerika); **in the United States** in den Vereinigten Staaten.

unity ['juːnətɪ] *n* - 1. [union] Einheit *die* - 2. [harmony] Einigkeit *die*.

universal [ˌjuːnɪ'vɜːsl] *adj* universal.

universe ['juːnɪvɜːs] *n* ASTRON Universum *das*.

university [ˌjuːnɪ'vɜːsətɪ] ◇ *n* Universität *die*. ◇ *comp* Universitäts-; **university student** Student *der*, -in *die*.

unjust [ˌʌn'dʒʌst] *adj* ungerecht.

unkempt [ˌʌn'kempt] *adj* [hair, beard, appearance] ungepflegt.

unkind [ʌn'kaɪnd] *adj* [uncharitable] gemein.

unknown [ˌʌn'nəʊn] *adj* unbekannt.

unlawful [ˌʌn'lɔːfʊl] *adj* ungesetzlich.

unleaded [ˌʌn'ledɪd] *adj* bleifrei.

unleash [ˌʌn'liːʃ] *vt liter* entfesseln.

unless [ən'les] *conj* es sei denn, wenn nicht; **unless you know more** es sei denn, Sie wissen mehr; **you'll be late unless you set off at once** wenn du dich nicht gleich auf den Weg machst, wirst du zu spät kommen; **unless I'm mistaken** wenn ich mich nicht irre; **unless there's a miracle** falls nicht ein Wunder geschieht.

unlike [ˌʌn'laɪk] *prep* - 1. [different from] nicht ähnlich (+ D) - 2. [in contrast to] im Gegensatz zu - 3. [not typical of]: **it's very unlike you to complain** es sieht dir gar nicht ähnlich, dich zu beschweren.

unlikely [ʌn'laɪklɪ] *adj* - 1. [not probable] unwahrscheinlich - 2. [bizarre] merkwürdig.

unlisted [ʌn'lɪstɪd] *adj US* [phone number]: **to be unlisted** nicht im Telefonbuch stehen.

unload [ˌʌn'ləʊd] *vt* - 1. [remove] auslladen - 2. [remove load from] entladen.

unlock [ˌʌn'lɒk] *vt* auf
schließen.

unlucky [ʌn'lʌkɪ] *adj* - 1. [unfortunate] unglücklich; [person] unglücksselig - 2. [bringing bad luck] Unglücks-.

unmarried [ˌʌn'mærɪd] *adj* unverheiratet.

unmistakable [ˌʌnmɪ'steɪkəbl] *adj* unverwechselbar.

unmitigated [ʌn'mɪtɪgeɪtɪd] *adj* vollkommen.

unnatural [ʌn'nætʃrəl] *adj* - 1. [unusual, strange] unnatürlich - 2. [affected] aufgesetzt.

unnecessary [ʌn'nesəsərɪ] *adj* unnötig.

unnerving [ˌʌn'nɜːvɪŋ] *adj* [experience] verunsichernd; [silence] beunruhigend.

unnoticed [ˌʌn'nəʊtɪst] *adj*: **to go** OR **pass unnoticed** nicht bemerkt werden.

unobtainable [ˌʌnəb'teɪnəbl] *adj* nicht erhältlich.

unofficial [ˌʌnə'fɪʃl] *adj* inoffiziell.

unorthodox [ˌʌn'ɔːθədɒks] *adj* unorthodox.

unpack [ˌʌn'pæk] *vt & vi* auslpacken.

unparalleled [ʌn'pærəleld] *adj* einmalig.

unpleasant [ʌn'pleznt] *adj* unangenehm.

unplug [ʌn'plʌg] *vt* ELEC: **to unplug sthg** den Stecker von etw herauslziehen.

unpopular [ˌʌn'pɒpjʊləʳ] *adj* unpopulär.

unprecedented [ʌn'presɪdəntɪd] *adj* beispiellos.

unpredictable [ˌʌnprɪ'dɪktəbl] *adj* unvorhersehbar; [person] unberechenbar.

unprofessional [ˌʌnprə'feʃənl] *adj* unprofessionell.

unqualified [ˌʌn'kwɒlɪfaɪd] *adj* - 1. [not qualified] unqualifiziert; [teacher, nurse] nicht ausgebildet - 2. [total, complete - success, support] uneingeschränkt; [- denial] vollständig.

unquestionable [ʌn'kwestʃənəbl] *adj* unbestreitbar.

unquestioning [ʌn'kwestʃənɪŋ] *adj* bedingungslos.

unravel [ʌn'rævl] (UK) (US) *vt* - 1. [undo - knitting] aufltrennen; [- threads] entwirren - 2. *fig* [solve] lösen.

unreal [ˌʌn'rɪəl] *adj* [strange] unwirklich.

unrealistic [ˌʌnrɪə'lɪstɪk] *adj* unrealistisch.

unreasonable [ʌn'riːznəbl] *adj* - 1. [person]: he's so unreasonable mit ihm kann man überhaupt nicht vernünftig reden - 2. [demand, decision] unangemessen.

unrelated [ˌʌnrɪ'leɪtɪd] *adj*: to be unrelated (to sthg) in keinem Zusammenhang (mit etw) stehen.

unrelenting [ˌʌnrɪ'lentɪŋ] *adj* [struggle, questions] unerbittlich; [pressure] unablässig.

unreliable [ˌʌnrɪ'laɪəbl] *adj* unzuverlässig.

unremitting [ˌʌnrɪ'mɪtɪŋ] *adj* [effort, activity] unablässig, unaufhörlich.

unrequited [ˌʌnrɪ'kwaɪtɪd] *adj* unerwidert.

unreserved [ˌʌnrɪ'zɜːvd] *adj* [admiration, support, approval] uneingeschränkt.

unresolved [ˌʌnrɪ'zɒlvd] *adj* ungelöst.

unrest [ˌʌn'rest] *n* (U) Unruhen *Pl*.

unrivalled UK, **unrivaled** US [ʌn'raɪvld] *adj* unübertroffen.

unroll [ˌʌn'rəʊl] *vt* auflrollen.

unruly [ʌn'ruːlɪ] *adj* - 1. [person, group] undiszipliniert; [child] unartig; [behaviour] ungezügelt - 2. [hair] widerspenstig.

unsafe [ʌn'seɪf] *adj* - 1. [dangerous] gefährlich - 2. [in danger] nicht sicher.

unsaid [ʌn'sed] *adj*: to leave sthg unsaid etw unausgesprochen lassen.

unsatisfactory [ˌʌnsætɪs'fæktərɪ] *adj* unbefriedigend.

unsavoury, unsavory US [ˌʌn'seɪvərɪ] *adj* - 1. [person] zwielichtig; [appearance] abstoßend; [reputation, behaviour, area] zweifelhaft - 2. [smell] widerwärtig.

unscathed [ˌʌn'skeɪðd] *adj* unversehrt.

unscrew [ˌʌn'skruː] *vt* - 1. [lid, bottle top] losldrehen - 2. [sign, mirror] ablschrauben.

unscrupulous [ʌn'skruːpjʊləs] *adj* skrupellos.

unseemly [ʌn'siːmlɪ] *adj* unpassend, unschicklich.

unselfish [ˌʌn'selfɪʃ] *adj* selbstlos.

unsettled [ʌn'setld] *adj* - 1. [disturbed - person] beunruhigt; [- weather] unbeständig - 2. [unfinished, unresolved - argument] nicht geregelt; [- issue] ungeklärt - 3. [account, bill] ausstehend.

unshak(e)able [ʌn'ʃeɪkəbl] *adj* [faith, belief] unerschütterlich; [decision] unumstößlich.

unshaven [ˌʌn'ʃeɪvn] *adj* unrasiert.

unsightly [ʌn'saɪtlɪ] *adj* unansehnlich.

unskilled [ˌʌn'skɪld] *adj* [worker] ungelernt; [work] einfach.

unsociable [ʌn'səʊʃəbl] *adj* ungesellig.

unsocial [ˌʌn'səʊʃl] *adj*: to work unsocial hours früh/morgens/nachts/am Wochenende arbeiten.

unsound [ˌʌn'saʊnd] *adj* - 1. [conclusion, theory, decision] zweifelhaft - 2. [building, structure] instabil.

unspeakable [ʌn'spiːkəbl] *adj* fürchterlich.

unstable [ʌn'steɪbl] *adj* - 1. [structure, government] instabil; [weather] wechselhaft - 2. [mentally, emotionally] labil.

unsteady [ˌʌn'stedɪ] *adj* wackelig.

unstoppable [ˌʌn'stɒpəbl] *adj* unaufhaltsam.

unstuck [ˌʌn'stʌk] *adj*: to come unstuck [notice, stamp, label] sich abllösen; *fig* [plan, system] schief gehen; [person] auf die Nase fallen.

unsuccessful [ˌʌnsək'sesfʊl] *adj* erfolglos; [attempt] vergeblich.

unsuccessfully [ˌʌnsək'sesfʊlɪ] *adv* erfolglos, vergeblich.

unsuitable [ˌʌn'suːtəbl] *adj* unpassend; to be unsuitable for sthg für etw ungeeignet sein.

unsure [ˌʌn'ʃɔːr] *adj* - 1. [not confident]: to be unsure of o.s. unsicher sein - 2. [not certain]: to be unsure (about/of sthg) sich (D) (einer Sache (G)) nicht sicher sein.

unsuspecting [ˌʌnsə'spektɪŋ] *adj* nichts ahnend.

unsympathetic ['ʌnˌsɪmpə'θetɪk] *adj* [unfeeling] nicht mitfühlend.

untangle [ˌʌn'tæŋgl] *vt* entwirren.

untapped [ˌʌn'tæpt] *adj* ungenutzt; [mineral resources] unerschlossen.

untenable [ˌʌn'tenəbl] *adj* unhaltbar.

unthinkable [ʌn'θɪŋkəbl] *adj* undenkbar, unvorstellbar.

untidy [ʌn'taɪdɪ] *adj* unordentlich.

untie [ˌʌn'taɪ] (cont untying) *vt* [string, knot, bonds] lösen; [package] auflbinden; [prisoner] loslbinden.

until [ən'tɪl] ◇ *prep* bis; until the evening/end bis zum Abend/Ende; not until erst; she won't come until two o'clock sie kommt erst um zwei Uhr. ◇ *conj* bis; **wait until he comes** warte, bis er kommt; **she won't come until she is invited** sie kommt erst, wenn sie eingeladen wird.

untimely [ʌn'taɪmlɪ] *adj* - **1.** [premature] vorzeitig - **2.** [inopportune] ungelegen, unpassend.

untold [ˌʌn'təʊld] *adj* [amount] ungezählt; [wealth] unermesslich; [suffering, joy] unsäglich.

untoward [ˌʌntə'wɔːd] *adj* [event] unglücklich; [behaviour] ungebührlich.

untrue [ˌʌn'truː] *adj* [inaccurate] unwahr, falsch.

unused *adj* - **1.** [ˌʌn'juːzd] [new] unbenutzt - **2.** [ʌn'juːst] [unaccustomed]: **to be unused to** sthg **an etw** *(A)* **nicht gewöhnt sein; to be unused to doing sthg** nicht daran gewöhnt sein, etw zu tun.

unusual [ʌn'juːʒl] *adj* ungewöhnlich.

unusually [ʌn'juːʒəlɪ] *adv* außergewöhnlich.

unveil [ˌʌn'veɪl] *vt liter & fig* enthüllen.

unwanted [ˌʌn'wɒntɪd] *adj* [clothes, furniture] ausrangiert; [child, pregnancy] ungewollt; **to feel unwanted** das Gefühl haben, unerwünscht zu sein.

unwelcome [ʌn'welkəm] *adj* - **1.** [news, experience] unerfreulich - **2.** [visitor] unwillkommen.

unwell [ˌʌn'wel] *adj*: **to be/feel unwell** sich unwohl fühlen.

unwieldy [ʌn'wiːldɪ] *adj* - **1.** [tool] unhandlich; [piece of furniture] sperrig - **2.** *fig* [system, method] umständlich; [organization] schwerfällig.

unwilling [ˌʌn'wɪlɪŋ] *adj* unwillig.

unwind [ˌʌn'waɪnd] *(pt & pp -wound)* ◇ *vt* abwickeln. ◇ *vi fig* [person] sich entspannen.

unwise [ˌʌn'waɪz] *adj* unklug.

unworkable [ˌʌn'wɜːkəbl] *adj* undurchführbar.

unworthy [ʌn'wɜːðɪ] *adj*: **to be unworthy of** sthg einer Sache *(G)* unwürdig sein.

unwound [ˌʌn'waʊnd] *pt & pp* ▷ **unwind**.

unwrap [ˌʌn'ræp] *vt* auspacken.

up [ʌp] ◇ *adv* - **1.** [towards higher position, level] hoch; **we walked up to the top** wir sind zum Gipfel gelaufen; **to throw sthg up** etw in die Höhe werfen; **prices are going up** die Preise steigen; **up and up** immer höher - **2.** [in higher position] oben; **she's up in her room** sie ist oben in ihrem Zimmer; **up here/there** hier/da OR dort oben - **3.** [into an upright position]: **to stand up** aufstehen; **to sit up** [from lying position] sich aufsetzen; [sit straight] sich gerade hinsetzen; **help me up** hilf mir auf - **4.** [northwards]: **to live up north** oben im Norden woh-

nen; **I'm going up to York** ich fahre hoch nach York - **5.** [facing upwards] nach oben gerichtet; **he was lying face up** er lag mit dem Gesicht nach oben - **6.** [along river] oben; **their house is a little further up** ihr Haus liegt ein bisschen weiter in dieser Richtung - **7.** [ahead]: **to be two goals up** mit zwei Toren führen. ◇ *prep* - **1.** [towards higher position]: **to walk up a hill** einen Hügel hinauflgehen; **I went up the stairs** ich ging die Treppe hinauf - **2.** [in higher position]: **to be up a hill** oben auf einem Hügel sein - **3.** [towards far end of]: **they live up the road from us** sie wohnen weiter oben in unserer Straße. ◇ *adj* - **1.** [out of bed] auf; **I was up at six today** ich war heute um sechs auf; **to be up all night** die ganze Nacht auflbleiben - **2.** [at an end] um, zu Ende; **time's up** die Zeit ist um - **3.** *inf* [wrong]: **there's something up** es liegt etwas in der Luft; **what's up (with you)?** was ist (mit dir) los? ◇ *n*: **ups and downs** Höhen und Tiefen *Pl.* ☞ **up and down** ◇ *adv*: **to walk/jump up and down** auf und ab gehen/springen. ◇ *prep* [backwards and forwards]: **we walked up and down the avenue** wir gingen die Allee auf und ab. ☞ **up to** *prep* - **1.** [indicating position, level] bis zu; **the water came up to my knees** das Wasser reichte mir bis an die Knie; **up to this point** bis zu diesem Punkt; **up to six weeks/ten people** bis zu sechs Wochen/zehn Personen - **2.** [in time] bis; **I felt fine up to last month** bis letzten Monat ging es mir gut - **3.** [well or able enough for]: **my French isn't up to much** *inf* mein Französisch ist nicht besonders gut; **to be up to a task** einer Aufgabe gewachsen sein; **I'm not up to going out tonight** ich schaffe es heute Abend nicht auszugehen - **4.** *phr*: **what are you up to?** *inf* [doing] was machst du da?; [planning] was hast du vor?; **they're up to something** sie haben etwas vor; **it's up to you** das liegt bei dir. ☞ **up until** *prep* bis; **up until ten o'clock** bis um zehn Uhr.

up-and-coming *adj* [athlete, actor] kommend; [business] aufstrebend.

upbringing [ʌp,brɪŋɪŋ] *n* Erziehung *die.*

update [ˌʌp'deɪt] *vt* aktualisieren.

upheaval [ʌp'hiːvl] *n* Aufruhr *der.*

upheld [ʌp'held] *pt & pp* ▷ **uphold**.

uphill [ˌʌp'hɪl] ◇ *adj* - **1.** [rising] ansteigend - **2.** *fig* [difficult] mühsam. ◇ *adv* bergauf.

uphold [ʌp'həʊld] *(pt & pp -held)* *vt* - **1.** [law] beilbehalten - **2.** [decision, system] unterstützen.

upholstery [ʌp'həʊlstərɪ] *n (U)* Polsterung *die.*

upkeep ['ʌpkiːp] *n* Instandhaltung *die;* [of garden] Pflege *die.*

uplifting [ʌp'lɪftɪŋ] *adj* [cheering] erhebend.

up-market *adj* [hotel, restaurant, area] vornehm; [goods] edel.

upon [ə'pɒn] *prep fml* - **1.** [on, on top of - indicating place, position] auf *(+ D)*; [- indicating direction] auf *(+ A)*; *(phrase)*: **summer/the weekend is upon us** es ist beinahe Sommer/ Wochenende - **2.** [when] als; **upon hearing the news, I rushed to the telephone** als ich die Neuigkeiten hörte, rannte ich sofort zum Telefon.

upper ['ʌpər] <> *adj* - **1.** [physically higher & GEOG] obere(r) (s); **upper lip** Oberlippe *die* - **2.** [higher in order, rank] höher. <> *n* [of shoe] Obermaterial *das*.

upper class *n*: **the upper class** die Oberschicht. <> **upper-class** *adj* vornehm.

upper-crust *adj* vornehm.

upper hand *n*: **to have the upper hand** die Oberhand haben; **to gain** OR **get the upper hand** die Oberhand gewinnen.

Upper House *n* POL Oberhaus *das*.

uppermost ['ʌpəməʊst] *adj* - **1.** [highest] oberste(r) (s) - **2.** [most important]: **my father's illness is uppermost in my mind at the moment** die Krankheit meines Vaters beschäftigt mich momentan am meisten.

upright ['ʌpraɪt] <> *adj liter* & *fig* aufrecht. <> *adv* aufrecht. <> *n* [of goal] Pfosten *der*; [of bookshelf] Seitenteil *das*; [of door] Türpfosten *der*.

uprising ['ʌp.raɪzɪŋ] *n* Aufstand *der*.

uproar ['ʌprɔːr] *n* Aufruhr *der*.

uproot [ʌp'ruːt] *vt* entwurzeln.

upset [ʌp'set] *(pt & pp inv)* <> *adj* - **1.** [distressed] aufgeregt; [shocked] bestürzt; [offended] beleidigt - **2.** MED: **to have an upset stomach** eine Magenverstimmung haben. <> *n* - **1.** MED: **to have a stomach upset** eine Magenverstimmung haben - **2.** [surprise result] Überraschungsergebnis *das*. <> *vt* - **1.** [distress] aufregen; **the news upset him** die Nachricht bestürzte ihn - **2.** [mess up] durcheinander bringen - **3.** [overturn, knock over] umlkippen, umlstoßen; [boat] zum Kentern bringen.

upshot ['ʌpʃɒt] *n* Ergebnis *das*.

upside down [,ʌpsaɪd-] <> *adj* [inverted] verkehrt herum. <> *adv* verkehrt herum; **to turn sthg upside down** *fig* [disorder] etw auf den Kopf stellen.

upstairs [,ʌp'steəz] <> *adj* oben, im oberen Stockwerk. <> *adv* - **1.** [not downstairs] oben; [with motion] nach oben - **2.** [on the floor above] oben, im oberen Stockwerk. <> *n* oberes Stockwerk.

upstart ['ʌpstɑːt] *n* Emporkömmling *der*.

upstream [,ʌp'striːm] <> *adj*: **upstream (from sthg)** stromaufwärts (von etw). <> *adv* stromaufwärts.

upsurge ['ʌpsɜːdʒ] *n*: **upsurge of/in sthg** Zunahme *die* an etw *(D)*.

uptake ['ʌpteɪk] *n*: **to be quick on the uptake** schnell verstehen; **to be slow on the uptake** schwer von Begriff sein.

uptight [ʌp'taɪt] *adj inf* verkrampft.

up-to-date *adj* - **1.** [machinery, methods] modern - **2.** [news, information] neueste(r) (s), aktuell; **to keep up-to-date with sthg** über etw *(A)* auf dem Laufenden bleiben.

upturn ['ʌptɜːn] *n*: **upturn (in sthg)** Aufschwung *der* (in etw *(D)*).

upward ['ʌpwəd] <> *adj* [movement, trend] Aufwärts-. <> *adv US* = **upwards**.

upwards ['ʌpwədz] *adv* - **1.** [to a higher place] nach oben - **2.** [to a higher number, degree, rate]: **to climb** OR **move upwards** anlsteigen. <> **upwards of** *prep* über (*+ A*), mehr als.

uranium [jʊ'reɪnjəm] *n* Uran *das*.

urban ['ɜːbən] *adj* städtisch; **urban development** Stadtentwicklung *die*.

urbane [ɜː'beɪn] *adj* gewandt.

Urdu ['ʊəduː] *n* Urdu *das*.

urge [ɜːdʒ] <> *n* Drang *der*; **to have an urge to do sthg** den Drang verspüren, etw zu tun. <> *vt* - **1.** [try to persuade]: **to urge sb to do sthg** jn drängen, etw zu tun - **2.** [advocate] eindringlich raten zu.

urgency ['ɜːdʒənsɪ] *n* Dringlichkeit *die*.

urgent ['ɜːdʒənt] *adj* - **1.** [pressing] dringend - **2.** [desperate] verzweifelt.

urinal [,jʊə'raɪnl] *n* [receptacle] Urinal *das*; [room] Pissoir *das*.

urinate ['jʊərɪneɪt] *vi* urinieren.

urine ['jʊərɪn] *n* Urin *der*.

urn [ɜːn] *n* - **1.** [for ashes] Urne *die* - **2.** [for tea, coffee] Heißwasserbehälter mit Zapfhahn.

Uruguay ['jʊərəgwaɪ] *n* Uruguay *nt*.

us [ʌs] *pers pron* uns; **they know us** sie kennen uns; **they like us** wir gefallen ihnen; **it's us** wir sinds; **send it to us** schicke es uns; **tell us** sag uns; **they're worse than us** sie sind schlimmer als wir; **you can't expect us to do it** du kannst nicht erwarten, dass **wir** das tun; **all of us** wir alle; **none of us** keiner von uns; **some/a few of us** einige von uns; **most of us** die meisten von uns; **both of us** wir beide; **there are three of us** wir sind zu dritt; **neither of us** keiner von uns.

US (*abbr of* **United States**) *n*: **the US** die USA *Pl*.

USA *n* (*abbr of* **United States of America**); **the USA** die USA *Pl*.

usage ['juːzɪdʒ] *n* - **1.** (U) [use of language] Gebrauch *der* - **2.** [meaning] Bedeutung *die* - **3.** (U) [treatment] Behandlung *die*; [handling] Gebrauch *der*.

use <> *n* [juːs] - **1.** [act of using] Gebrauch *der*, Benutzung *die*; [for specific purpose] Verwendung *die*; [of method] Anwendung *die*; **to be in/out of use** im/außer

Gebrauch sein; **to make use of sthg** von etw Gebrauch machen - **2.** [purpose, usefulness] Nutzen *der*; **can you find a use for this?** kannst du damit etwas anfangen?; **to be of use** nützlich sein; **it's no use!** es hat keinen Zweck!; **what's the use (of doing that)?** was hat es für einen Zweck(, das zu tun)? ◇ *aux vb* [ju:s]: **I used to go for a run every day** ich bin früher jeden Tag laufen gegangen; **he didn't use to be so fat** er war früher nicht so dick. ◇ *vt* [ju:z] - **1.** [utilize] gebrauchen, benutzen; [for specific purpose] verwenden; [method] an|wenden - **2.** *pej* [exploit] be- nutzen. ◆ **use up** *vt sep* auf|brauchen.

used *adj* - **1.** [ju:zd] [dirty] benutzt, schmut- zig - **2.** [ju:zd] [second-hand] gebraucht, Ge- braucht- - **3.** [ju:st] [accustomed]: **to be used to sthg** an etw *(A)* gewöhnt sein; **to be used to doing sthg** daran gewöhnt sein *OR* es ge- wöhnt sein, etw zu tun; **to get used to sthg** sich an etw *(A)* gewöhnen.

useful ['ju:sfʊl] *adj* [handy] nützlich.

useless ['ju:slɪs] *adj* - **1.** [unusable] nutzlos - **2.** [pointless] zwecklos, unnütz - **3.** *inf* [hope- less]: **to be useless** zu nichts zu gebrauchen sein.

user ['ju:zər] *n* Benutzer *der*, -in *die*; **drug user** Drogenkonsument *der*, -in *die*.

user-friendly *adj* benutzerfreundlich.

usher ['ʌʃər] ◇ *n* Platzanweiser *der*, -in *die*. ◇ *vt* führen.

usherette [ˌʌʃə'rèt] *n* Platzanweiserin *die*.

USSR (*abbr of* **Union of Soviet Socialist Re- publics**) *n* UdSSR *die*.

usual ['ju:ʒəl] *adj* üblich; **as usual** wie üblich.

usually ['ju:ʒəlɪ] *adv* normalerweise.

utensil [ju:'tensl] *n* Utensil *das*.

uterus ['ju:tərəs] (*pl* **-ri** [-raɪ] *OR* **-ruses**) *n* Uterus *der*, Gebärmutter *die*.

utility [ju:'tɪlətɪ] *n* - **1.** [usefulness] Nützlich- keit *die* - **2.** [company]: **(public) utility** (öffentli- cher) Versorgungsbetrieb - **3.** COMPUT Dienst- programm *das*.

utility room *n* ≈ Waschküche *die*.

utilize, -ise ['ju:təlaɪz] *vt* nutzen.

utmost ['ʌtməʊst] ◇ *adj* äußerste(r) (s). ◇ *n* - **1.** [best effort]: **to do one's utmost (to achieve sthg)** sein Möglichstes tun(, um etw zu erreichen) - **2.** [maximum] Äußerste *das*; **to the utmost** bis zum Äußersten.

utter ['ʌtər] ◇ *adj* völlig, komplett. ◇ *vt* [sound, cry] aus|stoßen; [word] sagen.

utterly ['ʌtəlɪ] *adv* völlig.

U-turn *n* - **1.** [turning movement] Wende *die* - **2.** *fig* [complete change] Kehrtwendung *die*.

V

v[1] (*pl* **v's** *OR* **vs**), **V** (*pl* **V's** *OR* **Vs**) [vi:] *n* [letter] v *das*, V *das*

v[2] *abbr of* **verse**, **versus**, **volt**.

vacancy ['veɪkənsɪ] *n* - **1.** [job, position] offene Stelle, freie Position - **2.** [room available] freies Zimmer; **'vacancies'** 'frei'; **'no vacancies'** 'be- legt'.

vacant ['veɪkənt] *adj* - **1.** [house] leer ste- hend; [chair] unbesetzt; [toilet] nicht besetzt; [room] frei - **2.** [post, job] offen, frei - **3.** [look] leer.

vacant lot *n* Baugrundstück *das*.

vacate [və'keɪt] *vt* - **1.** [post, job] auf|geben - **2.** [seat] frei machen - **3.** [hotel, room] aus|- ziehen aus.

vacation [və'keɪʃn] *n* - **1.** UNIV [period when closed] Ferien *Pl* - **2.** *US* [holiday] Ferien *Pl*, Ur- laub *der*.

vacationer [və'keɪʃənər] *n US* Urlauber *der*, -in *die*.

vaccinate ['væksɪneɪt] *vt*: **to vaccinate sb (against sthg)** jn (gegen etw) impfen.

vaccine [*UK* 'væksi:n, *US* væk'si:n] *n* Impf- stoff *der*.

vacuum ['vækjʊəm] ◇ *n* - **1.** TECH Vaku- um *das* - **2.** [cleaning machine] Staubsauger *der*. ◇ *vt & vi* Staub saugen.

vacuum cleaner *n* Staubsauger *der*.

vacuum-packed *adj* vakuumverpackt.

vagina [və'dʒaɪnə] *n* Scheide *die*, Vagi- na *die*.

vagrant ['veɪgrənt] *n* Landstreicher *der*, -in *die*.

vague [veɪg] *adj* - **1.** [imprecise, evasive] vage - **2.** [feeling] leicht - **3.** [absent-minded] zerstreut - **4.** [shape, outline] schemenhaft.

vaguely ['veɪglɪ] *adv* - **1.** [imprecisely] vage - **2.** [slightly, not very] leicht - **3.** [absent-mindedly] zerstreut - **4.** [indistinctly] undeutlich.

vain [veɪn] *adj* - **1.** *pej* [conceited] eitel - **2.** [at- tempt, hope] vergeblich. ◆ **in vain** *adv* ver- geblich, vergebens.

valentine card ['væləntaɪn-] *n* Grußkar- te *die* zum Valentinstag.

Valentine's Day ['væləntaɪnz-] *n*: **(St) Valentine's Day** Valentinstag *der*.

valet ['væleɪ, 'vælɪt] *n* Kammerdiener *der*.

valid ['vælɪd] *adj* - **1.** [argument] stichhaltig; [explanation] einleuchtend; [decision] begrün- det; [claim] berechtigt - **2.** [ticket, passport, driv- ing licence] gültig; [contract] rechtsgültig.

valley ['vælɪ] (*pl* **valleys**) *n* Tal *das*.

valour *UK,* **valor** *US* ['vælər] *n fml & liter* Heldenmut *der.*

valuable ['væljuəbl] *adj* wertvoll. ◆ **valuables** *npl* Wertsachen *Pl.*

valuation [,vælju'eɪʃn] *n* - **1.** *(U)* [pricing] Schätzung *die* - **2.** [estimated price] Schätzwert *der.*

value ['vælju:] ◇ *n (U)* Wert *der;* **to be good value** preisgünstig sein; **to be value for money** ein gutes Preis-Leistungs-Verhältnis haben. ◇ *vt* schätzen. ◆ **values** *npl* [morals] Werte *Pl,* Wertvorstellungen *Pl.*

value-added tax [-ædɪd-] *n* Mehrwertsteuer *die.*

valued ['vælju:d] *adj* geschätzt.

valve [vælv] *n* - **1.** [in pipe, tube] Absperrhahn *der* - **2.** [on tyre] Ventil *das.*

van [væn] *n* - **1.** AUT Transporter *der,* Lieferwagen *der* - **2.** *UK* RAIL Wagon *der,* Wagen *der.*

vandal ['vændl] *n* Vandale *der,* -lin *die.*

vandalism ['vændəlɪzm] *n* Vandalismus *der.*

vandalize, -ise ['vændəlaɪz] *vt* mutwillig beschädigen.

vanguard ['vænɡɑːd] *n*: **in the vanguard of sthg** an der Spitze einer Sache *(G).*

vanilla [və'nɪlə] *n* Vanille *die.*

vanish ['vænɪʃ] *vi* - **1.** [no longer be visible] verschwinden - **2.** [no longer exist - race, species] aussterben; [- hopes, chances] schwinden.

vanity ['vænətɪ] *n (U) pej* [of person] Eitelkeit *die.*

vapour *UK,* **vapor** *US* ['veɪpər] *n (U)* Dampf *der.*

variable ['veərɪəbl] *adj* - **1.** [changeable] unbeständig - **2.** [uneven - quality] unterschiedlich; [- performance] unbeständig.

variance ['veərɪəns] *n fml*: **to be at variance with sthg** mit etw nicht übereinstimmen.

variation [,veərɪ'eɪʃn] *n* - **1.** *(U)* [fact of difference] Unterschied *der* - **2.** [change in level or quantity] Schwankung *die* - **3.** [different version & MUS] Variation *die.*

varicose veins ['værɪkəus-] *npl* Krampfadern *Pl.*

varied ['veərɪd] *adj* [life] bewegt; [group] gemischt; [work, diet] abwechslungsreich.

variety [və'raɪətɪ] *n* - **1.** [difference in type] Abwechslung *die* - **2.** [selection] Auswahl *die* - **3.** [type] Art *die,* Sorte *die* - **4.** *(U)* THEAT Varietee *das.*

various ['veərɪəs] *adj* verschieden.

varnish ['vɑːnɪʃ] ◇ *n* [for wood, fingernails] Lack *der;* [for pottery] Glasur *die.* ◇ *vt* [wood, fingernails] lackieren; [pottery] glasieren.

vary ['veərɪ] ◇ *vt* verändern, variieren. ◇ *vi* [differ] sich unterscheiden; [fluctuate] sich ändern; [prices] schwanken.

vase [*UK* vɑːz, *US* veɪz] *n* Vase *die.*

vast [vɑːst] *adj* riesig; [expense, difference] enorm.

vat [væt] *n* [open] Bottich *der;* [closed] Fass *das.*

VAT [væt, viːeɪˈtiː] *(abbr of value added tax) n* Mehrwertsteuer *die,* MwSt.

Vatican ['vætɪkən] *n*: **the Vatican** der Vatikan.

vault [vɔːlt] ◇ *n* - **1.** [in bank] Tresorraum *der* - **2.** [under church] Gruft *die* - **3.** [roof] Gewölbe *das.* ◇ *vt* springen über *(+ A).* ◇ *vi*: **to vault over sthg** über etw *(A)* springen.

VCR *(abbr of video cassette recorder) n* Videorekorder *der.*

VD *n abbr of* **venereal disease**.

VDU *(abbr of visual display unit) n* Bildschirm *der.*

veal [viːl] *n* Kalbfleisch *das.*

veer [vɪər] *vi* - **1.** [vehicle] ausscheren; [road] eine Kurve machen; [wind] (sich) drehen - **2.** *fig* [conversation, mood] schwanken.

vegan ['viːgən] ◇ *adj* veganisch. ◇ *n* Veganer *der,* -in *die.*

vegetable ['vedʒtəbl] ◇ *n* Gemüse *das.* ◇ *adj* Gemüse-.

vegetarian [,vedʒɪ'teərɪən] ◇ *adj* vegetarisch. ◇ *n* Vegetarier *der,* -in *die.*

vegetation [,vedʒɪ'teɪʃn] *n* Vegetation *die.*

vehement ['viːəmənt] *adj* heftig; [denial, protest, defence] vehement; [debate] hitzig.

vehicle ['viːəkl] *n* [for transport] Fahrzeug *das.*

veil [veɪl] *n* Schleier *der;* **to draw a veil over sthg** *fig* etw verschweigen.

vein [veɪn] *n* [gen] Ader *die.*

velocity [vɪ'lɒsətɪ] *n* PHYS Geschwindigkeit *die.*

velvet ['velvɪt] *n* Samt *der.*

vendetta [ven'detə] *n* Blutrache *die;* [in the press] Hetzkampagne *die.*

vending machine ['vendɪŋ-] *n* Automat *der.*

vendor ['vendər] *n* Verkäufer *der,* -in *die;* **street vendor** Straßenhändler *der,* -in *die.*

veneer [və'nɪər] *n* - **1.** [of wood] Furnier *das* - **2.** *fig* [appearance]: **to give sthg a veneer of respectability** einer Sache *(D)* einen seriösen Anstrich geben.

venereal disease [vɪ'nɪərɪəl-] *n (U)* Geschlechtskrankheit *die.*

venetian blind [vɪ,niːʃn-] *n* Jalousie *die.*

Venezuela [,venɪz'weɪlə] *n* Venezuela *nt.*

vengeance ['vendʒəns] *n (U)* Vergeltung *die,* Rachung *die;* **with a vengeance** gewaltig; **to work with a vengeance** hart arbeiten.

venison ['venɪzn] *n (U)* Wild *das (Damwild).*

venom ['venəm] *n* - **1.** [poison] Gift *das* - **2.** *fig* [spite, bitterness] Gehässigkeit *die.*

vent [vent] ⟷ *n* Öffnung *die*; [in chimney, for ventilation] Abzug *der*; **to give vent to sthg** [feelings] etw *(D)* freien Lauf lassen; [anger] etw *(D)* Luft machen. ⟷ *vt* [express - feelings] freien Lauf lassen (+ *D*); [- anger] Luft machen (+ *D*); **to vent one's anger on sb** seinen Ärger an jm auslassen.

ventilate ['ventɪleɪt] *vt* (be)lüften.

ventilator ['ventɪleɪtər] *n* - 1. [in room, building] Ventilator *der* - 2. MED Beatmungsgerät *das*.

ventriloquist [ven'trɪləkwɪst] *n* Bauchredner *der*, -in *die*.

venture ['ventʃər] ⟷ *n* Unternehmen *das*. ⟷ *vt* [proffer - opinion, advice] zu äußern wagen; [- guess] wagen; [- suggestion, remark] sich *(D)* erlauben; **to venture to do sthg** sich *(D)* erlauben, etw zu tun. ⟷ *vi* - 1. [go somewhere dangerous] sich wagen - 2. [embark]: **to venture into politics** den Schritt in die Politik wagen.

venue ['venjuː] *n* [for concert, conference] Veranstaltungsort *der*; [for match] Austragungsort *der*.

veranda(h) [və'rændə] *n* Veranda *die*.

verb [vɜːb] *n* Verb *das*.

verbal ['vɜːbl] *adj* - 1. [spoken - agreement] mündlich; [- skills] sprachlich; **verbal abuse** Beschimpfung *die* - 2. GRAM Verb-, verbal.

verbatim [vɜː'beɪtɪm] *adj & adv* (wort)wörtlich.

verbose [vɜː'bəʊs] *adj fml* langatmig.

verdict ['vɜːdɪkt] *n* Urteil *das*; **what's your verdict on his new film?** was hältst du von seinem neuen Film?

verge [vɜːdʒ] *n* - 1. [edge, side] Rand *der*; [of road] Bankett *das* - 2. [brink]: **to be on the verge of sthg** [ruin, mental breakdown] am Rand einer Sache *(G)* stehen; [success] kurz vor etw *(D)* stehen; **to be on the verge of doing sthg** kurz davor stehen, etw zu tun. ➤ **verge (up)on** *vt insep* grenzen an (+ *A*).

verify ['verɪfaɪ] *vt* - 1. [check] prüfen, überprüfen - 2. [confirm] bestätigen.

veritable ['verɪtəbl] *adj fml & hum* wahr.

vermin ['vɜːmɪn] *npl* - 1. ZOOL [insects] Ungeziefer *das*; [rodents] Schädlinge *Pl* - 2. *pej* [people] Abschaum *der*.

vermouth [vɜː'muːθ] *n* Wermut *der*.

versatile ['vɜːsətaɪl] *adj* - 1. [person] vielseitig - 2. [machine, tool] vielseitig verwendbar.

verse [vɜːs] *n* - 1. (U) [poetry] Lyrik *die* - 2. [stanza] Strophe *die* - 3. [in Bible] Vers *der*.

version ['vɜːʃn] *n* [form, account of events] Version *die*.

versus ['vɜːsəs] *prep* - 1. SPORT gegen - 2. [as opposed to] im Gegensatz zu.

vertebra ['vɜːtɪbrə] (*pl* **-brae** [-briː]) *n* Rückenwirbel *der*.

vertical ['vɜːtɪkl] *adj* senkrecht, vertikal.

vertigo ['vɜːtɪgəʊ] *n* (U) Gleichgewichtsstörungen *Pl*.

verve [vɜːv] *n* Schwung *der*.

very ['verɪ] ⟷ *adv* sehr; **very much** sehr; **not very** nicht sehr. ⟷ *adj* genau; **the very opposite** genau das Gegenteil; **the very person I was looking for!** nach Ihnen habe ich gerade gesucht!; **that very afternoon** am selben Nachmittag; **the very next day** gleich am nächsten Tag; **my very own room** mein eigenes Zimmer; **the very best** das Allerbeste; **for the very first/last time** zum allerersten/allerletzten Mal; **at the very beginning** ganz am Anfang; **the very thought makes me shudder** mich schaudert beim bloßen Gedanken. ➤ **very well** *adv* - 1. [all right] schön, also gut - 2. *phr*: **I/you/etc can't very well say no** ich kann/du kannst/*etc* wohl kaum nein sagen.

vessel ['vesl] *n fml* - 1. [boat] Schiff *das* - 2. [container] Gefäß *das*.

vest [vest] *n* - 1. *UK* [undershirt] Unterhemd *das* - 2. *US* [waistcoat] Weste *die*.

vestibule ['vestɪbjuːl] *n fml* [entrance hall] Eingangshalle *die*.

vestige ['vestɪdʒ] *n fml* Spur *die*.

vestry ['vestrɪ] *n* Sakristei *die*.

vet [vet] ⟷ *n UK abbr of* **veterinary surgeon**. ⟷ *vt UK* [check] überprüfen.

veteran ['vetrən] ⟷ *adj* [experienced] mit langjähriger Erfahrung. ⟷ *n* Veteran *der*, -in *die*.

veterinarian [,vetərɪ'neərɪən] *n US* Tierarzt *der*, -ärztin *die*.

veterinary surgeon ['vetərɪnrɪ-] *n UK fml* Tierarzt *der*, -ärztin *die*.

veto ['viːtəʊ] (*pl* **-es**, *pt & pp* **-ed**, *cont* **-ing**) ⟷ *n* Veto *das*. ⟷ *vt* sein Veto einlegen gegen.

vex [veks] *vt fml* [annoy] (ver)ärgern.

VHF (*abbr of* very high frequency) *n* UKW.

VHS (*abbr of* video home system) *n* VHS.

via ['vaɪə] *prep* - 1. [travelling through] über (+ *A*), via (+ *A*) - 2. [by means of]: **via a friend** durch einen Freund; **via satellite** via *OR* per Satellit.

viable ['vaɪəbl] *adj* - 1. [plan, programme, scheme] durchführbar - 2. ECON lebensfähig.

Viagra® [vaɪ'ægrə] *n* Viagra® *das*.

vibrate [vaɪ'breɪt] *vi* vibrieren; PHYS schwingen.

vicar ['vɪkər] *n* Pfarrer *der*, -in *die*.

vicarage ['vɪkərɪdʒ] *n* Pfarrhaus *das*.

vicarious [vɪ'keərɪəs] *adj* [enjoyment, pleasure] indirekt.

vice [vaɪs] *n* - 1. [immorality, fault] Laster *das* - 2. [tool] Schraubstock *der*.

vice-chairman *n* stellvertretender Vorsitzender.

vice-chancellor n UNIV Leiter der Universitätsverwaltung und Vorsitzender des Senats.

vice-president n Vizepräsident der, -in die.

vice versa [,vaɪs'vɜ:sə] adv umgekehrt.

vicinity [vɪ'sɪnɪtɪ] n - 1. [neighbourhood] Umgebung die; **in the vicinity (of)** in der Nähe (von OR (+ G)) - 2. [approximate figures]: **in the vicinity of £80,000 a year** um die £80 000 pro Jahr.

vicious ['vɪʃəs] adj - 1. [attack, blow, killer] brutal - 2. [person, gossip] boshaft, gehässig - 3. [dog] bösartig.

vicious circle n Teufelskreis der.

victim ['vɪktɪm] n Opfer das; **to fall victim to sb/sthg** jm/etw zum Opfer fallen.

victimize, -ise ['vɪktɪmaɪz] vt schikanieren.

victor ['vɪktər] n Sieger der, -in die.

victorious [vɪk'tɔ:rɪəs] adj [winning] siegreich.

victory ['vɪktərɪ] n Sieg der; **to win a victory over sb/sthg** jn/etw bezwingen.

video ['vɪdɪəʊ] (pl -s, pt & pp -ed, cont -ing) ◇ n - 1. [gen] Video das; **I've got it on video** ich habe es auf Video - 2. [machine] Videorekorder der. ◇ comp Video-. ◇ vt - 1. [using videorecorder] (auf Video) aufnehmen - 2. [using camera] filmen.

video camera n Videokamera die.

video cassette n Videokassette die.

video game n Videospiel das.

videorecorder ['vɪdɪəʊrɪ,kɔ:dər] n Videorekorder der.

video shop n Videothek die.

videotape ['vɪdɪəʊteɪp] n Videoband das.

vie [vaɪ] (pt & pp vied, cont vying) vi: **to vie (with sb) for sthg** (mit jm) um etw wetteifern; **to vie with sb to do sthg** mit jm darum wetteifern, etw zu tun.

Vienna [vɪ'enə] n Wien nt.

Vietnam [UK ,vjet'næm, US ,vjet'nɑ:m] n Vietnam nt.

Vietnamese [,vjetnə'mi:z] ◇ adj vietnamesisch. ◇ n [language] Vietnamesisch(e) das. ◇ npl: **the Vietnamese** die Vietnamesen.

view [vju:] ◇ n - 1. [opinion] Ansicht die, Meinung die; **in my view** meiner Ansicht OR Meinung nach - 2. [vista] Aussicht die, Blick der - 3. [ability to see] Sicht die; **to come into view** in Sicht kommen. ◇ vt - 1. [consider] sehen; **he viewed her with suspicion** er betrachtete sie mit Argwohn - 2. fml [house] besichtigen. ◆ **in view of** prep angesichts (+ G). ◆ **with a view to** conj: **with a view to doing sthg** mit der Absicht, etw zu tun.

viewer ['vju:ər] n - 1. [person] Zuschauer der, -in die - 2. [for slides] Diabetrachter der.

viewfinder ['vju:,faɪndər] n Sucher der.

viewpoint ['vju:pɔɪnt] n - 1. [opinion] Standpunkt der - 2. [place] Aussichtspunkt der.

vigilante [,vɪdʒɪ'læntɪ] n (militante) Bürgerwehr.

vigorous ['vɪgərəs] adj - 1. [walk] flott; [shake, scrub] kräftig - 2. [protest, denial, attempt] energisch.

vile [vaɪl] adj [act, person] abscheulich; [food] scheußlich.

villa ['vɪlə] n Villa die.

village ['vɪlɪdʒ] n Dorf das.

villager ['vɪlɪdʒər] n Dorfbewohner der, -in die.

villain ['vɪlən] n - 1. [of film, book, play] Bösewicht der - 2. dated [criminal] Schurke der.

vindicate ['vɪndɪkeɪt] vt [confirm] bestätigen; [justify] rechtfertigen; **to vindicate o.s.** seine Unschuld beweisen.

vindictive [vɪn'dɪktɪv] adj rachsüchtig.

vine [vaɪn] n [grapevine] Weinrebe die.

vinegar ['vɪnɪgər] n Essig der.

vineyard ['vɪnjəd] n Weinberg der.

vintage ['vɪntɪdʒ] ◇ adj [wine] erlesen. ◇ n [wine] Jahrgang der.

vinyl ['vaɪnɪl] n Vinyl das.

viola [vɪ'əʊlə] n - 1. MUS Bratsche die - 2. BOT Veilchen das.

violate ['vaɪəleɪt] vt - 1. [human rights, law, treaty] verstoßen gegen - 2. [peace, privacy] stören - 3. [grave] schänden.

violence ['vaɪələns] n (U) - 1. [physical force] Gewalt die; [of people] Gewalttätigkeit die; [of actions] Brutalität die - 2. [of words, reaction] Heftigkeit die.

violent ['vaɪələnt] adj - 1. [person] gewalttätig; [attack] heftig; [crime] Gewalt-; [death] gewaltsam - 2. [intense] heftig.

violet ['vaɪələt] ◇ adj violett. ◇ n - 1. [flower] Veilchen das - 2. [colour] Violett das.

violin [,vaɪə'lɪn] n Violine die, Geige die.

violinist [,vaɪə'lɪnɪst] n Violinist der, -in die, Geiger der, -in die.

VIP (abbr of very important person) n Prominente der, die, VIP der.

viper ['vaɪpər] n Viper die.

virgin ['vɜ:dʒɪn] ◇ adj - 1. [gen] jungfräulich - 2. [forest, soil] unberührt. ◇ n Jungfrau die.

Virgo ['vɜ:gəʊ] (pl -s) n Jungfrau die.

virile ['vɪraɪl] adj männlich.

virtually ['vɜ:tʃʊəlɪ] adv [almost] so gut wie, praktisch.

virtual reality n virtuelle Realität.

virtue ['vɜ:tju:] n - 1. [goodness] Tugendhaftigkeit die - 2. [merit, quality] Tugend die - 3. [benefit] Vorteil der. ◆ **by virtue of** prep fml aufgrund (+ G).

virtuous ['vɜːtʃʊəs] *adj* tugendhaft.

virus ['vaɪrəs] *n* MED & COMPUT Virus *das*.

visa ['viːzə] *n* Visum *das*; **entry/exit visa** Einreise-/Ausreisevisum *das*.

vis-à-vis *prep fml* [in comparison to] gegenüber (+ D); [regarding] bezüglich (+ G).

viscose ['vɪskəʊs] *n* Viskose *die*.

visibility [ˌvɪzɪ'bɪlətɪ] *n* - **1.** [being visible] Sichtbarkeit *die* - **2.** [range of vision] Sichtweite *die*; **good/poor visibility** gute/schlechte Sicht.

visible ['vɪzəbl] *adj* - **1.** [which can be physically seen] sichtbar - **2.** [evident] sichtlich.

vision ['vɪʒn] *n* - **1.** [ability to see] Sehvermögen *das* - **2.** *fig* [foresight] Weitblick *der*; **a man of vision** ein Mann mit Weitblick - **3.** [impression, dream] Vision *die*.

visit ['vɪzɪt] <> *n* Besuch *der*; [stay] Aufenthalt *der*. <> *vt* besuchen.

visiting hours ['vɪzɪtɪŋ-] *npl* Besuchszeiten *Pl*.

visitor ['vɪzɪtər] *n* Besucher *der*, -in *die*; **she has visitors** sie hat Besuch.

visitors' book *n* Gästebuch *das*.

visor ['vaɪzər] *n* [on helmet] Visier *das*.

vista ['vɪstə] *n* [view] Ausblick *der*.

visual ['vɪʒʊəl] *adj* Seh-; [joke, memory, image] visuell.

visual display unit *n* Bildschirm *der*.

visualize, -ise ['vɪʒʊəlaɪz] *vt* sich (D) vorstellen.

vital ['vaɪtl] *adj* - **1.** [essential] unerlässlich, unbedingt notwendig; [essential to life] lebenswichtig - **2.** [full of life - person] vital.

vitally ['vaɪtəlɪ] *adv*: **vitally important** von entscheidender Bedeutung.

vitamin [UK 'vɪtəmɪn, US 'vaɪtəmɪn] *n* Vitamin *das*.

vivacious [vɪ'veɪʃəs] *adj* lebhaft, lebendig.

vivid ['vɪvɪd] *adj* - **1.** [colour] kräftig - **2.** [memory] lebhaft; [description] lebendig.

vividly ['vɪvɪdlɪ] *adv* - **1.** [painted] in kräftigen Farben - **2.** [remember] lebhaft; [describe] lebendig.

vixen ['vɪksn] *n* Füchsin *die*.

VLF (*abbr of* very low frequency) *n* VLF.

V-neck *n* - **1.** [sweater, dress] Pullover *der*/Kleid *das* mit V-Ausschnitt - **2.** [neck] V-Ausschnitt *der*.

vocabulary [və'kæbjʊlərɪ] *n* - **1.** [gen] Wortschatz *der*, Vokabular *das* - **2.** [list of words] Wörterverzeichnis *das*.

vocal ['vəʊkl] *adj* - **1.** [outspoken] lautstark - **2.** [of the voice] stimmlich.

vocal cords *npl* Stimmbänder *Pl*.

vocation [vəʊ'keɪʃn] *n* [calling] Berufung *die*.

vocational [vəʊ'keɪʃənl] *adj* berufsbezogen.

vociferous [və'sɪfərəs] *adj fml* lautstark.

vodka ['vɒdkə] *n* Wodka *der*.

vogue [vəʊg] *n* Mode *die*; **to be in vogue** in Mode sein.

voice [vɔɪs] <> *n* [gen] Stimme *die*. <> *vt* [opinion, emotion] zum Ausdruck bringen.

void [vɔɪd] <> *adj* - **1.** [contract, result] ungültig, nichtig, ⊳ **null** - **2.** *fml* [empty]: **void of interest** ohne jegliches Interesse. <> *n* - **1.** *liter* [feeling of emptiness]: **the void left by his death** die Lücke, die sein Tod hinterlassen hat - **2.** [chasm] Nichts *das*.

volatile [UK 'vɒlətaɪl, US 'vɒlətl] *adj* [situation] brisant; [person] aufbrausend; [market] unbeständig.

volcano [vɒl'keɪnəʊ] (*pl* -es OR -s) *n* Vulkan *der*.

volition [və'lɪʃn] *n fml*: **of one's own volition** aus freiem Willen.

volley ['vɒlɪ] (*pl* volleys) <> *n* - **1.** [of gunfire] Salve *die* - **2.** [of insults] Flut *die* - **3.** [in tennis] Volley *der*; [in football] Volleyschuss *der*. <> *vt* [in tennis] volley spielen; [in football] volley nehmen.

volleyball ['vɒlɪbɔːl] *n* SPORT Volleyball *das*.

volt [vəʊlt] *n* Volt *das*.

voltage ['vəʊltɪdʒ] *n* Spannung *die*.

voluble ['vɒljʊbl] *adj fml* redselig.

volume ['vɒljuːm] *n* - **1.** [of sound] Lautstärke *die* - **2.** [of container, object] Volumen *das*, Rauminhalt *der* - **3.** [of work] Umfang *der*; **volume of traffic** Verkehrsaufkommen *das* - **4.** [book] Band *der*.

voluntarily [UK 'vɒləntrɪlɪ, US ˌvɒlən'terəlɪ] *adv* freiwillig; [work] ehrenamtlich.

voluntary ['vɒləntrɪ] *adj* - **1.** [not obligatory] freiwillig - **2.** [unpaid] ehrenamtlich.

voluntary work *n* freiwillige OR ehrenamtliche Tätigkeit.

volunteer [ˌvɒlən'tɪər] <> *n* - **1.** [gen & MIL] Freiwillige *der*, *die* - **2.** [unpaid worker] freiwillige Helfer *der*, -in *die*. <> *vt* - **1.** [of one's free will]: **to volunteer to do sthg** sich bereit erklären, etw zu tun - **2.** [information] geben; **to volunteer advice** Ratschläge erteilen. <> *vi* sich freiwillig melden.

vomit ['vɒmɪt] <> *n* Erbrochene *das*. <> *vi* sich übergeben.

vote [vəʊt] <> *n* - **1.** [individual decision] Stimme *die*; **a vote for/against sb/sthg** eine Stimme für/gegen jn/etw - **2.** [session, ballot] Abstimmung *die* - **3.** [result of ballot]: **the vote** das Abstimmungsergebnis - **4.** [suffrage] Stimmrecht *das*. <> *vt* - **1.** [gen] wählen; **to vote to do sthg** (per Abstimmung) beschließen, etw zu tun - **2.** [suggest] vorschlagen. <> *vi* wählen; **to vote for/against sb/sthg** für/gegen jn/etw stimmen; **to vote on an issue** über eine Frage abstimmen.

voter ['vəʊtər] *n* Wähler *die*, -in *die*.

voting ['vəʊtɪŋ] *n* Wahl *die*, Abstimmung *die*.

vouch [vaʊtʃ] ➡ **vouch for** *vt insep* - 1. [person] bürgen für - 2. [character, accuracy] sich verbürgen für.

voucher ['vaʊtʃər] *n* Gutschein *der*.

vow [vaʊ] ◇ *n* Gelöbnis *das*; RELIG Gelübde *das*. ◇ *vt*: **to vow to do sthg** geloben, etw zu tun; **to vow (that)...** schwören(, dass)...

vowel ['vaʊəl] *n* Vokal *der*.

voyage ['vɔɪɪdʒ] *n* Reise *die*; [by sea] Seereise *die*; [through space] Flug *der*.

vs *abbr of* **versus**.

VSO (*abbr of* **Voluntary Service Overseas**) *n* britische Hilfsorganisation, die Freiwillige mit Berufsausbildung in Entwicklungsländern einsetzt.

vulgar ['vʌlgər] *adj* - 1. [tasteless - décor] geschmacklos; [- person] ordinär - 2. [rude] vulgär.

vulnerable ['vʌlnərəbl] *adj* - 1. [easily hurt - emotionally] verletzlich; [- physically] verwundbar - 2. [easily influenced]: **vulnerable (to sthg)** anfällig (für etw).

vulture ['vʌltʃər] *n liter & fig* Geier *der*.

w (*pl* **w's** OR **ws**), **W** (*pl* **W's** OR **Ws**) ['dʌblju:] *n* w *das*, W *das*. ➡ **W** (*abbr of* **west, watt**) W.

wad [wɒd] *n* - 1. [of cotton wool] Bausch *der* - 2. [of bank notes, documents] Bündel *das*.

waddle ['wɒdl] *vi* watscheln.

wade [weɪd] *vi* waten. ➡ **wade through** *vt insep fig* durchackern.

wading pool ['weɪdɪŋ-] *n US* Planschbecken *das*.

wafer ['weɪfər] *n* [thin biscuit] Waffel *die*.

waffle ['wɒfl] ◇ *n* - 1. CULIN Waffel *die* - 2. *UK inf* [vague talk] Geschwafel *das*. ◇ *vi* schwafeln.

wag [wæg] ◇ *vt* [tail] wedeln mit. ◇ *vi* [tail] wedeln.

wage [weɪdʒ] ◇ *n* Lohn *der*. ◇ *vt*: **to wage war against sb/sthg** einen Kampf gegen jn/etw führen. ➡ **wages** *npl* Lohn *der*.

wage packet *n* - 1. [envelope] Lohntüte *die* - 2. [pay] Lohn *der*.

wager ['weɪdʒər] *n* Wette *die*.

waggle ['wægl] *inf vt* [tail] wedeln mit; [ears] wackeln mit.

wagon, waggon *UK* ['wægən] *n* - 1. [horse-drawn vehicle] Fuhrwerk *das* - 2. *UK* RAIL Waggon *der*.

wail [weɪl] ◇ *n* - 1. [of baby] Geschrei *das*; [of mourner] Klagen *das* - 2. [of wind, siren] Heulen *das*. ◇ *vi* [baby] schreien; [mourner] klagen.

waist [weɪst] *n* Taille *die*.

waistcoat ['weɪskəʊt] *n UK* Weste *die*.

waistline ['weɪstlaɪn] *n* Taille *die*.

wait [weɪt] ◇ *n* Wartezeit *die*. ◇ *vi* warten; **to wait and see** abwarten(, was passiert). ◇ *vt* - 1. [person]: **I/he/she can't wait to do it** ich/er/sie kann es kaum erwarten, es zu tun - 2.: **to wait tables** kellnern. ➡ **wait for** *vt insep* warten auf (+ A); **to wait for sb to do sthg** darauf warten, dass jd etw tut. ➡ **wait on** *vt insep* [serve food to] bedienen. ➡ **wait up** *vi* aufbleiben.

waiter ['weɪtər] *n* Kellner *der*.

waiting list ['weɪtɪŋ-] *n* Warteliste *die*.

waiting room ['weɪtɪŋ-] *n* Warteraum *der*; [at doctor's] Wartezimmer *das*; [at railway station] Wartesaal *der*.

waitress ['weɪtrɪs] *n* Kellnerin *die*, Serviererin *die*.

waive [weɪv] *vt fml* [entrance fee] verzichten auf (+ A); [rule] nicht anwenden.

wake [weɪk] (*pt* woke OR -d, *pp* woken OR -d) ◇ *n* [of ship, boat] Kielwasser *das*. ◇ *vt* wecken. ◇ *vi* aufwachen. ➡ **wake up** ◇ *vt sep* aufwecken. ◇ *vi* [wake] aufwachen.

waken ['weɪkən] *fml* ◇ *vt* wecken. ◇ *vi* erwachen.

Wales [weɪlz] *n* Wales *nt*.

walk [wɔ:k] ◇ *n* - 1. [stroll] Spaziergang *der*; **to go for a walk** einen Spaziergang machen; **to take the dog for a walk** mit dem Hund spazieren gehen; **it's quite a long walk to the station** zu Fuß ist es ganz schön weit bis zum Bahnhof - 2. [gait] Gang *der*. ◇ *vt* - 1. [escort]: **I'll walk you back to the car park** ich gehe mit dir bis zum Parkplatz - 2. [dog] spazieren führen - 3. [cover on foot] laufen, (zu Fuß) gehen. ◇ *vi* gehen, laufen; [hike] wandern; **he walks to work** er geht zu Fuß zur Arbeit. ➡ **walk out** *vi* - 1. [leave suddenly] hinausgehen - 2. [go on strike] in Streik treten. ➡ **walk out on** *vt insep* sitzen lassen.

walker ['wɔ:kər] *n* [for pleasure] Spaziergänger *der*, -in *die*; [when hiking] Wanderer *der*, -derin *die*; SPORT Geher *der*, -in *die*.

walkie-talkie [ˌwɔ:kɪ'tɔ:kɪ] *n* Walkie-Talkie *das*.

walking ['wɔ:kɪŋ] *n* [for pleasure] Spazierengehen *das*; [hiking] Wandern *das*; SPORT Gehen *das*.

walking shoes *npl* Wanderschuhe *Pl.*

walking stick *n* Spazierstock *der*.

Walkman® ['wɔːkmən] n Walkman® der.

walkout ['wɔːkaʊt] n [of workers] Arbeitsniederlegung die.

walkover ['wɔːk,əʊvər] n UK inf [victory] spielender Sieg.

walkway ['wɔːkweɪ] n Fußweg der.

wall [wɔːl] n - 1. [inside building, of stomach, cell] Wand die - 2. [outside] Mauer die.

wallchart ['wɔːltʃɑːt] n Schautafel die.

walled [wɔːld] adj von Mauern umgeben.

wallet ['wɒlɪt] n [for money] Brieftasche die; [for documents] Etui das.

wallop ['wɒləp] inf vt [person] versohlen, verdreschen; [ball] dreschen.

wallow ['wɒləʊ] vi [in mud] sich wälzen, sich suhlen.

wallpaper ['wɔːl,peɪpər] ◇ n (U) Tapete die. ◇ vt tapezieren.

Wall Street n Wall Street die.

wally ['wɒlɪ] n UK inf Dussel der.

walnut ['wɔːlnʌt] n - 1. [nut] Walnuss die - 2. [tree] Walnussbaum der, Nussbaum der - 3. [wood] Nussbaumholz das.

walrus ['wɔːlrəs] (pl inv OR -es) n Walross das.

waltz [wɔːls] ◇ n Walzer der. ◇ vi [dance] Walzer tanzen.

wan [wɒn] adj [person, complexion] bleich; [smile] matt.

wand [wɒnd] n Zauberstab der.

wander ['wɒndər] vi - 1. [person] herumlaufen, umherwandern - 2. [thoughts] schweifen, wandern.

wane [weɪn] vi - 1. [popularity, enthusiasm] schwinden - 2. [moon] abnehmen.

wangle ['wæŋgl] vt inf organisieren; **to wangle sthg out of sb** jm etw aus dem Kreuz leiern.

want [wɒnt] ◇ vt - 1. [desire] wollen; **to want to do sthg** etw tun wollen; **to want sb to do sthg** wollen, dass jd etw tut; **what do you want to eat?** was möchtest du (zu) essen?; **you're wanted on the phone** Sie werden am Telefon verlangt - 2. [need] brauchen; **you want to be more careful** du solltest vorsichtiger sein - 3. [seek] suchen; **he is wanted by the police** er wird von der Polizei gesucht. ◇ n - 1. [need] Bedürfnis das - 2. [lack] Mangel der; **his want of understanding** seine mangelnde Einsicht; **for want of** aus Mangel an (+ D) - 3. [poverty] Not die; **to be in want** Not leiden.

wanted ['wɒntɪd] adj: **to be wanted (by the police)** (polizeilich) gesucht werden.

wanton ['wɒntən] adj fml [destruction] mutwillig; [neglect] sträflich.

WAP [wæp] n (abbr of wireless application protocol) WAP das.

war [wɔːr] n Krieg der; **to be at war** sich im Kriegszustand befinden.

ward [wɔːd] n - 1. [part of hospital] Station die; [room in hospital] Krankensaal der; **maternity ward** Entbindungsstation die - 2. UK POL Wahlbezirk der - 3. LAW Mündel das. ◆ **ward off** vt insep [blow, evil spirits] abwehren; [disease] schützen vor (+ D).

warden ['wɔːdn] n - 1. [of park] Aufseher der, -in die; [of game reserve] Wildhüter der, -in die - 2. UK [of youth hostel] Herbergsvater der, -mutter die; [of hall of residence] Heimleiter der, -in die - 3. US [prison governor] Gefängnisdirektor der, -in die.

warder ['wɔːdər] n [in prison] Wärter der, -in die.

wardrobe ['wɔːdrəʊb] n - 1. [piece of furniture] Kleiderschrank der, Schrank der - 2. [collection of clothes] Garderobe die.

warehouse ['weəhaʊs] (pl [-haʊzɪz]) n Lagerhaus das.

warfare ['wɔːfeər] n (U) [war] Krieg der; [technique] Kriegsführung die.

warhead ['wɔːhed] n Sprengkopf der.

warily ['weərəlɪ] adv [carefully] vorsichtig; [suspiciously] misstrauisch.

warm [wɔːm] ◇ adj - 1. [gen] warm; **are you warm enough?** ist dir warm genug? - 2. [friendly - person, feelings, welcome] herzlich; [- atmosphere] freundlich. ◇ vt [food, milk] warm machen. ◆ **warm to** vt insep [idea, place] Gefallen finden an (+ D). ◆ **warm up** ◇ vt sep - 1. [heat - food] warm machen; [- room] heizen - 2. [reheat] aufwärmen. ◇ vi - 1. [get warmer] wärmer werden - 2. [machine, engine] warm laufen; [audience] in Stimmung kommen - 3. [athlete, footballer] sich aufwärmen; [orchestra, musician] sich einspielen.

warm-hearted [-'hɑːtɪd] adj [person] warmherzig; [action, gesture] herzlich.

warmly ['wɔːmlɪ] adv - 1. [in warm clothes]: **to dress warmly** sich warm anziehen - 2. [in a friendly way] herzlich.

warmth [wɔːmθ] n - 1. [of temperature, clothes] Wärme die - 2. [of welcome, smile, support] Herzlichkeit die.

warn [wɔːn] vt - 1. [advise] warnen; **to warn sb of OR about sthg** jn vor etw (D) warnen - 2. [inform] Bescheid geben (+ D); **to warn sb that...** jn darauf hinlweisen, dass...

warning ['wɔːnɪŋ] n - 1. [cautionary advice] Warnung die - 2. [from police, judge] Verwarnung die - 2. [notice]: **to give sb warning** jm rechtzeitig Bescheid sagen.

warning light n Warnleuchte die.

warp [wɔːp] ◇ vt - 1. [wood]: **the sun will warp the wood** in der Sonne wird sich das Holz verziehen - 2. [mind] psychisch schwer schädigen. ◇ vi [wood] sich verziehen.

warrant ['wɒrənt] <> n LAW [written order] Befehl der; [for arrest] Haftbefehl der; [for search] Durchsuchungsbefehl der. <> vt fml [justify] rechtfertigen.

warranty ['wɒrəntɪ] n [guarantee] Garantie die.

warren ['wɒrən] n Kaninchenbau der.

warrior ['wɒrɪər] n liter Krieger der.

Warsaw ['wɔːsɔː] n Warschau nt.

warship ['wɔːʃɪp] n Kriegsschiff das.

wart [wɔːt] n Warze die.

wartime ['wɔːtaɪm] n Kriegszeit die; **in wartime** in Kriegszeiten.

wary ['weərɪ] adj [careful] vorsichtig; [suspicious] misstrauisch; **to be wary of sthg** sich vor etw (D) in Acht nehmen.

was (weak form [wəz], strong form [wɒz]) pt ⊳ **be**.

wash [wɒʃ] <> n - **1.** [act of washing]: **she/it needs a wash** sie/es muss gewaschen werden; **to have a wash** sich waschen; **to give sthg a wash** etw waschen - **2.** [clothes to be washed] Wäsche die - **3.** [from boat] Kielwasser das. <> vt [clean] waschen; [dishes] spülen, abwaschen. <> vi [clean o.s.] sich waschen.
◆ wash away vt sep wegspülen. **◆ wash up** <> vt sep UK [dishes] abwaschen, spülen. <> vi - **1.** UK [wash the dishes] abwaschen, spülen - **2.** US [wash o.s.] sich waschen.

washable ['wɒʃəbl] adj waschbar.

washbasin UK ['wɒʃ,beɪsn], **washbowl** US ['wɒʃbəʊl] n Waschbecken das.

washcloth ['wɒʃ,klɒθ] n US Waschlappen der.

washer ['wɒʃər] n - **1.** TECH Dichtungsring der - **2.** [washing machine] Waschmaschine die.

washing ['wɒʃɪŋ] n - **1.** [act] Waschen das - **2.** [clothes] Wäsche die.

washing line n Wäscheleine die.

washing machine n Waschmaschine die.

washing powder n UK Waschpulver das.

Washington ['wɒʃɪŋtən] n [city]: **Washington D.C.** Washington nt, Hauptstadt der USA.

washing-up n - **1.** UK [crockery, pans etc] Abwasch der - **2.** [act]: **to do the washing-up** spülen, den Abwasch machen.

washing-up liquid n UK Spülmittel das.

washout ['wɒʃaʊt] n inf Reinfall der.

washroom ['wɒʃrʊm] n US Toilette die.

wasn't ['wɒznt] abbr of **was not**.

wasp [wɒsp] n Wespe die.

wastage ['weɪstɪdʒ] n (U) [process] Verschwendung die; [amount] Verlust der.

waste [weɪst] <> adj [fuel] ungenutzt. <> n - **1.** [misuse] Verschwendung die; **a waste of time** eine Zeitverschwendung - **2.** [refuse] Abfall der. <> vt verschwenden; [opportunity] vertun.

wastebasket ['weɪst,bɑːskɪt] n US Papierkorb der.

waste disposal unit n Müllschlucker der.

wasteful ['weɪstfʊl] adj verschwenderisch.

waste ground n Ödland das.

wastepaper basket, wastepaper bin [,weɪst'peɪpər-], **wastebasket** US ['weɪst,bɑːskɪt] n Papierkorb der.

watch [wɒtʃ] <> n - **1.** [timepiece] Uhr die, Armbanduhr die - **2.** [act of guarding]: **to keep watch** Wache halten; **to keep (a) watch on sb/sthg** auf jn/etw aufpassen - **3.** [guard - person] Wachmann der; [- group] Wache die. <> vt - **1.** [observe] beobachten; [game, event] zusehen OR zuschauen bei; [film, play] sich (D) ansehen - **2.** [spy on] beobachten - **3.** [be careful about] aufpassen auf (+ A). <> vi [observe] zusehen, zuschauen. **◆ watch for** vt insep [person, thing] Ausschau halten nach; [opportunity] warten auf (+ A). **◆ watch out** vi - **1.** [be careful]: **to watch out (for sthg)** aufpassen (auf etw (A)), Acht geben (auf etw (A)); **watch out!** Achtung!, Vorsicht! - **2.** [keep a lookout]: **to watch out for sthg** nach etw Ausschau halten.

watchdog ['wɒtʃdɒg] n - **1.** [dog] Wachhund der - **2.** [organization] Aufsichtsbehörde die.

watchful ['wɒtʃfʊl] adj [vigilant] wachsam.

watchmaker ['wɒtʃ,meɪkər] n Uhrmacher der, -in die.

watchman ['wɒtʃmən] (pl -men [-mən]) n Wächter der.

water ['wɔːtər] <> n Wasser das. <> vt [plants] gießen; [garden, lawn] sprengen; [land, field] bewässern. <> vi - **1.** [eyes] tränen - **2.** [mouth]: **my mouth was watering** mir lief das Wasser im Munde zusammen. **◆ waters** npl [territory at sea] Gewässer Pl. **◆ water down** vt sep - **1.** [drink] verdünnen - **2.** [plan, criticism, novel] verwässern.

water bottle n Wasserflasche die.

watercolour ['wɔːtə,kʌlər] n - **1.** [picture] Aquarell das - **2.** [paint] Aquarellfarbe die.

watercress ['wɔːtəkres] n Brunnenkresse die.

waterfall ['wɔːtəfɔːl] n Wasserfall der.

water heater n Heißwassergerät das, Boiler der.

waterhole ['wɔːtəhəʊl] n Wasserstelle die.

watering can ['wɔːtərɪŋ-] n Gießkanne die.

water lily n Seerose die.

waterline ['wɔːtəlaɪn] n NAUT Wasserlinie die.

waterlogged ['wɔːtəlɒgd] adj - **1.** [land, sports] (völlig) aufgeweicht - **2.** [vessel] voll Wasser.

water main n Hauptwasserleitung die.

watermark ['wɔːtəmɑːk] n - **1.** [in paper] Wasserzeichen das - **2.** [showing water level] Wasserstandsmarke die.

watermelon ['wɔːtə,melən] n Wassermelone die.

water polo n Wasserball der.

waterproof ['wɔːtəpruːf] <> adj [watch] wasserdicht; [anorak, shoes] wasserundurchlässig. <> n: **waterproofs** Regenkleidung die.

watershed ['wɔːtəʃed] n [turning point] Wendepunkt der.

water skiing n Wasserskilaufen das.

water tank n Wassertank der.

watertight ['wɔːtətaɪt] adj - **1.** [waterproof] wasserdicht - **2.** [faultless] hieb- und stichfest.

waterworks ['wɔːtəwɜːks] (pl inv) n [building] Wasserwerk das.

watery ['wɔːtərɪ] adj - **1.** [food, juice] wässrig; [coffee, tea] dünn - **2.** [light, sun] blass.

watt [wɒt] n Watt das.

wave [weɪv] <> n - **1.** [gen] Welle die - **2.** [gesture]: **to give sb a wave** jm zuwinken. <> vt - **1.** [flag, handkerchief] schwenken; [baton] schwingen; [gun, stick] fuchteln; **to wave one's hand at sb** jm winken - **2.** [gesture to]: **to wave sb on/over** jn weiter-/herüberlwinken. <> vi - **1.** [with hand] winken; **to wave at** OR **to sb** jm zuwinken - **2.** [flag] wehen; [branches] sich hin und her bewegen, sich wiegen.

wavelength ['weɪvleŋθ] n Wellenlänge die; **to be on the same wavelength (as sb)** fig auf der gleichen Wellenlänge (wie jd) funken.

waver ['weɪvər] vi - **1.** [person, resolve, confidence] wanken - **2.** [voice] zittern - **3.** [flame, light] flackern.

wavy ['weɪvɪ] adj - **1.** [hair] wellig - **2.** [line] Schlangen-.

wax [wæks] <> n - **1.** [in candles, polish, for skis] Wachs das - **2.** [in ears] Ohrenschmalz das. <> vt - **1.** [floor, table, skis] wachsen - **2.** [legs] mit Wachs enthaaren. <> vi [moon] zulnehmen.

wax paper n US Wachspapier das.

waxworks ['wækswɜːks] (pl inv) n [museum] Wachsfigurenkabinett das.

way [weɪ] <> n - **1.** [means, method] Art und Weise die; **this/that way so; this is the best way to do it** man macht es am besten so - **2.** [manner, style] Art die; **I feel the same way as you** mir geht es wie Ihnen; **she's behaving in a very odd way** sie benimmt sich sehr seltsam; **if that's the way you feel** wenn du so denkst; **in the same way** auf die gleiche Weise - **3.** [thoroughfare, path] Weg der; **'give way'** UK AUT 'Vorfahrt beachten' - **4.** [route] Weg der; **which way is the station?** wie kommt man zum Bahnhof?; **what's the best way to the station?** wie kommt man am besten zum Bahnhof?; **to be in the way** im Weg sein; **to be in sb's way** jm im Wege stehen; **on the way**

(to the station) auf dem Weg (zum Bahnhof); **on the way home/to school** auf dem Heimweg/Schulweg; **on the way back/there** auf dem Rückweg/Hinweg; **out of the way** [place] abgelegen; **get out of the** OR **my way!** geh mir aus dem Weg!; **to go out of one's way to do sthg** sich (D) besondere Mühe geben, etw zu tun; **to keep out of sb's way** jm aus dem Wege gehen; **to be under way** [ship] in Fahrt sein; [project, meeting] im Gange sein; **to get under way** [ship] in Fahrt kommen; [project, meeting] in Gang kommen; **to lose one's way** sich verlaufen; [in car] sich verfahren; **make your way to the exit** begeben Sie sich zum Ausgang; **to make way for sb/sthg** jm/einer Sache Platz machen; **to stand in sb's way** fig jm im Wege stehen - **5.** [direction] Richtung die; **which way are you going?** in welche Richtung gehst du?; **this/that way** hier/dort entlang; **look this way, please** sehen Sie bitte hierher; **way in** Eingang der; **way out** Ausgang der - **6.** [side]: **the right way round** richtig herum; **the wrong way round** verkehrt herum; **the right/wrong way up** richtig/verkehrt herum; **the other way round** anders herum - **7.** [distance] Weg der; **all the way** den ganzen Weg; **we're with you all the way** fig wir stehen voll und ganz hinter dir; **it's a long way (away) from here** es liegt weit weg OR entfernt; **I have a long way to go** ich habe einen weiten Weg vor mir; **he's not as clever as her by a long way** er ist bei Weitem nicht so klug wie sie - **8.** phr: **to give way** [under weight, pressure] nachlgeben; **in many ways** in vieler Hinsicht; **no way!** auf keinen Fall! <> adv inf [far] viel; **way ahead** weit voraus; **way off** weit entfernt; **way back in 1930** damals, 1930. ➤ **ways** npl [customs, habits] Art die. ➤ **by the way** adv übrigens.

waylay [,weɪ'leɪ] (pt & pp **-laid** [-'leɪd]) vt ablfangen.

wayward ['weɪwəd] adj eigenwillig.

WC (abbr of water closet) n WC das.

we [wiː] pers pron & PI wir; **we British** wir Briten.

weak [wiːk] adj - **1.** [gen] schwach - **2.** [lacking knowledge, skill]: **to be weak on sthg** in etw (D) schwach sein.

weaken ['wiːkn] <> vt schwächen; [argument] entkräften. <> vi - **1.** [person] schwach werden - **2.** [influence, power & FIN] schwächer werden.

weakling ['wiːklɪŋ] n pej Schwächling der.

weakness ['wiːknɪs] n - **1.** [gen] Schwäche die; **to have a weakness for sthg** eine Schwäche für etw haben - **2.** [in plan, argument] Schwachpunkt der.

wealth [welθ] n - **1.** (U) [riches] Reichtum der - **2.** [abundance]: **a wealth of sthg** ein Reichtum an etw (D).

wealthy ['welθɪ] adj reich.

weapon ['wepən] *n* Waffe *die*.

weaponry ['wepənrɪ] *n* (U) Waffen *Pl*.

wear [weə^r] (*pt* wore, *pp* worn) ◇ *n* - 1. [type of clothes] Kleidung *die* - 2. [damage]: **wear (and tear)** Abnutzung *die*. ◇ *vt* - 1. [clothes, shoes, jewellery, spectacles] tragen - 2. [damage] ablnutzen. ◇ *vi* - 1. [deteriorate] sich ablnutzen - 2. [last]: **to wear well/badly** gut/nicht gut halten. ◆ **wear away** ◇ *vt sep* [steps] ausltreten; [inscription] verwittern; [grass] ablnutzen. ◇ *vi* [steps] ausgetreten werden; [inscription] verwittern; [grass] abgenutzt werden. ◆ **wear down** *vt sep* - 1. [reduce size of] ablnutzen; [heel] abllaufen - 2. [weaken] auslzehren; [resistance] zermürben. ◆ **wear off** *vi* nachllassen. ◆ **wear out** *vt sep* - 1. [clothing, machinery] ablnutzen - 2. [person, patience, strength] erschöpfen. ◇ *vi* [clothing, shoes] sich ablnutzen.

weary ['wɪərɪ] *adj* - 1. [exhausted] müde - 2. [fed up]: **to be weary of sthg** etw satt haben; **to be weary of doing sthg** es satt haben, etw zu tun.

weasel ['wɪːzl] *n* Wiesel *das*.

weather ['weðə^r] ◇ *n* Wetter *das*; **to be under the weather** nicht ganz auf der Höhe sein. ◇ *vt* [survive] überstehen.

weather-beaten [-,bɪːtn] *adj* [face, skin] wettergegerbt.

weather forecast *n* Wettervorhersage *die*.

weatherman ['weðəmæn] (*pl* -men [-men]) *n* Meterologe *der*.

weather vane [-veɪn] *n* Wetterfahne *die*.

weave [wiːv] (*pt* wove, *pp* woven) ◇ *vt* [using loom] weben. ◇ *vi* [move] sich durchlschlängeln.

weaver ['wiːvə^r] *n* Weber *der*, -in *die*.

web [web] *n* - 1. [cobweb] Spinnennetz *das* - 2. *fig* [of lies, intrigue] Netz *das*. ◆ **Web** *n*: **the Web** COMPUT das Netz, das Web.

webcam ['webkæm] *n* Webcam *die*.

webcast ['webkɑːst] *n* Webcast *der*.

website ['web,saɪt] *n* COMPUT Website *die*.

wed [wed] (*pt* & *pp* *inv* OR -ded) *liter* ◇ *vt* - 1. [marry] heiraten - 2. [subj: priest] trauen. ◇ *vi* heiraten.

we'd [wiːd] *abbr of* **we had**, **we would**.

wedding ['wedɪŋ] *n* Hochzeit *die*.

wedding anniversary *n* Hochzeitstag *der*.

wedding cake *n* Hochzeitskuchen *der*.

wedding dress *n* Hochzeitskleid *das*.

wedding ring *n* Ehering *der*.

wedge [wedʒ] *n* - 1. [gen] Keil *der* - 2. [of cheese, cake, pie] Stück *das*. ◇ *vt* - 1. [secure] festlklemmen - 2. [squeeze, push] zwängen.

Wednesday ['wenzdɪ] *n* Mittwoch *der*; *see also* **Saturday**.

wee [wiː] ◇ *adj Scotland* klein. ◇ *n vi inf*: **to do/have a wee** Pipi machen. ◇ *vi v inf* Pipi machen.

weed [wiːd] ◇ *n* - 1. [wild plant] Unkraut *das* - 2. *UK inf* [feeble person] Schwächling *der*. ◇ *vt*: **to weed the garden** im Garten Unkraut jäten.

weedkiller ['wiːd,kɪlə^r] *n* Unkrautvertilgungsmittel *das*.

weedy ['wiːdɪ] *adj UK inf* [feeble] schwächlich.

week [wiːk] *n* Woche *die*; **in three weeks' time** in drei Wochen; **a week last Saturday** Samstag vor einer Woche.

weekday ['wiːkdeɪ] *n* Wochentag *der*.

weekend [,wiːk'end] *n* Wochenende *das*; **at the weekend** am Wochenende.

weekly ['wiːklɪ] ◇ *adj* wöchentlich; [newspaper] Wochen-. ◇ *adv* wöchentlich. ◇ *n* Wochenzeitung *die*.

weep [wiːp] (*pt* & *pp* wept) *vt* & *vi* weinen.

weeping willow [,wiːpɪŋ-] *n* Trauerweide *die*.

weigh [weɪ] ◇ *vt* - 1. [find weight of] wiegen - 2. [consider carefully] ablwägen - 3. [raise]: **to weigh anchor** den Anker lichten. ◇ *vi* [have specific weight] wiegen. ◆ **weigh down** *vt sep* - 1. [physically]: **to be weighed down with sthg** mit etw beladen sein - 2. [mentally]: **to be weighed down by** OR **with sthg** mit etw belastet sein. ◆ **weigh up** *vt sep* [situation, pros and cons] ablwägen; [person, opposition] einlschätzen.

weight [weɪt] *n* - 1. [of person, package, goods & SPORT] Gewicht *das*; **to put on** OR **gain weight** zulnehmen; **to lose weight** ablnehmen - 2. *fig* [power, influence]: **the weight of public opinion** die Übermacht der öffentlichen Meinung; **to throw one's weight about** sich auflspielen - 3. *liter* & *fig* [burden] Last *die*; **it took a weight off my mind** damit ist mir ein Stein vom Herzen gefallen - 4. *phr*: **to pull one's weight** seinen Beitrag leisten.

weighted ['weɪtɪd] *adj*: **to be weighted in favour of/against sb/sthg** jn/etw bevorteilen/benachteiligen.

weighting ['weɪtɪŋ] *n* (U) Zulage *die*.

weight lifting *n* Gewichtheben *das*.

weighty ['weɪtɪ] *adj* [serious, important] schwerwiegend.

weir [wɪə^r] *n* Wehr *das*.

weird [wɪəd] *adj* seltsam.

welcome ['welkəm] ◇ *adj* - 1. [guest] willkommen - 2. [free]: **to be welcome to do sthg** etw gerne tun können - 3. [pleasant, desirable] angenehm - 4. [in reply to thanks]: **you're welcome** bitte, gern geschehen. ◇ *n* Willkommen *das*; **to get/receive a warm welcome**

herzlich aufgenommen werden. ◇ *vt*
- 1. [receive] empfangen - 2. [approve, support]
willkommen heißen. ◇ *excl* willkommen!

weld [weld] ◇ *n* Schweißnaht *die*. ◇ *vt*
schweißen.

welfare ['welfeər] ◇ *adj* sozial; [work, work-
er] Sozial-. ◇ *n* - 1. [state of wellbeing]
Wohl *das* - 2. *US* [income support] Sozialhilfe *die*.

well [wel] (*comp* better, *superl* best) ◇ *adj*
- 1. [in health] gesund; **how are you? - (I'm)**
well, thanks wie geht es Ihnen? – sehr gut,
danke; **to feel well** sich wohl fühlen; **to get**
well gesund werden; **get well soon!** gute Besserung! - 2. [good]: **all's well** alles ist in Ordnung; **it's just as well you stayed** nur gut, dass
du geblieben bist. ◇ *adv* - 1. [gen] gut; **the**
patient is doing well der Patient macht gute
Fortschritte; **to do well out of sthg** von etw
profitieren; **you did well to come immedi-**
ately gut, dass du sofort gekommen bist; **well**
done! gut gemacht!; **to speak well of sb** jn lo-
bend erwähnen; **you beaten** restlos geschlagen; **to go well** gut gehen - 2. [definitely, cer-
tainly]: **well within one's rights** voll im Recht;
you know perfectly well that... du weißt ganz
genau, dass...; **it's well worth it** es lohnt sich
unbedingt; **well after six o'clock** viel später
als sechs Uhr; **well over 50** weit über 50
- 3. [easily, possibly]: **it may well happen** es kann
durchaus passieren; **you may well laugh** lachen Sie nur!; **that may well be true** das mag
wahr sein. ◇ *n* - 1. [for water] Brunnen *der*
- 2. [oil well] Ölquelle *die*. ◇ *excl* - 1. [expres-
sing hesitation]: **well, I don't really know** tja,
das weiß ich nicht so recht - 2. [expressing
resignation]: **oh well!** na ja! - 3. [expressing sur-
prise]: **well, I didn't expect to see you here!** na
so was, ich habe nicht erwartet, Sie hier zu
sehen!; **well I never!** na, so was! - 4. [after in-
terruption]: **well, as I was saying** also, wie gesagt. ◆ **as well** *adv* [in addition] auch; **I might**
as well go home ich könnte genauso gut nach
Hause gehen. ◆ **as well as** *conj* sowohl …
als auch; **children as well as adults** sowohl
Kinder als auch Erwachsene. ◆ **well up** *vi*
[water] hochquellen.

we'll [wiːl] *abbr of* **we shall**, **we will**.

well-advised [-əd'vaɪzd] *adj* klug; **he/you**
would be well-advised to do sthg er täte/du
tätest gut daran, etw zu tun.

well-behaved [-bɪ'heɪvd] *adj* artig.

wellbeing [,wel'biːɪŋ] *n* Wohl *das*.

well-built *adj* [person] gut gebaut.

well-done *adj* [thoroughly cooked] durchgebraten.

well-dressed [-'drest] *adj* gut gekleidet.

well-earned [-ɜːnd] *adj* wohlverdient.

wellington (boot) ['welɪŋtən-] *n* Gummi-
stiefel *der*.

well-kept *adj* - 1. [garden, village] gepflegt
- 2. [secret] wohl gehütet.

well-known *adj* bekannt.

well-mannered [-'mænəd] *adj*: **to be well-**
mannered gute Manieren haben.

well-meaning *adj* [action, suggestion] gut gemeint; **she's very well-meaning** sie meint es
gut.

well-nigh [-naɪ] *adv* nahezu.

well-off *adj* - 1. [financially] wohlhabend
- 2. [in a good position]: **to be well-off for sthg**
mit etw gut versorgt sein.

well-read [-'red] *adj* belesen.

well-rounded [-'raundɪd] *adj* [varied] vielseitig.

well-timed [-'taɪmd] *adj* gut abgepasst.

well-to-do *adj* wohlhabend.

well-wisher [-,wɪʃər] *n* Sympathisant *der*,
-in *die*.

Welsh [welʃ] ◇ *adj* walisisch. ◇ *n* [lan-
guage] Walisisch(e) *das*.

Welshman ['welʃmən] (*pl* -men [-mən]) *n*
Waliser *der*.

Welshwoman ['welʃ,wumən] (*pl* -women
[-,wɪmɪn]) *n* Waliserin *die*.

went [went] *pt* ▷ **go**.

wept [wept] *pt & pp* ▷ **weep**.

were [wɜːr] *vb* ▷ **be**.

we're [wɪər] *abbr of* **we are**.

weren't [wɜːnt] *abbr of* **were not**.

west [west] ◇ *n* Westen *der*; **the west** der
Westen. ◇ *adj* - 1. [area] West-, westlich
- 2. [wind] West-. ◇ *adv* nach Westen, westwärts; **west of** westlich von. ◆ **West** *n* POL:
the West der Westen.

West Bank *n*: **the West Bank** das Westjor-
danland.

West Country *n*: **the West Country** der Südwesten Englands.

westerly ['westəlɪ] *adj* - 1. [direction] westlich - 2. [area] im Westen - 3. [wind] West-.

western ['westən] ◇ *adj* - 1. [part of country, continent] West- - 2. POL [relating to the West]
westlich. ◇ *n* [film] Western *der*.

West German ◇ *adj* westdeutsch. ◇ *n*
[person] Westdeutsche *der*, *die*.

West Germany *n*: (former) West Germany
(ehemaliges) Westdeutschland *nt*.

West Indies [-'ɪndiːz] *npl*: **the West Indies**
die Westindischen Inseln.

Westminster ['westmɪnstər] *n* - 1. [area]
Westminster *nt* - 2. *fig* [British parliament] *britisches Parlament*.

westward ['westwəd] ◇ *adj* nach Westen.
◇ *adv* = **westwards**.

westwards ['westwədz] *adv* nach Westen,
westwärts.

wet [wet] <> *adj* - **1.** [damp, soaked] nass - **2.** [rainy] regnerisch; [climate] feucht - **3.** [ink, concrete] feucht - **4.** *UK inf pej* [weak, feeble] lasch; **he's a wet** er ist ein Weichei. <> *n UK inf* POL Gemäßigte *der*, *die*. <> *vt* nass machen; **to wet the bed** ins Bett machen.

wet blanket *n inf pej* Spielverderber *der*.

wet suit *n* Taucheranzug *der*.

we've [wi:v] *abbr of* **we have**.

whack [wæk] *inf* <> *n* - **1.** [share] Teil *der* - **2.** [hit] Schlag *der*. <> *vt* einen Schlag geben (+ *D*).

whale [weɪl] *n* [animal] Wal *der*.

wharf [wɔ:f] (*pl* **-s** OR **wharves** [wɔ:vz]) *n* Kai *der*.

what [wɒt] <> *adj* - **1.** (in questions) welche(r) (s); **what colour is it?** welche Farbe hat es?; **he asked me what colour it was** er fragte mich, welche Farbe es hatte; **what time is it?** wie viel Uhr OR wie spät ist es?; **what sort of (an) animal is that?** was ist das für ein Tier? - **2.** (in exclamations) was für; **what a surprise!** was für eine Überraschung!; **what a beautiful day!** was für ein schöner Tag! <> *pron* - **1.** (in questions) was; **what is going on?** was ist los?; **what are they doing?** was tun sie da?; **what's your name?** wie heißt du?; **she asked me what happened** sie fragte mich, was passiert war; **what is it for?** wofür ist das?; **what are they talking about?** worüber reden Sie?; **what if it rains?** was geschieht, wenn es regnet?; **what did you say?** wie bitte? - **2.** (introducing relative clause) was; **I didn't see what happened** ich habe nicht gesehen, was passiert ist; **you can't have what you want** du kannst nicht haben, was du willst - **3.** *phr*: **what for?** wozu?; **what about going for a meal?** wie wäre es mit essen gehen?; **so what?** *inf* na und? <> *excl* was!

whatever [wɒt'evər] <> *adj*: **at whatever time you want** wann immer du willst; **they have no chance whatever** sie haben überhaupt keine Chance. <> *pron* - **1.** [no matter what]: **take whatever you want** nimm, was du willst; **whatever I do, I'll lose** was ich auch tue, ich verliere; **don't let go whatever happens** du darfst auf keinen Fall loslassen - **2.** [indicating vagueness]: **whatever that may be** was auch immer das sein mag - **3.** [indicating surprise]: **whatever did he say?** was hat er denn bloß gesagt? <> *excl US inf* von mir aus!

what's-his-name *n inf* Dingsda *der*, Dingsda *die*.

whatsit ['wɒtsɪt] *n inf* Dingsbums *das*.

whatsoever [,wɒtsəu'evər] *adj*: **I had no interest whatsoever** ich hatte keinerlei Interesse; **nothing whatsoever** überhaupt nichts.

wheat [wi:t] *n* Weizen *der*.

wheedle ['wi:dl] *vt*: **to wheedle sb into doing sthg** jn dazu kriegen, etw zu tun; **to wheedle sthg out of sb** jm etw ablschwatzen.

wheel [wi:l] <> *n* - **1.** [of bicycle, car, train] Rad *das* - **2.** AUT [steering wheel] Lenkrad *das*. <> *vt* schieben. <> *vi* [turn round]: **to wheel round** sich jäh umldrehen.

wheelbarrow ['wi:l,bærəu] *n* Schubkarre *die*.

wheelchair ['wi:l,tʃeər] *n* Rollstuhl *der*.

wheel clamp *n* Parkkralle *die*. ☛ **wheelclamp** *vt*: **my car was wheel clamped** an meinem Auto war eine Parkkralle.

wheeze [wi:z] *vi* pfeifend atmen.

whelk [welk] *n* Wellhornschnecke *die*.

when [wen] <> *adv* (in questions) wann; **when does the plane arrive?** wann kommt das Flugzeug an?; **he asked me when I would be in London** er fragte mich, wann ich in London sei. <> *conj* - **1.** [specifying time] wenn; [in the past] als; **on the day when it happened** an dem Tag, als es geschah - **2.** [although, seeing as] wo doch; **you said it was black when in fact it was white** du hast gesagt, es wäre schwarz, wo es doch weiß war.

whenever [wen'evər] <> *conj* [every time] (immer) wenn; **whenever you like** [no matter when] wann immer du willst. <> *adv*: **whenever did you find time to do it?** wann hast du bloß die Zeit dafür gefunden?; **next week or whenever** nächste Woche oder wann auch immer.

where [weər] <> *adv* (in questions) wo; **where do you come from?** woher kommst du?; **where are you going?** wohin gehst du? <> *conj* - **1.** [referring to place, situation] wo; **at the place where it happened** dort, wo es passiert ist; **that's (just) where you're wrong** (genau) da irren Sie sich - **2.** [whereas] während.

whereabouts <> *adv* [,weərə'bauts] wo. <> *npl* ['weərəbauts] Aufenthaltsort *der*.

whereas [weər'æz] *conj* während.

whereby [weə'baɪ] *conj fml* wodurch.

whereupon [,weərə'pɒn] *conj fml* woraufhin.

wherever [weər'evər] <> *conj* wo immer; [from any place] woher auch immer; [to any place] wohin auch immer; [everywhere] überall wo; **wherever that may be** wo immer das sein mag. <> *adv*: **wherever did you hear that?** wo hast du das bloß gehört?

whet [wet] *vt*: **to whet sb's appetite (for doing sthg)** jn auf den Geschmack bringen(, etw zu tun).

whether ['weðər] *conj* ob; **he didn't know whether to go or not** er wusste nicht, ob er gehen sollte oder nicht; **whether I want to or not** ob ich nun will oder nicht.

which [wɪtʃ] <> *adj* (in questions) welche(r) (s); **which room do you want?** welches Zimmer willst du?; **which one?** welches?; **she asked me which room I wanted** sie fragte mich, welches Zimmer ich wollte. <> *pron*

- 1. (in questions – subject) welche(r) (s); **which is the cheapest?** welches ist das billigste?; **he asked me which was the best** er fragte mich, welcher der beste sei **- 2.** (in questions – object) welche(n) (s); **which do you prefer?** welches gefällt dir besser?; **he asked me which I preferred** er fragte mich, welches ich bevorzugen würde **- 3.** (in questions – after prep + A) welche(n) (s); **which should I put the vase on?** auf welchen soll ich die Vase stellen? **- 4.** (in questions – after prep + D) welcher/welchem/welchem; **he asked me which I was talking about** er fragte mich, von welchem ich spreche **- 5.** (introducing relative clause – after subject) der/die/das, die pl; **the house which is on corner** das Haus, das an der Ecke steht **- 6.** (introducing relative clause – object, after prep + A) den/die/das, die pl; **the television which I bought** der Fernseher, den ich gekauft habe; **the book through which he became famous** das Buch, durch das er berühmt wurde **- 7.** (introducing relative clause – object, after prep + D) dem/der/dem, denen pl; **the settee on which I'm sitting** das Sofa, auf dem ich sitze; **ten apples, of which six are bad** zehn Äpfel, von denen OR wovon sechs faul sind **- 8.** (introducing relative clause – object, after prep + G) dessen/deren/dessen, deren pl **- 9.** (referring back) was; **he's late, which annoys me** er ist spät dran, was mich ärgert; **he's always late, which I don't like** er verspätet sich immer, was ich nicht leiden kann.

whichever [wɪtʃ'evər] ◇ adj **- 1.** [any] welche(r) (s); **take whichever book you like** nehmen Sie welches Buch Sie (auch immer) wollen **- 2.** [no matter which] egal welche; **whichever way you look** wo man auch hinsieht. ◇ pron [the one which] welche(r) (s); **take whichever you like** nimm welches du (auch) willst.

whiff [wɪf] n [smell] Hauch der.

while [waɪl] ◇ n: **a while** eine Weile; **for a while** eine Weile, eine Zeit lang; **in a while** bald; **a short while ago** vor Kurzem; **once in a while** hin und wieder. ◇ conj **- 1.** [gen] während; **he fell asleep while (he was) reading** er schlief beim Lesen ein **- 2.** [although] obgleich, während. ◆ **while away** vt sep: **to while away the time** sich (D) die Zeit vertreiben.

whilst [waɪlst] conj = **while**.

whim [wɪm] n Laune die.

whimper ['wɪmpər] vi [child] wimmern; [animal] winseln.

whimsical ['wɪmzɪkl] adj wunderlich.

whine [waɪn] vi [make sound] heulen; [dog] jaulen.

whinge [wɪndʒ] vi UK: **to whinge (about sb/sth)** (über jn/etw) jammern.

whip [wɪp] ◇ n **- 1.** [for hitting] Peitsche die **- 2.** UK POL Einpeitscher der. ◇ vt **- 1.** [beat with whip] auspeitschen **- 2.** [take quickly]: **to whip sth out** etw zücken; **to whip sth off** etw herunterreißen **- 3.** CULIN [whisk] schlagen.

whipped cream [wɪpt-] n Schlagsahne die.

whip-round n UK inf: **to have a whip-round** eine Sammlung machen.

whirl [wɜːl] ◇ n **- 1.** [rotating movement] Wirbel der **- 2.** fig [of activity] Trubel der. ◇ vt: **to whirl sb/sth round** jn etw herumwirbeln. ◇ vi [move around] wirbeln.

whirlpool ['wɜːlpuːl] n Strudel der.

whirlwind ['wɜːlwɪnd] n Wirbelsturm der.

whirr [wɜːr] vi [of wings] schwirren; [machinery, camera] surren.

whisk [wɪsk] ◇ n CULIN Schneebesen der. ◇ vt **- 1.** [put or take quickly]: **she was whisked into hospital** sie wurde schnellstens ins Krankenhaus gebracht **- 2.** CULIN (mit dem Schneebesen) schlagen.

whisker ['wɪskər] n [of animal] Schnurrhaar das. ◆ **whiskers** npl [of man] Backenbart der.

whisky UK, **whiskey** US Ireland (pl whiskeys) ['wɪskɪ] n Whisky der.

whisper ['wɪspər] ◇ vt flüstern; **to whisper sth to sb** jm etw zuflüstern. ◇ vi flüstern.

whistle ['wɪsl] ◇ n **- 1.** [through lips, from whistle] Pfiff der **- 2.** [of kettle, train] Pfeifen das **- 3.** [object] Pfeife die. ◇ vt pfeifen. ◇ vi: **to whistle at sb** jm nachpfeifen.

white [waɪt] ◇ adj **- 1.** [gen] weiß **- 2.** [coffee, tea] mit Milch **- 3.** [wine] Weiß-. ◇ n **- 1.** [colour] Weiß das **- 2.** [person] Weiße der, die **- 3.** [of egg] Eiweiß das **- 4.** [of eye] Weiße das.

white-collar adj: **white-collar worker** Büroangestellte der, die; phrase: **white-collar job** Schreibtischarbeit die.

white-hot adj weißglühend.

White House n [residence of president, US government]: **the White House** das Weiße Haus.

white lie n Notlüge die.

whiteness ['waɪtnɪs] n Weiße die.

white paper n POL Weißbuch das.

white sauce n Béchamelsoße die.

white spirit n (U) UK Terpentinersatz der.

whitewash ['waɪtwɒʃ] ◇ n **- 1.** (U) [paint] Tünche die **- 2.** pej [cover-up] Verschleierung die. ◇ vt [paint] tünchen.

Whitsun ['wɪtsn] n [day] Pfingstsonntag der.

whittle ['wɪtl] vt [reduce]: **to whittle sth away** OR **down** etw allmählich reduzieren.

whiz, whizz [wɪz] vi sausen.

whiz(z) kid n inf Senkrechtstarter der, -in die.

who [huː] pron **- 1.** (in questions) wer; (accusative) wen; (dative) wem; **who are you?** wer bist du/sind Sie?; **who does he think he is?**

was bildet er sich eigentlich ein? - **2.** *(in relative clauses)* der/die/das, die *Pl*; **the friend who came yesterday** der Freund, der gestern kam.

who'd [huːd] *abbr of* **who had**, **who would**.

whodu(n)nit [ˌhuːˈdʌnɪt] *n inf* Krimi *der*.

whoever [huːˈevər] *pron* [whichever person] wer immer; **whoever it is** wer es auch ist; **whoever could that be?** wer könnte das bloß sein?

whole [həʊl] <> *adj* - **1.** [entire, complete] ganz - **2.** *esp US* [for emphasis]: **a whole lot of questions** eine ganze Reihe von Fragen; **a whole lot bigger** viel größer. <> *adv esp US* [for emphasis] völlig. <> *n* - **1.** [all, entirety]: **the whole of the school** die ganze Schule; **the whole of the summer** den ganzen Sommer - **2.** [unit, complete thing] Ganze *das*. ✦ **as a whole** *adv* als Ganzes. ✦ **on the whole** *adv* im Großen und Ganzen.

whole-hearted [-'hɑːtɪd] *adj* [support, agreement] voll.

wholemeal *UK* ['həʊlmiːl], **whole wheat** *US adj* Vollkorn-.

wholesale ['həʊlseɪl] <> *adj* - **1.** [bulk] Großhandels- - **2.** *pej* [excessive] Massen-. <> *adv* - **1.** [in bulk] im Großhandel - **2.** *pej* [excessively] massenhaft.

wholesaler ['həʊlˌseɪlər] *n* Großhändler *der*, -in *die*.

wholesome ['həʊlsəm] *adj* gesund.

whole wheat *adj US* = **wholemeal**.

who'll [huːl] *abbr of* **who will**.

wholly ['həʊlɪ] *adv* völlig.

whom [huːm] *pron fml* - **1.** *(in direct, indirect questions)* wen; (dative) wem; **whom did you phone?** wen hast du angerufen?; **for/of/to whom?** nach/von/mit wem? - **2.** *(in relative clauses)* den/die/das, die *Pl*; (dative) dem/der/dem, denen *pl*; **the girl whom I married** das Mädchen, das er geheiratet hat; **the man to whom you were speaking** der Mann, mit dem du gesprochen hast; **several people came, none of whom I knew** es kamen verschiedene Leute, von denen ich keinen kannte.

whooping cough ['huːpɪŋ-] *n (U)* Keuchhusten *der*.

whopping ['wɒpɪŋ] *adj inf* Mords-; [lie] faustdick.

whore [hɔːr] *n pej* Hure *die*.

who're ['huːər] *abbr of* **who are**.

whose [huːz] <> *pron (in direct, indirect questions)* wessen; **whose is this?** wem gehört das?; <> *adj* - **1.** (in questions) wessen; **whose car is that?** wessen Auto ist das? - **2.** *(in relative clauses)* dessen/deren/dessen, deren *pl*; **that's the boy whose father's an MP** das ist der Junge, dessen Vater Abgeordneter ist.

who've [huːv] *abbr of* **who have**.

why [waɪ] <> *adv* warum; **why not?** warum nicht?; **I didn't ask why** ich habe nicht gefragt, weshalb. <> *conj* warum; **there are several reasons why he left** es gibt mehrere Gründe dafür, dass er wegging. <> *excl*: **why, it's David!** sieh da, (da kommt) David! ✦ **why ever** *adv*: **why ever did you do that?** warum hast du das bloß getan?

wick [wɪk] *n* [of candle] Docht *der*.

wicked ['wɪkɪd] *adj* - **1.** [evil] böse, schlecht - **2.** [mischievous] schelmisch.

wicker ['wɪkər] *adj*: **wicker chair** Korbstuhl *der*.

wicket ['wɪkɪt] *n* - **1.** CRICKET [stumps] Mal *das*, Wicket *das* - **2.** CRICKET [pitch] Spielbahn *die* - **3.** CRICKET [dismissal] Wicket *das*.

wide [waɪd] <> *adj* - **1.** [broad] breit - **2.** [variety, selection, gap, difference] groß - **3.** [coverage, knowledge] umfassend - **4.** [far-reaching] weit reichend. <> *adv* - **1.** [as far as possible] weit - **2.** [off-target] daneben.

wide-awake *adj* hellwach.

widely ['waɪdlɪ] *adv* - **1.** [broadly] breit - **2.** [extensively] weit; **widely read** belesen; **to be widely experienced** viel Erfahrung haben; **widely known** allgemein bekannt - **3.** [considerably] beträchtlich.

widen ['waɪdn] *vt* - **1.** [road, hole] verbreitern - **2.** [search, activity, range] auslweiten; [choice] erweitern - **3.** [gap, difference] vergrößern.

wide open *adj* - **1.** [window, door] weit offen - **2.** [eyes] weit aufgerissen.

wide-ranging [-'reɪndʒɪŋ] *adj* umfassend.

widescreen TV ['waɪdskriːn-] *n* - **1.** Breitwandfernsehen *das* - **2.** [TV set] Breitwandfernseher *der*.

widespread ['waɪdspred] *adj* weit verbreitet.

widow ['wɪdəʊ] *n* Witwe *die*.

widowed ['wɪdəʊd] *adj* verwitwet.

widower ['wɪdəʊər] *n* Witwer *der*.

width [wɪdθ] *n* Breite *die*; **3 metres in width** 3 Meter breit.

wield [wiːld] *vt* - **1.** [weapon] schwingen - **2.** [power] auslüben.

wife [waɪf] *(pl* wives) *n* Ehefrau *die*.

wig [wɪg] *n* Perücke *die*.

wiggle ['wɪgl] *inf vt*: **to wiggle one's ears/toes** mit seinen Ohren/Zehen wackeln.

wild [waɪld] *adj* - **1.** [gen] wild - **2.** [violent, dangerous] gewalttätig - **3.** [weather, sea] stürmisch - **4.** [hair, look] wirr. ✦ **wilds** *npl*: **the wilds** die Wildnis.

wilderness ['wɪldənɪs] *n* Wildnis *die*.

wild-goose chase *n inf* hoffnungslose Suche.

wildlife ['waɪldlaɪf] *n* Tierwelt *die*.

wildly ['waɪldlɪ] *adv* - **1.** [gen] wild - **2.** [talk, throw] aufs Geratewohl - **3.** [very] äußerst.

wilful *UK*, **willful** *US* ['wɪlfʊl] *adj* - **1.** [determined] stur - **2.** [deliberate] beabsichtigt.

will¹ [wɪl] ◇ *n* - **1.** [gen] Wille *der*; **against his will** gegen seinen Willen; **will to live** Lebenswille *der* - **2.** [document] Testament *das*. ◇ *vt*: **to will sb to do sthg** (sich (D)) mit aller Kraft wünschen, dass jd etw tut.

will² [wɪl] *aux vb* - **1.** [expressing future tense] werden; **will you be here next Friday?** bist du nächsten Freitag hier?; **will you do that for me?** – **no I won't/yes I will** wirst du das für mich tun? – nein(, werde ich nicht)/ja(, werde ich); **when will you have finished it?** wann seid ihr damit fertig?; **I think he will come** ich glaube schon, dass er kommt - **2.** [expressing willingness] wollen, werden; **I won't do it** ich werde das nicht tun; **no one will do it** keiner wird das machen - **3.** [expressing polite question]: **will you have some more tea?** möchten Sie noch mehr Tee? - **4.** [in commands, requests]: **will you please be quiet!** sei bitte ruhig!; **close that window, will you?** mach doch bitte das Fenster zu - **5.** [expressing possibility]: **the hall will hold up to 1,000 people** die Halle fasst bis zu 1000 Leute; **pensions will be paid monthly** Pensionen werden monatlich ausgezahlt - **6.** [expressing an assumption]: **that'll be your father** das wird dein Vater sein; **as you will have gathered, ...** wie Sie sich wohl gedacht haben, ... - **7.** [indicating irritation]: **well, if you will leave your toys everywhere** na ja, wenn ihr auch dauernd eure Spielsachen überall herumliegen lasst; **she will keep phoning me** sie ruft mich aber auch dauernd an.

willful *adj US* = **wilful**.

willing ['wɪlɪŋ] *adj* - **1.** [prepared]: **to be willing (to do sthg)** bereit sein(, etw zu tun) - **2.** [eager] bereitwillig.

willingly ['wɪlɪŋlɪ] *adv* bereitwillig, gerne.

willow (tree) ['wɪləʊ-] *n* Weide *die*.

willpower ['wɪlˌpaʊə*r*] *n* Willenskraft *die*.

willy-nilly [ˌwɪlɪ'nɪlɪ] *adv* - **1.** [at random] aufs Geratewohl - **2.** [wanting to or not] wohl oder übel.

wilt [wɪlt] *vi* - **1.** [plant] verwelken - **2.** *fig* [person] schlapp werden.

wily ['waɪlɪ] *adj* listig.

wimp [wɪmp] *n inf pej* Waschlappen *der*.

win [wɪn] (*pt & pp* **won**) ◇ *n* Sieg *der*. ◇ *vt* gewinnen. ◇ *vi* gewinnen; [in battle] siegen. ➤ **win over, win round** *vt sep* für sich gewinnen.

wince [wɪns] *vi*: **to wince at/with sthg** bei/vor etw (D) zusammenzucken.

winch [wɪntʃ] *n* Winde *die*.

wind¹ [wɪnd] ◇ *n* - **1.** METEOR Wind *der* - **2.** (U) [breath] Atem *der* - **3.** (U) [in stomach] Blähungen *Pl.* ◇ *vt* [knock breath out of]: **I was winded by the fall** durch den Sturz blieb mir die Luft weg.

wind² [waɪnd] (*pt & pp* **wound**) ◇ *vt* - **1.** [string, thread] wickeln - **2.** [clock] aufziehen. ◇ *vi* [river, road] sich schlängeln. ➤ **wind down** ◇ *vt sep* - **1.** [car window] herunterkurbeln - **2.** [production] allmählich einstellen. ◇ *vi* [relax] entspannen. ➤ **wind up** *vt sep* - **1.** [finish - meeting] abschließen; [- business] auflösen - **2.** [clock] aufziehen - **3.** [car window] heraufkurbeln - **4.** *UK inf* [deliberately annoy] aufziehen.

windfall ['wɪndfɔːl] *n* [unexpected gift] unerhoffter Gewinn.

winding ['waɪndɪŋ] *adj* kurvenreich; [river] gewunden.

wind instrument [wɪnd-] *n* Blasinstrument *das*.

windmill ['wɪndmɪl] *n* Windmühle *die*.

window ['wɪndəʊ] *n* - **1.** [gen & COMPUT] Fenster *das* - **2.** [of shop] Schaufenster *das* - **3.** [free time] freie Zeit.

window box *n* Blumenkasten *der*.

window cleaner *n* Fensterputzer *der*, -in *die*.

window ledge *n* [outside] Fenstersims *das*; [inside] Fensterbrett *das*.

windowpane ['wɪndəʊpeɪn] *n* Fensterscheibe *die*.

windowsill ['wɪndəʊsɪl] *n* [outside] Fenstersims *der* ODER *das*; [inside] Fensterbrett *das*.

windpipe ['wɪndpaɪp] *n* Luftröhre *die*.

windscreen *UK* ['wɪndskriːn], **windshield** *US* ['wɪndʃiːld] *n* Windschutzscheibe *die*.

windscreen washer *n* Scheibenwaschanlage *die*.

windscreen wiper *n* Scheibenwischer *der*.

windshield *n US* = **windscreen**.

windsurfing ['wɪndˌsɜːfɪŋ] *n* Windsurfen *das*.

windswept ['wɪndswept] *adj* [landscape] windgepeitscht.

windy ['wɪndɪ] *adj* windig.

wine [waɪn] *n* Wein *der*.

wine bar *n UK* Weinbar *die*.

wineglass ['waɪnglɑːs] *n* Weinglas *das*.

wine list *n* Weinkarte *die*.

wine tasting [-ˌteɪstɪŋ] *n* - **1.** [practice] Weinverkosten *das* - **2.** [event] Weinprobe *die*.

wine waiter *n* Weinkellner *der*.

wing [wɪŋ] *n* - **1.** [gen] Flügel *der* - **2.** [of plane] Tragfläche *die* - **3.** [of car] Kotflügel *der*. ➤ **wings** *npl* THEAT: **the wings** die Kulissen.

winger ['wɪŋə*r*] *n* SPORT Außenstürmer *der*, -in *die*.

wink [wɪŋk] ◇ *n* [of eye] Zwinkern *das*. ◇ *vi* [eye] zwinkern; **to wink at sb** jm zuzwinkern.

winkle ['wɪŋkl] *n* Strandschnecke *die*. ◆ **winkle out** *vt sep* herauslbekommen; **to winkle sth out of sb** *fig* etw aus jm herauslbekommen.

winner ['wɪnə'] *n* [person] Gewinner *der*, -in *die*; [in sport] Sieger *der*, -in *die*.

winning ['wɪnɪŋ] *adj* [victorious] siegreich; [successful] erfolgreich. ◆ **winnings** *npl* Gewinn *der*.

winning post *n* Zielpfosten *der*.

winter ['wɪntə'] <> *n* Winter *der*; **in winter** im Winter. <> *comp* Winter-.

winter sports *npl* Wintersport *der*.

wintertime ['wɪntətaɪm] *n* Winterzeit *die*.

wint(e)ry ['wɪntrɪ] *adj* winterlich.

wipe [waɪp] <> *n* [clean]: **he gave his face/ the table a wipe** er wischte sein Gesicht/den Tisch ab. <> *vt* - 1. [rub to clean - floor] wischen; [- face, table] ablwischen - 2. [rub to dry] abltrocknen. ◆ **wipe out** *vt sep* - 1. [erase] weglwischen - 2. [eradicate - one] vernichten; [- race] auslrotten. ◆ **wipe up** <> *vt sep* auflwischen. <> *vi* [dry dishes] abltrocknen.

wire ['waɪə'] <> *n* - 1. [gen] Draht *der*; [electrical] Leitung *die* - 2. *esp US* [telegram] Telegramm *das*. <> *vt* - 1. ELEC [plug] anlschließen - 2. *esp US* [send telegram to] ein Telegramm schicken.

wireless ['waɪəlɪs] *n dated* Radio *das*.

wireless network *n* Kabellose Netzwerk *das*.

wiring ['waɪərɪŋ] *n (U)* elektrische Leitungen *Pl*.

wiry ['waɪərɪ] *adj* - 1. [hair] borstig - 2. [body, man] drahtig.

wisdom ['wɪzdəm] *n* Weisheit *die*.

wisdom tooth *n* Weisheitszahn *der*.

wise [waɪz] *adj* [prudent] weise.

wish [wɪʃ] <> *n* Wunsch *der*; **wish to do sthg** der Wunsch, etw zu tun; **wish for sthg** der Wunsch nach etw (D). <> *vt* - 1. [want]: **to wish to do sthg** *fml* etw zu tun wünschen; **I wished (that) he'd come** wenn er nur käme - 2. [desire, request by magic]: **I wish (that) I had a million pounds** ich wünschte, ich hätte eine Million Pfund - 3. [in greeting]: **to wish sb sthg** jm etw wünschen. <> *vi* [by magic]: **to wish for sthg** sich etw herbeilwünschen. ◆ **wishes** *npl*: **best wishes** alles Gute; **(with) best wishes** [at end of letter] herzliche Grüße.

wishy-washy ['wɪʃɪ,wɒʃɪ] *adj inf pej* [person] kraftlos; [ideas] vage.

wisp [wɪsp] *n* - 1. [tuft] Büschel *das* - 2. [small cloud]: **wisp of smoke** Rauchfahne *die*.

wistful ['wɪstful] *adj* wehmütig.

wit [wɪt] *n* - 1. [humour] Witz *der* - 2. [intelligence]: **to have the wit to do sthg** klug genug sein, etw zu tun. ◆ **wits** *npl* [intelligence, mind]: **to have** OR **keep one's wits about one** geistesgegenwärtig sein.

witch [wɪtʃ] *n* Hexe *die*.

with [wɪð] *prep* - 1. [gen] mit; **come with me** komm mit mir; **a man with a beard** ein Mann mit Bart; **a room with a bathroom** ein Zimmer mit Bad; **be careful with that!** sei vorsichtig damit!; **bring it with you** bringen Sie es mit; **to argue with sb** (sich) mit jm streiten; **the war with Germany** der Krieg gegen Deutschland; **I can't do it with you watching me** ich kann es nicht tun, wenn du mir zuschaust - 2. [at house of, in the hands of] bei; **we stayed with friends** wir haben bei Freunden übernachtet; **the decision rests with you** die Entscheidung liegt bei dir - 3. [indicating emotion] vor (+ D); **to tremble with fear** vor Angst zittern - 4. [because of] bei; **with the weather as it is, we decided to stay at home** angesichts des Wetters beschlossen wir zu Hause zu bleiben; **with my luck, I'll probably lose** bei meinem Glück werde ich wahrscheinlich verlieren - 5. *phr*: **I'll be with you in a moment** ich komme gleich; **I'm not quite with you** [I don't understand] ich komme nicht ganz mit; **I'm with you there** [I'm on your side] da bin ich ganz deiner Ansicht.

withdraw [wɪð'drɔː] (*pt* -drew, *pp* -drawn) <> *vt* - 1. *fml* [remove] weglnehmen; **to withdraw sthg from sthg** etw von etw weglnehmen - 2. FIN [money] ablheben - 3. MIL [troops] zurücklziehen - 4. [retract] zurücklnehmen. <> *vi* - 1.: **to withdraw (from)** sich zurücklziehen (aus) - 2. [quit, give up] auflgeben; **to withdraw from sthg** aus etw auslscheiden.

withdrawal [wɪð'drɔːəl] *n* - 1. [removal] Zurückziehen *das* - 2. MIL Rückzug *der* - 3. [retraction] Zurücknahme *die* - 4. [leaving, quitting]: **withdrawal (from sthg)** Ausscheiden *das* (aus etw) - 5. FIN Abheben *das*.

withdrawal symptoms *npl* Entzugserscheinungen *Pl*.

withdrawn [wɪð'drɔːn] <> *pp* ▷ **withdraw**. <> *adj* [shy, quiet] verschlossen.

withdrew [wɪð'druː] *pt* ▷ **withdraw**.

wither ['wɪðə'] *vi* - 1. [dry up] verwelken - 2. [become weak] schwinden.

withhold [wɪð'həʊld] (*pt & pp* -held [-'held]) *vt* [information] zurücklhalten.

within [wɪ'ðɪn] <> *prep* innerhalb (+ G); **within sight** in Sichtweite; **within the next week** innerhalb der nächsten Woche; **within 10 miles** im Umkreis von 10 Meilen. <> *adv* innen.

without [wɪð'aʊt] *prep* ohne; **without doing sthg** ohne etw zu tun; **I left without him seeing me** ich ging (weg), ohne dass er mich sah.

withstand [wɪð'stænd] (*pt & pp* -stood [-'stʊd]) *vt* standlhalten (+ D).

witness ['wɪtnɪs] <> *n* - 1. [gen] Zeuge *der*, -gin *die* - 2.: **to bear witness to sthg** [be proof of] von etw zeugen. <> *vt* - 1.: **to witness sthg**

[murder, accident] Zeuge einer Sache (G) sein; [changes] etw erleben - **2.** [countersign] als Zeuge unterschreiben.

witness box UK, **witness stand** US n Zeugenstand der.

witticism ['wɪtɪsɪzm] n geistreiche Bemerkung.

witty ['wɪtɪ] adj geistreich und witzig.

wives [waɪvz] Pl ▷ **wife**.

wizard ['wɪzəd] n - **1.** [man with magic powers] Zauberer der - **2.** [skilled person] Genie das.

wobble ['wɒbl] vi wackeln.

woe [wəʊ] n liter Leid das.

woke [wəʊk] pt ▷ **wake**.

woken ['wəʊkn] pp ▷ **wake**.

wolf [wʊlf] (pl wolves) n [animal] Wolf der.

woman ['wʊmən] (pl women ['wɪmɪn]) ◇ n Frau die. ◇ comp: **woman doctor** Ärztin die; **woman teacher** Lehrerin die.

womanly ['wʊmənlɪ] adj fraulich.

womb [wu:m] n Gebärmutter die.

women ['wɪmɪn] Pl ▷ **woman**.

women's liberation n - **1.** [aim] Gleichstellung die der Frau - **2.** [movement] Frauenrechtsbewegung die.

won [wʌn] pt & pp ▷ **win**.

wonder ['wʌndə'] ◇ n - **1.** [amazement] Staunen das - **2.** [cause for surprise]: **it's a wonder that...** es ist ein Wunder, dass...; **no** OR **little** OR **small wonder** kein Wunder; **no wonder she left!** kein Wunder, dass sie gegangen ist! - **3.** [amazing thing] Wunder das. ◇ vt - **1.** [speculate] sich fragen; **to wonder if** OR **whether...** sich fragen, ob... - **2.** [in polite requests]: **I wonder whether you would mind shutting the window?** könnten Sie wohl bitte das Fenster schließen? ◇ vi [speculate] sich fragen; **to wonder about sthg** sich über etw (A) Gedanken machen.

wonderful ['wʌndəfʊl] adj wundervoll, wunderbar.

wonderfully ['wʌndəfʊlɪ] adv - **1.** [very well] wunderbar - **2.** [for emphasis] sehr.

won't [wəʊnt] abbr of **will not**.

woo [wu:] vt - **1.** liter [court - woman] den Hof machen (+ D) - **2.** fig [try to win over] umlwerben.

wood [wʊd] ◇ n - **1.** (U) [timber] Holz das - **2.** [group of trees] Wald der. ◇ comp Holz-. ◆ **woods** npl [forest] Wald der.

wooded ['wʊdɪd] adj [forested] bewaldet.

wooden ['wʊdn] adj - **1.** [of wood] Holz- - **2.** pej [actor] hölzern.

woodpecker ['wʊd,pekə'] n Specht der.

woodwind ['wʊdwɪnd] n: **the woodwind** die Holzbläser Pl.

woodwork ['wʊdwɜ:k] n - **1.** [wooden objects] Holzarbeiten Pl; [part of house or room] Holzteile Pl - **2.** [craft] Tischlerei die.

wool [wʊl] n - **1.** [gen] Wolle die - **2.** phr: **to pull the wool over sb's eyes** inf jn hinters Licht führen.

woollen UK, **woolen** US ['wʊlən] adj [garment] Woll-. ◆ **woollens** npl Wollwaren Pl.

woolly ['wʊlɪ] adj [woollen] Woll-.

word [wɜ:d] ◇ n - **1.** LING Wort das; **word for word** Wort für Wort; **in other words** mit anderen Worten; **in a word** kurz gesagt; **can I have a word (with you)?** kann ich Sie mal sprechen?; **I/you/etc couldn't get a word in edgeways** ich bin/du bist/etc nicht zu Wort gekommen - **2.** (U) [news] Nachricht die; **have you had word of John recently?** hast du in letzter Zeit etwas von John gehört? - **3.** [promise] Wort das; **to give sb one's word** jm sein Wort geben. ◇ vt formulieren.

wording ['wɜ:dɪŋ] n Wortlaut der.

word processing n Textverarbeitung die.

word processor [-,prəʊsesə'] n Textverarbeitungssystem das.

wore [wɔ:'] pt ▷ **wear**.

work [wɜ:k] ◇ n - **1.** (U) [gen] Arbeit die; **to be in work** Arbeit haben; **to be out of work** arbeitslos sein - **2.** ART & LIT [created product] Werk das. ◇ vt - **1.** [person, staff]: **he works his staff too hard** er verlangt zu viel von seinen Angestellten - **2.** [machine] bedienen - **3.** [wood, clay, land] bearbeiten. ◇ vi - **1.** [do a job] arbeiten - **2.** [function, be successful] funktionieren - **3.** [gradually become]: **to work loose** sich lockern. ◆ **works** ◇ n [factory] Werk das. ◇ npl - **1.** [mechanism] Innere das - **2.** [digging, building] Bauarbeiten Pl. ◆ **work on** vt insep - **1.** [concentrate on] arbeiten an (+ D) - **2.** [principle, assumption, belief] auslgehen von - **3.** [try to persuade] bearbeiten. ◆ **work out** ◇ vt sep - **1.** [formulate] auslarbeiten - **2.** [calculate] auslrechnen. ◇ vi - **1.** [figure, total]: **that works out at £10 each** das macht 10 Pfund pro Person - **2.** [turn out]: **to work out in sb's favour** für jn vorteilhaft sein - **3.** [be successful] gut auslgehen - **4.** [train, exercise] trainieren. ◆ **work up** vt sep - **1.** [excite]: **to work o.s. up into** sich hineinlsteigern in (+ A) - **2.** [generate - enthusiasm, courage] auflbringen; [- appetite] entwickeln.

workable ['wɜ:kəbl] adj [practicable] durchführbar.

workaholic [,wɜ:kə'hɒlɪk] n Workaholic der.

worked up [,wɜ:kt-] adj aufgeregt.

worker ['wɜ:kə'] n [employee] Arbeiter der, -in die.

workforce ['wɜ:kfɔ:s] n Belegschaft die.

working ['wɜ:kɪŋ] adj - **1.** [in operation] in Betrieb - **2.** [having employment] erwerbstätig - **3.** [relating to work] Arbeits-. ◆ **workings** npl [of system, machine] Funktionsweise die.

working class n: the working class die Arbeiterklasse. ◆ **working-class** adj Arbeiter-.

working order n: in working order funktionstüchtig.

workload ['wɜːkləʊd] n Arbeitsvolumen das.

workman ['wɜːkmən] (pl **-men** [-mən]) n [craftsman] Handwerker der; [worker] Arbeiter der.

workmanship ['wɜːkmənʃɪp] n (U) handwerkliches Können.

workmate ['wɜːkmeɪt] n Kollege der, -gin die.

work permit n Arbeitserlaubnis die.

workplace ['wɜːkpleɪs] n Arbeitsplatz der.

workshop ['wɜːkʃɒp] n - 1. [room, building] Werkstatt die - 2. [discussion] Workshop der.

workstation ['wɜːkˌsteɪʃn] n COMPUT Workstation die.

worktop ['wɜːktɒp] n UK Arbeitsfläche die.

world [wɜːld] ◇ n - 1. [gen]: **the world** die Welt; **to have the best of both worlds** die Vorteile beider Seiten genießen; **the next world** das Jenseits - 2. [great deal]: **to think the world of sb** große Stücke auf jn halten; **a world of difference** ein himmelweiter Unterschied. ◇ comp Welt-.

world-class adj Weltklasse-.

world-famous adj weltberühmt.

worldly ['wɜːldlɪ] adj [not spiritual] weltlich.

World War I n Erster Weltkrieg.

World War II n Zweiter Weltkrieg.

worldwide ['wɜːldwaɪd] adj & adv weltweit.

World Wide Web n: the World Wide Web COMPUT das World Wide Web.

worm [wɜːm] n [animal] Wurm der.

worn [wɔːn] ◇ pp ▷ **wear**. ◇ adj - 1. [threadbare - carpet] abgenutzt; [- clothes] abgetragen; [- tyre] abgefahren - 2. [tired] erschöpft.

worn-out adj - 1. [old, threadbare] ganz abgenutzt; [clothes, shoes] ganz abgetragen - 2. [tired] ausgelaugt.

worried ['wʌrɪd] adj besorgt; **I was worried he'd be angry** ich hatte Angst, er würde böse sein.

worry ['wʌrɪ] ◇ n Sorge die. ◇ vt [cause to be troubled] Sorgen machen (+ D). ◇ vi: **to worry about sb/sthg** sich um jn/etw sorgen OR Sorgen machen; **not to worry!** keine Sorge!

worrying ['wʌrɪɪŋ] adj beunruhigend.

worse [wɜːs] ◇ adj - 1. [not as good] schlechter; [situation] schlimmer; **to get worse** sich verschlechtern; [situation] sich verschlimmern - 2. [sicker]: **he's worse** es geht ihm schlechter; **she seemed to get worse** ihr Zustand schien sich zu verschlechtern. ◇ adv [more badly] schlechter; **worse off** [having less money] schlechter dran; [in a more unpleasant situation] schlimmer dran. ◇ n Schlimmeres das; **a change for the worse** eine Verschlimmerung; [of health, weather] eine Verschlechterung.

worsen ['wɜːsn] ◇ vt [situation, crisis] verschlimmern. ◇ vi [situation, crisis] sich verschlimmern; [weather, work] sich verschlechtern.

worship ['wɜːʃɪp] (UK) (US) ◇ vt - 1. RELIG anlbeten - 2. [admire, adore] vergöttern. ◇ n - 1. (U) RELIG Verehrung die; [service] Gottesdienst der - 2. (U) [adoration] Vergötterung die. ◆ **Worship** n: Your Worship Euer Ehren; Her/His Worship (the Mayoress/Mayor) die sehr verehrte Frau Bürgermeister/der sehr verehrte Herr Bürgermeister.

worst [wɜːst] ◇ adj schlimmste(r) (s), schlechteste(r) (s). ◇ adv am schlimmsten, am schlechtesten. ◇ n: the worst das Schlimmste; **if the worst comes to the worst** wenn alle Stricke reißen. ◆ **at (the) worst** adv schlimmstenfalls.

worth [wɜːθ] ◇ prep: **how much is it worth?** wie viel ist das wert?; **it's worth £50** es ist 50 Pfund wert; **it's worth seeing** es ist sehenswert; **it's not worth it** es lohnt sich nicht; **he's worth millions** er besitzt Millionen; **to run for all one is worth** fig rennen, was man nur rennen kann. ◇ n - 1. [amount]: **£50 worth of traveller's cheques** Reiseschecks im Wert von 50 Pfund; **a week's worth of groceries** Lebensmittel Pl für eine Woche - 2. [value] Wert der; **he proved his worth** er hat sich bewährt.

worthless ['wɜːθlɪs] adj - 1. [object] wertlos - 2. [person] nichtsnutzig.

worthwhile [ˌwɜːθ'waɪl] adj lohnend; **to be worthwhile** sich lohnen.

worthy ['wɜːðɪ] adj - 1. [deserving of respect] würdig; **for a worthy cause** für einen guten Zweck - 2. [deserving]: **to be worthy of sthg** etw verdienen - 3. pej [good but unexciting] ehrbar.

would [wʊd] modal vb - 1. [in reported speech]: **she said she would come** sie sagte, sie würde kommen - 2. [indicating condition]: **what would you do?** was würdest du tun?; **what would you have done?** was hättest du getan?; **I would be most grateful** ich wäre äußerst dankbar - 3. [indicating willingness]: **she wouldn't go** sie wollte einfach nicht gehen; **he would do anything for her** er würde alles für sie tun - 4. [in polite questions]: **would you like a drink?** möchtest du etwas trinken?; **would you mind closing the window?** könntest du das Fenster zumachen? - 5. [indicating inevitability]: **he would say that** er musste das sagen; **I quite forgot! – you would!** das habe

ich ganz vergessen! – das sieht dir ähnlich!
- 6. [giving advice]: **I would report it if I were
you** an deiner Stelle würde ich es melden
- 7. [expressing opinions]: **I would prefer coffee**
ich hätte lieber Kaffee; **I would prefer to go by
bus** ich würde lieber mit dem Bus fahren; **I
would have thought (that)...** ich hätte gedacht, dass... - 8. [describing habitual past actions]: **she would often come home tired out**
oft kam sie total erschöpft nach Hause.

would-be adj angehend.

wouldn't ['wʊdnt] abbr of **would not**.

would've ['wʊdəv] abbr of **would have**.

wound[1] [wuːnd] ⟨> n Wunde die. ⟨> vt
- 1. [physically] verwunden - 2. [emotionally] verletzen.

wound[2] [waʊnd] pt & pp ▷ **wind**[2].

wove [wəʊv] pt ▷ **weave**.

woven ['wəʊvn] pp ▷ **weave**.

WP n abbr of **word processing**, **word processor**.

wrangle ['ræŋgl] ⟨> n Streitigkeiten Pl.
⟨> vi sich streiten; **to wrangle with sb (over
sthg)** mit jm (über etw (A)) streiten.

wrap [ræp] vt [cover in paper or cloth] einlwickeln; [- worm] sich winden - 2. [twist]: **he
wriggled under the fence** er wand sich unter
dem Zaun hindurch; **to wriggle free** sich loslwinden.

wrap [ræp] vt [cover in paper or cloth] einlwickeln; **to wrap sthg in sthg** etw in etw (A)
einlwickeln; **to wrap sthg (a)round sthg** etw
um etw wickeln. ⬥ **wrap up** ⟨> vt sep [cover in paper or cloth] einlwickeln. ⟨> vi [put
warm clothes on]: **wrap up well** OR **warmly!** zieh
dich warm an!

wrapper ['ræpər] n Hülle die; [of sweets] Papier das.

wrapping ['ræpɪŋ] n Verpackung die.

wrapping paper n (U) Geschenkpapier das.

wreak [riːk] vt [destruction, havoc] anlrichten;
[revenge] üben.

wreath [riːθ] n [circle of flowers] Kranz der.

wreck [rek] ⟨> n Wrack das; **a nervous
wreck** ein Nervenbündel; **a car wreck** US ein
Autounfall. ⟨> vt - 1. [break, destroy] demolieren; [car] zu Schrott fahren - 2. NAUT [cause to
run aground] versenken; **to be wrecked** [person]
Schiffbruch erleiden - 3. [spoil, ruin] ruinieren.

wreckage ['rekɪdʒ] n [of plane, building]
Trümmer Pl; [of car] Wrack das.

wren [ren] n Zaunkönig der.

wrench [rentʃ] ⟨> n [tool] Schraubenschlüssel der. ⟨> vt - 1. [pull violently] reißen - 2. [twist
and injure]: **to wrench one's arm/leg** sich den
Arm/das Bein verrenken.

wrestle ['resl] vi - 1. [fight]: **to wrestle with sb**
mit jm ringen - 2. fig [struggle]: **to wrestle with
sthg** mit etw kämpfen.

wrestler ['reslər] n Ringer der, -in die; [as entertainer] Wrestler der, -in die.

wrestling ['reslɪŋ] n Ringen das; [as entertainment] Wrestling das.

wretch [retʃ] n [unhappy person]: **poor
wretch!** armer Tropf!

wretched ['retʃɪd] adj - 1. [miserable] elend;
[conditions] erbärmlich - 2. inf [damned] verflixt.

wriggle ['rɪgl] vi - 1. [move about - person]
zappeln; [- worm] sich winden - 2. [twist]: **he
wriggled under the fence** er wand sich unter
dem Zaun hindurch; **to wriggle free** sich loslwinden.

wring [rɪŋ] (pt & pp wrung) vt [squeeze out
water from] auslwringen.

wringing ['rɪŋɪŋ] adj: **wringing (wet)** tropfnass.

wrinkle ['rɪŋkl] ⟨> n - 1. [on skin] Falte die
- 2. [in cloth] Knitterfalte die. ⟨> vt [screw up
- nose] rümpfen; [- forehead] runzeln. ⟨> vi
[crease] knittern.

wrist [rɪst] n Handgelenk das.

wristwatch ['rɪstwɒtʃ] n Armbanduhr die.

writ [rɪt] n Verfügung die.

write [raɪt] (pt wrote, pp written) ⟨> vt
- 1. [gen] schreiben - 2. [cheque, prescription]
auslstellen - 3. COMPUT speichern. ⟨> vi
- 1. [gen] schreiben - 2. COMPUT ablspeichern.
⬥ **write down** vt sep auflschreiben.
⬥ **write off** vt sep - 1. [project] auflgeben
- 2. [debt, investment, person] ablschreiben
- 3. UK inf [vehicle] zu Schrott fahren.
⬥ **write up** vt sep [notes] auslarbeiten.

write-off n [car] Totalschaden der.

writer ['raɪtər] n - 1. [as profession] Schriftsteller der, -in die - 2. [of letter, article, story]
Verfasser der, -in die.

writhe [raɪð] vi sich winden; [with pain] sich
krümmen.

writing ['raɪtɪŋ] n - 1. [gen] Schrift die; **in
writing** schriftlich - 2. [activity] Schreiben das.

writing paper n (U) Briefpapier das.

written ['rɪtn] ⟨> pp ▷ **write**. ⟨> adj
schriftlich.

wrong [rɒŋ] ⟨> adj - 1. [amiss]: **there's nothing wrong with me** mir fehlt nichts; **is
something wrong?** stimmt etwas nicht?;
what's wrong? was ist los?; **there's something
wrong with the car** mit dem Auto stimmt etwas nicht - 2. [not suitable] falsch - 3. [not correct - answer, decision, turning] falsch, verkehrt; **to be wrong** [person] Unrecht haben; **I
was wrong to ask** ich hätte nicht fragen sollen
- 4. [morally bad] unrecht. ⟨> adv [incorrectly]
falsch, verkehrt; **to get sthg wrong** sich mit
etw vertun; **to go wrong** [make a mistake] einen Fehler machen; **the printer keeps going
wrong** der Drucker spielt ständig verrückt.
⟨> n Unrecht das; **to be in the wrong** Unrecht
haben. ⟨> vt liter Unrecht tun (+ D).

wrongful ['rɒŋfʊl] *adj* [unjust] ungerecht.

wrongly ['rɒŋlɪ] *adv* - **1.** [unsuitably] falsch - **2.** [mistakenly] zu Unrecht.

wrong number *n* falsche Nummer; **you've got the wrong number** Sie haben sich verwählt.

wrote [rəʊt] *pt* ▷ **write**.

wrung [rʌŋ] *pt & pp* ▷ **wring**.

wry [raɪ] *adj* [amused] ironisch; [humour, remark] trocken.

x (*pl* x's OR xs), **X** (*pl* X's OR Xs) [eks] *n* - **1.** [letter] x *das*, X *das* - **2.** [unknown name] X - **3.** [quantity, in algebra] x - **4.** [to mark place]: **X marks the spot** ein Kreuzchen markiert die Stelle - **5.** [at end of letter] *ein Kreuzchen am Ende eines Briefes, das einen Kuss bedeutet.*

xenophobic [ˌzenə'fəʊbɪk] *adj* fremdenfeindlich, xenophob.

Xmas ['eksməs] *n* Weihnachten *das*.

X-ray ◇ *n* - **1.** [ray] Röntgenstrahl *der* - **2.** [picture] Röntgenbild *das*. ◇ *vt* röntgen.

xylophone ['zaɪləfəʊn] *n* Xylofon *das*.

y (*pl* y's OR ys), **Y** (*pl* Y's OR Ys) [waɪ] *n* [letter] y *das*, Y *das*.

yacht [jɒt] *n* Jacht *die*.

yachting ['jɒtɪŋ] *n* Segeln *das*.

yachtsman ['jɒtsmən] (*pl* -men [-mən]) *n* Segler *der*.

Yank [jæŋk] *n UK inf pej* Ami *der*.

Yankee ['jæŋkɪ] *n UK inf pej* [American] Ami *der*.

yap [jæp] *vi* [dog] kläffen.

yard [jɑːd] *n* - **1.** [unit of measurement] Yard *das*, = 91,44 cm - **2.** [enclosed area] Hof *der*

- **3.** [place of work]: **ship yard** Schiffswerft *die*; **builder's yard** Bauhof *der* - **4.** *US* [attached to house] Garten *der*.

yardstick ['jɑːdstɪk] *n* Maßstab *der*.

yarn [jɑːn] *n (U)* [thread] Garn *das*.

yawn [jɔːn] ◇ *n* [when tired] Gähnen *das*. ◇ *vi* gähnen.

yd *abbr of* **yard**.

yeah [jeə] *adv inf* ja.

year [jɪəʳ] *n* Jahr *das*; **all (the) year round** das ganze Jahr über; **for seven years** sieben Jahre (lang). ◆ **years** *npl* [ages] Jahre *Pl*; **for years** jahrelang.

yearly ['jɪəlɪ] ◇ *adj* - **1.** [event, inspection, report] jährlich - **2.** [income, wage] Jahres-. ◇ *adv* jährlich.

yearn [jɜːn] *vi*: **to yearn for sthg** sich nach etw sehnen; **to yearn to do sthg** sich danach sehnen, etw zu tun.

yearning ['jɜːnɪŋ] *n*: **yearning (for sb/sthg)** Sehnsucht *die* (nach jm/etw).

yeast [jiːst] *n (U)* Hefe *die*.

yell [jel] ◇ *n* Schrei *der*. ◇ *vt & vi* schreien.

yellow ['jeləʊ] ◇ *adj* [in colour] gelb. ◇ *n* Gelb *das*.

yellow card *n* FTBL gelbe Karte.

yelp [jelp] *vi* aufjaulen; [of person] aufschreien.

yes [jes] ◇ *adv* - **1.** [gen] ja; **yes, please** ja, bitte; **to say yes to sthg** einer Sache (D) zustimmen - **2.** [to encourage further speech] so - **3.** [expressing disagreement] doch. ◇ *n* [vote in favour] Ja *das*.

yesterday ['jestədɪ] ◇ *n* Gestern *das*. ◇ *adv* gestern.

yet [jet] ◇ *adv* noch; *(in questions)* schon; **have you read the book yet?** hast du das Buch schon gelesen?; **not yet** noch nicht; **aren't you ready yet?** bist du bald fertig?; **as yet** bisher, bis jetzt; **I've yet to do it** ich muss es noch tun; **yet another delay** noch eine Verspätung; **yet again** schon wieder; **he'll win yet** er wird schon noch gewinnen. ◇ *conj* doch; **simple yet effective** einfach, aber wirksam; **and yet I like him** und doch OR dennoch mag ich ihn.

yew [juː] *n* Eibe *die*.

yield [jiːld] ◇ *n* Ertrag *der*. ◇ *vt* - **1.** [produce] hervorbringen; [fruit] tragen; [profits] abwerfen; [result, answer, clue] ergeben - **2.** [give up] abgeben. ◇ *vi* - **1.** [open, give way, break] nachgeben - **2.** *fml* [give up, surrender] sich ergeben - **3.** *US* AUT [give way]: **'yield'** 'Vorfahrt beachten'.

YMCA (*abbr of* **Young Men's Christian Association**) *n* CVJM *der*.

yoga ['jəʊgə] *n* Yoga *der* ODER *das*.

yoghourt, yoghurt, yogurt [UK 'jɒgət, US 'jəʊgərt] n Jogurt der ODER das ODER die.

yoke [jəʊk] n Joch das.

yolk [jəʊk] n Dotter der ODER das, Eigelb das.

you [juː] pers pron - 1. (subject – singular) du; (– plural) ihr; (– polite form) Sie; **you Germans** ihr Deutschen; **I'm shorter than you** ich bin kleiner als du/Sie/ihr - 2. (direct object, after prep + A – singular) dich; (– plural) euch; (– polite form) Sie; **I hate you!** ich hasse dich/Sie/euch!; **I did it for you** ich habe es für dich/Sie/euch getan - 3. (direct object, after prep + D – singular) dir; (– plural) euch; (– polite form) Ihnen; **I told you!** ich habe es dir/Ihnen/euch gesagt; **after you!** nach Ihnen! - 4. (indefinite use – subject) man; (– object) einen; (– indirect object) einem; **you never know** man kann nie wissen; **it does you good** es tut einem gut.

you'd [juːd] abbr of **you had, you would**.

you'll [juːl] abbr of **you will**.

young [jʌŋ] <> adj [not old] jung. <> npl - 1. [young people]: **the young** die Jugend - 2. [baby animals] Junge Pl.

younger ['jʌŋgər] adj jünger.

youngster ['jʌŋstər] n - 1. [child] Kind das - 2. [young person] Jugendliche der, die.

your [jɔːr] poss adj - 1. (singular subject) dein(e), deine Pl; (plural subject) euer/eure, eure Pl; (polite form) Ihr(e), Ihre Pl; **your dog** dein/euer/Ihr Hund; **your house** dein/euer/Ihr Haus; **your children** deine/eure/IhreKinder - 2. (indefinite subject): **it's good for your teeth** es ist gut für die Zähne; **your average Englishman** der durchschnittliche Engländer.

you're [jɔːr] abbr of **you are**.

yours [jɔːz] poss pron (singular subject) deiner/deine/deins, deine Pl; (plural subject) eurer/eure/eures, eure Pl; (polite form) Ihrer/Ihre/Ihres, Ihre Pl; **a friend of yours** ein Freund von dir/euch/Ihnen; **that money is yours** dieses Geld gehört dir/euch/Ihnen. ◆ **Yours** adv [in letter - gen] Dein/Deine; [- polite form] Ihr/Ihre.

yourself [jɔː'self] (pl **-selves** [-'selvz]) pron - 1. (reflexive, after prep + A – singular) dich; (– plural) euch; (– polite form) sich - 2. (reflexive, after prep + D – singular) dir; (– plural) euch; (– polite form) sich; **did you do it yourself?** hast du/haben Sie das selbst gemacht?; **did you do it yourselves?** habt ihr/haben Sie das selbst gemacht?; **by yourself/yourselves** allein.

youth [juːθ] n - 1. [period of life, young people] Jugend die - 2. [quality] Jugendlichkeit die - 3. [boy] Junge der; [young man] junger Mann.

youth club n Jugendklub der.

youthful ['juːθfʊl] adj jugendlich.

youth hostel n Jugendherberge die.

you've [juːv] abbr of **you have**.

Yugoslavia [ˌjuːgə'slɑːvɪə] n Jugoslawien das.

Yugoslavian [ˌjuːgə'slɑːvɪən] <> adj jugoslawisch. <> n Jugoslawe der, -win die.

yuppie, yuppy ['jʌpɪ] n Yuppie der.

YWCA (abbr of Young Women's Christian Association) n CVJF der.

Z

z (pl **z's** OR **zs**), **Z** (pl **Z's** OR **Zs**) [UK zed, US ziː] n [letter] z das, Z das.

zany ['zeɪnɪ] adj inf verrückt.

zeal [ziːl] n fml Eifer der.

zebra [UK 'zebrə, US 'ziːbrə] (pl inv OR **-s**) n Zebra das.

zebra crossing n UK Zebrastreifen der.

zenith [UK 'zenɪθ, US 'ziːnəθ] n liter & fig Zenit der.

zero [UK 'zɪərəʊ, US 'ziːrəʊ] (pl **-s** OR **-es**, pt & pp **-ed**, cont **-ing**) <> adj keinerlei; **zero growth** Nullwachstum das. <> n Null die.

zest [zest] n - 1. [excitement] Schwung der - 2. (U) [eagerness] Begeisterung die - 3. (U) [of orange, lemon] Schale der.

zigzag ['zɪgzæg] vi [person, vehicle] im Zickzack laufen/fahren; [path] im Zickzack verlaufen.

Zimbabwe [zɪm'bɑːbwɪ] n Simbabwe nt.

zinc [zɪŋk] n Zink das.

zip [zɪp] <> n UK [fastener] Reißverschluss der. <> vt COMPUT zippen. ◆ **zip up** vt sep den Reißverschluss zulmachen an (+ D).

zip code n US Postleitzahl die.

zip fastener n UK = **zip**.

zipper ['zɪpər] n US = **zip**.

zodiac ['zəʊdɪæk] n: **the zodiac** Tierkreis der.

zone [zəʊn] n [district] Zone die.

zoo [zuː] n Zoo der.

zoom [zuːm] vi inf [move quickly] sausen. ◆ **zoom off** vi inf ablrauschen.

zoom lens n Zoomobjektiv das.

zucchini [zuː'kiːnɪ] (pl inv OR **-s**) n US Zucchini die.